PRENTICE-HALL

·

Federal Income Tax REGULATIONS

·

VOLUME THREE

·

§1.1501-1 — END

PRENTICE-HALL, INC.

Englewood Cliffs, New Jersey

CONSOLIDATED RETURNS
RETURNS AND PAYMENT OF TAX

§ 1.1501 Statutory provisions; privilege to file consolidated returns. [Sec. 1501, IRC]

§ 1.1501-1 (T.D. 6140, filed 8-29-55; republished in T.D. 6500, filed 11-25-60.) **Privilege to file consolidated returns.**

For regulations relating to the privilege of filing consolidated returns, see § 1.1502-0 and following. For convenience, the several sections of the regulations under section 1502 have to the extent practicable, been given numbers corresponding, respectively, to the section numbers of prior consolidated returns regulations but preceded by the code number 1.1502.

§ 1.1502 Statutory provisions; regulations. [Sec. 1502, IRC]

§ 1.1502-0 (T.D. 6894, filed 9-7-66.) **Effective date.**

(a) The provisions of §§ 1.1502-1 through 1.1502-80 shall be applicable to taxable years beginning after December 31, 1965.

(b) The provisions of §§ 1.1502-0A through 1.1502-51A shall be applicable to taxable years beginning before January 1, 1966.[1]

§ 1.1502-1 (T.D. 6894, filed 9-7-66; amended by T.D. 7246, filed 12-29-72.) **Definitions.**

(a) *Group.* The term "group" means an affiliated group of corporations as defined in section 1504. See § 1.1502-75(d) as to when a group remains in existence.

(b) *Member.* The term "member" means a corporation (including the common parent) which is included within such group.

(c) *Subsidiary.* The term "subsidiary" means a corporation other than the common parent which is a member of such group.

(d) *Consolidated return year.* The term "consolidated return year" means a taxable year for which a consolidated return is filed or required to be filed by such group.

(e) *Separate return year.* The term "separate return year" means a taxable year of a corporation for which it files a separate return or for which it joins in the filing of a consolidated return by another group.

(f) *Separate return limitation year*—(1) *In general.* Except as provided in subparagraphs (2) and (3) of this paragraph, the term "separate return limitation year" means any separate return year of a member or of a predecessor of such member. The term "predecessor" means a transferor or distributor of assets to a member in a transaction to which section 381(a) applies.

(2) *Exceptions.* The term "separate return limitation year" shall not include—

(i) A separate return year of the corporation which is the common parent for the consolidated return year to which the tax attribute is to be carried (except as provided in § 1.1502-75(d)(2)(ii) and subparagraph (3) of this paragraph),

(ii) A separate return year of any corporation which was a member of the group for each day of such year, or

(iii) A separate return year of a predecessor of any member if such predecessor was a member of the group for each day of such year,

provided that an election under section 1562(a) (relating to the privilege to elect multiple surtax exemptions) was never effective (or is no longer effective as a result of a termination of such election) for such year. An election under section 1562 (a) which is effective for taxable year beginning in 1963 and ending in 1964 shall be disregarded.

(3) *Reverse acquisitions.* In the event of an acquisition to which § 1.1502-75(d)(3) applies. all taxable years of the first corporation and of each of its subsidiaries ending on or before the date of the acquisition shall be treated as separate return limitation years, and the separate return years (if any) of the second corporation and each of its subsidiaries shall not be treated as separate return limitation years (unless they were so treated immediately before the acquisition). For example, if corporation P merges into corporation T, and the persons who were stockholders of P immediately before the merger, as a result of owning the stock of P, own more than 50 percent of the fair market value of the outstanding stock of T, then a loss incurred before the merger by T (even though it is the common parent), or by a subsidiary of T, is treated as having been incurred in a separate return limitation year. Conversely, a loss incurred before the merger by P, or by a subsidiary of P in a separate return year during all of which such subsidiary was a member of the group of which P was the common parent and for which section 1562 was not effective, is treated as having been incurred in a year which is not a separate return limitation year.

(g) *Consolidated return change of ownership*—(1) *In general.* A consolidated return change of ownership occurs during any taxable year (referred to in this subparagraph as the "year of change") of the corporation which is the common parent for the taxable year to which the tax attributable is to be carried, if, at the end of the year of change—

(i) Any one or more of the persons described in section 382(a)(2) own a percentage of the fair market value of the outstanding stock of such corporation which is more than 50 percentage points greater than such person or persons owned at—

(a) The beginning of such taxable year, or

(b) The beginning of the preceding taxable year, and

(ii) The increase in percentage points at the end of such year is attributable to—

(a) A purchase (within the meaning of

---

(1) Regs. §§ 1.1502-0A through 1.1502-51A, applicable to taxable years beginning before January 1, 1966, appear (as amended) in *P-H Cumulative Changes.*

section 382(a)(4)) by such person or persons of such stock, the stock of another corporation owning stock in such corporation, or an interest in a partnership or trust owning stock in such corporation, or

(b) A decrease in the amount of such stock outstanding or the amount of stock outstanding of another corporation owning stock in such corporation, except a decrease resulting from a redemption to pay death taxes to which section 303 applies. For purposes of subdivision (i) *(a)* and *(b)* of this subparagraph, the beginning of the taxable years specified therein shall be the beginning of such taxable years or October 1, 1965, whichever occurs later.

(2) *Operating rules.* For purposes of this paragraph—

(i) The term "stock" means all shares except nonvoting stock which is limited and preferred as to dividends, and

(ii) Section 318 (relating to constructive ownership of stock) shall apply in determining the ownership of stock, except that section 318 (a) (2) (C) and (3) (C) shall be applied without regard to the 50 percent limitation contained therein.

(3) *Old members.* The term "old members" of a group means—

(i) Those corporations which were members of such group immediately preceding the first day of the taxable year in which the consolidated return change of ownership occurs, or

(ii) If the group was not in existence prior to the taxable year in which the consolidated return change of ownership occurs, the corporation which is the common parent for the taxable year to which the tax attribute is to be carried.

(4) *Reverse acquisitions.* If there has been a consolidated return change of ownership of a corporation under subparagraph (1) of this paragraph and the stock or assets of such corporation are subsequently acquired by another corporation in an acquisition to which § 1.1502-75 (d) (3) applies so that the group of which the former corporation is the common parent is treated as continuing in existence, then the "old members", as defined in subparagraph (3) of this paragraph, of such group immediately before the acquisition shall continue to be treated as "old members" immediately after the acquisition. For example, assume that corporations P and S comprise group PS, and PS undergoes a consolidated return change of ownership. Subsequently, the stock of P, the common parent, is acquired by corporation T, the common parent of group TU, in an acquisition to which section 368 (a) (1) (B) and § 1.1502-75 (d) (3) apply. The PS group is treated as continuing in existence with T as the common parent. P and S continue to be treated as old members, as defined in subparagraph (3) of this paragraph.

CONSOLIDATED TAX LIABILITY

O—➤ § 1.1502-2 (T.D. 6894, filed 9-7-66; amended by T.D. 7093, filed 3-12-71.) **Computation of tax liability.** The tax liability of a group for a consolidated return year shall be determined by adding together—

(a) The tax imposed by section 11 on the consolidated taxable income for such year (see § 1.1502-11 for the computation of consolidated taxable income);

(b) The tax imposed by section 541 on the consolidated undistributed personal holding company income;

(c) If paragraph (b) of this section does not apply, the aggregate of the taxes imposed by section 541 on the separate undistributed personal holding company income of the members which are personal holding companies;

(d) If paragraph (b) of this section does not apply, the tax imposed by section 531 on the consolidated accumulated taxable income;

(e) The tax imposed by section 594 (a) in lieu of the taxes imposed by section 11 or 1201 on the taxable income of a life insurance department of the common parent of a group which is a mutal savings bank;

(f) The tax imposed by section 802 (a) on consolidated life insurance company taxable income;

(g) The tax imposed by section 831 (a) on the consolidated insurance company taxable income of the members which are subject to such tax;

(h) The tax imposed by section 1201, in lieu of the taxes computed under paragraphs (a) and (g) of this section, computed by reference to the excess of the consolidated net long-term capital gain over the consolidated net short-term capital loss (see § 1.1502-41 for the determination of the consolidated net long-term capital gain and the consolidated net short-term capital loss);

(i) [Reserved]

(j) The tax imposed by section 1333 on war loss recoveries; and

by allowing as a credit against such taxes the investment credit under section 38 (see § 1.1502-3), and the foreign tax credit under section 33 (see § 1.1502-4). For purposes of this section, the surtax exemption of the group for a consolidated return year is $25,000, or if a lesser amount is allowed under section 1561, such lesser amount. See § 1.1561-2 (a) (2). For increase in tax due to the application of section 47, see § 1.1502-3(f). For amount of tax surcharge see section 51 and § 1.1502-7.

O—➤ § 1.1502-3 (T.D. 6894, filed 9-7-66; amended by T.D. 7246, filed 12-29-72.) **Consolidated investment credit.**

(a) *Determination of amount of credit*—(1) *In general.* The credit allowed by section 38 for a consolidated return year of a group shall be equal to the consolidated credit earned. The consolidated credit earned is equal to the aggregate of the credit earned (as determined under subparagraph (2) of this paragraph) by all members of the group for the consolidated return year.

(2) *Determination of credit earned.* The credit earned of a member is an amount equal to 7 percent of such member's qualified investment (determined under section 46 (c)). For purposes of computing a member's qualified investment, the basis of property shall not include any gain or loss realized with respect to such property by another member in an intercompany transaction (as defined in § 1.1502-13(a)(1)), whether or not such gain or loss is deferred. Thus, if section 38 property acquired in an intercompany transaction has a basis of $100 to the purchasing member, and if the selling member has a $20 gain with respect to such property, the basis of

such property for purposes of computing the purchaser's qualified investment is only $80. Such $80 basis shall also be used for purposes of applying section 47 to such property. See paragraph (f) of this section.

(3) *Consolidated limitation based on amount of tax.* (i) Notwithstanding the amount of the consolidated credit earned for the taxable year, the consolidated credit allowed by section 38 to the group for the consolidated return year is limited to—

(a) So much of the consolidated liability for tax as does not exceed $25,000, plus

(b) For taxable years ending on or before March 9, 1967, 25 percent of the consolidated liability for tax in excess of $25,000, or

(c) For taxable years ending after March 9, 1967, 50 percent of the consolidated liability for tax in excess of $25,000.

The $25,000 amount referred to in the preceding sentence shall be reduced by any part of such $25,000 amount apportioned under § 1.46-1 to component members of the controlled group (as defined in section 46 (a)(5)) which do not join in the filing of the consolidated return. For further rules for computing the limitation based on amount of tax with respect to the suspension period (as defined in section 48(j)), see section 46(a)(2). The amount determined under this subparagraph is referred to in this section as the "consolidated limitation based on amount of tax."

(ii) If an organization to which section 593 applies or a cooperative organization described in section 1381(a) joins in the filing of the consolidated return, the $25,000 amount referred to in subdivision (i) of this subparagraph (reduced as provided in such subdivision) shall be apportioned equally among the members of the group filing the consolidated return. The amount so apportioned equally to any such organization shall then be decreased in accordance with the provisions of section 46(d). Finally, the sum of all such equal portions (as decreased under section 46(d)) of each member of the group shall be substituted for the $25,000 amount referred to in subdivision (i) of this subparagraph.

(4) *Consolidated liability for tax.* For purposes of subparagraph (3) of this paragraph, the consolidated liability for tax shall be the income tax imposed for the taxable year upon the group by chapter 1 of the Code, reduced by the consolidated foreign tax credit allowable under § 1.1502-4. The tax imposed by section 56 (relating to minimum tax for tax preferences), section 531 (relating to accumulated earnings tax), section 541 (relating to personal holding company tax), and any additional tax imposed by section 1351(d)(1) (relating to recoveries of foreign expropriation losses) shall not be considered tax imposed by chapter 1 of the Code. In addition, any increase in tax resulting from the application of section 47 (relating to certain dispositions, etc., of section 38 property) shall not be treated as tax imposed by chapter 1 for purposes of computing the consolidated liability for tax.

(b) *Carryback and carryover of unused credits*—(1) *Allowance of unused credit* as consolidated carryback or carryover. A group shall be allowed to add to the amount allowable as a credit under paragraph (a)(1) of this section for any consolidated return year an amount equal to the aggregate of the consolidated investment credit carryovers and carrybacks to such year. The consolidated investment credit carryovers and carrybacks to the taxable year shall consist of any consolidated unused credits of the group, plus any unused credits of members of the group arising in separate return years of such members, which may be carried over or back to the taxable year under the principles of section 46(b). However, such consolidated carryovers and carrybacks shall not include any consolidated unused credits apportioned to a corporation for a separate return year pursuant to paragraph (c) of § 1.1502-79 and shall be subject to the limitations contained in paragraphs (c) and (e) of this section. A consolidated unused credit for any consolidated return year is the excess of the consolidated credit earned over the consolidated limitation based on amount of tax for such year.

(2) *Absorption rules.* For purposes of determining the amount, if any, of an unused credit (whether consolidated or separate) which can be carried to a taxable year (consolidated or separate), the amount of such unused credit which is absorbed in a prior consolidated return year under section 46(b) shall be determined by—

(i) Applying all unused credits which can be carried to such prior year in the order of the taxable years in which such unused credits arose, beginning with the taxable year which ends earliest, and

(ii) Applying all such unused credits which can be carried to such prior year from taxable years ending on the same date on a pro rata basis.

(c) *Limitation on investment credit carryovers and carrybacks from separate return limitation years*—(1) *General rule.* In the case of an unused credit of a member of the group arising in a separate return limitation year (as defined in paragraph (f) of § 1.1502-1) of such member (and in a separate return limitation year of any predecessor of such member), the amount which may be included under paragraph (b) of this section (computed without regard to the limitation contained in paragraph (e) of this section) shall not exceed the amount determined under subparagraph (2) of this paragraph.

(2) *Computation of limitation.* The amount referred to in subparagraph (1) of this paragraph with respect to a member of the group is the excess, if any, of—

(i) The limitation based on amount of tax of the group, minus such limitation recomputed by excluding the items of income, deduction, and foreign tax credit of such member, over

(ii) The sum of *(a)* the investment credit earned by such member for such consolidated return year, and *(b)* the unused credits attributable to such member which may be carried to such consolidated return year arising in unused credit years ending prior to the particular separate return limitation year.

(d) *Examples.* The provisions of paragraphs (a), (b), and (c) of this section may be illustrated by the following examples:

Example (1). Corporation P is incorporated on January 1, 1966. On that same day

Reg. § 1.1502-3(d)

P incorporates corporation S, a wholly owned subsidiary. P and S file a consolidated return for calendar years 1966 and 1967. P's and S's credit earned, the consolidated credit earned, and the consolidated limitation based on amount of tax for 1966 and 1967 are as follows:

		Credit earned	Consolidated credit earned	Consolidated limitation based on amount of tax
1966	P	$60,000	$90,000	$100,000
	S	$30,000		
1967	P	$40,000	$65,000	$ 50,000
	S	$25,000		

(i) P's and S's credit earned for 1966 are aggregated and the group's consolidated credit earned, $90,000, is allowable in full to the group as a credit under section 38 for 1966 since such amount is less than the consolidated limitation based on amount of tax for 1966, $100,000.

(ii) Since the consolidated limitation based on amount of tax for 1967 is $50,000, only $50,000 of the $65,000 consolidated credit earned for such year is allowable to the group under section 38 as a credit for 1967. The consolidated unused credit for 1967 of $15,000 ($65,000 less $50,000) is a consolidated investment credit carryback and carryover to the years prescribed in section 46(b). In this case the consolidated unused credit is a consolidated investment credit carryback to 1966 (since P and S were not in existence in 1964 and 1965) and a consolidated investment credit carryover to 1968 and subsequent years. The portion of the consolidated unused credit for 1967 which is allowable as a credit for 1966 is $10,000. This amount shall be added to the amount allowable as a credit to the group for 1966. The balance of the consolidated unused credit for 1967 to be carried to 1968 is $5,000.

These amounts are computed as follows:

Consolidated carryback to 1966		$15,000
1966 consolidated limitation based on tax		$100,000
Less: Consolidated credit earned for 1966 .... $90,000		
Consolidated unused credits attributable to years preceding 1967 0		90,000
Limit on amount of 1967 consolidated unused credit which may be added as a credit for 1966		10,000
Balance of 1967 consolidated unused credit to be carried to 1968		$ 5,000

Example (2). (i) Assume the same facts as in example (1), except that all the stock of corporation T, also a calendar year taxpayer, is acquired by P on January 1, 1968, and that P, S, and T file a consolidated return for 1968. In 1966 T had an unused credit of $10,000 which has not been absorbed and is available as an investment credit carryover to 1968. Such carryover is from a separate return limitation year. P's and S's credit earned for 1968 is $10,000 each and T's credit earned is $8,000; the consolidated credit earned is therefore $28,000. The group's consolidated limitation based on amount of tax for 1968 is $50,000. Such limitation recomputed by excluding the items of income, deduction, and foreign tax credit of T is $30,000. Thus, the amount determined under paragraph (c)(2)(i) of this section is $20,000 ($50,000 minus $30,000). Accordingly, the limitation on the carryover of T's unused credit is $12,000, the excess of $20,000 over $8,000 (the sum of T's credit earned for the taxable year and any carryovers from prior unused credit years (none in this case)). Therefore T's $10,000 unused credit from 1966 may be carried over to the consolidated return year without limitation.

(ii) The group's consolidated credit earned for 1968, $28,000, is allowable in full as a credit under section 38 since such amount is less than the consolidated limitation based on amount of tax, $50,000.

(iii) The group's consolidated investment credit carryover to 1968 is $15,000, consisting of the consolidated unused credits of the group ($5,000), plus T's separate return year unused credit ($10,000). The entire $15,000 consolidated carryover shall be added to the amount allowable to the group as a credit under section 38 for 1968, since such amount is less than $22,000 (the excess of the consolidated limitation based on tax, $50,000, over the sum of the consolidated credit earned for 1968, $28,000, and unused credits arising in prior unused credit years, zero).

Reg. § 1.1502-3(d)

Example (3). Assume the same facts as in example (2), except that the amount determined under paragraph (c)(2)(i) of this section is $12,000. Therefore, the limitation on the carryover of T's unused credit is $4,000. Accordingly, the consolidated investment credit carryover is only $9,000 since the amount of T's separate return year unused credit which may be added to the group's $5,000 consolidated unused credit is $4,000. These amounts are computed as follows:

T's carryover to 1968		$10,000
Consolidated limitation based on amount of tax minus recomputed limitation	$12,000	
Less: T's credit earned for 1968	$8,000	
Unused credits attributable to T arising in unused credit years preceding 1966	0	8,000
Limit on amount of 1966 unused credit of T which may be added to consolidated investment credit carryover		4,000
Balance of 1966 unused credit of T to be carried to 1969 (subject to the limitation contained in paragraph (c) of this section)		6,000

(e) *Limitation on investment credit carryovers where there has been a consolidated return change of ownership*—(1) *General rule.* If a consolidated return change of ownership (as defined in paragraph (g) of § 1.1502-1) occurs during the taxable year or an earlier taxable year, the amount which may be included under paragraph (b) of this section in the consolidated investment credit carryovers to the taxable year with respect to the aggregate unused credits attributable to old members of the group (as defined in paragraph (g)(3) of § 1.1502-1) arising in taxable years (consolidated or separate) ending on the same day and before the taxable year in which the consolidated return change of ownership occurred shall not exceed the amount determined under subparagraph (2) of this paragraph.

(2) *Computation of limitation.* The amount referred to in subparagraph (1) of this paragraph shall be the excess of the consolidated limitation based on the amount of tax for the taxable year, recomputed by including only the items of income, deduction, and foreign tax credit of the old members, over the sum of—

(i) The aggregate investment credits earned by the old members for the taxable year, and

(ii) The aggregate unused investment credits attributable to the old members which may be carried to the taxable year arising in unused credit years ending prior to the particular unused credit year or years.

(f) *Early dispositions, etc., of section 38 property*—(1) *Dispositions of section 38 property during and after consolidated return year.* If property is subject to section 47(a)(1) or (2) with respect to a member during a consolidated return year, any increase in tax shall be added to the tax liability of the group under § 1.1502-2 (regardless of whether the property was placed in service in a consolidated or separate return year). Also, if property is subject to section 47(a)(1) or (2) with respect to a corporation during a taxable year for which such corporation files on a separate return basis, any increase in tax shall be added to the tax liability of such corporation (regardless of whether such property was placed in service in a consolidated or separate return year).

(2) *Exception for transfer to another member.* (i) Except as provided in subdivisions (ii) and (iii) of this subparagraph, a transfer of section 38 property from one member of the group to another member of such group during a consolidated return year shall not be treated as a disposition of cessation within the meaning of section 47(a)(1). If such section 38 property is disposed of, or otherwise ceases to be section 38 property or becomes public utility property with respect to the transferee, before the close of the estimated useful life which was taken into account in computing qualified investment, then section 47 (a)(1) or (2) shall apply to the transferee with respect to such property (determined by taking into account the period of use, qualified investment, other dispositions, etc., of the transferor). Any increase in tax due to the application of section 47 (a)(1) or (2) shall be added to the tax liability of such transferee (or the tax liability of a group, if the transferee joins in the filing of a consolidated return).

(ii) Except as provided in subdivision (iii) of this subparagraph, if section 38 property is disposed of during a consolidated return year by one member of the group to another member of such group which is an organization to which section 593 applies or a cooperative organization described in section 1381 (a), the tax under chapter 1 of the Code for such consolidated return year shall be increased by an amount equal to the aggregate decrease in the credits allowed under section 38 for all prior taxable years which would result solely from treating such property, for purposes of determining qualified investment, as placed in service by such organization to which section 593 applies or such cooperative organization described in section 1381(a), as the case may be, but with due regard to the use of the property before such transfer.

(iii) Section 47(a)(1) shall apply to a transfer of section 38 property by a corporation during a consolidated return year if such corporation is liquidated in a transaction to which section 334(b)(2) applies.

(3) *Examples.* The provisions of this paragraph may be illustrated by the following examples:

Example (1). P, S, and T file a consolidated return for calendar year 1967. In such year S places in service section 38 property having an estimated useful life of more than 8 years. In 1968, P, S, and T file a consolidated return, and in such year S sells such property to T. Such sale will not cause section 47 (a) (1) to apply.

Example (2). Assume the same facts as in example (1), except that P, S, and T filed separate returns for 1967. The sale from S to T will not cause section 47 (a) (1) to apply.

Example (3). Assume the same facts as in example (1), except that P, S, and T continue to file a consolidated return through 1971, and in such year T disposes of the property to individual A. Section 47 (a) (1) will apply to the group and any increase in tax shall be added to the tax liability of the group. For the purposes of determining the actual period of use by T, such period shall include S's period of use.

Example (4). Assume the same facts as in example (3), except that T files a separate return in 1971. Again, the actual periods of use by S and T will be combined in applying section 47. If the disposition results in an increase in tax under section 47 (a) (1), such additional tax shall be added to the separate tax liability of T.

Example (5). Assume the same facts as in example (1), except that in 1969, P sells all the stock of T to a third party. Such sale will not cause section 47 (a) (1) to apply.

§ 1.1502-4 (T.D. 6894, filed 9-7-66.) **Consolidated foreign tax credit.**

(a) *In general.* The credit under section 901 for taxes paid or accrued to any foreign country or possession of the United States shall be allowed to the group only if the common parent corporation chooses to use such credit in the computation of the tax liability of the group for the consolidated return year. If this choice is made, no deduction may be taken on the consolidated return for such taxes paid or accrued by any member of the group. See section 275 (a) (4).

(b) *Limitation effective under section 904(a) for the group*—(1) *Common parent's limitation effective for group.* The determination of whether the overall limitation or the per-country limitation applies for a consolidated return year shall be made by reference to the limitation effective with respect to the common parent corporation for such year. If the limitation effective with respect to a member for its immediately preceding separate return year differs from the limitation effective with respect to the common parent corporation for the consolidated return year, then such member shall, if the overall limitation is effective with respect to the common parent, be deemed to have made an election to use such overall limitation, or, if the per-country limitation is effective with respect to the common parent, be deemed to have revoked its election to use the overall limitation. Consent of the Secretary or his delegate (if otherwise required) is hereby given to such member for such election or revocation. Any such election or revocation shall apply only prospectively beginning with such consolidated return year.

(2) *Limitation effective for subsequent years.* The limitation effective with respect to a member for the last year for which it joins in the filing of a consolidated return with a group shall remain in effect for a subsequent separate return year and may be changed by such corporation for such subsequent year only in accordance with the provisions of section 904(b) (and this paragraph if it joins in the filing of a consolidated return with another group). Any retroactive change in the limitation by the common parent corporation for such member's last consolidated return year shall change the election effective with respect to such member for such last period. Thus, if the common parent (P) elects the overall limitation with respect to calendar year 1966, such election would be effective with respect to its subsidiary S for 1966. If S leaves the group at the beginning of calendar year 1967, such election shall be effective for 1967 with respect to S (unless S revokes such election for 1967 or a subsequent year in accordance with section 904 (b), or this paragraph if it joins in the filing of a consolidated return with another group). However, if P retroactively changes back to the per-country limitation with respect to 1966, such limitation would be effective with respect to S for 1966 and subsequent years (unless S elects the overall limitation for any such subsequent year).

(c) *Computation of consolidated foreign tax credit.* The foreign tax credit for the consolidated return year shall be determined on a consolidated basis under the principles of sections 901 through 905 and section 960. For example, if the per-country limitation applies to the consolidated return year, taxes paid or accrued for such year (including those deemed paid or accrued under sections 902 and 960(a) and paragraph (e) of this section) to each foreign country or possession by the members of the group shall be aggregated. If the overall limitation applies, taxes paid or accrued for such year (including those deemed paid or accrued) to all foreign countries and possessions by members of the group shall be aggregated. If the overall limitation applies and a member of the group qualifies as a Western Hemisphere trade corporation, see section 1503(b).

(d) *Computation of limitation on credit.* For purposes of computing the group's applicable limitation under section 904(a), the following rules shall apply:

(1) *Computation of taxable income from foreign sources.* The numerator of the applicable limiting fraction under section 904 (a) shall be an amount (not in excess of the amount determined under subparagraph (2) of this paragraph) equal to the aggregate of the separate taxable

incomes of the members from sources within each foreign country or possession of the United States (if the per-country limitation is applicable), or from sources without the United States (if the overall limitation is applicable), determined under § 1.1502-12, adjusted for the following items taken into account in the computation of consolidated taxable income:

(i) The portion of the consolidated net operating loss deduction, the consolidated charitable contributions deduction, the consolidated dividends received deduction, and the consolidated section 922 deduction, attributable to such foreign source income;

(ii) Any such foreign source net capital gain (determined without regard to any net capital loss carryover);

(iii) Any such foreign source net capital loss and section 1231 net loss, reduced by the portion of the consolidated net capital loss attributable to such foreign source loss; and

(iv) The portion of any consolidated net capital loss carryover attributable to such foreign source income which is absorbed in the taxable year.

(2) *Computation of entire taxable income.* The denominator of the applicable limiting fraction under section 904 (a) (that is, the entire taxable income of the group) shall be the consolidated taxable income of the group computed in accordance with § 1.1502-11.

(3) *Computation of tax against which credit is taken.* The tax against which the limiting fraction under section 904 (a) is applied, shall be the consolidated tax liability of the group determined under § 1.1502-2, but without regard to paragraphs (b), (c), (d), and (j) thereof, and without regard to any credit against such liability.

(e) *Carryover and carryback of unused foreign tax*—(1) *Allowance of unused foreign tax as consolidated carryover or carryback.* The aggregate of the consolidated unused foreign tax carryovers and carrybacks to the taxable year, to the extent absorbed for such year under the principles of section 904(d), shall be deemed to be paid or accrued to a foreign country or possession for such year. The consolidated unused foreign tax carryovers and carrybacks to the taxable year shall consist of any consolidated unused foreign tax, plus any unused foreign tax of members for separate return years of such members, which may be carried over or back to the taxable year under the principles of section 904(d) and (e). However, such consolidated carryovers and carrybacks shall not include any consolidated unused foreign taxes apportioned to a corporation for a separate return year pursuant to § 1.1502-79(d) and shall be subject to the limitations contained in paragraphs (f) and (g) of this section. A consolidated unused foreign tax is the excess of the foreign taxes paid or accrued by the group (or deemed paid or accrued by the group, other than by reason of section 904 (d)) over the applicable limitation for the consolidated return year.

(2) *Absorption rules.* For purposes of determining the amount, if any, of an unused tax (consolidated or separate) which can be carried to a taxable year (consolidated or separate), the amount of such unused tax which is absorbed in a prior consolidated return year under section 904 (d) shall be determined by—

(i) Applying all unused foreign taxes which can be carried to such prior year in the order of the taxable years in which such unused taxes arose, beginning with the taxable year which ends earliest, and

(ii) Applying all such unused taxes which can be carried to such prior year from taxable years ending on the same date on a pro rata basis.

(f) *Limitation on unused foreign tax carryover or carryback from separate return limitation years*—(1) *General rule.* In the case of an unused foreign tax of a member of the group arising in a separate return limitation year (as defined in paragraph (f) of § 1.1502-1) of such member, the amount which may be included under paragraph (e) of this section (computed without regard to the limitation contained in paragraph (g) of this section) shall not exceed the amount determined under subparagraph (2) of this paragraph.

(2) *Computation of limitation.* The amount referred to in subparagraph (1) of this paragraph with respect to a member of the group is the excess, if any, of—

(i) The section 904(a) limitation of the group, minus such limitation recomputed by excluding the items of income and deduction of such member, over

(ii) The sum of (a) the foreign taxes paid (or deemed paid, other than by reason of section 904(d)) by such member for the consolidated return year, and (b) the unused foreign tax attributable to such member which may be carried to such consolidated return year arising in taxable years ending prior to the particular separate return limitation year.

(g) *Limitation on unused foreign tax carryover where there has been a consolidated return change of ownership*—(1) *General rule.* If a consolidated return change of ownership (as defined in paragraph (g) of § 1.1502.1) occurs during the taxable year or an earlier taxable year, the amount which may be included under paragraph (e) of this section in the consolidated unused foreign tax carryovers to the taxable year with respect to the aggregate unused credits attributable to the old members of the group (as defined in paragraph (g)(3) of § 1.1502-1) arising in taxable years (consolidated or separate) ending on the same day and before the taxable year in which the consolidated return change of ownership occurred shall not exceed the amount determined under subparagraph (2) of this paragraph.

(2) *Computation of limitation.* The amount referred to in subparagraph (1) of this paragraph shall be the excess of the section 904(a) limitation of the group for the taxable year, recomputed by including only the items of income and deduction of the old members of the group, over the sum of—

(i) The aggregate foreign taxes paid (or deemed paid, other than by reason of section 904(d)) by the old members for the taxable year, and

(ii) The aggregate unused foreign tax

attributable to the old members which can be carried to the taxable year arising in taxable years ending prior to the particular unused foreign tax year or years.

(h) *Amount of credit with respect to interest income.* If any member of the group has interest income described in section 904(f)(2) (for a year for which it filed on a consolidated or separate basis), the group's foreign tax credit with respect to such interest shall be computed separately in accordance with the principles of section 904(f) and this section.

(i) [Reserved]

(j) *Examples.* The provisions of this section may be illustrated by the following examples:

Example (1). Domestic corporation P is incorporated on January 1, 1966. On that same day it also incorporates domestic corporations S and T, wholly owned subsidiaries. P, S, and T file consolidated returns for 1966 and 1967 on the basis of a calendar year. T engages in business solely in country A. S transacts business soley in countries A and B. P does business solely in the United States. During 1966 T sold an item of inventory to P at a profit of $2,000. Under § 1.1502-13 such profit is deferred and none of the circumstances of restoration contained in paragraph (d), (e), or (f) of § 1.1502-13 have occurred as of the close of 1966. The taxable income for 1966 from foreign and United States sources, and the foreign taxes paid on such foreign income are as folows:

Corporation	U.S. Taxable income	Country A Taxable income	Country A Foreign tax paid	Country B Taxable income	Country B Foreign tax paid	Total Taxable income
P	$40,000					$40,000
T		$20,000	$12,000			20,000
S		10,000	6,000	$10,000	$3,000	20,000
						$80,000

Such taxable income was computed by taking into account the rules provided in § 1.1502-12. Thus, the $2,000 deferred profit is not included in T's taxable income for 1966 (but will be included for the taxable year for which one of the events specified in paragraph (d), (e), or (f) of § 1.1502-13 occurs). The consolidated taxable income of the group (computed in accordance with § 1.1502-11) is $80,000. The consolidated tax liability against which the credit may be taken (computed in accordance with paragraph (d)(3) of this section) is $31,900.

(i) Assuming P chooses to use the foreign taxes paid as a credit and the group is subject to the pre-country limitation, the group may take as a credit against the consolidated tax liability $1,962.50 of the amount paid to country A, plus the $3,000 paid to country B. Such amounts are computed as follows: he aggregate taxes paid to country A of $18,000 is limited to $11,962.50 ($31,900 times $20,000/$80,000). The unused foreign tax with respect to country A is $6,037.50 ($18,000 less $11,962.50) and is a consolidated unused foreign tax which shall be carried to the years prescribed by section 904(d). A credit of $3,000 is available with respect to the taxes paid to country B since such amount is less that the limitation of $3,987.50 ($31,900 times $10,000/$80,000).

(ii) Assuming the overall limitation is in effect for the taxable year, the group may take $15,950 as a credit, computed as follows: The aggregate taxes paid to all foreign countries of $21,000 is limited to $15,950 ($31,900 times $40,000/$80,000). The unused foreign tax is $5,050 ($21,000 less $15,950), and is a consolidated unused foreign tax which shall be carried to the years prescribed by section 904(d).

Example (2). Assume the same facts as in example (1), except that T has a $10,000 long-term capital gain (derived from a sale to a nonmember in country A) and P has a $10,000 long-term capital loss (derived from a sale to a nonmember in the United States). Notwithstanding that the consolidated net capital gain of the group is zero, T's capital gain shall be reflected in full in the computation of taxable income from foreign sources.

Example (3). Assume the same facts as in example (1), except that the group had a consolidated section 172 deduction of $8,000 which is attributable to a net operating loss sustained by T. The $8,000 consolidated net operating loss deduction is offset against T's income from country A, thus reducing T's taxable income from country A to $12,000.

§ 1.1502-5 (T.D. 6894, filed 9-7-66; amended by T.D. 7059, filed 9-16-70). Estimated tax.

(a) *General rule*—(1) *Consolidated estimated tax.* If a group files a consolidated return for two consecutive taxable years, it shall file its declaration of estimated tax on a consolidated basis for each subsequent taxable year, until such time as separate returns are properly filed under § 1.1502-75 (c). Until such time, the group shall be treated as a single corporation for purposes of sections 6016 and 6154 (relating to declaration and payment of estimated tax by corporations). If separate returns are filed by the members for a taxable year, the amount of any estimated tax payments made with respect to a consolidated declaration of estimated tax for such year shall be credited against the separate tax liabilities of the members in any manner designated by the common parent which is satisfactory to the Commissioner. The consolidated declaration of estimated tax shall be filed, and payments shall be made, to the district director with whom the

Reg. § 1.1502-5(a)(1)

common parent would file a separate return. A statement should be attached to the declaration setting forth the name, address, taxpayer account number, and district director of each member.

(2) *Estimated tax on a separate basis.* If a group is not required to file a consolidated declaration of estimated tax for a taxable year, then each member shall be treated as a separate corporation for such taxable year for purposes of sections 6016 and 6154, except as otherwise provided in section 243 (b) (3) (C) (v). If a consolidated return is filed for such year, the amount of any estimated tax payments made for such year shall be credited against the tax liability of the group.

(b) *Additions to tax for failure to pay estimated tax under section 6655*—(1) *Consolidated declaration of estimated tax required to be filed.* If a group is required to file a consolidated declaration of estimated tax for the taxable year under paragraph (a) (1) of this section, then—

(i) If such group files a consolidated return for the taxable year, it shall be limited to a single $100,000 exemption for purposes of applying section 6655 to payments of estimated tax for such year. For purposes of section 6655 (d)(1), the "tax shown on the return" shall be the tax shown on the consolidated return for the preceding taxable year, and for purposes of section 6655 (d) (2), the "facts shown on the return" shall be the facts shown on the consolidated return for the preceding taxable year.

(ii) If such group does not file a consolidated return for the taxable year, each member of the group shall, except as otherwise provided in section 243 (b) (3) (C) (v), be entitled to a separate $100,000 exemption for purposes of applying section 6655 to payments of estimated tax for such year. For purposes of section 6655 (b) (2), the "amount, if any, of the installment paid" by any member shall be an amount apportioned to such member in a manner designated by the common parent which is satisfactory to the Commissioner. For purposes of section 6655 (d) (1), the "tax shown on the return" for any member shall be the portion of the tax shown on the consolidated return for the preceding year allocable to such member under subparagraph (3) of this paragraph. For purposes of section 6655 (d) (2), the "facts shown on the return" shall be the facts shown on the consolidated return for the preceding year and the tax computed under such section shall be allocated under the rules of subparagraph (3) of this paragraph.

(2) *Separate declaration of estimated tax.* If the members of a group are treated as separate corporations for the taxable year under paragraph (a) (2) of this section, then, except as otherwise provided in section 243 (b) (3) (C) (v), each such member is entitled to a separate $100,000 exemption for purposes of applying section 6655 to payments of estimated tax for such year, whether or not the group files a consolidated return for such year. If the group files a consolidated return for such year, then for purposes of section 6655 (d) (1), the "tax shown on the return" for any member shall be the portion of the tax shown on the consolidated return allocable to such member under subparagraph (3) of this paragraph. If the group filed a consolidated return for the preceding taxable year, then for purposes of section 6655 (d) (1), the "tax shown on the return" for any member shall be the portion of the tax shown on the consolidated return for such preceding year allocable to such member under subparagraph (3) of this paragraph. For purposes of section 6655 (d) (2), the "facts shown on the return" shall be the facts shown on the consolidated return for the preceding year and the tax computed under such section shall be allocated under the rules of subparagraph (3) of this paragraph.

(3) *Rules for allocation of consolidated tax liability.* For purposes of subparagraphs (1) and (2) of this paragraph, the tax shown on a consolidated return shall be allocated to the members of the group under the method which the group has elected pursuant to section 1552.

(c) *Examples.* The provisions of this section may be illustrated by the following examples:

Example (1). Corporations P and S-1 file a consolidated return for the first time for calendar year 1966. P and S-1 also file consolidated returns for 1967 and 1968. For 1966 and 1967 P and S-1 may file separate declarations of estimated tax, and they are entitled to separate $100,000 exemptions. For 1968, however, the group must compute its estimated tax on a consolidated basis, and it is limited to a single $100,000 exemption. In determining whether P and S-1 come within the exception provided in section 6655 (d) (1) for 1968, the "tax shown on the return" is the tax shown on the consolidated return for 1967.

Example (2). Assume the same facts as in example (1). Assume further that corporation S-2 was a member of the group during 1967, and joined in the filing of the consolidated return for such year, but ceased to be a member of the group on September 15, 1968. In determining whether the group (which no longer includes S-2) comes within the exception provided in section 6655 (d) (1) for 1968, the "tax shown on the return" is the tax shown on the consolidated return for 1967.

Example (3). Assume the same facts as in example (1). Assume further that corporation S-2 becomes a member of the group on June 1, 1968, and joins in the filing of the consolidated return for 1968. In determining whether the group (which now includes S-2) comes within the exception provided in section 6655 (d) (1) for 1968, the "tax shown on the return" is the tax shown on the consolidated return for 1967. Any tax of S-2 for any separate return year is not included as a part of the "tax shown on the return" for purposes of applying section 6655 (d) (1).

Example (4). Corporations X and Y filed consolidated returns for the calendar years 1966 and 1967 and separate returns for 1968. X and Y are each entitled to a separate $100,000 exemption for 1968 for purposes of applying section 6655. In determining whether X or Y comes within the exception provided in section 6655 (d) (1) for 1968, the "tax shown on the return" is the amount of tax shown on the consolidated return for 1967 allocable to X and to

Y in accordance with paragraph (b) (3) of this section.

(d) *Cross reference.* For provisions relating to quick refunds of corporate estimated tax payments, see § 1.1502-78, and § 1.16425-1 through § 1.6425-3, of this chapter.

§ 1.1502-6 (T.D. 6894, filed 9-7-66.) **Liability for tax.**

(a) *Several liability of members of group.* Except as provided in paragraph (b) of this section, the common parent corporation and each subsidiary which was a member of the group during any part of the consolidated return year shall be severally liable for the tax for such year computed in accordance with the regulations under section 1502 prescribed on or before the due date (not including extensions of time) for the filing of the consolidated return for such year.

(b) *Liability of subsidiary after withdrawal.* If a subsidiary has ceased to be a member of the group and if such cessation resulted from a bona fide sale or exchange of its stock for fair value and occurred prior to the date upon which any deficiency is assessed, the district director may, if he believes that the assessment or collection of the balance of the deficiency will not be jeopardized, make assessment and collection of such deficiency from such former subsidiary in an amount not exceeding the portion of such deficiency which the district director may determine to be allocable to it. If the district director makes assessment and collection of any part of a deficiency from such former subsidiary, then for purposes of any credit or refund of the amount collected from such former subsidiary the agency of the common parent under the provisions of § 1.1502-77 shall not apply.

(c) *Effect of intercompany agreements.* No agreement entered into by one or more members of the group with any other member of such group or with any other person shall in any case have the effect of reducing the liability prescribed under this section.

§ 1.1502-7 (T.D. 7093, filed 3-12-71.) **Tax surcharge.**

(a) *Part-year affiliate.* If—
(1) A group files a consolidated return for any taxable year which includes any portion of the period beginning January 1, 1970, and ending June 30, 1970, and
(2) Any corporation (referred to in paragraph (b) of this section as a "part-year affiliate") which joins in the filing of such return is not a member of the group for each day during any such taxable year, the surcharge liability of the group under section 51 shall be determined under paragraph (b) of this section.

(b) *Amount of surcharge.* If paragraph (a) of this section applies, the surcharge liability imposed by section 51 on consolidated taxable income shall be the sum of—
(1) The surcharge which would be imposed under section 51 (a) (1) (B) or (2) if that portion of the consolidated tax liability allocable to any part-year affiliate were excluded from the consolidated tax liability of the group, and
(2) The surcharge which would be imposed under section 51 (a) (2) on any part-year affiliate if such part-year affiliate filed a separate return for the period for which its income was included in the consolidated return and if the tax imposed by this chapter for such period was the portion of consolidated tax liability allocable to such corporation.

Consolidated tax liability under subparagraphs (1) and (2) shall be determined under § 1.1502-2 without regard to the tax surcharge imposed by section 51, the minimum tax imposed by section 56, any increase in tax under section 47 (a), relating to early dispositions of investment credit property, or under section 614 (c) (4) (C), relating to an election to aggregate certain mineral interests.

(c) *Allocation of tax liability.* For purposes of this section, the portion of consolidated tax liability allocable to a member shall be determined under the method used in allocating the tax liability of the group under the provisions of section 1552 (a).

§§ 1.1502-8 to 1.1502-10 [Reserved]

COMPUTATION OF CONSOLIDATED TAXABLE INCOME

§ 1.1502-11 (T.D. 6894, filed 9-7-66; amended by T.D. 7246, filed 12-29-72.) **Consolidated taxable income.**

(a) *In general.* The consolidated taxable income for a consolidated return year shall be determined by taking into account—
(1) The separate taxable income of each member of the group (see § 1.1502-12 for the computation of separate taxable income);
(2) Any consolidated net operating loss deduction (see § 1.1502-21 for the computation of the consolidated net operating loss deduction);
(3) Any consolidated net capital gain (see § 1.1502-22 for the computation of the consolidated net capital gain);
(4) Any consolidated section 1231 net loss (see § 1.1502-23 for the computation of the consolidated section 1231 net loss);
(5) Any consolidated charitable contributions deduction (see § 1.1502-24 for the computation of the consolidated charitable contributions deduction);
(6) Any consolidated section 922 deduction (see § 1.1502-25 for the computation of the consolidated section 922 deduction);
(7) Any consolidated dividends received deduction (see § 1.1502-26 for the computation of the consolidated dividends received deduction); and
(8) Any consolidated section 247 deduction (see § 1.1502-27 for the computation of the consolidated section 247 deduction).

(b) *Disposition of stock of a subsidiary*—(1) *In general.* If there is a disposition (as defined in § 1.1502-19(b)) of stock (ignoring for this purpose stock which is limited and preferred as to dividends) of a subsidiary during the taxable year, the adjustments under § 1.1502-32(b) with respect to such stock and the amount of gain or loss on disposition shall be determined in accordance with this paragraph, and the amounts taken into account in computing consolidated taxable income shall be limited as provided in this paragraph.

Reg. § 1.1502-11 (b) (1)

(2) *Determination of amount of gain or loss on disposition.* For the purpose of determining gain or loss or disposition—

(i) Consolidated taxable income or consolidated net operating loss (and earnings and profits or deficit in earnings and profits) for the taxable year shall be determined tentatively without regard to gain or loss on disposition,

(ii) The adjustments under § 1.1502-32 (b) with respect to the stock disposed of shall be based upon the amounts determined under subdivision (i) of this subparagraph, and

(iii) Gain (including any amount included in income under § 1.1502-19(a)) or loss on disposition shall be determined in accordance with such adjustments to basis.

(3) *Limitation on carryovers.* If this paragraph applies—

(i) The portion of any consolidated net capital or net operating loss carryover attributable to the subsidiary whose stock is disposed of, and

(ii) The portion of any net capital or net operating loss carryover from a separate return year of such subsidiary, which may be carried to the taxable year shall not exceed the amount of any such carryover which could be carried to the taxable year if the tentative consolidated taxable income determined under subparagraph (2)(i) of this paragraph were consolidated taxable income for the year.

(4) *Limitation on loss.* If there is gain (including any amount included in income under § 1.1502-19(a)) on disposition—

(i) The amount of capital losses of the subsidiary whose stock is disposed of taken into account under § 1.1502-22 shall be reduced by an amount equal to the portion of any tentative consolidated net capital loss attributable to the subsidiary under § 1.1502-79(b)(2), and

(ii) The amount of the excess of deductions over gross income of such subsidiary taken into account under paragraph (a)(1) of this section and § 1.1502-21(f)(1) shall be reduced by an amount equal to the portion of any tentative consolidated net operating loss attributable to the subsidiary under § 1.1502-79(a)(3).

The amount of any loss or excess deductions not taken into account because of the limitations of subdivisions (i) and (ii) shall be treated as a net capital or net operating loss sustained in the taxable year and shall be carried to those taxable years (consolidated or separate) to which a consolidated net capital or net operating loss could be carried under §§ 1.1502-21, 1.1502-22, and 1.1502-79, but the portion of such loss which may be carried to a prior year shall not exceed the portion of the tentative consolidated net capital or net operating loss attributable to the subsidiary which could be carried to such year if the tentative consolidated net capital or net operating loss determined under subparagraph (2)(i) of this paragraph were the consolidated net capital or net operating loss for the year.

(5) *Adjustments to stock not disposed of.* If some of the stock of a subsidiary is disposed of but the subsidiary remains a member, the adjustments under § 1.1502-32 with respect to stock not disposed of shall include an allocable portion of the amount treated as a net capital or net operating loss under subparagraph (4) of this paragraph which is not carried back and absorbed in a prior taxable year.

(6) *Examples.* The provisions of this paragraph may be illustrated by the following examples:

Example (1). (a) Assume that corporation P and its wholly owned subsidiary S, both incorporated on January 1, 1969, comprise an affiliated group and file a consolidated return for the taxable years 1969 and 1970. In 1969, the group has consolidated taxable income of $30 and a consolidated net capital loss of $100, of which $50 is attributable to S. On January 1, 1970, the adjusted basis of the S stock is $300. In 1970, P has a net capital gain of $20 (computed without regard to any capital loss carryover and without regard to gain from the disposition of the S stock) and ordinary income of $30, and S has a deficit of $100. On December 31, 1970, P sells all of the stock of S for $280.

(b) Tentative consolidated taxable income consists of (1) net capital gain of zero ($20 capital gain reduced by $20 of the net capital loss carryover, of which $10 is attributable to S), and (2) a net operating loss of $70, all of which is attributable to S and $30 of which may be carried back and absorbed in 1969.

(c) Under § 1.1502-32(b) and (e) and subparagraph (2)(ii) of this paragraph there is a net negative adjustment to the basis of the S stock of $70 (negative adjustments of $100 for the deficit and $10 for the portion of the consolidated net capital loss for 1969 attributable to S which is carried over and absorbed in the taxable year, and a positive adjustment of $40 for the portion of the consolidated net operating loss attributable to S which is not carried back and absorbed in 1969). Accordingly, the adjusted basis of the S stock is $230 and a gain of $50 is realized on the sale.

(d) Under subparagraph (3)(i) of this paragraph, the consolidated net capital loss carryover is limited to $60 (all of the portion attributable to P ($50), plus the amount attributable to S included in the tentative computation ($10) under subdivision (b)(1) of this example). Under subparagraph (4)(i) of this paragraph, the excess of deductions over income of S ($100) taken into account is reduced by an amount equal to the portion of the tentative consolidated net operating loss attributable to S ($70). Accordingly, consolidated taxable income for 1970 is computed as follows:

Consolidated net capital gain:		
Capital gain for 1970	$70 i.e., 50 + 20	
Capital loss carryover from 1969 ..	60	$10
Income exclusive of capital gain:		
P	30	
S	(30) i.e., (100) − 70	0
Consolidated taxable income:		10

The amount by which the excess of deductions over income of S is reduced ($70) is treated as a net operating loss of S for the year; $30 of such amount is carried back and absorbed in 1969 and $40 may be carried over to a separate return year of S. In addition, S has a net capital loss carryover of $40 from 1969.

Example (2). (a) Assume that corporation P owns all 10 outstanding shares of corporation S and that P and S comprise an affiliated group which files a consolidated return for 1969, 1970, and 1971. Neither P nor S was in existence before January 1, 1969. In 1969, the group has consolidated taxable income of $100. On January 1, 1970, the adjusted basis of each of the 10 shares of S is $40. In 1970, P has a deficit of $80 (determined without regard to gain on the disposition of the S stock) and S has a deficit of $80. On December 31, 1970, P sells two shares of the S stock for $85 each.

(b) The tentative consolidated net operating loss for 1970 is $160 of which $80 is attributable to S. One hundred dollars of such tentative loss is carried back and absorbed in 1969 and of this amount the portion attributable to S is $50.

(c) Under § 1.1502-32(b) and (e) and subparagraph (2)(ii) of this paragraph, there is a net negative adjustment to each of the two shares of S stock sold by P of $5, i.e., an allocable portion of an aggregate net negative adjustment of $50 (a negative adjustment of $80 for the deficit and a positive adjustment of $30 for the portion of the consolidated net operating loss attributable to S which is not carried back and absorbed in 1969). Accordingly, the adjusted basis of each of the two shares of S stock disposed of by P is $35 and a gain of $100 is realized on the sale of the two shares of stock.

(d) Under subparagraph (4)(ii) of this paragraph, the excess of deductions over income of S ($80) taken into account is reduced by an amount equal to the portion of the tentative consolidated net operating loss attributable to S ($80). Accordingly, consolidated taxable income for 1970 is computed as follows:

Consolidated net
  capital gain: $100
Income exclusive
  of capital gain:
  P ($80)
  S   0 i.e., (80) − 80 .... (80)
Consolidated taxable
  income 20

The amount by which the excess of deductions over income of S is reduced ($80) is treated as a net operating loss of S for the taxable year. Because of the limitation of subparagraph (4) of this paragraph, only $50 of such loss may be carried back and absorbed in 1969, since the portion of such loss which may be carried back to a prior year may not exceed the portion of the tentative consolidated net operating loss attributable to S which was carried back to the prior year in the tentative computation under subparagraph (2)(i) of this paragraph. The remaining $30 may be carried over to 1971 and subsequent years.

(e) Under § 1.1502-32(b) and (e) and subparagraph (5) of this paragraph, there is a negative adjustment of $5 to the basis of each of the remaining 8 shares of S owned by P, i.e., an allocable portion of an aggregate net adjustment of $50 (see subdivision (c) of this example).

Example (3). (a) Assume that corporations P and S comprise an affiliated group and file a consolidated return for 1969. There is no income for years prior to 1969. In 1969, P has capital gain of $100 (determined without regard to loss on the disposition of the S stock) and S has a capital loss of $60. In addition to the capital loss, S has a deficit of $200. On January 1, 1969, the basis of the S stock is $400. On December 31, 1969, P sells all of the stock of S for $140.

(b) Tentative consolidated taxable income consists of (1) net capital gain of $40, and (2) a net operating loss of $160, all of which is attributable to S.

(c) Under § 1.1502-32(b) and (e) and subparagraph (2)(ii) of this paragraph, there is a net negative adjustment to the basis of the S stock of $100 (a negative adjustment of $260 for the deficit and a positive adjustment of $160 for the portion of the consolidated net operating loss attributable to S, none of which is carried back to a prior year). Accordingly, the adjusted basis of the S stock is $300 and P realizes a loss of $160 on the sale.

(d) Consolidated taxable income for 1969 is computed as follows:

Consolidated net
  capital loss:
  P ($60) i.e., 100 − (160)
  S (60) .... ($120)
Income exclusive of
  capital gain:
  P   0
  S (200) .... (200)
Consolidated net
  operating loss: .... (200)

Sixty dollars of the consolidated net capital loss is attributable to S and the entire consolidated net operating loss is attributable to S. Since S is no longer a member of the group, such amounts are apportioned to S under § 1.1502-79(a) and (b) and may be carried to a subsequent separate return year of S.

COMPUTATION OF SEPARATE TAXABLE INCOME

○→ § 1.1502-12 (T.D. 6894, filed 9-7-66; amended by T.D. 7192, filed 6-29-72 and T.D. 7246, filed 12-29-72.) **Separate taxable income.**

The separate taxable income of a member of a group shall be computed in accordance with the provisions covering the determination of taxable income of separate corporations except that—

(a) Transactions between members and transactions with respect to stock, bonds, or other obligations of members shall be reflected according to the provisions of §§ 1.1502-13 and 1.1502-14;

(b) Any deduction which is disallowed under § 1.1502-15 shall be taken into account as provided in that section;

(c) The limitation on deductions provided in section 615(c) or section 617(h) shall be taken into account as provided in § 1.1502-16;

(d) The method of accounting under which such computation is made and the adjustments to be made because of any change in method of accounting shall be determined under § 1.1502-17;

Reg. § 1.1502-12(d)

(e) Inventory adjustments shall be made as provided in § 1.1502-18;

(f) Any amount included in income under § 1.1502-19 shall be taken into account;

(g) In the computation of the deduction under section 167, property shall not lose its character as new property as a result of a transfer from one member to another member during a consolidated return year if—

(1) The transfer occurs on or before January 4, 1973, or

(2) The transfer occurs after January 4, 1973, and the transfer is a deferred intercompany transaction as defined in § 1.1502-13(a)(2) or the basis of the property in the hands of the transferee is determined (in whole or in part) by reference to its basis in the hands of the transferor;

(h) No net operating loss deduction shall be taken into account;

(i) [Reserved]

(j) No capital gains or losses shall be taken into account;

(k) No gains and losses subject to section 1231 shall be taken into account;

(l) No deduction under section 170 with respect to charitable contributions shall be taken into account;

(m) No deduction under section 922 (relating to the deduction for Western Hemisphere trade corporations) shall be taken into account; and

(n) No deductions under section 243 (a)(1), 244 (a), 245, or 247 (relating to deductions with respect to dividends received and dividends paid) shall be taken into account.

(o) Basis shall be determined under §§ 1.1502-31 and 1.1502-32, and earnings and profits shall be determined under § 1.1502-33. The term "separate taxable income" shall include a case in which the determination under this section results in an excess of deductions over gross income.

§ 1.1502-13 (T.D. 6894, filed 9-7-66; amended by T.D. 7246, filed 12-29-72.) Intercompany transactions.

(a) *Definitions.* For purposes of §§ 1.1502-1 through 1.1502-80—

(1) *"Intercompany transaction".* (i) Except as provided in subdivision (ii) of this subparagraph, the term "intercompany transaction" means a transaction during a consolidated return year between corporations which are members of the same group immediately after such transaction. Thus, for example, an intercompany transaction would include a sale of property by one member of a group (hereinafter referred to as the "selling member") to another member of the same group ("purchasing member"), the performance of services by one member of a group ("selling member") for another member of the same group ("purchasing member"), or the payment of interest by one member of a group ("purchasing member") to another member of the same group ("selling member"), during a consolidated return year.

(ii) The term "intercompany transaction" does not include a distribution by one member of a group to another member of the same group with respect to the distributing member's stock, or a contribution to capital on which no gain is realized. Thus, for example, dividend distributions, redemptions, and liquidations are not intercompany transactions. The term also does not include sales and other dispositions of, and bad debts with respect to obligations of other members of the group. See § 1.1502-14, relating to amounts received with respect to stock, bonds, or other obligations of a member of the group.

(2) *"Deferred intercompany transaction".* The term "deferred intercompany transactions" means—

(i) The sale or exchange of property,

(ii) The performance of services in a case where the amount of the expenditure for such services is capitalized (for example, a builder's fee, architect's fee, or other similar cost which is included in the basis of property), or

(iii) Any other expenditure in a case where the amount of the expenditure is capitalized (for example, prepaid rent, or interest which is included in the basis of property),

in an intercompany transaction.

(b) *Treatment of intercompany transactions other than deferred intercompany transactions.*—(1) *General rule.* Gain or loss on intercompany transactions (other than deferred intercompany transactions) shall not be deferred or eliminated. Thus, for example, if, during a consolidated return year, a purchasing member makes an interest payment on an indebtedness to a selling member in an intercompany transaction, the purchasing member shall take the deduction for interest into account and the selling member shall take the interest income into account.

(2) *Special rule.* If, in an intercompany transaction (other than a deferred intercompany transaction), one member would otherwise properly take an item of income or a deduction into account for a consolidated return year earlier than the year (whether consolidated or separate) for which another member of the group can properly take into account the corresponding item of income or deduction, then both the item of income and the deduction shall be taken into account for the later year (whether consolidated or separate). On the other hand, if one member properly takes an item of income or a deduction into account for a separate return year earlier than the consolidated return year for which the other member can properly take into account the corresponding item of income or deduction, then such other member shall take the corresponding deduction or item of income into account for such later consolidated return year.

(c) *Deferral of gain or loss on deferred intercompany transaction*—(1) *General rule.* (i) To the extent gain or loss on a deferred intercompany transaction is recognized under the Code for a consolidated return year, such gain or loss shall be deferred by the selling member (hereinafter referred to as "deferred gain or loss").

(ii) The following rules apply with respect to the deferral of gain or loss on deferred intercompany transactions:

(a) The selling member may not report gain on the installment method under section 453;

(b) A selling member shall take into account the gain or loss on a deferred intercompany transaction in accordance with the provisions of paragraphs (d), (e), and (f) of this section, notwithstanding that such selling member, under its method of accounting, would not otherwise recognize such gain or loss until a later taxable year. Thus, for example, a selling member must take into account its gain on a deferred intercompany transaction for the first taxable year for which the purchasing member is allowed a deduction for depreciation with respect to the property involved, even though the selling member, under its method of accounting, would not otherwise recognize such gain until a later taxable year.

(iii) See paragraphs (d), (e), and (f) of this section, relating to the time and manner of restoring deferred gain or loss. See paragraph (a) of § 1.1502-31, relating to basis of property acquired in a deferred intercompany transaction.

(2) *Determination of amount of deferred gain or loss.* In determining the amount of deferred gain or loss, the cost of property, services, or any other expenditure shall include both direct costs and indirect costs which are properly includible in the cost of goods sold or cost of the services or other expenditure. See § 1.471-3 for costs properly includible in cost of goods sold.

(3) *Election not to defer.* A group may elect with the consent of the Commissioner not to defer gain or loss on any deferred intercompany transactions with respect to all property or any class or classes of property. Applications for such consent must be filed with the Commissioner of Internal Revenue, Washington, D.C. 20224, on or before the due date of the consolidated return (not including extensions of time) for the taxable year to which the election is to apply. An election under this subparagraph shall, unless revoked with consent of the Commissioner, apply to all members of the group for the consolidated return year for which made and all subsequent consolidated return years ending prior to the first year for which such group does not file a consolidated return.

(4) *Character and source of deferred gain or loss.* (1) Except as provided in subdivision (ii) of this subparagraph, the character and source of deferred gain or loss on a deferred intercompany transaction shall be determined at the time of the deferred intercompany transaction as if such transaction had not occurred during a consolidated return year.

(ii) Deferred gain or loss taken into account by the selling member under paragraph (d)(1) of this section, or (as a result of abandonment) under paragraph (f) of this section, shall be treated as ordinary income or loss.

(5) *Accounting for deferred gain or loss.* The amount of deferred gain or loss shall be reflected on permanent records (including work papers). From such permanent records the group must be able to identify the character and source of the deferred gain or loss to the selling member, and must be able to apply the restoration rules of paragraphs (d), (e), and (f) of this section.

(6) *Inheritance of deferred gain or loss.* If the assets of a selling member are acquired by one or more other members in an acquisition to which section 391(a) applies, the member acquiring the greatest portion of the assets (measured by fair market value) of the selling member shall be subject to the provisions of paragraphs (d), (e), and (f) of this section with respect to the entire remaining balance of the deferred gain or loss. If two or more members acquire the same portion (which is greater than that acquired by any other members), the common parent shall select which such member shall be subject to the provisions of paragraphs (d), (e), and (f) of this section. For purposes of this section, a member which inherits the balance of the deferred gain or loss under this subparagraph shall be treated as the selling member.

(d) *Restoration of deferred gain or loss for property subject to depreciation, amortization, or depletion.*—(1) *General rule.* (i) If property (including a capitalized expenditure for services, or any other capitalized expenditure) acquired in a deferred intercompany transaction is, in the hands of any member of the group, subject to depreciation, amortization, or depletion, then, for each taxable year (whether consolidated or separate) for which a depreciation, amortization, or depletion deduction is allowed to any member of the group with respect to such property, a portion (as determined under subdivision (ii) of this subparagraph) of the deferred gain or loss attributable to such property shall be taken into account by the selling member.

(ii) The portion of the deferred gain or loss attributable to any property which shall be taken into account by the selling member shall be an amount equal to—

(a) The amount of gain or loss deferred by the selling member at the time the deferred intercompany transaction (and if a member has transferred the property to another member of the group, the remaining balance at the time of such transfer) multiplied by

(b) A fraction, the numerator of which is the amount of the depreciation, amortization, or depletion deduction with respect to such property allowed to any member of the group for the year (whether consolidated or separate), and the denominator of which is depreciable basis (i.e., basis reduced by salvage value required to be taken into account, if any) of such property in the hands of such member immediately after such property was transferred to such member.

(2) *Multiple asset accounts.* In the case of property contained in a multiple asset account (or in single asset accounts for which an average rate is used), for purposes of subparagraph (1)(ii)(b) of this paragraph the depreciation deduction allowed for a particular taxable year shall be determined by reference to the rate and method of depreciation applied to such multiple asset account (or average rate and method of depreciation applied to such single asset accounts).

Thus, if property with an estimated useful life of 3 years is placed in a multiple asset account which is depreciated on the straight-line method at a rate of 20 percent, the depreciation deduction allowed for each taxable year shall be assumed to be 20 percent of the basis of such property (reduced by the salvage value taken into account).

(3) *Reduction or deferred gain or loss.* The deferred gain or loss shall be reduced

Reg. § 1.1502-13(d)(3)

by the amount taken into account by the selling member under subparagraph (1) of this paragraph. If the deferred gain includes any ordinary income, the reduction shall first be applied against the ordinary income. Thus, for example, if the selling member has deferred gain of $100, of which $70 is capital gain and $30 is ordinary income, the first $30 taken into account by the selling member under subparagraph (1) of this paragraph shall be applied against the ordinary income, and any additional amounts so taken into account shall be applied against the capital gain.

(e) *Restoration of deferred gain or loss for installment obligations and sales*—(1) *Installment obligations*. If an installment obligation (within the meaning of section 453(d)) is transferred in a deferred intercompany transaction, then on each date on which the obligation is satisfied the selling member shall take into account an amount equal to the deferred gain or loss on such transfer, multiplied by a fraction, the numerator of which is the portion of such obligation satisfied on such date, and the denominator of which is the aggregate unpaid installments immediately after the deferred intercompany transaction.

(2) *Installment sales.* If—

(i) Property acquired in a deferred intercompany transaction is disposed of outside the group, and

(ii) The purchasing member-vendor reports its income on the installment method under section 453, then on each date on which the purchasing member-vendor receives an installment payment the selling member shall take into account an amount equal to the deferred gain or loss attributable to such property (after taking into account any prior reductions under paragraph (d)(3) of this section) multiplied by a fraction, the numerator of which is the installment payment received and the denominator of which is the total contract price. If the deferred gain includes any ordinary income, the ordinary income shall be taken into account first.

(3) *Reduction of deferred gain or loss.* The deferred gain or loss shall be reduced by the amount taken into account by the selling member under subparagraph (1) or (2) of this paragraph. If the deferred gain includes any ordinary income, the reduction shall first be applied against the ordinary income.

(f) *Restoration of deferred gain or loss on dispositions, etc.*—(1) *General rule.* The remaining balance (after taking into account any prior reductions under paragraphs (d)(3) and (e)(3) of this section) of the deferred gain or loss attributable to property, services, or other expenditure shall be taken into account by the selling member as of the earliest of the following dates:

(i) The date on which such property is disposed of outside the group (including abandoned) other than in a transaction described in paragraph (e)(2) of this section (but not including a normal retirement, as defined in paragraph (b) of § 1.167(a)-8, from an average-life multiple asset account or from a single asset account for which an average rate is used). If such property is of a kind which would properly be included in the inventory of a member if on hand at the close of its taxable year, such member shall determine whether or not such item of property has been disposed of outside the group by reference to its method of inventory identification (*e.g.*, first-in, first-out, last-in, first-out, or specific identification);

(ii) In the case of a transaction described in paragraph (e)(2) of this section, the date on which the installment debt is written off, satisfied, discharged, or disposed of outside the group or the property sold is repossessed (except as provided in section 1038), whichever occurs earliest;

(iii) Immediately preceding the time when either the selling member or the member which owns the property ceases to be a member of the group;

(iv) In the case of property which is stock in trade or other property of a kind which would be properly included in inventory of the member which owns the property if on hand at the close of such member's taxable year, or held primarily for sale to customers in the ordinary course of such member's trade or business, the first day of the first separate return year of the selling member or the member which owns the property;

(v) In the case of an obligation (other than an obligation of a member of the group), the date on which such obligation is satisfied or becomes worthless;

(vi) In the case of stock, the date on which such stock is redeemed (whether or not it is cancelled, retired, or held as treasury stock) or becomes worthless;

(vii) If consolidated returns are filed by the group for fewer than three consecutive taxable years immediately preceding a separate return year of the common parent, the first day of such separate return year; or

(viii) In the case of inventory, the date on which its value is written down market (if the lower-of-cost-or-marke method is used by the purchaser), but only to the extent of such writedown.

(2) *Exceptions.* (i) Subparagraph (1) of this paragraph shall not apply solely because of a termination of the group (hereinafter referred to as the "terminating group") resulting from—

(a) The acquisition by a nonmember corporation of (1) the assets of the common parent in a reorganization described in subparagraph (A), (C), or (D) (but only if the requirements of subparagraphs (A) and (B) of section 354(b)(1) are met) of section 368(a)(1), or (2) stock of the common parent, or

(b) The acquisition (in a transaction to which § 1.1502-75(d)(3) applies) by a member of (1) the assets of a nonmember corporation in a reorganization referred to in subdivision (a), or (2) stock of a nonmember corporation,

if all the members of the terminating group (other than such common parent if its assets are acquired) immediately before the acquisition are members immediately after the acquisition of another group (hereinafter referred to as the "succeeding group") which files a consolidated return for the first taxable year ending after the date of acquisition. The members of the succeeding group shall succeed to any deferred gain or loss of members of the ter-

Consolidated Returns (I.R.C.) 24,211

minating group and to the status of such members as selling or purchasing members. This subdivision shall not apply with respect to acquisitions occurring before August 25, 1971, except that in the case of an acquisition occurring after April 16, 1968, and before August 25, 1971, this subdivision shall apply if the terminating group and the succeeding group elect to apply § 1.1502-18(c)(4) (notwithstanding the last sentence thereof) with respect to such acquisition. The election shall be made in a joint statement filed by the terminating and succeeding groups on or before March 5, 1973, with the Internal Revenue Service Center or Centers with which the terminating and succeeding groups filed their consolidated returns for the taxable year which includes the date of the acquisition. Such election shall be irrevocable.

(ii) Subparagraph (1)(iii) of this paragraph shall not apply in a case where—

(a) The selling member or the member which owns the property, as the case may be, ceases to be a member of the group by reason of an acquisition to which section 381(a) applies, and the acquiring corporation is a member, or

(b) The group is terminated, and immediately after such termination the corporation which was the common parent (or a corporation which was a member of the affiliated group and has succeeded to and become the owner of substantially all of the assets of such former parent) owns the property involved and is the selling member or is treated as the selling member under paragraph (c)(6) of this section.

Paragraphs (d) and (e) of this section and this paragraph shall apply to such selling member. Thus, for example, subparagraph (1)(iii) of this paragraph does not apply in a case where corporation P, the common parent' of a group consisting of P and corporations S and T, sells an asset to S in a deferred intercompany transaction, and subsequently all of the assets of S are distributed to P in complete liquidation of S. Moreover, if, after the liquidation of S, P sold T, subparagraph (1)(iii) of this paragraph would not apply even though P ceased to be a member of the group.

(3) *Certain divestitures.* If, pursuant to a final judgment or a final order of a court or an agency of the Federal or a state government, any member or members are required to divest themselves of control of any other member and, as a result, any member ceases to be a member, the Commissioner may enter into a closing agreement under section 7121 with the group. Such closing agreement may provide that any deferred gain or loss which would otherwise be taken into account under subparagraph (1)(iii) of this paragraph shall instead be taken into account over an appropriate period of time related to the period of time within which the deferred income would have been taken into account had the divestiture not taken place, but not in excess of 10 years. Ordinarily, application for such closing agreement will not be granted where such divestiture is occasioned by the acquisition after August 31, 1966, of control of a corporation or of assets. In no event will any such application be granted unless the group establishes to the satisfaction of the Commissioner that the collection of the tax liability attributable to any deferred gain will not be jeopardized by the delay.

(g) *Holding period.* In determining the period for which a purchasing member has held property acquired in a deferred intercompany transaction, the period such property was held by the selling member shall not be included.

(h) *Examples.* This section may be illustrated by the following examples:

Example (1). (i) Corporations P and S file consolidated returns on a calendar year basis. On January 10, 1966, S sells land, which it has used in its trade or business, to P for $100,000. Immediately before the sale the basis of the land in S's hands is $60,000. P holds the land primarily for sale to customers in the ordinary course of its trade or business. On July 12, 1967, P sells the land to A, an individual.

(ii) The sale by S to P is a deferred intercompany transaction; S defers its $40,000 gain on the land ($100,000 less $60,000), which is gain from the sale of property described in section 1231. As of July 12, 1967, S takes the $40,000 deferred gain into account since on such date the property is disposed of outside the group. Such $40,000 gain is taken into account in determining the consolidated section 1231 net gain or loss for 1967 under § 1.1502-23.

Example (2). Corporations P and S file consolidated returns on a calendar year basis. On August 1, 1966, P transfers property with a fair market value of $100,000 and an adjusted basis in its hands of $85,000 to S in exchange for stock and $10,000 cash. Under section 351(b), only $10,000 of the $15,000 gain is recognized by P. The transfer is a deferred intercompany transaction; P defers the $10,000 gain recognized under section 351(b).

Example (3). Corporations P and S file consolidated returns on a calendar year basis and report income on the cash basis. On July 1, 1966, S pays P $1,000 interest on a loan made in 1961. The payment of interest is an intercompany transaction other than a deferred intercompany transaction; S does not defer or eliminate the $1,000 deduction for interest, and P does not defer or eliminate the $1,000 item of interest income. Thus, consolidated taxable income for 1966 reflects interest income of $1,000 and a corresponding deduction for interest of $1,000.

Example (4). (i) Corporations P, S, and T file consolidated returns on a calendar year basis. On January 1, 1966, S, which is in the business of manufacturing machinery, sells a machine to P for $1,000. The cost of the machine is $800. P uses the machine in its trade or business and depreciates it on the straight-line method over an estimated useful life of 10 years. Salvage value of $200 is taken into account. Thus, its annual depreciation deduction with respect to the machine is $80 ($800 ($1,000 less $200 salvage) divided by 10). On January 1, 1969, P sells the machine to A, an individual.

(ii) The sale by S to P is a deferred intercompany transaction; S defers its $200 gain on the machine ($1,000 less $800), which is characterized as ordinary income. For each of the 3 taxable years (1966, 1967, and 1968) prior to the sale to A, S takes into account $20 of its deferred gain, computed as follows:

Reg. § 1.1502-13(h)

$$\$200 \text{ deferred gain} \times \frac{\$80 \text{ depreciation deduction}}{\$800 \text{ basis to P subject to depreciation}}$$

Such $20 gain retains its character as ordinary income.

(iii) As of January 1, 1969, S takes the $140 remaining balance of the deferred gain ($200 less $60) into account since on such date the machine is disposed of outside the group. Such $140 gain retains its character as ordinary income.

Example (5). (i) The facts are the same as in example (4) except that beginning with 1968 P and S file separate returns.

(ii) Assuming that P, S, and T filed a consolidated return for 1965, the result is the same as in example (4). Thus, for each of the years 1966, 1967, and 1968 S takes into account $20 of its deferred gain and as of January 1, 1969, S takes the remaining $140 ($200 less $60) into account.

(iii) Assuming that P, S, and T filed separate returns for 1965, as of January 1, 1968 S takes the $160 remaining balance of the deferred gain ($200 less $40) into account since P filed a separate return for 1968 and the group had filed consolidated returns for only 2 consecutive years preceding 1968.

Example (6). (i) The facts are the same as in example (4) except that on January 1, 1969, P sells the machine to T for $660 in a transaction in which gain is recognized. T uses the machine in its trade or business and depreciates it on the straight-line method over an estimated useful life of 10 years. No salvage value is taken into account. Thus, T's annual depreciation deduction with respect to the machine is $66 ($660 divided by 10).

(ii) The sale by S to P is a deferred intercompany transaction; S defers its $200 gain on the machine ($1,000 less $800), which is characterized as ordinary income. For each of the 3 years (1966, 1967, and 1968) prior to the sale to T, S takes into account $20 of its deferred gain.

(iii) The sale by P to T is also a deferred intercompany transaction; P defers its $100 loss on the machine (adjusted basis of $760 ($1,000 less $240 total depreciation) less $660).

(iv) For 1969 S takes into account $14 of its deferred gain, computed as follows:

$$\$140 \text{ remaining balance of deferred gain} \times \frac{\$66 \text{ depreciation deduction}}{\$660 \text{ basis to T subject to depreciation}}$$

(v) For 1969 P takes into account $10 of its deferred loss, computed as follows:

$$\$100 \text{ deferred loss} \times \frac{\$66 \text{ depreciation deduction}}{\$660 \text{ basis to T subject to depreciation}}$$

Example (7). (i) Corporations P and S file consolidated returns on a calendar year basis. On May 2, 1966, S sells a machine with an adjusted basis of $50 to P for $100 in a transaction in which gain is recognized. S used the machine in its trade or business. For purposes of depreciation, P places the machine, which has an estimated useful life of 3 years, in an average life multiple asset account which is depreciated on the straight-line method at a rate of 20 percent. Under P's consistent depreciation practice it takes a full year's depreciation on all purchases made in the first half of its taxable year.

(ii) The sale by S to P is a deferred intercompany transaction; S defers its $50 gain on the machine ($100 less $50). For each of the taxable years 1966, 1967, 1968, 1969, and 1970 S takes into account $10 of its deferred gain, computed as follows:

$$\$50 \text{ deferred gain} \times \frac{\$20 \text{ depreciation deduction}}{\$100 \text{ basis to P subject to depreciation}}$$

Such $10 is characterized as gain from the sale or exchange of property which is neither a capital asset nor property described in section 1231, notwithstanding the character of the $50 gain determined at the time of the sale.

Example (8). The facts are the same as in example (7) and in addition during 1969 the machine is disposed of outside the group. Such disposal is treated as a normal retirement (as defined in paragraph (b) of § 1.167 (a)-8). The result is the same as in example (7). Thus, S takes into account $10 for each of the years 1966, 1967, 1968, 1969, and 1970 even though the property was disposed of in 1969.

Example (9). (i) The facts are the same as in example (7) except that the multiple asset account is depreciated over a 5-year average useful life on the double declining balance method.

(ii) For 1966 S takes into account $20 of its deferred gain, computed as follows:

$50 \text{ deferred gain} \times \dfrac{\$40 \ (\$100 \times 40\%) \text{ depreciation deduction}}{\$100 \text{ basis to P subject to depreciation}}$

For 1967 S takes into account $12 of its deferred gain, computed as follows:

$50 \text{ deferred gain} \times \dfrac{\$24 \ (\$60 \ (\$100 \text{ less } \$40) \times 40\%) \text{ depreciation deduction}}{\$100 \text{ basis to P subject to depreciation}}$

Example (10). (i) P Corporation and S Corporation, its wholly-owned subsidiary, file consolidated returns on a calendar year basis. On January 10, 1966, S sells land, with a basis of $60,000, to P for $100,000. As of the close of business on June 10, 1969, P sells 25 percent of the outstanding stock of S to A, an individual.

(ii) The sale by S to P is a deferred intercompany transaction; S defers its $40,000 gain on the land ($100,000 less $60,000). As of June 10, 1969, S takes the $40,000 gain into account for 1969 since it ceases to be a member of the group as of the close of business on such date.

Example (11). (i) Corporations P and S file consolidated returns on a calendar year basis. On January 15, 1966, P sells an obligation payable in installments, with a basis of $48 in its hands, to S for $60. At the time of the sale the debtor owes 3 annual installments of $20 payable each year on July 1. Such installments are paid timely.

(ii) The sale by P to S is a deferred intercompany transaction; P defers its $12 gain on the obligation ($60 less $48).

(iii) For each of the years 1966, 1967, and 1968 P takes into account $4 of its deferred gain, computed as follows:

$12 \text{ deferred gain} \times \dfrac{\$20 \text{ portion satisfied}}{\$60 \text{ aggregate unpaid portions}}$

Example (12). (i) Corporations P and S file consolidated returns on a calendar year basis. On January 2, 1966, S, a manufacturer, sells a machine to P, a distributor, for $2,000. The machine cost S $1,200. On February 1, 1966 P sells the machine to A, an individual, for $2,200 and, under section 453, reports its income thereon on the installment plan. A makes monthly payments of $110 starting with March 1966.

(ii) The sale by S to P is a deferred intercompany transaction; S defers its $800 gain ($2,000 less $1,200).

(iii) For 1966 S takes into account $400 of its deferred gain, computed as follows:

$800 \text{ deferred gain} \times \dfrac{\$1,100 \text{ installment payments received}}{\$2,200 \text{ total contract price}}$

Example (13). Corporations P and S file consolidated returns on a calendar year basis for 1966 and 1967. S reports income on the accrual method while P reports income on the cash method. On December 31, 1966, S would properly accrue interest of $1,000 which is payable to P. On February 1, 1967, S pays P the $1,000. Both the deduction and the item of income are taken into account for 1967, the later year. Thus, S takes the $1,000 interest deduction into account for 1967, which is the year P also takes the $1,000 item of interest income into account. Consolidated taxable income for 1967 reflects both interest income of $1,000 and a corresponding deduction for interest of $1,000.

Example (14). The facts are the same as in example (13) except that for 1967 S and P file separate returns. The result is the same as in example (13).

Example (15). (i) The facts are the same as in example (13) except that for 1966 P and S file separate returns.

(ii) For 1966 S takes into account the $1,000 deduction for interest; for 1967 P takes into account the $1,000 item of interest income.

Example (16). Corporations P and S file consolidated returns on a calendar year basis. On January 10, 1968, P sells an issue of its $100 par value bonds. S purchases a bond from P for $110. S does not elect under section 171 to amortize the $10 premium. P may not take the $10 premium into account as income until it redeems the bond since S cannot properly take a deduction for the $10 premium until the bond is redeemed.

Example (17). (i) Corporations P, S, and M file consolidated returns on a calendar year basis. On November 20, 1962, S sold land, with a basis of $60,000, to P for $100,000. Under paragraph (b) (1) of § 1.1502-31A the $40,000 gain was eliminated. Thus,

Reg. § 1.1502-13(h)

S did not take into account such $40,000 gain for 1962 and P's basis in the land is only $60,000. On February 10, 1966, P sells the land to A, an individual, for $104,000.

(ii) P takes the entire $44,000 gain ($104,000 less $60,000) on the land into account for 1966 since the deferral rules provided in paragraph (c) of this section, as well as the corresponding basis rules provided in paragraph (a) of § 1.1502-31, were not effective with respect to the sale of such land.

(iii) If, on February 10, 1966, P had sold the land to M for $104,000, P would defer its $44,000 gain on the land since the sale by P to M would be a deferred intercompany transaction.

Example (18). (i) Corporations P and S file separate returns on a calendar year basis for 1966 and file consolidated returns on a calendar year basis beginning with 1967. On January 2, 1966, S, a dealer in machinery, sells a machine to P for $2,000 and, under section 453, reports the income thereon on the installment plan. The machine cost S $1,200. P makes monthly payments of $100 starting with January 1966.

(ii) The sale by S to P is not an intercompany transaction since the sale did not occur during a consolidated return year. Therefore, S takes into account the gross profit on each of the 20 monthly payments under section 453.

(i) [Reserved]

(j) *Regulated public utilities.* Subject to the provisions of section 7121, the Commissioner may enter into a closing agreement which, notwithstanding the provisions of §§ 1.1502-13, 1.1502-31, and 1.1502-33, determines the consequences of deferred intercompany transactions or of any matters relating to or affected by such transactions, provided that—

(1) The purchasing members are domestic regulated public utilities as defined in section 7701 (a) (4) and (33),

(2) In the taxable year immediately preceding the first taxable year for which this section is effective there was in effect among the members an arrangement relating to intercompany transactions which had a significant effect upon regulated rates of the public utility members of the group, and the accounting of the public utility members under the arrangement was accepted or approved by a regulatory agency having jurisdiction over the accounts of such members, and

(3) The Commissioner is satisfied that the terms of such closing agreement will not for any taxable year result in a reduction of the tax liability of the group (including former members) or of the shareholders of any members (or former members).

A request for such an agreement must be made on or before November 15, 1966.

○➡ § 1.1502-14 (T.D. 6909 filed 12-29-66; amended by T.D. 7246, filed 12-29-72.) **Stock, bonds, and other obligations of members.**

(a) *Intercompany distributions with respect to stock*—(1) *Dividends.* A dividend distributed by one member to another member during a consolidated return year shall be eliminated. For purposes of this paragraph, the term "dividend" means a distribution which is described in section 301 (c) (1) other than a distribution described in section 243 (c) (1).

(2) *Nondividend distributions.* No gain shall be recognized to the distributee on a distribution with respect to stock, from one member to another member during a consolidated return year, which is described in section 301 (c) (2) or (3). Such distribution shall be applied against and reduce the adjusted basis (determined after taking into account any adjustment under § 1.1502-32) of such stock in the distributing corporation held by the distributee, and to the extent such distribution exceeds the adjusted basis, the excess shall be (or shall be added to) the excess loss account for such stock in the distributing corporation held by the distributee. (See §§ 1.1502-19 and 1.1502-32.)

(3) *Amount distributed.* For purposes of this paragraph, the amount of any distribution of property other than money shall be determined under section 301 (b) (1) (B) (ii).

(4) *Example.* This paragraph may be illustrated by the following example:

Example. Assume that corporation P and it wholly owned subsidiary, corporation S, are members of a group filing consolidated returns on a calendar year basis. On December 31, 1966, S distributed to P with respect to its stock $5,000 cash and land with an adjusted basis to S of $6,000 and a fair market value of $5,000. No part of the distribution constituted a dividend. On December 31, 1966, P had an adjusted basis of $3,000 in the stock of S. The amount distributed is $11,000. $3,000 of that amount is applied against and reduces the adjusted basis of the stock to zero, and the remaining $8,000 is treated as P's excess loss account for its stock in S. No gain is recognized by P. Pursuant to § 1.1502-31 (b) (1) P's basis in the land is $6,000.

(b) *Intercompany distributions in cancellation or redemption of all or part of the stock of the distributing corporation*—(1) *General rule.* Except as provided in subparagraph (2) of this paragraph and in § 1.1502-19, no gain or loss shall be recognized on the receipt, during a consolidated return year, by one member of property (including cash) distributed in cancellation or redemption of all or a part of the stock of another member. For purposes of this paragraph, a distribution is in cancellation or redemption of all or a part of stock only if—

(i) It is in complete liquidation of the distributing corporation,

(ii) It is in partial liquidation of the distributing corporation within the meaning of section 346, and such corporation remains a member of the group immediately after the distribution, or

(iii) It is a distribution in redemption of the stock of the distributing corporation to which section 302 (a) applies, and such corporation remains a member of the group immediately after the distribution.

(2) *Gain or loss recognized.* In the case of a distribution (other than a distribution to which section 332 applies) described in subparagraph (1) of this paragraph, the following rules shall apply—

(i) Gain shall be recognized to the extent that any cash distributed exceeds the sum of—

(*a*) The adjusted basis (determined

after taking into account any adjustment under § 1.1502-32) of the stock of the distributing corporation held by the distributee which was cancelled or redeemed, plus

(b) Any liabilities assumed by the distributee (or to which the property received is subject).

(ii) If the property distributed consists only of cash, loss shall be recognized to the extent that the sum of—

(a) The adjusted basis (determined after taking into account any adjustment under § 1.1502-32) of the stock of the distributing corporation held by the distributee which was cancelled or redeemed, plus

(b) Any liabilities assumed by the distributee,

exceeds the amount of cash distributed.

(iii) If the distribution is not in complete liquidation of the distributing corporation, any gain or loss recognized shall be deferred.

(3) *Restoration of gain or loss.* Gain or loss deferred under subparagraph (2) of this paragraph shall be taken into account immediately before the occurrence of the earliest of the following events:

(i) When the distributee corporation ceases to be a member, or

(ii) When the stock of the distributing corporation (or any successor member in an acquisition to which section 381(a) applies) is considered to be disposed of by any member under § 1.1502-19(b)(2) (other than subdivision (ii) thereof.

(c) *Treatment of distributing corporation*—(1) *Deferral in other than complete liquidations.* Except as provided in subparagraph (2) of this paragraph, to the extent gain or loss is recognized to the distributing corporation on a distribution described in paragraph (a) or (b) of this section (including any amount which is treated as gain under section 311, 336, 341 (f)(2), 453(d), 1245(a)(1), or 1250(a)(1)), such gain or loss shall be deferred by the distributing corporation. Such deferred gain or loss shall be taken into account by the distributing corporation at the time and in the manner specified in paragraphs (d), (e), and (f) of § 1.1502-13, as if such distributing corporation were a "selling member" and the distributee were a "purchasing member".

(2) *Complete liquidations.* Gain or loss shall be taken into account by the distributing corporation on a complete liquidation, in the same manner and to the same extent as if separate returns were filed.

(d) *Gains and losses on obligations of members*—(1) *Deferral of gain or loss.* To the extent gain or loss is recognized under the Code to a member during a consolidated return year because of a sale or other disposition (other than a redemption or cancellation) of an obligation of another member (referred to in this paragraph as the "debtor member"), whether or not such obligation is evidenced by a security, such gain or loss shall be deferred. For purposes of this paragraph, a deduction because of the worthlessness of, or a deduction for a reasonable addition to a reserve for bad debts with respect to, an obligation described in this subparagraph shall be considered a loss from the disposition of such obligation.

(2) *Restoration of gain or loss where obligation leaves group.* If an obligation described in subparagraph (1) of this paragraph is sold or disposed of to a nonmember (or if the member holding the obligation becomes a nonmember), each member with deferred gain or loss with respect to such obligation under subparagraph (1) of this paragraph shall, except as provided in subparagraph (3) of this paragraph, take such gain or loss into account ratably over the remaining term of the obligation.

(3) *Restoration of gain or loss on other events.* Each member's gain or loss deferred with respect to an obligation under subparagraph (1) which has not been taken into account under subparagraph (2) of this paragraph shall be taken into account immediately before the occurrence of the earliest of the following events:

(i) When such member ceases to be a member,

(ii) When the stock of the debtor member (or any successor in an acquisition to which section 381(a) applies) is considered to be disposed of by any member under § 1.1502-19(b)(2) (other than subdivision (ii) thereof), or

(iii) When the obligation is redeemed or cancelled.

(4) *Exception for obligations acquired in tax-free exchanges.* (i) If—

(a) A member received an obligation of another member in exchange for property,

(b) The basis of the obligation was determined in whole or in part by reference to the basis of the property exchanged, and

(c) The obligation has never been held by a nonmember,

then any gain or loss of any member on redemption or cancellation of such obligation shall be deferred, and subparagraph (3) of this paragraph shall not apply.

(ii) Gain or loss deferred by a member under subdivision (i) of this subparagraph, and under subparagraph (1) of this paragraph with respect to an obligation to which this subparagraph applies, shall be taken into account immediately before the occurrence of the earliest of the following events:

(a) When such member ceases to be a member, or

(b) When the stock of the debtor member is considered to be disposed of by any member under § 1.1502-19(b)(2) (other than subdivision (ii) thereof), determined without regard to § 1.1502-19(d) and (e).

(iii) This subparagraph may be illustrated by the following example.

Example. Corporation P forms a subsidiary, S, in a transaction to which section 351 applies and receives as a result of such transaction, in addition to stock, a security with a face value of $100 and a basis of $50. If the security is redeemed for $100, the $50 gain on redemption is deferred and is not taken into account until P ceases to be a member or the stock of S is treated as disposed of under this subparagraph.

(5) *Premium and discount.* For treatment of premium and discount with respect to obligations described in this subparagraph, see § 1.1502-13(b) and example 16 of § 1.1502-13(h).

(e) *Character and inheritance of de-*

Reg. § 1.1502-14(e)

24,216 (I.R.C.) Reg. § 1.1502-14(e)

ferred items.—(1) *Character.* The character of gain or loss deferred under paragraph (b)(2), (d)(1), or (d)(4) of this section shall be determined at the time of the transaction as if such transaction had not occurred during a consolidated return year.

(2) *Inheritance.* Paragraphs (b)(3)(i), (d)(3)(i), and (d)(4)(ii)(a) shall not apply if a member with deferred gain or loss ceases to be a member because its assets are acquired by one or more members in an acquisition to which section 381(a) applies. The member acquiring the greatest portion of the assets (measured by fair market value) of such member shall be subject to the appropriate restoration provisions of paragraphs (b) and (d) of this section.

(f) *Acquisition of group.* Paragraphs (b)(3), (c), and (d)(2), (3) and (4)(ii) of this section shall not apply solely because of a termination of the group (hereinafter referred to as the "terminating group") resulting from—

(1) The acquisition by a nonmember corporation of (i) the assets of the common parent in a reorganization described in subparagraph (A), (C), or (D) (but only if the requirements of subparagraphs (A) and (B) of section 354(b)(1) are met) of section 368(a)(1), or (ii) stock of the common parent, or

(2) The acquisition (in a transaction to which § 1.1502-75(d)(3) applies) by a member of (i) the assets of a nonmember corporation in a reorganization referred to in subparagraph (1) of this paragraph, or (ii) stock of a nonmember corporation, if all the members of the terminating group (other than such common parent if its assets are acquired) immediately before the acquisition are members immediately after the acquisition of another group (hereinafter referred to as the "succeeding group") which files a consolidated return for the first taxable year ending after the date of acquisition. The members of the succeeding group shall succeed to any deferred gain or loss of members of the terminating group and to the status of such members as distributing or distributee corporations. This paragraph shall not apply with respect to acquisitions occurring before August 25, 1971.

○→ § 1.1502-15 (T.D. 6894, filed 9-7-66; amended by T.D. 6909, filed 12-29-66 and T.D. 7246, filed 12-29-72.) **Limitations on certain deductions.**

(a) *Limitation on built-in deductions*— (1) *General rule.* Built-in deductions (as defined in subparagraph (2) of this paragraph for a taxable year shall be subject to the limitation of § 1.1502-21 (c) (determined without regard to such deductions and without regard to net operating loss carryovers to such year) and the limitation of § 1.1502-22(c) (determined without regard to such deductions and without regard to capital loss carryovers to such year). If as a result of applying such limitations, built-in deductions are not allowable in such consolidated return year, such deductions shall be treated as a net operating loss or net capital loss (as the case may be) sustained in such year and shall be carried to those taxable years (consolidated or separate) to which a consolidated net operating loss or a consolidated net capital loss could be carried under §§ 1.1502-21, 1.1502-22, and 1.1502-79, except that such losses shall be treated as losses subject to the limitations contained in § 1.1502-21(c) or § 1.1502-22(c) (as the case may be). Thus, for example, if member X sells a capital asset during a consolidated return year at a $1,000 loss and such loss is treated as a built-in deduction, then such loss shall be subject to the limitation contained in § 1.1502-22(c), which, in general, would allow such loss to be offset only against X's own net capital gain. Assuming X had no net capital gain reflected in such year (after taking into account its capital losses, other than capital loss carryovers and the built-in deduction), such $1,000 loss shall be treated as a net capital loss and shall be carried over for 5 years under § 1.1502-22, subject to the limitation contained in § 1.1502-22(c) for consolidated return years.

(2) *Built-in deductions.* (i) For purposes of this paragraph, the term "built-in deductions" for a consolidated return year means those deductions or losses of a corporation which are recognized in such year, or which are recognized in a separate return year and carried over in the form of a net operating or net capital loss to such year, but which are economically accrued in a separate return limitation year (as defined in § 1.1502-1(f)). Such term does not include deductions or losses incurred in rehabilitating such corporation. Thus, for example, assume P is the common parent of a group filing consolidated returns on the basis of a calendar year and that P purchases all of the stock of S on December 31, 1966. Assume further that on December 31, 1966, S owns a capital asset with an adjusted basis of $100 and a fair market value of $50. If the group files a consolidated return for 1967, and S sells the asset for $30, $50 of the $70 loss is treated as a built-in deduction, since it was economically accrued in a separate return limitation year. If S sells the asset for $80 instead of $30, the $20 loss is treated as a built-in deduction. On the other hand, if such asset is a depreciable asset and is not sold by S, depreciation deductions attributable to the $50 difference between basis and fair market value are treated as built-in deductions.

(ii) In determining, for purposes of subdivision (i) of this subparagraph, whether a deduction or loss with respect to any asset is economically accrued in a separate return limitation year, the term "predecessor" as used in § 1.1502-1(f)(1) shall include any transferor of such asset if the basis of the asset in the hands of the transferee is determined (in whole or in part) by reference to its basis in the hands of such transferor.

(3) *Transitional rule.* If the assets which produced the built-in deductions were acquired (either directly or by acquiring a new member) by the group on or before January 4, 1973, and the separate return limitation year in which such deductions were economically accrued ended before such date, then at the option of the taxpayer, the provisions of this paragraph before amendment by T.D. 7246 shall apply, and, in addition, if such assets were acquired on or before April 17, 1968, and the separate return limitation year in which the built-in deductions were economically accrued ended on or before such date, then at the option of the taxpayer,

the provisions of § 1.1502-31A(b)(9) shall apply in lieu of this paragraph.

(4) *Exceptions.* (i) Subparagraph (1), (2), and (3) of this paragraph shall not limit built-in deductions in a taxable year with respect to assets acquired (either directly or by acquiring a new member) by the group if—

(a) The group acquired the assets more than 10 years before the first day of such taxable year, or

(b) Immmediately before the group acquired the assets, the aggregate of the adjusted basis of all assets (other than cash, marketable securities, and goodwill) acquired from the transferor or owned by the new member did not exceed the fair market value of all such assets by more than 15 percent.

(ii) For purposes of subdivision (i)(b) of this subparagraph, a security is not a marketable security if immediately before the group acquired the assets—

(a) The fair market value of the security is less than 95 percent of its adjusted basis, or

(b) The transferor or new member had held the security for at least 24 months, or

(c) The security is stock in a corporation at least 50 percent of the fair market value of the outstanding stock of which is owned by the transferor or new member.

(b) *Other limitation.* No loss shall be allowed upon the sale or other disposition of stock, bonds, or other obligations of a member or former member to the extent that such loss is attributable to a distribution made in an affiliated year beginning before January 1, 1966 out of earnings and profits accumulated before the distributing corporation became a member.

○— § 1.1502-16 (T.D. 6894, filed 9-7-66; amended by T.D. 7192, filed 6-29-72.) **Mine exploration expenditures.**

(a) *Section 617*—(1) *In general.* If the aggregate amount of the expenditures to which section 617(a) applies, paid or incurred with respect to mines or deposits located outside the United States (as defined in section 638 and the regulations thereunder), does not exceed—

(i) $100,000 minus

(ii) all amounts deducted or deferred during the taxable year and all preceding taxable years under section 617 or section 615 of the Internal Revenue Code of 1954 and section 23(ff) of the Internal Revenue Code of 1939 by corporations which are members of the group during the taxable year (and individuals or corporations which have transferred any mineral property to any such member within the meaning of section 617(g)(2)(B)) for taxable years ending after December 31, 1950 and prior to the taxable year, then the deduction under section 617 with respect to such foreign expenditures and paragraph (c) of § 1.1502-12 for each member shall be no greater than an allocable portion of such amount hereinafter referred to as the "consolidated foreign exploration limitation." Such allocable portion shall be determined under subparagraph (2) of this paragraph. If the amount of such expenditures exceeds the consolidated foreign exploration limitation, no deduction shall be allowed with respect to such excess.

(2) *Allocable portion of limitation.* A member's allocable portion of the consolidated foreign exploration limitation for a consolidated return year shall be—

(i) The amount allocated by the common parent pursuant to an allocation plan adopted by the consolidated group, but in no event shall a member be allocated more than the amount it could have deducted had it filed a separate return. Such allocation plan must include a statement which also contains the total foreign exploration expenditures of each member which could have been deducted under section 617 if the member had filed a separate return. Such plan must be attached to a consolidated return filed on or before the due date of such return (including extensions of time), and may not be changed after such date, or

(ii) If no plan is filed in accordance with subdivision (i) of this subparagraph, then the portion of the consolidated foreign exploration limitation allocable to each member incurring such expenditures is an amount equal to such limitation multiplied by a fraction, the numerator of which is the amount of foreign exploration expenditures which could have been deducted under section 617 by such member had it filed a separate return and the denominator of which is the aggregate of such amounts for all members of the group.

(b) *Section 615*—(1) *In general.* If the aggregate amount of the expenditures, to which section 615(a) applies, which are paid or incurred by the members of the group during any consolidated return year exceeds the lesser of—

(i) $100,000, or

(ii) $400,000 minus all such expenditures deducted (or deferred) by corporations which are members of the group during the taxable year (and individuals or corporations which have transferred any mineral property to any such member within the meaning of section 615(c)(2)(B)) for taxable years ending after December 31, 1950, and prior to the taxable year, then the deduction (or amount deferrable) under section 615 and paragraph (c) of § 1.1502-12 for each member shall be no greater than an allocable portion of such lesser amount, hereinafter referred to as the "consolidated exploration limitation". Such allocable portion shall be determined under subparagraph (2) of this paragraph.

(2) *Allocable portion of limitation.* A member's allocable portion of the consolidated exploration limitation for a consolidated return year shall be—

(i) The amount allocated by the common parent pursuant to an allocation plan adopted by the consolidated group, but in no event shall a member be allocated more than the amount it could have deducted (or deferred) had it filed a separate return. Such allocation plan must include a statement which also contains the total exploration expenditures of each member for the taxable year, and the expenditures of each member which could have been deducted (or deferred) under section 615 if the member had filed a separate return. Such plan must be attached to a consolidated return filed on or before the due date of such return (including extensions of time), and may not be changed after such date, or

(ii) If no plan is filed in accordance with subdivision (i) of this subparagraph,

Reg. § 1.1502-16(b)(2)

24,218 (I.R.C.) Reg. § 1.1502-16(b)(2) 10-3-77

then the portion of the consolidated exploration limitation allocable to each member incurring such expenditures is an amount equal to such limitation multiplied by a fraction, the numerator of which is the amount which could have been deducted (or deferred) under section 615 by such member had it filed a separate return and the denominator of which is the aggregate of such amounts for all members of the group.

(c) *Examples.* The provisions of this section may be illustrated by the following examples:

Example (1). Corporation X and its wholly-owned subsidiaries, corporations Y and Z, file a consolidated return for the calendar year 1971. None of the corporations have incurred exploration expenditures described in section 617 in previous years. During 1971, X incurred foreign exploration expenditures of $30,000, Y of $20,000 and Z of $40,000. The amount of foreign exploration expenditures deductible under section 617 for purposes of computing separate taxable income under § 1.1502-12 will be the amount actually expended by each corporation.

Example (2). Assume the same facts as in example (1) except that prior to 1971, X, Y, and Z had deducted (or deferred) under section 615 and 617 a total of $300,000 of exploration expenditures. During 1971, with respect to deposits located outside the United States X incurred exploration expenditures of $25,000, Y of $75,000 and Z of $125,000. The consolidated exploration limitation under paragraph (a) of this section with respect to the foreign deposits (there is no limitation with respect to the domestic expenditures) is $100,000. X may allocate the $100,000 in any manner among the three members, except that X may not be allocated more than $25,000 nor Y more than $75,000, the amount actually expended by X and Y and which they could have deducted had they each filed a separate return. If the allocation is not made in accordance with paragraph (a)(2)(i) of this section, the $100,000 limitation will be allocated under paragraph (a)(2)(ii) of this section as follows:

Corporation	Expenditure	Fraction	Limitation	Allocable Portion
X	$ 25,000	$\frac{25,000}{200,000}$	× $100,000	= $12,500
Y	$ 75,000	$\frac{75,000}{200,000}$	× $100,000	= $37,500
Z	$125,000	$\frac{100,000}{200,000}$	× $100,000	= $50,000

The denominator of $200,000 was calculated as follows:
X = $ 25,000
Y = $ 75,000
Z = $100,000 (maximum amount allowed if filed separately)
Total $200,000

Example (3). Assume the same facts as in example (2) and that on January 1, 1971, X acquired all of the stock of corporation T which prior to its taxable year beginning January 1, 1971, had previously deducted (or deferred) $310,000 of exploration expenditures. Assume further that in 1971 X incurred $25,000 of foreign exploration expenditures, Y $50,000, T $50,000 and Z none. A consolidated return is filed for 1971. None of the expenditures may be deducted under section 617 since the consolidated exploration limitation is zero. The limitation is zero since the aggregate amount of previously deducted (or deferred) exploration expenditures by the members of the group exceeds $400,000. (The total of such expenditures is $410,000, of which $310,000 is attributable to T and, assuming the allocation of the limitation in example (2) is made under paragraph (a)(2)(ii) of this section. $12,500 is attributable to X, $37,500 to Y, and $50,000 to Z.)

Example (4). Assume the same facts as in example (3) except that on December 31, 1971, X sold all of the stock in Z to an unrelated party. The consolidated exploration limitation for 1972 will be $40,000, computed by subtracting from $400,000 the aggregate amount of previously deducted (or deferred) exploration expenditures incurred by the members of the group prior to 1972. (The total of such expenditures is $360,000, of which $12,500 is attributable to X, $37,500 to Y and $310,000 to T.) Amounts previously deducted (or deferred) by Z are not taken into account since it was not a member of the group at any time during 1972. Amounts previously deducted (or deferred) by Z shall be taken into account by it for subsequent separate return years.

○━▶ § 1.1502-17 (T.D. 6894, filed 9-7-66.) **Methods of accounting.**

(a) *General rule.* The method of accounting to be used by each member of the group shall be determined in accordance with the provisions of section 446 as if such member filed a separate return. For treatment of depreciable property after a transfer within the group, see paragraph (g) of § 1.1502-12.

(b) *Adjustments required where method of accounting changed.* In any case in which a member of a group changes its method of accounting for a consolidated return year, the provisions of section 481(a) shall be applicable. If the requirements of section 481(b) are met because the adjustments under section 481(a) are substantial, the increase in tax for any prior year shall be computed upon the basis of a consolidated return or a separate return, whichever was filed for such prior year.

(c) *Example.* The provisions of this section may be illustrated by the following example:

Example. X and its wholly owned subsidiary Y filed separate returns for their calendar years ending December 31, 1965.

During calendar year 1965, X employed an accrual method of accounting, established a reserve for bad debts, and elected under section 171 to amortize bond premiums with respect to its fully taxable bonds. During calendar year 1965, Y employed the cash receipts and disbursements method, used the specific charge-off method with respect to its bad debts, and did not elect to amortize bond premiums under section 171 with respect to its bonds. X and Y led a consolidated return for 1966. For 1966 X and Y must continue to compute income under their respective methods of accounting (unless a change in method under section 446 is made).

§ 1.1502-18 (T.D. 6894, filed 9-7-66; amended by T.D. 7246, filed 12-29-72.) **Inventory adjustments.**

(a) *Definition of intercompany profit amount.* For purposes of this section, the term "intercompany profit amount" for a taxable year means an amount equal to the profits of a corporation (other than those profits which such corporation has elected not to defer pursuant to § 1.1502-13(c)(3) or which have been taken into account pursuant to § 1.1502-13(f)(1)(viii)) arising in transactions with other members of the group with respect to goods which are, at the close of such corporation's taxable year, included in the inventories of any member of the group. See § 1.1502-13(c)(2) with respect to the determination of profits. See the last sentence of § 1.1502-13(f)(1)(i) for rules for determining which goods are considered to be disposed of outside the group and therefore not included in inventories of members.

(b) *Addition of initial inventory amount to taxable income.* If a corporation—

(1) Is a member of a group filing a consolidated return for the taxable year,
(2) Was a member of such group for its immediately preceding taxable year, and
(3) Filed a separate return for such preceding year,

then the intercompany profit amount of such corporation for such separate return year (hereinafter referred to as the "initial inventory amount") shall be added to the income of such corporation for the consolidated return year (or years) in which the goods to which the initial inventory amount is attributable are disposed of outside the group or such corporation becomes a nonmember. Such amount shall be treated as gain from the sale or exchange of property which is neither a capital asset nor property described in section 1231.

(c) *Recovery of initial inventory amount*—(1) *Unrecovered inventory amount.* The term "unrecovered inventory amount" for any consolidated return year means the lesser of—

(i) The intercompany profit amount for such year, or
(ii) The initial inventory amount.

However, if a corporation ceases to be a member of the group during a consolidated return year, its unrecovered inventory amount for such year shall be considered to be zero.

(2) *Recovery during consolidated return years.* (i) To the extent that the unrecovered inventory amount of a corporation for a consolidated return year is less than such amount for its immediately preceding year, such decrease shall be treated for such year by such corporation as a loss from the sale or exchange of property which is neither a capital asset nor property described in section 1231.

(ii) To the extent that the unrecovered inventory amount for a consolidated return year exceeds such amount for the preceding year, such increase shall be treated as gain from the sale or exchange of property which is neither a capital asset nor property described in section 1231.

(3) *Recovery during first separate return year.* For the first separate return year of a member following a consolidated return year, the unrecovered inventory amount for such consolidated return year (minus any part of the initial inventory amount which has not been added to income pursuant to paragraph (b) of this section) shall be treated as a loss from the sale or exchange of property which is neither a capital asset nor property described in section 1231.

(4) *Acquisition of group.* For purposes of this section, a member of a group shall not become a nonmember or be considered as filing a separate return solely because of a termination of the group (hereinafter referred to as the "terminating group") resulting from—

(i) The acquisition by a nonmember corporation of (a) the assets of the common parent in a reorganization described in subparagraph (A), (C), or (D) (but only if the requirements of subparagraphs (A) and (B) of section 354(b)(1) are met) of section 368(a)(1), or (b) stock of the common parent, or

(ii) The acquisition (in a transaction to which § 1.1502-75(d)(3) applies) by a member of (a) the assets of a nonmember corporation in a reorganization referred to in subdivision (i) of this subparagraph, or (b) stock of a nonmember corporation,

if all the members of the terminating group (other than such common parent if its assets are acquired) immediately before the acquisition are member immediately after the acquisition of another group (hereinafter referred to as the "succeeding group") which files a consolidated return for the first taxable year ending after the date of acquisition. The members of the succeeding group shall succeed to any initial inventory amount to any unrecovered inventory amount of members of the terminating group. This subparagraph shall not apply with respect to acquisitions occurring before August 25, 1971.

(d) *Examples.* The provisions of paragraphs (a), (b), and (c) of this section may be illustrated by the following examples:

Example (1). Corporations P, S, and T report income on the basis of a calendar year. Such corporations file separate returns for 1965. P manufactures widgets which it sells to both S and T, who act as distributors. The inventories of S and T at the close of 1965 are comprised of widgets which they purchased from P and with respect to which P derived profits of $5,000 and $8,000, respectively. P, S, and T file a consolidated return for 1966. During 1966, P sells widgets to S and T with respect to which it derives profits of $7,000 and $10,000, respectively. The inventories of S and T as of December 31, 1966, are

Reg. § 1.1502-18(d)

comprised of widgets on which P derived net profits of $4,000 and $8,000, respectively. P's initial inventory amount is $13,000, P's intercompany profit amount for 1965 (such $13,000 amount is the profits of P with respect to goods sold to S and T and included in their inventories at the close of 1965). Assuming that S and T identify their goods on a first-in, first-out basis, the entire opening inventory amount of $13,000 is added to P's income for 1966 as gain from the sale or exchange of property which is neither a capital asset nor property described in section 1231, since the goods to which the initial inventory amount is attributable were disposed of in 1966 outside the group. However, since P's unrecovered inventory amount for 1966, $12,000 (the intercompany profit amount for the year, which is less than the initial inventory amount), is less than the unrecovered inventory amount for 1965, $13,000, this decrease of $1,000 is treated by P for 1966 as a loss from the sale or exchange of property which is neither a capital asset nor property described in section 1231.

Example (2). Assume the same facts as in example (1) and that at the close of 1967, a consolidated return year, the inventories of S and T are comprised of widgets on which P derived profits of $5,000 and $3,000, respectively. Since P's unrecovered inventory amount for 1967, $8,000, is less than $12,000, the unrecovered inventory amount for 1966, this decrease of $4,000 is treated by P for 1967 as a loss from the sale or exchange of property which is neither a capital asset nor property described in section 1231.

Example (3). Assume the same facts as in examples (1) and (2) and that in 1968, a consolidated return year, P's intercompany profit amount is $11,000. P will report $3,000 (the excess of $11,000, P's unrecovered inventory amount for 1968, over $8,000, P's unrecovered inventory amount for 1967) for 1968 as a gain from the sale or exchange of property which is neither a capital asset nor property described in section 1231.

Example (4). Assume the same facts as in examples (1), (2), and (3) and that in 1969 P, S, and T file separate returns. P will report $11,000 (its unrecovered inventory amount for 1968, $11,000, minus the portion of the initial inventory amount which has not been added to income during 1966, 1967, and 1968, zero) as a loss from the sale or exchange of property which is neither a capital asset nor property described in section 1231.

Example (5). Corporations P and S file a consolidated return for the first time for the calendar year 1966. P manufactures machines and sells them to S, which sells them to users throughout the country. At the close of 1965, S has on hand 20 machines which it purchased from P and with respect to which P derived profits of $3,500. During 1966, P sells 6 machines to S on which it derives profits of $1,300, and S sells 5 machines which it had on hand at the beginning of the year (S specifically identifies the machines which it sells) and on which P had derived profits of $900. P's initial inventory amount is $3,500, of which $900 is added to P's income in 1966 as gain from the sale or exchange of property which is neither a capital asset nor property described in section 1231, since such $900 amount is attributable to goods disposed of in 1966 outside the group, which goods were included in S's inventory at the close of 1965. If P and S continue to file consolidated returns, the remaining $2,600 of the initial inventory amount will be added to P's income as the machines on which such profits were derived are disposed of outside the group.

Example (6). Assume that in example (5) S had elected to inventory its goods under section 472 (relating to last-in, first-out inventories). None of P's initial inventory amount of $3,500 would be added to P's income in 1966, since none of the goods to which such amount is attributable would be considered to be disposed of during such year under the last-in, first-out method of identifying inventories.

(e) *Section 381 transfer.* If a member of the group is a transferor or distributor of assets to another member of the group within the meaning of section 381 (a), then the acquiring corporation shall be treated as succeeding to the initial inventory amount of the transferor or distributor corporation to the extent that as of the date of distribution or transfer such amount has not yet been added to income. Such amount shall then be added to the acquiring corporation's income under the provisions of paragraph (b) of this section. For purposes of applying paragraph (c) of this section—

(1) The initial inventory amount of the transferor or distributor corporation shall be added to such amount of the acquiring corporation as of the close of the acquiring corporation's taxable year in which the date of distribution or transfer occurs, and

(2) The unrecovered inventory amount of the transferor or distributor corporation for its taxable year preceding the taxable year of the group in which the date of distribution or transfer occurs shall be added to such amount of the acquiring corporation.

(f) *Transitional rules*—(1) *In general.* If—

(i) A group filed a consolidated return for the taxable year immediately preceding the first taxable year to which this section applies,

(ii) Any member of such group made an opening adjustment to its inventory pursuant to paragraph (b) of § 1.1502-39A, and

(iii) Paragraph (c) of § 1.1502-39A has not been applicable for any taxable year subsequent to the taxable year for which such adjustment was made,

then subparagraphs (2) and (3) of this paragraph shall apply.

(2) *Closing adjustment to inventory.* (i) For the first consolidated return year to which this section applies, the increase in inventory prescribed in paragraph (c) of § 1.1502-39A shall be made as if such year were a separate return year.

(ii) For the first separate return year of a member to which this section applies, the adjustment to inventory (whether an increase or a decrease) prescribed in paragraph (c) of § 1.1502-39A, minus any adjustment already made pursuant to subdivision (i) of this subparagraph, shall be made to the inventory of such member.

(3) *Addition and recovery of initial inventory amount.* Each selling member shall treat as an initial inventory amount its share of the net amount by which the inventories of all members are increased pursuant to subparagraph (2) (i) of this paragraph for the first taxable year to which this section applies. A member's share shall be such net amount multiplied by a fraction, the numerator of which is its initial inventory amount (computed under paragraph (b) as if such taxable year were its first consolidated return year), and the denominator of which is the sum of such initial inventory amounts of all members. Such initial inventory amount shall be added to the income of such selling member and shall be recovered at the time and in the manner prescribed in paragraphs (b) and (c) of this section.

(4) *Example.* The provisions of this paragraph may be illustrated by the following examples:

Example. (i) Corporations P, S, and T file consolidated returns for calendar 1966, having filed consolidated returns continuously since 1962. P is a wholesale distributor of groceries selling to chains of supermarkets, including those owned by S and T. The opening inventories of S and T for 1962 were reduced by $40,000 and $80,000, respectively, pursuant to paragraph (b) of § 1.1502-39A. At the close of 1965, S and T have on hand in their inventories goods on which P derived profits of $80,000 and $90,000, respectively. The inventories of S and T at the close of 1966 include goods which they purchased from P during the year on which P derived profits of $85,000 and $105,000, respectively.

(ii) The opening inventories of S and T for 1966, the first year to which this section applies, are increased by $40,000 and $80,000, respectively, pursuant to the provisions of subparagraph (2) (i) of this paragraph. P will take into account (as provided in paragraphs (b) and (c) of this section) and initial inventory amount of $120,000 as of the beginning of 1966, the net amount by which the inventories of S and T were increased in such year. Since the increases in the inventories of S and T are the maximum allowable under paragraph (c) of § 1.1502-39A (i.e., the amount by which such inventories were originally decreased), no further adjustments will be made pursuant to subparagraph (2) (ii) of this paragraph to such inventories in the event that separate returns are subsequently filed.

(5) *Election not to eliminate.* If a group filed a consolidated return for the taxable year immediately preceding the first taxable year to which this section applies, and for such preceding year the members of the group did not eliminate gain or loss on intercompany inventory transactions pursuant to the adoption under § 1.1502-31A (b) (1) of a consistent accounting practice taking into account such gain or loss, then for purposes of this section each member shall be treated as if it had filed a separate return for such immediately preceding year.

○━▶ § 1.1502-19 (T.D. 6909, filed 12-29-66; amended by T.D. 7246, filed 12-29-72.) **Excess losses.**

(a) *Recognition of income*—(1) *In general.* Immediately before the disposition (as defined in paragraph (b) of this section) of stock of a subsidiary, there shall be included in the income of each member disposing of such stock that member's excess loss account (determined under §§ 1.-1502-14 and 1.1502-32) with respect to the stock disposed of.

(2) *Character of income.* (i) *In general.* Except to the extent otherwise provided in this subparagraph, the amount included in income under subparagraph (1) of this paragraph shall be treated as gain from the sale of stock (that is, as capital gain or ordinary income, as the case may be).

(ii) *Insolvency.* If, at the time of the disposition of stock of a subsidiary, the subsidiary is insolvent, then the amount included in income under subparagraph (1) of this paragraph, minus all amounts which increased the excess loss account under § 1.1502-14(a)(2) for any consolidated return year, shall be treated as ordinary income to the extent of such insolvency. For purposes of the preceding sentence, a subsidiary is insolvent to the extent that the sum of—

(a) All its liabilities,

(b) All its liabilities which were discharged during consolidated return years to the extent such discharge would have resulted in "cancellation of indebtedness income" but for the insolvency of such subsidiary, and

(c) The amount to which all stock of such subsidiary which is limited and preferred as to dividends is entitled in liquidation,

exceeds the fair market value of such subsidiary's assets. This subdivision shall not apply to the extent that the taxpayer establishes to the satisfaction of the Commissioner that the ordinary income portion of the excess loss account is attributable to losses of the subsidiary which reduced long-term capital gains of the group (without regard to section 1201).

(3) *Cancellation or redemption.* If stock of a subsidiary is considered to be disposed of under paragraph (b)(1)(ii) of this section other than in complete liquidation of such subsidiary, any amount which would otherwise be included in the income of the disposing member under subparagraph (1) of this paragraph shall be deferred and taken into account at the time provided in § 1.1502-14(b)(3).

(4) *Prior law.* To the extent the excess loss account is attributable to an adjustment under § 1.1502-32(f)(1) which was not subsequently reduced under § 1.1502-32(e)(2) or (3), it shall be taken into account in the same manner as it would have been taken into account under regulations effective for taxable years beginning before January 1, 1966. For example, assume that P is the common parent of a group which filed a consolidated return for 1965. During such taxable year a member of the group, corporation S, sustained a loss of $100, all of which was availed of in the consolidated return for 1965. P organized S on January 1, 1965, with a contribution to capital of $80 and a $10 loan. The group files a consolidated return for 1966. Under § 1.1502-32 (f)(1), P's basis for the stock in S as of January 1, 1966 is reduced to zero, and P has

Reg. § 1.1502-19(a)(4)

an excess loss account with respect to such stock of $20. No part of the reduction for losses availed of is applied to reduce the basis of the $10 obligation. During 1966, S has earnings and profits of $5, and under § 1.1502-32(e)(2) P's excess loss account for its stock of S is reduced to $15. On December 31, 1966 P sells the stock of S for $5. P realizes a $5 gain on such sale. In addition, the excess loss account of $15 is applied to reduce the basis of S's obligation to zero, and the balance is otherwise taken into account in the same manner and to the same extent as it would have been taken into account under the regulations applicable to 1965. If, on December 31, 1966, P had sold S's obligation instead of its stock, the excess loss account would be applied to reduce the basis of the obligation to zero, and P would then have an excess loss account of $5 with respect to the stock of S.

(5) *Foreign expropriation losses.* If there is a disposition of stock of a subsidiary, subparagraph (1) of this paragraph shall not apply to the excess loss account with respect to such stock to the extent such excess loss account is attributable to a foreign expropriation loss occurring in a taxable year beginning before January 1, 1966, which is absorbed as part of a consolidated net capital or net operating loss carryover in a taxable year ending before January 1, 1971, and the regulations applicable to taxable years beginning before January 1, 1966, shall apply to such disposition.

(6) *Election to reduce basis of other investment.* If there is a disposition (as defined in paragraph (b) of this section) after August 25, 1971, of stock of a subsidiary, all or any part of the excess loss account with respect to such stock may be applied to reduce the basis of any other stock or obligations of the subsidiary (whether or not evidenced by a security) held by the disposing member immediately before the disposition. Only the excess loss account which remains after such application shall be included in income under this paragraph. If subparagraph (4) of this paragraph applies to part of the excess loss account, such part must be applied to reduce the basis of stock or obligations under this subparagraph before the other part may be so applied.

(b) *Disposition*—(1) *Disposition of particular share.* Except as otherwise provided in paragraphs (d) and (e) of this section, a member shall be considered for purposes of this section as having disposed of a share of stock in a subsidiary—

(i) On the day such share is transferred to any person, or

(ii) On the days such member receives a distribution in cancellation or redemption of such stock (as defined in § 1.1502-14(b)(1)).

(2) *Disposition of all shares.* Except as otherwise provided in paragraphs (d) and (e) of this section, a member shall be considered for purposes of this section has having disposed of all of its shares of stock in a subsidiary—

(i) On the day such subsidiary ceases to be a member,

(ii) On the day such member ceases to be a member,

(iii) On the last day of each taxable year of such subsidiary in which any of its stock is wholly worthless (within the meaning of section 165(g)), or in which an indebtedness of the subsidiary is discharged if such discharge would have resulted in "cancellation of indebtedness income" but for the insolvency of the subsidiary,

(iv) On the last day of each taxable year of the subsidiary for which the Commissioner is satisfied that 10 percent or less of the face amount of any obligation for which the subsidiary is personally liable (primarily or secondarily) is recoverable at maturity by its creditors,

(v) On the day on which a member transfers an obligation for which the subsidiary is personally liable (primarily or secondarily) to any nonmember for an amount which is 25 percent or less of the face amount of such obligation, or

(vi) On the last day of the taxable year preceding the first taxable year for which the group does not file a consolidated return.

(c) *Effect of chain of ownership*—(1) *Multiple dispositions.* If the stock of more than one subsidiary is disposed of in the same transaction, paragraph (a) of this section shall be applied in the order of the tiers, from the lowest to the highest.

(2) *Examples.* The provisions of this paragraph may be illustrated by the following examples:

Example (1). (a) Assume that corporations P, S, T, and U first file a consolidated return for the taxable year beginning January 1, 1966. On that date, P owns all the stock of S with an adjusted basis of $15, S owns all the stock of T with an adjusted basis of $5, and T owns all the stock of U with an adjusted basis of $10. For the year 1966, the group has consolidated taxable income but U has a deficit in earnings and profits of $20. Under § 1.1502-32(b)(2). T reduces its basis with respect to the stock of U to zero and has an excess loss account of $10, S reduces its basis in T's stock to zero and has an excess loss account of $15, and P decreases its basis in S's stock to zero and has an excess loss account of $5.

(b) In 1967 the stock of U becomes worthless. T is considered as having disposed of such stock under paragraph (b) of this section and realizes income of $10. If the group has elected to adjust earnings and profits currently, T will have earnings and profits of $10 resulting from the disposition of the stock of U (see § 1.1502-33(c)(4)(ii)(b)); if the group has not so elected, T will have a deficit in earnings and profits of $10 resulting from the disposition (see § 1.1502-33(c)(4)(i)(b)). However, for purposes of the adjustment under § 1.1502-32(b) to the basis of stock owned by higher-tier members, T's earnings and profits on the disposition are $10 regardless of whether the group adjusts earnings and profits currently (see § 1.1502-32(d)(1)(i)). S's excess loss account with respect to T's stock will be reduced to $5 (see § 1.1502-32(b)(1)(i)). P's excess loss account with respect to S's stock will be reduced to zero and its basis for S's stock will be increased to $5 (see § 1.1502-32(b)(1)(i) or (iii)).

Example (2). Assume the same facts as in example (1) except that the stock of T, rather than the stock of U, becomes worthless and therefore S is considered as having disposed of its stock in T under paragraph (b) of this section and T is considered as having disposed of its stock in U. Since U is the lowest tier subsidiary, this section is applied first with respect to the excess loss account relating to the stock of U with the same result as in example (1). This section is then also applied with respect to the stock of T. Thus, in addition to the result in example (1), S will realize income of $5, and P's basis for S's stock will be increased by $5 to $10.

Example (3). Corporation P is the common parent of an affiliated group which filed a consolidated return for 1966. Corporations S1 and S2 are wholly owned subsidiaries of P organized on January 1, 1966. Corporation T was also organized on January 1, 1966, its stock being owned 75 percent by S2 and 25 percent by S1. P originally invested $300 in the stock of S1 and $200 in the stock of S2; S1 and S2 originally invested $50 and $150, respectively, in the stock of T. For the year 1966, there were the following undistributed earnings and profits or deficits, computed without regard to § 1.1502-33(c)(4):

S1	$50
S2	0
T	(400)

There were no consolidated net losses. Under § 1.1502-32(e) the basis and excess loss accounts would be as follows:

	S1 in T	S2 in T	P in S1	P in S2
Original basis	$50	$150	$300	$200
Deficit of T	(100)	(300)	(100)	(300)
Undistributed earnings and profits of S1			50	
Basis or (excess loss account)	($50)	($150)	$250	($100)

Assume that the group does not file a consolidated return for 1967. As of December 31, 1966, the following adjustments would be made:

	S1 in T	S2 in T	P in S1	P in S2
Basis or (excess loss account)	($50)	($150)	$250	($100)
Income to S1 Adjustment under § 1.1502-32(b)(1)	50		50	
Income to S2 Adjustment under § 1.1502-32(b)(1)		150		150
Basis of stock	0	0	$300	$ 50

(d) *Transfers of stock of subsidiary within the group*—(1) *In general.* A transfer of stock of a subsidiary from one member to another member in a consolidated return year shall not be treated as a disposition for purposes of paragraph (b) of this section if the basis of such stock in the hands of the transferee is determined by reference to the basis of such stock in the hands of the transferor. In such case, the transferee member shall succeed to the transferor member's excess loss account with respect to the transferred stock. See example (5) of paragraph (f) of this section.

(2) *Contributions to capital.* If the transferor in a transfer described in subparagraph (1) of this paragraph owns or receives stock in the transferee, the transferor's excess loss account for the transferred stock shall also be immediately applied to reduce the basis, if any, of the stock which the transferor owns or receives in the transferee. The excess, if any, over such basis shall be the transferor's excess loss account with respect to the stock owned or received. See example (5) of paragraph (f) of this section.

(e) *Nontaxable liquidations and reorganizations to which the subsidiary is a party.* If, in a consolidated return year, a member is the transferor or distributor corporation and another member is the acquiring corporation in a transaction to which section 381(a) applies, members owning stock in the transferor or distributor corporation shall not, by reason of such transaction (or by reason of an exchange under section 354 pursuant to such transaction), be considered for purposes of paragraph (b) of this section as having disposed of such stock. If the transaction is a distribution in liquidation to which section 334(b)(1) applies, the excess loss account in the stock of the distributor corporation shall be eliminated. If the transaction involves an exchange to which section 354 applies, the excess loss account in the stock of the transferor corporation surrendered in exchange shall be applied to reduce the basis (or to increase the excess loss account) of the stock received in the exchange or previously owned. If, immediately before a transfer described in section 381(a), the transferor corporation owned stock of the acquiring corporation, the excess loss account in such stock shall be eliminated. For example, assume that corporation P owns all of the stock of corporation S with an excess loss account of $20, and that S owns all of the stock of T with an excess loss account of $30. If S is merged into corporation U (another member) in a transaction described in section 368(a)(1)(A), P will apply the $20 excess loss account against and reduce the basis (or increase the excess loss account) of any stock of U which P owns or receives pursuant to the merger. However, if S is merged into T, the $30 excess loss account in the T stock is eliminated (and is not included in income), and the $20 excess loss account in the S stock becomes a $20 excess loss account in the T stock in the hands of P.

(f) *Examples.* This section may be illustrated by the following examples:

Example (1). Corporation P is the common parent of an affiliated group which files consolidated returns for 1966 through 1970. Included in the group for all such years are corporations S1 and S2 which are wholly owned by P, corporation T which is owned 40 percent by P, and 60 percent by S2, and corporation U which is wholly owned by T. S1, S2, T, and U

Reg. § 1.1502-19(f)

were each organized on January 1, 1966, with the following investments being made in their stock.

P in S1	$50
P in S2	150
P in T	40
S2 in T	60
T in U	50

During the period 1966-1970, S1, S2, T, and U made no distributions and had the following earnings and profits or deficits computed without regard to § 1.1502-33 (c) (4):

S1	($70)
S2	60
T	(120)
U	(80)

There were no consolidated net losses in 1966-1970. Under § 1.1502-32 (e) the basis and excess loss accounts for the stock of S1, S2, and T, and U would be as follows:

	T in U	P in T	S2 in T	P in S2	P in S1
Original basis	$50	$40	$60	$150	$50
Undistributed earnings and profits or (deficits)					
of U	(80)	(32)	(48)	(48)	
of T		(48)	(72)	(72)	
of S2				60	
of S1					(70)
Basis or (excess loss account)	($30)	($40)	($60)	$90	($20)

On January 1, 1971, P sells its stock in S1 to an unrelated person for $10. The group files a consolidated return for 1971. P must include in its income for 1971 the $20 in its excess loss account for S1 and the $10 gain from the sale of the stock of S1.

Example (2). Assume the same facts as in example (1) except that P does not sell its stock in S1, but on January 1, 1971, P sells its stock in S2 to an unrelated person for $170. Since S2, T, and U have ceased to be members of the group, the following adjustments must be made:

	T in U	P in T	S2 in T	P in S2
Basis or (excess loss account)	($30)	($40)	($60)	$90
T's excess loss account in U (see paragraph (c) of this section)	30	12	18	18
		($28)	($42)	$108
S2's excess loss account in T (see paragraph (c) of this section)			42	42
				$150
P's excess loss account in T		28		
Basis or (excess loss account)	0	0	0	$150

For the year 1971, P, S2, and T would include in their incomes $28, $42, and $30, respectively. In addition, P would have a gain of $20 from the sale of the stock of S2, zero bases for its stock in T and S1, and a $20 excess account for its stock in S1.

Example (3). Assume the same facts as in example (2), except that a consolidated return is not filed for 1971. As of December 31, 1970, P, S2, and T would include in their incomes $28, $42, and $30, respectively (see example (2)), and P would have a $150 basis for its stock in S2 and zero bases for its stock in T and S1. In addition, P would include in its income $20 with respect to its excess loss account in S1. In 1971, P would have a gain of $20 from the sale of its stock in S2.

Example (4). Assume the same facts as in example (1), except that P does not sell its stock in S1, but on January 1, 1971, T redeems for $30 cash, in a transaction qualifying under section 346, one half of its stock held by P. P has income in 1971 of $20, but such income is deferred; P's excess loss account for its remaining stock in T is reduced to 20. In addition, P recognizes a gain of $30 on the redemption of the stock of T, which gain is deferred.

Example (5). Assume the same facts as in example (1), except that instead of selling its stock in S1 to an unrelated person, P transfers its stock in S1 to T in exchange for stock in T in a transaction to which section 351 applies. P's excess loss account of $20 for the stock in S1 which was transferred to T increases P's excess loss account for its stock in T from $40 to $60. In addition, T has a zero basis and an excess loss account of $20 for the stock it acquired in S1.

Example (6). Assume the same facts as in example (1), except that P does not sell its stock in S1, but on January 1, 1971, S2 is liquidated into P in a liquidation to which section 334 (b) (1) applies. No income is realized by S2 by reason of its distribution to P of its stock in T. S2's excess loss account of $60 for its stock in T is added to, and is merged within, P's excess loss account for its stock in T. Thus, P has an excess loss account of $100 for all its stock in T.

Example (7). Assume the same facts as in example (6), except that S1, rather than S2, is liquidated into P in a liquidation to which section 334 (b) (1) applies. P's excess loss account for its stock in S1 is eliminated.

(g) *Acquisition of group*—(1) *In general.* Paragraph (b) of this section shall not apply solely because of a termination of the group (hereinafter referred to as the "terminating group") resulting from—

(i) The acquisition by a nonmember corporation of (a) the assets of the common parent in a reorganization described in subparagraph (A), (C), or (D) (but only if the requirements of subparagraphs (A) and (B) of section 354(b)(1) are met) of section 368(a)(1), or (b) stock of the common parent, or

(ii) The acquisition, in a transaction to which § 1.1502-75(d)(3) applies, by a member of (a) the assets of a nonmember corporation in a reorganization referred to in subdivision (i) of this subparagraph, or

(b) stock of a nonmember corporation, if all the members of the terminating group (other than such common parent if its assets are acquired) immediately before the acquisition are members immediately after the acquisition of another group (hereinafter referred to as the "succeeding group") which files a consolidated return for the first taxable year ending after the date of acquisition. The members of the succeeding group shall succeed to any excess loss accounts with respect to stock of members of the terminating group as of the date of acquisition. This paragraph shall not apply with respect to acquisitions occurring before August 25, 1971.

(2) *Adjustments*—(i) *In general.* If any stock of a member of the succeeding group is disposed of under this section, a higher tier limitation member (as defined in subdivision (ii) of this subparagraph) owning stock in the disposing member shall, in making the adjustment under § 1.1502-32 (b) with respect to stock of such disposing member, take into account the increase in earnings and profits attributable to inclusion of the excess loss account in the income of such member only to the extent that the amount of such excess loss account exceeds the amount of any excess loss account with respect to the stock disposed of at the time of the acquisition. If there are intervening members between the member disposing of stock under this section and a higher tier limitation member, and if a member owning stock in the disposing member is not a higher tier limitation member, then solely for the purpose of the adjustment under § 1.1502-32(b) by the higher tier limitation member with respect to stock of a subsidiary, the adjustments under § 1.1502-32(b) for such intervening members shall be computed as if members owning stock in the disposing member were higher tier limitation members.

(ii) *Limitation member.* A higher tier member of the succeeding group in a "higher tier limitation member" unless such member (a) was a member immediately before the acquisition of the same group as the member with respect to the stock of which the excess loss account existed, or (b) acquired the assets of the common parent of such group in a reorganization described in subparagraph (1) of this paragraph.

(3) *Examples.* The provisions of this paragraph may be illustrated by the following examples:

Example (1). (a) Assume there are two affiliated groups, one comprising P, S, and T, and the other comprising X and Y, both of which file consolidated returns for the calendar year 1971. P owns all the stock of S with an adjusted basis of $100, and S owns all the stock of T with an adjusted basis of zero and an excess loss account of $30. X owns all the stock of Y with an adjusted basis of $200. On January 1, 1972, Y acquires all the assets of P in exchange for 20 percent of the stock of X in a reorganization to which section 368 (a)(1)(C) applies. As a result of the acquisition of the assets of P by Y, the P-S-T group terminates. X, Y, S, and T file a consolidated return for the first taxable year ending after the date of the acquisition.

(b) Paragraph (b) of this section does not apply, merely because of the termination of the P group, to include in S's income its excess loss account with respect to the stock of T.

(c) If T has a deficit in earnings and profits of $10 for 1972, S would increase its excess loss account with respect to the stock of T to $40, Y would decrease the basis of its S stock (which is a carryover of P's basis) to $90, and X would decrease the basis of its Y stock to $190.

(d) Assume that the stock of T becomes worthless in 1973. S would include $40 in income. For purposes of the adjustments under § 1.1502-32(b), S would have earnings and profits of $40 resulting from the disposition of the stock of T (amount realized, $40, minus the adjusted basis of zero determined by taking into account the adjustments under § 1.1502-32(e)). If S had no other earnings and profits for the year, Y (which is not a higher tier limitation member) would adjust its basis for the stock of S under § 1.1502-32(b)(1)(i) by the full amount of S's earnings and profits, thus increasing the basis of the S stock to $130. The adjustment by Y with respect to the stock of S would ordinarily be reflected under § 1.1502-32(b)(1)(i) or (iii) in the adjustment by X with respect to the stock of Y. However, X is a higher tier limitation member, and, solely for the purpose of determining the adjustment by X with respect to the stock of Y, the adjustment by Y with respect to the stock of S must be recomputed by including only $10 (i.e., the amount by which S's excess loss account in the stock of T, $40, exceeds the excess loss account with respect to such stock at the time of the acquisition, $30) in the adjustment under § 1.1502-32(b)(1) (i). Thus, if there were no other adjustments under § 1.1502-32(b) with respect to the stock of S and Y, X would make a positive adjustment under § 1.1502-32(b)(1) (i) or (iii) and (e)(2) of $10 with respect to the stock of Y, increasing the basis of such stock to $200. The basis of the stock of S held by Y is not affected by the recomputation.

Example (2). Assume the same facts as in example (1) except that the shareholders of P receive more than 50 percent of the stock of X so that the transaction is a reverse acquisition under § 1.1502-75 (d)(3) with the X-Y group terminating and the P-S-T group surviving. The adjustments and limitations apply as in example (1).

Example (3). Assume the same facts as in example (1) except that subsequent to the acquisition T has earnings and profits of $100 in 1972 (thus eliminating the excess loss account with respect to the stock of T and increasing the basis of such stock to $70) and a deficit in earnings and profits of $110 in 1973, thereby decreasing the basis with respect to such stock to zero and creating an excess loss account of $40 which is included in S's income in 1973. The adjustments and limitations apply as in example (1).

§ 1.1502-20 [Reserved]

COMPUTATION OF CONSOLIDATED ITEMS

§ 1.1502-21 (T.D. 6894, filed 9-7-66.) Consolidated net operating loss deduction.

(a) *In general.* The consolidated net operating loss deduction shall be an amount equal to the aggregate of the consolidated net operating loss carryovers and carry-

Reg. § 1.1502-21(a)

backs to the taxable year (as determined under paragraph (b) of this section).

(b) *Consolidated net operating loss carryovers and carrybacks*—(1) *In general.* The consolidated net operating loss carryovers and carrybacks to the taxable year shall consist of any consolidated net operating losses (as determined under paragraph (f) of this section) of the group, plus any net operating losses sustained by members of the group in separate return years, which may be carried over or back to the taxable year under the principals of section 172(b). However, such consolidated carryovers and carrybacks shall not include any consolidated net operating loss apportioned to a corporation for a separate return year pursuant to paragraph (a) of § 1.1502-79, and shall be subject to the limitations contained in paragraphs (c), (d), and (e) of this section and to the limitation contained in § 1.1502-15.

(2) *Rules for applying section 172(b)(1)*—(i) Regulated transportation corporations. For purposes of applying section 172(b)(1)(C) (relating to net operating losses sustained by regulated transportation corporations), in the case of a consolidated net operating loss sustained in a taxable year for which a member of the group was a regulated transportation corporation (as defined in section 172(j)(1)), the portion, if any, of such consolidated net operating loss which is attributable to such corporation (as determined under paragraph (a)(4) of § 1.1502-79) shall be a carryover to the sixth taxable year following the loss year only if such corporation is a regulated transportation corporation for such sixth year, and shall be a carryover to the seventh taxable year following the loss year only if such corporation is a regulated transportation corporation for both such sixth and seventh years.

(ii) Trade expansion losses. In the case of a carryback of a consolidated net operating loss from a taxable year for which a member of the group has been issued a certification under section 317 of the Trade Expansion Act of 1962 and with respect to which the requirements of section 172(b)(3)(A) have been met, section 172(b)(1)(A)(ii) shall apply only to the portion of such consolidated net operating loss attributable to such member.

(iii) Foreign expropriation losses. An election under section 172(b)(3)(C) (relating to 10-year carryover of portion of net operating loss attributable to a foreign expropriation loss) may be made for a consolidated return year only if the sum of the foreign expropriation losses (as defined in section 172(k)) of the members of the group for such year equals or exceeds 50 percent of the consolidated net operating loss for such year. If such election is made, the amount which may be carried over under section 172(b)(1)(D) is the smaller of (a) the sum of such foreign expropriation losses, or (b) the consolidated net operating loss.

(3) *Absorption rules.* For purposes of determining the amount, if any, of a net operating loss (whether consolidated or separate) which can be carried to a taxable year (consolidated or separate), the amount of such net operating loss which is absorbed in a prior consolidated return year under section 172(b)(2) shall be determined by—

(i) Applying all net operating losses which can be carried to such prior year in the order of the taxable years in which such losses were sustained, beginning with the taxable year which ends earliest, and

(ii) Applying all such losses which can be carried to such prior year from taxable years ending on the same date on a pro rata basis, except that any portion of a net operating loss attributable to a foreign expropriation loss to which section 172(b)(1)(D) applies shall be applied last.

(c) *Limitation on net operating loss carryovers and carrybacks from separate return limitation years*—(1) *General rule.* In the case of a net operating loss of a member of the group arising in a separate return limitation year (as defined in paragraph (f) of § 1.1502-1) of such member (and in a separate return limitation year of any predecessor of such member), the amount which may be included under paragraph (b) of this section (computed without regard to the limitation contained in paragraph (d) of this section) in the consolidated net operating loss carryovers and carrybacks to a consolidated return year of the group shall not exceed the amount determined under subparagraph (2) of this paragraph.

(2) *Computation of limitation.* The amount referred to in subparagraph (1) of this paragraph with respect to a member of the group is the excess, if any, of—

(i) Consolidated taxable income (computed without regard to the consolidated net operating loss deduction), minus such consolidated taxable income recomputed by excluding the items of income and deduction of such member, over

(ii) The net operating losses attributable to such member which may be carried to the consolidated return year arising in taxable years ending prior to the particular separate return limitation year.

(3) *Examples.* The provisions of this paragraph and paragraphs (a) and (b) of this section may be illustrated by the following examples:

Example (1). (i) Corporation P formed corporations S and T on January 1, 1965. P, S, and T filed separate returns for the calendar year 1965, a year for which an election under section 1562 was effective. T's return for that year reflected a net operating loss of $10,000. The group filed a consolidated return for 1966 reflecting consolidated taxable income of $30,000 (computed without regard to the consolidated net operating loss deduction). Among the transactions occurring during 1966 were the following:

(a) P sold goods to T deriving deferred profits of $7,000 on such sales, $2,000 of which was restored to consolidated taxable income on the sale of such goods to outsiders;

(b) T sold a machine to S deriving a deferred profit of $5,000, $1,000 of which was restored to consolidated taxable income as a result of S's depreciation deductions;

(c) T distributed a $3,000 dividend to P; and

(d) In addition to the transactions described above, T had other taxable income of $6,000.

(ii) The carryover of T's 1965 net operating loss to 1966 is subject to the limitation contained in this paragraph, since 1965 was a separate return limitation year (an election under section 1562 was effective for such year). Thus, only $7,000 of T's $10,000 net operating loss is a consolidated net operating loss carryover to 1966, since such carryover is limited to consolidated taxable income (computed without regard to the consolidated net operating loss deduction), $30,000, minus such consolidated taxable income recomputed by excluding the items of income and deduction of T, $23,000 (i.e., consolidated taxable income computed without regard to the $1,000 restoration of T's deferred gain and T's $6,000 of other income). In making such recomputation, no change is made in the effect on consolidated taxable income of P's sale to T, or of the dividend from T to P.

Example (2). (i) Corporation P was formed on January 1, 1966. P filed separate returns for the calendar years 1966 and 1967 reflecting net operating losses of $4,000 and $12,000, respectively. P purchased corporation S on March 15, 1967. S was formed on February 1, 1966, and filed a separate return for the taxable year ending January 31, 1967. S also filed a short period return for the period from February 1 to December 31, 1967, and joined with P in filing a consolidated return for 1968. S sustained net operating losses of $5,000 and $6,000 for its taxable years ending January 31, 1967 and December 31, 1967, respectively. An election under section 1562 was not effective for P and S during the period involved. Consolidated taxable income for 1968 (computed without regard to the consolidated net operating loss deduction) was $16,000; such consolidated taxable income recomputed by disregarding the items of income and deduction of S was $9,000.

(ii) In order of time, the following losses are absorbed in 1968:

(a) P's $4,000 net operating loss for the calendar year 1966 (such loss is not subject to the limitation contained in this paragraph since P is the common parent corporation for 1968);

(b) S's $5,000 net operating loss for the year ended January 31, 1967. Such loss is subject to the limitation contained in this paragraph, since S was not a member of the group on each day of such year. However, such loss can be carried over and absorbed in full since such limitation is $7,000 (consolidated taxable income computed without regard to the consolidated net operating loss deduction, $16,000, minus such consolidated taxable income recomputed, $9,000); and

(c) $6,000 of P's net operating loss and $1,000 of S's net operating loss for the taxable years ending December 31, 1967. This is determined by applying the losses from such year which can be carried to 1968 (P's $12,000 loss and $2,000 of S's $6,000 loss, since such $6,000 loss is limited under this paragraph) on a pro rata basis against the amount of such losses which can be absorbed in that year, $7,000 (consolidated taxable income of $16,000 less the $9,000 of losses absorbed from prior years). The carryover of S's loss to 1968 is subject to the limitation contained in that paragraph, since S was not a member of the group on each day of its taxable year ending December 31, 1967. Such loss is limited to $2,000, the excess of $7,000 (as determined under (ii) (b)) over $5,000 (S's carryover from the year ended January 31, 1967). If a consolidated return is filed in 1969, the consolidated net operating loss carryovers will consist of P's unabsorbed loss of $6,000 ($12,000 minus $6,000) from 1967 and, subject to the limitation contained in this paragraph, S's unabsorbed loss of $5,000 ($6,000 minus $1,000) from its year ended December 31, 1967.

(d) *Limitation on carryovers where there has been a consolidated return change of ownership*—(1) *General rule.* If a consolidated return change of ownership (as defined in paragraph (g) of § 1.1502-1) occurs during the taxable year or an earlier taxable year, the amount which may be included under paragraph (b) of this section in the consolidated net operating loss carryovers to the taxable year with respect to the aggregate of the net operating losses attributable to old members of the group (as defined in paragraph (g) (3) of § 1.1502-1) arising in taxable years (consolidated or separate) ending on the same day and before the taxable year in which the consolidated return change of ownership occurred shall not exceed the amount determined under subparagraph (2) of this paragraph.

(2) *Computation of limitation.* The amount referred to in subparagraph (1) of this paragraph shall be the excess of—

(i) The consolidated taxable income for the taxable year (determined without regard to the consolidated net operating loss deduction) recomputed by including only the items of income and deduction of the old members of the group, over

(ii) The sum of the net operating losses attributable to the old members of the group which may be carried to the taxable year arising in taxable years ending prior to the particular loss year or years.

(3) *Example.* The provisions of this paragraph may be illustrated by the following example:

Example. (i) Corporation P is formed on January 1, 1967, and on the same day it forms corporation S. P and S file a consolidated return for the calendar year 1967, reflecting a consolidated net operating loss of $500,000. On January 1, 1968, individual X purchases all of the outstanding stock of P. X subsequently contributes $1,000,000 to P and P purchases the stock of corporation T. P, S, and T file a consolidated return for 1968 reflecting consolidated taxable income of $600,000 (computed without regard to the consolidated net operating loss deduction). Such consolidated taxable income recomputed by including only the items of income and deduction of P and S is $350,000.

(ii) Since a consolidated return change of ownership took place in 1968 (there was more than a 50 percent change of ownership of P), the amount of the consolidated net operating loss from 1967 which can be carried over to 1968 is limited to $350,000, the excess of $350,000 (consolidated taxable income recomputed by including only the items of income and deduction of the old members of the group, P and S) over zero (the amount of the consolidated net operating loss carryovers attributable to the old members of the group arising in taxable years ending before 1967).

Reg. § 1.1502-21 (d) (3)

24,228 (I.R.C.) Reg. § 1.1502-21(e)(1)

(e) *Limitations on net operating loss carryovers under section 382*—(1) *Section 382 (a).* (i) If at the end of a taxable year (consolidated or separate) there has been an increase in ownership of the stock of the common parent of a group (within the meaning of section 382 (a) (1) (A) and (B)), and any member of the group has not continued to carry on a trade or business substantially the same as that conducted before any such increase (within the meaning of section 382 (a) (1) (C)), then the portion of any consolidated net operating loss sustained in prior taxable years attributable to such member (as determined under paragraph (a) (3) of § 1.1502-79) shall not be allowed as a carryover to such taxable year or to any subsequent taxable year.

(ii) If the provisions of section 382(a) disallow the deduction of a net operating loss carryover from a separate return year of a member of the group to a subsequent taxable year, no amount shall be included under paragraph (b) of this section as a consolidated net operating loss carryover to such a subsequent consolidated return year with respect to such separate return year of such member.

(iii) The provisions of this subparagraph may be illustrated by the following example:

Example. P, S, and T file a consolidated return for the calendar year 196., reflecting a consolidated net operating loss attributable in part to each member. P owns 80 percent of S's stock and S owns 80 percent of T's stock. On January 1, 1970, A purchases 50 percent of P's stock. During 1970 T's business is discontinued. Since there has been a 50 percentage point increase in ownership of P, the common parent of the group, and since T has not continued to carry on the same trade or business after such increase, the portion of the 1969 consolidated net operating loss attributable to T shall not be included in any net operating loss deduction for 1970 or for any subsequent taxable years, whether consolidated or separate.

(2) *Section 382(b).* If a net operating loss carryover from a separate return year of a predecessor of a member of the group to the taxable year is reduced under the provisions of section 382(b), the amount included under paragraph (b) of this section with respect to such predecessor shall be so reduced.

(f) *Consolidated net operating loss.* The consolidated net operating loss shall be determined by taking into account the following:

(1) The separate taxable income (as determined under § 1.1502-12) of each member of the group, computed without regard to any deduction under section 242;

(2) Any consolidated net capital gain;

(3) Any consolidated section 1231 net loss;

(4) Any consolidated charitable contributions deduction;

(5) Any consolidated dividends received deduction (determined under § 1.1502-26 without regard to paragraph (a)(2) of that section); and

(6) Any consolidated section 247 deduction (determined under § 1.1502-27 without regard to paragraph (a)(1)(ii) of that section).

§ 1.1502-22 (T. D. 6894, filed 9-7-66.) **Consolidated net capital gain or loss.**

(a) *Computation*—(1) *Consolidated net capital gain.* The consolidated net capital gain for the taxable year shall be determined by taking into account—

(i) The aggregate of the capital gains and losses (determined without regard to gains or losses to which section 1231 applies or net capital loss carryovers) of the members of the group for the consolidated return year,

(ii) The consolidated section 1231 net gain for such year (computed in accordance with § 1.1502-23), and

(iii) The consolidated net capital loss carryovers to such year (as determined under paragraph (b) of this section).

(2) *Consolidated net capital loss.* The consolidated net capital loss shall be determined under subparagraph (1) of this paragraph but without regard to subdivision (iii) thereof.

(3) *Special rules.* For purposes of this section, capital gains and losses on intercompany transactions and transactions with respect to stock, bonds, and other obligations of a member of the group shall be reflected as provided in §§ 1.1502-13, 1.1502-14, and 1.1502-19, and capital losses shall be limited as provided in § 1.1502-15.

(4) [Reserved.]

(5) *Example.* The provisions of this paragraph may be illustrated by the following example:

Example. (i) Corporations P, S, and T file consolidated returns on a calendar year basis for 1966 and 1967. The members had the following transactions involving capital assets during 1967: P sold an asset with a $10,000 basis to S for $17,000 and none of the circumstances of restoration described in paragraph (d), (e), or (f) of § 1.1502-13 occurred by the end of the consolidated return year; S sold an asset to individual A for $7,000 which S had purchased during 1966 from P for $10,000, and with respect to which P had deferred a gain of $2,000; T sold an asset with a basis of $10,000 to individual B for $25,000. The group has a consolidated net capital loss carryover to the taxable year of $10,000.

(ii) The consolidated net capital gain of the group is $4,000, determined as follows: P's net capital gain of $2,000, representing the deferred gain on the sale to S during the taxable year 1966, restored into income during taxable year 1967 (the $7,000 gain on P's deferred intercompany transaction is not taken into account for the current year), plus T's net capital gain of $15,000, minus S's net capital loss of $3,000, and the consolidated net capital loss carryover of $10,000.

(b) *Consolidated net capital loss carryovers*— (1) *In general.* The consolidated net capital loss carryovers to the taxable year shall consist of any consolidated net capital losses of the group, plus any net capital losses of members of the group arising in separate return years of such members, which may be carried to the taxable year under the principles of section 1212 (a). However, such consolidated carryovers shall not include any consolidated net capital loss apportioned to a corporation for a separate return year pursuant to paragraph (b) of § 1.1502-79 and shall be subject to the limitations contained in paragraph (c) and (d) of this section. For purposes of section 1212 (a) (1), the portion of any consolidated net capital loss for any taxable year attributable to a foreign expropriation capital loss is the amount of the foreign expropriation capital losses of all the members for such year (but not in excess of the consolidated net capital loss for such year).

(2) *Absorption rules.* For purposes of determining the amount, if any, of a net capital loss (whether consolidated or separate) which can be carried to a taxable year (consolidated or separate), the amount of such net capital loss which is absorbed in a prior consolidated return year under section 1212 (a) (1) shall be determined by—

(i) Applying all net capital losses which can be carried to such prior year in the order of the taxable years in which such losses were sustained, beginning with the taxable year which ends earliest, and

(ii) Applying all such losses which can be carried to such prior year from taxable years ending on the same date on a pro rata basis, except that any portion of a net capital loss attributable to a foreign expropriation capital loss to which section 1212 (a) (1) (B) applies shall be applied last.

(c) *Limitation on net capital loss carryovers from separate return limitation years* —(1) *General rule.* In the case of a net capital loss of a member of the group arising in a separate return limitation year (as defined in a paragraph (f) of § 1.1502-1) of such member (and in a separate return limitation year of any predecessor of such member), the amount that may be included under paragraph (b) of this section (computed without regard to the limitation contained in paragraph (d) of this section) shall not exceed the amount determined under subparagraph (2) of this paragraph.

(2) *Computation of limitation.* The amount referred to in subparagraph (1) of this paragraph with respect to a member of the group is the excess, if any, of—

(i) The consolidated net capital gain for the taxable year (computed without regard to any net capital loss carryovers), minus such consolidated net capital gain for the taxable year recomputed by excluding the capital gains and losses and the gains and losses to which section 1231 applies of such member, over

(ii) The net capital losses attributable to such member which can be carried to the taxable year arising in taxable years ending prior to the particular separate return limitation year.

(d) *Limitation on capital loss carryovers where there has been a consolidated return change of ownership*—(1) *General rule.* If a consolidated return change of ownership (as defined in paragraph (g) of § 1.1502-1) occurs during the taxable year or an earlier taxable year, the amount which may be included under paragraph (b) of this section in the consolidated net capital loss carryovers to the taxable year with respect to the aggregate of the net capital losses attributable to old members of the group (as defined in paragraph (g) (3) of § 1.1502-1) arising in taxable years (consolidated or separate) ending on the same day and before the taxable year in which the consolidated return change of ownership occurred shall not exceed the amount determined under subparagraph (2) of this paragraph.

(2) *Computation of limitation.* The amount referred to in subparagraph (1) of this paragraph shall be the excess of—

(i) The consolidated net capital gain (determined without regard to any net capital loss carryovers for the taxable year) recomputed by including only capital gains and losses and gains and losses to which section 1231 applies of the old members of the group, over

(ii) The aggregate net capital losses attributable to the old members of the group which may be carried to the taxable year arising in taxable years ending prior to the particular loss year or years.

o—▸ § 1.1502-23 (T.D. 6894, filed 9-7-66; amended by T.D. 7246, filed 12-29-72.) **Consolidated section 1231 net gain or loss.**

The consolidated section 1231 net gain or loss for the taxable year shall be determined by taking into account the aggregate of the gains and losses to which section 1231 applies of the members of the group for the consolidated return year. Section 1231 gains and losses on intercompany transactions shall be reflected as provided in § 1.1502-13. Section 1231 losses that are "built-in deductions" shall be subject to the limitations of §§ 1.1502-21(c) and 1.1502-22(c) as provided in § 1.1502-15(a).

o—▸ § 1.1502-24 (T.D. 6894, filed 9-7-66.) **Consolidated charitable contributions deduction.**

(a) *Determination of amount of consolidated charitable contributions deduction.* The deduction allowed by section 170 for the taxable year shall be the lesser of—

(1) The aggregate deductions of the members of the group allowable under section 170 (determined without regard to section 170(b)(2)), plus the consolidated charitable contribution carryovers to such year, or

(2) Five percent of the adjusted consolidated taxable income as determined under paragraph (c) of this section.

(b) *Carryover of excess charitable contributions.* The consolidated charitable contribution carryovers to any consolidated return year shall consist of any excess consolidated charitable contributions of the group, plus any excess charitable contributions of members of the group arising in separate return years of such members, which may be carried over to the taxable year under the principles of section 170 (b) (2) and (3). However, such consolidated carryovers shall not include any excess charitable contributions apportioned to a corporation for a separate return year pursuant to paragraph (e) of § 1.1502-79.

(c) *Adjusted consolidated taxable income.* For purposes of this section, the adjusted consolidated taxable income of the group for any consolidated return year shall be the consolidated taxable income computed without regard to this section,

Reg. § 1.1502-24(c)

section 242, section 243 (a) (2) and (3), § 1.1502-25, § 1.1502-26, and § 1.1502-27, and without regard to any consolidated net operating loss carrybacks to such year.

○━━ § 1.1502-25 (T.D. 6909, filed 12-29-66.) **Consolidated section 922 deduction.**

(a) *In general.* The consolidated section 922 deduction for the taxable year shall be determined by multiplying the fraction specified in section 922 (2) by that portion of the consolidated taxable income attributable to those members of the group which are Western Hemisphere trade corporations for such year.

(b) *Definition of Western Hemisphere trade corporation.* For purposes of paragraph (a) of this section, in determining whether a member is a Western Hemisphere trade corporation, the definition contained in section 921 shall be applied to such member separately. For purposes of applying the gross income tests of section 921 to such member, the gross income of such member for a consolidated return year shall be determined as if such member had filed a separate return, except that—

(1) Gains and losses on intercompany transactions shall be reflected in gross income in the manner provided by § 1.1502-13;

(2) Gains (not including dividends) and losses on transactions with respect to stock, bonds, or other obligations of members of the group shall be reflected in gross income in the manner provided by §§ 1.1502-14 and 1.1502-19; and

(3) The adjustments prescribed by §§ 1.1502-18 and 1.1502-32 shall be made.

(c) *Portion of consolidated taxable income attributable to Western Hemisphere trade corporations.* (1) *In general.* For purposes of paragraph (a) of this section, the portion of the consolidated taxable income attributable to those members of the group which are Western Hemisphere trade corporations is an amount equal to the consolidated taxable income (computed without regard to the section 922 deduction) multiplied by a fraction, the numerator of which is the sum of the taxable incomes of those members which are Western Hemisphere trade corporations, and the denominator of which is the sum of the taxable incomes of all the members.

(2) *Taxable income.* For purposes of this paragraph, the taxable income of a member shall be the separate taxable income determined under § 1.1502-12, adjusted for the following items taken into account in the computation of consolidated taxable income:

(i) The portion of the consolidated net operating loss deduction, the consolidated charitable contributions deduction, and the consolidated dividends received deduction, attributable to such member;

(ii) Such member's net capital gain (determined without regard to any net capital loss carryover attributable to such member);

(iii) Such member's net capital loss and section 1231 net loss, reduced by the portion of the consolidated net capital loss attributable to such member; and

(iv) The portion of any consolidated net capital loss carryover attributable to such member which is absorbed in the taxable year.

If the computation of the taxable income of a member under this subparagraph results in an excess of deductions over gross income, then for purposes of subparagraph (1) of this paragraph such member's taxable income shall be zero.

○━━ § 1.1502-26 (T.D. 6894, filed 9-7-66; amended by T.D. 7246, filed 12-29-72.) **Consolidated dividends received deduction.**

(a) *In general.* The consolidated dividends received deduction for the taxable year shall be the lesser of—

(1) The aggregate of the deductions of the members of the group allowable under sections 243(a)(1), 244(a), and 245 (computed without regard to the limitation provided in section 246(b)), or

(2) 85 percent of the consolidated taxable income computed without regard to the consolidated net operating loss deduction, consolidated section 247 deduction, the consolidated dividends received deduction, and any consolidated net capital loss carryback to the taxable year.

Subparagraph (2) of this paragraph shall not apply for any consolidated return year for which there is a consolidated net operating loss. (See paragraph (f) of § 1.1502-21 for the definition of a consolidated net operating loss.) If section 593 applies to one or more members and any member computes additions to the reserve for losses on loans for a taxable year beginning after July 11, 1969, under the percentage of income method provided by section 593(b)(2), the deduction otherwise computed under this section shall be reduced by an amount determined by multiplying such deduction (determined without regard to this sentence and without regard to dividends received by the common parent if such parent does not use the percentage of income method provided by section 593(b)(2)) by the applicable percentage of the member with the highest applicable percentage (determined under subparagraphs (A) and (B) of section 593(b)(2)).

(b) *Intercompany dividends.* The amount determined under paragraph (a) of this section shall be determined without regard to dividends received from other members of the group during a consolidated return year. (See paragraph (a) (1) of § 1.1502-14 for rules relating to intercompany dividends.)

(c) *Examples.* The provisions of this section may be illustrated by the following examples:

Example (1). Corporations P, S, and S-1 filed a consolidated return for the calendar year 1966 showing consolidated taxable income of $100,000 (determined without regard to the consolidated net operating loss deduction, consolidated dividends received deduction, and the consolidated section 247 deduction). Such corporations received dividends during such year from nonmember domestic corporations as follows:

Corporation	Dividends
P	$ 6,000
S	10,000
S-1	34,000
Total	$50,000

The dividends received deduction allowable to each member under section 243 (a) (1) computed without regard to the limitation in section 246 (b)) is as follows: P has $5,100 (85 percent of $6,000), S has $8,500 (85 percent of $10,000), and S-1 has $28,900 (85 percent of $34,000), or a total of $42,500. Since $42,500 is less than $85,000 (85 percent of $100,000), the consolidated dividends received deduction is $42,500.

Example (2). Assume the same facts as in example (1) except that consolidated taxable income (computed without regard to the consolidated net operating loss deduction, consolidated dividends received deduction, and the consolidated section 247 deduction) was $40,000. The aggregate of the dividends received deductions, $42,500, computed without regard to section 246 (b), results in a consolidated net operating loss of $2,500. See section 172 (d) (6). Therefore, paragraph (a) (2) of this section does not apply and the consolidated dividends received deduction is $42,500.

○— § 1.1502-27 (T.D. 6894, filed 9-7-66.) **Consolidated section 247 deduction.**

(a) *Amount of deduction*. The consolidated section 247 deduction for the taxable year shall be an amount computed as follows:

(1) First, determine the amount which is the lesser of—

(i) The aggregate of the dividends paid (within the meaning of section 247 (a)) during such year by members of the group which are public utilities (within the meaning of section 247 (b) (1)) on preferred stock (within the meaning of section 247 (b) (2)), other than dividends paid to other members of the group, or

(ii) The aggregate of the taxable income (or loss) (as determined under paragraph (b) of this section) of each such member which is a public utility.

(2) Then, multiply the amount determined under subparagraph (1) of this paragraph by the fraction specified in section 247 (a) (2).

(b) *Computation of taxable income*. For purposes of paragraph (a) (1) (ii) of this section, the taxable income (or loss) of a member of the group described in paragraph (a) (1) (i) shall be determined under § 1.1502-12, adjusted for the following items taken into account in the computation of consolidated taxable income:

(1) The portion of the consolidated net operating loss deduction, the consolidated charitable contributions deduction, and the consolidated dividends received deduction, attributable to such member;

(2) Such member's net capital gain (determined without regard to any net capital loss carryover attributable to such member);

(3) Such member's net capital loss and section 1231 net loss, reduced by the portion of the consolidated net capital loss attributable to such member; and

(4) The portion of any consolidated net capital loss carryover attributable to such member which is absorbed in the taxable year.

○— §§ 1.1502-28 to 1.1502-30 [Reserved]

BASIS, STOCK OWNERSHIP, AND EARNINGS AND PROFITS RULES

○— § 1.1502-31 (T.D. 6909, filed 12-29-66; amended by T.D. 7246, filed 12-29-72.) **Basis of property.**

(a) *Deferred intercompany transactions*. The basis of property acquired by a purchasing member in a deferred intercompany transaction shall be determined as if separate returns were filed. Thus, if, in a deferred intercompany transaction, S sells property with an adjusted basis of $80 to P for $100, the basis of such property in the hands of P shall be $100 even though, under § 1.1502-13, S defers its $20 gain on the sale.

(b) *Basis after liquidation or intercompany distributions with respect to stock*— (1) *Distributions in kind*. The basis of property received in a distribution to which section 301 applies shall be determined under section 301(d)(2)(B).

(2) *Liquidations and redemptions*. (i) The basis of property acquired in a liquidation to which section 332 applies shall be determined as if separate returns were filed.

(ii) The aggregate basis of all property acquired in a distribution in cancellation or redemption of stock (as defined in § 1.1502-14(b)(1)) by a member to another member, other than a liquidation to which section 332 applies, shall be the same as the adjusted basis of the stock exchanged therefor (adjusted in accordance with the rules prescribed in § 1.1502-32(a)), increased by the amount of any liabilities of the distributing corporation assumed by the distributee or to which the property acquired is subject, and reduced by the amount of cash received in the distribution. Such aggregate basis shall be allocated among the assets received (except cash) in proportion to the fair market values of such assets on the date received.

○— § 1.1502-32 (T.D. 6909, filed 12-29-66; amended by T.D. 7246, filed 12-29-72.) **Investment adjustment.**

(a) *In general*. As of the end of each consolidated return year, each member owning stock in a subsidiary shall adjust the basis of such stock in the manner prescribed in this section. If a subsidiary owns stock in any other subsidiary, the adjustment with respect to the stock of the higher tier subsidiary shall not be made until after the adjustment is made with respect to the stock of the lower tier subsidiary. In the case of a disposition (as defined in § 1.1502-19(b)) of stock of a subsidiary before the end of the taxable year, the adjustment with respect to such stock shall be made as of the date of disposition. The amount of such adjustment shall be the difference between the positive adjustment described in paragraph (b)(1) or (c)(1) of this section, which ever is applicable, and the negative adjustment described

Reg. § 1.1502-32(a)

in paragraph (b)(2) or (c)(2) of this section, whichever is applicable. Such difference is referred to in this section as the "net positive adjustment" or the "net negative adjustment", as the case may be.

(b) *Stock which is not limited and preferred as to dividends*—(1) *Positive adjustment.* The positive adjustment with respect to a share of stock which is not limited and preferred as to dividends shall be the sum of—

(i) An allocable part of the undistributed earnings and profits of the subsidiary for the taxable year;

(ii) An allocable part of the portion of any consolidated net operating loss or consolidated net capital loss for the taxable year which is attributable to such subsidiary under § 1.1502-79(a)(3) or (b)(2), and which is not carried back and absorbed in a prior taxable year; and

(iii) If such subsidiary owns stock in another subsidiary and § 1.1502-33(c)(4)(i) applies to the taxable year, an allocable part of the net positive adjustment made by the higher tier subsidiary for the taxable year with respect to its stock in such other subsidiary.

(2) *Negative adjustment.* The negative adjustment with respect to a share of stock which is not limited and preferred as to dividends shall be the sum of—

(i) An allocable part of the deficit in earnings and profits of the subsidiary for the taxable year (determined under § 1.1502-33);

(ii) An allocable part of any net operating loss or net capital loss incurred by the subsidiary in a prior separate return year, and of any portion of a consolidated net operating loss or consolidated net capital loss incurred by the group in a prior consolidated return year which is attributable to such subsidiary under § 1.1502-79 (a) (3) or (b) (2), and which is carried over and absorbed in the taxable year;

(iii) Distributions made by the subsidiary during the taxable year with respect to such share out of earnings and profits of the subsidiary—

(a) Accumulated in prior consolidated return years beginning after December 31, 1965; or

(b) Accumulated in pre-affiliation years of the subsidiary; and

(iv) If such subsidiary owns stock in another subsidiary and § 1.1502-33(c)(4)(i) applies to the taxable year, an allocable part of the net negative adjustment made by the higher tier subsidiary for the taxable year with respect to its stock in such other subsidiary.

(c) *Limited and preferred stock* — (1) *Positive adjustment.* The positive adjustment with respect to a share of stock which is limited and preferred as to dividends shall be an allocable part of the undistributed earnings and profits of the subsidiary for the taxable year.

(2) *Negative adjustment.* The negative adjustment with respect to a share of stock which is limited and preferred as to dividends shall be the amount of distributions made by the subsidiary during the taxable year with respect to such share out of earnings and profits of the subsidiary—

(i) Accumulated in prior consolidated return years beginning after December 31, 1965; or

(ii) Accumulated in pre-affiliation years of the subsidiary.

(3) *Exception.* The negative adjustment under subparagraph (2)(i) of this paragraph shall not exceed—

(i) The sum of the positive adjustments under subparagraph (1) of this paragraph for all prior years, minus

(ii) The sum of the negative adjustments under subparagraph (2)(i) of this paragraph for all prior years.

The amount by which the adjustment under subparagraph (2)(i) of this paragraph (determined without regard to this subparagraph) exceeds the amount of such adjustment determined with regard to this subparagraph shall be treated for purposes of paragraph (b)(2)(iii)(a) of this section as a distribution with respect to stock which is not limited and preferred as to dividends.

(d) *Operating rules.* For purposes of paragraphs (b) and (c) of this section—

(1) *Earnings and profits.* (i) The earnings and profits (or deficit in earnings and profits) of a member shall be determined under § 1.1502-33, except that—

(a) The earnings and profits of a member resulting from the disposition of stock of a subsidiary shall be determined in accordance with § 1.1502-33(c)(4)(ii)(b) whether or not such section otherwise applies,

(b) Section 1.1502-33(c)(4)(ii)(c)(2) and (3) shall not apply, and

(c) In computing the earnings and profits of a member resulting from the disposition of stock or an obligation to which § 1.1502-19(a)(6) applies, the adjusted basis of such stock or obligation shall be determined by taking into account any adjustments under § 1.1502-19(a)(6).

(ii) The undistributed earnings and profits for the taxable year shall first be allocated to all the outstanding stock (including the stock held by nonmembers) which is limited and preferred as to dividends in an amount equal to the excess, if any, of—

(a) The cumulative dividends in arrears (determined as of the last day of the subsidiary's taxable year) for all consolidated return years beginning after December 31, 1965, over

(b) The accumulated earnings and profits of the subsidiary as of the first day of the taxable year,

but such amount shall not exceed the accumulated earnings and profits of the subsidiary as of the last day of the taxable year. The balance, if any, of the undistributed earnings and profits, and any net positive adjustment made by such subsidiary with respect to lower tier subsidiaries, for the taxable year shall be allocated among all the outstanding stock of such subsidiary (including stock held by nonmembers) which is not limited and preferred as to dividends.

(2) *Allocation of deficit.* A deficit in earnings and profits, and any net negative adjustments made by such subsidiary with respect to lower tier subsidiaries, for the taxable year, shall be allocated among all the outstanding stock of such subsidiary

(including stock held by nonmembers) which is not limited and preferred as to dividends.

(3) *Loss carryovers.* The amounts described in paragraphs (b) (1) (ii) and (b) (2) (ii) shall be allocated as if such amounts were deficits in earnings and profits for the current taxable year.

(4) *Portion of taxable year.* If an adjustment is required to be made under this section prior to the end of a taxable year of the subsidiary, the amounts referred to in paragraphs (b) (1), (b) (2) (i), (ii) and (iv), and (c) (1) of this section for the taxable year shall be prorated on a daily basis.

(5) *Built-in deductions.* For purposes of paragraphs (b) (1) (ii) and (b) (2) (ii) of this section, the amount of any built-in deductions (as defined in § 1.1502-15(a)) of a subsidiary which are not allowable in a consolidated return year shall be treated as a net operating loss or net capital loss attributable to such subsidiary.

(6) *Acquisitions of nonmembers.* If a subsidiary acquires the assets of a nonmember in a transaction to which section 381 (a) applies, the earnings and profits or deficit in earnings and profits carried over to the subsidiary pursuant to section 381 (c) (2) shall not be treated, for purposes of paragraphs (b) (2) (iii) and (c) (2) of this section, as earnings and profits accumulated in prior consolidated return years beginning after December 31, 1965 or in pre-affiliation years of the subsidiary.

(7) *Distributions from contiguous country corporations.* For purposes of paragraphs (b) (2) (iii) (b) and (c) (2) (ii), a distribution by a subsidiary for which an election has been made under section 1504 (d), out of earnings and profits accumulated during a taxable year on each day of which such subsidiary would have been a member but for section 1504(b)(3), shall not be treated as a distribution out of earnings and profits accumulated in pre-affiliation year.

(8) *Undistributed earnings and profits.* For purposes of this section, the term "undistributed earnings and profits for the taxable year" means earnings and profits for the taxable year after diminution by reason of distribution of dividends (as defined in § 1.1502-14(a)(1)).

(9) *Preaffiliation year.* The term "preaffiliation year" of a subsidiary means any taxable year which includes at least one day on which such subsidiary was not a member of the group, and each taxable year preceding such year.

(10) *Prior consolidated return years beginning after December 31, 1965.* The term "prior consolidated return years beginning after December 31, 1965" shall not include consolidated return years of a corporation which precede the most recent separate return year of such corporation. Thus, if P and its wholly owned subsidiary, S, filed a consolidated return for 1966, separate returns for 1967, and a consolidated return for 1968, P's basis in S's stock is not reduced under paragraph (b)(2)(iii) or (c) (2) of this section because of distributions by S after 1967 out of earnings and profits accumulated in 1966.

(e) *Application of adjust*ment—(1) *Net negative adjustment.* A member owning stock in a subsidiary shall apply its net negative adjustment to reduce its basis for such stock. Any excess of such adjustment over basis is herein referred to as such member's "excess loss account".

(2) *Net positive adjustment.* A member owning stock in a subsidiary shall apply its net positive adjustment with respect to such stock to reduce its excess loss account, if any, with respect to such stock. Any excess of such adjustment over the excess loss account shall be applied to increase the member's basis for such stock.

(3) *Subsequent investment.* If a member has an excess loss account with respect to stock in a subsidiary, any increase in the basis of such stock as a result of a contribution to the capital of the subsidiary (or any basis in stock of the same class or of a similar class acquired with respect to such contribution) shall be applied against and reduce the excess loss account. For example, if corporation P has an excess loss account of $100 in the stock of its wholly-owned subsidiary, S, and P transfers $150 to S in a transaction described in section 351, the excess loss account is reduced to zero and P has a $50 basis in the stock of S.

(4) *Excess loss account.* With respect to the time and manner for taking into account the excess loss account, see § 1.-1502-19.

(f) *Special rules* — (1) *Transitional rules.* (i) If any subsidiary joined in filing (or was required to join in filing) a consolidated return for a taxable year beginning before January 1, 1966 (whether or not with the same group), then for purposes of determining the basis of stock of such subsidiary as of the first day of the first taxable year to which this section applies § 1.1502-34A(b)(2) and (c) shall be applied with respect to the stock (other than stock which is limited and preferred as to dividends) of such subsidiary owned by each member as if such stock were disposed of on such date. If the amount of deductions for losses availed of under § 1.1502-34A(b)(2) or (c)(2) exceeds the sum of the aggregate bases of such stock owned by all members, such excess shall be treated as an excess loss account with respect to such stock. See § 1.1502-19(a)(4) with respect to the treatment of such excess loss account.

(ii) No adjustments to the basis of a subsidiary's stock shall be made under paragraph (b)(2)(ii) of this section on account of losses sustained in taxable years beginning before January 1, 1966, to the extent that the basis of such stock would have been higher as of the beginning of the first taxable year beginning after December 31, 1965, if this section had applied to taxable years beginning before January 1, 1966. For example, assume that subsidiary S was organized in 1961 with $100 capital by the parent of a group filing consolidated returns on a calendar year basis, that S earned $200 in 1961, had no income or losses in 1962 through 1964, and had a deficit of $225 in 1965 that was not absorbed by the parent in 1965 or prior years but was carried over to and absorbed in 1966. The basis of the stock on January 1, 1966, is $100, but if § 1.1502-32 had applied

Reg. § 1.1502-32(f)(1)

24,230.2-B *(I.R.C.)*   Reg. § 1.1502-32(f)(1)   1-15-73

for the years 1961 through 1965, the basis of the S stock on January 1, 1966, would have been $300. Therefore, to the extent of $200 there is no basis adjustment under paragraph (b)(2)(ii) of this section on account of the absorption, and the adjustment is only $25 ($225 minus $200).

(2) *Deemed dividend.* If all the stock of a subsidiary is owned on each day of the subsidiary's taxable year by members, then at the election of the group, such subsidiary shall be treated for all tax purposes as having made a distribution on the first day of such taxable year in an amount equal to, and out of, its accumulated earnings and profits on the day preceding such day. Each member owning stock in such subsidiary shall be treated for all tax purposes as having received an allocable share of such distribution, and as having immediately contributed such allocable share to the capital of the subsidiary. The election shall be made by submitting a statement, on or before the due date (including any extensions of time) of the consolidated return for such year, to the Internal Revenue Service Center with which the group files such return.

(g) *Adjustment on disposition* — (1) *Separate return year ending on or before January 4, 1973.* A member owning stock in a subsidiary shall, on the first day of the first separate return year ending on or before January 4, 1973, of the member or of the subsidiary, whichever occurs first, decrease its basis for such stock by the lesser of—

(i) The accumulated earnings and profits of the subsidiary, or

(ii) The excess, with respect to such stock, of—

(a) The net positive adjustments under paragraph (e)(2) of this section for all consolidated return years, over

(b) The net negative adjustments under paragraph (e)(1) of this section for all consolidated return years.

(2) *Separate return year ending after January 4, 1973.* A member owning stock in a subsidiary shall, on the first day of the first separate return year ending after January 4, 1973, of the member or of the subsidiary, whichever occurs first, decrease its basis for such stock by the excess, with respect to such stock, of

(i) The net positive adjustments under paragraph (e)(2) of this section for all consolidated return years, over

(ii) The net negative adjustments under paragraph (e)(1), plus any decreases under paragraph (f)(1)(i), of this section, for all consolidated return years.

If the amount referred to in the preceding sentence exceeds the basis of such stock, the amount of the excess shall, as of the day immediately preceding such first day, be included in the income of such member as income described in § 1.1502-19(a).

(3) *Example.* Assume that in 1967 corporation P organizes corporation S, investing $500 for all of S's stock. For the taxable year 1967, S has earnings and profits of $100, thus increasing P's basis in S's stock to $600 on the last day of 1967. On December 31, 1967, P sells one-half of its stock in S to a nonmember for $370. P recognizes a gain of $70 on such sale, and on January 1, 1968, P's basis for its remaining stock in S is reduced by $50 to $250.

(h) *Section 334(b)(2) adjustments.* If a subsidiary is liquidated pursuant to section 332 and the basis of the assets distributed is determined under section 334(b)(2), adjustments shall be made to the extent necessary to avoid duplications of adjustments otherwise required by section 334(b)(2) and the regulations thereunder.

(i) [Reserved]

(j) *Examples.* This section may be illustrated by the following examples:

Example (1). On January 1, 1967, corporation P acquired all of the stock of corporation S for $1,000. On that date S had accumulated earnings and profits of $200. In 1967 S had no earnings and profits and distributed $100; in 1968 S had earnings and profits of $150; in 1969 S had a deficit of $30 and made a distribution (on the last day of the year) of $200; in 1970 S had a deficit of $2,000; in 1971 S had earnings and profits of $5,000, and made a distribution of $1,000; in January–June 1972 S had no earnings and profits and made a distribution of $2,000. Consolidated returns were filed for 1967-1972 in which there were no consolidated net losses. On June 30, 1972 the stock of S was sold to an unrelated person. P's basis in S's stock on June 30, 1972 is computed as follows:

Cost		$1,000
1967-Distribution of pre-affiliation earnings		(100)
Basis		$ 900
1968-Undistributed earnings and profits		150
Basis		$1,050
1969-Deficit	($ 30)	
Distribution of 1967-1969 earnings	(120)	
Distribution of preaffiliation earnings	(80)	(230)
Basis		$ 820
1970-Deficit		(2,000)
Excess loss account		($1,180)
1971-Undistributed earnings and profits		4,000
Basis		$2,820
1972-Distribution of 1967-1971 earnings		(2,000)
Basis on June 30, 1972		$ 820

Example (2). On January 1, 1966, corporation P organized a wholly owned subsidiary, corporation S; on the same date S organized a wholly owned subsidiary, corporation T. P invested $1,000 in the stock of S; S invested $600 in the stock of T. Consolidated returns are filed for the years 1966-1969 for which there were no consolidated net losses. Earnings and profits and deficits of T were as follows:

	T
1966	($150)
1967	(900)
1968	600
1969	(100)

Earnings and profits and deficits of S, determined without regard to § 1.1502-33(c)(4), were as follows:

Consolidated Returns (I.R.C.) 24,230.2-C

	S
1966	$ 100
1967	200
1968	(1000)
1969	500

No distributions were made by S or T. On December 31, 1969, the adjusted bases for the stock of S and T would be computed as follows:

	S in T	P in S
Original basis	$600	$1,000
1966		
Deficit of T	(150)	(150)
Undistributed earnings and profits of S		100
Basis	$450	$ 950
1967		
Deficit of T	(900)	(900)
Undistributed earnings and profits of S		200
Basis or (excess loss account)	($450)	$ 250
1968		
Undistributed earnings and profits of T	600	600
Deficit of S		(1,000)
Basis or (excess loss account)	$150	($150)
1969		
Deficit of T	(100)	(100)
Undistributed earnings and profits of S		500
Basis	$ 50	$250

Example (3). Corporation P purchased all the stock of corporation S for $60,000 at the beginning of the calendar year. On August 15, P sold the stock of S for $70,000. A consolidated return is filed by P and S for the calendar year. S had a $40,000 net operating loss and deficit for the period it was included in the consolidated return, while P had $10,000 income for the taxable year (computed without regard to any gain or loss on the sale of S's stock). In computing P's gain on the sale of the stock, P's basis for such stock was decreased by $40,000, the amount of S's deficit, and increased by the portion of the consolidated net operating or capital loss for the taxable year attributable to S under § 1.1502-79(a)(3). Since there were no such consolidated losses for the taxable year, P's basis for S's stock was $20,000 and P's gain was $50,000.

Example (4). Assume the same facts as in example (3) except that P sold the stock of S for $30,000. In such case, there was a consolidated net capital loss for the taxable year none of which was attributable to S, and a consolidated net operating loss for the taxable year of $30,000, all of which was attributable to S. P's basis for its stock in S was $50,000 (original basis of $60,000, minus S's deficit of $40,000, plus the consolidated net operating loss attributable to S of $30,000), and P's loss on the sale of S's stock was $20,000.

○━━▶ § 1.1502-33 (T.D. 6909, filed 12-29-66; amended by T.D. 6493, filed 1-15-68; T.D. 6962, filed 7-2-68 and T.D. 7246, filed 12-29-72.) **Earnings and profits.**

(a) *Intercompany transactions.* Gain or loss on an inter company transaction shall be reflected in the earnings and profits of a member for its taxable year in which such gain or loss is taken into account under § 1.1502-13. Thus, for example, gain on a deferred intercompany transaction shall be reflected in the earnings and profits of a member for its taxable year in which such deferred gain is taken into account under paragraph (d), (e), or (f) of § 1.1502-13, rather than for the taxable year in which such gain or loss is deferred.

(b) *Effect of inventory adjustments.* There shall be reflected in the earnings and profits of a member for a taxable year gains and losses taken into account pursuant to § 1.1502-18 for such year.

(c) *Stock and obligations*—(1) *Dividend distributions.* Dividend distributions from one member to another member shall be reflected in the earnings and profits of such members.

(2) *Nondividend distributions.* Distributions to which section 301(c)(3) applies from one member to another member shall be reflected in earnings and profits only if subparagraph (4)(i) of this paragraph applies.

(3) *Gains or losses on dispositions.* Gains or losses on the disposition of stock or obligations of a subsidiary (including amounts determined under §§ 1.1502-14 and 1.1502-19) shall be reflected in the earnings and profits of a member for the taxable year in which such gain or loss is taken into account. Thus, for example, deferred gain resulting from a partial liquidation shall be reflected in the earnings and profits of a member for its taxable year in which such deferred gain is taken into account under § 1.1502-14(b)(3).

(4) *Investment adjustment*—(i) *Taxable years beginning before January 1, 1976.* Except as provided in subdivision (iii) of this subparagraph, for taxable years beginning before January 1, 1976—

(a) Adjustments made by a member under § 1.1502-32(e)(1) and (2) and (g) shall not be reflected in the earnings and profits of such member.

(b) For purposes of computing the earnings and profits of a member resulting from the disposition of stock of a subsidiary, the adjusted basis of such stock shall be—

(1) The adjusted basis determined without regard to adjustments under § 1.1502-32(e)(1) and (2) and (g), plus

(2) The amount of any excess loss account includible in income by such member under § 1.1502-19(a)(1) on such disposition.

(ii) *Taxable years beginning after December 31, 1975.* For taxable years beginning after December 31, 1975—

(a) There shall be reflected in the earnings and profits of each member for a taxable year an amount equal to any increase or decrease for such taxable year pursuant to § 1.1502-32(e)(1) and (2) and (g) in such member's basis or excess loss account for its stock in a subsidiary.

(b) For purposes of computing the earnings and profits of a member resulting from the disposition of stock of a subsidiary, the adjusted basis of such stock shall be determined by taking into account

Reg. § 1.1502-33(c)(4)

any adjustments under § 1.1502-32(e)(1) and (2) and (g).

(c) If subdivision (i) of this subparagraph applies for one or more taxable years before this subdivision applies—

(1) For purposes of computing the earnings and profits of a member resulting from the disposition of stock of a subsidiary, the adjusted basis of such stock shall be determined by taking into account any adjustments under § 1.1502-32(e)(1) and (2) and (g) for all consolidated return years;

(2) The negative adjustment applicable under § 1.1502-32(b)(2)(iii) (a) or (c)(2)(i) to distributions made in years for which this subdivision applies out of earnings and profits accumulated in years for which this subdivision did not apply shall be eliminated in computing earnings and profits; and

(3) The earnings and profits of a member disposing of stock of a subsidiary shall be (i) increased by an amount equal to the excess of the positive adjustments with respect to such stock under § 1.1502-32(b)(1) or (c)(1) for all years for which this subdivision did not apply, over the sum of the negative adjustments under § 1.1502-32(b)(2) or (c)(2) for all such years plus any adjustments under § 1.1502-32(b)(2)(iii) (a) or (c)(2)(i) which are described in (c)(2) of this subdivision, or (ii) decreased by an amount equal to the excess of the sum of the negative adjustments with respect to such stock under § 1.1502-32(b)(2) or (c)(2) for all years for which this subdivision did not apply plus any adjustments under § 1.1502-32(b)(2)(iii)(a) or (c) (2)(i) which are described in (c)(2) of this subdivision, over the positive adjustments with respect to such stock under § 1.1502-32(b)(1) or (c)(1) for all years for which this subdivision did not apply.

(iii) *Election to adjust currently.* For any taxable year beginning before January 1, 1970, the group may elect to apply the provisions of subdivision (ii) of this subparagraph. Such election shall be made by submitting a statement, on or before the due date (including any extensions of time) of the consolidated return for the first taxable year for which the election is to apply, to the internal revenue officer with whom the group files such return. However, such election may be made for any taxable year beginning after December 31, 1965, within 60 days after July 3, 1968, if it is made in conjunction with an election under paragraph (d) of this section. If an election is made under this subdivision for any taxable year, it may not thereafter be revoked and shall apply for all subsequent taxable years beginning before January 1, 1976.

(iv) *Example.* The application of subdivisions (i) and (ii) of this subparagraph may be illustrated by the following example:

Example. (a) Corporation P forms a wholly-owned subsidiary, S, on January 1, 1966, with a capital contribution of $100, and the PS group files consolidated returns for calendar years 1966 and 1967. S earns $100 in 1966 and has no earnings and profits or deficit in 1967. During 1967, S distributes a $50 dividend to P. On December 31, 1967, P sells all of the stock of S for $150.

(b) If the group has not elected under subdivision (iii) of this subparagraph, the $100 earned by S is not reflected in P's earnings and profits in 1966. However, P's earnings and profits are increased by $50 in 1967, since the dividend is reflected in earnings and profits under paragraph (c)(1) of this section and the corresponding negative adjustment under § 1.1502-32(b)(2)(iii)(a) is not reflected in earnings and profits. P's earnings and profits are further increased by $50 on the sale of the S stock since, for purposes of computing earnings and profits, the basis of such stock is $100 (the original basis without regard to adjustments under § 1.1502-32(e)(1) and (2)).

(c) If the group has elected under subdivision (iii) of this subparagraph, for 1966, the $100 earned by S, a net positive adjustment under § 1.1502-32(e)(2), is reflected in the earnings and profits of P for 1966. No additional earnings and profits result from the distribution in 1967, since there is a $50 increase under paragraph (c)(1) of this section, and the corresponding $50 negative adjustment under § 1.1502-32(b)(2)(iii)(a) is reflected as a decrease in earnings and profits. The subsequent sale of the S stock for $150 does not affect P's earnings and profits since the basis is $150 ($100 original basis plus $100 earnings and profits, minus the $50 distribution out of earnings and profits accumulated in consolidated return years beginning after December 31, 1965).

(d) If the group first elected under subdivision (iii) of this subparagraph for 1967 (so that subdivision (i) was applicable for 1966), the $100 earned by S in 1966 is not reflected in P's earnings and profits in 1966. However, P's earnings and profits are increased by $50 in 1967, since the dividend is reflected in earnings and profits under paragraph (c)(1) of this section, and the corresponding negative adjustment under § 1.1502-32(b)(2)(iii)(a) is eliminated under subdivision (ii)(c) of this subparagraph in computing earnings and profits. P's earnings and profits are further increased by $50 on the sale of the S stock, the amount by which the positive adjustment ($100) under § 1.1502-32(b)(1) for years for which subdivision (ii) did not apply exceeds the sum of the negative adjustments under § 1.1502-32(b)(2) for such years (zero) and the negative adjustment ($50) under § 1.1502-32(b)(2)(iii)(a) for years for which subdivision (ii) did apply.

(v) *Transitional rule.* (a) Adjustments under § 1.1502-32(f)(1) shall not be reflected in earnings and profits.

(b) For purposes of computing the earnings and profits of a member on the disposition of stock (or an obligation to which § 1.1502-19(a)(4) applies) of a subsidiary, the adjusted basis of such stock (or obligation) shall be (1) the adjusted basis determined without regard to adjustments under §§ 1.1502-32(f)(1), plus (2) the amount of any excess loss account includible in income by such member under § 1.1502-19(a)(4) on such disposition.

(vi) *Stock or obligations with reduced basis.* (a) Adjustments under § 1.1502-19(a)(6) shall not be reflected in earnings and profits.

(b) For purposes of computing the earnings and profits of a member on the disposition of stock or an obligation to which § 1.1502-19(a)(6) applies, the adjusted basis of such stock or obligation shall be determined by taking into account any adjustments under § 1.1502-19(a)(6) except such adjustments which were made for a taxable year to which subdivision (i) of this subparagraph applies.

(5) *Section 381 transactions.* The amount of earnings and profits or deficit of a transferor or distributor member which is carried over to the acquiring member in a transaction to which section 381(a) applies shall be adjusted so as not to duplicate any amount reflected in earnings and profits under subparagraph (4) of this paragraph.

(d) *Federal income tax liability*—(1) *In general.* For the purpose of determining the earnings and profits of each member of a group for a consolidated return year beginning after December 31, 1965, the tax liability of the group for such year may be allocated among the members in accordance with subparagraph (2)(i), (ii), or (iii) of this paragraph, if an election is made in accordance with subparagraph (3) of this paragraph. Allocations of tax liability made in accordance with subparagraph (2) of this paragraph shall be treated as allocations of the tax liability of the group for taxable years beginning after December 31, 1965, even though the sum of the amounts allocated for a taxable year may exceed the tax liability of the group as determined under paragraph (b)(1) of § 1.1552-1. See paragraph (b)(2) of § 1.1552-1 for the effect of the allocations.

(2) *Methods of allocation*—(i) The tax liability of the group, as determined under paragraph (b)(1) of § 1.1552-1, shall be allocated to the members in accordance with paragraph (a)(1), (2), or (3) of § 1.1552-1, whichever is applicable, but—

(a) The amount of tax liability allocated to any member for a taxable year to any member for a taxable year shall not exceed the excess of (1) the total of the tax liabilities of such member on a separate return basis for all taxable years to which the election under this paragraph applies, and for which such member joined in the filing of a consolidated return of such group (including the current taxable year), computed as if it had actually filed separate returns for all such years, over (2) the total of the portions of the tax liability of the group allocated to such member for all previous taxable years to which the election under this paragraph applies; and

(b) The amount of any excess tax liability which would be allocated to a member of a group but for (a) of this subdivision (i) shall be apportioned among the other members in direct proportion to, but limited to, the reduction in tax liability resulting to such other members. Such reduction for any member shall be the excess, if any, of (1) the total of its tax liabilities on a separate return basis for all taxable years to which the election under this paragraph applies, and for which such member joined in the filing of a consolidated return of such group (including the current taxable year), computed as if it had actually filed separate returns for all such years, over (2) the total of the portions of the tax liability of the group allocated to such member of all taxable years to which the election under this paragraph applies (including for the current taxable year only the amount allocated under § 1.1552-1(a)(1), (2), or (3). If any excess tax liability remains after being apportioned among members with a reduction in tax liability to the extent of such reduction, as provided in (b) of this subdivision (i), such remaining amount shall, notwithstanding (a) of this subdivision (i), be allocated to the members in accordance with § 1.1552-1(a)(1), (2), or (3), whichever is applicable. In computing the tax liability of a member on a separate return basis for purposes of (a)(1) and (b)(1) of this subdivision (i), its surtax exemption shall be an amount equal to $25,000 divided by the number of members in the group for such year (or such portion of $25,000 which is apportioned to such number pursuant to a schedule attached to the consolidated return for the taxable year), and an election under section 243(b)(2) shall be deemed to be in effect for the group. (However, if for the taxable year some or all of the members are component members of a controlled group of corporations (within the meaning of section 1563) and if there are other such component members which do not join in filing the consolidated return for such year, the amount to be divided among the members filing the consolidated return shall be (in lieu of $25,000) the sum of the amounts apportioned to the component members which join in filing the consolidated return (as determined under § 1.1561-2(a)(2) or § 1.1561-3, whichever is applicable).) If a group elects to use the method of allocation provided by this subdivision, it must maintain specific records to substantiate the tax liability of each member on a separate return basis for purposes of (a)(1) and (b)(1) of this subdivision (i).

(ii) *(a)* The tax liability of the group, as determined under paragraph (b)(1) of § 1.1552-1 shall be allocated to the members in accordance with paragraph (a)(1), (2) or (3) of § 1.1552-1, whichever is applicable;

(b) An additional amount shall be allocated to each member equal to a fixed percentage (which does not exceed 100 percent) of the excess, if any, of (1) the separate return tax liability of such member for the taxable year (computed as provided in paragraph (a)(2)(ii) of § 1.1552-1), over (2) the tax liability allocated to such member in accordance with (a) of this subdivision (ii); and

(c) The total of any additional amounts allocated pursuant to (b) of this subdivision (ii) (including amounts allocated as a result of a carryback) shall be credited to the earnings and profits of those members which had items of income, deductions, or credits to which such total is attributable pursuant to a consistent method which fairly reflects such items of income, deductions, or credits, and which is substantiated by specific records maintained by the group for such purpose.

(iii) Allocations of tax liability to the members shall be made in accordance with any other method approved by the Commissioner. A condition of any such approval shall be that the group maintains specific records to substantiate its computations pursuant to such method.

(3) *Method of election.* (i) In the event a group desires to allocate its tax liability in accordance with a method provided in subparagraph (2)(i) or (ii) of this para-

Reg. § 1.1502-33(d)(3)

graph, for a consolidated return year beginning after December 31, 1965, an election to that effect shall be made within the time prescribed by law for filing the consolidated return for the first taxable year to which the group desires the election to apply (including extensions thereof), or within 60 days after July 3, 1968, whichever is later. The election shall be made by attaching a statement to the consolidated return for the first taxable year to which the group desires the election to apply, or if such election is made within the time prescribed above but after such return is filed, by filing a statement with the internal revenue officer with whom such return was filed. Such statement shall indicate which method is elected, and which method under paragraph (a) (1), (2), or (3) of § 1.1552-1 is elected in conjunction with the election under this subparagraph; in addition, if the method elected is the method provided in subparagraph (2)(ii) of this paragraph, such statement shall state the percentage used pursuant to subparagraph (2)(ii)(b) of this paragraph. In the event a group desires to allocate its tax liability in accordance with a method pursuant to subparagraph (2)(iii) of this paragraph, approval of such method by the Commissioner must be obtained (or, for a taxable year ending before July 1, 1968, a request for approval must be made) within the time prescribed above. The request shall state fully the method which the group wishes to use. An election once made under this subparagraph shall be irrevocable and shall be binding upon the group with respect to the year for which made and for all future consolidated return years of the group unless the Commissioner authorizes a change to another method prior to the time prescribed by law for filing the return for the year in which such change is to be effective.

(ii) If a group does not make an election under this subparagraph for a taxable year ending before July 1, 1968, it may not thereafter make such an election without the approval of the Commissioner unless the election is made for the first consolidated return year of the group.

(iii) An election under this subparagraph shall not be effective unless the group has also made an election under paragraph (c)(4)(iii) of this section.

(4) *Examples.* The provisions of this paragraph may be illustrated by the following examples:

Example (1). (i) Corporation P is the common parent owning all of the stock of corporations S1 and S2, members of an affiliated group. A consolidated return is filed for the taxable year ending December 31, 1966, by P, S1, and S2. The group has made an election in accordance with subparagraph (3) of this paragraph to use the method of allocation provided in subparagraph (2)(i) of this paragraph in conjunction with paragraph (a)(1) of § 1.1552-1. For 1966, the corporations had the following taxable incomes or losses computed as if separate returns were actually filed for such year:

P .... $ 0
S1 2,000
S2 .... (1,000)

Assuming that each member's portion of consolidated taxable income attributable to it is the same as its taxable income computed as if separate returns were actually filed (see paragraph (a)(1) of § 1.1552-1), the tax liability of the group for the year (assuming a 22 percent rate) is $220, all of which is allocated to S1. S1 accordingly reduces its earnings and profits in the amount of $220, irrespective of who actually pays the tax liability. If S1 pays the $220 tax liability there will be no further effect upon the income, earnings and profits, or the basis of stock of any member. If, however, P pays the $220 tax liability (and such payment is not in fact a loan from P to S1), then P shall be treated as having made a contribution to the capital of S1 in the amount of $220. On the other hand, if S2 pays the $220 tax liability (and such payment is not in fact a loan from S2), then S2 shall be treated as having made a distribution with respect to its stock to P in the amount of $220, and P shall be treated as having made a contribution to the capital of S1 in the amount of $220. (See paragraph (b)(2) of § 1.1552-1.)

(ii) For the 1967 taxable year, P, S1, and S2 had the following taxable incomes computed as if separate returns were actually filed, but without regard to any carryover from 1966:

P .... $ 0
S1 1,000
S2 3,000

Assuming that each member's portion of the consolidated taxable income attributable to it is the same as its taxable income computed as if separate returns were actually filed, the tax liability of the group for 1967 is $880; $440 is allocated to S1 and $440 is allocated to S2, determined as follows: If S2 had filed separate returns for 1966 and 1967 it would have had no tax liability for 1966 and a tax liability for 1967 of $440 (taking into account a $1,000 net operating loss carryover from 1966). Thus, $440 is the maximum amount which may be allocated to S2 for 1967, pursuant to the method of allocation elected by the group. The entire excess of $220 (which would otherwise be allocated to S2 under § 1.1552-1(a)(1) is allocated to S1 because S1 had a $220 reduction in tax liability, as determined under subparagraph (2)(i)(b) of this paragraph. Such reduction is the excess of S1's 1966 and 1967 tax liabilities on a separate return basis ($660) over its allocated portion of the tax liability of the group for 1966 ($220) plus the amount allocated to it for 1967 under § 1.1552-1(a)(1) ($220). The effect of the allocation of $440 to S1 and $440 to S2 is determined under § 1.1552-1(b)(2).

Example (2). Assume the same facts as in example (1) except that the group elected in accordance with subparagraph (3) of this paragraph to use the method of allocation provided in subparagraph (2)(ii) of this paragraph, choosing a fixed percentage of 100 percent under subparagraph (2)(ii)(b) of this paragraph. Assume also that the taxable incomes and losses of the corporations shown in example (1) would be the same amount if computed as provided in paragraph (a)(2)(ii) of § 1.1552-1. Thus, for 1966, $440 is allocated to S1 (the $220 tax liability of the group, and an additional $220 pursuant to subparagraph (2)(ii)(b) of this paragraph). The earnings and profits of S1 are reduced in the amount of $440, and the earnings and profits of S2 are increased in the amount of $220 because the $220 allocated to S1 which is in addition to the tax liability of the group is attributable to deductions of S2. If S1 pays the $220 tax liability of the group and pays $220 to S2, no further adjustments will be made, as a result of the 1966 tax liability, to the income, earnings and profits, or basis of stock of any member. If S1 pays the $220 tax liability of the group, and pays the other $220 to P instead of S2, because, for example, of an agreement among P, S1, and S2, S2 is treated as having made a distribution with respect to its stock to P in the year that S1 makes the payment to P. See paragraph (b)(2) of § 1.1552-1.

For 1967, $220 is allocated to S1 and $660 is allocated to S2. No additional amounts are allocated pursuant to subparagraph (2)(ii)(b) of this paragraph.

○— § 1.1502-34 (T.D. 6894, filed 9-7-66.) **Special aggregate stock ownership rules.**

For purposes of §§ 1.1502-1 through 1.-1502-80, in determining the stock ownership of a member of the group in another corporation (the "issuing corporation") for purposes of determining the application of section 165(g)(3)(A), 332(b)(1), 333(b), 351(a), or 904(f), in a consolidated return year, there shall be included stock owned by all other members of the group in the issuing corporation. Thus, assume that members A, B, and C each own 33⅓ percent of the stock issued by D. In such case, A, B, and C shall each be treated as meeting the 80-percent stock ownership requirement for purposes of section 332, and no member can elect to have section 333 apply. Furthermore, the special rule for minority shareholders in section 337(d) cannot apply with respect to amounts received by A, B, or C in liquidation of D.

○— §§ 1.1502-35 to 1.1502-40 [Reserved]

SPECIAL TAXES AND TAXPAYERS

○— § 1.1502-41 (T.D. 6894, filed 9-7-66.) **Determination of consolidated net long-term capital gain and consolidated net short-term capital loss.**

(a) *Consolidated net long-term capital gain.* The consolidated net long-term capital gain shall be determined by taking into account (1) those gains and losses to which paragraph (a)(1) of § 1.1502-22 applies which are treated as long term under section 1222, and (2) the consolidated section 1231 net gain (computed in accordance with § 1.1502-23).

(b) *Consolidated net short-term capital loss.* The consolidated net short-term capital loss shall be determined by taking into account (1) those gains and losses to which paragraph (a)(1) of § 1.1502-22 applies which are treated as short term under section 1222, and (2) the consolidated net capital loss carryovers to the taxable year (as determined under paragraph (b) of § 1.-1502-22).

○— § 1.1502-42   (T.D. 7246, filed 12-29-72.)

Mutual savings banks, domestic building and loan associations, and cooperative banks.

In the case of mutual savings banks, domestic building and loan associations, and cooperative banks—

(a) In computing for purposes of section 593(b)(1)(B)(ii) total deposits or withdrawable accounts at the close of the taxable year, the total deposits or withdrawable accounts of other members shall be excluded, and

(b) For purposes of section 593(b)(2), a member's taxable income shall be the amount computed under § 1.1502-27(b) (computed without regard to the amount of any addition to the reserve for bad debts of any member determined under section 593(b)(2)). In the case of a taxable year beginning before July 12, 1969, such amount shall be computed without regard to any net operating loss carryback.

○— §§ 1.1502-43 to 1.1502-74 [Reserved]

ADMINISTRATIVE PROVISIONS AND OTHER RULES

○— § 1.1502-75 (T.D. 6894, filed 9-7-66; amended by T.D. 7016, filed 10-6-69; T.D. 7024, filed 2-9-70; T.D. 7244, filed 12-29-72 and T.D. 7246, filed 12-29-72.) **Filing of consolidated returns.**

(a) *Privilege of filing consolidated returns—(1) Exercise of privilege for first consolidated return year.* A group which did not file a consolidated return for the immediately preceding taxable year may file a consolidated return in lieu of separate returns for the taxable year, provided that each corporation which has been a member during any part of the taxable year for which the consolidated return is to be filed consents (in the manner provided in paragraph (b) of this section) to the regulations under section 1502. If a group wishes to exercise it privilege of

24,230.4 (I.R.C.)   Reg. § 1.1502-75(a)(1)   1-15-73

filing a consolidated return, such consolidated return must be filed not later than the last day prescribed by law (including extensions of time) for the filing of the common parent's return. Such consolidated return may not be withdrawn after such last day (but the group may change the basis of its return at any time prior to such last day).

(2) *Continued filing requirement.* A group which filed (or was required to file) a consolidated return for the immediately preceding taxable year is required to file a consolidated return for the taxable year unless it has an election to discontinue filing consolidated returns under paragraph (c) of this section.

(b) *How consent for first consolidated year exercised*—(1) *General rule.* The consent of a corporation referred to in paragraph (a) (1) of this section shall be made by such corporation joining in the making of the consolidated return for such year. A corporation shall be deemed to have joined in the making of such return for such year if it files a Form 1122 in the manner specified in paragraph (b) (2) of this section.

(2) *Consent under facts and circumstances.* If a member of the group fails to file Form 1122, the Commissioner may under the facts and circumstances determine that such member has joined in the making of a consolidated return by such group. The following circumstances, among others, will be taken into account in making this determination:

(i) Whether or not the income and deductions of the member were included in the consolidated return;

(ii) Whether or not a separate return was filed by the member for that taxable year; and

(iii) Whether or not the member was included in the affiliations schedule, Form 851.

If the Commissioner determines that the member has joined in the making of the consolidated return, such member shall be treated as if it had filed a Form 1122 for such year for purposes of paragraph (h) (2) of this section.

(3) *Failure to consent due to mistake.* If any member has failed to join in the making of a consolidated return under either subparagraph (1) or (2) of this paragraph, then the tax liability of each member of the group shall be determined on the basis of separate returns unless the common parent corporation establishes to the satisfaction of the Commissioner that the failure of such member to join in the making of the consolidated return was due to a mistake of law or fact, or to inadvertence. In such case, such member shall be treated as if it had filed a Form 1122 for such year for the purposes of paragraph (h)(2) of this section, and thus joined in the making of the consolidated return for such year.

(c) *Election to discontinue filing consolidated returns*—(1) *Good cause*—(i) *In general.* Notwithstanding that a consolidated return is required for a taxable year, the Commissioner, upon application by the common parent, may for good cause shown grant permission to a group to discontinue filing consolidated returns. Any such application shall be made to the Commissioner of Internal Revenue, Washington, D.C. 20224, and shall be made not later than the 90th day before the due date for the filing of the consolidated return (including extensions of time). In addition, if an amendment of the Code, or other law affecting the computation of tax liability, is enacted and the enactment is effective for a taxable year ending before or within 90 days after the date of enactment, then application for such a taxable year may be made not later than the 180th day after the date of enactment, and if the application is approved the permission to discontinue filing consolidated returns will apply to such taxable year notwithstanding that a consolidated return has already been filed for such year.

(ii) *Substantial adverse change in law affecting tax liability.* Ordinarily, the Commissioner will grant a group permission to discontinue filing consolidated returns if the net result of all amendments to the Code or regulations with effective dates commencing within the taxable year has a substantial adverse effect on the consolidated tax liability of the group for such year relative to what the aggregate tax liability would be if the members of the group filed separate returns for such year. Thus, for example, assume P and S filed a consolidated return for the calendar year 1966 and that the provisions of the Code have been amended by a bill which was enacted by Congress in 1966, but which is first effective for taxable years beginning on or after January 1, 1967. Assume further that P makes a timely application to discontinue filing consolidated returns. In order to determine whether the amendments have a substantial adverse effect on the consolidated tax liablity for 1967, relative to what the aggregate tax liability would be if the members of the group filed separate returns for 1967, the difference between the tax liability of the group computed on a consolidated basis and taking into account the changes in the law effective for 1967 and the aggregate tax liability of the members of the group computed as if each such member filed separate returns for such year (also taking into account such changes) shall be compared with the difference between the tax liability of such group for 1967 computed on a consolidated basis without regard to the changes in the law effective in such year and the aggregate tax liability of the members of the group computed as if separate returns had been filed by such members for such year without regard to the changes in the law effective in such year.

(iii) *Other factors.* In addition, the Commissioner will take into account other factors in determining whether good cause exists for granting permission to discontinue filing consolidated returns beginning with the taxable year, including—

(a) Changes in law or circumstances, including changes which do not affect Federal income tax liability.

(b) Changes in law which are first effective in the taxable year and which result in a substantial reduction in the consolidated net operating loss (or consolidated unused investment credit) for such year relative to what the aggregate net operating losses (or investment credits) would be if the members of the group filed separate returns for such year, and

(c) Changes in the Code or regulations which are effective prior to the taxable year but which first have a substantial adverse effect on the filing of a consolidated return relative to the filing of separate returns by members of the group in such year.

(2) *Discretion of Commissioner to grant blanket permission*—(i) Permission to all groups. The Commissioner, in his discretion, may grant all groups permission to dis-

continue filing consolidated returns if any provisions of the Code or regulations has been amended and such amendment is of the type which could have a substantial adverse effect on the filing of consolidated returns by substantially all groups, relative to the filing of separate returns. Ordinarily, the permission to discontinue shall apply with respect to the taxable year of each group which includes the effective date of such an amendment.

(ii) Permission to a class of groups. The Commissioner, in his discretion, may grant a particular class of groups permission to discontinue filing consolidated returns if any provision of the Code or regulations has been amended and such amendment is of the type which could have a substantial adverse effect on the filing of consolidated returns by substantially all such groups relative to the filing of separate returns. Ordinarily, the permission to discontinue shall apply with respect to the taxable year of each group within the class which includes the effective date of such an amendment.

(3) *Time and manner for exercising election.* If, under subparagraph (1) or (2) of this paragraph, a group has an election to discontinue filing consolidated returns for any taxable year and such group wishes to exercise such election, then the common parent must file a separate return for such year on or before the last day prescribed by law (including extensions of time) for the filing of the consolidated return for such year. See section 6081 (relating to extensions of time for filing returns).

(d) *When group remains in existence—*
(1) *General rule.* A group shall be considered as remaining in existence if the common parent corporation remains as the common parent and at least one subsidiary remains affiliated with it, whether or not such subsidiary was a member of the group in a prior year and whether or not one or more corporations have ceased to be subsidiaries at any time after the group was formed. Thus, for example, assume that individual A forms corporation P. P acquires 100 percent of the stock of corporation S on January 1, 1965, and P and S file a consolidated return for the calendar year 1965. On May 1, 1966, P acquires 100 percent of the stock of S-1, and on July 1, 1966, P sells the stock of S. The group (consisting originally of P and S) remains in existence in 1966 since P has remained as the common parent and at least one subsidiary (now S-1) remains affiliated with it.

(2) *Common parent no longer in existence—*(i) Mere change in identity. For purposes of this paragraph, the common parent corporation shall remain as the common parent irrespective of a mere change in identity, form, or place of organization of such common parent corporation (see section 368(a)(1)(F)).

(ii) *Transfer of assets to subsidiary.* The group shall be considered as remaining in existence notwithstanding that the common parent is no longer in existence if the members of the affiliated group succeed to and become the owners of substantially all of the assets of such former parent and there remains one or more chains of includible corporations connected through stock ownership with a common parent corporation which is an includible corporation and which was a member of the group prior to the date such former parent ceases to exist. For purposes of applying paragraph (f)(2)(i) of § 1.1502-1 to separate return years ending on or before the date on which the former parent ceases to exist, such former parent, and not the new common parent, shall be considered to be the corporation described in such paragraph.

(iii) *Taxable years.* If a transfer of assets described in subdivision (ii) of this subparagraph is an acquisition to which section 381(a) applies and if the group files a consolidated return for the taxable year in which the acquisition occurs, then for purposes of section 381—

(a) The former common parent shall not close its taxable year merely because of the acquisition, and all taxable years of such former parent ending on or before the date of acquisition shall be treated as taxable years of the acquiring corporation, and

(b) The corporation acquiring the assets shall close its taxable year as of the date of acquisition, and all taxable years of such corporation ending on or before the date of acquisition shall be treated as taxable years of the transferor corporation.

(iv) *Exception.* With respect to acquisitions occurring before January 1, 1971, subdivision (iii) of this subparagraph shall not apply if the group, in its income tax return, treats the taxable year of the former common parent as having closed as of the date of acquisition.

(3) *Reverse acquisitions*—(i) *In general.* If a corporation (hereinafter referred to as the "first corporation") or any member of a group of which the first corporation is the common parent acquires after October 1, 1965—

(a) Stock of another corporation (hereinafter referred to as the second corporation), and as a result the second corporation becomes (or would become but for the application of this subparagraph) a member of a group of which the first corporation is the common parent, or

(b) Substantially all the assets of the second corporation,

in exchange (in whole or in part) for stock of the first corporation, and the stockholders (immediately before the acquisition) of the second corporation, as a result of owning stock of the second corporation, own (immediately after the acquisition) more than 50 percent of the fair market value of the outstanding stock of the first corporation, then any group of which the first corporation was the common parent immediately before the acquisition shall cease to exist as of the date of acquisition, and any group of which the second corporation was the common parent immediately before the acquisition shall be treated as remaining in existence (with the first corporation becoming the common parent of the group). Thus, assume that corporations P and S comprised group PS (P being the common parent), that P was merged into corporation T (the common parent of a group composed of T and corporation U), and that the shareholders of P immediately before the merger, as a result of owning stock in P, own 90 percent of the fair market value of T's stock immediately after the merger. The group of which P was the common parent is treated as con-

Reg. § 1.1502-75(d)(3)

tinuing in existence with T and U being added as members of the group, and T taking the place of P as the common parent. For purposes of determining under (a) of this subdivision whether the second corporation becomes (or would become) a member of the group of which the first corporation is the common parent, and for purposes of determining whether the former stockholders of the second corporation own more than 50 percent of the outstanding stock of the first corporation, there shall be taken into account any acquisitions or redemptions of the stock of either corporation which are pursuant to a plan of acquisition described in (a) or (b) of this subdivision.

(ii) *Prior ownership of stock.* For purposes of subdivision (i) of this subparagraph, if the first corporation, and any members of a group of which the first corporation is the common parent, have continuously owned for a period of at least five years ending on the date of the acquisition an aggregate of at least 25 percent of the fair market value of the outstanding stock of the second corporation, then the first corporation (and any subsidiary which owns stock of the second corporation immediately before the acquisition) shall, as a result of owning such stock, be treated as owning (immediately after the acquisition) a percentage of the fair market value of the first corporation's outstanding stock which bears the same ratio to (a) the percentage of the fair market value of all the stock of the second corporation owned immediately before the acquisition by the first corporation and its subsidiaries as (b) the fair market value of the total outstanding stock of the second corporation immediately before the acquisition bears to (c) the sum of (1) the fair market value, immediately before the acquisition, of the total outstanding stock of the first corporation, and (2) the fair market value, immediately before the acquisition, of the total outstanding stock of the second corporation (other than any such stock owned by the first corporation and any of its subsidiaries). For example, assume that corporation P owns stock in corporation T having a fair market value of $100,000, that P acquires the remaining stock of T from individuals in exchange for stock of P, that immediately before the acquisition the total outstanding stock of T had a fair market value of $150,000, and that immediately before the acquisition the total outstanding stock of P had a fair market value of $200,000. Assuming P owned at least 25 percent of the fair market value of T's stock for five years, then for purposes of this subparagraph, P is treated as owning (immediately after the acquisition) 40 percent of the fair market value of its own outstanding stock, determined as follows:

$$\frac{\$150,000}{\$200,000 + \$50,000} \times 66\tfrac{2}{3}\% = 40\%$$

Thus, if the former individual stockholders of T own, immediately after the acquisition more than 10 percent of the fair market value of the outstanding stock of P as a result of owning stock of T, the group of which T was the common parent is treated as continuing in existence with P as the common parent, and the group of which P was the common parent before the acquisition ceases to exist.

(iii) *Election.* The provisions of subdivision (ii) of this subparagraph shall not apply to any acquisition occurring in a taxable year ending after October 7, 1969, unless the first corporation elects to have such subdivision apply. The election shall be made by means of a statement, signed by any officer who is duly authorized to act on behalf of the first corporation, stating that the corporation elects to have the provisions of § 1.1502-75(d)(3)(ii) apply and identifying the acquisition to which such provisions will apply. The statement shall be filed, on or before the due date (including extensions of time) of the return for the group's first consolidated return year ending after the date of the acquisition, with the internal revenue officer with whom such return is required to be filed.

(iv) *Transfer of assets to subsidiary.* This subparagraph shall not apply to a transaction to which subparagraph (2)(ii) of this paragraph applies.

(v) *Taxable years.* If, in a transaction described in subdivision (i) of this subparagraph, the first corporation files a consolidated return for the first taxable year ending after the date of acquisition, then—

(a) The first corporation, and each corporation which, immediately before the acquisition, is a member of the group of which the first corporation is the common parent, shall close its taxable year as of the date of acquisition, and each such corporation shall, immediately after the acquisition, change to the taxable year of the second corporation, and

(b) If the acquisition is a transaction described in section 381(a)(2), then for purposes of section 381—

(1) All taxable years ending on or before the date of acquisition, of the first corporation and each corporation which, immediately before the acquisition, is a member of the group of which the first corporation is the common parent, shall be treated as taxable years of the transfer corporation, and

(2) The second corporation shall not close its taxable year merely because of such acquisition, and all taxable years ending on or before the date of acquisition, of the second corporation and each corporation which, immediately before the acquisition, is a member of any group of which the second corporation is the common parent, shall be treated as taxable years of the acquiring corporation.

(vi) *Exception.* With respect to acquisitions occurring before April 17, 1968, subdivision (v) of this subparagraph shall not apply if the parties to the transaction, in their income tax returns, treat subdivision (i) as not affecting the closing of taxable years or the operation of section 381.

(e) *Failure to include subsidiary.* If a consolidated return is required for the taxable year under the provisions of paragraph (a)(2) of this section, the tax liability of all members of the group for such year shall be computed on a consolidated basis even though—

(1) Separate returns are filed by one or more members of the group, or

(2) There has been a failure to include in the consolidated return the income of any member of the group.

If subparagraph (1) of this paragraph applies, the amounts assessed or paid upon the basis of separate returns shall be considered as having been assessed or paid upon the basis of a consolidated return.

(f) *Inclusion of one or more corporations not members of the group*—(1) *Method of determining tax liability.* If a consolidated return includes the income of a corporation which was not a member of the group at any time during the consolidated return year, the tax liability of such corporation will be determined upon the basis of a separate return (or a consolidated return of another group, if paragraph (a) (2) or (b) (3) of this section applies), and the consolidated return will be considered as including only the income of the corporations which were members of the group during that taxable year. If a consolidated return includes the income of two or more corporations which were not members of the group but which constitute another group, the tax liability of such corporations will be computed in the same manner as if separate returns had been made by such corporations unless the Commissioner upon application approves the making of a consolidated return for the other group or unless under paragraph (a) (2) of this section a consolidated return is required for the other group.

(2) *Allocation of tax liability.* In any case in which amounts have been assessed and paid upon the basis of a consolidated return and the tax liability of one or more of the corporations included in the consolidated return is to be computed in the manner described in subparagraph (1) of this paragraph, the amounts so paid shall be allocated between the group composed of the corporations properly included in the consolidated return and each of the corporations the tax liability of which is to be computed on a separate basis (or on the basis of a consolidated return of another group) in such manner as the corporations which were included in the consolidated return may, subject to the approval of the Commissioner, agree upon or in the absence of an agreement upon the method used in allocating the tax liability of the members of the group under the provisions of section 1552 (a).

(g) *Computing periods of limitation*—(1) *Income incorrectly included in consolidated return.* If—

(i) A consolidated return is filed by a group for the taxable year, and

(ii) The tax liability of a corporation whose income is included in such return must be computed on the basis of a separate return (or on the basis of a consolidated return with another group),

then for the purpose of computing any period of limitation with respect to such separate return (or such other consolidated return), the filing of such consolidated return by the group shall be considered as the making of a return by such corporation.

(2) *Income incorrectly included in separate returns.* If a consolidated return is required for the taxable year under the provisions of paragraph (a) (2) of this section, the filing of separate returns by the members of the group for such year shall not be considered as the making of a return for the purpose of computing any period of limitation with respect to such consolidated return unless there is attached to each such separate return a statement setting forth—

(i) The most recent taxable year of the member for which its income was included in a consolidated return, and

(ii) The reasons for the group's belief that a consolidated return is not required for the taxable year.

(h) *Method of filing return and forms*—(1) *Consolidated return made by common parent corporation.* The consolidated return shall be made on Form 1120 for the group by the common parent corporation. The consolidated return, with Form 851 (affiliations schedule) attached, shall be filed with the district director with whom the common parent would have filed a separate return.

(2) *Filing of Form 1122 for first year.* If, under the provisions of paragraph (a) (1) of this section, a group wishes to exercise its privilege of filing a consolidated return, then a Form 1122 must be executed by each subsidiary and must be attached to the consolidated return for such year. Form 1122 shall not be required for a taxable year if a consolidated return was filed (or was required to be filed) by the group for the immediately preceding taxable year.

(3) *Persons qualified to execute returns and forms.* Each return or form required to be made or prepared by a corporation must be executed by the person authorized under section 6062 to execute returns of separate corporations.

(i) [Reserved]

(j) *Statements and schedules for subsidiaries.* The statement of gross income and deductions and the schedules required by the instructions on the return shall be prepared and filed in columnar form so that the details of the items of gross income, deductions, and credits for each member may be readily audited. Such statements and schedules shall include in columnar form a reconciliation of surplus for each corporation, and a reconciliation of consolidated surplus. Consolidated balance sheets as of the beginning and close of the taxable year of the group, taken from the books of the members, shall accompany the consolidated return and shall be prepared in a form similar to that required for reconciliation of surplus.

O—— § 1.1502-76 (T.D. 6894, filed 9-7-66; amended by T.D. 7244, filed 12-29-72 and T.D. 7246, filed 12-29-72.) **Taxable year of members of group.**

(a) *Taxable year of members of group*—(1) *Change to parent's taxable year.* The consolidated return of a group must be filed on the basis of the common parent's taxable year, and each subsidiary must adopt the common parent's annual accounting period for the first consolidated return year for which the subsidiary's income is includible in the consolidated return. If any member is on a 52-53-week taxable year, the rule of the preceding sentence shall, with the advance consent the Commissioner, be deemed satisfied if the taxable years of all members of the group end within the same 7-day period. Any request for such consent shall be filed with the

Reg. § 1.1502-76(a)(1)

Commissioner of Internal Revenue, Washington, D.C. 20224, not later than the thirtieth day before the due date (not including extensions of time) for the filing of the consolidated return.

(2) *Includible insurance company as member of group.* If an includible insurance company required by section 843 to file its return on the basis of a calendar year is a member of the group and if the common parent of such group files its return on the basis of a fiscal year, then the first consolidated return which includes the income of such insurance company may be filed on the basis of the common parent's fiscal year, provided, however, that if such insurance company is a member of the group on the last day of the common parent's taxable year, all members other than such insurance company change to a calendar year or to a 52-53 week taxable year ending within a 7-day period which includes December 31, effective immediately after the close of the common parent's taxable year. If any member changes to a 52-53 week taxable year, the advance consent of the Commissioner shall be obtained in accordance with subparagraph (1) of this paragraph.

(b) *Income to be included in returns for taxable year*—(1) *Inclusion of income in consolidated return.* The consolidated return of a group must include the income of the common parent for that corporation's entire taxable year (excluding any portion of such taxable year for which its income is properly included in the consolidated return of another group) and, except as provided in subparagraph (5) of this paragraph, the income of each subsidiary for the portion of such taxable year during which it was a member of the group. If § 1.1502-75(d)(2)(ii) applies to a group, then for purposes of this paragraph, the former common parent shall be deemed to continue in existence and shall be regarded as the common parent for the entire taxable year in which the acquisition occurs. If § 1.1502-75(d)(3)(v) applies to a group, then for purposes of the application of this paragraph (other than to a group which ceases to exist as a result of the application of § 1.1502-75(d)(3)(i)), the second corporation (whether or not it remains in existence) shall be treated as the common parent for the entire taxable year of such corporation in which the acquisition occurs, and the first corporation shall be treated as a subsidiary for the portion of such taxable year subsequent to the acquisition.

(2) *Separate return for period not included in a consolidated return.* If the consolidated return of a group properly includes the income of a corporation for only a portion of such corporation's taxable year (determined without regard to a change of its taxable year under paragraph (a) of this section), then the income for the portion of such taxable year not included in the consolidated return must be included in a separate return (or, if such corporation is a member of another group which files a consolidated return for such portion of such year, then in such consolidated return).

(3) *Examples.* The provisions of subparagraphs (1) and (2) of this paragraph may be illustrated by the following examples:

Example (1). Corporations X and Y filed separate returns for the calendar year 1965. As of the close of June 30, 1966, X acquired all of the stock of Y. If X files a consolidated return for 1966, it must include in such return its income for the entire taxable year and the income of Y for the period July 1, 1966, through December 31, 1966. Y must include its income for the period January 1, 1966, through June 30, 1966, in a separate return.

Example (2). Corporations P and S, a group of corporations, filed a consolidated return for the calendar year 1966. As of the close of June 30, 1967, all of the stock of S was sold to individual A. P must file a consolidated return for 1967 including P's income for the entire taxable year and the income of S for the period of January 1, 1967, through June 30, 1967. S must file a separate return for the period July 1, 1967, through December 31, 1967.

Example (3). Assume the same facts as in example (2) plus the additional fact that as of the close of July 31, 1967, P acquired all the stock of corporation T (which filed separate returns on the basis of a fiscal year ending November 30), and that P and T filed a consolidated return for 1967. P must file two consolidated returns for 1967. The consolidated return of P and S for 1967 must include P's income for the entire taxable year, excluding that portion of such year (August 1 through December 31) for which its income is includible in the consolidated return of P and T. The consolidated return of P and T for 1967 must include P's income for its entire taxable year, excluding that portion of the taxable year (January 1 through July 31) for which P's income is included in the consolidated return of P and S, and including the income of T for the period August 1 through December 31. T must file a separate return for the period December 1, 1966, through July 31, 1967.

(4) *Allocation of income between separate and consolidated returns.* (i) If the taxable income of a member for a taxable year (determined without regard to a change of its year under paragraph (a) of this section) must be included in part in a consolidated return and in part in a separate return (or a consolidated return of another group), the taxable income to be reported in each such return shall be determined on the basis of its income shown on its permanent records (including work papers).

(ii) If the portion of an item of income or deduction to be reported in each such return cannot be clearly determined from the permanent records, the portion of such item to be included in each such return shall be the amount of the item for the full taxable year (determined without regard to the change of year) multiplied by a fraction, the numerator of which is the number of days for which the member's income is to be included in such return and the denominator of which is the total number of days in such year.

(5) *Period of 30 days or less may be disregarded.* For purposes of the regulations under section 1502—

(i) If within a period of 30 days after the beginning of a corporation's taxable year (determined without regard to the required change to the parent's taxable year) it becomes a member of a group which files a consolidated return for a taxable year which includes such period, then such corporation may at its option be considered to have become a member of the group as of the beginning of the first day of such corporation's taxable year, or

(ii) If, during a consolidated return year of a group, a corporation (other than a corporation created or organized in such year by a member of the group) has been a member of such group for a period of 30 days or less, then such corporation may at its option be considered as not having been a member of the group during such year.

(6) *Examples.* The provisions of subparagraph (5) of this paragraph may be illustrated by the following examples:

Example (1). Corporation P, a common parent corporation, filed a consolidated return for the calendar year 1965. As of the close of July 14, 1966, P acquired all of the stock of corporation S. S filed its separate returns on the basis of the fiscal year ending June 30. P files a consolidated return for 1966. Since S became a member of the group within 30 days after the beginning of its taxable year, S may at its option include its income in such consolidated return for the period July 1, 1966 (the beginning of its taxable year), through December 31, 1966, in lieu of the period July 15, 1966, through December 31, 1966.

Example (2). Assume the same facts as in example (1) except that P acquired all of the stock of S as of the close of December 14, 1966. Since S has been a member of the group for a period of 30 days or less during the group's calendar year 1966, S may at its option not include any of its income in the consolidated return filed for 1966.

(c) *Time for making separate returns for periods not included in consolidated return*—(1) *Consolidated return filed by due date for separate return.* If the group has filed a consolidated return on or before the due date for the filing of a subsidiary's separate return (including extensions of time and determined without regard to any change of its taxable year required under paragraph (a) of this section), then the separate return for any portion of the subsidiary's taxable year for which its income is not included in the consolidated return of the group must be filed no later than the due date of such consolidated return (including extensions of time).

(2) *Consolidated return not filed by due date for separate return.* If the group has not filed a consolidated return on or before the due date for the filing of a subsidiary corporation's separate return (including extensions of time and determined without regard to any change of its taxable year required under paragraph (a) of this section), then on or before such due date such subsidiary shall file a separate return either for the portion of its taxable year for which its income would not be included in a consolidated return if such a return were filed, or for its complete taxable year. However, if a separate return is filed for such portion of its taxable year and the group subsequently does not file a consolidated return, such subsidiary corporation shall file a substituted return for its complete taxable year not later than the due date (including extensions of time) prescribed for the filing of the common parent's return. On the other hand, if the return is filed for the subsidiary's complete taxable year and the group later files a consolidated return, such subsidiary must file an amended return not later than the due date (including extensions of time) for the filing of the consolidated return of the group. Such amended return shall be for that portion of such subsidiary's taxable year which is not included in the consolidated return. If, under this subparagraph, a substituted return must be filed, then the return previously filed shall not be considered a return within the meaning of section 6011. If, under this subparagraph, a substituted or amended return must be filed, then, for purposes of sections 6513 (a) and 6601 (a), the last date prescribed for payment of tax shall be the due date (not including extensions of time) for the filing of the subsidiary's separate return (determined without regard to this subparagraph and without regard to any change of its taxable year required under paragraph (a) of this section).

(3) *Examples.* The provisions of this paragraph may be illustrated by the following examples:

Example (1). Corporation P, which filed a separate return for the calendar year 1966, acquires all of the stock of corporation S as of the close of December 31, 1966. Corporation S reports its income on the basis of a fiscal year ending March 31. On June 15, 1967, the due date for the filing of a separate return by S (assuming no extensions of time), a consolidated return has not been filed for the group (P and S). On such date S may either file a return for the period April 1, 1966, through December 31, 1966, or it may file a return for the complete fiscal year ending March 31, 1967. If S files a return for the short period ending December 31, 1966, and if the group elects not to file a consolidated return for the calendar year 1967, S, on or before March 15, 1968 (the due date of P's return, assuming no extensions of time), must file a substitute return for the complete fiscal year ending March 31, 1967, in lieu of the return previously filed for the short period. Interest is computed from June 15, 1967. If, however, S files a return for the complete fiscal year ending March 31, 1967, and the group elects to file a consolidated return for the calendar year 1967, then S must file an amended return covering the period from April 1, 1966, through December 31, 1966, in lieu of the return previously filed for the complete fiscal year. Interest is computed from June 15, 1967.

Example (2). Assume the same facts as in example (1) except that corporation P acquires all of the stock of corporation S at the close of September 30, 1967, and that P files a consolidated return for the group for 1967 on March 15, 1968 (not having obtained any extensions of time). Since a consolidated return has been filed on or before the due date (June 15, 1968) for the filing of the separate return for the taxable year ending March 31, 1968, the return of S for the short taxable year beginning April 1, 1967, and ending September 30, 1967, should be filed no later than March 15, 1968.

(d) *Taxable year of less than 12 months.* Any period of less than 12

Reg. § 1.1502-76(d)

24,230.10 (I.R.C.)   Reg. § 1.1502-76(d)   9-30-74

months for which either a separate return or a consolidated return is filed under the provisions of this section shall be considered as a separate taxable year.

○— § 1.1502-77 (T.D. 6894, filed 9-7-66; amended by T.D. 7323, filed 9-24-74.) **Common parent agent for subsidiaries.**

(a) *Scope of agency of common parent corporation.* The common parent, for all purposes (other than the making of the consent required by paragraph (a)(1) of § 1.1502-75, the making of an election to be treated as a DISC under § 1.992-2, and a change of the annual accounting period pursuant to paragraph (b)(3)(ii) of § 1.991-1) shall be the sole agent for each subsidiary in the group, duly authorized to act in its own name in all matters relating to the tax liability for the consolidated return year. Except as provided in the preceding sentence, no subsidiary shall have authority to act for or to represent itself in any such matter. For example, any election available to a subsidiary corporation in the computation of its separate taxable income must be made by the common parent, as must any change in an election previously made by the subsidiary corporation; all correspondence will be carried on directly with the common parent; the common parent shall file for all extensions of time including extensions of time for payment of tax under section 6164; notices of deficiencies will be mailed only to the common parent, and the mailing to the common parent shall be considered as a mailing to each subsidiary in the group; notice and demand for payment of taxes will be given only to the common parent and such notice and demand will be considered as a notice and demand to each subsidiary; the common parent will file petitions and conduct proceedings before the Tax Court of the United States, and any such petition shall be considered as also having been filed by each such subsidiary. The common parent will file claims for refund or credit, and any refund will be made directly to and in the name of the common parent and will discharge any liability of the Government in respect thereof to any such subsidiary; and the common parent in its name will give waivers, give bonds, and execute closing agreements, offers in compromise, and all other documents, and any waiver or bond so given, or bond so given, or agreement, offer in compromise, or any other document so executed, shall be considered as having also been given or executed by each such subsidiary. Nothwithstanding the provisions of this paragraph, any notice of deficiency, in respect of the tax for a consolidated return year, will name each corporation which was a member of the group during any part of such period (but a failure to include the name of any such member will not affect the validity of the notice of deficiency as to the other members); any notice and demand for payment will name each corporation which was a member of the group during any part of such period (but a failure to include the name of any such member will not affect the validity of the notice and demand as to the other members); and any levy, any notice of a lien, or any other proceeding to collect the amount of any assessment, after the assessment has been made, will name the corporation from which such collection is to be made. The provisions of this paragraph shall apply whether or not a consolidated return is made for any subsequent year, and whether or not one or more subsidiaries have become or have ceased to be members of the group at any time. Notwithstanding the provisions of this paragraph, the district director may, upon notifying the common parent, deal directly with any member of the group in respect of its liability, in which event such member shall have full authority to act for itself.

(b) *Notification of deficiency to corporation which has ceased to be a member of the group.* If a subsidiary has ceased to be a member of the group and if such subsidiary files written notice of such cessation with the district director with whom the consolidated return is filed, then such district director upon request of such subsidiary will furnish it with a copy of any notice of deficiency in respect of the tax for a consolidated return year for which it was a member and a copy of any notice and demand for payment of such deficiency. The filing of such written notification and request by a corporation shall not have the effect of limiting the scope of the agency of the common parent provided for in paragraph (a) of this section and a failure by such district director to comply with such written request shall not have the effect of limiting the tax liability of such corporation provided for in § 1.1502-6.

(c) *Effect of waiver given by common parent.* Unless the district director agrees to the contrary, an agreement entered into by the common parent extending the time within which an assessment may be made or levy or proceeding in court begun in respect of the tax for a consolidated return year shall be applicable—

(1) To each corporation which was a member of the group during any part of such taxable year, and

(2) To each corporation the income of which was included in the consolidated return for such taxable year, notwithstanding that the tax liability of any such corporation is subsequently computed on the basis of a separate return under the provisions of § 1.1502-75.

(d) *Effect of dissolution of common parent corporation.* If the common parent corporation contemplates dissolution, or is about to be dissolved, or if for any other reason its existence is about to terminate, it shall forthwith notify the district director with whom the consolidated return is filed of such fact and designate, subject to the approval of such district director, another member to act as agent in its place to the same extent and subject to the same conditions and limitations as are applicable to the common parent. If the notice thus required is not given by the common parent, or the designation is not approved by the district director the remaining members may, subject to the approval of such district director, designate another member to act as such agent, and notice of such designation shall be given to such district director. Until a notice in writing designating a new agent has been approved by such district director, any notice of deficiency or other communication mailed to the common parent shall be considered as having been properly mailed to the agent of the group; or, if such district director has reason to believe that the existence of the common parent has terminated, he may, if he deems it advisable, deal directly with any member in respect of its liability.

Consolidated Returns (I.R.C.) 24,230.11

§ 1.1502-78 (T.D. 6894, filed 9-7-66; amended by T.D. 7059, filed 9-16-70 and T.D. 7246, filed 12-29-72.) **Tentative carryback adjustments.**

(a) *General rule.* If a group has a consolidated net operating loss, a consolidated net capital loss, or a consolidated unused investment credit for any taxable year, then any application under section 6411 for a tentative carryback adjustment of the taxes for a consolidated return year or years preceding such year shall be made by the common parent corporation to the extent such loss or unused investment credit is not apportioned to a corporation for a separate return year pursuant to § 1.1502-79(a), (b), or (c). In the case of the portion of a consolidated net operating loss or consolidated net capital loss or consolidated unused investment credit to which the preceding sentence does not apply, and in the case of a net capital or net operating loss or unused investment credit arising in a separate return year which may be carried back to a consolidated return year, the corporation or corporations to which any such loss or credit is attributable shall make any application under section 6411.

(b) *Special rules*—(1) *Payment of refund.* Any refund allowable under an application referred to in paragraph (a) of this section shall be made directly to and in the name of the corporation filing the application, except that in all cases where a loss is deducted from the consolidated taxable income or a credit is allowed in computing the consolidated tax liability for a consolidated return year, any refund shall be made directly to and in the name of the common parent corporation. The payment of any such refund shall discharge any liability of the Government with respect to such refund.

(2) *Several liability.* If a group filed a consolidated return for a taxable year for which there was an adjustment by reason of an application under section 6411, and if a deficiency is assessed against such group under section 6213(b)(2), then each member of such group shall be severally liable for such deficiency including any interest or penalty assessed in connection with such deficiency.

(c) *Examples.* The provisions of paragraphs (a) and (b) of this section may be illustrated by the following examples:

Example (1). Corporations P, S, and S-1 filed a consolidated return for the calendar year 1966. P, S, and S-1 also filed a consolidated return for the calendar year 1969. The group incurred a consolidated net operating loss in 1969 attributable to S-1 which may be carried back to 1966 as a consolidated net operating loss carryback. If a tentative carryback adjustment is desired, P, the common parent, must file an application under section 6411 and any refund will be made to P.

Example (2). Assume the same facts as in example (1) except that P, S, and S-1 filed separate returns for the calendar year 1969, even though they were members of the same group for such year. S-1 incurred a net operating loss in 1969 which may be carried back to 1966. If a tentative carryback adjustment is desired, S-1 must file an application under section 6411 and any refund from such application will be made to P.

Example (3). Corporation X, Y, and Z filed a consolidated return for the calendar year 1966. Z ceased to be a member of the group in 1967. Z filed a separate return for 1968 while X and Y filed a consolidated return for such year. The group incurred a consolidated net operating loss in 1968 attributable to Y, which may be carried back to 1966. Z also incurred a net operating loss for 1968 which may be carried back to 1966. If a tentative carryback adjustment is claimed with respect to the consolidated net operating loss, X, the common parent, must file an application under section 6411. If a tentative carryback adjustment is desired with respect to Z's loss, Z must file an application. Any refunds attributable to either application will be made to X. If an assessment is made under section 6213 (b) (2) to recover an excessive tentative allowance made with respect to calendar year 1966, X, Y, and Z are severally liable for such assessment.

Example (4). Corporations L and M filed a consolidated return for the calendar year 1966. Corporation N filed a separate return for such year. Later, N became a member of the group and filed a consolidated return with the group for the calendar year 1968. The group incurred a consolidated net operating loss in 1968 attributable to N which may be carried back to N's separate return for 1966. If a tentative carryback adjustment is desired, N must file an application under section 6411 and any refund will be made directly to N.

(d) *Adjustments of overpayments of estimated income tax.* If a group paid its estimated income tax on a consolidated basis, then any application under section 6425 for an adjustment of overpayment of estimated income tax shall be made by the common parent corporation. If the members of a group paid estimated income taxes on a separate basis, then any application under section 6425 shall be made by the member of the group which claims an overpayment on a separate basis. Any refund allowable under an application under section 6425 shall be made directly to and in the name of the corporation filing the application.

§ 1.1502-79 (T.D. 6894, filed 9-7-66.) **Separate return years.**

(a) *Carryover and carryback of consolidated net operating losses to separate return years*—(1) *In general.* (i) If a consolidated net operating loss can be carried under the principles of section 172 (b) and paragraph (b) of § 1.1502-21 to a separate return year of a corporation (or could have been so carried if such corporation were in existence) which was a member in the year in which such loss arose, then the portion of such consolidated net operating loss attributable to such corporation (as determined under subparagraph (3) of this paragraph) shall be apportioned to such corporation (and any successor to such corporation in a transaction to which section 381 (a) applies) and shall be a net operating loss carryover or carryback to such separate return year; accordingly, such portion shall not be included in the

Reg. § 1.1502-79(a)(1)

24,230.12 *(I.R.C.)*   Reg. § 1.1502-79(a)(1)   [4]

consolidated net operating loss carryovers or carrybacks to the equivalent consolidated return year. Thus, for example, if a member filed a separate return for the third year preceding a consolidated return year in which a consolidated net operating loss was sustained and if any portion of such loss is apportioned to such member for such separate return year, such portion may not be carried back by the group to its third year preceding such consolidated return year.

(ii) If a corporation ceases to be a member during a consolidated return year, any consolidated net operating loss carryover from a prior taxable year must first be carried to such consolidated return year, notwithstanding that all or a portion of the consolidated net operating loss giving rise to the carryover is attributable to the corporation which ceases to be a member. To the extent not absorbed in such consolidated return year, the portion of the consolidated net operating loss attributable to the corporation ceasing to be a member shall then be carried to such corporation's first separate return year.

(2) *Nonapportionment to certain members not in existence.* Notwithstanding subparagraph (1) of this paragraph, the portion of a consolidated net operating loss attributable to a member shall not be apportioned to a prior separate return year for which such member was not in existence and shall be included in the consolidated net operating loss carryback to the equivalent consolidated return year of the group (or, if such equivalent year is a separate return year, then to such separate return year), provided that such member was a member of the group immediately after its organization.

(3) *Portion of consolidated net operating loss attributable to a member.* The portion of a consolidated net operating loss attributable to a member of a group is an amount equal to the consolidated net operating loss multiplied by a fraction, the numerator of which is the separate net operating loss of such corporation, and the denominator of which is the sum of the separate net operating losses of all members of the group in such year having such losses. For purposes of this subparagraph, the separate net operating loss of a member of the group shall be determined under § 1.1502-12 (except that no deduction shall be allowed under section 242), adjusted for the following items taken into account in the computation of the consolidated net operating loss:

(i) The portion of the consolidated dividends received deduction, the consolidated charitable contributions deductions, and the consolidated section 247 deduction, attributable to such member;

(ii) Such member's net capital gain (determined without regard to any net capital loss carryover attributable to such member);

(iii) Such member's net capital loss and section 1231 net loss, reduced by the portion of the consolidated net capital loss attributable to such member (as determined under paragraph (b)(2) of this section); and

(iv) The portion of any consolidated net capital loss carryover attributable to such member which is absorbed in the taxable year.

(4) *Examples.* The provisions of this paragraph may be illustrated by the following examples:

Example (1). (i) Corporation P was formed on January 1, 1966. P filed a separate return for the calendar year 1966. On March 15, 1967, P formed corporation S. P and S filed a consolidated return for 1967. On January 1, 1968, P purchased all the stock of corporation T, which had been formed in 1967 and had filed a separate return for its taxable year ending December 31, 1967.

(ii) P, S, and T join in the filing of a consolidated return for 1968, which return reflects a consolidated net operating loss of $11,000. $2,000 of such consolidated net operating loss is attributable to P, $3,000 to S, and $6,000 to T. Such apportionment of the consolidated net operating loss was made on the basis of the separate net operating losses of each member as determined under subparagraph (3) of this paragraph.

(iii) $5,000 of the 1968 consolidated net operating loss can be carried back to P's separate return for 1966. Such amount is the portion of the consolidated net operating loss attributable to P and S. Even though S was not in existence in 1966, the portion attributable to S can be carried back to P's separate return year, since S (unlike T) was a member of the group immediately after its organization. The 1968 consolidated net operating loss can be carried back against the group's income in 1967 except to the extent (i.e., $6,000) that it is apportioned to T for its 1967 separate return year and to the extent that it was absorbed in P's 1966 separate return year. The portion of the 1968 consolidated net operating loss attributable to T ($6,000) is a net operating loss carryback to its 1967 separate return.

Example (2). (i) Assume the same facts as in example (1). Assume further that on June 15, 1969, P sells all the stock of T to an outsider, that P and S file a consolidated return for 1969 (which includes the income of T for the period January 1 through June 15), and that T files a separate return for the period June 16 through December 31, 1969.

(ii) The 1968 consolidated net operating loss, to the extent not absorbed in prior years, must first be carried to the consolidated return year 1969. Any portion of the $6,000 amount attributable to T which is not absorbed in T's 1967 separate return year or in the 1969 consolidated return year shall then be carried to T's separate return year ending December 31, 1969.

(b) *Carryover of consolidated net capital loss to separate return years*—(1) *In general.* If a consolidated net capital loss can be carried under the principles of section 1212(a) and paragraph (b) of § 1.1502-22 to a separate return year of a corporation (or could have been so carried if such corporation were in existence) which was a member of the group in the year in which such consolidated net capital loss arose, then the portion of such consolidated net capital loss attributable to such corporation (as determined under subparagraph (2) of this paragraph) shall be apportioned to such corporation (and any successor to such corporation in a transaction to which section 381(a) applies) under the principles of paragraph (a)(1), (2) and (3) of this section and shall be a net capital loss carryover to such separate return year.

(2) *Portion of consolidated net capital loss attributable to a member.* The portion of a consolidated net capital loss attributable to a member of a group is an amount equal to such consolidated net capital loss multiplied by a fraction, the numerator of which is the net capital loss of such member, and the denominator of which is the sum of the net capital losses of those members of the group having net capital losses. For purposes of this subparagraph, the net capital loss of a member of the group shall be determined by taking into account the following:

(i) Such member's net capital gain or loss (determined without regard to any net capital loss carryover); and

(ii) Such member's section 1231 net loss, reduced by the portion of the consolidated section 1231 net loss attributable to such member.

(c) *Carryover and carryback of consolidated unused investment credit to separate return years*—(1) *In general.* If a consolidated unused investment credit can be carried under the principles of section 46 (b) and paragraph (b) of § 1.1502-3 to a separate return year of a corporation (or could have been so carried if such corporation were in existence) which was a member of the group in the year in which such unused credit arose, then the portion of such consolidated unused credit attributable to such corporation (as determined under subparagraph (2) of this paragraph) shall be apportioned to such corporation (and any successor to such corporation in a transaction to which section 381 (a) applies) under the principles of paragraph (a) (1) and (2) of this section and shall be an investment credit carryover or carryback to such separate return year.

(2) *Portion of consolidated unused investment credit attributable to a member.*
(i) Investment credit carryback. In the case of a consolidated unused credit which is an investment credit carryback, the portion of such consolidated unused credit attributable to a member of the group is an amount equal to such consolidated unused credit multiplied by a fraction, the numerator of which is the credit earned of such member for the consolidated unused credit year, and the denominator of which is the consolidated credit earned for such unused credit year.

(ii) Investment credit carryover. In the case of a consolidated unused credit which is an investment credit carryover, the portion of such consolidated unused credit attributable to a member of the group is an amount equal to such consolidated unused credit multiplied by a fraction, the numerator of which is the credit earned with respect to any section 38 property placed in service in the consolidated unused credit year and owned by such member (whether or not placed in service by such member) at the close of the last day as of which the taxable income of such member is included in a consolidated return filed by the group, and the denominator of which is the consolidated credit earned for such unused credit year.

(d) *Carryover and carryback of consolidated unused foreign tax*—(1) *In general.* If a consolidated unused foreign tax can be carried under the principles of section 904(d) and paragraph (e) of § 1.1502-4 to a separate return year of a corporation (or could have been so carried if such corporation were in existence) which was a member of the group in the year in which such unused foreign tax arose, then the portion of such consolidated unused foreign tax attributable to such corporation (as determined under subparagraph (2) of this paragraph) shall be apportioned to such corporation (and any successor to such corporation in a transaction to which section 381 (a) applies) under the principles of paragraph (a) (1) and (2) of this section and shall be deemed paid or accrued in such separate return year to the extent provided in section 904 (d).

(2) *Portion of consolidated unused foreign tax attributable to a member.* The portion of a consolidated unused foreign tax for any year attributable to a member of a group is an amount equal to such consolidated unused foreign tax multiplied by a fraction, the numerator of which is the foreign taxes paid or accrued for such year (including those taxes deemed paid or accrued, other than by reason of section 904(d)) to each foreign country or possession (or to all foreign countries or possessions if the overall limitation is effective) by such member, and the denominator of which is the aggregate of all such taxes paid or accrued for such year (including those taxes deemed paid or accrued, other than by reason of section 904(d)) to each such foreign country or possession (or to all foreign countries or possessions if the overall limitation is effective) by all the members of the group.

(e) *Carryover of consolidated excess charitable contributions to separate return years*—(1) *In general.* If the consolidated excess charitable contributions for any taxable year can be carried under the principles of section 170(b)(2) and paragraph (b) of § 1.1502-24 to a separate return year of a corporation (or could have been so carried if such corporation were in existence) which was a member of the group in the year in which such excess contributions arose, then the portion of such consolidated excess charitable contributions attributable to such corporation (as determined under subparagraph (2) of this paragraph) shall be apportioned to such corporation (and any successor to such corporation in a transaction to which section 381(a) applies) under the principles of paragraph (a) (1) and (2) of this section and shall be a charitable contribution carryover to such separate return year.

(2) *Portion of consolidated excess charitable contributions attributable to a member.* The portion of the consolidated excess charitable contributions attributable to a member of a group is an amount equal to such consolidated excess contributions multiplied by a fraction, the numerator of which is the charitable contributions paid by such member for the taxable year, and the denominator of which is the aggregate of all such charitable contributions paid for such year by all the members of the group.

(f) *Intercompany transactions*—(1) *In-*

Reg. § 1.1502-79(f)(1)

24,230.14 (I.R.C.) Reg. § 1.1502-79(f)(1) [4]

tercompany transactions other than deferred intercompany transactions. In certain cases a member of the group must take into account in a separate return year an item of income or a deduction which it otherwise would have taken into account in earlier consolidated return years. See paragraph (b) (2) of § 1.1502-13,

(2) *Deferred intercompany transactions.* See paragraphs (d), (e), and (f) of § 1.1502-13 for rules with respect to restoration of deferred gains and losses in separate return years.

○━ § 1.1502-80 (T.D. 6894, filed 9-7-66.) **Applicability of other provisions of law.**

The Code, or other law, shall be applicable to the group to the extent the regulations do not exclude its application. Thus, for example, in a transaction to which section 381 (a) applies, the acquiring corporation will succeed to the tax attributes described in section 381 (c). Furthermore, sections 269, 304, and 482 apply for any consolidated return year.

○━ § 1.1502-100 (T.D. 7183, filed 4-20-72.) *Includible tax exempt organizations.*

For taxable years beginning after December 31, 1969, two organizations exempt from taxation under section 501(a), one of which is described in section 501(c)(2) and the other of which derives income from such section 501(c)(2) organization, shall be considered as "includable corporations" for purposes of the application of subsection (a) of section 1504 to such organizations alone, despite the provisions of paragraph (1) of subsection (b) of section 1504. If such organizations satisfy the requirements of section 1504(a) (relating to the definition of an "affiliated group") and the other relevant provisions of chapter 6 of the Code, then such organizations may file a consolidated return.

TD 6894, filed 9-7-66, promulgated new consolidated return regulations under Sec. 1502: Reg. § 1.1502-0 through § 1.1502-80. The new regulations are applicable to taxable years beginning after Dec. 31, 1965. They are published on pages 24,196 through 24,230.14. The old regulations were redesignated as § 1.1502-0A through § 1.1502-51A. The old regulations are applicable to taxable years beginning before Jan. 1, 1966 and they appear in P-H Cumulative Changes.

○━ § 1.1503 **Statutory provisions; computation and payment of tax.** [Sec. 1503, IRC]
○━ § 1.1503-1 (T.D. 6140, filed 8-29-55; republished in T.D. 6500, filed 11-25-60; amended by T.D. 7244, filed 12-29-72.) **Computation and payment of tax.**

(a) *General rule.* In any case in which a consolidated return is filed or required to be filed, the tax shall be determined, computed, assessed, collected, and adjusted in accordance with the regulations prescribed under section 1502 promulgated prior to the last date prescribed by law for the filing of such return.

(b) *Limitation.* If the affiliated group includes one or more Western Hemisphere trade corporations (as defined in section 921) or one or more regulated public utilities (as defined in section 1503(c)) the increase in tax described in section 1503(a) shall be applied in a manner provided in the regulations under section 1502.

§ 1.1504 **Statutory provisions; definitions.** [Sec. 1504, IRC]

§ 1.1504-1 (T.D. 6140, filed 8-29-55; republished in T.D. 6500, filed 11-25-60.) **Definitions.**

The privilege of filing consolidated returns is extended to all includible corporations constituting affiliated groups as defined in section 1504. See the regulations under § 1.1502 for a description of an affiliated group and the corporations which may be considered as includible corporations.

§ 1.1505 **Statutory provisions; cross references.** [Sec. 1505, IRC]

RELATED RULES

§ 1.1551 **Statutory provisions; disallowance of surtax exemption and accumulated earnings credit.** [Sec. 1551, IRC]

§ 1.1551-1 (T.D. 6140; filed 8-29-55; amended by T.D. 6377, filed 5-12-59; and T.D. 6412, filed 9-10-59; republished in T.D. 6500, filed 11-25-60; amended by T.D. 6911, filed 2-23-67 and T.D. 7376, filed 9-15-75.) **Disallowance of surtax exemption and accumulated earnings credit.**

(a) *In general.* If—

(1) Any corporation transfers, on or after January 1, 1951, and before June 13, 1963, all or part of its property (other than money) to a transferee corporation,

(2) Any corporation transfers, directly or indirectly, after June 12, 1963, all or part of its property (other than money) to a transferee corporation, or

(3) Five or fewer individuals are in control of a corporation and one or more of them transfer, directly or indirectly, after June 12, 1963, property (other than money) to a transferee corporation,

and the transferee was created for the purpose of acquiring such property or was not actively engaged in business at the time of such acquisition, and if after such transfer the transferor or transferors are in control of the transferee during any part of the taxable year of the transferee, then for such taxable year of the transferee the Secretary or his delegate may disallow the surtax exemption defined in section 11(d) or the accumulated earnings credit of $150,000 ($100,000 in the case of taxable years beginning before January 1, 1975) provided in paragraph (2) or (3) of section 535 (c), unless the transferee establishes by the clear preponderance of the evidence that the securing of such exemption or credit was not a major purpose of the transfer.

(b) *Purpose of section 1551.* The purpose of section 1551 is to prevent avoidance or evasion of the surtax imposed by section 11(c) or of the accumulated earnings tax imposed by section 531. It is not intended, however, that section 1551 be interpreted as delimiting or abrogating any principle of law established by judicial decision, or any existing provisions of the Code, such as sections 269 and 482, which have the effect of preventing the avoidance or evasion of income taxes. Such principles of law and such provisions of the Code, including section 1551, are not mutually exclusive, and in appropriate cases they may operate together or they may operate separately.

(c) *Application of section 269(b) to cases covered by section 1551.* The provisions of section 269(b) and the authority of the district director thereunder, to the extent not inconsistent with the provisions of section 1551, are applicable to cases covered by section 1551. Pursuant to the authority provided in section 269(b) the district director may allow to the transferee any part of a surtax exemption or accumulated earnings credit for a taxable year for which such exemption or credit would otherwise be disallowed under section 1551(a); or he may apportion such exemption or credit among the corporations involved. For example, corporation A transfers on January 1, 1955, all of its property to corporations B and C in exchange for all of the stock of such corporations. Immediately thereafter, corporation A is dissolved and its stockholders become the sole stockholders of corporations B and C. Assuming that corporations B and C are unable to establish by the clear preponderance of the evidence that the securing of the surtax exemption defined in section 11(d) or the accumulated earnings credit provided in section 535, or both, was not a major purpose of the transfer, the district director is authorized under sections 1551 (c) and 269(b) to allow one such exemption and credit and to apportion such exemption and credit between corporations B and C.

(d) *Actively engaged in business.* For purposes of this section, a corporation maintaining an office for the purpose of preserving its corporate existence is not considered to be "actively engaged in business" even though such corporation may be deemed to be "doing business" for other purposes. Similarly, for purposes of this section, a corporation engaged in winding up its affairs, prior to an acquisition to which section 1551 is applicable, is not considered to be "actively engaged in business."

(e) *Meaning and application of the term "control"*—(1) *In general.* For purposes of this section, the term "control" means—

(i) With respect to a transferee corporation described in paragraph (a)(1) or (2) of this section, the ownership by the transferor corporation, its shareholders, or both, of stock possessing either (a) at least 80 percent of the total combined voting power of all classes of stock entitled to vote, or (b) at least 80 percent of the total value of shares of all classes of stock.

(ii) With respect to each corporation described in paragraph (a)(3) of this section, the ownership by five or fewer individuals of stock possessing (a) at least 80 percent of the total combined voting power of all classes of stock, entitled to vote or at least 80 percent of the total value of shares of all classes of the stock of each corporation, and (b) more than 50 percent of the total combined voting power of all classes of stock entitled to vote or more than 50 percent of the total value of shares of all classes of stock of each corporation, taking into account the stock ownership of

Reg. § 1.1551-1(e)(1)

each such individual only to the extent such stock ownership is identical with respect to each such corporation.

(2) *Special rules.* In determining for purposes of this section whether stock possessing at least 80 percent (or more than 50 percent in the case of subparagraph (1)(ii)(b) of this paragraph) of the total combined voting power of all classes of stock entitled to vote is owned, all classes of such stock shall be considered together; it is not necessary that at least 80 percent (or more than 50 percent) of each class of voting stock be owned. Likewise, in determining for purposes of this section whether stock possessing at least 80 percent (or more than 50 percent) of the total value of shares of all classes of stock is owned, all classes of stock of the corporation shall be considered together; it is not necessary that at least 80 percent (or more than 50 percent) of the value of shares of each class be owned. The fair market value of a share shall be considered as the value to be used for purposes of this computation. With respect to transfers described in paragraph (a)(2) or (3) of this section, the ownership of stock shall be determined in accordance with the provisions of section 1563(e) and the regulations thereunder. With respect to transfers described in paragraph (a)(1) of this section, the ownership of stock shall be determined in accordance with the provisions of section 544 and the regulations thereunder, except that constructive ownership under section 544(a)(2) shall be determined only with respect to the individual's spouse and minor children. In determining control, no stock shall be excluded because such stock was acquired before January 1, 1951 (the effective date of section 1551(a)(1), or June 13, 1963 (the effective date of section 1551(a)(2) and (3)).

(3) *Example.* This paragraph may be illustrated by the following example:

Example. On January 1, 1964 individual A, who owns 50 percent of the voting stock of corporation X, and individual B, who owns 30 percent of such voting stock, transfer property (other than money) to corporation Y (newly created for the purpose of acquiring such property) in exchange for all of Y's voting stock. After the transfer, A and B own the voting stock of corporations X and Y in the following proportions:

Individual	Corp. X	Corp. Y	Identical Ownership
A	50	30	30
B	30	50	30
Total —	80	80	60

The transfer of property by A and B to corporation Y is a transfer described in paragraph (a)(3) of this section since (i) A and B own at least 80 percent of the voting stock of corporations X and Y, and (ii) taking into account each such individual's stock ownership only to the extent such ownership is identical with respect to each such corporation. A and B own more than 50 percent of the voting stock of corporations X and Y.

(f) *Taxable year of allowance or disallowance*—(1) *In general.* The district director's authority with respect to cases covered by section 1551 is not limited to the taxable year of the transferee corporation in which the transfer of property occurs. Such authority extends to the taxable year in which the transfer occurs or any subsequent taxable year of the transferee corporation if, during any part of such year, the transferor or transferors are in control of the transferee.

(2) *Examples.* This paragraph may be illustrated by the following examples:

Example (1). On January 1, 1955, corporation D transfers property (other than money) to corporation E, a corporation not actively engaged in business at the time of the acquisition of such property, in exchange for 60 percent of the voting stock of E. During a later taxable year of E, corporation D acquires an additional 20 percent of such voting stock. As a result of such additional acquisition, D owns 80 percent of the voting stock of E. Accordingly, section 1551(a)(1) is applicable for the taxable year in which the later acquisition of stock occurred and for each taxable year thereafter in which the requisite control continues.

Example (2). On June 20, 1963, individual A, who owns all of the stock of corporation X, transfers property (other than money) to corporation Y, a corporation not actively engaged in business at the time of the acquisition of such property, in exchange for 60 percent of the voting stock of Y. During a later taxable year of Y, A acquires an additional 20 percent of such voting stock. After such acquisition A owns at least 80 percent of the voting stock of corporations X and Y. Accordingly, section 1551(a)(3) is applicable for the taxable year in which the later acquisition of stock occurred and for each taxable year thereafter in which the requisite control continues.

Example (3). Individuals A and B each owns 50 percent of the stock of corporation X. On January 15, 1964, A transfers property (other than money) to corporation Y (newly created by A for the purpose of acquiring such property) in exchange for all the stock of Y. In a subsequent taxable year of Y, individual B buys 50 percent of the stock which A owns in Y (or he transfers money to Y in exchange for its stock, as a result of which he owns 50 percent of Y's stock). Immediately thereafter the stock ownership of A and B in corporation Y is identical to their stock ownership in corporation X. Accordingly, section 1551(a)(3) is applicable for the taxable year in which B acquires stock in corporation Y (see paragraph (g)(3) of this section) and for each taxable year thereafter in which the requisite control continues. Moreover, if B's acquisition of stock in Y is pursuant to a preexisting agreement with A, A's transfer to Y and B's acquisition of Y's stock are considered a single transaction and section 1551(a)(3) also would be applicable for the taxable year in which A's transfer to Y took place and for each taxable year thereafter in which the requisite control continues.

(g) *Nature of transfer*—(1) *Corporate transfers before June 13, 1963.* A transfer made before June 13, 1963, by any corporation of all or part of its assets, whether or not such transfer qualifies as a reorganization under section 368, is within the scope of section 1551(a)(1), except that section 1551(a)(1) does not apply to a transfer of money only. For example, the transfer of cash for the purpose of expanding the business of the transferor corporation through the formation of a new corporation is not a transfer within the scope of section 1551(a)(1), irrespective of whether the new corporation uses the cash to purchase from the transferor corporation stock in trade or similar property.

(2) *Corporate transfers after June 12, 1963.* A direct or indirect transfer made after June 12, 1963, by any corporation of all or part of its assets to a transferee corporation, whether or not such transfer qualifies as a reorganization under section 368, is within the scope of section 1551(a)(2) except that section 1551(a)(2) does not apply to a transfer of money only. For example, if a transferor corporation transfers property to its shareholders or to a subsidiary, the transfer of that property by the shareholders or the subsidiary to a transferee corporation as part of the same transaction is a transfer of property by the transferor corporation to which section 1551(a)(2) applies. A transfer of property pursuant to a purchase by a transferee corporation from a transferor corporation controlling the transferee is within the scope of section 1551(a)(2), whether or not the purchase follows a transfer of cash from the controlling corporation.

(3) *Other transfers after June 12, 1963.* A direct or indirect transfer made after June 12, 1963, by five or fewer individuals to a transferee corporation, whether or not such transfer qualifies under one or more other provisions of the Code (for example, section 351), is within the scope of section 1551(a)(3) except that section 1551(a)(3) does not apply to a transfer of money only. Thus, if one of five or fewer individuals who are in control of a corporation transfers property (other than money) to a controlled transferee corporation, the transfer is within the scope of section 1551(a)(3) notwithstanding that the other individuals transfer nothing or transfer only money.

(4) *Examples.* This paragraph may be illustrated by the following examples:

Example (1). Individuals A and B each owns 50 percent of the voting stock of corporation X. On January 15, 1964, A and B each acquires property (other than money) from X and, as part of the same transaction, each transfers such property to his wholly owned corporation (newly created for the purpose of acquiring such property). A and B retain substantial continuing interests in corporation X. The transfers to the two newly created corporations are within the scope of section 1551(a)(2).

Example (2). Corporation W organizes corporation X, a wholly owned subsidiary, for the purpose of acquiring the properties of corporation Y. Pursuant to a reorganization qualifying under section 368(a)(1)(C), substantially all of the properties of corporation Y are transferred on June 15, 1963, to corporation X solely in exchange for voting stock of corporation W. There is a transfer of property from W to X within the meaning of section 1551(a)(2).

Example (3). Individuals A and B, each owning 50 percent of the voting stock of corporation X, organize corporation Y to which each transfers money only in exchange for 50 percent of the stock of Y. Subsequently, Y uses such money to acquire other property from A and B after June 12, 1963. Such acquisition is within the scope of section 1551(a)(3).

Example (4). Individual A owns 55 percent of the stock of corporation X. Another 25 percent of corporation X's stock is owned in the aggregate by individuals B, C, D, and E. On June 15, 1963, individual A transfers property to corporation Y (newly created for the purpose of acquiring such property) in exchange for 60 percent of the stock of Y, and B, C, and D acquire all of the remaining stock of Y. The transfer is within the scope of section 1551(a)(3).

(h) *Purpose of transfer.* In determining, for purposes of this section, whether the securing of the surtax exemption or accumulated earnings credit constituted "a major purpose" of the transfer, all circumstances relevant to the transfer shall be considered. "A major purpose" will not be inferred from the mere purchase of inventory by a subsidiary from a centralized warehouse maintained by its parent corporation or by another subsidiary of the parent corporation. For disallowance of the surtax exemption and accumulated earnings credit under section 1551, it is not necessary that the obtaining of either such credit or exemption, or both, have been the sole or principal purpose of the transfer of the property. It is sufficient if it appears, in the light of all the facts and circumstances, that the obtaining of such exemption or credit, or both, was one of the major considerations that prompted the transfer. Thus, the securing of the surtax exemption or the accumulated earnings credit may constitute "a major purpose" of the transfer, notwithstanding that such transfer was effected for a valid business purpose and qualified as a reorganization within the meaning of section 368. The taxpayer's burden of establishing by the clear preponderance of the evidence that the securing of either such exemption or credit or both was not "a major purpose" of the transfer may be met, for example, by showing that the obtaining of such exemption, or credit, or both, was not a major factor in relationship to the other consideration or considerations which prompted the transfer.

○→ § 1.1552 **Statutory provisions; earnings and profits.** [Sec. 1552, IRC]

○→ § 1.1552-1 (T.D. 6140, filed 8-29-55; republished in T.D. 6500, filed 11-25-60; amended by T.D. 6962, filed 7-2-68; T.D. 7528, filed 12-27-77.) **Earnings and profits.**

(a) *General rule.* For the purpose of determining the earnings and profits of each member of an affiliated group which is required to be included in a consolidated return for such group filed for a taxable year beginning after December 31, 1953,

Reg. § 1.1552-1(a)

and ending after August 16, 1954, the tax liability of the group shall be allocated among the members of the group in accordance with one of the following methods, pursuant to an election under paragraph (c) of this section:

(1) (i) The tax liability of the group shall be apportioned among the members of the group in accordance with the ratio which that portion of the consolidated taxable income attributable to each member of the group having taxable income bears to the consolidated taxable income.

(ii) For consolidated return years beginning after December 31, 1965, a member's portion of the tax liability of the group under the method of allocation provided by subdivision (i) of this subparagraph is an amount equal to the tax liability of the group multiplied by a fraction, the numerator of which is the taxable income of such member, and the denominator of which is the sum of the taxable incomes of all the members. For purposes of this subdivision the taxable income of a member shall be the separate taxable income determined under § 1.1502-12, adjusted for the following items taken into account in the computation of consolidated taxable income:

(a) The portion of the consolidated net operating loss deduction, the consolidated charitable contributions deduction, the consolidated dividends received deduction, the consolidated section 247 deduction, the consolidated section 582(c) net loss, and the consolidated section 922 deduction, attributable to such member;

(b) Such member's net capital gain (determined without regard to any net capital loss caryover attributable to such member);

(c) Such member's net capital loss and section 1231 net loss, reduced by the portion of the consolidated net capital loss attributable to such member; and

(d) The portion of any consolidated net capital loss carryover attributable to such member which is absorbed in the taxable year.

If the computation of the taxable income of a member under this subdivision results in an excess of deductions over gross income, then for purposes of this subdivision such member's taxable income shall be zero.

(2) (i) The tax liability of the group shall be allocated to the several members of the group on the basis of the percentage of the total tax which the tax of such member if computed on a separate return would bear to the total amount of the taxes for all members of the group so computed.

(ii) For consolidated return years beginning after December 31, 1965, a member's portion of the tax liability of the group under the method of allocation provided by subdivision (i) of this subparagraph is an amount equal to the tax liability of the group multiplied by a fraction, the numerator of which is the separate return tax liability of such member, and the denominator of which is the sum of the separate return tax liabilities of all the members. For purposes of this subdivision the separate return tax liability of a member is its tax liability computed as if it has filed a separate return for the year except that—

(a) Gains and losses on intercompany transactions shall be taken into account as provided in § 1.1502-13 as if a consolidated return had been filed for the year;

(b) Gains and losses relating to inventory adjustments shall be taken into account as provided in § 1.1502-18 as if a consolidated return had been filed for the year;

(c) Transactions with respect to stock, bonds, or other obligations of members shall be reflected as provided in § 1.1502-14 as if a consolidated return had been filed for the year;

(d) Excess losses shall be included in income as provided in § 1.1502-19 as if a consolidated return had been filed for the year;

(e) In the computation of the deduction under section 167, property shall not lose its character as new property as a result of a transfer from one member to another member during the year;

(f) A dividend distributed by one member to another member during the year shall not be taken into account in computing the deductions under section 243(a) (1), 244 (a), 245, or 247 (relating to deductions with respect to dividends received and dividends paid);

(g) Basis shall be determined under §§ 1.1502-32 and 1.1502-32, and earnings and profits shall be determined under § 1.1502-33, as if a consolidated return had been filed for the year;

(h) Subparagraph (2) of § 1.1502-3(f) shall apply as if a consolidated return had been filed for the year; and

(i) For purposes of subtitle A of the Code, the surtax exemption of the member shall be an amount equal to $25,000 ($50,000 in the case of a taxable year ending in 1975), divided by the number of members (or such portion of $25,000 or $50,000 which is apportioned to the member pursuant to a schedule attached to the consolidated return for the taxable year). (However, if for the taxable year some or all of the members are component members of a controlled group of corporations (within the meaning of section 1563) and if there are other such component members which do not join in filing the consolidated return for such year, the amount to be divided among the members filing the consolidated return shall be (in lieu of $25,000 or $50,000) the sum of the amounts apportioned to the component members which join in filing the consolidated return (as determined for taxable years beginning after December 31, 1974, under § 1.1561-2(a)(2) or § 1.1561-3, whichever is applicable, and for taxable years beginning before January 1, 1975, under § 1.1561-2A(a)(2) or § 1.1561-3A, whichever is applicable).)

If the computation of the separate return tax liability of a member under this subdivision does not result in a positive tax liability, then for purposes of this subdivision such member's separate return tax liability shall be zero.

(3) (i) The tax liability of the group (excluding the tax increases arising from the consolidation) shall be allocated on the basis of the contribution of each member

of the group to the consolidated taxable income of the group. Any tax increases arising from the consolidation shall be distributed to the several members in direct proportion to the reduction in tax liability resulting to such members from the filing of the consolidated return as measured by the difference between their tax liabilities determined on a separate return basis and their tax liabilities (determined without regard to the 2-percent increase provided by section 1503(a) and paragraph (a) of § 1.1502-30A for taxable years beginning before January 1, 1964) based on their contributions to the consolidated taxable income.

(ii) For consolidated return years beginning after December 31, 1965, a member's portion of the tax liability of the group under the method of allocation provided by subdivision (i) of this subparagraph shall be determined by—

(a) Allocating the tax liability of the group in accordance with subparagraph (1)(ii) of this paragraph, but

(b) The amount of tax liability allocated to any member shall not exceed the separate return tax liability of such member, determined in accordance with subparagraph (2)(ii) of this paragraph, and

(c) The sum of the amount which would be allocated to the members but for (b) of this subdivision (ii) shall be apportioned among the other members in direct proportion to, but limited to, the reduction in tax liability resulting to such other members. Such reduction for any member shall be the excess, if any, of (1) its separate return tax liability determined in accordance with subparagraph (2)(ii) of this paragraph, over (2) the amount allocated to such member under (a) of this subdivision (ii). If any amount remains after being apportioned among members with a reduction in tax liability to the extent of such reduction, as provided in (c) of this subdivision (ii), such remaining amount shall, notwithstanding (b) of this subdivision (ii), be allocated to the members in accordance with the fractions determined under subparagraph (1)(ii) of this paragraph.

(4) The tax liability of the group shall be allocated in accordance with any other method selected by the group with the approval of the Commissioner. No method of allocation may be approved under this subparagraph which may result in the allocation of a positive tax liability for a taxable year, among the members who are allocated a positive tax liability for such year, in a total amount which is more or less than the tax liability of the group for such year. (However, see paragraph (d) of § 1.1502-33.)

(b) *Application of rules*—(1) *Tax liability of the group.* For purposes of section 1552 and this section, the tax liability of the group for a taxable year shall consist of the Federal income tax liability of the group for such year determined in accordance with §1.1502-2 or § 1.1502-30A, whichever is applicable. Thus, in the case of a carryback of a loss or credit to such year, although the earnings and profits of the members of the group may not be adjusted until the subsequent taxable year from which the loss or credit was carried back, the effect of the carryback, for purposes of this section, shall be determined by allocating the amount of the adjustment as a part of the tax liability of the group for the taxable year to which the loss or credit is carried. For example, if a consolidated net operating loss is carried back from 1969 to 1967, the allocation of the tax liability of the group for 1967 shall be recomputed in accordance with the method of allocation used for 1967, and the changes resulting from such recomputation shall, for accrual method taxpayers' be reflected in the earnings and profits of the appropriate members in 1969.

(2) *Effect of allocation.* The amount of tax liability allocated to a corporation as its share of the tax liability of the group, pursuant to this section, shall (i) result in a decrease in the earnings and profits of such corporation in such amount, and (ii) be treated as a liability of such corporation for such amount. If the full amount of such liability is not paid by such corporation, pursuant to an agreement among the members of the group or otherwise, the amount which is not paid will generally be treated as a distribution with respect to stock, a contribution to capital, or a combination thereof, as the case may be.

(c) *Method of election.* (1) The election under paragraph (a)(1), (2), or (3) of this section shall be made not later than the time prescribed by law for filing the first consolidated return of the group for a taxable year beginning after December 31, 1953, and ending after August 16, 1954 (including extensions thereof). If the group elects to allocate its tax liability in accordance with the method prescribed in paragraph (a)(1), (2), or (3) of this section, a statement shall be attached to the return stating which method is elected. Such statement shall be made by the common parent corporation and shall be binding upon all members of the group. In the event that the group desires to allocate its tax liability in accordance with any other method pursuant to paragraph (a)(4) of this section, approval of such method by the Commissioner must be obtained within the time prescribed above. If such approval is not obtained in such time, the group shall allocate in accordance with the method prescribed in paragraph (a)(1) of this section. The request shall state fully the method which the group wishes to apply in apportioning the tax liability. Except as provided in subparagraph (2) of this paragraph, an election once made shall be irrevocable and shall be binding upon the group with respect to the year for which made and for all future years for which a consolidated return is filed or required to be filed unless the Commissioner authorizes a change to another method prior to the time prescribed by law for filing the return for the year in which such change is to be effective.

(2) Each group may make a new election to use any one of the methods prescribed in paragraph (a)(1), (2), or (3) of this section for its first consolidated return year beginning after December 31, 1965, or in conjunction with an election under paragraph (d) of § 1.1502-33, or may request the Commissioner's approval of a method under

Reg. § 1.1552-1(c)(1)

paragraph (a)(4) of this section for its first consolidated return year beginning after December 31, 1965, irrespective of its previous method of allocation under this section. If such new election is not made in conjunction with an election under paragraph (d) of § 1.1502-33, it shall be effective for the first consolidated return year beginning after December 31, 1965, and all succeeding years. (See paragraph (d)(3) of § 1.1502-33 for the method of making such new election in conjunction with an election under paragraph (d) of § 1.1502-33.) Any other such new election (or request for the Commissioner's approval of a method under paragraph (a)(4) of this section) shall be made within the time prescribed by law for filing the consolidated return for the first taxable year beginning after December 31, 1965 (including extensions thereof), or within 60 days after [insert date these regulations are published in final form in the Federal Register], whichever is later. Such new election shall be made by attaching a statement to the consolidated return for the first taxable year beginning after December 31, 1965, or if such election is made within the time prescribed above but after such return is filed, by filing a statement with the internal revenue officer with whom such return was filed.

(d) *Failure to elect.* If a group fails to make an election in its first consolidated return, or any other election, in accordance with paragraph (c) of this section, the method prescribed under paragraph (a)(1) of this section shall be applicable and shall be binding upon the group in the same manner as if an election had been made to so allocate.

(e) *Definitions.* Except as otherwise provided in this section, the terms used in this section shall have the same meaning as provided in the regulations under section 1502.

(f) *Example.* The provisions of this section may be illustrated by the following example:

Example. Corporation P is the common parent owning all of the stock of corporation S1 and S2, members of an affiliated group. A consolidated return is filed for the taxable year ending December 31, 1966, by P, S1, and S2. For 1966 such corporations had the following taxable incomes or losses computed in accordance with paragraph (a)(1)(ii) of this section:

P .... $ 0
S1 2,000
S2 .... (1,000)

The group has not made an election under paragraph (c) of this section or paragraph (d) of § 1.1502-33. Accordingly, the method of allocation provided by paragraph (a)(1) of this section is in effect for the group. Assuming that the consolidated taxable income is equal to the sum of the members' taxable income and losses, or $1,000, the tax liability of the group for the year (assuming a 22 percent rate) is $220 all of which is allocated to S1. S1 accordingly reduces its earnings and profits in the amount of $220, irrespective of who actually pays the tax liability. If S1 pays the $220 tax liability there will be no further effect upon the income, earnings and profits, or the basis of stock of any member. If, however, P pays the $220 tax liability (and such payment is not in fact a loan from P to S1), then P shall be treated as having made a contribution to the capital of S1 in the amount of $220. On the other hand, if S2 pays the $220 tax liability (and such payment is not in fact a loan from S2), then S2 shall be treated as having made a distribution with respect to its stock to P in the amount of $220, and P shall be treated as having made a contribution to the capital of S1 in the amount of $220.

CERTAIN CONTROLLED CORPORATIONS

§ 1.1561 [Deleted by TD 7528, filed 12-27-77.]

§ 1.1561-0 (T.D. 7528, filed 12-27-77.) **Effective date.**

(a) *Taxable years beginning after December 31, 1974.* The provisions of §§ 1.1561-1 through 1.1561-3 apply only to taxable years beginning after December 31, 1974.

(b) *Taxable years beginning before January 1, 1975.* The provisions of §§ 1.1561-1A through 1.1561-3A apply only to taxable years beginning before January 1, 1975.

§ 1.1561-1 (T.D. 7528, filed 12-27-77.) **Limitations on certain multiple tax benefits in the case of certain controlled corporations.**

(a) *In general.* Part II (section 1561 and following), subchapter B, chapter 6 of the Code, provides rules relating to certain controlled corporations. In general, section 1561 provides that the component members of a controlled group of corporations on a December 31, for their taxable years which include such December 31, shall be limited for purposes of subtitle A to

(1) One surtax exemption under section 11(d),

(2) One $150,000 amount for purposes of computing the accumulated earnings credit under section 535(c)(2) and (3), and

(3) One $25,000 amount for purposes of computing the limitation on the small business deduction of life insurance companies under sections 804(a)(4) and 809(d)(10).

For certain definitions (including the definition of a "controlled group of corporations" and a "component member") and special rules for purposes of part II of subchapter B, see section 1563 and the regulations thereunder.

(b) *Tax avoidance.* The provisions of part II, subchapter B, chapter 6 do not delimit or abrogate any principle of law established by judicial decision, or any existing provisions of the Code, such as sections 269, 482 and 1551, which have the effect of preventing the avoidance or evasion of income taxes.

(c) *Special rules.* (1) For purposes of sections 1561 and 1563 and the regulations thereunder, the term "corporation" includes an electing small business corporation (as defined in section 1371(b)). However, for the treatment of an electing small business corporation as an excluded member of a controlled group of corporations, see paragraph (b)(2)(ii) of § 1.1563-1.

(2) In the case of corporations electing a 52-53-week taxable year under section 441(f)(1), the provisions of sections 1561 and 1563 and the regulations thereunder shall be applied in accordance with the special rule of section 441(f)(2)(A). See paragraph (b)(1) of § 1.441-2.

§ 1.1561-2 (T.D. 7528, filed 12-27-77.) **Determination of amount of tax benefits.**

(a) *Surtax exemption.* (1) If a corporation is a component member of a controlled group of corporations on a December 31, the surtax exemption under section 11(d) of such corporation for the taxable year which includes such December 31 shall be an amount equal to—

(i) $50,000 divided by the number of corporations which are component members of such group on such December 31, or

(ii) If an apportionment plan is adopted under § 1.1561-3 which is effective with respect to such taxable year, such portion of $50,000 as is apportioned to such member in accordance with such plan.

(2) In the case of a controlled group of corporations which includes component members which join in the filing of a consolidated return and other component members which do not join in the filing of such a return, and where there is no apportionment plan effective under § 1.1561-3 apportioning the $50,000 amount among the component members filing the consolidated return and the other component members of the controlled group, each component member of the controlled group (including each component member which joins in filing the consolidated return) shall be treated as a separate corporation for purposes of equally apportioning the $50,000 amount under subparagraph (1)(i) of this paragraph. In such case, the surtax exemption of the corporations filing the consolidated return shall be the sum of the amounts apportioned to each component member which joins in filing the consolidated return.

(3) The provisions of section 1561 may reduce the surtax exemption of any corporation which is a component member of a controlled group of corporations and which is subject to the tax imposed by section 11, or by any other provision of subtitle A of the Code if the tax under such other provisions is computed by reference to the amount of the surtax exemption provided by section 11. Such other provisions include, for example, sections 511(a)(1), 594, 802, 831, 852, 857, 882, 1201, and 1378.

(4) This paragraph (a) shall not apply with respect to any component member of a controlled group of corporations on a December 31 if one or more component members of such controlled group has a taxable year including such December 31 which ends after December 31, 1978. Rules pertaining to the apportionment of the surtax exemption with respect to component members of controlled groups of corporations to which this paragraph does not apply are reserved.

(5) The application of this paragraph may be illustrated by the following examples:

Example (1). Corporations W, X, Y, and Z are component members of a controlled group of corporations on December 31, 1975, and each corporation files its income tax return on the basis of a calendar year. For their taxable years ending on December 31, 1975, W and X each incurs a net operating loss; Y has $5,250 of taxable income; and Z has $30,000 of taxable income. If an apportionment plan is not effective for such taxable years, the surtax exemption under section 11(d) of each corporation determined under subparagraph (1)(i) of this paragraph is $12,500 ($50,000 ÷ 4). However, the four corporations may avoid a pro rata division of the $50,000 amount by filing an apportionment plan in accordance with the provisions of § 1.1561-3 allocating the $50,000 amount in any manner they deem proper.

Example (2). Corporation A files its income tax return on the basis of a calendar year; corporation B files its income tax return on the basis of a fiscal year ending March 31. On December 31, 1975, A and B are the only component members of a controlled group of corporations. Under subparagraph (1)(i) of this paragraph, the surtax exemption of A for 1975, and the surtax exemption of B for its fiscal year ending March 31, 1976, is $25,000 ($50,000 ÷ 2). However, if an apportionment plan is filed in accordance with the provisions of § 1.1561-3, the surtax exemption of each such corporation will be the amount apportioned to the corporation pursuant to the plan.

Example (3). Corporations R, P, and S are component members of a controlled group of corporations on December 31, 1975. P and S file a consolidated return for their fiscal years ending June 30, 1976. R files a separate return for its taxable year ending on December 31, 1975. No apportionment plan is effective with respect to R's, P's, and S's taxable years which include December 31, 1975. Therefore, R, P, and S are each apportioned $16,666.67 ($50,000 ÷ 3) as their surtax exemption under section 11(d) for their taxable years including such date. The surtax exemption of the affiliated group filing a consolidated return (P and S) for the year ending June 30, 1976, is $33,333.34 (*i.e.*, the sum of the $16,666.67 amounts apportioned to P and S). However, if an apportionment plan is filed in accordance with the provisions of § 1.1561-3, the surtax exemption of the corporations which are members of the affiliated group filing a consolidated return and of each other corporation which is a component member of the controlled group of corporations will be the amount apportioned to such affiliated group and to each such other corporation pursuant to the plan.

(b) *Allocation of amounts of taxable income subject to normal tax.* (1) In the case of a taxable year of a corporation, if—

(i) The amount of normal tax under section 11(b) is equal to the sum of 20 percent of so much of the taxable income as does not exceed $25,000, plus 22 percent of so much of the taxable income as exceeds $25,000 for a taxable year, and

(ii) The amount of surtax exemption of the corporation is less than $50,000 under paragraph (a)(1)(i) or (ii) of this section, then for purposes of applying section 11(b),

Reg. § 1.1561-2(b)(1)

24,232-F (I.R.C.)   Reg. § 1.1561-2(b)(1)   12-30-77

the taxable income subject to taxation at the rate of 20 percent shall be (in lieu of the first $25,000 of taxable income) one-half of the amount of the surtax exemption allocated to such corporation under paragraph (a)(1)(i) or (ii) of this section. In addition, the amount of taxable income subject to taxation at the rate of 22 percent shall be (in lieu of the amount of taxable income in excess of $25,000) the taxable income that exceeds one-half of the amount of the surtax exemption allocated to such corporation under paragraph (a)(1)(i) or (ii) of this section for such year. In the case of an affiliated group of corporations filing a consolidated return for a taxable year, the preceding sentence shall be applied by substituting the term "affiliated group" for the term "corporation" each time it appears.

(2) The provisions of this paragraph may be illustrated by the following example:

Example. Corporations P and S are component members of a controlled group of corporations on December 31, 1975, and each corporation files a separate income tax return on the basis of a calendar year. For the taxable year ending on December 31, 1975, P incurs a net operating loss and S has $25,000 of taxable income. If an apportionment plan is not effective for that taxable year, the surtax exemption under section 11(d) of each corporation (determined under paragraph (a)(1)(i) of this section) is $25,000 ($50,000 ÷ 2). For purposes of applying section 11(b) to determine S's liability for tax for 1975, the amount of taxable income subject to taxation at the rate of 20 percent is limited to $12,500 (*i.e.*, one-half of the amount of the surtax exemption allocated to S under paragraph (a)(1)(i) of this section), and the amount of taxable income subject to taxation at the rate of 22 percent is $12,500 (*i.e.*, the amount of taxable income in excess of one-half of the amount of the surtax exemption). If, on the other hand, an apportionment plan is adopted by P and S effective for such taxable years apportioning the entire $50,000 surtax exemption to S, then, for purposes of applying section 11(b) to determine S's liability for tax for 1975, the amount of taxable income subject to taxation at the rate of 20 percent is $25,000.

(3) If an apportionment plan is adopted under § 1.1561-3 for a December 31, and if paragraph (b)(1) of this section applies to any component member whose taxable year includes such December 31, then the plan shall specify—

(i) The amount subject to taxation at the rate of 20 percent, and

(ii) The amount subject to taxation at the rate of 22 percent

as determined under paragraph (b)(1) of this section for each component member. The information required to be included in a plan by this subparagraph is in addition to the information required under § 1.1561-3 (a). Where an existing apportionment plan is effective under § 1.1561-3(a)(3) for such December 31, the additional information required under this subparagraph may be provided in an amendment of the existing plan as provided in § 1.1561-3(c).

(c) *Accumulated earnings credit.* (1) Except as provided in subparagraph (2) of this paragraph, if a corporation is a component member of a controlled group on a December 31, the amount for purposes of computing the accumulated earnings credit under section 535(c)(2) and (3) of such corporation shall be an amount equal to $150,000 divided by the number of corporations which are component members of such group on such December 31. In the case of a controlled group of corporations which includes component members which join in the filing of a consolidated return and other component members which do not join in the filing of such a return, each component member of the controlled group (including each component member which joins in filing the consolidated return) shall be treated as a separate corporation for purposes of equally apportioning the $150,000 amount under this subparagraph. In such case, the amount for purposes of computing the accumulated earnings credit for the component members filing the consolidated return shall be the sum of the amounts apportioned to each component member which joins in filing the consolidated return.

(2) If, with respect to any component member of the controlled group, the amount determined under subparagraph (1) of this paragraph exceeds the sum of (i) such member's accumulated earnings and profits as of the close of the preceding taxable year, plus (ii) such member's earnings and profits for the taxable year which are retained (within the meaning of section 535 (c)(1)), then any such excess shall be subtracted from the amount determined under subparagraph (1) of this paragraph with respect to such member and shall be divided equally among those remaining component members of the controlled group that do not have such an excess (until no such excess remains to be divided among those remaining members that have not had such an excess). The excess so divided among such remaining members shall be added to the amount determined under subparagraph (1) with respect to such members. If a controlled group of corporations includes component members which join in the filing of a consolidated return and other component members which do not join in filing such return, the component members filing the consolidated return shall be treated as a single corporation for purposes of this subparagraph.

(3) A controlled group may not adopt an apportionment plan, as provided in § 1.1561-3, with respect to the amounts computed under the provisions of this paragraph.

(4) The provisions of this paragraph may be illustrated by the following example:

Example. A controlled group is composed of four component member corporations, W, X, Y, and Z. Each corporation files a separate income tax return on the basis of a calendar year. The sum of the earnings and profits for the taxable year ending December 31, 1975, which are retained plus the sum of the accumulated earnings and profits (as of the close of the preceding taxable year) is $15,000, $75,000, $37,500, and $300,000 for W, X, Y, and Z, respectively. The amounts determined under this paragraph for W, X, Y, and Z for 1975 are $15,000, $48,750, $37,500, and $48,750, respectively, computed as follows:

	W	Component members X	Y	Z
Earnings and profits	$15,000	$75,000	$37,500	$300,000
Amount computed under subparagraph (1)	37,500	37,500	37,500	37,500
Excess	22,500	0	0	0
Allocation of excess	—	7,500	7,500	7,500
New excess	—	—	7,500	—
Reallocation of new excess	—	3,750	—	3,750
Amount to be used for purposes of section 535(c) (2) and (3)	15,000	48,750	37,500	48,750

(d) *Small business deduction of life insurance companies.* (1) Except as provided in subparagraph (2) of this paragraph, if two or more life insurance companies which are taxable under section 802 are component members of a controlled group of corporations on a December 31, the amount for purposes of computing the limitation on the small business deduction under sections 804(a)(4) and 809(d)(10) of such corporations for their taxable years which include such December 31 shall be an amount equal to $25,000 divided by the number of life insurance companies taxable under section 802 which are component members of such group on such December 31.

(2) If, with respect to any of the component members of the controlled group which are described in subparagraph (1) of this paragraph, the amount determined under such subparagraph exceeds 10 percent of such member's investment yield (as defined in section 804(c)), then any such excess shall be subtracted from the amount determined under subparagraph (1) of this paragraph with respect to such member and shall be divided equally among those remaining life insurance company members of the controlled group that do not have such an excess (until no such excess remains to be divided among those remaining members that have not had such an excess). The excess so divided among such remaining members shall be added to the amount determined under subparagraph (1) with respect to such members.

(3) A controlled group may not adopt an apportionment plan, as provided in § 1.1561-3, with respect to the amounts computed under the provisions of this paragraph.

(e) *Certain short taxable years.* (1) If the return of a corporation is for a short period which does not include a December 31, and such corporation is a component member of a controlled group of corporations with respect to such short period, then for purposes of Subtitle A of the Code —

(i) The surtax exemption under section 11(d) of such corporation for such short period shall be an amount equal to $50,000 ($25,000 in the case of certain taxable years), divided by the number of corporations which are component members of such controlled group on the last day of such short period;

(ii) The amount to be used in computing the accumulated earnings credit under section 535(c)(2) and (3) of such corporation for such short period shall be an amount equal to $150,000 divided by the number of corporations which are members of such controlled group on the last day of such short period; and

(iii) The amount to be used in computing the limitation on the small business deduction of life insurance companies under sections 804(a)(4) and 809(d)(10) of such corporation for such short period shall not exceed an amount equal to $25,000 divided by the number of life insurance companies taxable under section 802 which are component members of the controlled group on the last day of such short period.

For purposes of the preceding sentence, the term "short period" does not include any period if the income for such period is required to be included in a consolidated return under § 1.1502-76. The determination of whether a corporation is a component member of a controlled group of corporations on the last day of a short period is made by applying the definition of "component member" contained in section 1563 (b) and § 1.1563-1 as if the last day of such short period were a December 31 occurring after December 31, 1974.

(2) The provisions of this paragraph may be illustrated by the following examples:

Example (1). On January 2, 1975, corporation X transfers cash to newly formed corporation Y (which begins business on that date) and receives all of the stock of Y in return. X also owns all of the stock of corporation Z on each day of 1974 and 1975. X uses the calendar year as its taxable year and Z uses a fiscal year ending on March 31. Y adopts a fiscal year ending on June 30 as its annual accounting period, and, therefore, files a return for the short taxable year beginning on January 2, 1975, and ending on June 30, 1975. On June 30, 1975, Y is a component member of a parent-subsidiary controlled group of corporations of which X, Y, and Z are component members. Accordingly, the surtax exemption of Y for the short taxable year ending on June 30, 1975, is $16,666.67 ($50,000 ÷ 3). On December 31, 1975, X, Y, and Z are component members of a parent-subsidiary controlled group of corporations. Accordingly, the surtax exemption of each such corporation for its taxable year including December 31, 1975 (*i.e.,* X's calendar year ending December 31, 1975, Z's fiscal year ending March 31, 1976, and Y's fiscal year ending June 30, 1976) is $16,-666.67 ($50,000 ÷ 3), or, if an apportionment plan is filed under § 1.1561-3, the amount apportioned pursuant to such plan.

Example (2). On January 1, 1975, corporation P owns all of the stock of corporations S-1, S-2, and S-3. P, S-1, S-2, and S-3 file separate returns on a calendar year basis. On July 31, 1975, S-1 is liquidated and therefore files a return for the short taxable year beginning on January 1, 1975, and ending on July 31, 1975. On August 31, 1975, S-2 is liquidated and there-

Reg. § 1.1561-2(e)(2)

fore files a return for the short taxable year beginning on January 1, 1975, and ending on August 31, 1975. On July 31, 1975, S-1 is a component member of a parent-subsidiary controlled group of corporations of which P, S-1, S-2, and S-3 are component members. Accordingly, the surtax exemption under section 11(d) of S-1 for the short taxable year ending on July 31, 1975, is $12,500 ($50,000 ÷ 4). On August 31, 1975, S-2 is a component member of a parent-subsidiary controlled group of corporations of which P, S-2, and S-3 are component members. Accordingly, the surtax exemption of S-2 for the short taxable year ending on August 31, 1975, is $16,666.67 ($50,000 ÷ 3). On December 31, 1975, P and S-3 are component members of a parent-subsidiary controlled group of corporations. Accordingly, the surtax exemption of each such corporation for the calendar year 1975 is $25,000 ($50,000 ÷ 2), or, if an apportionment plan is filed under § 1.1561-3, the amount apportioned pursuant to such plan.

§ 1.1561-3 (T.D. 7528, filed 12-27-77.) **Apportionment of surtax exemption.**

(a) *In general.* (1) In the case of corporations which are component members of a controlled group of corporations on a December 31, the single $50,000 surtax exemption under section 11(d) may be apportioned among such members (for the taxable year of each such member which includes such December 31) if all such members consent, in the manner provided in paragraph (b) of this section, to an apportionment plan with respect to such December 31. Such plan shall provide for the apportionment of a fixed dollar amount to one or more of such members, but in no event shall the sum of the amounts so apportioned exceed $50,000. An apportionment plan shall not be considered as adopted with respect to a particular December 31 until each component member which is required to consent to the plan under paragraph (b)(1) of this section files the original of a statement described in such paragraph (or, the original of a statement incorporating its consent is filed on its behalf). In the case of a return filed before a plan is adopted, the surtax exemption for purposes of such return shall be equally apportioned in accordance with the rules provided in § 1.1561-2(a)(1)(i). (If a valid apportionment plan is adopted after the return is filed and within the time prescribed by subparagraph (2) of this paragraph, such return should be amended (or a claim for refund should be made) to reflect the change from equal apportionment.)

(2) A controlled group may adopt an apportionment plan with respect to a particular December 31 only if, at the time such plan is sought to be adopted, there is at least one year remaining in the statutory period (including any extensions thereof) for the assessment of a deficiency against any corporation the tax liability of which would be increased by the adoption of such plan. If there is less than one year remaining with respect to any such corporation, the director of the service center with which such corporation files its income tax return will ordinarily, upon request, enter into an agreement to extend such statutory period for the limited purpose of assessing any deficiency against such corporation attributable to the adoption of such apportionment plan.

(3)(i) The amount apportioned to a component member of a controlled group of corporations in an apportionment plan adopted with respect to a particular December 31 shall constitute such member's surtax exemption for its taxable year including the particular December 31, and for all taxable years of such members including succeeding December 31's, unless the apportionment plan is amended in accordance with paragraph (c) of this section or is terminated under subdivision (ii) of this subparagraph. Thus, the apportionment plan (including any amendments thereof) has a continuing effect and need not be renewed annually.

(ii) If an apportionment plan is adopted with respect to a paticular December 31, such plan shall terminate with respect to a succeeding December 31, if—

(a) The controlled group ceases to remain in existence during the calendar year ending on such succeeding December 31,

(b) Any corporation which was a component member of such group on the particular December 31 is not a component member of such group on such succeeding December 31, or

(c) Any corporation which was not a component member of such group on the particular December 31 is a component member of such group on such succeeding December 31.

An apportionment plan, once terminated with respect to a December 31, is no longer effective. Accordingly, unless a new apportionment plan is adopted, the surtax exemption of the component members of the controlled group for their taxable years which include such December 31 and all December 31's thereafter will be determined in accordance with the rules provided in paragraph (a)(1)(i) of § 1.1561-2.

(iii) For purposes of subdivision (ii) (a)—

(a) A parent-subsidiary controlled group of corporations shall be considered as remaining in existence as long as its common parent corporation remains as a common parent.

(b) A brother-sister controlled group of corporations shall be considered as remaining in existence as long as the requirements of paragraph (a)(3)(i) of § 1.1563-1 continue to be satisfied with respect to at least two corporations, taking into account the stock ownership of only those five or fewer persons whose stock ownership was taken into account at the time the apportionment plan adopted by the component members of such group first became effective.

(c) A combined group of corporations shall be considered as remaining in existence as long as the brother-sister controlled group of corporations referred to in paragraph (a)(4)(i) of § 1.1563-1 in respect of such combined group remains in existence (within the meaning of (b) of this subdivision), and at least one such corporation is a common parent of a parent-subsidiary controlled group of corporations refered to in such paragraph (a)(4)(i).

(d) If, by reason of paragraph (a)(5) (i) of § 1.1563-1, two or more insurance companies subject to taxation under section 802 are treated as an insurance group separate from any corporations which are members of a controlled group described in paragraph (a)(2), (3), or (4) of § 1.1563-1, such insurance group shall be considered as remaining in existence as long as the controlled group described in paragraph (a)(2), (3), or (4) of such section, as the case may be, remains in existence (within the meaning of (a), (b), or (c) of this subdivision), and there are at least two insurance companies which satisfy the requirements of paragraph (a)(5)(i) of such section.

(iv) If an apportionment plan is terminated with respect to a particular December 31 by reason of an occurrence described in subdivision (ii)(b) or (c) of this subparagraph, each corporation which is a component member of the controlled group on such particular December 31 should, on or before the date it files its income tax return for the taxable year which includes such particular December 31, notify the service center with which it files such return of such termination. If an apportionment plan is terminated with respect to a particular December 31 by reason of an occurrence described in subdivision (ii)(a) of this subparagraph, each corporation which was a component member of the controlled group on the preceding December 31 should, on or before the date it files its income tax return for the taxable year which includes such particular December 31, notify the service center with which it files such return of such termination.

(b) *Consents to plan.* (1)(i) The consent of a component member (other than a wholly-owned subsidiary) to an apportionment plan with respect to a particular December 31 shall be made by means of a statement, signed by any person who is duly authorized to act on behalf of the consenting member, stating that such member consents to the apportionment plan with respect to such December 31. The statement shall set forth the name, address, taxpayer account number, and taxable year of the consenting component member, the amount apportioned to such member under the plan, and the service center where the original of the statement is to be filed. The consent of more than one component member may be incorporated in a single statement. The original of a statement of consent shall be filed with the service center with which the component member of the group on such December 31 which has the taxable year ending first on or after such date filed its return for such taxable year. (If two or more component members have the same such taxable year, a statement of consent may be filed with the service center with which the return for any such taxable year is filed.) The original of a statement of consent shall have attached thereto information (referred to in this paragraph as "group identification") setting forth the name, address, taxpayer account number, and taxable year of each component member of the controlled group on such December 31 (including wholly-owned subsidiaries) and the amount apportioned to each such member under the plan. If more than one original statement is filed, a statement may incorporate the group identification by reference to the name, address, taxpayer account number, and taxable year of a component member of the group which has attached such group identification to the original of its statement.

(ii) Each component member of the group on such December 31 (other than wholly-owned subsidiaries) should attach a copy of its consent (or a copy of the statement incorporating its consent) to the income tax return, amended return, or claim for refund filed with its service center for the taxable year including such date. Such copy shall either have attached thereto information on group identification or shall incorporate such information by reference to the name, address, taxpayer account number, and taxable year of a component member of the group which has attached such information to its income tax return, amended return, or claim for refund filed with the same service center for the taxable year including such date.

(2)(i) Each component member of a controlled group which is a wholly-owned subsidiary of such group with respect to a December 31 shall be deemed to consent to an apportionment plan with respect to such December 31, provided each component member of the group which is not a wholly-owned subsidiary consents to the plan. For purposes of this section, a component member of a controlled group shall be considered to be a wholly-owned subsidiary of the group with respect to a December 31, if, on each day preceding such date during its taxable year which includes such date, all of its stock is owned directly by one or more corporations which are component members of the group on such December 31.

(ii) Each wholly-owned subsidiary of a controlled group with respect to a December 31 should attach a statement containing the information which is required to be set forth in a statement of consent to an apportionment plan with respect to such December 31 to the income tax return, amended return, or claim for refund filed with its service center for the taxable year which includes such date. Such statement should either have attached thereto information on group identification or incorporate such information by reference to the name, address, taxpayer account number, and taxable year of a component member of the group which has attached such information to its income tax return, amended return, or claim for refund filed with the same service center for the taxable year including such date.

(c) *Amendment of plan.* An apportionment plan adopted with respect to a December 31 by a controlled group of corporations may be amended with respect to such December 31, or with respect to any succeeding December 31 for which the plan is effective under paragraph (a)(3) of this section. An apportionment plan must be amended with respect to a particular December 31 and the amendments to the plan shall be effective only if adopted in accordance with the rules prescribed in this section for the adoption of an original plan with respect to such December 31.

(d) *Component members filing consolidated returns.* If the component members of a controlled group of corporations on a December 31 include corporations which join in the filing of a consolidated return, the corporations filing the consolidated return shall be treated as a single component member for purposes of this section. Thus, for example, only one consent, executed by the common parent, to an apportionment plan filed pursuant to this section is required on behalf of the component members filing the consolidated return.

§ 1.1561-1A (T.D. 6845, filed 8-4-65; redesignated and amended by T.D. 7528,

Reg. § 1.1561-1A

24,232-F.4 (I.R.C.)   Reg. § 1.1561-1A   2-14-78

filed 12-27-77.) **Surtax exemptions in case of certain controlled corporations.**

(a) In general. Part II (section 1561 and following), subchapter B, chapter 6 of the Code, deals with the surtax exemptions of certain controlled corporations. In general, section 1561 provides that for taxable years ending after December 31, 1963, the component members of a controlled group of corporations are entitled, in the aggregate, to only a single $25,000 ($50,000 in the case of a taxable year ending in 1975) surtax exemption (in lieu of the multiple surtax exemptions which may have been available to such corporations in prior taxable years). However, under section 1562 a controlled group of corporations has the privilege of electing to have each of its component members make its returns without regard to section 1561. In such case, each component member of the electing controlled group is generally liable for the additional tax imposed by section 1562(b). Section 1563 contains certain definitions (including the definition of a "controlled group of corporations", and "component member") and special rules for purposes of part II of subchapter B.

(b) Tax avoidance. The provisions of part II, subchapter B, chapter 6 do not delimit or abrogate any principle of law established by judicial decision, or any existing provisions of the Code, such as sections 269, 482, and 1551, which have the effect of preventing the avoidance or evasion of income taxes. Thus, for example, notwithstanding the fact that a corporation is a component member of a controlled group of corporations which has elected multiple surtax exemptions under section 1562, if property is transferred to such corporation under the circumstances described in section 1551(a), the Commissioner may disallow in whole or in part the surtax exemption of the transferee corporation unless such transferee corporation establishes by the clear preponderance of the evidence that the securing of such exemption was not a major purpose of the transfer.

(c) Special rules. (1) For purposes of sections 1561 through 1563 and the regulations thereunder, the term "corporation" includes an unincorporated business enterprise subject to tax as a corporation under section 1361 and an electing small business corporation (as defined in section 1371(b)). However, for the treatment of an electing small business corporation as an excluded member of a controlled group of corporations, see paragraph (b)(2)(ii) of § 1.1563-1.

(2) In the case of corporations electing a 52-53-week taxable year under section 441(f)(1), the provisions of sections 1561 through 1563 and the regulations thereunder shall be applied in accordance with the special rule of section 441(f)(2)(A). See paragraph (b)(1) of § 1.441-2.

(3) If—

(i) The surtax exemption of a corporation for a taxable year beginning in 1963 and ending in 1964 is less than $25,000 by reason of the application of section 1561, or

(ii) An additional tax is imposed by section 1562(b) on the taxable income of a corporation for any such taxable year,

the change in the surtax exemption, or the imposition of the additional tax, is treated as a change in a rate of tax taking effect on January 1, 1964, for purposes of section 21(a). See section 21(d)(2) and the regulations thereunder.

§ 1.1561-2A (T.D. 6845, filed 8-4-65; amended by T.D. 6960, filed 6-24-68; T.D. 7244, filed 12-29-72; redesignated and amended by T.D. 7528, filed 12-27-77.) **Reduction of surtax exemption.**

(a) Amount of surtax exemption—(1) General rule. Under section 1561(a), if a corporation is a component member of a controlled group of corporations on a December 31, then for purposes of subtitle A of the Code the surtax exemption of such corporation for the taxable year which includes such December 31 shall be an amount equal to—

(i) $25,000 ($50,000 in the case of a taxable year ending in 1975) divided by the number of corporations which are component members of such group on such December 31, or

(ii) If an apportionment plan is adopted under § 1.1561-3A which is effective with respect to such taxable year, such portion of $25,000 ($50,000 in the case of a taxable year ending in 1975) as is apportioned to such member in accordance with such plan.

(2) Consolidated returns. The surtax exemption, of a controlled group of corporations all of whose component members join in the filing of a consolidated return shall be $25,000 (or $50,000). If there are component members of the controlled group which do not join in the filing of a consolidated return, and there is no apportionment plan effective under § 1.1561-3A apportioning the $25,000 (or $50,000) amount among the component members filing the consolidated return and the other component members of the controlled group, each component member of the controlled group (including each component member which joins in filing the consolidated return) shall be treated as a separate corporation for purposes of equally apportioning the $25,000 (or $50,000) amount under subparagraph (1)(i) of this paragraph. In such case, the surtax exemption of the corporations filing the consolidated return shall be the sum of the amounts apportioned to each component member which joins in filing the consolidated return.

(3) Taxable years including December 31, 1974. (i) This subparagraph (3) applies if one or more component members of a controlled group of corporations on December 31, 1974, has a taxable year that ends on that date and one or more other component members has a taxable year ending in 1975.

(ii) If no apportionment plan is effective under § 1.1561-3A, then for purposes of applying paragraph (a)(1)(i) of this section each component member shall be taken into account for purposes of equally apportioning the $50,000 amount among component members whose taxable years end in 1975, and equally apportioning the $25,000 among component members whose taxable years end on December 31, 1974. In such case, the surtax exemption of each corporation whose taxable year ends in 1975 shall be $50,000 divided by the number of corporations which are component members of the controlled group on December 31, 1974 and the surtax exemption of each corporation whose taxable year ends on December 31, 1974, shall be $25,000 divided by the number of corporations which are component members on December 31, 1974.

(iii) If an apportionment plan is adopted under § 1.1561-3A, the single surtax exemption available to the controlled group may be divided proportionately among the component members under such plan. Thus, if ⅕ of the $25,000 surtax exemption available for 1974 is apportioned to members having taxable years ending on December 31, 1974, the remaining ⅘ of the $25,000 surtax/exemption available for 1974, as well as ⅘ of the $50,000 surtax exemption available for 1975, would be apportioned among members having taxable years ending in 1975. In the case of members having taxable years ending in 1975, the portion of the $50,000 surtax exemption available to such members for 1975 and the portion of the $25,000 surtax exemption available to such members for 1974 must be divided among such members in the same proportion.

(iv) For purposes of section 11(b)(2)(A) (relating to 20 percent rate of normal tax on first $25,000 of taxable income), the $25,000 amount referred to in such section shall be allocated among the members having taxable years ending in 1975 in the same proportion as the total amount of the surtax exemption available to such members is divided among such members.

(v) This subparagraph may be illustrated by the following examples:

Example (1). Corporations X, Y, and Z are component members of a controlled group of corporations on December 31, 1974. X has taxable income of $10,000 for the taxable year ending December 31, 1974. Y has taxable income of $60,000 for the taxable year ending June 30, 1975. Z has taxable income of $15,000 for the taxable year ending September 30, 1975. Section 1561 applies to the group. The group files an apportionment plan under § 1.1561-3A apportioning the amount of $5,000 (i.e., ⅕ of $25,000) to X, the calendar-year member. Of the remaining ⅘ of the surtax exemption available to the group, ¾ is apportioned to Y and ¼ to Z. The tax liabilities of Y and Z for their taxable years ending in 1975 are computed as follows: (Computation of X's tax liability for 1974, using a surtax exemption of $5,000, is not shown.)

1975 Tentative Tax

		Y		Z
Taxable income		$60,000		$15,000
Normal tax	20 percent of $15,000 (i.e., 3/4 of $20,000)	$ 3,000	20 percent of $ 5,000 (i.e., 1/4 of $20,000)	$ 1,000
	22 percent of $45,000	9,900	22 percent of $10,000	2,200
		$12,900		$ 3,200
Surtax Taxable income	$60,000		$15,000	
Surtax exemption	30,000 (i.e., 3/4 of $40,000)		10,000 (i.e., 1/4 of $40,000)	
	$30,000 x 26 percent	7,800	$ 5,000 x 26 percent	1,300
1975 tentative tax		$20,700		$ 4,500

1974 Tentative Tax

		Y		Z
Taxable income		$60,000		$15,000
Normal tax	22 percent x $60,000	$13,200	22 percent x $15,000	$ 3,300
Surtax Taxable income	$60,000		$15,000	
Surtax exemption	15,000 (i.e., 3/4 of $20,000)		5,000 (i.e., 1/4 of $20,000)	
	$45,000 x 26 percent	11,700	$10,000 x 26 percent	2,600
1974 tentative tax		$24,900		$5,900

Reg. § 1.1561-2A(a)(3)

24,232-F.6 (I.R.C.)   Reg. § 1.1561-2A(a)(3)   12-30-77

The 1974 and 1975 tentative taxes are apportioned as follows:

Corporation Y:
- 1974 184/365 of $24,900 .... $12,552
- 1975 181/365 of $20,700 10,265
- Total tax for taxable year .. $22,817

Corporation Z:
- 1974 92/365 of $ 5,900 .... $ 1,487
- 1975 273/365 of $ 4,500 3,366
- Total tax for taxable year .. $ 4,853

Example (2). The facts are the same as in Example (1) execpt that an election under section 1562 is effective for taxable years including December 31, 1974. The group selects corporation Y to receive the full surtax exemption. The tax liabilities of Y and Z for their taxable years ending in 1975 are computed as follows: (Computation of X's tax liability for 1974, using a surtax exemption of $4,167 and including an additional tax of 6 percent of $4,167, is not shown.)

1975 Tentative Tax

	Y		Z	
Taxable income	$60,000		$15,000	
Normal tax 20 percent of $25,000	$ 5,000	22 percent of $15,000	$ 3,300	
22 percent of $35,000	7,700			
	$12,700			
Surtax				
Taxable income $60,000		$15,000		
Surtax exemption 50,000		-0-		
$10,000 x 26 percent	2,600	$15,000 x 26 percent	3,900	
1975 tentative tax	$15,300		$ 7,200	

1974 Tentative Tax

	Y		Z	
Taxable income	$60,000		$15,000	
Normal tax 22 percent x $60,000	$13,200	22 percent x $15,000	$ 3,300	
Surtax				
Taxable income $60,000		$15,000		
Surtax exemption 25,000		4,167		
$35,000 x 26 percent	9,100	$10,833 x 26 percent	2,817	
Additional tax $25,000 x 6 percent	1,500	$4,167 x 6 percent	250	
1974 tentative tax	$23,800		$ 6,367	

The 1974 and 1975 tentative taxes are apportioned as follows:

Corporation Y:
- 1974 184/365 of $23,800 .... $11,998
- 1975 181/365 of $15,300 7,587
- Total tax for taxable year .. $19,585

Corporation Z:
- 1974 92/365 of $ 6,367 .... $ 1,605
- 1975 273/365 of $ 7,200 5,385
- Total tax for taxable year .. $ 6,990

(4) *Examples.* The provisions of this paragraph may be illustrated by the following examples:

Example (1). Corporations W, X, Y, and Z are component members of a controlled group of corporations on December 31, 1964, and each corporation files its income tax return on the basis of a calendar year. For their taxable years ending on December 31, 1964, W and X each incur a net operating loss, Y has $5,250 of taxable income; and Z has $30,000 of taxable income. If an apportionment plan is not effective for such taxable years the surtax exemption of each corporation, determined under subparagraph (1)(i) of this paragraph, is $6,250 ($25,000 ÷ 4). However, the four corporations may avoid a pro rata division of the $25,000 amount by filing an apportionment plan in accordance with the provisions of § 1.1561-3A allocating the $25,000 amount in any manner they deem proper.

Example (2). Corporation A files its income tax return on the basis of a calendar year; corporation B files its income tax return on the basis of a fiscal year ending on March 31. On December 31, 1964, A and B are the only component members of a controlled group of corporations. Under subparagraph (1)(i) of this paragraph, the surtax exemption of A for 1964, and the surtax exemption of B for its fiscal year ending March 31, 1965, is an amount equal to $12,500 ($25,000 ÷ 2). However, if an apportionment plan is filed in accordance with the provisions of § 1.1561-3A, the surtax exemption of each such corporation will be the amount apportioned to the corporation pursuant to the plan.

Example (3). Corporations B, P, and S are component members of a controlled group of corporations on December 31, 1964. P and S file a consolidated return for their fiscal years ending June 30, 1965. B files a separate return for its taxable year ending on December 31, 1964. No apportionment plan is effective with respect to B's, P's, and S's taxable years which include December 31, 1964. Therefore, B, P, and S are each apportioned $8,333.33 of the $25,000 amount ($25,000 ÷ 3) for their taxable years including such date. The surtax exemption for the affiliated group filing a consolidated return (P and S) for the year ending June 30, 1965, is $16,666.66 (i.e., the sum of the $8,333.33 amounts apportioned to P and S). However, if an apportionment plan is filed in accordance with the provisions of § 1.-1561-3A, the surtax exemption of the corporations which are members of the affiliated group filing a consolidated return and of each other corporation which is a component member of the controlled group of corporations will be the amount apportioned to such affiliated group and to each such other corporation pursuant to the plan.

(b) *Certain short taxable years*—(1) *General rule.* If (i) the return of a corporation is for a short period (ending after December 31, 1963) which does not include a December 31, and (ii) such corporation is a component member of a controlled group of corporations with respect to such short period, then for purposes of subtitle A of the Code the surtax exemption of such corporation for such short period shall be an amount equal to $25,000 divided by the number of corporations which are component members of such group on the last day of such short period. For purposes of the preceding sentence, the term "short period" does not include any period if the income for such period is required to be included in a consolidated return under § 1.1502-76. The determination of whether a corporation is a component member of a controlled group of corporations on the last day of a short period is made by applying the definition of "component member" contained in section 1563(b) and § 1.1563-1 as if the last day of such short period were a December 31 occurring after December 31, 1963.

(2) *Examples.* The provisions of this paragraph may be illustrated by the following examples:

Example (1). On January 2, 1964, corporation X transfers cash to newly formed corporation Y (which begins business on that date) and receives all the stock of Y in return. X also owns all the stock of corporation Z on each day of 1963 and 1964. X uses the calendar year as its taxable year and Z uses a fiscal year ending on August 31. Y adopts a fiscal year ending on June 30 as its annual accounting period and, therefore, files a return for the short taxable year beginning on January 2, 1964, and ending on June 30, 1964. On June 30, 1964, Y is a component member of a parent-subsidiary controlled group of corporations of which X, Y, and Z are component members. Accordingly, the surtax exemption of Y for the short taxable year ending on June 30, 1964, is $8,333.33 ($25,000 ÷ 3). On December 31, 1964, X, Y, and Z are component members of a parent-subsidiary controlled group of corporations. Accordingly, the surtax exemption of each such corporation for its taxable year including December 31, 1964 (i.e., X's calendar year ending December 31, 1964, Z's fiscal year ending August 31, 1965, and Y's fiscal year ending June 30, 1965) is $8,333.33 ($25,000 ÷ 3), or, if an apportionment plan is filed under § 1.1561-3A, the amount apportioned pursuant to such plan.

Example (2). On January 1, 1964, corporation P owns all the stock of corporations S-1, S-2, and S-3. P, S-1, S-2, and S-3 file separate returns on a calendar year basis. On July 31, 1964, S-1 is liquidated and therefore files a return for the short taxable year beginning on January 1, 1964, and ending on July 31, 1964. On August 31, 1964, S-2 is liquidated and therefore files a return for the short taxable year beginning on January 1, 1964, and ending on August 31, 1964. On July 31, 1964, S-1 is a component member of a parent-subsidiary controlled group of corporations of which P, S-1, S-2, and S-3 are component members. Accordingly, the surtax exemption of S-1 for the short taxable year ending on July 31, 1964, is $6,250 ($25,000 ÷ 4). On August 31, 1964, S-2 is a component member of a parent-subsidiary controlled group of corporations of which P, S-2, and S-3 are component members. Accordingly, the surtax exemption of S-2 for the short taxable year ending on August 31, 1964, is $8,333.33 ($25,000 ÷ 3). On December 31, 1964, P and S-3 are component members of a parent-subsidiary controlled group of corporations. Accordingly, the surtax exemption of each such corporation for the calendar year 1964 is $12,500 ($25,000 ÷ 2), or, if an apportionment plan is filed under § 1.1561-3A, the amount apportioned pursuant to such plan.

(c) *Corporations affected.* The provisions of section 1561 may result in the reduction of the surtax exemption of any corporation which is a component member of a controlled group of corporations and which is subject to the tax imposed by section 11, or by any other provision of subtitle A of the Code if the tax under such other provisions is computed by reference to the amount of the surtax exemption provided by section 11. Such other provisions include, for example, sections 511(a)(1), 594, 802, 831, 852, 857, 882, 1201, and 1378.

Reg. § 1.1561-2A(c)

§ 1.1561-3A (T.D. 6845, filed 8-4-65; redesignated and amended by T.D. 7528, filed 12-27-77.) **Apportionment of $25,000 surtax exemption.**

(a) Apportionment plan—(1) In general. In the case of corporations which are component members of a controlled group of corporations on a December 31, a single $25,000 ($50,000 in the case of a taxable year ending in 1975) surtax exemption may be apportioned among such members (for the taxable year of each such member which includes such December 31) if all such members consent, in the manner provided in paragraph (b) of this section, to an apportionment plan with respect to such December 31. Such plan shall provide for the apportionment of a fixed dollar amount to one or more of such members. See § 1.1561-2A(a)(3) for limitation on apportionable amount for taxable years including December 31, 1974, that end in 1975. An apportionment plan shall not be considered as adopted with respect to a particular December 31 until each component member which is required to consent to the plan under paragraph (b)(1) of this section files the original of a statement described in such paragraph (or, the original of a statement incorporating its consent is filed on its behalf). In the case of a return filed before a plan is adopted, the surtax exemption for purposes of such return, shall be equally apportioned in accordance with paragraph (a)(1)(i) of § 1.1561-2A. (If a valid apportionment plan is adopted after the return is filed and within the time prescribed in subparagraph (2) of this paragraph, such return should be amended (or a claim for refund should be made) to reflect the change from equal apportionment.)

(2) Time for adopting plan. A controlled group may adopt an apportionment plan with respect to a particular December 31 only if, at the time such plan is sought to be adopted, there is at least one year remaining in the statutory period (including any extensions thereof) for the assessment of a deficiency against any corporation the tax liability of which would be increased by the adoption of such plan. If there is less than one year remaining with respect to any such corporation, the district director with whom such corporation files its income tax return will ordinarily, upon request, enter into an agreement to extend such statutory period for the limited purpose of assessing any deficiency against such corporation attributable to the adoption of such apportionment plan.

(3) Years for which effective. (i) The amount apportioned to a component member of a controlled group of corporations in an apportionment plan adopted with respect to a particular December 31 shall constitute such member's surtax exemption for its taxable year including the particular December 31, and for all taxable years including succeeding December 31's, unless the apportionment plan is amended in accordance with paragraph (c) of this section or is terminated under subdivision (ii) of this subparagraph. Thus, the apportionment plan (including any amendments thereof) has a continuing effect and need not be renewed annually. For an exception to this rule in case of apportionment plans adopted with respect to December 31, 1963, see paragraph (e) of this section.

(ii) If an election is made under section 1562(a)(1) which is effective with respect to a December 31 for which an apportionment plan would otherwise be effective under subdivision (i) of this subparagraph, then such plan shall terminate with respect to such December 31. Furthermore, if an apportionment plan is adopted with respect to a particular December 31, such plan shall terminate with respect to a succeeding December 31, if—

(a) The controlled group goes out of existence with respect to such succeeding December 31 within the meaning of paragraph (b) of § 1.1562-5,

(b) Any corporation which was a component member of such group on the particular December 31 is not a component member of such group on such succeeding December 31, or

(c) Any corporation which was not a component member of such group on the particular December 31 is a component member of such group on such succeeding December 31.

An apportionment plan, once terminated with respect to a December 31, is no longer effective. Accordingly, unless a new apportionment plan is adopted or an election under section 1562(a)(1) is effective, the surtax exemption of the component members of the controlled group for their taxable years which include such December 31 and all December 31's thereafter will be determined under paragraph (a)(1)(i) of § 1.1561-2A.

(iii) If an apportionment plan is terminated with respect to a particular December 31 by reason of an occurrence described in subdivision (ii) *(b)* or *(c)* of this subparagraph, each corporation which is a component member of the controlled group on such particular December 31 should, on or before the date it files its income tax return for the taxable year which includes such particular December 31, notify the district director with whom it files such return of such termination. If an apportionment plan is terminated with respect to a particular December 31 by reason of an occurrence described in subdivision (ii) *(a)* of this subparagraph, each corporation which was a component member of the controlled group on the preceding December 31 should, on or before the date it files its income tax return for the taxable year which includes such particular December 31, notify the district director with whom it files such return of such termination.

(b) Consents to plan—(1) General. (i) The consent of a component member (other than a wholly-owned subsidiary) to an apportionment plan with respect to a particular December 31 shall be made by means of a statement, signed by any person who is duly authorized to act on behalf of the consenting member, stating that such member consents to the apportionment plan with respect to such December 31. The statement shall set forth the name, address, taxpayer account number, and taxable year of the consenting component member, the amount apportioned to such member under the plan, and the internal revenue district where the original of the statement is to be filed. The consent of more than one component member may be incorporated in a single statement. The original of a statement of consent shall be filed with the district director with whom

the component member of the group on such December 31 which has the taxable year ending first on or after such date filed its return for such taxable year. (If two or more component members have the same such taxable year, a statement of consent may be filed with the district director with whom the return for any such taxable year is filed.) The original of a statement of consent shall have attached thereto information (referred to in this paragraph as "group identification") setting for the name, address, taxpayer account number, and taxable year of each component member of the controlled group on such December 31 (including wholly-owned subsidiaries) and the amount apportioned to each such member under the plan. If more than one original statement is filed, a statement may incorporate the group identification by reference to the name, address, taxpayer account number, and taxable year of a component member of the group which has attached such group identification to the original of its statement.

(ii) Each component member of the group on such December 31 (other than wholly-owned subsidiaries) should attach a copy of its consent (or a copy of the statement incorporating its consent) to the income tax return, amended return, or claim for refund filed with its district director for the taxable year including such date. Such copy shall either have attached thereto information on group identification or shall incorporate such information by reference to the name, address, taxpayer account number, and taxable year of a component member of the group which has attached such information to its income tax return, amended return, or claim for refund filed with the same district director for the taxable year including such date.

(2) *Wholly-owned subsidiaries.* (i) Each component member of a controlled group which is a wholly-owned subsidiary of such group with respect to a December 31 shall be deemed to consent to an apportionment plan with respect to such December 31, provided each component member of the group which is not a wholly-owned subsidiary consents to the plan. For purposes of this section, a component member of a controlled group shall be considered to be a wholly-owned subsidiary of the group with respect to a December 31, if, on each day preceding such date during its taxable year which includes such date, all of its stock is owned directly by one or more corporations which are component members of the group on such December 31.

(ii) Each wholly-owned subsidiary of a controlled group with respect to a December 31 should attach a statement containing the information which is required to be set forth in a statement of consent to an apportionment plan with respect to such December 31 to an income tax return, amended return, or claim for refund filed with its district director for the taxable year which includes such date. Such statement should either have attached thereto information on group identification or incorporate such information by reference to the name, address, taxpayer account number, and taxable year of a component member of the group which has attached such information to its income tax return, amended return, or claim for refund filed with the same district director for the taxable year including such date.

(c) *Amendment of plan.* An apportionment plan adopted with respect to a December 31 by a controlled group of corporations may be amended with respect to such December 31, or with respect to any succeeding December 31 for which the plan is effective under paragraph (a)(3) of this section. An apportionment plan must be amended with respect to a particular December 31 and the amendments to the plan shall be effective only if adopted in accordance with the rules prescribed in this section for the adoption of an original plan with respect to such December 31.

(d) *Component members filing consolidated return.* If the component members of a controlled group of corporations on a December 31 include corporations which join in the filing of a consolidated return, the corporations filing the consolidated return shall be treated as a single component member for purposes of this section. Thus, for example, only one consent, executed by the common parent, to an apportionment plan filed pursuant to this section is required on behalf of the component members filing the consolidated return.

(e) *Apportionment plans with respect to December 31, 1963.* Any apportionment plan with respect to December 31, 1963, filed in accordance with Treasury Decision 6733, approved May 11, 1964 (29 F.R. 6320, C.B. 1964-1 (Part 1), 635) shall be deemed to satisfy the requirements of this section. However, any such plan shall not be effective under paragraph (a)(3) of this section with respect to taxable years including December 31, 1964 (or any succeeding December 31) unless the requirements of this section are actually satisfied. For example, if a component member of a controlled group of corporations on December 31, 1963, is deemed to consent to an apportionment plan with respect to such date filed in accordance with the provisions of Treasury Decision 6733, but would not be deemed to consent to such plan under the provisions of paragraph (b)(2) of this section, then although such plan is valid with respect to the taxable years of the component members of such group which include December 31, 1963, such plan is not effective under paragraph (a)(3) of this section with respect to taxable years including December 31, 1964 (or any succeeding December 31). Accordingly, if an apportionment plan is desired with respect to December 31, 1964 (or any succeeding December 31), new consents will be required.

§ 1.1562 Statutory provisions; privilege of groups to elect multiple surtax exemptions. [Sec. 1562, IRC]

§ 1.1562-0 (T.D. 7528, filed 12-27-77.) Effective date.

The provisions of §§ 1.1562-1 through 1.1562-7 apply only to taxable years beginning before January 1, 1975.

§ 1.1562-1 (T.D. 6845, filed 8-4-65; amended by T.D. 6960, filed 6-24-68 and T.D. 7181, filed 4-24-72.) Privilege of controlled group to elect multiple surtax exemptions.

(a) *Election*—(1) *In general.* (i) Under section 1562(a)(1) a controlled group of corporations has the privilege of electing to

Reg. § 1.1562-1(a)(1)

have each of its component members make its returns without regard to section 1561 (relating to single surtax exemption in the case of a controlled group of corporations). The election shall be made with respect to a particular December 31 and shall be valid only if each corporation which is required to consent to the election under the provisions of paragraph (a)(1) of § 1.1562-3 gives its consent in the manner and within the time prescribed in such section. An election shall not be considered as made with respect to a particular December 31 until each corporation which is required to consent to the election under paragraph (c)(1) of § 1.1562-3 files the original of a statement described in such paragraph (or, the original of a statement incorporating its consent is filed on its behalf). Accordingly, for purposes of returns filed before an election is made, the surtax exemption of component members of a controlled group of corporations shall be determined in accordance with section 1561 and the regulations thereunder. (If a valid election is made after the return is filed and within the time prescribed in § 1.1562-3, such return should be amended (or a claim for refund should be made) to reflect the change in the amount of the surtax exemption (and the imposition of the additional tax) resulting from the election.)

(ii) An election once made with respect to a particular December 31 may not thereafter be withdrawn unless such election is terminated with respect to such December 31 in accordance with the provisions of section 1562(c) and § 1.1562-2.

(iii) An election under section 1562(a)(1) may be made by a controlled group of corporations with respect to any December 31 (after December 31, 1962), unless—

(a) A component member of such group on such December 31 joins, or is required to join, in the filing of a consolidated return for its taxable year which includes such date, or

(b) Such controlled group is not eligible to make an election with respect to such December 31 by reason of section 1562(d). See also section 243(b)(3)(A), relating to effect of election of 100-percent dividends received deduction, which may prevent a controlled group from making an election under section 1562(a)(1) with respect to a particular December 31.

(2) *Years for which effective.* (i) A valid election under section 1562(a)(1) by a controlled group of corporations with respect to a particular December 31 is effective with respect to—

(a) The taxable year of each component member of such group on such December 31 which includes such December 31, and

(b) Any succeeding taxable year of any corporation which is a component member of such group (or a successor group) on a succeeding December 31 included within any such succeeding taxable year. Under section 1562(c) and § 1.1562-2, an election under section 1562(a)(1) may be terminated with respect to a December 31 referred to in either *(a)* or *(b)* of this subdivision. For years affected by termination, see paragraph (c) of § 1.1562-2.

(ii) For the application of an election under section 1562(a)(1) to certain short taxable years not including a December 31, see section 1562(f)(2) and § 1.1562-6.

(iii) The provisions of this subparagraph may be illustrated by the following example:

Example. Corporation P is the common parent of a parent-subsidiary controlled group of corporations of which corporations P, S-1, and S-2 are component members on December 31, 1964. On December 31, 1965, the controlled group of corporations consists of the same component members as on December 31, 1964, except that corporation S-3 is also a component member on December 31, 1965. On December 31, 1966, the controlled group of corporations consists of the same component members as on December 31, 1965, except that S-1 is no longer a component member on December 31, 1966. In January 1965, the controlled group makes a valid election under section 1562(a)(1) with respect to December 31, 1964. Under subdivision (i) *(a)* of this subparagraph, the election (unless terminated) is effective with respect to the taxable years of P, S-1, and S-2 which include December 31, 1964. Under subdivision (i) *(b)* of this subparagraph, the election (unless terminated) is also effective with respect to the taxable years of P, S-1, S-2, and S-3 which include December 31, 1965, and with respect to the taxable years of P, S-2, and S-3 which include December 31, 1966.

(b) *Effect of election*—*(1) General.* If an election under section 1562(a)(1) is effective with respect to a taxable year of a corporation, then—

(i) Section 1561 shall not apply to such corporation for such taxable year, but

(ii) The additional tax imposed by section 1562(b) shall apply to such corporation for such taxable year (except as otherwise provided in subparagraph (3) of this paragraph).

(2) *Additional tax.* The additional tax imposed by section 1562(b) is an amount equal to 6 percent of so much of a corporation's taxable income for the taxable year as does not exceed the amount of such corporation's surtax exemption for such taxable year. However, if a corporation computes its tax under section 1201 (relating to alternative tax) and is subject to the additional tax imposed by section 1562(b) for such taxable year, the additional tax applies only to an amount equal to the taxable income reduced by the excess of the net long-term capital gain over the net short-term capital loss for such taxable year (to the extent such amount does not exceed the amount of such corporation's surtax exemption for such taxable year).

(3) *Exceptions.* The additional tax imposed by section 1562(b) shall not apply to a corporation for any taxable year if—

(i) Such corporation is the only component member of a controlled group on the December 31 included within such taxable year which has taxable income for the taxable years including such date, or

(ii) Such corporation's surtax exemption is disallowed for such year under any provision of the Code. For purposes of this subdivision, if the component members of a controlled group of corporations on a December 31 are limited in the aggregate to a single $25,000 surtax exemption for their taxable years which include such date, then the surtax exemption of each such component member shall be considered to be disallowed for such taxable year regardless of how the $25,000 is allocated among such members. For example, if pursuant to the authority provided in section 269(b), the Commissioner allocates a single $25,000 surtax exemption equally between two corporations which are the only component members of an electing controlled group of corporations, the surtax exemption of each such corporation shall be considered to be disallowed.

The application of this subparagraph in respect of a taxable year of a component member of a controlled group of corporations does not constitute the termination of an election made under section 1562(a)(1). Accordingly, such election continues in effect for the subsequent taxable years of such corporation and the other corporations which are component members of the controlled group, unless the election is terminated under section 1562(c).

(4) *Taxable income defined.* For purposes of this paragraph, the term "taxable income" means—

(i) In the case of a corporation subject to tax under section 511(a) (relating to tax on unrelated business income of charitable, etc., organizations at corporation rates), its "unrelated business taxable income" (as defined in section 512),

(ii) In the case of a life insurance company, its "life insurance company taxable income" (as defined in section 802(b)),

(iii) In the case of a regulated investment company, its "investment company taxable income" (as defined in section 852(b)(2)),

(iv) In the case of a real estate investment trust, its "real estate investment trust taxable income" (as defined in section 857(b)(2)), and

(v) In the case of an electing small business corporation, its "taxable income" (as defined in section 1373(d)).

(5) *Tax treated as imposed by section 11, etc.* For purposes of applying other sections of the Code, if for a taxable year a corporation is subject to both the tax imposed by section 11 and to the additional tax imposed by section 1562(b), then the additional tax is treated as if it were imposed by section 11. If a corporation is subject to a tax imposed by any section of chapter 1 of the Code other than section 11 but such tax is computed by reference

to section 11, the additional tax is treated for purposes of the Code as imposed by such other section. (For example, the tax imposed by section 831(a) is "computed as provided in section 11"; therefore if a corporation is subject to both the tax imposed by section 831(a) and the additional tax imposed by section 1562(b) for any taxable year, the additional tax is treated as imposed by section 831(a) for such taxable year.) Accordingly, the credits against the tax imposed by chapter 1 of the Code allowable, for example, under sections 38 (relating to credit against tax for investment in certain depreciable property) and 33 (relating to credit against tax for investment in certain possessions of the United States) may be applied against the additional tax.

(6) Special rules. For purposes of sections 244 (relating to dividends received on certain preferred stock), 247 (relating to dividends paid on certain preferred stock of public utilities), 804(a)(3) (relating to deduction for partially tax-exempt interest in the case of a life insurance company), and 922 (relating to special deduction for Western Hemisphere trade corporations), the normal tax rate referred to in such sections shall be determined without regard to the additional tax imposed by section 1562(b). For example, in the case of a corporation subject to the additional tax imposed by section 1562(b) for its taxable year ending December 31, 1965, the percentage computed under section 244(a)(2)(B) for such taxable year would be 48 percent.

§ 1.1562-2 (T.D. 6845, filed 8-4-65.) **Termination of election.**

(a) In general. An election under section 1562(a)(1) is terminated by any one of the occurrences described in paragraph (b) of this section. For years affected by termination, see paragraph (c) of this section.

(b) Methods of termination—(1) Consent of the members. An election may be terminated with respect to a particular December 31 by consent of the component members of a controlled group of corporations. A termination by consent shall be made with respect to a particular December 31 and shall be valid only if each corporation which is required to consent to the termination under paragraph (a)(1) of § 1.1562-3 gives its consent in the manner and within the time prescribed in such section. A termination by consent shall not be considered as made with respect to a particular December 31 until each corporation which is required to consent to the termination under paragraph (c)(1) of § 1.1562-3 files the original of a statement described in such paragraph (or, the original of a statement incorporating its consent is filed on its behalf.).

(2) Refusal by new member to consent. (i) If on a December 31 a controlled group of corporations which has made an election under section 1562(a)(1) includes a new member which files a statement that it does not consent to the election with respect to such December 31, then such election shall terminate with respect to such date. Such statement shall be signed by any person who is dully authorized to act on behalf of the new member, and shall be attached to the income tax return of such new member for its taxable year which includes such December 31, filed on or before the date prescribed by law (including extensions of time) for the filing of such return. The statement shall set forth the name, address, taxpayer account number, and taxable year of each corporation which was a component member of the controlled group on such December 31. In the event of a termination under this subparagraph, each component member of the controlled group on such December 31 (other than such new member) should, within 30 days after such new member files the statement of refusal to consent, file notification of the termination with the district director with whom it filed (or will file) an income tax return for its taxable year which includes such December 31.

(ii) For purposes of subdivision (i) of this subparagraph, a corporation shall be considered to be a new member of a controlled group of corporations on a December 31 if such corporation—

(a) Is a component member of such group on such December 31, and

(b) Was not a member of such group on the January 1 immediately preceding such December 31.

(3) Consolidated returns. (i) If any corporations which is a component member of a controlled group of corporations on a December 31 joins, or is required to join, in the filing of a consolidated return for its taxable year which includes such date, then an election under section 1562(a)(1) which is effective with respect to preceding taxable years of component members of the group shall terminate with respect to such December 31. In the event of a termination under this subparagraph, each component member of the controlled group on such December 31 which does not join in the filing of a consolidated return for the taxable year which includes such date, should, within 30 days after such consolidated return is filed, file notification of the termination with the district director with whom it filed (or will file) an income tax return for its taxable year which includes such December 31.

(ii) The provisions of this subparagraph may be illustrated by the following example:

Example. On each day of 1964 and 1965 Brown, an individual, owns all the stock of corporations M and P. Corporation P, in turn, owns all the stock of corporation S. Each corporation files a separate return for its taxable year ending on December 31, 1964. On April 30, 1965, the controlled group of corporations consisting of M, P, and S makes an election under section 1562(a)(1) with respect to December 31, 1964. On March 15, 1966, P and S join in the filing of a consolidated return for their taxable years ending December 31, 1965, and M files a separate return for its taxable year ending on such date. Under this subparagraph, the election by the controlled

Reg. § 1.1562-2(b)(3)

group with respct to December 31, 1964, is terminated with respect to December 31, 1965. On or before April 14, 1966, M should file notification of the termination with the district director with whom it filed its income tax return for 1965.

(4) Controlled group no longer in existence. If a controlled group of corporations is considered as going out of existence with respect to a particular December 31 under paragraph (b) of § 1.1562-5, and if there is no successor group in respect of such controlled group under the rules provided in paragraph (c) of such section, then an election under section 1562(a)(1) with respect to such controlled group shall terminate with respect to such December 31.

(c) Effect of termination. A termination under subparagraph (1), (2), (3), or (4) of paragraph (b) of this section is effective with respect to the December 31 referred to in such subparagraph. An election, once terminated, is no longer effective. Thus, a termination is effective with respect to the taxable year of each component member of a controlled group of corporations which includes such December 31 and with respect to all succeeding taxable years of each corporation which is a component member of such group (or a successor group). Moreover, after a termination, the controlled group (and any successor group) may not make a new election except as provided in section 1562(d) and § 1.1562-4.

§ 1.1562-3 (T.D. 6845, filed 8-4-65.) **Consents to election and termination.**

(a) Consents required — (1) General. An election under paragraph (a)(1) of § 1.1562-1, or a termination by consent under paragraph (b)(1) of § 1.1562-2, may be made by a controlled group of corporation with respect to a particular December 31 only if each corporation, which was a component member of such group (or a successor group) on any December 31 falling within the period beginning on the particular December 31 and ending on the most recently past December 31, consents to the election or termination with in the time prescribed in paragraph (b) of this section and in the manner prescribed in paragraph (c) of this section. Such election or termination may be made with respect to a particular December 31 whether or not the electing or terminating group ceases to remain in existence under the principles of paragraph (a) of § 1.1562-5 before such election or termination is made. In the case of an election with respect to December 31, 1963, if each corporation which is required to consent to the election under the rules provided in Treasury Decision 6733, approved May 11, 1964 (29 F.R. 6320, C.B. 1964-1 (Part 1), 635) gives its consent in the manner provided in such Treasury Decision before December 31, 1964, then a valid election under section 1562(a)(1) shall be considered to have been made with respect to December 31, 1963.

(2) Examples. The provisions of subparagraph (1) of this paragraph may be illustrated by the following examples:

Example (1). P Corporation is the common parent of a parent-subsidiary controlled group of which corporations P, S-1, and S-2 are component members on December 31, 1965. On December 31, 1966, the controlled group consists of the same component members as on December 31, 1965, except that S-1 is no longer a component member on December 31, 1966. On December 31, 1967, the controlled group of corporations consists of the same component members as in December 31, 1966, except that corporation S-3 is also a component member on December 31, 1967. In January 1968, the controlled group desires to make an election under section 1562 (a) (1) with respect to December 31, 1965. Such election may be made only if P, S-1 (even though S-1 was not a component member of the group on December 1, 1966, or December 31, 1967), S-2 and S-3 (even though S-3 was not a component member of the group on December 31, 1965, or December 31, 1966) consent to the election.

Example (2). Assume to same facts as in example (1) and further assume that in January 1968, the controlled group makes a valid election with respect to December 31, 1965. If, in July 1968, the controlled group desires to terminate the election with respect to December 31, 1966, P, S-2, and S-3 must consent to the termination.

(b) Time for consents—(1) Consents to election. The consent of each component member of a controlled group of corprations which is required with respect to an election for a particular December 31, shall be made at any time after such December 31 and before the expiration of 3 years after the date on which the income tax return, for the taxable year of the component member of the group on such December 31 which has the taxable year ending first on or after such date, is required to be filed (determined without regard to any extensions of time for the filing of such return). See section 1562(e)(1).

(2) Consents to termination. The consent of each component member of a controlled group of corporations which is required with respect to a termination for a particular December 31, shall be made at any time after such December 31 and before the expiration of 3 years after such date. See section 1562(e)(2).

(3) Examples. The provisions of this paragraph may be illustrated by the following examples:

Example (1). The component members of a controlled group of corporations on December 31, 1965, consist of 2 calendar-year corporations, X and Y. The group desires to make an election under section 1562(a)(1) with respect to December 31, 1965. Under subparagraph (1) of this paragraph, the required consents to the election must be made after December 31, 1965, and on or before March 15, 1969. The result is the same whether or not X or Y (or both) ceases to be a component member of the group after December 31, 1965, and whether or not X or Y (or both) is granted an extension of time for the filing of its income tax return for 1965.

Example (2). Assume the same facts as in example (1) except that X files its income tax return on the basis of a fiscal year ending January 31, and Y files its income tax return on the basis of a fiscal year ending on June 30. Under subparagraph (1) of this paragraph, the last day on which the required consents may be made with respect to an election for December 31, 1965, is April 15, 1969.

Example (3). Assume the same facts as in example (1) or (2) except that an election under section 1562(a)(1) is effective for X's and Y's taxable years including December 31, 1965. Assume further that the group desires to terminate the election with respect to December 31, 1965. Under subparagraph (2) of this paragraph, the required consents to the termination must be made after December 31, 1965, and on or before December 31, 1968.

(c) *Manner of consenting*—(1) *General rule.* (i) The consent of a corporation to an election or termination with respect to a particular December 31, (other than a corporation which is a wholly-owned subsidiary in respect of such election or termination) shall be made by means of a statement, signed by any person who is duly authorized to act on behalf of the consenting corporation, stating that such corporation consents to an election or termination (as the case may be) with respect to such December 31. Such statement shall set forth the name, address and taxpayer account number of the consenting member and the internal revenue district where the original of the statement is to be filed. The consent of more than one component member may be incorporated in a single statement. The original of a statement of consent shall be filed with the district director with whom the component member of the group on the particular December 31 which has the taxable year ending first on or after such date filed its return for such taxable year. (If two or more component members have the same such taxable year, a statement of consent may be filed with the district director with whom the return for any such taxable year is filed.) The original of a statement shall have attached thereto information (referred to in this paragraph as "group identification") setting forth the name, address, taxpayer account number, and taxable year of each component member of the controlled group on such December 31 (including wholly-owned subsidiaries). If the particular December 31 is a December 31 other than the December 31 immediately preceding the date on which such statement is filed then, as part of the "group identification", the original of the statement shall also set forth the information required in the preceding sentence with respect to each other corporation which was a component member of the group (or a successor group) on any December 31 occurring after the particular December 31 on which the consenting corporation was a component member of such group. If more than one original statement is filed, a statement may incorporate the group identification by reference to the name, address, taxpayer account number, and taxable year of a component member of the group which has attached such group identification to the original of its statement.

(ii) Each corporation which was a component member of the electing (or terminating) controlled group (or a successor group) on a December 31 falling within the period beginning on the particular December 31 and ending on the most recently past December 31 (other than a wholly-owned subsidiary in respect of such election or termination) should attach a copy of its consent (or a copy of the statement incorporating its consent) to each income tax return, amended return, or claim for refund filed with its district director for a taxable year which includes any such December 31. Such copy should either have attached thereto information on group identification or incorporate such information by reference to the name, address, taxpayer account number, and taxable year of a component member of the group which has attached such information to its income tax return, amended return, or claim for refund filed with the same district director for a taxable year which includes any such December 31.

(2) *Wholly-owned subsidiaries.* (i) Each corporation which is a wholly-owned subsidiary of a controlled group of corporations in respect of an election or termination with respect to a particular December 31 shall be deemed to consent to such election or termination (as the case may be). For purposes of this section, a corporation shall be considered to be a wholly-owned subsidiary of a controlled group in respect of an election or termination with respect to a particular December 31 if, on each day falling within the period beginning on the first day of such corporation's taxable year which included such December 31 and ending on the day on which such election or termination is made (or, if such corporation was not in existence on each day of such period, on each day falling within such period during which the corporation was in existence), all the stock of such corporation is owned directly by one or more corporations which are component members of such group (or a successor group) on any December 31 falling within such period.

(ii) Each wholly-owned subsidiary should attach a statement to an income tax return, amended return, or claim for refund filed with its district director for each taxable year which contains a December 31 falling within the period described in the last sentence of subdivision (i) of this subparagraph, stating that an election or termination (as the case may be) is effective for such taxable year and containing the information which would be required to be set forth in a statement of consent to the election or termination filed pursuant to subparagraph (1)(i) of this paragraph. Information on group identification may either be attached to the statement or incorporated by reference to the name, address, taxpayer account number, and taxable year of a component member of the group which has attached such group identification to an income tax return, amended return, or claim for refund filed with the same district director for the taxable year including such date.

(d) *Effect of consent.* Under section 1562(e), any consent to an election under section 1562(a)(1) or a termination under section 1562(c)(1) is deemed to be a consent to the application of section 1562(g)(1) (relating to tolling of statute of limitations on assessment of deficiencies). See § 1.1562-7.

Reg. § 1.1562-3(d)

§ 1.1562-4 (T.D. 6845, filed 8-4-65.) Election after termination.

(a) *In general.* Under section 1562(d), if a controlled group of corporations has made a valid election under section 1562(a)(1), and such election is terminated by any one of the occurrences described in paragraph (b) of § 1.1562-2, then such group (or any controlled group which is a successor to such group within the meaning of paragraph (c) of § 1.1562-5) is not eligible to make an election under section 1562(a)(1) with respect to any December 31 before the sixth December 31 after the particular December 31 with respect to which such termination was effective. For the particular December 31 with respect to which a termination is effective, see paragraph (c) of § 1.1562-2.

(b) *Example.* The provisions of this section may be illustrated by the following example:

Example. In 1965, a controlled group of corporations makes a valid election under section 1562(a)(1) with respect to December 31, 1964. In 1967, the election is terminated with respect to December 31, 1964, by consent pursuant to paragraph (b)(1) of § 1.1562-2. The group (or any successor group) is not eligible to make another election with respect to any December 31 before December 31, 1970 (*i.e.,* the sixth December 31 after December 31, 1964, the particular December 31 with respect to which such termination was effective). If in this example the election had been terminated with respect to December 31, 1965, instead of December 31, 1964, the group (or any successor group) would not be eligible to make another election with respect to any December 31 before December 31, 1971.

§ 1.1562-5 (T.D. 6845, filed 8-4-65; amended by T.D. 7181, filed 4-24-72.) Continuing and successor controlled groups.

(a) *Controlled group continuing in existence.* For purposes of § 1.1561-3, and §§ 1.1562-1 through 1.1562-4—

(1) *Parent-subsidiary group.* A parent-subsidiary controlled group of corporations shall be considered as remaining in existence as long as (i) such group is not considered, under paragraph (c)(3) of this section, to be a successor controlled group in respect of another controlled group, and (ii) its common parent corporation remains as a common parent and satisfies the requirements of paragraph (a)(2)(i)*(b)* of § 1.1563-1 with respect to the ownership of stock of at least one corporation.

(2) *Brother-sister group.* A brother-sister controlled group of corporation shall be considered as remaining in existence as long as the requirements of paragraph (a)(3)(i) of § 1.1563-1 continue to be satisfied with respect to at least two corporations, taking into account the stock ownership of only those 5 or fewer persons whose stock ownership was taken into account with respect to the election under section 1562(a)(1).

(3) *Combined group.* A combined group of corporations shall be considered as remaining in existence as long as (i) the brother-sister controlled group of corporations referred to in paragraph (a)(4)(i) of § 1.1563-1 in respect of such combined group remains in existence (within the meaning of subparagraph (2) of this paragraph), and (ii) at least one such corporation is a common parent of a parent-subsidiary controlled group of corporations referred to in such paragraph (a)(4)(i).

(4) *Insurance group.* If, by reason of paragraph (a)(5)(i) of § 1.1563-1, two or more insurance companies subject to taxation under section 802 are treated as an insurance group separate from any corporations which are members of a controlled group described in paragraph (a)(2), (3), or (4) of § 1.1563-1, such insurance group shall be considered as remaining in existence as long as (i) the controlled group described in paragraph (a)(2), (3), or (4) of such section, as the case may be, remains in existence (within the meaning of subparagraph (1), (2), or (3) of this paragraph), and (ii) there are at least two insurance companies which satisfy the requirements of paragraph (a)(5)(i) of such section.

(b) *Controlled group no longer in existence*—(1) *General.* Except as provided in subparagraph (3) of this paragraph, a controlled group of corporations is considered as going out of existence with respect to a December 31 if such group ceases to remain in existence under the principles of paragraph (a) of this section during the calendar year ending on such date.

(2) *Examples.* The provisions of subparagraph (1) of this paragraph may be illustrated by the following examples, in which each corporation referred to uses the calendar year as its taxable year:

Example (1). Corporation P was organized on January 1, 1964, and acquired all the stock of corporation S-1 on February 1, 1964, and all the stock of corporation S-2 on March 1, 1965. On April 1, 1965, P sold all its S-1 stock to the public. Beginning on February 1, 1964, P is the common parent corporation of a parent-subsidiary controlled group of corporations. Under paragraph (a)(1) of this section, the controlled group remains in existence throughout the remainder of 1964 and throughout 1965 even though after April 1, 1965, P satisfies the stock ownership requirements of paragraph (a)(2)(i)*(b)* of § 1.1563-1 only with respect to the stock of S-2, a corporation which was not a member of the group at the time the group was formed, and even though S-1 ceased to be a member of the group after the group was formed. Accordingly, if the controlled group makes a valid election under section 1562(a)(1) with respect to December 31, 1964, such election will remain in effect with respect to December 31, 1965, unless terminated under section 1562(c)(1), (2), or (3). Moreover, if such election were made and subsequently terminated with respect to December 31, 1964, the group would not be eligible (by reason of section 1562(d)) to make an election under section 1562(a)(1) with respect to December 31, 1965.

Example (2). Assume the same facts as in example (1) except that corporation S-2 is a franchised corporation as defined in section 1563(f)(4) for its 1965 taxable year. On December 31, 1965, S-2 is treated as an excluded member of the parent-subsidiary controlled group of which P is the common parent. See section 1563(b)(2)(E). Nevertheless, such controlled group is considered as remaining in existence throughout 1965.

Example (3). Assume the same facts as in example (1) except that P sold its S-1 stock on February 28, 1965, instead of April 1, 1965. Under the principles of paragraph (a)(1) of this section, the parent-subsidiary controlled group ceases to remain in existence on February 28, 1965. Accordingly, under subparagraph (1) of this paragraph, such group is considered as going out of existence with respect to December 31, 1965. Thus, if the group makes a valid election under section 1562 (a)(1) with respect to December 31, 1964, such election terminates with respect to December 31, 1965. Moreover, the new controlled group of corporations consisting of P and S-2 is not precluded (by reason of section 1562(d)) from making an election under section 1562(a)(1) with respect to December 31, 1965.

Example (4). Smith, an individual, owns 80 percent of the only class of stock of corporations W and X on each day of 1966 and 1967. W, in turn, owns 80 percent of the only class of stock of corporation Y on each day of 1966. On April 15, 1967, X purchases 80 percent of the only class of corporation Z and on April 30, 1967, W sells all its stock in Y. Under paragraph (a) (3) of this section, the combined group remains in existence throughout 1966 and 1967 since (i) the brother-sister controlled group of corporations referred to in paragraph (a)(4)(i) of § 1.1563-1 in respect of such combined group remains in existence, and (ii) at least one corporation is a common parent of a parent-subsidiary controlled group referred to in such paragraph.

Example (5). Assume the same facts as in example (4) except that Y and Z are life insurance companies subject to taxation under section 802 of the Code. Further assume that throughout 1966 and 1967 Y owns all the stock of corporation S, and Z owns all the stock of corporation T. S and T are life insurance companies subject to taxation under section 802. Before April 15, 1967, under paragraph (a)(5)(i) of § 1.1563-1, Y and S are treated as an insurance group of corporations. After April 30, 1967, under paragraph (a)(4) of this section, Z and T are treated as an insurance group which remains in existence throughout 1966 and 1967, since the combined group remains in existence within the meaning of paragraph (a)(3) of this section throughout 1966 and 1967, and there are at all times at least two insurance companies which satisfy the requirements of paragraph (a)(5)(i) of § 1.1563-1. (However, after April 30, 1967, Y and S cease to be members of the combined group and are considered to be a new controlled group of corporations.)

Example (6). Jones, an individual, owns all the stock of corporations M and N on each day of 1966. On February 1, 1967, he gives all the stock of M to his 18-year-old son who continues to hold the M stock throughout the remainder of 1967. Since Jones (or his son) owns, or is considered as owning under paragraph (b)(6)(i) of § 1.1563-3, all the stock of M and N on each day of 1967, under paragraph (a)(2) of this section the brother-sister controlled group consisting of M and N remains in existence throughout 1967.

(3) *Special rule.* If—

(i) Under subparagraph (1) of this paragraph, a controlled group of corporations would (without regard to this subparagraph) be considered as going out of existence with respect to a December 31 because two or more corporations cease to be members of such group during the calendar year ending on such date,

(ii) Under paragraph (c) of this section, there is no successor group in respect of such group, and

(iii) At least two of such corporations are considered to be component members of such group on such December 31 by reason of the additional member rule of paragraph (b)(3) of § 1.1563-1,

then such group shall be considered as going out of existence with respect to the December 31 immediately succeeding such December 31. For example, assume that corporations P and S file their returns on the basis of the calendar year. P owns all the stock of S from January 1, 1965, through December 1, 1965. On December 2, 1965, P sells the stock of S to the public. Under subparagraph (1) of this paragraph the controlled group consisting of P and S would (without regard to this subparagraph) be considered as going out of existence with respect to December 31, 1965, because P and S ceased to be members of the group on December 2, 1965. However, since there is no successor group in respect of the controlled group, and P and S are considered to be component members of such group on December 31, 1965, by reason of the additional member rule of paragraph (b)(3) of § 1.1563-1, under this subparagraph the group is considered as going out of existence with respect to December 31, 1966, and not December 31, 1965.

(c) *Successor groups*—(1) *Transactions involving a former owner or owners.* If, as a result of the transfer of stock of a corporation or corporations (whether by sale, exchange, distribution, contribution to capital, or otherwise), a controlled group ("old group") goes out of existence, and a new controlled group ("new group") comes into existence, then the new group shall be considered to be a successor to the old group, provided one of the following applies:

(i) A person or persons who own stock of the new group that meets the more-than-50-percent stock ownership requirement of section 1563(a)(2)(B) owned stock which met such stock ownership requirement with respect to the old group;

(ii) A person or persons who owned more than 50 percent of the fair market value of the stock of the common parent of the old group owns, with respect to the new group, stock that meets the more-than-50-percent stock ownership requirement of section 1563(a)(2)(B); or

(iii) A person or persons who owned stock that met the more-than-50-percent stock ownership requirement of section 1563(a)(2)(B) with respect to the old group owns more than 50 percent of the fair market value of the stock of the common parent of the new group.

For purposes of this paragraph, the term "owns" includes direct ownership and ownership with the application of the rules contained in paragraph (b) of § 1.1563-3. For purposes of this subparagraph, if as

Reg. § 1.1562-5(c)(1)

24,232-L (I.R.C.)   Reg. § 1.1562-5(c)(1)

a result of the transfer of stock, a parent-subsidiary controlled group or a brother-sister controlled group becomes a part of a combined group, then such parent-subsidiary or brother-sister group shall be considered as going out of existence as a result of such transfer. Also for purposes of this subparagraph, if as a result of the transfer of stock, a combined group goes out of existence and a parent-subsidiary or brother-sister group which was part of such combined group remains, then such parent-subsidiary or brother-sister group shall be considered to be a new controlled group which came into existence as a result of such transfer.

(2) *Examples.* The principles of subparagraph (1) of this paragraph may be illustrated by the following examples:

Example (1). On each day of 1971, unrelated individuals Grey, Black, and Green own the following amounts of the only class of outstanding stock of each of corporations R and T: Grey owns 40 percent, Black owns 40 percent, and Green owns 20 percent. On March 1, 1972, Grey sells all his stock in both corporations to unrelated individual Clay. As a result of the transfer, the brother-sister controlled group consisting of R and T goes out of existence. Since Black and Green, who owned stock which met the more-than-50-percent stock ownership requirement of section 1563(a)(2)(B) with respect to the old group, own stock of the new group (consisting of R and T) that meets the more-than-50-percent stock ownership requirement of section 1563(a)(2)(B), the new group is considered to be the successor to the old group. If Green also sold all his stock in both corporations to unrelated individual Barnes, Black would be the only stockholder of the new group whose stock ownership was taken into account in meeting the more-than-50-percent stock ownership requirement of section 1563(a)(2)(B) with respect to the old group. Since Black would not own stock of the new group that meets the more-than-50-percent stock ownership requirement of section 1563(a)(2)(B), the new group would not be considered a successor to the controlled group which went out of existence.

Example (2). On each day of 1971, all the outstanding stock of corporation P is owned in the following manner: Smith owns 30 percent, Jones owns 30 percent, and White owns 40 percent. P owns all the stock of corporation S_1, S_2, W_1, and W_2. On December 31, 1971, P, S_1, S_2, W_1, and W_2 are component members of the same controlled group. If on March 1, 1972, P distributes all the stock of S_1 and S_2 equally to Smith and Jones and all the stock of W_1 and W_2 to White, the controlled group consisting of P, S_1, S_2, W_1, and W_2 goes out of existence. Since Smith and Jones, who together owned stock which met the more-than-50-percent stock ownership requirement of section 1563(a)(2)(B) with respect to the old group, now together own stock of the new group (consisting of S_1 and S_2) that meets the more-than-50-percent stock ownership requirement of section 1563(a)(2)(B), such new group is considered the successor to the old group. On the other hand, since White, the sole shareholder of W_1 and W_2, did not own stock which met such stock ownership requirement with respect to the old group, the new group consisting of W_1 and W_2 is not considered a successor of the old group.

(3) *Transactions involving two common parents.* If, as a result of the transfer of stock of a corporation or corporations (whether by sale, exchange, distribution, contribution to capital, or otherwise)—

(1) A parent-subsidiary controlled group of corporations goes out of existence because its common parent corporation ceases to be a common parent, and

(ii) The stockholders (immediately before the transfer) of such common parent corporation, as a result of owning stock in such common parent, own (immediately after the transfer) more than 50 percent of the fair market value of the stock of a corporation which is the common parent corporation of a controlled group of corporations immediately after the transfer, the resulting controlled group shall be considered to be a successor group in respect of the controlled group which went out of existence as a result of the transfer.

(4) *Example.* The provisions of subparagraph (3) of this paragraph may be illustrated by the following example:

Example. Corporation Y, the common parent of a parent-subsidiary controlled group, acquires the assets of corporation X, the common parent of another controlled group, in a statutory merger. The stockholders of X exchange their X stock for 60 percent of the fair market value of all of the outstanding shares of Y. Since, as a result of the exchange, (i) the parent-subsidiary controlled group of which X was the common parent goes out of existence because X ceases to be a common parent, and (ii) the stockholders of X, as a result of owning stock in X, own immediately after the exchange more than 50 percent of the fair market value of the stock of Y (the common parent of a controlled group of corporations immediately after the exchange), the controlled group of which Y is the common parent after the merger is considered to be a successor group in respect of the controlled group of which X was the common parent, and the group of which Y was the common parent before the merger is considered, under paragraph (a)(1) of this section, as no longer in existence. Thus, for example, if before the merger the controlled group of which X was the common parent was not eligible, by reason of the application of section 1562(d), to make an election under section 1562(a)(1) with respect to a December 31 occurring before December 31, 1970, then the successor controlled gzroup would also be ineligible to make an election with respect to a December 31 occurring before December 31, 1970, whether or not the controlled group of which Y was the common parent before the merger had an election in effect pursuant to section 1562(a)(1).

○─► § 1.1562-6 (T.D. 6845, filed 8-4-65.) **Election for short taxable years.**

(a) *Application of election to short taxable years*—*(1) General.* If the return of a corporation is for a short period which does not include a December 31, and if such corporation is a component member of a controlled group of corporations with respect to such short period, then an election under section 1562(a)(1) by such group shall apply with respect to such short period if—

(i) Such election is in effect with respect to both the December 31 immediately preceding such short period (hereinafter in this section referred to as the "preceding December 31") and the December 31 immediately succeeding such short period (hereinafter in this section referred to as the "succeeding December 31"), or

(ii) Such election is in effect with respect to either the preceding December 31 or the succeeding December 31, and each corporation which is a component member of such group with respect to a short period falling between such dates consents to the application of such election to such short period. See subparagraph (4) of this paragraph for rules relating to an election with respect to certain short taxable years ending during 1964.

(2) *Component members.* For purposes of this section, the determination of whether a corporation is a component member of a controlled group of corporations with respect to a short period shall be made by applying the definition of component member contained in section 1563(b) and paragraph (b) of § 1.1563-1 as if the last day of such short period were a December 31 occurring after December 31, 1963.

(3) *Example.* The provisions of this paragraph may be illustrated by the following example:

Example. On December 31, 1964, corporations P, S-1, and S-2 are component members of a parent-subsidiary controlled group of corporations. P, S-1, and S-2 each uses the calendar year as its taxable year. On February 1, 1965, S-1 transfers property to newly formed corporation S-3 (which begins business on that date) and receives all the stock of S-3 in return. S-3 adopts a fiscal year ending on November 30 as its taxable year and, therefore, files a return for the short taxable year beginning on February 1, 1965, and ending on November 30, 1965. On December 5, 1965, S-2 is liquidated, and therefore files a return for the short taxable year beginning on January 1, 1965, and ending on December 5, 1965. S-2 and S-3 are component members of the controlled group of corporations with respect to their short taxable years falling between December 31, 1964, and December 31, 1965, within the meaning of subparagraph (2) of this paragraph. Assume that the controlled group has an election under section 1562(a)(1) in effect with respect to either December 31, 1964, or December 31, 1965, but not both such dates. Under subparagraph (1)(ii) of this paragraph, S-2 and S-3 must both file consents to the application of the section 1562(a)(1) election with respect to their short periods in order for the election to be effective with respect to either such short period.

(4) *Election for certain short taxable years ending during 1964.* If—

(i) A corporation is a component member of a controlled group of corporations with respect to a short taxable year beginning and ending in 1964,

(ii) Each corporation which was a component member of such group on December 31, 1963 (determined without regard to paragraph (b)(2)(iii) of § 1.1563-1, relating to the treatment of a corporation which has a taxable year ending on December 31, 1963 as an excluded member of a controlled group on such date) filed its income tax return on the basis of the calendar year ending on such date, and

(iii) Such controlled group of corporations is considered as going out of existence with respect to December 31, 1964, pursuant to paragraph (b)(4) of § 1.1562-2,

then, for purposes of paragraph (a)(1)(ii) of this section, an election by such controlled group under section 1562(a)(1) shall be deemed to have been in effect for the preceding December 31. Each corporation which is a component member of such group with respect to a short period falling between such preceding and succeeding December 31's must, on or before November 3, 1965, consent to the application of such election to its short period falling between such December 31's.

(b) *Status at time of filing return.* If, on the date a corporation files its income tax return for a short period falling between a preceding and succeeding December 31 (with respect to which period it is a component member of a controlled group of corporations)—

(1) Election not effective. An election under section 1562(a)(1) is not effective with respect to either such preceding or succeeding December 31, then such member shall determine its surtax exemption for purposes of such return in accordance with section 1561(b).

(2) Election effective for preceding December 31. An election under section 1562 (a)(1) is effective with respect to such preceding December 31, and if on the date the return is filed the election has not been terminated with respect to such succeeding December 31, then such member may compute its tax for purposes of such return on the assumption that the conditions of paragraph (a)(1)(i) of this section are satisfied with respect to such short period.

(3) Election effective for preceding or succeeding December 31. An election under section 1562(a)(1) is effective with respect to either (but not both) such preceding or succeeding December 31, and the return is filed after such succeeding December 31, then the members' surtax exemption for purposes of such return shall be determined in accordance with section 1561(b) unless—

(i) It attaches to such return its consent to the application of such election to such short period, and

(ii) Each other corporation which is a component member of the group with respect to a short period falling between such December 31's files, within 30 days after such return is filed, a consent to the application of such election to its short period falling between such December 31's.

(c) Election or termination after returns filed—(1) Election. If, after each component member of a controlled group with respect to a short period falling between a preceding and succeeding December 31 files its return for such short period, the group makes an election under section 1562(a)(1) with respect to such succeeding December 31, then the election shall apply with respect to each such short period only if each such member files, within 30 days after such election is made, a consent to the application of such election to its short period.

(2) Termination. If, after each component member of a controlled group with respect to a short period falling between a preceding and succeeding December 31 files its return for such short period, an election under section 1562(a)(1) which is effective with respect to such group with respect to such preceding December 31 is terminated with respect to such succeeding December 31, then such election shall apply with respect to each such short period only if each such member files, within 30 days after the termination occurs, a consent to the application of such election to its short period. For purposes of the preceding sentence, (i) the termination of an election by consent under section 1562(c)(1) shall be considered to occur on the date the termination is made, and (ii) the termination of an election under section 1562(c)(2), (3), or (4) shall be considered to occur on the date the event causing termination occurs (for example, on the date a new member files a refusal to consent, or on the date a consolidated return is filed) unless the election is made after such date, in which case the termination shall be considered to occur on the date the election is made.

(d) Manner of consenting. A consent referred to in paragraph (b)(3) or (c) of this section shall be made by means of a statement, signed by any person who is duly authorized to act on behalf of the consenting corporation, stating that such corporation consents to the application of an election under section 1562(a)(1) with respect to its short period. Each such statement shall set forth the name, address, taxpayer account number, and taxable year of (1) each corporation which is a component member of the electing controlled group with respect to a short period falling between the preceding December 31 and the succeeding December 31, and (2) each corporation which is a component member of such group on either the preceding or succeeding December 31. Each consenting corporation shall file such statement with the district director with whom it files (or filed) its income tax return for the short period.

§ 1.1562-7 (T.D. 6845, filed 8-4-65.) Extension of statutory periods of limitation.

(a)(1) Under section 1562(g)(1), the statutory period for assessment of any deficiency against a corporation which is a component member of a controlled group of corporations with respect to any taxable year, to the extent such deficiency is attributable to an election under section 1562 (a)(1) or a termination by consent under section 1562(c)(1), shall not expire before the expiration of one year after the date such election or termination is made.

(2) Under section 1562(g)(2), the statutory period for allowing or making credit or refund of any overpayment of tax by a corporation which is a component member of a controlled group of corporations with respect to any taxable year, to the extent such overpayment is attributable to an election under section 1562(a)(1) or a termination by consent under section 1562 (c)(1), shall not expire before the expiration of one year after the date such election or termination is made.

(b) For purposes of this section, the deficiency or overpayment in tax attributable to an election under section 1562(a)(1) or a termination by consent under section 1562(c)(1) shall be that amount of the increase or decrease in tax over the amount previously determined (as defined in section 1314(a)) for any taxable year which results from the application or nonapplication of section 1562, as the case may be. In determining the amount of such increase or decrease, due regard shall be given to the effect of any change in the amount of the surtax exemption (or the application or nonapplication of the additional tax under section 1562(b)) on credits allowable for any taxable year. Thus, for example, as a result of such change it may be necessary to recompute the amount of the investment credit allowable under section 38 for a taxable year for which the election or termination is effective and for other taxable

years affected, or treated as affected, by an investment credit carryback or carryover (as defined in section 46(b)) determined with reference to the taxable years with respect to which such election or termination is effective.

(c) The provisions of this section shall not be construed to—

(1) Shorten the period within which an assessment of a deficiency may otherwise be made or the credit or refund of an overpayment may otherwise be allowed or made, or

(2) Apply to a deficiency or overpayment for a taxable year if the tax liability for such taxable year has been compromised under section 7122, or is the subject of a closing agreement under section 7121.

§ 1.1563 Statutory provisions; definitions and special rules. [Sec. 1563 IRC]

§ 1.1563-1 (T.D. 6845, filed 8-4-65; amended by T.D. 6960, filed 6-24-68 and T.D. 7293, filed 11-27-73.) **Definition of controlled group of corporations and component members.**

(a) *Controlled group of corporations—* (1) *In general.* For purposes of sections 1561 through 1563 and the regulations thereunder, the term "controlled group of corporations" means any group of corporations which is either a "parent-subsidiary controlled group" (as defined in subparagraph (2) of this paragraph), a "brother-sister controlled group" (as defined in subparagraph (3) of this paragraph), a "combined group" (as defined in subparagraph (4) of this paragraph), or an "insurance group" (as defined in subparagraph (5) of this paragraph). For the exclusion of certain stock for purposes of applying the definitions contained in this paragraph see section 1563(c) and § 1.1563-2.

(2) *Parent-subsidiary controlled group.* (i) The term "parent-subsidiary controlled group" means one or more chains of corporations connected through stock ownership with a common parent corporation if—

(a) Stock possessing at least 80 percent of the total combined voting power of all classes of stock entitled to vote or at least 80 percent of the total value of shares of all classes of stock of each of the corporations, except the common parent corporation, is owned (directly and with the application of paragraph (b)(1) of § 1.1563-3, relating to options) by one or more of the other corporations; and

(b) The common parent corporation owns (directly and with the application of paragraph (b)(1) of § 1.1563-3, relating to options) stock possessing at least 80 percent of the total combined voting power of all classes of stock entitled to vote or at least 80 percent of the total value of shares of all classes of stock of at least one of the other corporations, excluding, in computing such voting power or value, stock owned directly by such other corporations.

(ii) The definition of a parent-subsidiary controlled group of corporations may be illustrated by the following examples:

Example (1). P Corporation owns stock possessing 80 percent of the total combined voting power of all classes of stock entitled to vote of S Corporation. P is the common parent of a parent-subsidiary controlled group consisting of member corporations P and S.

Example (2). Assume the same facts as in example (1). Assume further that S owns stock possessing 80 percent of the total value of shares of all classes of stock of T Corporation. P is the common parent of a parent-subsidiary controlled group consisting of member corporations P, S, and T. The result would be the same if P, rather than S, owned the T stock.

Example (3). L Corporation owns 80 percent of the only class of stock of M Corporation and M, in turn, owns 40 percent of the only class of Stock of O Corporation. L also owns 80 percent of the only class of stock of N Corporation and N, in turn, owns 40 percent of the only class of stock of O. L is the common parent of a parent-subsidiary controlled group consisting of member corporations L, M, N, and O.

Example (4). X Corporation owns 75 percent of the only class of stock of Y and Z Corporations; Y owns all the remaining stock of Z; and Z owns all the remaining stock of Y. Since intercompany stockholdings are excluded (that is, are not treated as outstanding) for purposes of determining whether X owns stock possessing at least 80 percent of the voting power or value of at least one of the other corporations, X is treated as the owner of stock possessing 100 percent of the voting power and value of Y and of Z for purposes of subdivision (i) (b) of this subparagraph. Also, stock possessing 100 percent of the voting power and value of Y and Z is owned by the other corporations in the group within the meaning of subdivision (i)(a) of this subparagraph. (X and Y together own stock possessing 100 percent of the voting power and value of Z, and X and Z together own stock possessing 100 percent of the voting power and value of Y.) Therefore, X is the common parent of a parent-subsidiary controlled group of corporations consisting of member corporations X, Y, and Z.

(3) *Brother-sister controlled group—* (i) The term "brother-sister" controlled group" means two or more corporations if the same five or fewer persons who are individuals, estates, or trusts own (directly and with the application of the rules contained in paragraph (b) of § 1.1563-3), singly or in combination, stock possessing—

(a) At least 80 percent of the total combined voting power of all classes of stock entitled to vote or at least 80 perecent of the total value of shares of all classes of stock of each corporation; and

(b) More than 50 percent of the total combined voting power of all classes of stock entitled to vote or more than 50 percent of the total value of shares of all classes of stock of each corporation, taking into account the stock ownership of each such person only to the extent such stock ownership is identical with respect to each such corporation.

(ii) The principles of this subparagraph may be illustrated by the following examples:

Example (1). The outstanding stock of corporations P, Q, R, S, and T, which have only one class of stock outstanding, is owned by the following unrelated individuals:

Reg. § 1.1563-1(a)(3)

Individuals	Corporations				Identical Ownership
	P	Q	R	S	T	
A	60%	60%	60%	60%	100%	60%
B	40%	—	—	—	—	—
C	—	40%	—	—	—	—
D	—	—	40%	—	—	—
E	—	—	—	40%	—	—
Total	100%	100%	100%	100%	100%	60%

Corporations P, Q, R, S, and T are members of a brother-sister controlled group.

Example (3). The outstanding stock of corporations U and V, which have only one class of stock outstanding, is owned by the following unrelated individuals:

Individuals	Corporations		Identical Ownership
	U	V	
F	5%	—	—
G	10%	—	—
H	10%	—	—
I	20%	—	—
J	55%	55%	55%
K	—	10%	—
L	—	10%	—
M	—	10%	—
N	—	10%	—
O	—	5%	—
Total	100%	100%	55%

Corporations U and V are not members of a brother-sister controlled group because at least 80 percent of the stock of each corporation is not owned by the same 5 or fewer persons.

(4) *Combined group.* (i) The term "combined group" means any group of three or more corporations, if—

(a) Each such corporation is a member of either a parent-subsidiary controlled group of corporations or a brother-sister controlled group of corporations, and

(b) At least one of such corporations is the common parent of a parent-subsidiary controlled group and also is a member of a brother-sister controlled group.

(ii) The definition of a combined group of corporations may be illustrated by the following examples:

Example (1). Smith, an individual, owns stock possessing 80 percent of the total combined voting power of all classes of the stock of corporations X and Y. Y, in turn, owns stock possessing 80 percent of the total combined voting power of all classes of the stock of corporation Z. Since—

(a) X, Y, and Z are each members of either a parent-subsidiary or brother-sister controlled group of corporations, and

(b) Y is the common parent of a parent-subsidiary controlled group of corporations consisting of Y and Z, and also is a member of a brother-sister controlled group of corporations consisting of X and Y,

X, Y, and Z are members of the same combined group.

Example (2). Assume the same facts as in example (1), and further assume that corporation X owns 80 percent of the total value of shares of all classes of stock of corporation T. X, Y, Z, and T are members of the same combined group.

(5) *Insurance group.* (i) The term "insurance group" means two or more insurance companies subject to taxation under section 802 each of which is a member of a controlled group of corporations described in subparagraph (2), (3), or (4) of this paragraph. Such insurance companies shall be treated as a controlled group of corporations separate from any other corporations which are members of the controlled group described in such subparagraph (2), (3), or (4). For purposes of this section and § 1.1562-5, the common parent of the controlled group described in subparagraph (2) of this paragraph shall be referred to as the common parent of the insurance group.

(ii) The definition of an insurance group may be illustrated by the following example:

Example. Corporation P owns all the stock of corporation I which, in turn, owns all the stock of corporation X. P also owns all the stock of corporation Y which, in turn, owns all the stock of corporation J. I and J are life insurance companies subject to taxation under section 802 of the Code. Since I and J are members of a parent-subsidiary controlled group of corporations, such companies are treated as members of an insurance group separate from the parent-subsidiary controlled group consisting of P, X, and Y. For purposes of this section and § 1.1562-5, P is referred to as the common parent of the insurance group even though P is not a member of such group.

(6) *Voting power of stock.* For purposes of § 1.1562-5, this section, § 1.1563-2, and § 1.1563-3, in determining whether the stock owned by a person (or persons) possesses a certain percentage of the total combined voting power of all classes of stock entitled to vote of a corporation, consideration will be given to all the facts and circumstances of each case. A share of stock will generally be considered as possessing the voting power accorded to such share by the corporate charter, by-laws, or share certificate. On the other hand, if there is any agreement, whether express or implied, that a shareholder will not vote his stock in a corporation, the formal voting rights possessed by his stock may be disregarded in determining the percentage of the total combined voting power possessed by the stock owned by other shareholders in the corporation, if the result is that the corporation becomes a component member of a controlled group of corporations. Moreover, if a shareholder agrees to vote his stock in a corporation in the manner specified by another shareholder in the corporation, the voting rights possessed by the stock owned by the first shareholder may be considered to be possessed by the stock owned by such other shareholder if the result is that the corporation becomes a component member of a controlled group of corporations.

(b) *Component members—(1) In general.* For purposes of sections 1561 through 1563 and the regulations thereunder, a corporation is a component member of a controlled group of corporations on a December 31 (and with respect to the taxable year which includes such December 31) if such corporation—

(i) Is a member of such controlled group on such December 31 and is not treated as an excluded member under subparagraph (2) of this paragraph, or

(ii) Is not a member of such controlled group on such December 31 but is treated as an additional member under subparagraph (3) of this paragraph.

(2) *Excluded members.* (i) A corporation, which is a member of a controlled group of corporations on the December 31 included within its taxable year, but was a member of such group for less than one-half of the number of days in such taxable year which precede such December 31, shall be treated as an excluded member of such group on such December 31.

(ii) A corporation which is a member of a controlled group of corporations on any December 31 shall be treated as an excluded member of such group on such date if, for its taxable year including such date, such corporation is—

(a) Exempt from taxation under section 501(a) (except a corporation which has unrelated business taxable income for such taxable year which is subject to tax under section 511) or 521,

(b) A foreign corporation not subject to taxation under section 882(a) for the taxable year,

(c) An electing small business corporation (as defined in section 1371(b)) not subject to the tax imposed by section 1378,

(d) A franchised corporation (as defined in section 1563(f)(4) and § 1.1563-4), or

(e) An insurance company subject to taxation under section 802 or 821, except that an insurance company taxable under section 802 which (without regard to this subdivision) is a component member of an insurance group described in paragraph (a)(5) of this section shall not be treated as an excluded member of such insurance group.

(iii) A corporation which has a taxable year ending on December 31, 1963, shall be treated as an excluded member of a controlled group on such date.

(3) *Additional members.* A corporation which—

(i) Is not a member of a controlled group of corporations on the December 31 included within its taxable year, and

(ii) Is not described, with respect to such taxable year, in subparagraph (2)(ii) (a), (b), (c), (d), or (e), or (2)(iii) of this paragraph,

shall be treated as an additional member of such group on such December 31 if it was a member of such group for one-half (or more) of the number of days in such taxable year which precede such December 31.

(4) *Examples.* The provisions of this paragraph may be illustrated by the following examples:

Example (1). Brown, an individual, owns all of the stock of corporations W and X on each day of 1964. W and X each uses the calendar year as its taxable year. On January 1, 1964, Brown also owns all the stock of corporation Y (a fiscal year corporation with a taxable year beginning on July 1, 1964, and ending on June 30, 1965) which stock he sells on October 15, 1964. On December 1, 1964, Brown purchases all the stock of corporation Z (a fiscal year corporation with a taxable year beginning on September 1, 1964, and ending on August 31, 1965). On December 31, 1964, W, X, and Z are members of the same controlled group. However, the component members of the group on such December 31 are W, X, and Y. Under subparagraph (2)(i) of this paragraph, Z is treated as an excluded member of the group on December 31, 1964, since Z was a member of the group for less than one-half of the number of days (29 out of 121 days) during the period beginning on September 1, 1964 (the first day of its taxable year) and ending on December 30, 1964. Under subparagraph (3) of this paragraph, Y is treated as an additional member of the group on December 31, 1964, since Y was a member of the group for at least one-half of the number of days (107 out of 183 days) during the period beginning on July 1, 1964 (the first day of its taxable year) and ending on December 30, 1964.

Example (2). On January 1, 1964, corporation P owns all the stock of corporation S, which in turn owns all the stock of corporation S-1. On November 1, 1964, P purchases all of the stock of corporation X from the public and sells all of the stock of S to the public. Corporation X owns all the stock of corporation Y during 1964. P, S, S-1, X, and Y file their returns on the basis of the calendar year. On December 31, 1964, P, X, and Y are members of a parent-subsidiary controlled group of corporations; also, corporations S and S-1 are members of a different parent-subsidiary controlled group on such date. However, since X and Y have been members of the parent-subsidiary controlled group of which P is the common parent for less than one-half the number of days during the period January 1 through December 30, 1964, they are not component members of such group on such date. On the other hand, X and Y have been members of a parent-subsidiary controlled group of which X is the common parent for at least one-half the number of days during the period January 1 through December 30, 1964, and therefore they are component members of such group on December 31, 1964. Also since S and S-1 were members of the parent-subsidiary controlled group of which P is the common parent for at least one-half the number of days in the taxable years of each such corporation during the period January 1 through December 30, 1964, P, S, and S-1 are component members of such group on December 31, 1964.

Example (3). Throughout 1964, corporation M owns all the stock of corporation F which, in turn, owns all the stock of corporations L-1, L-2, X, and Y. M is a domestic mutual insurance company subject to taxation under section 821, F is a foreign corporation not engaged in trade or business within the United States, L-1 and L-2 are domestic life insurance companies subject to taxation under section 802, and X and Y are domestic corporations subject to tax under section 11 of the Code. Each corporation uses the calendar year as its taxable year. On December 31, 1964, M, F, L-1, L-2, X, and Y are members of a parent-subsidiary controlled group of corporations. However, under subparagraph (2)(ii) of this paragraph, M, F, L-1, and L-2 are treated as excluded members of the group on December 31, 1964. Thus, on December 31, 1964, the component members of the parent-subsidiary controlled group of which M is the common parent include only X and Y. Furthermore, since subparagraph (2)(ii)(e) of this paragraph does not result in L-1 and L-2 being treated as excluded members of an insurance group, L-1 and L-2 are component members of an insurance group on December 31, 1964.

(5) *Application of constructive owner-*

Reg. § 1.1563-1(b)(5)

ship rules. For purposes of subparagraphs (2)(i) and (3) of this paragraph, it is necessary to determine whether a corporation was a member of a controlled group of corporations for one-half (or more) of the number of days in its taxable year which precede the December 31 falling within such taxable year. Therefore, the constructive ownership rules contained in paragraph (b) of § 1.1563-3 (to the extent applicable in making such determination) must be applied on a day-by-day basis. For example, if P Corporation owns all the stock of X Corporation on each day of 1964, and on December 30, 1964, acquires an option to purchase all the stock of Y Corporation (a calendar-year taxpayer which has been in existence on each day of 1964), the application of paragraph (b)(1) of § 1.1563-3 on a day-by-day basis results in Y being a member of the brother-sister controlled group on only one day of Y's 1964 year which precedes December 31, 1964. Accordingly, since Y is not a member of such group for one-half or more of the number of days in its 1964 year preceding December 31, 1964, Y is treated as an excluded member of such group on December 31, 1964.

(c) *Overlapping groups*—(1) *In general.* If on a December 31 a corporation is a component member of a controlled group of corporations by reason of ownership of stock possessing at least 80 percent of the total value of shares of all classes of stock of the corporation, and if on such December 31 such corporation is also a component member of another controlled group of corporations by reason of ownership of other stock (that is, stock not used to satisfy the at-least-80-percent total value test) possessing at least 80 percent of the total combined voting power of all classes of stock of the corporation entitled to vote, then such corporation shall be treated as a component member only of the controlled group of which it is a component member by reason of the ownership of at least 80 percent of the total value of its shares.

(2) *Brother-sister controlled groups.* (i) If on a December 31, a corporation would, without application of this subparagraph, be a component member of more than one brother-sister controlled group on such date, such corporation shall be treated as a component member of only one such group on such date. Such a corporation may select which group in which it is to be included by filing an election as provided in this subparagraph. The election shall be in the form of a statement designating the group in which the corporation is to be included. The statement shall provide all the information with respect to stock ownership which is reasonably necessary to satisfy the Internal Revenue officer with whom is it filed that the corporation would, but for the election, be a component member of more than one controlled group. Once filed, the election is irrevocable and effective until such time that a change in the stock ownership of the corporation results in termination of membership in the controlled group in which such corporation has been included.

(ii) Except as provided in subdivision (iii) of this subparagraph, the statement shall be signed by a person duly authorized to act on behalf of such corporation and shall be filed on or before the due date (including extension of time) for the filing of the income tax return of such corporation for the taxable year. However, in the case of an election with respect to December 31, 1970, the statement shall be considered as timely filed if filed on or before December 15, 1971. In the event no election is filed in accordance with the provisions of this subdivision, then the district director with audit jurisdiction of such corporation's return for the taxable year which includes such December 31 shall determine the group in which such corporation is to be included, and such determination shall be binding for all subsequent years unless the corporation files a valid election with respect to any such subsequent year.

(iii) If more than one corporation would, without application of this subparagraph, be a component member of more than one controlled group, a single statement shall be signed by persons duly authorized to act on behalf of each such corporation. Such statement shall designate the group in which each corporation is to be included. The statement shall be attached to the income tax return of the corporation that, among those corporations which would (without the application of this subparagraph) belong to more than one group, has the taxable year including such December 31 which ends on the earliest date. However, in the case of an election with respect to December 31, 1970, the statement may be filed by December 15, 1971, with the service center director with whom such corporation's return is filed for the taxable year which includes such December 31. In the event no election is filed in accordance with the provisions of this subdivision, then the district director with audit jurisdicton of such corporaton's return for the taxable year that includes such December 31 shall determine the group in which each corporation is to be included, and such determination shall be binding for all subsequent years unless the corporations file a valid election with respect to any such subsequent year.

(iv) The provisions of this subparagraph may be illustrated by the following examples (in which it is assumed that all the individuals are unrelated):

Example (1). On each day of 1970 all the outstanding stock of corporations M, N, and P is held in the following manner:

Individuals	Corporations		
	M	N	P
A	60%	40%	0
B	40%	20%	40%
C	0	40%	60%

Since the more-than-50-percent stock ownership requirement of section 1563(a)(2)(B) is met with respect to corporations M and N and with respect to corporations N and P, but not with respect to corporations M, N, and P, corporation N would, without the application of this subparagraph, be a component member on December 31, 1970, of overlapping groups consisting of M and N and of N and P. If N does not file an election in accordance with subdivision (ii) of this subparagraph, the district director with audit jurisdiction of N's return will determine the group in which N is to be included.

Example (2). On each day of 1970, all the outstanding stock of corporations S, T, W, X, and Z is held in the following manner:

Indi-		Corporations			
viduals	S	T	W	X	Z
D	60%	60%	60%	60%	60%
E	40%	0	0	0	0
F	0	40%	0	0	0
G	0	0	40%	0	0
H	0	0	0	40%	0
I	0	0	0	0	40%

On December 31, 1970, the more-than-50-percent stock ownership requirement of section 1563(a)(2)(B) may be met with regard to any combination of the corporations but all five corporations cannot be included as component members of a single controlled group because the inclusion of all the corporations in a single group would be dependent upon taking into account the stock ownership of more than five persons. Therefore, if the corporations do not file a statement in accordance with subdivision (iii) of this subparagraph, the district director with audit jurisdiction of the return of the corporation whose taxable year ends on the earliest date will determine the group in which each corporation is to be included. The corporations or the district director, as the case may be, may designate that three corporations be included in one group and two corporations in another, or that any four corporations be included in one group and that the remaining corporation not be included in any group.

○— § 1.1563-2 (T.D. 6845, filed 8-4-65; amended by T.D. 7181, filed 4-24-72.) **Excluded stock.**

(a) *Certain stock excluded.* For purposes of sections 1561 through 1563 and the regulations thereunder, the term "stock" does not include—

(1) Nonvoting stock which is limited and preferred as to dividends, and

(2) Treasury stock.

(b) *Stock treated as excluded stock—* (1) *Parent-subsidiary controlled group.* If a corporation (hereinafter in this paragraph referred to as "parent corporation") owns 50 percent or more of the total combined voting power of all classes of stock entitled to vote or 50 percent or more of the total value of shares of all classes of stock in another corporation (hereinafter in this paragraph referred to as "subsidiary corporation"), the provisions of subparagraph (2) of this paragraph shall apply. For purposes of this subparagraph, stock owned by a corporation means stock owned directly plus stock owned with the application of the constructive ownership rules of paragraph (b) (1) and (4) of § 1.1563-3, relating to options and attribution from corporations. In determining whether the stock owned by a corporation possesses the requisite percentage of the total combined voting power of all classes of stock entitled to vote of another corporation, see paragraph (a)(6) of § 1.1563-1.

(2) *Stock treated as not outstanding.* If the provisions of this subparagraph apply, then for purposes of determining whether the parent corporation or the subsidiary corporation is a member of a parent-subsidiary controlled group of corporations within the meaning of paragraph (a) (2) of § 1.1563-1, the following stock of the subsidiary corporation shall, except as otherwise provided in paragraph (c) of this section, be treated as if it were not outstanding:

(i) Plan of deferred compensation. Stock in the subsidiary corporation held by a trust which is part of a plan of deferred compensation for the benefit of the employees of the parent corporation or the subsidiary corporation. The term "plan of same meaning such term has in section 406 (a)(3) and the regulations thereunder.

(ii) Principal stockholders and officers. Stock in the subsidiary corporation owned (directly and with the application of the rules contained in paragraph (b) of § 1.1563-3) by an individual who is a principal stockholder or officer of the parent corporation. A principal stockholder of the parent corporation is an individual who owns (directly and with the application of the rules contained in paragraph (b) of § 1.1563-3) 5 percent or more of the total combined voting power of all classes of stock entitled to vote or 5 percent or more of the total value of shares of all classes of stock of the parent corporation. An officer of the parent corporation includes the president, vice-presidents, general manager, treasurer, secretary, and comptroller of such corporation, and any other person who performs duties corresponding to those normally performed by persons occupying such positions.

(iii) Employees. Stock in the subsidiary corporation owned (directly and with the application of the rules contained in paragraph (b) of § 1.1563-3) by an employee of the subsidiary corporation if such stock is subject to conditions which substantially restrict or limit the employee's right (or if the employee constructively owns such stock, the direct owner's right) to dispose of such stock and which run in favor of the parent or subsidiary corporation. In general, any condition which extends, directly or indirectly, to the parent corporation or the subsidiary corporation preferential rights with respect to the acquisition of the employee's (or direct owner's) stock will be considered to be a condition described in the preceding sentence. It is not necessary, in order for a condition to be considered to be in favor of the parent corporation or the subsidiary corporation, that the parent or subsidiary be extended a discriminatory concession with respect to the price of the stock. For example, a condition whereby the parent corporation is given a right of first refusal with respect to any stock of the subsidiary corporation offered by an employee for sale is a condition which substantially restricts or limits the employee's right to dispose of such stock and runs in favor of the parent corporation. Moreover, any legally enforceable condition which prohibits the employee from disposing of his stock without the consent of the parent (or a subsidiary of the parent) will be considered to be a substantial limitation running in favor of the parent corporation.

(iv) Controlled exempt organization. Stock in the subsidiary corporation owned (directly and with the application of the rules contained in paragraph (b) of § 1.-1563-3) by an organization (other than the parent corporation)—

(a) To which section 501 (relating to certain educational and charitable organi-

Reg. § 1.1563-2(b)(2)

24,234.4 (I.R.C.) Reg. § 1.1563-2(b)(2)

zations which are exempt from tax) applies, and

(b) Which is controlled directly or indirectly by the parent corporation or subsidiary corporation, by an individual, estate, or trust that is a principal stockholder of the parent corporation, by an officer of the parent corporation, or by any combination thereof.

The terms "principal stockholder of the parent corporation" and "officer of the parent corporation" shall have the same meanings in this subdivision as in subdivision (ii) of this subparagraph. The term "control" as used in this subdivision means control in fact and the determination of whether the control requirement of (b) of this subdivision is met will depend upon all the facts and circumstances of each case, without regard to whether such control is legally enforceable and irrespective of the method by which such control is exercised or exercisable.

(3) *Brother-sister controlled group.* If 5 or fewer persons (hereinafter referred to as common owners) who are individuals, estates, or trusts own (directly and with the application of the rules contained in paragraph (b) of § 1.1563-3) stock possessing 50 percent or more of the total combined voting power of all classes of stock entitled to vote or 50 percent or more of the total value of shares of all classes of stock in a corporation, the provisions of subparagraph (4) of this paragraph shall apply. In determining whether the stock owned by such person or persons possesses the requisite percentage of the total combined voting power of all classes of stock entitled to vote of a corporation, see paragraph (a)(6) of § 1.1563-1.

(4) *Stock treated as not outstanding.* If the provisions of this subparagraph apply, then for purposes of determining whether a corporation is a member of a brother-sister controlled group of corporations within the meaning of paragraph (a) (3) of § 1.1563-1, the following stock of such corporation shall, except as otherwise provided in paragraph (c) of this section, be treated as if it were not outstanding:

(i) Exempt employees' trust. Stock in such corporation held by an employees' trust described in section 401(a) which is exempt from tax under section 501(a), if such trust is for the benefit of the employees of such corporation.

(ii) Employees. Stock in such corporation owned (directly and with the application of the rules contained in paragraph (b) of § 1.1563-3) by an employee of such corporation if such stock is subject to conditions which run in favor of a common owner of such corporation (or in favor of such corporation) and which substantially restrict or limit the employee's right (or if the employee constructively owns such stock, the record owner's right) to dispose of such stock. The principles of subparagraph (2)(iii) of this paragraph shall apply in determining whether a condition satisfies the requirements of the preceding sentence. Thus, in general, a condition which extends, directly or indirectly, to a common owner or such corporation preferential rights with respect to the acquisition of the employee's (or record owner's) stock will be considered to be a condition which satisfies such requirements. For purposes of this subdivision, if a condition which restricts or limits an employee's right (or record owner's right) to dispose of his stock also applies to the stock in such corporation held by such common owner pursuant to a bona fide reciprocal stock purchase arrangement, such condition shall not be treated as one which restricts or limits the employee's (or record owner's) right to dispose of such stock. An example of a reciprocal stock purchase arrangement is an agreement whereby a common owner and the employee are given a right of first refusal with respect to stock of the employer corporation owned by the other party. If, however, the agreement also provides that the common owner has the right to purchase the stock of the employer corporation owned by the employee in the event that the corporation should discharge the employee for reasonable cause, the purchase arrangement would not be reciprocal within the meaning of this subdivision.

(iii) Controlled exempt organization. Stock in such corporation owned (directly and with the application of the rules contained in paragraph (b) of § 1.1563-3) by an organization—

(a) To which section 501(c)(3) (relating to certain educational and charitable organizations which are exempt from tax) applies, and

(b) which is controlled directly or indirectly by such corporation, by an individual, estate, or trust that is a principal stockholder of such corporation, by an officer of such corporation, or by any combination thereof.

The terms "principal stockholder" and "officer" shall have the same meanings in this subdivision as in subparagraph (2)(ii) of this paragraph. The term "control" as used in this subdivision means control in fact and the determination of whether the control requirement of (b) of this subdivision is met will depend upon all the facts and circumstances of each case, without regard to whether such control is legally enforceable and irrespective of the method by which such control is exercised or exercisable.

(5) *Other controlled groups.* The provisions of subparagraphs (1), (2), (3), and (4) of this paragraph shall apply in determining whether a corporation is a member of a combined group (within the meaning of paragraph (a)(4) of § 1.1563-1) or an insurance group (within the meaning of paragraph (a)(5) of § 1.1563-1). For example, under paragraph (a)(4) of § 1.1563-1, in order for a corporation to be a member of a combined group, such corporation must be a member of a parent-subsidiary group or a brother-sister group. Accordingly, the excluded stock rules provided by this paragraph are applicable in determining whether the corporation is a member of such group.

(6) *Meaning of employee.* For purposes of this section, § 1.1563-3, and § 1.1563-4, the term "employee" has the same meaning such term is given in section 3306(i) of the Code (relating to definitions for purposes of the Federal Unemployment Tax Act). Accordingly, the term employee as used in such sections includes an officer of a corporation.

(7) *Examples.* The provisions of this paragraph may be illustrated by the following examples:

Example (1). Corporation P owns 70

of the 100 shares of the only class of stock of corporation S. The remaining shares of S are owned as follows: 4 shares by Jones (the general manager of P), and 26 shares by Smith (who also owns 5 percent of the total combined voting power of the stock of P). P satisfies the 50 percent stock ownership requirement of subparagraph (1) of this paragraph with respect to S. Since Jones is an officer of P and Smith is a principal stockholder of P, under subparagraph (2)(ii) of this paragraph, the S stock owned by Jones and Smith is treated as not outstanding for purposes of determining whether P and S are members of a parent-subsidiary controlled group of corporations within the meaning of paragraph (a)(2) of § 1.1563-1. Thus, P is considered to own stock possessing 100 percent (70 ÷ 70) of the total voting power and value of all the S stock. Accordingly, P and S are members of a parent-subsidiary controlled group of corporations.

Example (2). Assume the same facts as in example (1) and further assume that Jones owns 15 shares of the 100 shares of the only class of stock of corporation S-1, and corporation S owns 75 shares of such stock. P satisfies the 50 percent stock ownership requirement of subparagraph (1) of this paragraph with respect to S-1 since P is considered as owning 52.5 percent (70 percent × 75 percent) of the S-1 stock with the application of paragraph (b)(4) of § 1.1563-3. Since Jones is an officer of P, under subparagraph (2)(ii) of this paragraph, the S-1 stock owned by Jones is treated as not outstanding for purposes of determining whether S-1 is a member of the parent-subsidiary controlled group of corporations. Thus, S is considered to own stock possessing 88.2 percent (75 ÷ 85) of the voting power and value of the S-1 stock. Accordingly, P, S, and S-1 are members of a parent-subsidiary controlled group of corporations.

Example (3). Corporation X owns 60 percent of the only class of stock of corporation Y. Davis, the president of Y, owns the remaining 40 percent of the stock of Y. Davis has agreed that if he offers his stock in Y for sale he will first offer the stock to X at a price equal to the fair market value of the stock on the first date the stock is offered for sale. Since Davis is an employee of Y within the meaning of section 3306(i) of the Code, and his stock in Y is subject to a condition which substantially restricts or limits his right to dispose of such stock and runs in favor of X, under subparagraph (2)(iii) of this paragraph, such stock is treated as if it were not outstanding for purposes of determining whether X and Y are members of a parent-subsidiary controlled group of corporations. Thus, X is considered to own stock possessing 100 percent of the voting power and value of the stock of Y. Accordingly, X and Y are members of a parent-subsidiary controlled group of corporations. The result would be the same if Davis's wife, instead of Davis, owned directly the 40 percent stock interest in Y and such stock was subject to a right of first refusal running in favor of X.

(c) *Exception—(1) General.* If stock of a corporation is owned by a person directly or with the application of the rules contained in paragraph (b) of § 1.1563-3 and such ownership results in the corporation being a component member of a controlled group of corporations on a December 31, then the stock shall not be treated as excluded stock under the provisions of paragraph (b) of this section if the result of applying such provisions is that such corporation is not a component member of a controlled group of corporations on such December 31.

(2) *Illustration.* The provisions of this paragraph may be illustrated by the following example:

Example. On each day of 1965, corporation P owns directly 50 of the 100 shares of the only class of stock of corporation S. Jones, an officer of P, owns directly 30 shares of S stock and P has an option to acquire such 30 shares from Jones. The remaining shares of S are owned by unrelated persons. If, pursuant to the provisions of paragraph (b)(2)(ii) of this section, the 30 shares of S stock owned directly by Jones is treated as not outstanding, the result is that P would be treated as owning stock possessing only 71 percent (50 ÷ 70) of the total voting power and value of S stock, and S would not be a component member of a controlled group of corporations on December 31, 1965. However, since P is considered as owning the 30 shares of S stock with the application of paragraph (b)(1) of § 1.1563-3, and such ownership plus the S stock directly owned by P (50 shares) results in S being a component member of a controlled group of corporations on December 31, 1965, the provisions of this paragraph apply. Therefore, the provisions of paragraph (b)(2)(ii) of this section do not apply with respect to the 30 shares of S stock, and on December 31, 1965, S is a component member of a controlled group of corporations consisting of P and S.

§ 1.1563-3 T.D. 6845, filed 8-4-65; amended by T.D. 7181, filed 4-24-72.) **Rules for determining stock ownership.**

(a) *In general.* In determining stock ownership for purposes of § 1.1562-5, § 1.-1563-1, § 1.1563-2, and this section, the constructive ownership rules of paragraph (b) of this section apply to the extent such rules are referred to in such sections. The application of such rules shall be subject to the operating rules and special rules contained in paragraphs (c) and (d) of this section.

(b) *Constructive ownership—(1) Options.* If a person has an option to acquire any outstanding stock of a corporation, such stock shall be considered as owned by such person. For purposes of this subparagraph, an option to acquire such an option, and each one of a series of such options, shall be considered as an option to acquire such stock. For example, assume Smith owns an option to purchase 100 shares of the outstanding stock of M Corporation. Under this subparagraph, Smith is considered to own such 100 shares. The result would be the same if Smith owned an option to acquire the option (or one of a series of options) to purchase 100 shares of M stock.

(2) *Attribution from partnerships.* (i) Stock owned, directly or indirectly, by or

Reg. § 1.1563-3(b)(2)

24,234.6 (I.R.C.) Reg. § 1.1563-3(b)(2) 5-2-72

for a partnership shall be considered as owned by any partner having an interest of 5 percent or more in either the capital or profits of the partnership in proportion to his interest in capital or profits, whichever such proportion is the greater.

(ii) The provisions of this subparagraph may be illustrated by the following example:

Example. Green, Jones, and White, unrelated individuals, are partners in the GJW partnership. The partners' interests in the capital and profits of the partnership are as follows:

Partner	Capital	Profits
Green	36%	25%
Jones	60	71
White	4	4

The GJW partnership owns the entire outstanding stock (100 shares) of X Corporation. Under this subparagraph, Green is considered to own the X stock owned by the partnership in proportion to his interest in capital (36 percent) or profits (25 percent), whichever such proportion is the greater. Therefore, Green is considered to own 36 shares of the X stock. However, since Jones has a greater interest in the profits of the partnership, he is considered to own the X stock in proportion to his interest in such profits. Therefore, Jones is considered to own 71 shares of the X stock. Since White does not have an interest of 5 percent or more in either the capital or profits of the partnership, he is not considered to own any shares of the X stock.

(3) *Attribution from estates or trusts.* (i) Stock owned, directly or indirectly, by or for an estate or trust shall be considered as owned by any beneficiary who has an actuarial interest of 5 percent or more in such stock, to the extent of such actuarial interest. For purposes of this subparagraph, the actuarial interest of each beneficiary shall be determined by assuming the maximum exercise of discretion by the fiduciary in favor of such beneficiary and the maximum use of such stock to satisfy his rights as a beneficiary. A beneficiary of an estate or trust who cannot under any circumstances receive any interest in stock held by the estate or trust, including the proceeds from the disposition thereof, or the income therefrom, does not have an actuarial interest in such stock. Thus, where stock owned by a decedent's estate has been specifically bequeathed to certain beneficiaries and the remainder of the estate is bequeathed to other beneficiaries, the stock is attributable only to the beneficiaries to whom it is specifically bequeathed. Similarly, a remainderman of a trust who cannot under any circumstances receive any interest in the stock of a corporation which is a part of the corpus of the trust (including any accumulated income therefrom or the proceeds from a disposition thereof) does not have an actuarial interest in such stock. However, an income beneficiary of a trust does have an actuarial interest in stock if he has any right to the income from such stock even though under the terms of the trust instrument such stock can never be distributed to him. The factors and methods prescribed in § 20.2031-7 of this chapter (Estate Tax Regulations) for use in ascertaining the value of an interest in property for estate tax purposes shall be used for purposes of this subdivision in determining a beneficiary's actuarial interest in stock owned directly or indirectly by or for a trust.

(ii) For the purposes of this subparagraph, property of a decedent shall be considered as owned by his estate if such property is subject to administration by the executor or administrator for the purposes of paying claims against the estate and expenses of administration notwithstanding that, under local law, legal title to such property vests in the decedent's heirs, legatees, or devisees immediately upon death. With respect to an estate, the term "beneficiary" includes any person entitled to receive property of the decedent pursuant to a will or pursuant to laws of descent and distribution. A person shall no longer be considered a beneficiary of an estate when all the property to which he is entitled has been received by him, when he no longer has a claim against the estate arising out of having been a beneficiary, and when there is only a remote possibility that it will be necessary for the estate to seek the return of property or to seek payment from him by contribution or otherwise to satisfy claims against the estate or expenses of administration. When pursuant to the preceding sentence, a person ceases to be a beneficiary, stock owned by the estate shall not thereafter be considered owned by him.

(iii) Stock owned, directly or indirectly, by or for any portion of a trust of which a person is considered the owner under subpart E, part I, subchapter J of the Code (relating to grantors and others treated as substantial owners) is considered as owned by such person.

(iv) This subparagraph does not apply to stock owned by any employees' trust described in section 401(a) which is exempt from tax under section 501(a).

(4) *Attribution from corporations.* (i) Stock owned, directly or indirectly, by or for a corporation shall be considered as owned by any person who owns (within the meaning of section 1563(d)) 5 percent or more in value of its stock in that proportion which the value of the stock which such person so owns bears to the value of all the stock in such corporation.

(ii) The provisions of this subparagraph may be illustrated by the following example:

Example. Brown, an individual, owns 60 shares of the 100 shares of the only class of outstanding stock of corporation P. Smith, an individual, owns 4 shares of the P stock, and corporation X owns 36 shares of the P stock. Corporation P owns, directly and indirectly, 50 shares of the stock of corporation S. Under this subparagraph, Brown is considered to own 30 shares of the S stock (60/100 × 50), and X is considered to own 18 shares of the S stock (36/100 × 50). Since Smith does not own 5 percent or more in value of the P stock, he is not considered as owning any of the S stock owned by P. If, in this example, Smith's wife had owned directly 1 share of the P stock, Smith (and his wife) would each own 5 shares of the P stock, and therefore Smith (and his wife) would be considered as owning 2.5 shares of the S stock (5/100 × 50).

(5) *Spouse.* (i) Except as provided in subdivision (ii) of this subparagraph, an

individual shall be considered to own the stock owned, directly or indirectly, by or for his spouse, other than a spouse who is legally separated from the individual under a decree of divorce, whether interlocutory or final, or a decree of separate maintenance.

(ii) An individual shall not be considered to own stock in a corporation owned, directly or indirectly, by or for his spouse on any day of a taxable year of such corporation, provided that each of the following conditions are satisfied with respect to such taxable year:

(a) Such individual does not, at any time during such taxable year, own directly any stock in such corporation.

(b) Such individual is not a member of the board of directors or an employee of such corporation and does not participate in the management of such corporation at any time during such taxable year.

(c) Not more than 50 percent of such corporation's gross income for such taxable year was derived from royalties, rents, dividends, interest, and annuities.

(d) Such stock in such corporation is not, at any time during such taxable year, subject to conditions which substantially restrict or limit the spouse's right to dispose of such stock and which run in favor of the individual or his children who have not attained the age of 21 years. The principles of paragraph (b)(2)(iii) of § 1.1563-2 shall apply in determining whether a condition is a condition described in the preceding sentence.

(iii) For purposes of subdivision (ii)(c) of this subparagraph, the gross income of a corporation for taxable year shall be determined under section 61 and the regulations thereunder. The terms "royalties", "rents", "dividends", "interest", and "annuities" shall have the same meanings such terms are given for purposes of section 1244(c). See paragraph (g)(1)(ii), (iii), (iv), (v) and (vi) of § 1.1244(c)-1.

(6) *Children, grandchildren, parents, and grandparents.* (i) An individual shall be considered to own the stock owned, directly or indirectly, by or for his children who have not attained the age of 21 years, and, if the individual has not attained the age of 21 years, the stock owned, directly or indirectly, by or for his parents.

(ii) If an individual owns (directly, and with the application of the rules of this paragraph but without regard to this subdivision) stock possessing more than 50 percent of the total combined voting power of all classes of stock entitled to vote or more than 50 percent of the total value of shares of all classes of stock in a corporation, then such individual shall be considered to own the stock in such corporation owned, directly or indirectly, by or for his parents, grandparents, and children who have attained the age of 21 years. In determining whether the stock owned by an individual possesses the requisite percentage of the total combined voting power of all classes of stock entitled to vote of a corporation, see paragraph (a)(6) of § 1.1563-1.

(iii) For purposes of section 1563, and §§ 1.1563-1 through 1.1563-4, a legally adopted child of an individual shall be treated as a child of such individual by blood.

(iv) The provisions of this subparagraph may be illustrated by the following example:

Example — (a) Facts. Individual F owns directly 40 shares of the 100 shares of the only class of stock of Z Corporation. His son, M (20 years of age), owns directly 30 shares of such stock, and his son, A (30 years of age), owns directly 20 shares of such stock. The remaining 10 shares of the Z stock are owned by an unrelated person.

(b) F's ownership. Individual F owns 40 shares of the Z stock directly and is considered to own the 30 shares of Z stock owned directly by M. Since, for purposes of the more-than-50-percent stock ownership test contained in subdivision (ii) of this subparagraph, F is treated as owning 70 shares or 70 percent of the total voting power and value of the Z stock, he is also considered as owning the 20 shares owned by his adult son, A. Accordingly, F is considered as owning a total of 90 shares of the Z stock.

(c) M's ownership. Minor son, M, owns 30 shares of the Z stock directly, and is considered to own the 40 shares of Z stock owned directly by his father, F. However, M is not considered to own the 20 shares of Z stock owned directly by his brother, A, and constructively by F, because stock constructively owned by F by reason of family attribution is not considered as owned by him for purposes of making another member of his family the constructive owner of such stock. See paragraph (c)(2) of this section. Accordingly, M owns and is considered as owning a total of 70 shares of the Z stock.

(d) A's ownership. Adult son, A, owns 20 shares of the Z stock directly. Since, for purposes of the more-than-50-percent stock ownership test contained in subdivision (ii) of this subparagraph, A is treated as owning only the Z stock which he owns directly, he does not satisfy the condition precedent for the attribution of Z stock from his father. Accordingly, A is treated as owning only the 20 shares of Z stock which he owns directly.

(c) *Operating rules and special rules—* (1) *In general.* Except as provided in subparagraph (2) of this paragraph, stock constructively owned by a person by reason of the application of subparagraph (1), (2), (3), (4), (5), or (6) of paragraph (b) of this section shall, for purposes of applying such subparagraphs, be treated as actually owned by such person.

(2) *Members of family.* Stock constructively owned by an individual by reason of the application of subparagraph (5) or (6) of paragraph (b) of this section shall not be treated as owned by him for purposes of again applying such subparagraphs in order to make another the constructive owner of such stock.

(3) *Precedence of option attribution.* For purposes of this section, if stock may be considered as owned by a person under subparagraph (1) of paragraph (b) of this section (relating to option attribution) and under any other subparagraph of such paragraph, such stock shall be considered as

Reg. § 1.1563-3(c)(3)

owned by such person under subparagraph (1) of such paragraph.

(4) *Examples.* The provisions of this paragraph may be illustrated by the following examples:

Example (1). A, 30 years of age, has a 90 percent interest in the capital and profits of a partnership. The partnership owns all the outstanding stock of corporation X and X owns 60 shares of the 100 outstanding shares of corporation Y. Under subparagraph (1) of this paragraph, the 60 shares of Y constructively owned by the partnership by reason of subparagraph (4) of paragraph (b) of this section is treated as actually owned by the partnership for purposes of applying subparagraph (2) of paragraph (b) of this section. Therefore, A is considered as owning 54 shares of the Y stock (90 percent of 60 shares).

Example (2). Assume the same facts as in example (1). Assume further that B, who is 20 years of age and the brother of A, directly owns 40 shares of Y stock. Although the stock of Y owned by B is considered as owned by C (the father of A and B) under paragraph (b) (6) (i) of this section, under subparagraph (2) of this paragraph such stock may not be treated as owned by C for purposes of applying paragraph (b) (6) (ii) of this section in order to make A the constructive owner of such stock.

Example (3). Assume the same facts assumed for purposes of example (2), and further assume that C has an option to acquire the 40 shares of Y stock owned by his son, B. The rule contained in subparagraph (2) of this paragraph does not prevent the reattribution of such 40 shares to A because, under subparagraph (3) of this paragraph, C is considered as owning the 40 shares by reason of option attribution and not by reason of family attribution. Therefore, since A satisfies the more-than-50-percent stock ownership test contained in paragraph (b)(6)(ii) of this section with respect to Y, the 40 shares of Y stock constructively owned by C are reattributed to A, and A is considered as owning a total of 94 shares of Y stock.

(d) *Special rule of section 1563(f)(3) (B)*—(1) *In general.* If the same stock of a corporation is owned (within the meaning of section 1563(d)) by two or more persons, then such stock shall be treated as owned by the person whose ownership of such stock results in the corporation being a component member of a controlled group on a December 31 which has at least one other component member on such date.

(2) *Component member of more than one group.* (i) If, by reason of subparagraph (1) of this paragraph, a corporation would (but for this subparagraph) become a component member of more than one controlled group on a December 31, such corporation shall be treated as a component member of only one such controlled group on such date. The determination as to which group such corporation is treated as a component member of shall be made in accordance with the rules contained in subdivisions (ii), (iii), and (iv) of this subparagraph.

(ii) In any case in which a corporation is a component member of a controlled group of corporations on a December 31 as a result of treating each share of its stock as owned only by the person who owns such share directly, then each such share shall be treated as owned by the person who owns such share directly.

(iii) If the application of subdivision (ii) of this subparagraph does not result in a corporation being treated as a component member of only one controlled group on a December 31, then the stock of such corporation described in subparagraph (1) of this paragraph shall be treated as owned by the one person described in such subparagraph who owns, directly and with the application of the rules contained in paragraph (b)(1), (2), (3), and (4) of this section, the stock possessing the greatest percentage of the total value of shares of all classes of stock of the corporation.

(iv) If the application of subdivision (ii) or (iii) of this subparagraph does not result in a corporation being treated as a component member of only one controlled group of corporations on December 31, then the determination of that group of which such corporation is to be treated as a component member shall be made by the district director with audit jurisdiction of such corporation's return for the taxable year that includes such December 31 unless such corporation files an election as provided in this subdivision. The election shall be in the form of a statement, signed by a person authorized to act on behalf of such corporation, designating the group in which the corporation has elected to be included. The statement shall provide all the information with respect to stock ownership which is reasonably necessary to satisfy the district director that the corporation would, but for the election, be a component member of more than one controlled group. The statement shall be filed on or before the due date (including extensions of time) for the filing of the income tax return of such corporation for the taxable year. However, in the case of an election with respect to December 31, 1970, the statement shall be considered as timely filed if filed on or before December 15, 1971. Once filed, the election is irrevocable and effective until subdivision (ii) or (iii) of this subparagraph applies or until there is a substantial change in the stock ownership of such corporation.

(3) *Examples.* The provisions of this paragraph may be illustrated by the following examples, in which each corporation referred to uses the calendar year as its taxable year and the stated facts are assumed to exist on each day of 1970 (unless otherwise provided in the example):

Example (1). Jones owns all the stock of corporation X and has an option to purchase from Smith all the outstanding stock of corporation Y. Smith owns all the outstanding stock of corporation Z. Since the Y stock is considered as owned by two or more persons, under subparagraph (2) (ii) of this paragraph the Y stock is treated as owned only by Smith since he has direct ownership of such stock. Therefore, on December 31, 1970, Y and Z are component members of the same brother-sister controlled group. If, however, Smith had owned his stock in corporation Z for less than one-half of the number of days of Z's 1970 taxable year, then under subparagraph (1) of this paragraph the Y stock would be treated as owned only by Jones since his ownership results in Y

Example (2). Individual H owns directly all the outstanding stock of corporation M. W (the wife of H) owns directly all the outstanding stock of corporation N. Neither spouse is considered as owning the stock directly owned by the other because each of the conditions prescribed in paragraph (b)(5)(ii) of this section is satisfied with respect to each corporation's 1970 taxable year. H owns directly 60 percent of the only class of stock of Corporation P and W owns the remaining 40 percent of the P stock. Under subparagraph (2)(iii) of this paragraph, the stock of P is treated as owned only by H since H owns (directly and with the application of the rules contained in paragraph (b)(1), (2), (3), and (4) of this section) the stock possessing the greatest percentage of the total value of shares of all classes of stock of P. Accordingly, on December 31, 1970, P is treated as a component member of a brother-sister group consisting of M and P.

Example (3). Unrelated individuals A and B each owns one-half of all the outstanding stock of corporation R, which in turn owns 70 percent of the only class of outstanding stock of corporation S. The remaining 30 percent of the stock of corporation S is owned by unrelated individual C. Under the attribution rule of paragraph (b)(4) of this section, A and B each is considered as owning 35 percent of the stock of corporation S. Accordingly, since 5 or fewer persons own at least 80 percent of the stock of corporations R and S and also own more than 50 percent identically (A and B's identical ownership each is 35 percent), on December 31, 1970, corporations R and S are treated as component members of the same brother-sister controlled group.

O— § 1.1563-4 (T.D. 6845, filed 8-4-65.) Franchised corporations.

(a) In general. For purposes of paragraph (b) (2) (ii) (d) of § 1.1563-1, a member of a controlled group of corporations shall be considered to be a franchised corporation for a taxable year if each of the following conditions are satisfied for one-half (or more) of the number of days preceding the December 31 included within such taxable year (or, if such taxable year does not include a December 31, for one-half or more of the number of days in such taxable year preceding the last day of such year):

(1) Such member is franchised to sell the products of another member, or the common owner, of such controlled group.

(2) More than 50 percent (determined on the basis of cost) of all the goods held by such member primarily for sale to its customers are acquired from members or the common owner of the controlled group, or both.

(3) The stock of such member is to be sold to an employee (or employees) of such member pursuant to a bona fide plan designed to eliminate the stock ownership of the parent corporation (as defined in paragraph (b) (1) of § 1.1563-2) or of the common owner (as defined in paragraph (b) (3) of § 1.1563-2) in such member.

(4) Such employee owns (or such employees in the aggregate own) directly more than 20 percent of the total value of shares of all classes of stock of such member. For purposes of this subparagraph, the determination of whether an employee (or employees) owns the requisite percentage of the total value of the stock of the member shall be made without regard to paragraph (b) of § 1.1563-2, relating to certain stock treated as excluded stock. Furthermore, if the corporation has more than one class of stock outstanding, the relative voting rights as between each such class of stock shall be disregarded in making such determination.

(b) Plan for disposition of stock. (1) A plan referred to in paragraph (a)(3) of this section must—

(i) Provide a reasonable selling price for the stock of the member, and

(ii) Require that a portion of the employee's compensation or dividends, or both, from such member be applied to the purchase of such stock (or to the purchase of notes, bonds, debentures, or similar evidences of indebtedness of such member held by the parent corporation or the common owner). It is not necessary, in order to satisfy the requirements of subdivision (ii) of this subparagraph, that the plan require that a percentage of every dollar of the compensation and dividends be applied to the purchase of the stock (or the indebtedness). The requirements of such subdivision are satisfied if an otherwise qualified plan provides that under certain specified conditions (such as a requirement that the member earn a specified profit) no portion of the compensation and/or dividends need be applied to the purchase of the stock (or indebtedness), provided such conditions are reasonable.

(2) A plan for the elimination of the stock ownership of the parent corporation or of the common owner will satisfy the requirements of paragraph (a)(3) of this section and subparagraph (1) of this paragraph even though it does not require that the stock of the member be sold to an employee (or employees) if it provides for the redemption of the stock of the member held by the parent or common owner and under the plan the amount of such stock to be redeemed during any period is calculated by reference to the profits of such member during such period.

O— § 1.1564 Statutory provisions; transitional rules in the case of certain controlled corporations. [Sec. 1564, IRC]

O— § 1.1564-1 (T.D. 7181, filed 4-24-72.) Limitations on additional benefits for members of controlled groups.

(a) In general. Section 1564(a)(1) provides that, with respect to any December 31 after 1969 and before 1975, only one component menber of a controlled group of corporations (as defined in section 1563 (a)) shall be allowed the full amount of—

(1) The $25,000 surtax exemption under section 1562 (relating to election of multiple surtax exemptions),

(2) The $100,000 amount under section 535(c)(2) and (3) (relating to the accumulated earnings credit), and

(3) The $25,000 limitation on the small business deduction of ife insurance companies under sections 804(a)(4) and 809(d)(10).

The amounts otherwise allowed to the other component members of such controlled group for their taxable years which include such December 31 shall be reduced to the amounts set forth in the following schedule:

Reg. § 1.1564-1(a)(3)

24,234.10 (I.R.C.) Reg. § 1.1564-1(a)(3) 5-20-74

Taxable years including—	Surtax exemption	Amount under sec. 535(c)(2) and (3)	Small business deduction limitation
Dec. 31, 1970	$20,833	$83,333	$20,833
Dec. 31, 1971	16,667	66,667	16,667
Dec. 31, 1972	12,500	50,000	12,500
Dec. 31, 1973	8,333	33,333	8,333
Dec. 31, 1974	4,167	16,667	4,167

(b) *Election.* (1) Section 1564(a)(2) provides that, with respect to any December 31 after 1969 and before 1975, the component members of a controlled group of corporations shall elect which component member or members of such group shall be allowed for their taxable years which includes such December 31 the full amounts described in paragraph (a)(1), (2), and (3) of this section. In making such election, the members may allocate such full amounts among themselves in any manner they choose. For example, the group may select one of its members to receive the full amount of the $25,000 surtax exemption under section 1562 and another of its members to receive the full $100,000 amount under section 535(c)(2), or it may select one of its members to claim both such full amounts.

(2) The election shall be made with respect to a particular December 31 and shall be valid only if each corporation which is a component member of the controlled group on such December 31 gives its consent. The consents shall be made by means of a statement, signed by persons duly authorized to act on behalf of each of the component members (other than wholly-owned subsidiaries), stating which member has been selected to receive the amount which is not reduced under paragraph (a) of this section. The member so selected shall attach the statement to its income tax return for the taxable year including such December 31. The statement shall set forth the name, address, employer identification number, and taxable years of each of the other component members (including wholly-owned subsidiaries) of the controlled group. Such other members shall attach a copy of the statement to their income tax returns for their taxable years including such December 31. An election plan adopted by a controlled group with respect to a particular December 31 shall be valid only for the taxable year of each member of the group which includes such December 31.

(3) Each component member of a controlled group which is a wholly-owned subsidiary of such group with respect to a December 31 shall be deemed to consent to an election with respect to such December 31, provided each component member of the group which is not a wholly-owned subsidiary consents to the election plan. A component member of a controlled group shall be considered to be a wholly-owned subsidiary of the group with respect to a December 31 if, on each day preceding such date during its taxable year which includes such date, all of its stock is owned directly by one or more corporations which are component members of the group on such December 31.

COLLECTION OF INCOME TAX AT SOURCE ON WAGES

§ 31.3401(a) Statutory provisions; definitions; wages. [Sec. 3401(a), IRC]

§ 31.3401(a)-1 (T.D. 6155, filed 12-29-55; amended by T.D. 6259, filed 10-25-57; republished in T.D. 6516, filed 12-19-60; amended by T.D. 6654, filed 5-27-63; T.D. 6908, filed 12-30-66; T.D. 7001, filed 1-17-69; T.D. 7068, filed 11-10-70; T.D. 7277, filed 5-14-73; TD 7493, filed 6-29-77.) Wages.

(a) *In general.* (1) The term "wages" means all remuneration for services performed by an employee for his employer unless specifically excepted under section 3401(a) or excepted under section 3402(e).

(2) The name by which the remuneration for services is designated is immaterial. Thus, salaries, fees, bonuses, commissions on sales or on insurance premiums, pensions, and retired pay are wages within the meaning of the statute if paid as compensation for services performed by the employee for his employer.

(3) The basis upon which the remuneration is paid is immaterial in determining whether the remuneration constitutes wages. Thus, it may be paid on the basis of piecework, or a percentage of profits; and may be paid hourly, daily, weekly, monthly, or annually.

(4) Generally the medium in which remuneration is paid is also immaterial. It may be paid in cash or in something other than cash, as for example, stocks, bonds, or other forms of property. (See, however, § 31.3401(a)(11)-1, relating to the exclusion from wages of remuneration paid in any medium other than cash for services not in the course of the employer's trade or business, and § 31.3401(a)(16)-1, relating to the exclusion from wages of tips paid in any medium other than cash.) If services are paid for in a medium other than cash, the fair market value of the thing taken in payment is the amount to be included as wages. If the services were rendered at a stipulated price, in the absence of evidence to the contrary, such price will be presumed to be the fair value of the remuneration received. If a corporation transfers to its employees its own stock as remuneration for services rendered by the employee, the amount of such remuneration is the fair market value of the stock at the time of the transfer.

(5) Remuneration for services, unless such remuneration is specifically excepted by the statute, constitutes wages even though at the time paid the relationship of employer and employee no longer exists between the person in whose employ the services were performed and the individual who performed them.

Example. A is employed by R during the month of January 1955 and is entitled to receive remuneration of $100 for the services performed for R, the employer, during the month. A leaves the employ of R at the close of business on January 31, 1955. On February 15, 1955 (when A is no longer an employee of R), R pays A the remuneration of $100 which was earned for the services performed in January. The $100 is wages within the meaning of the statute.

(b) *Certain specific items*—(1) Pensions and retirement pay. (i) In general, pensions and retired pay are wages subject to withholding. However, no withholding is required with respect to amounts paid to an employee upon retirement which are taxable as annuities under the provisions of section 72 or 403. So-called pensions awarded by one to whom no services have been rendered are mere gifts or gratuities and do not constitute wages. Those payments of pensions or other benefits by the Federal Government under Title 38 of the United States Code which are excluded from gross income are not wages subject to withholding.

(ii) Amounts received as retirement pay for service in the Armed Forces of the United States, the Coast and Geodetic Survey, or the Public Health Service or as a disability annuity paid under the provisions of section 831 of the Foreign Service Act of 1946, as amended (22 U.S.C. 1081; 60 Stat. 1021), are subject to withholding unless such pay or disability annuity is excluded from gross income under section 104(a)(4), or is taxable as an annuity under the provisions of section 72. Where such retirement pay or disability annuity (not excluded from gross income under section 104(a)(4) and not taxable as an annuity under the provisions of section 72) is paid to a nonresident alien individual, withholding is required only in the case of such amounts paid to a nonresident alien individual who is a resident of Puerto Rico.

(2) *Traveling and other expenses.* Amounts paid specifically—either as advances or reimbursements—for traveling or other bona fide ordinary and necessary expenses incurred or reasonably expected to be incurred in the business of the employer are not wages and are not subject to withholding. Traveling and other reimbursed expenses must be identified either by making a separate payment or by specifically indicating the separate amounts where both wages and expense allowances are combined in a single payment.

(3) *Vacation allowances.* Amounts of so-called "vacation allowances" paid to an employee constitute wages. Thus, the salary of an employee on vacation, paid notwithstanding his absence from work, constitutes wages.

(4) *Dismissal payments.* Any payments made by an employer to an employee on account of dismissal, that is, involuntary separation from the service of the employer, constitute wages regardless of whether the employer is legally bound by contract, statute, or otherwise to make such payments.

(5) *Deductions by employer from remuneration of an employee.* Any amount deducted by an employer from the remuneration of an employee is considered to be a part of the employee's remuneration and is considered to be paid to the employee as remuneration at the time that the deduction is made. It is immaterial that any act of Congress, or the law of any State or of Puerto Rico, requires or permits such deductions and the payment of the amounts

Reg. § 31.3401(a)-1(b)(5)

thereof to the United States, a State, a Territory, Puerto Rico, or the District of Columbia, or any political subdivision of any one or more of the foregoing.

(6) *Payment by an employer of employee's tax, or employee's contributions under a State law.* The term "wages" includes the amount paid by an employer on behalf of an employee (without deduction from the remuneration of, or other reimbursement from, the employee) on account of any payment required from an employee under a State unemployment compensation law, or on account of any tax imposed upon the employee by any taxing authority, including the taxes imposed by sections 3101 and 3201.

(7) *Remuneration for services as employee of nonresident alien individual or foreign entity.* The term "wages" includes remuneration for services performed by a citizen or resident of the United States as an employee of a nonresident alien individual, foreign partnership, or foreign corporation whether or not such alien individual or foreign entity is engaged in trade or business within the United States. Any person paying wages on behalf of a nonresident alien individual, foreign partnership, or foreign corporation, not engaged in trade or business within the United States (including Puerto Rico as if a part of the United States), is subject to all the provisions of law and regulations applicable with respect to an employer. See § 31.-3401(d)-1, relating to the term "employer," and § 31.3401(a)(8)(C)-1, relating to remuneration paid for services performed by a citizen of the United States in Puerto Rico.

(8) *Amounts paid under wage continuation plans*—(i) *Amounts paid before January 1, 1956*—(a) *Amounts paid by employer for whom services are performed.*

(1) Withholding is not required upon amounts paid before January 1, 1956, to an employee by his employer under a wage continuation plan for a period during which the employee is absent from work on account of personal injuries or sickness, if such amounts are excludable from the gross income of the employee under section 105 (d) and the records maintained by the employer in accordance with the provisions of sections 6001 and 6051 and the provisions thereunder in subpart G of the regulations in this part—

(i) Separately show the amounts of such payments and distinguish such amounts from all other payments, and

(ii) Establish the facts necessary to show that the employee is entitled to the exclusion provided by section 105(d), either by means of a written statement from the employee as to the injury, illness, or hospitalization, or by any other information which the employer believes to be accurate and which he is willing to accept for purposes of payments under the wage continuation plan.

(2) For the purpose of section 6051 and the regulations thereunder, relating to the requirement of receipts for employees, amounts paid before January 1, 1956, which are excludable from gross income under the provisions of section 105(d) shall be included in the total wages required to be shown on Form W-2. The amount of any such wages on which the employer, in reliance on section 105(d), does not withhold must be shown separately, and properly identified, on Form W-2 in such manner that it may be read on each copy of the form.

(3) See sections 6001 and 6051 and the provisions thereunder in subpart G of the regulations in this part for rules with respect to the records which must be maintained in connection with wage continuation payments and for rules with respect to the statements which must be furnished an employee in connection with wage continuation payments respectively. See also section 105 and § 1.105-4 of this chapter (Income Tax Regulations).

(b) *Amounts paid by person other than employer for whom services are performed.* Withholding is not required upon any amounts paid before January 1, 1956, to an employee for a period during which the employee is absent from work on account of personal injuries or sickness, whether or not such amounts are excludable from the gross income of the employee, if such amounts are paid through accident or health insurance or under an accident or health plan by a person who is not the employer for whom the employee performs services but who is regarded as an employer under section 3401(d)(1). For example, no withholding is required in connection with accident or health benefits paid by an insurance company under an accident or health policy, by a separate trust under an accident or health plan, or by a State agency from a sickness and disability fund maintained under State law.

(ii) *Amounts paid after December 31, 1955 and before January 1, 1977*—(a) *In general.* The term "wage continuation payment", as used in this subdivision, means any payment to an employee which is made after December 31, 1955 and before January 1, 1977, under a wage continuation plan (as defined in paragraph (a) (2)(i) of § 1.105-4 and § 1.105-5 of Part 1 of this chapter (Income Tax Regulations)) for a period of absence from work on account of personal injuries or sickness, to the extent such payment is attributable to contributions made by the employer which were not includible in the employee's gross income or is paid by the employer. Any such payment, whether or not excluded from the gross income of the employee under section 105(d), constitutes "wages" (unless specifically excepted under any of the numbered paragraphs of section 3401 (a) or under section 3402(e)) and withholding thereon is required except as provided in (b) and (c) of this subdivision.

(b) *Amounts paid before January 1, 1977 by employer for whom services are performed for period of absence beginning after December 31, 1963.* (1) Withholding is not required upon the amount of any wage continuation payment for a period of absence beginning after December 31, 1963, paid before January 1, 1977, to an employee directly by the employer for whom he performs services to the extent that such payment is excludable from the gross income of the employee under the provisions of section 105(d) in effect with respect to such payments, provided the records maintained by the employer—

(i) Separately show the amount of each such payment and the excludable portion thereof, and

(ii) Contain data substantiating the

employee's entitlement to the exclusion provided in section 105(d) with respect to such amount, either by a written statement from the employee specifying whether his absence from work during the period for which the payment was made was due to a personal injury or to sickness and whether he was hospitalized for at least one day during this period; or by any other information which the employer reasonably believes establishes the employee's entitlement to the exclusion under section 105(d). Employers shall not be required to ascertain the accuracy of any written statement submitted by an employee in accordance with this subdivision (b)(1)(ii).

For purposes of this subdivision (b)(1), wage continuation payments reasonably expected by the employer to be made on behalf of the employer by another person after August 1, 1977, the thirtieth day after the publication of this regulation in the Federal Register as a Treasury decision (and, at the option of the employer, such payments reasonably expected to be made prior thereto) shall be taken into account in determining whether the 75 percent test contained in section 105(d) is met and in computing the amount of any wage continuation payment made directly by the employer for whom services are performed by the employee which is within the $75 or $100 weekly rate of exclusion from the gross income of the employee provided in section 105(d). In making this latter computation, the amount excludable under section 105(d) shall be applied first against payments reasonably expected to be made on behalf of the employer by the other person and then, to the extent any part of the exclusion remains, against the payments made directly by the employer. In a case in which wage continuation payments are not paid at a constant rate for the first 30 calendar days of the period of absence the determination of whether the 75 percent test contained in section 105(d) is met shall be based upon the length of the employee's absence as of the end of the period for which the payment by the employer is made, without regard to the effect which any further extension of such absence may have upon the excludability of the payment.

(2) The computation of the amount of any wage continuation payment with respect to which the employer may refrain from withholding may be illustrated by the following examples:

Example (1). A, an employee of B, normally works Monday through Friday and has a regular weekly rate of wages of $100. On Monday, November 5, 1974, A becomes ill, and as a result is absent from work for two weeks, returning to work on Monday, November 19, 1974. A is not hospitalized. Under B's noncontributory wage continuation plan, A receives no benefits for the first three working days of absence and is paid benefits directly by B at the rate of $85 a week thereafter ($34 for the last two days of the first week of absence and $85 for the second week of absence). No wage continuation payment is made by any other person. Since the benefits are entirely attributable to contributions to the plan by B, such benefits are wage continuation payments in their entirety. The wage continuation payments for the first seven calendar days of absence are not excludable from A's gross income because A was not hospitalized for at least one day during his period of absence, and therefor B must withhold with respect to such payments. Under section 105(d), the wage continuation payments attributable to absence after the first seven calendar days of absence are excludable to the extent that they do not exceed a rate of $75 a week. Under the principles stated in paragraph (e)(6)(iv) of § 1.105-4 of this chapter (Income Tax Regulations), the wage continuation payments in this case are at a rate not in excess of 75 percent (119/200 or 59.5 percent) of A's regular weekly rate of wages. Accordingly, B may refrain from withholding with respect to $75 of the wage continuation payment attributable to the second week of absence.

Example (2). Assume the facts in example (1) except that A is unable to return to work until Monday, February 11, 1975, and that, of the $85 a week of wage continuation payments $35 is paid directly by B and $50 is reasonably expected by B to be paid by C, an insurance company, on behalf of B. In such a case, both the $50 and the $35 payments constitute wage continuation payments and the amount of such payments which is attributable to the first 30 calendar days of absence is at a rate not in excess of 75 percent (323/440 or 73.4 percent) of A's regular weekly rate of wages. Therefore, under section 105(d), the portion of such payments which is attributable to absence after the first seven calendar days of absence is excludable to the extent that it does not exceed a rate of $75 a week for the eighth through the thirtieth calendar day of absence and does not exceed a rate of $100 a week thereafter. B may refrain from withholding with respect to $25 a week (the amount by which the $75 maximum excludable amount exceeds the $50 reasonably expected by B to be paid by C) of his direct payments for the eighth through the thirtieth calendar day of absence. Thereafter, B may refrain from withholding with respect to the entire $35 paid directly by him, since the maximum excludable amount ($100 a week) exceeds the total of payments made by B and payments which B reasonably expects will be made by C.

(c) Amounts paid by employer for whom services are performed for period of absence beginning before January 1, 1964. Withholding is not required upon the amount of any wage continuation payment for a period of absence beginning before January 1, 1964, made to an employee directly by the employer for whom he performs services to the extent that such payment is excludable from the gross income of the employee under the provisions of section 105(d) in effect with respect to such payments, provided the records maintained by the employer—

(1) Separately show the amount of each such payment and the excludable portion thereof, and

(2) Contain data substantiating the employee's entitlement to the exclusion provided in section 105(d) with respect to such amount, either by a written statement from the employee specifying whether his absence from work during the period for

Reg. § 31.3401(a)-1(b)(8)

which the payment was made was due to a personal injury or whether such absence was due to sickness, and, if the latter, whether he was hospitalized for at least one day during this period; or by any other information which the employer reasonably believes establishes the employee's entitlement to the exclusion under section 105(d). Employers shall not be required to ascertain the accuracy of the information contained in any written statement submitted by an employee in accordance with this subdivision (c)(2).

For purposes of this subdivision (c), the computation of the amount excludable from the gross income of the employee under section 105(d) may be made either on the basis of the wage continuation payments which are made directly by the employer for whom the employee performs services, or on the basis of such payments in conjunction with any wage continuation payments made on behalf of the employer by a person who is regarded as an employer under section 3401(d)(1).

(d) *Amounts paid before January 1, 1977 by person other than the employer for whom services are performed.* No tax shall be withheld upon any wage continuation payment made to an employee by or on behalf of a person who is not the employer for whom the employee performs services but who is regarded as an employer under section 3401(d)(1). For example, no tax shall be withheld with respect to wage continuation payments made on behalf of an employer by an insurance company under an accident or health policy, by a separate trust under an accident or health plan, or by a State agency from a sickness and disability fund maintained under State law.

(e) *Cross references.* See sections 6001 and 6051 and the regulations thereunder for rules with respect to the records which must be maintained in connection with wage continuation payments and for rules with respect to the statements which must be furnished an employee in connection with wage continuation payments, respectively. See also section 105 and § 1.105-4 of this chapter (Income Tax Regulations).

(9) *Value of meals and lodging.* The value of any meals or lodging furnished to an employee by his employer is not subject to withholding if the value of the meals or lodging is excludable from the gross income of the employee. See § 1.119-1 of this chapter (Income Tax Regulations).

(10) *Facilities or privileges.* Ordinarily, facilities or privileges (such as entertainment, medical services, or so-called "courtesy" discounts on purchases), furnished or offered by an employer to his employees generally, are not considered as wages subject to withholding if such facilities or privileges are of relatively small value and are offered or furnished by the employer merely as a means of promoting the health, good will, contentment, or efficiency of his employees.

(11) *Tips or gratuities.* Tips or gratuities paid, prior to January 1, 1966, directly to an employee by a customer of an employer, and not accounted for by the employee to the employer are not subject to withholding. For provisions relating to the treatment of tips received by an employee after December 31, 1965, as wages, see §§ 31.3401(f)-1 and 31.3402(k)-1.

(12) *Remuneration for services performed by permanent resident of Virgin Islands*—(i) *Exemption from withholding.* No tax shall be withheld for the United States under chapter 24 from a payment of wages by an employer, including the United States or any agency thereof, to an employee if at the time of payment it is reasonable to believe that the employee will be required to satisfy his income tax obligations with respect to such wages under section 28 (a) of the Revised Organic Act of the Virgin Islands (68 Stat. 508). That section provides that all persons whose permanent residence is in the Virgin Islands "shall satisfy their income tax obligations under applicable taxing statutes of the United States by paying their tax on income derived from all sources both within and outside the Virgin Islands into the treasury of the Virgin Islands."

(ii) *Claiming exemption.* If the employee furnishes to the employer a statement in duplicate that he expects to satisfy his income tax obligations under section 28 (a) of the Revised Organic Act of the Virgin Islands with respect to all wages subsequently to be paid to him by the employer during the taxable year to which the statement relates, the employer may, in the absence of information to the contrary, rely on such statement as establishing reasonable belief that the employee will so satisfy his income tax obligations. The employee's statement shall identify the taxable year to which it relates, and both the original and the duplicate copy thereof shall be signed and dated by the employee.

(iii) *Disposition of statement.* The original of the statement shall be retained by the employer. The duplicate copy of the statement shall be sent by the employer to the Director of International Operations, Washington 25, D. C., on or before the last day of the calendar year in which the employer receives the statement from the employee.

(iv) *Applicability of subparagraph.* This subparagraph has no application with respect to any payment of remuneration which is not subject to withholding by reason of any other provision of the regulations in this subpart.

(13) *Federal employees resident in Puerto Rico.* Except as provided in paragraph (d) of § 31.3401(a)(6)-1, the term "wages" includes remuneration for services performed by a nonresident alien individual who is a resident of Puerto Rico if such services are performed as an employee of the United States or any agency thereof. The place where the services are performed is immaterial for purposes of this subparagraph.

(14) *Supplemental unemployment compensation benefits.* (i) Supplemental unemployment compensation benefits paid to an individual after December 31, 1970, shall be treated (for purposes of the provisions of Subparts E, F, and G of this part which relate to withholding of income tax) as if they were wages, to the extent such benefits

are includible in the gross income of such individual.

(ii) For purposes of this subparagraph, the term "supplemental unemployment compensation benefits" means amounts which are paid to an employee, pursuant to a plan to which the employer is a party, because of the employee's involuntary separation from the employment of the employer, whether or not such separation is temporary, but only when such separation is one resulting directly from a reduction in force, the discontinuance of a plant or operation, or other similar conditions.

(iii) For the meanings of the terms "involuntary separation from the employment of the employer" and "other similar conditions", see subparagraphs (3) and (4) of § 1.501 (c) (17)-1 (b) of this chapter (Income Tax Regulations).

(iv) As used in this subparagraph, the term "employee" means an employee within the meaning of paragraph (a) of § 31.3401 (c)-1, the term "employer" means an employer within the meaning of paragraph (a) of § 31.3401 (d)-1, and the term "employment" means employment as defined under the usual common law rules.

(v) References in this chapter to wages as defined in section 3401 (a) shall be deemed to refer also to supplemental unemployment compensation benefits which are treated under this subparagraph as if they were wages.

(c) *Geographical definitions.* For definition of the term "United States" and for other geographical definitions relating to the continental shelf, see section 638 and § 1.638-1 of this chapter.

○— § 31.3401(a)-2 (T.D. 6259, filed 10-25-57; republished in T.D. 6516, filed 12-19-60; amended by T.D. 6654, filed 5-27-63 and T.D. 7096, filed 3-17-71.) **Exclusions from wages.**

(a) *In general.* (1) The term "wages" does not include any remuneration for services performed by an employee for his employer which is specifically excepted from wages under section 3401(a).

(2) The exception attaches to the remuneration for services performed by an employee and not to the employee as an individual; that is, the exception applies only to the remuneration in an excepted category.

Example. A is an individual who is employed part time by B to perform domestic service in his home (see § 31.3401(a)(3)-1). A is also employed by C part time to perform services as a clerk in a department store owned by him. While no withholding is required with respect to A's remuneration for services performed in the employ of B (the remuneration being excluded from wages), the exception does not embrace the remuneration for services performed by A in the employ of C and withholding is required with respect to the wages for such services.

(3) For provisions relating to the circumstances under which remuneration which is excepted is nevertheless deemed to be wages, and relating to the circumstances under which remuneration which is not excepted is nevertheless deemed not to be wages, see § 31.3402(e)-1.

(4) For provisions relating to payments with respect to which a voluntary withholding agreement is in effect, which are not defined as wages in section 3401(a) but which are nevertheless deemed to be wages, see §§ 31.3401(a)-3 and 31.3402(p)-1.

(b) *Fees paid a public official.* (1) Authorized fees paid to public officials such as notaries public, clerks of courts, sheriffs, etc., for services rendered in the performance of their official duties are excepted from wages and hence are not subject to withholding. However, salaries paid such officials by the Government, or by a Government agency or instrumentality, are subject to withholding.

(2) Amounts paid to precinct workers for services performed at election booths in State, county, and municipal elections and fees paid to jurors and witnesses are in the nature of fees paid to public officials and therefore are not subject to withholding.

○— § 31.3401(a)-3 (T.D. 7096, filed 3-17-71.) **Amounts deemed wages under voluntary withholding agreements.**

(a) *In general.* Notwithstanding the exceptions to the definition of wages specified in section 3401(a) and the regulations thereunder, the term "wages" includes the amounts described in paragraph (b)(1) of this section with respect to which there is a voluntary withholding agreement in effect under section 3402(p). References in this chapter to the definition of wages contained in section 3401(a) shall be deemed to refer also to this section (§ 31.3401(a)-3).

(b) *Remuneration for services.* (1) Except as provided in subparagraph (2) of this paragraph, the amounts referred to in paragraph (a) of this section include any remuneration for services performed by an employee for an employer which, without regard to this section, does not constitute wages under section 3401(a). For example, remuneration for services performed by an agricultural worker or a domestic worker in a private home (amounts which are specifically excluded from the definition of wages by section 3401(a)(2) and (3), respectively) are amounts with respect to which a voluntary withholding agreement may be entered into under section 3402(p). See §§ 31.3401.(c)-1 and 31.3401(d)-1 for the definitions of "employee" and "employer".

(2) For purposes of this paragraph, remuneration for services shall not include amounts not subject to withholding under § 31.3401(a)-1(b)(12) (relating to remuneration for services performed by a permanent resident of the Virgin Islands), § 31.3401 (a)-2(b) (relating to fees paid to a public official), section 3401(a)(5) (relating to remuneration for services for foreign government or international organization), section 3401(a)(8)(B) (relating to remuneration for services performed in a possession of the United States (other than Puerto Rico) by citizens of the United States), section 3401(a)(8)(C) (relating to remuneration for services performed in Puerto Rico by citizens of the United States), section 3401(a)(11) (relating to remuneration other than in cash for service not in the course of employer's trade or business), section 3401(a)(12) (relating to payments

Reg. § 31.3401(a)-3(b)(2)

24,236.4 (I.R.C.) Reg. § 31.3401(a)-3(b)(2)

from or to certain tax-exempt trusts, or under or to certain annuity plans or bond purchase plans), section 3401(a)(14) (relating to group-term life insurance), section 3401(a)(15) (relating to moving expenses), or section 3401(a)(16)(A) (relating to tips paid in any medium other than cash).

○→ § 31.3401(a)(1) **Statutory provisions; definitions; wages; certain remuneration of members of the Armed Forces.** [Sec. 3401(a)(1), IRC]

○→ § 31.3401(a)(1)-1 (T.D. 6259, filed 10-25-57; republished in T.D. 6516, filed 12-19-60.) **Remuneration of members of the Armed Forces of the United States for active service in combat zone or while hospitalized as a result of such service.**

Remuneration paid for active service as a member of the Armed Forces of the United States performed in a month during any part of which such member served in a combat zone (as determined under section 112) or is hospitalized at any place as a result of wounds, disease, or injury incurred while serving in such a combat zone is excepted from wages and is, therefore, not subject to withholding. The exception with respect to hospitalization is applicable, however, only if during all of such month there are combatant activities in some combat zone (as determined under section 112). See § 1.112-1 of this chapter (Income Tax Regulations).

○→ § 31.3401(a)(2) **Statutory provisions; definitions; wages; remuneration paid for agricultural labor.** [Sec. 3401(a)(2), IRC]

○→ § 31.3401(a)(2)-1 (T.D. 6259, filed 10-25-57; republished in T.D. 6516, filed 12-19-60.) **Agricultural labor.**

The term "wages" does not include remuneration for services which constitute agricultural labor as defined in section 3121(g). For regulations relating to the definitions of the term "agricultural labor", see § 31.3121(g)-1.

○→ § 31.3401(a)(3) **Statutory provisions; definitions; wages; remuneration paid for domestic service.** [See 3401(a), IRC]

○→ § 31.3401(a)(3)-1 (T.D. 6259, filed 10-25-57; republished in T.D. 6516, filed 12-19-60.) **Remuneration for domestic service.**

(a) *In a private home.* (1) Remuneration paid for services of a household nature performed by an employee in or about a private home of the person by whom he is employed is excepted from wages and hence is not subject to withholding. A private home is a fixed place of abode of an individual or family. A separate and distinct dwelling unit maintained by an individual in an apartment house, hotel, or other similar establishment may constitute a private home. If a dwelling house is used primarily as a boarding or lodging house for the purpose of supplying board or lodging to the public as a business enterprise, it is not a private home, and the remuneration paid for services performed therein is not within the exception.

(2) In general, services of a household nature in or about a private home include services performed by cooks, waiters, but-

lers, housekeepers, governesses, maids, valets, baby sitters, janitors, laundresses, furnacemen, caretakers, handymen, gardeners, footmen, grooms, and chauffeurs of automobiles for family use.

(b) *In a local college club or local chapter of a college fraternity or sorority.* (1) Remuneration paid for services of a household nature performed by an employee in or about the club rooms or house, of a local college club or of a local chapter of a college fraternity or sorority by which he is employed is excepted from wages and hence is not subject to withholding. A local college club or local chapter of a college fraternity or sorority does not include an alumni club or chapter. If the club rooms or house of a local college club or local chapter of a college fraternity or sorority is used primarily for the purpose of supplying board or lodging to the students or the public as a business enterprise, the remuneration paid for services performed therein is not within the exception.

(2) In general, services of a household nature in or about the club rooms or house of a local college club or local chapter of a college fraternity or sorority include services rendered by cooks, waiters, butlers, maids, janitors, laundresses, furnacemen, handymen, gardeners, housekeepers, and housemothers.

(c) *Remuneration not accepted.* Remuneration paid for services not of a household nature, such as services performed as a private secretary, tutor, or librarian, even though performed in the employer's private home or in a local college club or local chapter of a college fraternity or sorority, is not within the exception. Remuneration paid for services of a household nature is not within the exception if performed in or about rooming or lodging houses, boarding houses, clubs (except local college clubs), hotels, hospitals, eleemosynary institutions, or commercial offices or establishments.

○─► § 31.3401(a)(4) **Statutory provisions; definitions; wages; cash remuneration for service not in the course of employer's trade or business.** [Sec. 3401(a)(4), IRC]

○─► § 31.3401(a)(4)-1 (T.D. 6259, filed 10-25-57; republished in T.D. 6516, filed 12-19-60.) **Cash remuneration for service not in the course of employer's trade or business.**

(a) Cash remuneration paid for services not in the course of the employer's trade or business performed by an employee for an employer in a calendar quarter is excepted from wages and hence is not subject to withholding unless—

(1) The cash remuneration paid for such services performed by the employee for the employer in the calendar quarter is $50 or more, and

(2) Such employee is regularly employed in the calendar quarter by such employer to perform such services.

Unless the tests set forth in both subparagraphs (1) and (2) of this paragraph are met, cash remuneration for service not in the course of the employer's trade or business is excluded from wages. (For provisions relating to the exclusion from wages of remuneration paid in any medium other than cash for services not in the course of the employer's trade or business, see § 31.3401(a)(11)-1.)

(b) The term "services not in the course of the employer's trade or business" includes services that do not promote or advance the trade or business of the employer. As used in this section, the term does not include service not in the course of the employer's trade or business performed on a farm operated for profit or domestic service in a private home, local college club, or local chapter of a college fraternity or sorority. Accordingly, this exception does not apply with respect to remuneration which is excepted from wages under section 3401(a)(2) or section 3401(a)(3) (see §§ 31.3401(a)(2)-1 and 31.3401(a)(3)-1, respectively). Remuneration paid for service performed for a corporation does not come within the exception.

(c) The test relating to cash remuneration of $50 or more is based on the remuneration earned during a calendar quarter rather than on the remuneration paid in a calendar quarter. However, for purposes of determining whether the test is met, it is also required that the remuneration be paid, although it is immaterial when the remuneration is paid. Furthermore, in determining whether $50 or more has been paid for service not in the course of the employer's trade or business, only cash remuneration for such service shall be taken into account. The term "cash remuneration" includes checks and other monetary media of exchange. Remuneration paid in any other medium, such as lodging, food, or other goods or commodities, is disregarded in determining whether the cash-remuneration test is met.

(d) For purposes of this exception, an individual is deemed to be regularly employed by an employer during a calendar quarter only if—

(1) Such individual performs service not in the course of the employer's trade or business for such employer for some portion of the day on at least 24 days (whether or not consecutive) during such calendar quarter; or

(2) Such individual was regularly employed (as determined under subparagraph (1) of this paragraph) by such employer in the performance of service not in the course of the employer's trade or business during the preceding calendar quarter.

(e) In determining whether an employee has performed service not in the course of the employer's trade or business on at least 24 days during a calendar quarter, there shall be counted as one day—

(1) Any day or portion thereof on which the employee actually performs such service; and

(2) Any day or portion thereof on which the employee does not perform service of the prescribed character but with respect to which cash remuneration is paid or payable to the employee for such service, such as a day on which the employee is sick or on vacation.

An employee who on a particular day reports for work and, at the direction of his employer, holds himself in readiness to perform service not in the course of the employer's trade or business shall be considered to be engaged in the actual

Reg. § 31.3401(a)(4)-1(e)(2)

performance of such service on that day. For purposes of this exception, a day is a continuous period of 24 hours commencing at midnight and ending at midnight.

○→ § 31.3401(a)(5) Statutory provisions; definitions; wages; remuneration for services for foreign government or international organization. [Sec. 3401(a)(5), IRC]

○→ § 31.3401(a)(5)-1 (T.D. 6259, filed 10-25-57; republished in T.D. 6516, filed 12-19-60.) Remuneration for services for foreign government or international organization.

(a) *Services for foreign government.* (1) Remuneration paid for services performed as an employee of a foreign government is excepted from wages and hence is not subject to withholding. The exception includes not only remuneration paid for services performed by ambassadors, ministers, and other diplomatic officers and employees but also remuneration paid for services performed as a consular or other officer or employee of a foreign government or as a nondiplomatic representative of such a government. However, the exception does not include remuneration for services performed for a corporation created or organized in the United States or under the laws of the United States or any State (including the District of Columbia or the Territory of Alaska or Hawaii) or of Puerto Rico even though such corporation is wholly owned by such a government.

(2) The citizenship or residence of the employee and the place where the services are performed are immaterial for purposes of the exception.

(b) *Services for international organization.* (1) Subject to the provisions of section 1 of the International Organizations Immunities Act (22 U.S.C. 288), remuneration paid for services performed within or without the United States by an employee for an international organization as defined in section 7701(a)(18) is excepted from wages and hence is not subject to withholding. The term "employee" as used in the preceding sentence includes not only an employee who is a citizen or resident of the United States but also an employee who is a nonresident alien individual. The term "employee" also includes an officer. An organization designated by the President through appropriate Executive order as entitled to enjoy the privileges, exemptions, and immunities provided in the International Organizations Immunities Act may enjoy the benefits of the exclusion from wages with respect to remuneration paid for services performed for such organization prior to the date of the issuance of such Executive order, if (i) the Executive order does not provide otherwise and (ii) the organization is a public international organization in which the United States participates, pursuant to a treaty or under the authority of an Act of Congress authorizing such participation or making an appropriation for such participation, at the time such services are performed.

(2) Section 7701(a)(18) provides as follows:

"Sec. 7701. Definitions. (a) When used in this title, where not otherwise distinctly expressed or manifestly incompatible with the intent thereof—

* * * * * *

"(18) International organization. The term "international organization" means a public international organization entitled to enjoy privileges, exemptions, and immunities as an international organization under the International Organizations Immunities Act (22 U. S. C. 228-288f)."

(3) Section 1 of the International Organizations Immunities Act provides as follows:

"Sec. 1. [International Organizations Immunities Act.] For the purposes of this title [International Organizations Immunities Act], the term "international organization" means a public international organization in which the United States participates pursuant to any treaty or under the authority of any Act of Congress authorizing such participation or making an appropriation for such participation, and which shall have been designated by the President through appropriate executive order as being entitled to enjoy the privileges, exemptions, and immunities herein provided. The President shall be authorized, in the light of the functions performed by any such international organization, by appropriate Executive order to withhold or withdraw from any such organization or its officers or employees any of the privileges, exemptions, and immunities provided for in this title (including the amendments made by this title) or to condition or limit the enjoyment by any such organization or its officers or employees of any such privilege, exemption, or immunity. The President shall be authorized, if in his judgment such action should be justified by reason of the abuse by an international organization or its officers and employees of the privileges, exemptions, and immunities herein provided or for any other reason, at any time to revoke the designation of any international organization under this section, whereupon the international organization in question shall cease to be classed as an international organization for the purposes of this title."

○→ § 31.3401(a)(6) Statutory provisions; definitions; wages; remuneration for services of certain nonresident alien individuals. [Sec. 3401(a)(6), IRC]

○→ § 31.3401(a)(6)-1 (T.D. 6908, filed 12-30-66.) Remuneration for services of nonresident alien individuals paid after December 31, 1966.

(a) *In general.* All remuneration paid after December 31, 1966, for services performed by a nonresident alien individual, if such remuneration otherwise constitutes wages within the meaning of § 31.3401(a)-1, is subject to withholding under section 3402 unless excepted from wages under this section.

(b) *Remuneration for services performed outside the United States.* Remuneration paid to a nonresident alien individual (other than a resident of Puerto Rico) for services performed outside the United States is excepted from wages and hence is not subject to withholding.

(c) *Remuneration for services of residents of Canada or Mexico who enter and leave the United States at frequent intervals*—(1) *Transportation service.* Remuneration paid to a nonresident alien individual who is a resident of Canada or Mexico and who, in the performance of his duties in transportation service between points in the United States and points in such foreign country, enters and leaves the United States at frequent intervals, is excepted from wages and hence is not subject to withholding. This exception applies to personnel engaged in railroad, bus, truck, ferry, steamboat, aircraft, or other transporation services and applies whether the employer is a domestic or foreign entity. Thus, the remuneration of a nonresident alien individual who is a resident of Canada and an employee of a domestic railroad, for services as a member of the crew of a train operating between points in Canada and points in the United States, is not subject to wtihholding under section 3402.

(2) *Service on international projects.* Remuneration paid to a nonresident alien individual who is a resident of Canada or Mexico and who, in the performance of his duties in connection with the construction, maintenance, or operation of a waterway, viaduct, dam, or bridge traversed by, or traversing, the boundary between the United States and Canada or the boundary between the United States and Mexico, as the case may be, enters and leaves the United States at frequent intervals, is expected from wages and hence is not subject to withholding. Thus, the remuneration of a nonresident alien individual who is a resident of Canada, for services as an employee in connection with the construction, maintenance, or operation of the Saint Lawrence Seaway and who, in the performance of such services, enters and leaves the United States at frequent intervals, is not subject to withholding under section 3402.

(3) *Limitation.* The exceptions provided by this paragraph do not apply to the remuneration of a resident of Canada or of Mexico who is employed wholly within the United States as, for example, where such a resident is employed to perform service at a fixed points or points in the United States, such as a factory, store, office, or designated area or areas within the United States, and who commutes from his home in Canada or Mexico, in the pursuit of his employment within the United States.

(4) *Certificate required.* In order for an exception provided by this paragraph to apply for any taxable year, the nonresident alien employee must furnish his employer a statement in duplicate for the taxable year setting forth the employee's name, address, and taxpayer identifying number, and certifying (i) that he is not a citizen or resident of the United States, (ii) that he is a resident of Canada or Mexico, as the case may be, and (iii) that he expects to meet the requirements of subparagraph (1) or (2) of this paragraph with respect to remuneration to be paid during the taxable year in respect of which the statement is filed. The statement shall be dated, shall identify the taxable year to which it relates, shall be signed by the employee, and shall contain, or be verified by, a written declaration that it is made under the penalties of perjury. No particular form is prescribed for this statement. The duplicate copy of each statement filed during any calendar year pursuant to this paragraph shall be forwarded by the employer with, and attached to, the Form 1042S required by paragraph (c) of § 1.1461-2 with respect to such remuneration for such calendar year.

(d) *Remuneration for services performed by residents of Puerto Rico.* (1) Remuneration paid for services performed in Puerto Rico by a nonresident alien individual who is a resident of Puerto Rico for an employer (other than the United States or any agency thereof) is excepted from wages and hence is not subject to withholding.

(2) Remuneration paid for services performed outside the United States but not in Puerto Rico by a nonresident alien individual who is a resident of Puerto Rico for an employer (other than the United States or any agency thereof) is excepted from wages and hence is not subject to withholding if such individual does not expect to be a resident of Puerto Rico during the entire taxable year. In order for the exception provided by this subparagraph to apply for any taxable year, the nonresident alien employee must furnish his employer a statement for the taxable year setting forth the employee's name and address and certifying (i) that he is not a citizen or resident of the United States and (ii) that he is a resident of Puerto Rico but does not expect to be a resident of Puerto Rico during the entire taxable year. The statement shall be dated, shall identify the taxable year to which it relates, shall be signed by the employee, and shall contain, or be verified by, a written declaration that it is made under the penalties of perjury. No particular form is prescribed for this statement.

(3) Remuneration paid for services performed outside the United States by a nonresident alien individual who is a resident of Puerto Rico as an employee of the United States or any agency thereof is excepted from wages and hence is not subject to withholding if such individual does not expect to be a resident of Puerto Rico during the entire taxable year. In order for the exception provided by this subparagraph to apply for any taxable year, the nonresident alien employee must furnish his employer a statement for the taxable year setting forth the employee's name and address and certifying (i) that he is not a citizen or resident of the United States and (ii) that he is a resident of Puerto Rico but does not expect to be a resident of Puerto Rico during the entire taxable year. This statement shall be dated, shall identify the taxable year to which it relates, shall be signed by the employee, and shall contain, or be verified by, a written declaration that it is made under the penalties of perjury. No particular form is prescribed for this statement.

(e) *Income exempt from income tax.* Remuneration paid for services performed within the United States by a nonresident alien individual is excepted from wages and hence is not subject to withholding if such remuneration is, or will be, exempt from the income tax imposed by chapter 1 of the Code by reason of a provision of the Internal Revenue Code or an income tax convention to which the United States is a party. In order for the exception pro-

Reg. § 31.3401 (a) (6)-1 (e)

vided by this paragraph to apply for any taxable year, the nonresident alien employee must furnish his employer a statement in duplicate for the taxable year setting forth the employee's name, address, and taxpayer identifying number, and certifying (1) that he is not a citizen or resident of the United States, (2) that the remuneration to be paid to him during the taxable year is, or will be, exempt from the tax imposed by chapter 1 of the Code, and (3) the reason why such remuneration is so exempt from tax. If the remuneration is claimed to be exempt from tax by reason of a provision of an income tax convention to which the United States is a party, the statement shall also indicate the provision and tax convention under which the exemption is claimed, the country of which the employee is a resident, and sufficient facts to justify the claim to exemption. The statement shall be dated, shall identify the taxable year for which it is to apply and the remuneration to which it relates, shall be signed by the employee, and shall contain, or be verified by, a written declaration that it is made under the penalties of perjury. No particular form is prescribed for this statement. The duplicate copy of each statement filed during any calendar year pursuant to this paragraph shall be forwarded by the employer with, and attached to, the Form 1042S required by paragraph (c) of § 1.1461-2 with respect to such remuneration for such calendar year.

O—▸ § 31.3401(a)(6)A Statutory provisions; definitions; wages; remuneration for services of certain nonresident alien individuals. [Sec. 3401(a)(6)A, IRC]

O—▸ § 31.3401(a)(6)-1A (T.D. 6259, filed 10-25-57; republished in T.D. 6516, filed 12-19-60; amended by T.D. 6654, filed 5-27-63; T.D. 6727, filed 5-4-64 and T.D. 6908, filed 12-30-66.) Remuneration for services of certain nonresident alien individuals paid before January 1, 1967.

(a) Except in the case of certain nonresident alien individuals who are residents of Canada, Mexico, or Puerto Rico or individuals who are temporarily present in the United States as nonimmigrants under subparagraph (F) or (J) of section 101(a)(15) of the Immigration and Nationality Act (8 U.S.C. 1101), as amended, remuneration for services performed by nonresident alien individuals does not constitute wages subject to withholding under section 3402. For withholding of income tax on remuneration paid for services performed within the United States in the case of nonresident alien individuals generally, see § 1.1441-1 and following of this chapter (Income Tax Regulations).

(b) Remuneration paid to nonresident aliens who are residents of a contiguous country (Canada or Mexico) and who enter and leave the United States at frequent intervals is not excepted from wages under section 3401(a)(6). See, however, § 31.3401(a)(7)-1, relating to remuneration paid to such nonresident alien individuals when engaged in transportation service.

(c) Remuneration paid to a nonresident alien individual for services performed in Puerto Rico for an employer (other than the United States or any agency thereof) is excepted from wages and hence is not subject to withholding, even though such alien individual is a resident of Puerto Rico at the time when such services are performed. Wages paid for services performed by a nonresident alien individual who is a resident of Puerto Rico are subject to withholding if such services are performed as an employee of the United States or any agency thereof. The place of performance of such services is immaterial, provided such alien individual is a resident of Puerto Rico at the time of performance of the services. Wages representing retirement pay for services in the Armed Forces of the United States, the Coast and Geodetic Survey, or the Public Health Service, or a disability annuity paid under the provisions of section 831 of the Foreign Service Act of 1946, as amended (22 U.S.C. 1081; 60 Stat. 1021), are subject to withholding, under the limitations specified in paragraph (b)(1)(ii) of § 31.3401 (a)-1, in the case of an alien resident of Puerto Rico.

(d)(1) Remuneration paid after 1961 to a nonresident alien individual who is temporarily present in the United States as a nonimmigrant under subparagraph (F) or (J) of section 101(a)(15) of the Immigration and Nationality Act (8 U.S.C. 1101), as amended, is not excepted from wages under section 3401(a)(6) if the remuneration is exempt from withholding under section 1441(a) by reason of section 1441(c)(4)(B) and is not exempt from taxation under section 872(b)(3). See § 1.872-2 and § 1.1441-4 of this chapter (Income Tax Regulations). A nonresident alien individual who is temporarily present in the United States as a nonimmigrant under subparagraph (J) includes an alien individual admitted to the United States as an "exchange visitor" under section 201 of the United States Information and Educational Exchange Act of 1948 (22 U.S.C. 1446).

(2) Section 101 of the Immigration and Nationality Act (8 U.S.C. 1101), as amended, provides in part, as follows:

Sec. 101. *Definitions.* [Immigration and Nationality Act (66 Stat. 166)]

(a) As used in this chapter—* * *

(15) The term "immigrant" means every alien except an alien who is within one of the following classes of nonimmigrant aliens—

* * * * * * *

(F)(i) An alien having a residence in a foreign country which he has no intention of abandoning, who is a bona fide student qualified to pursue a full course of study and who seeks to enter the United States temporarily and solely for the purpose of pursuing such a course of study at an established institution of learning or other recognized place of study in the United States, particularly designated by him and approved by the Attorney General after consultation with the Office of Education of the United States, which institution or place of study shall have agreed to report to the Attorney General the termination of attendance of each nonimmigrant student, and if any such institution of learning or place of study fails to make reports promptly the approval shall be withdrawn, and (ii) the alien spouse and minor children of any such alien if accompanying him or following to join him;

* * * * * * *

(J) An alien having a residence in a foreign country which he has no intention of abandoning who is a bona fide student, scholar, trainee, teacher, professor, research assistant, specialist, or leader in a field of specialized knowledge or skill, or other person of similar description, who is coming temporarily to the United States as a participant in a program designated by the Secretary of State, for the purpose of teaching, instructing or lecturing, studying, observing, conducting research, consulting, demonstrating special skills, or receiving training, and the alien spouse and minor children of any such alien if accompanying him or following to join him.

(e) This section shall not apply with respect to remuneration paid after December 31, 1966. For rules with respect to such remuneration see § 31.3401(a)(6)-1.

○—▶ § 31.3401(a)(7) **Statutory provisions; definitions; wages; remuneration for services performed by nonresident alien individuals who are residents of a contiguous country and who enter and leave the United States at frequent intervals.** [Sec. 3401(a)(7), IRC]

○—▶ § 31.3401(a)(7)-1 (T.D. 6259, filed 10-25-57; republished in T.D. 6516, filed 12-19-60; amended by T.D. 6908, filed 12-30-66.) **Remuneration for services performed by nonresident alien individuals who are residents of a contiguous country and who enter and leave the United States at frequent intervals.**

(a) *Transportation service.* Remuneration paid to nonresident aliens who are residents of a contiguous country (Canada or Mexico) and who, in the performance of their duties in transportation service between points in the United States and points in a contiguous country, enter and leave the United States at frequent intervals is excepted from wages and hence is not subject to withholding. The exception applies to personnel engaged in railroad, bus, ferry, steamboat and aircraft services and applies alike whether the employer is a domestic or foreign entity. Thus, the remuneration of a nonresident alien individual who is a resident of Canada and an employee of a domestic railroad, for services as a member of the crew of a train operating between points in Canada and points in the United States, is not subject to withholding under section 3402.

(b) *Service on international projects.* Remuneration paid to nonresident aliens who are residents of a contiguous country (Canada or Mexico) and who, in the performance of their duties in connection with the construction, maintenance, or operation of a waterway, viaduct, dam, or bridge traversed by or traversing the boundary between the United States and Canada or the boundary between the United States and Mexico, as the case may be, enter and leave the United States at frequent intervals, is excepted from wages and hence is not subject to withholding. Thus, the remuneration of a nonresident alien individual who is a resident of Canada, for services as an employee in connection with the construction, maintenance, or operation of the Saint Lawrence Seaway and who, in the performance of such services, enters and leaves the United States at frequent intervals, is not subject to withholding under section 3402.

(c) *Limitation on application of section.* The exception provided by this section has no application to the remuneration of a resident of Canada or of Mexico who is employed wholly within the United States as, for example, where such a resident is employed to perform service at a fixed point or points in the United States, such as a factory, store, office, or designated area or areas within the United States, and who commutes from his home in Canada or Mexico in the pursuit of his employment within the United States.

(d) *Certificate required.* In order for the exception to apply, the nonresident alien employee must furnish his employer a statement setting forth the employee's name and address and certifying (1) that he is not a citizen of the United States, (2) that he is a resident of Canada or Mexico, as the case may be, and (3) the approximate period of time during which he has had such status. Such statement shall be dated, shall be signed by the employee, and shall contain, or be verified by, a written declaration that it is made under the penalties of perjury. No particular form is prescribed for this statement.

(e) *Effective date.* This section shall not apply with respect to remuneration paid after December 31, 1966. For rules with respect to such remuneration see § 31.3401(a)(6)-1.

○—▶ § 31.3401(a)(8)(A) **Statutory provisions; definitions; wages; remuneration paid for services performed by citizens outside the United States.** [Sec. 3401(a)(8)(A), IRC]

○—▶ § 31.3401(a)(8)(A)-1 (T.D. 6259, filed 10-25-57; republished in T.D. 6516, filed 12-19-60; amended by T.D. 6697, filed 12-16-63.) **Remuneration for services performed outside the United States by citizens of the United States.**

(a) *Remuneration excluded from gross income under section 911*—(1) (i) Remuneration paid for services performed outside the United States for an employer (other than the United States or any agency thereof) by a citizen of the United States does not constitute wages and hence is not subject to withholding, if at the time of payment it is reasonable to believe that such remuneration will be excluded from gross income under the provisions of section 911.

The reasonable belief contemplated by the statute may be based upon any evidence reasonably sufficient to induce such belief, even though such evidence may be insufficient upon closer examination by the district director or the courts finally to establish that the remuneration is excludable from gross income under the provisions of section 911.

The reasonable belief shall be based upon the application of section 911 and the regulations thereunder in Part 1 of this chapter (Income Tax Regulations).

(ii) Remuneration paid by an employer to an employee constitutes wages, and hence is subject to withholding, only to the extent that the remuneration is paid after the aggregate amount which is excludable from the employee's gross income for the taxable year under section 911(c)(1) is ex-

Reg. § 31.3401(a)(8)(A)-1(a)(1)

ceeded. For this purpose, an employer is not required to ascertain information with respect to amounts received by his employee from any other source; but, if the employer has such information, he shall take it into account in determining whether the earned income of the employee is in excess of the applicable limitation. For purposes of section 911(c)(6), relating to an employee who states to the authorities of a foreign country that he is not a resident of that country, the employer is not required to ascertain whether such a statement has been made; but, if an employer knows that such a statement has been made, he shall presume that the employee is not a bona fide resident of that country, unless the employer also knows that the authorities of the foreign country have determined, notwithstanding the statement, that the employee is a resident of that country. For purposes of section 911(a)(1) or (2), relating to bona fide residence in or presence in a foreign country, the reasonable belief contemplated by the statute may be based upon a presumption of such residence or presence, as set forth in subparagraph (2) or (3) of this paragraph.

(2)(i) The employer may, in the absence of cause for a reasonable belief to the contrary, presume that an employee will be a bona fide resident of a foreign country or countries, within the meaning of section 911 (a)(1), for an uninterrupted period which includes each taxable year, or applicable portion thereof, of the employee in respect of which the employee properly executes and furnishes to the employer a statement in the following form:

Statement for claiming benefits of section 911 (a)(1) for calendar year .... or fiscal year beginning .... and ending ....

I have been a bona fide resident of the following foreign country or countries, namely, ..., for an uninterrupted period which began on ...., 19.....

I expect to remain a bona fide resident of a foreign country or countries from the date of this statement until the end of the taxable year in respect of which this statement is executed or, if not for such period, from the date of this statement until the following date within such taxable year, namely, ..., 19.....

I have not stated to the authorities of any foreign country named above that I am not a resident of that country or, if I made such a statement, the authorities of that country thereafter made a determination to the effect that I am a resident of that country.

On the basis of the facts in my case I have good reason to believe that, with respect to the above period of foreign residence falling within the taxable year, I will satisfy the bona fide foreign-residence requirement prescribed by section 911(a)(1) of the Internal Revenue Code of 1954.

In the event I become disqualified for the exclusion provided by section 911(a)(1) in respect of all or part of the above period of foreign residence falling within the taxable year, I will immediately notify my employer, giving sufficient facts to indicate the part, if any, of such period falling within such year in respect of which I am qualified for such exclusion.

I understand that any exemption from withholding of tax permitted by reason of the furnishing of this statement is not a determination by the district director of internal revenue that any remuneration paid to me for any services performed during the taxable year is excludable from gross income under the provisions of section 911(a)(1).

I declare under the penalties of perjury that this statement has been examined by me and to the best of my knowledge and belief is true and correct.

....
(Signature of taxpayer)
Date: ...., 19......

(ii) If the employer was entitled to presume for the two consecutive taxable years immediately preceding an employee's current taxable year that such employee was a bona fide resident of a foreign country or countries for an uninterrupted period which includes such preceding taxable years, he may, if such employee is residing in a foreign country on the first day of such current taxable year, presume, in the absence of cause for a reasonable belief to the contrary, and without obtaining from the employee the statement prescribed in subdivision (i) of this subparagraph, that the employee will be a bona fide resident of a foreign country or countries in such current taxable year.

(3) The employer may, in the absence of cause for a reasonable belief to the contrary, presume that an employee will be present in a foreign country or countries during at least 510 full days during any period of 18 consecutive months, within the meaning of section 911 (a)(2), and that such period includes each taxable year of the employee, or applicable portion of such taxable year, in respect of which the employee properly executes and furnishes to the employer a statement in the following form:

Statement for claiming benefits of section 911(a)(2) for calendar year .... or fiscal year beginning .... and ending ....

Except for occasional absences which have not disqualified me for the benefit of section 911(a)(2) of the Internal Revenue Code of 1954, I have been present in the following foreign country or countries, namely ....
during the period of time which began on ...., 19......

I expect to be present in a foreign country or countries, except for occasional absences not disqualifying me for the benefit of section 911(a)(2), from the date of this statement until the end of the taxable year in respect of which this statement is executed, or, if not for such period, from the date of this statement until the following date within such taxable year, namely, ..., 19......

On the basis of the facts in my case I have good reason to believe that, with respect to the above period of presence in a foreign country or countries falling within the taxable year, I will satisfy the 510 full-day requirement prescribed by section 911(a)(2).

In the event I become disqualified for the exclusion provided by section 911(a) (2) in respect of all or part of the above period of presence in a foreign country or

5-15-72 Collection of Income Tax at Source of Wages **(I.R.C.) 24,240.3**

countries falling within the taxable year, I will immediately notify my employer, giving sufficient facts to indicate the part, if any, of such period falling within such year in respect of which I am qualified for such exclusion.

I understand that any exemption from withholding of tax permitted by reason of the furnishing of this statement is not a determination by the district director of internal revenue that any remuneration paid to me for any services performed during the taxable year is excludable from gross income under the provisions of section 911(a)(2).

I declare under the penalties of perjury that this statement has been examined by me and to the best of my knowledge and belief is true and correct.

....
(Signature of taxpayer)

Date: ...., 19....

(b) *Remuneration subject to withholding of income tax under law of a foreign country or a possession of the United States.* (1) Remuneration paid for services performed in a foreign country or in a possession of the United States for an employer (other than the United States or any agency thereof) by a citizen of the United States does not constitute wages and hence is not subject to withholding, if at the time of the payment of such remuneration the employer is required by the law of any foreign country or of any possession of the United States to withhold income tax upon such remuneration. This paragraph, insofar as it relates to remuneration paid for services performed in a possession of the United States, applies only with respect to remuneration paid on or after August 9, 1955.

(2) Remuneration is not exempt from withholding under this paragraph if the employer is not required by the law of a

Reg. § 31.3401(a)(8)(A)-1(b)(2)

foreign country or of a possession of the United States to withhold income tax upon such remuneration. Mere agreements between the employer and the employee whereby the estimated income tax of a foreign country or of a possession of the United States is withheld from the remuneration in anticipation of actual liability under the law of such country or possession will not suffice.

(3) The exemption from withholding provided by this paragraph does not apply by reason of withholding of income tax pursuant to the law of a territory of the United States, of a political subdivision of a possession of the United States, or of a political subdivision of a foreign state.

(4) For provisions relating to remuneration for services performed by a permanent resident of the Virgin Islands, see paragraph (b)(12) of § 31.3401(a)-1 of the regulations in this subpart.

(c) *Limitation on application of section.* This section has no application to the remuneration paid to a citizen of the United States for services performed outside the United States as an employee of the United States or any agency thereof.

○—→ **§ 31.3401(a)(8)(B) Statutory provisions; definitions; wages; remuneration for services performed in possession of the United States (other than Puerto Rico) by citizen of the United States.** [Sec. 3401(a)(8)(B), IRC]

○—→ **§ 31.3401(a)(8)(B)-1** (T. D. 6259, filed 10-25-57; republished in T.D. 6516, filed 12-19-60.) **Remuneration for services performed in possession of the United States (other than Puerto Rico) by citizen of the United States.**

(a) Remuneration paid for services for an employer (other than the United States or any agency thereof) performed by a citizen of the United States within a possession of the United States (other than Puerto Rico) does not constitute wages and hence is not subject to withholding, if it is reasonable to believe that at least 80 percent of the remuneration to be paid to the employee by such employer during the calendar year will be for such services. The reasonable belief contemplated by section 3401(a)(8)(B) may be based upon any evidence reasonably sufficient to induce such belief, even though such evidence may be insufficient upon closer examination by the district director or the courts finally to establish that at least 80 percent of the remuneration paid by the employer to the employee during the calendar year was for services performed within such a possession of the United States.

(b) This section has no application to remuneration paid to a citizen of the United States for services performed in any possession of the United States as an employee of the United States or any agency thereof.

(c) For provisions relating to remuneration for services performed by a permanent resident of the Virgin Islands, see paragraph (b)(12) of § 31.3401(a)-1.

○—→ **§ 31.3401 (a) (8) (C) Statutory provisions; definitions; wages; remuneration**

for services performed in Puerto Rico by citizen of the United States. [Sec. 3401(a)(8)(C), IRC]

○—→ **§ 31.3401(a)(8)(C)-1** (T.D. 6259, filed 10-25-57; republished in T.D. 6516, filed 12-19-60.) **Remuneration for services performed in Puerto Rico by citizen of the United States.**

(a) Remuneration paid for services performed within Puerto Rico for an employer (other than the United States or any agency thereof) by a citizen of the United States does not constitute wages and hence is not subject to withholding, if it is reasonable to believe that during the entire calendar year the employee will be a bona fide resident of Puerto Rico. The reasonable belief contemplated by section 3401(a)(8)(C) may be based upon any evidence reasonably sufficient to induce such belief, even though such evidence may be insufficient upon closer examination by the district director or the courts finally to establish that the employee was a bona fide resident of Puerto Rico for the entire calendar year.

(b) The employer may, in the absence of cause for a reasonable belief to the contrary, presume that an employee will be a bona fide resident of Puerto Rico during the entire calendar year—

(1) Unless the employee is known by the employer to have maintained his abode at a place outside Puerto Rico at some time during the current or the preceding calendar year; or

(2) In any case where the employee files with the employer a statement (containing a declaration under the penalties of perjury that such statement is true to the best of the employee's knowledge and belief) that such employee has at all times during the current calendar year been a bona fide resident of Puerto Rico and that he intends to remain a bona fide resident of Puerto Rico during the entire remaining portion of such current calendar year.

(c) This section has no application to remuneration paid to a citizen of the United States for services performed in Puerto Rico as an employee of the United States or any agency thereof.

○—→ **§ 31.3401(a)(9) Statutory provisions; definitions; wages; remuneration for services performed by a minister of a church or a member of a religious order.** [Sec. 3401(a)(9), IRC]

○—→ **§ 31.3401(a)(9)-1** (T.D. 6259, filed 10-25-57; republished in T.D. 6516, filed 12-19-60.) **Remuneration for services performed by a minister of a church or a member of a religious order.**

(a) *In general.* Remuneration paid for services performed by a duly ordained, commissioned, or licensed minister of a church in the exercise of his ministry, or by a member of a religious order in the exercise of duties required by such order, is excepted from wages and hence is not subject to withholding.

Reg. § 31.3401(a)(9)-1(a)

(b) *Service by a minister in the exercise of his ministry.* Except as provided in paragraph (c) (3) of this section, service performed by a minister in the exercise of his ministry includes the ministration of sacerdotal functions and the conduct of religious worship, and the control, conduct, and maintenance of religious organizations (including the religious boards, societies, and other integral agencies of such organizations), under the authority of a religious body constituting a church or church denomination. The following rules are applicable in determining whether services performed by a minister are performed in the exercise of his ministry:

(1) Whether service performed by a minister constitutes the conduct of religious worship or the ministration of sacerdotal functions depends on the tenets and practices of the particular religious body constituting his church or church denomination.

(2) Service performed by a minister in the control, conduct, and maintenance of a religious organization relates to directing, managing, or promoting the activities of such organization. Any religious organization is deemed to be under the authority of a religious body constituting a church or church denomination if it is organized and dedicated to carrying out the tenets and principles of a faith in accordance with either the requirements or sanctions governing the creation of institutions of the faith. The term "religious organization" has the same meaning and application as is given to the term for income tax purposes.

(3) (i) If a minister is performing service in the conduct of religious worship or the ministration of sacerdotal functions, such service is in the exercise of his ministry whether or not it is performed for a religious organization.

(ii) The rule in subdivision (i) of this subparagraph may be illustrated by the following example:

Example. M, a duly ordained minister, is engaged to perform service as chaplain at N University. M devotes his entire time to performing his duties as chaplain which include the conduct of religious worship, offering spiritual counsel to the university students, and teaching a class in religion. M is performing service in the exercise of his ministry.

(4) (i) If a minister is performing service for an organization which is operated as an integral agency of a religious organization under the authority of a religious body constituting a church or church denomination, all service performed by the minister in the conduct of religious worship, in the ministration of sacerdotal functions, or in the control, conduct, and maintenance of such organization (see subparagraph (2) of this paragraph) is in the exercise of his ministry.

(ii) The rule in subdivision (i) of this subparagraph may be illustrated by the following example:

Example. M, a duly ordained minister is engaged by the N Religious Board to serve as director of one of its departments. He performs no other service. The N Religious Board is an integral agency of O, a religious organization operating under the authority of a religious body constituting a church denomination. M is performing service in the exercise of his ministry.

(5) (i) If a minister, pursuant to an assignment or designation by a religious body constituting his church, performs service for an organization which is neither a religious organization nor operated as an integral agency of a religious organization, all service performed by him, even though such service may not involve the conduct of religious worship or the ministration

of sacerdotal functions, is in the exercise of his ministry.

(ii) The rule in subdivision (i) of this subparagraph may be illustrated by the following example:

Example. M, a duly ordained minister is assigned by X, the religious body constituting his church, to perform advisory service to Y Company in connection with the publication of a book dealing with the history of M's church denomination. Y is neither a religious organization nor operated as an integral agency of a religious organization. M performs no other service for X or Y. M is performing service in the exercise of his ministry.

(c) *Service by a minister not in the exercise of his ministry.* (1) Section 3401 (a) (9) does not except from wages remuneration for service performed by a duly ordained, commissioned, or licensed minister of a church which is not in the exercise of his ministry.

(2) (i) If a minister is performing service for an organization which is neither a religious organization nor operated as an integral agency of a religious organization and the service is not performed pursuant to an assignment or designation by his ecclesiastical superiors, then only the service performed by him in the conduct of religious worship or the ministration of sacerdotal functions is in the exercise of his ministry. See, however, subparagraph (3) of this paragraph.

(ii) The rule in subdivision (i) of this subparagraph may be illustrated by the following example:

Example. M, a duly ordained minister is engaged by N University to teach history and mathematics. He performs no other service for N although from time to time he performs marriages and conducts funerals for relatives and friends. N University is neither a religious organization nor operated as an integral agency of a religious organization. M is not performing the service for N pursuant to an assignment or designation by his ecclesiastical superiors. The service performed by M for N University is not in the exercise of his ministry. However, service performed by M in performing marriages and conducting funerals is in the exercise of his ministry.

(3) Service performed by a duly ordained, commissioned, or licensed minister of a church as an employee of the United States, or a State, Territory, or possession of the United States, or the District of Columbia, or a foreign government, or a political subdivision of any of the foregoing, is not considered to be in the exercise of his ministry for purposes of the collection of income tax at source on wages, even though such service may involve the ministration of sacerdotal functions or the conduct of religious worship. Thus, for example, service performed by an individual as a chaplain in the Armed Forces of the United States is considered to be performed by a commissioned officer in his capacity as such, and not by a minister in the exercise of his ministry. Similarly, service performed by an employee of a State as a chaplain in a State prison is considered to be performed by a civil servant of the State and not a minister in the exercise of his ministry.

(d) *Service in the exercise of duties required by a religious order.* Service performed by a member of a religious order in the exercise of duties required by such order includes all duties required of the member by the order. The nature or extent of such service is immaterial so long as it is a service which he is directed or required to perform by his ecclesiastical superiors.

○━ § 31.3401(a)(10) Statutory provisions; definitions; wages; remuneration for services in the delivery or distribution of newspapers, shopping news, or magazines. [Sec. 3401(a) (10), IRC]

○━ § 31.3401(a)(10)-1 (T.D. 6259, filed 10-25-57; republished in T.D. 6516, filed 12-19-60.) Remuneration for services in delivery or distribution of newspapers, shopping news, or magazines.

(a) *Services of individuals under age 18.* Remuneration for services performed by an employee under the age of 18 in the delivery or distribution of newspapers, or shopping news, not including delivery or distribution (as, for example, by a regional distributor) to any point for subsequent delivery or distribution, is excepted from wages and hence is not subject to withholding. Thus, remuneration for services performed by an employee under the age of 18 in making house-to-house delivery or sale of newspapers or shopping news, including handbills and other similar types of advertising material, is excepted from wages. The remuneration is excepted irrespective of the form or method thereof. Remuneration for incidental services by the employee who makes the house-to-house delivery, such as services in assembling newspapers, is considered to be within the exception. The exception continues only during the time that the employee is under the age of 18.

(b) *Services of individuals of any age.* Remuneration for services performed by an employee in, and at the time of, the sale of newspapers or magazines to ultimate consumers under an arrangement under which the newspapers or magazines are to be sold by him at a fixed price, his remuneration being based on the retention of the excess of such price over the amount at which the newspapers or magazines are charged to him, is excepted from wages and hence is not subject to withholding. The remuneration is excepted whether or not the employee is guaranteed a minimum amount of remuneration, or is entitled to be credited with the unsold newspapers or magazines turned back. Moreover, the remuneration is excepted without regard to the age of the employee. Remuneration for services performed other than at the time of sale to the ultimate consumer is not within the exception. Thus, remuneration for services of a regional distributor which are antecedent to but not immediately part of the sale to the ultimate consumer is not within the exception. However, remuneration for incidental services by the employee who makes the sale to the ultimate consumer, such as services in assembling newspapers or in taking newspapers or magazines to the place of sale, is considered to be within the exception.

○━ § 31.3401(a)(11) Statutory provisions; definitions; wages; remuneration other than

Reg. § 31.3401(a)(10)-1(b)

in cash for services not in the course of employer's trade or business. [Sec. 3401(a) (11), IRC]

○— § 31.3401(a)(11)-1 (T.D. 6259, filed 10-25-57; republished in T.D. 6516, filed 12-19-60.) **Remuneration other than in cash for service not in the course of employer's trade or business.**

(a) Remuneration paid in any medium other than cash for services not in the course of the employer's trade or business is expected from wages and hence is not subject to withholding. Cash remuneration includes checks and other monetary media of exchange. Remuneration paid in any medium other than cash, such as lodging, food, or other goods or commodities, for services not in the course of the employer's trade or business does not constitute wages. Remuneration paid in any medium other than cash for other types of services does not come within this exception from wages. For provisions relating to cash remuneration for service not in the course of employer's trade or business, see § 31.3401(a) (4)-1.

(b) As used in this section, the term "services not in the course of the employer's trade or business" has the same meaning as when used in § 31.3401(a)(4)-1.

○— § 31.3401(a)(12) **Statutory provisions; definitions; wages; payments from or to certain tax-exempt trusts, or under or to certain annuity plans or bond purchase plans.** [Sec. 3401(a)(12), IRC]

○— § 31.3401(a) (12)-1 (T.D. 6259, filed 10-25-57; republished in T.D. 6516, filed 12-19-60; amended by T.D. 6654, filed 5-27-63 and T.D. 7068, filed 11-10-70.) **Payments from or to certain tax-exempt trusts, or under or to certain annuity plans or bond purchase plans.**

(a) *Payments from or to certain tax-exempt trusts.* The term "wages" does not include any payment made—

(1) By an employer, on behalf of an employee or his beneficiary, into a trust, or

(2) To, or on behalf of, an employee or his beneficiary from a trust,

if at the time of such payment the trust is exempt from tax under section 501 (a) as an organization described in section 401 (a). A payment made to an employee of such a trust for services rendered as an employee of the trust and not as a beneficiary thereof is not within this exclusion from wages. Also, since supplemental unemployment compensation benefits are treated under paragraph (b) (14) of § 31.3401 (a)-1 as if they were wages for purposes of this chapter, this section does not apply to such benefits.

(b) *Payments under or to certain annuity plans.* (1) The term "wages" does not include any payment made after December 31, 1962,—

(i) By an employer, on behalf of an employee or his beneficiary, into an annuity plan, or

(ii) To, or on behalf of, an employee or his beneficiary under an annuity plan, if at the time of such payment the annuity plan is a plan described in section 403 (a).

(2) The term "wages" does not include any payment made before January 1, 1963,—

(i) By an employer, on behalf of an employee or his beneficiary, into an annuity plan, or

(ii) To, or on behalf of, an employee or his beneficiary under an annuity plan, if at the time of such payment the annuity plan meets the requirements of section 401 (a) (3), (4), (5), and (6).

(c) *Payments under or to certain bond purchase plans.* The term "wages" does not include any payment made after December 31, 1962,—

(1) By an employer, on behalf of an employee or his beneficiary, into a bond purchase plan, or

(2) To, or on behalf of, an employee or his beneficiary under a bond purchase plan,

if at the time of such payment the plan is a qualified bond purchase plan described in section 405 (a).

○— § 31.3401 (a) (13) **Statutory provisions; definitions; wages; remuneration for services performed by Peace Corps volunteers.** [Sec. 3401(a)(13), IRC.]

○— § 31.3401 (a) (13)-1 (T.D. 6654, filed 5-27-63; amended by TD 7493, filed 6-29-77.) **Remuneration for services performed by Peace Corps volunteers.**

(a) Remuneration paid after September 22, 1961, for services performed as a volunteer or volunteer leader within the meaning of the Peace Corps Act (22 U.S.C. 2501) is excepted from wages, and hence is not subject to withholding, unless the remuneration is paid pursuant to section 5 (c) or section 6 (1) of the Peace Corps Act.

(b) Sections 5 and 6 of the Peace Corps Act (22 U.S.C. 2504, 2505) provide, in part, as follows:

Sec. 5. *Peace Corps Volunteers* [Peace Corps Act (75 Stat. 613); as amended by sec. 2(b), Act of December 13, 1963 (P.L. 88-200, 77 Stat. 359); sec. 2(a), Act of August 24, 1965, (P.L. 89-134, 79 Stat. 549); sec. 3(a), Act of July 24, 1970 (P.L. 91-352, 84 Stat. 464)]

* * * * * * * *

(c) *Readjustment allowances.* Volunteers shall be entitled to receive a readjustment allowance at a rate not to exceed $75 for each month of satisfactory service as determined by the President; except that, in the cases of volunteers who have one or more minor children at the time of their entering a period of pre-enrollment training, one parent shall be entitled to receive a readjustment allowance at a rate not to exceed $125 for each month of satisfactory service as determined by the President. The readjustment allowance of each volunteer shall be payable on his return to the United States: *Provided, however,* That, under such circumstances as the President may determine, the accrued readjustment allowance, or any part thereof, may be paid to the volunteer, members of his family or others, during the period of his service, or prior to his return to the United States. In the event of the volunteer's death during the period of his service, the amount of any unpaid readjustment allowance shall be paid in accordance with the provisions of section 5582(b) of Title 5. For purposes of the Internal Revenue Code of 1954, a volunteer shall be deemed to be paid and to receive each amount of a readjustment allowance to which he is entitled after December 31, 1964, when such amount is trans-

7-11-77   Collection of Income Tax at Source on Wages   *(I.R.C.)* 24,245

ferred from funds made available under this chapter to the fund from which such readjusment allowance is payable.

* * * * * * * *

Sec. 6. *Peace Corps Volunteer Leaders; number; applicability of chapter; benefits* [Peace Corps Act (75 Stat. 615), as amended by sec. 3, Act of December 13, 1963 (P.L. 88-200, 77 Stat. 360)] The President may enroll in the Peace Corps qualified citizens or nationals of the United States whose services are required for supervisory or other special duties or responsibilities in connection with programs under this chapter (referred to in this Act as "volunteer leaders"). The ratio of the total number of volunteer leaders to the total number of volunteers in service at any one time shall not exceed one to twenty-five. Except as otherwise provided in this Act, all of the provisions of this Act applicable to volunteers shall be applicable to volunteer leaders, and the term "volunteers" shall include "volunteer leaders": *Provided, however,* That—

(1) Volunteer leaders shall be entitled to receive a readjustment allowance at a rate not to exceed $125 for each month of satisfactory service as determined by the President;

* * * * * * * *

O─➤ § 31.3401(a)(14) **Statutory provisions; definitions; wages; group-term life insurance.** [Sec. 3401(a)(14), IRC]

O─➤ § 31.3401(a)(14)-1 (TD 7493, filed 6-29-77.) **Group-term life insurance.**

(a) The cost of group-term life insurance on the life of an employee is excepted from wages, and hence is not subject to withholding. For provisions relating generally to such remuneration, and for reporting requirements with respect to such remuneration, see sections 79 and 6052, respectively, and the regulations thereunder in Part 1 of this chapter (Income Tax Regulations).

(b) The cost of group-term life insurance on the life of an employee's spouse or children is not subject to withholding if it is excludable from the employee's gross income because it is merely incidental. See paragraph (d)(2)(ii)(b) of § 1.61-2 in Part 1 of this chapter (Income Tax Regulations).

O─➤ § 31.3401(a)(15) **Statutory provisions; definitions; wages; moving expenses.** [Sec. 3401(a)(15), IRC]

O─➤ § 31.3401(a)(15)-1 (TD 7493, filed 6-29-77.) **Moving expenses.**

(a) An amount paid to or on behalf of an employee after March 4, 1964, either as an advance or a reimbursement, specifically for moving expenses incurred or expected to be incurred is excepted from wages, and hence is not subject to withholding, if (and to the extent that) at the time of payment it is reasonable to believe that a corresponding deduction is or will be allowable to the employee under section 217. The reasonable belief contemplated by the statute may be based upon any evidence reasonably sufficient to induce such belief, even though such evidence may be insufficient upon closer examination by the district director or the courts finally to establish that a deduction is allowable under section 217. The reasonable belief shall be based upon the application of section 217 and the regulations thereunder in Part 1 of this chapter (Income Tax Regulations). When used in this section, the term "moving expenses" has the same meaning as when used in section 217. See § 1.6041-2(a) in Part 1 of this chapter (Income Tax Regulations), relating to return of information as to payments to employees, and § 31.6051-1(e), relating to the reporting of reimbursements of or payments of certain moving expenses.

(b) Except as otherwise provided in paragraph (a) of this section, or in a numbered paragraph of section 3401(a), amounts paid to or on behalf of an employee for moving expenses constitute wages subject to withholding.

O─➤ § 31.3401(a)(16) **Statutory provisions; definitions; wages; tips.** [Sec. 3401(a)(16), IRC]

O─➤ § 31.3401(a)(16)-1 (T.D. 7001, filed 1-17-69.) **Tips.**

Tips paid to an employee are excepted from wages and hence not subject to withholding if—

(a) The tips are paid in any medium other than cash, or

(b) The cash tips received by an employee in any calendar month in the course of his employment by an employer are less than $20.

However, if the cash tips received by an employee in a calendar month in the course of his employment by an employer amount to $20 or more, none of the cash tips received by the employee in such calendar month are excepted from wages under this section. The cash tips to which this section applies include checks and other monetary media of exchange. Tips received by an employee in any medium other than cash, such as passes, tickets, or other goods or commodities do not constitute wages. If an employee in any calendar month performs services for two or more employers and receives tips in the course of his employment by each employer, the $20 test is to be applied separately with respect to the cash tips received by the employee in respect of his services for each employer and not to the total cash tips received by the employee during the month. As to the time tips are deemed paid, see § 31.3401(f)-1. For provisions relating to the treatment of tips received by an employee prior to 1966, see paragraph (b)(11) of § 31.3401(a)-1.

O─➤ § 31.3401(b) **Statutory provisions; definitions; payroll period.** [Sec. 3401(b), IRC]

O─➤ § 31.3401(b)-1 (T.D. 6259, filed 10-25-57; republished in T.D. 6516, filed 12-19-60 and amended by T.D. 7068, filed 11-10-70.) **Payroll period.**

(a) The term "payroll period" means the period of service for which a payment of wages is ordinarily made to an employee by his employer. It is immaterial that the wages are not always paid at regular intervals. For example, if an em-

Reg. § 31.3401(b)-1(a)

ployer ordinarily pays a particular employee for each calendar week at the end of the week, but if for some reason the employee in a given week receives a payment in the middle of the week for the portion of the week already elapsed and receives the remainder at the end of the week, the payroll period is still the calendar week; or if, instead, that employee is sent on a 3-week trip by his employer and receives at the end of the trip a single wage payment for three weeks' services, the payroll period is still the calendar week, and the wage payment shall be treated as though it were three separate weekly wage payments.

(b) For the purpose of section 3402, an employee can have but one payroll period with respect to wages paid by any one employer. Thus, if an employee is paid a regular wage for a weekly payroll period and in addition thereto is paid supplemental wages (for example, bonuses) determined with respect to a different period, the payroll period is the weekly payroll period. For computation of tax on supplemental wage payments, see § 31.3402(g)-1.

(c) The term "payroll period" also means the period of accrual of supplemental unemployment compensation benefits for which a payment of such benefits is ordinarily made. Thus if benefits are ordinarily accrued and paid on a monthly basis, the payroll period is deemed to be monthly.

(d) The term "miscellaneous payroll period" means a payroll period other than a daily, weekly, biweekly, semimonthly, monthly, quarterly, semiannual, or annual payroll period.

○━ § 31.3401(c) Statutory provisions; definitions; employee. [Sec. 3401(c), IRC]

○━ § 31.3401(c)-1 (T.D. 6259, filed 10-25-57; republished in T.D. 6516, filed 12-19-60; amended by T.D. 7068, filed 11-10-70.) Employee.

(a) The term "employee" includes every individual performing services if the relationship between him and the person for whom he performs such services is the legal relationship of employer and employee. The term includes officers and employees, whether elected or appointed, of the United States, a State, Territory, Puerto Rico, or any political subdivision thereof, or the District of Columbia, or any agency or instrumentality of any one or more of the foregoing.

(b) Generally the relationship of employer and employee exists when the person for whom services are performed has the right to control and direct the individual who performs the services, not only as to the result to be accomplished by the work but also as to the details and means by which that result is accomplished. That is, an employee is subject to the will and control of the employer not only as to what shall be done but how it shall be done. In this connection, it is not necessary that the employer actually direct or control the manner in which the services are performed; it is sufficient if he has the right to do so. The right to discharge is also an important factor indicating that the person possessing that right is an employer. Other factors characteristic of an employer, but not necessarily present in every case, are the furnishing of tools and the furnishing of a place to work to the individual who performs the services. In general, if an individual is subject to the control or direction of another merely as to the result to be accomplished by the work and not as to the means and methods for accomplishing the result, he is not an employee.

(c) Generally, physicians, lawyers, dentists, veterinarians, contractors, subcontractors, public stenographers, auctioneers, and others who follow an independent trade, business, or profession, in which they offer their services to the public, are not employees.

(d) Whether the relationship of employer and employee exists will in doubtful cases be determined upon an examination of the particular facts of each case.

(e) If the relationship of employer and employee exists, the designation or description of the relationship by the parties as anything other than that of employer and employee is immaterial. Thus, if such relationship exists, it is of no consequence that the employee is designated as a partner, coadventurer, agent, independent contractor, or the like.

(f) All classes or grades of employees are included within the relationship of employer and employee. Thus, superintendents, managers, and other supervisory personnel are employees. Generally, an officer of a corporation is an employee of the corporation. However, an officer of a corporation who as such does not perform any services or performs only minor services and who neither receives nor is entitled to receive, directly or indirectly, any remuneration is not considered to be an employee of the corporation. A director of a corporation in his capacity as such is not an employee of the corporation.

(g) The term "employee" includes every individual who receives a supplemental unemployment compensation benefit which is treated under paragraph (b) (14) of § 31.3401 (a)-1 as if it were wages.

(h) Although an individual may be an employee under this section, his services may be of such a nature, or performed under such circumstances, that the remuneration paid for such services does not constitute wages within the meaning of section 3401(a).

○━ § 31.3401(d) Statutory provisions; definitions; employer. [Sec. 3401(d), IRC]

○━ § 31.3401(d)-1 (T.D. 6259, filed 10-25-57; republished in T.D. 6516, filed 12-19-60; amended by T.D. 7068, filed 11-10-70.) Employer.

(a) The term "employer" means any person for whom an individual performs or performed any service, of whatever nature, as the employee of such person.

(b) It is not necessary that the services be continuing at the time the wages are paid in order that the status of employer exist. Thus, for purposes of withholding, a person for whom an individual has performed past services for which he is still receiving wages from such person is an "employer."

(c) An employer may be an individual, a corporation, a partnership, a trust, an estate, a joint-stock company, an association, or a syndicate, group, pool, joint venture, or other unincorporated organization, group, or entity. A trust or estate, rather than the fiduciary acting for or on behalf of the trust or estate, is generally the employer.

(d) The term "employer" embraces not only individuals and organizations engaged in trade or business, but organizations exempt from income tax, such as religious and charitable organizations, educational institutions, clubs, social organizations and societies, as well as the governments of the United States, the States, Territories, Puerto Rico, and the District of Columbia, including their agencies, instrumentalities, and political subdivisions.

(e) The term "employer" also means (except for the purpose of the definition of "wages") any person paying wages on behalf of a nonresident alien individual, foreign partnership, or foreign corporation, not engaged in trade or business within the United States (including Puerto Rico as if a part of the United States).

(f) If the person for whom the services are or were performed does not have legal control of the payment of the wages for such services, the term "employer" means (except for the purpose of the definition of "wages") the person having such control. For example, where wages, such as certain types of pensions or retired pay, are paid by a trust and the person for whom the services were performed has no legal control over the payment of such wages, the trust is the "employer."

(g) The term "employer" also means a person making a payment of a supplemental unemployment compensation benefit which is treated under paragraph (b) (14) of § 31.3401 (a)-1 as if it were wages. For example, if supplemental unemployment compensation benefits are paid from a trust which was created under the terms of a collective bargaining agreement, the trust shall generally be deemed to be the employer. However, if the person making such payment is acting solely as an agent

Reg. § 31.3401(d)-1(g)

for another person, the term "employer" shall mean such other person and not the person actually making the payment.

(h) It is a basic purpose to centralize in the employer the responsibility for withholding, returning, and paying the tax, and for furnishing the statements required under section 6051 and § 31.6051-1. The special definitions of the term "employer" in paragraphs (e), (f), and (g) of this section are designed solely to meet special or unusual situations. They are not intended as a departure from the basic purpose.

○━━ § 31.3401(e) Statutory provisions; definitions; number of withholding exemptions claimed. [Sec. 3401(e), IRC]

○━━ § 31.3401(e)-1 (T.D. 6259, filed 10-25-57; republished in T.D. 6516, filed 12-19-60; amended by T.D. 7423, filed 6-24-76.) Number of withholding exemptions claimed.

(a) The term "number of withholding exemptions claimed" means the number of withholding exemptions claimed in a withholding exemption certificate in effect under section 3402(f) or in effect under section 1622(h) of the Internal Revenue Code of 1939. If no such certificate is in effect, the number of withholding exemptions claimed shall be considered to be zero. The number of withholding exemptions claimed must be taken into account in determining the amount of tax to be deducted and withheld under Section 3402, whether the employer computes the tax in accordance with the provisions of subsection (a) or subsection (c) of section 3402.

(b) The employer is not required to ascertain whether or not the number of withholding exemptions claimed is greater than the number of withholding exemptions to which the employee is entitled. If, however, the employer has reason to believe that the number of withholding exemptions claimed by an employee is greater than the number to which such employee is entitled, the district director should be so advised. For rules relating to invalid withholding exemption certificates, see § 31.3402(f)(2)-1(e).

(c) As to the number of withholding exemptions to which an employee is entitled, see § 31.3402(f)(1)-1.

○━━ § 31.3401(f) Statutory provisions; definitions; tips. [Sec. 3401(f), IRC]

○━━ § 31.3401(f)-1 (T.D. 7001, filed 1-17-69.) Tips.

(a) *Tips considered wages.* Tips received after 1965 by an employee in the course of his employment are considered to be wages, and thus subject to withholding of income tax at source. For an exception to the rule that tips constitute wages, see §§ 31.3401(a)(16) and 31.3401(a)(16)-1, relating to tips paid in a medium other than cash and cash tips of less than $20. For definition of the term "employee", see §§ 31.3401(c) and 31.3401(c)-1.

(b) *When tips deemed paid.* Tips reported by an employee to his employer in a written statement furnished to the employer pursuant to section 6053(a) (see § 31.6053-1) shall be deemed to be paid to the employee at the time the written statement is furnished to the employer. Tips received by an employee which are not reported to his employer in a written statement furnished pursuant to section 6053(a) shall be deemed to be paid to the employee at the time the tips are actually received by the employee.

○━━ § 31.3402(a) Statutory provisions; income tax collected at source; requirement of withholding. [Sec. 3402(a), IRC]

○━━ § 31.3402(a)-1 (T.D. 6259, filed 10-25-57; republished in T.D. 6516, filed 12-19-60; amended by T.D. 7001, filed 1-17-69 and T.D. 7115, filed 5-20-71.) Requirement of withholding.

(a) Section 3402 provides alternative methods, at the election of the employer, for use in computing the amount of income tax to be collected at source on wages. Under the percentage method of withholding (see § 31.3402(b)-1), the employer is required to deduct and withhold a tax computed in accordance with the provisions of section 3402(a). Under the wage bracket method of withholding (see § 31.3402(c)-1), the employer is required to deduct and withhold a tax determined in accordance with the provisions of section 3402(c). The employer may elect to use the percentage method, the wage bracket method, or certain other methods (see § 31.3402(h)(4)-1). Different methods may be used by the employer with respect to different groups of employees.

(b) The employer is required to collect the tax by deducting and withholding the amount thereof from the employee's wages as and when paid, either actually or constructively. Wages are constructively paid when they are credited to the account of or set apart for an employee so that they may be drawn upon by him at any time although not then actually reduced to possession. To constitute payment in such a case, the wages must be credited to or set apart for the employee without any substantial limitation or restriction as to the time or manner of payment or condition upon which payment is to be made, and must be made available to him so that they may be drawn upon at any time, and their payment brought within his own control and disposition.

(c) Except as provided in sections 3402(j) and (k) (see §§ 31.3402(j)-1 and 31.3402(k)-1, relating to noncash remuneration paid to retail commission salesman and to tips received by an employee in the course of his employment, respectively), an employer is required to deduct and withhold the tax notwithstanding the wages are paid in something other than money (for example, wages paid in stocks or bonds; see § 31.3401(a)-1) and to pay over the tax in money. If wages are paid in property other than money, the employer should make necessary arrangements to insure that the amount of the tax required to be withheld is available for payment in money.

(d) For provisions relating to the circumstances under which tax is not required to be deducted and withheld from certain wage payments, see paragraph (b)(8) of § 31.3401(a)-1 relating to amounts paid under wage continuation plans.

(e) As a matter of business administration, certain of the mechanical details of the withholding process may be handled

Reg. § 31.3402(a)-1(e)

24,248 (I.R.C.)   Reg. § 31.3402(a)-1(e)   7-6-76

by representatives of the employer. Thus, in the case of an employer having branch offices, the branch manager or other representative may actually, as a matter of internal administration, withhold the tax or prepare the statements required under section 6051. Nevertheless, the legal responsibility for withholding, paying, and returning the tax and furnishing such statements rests with the employer. For provisions relating to statements under section 6051, see § 31.6051-1.

(f) The amount of any tax withheld and collected by the employer is a special fund in trust for the United States. See section 7501.

○──▶ § 31.3402(a)-2 (T.D. 6860, filed 11-3-65; amended by T.D. 7115, filed 5-20-71; and T.D. 7355, filed 4-22-75.) **Amount of tax to be withheld under percentage method of withholding.**

(a) *Wages paid after December 31, 1969.* (1) Except as otherwise provided in subparagraph (2) of this paragraph, with respect to wages paid after December 31, 1969, the amount of tax to be deducted and withheld under the percentage method of withholding shall be determined in accordance with the tables set forth in section 3402(a), as in effect when such wages are paid.

(2) With respect to wages paid after April 30, 1975, and before January 1, 1976, the amount of tax to be deducted and withheld under the percentage method of withholding shall be determined under the applicable percentage method withholding table contained in Circular E (Employer's Tax Guide).

(b) *Wages paid after April 30, 1966, and before January 1, 1970.* With respect to wages paid after April 30, 1966, and before January 1, 1970, the amount of tax to be deducted and withheld under the percentage method of withholding shall be determined in accordance with the following tables instead of in accordance with the tables set forth in section 3402(a). For purposes of applying such tables, the term "the amount of the wages" means the amount by which the wages exceed the number of withholding exemptions claimed, multiplied by the amount of one such exemption as shown in the table contained in paragraph (a)(1) of § 31.3402(b)-2:

(1) In the case of wages paid after July 13, 1968, and before January 1, 1970: [Tables appear with this Regulation in

P-H Cumulative Changes]

(2) In the case of wages paid after April 30, 1966, and before July 14, 1968: [Tables appear with this Regulation in

P-H Cumulative Changes]

(c) *Wages paid before May 1, 1966.* With respect to wages paid before May 1, 1966, instead of determining the amount of tax to be deducted and withheld in accordance with the tables set forth in section 3402(a), the amount of tax to be deducted and withheld under the percentage method of withholding shall be equal to—

(1) 14 percent with respect to wages paid after March 4, 1964, and before May 1, 1966, and

(2) 18 percent with respect to wages paid before March 5, 1964, of the amount by which the wages exceed the number of withholding exemptions claimed, multiplied by the amount of one such exemption as shown in the table contained in paragraph (a)(2) of § 31.3402(b)-2.

○──▶ § 31.3402(b) **Statutory provisions; income tax collected at source; percentage method of withholding.** [Sec. 3402(b), IRC]

○──▶ § 31.3402(b)-1 (T.D. 6259, filed 10-25-57; republished in T.D. 6516, filed 12-19-60; amended by T.D. 6860, filed 11-3-65 and T.D. 7115, filed 5-20-71.) **Percentage method of withholding.**

(a) *In general.* (1) With respect to wages paid after December 31, 1969, the percentage method of computing the amount of tax to be withheld makes use of the percentage method withholding table contained in section 3402(b)(1). This table shows with respect to each of the designated payroll periods the amount allowable for one withholding exemption. The amount of the withholding exemption allowable with respect to a particular payroll period depends upon the number of withholding exemptions claimed. The term "payroll period" is defined in section 3401 (b) (see § 31.3402(b)-1). The term "number of withholding exemptions claimed" is defined in section 3401(e) (see § 31.3401(e)-1). For tables relating to wages paid before January 1, 1970, see paragraph (a) of § 31.-3402(b)-2.

(2) The steps in computing the tax under the percentage method of withholding with respect to wages paid after December 31, 1969, are summarized as follows:

Step 1. Determine the amount of one withholding exemption for the particular payroll period from the applicable percentage method withholding table in section 3402(b)(1).

Step 2. Multiply the amount determined in Step 1 by the number of exemptions claimed by the employee.

Step 3. Subtract the amount determined in Step 2 from the employee's wages.

Step 4. Compute the income tax to be withheld by applying to the amount determined in Step 3 the amounts shown in the appropriate table in section 3402(a). For steps in computing the tax on wages paid before January 1, 1970, see paragraph (b) of § 31.3402(b)-2.

Example. On May 14, 1971, an employee who has a weekly payroll period is paid $150. He has in effect a withholding exemption certificate claiming three withholding exemptions and indicating that he is married. His employer, using the percentage method, computes the tax to be withheld as follows:

Step 1. Amount of one withholding exemption	$ 12.50
Step 2. Multiplied by number of exemptions claimed on Form W-4	X3
Total withholding exemption	37.50
Step 3. Total wage payment	150.00
Less amount determined in Step 2	37.50
Balance subject to tax	112.50
Step 4. Tax on $77.00 (from table 1(b) in section 3402(a)(3))	9.03
Tax on $35.50 (at 16 percent as determined by such table 1(b))	5.68
Total to be withheld	$ 14.71

(3) For provisions relating to the treatment of wages paid under wage continuation plans and wages paid other than in cash to retail commission salesmen, see paragraph (b)(8) of § 31.3401(a)-1 and § 31.3402(j)-1, respectively.

(b) *Established payroll periods, other than daily or miscellaneous, as shown in percentage method withholding table.* The amount of one withholding exemption and the amount of tax to be withheld, with respect to each of the established payroll periods other than daily or miscellaneous, is determined, respectively, by reference to the line in the percentage method withholding table in section 3402(b)(1) (paragraph (a) of § 31.3402(b)-2, in the case of wages paid before January 1, 1970) which is applicable to the payroll period and to the applicable table set forth in section 3402(a) (paragraph (b) of § 31.3402(a)-2, in the case of wages paid after April 30, 1966, and before January 1, 1970) which is applicable to the payroll period and without reference to the time the employee is actually engaged in the performance of services during the payroll period.

Example (1). Employee A has a semimonthly payroll period. The number of withholding exemptions claimed by A is two. A's wages are determined at the rate of $2 per hour. During a certain payroll period he works only 24 hours and earns $48, which he is paid on April 30, 1971. Although A worked only 24 hours during the semimonthly payroll period, the applicable withholding exemption is $27.10, and the amount of two withholding exemptions, or $54.20, is allowable. Since the amount of the wages paid for the semimonthly payroll period is less than the amount allowed for two withholding exemptions for such period, the employer is not required to withhold any tax.

Example (2). Employee B has a weekly

Reg. § 31.3402(b)-1(b)

Collection of Income Tax at Source on Wages (I.R.C.) 24,249

payroll period. He has in effect a withholding exemption certificate claiming two withholding exemptions and indicating that he is married. B's wages are determined at the rate of $3 per hour. During a certain payroll period B works 24 hours and earns $72, which he is paid on April 30, 1971. Although B worked only 24 hours during the weekly payroll period, the applicable withholding exemption is $12.50, and the amount of two withholding exemptions, or $25, is allowable. The amount of tax to be withheld on the balance of $47, determined in accordance with the applicable table 1(b) in section 3402(a)(3), is $3.93.

(c) *Periods to which the daily or miscellaneous table and withholding exemption are applicable.*—(1) *In general.* The tables designated "Table 8" in section 3402 (a) and paragraph (b) of § 31.3402(a)-2 show for a daily or miscellaneous payroll period for employees who are to be withheld from as single persons and for employees who are to be withheld from as married persons the amount of tax to be withheld with respect to an amount of wages subject to withholding for one day. The percentage method withholding table shows for a daily or miscellaneous payroll period the amount of one withholding exemption allowable with respect to one day. For the purpose of determining the amount of tax to be withheld with respect to wages paid for a particular miscellaneous payroll period (see paragraph (c) of § 31.3401(b)-1), the amount of one withholding exemption shown in the table for one day of such period and the wages paid for the period must be placed on a comparable basis. With respect to wages paid after December 31, 1969, the amount of tax to be withheld shall be determined by the following method:

Step 1. Divide the wages paid to the employee for the period by the number of days (including Sundays and holidays) in the period.

Step 2. Multiply the amount per day shown in the applicable percentage method withholding table by the number of withholding exemptions claimed by the employee.

Step 3. Subtract the amount determined in Step 2 from the amount determined in Step 1.

Step 4. Compute the income tax to be withheld for one day on the amount determined in Step 3 from the applicable table designated Table 8 ((a) or (b), depending on the marital status of the employee indicated on the withholding exemption certificate in effect).

Step 5. Multiply the amount determined in Step 4 by the number of days (including Sundays and holidays) in the period. See paragraph (c) of § 31.3402(b)-2 for the steps in computing the tax on wages paid before January 1, 1970.

(2) *Period not a payroll period.* If wages are paid for a period which is not a payroll period, the amount to be deducted and withheld under the percentage method shall be the amount applicable in the case of a miscellaneous payroll period containing a number of days (including Sundays and holidays) equal to the number of days (including Sundays and holidays) in the period with respect to which such wages are paid.

Example. An individual performs services for a contractor in connection with a construction project. He has in effect a withholding exemption certificate indicating that he claims two withholding exemptions and that he is married. Wages have been fixed at the rate of $36 per day, to be paid upon completion of the project. The project is completed before July 1, 1971, in 12 consecutive days, at the end of which period the individual is paid wages of $360 for 10 days' services performed during the period. Under the percentage method the amount of tax to be withheld is determined as follows:

Step 1. Wages per day ($360 divided by 12) $30.00
Step 2. Amount deducted for withholding exemptions (2 × $1.80) 3.60
Step 3. Balance per day subject to tax 26.40
Step 4. Tax per day 3.84
Step 5. Total tax to be withheld ($3.84 × 12) $46.08

(3) *Wages paid without regard to any period.* If wages are paid to an employee without regard to any particular period, as, for example, commissions paid to a salesman upon consummation of a sale, the amount of tax to be deducted and withheld shall be determined in the same manner as in the case of a miscellaneous payroll period containing a number of days (including Sundays and Holidays) equal to the number of days (including Sundays and Holidays) which have elapsed, beginning with the latest of the following days:

(i) The first day after the last payment of wages to the employee by the employer in the calendar year, or

(ii) The date on which the individual's employment with the employer began in the calendar year, or

(iii) January 1 of the calendar year, and ending with (and including) the date on which the wages are paid.

Example. On April 2, 1971, C is employed by the X Real Estate Co. to sell real estate on a commission basis, commissions to be paid only upon consummation of sales. C has in effect a withholding exemption certificate indicating that he claims one withholding exemption and that he is not married. On May 22, 1971, C receives a commission of $300, his first commission since April 2, 1971. Again, on June 19, 1971, C receives a commission of $420. Under the percentage method, the amount of tax to be deducted and withheld in respect of the commission paid on May 22, is $9.10, which amount is obtained by multiplying $0.182 (tax per day under table 8 (a) in section 3402(a)(3) on wages per day subject to tax of $4.20) by 50 (number of days elapsed); and the amount of tax to be withheld with respect to the commission paid on June 19 is $52.92 which amount is obtained by multiplying $1.89 (tax per day under such table 8(a) on wages per day subject to tax of $13.20) by 28 (number of days elapsed).

(d) *Period or elapsed time less than one week.* (1) It is the general rule that if wages are paid for a payroll period or other period of less than one week, the tax to be deducted and withheld under the per-

Reg. § 31.3402(b)-1(d)(1)

24,250 (I.R.C.) Reg. § 31.3402(b)-1(d)(1) 5-24-71

centage method shall be the amount computed for a daily payroll period, or for a miscellaneous payroll period containing the same number of days (including Sundays and holidays) as the payroll period, other period, for which such wages are paid. In the case of wages paid without regard to any period, if the elapsed time computed as provided in paragraph (c) of this section is less than one week, the same rule is applicable.

Example (1). On May 14, 1971, an employee who has a daily payroll period is paid wages of $20 per day. The employee has in effect a withholding exemption certificate indicating that he claims one withholding exemption and that he is not married. The amount of each such daily wage payment subject to withholding is $18.20 ($20.00 − $1.80). The amount of tax to be deducted and withheld from such payment of wages is $2.81.

Example (2). An employee works for a certain employer on four consecutive days, for which he is paid wages totalling $60 on July 25, 1971. The employee has in effect a withholding exemption certificate indicating that he claims two withholding exemptions and that he is married. The amount of tax to be deducted and withheld under the percentage method is $5.38 (4 × $1.344).

(2) Under certain conditions, if the payroll period, other period, or elapsed time where wages are paid without regard to any period, is less than one week, the employer may, at his election, compute the tax to be withheld as if the aggregate of the wages paid to the employee during the calendar week were paid for a weekly payroll period. Such election may be made by the employer only if he is the only employer for whom the employee works for wages during the calendar week. Any employer electing to compute the tax upon the excess of the wages paid during the calendar week over the weekly exemption must secure a statement in writing from the employee, stating that he works for wages for such employer only, and that if he should thereafter secure additional employment for wages, he will within 10 days after the beginning of such additional employment, notify such employer of that fact. Such statement shall be signed by the employee and shall contain or be verified by a written declaration that it is made under the penalties of perjury. No particular form is prescribed for the statement.

Example. An employee works for a certain employer on four consecutive days, for which he is paid wages totalling $60 on July 25, 1971. The employee has in effect a withholding exemption certificate claiming two withholding exemptions and indicating that he is married. The employer elects to use the weekly withholding exemption after securing the proper statement from the employee. In such case, the amount of the withholding exemption allowable is $25 (2 × $12.50). The amount of tax to be deducted and withheld is $2.10.

(3) If such employee secures additional employment for wages, the daily or miscellaneous exemption will take effect as of the beginning of the first payroll period ending, or the first payment of wages made without regard to a payroll period, on or after the thirtieth day following the date on which such employee notifies such employer that he has secured additional employment for wages. After the daily or miscellaneous exemption takes effect the employer may not thereafter use the weekly exemption in computing the amount of tax to be withheld from the wages of such employee.

(4) As used in this paragraph the term "calendar week" means a period of 7 consecutive days beginning with Sunday and ending with Saturday.

(e) *Rounding off of wage payment*. In determining the amount to be deducted and withheld under the percentage method, the last digit of the wage amount may, at the election of the employer, be reduced to zero, or the wage amount may, at the election of the employer, be computed to the nearest dollar. For the purpose of the computation to the nearest dollar, the payment of a fractional part of a dollar shall be disregarded unless it amounts to one-half dollar or more, in which case it shall be increased to $1.00. Thus, if the weekly wage is $45.37, the employer may, in determining the amount of tax to be deducted and withheld, determine the tax on the basis of a wage payment of $45.30 or on the basis of a wage payment of $45. If the weekly wage is $45.50, the employer may determine the tax to be deducted and withheld on the basis of a wage payment of $46.

§ 31.3402(b)-2 (T.D. 7115, filed 5-20-71.) **Wages paid before January 1, 1970.**

With respect to wages paid before January 1, 1970—

(a) *Percentage method withholding tables*—(1) *Table applicable to wages paid after April 30, 1966, and before January 1, 1970*. With respect to wages paid after April 30, 1966, and before January 1, 1970, the following table shall be used instead of that set forth in section 3402(b)(1):

Percentage Method Withholding Table

Payroll period	Amount of one Withholding exemption:
Weekly	$ 13.50
Biweekly	26.90
Semimonthly	29.20
Monthly	58.30
Quarterly	175.00
Semiannual	350.00
Annual	700.00
Daily or miscellaneous (per day or such period)	1.90

(2) *Table applicable to wages paid before May 1, 1966*. With respect to wages paid before May 1, 1966, the following table shall be used instead of that set forth in section 3402(b)(1):

Percentage Method Withholding Table

Payroll period	Amount of one withholding exemption:
Weekly	$ 13.00
Biweekly	26.00
Semimonthly	28.00
Monthly	56.00
Quarterly	167.00
Semiannual	333.00
Annual	667.00
Daily or miscellaneous (per day of such period)	1.80

(b) *Steps in computing tax*. The total tax to be withheld from wages shall be determined in accordance with the method set

Collection of Income Tax at Source on Wages (I.R.C.) 24,251

forth in paragraph (a)(2) of § 31.3402(b)-1 except that in applying Step 1 the table set forth in paragraph (a) of this section shall be used and that in lieu of Step 4 the amount of tax to be withheld shall be determined by multiplying the amount determined in Step 3 by the applicable percentage figure set forth in paragraph (c) of § 31.3402(a)-2.

(c) *Periods to which the daily or miscellaneous table and withholding exemption are applicable.* (1) The total tax to be withheld from wages paid with respect to a period to which the daily or miscelneous table and withholding exemption are applicable may be determined in accordance with the method set forth in paragraph (c)(1) of § 31.3402(b)-1 except that in applying Step 1 the table set forth in paragraph (a) of this section shall be used and that in lieu of Step 4 the amount of tax per day to be withheld shall be determined by multiplying the amount determined in Step 3 by the applicable percentage figure set forth in paragraph (c) of § 31.3402(a)-2.

(2) In lieu of the method described in the preceding subparagraph, the following method for determining the amount of tax to be withheld on wages paid with respect to a period to which the daily or miscellaneous table and withholding exemption are applicable may be used:

Step 1. Multiply the amount shown in the percentage method withholding table as applicable per day of a miscellaneous payroll period by the number of days (including Sundays and holidays) in such period.

Step 2. Multiply the amount determined in Step 1 by the number of withholding exemptions claimed by the employee.

Step 3. Subtract the amount determined in Step 2 from the employee's wages.

Step 4. Multiply the difference by the applicable percentage figure under paragraph (c) of § 31.3402(a)-2.

○─ § 31.3402(c) Statutory provisions; income tax collected at source; wage bracket withholding. [Sec. 3402(c), IRC]

○─ § 31.3402(c)-1 (T.D. 6259, filed 10-25-57; republished in T.D. 6516, filed 12-19-60; amended by T.D. 6860, filed 11-3-65 and T.D. 7115, filed 5-20-71.) **Wage bracket withholding.**

(a) *In general.* (1) The employer may elect to use the wage bracket method provided in section 3402(c) instead of the percentage method with respect to any employee. The tax computed under the wage bracket method shall be in lieu of the tax required to be deducted and withheld under section 3402(a). With respect to wages paid after July 13, 1968, the correct amount of withholding shall be determined under the applicable wage bracket withholding table contained in the Circular E (Employer's Tax Guide) issued for use with respect to the period in which such wages are paid. For tables relating to wages paid before July 14, 1968, see § 31.3402(c)-2.

(2) For provisions relating to the treatment of wages paid under wage continuation plans and wages paid other than in cash to retail commission salesmen, see paragraph (b)(8) of § 31.3401(a)-1 and § 31.3402(j)-1, respectively.

(b) *Established payroll periods, other than daily or miscellaneous, covered by wage bracket withholding tables.* The wage bracket withholding tables contained in Circular E (§ 31.3402(c)-2, in the case of wages paid before July 14, 1968) for established periods other than daily or miscellaneous should be used in determining the tax to be withheld for any such period without reference to the time the employee is actually engaged in the performance of services during such payroll period.

Example (1). On June 30, 1971, employee A is paid wages for a semimonthly payroll period. A has in effect a withholding exemption certificate indicating that he claims two withholding exemptions and that he is married. A's wages are determined at the rate of $2 per hour. During a certain payroll period he works only 24 hours and earns $48. Although A worked only 24 hours during the semimonthly payroll period, the applicable wage bracket withholding table contained in Circular E for a semimonthly payroll period for an employee who is married should be used in determining the tax to be withheld. Under this table it will be found that no tax is required to be withheld from a wage payment of $48 when two withholding exemptions are claimed.

Example (2). On May 14, 1971, employee B is paid wages for a weekly payroll period. B has in effect a withholding exemption certification indicating that he claims one withholding exemption and that he is single. B's wages are determined at the rate of $2 per hour. During a certain payroll period B works 18 hours and earns $36. Although B worked only 18 hours during the weekly payroll period, the applicable wage bracket withholding table for a weekly payroll period for an employee who is single should be used in determining the tax to be withheld. Under this table it will be found that $0.50 is the amount of tax to be withheld from a wage payment of $36 when one withholding exemption is claimed.

(c) *Periods to which the tables for a daily or miscellaneous payroll period are applicable*—(1) *In general.* The tables applicable to a daily or miscellaneous payroll period show the tax for employees who are to be withheld from as single persons and for employees who are to be withheld from as married persons and on the amount of wages for one day. Where the withholding is computed under the rules applicable to a miscellaneous payroll period, the wages and the amounts shown in the applicable table must be placed on a comparable basis. This may be accomplished by reducing the wages paid for the period to a daily basis by dividing the total wages by the number of days (including Sundays and holidays) in the period. The amount of the tax shown in the applicable table as the tax required to be withheld from the wages, as so reduced to a daily basis, should then be multiplied by the number of days (including Sundays and holidays) in the period.

(2) *Period not a payroll period.* If wages are paid for a period which is not a payroll period, the amount to be deducted and withheld under the wage bracket method shall be the amount applicable in the case of a miscellaneous payroll period containing a number of days (including Sundays and holidays) equal to the number

Reg. § 31.3402(c)-1(c)(2)

24,252 (I.R.C.)   Reg. § 31.3402(c)-1(c)(2)

of days (including Sundays and holidays) in the period with respect to which such wages are paid.

Example. An individual performs services for a contractor in connection with a construction project. He has in effect a withholding exemption certificate indicating that he claims two withholding exemptions and that he is married. Wages have been fixed at the rate of $36 per day, to be paid upon completion of the project. The project is completed before July 1, 1971, in 12 consecutive days, at the end of which period the individual is paid wages of $360 for 10 days' services performed during the period. Under the wage bracket method the amount to be deducted and withheld from such wages is determined by dividing the amount of the wages ($360) by the number of days in the period (12), the result being $30. The amount of tax required to be withheld is determined under the appropriate table applicable to a miscellaneous payroll period for an employee who is married. Under this table the tax required to be withheld is $47.40 (12 × $3.95).

(3) *Wages paid without regard to any period.* If wages are paid to an employee without regard to any particular period, as, for example, commissions paid to a salesman upon consummation of a sale, the amount of tax to be deducted and withheld shall be determined in the same manner as in the case of a miscellaneous payroll period containing a number of days (including Sundays and holidays) equal to the number of days (including Sundays and holidays) which have elapsed, beginning with the latest of the following days:

(i) The first day after the last payment of wages to such employee by such employer in the calendar year, or

(ii) The date on which such individual's employment with such employer began in the calendar year, or

(iii) January 1 of such calendar year, and ending with (and including) the date on which such wages are paid.

Example. On April 2, 1971, C is employed by the X Real Estate Company to sell real estate on a commission basis, commissions to be paid only upon consummation of sales. C has in effect a withholding exemption certificate indicating that he claims one withholding exemption and that he is not married. On May 22, 1971, C receives a commission of $300, his first commission since April 2, 1971. Again, on June 19, 1971, C receives a commission of $420. Under the wage bracket method, the amount of tax to be deducted and withheld in respect of the commission paid on May 22, is $10.00, which amount is obtained by multiplying $0.20 (tax per day under the appropriate wage bracket table applicable to a daily or miscellaneous payroll period for an employee who is not married where wages are at least $6 but less than $6.25 a day) by 50 (number of days elapsed); and the amount of tax to be withheld with respect to the commission paid on June 19 is $54.60, which amount is obtained by multiplying $1.95 (tax under the appropriate wage bracket table for a daily or miscellaneous payroll period where wages are at least $15 but less than $15.50 a day) by 28 (number of days elapsed).

(d) *Period of elapsed time less than one week.* (1) It is the general rule that if wages are paid for a payroll period or other period of less than one week, the tax to be deducted and withheld under the wage bracket method shall be the amount computed for a daily payroll period, or for a miscellaneous payroll period containing the same number of days (including Sundays and holidays) as the payroll period, or other period, for which such wages are paid. In the case of wages paid without regard to any period, if the elapsed time computed as provided in paragraph (c) of this section is less than 1 week, the same rule is applicable.

Example (1). On May 14, 1971, an employee who has a daily payroll period is paid wages of $15 per day. The employee has in effect a withholding exemption certificate indicating that he claims one wtihholding exemption and that he is not married. Under the applicable table for a daily payroll period for an employee who is not married, the amount of tax to be deducted and withheld from each such payment of wages is $1.95.

Example (2). An employee works for a certain employer on four consecutive days for which he is paid wages totalling $60 on July 25, 1971. The employee has in effect a withholding exemption certificate claiming two withholding exemptions and indicating that he is married. The amount of tax to be deducted and withheld under the wage bracket method is $5.60 (4 × $1.40).

(2) If the payroll period, other period, or elapsed time where wages are paid without regard to any period, is less than one week, the employer may, under certain conditions, elect to deduct and withhold the tax determined by the application of the wage table for a weekly payroll period to the aggregate of the wages paid to the employee during the calendar week. The election to use the weekly wage table in such cases is subject to the limitations and conditions prescribed in paragraph (d) of § 31.3402(b)-1 with respect to employers using the percentage method in similar cases.

(3) As used in this paragraph the term "calendar week" means a period of seven consecutive days beginning with Sunday and ending with Saturday.

(e) *Rounding off of wage payment.* In determining the amount to be deducted and withheld under the wage bracket method the wages may, at the election of the employer, be computed to the nearest dollar, provided such wages are in excess of the highest wage bracket of the applicable table. For the purpose of the computation to the nearest dollar, the payment of a fractional part of a dollar shall be disregarded unless it amounts to one-half dollar or more, in which case it shall be increased to $1.00. Thus, if the payroll period of an employee is weekly and the wage payment of such employee is $255.49, the employer may compute the tax on the excess over $200 as if the excess were $55 instead of $55.49. If the weekly wage payment is $255.50, the employer may, in computing the tax, consider the excess over $200 to be $56 instead of $55.50.

○─▶ § 31.3402(c)-2 (T.D. 6860, filed 11-3-65; amended by T.D. 7115, filed 5-20-71.) **Wages paid before July 14, 1968.**

5-24-71 Collection of Income Tax at Source on Wages (I.R.C.) 24,253

(a) With respect to wages paid after April 30, 1966, and before July 14, 1968, the following tables shall be used:

[Tables appear with this Regulation in *P-H Cumulative Changes*]

(b) With respect to wages paid after March 4, 1964, and before May 1, 1966, the following tables shall be used:

[Tables appear with this Regulation in *P-H Cumulative Changes*]

(c) With respect to wages paid before March 5, 1964, the following tables shall be used:

[Tables appear with this Regulation in *P-H Cumulative Changes*]

○― § 31.3402(d) **Statutory provisions; income tax collected at source; tax paid by recipient.** [Sec. 3402(d), IRC]

○― § 31.3402(d)-1 (T.D. 6259, filed 10-25-57; republished in T.D. 6516, filed 12-19-60.) **Failure to withhold.**

If the employer in violation of the provisions of section 3402 fails to deduct and withhold the tax, and thereafter the income tax against which the tax under section 3402 may be credited is paid, the tax under section 3402 shall not be collected from the employer. Such payment does not, however, operate to relieve the employer from liability for penalties or additions to the tax applicable in respect of such failure to deduct and withhold. The employer will not be relieved of his liability for payment of the tax required to be withheld unless he can show that the tax against which the tax under section 3402 may be credited has been paid. See § 31.3403-1, relating to liability for tax.

○― § 31.3402(e) **Statutory provisions, income tax collected at source; included and excluded wages.** [Sec. 3402(e), IRC]

○― § 31.3402(e)-1 (T.D. 6259, filed 10-25-57; republished in T.D. 6516, filed 12-19-60.) **Included and excluded wages.**

(a) If a portion of the remuneration paid by an employer to his employee for services performed during a payroll period of not more than 31 consecutive days constitutes wages, and the remainder does not constitute wages, all the remuneration paid the employee for services performed during such period shall for purposes of withholding be treated alike, that is, either all included as wages or all excluded. The time during which the employee performs services, the remuneration for which under section 3401(a) constitutes wages, and the time during which he performs services, the remuneration for which under such section does not constitute wages, determine whether all the remuneration for services performed during the payroll period shall be deemed to be included or excluded.

(b) If one-half or more of the employee's time in the employ of a particular employer in a payroll period is spent in performing services the remuneration for which constitutes wages, then all the remuneration paid the employee for services performed in that payroll period shall be deemed to be wages.

(c) If less than one-half of the employee's time in the employ of a particular employer in a payroll period is spent in performing services the remuneration for which constitutes wages, then none of the remuneration paid the employee for services performed in that payroll period shall be deemed to be wages.

(d) The application of the provisions of paragraphs (a), (b), and (c) of this section may be illustrated by the following examples:

Example (1). Employer B, who operates a store and a farm, employs A to perform services in connection with both operations. The remuneration paid A for services on the farm is excepted as remuneration for agricultural labor, and the remuneration for services performed in the store constitutes wages. Employee A is paid on a monthly basis. During a particular month, A works 120 hours on the farm and 80 hours in the store. None of the remuneration paid by B to A for services performed during the month is deemed to be wages, since the remuneration paid for less than one-half of the services performed during the month constitutes wages. During another month A works 75 hours on the farm and 120 hours in the store. All of the remuneration paid by B to A for services performed during the month is deemed to be wages since the remuneration paid for one-half or more of the services performed during the month constitutes wages.

Example (2). Employee C is employed as a maid by D, a physician, whose home and office are located in the same building. The remuneration paid C for services in the home is excepted as remuneration for domestic service, and the remuneration paid for her services in the office constitutes wages. C is paid on a weekly basis. During a particular week C works 20 hours in the home and 20 hours in the office. All of the remuneration paid by D to C for services performed during that week is deemed to be wages, since the remuneration paid for one-half or more of the services performed during the week constitutes wages. During another week C works 22 hours in the home and 15 hours in the office. None of the remuneration paid by D to C for services performed during that week is deemed to be wages, since the remuneration paid for less than one-half of the services performed during the week constitutes wages.

(e) The rules set forth in this section do not apply (1) with respect to any remuneration paid for services performed by an employee for his employer if the periods for which remuneration is paid by the employer vary to the extent that there is no period which constitutes a payroll period within the meaning of section 3401(b) (see § 31.3401(b)-1), or (2) with respect to any remuneration paid for services performed by an employee for his employer if the payroll period for which remuneration is paid exceeds 31 consecutive days. In any such case withholding is required with respect to that portion of such remuneration which constitutes wages.

○― § 31.3402(f)(1) **Statutory provisions; income tax collected at source; withholding exemptions.** [Sec. 3402(f)(1), IRC]

○― § 31.3402(f)(1)-1 (T.D. 6259, filed 10-25-57; republished in T.D. 6516, filed 12-19-60; amended by T.D. 6654, filed 5-27-63; T.D. 7065, filed 10-22-70; T.D. 7114, filed

Reg. § 31.3402(f)(1)-1

24,254 (I.R.C.)   Reg. § 31.3402(f)(1)-1

5-17-71 and T.D. 7115, filed 5-20-71.) **Withholding exemptions.**

(a) *In general.* (1) Except as otherwise provided in section 3402 (f) (6) (see § 31.3402 (f) (6)-1), an employee receiving wages shall on any day be entitled to withholding exemptions as provided in section 3402 (f) (1). In order to receive the benefit of such exemptions, the employee must file with his employer a withholding exemption certificate as provided in section 3402 (f) (2). See § 31.3402 (f) (2)-1.

(2) The number of exemptions to which an employee is entitled on any day depends upon his status as single or married, upon his status as to old age and blindness, upon the number of his dependents, upon the number of exemptions claimed by his spouse (if he is married), and upon the number of withholding allowances based on itemized deductions to which he is entitled under section 3402(m).

(b) *Withholding exemptions to which an employee is entitled in respect of himself.* An employee is entitled to one withholding exemption for himself. An employee shall on any day be entitled to an additional withholding exemption for himself if he will have attained the age of 65 before the close of his taxable year which begins in, or with, the calendar year in which such day falls. If the employee is blind, he may claim an additional withholding exemption for blindness. For purposes of claiming a withholding exemption for blindness, an individual shall be considered blind only if his central visual acuity does not exceed 20/200 in the better eye with correcting lenses or if his visual acuity is greater than 20/200 but is accompanied by a limitation in the fields of vision such that the widest diameter of the visual field subtends an angle no greater than 20 degrees. For definition of the term "blindness", see section 151(d)(3). An employee may also be entitled under section 3402(m) to withholding exemptions with respect to withholding allowances for itemized deductions (see § 31.3402(m)-1).

(c) *Withholding exemptions to which an employee is entitled in respect of his spouse.* (1) A married employee, whose spouse is an employee receiving wages, is entitled to claim any withholding exemption to which his spouse is entitled under paragraph (b) of this section, unless the spouse has in effect a withholding exemption certificate claiming such withholding exemption. A married employee, whose spouse is not an employee receiving wages, is entitled to claim any withholding exemption to which his spouse would be entitled under paragraph (b) of this section if the spouse were an employee receiving wages.

Example (1). Assume that both the husband and wife have attained the age of 65 and are employees receiving wages. Each spouse is entitled under paragraph (b) of this section to claim 2 withholding exemptions in respect of himself or herself. Either spouse may claim, in addition to the withholding exemptions to which he or she is entitled in respect of himself or herself, any withholding exemption to which the other spouse is entitled under such paragraph (b) but does not claim on a withholding exemption certificate.

Example (2). Assume the same facts as in Example (1) except that only the husband is an employee receiving wages. The husband is entitled to claim 4 withholding exemptions, that is, the 2 withholding exemptions to which he is entitled in respect of himself and the 2 withholding exemptions to which his spouse would be entitled under paragraph (b) of this section if she were an employee receiving wages.

(2) In determining the number of withholding exemptions to which an employee is entitled for himself and his spouse on any day, the employee's status as a single person or a married person and, if married, whether a withholding exemption is claimed by his spouse, shall be determined as of such day. However, in the case of an employee whose spouse dies in the taxable year of the employee which begins in, or with, the calendar year in which the spouse dies, any withholding exemption which would be allowable to the employee in respect of such spouse, if living and not an employee receiving wages, may be claimed by the employee for that portion of the calendar year which occurs after his spouse's death. For provisions applicable in the case of an employee whose taxable year is not a calendar year, and whose spouse dies in that portion of the calendar year which precedes the first day of the taxable year of the employee which begins in the calendar year, see paragraph (b) of § 31.3402(f)(2)-1. An employee legally separated from his spouse under a decree of divorce or of separate maintenance or an employee who is a surviving spouse (as defined in section 2 and the regulations thereunder) shall not be entitled to any withholding exemptions in respect of his spouse.

(d) *Withholding exemptions to which an employee is entitled in respect of dependents.* Subject to the limitations stated in this paragraph, an employee shall be entitled on any day to a withholding exemption for each individual who may reasonably be expected to be his dependent for his taxable year beginning in, or with, the calendar year in which such day falls. For purposes of the withholding exemption for an individual who may reasonably be expected to be a dependent, the following rules shall apply:

(1) The determination that an individual may or may not reasonably be expected to be a dependent shall be made on the basis of facts existing at the beginning of the day for which a withholding exemption for such individual is to be claimed. The individual in respect of whom an exemption is claimed by an employee must, on the day in question, be in existence and be within one of the categories listed in section 152(a), which defines the term "dependent." However, a withholding exemption for a dependent who dies continues for the portion of the calendar year which occurs after the dependent's death, except that, in the case of an employee whose taxable year is not a calendar year, the withholding exemption does not continue for a dependent, within the meaning of section 152(a)(9) or (10), whose death occurs before the first day of the employee's taxable year beginning in the calendar year of death.

(2) The determination that an individual may or may not reasonably be expected to be a dependent shall be made for the taxable year of the employee in respect of which amounts deducted and withheld in the calendar year in which the day in question falls are allowed as a credit. In

general, amounts deducted and withheld during any calendar year are allowed as a credit against the tax imposed by chapter 1 of the Code for the taxable year which begins in, or with, such calendar year. Thus, in order for an employee to be able to claim for a calendar year a withholding exemption with respect to a particular individual as a dependent there must be a reasonable expectation that the employee will be allowed an exemption with respect to such individual under section 151(e) for his taxable year which begins in, or with, such calendar year.

(3) For the employee to be entitled on any day of the calendar year to a withholding exemption for an individual as a dependent, such individual must on such day—

(i) Be an individual referred to in one of the numbered paragraphs in section 152(a),

(ii) Reasonably be expected to receive over one-half of his support, within the meaning of section 152, from the employee in the calendar year, and

(iii) Either *(a)* reasonably be expected to have gross income of less than the amount determined pursuant to § 1.151-2 of Part 1 of this chapter (Income Tax Regulations) applicable to the calendar year in which the taxable year of the taxpayer begins, or *(b)* be a child (son, stepson, daughter, stepdaughter, adopted son, or adopted daughter) of the employee who *(1)* will not have attained the age of 19 at the close of the calendar year or *(2)* is a student as defined in section 151.

(4) An employee is not entitled to claim a withholding exemption for an individual otherwise reasonably expected to be a dependent of the employee if such individual is not a citizen of the United States, unless such individual (i) is at any time during the calendar year a resident of the United States, Canada, Mexico, the Canal Zone, or the Republic of Panama, or (ii) is a child of the employee born to him or legally adopted by him, in the Philippine Islands before January 1, 1956, and the child is a resident of the Republic of the Philippines, and the employee was a member of the Armed Forces of the United States at the time the child was born to him or legally adopted by him.

○→ § 31.3402(f)(2) **Statutory provisions; income tax collected at source; withholding exemptions; exemption certificates.** [Sec. 3402(f)(2), IRC]

○→ § 31.3402(f)(2)-1 (T.D. 6259, filed 10-25-57; republished in T.D. 6516, filed 12-19-60; amended by T.D. 6606, filed 8-24-62; T.D. 6654, filed 5-27-63; T.D. 7048, filed 6-23-70; T.D. 7065, filed 10-22-70; T.D. 7423, filed 6-24-76.) **Withholding exemption certificates.**

(a) *On commencement of employment.* On or before the date on which an individual commences employment with an employer, the individual shall furnish the employer with a signed withholding exemption certificate relating to his marital status and the number of withholding exemptions which he claims, which number shall in no event exceed the number to which he is entitled, or, if the statements described in § 31.3402(n)-1 are true with respect to an individual, he may furnish his employer with a signed withholding exemption certificate which contains such statements in lieu of the first-mentioned certificate. For form and contents of such certificates, see § 31.3402 (f) (5)-1. The employer is required to request a withholding exemption certificate from each employee, but if the employee fails to furnish such certificate, such employee shall be considered as a single person claiming no withholding exemptions.

(b) *Change in status which affects calendar year.* (1) If, on any day during the calendar year, the number of withholding exemptions to which the employee is entitled is less than the number of withholding exemptions claimed by him on the withholding exemption certificate then in effect, the employee must within 10 days after the change occurs furnish the employer with a new withholding exemption certificate relating to the number of withholding exemptions which the employee then claims, which must in no event exceed the number to which he is entitled on such day. The number of withholding exemptions to which an employee is entitled decreases, for example, for any one of the following reasons:

(i) The employee's wife (or husband) for whom the employee has been claiming a withholding exemption (a) is divorced or legally separated from the employee, or (b) claims her (or his) own withholding exemption on a separate certificate.

(ii) In the case of an employee whose taxable year is not a calendar year, the employee's wife (or husband) for whom the employee has been claiming a withholding exemption dies in that portion of the calendar year which precedes the first day of the taxable year of the employee which begins in the calendar year in which the spouse dies.

(iii) The employee finds that no exemption for his taxable year which begins in, or with, the current calendar year will be allowable to him under section 151(e) in respect of an individual claimed as a dependent on the employee's withholding exemption certificate.

(iv) It becomes unreasonable for the employer to believe that his wages for an estimation year will not be more, or that his itemized deductions for an estimation year will not be less, than the corresponding figure used in connection with a claim by him under section 3402(m) of a withholding allowance for itemized deductions to such an extent that the employee would no longer be entitled to such withholding allowance.

(v) It becomes unreasonable for an employee who has in effect a withholding exemption certificate on which he claims a withholding allowance for itemized deductions under section 3402(m), computed on the basis of the preceding taxable year, to believe that his wages and itemized deductions in such preceding taxable year or in his present taxable year will entitle him to such withholding allowance in the present taxable year.

(2) If, on any day during the calendar year, the number of withholding exemptions to which the employee is entitled is more than the number of withholding exemptions claimed by him on the withholding exemption certificate then in effect, the employee may furnish the employer with a new withholding exemption certificate on which the employee must in no event claim

Reg. § 31.3402(f)(2)-1(b)(2)

24,254.2 (I.R.C.) Reg. § 31.3402(f)(2)-1(b)(2)   7-6-76

more than the number of withholding exemptions to which he is entitled on such day.

(3) If, on any day during the calendar year, the statements described in § 31.3402 (n)-1 are true with respect to an employee, such employee may furnish his employer with a withholding exemption certificate which contains such statements.

(4) If, on any day during the calendar year, it is not reasonable for an employee, who has furnished his employer with a withholding exemption certificate which contains the statements described in § 31.3402 (n)-1, to anticipate that he will incur no liability for income tax imposed under subtitle A (as defined in § 31.3402 (n)-1 for his current taxable year, the employee must within 10 days after such day furnish the employer with a new withholding exemption certificate which does not contain such statements. If, on any day during the calendar year, it is not reasonable for such an employee whose liability for income tax imposed under subtitle A is determined on a basis other than the calendar year to so anticipate with respect to his taxable year following his current taxable year, the employee must furnish the employer with a new withholding exemption certificate which does not contain such statements within 10 days after such day or on or before the first day of the last month of his current taxable year, whichever is later.

(c) *Change in status which affects next calendar year.* (1) If, on any day during the calendar year, the number of exemptions to which the employee will be, or may reasonably be expected to be, entitled under sections 151 and 3402(m) for his taxable year which begins in, or with, the next calendar year is different from the number to which the employee is entitled on such day, the following rules shall be applicable:

(i) If such number is less than the number of withholding exemptions claimed by the employee on a withholding exemption certificate in effect on such day, the employee must, on or before December 1 of the year in which the change occurs, unless such change occurs in December, furnish his employer with a new withholding exemption certificate reflecting the decrease in the number of withholding exemptions. If the change occurs in December, the new certificate must be furnished within 10 days after the change occurs. The number of exemptions to which an employee is entitled for his taxable year which begins in, or with, the next calendar year decreases, for example, for any of the following reasons:

(a) The spouse or a dependent of the employee dies.

(b) The employee finds that it is not reasonable to expect that an individual claimed as a dependent on the employee's withholding exemption certificate will qualify as a dependent of the employee for such taxable year.

(c) It becomes unreasonable for an employee who has in effect a withholding exemption certificate on which he claims a withholding allowance for itemized deductions under section 3402(m) to believe that his wages and itemized deductions for his taxable year which begins in, or with, the next calendar year will entitle him to such withholding allowance for such taxable year.

(ii) If such number is greater than the number of withholding exemptions claimed by the employee on a withholding exemption certificate in effect on such day, the employee, may, on or before December 1 of the year in which such change occurs, unless such change occurs in December, furnish his employer with a new withholding exemption certificate reflecting the increase in the number of withholding exemptions. If the change occurs in December, the certificate may be furnished on or after the date on which the change occurs.

(2) If, on any day during the calendar year, it is not reasonable for an employee, who has furnished his employer with a withholding exemption certificate which contains the statements described in § 31.3402 (n)-1 and whose liability for such tax is determined on a calendar-year basis, to anticipate that he will incur no liability for income tax imposed under subtitle A (as defined in § 31.3402 (n)-1) for his taxable year which begins with the next calendar year, the employee must furnish his employer with a new withholding exemption certificate which does not contain such statements, on or before December 1 of the first-mentioned calendar year. If it first becomes unreasonable for the employee to so anticipate in December, the new certificate must be furnished within 10 days after the day on which it first becomes unreasonable for the employee to so anticipate.

(3) Before December 1 of each year, every employer should request each of his employees to file a new withholding exemption certificate for the ensuing calendar year, in the event of change in the employee's exemption status since the filing of his latest certificate.

(d) *Inclusion of account number on withholding exemption certificate.* Every individual to whom an account number has been assigned shall include such number on any withholding exemption certificate filed with an employer. For provisions relating to the obtaining of an account number, see § 31.6011 (b)-2.

(e) *Invalid withholding exemption certificates.* Any alteration of or unauthorized addition to a withholding exemption certificate shall cause such certificate to be invalid; see paragraph (b) of § 31.3402(f) (5)-1 for the definitions of alteration and unauthorized addition. Any withholding exemption certificate which the employee clearly indicates to be false by an oral statement or by a written statement (other than one made on the withholding exemption certificates itself) made by him to the employer on or before the date on which the employee furnishes such certificate is also invalid. For purposes of the preceding sentence, the term "employer" includes any individual authorized by the employer either to receive withholding exemption certificates, to make withholding computations, or to make payroll distributions. If an employer receives an invalid withholding exemption certificate, he shall consider it a nullity for purposes of computing withholding; he shall inform the employee who submitted the certificate that it is invalid, and shall request another withholding exemption certificate from the employee. If the employee who submitted the invalid certificate fails to comply with the employer's request, the employer shall withhold from the employee as from a single person claiming no exemptions (see § 31.3402(f)(2)-1(a)); if, however, a prior certificate is in effect with respect to the employee, the employer shall continue to withhold in accordance with the prior certificate. For instructions to employers who receive valid withholding exemption certificates which they have reason to believe may be incorrect, see § 31.3401(e)-1(b) and § 31.3402(n)-1. This paragraph applies only with respect to withholding exemption certificates received by an employer after July 26, 1976.

○━ § 31.3402(f)(3) **Statutory provisions; income tax collected at source; withholding exemptions; when exemption certificate takes effect. [Sec. 3402(f)(3), IRC]**

○━ § 31.3402(f)(3)-1 (T.D. 6259, filed 10-25-57; republished in T.D. 6516, filed 12-19-60; further amended by T.D. 7048, filed 6-23-70; T.D. 7065, filed 10-22-70 and T.D. 7115, filed 5-20-71.) **When withholding exemption certificate takes effect.**

(a) A withholding exemption certificate furnished the employer in any case in which no previous withholding exemption certificate is in effect with such employer, shall take effect as of the beginning of the first payroll period ending, or the first payment of wages made without regard to a payroll period, on or after the date on which such certificate is so furnished.

(b) A withholding exemption certificate furnished the employer in any case in which a previous withholding exemption certificate is in effect with such employer shall, except as hereinafter provided, take effect with respect to the first payment of wages made on or after the first status determination date which occurs at least 30 days after the date on which such certificate is so furnished. However, at the election of the employer, except as hereinafter provided, such certificate may be made effective with respect to any payment of wages made on or after the date on which such certificate is so furnished and before such status determination date.

(c) A withholding exemption certificate furnished the employer pursuant to section 3402(f)(2)(C) (see paragraph (c) of § 31.3402(f)(2)-1 or paragraph (b)(2)(ii) of § 31.3402(1)-1)) which effects a change for the next calendar year, shall not take effect, and may not be made effective, with respect to the calendar year in which the certificate is furnished. A withholding exemption certificate furnished the employer by an employee who determines his income tax liability on a basis other than a calendar-year basis, as required by paragraph (b)(4) of § 31.3402(f)(2)-1, which effects a change for the employee's next taxable year, shall not take effect, and may not be made effective, with respect to the taxable year of the employee in which the certificate is furnished.

(d) For purposes of this section, the term "status determination date" means January 1, May 1, July 1, and October 1 of each year. However, with respect to dates before March 15, 1966, the term "status determination date" means January 1 and July 1 of each year.

(e) Notwithstanding paragraph (b) of this section, a withholding exemption certificate furnished the employer after March 15, 1966, and before May 1, 1966, shall take effect with respect to the first payment of wages made on or after May 1, 1966, or the 10th day after the date on which such certificate is furnished to the employer, whichever is later, and at the election of the employer, such certificate may be made effective with respect to any payment of wages made on or after the date on which such certificate is furnished.

○━ § 31.3402(f)(4) **Statutory provisions; income tax collected at source; withholding exemptions; period during which exemption certificate remains in effect. [Sec. 3402(f)(4), IRC]**

○━ § 31.3402(f)(4)-1 (T.D. 6259, filed 10-25-57; republished in T.D. 6516, filed 12-19-60; further amended by T.D. 7048, filed 6-23-70 and T.D. 7065, filed 10-22-70.) **Period during which withholding exemption certificate remains in effect.**

(a) *In general.* Except as provided in paragraphs (b) and (c) of this section, a withholding exemption certificate which takes effect under section 3402(f) of the Internal Revenue Code of 1954, or which on December 31, 1954, was in effect under section 1622(h) of the Internal Revenue Code of 1939, shall continue in effect with respect to the employee until another withholding exemption certificate takes effect under section 3402(f).

(b) *Withholding allowances under section 3402(m) for itemized deductions.* In no case shall the portion of a withholding exemption certificate relating to withholding allowances under section 3402(m) for itemized deductions be effective with respect to any payment of wages made to an employee—

(1) In the case of an employee whose liability for tax under subtitle A of the Code is determined on a calendar-year basis, after April 30 of the calendar year immediately following the calendar year which was his estimation year for purposes of determining the withholding allowance or allowances claimed on such exemption certificate, or

(2) In the case of an employee to whom subparagraph (1) of this paragraph does not apply, after the last day of the fourth month immediately following his taxable year which was his estimation year for purposes of determining the withholding allowance or allowances claimed on such exemption certificate.

(c) *Statements under section 3402(n) eliminating requirement of withholding.* The statements described in § 31.3402(n)-1 made by an employee with respect to his preceding taxable year and current taxable year shall be deemed to have been made also with respect to his current taxable year and his taxable year immediately thereafter, respectively, until either a new withholding exemption certificate furnished by the employee takes effect or the existing certificate which contains such statements expires. In no case shall a withholding exemption certificate which contains such statements be effective with respect to any payment of wages made to an employee—

(1) In the case of an employee whose liability for tax under subtitle A is determined on a calendar-year basis, after April 30 of the calendar year immediately following the calendar year which was his original current taxable year for purposes of such statements, or

Reg. § 31.3402(f)(4)-1(c)(1)

24,254.4 (I.R.C.)   Reg. § 31.3402(f)(4)-1(c)(2)   7-6-76

(2) In the case of an employee to whom subparagraph (1) of this paragraph does not apply, after the last day of the fourth month immediately following his original current taxable year for purposes of such statements.

○—▶ § 31.3402(f)(5) Statutory provisions; income tax collected at source; withholding exemptions; form and contents of exemption certificate. [Sec. 3402(f)(5), IRC]

○—▶ § 31.3402(f)(5)-1 (T.D. 6259, filed 10-25-57; republished in T.D. 6516, filed 12-19-60; amended by T.D. 7048, filed 6-23-70; T.D. 7423, filed 6-24-76.) Form and contents of withholding exemption certificate.

(a) Forms W-4 and W-4E are the forms prescribed for the withholding exemption certificate required to be filed under section 3402(f)(2). Form W-4 is the form to be used unless the employee desires, in accordance with the provisions of § 31.3402(f)(2)-1, to use a withholding exemption certificate which contains the statements described in § 31.3402(n)-1, in which case Form W-4E is the form to be used. A withholding exemption certificate shall be prepared in accordance with the instructions and regulations applicable thereto, and shall set forth fully and clearly the data therein called for. Blank copies of Forms W-4 and W-4E will be supplied employers upon request to the district director. In lieu of the prescribed form, employers may prepare and use a form the provisions of which are identical with those of the prescribed form.

(b) A Form W-4 or W-4E does not meet the requirements of section 3402(f)(5) or this section and is invalid if it contains an alteration or unauthorized addition. For purposes of § 31.3402(f)(2)-1(e) and this paragraph—

(1) An alteration of a withholding exemption certificate is any deletion of the language of the jurat or other similar provision of such certificate by which the employee certifies or affirms the correctness of the completed certificate, or any material defacing of such certificate;

(2) An unauthorized addition to a withholding exemption certificate is any writing on such certificate other than the entries requested (e.g., name, address, and number of exemptions claimed).

○—▶ § 31.3402(f)(6) Statutory provisions; income tax collected at source; withholding exemptions; certain nonresident aliens. [Sec. 3402 (f) (6), IRC]

○—▶ § 31.3402(f)(6)-1 (T.D. 6654, filed 5-27-63; amended by T.D. 6908, filed 12-30-66.) Withholding exemption for nonresident alien individuals.

A nonresident alien individual subject to withholding under section 3402 is on any 1 day entitled under section 3402(f)(1) and § 31.3402(f)(1)-1 to the number of withholding exemptions corresponding to the number of personal exemptions to which he is entitled on such day by reason of the application of section 873(a)(3) or section 876, whichever applies. Thus, a nonresident alien individual who is not a resident of Canada or Mexico and who is not a resident of Puerto Rico during the entire taxable year, is allowed under section 3402(f)(1) only one withholding exemption.

○—▶ § 31.3402(g) Statutory provisions; income tax collected at source; overlapping pay periods, and payment by agent or fiduciary. [Sec. 3402(g), IRC]

○—▶ § 31.3402(g)-1 (T.D. 6259, filed 10-25-57; republished in T.D. 6516, filed 12-19-60; amended by T.D. 6860, filed 11-3-65 and T.D. 6882, filed 4-11-66.) Supplemental wage payments.

(a) *In general.* (1) An employee's remuneration may consist of wages paid for a payroll period and supplemental wages, such as bonuses, commissions, and overtime pay, paid for the same or a different period, or without regard to a particular period. When such supplemental wages are paid (whether or not at the same time as the regular wages) the amount of the tax required to be withheld under section 3402-(a) (the percentage method) or under section 3402(c) (the wage bracket method) shall be determined in accordance with this paragraph or paragraph (b) of this section.

(2) The supplemental wages, if paid concurrently with wages for a payroll period, shall be aggregated with the wages paid for such payroll period. If not paid concurrently, the supplemental wages shall be aggregated with the wages paid or to be paid within the same calendar year for the last preceding payroll period or for the current payroll period. The amount of tax to be withheld shall be determined as if the aggregate of the supplemental wages and the regular wages constituted a single wage payment for the regular payroll period.

Example (1). A, a single person, is employed as a salesman at a monthly salary of $130 plus commissions on sales made during the month. The number of withholding exemptions claimed is one. During May 1966 A earns $300 in commissions, which together with the salary of $130 is paid on June 10, 1966. Under the wage bracket method the amount of the tax required to be withheld is shown in the table applicable to a monthly payroll period with respect to an employee who is not married. Under this table it will be found that the amount of tax required to be withheld is $58.40.

Example (2). B, a married person, is employed at a salary of $3,600 per annum paid semimonthly on the 15th day and the last day of each month, plus a bonus and commission determined at the end of each 3-month period. The bonus and commission for the 3-month period ending on September 30, 1966, amount to $250, which is paid on October 10, 1966. B has in effect a withholding exemption certificate on which he claimed four withholding exemptions and disclosed that he is married. Under the wage bracket method, the amount of tax required to be withheld on the aggregate of the bonus of $250 and the last preceding semimonthly wage payment of $150, or $400, is shown in the table applicable to a married person with a semimonthly payroll period to be $44.50. However, since tax in the amount of $3.50 was withheld on the semimonthly wage payment of $150, the amount to be withheld on October 10, 1966, the amount to be withheld on October 10, 1966, is $41.00.

If however, supplemental wages are paid and tax has been withheld from the employee's regular wages, the employer may determine the tax to be withheld—

(i) From supplemental wages paid prior

Collection of Income Tax at Source on Wages (I.R.C.) 24,255

to May 1, 1966, by using the rate in effect under section 3402(a) at the time the wages are paid, and

(ii) From supplemental wages paid after April 30, 1966, by using a flat percentage rate of 20 percent, without allowance for exemption and without reference to any regular payment of wages.

(3) For provisions relating to the treatment of wages paid other than in cash to retail commission salesmen, see: § 31.-3402(j)-1.

(b) *Special rule where aggregate withholding exemption exceeds wages paid.* (1) If supplemental wages are paid to an employee during a calendar year for a period which involves two or more consecutive payroll periods, for which other wages also are paid during such calendar year, and the aggregate of such other wages is less than the aggregate of the amounts determined under the table provided in section 3402(b)(1) as the withholding exemptions applicable for such payroll periods, the amount of the tax required to be withheld on the supplemental wages shall be computed as follows:

Step 1. Determine an average wage for each of such payroll periods by dividing the sum of the supplemental wages and the wages paid for such payroll periods by the number of such payroll periods.

Step 2. Determine a tax for each payroll period as if the amount of the average wage constituted the wages paid for such payroll period.

Step 3. From the sum of the amounts of tax determined in Step 2 subtract the total amount of tax withheld, or to be withheld, from the wages, other than the supplemental wages, for such payroll periods. The remainder, if any, shall constitute the amount of the tax to be withheld upon the supplemental wages.

Example. An employee has a weekly payroll period ending on Saturday of each week, the wages for which are paid on Friday of the succeeding week. On the 10th day of each month he is paid a bonus based upon production during the payroll periods for which wages were paid in the preceding month. The employee is paid a weekly wage of $64 on each of the five Fridays occurring in July 1966. On August 10, 1966, the employee is paid a bonus of $125 based upon production during the five payroll periods covered by the wages paid in July. On the date of payment of the bonus, the employee, who is married and has three children, has a withholding exemption certificate in effect indicating that he is married and claiming five withholding exemptions. The amount of the tax to be withheld from the bonus paid on August 10, 1966, is computed as follows:

Wages paid in July 1966 for 5 payroll periods (5 × $64)	$320.00
Bonus paid August 10, 1966	125.00
Aggregate of wages and bonus	$445.00
Average wage per payroll period ($445 ÷ 5)	$ 89.00
Computation of tax under percentage method: Withholding exemptions (5 × $13.50)	$ 67.50
Remainder subject to tax	$ 21.50
Tax on average wage for 1 week under percentage method of withholding (married person with weekly payroll period) (14 percent of $17.50 (excess over $4))	$ 2.45
Tax on average wage for 5 weeks	$ 12.25
Less: Tax previously withheld on weekly wage payments of $64	None
Tax to be withheld on supplemental wages	$ 12.25
Computation of tax under wage bracket method: Tax on $89 wage under weekly wage table for married person ($2.50 per week for 5 weeks)	$ 12.50
Less: Tax previously withheld on weekly wage payments of $64	None
Tax to be withheld on supplemental wages	$ 12.50

(2) The rules prescribed in this paragraph shall, at the election of the employer, be applied in lieu of the rules prescribed in paragraph (a) of this section except that this paragraph shall not be applicable in any case in which the payroll period of the employee is less than one week.

(c) *Vacation allowances.* Amounts of so-called "vacation allowances" shall be subject to withholding as though they were regular wage payments made for the period covered by the vacation. If the vacation allowance is paid in addition to the regular wage payment for such period, the rules applicable with respect to supplemental wage payments shall apply to such vacation allowance.

○━ § 31.3402(g)-2 (T.D. 6259, filed 10-25-57; republished in T.D. 6516, filed 12-19-60.) **Wages paid for payroll period of more than one year.**

If wages are paid to an employee for a payroll period of more than one year, for the purpose of determining the amount of tax required to be deducted and withheld in respect of such wages—

(a) Under the percentage method, the amount of the tax shall be determined as if such payroll period constituted an annual payroll period, and

(b) Under the wage bracket method, the amount of the tax shall be determined as if such payroll period constituted a miscellaneous payroll period of 365 days.

○━ § 31.3402(g)-3 (T.D. 6259, filed 10-25-57; republished in T.D. 6516, filed 12-19-60.) **Wages paid through an agent, fiduciary, or other person on behalf of two or more employers.**

(a) If a payment of wages is made to an employee by an employer through an agent, fiduciary, or other person who also has the control, receipt, custody, or disposal of, or pays the wages payable by another employer to such employee, the amount of the tax required to be withheld on each wage payment made through such agent, fiduciary, or person shall, whether the wages are paid separately on behalf

Reg. § 31.3402(g)-3(a)

of each employer or paid in a lump sum on behalf of all such employers, be determined upon the aggregate amount of such wage payment or payments in the same manner as if such aggregate amount had been paid by one employer. Hence, under either the percentage method or the wage bracket method the tax shall be determined upon the aggregate amount of the wage payment.

(b) In any such case, each employer shall be liable for the return and payment of a pro-rata portion of the tax so determined, such portion to be determined in the ratio which the amount contributed by the particular employer bears to the aggregate of such wages.

(c) For example, three companies maintain a central management agency which carries on the administrative work of the several companies. The central agency organization consists of a staff of clerks, bookkeepers, stenographers, etc., who are the common employees of the three companies. The expenses of the central agency, including wages paid to the foregoing employees, are borne by the several companies in certain agreed proportions. Company X pays 45 percent, Company Y pays 35 percent and Company Z pays 20 percent of such expenses. The amount of the tax required to be withheld on the wages paid to persons employed in the central agency should be determined in accordance with the provisions of this section. In such event, Company X is liable as an employer for the return and payment of 45 percent of the tax required to be withheld, Company Y is liable for the return and payment of 35 percent of the tax and Company Z is liable for the return and payment of 20 percent of the tax. (See § 31.3504-1, relating to acts to be performed by agents.)

§ 31.3402(h)(1) **Statutory provisions; income tax collected at source; alternative methods of computing amount to be withheld; withholding on basis of average wages.** [Sec. 3402(h)(1), IRC]

§ 31.3402(h)(1)-1 (Originally § 31.3402(h)-1 as added T.D. 6259, filed 10-25-57; republished in T.D. 6516, filed 12-19-60; amended by T.D. 7001, filed 1-17-69; redesignated and amended by T.D. 7053, filed 7-20-70.) **Withholding on basis of average wages.**

(a) *In general.* An employer may determine the amount of tax to be deducted and withheld upon a payment of wages to an employee on the basis of the employee's average estimated wages, with necessary adjustments, for any quarter. This paragraph applies only where the method desired to be used includes wages other than tips (whether or not tips are also included).

(b) *Withholding on the basis of average estimated tips*—(1) *In general.* Subject to certain limitations and conditions, an employer may, at his discretion, withhold the tax under section 3402 in respect of tips reported by an employee to the employer on an estimated basis. An employer who elects to make withholding of the tax on an estimated basis shall:

(i) In respect of each employee, make an estimate of the amount of tips that will be reported, pursuant to section 6053, by the employee to the employer in a calendar quarter.

(ii) Determine the amount which must be deducted and withheld upon each payment of wages (exclusive of tips) which are under the control of the employer to be made during the quarter by the employer to the employee. The total amount which must be deducted and withheld shall be determined by assuming that the estimated tips for the quarter represents the amount of wages to be paid to the employee in the form of tips in the quarter and that such tips will be ratably (in terms of pay periods) paid during the quarter.

(iii) Deduct and withhold from any payment of wages (exclusive of tips) which are under the control of the employer, or from funds referred to in section 3402(k) (see §§ 31.3402(k) and 31.3402(k)-1, such amount as may be necessary to adjust the amount of tax withheld on the estimated basis to conform to the amount required to be withheld in respect of tips reported by the employee to the employer during the calendar quarter in written statements furnished to the employer pursuant to section 6053(a). If an adjustment is required, the additional tax required to be withheld may be deducted upon any payment of wages (exclusive of tips) which are under the control of the employer during the quarter and within the first 30 days following the quarter or from funds turned over by the employee to the employer for such purpose within such period. For provisions relating to the repayment to an employee, or other disposition, of amounts deducted from an employee's remuneration in excess of the correct amount of tax, see § 31.6413(a)-1.

(2) *Estimating tips employee will report*—(i) *Initial estimate.* The initial estimate of the amount of tips that will be reported by a particular employee in a calendar quarter shall be made on the basis of the facts and circumstances surrounding the employment of that employee. However, if a number of employees are employed under substantially the same circumstances and working conditions, the initial estimate established for one such employee may be used as the initial estimate for other employees in that group.

(ii) *Adjusting estimate.* If the quarterly estimate of tips in respect of a particular employee continues to differ substantially from the amount of tips reported by the employee and there are no unusual factors involved (for example, an extended absence from work due to illness) the employer shall make an appropriate adjustment of his estimate of the amount of tips that will be reported by the employee.

(iii) *Reasonableness of estimate.* The employer must be prepared, upon request of the district director, to disclose the factors upon which he relied in making the estimate, and his reasons for believing that the estimate is reasonable.

Collection of Income Tax at Source on Wages (I.R.C.) 24,256.1

§ 31.3402(h)(2) Statutory provisions; income tax collected at source; alternative methods of computing amount to be withheld; withholding on basis of annualized wages. [Sec. 3402(h)(2), IRC]

§ 31.3402(h)(2)-1 (T.D. 7053, filed 7-20-70.) **Withholding on basis of annualized wages.**

An employer may determine the amount of tax to be deducted and withheld upon a payment of wages to an employee by taking the following steps:

Step 1. Multiply the amount of the employee's wages for the payroll period by the number of such periods in the calendar year.

Step 2. Determine the amount of tax which would be required to be deducted and withheld upon the amount determined in Step 1 if that amount constituted the actual wages for the calendar year and the payroll period of the employee were an annual payroll period.

Step 3. Divide the amount of tax determined in Step 2 by the number of periods by which the employee's wages were multiplied in Step 1.

Example. On July 1, 1970, A, a single person who is on a weekly payroll period and claims one exemption, receives wages of $100 from X Co., his employer. X Co. multiplies the weekly wage of $100 by 52 weeks to determine an annual wage of $5,200. It then subtracts $650 for A's withholding exemption and arrives at a balance of $4,550. The applicable table in section 3402(a) for annual payroll periods indicates that the amount of tax to be withheld thereon is $376 plus $314.50 (17 percent of excess over $2,700), or a total of $690.50. The annual tax of $690.50, when divided by 52 to arrive at the portion thereof attributable to the weekly payroll period, equals $13.28. X Co. may, if it chooses, withhold $13.28 rather than the amount specified in section 3402(a) or (c) for a weekly payroll period.

§ 31.3402(h)(3) Statutory provisions; income tax collected at source; alternative methods of computing amount to be withheld; withholding on basis of cumulative wages. [Sec. 3402(h)(3), IRC]

§ 31.3402(h)(3)-1 (T.D. 7053, filed 7-20-70.) **Withholding on basis of cumulative wages.**

(a) *In general.* In the case of an employee who has in effect a request that the amount of tax to be withheld from his wages to be computed on the basis of his cumulative wages, and whose wages since the beginning of the current calendar year have been paid with respect to the same category of payroll period (e.g., weekly or semimonthly), the employer may determine the amount of tax to be deducted and withheld upon a payment of wages made to the employee after December 31, 1969, by taking the following steps:

Step 1. Add the amount of the wages to be paid the employee for the payroll period to the total amount of wages paid by the employer to the employee during the calendar year.

Step 2. Divide the aggregate amount of wages computed in Step 1 by the number of payroll periods to which that amount relates.

Step 3. Compute the total amount of tax that would have been required to be deducted and withheld under section 3402(a) if the average amount of wages (as computed in Step 2) had been paid to the employee for the number of payroll periods to which the aggregate amount of wages (computed in Step 1) relates.

Step 4. Determine the excess, if any, of the amount of tax computed in Step 3 over the total amount of tax already deducted and withheld by the employer from wages paid to the employee during the calendar year.

Example. On July 1, 1970, Y. Co. employs B, a single person claiming one exemption. Y Co. pays B the following amounts of wages on the basis of a biweekly payroll period on the following pay days:

July 20	$1,000
August 3	300
August 17	300
August 31	300
September 14	300
September 28	300

On October 5, B requests that Y Co. withhold on the basis of his cumulative wages with respect to his wages to be paid on October 12 and thereafter. Y Co. adds the $300 in wages to be paid to B on October 12 to the payments of wages already made to B during the calendar year, and determines that the aggregate amount of wages is $2,800. The average amount of wages for the 7 biweekly payroll periods is $400. The total amount of tax required to be deducted and withheld for payments of $400 for each of 7 biweekly payroll periods is $485.87 under section 3402(a). Since the total amount of tax which has been deducted and withheld by Y Co. through September 28 is $484.86, Y Co. may, if it chooses, deduct and withhold $1.01 (the amount by which $485.87 exceeds the total amount already withheld by Y Co.) from the payment of wages to B on October 12 rather than the amount specified in section 3402(a) or (c).

(b) *Employee's request and revocation of request.* An employee's request that his employer withhold on the basis of his cumulative wages and a notice of revocation of such request shall be in writing and in such form as the employer may prescribe. An employee's request furnished to his employer pursuant to this section shall be effective, and may be acted upon by his employer, after the furnishing of such request and before a revocation thereof is effective. A revocation of such request may be made at any time by the employee furnishing his employer with a notice of revocation. The employer may give immediate effect to a revocation, but, in any event, a revocation shall be effective with respect to payments of wages made on or after the first "status determination date" (see section 3402(f)(3)(B)) which occurs at least 30 days after the date on which such notice is furnished.

§ 31.3402(h)(4) Statutory provisions; income tax collected at source; alternative methods of computing amount to be withheld; other methods. [Sec. 3402(h)(4), IRC]

§ 31.3402(h)(4)-1 (T.D. 7053, filed 7-20-70; amended by T.D. 7251, filed 12-29-72.)

(a) *Maximum permissible deviation.* An employer may use any other method of

Reg. § 31.3402(h)(4)-1(a)

24,256.2 (I.R.C.) Reg. § 31.3402(h)(4)-1(a) 1-15-73

withholding under which the employer will deduct and withhold upon wages paid to an employee after December 31, 1969, for a payroll period substantially the same amount as would be required to be deducted and withheld by applying section 3402(a) with respect to the payroll period. For purposes of section 3402(h)(4) and this section, an amount is substantially the same as the amount required to be deducted and withheld under section 3402(a) if its deviation from the latter amount is not greater than the maximum permissible deviation prescribed in this paragraph. The maximum permissible deviation under this paragraph is determined by annualizing wages as provided in Step 1 of § 31.3402(h)(2)-1 and applying the following table to the amount of tax required to be deducted and withheld under section 3402(a) with respect to such annualized wages, as determined under Step 2 of § 31.3402(h)(2)-1:

If the tax required to be withheld under the annual percentage rate schedule is—	The maximum permissible annual deviation is—
$10 to $100	$10, plus 10% of excess over $ 10
$100 to $1,000	$19, plus 3% of excess over $ 100
$1,000 or over	$46, plus 1% of excess over $1,000

In any case, an amount which is less than $10 more or less per year than the amount required to be deducted and withheld under section 3402(a) is substantially the same as the latter amount. If any method produces results which are not greater than the prescribed maximum deviations only with respect to some of his employees, the employer may use such method only with respect to such employees. An employer should thoroughly test any method which he contemplates using to ascertain whether it meets the tolerances prescribed by this paragraph. An employer may not use any method one of the principal purposes of which is to consistently produce amounts to be deducted and withheld which are less (though substantially the same) than the amount required to be deducted and withheld by applying section 3402(a).

(b) *Combined FICA and income tax withholding.* In addition to the methods authorized by paragraph (a) of this section, an employer may determine the amount of tax to be deducted and withheld under section 3402 upon a payment of wages to an employee by using tables prescribed by the Commissioner which combine the amounts of tax to be deducted under sections 3102 and 3402. Such tables shall provide for the deduction of the sum of such amounts, computed on the basis of the midpoints of the wage brackets in the tables prescribed under section 3402(c). The portion of such sum which is to be treated as the tax deducted and withheld under section 3402 shall be the amount obtained by subtracting from such sum the amount of tax required to be deducted by section 3102. Such tables may be used only with respect to payments which are wages under both sections 3121(a) and 3401(a).

(c) *Part-year employment method of withholding*—(1) *In general.* In addition to the methods authorized by other paragraphs of this section, in the case of part-year employment (as defined in subparagraph (4) of this paragraph) of an employee who determines his liability for tax under subtitle A of the Code on a calendar-year basis and who has in effect a request that the amount of tax to be withheld from his wages be computed according to the part-year employment method described in this paragraph, the employer may determine the amount of tax to be deducted and withheld upon a payment of wages made to the employee on or after January 5, 1973 by taking the following steps:

Step 1. Add the amount of wages to be paid to the employee for the current payroll period to the total amount of wages paid by the employer to the employee for all preceding payroll periods included in the current term of continuous employment (as defined in subparagraph (3) of this paragraph) of the employee by the employer;

Step 2. Divide the aggregate amount of wages computed in Step 1 by the total of the number of payroll periods to which that amount relates plus the equivalent number of payroll periods (as defined in subparagraph (2) of this paragraph) in the employee's term of continuous unemployment immediately preceding the current term of continuous employment, such term of continuous unemployment to be exclusive of any days prior to the beginning of the current calendar year;

Step 3. Determine the total amount of tax that would have been required to be deducted and withheld under section 3402 if the average amount of wages (as computed in Step 2) had been paid to the employee for the number of payroll periods determined in Step 2 (including the equivalent number of payroll periods); and

Step 4. Determine the excess, if any, of the amount of tax computed in Step 3 over the total amount of tax already deducted and withheld by the employer from wages paid to the employee for all payroll periods during the current term of continuous employment.

The use of the method described in this paragraph does not preclude the employee from claiming additional withholding allowances for estimated itemized deductions pursuant to section 3402(m) or the standard deduction allowance pursuant to section 3402(f)(1)(G).

(2) *Equivalent number of payroll periods.* For purposes of this paragraph, the equivalent number of payroll periods shall be determined by dividing the number of calendar days contained in the current payroll period into the number of calendar days between the later of (i) the day certified by the employee as his last day of employment prior to his current term of continuous employment during the calendar year in which such term commenced, or (ii) the last day of the calendar year immediately preceding the current calendar year, and the first day of the current term of continuous employment. For purposes of the preceding sentence, the term "calendar days" includes holidays, Saturdays,

and Sundays. In determining the equivalent number of payroll periods, any fraction obtained in the division described in the first sentence of this subparagraph shall be disregarded. An employee paid for a miscellaneous payroll period shall be considered to have a daily payroll period for purposes of this subparagraph. In a case in which an employee is paid for a daily or miscellaneous payroll period and the employer elects under paragraph (d)(2) of § 31.3402(b)-1 to compute the tax to be withheld as if the aggregate of the wages paid to the employee during the calendar week were paid for a weekly period, the employer shall determine the equivalent number of payroll periods for purposes of the computation of the tax to be withheld for the calendar week on the basis of a weekly payroll period (notwithstanding the fact that a determination of the equivalent number of payroll periods for purposes of the computation of the tax to be withheld upon wages paid for daily or miscellaneous payroll periods within such calendar week has been made on the basis of a daily or miscellaneous payroll period).

(3) *Term of continuous employment.* For purposes of this paragraph, a term of employment is continuous if it is either a single term of employment or two or more consecutive terms of employment with the same employer. A term of continuous employment begins on the first day on which any services are performed by the employee for the employer for which compensation is paid or payable. Such term ends on the earlier of (i) the last day during the current term of continuous employment on which any services are performed by the employee for the employer, or (ii) if the employee performs no services for the employer for a period of more than 30 calendar days, the last day preceding such period on which any services are performed by the employee for the employer. For example, a professional athlete who signs a contract on December 31, 1973, to perform services from July 1 through December 31 for the calendar years 1974, 1975 and 1976 has a new term of employment beginning each July 1 and accordingly may qualify for use of the part-year withholding method in each of such years. Likewise, a term of continuous employment is not broken by a temporary layoff of no more than 30 days. On the other hand, when an employment relationship is actually terminated the term of continuous employment is ended even though a new employment relationship is established with the same employer within 30 days. A "term of continuous employment" includes all days on which an employee performs any services for an employer and includes days on which services are not performed because of illness or vacation, or because such days are holidays or are regular days off (such as Saturdays and Sundays, or days off in lieu of Saturdays and Sundays), or other days for which the employee is not scheduled to work. For example, an employee who is employed two days a week for the same employer from March 1 through December 31 has a term of continuous employment of 306 days.

(4) *Part-year employment.* For purposes of this paragraph, the term "part-year employment" means a term of continuous employment (i) the total duration of which will not exceed 245 days, (ii) which, during the current calendar year, will not exceed 245 days, or (iii) which, during the calendar year will not entitle the employee to wages of more than $30,000. For example, A graduates from college in June and accepts a permanent position with X Co., beginning July 1. Since the total duration of A's term of continuous employment will exceed 245 days it does not qualify as part-year employment for purposes of this section.

(5) *Employee's request.* (i) An employee's request that his employer withhold according to the part-year employment method shall be in writing and in such form as the employer may prescribe. Such request shall be made under the penalties of perjury and shall contain the following information—

(*a*) The last day of employment (if any) by any employer prior to the current term of continuous employment during the calendar year in which such term commenced,

(*b*) A statement that the employee reasonably anticipates that he will have no more than $30,000 in gross income from all sources for the calendar year and that he will have no more than 245 days of employment, either based upon all employment during the current calendar year or based upon the current term of continuous employment during the current calendar year and the following year (for this purpose days of employment shall include all days on which an employee performs any services for an employer, and includes days on which services are not performed because of illness or vacation, or because such days are holidays or are regular days off (such as Saturdays and Sundays, or days off in lieu of Saturdays and Sundays) or other days for which the employee is not scheduled to work), and

(*c*) The employee uses a calendar-year accounting period.

An employee's request furnished to his employer pursuant to this section shall be effective, and may be acted upon by his employer, with respect to wages paid after the furnishing of such request, and shall cease to be effective with respect to any wages paid on or after the beginning of the payroll period during which the current calendar year will end.

(ii) If, on any day during the calendar year, any of the anticipations stated by the employee in his statement provided pursuant to subdivision (i)(*b*) of this subparagraph becomes unreasonable, the employee shall revoke the request described in this subparagraph before the end of the payroll period during which it becomes unreasonable. The revocation shall be effective as of the beginning of the payroll period during which it is made.

(6) *Examples.* The application of this paragraph may be illustrated by the following examples:

Example (1). A, a calendar-year taxpayer being unemployed for the period beginning on May 25, 1973, and ending on October 28, 1973, a period of 157 calendar days, is employed by X Co. X Co. anticipates that A's employment will last 8 calendar weeks, from October 29 to December 23, and A's wages therefor will not exceed

Reg. § 31.3402(h)(4)-1(c)(6)

24,258 (I.R.C.)   Reg. § 31.3402(h)(4)-1(c)(6)   6-1-75

$30,000. In the Form W-4 which A furnishes X Co., A claims 4 exemptions and married status. A makes a written request, incorporating the statements required under subparagraph (5)(i)(b), that X Co. withhold on the basis of the part-year employment method. A works for the period beginning October 29, 1973, and ending on November 11, 1973, and earns $1,800 in wages. Wages are paid on a biweekly basis. Using the part-year employment method, X Co. determines that $22.80 is required to be deducted and withheld from A's wages to be paid for his services from October 29 to November 11, 1973. The determination is made as follows:

Amount of wages to be paid for the payroll period (biweekly)	$1,800.00
Number of payroll periods:	
Payroll Period-October 29 to November 11	1
The equivalent number of payroll periods for the period of unemployment, disregarding the fractional payroll period	11
	12
Average amount of wages per payroll period including equivalent number of payroll periods ($1,800 ÷ 12)	$150.00
Amount required to be withheld from a payment of $150.00 for a biweekly payroll period to a married person with 4 exemptions according to the wage bracket tables	$1.90
Total amount required to be withheld under the wage bracket method with respect to all payroll periods (including equivalent number of payroll periods) ($1.90 × 12)	$22.80
Amount already withheld by employer	0
Amount to be withheld under part-year employment method ($22.80 − 0 (the amount previously withheld))	$22.80

Example (2). A works for X for another 2-week period beginning on November 12, 1973 and ending on November 25, 1973, for which he earns $2,100.00. X Co., using the part-year employment method, determines that $323.00 is required to be deducted and withheld with respect to the wages for the current payroll period, as follows:

Amount of wages to be paid for the payroll period (biweekly)	$2,100.00
Amount of wages previously paid by the employer	$1,800.00
Sum of amount of wages to be paid with respect to current payroll period and amount of wages already paid	$3,900.00
Number of payroll periods:	
Payroll periods—October 29 to November 11 and November 12 to November 25	2
The equivalent number of payroll periods for the period of unemployment	11
	13
Average amount of wages per payroll period ($3900 ÷ 13)	$300.00
Amount required to be withheld according to wage bracket tables from a payment of $300 for a biweekly payroll period to a married person with 4 exemptions	$26.60
Total amount required to be withheld under the wage bracket method with respect to all payroll periods (including equivalent number of payroll periods) ($26.60 × 13)	$345.80
Amount already withheld by employer	$22.80
Amount required to be withheld under the part-year employment method ($345.80 − $22.80)	$323.00

§ 31.3402(i)   Statutory provisions; income tax collected at source; additional withholding. [Sec. 3402(i), IRC]

§ 31.3402(i)-1 (T.D. 6259, filed 10-25-57; republished in T.D. 6516, filed 12-19-60; amended by T.D. 7065, filed 10-22-70.) **Additional withholding.**

(a) In addition to the tax required to be deducted and withheld in accordance with the provisions of section 3402, the employer and employee may agree that an additional amount shall be withheld from the employee's wages. The agreement shall be in writing and shall be in such form as the employer may prescribe. The agreement shall be effective for such period as the employer and employee mutually agree upon. However, unless the agreement provides for an earlier termination, either the employer or the employee, by furnishing a written notice to the other, may terminate the agreement effective with respect to the first payment of wages made on or after the first "status determination date" (see paragraph (d) of § 31.3402(f)(3)-1) which occurs at least 30 days after the date on which such notice is furnished.

(b) The amount deducted and withheld pursuant to an agreement between the employer and employee shall be considered as tax required to be deducted and withheld under section 3402. All provisions of law and regulations applicable with respect to the tax required to be deducted and withheld under section 3402 shall be applicable with respect to any amount deducted and withheld pursuant to the agreement.

§ 31.3402(j)   Statutory provisions; income tax collected at source; noncash remuneration to retail commission salesman. [Sec. 3402(j), IRC]

§ 31.3402(j)-1 (T.D. 6259, filed 10-25-57; republished in T.D. 6516, filed 12-19-60.) **Remuneration other than in cash for service performed by retail commission salesman.**

(a) *In general.* (1) An employer, in computing the amount to be deducted and withheld as tax in accordance with section 3402, may, at his election, disregard any wages paid, after August 9, 1955, in a medium other than cash for services performed for him by an employee if (i) the noncash remuneration is paid for services performed by the employee as a retail commission salesman and (ii) the employer ordinarily pays the employee remuneration solely by way of cash commissions for services performed by him as a retail commission salesman.

Collection of Income Tax at Source on Wages

(2) Section 3402(j) and this section are not applicable with respect to noncash wages paid to a retail commission salesman for services performed by him in a capacity other than as such a salesman. Such sections are not applicable with respect to noncash wages paid by an employer to an employee for services performed as a retail commission salesman if the employer ordinarily pays the employee remuneration other than by way of cash commissions for such services. Thus, noncash remuneration may not be disregarded in computing the amount to be deducted and withheld in a case where the employee, for services performed as a retail commission salesman, is paid both a salary and cash commissions on sales, or is ordinarily paid in something other than cash (stocks, bonds, or other forms of property) notwithstanding that the amount of remuneration paid to the employee is measured by sales.

(b) *Retail commission salesman.* For purposes of section 3402(j) and this section, the term "retail commission salesman" includes an employee who is engaged in the solicitation of orders at retail, that is, from the ultimate consumer, for merchandise or other products offered for sale by his employer. The term does not include an employee salesman engaged in the solicitation on behalf of his employer of orders from wholesalers, retailers, or others, for merchandise for resale. However, if the salesman solicits orders for more than one principal, he is not excluded from the term solely because he. solicits orders from wholesalers or retailers on behalf of one or more principals. In such case the salesman may be a retail commission salesman with respect to services performed for one or more principals and not with respect to services performed for his other principals.

(c) *Noncash remuneration.* The term "noncash remuneration" includes remuneration paid in any medium other than cash, such as goods or commodities, stocks, bonds, or other forms of property. The term does not include checks or other monetary media of exchange.

(d) *Cross reference.* For provisions relating to records required to be kept and statements which must be furnished an employee with respect to wage payments, see sections 6001 and 6051 and the regulations thereunder in Subpart G of this part.

§ 31.3402(k) Statutory provisions; income tax collected at source; tips. [Sec. 3402(k), IRC]

§ 31.3402(k)-1 (T.D. 7001, filed 1-17-69; amended by T.D. 7053, filed 7-20-70.) **Special rule for tips.**

(a) *Withholding of income tax in respect of tips*—(1) *In general.* Subject to the limitations set forth in subparagraph (2) of this paragraph, an employer is required to deduct and withhold from each of his employees tax in respect of those tips received by the employee which constitute wages. (For provisions relating to the treatment of tips as wages, see §§ 31.-3401(a)(16) and 31,3401(f).) The employer shall make the withholding by deducting or causing to be deducted the amount of the tax from wages (exclusive of tips) which are under the control of the employer or other funds turned over by the employee to the employer (see subparagraph (3) of this paragraph.) For purposes of this section the term "wages (exclusive of tips) which are under the control of the employer" means, with respect to a payment of wages, an amount equal to wages as defined in section 3401(a) except that tips and non-cash remuneration which are wages are not included, less the sum of—

(i) The tax under section 3101 required to be collected by the employer in respect of wages as defined in section 3121(a) (exclusive of tips);

(ii) The tax under section 3402 required to be collected by the employer in respect of wages as defined in section 3401 (a) (exclusive of tips); and

(iii) The amount of taxes imposed on the remuneration of an employee withheld by the employer pursuant to State and local law (including amounts withheld under an agreement between the employer and the employee pursuant to such law) except that the amount of taxes taken into account in this subdivision shall not include any amount attributable to tips.

(2) *Limitations*—An employer is required to deduct and withhold the tax on tips which constitute wages only in respect of those tips which are reported by the employee to the employer in a written statement furnished to the employer pursuant to section 6053(a). The employer is responsible for the collection of the tax on tips reported to him only to the extent that the employer can, during the period beginning at the time the written statement is submitted to him and ending at the close of the calendar year in which the statement was submitted, collect the tax by deducting it or causing it to be deducted as provided in subparagraph (1).

(3) *Furnishing of funds to employer.* If the amount of the tax in respect of tips reported by the employee to the employer in a written statement furnished pursuant to section 6053(a) exceeds the wages (exclusive of tips) which are under the control of the employer from which the employer is required to withhold the tax in respect of such tips, the employee may furnish to the employer, within the period specified in subparagraph (2) of this paragraph, an amount of money equal to the amount of such excess.

(b) *Less than $20 of tips.* Notwithstanding the provisions of paragraph (a) of this section, if an employee furnishes to his employer a written statement—

(1) Covering a period of less than one month, and

(2) The statement is furnished to the employer prior to the close of the 10th day of the month following the month in

which the tips were actually received by the employee, and

(3) The aggregate amount of tips reported in the statement and in all other statements previously furnished by the employee covering periods within the same month is less than $20, and such statements, collectively, do not cover the entire month,

the employer may deduct amounts equivalent to the tax on such tips from wages (exclusive of tips) which are under the control of the employer or other funds turned over by the employee to the employer. For provisions relating to the repayment to an employee, or other disposition, of amounts deducted from an employee's remuneration in excess of the correct amount of tax, see § 31.6413(a)-1. (As to the exclusion from wages of tips of less than $20, see § 31.3401(a)(16)-1.)

(c) *Priority of tax collection*—(1) *In general.* In the case of a payment of wages (exclusive of tips), the employer shall deduct or cause to be deducted in the following order:

(i) The tax under section 3101 and the tax under section 3402 with respect to such payment of wages.

(ii) Any tax under section 3101 which, at the time of the payment of the wages, the employer is required to collect—

(a) In respect of tips reported by the employee to the employer in a written statement furnished to the employer pursuant to section 6053(a), or

(b) By reason of the employer's election to make collection of the tax under section 3101 in respect of tips on an estimated basis, but which has not been collected by the employer and which cannot be deducted from funds turned over by the employee to the employer for such purpose. (See § 31.3102-3, relating to collection of, and liability for, employee tax on tips.)

(iii) Any tax under section 3402 which, at the time of the payment of the wages, the employer is required to collect—

(a) In respect of tips reported by the employee to the employer in a written statement furnished to the employer pursuant to section 6053(a), or

(b) By reason of the employer's election to make collection of the tax under section 3402 in respect of tips on an estimated basis, but which has not been collected by the employer and which cannot be deducted from funds turned over by the employee to the employer for such purpose. For provisions relating to the withholding of tax on the basis of average estimated tips, see paragraph (b) of § 31.3402(h)(1)-1.

(2) *Examples.* The application of subparagraph (1) of this paragraph may be illustrated by the following examples (The amounts used in the following examples are intended for illustrative purposes and do not necessarily reflect currently effective rates or amounts.):

Example (1). W is a waiter employed by R restaurant. W's principal remuneration for his services is in the form of tips received from patrons of R; however, he also receives a salary from R of $40 per week, which is paid to him every Friday. W is a member of a labor union which has a contract with R pursuant to which R is to collect dues for the union by withholding from the wages of its employees at the rate of $1 per week. In addition to the taxes required to be withheld under the Internal Revenue Code, W's wages are subject to withholding of a state income tax imposed upon both his regular wage and his tips received and reported to R.

On Monday of a given week W furnishes a written statement to R pursuant to section 6053(a) in which he reports the receipt of $160 in tips. The $40 wage to be paid to W on Friday of the same week is subject to the following items of withholding:

	Taxes With Respect To Regular Wage	Taxes with Respect to Tips	Total
§ 3101 (F.I.C.A.)	$1.76	$7.04	$8.80
§ 3402 (Income Tax at Source)	5.65	28.30	33.95
State Income Tax	1.20	4.80	6.00
Union Dues			1.00
Total			$49.75

W does not turn over any funds to R. R should satisfy the taxes imposed by sections 3101 and 3402 out of W's $40 wage as follows: The taxes imposed with respect to the regular wage (a total of $7.41) should be satisfied first. The taxes imposed with respect to tips are to be withheld only out of "wages (exclusive of tips) which are under the control of the employer" as that phrase is defined in §§ 31.3102-3(a)(1) and 31.3402(k)-1(a)(1). The amount of such wages under the control of employer in this example is $31.39, or $40, less the amounts applied in satisfaction of the Federal and state withholding taxes imposed with respect to the regular $40 wage ($8.61). This $31.39 is applied first in satisfaction of the tax under section 3101 with respect to tips ($7.04) and the balance of $24.35 is applied in partial satisfaction of the withholding of income tax at source under section 3402 with respect to tips. The amount of the tax with respect to tips under section 3402 which remains unsatisfied ($3.95) should be withheld from wages under the control of the employer the following week.

Example (2). During the week following the week dealt with in example (1), W furnishes a written statement to R pursuant to section 6053(a) in which he reports the receipt of $130 in tips. In addition, R receives a notice of garnishment of W's wages issued by the state court, pursuant to which R is required to withhold $10 per week from W's wages for a period of ten weeks. The $40 wage to be paid to W at the end of the week is subject to the following items of withholding:

5-24-71 Collection of Income Tax at Source on Wages (I.R.C.) 24,258.3

	Taxes with Respect to Regular Wage	Taxes with Respect to Tips	Total
§ 3101 (F.I.C.A.)	$1.76	$ 5.72	$ 7.48
§ 3402 (Income Tax at Source) Current week	5.65	22.30	27.95
Carryover from prior week		3.95	3.95
State Income Tax	1.20	3.90	5.10
Union Dues			1.00
Garnishment			10.00
Total			$55.48

As in example (1), the amount of "wages (exclusive of tips) which are under the control of the employer" is $31.39. This amount is applied first in satisfaction of the tax under section 3101 with respect to tips ($5.72) and the balance is applied in partial satisfaction of the withholding of income tax at source under section 3402 with respect to tips (a total of $26.25), including that portion of the amount required to be withheld from the prior weekly wages which remained unsatisfied. The amount of the tax with respect to tips under section 3402 which remains unsatisfied ($.58) should be withheld from wages under the control of the employer the following week.

○—▶ § 31.3402(l) Statutory provisions; income tax collected at source; determination and disclosure of marital status. [Sec. 3402(l), IRC]

○—▶ § 31.3402(l) (T.D. 7115, filed 5-20-71.) Determination and disclosure of marital staus.

(a) *Determination of status by employer.* An employer in computing the tax to be deducted and withheld from an employee's wages paid after April 30, 1966, shall apply the applicable percentage method or wage bracket method withholding table (see section 3402(a), (b), and (c) and the regulations thereunder) for the pertinent payroll period which relates to employees who are single persons, unless there is in effect with respect to such payment of wages a withholding exemption certificate furnished to the employer by the employee after March 15, 1966, indicating that the employee is married in which case the employer shall apply the applicable table relating to employees who are married persons.

(b) *Disclosure of status by employee.* (1) An employee shall be entitled to furnish the employer with a withholding exemption certificate indicating he is married only if, on the day of such furnishing, he is married (determined by application of the rules in paragraph (c) of this section). Thus, an employee who is contemplating marriage may not, prior to the actual marriage, furnish the employer with a withholding exemption certificate indicating that he is a married person.

(2)(i) If, on any day during the calendar year, the marital status (as determined by application of the rules in paragraph (c) of this section) of an employee who has in effect a withholding exemption certificate indicating that he is a married person, changes from married to single, the employee must within 10 days after the change occurs furnish the employer with a new withholding exemption certificate indicating that the employee is a single person.

(ii) If an employee who has in effect a withholding exemption certificate indicating that he is a married person, is considered married solely because of the application of subparagraph (2)(ii) of paragraph (c) of this section, and his spouse died during the taxable year which precedes by two years the current taxable year, the employee must, on or before December 1 of the current taxable year, furnish the employer with a new withholding exemption certificate indicating that he is a single person. Such certificate shall not, however, become effective until the next calendar year (see paragraph (c) of § 31.3402(f)(3)-1).

(3) If, on any day during the calendar year, the marital status (as determined by application of the rules in paragraph (c) of this section) of an employee who has in effect a withholding exemption certificate indicating that he is a single person changes from single to married, the employee may furnish the employer with a new withholding exemption certificate indicating that the employee is a married person.

(c) *Determination of marital status.* For the purposes of section 3402(1)(2) and paragraph (b) of this section, the following rules shall be applied in determining whether an employee is a married person or a single person—

(1) An employee shall on any day be considered as a single person if—

(i) He is legally separated from his spouse under a decree of divorce or separate maintenance, or

(ii) Either he or his spouse is, or on any preceding day within the same calendar year was, a nonresident alien.

(2) An employee shall on any day be considered as a married person if—

(i) His spouse (other than a spouse referred to in subparagraph (1) of this paragraph) died within the portion of his taxable year which precedes such day, or

(ii) His spouse died during one of the two taxable years immediately preceding the current taxable year and, on the basis of facts existing at the beginning of such day, he reasonably expects, at the close of his taxable year, to be a surviving spouse as defined in section 2 and the regulations thereunder.

○—▶ § 31.3402(m) Statutory provisions; income tax collected at source; withholding allowances based on itemized deductions. [Sec. 3402(m), IRC]

○—▶ § 31.3402(m)-1 (T.D. 7065, filed 10-22-70.) Withholding allowances for itemized deductions.

(a) *General rule*—(1) *In general.* An employee shall be entitled to claim, with respect to wages paid after December 31, 1966, a number of withholding allowances determined in accordance with the tables set forth in subparagraph (2) of this paragraph. The tables show the number of withholding allowances which an employee may claim with respect to various amounts of estimated itemized deductions and estimated wages. Such determination must be based on an estimation year beginning after December 31, 1966. In order to receive the benefits of such allowances, the employee must have in effect with his employer a withholding exemption certificate claiming such allowances.

(2) *Tables for determining number of withholding allowances.*

[Table 1 appears on page 24,258.4 and Table 2 appears on page 24,258.5].

Reg. § 31.3402(m)-1(a)(2)

TABLE 1—WAGES PAID AFTER DECEMBER 31, 1969

THE NUMBER OF ADDITIONAL WITHHOLDING ALLOWANCES SHALL BE—

IF THE EXPECTED WAGES ARE—		0	1	2	3	4	5	6
AT LEAST	BUT LESS THAN	UNDER	AT LEAST BUT LESS THAN	AT LEAST BUT LESS THAN	AT LEAST BUT LESS THAN	AT LEAST BUT LESS THAN	AT LEAST BUT LESS THAN	AT LEAST BUT LESS THAN

ALL EMPLOYEES WITH WAGES UNDER $16,000

0	$ 6,000	$1,375	$1,375–$2,125	$2,125–$2,875	$2,875–$3,625	$3,625–$4,375	$4,375–$5,125	$5,125–$5,875
$ 6,000	$ 8,000	1,425	1,425– 2,175	2,175– 2,925	2,925– 3,675	3,675– 4,425	4,425– 5,175	5,175– 5,925
$ 8,000	$10,000	1,725	1,725– 2,475	2,475– 3,225	3,225– 3,975	3,975– 4,725	4,725– 5,475	5,475– 6,225
$10,000	$12,000	2,025	2,025– 2,775	2,775– 3,525	3,525– 4,275	4,275– 5,025	5,025– 5,775	5,775– 6,525
$12,000	$14,000	2,325	2,325– 3,075	3,075– 3,825	3,825– 4,575	4,575– 5,325	5,325– 6,075	6,075– 6,825
$14,000	$16,000	2,625	2,625– 3,375	3,375– 4,125	4,125– 4,875	4,875– 5,625	5,625– 6,375	6,375– 7,125

SINGLE EMPLOYEES WITH WAGES $16,000 – $50,000

$16,000	$18,000	2,995	2,995– 3,745	3,745– 4,495	4,495– 5,245	5,245– 5,995	5,995– 6,745	6,745– 7,495
$18,000	$20,000	3,490	3,490– 4,240	4,240– 4,990	4,990– 5,740	5,740– 6,490	6,490– 7,240	7,240– 7,990
$20,000	$22,000	4,060	4,060– 4,810	4,810– 5,560	5,560– 6,310	6,310– 7,060	7,060– 7,810	7,810– 8,560
$22,000	$24,000	4,705	4,705– 5,455	5,455– 6,205	6,205– 6,955	6,955– 7,705	7,705– 8,455	8,455– 9,205
$24,000	$26,000	5,425	5,425– 6,175	6,175– 6,925	6,925– 7,675	7,675– 8,425	8,425– 9,175	9,175– 9,925
$26,000	$28,000	6,170	6,170– 6,920	6,920– 7,670	7,670– 8,420	8,420– 9,170	9,170– 9,920	9,920–10,670
$28,000	$30,000	6,960	6,960– 7,710	7,710– 8,460	8,460– 9,210	9,210– 9,960	9,960–10,710	10,710–11,460
$30,000	$35,000	8,430	8,430– 9,180	9,180– 9,930	9,930–10,680	10,680–11,430	11,430–12,180	12,180–12,930
$35,000	$40,000	10,620	10,620–11,370	11,370–12,120	12,120–12,870	12,870–13,620	13,620–14,370	14,370–15,120
$40,000	$45,000	13,065	13,065–13,815	13,815–14,565	14,565–15,315	15,315–16,065	16,065–16,815	16,815–17,565
$45,000	$50,000	15,510	15,510–16,260	16,260–17,010	17,010–17,760	17,760–18,510	18,510–19,260	19,260–20,010

MARRIED EMPLOYEES WITH WAGES $16,000 – $50,000

$16,000	$18,000	2,925	2,925– 3,675	3,675– 4,425	4,425– 5,175	5,175– 5,925	5,925– 6,675	6,675– 7,425
$18,000	$20,000	3,225	3,225– 3,975	3,975– 4,725	4,725– 5,475	5,475– 6,225	6,225– 6,975	6,975– 7,725
$20,000	$22,000	3,525	3,525– 4,275	4,275– 5,025	5,025– 5,775	5,775– 6,525	6,525– 7,275	7,275– 8,025
$22,000	$24,000	3,825	3,825– 4,575	4,575– 5,325	5,325– 6,075	6,075– 6,825	6,825– 7,575	7,575– 8,325
$24,000	$26,000	4,125	4,125– 4,875	4,875– 5,625	5,625– 6,375	6,375– 7,125	7,125– 7,875	7,875– 8,625
$26,000	$28,000	4,425	4,425– 5,175	5,175– 5,925	5,925– 6,675	6,675– 7,425	7,425– 8,175	8,175– 8,925
$28,000	$30,000	4,725	4,725– 5,475	5,475– 6,225	6,225– 6,975	6,975– 7,725	7,725– 8,475	8,475– 9,225
$30,000	$35,000	5,290	5,290– 6,040	6,040– 6,790	6,790– 7,540	7,540– 8,290	8,290– 9,040	9,040– 9,790
$35,000	$40,000	6,570	6,570– 7,320	7,320– 8,070	8,070– 8,820	8,820– 9,570	9,570–10,320	10,320–11,070
$40,000	$45,000	8,105	8,105– 8,855	8,855– 9,605	9,605–10,355	10,355–11,105	11,105–11,855	11,855–12,605
$45,000	$50,000	9,875	9,875–10,625	10,625–11,375	11,375–12,125	12,125–12,875	12,875–13,625	13,625–14,375

Collection of Income Tax at Source on Wages (I.R.C.) 24,258.5

TABLE 2—WAGES PAID AFTER DECEMBER 31, 1966, AND BEFORE JANUARY 1, 1970

THE NUMBER OF ADDITIONAL WITHHOLDING ALLOWANCES SHALL BE—

IF THE EXPECTED WAGES ARE—		0	1	2	3	4	5	6
AT LEAST	BUT LESS THAN	UNDER	AT LEAST BUT LESS THAN	AT LEAST BUT LESS THAN	AT LEAST BUT LESS THAN	AT LEAST BUT LESS THAN	AT LEAST BUT LESS THAN	AT LEAST BUT LESS THAN

ALL EMPLOYEES WITH WAGES UNDER $22,000

0	2,000	800	800– 1,500	1,500 or more				
2,000	4,000	1,000	1,000– 1,700	1,700– 2,400	2,400– 3,100	3,100– 3,800	3,800 or more	
4,000	6,000	1,200	1,200– 1,900	1,900– 2,600	2,600– 3,300	3,300– 4,000	4,000– 4,700	4,700– 5,400
6,000	8,000	1,400	1,400– 2,100	2,100– 2,800	2,800– 3,500	3,500– 4,200	4,200– 4,900	4,900– 5,600
8,000	10,000	1,705	1,705– 2,405	2,405– 3,105	3,105– 3,805	3,805– 4,505	4,505– 5,205	5,205– 5,905
10,000	12,000	2,045	2,045– 2,745	2,745– 3,445	3,445– 4,145	4,145– 4,845	4,845– 5,545	5,545– 6,245
12,000	14,000	2,385	2,385– 3,085	3,085– 3,785	3,785– 4,485	4,485– 5,185	5,185– 5,885	5,885– 6,585
14,000	16,000	2,725	2,725– 3,425	3,425– 4,125	4,125– 4,825	4,825– 5,525	5,525– 6,225	6,225– 6,925
16,000	18,000	3,065	3,065– 3,765	3,765– 4,464	4,464– 5,165	5,165– 5,865	5,865– 6,565	6,565– 7,265
18,000	20,000	3,405	3,405– 4,105	4,105– 4,805	4,805– 5,505	5,505– 6,205	6,205– 6,905	6,905– 7,605
20,000	22,000	3,745	3,745– 4,445	4,445– 5,145	5,145– 5,845	5,845– 6,545	6,545– 7,245	7,245– 7,945

SINGLE EMPLOYEES WITH WAGES $22,000 – $50,000

22,000	24,000	4,345	4,345– 5,045	5,045– 5,745	5,745– 6,445	6,445– 7,145	7,145– 7,845	7,845– 8,545
24,000	26,000	5,020	5,020– 5,720	5,720– 6,420	6,420– 7,120	7,120– 7,820	7,820– 8,520	8,520– 9,220
26,000	28,000	5,770	5,770– 6,470	6,470– 7,170	7,170– 7,870	7,870– 8,570	8,570– 9,270	9,270– 9,970
28,000	30,000	6,540	6,540– 7,240	7,240– 7,940	7,940– 8,640	8,640– 9,340	9,340–10,040	10,040–10,740
30,000	35,000	7,940	7,940– 8,640	8,640– 9,340	9,340–10,040	10,040–10,740	10,740–11,440	11,440–12,140
35,000	40,000	10,035	10,035–10,735	10,735–11,435	11,435–12,135	12,135–12,835	12,835–13,535	13,535–14,235
40,000	45,000	12,205	12,205–12,905	12,905–13,605	13,605–14,305	14,305–15,005	15,005–15,705	15,705–16,405
45,000	50,000	14,420	14,420–15,120	15,120–15,820	15,820–16,520	16,520–17,220	17,220–17,920	17,920–18,620

MARRIED EMPLOYEES WITH WAGES $22,000 – $50,000

22,000	24,000	4,085	4,085– 4,785	4,785– 5,485	5,485– 6,185	6,185– 6,885	6,885– 7,585	7,585– 8,285
24,000	26,000	4,425	4,425– 5,125	5,125– 5,825	5,825– 6,525	6,525– 7,225	7,225– 7,925	7,925– 8,625
26,000	28,000	4,765	4,765– 5,465	5,465– 6,165	6,165– 6,865	6,865– 7,565	7,565– 8,265	8,265– 8,965
28,000	30,000	5,105	5,105– 5,805	5,805– 6,505	6,505– 7,205	7,205– 7,905	7,905– 8,605	8,605– 9,305
30,000	35,000	5,700	5,700– 6,400	6,400– 7,100	7,100– 7,800	7,800– 8,500	8,500– 9,200	9,200– 9,900
35,000	40,000	6,550	6,550– 7,250	7,250– 7,950	7,950– 8,650	8,650– 9,350	9,350–10,050	10,050–10,750
40,000	45,000	7,400	7,400– 8,100	8,100– 8,800	8,800– 9,500	9,500–10,200	10,200–10,900	10,900–11,600
45,000	50,000	8,260	8,260– 8,960	8,960– 9,660	9,660–10,360	10,360–11,060	11,060–11,760	11,760–12,460

PRENTICE-HALL, Inc., Englewood Cliffs, N.J. Reg. § 31.3402(m)-1(a)(2)

24,258.6 (I.R.C.)   Reg. § 31.3402(m)-1(a)(3)   10-30-70

(3) *Marital status.* In determining the number of withholding allowances to which an employee is entitled on any day, the employee's status as a single person or a married person shall be determined as of such day under section 3402(l). For special rules applicable to married individuals filing separate returns, see paragraph (c)(1)(ii) of this section.

(4) *More than 6 allowances.* For purposes of applying the tables set forth in subparagraph (2), the following rule shall be applied if an employee's estimated itemized deductions exceed the maximum amount of estimated itemized deductions which would permit 6 allowances. The number of allowances permitted shall be the sum of—

(i) 6 allowances, plus

(ii) The number arrived at by dividing by $750 ($700 in the case of wages paid before January 1, 1970) the amount of estimated itemized deductions in excess of the maximum amount of estimated itemized deductions which would permit 6 allowances.

For purposes of subdivision (ii) of this subparagraph, any fractional number shall be increased to the next whole number.

(5) *Employees with wages over $50,000.* For purposes of applying the tables set forth in subparagraph (2) of this paragraph, the following rule shall be applied if an employee's wages exceed $50,000. Increase the minimum and maximum amounts of estimated itemized deductions shown for the $45,000-$50,000 bracket by an amount equal to—

(i) If the employee is single, 50 percent of the amount by which the employee's wages exceed $50,000, or

(ii) If the employee is married, 45 percent (40 percent in the case of wages paid before January 1, 1970) of the amount by which the employee's wages exceed $50,000.

(6) The provisions of subparagraphs (4) and (5) of this paragraph may be illustrated by the following examples:

Example (1). A, an unmarried calendar-year individual, has for 1970 estimated wages of $25,000 and estimated itemized deductions of $12,300. Under the provisions of subparagraph (4) of this paragraph, A may claim 10 additional withholding allowances. Pursuant to subdivision (i) of such subparagraph, A is allowed 6 allowances. Pursuant to subdivision (ii) of such subparagraph, A is allowed 4 more allowances computed as follows:

Amount of estimated itemized deductions ..	$12,300
Less: Maximum amount of estimated itemized deductions which would permit A to claim 6 allowances (see Table 1 of this paragraph)	9,925
	2,375
Divided by $750	3 1/6
Increased to next whole number	4

Example (2). B, an unmarried calendar-year individual, has for 1970 estimated wages of $53,000 and estimated itemized deductions of $18,000. Under the provisions of subparagraph (5) of this paragraph, the number of additional allowances which may be claimed is determined by increasing the minimum and maximum amounts of estimated itemized deductions for each allowance shown in the $45,000—$50,000 bracket on Table 1. In B's case these amounts are increased by $1,500 (50 percent of the amount by which his estimated wages exceeds $50,000). After this increase, the minimum and maximum amounts for 2 allowances in the $45,000—$50,000 bracket for a single taxpayer are $17,760 and $18,510. Accordingly, B may claim 2 additional withholding allowances.

Example (3). C, an unmarried calendar-year individual, has for 1970 estimated wages of $68,000 and estimated itemized deductions of $33,000. The number of additional allowances which may be claimed is determined by first increasing, under subparagraph (5) of this paragraph, the minimum and maximum amounts of estimated itemized deductions for each allowance shown in the $45,000—$50,000 bracket on Table 1. In C's case these amounts are increased by $9,000 (50 percent of the amount by which his estimated wages exceeds $50,000). After this increase, the maximum amount of estimated itemized deductions which would permit C to claim 6 allowances is $29,010. Under the provisions of subparagraph (4) of this paragraph, C may claim 12 additional withholding allowances. Pursuant to subdivision (i) of such subparagraph (4), C is allowed 6 allowances. Pursuant to subdivision (ii) of such subparagraph, C is allowed 6 more allowances computed as follows:

Amount of estimated itemized deductions ..		$33,000
Less: Maximum amount of estimated itemized deductions which would permit C to claim 6 allowances (as adjusted)	29,010	$3,990
Divided by $750		5 8/25
Increased to next whole number		6

(b) *Definitions.* For purposes of section 3402(m) and this section—

(1) *Estimated itemized deductions.* (i) Except as provided in subdivisions (ii) and (iii) of this subparagraph, the term "estimated itemized deductions" means with respect to an employee the aggregate amount of deductions which he reasonably expects will be allowed to him for the estimation year under chapter 1 of the Code other than the deductions referred to in sections 141 (relating to the standard deduction) and 151 (relating to the deductions for personal exemptions), and other than the deductions required to be taken into account by him in determining his adjusted gross income under section 62 (see § 1.62-1 of this chapter (Income Tax Regulations)).

(ii) In the case of wages paid after December 31, 1969, the amount of the estimated itemized deductions shall not exceed the sum of—

(a) The amount shown on the income tax return which the employee has filed for the taxable year preceding the estimation year of the deductions which are of the kind permitted to be taken into account in making the computation in the preceding subdivision (or if no such deductions were so shown, the amount determined under section 141(b) or (c) of the Code), and

(b) The amount of his determinable additional deductions for the estimation year, as defined in subparagraph (3) of this paragraph.

(iii) In the case of wages paid before January 1, 1970, the amount of the estimated itemized deductions shall not exceed—

(a) The amount shown on the income tax return which the employee has filed for the taxable year preceding the estimation year of the deductions which are of the kind permitted to be taken into account in making the computation in subdivision (i) of this subparagraph, or

(b) In the case of an employee who did not show such deductions on his income tax return for the taxable year preceding the estimation year, an amount equal to the lesser of $1,000 or 10 percent of the amount of wages shown on the employee's income tax return for such preceding taxable year.

(2) *Estimated wages.* The term "estimated wages" means with respect to an employee the aggregate amount which he reasonably expects will constitute wages for the estimation year. However, in the case of wages paid before January 1, 1970, such amount shall not be less than the amount of wages shown on his income tax return for the taxable year preceding the estimation year.

(3) *Determinable additional deductions.* (i) The term "determinable additional deductions" means with respect to an employee those estimated itemized deductions—

(a) Which are demonstrably attributable to identifiable events during the estimation year or the preceding taxable year, but only to the extent that they can reasonably be expected to cause an increase in the amount of itemized deductions on the employee's income tax return for the estimation year over the amount of corresponding deductions for the employee's taxable year preceding the estimation year, and

(b) Which, when added to the employee's other estimated itemized deductions for the estimation year, are in excess of the amount described in subparagraph (1)(ii)(a) of this paragraph.

(ii) Estimated itemized deductions are demonstrably attributable to an identifiable event if they relate—

(a) To payments already made (or items otherwise already deductible) during the estimation year,

(b) To binding obligations to make payments during the estimation year,

(c) To taxes deductible under section 164 for the estimation year (see subdivision (v) of this subparagraph), or

(d) To other transactions or occurrences, the implementation of which has begun and is verifiable at the time the employee files a withholding exemption certificate claiming withholding allowances for itemized deductions relating thereto.

(iii) For purposes of section 3402(m) and this section, where an itemized deduction which is demonstrably attributable to an identifiable event (as defined in subdivision (ii) of this subparagraph) is expected to result from a payment to be made by the employee, an identifiable event with respect to the deduction shall be deemed to occur in the taxable year in which the payment becomes due or is reasonably expected to be made, whichever is later, as well as in the taxable year in which the event giving rise to the payment took place. See the treatment of alimony payments in example (1) in paragraph (d) of this section.

(iv) Subdivision (ii)(b) and (d) of this subparagraph shall apply to estimated itemized deductions under section 170 only if at the time the employee files a withholding exemption certificate claiming withholding allowances for itemized deductions relating thereto he has made a written pledge to the donee with respect thereto.

(v) For purposes of subdivision (ii) of this subparagraph, no increase in the amount of taxes deductible under section 164 for the estimation year over the amount of such deductions for the employee's taxable year preceding the estimation year, which is based upon the imposition of a new tax, an increase in tax rates, or other change due to the official action of a governmental authority, shall be taken into account until such official action has been completed.

(4) *Estimation year.* The term "estimation year" means—

(i) In the case of an employee who files his income tax return on a calendar year basis—

(a) With respect to payments of wages after April 30 and on or before December 31 of any calendar year, such calendar year and

(b) With respect to payments of wages on or after January 1 and before May 1 of a calendar year, the preceding calendar year, except that with respect to an exemption certificate furnished by an employee after he has filed his return for the preceding calendar year, it means the current calendar year.

(ii) In the case of an employee who files his return on a basis other than the calendar year—

(a) With respect to payments of wages after the last day of the fourth month of the employee's taxable year and on or before the last day of the taxable year, such taxable year, or

(b) With respect to payments of wages on or after the first day of the employee's taxable year and before the first day of the

Reg. § 31.3402(m)-1(b)(4)

fifth month of the employee's taxable year, the preceding taxable year, except that with respect to an exemption certificate furnished by an employee after he has filed his return for the preceding taxable year, it means the current taxable year.

(c) *Special rules*—(1) *Married individuals.* (i) Except as provided in subdivision (ii) of this subparagraph, a husband and wife shall determine the number of withholding allowances to which they are entitled under section 3402(m) on the basis of their combined wages and deductions. The withholding allowances to which a husband and wife are entitled may be claimed by the husband, by the wife, or they may be allocated between them. However, they may not both have withholding exemption certificates in effect claiming the same withholding allowance.

(ii) If a husband and wife filed separate income tax returns for the taxable year preceding the estimation year and reasonably expect to file separate returns for the estimation year, the husband and wife shall determine the number of withholding exemptions to which they are entitled under section 3402(m) on the basis of their individual wages and deductions. For purposes of applying the tables in paragraph (a)(2) of this section, the husband and wife shall be considered as single.

(2) *Only one certificate to be in effect.* An employee who is entitled to one or more withholding allowances under section 3402 (m) and who has, at the same time, two or more employers, may claim such withholding allowance or allowances with only one of his employers.

(d) *Examples.* The provisions of this section may be illustrated by the following examples:

Example (1). Employee A, an unmarried calendar-year taxpayer, filed his income tax return for 1969 on March 20, 1970. A's estimation year with respect to withholding allowances claimed after the filing of his 1969 return is calendar-year 1970. He reasonably expects to be paid $21,000 in wages during 1970. The itemized deductions reflected on A's 1969 income tax return, and the items which he reasonably expects will be allowable as itemized deductions on his 1970 return, are as follows:

	1969	1970
alimony payments pursuant to terms of 1964 divorce decree	$2,000	$3,000
taxes	1,000	1,500
charitable contributions	500	500
deductible medical expenses	0	1,500
	$3,500	$6,500

The increase in deductible taxes expected for 1970 results from A's purchase of real estate. Approximately $1,000 of the $1,500 estimated deductible medical expenses for 1970 is reasonably expected by A to result from orthodontic services being received by his dependent daughter. She has had a diagnostic session with an orthodontist and arrangements have been made for treatments although there is no legal obligation to continue. The other $500 in deductible medical expenses expected for 1970 is not yet related to identifiable events. It is expected to arise in connection with minor cosmetic surgery which A, although he has not yet consulted a physician with respect thereto, contemplates undergoing in late 1970. Only $2,500 of A's estimated itemized deductions for 1970 qualifies as determinable additional deductions, i.e., estimated itemized deductions, in excess of his 1969 deductions which are demonstrably attributable to identifiable events occurring during 1969 or 1970, and reasonably expected to cause an increase in itemized deductions for 1970 over those for 1969. These items consist of: (a) the $1,000 in alimony payments which will be made by A during 1970 over the amount of such payments made during 1969 (an identifiable event with respect to each alimony payment occurs in the taxable year in which such payments becomes due or is made (if later)); (b) the $500 excess of deductible tax payments (over the amount deductible therefor in 1969) which A reasonably expects to pay during 1970 due to the purchase of real estate; and (c) the $1,000 expected to be deductible as a result of the orthodontic services. A's estimated itemized deductions for his 1970 estimation year are $6,000 ($3,500 plus $2,500). From Table 1 in paragraph (a)(2) of this section it is determined that A is entitled to three withholding allowances. A may file a withholding exemption certificate claiming the three withholding allowances.

Example (2). Assume the same facts as in example (1) except that the years in question were 1968 and 1969 rather than 1969 and 1970. In this case, with respect to wages paid during 1969, A's estimated itemized deductions for the estimation year would be limited to $3,500 (the amount of itemized deductions claimed for the preceding taxable year).

Example (3). Employee B, who is married and files a joint return based on a calendar year, has in effect which his employer, X Co., a withholding exemption certificate filed on May 1, 1970, on which he claimed one withholding allowance under section 3402(m) and this section. B's wife is employed but does not claim any withholding allowance. B had, on May 1, 1970, determined that based on his and his wife's combined estimated wages and estimated itemized deductions for the estimation year 1970 they were entitled to two withholding allowances under section 3402(m) and this section. On January 15, 1971, B, who is still employed by X Co. and has not yet filed his income tax return for 1970, begins work for Y Co. Even if B is still entitled to claim the two withholding allowances, he may not claim one or both such withholding allowances on the withholding exemption certificate filed with Y Co. unless he first files a new withholding exemption certificate with X Co. on which he claims no withholding allowances under section 3402(m) and this section. In any event, under paragraph (b)(1) of § 31.3402 (f)(4)-1 unless B files a new withholding exemption certificate, his claim for the withholding allowance expires and must be disregarded in determining the amount of tax to be withheld upon wages paid to B on or after May 1, 1971.

§ 31.3402(n) Statutory provisions; income tax collected at source; employees incurring no income tax liability. [Sec. 3402(n), IRC]

§ 31.3402(n)-1 (T.D. 7048, filed 6-23-70; amended by T.D. 7423, filed 6-24-76.) **Employees incurring no income tax liability.**

Notwithstanding any other provision of this subpart, an employer shall not deduct and withhold any tax under chapter 24 upon a payment of wages made to an employee after April 30, 1970, if there is in effect with respect to the payment a withholding exemption certificate furnished to the employer by the employee which contains statements that—

(1) The employee incurred no liability for income tax imposed under subtitle A of the Code for his preceding taxable year; and

(2) The employee anticipates that he will incur no liability for income tax imposed by subtitle A for his current taxable year.

For purposes of section 3402(n) and this section, an employee is not considered to incur liability for income tax imposed under subtitle A if the amount of such tax is equal to or less than the total amount of credits against such tax which are allowable to him under part IV of subchapter A of chapter 1 of the Code, other than those allowable under section 31 or 39. For purposes of this section, an employee who files a joint return under section 6013 is considered to incur liability for any tax shown on such return. An employee who is entitled to file a joint return under such section shall not certify that he anticipates that he will incur no liability for income tax imposed by subtitle A for his current taxable year if such statement would not be true in the event that he files a joint return for such year, unless he filed a separate return for his preceding taxable year and anticipates that he will file a separate return for his current taxable year. If the employer has reason to believe that the withholding exemption certificate contains any incorrect statement, the district director should be so advised. See § 31.3402 (f) (2)-1 (e) for rules relating to invalid withholding exemption certificates.

Example (1). Employee A, an unmarried, calendar-year basis taxpayer, files his income tax return for 1970 on April 15, 1971. A has adjusted gross income of $1,200 and is not liable for any tax. He had $180 of income tax withheld during 1970. A anticipates that his gross income for 1971 will be approximately the same amount, and that he will not incur income tax liability for that year. On April 20, 1971, A commences employment and furnishes his employer an exemption certificate stating that he incurred no liability for income tax imposed under subtitle A for 1970, and that he anticipates that he will incur no liability for income tax imposed under subtitle A for 1971. A's employer shall not deduct and withhold on payments of wages made to A on or after April 20, 1971. Under paragraph (c) of § 31.3402(f)(4)-1, unless A files a new exemption certificate with his employer, his employer is required to deduct and withhold upon payments of wages to A made on or after May 1, 1972. (Under § 31.3402(f)(3)-1(b), if A had been employed by his employer prior to April 20, 1971, and had furnished his employer a withholding exemption certificate not containing the statements described in § 31.-3402(n)-1 prior to furnishing the withholding exemption certificate containing such statements on April 20, 1971, his employer would not be required to give effect to the new certificate with respect to payments of wages made by him prior to July 1, 1971 (the first status determination date which occurs at least 30 days after April 20, 1971). However his employer could, if he chose, make the new certificate effective with respect to any payment of wages made on or after April 20 and before July 1, 1971.

Example (2). Assume the facts are the same as in example (1) except that for 1970 A has taxable income of $8,000, income tax liability of $1,630, and income tax withheld of $1,700. Although A received a refund of $70 due to income tax withholding of $1,700, he may not state on his exemption certificate that he incurred no liability for income tax imposed by subtitle A for 1970.

§ 31.3402(o) Statutory provisions; income tax collected at source; extension of withholding to certain payments other than wages. [Sec. 3402 (o), IRC]

§ 31.3402(o)-1 (T.D. 7068, filed 11-10-70.) **Extension of withholding to certain payments other than wages.**

(a) *Supplemental unemployment compensation benefits.* Withholding of income tax is required under section 3402(o) with respect to payments of supplemental unemployment compensation benefits made after December 31, 1970, which are treated under paragraph (b)(14) of § 31.3401(a)-1 as if they were wages.

(b) *Withholding exemption certificates.* For purposes of section 3402(f)(2) and (3) and the regulations thereunder (relating to withholding exemption certificates), in the case of supplemental unemployment compensation benefits an employment relationship shall be considered to commence with either the date on which such benefits begin to accrue or January 1, 1971, whichever is later, and the withholding exemption certificate furnished the employer with respect to such commencement of employment shall be considered the first certificate furnished the employer. The withholding exemption certificate furnished by the employee to his former employer (with whom his employment has been involuntary terminated, within the meaning of paragraph (b)(14)(ii) of § 31.3401(a)-1) shall be treated as meeting the requirements of section 3402(f)(2)(A) and the regulations thereunder if such former employer furnishes such certificate to the employee's current employer, as defined in paragraph (g) of § 31.3401(d)-1, or if such former employer is the agent of such current employer with respect to the employee's withholding exemption certificate. However, the preceding sentence shall not be applicable if such employee furnishes a new withholding exemption certificate to such current employer (or his agent), provided that such withholding exemption certificate meets the requirements of section 3402(f)(2)(A) and the regulations thereunder. See the definitions of payroll period in paragraph (c) of § 31.3401(b)-1 and of employee in paragraph (g) of § 31.3401(c)-1.

Reg. § 31.3402(o)-1(b)

24,258.10 (I.R.C.) Reg. § 31.3402(p) 7-6-76

○→ § 31.3402(p) Statutory provisions; income tax collected at source; voluntary withholding agreements. [Sec. 3402, IRC]

○→ § 31.3402(p)-1 (T.D. 7096, filed 3-17-71.) Voluntary withholding agreements.

(a) *In general.* An employee and his employer may enter into an agreement under section 3402(p) to provide for the withholding of income tax upon payments of amounts described in paragraph (b)(1) of § 31.3401(a)-3, made after December 31, 1970. An agreement may be entered into under this section only with respect to amounts which are includible in the gross income of the employee under section 61, and must be applicable to all such amounts paid by the employer to the employee. The amount to be withheld pursuant to an agreement under section 3402(p) shall be determined under the rules contained in section 3402 and the regulations thereunder.

(b) *Form and duration of agreement.* (1)(i) Except as provided in subdivision (ii) of this subparagraph, an employee who desires to enter into an agreement under section 3402(p) shall furnish his employer with Form W-4 (withholding exemption certificate) executed in accordance with the provisions of section 3402(f) and the regulations thereunder. The furnishing of such Form W-4 shall constitute a request for withholding.

(ii) In the case of an employee who desires to enter into an agreement under section 3402(p) with his employer, if the employee performs services (in addition to those to be the subject of the agreement) the remuneration for which is subject to mandatory income tax withholding by such employer, or if the employee wishes to specify that the agreement terminate on a specific date, the employee shall furnish the employer with a request for withholding which shall be signed by the employee, and shall contain—

(a) The name, address, and social security number of the employee making the request,

(b) The name and address of the employer,

(c) A statement that the employee desires withholding of Federal income tax, and

(d) If the employee desires that the agreement terminate on a specific date, the date of termination of the agreement. If accepted by the employer as provided in subdivision (iii) of this subparagraph, the request shall be attached to, and constitute part of, the employee's Form W-4. An employee who furnishes his employer a request for withholding under this subdivision shall also furnish such employer with Form W-4 if such employee does not already have a Form W-4 in effect with such employer.

(iii) No request for withholding under section 3402(p) shall be effective as an agreement between an employer and an employee until the employer accepts the request by commencing to withhold from the amounts with respect to which the request was made.

(2) An agreement under section 3402(p) shall be effective for such period as the employer and employee mutually agree upon. However, either the employer or the employee may terminate the agreement prior to the end of such period by furnishing a signed written notice to the other. Unless the employer and employee agree to an earlier termination date, the notice shall be effective with respect to the first payment of an amount in respect of which the agreement is in effect which is made on or after the first "status determination date" (January 1, May 1, July 1, and October 1 of each year) that occurs at least 30 days after the date on which the notice is furnished. If the employee executes a new Form W-4, the request upon which an agreement under section 3402(p) is based shall be attached to, and constitute a part of, such new Form W-4.

○→ § 31.3403 Statutory provisions; liability for tax. [Sec. 3403, IRC]

○→ § 31.3403-1 (T.D. 6259, filed 10-25-57; republished in T.D. 6516, filed 12-19-60.) Liability for tax.

Every employer required to deduct and withhold the tax under section 3402 from the wages of an employee is liable for the payment of such tax whether or not it is collected from the employee by the employer. If, for example, the employer deducts less than the correct amount of tax, or if he fails to deduct any part of the tax, he is nevertheless liable for the correct amount of the tax. See, however, § 31.3402(d)-1. The employer is relieved of liability to any other person for the amount of any such tax withheld and paid to the district director or deposited with a duly designated depository of the United States.

○→ § 31.3404 Statutory provisions; return and payment by governmental employer. [Sec. 3404, IRC]

○→ § 31.3404-1 (T.D. 6259, filed 10-25-57; republished in T.D. 6516, filed 12-19-60.) Return and payment by governmental employer.

If the United States, or a State, Territory, Puerto Rico, or a political subdivision thereof, or the District of Columbia, or any agency or instrumentality of any one or more of the foregoing, is an employer required to deduct and withhold tax under chapter 24, the return of the amount deducted and withheld as such tax may be made by the officer or employee having control of the payment of the wages or other officer or employee appropriately designated for that purpose. (For provisions relating to the execution and filing of returns, see Subpart G of the regulations in this part.)

GENERAL PROVISIONS RELATING TO EMPLOYMENT TAXES

○→ § 31.3502 Statutory provisions; nondeductibility of taxes in computing taxable income. [Sec. 3502, IRC]

○→ § 31.3502-1 (T.D. 6354, filed 1-13-59; republished in T.D. 6516, filed 12-19-60; amended by T.D. 6780, filed 12-21-64.) Nondeductibility of taxes in computing taxable income.

For provisions relating to the nondeductibility, in computing taxable income under subtitle A, of the taxes imposed by sections 3101, 3201, and 3211, and of the tax deducted and withheld under chapter 24, see §§ 1.164-2 and 1.275-1 of this chapter (Income Tax Regulations). For provisions relating to the credit allowable to the recipient of the income in respect of the tax deducted and withheld under chapter 24, see § 1.31-1 of this chapter (Income Tax Regulations).

§ 31.3504 Statutory provisions; acts to be performed by agents. [Sec. 3504, IRC]

§ 31.3504-1 (T.D. 6354, filed 1-13-59; republished in T.D. 6516, filed 12-19-60; amended by T.D. 7012, filed 5-14-69.) Acts to be performed by agents.

(a) *In general.* In the event wages as defined in chapter 21 or 24 of the Internal Revenue Code of 1954, or compensation as defined in chapter 22 of such Code, of an employee or group of employees, employed by one or more employers, is paid by a fiduciary, agent, or other person, or if such fiduciary, agent, or other person has the control, receipt, custody, or disposal of such wages or compensation, the district director, or director of a service center, may, subject to such terms and conditions as he deems proper, authorize such fiduciary, agent, or other person to perform such acts as are required of such employer or employers under those provisions of the Internal Revenue Code of 1954 and the regulations thereunder which have application, for purposes of the taxes imposed by such chapter or chapters, in respect of such wages or compensation. If the fiduciary, agent, or other person is authorized by the district director, or director of a service center, to perform such acts, all provisions of law including penalties) and of the regulations prescribed in pursuance of law applicable to employers in respect of such acts shall be applicable to such fiduciary, agent, or other person. However, each employer for whom such fiduciary, agent, or other person performs such acts shall remain subject to all provisions of law (including penalties) and of the regulations prescribed in pursuance of law applicable to an employer in respect of such acts. Any application for authorization to perform such acts, signed by such fiduciary, agent, or other person, shall be filed with the district director, or director of a service center, with whom the fiduciary, agent, or other person will, upon approval of such application, file returns in accordance with such authorization.

(b) *Prior authorizations continued.* An authorization in effect under section 1632 of the Internal Revenue Code of 1939 on December 31, 1954, continues in effect under section 3504 and is subject to the provisions of paragraph (a) of this section.

§ 31.3505 Statutory provisions; liability of third parties paying or providing for wages. [Sec. 3505, IRC]

§ 31.3505-1 (T.D. 7430, filed 8-19-76.) Liability of third parties paying or providing for wages.

(a) *Personal liability in case of direct payment of wages*—(1) *In general.* A lender, surety, or other person—

(i) Who is not an employer for purposes of section 3102 (relating to deduction of tax from wages under the Federal Insurance Contributions Act), section 3202 (relating to deduction of tax from compensation under the Railroad Retirement Tax Act), or section 3402 (relating to deduction of income tax from wages) with respect to an employee or group of employees, and

(ii) Who pays wages on or after January 1, 1967, directly to such employee or group of employees, employed by one or more employers, or to an agent on behalf of such employee or employees,

shall be liable in his own person and estate for payment to the United States of an amount equal to the sum of the taxes required to be deducted and withheld from those wages by the employer under subtitle C of the Code and interest from the due date of the employer's return relating to such taxes for the period in which the wages are paid.

(2) *Example.* The provisions of this paragraph may be illustrated by the following example:

Example. Pursuant to a wage claim of $200, A, a surety company, paid a net amount of $158 to B, an employee of the X Construction Company. This was done in accordance with A's payment bond covering a private construction job on which B was an employee. If X Construction Company fails to make timely payment or deposit of $42.00, the amount of tax required by subtitle C of the Code to be deducted and withheld from a $200 wage payment to B, A becomes personally liable for $42.00 (i.e., an amount equal to the unpaid taxes), plus interest upon this amount from the due date of X's return.

(b) *Personal liability where funds are supplied*—(1) *In general.* A lender, surety, or other person who—

(i) Advances funds to or for the account of an employer for the specific purpose of paying wages of the employees of that employer, and

(ii) At the time the funds are advanced, has actual notice or knowledge (within the meaning of section 6323(i)(1)) that the employer does not intend to, or will not be able to, make timely payment or deposit of the amounts of tax required by subtitle C of the Code to be deducted and withheld by the employer from those wages,

shall be liable in his own person and estate for payment to the United States of an amount equal to the sum of the taxes which are required by subtitle C of the Code to be deducted and withheld from wages paid on or after January 1, 1967, and which are not paid over to the United States by the employer, and interest from the due date of the employer's return relating to such taxes. However, the liability of the lender, surety, or other person for such taxes shall not exceed 25 percent of the amount supplied by him for the payment of wages. The preceding sentence and the second sentence of section 3505(b) limit the liability of a lender, surety, or other person arising solely by reason of section 3505, and they do not limit the liability which the lender, surety or other person may incur to the United States as a third-party beneficiary of an agreement between the lender, surety, or other person and the employer. The liability of a lender, surety, or other person does not include penalties imposed on the taxpayer.

Reg. § 31.3505-1(b)(1)

(2) *Examples.* The provisions of this paragraph may be illustrated by the following examples:

Example (1). D, a savings and loan association, advances $10,000 to Y for the specific purpose of paying the net wages of Y's employees. D advances those funds with knowledge that Y will not be able to make timely payment of the taxes required to be deducted and withheld from these wages by subtitle C of the Code. Y uses the $10,000 to pay the net wages of his employees but fails to remit withholding taxes under subtitle C in the amount of $2,600. D's liability, under this section, is limited to $2,500, 25 percent of the amount supplied for the payment of wages to Y's employees, plus interest thereon.

Example (2). E, a loan company, advances $15,000 to F, a contractor, for the specific purpose of paying $20,000 of net wages due to F's employees. E advances those funds with knowledge that F will not be able to make timely payment of the taxes required to be deducted and withheld from these wages by subtitle C of the Code. F applies $5,000 of its own funds toward payment of these wages. The amount of tax required to be deducted and withheld from the gross wages is $4,500. The limitation applicable to E's liability for withholding taxes is $3,750 (25% of $15,000). However, because E furnished only a portion of the total net wages, E is liable for $3,375 of the taxes required to be deducted and withheld ($4,500 × $15,000/$20,000) plus interest thereon.

(3) *Ordinary working capital loan.* The provisions of section 3505(b) do not apply in the case of an ordinary working capital loan made to an employer, even though the person supplying the funds knows that part of the funds advanced may be used to make wage payments in the ordinary course of business. Generally, an ordinary working capital loan is a loan which is made to enable the borrower to meet current obligations as they arise. The person supplying the funds is not obligated to determine the specific use of an ordinary working capital loan or the ability of the employer to pay the amounts of tax required by subtitle C of the Code to be deducted and withheld. However, section 3505(b) is applicable where the person supplying the funds has actual notice or knowledge (within the meaning of section 6323 (i)(1)) at the time of the advance that the funds, or a portion thereof, are to be used specifically to pay net wages, whether or not the written agreement under which the funds are advanced states a different purpose. Whether or not a lender has actual notice or knowledge that the funds are to be used to pay net wages, or merely that the funds may be so used, depends upon the facts and circumstances of each case. For example, a lender, who has actual notice or knowledge that the withheld taxes will not be paid, will be deemed to have actual notice or knowledge that the funds are to be used specifically to pay net wages where substantially all of the employer's ordinary operating expenses consist of salaries and wages even though funds for other incidental operating expenses may be supplied pursuant to an agreement described as a working capital loan agreement.

(c) *Definition of other person*—(1) *In general.* As used in this section, the term "other person" means any person who directly pays the wages or supplies funds for the specific purpose of paying the wages of an employee or group of employees of another employer. It does not include a person acting only as agent of the employer or as agent of the employees.

(2) *Examples.* The provisions of this paragraph may be illustrated by the following examples:

Example (1). Pursuant to an agreement between L, a labor union, and M, an employer, M makes monthly vacation payments (of a sum equal to a certain percentage of the remuneration paid to each union member employed by M during the previous month) to a union administered pool plan under which each employee's rights are fully vested and nonforfeitable from the time the money is paid by M. Vacation allowances are accumulated by the plan and distributed to eligible employees during their vacations. L, acting merely as a conduit with respect to these payments, would incur no liability under section 3505.

Example (2). N, a construction company, maintains a payroll account with the O Bank in which N deposits its own funds. Pursuant to an automated payroll service agreement between N and O, O prepares payroll checks and earnings statements for each of N's employees reflecting the net pay due each such employee. These checks are delivered to N for signature. After the checks are signed, O distributes them directly to N's employees on the regularly scheduled pay day. O, acting only in the capacity of a disbursing agent of N's funds, would incur no liability under section 3505 with respect to these payroll distributions. However, O may incur liability under section 3505 in the capacity of a lender if it supplies the funds for the payment of wages.

(d) *Payment of taxes and interest*—(1) *Procedure for payment.* A lender, surety, or other person may satisfy the personal liability imposed upon him by section 3505 by executing Form 4219 and filing it, accompanied by payment of the amount of tax and interest due the United States in accordance with the instructions for the form. In the event the lender, surety, or other person does not satisfy the liability imposed by section 3505, the United States may collect the liability by appropriate civil proceeding commenced within 6 years after assessment of the tax against the employer.

(2) *Effect of payment*—(i) *In general.* A person paying the amounts of tax required to be deducted and withheld by subtitle C of the Code as a result of section 3505 and this section is not required to pay the employer's portion of the payroll taxes upon those wages, or file an employer's tax return with respect to those wages, or furnish annual wage and tax statements to the employees.

(ii) *Amounts paid by a lender, surety, or other person.* Any amounts paid by the lender, surety, or other person to the United States pursuant to this section shall be credited against the liability of the employer on whose behalf those payments are made and shall also reduce the total liability imposed upon the lender, surety, or other person under section 3505 and this section.

(iii) *Amounts paid by the employer.* Any amounts paid to the United States by an employer and applied to his liability under subtitle C of the Code shall reduce the total liability imposed upon that employer by subtitle C. Such payments will also reduce the liability imposed upon a lender, surety, or other person under section 3505 except that such liability shall not be reduced by any portion of an employer's payment applied against the employer's liability under subtitle C which is in excess of the total liability imposed upon the lender, surety, or other person under section 3505. For example, if a lender supplies $1,000 to an employer for the payment of net wages, upon which $300 withholding tax liability is imposed, a part-payment of $25 by the employer which is applied to this liability would reduce the employer's total liability under subtitle C of the Code by that amount, but the liability imposed upon the lender by section 3505(b) in an amount equal to the withholding tax liability of the employer, which is limited to 25 percent of the amount supplied by him, would remain $250. However, if the employer makes another payment of $200 which is applied to his liability for the withholding taxes, the lender's liability under section 3505 attributable to the withholding taxes is reduced by $175 ($225 less $50 (the amount by which the employer's liability exceeds the lender's liability after application of the limitation)). Thus, after the second payment by the employer, the lender's liability under section 3505(b) is $75 ($250 less $175) plus interest due on the underpayment for the period of underpayment.

(e) *Returns required by employers and statements for employees.* This section does not relieve the employer of the responsibilities imposed upon him to file the returns and supply the receipts and statements required under subchapter A, Chapter 61 of the Code (relating to returns and records).

(f) *Time when liability arises.* The liability under section 3505 and this section of a lender, surety, or other person paying or supplying funds for the payment of wages is incurred on the last day prescribed for the filing of the employer's Federal employment tax return (determined without regard to any extension of time) in respect of such wages.

PRIVATE FOUNDATION EXCISE TAXES
Subpart A—Taxes on Investment Income

§ 53.4940 Statutory provisions; imposition of excise tax on investment income. [Sec. 4940, IRC]

§ 53.4940-1 (T.D. 7250, filed 12-29-72; amended by T.D. 7407, filed 3-3-76.) **Excise tax on net investment income.**

(a) *In general.* Section 4940 imposes an excise tax of 4 percent on the net investment income (as defined in section 4940(c) and paragraph (c) of this section) of a tax-exempt private foundation (as defined in section 509) for each taxable year beginning after December 31, 1969. This tax will be reported on the form the foundation is required to file under section 6033 for the taxable year, and will be paid annually at the time prescribed for filing such annual return (determined without regard to any extension of time for filing). In addition, an excise tax is imposed in the manner prescribed in paragraph (b) of this section on certain non-exempt private foundations (including certain non-exempt charitable trusts). Except as provided in the succeeding sentence, this tax is to be reported by means of a schedule attached to the organization's income tax return. For taxable years ending on or after December 31, 1975, the tax imposed by section 4940 (b) and paragraph (b) of this section on a trust described in section 4947 (a) (1) which is a private foundation shall be reported on Form 5227. The tax imposed by section 4940 (b) and this section is to be paid annually at the time the organization is required to pay its income taxes imposed under Subtitle A. Except as otherwise provided herein, no exclusions or deductions from gross investment income or credits against tax are allowable under this section.

(b) *Taxable foundations.* (1) The excise tax imposed under section 4940 on private foundations which are not exempt from taxation under section 501(a) is equal to:

(i) The amount (if any) by which the sum of

(a) The tax on net investment income imposed under section 4940(a), computed as if such private foundation were exempt from taxation under section 501(a) and described in section 501(c)(3) for the taxable year, plus

(b) The amount of the tax which would have been imposed under section 511 for such taxable year if such private foundation had been exempt from taxation under section 501(a), exceeds

(ii) The tax imposed under subtitle A on such private foundation for the taxable year.

(2) The provisions of this paragraph may be illustrated by the following examples:

Example (1). Assume that the tax liability under subtitle A for private foundation X, which is not exempt from taxation under section 501 (a) for 1970, is $10,000. Had X been exempt under section 501(a) for 1970, the tax imposed under section 4940(a) would have been $4,000 and the tax imposed under section 511 would have been $7,000. The excess of the sum of the taxes which would have been imposed under sections 4940(a) and 511 ($11,000) over the tax that was imposed under subtitle A ($10,000) is $1,000, the amount of the tax imposed on such organization under section 4940(b).

Example (2). Assume the facts stated in Example (1), except that the tax liability under subtitle A is $15,000 rather than $10,000. Because the sum of the taxes which would have been imposed under sections 4940(a) and 511 ($11,000) does not exceed the tax that was imposed under subtitle A ($15,000), there is no tax imposed under section 4940(b) with respect to such foundation.

Reg. § 53.4940-1(b)(2)

(c) *Net investment income defined*—(1) *In general.* For purposes of section 4940 (a), "net investment income" of a private foundation is the amount by which:

(i) The sum of the gross investment income (as defined in section 4940(c)(2) and paragraph (d) of this section) and the net capital gain (within the meaning of section 4940(c)(4) and paragraph (f) of this section) exceeds

(ii) The deductions allowed by section 4940(c)(3) and paragraph (e) of this section. Except to the extent inconsistent with the provisions of this section, net investment income shall be determined under the principles of subtitle A.

(2) *Tax-exempt income.* For purposes of computing net investment income under section 4940, the provisions of section 103 (relating to interest on certain governmental obligations) and section 265 (relating to expenses and interest relating to tax-exempt income) and the regulations thereunder shall apply.

(d) *Gross investment income*—(1) *In general.* For purposes of paragraph (c) of this section, "gross investment income" means the gross amounts of income from interest, dividends, rents, and royalties (including overriding royalties) received by a private foundation from all sources, but does not include such income to the extent included in computing the tax imposed by section 511. Under this definition, interest, dividends, rents, and royalties derived from assets devoted to charitable activities are includible in gross investment income. Therefore, for example, interest received on a student loan would be includible in the gross investment income of a private foundation making such loan.

(2) *Certain estate and trust disbursements.* In the case of a distribution from an estate or a trust described in section 4947(a)(1) or (2), such distribution shall not retain its character in the hands of the distributee for purposes of computing the tax under section 4940; except that, in the case of a distribution from a trust described in section 4947(a)(2), the income of such trust attributable to transfers in trust after May 26, 1969, shall retain its character in the hands of a distributee private foundation for purposes of section 4940 (unless such income is taken into account because of the application of section 671).

(3) *Treatment of certain distributions in redemption of stock.* For purposes of applying section 302(b)(1), any distribution made to a private foundation by a disqualified person (as defined in section 4946(a)), in redemption of stock held by such private foundation in a business enterprise shall be treated as not essentially equivalent to a dividend if all of the following conditions are satisfied: (i) such redemption is of stock which was owned by a private foundation on May 26, 1969 (or which is acquired by a private foundation under the terms of a trust which was irrevocable on May 26, 1969, or under the terms of a will executed on or before such date, which is in effect on such date and at all times thereafter, or would have passed under such a will but before that time actually passes under a trust which would have met the test of this subdivision but for the fact that the trust was revocable (but was not in fact revoked)); (ii) such foundation is required to dispose of such property in order not to be liable for tax under section 4943 (relating to taxes on excess business holdings); and (iii) such foundation receives in return an amount which equals or exceeds the fair market value of such property at the time of such disposition or at the time a contract for such disposition was previously executed in a transaction which would not constitute a prohibited transaction (within the meaning of section 503(b) or the corresponding provisions of prior law). In the case of a disposition before January 1, 1975, section 4943 shall be applied without taking section 4943(c)(4) into account. A distribution which otherwise qualifies under section 302 as a distribution in part or full payment in exchange for stock shall not be treated as essentially equivalent to a dividend because it does not meet the requirements of this subparagraph.

(e) *Deductions*—(1) *In general.* (i) For purposes of computing net investment income, there shall be allowed as a deduction from gross investment income all the ordinary and necessary expenses paid or incurred for the production or collection of gross investment income or for the management, conservation, or maintenance of property held for the production of such income, determined with the modifications set forth in subparagraph (2) of this paragraph. Such expenses include that portion of a private foundation's operating expenses which is paid or incurred for the production or collection of gross investment income. Taxes paid or incurred under this section are not paid or incurred for the production or collection of gross investment income. A private foundation's operating expenses include compensation of officers, other salaries and wages of employees, outside professional fees, interest, and rent and taxes upon property used in the foundation's operations. Where a private foundation's officers or employees engage in activities on behalf of the foundation for both investment purposes and for exempt purposes, compensation and salaries paid to such officers or employees must be allocated between the investment activities and the exempt activities. To the extent a private foundation's expenses are taken into account in computing the tax imposed by section 511, they shall not be deductible for purposes of computing the tax imposed by section 4940.

(ii) Where only a portion of property produces, or is held for the production of, income subject to the section 4940 excise tax, and the remainder of the property is used for exempt purposes, the deductions allowed by section 4940(c)(3) shall be apportioned between the exempt and non-exempt uses.

(iii) No amount is allowable as a deduction under this section to the extent it is paid or incurred for purposes other than those described in subdivision (i) of this subparagraph. Thus, for example, the deductions prescribed by the following sections are not allowable: (1) the charitable deduction prescribed under section 170 and 642(c); (2) the net operating loss deduction prescribed under section 172; and (3) the special deductions prescribed under Part VIII, subchapter B, chapter 1.

(2) *Deduction modifications.* The following modifications shall be made in determining deductions otherwise allowable under this paragraph:

(i) The depreciation deduction shall be allowed, but only on the basis of the straight line method provided in section 167(b)(1).

(ii) The depletion deduction shall be

allowed, but such deduction shall be determined without regard to section 613, relating to percentage depletion.

(iii) The basis to be used for purposes of the deduction allowed for depreciation or depletion shall be the basis determined under the rules of Part II of subchapter O of chapter 1, subject to the provisions of section 4940(c)(3)(B), and without regard to section 4940(c)(4)(B), relating to the basis for determining gain, or section 362(c). Thus, a private foundation must reduce the cost or other substituted or transferred basis by an amount equal to the straight line depreciation or cost depletion, without regard to whether the foundation deducted such depreciation or depletion during the period prior to its first taxable year beginning after December 31, 1969. However, where a private foundation has previously taken depreciation or depletion deductions in excess of the amount which would have been taken had the straight line or cost method been employed, such excess depreciation or depletion also shall be taken into account to reduce basis. If the facts necessary to determine the basis of property in the hands of the donor or the last preceding owner by whom it was not acquired by gift are unknown to a donee private foundation, then the original basis to such foundation of such property shall be determined under the rules of § 1.1015-1(a)(3).

(iv) The deduction for expenses paid or incurred in any taxable year for the production of gross investment income earned as an incident to a charitable function shall be no greater than the income earned from such function which is includible as gross investment income for such year. For example, where rental income is incidentally realized in 1971 from historic buildings held open to the public, deductions for amounts paid or incurred in 1971 for the production of such income shall be limited to the amount of rental income includible as gross investment income for 1971.

(f) *Capital gain and losses*—(1) *General rule.* In determining net capital gain for purposes of the tax imposed by section 4940, there shall be taken into account only capital gains and losses from the sale or other disposition of property held by a private foundation for investment purposes (other than program-related investments, as defined in section 4944(c)), and property used for the production of income included in computing the tax imposed by section 511 except to the extent gain or loss from the sale or other disposition of such property is taken into account for purposes of such tax. For taxable years beginning after December 31, 1972, property shall be treated as held for investment purposes even though such property is disposed of by the foundation immediately upon its receipt, if it is property of a type which generally produces interest, dividends, rents, royalties, or capital gains through appreciation (for example, rental real estate, stock, bonds, mineral interests, mortgages, and securities). Under this subparagraph, gains and losses from the sale or other disposition of property used for the exempt purposes of the private foundation are excluded. For example, gain or loss on the sale of the buildings used for the exempt activities of a private foundation would not be subject to the section 4940 tax. Where the foundation uses property for its exempt purposes, but also incidentally derives income from such property which is subject to the tax imposed by section 4940(a), any gain or loss resulting from the sale or other disposition of such property is not subject to the tax imposed by section 4940(a). For example, if a tax-exempt private foundation maintains buildings of a historical nature and keeps them open for public inspection, but requires a number of its employees to live in these buildings and charges the employees rent, the rent would be subject to the tax imposed by section 4940(a), but any gain or loss resulting from the sale of such property would not be subject to such tax. However, where the foundation uses property for both exempt purposes and (other than incidentally) for investment purposes (for example, a building in which the foundation's charitable and investment activities are carried on), that portion of any gain or loss from the sale or other disposition of such property which is allocable to the investment use of such property must be taken into account in computing net capital gain for such taxable year. For purposes of this paragraph, a distribution of property for purposes described in section 170(c)(1) or (2)(B) which is a qualifying distribution under section 4942 shall not be treated as a sale or other disposition of property.

(2) *Basis.* (i) The basis for purposes of determining gain from the sale or other disposition of property shall be the greater of:

(a) Fair market value on December 31, 1969, plus or minus all adjustments after December 31, 1969, and before the date of disposition under the rules of Part II of subchapter O of chapter 1, provided that the property was held by the private foundation on December 31, 1969, and continuously thereafter to the date of disposition, or

(b) Basis as determined under the rules of Part II of subchapter O of chapter 1, subject to the provisions of section 4940(c)(3)(B) (and without regard to section 362(c)).

(ii) For purposes of determining loss from the sale or other disposition of property, basis as determined in subdivision (i)(b) of this subparagraph shall apply.

(3) *Losses.* Where the sale or other disposition of property referred to in section 4940(c)(4)(A) results in a capital loss, such loss may be subtracted from capital gains from the sale or other disposition of other such property during the same taxable year, but only to the extent of such gains. Should losses from the sale or other disposition of such property exceed gains from the sale or other disposition of such property during the same taxable year, such excess may not be deducted from gross investment income under section 4940(c)(3) in any taxable year, nor may such excess be used to reduce gains in either prior or future taxable years, regardless of whether the foundation is a corporation or a trust.

(4) *Examples.* The provisions of this paragraph may be illustrated by the following examples:

Example (1). A private foundation holds certain depreciable real property on De-

Reg. § 53.4940-1(f)(4)

24,258.10-B.2-B *(I.R.C.)* Reg. § 53.4940-1(f)(4)

cember 31, 1969, having a basis of $102,000. The fair market value of such property on that date was $100,000. For its taxable year 1970 the foundation was allowed depreciation for such property of $5,100 on the straight line method, the allowable amount computed on the $102,000 basis. The property was sold on January 1, 1971, for $100,000. Because fair market value on December 31, 1969, less straight line depreciation of $5,100 ($94,900) is less than basis as determined by Part II of subchapter O of chapter 1, $96,900 ($102,000 less $5,100), a gain of $3,100 is recognized (*i.e.*, sales price of $100,000 less the greater of the two possible bases).

Example (2). Assume the same facts in Example (1), except that the sale price was $95,000. Because the sale price was $1,900 less than the basis for loss ($96,900 as determined by the application of subparagraph (2)(ii) of this paragraph), there is a capital loss of $1,900 which may be deducted against capital gains for 1971 (if any) in determining net capital gain.

Example (3). A private foundation holds certain depreciable real property on December 31, 1969, having a basis of $102,000. The fair market value of such property on that date was $110,000. For its taxable year 1970 the foundation was allowed depreciation for such property of $5,100 on the straight line method, the allowable amount computed on the $102,000 basis. The property was sold on January 1, 1971, for $100,000. Fair market value on December 31, 1969, less straight line depreciation of $5,100 ($104,900) exceeds basis as determined by Part II of subchapter O of chapter 1, $96,900 ($102,000 less $5,100), and will be used for purposes of determining gain. Because basis for purposes of determining gain exceeds sale price, there is no gain. There is no loss because basis for purposes of determining loss ($96,900) is less than sale price.

Taxes on Self-Dealing

§ 53.4941(a) **Statutory provisions; exempt organizations; private foundations; taxes on self-dealing.** [Sec. 4941(a), IRC]

§ 53.4941(a)-1 (T.D. 7270, filed 4-16-73; amended by T.D. 7299, filed 12-26-73.) **Imposition of initial taxes.**

(a) *Tax on self-dealer*—(1) *In general.* Section 4941(a)(1) of the Code imposes an excise tax on each act of self-dealing between a disqualified person (as defined in section 4946(a)) and a private foundation. Except as provided in subparagraph (2) of this paragraph, this tax shall be imposed on a disqualified person even though he had no knowledge at the time of the act that such act constituted self-dealing. Notwithstanding the preceding two sentences, however, a transaction between a disqualified person and a private foundation will not constitute an act of self-dealing if—

(i) The transaction is a purchase or sale of securities by a private foundation through a stockbroker where normal trading procedures on a stock exchange or recognized over-the-counter market are followed;

(ii) Neither the buyer nor the seller of the securities nor the agent of either knows the identity of the other party involved; and

(iii) The sale is made in the ordinary course of business, and does not involve a block of securities larger than the average daily trading volume of that stock over the previous four weeks.

However, the preceding sentence shall not apply to a trasaction involving a dealer who is a disqualified person acting as a principal or to a transaction which is an act of self-dealing pursuant to section 4941(d)(1)(B) and § 53.4941(d)-2(c)(1). The tax imposed by section 4941(a)(1) is at the rate of 5 percent of the amount involved (as defined in section 4941(e)(2) and § 53.4941(e)-1(b)) with respect to the act of self-dealing for each year or partial year in the taxable period (as defined in section 4941(e)(1)) and shall be paid by any disqualified person (other than a foundation manager acting only in the capacity of a foundation manager) who participates in the act of self-dealing. However, if a foundation manager is also acting as a self-dealer, he may be liable for both the tax imposed by section 4941(a)(1) and the tax imposed by section 4941(a)(2).

(2) *Government officials.* In the case of a government official (as defined in section 4946(c)), the tax shall be imposed upon such government official who participates in an act of self-dealing, only if he knows that such act is an act of self-dealing. See paragraph (b)(3) of this section for a definition of "knowing".

(3) *Participation.* For purposes of this paragraph, a disqualified person shall be treated as participating in an act of self-dealing in any case in which he engages or takes part in the transaction by himself or with others, or directs any person to do so.

(b) *Tax on foundation manager*—(1) *In general.* Section 4941(a)(2) of the Code imposes an excise tax on the participation of any foundation manager in an act of self-dealing between a disqualified person and a private foundation. This tax is imposed only in cases in which the following circumstances are present:

(i) A tax is imposed by section 4941(a)(1),

(ii) Such participating foundation manager knows that the act is an act of self-dealing, and

(iii) The participation by the foundation manager is willful and is not due to reasonable cause.

The tax imposed by section 4941(a)(2) is at the rate of 2½ percent of the amount involved with respect to the act of self-dealing for each year or partial year in the taxable period and shall be paid by any foundation manager described in subdivisions (ii) and (iii) of this subparagraph.

(2) *Participation.* The term "participation" shall include silence or inaction on the part of a foundation manager where he is under a duty to speak or act, as well as any affirmative action by such manager. However, a foundation manager will not be considered to have participated in an act of self-dealing where he has opposed such act in a manner consistent with the fulfillment of his responsibilities to the private foundation.

(3) *Knowing.* For purposes of section 4941, a person shall be considered to have participated in a transaction "knowing" that it is an act of self-dealing only if—

(i) He has actual knowledge of sufficient facts so that, based solely upon such facts, such transaction would be an act of self-dealing,

(ii) He is aware that such an act under these circumstances may violate the provisions of federal tax law governing self-dealing, and

(iii) He negligently fails to make reasonable attempts to ascertain whether the transaction is an act of self-dealing, or he is in fact aware that it is such an act. For purposes of this part and chapter 42, the term "knowing" does not mean "having reason to know." However, evidence tending to show that a person has reason to know of a particular fact or particular rule is relevant in determining whether he had actual knowledge of such fact or rule. Thus, for example, evidence tending to show that a person has reason to know of sufficient facts so that, based solely upon such facts, a transaction would be an act of self-dealing is relevant in determining whether he has actual knowledge of such facts.

(4) *Willful.* Participation by a foundation manager shall be deemed willful if it is voluntary, conscious, and intentional. No motive to avoid the restrictions of the law or the incurrence of any tax is necessary to make the participation willful. However, participation by a foundation manager is not willful if he does not know that the transaction in which he is participating is an act of self-dealing.

(5) *Due to reasonable cause.* A foundation manager's participation is due to reasonable cause if he has exercised his responsibility on behalf of the foundation with ordinary business care and prudence.

(6) *Advice of counsel.* If a person, after full disclosure of the factual situation to legal counsel (including house counsel), relies on the advice of such counsel expressed in a reasoned written legal opinion that an act is not an act of self-dealing under section 4941, although such act is subsequently held to be an act of self-dealing, the person's participation in such act will ordinarily not be considered "knowing" or "willful" and will ordinarily be considered "due to reasonable cause" within the meaning of section 4941(a)(2). For purposes of this subparagraph, a written legal opinion will be considered "reasoned" even if it reaches a conclusion which is subsequently determined to be incorrect so long as such opinion addresses itself to the facts and applicable law. However, a written legal opinion will not be considered "reasoned" if it does nothing more than recite the facts and express a conclusion. However, the absence of advice of counsel with respect to an act shall not, by itself, give rise to any inference that a person participated in such act knowingly, willfully, or without reasonable cause.

(c) *Burden of proof.* For provisions relating to the burden of proof in cases involving the issue whether a foundation manager or a government official has knowingly participated in an act of self-dealing, see section 7454(b).

§ 53.4941(b) Statutory provisions; private foundations; taxes on self-dealing; additional taxes. [Sec. 4941(b), IRC]

§ 53.4941(b)-1 (T.D. 7270 filed 4-16-73.) **Imposition of additional taxes.**

(a) *Tax on self-dealer.* Section 4941(b)(1) of the Code imposes an excise tax in any case in which an initial tax is imposed by section 4941(a)(1) on an act of self-dealing by a disqualified person with a private foundation and the act is not corrected within the correction period (as defined in § 53.4941(e)-1(d)). The tax imposed by section 4941(b)(1) is at the rate of 200 percent of the amount involved and shall be paid by any disqualified person (other than a foundation manager acting only in the capacity of a foundation manager) who participated in the act of self-dealing.

(b) *Tax on foundation manager.* Section 4941(b)(2) of the Code imposes an excise tax to be paid by a foundation manager in any case in which a tax is imposed by section 4941(b)(1) and the foundation manager refused to agree to part or all of the correction of the self-dealing act. The tax imposed by section 4941(b)(2) is at the rate of 50 percent of the amount involved and shall be paid by any foundation manager who refused to agree to part or all of the correction of the self-dealing act. For the limitations on liability of a foundation manager, see § 53.4941(c)-1(b).

§ 53.4941(c) Statutory provisions; private foundations; taxes on self-dealing; special rules. [Sec. 4941(c), IRC]

§ 53.4941(c)-1 (T.D. 7270, filed 4-16-73.) **Special rules.**

(a) *Joint and several liability.* (1) In any case where more than one person is liable for the tax imposed by any paragraph of section 4941(a) or (b), all such persons shall be jointly and severally liable for the taxes imposed under such paragraph with respect to such act of self-dealing.

(2) The provisions of this paragraph may be illustrated by the following example:

Example. A and B, who are managers of private foundation X, lend one of the foundation's paintings to G, a disqualified person, for display in G's office, in a transaction which gives rise to liability for tax under section 4941(a)(2) (relating to tax on foundation managers). An initial tax is imposed on both A and B with respect to the act of lending the foundation's painting to G. A and B are jointly and severally liable for the tax.

(b) *Limits on liability for management.* (1) The maximum aggregate amount of tax collectible under section 4941(a)(2) from all foundation managers with respect to any one act of self-dealing shall be $10,000, and the maximum aggregate amount of tax collectible under section 4941(b)(2) from all foundation managers with respect to any one act of self-dealing shall be $10,000.

(2) The provisions of this paragraph may be illustrated by the following example:

Example. A, a disqualified person with respect to private foundation Y, sells certain real estate having a fair market value of $500,000 to Y for $500,000 in cash. B, C, and D, all the managers of foundation Y, authorized the purchase on Y's behalf knowing that such purchase was an act of self-dealing. The actions of B, C, and D in approving the purchase were willful and not due to reasonable cause. Initial taxes are imposed upon the foundation managers under subsections (a)(2) and (c)(2) of section 4941. The tax to be paid by the foundation managers is $10,000 (the lesser of $10,000 or 2½% of the amount involved). The managers are jointly and severally liable for this $10,000, and this sum may be collected by the Internal Revenue Service from any one of them.

§ 53.4941(d) Statutory provisions; exempt organizations; private foundations; taxes on self-dealing, self-dealing defined. [Sec. 4941(d), IRC]

§ 53.4941(d)-1 (T.D. 7270, filed 4-16-73.) **Definition of self-dealing.**

(a) *In general.* For purposes of section 4941, the term "self-dealing" means

Reg. § 53.4941(d)-1(a)

24,258.10-B.4 (I.R.C.)   Reg. § 53.4941(d)-1(a)   4-30-73

any direct or indirect transaction described in § 53.4941(d)-2. For purposes of this section, it is immaterial whether the transaction results in a benefit or a detriment to the private foundation. The term "self-dealing" does not, however, include a transaction between a private foundation and a disqualified person where the disqualified person status arises only as a result of such transaction. For example, the bargain sale of property to a private foundation is not a direct act of self-dealing if the seller becomes a disqualified person only by reason of his becoming a substantial contributor as a result of the bargain element of the sale. For the effect of sections 4942, 4943, 4944, and 4945 upon an act of self-dealing which also results in the imposition of tax under one or more of such sections, see the regulations under those sections.

(b) *Indirect self-dealing*—(1) *Certain business transactions.* The term "indirect self-dealing" shall not include any transaction described in § 53.4941(d)-2 between a disqualified person and an organization controlled by a private foundation (within the meaning of subparagraph (5) of this paragraph) if—

(i) The transaction results from a business relationship which was established before such transaction constituted an act of self-dealing (without regard to this paragraph).

(ii) The transaction was at least as favorable to the organization controlled by the foundation as an arm's-length transaction with an unrelated person, and

(iii) Either—

(*a*) The organization controlled by the foundation could have engaged in the transaction with someone other than a disqualified person only at a severe economic hardship to such organization, or

(*b*) Because of the unique nature of the product or services provided by the organization controlled by the foundation, the disqualified person could not have engaged in the transaction with anyone else, or could have done so only by incurring severe economic hardship. See example (2) of subparagroph (8) of this paragraph.

(2) *Grants to intermediaries.* The term "indirect self-dealing" shall not include a transaction engaged in with a government official by an intermediary organization which is a recipient of a grant from a private foundation and which is not controlled by such foundation (within the meaning of subparagraph (5) of this paragraph) if the private foundation does not earmark the use of the grant for any named government official and there does not exist an agreement, oral or written, whereby the grantor foundation may cause the selection of the government official by the intermediary organization. A grant by a private foundation is earmarked if such grant is made pursuant to an agreement, either oral or written, that the grant will be used by any named individual. Thus, a grant by a private foundation shall not constitute an indirect act of self-dealing even though such foundation had reason to believe that certain government officials would derive benefits from such grant so long as the intermediary organization exercises control, in fact, over the selection process and actually makes the selection completely independently of the private foundation. See example (3) of subparagraph (8) of this paragraph.

(3) *Transactions during the administration of an estate or revocable trust.* The term "indirect self-dealing" shall not include a transaction with respect to a private foundation's interest or expectancy in property (whether or not encumbered) held by an estate (or revocable trust, including a trust which has become irrevocable on a grantor's death), regardless of when title to the property vests under local law, if—

(i) The administrator or executor of an estate or trustee of a revocable trust either—

(*a*) Possesses a power of sale with respect to the property.

(*b*) Has the power to reallocate the property to another beneficiary, or

(*c*) Is required to sell the property under the terms of any option subject to which the property was acquired by the estate (or revocable trust);

(ii) Such transaction is approved by the probate court having jurisdiction over the estate (or by another court having jurisdiction over the estate (or trust) or over the private foundation);

(iii) Such transaction occurs before the estate is considered terminated for Federal income tax purposes pursuant to paragraph (a) of § 1.641(b)-3 of this chapter (or in the case of a revocable trust, before it is considered subject to section 4947);

(iv) The estate (or trust) receives an amount which equals or exceeds the fair market value of the foundation's interest or expectancy in such property at the time of the transaction, taking into account the terms of any option subject to which the property was acquired by the estate (or trust); and

(v) With respect to transactions occurring after April 16, 1973, the transaction either—

(*a*) Results in the foundation receiving an interest or expectancy at least as liquid as the one it gave up,

(*b*) Results in the foundation receiving an asset related to the active carrying out of its exempt purposes, or

(*c*) Is required under the terms of any option which is binding on the estate (or trust).

(4) *Transactions with certain organizations.* A transaction between a private foundation and an organization which is not controlled by the foundation (within the meaning of subparagraph (5) of this paragraph), and which is not described in section 4946(a)(1)(E), (F), or (G) because persons described in section 4946(a)(1)(A), (B), (C), or (D) own no more than 35 percent of the total combined voting power or profits or beneficial interest of such organization, shall not be treated as an indirect act of self-dealing between the foundation and such disqualified persons solely because of the ownership interest of such persons in such organization.

(5) *Control.* For purposes of this paragraph, an organization is controlled by a private foundation if the foundation or one or more of its foundation managers (acting only in such capacity) may, only by aggregating their votes or positions of authority, require the organization to engage in a transaction which if engaged in with the private foundation would consti-

tute self-dealing. Similarly, for purposes of this paragraph, an organization is controlled by a private foundation in the case of such a transaction between the organization and a disqualified person, if such disqualified person, together with one or more persons who are disqualified persons by reason of such a person's relationship (within the meaning of section 4946(a)(1)(C) through (G)) to such disqualified person, may, only by aggregating their votes or positions of authority with that of the foundation, require the organization to engage in such a transaction. The "controlled" organization need not be a private foundation; for example, it may be any type of exempt or nonexempt organization including a school, hospital, operating foundation, or social welfare organization. For purposes of this paragraph, an organization will be considered to be controlled by a private foundation or by a private foundation and disqualified persons referred to in the second sentence of this subparagraph if such persons are able, in fact, to control the organization (even if their aggregate voting power is less than 50 percent of the total voting power of the organization's governing body) or if one or more of such persons has the right to exercise veto power over the actions of such organization relevant to any potential acts of self-dealing. A private foundation shall not be regarded as having control over an organization merely because it exercises expenditure responsibility (as defined in section 4945(d)(4) and (h)) with respect to contributions to such organization. See example (6) of subparagraph (8) of this paragraph.

(6) *Certain transactions involving limited amounts.* The term "indirect self-dealing" shall not include any transaction between a disqualified person and an organization controlled by a private foundation (within the meaning of subparagraph (5) of this paragraph) or between two disqualified persons where the foundation's assets may be affected by the transaction if—

(i) The transaction arises in the normal and customary course of a retail business engaged in with the general public,

(ii) In the case of a transaction between a disqualified person and an organization controlled by a private foundation, the transaction is at least as favorable to the organization controlled by the foundation as an arm's-length transaction with an unrelated person, and

(iii) The total of the amounts involved in such transactions with respect to any one such disqualified person in any one taxable year does not exceed $5,000.
See example (7) of subparagraph (8) of this paragraph.

(7) *Applicability of statutory exceptions to indirect self-dealing.* The term "indirect self-dealing" shall not include a transaction involving one or more disqualified persons to which a private foundation is not a party, in any case in which the private foundation, by reason of section 4941(d)(2), could itself engage in such a transaction. Thus, for example, even if a private foundation has control (within the meaning of subparagraph (5) of this paragraph) of a corporation, the corporation may pay to a disqualified person, except a government official, reasonable compensation for personal services.

(8) *Examples.* The provisions of this paragraph may be illustrated by the following examples:

Example (1). Private foundation P owns the controlling interest of the voting stock of corporation X, and as a result of such interest, elects a majority of the board of directors of X. Two of the foundation managers, A and B, who are also directors of corporation X, form corporation Y for the purpose of building and managing a country club. A and B receive a total of 40 percent of Y's stock, making Y a disqualified person with respect to P under section 4946(a)(1)(E). In order to finance the construction and operation of the country club, Y requested and received a loan in the amount of $4,000,000 from X. The making of the loan by X to Y shall constitute an indirect act of self-dealing between P and Y.

Example (2). Private foundation W owns the controlling interest of the voting stock of corporation X, a manufacturer of certain electronic computers. Corporation Y, a disqualified person with respect to W, owns the patent for, and manufactures, one of the essential component parts used in the computers. X has been making regular purchases of the patented component from Y since 1965, subject to the same terms as all other purchasers of such component parts. X could not buy similar components from another source. Consequently, X would suffer severe economic hardship if it could not continue to purchase these components from Y, since it would then be forced to develop a computer which could be constructed with other components. Under these circumstances, the continued purchase by X from Y of these components shall not be an indirect act of self-dealing between W and Y.

Example (3). Private foundation Y made a grant to M University, an organization described in section 170(b)(1)(A)(ii), for the purpose of conducting a seminar to study methods for improving the administration of the judicial system. M is not controlled by Y within the meaning of subparagraph (5) of this paragraph. In conducting the seminar, M made payments to certain government officials. By the nature of the grant, Y had reason to believe that government officials would be compensated for participation in the seminar. M, however, had completly independent control over the selection of such participants. Thus, such grant by Y shall not constitute an indirect act of self-dealing with respect to the government officials.

Example (4). A, a substantial contributor to P, a private foundation, bequeathed one-half of his estate to his spouse and one-half of his estate to P. Included in A's estate is a one-third interest in AB, a partnership. The other two-thirds interest in AB is owned by B, a disqualified person with respect to P. The one-third interest in AB was subject to an option agreement when it was acquired by the estate. The executor of A's estate sells the one-third interest in AB to B pursuant to such option agreement at the price fixed in such option agreement in a sale which meets the requirements of subparagraph (3) of this paragraph. Under these circumstances, the sale does not constitute an indirect act of self-dealing between B and P.

Reg. § 53.4941(d)-1(b)(8)

Example (5). A bequeathed $100,000 to his wife and a piece of unimproved real estate of equivalent value to private foundation Z, of which A was the creator and a foundation manager. Under the laws of State Y, to which the estate is subject, title to the real estate vests in the foundation upon A's death. However, the executor has the power under State law to reallocate the property to another beneficiary. During a reasonable period for administration of the estate, the executor exercises this power and distributes the $100,000 cash to the foundation and the real estate to A's wife. The probate court having jurisdiction over the estate approves the executor's action. Under these circumstances, the executor's action does not constitute an indirect act of self-dealing between the foundation and A's wife.

Example (6). Private foundation P owns 20 percent of the voting stock of corporation W. A, a substantial contributor with respect to P, owns 16 percent of the voting stock of corporation W. B, A's son, owns 15 percent of the voting stock of corporation W. The terms of the voting stock are such that P, A, and B could vote their stock in a block to elect a majority of the board of directors of W. W is treated as controlled by P (within the meaning of subparagraph (5) of this paragraph) for purposes of this example. A and B also own 50 percent of the stock of corporation Y, making Y a disqualified person with respect to P under section 4946(a)(1)(E). W makes a loan to Y of $1,000,000. The making of this loan by W to Y shall constitute an indirect act of self-dealing between P and Y.

Example (7). A, a disqualified person with respect to private foundation P, enters into a contract with corporation M, which is also a disqualified person with respect to P. P owns 20 percent of M's stock, and controls M within the meaning of subparagraph (5) of this paragraph. M is in the retail department store business. Purchases by A of goods sold by M in the normal and customary course of business at retail or higher prices are not indirect acts of self-dealing so long as the total of the amounts involved in all of such purchases by A in any one year does not exceed $5,000.

§ 53.4941(d)-2 (T.D. 7270, filed 4-16-73.) **Specific acts of self-dealing.**

Except as provided in § 53.4941(d)-3 or § 53.4941(d)-4—

(a) *Sale or exchange of property*—(1) *In general.* The sale or exchange of property between a private foundation and a disqualified person shall constitute an act of self-dealing. For example, the sale of incidental supplies by a disqualified person to a private foundation shall be an act of self-dealing regardless of the amount paid to the disqualified person for the incidental supplies. Similarly, the sale of stock or other securities by a disqualified person to a private foundation in a "bargain sale" shall be an act of self-dealing regardless of the amount paid for such stock or other securities. An installment sale may be subject to the provisions of both section 4941(d)(1)(A) and section 4941(d)(1)(B).

(2) *Mortgaged property.* For purposes of subparagraph (1) of this paragraph, the transfer of real or personal property by a disqualified person to a private foundation shall be treated as a sale or exchange if the foundation assumes a mortgage or similar lien which was placed on the property prior to the transfer, or takes subject to a mortgage or similar lien which a disqualified person placed on the property within the 10-year period ending on the date of transfer. For purposes of this subparagraph, the term "similar lien" shall include, but is not limited to, deeds of trust and vendors' liens, but shall not include any other lien if such lien is insignificant in relation to the fair market value of the property transferred.

(b) *Leases*—(1) *In general.* Except as provided in subparagraph (2) of this paragraph, the leasing of property between a disqualified person and a private foundation shall constitute an act of self-dealing.

(2) *Certain leases without charge.* The leasing of property by a disqualified person to a private foundation shall not be an act of self-dealing if the lease is without charge. For purposes of this subparagraph, a lease shall be considered to be without charge even though the private foundation pays for janitorial services, utilities, or other maintenance costs it incurs for the use of the property, so long as the payment is not made directly or indirectly to a disqualified person.

(c) *Loans*—(1) *In general.* Except as provided in subparagraphs (2), (3), and (4) of this paragraph, the lending of money or other extension of credit between a private foundation and a disqualified person shall constitute an act of self-dealing. Thus, for example, an act of self-dealing occurs where a third party purchases property and assumes a mortgage, the mortgagee of which is a private foundation, and subsequently the third party transfers the property to a disqualified person who either assumes liability under the mortgage or takes the property subject to the mortgage. Similarly, except in the case of the receipt and holding of a note pursuant to a transaction described in § 53.4941(d)-1(b)(3), an act of self-dealing occurs where a note, the obligor of which is a disqualified person, is transferred by a third party to a private foundation which becomes the creditor under the note.

(2) *Loans without interest.* Subparagraph (1) of this paragraph shall not apply to the lending of money or other extension of credit by a disqualified person to a private foundation if the loan or other extension of credit is without interest or other charge.

(3) *Certain evidences of future gifts.* The making of a promise, pledge, or similar arrangement to a private foundation by a disqualified person, whether evidenced by an oral or written agreement, a promissory note, or other instrument of indebtedness, to the extent motivated by charitable intent and unsupported by consideration, is not an extension of credit (within the meaning of this paragraph) before the date of maturity.

(4) *General banking functions.* Under section 4941(d)(2)(E) the performance by a bank or trust company which is a disqualified person of trust functions and certain general banking services for a private foundation is not an act of self-dealing, where the banking services are reasonable

and necessary to carrying out the exempt purposes of the private foundation, if the compensation paid to the bank or trust company, taking into account the fair interest rate for the use of the funds by the bank or trust company, for such services is not excessive. The general banking services allowed by this subparagraph are:

(i) Checking accounts, as long as the bank does not charge interest on any overwithdrawals,

(ii) Savings accounts, as long as the foundation may withdraw its funds on no more than 30-days' notice without subjecting itself to a loss of interest on its money for the time during which the money was on deposit, and

(iii) Safekeeping activities.
See example (3) of § 53.4941(d)-3(c)(2).

(d) *Furnishing goods, services, or facilities*—(1) *In general.* Except as provided in subparagraph (2) or (3) of this paragraph (or § 53.4941(d)-3(b)), the furnishing of goods, services, or facilities between a private foundation and a disqualified person shall constitute an act of self-dealing. This subparagraph shall apply, for example, to the furnishing of goods, services, or facilities such as office space, automobiles, auditoriums, secretarial help, meals, libraries, publications, laboratories, or parking lots. Thus, for example, if a foundation furnishes personal living quarters to a disqualified person (other than a foundation manager or employee) without charge, such furnishing shall be an act of self-dealing.

(2) *Furnishing of goods, services, or facilities to foundation managers and employees.* The furnishings of goods, services, or facilities such as those described in subparagraph (1) of this paragraph to a foundation manager in recognition of his services as a foundation manager, or to another employee (including an individual who would be an employee but for the fact that he receives no compensation for his services) in recognition of his services in such capacity, is not an act of self-dealing if the value of such furnishing (whether or not includible as compensation in his gross income) is reasonable and necessary to the performance of his tasks in carrying out the exempt purposes of the foundation and, taken in conjunction with any other payment of compensation or payment or reimbursement of expenses to him by the foundation, is not excessive. For example, if a foundation furnishes meals and lodging which are reasonable and necessary (but not excessive) to a foundation manager by reason of his being a foundation manager, then, without regard to whether such meals and lodging are excludable from gross income under section 119 as furnished for the convenience of the employer, such furnishing is not an act of self-dealing. For the effect of section 4945(d)(5) upon an expenditure for unreasonable administrative expenses, see § 53.4945-6(b)(2).

(3) *Furnishing of goods, services, or facilities by a disqualified person without charge.* The furnishing of goods, services, or facilities by a disqualified person to a private foundation shall not be an act of self-dealing if they are furnished without charge. Thus, for example, the furnishing of goods such as pencils, stationery, or other incidental supplies, or the furnishing of facilities such as a building, by a disqualified person to a foundation shall be allowed if such supplies or facilities are furnished without charge. Similarly, the furnishing of services (even though such services are not personal in nature) shall be permitted if such furnishing is without charge. For purposes of this subparagraph, a furnishing of goods shall be considered without charge even though the private foundation pays for transportation, insurance, or maintenance costs it incurs in obtaining or using the property, so long as the payment is not made directly or indirectly to the disqualified person.

(e) *Payment of compensation.* The payment of compensation (or payment or reimbursement of expenses) by a private foundation to a disqualified person shall constitute an act of self-dealing. See, however, § 53.4941(d)-3(c) for the exception for the payment of compensation by a foundation to a disqualified person for personal services which are reasonable and necessary to carry out the exempt purposes of the foundation.

(f) *Transfer or use of the income or assets of a private foundation*—(1) *In general.* The transfer to, or use by or for the benefit of, a disqualified person of the income or assets of a private foundation shall constitute an act of self-dealing. For purposes of the preceding sentence, the payment by a private foundation of any tax imposed on a disqualified person by chapter 42 shall be treated as a transfer of the income or assets of a private foundation for the benefit of a disqualified person. Similarly, the payment by a private foundation of the premiums for an insurance policy providing liability insurance to a foundation manager for chapter 42 taxes shall be an act of self-dealing under this paragraph unless such premiums are treated as part of the compensation paid to such manager.
In addition, the purchase or sale of stock or other securities by a private foundation shall be an act of self-dealing if such purchase or sale is made in an attempt to manipulate the price of the stock or other securities to the advantage of a disqualified person. Similarly, the indemnification (of a lender) or guarantee (of repayment) by a private foundation with respect to a loan to a disqualified person shall be treated as a use for the benefit of a disqualified person of the income or assets of the foundation (within the meaning of this subparagraph). In addition, if a private foundation makes a grant or other payment which satisfies the legal obligation of a disqualified person, such grant or payment shall ordinarily constitute an act of self-dealing to which this subparagraph applies. However, if a private foundation makes a grant or payment which satisfies a pledge, enforceable under local law, to an organization described in section 501(c)(3), which pledge is made on or before April 16, 1973, such grant or payment shall not constitute an act of self-dealing to which this subparagraph applies so long as the disqualified person obtains no substantial benefit, other than the satisfaction of his obligation, from such grant or payment.

(2) *Certain incidental benefits.* The fact that a disqualified person receives an incidental or tenuous benefit from the use by a foundation of its income or assets will not, by itself, make such use an act of self-

Reg. § 53.4941(d)-2(f)(2)

dealing. Thus, the public recognition a person may receive, arising from the charitable activities of a private foundation to which such person is a substantial contributor, does not in itself result in an act of self-dealing since generally the benefit is incidental and tenuous. For example, a grant by a private foundation to a section 509(a)(1), (2), or (3) organization will not be an act of self-dealing merely because such organization is located in the same area as a corporation which is a substantial contributor to the foundtion, or merely because one of the section 509(a)(1), (2), or (3) organization's officers, directors, or trustees is also a manager of or a substantial contributor to the foundation. Similarly, a scholarship or a fellowship grant to a person other than a disqualified person, which is paid or incurred by a private foundation in accordance with a program which is consistent with—

(i) The requirements of the foundation's exempt status under section 501(c)(3),

(ii) The requirements for the allowance of deductions under section 170 for contributions made to the foundation, and

(iii) The requirements of section 4945(g)(1), will not be an act of self-dealing under section 4941(d)(1) merely because a disqualified person indirectly receives an incidental benefit from such grant. Thus, a scholarship or a fellowship grant made by a private foundation in accordance with a program to award scholarships or fellowship grants to the children of employees of a substantial contributor shall not constitute an act of self-dealing if the requirements of the preceding sentence are satisfied. For an example of the kind of scholarship program with an employment nexus that meets the above requirements, see § 53.4945-4(b)(5) (Example 1).

(3) *Indemnification of foundation managers against liability for contesting chapter 42 taxes.* Except as provided in § 53.4941(d)-3(c), section 4941(d)(1) shall not apply to the indemification by a private foundation of a foundation manager, with respect to his defense in a judicial or administrative proceeding involving chapter 42 or state laws relating to mismanagement of funds of charitable organizations, against all expenses (other than taxes, penalties, or expenses of correction) including attorneys' fees, if—

(i) Such expenses are reasonably incurred by him in connection with such proceeding, and

(ii) He is successful in such defense, or such proceeding is terminated by settlement, and he has not acted willfully and without reasonable cause with respect to the act or failure to act which led to liability for tax under chapter 42. Similarly, except as provided in § 53.4941(d)-3(c), section 4941(d)(1) shall not apply to premiums for insurance to reimburse a foundation for an indemnification payment allowed pursuant to this subparagraph.

(4) *Examples.* The provisions of this paragraph may be illustrated by the following examples:

Example (1). M, a private foundation, makes a grant of $50,000 to the governing body of N City for the purpose of alleviating the slum conditions which exist in a particular neighborhood of N. Corporation P, a substantial contributor to M, is located in the same area in which the grant is to be used. Although the general improvement of the area may constitute an incidental and tenuous benefit to P, such benefit by itself will not constitute an act of self-dealing.

Example (2). Private foundation X established a program to award scholarship grants to the children of employees of corporation M, a substantial contributor to X. After disclosure of the method of carrying out such program, X received a determination letter from the Internal Revenue Service stating that X is exempt from taxation under section 501(c)(3), that contributions to X are deductible under section 170, and that X's scholarship program qualifies under section 4945(g)(1). A scholarship grant to a person not a disqualified person with respect to X paid or incurred by X in accordance with such program shall not be an indirect act of self-dealing between X and M.

Example (3). Private foundation Y owns voting stock in corporation Z, the management of which includes certain disqualified persons with respect to Y. Prior to Z's annual stockholder meeting, the management solicits and receives the foundation's proxies. The transfer of such proxies in and of itself shall not be an act of self-dealing.

Example (4). A, a disqualified person with respect to private foundation S, contributes certain real estate to S for the purpose of building a neighborhood recreation center in a particular underprivileged area. As a condition of the gift, S agrees to name the recreation center after A. Since the benefit to A is only incidental and tenuous, the naming of the recreation center, by itself, will not be an act of self-dealing.

(g) *Payment to a government official.* Except as provided in section 4941(d)(2)(G) or § 53.4941(d)-3(e), the agreement by a private foundation to make any payment of money or other property to a government official, as defined in section 4946(c), shall constitute an act of self-dealing. For purposes of this paragraph, an individual who is otherwise described in section 4946(c) shall be treated as a government official while on leave of absence from the government without pay.

○━ § 53.4941(d)-3 (T.D. 7270, filed 4-16-73.) Exceptions to self-dealing.

(a) *General rule.* In general, a transaction described in section 4941(d)(2)(B), (C), (D), (E), (F), or (G) is not an act of self-dealing. Section 4941(d)(2)(B) and (C) provides limited exceptions to certain specific transactions, as described in paragraphs (b)(2), (c)(2), and (d)(3) of § 53.-4941(d)-2. Section 4941(d)(2)(D), (E), (F), and (G) and paragraphs (b) through (e) of this section describe certain transactions which are not acts of self-dealing.

(b) *Furnishing of goods, services, or facilities to a disqualified person*—(1) *In general.* Under section 4941(d)(2)(D), the furnishing of goods, services, or facilities by a private foundation to a disqualified person shall not be an act of self-dealing if such goods, services, or facilities are made available to the general public on at least as favorable a basis as they are made available to the disqualified person. This subparagraph shall not apply, however, in the case of goods, services or facilities furnished later than May 16, 1973, unless such goods, services or facilities are functionally related, within the meaning of section 4942(j)(5), to the exercise or performance by a private foundation of its charitable, educational, or other purpose or function constituting the basis for its exemption under section 501(c)(3).

(2) *General public.* For purposes of this paragraph, the term "general public" shall include those persons who, because of the particular nature of the activities of the private foundation, would be reasonably expected to utilize such goods, services, or facilities. This paragraph shall not apply, however, unless there are a substantial number of persons other than disqualified persons who are actually utilizing such goods, services or facilities. Thus, a private foundation which furnishes recreational or park facilities to the general public may furnish such facilities to a disqualified person provided they are furnished to him on a basis which is not more favorable than that on which they are furnished to the general public. Similarly, the sale of a book or magazine by a private foundation to disqualified persons shall not be an act of self-dealing if the publication of such book or magazine is functionally related to a charitable or educational activity of the foundation and the book or magazine is made available to the disqualified persons and the general public at the same price. In addition, if the terms of the sale require, for example, payment within 60 days from the date of delivery of the book or magazine, such terms are consistent with normal commercial practices, and payment is made within the 60-day period, the transaction shall not be treated as a loan or other extension of credit under § 53.4941(d)-2(c)(1).

(c) *Payment of compensation for certain personal services*—(1) *In general.* Under section 4941(d)(2)(E), except in the case of a government official (as defined in section 4946(c)), the payment of compensation (and the payment or reimbursement of expenses, including reasonable advances for expenses anticipated in the immediate future) by a private foundation to a disqualified person for the performance of personal services which are reasonable and necessary to carry out the exempt purpose of the private foundation shall not be an act of self-dealing if such compensation (or payment or reimbursement) is not excessive. For purposes of this subparagraph the term "personal services" includes the services of a broker serving as agent for the private foundation, but not the services of a dealer who buys from the private foundation as principal and resells to third parties. For the determination whether compensation is excessive, see § 1.162-7 of this chapter (Income Tax Regulations). This paragraph applies without regard to whether the person who receives the compensation (or payment or reimbursement) is an individual. The portion of any payment which represents payment for property shall not be treated as payment of compensation (or payment or reimbursement of expenses) for the performance of personal services for purposes of this paragraph. For rules with respect to the performance of general banking services, see § 53.4941

(d)-2(c)(4). Further, the making of a cash advance to a foundation manager or employee for expenses on behalf of the foundation is not an act of self-dealing, so long as the amount of the advance is reasonable in relation to the duties and expense requirements of the foundation manager. Except where reasonably allowable pursuant to subdivision (iii) of this subparagraph, such advances shall not ordinarily exceed $500. For example, if a foundation makes an advance to a foundation manager to cover anticipated out-of-pocket current expenses for a reasonable period (such as a month) and the manager accounts to the foundation under a periodic reimbursement program for actual expenses incurred, the foundation will not be regarded as having engaged in an act of self-dealing—

(i) When it makes the advance,

(ii) When it replenishes the funds upon receipt of supporting vouchers from the foundation manager, or

(iii) If it temporarily adds to the advance to cover extraordinary expenses anticipated to be incurred in fulfillment of a special assignment (such as long distance travel).

(2) *Examples.* The provisions of this paragraph may be illustrated by the following examples:

Example (1). M, a partnership, is a firm of ten lawyers engaged in the practice of law. A and B, partners in M, serve as trustees to private foundation W and, therefore, are disqualified persons. In addition, A and B own more than 35 percent of the profits interest in M, thereby making M a disqualified person. M performs various legal services for W from time to time as such services are requested. The payment of compensation by W to M shall not constitute an act of self-dealing if the services performed are reasonable and necessary for the carrying out of W's exempt purposes and the amount paid by W for such services is not excessive.

Example (2). C, a manager of private foundation X, owns an investment counseling business. Acting in his capacity as an investment counselor, C manages X's investment portfolio for which he receives an amount which is determined to be not excessive. The payment of such compensation to C shall not constitute an act of self-dealing.

Example (3). M, a commercial bank, serves as a trustee for private foundation Y. In addition to M's duties as trustee, M maintains Y's checking and savings accounts and rents a safety deposit box to Y. The use of the funds by M and the payment of compensation by Y to M for such general banking services shall be treated as the payment of compensation for the performance of personal services which are reasonable and necessary to carry out the exempt purposes of Y if such compensation is not excessive.

Example (4). D, a substantial contributor to private foundation Z, owns a factory which manufactures microscopes. D contracts with Z to manufacture 100 microscopes for Z. Any payment to D under the contract shall constitute an act of

Reg. § 53.4941(d)-3(c)(2)

self-dealing, since such payment does not constitute the payment of compensation for the performance of personal services.

(d) *Certain transactions between a foundation and a corporation*—(1) *In general.* Under section 4941(d)(2)(F), any transaction between a private foundation and a corporation which is a disqualified person will not be an act of self-dealing if such transaction is engaged in pursuant to a liquidation, merger, redemption, recapitalization, or other corporate adjustment, organization, or reorganization, so long as all the securities of the same class as that held (prior to such transaction) by the foundation are subject to the same terms and such terms provide for receipt by the foundation of no less than fair market value. For purposes of this paragraph, all of the securities are not "subject to the same terms" unless, pursuant to such transaction, the corporation makes a bona fide offer on a uniform basis to the foundation and every other person who holds such securities. The fact that a private foundation receives property, such as debentures, while all other persons holding securities of the same class receive cash for their interests, will be evidence that such offer was not made on a uniform basis. This paragraph may apply even if no other person holds any securities of the class held by the foundation. In such event, however, the consideration received by holders of other classes of securities, or the interests retained by holders of such other classes, when considered in relation to the consideration received by the foundation, must indicate that the foundation received at least as favorable treatment in relation to its interests as the holders of any other class of securities. In addition, the foundation must receive no less than the fair market value of its interests.

(2) *Examples.* The provisions of this paragraph may be illustrated by the following examples:

Example (1). Private foundation X owns 50 percent of the Class A preferred stock of corporation M, which is a disqualified person with respect to X. The terms of such securities provide that the stock may be called for redemption at any time by M at 105 percent of the face amount of the stock. M exercises this right and calls all the Class A preferred stock by paying 105 percent of the face amount in cash. At the time of the redemption of the Class A preferred stock, it is determined that the fair market value of the preferred stock is equal to its face amount. In such case, the redemption by M of the preferred stock of X is not an act of self-dealing.

Example (2). Private foundation Y, which is on a calendar year basis, acquires 60 percent of the Class A preferred stock of corporation N by will on January 10, 1970. N, which is also on a calendar year basis, is a disqualified person with respect to Y. In 1971, N offers to redeem all of the Class A preferred stock for a consideration equal to 100 percent of the face amount of such stock by the issuance of debentures. The offer expires January 2, 1972. Both Y and all other holders of the Class A preferred stock accept the offer and enter into the transaction on January 2, 1972, at which time it is determined that the fair market value of the debentures is no less than the fair market value of the preferred stock. The transaction on January 2, 1972, shall not be treated as an act of self-dealing for 1972. However, because under § 53.4941(e)-1(e)(1)(i) an act of self-dealing occurs on the first day of each taxable year or portion of a taxable year that an extension of credit from a foundation to a disqualified person goes uncorrected, if such debentures are held by Y after December 31, 1972, except as provided in § 53.4941(d)-4(c)(4), such extension of credit shall not be excepted from the definition of an act of self-dealing by reason of the January 2, 1972, transaction. See § 53.4941(d)-4(c)(4) for rules indicating that under certain circumstances such debentures could be held by Y until December 31, 1979.

(e) *Certain payments to government officials.* Under section 4941(d)(2)(G), in the case of a government official, in addition to the exceptions provided in section 4941(d)(2)(B), (C), and (D), section 4941(d)(1) shall not apply to—

(1) A prize or award which is not includible in gross income under section 74(b), if the government official receiving such prize or award is selected from the general public;

(2) A scholarship or a fellowship grant which is excludable from gross income under section 117(a) and which is to be utilized for study at an educational institution described in section 151(e)(4);

(3) Any annuity or other payment (forming part of a stock-bonus, pension, or profit sharing plan) by a trust which constitutes a qualified trust under section 401;

(4) Any annuity or other payment under a plan which meets the requirements of section 404(a)(2);

(5) Any contribution or gift (other than a contribution or gift of money) to, or services or facilities made available to, any government official, if the aggregate value of such contributions, gifts, services, and facilities does not exceed $25 during any calendar year;

(6) Any payment made under 5 U.S.C. chapter 41 (relating to government employees' training programs);

(7) Any payment or reimbursement of traveling expenses (including amounts expended for meals and lodging, regardless of whether the government official is "away from home" within the meaning of section 162(a)(2), and including reasonable advances for such expenses anticipated in the immediate future) for travel solely from one point in the United States to another in connection with one or more purposes described in section 170(c)(1) or (2)(B), but only if such payment or reimbursement does not exceed the actual cost of the transportation involved plus an amount for all other traveling expenses not in excess of 125 percent of the maximum amount payable under 5 U.S.C. 5702(a) for like travel by employees of the United States;

(8) Any agreement to employ or make a grant to a government official for any period after the termination of his government service if such agreement is entered into within 90 days prior to such termination;

(9) If a government official attends or participates in a conference sponsored by a private foundation, the allocable portion of the cost of such conference and other non-monetary benefits (for example, benefits of a professional, intellectual, or psy-

chological nature, or benefits resulting from the publication or the distribution to participants of a record of the conference), as well as the payment or reimbursement of expenses (including reasonable advances for expenses anticipated in connection with such a conference in the near future), received by such government official as a result of such attendance or participation shall not be subject to section 4941(d)(1), so long as the conference is in furtherance of the exempt purposes of the foundation; or

(10) In the case of any government official who was on leave of absence without pay on December 31, 1969, pursuant to a commitment entered into on or before such date for the purpose of engaging in certain activities for which such individual was to be paid by one or more private foundations, any payment of compensation (or payment or reimbursement of expenses, including reasonable advances for expenses anticipated in the immediate future) by such private foundations to such individual for any continuous period after December 31, 1969, and prior to January 1, 1971, during which such individual remains on leave of absence to engage in such activities. A commitment is considered entered into on or before December 31, 1969, if on or before such date, the amount and nature of the payments to be made and the name of the individual receiving such payments were entered on the records of the payor, or were otherwise adequately evidenced, or the notice of the payment to be received was communicated to the payee orally or in writing.

§ 53.4941(d)-4 (T.D. 7270, filed 4-16-73.) **Transitional rules.**

(a) *Certain transactions involving securities acquired by a foundation before May 27, 1969*—(1) *In general.* Under section 101(l)(2)(A) of the Tax Reform Act of 1969 (83 Stat. 533), any transaction between a private foundation and a corporation which is a disqualified person shall not be an act of self-dealing if such transaction is pursuant to the terms of securities of such corporation, if such terms were in existence at the time such securities were acquired by the foundation, and if such securities were acquired by the foundation before May 27, 1969.

(2) *Example.* The provisions of this paragraph may be illustrated by the following example:

Example. Private foundation X purchased preferred stock of corporation M a disqualified person with respect to X, on March 15, 1969. The terms of such securities on such date provided that the stock could be called by M at any time if M paid the outstanding shareholders cash equal to 105 percent of the face amount of the stock. If M exercises this right and calls the stock owned by X on February 15, 1970, such call shall not constitute an act of self-dealing even if such price is not equivalent to fair market value on such date and even if not all of the securities of that class are called.

(b) *Disposition of certain business holdings*—(1) *In general.* Under section 101(l)(2)(B) of the Tax Reform Act of 1969 (83 Stat. 533), the sale, exchange, or other disposition of property which is owned by a private foundation on May 26, 1969, to a disqualified person shall not be an act of self-dealing if the foundation is required to dispose of such property in order not to be liable for tax under section 4943 (determined without regard to section 4943(c)(2) (C) and as if every disposition by the foundation were made to disqualified persons) and if such disposition satisfies the requirements of subparagraph (2) of this paragraph. In determining the amount of excess business holdings for purposes of applying this paragraph in the case of a disposition completed before January 1, 1975, section 4943 shall be applied without taking section 4943(c)(4) into account.

(2) *Terms of the disposition.* Subparagraph (1) of this paragraph shall not apply unless—

(i) The private foundation receives an amount which equals or exceeds the fair market value of the business holdings at the time of disposition or at the time a contract for such disposition was previously executed; and

(ii) At the time with respect to which subdivision (i) of this subparagraph is applied, the transaction would not have constituted a prohibited transaction within the meaning of section 503(b) or the corresponding provisions of prior law if such provisions had been applied at such time.

(3) *Property received under a trust or will.* For purposes of this paragraph, property shall be considered as owned by a private foundation on May 26, 1969, if such property is acquired by such foundation under the terms of a will executed on or before such date, under the terms of a trust which was irrevocable on such date, or under the terms of a revocable trust executed on or before such date if the property would have passed under a will which would have met the requirements of this subparagraph but for the fact that a grantor dies without having revoked the trust. An amendment or republication of a will which was executed on or before May 26, 1969, does not prevent any interest in a business enterprise which was to pass under the terms of such will (which terms were in effect on May 26, 1969, and at all times thereafter) from being treated as owned by a private foundation on or before May 26, 1969, solely because—

(i) There is a reduction in the interest in the business enterprise which the foundation was to receive under the terms of the will (for example, if the foundation is to receive the residuary estate and one class of stock is disposed of by the decedent during his lifetime or by a subsequent codicil),

(ii) Such amendment or republication is necessary in order to comply with section 508(e) and the regulations thereunder,

(iii) There is a change in the executor of the will, or

(iv) There is any other change which does not otherwise change the rights of the foundation with respect to such interest in the business enterprise.

However, if under such amendment or republication there is an increase of the interest in the business enterprise which the foundation was to receive under the terms of the will in effect on May 26, 1969, such increase shall not be treated as owned by

Reg. § 53.4941(d)-4(b)(3)

24,258.10-B.12 (I.R.C.) Reg. § 53.4941(d)-4(b)(3) 4-23-73

the private foundation on or before May 26, 1969, but under such circumstances the interest which would have been acquired before such increase shall be treated as owned by the private foundation on or before May 26, 1969.

(4) *Examples.* The provisions of this paragraph may be illustrated by the following examples:

Example (1). On May 26, 1969, private foundation X owns 10 percent of corporation Y's voting stock, which is traded on the New York Stock Exchange. Disqualified persons with respect to X own an additional 40 percent of such voting stock. X is on a calendar year basis. Prior to January 1, 1975, X privately sold its entire 10 percent for cash to B, a disqualified person, at the price quoted on the stock exchange at the close of the day less commissions. Since the 10 percent owned by X would constitute excess business holdings without the application of section 4943(c)(2)(C) or (4), the disposition will not constitute an act of self-dealing.

Example (2). Assume the facts as stated in Example (1), except that the only stock of corporation Y which X owns is 1.5 percent of Y's voting stock. Since the 1.5 percent owned by X would constitute excess business holdings without the application of section 4943(c)(2)(C) or (4), the disposition of the stock to B for cash will not constitute an act of self-dealing.

Example (3). Assume the facts as stated in Example (1), except that B, instead of paying cash as consideration for the stock, issued a 10-year secured promissory note as consideration for the stock. The issuance of such promissory note will not be treated as an act of self-dealing until taxable years beginning after December 31, 1979, unless such issuance would have been a prohibited transaction under section 503(b), or unless the transaction does not remain throughout its life at least as favorable as an arm's-length contract negotiated currently. See paragraph (c) of this section.

(c) *Existing leases and loans*—(1) *In general.* Under section 101(l)(2)(C) of the Tax Reform Act of 1969 (83 Stat. 533), the leasing of property or the lending of money (or other extension of credit) between a disqualified person and a private foundation pursuant to a binding contract which was in effect on October 9, 1969 (or pursuant to a renewal or modification of such a contract, as described in subparagraph (2) of this paragraph), shall not be an act of self-dealing until taxable years beginning after December 31, 1979, if—

(i) At the time the contract was executed, such contract was not a prohibited transaction (within the meaning of section 503(b) or the corresponding provisions of prior law), and

(ii) The leasing or lending of money (or other extension of credit) remains throughout the term of the lease or extension of credit at least as favorable as a current arm's-length transaction with an unrelated person.

(2) *Renewal or modification of existing contracts.* A renewal or a modification of an existing contract is referred to in subparagraph (1) of this paragraph only if any modifications of the terms of such contract are not substantial and the relative advantages of the modified contract compared with contracts entered into at arm's-length with an unrelated person at the time of the renewal or modification are at least as favorable to the private foundation as the relative advantages of the original contract compared with contracts entered into at arm's-length with an unrelated person at the time of execution of the original contract. Such renewal or modification need not be provided for in the original contract; it may take place before or after the expiration of the original contract and at any time before the first day of the first taxable year of the private foundation beginning after December 31, 1979. Where, in a normal commercial setting, an unrelated party in the position of a private foundation could be expected to insist upon a renegotiation or termination of a binding contract, the private foundation must so act. Thus, for example, if a disqualified person leases office space from a private foundation on a month-to-month basis, and a party in the position of the private foundation could be expected to renegotiate the rent required in such contract because of a rise in the fair market value of such office space, the private foundation must so act in order to avoid participation in an act of self-dealing. Where the private foundation has no right to insist upon renegotiation, an act of self-dealing shall occur if the terms of the contract become less favorable to the foundation than an arm's-length contract negotiated currently, unless —

(i) The variation from current fair market value is de minimis, or

(ii) The contract is renegotiated by the foundation and the disqualified person so that the foundation will receive no less than fair market value.

For purposes of subdivision (i) of this subparagraph de minimis ordinarily shall be no more than one-half of 1 percent in the rate of return in the case of a loan, or 10 percent of the rent in the case of a lease.

(3) *Example.* The provisions of subparagraphs (1) and (2) of this paragraph may be illustrated by the following example.

Example. Under a binding contract entered into on January 1, 1964, X, a private foundation, leases a building for 10 years from Z, a disqualified person. At the time the contract was executed, the lease was not a "prohibited transaction" within the meaning of section 503(b), since the rent charged X was only 50 percent of the rent which would have been charged in an arm's-length transaction with an unrelated person. On January 1, 1974, X renewed the lease for 5 additional years. The terms of the renewal agreement provided for a 20 percent increase in the amount of rent charged X. However, at the time of such renewal, the rent which would have been charged in an arm's-length transaction had also increased by 20 percent from that of 1964. The renewal agreement shall not be treated as an act of self-dealing.

(4) *Certain exchanges of stock or securities for bonds, debentures or other indebtedness.* (i) In the case of a transaction described in paragraph (a) or (b) of this section or paragraph (d) of § 53.-4941(d)-3, where a bond, debenture, or other indebtedness of a disqualified person is acquired by a private foundation in exchange for stock or securities which it

held on October 9, 1969, and at all times thereafter, such indebtedness shall be treated as an extension of credit pursuant to a binding contract in effect on October 9, 1969, to which this paragraph applies. Thus, so long as the extension of credit remains at least as favorable as an arm's-length transaction with an unrelated person and neither the acquisition of the securities which were exchanged for the indebtedness nor the exchange of such securities for the indebtedness was a prohibited transaction within the meaning of section 503(b) (or the corresponding provisions of prior law) at the time of such acquisition, such extension of credit shall not be an act of self-dealing until taxable years beginning after December 31, 1979.

(ii) The provisions of this subparagraph may be illustrated by the following examples:

Example (1). Assume the facts as stated in Example (2) of § 53.4941(d)-3(d)(2), except that the preferred stock was held by Y on October 9, 1969, and at all times thereafter until the redemption occurred on January 2, 1972. In addition, assume that the acquisition of the preferred stock was not a prohibited transaction within the meaning of section 503(b) at the time of such acquisition and the exchange of the preferred stock for the debentures would not have been a prohibited transaction within the meaning of section 503(b). For 1973 through 1979, the extension of credit arising from the holding of the debentures is not an act of self-dealing so long as the extension of credit remains at least as favorable as an arm's-length transaction with an unrelated person. See, however, Example (3) of § 53.-4941(e)-1(e)(1)(ii).

Example (2). Assume the same facts as stated in Example (1) of § 53.4941(d)-4(b)(4), except that private foundation X sold its entire 10 percent of corporation Y's voting stock in exchange for Y's secured notes which mature on December 31, 1985. For taxable years beginning before January 1, 1980, the extension of credit arising from the holding of such notes by X is not an act of self-dealing so long as the extension of credit remains at least as favorable as an arm's-length transaction with an unrelated person and neither the acquisition of the securities which were exchanged for the indebtedness nor the exchange of such securities for the indebtedness was a prohibited transaction within the meaning of section 503(b) (or the corresponding provisions of prior law). Under § 53.4941(e)-1, a new extension of credit occurs on the first day of each taxable year in which an indebtedness is outstanding; therefore, if the secured notes are held by X after December 31, 1979, a new extension of credit not excepted from the definition of an act of self-dealing will occur on the first day of the first taxable year beginning after December 31, 1979, and on the first day of each succeeding taxable year in which X holds such secured notes.

(d) *Sharing of goods, services, or facilities before January 1, 1980*. (1) Under section 101(l)(2)(D) of the Tax Reform Act of 1969 (83 Stat. 533), the use (other than leasing) of goods, services, or facilities which are shared by a private foundation and a disqualified person shall not be an act of self-dealing until taxable years beginning after December 31, 1979, if—

(i) The use is pursuant to an arrangement in effect before October 9, 1969, and at all times thereafter;

(ii) The arrangement was not a prohibited transaction (within the meaning of section 503(b) or the corresponding provisions of prior law) at the time it was made; and

(iii) The arrangement would not be a prohibited transaction if section 503(b) continued to apply.

For purposes of this paragraph, such arrangement need not be a binding contract.

(2) The provisions of this paragraph may be illustrated by the following example:

Example. In 1964 X, a private foundation, and B, a disqualified person, arranged for the sharing of computer time in B's son's company for a 10-year period commencing January 1, 1965. B's son has the unilateral right to terminate the arrangement at any time. X uses the computer facilities in connection with an analysis of its grant-making activities, while B's use is related to his business affairs. Both X and B make reasonable fixed payments to the computer company based on the number of hours of computer use and comparable to fees charged in arm's length transactions with unrelated parties. The company imposes a maximum limit per month on the sum of the number of hours for which X and B use the computer facilities. Under these circumstances, the sharing of computer time is not an act of self-dealing.

(e) *Use of certain property acquired before October 9, 1969*. (1) Under section 101(l)(2)(E) of the Tax Reform Act of 1969 (83 Stat. 533), the use of property in which a private foundation and a disqualified person have a joint or common interest will not be an act of self-dealing if the interests of both in such property were acquired before October 9, 1969.

(2) The provisions of this paragraph may be illustrated by the following example:

Example. Prior to October 9, 1969, C, a disqualified person, gave beachfront property to private foundation X for use as a recreational facility for underprivileged, inner-city children during the summer months. However, C retained the right to use such property for his life. The use of such property by C or X is not an act of self-dealing.

० § 53.4941(e) **Statutory provisions; exempt organizations; private foundations; taxes on self-dealing, other definitions.** [Sec. 4941(e), IRC]

० § 53.4941(e)-1 (T.D. 7270, filed 4-16-73.) **Definitions.**

(a) *Taxable period* — (1) *In general*. For purposes of any act of self-dealing, the term "taxable period" means the period beginning with the date on which the act of self-dealing occurs and ending on the earlier of:

(i) The date of mailing of a notice of deficiency under section 6212 with respect to the tax imposed by section 4941(a)(1), or

Reg. § 53.4941(e)-1(a)(1)

(ii) The date on which correction of the act of self-dealing is completed.

(2) *Date of occurrence.* An act of self-dealing occurs on the date on which all the terms and conditions of the transaction and the liabilities of the parties have been fixed. Thus, for example, if a private foundation gives a disqualified person a binding option on June 15, 1971, to purchase property owned by the foundation at any time before June 15, 1972, the act of self-dealing has occurred on June 15, 1971. Similarly, in the case of a conditional sales contract, the act of self-dealing shall be considered as occurring on the date the property is transferred subject only to the condition that the buyer make payment for receipt of such property.

(3) *Special rule.* Where a notice of deficiency referred to in subparagraph (1)(i) of this paragraph is not mailed because a waiver of the restrictions on assessment and collection of a deficiency has been accepted, or because the deficiency is paid, the date of filing of the waiver or the date of such payment, respectively, shall be treated as the end of the taxable period.

(4) *Examples.* The provisions of this paragraph may be illustrated by the following examples:

Example (1). On July 16, 1970, F, a manager of private foundation X acting on behalf of the foundation, knowing his act to be one of self-dealing, willfully and without reasonable cause engaged in an act of self-dealing by selling certain real estate to A, a disqualified person. On March 25, 1973, the Internal Revenue Service mailed a notice of deficiency to A with respect to the tax imposed on the sale under section 4941(a)(1). The taxable period with respect to the act of self-dealing for both A and F is July 16, 1970, through March 25, 1973.

Example (2). Assume the facts as stated in Example (1), except that the act of self-dealing is corrected by A on March 17, 1971. The taxable period with respect to the act of self-dealing for both A and F is July 16, 1970, through March 17, 1971.

Example (3). Assume the facts as stated in Example (1), except that on August 20, 1972, A files a waiver of the restrictions on asessment and collection of the tax imposed on the sale under section 4941(a)(1) which is accepted. The taxable period with respect to the act of self-dealing for both A and F is July 16, 1970, through August 20, 1972.

(b) *Amount involved*—(1) *In general.* Except as provided in subparagraph (2) of this paragraph, for purposes of any act of self-dealing, the term "amount involved" means the greater of the amount of money and the fair market value of the other property given or the amount of money and the fair market value of the other property received.

(2) *Exceptions.* (i) In the case of the payment of compensation for personal services to persons other than government officials, the amount involved shall be only the excess compensation paid by the private foundation.

(ii) Where the use of money or other property is involved, the amount involved shall be the greater of the amount paid for such use or the fair market value of such use for the period for which the money or other property is used. Thus, for example, in the case of a lease of a building by a private foundation to a disqualified person, the amount involved is the greater of the amount of rent received by the private foundation from the disqualified person or the fair rental value of the building for the period such building is used by the disqualified person.

(iii) In cases in which a transaction would not have been an act of self-dealing had the private foundation received fair market value, the amount involved is the excess of the fair market value of the property transferred by the private foundation over the amount which the private foundation receives, but only if the parties have made a good faith effort to determine fair market value. For purposes of this subdivision a good faith effort to determine fair market value shall ordinarily have been made where—

(a) The person making the valuation is not a disqualified person with respect to the foundation and is both competent to make the valuation and not in a position, whether by stock ownership or otherwise, to derive an economic benefit from the value utilized, and

(b) The method utilized in making the valuation is a generally accepted method for valuing comparable property, stock, or securities for purposes of arm's-length business transactions where valuation is a significant factor.

See section 4941(d)(2)(F) and §§ 53.4941(d)-1(b)(3), 53.4941(d)-3(d)(1) and 53.4941(d)-4(b).

Thus, for example, if a corporation which is a disqualified person with respect to a private foundation recapitalizes in a transaction which would be described in section 4941(d)(2)(F) but for the fact that the private foundation receives new stock worth only $95,000 in exchange for the stock which it previously held in the corporation and which has a fair market value of $100,000 at the time of the recapitalization, the amount involved would be $5,000 ($100,000 — $95,000) if there had been a good faith attempt to value the stock. Similarly, if an estate enters into a transaction with a disqualified person with respect to a foundation and such transaction would be described in § 53.4941(d)-1(b)(3) but for the fact that the estate receives less than fair market value for the property exchanged, the amount involved is the excess of the fair market value of the property the estate transfers to the disqualified person over the money and the fair market value of the property received by the estate.

(3) *Time for determining fair market value.* The fair market value of the property or the use thereof, as the case may be, shall be determined as of the date on which the act of self-dealing occurred in the case of the initial taxes imposed by section 4941(a) and shall be the highest fair market value during the correction period in the case of the additional taxes imposed by section 4941(b).

(4) *Examples.* The provisions of this paragraph may be illustrated by the following examples:

Example (1). A, a disqualified person with respect to private foundation M, uses an airplane owned by M on June 15 and June 16, 1970, for a two-day trip to New York City on personal business and pays M $500 for the use of such airplane. The fair rental value for the use of the airplane for those two days is $3,000. For purposes of section 4941(a), the amount involved with respect to the act of self-dealing is $3,000.

Example (2). On April 10, 1970, B, a manager of private foundation P, borrows $100,000 from P at 6 percent interest per annum. Both principal and interest are to be paid one year from the date of the loan. The fair market value of the use of the money on April 10, 1970, is 10 percent per annum. Six months later, B and P terminate the loan, and B repays the $100,000 principal plus $3,000 ($100,000 × 6 percent for one-half year) interest. For purposes of section 4941(a), the amount involved with respect to the act of self-dealing is $5,000 ($100,000 × 10 percent for one-half year) for each year or partial year in the taxable period.

Example (3). C, a substantial contributor to private foundation S, leases office space in a building owned by S for $3,600 for 1 year beginning on January 1, 1971. The fair rental value of the building for a one-year lease on January 1, 1971, is $5,600. On December 31, 1971, the lease is terminated. For purposes of section 4941(a), the amount involved with respect to the act of self-dealing is $5,600 for each year or partial year in the taxable period.

Example (4). D, a disqualified person with respect to private foundation T, purchases 100 shares of stock from T for $5,000 on June 15, 1972. The fair market value of the 100 shares of stock on such date is $4,800. D sells the 100 shares of stock on December 20, 1973, for $6,000. Subsequently, D receives a notice of deficiency with respect to the taxes imposed under subsections (a) and (b) of section 4941. D fails to correct during the correction period. Between June 15, 1972, and the end of the correction period, the stock was quoted on the New York Stock Exchange at a high of $67 per share. The amount involved with respect to the tax imposed under subsection (a) is $5,000, and the amount involved with respect to the tax imposed under subsection (b) for failure to correct is $6,700 (100 shares at $67 per share), the highest fair market value during the correction period.

Example (5). Corporation M, a disqualified person with respect to private foundation V, redeems all of its Class B common stock, some of which is held by V. The redemption of V's stock would be described in section 4941(d)(2)(F) but for the fact that V receives only $95,000 in exchange for stock which has a fair market value of $100,000 at the time of the transaction. The $95,000 value of V's stock, which is not publicly traded, was determined by investment bankers in accordance with accepted methods of valuation that would be utilized if the M stock held by V were to be offered for sale to the public. Therefore, the amount involved with respect to the transaction will ordinarily be limited to $5,000 ($100,000 − $95,000).

(c) *Correction*—(1) *In general.* Correction shall be accomplished by undoing the transaction which constituted the act of self-dealing to the extent possible, but in no case shall the resulting financial position of the private foundation be worse than that which it would be if the disqualified person were dealing under the highest fiduciary standards. For example, where a disqualified person sells property to a private foundation for cash, correction may be accomplished by recasting the transaction in the form of a gift by returning the cash to the foundation. Subparagraphs (2) through (6) of this paragraph illustrate the minimum standards of correction in the case of certain specific acts of self-dealing. Principles similar to the principles contained in such subparagraphs shall be applied with respect to other acts of self-dealing. Any correction pursuant to this paragraph and section 4941 shall not be an act of self-dealing.

(2) *Sales by foundation.* (i) In the case of a sale of property by a private foundation to a disqualified person for cash, undoing the transaction includes, but is not limited to, requiring rescission of the sale where possible. However, in order to avoid placing the foundation in a position worse than that in which it would be if rescission were not required, the amount returned to the disqualified person pursuant to the rescission shall not exceed the lesser of the cash received by the private foundation or the fair market value of the property received by the disqualified person. For purposes of the preceding sentence, fair market value shall be the lesser of the fair market value at the time of the act of self-dealing or the fair market value at the time of rescission. In addition to rescission, the disqualified person is required to pay over to the private foundation any net profits he realized after the original sale with respect to the property he received from the sale. Thus, for example, the disqualified person must pay over to the foundation any income derived by him from the property he received from the original sale to the extent such income during the correction period exceeds the income derived by the foundation during the correction period from the cash which the disqualified person originally paid to the foundation.

(ii) If, prior to the end of the correction period, the disqualified person resells the property in an arm's-length transaction to a bona fide purchaser who is not the foundation or another disqualified person, no rescission is required. In such case, the disqualified person must pay over to the foundation the excess (if any) of the greater of the fair market value of such property on the date on which correction of the act of self-dealing occurs or the amount realized by the disqualified person from such arm's length resale over the amount which would have been returned to the disqualified person pursuant to subdivision (i) of this subparagraph if rescission had been required. In addition, the disqualified person is required to pay over to the foundation any net profits he realized, as described in subdivision (i) of this subparagraph.

(iii) *Examples.* The provisions of this subparagraph may be illustrated by the following examples:

Example (1). On July 1, 1970, private foundation M sold a painting to A, a disqualified person, for $5,000, in a transaction not within any of the exceptions to self-dealing. The fair market value of the painting on such date was $6,000. On March 25, 1971, the painting is still owned by A and has a fair market value of $7,200.

Reg. § 53.4941(e)-1(c)(2)

A did not derive any income as a result of purchasing the painting. In order to correct the act of self-dealing under this subparagraph on March 25, 1971, the sale must be rescinded by the return of the painting to M. However, pursuant to such rescission, M must not pay A more than $5,000, the original consideration received by M.

Example (2). Assume the facts as stated in Example (1), except that A sold the painting on December 15, 1970, in an arm's-length transaction to C, a bona fide purchaser who is not a disqualified person, for $6,100. In addition, assume that the fair market value of the painting on March 25, 1971, is $7,600. In order to correct the act of self-dealing under this subparagraph on March 25, 1971, A must pay M $2,600 ($7,600, the fair market value at the time of correction, less $5,000, the amount which would have been returned to A if rescission had been required). Since the painting was sold to C in an arm's-length transaction prior to correction, no rescission is required.

(3) *Sales to foundation.* (i) In the case of a sale of property to a private foundation by a disqualified person for cash, undoing the transaction includes, but is not limited to, requiring rescission of the sale where possible. However, in order to avoid placing the foundation in a position worse than that in which it would be if rescission were not required, the amount received from the disqualified person pursuant to the rescission shall be the greatest of the cash paid to the disqualified person, the fair market value of the property at the time of the original sale, or the fair market value of the property at the time of rescission. In addition to rescission, the disqualified person is required to pay over to the private foundation any net profits he realized after the original sale with respect to the consideration he received from the sale. Thus, for example, the disqualified person must pay over to the foundation any income derived by him from the cash he received from the original sale to the extent such income during the correction period exceeds the income derived by the foundation during the correction period from the property which the disqualified person originally transferred to the foundation.

(ii) If, prior to the end of the correction period, the disqualified person resells the property in an arms'-length transaction to a bona fide purchaser who is not a disqualified person, no rescission is required. In such case, the disqualified person must pay over to the foundation the excess (if any) of the amount which would have been received from the disqualified person pursuant to subdivision (i) of this subparagraph, if rescission had been required over the amount realized by the foundation upon resale of the property. In addition, the disqualified person is required to pay over to the foundation any net profits he realized, as described in subdivision (i) of this subparagraph.

(iii) *Examples.* The provisions of this subparagraph may be illustrated by the following examples:

Example (1). On February 10, 1972, D, a disqualified person with respect to private foundation P, sells 100 shares of X stock to P for $2,500 in a transaction which does not fall within any of the exceptions to self-dealing. The fair market value of the 100 shares of X stock on February 10, 1972, is $3,200. On June 1, 1973, the 100 shares of X stock have a fair market value of $2,900. From February 10, 1972, through June 1, 1973, P has received dividends of $90 from the stock, and D has received interest of $300 from the $2,500 which D received as consideration for the stock. In order to correct the act of self-dealing under this subparagraph on June 1, 1973, the sale must be rescinded by the return of the stock to D. However, pursuant to such rescission, D must pay P $3,200, the fair market value of the stock on the date of sale. In addition, D must pay P $210, the amount of income derived by D during the correction period from the $2,500 received from P ($300) minus the income derived by P during the correction period from the stock sold to P ($90).

Example (2). Assume the facts as stated in Example (1), except that on September 1, 1972, P sells the 100 shares of X stock to E, a bona fide purchaser who is not a disqualified person, in an arm's length transaction for $2,750. Assume further that P has not received any dividends from the stock prior to the sale to E, but that P receives interest of $260 from the $2,750 received as consideration for the stock for the period from September 1, 1972, to June 1, 1973. In order to correct the act of self-dealing under this subparagraph on June 1, 1973, D must pay P $450 ($3,200, the amount which would have been received from D if rescission had been required, less $2,750, the amount realized by P from the sale to E). In addition, D must pay P $40, the amount of income derived by D during the correction period from the $2,500 received from P ($300) minus the income derived by P during the correction period from the stock sold to P ($260) from the $2,750 received as consideration for the stock). Since the stock was sold to E in an arm's length transaction prior to correction, no rescission is required.

(4) *Use of property by a disqualified person.* (i) In the case of the use by a disqualified person of property owned by a private foundation, undoing the transaction includes, but is not limited to, terminating the use of such property. In addition to termination, the disqualified person must pay the foundation—

(*a*) The excess (if any) of the fair market value of the use of the property over the amount paid by the disqualified person for such use until such termination, and

(*b*) The excess (if any) of the amount which would have been paid by the disqualified person for the use of the property on or after the date of such termination, for the period such disqualified person would have used the property (without regard to any further extensions or renewals of such period) if such termination had not occurred, over the fair market value of such use for such period.

In applying (*a*) of this subdivision the fair market value of the use of property shall be the higher of the rate (that is, fair rental value per period in the case of use of property other than money or fair interest rate in the case of use of money) at the time of the act of self-dealing (within the meaning of paragraph (e)(1) of this section) or such rate at the time of correction of such act of self-dealing. In applying (*b*) of this subdivision the fair market value of the use of property shall be the rate at the time of correction.

(ii) The provisions of this subparagraph may be illustrated by the following examples:

Example (1). On January 1, 1972, private foundation S rented the third story of its office building to A, a disqualified person, for one year at an annual rent of $10,000, in a transaction not within any of the exceptions to self-dealing. Both S and A are on the calendar year basis. The fair rental value of such office space for a one-year period on January 1, 1972, is $12,000. On June 30, 1972, the fair rental value of such office space for a one-year period is $13,000. In order to correct the act of self-dealing under this subparagraph on June 30, 1972, A must terminate his use of the property. In addition, A must pay S $1,500, the excess of $6,500 (the fair rental value for six months as of June 30, 1972) over $5,000 (the amount paid to S from January 1, 1972, to June 30, 1972).

Example (2). On January 1, 1972, private foundation R rented the fourth story of its office building to B, a disqualified person, for one year at an annual rent of $10,000, in a transaction not included in any of the exceptions to self-dealing. Both R and B are on the calendar year basis. On January 1, 1973, B continues to rent the office space as a periodic tenant paying his rent monthly at an annual rate of $10,000. The fair rental value of such office space for a one-year period on January 1, 1972, is $12,000, and as of January 1, 1973, is $1,250 per month. As of December 31, 1973, the fair rental value of such office space is $14,000 for a one-year period and $1,200 on a monthly basis. In order to correct his acts of self-dealing (within the meaning of paragraph (e)(1) of this section) under this subparagraph on December 31, 1973, B must terminate his use of the property. In addition, B must pay R $9,000, $4,000 for his use of the property for 1972 (the excess of $14,000, the fair rental value for one year as of December 31, 1973, over $10,000, the amount B paid R for his use of the property for 1972) and $5,000 for his use of the property for 1973 (the excess of $15,000, the fair rental value for 12 months as of January 1, 1973, over $10,000, the amount B paid R for his use of the property for 1973).

Example (3). B, a substantial contributor to private foundation T, leases office space in a building owned by T for $5,000 for one year beginning on November 10, 1972, in a transaction not included in any of the exceptions to self-dealing. The fair rental value of the building for a one-year period on November 10, 1972, is $4,000. On May 10, 1973, the fair rental value of the building for the remaining period of the lease is $2,200. In order to correct the acts of self-dealing under this subparagraph on May 10, 1973, B and T must terminate the lease. In addition, B must pay T $300 (the excess of $2,500, the amount which would have been paid by B for the remaining period of the lease if it had not been terminated, over $2,200, the fair rental value at the time of correction for the remaining period of the lease).

(5) *Use of property by a private foundation.* (i) In the case of the use by a private foundation of property owned by a disqualified person, undoing the transaction includes, but is not limited to, terminating the use of such property. In addition to termination, the disqualified person must pay the foundation—

(*a*) The excess (if any) of the amount paid to the disqualified person for such use until such termination over the fair market value of the use of the property, and

(*b*) The excess (if any) of the fair market value of the use of the property, for the period the foundation would have used the property (without regard to any further extensions or renewals of such period) if such termination had not occurred, over the amount which would have been paid to the disqualified person on or after the date of such termination for such use for such period.

In applying (*a*) of this subdivision the fair market value of the use of property shall be the lesser of the rate (that is, fair rental value per period in the case of use of property other than money or fair interest rate in the case of use of money) at the time of the act of self-dealing (within the meaning of paragraph (e)(1) of this section) or such rate at the time of correction of such act of self-dealing. In applying (*b*) of this subdivision the fair market value of the use of property shall be the rate at the time of correction.

(ii) The provisions of this subparagraph may be illustrated by the following examples:

Example (1). On July 1, 1972, private foundation X leases office space in a building owned by C, a disqualified person, for one year at an annual rent of $6,000. Both X and C are on the calendar year basis. The fair rental value of such office space for a one-year period as of July 1, 1972, is $4,200. As of January 1, 1973, the fair rental value of such office space for a one-year period is $5,400, and as of June 30, 1973, the fair rental value of such office space for a one-year period is $4,800. In order to correct his acts of self-dealing (within the meaning of paragraph (3)(1) of this section) under this subparagraph on June 30, 1973, C must terminate X's use of the property. In addition, C must pay X $1,500, $9000 (the excess of $3,000, the amount paid to C from July 1, 1972, through December 31, 1972, over $2,100, the fair rental value for six months as of July 1, 1972) plus $600 (the excess of $3,000, the amount paid to C from January 1, 1973, through June 30, 1973, over $2,400, the fair rental value for six months as of June 30, 1973).

Example (2). On April 1, 1973, D, a disqualified person with respect to private foundation Y, loans $100,000 to Y at 6 percent interest per annum. Both principal and interest are to be paid on April 1, 1978. The fair market value of the use of the money on April 1, 1973, is 9 percent per annum. On April 1, 1974, D and Y terminate the loan. On such date, the fair market value of the use of $100,000 is 10 percent per annum. In order to correct the act of self-dealing on April 1, 1974, in addition to the termination of the loan from D to Y, D must pay Y $16,000, the excess of $40,000 ($100,000 × 10 percent, the fair market value of the use determined at the time

Reg. § 53.4941(e)-1(c)(5)

of correction, from April 1, 1974, to April 1, 1978) over $24,000 (the amount of interest Y would have paid to D from April 1, 1974, to April 1, 1978, if the loan from D to Y had not been terminated).

(6) *Payment of compensation to a disqualified person.* In the case of the payment of compensation by a private foundation to a disqualified person for the performance of personal services which are reasonable and necessary to carry out the exempt purpose of such foundation, undoing the transaction requires that the disqualified person pay to the foundation any amount which is excessive. However, termination of the employment or independent contractor relationship is not required.

(7) *Special rule for correction of valuation errors.* (i) In the case of a transaction described in paragraph (b)(2)(iii) of this section, a "correction" of the act of self-dealing shall ordinarily be deemed to occur if the foundation is paid an amount of money equal to the amount involved (as defined in paragraph (b)(2)(iii) of this section) plus such additional amounts as are necessary to compensate it for the loss of the use of the money or other property during the period commencing on the date of the act of self-dealing and ending on the date the transaction is corrected pursuant to this subparagraph.

(ii) The provisions of this subparagraph may be illustrated by the following example:

Example. Assume the same facts as in Example (5) of paragraph (b)(4) of this section. Such transaction shall be considered as corrected by a payment of $5,000 by M to V, together with an additional payment to V of an amount equal to the interest which V could have obtained on $5,000 for the period commencing on the date of the redemption and ending on the date the act is corrected.

(d) *Correction period*—(1) *In general.* For purposes of section 4941, the correction period shall begin with the date on which the act of self-dealing occurs and end 90 days after the date of mailing of a notice of deficiency under section 6212 with respect to the tax imposed by section 4941(b)(1).

(2) *Extensions of correction period.* (i) The correction period referred to in subparagraph (1) of this paragraph shall be extended by any period in which a deficiency cannot be assessed under section 6213(a). In addition, the correction period referred to in subparagraph (1) of this paragraph shall be extended in accordance with subdivisions (ii), (iii), and (iv) of this subparagraph, except that such subdivision (iii) or (iv) shall not operate to extend a correction period with respect to which a taxpayer has filed a petition with the United States Tax Court for redetermination of a deficiency within the time prescribed by section 6213(a).

(ii) The correction period referred to in subparagraph (1) of this paragraph may be extended by any period which the Commissioner determines is reasonable and necessary to bring about correction of the act of self-dealing. The Commissioner ordinarily will not extend the correction period pursuant to this subdivision unless the following factors are present:

(a) The foundation or an appropriate State officer (as defined in section 6104(c)(2)) is actively seeking in good faith to correct the act of self-dealing;

(b) Adequate corrective action cannot reasonably be expected to result during the unextended correction period; and

(c) The act of self-dealing appears to have been an isolated occurrence and it appears unlikely that similar acts of self-dealing will occur in the future.

(iii) If, within the unextended correction period, the tax imposed by section 4941(a)(1) is paid, the Commissioner shall extend the correction period to the later of—

(a) A period of 90 days after the payment of such tax, or

(b) The correction period determined without regard to this subdivision.

(iv) If prior to the expiration of the correction period (including extensions) a claim for refund with respect to a tax imposed by section 4941(a)(1) is filed, the Commissioner shall extend the correction period during the pendency of the claim plus an additional 90 days. If within such time, a suit or proceeding referred to in section 7422(g) with respect to such claim is filed, the Commissioner shall extend the correction period during the pendency of such suit or proceeding. See § 301.7422-1 of this chapter (Regulations on Procedure and Administration) for rules relating to pendency of such suit or proceeding.

(e) *Act of self-dealing*—(1) *Number of acts; use of money or property*—(i) *In general.* If a transaction between a private foundation and a disqualified person is determined to be self-dealing (as defined in section 4941(d)), for purposes of section 4941 there is generally one act of self-dealing. For the date on which such act is treated as occurring, see paragraph (a)(2) of this section. If, however, such transaction relates to the leasing of property, the lending of money or other extension of credit, other use of money or property, or payment of compensation, the transaction will generally be treated (for purposes of section 4941 but not section 507 or 6684) as giving rise to an act of self-dealing on the day the transaction occurs plus an act of self-dealing on the first day of each taxable year or portion of a taxable year which is within the taxable period and which begins after the taxable year in which the transaction occurs.

(ii) *Examples.* The provisions of this subparagraph may be illustrated by the following examples:

Example (1). On August 31, 1970, X, a private foundation, sells a building to A, a disqualified person with respect to X. A is on the calendar year basis. Under these circumstances, the transaction between A and X is one act of self-dealing which is treated for purposes of section 4941 as occurring on August 31, 1970.

Example (2). Assume the facts as stated in Example (1), except that, instead of selling the building to A, X leases the building to A for a term of four years beginning July 31, 1970, at an annual rental of $12,000. The fair rental value of the building is also $12,000 per annum as of July 31, 1970, and throughout the next four years. This transaction is corrected on September 30, 1973, in accordance with paragraph (c)(4) of this section. Under these circumstances, the transaction between A and X constitutes four separate acts of self-dealing, which are treated for purposes of section 4941 as occurring on July 31, 1970, January 1, 1971, January 1, 1972, and January 1, 1973. Consequently, there are four taxable periods. The first taxable period is from July 31, 1970, to September 30, 1973; the second is from January 1, 1971, to September 30, 1973; the third is from January 1, 1972 to September 30, 1973; and the fourth is from January 1, 1973, to September 30, 1973. For purposes of the initial taxes in section 4941(a), the amount involved is $5,000 for the first taxable period, $12,000 for the second, $12,000 for the third, and $9,000 for the fourth. The initial taxes to be paid by A are thus $1,000 ($5,000 × 5% × 4 taxable years or partial taxable years in the taxable period) for the first act; $1,800 ($12,000 × 5% × 3) for the second act; $1,200 ($12,000 × 5% × 2) for the third act; and $450 ($9,000 × 5% × 1) for the fourth act.

Example (3). Assume the facts as stated in Example (1) of § 53.4941(d)-4(c)(4)(ii). If the debentures are held by Y after December 31, 1979, the extension of credit will not be excepted from the definition of an act of self-dealing, because a new act of self-dealing will be treated (for purposes of section 4941) as occurring on January 1, 1980.

(2) *Number of acts; joint participation by disqualified persons*—(i) *In general.* If joint participation in a transaction by two or more disqualified persons constitues self-dealing (such as a joint sale of property to a private foundation or joint use of its money or property), such transaction shall generally be treated as a separate act of self-dealing with respect to each disqualified person for purposes of section 4941. For purposes of section 507 and, in the case of a foundation manager, section 6684, however, such transaction shall be treated as only one act of self-dealing. For purposes of this subparagraph, an individual and one or more members of his family (within the meaning of section 4946(d)) shall be treated as one person, regardless of whether a member of the family is a disqualified person not only by reason of section 4946(a)(1)(D) but also by reason of another subparagraph of section 4946(a)(1). However, the liability imposed on a disqualified person and one or more members of his family for joint participation in an act of self-dealing shall be joint and several in accordance with section 4941(c)(1) and § 53.4941(c)-1(a).

(ii) *Examples.* The provisions of this subparagraph may be illustrated by the following examples:

Example (1). Private foundation X permits A, a substantial contributor to X, and her spouse, H, to use an automobile owned by X and normally used in its foundation activities to travel from State Z to State Y for a vacation on December 1, 1971. The automobile is then returned to X until December 21, 1971, when X again permits them to use the automobile to return to their home in State Z. Under these circumstances, there is one act of self-dealing on December 1, 1971, and a second act of self-dealing on December 21, 1971.

Example (2). Assume the facts as stated in Example (1), except that B joined A and H on their vacation and travelled with them both to and from State Y. B is a disqualified person with respect to X, but he is not related by blood or marriage to A or H. Assume also that X is not paid for the use of its automobile, but that the fair rental value during the correction period is $300 (or $100 per person) for a one-way trip between State Y and State Z. Under these circumstances, there are four acts of self-dealing, two with respect to A and H and two with respect to B. The amount involved with respect to A and H is $200 for each act, and the amount involved with respect to B is $100 for each act.

(f) *Fair market value.* For purposes of §§ 53.4941(a)-1 through 53.4941(f)-1, fair market value shall be determined pursuant to the provisions of § 53.4942(a)-2(c)(4).

○━━ § 53.4941(f)-1 (T.D. 7270, filed 4-16-73.) Effective dates.

(a) *In general.* Except as provided in paragraph (b) of this section, §§ 53.4941(a)-1 through 53.4941(e)-1 shall apply to all acts of self-dealing engaged in after December 31, 1969.

(b) *Transitional rules*—(1) *Commitments made prior to January 1, 1970, between private foundations and government officials.* Section 4941 shall not apply to a payment for one or more purposes described in section 170(c)(1) or (2)(B) made on or after January 1, 1970, by a private foundation to a government official, if such payment is made pursuant to a commitment entered into prior to such date, but only if such commitment was made in accordance with the foundation's usual practices and is reasonable in amount in light of the purposes of the payment. For purposes of this subparagraph, a commitment will be considered entered into prior to January 1, 1970, if prior to such date, the amount and nature of the payments to be made and the name of the payee were entered on the records of the payor, or were otherwise adequately evidenced, or the notice of the payment to be received was communicated to the payee in writing.

(2) *Special transitional rule.* In the case of an act of self-dealing engaged in prior to July 5, 1971, section 4941(a)(1) shall not apply if—

(i) The participation (as defined in § 53.4941(a)-1(a)(3)) by the disqualified person in such act is not willful and is due to reasonable cause (as defined in § 53.4941(a)-1(b)(4) and (5)),

(ii) The transaction would not be a prohibited transaction if section 503(b) applied, and

(iii) The act is corrected (within the meaning of § 53.4941(e)-1(c)) within a period ending July 16, 1973, extended (prior to the expiration of the original period) by any period which the Commissioner determines is reasonable and necessary (within the meaning of § 53.4941(e)-1(d)) to bring about correction of the act of self-dealing.

Reg. § 53.4941(f)-1(b)(2)

24,258.10-D (I.R.C.)   Reg. § 53.4942   4-23-73

Distribution of Foundation Income

§ 53.4942 **Statutory provisions; taxes on failure to distribute income.** [Sec. 4942, IRC]

§ 53.4942(a)-1 (T.D. 7256, filed 2-2-73.) **Taxes for failure to distribute income.**

(a) *Imposition of tax*—(1) *Initial tax.* Except as provided in paragraph (b) of this section, section 4942(a) imposes an excise tax of 15 percent on the undistributed income (as defined in paragraph (a) of § 53.4942(a)-2) of a private foundation for any taxable year which has not been distributed before the first day of the second (or any succeeding) taxable year following such taxable year (if such first day falls within the taxable period as defined in paragraph (c)(1) of this section). For purposes of section 4942 and this section, the term "distributed" means distributed as qualifying distributions under section 4942 (g). See paragraph (d)(2) of § 53.4942(a)-3 with respect to correction of deficient distributions for prior taxable years.

(2) *Additional tax.* In any case in which an initial excise tax is imposed by section 4942(a) on the undistributed income of a private foundation for any taxable year, section 4942(b) imposes an additional excise tax on any portion of such income remaining undistributed at the close of the correction period (as defined in paragraph (c)(3) of this section). The tax imposed by section 4942(b) is equal to 100 percent of the amount remaining undistributed at the close of the correction period.

(3) *Payment of tax.* Payment of the excise taxes imposed by section 4942(a) or (b) is in addition to, and not in lieu of, making the distribution of such undistributed income as required by section 4942. See section 507(a)(2) and the regulations thereunder.

(4) *Examples.* The provisions of this paragraph may be illustrated by the following examples:

Example (1). M, a private foundation which uses the calendar year as the taxable year, has at the end of 1971 $50,000 of undistributed income (as defined in paragraph (a) of § 53.4942(a)-2) for 1971. As of January 1, 1973, $40,000 of such sum is still undistributed and on August 15, 1973, a notice of deficiency with respect to the excise taxes imposed by section 4942(a) and (b) is mailed to M under section 6212(a). Thus, under the given facts, an initial excise tax of $6,000 (15 percent of $40,000) is imposed upon M.

Example (2). Assume the facts as stated in example (1), except that as of November 13, 1973 (the close of the correction period), there remains undistributed income of $20,000 from 1971. Hence, an additional excise tax of $20,000 (100 percent of $20,000) is imposed by section 4942(b).

Example (3). Assume the facts as stated in example (1), except that the notice of deficiency is not mailed to M until September 1, 1974, and as of January 1, 1974, only $10,000 of the $50,000 of undistributed income with respect to 1971 is undistributed. Therefore, initial excise taxes of $6,000 (15 percent of $40,000, M's undistributed income from 1971, as of January 1, 1973) and $1,500 (15 percent of $10,000, M's undistributed income from 1971, as of January 1, 1974) are imposed by section 4942(a).

Example (4). Assume the facts as stated in example (3) and that at the end of the correction period, November 30, 1974, the $10,000 of undistributed income from 1971 remains undistributed. Thus, an additional tax of $10,000 (100 percent of $10,000, M's undistributed income from 1971, as of November 30, 1974, the last day of the correction period) is imposed by section 4942 (b).

(b) *Exceptions*—(1) *In general.* The initial excise tax imposed by section 4942 (a) shall not apply to the undistributed income of a private foundation—

(i) For any taxable year for which it is an operating foundation (as defined in section 4942(j)(3) and the regulations thereunder), or

(ii) To the extent that the foundation failed to distribute any amount solely because of an incorrect valuation of assets under paragraph (c)(4) of § 53.4942(a)-2, if—

(a) The failure to value the assets properly was not willful and was due to reasonable cause,

(b) Such amount is distributed as qualifying distributions (within the meaning of paragraph (a) of § 53.4942(a)-3) by the foundation during the allowable distribution period (as defined in paragraph (c)(2) of this section),

(c) The foundation notifies the Commissioner that such amount has been distributed (within the meaning of subdivision (ii)(b) of this subparagraph) to correct such failure, and

(d) Such distribution is treated under paragraph (d)(2) of § 53.4942(a)-3 as made out of the undistributed income for the taxable year for which a tax would (except for this subdivision) have been imposed by section 4942(a).

(2) *Improper valuation.* For purposes of subparagraph (1)(ii) of this paragraph, failure to value an asset properly shall be regarded as "not willful" and "due to reasonable cause" whenever, under all the facts and circumstances, the foundation can show that it has made all reasonable efforts in good faith to value such an asset in accordance with the provisions of paragraph (c)(4) of § 53.4942(a)-2. If a foundation, after full disclosure of the factual situation, obtains a bona fide appraisal of the fair market value of an asset by a person qualified to make such an appraisal (whether or not such a person is a disqualified person with respect to the foundation), and such foundation relies upon such appraisal, then failure to value the asset properly shall ordinarily be regarded as "not willful" and "due to reasonable cause". Notwithstanding the preceding sentence, the failure to obtain such a bona fide appraisal shall not, by itself, give rise to any inference that a foundation's failure to value an asset properly was willful or not due to reasonable cause.

(3) *Example.* The provisions of this paragraph may be illustrated by the following example:

Example. In 1976 M, a private foundation which was established in 1975 and which uses the calendar year as the taxable year, incorrectly values its assets under paragraph (c)(4) of § 53.4942(a)-2 in a manner which is not willful and is due to reasonable cause. As a result of the incorrect valuation of assets, $20,000 which should be distributed with respect to 1976 is not distributed, and as of January 1, 1978, such amount is still undistributed. On March 29, 1978, a notice of deficiency with respect to the excise taxes imposed by section 4942(a) and (b) is mailed to M under section 6212(a). On May 5, 1978 (within the allowable distribution period), M makes a qualifying distribution of $20,000 which is treated under paragraph (d)(2) of § 53.4942 (a)-3 as made out of M's undistributed income for 1976. M notifies the Commissioner of its action. Under the stated facts, an initial excise tax of $3,000 (15 percent of $20,000) would (except for the exception contained in subparagraph (1)(ii) of this paragraph) have been imposed by section 4942(a), but since all of the requirements of such subparagraph are satisfied no tax is imposed by section 4942(a).

(c) *Certain periods.* For purposes of this section—

(1) *Taxable period.* (i) The term "taxable period" means, with respect to the undistributed income of a private foundation for any taxable year, the period beginning with the first day of the taxable year and ending on the date of mailing of a notice of deficiency under section 6212(a) with respect to the initial excise tax imposed by section 4942(a). For example, assume M, a private foundation which uses the calendar year as the taxable year, has $15,000 of undistributed income for 1971. A notice of deficiency is mailed to M under section 6212(a) on March 1, 1973. With respect to the undistributed income of M for 1971, the taxable period began on January 1, 1971, and ended on March 1, 1973.

(ii) Where a notice of deficiency referred to in subdivision (i) of this subparagraph is not mailed because there is a waiver of the restrictions on assessment and collection of a deficiency, or because the deficiency is paid, the date of filing of the waiver or the date of such payment, respectively, shall be treated as the end of the taxable period.

(2) *Allowable distribution period.* (i) The term "allowable distribution period" means the period beginning with the first day of the first taxable year following the taxable year in which the incorrect valuation of foundation assets (described in paragraph (b)(1)(ii) of this section) occurred and ending 90 days after the date of mailing of a notice of deficiency under section 6212(a) with respect to the initial excise tax imposed by section 4942(a). This period shall be extended by any period in which a deficiency cannot be assessed under section 6213(a), and any other period which the Commissioner determines is reasonable and necessary to permit a distribution of undistributed income under section 4942.

(ii) Where a notice of deficiency referred to in subdivision (i) of this subparagraph is not mailed because there is a waiver of the restrictions on assessment and collection of a deficiency, or because the deficiency is paid, the date of filing of the waiver or the date of such payment, respectively, shall be treated as the end of the allowable distribution period.

(3) *Correction period.* (i) The term "correction period" means the period beginning with the first day of the taxable year and ending 90 days after the date of mailing of a notice of deficiency under section 6212(a) with respect to the additional excise tax imposed by section 4942(b).

(ii) The correction period referred to in subdivision (i) of this subparagraph shall be extended by any period in which a deficiency cannot be assessed under section 6213(a). In addition, the correction period shall be extended in accordance with subdivisions (iii), (iv), and (v) of this subparagraph, except that such subdivision (iv) or (v) shall not operate to extend a correction period where a foundation has filed a petition with the Tax Court for redetermination of a deficiency within the time prescribed by section 6213(a).

(iii) The correction period referred to in subdivision (i) of this subparagraph may be extended by any period which the Commissioner determines is reasonable and necessary to permit a distribution of undistributed income under section 4942. The Commissioner ordinarily will not extend the correction period pursuant to this sub-

Reg. § 53.4942(a)-1(c)(3)

division unless the following factors are present:

(a) The foundation or an appropriate State officer (as defined in section 6104(c)(2)) is in good faith actively seeking to take adequate corrective action;

(b) Adequate corrective action cannot reasonably be expected to result during the unextended correction period; and

(c) The failure to distribute appears to have been an isolated occurrence which is unlikely to recur in the future.

(iv) If, within the unextended correction period, the tax imposed by section 4942(a) is paid, then the Commissioner shall extend the correction period to the later of—

(a) A period of 90 days after the payment of such tax, or

(b) A period determined without regard to this subdivision.

(v) If prior to the expiration of the correction period (including extensions) a claim for refund with respect to a tax imposed by section 4942(a) is filed, the Commissioner shall extend the correction period during the pendency of the claim plus an additional 90 days. If within such time, a suit or proceeding referred to in section 7422(g) with respect to such claim is filed, the Commissioner shall extend the correction period during the pendency of such suit or proceeding. See § 301.7422-1 of this chapter (Regulations on Procedure and Administration) for rules relating to pendency of such suit or proceeding.

(4) *Examples.* The provisions of this paragraph may be illustrated by the following examples:

Example (1). In 1975 M, a private foundation which uses the calendar year as the taxable year, made an error in valuing its assets which was not willful and was due to reasonable cause. The error caused M not to distribute $25,000 that should have been distributed with respect to 1975. On March 1, 1978, a notice of deficiency with respect to the excise taxes imposed by section 4942(a) and (b) was mailed to M under section 6212(a). With respect to the undistributed income for 1975, the "taxable period" is the period from January 1, 1975, through March 1, 1978, and the "allowable distribution period" is the period from January 1, 1976, through May 30, 1978 (90 days after the mailing of the notice of deficiency).

Example (2). Assume the facts as stated in example (1), except that the Commissioner determines that it is reasonable and necessary to extend the period for distribution through June 15, 1978. Thus, the "allowable distribution period" is from January 1, 1976, through June 15, 1978.

Example (3). Assume the facts as stated in example (1) and that M has not filed a petition with the Tax Court for a redetermination of the deficiency, nor paid the initial excise tax imposed by section 4942(a). Thus, the "correction period" is from January 1, 1975, through May 30, 1978, unless the Commissioner determines it is reasonable and necessary to extend the correction period to permit M to distribute the undistributed income for 1975.

(d) *Effective date.* Except as otherwise specifically provided, section 4942 and the regulations thereunder shall only apply with respect to taxable years beginning after December 31, 1969.

§ 53.494(a)-2 (T.D. 7256, filed 2-2-73; amended by T.D. 7486, filed 5-12-77.) **Computation of undistributed income.**

(a) *Undistributed income.* For purposes of section 4942, the term "undistributed income" means, with respect to any private foundation for any taxable year as of any time, the amount by which—

(1) The distributable amount (as defined in paragraph (b) of this section) for such taxable year, exceeds

(2) The qualifying distributions (as defined in § 53.4942(a)-3) made before such time out of such distributable amount.

(b) *Distributable amount*—(1) *In general.* For purposes of paragraph (a) of this section, the term "distributable amount" means an amount equal to the greater of the minimum investment return (as defined in paragraph (c) of this section) or the adjusted net income (as defined in paragraph (d) of this section), reduced by the sum of the taxes imposed on such private foundation for such taxable year under subtitle A of the Code and section 4940, and increased by the amounts received from trusts described in subparagraph (2) of this paragraph.

(2) *Certain trust amounts*—(i) *In general.* The distributable amount shall be increased by the income portion (as defined in subdivision (ii) of this subparagraph) of distributions from trusts described in section 4947(a)(2) with respect to amounts placed in trust after May 26, 1969. If such distributions are made with respect to amounts placed in trust both on or before and after May 26, 1969, such distributions shall be allocated between such amounts to determine the extent to which such distributions shall be included in the foundation's distributable amount. For rules relating to the segregation of amounts placed in trust on or before May 26, 1969, from amounts placed in trust after such date and to the allocation of income derived from such amounts, see paragraph (c)(5) of § 53.4947-1.

(ii) *Income portion of distributions to private foundations.* For purposes of subdivision (i) of this subparagraph, the income portion of a distribution from a section 4947(a)(2) trust to a private foundation in a particular taxable year of such foundation shall be the greater of:

(a) The amount of such distribution which is treated as income (within the meaning of section 643(b)) of the trust, or

(b) The guaranteed annuity, or fixed percentage of the fair market value of the trust property (determined annually), which the private foundation is entitled to receive for such year, regardless of whether such amount is actually received in such year or in any prior or subsequent year.

(iii) *Limitation.* Notwithstanding subdivisions (i) and (ii) of this subparagraph, a private foundation shall not be required to distribute a greater amount for any taxable year than would have been required (without regard to this subparagraph) for such year had the corpus of the section 4947(a)(2) trust to which the distribution described in subdivision (ii) of this subparagraph is attributable been taken into account by such foundation as an asset described in paragraph (c)(1)(i) of this section.

(c) *Minimum investment return*—(1) *In general.* For purposes of paragraph (b) of this section, the "minimum investment return" for any private foundation for any taxable year is the amount determined by multiplying—

(i) The excess of the aggregate fair market value of all assets of the foundation, other than those described in subparagraph (2) or (3) of this paragraph, over the amount of the acquisition indebtedness with respect to such assets (determined under section 514(c)(1), but without regard to the taxable year in which the indebtedness was incurred), by

(ii) The applicable percentage (as defined in subparagraph (5) of this paragraph) for such taxable year.

For purposes of subdivision (i) of this subparagraph, the aggregate fair market value of all assets of the foundation shall include the average of the fair market values on a monthly basis of securities for which market quotations are readily available (within the meaning of subparagraph (4)(i)(a) of this paragraph), the average of the foundation's cash balances on a monthly basis (less the cash balances excluded from the computation of the minimum investment return by operation of subparagraph (3)(iv) of this paragraph), and the fair market value of all other assets (except those assets described in subparagraph (2) or (3) of this paragraph) for the period of time during the taxable year for which such assets are held by the foundation. Any determination of the fair market value of an asset required pursuant to the provisions of this subparagraph shall be made in accordance with the rules of subparagraph (4) of this paragraph.

(2) *Certain assets excluded.* For purposes of this paragraph, the assets taken into account in determining minimum investment return shall not include the following:

(i) Any future interest (such as a vested or contingent remainder, whether legal or equitable) of a foundation in the income or corpus of any real or personal property until all intervening interests in, and rights to the actual possession or enjoyment of, such property have expired, or, although not actually reduced to the foundation's possession, until such future interest has been constructively received by the foundation, as where it has been credited to the foundation's account, set apart for the foundation, or otherwise made available so that the foundation may acquire it at any time or could have acquired it if notice of intention to acqiure had been given;

(ii) The assets of an estate until such time as such assets are distributed to the foundation or, due to a prolonged period of administration, such estate is considered terminated for Federal income tax purposes by operation of paragraph (a) of § 1.641(b)-3 of this chapter (Income Tax Regulations);

(iii) Any present interest of a foundation in any trust created and funded by another person (see, however, paragraph (b)(2) of this section with respect to amounts received from certain trusts described in section 4947(a)(2));

(iv) Any pledge to the foundation of money or property (whether or not the pledge may be legally enforced); and

(v) Any assets used (or held for use) directly in carrying out the foundation's exempt purpose.

(3) *Assets used (or held for use) in carrying out the exempt purpose*—(i) *In general.* For purposes of subparagraph (2)(v) of this paragraph, an asset is "used (or held for use) directly in carrying out the foundation's exempt purpose" only if the asset is actually used by the foundation in carrying out the charitable, educational, or other similar purpose which gives rise to the exempt status of the foundation, or if the foundation owns the asset and establishes to the satisfaction of the Commissioner that its immediate use for such exempt purpose is not practical (based on the facts and circumstances of the particular case) and that definite plans exist to commence such use within a reasonable period of time. Consequently, assets which are held for the production of income or for investment (for example, stocks, bonds, interest-bearing notes, endowment funds, or, generally, leased real estate) are not being used (or held for use) directly in carrying out the foundation's exempt purpose, even though the income from such assets is used to carry out such exempt purpose. Whether an asset is held for the production of income or for investment rather than used (or held for use) directly by the foundation to carry out its exempt purpose is a question of fact. For example, an office building used for the purpose of providing offices for employees engaged in the management of endowment funds of the foundation is not being used (or held for use) directly by the foundation to carry out its charitable, educational, or other similar exempt purpose. However, where property is used both for charitable, educational, or other similar exempt purposes and for other purposes, if such exempt use represents 95 percent or more of the total use, such property shall be considered to be used exclusively for a charitable, educational, or other similar exempt purpose. If such exempt use of such property represents less than 95 percent of the total use, reasonable allocation between such exempt and nonexempt use must be made for purposes of this paragraph. Property acquired by the foundation to be used in carrying out its charitable, educational, or other similar exempt purpose may be considered as used (or held for use) directly to carry out such exempt purpose even though the property, in whole or in part, is leased for a limited period of time during which arrangements are made for its conversion to the use for which it was acquired, provided such income-producing use of the property does not exceed a reasonable period of time. Generally, one year shall be deemed to be a reasonable period of time for purposes of the immediately preceding sentence. For treatment of the income derived from such income-producing use, see paragraph (d)(2)(viii) of this section. Where the income-producing use continues beyond a reasonable period of time, the property shall not be deemed to be used by the foundation to carry out its charitable, educational, or other similar exempt purpose, but, instead, as of the time the income-producing use becomes unreasonable, such property shall be treated as disposed of within the mean-

Reg. § 53.4942(a)-2(c)(3)

ing of paragraph (d)(2)(iii)(b) of this section to the extent that the acquisition of the property was taken into account as a qualifying distribution (within the meaning of paragraph (a)(2) of § 53.4942(a)-3) for any taxable year. If, subsequently, the property is used by the foundation directly in carrying out its charitable, educational, or other similar exempt purpose, a qualifying distribution in the amount of its then fair market value, determined in accordance with the rules contained in subparagraph (4) of this paragraph, shall be deemed to have been made as of the time such exempt use begins.

(ii) *Illustrations.* Examples of assets which are "used (or held for use) directly in carrying out the foundation's exempt purpose" include, but are not limited to, the following:

(*a*) Administrative assets, such as office equipment and supplies, which are used by employees or consultants of the foundation, to the extent such assets are devoted to and used directly in the administration of the foundation's charitable, educational, or other similar exempt activities;

(*b*) Real estate or the portion of a building used by the foundation directly in its charitable, educational, or other similar exempt activities;

(*c*) Physical facilities used in such activities, such as paintings or other works of art owned by the foundation which are on public display, fixtures and equipment in classrooms, and research facilities and related equipment, which under the facts and circumstances serve a useful purpose in the conduct of such activities;

(*d*) Any interest in a functionally related business (as defined in subdivision (iii) of this subparagraph) or in a program-related investment (as defined in section 4944(c));

(*e*) The reasonable cash balances (as described in subdivision (iv) of this subparagraph) necessary to cover current administrative expenses and other normal and current disbursements directly connected with the foundation's charitable, educational, or other similar exempt activities; and

(*f*) Any property leased by a foundation in carrying out its charitable, educational, or other similar exempt purpose at no cost (or at a nominal rent) to the lessee or for a program-related purpose (within the meaning of section 4944(c)), such as the leasing of renovated apartments to low-income tenants at a low rental as part of the lessor-foundation's program for rehabilitating a blighted portion of a community. For treatment of the income derived from such use, see paragraph (d)(2)(viii) of this section.

(iii) *Functionally related business*—(*a*) *In general.* The term "functionally related business" means—

(*1*) A trade or business which is not an unrelated trade or business (as defined in section 513), or

(*2*) An activity which is carried on within a larger aggregate of similar activities or within a larger complex of other endeavors which is related (aside from the need of the organization for income or funds or the use it makes of the profits derived) to the charitable, educational, or other similar exempt purpose of the organization.

(*b*) *Examples.* The provisions of this subdivision may be illustrated by the following examples:

Example (1). X, a private foundation, maintains a community of historic value which is open to the general public. For the convenience of the public, X, through a wholly owned, separately incorporated, taxable entity, maintains a restaurant and hotel in such community. Such facilities are within the larger aggregate of activities which makes available for public enjoyment the various buildings of historic interest and which is related to X's exempt purpose. Thus, the operation of the restaurant and hotel under such circumstances constitutes a functionally related business.

Example (2). Y, a private foundation, as part of its medical research program under section 501(c)(3), publishes a medical journal in carrying out its exempt purpose. Space in the journal is sold for commercial advertising. Notwithstanding the fact that the advertising activity may be subject to the tax imposed by section 511, such activity is within a larger complex of endeavors which makes available to the scientific community and the general public developments with respect to medical research and is therefore a functionally related business.

(iv) *Cash held for charitable, etc. activities.* For purposes of subdivision (ii) (*e*) of this subparagraph, the reasonable cash balances which a private foundation needs to have on hand to cover expenses and disbursements described in such subdivision will generally be deemed to be an amount, computed on an annual basis, equal to one and one-half percent of the fair market value of all assets described in subparagraph (1)(i) of this paragraph, without regard to subdivision (ii)(*e*) of this subparagraph. However, if the Commissioner is satisfied that under the facts and circumstances an amount in addition to such one and one-half percent is necessary for payment of such expenses and disbursements, then such additional amount may also be excluded from the amount of assets described in subparagraph (1)(i) of this paragraph. All remaining cash balances, including amounts necessary to pay any tax imposed by section 511 or any section of chapter 42 of the Code except section 4940, are to be included in the assets described in subparagraph (1)(i) of this paragraph.

(4) *Valuation of assets*—(i) *Certain securities.* (*a*) For purposes of subparagraph (1)(i) of this paragraph, a private foundation may use any reasonable method to determine the fair market value on a monthly basis of securities for which market quotations are readily available, as long as such method is consistently used. For purposes of this subparagraph, market quotations are readily available if a security is:

(*1*) Listed on the New York Stock Exchange, the American Stock Exchange, or any city or regional exchange in which quotations appear on a daily basis, including foreign securities listed on a recognized foreign national or regional exchange;

(*2*) Regularly traded in the national or regional over-the-counter market, for which published quotations are available; or

(3) Locally traded, for which quotations can readily be obtained from established brokerage firms.

(b) For purposes of this subdivision, commonly accepted methods of valuation must be used in making an appraisal. Valuations made in accordance with the principles stated in the regulations under section 2031 constitute acceptable methods of valuation.

(c) In the case of securities described in subdivision (i)(a) of this subparagraph, which are held in trust for, or on behalf of, a foundation by a bank or other financial institution which values such securities periodically by use of a computer, a foundation may determine the correct value of securities by use of such computer pricing system, provided the Comissioner has accepted such computer pricing system as a valid method for valuing securities for Federal estate tax purposes.

(d) This subdivision may be illustrated by the following examples:

Example (1). U, a private foundation, owns 1,000 shares of the stock of M Corporation. M stock is regularly traded on the New York Stock Exchange. U consistently follows a practice of valuing its 1,000 shares of M stock on the last trading day of each month based upon the quoted closing price for M stock. U's method of valuing its M Corporation stock is permissible under the rules contained in subdivision (i)(a) of this subparagraph.

Example (2). Assume the facts as stated in example (1), except that U consistently follows a practice of valuing its 1,000 shares of M stock by taking the mean of the closing prices for M stock on the first and last trading days of each month and the trading day nearest the 15th day of each month. U's method of valuing its M stock is permissible under the rules contained in subdivision (i)(a) of this subparagraph.

Example (3). Assume the facts as stated in example (1), except that U consistently follows a practice of valuing its M stock by taking the mean of the highest and lowest quoted prices for the stock on the last trading day of each month. U's method of valuing its M stock is permissible under the rules contained in subdivision (1)(a) of this subparagraph.

Example (4). V, a private foundation, owns 1,000 shares of the stock of N Corporation. N stock is regularly traded in the national over-the-counter market and published quotations of the bid and asked prices for the stock are available. V consistently follows a practice of valuing its 1,000 shares of N stock on the first trading day of each month by taking the mean of the bid and asked prices on that day. V's method of valuing its N Corporation stock is permissible under the rules contained in subdivision (i)(a) of this subparagraph.

Example (5). W, a private foundation, owns 1,000 shares of the stock of O Corporation. O stock is locally traded and quotations can readily be obtained from established brokerage firms. W consistently follows a practice of valuing its O stock on the 15th day of each month by obtaining a bona fide quotation of bid and asked prices for the stock from an established brokerage firm and taking the mean of such prices on that day. If a quotation is unavailable on the regular valuation date, W values its O stock based upon a bona fide quotation on the first day thereafter on which such a quotation is available. W's method of valuing its O Corporation stock is permissible under the rules contained in subdivision (i)(a) of this subparagraph.

(ii) *Cash.* In order to determine the amount of a foundation's cash balances, the foundation shall value its cash on a monthly basis by averaging the amount of cash on hand as of the first day of each month and as of the last day of each month.

(iii) *Common trust funds.* If a private foundation owns a participating interest in a common trust fund (as defined in section 584) established and administered under a plan providing for the periodic valuation of participating interests during the fund's taxable year and the reporting of such valuations to participants, the value of the foundation's interest in the common trust fund based upon the average of the valuations reported to the foundation during its taxable year will ordinarily constitute an acceptable method of valuation.

(iv) *Other assets.* (a) Except as otherwise provided in subdivision (iv)(b) of this subparagraph, the fair market value of assets other than those described in subdivisions (i) through (iii) of this subparagraph shall be determined annually. Thus, the fair market value of securities other than those described in subdivision (i) of this subparagraph shall be determined in accordance with this subdivision (a). Such determination may be made by employees of the private foundation or by any other person, without regard to whether such person is a disqualified person with respect to the foundation. A valuation made pursuant to the provisions of this subdivision, if accepted by the Commissioner, shall be valid only for the taxable year for which it is made. A new valuation made in accordance with these provisions is required for the succeeding taxable year.

(b) If the requirements of this subdivision are met, the fair market value of any interest in real property, including any improvements thereon, may be determined on a five-year basis. Such value must be determined by means of a certified, independent appraisal made in writing by a qualified person who is neither a disqualified person with respect to, nor an employee of, the private foundation. The appraisal is certified only if it contains a statement at the end thereof to the effect that, in the opinion of the appraiser, the values placed on the assets appraised were determined in accordance with valuation principles regularly employed in making appraisals of such property using all reasonable valuation methods. The foundation shall retain a copy of the independent appraisal for its records. If a valuation made pursuant to the provisions of this subdivision in fact falls within the range of reasonable values for the appraised property, such valuation may be used by the foundation for the taxable year for which the valuation is made and for each of the succeeding four taxable years. Any valuation made pursuant to the provisions of this subdivision may be replaced during

Reg. § 53.4942(a)-2(c)(4)

the five-year period by a subsequent five-year valuation made in accordance with the rules set forth in this subdivision, or with an annual valuation made in accordance with subdivision (iv)(a) of this subparagraph, and the most recent such valuation of such assets shall be used in computing the foundation's minimum investment return. In the case of a foundation organized before May 27, 1969, a valuation made in accordance with this subdivision applicable to the foundation's first taxable year beginning after December 31, 1972 and the four succeeding taxable years must be made no later than the last day of such first taxable year. In the case of a foundation organized after May 26, 1969, a valuation made in accordance with this subdivision applicable to the foundation's first taxable year beginning after [insert date these regulations are published as a Treasury decision] and the succeeding four taxable years must be made no later than the last day of such first taxable year. Any subsequent valuation made in accordance with this subdivision must be made no later than the last day of the first taxable year for which such new valuation is applicable. A valuation, if properly made in accordance with the rules set forth in this subdivision, will not be disturbed by the Commissioner during the five-year period for which it applies even if the actual fair market value of such property changes during such period.

(c) For purposes of this subdivision, commonly accepted methods of valuation must be used in making an appraisal. Valuations made in accordance with the principles stated in the regulations under section 2031 constitute acceptable methods of valuation. The term "appraisal," as used in this subdivision, means a determination of fair market value and is not to be construed in a technical sense peculiar to particular property or interests therein, such as, for example, mineral interests in real property.

(v) *Definition of "securities".* For purposes of this subparagraph, the term "securities" includes, but is not limited to, common and preferred stocks, bonds, and mutual fund shares.

(vi) *Valuation date.* (a) In the case of an asset which is required to be valued on an annual basis as provided in subdivision (iv)(a) of this subparagraph, such asset may be valued as of any day in the private foundation's taxable year to which such valuation applies, provided the foundation follows a consistent practice of valuing such asset as of such date in all taxable years.

(b) A valuation described in subdivision (iv)(b) of this subparagraph may be made as of any day in the first taxable year of the private foundation to which such valuation is to be applied.

(vii) *Assets held for less than a taxable year.* For purposes of this paragraph, any asset described in subparagraph (1)(i) of this paragraph which is held by a foundation for only part of a taxable year shall be taken into account for purposes of determining the foundation's minimum investment return for such taxable year by multiplying the fair market value of such asset (as determined pursuant to this subparagraph) by a fraction, the numerator of which is the number of days in such taxable year that the foundation held such asset and the denominator of which is the number of days in such taxable year.

(5) *Applicable percentage*—(i) *In general.* For purposes of subparagraph (1)(ii) of this paragraph, except as provided in subdivision (ii) or (iii) of this subparagraph, the applicable percentage is:

(a) 6 percent for a taxable year beginning in calendar years 1970 and 1971; and

(b) 5½ percent for a taxable year beginning in calendar year 1972 and in any subsequent calendar year, unless another percentage has been determined and published by the Secretary or his delegate.

Any determination that a new applicable percentage is to be used for taxable years beginning in a calendar year subsequent to 1972 will be published by May 1st of such calendar year. The latest published percentage shall apply for any taxable year beginning in the calendar year with respect to which publication is made and for any subsequent taxable year. The applicable percentage shall bear a relationship to 6 percent which the Secretary or his delegate determines to be comparable to the relationship which the money rates and investment yields for the calendar year immediately preceding the beginning of the taxable year bear to the money rates and investment yields for the calendar year 1969. Any adjustment in the applicable percentage shall be made only to the nearest one-fourth of one percent.

(ii) *Transitional rule.* In the case of organizations organized before May 27, 1969 (including organizations deemed to be so organized by virtue of the provisions of paragraph (e)(2) of this section), section 4942 shall, for all purposes other than the determination of the minimum investment return under section 4942(j)(3)(B)(ii), for taxable years—

(a) Beginning before January 1, 1972, apply without regard to section 4942(e),

(b) Beginning in 1972, apply with an applicable percentage of 4⅛ percent,

(c) Beginning in 1973, apply with an applicable percentage which is the lesser of 5 percent or 5/6 of the applicable percentage prescribed in subdivision (i) of this subparagraph for 1973, and

(d) Beginning in 1974, apply with an applicable percentage which is the lesser of 5½ percent or 11/12 of the applicable percentage prescribed in subdivision (i) of this subparagraph for 1974.

(iii) *Short taxable periods.* In any case in which a taxable year referred to in this subparagraph is a period less than 12 months, the applicable percentage to be applied to the amount determined under the provisions of subparagraph (1) of this paragraph shall be equal to the applicable percentage for the calendar year in which the short taxable period began multiplied by a fraction, the numerator of which is the number of days in such short taxable period and the denominator of which is 365.

(d) *Adjusted net income*—(1) *Definition.* For purposes of paragraph (b) of this section, the term "adjusted net income" means the excess (if any) of—

(i) The gross income for the taxable year (including gross income from any unrelated trade or business) determined with the income modifications provided by subparagraph (2) of this paragraph, over

(ii) The sum of the deductions (including deductions directly connected with the carrying on of any unrelated trade or business), determined with the deduction modifications provided by subparagraph (4) of this paragraph, which would be allowed to a corporation subject to the tax imposed by section 11 for the taxable year.

In computing the income includible under this paragraph as gross income and the deductions allowable under this paragraph from such income, the principles of subtitle A of the Code shall apply except to the extent such principles conflict with section 4942 and the regulations thereunder (without regard to this sentence). Except as otherwise provided in this paragraph, no exclusions or deductions from gross income or credits against tax are allowable under this paragraph. For purposes of subdivision (i) of this subparagraph, the term "gross income" does not include gifts, grants, or contributions received by the private foundation but does include income from a functionally related business (as defined in paragraph (c)(3)(iii) of this section).

(2) *Income modifications.* The income modifications referred to in subparagraph (1)(i) of this paragraph are as follows:

(i) Section 103 (relating to interest on certain governmental obligations) shall not apply. Hence, interest which would have been excluded from gross income by section 103 shall be included in gross income.

(ii) Capital gains and losses from the sale or other disposition of property shall be taken into account only in an amount equal to any net short-term capital gain (as defined in section 1222(5)) for the taxable year. Long-term capital gain or loss is not included in the computation of adjusted net income. Similarly, net section 1231 gains shall be excluded from the computation of adjusted net income. However, net section 1231 losses shall be included in the computation of adjusted net income, if such losses are otherwise described in subparagraph (1)(ii) of this paragraph. Any net short-term capital loss for a given taxable year shall not be taken into account in computing adjusted net income for such year or in computing net short-term capital gain for purposes of determining adjusted net income for prior or future taxable years regardless of whether the foundation is a corporation or a trust.

(iii) The following amounts shall be included in gross income for the taxable year—

(a) Amounts received or accrued as repayments of amounts which were taken into account as a qualifying distribution within the meaning of paragraph (a)(2)(i) of § 53.4942(a)-3 for any taxable year;

(b) Notwithstanding subdivision (ii) of this subparagraph, gross amounts received or accrued from the sale or other disposition of property to the extent that the acquisition of such property was taken into account as a qualifying distribution (within the meaning of paragraph (a)(2)(ii) of § 53.4942(a)-3) for any taxable year; and

(c) Any amount set aside under paragraph (b) of § 53.4942(a)-3 to the extent it is determined that such amount is not necessary for the purposes for which it was set aside.

(iv) Any distribution received by a private foundation from a disqualified person in redemption of stock held by such private foundation in a business enterprise shall be treated as not essentially equivalent to a dividend under section 302(b)(1) if all of the following conditions are satisfied:

(a) Such redemption is of stock which was owned by a private foundation on May 26, 1969 (or which is acquired by a private foundation under the terms of a trust which was irrevocable on May 26, 1969, or under the terms of a will executed on or before such date which are in effect on such date and at all times thereafter);

(b) Such foundation is required to dispose of such property in order not to be liable for tax under section 4943 (relating to taxes on excess business holdings) applied, in the case of a disposition before January 1, 1975, without taking section 4943 (c)(4) into account; and

(c) Such foundation receives in return an amount which equals or exceeds the fair market value of such property at the time of such disposition or at the time a contract for such disposition was previously executed in a transaction which would not constitute a prohibited transaction (within the meaning of section 503(b) or the corresponding provisions of prior law).

(v) If, as of the date of distribution of property for purposes described in section 170(c)(1) or (2)(B), the fair market value of such property exceeds its adjusted basis, such excess shall not be deemed an amount includible in gross income.

(vi) The income received by a private foundation from an estate during the period of administration of such estate shall not be included in such foundation's gross income, unless, due to a prolonged period of administration, such estate is considered terminated for Federal income tax purposes by operation of paragraph (a) of § 1.641(b)-3 of this chapter (Income Tax Regulations).

(vii) Distributions received by a private foundation from a trust created and funded by another person shall not be included in the foundation's gross income. However, with respect to distributions from certain trusts described in section 4947(a)(2), see paragraph(b)(2) of this section.

(viii) Gross income shall include all amounts derived from, or in connection with, property held by the foundation, even though the fair market value of such property may not be included in such foundation's assets for purposes of determining minimum investment return by operation of paragraph (c)(3) of this section.

(ix) Gross income shall include amounts treated in a preceding taxable year as a "qualifying distribution" by operation of paragraph (c) of § 53.4942(a)-3 where such amounts are not redistributed by the close of the donee organization's succeeding taxable year in accordance with the rules prescribed in such paragraph (c). In such cases, such amounts shall be included in the donor foundation's gross income for such foundation's first taxable year beginning after the close of the donee organization's first taxable year following the donee organization's taxable year of receipt.

(3) *Adjusted basis*—(i) *In general.* For purposes of subparagraph (2)(ii) of this paragraph, the adjusted basis for purposes of determining gain from the sale or other

Reg. § 53.4942(a)-2(d)(3)

disposition of property shall be determined in accordance with the rules set forth in subdivision (ii) of this subparagraph and the adjusted basis for purposes of determining loss from such disposition shall be determined in accordance with the rules set forth in subdivision (iii) of this subparagraph. Further, the provisions of this subparagraph do not apply for any purpose other than for purposes of subparagraph (2)(ii) of this paragraph. For example, the determination of gain pursuant to the provisions of section 341 is determined without regard to this subparagraph.

(ii) *Gain from sale or other disposition.* The adjusted basis for purposes of determining gain from the sale or other disposition of property shall be the greater of:

(a) The fair market value of such property on December 31, 1969, plus or minus all adjustments after December 31, 1969, and before the date of sale or other disposition under the rules of Part II, subchapter O, chapter 1 of the Code, provided that the property was held by the private foundation on December 31, 1969, and continuously thereafter to such date of sale or other disposition; or

(b) The adjusted basis as determined under the rules of Part II, subchapter O, chapter 1 of the Code, subject to the provisions of section 4940(c)(3)(B) and the regualtions thereunder (and without regard to section 362(c)). With respect to assets acquired prior to December 31, 1969, which were subject to depreciation or depletion, for purposes of determining the adjustments to be made to basis between the date of acquisition and December 31, 1969, an amount equal to straight-line depreciation or cost depletion shall be taken into account. In addition, in determining such adjustments to basis, if any other adjustments would have been made during such period (such as a change in useful life based upon additional data or a change in facts), such adjustments shall also be taken into account.

(iii) *Loss from sale or other disposition.* For purposes of determining loss from the sale or other disposition of property, adjusted basis as determined in subdivision (ii)(b) of this subparagraph shall apply.

(iv) *Examples.* The provisions of this subparagraph may be illustrated by the following examples:

Example (1). A private foundation, which uses the cash receipts and disbursements method of accounting, purchased certain depreciable real property on December 1, 1969. On December 31, 1969, the fair market value of such property was $100,000 and its adjusted basis (determined under the provisions of this subparagraph) was $102,000. The property was sold on January 2, 1970, for $105,000. Because fair market value on December 31, 1969, $100,000, is less than the adjusted basis as determined by Part II, subchapter O, chapter 1 of the Code, $102,000, a short-term gain of $3,000 is recognized (i.e., sale price of $105,000 less the greater of the two possible bases) for purposes of subparagraph (2)(ii) of this paragraph.

Example (2). Assume the facts as stated in example (1), except that the sale price was $95,000. Because the sale price was $7,000 less than the adjusted basis for loss ($102,000, as determined by the application of subdivision (iii) of this subparagraph), there is a capital loss of $7,000 which may be deducted against short-term capital gains for 1970 (if any) in determining net short-term capital gain.

Example (3). A private foundation, which uses the cash receipts and disbursement method of accounting, purchased unimproved land on December 1, 1969. On December 31, 1969, the fair market value of such property was $110,000 and its adjusted basis (determined under the provisions of this subparagraph) was $102,000. The property was sold on January 2, 1970, for $105,000. Since the fair market value on December 31, 1969, $110,000, exceeds the adjusted basis as determined by Part II, subchapter O, chapter 1 of the Code, $102,000, such fair market value will be used for purposes of determining gain. However, because the adjusted basis for purposes of determining gain exceeds the sale price, there is no gain. Furthermore, because the adjusted basis for purposes of determining loss, $102,000, is less than the sale price, there is no loss.

(4) *Deduction modifications* — (i) *In general.* For purposes of computing adjusted net income under subparagraph (1) of this paragraph, no deduction shall be allowed other than all the ordinary and necessary expenses paid or incurred for the production or collection of gross income or for the management, conservation, or maintenance of property held for the production of such income, except as provided in subdivision (ii) of this subparagraph. Such expenses include that portion of a private foundation's operating expenses which is paid or incurred for the production or collection of gross income. Operating expenses include compensation of officers, other salaries and wages of employees, interest, rent, and taxes. Where only a portion of the property produces (or is held for the production of) income subject to the provisions of section 4942, and the remainder of the property is used for charitable, educational, or other similar exempt purposes, the deductions allowed by this subparagraph shall be apportioned between such exempt and non-exempt uses. Similarly, where the deductions with respect to property used for a charitable, educational, or other similar exempt purpose exceed the income derived from such property, such excess shall not be allowed as a deduction, but may be treated as a qualifying distribution described in paragraph (a)(2)(ii) of § 53.4942(a)-3. Furthermore, this subdivision does not allow deductions which are not paid or incurred for the purposes herein prescribed. Thus, for example, the deductions prescribed by the following sections are not allowable: (a) the charitable contributions deduction prescribed under sections 170 and 642(c); (b) the net operating loss deduction prescribed under section 172; and (c) the special deductions prescribed under Part VIII, subchapter B, chapter 1 of the Code.

(ii) *Special rules.* For purposes of computing adjusted net income under subparagraph (1) of this paragraph: (a) the allowances for depreciation and depletion as determined under section 4940(c)(3)(B) and the regulations thereunder shall be taken into account, and (b) section 265 (relating to expenses and interest relating to tax-exempt interest) shall not apply.

(e) *Certain transitional rules* —(1) *In general.* In the case of organizations organized before May 27, 1969, section 4942 shall—

(i) Not apply to an organization to the extent its income is required to be accumulated pursuant to the mandatory terms (as in effect on May 26, 1969, and at all times thereafter) of an instrument executed before May 27, 1969, with respect to the transfer of income producing property to such organization, except that section 4942 shall apply to such organization if the organization would have been denied exemption had section 504(a) not been repealed, or would have had its deductions under section 642(c) limited had section 681(c) not been repealed. In applying the preceding sentence, in addition to the limitations contained in section 504(a) or 681 (c) before its repeal, section 504(a)(1) or 681(c)(1) shall be treated as not applying to an organization to the extent its income is required to be accumulated pursuant to the mandatory terms (as in effect on January 1, 1951, and at all times thereafter) of an instrument executed before January 1, 1951, with respect to the transfer of income producing property to such organization before such date, if such transfer was irrevocable on such date; and

(ii) Not apply to an organization which is prohibited by its governing instrument or other instrument from distributing capital or corpus to the extent the requirements of section 4942 are inconsistent with such prohibition.

(2) *Certain existing organizations.* For purposes of this section, an organization will be deemed to be organized prior to May 27, 1969, if it is either a testamentary trust created under the will of an individual who died prior to such date or an inter vivos trust which was in existence and irrevocable prior to such date, even though it is not funded until after May 26, 1969. Similarly, a split-interest trust, as described in section 4947(a)(2) (without regard to section 4947(a)(2)(c)), which became irrevocable prior to May 27, 1969, and which is treated as a private foundation under section 4947(a)(1) subsequent to such date, likewise shall be treated as an organization organized prior to such date. See section 507(b)(2) and the regulations thereunder with respect to the applicability of transitional rules where there has been a merger of two or more private foundations or a reorganization of a private foundation.

(3) *Limitation.* With respect to taxable years beginning after December 31, 1971, subparagraph (1)(i) and (ii) of this paragraph shall apply only for taxable years during which there is pending any judicial proceeding by the private foundation which is necessary to reform, or to excuse such foundation from compliance with, its governing instrument or any other instrument (as in effect on May 26, 1969) in order to comply with the provisions of section 4942, and in the case of subparagraph (1)(i) of this paragraph for all taxable years following the taxable year in which such judicial proceeding is terminated during which the governing instrument or any other instrument does not permit compliance with such provisions. Thus, the execption described in subparagraph (1)(ii) of this paragraph applies after 1971 only for taxable years during which such judicial proceeding is pending. Accordingly, beginning with the first taxable year following the taxable year in which such judicial proceeding is terminated, such foundation will be required to meet the requirements of section 4942 and the regulations thereunder (and be subject to the taxes provided upon failure to do so) except to the extent such foundation is required to accumulate income as described in subparagraph (1)(i) of this paragraph, even if the governing instrument continues to prohibit invasion of capital or corpus. In any case where a foundation's governing instrument or any other instrument requires accumulation of income as described in subparagraph (1)(i) of this paragraph beginning with the first taxable year following the taxable year in which such judicial proceeding is terminated, the distributable amount (as defined in paragraph (b) of this section) for such foundation shall be reduced by the amount of the income required to be accumulated. Therefore, if the foundation's adjusted net income for any taxable year equals or exceeds its minimum investment return for such year, the accumulation provision will be given full effect. However, if the minimum investment return exceeds the adjusted net income for any taxable year, the foundation will be required to distribute such excess for such year. For purposes of this paragraph, a judicial proceeding will be treated as pending only if the foundation is diligently pursuing its judicial remedies and there is no unreasonable delay in such proceeding for which the private foundation is responsible.

(4) *Examples.* The provisions of this paragraph may be illustrated by the following examples:

Example (1). X, a private foundation organized in 1930, is required by the mandatory terms of its governing instrument to accumulate 25 percent of its adjusted net income and to add such accumulations to corpus. The instrument also prohibits distribution of corpus for any purpose. On July 13, 1971, X instituted an action in the appropriate State court to reform the instrument by deleting the accumulation and corpus provisions described above. If the court's final order reforms the accumulation provision to allow distributions of income sufficient to avoid the imposition of a tax under section 4942, then section 4942 applies to X, regardless of the court's action with respect to the corpus provision. However, if the court rules that the accumulation provision may not be reformed, section 4942 applies to X only to the extent provided for in subparagraph (3) of this paragraph, regardless of the court's action with respect to the corpus provision.

Example (2). Private foundation Y was created by the will of A who died in 1940. Y's governing instrument requires that 40 percent of Y's adjusted net income be added to corpus each year. In an action commenced prior to December 31, 1971, a court of competent jurisdiction ruled that this accumulation provision must be complied with. In Y's succeeding taxable year its adjusted net income is $120,000, and its minimum investment return is $140,000. Thus, Y is required to accumulate $48,000

Reg. § 53.4942(a)-2(e)(4)

24,258.10-D.10 (I.R.C.)   Reg. § 53.4942(a)-2(e)(4)

(40% of $120,000) and shall be allowed to do so. Therefore, Y's distributable amount for such taxable year shall be the greater of its adjusted net income ($120,000) or its minimum investment return ($140,000), reduced by the amount of the income required to be accumulated ($48,000) and the taxes imposed by subtitle A of the Code and section 4940 and increased by any trust distributions described in paragraph (b)(2) of this section. Accordingly, Y's distributable amount for such taxable year is $92,000 ($140,000 reduced by $48,000), before other adjustments. If Y's minimum investment return had been $120,000 instead of $140,000, its distributable amount for such taxable year would hvae been $72,000 ($120,000 reduced by $48,000), before other adjustments. Similarly, if Y's minimum investment return had been $100,000 instead of $140,000, its distributable amount for such taxable year would also have been $72,000, before other adjustments.

○—▶ § 53.4942(a)-3   (T.D. 7256, filed 2-2-73; amended by T.D. 7486, filed 5-12-77.) **Qualifying distributions defined.**

(a) *In general*—(1) *Distributions generally.* For purposes of section 4942 and the regulations thereunder, the amount of a qualifying distribution of property (as defined in subparagraph (2) of this paragraph) is the fair market value of such property as of the date such qualifying distribution is made. The amount of an organization's qualifying distributions will be determined solely on the cash receipts and disbursements method of accounting described in section 446(c)(1).

(2) *Definition.* The term "qualifying distribution" means—

(i) Any amount (including program-related investments, as defined in section 4944(c), and reasonable and necessary administrative expenses) paid to accomplish one or more purposes described in section 170(c)(1) or (2)(B), other than any contribution to—

(a) A private foundation which is not an operating foundation (as defined in section 4942(j)(3)), except as provided in paragraph (c) of this section, or

(b) An organization controlled (directly or indirectly) by the contributing private foundation or one or more disqualified persons with respect to such foundation, except as provided in paragraph (c) of this section;

(ii) Any amount paid to acquire an asset used (or held for use) directly in carrying out one or more purposes described in section 170(c)(1) or (2)(B) (see paragraph (c)(3) of § 53.4942(a)-2 for the definition of "used (or held for use)"); or

(iii) Any amount set aside within the meaning of paragraph (b) of this section.

(3) *Control.* For purposes of subparagraph (2)(i)(b) of this paragraph, an organization is "controlled" by a foundation of one or more disqualified persons with respect to the foundation if any of such persons may, by aggregating their votes or positions of authority, require the donee organization to make an expenditure, or prevent the donee organization from making an expenditure, regardless of the method by which the control is exercised or exercisable. "Control" of a donee organization is determined without regard to any conditions imposed upon the donee as part of the distribution or any other restrictions accompanying the distribution as to the manner in which the distribution is to be used, unless such conditions or restrictions are described in paragraph (a)(8) of § 1.507-2 of this chapter (Income Tax Regulations). In general, it is the donee, not the distribution, which must be "controlled" by the distributing private foundation for the provisions of subparagraph (2)(i)(b) of this paragraph to apply. Thus, the furnishing of support to an organization and the consequent imposition of budgetary procedures upon that organization with respect to such support shall not in itself be treated as subjecting that organization to the distributing foundation's control within the meaning of this subparagraph. Such "budgetary procedures" include expenditure responsibility requirements under section 4945(d)(4). The "controlled" organization need not be a private foundation; it may be any type of exempt or nonexempt organization including a school, hospital, operating foundation, or social welfare organization.

(4) *Borrowed funds*—(i) *In general.* For purposes of this paragraph, if a private foundation borrows money in a particular taxable year to make expenditures for a specific charitable, educational, or other similar exempt purpose, a qualifying distribution out of such borrowed funds will, except as otherwise provided in subdivision (ii) of this subparagraph, be deemed to have been made only at the time that such borrowed funds are actually distributed for such exempt purpose.

(ii) *Funds borrowed before 1970.* (a) If a private foundation has borrowed money in a taxable year beginning before January 1, 1970, or subsequently borrows money pursuant to a written commitment which was binding as of the last day of such taxable year, to make expenditures for a specific charitable, educational, or other similar exempt purpose, if such borrowed funds are in fact expended for such purpose in any taxable year, and if such loan is thereafter repaid, in whole or in part, in a taxable year beginning after December 31, 1969, then, at the election of the foundation as provided in subdivision (ii)(b) of this subparagraph, a qualifying distribution will be deemed to have been made at such time or times that such loan principal is so repaid rather than at the earlier time that the borrowed funds were actually distributed for such exempt purpose.

(b) The election described in subdivision (ii)(a) of this subparagraph is to be made by attaching a statement to the form the private foundation is required to file under section 6033 for the first taxable year beginning after December 31, 1969 in which a repayment of loan principal is made. Such statement shall be made a part of such form and shall be attached to such form in each succeeding taxable year in which any repayment of loan principal is made. The statement shall set forth the name and address of the lender, the amount borrowed, the specific use made of such borrowed funds, and the private foundation's election to treat repayments of loan principal as qualifying distributions.

(iii) *Interest.* Any payment of interest with respect to a loan described in subdivision (i) or (ii) of this subparagraph shall be treated as a deduction under paragraph (d)(1)(ii) of § 53.4942(a)-2 in the taxable year in which it is made.

(5) *Changes in use of an asset.* If an asset not used (or held for use) directly in carrying out one or more purposes described in section 170 (c)(1) or (2)(B) is subsequently converted to such a use, the foundation may treat such conversion as a qualifying distribution. The amount of such qualifying distribution shall be the fair market value of the converted asset as of the date of its conversion. For purposes of the preceding sentence, fair market value shall be determined by making a valuation of the converted asset as of the date of its conversion in accordance with the rules set forth in paragraph (c)(4) of § 53.4942(a)-2.

(6) *Certain foreign organizations*—(i) *In general.* Distributions for purposes described in section 170(c)(2)(B) to a foreign organization, which has not received a ruling or determination letter that it is an organization described in section 509(a)(1), (2), or (3) or 4942(j)(3), will be treated as a distribution made to an organization described in section 509(a)(1), (2), or (3) or 4942(j)(3) if the distributing foundation has made a good faith determination that the donee organization is an organization described in section 509(a)(1), (2), or (3) or 4942(j)(3). Such a "good faith determination" ordinarily will be considered as made where the determination is based on an affidavit of the donee organization or an opinion of counsel (of the distributing foundation or the donee organization) that the donee is an organization described in section 509(a)(1), (2), or (3) or 4942(j)(3). Such an affidavit or opinion must set forth sufficient facts concerning the operations and support of the donee organization for the Internal Revenue Service to determine that the donee organization would be likely to qualify as an organization described in section 509(a)(1), (2), or (3) or 4942(j)(3).

(ii) *Definition.* For purposes of this subparagraph, the term "foreign organization" means any organization which is not described in section 170(c)(2)(A).

(7) *Payment of tax.* The payment of any tax imposed under chapter 42 of the Code shall not be treated as a qualifying distribution.

(8) *Examples.* The provisions of this paragraph may be illustrated by the following examples:

Example (1). M, a private foundation which uses the calendar year as the taxable year, makes the following payments in 1970: (i) a payment of $44,000 to five employees for conducting a foundation program of educational grants for research and study; (ii) $20,000 for various items of overhead, 10 percent of which is attributable to the activities of the employees mentioned in payment (i) of this example and the other 90 percent of which is attributable to administrative expenses which were not paid to accomplish any section 170 (c)(1) or (2)(B) purpose; and (iii) a $100,000 general purpose grant paid to an educational institution described in section 170(b)(1)(A)(ii) which is not controlled by M or any disqualified persons with respect to M. Payments (i) and (ii) of this example are qualifying distributions to the extent of $46,000 ($44,000 of salaries and 10 percent of the overhead, both of which are reasonable administrative expenses paid to accomplish section 170(c)(1) or (2)(B) purposes). Payment (iii) of this example is also a qualifying distribution, since it is a contribution for section 170(c)(2)(B) purposes to an organization which is not described in subparagraph (2)(i)(*a*) or (*b*) of this paragraph. The other 90 percent of payment (ii) of this example may constitute items of deduction under paragraph (d)(1)(ii) of § 53.4942(a)-2 if such items otherwise qualify under such paragraph.

Example (2). On February 21, 1972, N, a private foundation which uses the calendar year as the taxable year, pays $500,000 for real property on which it plans to build hospital facilities to be used for medical care and education. The real property produces no income and the hospital facilities will not be constructed until 1974 according to the set-aside plan submitted to and approved by the Commissioner pursuant to paragraph (b) of this section. The purchase of the land is a qualifying distribution under subparagraph (2)(ii) of this paragraph. If, however, the property were used to produce rental income for more than a reasonable period of time before construction of the hospital is begun, then as of the time such rental use becomes unreasonable (i) such purchase would no longer be deemed to constitute a qualifying distribution under subparagraph (2)(ii) of this paragraph and (ii) the amount of the qualifying distribution would be included in N's gross income. See paragraphs (c)(3)(i) and (d)(2)(iii)(*b*) of § 53.4942(a)-2.

Example (3). In 1971, X, a private foundation engaged in holding paintings and exhibiting them to the public, purchases an additional building to be used to exhibit the paintings. Such expenditure is a qualifying distribution under subparagraph (2)(ii) of this paragraph. In 1975, X sells the building. Under paragraph (d)(2)(iii)(*b*) of § 53.4942(a)-2, all of the proceeds of the sale (less direct costs of the sale) are included in X's gross income for 1975.

Example (4). In January, 1969, M, a private foundation which uses the calendar year as the taxable year, borrows $10 million to give to N, a private college, for the construction of a science center. M borrowed the money from X, a commercial bank. M is to repay X at the rate of $1.1 million per year ($1 million principal plus $0.1 million interest) for 10 years beginning in January, 1973. M distributed $5 million of the borrowed funds to N in February 1969, and the other $5 million in March 1970. M files a statement with the form it is required to file under section 6033 for 1973 which contains the information required by subparagraph (4)(ii) (*b*) of this paragraph. Pursuant to M's election, each repayment of loan principal constitutes a qualifying distribution in the year of repayment. Accordingly, the distribution of $5 million to N in March, 1970 will not be treated as a qualifying distribution. Each payment of interest ($0.1 million annually)

Reg. § 53.4942(a)-3(a)(8)

24,258.10-D.12 *(I.R.C.)*   Reg. § 53.4942(a)-3(a)(8)   3-25-74

with respect to M's loan from X is treated as a deduction under paragraph (d)(1)(ii) of § 53.4942(a)-2 in the taxable year in which it is made.

Example (5). Private foundation Y engages in providing care for the aged. Y makes a distribution of cash to H, a hospital described in section 170(b)(1)(A)(iii) which is not controlled by Y or any disqualified person with respect to Y. The distribution is made subject to the conditions that H will invest the money as a separate fund which will bear a name commemorating the creator of Y and will use the income from such fund only for H's exempt hospital purposes which relate to care for the aged. Under these circumstances, the distribution from Y to H is a qualifying distribution pursuant to subparagraph (2)(i) of this paragraph.

(b) *Certain set-asides*—(1) *In general.* An amount set-aside for a specific project which is for one or more of the purposes described in section 170(c)(1) or (2)(B) may be treated as a qualifying distribution, but only if, at the time of the set-aside, the private foundation establishes to the satisfaction of the Commissioner that—

(i) The amount will actually be paid for the specific project within 60 months from the date of the first set-aside, and

(ii) The project is one which can be better accomplished by such set-aside than by the immediate payment of funds.

(2) *Specific project defined.* For purposes of this paragraph, a "specific project" includes, but is not limited to, situations where relatively long-term grants or expenditures must be made in order to assure the continuity of particular charitable projects or program-related investments, as defined in section 4944(c), or where grants are made as part of a matching-grant program. Such term may include, for example, a plan to erect a building to house a direct charitable, educational, or other similar exempt activity of the foundation (for example, a museum building in which paintings are to be hung), even though the exact location and architectural plans have not been finalized; a plan to purchase an additional group of paintings offered for sale only as a unit which requires an expenditure of more than one year's income; or a plan to fund a specific research program which is of such magnitude as to require an accumulation prior to commencement of the research, even though not all of the details of the program have been finalized. For good cause shown, the period for paying the amount set aside may be extended by the Commissioner.

(3) *Approval requirements.* The approval by the Commissioner must be applied for not later than the end of the taxable year in which the amount is to be set aside, and in all cases the Commissioner will either approve or disapprove the set-aside in writing. An otherwise proper set-aside will not be a qualifying distribution under subparagraph (1) of this paragraph with respect to a specific taxable year if approval by the Commissioner is not sought prior to the end of the taxable year in which the amount is actually set aside. To obtain approval by the Commissioner for a set-aside, the foundation must write to Commissioner of Internal Revenue, T:MS:EO, 1111 Constitution Avenue, N.W., Washington, D.C. 20224, stating specifically—

(i) The nature and purposes of the specific project and the amount of the set-aside for which such approval is requested;

(ii) The amounts and approximate dates of any planned additions to the set-aside after its initial establishment;

(iii) The reasons why the project can be better accomplished by such set-aside than by the immediate payment of funds;

(iv) A detailed description of the project, including estimated costs, sources of any future funds expected to be used for completion of the project, and the location or locations (general or specific) of any physical facilities to be acquired or constructed as part of the project; and

(v) A statement by an appropriate foundation manager (as defined in section 4946(b)) that the amounts to be set aside will actually be paid for the specific project within a specified period of time which ends not more than 60 months after the date of the first set-aside, or a statement showing good cause why the period for paying the amount set aside should be extended (including a showing that the proposed project could not be divided into two or more projects covering periods of no more than 60 months each) and setting forth the extension of time requested.

(4) *Evidence of set-aside.* A set-aside approved by the Commissioner shall be evidenced by the entry of a dollar amount on the books and records of a private foundation as a pledge or obligation to be paid at a future date or dates. Any amount which is set aside shall be taken into account for purposes of determining the foundation's minimum investment return under paragraph (c)(1) of § 53.4942 (a)-2, and any income attributable to such set-aside shall be taken into account in computing adjusted net income under paragraph (d) of § 53.4942(a)-2.

(5) *Contingent set-aside.* Except as provided in paragraph (e)(1)(i) or (ii) of § 53.4942 (a)-2, with respect to amounts held by, or on behalf of, a foundation which may not be distributed pending the outcome of litigation because of a court order, a foundation may seek and obtain a set-aside for a purpose described in paragraph (a)(2) of this section equal to the amount in controversy, multiplied by the applicable percentage or percentages during the pendency of litigation, with the use of the funds contingent upon a disposition of the controversy favorable to the foundation.

In the event that the litigation encompasses more than one taxable year, the foundation may seek additional contingent set-asides. Such amounts must actually be distributed by the last day of the taxable year following the taxable year in which such proceedings are terminated. Amounts not distributed by the close of the appropriate taxable year shall be treated as described in paragraph (d)(2)(iii)(c) of § 53.4942(a)-2 for the succeeding taxable year.

(c) *Certain contributions to section 501 (c)(3) organizations*—(1) *In general.* For purposes of this section, the term "qualifying distribution" includes (in the year in which it is paid) a contribution to an exempt organization described in section 501 (c)(3) and in paragraph (a)(2)(i)(a) or (b) of this section if—

(i) Not later than the close of the first taxable year after the donee organization's taxable year in which such contribution is received, such donee organization makes a distribution equal to the full amount of such contribution and such distribution is a qualifying distribution (within the meaning of paragraph (a) of this section, without regard to this paragraph) which is treated under paragraph (d) of this section as a distribution out of corpus (or would be so treated if such section 501 (c)(3) organization were a private foundation which is not an operating foundation); and

(ii) The private foundation making the contribution obtains adequate records or other sufficient evidence from such donee organization (such as a statement by an appropriate officer, director, or trustee of such donee organization) showing (except as otherwise provided in this subparagraph) (a) that the qualifying distribution described in subdivision (i) of this subparagraph has been made by such organization, (b) the names and addresses of the recipients of such distribution and the amount received by each, and (c) that the distribution is treated as a distribution out of corpus under paragraph (d) of this section (or would be so treated if the donee organization were a private foundation which is not an operating foundation). Where a distribution is for an administrative expense which is part of a section 170 (c)(1) or (2)(B) expenditure or is part of another section 170 (c)(1) or (2)(B) ependiture that cannot reasonably be separately accounted for, the provisions of subdivision (ii) of this subparagraph may be satisfied by the submission by the donee organization of a statement setting forth the general purpose for which such expenditure was made and that the amount was distributed as a qualifying distribution described in subdivision (ii) (c) of this subparagraph.

(2) *Distribution requirements.* (i) In order for a donee organization to meet the distribution requirements of subparagraph (1)(i) of this paragraph, it must, not later than the close of the first taxable year after its taxable year in which any contributions are received, distribute (within the meaning of this subparagraph) an amount equal in value to the contributions received in such prior taxable year and have no remaining undistributed income for such prior taxable year. In the event that a donee organization redistributes less than an amount equal to the total contributions from donor organizations which are required to be redistributed by such donee organization by the close of the first taxable year following the taxable year in which such contributions were received, amounts treated as redistribution of such contributions shall be deemed to have been made pro rata out of all such contributions, regardless of any earmarking or identification made by such donee organization with respect to the source of such distributions. See paragraph (d)(2)(ix) of § 53.4942(a)-2 for the treatment of amounts deemed not to have been so redistributed. For purposes of this paragraph, the term "contributions" means all contributions, whether of cash or property, and the fair market value of contributed property determined as of the date of the contribution must be used in determining whether an amount equal in value to the contributions received has been redistributed.

(ii) For purposes of this paragraph, the characterization of qualifying distributions made during the taxable year (*i.e.*, whether out of the prior year's undistributed income, the current year's undistributed income, or corpus) is to be made as of the close of the taxable year in question, except to the extent that a different characterization is effected by means of the election provided for by paragraph (d)(2) of this section or by subdivsiion (iv) of this subparagraph. Once it is determined that a qualifying distribution is attributable to corpus, such distribution will first be charged to distributions which are required to be redistributed under this paragraph.

(iii) All amounts contributed to a specific exempt organization described in section 501(c)(3) and in paragraph (a)(2)(i) (a) or (b) of this section within any one taxable year of such organization shall be treated (with respect to the contributing private foundation) as one "contribution". If subparagraph (1)(i) or (ii) of this paragraph is not completely satisfied with respect to such contribution within the meaning of such subparagraph, only that portion of such contribution which was redistributed (within the meaning of subparagraph (1)(i) and (ii) of this paragraph) shall be treated as a qualifying distribution.

(iv) In order to satisfy distribution requirements under section 170(b)(1)(E) (ii) or this paragraph, a donee organization may elect to treat as a current distribution out of corpus any amount distributed in a prior taxable year which was treated as a distribution out of corpus under paragraph (d)(1)(iii) of this section, provided that (a) such amount has not been availed of for any other purpose, such as a carryover under paragraph (e) of this section or a redistribution under this paragraph for a prior year, (b) such corpus distribution occurred within the preceding five years, and (c) such amount is not later availed of for any other purpose. Such election must be made by attaching a statement to the return the foundation is required to file under section 6033 with respect to the taxable year for which such election is to apply. Such statement must contain a declaration by an appropriate foundation manager (within the meaning of section 4946(b)(1)) that the foundation is making an election under this subdivision and it must specify that the distribution was treated under paragraph (d)(1)(iii) of this section as a distribution out of corpus in a designated prior taxable year (or years). For purposes of elections made under this subdivision, see § 1.9100-1 of this chapter (Income Tax Regulations) relating to extensions of time for making certain elections.

(3) *Examples.* The provisions of subparagraphs (1) and (2) of this paragraph

Reg. § 53.4942(a)-3(c)(3)

may be illustrated by the following examples. It is assumed in these examples that all private foundations described use the calendar year as the taxable year.

Example (1). In 1972 M, a private foundation, makes a contribution out of 1971 income to X, another private foundation which is not an operating foundation. The contribution is the only one received by X in 1972. In 1973, X makes a qualifying distribution to an art museum maintained by an operating foundation in an amount equal to the amount of the contribution received from M. X also distributes all of its undistributed income for 1972 and 1973 for other purposes described in section 170(c)(2)(B). Under the provisions of paragraph (d) of this section, such distribution to the museum is treated as a distribution out of corpus. Thus, M's contribution to X is a qualifying distribution out of M's 1971 income provided M obtains adequate records or other sufficient evidence from X showing the nature and amount of the distribution made by X, the identity of the recipient, and the fact that the distribution is treated as made out of corpus. If X's qualifying distributions during 1973 had been equal only to M's contribution to X and X's undistributed income for 1972, X could have made an election under paragraph (d)(2) of this section to treat the amount distributed in excess of its 1972 undistributed income as a distribution out of corpus and in that manner satisfied the requirements of this paragraph.

Example (2). Assume the facts stated in example (1), except that X is a private college described in section 170(b)(1)(A)(ii) which is controlled by disqualified persons with respect to M and that the records which X furnishes to M show that the distribution would have been treated as made out of corpus if X were a private non-operating foundation. Under these circumstances, the result is the same as in example (1).

Example (3). Assume the facts stated in example (1), except that X makes a distribution to the museum equal only to one-half of the contribution from M, that the remainder of such contribution is added to X's funds and used to pay charitable administrative expenses, and that the records obtained by M from X are not sufficient to show the amounts distributed or the identities of the recipients of the distributions. The contribution by M to X will be a qualifying distribution only to the extent that M can obtain (i) other sufficient evidence (such as statements from officers or employees of X or from the museum) showing the facts required by subparagraph (1)(ii)(*a*), (*b*), and (*c*) of this paragraph and (ii) a statement from X setting forth that the remainder of the contribution was used for charitable administrative expenses which constituted qualifying distributions described in paragraph (a)(2)(i) of this section.

Example (4). X and Y are private non-operating foundations. A is an exempt organization which is not described in section 501(c)(3) but which supervises and conducts a program described in section 170(c)(2)(B). Y, but not X, controls A within the meaning of paragraph (a)(3) of this section. In 1972, X and Y each makes a grant to A of $100, specifically designated for use in the operation of A's section 170(c)(2)(B) program. X has made a qualifying distribution to A because the distribution is one described in paragraph (a)(2)(i) of this section. However, because A is controlled by Y, Y's grant of $100 to A does not constitute a qualifying distribution within the meaning of such paragraph (a)(2)(i). Furthermore, because A is not an exempt organization described in section 501(c)(3), Y's grant to A does not constitute a qualifying distribution by operation of the provisions of this paragraph.

Example (5). N, a private non-operating foundation, had distributable amounts of $100 in 1970 and $125 in 1971. In 1970 N received total contributions of $540: $150 from Y, a public charity; $70 from Z, a private foundation; $140 from Q, a private foundation, subject to the requirement that N earmark the amount and distribute it before distributing Z's contribution; and, $180 from R, also a private foundation. However, R specifically instructed N that such contribution did not have to be redistributed because R already had made enough qualifying distributions to avoid all section 4942 taxes. N is not controlled by Y, Z, Q, or R, and N made no qualifying distributions in 1970. By the close of 1971, N had made qualifying distributions of $420, earmarking $140 as having been a distribution of Q's contribution, but had made no election under paragraph (d)(2) of this section to have any amount distributed which was in excess of N's 1970 undistributed income treated as distributed out of corpus. Therefore, the first $225 of qualifying distributions made in 1971 (the sum of $100 and $125, N's distributable amounts for 1970 and 1971, respectively) are treated as amounts described in paragraph (d)(1)(i) and (ii) of this section. Since Y's contribution is a contribution from a public charity and does not have to be "redistributed" and since R specifically instructed N that its contribution need not be "redistributed", the remaining $195 of qualifying distributions will be treated as distributed pro rata from Z's and Q's contributions, regardless of N's earmarking. Accordingly, of Z's original qualifying distribution of $70 only $65 ($195 multiplied by $70, Z's contribution, over $210, the total ($70 plus $140) of Z's and Q's contributions) will be treated as redistributed by N. Similarly, of Q's original qualifying distribution of $140 only $130 ($195 multiplied by $140 over $210) will be treated as redistributed by N. Thus, Z's gross income for 1972 will be increased by $5 ($70 less the $65 actually redistributed), and Q's gross income for 1972 will be increased by $10 ($140 less the $130 actually redistributed).

(4) *Limitation.* A contribution by a private foundation to a donee organization which the donee uses to make payments to another organization (the secondary donee) shall not be regarded as a contribution by the private foundation to the secondary donee if the distributing foundation does not earmark the use of the contribution for any named secondary donee and does not retain power to cause the selection of the secondary donee by the organization to which such foundation has made the contribution. For purposes of this subparagraph, a contribution described herein shall not be regarded as a contribution by the foundation to the sec-

ondary donee even though such foundation has reason to believe that certain organizations would derive benefits from such contribution so long as the original donee organization exercises control, in fact, over the selection process and actually makes the selection completely independently of such foundation.

(5) *Transitional rule.* (i) For purposes of this paragraph, a contribution to a private foundation which is not an operating foundation and which is not controlled (directly or indirectly) by the distributing foundation or one or more disqualified persons with respect to the distributing foundation will be treated as a contribution to an operating foundation if—

(*a*) Such contribution is made pursuant to a written commitment which was binding on May 26, 1969, and at all times thereafter,

(*b*) Such contribution is made for one or more of the purposes described in section 170(c)(1) or (2)(B), and

(*c*) Such contribution is to be paid out to the donee private foundation on or before December 31, 1974.

(ii) For purposes of this subparagraph, a written commitment will be considered to have been binding prior to May 27, 1969, only if the amount and nature of the contribution and the name of the donee foundation were entered in the records of the distributing foundation, or were otherwise adequately evidenced, prior to May 27, 1969, or notice of the contribution was communicated in writing to such donee prior to May 27, 1969.

(d) *Treatment of qualifying distributions*—(1) *In general.* Except as provided in subparagraph (2) of this paragraph, any qualifying distribution made during a taxable year shall be treated as made—

(i) First out of the undistributed income (as defined in paragraph (a) of § 53.-4942(a)-2) of the immediately preceding taxable year (if the private foundation was subject to the initial excise tax imposed by section 4942(a) for such preceding taxable year) to the extent thereof;

(ii) Second out of the undistributed income for the taxable year to the extent thereof; and

(iii) Then out of corpus.

(2) *Election.* In the case of any qualifying distribution which (under subparagraph (1) of this paragraph) is not treated as made out of the undistributed income of the immediately preceding taxable year, the foundation may elect to treat any portion of such distribution as made out of the undistributed income of a designated prior taxable year or out of corpus. Such election must be made by filing a statement with the Commissioner during the taxable year in which such qualifying distribution is made or by attaching a statement to the return the foundation is required to file under section 6033 with respect to the taxable year in which such qualifying distribution was made. Such statement must contain a declaration by an appropriate foundation manager (within the meaning of section 4946(b)(1)) that the foundation is making an election under this subparagraph, and it must specify whether the distribution is made out of the undistributed income of a designated prior taxable year (or years) or is made out of corpus.

In any case where the election described in this subparagraph is made during the taxable year in which the qualifying distribution is made, such election may be revoked in whole or in part by filing a statement with the Commissioner during such taxable year revoking such election in whole or in part or by attaching a statement to the return the foundation is required to file under section 6033 with respect to the taxable year in which the qualifying distribution was made revoking such election in whole or in part. Such statement must contain a declaration by an appropriate foundation manager (within the meaning of section 4946(b)(1)) that the foundation is revoking an election under this subparagraph in whole or in part, and it must specify the election or part thereof being revoked. For purposes of elections made under this subparagraph, see § 1.9100-1 of this chapter (Income Tax Regulations) relating to extensions of time for making certain elections.

(3) *Examples.* The provisions of this paragraph may be illustrated by the following examples:

Example (1). M, a private foundation which was created in 1968 and which uses the calendar year as the taxable year, has distributable amounts and qualifying distributions for 1970 through 1976 as follows:

Year	1970	1971	1972	1973
Distributable amount	$100	$100	$100	$100
Qualifying distribution	$ 0	$100	$250	$100

Year	1974	1975	1976
Distributable amount	$100	$100	$100
Qualifying distribution	$100	$100	$100

In 1971 the qualifying distribution of $100 is treated under subparagraph (1)(i) of this paragraph as made out of the $100 of undistributed income for 1970. The qualifying distribution of $250 in 1972 is treated as made: (i) $100 out of the undistributed income for 1971 under subparagraph (1)(i) of this paragraph; (ii) $100 out of the undistributed income for 1972 under subparagraph (1)(ii) of this paragraph; and (iii) $50 out of corpus in 1972 under subparagraph (1)(iii) of this paragraph. The qualifying distribution of $100 in each of the years 1973 through 1976 is treated as made out of the undistributed income for each of those respective years under subparagraph (1)(ii) of this paragraph. See paragraph (e) of this section for rules relating to the carryover of qualifying distributions out of corpus.

Example (2). M, a private foundation which uses the calendar year as the taxable year, has undistributed income of $300 for 1971, $200 for 1972, and $400 for 1973. On January 14, 1973, M makes its first qualifying distribution in 1973 when it sets aside (within the meaning of paragraph (b) of this section) $700 for construction of a hospital. On February 24, 1973, a notice of deficiency with respect to the excise taxes imposed by section 4942(a) and (b) in regard to M's undistributed income for 1971 is mailed to M under section 6212(a). M notifies the Commissioner in writing on March 20, 1973, that it is making an elec-

Reg. § 53.4942(a)-3(d)(3)

tion under subparagraph (2) of this paragraph, and that its distribution of January 14th (to the extent it exceeds undistributed income for 1972) is to be applied first against undistributed income for 1971. Thus, under these facts and circumstances, an initial excise tax of $45 (15 percent of $300) is imposed by section 4942(a). Since M made the election described above, the $300 of undistributed income for 1971 is treated as distributed during the correction period (as defined in paragraph (c)(3) of § 53.4942(a)-1), and therefore no additional excise tax will be imposed. In addition, $200 ($700 minus $500) of the $700 qualifying distribution is treated as made out of undistributed income for 1973.

(e) *Carryover of excess qualifying distributions*—(1) *In general.* If in any taxable year for which an organization is subject to the initial excise tax imposed by section 4942(a) there is created an excess of qualifying distributions (as determined under subparagraph (2) of this paragraph), such excess may be used to reduce distributable amounts in any taxable year of the adjustment period (as defined subparagraph (3) of this paragraph). For purposes of section 4942, including paragraph (d) of this section, the distributable amount for a taxable year in the adjustment period shall be reduced to the extent of the lesser of (i) the excess of qualifying distributions made in prior taxable years to which such adjustment period applies or (ii) the remaining undistributed income at the close of such taxable year after applying any qualifying distributions made in such taxable year to the distributable amount for such taxable year (determined without regard to this paragraph). If during any taxable year of the adjustment period there is created another excess of qualifying distributions, such excess shall not be taken into account until any earlier excess of qualifying distributions has been completely applied against distributable amounts during its adjustment period.

(2) *Excess qualifying distributions.* An excess of qualifying distributions is created for any taxable year beginning after December 31, 1969, if—

(i) The total qualifying distributions treated (under paragraph (d) of this section) as made out of the undistributed income for such taxable year or as made out of corpus with respect to such taxable year (other than amounts distributed by an organization in satisfaction of section 170(b)(1)(E)(ii) or paragraph (c) of this section, or applied to a prior taxable year by operation of the elections contained in paragraphs (c)(2)(iv) and (d)(2) of this section), exceeds

(ii) The distributable amount for such taxable year (determined without regard to this paragraph).

(3) *Adjustment period.* For purposes of this paragraph, the taxable years in the adjustment period are the five taxable years immediately following the taxable year in which the excess of qualifying distributions is created. Thus, an excess (within the meaning of subparagraph (2) of this paragraph) for any one taxable year can not be carried over beyond the succeeding five taxable years. However, if during any taxable year in the adjustment period an organization ceases to be subject to the initial excise tax imposed by section 4942(a), any portion of the excess of qualifying distributions, which prior to such taxable year has not been applied against distributable amounts, may not be carried over to such taxable year or subsequent taxable years in the adjustment period, even if during any of such taxable years the organization again becomes subject to the initial excise tax imposed by section 4942(a).

(4) *Examples.* The provisions of this paragraph may be illustrated by the following examples:

Example (1). (i) F, a private foundation which was created in 1967 and which uses the calendar year as the taxable year, has distributable amounts and qualifying distributions for 1970 through 1976 as follows:

Year	1970	1971	1972	1973
Distributable amount	$100	$100	$100	$100
Qualifying distribution	0	$250	$70	$140

Year	1974	1975	1976
Distributable amount	$100	$100	$100
Qualifying distribution	$60	$75	$105

(ii) The qualifying distributions made in 1971 will be treated under paragraph (d) of this section as $100 made out of the undistributed income for 1970, then as $100 made out of the undistributed income for 1971, and finally as $50 out of corpus in 1971. Since the total qualifying distributions for 1971 ($150) exceed the distributable amount for 1971 ($100), there exists a $50 excess of qualifying distributions which F may use to reduce its distributable amounts for the years 1972 through 1976 (the taxable years in the adjustment period with respect to the 1971 excess). Therefore, the $100 distributable amount for 1972 is reduced by $30 (the lesser of the 1971 excess ($50) and the remaining undistributed income at the close of 1972 ($30), after the qualifying distributions of $70 for 1972 were applied to the original distributable amount for 1972 of $100). Since the distributable amount for 1972 was reduced to $70, there is no remaining undistributed income for 1972. Accordingly, the qualifying distributions made in 1973 will be treated as $100 made out of the undistributed income for 1973 and as $40 out of corpus in 1973. Since this amount ($140) exceeds the distributable amount for 1973 ($100), there exists a $40 excess which F may use to reduce its distributable amounts for the years 1974 through 1978 (the taxable years in the adjustment period with respect to the 1973 excess). However, in accordance with subparagraph (1) of this paragraph such excess may not be used to reduce F's distributable amounts for the years 1974 through 1976 until the excess created in 1971 has been completely applied against distributable amounts during such years. The distributable amount for 1974 is reduced by $40 (the lesser of the unused portion of the 1971 excess ($20) plus the 1973 excess ($40) and the remaining undistributed income at the close of 1974 ($40), after the qualifying distributions of $60 for 1974 were applied to the original distributable amount for 1974 of $100). The distributable amount for 1975 is reduced by $20 (the lesser of the unused portion of the 1973 excess of qualifying distributions ($20) and the remaining undistributed income at the close of 1975 ($25), after the qualifying distributions of $75 for 1975 were applied to the original distributable amount for 1975 of $100). Consequently, qualifying distributions made in 1976 will be treated as made first out of the $5 of remaining undistributed income for 1975 and then as $100 made out of the undistributed income for 1976.

Example 2. Assume the facts as stated in example (1), except that in 1974 F receives a contribution of $300 from G, a private foundation which controls F (within the meaning of paragraph (a)(3) of this section), and F distributes such contribution in 1975 in satisfaction of paragraph (c) of this seection. Under these circumstances, there would be no excess of qualifying distributions for 1975 with respect to such distribution, since such distribution is excluded from the computation of an excess of qualifying distributions by operation of subparagraph (2)(i) of this paragraph.

Example (3). Assume the facts as stated in example (1), except that in 1972 F is treated as an operating foundation (as such term is defined in section 4942(j)(3)). In accordance with subparagraph (3) of this paragraph since F is not subject to the initial excise tax imposed by section 4942(a) for 1972, the 1971 excess can not be carried forward to 1972 or any subsequent year in the adjustment period with respect to the 1971 excess, even if F is subsequently treated as a private non-operating foundation for any year during the period 1973 through 1976.

§ 53.4942(b)-1 (T.D. 7249, filed 12-29-72.) **Operating foundations.**

(a) *In general.* For purposes of section 4942 and the regulations thereunder, the term "operating foundation" means any private foundation which makes qualifying distributions (within the meaning of paragraph (a)(2) of § 53.4942(a)-3) directly for the active conduct of activities constituting its charitable, educational, or other similar exempt purpose equal in value to substantially all of its adjusted net income (as defined in paragraph (d) of § 53.4942(a)-2) and which, in addition, satisfies either the assets test set forth in paragraph (a) of § 53.4942(b)-2, the endowment test set forth in paragraph (b) of such section, or the support test set forth in paragraph (c) of such section.

(b) *Active conduct of activities constituting the exempt purpose*—(1) *In general.* For purposes of this section, except as provided in subparagraph (2) or (3) of this paragraph, qualifying distributions are not made by a foundation "directly for the active conduct of activities constituting its charitable, educational, or other similar exempt purpose" unless such qualifying distributions are used by the foundation itself, rather than by or through one or more grantee organizations which receive such qualifying distributions directly or indirectly from such foundation. Thus, grants made to other organizations to assist them in conducting activities which help to accomplish their charitable, educational, or other similar exempt purpose are considered an indirect, rather than direct, means of carrying out activities constituting the charitable, educational, or other similar exempt purpose of the grantor foundation, regardleses of the fact that the exempt activities of the grantee organization may assist the grantor foundation in carrying out its own exempt activities. However, amounts paid to acquire or maintain assets which are used directly in the conduct of the foundation's exempt activities, such as the operating assets of a museum, public park, or historic site, are considered direct expenditures for the active conduct of the foundation's exempt activities. Likewise, administrative expenses (such as staff salaries and traveling expenses) and other operating costs necessary to conduct the foundation's exempt activities (regardless of whether they are "directly for the active conduct" of such exempt activities) shall be treated as qualifying distributions expended directly for the active conduct of such exempt activities if such expenses and costs are reasonable in amount. Conversely, administrative expenses and operating costs which are not attributable to exempt activities, such as expenses in connection with the production of investment income, are not treated as such qualifying distributions. Expenses attributable to both exempt and nonexempt activities shall be allocated to each such activity on a reasonable and consistently applied basis. Any amount set aside by a foundation for a specific project, such as the acquisition and restoration, or construction, of additional buildings or facilities which are to be used by the foundation directly for the active conduct of the foundation's exempt activities, shall be deemed to be qualifying distributions expended directly for the active conduct of the foundation's exempt activities if the initial setting aside of the funds constitutes a set-aside within the meaning of paragraph (b) of § 53.4942 (a)-3.

(2) *Payments to individual beneficiaries*—(i) *In general.* If a foundation makes or awards grants, scholarships, or other payments to individual beneficiaries (including program related investments within the meaning of section 4944(c) made to individuals or corporate enterprises) to support active programs conducted to carry out the foundation's charitable, educational, or other similar exempt purpose, such grants, scholarships, or other payments will be treated as qualifying distributions made directly for the active conduct of exempt activities for purposes of paragraph (a) of this section only if the foundation, apart from the making or awarding of the grants, scholarships, or other payments, otherwise maintains some significant involvement (as defined in subdivision (ii) of this subparagraph) in the active programs in support of which such grants, scholarships, or other payments were made or awarded. Whether the making or awarding of grants, scholarships, or other payments constitutes qualifying distributions made directly for the active conduct of the foundation's exempt activities is to be determined on the basis of the facts and circumstances of each particular case. The test applied is a qualitative,

Reg. § 53.4942(b)-1(b)(2)

rather than a strictly quantitative, one. Therefore, if the foundation maintains a significant involvement (as defined in subdivision (ii) of this subparagraph) it will not fail to meet the general rule of subparagraph (1) of this paragraph solely because more of its funds are devoted to the making or awarding of grants, scholarships, or other payments than to the active programs which such grants, scholarships, or other payments support. However, if a foundation does no more than select, screen, and investigate applicants for grants or scholarships, pursuant to which the recipients perform their work or studies alone or exclusively under the direction of some other organization, such grants or scholarships will not be treated as qualifying distributions made directly for the active conduct of the foundation's exempt activities. The administrative expenses of such screening and investigation (as opposed to the grants or scholarships themselves) may be treated as qualifying distributions made directly for the active conduct of the foundation's exempt activities.

(ii) *Definition.* For purposes of this subparagraph, a foundation will be considered as maintaining a "significant involvement" in a charitable, educational, or other similar exempt activity in connection with which grants, scholarships, or other payments are made or awarded if—

(a) An exempt purpose of the foundation is the relief of poverty or human distress, and its exempt activities are designed to ameliorate conditions among a poor or distressed class of persons or in an area subject to poverty or national disaster (such as providing food or clothing to indigents or residents of a disaster area), the making or awarding of the grants or other payments to accomplish such exempt purpose is direct and without the assistance of an intervening organization or agency, and the foundation maintains a salaried or voluntary staff of administrators, researchers, or other personnel who supervise and direct the activities described in this subdivision (a) on a continuing basis; or

(b) The foundation has developed some specialized skills, expertise, or involvement in a particular discipline or substantive area (such as scientific or medical research, social work, education, or the social sciences), it maintains a salaried staff of administrators, researchers, or other personnel who supervise or conduct programs or activities which support and advance the foundation's work in its particular area of interest, and, as a part of such programs or activities, the foundation makes or awards grants, scholarships, or other payments to individuals to encourage and further their involvement in the foundation's particular area of interest and in some segment of the programs or activities carried on by the foundation (such as grants under which the recipients, in addition to independent study, attend classes, seminars, or conferences sponsored or conducted by the foundation, or grants to engage in social work or scientific research projects which are under the general direction and supervision of the foundation).

(3) *Payment of section 4940 tax.* For purposes of section 4942(j)(3)(A) and (B)(ii), payment of the tax imposed upon a foundation under section 4940 shall be considered a qualifying distribution which is made directly for the active conduct of activities constituting the foundation's charitable, educational, or other similar exempt purpose.

(c) *Substantially all.* For purposes of this section, the term "substantially all" shall mean 85 percent or more. Thus, if a foundation makes qualifying distributions directly for the active conduct of activities constituting its charitable, educational, or other similar exempt purpose in an amount equal to at least 85 percent of its adjusted net income, it will be considered as satisfying the income test described in this section even if it makes grants to organizations or engages in other activities with the remainder of its adjusted net income and with other funds. In determining whether the amount of qualifying distributions made directly for the active conduct of such exempt activities equals at least 85 percent of a foundation's adjusted net income, a foundation is not required to trace the source of such expenditures to determine whether they were derived from income or from contributions.

(d) *Examples.* The provisions of this section may be illustrated by the following examples. It is assumed that none of the organizations described in these examples is described in section 509(a)(1), (2), or (3).

Example (1). N, an exempt museum described in section 501(c)(3), was founded by the gift of an endowment from a single contributor. N uses 90 percent of its adjusted net income to operate the museum. If N satisfies one of the tests set forth in § 53.4942(b)-2 it may be classified as an operating foundation since substantially all of the qualifying distributions made by N are used directly for the active conduct of N's exempt activities within the meaning of paragraph (b)(1) of this section.

Example (2). M, an exempt organization described in section 501(c)(3), was created to improve conditions in a particular urban ghetto. M receives its funds primarily from a limited number of wealthy contributors interested in helping carry out its exempt purpose. M's program consists of making a survey of the problems of the ghetto to determine the areas in which its funds may be applied most effectively. Approximately 10 percent of M's adjusted net income is used to conduct this survey. The balance of its income is used to make grants to other nonprofit organizations doing work in the ghetto in those areas determined to have the greatest likelihood of resulting in improved conditions. Under these circumstances, since only 10 percent of M's adjusted net income may be considered as constituting qualifying distributions made directly for the active conduct of M's exempt activities, M cannot qualify as an operating foundation.

Example (3). Assume the facts as stated in example (2), except that M uses the remaining 90 percent of its adjusted net income for the following purposes: (1) M maintains a salaried staff of social workers and researchers who analyze its surveys and make recommendations as to methods for improving ghetto conditions; (2) M makes grants to independent social scientists who assist in these analyses and recommendations; (3) M publishes periodic

Reg. § 53.4942(b)-1(d)

reports indicating the results of its surveys and recommendations; (4) M makes grants to social workers and others who act as advisors to nonprofit organizations, as well as small business enterprises, functioning in the community (these advisors acting under the general direction of M attempt to implement M's recommendations through their advice and assistance to the nonprofit organizations and small business enterprises); and (5) M makes grants to other social scientists who study and report on the success of the various enterprises which attempt to implement M's recommendations. Under these circumstances, M satisfies the requirements of paragraph (b)(2) of this section, and the various grants it makes constitute qualifying distributions made directly for the active conduct of its exempt activities. Thus, if M satisfies one of the tests set forth in § 53.4942(b)-2 it may be classified as an operating foundation.

Example (4). P, an exempt educational organization described in section 501(c)(3), was created for the purpose of training teachers for institutions of higher education. Each year P awards a substantial number of fellowships to students for graduate study leading towards their M.A. or Ph.D. degrees. The applicants for these fellowships are carefully screened by P's staff, and only those applicants who indicate a strong interest in teaching in colleges or universities are chosen. P publishes and circulates various pamphlets encouraging a development of interest in college teaching and describing its fellowships. P also conducts annual summer seminars which are attended by its fellowship recipients, its staff, consultants and other interested parties. The purpose of these seminars is to foster and encourage the development of college teaching. P publishes a report of the seminar proceedings along with related studies written by those who attended. Despite the fact that a substantial portion of P's adjusted net income is devoted to granting fellowships, its commitment to encouraging individuals to become teachers at institutions of higher learning, its maintenance of a staff and programs designed to further this purpose, and the granting of fellowships to encourage involvement both in its own seminars and in its exempt purpose indicate a significant involvement by P beyond the mere granting of fellowships. Thus, the fellowship grants made by P constitute qualifying distributions made directly for the active conduct of P's exempt activities within the meaning of paragraph (b)(2) of this section.

Example (5). Q, an exempt organization described in section 501(c)(3), is composed of professional organizations interested in different branches of one academic discipline. Q trains its own professional staff, conducts its own program of research, selects research topics, screens and investigates grant recipients, makes grants to those selected, and sets up and conducts conferences and seminars for the grantees. Q has particular knowledge and skill in the given discipline, carries on activities to advance its study of that discipline, and makes grants to individuals to enable them to participate in activities which it conducts in carrying out its exempt purpose. Under these circumstances, Q's grants constitute qualifying distributions made directly for the active conduct of Q's exempt activities within the meaning of paragraph (b)(2) of this section.

Example (6). R, an exempt medical research organization described in section 501(c)(3), was created to study and perform research concerning heart disease. R has its own research center in which it carries on a broad number of research projects in the field of heart disease with its own professional staff. Physicians and scientists who are interested in special projects in this area present the plans for their projects to R. The directors of R study these plans and decide if the project is feasible and will further the work being done by R. If it is, R makes a grant to the individual to enable him to carry out his project, either at R's facilities or elsewhere. Reports of the progress of the project are made periodically to R, and R exercises a certain amount of supervision over the project. The resulting findings of these projects are usually published by R. Under these circumstances, the grants made by R constitute qualifying distributions made directly for the active conduct of R's exempt activities within the meaning of paragraph (b)(2) of this section.

Example (7). S, an exempt organization described in section 501(c)(3), maintains a large library of manuscripts and other historical reference material relating to the history and development of the region in which the collection is located. S makes a limited number of annual grants to enable post-doctoral scholars and doctoral candidates to use its library. Sometimes S obtains the right to publish the scholar's work, although this is not a prerequisite to the receipt of a grant. The primary criterion for selection of grant recipients is the usefulness of the library's resources to the applicant's field of study. Under these circumstances, the grants made by S constitute qualifying distributions made directly for the active conduct of S's exempt activities within the meaning of paragraph (b)(2) of this section.

Example (8). T, an exempt charitable organization described in section 501(c)(3), was created by the members of one family for the purpose of relieving poverty and human suffering. T has a large salaried staff of employees who operate offices in various areas throughout the country. Its employees make gifts of food and clothing to poor persons in the area serviced by each office. On occasion, T also provides temporary relief in the form of food and clothing to persons in areas striken by natural disasters. If conditions improve in one poverty area, T transfers the resources of the office in that area to another poverty area. Under these circumstances, the gifts of food and clothing made by T constitute qualifying distributions made directly for the active conduct of T's exempt activities within the meaning of paragraph (b)(2) of this section.

Example (9). U, an exempt scientific organization described in section 501(c)(3), was created for the principal purpose of studying the effects of early childhood brain damage. U conducts an active and continuous research program in this area through a salaried staff of scientists and physicians. As part of its research program, U awards scholarships to young people suffering mild brain damage to enable them to attend special schools equipped to handle such problems. The recipients are periodically tested to determine the effect of such schooling upon them. Under these circumstances, the scholarships awarded by U constitute qualifying distributions made directly for the active conduct of U's exempt activities within the meaning of paragraph (b)(2) of this section.

Example (10). O, an exempt charitable organization described in section 501(c)(3), was created for the purpose of giving scholarships to children of the employees of X Corporation who meet the standards set by O. O not only screens and investigates each applicant to make sure that he complies with the academic and financial requirements set for scholarship recipients, but also administers an examination which each applicant must take. 90 percent of O's adjusted net income is used in awarding these scholarships to the chosen applicants. O does not conduct any activities of an educational nature on its own. Under these circumstances, O is not using substantially all of its adjusted net income directly for the active conduct of its exempt activities within the meaning of paragraph (b) of this section. Thus, O is not an operating foundation because it fails to satisfy the income test set forth in paragraph (a) of this section.

O— § 53.4942(b)-2 (T.D. 7249, filed 12-29-72.) **Alternative Tests.**

(a) *Assets test*—(1) *In general.* A private foundation will satisfy the assets test under the provisions of this paragraph if substantially more than half of the foundation's assets:

(i) Are devoted directly *(a)* to the active conduct of activities constituting the foundation's charitable, educational, or other similar exempt purpose, *(b)* to functionally related businesses (as defined in paragraph (c)(3)(iii) of § 53.4942(a)-2), or *(c)* to any combination thereof;

(ii) Are stock of a corporation which is controlled by the foundation (within the meaning of section 368(c)) and substantially all the assets of which (within the meaning of paragraph (c) of § 53.4942(b)-1) are so devoted; or

(iii) Are in part assets which are described in subdivision (i) of this subparagraph and in part stock which is described in subdivision (ii) of this subparagraph.

(2) *Qualifying assets*—(i) *In general.* For purposes of subparagraph (1) of this paragraph, an asset is "devoted directly to the active conduct of activities constituting the foundation's charitable, educational, or other similar exempt purpose" only if the asset is actually used by the foundation directly for the active conduct of activities constituting its charitable, educational, or other similar exempt purpose. Thus, such assets as real estate, physical facilities or objects (such as museum assets, classroom fixtures and equipment, and research facilities), and intangible assets (such as patents, copyrights and trademarks) will be considered qualifying assets for purposes of this paragraph to the extent they are used directly for the active conduct of the foundation's exempt activities. However, assets which are held for the production of income, for investment, or for some other similar use (for example, stocks, bonds, interest-bearing notes, endowment funds, or, generally, leased real estate) are not devoted directly to the active conduct of the foundation's exempt activities, even though the income derived from such assets is used to carry out such exempt activities. Whether an asset is held for the production of income, for investment, or for some other similar use rather than being used for the active conduct of the foundation's exempt activities is a question of fact. For example, an office building used for the purpose of providing offices for employees engaged in the management of endowment funds of the foundation is not devoted to the active conduct of the foundation's exempt activities. However, where property is used both for exempt purposes and for other purposes, if such exempt use represents 95 percent or more of the total use, such property shall be considered to be used exclusively for an exempt purpose. Property acquired by a foundation to be used in carrying out the foundation's exempt purpose may be considered as devoted directly to the active conduct of such purpose even though the property, in whole or in part, is leased for a limited period of time during which arrangements are made for its conversion to the use for which it was acquired, provided such income-producing use of the property does not exceed a reasonable period of time. Generally, one year shall be deemed to be a reasonable period of time for purposes of the immediately preceding sentence. Similarly, where property is leased by a foundation in carrying out its exempt purpose and where the rental income derived from such property by the foundation is less than the amount which would be required to be charged in order to recover the cost of purchase and maintenance of such property (taking into account the deductions permitted by paragraph (d)(4) of § 53.4942(a)-2), such property shall be considered devoted directly to the active conduct of the foundation's exempt activities.

(ii) *Limitations.* (a) Assets which are held for the purpose of extending credit or making funds available to members of a charitable class (including any interest in a program related-investment, except as provided in paragraph (b)(2) of § 53.4942 (b)-1) are not considered assets devoted directly to the active conduct of activities constituting the foundation's charitable, educational, or other similar exempt purpose. For example, assets which are set aside in special reserve accounts to guarantee student loans made by lending institutions will not be considered assets devoted directly to the active conduct of the foundation's exempt activities.

(b) Any amount set aside by a foundation within the meaning of paragraph (b) (1) of § 53.4942(b)-1 shall not be treated as an asset devoted directly to the active conduct of the foundation's exempt activities.

(3) *Assets held for less than a taxable year.* For purposes of this paragraph, any asset which is held by a foundation for part of a taxable year shall be taken into account for such taxable year by multiplying the fair market value of such asset (as determined pursuant to subparagraph (4) of this paragraph) by a fraction, the numerator of which is the number of days in such taxable year that the foundation held such

Reg. § 53.4942(b)-2(a)(3)

24,258.10-H (I.R.C.)   Reg. § 53.4942(b)-2(a)(3)   1-15-73

asset and the denominator of which is the number of days in such taxable year.

(4) *Valuation*. For purposes of this paragraph, all assets shall be valued at their fair market value. Fair market value shall be determined in accordance with the rules set forth in paragraph (c)(4) of § 53.4942(a)-2, except in the case of assets which are devoted directly to the active conduct of the foundation's exempt activities and for which neither a ready market nor standard valuation methods exist (such as historical objects or buildings, certain works of art, and botanical gardens). In such cases, the historical cost (unadjusted for depreciation) shall be considered equal to fair market value unless the foundation demonstrates that fair market value is other than cost. In any case in which the foundation so demonstrates that the fair market value of an asset is other than historical cost, such substituted valuation may be used for the taxable year for which such new valuation is demonstrated and for each of the succeeding four taxable years if the valuation methods and procedures prescribed by paragraph (c)(4)(iv) (b) of § 53.4942(a)-2 are followed.

(5) *Substantially more than half*. For purposes of this paragraph, the term "substantially more than half" shall mean 65 percent or more.

(6) *Examples*. The provisions of this paragraph may be illustrated by the following examples. It is assumed that none of the organizations described in these examples is described in section 509(a)(1), (2), or (3).

Example (1). W, an exempt organization described in section 501(c)(3), is devoted to the maintenance and operation of a historic area for the benefit of the general public. W has acquired and erected facilities for lodging and other visitor accommodations in such area, which W operates through a wholly owned, separately incorporated, taxable entity. These facilities comprise substantially all of the subsidiary's assets. The operation of such accommodations constitutes a functionally related business within the meaning of paragraph (c)(3)(iii) of § 53.4942(a)-2. Under these circumstances, the stock of the subsidiary will be considered as part of W's assets which may be taken into account by W in determining whether it satisfies the assets test described in this paragraph.

Example (2). M, an exempt conservation organization described in section 501(c)(3), is devoted to acquiring, preserving, and otherwise making available for public use geographically diversified areas of natural beauty. M has acquired and erected facilities for lodging and other visitor accommodations in National Park areas. The operation of such accommodations constitutes a functionally related business within the meaning of paragraph (c)(3)(iii) of § 53.4942(a)-2. Therefore, M's assets which are directly devoted to such visitor accommodations may be taken into account by M in determining whether it satisfies the assets test described in this paragraph.

Example (3). P, an exempt organization described in section 501(c)(3), is devoted to acquiring and restoring historic houses. To insure that the restored houses will be kept in the restored condition, and to make the houses more readily available for public display, P rents the houses rather than sells them once they have been restored. The rental income derived by P is substantially less than the amount which would be required to be charged in order to recover the cost of purchase, restoration, and maintenance of such houses. Therefore, such houses may be taken into account by P in determining whether it satisfies the assets test described in this paragraph.

Example (4). Z, an exempt organization described in section 501(c)(3), is devoted to improving the public's understanding of Renaissance art. Z's principal assets are a number of paintings of this period which it circulates on an active and continuing basis to museums and schools for public display. These paintings constitute 80 percent of Z's assets. Under these circumstances, although Z does not have a building in which it displays these paintings, such paintings are devoted directly to the active conduct of activities constituting Z's exempt purpose. Therefore, Z has satisfied the assets test described in this paragraph.

(b) *Endowment test*—(1) *In general*. A foundation will satisfy the endowment test under the provisions of this paragraph if it normally makes qualifying distributions (within the meaning of paragraph (a)(2) of § 53.4942(a)-3) directly for the active conduct of activities constituting its charitable, educational, or other similar exempt purpose in an amount not less than two-thirds of its minimum investment return (as defined in paragraph (c) of § 53.4942(a)-2). In determining whether the amount of such qualifying distributions is not less than an amount equal to two-thirds of the foundation's minimum investment return, the foundation is not required to trace the source of such expenditures to determine whether they were derived from investment income or from contributions.

(2) *Definitions*. For purposes of this paragraph, the phrase "directly for the active conduct of activities constituting the foundation's charitable, educational, or other similar exempt purpose" shall have the same meaning as in paragraph (b) of § 53.4942(b)-1.

(3) *Example*. This paragraph may be illustrated by the following example:

Example. X, an exempt organization described in section 501(c)(3) and not described in section 509(a)(1), (2), or (3), was created on July 15, 1970. X uses the cash receipts and disbursements method of accounting. For 1971, the fair market value of X's assets not described in paragraph (c)(2) or (3) of § 53.4942(a)-2 is $400,000. X makes qualifying distributions for 1971 directly for the active conduct of its exempt activities of $17,000. For 1971 two-thirds of X's minimum investment return is $16,000 (6 percent × $400,000 = $24,000; ⅔ × $24,000 = $16,000). Under these circumstances, X has satisfied the endowment test described in this paragraph for 1971. However, if X's qualifying distributions for 1971 directly for the active conduct of its exempt activities were only $15,000, X would not satisfy the endowment test for 1971, unless the fair market value of its assets not described in paragraph (c)(2) or (3) of § 53.4942(a)-2 were no greater than $375,000 (6 percent × $375,000 = $22,500; ⅔ × $22,500 = $15,000).

(c) *Support test*—(1) *In general*. A

foundation will satisfy the support test under the provisions of this paragraph if:

(i) Substantially all of its support (other than gross investment income as defined in section 509(e)) is normally received from the general public and from five or more exempt organizations which are not described in section 4946(a)(1)(H) with respect to each other or the recipient foundation;

(ii) Not more than 25 percent of its support (other than gross investment income) is normally received from any one such exempt organization; and

(iii) Not more than half of its support is normally received from gross investment income.

(2) *Definitions and special rules.* For purposes of this paragraph—

(i) *Support.* The term "support" shall have the same meaning as in section 509(d).

(ii) *Substantially all.* The term "substantially all" shall have the same meaning as in paragraph (c) of § 53.4942(b)-1.

(iii) *Support from exempt organizations.* The support received from any one exempt organization may be counted towards satisfaction of the support test described in this paragraph only if the foundation receives support from no fewer than five exempt organizations. For example, a foundation which normally receives 20 percent of its support (other than gross investment income) from each of five exempt organizations may qualify under this paragraph even though it receives no support from the general public. However, if a foundation normally received 10 percent of its support from each of three exempt organizations and the balance of its support from sources other than exempt organizations, such support could not be taken into account in determining whether the foundation had satisfied the support test set forth in this paragraph.

(iv) *Support from the general public.* "Support" received from an individual, or from a trust or corporation (other than an exempt organization), shall be taken into account as support from the general public only to the extent that the total amount of the support received from any such individual, trust, or corporation during the period for determining the normal sources of the foundation's support (as set forth in § 53.4942(b)-3) does not exceed one percent of the foundation's total support (other than gross investment income) for such period. In applying this one-percent limitation, all support received by the foundation from any person and from any other person or persons standing in a relationship to such person which is described in section 4946 (a)(1)(C) through (G) and the regulations thereunder shall be treated as received from one person. For purposes of this paragraph, support received from a governmental unit described in section 170(c)(1) shall be treated as support received from the general public, but shall not be subject to the one-percent limitation.

○━▶ § 53.4942(b)-3 (T.D. 7249, filed 12-29-72.) **Determination of compliance with operating foundation tests.**

(a) *In general.* A foundation may satisfy the income test and either the assets, endowment, or support test by satisfying such tests for any three taxable years during a four-year period consisting of the taxable year in question and the three immediately preceding taxable years or on the basis of an aggregation of all pertinent amounts of income or assets held, received, or distributed during such four-year period. A foundation may not use one method for satisfying the income test described in paragraph (a) of § 53.4942(b)-1 and another for satisfying either the assets, endowment, or support test described in § 53.4942(b)-2. Thus, if a foundation satisfies the income test on the three-out-of-four-year basis for a particular taxable year, it may not use the aggregation method for satisfying either the assets, endowment, or support test for such particular taxable year. However, the fact that a foundation has chosen one method for satisfying the tests under §§ 53.4942(b)-1 and 53.4942(b)-2 for one taxable year will not preclude it from satisfying such tests for a subsequent taxable year by the alternate method. If a foundation fails to satisfy the income test and either the assets, endowment, or support test for a particular taxable year under either the three-out-of-four-year method or the aggregation method, it shall be treated as a non-operating foundation for such taxable year and for all subsequent taxable years until it satisfies the tests set forth in §§ 53.4942(b)-1 and 53.4942(b)-2 for a taxable year occurring after the taxable year in which it was treated as a non-operating foundation.

(b) *New organizations*—(1) *In general.* Except as provided in subparagraph (2) of this paragraph, an organization organized after December 31, 1969, will be treated as an operating foundation only if it has satisfied the tests set forth in §§ 53.4942(b)-1 and 53.4942(b)-2 for its first taxable year of existence. If an organization satisfies such tests for its first taxable year, it will be treated as an operating foundation from the beginning of such taxable year. If such is the case, the organization will be treated as an operating foundation for its second and third taxable years of existence only if it satisfies the tests set forth in §§ 53.4942 (b)-1 and 53.4942(b)-2 by the aggregation method for all such taxable years that it has been in existence.

(2) *Special rule.* An organization organized after December 31, 1969, will be treated as an operating foundation prior to the end of its first taxable year if such organization has made a good faith determination that it is likely to satisfy the income test set forth in paragraph (a) of § 53.4942 (b)-1 and one of the tests set forth in § 53.4942(b)-2 for such first taxable year pursuant to subparagraph (1) of this paragraph. Such a "good faith determination" ordinarily will be considered as made where the determination is based on an affidavit or opinion of counsel of such organization that such requirements will be satisfied. Such an affidavit or opinion must set forth sufficient facts concerning the operations and support of such organization for the Commissioner to be able to determine that such organization is likely to satisfy such requirements. An organization which, pursuant to this subparagraph, has been treated as an operating foundation for its first taxable year, but actually fails to qualify as an operating foundation under subparagraph (1) of this paragraph for such taxable year, will be treated as a pri-

Reg. § 53.4942(b)-3(b)(2)

vate foundation which is not an operating foundation as of the first day of its second taxable year for purposes of making any determination under the internal revenue laws with respect to such organization. The preceding sentence shall not apply if such organization establishes to the satisfaction of the Commissioner that it is likely to qualify as an operating foundation on the basis of its second, third and fourth taxable years. Thus, if such an organization fails to qualify as an operating foundation in its second, third and fourth taxable year after having failed in its first taxable year, it will be treated as a private foundation which is not an operating foundation as of the first day of such second, third or fourth taxable year in which it fails to qualify as an operating foundation, except as otherwise provided by paragraph (d) of this section. Such status as a private foundation which is not an operating foundation will continue until such time as the organization is able to satisfy the tests set forth in §§ 53.4942(b)-1 and 53.4942(b)-2 by either the three-out-of-four-year method or the aggregation method. For the status of grants or contributions made to such an organization with respect to sections 170 and 4942, see paragraph (d) of this section.

(c) *Transitional rule for existing organizations.* An organization organized before December 31, 1969 (including organizations deemed to be so organized by virtue of the principles of paragraph (e)(2) of § 53.4942(a)-2), but which is unable to satisfy the tests under §§ 53.4942(b)-1 and 53.4942(b)-2 for its first taxable year beginning after December 31, 1969 on the basis of its operations for taxable years prior to such taxable year by either the three-out-of-four-year method or the aggregation method, will be treated as a new organization for purposes of paragraph (b) of this section only if:

(1) The organization changes its methods of operation prior to its first taxable year beginning after December 31, 1972 to conform to the requirements of §§ 53.4942(b)-1 and 53.4942(b)-2;

(2) The organization has made a good faith determination (within the meaning of paragraph (b)(2) of the section) that it is likely to satisfy the tests set forth in §§ 53.4942(b)-1 and 53.4942(b)-2 prior to its first taxable year beginning after December 31, 1972 on the basis of its income or assets held, received, or distributed during its taxable years beginning in 1970 through 1972; and

(3) Such good faith determination is attached to the return the organization is required to file under section 6033 for its taxable year beginning in 1972.

(d) *Treatment of contributions*—(1) *In general.* The status of grants or contributions made to an operating foundation with respect to sections 170 and 4942 will not be affected until notice of change of status of such organization is made to the public (such as by publication in the Internal Revenue Bulletin), unless the grant or contribution was made after:

(i) The act or failure to act that resulted in the organization's inability to satisfy the requirements of §§ 53.4942(b)-1 and 53.4942(b)-2, and the grantor or contributor was responsible for, or was aware of, such act or failure to act, or

(ii) The grantor or contributor acquired knowledge that the Commissioner had given notice to such organization that it would be deleted from classification as an operating foundation.

(2) *Exception.* For purposes of subparagraph (1)(i) of this paragraph, a grantor or contributor will not be considered to be responsible for, or aware of, the act or failure to act that resulted in the grantee organization's inability to satisfy the requirements of §§ 53.4942(b)-1 and 53.4942(b)-2 if such grantor or contributor has made his grant or contribution in reliance upon a written statement by the grantee organization that such grant or contribution would not result in the inability of such grantee organization to qualify as an operating foundation. Such a statement must be signed by a foundation manager (as defined in section 4946(b)) of the grantee organization and must set forth sufficient facts concerning the operations and support of such grantee organization to assure a reasonably prudent man that his grant or contribution will not result in the grantee organization's inability to qualify as an operating foundation.

SUBPART D—MISCELLANEOUS EXCISE TAXES

§ 53.4943 Statutory provisions; imposition of excise tax on excess business holdings. [Sec. 4943, IRC]

§ 53.4943-1 (TD 7496, filed 7-5-77.) General rule; purpose.

Generally, under section 4943, the combined holdings of a private foundation and all disqualified persons (as defined in section 4946(a)) in any corporation conducting a business which is not substantially related (aside from the need of the foundation for income or funds or the use it makes of the profits derived) to the exempt purposes of the foundation are limited to 20 percent of the voting stock in such corporation. In addition, the combined holdings of a private foundation and all disqualified persons in any unincorporated business (other than a sole proprietorship) which is not substantially related (aside from the need of the foundation for income or funds or the use it makes of the profits derived) to the exempt purposes of such foundation are limited to 20 percent of the beneficial or profits interest in such business. In the case of a sole proprietorship which is not substantially related (within the meaning of the preceding sentence), section 4943 provides that a private foundation shall have no permitted holdings. These general provisions are subject to a number of exceptions and special provisions which will be described in following sections.

§ 53.4943-2 (TD 7496, filed 7-5-77.) Imposition of tax on excess business holdings of private foundations.

(a) *Imposition of initial tax*—(1) *In general*—(i) *Initial tax.* Section 4943(a)(1) imposes an initial excise tax (the "initial tax") on the excess business holdings of a private foundation for each taxable year of the foundation which ends during the taxable period defined in section 4943(d)(2). The amount of such tax is equal to 5 percent of the total value of all the private foundation's excess business holdings in each of its business enterprises. In determining the value of the excess business holdings of the foundation subject to tax under section 4943, the rules set forth in §§ 20.2031-1 through 20.2031-3 of this chapter (Estate Tax Regulations) shall apply.

(ii) *Disposition of certain excess business holdings within ninety days.* In any case in which a private foundation acquires excess business holdings, other than as a result of a purchase by the foundation, the foundation shall not be subject to the taxes imposed by section 4943, but only if it disposes of an amount of its holdings so that it no longer has such excess business holdings within 90 days from the date on which it knows, or has reason to know, of the event which caused it to have such excess business holdings. Similarly, a private foundation shall not be subject to the taxes imposed by section 4943 because of its purchase of holdings where it did not know, or have reason to know, of prior acquisitions by disqualified persons, but only if the foundation disposes of its excess holdings within the 90-day period described previously, and its purchase would not have created excess business holding but for such prior acquisitions by disqualified persons. In determining whether for purposes of this (ii) the foundation has disposed of such excess business holdings during such 90-day period, any disposition of holdings by a disqualified person during such period shall be disregarded.

(iii) *Extension of ninety day period.* The period described in paragraph (a)(1)(ii) of this section, during which no tax shall be imposed under section 4943, shall be extended to include the period during which a foundation is prevented by federal or state securities laws from disposing of such excess business holdings.

(iv) *Effect of disposition subject to material restrictions.* If a private foundation disposes of an interest in a business enterprise but imposes any material restrictions or conditions that prevent the transferee from freely and effectively using or disposing of the transferred interest, then the transferor foundation will be treated as owning such interest until all such restrictions or conditions are eliminated (regardless of whether the transferee is treated for other purposes of the Code as owning such interest from the date of the transfer). However, a restriction or condition imposed in compliance with federal or state securities laws, or in accordance with the terms or conditions of the gift or bequest through which such interest was acquired by the foundation, shall not be considered a material restriction or condition imposed by a private foundation.

(v) *Foundation knowledge of acquisitions made by disqualified persons.* (A) For purposes of paragraph (a)(1)(ii) of this section, whether a private foundation will be treated as knowing, or having reason to know, of the acquisition of holdings by a disqualified person will depend on the facts and circumstances of each case. Factors which will be considered relevant to a determination that a private foundation did not know or had no reason to know of an acquisition are: the fact that it did not discover acquisitions made by disqualified persons through the use of procedures reasonably calculated to discover such holdings; the diversity of foundation holdings; and the existence of large numbers of disqualified persons who have little or no contact with the foundation or its managers.

(B) The provisions of paragraph (a)(1)(v)(A) of this section may be illustrated by the following example:

Example. By the fifteenth day of the fifth month after the close of each taxable year, the F Foundation sends to each foundation manager, substantial contributor, person holding more than a 20% interest (as described in section 4946(a)(1)(C)) in a substantial contributor, and foundation described in section 4946(a)(1)(H), a questionnaire asking such persons to list all holdings, actual or constructive, in each business enterprise in which F had holdings during the taxable year in excess of those permitted by the 2 percent de minimis rule of section 4943(c)(2)(C). In preparing the list of such enterprises, F takes into account its constructive holdings only if, during the taxable year, F (along with all related foundations described in section 4946(a)(1)(H)) owned over 2% of the voting

Reg. § 53.4943-2(a)(1)

stock, profits interest or beneficial interest in the entity actually owning the holdings constructively held by F. The questionnaire asks each such person to list the holdings in such enterprises of any persons who, because of their relationship to such disqualified person, were themselves disqualified persons (i.e., members of the family (as defined in section 4946(d)), and any corporations, partnerships trusts and estates described in section 4946(a)(1)(E) through (G) in which such person, or members of his family, had an interest). The questionnaire asks that constructive holdings be listed only if, during the taxable year, the disqualified person owned over 2% of the voting stock, profits interest or beneficial interest in the entity actually owning the holdings constructively held by such person. (Thus a disqualified person owning less than 2% of a mutual fund is not required to list his attributed share of all the securities in the portfolio of the fund.) If no response to the questionnaire is received, the foundation seeks the information requested by the questionnaire by mailing a second (but not a third) questionnaire. If a questionnaire which is returned to the foundation indicates that certain information was unavailable to the person completing the questionnaire, the foundation seeks that information directly. For example, if a disqualified person indicates that he could not find out whether a corporation described in section 4946(a)(1)(E) had holdings in the enterprise listed in the questionnaire, the foundation seeks to obtain this information directly from the corporation by mailing it a questionnaire. In such a case, F may be found not to have reason to know of the acquisition of holdings by a disqualified person.

(vi) *Holdings acquired other than by purchase.* See section 4943(c)(6) and § 53.-4943-6 for rules relating to the acquisition of certain holdings other than by purchase by the foundation or a disqualified person.

(2) *Special rules.* In applying subparagraph (1) of this paragraph, the tax imposed by section 4943(a)(1)—

(i) shall be imposed on the last day of the private foundation's taxable year, but

(ii) the amount of such tax and the value of the excess business holdings subject to such tax shall be determined with respect to the foundation's holdings (based upon voting power, profits or beneficial interest, or value, whichever is applicable) in any business enterprise as of that day during the foundation's taxable year when the foundation's excess holdings in such enterprise were the greatest.

In applying subdivision (ii) of this subparagraph, if a foundation's excess business holdings in a business enterprise which constitute such foundation's greatest excess holdings in such enterprise for any taxable year are maintained for two or more days during such taxable year, the value of such excess holdings which is subject to tax under section 4943(a)(1) shall be the greatest value of such excess holdings in such enterprise as of any day on which such greatest excess holdings are maintained during such taxable year.

(3) *Examples.* The provisions of this paragraph may be illustrated by the following examples:

Example (1). Y is a private foundation reporting on a calendar year basis. On January 1, 1973, Y has 20 shares of common stock in Corporation N, of which 5 shares constitute excess business holdings. On June 1, 1973, Y disposes of such 5 shares; however, because of additional acquisitions of N common stock on such date by disqualified persons with respect to Y, the remaining 15 shares of N common stock held by Y now constitute excess business holdings. There are no further acquisitions or dispositions of N common stock during 1973 by Y or its disqualified persons. Although Y's greatest holdings in N during 1973 are held between January 1, 1973, and May 31, 1973, Y's greatest excess holdings in N during 1973 are held between June 1, 1973, and December 31, 1973. Therefore, the tax specified in section 4943(a)(1) shall be computed on the basis of the greatest value of such greatest excess holdings as of any day between June 1 and December 31, 1973.

Example (2). X is a private foundation reporting on a calendar year basis. On January 1, 1972, X has 100 shares of common stock in M corporation which are excess business holdings. On such date each share of M common stock has a fair market value of $100. On February 28, 1972, in an effort to dispose of such excess business holdings, X sells 70 shares of M common stock for $120 per share (the fair market an individual who is not a disqualified per value of each share on such date) to A, son within the meaning of section 4946(a). The value of $120 per share is the highest fair market value between January 1, and February 28, 1972. X disposes of no more stock in M for the remainder of calendar year 1972. On December 31, 1972, the fair market value of each share of M common stock is $80. X calculates its tax on its excess business holdings in M for 1972 as follows:

100 shares of M common stock times $120 fair market value per share as of February 28, 1972	$12,000
$12,000 multiplied by rate of tax .	5%
Amount of tax on X foundation's excess business holdings for 1972	$ 600

Example (3). Assume the same facts as in Example (2) except that the sale by X to A occurs on January 7, 1973, when the fair market value of each share of M corporation common stock equals $70. A value of $100 per share is the highest fair market value of the M common stock between January 1, 1973 and January 7, 1973. On May 9, 1973, X for the first time has excess business holdings in N corporation in the form of 200 shares of N common stock. The value per share of N common stock on May 9, 1973, equals $200. X makes no disposition of the N common stock during 1973, and the value of each share of N common stock as of December 31, 1973 equals $250 (the highest value of N common stock during 1973). X calculates its tax on its excess business holdings in both M and N for 1973 as follows:

100 shares of M common stock times $100 fair market value per share	$10,000
200 shares of N common stock times $250 fair market value per share	$50,000
Total	$60,000
$60,000 multiplied by rate of tax .	5%

Amount of tax on X foundation's excess business holdings for 1973 .... $ 3,000

(b) *Additional tax.* In any case in which the initial tax is imposed under section 4943(a) with respect to the holdings of a private foundation in any business enterprise, if, at the close of the correction period (as defined in section 4943(d)(3) and § 53.4943-9) with respect to such holdings the foundation still has excess business holdings in such enterprise, there is imposed a tax under section 4943(b) equal to 200 percent of the value of such excess holdings as of the last day of such correction period (determined without regard to extensions).

§ 53.4943-3 (TD 7496, filed 7-5-77.) Determination of excess business holdings.

(a) *Excess business holdings*—(1) *In general.* For purposes of section 4943, the term "excess business holdings" means, with respect to the holdings of any private foundation in any business enterprise (as described in section 4943(d)(4)), the amount of stock or other interest in the enterprise which, except as provided in § 53.4943-2(a)(1), the foundation, or a disqualified person, would have to dispose of, or cause the disposition of, to a person other than a disqualified person (as defined in section 4946(a)) in order for the remaining holdings of the foundation in such enterprise to be permitted holdings (as defined in paragraphs (b) and (c) of this section). If a private foundation is required by section 4943 and the regulations thereunder to dispose of certain shares of a class of stock in a particular period of time and other shares of the same class of stock in a shorter period of time, any stock disposed of shall be charged first against those dispositions which must be made in such shorter period.

(2) *Example.* The provisions of this paragraph may be illustrated by the following example:

Example. Corporation X has outstanding 100 shares of voting stock, with each share entitling the holder thereof to one vote. F, a private foundation, possesses 20 shares of X voting stock representing 20 percent of the voting power in X. Assume that the permitted holdings of F in X under paragraph (b)(1) of this section are 11 percent of the voting stock in X. F, therefore, possesses voting stock in X representing a percentage of voting stock in excess of the percentage permitted by such paragraph. Such excess percentage is 9 percent of the voting stock in X, determined by subtracting the percentage of voting stock representing the permitted holdings of F in X (i.e., 11 percent) from the percentage of voting stock held by F in X (i.e., 20 percent). (20%−11%=9%). The excess business holdings of F in X are an amount of voting stock representing such excess percentage, or 9 shares of X voting stock (9 percent of 100).

(b) *Permitted holdings in an incorporated business enterprise*—(1) *In general*—(i) *Permitted holdings defined.* Except as otherwise provided in section 4943(c)(2) and (4), the permitted holdings of any private foundation in an incorporated business enterprise (including a real estate investment trust, as defined in section 856) are—

(A) 20 percent of the voting stock in such enterprise reduced (but not below zero) by

(B) The percentage of voting stock in such enterprise actually or constructively owned by all disqualified persons.

(ii) *Voting stock.* For purposes of this section, the percentage of voting stock held by any person in a corporation is normally determined by reference to the power of stock to vote for the election of directors, with treasury stock and stock which is authorized but unissued being disregarded. Thus, for example, if a private foundation holds 20 percent of the shares of one class of stock in a corporation, which class is entitled to elect three directors, and such foundation holds no stock in the other class of stock, which is entitled to elect five directors, such foundation shall be treated as holding 7.5 percent of the voting stock because the class of stock it holds has 37.5 percent of such voting power, by reason of being able to elect three of the eight directors, and the foundation holds one-fifth of the shares of such class (20 percent of 37.5 percent is 7.5 percent). The fact that extraordinary corporate action (e.g., charter or by-law amendments) by a corporation may require the favorable vote of more than a majority of the directors, or of the outstanding voting stock, of such corporation shall not alter the determination of voting power of stock in such corporation in accordance with the two preceding sentences.

(2) *Nonvoting stock as permitted holdings*—(i) *In general.* In addition to those holdings permitted by paragraph (b)(1) of this section, the permitted holdings of a private foundation in an incorporated business enterprise shall include any share of nonvoting stock in such enterprise held by the foundation in any case in which all disqualified persons hold, actually or constructively, no more than 20 percent (35 percent where third persons have effective control as defined in paragraph (b)(3)(ii) of this section) of the voting stock in such enterprise. All equity interests which do not have voting power attributable to them shall, for purposes of section 4943, be classified as nonvoting stock. For this purpose, evidences of indebtedness (including convertible indebtedness), and warrants and other options or rights to acquire stock shall not be considered equity interests.

(ii) *Stock with contingent voting rights and convertible nonvoting stock.* Stock carrying voting rights which will vest only when conditions, the occurrence of which are indeterminate, have been met, such as preferred stock which gains such voting rights only if no dividends are paid thereon, will be treated as nonvoting stock until the conditions have occurred which cause the voting rights to vest. When such rights vest, the stock will be treated as voting stock that was acquired other than by purchase, but only if the private foundation or disqualified persons had no control over whether the conditions would occur. Similarly, nonvoting stock which may be converted into voting stock will not be treated as voting stock until such conversion occurs. For special rules where stock is acquired other than by purchase, see section 4943(c)(6) and the regulations thereunder.

Reg. § 53.4943-3(b)(2)

§ 53.4943-3(b)(2)

(iii) *Example.* The provisions of this paragraph (2) may be illustrated by the following example:

Example. Assume that F, a private foundation, holds 10 percent of the single class of voting stock of corporation X, and owns 20 shares of nonvoting stock in X. Assume further that A and B, the only disqualified persons with respect to F, hold 10 percent of the voting stock of X. Under the provisions of paragraph (b)(1) of this section, the 10 percent of X voting stock held by F will be classified as permitted holdings of F in X since 20 percent less the percentage of voting stock held by A and B in X is 10 percent. In addition, under the provisions of this (2), the 20 shares of X nonvoting stock will qualify as permitted holdings of F in X since the percentage of voting stock held by A and B in X is no greater than 20 percent.

(3) *Thirty-five-percent rule where third person has effective control of enterprise*—(i) *In general.* Except as provided in section 4943(c)(4), paragraph (b)(1) of this section shall be applied by substituting 35 percent for 20 percent if—

(A) The private foundation and all disqualified persons together do not hold, actually or constructively, more than 35 percent of the voting stock in the business enterprise, and

(B) The foundation establishes to the satisfaction of the Commissioner that effective control (as defined in paragraph (b)(3)(ii) of this section) of the business enterprise is in one or more persons (other than the foundation itself) who are not disqualified persons.

(ii) *"Effective control" defined.* For purposes of this subparagraph, the term "effective control" means the possession, directly or indirectly, of the power to direct or cause the direction of the management and policies of a business enterprise, whether through the ownership of voting stock, the use of voting trusts, or contractual arrangements, or otherwise. It is the reality of control which is decisive and not its form or the means by which it is exercisable. Thus, where a minority interest held by individuals who are not disqualified persons has historically elected the majority of a corporation's directors, effective control is in the hands of those individuals.

(4) *Two percent de minimis rule*—(i) *In general.* Under section 4943(c)(2)(C), a private foundation is not treated as having excess business holdings in any incorporated business enterprise in which it (together with all other private foundations (including trusts described in section 4947(a)(2)) which are described in section 4946(a)(1)(H)) actually or constructively owns not more than 2 percent of the voting stock and not more than 2 percent in value of all outstanding shares of all classes of stock. If, however, the private foundation, together with all other private foundations which are described in section 4946(a)(1)(H), actually or constructively owns more than 2 percent of either the voting stock or the value of the outstanding shares of all classes of stock in any incorporated business enterprise, all the stock in such business enterprise classified as excess business holding under section 4943 is treated as excess business holdings. For purposes of this paragraph, any stock owned by a private foundation which is treated as held by a disqualified person under section 4943(c)(4)(B), (5), or (6) shall be treated as actually owned by the private foundation. See paragraph (b)(1) of § 53.4941(d)-4 for the determination of excess business holdings without regard to section 4943(c)(2)(C) for purposes of applying section 101(*l*)(2)(B) of the Tax Reform Act of 1969 (83 Stat. 533).

(ii) *Examples.* The provisions of this subparagraph may be illustrated by the following examples:

Example (1). F, a private foundation, owns 1 percent of the single class of voting stock and 1 percent in value of all the outstanding shares of all classes of stock in X corporation. No other private foundation described in section 4946(a)(1)(H) owns any stock in X. All of the stock owned by F in X would be excess business holdings under section 4943(c)(1) if section 4943(c)(2)(C) were inapplicable. F owns no other shares of stock in X. Since F owns no more than 2 percent of the voting stock and no more than 2 percent in value of all outstanding shares of all classes of stock in X, under section 4943(c)(2)(C) none of the stock in X owned by F is treated as excess business holdings.

Example (2). Assume the facts as stated in Example (1), except that F and T, a controlled private foundation under section 4946(a)(1)(H), together own 1 percent of all the voting stock and 1 percent in value of all the outstanding shares of all classes of stock in X. All of the stock in X owned by F and T would be excess business holdings under section 4943(c)(1) if section 4943(c)(2)(C) were inapplicable. Since F and T together own no more than 2 percent of the voting stock and no more than 2 percent in value of all outstanding shares of all classes of stock in X, under section 4943(c)(2)(C) none of the stock in X owned by either F or T is treated as excess business holdings.

Example (3). Assume the facts as stated in Example (1), except that F owns 3 percent of the voting stock in X, 2 percent of which is treated as held by P, a disqualified person of F, under section 4943(c)(4)(B). Under subdivision (i) of this subparagraph, the 2 percent of the stock in X owned by F which is treated as held by P under section 4943(c)(4)(B) is treated as actually owned by F for purposes of section 4943(c)(2)(C). Consequently, all of the X stock owned by F is treated as excess business holdings under section 4943(c)(2)(C). However, only 1 percent of the stock in X is subject to tax under section 4943(a), since the other 2 percent is treated as owned by a disqualified person under section 4943(c)(4)(B) for purposes of determining the tax upon F under section 4943(a).

(c) *Permitted holdings in an unincorporated business enterprise*—(1) *In general.* The permitted holdings of a private foundation in any business enterprise which is not incorporated shall, subject to the provisions of subparagraphs (2), (3), and (4) of this paragraph, be determined under the principles of paragraph (b) of this section.

(2) *Partnership or joint venture.* In the case of a partnership (including a limited partnership) or joint venture, the terms "profits interest" and "capital interest" shall be substituted for "voting stock" and

"nonvoting stock," respectively, wherever those terms appear in paragraph (b) of this section. The interest in profits of such foundation (or such disqualified person) shall be determined in the same manner as its distributive share of partnership taxable income. See section 704(b) (relating to the determination of the distributive share by the income or loss ratio) and the regulations thereunder. In the absence of a provision in the partnership agreement, the capital interest of such foundation (or such disqualified person) in a partnership shall be determined on the basis of its interest in the assets of the partnership which would be distributable to such foundation (or such disqualified person) upon its withdrawal from the partnership, or upon liquidation of the partnership, whichever is the greater.

(3) *Sole proprietorship.* For purposes of section 4943, a private foundation shall have no permitted holdings in a sole proprietorship. In the case of a transfer by a private foundation of a portion of a sole proprietorship, see paragraph (c)(2) of this section (relating to permited holdings in partnerships). For the treatment of a private foundation's ownership of a sole proprietorship prior to May 26, 1969, see § 53.4943-4.

(4) *Trusts and other unincorporated business enterprises*—(1) *In general.* In the case of any unincorporated business enterprise which is not described in paragraph (c)(2) or (3) of this section, the term "beneficial interest" shall be substituted for "voting stock" wherever the term appears in paragraph (b) of this section. Any and all references to nonvoting stock in paragraph (b) of this section shall be inapplicable with respect to any unincorporated business enterprise described in this subparagraph.

(ii) *Trusts.* For purposes of section 4943, the beneficial interest of a private foundation or any disqualified person in a trust shall be the beneficial remainder interest of such foundation or person determined as provided in paragraph (b) of § 53.4943-8.

(iii) *Other unincorporated business enterprises.* For purposes of section 4943, the beneficial interest of a private foundation or any disqualified person in an unincorporated business enterprise (other than a trust or an enterprise described in paragraph (c) (2) or (3) of this section) includes any right to receive a portion of distributions of profits of such enterprise, and, if the portion of distributions is not fixed by an agreement among the participants, any right to receive a portion of the assets (if any) upon liquidation of the enterprise, except as a creditor or employee. For purposes of this subparagraph, a right to receive distributions of profits includes a right to receive any amount from such profits (other than as a creditor or employee), whether as a sum certain or as a portion of profits realized by the enterprise. Where there is no agreement fixing the rights of the participants in such enterprise, the interest of such foundation (or such disqualified person) in such enterprise shall be determined by dividing the amount of all equity investments or contributions to the capital of the enterprise made or obligated to be made by such foundation (or such disqualified person) by the amount of all equity investments or contributions to capital made or obligated to be made by all participants in the enterprise.

(d) *Examples.* The provisions of this section may be illustrated by the following examples:

Example (1). Corporation X has outstanding 100 shares of voting stock, with each share entitling the holder thereof to one vote. Assume that F, a private foundation, possesses 30 shares of X voting stock, and that A and B, the only disqualified persons with respect to F, together own 10 shares of X voting stock. The excess business holdings of F in X are 20 shares of X voting stock, determined as follows:

(i) Determination of voting stock percentages:
  (a) Total number of outstanding votes in X 100
  (b) Total number of votes in X held by F 30
  (c) Total number of votes in X held by A and B 10
  (d) Percentage of voting stock in X held by F (item (b) divided by Item (a)) (percent) 30
  (e) Percentage of voting stock in X held by A and B (item (c) divided by item (a)) (percent) 10

(ii) Determination of permitted holdings of voting stock:
  (a) Percentage of voting stock in X held by A and B (percent) 10
  (b) Permitted holdings of voting stock by F in X (20% less item (a)) (percent) 10

(iii) Determination of excess business holdings:
  (a) Percentage of voting stock in X held by F (percent) 30
  (b) Permitted holdings of voting stock by F in X (percent) 10
  (c) Item (a) less item (b) (percent) 20
  (d) Excess business holdings of F in X (i.e., an amount of X voting stock representing a percentage of voting stock equivalent to that in item (c)) (shares) 20

Example (2). F, a private foundation, is a partner in P partnership. In addition, A and B, the only disqualified persons with respect to F, are partners in P. The partnership agreement of P contains no provisions regarding the sharing of profits by, and the respective capital interests of, the partners.

(i) Assume that, under section 704(b), F's distributive share of P taxable income is determined to be 20 percent. In addition, assume that under such section, A and B are determined to have a 4 percent distributive share each of P taxable income. Accordingly, F holds a 20 percent profits interest in P, and A and B hold an 8 percent profits interest in P. Assuming that the provisions of section 4943(c)(2)(B) do not apply, the permitted holdings of F in P are 12 percent of the profits interest in P, determined by subtracting the percentage of the profits interest held by A and B in P (i.e., 8 percent) from 20 percent. (20% − 8% = 12%.) F, therefore,

Reg. § 53.4943-3(d)

holds a percentage of the profits interest in P in excess of the percentage permitted by § 53.4943-3(b)(1). The excess business holdings of F in P are a percentage of the profits interest in P equivalent to such excess percentage, or 8 percent of the profits interest in P, determined by subtracting the permitted holdings of F in P (i.e., 12 percent) from the percentage of the profits interest held by F in P (i.e., 20 percent) (20% − 12% = 8%).

(ii) Assume that, under the partnership agreement, F would be entitled to a distribution of 20 percent of P's assets upon F's withdrawal from P and to a distribution of 30 percent of P's assets upon the liquidation of P. F, therefore, holds a 30 percent capital interest in P; that is, the greater of the percentage of the assets of P distributable to F upon F's withdrawal from P, or the percentage of such assets distributable to F upon the liquidation of P. Since the percentage of the profits interest held by A and B in P is less than 20 percent, such 30 percent capital interest will be included in the permitted holdings of F in P.

○━ § 53.4943-4 (TD 7496, filed 7-5-77.) **Present holdings.**

(a) *Introduction*—(1) *Section 4943(c)(4) in general.* (i) Paragraph (4) of section 4943(c) prescribes transition rules for a private foundation which, but for such paragraph, would have excess business holdings on May 26, 1969. Section 4943(c)(4) provides such a foundation with protection from the initial tax on excess business holdings in two ways. First, the entire interest of such a foundation in any business enterprise in which such a foundation, but for section 4943(c)(4), would have had excess business holdings on May 26, 1969, is treated under section 4943(c)(4)(B) as held by disqualified persons for a certain period of time (the "first phase"). The effect of such treatment is to prevent a private foundation from being subject to the initial tax with respect to its May 26, 1969, interest during the first phase holding period and also to prevent the foundation from purchasing any additional business holdings in such business enterprise during such period (unless the combined holdings of the foundation and all disqualified persons fall below the 20 percent (or 35 percent, if applicable) figure prescribed by section 4943(c)(2)). Second, section 4943(c)(4)(A)(i) initially increases the percentage of permitted holdings of such a foundation to a percentage equal to the difference between—

(A) The percentage of combined holdings of the foundation and all disqualified persons in such business enterprise on May 26, 1969 (subject to a 50 percent maximum), and

(B) The percentage of holdings of all disqualified persons.

The percentage referred to in paragraph (a)(1)(i)(A) of this section is referred to in this section as the "substituted level". This "substituted level" is then reduced by the "downward ratchet rule" prescribed by section 4943(c)(4)(A)(ii) and paragraph (d)(3) of this section for certain dispositions by such foundation or by disqualified persons. The primary purpose of the substituted level is to indicate what the permitted holdings in such business enterprise will be immediately after the expiration of the first phase holding period. Thereafter, the permitted holdings of a private foundation itself are further limited to a maximum 25 percent interest in such business enterprise by section 4943(c)(4)(D) as soon as the combined holdings of all disqualified persons in such business enterprise exceed 2 percent (of the voting stock). If the combined holdings of all disqualified persons at no time exceed 2 percent (of the voting stock) during the 15 years following the first phase (the "second phase"), then the substituted level is reduced to a 35 percent maximum after the second phase.

(ii) Paragraph (a)(1)(i) of this section may be illustrated by the following example:

Example. On May 26, 1969, private foundation P held a 5 percent interest in corporation X (voting stock and value). On such date disqualified persons held a 16 percent interest in X (voting stock and value). Assume that except for section 4943(c)(4), P would have had a 1 percent interest in X which would have constituted excess business holdings. Therefore, section 4943(c)(4)(B) applies and P's 5 percent interest in X is treated as held by a disqualified person during the 10-year period beginning May 26, 1969. Since the entire 21 percent held by P and disqualified persons is now treated as held by disqualified persons, P's substituted level is 21 percent and its permitted holdings are zero (21% − 21%). However, P has no excess business holdings in X, because during the 10-year period P is not treated as holding such interest. The only change in the interest in X occurs on January 2, 1972, when P disposes of 2 percent of its interest in X to A, an unrelated person. Since the interest held by P and all disqualified persons (21% − 2% = 19%) has decreased below 20 percent, P's substituted level is reduced to 20 percent and its permitted holdings are 1 percent (20% − 19%) on such date. Therefore, if the other interests in X do not change, P will not have excess business holdings if P purchases no more than an additional 1 percent interest in X.

(2) *Interaction of provisions of Section 4943(c)(4), (5), and (6).* During the first phase, a private foundation may acquire additional interests in a business enterprise, other than by purchase, which are entitled to be treated as held by disqualified persons for varying holding periods under section 4943(c)(5) or (6) (relating respectively to certain holdings acquired pursuant to the terms of a trust or will in effect on May 26, 1969, and to the 5-year period to dispose of certain gifts, bequests, etc.). In any case, holdings which the private foundation disposes of shall be charged first against those holdings which it must dispose of in the shortest period in order to avoid the initial tax thereon. Further, acquisitions of a private foundation under a pre-May 27, 1969 will or trust described in section 4943(c)(5) are treated in a manner similar to the treatment of interests actually held by a private foundation on May 26, 1969. See §§ 53.4943-5 and 53.4943-6.

(b) *Present holdings in general.* (1) Section 4943(c)(4)(B) provides that any interest in a business enterprise held by a private foundation on May 26, 1969, if the foundation on such date has excess business holdings (determined without regard to section 4943(c)(4)), shall (while held by the foundation) be treated as held by a disqualified person during a first phase. Therefore, no interest of a private foundation shall be treated as held by a disqualified person under section 4943(c)(4)(B) and this section unless:

(i) The private foundation was an entity (not including a revocable trust) in existence on May 26, 1969, even though it was not then treated as a private foundation under section 509 or section 4947;

(ii) Such interest was actually or constructively owned by such entity on such date; and

(iii) Without regard to section 4943(c)(4), such entity had on such date an interest (considered in connection with the interests actually or constructively owned by all disqualified persons with respect to such entity on that date in the same business enterprise, determined as if the entity were then a private foundation) which exceeded the permitted holdings prescribed by section 4943(c)(2) or (3).

(See, however, section 4943(c)(5) and § 53-4943-5 for similar treatment for certain interests acquired by a private foundation under the terms of a trust or a will which were in effect on May 26, 1969.) If a private foundation owns an interest described by section 4943(c)(4)(B), then the length of the first phase for such an interest is prescribed by paragraph (c) of this section and shall not be affected by any interest acquired by the private foundation or any disqualified person in such business enterprise after May 26, 1969. In addition, the amount of permitted holdings in such business enterprise is prescribed by paragraph (d) of this section. An interest constructively held by a private foundation (or a disqualified person) on May 26, 1969, shall not cease to be an interest to which section 4943(c)(4) applies merely because it is later distributed to such foundation (or to such disqualified person). Nor shall an interest directly held by a private foundation (or disqualified person) on May 26, 1969, cease to be treated as an interest to which section 4943(c)(4) applies to the extent it remains actually or constructively held by such foundation (or such disqualified person) upon transfer of such interest, such as upon the incorporation of a sole proprietorship.

(2) The provisions of this paragraph may be illustrated by the following example:

Example. A, a nonprofit research organization described in section 501(c)(3), was organized in 1966. On May 26, 1969, A held 50 percent of the stock of corporation B. For its taxable years 1970, 1971, and 1972, A is classified as an organization described in section 509(a)(2). However, for 1973 and subsequent years, A fails to satisfy the gross investment income limitation of section 509(a)(2)(B), and is thus classified as a private foundation. In such a case, section 4943(c)(4) applies, and a disqualified person shall be treated as holding A's stock in B during a first phase that begins on May 26, 1969.

(c) *First phase holding periods*—(1) *In general.* If, on May 26, 1969, a private foundation has excess business holdings in any business enterprise (determined without regard to the 20 or 35 percent permitted holdings of section 4943(c)(2)), then all interests which such foundation holds, actually or constructively, in such enterprise on May 26, 1969, shall (while held by such foundation) be deemed held by a disqualified person during the following periods:

(i) The 20-year period beginning on May 26, 1969, if the private foundation holds, actually or constructively, more than 95 percent of the voting stock (or more than a 95 percent profits or beneficial interest in the case of an unincorporated enterprise) in such enterprise on such date;

(ii) Except as provided in paragraph (c)(1)(i) of this section, the 15-year period beginning on May 26, 1969, if the private foundation and all disqualified persons hold, actually or constructively on such date, more than 75 percent of the voting stock (or more than a 75 percent profits or beneficial interest in the case of any unincorporated enterprise) or 75 percent of the value of all outstanding shares of all classes of stock in such enterprise (or more than a 75 percent profits and capital interest in the case of a partnership or joint venture); or

(iii) The 10-year period beginning on May 26, 1969, in any case not described in paragraph (c)(1)(i) or (ii) of this section. The 20-year, 15-year, or 10-year period described in this subdivision (whichever applies) shall, for purposes of section 4943 and this section, be known as the "first phase".

(2) *Sole proprietorships.* The 20-year period described in paragraph (c)(1) of this section shall apply with respect to any interest which a private foundation holds in a sole proprietorship on May 26, 1969. See paragraph (b) of this section for the effect of converting such an enterprise to a corporate, partnership, or other form.

(3) *Suspension of first-phase periods.* The 20-year, 15-year, or 10-year period described in paragraph (c)(1) of this section shall be suspended during the pendency of any judicial proceeding which is brought and diligently litigated by the private foundation and which is necessary to reform, or to excuse the foundation from compliance with, its governing instrument or any other instrument (as in effect on May 26, 1969) in order to allow disposition of any excess business holdings held by the foundation on May 26, 1969.

(4) *Election to shorten the period during which certain holdings of private foundations are treated as held by disqualified persons.* If, on May 26, 1969, the combined holdings of a private foundation and all disqualified persons in any one business enterprise are such as to make applicable the 15-year period referred to in paragraph (c)(1)(ii) of this section, and if, on such date, the foundation's holdings do not exceed 95 percent of the voting stock in such enterprise, then such 15-year period is shortened to the 10-year period referred to in paragraph (c)(1)(iii), if at any time before January 1, 1971, one or more individuals—

(i) Who are substantial contributors (as described in section 507(d)(2)), or members of the family within the meaning of section 4946(d) of one or more substantial contributors, to such private foundation, and

24,258.10-R (I.R.C.)   Reg. § 53.4943-4(c)(4)   7-18-77

(ii) Who on May 26, 1969, held in the aggregate more than 15 percent of the voting stock in the enterprise,

made an election in the manner described in 26 CFR 143.6 (rev. as of Apr. 1, 1974).

(5) *Examples.* The provisions of this paragraph (c) may be illustrated by the following examples:

Example (1). Assume that F, a private foundation, owns, on May 26, 1969, 50 shares of voting stock in corporation X representing 50 percent of the voting power in X and 25 percent of the value of all outstanding shares of all classes of stock in X. Assume further that A and B, the only disqualified persons with respect to F, own five shares each of voting stock in X on such date. The 10 shares of voting stock in X owned by A and B together represent 10 percent of the voting power in X and 5 percent of the value of all outstanding shares of all classes of stock in X. Under the provisions of § 53.4943-3, the excess business holdings of F in X (determined without regard to section 4943(c)(4)) as of such date are, therefore, 40 percent of X voting stock. Accordingly, since the combined holdings of F, A, and B in X are, on such date, less than 75 percent of the voting stock in X and less than 75 percent of the value of all outstanding shares of all classes of stock in X, under the provisions of section 4943(c)(4)(B)(iii), all holdings of F in X (*i.e.,* 50 percent of X voting stock) will be treated as held by a disqualified person through May 25, 1979.

Example (2). Assume the facts as stated in Example (1), except that F, on December 15, 1969, purchases an additional 10 shares of voting stock in X representing 10 percent of X voting power. Assume, further, that there were no other transactions in the stock in X during 1969. While the 50 percent of X voting stock held by F on May 26, 1969, will be deemed held by a disqualified person through May 25, 1979, the additional 10 shares of X voting stock acquired by purchase by F on December 15, 1969, will not be deemed to be so held. Accordingly, since, under the provisions of § 53.4943-3, such 10 shares represent excess business holding of F in X, such 10 shares will be subject to the imposition of tax under the provisions of section 4943(a).

Example (3). Assume the facts as stated in Example (1), except that F, on December 15, 1971, acquires an additional 10 shares of voting stock in X (representing 10 percent of X voting power) under the terms of a will which was executed before May 26, 1969, to which section 4943 (c)(5) applies. While the 50 percent of X voting stock held by F on May 26, 1969, will be deemed held by a disqualified person through May 25, 1979, the additional 10 percent of X voting stock acquired by F on December 15, 1971, will, under the provisions of section 4943(c)(5), be deemed held by a disqualified person through December 14, 1981. See § 53.4943-5.

Example (4). Assume that F, a private foundation, owns on May 26, 1969, 50 shares of voting stock in corporation Y representing 50 percent of the voting power in Y. Assume further that C and D, the only disqualified persons with respect to F, own on such date 15 shares each of Y voting stock and that the 30 shares of Y voting stock owned by C and D together represent 30 percent of the voting power in Y. Under the provisions of § 53.4943-3 the excess business holdings of F in Y (determined without regard to section 4943(c)(4)) as of such date are, therefore, 50 percent of Y voting stock. Accordingly, since the combined holdings of F, C, and D in Y represent, on such date, more than 75 percent of the voting stock in Y, under the provisions of section 4943(c)(4)(B)(ii), all holdings of F in Y (i.e., 50 percent of Y voting stock) will be treated as held by a disqualified person through May 25, 1984.

Example (5). M, a private foundation, owns on May 26, 1969, sole proprietorship S. Since, under the provisions of § 53.5954-3, M's ownership of S constitutes excess business holdings (determined without regard to section 4943(c)(4)) as of May 26, 1969, and since M's interest in S is greater than 95 percent on such date, under the provisions of this paragraph a disqualified person will be treated as the owner of S for the 20-year period beginning on such date. If S is later incorporated, that percentage of the interest in S retained by M, even though less than a 95-percent interest, shall continue to be treated as held by a disqualified person through May 25, 1989.

Example (6). A and B, individuals, together own on May 26, 1969, 40 shares of voting stock in corporation X representing 40 percent of the voting power in X and 20 percent of the value of all outstanding shares of all classes of stock in X. A and B are both disqualified persons with respect to F, a private foundation, which owns no stock in X on May 26, 1969. On January 1, 1973, A and B donate the 40 shares of X voting stock held by them to F. Since F had no excess business holdings on May 26, 1969, section 4943(c)(4) does not apply. See however, section 4943(c)(6) and § 53-.4943-6.

Example (7). Assume the facts as stated in Example (6), except that F, on May 26, 1969, owns 50 shares of voting stock in X, representing 50 percent of the voting power in X and 25 percent of the value of all outstanding shares of all classes of stock in X. Under the provisions of this paragraph, the 50 shares of X voting stock held by F on May 26, 1969 shall be treated in accordance with the provisions of section 4943(c)(4), while the 40 shares of X voting stock acquired by F on January 1, 1973 shall be treated in accordance with the provisions of section 4943(c)(6). See § 53.4943-6.

(d) *Permitted holdings under section 4943(c)(4)*—(1) *In general.* The permitted holdings of a private foundation to which section 4943(c)(4) applies in a business enterprise shall be as follows:

(i) The excess of the substituted combined voting level over the disqualified person voting level, and separately,

(ii) The excess of the substituted combined value level over the disqualified person value level.

(2) *Definitions.* For purposes of paragraph (d) of this section—

(i) The term "disqualified person voting level" on any given date means the percentage of voting stock held by all disqualified persons together on such date (including stock deemed held by such a person by reason of section 4943(c)(4), (5), or (6)).

(ii) The term "disqualified person value level" on any given date means the percentage of the total value of all outstanding shares of all classes of stock in a business enterprise held by all disqualified persons together on such date (including stock deemed held by such a person by reason of section 4943(c)(4), (5), or (6)).

(iii) The term "foundation voting level" prior to the second phase is equal to zero. After the first phase, such term on any given date means the lowest percentage of voting stock held by a private foundation (without regard to section 4943(c)(4)(B)) in a business enterprise on May 26, 1969, and at all times thereafter up to such date. See section 4943(c)(5) and § 53.4943-5 for the effect of interests acquired pursuant to the terms of certain wills or trusts in effect on May 26, 1969.

(iv) The term "foundation value level" prior to the second phase is equal to zero. After the first phase, such term on any given date means the lowest percentage of the total value of all outstanding shares of all classes of stock held by a private foundation (without regard to section 4943(c)(4)(B)) in a business enterprise on May 26, 1969, and at all times thereafter up to such date. See section 4943(c)(5) and § 53.4943-5 for the effect of interests acquired pursuant to the terms of certain wills or trusts in effect on May 26, 1969.

(v) The term "substituted combined voting level" means the lowest percentage to which the sum of the foundation voting level plus the disqualified person voting level has been reduced since May 26, 1969, by paragraph (d)(4) of this section (the "downward ratchet rule"), subject to the following modifications:

(A) In no event shall such substituted level exceed 50 percent; and

(B) Such substituted level shall be increased (but not above 50 percent) in accordance with section 4943(c)(5) and § 53.4943-5 for certain interests acquired by such foundation pursuant to the terms of a will or trust in effect on May 26, 1969.

(vi) The term "substituted combined value level" means the lowest percentage to which the sum of the foundation value level plus the disqualified person value level has been reduced since May 26, 1969, by paragraph (d)(4) of this section (the "downward ratchet rule"), subject to the following modifications:

(A) In no event shall such substituted level exceed 50 percent; and

(B) Such substituted level shall be increased (but not above 50 percent) in accordance with section 4943(c)(5) and § 53.4943-5 for certain interests acquired by such foundation pursuant to the terms of a will or trust in effect on May 26, 1969.

(vii) In the case of an interest in a partnership or joint venture, definitions (i) through (iv) of this subparagraph shall be applied by substituting "profit interests" for "voting stock" and "all partnership interests" for "all outstanding shares of all classes of stock."

(viii) In the case of an interest in a business enterprise other than a corporation, partnership or joint venture, definitions (i) through (iv) of this subparagraph shall be applied by substituting "beneficial remainder interests" for "voting stock" and "all beneficial remainder interests" for "all outstanding shares of all classes of stock."

(ix) Each level defined in paragraph (d)(2)(iii), (iv), (v), and (vi) as of any date shall be carried over to the subsequent date subject to any adjustments prescribed for such level.

(3) *Permitted holdings—First phase.* Since during the first phase the substituted combined voting level generally does not exceed the disqualified person voting level, and the substituted combined value level generally does not exceed the disqualified person value level, the permitted holdings during the first phase are generally equal to zero. The permitted holdings during the first phase exceed zero only where the 20 percent (or 35 percent) limitation on the downward ratchet rule contained in paragraph (d)(4)(ii)(B) of this section applies.

(4) *Downward ratchet rule*—(i) *In general.* Except as provided in paragraph (d)(4)(ii) of this section and section 4943(c)(5)—

(A) *Scope of rule.* In general, when the percentage of the holdings in a business enterprise held by a private foundation and all disqualified persons together to which section 4943(c)(4) applies decreases, or when the percentage of the holdings of the private foundation alone in such business enterprise decreases, such holdings may not be increased (except as provided under section 4943(c)(5) or (6)). This so-called "downward ratchet rule" is designed to prevent the private foundation from purchasing additional holdings in the business enterprise until the substituted combined voting level is reduced to the 20-percent (or 35 percent) figure prescribed by section 4943(c)(2).

(B) *Levels affected.* Under the downward ratchet rule any decrease after May 26, 1969, in the percentage of holdings comprising either the substituted combined voting level, the substituted combined value level, the foundation voting level or the foundation value level shall cause the respective level to be decreased to such decreased percentage for purposes of determining the foundation's permitted holdings.

(C) *Implementation of reductions.* Thus, if at any time the sum of the foundation voting level and the disqualified person voting level is less than the immediately preceding substituted combined voting level, the substituted level shall be decreased so that it equals such sum. For example, if on May 26, 1969, a foundation and all disqualified persons together have holdings in a business enterprise equal to 50 percent, on such date the substituted combined voting level and the disqualified person voting level equal 50 percent (since such holdings of the foundation are treated as held by a disqualified person). If the private foundation or a disqualified person on May 27, 1969, sold 2 percent of such holdings to a nondisqualified person, the disqualified person voting level would be decreased to 48 percent (50% − 2%), causing the substituted combined voting level to be decreased to 48 percent. As a further example, assume that on May 26, 1969, a foundation and all disqualified persons together have holdings in a business enterprise equal to 50 percent, and when the first phase expires on May 26, 1979, the substituted combined voting level is still 50 percent, the foundation voting level is 10 percent, and the disqualified person voting level is 40

Reg. § 53.4943-4(d)(4)

24,258.10-T *(I.R.C.)* Reg. § 53.4943-4(d)(4)

percent. If a disqualified person thereafter sells 2 percent to a nondisqualified person so that the sum of the disqualified person voting level (40% − 2% = 38) and the foundation voting level (10%) equals 48 percent (38% + 10%), then the substituted combined voting level is decreased to 48 percent. Similarly, if at any time the sum of the foundation value level and the disqualified person value level is less than the immediately preceding substituted combined value level, the substituted combined value level shall be decreased so that it equals such sum.

(D) *Restrictions on increases in levels.* In addition, none of the four levels referred to in paragraph (d)(4)(i)(B) of this section may be adjusted upward to reflect any increase in the holdings comprising such level, except as provided in section 4943(c)(5) and § 53.4943-5. As a result, any transfer of May 26, 1969, holdings from a disqualified person to a private foundation shall not increase the foundation voting level or the foundation value level (unless the transfer qualifies under section 4943(c)(5)), and thus may reduce the substituted combined value level (and, where appropriate, the substituted combined voting level). Thus, in the last preceding example, if the disqualified person, instead of selling the 2 percent interest to a nondisqualified person, had sold such interest to the foundation, the substituted combined voting level would still be reduced to 48 percent, since the disqualified person voting level would be reduced by 2 percent (to 38%) but the foundation voting level would not be increased by 2 percent (remaining at 10%). However, any transfer of May 26, 1969, holdings from a private foundation to a disqualified person under section 101(*l*)(2)(B) of the Tax Reform Act of 1969, shall reduce the foundation value level (and, where appropriate, the foundation voting level), but will not reduce the substituted combined value level or the substituted combined voting level. The disqualified person voting level and disqualified person value level are correspondingly increased, not being limited to interests held since May 26, 1969. In addition, a transfer of May 26, 1969, holdings from one disqualified person to another, for example, by bequest, shall not reduce the substituted combined voting level nor the substituted combined value level.

(ii) *Exceptions*—(A) *One percent de minimus rule.* If after May 26, 1969, there are one or more decreases in the holdings comprising any of the four levels referred to in paragraph (d)(4)(i)(B) of this section during any taxable year of a private foundation, and if such decreases are attributable to issuances of stock (or such issuances coupled with redemptions), then, unless the aggregate of such decreases equals or exceeds 1 percent, the determination of whether there is a decrease in such level for purposes of this paragraph (d)(4) shall be made only at the close of such taxable year. If, however, the aggregate of such decreases equals or exceeds 1 percent, such level shall be decreased at that time as if the previous sentence had never applied.

(B) *Twenty percent (or 35 percent) floor.* In no event shall the downward rachet rule contained in paragraph (d)(4)(i) of this section decrease the substituted combined voting level or the substituted combined value level below 20 percent, or, for purposes of section 4943(c)(2)(B), below 35 percent.

(iii) *Special rules*—(A) *Change of foundation managers.* In the case of a foundation manager (as defined in section 4946(b)) who on May 26, 1969, owns holdings in a business enterprise and who is replaced by another foundation manager, the decrease in the substituted combined voting or value levels shall be limited to the excess, if any, of the departing foundation manager's holdings over his successor's holdings.

(B) *Termination of private foundation status under section 507.* If an organization gives the notification described in section 507(b)(1)(B)(ii) of the commencement of a 60-month termination period and fails to meet the requirements of section 509(a)(1), (2) or (3) for the entire period, then such organization will be treated as a private foundation during the entire 60-month period for purposes of this paragraph (d)(4) and section 4946(a)(1)(H). For example, X, a private foundation gives notification of the commencement of a 60-month termination commencing on January 1, 1972. X and Y, another private foundation, are effectively controlled by the same persons within the meaning of section 4946(a)(1)(H). X and Y hold 25 percent each of the voting stock of Z corporation on May 26, 1969, so that the substituted combined voting level for X or Y is 50 percent on such date. If X meets the requirements of section 509(a)(1), (2), or (3) for the entire 60-month period, section 4946(a)(1)(H) is inapplicable to X, and, under the downward ratchet rule, the substituted combined voting level for Y is decreased by 25 percent. On the other hand, if X meets the requirements of section 509(a)(2) for its taxable years 1972 and 1973, but fails to meet the requirements of section 509(a)(1), (2), or (3) in 1974, 1975, and 1976, then solely for purposes of section 4943(c)(4)(A)(ii) and this paragraph (d)(4), X will be treated as a disqualified person with respect to Y, and Y will be treated as a disqualified person with respect to X, for taxable years 1972 through 1976 pursuant to section 4946(a)(1)(H). Thus, for purposes of section 4943(c)(4)(A)(ii), the substituted combined voting level for X or Y will not be decreased by reason of the fact that X was attempting to terminate under section 507(b)(1)(B), and assuming no other transactions, such level will remain at 50 percent.

(iv) *Examples.* The provisions of this paragraph (d)(4) may be illustrated by the following examples:

Example (1). F, a private foundation, owns on May 26, 1969, 50 shares of voting stock in corporation X representing 50 percent of the voting stock in X and 25 percent of the value of all outstanding shares of all classes of stock in X. A and B, the only disqualified persons with respect to F, together own, on such date, 2 shares of voting stock in X representing 2 percent of the voting stock in X and 1 percent of the value of all outstanding shares of all classes of stock in X. In addition, on such date, F owns 30 shares of nonvoting stock in X, representing 30 percent of the value of all outstanding shares of all classes of stock in X, and A and B together own 15 shares of nonvoting stock in X representing 15 percent of the value of all outstanding shares of all classes of stock in X. The provisions of section 4943(c)(4)(B)(iii) apply and during the 10-year period beginning on May 26, 1969, a disqualified person is deemed to hold all interests of F in X. Assume that on February 1, 1972, F sells to C, an unrelated individual, 12 shares of voting stock in X representing 12 percent of the voting stock in X and 6 percent of the value of all outstanding shares of all classes of stock in X.

(i) Beginning on May 26, 1969, the disqualified person voting level is 52 percent, the foundation voting level is zero, and the substituted combined voting level is 50 percent; the disqualified person value level is 71 percent, the foundation value level is zero, and the substituted combined value level is 50 percent.

(ii) Beginning on February 1, 1972, the disqualified person voting level is 40 percent (52% — 12%), the foundation voting level is zero, and the substituted combined voting level is 40 percent; the disqualified person value level is 65 percent (71% — 6%), the foundation value level is zero and the substituted combined value level is 50 percent.

Example (2). F, a private foundation on the calendar year basis, holds, on May 26, 1969, 30 percent of the voting stock in corporation Y. C and D, the only disqualified persons with respect to F, together hold, on such date, 10 percent of the voting stock in Y. The provisions of section 4943 (c)(4)(B)(iii) apply with respect to F, and disqualified persons are deemed to hold all interests of F in Y for the 10-year period beginning on May 26, 1969, so that the substituted combined voting level as of such date is 40 percent. On February 1, 1973, a stock issuance by Y causes the combined holdings of voting power by F, C, and D in Y to decrease by 0.3 percent. On June 1, 1973, another such issuance causes such combined holdings to decrease by 0.5 percent. In September 1, 1973, an unrelated stock redemption by Y causes such combined holdings to increase by 0.4 percent. Under this paragraph the determination whether there is a decrease in the substituted combined voting level for purposes of the downward ratchet rule shall not be made before January 1, 1974, since the aggregate of the decreases occurring on February 1 and June 1 of 1973 is less than 1 percent (0.3% + 0.5%). Therefore, the substituted combined voting level as of January 1, 1974, is 39.6 percent (40% — [0.3% + 0.5%) — 0.4%].)

Example (3). Assume the facts as stated in Example (2), except that, on October 1, 1973, a stock issuance by Y causes the combined holdings of voting power by F, C, and D in Y to decrease by 0.3 percent. Since the aggregate of the decreases occurring on February 1, June 1, and October 1, of 1973 exceeds 1 percent, the determination whether there is a decrease in the substituted combined voting level shall be made as of October 1, 1973. At that time the substituted combined voting level shall be reduced to 39.2 percent (40% — 0.3% — 0.5%), the lowest actual combined holdings during the period that the *de minimis* rule was in effect.

(5) *Permitted holdings—Second phase* —(i) *In general.* For purposes of section 4943 and this section, the term "second phase" means the 15-year period immediately following the first phase. Upon the expiration of the first phase with respect to an interest to which section 4943(c)(4) applies, such interest shall no longer be treated as held by a disqualified person under section 4943(c)(4)(B). During the second phase, the manner of determining the permitted holdings of a private foundation to which section 4943(c)(4) applies shall be the same as applicable to the first phase, except that a 25 percent maximum shall apply under certain conditions specified in paragraph (d)(5)(ii) of this section. For these purposes the substituted combined voting level and the substituted combined value level in effect for the foundation at the end of the first phase shall be carried over to the second phase. The substituted levels are carried over because although there is a decrease in the disqualified person levels (since holdings are no longer treated as held by disqualified persons under section 4943(c)(4)(B)), a corresponding increase in the foundation levels occurs. For example, if a private foundation on May 26, 1969, held 10 percent of the voting stock in a corporation and disqualified persons held 40 percent of the voting stock, both the disqualified person voting level and the substituted combined voting level equal 50 percent (10% + 40%). Assuming no transactions during the first phase, on May 26, 1979, the disqualified person voting level would be decreased to 40 percent (50% — 10%), but the foundation voting level would be increased to 10 percent so that the substituted combined voting level would remain at 50 percent. In addition, the downward ratchet rule of paragraph (d)(4) of this section shall continue to apply, to prevent the foundation and disqualified persons from purchasing any additional interest in the same enterprise until the substituted combined voting level decreases below 20 percent.

(ii) *25 percent maximum on foundation holdings.* If, or as soon as, the disqualified person voting level exceeds 2 percent after the expiration of the first phase, the permitted holdings shall not thereafter exceed 25 percent of the voting stock or 25 percent of the value of all outstanding shares of all classes of stock, even though the holdings of the foundation and all disqualified persons combined do not exceed the substituted level. Solely for purposes of determining whether the 25 percent limitation of this subdivision (ii) applies, the disqualified person voting level shall not be treated as exceeding 2 percent solely as a result of the holdings of a private foundation which are treated as held by a disqualified person by reason of section 4943 (c)(5) or (6). For example, where under the constructive ownership rules for trusts in § 53.4943-8(b), a private foundation is deemed to own more than 2 percent of the voting stock of a business enterprise but such stock is treated as held by a disqualified person under section 4943(c)(5), the determination of the substituted percentage for permitted holdings in the second phase will be as if the foundation owned the stock held by the trust. Similarly, where a private foundation is the only remainder beneficiary of a trust that is a disqualified person under section 4946(a)(1)H), the disqualified person voting level shall not be treated as exceeding 2 percent solely as a result of the holdings of such a trust.

Reg. § 53.4943-4(d)(5)

24,258.10-V (I.R.C.) Reg. § 53.4943-4(d)(5) 7-18-77

(6) *Permitted holdings—Third phase.* For purposes of section 4943 and this section, the term "third phase" means the entire period following the second phase. During the third phase the manner of determining the permitted holdings of a private foundation to which section 4943(c)(4) applies shall be the same as applicable to the second phase under paragraph (d)(5) of this section (including the carryover of levels from the earlier phase). However, if the 25 percent limit of paragraph (d)(5)(ii) of this section never applied during the second phase, the substituted combined voting level and the substituted combined value level each shall not exceed 35 percent during the third phase.

(7) *Examples.* The provisions of this paragraph may be illustrated by the following examples:

Example (1). F, a private foundation, owns, on May 26, 1969, 30 shares of voting stock in corporation Z representing 30 percent of the voting power in Z and 15 percent of the value of all outstanding shares of all classes of stock in Z, and owns, on such date, 10 shares of nonvoting stock in Z representing 10 percent of the value of all outstanding shares of all classes of stock in Z. E and G, the only disqualified persons with respect to F, own, on such date, 5 shares each of nonvoting stock in Z. The 10 shares of nonvoting stock in Z owned by E and G together represent 10 percent of the value of all outstanding shares of all classes of stock in Z. Assume further that F cannot meet the requirements for the 35 percent test of section 4943(c)(2)(B). For purposes of applying section 4943(c)(4)(B) and this paragraph, F has excess business holdings in Z (determined without regard to section 4943(c)(4)), because under section 4943(c)(2)(A) F's permitted holdings are 20 percent (20%—0%) of the voting stock since disqualified persons have no holdings of voting stock. Therefore, section 4943(c)(4)(B) and this paragraph apply, and a disqualified person is treated as holding F's shares of both voting and nonvoting stock in Z for the 10-year period through May 25, 1979. Thus, since all holdings by F in Z are treated as held by a disqualified person during the first phase, F can not be subject to tax under section 4943(a) on its May 26, 1969, holdings prior to the termination of the first phase, regardless of whether or not disqualified persons purchase additional shares of Z during the first phase.

Example (2). Assume the same facts as in Example (1), and further assume that there were no transactions in the stock of Z during the first phase (May 26, 1969 through May 25, 1979). During the first phase the permitted holdings by F in Z for both the voting stock and the value is zero. The disqualified person voting level and the substituted combined voting level are each 30 percent, and the disqualified person value level and the substituted combined value level are each 35 percent (15% + 10% + 10%). The substituted levels are carried over into the second phase. The disqualified person voting level on May 26, 1979, the beginning of the second phase, is zero, because the voting shares held by F are no longer treated as held by a disqualified person. Therefore, F's permitted holdings on such date are 30 percent of the voting stock, because such percentage is equal to the excess of the substituted combined voting level (30%) over the disqualified person voting level (0%). The disqualified person value level on May 26, 1979, is 10 percent, because the voting and nonvoting shares held by F are no longer treated as held by a disqualified person. Therefore, F's permitted holdings on such date are 25 percent of the value of Z stock, because such percentage is equal to the excess of the substituted combined value level (35%) over the disqualified person value level (10%) as of such date.

Example (3). Assume the facts as stated in Example (2), except that E and G acquire, on February 1, 1970, 10 shares of Z voting stock representing 10 percent of the voting power in Z and 5 percent of the value of all outstanding shares of all classes of stock in Z. During the first phase such permitted holdings remain zero, and prior to May 25, 1979, the substituted combined voting level and substituted combined value level remain 30 and 35 percent, respectively, because such levels may not be increased by acquisitions by disqualified persons. However, the disqualified person voting level and the disqualified person value level are each increased to 40 percent (30% + 10%) and 40 percent (35% + 5%), respectively. During the first phase the excess of the disqualified person voting level over the substituted combined voting level (40% — 30%) and the excess of the disqualified person value level over the substituted combined value level (40% — 35%) indicate how much stock F must dispose of during the first phase to avoid the initial tax when it expires. On May 25, 1979, the last day of the first phase, F disposes of 12 shares of Z voting stock, representing 12 percent of the voting power in Z and 6 percent of the value of all such outstanding shares. The disposition by F reduces the interest F owns to 18 percent (30% — 12%) of the voting power, and 19 percent (25% — 6%) of the value of all outstanding shares of all classes of stock, in Z. Since the disqualified person voting level decreases to 28 percent (40% — 12%), the substituted combined voting level as of May 25, 1979, accordingly is decreased to 28 percent under the downward ratchet rule. Similarly, the substituted combined value level is decreased to 34 percent, as the disqualified person value level as of such date is 34 percent (40% — 6%). On May 26, 1979, the disqualified person voting level is 10 percent (28% — 18%), and the disqualified person value level is 15 percent (34% — 19%), since the shares owned by F are no longer treated as held by a disqualified person as of such date. Accordingly, on May 26, 1979, the permitted holdings by F and Z are 18 percent of the voting power in Z, because such percentage is equal to the excess of the substituted combined voting level (28%) over the disqualified person voting level (10%) as of such date. Similarly, the permitted holdings of F in Z by value are 19 percent (34% — 15%). If F had not disposed of the 12 shares, then on May 26, 1979, F's permitted holdings in voting power and value would be 20 percent (30% — 10%) and 20 percent (35% — 15%), respectively.

Example (4). F, a private foundation, owns on May 26, 1969, 35 shares of voting stock in corporation Y representing 35 percent of the voting stock in Y and 17.5 percent of the value of all classes of stock in Y, and owns on such date 45 shares of nonvoting stock representing 22.5 percent of the value of all outstanding shares of all classes of stock in Y. No disqualified person with respect to F owns, on such date, any stock in Y. Assume further that Y cannot meet the requirements of the 35 percent test of section 4943(c)(2)(B). For purposes of applying section 4943(c)(4)(B) and this paragraph, F has excess business holdings in Y (determined without regard to section 4943(c)(4)), because under section 4943(c)(2)(A) F's permitted holdings are 20 percent (20% − 0%) of the voting stock since disqualified persons have no holdings of voting stock. Therefore, section 4943(c)(4)(B) and this paragraph apply, and a disqualified person is treated as holding F's shares of both voting and nonvoting stock in Y for the 10-year period through May 25, 1979. During the first phase the permitted holdings by F in Y of both the voting stock and of value are zero. The disqualified person voting level and the substituted combined voting level are each 35 percent, and the disqualified person value level and the substituted combined value level are each 40 percent (17.5% + 22.5%). The substituted levels are carried over into the second phase. The disqualified person voting level and value level on May 26, 1979, are both zero, because the shares held by F are no longer treated as held by a disqualified person. Therefore, F's permitted holdings on such date are 35 percent of the voting power (35% − 0%) and 40 percent of the value (40% − 0%). Assume that on February 1, 1981, A, a disqualified person, acquires 6 percent of the voting stock in Y representing 3 percent of the value of all outstanding shares of all classes of stock in Y. The permitted holdings by F in Z on February 1, 1981, are thus reduced to 25 percent of the voting stock (the lesser of the separate 25% second phase limitation or 29% (35% substituted combined voting level minus 6% disqualified person voting level)) and 25 percent of the value (the lesser of the separate 25% second phase limitation or 37% (40% substituted combined value level minus 3% disqualified person value level)). But see paragraph (d)(8) of this section for limitations on restrictions with respect to nonvoting stock.

Example (5). Assume the same facts as in Example (4) except that A does not acquire the 6 shares of voting stock until February 1, 1996 (in the third phase), rather than on February 1, 1981. Thus, F's permitted holdings in Y would remain at 35 percent of the voting stock and 40 percent of the value during the second phase, which expired on May 25, 1994. Assume that on May 25, 1994, the last day of the second phase, F disposes of 10 shares of nonvoting stock representing 5 percent of the value of all outstanding shares in Y to meet the 35 percent third phase limit. In accordance with the downward ratchet rule, the substituted combined value level and F's permitted holdings in Y would be reduced to 35 percent of value. On February 1, 1996, F's permitted holdings in Y would be reduced to 25 percent of the voting stock (the lesser of the separate 25% third phase limitation or 29% (35% substituted combined voting level minus 6% disqualified person level)) and 25 percent of the value (the lesser of the separate 25% third phase limitation or 32% (35% substituted combined value level minus 3% disqualified person value level)). But see paragraph (d)(8) of this section for limitations on restrictions with respect to nonvoting stock.

(8) *Special rule where all holdings are permitted under section 4943(c)(2).* (i) Since section 4943(c)(4) and this paragraph provide transitional rules for foundations which would otherwise have had excess business holdings on May 26, 1969, no holdings shall cease to be permitted holdings under this paragraph where such holdings would be permitted holdings under section 4943(c)(2) and § 53.4943-3. Thus, for example, where the substituted combined voting level has been reduced to 20 percent, the provisions of § 53.4943-3(b)(2) concerning nonvoting stock as permitted holdings generally apply.

(ii) The provisions of this paragraph (d)(8) my be illustrated by the following example:

Example. (A) F, a private foundation, owns, on May 26, 1969, 40 shares of voting stock in corporation X representing 40 percent of the voting stock in X and 20 percent of the value of all outstanding shares of all classes of stock in X, and owns, on such date, 60 shares of nonvoting stock in X, representing 30 percent of the value of all outstanding shares of all classes of stock in X. A, the only disqualified person with respect to F, owns, on such date, 10 shares of voting stock in X, representing 10 percent of the voting stock in X and 5 percent of the value of all outstanding shares of all classes of stock in X. Under section 4943(c)(4)(B)(iii), a disqualified person is deemed the owner of all holdings by F in X for the 10-year period beginning on May 26, 1969.

(B) Assume that the only transaction in X stock during the first phase is the disposition of 30 shares of voting stock by F on May 1, 1975. The voting stock held by F is permitted holdings under § 53.4943-3 and under such section since all disqualified persons together do not own more than 20 percent of the voting stock in X, all nonvoting stock held by F shall also be treated as permitted holdings. Therefore, all the stock held by F is permitted holdings.

(C) Assume that on May 1, 1975, F had disposed of only 15 shares of voting stock and also had disposed of 35 shares of nonvoting stock. On May 26, 1979, at the beginning of the second phase, this paragraph (d)(8) would not apply since F would have excess business holdings under § 53.4943-3. Under the provisions of this section, the permitted holdings by F in X on such date are 25 percent of the voting stock (35% substituted combined voting level minus 10% disqualified person voting level) and 25 percent of the value (30% substituted combined value level minus 5% disqualified person value level).

(9) *Special rule for certain private foundations.* In the case of a private foundation—

(i) Which was incorporated before January 1, 1951;

(ii) Substantially all of the assets of which on May 26, 1969, consisted of more than 90 percent of the stock of an incorpo-

Reg. § 53.4943-4(d)(9)

rated business enterprise which is licensed and regulated, the sales or contracts of which are regulated, and the professional representatives of which are licensed, by State regulatory agencies in at least 10 States;

(iii) Which acquired such stock solely by gift, devise, or bequest;

(iv) Which does not purchase any stock or other interest in such enterprise after May 26, 1969, and does not acquire any stock or other interest in any other business enterprise which constitutes excess business holdings under § 53.4943-3; and

(v) Which, in the last 5 taxable years ending on or before December 31, 1970, expended substantially all of its adjusted net income (as defined in section 4942(f)) for the purpose or function for which it is organized and operated;

paragraph (d)(1) through (5) of this section (permitted holdings during the first and second phase) shall be applied with respect to the holdings of such foundation in such incorporated business enterprise by substituting "51 percent" for "50 percent," and section 4943(c)(4)(D) (third phase) shall not apply with respect to such holdings. For purposes of the preceding sentence, stock of such enterprise in a trust created before May 27, 1969, of which the foundation is the remainder beneficiary shall be deemed to be held by such foundation on May 26, 1969, if such foundation held (without regard to such trust) more than 20 percent of the stock of such enterprise on May 26, 1969.

○━➤ § 53.4943-5 (TD 7496, filed 7-5-77.) **Present holdings acquired by trust or a will.**

(a) *Interests to which section 4943(c) (5) applies*—(1) *In general.* Section 4943 (c)(5) provides that section 4943(c)(4) (other than the 20-year first phase holding period) applies to an interest in a business enterprise acquired after May 26, 1969 by a private foundation under the terms of a trust which was irrevocable on May 26, 1969, or under the terms of a will executed on or before May 26, 1969, which were in effect on May 26, 1969, and at all times thereafter, as if such interest were held on May 26, 1969. However, the first phase holding period prescribed by § 53.4943-4(c)(1) (ii) or (iii) shall commence for such an interest on the date of distribution to the foundation. Unlike section 4943(c)(4) and § 53.4943-4, section 4943(c)(5) and this section treat only the interest so acquired (and not the entire interest held by the foundation in such enterprise on the date of distribution) as held by a disqualified person during a first phase holding period. (See, however, section 4943(c)(6) and paragraph (b)(2) of § 53.4943-6 for the treatment of other holdings of the foundation in the same enterprise if an interest to which section 4943(c)(5) applies is acquired from a person who was not a disqualified person prior to the acquisition.) In addition, section 4943(c)(5) and this section shall not apply if after the acquisition of such an interest the foundation would not have excess business holdings (determined without regard to section 4943(c)(4), (5), or (6)).

(2) *After-acquired interests.* Section 4943(c)(5) and this section shall not apply to any interest acquired after May 26, 1969, by an estate or trust, other than by reason of the death of the decedent. For example, where a foundation is a residuary beneficiary under the terms of a will executed before May 26, 1969, and the residue of the estate consists of cash, then stock subsequently purchased with this cash for distribution to the foundation will not be treated as an interest acquired under the terms of a will executed on or before May 26, 1969.

(3) *Certain revocable trusts.* If an interest in a business enterprise actually passes to a private foundation under a trust which would have met the tests referred to in paragraph (a)(1) of this section but for the fact that the trust was revocable (even though it was not in fact revoked) and such interest would have passed to such foundation under a will that meets those tests but for the fact that the grantor died without having revoked the trust, then for purposes of section 4943(c) (5) and this section, such an interest shall be treated as having been acquired by the foundation under the will.

(4) *Modification of will*—(i) *In general.* For purposes of section 4943(c)(5) and this section, an amendment or republication of a will which was executed on or before May 26, 1969, does not prevent any interest in a business enterprise which was to pass under the terms (which were in effect on May 26, 1969, and at all times thereafter) of such will from being treated as a present holding under section 4943(c) (4) or (5)—

(A) Solely because there is a reduction in the interest in the business enterprise which the foundation was to receive under the terms of the will (for example, if the foundation is to receive the residuary estate, and if one class of stock is disposed of by the decedent during his lifetime or by a subsequent codicil);

(B) Solely because such amendment or republication is necessary in order to comply with section 508(e) and the regulations thereunder;

(C) Solely because there is a change in the executor of the will; or

(D) Solely because of any other change which does not otherwise change the rights of the foundation with respect to such interest in the business enterprise.

However, if under such amendment or republication there is an increase in the interest in the business enterprise which the foundation was to receive under the terms of the will in effect on May 26, 1969, such increase shall not be treated as present holdings under section 4943(c)(4) or (5). Under such circumstances the interest which would have been acquired before such increase shall remain present holdings. See section 4943(c)(6) and § 53.4943-6 with respect to the treatment of such increase in holdings of a private foundation.

(ii) *Examples.* The provisions of this paragraph (a)(4) may be illustrated by the following examples:

Example (1). On May 9, 1985, A modifies by codicil his will which was in effect on May 26, 1969, and was unchanged until such modification. The purpose of the codicil was, in the event of A's death, to increase the number of shares in X Corporation that would pass to the W foundation from 70 percent of all the voting power and value to 80 percent. Under these facts, if A dies without further modifying the terms of the will which apply to W's interest in X, section 4943(c)(5) will apply to 70 percent of the X voting power and value and section 4943(c)(6) will apply to 10 percent of the X voting power and value, since 10 percent of the X voting power and value would not pass under a provision of the will which was in effect on May 26, 1969, and at all times thereafter. Accordingly, if the stock is distributed to W on July 6, 1988, then, asuming that on May 26, 1969, W and all disqualified persons owned less than 75% of the voting stock in X, an amount of such stock representing 70 percent of X voting power and value shall be treated as held by a disqualified person through July 5, 1998, and an amount of such stock representing 10 percent of X voting power and value shall be treated as held by a disqualified person through July 5, 1993.

Example (2). Assume the facts as stated in Example (1), except that the sole purpose of the codicil was to change the executor of the will. Under paragraph (a)(4)(i) of this section, such codicil will not prevent the X voting stock which was bequeathed to W from being treated as held by a disqualified person through July 5, 1998.

(b) *Holding periods* (1) *In general.* An interest to which section 4943(c)(5) applies shall be entitled to a 15-year holding period starting on the date of distribution only if the interests actually or constructively owned by a private foundation and all disqualified persons on May 26, 1969, in a business enterprise exceed 75 percent of the voting stock (or of the profits or beneficial interest) or 75 percent of the value of all outstanding shares of all classes of stock (or of the profits and capital interest) in such enterprise. For purposes of the preceding sentence, interests held by the foundation on May 26, 1969, shall be deemed to include an interest to which section 4943(c)(5) applies and which has been acquired (on or before the date of distribution for the interest in question) from a person who was not a disqualified person on May 26, 1969. Therefore, if under the terms of a will in effect on May 26, 1969, and at all times thereafter, a private foundation is created on July 1, 1975, and receives 76 percent of the voting stock of a business enterprise on that date, such stock shall be treated as held by a disqualified person until June 30, 1990. Any interest to which section 4943(c)(5) applies but which is not entitled to a 15-year holding period shall be entitled to a 10-year holding period starting on the date of distribution. For purposes of this paragraph the date of distribution shall be deemed to occur no later than the date on which the trust or estate is considered to be terminated under § 1.641(b)-3 of this chapter (Income Tax Regulations).

(2) *Constructive ownership prior to date of distribution.* To the extent that an interest to which section 4943(c)(5) applies is constructively held by a private foundation under section 4943(d)(1) and § 53.4943-8 prior to the date of distribution, it shall be treated as held by a disqualified person prior to such date by reason of section 4943(c)(5). In addition, in the case of a foundation's interest in a trust which was irrevocable on May 26, 1969, and to which both sections 4943(c)(4) and (c)(5) apply, the first phase holding period for such interest shall end with whichever such period under section 4943(c)(4) or (5) ends later. For example, if under the terms of such a trust, 96 percent of the voting stock in a business enterprise was constructively held by a private foundation on May 26, 1969, and was distributed to such foundation on June 30, 1970, such interest is entitled to a 20-year holding period beginning on May 26, 1969.

(c) *Permitted holdings*—(1) *In general.* The permitted holdings of a private foundation which has an interest in a business enterprise to which section 4943(c)(5) applies shall be determined in accordance with the rules of paragraph (d) of § 53.4943-4. The levels referred to in such paragraph shall be adjusted to take into account the acquisition of such an interest as if it were treated as held by a disqualified person from May 26, 1969, until the date of acquisition. See also § 53.4943-6(b)(2) for the special rule for interests held by a private foundation at the time it acquires a section 4943(c)(5) interest from a nondisqualified person. Thus, for example, if on June 30, 1975, the disqualified person voting level and the substituted combined voting level in corporation X with respect to foundation F are 45 percent, and a nondisqualified person's 10 percent voting interest in X is acquired by F on July 1, 1975, in a transaction to which section 4943(c)(5) applies, the above-mentioned levels shall be increased to 55 and 50 percent respectively, on July 1, 1975. However, if such interest had been acquired from a person who was a disqualified person on May 26, 1969, rather than from a nondisqualified person, no adjustments in such levels would have taken place on July 1, 1975. In such a case, though, at the beginning of the second phase on July 1, 1985, the foundation voting level would be increased by 10 percent, and the disqualified person voting level decreased by 10 percent (assuming that none of the acquired stock had been disposed of prior to such date).

(2) *Separate phases.* The phases for each interest to which section 4943(c)(5) applies start independently from those for any other interest of the foundation in the same enterprise to which section 4943(c)(4) or (5) applies. Therefore, until an interest enters its own second phase, the 25 percent limit described in paragraph (d)(5) of § 53.-4943-4 shall not apply to such interest since such interest (and any subsequently acquired section 4943(c)(5) interest in the first phase) is still treated as held by a disqualified person for purposes of that 25 percent limit. In addition, if such an interest enters its second phase and at such time all disqualified persons together do not have holdings in excess of 2 percent of the voting stock in the same business enterprise, then the 25 percent limit of section 4943(c)(4)(D)(i) shall not then apply to such interest, even though such limit may have been applicable to an interest with an earlier second phase. Moreover, the 35 percent limit of section 4943(c)(4)(D)(ii) shall cause only interests which have entered the third phase to become excess business holdings, taking into account, however, interests in prior phases in determining the holdings subject to such limit.

(3) *Examples.* The provisions of this paragraph may be illustrated by the following examples: (After each example is a

Reg. § 53.4943-5(c)(2)

24,258.10-Z (I.R.C.) Reg. § 53.4943-5(c)(2) 7-18-77

chart setting forth the chronological changes in the various levels referred to in paragraph (d) of § 53.4943-4.)

Example (1). On May 26, 1969, F, a private foundation, owns no stock in M Corporation, and A, a disqualified person owns 40 percent of the voting stock (voting power and value) in M. A dies on May 1, 1971, leaving 30 percent of the voting stock in M to F and leaving the other 10 percent to a disqualified person. Distribution is made on June 1, 1972, and assume that section 4943(c)(5) applies. No transactions in the stock of M, other than those described in this example, occur. On May 26, 1969, the substituted combined voting level is 40 percent, the disqualified person voting level is deemed to be 40 percent, and the permitted holdings by F in M is deemed to be 0 percent (40% − 40%). On May 1, 1971 (the date that F acquired the M stock by reason of its constructive ownership of A's estate), the various levels remain unchanged. On May 1, 1971, the 30 percent interest is treated as held by a disqualified person for a period extending through May 31, 1982. On June 1, 1981, F disposes of 6 percent of the voting stock to a nondisqualified person. The substituted combined voting level and the disqualified person voting level thereby are reduced to 34 percent (40% − 6%) each. On June 1, 1982, at the beginning of the second phase, the foundation voting level increases to 24 percent (30% − 6%) and the disqualified person voting level is reduced to 10 percent (34% − 24%). The substituted combined voting level as of June 1, 1982, remains at 34 percent. The permitted holdings as of such date are 24 percent (34% − 10%). If F had not disposed of any holdings prior to June 1, 1982, F's permitted holdings would have been 25 percent, the lesser of 25 percent (the limitation of section 4943(c)(4)(D)(i)), or 30 percent (40% − 10%). Since on such date the 30 percent interest would no longer have been treated as held by a disqualified person, F would have had excess business holdings of 5 percent (30% − 25%).

[Table appears on page 24,258.10-Z.1 (*I.R.C.*)]

Example (2). (i) On May 26, 1969, F, a private foundation, owns 30 percent of the voting stock of N Corporation (voting power and value) and disqualified persons own 20 percent of the voting stock of N Corporation. On May 1, 1971, B, a disqualified person, dies leaving 15 percent of the voting stock to F. Assume that distribution was made on June 1, 1972, and that section 4943(c)(5) applies. On May 26, 1969, the substituted combined voting level and the disqualified person voting levels are each 50 percent and the permitted holdings are 0 percent (50% − 50%). On May 1, 1971, and June 1, 1972, these levels remain unchanged. On May 1, 1971, the 15 percent interest is treated as held by a disqualified person for a period extending through May 31, 1982.

(ii) On July 1, 1978, F sells 6 percent of the F stock to a nondisqualified person, thereby reducing the disqualified person voting level and the substituted combined voting level to 44 percent (50% − 6%). On May 26, 1979, at the beginning of the second phase for F's 1969 holdings, the foundation voting level is 24 percent (30% − 6%), the substituted combined voting level is still 44 percent, and the disqualified person voting level is 20 percent (44% − 24%). The permitted holdings are 24 percent (44% − 20%). In addition F's 24 percent holdings do not exceed the 25 percent limitation of section 4943(c)(4)(D)(i) and paragraph (d)(5)(ii) of § 53.4943-4.

(iii) On August 1, 1981, F sells 16 percent of the N stock to a nondisqualified person, thereby reducing the foundation voting level to 8 percent (24% − 16%), and reducing the substituted combined voting level to 28 percent (44% − 16%). The disqualified person voting level remains at 20 percent. On June 1, 1982, at the beginning of the second phase for F's holdings acquired by will, the substituted combined voting level is still 28 percent, the foundation voting level is 23 percent (8% + 15%), the disqualified person voting level is 5 percent (20% − 15%), and the permitted holdings are 23 percent (28% − 5%).

(iv) If F had not disposed of the 6 percent on July 1, 1978, then on May 26, 1979, at the beginning of the second phase for F's 1969 holdings, F's permitted holdings would have been 25 percent, the lesser of 25 percent (the limitation of section 4943(c)(4)(D)(i)), or 30 percent (50% − 20%). Since F's 30 percent interest would no longer have been treated as held by a disqualified person on May 26, 1979, F would have had excess business holdings of 5 percent (30% − 25%). Similarly, if F had not disposed of the 16 percent interest on August 1, 1981 (but had disposed of the 6 percent interest), on July 1, 1982, at the beginning of the second phase for F's holdings acquired by will, F's permitted holdings would have been 25 percent, the lesser of 25 percent (under section 4943(c)(4)(D)(ii)), or 39 percent (44% − 5%). Since as of such date F's entire holdings of 39 percent would no longer have been treated as held by a disqualified person, F would have had excess business holdings of 14 percent (39% − 25%).

[Table appears on page 24,258.10-Z.2 (*I.R.C.*)]

Example (3). (i) On May 26, 1969, F, a private foundation owns 5 percent of the voting stock of O Corporation (voting power and value), and disqualified persons own 45 percent of the voting stock. C, a disqualified person, dies on May 1, 1971, and leaves 41 percent of the voting stock of O to F. Assume that distribution is made on June 1, 1972, and that section 4943(c)(5) applies. On May 26, 1969, the substituted combined voting level and the disqualified person voting level are 50 percent and the permitted holdings are 0 percent (50% − 50%). On May 1, 1971, and June 1, 1972, the various levels remain unchanged. On May 1, 1971, the 41 percent interest is treated as held by a disqualified person for a period extending through May 31, 1982. On May 26, 1979, at the beginning of the second phase for F's 1969 holdings of 5 percent, the 5 percent is no longer treated as held by a disqualified person, the foundation voting level is 5 percent, the disqualified person voting level is reduced to 45 percent (50% − 5%), and the substituted combined voting level remains at 50 percent. On such date F's permitted holdings are 5 percent (50% − 45%). Since the 41 percent interest is treated as held by a disqualified person, the interest treated as held by F (5%) does not exceed the 25 percent limitation of section 4943(c)(4)(D)(i).

(ii) On August 1, 1981, F sells 22 percent of the O stock to a nondisqualified person, thereby reducing the foundation voting level to 0 percent. Since the reductions are first applied to the 1969 holdings of 5 percent, 17 percent (22% − 5%) applies to the 41 percent interest, reducing such in-

Private Foundations (I.R.C.) 24,258.10-Z.1

Date	F owns	interest treated as held by disqualified person	disqualified persons own	foundation voting level	substituted combined voting level	disqualified person voting level	permitted holdings	comments
5/26/69	0%	0%	40%	0%	40%	40%	0%	
5/1/71	+30%	+30%	-30%	0%	40%	40%	0%	A dies
5/1/71	30%	30%	10%	0%	40%	40%	0%	distribution
6/1/72	30%	30%	10%	0%	40%	40%	0%	
6/1/81	-6%	-6%	10%	0%	-6%	-6%	0%	F sells 6%
6/1/81	24%	24%	10%	0%	34%	34%	0%	
6/1/82	24%	-24%	10%	+24%	-24%	-24%	+24%	2nd phase begins
6/1/82	24%	0%	10%	24%	34%	10%	24%	

Reg. § 53.4943-5(c)(2)

24,258.10-Z.2 (I.R.C.)   Reg. § 53.4943-5(c)(2)   7-18-77

Date	F owns	F's interest 1969	F's interest 1971	interest treated as held by disqualified person	disqualified persons own	foundation voting level	substituted combined voting level	disqualified person voting level	permitted holdings	comments
5/26/69	30%	30%		30%	20%	0%	50%	50%	0%	
5/1/71	+15%		+15%	+15%	-15%	0%	50%	50%	0%	B dies
5/1/71	45%	30%	15%	45%	5%	0%	50%	50%	0%	
6/1/72	45%	30%	15%	45%	5%	0%	50%	50%	0%	distribution
7/1/78	-6%	-6%		-6%			-6%	-6%		F sells 6%
7/1/78	39%	24%	15%	39%	5%	0%	44%	44%	0%	
5/26/79				-24%		+24%		-24%	+24%	2nd phase for 24%
5/26/79	39%	24%	15%	15%	5%	24%	44%	20%	24%	
8/1/81	-16%	-16%				-16%	-16%		-16%	F sells 16%
8/1/81	23%	8%	15%	15%	5%	8%	28%	20%	8%	
7/1/82				-15%		+15%		-15%	+15%	All in 2nd phase
7/1/82	23%	8%	15%	0%	5%	23%	28%	5%	23%	

Private Foundations   *(I.R.C.)* 24,258.10-Z.3

terest to 24 percent (41% — 17%), and reducing the disqualified person voting level to 28 percent (45% — 17%). The substituted combined voting level is reduced to 28 percent (0% + 28%). On June 1, 1982, at the beginning of the second phase for F's holdings acquired by will, the substituted combined voting level remains at 28 percent, the foundation voting level is 24 percent, the disqualified person voting level is reduced to 4 percent (28% — 4%).

(iii) If F had not disposed of the 22 percent interest prior to June 1, 1982, F's permitted holdings would have been 25 percent, the lesser of 25 percent (under section 4943(c)(4)(D)(i)), or 46 percent (50% — 4%). Since as of such date, F's entire holdings of 46 percent would no longer have been treated as held by a disqualified person, F would have had excess business holdings of 21 percent (46% — 25%).

Date	F owns	F's interest 1969	F's interest 1971	interest treated as held by disqualified person	disqualified persons own	foundation voting level	substituted combined voting level	disqualified person voting level	permitted holdings	comments
5/26/69	5%	5%		5%	45%	0%	50%	50%	0%	
5/ 1/71	+41%		+41%	+41%	—41%					C dies
5/ 1/71	46%	5%	41%	46%	4%	0%	50%	50%	0%	
6/ 1/72	46%	5%	41%	46%	4%	0%	50%	50%	0%	distribution
5/26/79				—5%		+5%		—5%	+5%	2nd phase for 5%
5/26/79	46%	5%	41%	41%	4%	5%	50%	45%	5%	
8/ 1/81	—22%	—5%	—17%	—17%		—5%	—22%	—17%	—5%	F sells 22%
8/ 1/81	24%	0%	24%	24%	4%	0%	28%	28%	0%	
6/ 1/82				—24%		+24%		—24%	+24%	2nd phase for 24%
6/ 1/82	24%	0%	24%	0%	4%	24%	28%	4%	24%	

Example (4). (i) On May 26, 1969, F, a private foundation, owns 30 percent of the voting stock in P Corporation (voting power and value), and disqualified persons own 20 percent. On May 1, 1971, D, a disqualified person, dies leaving 18 percent of the voting stock to F. Assume that distribution was made on June 1, 1972, and that section 4943(c)(5) applies. On May 26, 1969, the substituted combined voting level and the disqualified person voting level are each 50 percent and the permitted holdings are 0 percent (50%—50%). On May 1, 1971, and June 1, 1972, these levels remain unchanged. On May 1, 1971, the 18 percent interest is treated as held by a disqualified person for a period extending through May 31, 1982. On May 26, 1979, the foundation voting level increases to 30 percent, the disqualified person voting level decreases to 20 percent (50% — 30%), and the permitted holdings are 30 percent (50% — 20%). On June 1, 1982, the foundation voting level increases to 48 percent, the disqualified person voting level decreases to 2 percent and the permitted holdings are 48 percent (50% — 2%). Since at no time during the second phase for F's 1969 holdings did all disqualified persons together have holdings in excess of 2 percent of the voting stock of P, the 25 percent limitation of section 4943(c)(4)(D)(i) did not apply to F's 1969 holdings.

(ii) On July 1, 1993, F disposes of 16 percent of the stock in P, thereby reducing the substituted combined voting level to 34 percent (50%—16%), and reducing the permitted holdings to 32 percent (34% — 2%). If F had not disposed of the 16 percent of the stock of P prior to May 26, 1994, on such date, under section 4943(c)(4)(D)(ii), F's substituted combined voting level for its 1969 holdings would have been 35 percent, and the permitted holdings would have been 33 percent (35% — 2%). Since none of F's holdings of 48 percent would have been treated as held by a disqualified person on such date (the beginning of the third phase for F's 1969 holdings), F would have had excess business holdings of 15 percent, the lesser of 30 percent (F's 1969 holdings in the third phase), or 15 percent (the excess of F's 48 percent holdings over the permitted holdings of 33 percent).

Date	F owns	1969 F's interest	1971 F's interest	interest treated as held by disqualified person	disqualified persons own	foundation voting level	substituted combined voting level	disqualified person voting level	permitted holdings	comments
5/26/69	30%	30%		30%	20%	0%	50%	50%	0%	
5/ 1/71	+18%		+18%	+18%	—18%					D dies
5/ 1/71	48%	30%	18%	48%	2%	0%	50%	50%	0%	
6/ 1/71	48%	30%	18%	48%	2%	0%	50%	50%	0%	distribution
5/26/79				—30%		+30%		—30%	+30%	2nd phase for 30%
5/26/79	48%	30%	18%	18%	2%	30%	50%	20%	30%	
6/ 1/82				—18%		+18%		—18%	+18%	2nd phase for 18%
6/ 1/82	48%	30%	18%	0%	2%	48%	50%	2%	48%	
7/ 1/93	—16%	—16%				—16%	—16%		—16%	F disposes of 16%
7/ 1/93	32%	14%	18%	0%	2%	32%	34%	2%	32%	
5/26/94	32%	14%	18%	0%	2%	32%	34%	2%	32%	3rd phase for 14%
6/ 1/97	32%	14%	18%	0%	2%	32%	34%	2%	32%	3rd phase for 18%

Example (5). (i) On May 26, 1969, F, a private foundation, owns 5 percent of the voting stock in Q Corporation (voting power and value), and disqualified persons own 45 percent. On May 1, 1971, E, a disqualified person, dies leaving 43 percent of the

Reg. § 53.4943-5(c)(3)

voting stock to F. Assume that distribution was made on June 1, 1972, and that section 4943(c)(5) applies. On May 26, 1969, the substituted combined voting level and the disqualified person voting level are each 50 percent and the permitted holdings are 0 percent (50% — 50%). On May 1, 1971, and June 1, 1972, these levels remain unchanged. On May 1, 1971, the 43 percent interest is treated as held by a disqualified person for a period extending through May 31, 1982. On May 26, 1979, the foundation voting level increases to 5 percent, the disqualified person voting level decreases to 45 percent, and the permitted holdings are 5 percent (50% — 45%). On June 1, 1982, the foundation voting level increases to 48 percent, the disqualified person voting level decreases to 2 percent, and the permitted holdings are 48 percent (50% — 2%). At no time during the second phase for F's 1969 holdings did all disqualified persons together have holdings in excess of 2 percent of the voting stock of Q. Therefore, the 25 percent limitation of section 4943(c)(4)(D)(i) did not apply.

(ii) On July 1, 1993, F sells 6 percent of the stock in Q to a nondisqualified person. This reduces the substituted combined voting level to 44 percent and reduces the permitted holdings to 42 percent (44% — 2%). If F had not disposed of the 6 percent of the stock in 1993, on May 26, 1994, at the beginning of the third phase for F's 1969 holdings, F would have had 5 percent excess business holdings. The excess business holdings are 5 percent because although the excess business holdings computed for the third phase are 15 percent (the excess of F's actual holdings (48%) over the permitted holdings of 33 percent (35% — 2%)), only 5 percent of the holdings are in this phase and subject to the 35 percent combined holdings limitation.

(iii) On July 1, 1995, F sells 10 percent of the stock in Q, thereby reducing the substituted combined voting level to 34 percent and reducing the permitted holdings to 32 percent (34% — 2%). If F had not disposed of the 10 percent of the stock, on June 1, 1997, at the beginning of the third phase for F's acquired holdings, F would have had 9 percent excess business holdings (the excess of F's total holdings in the third phase (42%) over the permitted holdings of 33 percent (35% — 2%)).
[Table appears on page 24,258.10-Z.5 (I.R.C.)]

Example (6). (i) On May 26, 1969, F, a private foundation, owns 30 percent of the voting stock in R Corporation (voting power and value), and disqualified persons own 20 percent. On August 1, 1978, F disposes of 6 percent of the stock to a nondisqualified person. On May 1, 1981, G, a disqualified person, dies leaving 15 percent of the voting stock to F. Assume that distribution was made on June 1, 1982, and that section 4943(c)(5) applies. On May 26, 1969, the substituted combined voting level and the disqualified person voting level are each 50 percent, and the permitted holdings are 0 percent (50% — 50%). On August 1, 1978, these levels decrease to 44 percent (50% — 6%). On May 26, 1979, the foundation voting level increases to 24 percent (30% — 6%), the disqualified person voting level decreases to 20 percent (44% — 24%), and the permitted holdings are 24 percent (44% — 20%). If F had not disposed of the 6 percent of the stock prior to May 26, 1979, on May 26, 1979, the beginning of the second phase for F's 1969 holdings, F's permitted holdings would have been 25 percent, the lesser of 25 percent (under section 4943(c)(4)(D)(i)) or 30 percent (50% — 20%). Since the 30 percent interest would no longer have been treated as held by a disqualified person on such date, F would have had excess business holdings of 5 percent (30% — 25%).

(ii) On May 1, 1981, and June 1, 1982 (assuming F had disposed of the 6 percent holdings), the foundation voting level, the disqualified person voting level, the substituted combined voting level and permitted holdings remain respectively 24 percent, 20 percent, 44 percent and 24 percent. On May 1, 1981, the 15 percent interest is treated as held by a disqualified person for a period extending through May 31, 1992. On July 1, 1991, F sells 16 percent of the voting stock in R to a nondisqualified person, thereby reducing the substituted combined voting level to 28 percent (44% — 16%), and reducing the foundation voting level to 8 percent (24% — 16%). The disqualified person voting level remains at 20 percent. On June 1, 1992, at the beginning of the second phase for F's holdings acquired by will, the substituted combined voting level remains at 28 percent, the foundation voting level increases to 23 percent (8% + 15%) and the disqualified person voting level decreases to 5 percent (20% — 15%). The permitted holdings on such date are 23 percent (28% — 5%). If F had not disposed of the 16 percent interest prior to June 1, 1992, F's permitted holdings would have been 25 percent, the lesser of 25 percent (under section 4943(c)(4)(D)(i)) or 39 percent (44% — 5%). Since as of such date, F's entire holdings of 39 percent would no longer have been treated as held by a disqualified person, F would have had excess business holdings of 14 percent (39% — 25%).
[Table appears on page 24,258.10-Z.6 (I.R.C.)]

Example (7). On May 26, 1969, F, a private foundation, owns 5 percent of the voting stock in S Corporation (voting power and value), and disqualified persons own 45 percent. On May 1, 1980, H, a disqualified person, dies leaving 41 percent of the voting stock to F. Assume that distribution is made on June 1, 1981, and that section 4943(c)(5) applies. On May 26, 1969, the substituted combined voting level and disqualified person voting levels are each 50 percent. On May 26, 1979, the disqualified person voting level decreases to 45 percent, the foundation voting level increases to 5 percent, and the permitted holdings are 5 percent (50% — 45%). On May 1, 1980, and June 1, 1981, the levels remain the same. Since the 41 percent holdings are treated as held by a disqualified person for the period beginning on May 1, 1980, and extending through May 31, 1991, F's remaining holdings of 5 percent do not exceed the 25 percent limitation of section 4943(c)(4)(D)(i).

(ii) On August 1, 1990, F sells 22 percent of the voting stock of S to a nondisqualified person, reducing the 5 percent foundation voting level to zero, leaving 17 percent (22% — 5%) to reduce the disqualified person voting level to 28 percent (45% — 17%) so that the substituted combined voting level equals 28 percent (50% — 22%). On June 1, 1991, the beginning of the second phase for the remaining 24 percent (41% — 17%) of F's holdings acquired by will, the foundation voting level increases from zero to 24 percent, the disqualified person voting level decreases to 4 percent (28% — 24%), the substituted combined voting level remains

Date	F owns	1969 F's interest	1971 F's interest	interest treated as held by disqualified person	disqualified persons own	foundation voting level	substituted combined voting level	disqualified person voting level	permitted holdings	comments
5/26/69	5%	5%		5%	45%	0%	50%	50%	0%	
5/1/71	+4.3%		+4.3%	+4.3%	-4.3%	0%	50%	50%	0%	E dies
5/1/71	48	5%	43%	48%	2%	0%	50%	50%	0%	
6/1/72	48	5%	43%	48%	2%	0%	50%	50%	0%	distribution
5/26/79		5%	43%	-5%		+5%	50%	-5%	+5%	2nd phase for 5%
5/26/79	48	5%	43%	43%	2%	5%	50%	45%	5%	
6/1/82			43%	-4.3%		+4.3%		-4.3%	+4.3%	2nd phase for 43%
6/1/82	48	5%	43%	0%	2%	48%	50%	2%	48%	
7/1/93	-6%	-5%	-1%			-6%	-6%		-6%	F sells 6%
7/1/93	42%	0%	42%	0%	2%	42%	44%	2%	42%	
7/1/95	-10%		-10%			-10%	-10%		-10%	F sells 10%
7/1/95	32%	0%	32%	0%	2%	32%	34%	2%	32%	
6/1/97	32%	0%	32%	0%	2%	32%	34%	2%	32%	3rd phase for 32%

Reg. § 53.4943-5(c)(2)

24,258.10-Z.6 *(I.R.C.)* Reg. § 53.4943-5(c)(2) 7-18-77

Date	F owns	1969 F's interest	1981 F's interest	interest treated as held by dis-qualified person	dis-qualified persons own	founda-tion voting level	substi-tuted com-bined voting level	dis-quali-fied person voting level	per-mitted hold-ings	comments
5/26/69	30%	30%		30%	20%	0%	50%	50%	0%	
8/1/78	-6%	-6%		-6%			-6%	-6%		F disposes of 6%
8/1/78	24%	24%		24%	20%	0%	44%	44%	0%	
5/26/79	24%			-24%		+24%		-24%	+24%	2nd phase for 24%
5/26/79	24%	24%		0%	20%	24%	44%	20%	24%	
5/1/81	+15%		+15%	+15%	-15%					
5/1/81	39%	24%	15%	15%	5%	24%	44%	20%	24%	
6/1/82	39%	24%	15%	15%	5%	24%	44%	20%	24%	G dies distribution
7/1/91	-16%	-16%		-15%		-16%	-16%	-15%	-16%	F disposes of 16%
7/1/91	23%	8%	15%	15%	5%	8%	28%	20%	8%	
6/1/92				-15%		+15%		-15%	+15%	2nd phase for 15%
6/1/92	23%	8%	15%	0%	5%	23%	28%	5%	23%	

at 28 percent, and the permitted holdings equal 24 percent (28% — 4%).

(iii) If F had not disposed of the 22 percent holdings prior to June 1, 1991, F's permitted holdings would have been 25 percent, the lesser of 25 percent (under section 4943(c)(4)(D)(i)) or 46 percent (50% — 4%). Since as of such date, F's entire holdings of 46 percent would no longer have been treated as held by a disqualified person, F would have had excess business holdings of 21 percent (46% — 25%).

[Table appears on page 24,258.10-Z.8 (I.R.C.)]

○— § 53.4943-6 (TD 7496, filed 7-5-77.) **Five-year period to dispose of gifts, bequests, etc.**

(a) *In general* — (1) *Application.* (i) Paragraph (6) of section 4943(c) prescribes transition rules for a private foundation, which, but for such paragraph, would have excess business holdings as a result of a change in the holdings in a business enterprise after May 26, 1969 (other than by purchase by such private foundation or by a disqualified person) to the extent that section 4943(c)(5) (relating to certain holdings acquired under a pre-May 27, 1969, will or trust) does not apply.

(ii) Subparagraph (A) of section 4943 (c)(6) applies where, immediately prior to a change in holdings described in paragraph (a)(1)(i) of this section, the foundation has no excess business holdings in such enterprise (determined without regard to section 4943(c)(4), (5), or (6)). In such a case, the entire interest of the foundation in such enterprise (immediately after such change) shall (while held by the foundation) be treated as held by a disqualified person (rather than by the foundation) during the five-year period beginning on the date of such change.

(iii) Subparagraph (B) of section 4943 (c)(6) applies where the foundation has excess business holdings in such enterprise (determined without regard to section 4943 (c)(4), (5), or (6)) immediately prior to a change in holdings described in paragraph (a)(1)(i) of this section. In such a case, the interest of the foundation in such enterprise (immediately after such change) shall (while held by the foundation) be treated as held by a disqualified person (rather than the foundation) during the five-year period beginning on the date of such change, except that if and as soon as any holdings in such enterprise become excess business holdings during such period (determined without regard to such change (and the resulting application of section 4943 (c)(6) to the foundation's interest in such enterprise)), such holdings shall no longer be treated as held by a disqualified person under this section, but shall constitute excess business holdings subject to the initial tax. In applying the preceding sentence, if holdings of the foundation which (but for such change in holding (and the resulting application of section 4943(c)(6) to the foundation's interest in such enterprise)) would be subject to the 25 percent limit prescribed by section 4943(c)(4)(D) after the expiration of the first phase, such holdings shall be treated as subject to such percentage limitation for purposes of determining excess business holdings. For example, if a private foundation in 1978 has present holdings of 28 percent in a business enterprise to which section 4943(c)(4) applies, and such holdings would exceed the 25 percent limit of section 4943(c)(4)(D)(i) on May 26, 1979, a gift of 5 percent to the foundation in 1978 of an interest in such enterprise shall not prevent the 3 percent (28% — 25%) excess over the 25 percent limit from constituting excess business holdings on May 26, 1979, if on such date disqualified persons hold more than a 2 percent interest in such enterprise (and no other transaction has taken place).

(2) *"Purchase" defined.* [Reserved]

(3) *Examples.* The provisions of paragraph (a) of this section may be illustrated by the following examples:

Example (1). On January 4, 1985, A, an individual, makes a contribution to F, a private foundation, of 200 shares of X Corporation common stock. Assume that F had no X stock before January 4, 1985, and under section 4943(c)(1) the receipt of the X stock by F would cause some or all of the 200 shares of the X stock to be classified as excess business holdings. Under the provisions of section 4943(c)(6)(A) and this paragraph (a), since the contribution of the X stock to F is a gift and not a purchase, the X stock in F's hands is treated as held by disqualified persons and not by F through January 3, 1990.

Example (2). Assume the facts as stated in Example (1) except that F receives the X stock as a bequest pursuant to the terms of A's will executed on April 1, 1980. A dies on June 3, 1984, and the stock is distributed to F on February 16, 1985. As in Example (1), the bequest of X to F is not a purchase under this paragraph (a). Consequently, the X stock in F's hands is treated as held by disqualified persons and not by F through February 15, 1990.

Example (3). On February 1, 1980, F, a private foundation, owns 15 percent of the voting stock of X Corporation, and disqualified persons own 4 percent of the voting stock of X Corporation. On February 2, 1980, B, a nondisqualified person, contributes 8 percent of the voting stock of X to F in a transaction to which section 4943(c) (5) does not apply. Assuming that the 35 percent limit of section 4943(c)(2)(B) does not apply, under the proviisons of section 4943(c)(6)(A) and paragraph (a) of this section the 23 percent voting stock owned by F on such date is treated as held by a disqualified person through February 1, 1985, since F would have had excess business holdings of 7 percent as a result of the contribution (23% actual holdings less 16% (20% — 4%) permitted holdings). On March 1, 1984, C, another nondisqualified person, contributes 6 percent of the voting stock of X Corporation to F. But for this second contribution and the resulting application of section 4943(c)(6) to F's interest in X, F would have excess business holdings of 7 percent (23% — 16%) within the five-year period beginning on the date of such contribution. Accordingly, under section 4943 (c)(6)(B) and paragraph (a) of this section, all 29 percent (6% + 23%) of the stock held by F on March 1, 1984, will be treated as held by a disqualified person until March 1, 1989, except that 7 percent will cease to be so treated on February 2, 1985. If prior to February 2, 1985, no further transactions occurred in the stock of X, F would have excess business holdings of 7 percent sub-

Reg. § 53.4943-6(a)(3)

24,258.10-Z.8 (I.R.C.) Reg. § 53.4943-5(c)(2)   7-18-77

Date	F owns	1969 F's interest	1980 F's interest	interest treated as held by disqualified person	disqualified persons own	foundation voting level	substituted combined voting level	disqualified person voting level	permitted holdings	comments
5/26/69	5%	5%		5%	45%	0%	50%	50%	0%	
5/26/79	5%	5%		-5%		+5%		-5%	+5%	2nd phase for 5%
5/26/79	5%	5%		0%	45%	5%	50%	45%	5%	
5/1/80	+41%		+41%	+41%	-41%					
5/1/80	46%	5%	41%	41%	4%	5%	50%	45%	5%	H dies
6/1/81	46%	5%	41%	41%	4%	5%	50%	45%	5%	
8/1/90	-22%	-5%	-17%	-17%		-5%	-22%	-17%	-5%	distribution
8/1/90	24%	0%	24%	24%	4%	0%	28%	28%	0%	F disposes of 22%
6/1/91				-24%		+24%		-24%	+24%	2nd phase for 24%
6/1/91	24%	0%	24%	0%	4%	24%	28%	4%	24%	

ject to the initial tax, since the amount still treated as held by disqualified persons (29% − 7%) plus the amount actually held by disqualified persons (4%) already exceed 20 percent.

Example (4). [Reserved]

(b) *Special rules for acquisitions by will or trust*—(1) *In general.* In the case of an acquisition of holdings in a business enterprise by a private foundation pursuant to the terms of a will or trust, the five-year period described in section 4943(c)(6) in this section shall not commence until the date on which the distribution of such holdings from the estate or trust to the foundation occurs. See § 53.4943-5(b)(1) for rules relating to the determination of the date of distribution under the terms of a will or trust. To the extent that an interest to which 4943(c)(6) applies is constructively held by a private foundation under section 4943(d)(1) and § 53.4943-8 prior to the date of distribution, it shall be treated as held by a disqualified person prior to such date by reason of section 4943(c)(6). See § 53.-4943-8 for rules relating to constructive ownership by a private foundation of business holdings held in an estate or trust for the benefit of the foundation.

(2) *Special rule for section 4943(c)(5) interests acquired from a nondisqualified person.* (i) In the case of holdings of a private foundation in a business enterprise to which section 4943(c)(5) (relating to certain holdings acquired under a pre-May 27, 1969, will or trust) applies which are acquired from a nondisqualified person, the interest of the foundation in such enterprise (immediately after such acquisition) shall (while held by the foundation) be treated as held by a disqualified person (rather than the foundation) under section 4943(c)(6)(B) and paragraph (a)(1)(iii) of this section from the date of acquisition until the end of the fifth year following the date of distribution of such holdings. Thereafter, only the holdings to which section 4943(c)(5) and § 53.4943-5(a)(1) apply shall continue to be treated as held by a disqualified person until the end of the first phase with respect thereto.

(ii) The provisions of paragraph (b)(2)(i) of this section may be illustrated by the following examples:

Example (1). On May 26, 1969, F, a private foundation, owns 5 percent of the voting stock of Corporation X and no disqualified persons own any stock in X. On June 30, 1977, a nondisqualified person bequeaths to F 33 percent of the voting stock in X to which section 4943(c)(5) applies. This 33 percent interest is distributed to F on August 17, 1978. Under section 4943(c)(6)(A) the entire 38 percent (5% + 33%) of the X voting stock shall be treated as held by a disqualified person from June 30, 1977 (the date the 33 percent interest is constructively acquired by F) until August 17, 1983 (five years after the date of distribution of the 33 percent interest to F). However, assuming that the 35 percent limit of section 4943(c)(2)(B) does not apply, the substituted combined voting level on June 30, 1977 is only 33 percent because there was no interest to which section 4943(c)(4) or (5) applied immediately before that date and thus there was no substituted combined voting level at that time. In that case, since the 3-phase holding period is only available for the interest acquired by will (33%) under section 4943(c)(5), the substituted combined voting level on June 30, 1977 is only 33 percent, not 38 percent. Assuming that the substituted combined voting level remains 33 percent at all relevant times, and prior to August 17, 1983, no further transactions occur in the stock of X, F on that date would have excess business holdings of 5 percent subject to the initial tax. The amount treated as held by disqualified persons at that time (33%) would equal the substituted combined voting level at that time (33%), and thus permitted holdings would be zero. Under section 4943(c)(5) the 33 percent interest will continue to be treated as held by a disqualified person until August 17, 1988 (10 years after the date of distribution).

Example (2). On May 26, 1969, F, a private foundation, owns 29 percent of the stock (voting power and value) of Corporation X, and on June 30, 1977, a nondisqualified person bequeaths to F 23 percent of the stock (voting power and value) in X to which section 4943(c)(5) does apply. This 23 percent interest is distributed to F on August 17, 1978. Disqualified persons hold no stock of X. Although the substituted combined voting and value levels cannot exceed 50 percent on May 26, 1979 (at the start of the second phase with respect to the 29 percent interest), under section 4943(c)(6)(B) the entire 52 percent (29% + 23%) of the X voting stock shall be treated as held by a disqualified person from June 30, 1977 (the date the 23% interest is constructively acquired by F) until August 17, 1983 (five years after the date of distribution of the 23% interest to F). On June 1, 1980, during such second phase, D, a disqualified person, purchases 3 percent of the X stock (voting power and value). On such date, but for the acquisition by F of the 23 percent interest, F would have had excess business holdings of 4 percent. The purchase by D of more than 2 percent of the voting stock of X causes the 25 percent limit of section 4943(c)(4)(D)(i) to apply to the 29 percent interest (29% − 25% = 4%). Thus, on June 1, 1980, 4 percent of the X voting stock held by F since May 27, 1969, shall cease to be treated as held by a disqualified person under section 4943(c)(6)(B) and become excess business holdings subject to the initial tax. See § 53.4943-2(a)(1)(ii) for the 90-day period in which to dispose of these excess business holdings resulting from the purchase by the disqualified person.

(c) *Exceptions.* (1) Section 4943(c)(6) and this section shall not apply to any transfer of holdings in a business enterprise by one private foundation to another private foundation which is related to the first foundation within the meaning of section 4946(a)(1)(H).

(2) Section 4943(c)(6) and this section shall not apply to an increase in the holdings of a private foundation in a business enterprise that is part of a plan whereby disqualified persons will purchase additional holdings in the same enterprise during the five-year period beginning on the date of such change, *e.g.*, to maintain control of such enterprise, since such increase shall be treated as caused in part by the purchase of such additional holdings.

(3) The purchase of holdings by an entity whose holdings are treated as construc-

tively owned by a foundation or a disqualified person under section 4943(d)(1) shall be treated as purchased by such foundation or disqualified person. Thus, if a foundation receives a specific bequest of 40 percent of the voting stock of a corporation and $20,000 in cash, and the estate uses the cash to purchase additional voting stock of the same corporation, the provisions of this section shall only apply to the 40 percent originally held by the estate, and the additional stock will be treated as if purchased by the foundation.

○━━ § 53.4943-7 (TD 7496, filed 7-5-77.) **Special rules for corporate organizations, reorganizations, redemptions, and distributions.**

[Reserved]

○━━ § 53.4943-8 (TD 7496, filed 7-5-77.) **Business holdings; constructive ownership.**

(a) *Constructive ownership*—(1) *In general.* For purposes of section 4943, in computing the holdings in a business enterprise of a private foundation, or a disqualified person (as defined in section 4946), any stock or other interest owned, directly or indirectly, by or for a corporation, partnership, estate or trust shall be considered as being owned proportionately by or for its shareholders, partners, or beneficiaries except as otherwise provided in paragraphs (b), (c) and (d) of this section. Any interest in a business enterprise actually or constructively owned by a shareholder of a corporation, a partner of a partnership, or a beneficiary of an estate or trust shall not be considered as constructively held by the corporation, partnership, trust or estate. Further, if any corporation, partnership, estate or trust has a warrant or other option to acquire an interest in a business enterprise, such interest is not deemed to be constructively owned by such entity until the option is exercised. (See paragraph (b)(2) of § 53.4943-3 for rules that options are not stock for purposes of determining excess business holdings.)

(2) *Powers of appointment.* Any interest in a business enterprise over which a foundation or a disqualified person has a power of appointment exercisable in favor of the foundation or a disqualified person shall be considered owned by the foundation or disqualified person holding such power of appointment.

(b) *Estates and trusts*—(1) *In general.* Any interest actually or constructively owned by an estate or trust is deemed constructively owned, in the case of an estate, by its beneficiaries or, in the case of a trust, by its remainder beneficiaries except as provided in paragraphs (b)(2), (3) and (4) of this section (relating to certain split-interest trusts described in section 4947(a)(2), to trusts of qualified pension, profit-sharing, and stock bonus plans described in section 401(a) and to revocable trusts). Thus, if a trust owns 100 percent of the stock of a corporation A, and if, on an actuarial basis, W's life interest in the trust is 15 percent, Y's life interest is 25 percent, and Z's remainder interest is 60 percent, under this paragraph (b), Z will be considered to be the owner of 100 percent of the stock of corporation A. See § 53.4943-4, § 53.4943-5 and § 53.4943-6 for rules relating to certain actual or constructive holdings of a foundation being treated as held by a disqualified person. For the treatment of certain property acquired by an estate or trust after May 26, 1969, see paragraph (a)(2) of § 53.4943-5.

(2) *Split-interest trusts*—(i) *Amounts transferred in trust after May 26, 1969.* In the case of an interest in a business enterprise which was transferred to a trust described in section 4947(a)(2) after May 26, 1969, for the benefit of a private foundation, no portion of such interest shall be considered as owned by the private foundation—

(A) If the foundation holds only an income interest in the trust, or

(B) If the foundation holds only a remainder interest in the trust (unless the foundation can exercise primary investment discretion with respect to such interest)

until such trust ceases to be so described. See section 4947(a)(2) and (b)(3) and the regulations thereunder for rules relating to such trusts. See also sections 4946(a)(1)(G) and (H) and the regulations thereunder for rules relating to when a trust described in this paragraph (b)(2) is itself a disqualified person.

(ii) *Amounts transferred in trust on or before May 26, 1969.* In the case of an interest in a business enterprise which was transferred to a trust described in section 4947(a)(2) (without regard to section 4947(a)(2)(C)) on or before May 26, 1969, for the benefit of a private foundation, no portion of such interest shall be considered as owned by the foundation until it is actually distributed to the foundation or until the trust ceases to be so described. See section 4943(c)(5) and § 53.4943-5 for rules relating to certain trusts which were irrevocable on May 26, 1969.

(3) *Employee benefit trusts.* An interest in a business enterprise owned by a trust described in section 401(a) (pension and profit-sharing plans) shall not be considered as owned by its beneficiaries, unless disqualified persons (within the meaning of section 4946) control the investment of the trust assets.

(4) *Revocable trusts.* An interest in a business enterprise owned by a revocable trust shall be treated as owned by the grantor of such trust.

(5) *Estates.* For purposes of applying section 4943(d)(1) to estates, the term "beneficiary" includes any person (including a private foundation) entitled to receive property of a decedent pursuant to a will or pursuant to laws of descent and distribution. However, a person shall no longer be considered a beneficiary of an estate when all the property to which he is entitled has been received by him, when he no longr has a claim against the estate and when there is only a remote possibility that it will be necessary for the estate to seek the return of property or to seek payment from him by contribution or otherwise to satisfy claims against the estate or expenses of administration. When pursuant to the preceding sentence, a person (including a private foundation) ceases to be a beneficiary, stock or another interest in a business enterprise owned by the estate shall not thereafter be considered owned by such person. If any person is the constructive owner of an interest in an business enter-

prise actually held by an estate, the date of death of the testator or decedent intestate shall be the first day on which such person shall be considered a constructive owner of such interest. See § 53.4943-5 for rules relating to wills executed on or before May 26, 1969.

(c) *Corporation actively engaged in a trade or business.* [Reserved]

(d) *Partnerships.* [Reserved]

(e) *Examples.* [Reserved]

§ 53.4943-9 (TD 7496, filed 7-5-77.) **Business holdings; certain periods.**

(a) *Taxable period*—(1) *In general.* For purposes of section 4943, the term "taxable period" means, with respect to any excess business holdings of a private foundation in a business enterprise, the period beginning with the first day on which there are such excess business holdings and ending on whichever of the following is the earlier:

(i) The date of mailing of a notice of deficiency under section 6212 with respect to the tax imposed on such holdings by section 4943(a); or

(ii) The date on which such excess is eliminated.

For example, M, a private foundation, first has excess business holdings in X, a corporation, on February 5, 1972. A notice of deficiency is mailed under section 6212 to M on June 1, 1974. With respect to M's excess business holdings in X, the taxable period begins on February 5, 1972, and ends on June 1, 1974.

(2) *Special rule.* Where a notice of deficiency referred to in subparagraph (1) (i) of this paragraph is not mailed because there is a waiver of the restrictions on assessment and collection of a deficiency, or because the deficiency is paid, the date of filing of the waiver or the date of such payment, respectively, shall be treated as the end of the taxable period.

(3) *Suspension of taxable period for 90 days.* In any case in which a private foundation has excess business holdings solely because of the acquisition of an interest in a business enterprise to which paragraph (a)(1)(ii) or (iii) of § 53.4943-2 applies, the taxable period described in paragraph (a) of this section shall be suspended for the 90-day period (as extended) starting with the date on which the foundation knows or has reason to know of the acquisition, provided that at the end of such period the foundation has disposed of such excess holdings.

(b) *Correction period*—(1) *In general.* For purposes of section 4943, the correction period shall begin with the first day on which the private foundation has excess business holdings in a business enterprise and end 90 days after the date of mailing of a notice of deficiency under section 6212 with respect to the tax imposed by section 4943(b).

(2) *Extensions of correction period.* (i) The correction period referred to in subparagraph (1) of this paragraph shall be extended by any period in which a deficiency cannot be assessed under section 6213(a). In addition, the correction period shall be extended in accordance with subdivisions (ii), (iii), and (iv) of this subparagraph, except that such subdivision (iii) or (iv) shall not operate to extend a correction period with respect to which a taxpayer has filed a petition with the Tax Court for redetermination of a deficiency within the time prescribed by section 6213(a).

(ii) The correction period referred to in subparagraph (1) of this paragraph may be extended by any period which the Commissioner determines is reasonable and necessary to permit orderly disposition of excess business holdings. The Commissioner ordinarily will not extend the correction period pursuant to this subdivision unless the following factors are present:

(a) The foundation or an appropriate State officer (as defined in section 6104(c) (2)) is actively in good faith seeking to dispose of such holdings;

(b) Orderly disposition of such holdings cannot reasonably be expected to result during the unextended correction period; and

(c) The failure to divest appears to have been an isolated occurrence which is unlikely to recur in the future.

(iii) If, within the unextended correction period, the tax imposed by section 4943(a) is paid and is accompanied by a statement of the taxpayer's intent to file a claim for refund with respect to such tax, then the Commissioner shall extend the correction period to the later of—

(a) A period of 90 days after the payment of such tax, or

(b) The period determined without regard to this subdivision.

(iv) If prior to the expiration of the correction period (including extensions) a claim for refund with respect to a tax imposed by section 4943(a) is filed, the Commissioner shall extend the correction period during the pendency of the claim plus an additional 90 days. If within such time, a suit or proceeding referred to in section 7422(b) with respect to such claim is filed, the Commissioner shall extend the correction period during the pendency of such suit or proceeding. (See § 301.7422-1(d) of this chapter (Regulations on Procedure and Administration) for rules relating to pendency of such suit or proceeding).

(c) *Correction.* For purposes of section 4943, correction shall be considered as made when no interest in the enterprise held by the foundation is classified as an excess business holding under section 4943 (c) (1). In any case where the private foundation has excess business holdings which are constructively held for it under section 4943 (c) (1), correction shall be considered made when either a corporation, partnership, estate, or trust in which holdings in such enterprise are constructively held for the foundation or a disqualified person; the foundation itself; or a disqualified person disposes of a sufficient interest in the enterprise held by the foundation is classified as excess business holdings under section 4943 (c) (1).

§ 53.4943-10 TD 7496, filed 7-5-77.) **Business enterprise; definition.**

(a) *In general.* (1) Except as provided in paragraph (b) or (c) of this section, under section 4943(d)(4) the term "business enterprise" includes the active conduct of a trade or business, including any activity

Reg. § 4943-10(a)(1)

24,258.10-Z.12 *(I.R.C.)* Reg. § 53.4943-10(a)(1) 7-18-77

which is regularly carried on for the production of income from the sale of goods or the performance of services and which constitutes an related trade or business under section 513. For purposes of the preceding sentence, where an activity carried on for profit constitutes an unrelated trade or business, no part of such trade or business shall be excluded from the classification of a business enterprise merely because it does not result in a profit.

(2) Notwithstanding paragraph (a)(1) of this section, a bond or other evidence of indebtedness does not constitute a holding in a business enterprise unless such bond or evidence of indebtedness is otherwise determined to be an equitable interest in such enterprise. Similarly, a leasehold interest in real property does not constitute an interest in a business enterprise, even though rent payable under such lease is dependent, in whole or in part, upon the income or profits derived by another from such property, unless such leasehold interest constitutes an interest in the income or profits of an unrelated trade or business under section 513.

(b) *Certain program-related activities.* For purposes of section 4943(d)(4) the term "business enterprise" does not include a functionally related business as defined in section 4942(j)(5). See § 53.4942(a)-2(c)(3)(iii). In addition, business holdings do not include program-related investments (such as investments in small businesses in central cities or in corporations to assist in neighborhood renovation) as defined in section 4944(c) and the regulations thereunder.

(c) *Income derived from passive sources* —(1) *In general.* For purposes of section 4943(d)(4), the term "business enterprise" does not include a trade or business at least 95 percent of the gross income of which is derived from passive sources; except that if in the taxable year in question less than 95 percent of the income of a trade or business is from passive sources, the foundation may, in applying this 95 percent test, substitute for the passive source gross income in such taxable year the average gross income from passive sources for the 10 taxable years immediately preceding the taxable year in question (or for such shorter period as the entity has been in existence). Thus, stock in a passive holding company is not to be considered a holding in a business enterprise even if the company is controlled by the foundation. Instead, the foundation is treated as owning its proportionate share of any interests in a business enterprise held by such company under section 4943(d)(1).

(2) *Gross income from passive sources.* Gross income from passive sources, for purposes of this paragraph, includes the items excluded by sections 512(b)(1) (relating to dividends, interest, and annuities), 512(b)(2) (relating to royalties), 512(b)(3) (relating to rent) and 512(b)(5) (relating to gains or losses from the disposition of certain property). Any income classified as passive under this paragraph does not lose its character merely because section 512(b)(4) or 514 (relating to unrelated debt-financed income) applies to such income. In addition, income from passive sources includes income from the sale of goods (including charges or costs passed on at cost to purchasers of such goods or income received in settlement of a dispute concerning or in lieu of the exercise of the right to sell such goods) if the seller does not manufacture, produce, physically receive or deliver, negotiate sales of, or maintain inventories in such goods. Thus, for example, where a corporation purchases a product under a contract with the manufacturer, resells it under contract at a uniform markup in price, and does not physically handle the product, the income derived from that markup meets the definition of passive income for purposes of this paragraph. On the other hand, income from individually negotiated sales, such as those made by a broker, would not meet such definition even if the broker did not physically handle the goods.

(d) *Application of section 4943(c)(6)*— (1) *Program related activities.* If a private foundation holds an interest which is not an interest in a business enterprise because of paragraph (b) of this section (relating to program related activities), and such interest later becomes an interest in a business enterprise solely by reason of failing to meet the requirements of such paragraph (b), such interest will then be subject to section 4943(c)(6) (regardless of when it was originally acquired) and will be treated as having been acquired other than by purchase for purposes of section 4943(c)(6).

(2) *Holding companies.* [Reserved]

○━ § 53.4943-11 (TD 7496, filed 7-5-77.) Effective date.

(a) *In general.* Section 4943 and §§ 53.-4943-1 through 53.4943-11 shall take effect for taxable years beginning after December 31, 1969, except as otherwise provided by such sections.

(b) *Special transitional rule.* In the case of any acquisition of excess holdings prior to February 2, 1973, section 4943(a)(1) shall not apply if correction occurs (within the meaning of paragraph (c) of § 53.4943-9) within a period ending 90 days after July 5, 1977, extended (prior to the expiration of the original period) by any period which the Commissioner determines is reasonable and necessary (within the meaning of paragraph (b) of § 53.4943-9) to bring about such correction.

SUBPART E—TAXES ON INVESTMENTS WHICH JEOPARDIZE CHARITABLE PURPOSE

§ 53.4944. Statutory provisions; private foundations; taxes on investments which jeopardize charitable purpose. [Sec. 4944, IRC]

§ 53.4944-1 (T.D. 7240, filed 12-28-72; amended by T.D. 7299, filed 12-26-73.) Initial taxes.

(a) *On the private foundation*—(1) *In general.* If a private foundation (as defined in section 509) invests any amount in such a manner as to jeopardize the carrying out of any of its exempt purposes, section 4944 (a)(1) of the Code imposes an excise tax on the making of such investment. This tax is to be paid by the private foundation and is at the rate of 5 percent of the amount so invested for each taxable year (or part thereof) in the taxable period (as defined in section 4944(e)(1). The tax imposed by section 4944(a)(1) and this paragraph shall apply to investments of either income or principal.

(2) *Jeopardizing investments.* (i) Except as provided in section 4944(c), § 53,4944-3, § 53.4944-6(a), and subdivision (ii) of this subparagraph, an investment shall be considered to jeopardize the carrying out of the exempt purposes of a private foundation if it is determined that the foundation managers, in making such investment, have failed to exercise ordinary business care and prudence, under the facts and circumstances prevailing at the time of making the investment, in providing for the long- and short-term financial needs of the foundation to carry out its exempt purposes. In the exercise of the requisite standard of care and prudence the foundation managers may take into account the expected return (including both income and appreciation of capital), the risks of rising and falling price levels, and the need for diversification within the investment portfolio (for example, with respect to type of security, type of industry, maturity of company, degree of risk and potential for return). The determination whether the investment of a particular amount jeopardizes the carrying out of the exempt purposes of a foundation shall be made on an investment by investment basis, in each case taking into account the foundation's portfolio as a whole. No category of investments shall be treated as a *per se* violation of section 4944. However, the following are examples of types or methods of investment which will be closely scrutinized to determine whether the foundation managers have met the requisite standard of care and prudence: Trading in securities on margin, trading in commodity futures, investments in working interests in oil and gas wells, the purchase of "puts" and "calls", and "straddles," the purchase of warrants, and selling short. The determination whether the investment of any amount jeopardizes the carrying out of a foundation's exempt purposes is to be made as of the time that the foundation makes the investment and not subsequently on the basis of hindsight. Therefore, once it has been ascertained that an investment does not jeopardize the carrying out of a foundation's exempt purposes, the investment shall never be considered to jeopardize the carrying out of such purposes, even though as a result of such investment, the foundation subsequently realizes a loss. The provisions of section 4944 and the regulations thereunder shall not exempt or relieve any person from compliance with any Federal or State law imposing any obligation, duty, responsibility, or other standard of conduct with respect to the operation or administration of an organization or trust to which section 4944 applies. Nor shall any State law exempt or relieve any person from any obligation, duty, responsibility, or other standard of conduct provided in section 4944 and the regulations thereunder.

(ii) *(a)* Section 4944 shall not apply to an investment made by any person which is later gratuitously transferred to a private foundation. If such foundation furnishes any consideration to such person upon the transfer, the foundation will be treated as having made an investment (within the meaning of section 4944(a)(1)) in the amount of such consideration.

(b) Section 4944 shall not apply to an investment which is acquired by a private foundation solely as a result of a corporate reorganization within the meaning of section 368(a).

(iii) For purposes of section 4944, a private foundation which, after December 31, 1969, changes the form or terms of an investment (regardless of whether subdivision (ii) of this subparagraph applies to such investment), will be considered to have entered into a new investment on the date of such change, except as provided in subdivision (ii) *(b)* of this subparagraph. Accordingly, a determination, under subdivision (i) of this subparagraph, whether such change in the investment jeopardizes the carrying out of the foundation's exempt purposes shall be made at such time.

(iv) It is not intended that the taxes imposed under chapter 42 be exclusive. For example, if a foundation purchases a sole proprietorship in a business enterprise within the meaning of section 4943(d)(4), in addition to tax under section 4943, the foundation may be liable for tax under section 4944 if the investment jeopardizes the carrying out of any of its exempt purposes.

(b) *On the management*—(1) *In general.* In any case in which a tax is imposed by section 4944(a)(1) and paragraph (a) of this section, section 4944(a)(2) of the Code imposes on the participation of any foundation manager in the making of the investment, knowing that it is jeopardizing the carrying out of any of the foundation's exempt purposes, a tax equal to 5 percent of the amount so invested for each taxable year of the foundation (or part thereof) in the taxable period (as defined in section 4944(e)(1)), subject to the provisions of section 4944(d) and § 53.4944-4, unless such participation is not willful and is due to reasonable cause. The tax imposed under section 4944(a)(2) shall be paid by the foundation manager.

(2) *Definitions and special rules*—(i) *Knowing.* For purposes of section 4944, a

foundation manager shall be considered to have participated in the making of an investment "knowing" that it is jeopardizing the carrying out of any of the foundation's exempt purposes only if—

(a) He has actual knowledge of sufficient facts so that, based solely upon such facts, such investment would be a jeopardizing investment under paragraph (a)(2) of this section,

(b) He is aware that such an investment under these circumstances may violate the provisions of federal tax law governing jeopardizing investments, and

(c) He negligently fails to make reasonable attempts to ascertain whether the investment is a jeopardizing investment, or he is in fact aware that it is such an investment.

For purposes of this part and chapter 42, the term "knowing" does not mean "having reason to know". However, evidence tending to show that a foundation manager has reason to know of a particular fact or particular rule is relevant in determining whether he had actual knowledge of such fact or rule. Thus, for example, evidence tending to show that a foundation manager has reason to know of sufficient facts so that, based solely upon such facts, an investment would be a jeopardizing investment is relevant in determining whether he has actual knowledge of such facts.

(ii) *Willful.* A foundation manager's participation in a jeopardizing investment is willful if it is voluntary, conscious, and intentional. No motive to avoid the restrictions of the law or the incurrence of any tax is necessary to make such participation willful. However, a foundation manager's participation in a jeopardizing investment is not willful if he does not know that it is a jeopardizing investment under paragraph (a)(2) of this section.

(iii) *Due to reasonable cause.* A foundation manager's actions are due to reasonable cause if he has exercised his responsibility on behalf of the foundation with ordinary business care and prudence.

(iv) *Participation.* The participation of any foundation manager in the making of an investment shall consist of any manifestation of approval of the investment.

(v) *Advice of counsel.* If a foundation manager, after full disclosure of the factual situation to legal counsel (including house counsel), relies on the advice of such counsel expressed in a reasoned written legal opinion that a particular investment would not jeopardize the carrying out of any of the foundation's exempt purposes (because, as a matter of law, the investment is excepted from such classification, for example, as a program-related investment under section 4944(c)), then although such investment is subsequently held to be a jeopardizing investment under paragraph (a)(2) of this section, the foundation manager's participation in such investment will ordinarily not be considered "knowing" or "willful" and will ordinarily be considered "due to reasonable cause" within the meaning of section 4944(a)(2). In addition, if a foundation manager, after full disclosure of the factual situation to qualified investment counsel, relies on the advice of such counsel, such advice being derived in a manner consistent with generally accepted practices of persons who are such a qualified investment counsel and being expressed in writing that a particular investment will provide for the long- and short-term financial needs of the foundation under paragraph (a)(2) of this section, then although such investment is subsequently held not to provide for such long- and short-term financial needs, the foundation manager's participation in failing to provide for such long- and short-term financial needs will ordinarily not be considered "knowing" or "willful" and will ordinarily be considered "due to reasonable cause" within the meaning of section 4944(a)(2). For purposes of this subdivision, a written legal opinion will be considered "reasoned" even if it reaches a conclusion which is subsequently determined to be incorrect so long as such opinion addresses itself to the facts and applicable law. However, a written legal opinion will not be considered "reasoned" if it does nothing more than recite the facts and express a conclusion. However, the absence of advice of legal counsel or qualified investment counsel with respect to the investment shall not, by itself, give rise to any inference that a foundation manager participated in such investment knowingly, willfully, or without reasonable cause.

(vi) *Cross reference.* For provisions relating to the burden of proof in cases involving the issue whether a foundation manager has knowingly participated in the making of a jeopardizing investment, see section 7454(b).

(c) *Examples.* The provisions of this section may be illustrated by the following examples:

Example (1). A is a foundation manager of B, a private foundation with assets of $100,000. A approves the following three investments by B after taking into account with respect to each of them B's portfolio as a whole: (1) An investment of $5,000 in the common stock of corporation X; (2) an investment of $10,000 in the common stock of corporation Y; and (3) an investment of $8,000 in the common stock of corporation Z. Corporation X has been in business a considerable time, its record of earnings is good and there is no reason to anticipate a diminution of its earnings. Corporation Y has a promising product, has had earnings in some years and substantial losses in others, has never paid a dividend, and is widely reported in investment advisory services as seriously undercapitalized. Corporation Z has been in business a short period of time and manufactures a product that is new, is not sold by others, and must compete with a well-established alternative product that serves the same purpose. Z's stock is classified as a high-risk investment by most investment advisory services with the possibility of substantial long-term appreciation but with little prospect of a current return. A has studied the records of the three corporations and knows the foregoing facts. In each case the price per share of common stock purchased by B is favorable to B. Under the standards of paragraph (a)(2)(i) of this section, the investment of $10,000 in the common stock of Y and the investment of $8,000 in the common stock of Z may be classified as jeopardizing investments, while the investment of $5,000 in the common stock of X will not be so classified. B would then be liable for an initial tax of $500 (i.e., 5 percent of $10,000) for each year (or part thereof) in the taxable period for the investment in Y, and an initial tax of $400 (i.e., 5 percent of $8,000) for each year (or part thereof) in the taxable period for the investment in Z. Further, A had actual knowledge that the investments in the common stock of Y and Z were jeopardizing investments and would be, therefore, liable for the same amount of initial taxes as B.

Example (2). Assume the facts as stated in Example (1), except that: (1) in the case of corporation Y, B's investment will be made for new stock to be issued by Y and there is reason to anticipate that B's investment, together with investments required by B to be made concurrently with its own, will satisfy the capital needs of corporation Y and will thereby overcome the difficulties that have resulted in Y's uneven earnings record; and (2) in the case of corporation Z, the management has a demonstrated capacity for getting new businesses started successfully and Z has received substantial orders for its new product. Under the standards of paragraph (a)(2)(i) of this section, neither the investment in Y nor the investment in Z will be classified as a jeopardizing investment and neither A nor B will be liable for an initial tax on either of such investments.

Example (3). D is a foundation manager of E, a private foundation with assets of $200,000. D was hired by E to manage E's investments after a careful review of D's training, experience and record in the field of investment management and advice indicated to E that D was well qualified to provide professional investment advice in the management of E's investment assets. D, after careful research into how best to diversify E's investments, provide for E's long-term financial needs, and protect against the effects of long-term inflation, decides to allocate a portion of E's investment assets to unimproved real estate in selected areas of the country where population patterns and economic factors strongly indicate continuing growth at a rapid rate. D determines that the short-term financial needs of E can be met through E's other investments. Under the standards of paragraph (a)(2)(i) of this section, the investment of a portion of E's investment assets in unimproved real estate will not be classified as a jeopardizing investment and neither D nor E will be liable for an initial tax on such investment.

§ 53.4944-2 (T.D. 7240, filed 12-28-72.) Additional taxes.

(a) *On the private foundation.* Section 4944(b)(1) of the Code imposes an excise tax in any case in which an initial tax is imposed by section 4944(a)(1) and § 53.4944-1(a) on the making of a jeopardizing investment by a private foundation and such investment is not removed from jeopardy within the correction period (as defined in section 4944(e)(3)). The tax imposed under section 4944(b)(1) is to be paid by the private foundation and is at the rate of 25 percent of the amount of the investment. This tax shall be imposed upon the portion of the investment which has not been removed from jeopardy within the correction period.

(b) *On the management.* Section 4944(b)(2) of the Code imposes an excise tax in any case in which an additional tax is imposed by section 4944(b)(1) and paragraph (a) of this section and a foundation manager has refused to agree to part or all of the removal of the investment from jeopardy. The tax imposed under section 4944(b)(2) is at the rate of 5 percent of the amount of the investment, subject to the provisions of section 4944(d) and § 53.4944-4. This tax is to be paid by any foundation manager who has refused to agree to the removal of part or all of the investment from jeopardy, and shall be imposed upon the portion of the investment which has not been removed from jeopardy within the correction period.

(c) *Examples.* The provisions of this section may be illustrated by the following examples:

Reg. § 53.4944-2(c)

Example (1). X is a foundation manager of Y, a private foundation. On the advice of X, Y invests $5,000 in the common stock of corporation M. Assume that both X and Y are liable for the taxes imposed by section 4944(a) on the making of the investment. Assume further that no part of the investment is removed from jeopardy within the correction period and that X refused to agree to such removal. Y will be liable for an additional tax of $1,250 (i.e., $5,000 × 25%). X will be liable for an additional tax of $250 (i.e., $5,000 × 5%).

Example (2). Assume the facts as stated in Example (1), except that X is not liable for the tax imposed by section 4944(a)(2) for his participation in the making of the investment, because such participation was not willfull and was due to reasonable cause. X will nonetheless be liable for the tax of $250 imposed by section 4944(b)(2) since an additional tax has been imposed upon Y and since X refused to agree to the removal of the investment from jeopardy.

Example (3). Assume the facts as stated in Example (1), except that Y removes $2,000 of the investment from jeopardy within the correction period, with X refusing to agree to the removal from jeopardy of the remaining $3,000 of such investment. Y will be liable for an additional tax of $750, imposed upon the portion of the investment which has not been removed from jeopardy within the correction period (i.e., $3,000 × 25%). Further, X will be liable for an additional tax of $150, also imposed upon the same portion of the investment (i.e., $3,000 × 5%).

○→ § 53.4944-3 (T.D. 7240, filed 12-28-72.) **Exception for program-related investments.**

(a) *In general.* (1) For purposes of section 4944 and §§ 53.4944-1 through 53.4944-6, a "program-related investment" shall not be classified as an investment which jeopardizes the carrying out of the exempt purposes of a private foundation. A "program-related investment" is an investment which possesses the following characteristics:

(i) The primary purpose of the investment is to accomplish one or more of the purposes described in section 170(c)(2)(B);

(ii) No significant purpose of the investment is the production of income or the appreciation of property; and

(iii) No purpose of the investment is to accomplish one or more of the purposes described in section 170(c)(2)(D).

(2) (i) An investment shall be considered as made primarily to accomplish one or more of the purposes described in section 170(c)(2)(B) if it significantly furthers the accomplishment of the private foundation's exempt activities and if the investment would not have been made but for such relationship between the investment and the accomplishment of the foundation's exempt activities. For purposes of section 944 and §§ 53.4944-1 through 53.4944-6, the term "purposes described in section 170(c)(2)(B)" shall be treated as including purposes described in section 170(c)(2)(B) whether or not carried out by organizations described in section 170(c).

(ii) In investment in an activity described in section 4942(j)(5)(B) and the regulations thereunder shall be considered, for purposes of this paragraph, as made primarily to accomplish one or more of the purposes described in section 170(c)(2)(B).

(iii) In determining whether a significant purpose of an investment is the production of income or the appreciation of property, it shall be relevant whether investors solely engaged in the investment for profit would be likely to make the investment on the same terms as the private foundation. However, the facts that an investment produces income or capital appreciation shall not, in the absence of other factors, be conclusive evidence of a significant purpose involving the production of income or the appreciation of property.

(iv) An investment shall not be considered as made to accomplish one or more of the purposes described in section 170(c)(2)(D) if the recipient of the investment appears before, or communicates to, any legislative body with respect to legislation or proposed legislation of direct interest to such recipient, provided that the expense of engaging in such activities would qualify as a deduction under section 162.

(3)(i) Once it has been determined that an investment is "program-related" it shall not cease to qualify as a "program-related investment" provided that changes, if any, in the form or terms of the investment are made primarily for exempt purposes and not for any significant purpose involving the production of income or the appreciation of property. A change made in the form or terms of a program-related investment for the prudent protection of the foundation's investment shall not ordinarily cause the investment to cease to qualify as program-related. Under certain conditions, a program-related investment may cease to be program-related because of a critical change in circumstances, as, for example, where it is serving an illegal purpose or the private purpose of the foundation or its managers. For purposes of the preceding sentence, an investment which ceases to be program-related because of a critical change in circumstances shall in no event subject the foundation making the investment to the tax imposed by section 4944(a)(1) before the thirtieth day after the date on which such foundation (or any of its managers) has actual knowledge of such critical change in circumstances.

(ii) If a private foundation changes the form or terms of an investment, and if, as a result of the application of subdivision (i) of this subparagraph, such investment no longer qualifies as program-related, the determination whether the investment jeopardizes the carrying out of exempt purposes shall be made pursuant to the provisions of § 53.4944-1(a)(2).

(b) *Examples.* The provisions of this section may be illustrated by the following examples:

Example (1). X is a small business enterprise located in a deteriorated urban area and owned by members of an economically disadvantaged minority group. Conventional sources of funds are unwilling or unable to provide funds to X on terms it considers economically feasible. Y, a private foundation, makes a loan to X bearing interest below the market rate for commercial loans of comparable risk. Y's primary purpose for making the loan is to encourage the economic development of such minority groups. The loan has no significant purpose involving the production of income or the appreciation of property. The loan significantly furthers the accomplishment of Y's exempt activities and would not have been made but for such relationship between the loan and Y's exempt activities. Accordingly, the loan is a program-related investment even though Y may earn income from the investment in an amount comparable to or higher than earnings from conventional portfolio investments.

Example (2). Assume the facts as stated in Example (1), except that after the date of execution of the loan Y extends the due date of the loan. The extension is granted in order to permit X to achieve greater financial stability before it is required to repay the loan. Since the change in the terms of the loan is made primarily for exempt purposes and not for any significant purpose involving the production of income or the appreciation of property, the loan shall continue to qualify as a program-related investment.

Example (3). X is a small business enterprise located in a deteriorated urban area and owned by members of an economically disadvantaged minority group. Conventional sources of funds are unwilling to provide funds to X at reasonable interest rates unless it increases the amount of its equity capital. Consequently, Y, a private foundation purchases shares of X's common stock. Y's primary purpose in purchasing the stock is to encourage the economic development of such minority group, and no significant purpose involves the production of income or the appreciation of property. The investment significantly furthers the accomplishment of Y's exempt activities and would not have been made but for such relationship between the investment and Y's exempt activities. Accordingly, the purchase of the common stock is a program-related investment, even though Y may realize a profit if X is successful and the common stock appreciates in value.

Example (4). X is a business enterprise which is not owned by low-income persons or minority group members, but the continued operation of X is important to the economic well-being of a deteriorated urban area because X employs a substantial number of low-income persons from such area. Conventional sources of funds are unwilling or unable to provide funds to X at reasonable interest rates. Y, a private foundation, makes a loan to X at an interest rate below the market rate for commercial loans of comparable risk. The loan is made pursuant to a program run by Y to assist low-income persons by providing increased economic opportunities and to prevent community deterioration. No significant purpose of the loan involves the production of income or the appreciation of property. The investment significantly furthers the accomplishment of Y's exempt activities and would not have been made but for such relationship between the loan and Y's exempt activities. Accordingly, the loan is a program-related investment.

Example (5). X is a business enterprise which is financially secure and the stock of which is listed and traded on a national exchange. Y, a private foundation, makes a loan to X at an interest rate below the market rate in order to induce X to establish a new plant in a deteriorated urban area which, because of the high risks involved, X would be unwilling to establish absent such inducement. The loan is made pursuant to a program run by Y to enhance the economic development of the area by, for example, providing employment opportunities for low-income persons at the new plant, and no significant purpose involves the production of income or the appreciation of property. The loan significantly furthers the accomplishment of Y's exempt activities and would not have been made but for such relationship between the loan and Y's exempt activities. Accordingly, even though X is large and established, the investment is program-related.

Example (6). X is a business enterprise which is owned by a nonprofit community development corporation. When fully operational, X will market agricultural products, thereby providing a marketing outlet for low-income farmers in a depressed rural area. Y, a private foundation, makes a loan to X bearing interest at a rate less than the rate charged by financial institutions which have agreed to lend funds to X if Y makes the loan. The loan is made pursuant to a program run by Y to encourage economic redevelopment of depressed areas, and no significant purpose involves the production of income or the appreciation of property. The loan significantly furthers the accomplishment of Y's exempt activities and would not have been made but for such relationship between the loan and Y's exempt activities. Accordingly, the loan is a program-related investment.

Example (7). X, a private foundation, invests $100,000 in the common stock of corporation M. The dividends received from such investment are later applied by X in furtherance of its exempt purposes. Although there is a relationship between the return on the investment and the accomplishment of X's exempt activities, there is no relationship between the investment per se and such accomplishment. Therefore, the investment cannot be considered as made primarily to accomplish one or more of the purposes described in section 170(c)(2)(B) and cannot qualify as program-related.

Example (8). S, a private foundation, makes an investment in T, a business corporation, which qualifies as a program-related investment under section 4944(c) at the time that it is made. All of T's voting stock is owned by S. T experiences financial and management problems which, in the judgment of the foundation, require changes in management, in financial structure or in the form of the investment. The following three methods of resolving the problems appear feasible to S, but each of the three methods would result in reduction of the exempt purposes for which the program-related investment was initially made:

(a) Sales of stock or assets. The foundation sells its stock to an unrelated person. Payment is made in part at the time of sale; the balance is payable over an extended term of years with interest on the amount outstanding. The foundation receives a purchase-money mortgage.

(b) Lease. The corporation leases its assets for a term of years to an unrelated person, with an option in the lessee to buy the assets. If the option is exercised, the

Reg. § 53.4944-3(b)

terms of payment are to be similar to those described in (a) of this example.

(c) Management contract. The corporation enters into a management contract which gives broad operating authority to one or more unrelated persons for a term of years. The foundation and the unrelated persons are obligated to contribute toward working capital requirements. The unrelated persons will be compensated by a fixed fee or a share of profits, and they will receive an option to buy the stock held by S or the assets of the corporation. If the option is exercised, the terms of payment are to be similar to those described in (a) of this example.

Each of the three methods involves a change in the form or terms of a program-related investment for the prudent protection of the foundation's investment. Thus, under § 53.4944-3(a)(3)(i), none of the three transactions (nor any debt instruments or other obligations held by S as a result of engaging in one of these transactions) would cause the investment to cease to qualify as program-related.

Example (9). X is a socially and economically disadvantaged individual. Y, a private foundation, makes an interest-free loan to X for the primary purpose of enabling X to attend college. The loan has no significant purpose involving the production of income or the appreciation of property. The loan significantly furthers the accomplishment of Y's exempt activities and would not have been made but for such relationship between the loan and Y's exempt activities. Accordingly, the loan is a program-related investment.

Example (10). Y, a private foundation, makes a high-risk investment in low-income housing, the indebtedness with respect to which is insured by the Federal Housing Administration. Y's primary purpose in making the investment is to finance the purchase, rehabilitation, and construction of housing for low-income persons. The investment has no significant purpose involving the production of income or the appreciation of property. The investment significantly furthers the accomplishment of Y's exempt activities and would not have been made but for such relationship between the investment and Y's exempt activities. Accordingly, the investment is program-related.

O→ § 53.4944-4 (T.D. 7240, filed 12-28-72.) **Special rules.**

(a) *Joint and several liability.* In any case where more than one foundation manager is liable for the tax imposed under section 4944(a)(2) or (b)(2) with respect to any one jeopardizing investment, all such foundation managers shall be jointly and severally liable for the tax imposed under each such paragraph with respect to such investment.

(b) *Limits on liability for management.* With respect to any one jeopardizing investment, the maximum aggregate amount of tax collectible under section 4944(a)(2) from all foundation managers shall not exceed $5,000, and the maximum aggregate amount of tax collectible under section 4944(b)(2) from all foundation managers shall not exceed $10,000.

(c) *Examples.* The provisions of this section may be illustrated by the following examples:

Example (1). A, B, and C are foundation managers of X, a private foundation. Assume that A, B, and C are liable for both initial and additional taxes under sections 4944(a)(2) and 4944(b)(2), respectively, for the following investments by X: an investment of $5,000 in the common stock of corporation M, and an investment of $10,000 in the common stock of corporation N. A, B, and C will be jointly and severally liable for the following initial taxes under section 4944(a)(2): a tax of $250 (i.e., 5% of $5,000) for each year (or part thereof) in the taxable period (as defined in section 4944(e)(1) for the investment in M, and a tax of $500 (i.e., 5% of $10,000) for each year (or part thereof) in the taxable period for the investment in N. Further, A, B, and C will be jointly and severally liable for the following additional taxes under section 4944(b)(2): a tax of $250 (i.e., 5% of $5,000) for the investment in M, and a tax of $500 (i.e., 5% of $10,000) for the investment in N.

Example (2). Assume the facts as stated in Example (1), except that X has invested $500,000 in the common stock of M, and $1,000,000 in the common stock of N. A, B, and C will be jointly and severally liable for the following initial taxes under section 4944(a)(2): a tax of $5,000 for the investment in M, and a tax of $5,000 for the investment in N. Further, A, B, and C will be jointly and severally liable for the following additional taxes under section 4944(b)(2): a tax of $10,000 for the investment in M, and a tax of $10,000 for the investment in N.

O→ § 53.4944-5 (T.D. 7240, filed 12-28-72.) **Definitions.**

(a) *Taxable period*—(1) *In general.* For purposes of section 4944, the term "taxable period" means, with respect to any investment which jeopardizes the carrying out of a private foundation's exempt purposes, the period beginning with the date on which the amount is so invested and ending on whichever of the following is the earlier:

(i) The date of mailing of a notice of deficiency under section 6212 with respect to the tax imposed on the making of the investment by section 4944(a)(1); or

(ii) The date on which the amount so invested is removed from jeopardy.

(2) *Special rule.* Where a notice of deficiency referred to in subparagraph (1)(i) of this paragraph is not mailed because there is a waiver of the restrictions on assessment and collection of a deficiency, or because the deficiency is paid, the date of filing of the waiver or the date of such payment, respectively, shall be treated as the end of the taxable period.

(b) *Removal from jeopardy.* An investment which jeopardizes the carrying out of a private foundation's exempt purposes shall be considered to be removed from jeopardy when—

(1) The foundation sells or otherwise disposes of the investment, and

(2) the proceeds of such sale or other disposition are not themselves investments which jeopardize the carrying out of such foundation's exempt purposes.

A change by a private foundation in the form or terms of a jeopardizing investment shall result in the removal of the investment from jeopardy if, after such change, the investment no longer jeopardizes the carrying out of such foundation's exempt purposes. For purposes of section 4944, the making by a private foundation of one jeopardizing investment and a subsequent exchange by the foundation of such investment for another jeopardizing investment will be treated as only one jeopardizing investment, except as provided in § 53-.4944-6(b) and (c). For the treatment of a jeopardizing investment which is removed from jeopardy or otherwise transferred by a private foundation by the making of a grant or by bargain-sale, see sections 4941 and 4945 and the regulations thereunder. A jeopardizing investment cannot be removed from jeopardy by a transfer from a private foundation to another private foundation which is related to the transferor foundation within the meaning of section 4946(a)(1)(H)(i) or (ii), unless the investment is a program-related investment in the hands of the transferee foundation.

(c) *Examples.* The provisions of this section may be illustrated by the following examples:

Example (1) X, a private foundation on the calendar year basis, makes a $1,000 jeopardizing investment on January 1, 1970. X thereafter sells the investment for $1,000 on January 3, 1971. The taxable period is from January 1, 1970, to January 3, 1971. X will be liable for an initial tax of $100, that is, a tax of 5 percent of the amount of the investment for each year (or part thereof) in the taxable period.

Example (2). Assume that both C and D are investments which jeopardize exempt purposes. X, a private foundation, purchases C in 1971 and later exchanges C for D. Such exchange does not constitute a removal of C from jeopardy. In addition, no new taxable period will arise with respect to D, since, for purposes of section 4944, only one jeopardizing investment has been made.

Example (3). Assume the facts as stated in Example (2), except that X sells C for cash and later reinvests such cash in D. Two separate investments jeopardizing exempt purposes have resulted. Since the cash received in the interim is not of a jeopardizing nature, the amount invested in C has been removed from jeopardy and, thus, the taxable period with respect to C has been terminated. The subsequent reinvestment of such cash in D gives rise to a new taxable period with respect to D.

(d) *Correction period*—(1) *In general.* For purposes of section 4944, the correction period shall begin with the date on which the investment which jeopardizes the exempt purposes of the private foundation is entered into and end 90 days after the date of mailing of a notice of deficiency under section 6212 with respect to the tax imposed by section 4944(b)(1).

(2) *Extensions of correction period.* (i) The correction period referred to in subparagraph (1) of this paragraph shall be extended by any period in which a deficiency cannot be assessed under section 6213(a). In addition, the correction period shall be extended in accordance with subdivisions (ii), (iii), and (iv) of this subparagraph, except that such subdivision (iii) or (iv) shall not operate to extend a correction period with respect to which a taxpayer has filed a petition with the Tax Court for redetermination of a deficiency within the time prescribed by section 6213(a).

(ii) The correction period referred to in subparagraph (1) of this paragraph may be extended by any period which the Commissioner determined is reasonable and necessary to bring about removal of an investment from jeopardy. The Commissioner ordinarily will not extend the correction period pursuant to this subdivision unless all of the following factors are present:

(*a*) The foundation or an appropriate State officer (as defined in section 6104(c) (2)) is actively in good faith seeking to remove the investment from jeopardy;

(*b*) The investment cannot reasonably be expected to be removed from jeopardy during the unextended correction period; and

(*c*) The jeopardizing investment appears to have been an isolated occurrence and it appears unlikely that the foundation will make similar investments in the future.

The fact that a jeopardizing investment is decreasing in value shall not, by itself, prevent an extension of the correction period with respect to such investment.

(iii) If, within the unextended correction period, the tax imposed by section 4944(a)(1) is paid, then the Commissioner shall extend the correction period to the later of—

(*a*) A period of 90 days after the payment of such tax, or

(*b*) The correction period determined without regard to this subdivision.

(iv) If prior to the expiration of the correction period (including extensions) a claim for refund with respect to a tax imposed by section 4944(a)(1) is filed, the Commissioner shall extend the correction period during the pendency of the claim plus an additional 90 days. If within such time, a suit or proceeding referred to in section 7422(g) with respect to such claim is filed, the Commissioner shall extend the correction period during the pendency of such suit or proceeding. See § 301.7422-1 of this chapter (Regulations of Procedure and Administration) for rules relating to pendency of such suit or proceeding.

§ 53.4944-6 (T.D. 7240, filed 12-28-72.) **Special rules for investments made prior to January 1, 1970.**

(a) Except as provided in paragraph (b) or (c) of this section, an investment made by a private foundation prior to January 1, 1970, shall not be subject to the provisions of section 4944.

(b) If the form or terms of an investment made by a private foundation prior to January 1, 1970, are changed (other than as described in paragraph (c) of this section) on or after such date, the provisions of § 53.4944-1(a)(2)(iii) shall apply with respect to such investment.

(c) In the case of an investment made by a private foundation prior to January 1, 1970, which is exchanged on or after

Reg. § 53.4944-6(c)

such date for another investment, for purposes of section 4944 the foundation will be considered to have made a new investment on the date of such exchange, unless the post-1969 investment is described in § 53.4944-1(a)(2)(ii)(b). Accordingly, a determination, under § 53.4944-1(a)(2)(i), whether the investment jeopardizes the carrying out of the foundation's exempt purposes shall be made at such time.

SUBPART F—TAXES ON TAXABLE EXPENDITURES

§ 53.4945 **Statutory provisions; imposition of excise taxes on taxable expenditures.** [Sec. 4945, IRC]

§ 53.4945-1 (T.D. 7215, filed 10-30-72; amended by T.D. 7299, filed 12-26-73; T.D. 7527, filed 12-23-77.) **Taxes on taxable expenditures.**

(a) *Imposition of initial taxes*—(1) *Tax on private foundation.* Section 4945(a)(1) of the Code imposes an excise tax on each taxable expenditure (as defined in section 4945(d)) of a private foundation. This tax is to be paid by the private foundation and is at the rate of 10 percent of the amount of each taxable expenditure.

(2) *Tax on foundation manager*—(i) *In general.* Section 4945(a)(2) of the Code imposes, under certain circumstances, an excise tax on the agreement of any foundation manager to the making of a taxable expenditure by a private foundation. This tax is imposed only in cases in which the following circumstances are present:

(a) A tax is imposed by section 4945 (a)(1),

(b) Such foundation manager knows that the expenditure to which he agrees is a taxable expenditure, and

(c) Such agreement is willful and is not due to reasonable cause.
However, the tax with respect to any particular expenditure applies only to the agreement of those foundation managers who are authorized to approve, or to exercise discretion in recommending approval of, the making of the expenditure by the foundation and to those foundation managers who are members of a group (such as the foundation's board of directors or trustees) which is so authorized. For the definition of the term "foundation manager", see section 4946(b) and the regulations thereunder.

(ii) *Agreement.* The agreement of any foundation manager to the making of a taxable expenditure shall consist of any manifestation of approval of the expenditure which is sufficient to constitute an exercise of the foundation manager's authority to approve, or to exercise discretion in recommending approval of, the making of the expenditure by the foundation, whether or not such manifestation of approval is the final or decisive approval on behalf of the foundation.

(iii) *Knowing.* For purposes of section 4945, a foundation manager shall be considered to have agreed to an expenditure "knowing" that it is a taxable expenditure only if—

(a) He has actual knowledge of sufficient facts so that, based solely upon such facts, such expenditure would be a taxable expenditure,

(b) He is aware that such an expenditure under these circumstances may violate the provisions of federal tax law governing taxable expenditures, and

(c) He negligently fails to make reasonable attempts to ascertain whether the expenditure is a taxable expenditure, or he is in fact aware that it is such an expenditure.
For purposes of this part and chapter 42, the term "knowing" does not mean "having reason to know". However, evidence tending to show that a foundation manager has reason to know of a particular fact or particular rule is relevant in determining whether he had actual knowledge of such fact or rule. Thus, for example, evidence tending to show that a foundation manager has reason to know of sufficient facts so that, based solely upon such facts, an expenditure would be a taxable expenditure is relevant in determining whether he has actual knowledge of such facts.

(iv) *Willful.* A foundation manager's agreement to a taxable expenditure is willful if it is voluntary, conscious, and intentional. No motive to avoid the restrictions of the law or the incurrence of any tax is necessary to make an agreement willful. However, a foundation manager's agreement to a taxable expenditure is not willful if he does not know that it is a taxable expenditure.

(v) *Due to reasonable cause.* A foundation manager's actions are due to reasonable cause if he has exercised his responsibility on behalf of the foundation with ordinary business care and prudence.

(vi) *Advice of counsel.* If a foundation manager, after full disclosure of the factual situation to legal counsel (including house counsel), relies on the advice of such counsel expressed in a reasoned written legal opinion that an expenditure is not a taxable expenditure under section 4945 (or that expenditures conforming to certain guidelines are not taxable expenditures), although such expenditure is subsequently held to be a taxable expenditure (or that certain proposed reporting procedures with respect to an expenditure will satisfy the tests of section 4945(h), although such procedures are subsequently held not to satisfy such section), the foundation manager's agreement to such expenditure (or to grants made with provision for such reporting procedures which are taxable solely because of such inadequate reporting procedures) will ordinarily not be considered "knowing" or "willful" and will ordinarily be considered "due to reasonable cause" within the meaning of section 4945(a)(2). For purposes of the subdivision, a written legal opinion will be considered "reasoned" even if it reaches a conclusion which is subsequently determined to be incorrect so long as such opinion addresses itself to the facts and applicable law. However, a written legal opinion will not be considered "reasoned" if it does nothing more than recite the facts and express a conclusion. However, the absence of advice of counsel with respect to an expenditure shall not, by itself, give rise to any inference that a foundation manager agreed to the making of the expenditure knowingly, willfully, or without reasonable cause.

(vii) *Rate and incidence of tax.* The tax imposed under section 4945(a)(2) is at the rate of 2½ percent of the amount of each taxable expenditure to which the foundation manager has agreed. This tax shall be paid by the foundation manager.

(viii) *Cross reference.* For provisions relating to the burden of proof in cases involving the issue whether a foundation manager has knowingly agreed to the making of a taxable expenditure, see section 7454(b).

(b) *Imposition of additional taxes*—(1) *Tax on private foundation.* Section 4945 (b)(1) of the Code imposes an excise tax in any case in which an initial tax is imposed under section 4945(a)(1) on a taxable expenditure of a private foundation and the expenditure is not corrected within the correction period (as defined in section 4945(i)(2)). The tax imposed under section 4945(b)(1) is to be paid by the private foundation and is at the rate of 100 percent of the amount of each taxable expenditure.

(2) *Tax on foundation manager.* Section 4945(b)(2) of the Code imposes an excise tax in any case in which a tax is imposed under section 4945(b)(1) and a foundation manager has refused to agree to part or all of the correction of the taxable expenditure. The tax imposed under section 4945(b)(2) is at the rate of 50 percent of the amount of the taxable expenditure. This tax is to be paid by any foundation manager who has refused to agree to part or all of the correction of the taxable expenditure.

(c) *Special rules*—(1) *Joint and several liability.* In any case where more than one foundation manager is liable for the tax imposed under section 4945(a)(2) or (b) (2) with respect to the making of a taxable expenditure, all such foundation managers shall be jointly and severally liable for the tax imposed under such paragraph with respect to such taxable expenditure.

(2) *Limits on liability for management.* The maximum aggregate amount of tax collectible under section 4945(a)(2) from all foundation managers with respect to any one taxable expenditure shall be $5,000, and the maximum aggregate amount of tax collectible under section 4945(b)(2) from all foundation managers with respect to any one taxable expenditure shall be $10,000.

(3) *Examples.* The provisions of this paragraph may be illustrated by the following examples:

Example (1). A, B, and C comprise the board of directors of Foundation M. They vote unanimously in favor of a grant of $100,000 to D, a business associate of each of the directors. The grant is to be used by D for travel and educational purposes and is not made in accordance with the requirements of section 4945 (g). Each director knows that D was selected as the recipient of the grant solely because of his friendship with the directors and is aware that some grants made for travel, study, or other similar purposes may be taxable expenditures. Also, none of the directors makes any attempt to consult counsel, or to otherwise determine, whether this grant is a taxable expenditure. Initial taxes are imposed under paragraphs (1) and (2) of section 4945 (a). The tax to be paid by the foundation is $10,000 (10 percent of $100,000). The tax to be paid by the board of directors is $2,500 (2½ percent of $100,000). A, B, and C are jointly and severally liable for this $2,500 and this sum may be collected by the Service from any one of them.

Example (2). Assume the same facts as in Example (1). Further assume that within the correction period A makes a motion to correct the taxable expenditure at a meeting of the board of directors. The motion is defeated by a two-to-one vote, A voting for the motion and B and C voting against it. In these circumstances an additional tax would be paid by the private foundation in the amount of $100,000 (100 percent of $100,000). The additional tax to be paid by B and C is $10,000 (50 percent of $100,000, subject to a maximum of $10,000). B and C are jointly and severally liable for the $10,000, and this sum may be collected by the Service from either of them.

(d) *Correction*—(1) *In general.* Except as provided in paragraph (d)(2) or (3) of this section, correction of a taxable expenditure shall be accomplished by recovering part or all of the expenditure to the extent recovery is possible, and, where full recovery cannot be accomplished, by any additional corrective action which the Commissioner may prescribe. Such additional corrective action is to be determined by the circumstances of each particular case and may include the following:

(i) Requiring that any unpaid funds due the grantee be withheld;

(ii) Requiring that no further grants be made to the particular grantee;

(iii) In addition to other reports that are required, requiring periodic (e.g., quarterly) reports from the foundation with respect to all expenditures of the foundation (such reports shall be equivalent in detail to the reports required by section 4945(h)(3) and § 53.4945-5(d));

(iv) Requiring improved methods of exercising expenditure responsibility;

(v) Requiring improved methods of selecting recipients of individual grants; and

(vi) Requiring such other measures as the Commission may prescribe in a particular case.

The foundation making the expenditure shall not be under any obligation to attempt to recover the expenditure by legal action if such action would in all probability not result in the satisfaction of execution on a judgment.

(2) *Correction for inadequate reporting.* If the expenditure is taxable only because of a failure to obtain a full and complete report as required by section 4945 (h)(2) or because of a failure to make a full and detailed report as required by section 4945(h)(3), correction may be accomplished by obtaining or making the report in question. In addition, if the expenditure is taxable only because of a failure to obtain a full and complete report as required by section 4945(h)(2) and an investigation indicates that no grant funds

Reg. § 53.4945-1 (d) (2)

have been diverted to any use not in furtherance of a purpose specified in the grant, correction may be accomplished by exerting all reasonable efforts to obtain the report in question and reporting the failure to the Internal Revenue Service, even though the report is not finally obtained.

(3) *Correction for failure to obtain advance approval.* Where an expenditure is taxable under section 4945(d)(3) only because of a failure to obtain advance approval of procedures with respect to grants as required by section 4945(g), correction may be accomplished by obtaining approval of the grant making procedures and establishing to the satisfaction of the Commissioner that:

(i) no grant funds have been diverted to any use not in furtherance of a purpose specified in the grant;

(ii) the grant making procedures instituted would have been approved if advance approval of such procedures had been properly requested; and

(iii) where advance approval of grant making procedures is subsequently required, such approval will be properly requested.

(e) *Correction period*—(1) *In general.* For purposes of section 4945, the correction period shall begin with the date on which the taxable expenditure occurs and end 90 days after the date of mailing of a notice of deficiency under section 6212 with respect to the tax imposed under section 4945 (b)(1).

(2) *Extensions of correction period.* (i) The correction period referred to in subparagraph (1) of this paragraph shall be extended by any period in which a deficiency cannot be assessed under section 6213(a). In addition, the correction period referred to in subparagraph (1) of this paragraph shall be extended in accordance with subdivisions (ii), (iii), and (iv) of the subparagraph, except that such subdivision (iii) or (iv) shall not operate to extend a correction period with respect to which a taxpayer has filed a petition with the Tax Court for redetermination of a deficiency within the time prescribed by section 6213(a).

(ii) The correction period referred to in subparagraph (1) of this paragraph may be extended by any period which the Commissioner determines is reasonable and necessary to bring about correction of the taxable expenditure. The Commissioner ordinarily will not extend the correction period pursuant to this subdivision unless the following factors are present:

(a) The foundation (or, with respect to any taxable expenditure within the meaning of section 4945(d)(5), an appropriate State officer as defined in section 6104(c)(2)) is actively in good faith seeking to correct the taxable expenditure.

(b) Adequate corrective action cannot reasonably be expected to result during the unextended correction period; and

(c) The taxable expenditure appears to have been an isolated occurrence and it appears unlikely that the foundation will pay or incur similar taxable expenditures in the future.

The Commissioner shall not make a determination extending the correction period with respect to any taxable expenditure within the meaning of section 4945(d)(1), (2), (3), or (4) because of any action by an appropriate State officer (as defined in section 6104(c)(2)), unless the expenditure is also taxable by reason of section 4945 (d)(5).

(iii) If, within the unextended correction period, the tax imposed by section 4945(a)(1) is paid, then the Commissioner shall extend the correction period to the later of—

(a) A period of 90 days after the payment of such tax, or

(b) The correction period determined without regard to this subdivision.

(iv) If prior to the expiration of the correction period (including extensions) a claim for refund with respect to a tax imposed by section 4945(a)(1) is filed, the Commissioner shall extend the correction period during the pendency of the claim plus an additional 90 days. If within such time, a suit or proceeding referred to in section 7422(g) with respect to such claim is filed, the Commissioner shall extend the correction period during the pendency of such suit or proceeding. See § 301.7422-1 of this chapter (Regulations on Procedure and Administration) for rules relating to pendency of such suit or proceeding.

§ 53.4945-2 (T.D. 7215, filed 10-30-72.) **Propaganda influencing legislation.**

(a) *Propaganda influencing legislation, etc.*—(1) *In general.* Under section 4945 (d)(1) the term "taxable expenditure" includes any amount paid or incurred by a private foundation to carry on propaganda, or otherwise to attempt, to influence legislation. Attempts to influence legislation may include communications with a member or employe of a legislative body or with an official of the executive department of a government or efforts to affect the opinion of the general public with respect to legislation being considered by, or to be submitted imminently to, a legislative body. For purposes of this section, a proposed treaty required to be submitted by the President to the Senate for its advice and consent shall be considered "legislation being considered by, or to be submitted imminently to, a legislative body" at the time the President's representative begins to negotiate its position with the prospective parties to the proposed treaty. See, however, paragraph (d) of this section for exceptions to the general rule.

(2) *Legislation defined.* For purposes of this section, the term "legislation" includes action by the Congress, by any State legislature, by any local council or similar governing body, or by the public in a referendum, initiative, constitutional amendment, or similar procedure. Such term does not include actions by executive, judicial, or administrative bodies. For purposes of the preceding sentence, school boards, housing authorities, sewer and water districts, zoning boards and other similar federal, state, or local special purpose bodies, whether elective or appointive, shall be considered administrative bodies. The word "action" includes the introduction, enactment, defeat, or repeal of legislation. Thus, for example, for purposes of section 4945, the term "any attempt to influence legislation" does not include attempts by a private foundation to persuade an executive body or department to form, support the formation of, expand or support the ex-

pansion of, or to acquire property to be used for the formation or expansion of, a public park or equivalent preserves (such as public recreation areas, game or forest preserves, and soil demonstration areas) established or to be established by act of Congress, by executive action in accordance with an act of Congress, or by State, municipality or other governmental unit described in section 170(c)(1), as compared with attempts to persuade a legislative body, a member thereof, or other governmental official or employee, to promote the appropriation of funds for such an acquisition or other legislative authorization of such an acquisition. Therefore, a private foundation could under this subdivision, for example, propose to a Park Authority that it purchase a particular tract of land for a new park, even though such an attempt would necessarily require the Park Authority eventually to seek appropriations to support a new park. However, in such a case, the foundation could not provide the Park Authority with a proposed budget to be submitted to a legislative body, unless such submission could qualify under paragraph (d) of this section.

(3) *Jointly funded projects.* A private foundation will not be treated as having paid or incurred any amount to attempt to influence legislation merely because it makes a grant to another organization upon the condition that the recipient obtain a matching support appropriation from a governmental body. In addition, a private foundation will not be treated as having made taxable expenditures of amounts paid or incurred in carrying on discussions with officials of governmental bodies provided that:

(i) The subject of such discussions is a program which is jointly funded by the foundation and the government or is a new program which may be jointly funded by the foundation and the government,

(ii) The discussions are undertaken for the purpose of exchanging data and information on the subject matter of the program, and

(iii) Such discussions are not undertaken by foundation managers in order to make any direct attempt to persuade governmental officials or employees to take particular positions on specific legislative issues other than such program.

(4) *Certain expenditures by recipients of program-related investments.* Any amount paid or incurred by a recipient of a program-related investment (as defined in § 53.4944-3) in connection with an appearance before, or communication with, any legislative body with respect to legislation or proposed legislation of direct interest to such recipient shall not be attributed to the investing foundation, if—

(i) The foundation does not earmark its funds to be used for any activities described in section 4945(d)(1) and

(ii) A deduction under section 162 is allowable to the recipient for such amount.

(5) *Grants to public organizations*—(i) *In general.* A grant by a private foundation to an organization described in section 509 (a)(1), (2) or (3) does not constitute a taxable expenditure by such foundation under section 4945(d) if the grant by the private foundation is not earmarked to be used for any activity described in section 4945(d) (1), (2), or (5), is not earmarked to be used in a manner which would violate section 4945(d)(3) or (4), and there does not exist an agreement, oral or written, whereby such grantor foundation may cause the grantee to engage in any such prohibited activity or to select the recipient to which the grant is to be devoted. For purposes of this subdivision, a grant by a private foundation is earmarked if such grant is given pursuant to an agreement, oral or written, that the grant will be used for specific purposes. For the expenditure responsibility requirements with respect to organizations other than those described in section 509(a)(1), (2) or (3), see § 53.4945-5.

(ii) *Certain "public" organizations.* For purposes of this section, an organization shall be considered a section 509(a)(1) organization if it is treated as such under paragraph (4) of § 53.4945-5(a).

(iii) *Examples.* The provisions of this subparagraph may be illustrated by the following examples:

Example (1). M, a private foundation, makes a general purpose grant to Z, an organization described in section 509(a)(1). As an insubstantial portion of its activities, Z makes some attempts to influence the State legislature with regard to changes in the mental health laws. The use of the grant is not earmarked by M to be used in a manner which would violate section 4945 (d). In addition, there is no oral or written agreement whereby M may influence the choice by Z of the activity or recipient to which the grant is to be devoted. Even if the grant is subsequently devoted by Z to its legislative activities, the grant by M is not a taxable expenditure under section 4945(d).

Example (2). X, a private foundation, makes a grant to Y University for the purpose of conducting research on the potential environmental effects of certain pesticides. X does not earmark the grant for any purpose which would violate section 4945(d) and there is no oral or written agreement whereby X may cause Y to engage in any activity described in section 4945(d)(1), (2), or (5), or to select any recipient to which the grant may be devoted. Y uses most of the funds for the research project; however, on its own volition, Y expends a portion of the grant funds to send a representative to testify at Congressional hearings on a specific bill proposing certain pesticide control measures. The portion of the grant funds expended with respect to the Congressional hearings is not treated as a taxable expenditure by X under section 4945(d).

Reg. § 53.4945-2(a)(5)

(b) *Attempts to affect the opinion of the general public.* Except as provided in paragraphs (d)(1) (relating to the making available of nonpartisan analysis, study or research) and (d)(4) (relating to examination and discussion of broad social, economic and similar problems) of this section, any expenditure paid or incurred by a private foundation in an attempt to influence any legislation through an attempt to affect the opinion of the general public or any segment thereof is a taxable expenditure.

(c) *Lobbying activities.* Except as provided in paragraph (d) of this section, any expenditure for the purpose of influencing legislation through communication with any member or employee of a legislative body, or with any government official or employee who may participate in the formulation of the legislation, is a taxable expenditure.

(d) *Exceptions*—(1) *Nonpartisan analysis, study, or research*—(i) *In general.* Engaging in nonpartisan analysis, study, or research and making available to the general public or a segment or members thereof or to governmental bodies, officials, or employees the results of such work do not constitute carrying on propaganda, or otherwise attempting, to influence legislation.

(ii) *Nonpartisan analysis, study or research.* For purposes of section 4945(e), "nonpartisan analysis, study, or research" means an independent and objective exposition of a particular subject matter, including any activity which is "educational" within the meaning of § 1.501(c)(3)-1(d)(3). Thus, "nonpartisan analysis, study, or research" may advocate a particular position or viewpoint so long as there is a sufficiently full and fair exposition of the pertinent facts to enable the public or an individual to form an independent opinion or conclusion. On the other hand, the mere presentation of unsupported opinion does not qualify as "nonpartisan analysis, study, or research". Activities of a noncommercial educational broadcasting station or network (television or radio) constitute "nonpartisan analysis, study, or research" if the station or network adheres to the Federal Communications Commission regulations and its "fairness doctrine" (requiring balanced, fair, and objective presentation of issues). Ordinarily, if no determination has been made by the Federal Communications Commission that the "fairness doctrine" (as stated above) has been violated, the activities of the station or network will be treated as "nonpartisan analysis, study, or research."

(iii) *Presentation as part of a series.* Normally, whether a publication or broadcast qualifies as "nonpartisan analysis, study, or research" will be determined on a presentation-by-presentation basis. However, if a publication or broadcast is one of a series prepared or supported by a private foundation and the series as a whole meets the standards of subdivision (ii) of this subparagraph, then any individual publication or broadcast within the series will not result in a taxable expenditure even though such individual broadcast or publication does not, by itself, meet the standards of subdivision (ii) of this subparagraph. Whether a broadcast or publication is considered part of a series will ordinarily depend on all the facts and circumstances of each particular situation. However, with respect to broadcast activities, all broadcasts within any period of 6 consecutive months will ordinarily be eligible to be considered as part of a series. If a private foundation times or channels a part of a series which is described in this subdivision in a manner designed to influence the general public or the action of a legislative body with respect to a specific legislative proposal in violation of section 4945(d)(1), the expenses of preparing and distributing such part of the analysis, study, or research will be a taxable expenditure under this section.

(iv) *Making available results of analysis, study, or research.* A private foundation may choose any suitable means, including oral or written presentations, to distribute the results of its nonpartisan analysis, study, or research, with or without charge. Such means include distribution of reprints of speeches, articles and reports (including the report required under section 6056); presentation of information through conferences, meetings and discussions; and dissemination to the news media, including radio, television and newspapers, and to other public forums. For purposes of this subparagraph, such presentations may not be limited to or directed toward persons who are interested solely in one side of a particular issue.

(v) *Examples.* The provisions of this paragraph may be illustrated by the following examples:

Example (1). M, a private foundation, establishes a research project to collect information for the purpose of showing the dangers of the use of pesticides in raising crops. The information collected includes data with respect to proposed legislation, pending before several State legislatures, which would ban the use of pesticides. The project takes favorable positions on such legislation without producing a sufficiently full and fair exposition of the pertinent facts to enable the public or an individual to form an independent opinion or conclusion on the pros and cons of the use of pesticides. This project is not within the exception for nonpartisan analysis, study, or research because it is designed to present information merely on one side of the legislative controversy.

Example (2). N, a private foundation, establishes a research project to collect information concerning the dangers of the use of pesticides in raising crops for the ostensible purpose of examining and reporting information as to the pros and cons of the use of pesticides in raising crops. The information is collected and distributed in the form of a published report which analyzes the effects and costs of the use and nonuse of various pesticides under various conditions on humans, animals and crops. The report also presents the advantages, disadvantages, and economic cost of allowing the continued use of pesticides unabated, of controlling the use of pesticides, and of developing alternatives to pesticides. Even if the report sets forth conclusions that the disadvantages as a result of using pesticides are greater than the advantages of using pesticides and that prompt legislative regulation of the use of

Reg. § 53.4945-2(d)(1)

pesticides is needed, the project is within the exception for nonpartisan analysis, study or research since it is designed to present information on both sides of the legislative controversy and presents a sufficiently full and fair exposition of the pertinent facts to enable the public or an individual to form an independent opinion or conclusion.

Example (3). O, a private foundation, establishes a research project to collect information on the presence or absence of disease in humans from eating food grown with pesticides and the presence or absence of disease in humans from eating food not grown with pesticides. As part of the research project, O hires a consultant who prepares a "fact sheet" which calls for the curtailment of the use of pesticides and which addresses itself to the merits of several specific legislative proposals to curtail the use of pesticides in raising crops which are currently pending before State Legislatures. The "fact sheet" presents reports of experimental evidence tending to support its conclusions but omits any reference to reports of experimental evidence tending to dispute its conclusions. O distributes ten thousand copies to citizens' groups. Expenditures by O in connection with this work of the consultant are not within the exception for nonpartisan analysis, study, or research.

Example (4). P, a private foundation, publishes a bi-monthly newsletter to collect and report all published materials, ongoing research, and new developments with regard to the use of pesticides in raising crops. The newsletter also includes notices of proposed pesticide legislation with impartial summaries of the provisions of and debates on such legislation. The newsletter is designed to present information on both sides of the legislative controversy and does present such information fully and fairly. It is within the exception for nonpartisan analysis, study, or research.

Example (5). X, a private foundation, is satisfied that A, a member of the faculty of Y University, is exceptionally well qualified to undertake a project involving a comprehensive study of the effect of pesticides on crop yields. Consequently, X makes a grant to A to underwrite the cost of the study and of the preparation of a book on the effect of pesticides on crop yields. X does not take any position on the issues or control the content of A's output. A produces a book which concludes that the use of pesticides often has a favorable effect on crop yields, and on that basis argues against pending bills which would ban the use of pesticides. A's book contains a sufficiently full and fair exposition of the pertinent facts, including known or potential disadvantages of the use of pesticides, to enable the public or an individual to form an independent opinion or conclusion as to whether pesticides should be banned as provided in the pending bills. Consequently, the book is within the exception for nonpartisan analysis, study, or research.

Example (6). Assume the same facts as Example (2), except that, instead of issuing a report, X presents within a period of 6 consecutive months a two-program television series relating to the pesticide issue. The first program contains information, arguments, and conclusions favoring legislation to restrict the use of pesticides. The second program contains information, arguments, and conclusions opposing legislation to restrict the use of pesticides. The programs are broadcast within 6 months of each other during commensurate periods of prime time. X's programs are within the exception for nonpartisan analysis, study, or research. Although neither program individually could be regarded as nonpartisan, the series of two programs constitutes a balanced presentation.

Example (7). Assume the same facts as Example (6), except that X arranged for televising the program favoring legislation to restrict the use of pesticides at 8:00 p.m. on a Thursday evening and for televising the program opposing such legislation at 7:00 a.m. on a Sunday morning. X's presentation is not within the exception for nonpartisan analysis, study, or research, since X disseminated its information in a manner prejudicial to one side of the legislative controversy.

(2) *Technical advice or assistance*—(i) *In general.* Amounts paid or incurred in connection with providing technical advice or assistance to a governmental body, a governmental committee, or a subdivision of either of the foregoing, in response to a written request by such body, committee, or subdivision do not constitute taxable expenditures for purposes of this section. Under this exception, the request for assistance or advice must be made in the name of the requesting governmental body, committee or subdivision rather than an individual member thereof. Similarly, the response to such request must be available to every member of the requesting body, committee or subdivision. For example, in the case of a written response to a request for technical advice or assistance from a Congressional committee, the response will be considered available to every member of the requesting committee if the response is submitted to the person making such request in the name of the committee and it is made clear that the response is for the use of all the members of the committee.

(ii) *Nature of technical advice or assistance.* "Technical advice or assistance" may be given as a result of knowledge or skill in a given area. Because such assistance or advice may be given only at the express request of a governmental body, committee or subdivision, the oral or written presentation of such assistance or advice need not qualify as nonpartisan analysis, study, or research. The offering of opinions or recommendations will ordinarily qualify under this exception only if such opinons or recommendations are specifically requested by the governmental body, committee or subdivision or are directly related to the materials so requested.

(iii) *Examples.* The provisions of this subparagraph may be illustrated by the following examples:

Example (1). A Congressional committee is studying the feasibility of legislation to provide funds for scholarships to United States students attending schools abroad. X, a private foundation which has engaged in a private scholarship program of this type, is asked, in writing, by the committee to describe the manner in which it selects candidates for its program. X's response disclosing its methods of selection constitutes technical advice or assistance.

Example (2). Assume the same facts as Example (1), except that X's response not only includes a description of its own grant-making procedures, but also its views regarding the wisdom of adopting such a program. Since such views are directly related to the subject matter of the request for technical advise or assistance, expenditures paid or incurred with respect to the presentation of such views would not constitute taxable expenditures. However, expenditures paid or incurred with respect to a response which is not directly related to the subject matter of the request for technical advice or assistance would constitute taxable expenditures unless the presentation can qualify as the making available of nonpartisan analysis, study or research.

Example (3). Assume the same facts as Example (1), except that X is requested, in addition, to give any views it considers relevant. A response to this request giving opinions which are relevant to the committee's consideration of the scholarship program but which are not necessarily directly related to X's scholarship program, such as discussions of alternative scholarship programs and their relative merits, would qualify as "technical advice or assistance", and expenditures paid or incurred with respect to such response would not constitute taxable expenditures.

Example (4). A, an official of the State Department, makes a written request in his official capacity for information from Foundation Y relating to the economic development of Country M and for the opinions of Y as to the proper position of the United States in pending negotiations with M concerning a proposed treaty involving a program of economic and technical aid to M. Y's furnishing of such information and opinions constitutes technical advice or assistance.

(3) *Decisions affecting the powers, duties, etc., of a private foundation*—(i) *In general.* Paragraph (c) of this section does not apply to any amount paid or incurred in connection with an appearance before, or communication with, any legislative body with respect to a possible decision of such body which might affect the existence of the private foundation, its powers and duties, its tax-exempt status, or the deductibility of contributions to such foundation. Under this exception, a foundation may communicate with the entire legislative body, committees or subcommittees of such legislative body, individual congressmen or legislators, members of their staffs, or representatives of the executive branch, who are involved in the legislative process, if such communication is limited to the prescribed subjects. Similarly, the foundation may make expenditures in order to initiate legislation if such legislation concerns only matters which might affect the existence of the private foundation, its powers and duties, its tax-exempt status, or the deductibility of contributions to such foundation.

(ii) *Examples.* The provisions of this subparagraph may be illustrated by the following examples:

Example (1). A bill is being considered by Congress which would, if enacted, restrict the power of a private foundation to engage in transactions with certain related persons. Under the proposed bill a private foundation would lose its exemption from taxation if it engages in such transactions. W, a private foundation, writes to the Congressional committee considering the bill, arguing that the enactment of such a bill would not be advisable, and subsequently appears before such committee to make its arguments. In addition, W requests that the Congressional committee consider modification of the 2 percent *de minimis* rule of section 4943(c)(2)(C). Expenditures paid or incurred with respect to such submissions do not constitute taxable expenditures since they are made with respect to a possible decision of Congress which might affect the existence of the private foundation, its powers and duties, its tax-exempt status, or the deduction of contributions to such foundation.

Example (2). A bill being considered in a State legislature is designed to implement the requirements of section 508(e) of the Internal Revenue Code of 1954. Under such section, a private foundation is required to make certain amendments to its government instrument. X, a private foundation, makes a submission to the legislature which proposes alternative measures which might be taken in lieu of the proposed bill. X also arranges to have its president contact certain State legislators with regard to this bill. Expenditures paid or incurred in making such submission and in contacting the State legislators do not constitute taxable expenditures since they are made with respect to a possible decision of such State legislature which might affect the existence of the private foundation, its powers and duties, its tax-exempt status, or the deduction of contributions to such foundation.

Example (3). A bill is being considered by a State legislature under which the State would assume certain responsibilities for nursing care of the aged. Y, a private foundation which hitherto has engaged in such activities, appears before the State legislature and contends that such activities can be better performed by privately supported organizations. Expenditures paid or incurred with respect to such appearance are not made with respect to possible decisions of the State legislature which might affect the existence of the private foundation, its powers and duties, its tax-exempt status, or the deduction of contributions to such foundation, but rather merely affect the scope of the private foundation's future activities.

Example (4). A State legislature is considering the annual appropriations bill. Z, a private foundation which had hitherto performed contract research for the State, appears before the appropriations committee in order to attempt to persuade the committee of the advisability of continuing the program. Expenditures paid or incurred with respect to such appearance are not made with respect to possible decisions of the State legislature which might affect the existence of the private foundation, its powers and duties, its tax-exempt status, or the deduction of contributions to such foundation, but rather merely affect the scope of the private foundation's future activities.

Reg. § 53.4945-2(d)(3)

(4) *Examinations and discussions of broad social, economic, and similar problems.* Expenditures for examinations and discussions of broad social, economic, and similar problems are not taxable even if the problems are of the type with which government would be expected to deal ultimately. Thus, the term "any attempt to influence any legislation" does not include public discussion, or communications with members of legislative bodies or governmental employees, the general subject of which is also the subject of legislation before a legislative body, so long as such discussion does not address itself to the merits of a specific legislative proposal. For example, a private foundation may, without incurring tax under section 4945, present discussions of problems such as environmental pollution or population growth which are being considered by Congress and various State legislatures, but only if the discussions are not directly addressed to specific legislation being considered.

§ 53.4945-3 (T.D. 7215, filed 10-30-72.) **Influencing elections and carrying on voter registration drives.**

(a) *Expenditures to influence elections or carry on voter registration drives*—(1) *In general.* Under section 4945(d)(2), the term "taxable expenditure" includes any amount paid or incurred by a private foundation to influence the outcome of any specific public election or to carry on, directly or indirectly, any voter registration drive, unless such amount is paid or incurred by an organization described in section 4945 (f). However, for treatment of non-earmarked grants to public organizations, see § 53.4945-2(a)(5) and for treatment of certain earmarked grants to organizations described in section 4945(f), see paragraph (b)(2) of this section.

(2) *Influencing the outcome of a specific public election.* For purposes of this section, an organization shall be considered to be influencing the outcome of any specific public election if it participates or intervenes, directly or indirectly, in any political campaign on behalf of or in opposition to any candidate for public office. The term "candidate for public office" means an individual who offers himself, or is proposed by others, as a contestant for an elective public office, whether such office be national, State or local. Activities which constitute participation or intervention in a political campaign on behalf of or in opposition to a candidate include, but are not limited to:

(i) Publishing or distributing written or printed statements or making oral statements on behalf of or in opposition to such a candidate;

(ii) Paying salaries or expenses of campaign workers; and

(iii) Conducting or paying the expenses of conducting a voter registration drive limited to the geographic area covered by the campaign.

(b) *Nonpartisan activities carried on by certain organizations*—(1) *In general.* If an organization meets the requirements described in section 4945(f), an amount paid or incurred by such organization shall not be considered a taxable expenditure even though the use of such amount is otherwise described in section 4945(d)(2). Such requirements are:

(i) The organization is described in section 501(c)(3) and exempt from taxation under section 501(a);

(ii) The activities of the organization are nonpartisan, are not confined to one specific election period, and are carried on in five or more States;

(iii) The organization expends at least 85 percent of its income directly for the active conduct (within the meaning of section 4942(j)(3) and the regulations thereunder) of the activities constituting the purpose or function for which it is organized and operated;

(iv) The organization receives at least 85 percent of its support (other than gross investment income as defined in section 509(e)) from exempt organizations, the general public, governmental units described in section 170(c)(1), or any combination of the foregoing; the organization does not receive more than 25 percent of its support (other than gross investment income) from any one exempt organization (for this purpose treating private foundations which are described in section 4946(a)(1)(H) with respect to each other as one exempt organization); and not more than half of the support of the organization is received from gross investment income; and

(v) Contributions to the organization for voter registration drives are not subject to conditions that they may be used only in specified States, possessions of the United States, or political subdivisions or other areas of any of the foregoing, or the District of Columbia, or that they may be used in only one specific election period.

(2) *Grants to section 4945(f) organizations.* If a private foundation makes a grant to an organization described in section 4945(f) (whether or not such grantee is a private foundation as defined in section 509(a)), such grant will not be treated as a taxable expenditure under section 4945(d)(2) or (4). Even if a grant to such an organization is earmarked for voter registration purposes generally, such a grant will not be treated as a taxable expenditure under section 4945(d)(2) or (4) as long as such earmarking does not violate section 4945(f)(5).

(3) *Period for determining support*—(i) *In general.* The determination whether an organization meets the support test in section 4945(f)(4) for any taxable year is to be made by aggregating all amounts of support received by the organization during the taxable year and the immediately preceding four taxable years. However, the support received in any taxable year which begins before January 1, 1970, shall be excluded.

(ii) *New organizations and organizations with no preceding taxable years beginning after December 31, 1969.* Except as provided in subparagraph (4) of this paragraph, in the case of a new organization or an organization with no taxable years that begin after December 31, 1969, and immediately precede the taxable year in question, the requirements of the support test in section 4945(f)(4) will be considered as met for the taxable year if such requirements are met by the end of the taxable year.

(iii) *Organization with three or fewer preceding taxable years.* In the case of an organization which has been in existence for at least one but fewer than four preceding taxable years beginning after December 31, 1969, the determination whether such organization meets the requirements of the support test in section 4945(f)(4) for the taxable year is to be made by taking into account all the support received by such organization during the taxable year and during each preceding taxable year beginning after December 31, 1969.

(4) *Advance rulings.* An organization will be given an advance ruling that it is an organization described in section 4945(f) for its first taxable year of operation beginning after [insert date these final regulations are filed by the Office of the Federal Register] or for its first taxable year of operation beginning after December 31, 1969, if it submits evidence establishing that it can reasonably be expected to meet the tests under section 4945(f) for such taxable year. An organization which, pursuant to this subparagraph, has been treated as an organization described in section 4945(f) for a taxable year (without withdrawal of such treatment by notification from the Internal Revenue Service during such year), but which actually fails to meet the requirements of section 4945(f) for such taxable year, will not be treated as an organization described in section 4945(f) as of the first day of its next taxable year (for purposes of making any determination under the internal revenue laws with respect to such organization) and until such time as the organization does meet the requirements of section 4945(f). For purposes of section 4945, the status of grants or contributions with respect to grantors or contributors to such organization will not be affected until notice of change of status of such organization is made to the public (such as by publication in the Internal Revenue Bulletin). The preceding sentence shall not apply, however, if the grantor or contributor was responsible for, or was aware of, the fact that the organization did not satisfy section 4945(f) at the end of the taxable year with respect to which the organization had obtained an advance ruling or a determination letter that it was a section 4945(f) organization, or acquired knowledge that the Internal Revenue Service had given notice to such organization that it would be deleted from classification as a section 4945(f) organization.

○― § 53.4945-4 (T.D. 7215, filed 10-30-72.) **Grants to individuals.**

(a) *Grants to individuals*—(1) *In general.* Under section 4945(d)(3) the term "taxable expenditure" includes any amount paid or incurred by a private foundation as a grant to an individual for travel, study, or other similar purposes by such individual unless the grant satisfies the requirements of section 4945(g). Grants to individuals which are not taxable expenditures because made in accordance with the requirements of section 4945(g) may result in the imposition of excise taxes under other provisions of chapter 42.

(2) *"Grants" defined.* For purposes of section 4945, the term "grants" shall include, but is not limited to, such expenditures as scholarships, fellowships, internships, prizes, and awards. Grants shall also include loans for purposes described in section 170(c)(2)(B) and "program related investments" (such as investments in small businesses in central cities or in businesses which assist in neighborhood renovation). Similarly, "grants" include such expenditures as payments to exempt organizations to be used in furtherance of such recipient organizations' exempt purposes whether or not such payments are solicited by such recipient organizations. Conversely, "grants" do not ordinarily include salaries or other compensation to employees. For example, "grants" do not ordinarily include educational payments to employees which are includible in the employees' incomes pursuant to section 61. In addition, "grants" do not ordinarily include payments (including salaries, consultants' fees and reimbursement for travel expenses such as transportation, board, and lodging) to persons (regardless of whether such persons are individuals) for personal services in assisting a foundation in planning, evaluating or developing projects or areas of program activity by consulting, advising, or participating in conferences organized by the foundation.

(3) *Requirements for individual grants*—(i) *Grants for other than section 4945(d)(3) purposes.* A grant to an individual for purposes other than those described in section 4945(d)(3) is not a taxable expenditure within the meaning of section 4945(d)(3). For example, if a foundation makes grants to indigent individuals to enable them to purchase furniture, such grants are not taxable expenditures within the meaning of section 4945(d)(3) even if the requirements of section 4945(g) are not met.

(ii) *Grants for section 4945(d)(3) purposes.* Under section 4945(g), a grant to an individual for travel, study, or other similar purposes is not a "taxable expenditure" only if:

(a) The grant is awarded on an objective and nondiscriminatory basis (within the meaning of paragraph (b) of this section);

(b) The grant is made pursuant to a procedure approved in advance by the Commissioner; and

(c) It is demonstrated to the satisfaction of the Commissioner that:

(1) The grant constitutes a scholarship or fellowship grant which is excluded from gross income under section 117(a) and is to be utilized for study at an educational institution described in section 151(e)(4);

(2) The grant constitutes a prize or award which is excluded from gross income under section 74(b), and the recipient of such prize or award is selected from the general public (within the meaning of section 4941(d)(2)(G)(i) and the regulations thereunder); or

(3) The purpose of the grant is to achieve a specific objective, produce a report or other similar product, or improve or enhance a literary, artistic, musical, scientific, teaching, or other similar capacity, skill, or talent of the grantee.

If a grant is made to an indivvidual for a purpose described in section 4945(g)(3) and such grant otherwise meets the requirements of section 4945(g), such grant shall not be treated as a taxable expenditure even if it is a scholarship or a fellowship

Reg. § 53.4945-4(a)(3)

grant which is not excludable from income under section 117 or if it is a prize or award which is includable in income under section 74.

(iii) *Renewals.* A renewal of a grant which satisfied the requirements of subdivision (ii) of this subparagraph shall not be treated as a grant to an individual which is subject to the requirements of this section, if—

(a) The grantor has no information indicating that the original grant is being used for any purpose other than that for which it was made,

(b) Any reports due at the time of the renewal decision pursuant to the terms of the original grant have been furnished, and

(c) Any additional criteria and procedures for renewal are objective and nondiscriminatory.

For purposes of this section, an extension of the period over which a grant is to be paid shall not itself be regarded as a grant or a renewal of a grant.

(4) *Certain designated grants*—(i) *In general.* A grant by a private foundation to another organization, which the grantee organization uses to make payments to an individual for purposes described in section 4945(d)(3), shall not be regarded as a grant by the private foundation to the individual grantee if the foundation does not earmark the use of the grant for any named individual and there does not exist an agreement, oral or written, whereby such grantor foundation may cause the selection of the individual grantee by the grantee organization. For purposes of this subparagraph, a grant described herein shall not be regarded as a grant by the foundation to an individual grantee even though such foundation has reason to believe that certain individuals would derive benefits from such grant so long as the grantee organization exercises control, in fact, over the selection process and actually makes the selection completely independently of the private foundation.

(ii) *Certain grants to "public charities".* A grant by a private foundation to an organization described in section 509(a)(1), (2), or (3), which the grantee organization uses to make payments to an individual for purposes described in section 4945(d)(3), shall not be regarded as a grant by the private foundation to the individual grantee (regardless of the application of subdivision (i) of this subparagraph) if the grant is made for a project which is to be undertaken under the supervision of the section 509(a)(1), (2), or (3) organization and such grantee organization controls the selection of the individual grantee. This subdivision shall apply regardless of whether the name of the individual grantee was first proposed by the private foundation, but only if there is an objective manifestation of the section 509(a)(1), (2), or (3) organization's control over the selection process, although the selection need not be made completely independently of the private foundation. For purposes of this subdivision, an organization shall be considered a section 509(a)(1) organization if it is treated as such under subparagraph (4) of § 53.4945-5(a).

(iii) *Grants to governmental agencies.* If a private foundation makes a grant to an organization described in section 170 (c)(1) (regardless of whether it is described in section 501(c)(3)) and such grant is earmarked for use by an individual for purposes described in section 4945(d)(3), such grant is not subject to the requirements of section 4945(d)(3) and (g) and this section (regardless of the application of subdivision (i) of this subparagraph) if the section 170(c)(1) organization satisfies the Commissioner in advance that its grant-making program:

(a) Is in furtherance of a purpose described in section 170(c)(2)(B),

(b) Requires that the individual grantee submit reports to it which would satisfy paragraph (c)(3) of this section, and

(c) Requires that the organization investigate jeopardized grants in a manner substantially similar to that described in paragraph (c)(4) of this section.

(iv) *Examples.* The provisions of this subparagraph may be illustrated by the following examples:

Example (1). M, a university described in section 170(b)(1)(A)(ii), requests that P, a private foundation, grant it $100,000 to enable M to obtain the services of a particular scientist for a research project in a special field of biochemistry in which he has exceptional qualifications and competence. P, after determining that the project deserves support, makes the grant to M to enable it to obtain the services of this scientist. M is authorized to keep the funds even if it is unsuccessful in attempting to employ the scientist. Under these circumstances P will not be treated as having made a grant to the individual scientist for purposes of section 4945(d)(3) and (g), since the requirements of subdivision (i) of this subparagraph have been satisfied. Even if M were not authorized to keep the funds if it is unsuccessful in attempting to employ the scientist, P would not be treated as having made a grant to the individual scientist for purposes of section 4945(d)(3) and (g), since it is clear from the facts and circumstances that the selection of the particular scientist was made by M and thus the requirements of subdivision (ii) of this subparagraph would have been satisfied.

Example (2). Assume the same facts as Example (1), except that there are a number of scientists who are qualified to administer the research project, P suggests the name of the particular scientist to be employed by M, and M is not authorized to keep the funds if it unsuccessful in attempting to employ the particular scientist. For purposes of section 4945(d)(3) and (g), P will be treated as having made a grant to the individual scientist whose name it suggested, since it is clear from the facts and circumstances that selection of the particular scientist was made by P.

Example (3). X, a private foundation, is aware of the exceptional research facilities at Y University, an organization described in section 170(b)(1)(A)(ii). Officials of X approach officials of Y with an offer to give Y a grant of $100,000 if Y will engage an adequately qualified physicist to conduct a specific research project. Y's officials accept this proposal, and it is agreed that Y will administer the funds. After examining the qualifications of several research physicists, the officials of Y agree that A, whose name was first suggested by officials of X and who first suggested the specific research project to

X, is uniquely qualified to conduct the project. X's grant letter provides that X has the right to renegotiate the terms of the grant if there is a substantial deviation from such terms, such as breakdown of Y's research facilities or termination of the conduct of the project by an adequately qualified physicist. Under these circumstances, X will not be treated as having made a grant to A for purposes of section 4945(d)(3) and (g), since the requirements of subdivision (ii) of this subparagraph have been satisfied.

Example (4). Professor A, a scholar employed by University Y, an organization described in section 170(b)(1)(A)(ii), approaches Foundation X to determine the availability of grant funds for a particular research project supervised or conducted by Professor A relevant to the program interests of Foundation X. After learning that Foundation X would be willing to consider the project if University Y were to submit the project to X, Professor A submits his proposal to the appropriate administrator of University Y. After making a determination that it should assume responsibility for the project, that Professor A is qualified to conduct the project, and that his participation would be consistent with his other faculty duties, University Y formally adopts the grant proposal and submits it to Foundation X. The grant is made to University Y which, under the terms of the grant, is responsible for the expenditure of the grant funds and the grant project. In such a case, and even if Foundation X retains the right to renegotiate the terms of the grant if the project ceases to be conducted by Professor A, the grant shall not be regarded as a grant by Foundation X to Professor A since University Y has retained control over the selection process within the meaning of subdivision (ii) of this subparagraph.

(5) *Earmarked grants to individuals.* A grant by a private foundation to an individual, which meets the requirements of section 4945(d)(3) and (g), is a taxable expenditure by such foundation under section 4945(d) only if—

(i) The grant is earmarked to be used for any activity described in section 4945(d)(1), (2), or (5), or is earmarked to be used in a manner which would violate section 4945(d)(3) or (4),

(ii) There is an agreement, oral or written, whereby such grantor foundation may cause the grantee to engage in any such prohibited activity and such grant is in fact used in a manner which violates section 4945(d), or

(iii) The grant is made for a purpose other than a purpose described in section 170(c)(2)(B).

For purposes of this subdivision, a grant by a private foundation is earmarked if such grant is given pursuant to an agreement, oral or written, that the grant will be used for specific purposes.

(b) *Selection of grantees on "an objective and nondiscriminatory basis*—(1) *In general.* For purposes of this section, in order for a foundation to establish that its grants to individuals are made on an objective and nondiscriminatory basis, the grants must be awarded in accordance with a program which, if it were a substantial part of the foundation's activities, would be consistent with:

(i) The existence of the foundation's exempt status under section 501(c)(3);

(ii) The allowance of deductions to individuals under section 170 for contributions to the granting foundation; and

(iii) The requirements of subparagraphs (2), (3), and (4) of this paragraph.

(2) *Candidates for grants.* Ordinarily, selection of grantees on an objective and nondiscriminatory basis requires that the group from which grantees are selected be chosen on the basis of criteria reasonably related to the purposes of the grant. Furthermore, the group must be sufficiently broad so that the giving of grants to members of such group would be considered to fulfill a purpose described in section 170(c)(2)(B). Thus, ordinarily the group must be sufficiently large to constitute a charitable class. However, selection from a group is not necessary where taking into account the purposes of the grant, one or several persons are selected because they are exceptionally qualified to carry out these purposes or it is otherwise evident that the selection is particularly calculated to effectuate the charitable purpose of the grant rather than to benefit particular persons or a particular class of persons. Therefore, consistent with the requirements of this subparagraph, the foundation may impose reasonable restrictions on the group of potential grantees. For example, selection of a qualified research scientist to work on a particular project does not violate the requirements of section 4945(d)(3) merely because the foundation selects him from a group of three scientists who are experts in that field.

(3) *Selection from within group of potential grantees.* The criteria used in selecting grant recipients from the potential grantees should be related to the purpose of the grant. Thus, for example, proper criteria for selecting scholarship recipients might include (but are not limited to) the following: prior academic performance; performance on tests designed to measure ability and aptitude for college work; recommendations from instructors; financial need; and the conclusions which the selection committee might draw from a personal interview as to the individual's motivation, character, ability and potential.

(4) *Persons making selections.* The person or group of persons who select recipients of grants should not be in a position to derive a private benefit, directly or indirectly, if certain potential grantees are selected over others.

(5) *Examples.* The provisions of this paragraph may be illustrated by the following examples:

Example (1). X Company employs 100,000 people of whom 1,000 are classified by the company as executives. The company has organized the X Company Foundation which, as its sole activity, provides 100 four-year college scholarships per year for children of the company's employees. Children of all employees (other than disqualified persons with respect to the foundation) who have worked for the X Company for at least two years are eligible to apply for these scholarships. In previous years,

Reg. § 53.4945-4(b)(5)

the number of children eligible to apply for such scholarships has averaged 2,000 per year. Selection of scholarship recipients from among the applicants is made by three prominent educators, who have no connection (other than as members of the selection committee) with the company, the foundation or any of the employees of the company. The selections are made on the basis of the applicants' prior academic performance, performance on certain tests designed to measure ability and aptitude for college work, and financial need. No disproportionate number of scholarships has been granted to relatives of executives of X Company. Under these circumstances, the operation of the scholarship program by the X Company Foundation: (1) is consistent with the existence of the foundation's exempt status under section 501(c)(3) and with the allowance of deductions under section 170 for contributions to the foundation; (2) utilizes objective and nondiscriminatory criteria in selecting scholarship recipients from among the applicants; and (3) utilizes a selection committee which appears likely to make objective and nondiscriminatory selections of grant recipients.

Example (2). Assume the same facts as Example (1), except that the foundation establishes a program to provide 20 college scholarships per year for members of a certain ethnic minority. All members of this minority group (other than disqualified persons with respect to the foundation) living in State Z are eligible to apply for these scholarships. It is estimated that at least 400 persons will be eligible to apply for these scholarships each year. Under these circumstances, the operation of this scholarship program by the foundation: (1) is consistent with the existence of the foundation's exempt status under section 501(c)(3) and with the allowance of deductions under section 170 for contributions to the foundation; (2) utilizes objective and nondiscriminatory criteria in selecting scholarship recipients from among the applicants; and (3) utilizes a selection committee which appears likely to make objective and nondiscriminatory selections of grant recipients.

(c) *Requirements of a proper procedure*—(1) *In general.* Section 4945(g) requires that grants to individuals must be made pursuant to a procedure approved in advance. To secure such approval, a private foundation must demonstrate to the satisfaction of the Commissioner that—

(i) Its grant procedure includes an objective and nondiscriminatory selection process (as described in paragraph (b) of this section);

(ii) Such procedure is reasonably calculated to result in performance by grantees of the activities that the grants are intended to finance; and

(iii) The foundation plans to obtain reports to determine whether the grantees have performed the activities that the grants are intended to finance.

No single procedure or set of procedures is required. Procedures may vary depending upon such factors as the size of the foundation, the amount and purpose of the grants and whether one or more recipients are involved.

(2) *Supervision of scholarship and fellowship grants.* Except as provided in subparagraph (5) of this paragraph, with respect to any scholarship or fellowship grants, a private foundation must make arrangements to receive a report of the grantee's courses taken (if any) and grades received (if any) in each academic period. Such a report must be verified by the educational institution attended by the grantee and must be obtained at least once a year. In cases of grantees whose study at an educational institution does not involve the taking of courses but only the preparation of research papers or projects, such as the writing of a doctoral thesis, the foundation must receive a brief report on the progress of the paper or project at least once a year. Such a report must be approved by the faculty member supervising the grantee or by another appropriate university official. Upon completion of a grantee's study at an educational institution, a final report must also be obtained.

(3) *Grants described in section 4945(g)(3).* With respect to a grant made under section 4945(g)(3), the private foundation shall require reports on the use of the funds and the progress made by the grantee toward achieving the purposes for which the grant was made. Such reports must be made at least once a year. Upon completion of the undertaking for which the grant was made, a final report must be made describing the grantee's accomplishments with respect to the grant and accounting for the funds received under such grant.

(4) *Investigation of jeopardized grants.* (i) Where the reports submitted under this paragraph or other information (including the failure to submit such reports) indicates that all or any part of a grant is not being used in furtherance of the purposes of such grant, the foundation is under a duty to investigate. While conducting its investigation, the foundation must withhold further payments to the extent possible until any delinquent reports required by this paragraph have been submitted and where required by subdivision (ii) or (iii) of this subparagraph.

(ii) In cases in which the grantor foundation determines that any part of a grant has been used for improper purposes and the grantee has not previously diverted grant funds to any use not in furtherance of a purpose specified in the grant, the foundation will not be treated as having made a taxable expenditure solely because of the diversion so long as the foundation—

(a) Is taking all reasonable and appropriate steps either to recover the grant funds or to insure the restoration of the diverted funds and the dedication (consistent with the requirements of (b)(1) and (2) of this subdivision) of other grant funds held by the grantee to the purposes being financed by the grant, and

(b) Withholds any further payments to the grantee after the grantor becomes aware that a diversion may have taken place (hereinafter referred to as "further payments") until it has—

(1) Received the grantee's assurances that future diversions will not occur, and

(2) Required the grantee to take extraordinary precautions to prevent future diversions from occurring.

If a foundation is treated as having made a taxable expenditure under this subparagraph in a case to which this subdivision applies, then unless the foundation meets the requirements of (a) of this subdivision the amount of the taxable expenditure shall be the amount of the diversion plus the amount of any further payments to the same grantee. However, if the foundation complies with the requirements of (a) of this subdivision but not the requirements of (b) of this subdivision, the amount of the taxable expenditure shall be the amount of such further payments.

(iii) In cases where a grantee has previously diverted funds received from a grantor foundation, and the grantor foundation determines that any part of a grant has again been used for improper purposes, the foundation will not be treated as having made a taxable expenditure solely by reason of such diversion so long as the foundation—

(a) Is taking all reasonable and appropriate steps to recover the grant funds or to insure the restoration of the funds and the dedication (consistent with the requirements of (b) (2) and (3) of this subdivision) of other grant funds held by the grantee to the purposes being financed by the grant, and

(b) Withholds further payments until—

(1) Such funds are in fact so recovered or restored,

(2) It has received the grantee's assurances that future diversions will not occur, and

(3) It requires the grantee to take extraordinary precautions to prevent future diversions from occurring.

If a foundation is treated as having made a taxable expenditure under this subparagraph in a case to which this subdivision applies, then unless the foundation meets the requirements of (a) of this subdivision, the amount of the taxable expenditure shall be the amount of the diversion plus the amount of any further payments to the same grantee. However, if the foundation complies with the requirements of (a) of this subdivision, but fails to withhold further payments until the requirements of (b) of this subdivision are met, the amount of the taxable expenditure shall be the amount of such further payments.

(iv) The phrase "all reasonable and appropriate steps" in subdivisions (ii) and (iii) of this subparagraph includes legal action where appropriate but need not include legal action if such action would in all probability not result in the satisfaction of execution on a judgment.

(5) *Supervision of certain scholarship and fellowship grants.* Subparagraph (2) and (4) of this paragraph shall be considered satisfied with respect to scholarship or fellowship grants under the following circumstances:

(i) The scholarship or fellowship grants are described in section 4945(g)(1);

(ii) The grantor foundation pays the scholarship or fellowship grants to an educational institution described in section 151(e)(4); and

(iii) Such educational institution agrees to use the grant funds to defray the recipient's expenses or to pay the funds (or a portion thereof) to the recipient only if the recipient is enrolled at such educational institution and his standing at such educational institution is consistent with the purposes and conditions of the grant.

(6) *Retention of records.* A private foundation shall retain records pertaining to all grants to individuals for purposes described in section 4945(d)(3). Such records shall include:

(i) All information the foundation secures to evaluate the qualification of potential grantees;

(ii) Identification of grantees (including any relationship of any grantee to the foundation sufficient to make such grantee a disqualified person of the private foundation within the meaning of section 4946(a)(1));

(iii) Specification of the amount and purpose of each grant; and

(iv) The follow-up information which the foundation obtains in complying with subparagraphs (2), (3) and (4) of this paragraph.

(7) *Example.* The provisions of paragraphs (b) and (c) of this section may be illustrated by the following example:

Example. The X Foundation grants ten scholarships each year to graduates of high schools in its area to permit the recipients to attend college. It makes the availability of its scholarships known by oral or written communications each year to the principals of three major high schools in the area. The foundation obtains information from each high school on the academic qualifications, background, and financial need of applicants. It requires that each applicant be recommended by two of his teachers or by the principal of his high school. All application forms are reviewed by the foundation officer responsible for making the awards and scholarships are granted on the basis of the academic qualifications and financial need of the grantees. The foundation obtains annual reports on the academic performance of the scholarship recipient from the college or university which he attends. It maintains a file on each scholarship awarded, including the original application, recommendations, a record of the action taken on the application, and the reports on the recipient from the institution which he attends. The described procedures of the X Foundation for the making of grants to individuals qualify for Internal Revenue Service approval under section 4945(g). Furthermore, if the X Foundation's scholarship program meets the requirements of subparagraph (5) of this paragraph, X Foundation will not have to obtain reports on the academic performance of the scholarship recipients.

(d) *Submission of grant procedure*—(1) *Contents of request for approval of grant procedures.* A request for advance approval of a foundation's grant procedures must fully describe the foundation's procedures for awarding grants and for ascertaining that such grants are used for the proper purposes.

The approval procedure does not contemplate specific approval of particular grant programs but instead one-time approval of a system of standards, procedures, and follow-up designed to result in grants which meet the requirements of section 4945(g). Thus, such approval shall apply to a sub-

Reg. § 53.4945-4(c)(7)

sequent grant program as long as the procedures under which it is conducted do not differ materially from those described in the request to the Commissioner. The request must contain the following items:

(i) A statement describing the selection process. Such statement shall be sufficiently detailed for the Commissioner to determine whether the grants are made on an objective and nondiscriminatory basis under paragraph (b) of this section.

(ii) A description of the terms and conditions under which the foundation ordinarily makes such grants, which is sufficient to enable the Commissioner to determine whether the grants awarded under such procedures would meet the requirements of paragraph (1), (2), or (3) of section 4945(g).

(iii) A detailed description of the private foundation's procedure for exercising supervision over grants, as described in paragraph (c)(2) and (3) of this section.

(iv) A description of the foundation's procedures for review of grantee reports, for investigation where diversion of grant funds from their proper purposes is indicated, and for recovery of diverted grant funds, as described in paragraph (c)(4) of this section.

(2) *Place of submission.* Request for approval of grant procedures shall be submitted to the District Director.

(3) *Internal Revenue Service action on request for approval of grant procedures.* If, by the 45th day after a request for approval of grant procedures has been properly submitted to the Internal Revenue Service, the organization has not been notified that such procedures are not acceptable, such procedures shall be considered as approved from the date of submission until receipt of actual notice from the Internal Revenue Service that such procedures do not meet the requirements of this section. If a grant to an individual for a purpose described in section 4945(d)(3) is made after notification to the organization by the Internal Revenue Service that the procedures under which the grant is made are not acceptable, such grant is a taxable expenditure under this section.

(e) *Effective dates* — (1) *In general.* This section shall apply to all grants to individuals for travel, study or other similar purposes which are made by private foundations more than 90 days after October 30, 1972.

(2) *Transitional rules*—(i) *Grants committed prior to January 1, 1970.* Section 4945(d)(3) and (g) and this section shall not apply to a grant for section 170(c)(2)(B) purposes made on or after January 1, 1970, if the grant was made pursuant to a commitment entered into prior to such date, but only if such commitment was made in accordance with the foundation's usual practices and is reasonable in amount in light of the purposes of the grant. For purposes of this subdivision, a commitment will be considered entered into prior to January 1, 1970, if prior to such date, the amount and nature of the payments to be made and the name of the payee were entered on the records of the payor, or were otherwise adequately evidenced, or the notice of the payment to be received was communicated to the payee in writing.

(ii) *Grants awarded on or after January 1, 1970.* In the case of a grant awarded on or after January 1, 1970, but prior to the expiration of 90 days after October 30, 1972, and paid within 48 months after the award of such grant, the requirements of section 4945(g) that an individual grant be awarded on an objective and nondiscriminatory basis pursuant to a procedure approved in advance by the Commissioner will be deemed satisfied if the grantor utilizes any procedure in good faith in awarding a grant to an individual which, in fact, is reasonably calculated to provide objectivity and nondiscrimination in the awarding of such grant and to result in a grant which complies with the conditions of section 4945(g)(1), (2) or (3).

O→ § 53.4945-5 (T.D. 7215, filed 10-30-72; amended by T.D. 7233, filed 12-20-72 and T.D. 7290, filed 11-16-73.) **Grants to organizations.**

(a) *Grants to nonpublic organizations*—(1) *In general.* Under section 4945(d)(4) the term "taxable expenditure" includes any amount paid or incurred by a private foundation as a grant to an organization (other than an organization described in section 509(a)(1), (2) or (3)), unless the private foundation exercises expenditure responsibility with respect to such grant in accordance with section 4945(h). However, the granting foundation does not have to exercise expenditure responsibility with respect to amounts granted to organizations described in section 4945(f).

(2) *"Grants" described.* For a description of the term "grants", see § 53.4945-4 (a)(2).

(3) *Section 509(a)(1), (2) and (3) organizations.* See section 508(b) and the regulations thereunder for rules relating to when a grantor may rely on a potential grantee's characterization of its status as set forth in the notice described in section 508(b).

(4) *Certain "public" organizations.* For purposes of this section, an organization will be treated as a section 509(a)(1) organization if:

(i) It qualifies as such under paragraph (a) of § 1.509(a)-2;

(ii) It is an organization described in section 170(c)(1) or 511(a)(2)(B), even if it is not described in section 501(c)(3); or

(iii) It is a foreign government, or any agency or instrumentality thereof, or an international organization designated as such by Executive Order under 22 U.S.C. 288, even if it is not described in section 501(c)(3).

However, any grant to an organization referred to in this subparagraph must be made exclusively for charitable purposes as described in section 170(c)(2)(B).

(5) *Certain foreign organizations.* If a private foundation makes a grant to a foreign organization which does not have a ruling or determination letter that it is an organization described in section 509(a)(1), (2), or (3), such grant will not be treated as a grant made to an organization other than an organization described in section 509(a)(1), (2), or (3) if the grantor private foundation has made a good faith determination that the grantee organization is an organization described in section 509(a)(1), (2) or (3). Such a "good faith determination" ordinarily will be considered as made where the determination is based on an affidavit of the grantee organization

or an opinion of counsel (of the grantor or the grantee) that the grantee is an organization described in section 509(a)(1), (2) or (3). Such an affidavit or opinion must set forth sufficient facts concerning the operations and support of the grantee for the Internal Revenue Service to determine that the grantee would be likely to qualify as an organization described in section 509(a)(1), (2) or (3). See paragraphs (b)(5) and (b)(6) of this section for other special rules relating to foreign organizations.

(6) *Certain earmarked grants*—(i) *In general.* A grant by a private foundation to a grantee organization which the grantee organization uses to make payments to another organization (the secondary grantee) shall not be regarded as a grant by the private foundation to the secondary grantee if the foundation does not earmark the use of the grant for any named secondary grantee and there does not exist an agreement, oral or written, whereby such grantor foundation may cause the selection of the secondary grantee by the organization to which it has given the grant. For purposes of this subdivision, a grant described herein shall not be regarded as a grant by the foundation to the secondary grantee even though such foundation has reason to believe that certain organizations would derive benefits from such grant so long as the original grantee organization exercises control, in fact, over the selection process and actually makes the selection completely independently of the private foundation.

(ii) *To governmental agencies.* If a private foundation makes a grant to an organization described in section 170(c)(1) and such grant is earmarked for use by another organization, the granting foundation need not exercise expenditure responsibility with respect to such grant if the section 170(c)(1) organization satisfies the Commissioner in advance that:

(a) Its grant-making program is in furtherance of a purpose described in section 170(c)(2)(B), and

(b) The section 170(c)(1) organization exercises "expenditure responsibility" in a manner that would satisfy this section if it applied to such section 170(c)(1) organization.

However, with respect to such grant, the granting foundation must make the reports required by section 4945(h)(3) and paragraph (d) of this section, unless such grant is earmarked for use by an organization described in section 509(a)(1), (2), or (3).

(b) *Expenditure responsibility*—(1) *In general.* A private foundation is not an insurer of the activity of the organization to which it makes a grant. Thus, satisfaction of the requirements of sections 4945(d)(4) and (h) and of subparagraph (3) or (4) of this paragraph, will ordinarily mean that the grantor foundation will not have violated section 4945(d)(1) or (2). A private foundation will be considered to be exercising "expenditure responsibility" under section 4945(h) as long as it exerts all reasonable efforts and establishes adequate procedures—

(i) To see that the grant is spent solely for the purpose for which made,

(ii) To obtain full and complete reports from the grantee on how the funds are spent, and

(iii) To make full and detailed reports with respect to such expenditures to the Commissioner.

In cases in which pursuant to paragraph (a)(6) of this section a grant is considered made to a secondary grantee rather than the primary grantee, the grantor foundation's obligation to obtain reports from the grantee pursuant to section 4945(h)(2) and this section will be satisfied if appropriate reports are obtained from the secondary grantee. For rules relating to expenditure responsibility with respect to transfers of assets described in section 507(b)(2), see section 507(b)(2) and the regulations thereunder.

(2) *Pre-grant inquiry*—(i) Before making a grant to an organization with respect to which expenditure responsibility must be exercised under this section, a private foundation should conduct a limited inquiry concerning the potential grantee. Such inquiry should be complete enough to give a reasonable man assurance that the grantee will use the grant for the proper purposes. The inquiry should concern itself with matters such as: *(a)* the identity, prior history and experience (if any) of the grantee organization and its managers; and *(b)* any knowledge which the private foundation has (based on prior experience or otherwise) of, or other information which is readily available concerning, the management, activities, and practices of the grantee organization.

The scope of the inquiry might be expected to vary from case to case depending upon the size and purpose of the grant, the period over which it is to be paid, and the prior experience which the grantor has had with respect to the capacity of the grantee to use the grant for the proper purposes. For example, if the grantee has made proper use of all prior grants to it by the grantor and filed the required reports substantiating such use, no further pre-grant inquiry will ordinarily be necessary. Similarly, in the case of an organization, such as a trust described in section 4947(a)(2), which is required by the terms of its governing instrument to make payments to a specified organization exempt from taxation under section 501(a), a less extensive pre-grant inquiry is required than in the case of a private foundation possessing discretion with respect to the distribution of funds.

(ii) The provisions of this subparagraph may be illustrated by the following examples:

Example (1). Officials of M, a newly established organization which is described in section 501(c)(4), request a grant from X Foundation to be used for a proposed program to combat drug abuse by establishing neighborhood clinics in certain ghetto areas of a city. Before making a grant to M, X makes an inquiry concerning the identity, prior history and experience of the officials of M. X obtains information pertaining to the officials of M from references supplied by these officials. Since one of the references indicated that A, an official of M, has an arrest record, police records are also checked and A's probation officer is interviewed.

Reg. § 53.4945-5(b)(2)

The inquiry also shows M has no previous history of administering grants and that the officials of M have had no experience in administering programs of this nature. However, in the opinion of X's managers, M's officials (including A who appears to be fully rehabilitated after having been convicted of a narcotics violation several years ago) are well qualified to conduct this program since they are members of the communities in which the clinics are to be established and are more likely to be trusted by drug users in these communities than are outsiders. Under these circumstances X has complied with the requirements of this subparagraph and a grant to M for its proposed program will not be treated as a taxable expenditure solely because of the operation of this subparagraph.

Example (2). Foundation Y wishes to make a grant to Foundation R for use in R's scholarship program. Y has made similar grants to R annually for the last several years and knows that R's managers have observed the terms of the previous grants and have made all requested reports with respect to such grants. No changes in R's management have occurred during the past several years. Under these circumstances, Y has enough information to have such assurance as a reasonable man would require that the grant to R will be used for proper purposes. Consequently, Y is under no obligation to make any further pre-grant inquiry pursuant to this subparagraph.

Example (3). S Foundation requests a grant from Z Foundation for use in S's program of providing medical research fellowships. S has been engaged in this program for several years and has received large numbers of grants from other foundations. Z's managers know that the reputations of S and of S's officials are good. Z's managers also have been advised by managers of W Foundation that W had recently made a grant to S and that W's managers were satisfied that such grant has been used for the purposes for which it was made. Under these circumstances Z has enough information to have such assurance as a reasonable man would require that the grant to S will be used for proper purposes. Consequently, Z is under no obligation to make any further pre-grant inquiry pursuant to this subparagraph.

(3) *Terms of grants.* Except as provided in subparagraph (4) of this paragraph, in order to meet the expenditure responsibility requirements of section 4945 (h), a private foundation must require that each grant to an organization, with respect to which expenditure responsibility must be exercised under this section, be made subject to a written commitment signed by an appropriate officer, director or trustee of the grantee organization. Such commitment must include an agreement by the grantee—

(i) To repay any portion of the amount granted which is not used for the purposes of the grant,

(ii) To submit full and complete annual reports on the manner in which the funds are spent and the progress made in accomplishing the purposes of the grant, except as provided in paragraph (c)(2) of this section,

(iii) To maintain records of receipts and expenditures and to make its books and records available to the grantor at reasonable times, and

(iv) Not to use any of the funds—

(a) To carry on propaganda, or otherwise to attempt, to influence legislation (within the meaning of section 4945(d)(1)),

(b) To influence the outcome of any specific public election, or to carry on, directly or indirectly, any voter registration drive (within the meaning of section 4945 (d)(2)),

(c) To make any grant which does not comply with the requirements of section 4945(d)(3) or (4), or

(d) To undertake any activity for any purpose other than one specified in section 170(c)(2)(B).

The agreement must also clearly specify the purposes of the grant. Such purposes may include contributing for capital endowment, for the purchase of capital equipment, or for general support provided that neither the grants nor the income therefrom may be used for purposes other than those described in section 170(c)(2) (B).

(4) *Terms of program-related investments.* In order to meet the expenditure responsibility requirements of section 4945 (h), with regard to the making of a program-related investment (as defined in section 4944 and the regulations thereunder), a private foundation must require that each such investment with respect to which expenditure responsibility must be exercised under section 4945(d)(4) and (h) and this section be made subject to a written commitment signed by an appropriate officer, director or trustee of the recipient organization. Such commitment must specify the purpose of the investment and must include an agreement by the organization—

(i) To use all the funds received from the private foundation (as determined under paragraph (c)(3) of this section) only for the purposes of the investment and to repay any portion not used for such purposes, provided that, with respect to equity investments, such repayment shall be made only to the extent permitted by applicable law concerning distributions to holders of equity interests,

(ii) At least once a year during the existence of the program-related investment, to submit full and complete financial reports of the type ordinarily required by commercial investors under similar circumstances and a statement that it has complied with the terms of the investment,

(iii) To maintain books and records adequate to provide information ordinarily required by commercial investors under similar circumstances and to make such books and records available to the private foundation at reasonable times, and

(iv) Not to use any of the funds—

(a) To carry on propaganda, or otherwise to attempt, to influence legislation (within the meaning of section 4945(d)(1)),

(b) To influence the outcome of any specific public election, or to carry on, directly or indirectly, any voter registration drive (within the meaning of section 4945 (d)(2)), or

(c) With respect to any recipient which is a private foundation (as defined in section 509(a)), to make any grant which does not comply with the requirements of section 4945(d)(3) or (4).

(5) *Certain grants to foreign organizations.* With respect to a grant to a foreign organization (other than an organization described in section 509(a)(1), (2), or (3) or treated as so described pursuant to paragraph (a)(4) or (a)(5) of this section), subparagraph (3)(iv) or (4)(iv) of this paragraph shall be deemed satisfied if the agreement referred to in subparagraph (3) or (4) of this paragraph imposes restrictions on the use of the grant substantially equivalent to the limitations imposed on a domestic private foundation under section 4945(d). Such restrictions may be phrased in appropriate terms under foreign law or custom and ordinarily will be considered sufficient if an affidavit or opinion of counsel (of the grantor or grantee) is obtained stating that, under foreign law or custom, the agreement imposes restrictions on the use of the grant substantially equivalent to the restrictions imposed on a domestic private foundation under subparagraph (3) or (4) of this paragraph.

(6) *Special rules for grants by foreign private foundations.* With respect to activities in jurisdictions other than those described in section 170(c)(2)(A), the failure of a foreign private foundation which is described in section 4948(b) to comply with subparagraph (3) or (4) of this paragraph with respect to a grant to an organization shall not constitute an act or failure to act which is a prohibited transaction (within the meaning of section 4948(c)(2)).

(7) *Expenditure responsibility with respect to certain transfers of assets described in section 507*—(i) Transfers of assets described in section 507(b)(2). For rules relating to the extent to which the expenditures responsibility rules contained in sections 4945(d)(4) and (h) and this section apply to transfers of assets described in section 507(b)(2), see §§ 1.507-3(a)(7), 1.507-3(a)(8)(ii)(f), and 1.507-3(a)(9).

(ii) Certain other transfers of assets. For rules relating to the extent to which the expenditure responsibility rules contained in sections 4945(d)(4) and (h) and this section apply to certain other transfers of assets described in § 1.507-3(b), see § 1.507-3(b).

(8) *Restrictions on grants (other than program-related investments) to organizations not described in section 501(c)(3).* For other restrictions on certain grants (other than program-related investments) to organizations which are not described in section 501(c)(3), see § 53.4945-6(c).

(c) *Reports from grantees*—(1) *In general.* In the case of grants described in section 4945(d)(4), except as provided in subparagraph (2) of this paragraph, the granting private foundation shall require reports on the use of the funds, compliance with the terms of the grant, and the progress made by the grantee toward achieving the purposes for which the grant was made. The grantee shall make such reports as of the end of its annual accounting period within which the grant or any portion thereof is received and all such subsequent periods until the grant funds are expended in full or the grant is otherwise terminated. Such reports shall be furnished to the grantor within a reasonable period of time after the close of the annual accounting period of the grantee for which such reports are made. Within a reasonable period of time after the close of its annual accounting period during which the use of the grant funds is completed, the grantee must make a final report with respect to all expenditures made from such funds (including salaries, travel, and supplies) and indicating the progress made toward the goals of the grant. The grantor need not conduct any independent verification of such reports unless it has reason to doubt their accuracy or reliability.

(2) *Capital endowment grants to exempt private foundations.* If a private foundation makes a grant described in section 4945(d)(4) to a private foundation which is exempt from taxation under section 501(a) for endowment, for the purchase of capital equipment, or for other capital purposes, the grantor foundation shall require reports from the grantee on the use of the principal and the income (if any) from the grant funds. The grantee shall make such reports annually for its taxable year in which the grant was made and the immediately succeeding two taxable years. Only if it is reasonably apparent to the grantor that, before the end of such second succeeding taxable year, neither the principal, the income from the grant funds, nor the equipment purchased with the grant funds has been used for any purpose which would result in liability for tax under section 4945(d), the grantor may then allow such reports to be discontinued.

(3) *Grantee's accounting and record-keeping procedures.* (i) A private foundation grantee exempt from taxation under section 501(a) (or the recipient of a program-related investment) need not segregate grant funds physically nor separately account for such funds on its books unless the grantor requires such treatment of the grant funds. If such a grantee neither physically segregates grant funds nor establishes separate accounts on its books, grants received within a given taxable year beginning after December 31, 1969, shall be deemed, for purposes of section 4945, to be expended before grants received in a succeeding taxable year. In such case expenditures of grants received within any such taxable year shall be prorated among all such grants. In accounting for grant expenditures, private foundations may make the necessary computations on a cumulative annual basis (or, where appropriate, as of the date for which the computations are made). The rules set forth in the preceding three sentences shall apply to the extent they are consistent with the available records of the grantee and with the grantee's treatment of qualifying distributions under section 4942(h) and the regulations thereunder. The records of expenditures, as well as copies of the reports submitted to the grantor, must be kept for at least 4 years after completion of the use of the grant funds.

(ii) For rules relating to accounting and record-keeping requirements for grantees other than those described in subdivision (i) of this subparagraph, see §§ 53.4945-5(b)(8) and 53.4945-6(c).

(4) *Reliance on information supplied by grantee.* A private foundation exercising expenditure responsibility with respect to its grants may rely on adequate records or

Reg. § 53.4945-5(c)(4)

other sufficient evidence supplied by the grantee organization (such as a statement by an appropriate officer, director or trustee of such grantee organization) showing, to the extent applicable, the information which the grantor must report to the Internal Revenue Service in accordance with paragraph (d)(2) of this section.

(d) *Reporting to Internal Revenue Service by grantor*—(1) *In general.* To satisfy the report-making requirements of section 4945(h)(3), a granting foundation must provide the required information on its annual information return, required to be filed by section 6033, for each taxable year with respect to each grant made during the taxable year which is subject to the expenditure responsibility requirements of section 4945(h). Such information must also be provided on such return with respect to each grant subject to such requirements upon which any amount or any report is outstanding at any time during the taxable year. However, with respect to any grant made for endowment or other capital purposes, the grantor must provide the required information only for any taxable year for which the grantor must require a report from the grantee under paragraph (c)(2) of this section. The requirements of this subparagraph with respect to any grant may be satisfied by submission with the foundation's information return of a report received from the grantee, if the information required by subparagraph (2) of this paragraph is contained in such report.

(2) *Contents of report.* The report required by this paragraph shall include the following information:

(i) The name and address of the grantee,

(ii) The date and amount of the grant,

(iii) The purpose of the grant,

(iv) The amounts expended by the grantee (based upon the most recent report received from the grantee),

(v) Whether the grantee has diverted any portion of the funds (or the income therefrom in the case of an endowment grant) from the purpose of the grant (to the knowledge of the grantor),

(vi) The dates of any reports received from the grantee, and

(vii) The date and results of any verification of the grantee's reports undertaken pursuant to and to the extent required under paragraph (c)(1) of this section by the grantor or by others at the direction of the grantor.

(3) *Record-keeping requirements.* In addition to the information included on the information return, a granting foundation shall make available to the Internal Revenue Service at the foundation's principal office each of the following items:

(i) A copy of the agreement covering each "expenditure responsibility" grant made during the taxable year,

(ii) A copy of each report received during the taxable year from each grantee on any "expenditure responsibility" grant, and

(iii) A copy of each report made by the grantor's personnel or independent auditors of any audits or other investigations made during the taxable year with respect to any "expenditure responsibility" grant.

(4) *Reports received after the close of grantor's accounting year.* Data contained in reports required by this paragraph, which reports are received by a private foundation after the close of its accounting year but before the due date of its information return for that year, need not be reported on such return, but may be reported on the grantor's information return for the year in which such reports are received from the grantee.

(e) *Violations of expenditure responsibility requirements*—(1) *Diversions by grantee* (i) Any diversion of grant funds (including the income therefrom in the case of an endowment grant) by the grantee to any use not in furtherance of a purpose specified in the grant may result in the diverted portion of such grant being treated as a taxable expenditure of the grantor under section 4945(d)(4). However, for purposes of this section, the fact that a grantee does not use any portion of the grant funds as indicated in the original budget projection shall not be treated as a diversion if the use to which the funds are committed is consistent with the purpose of the grant as stated in the grant agreement and does not result in a violation of the terms of such agreement required to be included by paragraph (b)(3) or (b)(4) of this section.

(ii) In any event, a grantor will not be treated as having made a taxable expenditure under section 4945(d)(4) solely by reason of a diversion by the grantee, if the grantor has complied with subdivision (iii)(*a*) and (*b*) or (iv)(*a*) and (*b*) of this subparagraph, whichever is applicable.

(iii) In cases in which the grantor foundation determines that any part of a grant has been used for improper purposes and the grantee has not previously diverted grant funds, the foundation will not be treated as having made a taxable expenditure solely by reason of the diversion so long as the foundation—

(*a*) Is taking all reasonable and appropriate steps either to recover the grant funds or to insure the restoration of the diverted funds and the dedication (consistent with the requirements of (*b*)(*1*) and (*2*) of this subdivision) of the other grant funds held by the grantee to the purposes being financed by the grant, and

(*b*) Withholds any further payments to the grantee after the grantor becomes aware that a diversion may have taken place (hereinafter referred to as "further payments") until it has—

(*1*) Received the grantee's assurances that future diversions will not occur, and

(*2*) Required the grantee to take extraordinary precautions to prevent future diversions from occurring.

If a foundation is treated as having made a taxable expenditure under this subparagraph in a case to which this subdivision applies, then unless the foundation meets the requirements of (*a*) of this subdivision the amount of the taxable expenditure shall be the amount of the diversion (for example, the income diverted in the case of an endowment grant, or the rental value of capital equipment for the period of time for which diverted) plus the amount of any further payments to the same grantee. However, if the foundation complies with the requirements of (*a*) of this subdivision but not the requirements of (*b*) of this subdivision, the amount of the taxable expenditure shall be the amount of such further payments.

(iv) In cases where a grantee has previously diverted funds received from a grantor foundation, and the grantor foundation determines that any part of a grant has again been used for improper purposes, the foundation will not be treated as having made a taxable expenditure solely by reason of such diversion so long as the foundation—

(a) Is taking all reasonable and appropriate steps to recover the grant funds or to insure the restoration of the diverted funds and the dedication (consistent with the requirements of *(b)(2)* and *(3)* of this subdivision) of other grant funds held by the grantee to the purposes being financed by the grant, except that if, in fact, some or all of the diverted funds are not so restored or recovered, then the foundation must take all reasonable and appropriate steps to recover all of the grant funds, and

(b) Withholds further payments until—

(1) Such funds are in fact so recovered or restored,

(2) It has received the grantee's assurances that future diversions will not occur, and

(3) It requires the grantee to take extraordinary precautions to prevent future diversions from occurring.

If a foundation is treated as having made a taxable expenditure under this subparagraph in a case to which this subdivision applies, then unless the foundation meets the requirements of *(a)* of this subdivision, the amount of the taxable expenditure shall be the amount of the diversion plus the amount of any further payments to the same grantee. However, if the foundation complies with the requirements of *(a)* of this subdivision, but fails to withhold further payments until the requirements of *(b)* of this subdivision are met, the amount of the taxable expenditure shall be the amount of such further payments.

(v) The phrase "all reasonable and appropriate steps" (as used in subdivisions (iii) and (iv) of this subparagraph) includes legal action where appropriate but need not include legal action if such action would in all probability not result in the satisfaction of execution on a judgment.

(2) *Grantee's failure to make reports.* A failure by the grantee to make the reports required by paragraph (c) of this section (or the making of inadequate reports) shall result in the grant's being treated as a taxable expenditure by the grantor unless the grantor:

(i) Has made the grant in accordance with paragraph (b) of this section,

(ii) Has complied with the reporting requirements contained in paragraph (d) of this section,

(iii) Makes a reasonable effort to obtain the required report, and

(iv) Withholds all future payments on this grant and on any other grant to the same grantee until such report is furnished.

(3) *Violations by the grantor.* In addition to the situations described in subparagraphs (1) and (2) of this paragraph, a grant which is subject to the expenditure responsibility requirements of section 4945 (h) will be considered a taxable expenditure of the granting foundation if the grantor—

(i) Fails to make a pre-grant inquiry as described in paragraph (b)(2) of this section,

(ii) Fails to make the grant in accordance with a procedure consistent with the requirements of paragraph (b)(3) or (4) of this section, or

(iii) Fails to report to the Internal Revenue Service as provided in paragraph (d) of this section.

(f) *Effective dates*—(1) *In general.* This section shall apply to all grants which are subject to the expenditure responsibility requirements of section 4945(d)(4) and (h) and which are made by private foundations more than 90 days after October 30, 1972.

(2) *Transitional rules*—(i) *Certain grants awarded prior to May 27, 1969.* Section 4945(d)(4) and (h) and this section shall not apply to a grant to a private foundation which is not controlled, directly or indirectly, by the grantor foundation or one or more disqualified persons (as defined in section 4946) with respect to the grantor foundation, provided that such grant—

(a) Is made pursuant to a written commitment which was binding on May 26, 1969, and at all times thereafter,

(b) Is made for one or more of the purposes described in section 170(c)(2)(B), and

(c) Is to be paid out to such grantee foundation on or before December 31, 1974.

(ii) *Grants or expenditures committed prior to January 1, 1970.* Except as provided in paragraph (e)(2)(i) of § 53.4945-4, section 4945 shall not apply to a grant or an expenditure for section 170(c)(2)(B) purposes made on or after January 1, 1970, if the grant or expenditure was made pursuant to a commitment entered into prior to such date, but only if (in the case of a grant or an expenditure other than an unlimited general-purpose grant to an organization) such commitment is reasonable in amount in light of the purposes of the grant. For purposes of this subdivision, a commitment will be considered entered into prior to January 1, 1970, if prior to such date, the amount and nature of the payments to be made and the name of the payee were entered on the records of the payor, or were otherwise adequately evidenced, or the notice of the payment to be received was communicated to the payee in writing.

(iii) *Grants awarded on or after January 1, 1970.* Paragraphs (b), (c), and (d) of this section shall not apply to grants awarded on or after January 1, 1970, but prior to the expiration of 90 days after October 30, 1972, if the grantor has made reasonable efforts, and has established adequate procedures such as a prudent man would adopt in managing his own property, to see that the grant is spent solely for the purpose for which made, to obtain full and complete reports from the grantee on how the funds are spent, and to make full and detailed reports with respect to such grant to the Commissioner. With respect

Reg. § 53.4945-5(f)(2)

to any return filed with the Internal Revenue Service before the expiration of 90 days after October 30, 1972, the grantor may treat reports which satisfy the requirements of the statement to be attached to Form 4720 for the year 1970 under "Specific Instructions—Question B" (items (1) through (5)) as satisfying the grantor reporting requirements with respect to "expenditure responsibility" grants. In the case of a private foundation required to file an annual return for a taxable year ending after January 1, 1970, and before December 31, 1970, the reporting requirements imposed by section 4945(h)(3) for such period shall be regarded as satisfied if such reports are made on the annual return for its first taxable year beginning after December 31, 1969.

§ 53.4945-6 (T.D. 7215, filed 10-30-72; amended by T.D.7233, filed 12-20-72.) Expenditures for noncharitable purposes.

(a) *In general.* Under section 4945(d)(5) the term "taxable expenditure" includes any amount paid or incurred by a private foundation for any purpose other than one specified in section 170(c)(2)(B). Thus, ordinarily only an expenditure for an activity which, if it were a substantial part of the organization's total activities, would cause loss of tax exemption is a taxable expenditure under section 4945(d)(5). For purposes of this section and §§ 53.4945-1 through 53.4945-5, the term "purposes described in section 170(c)(2)(B)" shall be treated as including purposes described in section 170(c)(2)(B) whether or not carried out by an organization described in section 170(c).

(b) *Particular expenditures.* (1) The following types of expenditures ordinarily will not be treated as taxable expenditures under section 4945(d)(5):

(i) Expenditures to acquire investments entered into for the purpose of obtaining income or funds to be used in furtherance of purposes described in section 170(c)(2)(B),

(ii) Reasonable expenses with respect to investments described in subdivision (i) of this subparagraph,

(iii) Payment of taxes,

(iv) Any expenses which qualify as deductions in the computation of unrelated business income tax under section 511,

(v) Any payment which constitutes a qualifying distribution under section 4942(g) or an allowable deduction under section 4940,

(vi) Reasonable expenditures to evaluate, acquire, modify, and dispose of program-related investments, or

(vii) Business expenditures by the recipient of a program-related investment.

(2) Conversely, any expenditures for unreasonable administrative expenses, including compensation, consultant fees and other fees for services rendered, will ordinarily be taxable expenditures under section 4945(d)(5) unless the foundation can demonstrate that such expenses were paid or incurred in the good faith belief that they were reasonable and that the payment or incurrence of such expenses in such amounts was consistent with ordinary business care and prudence. The determination whether an expenditure is unreasonable shall depend upon the facts and circumstances of the particular case.

(c) *Grants to "noncharitable" organizations*—(1) *In general.* Since a private foundation cannot make an expenditure for a purpose other than a purpose described in section 170(c)(2)(B), a private foundation may not make a grant to an organization other than an organization described in section 501(c)(3) unless

(i) The making of the grant itself constitutes a direct charitable act or the making of a program-related investment, or

(ii) Through compliance with the requirements of subparagraph (2) of this paragraph, the grantor is reasonably assured that the grant will be used exclusively for purposes described in section 170(c)(2)(B).

For purposes of this paragraph, an organization treated as a section 509(a)(1) organization under § 53.4945-5(a)(4) shall be treated as an organization described in section 501(c)(3).

(2) *Grants other than transfers of assets described in § 1.507-3(c)(1).* (i) If a private foundation makes a grant which is not a transfer of assets pursuant to any liquidation, merger, redemption, recapitalization, or other adjustment, organization or reorganization to any organization other than an organization described in section 501(c)(3) (except an organization described in section 509(a)(4)), the grantor is reasonably assured (within the meaning of subparagraph (1)(ii) of this paragraph) that the grant will be used exclusively for purposes described in section 170(c)(2)(B) only if the grantee organization agrees to maintain and, during the period in which any portion of such grant funds remain unexpended, does continuously maintain the grant funds (or other assets transferred) in a separate fund dedicated to one or more purposes described in section 170(c)(2)(B). The grantor of a grant described in this paragraph must also comply with the expenditure responsibility provisions contained in sections 4945(d) and (h) and § 53.4945-5.

(ii) For purposes of this paragraph, a foreign organization which does not have a ruling or determination letter that it is an organization described in section 501(c)(3) (other than section 509(a)(4)) will be treated as an organization described in section 501(c)(3) (other than section 509(a)(4)) if in the reasonable judgment of a foundation manager of the transferor private foundation, the grantee organization is an organization described in section 501(c)(3) (other than section 509(a)(4)). The term "reasonable judgment" shall be given its generally accepted legal sense within the outlines developed by judicial decisions in the law of trusts.

(3) *Transfers of assets described in § 1.507-3(c)(1).* If a private foundation makes a transfer of assets (other than a transfer described in subparagraph (1)(i) of this paragraph) pursuant to any liquidation, merger, redemption, recapitalization, or other adjustment, organization, or reorganization to any person, the transferred assets will not be considered used exclusively for purposes described in section 170(c)(2)(B) unless the assets are transferred to a fund or organization described in section 501(c)(3) (other than an organization described in section 509(a)(4)) or treated as so described under section 4947(a)(1).

SUBPART G—DEFINITIONS AND SPECIAL RULES

§ 53.4946 Statutory provisions; Definitions and special rules. [Sec. 4946, IRC].

§ 53.4946-1 (T.D. 7241, filed 12-28-72.) Definitions and special rules.

(a) *Disqualified person.* (1) For purposes of chapter 42 and the regulations thereunder, the following are disqualified persons with respect to a private foundation—

(i) All substantial contributors to the foundation, as defined in section 507(d)(2) and the regulations thereunder.

(ii) All foundation managers of the foundation as defined in section 4946(b)(1) and paragraph (f)(1)(i) of this section.

(iii) An owner of more than 20 percent of—

(a) The total combined voting power of a corporation,

(b) The profits interest of a partnership,

(c) The beneficial interest of a trust or unincorporated enterprise, which is (during such ownership) a substantial contributor to the foundation, as defined in section 507(d)(2) and the regulations thereunder,

(iv) A member of the family, as defined in section 4946(d) and paragraph (h) of this section, of any of the individuals described in subdivision (i), (ii) or (iii) of this subparagraph,

(v) A corporation of which more than 35 percent of the total combined voting power is owned by persons described in subdivision (i), (ii), (iii) or (iv) of this subparagraph,

(vi) A partnership of which more than 35 percent of the profits interest is owned by persons described in subdivision (i), (ii), (iii), or (iv) of this subparagraph, and

(vii) A trust, estate, or unincorporated enterprise of which more than 35 percent of the beneficial interest is owned by persons described in subdivision (i), (ii), (iii), or (iv) of this subparagraph.

(2) For purposes of subparagraphs (1) (iii)(b) and (1)(vi) of this paragraph, the profits interest of a partner shall be equal to his distributive share of income of the partnership, as determined under section 707(b)(3) and the regulations thereunder as modified by section 4946(a)(4).

(3) For purposes of subparagraphs (1) (iii)(c) and (1)(vii) of this paragraph, the beneficial interest in an unincorporated enterprise (other than a trust or estate) includes any right to receive a portion of distributions from profits of such enterprise, and, if the portion of distributions is not fixed by an agreement among the participants, any right to receive a portion of the assets (if any) upon liquidation of the enterprise, except as a creditor or employee. For purposes of this subparagraph, a right to receive distributions of profits includes a right to receive any amount from such profits other than as a creditor or employee, whether as a sum certain or as a portion of profits realized by the enterprise. Where there is no agreement fixing the rights of the participants in such enterprise, the fraction of the respective interests of each participant in such enterprise shall be determined by dividing the amount of all investments or contributions to the capital of the enterprise made or obligated to be made by such participant by the amount of all investments or contributions to capital made or obligated to be made by all of them.

(4) For purposes of subparagraphs (1) (iii)(c) and (1)(vii) of this paragraph, a person's beneficial interest in a trust shall be determined in proportion to the actuarial interest of such person in the trust.

(5) For purposes of subparagraph (1) (iii)(a) and (v) of this paragraph, the term "combined voting power" includes voting power represented by holdings of voting stock, actual or constructive (under section 4946(a)(3)), but does not include voting rights held only as a director or trustee.

(6) For purposes of subparagraph (1) (iii)(a) and (v) of this paragraph, the term "voting power" includes outstanding voting power and does not include voting power obtainable but not obtained, such as, for example, voting power obtainable by converting securities or nonvoting stock into voting stock or by exercising warrants or options to obtain voting stock, and voting power which will vest in preferred stockholders only if and when the corporation has failed to pay preferred dividends for a specified period of time or has otherwise failed to meet specified requirements. Similarly, for purposes of subparagraph (1)(iii)(b) and (c), (vi), and (vii) of this paragraph, the terms "profits interest" and "beneficial interest" include any such interest that is outstanding, but do not include any such interest that is obtainable but has not been obtained.

(7) For purposes of sections 170(b)(1) (E)(iii), 507(d)(1), 508(d), 509(a)(1) and (3), and chapter 42, the term "disqualified person" shall not include an organization which is described in section 509(a)(1), (2), or (3), or any other organization which is wholly owned by such section 509(a)(1), (2), or (3) organization.

(8) For purposes of section 4941 only, the term "disqualified person" shall not include any organization which is described in section 501(c)(3) (other than an organization described in section 509(a)(4)).

(b) *Section 4943.* (1) For purposes of section 4943 only, the term "disqualified person" includes a private foundation—

(i) Which is effectively controlled (within the meaning of § 1.482-1(a)(3)), directly or indirectly, by the same person or persons (other than a bank, trust company, or similar organization acting only as a foundation manager) who control the private foundation in question, or

(ii) Substantially all the contributions to which were made, directly or indirectly, by persons described in subdivision (i), (ii), (iii), or (iv) of paragraph (a)(1) of this section who made, directly or indirectly, substantially all of the contributions to the private foundation in question.

(2) For purposes of subparagraph (1) (ii) of this paragraph, one or more persons will be considered to have made substantially all of the contributions to a private

Reg. § 53.4946-1 (b) (2)

24,258.32 (I.R.C.) Reg. § 53.4946-1(b)(2) 1-15-73

foundation, if such persons have contributed or bequeathed at least 85 percent (and each such person has contributed or bequeathed at least 2 percent) of the total contributions and bequests (within the meaning of section 507(d)(2) and the regulations thereunder) which have been received by such private foundation during its entire existence.

(3) *Examples.* The provisions of this paragraph may be illustrated by the following examples:

Example (1). A, a private foundation, has a board of directors made up of X, Y, Z, M, N, and O. Foundation B's board of directors is made up of Y, M, N, and O. The board of directors in each case has plenary power to determine the manner in which the foundation is operated. For purposes of section 4943, foundation A is a disqualified person with respect to foundation B, and foundation B is a disqualified person with respect to foundation A.

Example (2). Private foundation A has received contributions of $100,000 throughout its existence: $35,000 from X, $51,000 from Y (who is X's father), and $14,000 from Z (an unrelated person). Private foundation B has received $100,000 in contributions during its existence: $50,000 from X and $50,000 from W, X's wife. For purposes of section 4943, private foundation A is a disqualified person with respect to private foundation B, and private foundation B is a disqualified person with respect to private foundation A.

(c) *Section 4941.* For purposes of section 4941, a government official, as defined in section 4946(c) and paragraph (g) of this section, is a disqualified person.

(d) *Attribution of stockholdings.* (1) For purposes of paragraph (a)(1)(iii)(a) and (v) of this section, indirect stockholdings shall be taken into account under section 267(c) and the regulations thereunder. However, for purposes of this paragraph—

(i) Section 267(c)(4) shall be treated as though it provided that the members of the family of an individual are the members within the meaning of section 4946(d) and paragraph (h) of this section; and

(ii) Any stockholdings which have been counted once (whether by reason of actual or constructive ownership) in applying section 4946(a)(1)(E) shall not be counted a second time.

For purposes of paragraph (a)(1)(v) of this section, section 267(c) shall be applied without regard to section 267(c)(3), and stock constructively owned by an individual by reason of the application of section 267(c)(2) shall not be treated as owned by him if he is described in section 4946(a)(1)(D) but not also in section 4946(a)(1)(A), (B), or (C).

(2) *Examples.* The provisions of this paragraph may be illustrated by the following examples:

Example (1). D is a substantial contributor to private foundation Y. D owns 20 percent of the outstanding stock of corporation P. E, D's wife, owns none of the outstanding stock of P. F, E's father, owns 10 percent of the outstanding stock of P. E is treated under section 507(d)(2) as a substantial contributor to Y. E is also treated under section 267(c)(2) as owning both D's 20 percent and F's 10 percent of P, but E is treated as owning nothing for purposes of section 4946(a)(1)(E) because D's 20 percent and F's 10 percent have already been taken into account once (because of their actual ownership of the stock of P) for such purposes. Hence, corporation P is not a disqualified person under section 4946(a)(1)(E) with respect to private foundation Y because persons described in section 4946(a)(1)(A), (B), (C), and (D) own only 30 percent of the stock of P.

Example (2). I, a substantial contributor to private foundation X, is the son of J. I owns 100 percent of the stock of corporation R, which in turn owns 18 percent of the stock of corporation S. J owns 18 percent of the stock of S. I constructively owns 36 percent of the stock of S (J's 18 percent plus R's 18 percent). Both J's actual holdings and R's actual holdings are counted in determining I's constructive holdings because this does not result in counting either of the holdings more than once for purposes of section 4946(a)(1)(E). Therefore, S is a disqualified person with respect to private foundation X, since I, a substantial contributor, constructively owns more than 35 percent of S's stock.

(e) *Attribution of profits or beneficial interests.* (1) For purposes of paragraph (a)(1)(iii)(b), (iii)(c), (vi), and (vii) of this section, ownership of profits or beneficial interests shall be taken into account as though such ownership related to stockholdings, if such stockholdings would be taken into account under section 267(c) and the regulations thereunder, except that section 267(c)(3) shall not apply to attribute the ownership of one partner to another solely by reason of such partner relationship. However, for purposes of this paragraph—

(i) Section 267(c)(4) shall be treated as though it provided that the members of the family of an individual are the members within the meaning of section 4946(d) and paragraph (h) of this section; and

(ii) Any profits interest or beneficial interest which has been counted once (whether by reason of actual or constructive ownership) in applying section 4946(a)(1)(F) or (G) shall not be counted a second time.

For purposes of paragraph (a)(1)(vi) and (vii) of this section, profits or beneficial interests constructively owned by an individual by reason of the application of section 267(c)(2) shall not be treated as owned by him if he is described in section 4946(a)(1)(D) but not in section 4946(a)(1)(A), (B) or (C).

(2) *Example.* The provisions of this paragraph may be illustrated by the following example:

Example. Partnership S is a substantial contributor to private foundation X. Trust T, of which G is sole beneficiary, owns 12 percent of the profits interest of S. G's husband, H, owns 10 percent of the profits interest of S. H is a disqualified person with respect to X (under section 4946(a)(1)(C)) because he is considered to own 22 percent of the profits interest of S (10 percent actual ownership, plus G's 12 percent constructively under section 267(c) (2)). G is a disqualified person with respect to X (under section 4946(a)(1)(C)) because she is considered to own 22 percent of the profits interest of S (12 percent constructively by reason of her beneficial interest in trust T, plus 10 percent constructively under section 267(c)(2) by reason of being a member of the family of H).

(f) *Foundation manager.* (1) For purposes of chapter 42 and the regulations thereunder, the term "foundation manager" means—

(i) An officer, director, or trustee of a foundation (or a person having powers or responsibilities similar to those of officers, directors, or trustees of the foundation), and

(ii) With respect to any act or failure to act, any employee of the foundation having final authority or responsibility (either officially or effectively) with respect to such act or failure to act.

(2) For purposes of subparagraph (1)(i) of this paragraph, a person shall be considered an officer of a foundation if—

(i) He is specifically so designated under the certificate of incorporation, by-laws, or other constitutive documents of the foundation; or

(ii) He regularly exercises general authority to make administrative or policy decisions on behalf of the foundation.

With respect to any act or failure to act, any person described in subdivision (ii) of this subparagraph who has authority merely to recommend particular administrative or policy decisions, but not to implement them without approval of a superior, is not an officer. Moreover, such independent contractors as attorneys, accountants, and investment managers and advisors, acting in their capacities as such, are not officers within the meaning of subparagraph (1)(i) of this paragraph.

(3) For purposes of subparagraph (1)(ii) of this paragraph, an individual rendering services to a private foundation shall be considered an employee of the foundation only if he is an employee within the meaning of section 3121(d)(2).

(4) Since the definition of the term "disqualified person" contained in section 4946(a)(1)(B) incorporates only so much of the definition of the term "foundation manager" as is found in section 4946(b)(1) and subparagraph (1)(i) of this paragraph, any references, in section 4946 and this section, to "disqualified persons" do not constitute references to persons who are "foundation managers" solely by reason of the definition of that term contained in section 4946(b)(2) and subparagraph (1)(ii) of this paragraph.

(g) *Government official*—(1) *In general.* Except as provided in subparagraph (3) of this paragraph, for purposes of section 4941 and paragraph (c) of this section, the term "government official" means, with respect to an act of self-dealing described in section 4941, an individual who, at the time of such act, is described in subdivision (i), (ii), (iii), (iv) or (v) of this subparagraph (other than a "special Government employee" as defined in 18 U.S.C. 202(a)):

(i)(a) An individual who holds an elective public office in the executive or legislative branch of the Government of the United States.

(b) An individual who holds an office in the exeutive or judicial branch of the Government of the United States appointment to which was made by the President.

(ii) An individual who holds a position in the executive, legislative or judicial branch of the Government of the United States—

(a) which is listed in schedule C of rule VI of the Civil Service Rules, or

(b) the compensation for which is equal to or greater than the lowest rate prescribed for GS-16 of the General Schedule under 5 U.S.C. 5332.

(iii) An individual who holds a position under the House of Representatives or the Senate of the United States, as an employee of either of such bodies, who receives gross compensation therefrom at an annual rate of $15,000 or more.

(iv) The holder of an elective or appointive public office in the executive, legislative, or judicial branch of the government of a State, possession of the United States, or political subdivision or other area of any of the foregoing, or of the District of Columbia, for which the gross compensation is at an annual rate of $15,000 or more, who is described in subparagraph (2) of this paragraph.

(v) The holder of a position as personal or executive assistant or secretary to any individual described in subdivision (i), (ii), (iii) or (iv) of this subparagraph.

(2) *Public office*—(i) Definition. In defining the term "public office" for purposes of section 4946(c)(5) and subparagraph (1)(iv) of this paragraph, such term must be distinguished from mere public employment. Although holding a public office is one form of public employment, not every position in the employ of a State or other governmental subdivision (as described in section 4946(c)(5)) constitutes a "public office". Although a determination whether a public employee holds a public office depends on the facts and circumstances of the case, the essential element is whether a significant part of the activities of a public employee is the independent performance of policy-making functions. In applying this subparagraph, several factors may be considered as indications that a position in the executive, legislative, or judicial branch of the government of a State, possession of the United States, or political subdivision or other area of any of the foregoing, or of the District of Columbia, constitutes a "public office". Among such factors to be considered in addition to that set forth above, are that the office is created by the Congress, a State constitution, or the State legislature, or by a municipality or other governmental body pursuant to authority conferred by the Congress, State constitution, or State legislature, and the powers conferred on the office and the duties to be discharged by such office are defined either directly or indirectly by the Congress, State constitution, or State legislature, or through legislative authority.

(ii) Illustrations. The following are illustrations of positions of public employment which do not involve policy-making functions within the meaning of subdivision (i) of this subparagraph and which are thus not a "public office" for purposes of section 4946(c)(5) and subparagraph (1)(iv) of this paragraph:

(a) The chancellor, president, provost, dean, and other officers of a State university who are appointed, elected, or otherwise hired by a State Board of Regents or

Reg. § 53.4946-1(g)(2)

equivalent public body and who are subject to the direction and supervision of such body;

(b) Professors, instructors, and other members of the faculty of a State educational institution who are appointed, elected, or otherwise hired by the officers of the institution or by the State Board of Regents or equivalent public body;

(c) The superintendent of public schools and other public officials who are appointed, elected, or otherwise hired by a Board of Education or equivalent public body and who are subject to the direction and supervision of such body;

(d) Public school teachers who are appointed, elected, or otherwise hired by the superintendent of public schools or by a Board of Education or equivalent public body;

(e) Physicians, nurses, and other professional persons associated with public hospitals and State boards of health who are appointed, elected, or otherwise hired by the governing board or officers of such hospitals or agencies; and

(f) Members of police and fire departments, except for those department heads who, under the facts and circumstances of the case, independently perform policy-making functions as a significant part of their activities.

(3) *Certain government officials on leave of absence.* For purposes of this paragraph, an individual who is otherwise described in section 4946(c) and this paragraph who was on leave of absence without pay on December 31, 1969, from his position or office pursuant to a commitment entered into on or before such date to engage in certain activities/for which he is paid by one or more private foundations, is not to be treated as holding such position or office for any continuous period after December 31, 1969, and prior to January 1, 1971, during which such individual remains on leave of absence to engage in the same activities for which he is paid by such foundations. For purposes of this subparagraph, a commitment is considered entered into on or before December 31, 1969, if on or before such date, the amount and nature of the payments to be made and the name of the individual receiving such payments were entered on the records of the payor, or were otherwise adequately evidenced, or the notice of the payment to be received was communicated to the payee orally or in writing.

(h) *Members of the family.* For purposes of this section, the members of the family of an individual include only—

(1) his spouse,

(2) his ancestors,

(3) his lineal descendants, and

(4) spouses of his lineal descendants. For example, a brother or sister of an individual is not a member of his family for purposes of this section. However, for example, the wife of a grandchild of an individual is a member of his family for such purposes. For purposes of this paragraph, a legally adopted child of an individual shall be treated as a child of such individual by blood.

SUBPART H. APPLICATION TO CERTAIN NONEXEMPT TRUSTS.

§ 53.4947 Statutory provisions; application of taxes to certain nonexempt trusts. [Sec. 4947, IRC]

§ 53.4947-1 (T.D. 7431, filed 8-20-76.) **Application of tax.**

(a) *In general.* Section 4947 subjects trusts which are not exempt from taxation under section 501(a), all or part of the unexpired interests in which are devoted to one or more of the purposes described in section 170(c)(2)(B), and which have amounts in trust for which a deduction was allowed under section 170, 545(b)(2), 556(b)(2), 642(c), 2055, 2106(a)(2) or 2522 to the same requirements and restrictions as are imposed on private foundations. The basic purpose of section 4947 is to prevent these trusts from being used to avoid the requirements and restrictions applicable to private foundations. For purposes of this section, a trust shall be presumed (in the absence of proof to the contrary) to have amounts in trust for which a deduction was allowed under section 170, 545(b)(2), 556(b)(2), 642(c), 2055, 2106(a)(2), or 2522 if a deduction would have been allowable under one of these sections. Also for purposes of this section and § 53.4947-2, the term "purposes described in section 170(c)(2)(B)" shall be treated as including purposes described in section 170(c)(1).

(b) *Charitable trusts* — (1) *General rule.* (i) For purposes of this section and § 53.4947-2, a "charitable trust", within the meaning of section 4947(a)(1), is a trust which is not exempt from taxation under section 501(a), all of the unexpired interests in which are devoted to one or more of the purposes described in section 170(c)(2)(B), and for which a deduction was allowed under section 170, 545(b)(2), 556(b)(2), 642(c), 2055, 2106(a)(2) or 2522 (or the corresponding provisions of prior law). A trust is one for which a deduction was allowed under section 642(c), within the meaning of section 4947(a)(1), once a deduction is allowed under section 642(c) to the trust for any amount paid or permanently set aside. (See section 642(c) and § 1.642-4 for the limitation on such deduction in certain cases.) A charitable trust (as defined in this paragraph) shall be treated as an organization described in section 501(c)(3) and, if it is determined under section 509 that the trust is a private foundation, then Part II of subchapter F of chapter 1 of the Code (other than section 508(a), (b) and (c)) and chapter 42 shall apply to the trust. However, the charitable trust is not treated as an organization described in section 501(c)(3) for purposes of exemption from taxation under section 501(a). Thus, the trust is subject to the excise tax on its investment income under section 4940(b) rather than the tax imposed by section 4940(a). For purposes of satisfying the organizational test described in § 1.501(c)(3)-1(b) when a charitable trust seeks an exemption from taxation under section 501(a), a charitable trust (as defined in this paragraph) shall be considered organized on the day it first becomes subject to section 4947(a)(1). However, for purposes of the special and transitional rules in sections 4940(c)(4)(B), 4942(f)(4), 4943(c)(4)(A)(i) and (B) and section 101(l)(2),(A), (B), (C), and (D), and (l)(3) of the Tax Reform Act of 1969, a charitable trust (as defined in this paragraph) shall be considered organized on the first day it has amounts in trust for which a deduction was allowed (within the meaning of paragraph (a) of this section) under section 170, 545(b)(2), 556(b)(2), 642(c), 2055, 2106(a)(2), or 2522. Thus, under this rule, a trust may be treated as a private foundation in existence on a date governing one of the applicable special and transitional rules even though the trust did not otherwise become subject to the provisions of chapter 42 until a later date.

(ii) The provisions of paragraph (b)(1) of this section may be illustrated by the following examples:

Example (1). On January 30, 1970, X creates an *inter vivos* trust under which M receives 50 percent and N receives 50 percent of the trust's income for 10 years, and upon the termination of which, at the end of the 10-year period, the corpus is to be distributed to O. M, N and O are all organizations described in section 501(c)(3), and X is allowed a deduction under section 170 for the value of all interests placed in trust. The trustees of the trust do not give notice to the Internal Revenue Service under the provisions of section 508(a), and the trust will therefore not be exempt from taxation under section 501(a). The trust is a charitable trust within the meaning of section 4947(a)(1) from the date of its creation.

Example 2. On March 1, 1971, Y creates a charitable remainder annuity trust described in section 664(d)(1) under which Z, Y's son, receives $10,000 per year for life, remainder to be held in trust for P, an organization described in section 501(c)(3). Y is allowed a deduction under section 170 for the present value of the remainder interest to P. During Z's lifetime, the trust is a split-interest trust described in section 4947(a)(2) and paragraph (c) of this section. Upon the death of Z, all unexpired interests (consisting of P's remainder interest) will be devoted to section 170(c)(2)(B) purposes. Except as provided in § 53.4947-1(b)(2)(iv) (relating to a reasonable period of settlement) the trust will be treated as a charitable trust within the meaning of section 4947(a)(1) from the date of the death of Z unless the trustees of the trust apply for recognition of section 501(c)(3) status under the provisions of section 508(a).

(2) *Scope of application of section 4947 (a)(1).*—(i) *In general.* Subject to paragraph (b)(2)(ii) through (vii) of this section, section 4947(a)(1) applies to nonexempt trusts in which all unexpired interests are charitable. For purposes of this section, the term "charitable" when used to describe an interest or beneficiary refers to the purposes described in section 170(c)(2)(B). An estate from which the executor or administrator is required to distribute all of the net assets in trust to such beneficiaries will not be considered a charitable trust under section 4947(a)(1) during the period of estate administration or settlement, except as provided in paragraph (b)(2)(ii) of this section. A charitable trust created by will shall be considered a charitable trust under section 4947(a)(1) as of the date of death of the decedent-grantor, except as provided in paragraph (b)(2)(v) of this section (relating to trusts which wind up). For the circumstances under which segregated amounts are treated as charitable trusts, see § 53.4947-1(c)(3)(iii).

(ii) *Estates.* (A) When an estate from which the executor or administrator is required to distribute all of the net assets in trust for charitable beneficiaries, or free of trust to such beneficiaries, is considered terminated for Federal income tax purposes under § 1.641(b)-3(a), then the estate will be treated as a charitable trust under section 4947(a)(1) between the date on which the estate is considered terminated under § 1.641(b)-3(a) and the date final distribution of all of the net assets is made to or for the benefit of the charitable beneficiaries. This (ii) does not affect the determination of the tax liability under subtitle A of the beneficiaries of the estates.

(B) The provisions of this (ii) may be illustrated by the following example:

Example. X bequeaths his entire estate, including 100 percent of the stock of a wholly-owned corporation, to M, an organization described in section 501(c)(3), under a will which gives his executor authority to hold the stock and manage the corporation for a period of up to 10 years for the benefit of M prior to its ultimate disposition. A deduction for the charitable bequest was allowed to X's estate under section 2055. The executor is vested with a full range of powers, including the power of sale. Upon the death of X, his executor distributes X's assets to M except for the stock of the corporation, which he holds for 5 years prior to its disposition. The continued holding of the stock of the corporation by the executor after the expiration of a reasonable time for performance of all the ordinary duties of administration causes the estate to be considered terminated for Federal income tax purposes pursuant to § 1.641(b)-3(a) and thereby subjects it to the provisions of section 4947(a)(1) from the date of such termination to the date of final disposition of the stock of the corporation.

(iii) *Certain split-interest trusts which wind up.* A split-interest trust (as defined in paragraph (c) of this section) in which all of the unexpired interests are charitable remainder interests and in which the charitable beneficiaries have become entitled to distributions of corpus in trust or free of trust shall continue to be treated as a split-interest trust under section 4947(a)(2) until the date on which final distribution of all the net assets is made. However, if after the expiration of any intervening interests the trust is considered terminated for Federal income tax purposes under § 1.641(b)-3(b), then the trust will be treated as a charitable trust under section 4947(a)(1), rather than a split-interest trust under section 4947(a)(2), between the date on which the trust is considered terminated under § 1.641(b)-3(b) and the date on which such final distribution of all of the net assets is made to or for the benefit of the charitable remainder beneficiaries. This (iii) does not affect the determination of the tax liability under subtitle A of the beneficiaries of the trusts.

Reg. § 53.4947-1 (b) (2)

(iv) *Split-interest trusts which become charitable trusts.* (A) A split-interest trust (as defined in paragraph (c) of this section) in which all of the unexpired interests are charitable remainder interests and in which some or all of the charitable beneficiaries are not entitled to distributions of corpus within the meaning of paragraph (b)(2)(iii) of this section shall continue to be treated as a split-interest trust under section 4947(a)(2) rather than a charitable trust under section 4947(a)(1) for a reasonable period of settlement after the expiration of the noncharitable interest. Thus, a split-interest trust which under its terms is to continue to hold assets for charitable beneficiaries after the expiration of the noncharitable interest rather than distributing them as in paragraph (b)(2)(iii) of this section is given a reasonable period of settlement before being treated as a charitable trust. For purposes of this paragraph, the term "reasonable period of settlement" means that period reasonably required (or if shorter, actually required) by the trustee to perform the ordinary duties of administration necessary for the settlement of the trust. These duties include, for example, the collection of assets, the payment of debts, taxes, and distributions, and the determination of the rights of the subsequent beneficiaries.

(B) This (iv) may be illustrated by the following example:

Example. On January 15, 1971, A creates a charitable remainder annuity trust described in section 664(d)(1) under which the trustees are required to distribute $10,000 a year to B, A's wife, for life, remainder to be held in trust for the use of M, an organization described in section 501(c)(3). A is allowed a deduction under section 170 for the amount of the charitable interest, and the trust is, therefore, treated as a split-interest trust under section 4947(a)(2) from the date of its creation. B dies on February 10, 1975. On April 15, 1975, the trustees complete performance of the ordinary duties of administration necessary for the settlement of the trust brought about by the death of B. These duties include, for example, an accounting for and payment to the estate of B of amounts accrued by B while alive during 1975. However, the trustees do not distribute the corpus to M by April 15, 1975. The trust shall continue to be treated as a split-interest trust under section 4947(a)(2) until April 15, 1975. After April 15, 1975, the trust shall be treated as a charitable trust under section 4947(a)(1).

(v) *Certain revocable and testamentary trusts which wind up.* A revocable trust that becomes irrevocable upon the death of the decedent-grantor, or a trust created by will, from which the trustee is required to distribute all of the net assets in trust for or free of trust to charitable beneficiaries is not considered a charitable trust under section 4947(a)(1) for a reasonable period of settlement (within the meaning of paragraph (b)(2)(iv) of this section) after becoming irrevocable. After that period the trust is considered a charitable trust under section 4947(a)(1).

(vi) *Revocable trusts which become charitable trusts.* A revocable trust that becomes irrevocable upon the death of the decedent-grantor in which all of the unexpired interests are charitable and under the terms of the governing instrument of which the trustee is required to hold some or all of the net assets in trust after becoming irrevocable solely for charitable beneficiaries is not considered a trust under section 4947(a)(1) for a reasonable period of settlement (within the meaning of paragraph (b)(2)(iv) of this section) after becoming irrevocable except that section 4941 may apply if the requirements of § 53.4941(d)-1 (b)(3) are not met. After that period, the trust is considered a charitable trust under section 4947(a)(1).

(vii) *Trust devoted to 170(c) purposes.* (A) A trust all of the unexpired interests in which are devoted to section 170(c)(3) or (5) purposes together with section 170(c)(2)(B) purposes shall be considered a charitable trust except that payments under the terms of the governing instrument to an organization described in section 170(c)(3) or (5) shall not be considered a violation of section 4945(d)(5) or any other provisions of chapter 42 and shall be considered qualifying distributions under section 4942.

(B) *Example.* The application of paragraph (b)(2)(vii) of this section may be illustrated by the following example:

Example. On January 30, 1970, H creates an *inter vivos* trust under the terms of the governing instrument of which M, an organization described in section 170(c)(3), and N, an organization described in section 501(c)(3), are each to receive 50 percent of the income for a period of 10 years. At the end of the 10 year period, the corpus is to be distributed to O, an organization also described in section 501(c)(3). H is allowed a deduction under section 170 for the value of all interests placed in trust. The payments to M do not constitute a violation of section 4945(d)(5) or any other provision of chapter 42 and constitute qualifying distributions under section 4942. However, except as provided in the previous sentence, the trust shall be considered a charitable trust.

(3) *Charitable trusts described in section 509(a)(3).* For purposes of section 509(a)(3)(A), a charitable trust shall be treated as if organized on the day on which it first becomes subject to section 4947(a)(1). However, for purposes of applying §§ 1.509(a)-4(d)(2)(iv)(a), and 1.509(a)-4(i)(1)(ii) and (iii)(c) the previous relationship between the charitable trust and the section 509(a)(1) or (2) organizations it benefits or supports may be considered. If the charitable trust otherwise meets the requirements of section 509(a)(3), it may obtain recognition of its status as a section 509(a)(3) organization by requesting a ruling from the Internal Revenue Service. For the special rules pertaining to the application of the organizational test to organizations terminating their private foundation status under the 12-month or 60-month termination period provided under section 507(b)(1)(B) by becoming "public" under section 509(a)(3), see the regulations under section 507(b)(1).

(c) *Split-interest trusts*—(1) *General rule*—(i) *Definition.* For purposes of this section and § 53.4947-2, a "split-interest trust", within the meaning of section 4947(a)(2), is a trust which is not exempt from taxation under section 501(a), not all of the unexpired interests in which are devoted to one or more of the purposes described in section 170(c)(2)(B), and which has amounts in trust for which a deduction was allowed (within the meaning of paragraph (a) of this section) under section 170, 545 (b)(2), 556(b)(2), 642(c), 2055, 2106(a)(2), or 2522. A trust is one which has amounts in trust for which a deduction was allowed under section 642(c) within the meaning of section 4947(a)(2) once a deduction is allowed under section 642(c) to the trust for any amount permanently set aside. This (i) also includes any trust which is not treated as a charitable trust by operation of paragraph (b)(2)(iii) or (iv) of this section (relating to split-interest trusts in the process of winding up or during a reasonable period of settlement). Section 4947(a)(1) shall apply to a trust described in this (i) (without regard to section 4947(a)(2)(A), (B), or (C)) from the first date upon which the provisions of paragraph (b)(2)(iii) or (iv) of this section are satisfied. For the circumstances under which a trust all of the unexpired interests in which are devoted to section 170(c)(3) or (5) purposes together with section 170(c)(2)(B) purposes is considered a charitable trust, see § 53.4947-1(b)(2)(vii).

(ii) *Applicability of statutory rules.* A split-interest trust is subject to the provisions of section 507 (except as provided in paragraph (e) of this section), 508(e) (to the extent applicable to a split-interest trust), 494, 4943 (except as provided in section 4947(b)(3)), 4944 (except as provided in section 4947(b)(3)), and 4945 in the same manner as if such trust were a private foundation.

(iii) *Special rules.* A newly created trust shall, for purposes of section 4947(a)(2), be treated as having amounts in trust for which a deduction was allowed under section 170, 545(b)(2), 556(b)(2), 642(c), 2055, 2106(a)(2), or 2522 from the date of its creation, even if a deduction was allowed for such amounts only at a later date. For purposes of this (iii), the date of creation of a charitable remainder trust shall be determined by applying the rules in § 1.664-1(a)(4).

(2) *Exception for amounts payable to income beneficiaries.*—(i) Under section 4947(a)(2)(A), paragraph (c)(1)(ii) of this section does not apply to any amounts payable under the terms of a split-interest trust to income beneficiaries unless a deduction was allowed under section 170(f)(2)(B), 2055(e)(2)(B), or 2522(c)(2)(B) with respect to the income interest of any such beneficiary. See § 1.170A-6(c), § 20.2055-2(e)(2), and § 25.2522(c)-3(c)(2) for rules regarding the allowance of these deductions. However, section 4947(a)(2)(A) does not apply when the value of all interests in property transferred in trust are deductible under section 170, 545(b)(2), 556(b)(2), 642(c), 2055, 2106(a)(2), or 2522.

(ii) The application of this subparagraph may be illustrated by the following examples:

Example (1). H creates a charitable remainder unitrust (described in section 664(d)(2)) which is required annually to pay W, H's wife, 5 percent of the net fair market value of the trust assets, valued annually, for her life; and to pay the remainder to Y, a section 501(c)(3) organization. A deduction under section 170(f)(2)(A) was allowed with respect to the remainder interest of Y. Under section 4947 (a)(2)(A), each annual amount which becomes payable to W during her life is not subject to paragraph (c)(1)(ii) of this section on or after the date upon which it becomes so payable and the payment of each amount to W is not an act of self-dealing under section 4941(d)(1) and does not violate any other provision of chapter 42. However, except as provided in the preceding sentence, the trust is subject to paragraph (c)(1)(ii) of this section in the same manner as any other split-interest trust.

Example (2). H bequeaths the residue of his estate in trust for the benefit of S, his son, and Y, an organization described in section 501(c)(3). A guaranteed annuity interest of $10,000 is to be paid to S for 20 years. A guaranteed annuity interest of $5,000 which meets the requirements contained in § 20.2055-2(e)(2)(v)(a) is also to be paid to Y for 20 years. Upon termination of the 20-year term, the corpus is to be distributed to Z, another organization described in section 501(c)(3). The trust is a charitable remainder annuity trust as described in section 664(d)(1) and the regulations thereunder, and a deduction under section 2055(e)(2)(A) was allowed with respect to the remainder interest of Z. A deduction was also allowed under section 2055(e)(2)(B) with respect to the guaranteed annuity interest of Y. The assets in the trust are not segregated under section 4947(a)(2)(B) and paragraph (c)(3) of this section. Under section 4947(a)(2)(A), each payment of $10,000 to S is not subject to section 4947(a)(2) and paragraph (c)(1)(ii) of this section. The payment of each amount to S is not an act of self-dealing under section 4941(d)(1) and does not violate any other provision of chapter 42. However, except as provided in the preceding sentence, the trust is subject to section 4947(a)(2) and paragraph (c)(1)(ii) of this section in the same manner as any other split-interest trust.

Example (3). H creates a trust under which the trustees are required to pay over an annuity interest of $20,000 to W, H's wife, for her life. A guaranteed annuity interest of $10,000 which meets the requirements contained in § 25.2522(c)-3(c)(2)(v) is also to be paid to X, an organization described in section 501(c)(3), for the life of W. Upon the death of W, the corpus of the trust, which consists of office buildings M and N, is to be distributed to S, H's son. H received a deduction under section 2522(c)(2)(B) for the value of X's income interest in the trust. The assets in the trust are not segregated under section 4947(a)(2)(B) and paragraph (c)(3) of this section. Under section 4947(a)(2)(A), each payment of $20,000 to W is not subject to section 4947(a)(2) and paragraph (c)(1)(ii) of this section. The payment of each amount to W is not an act of self-dealing under section 4941(d)(1) and does not violate any other provision of chapter 42. However, except as provided in the preceding sentence, the trust is subject to paragraph (c)(1)(ii) of this section in the same manner as any other split-interest trust. See example (1) of paragraph (c)(3)(v) of this section for the application of section 4947(a)(2)(B) to a similar trust where the trustees segregate the assets of the trust.

Reg. § 53.4947-1(c)(2)

24,258.38 (I.R.C.)   Reg. § 53.4947-1(c)(3)   8-30-76

(3) *Exception for certain segregated amounts.*—(i) *In general.* Under section 4947(a)(2)(B), paragraph (c)(1)(ii) of this section does not apply to assets held in trust (together with the income and capital gains derived from the assets), which are segregated from other assets held in trust for which a deduction was allowed for an income or remainder interest under section 170, 545(b)(2), 556(b)(2), 642(c), 2055, 2106 (a)(2), or 2522.

(ii) *Segregation of amounts.* Amounts will generally be considered segregated (within the meaning of section 4947(a)(2) (B)) if:

(A) assets with respect to which no deduction was allowed (for an income or remainder interest) under section 170, 545(b) (2), 556(b)(2), 642(c), 2055, 2106(a)(2), or 2522, are separately accounted for under section 4947(a)(3) and paragraph (c)(4) of this section from assets for which such a deduction was allowed for any income or remainder interest and,

(B) by reason of the separate accounting the trust can be treated as two separate trusts, one of which is devoted exclusively to noncharitable income and remainder interests and the other of which is a charitable trust described in section 4947(a)(1) or a split-interest trust described in section 4947(a)(2). Under these circumstances, only the "trust" which is devoted exclusively to noncharitable income and remainder interests will be considered a segregated amount which, under section 4947(a)(2)(B), is not subject to section 4947 (a)(2) and paragraph (c)(1)(ii) of this section.

(iii) *Exclusively charitable amounts.* If, under section 4947(a)(2)(B),

(A) an amount held in trust which is devoted exclusively to noncharitable income and remainder interests is segregated from

(B) an amount held in trust which is devoted exclusively to charitable income and remainder interests,
then for purposes of this section the amount described in paragraph (c)(3)(iii) (B) of this section will be treated as a charitable trust which is subject to the provisions of section 4947(a)(1).

(iv) *Charitable and noncharitable amounts.* If, under section 4947(a)(2)(B),

(A) an amount held in trust which is devoted exclusively to noncharitable income and remainder interests is segregated from

(B) an amount held in trust which is devoted to both charitable income or remainder interests and noncharitable income or remainder interests,
then for purposes of this section the amount described in paragraph (c)(3)(iv) (B) of this section will be treated as a split-interest trust which is subject to the provisions of section 4947(a)(2).

(v) *Examples.* The application of paragraph (c)(3) of this section may be illustrated by the following examples:

Example (1). H creates a trust under which the trustees are required to pay over annually 5 percent of the net fair market value of M building, valued annually, to W, H's wife, for life, remainder to S, H's son. The other asset in the trust is N building, with respect to which the trustees are required to pay over annually 5 percent of the net fair market value of the buildings, valued annually, to X, a section 501(c)(3) organization, for a period of 15 years, remainder to S. Each asset is separately accounted for under section 4947(a)(3) and paragraph (c)(4) of this section. H received a deduction under section 2522 for the value of X's income interest in N building. Under these circumstances, M building is considered segregated (within the meaning of section 4947(a)(2)(B)) from N building and is not subject to section 4947 (a)(2). The remainder interest of S in N building is not considered segregated from the income interest of X in N building, since both are interests in the same asset. N building is considered held in a split-interest trust which is subject to section 4947(a)(2) and paragraph (c)(1)(ii) of this section.

Example (2). H transfers $50,000 in trust to pay $2,500 per year to Z, a section 501(c)(3) organization, for a term of 20 years, remainder to S, H's son. H is allowed a deduction under section 2522 for the present value of Z's income interest. The income interest of Z in the trust asset cannot be segregated (within the meaning of section 4947(a)(2)(B)) from the remainder interest of S since both are interests in the same asset. Therefore, the entire trust is subject to section 4947(a)(2) and paragraph (c)(1)(ii) of this section.

(4) *Accounting for segregated amounts* —(i) *General rule.* Under section 4947(a) (2)(B), a trust with respect to which amounts are segregated within the meaning of paragraph (c)(3) of this section must separately account for the various income, deduction, and other items properly attributable to each segregated amount in the books of account and separately account to each of the beneficiaries of the trust.

(ii) *Method.* Separate accounting shall be made—

(A) According to the method regularly employed by the trust, if the method is reasonable, and

(B) In all other cases in a manner which, in the opinion of the Commissioner, is reasonable.

A method of separate accounting will be considered "regularly employed" by a trust when the method has been consistently followed in prior taxable years or when a trust which has never before maintained segregated amounts initiates a reasonable method of separate accounting for its segregated amounts and consistently follows such method thereafter. The trust shall keep permanent records and other data relating to the segregated amounts as are necessary to enable the district director to determine the correctness of the application of the rules prescribed in paragraph (c)(3) and (4) of this section.

(5) *Amounts transferred in trust before May 27, 1969*—(i) *General rule.* Under section 4947(a)(2)(C), paragraph (c)(1)(ii) of this section does not apply to any amounts transferred in trust before May 27, 1969. For purposes of this (5), an amount shall be considered to be transferred in trust only when the transfer is one which meets the requirements for the allowance of a deduction under section 170, 545(b)(2), 556(b)(2), 642(c), 2055, 2106(a) (2), or 2522 (or the corresponding provisions of prior law). Income and capital

gains which are derived at any time from amounts transferred in trust before May 27, 1969, shall also be excluded from the application of paragraph (c)(1)(ii) of this section. If an asset which was transferred in trust before May 27, 1969, is sold or exchanged after May 26, 1969, any asset received by the trust upon the sale or exchange shall be treated as an asset which was transferred in trust before May 27, 1969.

(ii) *Requirement for separate accounting for amounts transferred in trust before May 27, 1969.* If:

(A) Amounts are transferred in trust after May 26, 1969, and the trust to which the amounts are transferred also contains

(B) Amounts transferred in trust before May 27, 1969,

the general rule of paragraph (c)(5)(i) of this section applicable to the amounts described in paragraph (c)(5)(ii)(B) of this section will apply only if the amounts described in paragraph (c)(5)(ii)(A) of this section (together with all income and capital gains derived therefrom) are separately accounted for (within the meaning of paragraph (c)(4) of this section) from the amounts described in paragraph (c)(5)(ii)(B) of this section, together with all income and capital gains derived therefrom. For the application of section 508(e) to a trust with respect to which amounts were transferred both before and after May 27, 1969, see section 508(e) and the regulations thereunder.

(iii) *Exception for certain testamentary trusts.* (A) Amounts transferred in trust before May 27, 1969 include amounts transferred in trust after May 26, 1969 when the transfer is made under the terms of a testamentary trust created by the will of a decedent who died before May 27, 1969, (regardless of whether the executors or the testamentary trustees are required to execute testamentary trusts by court order under applicable local law). Amounts transferred in trust before May 27, 1969, also include amounts transferred to a testamentary trust created by the will of a decedent who died after May 26, 1969 if the will was executed before May 27, 1969 and no dispositive provision of the will was amended (within the meaning of § 20.2055-2(e)(4) and (5)) by the decedent by codicil or otherwise, after May 26, 1969, and the decedent was on May 27, 1969, and at all times thereafter under a mental disability (as defined in § 1.642(c)-2(b)(3)(ii)) to amend the will by codicil or otherwise.

(B) The provisions of this (iii) may be illustrated by the following example:

Example. X executed a will in 1960 which provided for the creation of a testamentary trust which meets the description of a split-interest trust under section 4947 (a)(2). X died on April 15, 1969. Under the provisions of his will, the probate court permitted certain property in X's estate to be transferred to the testamentary trust at fixed intervals over a period of two years during the administration of the estate. Section 4947(a)(2) does not apply to any amount described in this example, including the amounts transferred after May 26, 1969, because, for purposes of section 4947(a)(2)(C), each such transfer will be treated as an amount transferred in trust before May 27, 1969, within the meaning of section 4947(a)(2)(C).

(6) *Scope of application of section 4947(a)(2)*—(i) *In general.* Subject to paragraph (c)(6)(ii), (iii), and (iv) of this section, section 4947(a)(2) applies to trusts in which some but not all unexpired interests are charitable. An estate from which the executor or administrator is required to distribute all of the net assets in trust or free of trust to both charitable and noncharitable beneficiaries will not be considered to be a split-interest trust under section 4947(a)(2) during the period of estate administration or settlement, except as provided in paragraph (c)(6)(ii) of this section. A split-interest trust created by will shall be considered a split-interest trust under section 4947(a)(2) as of the date of death of the decedent-grantor, except as provided in paragraph (c)(6)(iv) of this section.

(ii) *Estates.* (A) When an estate from which the executor or administrator is required to distribute all of the net assets in trust or free of trust to both charitable and noncharitable beneficiaries is considered terminated for Federal income tax purposes under § 1.641(b)-3(a), then the estate will be treated as a split-interest trust under section 4947(a)(2) (or a charitable trust under section 4947(a)(1), if applicable) between the date on which the estate is considered terminated under § 1.641(b)-3(a) and the date on which final distribution of the net assets to the last remaining charitable beneficiary is made. This (ii) does not affect the determination of the tax liability under subtitle A of either charitable or noncharitable beneficiaries of the estates.

(B) The provisions of this (ii) may be illustrated by the following example:

Example. X dies on January 15, 1973 and bequeaths $10,000 to M, an organization described in section 501(c)(3), and the residue of his estate to W, his wife. A deduction for the charitable bequest was allowed to X's estate under section 2055. Substantially all of X's estate consists of 100 percent of the stock of a wholly owned corporation, certain liquid assets such as marketable stocks and securities and bank accounts, and X's home, automobile, and other personal property. X's will gives his executor a full range of powers, including the power to sell the stock of the wholly owned corporation. After the death of X, his executor continues to manage the wholly owned corporation while attempting to sell the stock of the corporation. During this period, the executor makes no distributions to M. On May 24, 1978, the Internal Revenue Service determines under § 1.641(b)-3(a) that the administration of the estate has been unduly prolonged and the estate is considered terminated as of that date for Federal income tax purposes. X's estate will be treated as a split-interest trust described in section 4947(a)(2) between May 24, 1978 and the date on which the $10,000 bequest to M is satisfied. X's estate will therefore be subject to the applicable private foundation provisions during that period and, for example, a sale of the house by the estate to any disqualified person (as defined in section 4946) will be an act of self-dealing under section 4941.

(iii) *Revocable trusts which become split-interest trusts.* A revocable trust that

Reg. § 53.4947-1(c)(6)

24,258.40 (I.R.C.)   Reg. § 53.4947-1(c)(6)   8-30-76

becomes irrevocable upon the death of the decedent-grantor under the terms of the governing instrument of which the trustee is required to hold some or all of its net assets in trust after becoming irrevocable for both charitable and noncharitable beneficiaries is not considered a split-interest trust under section 4947(a)(2) for a reasonable period of settlement after becoming irrevocable except that section 4941 may apply if the requirements of § 53.4941(d)-1 (b)(3) are not met. After that period, the trust is considered a split-interest trust trust under section 4947(a)(2). For purposes of this (iii), the term "reasonable period of settlement" means that period reasonably required (or if shorter, actually required) by the trustee to perform the ordinary duties of administration necessary for the settlement of the trust. These duties include, for example, the collection of assets, the payment of debts, taxes, and distributions, and the determination of rights of the subsequent beneficiaries.

(iv) *Certain revocable and testamentary trusts which wind up.* A revocable trust that becomes irrevocable upon the death of the decedent-grantor, or a trust created by will, from which the trustee is required to distribute all of the net assets in trust or free of trust to both charitable and noncharitable beneficiaries is not considered a split-interest trust under section 4947(a)(2) for a reasonable period of settlement (within the meaning of paragraph (c)(6)(iii) of this section) after becoming irrevocable. After that period, the trust is considered a split-interest trust under section 4947(a)(2) (or a charitable trust under section 4947(a)(1), if applicable).

(d) *Cross references; Governing instrument requirements and charitable deduction limitations.* For the application of section 642(c)(6) (relating to section 170 limitations on charitable deductions of nonexempt private foundation trusts) to a trust described in section 4947(a)(1), see § 1.642 (c)-4. For the denial of a deduction under section 170, 545(b)(2), 556(b)(2), 642(c), 2055, 2106(a)(2), or 2522 for a gift, a bequest for an amount paid to (and the denial of a deduction under section 642(c) for an amount set aside in) a trust described in section 4947(a)(1) or (2) that fails to meet the applicable governing instrument requirements of section 508(e) by the end of the taxable year of the trust, see section 508 (d)(2) and § 1.508-2(b). Since a charitable remainder trust (as defined in section 664) is not exempt under section 501(a), it is subject to section 4947(a)(2), and thus to the governing instrument requirements of section 508(e) to the extent they are applicable.

(e) *Application of section 507(a).*—(1) *General rule.* The provisions of section 507(a) shall not apply to a trust described in section 4947(a)(1) or (2) by reason of any payment to a beneficiary that is directed by the terms of the governing instrument of the trust and is not discretionary with the trustee or, in the case of a discretionary payment, by reason of, or following, the expiration of the last remaining charitable interest in the trust.

(2) *Examples.* The provisions of this (e) may be illustrated by the following examples:

Example (1). H creates a section 4947 (a)(1) trust under which the income is to be paid for 15 years to R, a section 501 (c)(3) organization. Upon the expiration of 15 years, the trust is to terminate and distribute all of its assets to S, another section 501(c)(3) organization. Distribution of the corpus of the trust to S will not be considered a termination of the trust's private foundation status within the meaning of section 507(a).

Example (2). H creates a trust under which X, a section 501(c)(3) organization, receives $20,000 per year for a period of 20 years, remainder to S, H's son. H is allowed a deduction under section 2522 for the present value of X's interest. When the final payment to X has been made at the end of the 20-year period in accordance with the terms of the trust, the provisions of section 4947(a)(2) will cease to apply to the trust because the trust no longer retains any amounts for which the deduction under section 2522 was allowed. However, the final payment to X will not be considered a termination of the trust's private foundation status within the meaning of section 507(a).

Example (3). J creates a charitable remainder annuity trust described in section 664(d)(1) under which S, J's son, receives $10,000 per year for life, remainder to be distributed outright to P, an organization described in section 501(c)(3). J is allowed a deduction under section 170 for the value of the remainder interest placed in trust for the benefit of P, and the provisions of section 4947(a)(2) apply to the trust. At the death of S, the trust will terminate and all assets will be distributed to P. However, such final distribution to P will not be considered a termination of the trust's private foundation status within the meaning of section 507(a).

§ 53.4947-2 (T.D. 7431, filed 8-20-76.) **Special rules.**

(a) *Limit to segregated amounts.* If any amounts held in trust are segregated within the meaning of § 53.4947-1(c)(3), the value of the net assets for purposes of section 507(c)(2) and (g) shall be limited to the segregated amounts with respect to which a deduction under section 170, 545 (b)(2), 556(b)(2), 642(c), 2055, 2106(a)(2), or 2522 was allowed. See the regulations under section 507(c)(2) and (g).

(b) *Applicability of sections 4943 and 4944 to split-interest trusts*—(1) *General rule.* Under section 4947(b)(3), sections 4943 and 4944 do not apply to a split-interest trust described in section 4947(a)(2) if:

(i) all the income interest (and none of the remainder interest) of the trust is devoted solely to one or more of the purposes described in section 170(c)(2)(B) and all amounts in the trust for which a deduction was allowed under section 170, 545 (b)(2), 556(b)(2), 642(c), 2055, 2106(a)(2), or 2522 have an aggregate value (at the time for which the deduction was allowed) of not more than 60 percent of the aggregate fair market value of all amounts in the trust (after the payment of estate taxes and all other liabilities), or

(ii) a deduction was allowed under section 170, 545(b)(2), 556(b)(2), 642(c), 2055, 2106(a)(2) or 2522 for amounts payable under the terms of the trust to every remainder beneficiary, but not to any income beneficiary.

This (1) shall apply to a trust described in paragraph (b)(1)(ii) of this section only if all amounts payable under the terms of the trust to every remainder beneficiary are to be devoted solely to one or more of the purposes described in section 170(c)(2)(B). After the expiration of all income interests in a trust described in paragraph (b)(1)(ii) of this section, the trust shall become subject to section 4947(a)(1) under § 53-.4947-1(b)(2), and section 4947(b)(3) shall no longer apply to the trust. A pooled income fund described in section 642(c)(5) will generally meet the requirements of paragraph (b)(1)(ii) of this section, as will a charitable remainder trust described in section 664(d)(1), if in either case it does not make payments to any income beneficary described in section 170(c).

(2) *Definitions.* (i) For purposes of section 4947(b)(3)(A), the term "income interest" shall include an interest in property transferred in trust which is in the form of a guaranteed annuity interest or unitrust interest as described in § 1.170A-6(c), § 20.2055-2(e)(2) or § 25.2522(c)-3(c)(2) and the term "remainder interest" shall include an interest which succeeds an "income interest" within the meaning of this (i).

(ii) For purposes of section 4947(b)(3)(B), the term "income beneficiary" shall include a recipient of payments described in section 642(c)(5)(F) from a pooled income fund, payments described in section 664(d)(1)(A) from a charitable remainder annuity trust, or payments described in section 664(d)(2)(A) or (3) from a charitable remainder unitrust. The term "remainder beneficiary" shall include a beneficiary of a remainder interest described in section 642(c)(5) or 664(d)(1)(C) or (2)(C).

(c) *Effective date.* Except as otherwise provided in §§ 53.4947-1 and 53.4947-2 and the regulations under sections 508(d) and (e), §§ 53.4947-1 and 53.4947-2 shall take effect on January 1, 1970.

[The page following is 24,258.71]

§ 53.4947-2(c)

SUBPART I—TAX ON INVESTMENT INCOME OF AND DENIAL OF EXEMPTION TO CERTAIN FOREIGN ORGANIZATIONS

§ 53.4948 Statutory provisions; tax on investment income and denial of exemption.
[Sec. 4948, IRC]

§ 53.4948-1 (T.D. 7218, filed 11-9-72.) Application of taxes and denial of exemption with respect to certain foreign organizations.

(a) *Tax on income of certain foreign organizations.* (1) In lieu of the tax imposed by section 4940 and the regulations thereunder, there is hereby imposed for each taxable year beginning after December 31, 1969, on the gross investment income (within the meaning of section 4940(c)(2) and the regulations thereunder) derived from sources within the United States (within the meaning of section 861 and the regulations thereunder) by every foreign organization which is a private foundation (within the meaning of section 509 and the regulations thereunder) and exempt from taxation under section 501(a) for the taxable year a tax equal to 4 percent of such income, except as provided in subparagraph (3) of this paragraph. The tax (if any) will be reported on the form the foundation is required to file under section 6033 for the taxable year, and will be paid annually at the time prescribed for filing such annual return (determined without regard to any extension of time for filing). For purposes of this section, the term "foreign organization" means any organization which is not described in section 170(c)(2)(A).

(2) With respect to the deduction and withholding of tax imposed by section 4948(a), see section 1443(b) and the regulations thereunder.

(3) Whenever there exists a tax treaty between the United States and a foreign country, and a foreign private foundation subject to section 4948(a) is a resident of such country or is otherwise entitled to the benefits of such treaty (whether or not such benefits are available to all residents), if the treaty provides that any item or items (or all items with respect to an organization exempt from income taxation) of gross investment income (within the meaning of section 4940(c)(2)) shall be exempt from income tax, such item or items shall not be taken into account by such foundation in computing the tax to be imposed under section 4948(a) for any taxable year for which the treaty is effective.

(b) *Certain sections inapplicable.* Section 507 (relating to termination of private foundation status), section 508 (relating to special rules with respect to section 501(c)(3) organizations), and chapter 42 (other than section 4948) of the Code shall not apply to any foreign organization which from the date of its creation has received at least 85 percent of its support (as defined in section 509(d), other than section 509(d)(4)) from sources outside the United States. For purposes of this paragraph, gifts, grants, contributions, or membership fees directly or indirectly from a U.S. person (as defined in section 7701(a)(30)) are from sources within the United States.

(c) *Denial of exemption to foreign organizations engaged in prohibited transactions*—(1) In general. A foreign private foundation described in section 4948(b) and paragraph (b) of this section shall not be exempt from taxation under section 501(a) if it has engaged in a prohibited transaction (within the meaning of subparagraph (2) of this paragraph) after December 31, 1969.

(2) *Prohibited transactions.* (i) For purposes of this section, the term "prohibited transaction" means any act or failure to act (other than with respect to section 4942(e), relating to minimum investment return) which would subject a foreign private foundation described in paragraph (b) of this section, or a disqualified person (as defined in section 4946) with respect thereto, to liability for a penalty under section 6684 (relating to assessable penalties with respect to liability for tax under chapter 42) or a tax under section 507 (relating to termination of private foundation status) if such foreign private foundation were a domestic private foundation.

(ii) For purposes of subdivision (i) of this subparagraph—

(a) Approval by an appropriate foreign government of grants by the foreign private foundation to individuals is sufficient to satisfy the requirements of section 4945(g) and the regulations thereunder.

(b) In determining whether a grantee of the foreign organization is a private foundation which is not an operating foundation for purposes of section 4942(g)(1)(A)(ii) or is an organization which is not described in section 509(a)(1), (2), or (3) for purposes of section 4945(d)(4) and (h), a determination made by such foreign organization will be accepted if such determination is made in good faith after a reasonable effort to identify the status of its grantee.

(iii) For purposes of subdivision (i) of this subparagraph, in order for an act or failure to act (without regard to section 4942(e)) to be treated as a prohibited transaction under section 4948(c)(2) by reason of the application of section 6684(1), there must have been a prior act or failure to act (without regard to section 4942(e)), which—

(a) Would have resulted in liability for tax under chapter 42 (other than section 4940 or 4948(a)) if the foreign private foundation had been a domestic private foundation, and

(b) Had been the subject of a warning from the Commissioner that a second act or failure to act (without regard to section 4942(e)) would result in a prohibited transaction.

The second act or failure to act (with respect to which a warning described in subparagraph (3)(i) of this paragraph is given) need not be related to the prior act or failure to act with respect to which a warning from the Commissioner was given under (b) of this subdivision.

(3) *Taxable years affected.* (i) Except as provided in subdivision (ii) of this subparagraph, a foreign private foundation described in paragraph (b) of this section shall be denied exemption from taxation

Reg. § 53.4948-1(c)(3)

under section 501(a) by reason of subparagraph (1) of this paragraph for all taxable years beginning with the taxable year during which it is notified by the Commissioner that it has engaged in a prohibited transaction. The Commissioner shall publish such notice in the Federal Register on the day on which he so notifies such foreign private foundation. In the case of an act or failure to act (without regard to section 4942(e)) which would result in a penalty under section 6684(1) if the foreign private foundation were a domestic private foundation, before giving notice under this subdivision the Commissioner shall warn such foreign private foundation that such act or failure to act may be treated as a prohibited transaction. However, such act or failure to act will not be treated as a prohibited transaction if it is corrected (within the meaning of chapter 42 and the regulations thereunder) within 90 days after the making of such warning.

(ii) *(a)* Any foreign private foundation described in paragraph (b) of this section which is denied exemption from taxation under section 501(a) by reason of subparagraph (1) of this paragraph may, with respect to the second taxable year following the taxable year in which notice is given under subdivision (i) of this subparagraph (or any taxable year subsequent to such second taxable year), file a request for exemption from taxation under section 501(a) on Form 1023. In addition to the information generally required of an organization requesting exemption as an organization described in section 501(a), a request under this subdivision must contain or have attached to it a written declaration, made under the penalties of perjury, by a principal officer of such organization authorized to make such declaration, that the organization will not knowingly again engage in a prohibited transaction.

(b) If the Commissioner is satisfied that such organization will not knowingly again engage in a prohibited transaction and that the organization has satisfied all other requirements under section 501, the organization will be so notified in writing. In such case the organization shall not, with respect to taxable years beginning with the taxable year with respect to which a request under this subdivision is filed, be denied exemption from taxation under section 501(a) by reason of any prohibited transaction which was engaged in before the date on which notice was given under subdivision (i) of this subparagraph. Section 4948(c) provides that an organization denied exemption under such section will not be exempt from taxation under section 501(a) for the taxable year in which notice of loss of exemption is given and at least one immediately subsequent taxable year.

(d) *Disallowance of certain charitable deductions.* No gift, bequest, legacy, devise, or transfer shall be allowed as a deduction under section 170, 545(b)(2), 556(b)(2), 642(c), 2055, 2106(a)(2), or 2522, if made:

(1) To a foreign private foundation described in paragraph (b) of this section after the date on which the Commissioner publishes notice under paragraph (c)(3)(i) of this section that he has notified such organization that it has engaged in a prohibited transaction, and

(2) In a taxable year of such organization for which it is not exempt from taxation under section 501(a) by reason of paragraph (c)(1) of this section.

For purposes of this paragraph, a bequest, legacy, devise, or transfer under section 2055 or 2106(a)(2) shall be treated as made on the date of death of the decedent. For example, assume that an individual gives money to a foreign private foundation described in section 4948(b) in January 1970, January 1971, and January 1972. The organization has a taxable year from June 1 through May 31. In February 1970, notice is duly published that the foreign organization has engaged in a prohibited transaction. In December 1970, the organization duly submits a request for exemption under paragraph (c)(3)(ii)(a) of this section which is granted for the taxable year ending May 31, 1972. The January 1970 gift is allowable as a deduction under section 2522 since it was made before the notice (February 1970). The January 1971 gift is not allowable as a deduction because the taxable year ending May 31, 1971, is a non-exempt year (the first taxable year subsequent to the taxable year of the notice) for the foreign organization. The January 1972 gift is allowable as a deduction under section 2522 because the taxable year ending May 31, 1972, is an exempt year for the organization.

QUALIFIED PENSION, ETC., PLANS

§ 54.4975-6 (T.D. 7491, filed 6-21-77.) **Statutory exemptions for office space or services and certain transactions involving financial institutions.**

(a) *Exemption for office space or services*—(1) *In general.* Section 4975(d)(2) exempts from the excise taxes imposed by section 4975 payment by a plan to a disqualified person, including a fiduciary, for office space or any service (or a combination of services), if (i) such office space or service is necessary for the establishment or operation of the plan; (ii) such office space or service is furnished under a contract or arrangement which is reasonable; and (iii) no more than reasonable compensation is paid for such office space or service. However, section 4975(d)(2) does not contain an exemption for acts described in section 4975(c)(1)(E) (relating to fiduciaries dealing with the income or assets of plans in their own interest or for their own account) or acts described in section 4975(c)(1)(F) (relating to fiduciaries receiving consideration for their own personal account from any party dealing with a plan in connection with a transaction involving the income or assets of the plan). Such acts are separate transactions not described in section 4975 (d)(2). See §§ 54.4975-6(a)(5) and 54.4975-6(a)(6) for guidance as to whether transactions relating to the furnishing of office space or services by fiduciaries to plans involve acts described in section 4975(c)(1)(E). Section 4975(d)(2) does not contain an exemption from other provisions of the Code, such as section 401, or other provisions of law which may impose requirements or restrictions relating to the transactions which are exempt under section 4975(d)(2). See, for example, the general fiduciary responsibility provisions of section 404 of the Employee Retirement Income Security Act of 1974 (the Act) (88 Stat. 877). The provisions of section 4975 (d)(2) are further limited by the flush language at the end of section 4975(d) (relating to transactions with owner-employees and related persons).

(2) *Necessary service.* A service is necessary for the establishment or operation of a plan within the meaning of section 4975(d)(2) and § 54.4975-6(a)(1)(i) if the service is appropriate and helpful to the plan obtaining the service in carrying out the purposes for which the plan is established or maintained. A person providing such a service to a plan (or a person who is a disqualified person solely by reason of a relationship to such a service provider described in section 4975(e)(2)(F), (G), (H) or (I)) may furnish goods which are necessary for the establishment or operation of the plan in the course of, and incidental to, the furnishing of such service to the plan.

(3) *Reasonable contract or arrangement.* No contract or arrangement is reasonable within the meaning of section 4975 (d)(2) and § 54.4975-6(a)(1)(ii) if it does not permit termination by the plan without penalty to the plan on reasonably short notice under the circumstances to prevent the plan from becoming locked into an arrangement that has become disadvantageous. A long-term lease which may be terminated prior to its expiration (without penalty to the plan) on reasonably short notice under the circumstances is not generally an unreasonable arrangement merely because of its long term. A provision in a contract or other arrangement which reasonably compensates the service provider or lessor for loss upon early termination of the contract, arrangement or lease is not a penalty. For example, a minimal fee in a service contract which is charged to allow recoupment of reasonable start-up costs is not a penalty. Similarly, a provision in a lease for a termination fee that covers reasonably foreseeable expenses related to the vacancy and reletting of the office space upon early termination of the lease is not a penalty. Such a provision does not reasonably compensate for loss if it provides for payment in excess of actual loss or if it fails to require mitigation of damages.

(4) *Reasonable compensation.* Section 4975(d)(2) and § 54.4975-6(a)(1)(iii) permit a plan to pay a disqualified person reasonable compensation for the provision of office space or services described in section 4975(d)(2). Paragraph (e) of this section contains regulations relating to what constitutes reasonable compensation for the provision of services.

(5) *Transactions with fiduciaries*—(i) *In general.* If the furnishing of office space or a service involves an act described in section 4975(c)(1)(E) or (F) (relating to acts involving conflicts of interest by fiduciaries), such an act constitutes a separate transaction which is not exempt under section 4975(d)(2). The prohibitions of sections 4975(c)(1)(E) and (F) supplement the other prohibitions of section 4975(c)(1) by imposing on disqualified persons who are fiduciaries a duty of undivided loyalty to the plans for which they act. These prohibitions are imposed upon fiduciaries to deter them from exercising the authority, control or responsibility which makes such persons fiduciaries when they have interests which may conflict with the interests of the plans for which they act. In such cases, the fiduciaries have interests in the transactions which may affect the exercise of their best judgment as fiduciaries. Thus, a fiduciary may not use the authority, control or responsibility which makes such person a fiduciary to cause a plan to pay an additional fee to such fiduciary (or to a person in which such fiduciary has an interest which may affect the exercise of such fiduciary's best judgment as a fiduciary) to provide a service. Nor may a fiduciary use such authority, control or responsibility to cause a plan to enter into a transaction involving plan assets whereby such fiduciary (or a person in which such fiduciary has an interest which may affect the exercise of such fiduciary's best judgment as a fiduciary) will receive consideration from a third party in connection with such transaction. A person in which a fiduciary has an interest which may affect the exercise of such fiduciary's best judgment as a fiduciary includes, for example, a person who is a disqualified person by reason of a relationship to such fiduciary described in section 4975(e)(2)(E), (F), (G), (H) or (I).

(ii) *Transactions not described in section 4975(c)(1)(E).* A fiduciary does not engage in an act described in section 4975 (c)(1)(E) if the fiduciary does not use any of the authority, control or responsibility which makes such person a fiduciary to cause a plan to pay additional fees for a service furnished by such fiduciary or to pay a fee for a service furnished by a person in which such fiduciary has an interest which may affect the exercise of such fiduciary's best judgment as a fiduciary. This may occur, for example, when one fiduciary is retained on behalf of a plan by a second fiduciary to provide a service for an additional fee. However, because the authority, control or responsibility which makes a person a fiduciary may be exercised "in effect" as well as in form, mere approval of the transaction by a second fiduciary does not mean that the first fiduciary has not used any of the authority, control or responsibility which makes such person a fiduciary to cause the plan to pay the first fiduciary an additional fee for a service.

(iii) *Services without compensation.* If a fiduciary provides services to a plan without the receipt of compensation or other consideration (other than reimbursement of direct expenses properly and actually incurred in the performance of such services within the meaning of paragraph (e) (4) of this section), the provision of such services does not, in and of itself, constitute an act described in section 4975(c)(1)(E) or (F). The allowance of a deduction to an employer under section 162 or 212 for the expense incurred in furnishing office space or services to a plan established or maintained by such employer does not constitute compensation or other consideration.

(6) *Examples.* The provisions of § 54.4975-6(a)(5) may be illustrated by the following examples.

Example (1). E, an employer whose employees are covered by plan P, is a fiduciary of P. I is a professional investment adviser in which E has no interest which may affect the exercise of E's best judgment as a fiduciary. E causes P to retain I to provide certain kinds of investment advisory services of a type which causes I to be a fiduciary of P under section 4975(e)(3)(B). Thereafter, I proposes to perform for additional fees portfolio evaluation services in addition to the services currently provided. The provision of such services is arranged by I and approved on behalf of the plan by E. I has not engaged in an act described in section 4975(c)(1)(E), because I did not use any of the authority, control or responsibility which makes I a fiduciary (the provision of investment advisory services) to cause the plan to pay I additional fees for the provision of the portfolio evaluation services. E has not engaged in an act which is described in section 4975(c)(1)(E). E, as the fiduciary who has the responsibility to be prudent in his selection and retention of I and the other investments advisers of the plan, has an interest in the purchase by the plan of portfolio evaluation services. However, such an interest is not an interest which may affect the exercise of E's best judgment as a fiduciary.

Example (2). D, a trustee of plan P with discretion over the management and disposition of plan assets, relies on the advice of C, a consultant to P, as to the investment of plan assets, thereby making C a fiduciary of the plan. On January 1, 1978, C recommends to D that the plan purchase an insurance policy from U, an insurance company which is not a disqualified person with respect to P. C thoroughly explains the reasons for the recommendation and makes a full disclosure concerning the fact that C will receive a commission from U upon the purchase of the policy by P. D considers the recommendations and approves the purchase of the policy by P. C receives a commission. Under such circumstances, C has engaged in an act described in section 4975(c)(1)(E) (as well as section 4975(c)(1)(F)), because C is in fact exercising the authority, control or responsibility which makes C a fiduciary to cause the plan to purchase the policy. However, the transaction is exempt from the prohibited transaction provisions of section 4975(c)(1) if the requirements of Prohibited Transaction Exemption 77-9 are met.

Example (3). Assume the same facts as in Example (2) except that the nature of C's relationship with the plan is not such that C is a fiduciary of P. The purchase of the insurance policy does not involve an act described in section 4975(c)(1)(E) or (F), because such sections only apply to acts by fiduciaries.

Example (4). E, an employer whose employees are covered by plan P, is a fiduciary with respect to P. A, who is not a disqualified person with respect to P, persuades E that the plan needs the services of a professional investment adviser and that A should be hired to provide the investment advice. Accordingly, E causes P to hire A to provide investment advice of the type which makes A a fiduciary under § 54.4975-9(c)(1)(ii)(B). Prior to the expiration of A's first contract with P, A persuades E to cause P to renew A's contract with P to provide the same services for additional fees in view of the increased costs in providing such services. During the period of A's second contract, A provides additional investment advice services for which no additional charge is made. Prior to the expiration of A's second contract, A persuades E to cause P to renew his contract for additional fees in view of the additional services A is providing. A has not engaged in an act described in section 4975(c)(1)(E), because A has not used any of the authority, control or responsibility which makes A a fiduciary (the provision of investment advice) to cause the plan to pay additional fees for A's services.

Example (5). F, a trustee of plan P with discretion over the management and disposition of plan assets, retains C to provide administrative services to P of the type which makes C a fiduciary under section 4975(e)(3)(C). Thereafter, C retains F to provide, for additional fees, actuarial and various kinds of administrative services in addition to the services F is currently providing to P. Both F and C have engaged in an act described in section 4975(c)(1)(E). F, regardless of any intent which he may have had at the time he retained C, has engaged in such an act because F has, in effect, exercised the authority, control or responsibility which makes F a fiduciary to cause the plan to pay F additional fees for the services. C, whose continued employment by P depends on F, has also engaged in such an act, because C has an interest in the transaction which might affect the exercise of C's best judgment as a fiduciary. As a result, C has dealt with plan assets in his own interest under section 4975(c)(1)(E).

Example (6). F, a fiduciary of plan P with discretionary authority respecting the management of P, retains S, the son of F, to provide for a fee various kinds of administrative services necessary for the operation of the plan. F has engaged in an act described in section 4975(c)(1)(E), because S is a person in whom F has an interest which may affect the exercise of F's best judgment as a fiduciary. Such act is not exempt under section 4975(d)(2) irrespective of whether the provision of the services by S is exempt.

Example (7). T, one of the trustees of plan P, is president of bank B. The bank proposes to provide administrative services to P for a fee. T physically absents himself from all consideration of B's proposal and does not otherwise exercise any of the authority, control or responsibility which makes T a fiduciary to cause the plan to retain B. The other trustees decide to retain B. T has not engaged in an act described in section 4975(c)(1)(E). Further, the other trustees have not engaged in an act described in section 4975(c)(1)(E) merely because T is on the board of trustees of P. This fact alone would not make them have an interest in the transaction which might affect the exercise of their best judgment as fiduciaries.

(b) *Exemption for bank deposits*—(1) *In general.* Section 4975(d)(4) exempts from the excise taxes imposed by section 4975 investment of all or a part of a plan's assets in deposits bearing a reasonable rate of interest in a bank or similar financial institution supervised by the United States or a State, even though such bank or similar financial institution is a fiduciary or other disqualified person with respect to the plan, if the conditions of either § 54.4975-6(b)(2) or § 54.4975-6(b)(3) are met. Section 4975 (d)(4) provides an exemption from section 4975(c)(1)(E) (relating to fiduciaries dealing with the income or assets of plans in their own interest or for their own account), as well as sections 4975(c)(1)(A) through (D), because section 4975(d)(4) contemplates a bank or similar financial institution causing a plan for which it acts as a fiduciary to invest plan assets in its own deposits if the requirements of section 4975(d)(4) are met. However, it does not provide an exemption from section 4975 (c)(1)(F) (relating to fiduciaries receiving consideration for their own personal account from any party dealing with a plan in connection with a transaction involving the income or assets of the plan). The receipt of such consideration is a separate transaction not described in the exemption. Section 4975(d)(4) does not contain an exemption from other provisions of the Code, such as section 401, or other provisions of law which may impose requirements or restrictions relating to the transactions which are exempt under section 4975(d)(4). See, for example, the general fiduciary responsibility provisions of section 404 of the Act. The provisions of section 4975(d)(4) are further limited by the flush language at the end of section 4975(d) (relating to transactions with owner-employees and related persons).

(2) *Plan covering own employees.* Such investment may be made if the plan is one which covers only the employees of the bank or similar financial institution, the employees of any of its affiliates, or the employees of both.

(3) *Other plans*—(i) *General rule.* Such investment may be made if the investment is expressly authorized by a provision of the plan or trust instrument or if the investment is expressly authorized (or made) by a fiduciary of the plan (other than the bank or similar financial institution or any of its affiliates) who has authority to make such investments, or to instruct the trustee or other fiduciary with respect to investments, and who has no interest in the transaction which may affect the exercise of such authorizing fiduciary's best judgment as a fiduciary so as to cause such authorization to constitute an act described in section 4975(c)(1)(E) or (F). Any authorization to make investments contained in a plan or trust instrument will satisfy the requirement of express authorization for investments made prior to November 1, 1977. Effective November 1, 1977, in the case of a bank or similar financial institution that invests plan assets in deposits in itself or its affiliates under an authorization contained in a plan or trust instrument, such authorization must name such bank or similar financial institution and must state that such bank or similar financial institution may make investments in deposits which bear a reasonable rate of interest in itself (or in an affiliate).

(ii) *Example.* B, a bank, is the trustee of plan P's assets. The trust instruments give the trustee the right to invest plan assets in its discretion. B invests in the certificates of deposit of bank C, which is a fiduciary of the plan by virtue of performing certain custodial and administrative services. The authorization is sufficient for the plan to make such investment under section 4975(d)(4). Further, such authorization would suffice to allow B to make investments in deposits in itself prior to November 1, 1977. However, subsequent to October 31, 1977, B may not invest in deposits in itself, unless the plan or trust instrument specifically authorizes it to invest in deposits of B.

(4) *Definitions.* (i) The term "bank or similar financial institution" includes a bank (as defined in section 581), a domestic building and loan association (as defined in section 7701(a)(19)), and a credit union (as defined in section 101(6) of the Federal Credit Union Act).

(ii) A person is an affiliate of a bank or similar financial institution if such person and such bank or similar financial institution would be treated as members of the same controlled group of corporations or as members of two or more trades or businesses under common control within the meaning of section 414(b) or (c) and regulations thereunder.

(iii) The term "deposits" includes any account, temporary or otherwise, upon which a reasonable rate of interest is paid, including a certificate of deposit issued by a bank or similar financial institution.

(c) *Exemption for ancillary bank services*—(1) *In general.* Section 4975(d)(6) exempts from the excise taxes imposed by section 4975 the provision of certain ancillary services by a bank or similar financial institution (as defined in § 54.4975-6(b)(4) (i)) supervised by the United States or a State to a plan for which it acts as a fiduciary if the conditions in § 54.4975-6(c)(2)

Reg. § 54.4975-6 (c) (1)

are met. Such ancillary services include services which do not meet the requirements of section 4975(d)(2), because the provision of such services involves an act described in section 4975(c)(1)(E) (relating to fiduciaries dealing with the income or assets of plans in their own interest or for their own account) by the fiduciary bank or similar financial institution. Section 4975 (d)(6) provides an exemption from section 4975(c)(1)(E), because section 4975(d)(6) contemplates the provision of such ancillary services without the approval of a second fiduciary (as described in § 54.4975-6 (a)(5)(ii)) if the conditions of § 54.4975-6 (c)(2) are met. Thus, for example, plan assets held by a fiduciary bank which are reasonably expected to be needed to satisfy current plan expenses may be placed by the bank in a non-interest-bearing checking account in the bank if the conditions of § 54.4975-6(c)(2) are met, notwithstanding the provisions of section 4975(d)(4) (relating to investments in bank deposits). However, section 4975(d)(6) does not provide an exemption for an act described in section 4975(c)(1)(F) (relating to fiduciaries receiving consideration for their own personal account from any party dealing with a plan in connection with a transaction involving the income or assets of the plan). The receipt of such consideration is a separate transaction not described in section 4975(d)(6). Section 4975(d)(6) does not contain an exemption from other provisions of the Code, such as section 401, or other provisions of law which may impose requirements or restrictions relating to the transactions which are exempt under section 4975(d)(6). See, for example, the general fiduciary responsibility provisions of section 404 of the Act. The provisions of section 4975(d)(6) are further limited by the flush language at the end of section 4975(d) (relating to transactions with owner-employees and related persons).

(2) *Conditions.* Such service must be provided—

(i) At not more than reasonable compensation;

(ii) Under adequate internal safeguards which assure that the provision of such service is consistent with sound banking and financial practice, as determined by Federal or State supervisory authority; and

(iii) Only to the extent that such service is subject to specific guidelines issued by the bank or similar financial institution which meet the requirements of § 54.4975-6 (c)(3).

(3) *Specific guidelines.* [Reserved]

(d) *Exemption for services as a fiduciary.* [Reserved]

(e) *Compensation for services*—(1) *In general.* Section 4975(d)(2) refers to the payment of reasonable compensation by a plan to a disqualified person for services rendered to the plan. Section 4975(d)(10) and §§ 54.4975-6(e)(2) through 54.4975-6(e) (5) clarify what constitutes reasonable compensation for such services.

(2) *General rule.* Generally, whether compensation is "reasonable" under sections 4975(d)(2) and (10) depends on the particular facts and circumstances of each case.

(3) *Payments to certain fiduciaries.* Under sections 4975(d)(2) and (10), the term "reasonable compensation" does not include any compensation to a fiduciary who is already receiving full-time pay from an employer or association of employers (any of whose employees are participants in the plan) or from an employee organization (any of whose members are participants in the plan), except for the reimbursement of direct expenses properly and actually incurred and not otherwise reimbursed. The restrictions of this paragraph (e)(3) do not apply to a disqualified person who is not a fiduciary.

(4) *Certain expenses not direct expenses.* An expense is not a direct expense to the extent it would have been sustained had the service not been provided or if it represents an allocable portion of overhead costs.

(5) *Expense advances.* Under sections 4975(d)(2) and (10), the term "reasonable compensation", as applied to a fiduciary or an employee of a plan, includes an advance to such a fiduciary or employee by the plan to cover direct expenses to be properly and actually incurred by such person in the performance of such person's duties with the plan if—

(i) The amount of such advance is reasonable with respect to the amount of the direct expense which is likely to be properly and actually incurred in the immediate future (such as during the next month); and

(ii) The fiduciary or employee accounts to the plan at the end of the period covered by the advance for the expenses properly and actually incurred.

(6) *Excessive compensation.* Under sections 4975(d)(2) and (10), any compensation which would be considered excessive under § 1.162-7 (relating to compensation for personal services which constitutes an ordinary and necessary trade or business expense) will not be "reasonable compensation". Depending upon the facts and circumstances of the particular situation, compensation which is not excessive under § 1.162-7 may, nevertheless, not be "reasonable compensation" within the meaning of sections 4975(d)(2) and (10).

○━ § 54.4975-7 (T.D. 7506, filed 8-30-77.) Other statutory exemptions.

(a) [Reserved]

(b) *Loans to employee stock ownership plans*—

(1) *Definitions.* When used in this paragraph (b) and § 54.4975-11, the terms listed below have the following meanings:

(i) *ESOP.* The term "ESOP" refers to an employee stock ownership plan that meets the requirements of section 4975(e) (7) and § 54.4975-11. It is not synonymous with "stock bonus plan." A stock bonus plan must, however, be an ESOP to engage in an exempt loan. The qualification of an ESOP under section 401(a) and § 54.4975-11 will not be adversely affected merely because it engages in a nonexempt loan.

(ii) *Loan.* The term "loan" refers to a loan made to an ESOP by a disqualified person or a loan to an ESOP which is guaranteed by a disqualified person. It includes a direct loan of cash, a purchase-money transaction, and an assumption of the obligation of an ESOP. "Guarantee" includes an unsecured guarantee and the use of assets of a disqualified person as collateral for a loan, even though the use of assets may not be a guarantee under applicable state law. An amendment of a loan in order to qualify as an exempt loan is not a refinancing of the loan or the making of another loan.

(iii) *Exempt loan.* The term "exempt loan" refers to a loan that satisfies the provisions of this paragraph (b). A "non-exempt loan" is one that fails to satisfy such provisions.

(iv) *Publicly traded.* The term "publicly traded" refers to a security that is listed on a national securities exchange registered under section 6 of the Securities Exchange Act of 1934 (15 U.S.C. 78f) or that is quoted on a system sponsored by a national securities association registered under section 15A(b) of the Securities Exchange Act (15 U.S.C. 78o).

(v) *Qualifying employer security.* The term "qualifying employer security" refers to a security described in § 54.4975-12.

(2) *Statutory exemption*—(1) *Scope.* Section 4975(d)(3) provides an exemption from the excise tax imposed under section 4975(a) and (b) by reason of section 4975 (c)(1)(A) through (E). Section 4975(d)(3) does not provide an exemption from the imposition of such tax by reason of section 4975(c)(1)(F), relating to fiduciaries receiving consideration for their own personal account from any party dealing with a plan in connection with a transaction involving the income or assets of the plan.

(ii) *Special scrutiny of transaction.* The exemption under section 4975(d)(3) includes within its scope certain transactions in which the potential for self-dealing by fiduciaries exists and in which the interests of fiduciaries may conflict with the interests of participants. To guard against these potential abuses, the Internal Revenue Service will subject these transactions to special scrutiny to ensure that they are primarily for the benefit of participants and their beneficiaries. Although the transactions need not be arranged and approved by an independent fiduciary, fiduciaries are cautioned to exercise scrupulously their discretion in approving them. For example, fiduciaries should be prepared to demonstrate compliance with the net effect test and the arm's-length standard under paragraph (b)(3)(ii) and (iii) of this section. Also, fiduciaries should determine that the transaction is truly arranged primarily in the interest of participants and their beneficiaries rather than, for example, in the interest of certain selling shareholders.

(3) *Primary benefit requirement*—(i) *In general.* An exempt loan must be primarily for the benefit of the ESOP participants and their beneficiaries. All the surrounding facts and circumstances, including those described in paragraph (b) (3)(ii) and (iii) of this section, will be considered in determining whether the loan satisfies this requirement. However, no loan will satisfy the requirement unless it satisfies the requirements of paragraph (b) (4), (5), and (6) of this section.

(ii) *Net effect on plan assets.* At the time that a loan is made, the interest rate for the loan and the price of securities to be acquired with the loan proceeds should not be such that plan assets might be drained off.

(iii) *Arm's-length standard.* The terms of a loan, whether or not between independent parties, must, at the time the loan is made, be at least as favorable to the ESOP as the terms of a comparable loan resulting from arm's-length negotiations between independent parties.

(4) *Use of loan proceeds.* The proceeds of an exempt loan must be used within a reasonable time after their receipt by the borrowing ESOP only for any or all of the following purposes:

(i) To acquire qualifying employer securities.

(ii) To repay such loan.

(iii) To repay a prior exempt loan. A new loan, the proceeds of which are so used, must satisfy the provisions of this paragraph (b).

Except as provided in paragraph (b)(9) and (10) of this section or as otherwise required by applicable law, no security acquired with the proceeds of an exempt loan may be subject to a put, call, or other option, or buy-sell or similar arrangement while held by and when distributed from a plan, whether or not the plan is then an ESOP.

(5) *Liability and collateral of ESOP for loan.* An exempt loan must be without recourse against the ESOP. Furthermore, the only assets of the ESOP that may be given as collateral on an exempt loan are qualifying employer securities of two classes: those acquired with the proceeds of the loan and those that were used as collateral on a prior exempt loan repaid with the proceeds of the current exempt loan. No person entitled to payment under the exempt loan shall have any right to assets of the ESOP other than:

(i) Collateral given for the loan,

(ii) Contributions (other than contributions of employer securities) that are made under an ESOP to meet its obligations under the loan, and

(iii) Earnings attributable to such collateral and the investment of such contributions.

The payments made with respect to an exempt loan by the ESOP during a plan year must not exceed an amount equal to the sum of such contributions and earnings received during or prior to the year less such payments in prior years. Such contributions and earnings must be accounted for separately in the books of account of the ESOP until the loan is repaid.

(6) *Default.* In the event of default upon an exempt loan, the value of plan assets transferred in satisfaction of the loan must not exceed the amount of default. If the lender is a disqualified person, a loan must provide for a transfer of plan assets upon default only upon and to the extent of the failure of the plan to meet the payment schedule of the loan. For purposes of this subparagraph (6), the making of a guarantee does not make a person a lender.

(7) *Reasonable rate of interest.* The interest rate of a loan must not be in excess of a reasonable rate of interest. All relevant factors will be considered in determining a reasonable rate of interest, including the amount and duration of the loan, the security and guarantee (if any) involved, the credit standing of the ESOP and the guarantor (if any), and the interest rate prevailing for comparable loans. When these factors are considered, a variable interest rate may be reasonable.

Reg. § 54.4975-7(b)(7)

(8) *Release from encumbrance*—(i) *General rule.* In general, an exempt loan must provide for the release from encumbrance under this subdivision (i) of plan assets used as collateral for the loan. For each plan year during the duration of the loan, the number of securities released must equal the number of encumbered securities held immediately before release for the current plan year multiplied by a fraction. The numerator of the fraction is the amount of principal and interest paid for the year. The denominator of the fraction is the sum of the numerator plus the principal and interest to be paid for all future years. See § 54.4975-7(b)(8)(iv). The number of future years under the loan must be definitely ascertainable and must be determined without taking into account any possible extensions or renewal periods. If the interest rate under the loan is variable, the interest to be paid in future years must be computed by using the interest rate applicable as of the end of the plan year. If collateral includes more than one class of securities, the number of securities of each class to be released for a plan year must be determined by applying the same fraction to each class.

(ii) *Special rule.* A loan will not fail to be exempt merely because the number of securities to be released from encumbrance is determined solely with reference to principal payments. However, if release is determined with reference to principal payments only, the following three additional rules apply. The first rule is that the loan must provide for annual payments of principal and interest at a cumulative rate that is not less rapid at any time than level annual payments of such amounts for 10 years. The second rule is that interest included in any payment is disregarded only to the extent that it would be determined to be interest under standard loan amortization tables. The third rule is that this subdivision (ii) is not applicable from the time that, by reason of a renewal, extension, or refinancing, the sum of the expired duration of the exempt loan, the renewal period, the extension period, and the duration of a new exempt loan exceeds 10 years.

(iii) *Caution against plan disqualification.* Under an exempt loan, the number of securities released from encumbrance may vary from year to year. The release of securities depends upon certain employer contributions and earnings under the ESOP. Under § 54.4975-11(d)(2) actual allocations to participants' accounts are based upon assets withdrawn from the suspense account. Nevertheless, for purposes of applying the limitations under section 415 to these allocations, under § 54.974-11(a)(8)(ii) contributions used by the ESOP to pay the loan are treated as annual additions to participants' accounts. Therefore, particular caution must be exercised to avoid exceeding the maximum annual additions under section 415. At the same time, release from encumbrance in annually varying numbers may reflect a failure on the part of the employer to make substantial and recurring contributions to the ESOP which will lead to loss of qualification under section 401(a). The Internal Revenue Service will observe closely the operation of ESOP's that release encumbered securities in varying annual amounts, particularly those that provide for the deferral of loan payments or for balloon payments.

(iv) *Illustration.* The general rule under paragraph (b)(8)(i) of this section operates as illustrated in the following example:

Example. Corporation X establishes an ESOP that borrows $750,000 from a bank. X guarantees the loan, which is for 15 years at 5% interest and is payable in level annual amounts of $72,256.72. Total payments on the loan are $1,083,850.80. The ESOP uses the entire loan proceeds to acquire 15,000 shares of X stock which is used as collateral for the loan. The number of securities to be released for the first year is 1,000 shares, *i.e.*, 15,000 shares × $72,256.72/$1,083,850.80 = 15,000 shares × 1/15. The number of securities to be released for the second year is 1,000 shares, *i.e.*, 14,000 shares × $72,256.72/$1,011.594.08 = 14,000 shares × 1/14. If all loan payments are made as originally scheduled, the number of securities released in each succeeding year of the loan will also be 1,000.

(9) *Right of first refusal.* Qualifying employer securities acquired with proceeds of an exempt loan may, but need not, be subject to a right of first refusal. However, any such right must meet the requirements of this subparagraph (9). Securities subject to such right must be stock or an equity security, or a debt security convertible into stock or an equity security. Also, the securities must not be publicly traded at the time the right may be exercised. The right of first refusal must be in favor of the employer, the ESOP, or both in any order of priority. The selling price and other terms under the right must not be less favorable to the seller than the greater of the value of the security determined under § 54.4975-11(d)(5), or the purchase price and other terms offered by a buyer, other than the employer or the ESOP, making a good faith offer to purchase the security. The right of first refusal must lapse no later than 14 days after the security holder gives written notice to the holder of the right that an offer by a third party to purchase the security has been received.

(10) *Put option.* A qualifying employer security acquired with the proceeds of an exempt loan by an ESOP after September 30, 1976, must be subject to a put option if it is not publicly traded when distributed or if it is subject to a trading limitation when distributed. For purposes of this subparagraph (10), a "trading limitation" on a security is a restriction under any Federal or state securities law, any regulation thereunder, or an agreement, not prohibited by this paragraph (b), affecting the security which would make the security not as freely tradable as one not subject to such restriction. The put option must be exercisable only by a participant, by the participant's donees, or by a person (including an estate or its distributee) to whom the security passes by reason of a participant's death. (Under this subparagraph (10), "participant" means a participant and beneficiaries of the participant under the ESOP.) The put option must permit a participant to put the security to the employer. Under no circumstances may the put option bind the ESOP. However, it may grant the ESOP an option to assume the rights and obligations of the employer at the time that the put option is exercised. If it is known at the

time a loan is made that Federal or state law will be violated by the employer's honoring such put option, the put option must permit the security to be put, in a manner consistent with such law, to a third party (e.g., an affiliate of the employer or a shareholder other than the ESOP) that has substantial net worth at the time the loan is made and whose net worth is reasonably expected to remain substantial.

(11) *Duration of put option*—(i) *General rule.* A put option must be exercisable at least during a 15-month period which begins on the date the security subject to the put option is distributed by the ESOP.

(ii) *Special rule.* In the case of a security that is publicly traded without restriction when distributed but ceases to be so traded within 15 months after distribution, the employer must notify each security holder in writing on or before the tenth day after the date the security ceases to be so traded that for the remainder of the 15-month period the security is subject to a put option. The number of days between such tenth day and the date on which notice is actually given, if later than the tenth day, must be added to the duration of the put option. The notice must inform distributees of the terms of the put options that they are to hold. Such terms must satisfy the requirements of paragraph (b)(10) through (12) of this section.

(12) *Other put option provision*—(i) *Manner of exercise.* A put option is exercised by the holder notifying the employer in writing that the put option is being exercised.

(ii) *Time excluded from duration of put option.* The period during which a put option is exercisable does not include any time when a distributee is unable to exercise it because the party bound by the put option is prohibited from honoring it by applicable Federal or state law.

(iii) *Price.* The price at which a put option must be exercisable is the value of the security, determined under § 54.4975-11(d)(5).

(iv) *Payment terms.* The provisions for payment under a put option must be reasonable. The deferral of payment is reasonable if adequate security and a reasonable interest rate are provided for any credit extended and if the cumulative payments at any time are no less than the aggregate of reasonable periodic payments as of such time. Periodic payments are reasonable if annual installments, beginning with 30 days after the date the put option is exercised, are substantially equal. Generally, the payment period may not end more than 5 years after the date the put option is exercised. However, it may be extended to a date no later than the earlier of 10 years from the date the put option is exercised or the date the proceeds of the loan used by the ESOP to acquire the security subject to the put option are entirely repaid.

(v) *Payment restrictions.* Payment under a put option may be restricted by the terms of a loan, including one used to acquire a security subject to a put option, made before Nov. 1, 1977. Otherwise, payment under a put option must not be restricted by the provisions of a loan or any other arrangement, including the terms of the employer's articles of incorporation, unless so required by applicable state law.

(13) *Other terms of loan.* An exempt loan must be for a specific term. Such loan may not be payable at the demand of any person, except in the case of default.

(14) *Status of plan as ESOP.* To be exempt, a loan must be made to a plan that is an ESOP at the time of such loan. However, a loan to a plan formally designated as an ESOP at the time of the loan that fails to be an ESOP because it does not comply with section 401(a) of the Code or § 54.4975-11 will be exempt as of the time of such loan if the plan is amended retroactively under section 401(b) or § 54.-4975-11(a)(4).

(15) *Special rules for certain loans*— (i) *Loans made before January 1, 1976.* A loan made before January 1, 1976, or made afterwards under a binding agreement in effect on January 1, 1976 (or under renewals permitted by the terms of the agreement on that date) is exempt for the entire period of the loan if it otherwise satisfies the provisions of this paragraph (b) for such period, even though it does not satisfy the following provisions of this section: the last sentence of paragraph (b)(4) and all of paragraph (b)(5), (6), (8)(i) and (ii), and (9) through (13), inclusive.

(ii) *Loans made after December 31, 1975, but before Nov. 1, 1977.* A loan made after December 31, 1975, but before Nov. 1, 1977 or made afterwards under a binding agreement in effect on Nov. 1, 1977 (or under renewals permitted by the terms of the agreement on that date) is exempt for the entire period of the loan if it otherwise satisfies the provisions of this paragraph (b) for such period even though it does not satisfy the following provisions of this section: paragraph (b)(6) and (9) and the three additional rules listed in paragraph (b)(8)(ii).

(iii) *Release rule.* Notwithstanding paragraph (b)(15)(i) and (ii) of this section, if the proceeds of a loan are used to acquire securities after Nov. 1, 1977, the loan must comply by such date with the provisions of paragraph (b)(8) of this section.

(iv) *Default rule.* Notwithstanding paragraph (b)(15)(i) and (ii) of this section, a loan by a disqualified person other than a guarantor must meet the requirements of paragraph (b)(6) of this section. A loan will meet these requirements if it is retroactively amended before Nov. 1, 1977 to meet these requirements.

(v) *Put option rule.* With respect to a security distributed before Nov. 1, 1977, the put option provisions of paragraph (b)(10), (11), and (12) of this section will be deemed satisfied as of the date the security is distributed if by December 31, 1977, the security is subject to a put option satisfying such provisions. For purposes of satisfying such provisions, the security will be deemed distributed on the date the put option is issued. However, the put option provisions need not be satisfied with respect to a security that is not owned on Nov. 1, 1977 by a person in whose hands a put option must be exercisable.

§ 54.4975-9 (T.D. 7386, filed 10-28-75.) Definition of "Fiduciary".

(a) [Reserved]
(b) [Reserved]

Reg. § 54.4975-9(b)

(c) *Investment advice.* (1) A person shall be deemed to be rendering "investment advice" to an employee benefit plan, within the meaning of section 4975 (e) (3) (B) and this paragraph, only if:

(i) Such person renders advice to the plan as to the value of securities or other property, or makes recommendations as to the advisability of investing in, purchasing, or selling securities or other property; and

(ii) Such person either directly or indirectly (e.g., through or together with any affiliate)—

(A) Has discretionary authority or control, whether or not pursuant to agreement, arrangement or understanding, with respect to purchasing or selling securities or other property for the plan; or

(B) Renders any advice described in paragraph (c) (1) (i) of this section on a regular basis to the plan pursuant to a mutual agreement, arrangement or understanding, written or otherwise, between such person and the plan or a fiduciary with respect to the plan, that such services will serve as a primary basis for investment decisions with respect to plan assets, and that such person will render individualized investment advice to the plan based on the particular needs of the plan regarding such matters as, among other things, investment policies or strategy, overall portfolio composition, or diversification of plan investments.

(2) A person who is a fiduciary with respect to a plan by reason of rendering investment advice (as defined in paragraph (c) (1) of this section) for a fee or other compensation, direct or indirect, with respect to any moneys or other property of such plan, or having any authority or responsibility to do so, shall not be deemed to be a fiduciary regarding any assets of the plan with respect to which such person does not have any discretionary authority, discretionary control or discretionary responsibility, does not exercise any authority or control, does not render investment advice (as defined in paragraph (c) (1) of this section) for a fee or other compensation, and does not have any authority or responsibility to render such investment advice, provided that nothing in this paragraph shall be deemed to:

(i) Exempt such person from the provisions of section 405 (a) of the Employee Retirement Income Security Act of 1974 concerning liability for fiduciary breaches by other fiduciaries with respect to any assets of the plan; or

(ii) Exclude such person from the definition of the term "disqualified person" (as set forth in section 4975 (e) (2)) with respect to any assets of the plan.

(d) *Execution of securities transactions.* (1) A person who is a broker or dealer registered under the Securities Exchange Act of 1934, a reporting dealer who makes primary markets in securities of the United States Government or of an agency of the United States Government and reports daily to the Federal Reserve Bank of New York its positions with respect to such securities and borrowings thereon, or a bank supervised by the United States or a State, shall not be deemed to be fiduciary, within the meaning of section 4975 (e) (3), with respect to an employee benefit plan solely because such person executes transactions for the purchase or sale of securities on behalf of such plan in the ordinary course of its business as a broker, dealer, or bank, pursuant to instructions of a fiduciary with respect to such plan, if:

(i) Neither the fiduciary nor any affiliate of such fiduciary is such broker, dealer, or bank; and

(ii) The instructions specify (A) the security to be purchased or sold, (B) a price range within which such security is to be purchased or sold, or, if such security is issued by an open-end investment company registered under the Investment Company Act of 1940 (15 U.S.C. 80a–1, et seq.), a price which is determined in accordance with Rule 22c–1 under the Investment Company Act of 1940 (17 CFR 270.22c–1), (C) a time span during which such security may be purchased or sold (not to exceed five business days), and (D) the minimum or maximum quantity of such security which may be purchased or sold within such price range, or, in the case of a security issued by an open-end investment company registered under the Investment Company Act of 1940, the minimum or maximum quantity of such security which may be purchased or sold, or the value of such security in dollar amount which may be purchased or sold, at the price referred to in paragraph (d)(1)(ii)(B) of this section.

(2) A person who is a broker-dealer, reporting dealer, or bank which is a fiduciary with respect to an employee benefit plan solely by reason of the possession or exercise of discretionary authority or discretionary control in the management of the plan or the management or disposition of plan assets in connection with the execution of a transaction or transactions for the purchase or sale of securities on behalf of such plan which fails to comply with the provisions of paragraph (d)(1) of this section, shall not be deemed to be a fiduciary regarding any assets of the plan with respect to which such broker-dealer, reporting dealer or bank does not have any discretionary authority, discretionary control or discretionary responsibility, does not exercise any authority or control, does not render investment advice (as defined in paragraph (c)(1) of this section) for a fee or other compensation, and does not have any authority or responsibility to render such investment advice, provided that nothing in this paragraph shall be deemed to:

(i) Exempt such broker-dealer, reporting dealer, or bank from the provisions of section 405(a) of the Employee Retirement Income Security Act of 1974 concerning liability for fiduciary breaches by other fiduciaries with respect to any assets of the plan; or

(ii) Exclude such broker-dealer, reporting dealer, or bank from the definition of the term "disqualified person" (as set forth in section 4975(e)(2)) with respect to any assets of the plan.

(e) *Affiliate and control.* (1) For purposes of paragraphs (c) and (d) of this section, an "affiliate" of a person shall include:

(i) Any person directly or indirectly, through one or more intermediaries, controlling, controlled by, or under common control with such person;

(ii) Any officer, director, partner, employee or relative (as defined in section 4975(e)(6)) of such person; and

(iii) Any corporation or partnership of which such person is an officer, director or partner.

(2) For purposes of this paragraph, the term "control" means the power to exercise a controlling influence over the management or policies of a person other than an individual.

§ 54.4975-11 (T.D. 7506, filed 8-30-77.) "ESOP" requirements.

(a) *In general*—(1) *Type of plan.* To be an "ESOP" (employee stock ownership plan), a plan described in section 4975(e)(7)(A) must meet the requirements of this section. See section 4975(e)(7)(B).

(2) *Designation as ESOP.* To be an ESOP, a plan must be formally designated as such in the plan document.

(3) *Non-terminable provisions.* [Reserved]

(4) *Retroactive amendment.* A plan meets the requirements of this section as of the date that it is designated as an ESOP if it is amended retroactively to meet, and in fact does meet, such requirements at any of the following times:

(i) 12 months after the date on which the plan is designated as an ESOP;

(ii) 90 days after a determination letter is issued with respect to the qualification of the plan as an ESOP under this section, but only if the determination is requested by the time in paragraph (a)(4)(i) of this section; or

(iii) A later date approved by the district director.

(5) *Addition to other plan.* An ESOP may form a portion of a plan the balance of which includes a qualified pension, profit-sharing, or stock bonus plan which is not an ESOP. A reference to an ESOP includes an ESOP that forms a portion of another plan.

(6) *Conversion of existing plan to an ESOP.* If an existing pension, profit-sharing, or stock bonus plan is converted into an ESOP, the requirements of section 404 of the Employee Retirement Income Security Act of 1974 (ERISA) (88 Stat. 877), relating to fiduciary duties, and section 401(a) of the Code, relating to requirements for plans established for the exclusive benefit of employees, apply to such conversion. A conversion may constitute a termination of an existing plan. For definition of a termination, see the regulations under section 411(d)(3) of the Code and section 4041(f) of ERISA.

(7) *Certain arrangements barred*—(i) *Buy-sell agreements.* An arrangement involving an ESOP that creates a put option must not provide for the issuance of put options other than as provided under § 54.-4975-7(b)(10), (11), and (12). Also, an ESOP must not otherwise obligate itself to acquire securities from a particular security holder at an indefinite time determined upon the happening of an event such as the death of the holder.

(ii) *Integrated plans.* [Reserved]

(8) *Effect of certain ESOP provisions on section 401(a) status*—(i) *Exempt loan requirements.* An ESOP will not fail to meet the requirements of section 401(a)(2) merely because it gives plan assets as collateral for an exempt loan under § 54.4975-7(b)(5) or uses plan assets under § 54.4975-7(b)(6) to repay an exempt loan in the event of default.

(ii) *Individual annual contribution limitation.* And ESOP will not fail to meet the requirements of section 401(a)(16) merely because annual additions under section 415(c) are calculated with respect to employer contributions issued to repay an exempt loan rather than with respect to securities allocated to participants.

(iii) *Income pass-through.* [Reserved]

(9) *Transitional rules for ESOP's established before Nov. 1, 1977.* A plan established before Nov. 1, 1977 that otherwise satisfies the provisions of this section constitutes an ESOP if it is amended by December 31, 1977, to comply from Nov. 1, 1977 with this section even though before Nov. 1, 1977 the plan did not satisfy paragraphs (c) and (d)(2), (4), and (5) of this section.

(10) *Additional transitional rules.* [Reserved]

(b) *Plan designed to invest primarily in qualifying employer securities.* A plan constitutes an ESOP only if the plan specifically states that it is designed to invest primarily in qualifying employer securities. Thus, a stock bonus plan or a money purchase pension plan constituting an ESOP may invest part of its assets in other than qualifying employer securities. Such plan will be treated the same as other stock bonus plans or money purchase pension plans qualified under section 401(a) with respect to those investments.

(c) *Suspense account.* All assets acquired by an ESOP with the proceeds of an exempt loan under section 4975(d)(3) must be added to and maintained in a suspense account. They are to be withdrawn from the suspense account by applying § 54.4975-7(b)(8) and (15) as if all securities in the suspense account were encumbered. Such assets acquired before Nov. 1, 1977, must be withdrawn by applying § 54.4975-7(b)(8) or the provision of the loan that controls release from encumbrance. Assets in such suspense accounts are assets of the ESOP. Thus, for example, such assets are subject to section 401(a)(2).

(d) *Allocations to accounts of participants*—(1) *In general.* Except as provided in this section, amounts contributed to an ESOP must be allocated as provided under § 1.401-1(b)(ii) and (iii) of this chapter, and securities acquired by an ESOP must be accounted for as provided under § 1.402(a)-1(b)(2)(ii) of this chapter.

(2) *Assets withdrawn from suspense account.* As of the end of each plan year, the ESOP must consistently allocate to the participants' accounts non-monetary units representing participants' interests in assets withdrawn from the suspense account.

(3) *Income.* Income with respect to securities acquired with the proceeds of an exempt loan must be allocated as income of the plan except to the extent that the ESOP provides for the use of income from such securities to repay the loan.

(4) *Forfeitures.* If a portion of a participant's account is forfeited, qualifying employer securities allocated under paragraph (d)(2) of this section must be forfeited only after other assets. If interests

Reg. § 54.4975-11 (d)(4)

in more than one class of qualifying employer securities have been allocated to the participant's account, the participant must be treated as forfeiting the same proportion of each such class.

(5) *Valuation.* For purposes of § 54.-4975-7(b)(9) and (12) and this section, valuations must be made in good faith and based on all relevant factors for determining the fair market value of securities. In the case of a transaction between a plan and a disqualified person, value must be determined as of the date of the transaction. For all other purposes under this subparagraph (5), value must be determined as of the most recent valuation date under the plan. An independent appraisal will not in itself be a good faith determination of value in the case of a transaction between a plan and a disqualified person. However, in other cases, a determination of fair market value based on at least an annual appraisal independently arrived at by a person who customarily makes such appraisals and who is independent of any party to a transaction under § 54.4975-7(b)(9) and (12) will be deemed to be a good faith determination of value.

(e) *Multiple plans*—(1) *General rule.* An ESOP may not be considered together with another plan for purposes of applying section 401(a)(4) and (5) or section 410 (b) unless—

(i) The ESOP and such other plan exist on Nov. 1, 1977; or

(ii) Paragraph (e)(2) of this section is satisfied.

(2) *Special rule for combined ESOP's.* [Reserved]

(f) *Distribution*—(1) *In general.* Except as provided in paragraph (f)(2) and (3) of this section, with respect to distributions, a portion of an ESOP consisting of a stock bonus plan or a money purchase pension plan is not to be distinguished from other such plans under section 401(a). Thus, for example, benefits distributable from the portion of an ESOP consisting of a stock bonus plan are distributable only in stock of the employer. Also, benefits distributable from the money-purchase portion of the ESOP may be, but are not required to be, distributable in qualifying employer securities.

(2) *Exempt loan proceeds.* If securities acquired with the proceeds of an exempt loan available for distribution consist of more than one class, a distributee must receive substantially the same proportion of each such class. However, as indicated in paragraph (f)(1) of this section, benefits distributable from the portion of an ESOP consisting of a stock bonus plan are distributable only in stock of the employer.

(3) *Income.* [Reserved]

○━ § 54.4975-12 (T.D. 7506, filed 8-30-77.) Definition of the term "qualifying employer security".

(a) *In general.* For purposes of section 4975(e)(8) and this section, the term "qualifying employer security" means an employer security which is—

(1) Stock or otherwise an equity security, or

(2) A bond, debenture, note, or certificate or other evidence of indebtedness which is described in paragraphs (1), (2), and (3) of section 503(e).

(b) *Special rule.* In determining whether a bond, debenture, note, or certificate or other evidence of indebtedness is described in paragraphs (1), (2), and (3) of section 503(e), any organization described in section 401(a) shall be treated as an organization subject to the provisions of section 503.

○━ § 54.4975-14 (T.D. 7489, filed 5-26-77.) Election to pay an excise tax for certain pre-1975 prohibited transactions.

(a) *In general.* Section 2003(c)(1)(B) of the Employee Retirement Income Security Act of 1974 (88 Stat. 978) provides an election to pay an excise tax by certain persons involved prior to 1975 in prohibited transactions within the meaning of section 503(b) or (g).

(b) *Effect of election.* If a valid election is made under this section with respect to a particular transaction, any loss of exemption under section 501(a) because of a prohibited transaction within the meaning of section 503(b) or (g) shall not apply. Instead, the person who made the election referred to in this section shall be subject to the taxes which would have been imposed by section 4975(a) or (b) as though section 4975 had imposed a tax in respect of the transaction. (However, section 4975(f)(1), relating to joint and several liability, shall not apply to any person who has not made an election under this section, and interest for late payment of tax shall not begin to accrue until after the date of the election.) Such an election is irrevocable. However, the making of the election does not affect the application of section 6501 for purposes of assessment and collection of tax and section 6511 for purposes of filing a claim for credit or refund with respect to taxpayers and to taxable years of taxpayers whose tax liability is or may be affected by reason of the nonapplication of a denial of exempt status.

(c) *Method of election.* A person shall make the election referred to in this section by filing the form issued for such purpose by the Internal Revenue Service, including therein the information required by such form and the instructions issued with respect thereto, and by paying the tax which the taxpayer indicates is due at the time the return is filed. To be valid the election must be made prior to the later of December 6, 1976, or 120 days after the date of notification referred to in § 1.503(a)-1(b) of this chapter (Income Tax Regulations), relating to loss of exemption for certain prohibited transactions. If there has been no notification of loss of exemption, the election may be made at any time. However, these limitations do not preclude an agreement between the disqualified person and the district director to extend the time within which the election is permitted.

(d) *Computation of section 4975 excise tax.* To the extent applicable, and solely for purposes associated with the payment of a section 4975 excise tax under the election referred to in this section, § 53.4941(e)-1 of this chapter (Foundation Excise Tax Regulations) is controlling.

○━ § 54.4975-15 (T.D. 7491, filed 6-21-77.) Other transitional rules.

(a) [Reserved]

(b) [Reserved]

(c) [Reserved]

(d) *Provision of certain services until June 30, 1977*—(1) *In general.* Section 2003(c)(2)(D) of the Employee Retirement Income Security Act of 1974 (the Act) (88 Stat. 979) provides that section 4975 shall not apply to the provision of services before June 30, 1977, between a plan and a disqualified person if the three requirements contained in section 2003(c)(2)(D) of the Act are met. The first requirement is that such services must be provided either (i) under a binding contract in effect on July 1, 1974 (or pursuant to a renewal or modification of such contract); or (ii) by a disqualified person who ordinarily and customarily furnished such services on June 30, 1974. The second requirement is that the services be provided on terms that remain at least as favorable to the plan as an arm's-length transaction with an unrelated party would be.

For this purpose, such services are provided on terms that remain at least as favorable to the plan as an arm's-length transaction with an unrelated party would be if, at the time of execution (or renewal) of such binding contract, the contract (or renewal) is on terms at least as favorable to the plan as an arm's-length transaction with an unrelated party would be. However, if in a normal commercial setting an unrelated party in the position of the plan could be expected to insist upon a renegotiation or termination of a binding contract, the plan must so act. Thus, for example, if a disqualified person provides services to a plan on a month-to-month basis, and a party in the position of the plan could be expected to renegotiate the price paid under such contract because of a decline in the fair market value of such services, the plan must so act in order to avoid participation in a prohibited transaction. The third requirement is that the provision of services must not be, or have been, at the time of such provision a prohibited transaction within the meaning of section 503(b) or the corresponding provisions of prior law. If these three requirements are met, section 4975 will apply neither to services provided before June 30, 1977 (both to customers to whom such services were being provided on June 30, 1974, and to new customers) nor to the receipt of compensation therefor. Thus, if these three requirements are met, section 4975 will not apply until June 30, 1977, to the provision of services to a plan by a disqualified person (including a fiduciary) even if such services could not be furnished pursuant to the exemption provisions of sections 4975(d)(2) or (6) and § 54.4975-6. For example, if the three requirements of section 2003(c)(2)(D) of the Act are met, a person serving as fiduciary to a plan who already receives full-time pay from an employer or an association of employers, whose employees are participants in such plan, or from an employee organization whose members are participants in such plan, may continue to receive reasonable compensation from the plan for services rendered to the plan before June 30, 1977. Similarly, until June 30, 1977, a plan consultant who may be a fiduciary because of the nature of the consultative and administrative services being provided may, if these three requirements are met, continue to cause the sale of insurance to the plan and continue to receive commissions for such sales from the insurance company writing the policy. Further, if the three requirements of section 2003(c)(2)(D) of the Act are met, a securities broker-dealer who renders investment advice to a plan for a fee, thereby becoming a fiduciary, may furnish other services to the plan, such as brokerage services, and receive compensation therefor. Also, if a registered representative of such a broker-dealer were a fiduciary, the registered representative may receive compensation, including commissions, for brokerage services performed before June 30, 1977.

(2) *Persons deemed to be June 30, 1974 service providers.* A disqualified person with respect to a plan which did not, on June 30, 1974, ordinarily and customarily furnish a particular service, will nevertheless be considered to have ordinarily and customarily furnished such service on June 30, 1974, for purposes of this section and section 2003(c)(2)(D) of the Act, if either of the following conditions are met:

(i) At least 50 percent of the outstanding beneficial interests of such disqualified person are owned directly or through one or more intermediaries by the same person or persons who owned, directly or through one or more intermediaries, at least 50 percent of the outstanding beneficial interests of a person who ordinarily and customarily furnished such service on June 30, 1974; or

(ii) Control or the power to exercise a controlling influence over the management and policies of such disqualified person is possessed, directly or through one or more intermediaries, by the same person or persons who possessed, directly or through one or more intermediaries, control or the power to exercise a controlling influence over the management and policies of a person who ordinarily and customarily furnished such service on June 30, 1974.

For purposes of this paragraph (d)(2) a person shall be deemed to be an "intermediary" of another person if at least 50 percent of the outstanding beneficial interests of such person are owned by such other person, directly or indirectly or if such other person controls or has the power to exercise a controlling influence over the management and policies of such person.

(3) *Examples.* The principals of § 54.4975-15(d)(2) may be illustrated by the following examples.

Example (1). A owns 50 percent of the outstanding beneficial interests of ABC Partnership which ordinarily and customarily furnished certain services on June 30, 1974. On July 2, 1974, ABC Partnership was incorporated into ABC Corporation with one class of stock outstanding. A owns 50 percent of the shares of such stock. ABC Corporation furnishes the same services that were furnished by ABC Partnership on June 30, 1974. ABC Corporation will be deemed to have ordinarily and customarily furnished such services on June 30, 1974, for purposes of section 2003(c)(2)(D) of the Act.

Example (2). A and B together own 100 percent of the beneficial interests of AB Partnership, which ordinarily and customarily furnished certain services on June 30, 1974. On September 1, 1974, AB Partnership was incorporated into AB Corporation with one class of stock outstanding. A and B each own 20 percent of such out-

Reg. § 54.4975-15(d)(3)

24,258.112 (I.R.C.)   Reg. § 54.4975-15(d)(3)

standing class of stock and together have control over the management and policies of AB Corporation. AB Corporation furnishes the same services that were furnished by AB Partnership on June 30, 1974. AB Corporation will be deemed to have ordinarily and customarily furnished such services on June 30, 1974, for purposes of section 2003(c)(2)(D) of the Act.

Example (3). On June 30, 1974, M Corporation was ordinarily and customarily furnishing certain services. On that date, X, Y and Z together owned 50 percent of all classes of the outstanding shares of M Corporation. On January 28, 1975, all of the shareholders of M Corporation exchanged their shares in M Corporation for shares of a new N Corporation. As a result of that exchange, X, Y and Z together own 50 percent of the common stock of N Corporation, the only class of N Corporation stock outstanding after the exchange. N Corporation furnishes the services formerly furnished by M Corporation. N Corporation will be deemed to have ordinarily and customarily furnished such services on June 30, 1974, for purposes of section 2003(c)(2)(D) of the Act.

Example (4). I Corporation ordinarily and customarily furnished certain services on June 30, 1974. On November 3, 1975, I Corporation organizes a wholly owned subsidiary, S Corporation, which furnishes the same services ordinarily and customarily furnished by I Corporation on June 30, 1974. S Corporation will be deemed to have ordinarily and customarily furnished such services on June 30, 1974, for purposes of section 2003(c)(2)(D) of the Act.

Example (5). X Corporation, wholly-owned and controlled by A, ordinarily and customarily furnished certain services on June 30, 1974. Y Corporation did not perform such services on that date. On January 2, 1976, X Corporation is merged into Y Corporation and, although A received less than 50 percent of the total outstanding shares of Y Corporation, after such merger A has control over the management and policies of Y Corporation. Y Corporation furnishes the same services that were formerly furnished by X Corporation. Y Corporation will be deemed to have ordinarily and customarily furnished such services on June 30, 1974, for purposes of section 2003(c)(2)(D) of the Act.

PROCEDURE AND ADMINISTRATION

INFORMATION AND RETURNS

RETURNS AND RECORDS

Records, Statements, and Special Returns

○━ § 1.6001 **Statutory provisions; notice or regulations requiring records, statements, and special returns.** [Sec. 6001, IRC]

○━ § 1.6001-1 (T.D. 6364, filed 2-13-59; republished in T.D. 6500, filed 11-25-60; amended by T.D. 7122, filed 6-7-71.) **Records.**

(a) *In general.* Except as provided in paragraph (b) of this section, any person subject to tax under subtitle A of the Code, or any person required to file a return of information with respect to income, shall keep such permanent books of account or records, including inventories, as are sufficient to establish the amount of gross income, deductions, credits, or other matters required to be shown by such person in any return of such tax or information.

(b) *Farmers and wage-earners.* Individuals deriving gross income from the business of farming, and individuals whose gross income includes salaries, wages, or similar compensation for personal services rendered, are required with respect to such income to keep such records as will enable the district director to determine the correct amount of income subject to the tax. It is not necessary, however, that with respect to such income individuals keep the books of account or records required by paragraph (a) of this section. For rules with respect to the records to be kept in substantiation of traveling and other business expenses of employees, see § 1.162-17.

(c) *Exempt organizations.* In addition to such permanent books and records as are required by paragraph (a) of this section with respect to the tax imposed by section 511 on unrelated business income of certain exempt organizations, every organization exempt from tax under section 501(a) shall keep such permanent books of account or records, including inventories, as are sufficient to show specifically the items of gross income, receipts and disbursements. Such organizations shall also keep such books and records as are required to substantiate the information required by section 6033. See section 6033 and § 1.6033-1.

(d) *Notice by district director requiring returns, statements, or the keeping of records.* The district director may require any person, by notice served upon him, to make such returns, render such statements, or keep such specific records as will enable the district director to determine whether or not such person is liable for tax under subtitle A of the Code.

(e) *Retention of records.* The books or records required by this section shall be kept at all times available for inspection by authorized internal revenue officers or employees, and shall be retained so long as the contents thereof may become material in the administration of any internal revenue law.

○━ § 31.6001 **Statutory provisions; notice of regulations requiring records, statements, and special returns.** [Sec. 6001, IRC]

○━ § 31.6001-1 (T.D. 6354, filed 1-13-59; republished in T.D. 6516, filed 12-19-60.) **Records in general.**

(a) *Form of records.* The records required by the regulations in this part shall be kept accurately, but no particular form is required for keeping the records. Such forms and systems of accounting shall be used as will enable the district director to ascertain whether liability for tax is incurred and, if so, the amount thereof.

(b) *Copies of returns, schedules, and statements.* Every person who is required, by the regulations in this part or by instructions applicable to any form prescribed thereunder, to keep any copy of any return, schedule, statement, or other document, shall keep such copy as a part of his records.

(c) *Records of claimants.* Any person (including an employee) who, pursuant to the regulations in this part, claims a refund, credit, or abatement, shall keep a complete and detailed record with respect to the tax, interest, addition to the tax, additional amount, or assessable penalty to which the claim relates. Such record shall include any records required of the claimant by paragraph (b) of this section and by §§ 31.6001-2 to 31.6001-5, inclusive, which relate to the claim.

(d) *Records of employees.* While not mandatory (except in the case of claims), it is advisable for each employee to keep permanent, accurate records showing the name and address of each employer for whom he performs services as an employee, the dates of beginning and termination of such services, the information with respect to himself which is required by the regulations in this subpart to be kept by employers, and the statements furnished in accordance with the provisions of § 31.6051-1.

(e) *Place and period for keeping records.* (1) All records required by the regulations in this part shall be kept, by the person required to keep them, at one or more convenient and safe locations accessible to internal revenue officers, and shall at all times be available for inspection by such officers.

(2) Except as otherwise provided in the following sentence, every person required by the regulations in this part to keep records in respect of a tax (whether or not such person incurs liability for such tax) shall maintain such records for at least four years after the due date of such tax for the return period to which the records relate, or the date such tax is paid, whichever is the later. The records of claimants required by paragraph (c) of this section shall be maintained for a period of at least four years after the date the claim is filed.

(f) *Cross reference.* See §§ 31.6001-2 to 31.6001-5, inclusive, for additional records re-

Reg. § 31.6001-1 (f)

24,260 (I.R.C.) Reg. § 31.6001-1(f)

quired with respect to the Federal Insurance Contributions Act, the Railroad Retirement Tax Act, the Federal Unemployment Tax Act, and the collection of income tax at source on wages, respectively.

○→ § 31.6001-5 (T.D. 6155, filed 12-29-55; amended by T.D. 6354, filed 1-13-59; republished in T.D. 6516, filed 12-19-60; amended by T.D. 6606, filed 8-24-62; T.D. 6908, filed 12-30-66; T.D. 7001, filed 1-17-69; T.D. 7048, filed 6-23-70 and T.D. 7053, filed 7-20-70.) **Additional records in connection with collection of income tax at source on wages.**

(a) Every employer required under section 3402 to deduct and withhold income tax upon the wages of employees shall keep records of all remuneration paid to (including tips reported by) such employees. Such records shall show with respect to each employee—

(1) The name and address of the employee, and, after December 31, 1962, the account number of the employee.

(2) The total amount and date of each payment of remuneration (including any sum withheld therefrom as tax or for any other reason) and the period of services covered by such payment.

(3) The amount of such remuneration payment which constitutes wages subject to withholding.

(4) The amount of tax collected with respect to such remuneration payment, and, if collected at a time other than the time such payment was made, the date collected.

(5) If the total remuneration payment (subparagraph (2) of this paragraph) and the amount thereof which is taxable (subparagraph (3) of this paragraph) are not equal, the reason therefore.

(6) Copies of any statements furnished by the employee pursuant to paragraph (b)(12) of § 31.3401 (a)-1 (relating to permanent residents of the Virgin Islands).

(7) Copies of an statements furnished by the employee pursuant to §§ 31.3401(a) (6)-1 and 31.3401(a)(7)-1, relating to nonresident alien individuals.

(8) Copies of any statements furnished by the employee pursuant to § 31.3401(a) (8)(A)-1 (relating to residence or physical presence in a foreign country).

(9) Copies of any statements furnished by the employee pursuant to § 31.3401(a) (8)(C)-1 (relating to citizens resident in Puerto Rico).

(10) The fair market value and date of each payment of noncash remuneration, made to an employee after August 9, 1955, for services performed as a retail commission salesman, with respect to which no income tax is withheld by reason of § 31.3402(j)-1.

(11) With respect to payments made in 1955 under a wage continuation plan (as defined in paragraph (a)(2)(i) of § 1.105-4 and § 1.105-5 of this chapter (Income Tax Regulations)), the records required to be kept in respect of such payments are those prescribed under paragraph (b)(8)(i) of § 31.3401(a)-1.

(12) In the case of the employer for whom services are performed, with respect to payments made directly by him after December 31, 1955, under a wage continuation plan (as defined in paragraph (a)(2) (i) of § 1.105-4 and § 1.105-5 of this chapter (Income Tax Regulations))—

(i) The beginning and ending dates of each period of absence from work for which any such payment was made; and

(ii) Sufficient information to establish the amount and weekly rate of each such payment.

(13) The withholding exemption certificates (Forms W-4 and W-4E) filed with the employer by the employee.

(14) The agreement, if any, between the employer and the employee for the withholding of additional amounts of tax pursuant to § 31.3402(i)-1.

(15) To the extent material to a determination of tax liability, the dates, in each calendar quarter, on which the employee performed services not in the course of the employer's trade or business, and the amount of cash remuneration paid at any time for such services performed within such quarter. See § 31.3401(a)(4)-1. The term "remuneration," as used in this paragraph, includes all payments whether in cash or in a medium other than cash, except that the term does not include payments in a medium other than cash for services not in the course of the employer's trade or business. See § 31.3401 (a)(11)-1.

(16) In the case of tips received by an employee after 1965 in the course of his employment, copies of any statements furnished by the employee pursuant to section 6053(a) unless the information disclosed by such statements is recorded on another document retained by the employer pursuant to the provisions of this paragraph.

(17) Any request of an employee under section 3402(h)(3) and § 31.3402(h)(3)-1 to have the amount of tax to be withheld from his wages computed on the basis of his cumulative wages, and any notice of revocation thereof.

The term "remuneration," as used in this paragraph, includes all payments whether in cash or in a medium other than cash, except that the term does not include payments in a medium other than cash for services not in the course of the employer's trade or business, and does not include tips received by an employee in any medium other than cash or in cash if such tips amount to less than $20 for any calendar month. See §§ 31.3401(a)(11)-1 and 31.3401 (a)(16)-1, respectively.

(b) The employer shall keep records of the details of each adjustment or settlement of income tax withheld under section 3402 made pursuant to the regulations in this part.

○→ § 31.6001-6 (T.D. 6472, filed 6-22-60; republished in T.D. 6516, filed 12-19-60.) **Notice by district director requiring returns, statements, or the keeping of records.**

The district director may require any person, by notice served upon him, to make such returns, render such statements, or keep such specific records as will enable

Records, Statements and Special Returns *(I.R.C.)* 24,261

the district director to determine whether or not such person is liable for any of the taxes to which the regulations in this part have application.

○━► **§ 53.6001 Statutory provisions; notice or regulations requiring records, statements, and special returns.** [Sec. 6001, IRC]

○━► **§ 53.6001-1** (T.D. 7368, filed 7-15-75.) **Notice or regulations requiring records, statements, and special returns.**

(a) *In general.* Any person subject to tax under chapter 42, Subtitle D, of the Code shall keep such complete and detailed records as are sufficient to enable the district director to determine accurately the amount of liability under chapter 42.

(b) *Notice by district director requiring returns, statements, or the keeping of records.* The district director may require any person, by notice served upon him, to make such returns, render such statements, or keep such specific records as will enable the district director to determine whether or not such person is liable for tax under chapter 42.

(c) *Retention of records.* The records required by this section shall be kept at all times available for inspection by authorized internal revenue officers or employees, and shall be retained so long as the contents thereof may become material in the administration of any internal revenue law.

○━► **§ 301.6001 Statutory provisions; notice or regulations requiring records, statements, and special returns.** [Sec. 6001, IRC]

○━► **§ 301.6001-1** (T.D. 6498, filed 10-24-60.) **Notice or regulations requiring records, statements, and special returns.**

For provisions requiring records, statements, and special returns, see the regulations relating to the particular tax.

Tax Returns or Statements

○━► **§ 1.6011-1** (T.D. 6364, filed 2-13-59; republished in T.D. 6500, filed 11-25-60; amended by T.D. 6922, filed 6-16-67.) **General requirement of return, statement, or list.**

(a) *General rule.* Every person subject to any tax, or required to collect any tax, under subtitle A of the Code, shall make such returns or statements as are required by the regulations in this chapter. The return or statement shall include therein the information required by the applicable regulations or forms.

(b) *Use of prescribed forms.* Copies of the prescribed return forms will so far as possible be furnished taxpayers by district directors. A taxpayer will not be excused from making a return, however, by the fact that no return form has been furnished to him. Taxpayers not supplied with the proper forms should make application therefor to the district director in ample time to have their returns prepared, verified, and filed on or before the due date with the internal revenue office where such returns are required to be filed. Each taxpayer should carefully prepare his return and set forth fully and clearly the information required to be included therein. Returns which have not been so prepared will not be accepted as meeting the requirements of the Code. In the absence of a prescribed form, a statement made by a taxpayer disclosing his gross income and the deductions therefrom may be accepted as a tentative return, and, if filed within the prescribed time, the statement so made will relieve the taxpayer from liability for the addition to tax imposed for the delinquent filing of the return, provided that without unnecessary delay such a tentative return is supplemented by a return made on the proper form.

(c) *Tax withheld on nonresident aliens and foreign corporations.* For requirements respecting the return of the tax required to be withheld under chapter 3 of the Code on nonresident aliens and foreign corporations and tax-free covenant bonds, see § 1.1461-2.

○━► **§ 1.6011-2** (T.D. 7533, filed 2-14-78.) **Returns, etc., of DISC's and former DISC's.**

(a) *Records and information.* Every DISC and former DISC (as defined in section 992(a)) must comply with section 6001 and the regulations thereunder, relating to required records, statements, and special returns. Thus, for example, a DISC is required to maintain the books of account or records described in § 1.6001-1(a). In addition, every DISC must furnish to each of its shareholders on or before the last day of the second month following the close of the taxable year of the DISC a copy of Schedule K (Form 1120-DISC) disclosing the amounts of actual distributions and deemed distributions from the DISC to such shareholder for the taxable year of the DISC. In the case of a deficiency distribution to meet qualification requirements, see § 1.992-3(a)(4) for requirements that distribution be designated in the form of a communication sent to a shareholder and service center at the time of distribution.

(b) *Returns*—(1) *Requirement of return.* Every DISC (as defined in section 992(a)(1)) shall make a return of income. A former DISC (as defined in section 992 (a)(3)) shall also make a return of income in addition to any other return required. The return required of a DISC or former DISC under this section shall be made on Form 1120-DISC. The provisions of § 1.6011-1 shall apply with respect to a DISC and former DISC. A former DISC should indicate clearly on Form 1120-DISC that it is making a return of income as a former DISC (for example, by labeling at the top of the Form 1120-DISC "FORMER DISC"). In the case of a former DISC, those items on the form which pertain to the computation of taxable income shall not be completed, but Schedules J, K, L, and M must be completed. Except as otherwise specifically provided in the Code or regulations, the return of a DISC or former DISC is considered to be an income tax return.

(2) *Existence of DISC.* A corporation which is a DISC and which is in existence during any portion of a taxable year is required to make a return for that fractional part of its taxable year during which it was in existence.

○━► **§ 31.6011(a)-4** (T.D. 6354, filed 1-13-59; republished in T.D. 6516, filed 12-19-60; amended by T.D. 7096, filed 3-17-71; T.D. 7200, filed 8-15-72 and T.D. 7351, filed 4-16-75.) **Returns of income tax withheld from wages.**

(a) *In general.* (1) Except as otherwise provided in subparagraph (3) of this paragraph and in § 31.6011(a)-5, every person required to make a return of income tax withheld from wages pursuant to sec-

Reg. § 31.6011(a)-4(a)(1)

24,262 (I.R.C.) Reg. § 31.6011(a)-4(a)(1) 2-21-78

tion 1622 of the Internal Revenue Code of 1939 for the calendar quarter ended December 31, 1954, shall make a return for each subsequent calendar quarter (whether or not wages are paid therein) until he has filed a final return in accordance with § 31.6011(a)-6. Except as otherwise provided in subparagraph (3) of this paragraph and in § 31.6011(a)-5, every person not required to make a return for the calendar quarter ended December 31, 1954, shall make a return of income tax withheld from wages pursuant to section 3402 for the first calendar quarter thereafter in which he is required to deduct and withhold such tax and for each subsequent calendar quarter (whether or not wages are paid therein) until he has filed a final return in accordance with § 31.6011(a)-6. Except as otherwise provided in § 31.6011(a)-8 and in subparagraphs (2) and (3) of this paragraph, Form 941 is the form prescribed for making the return required under this paragraph.

(2) Form 942 is the form prescribed for making the return required under subparagraph (1) of this paragraph with respect to income tax withheld, pursuant to an agreement under section 3402(p), from wages paid for domestic service in a private home of the employer not on a farm operated for profit. The preceding sentence shall not apply in the case of an employer who has elected under paragraph (a)(3) of § 31.-6011(a)-1 to use Form 941 as his return with respect to such payments for purposes of the Federal Insurance Contributions Act.

(3) Every person shall make a return of income tax withheld, pursuant to an agreement under section 3402(p), from wages paid for agricultural labor for the first calendar year in which he is required (by reason of such agreement) to deduct and withhold such tax and for each subsequent calendar year (whether or not wages for agricultural labor are paid therein) until he has filed a final return in accordance with § 31.6011(a)-6. Form 943 is the form prescribed for making the return required under this subparagraph.

(b) *Internal Revenue Service copies of Forms W-2 on domestic workers.* (1) Every employer who makes a return of tax on Form 942 pursuant to paragraph (a)(2) of this section shall submit as part of such return for a period ending December 31, or for any period for which such return is made as a final return, the Internal Revenue Service copy of a Form W-2 for each employee with respect to whose wages tax is reported thereon.

(2) The Internal Revenue Service copies of corrected Forms W-2 previously filed with a Form 942 for the calendar year shall be submitted with an explanatory statement to the service center on or before the date fixed for filing the employer's Form 942 for the calendar quarter in which the correction is made.

(3) For provisions relating to extensions of time for filing the Internal Revenue Service copies of Form W-2, see paragraph (a)(3) of § 31.6081(a)-1.

(2) The copies of withholding statements for the current calendar year transmitted with the return required under paragraph (a) of this section shall be accompanied by an information statement on Form W-3. This subparagraph has no application to any return filed under this section in 1955.

(3) The copies of withholding statements for the current calendar year transmitted with the return shall be accompanied by a list (preferably in the form of an adding machine tape) of the amounts of income tax withheld shown on such statements. If an employer's total payroll is made up on the basis of a number of separate units or establishments, the statements may be assembled accordingly and a separate list or tape submitted for each unit. In such case, a summary list or tape should be submitted, the total of which will agree with the corresponding entry to be made on Form W-3. If the number of statements is large, they may be forwarded in packages of convenient size. When this is done, the packages should be identified with the name of the employer and consecutively numbered, and Form W-3 should be placed in package No. 1. The number of packages should be indicated immediately after the employer's name on Form W-3. The return, Form 941, and remittance in cases of this kind should be submitted in the usual manner, accompanied by a brief statement that the district director's copies of Form W-2 and Form W-3 are in separate packages.

(4) The district director's copies of corrected Forms W-2 for a prior calendar year shall be submitted to the district director on or before the date fixed for filing the employer's return of income tax withheld from wages for the period ending December 31 of the year in which the correction is made, or for any period in such year for which the return is made as a final return. Such copies of corrected Forms W-2 shall be accompanied by a statement explaining the corrections and, if submitted with the employer's return for such period ending December 31 or with such final return, shall be assembled separately from the district director's copies of Forms W-2 for the current calendar year (see subparagraph (1) of this paragraph).

(5) For provisions relating to extensions of time for filing the district director's copies of Form W-2 and Form W-3, see paragraph (a)(3) of § 31.6081 (a)-1.

(c) *Time and place for filing returns.* For provisions relating to the time and place for filing returns, see §§ 31.6071 (a)-1 and 31.6091-1, respectively.

○─▬ § 31.6011(a)-5 (T.D. 6354, filed 1-13-59; republished in T.D. 6516, filed 12-19-60; amended by T.D. 7351, filed 4-16-75.) **Monthly returns.**

(a) *In general*—(1) *Requirement.* The provisions of this section are applicable in respect of the taxes reportable on Form 941, Form 941PR, or Form 941VI pursuant to § 31.6011(a)-1 or § 31.6011(a)-4. An employer who is required by § 31.6011(a)-1 or § 31.6011(a)-4 to make quarterly returns on any such form shall, in lieu of making such quarterly returns, make returns of such taxes in accordance with the provisions of this section if he is so notified in writing by the district director. The district director may so notify any employer (i) who, by reason of notification as provided in § 301.7512-1 of this chapter (Regulations on Procedure and Administration), is required to comply with the provisions of such § 301.7512-1, or (ii) who has failed to (a) make any such return on Form 941, Form 941PR, or Form 941VI, (b) pay tax reportable on any such form, or (c) deposit any such tax as required under the provisions of § 31.6302(c)-1. Every employer so notified by the district director shall make a return for the calendar month in which the notice is received and for each calendar month thereafter (whether or not wages are paid in any such month) until he has filed a final return or is required to make quarterly returns pursuant to notification as provided in subparagraph (2) of this paragraph. However, if the notice provided for in this subparagraph is received after the close of the first calendar month of a calendar quarter, the first returns under this section shall be made for the period beginning with the first day of such quarter and ending with the last day of the month in which the notice is received. Each return required under this section shall be made on the form prescribed for making the return which would otherwise be required of the employer under the provisions of § 31.6011(a)-1 or § 31.6011(a)-4, except that, if some other form is furnished by the district director for use in lieu of such prescribed form, the return shall be made on such other form.

(2) *Termination of requirement.* The district director, in his discretion, may notify the employer in writing that he shall discontinue the filing of monthly returns under this section. If the employer is so notified, the last month for which a return shall be made under this section is the last month of the calendar quarter in which such notice of discontinuance is received. Thereafter, the employer shall make quarterly returns in accordance with the provisions of § 31.6011(a)-1 or § 31.6011(a)-4.

(b) *Information returns.*
(1) *Federal Insurance Contributions Act.* * * *

* * * * * *

(2) *Information returns on Form W-3 and Internal Revenue Service copies of Form W-2.* See § 31.6051-2 for requirements with respect to information returns on Form W-3 and Internal Revenue Service copies of Form W-2.

O— § 31.6011(a)-6 (T.D. 6354, filed 1-13-59; republished in T.D. 6516, filed 12-19-60; amended by T.D. 7396, filed 1-12-76.) **Final returns.**

(a) *In general*—(1) *Federal Insurance Contributions Act; income tax withheld from wages.* An employer who is required to make a return on a particular form pursuant to § 31.6011(a)-1, § 31.6011(a)-4, or § 31.6011(a)-5, and who in any return period ceases to pay wages in respect of which he is required to make a return on such form, shall make such return for such period as a final return. Each return made as a final return shall be marked "Final return" by the person filing the return. Every such person filing a final return (other than a final return on Form 942 or Form 943) shall furnish information showing the date of the last payment of wages, as defined in section 3121(a) or section 3401(a). An employer (other than an employer making returns on Form 942) who has only temporarily ceased to pay wages, because of seasonal activities or for other reasons, shall not make a final return but shall continue to file returns. If (i) for any return period an employer makes a final return on a particular form, and (ii) after the close of such period the employer pays wages, as defined in section 3121(a) or section 3401(a), in respect of which the same or a different return form is prescribed, such employer shall make returns on the appropriate return form. For example, if an employer who has filed a final return on Form 941 pays wages only for domestic service in his private home not on a farm operated for profit, the employer is required to make returns on Form 942 in respect of such wages.

(2) *Railroad Retirement Tax Act*—* * *

* * * * * *

(b) *Statement to accompany final return.* There shall be executed as a part of each final return, except in the case of a final return on Form 942, a statement showing the address at which the records required by the regulations in this part will be kept, the name of the person keeping such records, and, if the business of an employer has been sold or otherwise transferred to another person, the name and address of such person and the date on which such sale or other transfer took place. If no such sale or transfer occurred or the employer does not know the name of the person to whom the business was sold or transferred, that fact should be included in the statement. Such statement shall include any information required by this section as to the date of the last payment of wages or compensation. If the statement is executed as a part of a final return on Form CT-1 or Form CT-2, such statement shall be furnished in duplicate.

(c) *Time and place for filing returns.* For provisions relating to the time and place for filing returns, see §§ 31.6071(a)-1 and 31.6091-1, respectively.

O— § 31.6011(a)-7 (T.D. 6354, filed 1-13-59; amended by T.D. 6472, filed 6-22-60; republished in T.D. 6516, filed 12-19-60; amended by T.D. 6606, filed 8-24-62; T.D. 6883, filed 5-2-66; T.D. 7276, filed 5-4-73; T.D. 7396, filed 1-12-76.) **Execution of returns.**

(a) *In general.* Each return required under the regulations in this part, together with any prescribed copies or supporting data, shall be filled in and disposed of in accordance with the forms, instructions, and regulations applicable thereto. The return shall be carefully prepared so as fully and accurately to set forth the data required to be furnished therein. Returns which have not been so prepared will not be accepted as meeting the requirements of the regulations in this part. The return may be made by an agent in the name of the person required to make the return if an acceptable power of attorney is filed with the internal revenue office with which such person is required to file his returns and if such return includes all taxes required to be reported by such person on such return for the period covered by the return. Only one return on any one prescribed form for a return period shall be filed by or for a taxpayer. Any supplemental return made on such form in accordance with § 31.6205-1 shall constitute a part of the return which it supplements. Except as may be provided under procedures authorized by the Commissioner with respect to taxes imposed by the Railroad Retirement Tax Act, consolidated returns of two or more employers are not permitted, as for example, returns of a parent and a subsidiary corporation. For provisions relating to the filing of returns of the taxes imposed by the Federal Insurance Contributions Act and of income tax withheld under section 3402 in the case of governmental employers, see § 31.3122 and § 31.3404-1.

(b) *Use of prescribed forms*—(1) *In general.* Copies of the prescribed return forms will so far as possible be regularly

Reg. § 31.6011(a)-7(b)(1)

24,262.2 (I.R.C.)   Reg. § 31.6011(a)-7(b)(1)   2-21-78

furnished taxpayers by the Internal Revenue Service. A taxpayer will not be excused from making a return, however, by the fact that no return form has been furnished to him. Taxpayers not supplied with the proper forms should make application therefor to an internal revenue office in ample time to have their returns prepared, verified, and filed on or before the due date with the internal revenue office with which they are required to file their returns. See §§ 31.6071(a)-1 and 31.6091-1, relating, respectively, to the time and place for filing returns. In the absence of a prescribed return form, a statement made by a taxpayer disclosing the aggregate amount of wages or compensation reportable on such form for the period in respect of which a return is required and the amount of taxes due may be accepted as a tentative return. If filed within the prescribed time, the statement so made will relieve the taxpayer from liability for the addition to tax imposed for the delinquent filing of the return, provided that without unnecessary delay such tentative return is supplemented by a return made on the proper form. For additions to the tax in case of failure to file a return within the prescribed time, see the provisions of § 301.6651-1 of this chapter (Regulations on Procedure and Administration).

(2) *Permission for use of magnetic tape*—(i) *Form W-2.* In any case where an employer is required by the regulations under this part to submit a copy of a Form W-2 as part of a return or together with an information statement, such requirement may be satisfied by submitting the information required by such form on magnetic tape or by other media, provided that the prior consent of the Commissioner or other authorized officer or employee of the Internal Revenue Service has been obtained. Applications for such consent must be filed in accordance with procedures established by the Internal Revenue Service. See § 1.9101-1 of this chapter (Income Tax Regulations) for additional rules relating to Form W-2.

(ii) *Schedule A of Form 941 or 943.* In any case where the use of a Schedule A of Form 941 or 943 is required by such Forms or the regulations under this part for the purpose of making a return, such requirement may be satisfied, to the extent prior consent is obtained from the Commissioner or other authorized officer or employee of the Internal Revenue Service, by submitting selected items of the information required by such Schedule on magnetic tape or by other media. Applications for such consent must be filed in accordance with procedures established by the Internal Revenue Service.

(c) *Signing and verification.* For provisions relating to the signing of returns, see § 31.6061-1. For provisions relating to the verifying of returns, see § 31.6065(a)-1.

(d) *Reporting of identifying numbers.* For provisions relating to the reporting of identifying numbers on returns required under the regulations in this part, see § 31.6109-1.

O—⚡ § 31.6011 (a)-8 (T.D. 7200, filed 8-15-72.) **Composite return in lieu of specified form.**

The Commissioner may authorize the use, at the option of the employer, of a composite return in lieu of any form specified in this part for use by an employer, subject to such conditions, limitations, and special rules governing the preparation, execution, filing, and correction thereof as the Commissioner may deem appropriate. Such composite return shall consist of a form prescribed by the Commissioner and an attachment or attachments of magnetic tape or other approved media. Notwithstanding any provisions in this part to the contrary, a single form and attachment may comprise the returns of more than one employer. To the extent that the use of a composite return has been authorized by the Commissioner, references in this part to a specific form for use by the employer shall be deemed to refer also to a composite return under this section.

O—⚡ § 31.6011(a)-9 (T.D. 7351, filed 4-16-75.) **Instructions to forms control as to which form is to be used.**

Notwithstanding provisions in this part which specify the use of a particular form for a return or other document required by this part, the use of a different form may be required by the latter form's instructions. In such case, the latter form shall be completed in accordance with its instructions.

O—⚡ § 31.6011 (b) **Statutory provisions; identification of taxpayer.** [Sec. 6011(b), IRC]

O—⚡ § 31.6011 (b)-1 (T.D. 6472, filed 6-22-60; republished in T.D. 6516, filed 12-19-60; amended by T.D. 6606, filed 8-24-62. and T.D. 7012, filed 5-14-69.) **Employers identification numbers.**—

(a) *Requirement of application*—(1) *In general.*—(i) *Before October 1, 1962.* Except as provided in paragraph (b) of this section, every employer who on any day after December 31, 1954, and before October 1, 1962, has in his employ one or more individuals in employment for wages subject to the taxes imposed by the Federal Insurance Contributions Act, but who prior to such day has neither assigned an identification number nor has applied therefor, shall make an application on Form SS-4 for an identification number.

(ii) *On or after October 1, 1962.* Except as provided in paragraph (b) of this section, every employer who on any day after September 30, 1962, has in his employ one or more individuals in employment for wages which are subject to the Federal Insurance Contributions Act or which are subject to the withholding of income tax from wages under section 3402, but who prior to such day neither has been assigned an identification number nor has applied therefor, shall make an application of Form SS-4 for an identification number.

(iii) *Method of application.* The application, together with any supplementary statement, shall be prepared in accordance with the form, instructions, and regulations applicable thereto, and shall set forth fully and clearly the data therein called for. Form SS-4 may be obtained from any district director or director of a service center or any district office of the Social Security Administration. The application shall be filed with the internal revenue officer designated in the instructions applicable to Form SS-4, or with the nearest district office of the Social Security Administration. The application shall be signed by (a) the individual, if the employer is an individual; (b) the president, vice president, or other principal officer, if the employer is a corporation; (c) a responsible and duly authorized member or officer having knowledge of its affairs, if the employer is a partnership or other unincorporated organization; or (d) the fiduciary, if the employer is a trust or estate. An identification number will be assigned to the employer in due course.

(2) *Time for filing Form SS-4.* The application for an identification number shall be filed on or before the seventh day after the first payment of wages, to which reference is made in subparagraph (1) of this paragraph. For provisions relating to the time when wages are paid, see § 31.3121 (a)-2 and paragraph (b) of § 31.3402(a)-1.

(b) *Employers who are assigned identification numbers without application.* An identification number may be assigned, without application by the employer, in the case of an employer who has in his employ only employees who are engaged exclusively in the performance of domestic service in his private home not on a farm operated for profit (see § 31.3121(a)(7)-1). If an identification number is so assigned, the employer is not required to make an application on Form SS-4 for the number.

(c) *Crew leaders.* Any person who, as a crew leader within the meaning of section 3121(o), furnishes individuals to perform agricultural labor for another person shall, on or before the first date on which he furnishes such individuals to perform such labor for such other person, advise such other person of his name; permanent mailing address, or if none, present address; and identification number, if any.

(d) *Use of identification number.* The identification number assigned to an employer (other than a household employer referred to in paragraph (b) of this section) shall be shown in the employer's records, and shall be shown in his claims to the extent required by the applicable forms, regulations and instructions. For provisions relating to the inclusion of identification numbers in returns, statements on Form W-2, and depository receipts, see § 31.6109-1.

○— § 31.6011(b)-2 (T.D. 6354, filed 1-13-59 amended by T.D. 6606, filed 8-24-62.) **Employees' account numbers.**

(a) *Requirement of application*—(1) *In general*—(i) *Before November 1, 1962.* Every employee who on any day after December 31, 1954, and before November 1, 1962, is in employment for wages subject to the taxes imposed by the Federal Insurance Contributions Act, but who prior to such day has neither secured an account number nor made application therefor, shall make an application on Form SS-5 for an account number.

(ii) *On or after November 1, 1962.* Every employee who on any day after October 31, 1962, is in employment for wages which are subject to the taxes imposed by the Federal Insurance Contributions Act or which are subject to the withholding of income tax from wages under section 3402, but who prior to such day has neither secured an account number nor made application therefor, shall make an application on Form SS-5 for an account number.

(iii) *Method of application.* The application shall be prepared in accordance with the form, instructions, and regulations applicable thereto, and shall set forth fully and clearly the data therein called for.

The employee shall file the application with any district office of the Social Security Administration or, if the employee is not working within the United States, with the district office of the Social Security Administration at Baltimore, Maryland. Form SS-5 may be obtained from any district office of the Social Security Administration or from an district director. An account number will be assigned to the employee by the Social Security Administration in due course upon the basis of information reported on the application required under this section. A card showing the name and account number of the employee to whom an account number has been assigned will be furnished to the employee by the Social Security Administration.

(2) *Time for filing Form SS-5.* The application shall be filed on or before the seventh day after the occurrence of the first day of employment to which reference is made in subparagraph (1) of this paragraph, unless the employee leaves the employ of his employer before such seventh day, in which case the application shall be filed on or before the date on which the employee leaves the employ of his employer.

(3) *Changes and corrections.* Any employee may have his account number changed at any time by applying to a district office of the Social Security Administration and showing good reasons for a change. With that exception, only one account number will be assigned to an employee. Any employee whose name is changed by marriage or otherwise, or who has stated incorrect information on Form SS-5, should report such change or correction to a district office of the Social Security Administration. Copies of the form for making such reports may be obtained from any district office of the Administration.

(b) *Duties of employee with respect to his account number*—(1) *Information to be furnished to employer.* An employee shall, on the day on which he enters the employ of any employer for wages, comply with the provisions of subdivision (i), (ii), (iii), or (iv) of this subparagraph, except that, if the employee's services for the employer consist solely of agricultural labor, domestic service in a private home of the employer not on a farm operated for profit, or service not in the course of the employer's trade or business, the employee shall comply with such provisions on the first day on which wages are paid to him by such employer, within the meaning of § 31.3121(a)-2:

(i) *Employee who has account number card.* If the employee has been issued an account number card by the Social Security Administration and has the card available, the employee shall show it to the employer.

(ii) *Employee who has number but card not available.* If the employee does not have available the account number card issued to him by the Social Security Administration but knows what his account number is, and what his name is, exactly as shown on such card, the employee shall advise the employer of such number and name. Care must be exercised that the em-

Reg. § 31.6011(b)-2(b)(1)

ployer is correctly advised of such number and name.

(iii) *Employee who has receipt acknowledging application.* If the employee does not have an account number card but has available a receipt issued to him by an office of the Social Security Administration acknowledging that an application for an account number has been received, the employee shall show such receipt to the employer.

(iv) *Employee who is unable to furnish number or receipt.* If an employee is unable to comply with the requirement of subdivision (i), (ii), or (iii) of this subparagraph, the employee shall furnish to the employer a statement in writing, signed by the employee, setting forth the date of the statement, the employee's full name, present address, date and place of birth, father's full name, mother's full name before marriage, and the employee's sex, including a statement as to whether the employee has previously filed an application on Form SS-5 and, if so, the date and place of such filing. The information required by this subdivision shall be furnished on Form SS-5, if a copy of Form SS-5 is available. The furnishing of such a Form SS-5 or other statement by the employee to the employer does not relieve the employee of his obligation to make an application on Form SS-5 and file it with a district office of the Social Security Administration as required by paragraph (a) of this section. The foregoing provisions of this subdivision are not applicable to an employee engaged exclusively in the performance of domestic service in a private home of his employer not on a farm operated for profit, or in the performance of agricultural labor, if the services are performed for an employer required to file returns of the taxes imposed by the Federal Insurance Contributions Act with the office of the United States Internal Revenue Service in Puerto Rico. However, such employee shall advise the employer of his full name and present address.

For provisions relating to the duties of an employer when furnished the information required by subdivision (i), (ii), (iii), or (iv) of this subparagraph, see paragraph (c) of this section.

(2) *Additional information to be furnished by employee to employer.* Every employee who, on the day on which he is required to comply with subdivision (i), (ii), (iii), or (iv) of subparagraph (1) of this paragraph, has an account number card but for any reason does not show such card to the employer on such day shall promptly thereafter show the card to the employer. An employee who does not have an account number card on such day shall, upon receipt of an account number card from the Social Security Administration, promptly show such card to the employer, if he is still in the employ of that employer. If the employee has left the employ of the employer when the employee receives an account number card from the Social Security Administration, he shall promptly advise the employer of his account number and name exactly as shown on such card. The account number originally assigned to an employee (or the number as changed in accordance with paragraph (a)(3) of this section) shall be used by the employee as required by this paragraph even though he enters the employ of other employers.

(3) *Furnishing of account number by employee to employer.* See § 31.6109-1 for additional provisions relating to the furnishing of an account number by the employee to his employer.

(c) *Duties of employer with respect to employees' account numbers*—(1) *Employee who shows account number.* Upon being shown the account number card issued to an employee by the Social Security Administration, the employer shall enter the account number and name, exactly as shown on the card, in the employer's records, returns, statements for employees, and claims to the extent required by the applicable forms, regulations, and instructions.

(2) *Employee who does not show account number card.* With respect to an employee who, on the day on which he is required to comply with subdivision (i), (ii), (iii), or (iv) of paragraph (b)(1) of this section, does not show the employer an account number card issued to the employee by the Social Security Administration, the employer shall request such employee to show him such card. If the card is not shown, the employer shall comply with the applicable provisions of subdivision (i), (ii), (iii), (iv), or (v) of this subparagraph:

(i) *Employee who has not applied for account number.* If the employee has not been assigned an account number and has not made application therefor with a district office of the Social Security Administration, the employer shall inform the employee of his duties under this section.

(ii) *Employee who has account number.* If the employee advises the employer of his number and name as shown on his account number card, as provided in paragraph (b)(1)(ii) of this section, the employer shall enter such number and name in his records.

(iii) *Employee who has receipt for application.* If the employee shows the employer, as provided in paragraph (b)(1)(iii) of this section, a receipt issued to him by an office of the Social Security Administration acknowledging that an application for an account number has been received from the employee, the employer shall enter in his records with respect to such employee the name and address of the employee exactly as shown on the receipt, the expiration date of the receipt, and the address of the issuing office. The receipt shall be retained by the employee.

(iv) *Employee who furnishes Form SS-5 or statement.* If the employee furnishes information to the employer as provided in paragraph (b)(1)(iv) of this section, the employer shall retain such information for use as provided in subparagraph (3)(ii) of this paragraph.

(v) *Household or agricultural employees.* If the employee advises the employer of his full name and present address in accordance with those provisions of paragraph (b)(1)(iv) of this section which are applicable in the case of employees engaged exclusively in the performance of domestic service in a private home of the employer not on a farm operated for profit, or agricultural labor, the employer shall enter such name and address in his records.

(3) *Account number unknown when return is filed.* In any case in which the employee's account number is for any reason unknown to the employer at the time the employer's return is filed for any return period with respect to which the employer is required to report the wages paid to such employee—

(i) *If employee has shown receipt for application.* If the employee has shown to the employer, as provided in paragraph (b)(1)(iii) of this section, a receipt issued to him by an office of the Social Security Administration acknowledging that an application for an account number has been received from the employee, the employer shall enter on the return, with the entry with respect to the employee, the name and address of the employee exactly as shown on the receipt, the expiration date of the receipt, and the address of the issuing office.

(ii) *If employee furnished Form SS-5 or statement.* If the employee has furnished information to the employer as provided in paragraph (b)(i)(iv) of this section, the employer shall prepare a copy of the Form SS-5 or statement furnished by the employee and attach the copy to the return.

(iii) *If employee did not furnish receipt, Form SS-5, or statement.* If neither subdivision (i) nor (ii) of this subparagraph is applicable, the employer shall, except as provided in subparagraph (4) of this paragraph, attach to the return a Form SS-5 or statement, signed by the employer, setting forth as fully and clearly as practicable the employee's full name, his present or last known address, date and place of birth, father's full name, mother's full name before marriage, the employee's sex, and a statement as to whether an application for an account number has previously been filed by the employee and, if so, the date and place of such filing. The employer shall also insert in such Form SS-5 or statement an explanation of why he has not secured from the employee the information referred to in paragraph (b)(1)(iv) of this section, and shall insert the word "Employer" as part of his signature.

(4) *Household or agricultural employees.* The provisions of subparagraph (3)(iii) of this paragraph are not applicable with respect to an employee engaged exclusively in the performance of domestic service in a private home of his employer not on a farm operated for profit, or in the performance of agricultural labor, if the services are performed for an employer other than an employer required to file returns of the taxes imposed by the Federal Insurance Contributions Act with the office of the United States Internal Revenue Service in Puerto Rico. If any such employee has not furnished to the employer the information required by paragraph (b)(1)(i), (ii), or (iii) of this section prior to the time the employer's return is filed for any return period with respect to which the employer is required to report wages paid to such employee, the employer shall enter the word "Unknown" in the account number column of the return and (i) file with the return a statement showing the employee's full name and present or last known address, or (ii) enter such address on the return form immediately below the name of the employee.

(5) *Where to obtain Form SS-5.* Employers may obtain copies of Form SS-5 from any district office of the Social Security Administration or from any district director.

(6) *Prospective employees.* While not mandatory, it is suggested that the employer advise any prospective employee who does not have an account number of the requirements of paragraphs (a) and (b) of this section.

○━━ § 53.6011 **Statutory provisions; general requirement of return, statement, or list.** [Sec. 6011, IRC]

○━━ § 53.6011-1 (T.D. 7368, filed 7-15-75; amended by T.D. 7407, filed 3-3-76.) **General requirement of return, statement, or list.**

(a) Every private foundation liable for tax under section 4940 or 4948(a) shall file an annual return with respect to such tax on the form prescribed by the Internal Revenue Service for such purpose and shall include therein the information required by such form and the instructions issued with respect thereto.

(b) Every person liable for tax imposed by section 4941(a), 4942(a), 4943(a), 4944(a) or 4945(a), and every private foundation and every trust described in section 4947(a)(2) which has engaged in an act of self-dealing (as defined in section 4941(d)) (other than an act giving rise to no tax under section 4941(a)) shall file an annual return on Form 4720 and shall include therein the information required by such form and the instructions issued with respect thereto. In the case of any tax imposed by sections 4941(a), 4942(a), 4943(a), and 4944(a), the annual return shall be filed with respect to each act (or failure to act) for each year (or part thereof) in the taxable period (as defined in sections 4941(e)(1), 4942(j)(1), 4943(d)(2), and 4944(e)(1)). In the case of a tax imposed by section 4945(a), the annual return shall be filed with respect to each act for the year in which such act giving rise to liability occurred.

(c) If a Form 4720 is filed by a private foundation or trust described in section 4947(a)(2) with respect to a transaction to which other persons are required to file under paragraph (b) of this section, such persons may by their signature designate such organization's Form 4720 (to the extent applicable) as their return for purposes of compliance with such paragraph. However, this paragraph shall not apply to a person whose taxable year is other than the taxable year of the foundation or trust.

(d) For taxable years ending on or after December 31, 1975, every trust de-

Reg. § 53.6011-1(d)

scribed in section 4947(a)(1) which is a private foundation and every trust described in section 4947(a)(2) which is subject to any of the provisions of Chapter 42 as if it were a private foundation shall file an annual return on Form 5227.

○━▶ § 301.6011-1 (T.D. 6498, filed 10-24-60.) General requirement of return, statement, or list.

For provisions requiring returns, statements, or lists, see the regulations relating to the particular tax.

○━▶ § 1.6012 Statutory provisions; persons required to make returns of income. [Sec. 6012, IRC]

○━▶ § 1.6012-1 (T.D. 6364, filed 2-13-59; amended by T.D. 6455, filed 3-1-60; republished in T.D. 6500, filed 11-25-60; amended by T.D. 6533, filed 1-18-61; T.D. 6581, filed 12-5-61; T.D. 6777, filed 12-15-64; T.D. 6817, filed 4-7-65; T.D. 6856, filed 10-19-65; T.D. 6885, filed 6-1-66; T.D. 7069, filed 11-10-70; T.D. 7269, filed 4-12-73; T.D. 7274, filed 5-4-73 and T.D. 7332, filed 12-20-74). **Individuals required to make returns of income.**

(a) *Individual citizen or resident—* (1) *In general.* Except as provided in subparagraph (2) of this paragraph, an income tax return must be filed by every individual for each taxable year beginning before January 1, 1973, during which he receives $600 or more of gross income, and for each taxable year beginning after December 31, 1972, during which he receives $750 or more of gross income, if such individual is—

(i) A citizen of the United States, whether residing at home or abroad,

(ii) A resident of the United States even though not a citizen thereof, or

(iii) An alien bona fide resident of Puerto Rico during the entire taxable year.

(2) *Special rules.* (i) For taxable years beginning before January 1, 1970, an individual who is described in subparagraph (1) of this paragraph and who has attained the age of 65 before the close of his taxable year must file an income tax return only if he receives $1,200 or more of gross income during his taxable year.

(ii) For taxable years beginning after December 31, 1969, and before January 1, 1973, an individual described in subparagraph (1) of this paragraph (other than an individual referred to in section 142 (b))—

(a) Who is not married (as determined by applying section 143 (a) and the regulations thereunder) must file an income tax return only if he receives $1,700 or more of gross income during his taxable year, except that if such an individual has attained the age of 65 before the close of his taxable year an income tax return must be filed by such individual only if he receives $2,300 or more of gross income during his taxable year.

(b) Who is entitled to make a joint return under section 6013 and the regulations thereunder must file an income tax return only if his gross income received during his taxable year, when combined with the gross income of his spouse received during his taxable year, is $2,300 or more. However, if such individual or his spouse has attained the age of 65 before the close of the taxable year an income tax return must be filed by such individual only if their combined gross income is $2,900 or more. If both the individual and his spouse have attained the age of 65 before the close of the taxable year such return must be filed only if their combined gross income is $3,500 or more. However, this subdivision (ii)(b) shall not apply if the individual and his spouse did not have the same household as their home at the close of their taxable year, if such spouse files a separate return for a taxable year which includes any part of such individual's taxable year, or if any other taxpayer is entitled to an exemption for such individual or his spouse under section 151(e) for such other taxpayer's taxable year beginning in the calendar year in which such individual's taxable year begins. For example, a married student more than half of whose support is furnished by his father must file an income tax return if he receives $600 or more of gross income during his taxable year.

(iii) For taxable years beginning after December 31, 1972, an individual described in subparagraph (1) of this paragraph (other than an individual referred to in section 142(b))—

(a) Who is not married (as determined by applying section 143(a) and the regulations thereunder) must file an income tax return only if he receives $1,750 or more of gross income during his taxable year, except that if such an individual has attained the age of 65 before the close of his taxable year an income tax return must be filed by such individual only if he receives $2,500 or more of gross income during his taxable year.

(b) Who is entitled to make a joint return under section 6013 and the regulations thereunder must file an income tax return only if his gross income received during his taxable year, when combined with the gross income of his spouse received during his taxable year, is $2,500 or more. However, if such individual or his spouse has attained the age of 65 before the close of the taxable year an income tax return must be filed by such individual only if their combined gross income is $3,250 or more. If both the individual and his spouse attain the age of 65 before the close of the taxable year such return must be filed only if their combined gross income is $4,000 or more. However, this subdivision (iii)(b) shall not apply if the individual and his spouse did not have the same household as their home at the close of their taxable year, if such spouse files a separate return for a taxable year which includes any part of such individual's taxable year, or if any other taxpayer is entitled to an exemption for the taxpayer or his spouse under section 151(e) for such other taxpayer's taxable year beginning in the calendar year in which such individual's taxable year begins. For example, a married student more than half of whose support is furnished by his father must file an income tax return if he receives $750 or more of gross income during the taxable year.

(iv) For purposes of section 6012(a)(1)(A)(ii) and subdivisions (ii)(b) and (iii)(b) of this subparagraph, an individual and his spouse are considered to have the same household as their home at the close of a taxable year if the same household constituted the principal place of abode of both the individual and his spouse at the close of such taxable year (or on the date of death, if the individual or his spouse died within the taxable year). The individual and his spouse will be considered to have the same household as their home at the close of the taxable year notwithstanding a temporary absence from the household due to special circumstances, as, for example, in the case of a nonpermanent failure on the part of the individual and his spouse to have a common abode by reason of illness, education, business, vacation, or military service. For example, A, a calendar-year individual under 65 years of age, is married to B, also under 65 years of age, and is a member of the Armed Forces of the United States. During 1970 A is transferred to an overseas base. A and B give up their home, which they had jointly occupied until that time; B moves to the home of her parents for the duration of A's absence. They fully intend to set up a new joint household upon A's return. Neither A nor B must file a return for 1970 if their combined gross income for the year is less than $2,300 and if no other taxpayer is entitled to a dependency exemption for A or B under section 151(e).

(v) In the case of a short taxable year referred to in section 443(a)(1), an individual described in subparagraph (1) of this paragraph shall file an income tax return if his gross income received during such short taxable year equals or exceeds his own personal exemption allowed by section 151(b) (prorated as provided in section 443(c)) and, when applicable, his additional exemption for age 65 or more allowed by section 151(c)(1) (prorated as provided in section 443(c)).

(3) *Earned income from without the United States and gain from sale of residence.* For the purpose of determining whether an income tax return must be filed for any taxable year beginning after December 31, 1957, gross income shall be computed without regard to the exclusion provided for in section 911 (relating to earned income from sources without the United States). For the purpose of determining whether an income tax return must be filed for any taxable year ending after December 31, 1963, gross income shall be computed without regard to the exclusion provided for in section 121 (relating to sale of residence by individual who has attained age 65). In the case of an individual claiming an exclusion under section 121, he shall

Reg. § 1.6012-1(a)(3)

attach Form 2119 to the return required under this paragraph and in the case of an individual claiming an exclusion under section 911, he shall attach Form 2555 to the return required under this paragraph.

(4) *Return of income of minor.* A minor is subject to the same requirements and elections for making returns of income as are other individuals. Thus, for example, for a taxable year beginning after December 31, 1972, a return must be made by or for a minor who has an aggregate of $1,750 of gross income from funds held in trust for him and from his personal services, regardless of the amount of his taxable income. The return of a minor must be made by the minor himself or must be made for him by his guardian or other person charged with the care of the minor's person or property. See paragraph (b)(3) of § 1.6012-3. See § 1.73-1 for inclusion in the minor's gross income of amounts received for his personal services. For the amount of tax which is considered to have been properly assessed against the parent, if not paid by the child, see section 6201(c) and paragraph (c) of § 301.6201-1 of this chapter (Regulations on Procedure and Administration).

(5) *Returns made by agents.* The return of income may be made by an agent if, by reason of disease or injury, the person liable for the making of the return is unable to make it. The return may also be made by an agent if the taxpayer is unable to make the return by reason of continuous absence from the United States (including Puerto Rico as if a part of the United States) for a period of at least 60 days prior to the date prescribed by law for making the return. In addition, a return may be made by an agent if the taxpayer requests permission, in writing, of the district director for the internal revenue district in which is located the legal residence or principal place of business of the person liable for the making of the return, and such district director determines that good cause exists for permitting the return to be so made. However, assistance in the preparation of the return may be rendered under any circumstances. Whenever a return is made by an agent it must be accompanied by a power of attorney (or copy thereof) authorizing him to represent his principal in making, executing, or filing the return. A Form 2848, when properly completed, is sufficient. In addition, where one spouse is physically unable by reason of disease or injury to sign a joint return, the other spouse may, with the oral consent of the one who is incapacitated, sign the incapacitated spouse's name in the proper place on the return followed by the words "By .... Husband (or Wife)", and by the signature of the signing spouse in his own right, provided that a dated statement signed by the spouse who is signing the return is attached to and made a part of the return stating—

(i) The name of the return being filed,
(ii) The taxable year,
(iii) The reason for the inability of the spouse who is incapacitated to sign the return, and
(iv) That the spouse who is incapacitated consented to the signing of the return. The taxpayer and his agent, if any, are responsible for the return as made and incur liability for the penalties provided for erroneous, false, or fraudulent returns. For a return of an agent for a nonresident alien individual, see paragraph (b)(6) of this section. For the requirements regarding signing of returns, see § 1.6061-1.

(6) *Form of return.* Form 1040 is prescribed for general use in making the return required under this paragraph. Form 1040A is an optional short form which, in accordance with paragraph (a)(7) of this section, may be used by certain taxpayers. A taxpayer otherwise entitled to use Form 1040A as his return for any taxable year may not make his return on such form if he elects not to take the standard deduction provided in section 141, and in such case he must make his return on Form 1040. For taxable years beginning before January 1, 1970, a taxpayer entitled under section 6014 and § 1.6014-1 to elect not to show his tax on his return must, if he desires to exercise such election, make his return on Form 1040A. Form 1040W is an optional short form which, in accordance with paragraph (a)(8) of this section, may be used only with respect to taxable years beginning after December 31, 1958 and ending before December 31, 1961.

(7) (i) *Use of Form 1040A.* Form 1040A may be filed only by those individuals entitled to use such form as provided by and in accordance with the instructions for such form.

(ii) *Computation and payment of tax.* Unless a taxpayer is entitled to elect under section 6014 and § 1.6014-1 not to show the tax on Form 1040A and does so elect, he shall compute and show on his return on Form 1040A the amount of the tax imposed by subtitle A of the Code and shall, without notice and demand therefor, pay any unpaid balance of such tax not later than the date fixed for filing the return.

(iii) *Change of election to use Form 1040A.* A taxpayer who has elected to make his return on Form 1040A may change such election. Such change of election shall be within the time and subject to the conditions prescribed in section 144 (b) and § 1.144-2 relating to change of election to take, or not to take the standard deduction.

(8) *Use of Form 1040W for certain taxable years*—(i) *In general.* An individual may use Form 1040W as his return for any taxable year beginning after December 31, 1958, and ending before Decembar 31, 1961, in which the gross income of the individual regardless of the amount thereof—

(a) Consists entirely of remuneration for personal services performed as an employee (whether or not such remuneration constitutes wages as defined in section 3401 (a)), dividends, or interest, and

(b) Does not include more than $200 from dividends and interest.

For purposes of determining whether gross income from dividends and interest exceeds $200, dividends from domestic corporations are taken into account to the extent that they are includible in gross income.

For purposes of this subparagraph, any reference to Form 1040 in §§ 1.4-2, 1.142-1, and 1.144-1 and this section shall also be deemed a reference to Form 1040W.

(ii) *Change of election to use Form 1040W.* A taxpayer who has elected to make his return on Form 1040W may

Reg. § 1.6012-1 (a) (8)

change such election. Such change of election shall be within the time and subject to the conditions prescribed in section 144(b) and § 1.144-2, relating to change of election to take, or not to take, the standard deduction.

(iii) *Joint return of husband and wife on Form 1040W.* A husband and wife, eligible under section 6013 and the regulations thereunder to file a joint return for the taxable year, may, subject to the provisions of this subparagraph, make a joint return on Form 1040W for any taxable year beginning after December 31, 1958, and ending before December 31, 1961, in which the aggregate gross income of the spouses (regardless of amount) consists entirely of remuneration for personal services performed as an employee (whether or not such remuneration constitutes wages as defined in section 3401(a)), dividends, or interest, and does not include more than $200 from dividends and interest. For purposes of determining whether gross income from sources to which the $200 limitation applies exceeds such amount in cases where both spouses receive dividends from domestic corporations, the amount of such dividends received by each spouse is taken into account to the extent that such dividends are includible in gross income. See section 116 and §§ 1.116-1 and 1.116-2. If a joint return is made by husband and wife on Form 1040W, the liability for the tax shall be joint and several.

(9) [Deleted.]
(10) [Deleted.]

(b) *Return of nonresident alien individual*—(1) *Requirement of return*—(i) *In general.* Except as otherwise provided in subparagraph (2) of this paragraph, every nonresident alien individual who is engaged in trade or business in the United States at any time during the taxable year or who has income which is subject to taxation under subtitle A of the Code shall make a return on Form 1040NR. For this purpose it is immaterial that the gross income for the taxable year is less than the minimum amount specified in section 6012 (a) for making a return. Thus, a nonresident alien individual who is engaged in a trade or business in the United States at any time during the taxable year is required to file a return on Form 1040NR even though *(a)* he has no income which is effectively connected with the conduct of a trade or business in the United States, *(b)* he has no income from sources within the United States, or *(c)* his income is exempt from income tax by reason of an income tax convention or any section of the Code. However, if the nonresident alien individual has no gross income for the taxable year, he is not required to complete the return schedules but must attach a statement to the return indicating the nature of any exclusions claimed and the amount of such exclusions to the extent such amounts are readily determinable.

(ii) *Treaty income.* If the gross income of a nonresident alien individual includes treaty income, as defined in paragraph (b)(1) of § 1.871-12, a statement shall be attached to the return on Form 1040NR showing with respect to that income—

(a) The amounts of tax withheld,

(b) The names and post office addresses of withholding agents, and

(c) Such other information as may be required by the return form, or by the instructions issued with respect to the form, to show the taxpayer's entitlement to the reduced rate of tax under the tax convention.

(2) *Exceptions*—(i) Return not required when tax is fully paid at source. A nonresident alien individual who at no time during the taxable year is engaged in a trade or business in the United States is not required to make a return for the taxable year if his tax liability for the taxable year is fully satisfied by the withholding of tax at source under chapter 3 of the Code. This subdivision does not apply to a nonresident alien individual who has income for the taxable year which is treated under section 871(c) or (d) and § 1.871-9 (relating to students or trainees) or § 1.871-10 (relating to real property income) as income which is effectively connected for the taxable year with the conduct of a trade or business in the United States by that individual, or to a nonresident alien individual making a claim under § 301.6402-3 of this chapter (Procedure and Administration Regulations) for the refund of an overpayment of tax for the taxable year. For purposes of this subdivision, some of the items of income from sources within the United States upon which the tax liability will not have been fully satisfied by the withholding of tax at source under chapter 3 of the Code are:

(a) Interest upon so-called tax-free covenant bonds upon which, in accordance with section 1451 and § 1.1451-1, a tax of only 2 percent is required to be withheld at the source,

(b) In the case of bonds or other evidences of indebtedness issued after September 28, 1965, amounts described in section 871(a)(1)(C),

(c) Capital gains described in section 871(a)(2) and paragraph (d) of § 1.871-7, and

(d) Accrued interest received in connection with the sale of bonds between interest dates, which, in accordance with paragraph (h) of § 1.1441-4, is not subject to withholding of tax at the source.

(ii) *Return of individual for taxable year of change of U.S. citizenship or residence.* (a) If an alien individual becomes a citizen or resident of the United States during the taxable year and is a citizen or resident of the United States on the last day of such year, he must make a return on Form 1040 for the taxable year. However, a separate schedule is required to be attached to this return to show the income tax computation for the part of the taxable year during which the alien was neither a citizen nor resident of the United States. A Form 1040NR, clearly marked "Statement" across the top, may be used as such a separate schedule.

(b) If an individual abandons his U.S. citizenship or residence during the taxable year and is not a citizen or resident of the United States on the last day of such year, he must make a return on Form 1040NR for the taxable year. However, a separate schedule is required to be attached to this return to show the income tax computation for the part of the taxable year during which the individual was a citizen or resident of the United States. A Form 1040, clearly marked "Statement" across the top, may be used as such a separate schedule.

(c) A return is required under this subdivision (ii) only if the individual is otherwise required to make a return for the taxable year.

(iii) *Beneficiaries of estates or trusts.* A nonresident alien individual who is a beneficiary of an estate or trust which is engaged in trade or business in the United States is not required to make a return for the taxable year merely because he is deemed to be engaged in trade or business within the United States under section 875 (2). However, such nonresident alien beneficiary will be required to make a return if he otherwise satisfies the conditions of subparagraph (1)(i) of this paragraph for making a return.

(iv) *Certain alien residents of Puerto Rico.* This paragraph does not apply to a nonresident alien individual who is a bona fide resident of Puerto Rico during the taxable year. See section 876 and paragraph (a)(1)(iii) of this section.

(3) *Representative or agent for nonresident alien individual*—(i) Cases where power of attorney is not required. The responsible representative or agent within the United States of a nonresident alien individual shall make on behalf of his nonresident alien principal a return of, and shall pay the tax on, all income coming within his control as representative or agent which is subject to the income tax under subtitle A of the Code. The agency appointment will determine how completely the agent is substituted for the principal for tax purposes. Any person who collects interest or dividends on deposited securities of a nonresident alien individual, executes ownership certificates in connection therewith, or sells such securities under special instructions shall not be deemed merely by reason of such acts to be the responsible representative or agent of the nonresident alien individual. If the responsible representative or agent does not have a specific power of attorney from the nonresident alien individual to file a return in his behalf, the return shall be accompanied by a statement to the effect that the representative or agent does not possess specific power of attorney to file a return for such individual but that the return is being filed in accordance with the provisions of this subdivision.

(ii) *Cases where power of attorney is required.* Whenever a return of income of a nonresident alien individual is made by an agent acting under a duly authorized power of attorney for that purpose, the return shall be accompanied by the power of attorney in proper form, or a copy thereof, specifically authorizing him to represent his principal in making, executing, and filing the income tax return. Form 2848 may be used for this purpose. The agent, as well as the taxpayer, may incur liability for the penalties provided for erroneous, false, or fraudulent returns. For the requirements regarding signing of returns, see § 1.6061-1. The rules of paragraph (e) of § 601.504 of this chapter (Statement of Procedural Rules) shall apply under this subparagraph in determining whether a copy of a power of attorney must be certified.

(iii) *Limitation.* A return of income shall be required under this subparagraph only if the nonresident alien individual is otherwise required to make a return in accordance with this paragraph.

(4) *Disallowance of deductions and credits.* For provisions disallowing deductions and credits when a return of income has not been filed by or on behalf of a nonresident alien individual, see section 874 (a) and the regulations thereunder.

(5) *Effective date.* This paragraph shall apply for taxable years beginning after December 31, 1966, except that it shall not be applied to require (i) the filing of a return for any taxable year ending before January 1, 1974, which, pursuant to instructions applicable to the return, is not required to be filed or (ii) the amendment of a return for such a taxable year which, pursuant to such instructions, is required to be filed. For corresponding rules applicable to taxable years beginning before January 1, 1967, see 26 CFR 1.6012-1(b) (Rev. as of Jan. 1, 1967).

(c) *Cross reference.* For returns by fiduciaries for individuals, estates, and trusts, see § 1.6012-3.

§ 1.6012-2 (T.D. 6301, filed 7-8-58; amended by T.D. 6364, filed 2-13-59, T.D. 6427, filed 12-2-59; republished in T.D. 6500, filed 11-25-60; amended by T.D. 6523, filed 12-28-60; T.D. 6533, filed 1-18-61; T.D. 6628, filed 12-28-62; T.D. 6643, filed 4-1-63; T.D. 6960, filed 6-24-68; T.D. 7244, filed 12-29-72; T.D. 7293, filed 11-27-73 and T.D. 7332, filed 12-20-74.) **Corporations required to make returns of income.**

(a) *In general*—(1) *Requirement of return.* Except as provided in paragraphs (e) and (g)(1) of this section with respect to charitable and other organizations having unrelated business income and to certain foreign corporations, respectively, every corporation, as defined in section 7701(a)(3), subject to taxation under subtitle A of the Code shall make a return of income regardless of whether it has taxable income or regardless of the amount of its gross income.

(2) *Existence of corporation.* A corporation in existence during any portion of a taxable year is required to make a return. If a corporation was not in existence throughout an annual accounting period (either calendar year or fiscal year), the corporation is required to make a return for that fractional part of a year during which it was in existence. A corporation is not in existence after it ceases business and dissolves, retaining no assets, whether or not under State law it may thereafter be treated as continuing as a corporation for certain limited purposes connected with winding up its affairs, such as for the purpose of suing and being sued. If the corporation has valuable claims for which it will bring suit during this period, it has retained assets and therefore continues in existence. A corporation does not go out of existence if it is turned over to receivers or trustees who continue to operate it. If a corporation has received a charter but has never perfected its organization and has transacted no business and has no income from any source, it may upon pre-

Reg. § 1.6012-2(a)(2)

sentation of the facts to the district director be relieved from the necessity of making a return. In the absence of a proper showing of such facts to the district director, a corporation will be required to make a return.

(3) *Form of return.* The return required of a corporation under this section shall be made on Form 1120 unless the corporation is of a type for which a special form is prescribed. The special forms of returns and schedules required of particular types of corporations are set forth in paragraphs (b) to (g), inclusive, of this section.

(b) *Personal holding companies.* A personal holding company, as defined in section 542, including a foreign corporation within the definition of such section, shall attach Schedule PH, Computation of U. S. Personal Holding Company Tax, to the return required by paragraph (a) or (g), as the case may be, of this section.

(c) *Insurance companies*—(1) *Life insurance companies.* A life insurance company subject to tax under section 802 or 811 shall make a return on Form 1120L. There shall be filed with the return (i) a copy of the annual statement, the form of which has been approved by the National Association of Insurance Commissioners, which is filed by the company for the year covered by such return with the Insurance Departments of States, Territories, and the District of Columbia, and which shows the reserves used by the company in computing the taxable income reported on its return, and (ii) copies of Schedule A (real estate) and Schedule D (bonds and stocks) of such annual statement.

(2) *Mutual insurance companies.* A mutual insurance company (other than a life or marine insurance company and other than a fire insurance company subject to the tax imposed by section 831) or an interinsurer or reciprocal underwriter subject to tax under section 821 shall make a return on Form 1120M. See paragraph (a)(3) of § 1.821-1. There shall be filed with the return (i) a copy of the annual statement, the form of which has been approved by the National Association of Insurance Commissioners, which is filed by the company for the year covered by such return with the Insurance Departments of States, Territories, and the District of Columbia, and (ii) copies of Schedule A (real estate) and Schedule D (bonds and stocks) of such annual statement.

(3) *Other insurance companies.* Every insurance company (other than a life or mutual insurance company), every mutual marine insurance company, and every mutual fire insurance company, subject to tax under section 831, and every mutual savings bank conducting a life insurance business and subject to tax under section 594, shall make a return on Form 1120. See paragraph (c) of § 1.831-1. There shall be filed with the return a copy of the annual statement, the form of which has been approved by the National Association of Insurance Commissioners, which contains the underwriting and investment exhibit for the year covered by such return.

(4) *Foreign insurance companies.* The provisions of subparagraphs (1), (2), and (3) of this paragraph concerning the returns and statements of insurance companies subject to tax under section 802 or 811, section 821, and section 831, respectively, are applicable to foreign insurance companies subject to tax under such sections, except that the copy of the annual statement, the form of which has been approved by the National Association of Insurance Commissioners, required to be submitted with the return shall, in the case of a foreign insurance company, be a copy of the statement relating to the United States business of such company.

(d) *Affiliated groups.* For the forms to be used by affiliated corporations filing a consolidated return, see § 1.1502-75.

(e) *Charitable and other organizations with unrelated business income.* Every organization, described in section 501(c) (2), (3), (5), and (6), which is otherwise exempt from tax under section 501(a), and which is subject to the tax imposed on unrelated business taxable income by section 511(a) (1), shall make a return on Form 990-T for each taxable year if it has gross income, included in computing unrelated business taxable income for such taxable year, of $1,000 or more. A return on Form 990-T shall also be made for each taxable year by every governmental college or university and by every corporation wholly owned by such a college or university, which is subject to the tax on unrelated business taxable income and which has gross income included in computing unrelated business taxable income for such taxable year, of $1,000 or more. The filing of a return of unrelated business income does not relieve the organization of the duty of filing other required returns.

(f) *Farmers' cooperatives.* Farmers' cooperative organizations described in section 521 are required to make a return of income whether or not such organizations are subject to the taxes imposed by sections 11 and 1201 as prescribed in section 522 or 1381. The return shall be made on Form 990-C.

(g) *Returns by foreign corporations—* (1) *Requirement of return* — (i) *In general.* Except as otherwise provided in subparagraph (2) of this paragraph, every foreign corporation which is engaged in trade or business in the United States at any time during the taxable year or which has income which is subject to taxation under subtitle A of the Code (relating to income taxes) shall make a return on Form 1120-F. Thus, for example, a foreign corporation which is engaged in trade or business in the United States at any time during the taxable year is required to file a return on Form 1120-F even though *(a)* it has no income which is effectively connected with the conduct of a trade or business in the United States, *(b)* it has no income from sources within the United States, or *(c)* its income is exempt from income tax by reason of an income tax convention or any section of the Code. However, if the foreign corporation has no gross income for the taxable year, it is not required to complete the return schedules but must attach a statement to the return indicating the nature of any exclusions claimed and the amount of such exclusions to the extent such amounts are readily determinable.

(ii) *Treaty income.* If the gross income of a foreign corporation includes treaty income, as defined in paragraph (b) (1) of § 1.871-12, a statement shall be attached to the return on Form 1120-F showing with respect to that income—

(a) The amounts of tax withheld.

(b) The names and post office addresses of withholding agents, and

(c) Such other information as may be required by the return form or by the instructions issued with respect to the form, to show the taxpayer's entitlement to the reduced rate of tax under the tax convention.

(iii) *Balance sheet and reconciliation of income.* At the election of the taxpayer, the balance sheets and reconciliation of income, as shown on Form 1120-F, may be limited to—

(a) The assets of the corporation located in the United States and to its other assets used in the trade or business conducted in the United States, and

(b) Its income effectively connected with the conduct of a trade or business in the United States and its other income from sources within the United States.

(2) *Exceptions.* (i) Return not required when tax is fully paid at source—
(a) *In general.* A foreign corporation which at no time during the taxable year is engaged in a trade or business in the United States is not required to make a return for the taxable year if its tax liability for the taxable year is fully satisfied by the withholding of tax at source under chapter 3 of the Code. For purposes of this subdivision, some of the items of income from sources within the United States upon which the tax liability will not have been fully satisfied by the withholding of tax at source under chapter 3 of the Code are:

(1) Interest upon so-called tax-free convenant bonds upon which, in accordance with section 1451 and § 1.1451-1, a tax of only 2 percent is required to be withheld at source,

(2) In the case of bonds or other evidence of indebtedness issued after September 25, 1965, amounts described in section 881(a)(3),

(3) Accrued interest received in connection with the sale of bonds between interest dates, which, in accordance with paragraph (h) of § 1.1441-4, is not subject to withholding of tax at source.

(b) *Corporations not included.* This subdivision (i) shall not apply—

(1) To a foreign corporation which has income for the taxable year which is treated under section 882(d) or (e) and § 1.882-2 as income which is effectively connected for the taxable year with the conduct of a trade or business in the United States by that corporation,

(2) To a foreign corporation making a claim under § 301.6402-3 of this chapter (Procedure and Administration Regulations) for the refund of an overpayment of tax for the taxable year, or

(3) To a foreign corporation described in paragraph (c)(2)(i) of § 1.532-1 whose accumulated taxable income for the taxable year is determined under paragraph (b)(2) of § 1.535-1.

(ii) *Beneficiaries of estates or trusts.* A foreign corporation which is a beneficiary of an estate or trust which is engaged in trade or business in the United States is not required to make a return for the taxable year merely because it is deemed to be engaged in trade or business within the United States under section 875(2). However, such foreign corporation will be required to make a return if it otherwise satisfies the conditions of subparagraph (1)(i) of this paragraph for making a return.

(iii) *Special returns and schedules.* The provisions of paragraphs (b) through (f) of this section shall apply to a foreign corporation except that a foreign corporation which is an insurance company to which paragraph (c)(3) of this section applies shall make a return on Form 1120-F and not on Form 1120. If a foreign corporation which is an insurance company to which paragraph (c)(1) or (2) of this section applies has income for the taxable year from sources within the United States which is not effectively connected for that year with the conduct of a trade or business in the United States by that corporation, the corporation shall attach to its return on Form 1120L or 1120M, as the case may be, a separate schedule showing the nature and amount of the items of such income, the rate of tax applicable thereto, and the amount of tax withheld therefrom under chapter 3 of the Code.

(3) *Representative or agent for foreign corporation*—(i) Cases where power of attorney is not required. The responsible representative or agent within the United States of a foreign corporation shall make on behalf of his principal a return of, and shall pay the tax on, all income coming within his control as representative or agent which is subject to the income tax under subtitle A of the Code. The agency appointment will determine how completely the agent is substituted for the principal for tax purposes. Any person who collects interest or dividends on deposited securities of a foreign corporation, executes ownership certificates in connection therewith, or sells such securities under special instructions shall not be deemed merely by reason of such acts to be the responsible representative or agent of the foreign corporation. If the responsible representative or agent does not have a specific power of attorney from the foreign corporation to file a return in its behalf, the return shall be accompanied by a statement to the effect that the representative or agent does not possess specific power of attorney to file a return for such corporation but that the return is being filed in accordance with the provisions of this subdivision.

(ii) *Cases where power of attorney is required.* Whenever a return of income of a foreign corporation is made by an agent acting under a duly authorized power of attorney for that purpose, the return shall be accompanied by the power of attorney in proper form, or a copy thereof, specifically authorizing him to represent his principal in making, executing, and filing the income tax return. Form 2848 may be used for this purpose. The agent, as well as the taxpayer, may incur liability for the penalties provided for erroneous, false, or fraudulent returns. For the requirements regarding signing of returns, see § 1.6062-1. The rules of paragraph (e) of § 601.504 of this chapter (Statement of Procedural Rules) shall apply under this subparagraph

Reg. § 1.6012-2(g)(3)

in determining whether a copy of a power of attorney must be certified.

(iii) *Limitation.* A return of income shall be required under this subparagraph only if the foreign corporation is otherwise required to make a return in accordance with this paragraph.

(4) *Disallowance of deductions and credits.* For provisions disallowing deductions and credits when a return of income has not been filed by or on behalf of a foreign corporation, see section 882(c)(2) and the regulations thereunder, and paragraph (b)(2) and (3) of § 1.535-1.

(5) *Effective date.* This paragraph shall apply for taxable years beginning after December 31, 1966, except that it shall not be applied to require (i) the filing of a return for any taxable year ending before January 1, 1974, which, pursuant to instructions applicable to the return, is not required to be filed or (ii) the amendment of a return for such a taxable year which, pursuant to such instructions, is required to be filed. For corresponding rules applicable to taxable years beginning before January 1, 1967, see 26 CFR 1.6012-2(g) (Rev. as of Jan. 1, 1967).

(h) *Electing small business corporations.* An electing small business corporation, whether or not subject to the tax imposed by section 1378, shall make a return on Form 1120-S. See also section 6037 and the regulations thereunder.

(i) *Other provisions.* For returns by fiduciaries for corporations, see § 1.6012-3. For information returns by corporations regarding payments of dividends, see §§ 1.6042-1 to 1.6042-3, inclusive; regarding corporate dissolutions or liquidations, see § 1.6043-1; regarding distributions in liquidation, see § 1.6043-2; regarding payments of patronage dividends, see §§ 1.6044-1 to 1.6044-4, inclusive; and regarding certain payments of interest, see §§ 1.6049-1 and 1.6049-2. For information returns of officers, directors, and shareholders of foreign personal holding companies, as defined in section 552, see §§ 1.6035-1 and 1.6035-2. For returns as to formation or reorganization of foreign corporations, see §§ 1.6046-1 to 1.6046-3, inclusive.

○━▶ § 1.6012-3 (T.D. 6301, filed 7-8-58; amended by T.D. 6364, filed 2-13-59, republished in T.D. 6500, filed 11-25-60; amended by T.D. 6628, filed 12-27-62; T.D. 6972, filed 9-11-68; T.D. 7200, filed 8-15-72; T.D. 7202, filed 8-22-72; T.D. 7332, filed 12-20-74; T.D. 7407, filed 3-3-76.)

Returns by fiduciaries.

(a) *For estates and trusts*—(1) *In general.* Except as otherwise provided in this paragraph, every fiduciary, or at least one of joint fiduciaries, must make a return of income on Form 1041 (or by use of a composite return pursuant to § 1.6012-5)—

(i) For each estate for which he acts if the gross income of such estate for the taxable year is $600 or more;

(ii) For each trust for which he acts, except a trust exempt under section 501(a), if such trust has for the taxable year any taxable income, or has for the taxable year gross income of $600 or more regardless of the amount of taxable income; and

(iii) For each estate and each trust for which he acts, except a trust exempt under section 501(a), regardless of the amount of income for the taxable year, if any beneficiary of such estate or trust is a nonresident alien.

(2) *Gross income of $5,000 or more.* In cases in which the gross income of the estate or trust is $5,000 or over for any taxable year, a copy of the will or trust instrument, accompanied by a written declaration of the fiduciary under the penalties of perjury that it is a true and complete copy, must be filed with the fiduciary return of the estate or trust, together with a statement by the fiduciary indicating the provisions of the will or trust instrument which, in his opinion, determine the extent to which the income of the estate or trust is taxable to the estate or trust, the beneficiaries, or the grantor, respectively. If, however, a copy of the will or trust instrument, and statement relating to the provisions of the will or trust instrument, have once been filed, they need not again be filed if the fiduciary return contains a statement showing when and where they were filed. If the trust instrument is amended in any way after such copies have been filed, a copy of the amendment must be filed by the fiduciary with the return for the taxable year in which the amendment was made. The fiduciary must also file with such amendment a statement indicating the effect, if any, in his opinion, of the amendment on the extent to which the income of the estate or trust is taxable to the estate or trust, the beneficiaries, or the grantor, respectively.

(3) *Domiciliary and ancillary representatives.* In the case of an estate required to file a return under subparagraph (1) of this paragraph, having both domiciliary and ancillary representatives, the domiciliary and ancillary representatives must each file a return on Form 1041. The domiciliary representative is required to include in the return rendered by him as such domiciliary representative the entire income of the estate. The return of the ancillary representative shall be filed with the district director for his internal revenue district and shall show the name and address of the domiciliary representative, the amount of gross income received by the ancillary representative, and the deductions to be claimed against such income, including any amount of income properly paid or credited by the ancillary representative to any legatee, heir, or other beneficiary. If the ancillary representative for the estate of a nonresident alien is a citizen or resident of the United States, and the domiciliary representative is a nonresident alien, such ancillary representative is required to render the return otherwise required of the domiciliary representative.

(4) *Two or more trusts.* A trustee of two or more trusts must make a separate return for each trust, even through such trusts were created by the same grantor for the same beneficiary or beneficiaries.

(5) *Trusts with unrelated business income.* Every fiduciary for a trust, described in section 501(c)(3) or (17), or section 401(a), which is otherwise exempt from tax under section 501(a), and which is subject to the tax imposed on unrelated business taxable income by section 511(b)(1), shall make a return on Form 990-T for each

taxable year if the trust has gross income, included in computing unrelated business taxable income for such taxable year, of $1,000 or more. The filing of a return of unrelated business income does not relieve the fiduciary of such trust from the duty of filing other required returns.

(6) *Charitable remainder trusts.* Every fiduciary for a charitable remainder annuity trust as defined in § 1.664-2) or a charitable remainder unitrust (as defined in § 1.664-3) shall make a return on Form 1041-B for each taxable year of the trust even though it is nonexempt because it has unrelated business taxable income. The return on Form 1041-B shall be made in accordance with the instructions for the form and shall be filed with the designated Internal Revenue office on or before the 15th day of the fourth month following the close of the taxable year of the trust. A copy of the instrument governing the trust, accompanied by a written declaration of the fiduciary under the penalties of perjury that it is a true and complete copy, shall be attached to the return for the first taxable year of the trust.

(7) *Certain trusts described in section 4947(a).* For taxable years ending on or after December 31, 1975, in the case of a trust described in section 4947(a)(1) which is a private foundation, and which has no taxable income for a taxable year, the filing requirement of section 6012 and this section shall be satisfied by the fiduciary of such trust filing Form 5227 pursuant to § 53.6011-1 of this chapter (Foundation Excise Tax Regulations). When the provisions of this (7) are met, the fiduciary shall not be required to file Form 1041.

(b) *For other persons*—(1) *Decedents.* The executor or adminstrator of the estate of a decedent, or other person charged with the property of a decedent, shall make the return of income required in respect of such decedent. For the decedent's taxable year which ends with the date of his death, the return shall cover the period during which he was alive. For the filing of returns of income for citizens and alien residents of the United States, and alien residents of Puerto Rico, see paragraph (a) of § 1.6012-1. For the filing of a joint return after death of spouse, see paragraph (d) of § 1.6013-1.

(2) *Nonresident alien individuals*—(i) *In general.* A resident or domestic fiduciary or other person charged with the care of the person or property of a nonresident alien individual shall make a return for that individual and pay the tax unless—

(a) The nonresident alien individual makes a return of, and pays the tax on, his income for the taxable year,

(b) A responsible representative or agent in the United States of the nonresident alien individual makes a return of, and pays the tax on, the income of such alien individual for the taxable year, or

(c) The nonresident alien individual has appointed a person in the United States to act as his agent for the purpose of making a return of income and, if such fiduciary is required to file a Form 1041 for an estate or trust of which such alien individual is a beneficiary, such fiduciary attaches a copy of the agency appointment to his return on Form 1041.

(ii) *Income to be returned.* A return of income shall be required under this subparagraph only if the nonresident alien individual is otherwise required to make a return in accordance with paragraph (b) of § 1.6012-1. The provisions of that section shall apply in determining the form of return to be used and the income to be returned.

(iii) *Disallowance of deductions and credits.* For provisions disallowing deductions and credits when a return of income has not been filed by or on behalf of a nonresident alien individual, see section 874 and the regulations thereunder.

(iv) *Alien resident of Puerto Rico.* This subparagraph shall not apply to the return of a nonresident alien individual who is a bona fide resident of Puerto Rico during the entire taxable year. See § 1.876-1.

(v) *Cross reference.* For requirements of withholding tax at source on nonresident alien individuals and of returns with respect to such withheld taxes, see §§ 1.-1441-1 to 1.1465-1, inclusive.

(3) *Persons under a disability.* A fiduciary acting as the guardian of a minor, or as the guardian or committee of an insane person, must make the return of income required in respect of such person unless, in the case of a minor, the minor himself makes the return or causes it to be made.

(4) *Corporations.* A receiver, trustee in dissolution, trustee in bankruptcy, or assignee, who, by order of a court of competent jurisdiction, by operation of law or otherwise, has possession of or holds title to all or substantially all the property or business of a corporation, shall make the return of income for such corporation in the same manner and form as corporations are required to make such returns. Such return shall be filed whether or not the receiver, trustee, or assignee is operating the property or business of the corporation. A receiver in charge of only a small part of the property of a corporation, such as a receiver in mortgage foreclosure proceedings involving merely a small portion of its property, need not make the return of income. See also § 1.6041-1, relating to returns regarding information at source; §§ 1.6042-1 to 1.6042-3, inclusive, relating to returns regarding payments of dividends; §§ 1.6044-1 to 1.6044-4, inclusive, relating to returns regarding payments of patronage dividends; §§ 1.6049-1 and 1.6049-2, relating to returns regarding certain payments of interest.

(5) *Individuals in receivership.* A receiver who stands in the place of an individual must make the return of income required in respect of such individual. A receiver of only part of the property of an individual need not file a return, and the individual must make his own return.

(c) *Joint fiduciaries.* In the case of joint fiduciaries, a return is required to be made by only one of such fiduciaries. A return made by one of joint fiduciaries shall contain a statement that the fiduciary has sufficient knowledge of the affairs of the person for whom the return is made to enable him to make the return, and that the return is, to the best of his knowledge and belief, true and correct.

Reg. § 1.6012-3(c)

24,270.4 (I.R.C.) Reg. § 1.6012-3(d) 11-7-77

(d) *Other provisions.* For the definition of the term "fiduciary", see section 7701(a) (6) and the regulations thereunder. For information returns required to be made by fiduciaries under section 6041, see § 1.6041-1. As to further duties and liabilities of fiduciaries, see section 6903 and § 301.6903-1 of this chapter. (Regulations on Procedure and Administration).

○━► § 1.6012-4 (T.D. 6364, filed 2-13-59; republished in T.D. 6500, filed 11-25-60; amended by T.D. 7332, filed 12-20-74.) **Miscellaneous returns.**

For returns by regulated investment companies of tax on undistributed capital gain designated for special treatment under section 852(b)(3)(D), see § 1.852-9. For returns with respect to tax withheld on nonresident aliens and foreign corporations and on tax-free covenant bonds, see §§ 1.-1461-1 to 1.1465-1, inclusive. For returns of tax on transfers to avoid income tax, see § 1.1494-1. For the requirement of an annual report by persons completing a Government contract, see 26 CFR (1939) 17.16 (Treasury Decision 4906, approved June 23, 1939), and 26 CFR (1939) 16.15 (Treasury Decision 4909, approved June 28, 1939), as made applicable to section 1471 of the 1954 Code by Treasury Decision 6091, approved August 16, 1954 (19 F.R. 5167, C.B. 1954-2, 47). See also § 1.1471-1.

○━► § 1.6012-5 (T.D. 7200, filed 8-15-72.) **Composite return in lieu of specified form.**

The Commissioner may authorize the use, at the option of a person required to make a return, of a composite return in lieu of any form specified in this part for use by such a person, subject to such conditions, limitations, and special rules governing the preparation, execution, filing, and correction thereof as the Commissioner may deem appropriate. Such composite return shall consist of a form prescribed by the Commissioner and an attachment or attachments of magnetic tape or other approved media. Notwithstanding any provisions in this part to the contrary, a single form and attachment may comprise the returns of more than one such person. To the extent that the use of a composite return has been authorized by the Commissioner, references in this part to a specific form for use by such a person shall be deemed to refer also to a composite return under this section.

○━► § 1.6012-6 (T.D. 7516, filed 11-1-77.) **Returns by political organizations.**

(a) *Requirement of return*—(1) *In general.* For taxable years beginning after December 31, 1974, every political organization described in section 527 (e) (1), and every fund described in section 527 (f) (3) or section 527 (g), and every organization described in section 501 (c) and exempt from taxation under section 501 (a) shall make a return of income within the time provided in section 6072 (b), if a tax is imposed on such an organization or fund by section 527 (b).

(2) *Taxable years beginning after December 31, 1971, and before January 1, 1975.* For taxable years beginning after December 31, 1971, and before January 1, 1975, any political organization which would be described in section 527 (e) (1) if such section applied to such years shall not be required to make a return if such organization would not be required to make a return under paragraph (a) (1) of this section.

(b) *Form of return.* The return required by an organization or fund upon which a tax is imposed by section 527 (b) shall be made on Form 1120-POL.

○━► § 301.6012 **Statutory provisions; persons required to make returns of income.** [Sec. 6012, IRC]

○━► § 301.6012-1 (T.D. 6498, filed 10-24-60.) **Persons required to make returns of income.**

For provisions with respect to persons required to make returns of income, see §§ 1.6012-1 to 1.6012-4, inclusive, of this chapter (Income Tax Regulations).

○━► § 1.6013 **Statutory provisions; joint returns of income tax by husband and wife.** [Sec. 6013, IRC]

○━► § 1.6013-1 (T.D. 6364, filed 2-13-59; republished in T.D. 6500, filed 11-25-60; amended by T.D. 7274, filed 5-4-73.) **Joint returns.**

(a) *In general.* (1) A husband and wife may elect to make a joint return under section 6013(a) even though one of the spouses has no gross income or deductions. For rules for determining whether individuals occupy the status of husband and wife for purposes of filing a joint return, see paragraph (a) of § 1.6013-4. For any taxable year with respect to which a joint return has been filed, separate returns shall not be made by the spouses after the time for filing the return of either has expired. See, however, paragraph (d)(5) of this section for the right of an executor to file a late separate return for a deceased spouse and thereby disaffirm a timely joint return made by the surviving spouse.

(2) A joint return of a husband and wife (if not made by an agent of one or both spouses) shall be signed by both spouses. The provisions of paragraph (a) (5) of § 1.6012-1, relating to returns made by agents, shall apply where one spouse signs a return as agent for the other, or where a third party signs a return as agent for one or both spouses.

(b) *Nonresident alien.* A joint return shall not be made if either the husband or wife at any time during the taxable year is a nonresident alien.

(c) *Different taxable years.* Except as otherwise provided in this section, a husband and wife shall not file a joint return if they have different taxable years.

(d) *Joint return after death.* (1) Section 6013(a)(2) provides that a joint return may be made for the survivor and the deceased spouse or for both deceased spouses if the taxable years of such spouses begin on the same day and end on different days only because of the death of either or both. Thus, if a husband and wife make their returns on a calendar year basis, and the wife dies on August 1, 1956, a joint return may be made with respect to the calendar year 1956 of the husband and the taxable year of the wife beginning on January 1, 1956, and ending with her death on August 1, 1956. Similarly, if husband and wife both make their returns on the basis of a fiscal year beginning on July 1 and the wife dies on October 1, 1956, a joint return may be made with respect to the fiscal year of the husband beginning on July 1, 1956, and ending on June 30, 1957, and with respect to the taxable year of the wife beginning on July 1, 1956, and ending with her death on October 1, 1956.

(2) The provision allowing a joint return to be made for the taxable year in which the death of either or both spouses occurs is subject to two limitations. The first limitation is that if the surviving spouse remarries before the close of his taxable year, he shall not make a joint return with the first spouse who died during the taxable year. In such a case, however, the surviving spouse may make a joint return with his new spouse provided the other requirements with respect to the filing of a joint return are met. The second limitation is that the surviving spouse shall not make a joint return with the deceased spouse if the taxable year of either spouse is a fractional part of a year under section 443(a)(1) resulting from a change of accounting period. For example, if a husband and wife make their returns on the calendar year basis and the wife dies on March 1, 1956, and thereafter the husband receives permission to change his annual accounting period to a fiscal year beginning July 1, 1956, no joint return shall be made for the short taxable year ending June 30, 1956. Similarly, if a husband and wife who make their returns on a calendar year basis receive permission to change to a fiscal year beginning July 1, 1956, and the wife dies on June 1, 1956, no joint return shall be made for the short taxable year ending June 30, 1956.

(3) Section 6013(a)(3) provides for the method of making a joint return in the case of death of one spouse or both spouses. The general rule is that, in the case of the death of one spouse, or of both spouses, the joint return with respect to the decedent may be made only by this executor or administrator, as defined in paragraph (c) of § 1.6013-4. An exception is made to this general rule whereby, in the case of the death of one spouse, the joint return may be made by the surviving spouse with respect to both him and the decedent if all the following conditions exist:

(i) No return has been made by the decedent for the taxable year in respect of which the joint return is made;

(ii) No executor or administrator has been appointed at or before the time of making such joint return; and

(iii) No executor or administrator is appointed before the last day prescribed by law for filing the return of the surviving spouse.

These conditions are to be applied with respect to the return for each of the taxable years of the decedent for which a joint return may be made if more than one such taxable year is involved. Thus, in the case of husband and wife on the calendar year basis, if the wife dies in February 1957, a joint return for the husband and wife for 1956 may be made if the conditions set forth in this subparagraph are satisfied with respect to such return. A joint return also may be made by the survivor for both himself and the deceased spouse for the calendar year 1957 if it is separately determined that the conditions set forth in this subparagraph are satisfied with respect to the return for such year. If, however, the deceased spouse should, prior to her death, make a return for 1956, the surviving spouse may not thereafter make a joint return for himself and the deceased spouse for 1956.

(4) If an executor or administrator is appointed at or before the time of making the joint return or before the last day prescribed by law for filing the return of the surviving spouse, the surviving spouse cannot make a joint return for himself and the deceased spouse whether or not a separate return for the deceased spouse is made by such executor or administrator. In such a case, any return made solely by the surviving spouse shall be treated as his separate return. The joint return, if one is to be made, must be made by both the surviving spouse and the executor or administrator. In determining whether an executor or administrator is appointed before the last day prescribed by law for filing the return of the surviving spouse, an extension of time for making the return is included.

(5) If the surviving spouse makes the joint return provided for in subparagraph (3) of this paragraph and thereafter an executor or administrator of the decedent is appointed, the executor or administrator may disaffirm such joint return. This disaffirmance, in order to be effective, must be made within one year after the last day prescribed by law for filing the return of the surviving spouse (including any extension of time for filing such return) and must be made in the form of a separate return for the taxable year of the decedent with respect to which the joint return was made. In the event of such proper disaffirmance the return made by the survivor shall constitute his separate return, that is, the joint return made by him shall be treated as his return and the tax thereon shall be computed by excluding all items properly includible in the return of the deceased spouse. The separate return made by the executor or administrator shall constitute the return of the deceased spouse for the taxable year.

(6) The time allowed the executor or administrator to disaffirm the joint return by the making of a separate return does not establish a new due date for the return of the deceased spouse. Accordingly, the provisions of sections 6651 and 6601, relating to delinquent returns and delinquency in payment of tax, are applicable to such return made by the executor in disaffirmance of the joint return.

(e) *Return of surviving spouse treated as joint return.* For provisions relating to the treatment of the return of a surviving spouse as a joint return for each of the next two taxable years following the year of the death of the spouse, see section 2 and § 1.2-2.

○━▶ § 1.6013-2 (T.D. 6364, filed 2-13-59; republished in T.D. 6500, filed 11-25-60.) **Joint return after filing separate return.**

(a) *In general.* (1) Where an individual has filed a separate return for a taxable year for which a joint return could have been made by him and his spouse under section 6013(a), and the time prescribed by law for filing the return for such taxable year has expired, such individual and his spouse may, under conditions hereinafter set forth, make a joint return for such taxable year. The joint return filed pursuant to section 6013(b) shall constitute the return of the husband and wife for such year, and all payments, credits, refunds, or other repayments, made or al-

Reg. § 1.6013-2(a)(1)

24,272 (I.R.C.)   Reg. § 1.6013-2(a)(1)   8-12-74

lowed with respect to the separate return of either spouse are to be taken into account in determining the extent to which the tax based on the joint return has been paid.

(2) If a joint return is made under section 6013(b), any election, other than the election to file a separate return, made by either spouse in his separate return for the taxable year with respect to the treatment of any income, deduction, or credit of such spouse shall not be changed in the making of the joint return where such election would have been irrevocable if the joint return had not been made. Thus, if one spouse has made an irrevocable election to adopt and use the last-in, first-out inventory method under section 472, this election may not be changed upon making the joint return under section 6013(b).

(3) A joint return made under section 6013(b) after the death of either spouse shall, with respect to the decedent, be made only by his executor or administrator. Thus, where no executor or administrator has been appointed, a joint return cannot be made under section 6013(b).

(b) *Limitations with respect to making of election.* A joint return shall not be made under section 6013(b)(1) with respect to a taxable year—

(1) Unless there is paid in full at or before the time of the filing of the joint return the amount shown as tax upon such joint return; or

(2) After the expiration of three years from the last day prescribed by law for filing the return for such taxable year determined without regard to any extension of time granted to either spouse; or

(3) After there has been mailed to either spouse, with respect to such taxable year, a notice of deficiency under section 6212, if the spouse, as to such notice, files a petition with the Tax Court of the United States within the time prescribed in section 6213; or

(4) After either spouse has commenced a suit in any court for the recovery of any part of the tax for such taxable year; or

(5) After either spouse has entered into a closing agreement under section 7121 with respect to such taxable year, or after any civil or criminal case arising against either spouse with respect to such taxable year has been compromised under section 7122.

(c) *When return deemed filed; assessment and collection; credit or refund.* (1) For the purpose of section 6501, relating to the period of limitations upon assessment and collection, and section 6651, relating to delinquent returns, a joint return made under section 6013(b) shall be deemed to have been filed, giving due regard to any extension of time granted to either spouse, on the following date:

(i) Where both spouses filed separate returns, prior to making the joint return under section 6013(b), on the date the last separate return of either spouse was filed for the taxable year, but not earlier than the last date prescribed by law for the filing of the return of either spouse;

(ii) Where only one spouse was required and did file a return prior to the making of the joint return under section 6013(b), on the date of the filing of the separate return, but not earlier than the last day prescribed by law for the filing of such return; or

(iii) Where both spouses were required to file a return, but only one spouse did so file, on the date of the filing of the joint return under section 6013(b).

(2) For the purpose of section 6511, relating to refunds and credits, a joint return made under section 6013(b) shall be deemed to have been filed on the last date prescribed by law for filing the return for such taxable year, determined without regard to any extension of time granted to either spouse for filing the return or paying the tax.

(d) *Additional time for assessment.* In the case of a joint return made under section 6013(b), the period of limitations provided in sections 6501 and 6502 shall not be less than one year after the date of the actual filing of such joint return. The expiration of the one year is to be determined without regard to the rules provided in paragraph (c)(1) of this section, relating to the application of sections 6501 and 6651 with respect to a joint return made under section 6013(b).

(e) *Additions to the tax and penalties.* (1) Where the amount shown as the tax by the husband and wife on a joint return made under section 6013(b) exceeds the aggregate of the amounts shown as tax on the separate return of each spouse, and such excess is attributable to negligence, intentional disregard of rules and regulations, or fraud at the time of the making of such separate return, there shall be assessed, collected, and paid in the same manner as if it were a deficiency an additional amount as provided by the following:

(i) If any part of such excess is attributable to negligence, or intentional disregard of rules and regulations, at the time of the making of such separate return, but without any intent to defraud, this additional amount shall be 5 percent of the total amount of the excess.

(ii) If any part of such excess is attributable to fraud with intent to evade tax at the time of the making of such separate return, this additional amount shall be 50 percent of the total amount of the excess. The latter addition is in lieu of the 50 percent addition to the tax provided in section 6653(b).

(2) For purposes of section 7206(1) and (2) and section 7207 (relating to criminal penalties in the case of fraudulent returns), the term "return" includes a separate return filed by a spouse with respect to a taxable year for which a joint return is made under section 6013(b) after the filing of a separate return.

○━▶ § 1.6013-3 (T.D. 6364, filed 2-13-59; republished in T.D. 6500, filed 11-25-60.) **Treatment of joint return after death of either spouse.**

For purposes of section 21 (relating to change in rates during a taxable year), section 443 (relating to returns for a period of less than 12 months), and section 7851(a)(1)(A) (relating to the applicability of certain provisions of the Internal Revenue Code of 1954 and the Internal Revenue Code of 1939), where the husband and wife have different taxable years because of death of either spouse, the joint return shall be treated as if the taxable years of both ended on the date of the closing of the surviving spouse's taxable year. Thus, in cases where the Internal Revenue Code of 1939 otherwise would apply to the taxable year of the decedent spouse and the Internal Revenue Code of 1954 would apply to the taxable year of the surviving spouse, this provision makes the Internal Revenue Code of 1954 applicable to the taxable years of both spouses if a joint return is filed.

○— § 1.6013-4 (T.D. 6364, filed 2-13-59; republished in T.D. 6500, filed 11-25-60; amended by T.D. 7102, filed 3-23-71.) Applicable rules.

(a) *Status as husband and wife.* For the purpose of filing a joint return under section 6013, the status as husband and wife of two individuals having taxable years beginning on the same day shall be determined—

(1) If the taxable year of each individual is the same, as of the close of such year; and

(2) If the close of the taxable year is different by reason of the death of one spouse, as of the time of such death.

An individual legally separated from his spouse under a decree of divorce or of separate maintenance shall not be considered as married. However, the mere fact that spouses have not lived together during the course of the taxable year shall not prohibit them from making a joint return. A husband and wife who are separated under an interlocutory decree of divorce retain the relationship of husband and wife until the decree becomes final. The fact that the taxpayer and his spouse are divorced or legally separated at any time after the close of the taxable year shall not deprive them of their right to file a joint return for such taxable year under section 6013.

(b) *Computation of income, deductions, and tax.* If a joint return is made, the gross income and adjusted gross income of husband and wife on the joint return are computed in an aggregate amount and the deductions allowed and the taxable income are likewise computed on an aggregate basis. Deductions limited to a percentage of the adjusted gross income, such as the deduction for charitable, etc., contributions and gifts, under section 170, will be allowed with reference to such aggregate adjusted gross income. A similar rule is applied in the case of the limitation of section 1211(b) on the allowance of losses resulting from the sale or exchange of capital assets (see § 1.1211-1). Although there are two taxpayers on a joint return, there is only one taxable income. The tax on the joint return shall be computed on the aggregate income and the liability with respect to the tax shall be joint and several. For computation of tax in the case of a joint return, see § 1.2-1. For tax in the case of a joint return of husband and wife electing to pay the optional tax under section 3, see § 1.3-1. For the election not to show on a joint return the amount of tax due in connection therewith, see paragraph (c) of § 1.6014-1 and paragraph (d) of § 1.6014-2. For separate computations of the self-employment tax of each spouse on a joint return, see paragraph (b) of § 1.6017-1.

(c) *Definition of executor or administrator.* For purposes of section 6013 the term "executor or administrator" means the person who is actually appointed to such office and not a person who is merely in charge of the property of the decedent.

○— § 1.6013-5 (T.D. 7320, filed 8-5-74.) Spouse relieved of liability in certain cases.

(a) *In general.* A person shall be relieved from liability for any tax, penalties, additions to tax, interest, or other amounts, to the extent that such liability is attributable to an omission from gross income in a taxable year, and—

(1) He filed a joint return with a spouse in such taxable year,

(2) An amount of income which exceeds 25 percent of the amount of gross income which is started in the return (as determined in a manner provided by section 6501 (e)(1)(A) of the Code) and which is attributable to such person's spouse was omitted from the return, and should have been, under chapter 1 of the Code, included in the return,

(3) He establishes that he did not know of, and had no reason to know of such omission, and

(4) It is inequitable to hold the taxpayer liable for the deficiency in tax for such taxable year attributable to such omission.

(b) *Inequitable defined.* Whether it is inequitable to hold a person liable for the deficiency in tax, within the meaning of paragraph (a)(4) of this section, is to be determined on the basis of all the facts and circumstances. In making such a determination a factor to be considered is whether the person seeking relief significantly benefited, directly or indirectly, from the items omitted from gross income. However, normal support is not a significant "benefit" for purposes of this determination. Evidence of direct or indirect benefit may consist of transfers of property, including transfers which may be received several years after the year in which the omitted item of income should have been included in gross income. Thus, for example, if a person seeking relief receives from his spouse an inheritance of property or life insurance proceeds which are traceable to items omitted from gross income by his spouse, that person will be considered to have benefited from those items. Other factors which may also be taken into account, if the situation warrants, include the fact that the person seeking relief has been deserted by his spouse or the fact that he has been divorced or separated from such spouse.

(c) *Community property laws.* The determination of the spouse to whom items of gross income (other than gross income from property) are attributable shall be made without regard to any applicable community property laws.

(d) *Omission of income.* Section 6013(e) of the Code shall apply only to income which is properly includible as gross income under chapter 1 of the Code, which was, in fact, omitted from a joint return. Section 6013(e) shall not apply to a tax deficiency resulting from erroneous or fraudulent deductions, claims, or other evasions or avoidances of tax.

(e) *Scope of section.* This section does not apply to any taxable year for which a claim for credit or refund is barred by operation of any law or rule of law.

Reg. § 1.6013-5(e)

24,274 (I.R.C.) Reg. § 301.6013

○━━ § 301.6013 **Statutory provisions; joint returns of income tax by husband and wife.** [Sec. 6013, IRC]

○━━ § 301.6013-1 (T.D. 6498, filed 10-24-60.) **Joint returns of income tax by husband and wife.**

For provisions with respect to joint returns of income tax by husband and wife, see §§ 1.6013-1 to 1.6013-4, inclusive, of this chapter (Income Tax Regulations).

○━━ § 1.6014 **Statutory provisions; income tax return—tax not computed by taxpayer.** [Sec. 6014, IRC]

○━━ § 1.6014-1 (T.D. 6364, filed 2-13-59; amended by T.D. 6455, filed 3-1-60; republished in T.D. 6500, filed 11-25-60; amended by T.D. 6581, filed 12-5-61; T.D. 6792, filed 1-14-65 and T.D. 7102, filed 3-23-71.) **Tax not computed by taxpayer for taxable years beginning before January 1, 1970.**

(a) *In general.* If an individual is entitled under paragraph (a)(7) of § 1.6012-1 to use as his return Form 1040A, he may elect not to show thereon the amount of the tax due in connection with such return if his gross income is less than $5,000.

(b) *Computation and payment of tax.* A taxpayer who, in accordance with paragraph (a) of this section, elects not to show the tax on Form 1040A is not required to pay the unpaid balance of such tax at the time he files the return. In such case, the tax will be computed for the taxpayer by the Internal Revenue Service, and a notice will be mailed to the taxpayer stating the amount of tax due. Where it is determined that a refund of tax is due, the Internal Revenue Service will send such refund to the taxpayer. See paragraph (c) of § 301.6402-3 of this chapter (Regulations on Procedure and Administration).

(c) *Joint return.* (1) A husband and wife who, pursuant to paragraph (a)(7) of § 1.6012-1, file a joint return on Form 1040A may elect not to show the tax on such return if their aggregate gross income for the taxable year is less than $5,000.

(2) The tax computed for the taxpayer who files Form 1040A and elects not to show thereon the tax due shall be the lesser of the following amounts:

(i) A tax computed as though the return on Form 1040A constituted the separate returns of the spouses, or

(ii) A tax computed as though the return on Form 1040A constituted a joint return.

(d) *Married individual filing separate returns.* In the case of a married individual who files a separate return and who elects under this section not to show his tax on Form 1040A his tax shall be computed with reference to the 10-percent standard deduction rather than the minimum standard deduction.

(e) This section shall apply to taxable years beginning before January 1, 1970.

○━━ § 1.6014-2 (T.D. 7102, filed 3-23-71; amended by T.D. 7298, filed 12-21-73; T.D. 7391, filed 12-1-75.) **Tax not computed by taxpayer for taxable years beginning after December 31, 1969.**

(a) *In general.* An individual subject to the tax imposed by section 1 of the Code may, in accordance with the instructions applicable to the income tax return to be filed, elect, for any taxable year beginning after December 31, 1969, not to show on his income tax return for such year the amount of tax due in connection with such return.

(b) *Restriction on making an election.* The election pursuant to this section shall not be made by an individual who does not file his return (or amended return) making such election on or before the date prescribed in section 6072(a) for the filing of the original return (determined without regard to any extension of time).

(c) *Effects of election.* (1) A taxpayer who, in accordance with the provisions of this section, elects not to show the tax on his income tax return is not required to pay the unpaid balance of such tax at the time he files the return. In such case, the tax will be computed for the taxpayer by the Internal Revenue Service, and a notice will be mailed to the taxpayer stating the amount of tax due. Where it is determined that a refund of tax is due, the Internal Revenue Service will send such refund to the taxpayer. See paragraph (c) of § 301.6402-3 of this chapter (Regulations on Procedure and Administration). The computation of tax by the Internal Revenue Service shall be treated for purposes of this chapter as if made by the taxpayer, and such computation or the issuance of a notice or refund pursuant thereto shall not relieve the taxpayer of liability for any deficiency (although the deficiency is based upon an amount of tax different from that computed for the taxpayer by the Internal Revenue Service) or affect the rights of the Internal Revenue Service with respect to any subsequent audit or other review of the taxpayer's return.

(2) Where the election provided for in this section is made by a taxpayer who takes the standard deduction and who has adjusted gross income of less than $10,000, such election constitutes an election to pay the tax imposed by section 3.

(3) A taxpayer who makes an election under section 6014 shall not be precluded from claiming—

(i) Status as a head of household or a surviving spouse;

(ii) The credit under section 31 (relating to tax withheld on wages);

(iii) The credit under section 37 (relating to retirement income);

(iv) The credit under section 38 (relating to investment in certain depreciable property);

(v) The credit under section 39 (relating to certain uses of gasoline and lubricating oil);

(vi) The credit under section 41 (relating to contributions to candidates for public office);

(vii) The credit under section 42 (relating to personal exemptions);

(viii) The credit under section 43 (relating to earned income);

(ix) The credit under section 44 (relating to purchase of new principal residence), or

(x) The credit under section 45 (relating to overpayments of tax).

(d) *Joint returns.* (1) A husband and wife who file a joint return may elect not to show the tax on such return in accordance with the rules prescribed in paragraphs (a) and (b) of this section.

(2) The tax computed for a husband and wife who elect pursuant to this section not to show their tax on their joint income tax return shall be the lesser of the following amounts:

(i) A tax computed as though the return of income constituted a joint return, or

(ii) If sufficient information is provided for the taxable income of each spouse to be determined, a tax computed as though the return of income constituted the separate returns of the spouses.

(e) *Married individuals filing separate returns.* This section shall apply to married individuals filing separate returns unless otherwise provided in the instructions accompanying a return. The instructions may require the taxpayer to attach to his return a statement to the effect that his tax and the tax of his spouse were determined in accordance with the rules of sections 141(d) and 142(a).

(f) *Revocation of election.* An election pursuant to this section may be revoked on an amended return (whether such return is filed before or after the date prescribed in section 6072(a) for filing the original return).

§ 301.6014 **Statutory provisions; income tax return—tax not computed by taxpayer.** [Sec. 6014, IRC]

§ 301.6014-1 (T.D. 6498, filed 10-24-60); amended by T.D. 7102, filed 3-23-71.) **Income tax return—tax not computed by taxpayer.**

For provisions relating to the election not to show on an income tax return the amount of tax due in connection therewith, see §§ 1.6014-1 and 1.6014-2 of this chapter (Income Tax Regulations).

§ 1.6015(a) **Statutory provisions; declaration of estimated income tax by individuals; requirement of declaration.** [Sec. 6015(a), IRC]

§ 1.6015(a)-1 (T.D. 6267, filed 11-13-57; republished in T.D. 6500, filed 11-25-60; amended by T.D. 6523, filed 12-28-60; T.D. 6817, filed 4-7-65; T.D. 7117, filed 5-24-71; T.D. 7274, filed 5-4-73; T.D. 7282, filed 7-16-73 and T.D. 7332, filed 12-20-74.) **Declaration of estimated income tax by individuals.**

(a) *Requirement*—(1) *Taxable years beginning after December 31, 1971.* With respect to taxable years beginning after December 31, 1971, a declaration of estimated income tax by an individual is not required if the estimated tax (as defined in section 6015(c)) can reasonably be expected to be less than $100. In all other cases a declaration of estimated income tax shall be made by every individual if the following conditions are met and if such individual is not a nonresident alien individual who is excepted under section 6015(i) of § 1.6015(i)-1 from the requirements of making a declaration:

(i) The gross income for the taxable year can reasonably be expected to exceed —

(a) $20,000, in the case of—

(1) A single individual including a head of a household (as defined in section 2(b)) or a surviving spouse (as defined in section 2(a)); or

(2) A married individual entitled under section 6015(b) to file a joint declaration with his spouse, if his spouse has not received wages (as defined in section 3401(a)) for the taxable year; or

(b) $10,000, in the case of a married individual entitled under section 6015(b) to file a joint declaration with his spouse, if both he and his spouse have received wages (as defined in section 3401(a)) for the taxable year; or

(c) $5,000, in the case of a married individual not entitled under section 6015(b) to file a joint declaration with his spouse; or

(ii) The gross income can reasonably be expected to include more than $500 from sources other than wages (as defined in section 3401(a)).

(2) *Taxable years beginning after December 31, 1966, and before January 1, 1972.* With respect to taxable years beginning after December 31, 1966, and before January 1, 1972, a declaration of estimated income tax by an individual is not required if the estimated tax (as defined in section 6015(c)) can reasonably be expected to be less than $40. In all other cases a declaration of estimated income tax shall be made by every individual if the following conditions are met and if such individual is not a nonresident alien individual who is excepted under section 6015(i) and § 1.6015(i)-1 from the requirement of making a declaration:

(i) The gross income for the taxable year can reasonably be expected to exceed —

(a) $5,000, in the case of—

(1) A single individual other than a head of a household (as defined in section 1(b)(2) for taxable years ending before January 1, 1971, or as defined in section 2(b) of the Code as amended by the Tax Reform Act of 1969 for taxable years beginning after December 31, 1970) or a surviving spouse (as defined in section 2(b) for taxable years ending before January 1, 1971, or as defined in section 2(a) of the Code as amended by the Tax Reform Act of 1969 for taxable years beginning after December 31, 1970);

(2) A married individual not entitled under section 6015(b) to file a joint declaration with his spouse; or

(3) A married individual entitled under section 6015(b) to file a joint declaration with his spouse, but only if the aggregate gross income of such individual and his spouse for the taxable year can reasonably be expected to exceed $10,000; or

(b) $10,000, in the case of—

(1) A head of household (as defined in section 1(b)(2) for taxable years ending before January 1, 1971, or as defined in section 2(b) of the Code as amended by the Tax Reform Act of 1969 for taxable years beginning after December 31, 1970); or

(2) A surviving spouse (as defined in section 2(b) for taxable years ending before January 1, 1971, or as defined in section 2(a) of the Code as amended by the Tax Reform Act of 1969 for taxable years

Reg. § 1.6015(a)-1(a)(2)

beginning after December 31, 1970; or

(ii) The gross income can reasonably be expected to include more than $200 from sources other than wages (as defined in section 3401(a)).

(3) *Taxable years beginning before January 1, 1967.* With respect to taxable years beginning before January 1, 1967, and after December 31, 1960, a declaration of estimated income tax by an individual is not required if the estimated tax (as defined in section 6015(c)) can reasonably be expected to be less than $40. In all other cases a declaration shall be made by every citizen of the United States, whether residing at home or abroad, every individual residing in the United States though not a citizen thereof, every nonresident alien who is a resident of Canada, Mexico, or Puerto Rico and who has wages subject to withholding at the source under section 3402, and every nonresident alien who has been, or expects to be, a resident of Puerto Rico during the entire taxable year, if—

(i) The gross income for the taxable year can reasonably be expected to exceed

(a) $5,000, in the case of—

(1) A single individual other than a head of a household (as defined in section 1(b)(2)); or

(2) A married individual not entitled under section 6015(b) to file a joint declaration with his spouse; or

(3) A married individual entitled under section 6015(b) to file a joint declaration with his spouse, but only if the aggregate gross income of such individual and his spouse for the taxable year can reasonably be expected to exceed $10,000; or

(b) $10,000, in the case of—

(1) A head of a household (as defined in section 1(b)(2)); or

(2) A surviving spouse (as defined in section 2(b)); or

(ii) The gross income can reasonably be expected to include more than $200 from sources other than wages (as defined in section 3401(a)).

(b) *Income of child.* In estimating his gross income for the taxable year a parent should not take into account the income of his minor child. Such income is not includible in the gross income of the parent. See section 73 and § 1.73-1.

(c) *Exemption of spouse.* For the purpose of determining whether a declaration of estimated tax is required under the provisions of paragraph (a)(3) of this section, a married person filing a separate declaration may not take into account the exemption of his spouse, if his spouse has, or is reasonably expected to have, gross income, or is reasonably expected to be the dependent of another taxpayer for the taxable year.

(d) *Nonresident alien individuals.* For the rules exempting certain nonresident alien individuals from the requirement of making a declaration of estimated income tax, see § 1.6015(i)-1.

(e) *Examples.* The application of the provisions of this section may be illustrated by the following examples:

Example (1). H maintains as his home a household which is the principal place of abode of himself and his two dependent children. H's wife died in 1970 and he has not remarried. H and his wife filed a joint return for 1970. H's salary from January 1 to June 30, 1972, is at the annual rate of $18,000. However, effective July 1, 1972, his annual salary is increased to $24,000, and under the facts then existing it is reasonable to assume that his salary for the remaining portion of 1972 will remain unchanged and that his total salary for the year will, therefore, be $21,000. Since H is a surviving spouse (as defined in section 2(a)) and his gross income can reasonably be expected to exceed $20,000, he is required to file a declaration of estimated tax for 1972. Since it was not reasonable to assume that H's gross income for 1972 would exceed $20,000 until July 1972 (after June 1 and before September 2), H is not required to file a declaration until September 15, 1972. However, if H's estimated tax (as defined in section 6015(c)) can reasonably be expected to be less than $100, he is not required to file a declaration of estimated tax. See section 6073 and §§ 1.6073-1 to 1.6073-4, inclusive, for rules as to when a declaration must be filed.

Example (2). H, a taxpayer making his return on the calendar year basis, has an annual salary of $12,000 in 1972. W, H's wife, received wages (as defined in section 3401(a)) in December 1972. W did not receive wages prior to December. Assuming that H and W are entitled to file a joint declaration of estimated tax under section 6015(b), H would not be required to file a declaration for 1972 until January 15, 1973, since prior to December 1972 W had not received wages. Since W received wages after September 1, 1972, H must file a declaration on or before January 15, 1973, because, under the rule contained in paragraph (a)(1)(i)(b) of this section, H's gross income could reasonably be expected to exceed $10,000 for 1972. However, no declaration would be required if H's estimated tax (as defined in section 6015(c)) could reasonably be expected to be less than $100. No declaration is required prior to January 15, 1973, because, under the rule contained in paragraph (a)(1)(i)(a)(2) of this section, H's gross income for 1972 could not reasonably be expected to exceed $20,000.

Example (3). P is a taxpayer making his return on the calendar year basis. P is engaged in the practice of his profession on his own account and has gross income of $2,000 from such profession for the two months of January and February 1972. He reasonably expects that his gross income from his profession will continue to average $1,000 each month throughout the year and that he will have no income from any other source during 1972. Since P has gross income which does not constitute wages subject to withholding, he is required to file a declaration of estimated tax for that year since he has income of more than $500 from sources other than wages, unless he reasonably expects his estimated tax to be less than $100.

Example (4). S, a married taxpayer, has been regularly employed for many years. As of January 1, 1972, his weekly wages are $305. For many years, S has also owned stock in a corporation which has regularly paid him annual dividends ranging from $575 to $600. Because his gross income can reasonably be expected to include more than $500 from sources other than wages, S is required to make a declaration of estimated tax for 1972, unless he reasonably expects his estimated tax to be less than $100.

(f) *Declarations made by agents.* The declaration of income may be made by an agent if, by reason of disease or injury, the person liable for the making of the declaration is unable to make it. The declaration may also be made by an agent if the taxpayer is unable to make the declaration by reason of continuous absence from the United States (including Puerto Rico as if a part of the United States) for a period of at least 60 days prior to the date prescribed by law for making the declaration. In addition, a declaration may be made by an agent if the taxpayer requests permission, in writing, of the district director for the internal revenue district in which is located the legal residence or principal place of business of the person liable for the making of the declaration, and such district director determines that good cause exists for permitting the declaration to be so made. However, assistance in the preparation of the declaration may be rendered under any circumstances. Whenever a declaration is made by an agent it must be accompanied by a power of attorney (or copy thereof) authorizing him to represent his principal in making, executing, or filing the declaration. A Form 2848, when properly completed, is sufficient. In addition, where one spouse is physically unable by reason of disease or injury to sign a joint declaration, the other spouse may, with the oral consent of the one who is incapacitated, sign the incapacitated spouse's name in the proper place in the declaration followed by the words "By ———— Husband (or Wife)", and by the signature of the signing spouse in his own right, provided that a dated statement signed by the spouse who is signing the declaration is attached to and made a part of the declaration stating—

(1) The name of the declaration being filed,
(2) The taxable year,
(3) The reason for the inability of the spouse who is incapacitated to sign the declaration, and
(4) That the spouse who is incapacitated consented to the signing of the declaration.

The taxpayer and his agent, if any, are responsible for the declaration as made and incur liability for the penalties provided for erroneous, false, or fraudulent declarations.

§ 1.6015(b) Statutory provisions; declaration of estimated income tax by individuals; joint declaration by husband and wife. [Sec. 6015(b), IRC]

§ 1.6015(b)-1 (T.D. 6267, filed 11-13-57; republished in T.D. 6500, filed 11-25-60; amended by T.D. 7274, filed 5-4-73; T.D. 7427, filed 8-9-76.) **Joint declaration by husband and wife.**

(a) *In general.* A husband and wife may make a joint declaration of estimated tax even though they are not living together. However, a joint declaration may not be made if they are separated under a decree of divorce or of separate maintenance. A joint declaration may not be made if the taxpayer's spouse is a nonresident alien (including a nonresident alien who is a bona fide resident of Puerto Rico during the entire taxable year) or if his spouse has a different taxable year. If the gross income of each spouse meets the requirements of section 6015(a), either a joint declaration must be made or a separate declaration must be made by each. If a joint declaration is made, the amount estimated as the income tax imposed by chapter 1 (other than by section 56) must be computed on the aggregate estimated taxable income of the spouses (see section 6013(d)(3) and § 1.2-1), while (for taxable years beginning after December 31, 1966) the amount estimated as the self-employment tax imposed by chapter 2 must be computed on the separate estimated self-employment income of each spouse. See sections 1401 and 1402 and § 1.6017-1(b)(1). The liability with respect to the estimated tax, in the case of a joint declaration, shall be joint and several.

(b) *Application to separate returns.* The fact that a joint declaration of estimated tax is made by them will not preclude a husband and his wife from filing separate returns. In case a joint declaration is made but a joint return is not made for the same taxable year, the payments made on account of the estimated tax for such year may be treated as payments on account of the tax liability of either the husband or wife for the taxable year or may be divided between them in such manner as they may agree. In the event the husband and wife fail to agree to a division, such payments shall be allocated between them in accordance with the following rule. The portion of such payments to be allocated to a spouse shall be that portion of the aggregate of all such payments as the amount of tax imposed by chapter 1 (other than by section 56) shown on the separate return of the taxpayer (plus, for taxable years beginning after December 31, 1966, the amount of tax imposed by chapter 2 shown on the return of the taxpayer) bears to the sum of the taxes imposed by chapter 1 (other than by section 56) shown on the separate returns of the taxpayer and his spouse (plus, for taxable years beginning after December 31, 1966, the sum of the taxes imposed by chapter 2 shown on the returns of the taxpayer and his spouse). For example, assume that for calendar year 1972 H and his spouse W make a joint declaration of estimated tax and, pursuant thereto, pay a total of $19,500 of estimated tax. H and W subsequently file separate returns for 1972 showing tax imposed by chapter 1 (other than by section 56) in the amount of $11,500 and $8,000, respectively. In addition, H's return shows a tax imposed by chapter 2 in the amount of $500. H and W fail to agree to a division of the estimated tax paid. The amount of the aggregate estimated tax payments allocated to H is computed as follows:

(1) Amount of tax imposed by chapter 1 (other than by section 56) shown on H's return $11,500
(2) Plus: Amount of tax imposed by chapter 2 shown on H's return 500
(3) Total taxes imposed by chapter 1 (other than by section 56) and by chapter 2 shown on H's return $12,000

Reg. § 1.6015(b)-1(b)

24,278 (I.R.C.)   Reg. § 1.6015(b)-1(b)   8-16-76

(4) Amount of tax imposed by chapter 1 (other than by section 56) shown on W's return 8,000

(5) Total taxes imposed by chapter 1 (other than by section 56) and by chapter 2 shown on both H's and W's returns $20,000

(6) Proportion of such taxes shown on H's return to total amount of such taxes shown on both H's and W's returns ($12,000 ÷ 20,000) 60%

(7) Amount of estimated tax payments allocated to H (60% of $19,500) $11,700

Accordingly, H's return would show remaining tax liability in the amount of $300 ($12,000 taxes shown less $11,700 estimated tax allocated).

(c) *Death of spouse.* (1) A joint declaration may not be made after the death of either the husband or wife. However, if it is reasonable for a surviving spouse to assume that there will be filed a joint return for himself and the deceased spouse for his taxable year and the last taxable year of the deceased spouse he may, in making a separate declaration for his taxable year which includes the period comprising such last taxable year of his spouse, estimate the amount of the tax imposed by chapter 1 (other than by section 56) on his and his spouse's taxable income on an aggregate basis and compute his estimated tax with respect to such chapter 1 tax in the same manner as though a joint declaration had been filed.

(2) If a joint declaration is made by husband and wife and thereafter one spouse dies, no further payments of estimated tax on account of such joint declaration are required from the estate of the decedent. The surviving spouse, however, shall be liable for the payment of any subsequent installments of the joint estimated tax unless an amended declaration setting forth the separate estimated tax for the taxable year is made by such spouse. Such separate estimated tax shall be paid at the times and in the amounts determined under the rules prescribed in section 6153. For purposes of (i) the making of such an amended declaration by the surviving spouse, and (ii) the allocation of payments made pursuant to a joint declaration between the surviving spouse and the legal representative of the decedent in the event a joint return is not filed, the payments made pursuant to the joint declaration may be divided between the decedent and the surviving spouse in such proportion as the surviving spouse and the legal representative of the decedent may agree. In the event the surviving spouse and the legal representative of the decedent fail to agree to a division, such payments shall be allocated in accordance with the following rule. The portion of such payments to be allocated to the surviving spouse shall be that portion of the aggregate amount of such payments as the amount of tax imposed by chapter 1 (other than by section 56) shown on the separate return of the surviving spouse (plus, for taxable years beginning after December 31, 1966, the amount of tax imposed by chapter 2 shown on the return of the surviving spouse) bears to the sum of the taxes imposed by chapter 1 (other than by section 56) shown on the separate returns of the surviving spouse and of the decedent (plus, for taxable years beginning after December 31, 1966, the sum of the taxes imposed by chapter 2 shown on the returns of the surviving spouse and of the decedent); and the balance of such payments shall be allocated to the decedent. This rule may be illustrated by analogizing the surviving spouse described in this rule to H in the example contained in paragraph (b) of this section and the decedent in this rule to W in that example.

(d) *Signing of declaration.* A joint declaration of a husband and wife (if not made by an agent of one or both spouses) shall be signed by both spouses. The provisions of paragraph (f) of § 1.6015(a)-1, relating to returns made by agents, shall apply where one spouse signs a declaration as agent for the other, or where a third party signs a declaration as agent for one or both spouses.

○── § 1.6015(c) **Statutory provisions; declaration of estimated income tax by individuals; estimated tax.** [Sec. 6015(c), IRC]

○── § 1.6015(c)-1 (T.D. 6267, filed 11-13-57; republished in T.D. 6500, filed 11-25-60; amended by T.D. 6777, filed 12-15-64; T.D. 7427, filed 8-9-76.) **Definition of estimated tax.**

In the case of an individual, the term "estimated tax" means—

(a) The amount which the individual estimates as the amount of the income tax imposed by chapter 1 (other than the tax imposed by section 56 or, for taxable years ending before September 30, 1968, the tax surcharge imposed by section 51) for the taxable year, plus

(b) For taxable years beginning after December 31, 1966, the amount which the individual estimates as the amount of the self-employment tax imposed by chapter 2 for the taxable year, minus

(c) The amount which the individual estimates as the sum of any credits against tax provided by part IV of subchapter A of chapter 1. These credits are those provided by section 31 (relating to tax withheld on wages), section 32 (relating to tax withheld at source on nonresident aliens and foreign corporations and on tax-free covenant bonds), section 33 (relating to foreign taxes), section 34 (relating to the credit for dividends received on or before December 31, 1964), section 35 (relating to partially tax-exempt interest), section 37 (relating to retirement income), section 38 (relating to the investment credit), section 39 (relating to certain uses of gasoline, special fuels, and lubricating oils), section 40 (relating to expenses of work incentive programs), section 41 (relating to contributions to candidates), and section 42 (relating to overpayments of tax). An individual who expects to elect to pay the optional tax imposed by section 3, or one who expects to elect to take the standard deduction allowed by section 144, should disregard any credits otherwise allowable under sections 32, 33, and 35 in computing his estimated tax since, if he so elects, these credits are not allowed in computing his tax liability. See section 36.

For example, if a self-employed individual estimates that his liabilities for income tax and self-employment tax for 1973 will be

$1,600 and $400, respectively, he is required to declare and pay an estimated tax of $2,000 for that year.

○― § 1.6015(d) Statutory provisions; declaration of estimated income tax by individuals; contents of declaration. [Sec. 6015(d), IRC]

○― § 1.6015(d)-1 (T.D. 6267, filed 11-13-57; republished in T.D. 6500, filed 11-25-60; amended by T.D. 7427, filed 8-9-76.) Contents of declaration of estimated tax.

(a) *In general*. (1) The declaration of estimated tax by an individual shall be made on Form 1040-ES. For the purpose of making the declaration, the amount of gross income which the taxpayer can reasonably be expected to receive or accrue, depending upon the method of accounting upon which taxable income is computed, and the amount of the estimated allowable deductions and credits to be taken into account in computing the amount of estimated tax shall be determined upon the basis of the facts and circumstances existing as at the time prescribed for the filing of the declaration as well as those reasonably to be anticipated for the taxable year. If, therefore, the taxpayer is employed at the date prescribed for filing his declaration at a given wage or salary, it should, in the absence of circumstances indicating the contrary, be presumed by him for the purpose of the declaration that such employment will continue to the end of the taxable year at the wage or salary received by him as of such date. In the case of income other than wages and salary the regularity in the payment of income, such as dividends, interests, rents, royalties, and income arising from estates and trusts is a factor to be taken into consideration. Thus, if the taxpayer owns shares of stock in a corporation and dividends have been paid regularly for several years upon such stock, the taxpayer in the preparation of his declaration should, in the absence of information indicating a change in the dividend policy, include the prospective dividends from the corporation for the taxable year as well as those actually received in such year prior to the filing of the declaration. In the case of a taxpayer engaged in business on his own account, there shall be made an estimate of gross income and deductions and credits in the light of the best available information affecting the trade, business, or profession.

(2) In the case of any individual who can, at the time of the preparation of his declaration, reasonably anticipate that his gross income will be of such amount and character as to enable him to elect upon his return for such year to compute the tax under section 3 (relating to optional tax), in lieu of the tax imposed by section 1, the declaration of estimated tax may be made upon the basis set forth in section 3 and § 1.3-1. The filing of a declaration computed upon the basis of section 3 shall not constitute the making of an election under section 4 (relating to rules for optional tax) nor will it permit the filing of a return on the basis of the optional tax under section 3 unless the taxpayer otherwise comes within the provisions of sections 3 and 4. For the purpose of computing the tax liability in the case of married persons, if the taxable income of one spouse is determined without regard to the standard deduction, **the standard deduction is not allowed to** either. (See, however, paragraph (c) of § 1.142-1 for exceptions where spouses are legally separated under a decree of divorce or separate maintenance.) Hence, where separate declarations are filed, one spouse should not use section 3 in computing the estimated tax unless the other spouse also uses section 3 or employs the standard deduction in computing the estimated tax.

(b) *Computation of estimated tax*. In computing the estimated tax the taxpayer should take into account the following:

(1) The amount estimated as the income tax imposed by chapter 1 (other than by section 56) for the taxable year after the application of any allowable amounts estimated as the credit for foreign taxes, the dividends received credit (for dividends received on or before December 31, 1964), the credit for partially tax-exempt interest, the retirement income credit, the investment credit, the credit for expenses of work incentive programs, the credit for contributions to candidates, the credit for overpayments of tax, but without regard to the credit under section 31 for tax withheld on wages or to the credit under section 39 for certain uses of gasoline, special fuels, and lubricating oils;

(2) For taxable years beginning after December 31, 1966 (and, if the taxpayer so desires, for an earlier taxable year), the amount estimated as the tax on self-employment income imposed by chapter 2;

(3) The amounts estimated by the taxpayer as the credits under section 31 for tax withheld on wages and under section 39 for certain uses of gasoline, special fuels, and lubricating oils; and

(4) The excess, if any, of the sum of the amounts shown under subparagraphs (1) and (2) of this paragraph over the amount shown under subparagraph (3) of this paragraph, which excess shall be the estimated tax for such taxable year.

(c) *Use of prescribed form*. Copies of Form 1040-ES will so far as possible be furnished taxpayers by district directors. A taxpayer will not be excused from making a declaration, however, by the fact that no form has been furnished to him. Taxpayers not supplied with the proper form should make application therefor to the district director in ample time to have their declarations prepared, verified, and filed with the district director on or before the date prescribed for filing the declaration. If the prescribed form is not available, a statement disclosing the amount estimated as the tax, the estimated credits, and the estimated tax after deducting such credits should be filed as a tentative declaration within the prescribed time, accompanied by the payment of the required installment. Such tentative declaration should be supplemented, without unnecessary delay, by a declaration made on the proper form.

○― § 1.6015(e) Statutory provisions; declaration of estimated income tax by individuals; amendment of declaration. [Sec. 6015(e), IRC]

○― § 1.6015(e)-1 (T.D. 6267, filed 11-13-57; republished in T.D. 6500, filed 11-25-60; amended by T.D. 7427, filed 8-9-76.) **Amendment of declaration.**

Reg. § 1.6015(e)-1

24,280 (I.R.C.)

In the making of a declaration of estimated tax, the taxpayer is required to take into account the then existing facts and circumstances as well as those reasonably to be anticipated relating to prospective gross income, allowable deductions, and estimated credits for the taxable year. Amended or revised declarations may be made in any case in which the taxpayer estimates that his gross income, deductions, or credits will differ from the gross income, deductions, or credits reflected in the previous declaration. An amended declaration may also be made based upon a change in the number of exemptions to which the taxpayer may be entitled for the then current taxable year. However, only one amended declaration may be filed during any interval between installment dates. See paragraph (d) of § 1.6073-1. An amended declaration may be filed jointly by husband and wife even though separate declarations have previously been filed. An amended declaration must be made on Form 1040-ES (marked "Amended"). See, however, paragraph (c) of § 1.6015(d)-1 for procedure to be followed if the prescribed form is not available.

○━━ § 1.6015(f) **Statutory provisions; declaration of estimated income tax by individuals; return as declaration or amendment.** [Sec. 6015(f), IRC]

○━━ § 1.6015(f)-1 (T.D. 6267, filed 11-13-57; republished in T.D. 6500, filed 11-25-60; amended by T.D. 6678, filed 9-30-63 and T.D. 7028, filed 2-26-70.) **Return as declaration or amendment.**

(a) *Time for filing return.* (1)(i) If a taxpayer pays in full the amount computed on the return as payable, and

(*a*) If a taxpayer (other than a taxpayer referred to in (*b*) of this subdivision)—

(*1*) On the calendar year basis, files his return on or before January 31 of the succeeding calendar year, or

(*2*) On a fiscal year basis, files his return on or before the last day of the first month immediately succeeding the close of such fiscal year, or

(*b*) If an individual referred to in section 6073(b), relating to income from farming, or, with respect to taxable years beginning after December 31, 1962, from fishing—

(*1*) On the calendar year basis, for taxable years beginning before January 1, 1969, files his return on or before February 15, or

(*2*) On a fiscal year basis, for taxable years beginning before January 1, 1969, files his return on or before the fifteenth day of the second month after the close of his fiscal year, or

(*3*) On the calendar year basis, for taxable years beginning after December 31, 1968, files his return on or before March 1, or

(*4*) On a fiscal year basis, for taxable years beginning after December 31, 1968, files his return on or before the first day of the third month after the close of his fiscal year, then—

(ii) (*a*) If the declaration is not required to be filed during the taxable year, but is required to be filed on or before January 15 of the succeeding year (or the date corresponding thereto in the case of a fiscal year), such return shall be considered as such declaration; or

(*b*) If a declaration was filed during the taxable year, such return shall be considered as the amendment of the declaration permitted by section 6015(c) to be filed on or before January 15 of the succeeding year (or the date corresponding thereto in the case of a fiscal year).

Hence, for example, an individual taxpayer on the calendar year basis who, subsequent to September 1, 1963, first meets the requirements of section 6015(a) which necessitate the filing of a declaration for 1963, may satisfy the requirements as to the filing of such declaration by filing his return for 1963 on or before January 31, 1964 (February 15, 1964, in the case of a farmer or fisherman), and paying in full at the time of such filing the tax shown thereon to be payable. Likewise, if a taxpayer files on or before September 15, 1963, a timely declaration for such year and subsequent thereto and on or before January 31, 1964, files his return for 1963, and pays at the time of such filing the tax shown by the return to be payable, such return shall be treated as an amended declaration timely filed.

(2) For the purpose of section 6015(f) a taxpayer may file his return on or before the last day of the first month following the close of the taxable year even though he has not been furnished Form W-2 by his employer. In such case the taxpayer shall compute, as accurately as possible, his wages for such year and the tax withheld for which he is entitled to a credit, reporting such wages and tax on his return, together with all other pertinent information necessary to the determination of his tax liability for such year.

(b) *Effect on addition to the tax.* Compliance with the provisions of section 6015(f) will enable a taxpayer to avoid the addition to the tax imposed by section 6654 with respect to an underpayment of the installment not required to be paid until January 15 of the succeeding calendar year (or the corresponding date in the case of a fiscal year). With respect to an underpayment of any earlier installment, compliance with section 6015(f) will not relieve the taxpayer from the addition to the tax imposed by section 6654. However, installment, will terminate on January 15 of the succeeding calendar year (or the period of the underpayment under section 6654(c), with respect to any earlier corresponding date in the case of a fiscal year). For example, a taxpayer discovers on January 14, 1956, that he has underpaid his estimated tax for the calendar year 1955. He may, in lieu of filing an amended declaration on January 15, 1956, and paying the balance of the estimated tax determined thereon, file his final return on January 31, 1956, and pay in full the amount computed thereon as payable. By so doing, he will avoid the addition to the tax with respect to the underpayment of the installment required to be paid by January 15, 1956. The periods of underpayment under section 6654(c), as to the installments required to be paid on April 15, 1955, June 15, 1955, and September 15, 1955, also terminate on January 15, 1956.

○━━ § 1.6015(g) **Statutory provisions; declaration of estimated income tax by in-**

dividuals; short taxable years. [Sec. 6015 (g), IRC]

○━▶ § 1.6015(g)-1 (T.D. 6267, filed 11-13-57; republished in T.D. 6500, filed 11-25-60; amended by T.D. 7427, filed 8-9-76.) **Short taxable years of individuals.**

(a) *Requirement of declaration.* No declaration may be made for a period of more than 12 months. For purposes of this section a taxable year of 52 or 53 weeks, in the case of a taxpayer who computes his taxable income in accordance with the election permitted by section 441(f) shall be deemed a period of 12 months. For the special rules affecting the time for filing declarations and paying estimated tax by such a taxpayer, see paragraph (b) of § 1.441-2. A separate declaration for a fractional part of a year is required where, for example, there is a change, with the approval of the Commissioner, in the basis of computing taxable income from one taxable year to another taxable year. The periods to be covered by such separate declarations in the several cases are those set forth in section 443. No declaration is required of the short taxable year is—

(1) A period of less than four months,

(2) A period of at least four months but less than six months and the requirements of section 6015(a) are first met after the 1st day of the fourth month,

(3) A period of at least six months but less than nine months and the requirements of section 6015(a) are first met after the 1st day of the sixth month, or

(4) A period of nine months or more and the requirements of section 6015(a) are first met after the 1st day of the ninth month.

In the case of a decedent, no declaration need be filed subsequent to the date of death. As to the requirement for an amended declaration if death of one spouse occurs after filing a joint declaration, see paragraph (c) of § 1.6015(b)-1.

(b) *Income and income tax placed on annual basis.* For the purpose of determining whether the anticipated income and tax for a short taxable year resulting from a change of annual accounting period necessitates the filing of a declaration, income and income tax imposed by chapter 1 (other than by section 56) shall be placed on an annual basis in the manner prescribed in section 443(b)(1). Thus, for example, an unmarried taxpayer who changes from a fiscal year basis to a calendar year basis beginning January 1, 1973, will have a short taxable year beginning July 1, 1972, and ending December 31, 1972. If his anticipated gross income for such short taxable year consists solely of wages (as defined in section 3401(a)) in the amount of $11,000, his total gross income and his gross income from such wages for the purpose of determining whether a declaration is required is $22,000, the amount obtained by placing anticipated income of $11,000 upon an annual basis. Since the taxpayer's anticipated gross income from wages when placed upon an annual basis is in excess of $20,000, he is required to file a declaration of estimated tax for the short taxable year unless the estimated tax can reasonably be expected to be less than $100. However, for taxable years beginning after December 31, 1966, the amount which the individual estimates as the amount of self-employment tax imposed by chapter 2 shall be computed on the actual self-employment income for the short period.

○━▶ § 1.6015(h) **Statutory provisions; declaration of estimated income tax by individuals; estates and trusts.** [Sec. 6015(h), IRC]

○━▶ § 1.6015(h)-1 (T.D. 6276, filed 11-13-57; republished in T.D. 6500, filed 11-25-60.) **Estates and trusts.**

An estate or trust, though generally taxed as an individual, is not required to file a declaration.

○━▶ § 1.6015(i) **Statutory provisions; declaration of estimated income tax by individuals; nonresident alien individuals.** [Sec. 6015(i), IRC]

○━▶ § 1.6015(i)-1 T.D. 7332, filed 12-20-74.) **Nonresident alien individuals.**

(a) *Exception from requirement of making a declaration.* No declaration of estimated income tax is required to be made under section 6015(a) and § 1.6015(a)-1 by a nonresident alien individual unless—

(1) Such individual has wages, as defined in section 3401(a), and the regulations thereunder, upon which tax is required to be withheld under section 3402,

(2) Such individual has income (other than compensation for personal services upon which tax is required to be withheld at source under section 1441) which is effectively connected for the taxable year with the conduct of a trade or business in the United States by such individual, or

(3) Such individual has been, or expects to be, a resident of Puerto Rico during the entire taxable year.

(b) *Rules applicable to nonresident alien individuals required to make a declaration*—(1) *Tests to be applied.* A nonresident alien individual who is not excepted by paragraph (a) of this section from the requirement of making a declaration of income tax is required to file a declaration if his gross income meets the requirements of section 6015(a) and § 1.6015(a)-1. In making the determination under section 6015(a)(1) as to whether the amount of the gross income of a nonresident alien individual is such as to require making a declaration of estimated income tax, only the tests relating to a single individual (other than a head of household) or to a married individual not entitled to file a joint declaration with his spouse shall apply, since a nonresident alien individual may not make a joint declaration by reason of section 6015(b) and is not a head of household. Only in a rare case would a nonresident alien individual be a surviving spouse.

(2) *Determination of gross income.* To determine the gross income of a nonresident alien individual who is not, or does not expect to be, a resident of Puerto Rico during the entire taxable year, see section 872 and §§ 1.872-1 and 1.872-2. To determine the gross income of a nonresident alien individual who is, or expects to be, a resident of Puerto Rico during the entire taxable year, see section 876 and § 1.876-1.

Reg. § 1.6015(i)-1(b)(2)

For purposes of applying paragraph (a)(2) of this section, income which is effectively connected for the taxable year with the conduct of a trade or business in the United States includes all income which is treated under section 871(c) or (d) and § 1.871-9 (relating to students and trainees) or § 1.871-10 (relating to real property income) as income which is effectively connected for such year with the conduct of a trade or business in the United States.

(c) *Effective date.* This section shall apply for aaxable years beginning after December 31, 1966. For corresponding rules applicable to taxable years beginning before January 1, 1967, see 26 CFR 1.6015(a)-1(d) (Rev. as of Jan. 1, 1971).

○━ § 1.6015(j) **Statutory provisions; declaration of estimated income tax by individuals; applicability.** [Sec. 6015(j), IRC]

○━ § 1.6015(j)-1 (Originally § 1.6015(i)-1 as promulgated by T.D. 6267, filed 11-13-57; republished in T.D. 6500, filed 11-25-60; redesignated and amended by T.D. 7332, filed 12-20-74.) **Applicability.**

Section 6015 is applicable only with respect to taxable years beginning after December 31, 1954. Sections 58, 59, and 60 of the Internal Revenue Code of 1939 and the regulations thereunder, shall continue in force with respect to taxable years beginning before January 1, 1955.

○━ § 301.6015 **Statutory provisions; declaration of estimated income tax by individuals.** [Sec. 6015, IRC]

○━ § 301.6015-1 (T.D. 6498, filed 10-24-60; amended by T.D. 7332, filed 12-20-74; T.D. 7427, filed 8-9-76.) **Declaration of estimated income tax by individuals.**

For provisions relating to requirement of declarations of estimated income tax by individuals, see § 1.6015 of this chapter (Income Tax Regulations).

○━ § 1.6016 **Statutory provisions; declarations of estimated income tax by corporations.** [Sec. 6016, IRC]

○━ § 1.6016-1 (T.D. 6267, filed 11-13-57; republished in T.D. 6500, filed 11-25-60; amended by T.D. 6768, filed 11-3-64.) **Corporations.**

(a) *Requirement.* For taxable years ending on or after December 31, 1955, a declaration of estimated tax shall be made by every corporation (including unincorporated business enterprises electing to be taxed as domestic corporations under section 1361), which is subject to taxation under section 11 or 1201 (a), or subchapter L, chapter 1 of the Code (relating to insurance companies), if its income tax under such sections or such subchapter L for the taxable year can reasonably be expected to exceed the sum of $100,000 plus the amount of any estimated credits allowable under section 32 (relating to tax withheld at source on nonresident aliens and foreign corporations and on tax-free covenant bonds), section 33 (relating to taxes of foreign countries and possessions of the United States), and section 38 (relating to investment in certain depreciable property).

(b) *Definition of estimated tax.* The term "estimated tax", in the case of a corporation, means the excess of the amount which such corporation estimates as its income tax liability for the taxable year under section 11 or 1201(a), or subchapter L, chapter 1 of the Code, over the sum of $100,000 and any estimated credits under sections 32, 33, and 38. However, for the rule with respect to the limitation upon the $100,000 exemption for members of certain electing affiliated groups, see section 243(b)(3)(C)(v) and the regulations thereunder.

(c) *Examples.* The application of this section may be illustrated by the following examples:

Example (1). M, a corporation subject to tax under section 11, reasonably anticipates that it will have taxable income of $224,000 for the calendar year 1964. The normal tax and surtax result in an expected liability of $105,000. M determines that it will not have any allowable credits under sections 32, 33, and 38 for 1964. Since M's expected tax ($105,000) exceeds the exemption ($100,000), a declaration of estimated tax is required to be filed, reporting an estimated tax of $5,000 ($105,000—100,000) for the calendar year 1964.

Example (2). Under the facts stated in example (1), except that M estimates it will have an allowable foreign tax credit under section 33 in the amount of $4,000 and an allowable investment credit under section 38 in the amount of $3,000, no declaration is required, since M's expected tax ($105,000) does not exceed the $100,000 plus the allowable credits totaling $7,000.

○━ § 1.6016-2 (T.D. 6267, filed 11-13-57; republished in T.D. 6500, filed 11-25-60.) **Contents of declaration of estimated tax.**

(a) *In general.* The declaration of estimated tax by a corporation shall be made on Form 1120-ES. For the purpose of making the declaration, the estimated tax should be based upon the amount of gross income which the taxpayer can reasonably be expected to receive or accrue as the case may be, depending upon the method of accounting upon the basis of which the taxable income is computed, and the amount of the estimated allowable deductions and credits to be taken into account. Such amounts of gross income, deductions, and credits should be determined upon the basis of facts and circumstances existing as at the time prescribed for the filing of the declaration as well as those reasonably to be anticipated for the taxable year.

(b) *Use of prescribed form.* Copies of Form 1120-ES will so far as possible be furnished taxpayers by district directors. A taxpayer will not be excused from making a declaration, however, by the fact that no form has been furnished. Taxpayers not supplied with the proper form should make application therefor to the district director in ample time to have their declarations prepared, verified, and filed with the district director on or before the date prescribed for filing the declaration. If the prescribed form is not available a statement disclosing the estimated income tax after the exemption and the credits, if any, should be filed as a tentative declaration within the prescribed time, accompanied by the payment of the required installment. Such tentative declaration should be supplemented, without unnecessary delay, by a declaration made on the proper form.

○— § 1.6016-3 (T.D. 6267, filed 11-13-57; republished in T.D. 6500, filed 11-25-60; amended by T.D. 6768, filed 11-3-64.) **Amendment of declaration.**

In the making of a declaration of estimated tax the corporation is required to take into account the then existing facts and circumstances as well as those reasonably to be anticipated relating to prospective gross income, allowable deductions, and estimated credits for the taxable year. Amended or revised declarations may be made in any case in which the corporation estimates that its gross income, deductions, or credits will materially change the estimated tax reported in the previous declaration. However, for the rule with respect to the number of amended declarations which may be filed for taxable years beginning after December 31, 1963, see paragraph (d) (2) of § 1.6074-1. Such amended declaration may be made on either Form 1120-ES (marked "Amended") or on the reverse side of the installment notice furnished the corporation by the district director. See, however, paragraph (b) of § 1.6016-2 for procedure to be followed if the prescribed form is not available.

○— § 1.6016-4 (T.D. 6267, filed 11-13-57; republished in T.D. 6500, filed 11-25-60; amended by T.D. 6768, filed 11-3-64.) **Short taxable year.**

(a) *Requirement of declaration.* No declaration may be made for a period of more than 12 months. For purposes of this section a taxable year of 52 or 53 weeks, in the case of a corporation which computes its taxable income in accordance with the election permitted by section 441 (f), shall be deemed a period of 12 months. For special rules affecting the time for filing declarations and paying estimated tax by such corporation, see paragraph (b) of § 1.441-2. A separate declaration is required where a corporation is required to submit an income tax return for a period of less than 12 months, but only if such short period ends on or after December 31, 1955. However, no declaration is required if the short taxable year—

(1) Begins on or before December 31, 1963, and is—

  (i) A period of less than 9 months, or

  (ii) A period of 9 or more months but less than 12 months and the requirements of section 6016 (a) are not met before the 1st day of the last month in the short taxable year, or

(2) Begins after December 31, 1963, and is—

  (i) A period of less than 4 months, or

  (ii) A period of 4 or more months but less than 12 months and the requirements of section 6016 (a) are not met before the 1st day of the last month in the short taxable year.

(b) *Income placed on an annual basis.* In cases where the short taxable year results from a change of annual accounting period, for the purpose of determining whether the anticipated income for a short taxable year will result in an estimated tax liability requiring the filing of a declaration, such income shall be placed on an annual basis in the manner prescribed in section 443(b) (1). If a tax computed on such annualized income exceeds the sum of $100,000 and any credits under part IV, of subchapter A, chapter 1 of the Code, the estimated tax shall be the same part of the excess so computed as the number of months in the short period is of 12 months. Thus, for example, a corporation which changes from a calendar year basis to a fiscal year basis beginning October 1, 1956, will have a short taxable year beginning January 1, 1956, and ending September 30, 1956. If on or before August 31, 1956, the taxpayer anticipates that it will have income of $264,000 for the 9-month taxable year the estimated tax is computed as follows:

(1) Anticipated taxable income for
    9 months $264,000
(2) Annualized income ($264,000 ×
    12 ÷ 9) 352,000
(3) Tax liability on item (2) 177,540
(4) Item (3) reduced by $100,000
    (there are no credits under part
    IV, subchapter A, chapter 1 of the
    Code) 77,540
(5) Estimated tax for 9-month period ($77,540 × 9 ÷ 12) 58,155

Since the tax liability on the annualized income is in excess of $100,000, a declaration is required to be filed, reporting an estimated tax of $58,155 for the 9-month taxable period. This paragraph has no application where the short taxable year does not result from a change in the taxpayer's annual accounting period.

○— § 301.6016 **Statutory provisions; declarations of estimated income tax by corporations.** [Sec. 6016, IRC]

○— § 301.6016-1 (T.D. 6498, filed 10-24-60.) **Declarations of estimated income tax by corporations.**

For provisions concerning the requirement of declarations of estimated income tax by corporations, see §§ 1.6016-1 to 1.6016-4, inclusive, of this chapter (Income Tax Regulations).

○— 1.6017 **Statutory provisions; self-employment tax returns.** [Sec. 6017, IRC]

○— § 1.6017-1 (T.D. 6364, filed 2-13-59; republished in T.D. 6500, filed 11-25-60; amended by T.D. 6691, filed 12-2-63; T.D. 7427, filed 8-9-76.) **Self-employment tax returns.**

(a) *In general.* (1) Every individual, other than a nonresident alien, having net earnings from self-employment, as defined in section 1402, of $400 or more for the taxable year shall make a return of such earnings. For purposes of this section, an individual who is a resident of the Virgin Islands, Puerto Rico, or (for any taxable year beginning after 1960) Guam or American Samoa is not to be considered a nonresident alien individual. See paragraph (d) of § 1.1402(b)-1. A return is required under this section if an individual has self-employment income, as defined in section 1402(b), even though he may not be required to make a return under section 6012 for purposes of the tax imposed by section 1 or 3. Provisions applicable to returns under section 6012(a) shall be applicable to returns under this section.

Reg. § 1.6017-1(a)(1)

24,282.2 (I.R.C.) Reg. § 1.6017-1(a)(2) 8-16-76

(2) Except as otherwise provided in this subparagraph, the return required by this section shall be made on Form 1040. The form to be used by residents of the Virgin Islands, Guam, or American Samoa is Form 1040SS. In the case of a resident of Puerto Rico who is not required to make a return of income under section 6012(a), the form to be used is Form 1040SS, except that Form 1040PR shall be used if it is furnished by the Internal Revenue Service to such resident for use in lieu of Form 1040SS.

(b) *Joint returns.* (1) In the case of a husband and wife filing a joint return under section 6013, the tax on self-employment income is computed on the separate self-employment income of each spouse, and not on the aggregate of the two amounts. The requirement of section 6013 (d)(3) that in the case of a joint return the tax is computed on the aggregate income of the spouses is not applicable with respect to the tax on self-employment income. Where the husband and wife each has net earnings from self-employment of $400 or more, it will be necessary for each to complete separate schedules of the computation of the self-employment tax with respect to the net earnings of each spouse, despite the fact that a joint return is filed. If the net earnings from self-employment of either the husband or the wife are less than $400, such net earnings are not subject to the tax on self-employment income, even though they must be shown on the joint return for purposes of the tax imposed by section 1 or 3.

(2) Except as otherwise expressly provided, section 6013 is applicable to the return of the tax on self-employment income; therefore, the liability with respect to such tax in the case of a joint return is joint and several.

(c) *Social security account numbers.* (1) Every individual making a return of net earnings from self-employment for any period commencing before January 1, 1962, is required to show thereon his social security account number, or, if he has no such account number, to make application therefor on Form SS-5 before filing such return. However, the failure to apply for or receive a social security account number will not excuse the individual from the requirement that he file such return on or before the due date thereof. Form SS-5 may be obtained from any district office of the Social Security Administration or from any district director. The application shall be filed with a district office of the Social Security Administration or, in the case of an individual not in the United States, with the district office of the Social Security Administration at Baltimore, Maryland. An individual who has previously secured a social security account number as an employee shall use that account number on his return of net earnings from self-employment.

(2) For provisions applicable to the securing of identifying numbers and the reporting thereof on returns and schedules for periods commencing after December 31, 1961, see § 1.6109-1.

(d) *Declaration of estimated tax with respect to taxable years beginning after December 31, 1966.* For taxable years beginning after December 31, 1966, section 6015 provides that the term "estimated tax" includes the amount which an individual estimates as the amount of self-employment tax imposed by chapter 2 for the taxable year. Thus, individuals upon whom self-employment tax is imposed by section 1401 must make a declaration of estimated tax if they meet the requirements of section 6015(a), except as otherwise provided under section 6015(i).

○→ § 301.6017 Statutory provisions; self-employment tax returns. [Sec. 6017, IRC]

○→ § 301.6017-1 (T.D. 6498, filed 10-24-60.) Self-employment tax returns.

For provisions relating to the requirement of self-employment tax returns, see § 1.6017-1 of this chapter (Income Tax Regulations).

○→ § 301.6020 Statutory provisions; returns prepared for or executed by Secretary [Sec. 6020, IRC]

○→ § 301.6020-1 (T.D. 6498, filed 10-24-60.) Returns prepared or executed by district directors or other internal revenue officers.

(a) *Preparation of returns*—(1) *In general.* If any person required by the Code or by the regulations prescribed thereunder to make a return fails to make such return, it may be prepared by the district director or other authorized internal revenue officer or employee provided such person consents to disclose all information necessary for the preparation of such return. The return upon being signed by the person required to make it shall be received by the district director as the return of such person.

(2) *Responsibility of person for whom return is prepared.* A person for whom a return is prepared in accordance with subparagraph (1) of this paragraph shall for all legal purposes remain responsible for the correctness of the return to the same extent as if the return had been prepared by him.

(b) *Execution of returns*—(1) *In general.* If any person required by any internal revenue law or by the regulations prescribed thereunder to make a return (other than a declaration of estimated tax required under section 6015 or 6016) fails to make such return at the time prescribed therefor, or makes, willfully or otherwise, a false or fraudulent return, the district director or other authorized internal revenue officer or employee shall make such return from his own knowledge and from such information as he can obtain through testimony or otherwise.

(2) *Status of returns.* Any return made in accordance with subparagraph (1) of this paragraph and subscribed by the district director or other authorized internal revenue officer or employee shall be prima facie good and sufficient for all legal purposes.

(3) *Deficiency procedures.* For deficiency procedures in the case of income, estate, and gift taxes, see sections 6211 to 6216, inclusive, and §§ 301.6211-1 to 301.6215-1, inclusive.

(c) *Cross references.* (1) For provisions that a return executed by a district director or other authorized internal revenue officer or employee will not start the running of the period of limitations on assessment and collection, see section 6501(b) (3) and paragraph (c) of § 301.-6501(b)-1.

(2) For additions to the tax and additional amounts for failure to file returns, see section 6651 and § 301.6651-1, and section 6652 and § 301.6652-1, respectively.

(3) For additions to the tax for failure to pay tax, see section 6653 and § 301.-6653-1.

(4) For criminal penalties for willful failure to make returns, see sections 7201, 7202, and 7203.

(5) For criminal penalties for willfully making false or fraudulent returns, see sections 7206 and 7207.

(6) For authority to examine books and witnesses, see section 7602 and § 301.-7602-1.

§ 301.6021 **Statutory provisions; listing by Secretary of taxable objects owned by nonresidents of internal revenue districts.** [Sec. 6021, IRC]

§ 301.6021-1 (TD 6498, filed 10-24-60.) **Listing by district directors of taxable objects owned by nonresidents of internal revenue districts.**

Whenever there are in any internal revenue district any articles subject to tax, which are not owned or possessed by or under the care or control of any person within such district, and of which no list has been transmitted to the district director, as required by law or by regulations prescribed pursuant to law, the district director, or other authorized internal revenue officer or employee, shall enter the premises where such articles are situated, shall make such inspection of the articles as may be necessary, and shall make lists of the same according to the forms prescribed. Such lists, being subscribed by the district director or other authorized internal revenue officer or employee, shall be sufficient lists of such articles for all purposes.

Information Returns

§ 1.6031 **Statutory provisions; return of partnership income.** (Sec. 6031, IRC]

§ 1.6031-1 (TD 6364, filed 2-13-59; republished in TD 6500, filed 11-25-60; amended by TD 7012, filed 5-14-69; TD 7208, filed 10-2-72; TD 7495, filed 6-29-77.) **Return of partnership income.**

(a) *In general*—(1) *General rule.* Except as provided in paragraphs (b) and (d) of this section with respect to certain organizations excluded from the application of subchapter K of chapter 1 of the Code and certain partnerships having no United States business, an unincorporated organization defined as a partnership in section 761(a), through or by means of which any business, financial operation, or venture is carried on, shall make a return for each taxable year on Form 1065. For purposes of filing a partnership return, an unincorporated organization will not be considered, within the meaning of section 761(a), to carry on a business, financial operation, or venture as a partnership before the first taxable year in which such organization receives income or makes or incurs any expenditures treated as deductions for Federal income tax purposes. Such return shall state specifically the items of partnership gross income and the deductions allowable by subtitle A of the Code and shall include the names and addresses of all the partners and the amount of the distributive shares of income, gain, loss, deduction, or credit allocated to each partner. Such return shall be made for the taxable year of the partnership, irrespective of the taxable years of the partners. For taxable years of a partnership and of a partner, see section 706 and § 1.706-1. For signing of a partnership return, see § 1.6063-1.

(2) *Special rule.* Except in the case of an unincorporated organization deemed to be excluded from the application of subchapter K in the manner described in paragraph (b)(2)(ii) of § 1.761-2 for the first year of its existence, an unincorporated organization described in paragraph (a) of § 1.761-2 shall file a partnership return for the first taxable year in which the participants by a formal agreement undertake to engage in joint operations, or in the absence of a formal agreement for the first taxable year in which the participants with respect to the joint use of property jointly have income, or make or incur any expenditures treated as deductions for Federal income tax purposes. Additionally, if an organization described in paragraph (a) of § 1.761-2 does not elect under section 761 and the regulations thereunder to be excluded from the application of subchapter K of chapter 1 of the Code, it is required to file a return for each taxable year subsequent to its first taxable year in accordance with the requirements of this section until an election is made in accordance with paragraph (b)(2)(i) of § 1.761-2. Where no annual accounting period has been adopted by an organization described in paragraph (a) of § 1.761-2, its taxable year shall be the calendar year in accordance with section 441(g). For special rules in the case of an organization making the election for exclusion under section 761, see paragraphs (b)(2)(i) and (c) of § 1.761-2 and paragraph (b) of this section.

(b) *Unincorporated organizations excluded from the application of subchapter K*—(1) *Wholly excluded.* (i) Any unincorporated organization with respect to which under section 761(a) an election to be excluded from all the provisions of subchapter K of chapter 1 of the Code has been made in the manner described in paragraph (b)(2)(i) of § 1.761-2 shall file Form 1065 for the first year with respect to which such an election has been made and such return shall, in lieu of the information therein required, contain or be accompanied by the information required by such paragraph.

(ii) Except as otherwise provided in subdivision (i) of this subparagraph, an unincorporated organization which is wholly excluded from the application of subchapter K need not file a partnership return.

(2) *Partially excluded.* Any unincorporated organization excluded from the application of part of subchapter K of chapter 1 of the Code shall file a return on Form 1065 containing such information as the Commissioner may require. See section 761 and paragraph (c) of § 1.761-2.

(c) *Partnerships having business or source of income within the United States.* Every partnership engaged in trade or busi-

24,284 (I.R.C.)   Reg. § 1.6031-1(c)   7-18-77

ness, or having income from sources, within the United States shall file a partnership return in accordance with this section, whether or not its principal place of business is outside of the United States, and whether or not all its members are nonresident aliens.

(d) *Partnerships having no United States business*—(1) *No return required from partnership.* A partnership carrying on no business in the United States and deriving no income from sources within the United States need not file a partnership return.

(2) *Returns of information with respect to partnership required of citizen or resident partners.* Where a U.S. citizen or resident is a partner in a partnership described in subparagraph (1) of this paragraph which is not required to file a partnership return, the district director or director of the service center may require such person to render such statements or provide such information as is necessary to show whether or not such person is liable for tax on income derived from such partnership. In addition, if an election in accordance with the provisions of section 703 (relating to elections affecting the computation of taxable income derived from a partnership) or section 761 (relating to the election to be excluded from the application of all or part of subchapter K, chapter 1 of the Code) is to be made by or for the partnership, a return on Form 1065 shall be filed for such partnership. See section 6063 and § 1.6063-1, relating to the authority of a partner to sign a partnership return. The filing of one such return for a taxable year of the partnership by a citizen or resident partner shall constitute a filing for the partnership of such partnership return.

(e) *Place and time for filing returns*—(1) *Place for filing*—(i) Returns filed with district director or Director of International Operations. The returns of partnerships doing business, or having income from sources, within the United States shall be filed with the district director for the internal revenue district in which the partnership has its principal office or principal place of business within the United States. If a partnership has no office, place of business, or agency within the United States, the return shall be filed with the Director of International Operations, Internal Revenue Service, Washington, D.C. 20225. A partnership return filed under the authority of paragraph (d)(2) of this section shall be filed with the internal revenue officer with whom the citizen or resident partner files his separate income tax return.

(ii) Returns filed with service centers. Notwithstanding subdivision (i) of this subparagraph, unless a return is filed by hand carrying, whenever instructions applicable to partnership returns provide that the return be filed with a service center, the return must be so filed in accordance with the instructions. Returns which are filed by hand carrying shall be filed with the district director (or with any person assigned the administrative supervision of an area, zone or local office constituting a permanent post of duty within the internal revenue district of such director) in accordance with paragraph (e) (1) (i) of this section.

(2) *Time for filing.* The return of a partnership shall be filed on or before the fifteenth day of the fourth month following the close of the taxable year of the partnership, except that the return of a partnership consisting entirely of nonresident aliens shall be filed on or before the fifteenth day of the sixth month following the close of the taxable year of the partnership.

○━ § 301.6031 Statutory provisions; return of partnership income. [Sec. 6031, IRC]

○━ § 301.6031-1 (TD 6498, filed 10-24-60.) Return of partnership income.

For provisions relating to the requirement of returns of partnership income, see § 1.6031-1 of this chapter (Income Tax Regulations).

○━ § 1.6032 Statutory provisions; returns of banks with respect to common trust funds. [Sec. 6032, IRC]

○━ § 1.6032-1 (TD 6364, filed 2-13-59; republished in TD 6500, filed 11-25-60.) Returns of banks with respect to common trust funds.

Every bank (as defined in section 581) maintaining a common trust fund shall make a return of income of the common trust fund, regardless of the amount of its taxable income. If a bank maintains more than one common trust fund, a separate return shall be made for each. No particular form is prescribed for making the return under this section, but Form 1065 may be used if it is designated by the bank as the return of a common trust fund. The return shall be made for the taxable year of the common trust fund and shall be filed on or before the fifteenth day of the fourth month following the close of such taxable year with the district director for the district in which the income tax return of the bank is filed. Such return shall state specifically with respect to the fund the items of gross income and the deductions allowed by subtitle A of the Code, and shall include each participant's name and address, the participant's proportionate share of taxable income or net loss (exclusive of gains and losses from sales or exchanges of capital assets), and the participant's proportionate share of gains and losses from sales or exchanges of capital assets. See § 1.584-2. A copy of the plan of the common trust fund must be filed with the return. If, however, a copy of such plan has once been filed with a return, it need not again be filed if the return contains a statement showing when and where it was filed. If the plan is amended in any way after such copy has been filed, a copy of the amendment must be filed with the return for the taxable year in which the amendment was made. For the signing of a return of a bank with respect to common trust funds, see § 1.6062-1, relating to the manner prescribed for the signing of a return of a corporation.

○━ § 301.6032 Statutory provisions; returns of banks with respect to common trust funds. [Sec. 6032, IRC]

○━ § 301.6032-1 (TD 6498, filed 10-24-60.) Returns of banks with respect to common trust funds.

For provisions relating to requirement of returns of banks with respect to common trust funds, see § 1.6032-1 of this chapter (Income Tax Regulations).

§ 1.6033 Statutory provisions; returns by exempt organizations. [Sec. 6033, IRC]

§ 1.6033-1 (TD 6203, filed 9-24-56; amended by TD 6301, filed 7-8-58; republished in TD 6500, filed 11-25-60; amended by TD 6645, filed 4-1-63; TD 6722, filed 4-13-64; TD 6972, filed 9-11-68; TD 6980, filed 11-8-68; TD 7122, filed 6-7-71.) **Returns by exempt organizations; taxable years beginning before January 1, 1970.**

(a) *In general.* (1) Except as provided in section 6033(a) and paragraph (g) of this section, every organization exempt from taxation under section 501(a) shall file an annual return of information specifically stating its items of gross income, receipts and disbursements, and such other information as may be prescribed in the instructions issued with respect to the return. Such information return shall be filed annually regardless of the amount or source of the income or receipts of the organization. Except as provided in paragraph (d) of this section, such return shall be filed annually regardless of whether such organization is chartered by, or affiliated or associated with, any central, parent, or other organization.

(2)(i) Except as otherwise provided in this subparagraph, every organization exempt from taxation under section 501(a), and required to file a return under section 6033 and this section, other than an organization described in section 401(a), 501(c) (3), or 501(d), shall file its annual return on Form 990. However, such an exempt organization, instead of filing Form 990, may file its annual return on Form 990(SF), a short form, if its gross receipts for the taxable year do not exceed $10,000 and its total assets on the last day of its taxable year do not exceed $10,000.

(ii) For purposes of this subparagraph and subparagraph (4) of this paragraph, "gross receipts" means the gross amount received by the organization during its annual accounting period from all sources without reduction for any costs or expenses including, for example, cost of goods or assets sold, cost of operations, or expenses of earning, raising, or collecting such amounts. Thus, "gross receipts" includes, but is not limited to, (a) the gross amount received as contributions, gifts, grants, and similar amounts without reduction for the expenses of raising and collecting such amounts, (b) the gross amount received as dues or assessments from members or affiliated organizations without reduction for expenses attributable to the receipt of such amounts, (c) gross sales or receipts from business activities (including business activities unrelated to the purpose for which the organization received an exemption, the net income or loss from which may be required to be reported on Form 990-T), (d) the gross amount received from the sale of assets without reduction for cost or other basis and expenses of sale, and (e) the gross amount received as investment income such as interest, dividends, rents, and royalties.

(3) Every employees' trust described in section 401(a) which is exempt from taxation under section 501(a) shall file an annual return on Form 990-P. The return shall include the information required by paragraph (b)(5)(ii) of § 1.401-1. In addition, the trust must file the information required to be filed by the employer pursuant to the provisions of § 1.404(a)-2, unless the employer has notified the trustee in writing that he has or will timely file such information. If the trustee has received such notification from the employer, then such notification, or a copy thereof, shall be retained by the trust as a part of its records.

(4) Except as otherwise provided in this subparagraph, every organization described in section 501(c)(3), which is required to file a return under section 6033 and this section, shall file its annual return on Form 990-A. However, such an exempt organization, instead of filing Form 990-A, may file its annual return on Form 990-A (SF), a short form, if its gross receipts for the taxable year do not exceed $10,000 and its total assets on the last day of its taxable year do not exceed $10,000. For purposes of this subparagraph, "gross receipts" shall be defined in the manner prescribed in subparagraph (2)(ii) of this paragraph. The forms prescribed by this subparagraph shall be as follows:

(i) Form 990-A shall consist of Parts I and II. Part I shall contain, in addition to information required in Part II, such information as may be prescribed in the return and instructions which is required to be furnished by section 6033(a) or which is necessary to show whether or not such organization is exempt from tax under section 501(a). Part II, which shall be open to public inspection pursuant to section 6104 and other applicable sections and the regulations thereunder, shall contain principally the information required by section 6033(b) and the regulations thereunder. The information contained in Part II, to be furnished by the organization in duplicate in the manner prescribed by the instructions issued with respect to the return, is as follows:

(a) Its gross income for the year. For this purpose, gross income includes tax-exempt income, but does not include contributions, gifts, grants, and similar amounts received. Whether or not an item constitutes a contribution, gift, grant, or similar amount, depends upon all the surrounding facts and circumstances.

(b) Its expenses attributable to such income and incurred within the year.

(c) Its disbursements out of income (including prior years' accumulations) made within the year for the purposes for which it is exempt. Information shall be included as to the class of activity with a separate total for each activity as well as the name, address, and amount received by each individual or organization receiving cash, other property, or services within the taxable year. If the donee is related by blood, marriage, adoption, or employment (including children of employees) to any person or corporation having an interest in the exempt organization, such as a creator, donor, director, trustee, or officer, the relationship of the donee shall be stated. Activities shall be classified according to purpose in greater detail than merely charitable, educational, religious, or scientific. For example, payments for nursing service, for

Reg. § 301.6033-1(a)(4)

laboratory construction, for fellowships, or for assistance to indigent families shall be so identified. Where the fair market value of the property at the time of disbursement is used as the measure of the disbursement, the book value of such property (and a statement of how book value was determined) shall also be furnished, and any difference between the fair market value at the time of disbursement and the book value should be reflected in the books of account. The expenses allocable to making the disbursements shall be set forth in such detail as is prescribed by the form or instructions.

(d) Its accumulation of income within the year. The amount of such accumulation is obtained by subtracting from the amount in (a) of this subdivision the sum of the amounts determined in (b) and (c) of this subdivision and the expenses allocable to carrying out the purposes for which it is exempt.

(e) Its aggregate accumulation of income at the beginning and end of the year. The aggregate accumulation of income shall be divided between that which is attributable to the gain or loss on the sale of assets (excluding inventory items) and that which is attributable to all other income. For this purpose expenses and disbursements shall be allocated on the basis of accounting records, the governing instrument, or applicable local law.

(f) Its disbursements out of principal in the current and prior years for the purposes for which it is exempt. In addition, the same type of information shall be required with respect to disbursements out of principal made in the current year as is prescribed by (c) of this subdivision with respect to disbursements out of income.

(g) A balance sheet showing its assets, liabilities, and net worth as of the beginning and end of such year. Detailed information on the assets, liabilities, and net worth shall be furnished on the schedule provided for this purpose on the Form 990-A. Such schedule shall be supplemented by attachments where appropriate.

(h) The total of the contributions and gifts received by it during the year. A statement shall be included showing the gross amount of contributions and gifts collected by the organization, the expenses incurred by the organization in collecting such amount, and the net proceeds.

(i) In addition to the information required in (a) through (h) of this subdivision, the organization shall furnish such specific information and answer such specific questions as are required by the form or instructions.

(ii) Form 990-A(SF) is a short form consisting of a single part which contains such information as may be prescribed in the return and instructions which is required to be furnished by section 6033(a) or which is necessary to show whether or not such organization is exempt from tax under section 501(a). In addition, Form 990-A(SF) shall contain the information required by section 6033(b) which must be furnished in the manner prescribed in the instructions issued with respect to the return. Form 990-A(SF) shall be open to public inspection pursuant to section 6104 and other applicable sections and the regulations thereunder.

(5) (i) Every religious or apostolic association or corporation described in section 501(d) which is exempt from taxation under section 501(a) shall file a return on Form 1065 for each taxable year, stating specifically the items of gross income and deductions, and its taxable income. There shall be attached to the return as a part thereof a statement showing the name and address of each member of the association or corporation and the amount of his distributive share of the taxable income of the association or corporation for such year.

(ii) If the taxable year of any member is different from the taxable year of the association or corporation, the distributive share of the taxable income of the association or corporation to be included in the gross income of the member for his taxable year shall be based upon the taxable income of the association or corporation for its taxable year ending with or within the taxable year of the member.

(b) *Accounting period for filing return.* A return on Form 990, 990-A, 990(SF), 990-A(SF), or 990-P shall be on the basis of the established annual accounting period of the organization. If the organization has no such established accounting period, such return shall be on the basis of the calendar year.

(c) *Returns when exempt status not established.* An information return on Form 990, 990-A, 990(SF), or 990-A(SF) is not required to be filed by an organization claiming an exempt status under section 501(a) prior to the establishment by the organization of such exempt status under section 501 and § 1.501(a)-1. If the date for filing an income tax return and paying the tax occurs before the tax-exempt status of the organization has been established, the organization is required to file the income tax return and pay the tax. However, see sections 6081 and 6161 and the regulations thereunder for extensions of time for filing the return and paying the tax. Upon establishment of its exempt status, the organization may file a claim for a refund of income taxes paid for the period for which its exempt status is established.

(d) *Group returns.* (1) A central parent, or like organization (referred to in this paragraph as "central organization"), exempt under section 501(a) and described in section 501(c), although required to file a separate annual return for itself under section 6033 and paragraph (a) of this section, may file annually, in addition to such separate annual return, a group return on Form 990 or 990-A, 990(SF), or 990-A(SF), as may be appropriate. Form 990(SF) or 990-A(SF) may be used where each local organization qualifies under paragraph (a) of this section. Such group return may be filed for two or more of the local organizations, chapters, or the like (referred to in this paragraph as "local organizations") which are (i) affiliated with such central organization at the close of its annual accounting period, (ii) subject to the general supervision or control of the central organization, and (iii) exempt from taxation under the same paragraph of section 501(c) of the Code, although the local organizations are not necessarily exempt under the paragraph under which the central organization is exempt.

Reg. § 1.6033-1 (d) (1)

(2) (i) The filing of the group return shall be in lieu of the filing of a separate return by each of the local organizations included in the group return. The group return shall include only those local organizations which in writing have authorized the central organization to include them in the group return, and which have made and filed, with the central organization, their statements, specifically stating their items of gross income, receipts, and disbursements, and such other information relating to them as is required to be stated in the group return. Such an authorization by a local organization shall be made annually, under the penalties of perjury, and shall be signed by a duly authorized officer of the local organization in his official capacity and shall contain the following statement, or a statement of like import: "I hereby declare under the penalties of perjury that this authorization (including any accompanying schedules and statements) has been examined by me and to the best of my knowledge and belief is true, correct and complete and made in good faith for the taxable year stated." Such authorizations and statements shall be permanently retained by the central organization.

(ii) There shall be attached to the group return and made a part thereof a schedule showing the name and address of each of the local organizations and the total number thereof included in such return, and a schedule showing the name and address of each of the local organizations and the total number thereof not included in the group return.

(3) The group return shall be on the basis of the established annual accounting period of the central organization. Where such central organization has no established annual accounting period, such return shall be on the basis of the calendar year. The same income, receipts, and disbursements of a local organization shall not be included in more than one group return.

(4) The group return shall be filed in accordance with these regulations and the instructions issued with respect to Form 990, 990-A, 990(SF), or 990-A(SF), whichever is appropriate, and shall be considered the return of each local organization included therein. The tax-exempt status of a local organization must be established under a group exemption letter issued to the central organization before a group return including the local organization will be considered as the return of the local organization. See § 1.501(a)-1 for requirements for establishing a tax-exempt status.

(e) *Time and place for filing.* The annual return of information on Form 990, 990-A, 990(SF), 990-A(SF), or 990-P shall be filed on or before the fifteenth day of the fifth calendar month following the close of the period for which the return is required to be filed. The annual return on Form 1065 required to be filed by a religious or apostolic association or corporation shall be filed on or before the fifteenth day of the fourth month following the close of the taxable year for which the return is required to be filed. Each such return shall be filed in accordance with the instructions applicable thereto.

(f) *Penalties.* For criminal penalties for failure to file a return and filing a false or fraudulent return, see sections 7203, 7206, and 7207.

(g) *Organizations not required to file annual returns.* (1) (i) Annual returns on Form 990-A or Form 990-A (SF) are not required to be filed by an organization described in Section 501(c)(3) which has established its right to exemption from taxation under section 501(a) and which is—

(a) Organized and operated exclusively for religious purposes;

(b) Operated, supervised, or controlled by or in connection with an organization which is organized and operated exclusively for religious purposes;

(c) An educational organization which normally maintains a regular faculty and curriculum and normally has a regularly organized body of pupils or students in attendance at the place where its educational activities are regularly carried on; or

(d) A charitable organization, or an organization for the prevention of cruelty to children or animals, which is supported, in whole or in part, by funds contributed by the United States or any State or political subdivision thereof, or which is primarily supported by contributions of the general public.

(ii) An educational organization which normally maintains and has a regular faculty, curriculum, and student body and meets the conditions of subdivision (i) (c) of this subparagraph, which relieves it from the requirement of filing annual returns, shall not be considered as having thereafter failed to continue meeting such conditions if it is temporarily compelled to curtail or discontinue its normal and regular activities during the existence of abnormal circumstances and conditions.

(iii) An organization organized and operated exclusively for charitable purposes or for the prevention of cruelty to children or animals is "primarily supported by contributions of the general public" for any accounting period if more than 50 percent of its income and receipts for such period is actually derived from voluntary contributions and gifts made by the general public, as distinguished from a few contributors or donors or from related or associated persons. For purposes of this subdivision, the words "related or associated persons" refer to persons of a particular group who are connected with or are interested in the activities of the organization, such as founders, incorporators, shareholders, members, fiduciaries, officers, employees, or the like, or who are connected with such persons by family or business relationships. An organization claiming an exception from the filing of an information return under this subdivision must maintain adequate records in order to substantiate such claim. Furthermore, if it is doubtful to an organization that it falls within this exception for filing annual information returns, it must file the return on Form 990-A or Form 990-A(SF).

(2) The annual return on Form 990 or Form 990(SF) need not be filed by—

(i) A fraternal beneficiary society,

order, or association, described in section 501(c)(8), or

(ii) An organization described in section 501(c)(1) if it is a corporation wholly owned by the United States or any agency or instrumentality thereof, or is a wholly owned subsidiary of such a corporation, which has established its exemption from tax under section 501(a).

(3) The provisions of section 6033(a) relieving certain specified types of organizations exempt from tax under section 501(a) from filing annual returns do not abridge or impair in any way the powers and authority of district directors or directors of service centers provided for in other provisions of the Code and in the regulations thereunder to require the filing of such returns by such organizations. See section 6001 and § 1.6001-1.

(h) *Records, statements, and other returns of tax-exempt organizations.* (1) An organization which has established its right to exemption from tax under section 501(a) and has also established that it is not required to file annually the return of information on Form 990, 990-A, 990(SF) or 990-A (SF) shall immediately notify in writing the district director for the internal revenue district in which its principal office is located of any changes in its character, operations, or purpose for which it was originally created.

(2) Every organization which has established its right to exemption from tax, whether or not it is required to file an annual return of information, shall submit such additional information as may be required by the district director for the purpose of enabling him to inquire further into its exempt status and to administer the provisions of subchapter F (section 501 and following), chapter 1 of the Code, and of section 6033. See section 6001 and § 1.-6001-1 with respect to the authority of the district director or directors of service centers to require such additional information and with respect to the permanent books of account or records to be kept by such organizations.

(3) An organization which has established its right to exemption from tax under section 501(a), including an organization which is relieved under section 6033 and this section from filing annual returns of information, is not, however, relieved from

Reg. § 1.6033-1(h)(3)

the duty of filing other returns of information. See, for example, sections 6041 and 6051 and the regulations thereunder.

(i) *Unrelated business tax returns.* In addition to the foregoing requirements of this section, certain organizations otherwise exempt from tax under section 501(a) and described in section 501(c)(2), (3), (5), (6), or (17) or section 401(a) which are subject to tax on unrelated business taxable income are also required to file returns on Form 990-T. See paragraph (e) of § 1.6012-2 and paragraph (a)(5) § 1.6012-3 for requirements with respect to such returns.

(j) *Effective date.* The provisions of this section shall apply with respect to returns filed for taxable years beginning before January 1, 1970.

§ 1.6033-2 (T.D. 7122, filed 6-7-71; amended by T.D. 7168, filed 3-8-72; T.D. 7223, filed 11-20-72; T.D. 7290, filed 11-16-73; T.D. 7454, filed 12-29-76.) **Returns by exempt organizations; taxable years beginning after December 31, 1969.**

(a) *In general.* (1) Except as provided in section 6033(a)(2) and paragraph (g) of this section, every organization exempt from taxation under section 501(a) shall file an annual information return specifically setting forth its items of gross income, gross receipts and disbursements, and such other information as may be prescribed in the instructions issued with respect to the return. Except as provided in paragraph (d) of this section, such return shall be filed annually regardless of whether such organization is chartered by, or affiliated or associated with, any central, parent, or other organization.

(2)(i) Except as otherwise provided in this paragraph and paragraph (g) of this section, every organization exempt from taxation under section 501(a), and required to file a return under section 6033 and this section (including, for taxable years ending before December 31, 1972, private foundations, as defined in section 509(a)), other than an organization described in section 401(a) or 501(d), shall file its annual return on Form 990. For taxable years ending on or after December 31, 1972, every private foundation shall file Form 990-PF as its annual information return.

(ii) The information generally required to be furnished by an organization exempt under section 501(a) is:

(*a*) Its gross income for the year. For this purpose, gross income includes tax-exempt income, but does not include contributions, gifts, grants, and similar amounts received. Whether an item constitutes a contribution, gift, grant, or similar amount depends upon all the surrounding facts and circumstances. The computation of gross income shall be made by subtracting the cost of goods sold from all receipts other than gross contributions, gifts, grants and similar amounts received and noninclludible dues and assessments from members and affiliates.

(*b*) To the extent not included in gross income, its dues and assessments from members and affiliates for the year.

(*c*) Its expenses incurred within the year attributable to gross income.

(*d*) Its disbursements (including prior years' accumulations) made within the year for the purposes for which it is exempt.

(*e*) A balance sheet showing its assets, liabilities, and net worth as of the beginning and end of such year. Detailed information relating to the assets, liabilities, and net worth shall be furnished on the schedule provided for this purpose on the return required by this section. Such schedule shall be supplemented by attachments where appropriate.

(*f*) The total of the contributions, gifts, grants and similar amounts received by it during the taxable year, and the names and addresses of all persons who contributed, bequeathed, or devised $5,000 or more (in money or other property) during the taxable year. In the case of a private foundation (as defined in section 509(a)), the names and addresses of all persons who became substantial contributors (as defined in section 507(d)(2)) during the taxable year shall be furnished. In addition, for its first taxable year beginning after December 31, 1969, each private foundation shall furnish the names and addresses of all persons who became substantial contributors before such taxable year. For special rules with respect to contributors and donors, see subdivision (iii) of this subparagraph.

(*g*) The names and addresses of all officers, directors, or trustees (or any person having responsibilities or powers similar to those of officers, directors or trustees) of the organization, and, in the case of a private foundation, all persons who are foundation managers, within the meaning of section 4946(b)(1). Organizations described in section 501(c)(3) must also attach a schedule showing the names and addresses of the five employees (if any) who received the greatest amount of annual compensation in excess of $30,000; the total number of other employees who received annual compensation in excess of $30,000; the names and addresses of the five independent contractors (if any) who performed personal services of a professional nature for the organization (such as attorneys, accountants, and doctors, whether such services are performed by such persons in their individual capacity or as employees of a professional service corporation) and who received the greatest amount of compensation in excess of $30,000 from the organization for the year for the performance of such services; and the total number of other such independent contractors who received in excess of $30,000 for the year for the performance of such services.

(*h*) A schedule showing the compensation and other payments made during the organization's annual accounting period (or during the calendar year ending within such period) which are includible in the gross income of each individual whose name is required to be listed in (*g*) of this subdivision.

(*i*) For any taxable year ending on or after December 31, 1971, such information as is required by Forms 4848 and 4849 and, only with respect to any such taxable year ending before December 31, 1972, such information as is required by Form 2950. Such forms are required by this section to be filed by an organization exempt from tax under section 501(a) which is an employer who maintains a funded pension or annuity plan for its employees. See paragraph (g) of this section for exceptions from fil-

Reg. § 1.6033-2(a)(2)

ing. Form 4849 need not be filed by the organization if the fiduciary for the plan has given written notification to the organization that such form will be filed as an attachment to Form 990-P filed by the fiduciary. Form 4848 (and Form 4849 if required to be filed by the organization) shall be filed as a separate return on or before the due date for Form 990. For rules relating to the extension of time for filing, see section 6081 and the regulations thereunder and the instructions for Form 4848. A central organization which files Form 990 as a group return under paragraph (d) of this section may also file Form 4848 as a group return. The rules provided by paragraph (d) of this section with respect to a group return filed on Form 990 shall apply to a group return filed on Form 4848. Unless otherwise expressly provided therein, an authorization to include a local organization in a group for purposes of filing Form 990 as a group return shall be treated as an authorization to include such local organization in a group for purposes of filing Form 4848 as a group return. A group return on Form 4848 shall be filed in accordance with this section and the instructions to Form 4848 and shall be considered the return of each local organization included therein. In addition to the information required to be furnished by Forms 4848 and 4849, the district director may require any further information that he considers necessary to determine qualification of the plan under section 401 or the taxability under section 403(b) of a beneficiary under an annuity purchased by a section 501(c)(3) organization.

(iii) *Special rules.* In providing the names and addresses of contributors and donors under subdivision (ii)(*f*) of this subparagraph —

(*a*) An organization described in section 501(c)(3) which meets the 33⅓ percent-of-support test of the regulations under section 170(b)(1)(A)(vi) (without regard to whether such organization otherwise qualifies as an organization described in section 170(b)(1)(A)) is required to provide the name and address of a person who contributed, bequeathed, or devised $5,000 or more during the year only if his amount is in excess of 2 percent of the total contributions, bequests and devises received by the organization during the year.

(*b*) An organization other than a private foundation is required to report only the names and addresses of contributors of whom it has actual knowledge. For instance, an organization need not require an employer who withholds contributions from the compensation of employees and pays over to the organization periodically the total amounts withheld, to specify the amounts paid over with respect to a particular employee. In such case, unless the organization has actual knowledge that a particular employee gave more than $5,000 (and in excess of 2 percent if (*a*) of this subdivision is applicable), the organization need report only the name and address of the employer, and the total amount paid over by him.

(*c*) Separate and independent gifts made by one person in a particular year need be aggregated to determine if his contributions and bequests exceed $5,000 (and in excess of 2 percent if (*a*) of this subdivision is applicable), only if such gifts are of $1,000 or more.

(*d*)(*1*) Organizations described in section 501(c)(8) or (10) (and, for taxable years beginning after December 31, 1970, organizations described in section 501(c)(7)) that receive contributions or bequests to be used exclusively for purposes described in section 170(c)(4), 2055(a)(3), or 2522(a)(3), must attach a schedule with respect to all gifts which aggregate more than $1,000 from any one person showing the name of the donor, the amount of the contribution or bequest, the specific purpose for which such amount was received, and the specific use to which such amount was put. In the case of an amount set aside for such purposes, the organization shall indicate the manner in which such amount is held (for instance, whether such amount is commingled with amounts held for other purposes). If the contribution or bequest was transferred to another organization, the schedule must include the name of the transferee organization, a description of the nature of such organization, and a description of the relationship between the transferee and transferor organizations.

(*2*) For taxable years beginning after December 31, 1970, such organizations must also attach a statement showing the total dollar amount of contributions and bequests received for such purposes which are $1,000 or less.

(iv) *Listing of States.* A private foundation is required to attach to its return required by this section a list of all States—

(*a*) To which the organization reports in any fashion concerning its organization, assets, or activities, or

(*b*) With which the organization has registered (or which it has otherwise notified in any manner) that it intends to be, or is, a charitable organization or a holder of property devoted to a charitable purpose.

(3)(i) For taxable years beginning after December 31, 1969, and ending before December 31, 1971, every employee's trust described in section 401(a) which is exempt from taxation under section 501(a) shall file an annual return on Form 990-P. The return shall include the information required by paragraph (b)(5)(ii) of § 1.401-1. For such years, in addition, the trust must file the information required to be filed by the employer pursuant to the provisions of § 1.404(a)-2, unless the employer has notified the trustee in writing that he has filed or will timely file such information. If the trustee has received such notification from the employer, then such notification, or a copy thereof, shall be retained by the trust as a part of its records.

(ii) For taxable years ending on or after December 31, 1971, every employee's trust described in section 401(a) which is exempt from taxation under section 501(a) shall file an annual return on Form 990-P. The trust shall furnish such information as is required by such form and the instructions issued with respect thereto.

(b) *Accounting period for filing return.* A return required by this section shall be on the basis of the established annual accounting period of the organization. If the organization has no such established accounting period, such return shall be on the basis of the calendar year.

(c) *Returns when exempt status not established.* An organization claiming an exempt status under section 501(a) prior to the establishment of such exempt status under section 501 and § 1.501(a)-1, shall file a return required by this section in accordance with the instructions applicable thereto. In such case the organization must indicate on such return that it is being filed in the belief that the organization is exempt under section 501(a), but that the Internal Revenue Service has not yet recognized such exemption.

(d) *Group returns.* (1) A central, parent, or like organization (referred to in this paragraph as "central organization"), exempt under section 501(a) and described in section 501(c) (other than a private foundation), although required to file a separate annual return for itself under section 6033 and paragraph (a) of this section, may file annually, in addition to such separate annual return, a group return on Form 990. Such group return may be filed for two or more of the local organizations, chapters, or the like (referred to in this paragraph as "local organizations") which are (i) affiliated with such central organization at the close of its annual accounting period, (ii) subject to the general supervision or control of the central organization, and (iii) exempt from taxation under the same paragraph of section 501 (c) of the Code, although the local organizations are not necessarily exempt under the paragraph under which the central organization is exempt. Such group return may not be filed for a local organization which is a private foundation.

(2)(i) The filing of the group return shall be in lieu of the filing of a separate return by each of the local organizations included in the group return. The group return shall include only those local organizations which in writing have authorized the central organization to include them in the group return, and which have made and filed, with the central organization, their statements, specifically stating their items of gross income, receipts, and disbursements, and such other information relating to them as is required to be stated in the group return. Such an authorization and statement by a local organization shall be made under the penalties of perjury, shall be signed by a duly authorized officer of the local organization in his official capacity, and shall contain the following statement, or a statement of like import: "I hereby declare under the penalties of perjury that this authorization (including any accompanying schedules and statements) has been examined by me and to the best of my knowledge and belief is true, correct and complete and made in good faith." Such authorization and statement with respect to a local organization shall be retained by the central organization until the expiration of six years after the last taxable year for which a group return filed by such central organization includes such local organization.

(ii) There shall be attached to the group return and made a part thereof a schedule showing the name, address, and employer identification number of each of the local organizations and the total number thereof included in such return, and a schedule showing the name, address, and employer identification number of each of the local organizations and the total number thereof not included in the group return.

(3) The group return shall be on the basis of the established annual accounting period of the central organization. Where such central organization has no established annual accounting period, such return shall be on the basis of the calendar year. The same income, receipts, and disbursements of a local organization shall not be included in more than one group return.

(4) The group return shall be filed in accordance with these regulations and the instructions issued with respect to Form 990, and shall be considered the return of each local organization included therein. The tax exempt status of a local organization must be established under a group exemption letter issued to the central organization before a group return including the local organization will be considered as the return of the local organization. See § 1.501(a)-1 for requirements for establishing a tax-exempt status.

(5) In providing the information required by paragraph (a)(2)(ii)(f), and (h) of this section, such information may be provided—

(i) with respect to the central or parent organization on its Form 990, and with respect to the local organizations on separate schedules attached to the group return for the year, or

(ii) on a consolidated basis for all the local organizations and the central or parent organization on the group return.

Such information need be provided only with respect to those local organizations which are not excepted from filing under the provisions of paragraph (g) of this section. A central or parent organization shall indicate whether it has provided such information in the manner described in subdivision (i) or in subdivision (ii) of this subparagraph, and may not change the manner in which it provides such information without the consent of the Commissioner.

(e) *Time and place for filing.* The annual return required by this section shall be filed on or before the 15th day of the fifth calendar month following the close of the period for which the return is required to be filed. The annual return on Form 1065 required to be filed by a religious or apostolic association or corporation shall be filed on or before the 15th day of the fourth month following the close of the taxable year for which the return is required to be filed. Each such return shall be filed in accordance with the instructions applicable thereto.

(f) *Penalties and additions to tax.* For penalties and additions to tax for failure to file a return and filing a false or fraudulent return, see sections 6652, 7203, 7206 and 7207.

(g) *Organizations not required to file annual returns.* (1) Annual returns required by this section are not required to be filed by an organization exempt from taxation under section 501(a) which is—

(i) A church, an interchurch organization of local units of a church, a convention or association of churches, or an integrated auxiliary of a church;

Reg. § 1.6033-2(g)(1)

(ii) An exclusively religious activity of any religious order;

(iii) An organization (other than a private foundation) the gross receipts of which in each taxable year are normally not more than $5,000 (as described in subparagraph (3) of this paragraph);

(iv) A mission society sponsored by or affiliated with one or more churches or church denominations, more than one-half of the activities of which society are conducted in, or directed at persons in, foreign countries;

(v) A State institution, the income of which is excluded from gross income under section 115(a);

(vi) An organization described in section 501(c)(1); or

(vii) An educational organization (below college level) which is described in section 170(b)(1)(A)(ii), which has a program of a general academic nature, and which is affiliated (within the meaning of paragraph (g)(5)(iii) of this section) with a church or operated by a religious order.

(2) The provisions of section 6033(a) relieving certain specified types of organizations exempt from taxation under section 501(a) from filing annual returns do not abridge or impair in any way the powers and authority of district directors or directors of service centers provided for in other provisions of the Code and in regulations thereunder to require the filing of returns or notices by such organizations. See section 6001 and § 1.6001-1.

(3) For purposes of subparagraph (1)(iii) of this paragraph, the gross receipts (as defined in subparagraph (4) of this paragraph) of an organization are normally not more than $5,000 if—

(i) In the case of an organization which has been in existence for one year or less, the organization has received, or donors have pledged to give, gross receipts of $7,500 or less during the first taxable year of the organization,

(ii) In the case of an organization which has been in existence for more than one but less than three years, the average of the gross receipts received by the organization in its first two taxable years is $6,000 or less, and

(iii) In the case of an organization which has been in existence for three years or more, the average of the gross receipts received by the organization in the immediately preceding three taxable years, including the year for which the return would be required to be filed, is $5,000 or less.

(4) For purposes of this paragraph and paragraph (a)(2) of this section, "gross receipts" means the gross amount received by the organization during its annual accounting period from all sources without reduction for any costs or expenses including, for example, cost of goods or assets sold, cost of operations, or expenses of earning, raising, or collecting such amounts. Thus "gross receipts" includes, but is not limited to (i) the gross amount received as contributions, gifts, grants, and similar amounts without reduction for the expenses of raising and collecting such amounts, (ii) the gross amount received as dues or assessments from members or affiliated organizations without reduction for expenses attributable to the receipt of such amounts, (iii) gross sales or receipts from business activities (including business activities unrelated to the purpose for which the organization qualifies for exemption, the net income or loss from which may be required to be reported on Form 990-T), (iv) the gross amount received from the sale of assets without reduction for cost or other basis and expenses of sale, and (v) the gross amount received as investment income, such as interest, dividends, rents, and royalties.

(5)(i) For purposes of this title, the term "integrated auxiliary of a church" means an organization—

(a) Which is exempt from taxation as an organization described in section 501(c)(3);

(b) Which is affiliated (within the meaning of paragraph (g)(5)(iii) of this section) with a church; and

(c) Whose principal activity is exclusively religious.

(ii) An organization's principal activity will not be considered to be exclusively religious if that activity is educational, literary, charitable, or of another nature (other than religious) that would serve as a basis for exemption under section 501(c)(3).

(iii) For purposes of paragraph (g)(5) of this section, the term "affiliated" means either controlled by or associated with a church or with a convention or association of churches. For example, an organization, a majority of whose officers or directors are appointed by a church's governing board or by officials of a church, is controlled by a church within the meaning of this paragraph. An organization is associated with a church or with a convention or association of churches if it shares common religious bonds and convictions with that church or convention or association of churches.

(iv) Organizations which are integrated auxiliaries include a men's or women's organization, a religious school (such as a seminary), a mission society, or a youth group. The types of organizations which are not integrated auxiliaries may be illustrated by the following examples:

Example (1). Hospital A is a nonprofit corporation exempt from Federal income tax as an organization described in section 501(c)(3). Hospital A is affiliated (within the meaning of pararaph (g)(5)(iii) of § 1.6033-2) with a church which is also exempt as an organization described in section 501(c)(3). The hospital provides medical care for the community in which it is located, and the provision of such medical care is its principal activity. Since this activity could serve as the basis for Hospital A's exemption under section 501(c)(3) if it were not affiliated with a church, A is not an integrated auxiliary of a church within the meaning of paragraph (g)(5) of § 1.6033-2.

Example (2). School B, an elementary grade school exempt from Federal income tax as an organization described in section 501(c)(3), is affiliated (within the meaning of paragraph (g)(5)(iii) of § 1.6033-2) with a church which is also exempt from Federal income tax as an organization described in section 501(c)(3). School B has a separate legal identity from that of the church. The school property, including building and grounds, is owned by the church. The school's supervisory and managerial personnel are appointed by church officials. The school's budget is prepared subject to approval by a church official responsible for the overall supervision of the school. The school's program corresponds with the public school program for the same grades and complies with State law requirements for public education. The principal activity of school B is education. Since this activity could serve as the basis for School B's exemption under section 501(c)(3) if it were not affiliated with a church, B is not an integrated auxiliary of a church within the meaning of paragraph (g)(5) of § 1,6033-2. However, since School B is excluded from filing under § 1.6033-2(g)(1)(vii), it is not required to file an annual information return.

Example (3). Orphanage C, exempt from Federal income tax as an organization described in section 501(c)(3), is a nonprofit corporation organized and operated as an orphanage. It is affiliated (within the meaning of paragraph (g)(5)(iii) of § 1,6033-2) with a church which is also exempt as an organization described in section 501(c)(3). The orphanage is dedicated to the service of the entire community in which it is located. The principal activity of the orphanage is to provide children with housing, medical care, guidance, and similar services and facilities on a non-sectarian basis. Since this activity could serve as the basis for Orphanage C's exemption under section 501(c)(3) if it were not affiliated with a church, Orphanage C is not an integrated auxiliary of a church within the meaning of paragraph (g)(5) of § 1.6033-2.

Example (4). Organization D, exempt from Federal income tax as an organization described in section 501(c)(3) of the Code, is a trust operating an old age home. It is affiliated (within the maning of paragraph (g)(5)(iii) of § 1,6033-2) with a church which is also exempt from income tax as an organization described in section 501(c)(3). The home provides services exclusively to the elderly members of the church's denomination. The principal activity of the home is to provide the residents with housing, limited nursing care, and similar services and facilities. Since this activity could serve as the basis for Organization D's exemption under section 501(c)(3) if it were not affiliated with a church, D is not an integrated auxiliary of a church within the meaning of paragraph (g)(5) of § 1.6033-2.

Example (5). University E is a nonprofit corporation exempt from Federal income tax as an organization described in section 501(c)(3) of the Code. It is affiliated (within the meaning of paragraph (g)(5)(iii) of section 1.6033-2) with a church which is also exempt from income tax as an organization described in section 501(c)(3). The university provides a program of general academic studies on the undergraduate level and graduate education in the arts, humanities, and sciences. Although it offers courses in religion, it does not provide religious training in the sense that a seminary offers such training.

The principal activity of the university is to provide college and graduate level education of a general academic nature. Since this activity could serve as the basis for University E's exemption under section 501(c)(3) if it were not affiliated with a church, E is not an integrated auxiliary of a church within the meaning of paragraph (g)(5) of this section. In addition, because E is a college level institution, paragraph (g)(1)(vii) of this section does not apply and E is required to file a return under section 6033.

Example (6). Orphanage F performs functions similar to those of Orphanage C described in example (3). However, Orphanage F does not have a legal identity separate from that of the church. Thus Orphanage F is not itself exempt from tax as an organization described in section 501(c)(3), and is not an integrated auxiliary of a church. The exception from filing a return under section 6033 accorded to the church of which Orphanage F is a part also applies to Orphanage F itself. Accordingly, Orphanage F is not required to file a return under section 6033.

(6) The Commissioner may relieve any organization or class of organizations from filing, in whole or in part, the annual return required by this section where he determines that such returns are not necessary for the efficient administration of the internal revenue laws.

(h) *Records, statements, and other returns of tax-exempt organizations.* (1) An organization which is exempt from taxation under section 501(a) and is not required to file annually an information return required by this section shall immediately notify in writing the district director for the internal revenue district in which its principal office is located of any changes in its character, operations, or purpose for which it was originally created.

(2) Every organization which is exempt from tax, whether or not it is required to file an annual information return, shall submit such additional information as may be required by the Internal Revenue Service for the purpose of inquiring into its exempt status and administering the provisions of subchapter F (section 501 and following), chapter 1 of subtitle A of the Code, section 6033, and chapter 42 of subtitle D of the Code. See section 6001 and § 1.6001-1 with respect to the authority of the district director or directors of service centers to require such additional information and with respect to the books of account or records to be kept by such organizations.

(3) An organization which has established its exemption from taxation under section 501(a), including an organization which is relieved under section 6033 and this section from filing annual returns of information, is not relieved of the duty of filing other returns of information. See, for example, sections 6041, 6043, and 6051 and the regulations thereunder.

(i) *Unrelated business tax returns.* In addition to the foregoing requirements of this section, certain organizations otherwise exempt from tax under section 501(a) which are subject to tax on unrelated

Reg. § 1.6033-2(i)

business taxable income are also required to file returns on Form 990-T. See paragraph (e) of § 1.6012-2 and paragraph (a) (5) of § 1.6012-3 for requirements with respect to such returns.

(j) *Special rule for private foundations.* A private foundation shall attach to each copy of the annual report required by section 6056 which its foundation managers send to a State Attorney General a copy of the return required by this section, and a copy of the Form 4720, if any, filed by the foundation with the Internal Revenue Service for the year. For provisions relating to annual reports, see section 6056 and the regulations thereunder.

(k) *Effective date.* The provisions of this section shall apply with respect to returns filed for taxable years beginning after December 31, 1969.

○— § 301.6033 Statutory provisions; returns by exempt organizations. [Sec. 6033, IRC]

○— § 301.6033-1 (T.D. 6498, filed 10-24-60.) Returns by exempt organizations.

For provisions relating to the requirement of returns by exempt organizations, see § 1.6033-1 of this chapter (Income Tax Regulations).

○— § 1.6034 Statutory provisions; returns by trusts claiming charitable deductions under section 642(c). [Sec. 6034, IRC]

○— § 1.6034-1 (T.D. 6364, filed 2-13-59; republished in T.D. 6500, filed 11-25-60; amended by T.D. 7012, filed 5-14-69.) Information returns required of certain trusts claiming charitable or other deductions under section 642(c).

(a) *In general.* Every trust (other than a trust described in paragraph (b) of this section) claiming a charitable or other deduction under section 642(c) shall file, with respect to the taxable year for which such deduction is claimed, a return of information on Form 1041A. The return shall set forth the name and address of the trust and the following information concerning the trust in such detail as is prescribed by the form or in the instructions issued with respect to such form:

(1) The amount of the charitable or other deduction taken under section 642(c) for the taxable year, showing separately for each class of activity for which disbursements were made (or amounts were permanently set aside) the amounts which, during such year, were paid out (or which were permanently set aside) for charitable or other purposes under section 642(c);

(2) The amount paid out during the taxable year which represents amounts permanently set aside in prior years for which charitable or other deductions have been taken under section 642(c), and separately listing for each class of activity, for which disbursements were made, the total amount paid out;

(3) The amount for which charitable or other deductions have been taken in prior years under section 642(c) and which had not been paid out at the beginning of the taxable year;

(4) (i) The amount paid out of principal in the taxable year for charitable, etc., purposes, and separately listing for each such class of activity, for which disbursements were made, the total amount paid out;

(ii) The total amount paid out of principal in prior years for charitable, etc., purposes;

(5) The gross income of the trust for the taxable year and the expenses attributable thereto, in sufficient detail to show the different categories of income and of expense; and

(6) A balance sheet showing the assets, liabilities, and net worth of the trust as of the beginning of the taxable year.

(b) *Exception.* A trust is not required to file a Form 1041A for any taxable year with respect to which the trustee is required by the terms of the governing instrument and applicable local law to distribute currently all of the income of the trust. For this purpose, the income of the trust shall be determined in accordance with section 643(b) and §§ 1.643(b)-1 and 1.643(b)-2.

(c) *Time and place for filing return.* The return on Form 1041-A shall be filed on or before the 15th day of the fourth month following the close of the taxable year of the trust, with the internal revenue officer designated by the instructions applicable to such form.

(d) *Other provisions.* For publicity of information on Form 1041A, see section 6104 and the regulations thereunder in Part 301 of this chapter. For the criminal penalties for failure to file a return and filing a false or fraudulent return, see sections 7203, 7206, and 7207.

○— § 301.6034 Statutory provisions; returns by trusts claiming charitable deductions under section 642(c). [Sec. 6034, IRC]

○— § 301.6034-1 (T.D. 6498, filed 10-24-60.) Returns by trusts claiming charitable or other deductions under section 642(c).

For provisions relating to the requirement of returns by trusts claiming charitable or other deductions under section 642 (c), see § 1.6034-1 of this chapter (Income Tax Regulations).

○— § 1.6035 Statutory provisions; returns of officers, directors, and shareholders of foreign personal holding companies. [Sec. 6035, IRC]

○— § 1.6035-1 (T.D. 6364, filed 2-13-59; republished in T.D. 6500, filed 11-25-60; amended by T.D. 7322, filed 8-23-74; T.D. 7517, filed 11-11-77.) Returns of officers and directors of foreign personal holding companies for taxable years beginning after December 31, 1958.

(a) *Requirement of returns*—(1) *Form 957.* For taxable years beginning after December 31, 1958, on the fifteenth day of the first month after the close of each such taxable year of a foreign personal holding company (as defined in section 552) each United States citizen or resident who on such day is an officer or director of such company shall file an information return on Form 957 with respect to the stock and securities of the company setting forth the following information with respect to the taxable year:

(i) The name and address of the corporation;

(ii) The kind of business in which the corporation is engaged;

(iii) The date of incorporation;

(iv) The country under the laws of which the corporation is incorporated;

(v) The number of shares and par value of common stock of the corporation outstanding as of the beginning and end of the taxable year;

(vi) The number of shares and par value of preferred stock of the corporation outstanding as of the beginning and end of the taxable year, the rate of dividend on such stock, and whether such dividend is cumulative or noncumulative;

(vii) A description of the convertible securities issued by the corporation, including a statement of the face value of, and rate of interest on, such securities;

(viii) The name and address of each person who was a shareholder during the taxable year and the class and number of shares held by each, together with an explanation of any changes in stockholdings during the taxable year;

(ix) The name and address of each holder during the taxable year of securities convertible into stock of the corporation, and the class, number, and face value of the securities held by each, together with an explanation of any changes in the holdings of such securities during the taxable year;

(x) If any resolution or plan in respect of the dissolution of the corporation or the liquidation of the whole or any part of its capital stock was adopted during the taxable year, a certified copy of such resolution or plan and of any amendments thereof or supplements thereto;

(xi) If the return is for any taxable year in which the corporation was organized or reorganized—

(a) The classes and kinds of assets transferred to the corporation for stock or securities of the corporation in connection with its formation, organization, or reorganization;

(b) A detailed list of any stock or securities included in the assets transferred to the corporation for stock or securities of the corporation; and

(c) The names and addresses of the persons who were the owners of assets transferred to the corporation for stock or securities of the corporation immediately prior to such transfer; and

(xii) Such other information with respect to the stock or securities of the company as may be required by the return form.

(2) *Form 958.* For taxable years beginning after December 31, 1958, and ending before December 31, 1977, on the sixtieth day after the close of the taxable year of a foreign personal holding company (as defined in section 552), each United States citizen or resident who on such day is an officer or director of such company shall file an information return on Form 958 with respect to the income of the corporation for the taxable year setting forth the following information:

(i) The gross income, deductions and credits, taxable income, foreign personal holding company income, and undistributed foreign personal holding company income for such taxable year, in complete detail;

(ii) The same information with respect to such taxable year as is required in subparagraph (1) of this paragraph, except that if all the information required under subparagraph (1) of this paragraph has been submitted, such information need not be set forth in the return on Form 958; and

(iii) Such other information as is required by the return form.

Reg. § 1.6035-1(a)(2)

(b) *Returns jointly made.* If two or more officers or directors of a foreign personal holding company are required to file information returns for any taxable year under section 6035(a) and this section, any two or more of such officers or directors may, in lieu of filing separate returns for such year, jointly execute and file the return on Form 957 and the return on Form 958.

(c) *Separate returns for each corporation.* If a person is required to file returns under section 6035(a) and this section with respect to more than one foreign personal holding company, separate returns must be filed with respect to each company.

(d) *Place for filing returns.* Returns required under section 6035(a) and this section shall be filed with the Internal Revenue Service Center designated in the instructions of the applicable form.

(e) *Penalties.* For criminal penalties for failure to file a return and filing a false or fraudulent return, see sections 7203, 7206, and 7207.

○━ § 1.6035-2 (T.D. 6364, filed 2-13-59; republished in T.D. 6500, filed 11-25-60; amended by T.D. 7322, filed 8-23-74.) **Returns of shareholders of foreign personal holding companies for taxable years beginning after December 31, 1958.**

(a) *Requirement of return.* For taxable years beginning after December 31, 1958, on the fifteenth day of the first month after the close of each such taxable year of a foreign personal holding company (as defined in section 552) each United States shareholder, by or for whom on such day 50 percent or more in value of the outstanding stock of such company is owned directly or indirectly, shall file an information return on Form 957 for such taxable year. For purposes of this section, an individual shall be considered as owning the stock owned by members of his family, as described in section 544(a)(2). The return shall set forth for the taxable year the same information as is required under paragraph (a)(1) of 1.6035-1.

(b) *Duplicate returns.* If a shareholder of a foreign personal holding company is required to file a return as an officer or a director of such company under section 6035(a) and paragraph (a)(1) of § 1.6035-1, he shall file such return and not the return required to be filed under section 6035(b) and this section.

(c) *Separate return for each corporation.* If a person is required to file a return under section 6035(b) and this section with respect to more than one foreign personal holding company, a separate return must be filed with respect to each company.

(d) *Place for filing return.* The return required under section 6035(b) and this section shall be filed with the Internal Revenue Service Center designated in the instructions of the applicable form.

(e) *Penalties.* For criminal penalties for failure to file a return and filing a false or fraudulent return, see sections 7203, 7206, and 7207.

○━ § 1.6035-3 (T.D. 6364, filed 2-13-59; republished in T.D. 6500, filed 11-25-60.) **Returns of officers, directors, and shareholders of foreign personal holding companies for periods within or for taxable years beginning before January 1, 1959.**

(a) For rules relating to information returns required to be filed by officers and directors of foreign personal holding companies for periods within or for taxable years beginning before January 1, 1959, see 26 CFR (1939) 39.338-1 and 39.338-2 (Regulations 118) as made applicable under the Internal Revenue Code of 1954 by Treasury Decision 6091, approved August 16, 1954 (19 F.R. 5167, C.B. 1954-2, 47).

(b) For rules relating to information returns required to be filed by shareholders of foreign personal holding companies for taxable years beginning before January 1, 1959, see 26 CFR (1939) 39.339-1 and 39.339-2 (Regulations 118) as made applicable under the Internal Revenue Code of 1954 by Treasury Decision 6091, approved August 16, 1954 (19 F.R. 5167, C.B. 1954-2, 47).

○━ § 301.6035 **Statutory provisions; returns of officers, directors, and shareholders of foreign personal holding companies.** [Sec. 6035, IRC]

○━ § 301.6035-1 (T.D. 6498, filed 10-24-60.) **Returns of officers, directors, and shareholders of foreign personal holding companies.**

For provisions relating to the requirement of returns by officers, directors, and shareholders of foreign personal holding companies, see §§ 1.6035-1 to 1.6035-3, inclusive, of this chapter (Income Tax Regulations).

○━ § 1.6036 **Statutory provisions; notice of qualification as executor or receiver.** [Sec. 6036, IRC]

○━ § 1.6036-1 (T.D. 6455, filed 3-1-60; republished in T.D. 6500, filed 11-25-60.) **Notice of qualification as executor or receiver.**

For provisions relating to the notice required of fiduciaries, see the regulations under section 6036 contained in Part 301 of this chapter (Regulations on Procedure and Administration).

○━ § 301.6036 **Statutory provisions; notice of qualification as executor or receiver.** [Sec. 6036, IRC]

○━ § 301.6036-1 (T.D. 6517, filed 12-20-60; amended by T.D. 7222, filed 11-20-72 and T.D. 7238, filed 12-28-72.) **Notice required of executor or of receiver or other like fiduciary.**

(a) *Receivers and other like fiduciaries*—(1) *Bankruptcy proceedings.* The receiver or the trustee in bankruptcy, the debtor in possession, or other person, designated as in control of the assets of a debtor in any bankruptcy proceeding by order of the court in which such proceeding is pending, shall on, or within 10 days of, the date of his appointment or authorization to act, give notice thereof in writing to the district director for the internal revenue district in which such debtor is or was required to make returns. Notice under this subparagraph shall not be required if, prior

Reg. § 301.6036-1(a)(1)

24,290 (I.R.C.) Reg. § 301.6036-1(a)(1) 9-3-74

to, on, or within 10 days of, the date of such appointment or authorization to act, any notice regarding such proceeding has been given under any provision of the Bankruptcy Act (Title 11 of the United States Code) to the Secretary or other proper officer of the Treasury Department.

(2) *Proceedings other than bankruptcy.* A receiver in a receivership proceeding or a similar fiduciary in any proceeding (including a fiduciary in aid of foreclosure), designated by order of any court of the United States or of any State or Territory or of the District of Columbia as in control of all or substantially all the assets of a debtor or other party to such proceeding shall, on, or within 10 days of, the date of his appointment or authorization to act, give notice thereof in writing to the district director for the internal revenue district in which the debtor, or such other party, is or was required to make returns. Moreover, any fiduciary in aid of foreclosure not appointed by order of any such court, if he takes possession of all or substantially all the assets of the debtor, shall, on, or within 10 days of, the date of his taking possession, give notice thereof in writing to such district director.

(3) *Assignment for benefit of creditors.* An assignee for the benefit of a creditor or creditors shall, on, or within 10 days of, the date of an assignment, give notice thereof in writing to the district director for the internal revenue district in which the debtor is or was required to make returns. For purposes of this subparagraph, an assignee for the benefit of creditors shall be any person who, by authority of law, by the order of any court, by oral or written agreement, or in any other manner acquires control or possession of or title to all or substantially all the assets of a debtor, and who under such acquisition is authorized to use, reassign, sell, or in any manner dispose of such assets so that the proceeds from the use, sale, or other disposition may be paid to or may inure directly or indirectly to the benefit of a creditor or creditors of such debtor.

(4) *Contents of notice*—(i) Bankruptcy and other proceedings. The written notice required under subparagraph (1) or (2) of this paragraph shall contain—

(a) The name and address of the person making such notice and the date of his appointment or his taking possession of the assets of the debtor or other person whose assets are controlled,

(b) The name, address, and, for notices filed after December 21, 1972, the taxpayer identification number of the debtor or other person whose assets are controlled.

(c) In the case of a court proceeding—

(1) The name and location of the court in which the proceedings are pending,

(2) The date on which such proceedings were instituted,

(3) The number under which such proceedings are docketed, and

(4) When possible, the date, time, and place of any hearing, meeting of creditors, or other scheduled action with respect to such proceedings.

(ii) Assignment for benefit of creditors. The written notice required under subparagraph (3) of this paragraph shall contain—

(a) The name and address of, and the date the asset or assets were assigned to, the assignee,

(b) The name, address, and, for notices filed after December 21, 1972, the taxpayer identification number oof the debtor whose assets were assigned.

(c) A brief description of the assets assigned,

(d) An explanation of the action expected to be taken with respect to such assets, and

(e) When possible, the date, time, and place of any hearing, meeting of creditors, sale, or other scheduled action with respect to such assets.

(iii) The notice required by this section shall be sent to the attention of the Chief, Special Procedure Staff, of the District office to which it is required to be sent.

(b) *Executors, administrators, and persons in possession of property of decedent.* For provisions relating to the requirement of filing, by an executor, administrator, or person in possession of property of a decedent, of a preliminary notice in the case of the estate of a decedent dying before January 1, 1971, see § 20.6036-1 of this chapter (Estate Tax Regulations).

(c) *Notice of fiduciary relationship.* When a notice is required under § 301.6903-1 of a person acting in a fiduciary capacity and is also required of such person under this section, notice given in accordance with the provisions of this section shall be considered as complying with both sections.

(d) *Suspension of period on assessment.* For suspension of the running of the period of limitations on the making of assessments from the date a proceeding is instituted to a date 30 days after receipt of notice from a fiduciary in any proceeding under the Bankruptcy Act or from a receiver in any other court proceeding, see section 6872 and § 301.6872-1.

(e) *Applicability.* The provisions of this section shall apply to those persons referred to in this section whose appointments, authorizations, or assignments occur on or after December 21, 1960.

(f) *Cross references.* (1) For criminal penalty for willful failure to supply information, see section 7203.

(2) For criminal penalties for willfully making false or fraudulent statements, see sections 7206 and 7207.

(3) For time for performance of acts where the last day falls on a Saturday, Sunday, or legal holiday, see section 7503 and § 301.7503-1.

○━━ **§ 1.6037 Statutory provisions; return of electing small business corporation.** [Sec. 6037, IRC]

○━━ **§ 1.6037-1** (T.D. 6432, filed 12-18-59; republished in T.D. 6500, filed 11-25-60; amended by T.D. 7012, filed 5-14-69.) **Return of electing small business corporation.**

(a) *In general.* Every small business corporation (as defined in section 1371 (a)) which has made an election under section 1372(a) not to be subject to the tax imposed by chapter 1 of the Code shall file, with respect to each taxable year for which the election is in effect, a return of income on Form 1120-S. The return shall set forth the items of gross income and the deductions allowable in computing taxable income as required by the return form or in the instructions issued with respect thereto and shall be signed in accordance with section 6062 by the person authorized to sign a return. The return shall also set forth the following information concerning the electing small business corporation:

(1) The names and addresses of all persons owning stock in the corporation at any time during the taxable year;

(2) The number of shares of stock owned by each shareholder at all times during the taxable year;

(3) The amount of money and other property distributed by the corporation during the taxable year to each shareholder;

(4) The date of each distribution of money and other property; and

(5) Such other information as is required by the form or by the instructions issued with respect to such form.

(b) *Time and place for filing return.* The return shall be filed on or before the 15th day of the third month following the close of the taxable year with the internal revenue officer designated in the instructions applicable to Form 1120-S. (See section 6072.)

(c) *Other provisions.* The return on Form 1120-S will be treated as a return filed by the corporation under section 6012, relating to persons required to make returns of income, for purposes of the provisions of chapter 66 of the Code, relating to limitations. Thus, for example, the period of limitation on assessment and collection of any corporate tax found to be due upon a subsequent determination that the corporation was not entitled to the benefits of subchapter S, chapter 1 of the Code, will run from the date of filing the return under section 6037, or from the date prescribed for filing such return, whichever is the later.

(d) *Penalties.* For criminal penalties for failure to file a return, supply information, or pay tax, and for filing a false or fraudulent return, statement, or other document, see sections 7203, 7206, 7207.

§ 301.6037 **Statutory provisions; return of electing small business corporation.** [Sec. 6037, IRC]

§ 301.6037-1 (T.D. 6498, filed 10-24-60.) **Return of electing small business corporation.**

For provisions relating to requirement of return of electing small business corporation, see § 1.6037-1 of this chapter (Income Tax Regulations).

§ 1.6038 **Statutory provisions; information with respect to certain foreign corporations.** [Sec. 6038, IRC]

§ 1.6038-1 (T.D. 6506, filed 11-29-60; amended by T.D. 6621, filed 11-30-62.) **Information returns required of domestic corporations with respect to annual accounting periods of certain foreign corporations beginning before January 1, 1963.**

(a) *Requirement of return.* For taxable years beginning after December 31, 1960, every domestic corporation shall make a separate annual information return on Form 2952, in duplicate, with respect to each foreign corporation which it controls, as defined in paragraph (b) of this section, and with respect to each foreign subsidiary as defined in paragraph (c) of this section for each annual accounting period (described in paragraph (d) of this section) of each such controlled foreign corporation or foreign subsidiary beginning after December 31, 1960, and before January 1, 1963. Such information shall not be required to be furnished, however, with respect to a corporation defined in section 1504(d) of the Code which makes a consolidated return for the taxable year. For annual accounting periods beginning after December 31, 1962, see § 1.6038-2.

(b) *Control.* A domestic corporation shall be deemed to be in control of a foreign corporation if at any time during its taxable year it owns more than 50 percent of the voting stock of such foreign corporation.

(c) *Foreign subsidiary.* A foreign corporation more than 50 percent of the voting stock of which is owned by a controlled foreign corporation at any time during the annual accounting period of such controlled foreign corporation shall be considered a foreign subsidiary.

(d) *Period covered by return*—(1) *Controlled foreign corporation.* The information with respect to a controlled foreign corporation shall be furnished for its annual accounting period ending with or within the domestic corporation's taxable year.

(2) *Foreign subsidiary.* The information with respect to a foreign subsidiary shall be furnished for such subsidiary's annual accounting period ending with or within the controlled foreign corporation's annual accounting period.

(3) *Annual accounting period defined.* For purposes of this section, the annual accounting period of a controlled foreign corporation or of a foreign subsidiary is the annual period on the basis of which the controlled foreign corporation or foreign subsidiary regularly computes its income in keeping its books. The term "annual accounting period" may refer to a period of less than 1 year, where for example the foreign income, war profits, and excess profits taxes are determined on the basis of an accounting period of less than 1 year as described in section 902(c)(2).

(e) *Contents of return.* The return on Form 2952 shall contain the following in-

Reg. § 1.6038-1 (e)

formation with respect to each controlled foreign corporation and each foreign subsidiary:

(1) The name and address of the corporation;

(2) The principal place of business of the corporation;

(3) The date of incorporation and the country under whose laws incorporated;

(4) The nature of the corporation's business;

(5) As regards the outstanding stock of the corporation—

(i) A description of each class of the corporation's stock, and

(ii) The number of shares of each class outstanding at the beginning and the end of the annual accounting period;

(6) A list showing the name and address of, and the number of shares of each class of the corporation's stock held by, each citizen or resident of the United States, and each domestic corporation, who is a shareholder of record owning at any time during the annual accounting period 5 percent or more in value of any class of the corporation's outstanding stock;

(7) The amount of the corporation's gross receipts, net profits before taxes and provision for foreign income taxes, for the annual accounting period, as reflected on the financial statements required under paragraph (f) of this section to be filed with the return; and

(8) A summary showing the total amount of each of the following types of transactions of the corporation, which took place during the annual accounting period, with the domestic corporation or any shareholder of the domestic corporation owning at the time of the transaction 10 percent or more of the value of any class of stock outstanding of the domestic corporation:

(i) Sales and purchases of stock in trade;

(ii) Purchases of property of a character which is subject to the allowance for depreciation;

(iii) Compensation paid and compensation received for the rendition of technical, managerial, engineering, construction, scientific, or like services;

(iv) Commissions paid and commissions received;

(v) Rents and royalties paid and rents and royalties received;

(vi) Amounts loaned and amounts borrowed (other than open accounts which arise and are collected in the ordinary course of business);

(vii) Dividends paid and dividends received;

(viii) Interest paid and interest received; and

(ix) Premiums received for insurance or reinsurance.

If the domestic corporation is a bank, as defined in section 581, or is controlled within the meaning of section 368 (c) by a bank, the term "transactions" shall not, as to a corporation with respect to which a return is filed, include banking transactions entered into on behalf of customers; in any event, however, deposits in accounts between a controlled foreign corporation or a foreign subsidiary and the domestic corporation or a 10-percent shareholder described in this subparagraph and withdrawals from such accounts shall be summarized by reporting end-of-month balances.

(f) *Financial statements.* The following information with respect to each controlled foreign corporation and each foreign subsidiary shall be attached to and filed as part of the return required by this section:

(1) A statement of the corporation's profit and loss for the annual accounting period;

(2) A balance sheet as of the end of the annual accounting period of the corporation showing—

(i) The corporation's assets,

(ii) The corporation's liabilities, and

(iii) The corporation's net worth; and

(3) An analysis of changes in the corporation's surplus accounts during the annual accounting period including both opening and closing balances.

The statements listed in subparagraphs (1), (2), and (3) of this paragraph shall be prepared in conformity with generally accepted accounting principles, and in such form and detail as is customary for the corporation's accounting records.

(g) *Method of reporting.* All amounts furnished under paragraphs (e) and (f) of this section shall be expressed in United States currency with a statement of the exchange rates used.

(h) *Time and place for filing return.* Returns on Form 2952 required under paragraph (a) of this section shall be filed with the domestic corporation's income tax return on or before the fifteenth day of the third month following the close of such corporation's taxable year.

(i) *Extensions of time for filing.* District directors are authorized to grant reasonable extensions of time for filing returns on Form 2952 in accordance with the applicable provisions of § 1.6081-1 of this chapter. An application by a domestic corporation for an extension of time for filing a return of income shall also be considered as an application for an extension of time for filing returns on Form 2952.

(j) *Failure to furnish information*—(1) *Effect on foreign tax credit.* (i) Failure by a domestic corporation to furnish, in accordance with the provisions of this section, any return or any information in any return, required to be filed for a taxable year under authority of section 6038 on or before the date prescribed in paragraph (h) of this section (determined with regard to any extension of time for such filing) shall affect the application of section 902 as provided in subparagraph (2) of this paragraph. Such failure shall affect the application of section 902 to such domestic corporation or to any person who acquires from any person any portion (but only to the extent of such portion) of the interest of such domestic corporation in any controlled foreign corporation or foreign subsidiary.

Reg. § 1.6038-1 (j) (1)

(ii) Where the domestic corporation, having filed the return required by this section except for an omission of, or error with respect to, some of the information referred to in paragraphs (e) and (f) of this section, establishes to the satisfaction of the Commissioner that such omission or error was inadvertent or for reasonable cause and that such domestic corporation has substantially complied with this section, such omission or error shall not constitute a failure under this section.

(2) *Reduction of foreign taxes.* In the application of section 902 to the domestic corporation or person referred to in subdivision (i) of subparagraph (1) of this paragraph for any taxable year, the amount of taxes paid or deemed paid by each controlled foreign corporation and each foreign subsidiary for the accounting period or periods for which the domestic corporation was required for the taxable year of the failure to furnish information under this section shall be reduced by 10 percent. The 10 percent reduction is not limited to the taxes paid or deemed paid by the controlled foreign corporation or foreign subsidiary with respect to which there is a failure to file information but shall apply to the taxes paid or deemed paid by all controlled foreign corporations and foreign subsidiaries.

(3) *Reduction for continued failure.* (i) If the failure, referred to in subdivision (i) of subparagraph (1) of this paragraph, continues for 90 days or more after date of written notice by the district director to the domestic corporation, then the amount of the reduction referred to in subparagraph (2) of this paragraph shall be 10 percent plus an additional 5 percent for each 3-month period, or fraction thereof, during which such failure continues after the expiration of such 90-day period.

(ii) Taxes paid by a foreign subsidiary when once reduced for a failure shall not be reduced again for the same failure in their status as taxes deemed paid by a controlled foreign corporation. Where a failure continues, each additional periodic 5 percent reduction, referred to in subdivision (i) of this subparagraph, shall be considered as part of the one reduction.

(4) *Reasonable cause.* (i) For purposes of subsection (b) of section 6038 and this section the time prescribed for furnishing information under this paragraph, and the beginning of the 90-day period after notice by the district director, shall be treated as being not earlier than the last day on which (as shown to the satisfaction of the district director) reasonable cause existed for failure to furnish such information.

(ii) A domestic corporation, which wishes to avoid a reduction in foreign tax credit as provided in subparagraphs (2) and (3) of this paragraph for failure to furnish information in accordance with this section, must make an affirmative showing of all facts alleged as a reasonable cause for such failure in the form of a written statement containing a declaration that it is made under the penalties of perjury.

(5) *Penalties.* — The information required by section 6038 of the Code must be furnished even though there are no foreign taxes which would be reduced under the provisions of subparagraph (2) of this paragraph. For criminal penalties for failure to file a return and filing a false or fraudulent return, see sections 7203, 7206, and 7207 of the Code.

0— § 301.6038 Statutory provisions; information with respect to certain foreign corporations. [Sec. 6038, IRC]

0— § 301.6038-1 (T.D. 6555, filed 3-14-61; amended by T.D. 6700, filed 1-6-64.) Information returns required of United States persons with respect to certain foreign corporations.

For provisions relating to information returns required of United States persons with respect to certain foreign corporations, see §§ 1.6038-1, 1.6038-2 of this chapter (Income Tax Regulations).

0— § 1.6038-2 (T.D. 6621, filed 11-30-62; amended by T.D. 6969, filed 8-22-68; amended by T.D. 6997, filed 1-17-69.) Information returns required of United States persons with respect to annual accounting periods of certain foreign corporations beginning after December 31, 1962.

(a) *Requirement of return.* Every United States person shall make a separate annual information return on Form 2952 with respect to each annual accounting period (described in paragraph (e) of this section) beginning after December 31, 1962, of each foreign corporation which that person controls (as defined in paragraph (b) of this section) for an uninterrupted period of 30 days or more during such annual accounting period. Such information shall not be required to be furnished, however, with respect to a corporation defined in section 1504(d) of the Code which makes a consolidated return for the taxable year.

(b) *Control.* A person shall be deemed to be in control of a foreign corporation if at any time during that person's taxable year it owns stock possessing more than 50 percent of the total combined voting power of all classes of stock entitled to vote, or more than 50 percent of the total value of shares of all classes of stock of the foreign corporation. A person in control of a corporation which, in turn, owns more than 50 percent of the combined voting power, or of the value, of all classes of stock of another corporation is also treated as being in control of such other corporation. The provisions of this paragraph may be illustrated by the following example:

Example. Corporation A owns 51 percent of the voting stock in Corporation B. Corporation B owns 51 percent of the voting stock in Corporation C. Corporation C in turn owns 51 percent of the voting stock in Corporation D. Corporation D is controlled by Corporation A.

(c) *Attribution rules.* For the purpose of determining control of domestic or foreign corporations the constructive ownership rules of section 318(a) shall apply, except that:

(1) Stock owned by or for a partner or a beneficiary of an estate or trust shall not be considered owned by the partnership, estate, or trust when the effect is to consider a United States person as owning stock owned by a person who is not a United States person;

(2) A corporation will not be considered as owning stock owned by or for a 50 percent or more shareholder when the effect is to consider a United States person as owning stock owned by a person who is not a United States person; and

(3) If 10 percent or more in value of the stock in a corporation is owned, directly or indirectly, by or for any person, section 318(a)(2)(C) shall apply.

The constructive ownership rules of section 318(a) apply only for purposes of determining control as defined in paragraph (b) of this section.

(d) *United States person.* For purposes of section 6038 and this section, the term "United States person" has the meaning assigned to it by section 7701(a)(30) of the Code, except that—

(1) With respect to a corporation organized under the laws of the Commonwealth of Puerto Rico, such term does not include an individual who is a bona fide resident of Puerto Rico, if a dividend received by such individual during the taxable year from such corporation would, for purposes of section 933(1), be treated as income derived from sources within Puerto Rico,

(2) With respect to a corporation organized under the laws of the Virgin Islands, such term does not include as individual who is a bona fide resident of the Virgin Islands and whose income tax obligation under subtitle A (relating to income taxes) of the Code for the taxable year is satisfied pursuant to section 28(a) of the Revised Organic Act of the Virgin Islands, approved July 22, 1954 (48 U.S.C. 1642), by paying tax on income derived from all sources both within and outside the Virgin Islands into the treasury of the Virgin Islands, and

(3) With respect to a corporation organized under the laws of any possession of the United States (other than Puerto Rico or the Virgin Islands), such term does not include an individual who is a bona fide resident of such possession and whose income derived from sources within any possession of the United States is not, by reason of section 931(a), includible in gross income under subtitle A (relating to income taxes) of the Code for the taxable year.

The provisions of paragraph (b), (c), or (d), respectively, of § 1.957-4 shall apply for purposes of determining whether an individual is excepted under subparagraph (1), (2), or (3), respectively, of this paragraph from being a United States person with respect to a corporation described in such subparagraph.

(e) *Period covered by return.* The information required under paragraphs (f) and (g) of this section with respect to a foreign corporation shall be furnished for the annual accounting period of the foreign corporation ending with or within the United States person's taxable year. For purposes of this section, the annual accounting period of a foreign corporation is the annual period on the basis of which that corporation regularly computes its income in keeping its books. The term "annual accounting period" may refer to a period of less than one year, where, for example, the foreign income, war profits, and excess profits taxes are determined on the basis of an accounting period of less than one year as described in section 902(c)(2). If more than one annual accounting period ends with or within the United States person's taxable year, separate annual information returns shall be submitted for each annual accounting period.

(f) *Contents of return.* The return on Form 2952 shall contain the following information with respect to each foreign corporation:

(1) The name, address, and employer identification number, if any, of the corporation;

(2) The principal place of business of the corporation;

(3) The date of incorporation and the country under whose laws incorporated;

(4) The name and address of the foreign corporation's statutory or resident agent in the country of incorporation;

(5) The name, address, and identifying number of any branch office or agent of the foreign corporation located in the United States;

(6) The name and address of the person (or persons) having custody of the books of account and records of the foreign corporation, and the location of such books and records if different from such address;

(7) The nature of the corporation's business and the principal places where conducted;

(8) As regards the outstanding stock of the corporation—

(i) A description of each class of the corporation's stock, and

(ii) The number of shares of each class outstanding at the beginning and end of the annual accounting period;

(9) A list showing the name, address, and identifying number of, and the number of shares of each class of the corporation's stock held by, each United States person who is a shareholder owning at any time during the annual accounting period 5 percent or more in value of any class of the corporation's outstanding stock;

(10) For the annual accounting period, the amount of the corporation's:

(i) Current earnings and profits;

(ii) Foreign income, war profits, and excess profits taxes paid or accrued;

(iii) Distributions out of current earnings and profits for the period;

(iv) Distributions other than those described in subdivision (iii) of this subparagraph and the source thereof:

(11) A summary showing the total amount of each of the following types of transactions of the corporation, which took

24,292.2 (I.R.C.) Reg. § 1.6038-2(f)(11) 1-27-69

place during the annual accounting period, with the person required to file this return, any other corporation controlled by that person, or any United States person owning at the time of the transaction 10 percent or more in value of any class of stock outstanding of the foreign corporation, or of any corporation controlling that foreign corporation:

(i) Sales and purchases of stock in trade, except in the ordinary course of business where neither party to the transaction is a United States person;

(ii) Purchases of tangible property other than stock in trade, except where neither party to the transaction is a United States person;

(iii) Sales and purchases of patents, inventions, models, or designs (whether or not patented), copyrights, trademarks, secret formulas or processes, or any other similar property rights;

(iv) Compensation paid and compensation received for the rendition of technical, managerial, engineering, construction, scientific, or like services;

(v) Commissions paid and commissions received;

(vi) Rents and royalties paid and rents and royalties received;

(vii) Amounts loaned and amounts borrowed (other than open accounts which arise and are collected in the ordinary course of business);

(viii) Dividends paid and dividends received;

(ix) Interest paid and interest received;

(x) Premiums received for insurance or reinsurance.

If the United States person is a bank, as defined in section 581, or is controlled within the meaning of section 368(c) by a bank, the term "transactions" shall not, as to a corporation with respect to which a return is filed, include banking transactions entered into on behalf of customers; in any event, however, deposits in accounts between a foreign corporation, controlled (within the meaning of paragraph (b) of this section) by a United States person, and a person described in this subparagraph and withdrawals from such accounts shall be summarized by reporting end-of-month balances.

(g) *Financial statements.* The following information with respect to the foreign corporation shall be attached to and filed as part of the return required by this section:

(1) A statement of the corporation's profit and loss for the annual accounting period;

(2) A balance sheet as of the end of the annual accounting period of the corporation showing—

(i) The corporation's assets,

(ii) The corporation's liabilities,

(iii) The corporation's net worth;

(3) An analysis of changes in the corporation's surplus accounts during the annual accounting period including both opening and closing balances.

The statements listed in subparagraphs (1), (2), and (3) of this paragraph shall be prepared in conformity with generally accepted accounting principles, and in such form and detail as is customary for the corporation's accounting records.

(h) *Method of reporting.* All amounts furnished under paragraphs (f) and (g) of this section shall be expressed in United States currency with a statement of the exchange rates used. All statements submitted on or with the return required under this section shall be rendered in the English language.

(i) *Time and place for filing return.* Returns on Form 2952 required under paragraph (a) of this section shall be filed with the United States person's income tax return on or before the date required by law for the filing of that person's income tax return.

(j) *Extension of time for filing.* District directors are authorized to grant reasonable extensions of time for filing returns on Form 2952 in accordance with the applicable provisions of § 1.6081-1 of this chapter. An application for an extension of time for filing a return of income shall also be considered as an application for an extension of time for filing returns on Form 2952.

(k) *Two or more persons required to submit the same information*—(1) *Return jointly made.* If two or more persons are required to furnish information with respect to the same foreign corporation for the same period, such persons may, in lieu of making separate returns, jointly make one return. Such joint return shall be filed with the income tax return of any one of the persons making such joint return.

(2) *Persons excepted from furnishing information.* Any person required to furnish information under this section with respect to a foreign corporation need not furnish that information provided all of the following conditions are met:

(i) Such person does not directly own an interest in the foreign corporation;

(ii) Such person is required to furnish the information solely by reason of attribution of stock ownership from a United States person under paragraph (c) of this section;

(iii) The person from whom the stock ownership is attributed furnishes all of the information required under this section of the person to whom the stock ownership is attributed.

The rule of this subparagraph may be illustrated by the following examples:

Example (1). A, a United States person, owns 100 percent of the stock of M, a domestic corporation. A also owns 100 percent of the stock of N, a foreign corporation organized under the laws of foreign country Y. A, in filing the information return required by this section with respect to N Corporation, in fact furnishes all of the information required of M Corporation with respect to N Corporation. M Corporation need not file the information.

Example (2). X, a domestic corporation, owns 100 percent of the stock of Y, a domestic corporation. Y Corporation owns 100 percent of the stock of Z, a foreign corporation. X Corporation is not excused by this subparagraph from filing information with respect to Z Corporation because X Corporation is deemed to control Z Corporation under the provisions of paragraph (b) of this section without recourse to the attribution rules in paragraph (c).

(3) *Statement required.* Any United States person required to furnish information under this section with his return who does not do so by reason of the provisions of subparagraph (1) or (2) of this paragraph shall file a statement with his return indicating that such liability has been (or, in the case of a joint return made under subparagraph (1) of this paragraph, will be) satisfied and identifying the return with which the information was or will be filed and the place of filing.

(l) *Failure to furnish information*—(1) *Effect on foreign tax credit.* (i) Failure of a United States person to furnish, in accordance with the provisions of this section, any return or any information in any return, required to be filed for a taxable year under authority of section 6038 on or before the date prescribed in paragraph (i) of this section (determined with regard to any extension of time for such filing) shall affect the application of section 901 as provided in subparagraph (2) of this paragraph and shall affect the application of sections 902 and 960 as provided in subparagraph (3) of this paragraph. Such failure shall affect the application of sections 902 and 960 to any such United States person which is a corporation or to any person who acquires from any other person any portion (but only to the extent of such portion) of the interest of such other person in any such foreign corporation.

(ii) Where a United States person, fails to file a return, or having filed the return required by this section except for an omission of, or error with respect to, some of the information referred to in paragraphs (f) and (g) of this section, establishes to the satisfaction of the Commissioner that such failure, omission or error was inadvertent or for reasonable cause and that such person has substantially complied with this section, such omission or error shall not constitute a failure under this section.

(2) *Application of section 901.* In the application of section 901 to a United States person referred to in subdivision (i) of subparagraph (1) of this paragraph, the amount of taxes paid or deemed paid by such person for any taxable year, with or within which the annual accounting period of a foreign corporation for which such person failed to furnish information required under this section ended, shall be reduced by 10 percent. However, no tax reduced under subparagraph (3) of this paragraph or deemed paid under section 904 (d) shall be reduced under the provisions of this subparagraph.

(3) *Application of sections 902 and 960.* In the application of sections 902 and 960 to a United States person referred to in subdivision (i) of subparagraph (1) of this paragraph for any taxable year, the amount of taxes paid or deemed paid by each foreign corporation for the accounting period or periods for which such person was required for the taxable year of the failure to furnish information under this section shall be reduced by 10 percent. The 10-percent reduction is not limited to the taxes paid or deemed paid by the foreign corporation with respect to which there is a failure to file information but shall apply to the taxes paid or deemed paid by all foreign corporations controlled by that person. In applying subsections (a) and (b) of section 902, and in applying subsection (a) of section 960, the reduction provided by this paragraph shall not apply for purposes of determining the amount of accumulated profits in excess of income, war profits, and excess profits taxes.

(4) *Reduction for continued failure.* (i) If the failure referred to in subdivision (i) of subparagraph (1) of this paragraph continues for 90 days or more after date of written notice by the district director to such United States person, then the amount of the reduction referred to in subparagraphs (2) and (3) of this paragraph shall be 10 percent plus an additional 5 percent for each 3-month period, or fraction thereof, during which such failure continues after the expiration of such 90-day period.

(ii) No taxes shall be reduced under this paragraph more than once for the same failure. Taxes paid by a foreign corporation when once reduced for a failure shall not be reduced again for the same failure in their status as taxes deemed paid by a corporate shareholder. Where a failure continues, each additional periodic 5-percent reduction, referred to in subdivision (i) of this subparagraph, shall be considered as part of the one reduction.

(iii) The effects of section 6038(b) and of this paragraph on the computation of foreign tax credit under section 902(a) of the Code and, where applicable, on the computation of the amount equal to taxes deemed paid which is includible in gross income under section 78 of the Code, may be illustrated by the following examples:

Example (1). M, a domestic corporation, owns 100 percent of the stock of N, a foreign corporation which is a less developed country corporation within the meaning of section 902(d) of the Code. Both M and N use the calendar year as a taxable year and all of the following events occur after January 1, 1965. The dividend from N Corporation is the only dividend from a foreign corporation received by M Corporation during the taxable year.

(a) Gains, profits, and income of N Corporation. $100,000

(b) Foreign tax paid with respect to such gains, profits, and income by N Corporation. 40,000

(c) Reduction of foreign tax paid by N Corporation resulting from M Corporation's failure to file information with respect to N Corporation as required under section 6038(a): 90-day failure to file, 10-percent reduction; additional 3 months failure to file, 5-percent reduction; total reduction, 15 percent. ($40,000 times 15 percent) 6,000

(d) Foreign tax paid by N Corporation after section 6038(b)(1)(B) reduction. 34,000

(e) Dividend paid by N Corporation to M Corporation. 45,000

(f) Accumulated profits of N Corporation as defined in section 902(c)(1)(B) (determined without regard to the section 6038(a)(1)(B) reduction). 60,000

(g) M Corporation is deemed to have paid the same proportion of foreign taxes paid (reduced as provided under section 6038(b)) on or with respect to the accumulated profits (determined without regard to the reduction provided under section 6038(b)) as the amount of dividends bears to the amount of such accumulated profits. .... $ 15,300

$$\frac{60,000}{100,000} \times \frac{45,000}{60,000} \times 34,000$$

The above example illustrates that the reduction in foreign taxes paid by the foreign corporation provided under section 6038(b) and this paragraph are not taken into account in computing accumulated profits for purposes of determining the amount of foreign taxes deemed paid with respect to a particular dividend.

Example (2). The facts are the same as in example (1) except that N Corporation is not a less developed country corporation within the meaning of section 902(d) of the Code.

(a) Gains, profits, and income of N Corporation. $100,000

(b) Foreign tax paid by N Corporation with respect to such gains, profits, and income. 40,000

Reg. § 1.6038-2(l)(4)

24,294 (I.R.C.) Reg. § 1.6038-2(l)(4)

(c) Reduction of foreign tax paid by N Corporation resulting from M Corporation's failure to file information with respect to N Corporation as required under section 6038(a): 90-day failure to file, 10-percent reduction; additional 3 months failure to file, 5-percent reduction; total reduction, 15 percent. ($40,000 times 15 percent). .... $ 6,000

(d) Foreign tax paid by N Corporation after section 6038(b)(1)(B) reduction. 34,000

(e) Dividend paid by N Corporation to M Corporation. 45,000

(f) Accumulated profits of N Corporation as defined in section 902(c)(1)(A) (determined without regard to the section 6038(b)(1)(B) reduction). 100,000

(g) Accumulated profits of N Corporation as described in section 902(a)(1) (determined without regard to the section 6038(b)(1)(B) reduction). 60,000

(h) M Corporation is deemed to have paid the same proportion of foreign taxes paid (reduced as provided under section 6038(b)) with respect to the accumulated profits (determined without regard to the reduction provided under section 6038(b)) as the amount of the dividend (determined without regard to section 78) bears to such amount of accumulated profits. .... $ 25,500

$$\frac{45,000}{60,000} \times 34,000$$

M Corporation must include $25,500 in gross income as a dividend under the provisions of section 78 of the Code. The above example illustrates that the reductions in foreign taxes paid by the foreign corporation provided under section 6038(b) are taken into account in determining the amount included in gross income of the domestic corporation as foreign taxes deemed paid under section 78 of the Code but such reductions are not taken into account in computing accumulated profits for purposes of determining the amount of foreign taxes deemed paid with respect to a particular dividend.

(5) *Limitation on reduction.* The amount of the reduction under this paragraph for each failure to furnish information with respect to a foreign corporation as required under this section shall not exceed the greater of:

(i) $10,000, or

(ii) The income of the foreign corporation for its annual accounting period with respect to which the failure occurs. For purposes of this section if a person is required to furnish information with respect to more than one foreign corporation, controlled (within the meeting of paragraph (b) of this section) by that person, each failure to submit information for each such corporation constitutes a separate failure.

(6) *Reasonable cause.* For purposes of subsection (b) of section 6038 and this section, the time prescribed for furnishing information under this paragraph, and the beginning of the 90-day period after notice by the district director, shall be treated as being not earlier than the last day on which (as shown to the satisfaction of the district director) reasonable cause existed for failure to furnish such information.

(7) A person, who wishes to avoid the reductions provided in subparagraphs (2), (3), and (4) of this paragraph for failure to furnish information in accordance with this section, must make an affirmative showing under subparagraph (1)(ii) or (6) of this paragraph of all facts alleged as a reasonable cause for such failure in the form of a written statement containing a declaration that it is made under the penalties of perjury.

(8) *Penalties.* The information required by section 6038 of the Code must be furnished even though there are no foreign taxes which would be reduced under the provisions of this section. For criminal penalties for failure to file a return and filing a false or fraudulent return, see sections 7203, 7206, and 7207 of the Code.

§ 1.6039 Statutory provisions; returns required in connection with certain stock options. [Sec. 6039, IRC]

§ 1.6039-1 (T.D. 6887, filed 6-23-66.) **Information returns required of corporations with respect to certain stock option transactions occurring on or after January 1, 1964.**

(a) *Requirement of return under section 6039(a)(1).* Every corporation which transfers stock to any person pursuant to such person's exercise on or after January 1, 1964, of a qualified stock option described in section 422(b), or a restricted stock option described in section 424(b), shall make, for each calendar year in which such a transfer occurs, an information return on Form 3921 with respect to each transfer made during such year. The return shall include the following information:

(1) The name, address and employer identification number of the corporation transferring the stock;

(2) The name, address and identifying number of the person to whom the share or shares of stock were transferred;

(3) The name and address of the corporation the stock of which is the subject of the option (if other than the corporation transferring the stock);

(4) The date the option was granted;

(5) The date the shares were transferred to the person exercising the option;

(6) The fair market value of the stock at the time the option was exercised;

(7) The number of shares of stock transferred pursuant to the option;

(8) The type of option under which the transferred shares were acquired; and

(9) Such other information as may be required by the return or by the instructions issued with respect thereto.

(b) *Requirement of return under section 6039(a)(2).* (1) Every corporation which records, or has by its agent recorded, a transfer of the title to stock acquired by the transferor pursuant to his exercise on or after January 1, 1964, of—

(i) An option granted under an employee stock purchase plan which meets the requirements of section 423(b), and with respect to which the special rule of section 423(c) applied, or

(ii) A restricted stock option which meets the requirements of section 424(b), and with respect to which the special rule of section 424(c)(1) applies, shall make, for each calendar year in which such a recorded transfer of title to such stock occurs, an information return on Form 3922 with respect to each transfer containing the information required by subparagraph (2) of this paragraph.

(2) The return required by subparagraph (1) of this paragraph shall contain the following information:

(i) The name and address of the corporation whose stock is being transferred;

(ii) The name, address, and identifying number of the transferor;

(iii) The date such stock was transferred to the transferor;

(iv) The number of shares to which title is being transferred; and

(v) The type of option under which the transferred shares were acquired.

(3) If the return required by this paragraph is made by the authorized "transfer agent" of the corporation, it shall be deemed to have been made by the corporation. The term "transfer agent", as used in this paragraph, means any designee authorized to keep the stock ownership records of a corporation and to record a transfer of title of the stock of such corporation on behalf of such corporation.

(4) Where a corporation is required by this paragraph to make an information return for the calendar year, such return will only have to supply information relating to the first recorded transfer of title to the share or shares of stock. Thus, for example, if the owner has record title to a share or shares of stock transferred to a recognized broker or financial institution and the stock is subsequently sold by such broker or institution (on behalf of the owner) the corporation is only required to report information relating to the transfer of record title to the broker or financial institution. Similarly, a return is required when a share of stock is transferred by the optionee to himself and another person (or persons) as joint tenants, tenants by the entireties or tenants in common. However, when stock is originally issued to the optionee and another person (or persons) as joint tenants, or as tenants by the entirety, and a stock certificate was not previously actually issued to the optionee as a sole owner, the return required by this paragraph shall be made (at such time and in such manner as is provided by this section with respect to a transfer by the optionee) in respect of the first transfer of the title to such stock by the optionee.

(5) Every corporation which transfers any share of stock pursuant to the exercise of an option described in this paragraph shall identify such stock in a manner sufficient to enable the accurate reporting of the transfer of record title to such shares. Such identification may be accomplished by assigning to the certificates of stock issued pursuant to the exercise of such options a special serial number, or color.

(c) *Time, place and manner of filing.* (1) The returns on Forms 3921 and 3922 required by section 6039(a)(1) and (2) and paragraphs (a) and (b) of this section shall be filed as attachments to a summary report on Form 4067 which must be signed by the person required to file the returns or its duly authorized agent. With respect to returns on Form 3921, the summary report on Form 4067 shall indicate the number of returns filed, the number of shares transferred pursuant to exercise of options, the dates on which the options exercised were offered or granted, the fair market value of shares subject to option on such dates, the method by which such value was determined, the type of options under which the transferred shares were acquired, and such other information as may be required by the form or by the instructions issued with respect thereto. With respect to returns on Form 3922, the summary report on Form 4067 shall indicate the number of returns filed, the number of shares transferred, the type of options under which the transferred shares were acquired and such other information as may be required by the form or by the instructions issued with respect thereto. The summary report on Form 4067 and the attached returns on Forms 3921 and 3922 required for any calendar year shall be filed on or before February 28 of the following year with any of the Internal Revenue Service Centers.

(2) If a return is made by the authorized "transfer agent" of the corporation, as described in paragraph (b)(3) of this section, it shall be filed with the district director for the district where the income tax return of the principal corporation is filed after the close of the calendar year for which the return is required, but on or before February 28th of the following calendar year.

(3) For provisions relating to the extension of time for filing the returns required by this section, see § 1.6081-1.

(4) For provisions relating to the time for performance of an act when the last day prescribed for performance falls on Saturday, Sunday, or a legal holiday, see § 301.7503-1 of this chapter (Regulations on Procedure and Administration).

(d) *Stock to which this section applies.* The rules of this section shall apply to any full share of stock acquired pursuant to the exercise of any qualified or restricted stock option, or any option granted under an employee stock purchase plan, irrespective of whether the transfer of stock pursuant to such exercise qualified for the special tax treatment of section 421 and the regulations thereunder. In addition, the rules of paragraph (b) of this section shall apply to any full shares of stock received in respect of stock which was originally acquired pursuant to the exercise of an option described in the preceding sentence. See section 425(b). For definitions of the terms "exercise" and "transfer" see para-

Reg. § 1.6039-1(d)

24,296 (I.R.C.)   Reg. § 1.6039-1(d)   8-20-73

graphs (f) and (g) of § 1.421-7. A return is required under paragraph (b) of this section irrespective of whether the transfer of title constitutes a disposition of such stock as defined by section 425(c).

0→ § 1.6039-2 (T.D. 6887, filed 6-23-66.) **Statements to persons with respect to whom information is furnished.**

(a) *Requirement and form of statement.* Every corporation required to make a return on Form 3921 or 3922 under section 6039(a) and § 1.6039-1 shall furnish to each person whose identifying number is (or should be) shown on such return a written statement containing the information required to be shown on such return. This requirement may be met by furnishing a copy of the appropriate return to such person. A statement shall be considered to be furnished to a person within the meaning of this section if it is mailed to such person at his last known address.

(b) *Time for furnishing statements*—(1) *In general.* Each statement required by this section to be furnished to any person for a calendar year shall be furnished to such person on or before January 31 of the year following the year for which the statement is required.

(2) *Extension of time.* For good cause shown upon written application of the corporation required to furnish statements under this section, the district director may grant an extension of time not exceeding 30 days in which to furnish such statements. The application shall be addressed to the district director with whom the income tax returns of the applicant-corporation are filed and shall contain a full recital of the reasons for requesting the extension to aid the district director in determining the period of the extension, if any, which will be granted. Such a request in the form of a letter to the district director signed by the applicant (or its agent) will suffice as an application. The application shall be filed on or before the date prescribed in subparagraph (1) of this paragraph for furnishing the statements required by this section.

(3) *Last day for furnishing statement.* For provisions relating to the time for performance of an act when the last day prescribed for performance falls on Saturday, Sunday, or a legal holiday, see § 301.7503-1 of this chapter (Regulations on Procedure and Administration).

(c) *Penalty.* For provisions relating to the penalty provided for failure to furnish a statement under this section, see § 301.-6678-1 of this chapter (Regulations on Procedure and Administration).

0→ § 301.6039 Statutory provisions; information required in connection with certain options. [Sec. 6039, IRC]

0→ § 301.6039-1 (T.D. 7275, filed 5-4-73.) **Information returns and statements required in connection with certain options.**

For provisions relating to information returns and statements required in connection with certain options, see §§ 1.6039-1 and 1.6039-2 of this chapter (Income Tax Regulations).

0→ § 301.6040 Statutory provisions; Cross references. [Sec. 6040, IRC]

0→ § 1.6041 Statutory provisions; information at source. [Sec. 6041, IRC]

0→ § 1.6041-1 (T.D. 6364, filed 2-13-59; republished in T.D. 6500, filed 11-25-60; amended by T.D. 6628, filed 12-27-62; T.D. 6677, filed 9-16-63; T.D. 6888, filed 7-5-66 and T.D. 7284, filed 8-2-73.) **Return of information as to payments of $600 or more.**

(a) *General rule.* (1) Except as provided in § 1.6041-3, every person engaged in a trade or business shall make an information return for each calendar year with respect to payments made by him during the calendar year in the course of his trade or business to another person of fixed or determinable—

(i) Salaries, wages, commissions, fees, and other forms of compensation for services rendered aggregating $600 or more;

(ii) Interest, rents, royalties, annuities, pensions, and other gains, profits, and income aggregating $600 or more; or

(iii) Foreign items, as defined in § 1.-6041, aggregating $600 or more.

The payments described in subdivisions (i), (ii), and (iii) of this subparagraph shall not include any payments with respect to which a statement is required by, or may be required under authority of, section 6042(a) (relating to dividends), section 6043(a)(2) (relating to distributions in liquidation) section 6044(a) (relating to patronage dividends), section 6045 (relating to brokers' transactions with customers), or section 6049(a)(1) and (2) (relating to interest). Thus, the term "interest", as used in subdivision (ii) of this subparagraph, includes all interest other than that coming within the definition of interest provided in § 1.6049-2. For example, a closely held corporation borrows money from one of its officers on a promissory note not in registered form the yearly interest on which is $300. It also pays royalties to such officer amounting to $400 a year. An information return is required under subdivision (ii) of this subparagraph with respect to the payments to such officer since the interest does not come within the definition of interest provided in § 1.6049-2 and the aggregate of the interest and royalty payments is in excess of $600.

(2) *Prescribed form.* The return required by subparagraph (1) of this paragraph shall be made on Forms 1096 and 1099 except that (i) the return with respect to distributions to beneficiaries of a trust or of an estate shall be made on Form 1041, and (ii) the return with respect to certain payments of compensation to an employee by his employer shall be made on Forms W-3 and W-2 under the provisions of § 1.-6041-2 (relating to return of information as to payments to employees). See, however, § 1.6041-2(a)(2) for special election applicable to the reporting of commissions paid to full-time life insurance salesmen. Where Form 1099 is required to be filed under this section, a separate Form 1099 shall be furnished for each person to whom payments described in subdivision (i), (ii), or (iii) of subparagraph (1) of this paragraph are made. For time and place for filing Forms 1096 and 1099, see § 1.6041-6.

(b) *Persons engaged in trade or business.* The term "all persons engaged in a trade or business", as used in section

6041(a), includes not only those so engaged for gain or profit, but also organizations the activities of which are not for the purpose of gain or profit. Thus, the term includes the organizations referred to in sections 401(a), 501(c), 501(d) and 521 and in paragraph (g) of this section. On the other hand, section 6041(a) applies only to payments in the course of trade or business; hence it does not apply to an amount paid by the proprietor of a business to a physician for medical services rendered by the physician to the proprietor's child.

(c) *Fixed or determinable income.* Income is fixed when it is to be paid in amounts definitely predetermined. Income is determinable whenever there is a basic of calculation by which the amount to be paid may be ascertained. The income need not be paid annually or at regular intervals. The fact that the payments may be increased or decreased in accordance with the happening of an event does not for purposes of this section make the payments any the less determinable. A salesman working by the month for a commission on sales which is paid or credited monthly receives determinable income.

(d) *Payments specifically included.* (1) Sums paid in respect of life insurance, endowment, or annuity contracts are required to be reported in returns of information under this section—

(i) Unless the payment is made in respect of a life insurance or endowment contract by reason of the death of the insured and is not required to be reported by paragraph (b) of § 1.6041-2,

(ii) Unless the payment is made by reason of the surrender prior to maturity or lapse of a policy, other than a policy which was purchased (a) by a trust described in section 401(a) which is exempt from tax under section 501(a), (b) as part of a plan described in section 403(a), or (c) by an employer described in section 403(b)(1)(A),

(iii) Unless the payment is interest as defined in § 1.6049-2 and is made after December 31, 1962,

(iv) Unless the payment is a payment with respect to which a return is required by § 1.6047-1, relating to employee retirement plans covering owner-employees,

(v) Unless the payment is with respect to which a return is required by § 1.6052-1, relating to payment of wages in the form of group-term life insurance.

(2) Fees for professional services paid to attorneys, physicians, and members of other professions are required to be reported in returns of information if paid by persons engaged in a trade or business and paid in the course of such trade or business.

(3) Amounts paid as prizes and awards which are required to be included in gross income under section 74 and § 1.74-1 when paid in the course of a trade or business shall be reported in returns of information.

(e) *Payment made in medium other than cash.* If any payment required to be reported on Form 1099 is made in property other than money, the fair market value of the property at the time of payment is the amount to be included on such form.

(f) *When payment deemed made.* For purposes of a return of information, an amount is deemed to have been paid when it is credited or set apart to a person without any substantial limitation or restriction as to the time or manner of payment or condition upon which payment is to be made, and is made available to him so that it may be drawn at any time, and its receipt brought within his own control and disposition.

(g) *Payments made by United States or a State.* Information returns on—

(1) Forms 1096 and 1099 and

(2) Forms W-3 and W-2 (when made under the provisions of § 1.6041-2) of payments made by the United States or a State, or political subdivision thereof, or the District of Columbia, or any agency or instrumentality of any one or more of the foregoing, shall be made by the officer or employee of the United States, or of such State, or political subdivision, or of the District of Columbia, or of such agency or instrumentality, as the case may be, having control of such payments or by the officer or employee appropriately designated to make such returns.

O—— § 1.6041-2 (T.D. 6364, filed 2-13-59; republished in T.D. 6500, filed 11-25-60; amended by T.D. 6677, filed 9-16-63; T.D. 6972, filed 9-11-68; T.D. 7068, filed 11-10-70 and T.D. 7284, filed 8-2-73.) **Return of information as to payments to employees.**

(a)(1) *In general.* Wages, as defined in section 3401, paid to an employee are required to be reported on Form W-2. See section 6011 and the Employment Tax Regulations thereunder. Except as otherwise provided in subparagraph (2) of this paragraph, all other payments of compensation, including the cash value of payments made in any medium other than cash, to an employee by his employer in the course of the trade or business of the employer must also be reported on Form W-2 if the total of such payments and the amount of the employee's wages (as defined in section 3401), if any, required to be reported on Form W-2 aggregates $600 or more in a calendar year. For example, if a payment of $700 was made to an employee and $400 thereof represents wages subject to withholding under section 3402 and the remaining $300 represents compensation not subject to withholding, such wages and compensation must both be reported on Form W-2. A separate Form W-2 shall be furnished for each employee for whom a return must be made. At the election of the employer, components of amounts required to be reported on Form W-2 pursuant to the provisions of this subparagraph may be reported on more than one Form W-2.

(2) *Certain payments by a life insurance company.* All payments of commissions by a life insurance company to its full-time life insurance salesmen (within the meaning of section 3121(d)(3)(B)) may, at the election of the payer, be reported on Forms 1096 and 1099 rather than on Forms W-3 and W-2. A separate Form 1099 shall be furnished for each employee for whom a return must be made. For contents and time and place for filing Forms 1096 and 1099, see § 1.6041-6.

(3) *Transmittal form.* The transmittal form for a return on Form W-2 made pursuant to the provisions of subparagraph (1) of this paragraph shall be Form W-3. In a case where an employer must file a Form W-3 under this paragraph and also under § 31.6011(a)-4 or § 31.6011(a)-5 of this

Reg. § 1.6041-2(a)(3)

chapter (Employment Tax Regulations), the Form W-3 filed under such § 31.6011(a)-4 or § 31.6011(a)-5 shall also be used as the transmittal form for a return on Form W-2 made pursuant to the provisions of this paragraph.

(4) *Time for filing*—(i) *General rule.* In a case where an employer must file Forms W-3 and W-2 under this paragraph and also under § 31.6011(a)-4 or § 31.6011(a)-5 of this chapter (Employment Tax Regulations), the time for filing such forms under this paragraph shall be the same as the time (including extensions thereof) for filing such forms under § 31.6011(a)-4 or § 31.6011(a)-5.

(ii) *Exception.* In a case where an employer is not required to file Forms W-3 and W-2 under § 31.6011(a)-4 or § 31.6011(a)-5 of this chapter (Employment Tax Regulations), returns on Forms W-3 and W-2 required under this paragraph for any calendar year shall be filed on or before February 28 of the following year.

(iii) *Cross reference.* For extensions of time for filing returns, see section 6081 and the regulations thereunder.

(5) *Place for filing.* The returns on Forms W-3 and W-2 required under this paragraph shall be filed pursuant to the rules contained in § 31.6091-1 of this chapter (Employment Tax Regulations), relating to the place for filing certain returns.

(b) *Distributions under employees' trust or plan.* (1) Amounts which are—

(i) Distributed or made available to a beneficiary, and to which section 402 (relating to employees' trusts) or section 403 (relating to employee annuity plans) applies, or

(ii) Described in section 72(m)(3)(B), shall be reported on Forms 1096 and 1099 to the extent such amounts are includible in the gross income of such beneficiary if the amounts so includible aggregate $600 or more in any calendar year. In addition, every trust described in section 501(c)(17) which makes one or more payments (including separation and sick and accident benefits) totaling $600 or more in 1 year to an individual must file an annual information return on Form 1096, accompanied by a statement on Form 1099, for each such individual. Payments made by an employer or a person other than the trustee of the trust should not be considered in determining whether the $600 minimum has been paid by the trustee. The provisions of this subparagraph shall not be applicable to payments of supplemental unemployment compensation benefits made after December 31, 1970, which are treated as if they were wages for purposes of section 3401(a). Such amounts are required to be reported on Forms W-3 and W-2. See paragraph (b)(14) of § 31.3401(a)-1 of this chapter (Employment Tax Regulations).

(2) Any amount with respect to which a statement is required by § 1.6047-1, relating to employee retirement plans covering owner-employees, shall not be included in amounts required to be reported under section 6041.

(c) *Special rule for calendar years before 1972.* For calendar years before 1972, the provisions of this section will be deemed to have been complied with if the returns for such years were filed in accordance with the provisions of this section in effect prior to August 3, 1973 or with the instructions applicable to the appropriate forms.

§ 1.6041-3 (T.D. 6364, filed 2-13-59; republished in T.D. 6500, filed 11-25-60; amended by T.D. 6628, filed 12-27-62; T.D. 6966, filed 8-7-68; T.D. 7000, filed 1-17-69; T.D. 7119, filed 6-1-71 and T.D. 7284, filed 8-2-73.) **Payments for which no return of information is required under section 6041.**

Returns of information are not required under section 6041 and §§ 1.6041-1 and 1.6041-2 with respect to payments of the following character—

(a) Payments of income required to be reported on Forms 1042, 1042S, 1000, 1001 (including all special variations thereof), 1120-S, 941, W-3, and W-2 (however, see § 1.6041-2 with respect to Forms W-3 and W-2);

(b) Payments by a broker to his customer (but for reporting requirements as to certain of such payments made after December 31, 1962, see sections 6042 and 6049 and the regulations thereunder in this part);

(c) Payments to a corporation, except payments made after December 31, 1970, to a corporation engaged in providing medical and health care services or engaged in the billing and collecting of payments in respect to the providing of medical and health care services, other than payments to—

(1) A hospital or extended care facility described in section 501(c)(3) which is exempt from taxation under section 501(a) or

(2) A hospital or extended care facility owned and operated by the United States, a State, the District of Columbia, a possession of the United States, or a political subdivision, agency or instrumentality of any of the foregoing.

For reporting requirements as to payments by cooperatives, and to certain other payments, see sections 6042, 6044, and 6049 and the regulations thereunder in this part;

(d) Payments of bills for merchandise, telegrams, telephone, freight, storage, and similar charges;

(e) Payments of rent made to real estate agents (but the agent is subject to the requirements of paragraph (a)(1)(ii) and (2)(ii) of § 1.6041-1);

(f) Payments representing earned income for services rendered without the United States made to a citizen of the United States, if it is reasonable to believe that such amounts will be excluded from gross income under the provisions of section 911 and the regulations thereunder;

(g) Salaries and profits paid or distributed by a partnership to the individual partners;

(h) Payments of commissions to general agents by fire insurance companies or other companies insuring property, except when specifically directed by the Commissioner to be filed;

(i) Advances, reimbursements, or charges for traveling and other business expenses of an employee to the extent that the employee is required to account (within the meaning of the term "account" as set forth in paragraph (b)(4) of § 1.162-17) and does so account to his employer for such expenses;

(j) Amounts paid to persons in the military or civil service of the United States or a State, Territory or political subdivision thereof, or the District of Columbia as an allowance or reimbursement for traveling or other bona fide ordinary and necessary expenses, including an allowance for meals and lodging or a per diem allowance in lieu of subsistence;

(k) Payments of interest on obligations of the United States, or a State, Territory, or political subdivision thereof, or the District of Columbia, or any agency or instrumentality of any one or more of the foregoing (but for requirements for reporting certain such payments by the United States or any agency or instrumentality thereof, see §§ 1.1461-1 to 1.1461-3, inclusive);

(l) Payments of interest on corporate bonds (but for reporting requirements as to payments made after December 31, 1962, of interest on certain corporate bonds, see § 1.6049-1 to § 1.6049-3, inclusive; and as to payments of interest on bonds, mortgages, deeds of trust, or other similar obligations issued before January 1, 1934, and containing a tax-free covenant, see §§ 1.1461-1 to 1.1461-3, inclusive);

(m) Payments made to employees for services in Puerto Rico;

(n) Amounts paid to persons in the service of an international organization, as defined in section 7701(a)(18), as an allowance or reimbursement for traveling or other bona fide ordinary and necessary expenses, including an allowance for meals and lodging or a per diem allowance in lieu of subsistence;

(o) A payment of a type determined by the Commissioner to be paid as an award to an informer or other payment of a similar character made by the United States, a State, Territory, or political subdivision thereof, or the District of Columbia, or any agency or instrumentality of any one or more of the foregoing; and

(p) On and after September 9, 1968, payments by a person carrying on the banking business of interest on a deposit evidenced by a negotiable time certificate of deposit (but for reporting requirements as to payments made after December 31, 1962, of interest on certain deposits, see section 6049 and the regulations thereunder in this part).

(q) Payments made to principals by persons carrying on the banking business, and by persons which are mutual savings banks, cooperative banks, building and loan associations, homestead associations, credit unions, or similar organizations chartered and supervised by Federal or State law, of funds collected when acting in the capacity of collection agents. This exception does not apply to collection of items on a regular and continuing basis under a so-called escrow, trust, custody or investment advisory agreement. However, returns of information are not required unless payment is of the type with respect to which such returns would otherwise be required under section 6041 if the payer were engaged in a trade or business; nor are returns of information required on payments pursuant to a trust with respect to which Form 1041 is required to be filed by the trustee. The exception from reporting set forth in this paragraph shall apply until such time as the Commissioner determines that it is feasible for such persons to report the payments, and this paragraph is amended accordingly to require such reporting.

O— § 1.6041-4 (T.D. 6364, filed 2-13-59; republished in T.D. 6500, filed 11-25-60.) Returns of information as to foreign items.

(a) *In general.* If the amount of foreign items, as defined in paragraph (b) of this section, paid in any calendar year to a citizen or resident of the United States (individual or fiduciary), or a partnership any member of which is a citizen or resident of the United States, is $600 or more, an information return on Form 1099 setting forth the amount of such items is required to be filed by any person who accepts the item for collection as a matter of business or for profit, such as a bank. As used in this section, the term "collection" includes (1) payment of the foreign item in cash; (2) the crediting of the account of the person presenting the foreign item; (3) the tentative crediting of the account of the person presenting the foreign item until the amount of the foreign item is received by the bank or collecting agent from abroad; and (4) the receipt of foreign items for the purpose of transmitting them abroad for deposits.

(b) *Foreign items defined.* The term "foreign items", as used in this section, means any item of interest upon the bonds of a foreign country or of a nonresident foreign corporation not having a fiscal or paying agent in the United States (including Puerto Rico as if a part of the United States), or any item of dividends upon the stock of such corporation.

(c) *License to collect foreign items.* A bank or agent collecting foreign items is required to obtain a license pursuant to the provisions of section 7001 and the regulations thereunder in Part 301 of this chapter. (Regulations on Procedure and Administration).

O— § 1.6041-5 (T.D. 6364, filed 2-13-59; republished in T.D. 6500, filed 11-25-60.) Information as to actual owner.

When a person receiving a payment described in section 6041 is not the actual owner of the income received, the name and address of the actual owner shall be furnished upon demand of the person paying the income, and in default of compliance with such demand the payee becomes liable for the penalties provided. See section 7203.

O— § 1.6041-6 (T.D. 6364, filed 2-13-59; republished in T.D. 6500, filed 11-25-60; amended by T.D. 6628, filed 12-27-62 and T.D. 7284, filed 8-2-73.) Returns under section 6041; contents and time and place for filing.

Returns made under section 6041 on Forms 1096 and 1099 for any calendar year shall be filed on or before February 28 of the following year with any of the Internal Revenue Service Centers, the addresses of which are listed in the instructions for such forms. The name and address of the person making the payment and the name and

Reg. § 1.6041-6

address of the recipient of the payment shall be stated on Form 1099. If the present address of the recipient is not available, the last known post office address must be given. See section 6109 and the regulations thereunder for rules requiring the inclusion of identifying numbers in Form 1099.

○— § 1.6041-7 (T.D. 6883, filed 5-2-66; amended by T.D. 7106, filed 4-2-71.) **Permission to submit information required by Form 1099 or W-2 on magnetic tape.**

(a) *General.* For rules relating to permission to submit the information required by Form 1099 or W-2 on magnetic tape or other media, see § 1.9101-1. See also paragraph (b)(2) of § 31,6011(a)-7 of this chapter (Employment Tax Regulations) for additional rules relating to Form W-2.

(b) *Returns on magnetic tape by departments of health care carriers.* (1) For calendar years beginning on or after January 1, 1971, a health care carrier, or an agent thereof, making payment of fees or other compensation to providers of medical and health care services, may make a separate return on magnetic tape for each separate department within a specific line of such carrier's business, so long as all of such returns taken together contain all of the information required by section 6041 with respect to each provider of medical and health care services to whom such health care carrier makes payments aggregating $600 or more during the calendar year. Examples of separate departments within a specific line of such carrier's business (such as health and accident insurance) include, but are not limited to, separate departments to process claims of individual and group policyholders; and separate departments established along geographic lines.

(2) For purposes of this paragraph, the term "health care carrier" means any person making health care payments: (i) in exchange for the payment of a premium, (ii) in accordance with an employee benefit program, or (iii) in connection with a government-sponsored health care program.

○— § 301.6041 **Statutory provisions; information at source.** [Sec. 6041, IRC]

○— § 301.6041-1 (T.D. 6498, filed 10-24-60.) **Returns of information regarding certain payments.**

For provisions relating to the requirement of returns of information regarding certain payments, see §§ 1.6041-1 to 1.6041-6, inclusive, of this chapter (Income Tax Regulations).

○— § 1.6042 **Statutory provisions; returns regarding corporate dividends, earnings, and profits.** [Sec. 6042, IRC]

○— § 1.6042-1 (T.D. 6364, filed 2-13-59; republished in T.D. 6500, filed 11-25-60; amended by T.D. 6628, filed 12-27-62.) **Return of information as to dividends paid in calendar years before 1963.**

(a) *Requirement of return* — (1) *In general.* Except as provided in subparagraphs (2) and (3) of this paragraph, every domestic corporation, or foreign corporation engaged in business within the United States or having an office or place of business or a fiscal or paying agent in the United States, making payments during any calendar year before 1963 of $10 or more of dividends and distributions (other than distributions in liquidation) to any shareholder who is an individual (citizen or resident of the United States), a resident fiduciary, or a resident partnership any member of which is a citizen or resident shall file for the calendar year a return setting forth the amount of such payments for such calendar year. A separate return on Form 1099, showing the name and address of the payor and the shareholder, and the amount paid, shall be prepared with respect to each shareholder. These returns shall be accompanied by transmittal Form 1096.

(2) *Federal land bank associations and certain other corporations.* A corporation described in section 501(c)(12), (15), or (16), or section 521(b)(1), or a Federal land bank association or a production credit association, making a payment of a dividend, or a distribution, to any shareholder in any calendar year before 1963 shall file an information return with respect to such payments when they total $100 or more during the calendar year.

(3) *Savings and loan associations, etc.* A savings and loan association, a cooperative bank, a homestead association, a credit union, or a building and loan association is required to file an information return with respect to distributions made to a shareholder during any calendar year before 1963 only if the amount thereof paid to the shareholder during the calendar year, or such amount when aggregated with other payments made to the shareholder during such year of interest, rents, royalties, annuities, pensions, and other gains, profits, and income, as described in paragraph (a)(2)(ii) of § 1.6041-1, totals $600 or more. For this purpose, the term "distributions to a shareholder" includes periodical distributions of earnings on running installment shares of stock paid or credited by a building and loan association to its holders of that class of stock, and the sum received upon withdrawal from a building and loan association in excess of the amounts paid in on account of membership fees and stock subscriptions, consisting of accumulated profits.

(b) *Nontaxable or partly nontaxable distributions.* In the case of a distribution which is made from a depletion or depreciation reserve, or which for any other reason is deemed by the corporation to be nontaxable or partly nontaxable to its shareholders, the corporation shall fill in the information on both sides of Form 1096.

(c) *Information as to actual owner—* (1) *In general.* When the person receiving a payment with respect to which an information return is required under authority of the Code is not the actual owner of the income received, the name and address of the actual owner or payee shall be furnished upon demand of the person paying the income, and in default of a compliance with such demand the payee becomes liable for the penalties provided. See section 7203. Dividends on stock are prima facie the income of the record owner of the stock. If a record owner of stock who is not the actual owner thereof receives dividends on such stock in any calendar year before 1963, he shall file a Form 1087 disclosing the name and address of the actual owner or payee, the name of the issuing corporation, the number of shares of such stock, and the amount of dividends received with respect to such stock during the calendar year. (For the reporting by a nominee of dividends received by him on behalf of another person in any calendar year after 1962, see § 1.6042-2.) Unless such a disclosure is made the record owner will be held liable for any tax based upon such dividends. A separate Form 1087 shall be filed by the record owner for each of the stockholdings of each actual owner for whom he acts as nominee. However, where the record owner is a banking institution, trust company, or brokerage firm, it may, provided it maintains such records as will permit a prompt substantiation of each payment of dividends made to the actual owner, file one Form 1087 for each actual owner for whom it acts as nominee and report thereon the total amount of the dividends paid to such actual owner (without itemization as to the issuing company, class of stock, etc.).

(2) *Exceptions.* The filing of Form 1087 is not required if—

(i) The record owner is required to file a fiduciary return on Form 1041, or a withholding return on Form 1042, disclosing the name and address of the actual owner or payee;

(ii) The actual owner or payee is a nonresident alien individual, foreign partnership, or foreign corporation and the tax has been withheld at the source before receipt of the dividends by the record owner;

(iii) The record owner is a banking institution, a trust company, or a brokerage firm which prepares the individual income tax return of the actual owner, provided the verification on the return with respect to the preparation thereof is executed by such record owner;

(iv) The record owner is a nominee of a banking institution or trust company exercising trust powers, and such banking institution or trust company is required to file a fiduciary return on Form 1041 which reflects the name and address of the actual owner or payee;

(v) The actual owner is an organization exempt from taxation under section 501(a) and is exempt from the requirement of filing a return under section 6033 and paragraph (g) of § 1.6033-1; or

(vi) The record owner is a banking institution or trust company exercising trust powers, or a nominee thereof, and the actual owner is an organization exempt from taxation under section 501(a) for which such banking institution or trust company files an annual return.

See § 1.1441-1, relating to withholding of tax on nonresident alien individuals, and § 1.1442-1, relating to withholding of tax on nonresident foreign corporations.

(d) *Time and place for filing.* Returns made under this section on Forms 1096 and 1099 and Form 1087 for any calendar year shall be filed on or before February 28 of the following year with any of the Internal Revenue Service Centers, the addresses of which are listed in the instructions for such forms.

O→ § 1.6042-2 (T.D. 6628, filed 12-27-62; amended by T.D. 6677, filed 9-16-63; T.D. 6879, filed 3-7-66; T.D. 6883, filed 5-2-66; T.D. 6891, filed 8-3-66; T.D. 7000, filed 1-17-69 and T.D. 7187, filed 7-5-72.) **Returns of information as to dividends paid in calendar years after 1962.**

(a) *Requirement of reporting*—(1) *In general.* (i) Every person who makes payments of dividends (as defined in § 1.6042-3) aggregating $10 or more to any other person during a calendar year after 1962 shall make an infomation return on Forms 1096 and 1099 for such calendar year showing the aggregate amount of such payments, the name and address of the person to whom paid, the total of such payments for all persons, and such other information as is required by the forms. In the case of dividends paid during the calendar year 1963 or 1964, the requirement of this subdivision for the filing of Form 1099 will be met if a person making payments of dividends to another person on two or more classes of stock files a separate Form 1099 with respect to each such class of stock on which $10 or more of dividends are paid to such other person during the calendar year. Thus, if during 1963 a corporation pays to a person dividends totaling $15 on its common stock and $20 on its preferred stock, it may file separate Forms 1099 with respect to the payments of $15 and $20. If the dividends on the preferred stock totaled $5 instead of $20, no return would be required with respect to the $5. In addition, in the case of dividends paid during calendar years beginning with 1965 and continuing until such time as the Commissioner determines that it is feasible to aggregate payments on two or more separate stock ownership accounts and this subdivision is amended accordingly to provide for reporting on an aggregate basis, the requirement of this subdivision for the filing of Form 1099 will be met if a person making payments of dividends to another person on two or more such separate stock ownership accounts (regardless of whether the payments are made on only one class of stock) files a separate Form 1099 with respect to each such stock ownership account on which $10 or more of dividends are paid to such other person during the calendar year.

(ii) Every person, except to the extent that he acts as a nominee described in subdivision (iii) of this subparagraph, who during a calendar year after 1962 receives payments of dividends as a nominee on behalf of another person aggregating $10 or more shall make an information return on Forms 1096 and 1087 for such calendar year showing the aggregate amount of such dividends, the name and address of the person on whose behalf received, the total of such dividends received on behalf of all persons, and such other information as is required by the forms. Notwithstanding the preceding sentence, the filing of Form 1087 is not required if—

(a) The record owner is required to file a fiduciary return on Form 1041 disclosing the name, address, and identifying number of the actual owner;

(b) The record owner is a nominee of a banking institution or trust company exercising trust powers, and such banking institution or trust company is required to file a fiduciary return on Form 1041 disclosing the name, address, and identifying number of the actual owner; or

(c) The record owner is a banking institution or trust company exercising trust

Reg. § 1.6042-2 (a) (1)

24,296.6 (I.R.C.) Reg. § 1.6042-2(a).(1) 8-6-73

powers, or a nominee thereof, and the actual owner is an organization exempt from taxation under section 501(a) for which such banking institution or trust company files an annual return;
but only if the name, address, and identifying number of the record owner are included on or with the Form 1041 fiduciary return filed for the estate or trust or the annual return filed for the tax-exempt organization.

(iii) Every person who is a nominee acting as a custodian of a unit investment trust described in section 851(f)(1) and paragraph (d) of § 1.851-7 who, during a calendar year after 1968, receives payments of dividends in such capacity, shall make an information return on Forms 1096 and 1099M, for such calendar year showing the information required by such forms and instructions thereto and the name, address, and identifying number of the nominee identified as such. This subdivision shall not apply if the regulated investment company agrees with the nominee to satisfy the requirements of section 6042 and the regulations thereunder with respect to each holder of an interest in the unit investment trust whose shares are being held by the nominee as custodian and within the time limit for furnishing statements prescribed by § 1.6042-4, files with the Internal Revenue Service office where such company's return is to be filed for the taxable year, a statement that the holders of the unit investment trust with whom the agreement was made have been directly notified by the regulated investment company. Such statement shall include the name, sponsor, and custodian of each unit investment trust whose holders have been directly notified. The nominee's requirements under this subdivision shall be deemed met if the regulated investment company transmits a copy of such statement to the nominee within such period; provided, however, if the regulated investment company fails or is unable to satisfy the requirements of section 6042 with respect to the holders of interest in the unit investment trust, it shall so notify the Internal Revenue Service within 45 days following the close of its taxable year. The custodian shall, upon notice by the Internal Revenue Service that the regulated investment company has failed to comply with the agreement, satisfy the requirements of this subdivision within 30 days of such notice.

(2) *Definitions.* The term "person" when used in this section does not include the United States, a State, the District of Columbia, a foreign government, a political subdivision of a State or of a foreign government, or an international organization. Therefore, dividends paid by or to one of these entities need not be reported. For purposes of this section, a person who receives a dividend shall be considered to have received it as a nominee if he is not the actual owner of such dividend and if he was required under § 1.6109-1 to furnish his identifying number to the payer of the dividend (or would have been so required if the total of such dividends for the year had been $10 or more), and such number was (or would have been required to be included on an information return filed by the payer with respect to the dividend. However, a person shall not be considered to be a nominee as to any portion of a dividend which is actually owned by another person whose name is also shown on the information return filed by the payer or nominee with respect to such dividend. Thus, in the case of stock jointly owned by a husband and wife, the husband will not be considered as receiving any portion of a dividend on that stock as a nominee for his wife if his wife's name is included on the information return filed by the payer with respect to the dividend.

(3) *Determination of person to whom a dividend is paid or for whom it is received.* For purposes of applying the provisions of this section, the person whose identifying number is required to be included by the payer of a dividend on an information return with respect to such dividend shall be considered the person to whom the dividend is paid. In the case of a dividend received by a nominee on behalf of another person, the person whose identifying number is required to be included on an information return made by the nominee with respect to such dividend shall be considered the person on whose behalf such dividend is received by the nominee. Thus, in the case of a dividend made payable to a person other than the record owner of the stock with respect to which the dividend is paid, the record owner of the stock shall be considered the

person to whom the dividend is paid for purposes of applying the reporting requirements in this section, since his identifying number is required to be included on the information return filed under such section by the payer of the dividend. Similarly, if a stockbroker receives a dividend on stock held in street name for the joint account of a husband and wife, the dividend is considered as received on behalf of the husband since his identifying number should be shown on the information return filed by the nominee under this section. Thus, if the wife has a separate account with the same stockbroker, any dividends received by the stockbroker for her separate account should not be aggregated with the dividends received for the joint account for purposes of information reporting. For regulations relating to the use of identifying numbers, see § 1.6109-1.

(4) *Inclusion of other payments.* The Form 1099 filed by any person with respect to payments of dividends to another person during a calendar year may, at the election of the maker, include other payments made by him to such other person during such year which are required to be reported on Form 1099. Similarly, the Form 1087 filed by a nominee with respect to payments of dividends received by him on behalf of any other person during a calendar year may include payments of interest received by him on behalf of such person during such year which are required to be reported on Form 1087. In addition, any person required to report payments on both Forms 1087 and 1099 for any calendar year may use one Form 1096 to summarize and transmit such Forms.

(b) *When payment deemed made.* For purposes of a return of information, an amount is deemed to have been paid when it is credited or set apart to a person without any substantial limitation or restriction as to the time or manner of payment or condition upon which payment is to be made, and is made available to him so that it may be drawn at any time, and its receipt brought within his own control and disposition.

(c) *Time and place for filing.* The returns required under this section for any calendar year shall be filed after September 30 of such year, but not before the payer's final payment for the year, and on or before February 28 of the following year with any of the Internal Revenue Service Centers, the addresses of which are listed in the instructions for Form 1096. For extensions of time for filing returns under this section, see § 1.6081-1.

(d) *Penalty.* For penalty for failure to file the statements required by this section, see § 301.6652-1 of this chapter (Regulations on Procedure and Administration).

(e) *Permission to submit information required by Form 1087 or 1099 on magnetic tape.* For rules relating to permission to submit the information required by Form 1087 or 1099 on magnetic tape or other media, see § 1.9101-1.

O—☛ § 1.6042-3 (T.D. 6628, filed 12-27-62; amended by T.D. 6908, filed 12-30-66.) **Dividends subject to reporting.**

(a) *In general.* Except as provided by paragraph (b) of this section, the term "dividend" for purposes of this section and §§ 1.6042-2 and 1.6042-4 means—

(1) Any distribution made by a corporation to its shareholders which is a dividend as defined in section 316; and

(2) Any payment made by a stockbroker to any person as a substitute for a dividend (as so defined).

A "dividend" paid by an insurance company to a policy holder, other than a dividend upon its capital stock, is not a dividend for purposes of this section. Similarly, payments (however denominated) by a mutual savings bank, savings and loan association, or similar organization, in respect of deposits, investment certificates, or withdrawable or repurchasable shares are not dividends for purposes of this section (but, for provisions requiring reporting of such payments, see §§ 1.6049-1 to 1.6049-3, inclusive). The payments by a stockbroker which are defined as dividends in subparagraph (2) of this paragraph include any payment made in lieu of a dividend to a person whose stock has been borrowed in connection with a short sale or other similar transaction.

(b) *Exceptions.* The term "dividend" does not include—

(1) Any distribution or payment by a foreign corporation if it is not engaged in business within the United States and does not have an office or place of business or a fiscal or paying agent in the United States,

(2) Any distribution or payment which is subject to withholding under section 1441 or 1442 (relating to withholding of tax on nonresident aliens and foreign corporations, respectively) by the person making the distribution or payment, or which would be so subject to withholding but for the provisions of a treaty, or for the fact that it is attributable to income from sources outside the United States, or for the fact that withholding is not required by reason of paragraph (a) or (f) of § 1.1441-4.

(3) In the case of a nominee, any distribution or payment which he receives and with respect to which he is required to withhold under section 1441 or 1442, or would be so required to withhold but for the provisions of a treaty, or for the fact that the distribution or payment is attributable to income from sources outside the United States, or for the fact that withholding is not required by reason of paragraph (a) or (f) of § 1.1441-4.

(4) Any amount which is treated under section 1373 (relating to undistributed taxable income of electing small business corporations) as an amount distributed as a dividend.

(c) *Special rule.* If a person makes a payment which may be a dividend, or if a nominee receives a payment which may be a dividend, but such person or nominee is unable to determine the portion of the payment which is a dividend (as defined in paragraphs (a) and (b) of this section) at the time he files his return under § 1.6042-2, he shall, for purposes of such section treat the entire amount of such payment as a dividend.

O—☛ § 1.6042-4 (T.D. 6628, filed 12-27-62; amended by T.D. 6879, filed 3-7-66 and T.D. 7187, filed 7-5-72.) **Statements to recipients of dividend payments.**

Reg. § 1.6042-4

24,298 (I.R.C.) Reg. § 1.6042-4(a) 7-10-72

(a) *Requirement.* Every person filing a Form 1099 or 1087 under section 6042(a)(1) and § 1.6042-2 with respect to payments of dividends shall furnish to the person whose identifying number is (or should be) shown on the form a written statement showing the information required by paragraph (b) of this section. However, no statement is required to be furnished under section 6042(c) or this section to any person if the aggregate of the payments to (or received on behalf of) such person shown on the form is less than $10.

(b) *Form of statement.* The written statement required to be furnished to a person under paragraph (a) of this section shall—

(1) Show the aggregate amount of payments shown on the Form 1099 or 1087 as having been made to (or received on behalf of) such person and include a legend stating that such amount is being reported to the Internal Revenue Service, and

(2) Show the name and address of the person filing the form.

The requirement of this section for the furnishing of a statement to any person, including the legend requirement of this paragraph, may be met by the furnishing to such person of a copy of the Form 1099 or 1087 filed pursuant to § 1.6042-2, or a reasonable facsimile thereof, in respect of such person. A statement shall be considered to be furnished to a person within the meaning of this section if it is mailed to such person at his last known address.

(c) *Time for furnishing statements—*(1) *In general.* Each statement required by this section to be furnished to any person for a calendar year shall be furnished to such person after November 30 of the year and on or before January 31 (February 10 in the case of a nominee filing under § 1.6042-2(a)(1)(iii) of the following year, but no statement may be furnished before the final dividend for the calendar year has been paid. However, the statement may be furnished at any time after September 30 if it is furnished with the final dividend for the calendar year.

(2) *Extensions of time.* For good cause shown upon written application of the person required to furnish statements under this section, the district director may grant an extension of time not exceeding 30 days in which to furnish such statements. The application shall be addressed to the district director with whom the income tax returns of the applicant are filed and shall contain a full recital of the reasons for requesting the extension to aid the district director in determining the period of the extension, if any, which will be granted. Such a request in the form of a letter to the district director signed by the applicant will suffice as an application. The application shall be filed on or before the date prescribed in subparagraph (1) of this paragraph for furnishing the statements required by this section.

(3) *Last day for furnishing statement.* For provisions relating to the time for performance of an act when the last day prescribed for performance falls on Saturday, Sunday, or a legal holiday, see § 301.-7503-1 of this chapter (Regulations on Procedure and Administration).

(d) *Penalty.* For provisions relating to the penalty provided for failure to furnish a statement under this section, see § 301.6678-1 of this chapter (Regulations on Procedure and Administration).

§ 301.6042 **Statutory provisions; returns regarding payments of dividends and corporate earnings and profits.** [Sec. 6042, IRC]

§ 301.6042-1 (T.D. 6498, filed 10-24-60; amended by T.D. 6700, filed 1-6-64.) **Returns of information regarding payments of dividends and corporate earnings and profits.**

For provisions relating to the requirement of returns of information regarding payments of dividends and corporate earnings and profits, see §§ 1.6042-1 to 1.6042-4, inclusive, of this chapter (Income Tax Regulations).

§ 1.6043 **Statutory provisions; return regarding corporate dissolution or liquidation.** [Sec. 6043, IRC]

§ 1.6043-1 (T.D. 6364, filed 2-13-59; republished in T.D. 6500, filed 11-25-60; amended by T.D. 6949, filed 4-8-68.) **Return regarding corporate dissolution of liquidation.**

(a) *Requirement of returns.* Within 30 days after the adoption of any resolution or plan for or in respect of the dissolution of a corporation or the liquidation of the whole or any part of its capital stock, the corporation shall file a return on Form 966, containing the information required by paragraph (b) of this section and by such form. Such return shall be filed with the district director for the district in which the income tax return of the corporation is filed. Further, if after the filing of a Form 966 there is an amendment of or supplement to the resolution or plan, an additional Form 966, based on the resolution or plan as amended or supplemented, must be filed within 30 days after the adoption of such amendment or supplement. A return must be filed under section 6043 and this section in respect of a liquidation whether or not any part of the gain or loss to the shareholders upon the liquidation is recognized under the provisions of section 1002.

(b) *Contents of return*—(1) *In general.* There shall be attached to and made a part of the return required by section 6043 and paragraph (a) of this section of a certified copy of the resolution or plan, together with any amendments thereof or supplements thereto, and such return shall in addition contain the following information:

(i) The name and address of the corporation;

(ii) The place and date of incorporation;

(iii) The date of the adoption of the resolution or plan and the dates of any amendments thereof or supplements thereto; and

(iv) The internal revenue district in which the last income tax return of the corporation was filed and the taxable year covered thereby.

(2) *Liquidation within one calendar month.* If the corporation is a domestic corporation, and the plan of liquidation provides for a distribution in complete cancellation or redemption of all of the capital stock of the corporation, and for the transfer of all the property of the corporation under the liquidation entirely within some one calendar month pursuant to section 333, and any shareholder claims the benefit of such section, such return shall, in addition to the information required by subparagraph (1) of this paragraph, contain the following:

(i) A statement showing the number of shares of each class of stock outstanding at the time of the adoption of the plan of liquidation, together with a description of the voting power of each such class;

(ii) A list of all the shareholders owning stock at the time of the adoption of the plan of liquidation, together with the number of shares of each class of stock owned by each shareholder, the certificate numbers thereof, and the total number of votes to which entitled on the adoption of the plan of liquidation;

(iii) A list of all corporate shareholders as of January 1, 1954, together with the number of shares of each class of stock owned by each such shareholder, the certificate numbers thereof, the total number of votes to which entitled on the adoption of the plan of liquidation, and a statement of all changes in ownership of stock by corporate shareholders between January 1,

1954, and the date of the adoption of the plan of liquidation, both dates inclusive; and

(iv) If the liquidation is pursuant to section 333(g), a computation indicating that the corporation was not a personal holding company for at least one of its two most recent taxable years ending before February 26, 1964, but that it would have been a personal holding company under section 542 if the law applicable for the first taxable year beginning after December 31, 1963, had been applicable to such year.

(3) *Returns in respect of amendments or supplements.* If a return has been filed pursuant to section 6043 and this section, any additional return made necessary by an amendment of or a supplement to the resolution or plan will be deemed sufficient if it gives the date the prior return was filed and contains a duly certified copy of the amendment or supplement and all other information required by this section and by Form 966 which was not given in the prior return.

o—→ § 1.6043-2 (T.D. 6364, filed 2-13-59; republished in T.D. 6500, filed 11-25-60; amended by T.D. 6949, filed 4-8-68). Return of information respecting distributions in liquidation.

(a) Unless the distribution is one in respect of which information is required to be filed pursuant to paragraph (b) of § 1.332-6, paragraph (a) of § 1.368-3, or § 1.1081-11, every corporation making any distribution of $600 or more during a calendar year to any shareholder in liquidation of the whole or any part of its capital stock shall file a return of information on Forms 1096 and 1099L, giving all the information required by such forms and by the regulations in this part. A separate Form 1099L must be prepared for each shareholder to whom such distribution was made, showing the name and address of such shareholder, the number and class of shares owned by him in liquidation of which such distribution was made, and total amount distributed to him on each class of stock. If the amount distributed to such shareholder on any class of stock consisted in whole or in part of property other than money, the return on such form shall in addition show the amount of money distributed, if any, and shall list separately each class of property other than money distributed, giving a description of the property in each such class and a statement of its fair market value at the time of the distribution. Such forms, accompanied by transmittal Form 1096 showing the number of Forms 1099L filed therewith, shall be filed on or before February 28 of the year following the calendar year in which such distribution was made with any of the Internal Revenue Service Centers, the addresses of which are listed in the instructions for such forms.

(b) If the distribution is in complete liquidation of a domestic corporation pursuant to a plan of liquidation in accordance with which all the capital stock of the corporation is cancelled or redeemed, and the transfer of all the property under the liquidation occurs within some one calendar month pursuant to section 333, and any shareholder claims the benefits of such

Reg. § 1.6043-2(b)

section, the return on Form 1096 shall show:

(1) The amount of earnings and profits of the corporation accumulated after February 28, 1913, determined as of the close of such calendar month, without diminution by reason of distributions made during such calendar month, but including in such computation all items of income and expense accrued up to the date on which the transfer of all the property under the liquidation is completed;

(2) The ratable share of such earnings and profits of each share of stock canceled or redeemed in the liquidation;

(3) The date and circumstances of the acquisition by the corporation of any stock or securities distributed to shareholders in the liquidation;

(4) If the liquidation is pursuant to section 333(g), a schedule showing the amount of earnings and profits to which the corporation has succeeded after December 31, 1963, pursuant to any corporate reorganization or pursuant to a liquidation to which section 332 applies, except earnings and profits which on December 31, 1963, constituted earnings and profits of a corporation referred to in section 333(g)(3), and except earnings and profits which were earned after such date by a corporation referred to in section 333(g)(3); and

(5) If the liquidation occurs after December 31, 1966, and is pursuant to section 333(g)(2), the amount of earnings and profits of the corporation accumulated after February 28, 1913, and before January 1, 1967, and the ratable share of such earnings and profits of each share of stock canceled or redeemed in the liquidation.

§ 301.6043 Statutory provisions; return regarding corporate dissolution or liquidation. [Sec. 6043, IRC]

§ 301.6043-1 (T.D. 6498, filed 10-24-60.) Returns of information regarding corporate dissolutions or liquidations.

For provisions relating to the requirement of returns of information regarding corporate dissolutions or liquidations, see §§ 1.6043-1 and 1.6043-2 of this chapter (Income Tax Regulations).

§ 1.6044 Statutory provisions; returns regarding payments of patronage dividends. [Sec. 6044, IRC]

§ 1.6044-1 (T.D. 6364, filed 2-13-59; republished in T.D. 6500, filed 11-25-60; amended by T.D. 6628, filed 12-27-62.) Returns of information as to patronage dividends with respect to patronage occurring in taxable years beginning before 1963.

(a) *Requirement*—(1) *In general.* Except as provided in subparagraph (2) of this paragraph, any corporation allocating to any patron in respect of patronage occurring in any taxable year of the corporation beginning before January 1, 1963, amounts aggregating $100 or more during the calendar year as patronage dividends, rebates, or refunds (whether in cash, merchandise, capital stock, revolving fund certificates, retain certificates, letters of advice or in some other manner that discloses to each patron the amount of such dividend, rebate, or refund) shall for each such calendar year file a return of information with respect to such allocation on Forms 1096 and 1099. A separate Form 1099 shall be prepared for each patron showing the name and address of the patron to whom such allocation is made, and the amount of the allocation. The allocation shall be reported for the calendar year during which the allocation is made, regardless of whether the allocation is deemed for the purpose of section 522 to be made at the close of a preceding taxable year of the corporation.

(2) *Exception.* A return is not required under this section in the case of any corporation (including any cooperative or nonprofit corporation engaged in rural electrification) described in section 501(c)(12) or (15) which is exempt from tax under section 501(a), or in the case of any corporation subject to a tax imposed by subchapter L, chapter 1, of the Code.

(b) *Time and place for filing.* Returns made under this section on Forms 1096 and 1099 for any calendar year shall be filed on or before February 28 of the following year with any of the Internal Revenue Service Centers, the addresses of which are listed in the instructions for such forms.

(c) *Definitions.* The terms "cooperative association", "patron", "patronage dividends, rebates, and refunds", and "allocation" are defined, for the purpose of this section, in paragraph (b) of § 1.522-1.

§ 1.6044-2 (T.D. 6628, filed 12-27-62; amended by T.D. 6677, filed 9-16-63; T.D. 6879, filed 3-7-66 and T.D. 6883, filed 5-2-66.) Returns of information as to payments of patronage dividends with respect to patronage occurring in taxable years beginning after 1962.

(a) *Requirement of reporting*—(1) *In general.* Except as provided in § 1.6044-4, every organization described in paragraph (b) of this section which makes payments with respect to patronage occurring on or after the first day of the first taxable year of the organization beginning after December 31, 1962, of amounts described in § 1.6044-3 aggregating $10 or more to any person during any calendar year shall make an information return on Forms 1096 and 1099 for the calendar year showing the aggregate amount of such payments, the name and address of the person to whom paid, the total of such payments for all persons, and such other information as is required by the forms.

(2) *Definitions.* The term "person" when used in this section does not include the United States, a State, the District of Columbia, a foreign government, a political subdivision of a State or of a foreign government, or an international organization. Therefore, payment of amounts described in § 1.6044-3 to one of these entities need not be reported.

(3) *Determination of person to whom a patronage dividend is paid.* For purposes of applying the provisions of this section, the person whose identifying number is required to be included by the cooperative on an information return with respect to a patronage dividend shall be considered the person to whom such dividend is paid. For regulations relating

PRENTICE-HALL, Inc., Englewood Cliffs, N. J.

to the use of identifying numbers, see § 1.6109-1.

(4) *Inclusion of other payments.* The Form 1099 filed by an organization with respect to payments of patronage dividends made to any person during a calendar year may, at the election of the organization, include other payments made by it to such person during such year which are required to be reported on Form 1099.

(b) *Organizations subject to reporting requirement.* The organizations subject to the reporting requirements of paragraph (a) of this section are—

(1) Any organization exempt from tax under section 521 (relating to exemption of farmers' cooperatives from tax), and

(2) Any corporation operating on a cooperative basis other than an organization—

(i) Which is exempt from tax under chapter 1 (other than section 521), or

(ii) Which is subject to the provisions of part II of subchapter H of chapter 1 (relating to mutual savings banks, etc.), or subchapter L of chapter 1 (relating to insurance companies), or

(iii) Which is engaged in furnishing electric energy, or providing telephone service, to persons in rural areas.

(c) *When payment deemed made.* For purposes of this section, money or other property (except written notices of alloca-

tion) is deemed to have been paid when it is credited or set apart to a person without any substantial limitation or restriction as to the time or manner of payment or condition upon which payment is to be made, and is made available to him so that it may be drawn at any time, and its receipt brought within his own control and disposition. A written notice of allocation is considered to have been paid when it is issued by the organization to the distributee. Similarly, a qualified check (as defined in section 1388(d)(4)) is considered to have been paid when it is issued to the distributee.

(d) *Time and place for filing.* The return required under this section on Forms 1096 and 1099 for any calendar year shall be filed after September 30 of such year, but not before the payer's final payment for the year, and on or before February 28 of the following year, with any of the Internal Revenue Service Centers, the addresses of which are listed in the instructions for such forms. For extensions of time for filing returns under this section, see § 1.6081.1.

(e) *Penalty.* For penalty for failure to file the statements required by this section, see § 301.6652-1 of this chapter (Regulations on Procedure and Administration).

(f) *Permission to submit information required by Form 1099 on magnetic tape.* For rules relating to permission to submit the information required by Form 1099 on magnetic tape or other media, see § 1.9101-1.

§ 1.6044-3 (T.D. 6628, filed 12-27-62.) **Amounts subject to reporting.**

(a) *In general.* Except as provided in paragraph (c) of this section, the amounts subject to reporting under § 1.6044-2 are—

(1) Payments by all organizations subject to such reporting requirements of—

(i) Patronage dividends (as defined in section 1388 (a)) paid in money, qualified written notices of allocation (as defined in section 1388 (c)), or other property (except nonqualified written notices of allocation as defined in section 1388 (d)); and

(ii) Amounts described in section 1382 (b)(2) (relating to redemption of nonqualified written notices of allocation previously paid as patronage dividends) paid in money or property (except written notices of allocations); and

(2) Payments by farmers' cooperatives exempt from tax under section 521 of—

(i) Amounts described in section 1382 (c)(2)(A) (relating to distributions with respect to earnings derived from sources other than patronage) paid in money, qualified written notices of allocation, or other property (except nonqualified written notices of allocation); and

(ii) Amounts described in section 1382 (c)(2)(B) (relating to redemption of nonqualified written notices of allocation previously paid as distributions with respect to earnings derived from sources other than patronage) paid in money or other property (except written notices of allocation).

(b) *Special rules.* (1) If an organization makes a distribution consisting in whole or in part of a written notice of allocation and a qualified check and, at the time it files its return under § 1.6044-2, is unable to determine whether such written notice of allocation and such check constitute nonqualified written notices of allocation, such organization shall for purposes of such return treat such written notice of allocation as a qualified written notice of allocation and such qualified check as a payment in money.

(2) An amount described in paragraph (a) of this section is subject to reporting even though the organization paying such amount is allowed no deduction for it because it was not paid within the time prescribed in section 1382. Thus, a patronage dividend of $25 paid by a marketing cooperative must be reported even though it is paid after the end of the payment period (see section 1382(d)) for the organization's taxable year in which the patronage occurred.

(c) *Exceptions.* Reporting under § 1.6044-2 of payments of amounts described in paragraph (a) of this section is not required—

(1) If such payments are made by a foreign corporation which is not engaged in business within the United States and does not have an office or place of business or a fiscal or paying agent in the United States, or

(2) If such payments are subject to withholding under section 1441 or 1442 (relating to withholding of tax on nonresident aliens and foreign corporations, respectively) by the person making the distribution or payment, or would be so subject to withholding but for the provisions of a treaty, or for the fact that it is attributable to income from sources outside the United States.

(d) *Determination of amount paid.* For purposes of § 1.6044-2 and this section, in determining the amount of any payment subject to reporting under paragraph (a) of this section—

(1) Property (other than a qualified written notice of allocation) shall be taken into account at its fair market value, and

(2) A qualified written notice of allocation shall be taken into account at its stated dollar amount.

§ 1.6044-4 (T.D. 6628, filed 12-27-62) **Exemption for certain consumer cooperatives.**

(a) *In general*—(1) *Determination of exemption.* Exemption from the reporting requirements of § 1.6044-2 shall, upon application therefor, be granted by the district director to any cooperative which he determines is primarily engaged in selling at retail goods or services of a type which is generally for personal, living, or family use. A cooperative is not exempt from the reporting requirements merely because it is an organization of a type to which section 6044(c) and this section relate. In order for the exemption from reporting to apply, it is necessary that the cooperative file an application in accordance with this section and obtain a determination of exemption.

(2) *Basis for exemption.* For a cooperative to qualify for the exemption from reporting provided by section 6044(c) and this section 85 percent of its gross receipts for the preceding taxable year, or 85 percent of its aggregate gross receipts for the preced-

Reg. § 1.6044-4(a)(2)

24,300 (I.R.C.)   Reg. § 1.6044-4(a)(2)   1-9-78

ing three taxable years, must have been derived from the sale at retail of goods or services of a type which is generally for personal, living, or family use. In determining whether an item is of a type that is generally for personal living, or family use, an item which may be purchased either for such use or for business use and which when acquired for business purposes is generally purchased at wholesale will, when sold by a cooperative at retail, be treated as goods or services of a type generally for personal, living, or family use.

(3) *Period of exemption.* A determination of exemption from reporting shall apply beginning with the payments made during the calendar year in which the determination is made and shall automatically cease to be effective beginning with payments made after the close of the first taxable year of the cooperative in which less than 70 percent of its gross receipts is derived from the sale at retail of goods or services of a type which is generally for personal, living, or family use.

(b) *Application for exemption.* Application for exemption from the reporting requirements of section 6044 shall be made on Form 3491, and shall be filed with the district director for the internal revenue district in which the cooperative has its principal place of business.

O— § 1.6044-5 (T.D. 6628, filed 12-27-62; amended by T.D. 6879, filed 3-7-66; T.D. 7529, filed 12-27-77.) **Statements to recipients of patronage dividends.**

(a) *Requirement.* Every cooperative making a return under section 6044(a)(1) and § 1.6044-2 with respect to payments made by such cooperative to its patrons shall furnish to each patron named in the return a written statement showing the information required by paragraph (b) of this section. However, no statement is required to be furnished under section 6044 (e) and this section to any person if the aggregate of the payments to such person shown in the return is less than $10.

(b) *Form of statements.* The written statement required to be furnished to a person with respect to whom a return of information is made under § 1.6044-2 shall—

(1) Show the aggregate amount of payments shown on the return as having been made to such person and include a legend stating that such amount is being reported to the Internal Revenue Service, and

(2) Show the name and address of the cooperative making the return.

The requirement of this section for the furnishing of a statement to any person, including the legend requirement of this paragraph, may be met by the furnishing to such person of a copy of the Form 1099 filed pursuant to § 1.6044-2, or a reasonable facsimile thereof, in respect of such person. A statement shall be considered to be furnished to a person within the meaning of this section if it is mailed to such person at his last known address.

(c) *Time for furnishing statements.*—(1) *In general.* Each statement required by this section to be furnished to any person for a calendar year shall be furnished after November 30th of the year and on or before January 31 of the following year. However, the statement may be furnished before December 1 if it is furnished with the final payment for the calendar year. No statement may be furnished before the final payment for the calendar year of an amount described in § 1.6044-3.

(2) *Extensions of time.* For good cause shown upon written application of the person required to furnish statements under this section, the district director may grant an extension of time not exceeding 30 days in which to furnish such statements. The application shall be addressed to the district director for the internal revenue district in which the cooperative has its principal place of business and shall contain a full recital of the reasons for requesting the extension to aid the district director in determining the period of the extension, if any, which will be granted. Such a request in the form of a letter to the district director signed by the applicant will suffice as an application. The application shall be filed on or before the date prescribed in subparagraph (1) of this paragraph for furnishing the statements required by this section.

(3) *Last day for furnishing statement.* For provisions relating to the time for performance of an act when the last day prescribed for performance falls on Saturday, Sunday, or a legal holiday, see § 301.7503-1 of this chapter (Regulations on Procedure and Administration).

(d) *Penalty.* For provisions relating to the penalty provided for failure to furnish a statement under this section, § 301.-6678-1 of this chapter (Regulations on Procedure and Administration).

O— § 301.6044 **Statutory provisions; returns regarding payments of patronage dividends.** [Sec. 6044, IRC]

O— § 301.6044-1 (T.D. 6498, filed 10-24-60; amended by T.D. 6700, filed 1-6-64.) **Returns of information regarding payments of patronage dividends.**

For provisions relating to the requirement of returns of information regarding payments of patronage dividends, see §§ 1.6044-1 to 1.6044-5, inclusive, of this chapter (Income Tax Regulations).

O— § 1.6045 **Statutory provisions; returns of brokers.** [Sec. 6045, IRC]

O— § 301.6045 **Statutory provisions; returns of brokers.** [Sec. 6045, IRC]

O— § 1.6046 **Statutory provisions; returns as to organization or reorganization of foreign corporations and as to acquisitions of their stock.** [Sec. 6046, IRC]

O— § 1.6046-1 (T.D. 6623, filed 11-30-62; amended by T.D. 6997, filed 1-17-69 and T.D. 7322, filed 8-23-74.) **Returns as to organization or reorganization of foreign corporations and as to acquisitions of their stock, on or after January 1, 1963.**

(a) *Officers or directors*—(1) *When liability arises on January 1, 1963.* Each United States citizen or resident who is on January 1, 1963, an officer or director of a foreign corporation shall make a return on Form 959 showing the name, address, and identifying number of each United States person who, on January 1, 1963, owns 5 percent or more in value of the outstanding stock of such foreign corporation.

(2) *When liability arises after January 1, 1963*—(i) Requirement of return. Each United States citizen or resident who is at any time after January 1, 1963, an officer or director of a foreign corporation shall make a return on Form 959 setting forth the information described in subdivision (ii) of this subparagraph with respect to each United States person who, during the time such citizen or resident is such an officer or director—

(a) Acquires (whether in one or more transactions) outstanding stock of such corporation which has, or which when added to any such stock then owned by him (excluding any stock owned by him on January 1, 1963, if on that date he owned 5 percent or more in value of such stock) has, a value equal to 5 percent or more in value of the outstanding stock of such foreign corporation, or

(b) Acquires (whether in one or more transactions) an additional 5 percent or more in value of the outstanding stock of such foreign corporation.

(ii) *Information required to be shown on return.* The return required under subdivision (i) of this subparagraph shall contain the following information:

(a) Name, address, and identifying number of each shareholder with respect to whom the return is filed;

(b) A statement showing that the shareholder is either described in subdivision (i) *(a)* or (i) *(b)* of this subparagraph; and

(c) The date on which the shareholder became a person described in subdivision (i) *(a)* or (i) *(b)* of this subparagraph.

(3) *Application of rules.* The provisions of this paragraph may be illustrated by the following examples:

Example (1). A, a United States citizen, is, on January 1, 1963, a director of M, a foreign corporation. X, on January 1, 1963, is a United States person owning 5 percent in value of the outstanding stock of M Corporation. A must file a return under the provisions of subparagraph (1) of this paragraph.

Example (2). The facts are the same as in Example (1) except that X owns only 2 percent in value of the outstanding stock of M Corporation on January 1, 1963. On July 1, 1963, X acquires 2 percent in value of the outstanding stock of M Corporation and on September 1, 1963, he acquires an additional 2 percent in value of such stock. The July 1, 1963, transaction does not give rise to liability to file a return; however, A must file a return as a result of the September 1, 1963, transaction because X's holdings now exceed 5 percent.

Example (3). The facts are the same as in Example (2) and, on September 15, 1963, X acquires an additional 4 percent in value of the outstanding stock of M Corporation (X's total holdings are now 10 percent). On November 1, 1963, X acquires an additional 2 percent in value of the outstanding stock of M Corporation. The September 15, 1963, transaction does not give rise to liability to file a return since X has not acquired 5 percent in value of the outstanding stock of M Corporation since A last became liable to file a return. However, A must file a return as a result of the November 1, 1963, transaction because X has now acquired an additional 5 percent in value of the outstanding stock of M Corporation.

Example (4). The facts are the same as in Examples (2) and (3) and, in addition, B, a United States citizen, becomes an officer of M Corporation on October 1, 1963. B is not required to file a return either as a result of the facts set forth in Example (2) or as a result of the September 15, 1963, transaction described in Example (3). However, B is required to file a return as a result of the November 1, 1963, transaction described in Example (3) because X has acquired an additional 5 percent in value of the outstanding stock of M Corporation while B is an officer or director.

(b) *Returns required of United States persons when liability to file arises on January 1, 1963.* Each United States person who, on January 1, 1963, owns 5 percent or more in value of the outstanding stock of a foreign corporation, shall make a return on Form 959 with respect to such foreign corporation setting forth the following information:

(1) The name, address, and identifying number of the shareholder (or shareholders) filing the return, and the internal revenue district in which such shareholder filed his most recent United States income tax return;

(2) The name, business address, and employer identification number, if any, of the foreign corporation, the name of the country under the laws of which it is incorporated, and the name of the country in which is located its principal place of business;

(3) The date of organization and, if any, of each reorganization of the foreign corporation if such reorganization occurred on or after January 1, 1960, while the shareholder owned 5 percent or more in value of the outstanding stock of such corporation;

(4) The name and address of the foreign corporation's statutory or resident agent in the country of incorporation;

(5) The name, address, and identifying number of any branch office or agent of the foreign corporation located in the United States;

(6) If the foreign corporation has filed a United States income tax return, or participated in the filing of a consolidated return, for any of its last three calendar or fiscal years immediately preceding January 1, 1963, state each year for which a return was filed (including, in the case of a consolidated return, the name of the corporation filing such return), the type of form used, the internal revenue office to which it was sent, and the amount of tax, if any, paid;

(7) The name and address of the person (or persons) having custody of the books of account and records of the foreign corporation, and the location of such books and records if different from such address;

(8) The names, addresses, and identifying numbers of all United States persons who are principal officers (for example, president, vice president, secretary, treasurer, and comptroller) or members of the board of directors of the foreign corporation as of January 1, 1963;

(9) A complete description of the principal business activities in which the foreign corporation is actually engaged and,

Reg. § 1.6046-1 (b) (9)

24,300.2 (I.R.C.)   Reg. § 1.6046-1(b)(9)   9-3-74

if the foreign corporation is a member of a group constituting a chain of ownership with respect to each unit of which the shareholder owns 5 percent or more in value of the outstanding stock, a chart showing the foreign corporation's position in the chain of ownership and the percentages of ownership;

(10) A copy of the following statements prepared in accordance with generally accepted accounting principles and in such form and detail as is customary for the corporation's accounting records:

(i) The corporation's profit and loss statement for the most recent complete annual accounting period; and

(ii) The corporation's balance sheet as of the end of the most recent complete annual accounting period;

(11) A statement showing as of January 1, 1963, the amount and type of any indebtedness of the foreign corporation—

(i) To any United States person owning 5 percent or more in value of its stock, or

(ii) To any other foreign corporation owning 5 percent or more in value of the outstanding stock of the foreign corporation with respect to which the return is filed provided that the shareholder filing the return owns 5 percent or more in value of the outstanding stock of such other foreign corporation, together with the name, address, and identifying number, if any, of each such shareholder or entity;

(12) A statement, as of January 1, 1963, showing the name, address, and identifying number, if any, of each person who is, on January 1, 1963, a subscriber to the stock of the foreign corporation, and the number of shares subscribed to by each;

(13) A statement showing the number of shares of each class of stock of the foreign corporation owned by each shareholder filing the return and—

(i) If such stock was acquired after December 31, 1953, the dates of acquisition, the amounts paid or value given therefor, the method of acquisition, i.e., by original issue, purchase on open market, direct purchase, gift, inheritance, etc., and from whom acquired; or

(ii) If such stock was acquired before January 1, 1954, a statement that such stock was acquired before such date, and the value at which such stock is carried on the books of such shareholder;

(14) A statement showing as of January 1, 1963, the name, address, and identifying number of each United States person who owns 5 percent or more in value of the outstanding stock of the foreign corporation, the classes of stock held, the number of shares of each class held, including the name, address, and identifying number, if any, of each actual owner if such person is different from the shareholder of record and a statement of the nature and amount of the interests of each such actual owner; and

(15) The total number of shares of each class of outstanding stock of the foreign corporation (or other data indicating the shareholder's percentage of ownership).

(c) *Returns required of United States persons when liability to file arises after January 1, 1963*—(1) *United States persons required to file.* A return on Form 959, containing the information required by subparagraph (3) of this paragraph, shall be made by each United States person when at any time after January 1, 1963—

(i) Such person acquires (whether in one or more transactions) outstanding stock of such foreign corporation which has, or which when added to any such stock then owned by him (excluding any stock owned by him on January 1, 1963, if on that date he owned 5 percent or more in value of such stock) has, a value equal to 5 percent or more in value of the outstanding stock of such foreign corporation, or

(ii) Such person, having already acquired the interest referred to in paragraph (b) of this section or in subdivision (i) of this subparagraph—

(a) Acquires (whether in one or more transactions) an additional 5 percent or more in value of the outstanding stock of such foreign corporation,

(b) Owns 5 percent or more in value of the outstanding stock of such foreign corporation when such foreign corporation is reorganized (as defined in paragraph (f)), or

(c) Disposes of sufficient stock in such foreign corporation to reduce his interest to less than 5 percent in value of the outstanding stock of such foreign corporation. The provisions of this subparagraph may be illustrated by the following examples:

Example (1). On January 15, 1963, A, a United States person, acquires 5 percent in value of the outstanding stock of M, a foreign corporation. A must file a return under the provisions of this subparagraph.

Example (2). On January 1, 1963, B, a United States person, owns 2 percent in value of the outstanding stock of M, a foreign corporation. B is not required to file a return under the provisions of this section because he does not own 5 percent or more in value of the outstanding stock of M Corporation. On February 1, 1963, B acquires an additional 3 percent in value of the oustanding stock of M Corporation.

B must file a return under the provisions of this subparagraph.

Example (3). On January 1, 1963, C, a United States person, owns 6 percent in value of the outstanding stock of M, a foreign corporation. C must file a return under the provisions of paragraph (b) of this section. On February 1, 1963, C acquires an additional 2 percent in value of the outstanding stock of M Corporation in a transaction not involving a reorganization. C is not required to file a return under the provisions of this subparagraph.

Example (4). The facts are the same as in Example (3) except that, in addition, on April 1, 1963, C acquires 2 percent in value of the outstanding stock of M Corporation in a transaction not involving a reorganization. (C's total holdings are now 10 percent.) C is not required to file a return under the provisions of this subparagraph because he has not acquired 5 percent or more in value of the outstanding stock of M Corporation since he last became liable to file a return. On May 1, 1963, C acquires 1 percent in value of the outstanding stock of M Corporation. C must file a return under the provisions of this subparagraph.

Example (5). On June 1, 1963, D, a United States person, owns 12 percent in value of the outstanding stock of M, a foreign corporation. Also, on June 1, 1963, M Corporation is reorganized and, as a result of such reorganization, D owns only 6 percent of the outstanding stock of such foreign corporation. D must file a return under the provisions of this subparagraph.

Example (6). The facts are the same as in Example (5) except that, in addition, on November 1, 1970, D donates 2 percent of the outstanding stock of M Corporation to a charity. Since D has disposed of sufficient stock to reduce his interest in M Corporation to less than 5 percent in value of the outstanding stock of such corporation, D must file a return under the provisions of this subparagraph.

(2) *Shareholders who become United States persons.* A return on Form 959, containing the information required by subparagraph (3) of this paragraph, shall be made by each person who at any time after January 1, 1963, becomes a United States person while owning 5 percent or more in value of the outstanding stock of such foreign corporation.

(3) *Information required to be shown on return*—(i) *In general.* The return on Form 959, required to be filed by persons described in subparagraph (1) or (2) of this paragraph, shall set forth the same information as is required by the provisions of paragraph (b) of this section except that where such provisions require information with respect to January 1, 1963, such information shall be furnished with respect to the date on which liability arises to file the return required under this paragraph.

(ii) *Additional information.* In addition to the information required under subdivision (i) of this subparagraph, the following information shall also be furnished in the return required under this paragraph:

(a) The date on or after January 1, 1963, if any, on which such shareholder (or shareholders) last filed a return under this section with respect to the corporation;

(b) If a return is filed by reason of becoming a United States person, the date the shareholder became a United States person;

(c) If a return is filed by reason of the disposition of stock, the date and method of such disposition and the person to whom such disposition was made; and

(d) If a return is filed by reason of the organization or reorganization of the foreign corporation on or after January 1, 1963, the following information with respect to such organization or reorganization:

(1) A statement showing a detailed list of the classes and kinds of assets transferred to the foreign corporation including a description of the assets (such as a list of patents, copyrights, stock, securities, etc.), the fair market value of each asset transferred (and, if such asset is transferred by a United States person, its adjusted basis), the date of transfer, the name, address, and identifying number, if any, of the owner immediately prior to the transfer, and the consideration paid by the foreign corporation for such transfer;

(2) A statement showing the assets transferred and the notes or securities issued by the foreign corporation, the name, address, and identifying number, if any, of each person to whom such transfer or issue was made, and the consideration paid to the foreign corporation for such transfer or issue; and

(3) An analysis of the changes in the corporation's surplus accounts occurring on or after January 1, 1963.

(iii) *Exclusion of information previously furnished.* In any case where any identical item of information required to be filed under this paragraph by a shareholder with respect to a foreign corporation has previously been furnished by such shareholder in any return made in accordance with the provisions of this section, such shareholder may satisfy the requirements of this paragraph by filing Form 959, identifying such item of information, the date furnished, and stating that it is unchanged.

(d) *Associations, etc.* Returns are required to be filed in accordance with the provisions of this section with respect to any foreign association, foreign joint-stock company, or foreign insurance company, etc., which would be considered to be a corporation under § 301.7701-2 of this chapter (Regulations on Procedure and Administration). Persons who would qualify by the nature of their functions and ownership in such associations, etc., as officers, directors, or shareholders thereof will be treated as such for purposes of this section without regard to their designations under local law.

(e) *Special provisions* — (1) *Return jointly made.* Any two or more persons required under paragraph (a) of this section to make a return with respect to one or more shareholders of the same corporation, or under paragraph (b) or (c) of this section to make a return with respect to the same corporation, may in lieu of making several returns, jointly make one return.

(2) *Separate return for each corporation.* When returns are required with respect to more than one foreign corporation, a separate return must be made for each corporation.

(3) *Use of power of attorney by officers or directors*—(i) *In general.* Any two or more persons required under paragraph (a) of this section to make a return with respect to one or more shareholders of the same corporation may, by means of one or more duly executed powers of attorney, constitute one of their number as attorney in fact for the purpose of making such returns or for the purpose of making a joint return under subparagraph (1) of this paragraph.

(ii) *Nature of power of attorney.* The power of attorney referred to in subdivision (i) of this subparagraph shall be limited to the making of returns required under paragraph (a) of this section and shall be limited to a single calendar year with respect to which such returns are required.

(iii) *Manner of execution of power of attorney.* The use of technical language in the preparation of the power of attorney referred to in subdivision (i) of this subparagraph is not necessary. Such power of attorney shall be signed by the individual United States citizen or resident required to file a return or returns under paragraph (a) of this section. Such power of attorney must be acknowledged before a notary public or, in lieu thereof, witnessed by two disinterested persons. The notarial seal must be affixed unless such seal is not required under the laws of the state or country wherein such power of attorney is executed.

(iv) *Manner of execution of return under authority of power of attorney.* A return made under authority of one or more powers of attorney referred to in subdivision (i) of this subparagraph shall be signed by the attorney in fact for each principal for which such attorney in fact is acting. A copy of such one or more powers of attorney shall be kept at a convenient and safe location accessible to internal revenue officers, and shall at all times be available for inspection by such officers.

(v) *Effect on penalties.* The fact that a return is made under authority of a power of attorney referred to in subdivision (i) of this subparagraph shall not affect the principal's liability for penalties provided for failure to file a return required under paragraph (a) of this section or for filing a false or fraudulent return.

(4) *Persons excepted from filing returns*—(i) *Return required of officer or director under paragraph (a)(1).* Notwithstanding paragraph (a)(1) of this section, any United States citizen or resident required to make a return under such paragraph with respect to shareholders of a foreign corporation, need not make such return if, on January 1, 1963, three or fewer United States persons own 95 percent or more in value of the outstanding stock of such foreign corporation and file a return or returns with respect to such corporation under paragraph (b) of this section.

(ii) *Return required of officer or director under paragraph (a)(2).* Notwithstanding paragraph (a)(2) of this section, any United States citizen or resident required to make a return under such paragraph with respect to a person acquiring stock of a foreign corporation in an acquisition described in subdivision (i)(a) or (b) of such paragraph need not make such return, if—

(a) As a result of such acquisition of stock of such foreign corporation, a United States person files a return as a shareholder under paragraph (c)(1) of this section, and

(b) Immediately after such acquisition of stock, three or fewer United States persons own 95 percent or more in value of the outstanding stock of such foreign corporation.

(iii) *Return required by reason of attribution rules.* Notwithstanding paragraph (b) or (c) of this section, any person required to make a return under such paragraph with respect to a foreign corporation need not make such return, if—

(a) Such person does not directly own an interest in the foreign corporation,

(b) Such person is required to furnish the information solely by reason of attribution of stock ownership from a United States person under paragraph (i) of this section, and

(c) The person from whom the stock ownership is attributed furnishes all of the information required under paragraph (b) or (c) of this section of the person to whom such stock ownership is attributed.

(iv) *Return required of officer or director with respect to person described in subdivision (iii).* Notwithstanding paragraph (a) of this section, any United States citizen or resident required to make a return under such paragraph with respect to a person exempted under subdivision (iii) of this subparagraph from making a return need not make a return with respect to such person.

(5) *Persons excepted from furnishing items of information.* Any person required to furnish any item of information under paragraph (b) or (c) of this section with respect to a foreign corporation, may, if such item of information is furnished by another person having an equal or greater stock interest (measured in terms of value of such stock) in such foreign corporation, satisfy such requirement by filing a statement with his return on Form 959 indicating that such liability has been satisfied and identifying the return in which such item of information was included.

(f) *Meaning of terms.* For purposes of this section—

(1) *Acquisition.* Stock in a foreign corporation shall be considered acquired when a person has an unqualified right to receive such stock, even though such stock is not actually issued. For example, when under the law of a foreign country, all the necessary steps for incorporation are completed but stock in the corporation will not be is-

sued within 30 days, every United States citizen or resident who is an officer or a director of such corporation, provided a United States person has an interest of 5 percent or more in such corporation, and every such United States person shall, within 90 days of the date of incorporation, file the returns required under section 6046 and this section. In the case of a reorganization, new stock may be acquired, depending on the type of reorganization, whether or not any stock certificates are surrendered or exchanged or the designation of such stock is altered.

(2) *Reorganization.* With respect to a foreign corporation, the term "reorganization" shall mean not only a transaction described in section 368(a)(1) and the regulations thereunder but also any other transaction or series of transactions which has the same effect.

(3) *United States person.* For purposes of section 6046 and this section the term "United States person" has the meaning assigned to it by section 7701(a)(30) of the Code, except that—

(i) With respect to a corporation organized under the laws of the Commonwealth of Puerto Rico, such term does not include an individual who is a bona fide resident of Puerto Rico, if a dividend received by such individual during the taxable year from such corporation would, for purposes of section 933(1), be treated as income derived from sources within Puerto Rico,

(ii) With respect to a corporation organized under the laws of the Virgin Islands such term does not include an individual who is a bona fide resident of the Virgin Islands and whose income tax obligation under subtitle A (relating to income taxes) of the Code for the taxable year is satisfied pursuant to section 28(a) of the Revised Organic Act of the Virgin Islands, approved July 22, 1954 (48 U.S.C. 1642), by paying tax on income derived from all sources both within and outside the Virgin Islands into the treasury of the Virgin Islands, and

(iii) With respect to a corporation organized under the laws of any possession of the United States (other than Puerto Rico or the Virgin Islands), such term does not include an individual who is a bona fide resident of such possession and whose income derived from sources within any possession of the United States is not, by reason of section 931(a), includible in gross income under subtitle A (relating to income taxes) of the Code for the taxable year.

The provisions of paragraph (b), (c), or (d), respectively, of § 1.957-4 shall apply for purposes of determining whether an individual is excepted under subdivision (i), (ii), or (iii), respectively, of this subparagraph from being a United States person with respect to a corporation described in such subdivision.

(4) *Applicable Form 959.* The Form 959 which shall be used for purposes of this section is Form 959 (Rev. Jan. 1963) or such subsequent revision of such form as may be in use at the time the liability to file a return on Form 959 arises.

(g) *Method of reporting.* All amounts furnished in returns prescribed under this section shall be expressed in United States currency with a statement of the exchange rates used. All statements required to be submitted on or with returns under this section shall be rendered in the English language.

(h) *Actual ownership of stock.* If any shareholder, referred to in this section, is not the actual owner of the stock of the foreign corporation, the information required under this section shall be furnished in the name of and by such actual owner. For example, in the case of stock held by a nominee, the information required under this section shall be furnished by the actual owner of such stock.

(i) *Constructive ownership of stock*—(1) *In general.* Stock owned directly or indirectly by or for a foreign corporation or a foreign partnership shall be considered as being owned proportionately by its shareholders or partners. Thus, any United States person who is a member of a nonresident foreign partnership which becomes a shareholder in a foreign corporation shall be considered to be a shareholder in such foreign corporation to the extent of his proportionate share in such partnership.

(2) *Members of family.* An individual shall be considered as owning the stock owned directly or indirectly by or for his brothers and sisters (whether by the whole or half blood), his spouse, his ancestors, and his lineal descendants. However, when stock is treated as owned by an individual under the rule provided in this subparagraph, it shall not be treated as owned by him for the purposes of again applying such rule in order to make another the constructive owner of such stock. The provisions of this subparagraph may be illustrated by the following example:

Example. H, W, and HF are United States citizens. W, wife of H, owns 20 percent of the value of the outstanding stock of X, a foreign corporation. X Corporation owns 90 percent of the value of the outstanding stock of Y, a foreign corporation. Y Corporation becomes the owner of 50 percent of the value of the outstanding stock of each of two newly organized foreign corporations, M and N. In applying the "members of family" rule, H is considered to own 20 percent of the value of the outstanding stock of X Corporation, and 18 percent of the value of the outstanding stock of Y Corporation, and 9 percent of M Corporation and N Corporation. However, HF, the father of H, is not considered to own stock of X, Y, M, or N since his son, H, is not treated as the owner of such stock for purposes of again applying the "members of family" rule.

(j) *Time and place for filing return*—(1) *Time for filing.* Any return required by section 6046 and this section shall be filed on or before the 90th day after the date on which a United States citizen, resident, or person becomes liable to file such return under any provision of section 6046(a) and of paragraph (a), (b), or (c) of this section. The Director of the Internal Revenue Service Center where the return is required to be filed is authorized to grant reasonable extensions of time for filing returns under section 6046 and this section in accordance with the applicable provisions of section 6081(a) and § 1.6081-1.

(2) *Place for filing.* Returns required by section 6046 and this section shall be filed

Reg. § 1.6046-1 (j) (2)

24,300.4 (I.R.C.)   Reg. § 1.6046-1(j)(2)   9-3-74

with the Internal Revenue Service Center designated in the instructions of the applicable form.

(k) *Penalties.* (1) for criminal penalties for failure to file a return and filing a false or fraudulent return, see sections 7203, 7206, and 7207.

(2) For civil penalty for failure to file return, or failure to show information required on a return, under this section, see section 6679.

○━ § 1.6046-2 (T.D. 6623, filed 11-30-62 amended by T.D. 7322, filed 8-23-74.) **Returns as to foreign corporations which are created or organized, or reorganized, on or after September 15, 1960, and before January 1, 1963.**

(a) *Requirement of returns.* In the case of any foreign corporation which is created or organized, or reorganized, on or after September 15, 1960, and before January 1, 1963—

(1) Each United States citizen or resident who was an officer or director of such corporation at any time within 60 days after such creation or organization, or reorganization, and

(2) Each United States shareholder of such corporation by or for whom, at any time within 60 days after such creation or organization, or reorganization, 5 percent or more in value of such corporation's then outstanding stock was owned directly or indirectly (including, in the case of an individual stock owned by members of his family), shall file a return on Form 959 (Rev. Oct. 1960), United States Information Return With Respect to the Creation or Organization, or Reorganization, of a Foreign Corporation.

(b) *Information required to be shown on return.* The return required by section 6046, prior to its amendment by section 20 (b) of the Revenue Act of 1962, and this section shall set forth the following information:

(1) The name and address of the person (or persons) filing the return, and an indication that he is a United States shareholder, officer, or director;

(2) The name and business address of the foreign corporation;

(3) The name of the country under the laws of which the foreign corporation was created or organized, or reorganized;

(4) The name and address of the foreign corporation's statutory or resident agent in the country of incorporation;

(5) The date of the foreign corporation's creation or organization, or reorganization;

(6) A statement of the manner in which the creation or organization, or reorganization, of the foreign corporation was effected;

(7) A complete statement of the reasons for, and the purposes sought to be accomplished by, the creation or organization, or reorganization, of the foreign corporation;

(8) A statement showing the classes and kinds of assets transferred to the foreign corporation in connection with its creation or organization, or reorganization, including a list completely describing each asset or group of assets, its value, date of transfer, and the name and address of person (or persons) owning such asset or group immediately prior to the transfer;

(9) A statement showing the assets transferred and the securities issued by the foreign corporation in its creation or organization or reorganization, as well as the name and address of each person to whom such a transfer or issuance was made;

(10) A statement specifying the amount and type of any indebtedness due from the foreign corporation to each of its shareholders and the name of each such shareholder;

(11) The names and addresses of the shareholders of the foreign corporation at the time of its creation or organization, or reorganization, and the classes of stock and number of shares held by each;

(12) The names and addresses of subscribers to the stock of the foreign corporation, and the number of shares subscribed to by each; and

(13) The name and address of the person (or persons) having custody of the books of account and records of the foreign corporation, and the location of such books and records if different from such address.

(c) *Time and place for filing return.* The return required by section 6046, prior to its amendment by section 20 (b) of the Revenue Act of 1962, and this section shall be filed with the Internal Revenue Service Center designated in the instructions of the applicable form. Such return shall be filed on or before the 90th day after the date such foreign corporation is created or organized, or reorganized.

○━ § 1.6046-3 (Originally § 1.6046-1, T.D. 6364, filed 2-13-59; republished in T.D. 6500, filed 11-25-60; renumbered and amended by T.D. 6623, filed 11-30-62; T.D. 6677, filed 9-16-63; and T.D. 7322, filed 8-23-74.) **Returns as to formation or reorganization of foreign corporations prior to September 15, 1960.**

(a) *Requirement of returns.* Every attorney, accountant, fiduciary, bank, trust company, financial institution, or other person, who, on or before September 14, 1960, aids, assists, counsels, or advises in, or with respect to, the formation, organization, or reorganization of any foreign corporation shall file an information return on Form 959 (as in use prior to the October 1960 revision). The return must be filed in every such case regardless of—

(1) The nature of the counsel or advice given, whether for or against the formation, organization, or reorganization of the foreign corporation, or the nature of the aid or assistance rendered, and

(2) The action taken upon the advice or counsel, that is, whether the foreign corporation is actually formed, organized or reorganized.

(b) *Special provisions*—(1) *Employers.* In the case of aid, assistance, counsel, or advice in, or with respect to, the formation, organization, or reorganization of a foreign corporation given by a person in whole or in part through the medium of employees (including, in the case of a corporation, the officers thereof), the return made by the employer must set forth in detail the information required by this section including that which, as an incident to such employment, is within the possession or knowledge or under the control of such employees.

(2) *Employees.* The obligation of an employee (including, in the case of a corporation, the officers thereof) to file a return with respect to any aid, assistance, counsel, or advice in or with respect to the formation, organization, or reorganization of a foreign corporation, given as an incident to his employment, will be satisfied if a return as prescribed by this section is duly filed by the employer. Clerks, stenographers, and other employees rendering aid or assistance solely of a clerical or mechanical character in or with respect to the formation, organization, or reorganization of a foreign corporation are not required to file returns by reason of such services.

(3) *Partners.* In the case of aid, assistance, counsel, or advice in, or with respect to, the formation, organization, or reorganization of a foreign corporation given by one or more members of a partnership in the course of its business, the obligation of each such individual member to file a return will be satisfied if a return as prescribed by this section is duly filed by the partnership executed by all the members of the firm who gave any such aid, assistance, counsel, or advice. If, however, the partnership has been dissolved at the time the return is due, individual returns must be filed by each member of the former partnership who gave any such aid, assistance, counsel, or advice.

(4) *Return jointly made.* If two or more persons aid, assist, counsel, or advise in, or with respect to, the formation, organization, or reorganization of a particular foreign corporation, any two or more of such persons may, in lieu of filing several returns, jointly execute and file one return.

(5) *Separate return for each corporation.* If a person aids, assists, counsels, or advises in, or with respect to, the formation, organization, or reorganization of more than one foreign corporation, a separate return must be filed with respect to each foreign corporation.

(c) *Information required to be shown on return.* The return required by section 6046, prior to its amendment by section 7(a) of the Act of September 14, 1960, and this section shall set forth the following information to the extent the information is within the possession or knowledge, or under the control, of the person filing the return:

(1) The name and address of the person (or persons) to whom, and the person (or persons) for whom, or on whose behalf, the aid, assistance, counsel, or advice was given;

(2) The name and address of the foreign corporation and the country under the laws of which it was formed, organized, or reorganized;

(3) The month and year when the foreign corporation was formed, organized, or reorganized;

(4) A statement of the manner in which the formation, organization, or reorganization of the foreign corporation was effected;

(5) A complete statement of the reasons for, and the purposes sought to be accomplished by, the formation, organization, or reorganization of the foreign corporation;

(6) A statement showing the classes and kinds of assets transferred to the foreign corporation in connection with its formation, organization, or reorganization, including a detailed list of any stock or securities included in such assets, and a statement showing the names and addresses of the persons who were the owners of such assets immediately prior to the transfer;

(7) The names and addresses of the shareholders of the foreign corporation at the time of the completion of its formation, organization, or reorganization, showing the classes of stock and number of shares held by each and, in the case of Forms 959 filed after December 31, 1958, the names and addresses of the subscribers to the stock of the foreign corporation and the number of shares subscribed to by each;

(8) The name and address of the person (or persons) having custody of the books of account and records of the foreign corporation; and

(9) Such other information as is required by the return form.

(d) *Privileged communications.* An attorney-at-law is not required to file a return with respect to any advice given or information obtained through the relationship of attorney and client.

(e) *Time and place for filing return*—(1) *Time for filing.* Returns required by section 6046, prior to its amendment by section 7(a) of the Act of September 14, 1960, and this section shall be filed within 30 days after the first performance of any of the functions referred to in paragraph (a) of this section. If in a particular case, the aid, assistance, counsel, or advice given by any person extends over a period of more than one day, such person, to avoid multiple filings of returns, shall file a return within 30 days after either of the following events:

(i) The formation, organization, or reorganization of the foreign corporation, or

(ii) The termination of his aid, assistance, counsel, or advice in, or with respect to, the formation, organization, or reorganization of the foreign corporation.

(2) *Place for filing.* Returns required by section 6046 and this section shall be filed with the Internal Revenue Service Center designated in the instructions of the applicable form.

(f) *Penalties.* For criminal penalties for failure to file a return and filing a false or fraudulent return, see sections 7203, 7206, and 7207.

○━▶ **§ 301.6046 Statutory provisions; returns as to organization or reorganization of foreign corporations and as to acquisitions of their stock. [Sec. 6046, IRC]**

○━▶ § 301.6046-1 (T.D. 6498, filed 10-24-60 and T.D. 6555, filed 3-14-61; amended by T.D. 6700, filed 1-6-64.) **Returns as to organiza-**

Reg. § 301.6046-1

24,300.6 (I.R.C.)   Reg. § 301.6046-1   9-3-74

tion or reorganization of foreign corporations and as to acquisitions of their stock.

For provisions relating to requirement of returns as to organization or reorganization of foreign corporations and as to acquisitions of their stock, see §§ 1.6046-1 to 1.6046-3, inclusive, of this chapter (Income Tax Regulations).

○→ § 1.6047 Statutory provisions; information relating to certain trusts and annuity and bond purchase plans. [Sec. 6047, IRC]

○→ § 1.6047-1 (T.D. 6677, filed 9-16-63; amended by T.D. 6883, filed 5-2-66.) Information to be furnished with regard to employee retirement plan covering an owner-employee.

(a) *Trustees and insurance companies* —(1) *Requirement of return.* (i) Every trustee of a trust described in section 401(a) and exempt from tax under section 501(a) which makes payments of amounts described in subparagraph (2) of this paragraph aggregating $10 or more during any calendar year to an individual (or his beneficiary) who was covered, within the meaning of paragraph (a)(2) of § 1.401-10, as an owner-employee under the plan of which such trust is a part shall make a return on Forms 1096 and 1099 for such year showing the name and address of the person to whom paid, the aggregate amount of such payments, specifically identified as an amount to which this paragraph applies, and such other information as is required by the forms. A separate Form 1099 shall be filed with respect to each payee. The term "owner-employee" means an owner-employee as defined in section 401(c)(3) and paragraph (d) of § 1.401-10. Any custodial account which satisfies the requirements of section 401(f) shall be treated as a qualified trust and the custodian of such a custodial account must comply with the requirements of this section as if he were the trustee.

(ii) Every issuer of a contract which is treated as an annuity contract under sections 401 through 404 purchased by a trust described in section 401(a) and exempt from tax under section 501(a) or under a plan described in section 403(a) which makes payments of amounts described in subparagraph (2) of this paragraph aggregating $10 or more during any calendar year to an individual (or his beneficiary) who was covered, within the meaning of paragraph (a)(2) of § 1.401-10, as an owner-employee under the plan of which such trust is a part or under which such contract was purchased shall make a return on Forms 1096 and 1099 for such year showing the name and address of the person to whom paid, the aggregate amount of such payments, specifically identified as an amount to which this paragraph applies, and such other information as is required by the form. A separate Form 1099 shall be filed with respect to each payee.

(2) *Amounts subject to this section.* The amounts subject to reporting under subparagraph (1) of this paragraph include all amounts distributed or made available to which section 402(a) (relating to employees' trusts) or section 403(a) (relating to employee annuity plans) applies, whether or not such amounts are includible in gross income and whether or not attributable to contributions made while the individual to whom they relate was an owner-employee. However, amounts subject to reporting do not include any amounts distributed or made available by the trustee of any trust or the issuer of any contract under any plan with respect to which he has not received the notification provided in either subparagraph (3) of this paragraph or paragraph (b) of this section. Amounts distributed or made available

under the plan include, for example, amounts received by the individual as loans on contracts purchased under the plan, and payments made to the individual by reason of the surrender of contracts purchased under the plan, whether or not prior to their maturity.

(3) *Notification by trustee.* The trustee of any trust described in section 401(a) and exempt from tax under section 501(a) who receives notification from any owner-employee that contributions have been made to the trust on behalf of that owner-employee as an owner-employee shall notify in writing the issuer of any contract which is treated as an annuity contract under sections 401 through 404 purchased by the trust for the benefit of that owner-employee that such contributions have been made to such trust. Such notification shall be delivered to such issuer at the time such contract is purchased or within 90 days after the notification required by paragraph (b) of this section is received by the trustee, whichever is later. Only one such notification must be made with respect to any contract.

(4) *Record keeping.* Any trustee, insurance company, or other person, which is referred to in subparagraph (1) of this paragraph and which is notified under section 6047(b) that contributions to the trust or under the plan have been made on behalf of an owner-employee shall maintain a record of such notification until all funds of the trust or under the plan on behalf of the owner-employee have been distributed.

(5) *Inclusion of other payments.* The Form 1099 filed under this section by any person with respect to payments to another person during a calendar year may, at the election of the maker, include other payments made by him to such other person during such year which are required to be reported on Form 1099.

(6) *Time and place for filing.* The return required under this section for any calendar year shall be filed after the close of that year and on or before February 28 of the following year with any of the Internal Revenue Service Centers, the addresses of which are listed in the instructions for Form 1096. For extensions of time for filing returns under this section, see § 1.6081-1.

(b) *Notification by owner-employee.* Any owner-employee on behalf of whom contributions are made to a trust described in section 401(a) and exempt under section 501(a) or under a plan described in section 403(a) shall notify in writing—

(1) The trustee of such a trust, or
(2) The issuer of any contract which is treated as an annuity contract under sections 401 through 404 under such plan, that such contributions have been made to such trust or plan. Such notification shall be delivered to such trustee or such issuer during the first calendar year in which such contributions are made on or before February 28 of the year following such year. Only one such notification must be made with respect to any contract or any trust.

(c) *Penalty.* For criminal penalty for furnishing fraudulent information under this section, see § 301.7207-1 of this chapter Regulations on Procedure and Administration).

(d) *Permission to submit information required by Form 1099 on magnetic tape.* For rules relating to permission to submit the information required by Form 1099 on magnetic tape or other media, see § 1.9101-1.

○→ § 301.6047 **Statutory provisions; information relating to certain trusts and annuity and bond purchase plans.** [Sec. 6047, IRC]

○→ § 301.6047-1 (T.D. 6700, filed 1-6-64.) **Information relating to certain trusts and annuity and bond purchase plans.**

For provisions relating to the requirement of returns of information regarding certain trusts and annuity and bond purchase plans, see § 1.6047-1 of this chapter (Income Tax Regulations).

○→ § 301.6048 **Statutory provisions; returns as to creation of or transfers to certain foreign trusts.** [Sec. 6048, IRC]

○→ § 301.6048-1 (T.D. 6700, filed 1-6-64.) **Returns as to creation of or transfers to certain foreign trusts.**

For provisions relating to the requirement of returns as to creation of or transfers to certain foreign trusts, see § 16.3-1 of this chapter (Temporary Regulations under the Revenue Act of 1962).

○→ § 1.6049 **Statutory provisions; returns regarding payments of interest.** [Sec. 6049, IRC]

○→ § 1.6049-1 (T.D. 6628, filed 12-27-62; amended by T.D. 6677, filed 9-16-63; T.D. 6879, filed 3-7-66; T.D. 6883, filed 5-2-66; T.D. 6891, filed 8-3-66; T.D. 7000, filed 1-17-69; T.D. 7154, filed 12-27-71 and T.D. 7311, filed 3-29-74.) **Returns of information as to interest paid in calendar years after 1962 and original issue discount includible in gross income for calendar years after 1970.**

(a) *Requirement of reporting*—(1) *In general.* (i) Every person who makes payments of interest (as defined in § 1.6049-3) aggregating $10 or more to any other person during a calendar year after 1962 shall make an information return on Forms 1096 and 1099 for such calendar year showing the aggregate amount of such payments, the name and address of the person to whom paid, the total of such payments for all persons, and such other information as is required by the forms. In the case of interest paid during calendar years beginning with 1963 and continuing until such time as the Commissioner determines that it is feasible to aggregate payments on two or more accounts, insurance contracts, or investment certificates and this subdivision is amended accordingly to provide for reporting on an aggregate basis, the requirement of this subdivision for the filing of Form 1099 will be met if a person making payments of interest to another person on two or more such accounts, insurance contracts, or investment certificates, files a separate Form 1099 with respect to each such account, contract, or certificate on which $10 or more of interest is paid to such other person during the calendar year. In the case of evidences of indebtedness described in section 6049 (b) (1) (A), separate Forms 1099 may be filed as provided in the pre-

Reg. § 1.6049-1(a)(1)

ceding sentence with respect to holdings in different issues. Thus, if a bank pays to a person interest totaling $15 on one account and $20 on a second account, it may file separate Forms 1099 with respect to the payments of $15 and $20. If the interest on the second account totaled $5 instead of $20, no return would be required with respect to the $5.

(ii) (a) Every person which is a corporation that has outstanding any bond, debenture, note, or certificate or other evidence of indebtedness (referred to in this section and § 1.6049-2 as an obligation) in "registered form" (as defined in paragraph (d) of § 1.6049-2) issued after May 27, 1969 (other than an obligation issued by a corporation pursuant to a written commitment which was binding on May 27, 1969, and at all times thereafter), as to which there is during any calendar year after 1970 an amount of original issue discount (as defined in § 1.6049-2) aggregating $10 or more includible as interest in the gross income for such calendar year of any holder (determined, if semiannual record date reporting is being used under *(b)(1)* of this subdivision, by treating each holder as holding the obligation on every day it was outstanding during the calendar year), shall make an information return on Forms 1096 and 1099-OID for such calendar year showing the following:

(1) The name and address of each record holder for whom such aggregate amount of original issue discount is $10 or more and, for calendar years subsequent to 1972, the account, serial, or other identifying number of each obligation for which a return is being made.

(2) The aggregate amount of original issue discount includible by each such holder for the period during the calendar year for which the return is made (or, if the aggregation rules of *(b)(2)* of this subdivision are being used, that he held the obligations). If, however, the semiannual record date reporting rules are being used under *(b)(1)* of this subdivision, such aggregate amount shall be determined by treating each such record date holder as if he held each such obligation on every day it was outstanding during the calendar year. For purposes of this section, an obligation shall be considered to be outstanding from the date of original issue (as defined in paragraph (b)(3) of § 1.1232-3). In the case of a time deposit open account arrangement to which paragraph (e)(5) of § 1.1232-3A applies, for example, the amount to be shown under this subdivision *(2)* on the Forms 1096 and 1099-OID is the sum (computed under such paragraph (e)(5)) of the amounts separately computed for each deposit made pursuant to the arrangement.

(3) The issue price of the obligation (as defined in paragraph (b)(2) of § 1.1232-3).

(4) The stated redemption price of the obligation at maturity (as defined in paragraph (b)(1)(iii) of § 1.1232-3).

(5) The ratable monthly portion of original issue discount with respect to the obligation as defined in section 1232(a)(3)(A) (determined without regard to a reduction for a purchase allowance or whether the holder purchased at a premium).

(6) The name and address of the person filing the form.

(7) Such other information as is required by the form. And,

(8) The sum, for all such holders of the aggregate amounts of such original issue discount includible for such calendar year for each such holder.

(b) With respect to any obligation (other than an obligation to which paragraph (e) or (f) of § 1.1232-3A applies (relating respectively to deposits in banks and similar financial institutions and to face-amount certificates)), the issuing corporation (or an agent acting on its behalf)—

(1) Shall be permitted (until this subdivision *(1)* is amended) to prepare a Form 1099-OID only for each person who is a holder of record of the obligation on the semiannual record date (if any) used by the corporation (or agent) for the payment of stated interest or, if there is no such date, the semiannual record dates shall be considered to be June 30, and December 31.

(2) Shall be permitted to aggregate all original issue discount with respect to 2 or more obligations of the same issue for which the amounts specified in *(a)(2)*, *(a)(3)*, *(a)(4)*, and *(a)(5)* of this subdivision are proportional and, therefore, may file one Form 1099-OID for all such obligations being aggregated, except that for calendar year 1971 this aggregation rule shall apply only where such specified amounts are identical. For an illustration of proportional aggregation, see example *(4)* in (d) of this subdivision.

(c) In any case in which any one holder of a particular obligation for the calendar year held such obligation on more than one record date, only one Form 1099-OID shall be filed for that year with respect to that holder and that obligation. This provision applies only in the case in which any corporation prepares Forms 1099-OID in accordance with the record date reporting rule of *(b)(1)* of this subdivision.

(d) The requirements of (a)(3), (a)(4) and (a)(5) of this subdivision shall not apply to a time deposit open account arrangement to which paragraph (e)(5) of § 1.1232-3A applies, or to a face-amount certificate to which paragraph (f) of § 1.1232-3A applies.

(e) The provisions of this subdivision (ii) may be illustrated by the following examples:

Example (1). On January 1, 1971, a corporation issued a 10-year bond in registered form which pays stated interest to the holder of record on June 30 and December 31. The bond has an issue price (as defined in paragraph (b)(2) of § 1.1232-3) of $7,600, a stated redemption price (as defined in paragraph (b)(1) of § 1.1232-3) at maturity of $10,000, and a ratable monthly portion of original issue discount (as defined in section 1232(a)(3)(A)) of $20. The corporation's books indicate that A was the holder of record on June 30, 1971, and B was the holder of record on December 31, 1971. Under *(b)(1)* of this subdivision, the corporation is permitted to file separate Forms 1099-OID for both A and B showing, on each form, all items required by *(a)* of this subdivision, including the total original issue discount of $240 for the entire calendar year (which includes original issue discount for all holders), the issue price of $7,600, the stated redemption price at maturity of $10,000, and the ratable monthly portion of original issue discount of $20.

Example (2). Assume the facts stated

in Example (1), except that A is recorded on the books of the corporation as holding the bond on June 30 and December 31, 1971. The corporation shall complete and file only one Form 1099-OID for A.

Example (3). Assume the facts stated in Example (1), except that the books of the corporation show that A held 2 of the bonds at all times in 1971. The amounts of the items listed in *(a)(2), (a)(3), (a)(4),* and *(a)(5)* of this subdivision are identical for the 2 bonds. Under *(b)(2)* of this subdivision, the corporation is permitted to treat the 2 bonds as one for purposes of completing and filing a Form 1099-OID for 1971 and aggregate the amounts being reported.

Example (4). On January 1, 1972, a corporation issued to C 3 bonds in registered form of the same issue with stated redemption prices of $1,000, $5,000, and $10,000. The aggregate amounts of original issue discount for each year, the issue prices, the stated redemption prices, and the monthly portions of original issue discount are the same for each $1,000 of stated redemption price. Thus, all relevant amounts for any one bond are proportional to such amounts for any other bond. Therefore, so long as C holds the bonds the corporation shall be permitted to aggregate on one Form 1099-OID all original issue discount with respect to such obligations in accordance with *(b)(2)* of this subdivision.

Example (5). On June 1, 1971, a corporation issues a 10-year bond to D, for which the ratable monthly portion of original issue discount is $10. For 1971, the corporation uses the record date reporting system permitted by *(b)(1)* of this subdivision. The corporation's books show that E held the bond on June 30, 1971, and that F held the bond on December 31, 1971, the dates on which the corporation pays stated interest on the bond. The corporation shall file a Form 1099-OID for both E and F showing on each form the aggregate amount of original issue discount includible for 1971 of $70 since E and F are each treated as if each held the bond every day it was outstanding and it was outstanding 7 months in 1971. As to D, the corporation is not required to file a Form 1099-OID since D did not hold the bond on either of the 2 record dates.

(iii) Every person who during a calendar year after 1962 receives payments of interest as a nominee on behalf of another person aggregating $10 or more shall make an information return on Forms 1096 and 1087 for such calendar year showing the aggregate amount of such interest, the name and address of the person on whose behalf received, the total of such interest received on behalf of all persons, and such other information as is required by the forms.

(iv) Except with respect to an obligation to which paragraph (e) or (f) of § 1.1232-3A applies (relating respectively to deposits in banks and similar financial institutions and to face-amount certificates), every person who is a nominee on behalf of the actual owner of an obligation as to which there is original issue discount aggregating $10 or more includible in the gross income of such owner during a calendar year after 1970, regardless of whether he receives a Form 1099-OID with respect to such discount, shall make an information return on Forms 1096 and 1087-OID for such calendar year showing in the manner prescribed on such forms the same information for the actual owner as is required or permitted in subdivision (ii) of this subparagraph for the record holder.

(v) Notwithstanding the provisions of subdivisions (iii) and (iv) of this subparagraph, the filing of Form 1087 or Form 1087-OID is not required if—

(a) The record owner is required to file a fiduciary return on Form 1041 disclosing the name, address, and identifying number of the actual owner;

(b) The record owner is a nominee of a banking institution or trust company exercising trust powers, and such banking institution or trust company is required to file a fiduciary return on Form 1041 disclosing the name, address, and identifying number of the actual owner; or

(c) The record owner is a banking institution or trust company exercising trust powers, or a nominee thereof, and the actual owner is an organization exempt from taxation under section 501(a) for which such banking institution or trust company files an annual return, but only if the name, address, and identifying number of the record owner are included on or with the Form 1041 fiduciary return filed for the estate or trust or the annual return filed for the tax exempt organization.

(2) *Definitions.* (i) The term "person" when used in this section does not include the United States, a State, the District of Columbia, a foreign government, a political subdivision of a State or of a foreign government, or an international organization. Therefore, interest paid by or to one of these entities need not be reported. Similarly, original issue discount in respect of an obligation issued by or to one of these entities need not be reported.

(ii) For purposes of this section, a person who receives interest shall be considered to have received it as a nominee if he is not the actual owner of such interest and if he was required under § 1.6109-1 to furnish his identifying number to the payer of the interest (or would have been so required if the total of such interest for the year had been $10 or more), and such number was (or would have been) required to be included on an information return filed by the payer with respect to the interest. However, a person shall not be considered to be a nominee as to any portion of an interest payment which is actually owned by another person whose name is also shown on the information return filed by the payer or nominee with respect to such interest payment. Thus, in the case of a savings account jointly owned by a husband and wife, the husband will not be considered as receiving any portion of the interest on that account as a nominee for his wife if his wife's name is included on the information return filed by the payer with respect to the interest.

(iii) For purposes of this section, in the case of a person who receives a Form 1099-OID, the determination of who is considered a nominee shall be made in a manner consistent with the principles of subdivision (ii) of this subparagraph.

(iv) For purposes of this section and

Reg. § 1.6049-1(a)(2)

§ 1.6049-3, the term "Form 1099-OID" means the appropriate Form 1099 for original issue discount prescribed for the calendar year.

(3) *Determination of person to whom interest is paid or for whom it is received.* For purposes of applying the provisions of this section, the person whose identifying number is required to be included by the payer of interest on an information return with respect to such interest shall be considered the person to whom the interest is paid. In the case of interest received by a nominee on behalf of another person, the person whose identifying number is required to be included on an information return made by the nominee with respect to such interest shall be considered the person on whose behalf such interest is received by the nominee. Thus, in the case of interest made payable to a person other than the record owner of the obligation with respect to which the interest is paid, the record owner of the obligation shall be considered the person to whom the interest is paid for purposes of applying the reporting requirements of this section, since his identifying number is required to be included on the information return filed under such section by the payer of the interest. Similarly, if a stockbroker receives interest on a bond held in street name for the joint account of a husband and wife, the interest is considered as received on behalf of the husband since his identifying number should be shown on the information return filed by the nominee under this section. Thus if the wife has a separate account with the same stockbroker, any interest received by the stockbroker for her separate account should not be aggregated with the interest received for the joint account for purposes of information reporting. For regulations relating to the use of identifying numbers, see § 1.6109-1.

(4) *Determination of person by whom original issue discount is includible or for whom a Form 1099-OID showing original issue discount is received.* For purposes of applying the provisions of this section, the determination of the person by whom original issue discount is includible or for whom a Form 1099-OID is received shall be made in a manner consistent with the principles of subparagraph (3) of this paragraph.

(5) *Inclusion of other payments.* The Form 1099 filed by any person with respect to payments of interest to another person during a calendar year prior to 1972 may, at the election of the maker, include payments other than interest made by him to such other person during such year which are required to be reported on Form 1099. Similarly, the Form 1087 filed by a nominee with respect to payments of interest received by him on behalf of any other person during a calendar year prior to 1972 may include payments of dividends received by him on behalf of such person during such year which are required to be reported on Form 1087. However, except as provided in subparagraph (1)(ii)(b) of this paragraph, a separate Form 1087-OID or 1099-OID shall be filed for each obligation in respect of which original issue discount is required to be reported for any calendar year after 1970. In addition, any person required to report payments on both Forms 1087, 1087-OID, 1099, and 1099-OID, for any calendar year may use one Form 1096 to summarize and transmit such forms.

(b) *When payment deemed made.* For purposes of section 6049, interest is deemed to have been paid when it is credited or set apart to a person without any substantial limitation or restriction as to the time or manner of payment or condition upon which payment is to be made, and is made available to him so that it may be drawn at any time, and its receipt brought within his own control and disposition.

(c) *Time and place for filing.* (1) *Payments of interest.* The returns required under this section for any calendar year for the payment of interest shall be filed after September 30 of such year, but not before the payer's final payment for the year, and on or before February 28 of the following year with any of the Internal Revenue Service Centers, the addresses of which are listed in the instructions for Form 1096. For extensions of time for filing returns under this section, see § 1.6081-1.

(2) *Original issue discount.* (i) The returns required under this section for any calendar year for original issue discount shall be filed after December 31 of such year and on or before February 28 of the following year with any of the Internal Revenue Service Centers, the addresses of which are listed in the instructions for Form 1096. For extensions of time for filing returns under this section, see § 1.6081-1.

(ii) The time for filing returns for the calendar year 1971 required under this section for original issue discount in respect of obligations to which paragraph (e) of § 1.1232-3A applies (relating to deposits in banks and other similar financial institutions) is extended to April 15, 1972.

(d) *Penalty.* For penalty for failure to file the statements required by this section, see § 301.6652-1 of this chapter (Regulations on Procedure and Administration).

(e) *Permission to submit information required by Form 1087 or 1099 on magnetic tape.* For rules relating to permission to submit the information required by Form 1087 or 1099 on magnetic tape or other media, see § 1.9101-1.

○— § 1.6049-2 (T.D. 6628, filed 12-27-62; amended by T.D. 6908, filed 12-30-66; T.D. 6966, filed 8-7-68 and T.D. 7154, filed 12-27-71.) **Interest and original issue discount subject to reporting.**

(a) *Interest in general.* Except as provided in paragraph (b) of this section, the term "interest" when used in this section and §§ 1.6049-1 and 1.6049-3 means:

(1) Interest on evidences of indebtedness issued by a corporation in "registered form" (as defined in paragraph (d) of this section). The phrase "evidences of indebtedness" includes bonds, debentures, notes, certificates and other similar instruments regardless of how denominated.

(2) (i) Before September 9, 1968, interest on deposits (except deposits evidenced by negotiable time certificates of deposits) paid (or credited) by persons carrying on the banking business.

(ii) On and after September 9, 1968, interest on deposits (except deposits evidenced by negotiable time certificates of deposit issued either in bearer form or in an amount of $100,000 or more) paid (or credited) by persons carrying on the banking business. For purposes of this subdivision, a negotiable time certificate of deposit shall not be considered as issued in bearer form if it has been indorsed by the purchaser as payable to his order, and has not been indorsed by any other person (other than a banking institution).

(3) Amounts, whether or not designated as interest, paid (or credited) by mutual savings banks, savings and loan associations, building and loan associations, cooperative banks, homestead associations, credit unions, or similar organizations in respect of deposits, face amount certificates, investment certificates, or withdrawable or repurchasable shares. Thus, even though amounts paid or credited by such organizations with respect to deposits are designated as "dividends", such amounts are included in the definition of interest for purposes of section 6049.

(4) Interest on amounts held by insurance companies under agreements to pay interest thereon. This includes interest paid by insurance companies with respect to policy "dividend" accumulations (see sections 61 and 451 and the regulations thereunder for rules as to when such interest is considered paid), and interest paid with respect to the proceeds of insurance policies left with the insurer. The so-called "interest element" in the case of annuity or installment payments under life insurance or endowment contracts does not constitute interest for purposes of this section.

(5) Interest on deposits with stockbrokers, bondbrokers, and other persons engaged in the business of dealing in securities.

(b) *Exceptions.* The term "interest" when used in section 6049 does not include—

(1) Interest on obligations described in section 103(a)(1) or (3), relating to certain governmental obligations.

(2) Any payment by—
(i) A foreign corporation,
(ii) A nonresident alien individual, or
(iii) A partnership composed in whole or in part of nonresident aliens,

if such corporation, individual, or partnership is not engaged in trade or business within the United States and does not have an office or place of business or a fiscal or paying agent in the United States.

(3) Any interest which is subject to withholding under section 1441 or 1442 (relating to withholding of tax on nonresident aliens and foreign corporations, respectively) by the person making the payment, or which would be so subject to withholding but for the provisions of a treaty, or for the fact that under section 861(a)(1) it is not from sources within the United States, or for the fact that withholding is not required by reason of paragraph (a) or (f) of § 1.1441-4.

(4) In the case of a nominee, any interest which he receives and with respect to which he is required to withhold under section 1441 or 1442, or would be so required to withhold but for the provisions of a treaty, or for the fact that under section 861(a)(1) it is not from sources within the United States, or for the fact that withholding is not required by reason of paragraph (a) or (f) of § 1.1441-4.

(5) Any amount on which the person making the payment is required to deduct and withhold a tax under section 1451 (relating to tax-free covenant bonds), or would be so required but for section 1451 (d) (relating to benefit of personal exemptions).

(6) Any amount which is subject to reporting as original issue discount.

(c) *Original issue discount.* (1) *In general.* The term "original issue discount" when used in this section and §§ 1.6049-1 and 1.6049-3 means original issue discount subject to the ratable inclusion rules of paragraph (a) of § 1.1232-3A, determined without regard to any reduction by reason of a purchase allowance under paragraph (a)(2)(ii) of § 1.1232-3A or a purchase at a premium as defined in paragraph (d)(2) of § 1.1232-3.

(2) *Coordination with interest reporting.* In the case of an obligation issued after May 27, 1969 (other than an obligation issued pursuant to a written commitment which was binding on May 27, 1969, and at all times thereafter), original issue discount which is not subject to the ratable inclusion rules is interest within the meaning of paragraph (a) of this section and original issue discount which is subject to the ratable inclusion rules is not interest within the meaning of such paragraph (a). Thus, for example, if such an obligation has a fixed maturity date not exceeding one year from the date of original issue (as defined in paragraph (b)(3) of § 1.1232-3), the amount of the original issue discount in respect of the obligation shall be reported as interest upon its retirement.

(3) *Exceptions.* Reporting of original issue discount is not required in respect of an obligation which paragraph (b)(2) of this section except from interest reporting.

(d) *Definition of "in registered form."* For purposes of § 1.6049-1 and this section, an evidence of indebtedness is registered form if it is registered as to both principal and interest (or, for purposes of reporting with respect to original issue discount, if it is registered as to principal) and if its transfer must be effected by the surrender of the old instrument and either the reissuance by the corporation of the old instrument to the new holder or the issuance by the corporation of a new instrument to the new holder.

○→ § 1.6049-3 (T.D. 6628, filed 12-27-62; amended by T.D. 6879, filed 3-7-66 and T.D. 7154, filed 12-27-71.) **Statements to recipients of interest payments and holders of obligations to which there is attributed original issue discount.**

(a) *Requirement.* Every person filing (1) a Form 1099 or 1087 under section 6049 (a)(1) and § 1.6049-1 with respect to payments of interest or (2) a Form 1099-OID or 1087-OID with respect to original issue discount includible in gross income, shall furnish to the person whose identifying number is (or should be) shown on the form a written statement showing the information required by paragraph (b) of this section. With respect to interest, no

Reg. § 1.6049-3(a)

24,302.4 (I.R.C.)   Reg. § 1.6049-3(a)   5-2-72

statement is required to be furnished under section 6049(c) and this section to any person if the aggregate of the payments to (or received on behalf of) such person shown on the form would be less than $10. With respect to original issue discount, no statement is required to be furnished under section 6049(c) and this section to any person if the aggregate amount of original issue discount on the statement to such person with respect to the obligation would be less than $10.

(b) *Form of statement*—(1) *In general.* The written statement required to be furnished to a person under paragraph (a) of this section shall show—

(i) With respect to payments of interest (as defined in § 1.6049-2) aggregating $10 or more to any person during a calendar year after 1962—

(a) The aggregate amount of payments shown on the Form 1099 or 1087 as having been made to (or received on behalf of) such person and a legend stating that such amount is being reported to the Internal Revenue Service, and

(b) The name and address of the person filing the form, and

(ii) With respect to original issue discount (as defined in § 1.6049-2) which would aggregate $10 or more on the statement to the holder during a calendar year after 1970—

(a) The aggregate amount or original issue discount includible by (or on behalf of) such person with respect to the obligation, as shown on Form 1099-OID or Form 1087-OID for such calendar year (determined by applying the rules of paragraph (a)(1)(ii) of § 1.6049-1 for purposes of completing either form),

(b) All other items shown on such Form 1099-OID or Form 1087-OID for such calendar year (so determined), and

(c) A legend stating that such amount and such items are being reported to the Internal Revenue Service.

(2) *Special rule.* The requirements of this section for the furnishing of a statement to any person, including the legend requirement of this paragraph, may be met by the furnishing to such person of a copy of the Form 1099, 1099-OID, 1087, or 1087-OID filed pursuant to § 1.6049-1, or a reasonable facsimile thereof, in respect of such person. However, in the case of Form 1087-OID or 1099-OID, a copy of the instructions must also be sent to such person. A statement shall be considered to be furnished to a person within the meaning of this section if it is mailed to such person at his last known address.

(c) *Time for furnishing statements*—(1) *In general*—(i) *Payment of interest.* Each statement required by this section to be furnished to any person for a calendar year for the payment of interest shall be furnished to such person after November 30 of the year and on or before January 31 of the following year, but no statement may be furnished before the final interest payment for the calendar year has been paid. However, the statement may be furnished at any time after September 30 if it is furnished with the final interest payment for the calendar year.

(ii) *Original issue discount.* (a) Except as otherwise provided in this subdivision (ii) each statement required by this section to be furnished to any person for a calendar year for original issue discount shall be furnished to such person after December 31 of the year and on or before January 31 of the following year.

(b) The time for furnishing each statement required by this section to be furnished to any person for the calendar year 1971 for original issue discount in respect of obligations to which paragraph (e) of § 1.1232-3A applies (relating to deposits in banks and other similar financial institutions) is extended to March 15, 1972.

(c) The time for furnishing each statement required by this section to be furnished by a nominee to any person for the calendar year 1971 for original issue discount is extended to February 28, 1972.

(2) *Extensions of time.* For good cause shown upon written application of the person required to furnish statements under this section, the district director may grant an extension of time not exceeding 30 days in which to furnish such statements. The application shall be addressed to the district director with whom the income tax returns of the applicant are filed and shall contain a full recital of the reasons for requesting the extension to aid the district director in determining the period of the extension, if any, which will be granted. Such a request in the form of a letter to the district director signed by the applicant will suffice as an application. The application shall be filed on or before the date prescribed in subparagraph (1) of this paragraph for furnishing the statements required by this section.

(3) *Last day for furnishing statement.* For provisions relating to the time for performance of an act when the last day prescribed for performance falls on Saturday, Sunday, or a legal holiday, see § 301.-7503-1 of this chapter (Regulations on Procedure and Administration).

(d) *Penalty.* For provisions relating to the penalty provided for failure to furnish a statement under this section, see § 301.6678-1 of this chapter (Regulations on Procedure and Administration).

O— § 301.6049 Statutory provisions; returns regarding payments of interest. [Sec. 6049, IRC.]

O— § 301.6049-1 (T.D. 6700, filed 1-6-64.) Returns regarding payments of interest.

For provisions relating to the requirement of returns regarding payments of interest, see §§ 1.6049-1 to 1.6049-3, inclusive. of this chapter (Income Tax Regulations).

O— § 1.6050 Statutory provisions; returns relating to certain transfers to exempt organizations. [Sec. 6050, IRC]

O— § 1.6050-1 (T.D. 7183, filed 4-20-72.) Returns relating to certain transfers to exempt organizations.

(a) *Requirement of reporting.* Any person (individual, corporation, partnership, etc.) who, after December 31, 1969, sells, exchanges, gives, bequeaths or otherwise transfers income producing property with a fair market value in excess of $50,000 (without regard to any lien thereon) to any organization or trust which is known by such person to be an organization or trust exempt from taxation by reason of section 501(a) (excluding organizations described in section 501(c)(1)), or to be an organization referred to in section 511(a)(2)(B), shall make a separate return on

Form 4629 with respect to each such organization or trust. The return shall include the following information:

(1) Name, address, and identifying number (as defined in § 1.6109-1) of the transferor.

(2) Name and address of the transferee.

(3) Description of property transferred.

(4) Date of transfer of the property.

(5) Fair market value of the property (without regard to any lien thereon) on the date of transfer.

(6) Whether the property was transferred subject to a mortgage or other similar lien.

(7) Amount of a mortgage or other similar lien (if any) on the property immediately after the transfer.

(b) *Time and place for filing.* The return required by this section shall be filed on or before the later of July 20, 1972 or the 90th day after the date of transfer of the property with the Mid-Atlantic Service Center, Philadelphia, Pennsylvania. For extensions of time for filing returns under this section, see § 1.6081-1.

(c) *Last day for filing return.* For provisions relating to the time for performance of an act when the last day prescribed for performance falls on Saturday, Sunday, or a legal holiday, see § 301.7503-1 of this chapter (Regulations on Procedure and Administration).

○— § 301.6050 **Statutory provisions; returns relating to certain transfers to exempt organizations.** [Sec. 6050, IRC]

○— § 301.6050-1 (T.D. 7183, filed 4-20-72.) **Returns relating to certain transfers to exempt organizations.**

For provisions regarding the requirement of returns relating to certain transfers to exempt organizations, see § 1.6050-1 of this chapter (Income Tax Regulations).

○— § 31.6051 **Statutory provisions; receipts for employees.** [Sec. 6051, IRC]

○— § 31.6051-1 (T.D. 6155, filed 12-29-55; amended by T.D. 6472, filed 6-22-60; republished in T.D. 6516, filed 12-19-60; further amended by T.D. 6606, filed 8-24-62; T.D. 6983, filed 12-3-68; T.D. 7001, filed 1-17-69; T.D. 7048, filed 6-23-70; T.D. 7115, filed 5-20-71; T.D. 7195, filed 7-10-72; T.D. 7351, filed 4-16-75 and T.D. 7374, filed 7-23-75.) **Statements for employees.**

(a) *Requirement if wages are subject to withholding of income tax*—(1) *General rule.* (i) Every employer, as defined in section 3401(d), required to deduct and withhold from an employee a tax under section 3402, or who would have been required to deduct and withhold a tax under section 3402 (determined without regard to section 3402(n)) if the employee had claimed no more than one withholding exemption, shall furnish to each such employee, in respect of the renumeration paid by such employer to such employee during the calendar year, the tax return copy and the employee's copy of a statement on Form W-2. For example, if the wage bracket method of withholding provided in section 3402(c)(1) is used, a statement on Form W-2 must be furnished to each employee whose wages during any payroll period are equal to or in excess of the smallest wage from which tax must be withheld in the case of an employee claiming one exemption. If the percentage method is used, a statement on Form W-2 must be furnished to each employee whose wages during any payroll period, reduced by the amount of one withholding exemption, are equal to or in excess of the smallest amount of wages from which tax must be withheld. See section 3402(a) and (b) and the regulations thereunder. Each statement on Form W-2 shall show the following:

(a) The name, address, and identification number of the employer,

(b) The name and address of the employee, and his social security account number if wages as defined in section 3121 (a) have been paid or if the Form W-2 is required to be furnished to the employee for a period commencing after December 31, 1962,

(c) The total amount of wages as defined in section 3401(a),

(d) The total amount deducted and withheld as tax under section 3402,

(e) The total amount of wages as defined in section 3121(a), and

(f) The total amount of employee tax under section 3101 deducted and withheld (increased by any adjustment in the calendar year for overcollection, or decreased by any adjustment in such year for undercollection, of such tax during any prior year) and the proportion thereof (expressed either as a dollar amount, as a percentage of the total amount of wages as defined in section 3121(a), or as a percentage of the total amount of employee tax under section 3101) withheld as tax under section 3101(b) for financing the cost of hospital insurance benefits.

See paragraph (d) of this section for provisions relating to the time for furnishing the statement required by this subparagraph. See paragraph (f) of this section for an exception for employers filing composite returns from the requirement that statements for employees be on Form W-2.

(ii) Payments made in 1955 under a wage continuation plan shall be reported on Form W-2 to the extent, and in the manner, provided in paragraph (b)(8)(i) of § 31.3401(a)-1.

(iii) In the case of statements furnished by the employer for whom services are performed, with respect to wages paid after December 31, 1955, "the total amount of wages as defined in section 3401(a)", as used in section 6051(a)(3), shall include all payments made directly by such employer under a wage continuation plan which constitute wages in accordance with paragraph (b)(8)(ii)(a) of § 31.3401(a)-1, without regard to whether tax has been withheld on such amounts.

(iv) Form W-2 is not required in respect of any wage continuation payment made to an employee by or on behalf of a person who is not the employer for whom the employee performs services but who is regarded as an employer under section 3401(d)(1). See paragraph (b)(8) of § 31.3401(a)-1.

(v) In the case of remuneration paid for service described in section 3121(m), relating to service in the uniformed services, performed after 1956, "wages as defined in section 3121(a)", as used in section 6051(a)(2) and (5), shall be determined in accordance with section 3121 (i)(2) and section 3122.

Reg. § 31.6051-1(a)(1)

(vi) In the case of remuneration in the form of tips received by an employee in the course of his employment, the amounts required to be shown by paragraphs (3) and (5) of section 6051(a) (see subdivision (i)(c) and (e) of this subparagraph) shall include only such tips as are reported by the employees to the employer in a written statement furnished to the employer pursuant to section 6053(a).

(2) *Statements for members of the Armed Forces of the United States.* Section 6051(b) contains certain special provisions which are applicable in the case of members of the Armed Forces of the United States in active service. In such case, Form W-2 shall be furnished to each such member of the Armed Forces if any tax has been withheld under section 3402 during the calendar year from the remuneration of such member or if any of the remuneration paid during the calendar year for such active service is includible under chapter 1 of the Code in the gross income of such member. Form W-2, in the case of such member, shall show, as "the total amount of wages as defined in section 3401(a)", as used in section 6501(a) (3), the amount of the remuneration paid during the calendar year which is not excluded under chapter 1 from the gross income of such member, whether or not such remuneration constitutes wages as defined in section 3401(a) and whether or not paid for such active service.

(3) *Undelivered statements for employees.* The Internal Revenue Service copy and the employee's copy of each withholding statement for the calendar year which the employer is required to furnish to the employee and which after reasonable effort he is unable to deliver to the employee shall be retained by the employer for the 4-year period prescribed in paragraph (e)(2) of § 31.6001-1.

(b) *Requirement if wages are not subject to withholding of income tax*—(1) *General rule.* If during the calendar year an employer pays to an employee wages subject to the employee tax imposed by section 3101, but not subject to income tax withholding under section 3402, the employer shall furnish to such employee the tax return copy and the employee's copy of a statement on Form W-2 for such calendar year. Such statement shall show the following:

(i) The name and address of the employer,

(ii) The name, address, and social security account number of the employee,

(iii) The total amount of wages as defined in section 3121(a), and

(iv) The total amount of employee tax deducted and withheld from such wages (increased by any adjustment in such year for overcollection, or decreased by any adjustment in such year for undercollection, of employee tax during any prior year) and the proportion thereof (expressed either as a dollar amount, as a percentage of the total amount of wages as defined in section 3121(a), or as a percentage of the total amount of employee tax under section 3101) withheld as tax under section 3101(b) for financing the cost of hospital insurance benefits.

See paragraph (d) of this section for provisions relating to the time for furnishing the statement required by this paragraph.

(2) *Uniformed services.* In the case of remuneration paid for service described in section 3121(m), relating to service in the uniformed services, performed after 1956, "wages as defined in section 3121 (a)", as used in section 6051(a)(5), shall be determined in accordance with section 3121(i)(2) and section 3122.

(c) *Correction of statements.*—(1) *Federal Insurance Contributions Act.* * * *

(2) *Income tax withholding.* A corrected statement shall be furnished to the employee with respect to a prior calendar year (i) to show the correct amount of wages, as defined in section 3401(a), paid during the prior calendar year if the amount of such wages entered on a statement furnished to the employee for such prior year is incorrect, or (ii) to show the amount actually deducted and withheld as tax under section 3402 if such amount is less or greater than the amount entered as tax withheld on the statement furnished the employee for such prior year. Such statement shall be indicated as corrected.

(3) *Cross reference.* For provisions relating to the disposition of the Internal Revenue Service copy of a corrected statement, see paragraph (b)(2) of § 31.-6011(a)-4 and paragraph (b) of § 31.6051-2.

(d) *Time for furnishing statements*—(1) *In general.* Each statement required by this section for a calendar year and each corrected statement required for the year shall be furnished to the employee on or before January 31 of the year succeeding such calendar year, or, if his employment is terminated before the close of such calendar year, on or before the 30th day after the day on which the last payment of wages is made. For provisions relating to the filing of the Internal Revenue Service copies of the statement, see § 31.6051-2.

(2) *Extensions of time.* (i) For good cause shown upon written application by an employer, the district director or director of a service center may grant an extension of time not exceeding 30 days in which to furnish to employees the statements required by this section. Each application for an extension of time under this subdivision shall be made in writing, properly signed by the employer or his duly authorized agent; shall be addressed to the internal revenue office with which the employer is required to file the Internal Revenue Service copies of the statements; and shall contain a full recital of the reasons for requesting the extension, to aid the internal revenue office in determining the period of extension, if any, which will be granted. Such a request in the form of a letter to the internal revenue office will suffice as an application. The application shall be filed on or before the date prescribed in subparagraph (1) of this paragraph for furnishing the statements required by this section. In any case in which an employer is unable, by reason of illness, absence, or other good cause, to sign a request for an extension, any person standing in close personal or business relationship to the employer may sign the request on his behalf, and shall be considered as a duly authorized agent for this purpose, provided the request sets forth a reason for a signature other than the employer's and the relationship existing between the employer and the signer. For provisions relating to extensions of time for filing the Internal Revenue Service copies of the statements, see paragraph (a)(3) of § 31.6081(a)-1.

(ii) An extension of time, not exceeding 30 days, within which to furnish any statement required by this section upon termination of employment is hereby granted to any employer with respect to any employee whose employment is terminated during the calendar year. In the case of intermittent or interrupted employment where there is reasonable expectation on the part of both employer and employee of further employment, there is no requirement that a written statement be immediately furnished the employee; but when such expectation ceases to exist, the statement must be furnished within 30 days from that time.

(e) *Reporting of reimbursements of or payments of expenses of moving from one residence to another residence after July 23, 1971.* Every employer who after July 23, 1971, makes reimbursement to, or payment to (other than direct cash reimbursement), an employee for his expenses of moving from one residence to another residence which is includible in gross income under section 82 shall furnish to the best of his ability to such employee information sufficient to assist the employee in the computation of any deduction allowable under section 217 with respect to such reimbursement or payment. The information required under this paragraph may be furnished on Form 4782 provided by the Internal Revenue Service or may be furnished on forms provided by the employer so long as the employee receives the same information he would have received had he been furnished with a completed Form 4782. The information shall include the amount of the reimbursement or payment and whether the reimbursement or payment was made directly to a third party for the benefit of an employee or furnished in kind to the employee. In addition, information shall be furnished as to whether the reimbursement or payment represents an expense described in subparagraphs (A) through (E) of section 217(b)(1), and if so, the amount and nature of the expenses described in each such subparagraph. The information described in this paragraph shall be furnished at the same time or before the written statement required by section 6051(a) is furnished in respect of the calendar year for which the information provided under this paragraph is required. The information required under this paragraph shall be provided for the taxable year in which the payment or reimbursement is received by the employee. For determining the taxable year in which a payment or reimbursement is received, see section 82 and § 1.82-1.

(f) *Employers filing composite returns.* Every employer who files a composite return pursuant to § 31.6011(a)-8 shall furnish to his employees the statements required under this section, except that in lieu of Form W-2 the statements may be in any form which is suitable for retention by the employee and which contains all information required to be shown on Form W-2.

(g) *Statements with respect to compensation, as defined in the Railroad Retirement Tax Act, paid after December 31, 1967*—(1) *Required information relating to excess medicare tax on compensation paid after December 31, 1971*—(i) Notification of possible credit or refund. With respect to compensation (as defined in section 3231 (e)) paid after December 31, 1971, every employer (as defined in section 3231(a)) who is required to deduct and withhold from an employee (as defined in section 3231(b)) a tax under section 3201, shall include on or with the statement required to be furnished such employee under section 6051(a), a notice concerning the provisions of this title with respect to the allowance of a credit or refund of the tax on wages imposed by section 3101(b) and the tax on compensation imposed by section 3201 or 3211 which is treated as a tax on wages imposed by section 3101(b). Such notice shall inform such employee of the eligibility of persons having a second employment, in addition to railroad employment, for a credit or refund of any excess hospital insurance tax which such persons have paid because of employment under both social security (including employee and self-employment coverage) and railroad retirement. See section 6413 (c)(3) and paragraph (c) of § 31.6413(c)-1, relating to special refunds with respect to compensation as defined in the Railroad Retirement Tax Act.

(ii) Information to be supplied to employees upon request. With respect to compensation (as defined in section 3231(e)) paid after December 31, 1971, every employer (as defined in section 3231(a)) who is required to deduct and withhold tax under section 3201 from an employee (as defined in section 3231(b)) who has also received wages during such year subject to the tax imposed by section 3101(b), shall upon request of such employee furnish to him a written statement showing—

(a) The total amount of compensation with respect to which the tax imposed by section 3101(b) was deducted,

(b) The total amount of employee tax under section 3201 deducted and withheld (increased by any adjustment in the calendar year for overcollection, or decreased by any adjustment in such year for undercollection, of such tax during any prior year), and

(c) The proportion thereof (expressed either as a dollar amount, or a percentage of the total amount of compensation as defined in section 3231(e), or as a percentage of the total amount of employee tax under section 3201) withheld as tax under section 3201 for financing the cost of hospital insurance benefits.

(2) *Statements on Form W-2 (RR).* (i) *Compensation paid during 1970 or 1971.* With respect to compensation (as defined in section 3231(e)) paid during 1970 or 1971, every employer (as defined in section 3231(a)) who is required to deduct and withhold from an employee (as defined in section 3231(b)) a tax under section 3402 with respect to compensation, or who would have been required to deduct and withhold a tax under section 3402 (determined without regard to section 3402(n)) if the employee had claimed no more than one withholding exemption, shall furnish to each such employee in respect of such compensation the tax return copy and the employee's copy of a statement on Form W-2 (RR) instead of Form W-2, unless such employers are permitted by the Internal Revenue Service to continue to use Form W-2 in lieu of Form W-2 (RR). If the wage bracket method of withholding provided in section 3402(c)(1) is used in respect of such compensation, a statement on Form W-2 (RR) must be furnished to each employee

Reg. § 31.6051-1 (g) (2)

24,304 (I.R.C.) Reg. § 31.6051-1(g)(2) 7-28-75

whose wages during any payroll period are equal to or in excess of the smallest wage from which tax must be withheld in the case of an employee claiming one exemption. If the percentage method is used, a statement on Form W-2 (RR) must be furnished to each employee whose wages during any payroll period are in excess of one withholding exemption for such payroll period as shown in the percentage method withholding table contained in section 3402 (b)(1). Each statement on Form W-2 (RR) shall show the following:

(a) The name, address, and identification number of the employer,

(b) The name and address of the employee and his social security account number,

(c) The total amount of wages as defined in section 3401(a),

(d) The total amount deducted and withheld as tax under section 3402,

(e) The total amount of compensation as defined in section 3231(e), and

(f) The total amount of employee tax under section 3201 deducted and withheld (increased by any adjustment in the calendar year for overcollection, or decreased by any adjustment in such year for undercollection, of such tax during any prior year) and the proportion thereof (expressed either as a dollar amount, as a percentage of the total amount of compensation as defined in section 3231(e), or as a percentage of the total amount of employee tax under section 3201) withheld as tax under section 3201 for financing the cost of hospital insurance benefits. The provisions of this chapter applicable to Form W-2, other than those relating solely to the Federal Insurance Contributions Act, are hereby made applicable to Form W-2(RR). See paragraph (d) of this section for provisions relating to the time and place for furnishing the statement required by this subparagraph.

(ii) Compensation paid during 1968 or 1969. At the option of the employer, the provisions of subdivision (i) of this subparagraph may apply with respect to compensation paid during 1968 or 1969.

(iii) Every employer who, pursuant to subdivision (i) or (ii) of this subparagraph, does not provide Form W-2 (RR) with respect to compensation must furnish the additional information required by Form W-2 (RR) upon request by the employee.

(h) *Cross references.* For provisions relating to the penalties provided for the willful furnishing of a false or fraudulent statement, or for the willful failure to furnish a statement, see § 31.6674-1 and section 7204. For additional provisions relating to the inclusion of identification numbers and account numbers in statements on Form W-2, see § 31.6109-1. For provisions relating to the penalty for failure to report an identification number or an account number, as required by § 31.6109-1, see § 301.6676-1 of this chapter (Regulations on Procedure and Administration).

○→ § 301.6051 **Statutory provisions; receipts for employees.** [Sec. 6051, IRC]

○→ 301.6051-1 (T.D. 6498, filed 10-24-60.) **Receipts for employees.**

For provisions relating to statements for employees regarding remuneration paid during calendar year, see § 31.6051-1 of this chapter (Employment Tax Regulations).

○→ § 31.6051-2 (T.D. 7351, filed 4-16-75.) **Information returns on Form W-3 and Internal Revenue Service copies of Forms W-2.**

(a) *In general.* Every employer who is required to make a return of tax under § 31.6011(a)-1 (relating to returns under the Federal Insurance Contributions Act), § 31.6011(a)-4 (relating to returns of income tax withheld from wages), or § 31.6011(a)-5 (relating to monthly returns) for a calendar year or any period therein shall file the Internal Revenue Service copy of each Form W-2 required under § 31.6051-1 to be furnished by the employer with respect to wages paid during the calendar year (other than Forms W-2 which are filed as part of a return of tax on Form 942). Each Form W-2 and the transmittal Form W-3 shall together constitute an information return to be filed with the internal revenue office with which the employer is required to file such return of tax. However, in the case of an employer who elects to file a composite return pursuant to § 31.6011(a)-8, the information return required by this section shall consist of magnetic tape (or other approved media) containing all information required to be on the employee statement, together with transmittal Form 4804.

(b) *Corrected returns.* The Internal Revenue Service copies of corrected Forms W-2 (or magnetic tape or other approved media) for employees for the calendar year shall be submitted with Form W-3 (or Form 4804) and an explanatory statement, on or before the date on which information returns for the period in which the correction is made would be due under paragraph (a)(3)(ii) of § 31.6071(a)-1, to the internal revenue office with which such returns are required to be filed.

(c) *Cross references.* (For provisions relating to the time for filing the information returns required by this section and to extensions of the time for filing, see paragraph (a)(3)(ii) of § 31.6071(a)-1 and paragraph (a)(3) of § 31.6081(a)-1, respectively. For the penalty provided in case of each failure to file, see paragraph (a) of § 301.6652-1 of this chapter (Regulations on Procedure and Administration).

○→ § 1.6052 **Statutory provisions; returns regarding payment of wages in the form of group-term life insurance.** [Sec. 6052, IRC]

○→ § 1.6052-1 (T.D. 6888, filed 7-5-66; amended by T.D. 7284, filed 8-2-73.) **Information returns regarding payment of wages in the form of group-term life insurance.**

(a) *Requirement of reporting*—(1) *In general.* (i) Every employer, who during any calendar year provides any one of his employees remuneration for services in the form of group-term life insurance on the life of such employee any part of the cost of which is to be included in such employee's gross income as set forth in paragraph (a)(2) of § 1.79-1, shall make a separate return on Form W-2 with respect to each such employee for such year which includes the following information:

(a) Name, address, and identifying number of the employer;

(b) Name, address, and social security number of the employee; and

(c) Total amount includible in the employee's gross income by reason of the pro-

visions of section 79(a), computed as if each employee reported his income on the basis of a calendar year (determined as if the employer making such return is the only employer paying the employee remuneration in the form of group-term life insurance on his life which is includible in his gross income under section 79(a)).

Returns on Form W-2 required to be filed pursuant to the provisions of this section shall be transmitted by Form W-3. In a case where, with respect to the same employee, an employer must make a return on Form W-2 under this section and also under § 31.6011(a)-4 or § 31.6011(a)-5 of this chapter (Employment Tax Regulations), or under § 1.6041-2 (relating to return of information as to payments to employees), such employer may make such returns on the same Form W-2 or on separate Forms W-2. In a case where an employer must file a Form W-3 under this section and also under § 31.6011(a)-4 or § 31.6011(a)-5 of this chapter (Employment Tax Regulations), the Form W-3 filed under such § 31.6011(a)-4 or § 31.6011(a)-5 shall also be used as the transmittal form for a return on Form W-2 made pursuant to the provisions of this section.

(ii) Notwithstanding subdivision (i) of this subparagraph, if a life insurance company has elected, as provided by § 1.6041-2(a)(2), to report all payments of commissions to its full-time life insurance salesmen on Forms 1096 and 1099 rather than on Forms W-3 and W-2, remuneration for services in the form of group-term life insurance on the lives of such salesmen shall be reported on Forms 1096 and 1099. Returns on Form 1099 required to be filed pursuant to the provisions of this section shall include the information prescribed by subdivision (i)(c) of this subparagraph and shall be transmitted by Form 1096. In a case where, with respect to the same full-time life insurance salesman, a life insurance company is required to make a return on Form 1099 under this section and also under § 1.6041-2(a)(2) (relating to return of information as to payments to employees), the life insurance company may make such returns on the same Form 1099 or on separate Forms 1099. See § 1.6041-6 for contents and time and place for filing Forms 1096 and 1099.

(2) *Definitions.* Terms used in subparagraph (1) of this paragraph which are defined in paragraph (b) of § 1.79-1 have the meaning ascribed to them in such paragraph (b).

(b) *Time and place for filing*—(1) *Time for filing*—(i) *General rule.* In a case where an employer must file Forms W-3 and W-2 under this section and also under § 31.6011(a)-4 or § 31.6011(a)-5 of this chapter (Employment Tax Regulations), the time for filing such forms under this section shall be the same as the time (including extensions thereof) for filing such forms under § 31.6011(a)-4 or § 31.6011(a)-5.

(ii) *Exception.* In a case where an employer is not required to file Forms W-3 and W-2 under § 31.6011(a)-4 or § 31.6011(a)-5 of this chapter (Employment Tax Regulations), returns on Forms W-3 and W-2 required under paragraph (a) of this section for any calendar year shall be filed on or before February 28 of the following year.

(iii) *Cross reference.* For extensions of time for filing returns, see section 6081 and the regulations thereunder.

(2) *Place for filing.* The returns on Forms W-3 and W-2 required under paragraph (a) of this section shall be filed pursuant to the rules contained in § 31.6091-1 of this chapter (Employment Tax Regulations), relating to the place for filing certain returns.

(c) *Special rule for calendar years before 1972.* For calendar years before 1972, the provisions of this section will be deemed to have been complied with if the returns for such years were filed in accordance with the provisions of this section in effect prior to August 3, 1973 or with the instructions applicable to the appropriate forms.

(d) *Last day for filing return.* For provisions relating to the time for performance of an act when the last day prescribed for performance falls on Saturday, Sunday, or a legal holiday, see § 301.7503-1 of this chapter (Regulations on Procedure and Administration).

(e) *Penalty.* For provisions relating to the penalty provided for failure to file the information returns required by this section, see section 6652 and the regulations thereunder.

O— § 1.6052-2 (T.D. 6888, filed 7-5-66; amended by T.D. 7284, filed 8-2-73.) **Statements to be furnished employees with respect to wages paid in the form of group-term life insurance.**

(a) *Requirement.* Every employer filing a return under section 6052(a) and § 1.6052-1 with respect to group-term life insurance on the life of an employee shall furnish to the employee whose name is set forth in such return a written statement showing the information required by paragraph (b) of this section.

(b) *Form of statement.* The written statement required to be furnished to an employee under paragraph (a) of this section shall show—

(1) The total amount includible in the employee's gross income by reason of the provisions of section 79(a), but determined as if the employer furnishing such statement is the only employer paying the employee remuneration in the form of group-term life insurance on his life which is includible in his gross income under section 79(a).

(2) The name, address, and identifying number of the employer filing the statement. The requirement of this section for the furnishing of a statement to an employee may be satisfied by the furnishing to such employee of a copy of the return filed pursuant to § 1.6052-1 in respect of such employee. A statement shall be con-

Reg. § 1.6052-2(b)(2)

sidered to be furnished to a person within the meaning of this section if it is mailed to such person at his last known address.

(c) *Time for furnishing statements*—(1) *In general.* Each statement required by this section to be furnished to any employee for a calendar year shall be furnished to such person after the close of that year and on or before January 31 of the following year.

(2) *Extensions of time.* For good cause shown upon written application of the employer required to furnish statements under this section, the district director may grant an extension of time not exceeding 30 days in which to furnish such statements. The application shall be addressed to the district director with whom the income tax returns of the applicant are filed and shall contain a full recital of the reasons for requesting the extension to aid the district director in determining the period of the extension, if any, which will be granted. Such a request in the form of a letter to the district director signed by the applicant will suffice as an application. The application shall be filed on or before the date prescribed in subparagraph (1) of this paragraph for furnishing the statements required by this section.

(3) *Last day for furnishing statement.* For provisions relating to the time for performance of an act when the last day prescribed for performance falls on Saturday, Sunday, or a legal holiday, see § 301.-7503-1 of this chapter (Regulations on Procedure and Administration).

(d) *Special rule where Form W-2 or Form 1099 is used.* The provisions of this paragraph shall apply notwithstanding anything to the contrary in paragraph (b) or (c) of this section. The requirement of this section for the furnishing of a statement to an employee may be satisfied by furnishing to such employee the employee's copy of Form W-2 filed pursuant to § 1.6052-1 in respect of such employee, or, in the case of an election by a life insurance company pursuant to the provisions of § 1.6041-2(a)(2), by furnishing to the full-time life insurance salesman a copy of Form 1099 filed pursuant to § 1.6052-1(a)(1). In a case where the statement furnished by an employer to an employee for purposes of complying with this section is the employee's copy of a Form W-2, or in the case of certain full-time life insurance salesmen a copy of Form 1099, then the rules in § 31.-6051-1 of this chapter (Employment Tax Regulations) shall apply with respect to the means and time (including extensions thereof) for furnishing such statements to the employee and making corrections on such form.

(e) *Definitions.* Terms used in this section which are defined in paragraph (b) of § 1.79-1 have the meaning ascribed to them in such paragraph (b).

(f) *Penalty.* For provisions relating to the penalty provided for failure to furnish a statement under this section, see section 6678 and the regulations thereunder.

(g) *Special rule for calendar years before 1972.* For calendar years before 1972, the provisions of this section will be deemed to have been complied with if the statements for such years were furnished in accordance with the provisions of this section in effect prior to August 3, 1973 or with the instructions applicable to the appropriate forms.

§ 301.6052 Statutory provisions; returns regarding payment of wages in the form of group-term life insurance. [Sec. 6052, IRC]

§ 301.6052-1 (T.D. 7275, filed 5-4-73.) Information returns and statements regarding payment of wages in the form of group-term life insurance.

For provisions relating to information returns and statements required in connection with the payment of wages in the form of group-term life insurance, see §§ 1.6052-1 and 1.6052-2 of this chapter (Income Tax Regulations).

§ 31.6053 Statutory provisions; reporting of tips. [Sec. 6053, IRC]

§ 31.6053-1 (T.D. 7001, filed 1-17-69.) Report of tips by employee to employer.

(a) *Requirement that tips be reported.* An employee who receives after 1965, in the course of his employment by an employer, tips which constitutes wages as defined in section 3121(a) or section 3401 shall furnish to his employer a written statement, or statements, disclosing the total amount of such tips received by the employee in the course of his employment by such employer. For provisions relating to the treatment of tips as wages for purposes of the tax under section 3101, see §§ 31.3121 (a) (12) and 31.3121 (q). For provisions relating to the treatment of tips as wages for purposes of the tax under section 3402, see §§ 31.3401(a)(16) and 31.3401(f). Tips received by an employee in a calendar month in the course of his employment by an employer which are required to be reported to the employer must be so reported on or before the 10th day of the following month. Thus, tips received by an employee in January 1966, are required to be reported by the employee to his employer on or before February 10, 1966.

(b) *Statement for use in reporting tips* —(1) *In general.* The written statement furnished by the employee to the employer in respect of tips received by the employee shall be signed by the employee and disclose:

(i) The name, address, and social security number of the employee.

(ii) The name and address of the employer.

(iii) The period for which, and the date on which, the statement is furnished. If the statement is for a calendar month, the month and year should be specified. If the statement is for a period of less than one calendar month, the beginning and ending dates of the period should be shown (for example, Jan. 1 through Jan. 8, 1966).

(iv) The total amount of tips received by the employee during the period covered by the statement which are required to be reported to the employer (see paragraph (a) of this section).

(2) *Form of statement*—(i) *In general.* No particular form is prescribed which must be used in all cases in furnishing the statement required by this section. Unless some other form is provided by the employer for use by the employee in re-

Reg. § 31.6053-1 (b) (2)

porting tips received by him, Form 4070 may be used by the employee. Copies of Form 4070 will be furnished by district directors upon request.

(ii) *Forms provided by employers.* Subject to certain conditions and limitations, an employer may provide a form or forms for use by his employees in reporting tips received by them. Any such form provided for use by an employee, which is to be used solely for the purpose of reporting tips, shall meet all the requirements of subparagraph (1) of this paragraph, and a blank copy of the form shall be made available to the employee for completion and retention by him. In lieu of a special form for tip reporting, an employer may provide regularly used forms (such as time cards) for use by employees in reporting tips. Any such regularly used form must meet the requirements of subparagraph (1) (iii) and (iv) of this paragraph and shall contain identifying information which will assure accurate identification of the employee by the employer. However, a regularly used form may be used for the purpose of reporting tips only if, at the time of the first payment of wages (or within a short period thereafter) following the reporting of tips by the employee, the employee is furnished a statement suitable for retention by him showing the amount of tips reported by the employee for the period. This requirement may be met, for example, through the use of a payroll check stub or other payroll document regularly furnished by the employer to the employee showing gross pay, deductions, etc.

(c) *Period covered by, and due date of, tip statement*—(1) *In general.* In no event shall the written statement furnished by the employee to the employer in respect of tips received by him cover a period in excess of one calendar month. An employer may, in his discretion, require the submission of a written statement in respect of a specified period of time, for example, on a weekly or biweekly basis, regular payroll period, etc. An employer may specify, subject to the limitation in paragraph (a) of this section, the time within which, or the date on which, the statement for a specified period of time should be submitted by the employee. For example, a statement covering a payroll period may be required to be submitted on the first (or second) day following the close of such payroll period. However, a written statement submitted by an employee after the date specified by the employer for its submission shall be considered as a statement furnished pursuant to section 6053 (a) and this section if it is submitted to the employer on or before the 10th day following the month in which the tips were received.

(2) *Termination of employment.* If an employee's employment is being terminated, a written statement in respect of tips shall be furnished by the employee to the employer at the time the employee ceases to perform services for the employer. However, a written statement submitted by an employee after the date on which he ceases to perform services for the employer shall be considered as a statement furnished pursuant to section 6053 (a) and this section if the statement is submitted to the employer prior to the day on which the final payment of wages is made by the employer to the employee and on or before the 10th day following the month in which the tips were received.

O—☛ § 31.6053-2 (T.D. 7001, filed 1-17-69; amended by T.D. 7351, filed 4-16-75.) **Employer statement of uncollected employee tax.**

(a) *Requirement that statement be furnished. If*—

(1) The amount of the employee tax imposed by section 3101 in respect of tips reported by an employee to his employer pursuant to section 6053(a) (see § 31.6053-1) exceeds

(2) The amount of employee tax imposed by section 3101 in respect of such tips which can be collected by the employer from wages (exclusive of tips) of such employee or from funds furnished to the employer by the employee, the employer shall furnish to the employee a statement showing the amount of the excess. For provisions relating to the collection of, and liability for, employee tax on tips, see § 31.3102-3.

(b) *Form of statement.* Form W-2 is the form prescribed for use in furnishing the statement required by paragraph (a) of this section, except that if an employer files a composite return pursuant to § 31.6011(a)-8 he may furnish to the employee, in lieu of Form W-2, a statement containing the required information in a form suitable for retention by the employee. A statement is required under this section in respect of an excess referred to in paragraph (a) of this section, even though the employer may not be required to furnish a statement to the employee under § 31.6051. Provisions applicable to the furnishing of a statement under § 31.6051 shall be applicable to statements under this section.

(c) *Excess to be shown on statement.* If there is an excess in respect of the tips reported by an employee in two or more statements furnished pursuant to section 6053(a), only the total excess for the period covered by the employer statement shall be shown on such statement.

O—☛ § 1.6056 **Statutory provisions; annual reports by private foundations.** [Sec. 6056, IRC]

O—☛ § 1.6056-1 (T.D. 7122, filed 6-7-71; amended by T.D. 7290, filed 11-16-73.) **Annual reports by private foundations.**

(a) *Annual reports*—(1) *In general.* The foundation managers (as defined in section 4946(b)) of every organization (including a trust described in section 4947 (a)(1)) which is (or is treated as) a private foundation (as defined in section 509(a)) the assets of which are at least $5,000 at any time during a taxable year shall file an annual report setting forth the information described in subparagraphs (2) and (3) of this paragraph.

(2) *Form of annual report, time and place of filing.* The annual report required by this paragraph may be in printed, typewritten, or other form, provided that it readily and legibly discloses the information required by section 6056 and this section. Form 990-AR, Annual Report of Private Foundation, may be used for this purpose. The annual report shall be filed

at the place specified in the instructions applicable to the return required by section 6033 at the same time as such return.

(3) *Foundation managers not using Form 990-AR.* Foundation managers not choosing to use Form 990-AR as the annual report required by this paragraph shall file a report in accordance with subparagraphs (1) and (2) of this paragraph, setting forth the information required by section 6056(b) and in accordance with the instructions applicable to Form 990-AR. For purposes of section 6056(b)(1), gross income shall be as defined in the regulations under section 6033(b)(1), and for purposes of section 6056(b)(2), expenses attributable to such income shall be as defined in the regulations under section 6033 (b)(2). For purposes of section 6056(b)(7), the term "relationship" shall include, but is not limited to, any case in which an individual recipient of a grant or contribution by a private foundation is (i) a member of the family (as defined in section 4946(d)) of a substantial contributor or foundation manager of such foundation, (ii) a partner of such substantial contributor or foundation manager, or (iii) an employee of such substantial contributor or foundation manager or of an organization which is effectively controlled (directly or indirectly) by one or more such substantial contributors or foundation managers (within the meaning of section 4946(a)(1)(H)(i) and the regulations thereunder. For purposes of section 6056(b)(7) and (9), the business address of an individual grant recipient or foundation manager may be used by the foundation in its annual report in lieu of the home address of such recipient or manager. For purposes of section 6056(b)(9), the term "foundation managers" shall have the same meaning as such term has in section 6033(b)(6).

(4) *Notice to public of availability of annual report.* A copy of the notice required by section 6104(d) (relating to public inspection of private foundations' annual reports), and proof of publication thereof, shall be filed with the annual report required by this paragraph. A copy of such notice as published, and a statement signed by a foundation manager stating that such notice was published, setting forth the date of publication and the publication in which it appeared, shall be sufficient proof of publication for purposes of this subparagraph.

(b) *Special rules* — (1) *Manner of making annual report available for public inspection.* The foundation managers of a private foundation may satisfy the requirement that the annual report be made available for public inspection at the foundation's principal office by furnishing a copy free of charge to persons who request inspection in the manner and at the time prescribed therefor in section 6104(d) and the regulations thereunder.

(2) *Furnishing copies to libraries and depositories.* The Commissioner may designate one or more appropriate libraries or depositories to which the foundation managers will be required to send copies of their annual reports, in addition to, and not in lieu of, filing such annual reports with the Internal Revenue Service and making such annual reports available for public inspection at the principal office of the foundation.

(3) *Furnishing of copies to State Officers.* The foundation managers of a private foundation shall furnish a copy of the annual report required by section 6056 and this section to the Attorney General of (i) each State which the foundation is required to list on its return pursuant to § 1.6033-2 (a)(2)(iv), (ii) the State in which is located the principal office of the foundation, and (iii) the State in which the foundation was incorporated or created. The annual report shall be sent to each Attorney General described in subdivision (i), (ii), or (iii) of this subparagraph at the same time as it is sent to the Internal Revenue Service. Upon request the foundation managers shall also furnish a copy of the annual report to the Attorney General or other appropriate State officer (within the meaning of section 6104(c)(2)) of any State. The foundation managers shall attach to each copy of the annual report sent to State officers under this subparagraph a copy of the returns required by section 6033, and a copy of the Form 4720, if any, filed by the foundation for the year.

(c) *Special rules for certain foreign organizations.* The provisions of paragraphs (a)(4), (b)(1) and (b)(3) of this section shall not apply with respect to an organization described in section 4948(b). The foundation managers of such organizations are not required to publish notice of availability of the annual report for inspection, to make the annual report available at the principal office of the foundation for public inspection under section 6104(d), or to send copies of the annual report to State officers. Such foundation managers may be required to furnish copies of their annual reports to libraries and depositories in accordance with the provisions of paragraph (b)(2) of this section.

O→ § 1.6060-1 (T.D. 7519, filed 11-17-77.) **Information returns of income tax return preparers.**

(a) *In general.* (1) Each person who employs (or engages) one or more income tax return preparers to prepare any return of tax under subtitle A of the Internal Revenue Code of 1954 or claim for refund of tax under subtitle A of the Internal Revenue Code of 1954, other than for the person, at any time during a return period shall file an information return setting forth the name, taxpayer identification number, and principal place of work during the return period of each income tax return preparer employed (or engaged) by the person at any time during such period.

(2) For the definition of the term "income tax return preparer", see section 7701 (a)(36) and § 301.7701-15. For the definition of the term "return period", see section 6060(c) and paragraph (c) of this section.

(3)(i) For purposes of this section, any individual who, in acting as an income tax return preparer, is not employed by another income tax return preparer shall be treated as his own employer. Thus, a sole proprietor shall file the information return.

(ii) A partnership shall, for purposes of this section, be treated as the employer of the partners of the partnership and shall file the information return.

(4) Form 5717 is the return form prescribed for filing the information required

Reg. § 1.6060-1 (a) (4)

under this paragraph. The information return shall be filed with the Internal Revenue Service Center on or before the first July 31 following the end of the return period to which the return relates.

(5)(i) Any person required to file an information return under this paragraph on Form 5717 may request approval of a different reporting method which the person wishes to use to comply with this paragraph. Such a requested reporting method may include, for example, the filing, on a consistent basis, of the information required on magnetic tape. However, no approval will be given to a reporting method that does not require some form of annual filing of all the information required by this paragraph.

(ii) Any request for approval of a different reporting method shall be in writing, shall be filed at least 90 days prior to the date the return is due, and shall be directed, in the case of requested reporting not involving magnetic tape, to the Office of the Assistant Commissioner (Accounts, Collection, and Taxpayer Service), Internal Revenue Service, 1111 Constitution Avenue, N.W., Washington, D.C. 24224 (Attention: ACTS:T) and, in the case of requested reporting involving magnetic tape, to the Director of the Internal Revenue Service Center where the applicant would file Form 5717. The information required shall be filed when due on Form 5717 if the request is denied (or not approved) by the date when the return is due. If the request is approved, the approval shall continue in effect with respect to all return periods until modified or revoked by written notice to the person required to file the return or until the person no longer follows the different reporting method for which approval was given.

(b) *Return period defined.* For purposes of this section, the term "return period" means the 12-month period beginning on July 1 of each year, except that the first return period shall be the 6-month period beginning on January 1, 1977, and ending on June 30, 1977.

(c) *Penalty.* For the civil penalty for failure to file an information return as required under this section, or for failure to set forth an item in the return as required under this section, see section 6695(e) and § 1.6695-1(e).

Signing and Verifying of Returns and Other Documents

O—☞ § 1.6061 Statutory provisions; signing of returns and other documents. [Sec. 6061, IRC]

O—☞ § 1.6061-1 (T.D. 6364, filed 2-13-59; republished in T.D. 6500, filed 11-25-60; amended by T.D. 7332, filed 12-20-74.) Signing of returns and other documents by individuals.

(a) *Requirement.* Each individual (including a fiduciary) shall sign the income tax return required to be made by him, except that the return may be signed for the taxpayer by an agent who is duly authorized in accordance with paragraph (a)(5) or (b) of § 1.6012-1 to make such return. Other returns, statements, or documents required under the provisions of subtitle A or F of the Code or of the regulations thereunder to be made by any person with respect to any tax imposed by subtitle A of the Code shall be signed in accordance with any regulations contained in this chapter, or any instructions, issued with respect to such returns, statements, or other documents.

(b) *Cross references.* For provisions relating to the signing of returns, statements, or other documents required to be made by corporations and partnerships with respect to any tax imposed by subtitle A of the Code, see §§ 1.6062-1 and 1.6063-1, respectively. For provisions relating to the making of returns by agents, see paragraphs (a)(5) and (b) of § 1.6012-1; and to the making of returns for minors and persons under a disability, see paragraph (a)(4) of § 1.6012-1 and paragraph (b) of § 1.6012-3.

O—☞ § 31.6061 Statutory provisions; signing of returns and other documents. [Sec. 6061 IRC]

O—☞ § 31.6061-1 (T.D. 6472, filed 6-22-60; republished in T.D. 6516, filed 12-19-60.) Signing of returns.

Each return required under the regulations in this subpart shall, if signature is called for by the form or instructions relating to the return, be signed by (a) the individual, if the person required to make the return is an individual; (b) the president, vice president, or other principal officer, if the person required to make the return is a corporation; (c) a responsible and duly authorized member or officer having knowledge of its affairs, if the person

Signing & Verifying Returns & Documents *(I.R.C.)* 24,304.3

required to make the return is a partnership or other unincorporated organization; or (d) the fiduciary, if the person required to make the return is a trust or estate. The return may be signed for the taxpayer by an agent who is duly authorized in accordance with § 31.6011(a)-7 to make such return.

○→ § 53.6061 Statutory provisions; signing of returns and other documents. [Sec. 6061, IRC]

○→ § 53.6061-1 (T.D. 7368, filed 7-15-75.) Signing of returns and other documents.

Any return, statement, or other document required to be made with respect to a tax imposed by chapter 42 or the regulations thereunder shall be signed by the person required to file such return, statement or document, or by such other persons required or duly authorized to sign in accordance with the regulations, forms or instructions prescribed with respect to such return, statement or other document. The person required or duly authorized to make the return may incur liability for penalties provided for erroneous, false or fraudulent returns, for criminal penalties see sections 7201, 7203, 7206, and 7207.

○→ § 301.6061 Statutory provisions; signing of returns and other documents. [Sec. 6061, IRC]

○→ § 301.6061-1 (T.D. 6498, filed 10-24-60.) Signing of returns and other documents.

For provisions concerning the signing of returns and other documents, see the regulations relating to the particular tax.

○→ § 1.6062 Statutory provisions; signing of corporation returns. [Sec. 6062, IRC]

○→ § 1.6062-1 (T.D. 6364, filed 2-13-59 as amended by T.D. 6455, filed 3-1-60; republished in T.D. 6500, filed 11-25-60; amended by T.D. 7293, filed 11-27-73.) Signing of returns, statements, and other documents made by corporations.

(a) *Returns*—(1) *In general.* Returns required to be made by corporations under the provisions of subtitle A or F of the Code, or the regulations thereunder, with respect to any tax imposed by subtitles A of the Code, shall be signed for the corporation by the president, vice-president, treasurer, assistant treasurer, chief accounting officer, or any other officer duly authorized to sign such returns. It is not necessary that the corporate seal be affixed to the return. Spaces provided on return forms for affixing the corporate seal are for the convenience of corporations required by charter, or by the law of the jurisdiction in which they are incorporated, to affix their corporate seals in the execution of instruments.

(2) *By fiduciaries.* A return with respect to income required to be made for a corporation by a fiduciary, pursuant to the provisions of section 6012(b)(3), shall be signed by such fiduciary. See paragraph (b)(4) of § 1.6012-3.

(3) *By agents.* A return with respect to income required to be made by an agent for a foreign corporation shall be signed by such agent. See paragraph (g) of § 1.6012-2.

(b) *Statements and other documents.* Statements and other documents required to be made by or for corporations under the provisions of subtitle A or F of the Code, or the regulations thereunder, with respect to any tax imposed by subtitle A, shall be signed in accordance with the regulations contained in this chapter, or the forms and instructions, issued with respect to such statements or other documents.

(c) *Evidence of authority to sign.* An individual's signature on a return, statement, or other document made by or for a corporation shall be prima facie evidence that such individual is authorized to sign such return, statement, or other document.

(d) *Related provisions.* For the rules relating to the verification of returns, see § 1.6065-1.

○→ § 301.6062 Statutory provisions; signing of corporations returns. [Sec. 6062, IRC]

○→ § 301.6062-1 (T.D. 6498, filed 10-24-60.) Signing of corporation returns.

For provisions relating to the signing of corporation income tax returns, see § 1.6062-1 of this chapter (Income Tax Regulations).

○→ § 1.6063 Statutory provisions; signing of partnership returns. [Sec. 6063, IRC]

○→ § 1.6063-1 (T.D. 6364, filed 2-13-59; republished in T.D. 6500, filed 11-25-60.) Signing of returns, statements, and other documents made by partnerships.

(a) *In general.* Returns, statements, and other documents required to be made by partnerships under the provisions of subtitle A or F of the Code, or the regulations thereunder, with respect to any tax imposed by subtitle A of the Code shall be signed by any one of the partners. However, with respect to the signing of powers of attorney, see paragraph (a)(2) of § 601.-504 of this chapter. (Statement of Procedural Rules.)

(b) *Evidence of authority to sign.* A partner's signature on a return, statement, or other document made by or for a partnership of which he is a member shall be prima facie evidence that such partner is authorized to sign such return, statement, or other document.

○→ § 301.6063 Statutory provisions; signing of partnership returns. [Sec. 6063, IRC]

○→ § 301.6063-1 (T.D. 6498, filed 10-24-60.) Signing of partnership returns.—For provisions relating to the signing of returns of partnership income, see § 1.6063-1 of this chapter (Income Tax Regulations).

○→ § 301.6064 Statutory provisions; signature presumed authentic. [Sec. 6064, IRC]

○→ § 301.6064-1 (T.D. 6498, filed 10-24-60.) Signature presumed authentic.—An individual's name, signed to a return, statement, or other document shall be prima facie evidence for all purposes that the return, statement, or other document was actually signed by him.

○→ § 1.6065 Statutory provisions; verification of returns. [Sec. 6065, IRC]

Reg. § 1.6065

24,304.4 (I.R.C.) Reg. § 1.6065-1

○→ § 1.6065-1 (T.D. 6364, filed 2-13-59; republished in T.D. 6500, filed 11-25-60.) Verification of returns.

(a) *Persons signing returns.* If a return, declaration, statement, or other document made under the provisions of subtitle A or F of the Code, or the regulations thereunder, with respect to any tax imposed by subtitle A of the Code is required by the regulations contained in this chapter, or the form and instructions, issued with respect to such return, declaration, statement, or other document, to contain or be verified by a written declaration that it is made under the penalties of perjury, such return, declaration, statement, or other document shall be so verified by the person signing it.

(b) *Persons preparing returns*—(1) *In general.* Except as provided in subparagraph (2) of this paragraph, if a return, declaration, statement, or other document is prepared for a taxpayer by another person for compensation or as an incident to the performance of other services for which such person receives compensation, and the return, declaration, statement, or other document requires that it shall contain or be verified by a written declaration that it is prepared under the penalties of perjury, the preparer must so verify the return, declaration, statement, or other document. A person who renders mere mechanical assistance in the preparation of a return, declaration, statement, or other document as, for example, a stenographer or typist, is not considered as preparing the return, declaration, statement, or other document.

(2) *Exception.* The verification required by subparagraph (1) of this paragraph is not required on returns, declarations, statements, or other documents which are prepared—

(i) For an employee either by his employer or by an employee designated for such purpose by the employer, or

(ii) For an employer as a usual incident of the employment of one regularly or continuously employed by such employer.

○→ § 31.6065 (a) Statutory provisions; verification of returns. [Sec. 6065(a), IRC]

○→ § 31.6065 (a)-1 (T.D. 6472, filed 6-22-60; republished in T.D. 6516, filed 12-19-60.)

Verification of returns or other documents. If a return, statement, or other document made under the regulations in this part is required by the regulations contained in this part, or the form and instructions issued with respect to such return, statement, or other document, to contain or be verified by a written declaration that it is made under the penalties of perjury, such return, statement, or other document shall be so verified by the person signing it.

○→ § 53.6065 Statutory provisions; verification of returns. [Sec. 6065, IRC]

○→ § 53.6065-1 (T.D. 7368, filed 7-15-75.) Verification of returns.

(a) *Penalties of perjury.* If a return, statement, or other document made under the provisions of chapter 42 or subtitle F of the Code or the regulations thereunder with respect to any tax imposed by chapter 42 of the Code, or the form and instructions issued with respect to such return, statement, or other document, requires that it shall contain or be verified by a written declaration that it is made under the penalties of perjury, it must be so verified by the person or persons required to sign such return, statement, or other document. In addition, any other statement or document submitted under any provision of chapter 42 or subtitle F of the Code or regulations thereunder with respect to any tax imposed by chapter 42 of the Code may be required to contain or be verified by a written declaration that it is made under the penalties of perjury.

(b) *Oath.* Any return, statement, or other document required to be submitted under chapter 42 or subtitle F of the Code or regulations prescribed thereunder with respect to any tax imposed by chapter 42 of the Code may be required to be verified by an oath.

○→ § 301.6065 Statutory provisions; verification of returns. [Sec. 6065, IRC]

○→ § 301.6065-1 (T.D. 6498, filed 10-24-60.) Verification of returns.—For provisions concerning the verification of returns and other documents, see the regulations relating to the particular tax.

Time for Filing Returns and Other Documents

C→ § 1.6071 Statutory provisions; time for filing returns and other documents. [Sec. 6071(a), IRC]

○→ § 1.6071-1 (T.D. 6364, filed 2-13-59; republished in T.D. 6500, filed 11-25-60; amended by T.D. 6628, filed 12-27-62; T.D. 6887, filed 6-23-66; T.D. 6908, filed 12-30-66; T.D. 7284, filed 8-2-73; T.D. 7533, filed 2-14-78.) Time for filing returns and other documents.

(a) *In general.* Whenever a return, statement, or other document is required to be made under the provisions of subtitle A or F of the Code, or the regulations thereunder, with respect to any tax imposed by subtitle A of the Code, and the time for filing such return, statement, or other document is not provided for by the Code, it shall be filed at the time prescribed by the regulations contained in this chapter with respect to such return, statement, or other document.

(b) *Return for a short period.* In the case of a return with respect to tax under subtitle A of the Code for a short period (as defined in section 443), the district director or director of the Internal Revenue Service Center may, upon a showing by the taxpayer of unusual circumstances, prescribe a time for filing the return for such period later than the time when such return would otherwise be due. However, the district director or director of the Internal Revenue Service Center may not extend the time when the return for a DISC (as defined in section 992(a)(1)) must be filed, as specified in section 6072 (b).

(c) *Time for filing certain information returns.* (1) For provisions relating to the time for filing returns of partnership income, see paragraph (e)(2) of § 1.6031-1.

(2) For provisions relating to the time for filing information returns by banks with

2-21-78 Time for Filing Returns and Other Documents *(I.R.C.)* 24,304.5

respect to common trust funds, see § 1.6032-1.

(3) For provisions relating to the time for filing information returns by certain organizations exempt from taxation under section 501(a), see paragraph (e) of § 1.6033-1.

(4) For provisions relating to the time for filing returns by trusts claiming charitable deductions under section 642(c), see paragraph (c) of § 1.6034-1.

(5) For provisions relating to the time for filing information returns by officers, directors, and shareholders of foreign personal holding companies, see §§ 1.6035-1 and 1.6035-2.

(6) For provisions relating to the time for filing information returns with respect to certain stock option transactions, see paragraph (c) of § 1.6039-1.

(7) For provisions relating to the time for filing information returns by persons making certain payments, see paragraph (a)(4) of § 1.6041-2 and § 1.6041-6.

(8) For provisions relating to the time for filing information returns regarding payments of dividends, see paragraph (d) of § 1.6042-1, and paragraph (c) of § 1.6042-2 (relating to returns for calendar years after 1962).

(9) For provisions relating to the time for filing information returns by corporations with respect to contemplated dissolution or liquidations, see paragraph (a) of § 1.6043-1.

(10) For provisions relating to the time for filing information returns by corporations with respect to distributions in liquidation, see paragraph (a) of § 1.6043-2.

(11) For provisions relating to the time for filing information returns with respect to payments of patronage dividends, see paragraph (b) of § 1.6044-1, and paragraph (d) of § 1.6044-2 (relating to returns for calendar years after 1962).

(12) For provisions relating to the time for filing information returns with respect to formation or reorganization of foreign corporations, see § 1.6046-1.

(13) For provisions relating to the time for filing information returns regarding certain payments of interest, see paragraph (c) of § 1.6049-1.

(14) For provisions relating to the time for filing information returns with respect to payment of wages in the form of group-term life insurance, see paragraph (b) of § 1.6052-1.

(15) For provisions relating to the time for filing ownership certificates with respect to interest payments on certain bonds, mortgages, deeds of trust, and other similar obligations, see § 1.1461-1.

(16) For provisions relating to the time for filing the annual information return on Form 1042S of the tax withheld under chapter 3 of the Code (relating to withholding of tax on nonresident aliens and foreign corporations and tax-free covenant bonds), see paragraph (c) of §1.1461-2.

○→ § 31.6071(a) Statutory provisions; time for filing returns and other documents. [Sec. 6071, IRC]

○→ § 31.6071(a)-1 (T.D. 6354, filed 1-13-59; republished in T.D. 6516, filed 12-19-60; amended by T.D. 6893, filed 8-29-66; T.D. 6941, filed 12-15-67; T.D. 7001, filed 1-17-69; T.D. 7078, filed 12-4-70 and T.D. 7351, filed 4-16-75.) Time for filing returns and other documents.

(a) *Federal Insurance Contributions Act and income tax withheld from wages—* (1) *Quarterly or annual returns.* Except as provided in subparagraph (4) of this paragraph each return required to be made under § 31.6011(a)-1, in respect of the taxes imposed by the Federal Insurance Contributions Act, or required to be made under § 31.6011(a)-4, in respect of income tax withheld, shall be filed on or before the last day of the first calendar month following the period for which it is made. However, a return may be filed on or before the 10th day of the second calendar month following such period if timely deposits under section 6302(c) of the Code and the regulations thereunder have been made in full payment of such taxes due for the period. For the purpose of the preceding sentence, a deposit which is not required by such regulations in respect of the return period may be made on or before the last day of the first calendar month following the close of such period, and the timeliness of any deposit will be determined by the earliest date stamped on the applicable deposit form by an authorized commercial bank or by a Federal Reserve bank.

(2) *Monthly tax returns.* Each return in respect of the taxes imposed by the Federal Insurance Contributions Act or of income tax withheld which is required to be made under paragraph (a) of § 31.6011(a)-5 shall be filed on or before the fifteenth day of the first calendar month following the period for which it is made.

(3) *Information returns.*—(i) Returns on Form 941. Each information return in respect of wages as defined in the Federal Insurance Contributions Act which is required to be made under paragraph (b)(1) of § 31.6011(a)-5 shall be filed on or before the fifteenth day following the calendar quarter for which it is made, except that, if a tax return under paragraph (a) of § 31.6011(a)-5 is made as a final return for a period ending prior to the last day of a calendar quarter, the information return shall be filed on or before the fifteenth day of the first calendar month following the period for which the tax return is filed.

(ii) *Returns on Forms W-2 and W-3.* Each information return in respect of wages as defined in the Federal Insurance Contributions Act or of income tax withheld from wages which is required to be made under § 31.6051-2 shall be filed on or before the last day of February following the calendar year for which it is made, except that, if a tax return under paragraph (a) of § 31.6011(a)-5 is filed as a final return for a period ending prior to December 31, the information statement shall be filed on or before the last day of the second calendar month following the period for which the tax return is filed.

(4) *Employee returns under Federal Insurance Contributions Act.* A return of employee tax under section 3101 required under paragraph (d) of § 31.6011(a)-1 to

Reg. § 31.6071(a)-1(a)(4)

24,304.6 (I.R.C.)   Reg. § 31.6071(a)-1(a)(4)   2-21-78

be made by an individual for a calendar year on Form 1040 shall be filed on or before the due date of such individual's return of income (see § 1.6012-1 of this chapter (Income Tax Regulations)) for the calendar year, or, if the individual makes his return of income on a fiscal year basis, on or before the due date of his return of income for the fiscal year beginning in the calendar year for which a return of employee tax is required. A return of employee tax under section 3101 required under paragraph (d) of § 31.6011 (a)-1 to be made for a calendar year—

(i) On Form 1040SS or Form 1040PR, or

(ii) On Form 1040 by an individual who is not required to make a return of income for the calendar year or for a fiscal year beginning in such calendar year,

shall be filed on or before the 15th day of the fourth month following the close of the calendar year.

* * * * * * * *

(b) *Railroad Retirement Act.*—* * *

(c) *Federal Unemployment Tax Act.*— * * *

(d) *Last day for filing.* For provisions relating to the time for filing a return when the prescribed due date falls on Saturday, Sunday, or a legal holiday, see the provisions of § 301.7503-1 of this chapter (Regulations on Procedure and Administration).

(e) *Late filing.* For additions to the tax in case of failure to file a return within the prescribed time, see the provisions of § 301.6651-1 of this chapter (Regulations on Procedure and Administration).

(f) *Cross reference.* For extensions of time for filing return and other documents, see § 31.6081(a)-1.

○━━ § 53.6071 Statutory provisions; time for filing returns and other documents. [Sec. 6071, IRC]

○━━ § 53.6071-1 (T.D. 7368, filed 7-15-75; amended by T.D. 7407, filed 3-3-76.) **Time for filing returns.**

(a) *General rule.* Except as provided in paragraphs (b) and (c) of this section, a return required by § 53.6011-1 shall be filed at the time the private foundation or trust described in section 4947(a)(2) is required to file its annual information or tax return under section 6033 or 6012 (as may be applicable).

(b) *Exception.* The Form 4720 of a person whose taxable year ends on a date other than that on which the taxable year of the foundation or trust ends shall be filed on or before the 15th day of the fifth month following the close of such person's taxable year.

(c) *Form 5227.* A Form 5227 required to be filed by paragraph (d) of § 53.6011-1 for a trust described in section 4947(a) shall be filed on or before the 15th day of the fourth month following the close of the trust's taxable year.

○━━ § 301.6071 Statutory provisions, time for filing returns and other documents. [Sec. 6071, IRC]

○━━ § 301.6071-1 (T.D. 6498, filed 10-24-60.) **Time for filing returns and other documents.** For provisions concerning the time for filing returns and other documents, see the regulations relating to the particular tax.

○━━ § 1.6072-1 (T.D. 6364, filed 2-13-59; republished in T.D. 6500, filed 11-25-60; amended by T.D. 7426, filed 8-6-76.) **Time for filing returns of individuals, estates and trusts.**

(a) *In general.* Except as provided in paragraphs (b) and (c) of this section, returns of income required under sections 6012, 6013, 6014, and 6017 of individuals, estates, domestic trusts, and foreign trusts having an office or place of business in the United States (including unrelated business tax returns of such trusts referred to in section 511(b)(2)) shall be filed on or before the fifteenth day of the fourth month following the close of the taxable year.

(b) *Decedents.* In the case of a final return of a decedent for a fractional part of a year, the due date of such return shall be the fifteenth day of the fourth month following the close of the 12-month period which began with the first day of such fractional part of the year.

(c) *Nonresident alien individuals and foreign trusts.* The income tax return of a nonresident alien individual and of a foreign trust which does not have an office or place of business in the United States (including unrelated business tax returns of such trusts referred to in section 511 (b)(2)) shall be filed on or before the fifteenth day of the sixth month following the close of the taxable year. However, a nonresident alien individual who for the taxable year has wages subject to withholding under chapter 24 of the Code shall file his income tax return on or before the fifteenth day of the fourth month following the close of the taxable year.

(d) *Last day for filing return.* For provisions relating to the time for filing a return where the last day for filing falls on Saturday, Sunday, or a legal holiday, see section 7503 and § 301.7503-1 of this chapter (Regulations on Procedure and Administration).

○━━ § 1.6072-2 (T.D. 6346, filed 2-13-59; republished in T.D. 6500, filed 11-25-60; amended by T.D. 6643, filed 4-1-63 and T.D. 7244, filed 12-29-72; T.D. 7533, filed 2-14-78.) **Time for filing returns of corporations.**

(a) *Domestic and certain foreign corporations.* The income tax return required under section 6012 of a domestic corporation or of a foreign corporation having an office or place of business in the United States shall be filed on or before the fifteenth day of the third month following the close of the taxable year.

(b) *Foreign corporations not having an office or place of business in the United States.* The income tax return of a foreign corporation which does not have an office or place of business in the United States shall be filed on or before the fifteenth day of the sixth month following the close of the taxable year.

Time for Filing Returns and Other Documents (I.R.C.) 24,305

(c) *Organizations having unrelated business income taxable at corporation rates.* The provisions of paragraphs (a) or (b) of this section apply to organizations referred to in section 511(a)(2) and required to file a return of unrelated business taxable income.

(d) *Cooperative organizations.* The income tax return of the following cooperative organizations shall be filed on or before the fifteenth day of the ninth month following the close of the taxable year:

(1) A farmers', fruit growers', or like association, organized and operated in compliance with the requirements of section 521 and § 1.521-1; and

(2) For a taxable year beginning after December 31, 1962, a corporation described in section 1381(a)(2), which is under a valid enforceable written obligation to pay patronage dividends (as defined in section 1388(a) and paragraph (a) of § 1.1388-1) in an amount equal to at least 50 percent of its net earnings from business done with or for its patrons, or which paid patronage dividends in such an amount out of the net earnings from business done with or for patrons during the most recent taxable year for which it had such net earnings. Net earnings for this purpose shall not be reduced by any taxes imposed by subtitle A of the Code and shall NOT be reduced by dividends paid on capital stock or other proprietary interest.

(e) *DISC's and former DISC's.* The return required under section 6011(c)(2) of a corporation which is a DISC (as defined in section 992(a)) shall be filed on or before the 15th day of the 9th month following the close of the taxable year. For the rule that a DISC may not have an extension of time in which to file such return, see §§ 1.6071-1(b), 1.6081-1(a), and 1.6081-3(e). The return required under § 1.6011-2(b)(1) by a former DISC shall be filed at the time it is required to file its income tax return.

(f) *Cross references.* For provisions relating to the time for filing a return where the last day for filing falls on Saturday, Sunday, or a legal holiday, see section 7503 and § 301.7503-1 of this chapter (Regulations on Procedure and Administration). For provisions relating to the fixing of a later time for filing in the case of a return for a short period, see paragraph (b) of § 1.6071-1. For provisions relating to time for filing consolidated returns and separate returns for short periods not included in consolidated returns, see §§ 1.1502-75 and 1.1502-76.

○── § 1.6072-3 (T.D. 6364, filed 2-13-59; republished in T.D. 6500, filed 11-25-60.) **Income tax due dates postponed in case of China Trade Act corporations.**

(a) With respect to a taxable year beginning after December 31, 1948, and ending before October 1, 1956, the income tax return of any corporation organized under the China Trade Act of 1922 (15 U.S.C. ch. 4); as amended, shall not become due until December 31, 1956, provided that during any such taxable year conditions in China have been generally so unsettled as to militate against the normal commercial operations and corporate activities of such corporation. However, the postponement of the due date shall not apply to an income tax return for any such taxable year if—

(1) The books of account and business records are available so as to permit the filing of a proper return, and the corporation has otherwise been in a position to carry on its commercial operations and corporate activities and to make a proper distribution of its earnings or profits, if any, so as to permit the certification required by section 941(b); or

(2) All the commercial operations and corporate activities of such corporation have been carried on in Hong Kong, Macao, or Taiwan (Formosa).

(b) Notwithstanding the provisions of paragraph (a)(1) or (2) of this section, the postponed due date referred to in this section will apply if a corporation satisfies the Commissioner that special circumstances exist, related to the unsettled conditions in China, which warrant such postponement.

(c) The postponed due date provided for in this section is expressly subject to the power of the Commissioner to extend, as in other cases, the time for filing the income tax return. See section 6081 and the regulations thereunder.

○── § 1.6072-4 (T.D. 6364, filed 2-13-59; republished in T.D. 6500, filed 11-25-60; amended by T.D. 6908, filed 12-30-66.) **Time for filing other returns of income.**

(a) *Reports for recovery of excessive profits on Government contracts.* For the time for filing annual reports by persons completing Government contracts, see 26 CFR (1939) 17.16 (Treasury Decision 4906, approved June 23, 1939), and 26 CFR (1939) 16.15 (Treasury Decision 4909, approved June 28, 1939), as made applicable to section 1471 of the Internal Revenue Code of 1954 by Treasury Decision 6091, approved August 16, 1954 (19 F.R. 5167, C.B. 1954-2, 47).

(b) *Returns of tax on transfers to avoid income tax.* For the time for filing returns of tax under chapter 5 of the Code, see § 1.1494-1.

○── § 301.6072-1 (T.D. 6498, filed 10-24-60.) **Time for filing income tax returns.**—For provisions relating to time for filing income tax returns, see §§ 1.6072-1 to 1.6072-4, inclusive, of this chapter (Income Tax Regulations).

○── § 1.6073 **Statutory provisions; time for filing declarations of estimated income tax by individuals.** [Sec. 6073, IRC]

○── § 1.6073-1 (T.D. 6267, filed 11-13-57; republished in T.D. 6500, filed 11-25-60; amended by T.D. 6678, filed 9-30-63 and T.D. 6950, filed 4-3-68.) **Time and place for filing declarations of estimated income tax by individuals.**

(a) *Individuals other than farmers or fishermen.* Declarations of estimated tax for the calendar year shall be made on or before April 15th of such calendar year by every individual whose anticipated income for the year meets the requirements of section 6015(a). If, however, the requirements necessitating the filing of the declaration are first met, in the case of an individual on the calendar year basis, after April 1st, but before June 2d of the calendar year, the declaration must be filed on or before

Reg. § 1.6073-1(a)

24,306 (I.R.C.) Reg. § 1.6073-1(a)

June 15th; if such requirements are first met after June 1st and before September 2d, the declaration must be filed on or before September 15th; and if such requirements are first met after September 1st, the declaration must be filed on or before January 15th of the succeeding calendar year. In the case of an individual on the fiscal year basis, see § 1.6073-2.

(b) *Farmers or fishermen*—(1) *In general.* In the case of an individual on a calendar year basis, whose estimated gross income from farming (including oyster farming) or, with respect to taxable years beginning after December 31, 1962, from fishing for the calendar year is at least two-thirds of his total estimated gross income from all sources for such year, his declaration may be filed on or before the 15th day of January of the succeeding calendar year in lieu of the time prescribed in paragraph (a) of this section. For the filing of a return in lieu of a declaration, see paragraph (a) of § 1.6015 (f)-1.

(2) *Farmers.* The estimated gross income from farming is the estimated income resulting from oyster farming, the cultivation of the soil, the raising or harvesting of any agricultural or horticultural commodities, and the raising of livestock, bees, or poultry. In other words, the requisite gross income must be derived from the operations of a stock, dairy, poultry, fruit, or truck farm, or plantation, ranch, nursery, range, orchard, or oyster bed. If an individual receives for the use of his land income in the form of a share of the crops produced thereon such income is from farming. As to determination of income of farmers, see sections 61 and 162 and the regulations thereunder.

(3) *Fishermen.* The estimated gross income from fishing is the estimated income resulting from the catching, taking, harvesting, cultivating, or farming of any kind of fish, **shellfish** (for example, clams and mussels), crustacea (for example, lobsters, crabs, and shrimps), sponges, seaweeds, or other aquatic forms of animal and vegetable life. The estimated gross income from fishing includes the income expected to be received by an officer or member of the crew of a vessel while the vessel is engaged in any such activity, whether or not the officer or member of the crew is himself so engaged, and, in the case of an individual who is engaged in any such activity in the employ of any person, the income expected to be received by such individual from such employment. In addition, income expected to be received for services performed as an ordinary incident to any such activity is estimated gross income from fishing. Similarly, for example, the estimated gross income from fishing includes income expected to be received from the shore services of an officer or member of the crew of a vessel engaged in any such activity, if such services are an ordinary incident to any such activity. Services performed as an ordinary incident to such activities include, for example, services performed in such cleaning, icing, and packing of fish as are necessary for the immediate preservation of the catch.

(c) *Place for filing declaration.* Except as provided in paragraph (b) of § 301.6091-1 (relating to hand-carried documents), the declaration of estimated tax shall be filed at the place prescribed by the instructions applicable to such declaration. For example, if the instructions applicable to a declaration provide that the declaration of a taxpayer located in North Carolina be filed with the Director, Internal Revenue Service Center, Chamblee, Ga., such declaration shall be filed with the service center.

(d) *Amendment of declaration.* An amended declaration of estimated tax may be filed during any interval between installment dates prescribed for the taxable year. However, no amended declaration may be filed until after the installment date on or before which the original declaration was filed and only one amended declaration may be filed during each interval between installment dates. Except as provided in paragraph (b) of § 301.6091-1 (relating to hand-carried documents), an amended declaration shall be filed with the internal revenue officer with whom the original declaration was filed.

§ 1.6073-2 (T.D. 6267, filed 11-13-57; republished in T.D. 6500, filed 11-25-60; amended by T.D. 6678, filed 9-30-63.) **Fiscal years.**

(a) *Individuals other than farmers or fishermen.* In the case of an individual on the fiscal year basis, the declaration must be filed on or before the 15th day of the 4th month of the taxable year. If, however, the requirements of section 6015(a) are first met after the 1st day of the 4th month and before the 2d day of the 6th month, the declaration must be filed on or before the 15th day of the 6th month of the taxable year. If such requirements are first met after the 1st day of the 6th month, and before the 2d day of the 9th month, the declaration must be filed on or before the 15th day of the 9th month of the taxable year. If such requirements are first met after the 1st day of the 9th month, the declaration must be filed on or before the 15th day of the 1st month of the succeeding fiscal year. Thus, if an individual taxpayer has a fiscal year ending on June 30, 1956, his declaration must be filed on or before October 15, 1955, if the requirements of section 6015(a) are met on or before October 1, 1955. If, however, such requirements are not met until after October 1, 1955, and before December 2, 1955, the declaration need not be filed until December 15, 1955.

(b) *Farmers or fishermen.* An individual on the fiscal year basis whose estimated gross income from farming or, with respect to taxable years beginning after December 31, 1962, from fishing (as defined in paragraph (b) of § 1.6073-1) is at least two-thirds of his total estimated gross income from all sources for such taxable year may file his declaration on or before the 15th day of the month immediately following the close of his taxable year.

O—► § 1.6073-3 (T.D. 6267, filed 11-13-57; republished in T.D. 6500, filed 11-25-60; amended by T.D. 6678, filed 9-30-63.) **Short taxable years.**

(a) *Individuals other than farmers or fishermen.* In the case of short taxable years the declaration shall be filed on or before the 15th day of the 4th month of such taxable year if the requirements of section 6015(a) are met on or before the 1st day of the 4th month of such year. If such requirements are first met after the 1st day of the 4th month but before the 2nd day of the 6th month, the declaration must be filed on or before the 15th day of the 6th month. If such requirements are first met after the 1st day of the 6th month but before the 2d day of the 9th month, the declaration must be filed on or before the 15th day of the 9th month. If, however, the period for which the declaration is filed is one of 4 months, or one of 6 months and the requirements of section 6015(a) are not met until after the 1st day of the 4th month, or one of 9 months and such requirements are not met until after the 1st day of the 6th month, the declaration may be filed on or before the 15th day of the succeeding taxable year.

(b) *Farmers or fishermen* In the case of an individual whose estimated gross income from farming or, with respect to taxable years beginning after December 31, 1962, from fishing (as defined in paragraph (b) of § 1.6073-1) for a short taxable years is at least two-thirds of his total estimated gross income from all sources of such taxable year, his declaration may be filed on or before the 15th day of the month immediately following the close of such taxable year.

O—► § 1.6073-4 (T.D. 6267, filed 11-13-57; amended by T.D. 6371, filed 4-6-59; republished in T.D. 6500, filed 11-25-60; amended by T.D. 6638, filed 2-25-63 and T.D. 6950, filed 4-3-68.) **Extension of time for filing declarations by individuals.**

(a) *In general.* District directors and directors of service centers are authorized to grant a reasonable extension of time for filing a declaration or an amended declaration. Except as provided in paragraph (b) of § 301.6091-1 (relating to hand-carried documents), an application for an extension of time for filing such a declaration shall be addressed to the internal revenue officer with whom the taxpayer is required to file his declaration, and must contain a full recital of the causes for the delay. Except in the case of taxpayers who are abroad, no extension for filing declarations may be granted for more than 6 months.

(b) *Citizens outside of the United States.* In the case of a United States citizen outside the United States and Puerto Rico on the 15th day of the 4th month of his taxable year, an extension of time for filing his declaration of estimated tax otherwise due on or before the 15th day of the 4th month of the taxable year is granted to and including the 15th day of the 6th month of the taxable year. For purposes of applying this paragraph to taxable years beginning prior to January 1, 1964, Alaska shall be considered outside the United States.

(c) *Addition to tax applicable.* An extension of time for filing the declaration of estimated tax automatically extends the time for paying the estimated tax (without interest) for the same period. However, such extension does not relieve the taxpayer from the addition to the tax imposed by section 6654, and the period of the underpayment will be determined under section 6654(c) without regard to such extension.

O—► § 301.6073 **Statutory provisions; time for filing declarations of estimated income tax by individuals.** [Sec. 6073. IRC]

O—► § 301.6073-1 (T.D. 6498, filed 10-24-60.) **Time for filing declarations of estimated income tax by individuals.**—For provisions relating to time for filing declarations of estimated income tax by individuals, see §§ 1.6073-1 to 1.6073-4, inclusive, of this chapter (Income Tax Regulations).

O—► § 1.6074 **Statutory provisions; time for filing declarations of estimated income tax by corporations.** [Sec. 6074, IRC]

O—► § 1.6074-1 (T.D. 6267, filed 11-13-57; republished in T.D. 6500, filed 11-25-60; amended by T.D. 6768, filed 11-3-64 and T.D. 6950, filed 4-3-68.) **Time and place for filing declarations of estimated income tax by corporations.**

(a) *Taxable years beginning on or before December 31, 1963.* For taxable years ending on or after December 31, 1955, and beginning on or before December 31, 1963, declarations of estimated tax for the taxable year shall be filed on or before the 15th day of the 9th month of such year by every corporation whose then anticipated income tax liability under section 11 or 1201 (a), or subchapter L, chapter 1 of the Code, for the year meets the requirements of section 6016 (a). If, however, the requirements necessitating the filing of a declaration are first met after the last day of the 8th month and before the first day of the 12th month of the taxable year the declaration shall be filed on or before the 15th day of the 12th month of the taxable year. If, however, the requirements of section 6016 (a) are not met before the first day of the 12th month of the taxable year, no declaration need be filed for such year.

(b) *Taxable years beginning after December 31, 1963.* A declaration of estimated tax for a taxable year beginning after December 31, 1963, required of a corporation by section 6016 shall be filed as follows:

Reg. § 1.6074-1 (b)

24,308 (I.R.C.)   Reg. § 1.6074-1(b)   4-8-68

If the requirements of section 6016 are first met—	The declaration shall be filed on or before—
before the 1st day of the 4th month of the taxable year	the 15th day of the 4th month of the taxable year
after the last day of the 3d month and before the 1st day of the 6th month of the taxable year	the 15th day of the 6th month of the taxable year
after the last day of the 5th month and before the 1st day of the 9th month of the taxable year	the 15th day of the 9th month of the taxable year
after the last day of the 8th month and before the 1st day of the 12th month of the taxable year	the 15th day of the 12th month of the taxable year

(c) *Place for filing declaration.* Except as provided in paragraph (b) of § 301.6091-1 (relating to hand-carried documents), the declaration of estimated tax shall be filed at the place prescribed by the instructions applicable to such declaration. For example, if the instructions applicable to a declaration provide that the declaration of a corporation located in North Carolina be filed with the Director, Internal Revenue Service Center, Chamblee, Ga., such declaration shall be filed with the service center.

(d) *Amendment of declaration* — (1) *Taxable years beginning on or before December 31, 1963.* A declaration of estimated tax for a taxable year beginning on or before December 31, 1963, which is filed by a corporation prior to the 15th day of the 12th month of the taxable year may be amended in the manner prescribed in § 1.6016-3, at any time on or before such 15th day. An amended declaration shall be filed with the internal revenue officer with whom the original declaration was filed.

(2) *Taxable years beginning after December 31, 1963.* In any case where a declaration of estimated tax for a taxable year beginning after December 31, 1963, has been filed, an amended declaration of estimated tax may be filed during any interval between installment dates prescribed for the taxable year. However, no amended declaration may be filed until after the installment date on or before which the original declaration was filed and only one amended declaration may be filed during each interval between installment dates. See § 1.6016-3 for the manner of making an amended declaration. Except as provided in paragraph (b) of § 301.6091-1 (relating to hand-carried documents), an amended declaration shall be filed with the internal revenue officer with whom the original declaration was filed.

○→ § 1.6074-2 (T.D. 6267, filed 11-13-57; republished in T.D. 6500, filed 11-25-60; amended by T.D. 6768, filed 11-3-64.) **Time for filing declarations by corporations in case of a short taxable year.**

(a) *Taxable years beginning on or before December 31, 1963*—(1) *In general.* In the case of a short taxable year of 9 months or more beginning on or before December 31, 1963, where the requirements of section 6016 (a) are met before the 1st day of the 9th month of the short taxable year, the declaration shall be filed on or before the 15th day of the 9th month of such short year. In the case of a short taxable year of more than 9 months, where the requirements of section 6016 (a) are first met after the last day of the 8th month of the short taxable year, the declaration shall be filed on or before the 15th day of the last month of such short year. See § 1.6016-4, relating to the requirement of a declaration in the case of a short taxable year, and paragraph (a) of § 1.6154-2, relating to the time for payment of the estimated tax in case of a short taxable year.

(2) *Example.* The application of the provisions of this paragraph may be illustrated by the following example:

Example. A corporation which changes from a calendar year basis to a fiscal year basis beginning November 1, 1960, will have a short taxable year beginning January 1, 1960, and ending October 31, 1960. If the requirements of section 6016 (a) are met before September 1, 1960 (the 1st day of the 9th month), the corporation is required to file its declaration on or before September 15, 1960 (the 15th day of the 9th month). However, if the requirements of section 6016 (a) are first met after August 31, 1960 (the last day of the 8th month), but before October 1, 1960 (the 1st day of the last month of the short year), the corporation is required to file its declaration on or before October 15, 1960 (the 15th day of the last month of the short year).

(b) *Taxable years beginning after December 31, 1963*—(1) *In general.* In the case of a short taxable year of 4 or more months which begins after December 31, 1963, the declaration shall be filed on or before the applicable date specified in paragraph (b) of § 1.6074-1, except that in the case of a short taxable year ending after November 30, 1964, the declaration shall be filed on or before the 15th day of the last month of the short taxable year if the requirements of section 6016(a) are first met before the first day of such last month and the date specified in such paragraph (b) as applicable is not within the short taxable year. See § 1.6016-4, relating to the requirement of a declaration in the case of a short taxable year, and paragraph (b) of § 1.6154-2, relating to the time for payment of the estimated tax in case of a short taxable year.

(2) *Examples.* The application of the provisions of this paragraph may be illustrated by the following examples:

Example (1). A corporation filing on a

Reg. § 1.6074-1   PRENTICE-HALL, Inc., Englewood Cliffs, N. J.

Time for Filing Returns and Other Documents (I.R.C.) 24,309

calendar year basis which changes to a fiscal year beginning September 1, 1965, will have a short taxable year beginning January 1, 1965, and ending August 31, 1965. If the requirements of section 6016(a) are met before April 1, 1965 (the 1st day of the 4th month), the declaration of estimated tax must be filed on or before April 15, 1965 (the 15th day of the 4th month).

Example (2). If, in the first example, the corporation first meets the requirements of section 6016(a) during July 1965, then the requirements of section 6016(a) were met before the first day of the last month of the short taxable year, and a declaration of estimated tax is required to be filed on or before August 15, 1965, for the short taxable year. However, if the corporation does not meet the requirements of section 6016(a) until August 1, 1965, then the requirements of section 6016(a) were not met before the first day of the last month of the short taxable year, and no declaration of estimated tax is required to be filed for the short taxable year.

(c) *Amendment of declaration* — (1) *Taxable years beginning on or before December 31, 1963.* Where a declaration of estimated tax for a short taxable year of more than 9 months beginning on or before December 31, 1963, is filed before the 15th day of the last month of the short taxable year, an amended declaration may be filed any time on or before such 15th day.

(2) *Taxable years beginning after December 31, 1963.* Where a declaration of estimated tax for a short taxable year beginning after December 31, 1963, has been filed, an amended declaration may be filed during any interval between installment dates. However, no amended declaration for a short taxable year may be filed until after the installment date on or before which the original declaration was filed and only one amended declaration may be filed during each interval between installment dates. For purposes of this subparagraph the term "installment date" includes the 15th day of the last month of a short taxable year if such 15th day does not fall on a prescribed installment date.

○─▶ § 1.6074-3 (T.D. 6267, filed 11-13-57; republished in T.D. 6500, filed 11-25-60; amended by T.D. 6950, filed 4-3-68.) **Extension of time for filing declarations by corporations.**

(a) *In general.* District directors and directors of service centers are authorized to grant a reasonable extension of time for filing a declaration or an amended declaration. Except as provided in paragraph (b) of § 301.6091-1 (relating to hand-carried documents), an application by a corporation for an extension of time for filing such a declaration shall be addressed to the internal revenue officer with whom the corporation is required to file its declaration and must contain a full recital of the causes for the delay.

(b) *Addition to tax applicable.* An extension of time granted to a corporation for filing a declaration of estimated tax automatically extends the time for paying the estimated tax (without interest) for the same period. However, such extension does not relieve the corporation from the addition to the tax imposed by section 6655, and the period of the underpayment will be determined under section 6655(c) without regard to such extension.

○─▶ § 301.6074 **Statutory provisions; time for filing declarations of estimated income tax by corporations.** [Sec. 6074, IRC]

○─▶ § 301.6074-1 (T.D. 6498, filed 10-24-60.) **Time for filing declarations of estimated income tax by corporations.**—For provisions relating to time for filing declarations of estimated income tax by corporations, see §§ 1.6074-1 to 1.6074-3, inclusive, of this chapter (Income Tax Regulations).

EXTENSION OF TIME FOR FILING RETURNS

○─▶ § 1.6081 **Statutory provisions; extension of time for filing returns.** [Sec. 6081, IRC]

○─▶ § 1.6081-1 (T.D. 6364, filed 2-13-59, amended by T.D. 6371, filed 4-6-59; and T.D. 6436, filed 12-30-59; republished in T.D. 6500, filed 11-25-60; amended by T.D. 6581, filed 12-5-61; T.D. 6950, filed 4-3-68; T.D. 7133, filed 7-21-71; T.D. 7160, filed 2-1-72; T.D. 7260, filed 2-9-73; T.D. 7533, filed 2-14-78.) **Extension of time for ling returns.**

(a) *In general.* District directors and directors of service centers are authorized to grant a reasonable extension of time for filing any return, declaration, statement, or other document which relates to any tax imposed by subtitle A of the Code and which is required under the provisions of subtitle A or F of the Code or the regulations thereunder. However, other than in the case of taxpayers who are abroad, such extensions of time shall not be granted for more than 6 months, and an extension of time for the filing of a return of a DISC (as defined in section 992(a)), as specified in section 6072(b), shall not be granted. Except in the case of an extension of time pursuant to § 1.6081-2, an extension of time for filing an income tax return shall not operate to extend the time for the payment of the tax or any installment thereof unless specified to the contrary in the extension. In the case of an extension of time pursuant to § 1.6081-2, an extension of time for filing an income tax return shall operate to extend the time for the payment of the tax or any installment thereof unless specified to the contrary in the extension. For extension of time for filing of declarations of estimated tax, see § 1.6073-4. For rules relating to extension of time for paying tax, see § 1.6161-1.

(b) *Application for extension of time*—(1) *In general.* A taxpayer desiring an extension of the time for filing a return, statement, or other document shall submit an application therefor on or before the due date of such return, statement, or other document. Except as provided in subparagraph (3) of this paragraph and, except as provided in paragraph (b) of § 301.6091-1 (relating to hand-carried documents), such application shall be made to the internal revenue officer with whom such return, statement, or other document is required to be filed. Such application shall be in writing, properly signed by the taxpayer or his duly authorized agent, and

Reg. § 1.6081-1(b)(1)

shall clearly set forth (i) the particular tax return, information return, statement, or other document, including the taxable year or period thereof, with respect to which the extension of the time for filing is desired, and (ii) a full recital of the reasons for requesting the extension to aid such internal revenue officer in determining the period of extension, if any, which will be granted.

(2) *Additional information in the case of Form 1040.* In addition to the information required under subparagraph (1) of this paragraph, the application of a taxpayer desiring an extension of the time for filing an individual income tax return on Form 1040 for any taxable year beginning after December 31, 1958, shall also set forth (i) whether an income tax return has been filed on or before its due date for each of the three taxable years immediately preceding the taxable year of such return, and if not, the reason for each failure, and (ii) whether the taxpayer was required to file a declaration of estimated tax for the taxable year of such return, and if so, whether each required estimated tax payment was made on or before its due date. For purposes of this subparagraph a return is considered as filed on or before its due date if it is filed on or before the applicable date provided in section 6072 or on or before the last day of the period covered by an extension of time granted pursuant to the provisions of section 6081, and each required payment of estimated tax is considered as paid on or before its due date if it is paid on or before the applicable date provided in section 6153 or on or before the last day of the period covered by an extension of time granted pursuant to the provisions of section 6161.

(3) *Information returns filed with Service Center.* An application for an extension of the time for filing any information return required to be filed with an Internal Revenue Service Center shall state the location of the Service Center with which such return will be filed. Except as provided in paragraph (b) of § 301.6091–1 (relating to hand-carried documents), such application shall be made to the internal revenue officer with whom the applicant is required to file an income tax return or with whom the applicant would be required to file an income tax return if such a return were required of him.

(4) *Taxpayer unable to sign.* In any case in which a taxpayer is unable, by reason of illness, absence, or other good cause, to sign a request for an extension, any person standing in close personal or business relationship to the taxpayer may sign the request on his behalf and shall be considered as a duly authorized agent for this purpose, provided the request sets forth the reasons for a signature other than the taxpayer's and the relationship existing between the taxpayer and the signer.

(5) *Form of application.* The application for an extension of the time for filing a return, statement, or other document may be made in the form of a letter. However, in the case of an individual income tax return on Form 1040, the application for an extension of the time for filing may be made either on Form 2688 or in the form of a letter.

O— § 1.6081–2 (T.D. 6364, filed 2-13-59; republished in T.D. 6500, filed 11-25-60; amended by T.D. 6638, filed 2-25-63.) Extensions of time in the case of certain partnerships, certain domestic corporations, foreign organizations, and United States citizens residing or traveling outside the United States and Puerto Rico.

(a) *In general.* An extension of time for filing returns of income is hereby granted to and including the fifteenth day of the sixth month following the close of the taxable year in the case of:

(1) Partnerships which are required under paragraph (e)(2) of § 1.6031–1 to file returns on the fifteenth day of the fourth month following the close of the taxable year of the partnership, and which keep their records and books of account outside the United States and Puerto Rico;

(2) Domestic corporations which transact their business and keep their records and books of account outside the United States and Puerto Rico;

(3) Foreign corporations which maintain an office or place of business within the United States;

(4) Domestic corporations whose principal income is from sources within the possessions of the United States; and

(5) United States citizens residing or traveling outside the United States and Puerto Rico, including persons in military or naval service on duty outside the United States and Puerto Rico.

In all such cases a statement must be attached to the return showing that the person for whom the return is made is a person described in this section.

(b) *Limitation.* In applying paragraph (a) of this section to taxable years beginning prior to January 1, 1963, the term "United States", as used in subparagraphs (1), (2) and (5) of such paragraph, does not include Alaska.

O— § 1.6081–3 (T.D. 6364, filed 2-13-59; republished in T.D. 6500, filed 11-25-60; amended by T.D. 6914, filed 3-7-67; T.D. 6950, filed 4-3-68; T.D. 7138, filed 8-10-71; T.D. 7260, filed 2-9-73; T.D. 7533, filed 2-14-78.) Automatic extension of time for filing corporation income tax returns.

(a) *In general.* A corporation shall be allowed an automatic extension of time to the fifteenth day of the third month following the month in which falls the date prescribed for the filing of its income tax return provided the following requirements are met:

(1) An application must be prepared in duplicate on Form 7004, "Application for Automatic Extension of Time to file U.S. Corporation Income Tax Return", and must be signed by a person authorized by the corporation to request such extension. Such person must be a person authorized under section 6062 to execute the return of the corporation; a person currently enrolled to practice before the Treasury Department; or after November 7, 1965 either an attorney who is a member in good standing of the bar of the highest court of a State, possession, territory, commonwealth, or the District of Columbia; or a certified public accountant duly qualified to practice in a State, possession, territory, commonwealth, or the District of Columbia.

(2) The original of the application must be filed on or before the date prescribed for the filing of the return of the corporation with the internal revenue officer with whom the corporation is required to file its income tax return. The corporation shall

make a remittance of an estimated amount of tax which shall not be less than would be required as the first installment under section 6152(a)(1) should the corporation elect to pay the tax in installments. Upon the timely filing of Form 7004, properly prepared, the three-month extension shall be considered as allowed. If the taxpayer elects to pay in installments the tax shown on Form 7004, the installment privilege provided in section 6152(a)(1) is limited to the amount shown on the form. The duplicate Form 7004 shall be attached to the completed income tax return when filed as evidence of the extension.

(b) *Consolidated returns.* An application for an automatic extension of time for filing a consolidated return shall be made by a person authorized by the parent corporation to request such extension. Such person must be a person authorized under section 6062 to execute the return of the parent corporation; a person currently enrolled to practice before the Treasury Department; or after November 7, 1965 either an attorney who is a member in good standing of the bar of the highest court of a State, possession, territory, commonwealth, or the District of Columbia; or a certified public accountant duly qualified to practice in a State, possession, territory, commonwealth, or the District of Columbia. There shall be attached to such application a statement listing the name and address of each member of the affiliated group for which such consolidated return will be made. For taxable years beginning after December 31, 1970, the original of such application shall be filed with the internal revenue officer with which the parent corporation will file its income tax return. Upon the timely filing of Form 7004 with the internal revenue officer with which such corporation files its return, the three month extension shall be considered as granted to the affiliated group for the filing of its consolidated return or for the filing of each member's separate return. For taxable years beginning after December 31, 1970, in the event that the privilege of filing a consolidated return is not exercised, the parent corporation, and members of the affiliated group shall attach to their completed separate income tax returns a copy of the application (Form 7004).

(c) *Special rule for the extension of time for the payment of tax.* Notwithstanding the application of § 1.6081-1(a), any automatic extension of time for filing a corporation income tax return granted under paragraph (a) or (b) of this section shall not operate to extend the time for payment of any tax due on such return.

(d) *Termination of automatic extension.* The district director, including the Director of International Operations, or the director of a service center may, in his discretion, terminate at any time an automatic extension by mailing to the corporation (parent corporation in the case of an affiliated group), or the person who requested such extension for the corporation, a notice of termination. The notice shall be mailed at least ten days prior to the termination date designated in such notice. The notice of termination shall be sufficient for all purposes when mailed to the corporation at its address shown on Form 7004 or to the person who requested such extension for the corporation at his last known address or last known place of business, even if such corporation has terminated its existence, or such person is deceased or is under a legal disability.

(e) Paragraph (a) through (d) of this section shall not apply to returns filed by a DISC pursuant to section 6011(c)(2).

§ 1.6081-4 (T.D. 7160, filed 2-1-72.) Automatic extension of time for filing individual income tax return.

(a) *In general.* (1) An individual who is required to file an income tax return on Form 1040 for any taxable year ending on or after December 31, 1971, shall be allowed an automatic two-month extension of time to file such return after the date prescribed for filing of the return only if the requirements contained in subparagraph (2)(3) and (4) of this paragraph are met.

(2) An application must be prepared in duplicate on Form 4868 "Application for Automatic Extension of Time to File U.S. Individual Income Tax Return", and must be signed by the taxpayer or other person duly authorized by the taxpayer to request such extension. Such other person must either be an attorney who is a member in good standing of the bar of the highest court of a State, possession, territory, commonwealth, or the District of Columbia; a certified public accountant duly qualified to practice in a State, possession, territory, commonwealth, or the District of Columbia; a person currently enrolled to practice before the Treasury Department; a duly authorized agent holding a power of attorney with respect to the filing of income tax returns; or a person standing in a close personal or business relationship to the taxpayer where such taxpayer is unable to sign the application because of illness, absence, or other good cause.

(3) The original of the application must be filed on or before the date prescribed for the filing of the return of the individual with the internal revenue officer with whom the individual is required to file his income tax return.

(4) Such application for extension must show the full amount properly estimated as tax for such taxpayer for such taxable year, and such application must be accompanied by the full remittance of the amount properly estimated as tax which is unpaid as of the date prescribed for the filing of the return.

(5) Upon the timely filing of Form 4868, properly prepared, and accompanied by remittance of the full amount of the estimated unpaid tax liability, the two-month extension shall be considered as allowed. The duplicate Form 4868 shall be attached to the face of the completed income tax return when filed as evidence of the extension. Except in undue hardship cases, no extension of time for filing an individual income tax return shall be granted under § 1.6081-1 until an individual has properly availed himself of the provisions of this paragraph.

(b) *Special rule for the extension of time for the payment of tax.* Notwithstanding the application of § 1.6081-1(a), any automatic extension of time for filing an individual income tax return granted under paragraph (a) of this section shall not operate to extend the time for the pay-

Reg. § 1.6081-4(b)

ment of any tax due on such return.

(c) *Termination of automatic extension.* The district director, including the Director of International Operations, or the director of a service center may, in his discretion, terminate at any time an automatic extension by mailing to the taxpayer, or the person who requested such extension for the taxpayer, a notice of termination. The notice shall be mailed at least 10 days prior to the termination date designated in such notice. The notice of termination shall be sufficient for all purposes when mailed to the taxpayer at his address shown on Form 4868 or to the person who requested such extension for the taxpayer at his last known address or last known place of business, even if such person is deceased or is under a legal disability.

O—☛ § 31.6081(a) Statutory provisions; extension of time for filing returns. [Sec. 6081(a), IRC]

O—☛ § 31.6081(a)-1 (T.D. 6354, filed 1-13-59; republished in TD. 6516, filed 12-19-60; amended by T.D. 6950, filed 4-3-68 and T.D. 7351, filed 4-16-75.) **Extensions of time for filing returns and other documents.**

(a) *Federal Insurance Contributions Act; income tax withheld from wages; and Railroad Retirement Tax Act*—(1) *In general.* Except as otherwise provided in subparagraphs (2) and (3) of this paragraph no extension of time for filing any return or other document required in respect of the Federal Insurance Contributions Act, income tax withheld from wages, or the Railroad Retirement Tax Act will be granted.

(2) *Information returns of employers required to file monthly returns of tax under the Federal Insurance Contributions Act.* The district director or director of a service center may, upon application of the employer, grant an extension of time in which to file any information return required under paragraph (b)(1) of § 31.6011 (a)-5. Such extension of time shall not extend beyond the last day of the calendar month in which occurs the due date prescribed in paragraph (a)(3)(i) of § 31.6071 (a)-1 for filing the information return. Each application for an extension of time for filing an information return shall be made in writing, properly signed by the employer or his duly authorized agent. Except as provided in paragraph (b) of § 301.6091-1 (relating to hand-carried documents), each application shall be addressed to the internal revenue officer with whom the employer will file the return. Each application shall contain a full recital of the reasons for requesting the extension, to aid the officer in determining the period of the extension, if any, which will be granted. Such a request in the form of a letter to such internal revenue officer will suffice as an application. The application shall be filed on or before the due date prescribed in paragraph (a)(3)(i) of § 31.6071(a)-1 for filing the information return.

(3) *Information returns of employers on Forms W-2 and W-3.* For good cause shown upon application by an employer, the district director or director of a service center may grant an extension of time not exceeding 30 days in which to file (i) the copies of withholding statements (Form W-2) which are part of a return on Form 942 under paragraph (b) of § 31.6011(a)-4, or (ii) copies of withholding statements and the accompanying transmittal which constitute information returns under paragraph (a) of § 31.6051-2. Each application for an extension of time under this subparagraph shall be made in writing, properly signed by the employer or his duly authorized agent. Except as provided in paragraph (b) of § 301.6091-1 (relating to hand-carried documents), each application shall be addressed to the internal revenue office with whom the employer is required to file the Forms W-2. Each application shall contain a full recital of the reasons for requesting the extension, to aid such office in determining the period of the extension, if any, which will be granted. Such a request in the form of a letter to such internal revenue office will suffice as an application. The application shall be filed on or before the date on which the employer is required to file the withholding statements without regard to this subparagraph.

(b) *Federal Unemployment Tax Act.* The district director or director of a service center may, upon application of the employer, grant a reasonable extension of time (not to exceed 90 days) in which to file any return required in respect of the Federal Unemployment Tax Act. Any application for an extension of time for filing the return shall be in writing, properly signed by the employer or his duly authorized agent. Except as provided in paragraph (b) of § 301.6091-1 (relating to hand-carried documents), each application shall be addressed to the internal revenue officer with whom the employer will file the return. Each application shall contain a full recital of the reasons for requesting the extension, to aid such officer in determining the period of the extension, if any, which will be granted. Such a request in the form of a letter to such internal revenue officer will suffice as an application. The application shall be filed on or before the due date prescribed in paragraph (c) of § 31.6071 (a)-1 for filing the return, or on or before the date prescribed for filing the return in any prior extension granted. An extension of time for filing a return does not operate to extend the time for payment of the tax or any part thereof.

(c) *Duly authorized agent.* In any case in which an employer is unable, by reason of illness, absence or other good cause, to sign a request for an extension, any person standing in close personal or business relationship to the employer may sign the request on his behalf, and shall be considered as a duly authorized agent for this purpose, provided the request sets forth the reasons for a signature other than the employer's and the relationship existing between the employer and the signer.

O—☛ § 53.6081 Statutory provisions; extension of time for filing the return. [Sec 6081, IRC]

O—☛ § 53.6081-1 (T.D. 7368, filed 7-15-75.) **Extension of time for filing the return.**

(a) District directors and directors of service centers are authorized to grant a reasonable extension of time for filing any return, statement, or other document which relates to any tax imposed by chapter 42 and which is required under the provisions of chapter 42 or the regulations thereunder. However, except in the case of taxpayers who are abroad, such extensions of time shall not be granted for more than 6 months. An extension of time for filing a return shall not operate to extend the time for the payment of the tax or any part thereof unless specified to the contrary in the extension.

(b) The application for an extension of time for filing the return shall be addressed to the district director or director of the service center with whom the return is to be filed and must contain a full recital of the causes for the delay. It should be made before the expiration of the time within which the return otherwise must be filed, and failure to do so may indicate negligence and constitute sufficient cause for denial. It should, where possible, be made sufficiently early to permit consideration of the matter and reply before what otherwise would be the due date of the return.

(c) If an extension of time for filing the return is granted, a return shall be filed before the expiration of the period of extension.

○━━▶ § 301.6081 **Statutory provisions; extension of time for filing returns.** [Sec. 6081 IRC]

○━━▶ § 301.6081-1 (TD 6498, filed 10-24-60.) **Extension of time for filing returns.**

For provisions concerning extensions of time for filing returns or other documents, see the regulations relating to the particular tax.

PLACE FOR FILING RETURNS OR OTHER DOCUMENTS

○━━▶ § 1.6091 **Statutory provisions; place for filing returns or other documents.** [Sec. 6091, IRC]

○━━▶ § 1.6091-1 (TD 6364, filed 2-13-59; republished in TD 6500, filed 11-25-60; amended by TD 6628, filed 12-27-62; TD 6887, filed 6-23-66; TD 6922, filed 6-16-67; TD 7284, filed 8-2-73; TD 7385, filed 10-28-75.) **Place for filing returns or other documents.**

(a) *In general.* Except as provided in § 1.6091-4, whenever a return, statement, or other document is required to be made under the provisions of subtitle A or F of the Code, or the regulations thereunder, with respect to any tax imposed by subtitle A of the Code, and the place for filing such return, statement, or other document is not provided for by the Code, it shall be filed at the place prescribed by the regulations contained in this chapter.

(b) *Place for filing certain information returns.* (1) For the place for filing returns of partnership income, see paragraph (e)(1) of § 1.6031-1.

(2) For the place for filing information returns by banks with respect to common trust funds, see § 1.6032-1.

(3) For the place for filing information returns by certain organizations exempt from taxation under section 501 (a), see paragraph (e) of § 1.6033-1.

(4) For the place for filing information returns by trusts claiming charitable deductions under section 642 (c), see paragraph (c) of § 1.6034-1.

(5) For the place for filing information returns by officers, directors, and shareholders of foreign personal holding companies see paragraph (d) of § 1.6035-1 and paragraph (d) of § 1.6035-2.

(6) For the place for filing information returns relating to certain stock option transactions, see paragraph (c) of § 1.6039-1.

(7) For the place for filing returns of information reporting certain payments, see paragraph (a)(5) of § 1.6041-2 and § 1.-6041-6.

(8) For the place for filing returns of information regarding payments of dividends, see paragraph (d) of § 1.6042-1 and paragraph (c) of § 1.6042-2 (relating to returns for calendar years after 1962).

(9) For the place for filing information returns by corporations relating to contemplated dissolution or liquidation, see paragraph (a) of § 1.6043-1.

(10) For the place for filing information returns by corporations relating to distributions in liquidation, see paragraph (a) of § 1.6043-2.

(11) For the place for filing returns of information regarding payments of patronage dividends, see paragraph (b) of § 1.6044-1, and paragraph (d) of § 1.6044-2 (relating to returns for calendar years after 1962).

(12) For the place for filing information returns relating to formation or reorganization of foreign corporations, see paragraph (e) of § 1.6046-1.

(13) For the place for filing information returns regarding certain payments of interest, see paragraph (c) of § 1.6049-1.

(14) For the place for filing information returns with respect to payment of wages in the form of group-term life insurance, see paragraph (b) of § 1.6052-1.

(15) For the place for filing information returns on Form 1042S with respect to certain amounts paid to nonresident alien individuals, foreign partnerships, or foreign corporations, see paragraph (c) of § 1.1461-2.

(16) For the place for filing information returns on Form 5074 with respect to the allocation of individual income tax to Guam, see paragraph (b)(3) of § 1.935-1 and paragraph (d) of § 301.7654-1 of this chapter (Regulations on Procedure and Administration).

○━━▶ § 1.6091-2 (TD 6364, filed 2-13-59; republished in TD 6500, filed 11-25-60; amended by TD 6950, filed 4-3-68; TD 7012, filed 5-14-69; TD 7495, filed 6-29-77.) **Place for filing income tax returns.**

Except as provided in § 1.6091-3 (relating to income tax returns required to be filed with the Director of International Operations) and § 1.6091-4 (relating to exceptional cases)—

(a) *Individuals, estates, and trusts.* (1) Except as provided in paragraph (c) of this section, income tax returns of individuals, estates, and trusts shall be filed with the district director for the internal revenue district in which is located the legal residence or principal place of business of the person required to make the return, or, if such person has no legal residence or principal place of business in any internal revenue district, with the District Director at Baltimore, Maryland 21202.

(2) An individual employed on a salary or commission basis who is not also engaged in conducting a commercial or professional enterprise for profit on his own account does not have a "principal place of business" within the meaning of this section.

(b) *Corporations.* Except as provided in paragraph (c) of this section, income tax returns of corporations shall be filed with

Reg. § 1.6091-2(b)

the district director for the internal revenue district in which is located the principal place of business or principal office or agency of the corporation.

(c) *Returns filed with service centers.* Notwithstanding paragraphs (a) and (b) of this section, whenever instructions applicable to income tax returns provide that the returns be filed with a service center, the returns must be so filed in accordance with the instructions.

(d) *Hand-carried returns.* Notwithstanding paragraphs (1) and (2) of section 6091(b) and paragraph (c) of this section—

(1) *Persons other than corporations.* Returns of persons other than corporations which are filed by hand carrying shall be filed with the district director (or with any person assigned the administrative supervision of an area, zone or local office constituting a permanent post of duty within the internal revenue district of such director) as provided in paragraph (a) of this section.

(2) *Corporations.* Returns of corporations which are filed by hand carrying shall be filed with the district director (or with any person assigned the administrative supervision of an area, zone or local office constituting a permanent post of duty within the internal revenue district of such director) as provided in paragraph (b) of this section.

See § 301.6091-1 of this chapter (Regulations on Procedure and Administration) for provisions relating to the definition of hand carried.

(e) *Amended returns.* In the case of amended returns filed after April 14, 1968, except as provided in paragraph (d) of this section—

(1) *Persons other than corporations.* Amended returns of persons other than corporations shall be filed with the service center serving the internal revenue district referred to in paragraph (a) of this section.

(2) *Corporations.* Amended returns of corporations shall be filed with the service center serving the internal revenue district referred to in paragraph (b) of this section.

O— § 1.6091-3 (TD 6364, filed 2-13-59; republished in TD 6500, filed 11-25-60; amended by TD 6872, filed 1-5-66; TD 6922, filed 6-16-67; TD 6950, filed 4-3-68; TD 7012, filed 5-14-69.) **Income tax returns required to be filed with Director of International Operations.**

The following income tax returns shall be filed with the Director of International Operations, Internal Revenue Service, Washington, D.C. 20225, or the district director, or the director of the service center, depending on the appropriate officer designated on the return form or in the instructions issued with respect to such form:

(a) Income tax returns on which all, or a portion, of the tax is to be paid in foreign currency. See §§ 301.6316-1 to 301.6316-6 inclusive, and §§ 301.6316-8 and 301.6316-9 of this chapter (Regulations on Procedure and Administration).

(b) Income tax returns on an individual citizen of the United States whose principal place of abode for the period with respect to which the return is filed is outside the United States. A taxpayer's principal place of abode will be considered to be outside the United States if his legal residence is outside the United States or if his return bears a foreign address.

(c) Income tax returns of an individual citizen of a possession of the United States (whether or not a citizen of the United States) who has no legal residence or principal place of business in any internal revenue district in the United States.

(d) Except in the case of any departing alien return under section 6851 and § 1.6851-2, the income tax return of any nonresident alien.

(e) The income tax return of an estate or trust the fiduciary of which is outside the United States and has no legal residence or principal place of business in any internal revenue district in the United States.

(f) Income tax returns of foreign corporations.

(g) The return by a withholding agent of the income tax required to be withheld at source under chapter 3 of the Code on nonresident aliens and foreign corporations and tax-free covenant bonds, as provided in § 1.1461-2.

(h) Income tax returns of persons who claim the benefits of section 911 (relating to earned income from sources without the United States).

(i) Income tax returns of corporations which claim the benefits of section 922 (relating to special deduction for Western Hemisphere trade corporations) except in the case of consolidated returns filed pursuant to the regulations under section 1502.

(j) Income tax returns of persons who claim the benefits of section 931 (relating to income from sources within possessions of the United States).

(k) Income tax returns of persons who claim the benefits of section 933 (relating to income from sources within Puerto Rico).

(l) Income tax returns of corporations which claim the benefits of section 941 (relating to the special deduction for China Trade Act corporations.)

O— § 1.6091-4 (TD 6364, filed 2-13-59; republished in TD 6500, filed 11-25-60; amended by TD 6793, filed 1-21-65; TD 7385, filed 10-28-75.) **Exceptional cases.**

(a) *Permission to file in district other than required district.* (1) The Commissioner may permit the filing of any income tax return required to be made under the provisions of subtitle A or F of the Code, or the regulations in this part, in any internal revenue district, notwithstanding the provisions of paragraphs (1) and (2) of section 6091(b) and §§ 1.6091-1 to 1.6091-3, inclusive.

(2) In cases where the Commissioner authorizes (for all purposes except venue) a director of an internal revenue service center to receive returns, such returns pursuant to instructions issued with respect thereto, may be sent directly to the director and are thereby filed with him for all purposes except as a factor in determining venue. However, after initial processing all such returns shall be forwarded by the di-

rector of a service center to the office with which such returns are, without regard to this subparagraph, required to be filed. For the sole purpose of determining venue, such returns are filed only with such office.

(3) Notwithstanding the provisions of other sections of this chapter or any rule issued under this chapter—

(i) In cases where, in accordance with subparagraph (2) of this paragraph, a return is filed with the director of a service center, the authority of the district director with whom such return would, without regard to such subparagraph, be required to be filed shall remain the same as if the return had been so filed;

(ii) Unless a return or other document is a proper attachment to, or is, a return which the director of a service center is expressly authorized to receive, such return or other document shall be filed as if all returns sent directly to the service centers, in accordance with subparagraph (2) of this paragraph, were filed in the office where such returns are, without regard to such subparagraph, required to be filed; and

(iii) Unless the performance of an act is directly related to the sending of a return directly to the director of a service center, such act shall be performed as if all returns sent directly to the service centers, in accordance with subparagraph (2) of this paragraph, were filed in the office where such returns are, without regard to such subparagraph, required to be filed.

(4) The application of subparagraphs (2) and (3) of this subparagraph may be illustrated by the following examples:

Example (1). The Commissioner has authorized the Director, Internal Revenue Service Center, Chamblee, Georgia, (for all purposes except venue) to receive Forms 1040 and 1040A. A, a resident of Greensboro, North Carolina, is required to file his Form 1040 for the calendar year 1964 with the District Director, Greensboro, North Carolina. In addition, A is required to file his declaration of estimated tax, Form 1040ES, for the calendar year 1965, which under paragraph (c) of § 1.6073-1 must be filed with the district director for the district in which A expects to file his income tax return. Under subparagraph (2) of this paragraph A may send his Form 1040 to either the director of the service center or to his district director. However, since his Form 1040ES is not a proper attachment to his income tax return, he shall send his Form 1040ES to his district director (with whom he is, without regard to subparagraph (2) of this paragraph, required to file his income tax return).

Example (2). Assume the same facts as in Example (1), and in addition, that A is required to attach copies of his Forms W-2 to his income tax return, Form 1040. Therefore, A must attach copies of his Forms W-2 to his Form 1040 and send both to either his district director or the director of the service center.

Example (3). Assume the facts in Example (1) and in addition, that A sends his Form 1040 to the director of the service center. Assume further that A is entitled to file a claim under section 6421 for refund of certain taxes paid for gasoline used for certain nonhighway uses. Under paragraph (c) of § 48.6421 (c)-1 of this chapter the claim on Form 843 shall be filed with the district director with whom the claimant filed his latest income tax return. Since Form 843 is not a proper attachment to A's Form 1040, the claim shall be sent to A's district director since his is the office with which A would, without regard to subparagraph (2) of this paragraph, be required to file his Form 1040.

Example (4). Taxpayer B sends his Form 1040 to the director of a service center. B wishes to apply for an extension of the period of replacement for involuntarily converted property pursuant to section 1033 of the Code. Under paragraph (c) (3) of § 1.1033 (a)-2 of this chapter such application is to be made to the district director for the internal revenue district in which the income tax return is filed for the first taxable year during which any of the gain from the involuntary conversion is realized. Pursuant to subparagraph (3) of this paragraph, B shall apply to the district director for the internal revenue district in which such income tax return is, without regard to subparagraph (2) of this paragraph, required to be filed. Such district director is authorized to grant or withhold such extension of the period of replacement.

Example (5). Taxpayer C sends his return directly to the director of a service center. C wishes to receive certain information concerning the value of a reversionary interest with respect to his charitable contribution under section 170 of the Code. Under paragraph (d) (2) of § 1.170-2 of this chapter, C may upon request, obtain the information from the district director with whom he files his income tax return. Under subparagraph (3) of this paragraph, C shall request such information from the district director with whom he would, without regard to subparagraph (2) of this paragraph, be required to file his return.

(b) *Returns of officers and employees of the Internal Revenue Service.* The commissioner may require any officer or employee of the Internal Revenue Service to file his income tax return in any district selected by the Commissioner.

(c) *Residents of Guam.* Income tax returns of an individual citizen of the United States who is a resident of Guam shall be filed with Guam, as provided in paragraph (b)(1) of § 1.935-1.

○─▶ § 31.6091 Statutory provisions; place for filing returns. [See Sec. 6091, IRC]

○─▶ § 31.6091-1 (T.D. 6472, filed 6-22-60; republished in T.D. 6516, filed 12-19-60; amended by TD 6915, filed 3-28-67; TD 7495, filed 6-29-77.) **Place for filing returns.**

(a) *Persons other than corporations.* The return of a person other than a corporation shall be filed with the district director for the internal revenue district in which is located the principal place of business or legal residence of such person. If such person has no principal place of business or legal residence in any internal revenue district, the return shall be filed with the District Director at Baltimore, Maryland, except as provided in paragraph (c) of this section.

Reg. § 31.6091-1 (a)

24,314.2 (I.R.C.) Reg. § 31.6091-1(b) 7-18-77

(b) *Corporations.* The return of a corporation shall be filed with the district director for the district in which is located the principal place of business or principal office or agency of the corporation, except as provided in paragraph (c) of this section.

(c) *Returns of taxpayers outside the United States.* The return of a person (other than a corporation) outside the United States having no legal residence or principal place of business in any internal revenue district, or the return of a corporation having no principal place of business or principal office or agency in any internal revenue district, shall be filed with the Director of International Operations, Internal Revenue Service, Washington, D.C. 20225, unless the principal place of business or legal residence of such person, or the principal place of business or principal office or agency of such corporation, is located in the Virgin Islands or Puerto Rico, in which case the return shall be filed with the Director of International Operations, United States Internal Revenue Service, Hato Rey, Puerto Rico 00917.

(d) *Returns filed with service centers.* Notwithstanding paragraphs (a), (b), and (c) of this section, whenever instructions applicable to such returns provide that the returns shall be filed with a service center, such returns shall be so filed in accordance with such instructions.

(e) *Hand-carried returns.* Except as provided in subparagraph (3) of this paragraph, and notwithstanding paragraphs (1) and (2) of section 6091(b) and paragraph (d) of this section—

(1) *Persons other than corporations.* Returns of persons other than corporations which are filed by hand carrying shall be filed with the district director (or with any person assigned the administrative supervision of an area, zone or local office constituting a permanent post of duty within the internal revenue district of such director) as provided in paragraph (a) of this section.

(2) *Corporations.* Returns of corporations which are filed by hand carrying shall be filed with the district director (or with any person assigned the administrative supervision of an area, zone or local office constituting a permanent post of duty within the internal revenue district of such director) as provided in paragraph (b) of this section.

(3) *Exceptions.* This paragraph shall not apply to returns of—

(i) Persons who have no legal residence, no principal place of business, nor principal office or agency in any internal revenue district,

(ii) Citizens of the United States whose principal place of abode for the period with respect to which the return is filed is outside the United States,

(iii) Persons who claim the benefits of section 911 (relating to earned income from sources without the United States), section 922 (relating to special deduction for Western Hemisphere trade corporations), section 931 (relating to income from sources within possessions of the United States), section 933 (relating to income from sources within Puerto Rico), or section 941 (relating to the special deduction for China Trade Act corporations), and

(iv) Nonresident alien persons and foreign corporations.

(f) *Permission to file in district other than required district.* The Commissioner may permit the filing of any return required to be made under the regulations in this subpart in any internal revenue district, notwithstanding the provisions of paragraphs (1), (2), and (4) of section 6091(b) and paragraphs (a), (b), (c), (d) and (e) of this section.

(g) *Returns of officers and employees of the Internal Revenue Service.* The Commissioner may require any officer or employee of the Internal Revenue Service to file any return required of him under the regulations in this subpart in any internal revenue district selected by the Commissioner, notwithstanding the provisions of paragraphs (1), (2), and (4) of section 6091 (b) and paragraphs (a), (b), (c), (d) and (e) of this section.

○━▶ § 53.6091 **Statutory provisions; place for filing returns or other documents.** [Sec. 6091, IRC]

○━▶ § 53.6091-1 (TD 7368, filed 7-15-75; amended by TD 7495, filed 6-29-77.) **Place for filing chapter 42 tax returns.**

Except as provided in § 53.6091-2 (relating to exceptional cases)—

(a) *Persons other than corporations.* Chapter 42 tax returns of persons other than corporations shall be filed with the district director for the internal revenue district in which is located the legal residence or principal place of business of the person required to make the return.

(b) *Corporations.* Chapter 42 tax returns of corporations shall be filed with the district director for the internal revenue district in which is located the principal place of business or principal office or agency of the corporation.

(c) *Returns filed with service centers.* Notwithstanding paragraphs (a) and (b) of this section, unless a return is filed by hand-carrying, whenever instructions applicable to chapter 42 tax returns provide that the returns be filed with a service center, the returns must be so filed in accordance with the instructions. Returns which are filed by hand carrying shall be filed with the district director (or with any person assigned the administrative supervision of an area, zone or local office constituting a permanent post of duty within the internal revenue district of such director) in accordance with paragraph (a) or (b) of this section, whichever is applicable.

○━▶ § 53.6091-2 (T.D. 7368, filed 7-15-75.) **Exceptional cases.**

Notwithstanding the provisions of § 53.6091-1, the Commissioner may permit the filing of any chapter 42 tax return in any internal revenue district.

○━▶ § 301.6091 **Statutory provisions; place for filing returns or other documents.** [Sec. 6091, IRC]

○━▶ § 301.6091-1 (T.D. 6498, filed 10-24-60; amended by T.D. 6950, filed 4-3-68; T.D. 7008, filed 2-28-69; T.D. 7012, filed 5-14-69; T.D. 7188, filed 6-28-72; T.D. 7238, filed 12-28-72; TD 7495, filed 6-29-77.) **Place for filing returns and other documents.**

(a) *General rule.* For provisions concerning the place for filing returns, including hand-carried returns, see the regulations relating to the particular tax. Except as provided in paragraph (b) of this section, for provisions concerning the place for filing documents other than returns, see the regulations relating to the particular tax.

(b) *Exception for hand-carried documents other than returns.* Notwithstanding any other provisions of this chapter—

(1) *Persons other than corporations.* If a document, other than a return, of a person (other than a corporation) is hand carried, and if the document is otherwise required to be filed with a service center, such document may be filed with the district director (or with any person assigned the administrative supervision of an area, zone or local office constituting a permanent post of duty within the internal revenue district of such director) for the internal revenue district in which is located the legal residence or principal place of business of such person, or, in the case of an estate, the internal revenue district in which was the domicile of the decedent at the time of his death. A document may also be filed by hand carrying such document to the appropriate service center, or, in the case of a document required to be filed (i) with the Office of International Operations, by hand carrying to such Office, or (ii) with the office of the assistant regional commissioner (alcohol, tobacco and firearms), by hand carrying to such office.

(2) *Corporations.* If a document, other than a return, of a corporation is hand carried, and if the document is otherwise required to be filed with a service center, such document may be filed with the district director (or with any person assigned the administrative suprevision of an area, zone or local office constituting a permanent post of duty within the internal revenue district of such director) for the internal revenue district in which is located the principal place of business or principal office or agency of the corporation. A document may also be filed by hand carrying such document to the appropriate service center, or, in the case of a document required to be filed (i) with the office of International Operations, by hand carrying to such Office, or (ii) with the office of the assistant regional commissioner (alcohol, tobacco and firearms), by hand carrying to such office.

(c) *Definition of hand carried.* For purposes of this section and section 6091 (b)(4) and the regulations issued thereunder, a return or document will be considered to be hand carried if it is brought to the district director by the person required to file the return or other document, or by his agent. Examples of persons who will be considered to be agents, for purposes of the preceding sentence, are: Members of the taxpayer's family, an employee of the taxpayer, the taxpayer's attorney, accountant, or tax advisor, and messengers employed by the taxpayer. A return or document will not be considered to be hand carried if it is sent to the Internal Revenue Service through the U.S. Mail.

DESIGNATION OF INCOME TAX PAYMENTS TO PRESIDENTIAL ELECTION CAMPAIGN FUND

○─ § 301.6096 **Statutory provisions; designation by individuals.** [Sec. 6096, IRC]

○─ § 301.6096-1 (T.D. 7304, filed 2-1-74; as amended by T.D. 7391, filed 12-1-75.) **Designation by individuals for taxable years beginning after December 31, 1972.**

(a) *In general.* Every individual (other than a nonresident alien) whose income tax liability, as defined in paragraph (b) of this section, is one dollar or more may, at his option, designate that one dollar shall be paid over to the Presidential Election Campaign Fund, in accordance with the provisions of section 9006. In the case of a joint return of a husband and wife, each spouse may designate that one dollar be paid to the fund as provided in this paragraph only if the joint income tax liability of the husband and wife is two dollars or more.

(b) *Income tax liability.* For purposes of paragraph (a) of this section, the income tax liability of an individual for any taxable year is the amount of the tax imposed by chapter 1 on such individual for such taxable year (as shown on his return), reduced by the sum of the credits (as shown on his return) allowable under sections 33, 37, 38, 40, 41, 42, and 44.

(c) *Manner and time of designation.* (1) A designation under paragraph (a) of this section may be made with respect to any taxable year at the time of the filing of the return of the tax imposed by chapter 1 for such taxable year, and shall be made either on the first page of the return or on the page bearing the taxpayer's signature, in accordance with the instructions applicable thereto.

(2) With respect to any taxable year beginning after December 31, 1972 for which no designation was made under subparagraph (1) of this paragraph, a designation may be made on the form furnished by the Internal Revenue Service for such purpose, filed within 20 and one-half months after the due date for the original return for such taxable year. In the case of a joint return where neither spouse made a designation or where only one spouse made a designation, a designation may be made, as provided in this subparagraph, by the spouse or spouses who had not previously made a designation.

(3) A designation once made, whether by an original return or otherwise, may not be revoked.

(d) *Effective date.* This section shall apply to taxable years beginning after December 31, 1972.

○─ § 301.6096-2 (T.D. 7304, filed 2-1-74.) **Designation by individuals for taxable years ending on or after December 31, 1972 and beginning before January 1, 1973.**

(a) *In general.* (1) For taxable years ending on or after December 31, 1972 and beginning before January 1, 1973, every individual (other than a non-resident alien) whose income tax liability, as defined in paragraph (b) of this section, is one dollar or more, may, at his option, designate that

Reg. § 301.6096-2(a)

one dollar shall be paid over to the Presidential Election Campaign Fund, referred to in § 301.6096-1(a). Where in accordance with prior law, such a designation was made for the account of any candidate of any specified political party, or for a general account for all candidates for election to the offices of President and Vice President of the United States, such a designation shall be treated solely as a designation to such fund.

(2) In the case of a joint return of a husband and wife, each spouse may designate that one dollar be paid to the fund as provided in subparagraph (1) of this paragraph only if the joint income tax liability of the husband and wife is two dollars or more.

(b) *Income tax liability.* For purposes of paragraph (a) of this section, the income tax liability of an individual for any taxable year is the amount of the tax imposed by chapter 1 on such individual for such taxable year (as shown on his return), reduced by the sum of the credits (as shown on his return).

(c) *Manner and time of designation.* (1) A designation under paragraph (a) of this section may be made with respect to any such taxable year at the time of the filing of the return of the tax imposed by chapter 1 for such taxable year. If such designation is made at the time of filing the original return for such year, it shall be made by the individual on the form furnished by the Internal Revenue Service for such purpose in accordance with the instructions applicable thereto.

(2) With respect to any taxable year ending on or after December 31, 1972 and beginning before January 1, 1973, for which no designation was made under subparagraph (1) of this paragraph, a designation may be made on the form furnished by the Internal Revenue Service for such purpose, filed within 20 and one-half months after the due date for the original return for such taxable year. In the case of a joint return where neither spouse made a designation or where only one spouse made a designation, a designation may be made, as provided in this subparagraph, by the spouse or spouses who had not previously made a designation.

(3) A designation once made, whether by an original return or otherwise, may not be revoked.

MISCELLANEOUS PROVISIONS

§ 31.6101 Statutory provisions; period covered by returns or other documents. [Sec. 6101, IRC]

§ 31.6101-1 (T.D. 6472, filed 6-22-60; republished in T.D. 6516, filed 12-19-60.) Period covered by returns. The period covered by any return required under the regulations in this subpart shall be as provided in those provisions of the regulations under which the return is required to be made. See § 31.6011(a)-1, relating to returns of taxes under the Federal Insurance Contributions Act; § 31.6011(a)-2, relating to returns of taxes under the Railroad Retirement Tax Act; § 31.6011(a)-3, relating to returns of tax under the Federal Unemployment Tax Act; § 31.6011(a)-4, relating to returns of income tax withheld under section 3402; and § 31.6011(a)-5, relating to monthly returns of taxes under the Federal Insurance Contributions Act and of income tax withheld under section 3402.

§ 301.6101 Statutory provisions; period covered by returns or other documents. [Sec. 6101, IRC]

§ 301.6101-1 (T.D. 6498, filed 10-24-60.) Period covered by returns or other documents. — For provisions concerning the period covered by returns or other documents, see the regulations relating to the particular tax.

§ 1.6102 Statutory provisions; computations on returns or other documents. [Sec. 6102, IRC]

§ 1.6102-1 (T.D. 6364, filed 2-13-59; republished in T.D. 6500, filed 11-25-60.) Computations on returns or other documents.

For provisions with respect to the rounding off to whole-dollar amounts of money items on returns and accompanying schedules, see § 301.6102-1 of this chapter (Regulations on procedure and administration).

§ 301.6102 Statutory provisions; computations on returns or other documents. [Sec. 6102, IRC]

§ 301.6102-1 (T.D. 6142, filed 9-2-55; republished in T.D. 6498, filed 10-24-60.) Computations on returns or other documents.

(a) *Amounts shown on forms.* To the extent permitted by any internal revenue form or instructions prescribed for use with respect to any internal revenue return, declaration, statement, other document, or supporting schedules, any amount required to be reported on such form shall be entered at the nearest whole dollar amount. The extent to which, and the conditions under which, such whole dollar amounts shall be entered on any form will be set forth in the instructions issued with respect to such form. For the purpose of the computation to the nearest dollar, a fractional part of a dollar shall be disregarded unless it amounts to one-half dollar or more, in which case the amount (determined without regard to the fractional part of a dollar) shall be increased by $1. The following illustrates the application of this paragraph:

Exact amount:	To be reported as—
$18.49	$18
18.50	19
18.51	19

(b) *Election not to use whole dollar amounts.*—(1) *Method of election.* Where any internal revenue form, or the instructions issued with respect to such form, provide that whole dollar amounts shall be reported, any person making a return, declaration, statement, or other document on such form may elect not to use whole dollar amounts by reporting thereon all amounts in full, including cents.

(2) *Time of election.* The election not to use whole dollar amounts must be made at the time of filing the return, declaration, statement, or other document. Such election may not be revoked after the time

prescribed for filing such return, declaration, statement, or other document, including extensions of time granted for such filing. Such election may be made on any return, declaration, statement, or other document which is filed after the time prescribed for filing (including extensions of time), and such an election is irrevocable.

(3) *Effect of election.* The taxpayer's election shall be binding only on the return, declaration, statement, or other document filed for a taxable year or period, and a new election may be made on the return, declaration, statement, or other document filed for a subsequent taxable year or period. An election by either a husband or a wife not to report whole dollar amounts on a separate income tax return shall be binding on any subsequent joint return filed under the provisions of section 6013(b).

(4) *Fractional part of a cent.* For treatment of the fractional part of a cent in the payment of taxes, see section 6313 and § 301.6313-1.

(c) *Inapplicability to computation of amount.* The provisions of paragraph (a) of this section apply only to amounts required to be reported on a return, declaration, statement, or other document. They do not apply to items which must be taken into account in making the computations necessary to determine such amounts. For example, each item of receipt must be taken into account at its exact amount, including cents, in computing the amount of total receipts required to be reported on an income tax return or supporting schedule. It is the amount of total receipts, so computed, which is to be reported at the nearest whole dollar on the return or supporting schedule.

(d) *Effect on accounting method.* Section 6102 and this section have no effect on any authorized accounting method.

○━➤ § 301.6103 (a) Statutory provisions; **publicity of returns and lists of taxpayers; public record and inspection.** [Sec. 6103, IRC]

○━➤ § 301.6103(a)-1 (T.D. 6543, filed 1-18-61; amended by T.D. 6646, filed 4-5-63; T.D. 6809, filed 3-22-65; T.D. 7162, filed 2-18-72 and T.D. 7266, filed 3-9-73.) **Inspection of returns by certain classes of persons and State and Federal government establishments pursuant to Executive order.**

(a) *In general*—(1) *Authority.* The President is authorized by subsection (a) of section 6103 to open to public examination and inspection returns in respect of the taxes described in paragraphs (1) and (2) of such subsection. In addition, section 6106 provides that returns in respect of the tax described therein (unemployment tax imposed by chapter 23 of the Code) shall be open to inspection in the same manner, to the same extent, and subject to the same provisions of law, including penalties, as returns of the taxes described in section 6103, except that subsections (a) (2) and (b) (2) of section 6103, and subsection (a) (2) of section 7213 (relating to unauthorized disclosure of information) shall not apply.

(2) *Scope.* This section and the Executive orders pursuant to which this section is prescribed govern the inspection of returns by the classes of persons and State and Federal government establishments designated in the succeeding paragraphs of this section insofar as such inspection is permissible only upon order of the President and under regulations approved by the President. Specifically, this section relates to inspection of returns made in respect of the taxes imposed by the following subdivisions of the Code: Chapters 1, 2, 3, and 6 (income taxes); chapter 5 (tax on transfers to avoid income tax); chapter 11 (estate tax); chapter 12 (gift tax); chapter 23 (unemployment tax); chapter 32 (manufacturers excise taxes); subchapters B, C, and D of chapter 33 (communications tax, transportation taxes, and tax on safe deposit boxes, respectively); subchapter B of chapter 37 (tax on coconut and palm oil); and chapter 41 (interest equalization tax).

(3) *Terms used*—(i) *Return.* For purposes of section 6103(a), the term "return" includes—

(a) Information returns, schedules, lists, and other written statements filed by or on behalf of the taxpayer with the Internal Revenue Service which are designed to be supplemental to or become a part of the return, and

(b) Other records, reports, information received orally or in writing, factual data, documents, papers, abstracts, memoranda, or evidence taken, or any portion thereof, relating to the items included under (a) of this subdivision. The items listed in (b) of this subdivision may be open to inspection in any case where inspection of the return is authorized by section 6103(a) and these regulations only in the discretion of the Secretary or the Commissioner or the delegate of either. The above rules and procedures also apply to any reproductions or recordings by whatever means made of any such documents or portion thereof. A notice of acquisition filed under section 4917 is a return for purposes of section 6103. An application for exemption from income tax under section 501(a) filed by an organization described in section 501(c) or (d) in order to establish its exemption is not a return for purposes of section 6103. For provisions opening to public inspection exemption applications with respect to which a determination has been made that the organization is entitled to exemption from income tax under section 501(a), see section 6104(a) and § 301.6104-1.

(ii) *Other terms.*—Any word or term used in this section, other than the word "return", which is defined in any chapter of the Code shall be given the definition contained in the chapter which is applicable to the particular return made.

(4) *Cross references.* For special provisions relating to inspection of returns pursuant to Executive order by committees of Congress other than those enumerated in section 6103 (d) or by certain designated Federal Government establishments, see the regulations under section 6103 (a) in §§ 301.6103 (a)-100, et seq.

(b) *Procedure for inspection*—(1) *Authority to permit inspection.* The Secretary or the Commissioner or the delegate

Reg. § 301.6103(a)-1(a)(3)

24,314.4-B *(I.R.C.)*   Reg. § 301.6103(a)-1(a)(3)   7-18-77

of either may grant permission for the inspection of returns in accordance with this section.

(2) *Place of inspection.* Generally, returns may be inspected in the Internal Revenue Service office in which they were filed or in the national office. In appropriate cases, inspection may also be made in other offices of the Internal Revenue Service as designated by the Commissioner. Such inspection shall be made only in the presence of an internal revenue officer or employee and only during the regular hours of business of the Internal Revenue Service office.

(3) *Penalties.* For penalties for unauthorized disclosure of information, see section 7213.

(c) *Inspection by certain classes of persons*—(1) *Returns in respect of income tax, unemployment tax, and certain excise taxes*—(i) *In general.* Returns in respect of the taxes imposed by chapters 1, 2, 3, and 6 (income taxes), chapter 5 (tax on transfers to avoid income tax), chapter 23 (unemployment tax), chapter 32 (manufacturers excise taxes), subchapters B, C, and D of chapter 33 (communications tax, transportation taxes, and tax on safe deposit boxes, respectively), subchapter B of chapter 37 (tax on coconut and palm oil), and chapter 41 (interest equalization tax) of the Code shall be open to inspection as hereinafter provided in this subparagraph by certain persons having a material interest which will be affected by information contained in such returns. The word "return", as used in the succeeding subdivisions of this subparagraph, refers to a return made in respect of any of the taxes described in the preceding sentence except as such word is expressly limited in any such subdivision to the return of a particular tax.

(ii) Return of individual. A return of an individual shall be open to inspection—

(a) By the individual for whom the return was made;

(b) If the individual for whom the return was made is legally incompetent, by the committee, trustee, or guardian of his estate;

(c) If the individual for whom the return was made has died, (1) by the administrator, executor, or trustee of his estate, (2) in the discretion of the Secretary or the Commissioner or the delegate of either, by any heir at law, next of kin, or beneficiary under the will, of such decedent, upon submission of satisfactory evidence that such heir at law, next of kin, or beneficiary has a material interest which will be affected by information contained in the return;

(d) If the property of the individual for whom the return was made is in the hands of a receiver or trustee in bankruptcy, by such receiver or trustee; and

(e) By the duly constituted attorney in fact of any of the foregoing persons, subject to the conditions of inspection prescribed for such person.

(iii) Joint return of income tax. A joint income tax return of husband and wife shall be open to inspection—

(a) By either of the individuals for whom the return was made;

(b) If either of the individuals for whom the return was made is legally incompetent, by the committee, trustee, or guardian of the estate of such individual;

(c) If either of the individuals for whom the return was made has died, (1) by the administrator, executor, or trustee of the estate of such decedent, and (2) in the discretion of the Secretary or the Commissioner or the delegate of either, by any heir at law, next of kin, or beneficiary under the will, of such decedent, upon submission of satisfactory evidence that such heir at law, next of kin, or beneficiary has a material interest which will be affected by information contained in the return;

(d) If the property of either of the individuals for whom the return was made is in the hands of a receiver or trustee in bankruptcy, by such receiver or trustee; and

(e) By the duly constituted attorney in fact of any of the foregoing persons, subject to the conditions of inspection prescribed for such person.

(iv) Return of partnership. A return of a partnership shall be open to inspection—

(a) By any person who was a member of the partnership during any part of the period covered by the return upon submission of satisfactory evidence of such membership;

(b) If an individual who was a member of the partnership during any part of the period covered by the return is legally incompetent, by the committee, trustee, or guardian of his estate;

(c) If an individual who was a member of the partnership during any part of the period covered by the return has died, (1) by the administrator, executor, or trustee of his estate, and (2) in the discretion of the Secretary or the Commissioner or the delegate of either, by any heir at law, next of kin, or beneficiary under the will, of such decedent, upon submission of satisfactory evidence that such heir at law, next of kin, or beneficiary has a material interest which will be affected by information contained in the return;

(d) If the property of the partnership is in the hands of a receiver or trustee in bankruptcy, by such receiver or trustee; and

(e) By the duly constituted attorney in fact of any of the foregoing persons, subject to the conditions of inspection prescribed for such person.

(v) Return of estate. A return of an estate shall be open to inspection—

(a) By the administrator, executor, or trustee of the estate;

(b) In the discretion of the Secretary or the Commissioner or the delegate of either, by any heir at law, next of kin, or beneficiary under the will, of the decedent for whose estate the return was made, upon submission of satisfactory evidence that such heir at law, next of kin, or beneficiary has a material interest which will be affected by information contained in the return, or, if any such heir at law, next of kin, or beneficiary has died or is legally incompetent, by the administrator, executor, committee, trustee, or guardian of his estate, upon a like submission of evidence; and

(c) By the duly constituted attorney in fact of any of the foregoing persons, subject to the conditions of inspection prescribed for such person.

(vi) Return of trust. A return of a trust shall be open to inspection—

(a) By the trustee or trustees, jointly or severally;

(b) By any person who was a beneficiary of the trust during any part of the period covered by the return, upon submission of satisfactory evidence that the person was such a beneficiary;

(c) If any individual who was a beneficiary of the trust during any part of the period covered by the return is legally incompetent, by the committee, trustee, or guardian of his estate;

(d) If any individual who was a beneficiary of the trust during any part of the period covered by the return has died, (1) by the administrator, executor, or trustee of his estate, and (2) in the discretion of

Reg. § 301.6103(a)-1(c)(1)

the Secretary or the Commissioner or the delegate of either, by any heir at law, next of kin, or beneficiary under the will, of such decedent, upon submission of satisfactory evidence that such heir at law, next of kin, or beneficiary has a material interest which will be affected by information contained in the return; and

(e) By the duly constituted attorney in fact of any of the foregoing persons, subject to the conditions of inspection prescribed for such person.

(vii) Return of corporation. A return of a corporation shall be open to inspection—

(a) By any person designated by action of its board of directors, or other similar governing body, upon submission of satisfactory evidence of such action;

(b) By any officer or employee of the corporation upon written request signed by any principal officer and attested by the secretary, or other officer, under the corporate seal, if any;

(c) By the duly constituted attorney in fact of the corporation;

(d) If the property of the corporation is in the hands of a receiver or trustee in bankruptcy, by such receiver or trustee, or by the duly constituted attorney in fact of such receiver or trustee; and

(e) In the discretion of the Secretary or the Commissioner or the delegate of either, if the corporation has been dissolved, by any person who under the regulations in this subdivision (vii) might have inspected the return at the date of dissolution.

For provisions relating to inspection of corporation income or unemployment tax returns by shareholders, see section 6103 (c) and § 301.6103 (c)-1.

(2) *Returns in respect of estate tax.* A return or notice in respect of estate tax imposed by chapter 11 of the Code shall be open to inspection—

(i) By the executor, or his successor in office, or the duly constituted attorney in fact of such executor or successor; and

(ii) In the discretion of the Secretary or the Commissioner or the delegate of either, by any other person upon submission of satisfactory evidence that such person has a material interest either in ascertaining any fact disclosed by the return or notice or in obtaining information as to the payment of the tax.

(3) *Returns in respect of gift tax.* A return in respect of gift tax imposed by chapter 12 of the Code shall be open to inspection—

(i) By the donor or his duly constituted attorney in fact; and

(ii) In the discretion of the Secretary or the Commissioner or the delegate of either, by any other person upon submission of satisfactory evidence that such person has a material interest either in ascertaining any fact disclosed by the return or in obtaining information as to the payment of the tax.

(4) *Applications for inspection.* Applications for permission to inspect returns under this paragraph shall be made in writing to the internal revenue officer (district director or Director of International Operations) with whom the return was filed and shall set forth (i) the name and address of the person for whom the return was made, (ii) the kind of tax reported on the return, (iii) the taxable period covered by the return, (iv) the reason why inspection is desired, and (v) a statement showing that the applicant is a person entitled under this paragraph to make the inspection requested.

(d) *Inspection by States, the District of Columbia, the Commonwealth of Puerto Rico, and possessions of returns in respect of certain taxes*—(1) *Inspection of estate and gift tax returns by States, the District of Columbia, the Commonwealth of Puerto Rico, and possessions.* Returns and notices in respect of estate tax imposed by chapter 11 of the Code and returns in respect of the gift tax imposed by chapter 12 of the Code may, in the discretion of the Secretary or the Commissioner or the delegate of either, be made available for inspection by any properly authorized official, body, or commission, lawfully charged with the administration of any tax law of a State, the District of Columbia, the Commonwealth of Puerto Rico, or a possession of the United States, for the purpose of such administration, provided a like cooperation is given by the State, District of Columbia, the Commonwealth of Puerto Rico, or the possession to the Commissioner and his representatives with respect to the inspection of returns of estate, inheritance, legacy, succession, gift, or other tax of the State, District of Columbia, Commonwealth of Puerto Rico, or possession for use in the administration of the Federal tax laws.

(2) *Inspection of unemployment tax returns by States, the District of Columbia, the Commonwealth of Puerto Rico, and possessions.* Returns in respect of the unemployment tax imposed by chapter 23 of the Code may, in the discretion of the Secretary or the Commissioner or the delegate of either, be made available for inspection by any properly authorized official of a State, the District of Columbia, the Commonwealth of Puerto Rico, or a possession of the United States, provided (i) such government has a law certified to the Secretary as having been approved in accordance with section 3304, and (ii) the inspection is solely for the purpose of administering such law.

(3) *Inspection of excise tax returns by States, the District of Columbia, the Commonwealth of Puerto Rico, and possessions.* Returns in respect of the excise taxes imposed by chapter 5 (tax on transfers to avoid income tax); chapter 32 (manufacturers excise taxes); subchapters B, C, and D of chapter 33 (communications tax, transportation taxes, and tax on safe deposit boxes, respectively); subchapter B of chapter 37 (tax on coconut and palm oil); and chapter 41 (interest equalization tax) may, in the discretion of the Secretary or the Commissioner or the delegate of either, be made available for inspection by any properly authorized official, body, or commission, lawfully charged with the administration of any tax law of a State, the District of Columbia, the Commonwealth of Puerto Rico, or a possession of the United States, for the purpose of such administration.

Reg. § 301.6103(a)-1(d)(3)

(4) Inspection of income tax returns by the District of Columbia, the Commonwealth of Puerto Rico, or possessions. Returns in respect of income tax imposed by chapters 1, 2, 3, or 6 of the Code, may, in the discretion of the Secretary or the Commissioner or the delegate of either, be made available for inspection by any properly authorized official, body, or commission, lawfully charged with the administration of any tax law of the District of Columbia, the Commonwealth of Puerto Rico, or a possession of the United States, for the purpose of such administration.

(5) Application for inspection—(i) *In general.* Application for the inspection provided for in subparagraphs (1), (2), (3), or (4) of this paragraph shall be made in writing and signed by the governor of the State or the executive head of the District of Columbia, the Commonwealth of Puerto Rico, or possession, and shall be addressed to the Commissioner of Internal Revenue, Washington, D. C. 20224. The application shall state—

(a) The title of the official, body, or commission by whom or which inspection is to be made;

(b) By specific reference, the law of the State, District of Columbia, Commonwealth of Puerto Rico, or possession which such official, body, or commission is charged with administering and the law under which he or it is so charged;

(c) The purpose for which the inspection is to be made; and

(d) If inspection of estate or gift tax returns is requested, that the State, District of Columbia, Commonwealth of Puerto Rico, or possession, as the case may be, gives to the Commissioner and his representatives like cooperation with respect to the inspection of returns of estate, inheritance, legacy, succession, gift, or other tax of the State, District of Columbia, Commonwealth of Puerto Rico, or possession, for use in the administration of the Federal tax laws.

(ii) *Returns filed in internal revenue district within or including State or other entity requesting inspection—(a) General inspection.* Upon application by a State, the District of Columbia, the Commonwealth of Puerto Rico, or a possession of the United States, permission may be granted for general inspection of returns of the taxes specified in subparagraph (1), (2), (3), or (4) of this paragraph which are filed in an internal revenue district within or including such State or District or, in the case of the Commonwealth of Puerto Rico, or a possession, with the Director of International Operations. If such general inspection is desired, the application made to the Commissioner in accordance with subdivision (i) of this subparagraph shall include a statement that general inspection is desired of a specified class or classes of returns (for example, estate tax returns, gift tax returns, etc.). Permission granted, to a State, the District of Columbia, the Commonwealth of Puerto Rico, or a possession for the general inspection provided for in this subdivision shall, except as hereinafter provided in the case of unemployment tax returns, continue in effect until such time as the Secretary or the Commissioner or the delegate of either, by written notice to the governor of the State or the executive head of the District of Columbia, the Commonwealth of Puerto Rico, or possession, provides that such inspection will be permitted only on the basis of periodic applications therefor. Permission for general inspection of unemployment tax returns will terminate without notice at such time as the State, District of Columbia, Commonwealth of Puerto Rico, or possession ceases to have a law certified to the Secretary as having been approved in accordance with section 3304. The governor of the State or the executive head of the District of Columbia, the Commonwealth of Puerto Rico, or possession, as the case may be, shall supply in writing to the internal revenue officer (district director or Director of International Operations) with whom the returns to be inspected were filed a list of the names of the individuals designated to make the inspection on behalf of the official, body, or commission named in the application to the Commissioner, and shall keep such list current by appropriate deletions or additions as may be necessary.

(b) Inspection of specific returns. Permission granted pursuant to *(a)* of this subdivision for general inspection of returns of a particular tax includes permission to inspect specifically identified returns of such tax when desired. However, if a State, the District of Columbia, the Commonwealth of Puerto Rico, or possession is interested only in examining certain returns of particular taxpayers, the application for inspection of such returns shall be made to the Commissioner as provided in subdivision (i) of this subparagraph and, in addition to the information outlined in such subdivision, shall state the name and address of each taxpayer whose return or returns it is desired to inspect, the kind of tax reported on each such return, the taxable period covered by each such return, and the names of the individuals designated to make the inspection on behalf of the official, body, or commission named in the application.

(iii) *Returns filed in other internal revenue districts.* In the case of returns filed in an internal revenue district other than one within or including the State or District of Columbia requesting inspection or, if the inspection is requested by the Commonwealth of Puerto Rico, or a possession, filed elsewhere than with the Director of International Operations, permission for the inspection provided for in subparagraphs (1), (2), (3), and (4) of this paragraph will be granted only with respect to specifically identified returns. The application for such inspection shall be made to the Commissioner as provided in subdivision (i) of this subparagraph and, in addition to the information outlined in such subdivision and in subdivision (ii) *(b)* of this subparagraph, shall specify the internal revenue district or office in which the returns to be inspected are believed to have been filed.

(6) *Time and place of inspection.* A

convenient time and place for the inspection of returns permitted under this paragraph will be arranged by the internal revenue officer (district director or Director of International Operations) with whom the returns were filed.

(7) *Cross reference.* For other provisions relating to inspection of returns on behalf of States or political subdivisions thereof, see section 6103 (b) and § 301.6103 (b)-1.

(e) *Inspection of returns by Department of the Treasury.* Officers and employees of the Department of the Treasury whose official duties require inspection of returns made in respect of any tax described in paragraph (a)(2) of this section may inspect any such returns without making written application therefor. If the head of a bureau or office in the Department of the Treasury, not a part of the Internal Revenue Service, desires to inspect, or to have an employee of his bureau or office inspect, any such return in connection with some matter officially before him for reasons other than tax administration purposes, the inspection may, in the discretion of the Secretary or the Commissioner or the delegate of either, be permitted upon written application by the head of the bureau or office desiring the inspection. The application shall be made to the Commissioner of Internal Revenue, **Washington, D. C. 20224, and shall show (1)** the name and address of the person for whom the return was made, (2) the kind of tax reported on the return, (3) the taxable period covered by the return, and (4) the reason why inspection is desired. The information obtained from inspection pursuant to this paragraph may be used as evidence in any proceeding, conducted by or before any department or establishment of the United States, or to which the United States is a party.

(f) *Inspection of returns by executive departments other than the Department of the Treasury and by other establishments of the Federal Government.* Except as provided in paragraphs (d) and (g) of this section, if the head of an executive department (other than the Department of the Treasury), or of any other establishment of the Federal Government, desires to inspect, or to have some other officer or employee of his department or establishment inspect, a return in respect of any tax described in paragraph (a)(2) of this section in connection with some matter officially before him, the inspection may, in the discretion of the Secretary of the Treasury or the Commissioner or the delegate of either, be permitted upon written application signed by the head of the executive department or other Government establishment desiring the inspection. The application shall be made to the Commissioner of Internal Revenue, **Washington, D. C. 20224, and shall set forth** (1) the name and address of the person for whom the return was made, (2) the kind of tax reported on the return, (3) the taxable period covered by the return, (4) the reason why inspection is desired, and (5) the name and the official designation of the person by whom the inspection is to be made. The information obtained from inspection pursuant to this paragraph may be used as evidence in any proceeding, conducted by or before any department or establishment of the United States, or to which the United States is a party.

(g) *Inspection of returns by U.S. attorneys and attorneys of Department of Justice.* A return in respect of any tax described in paragraph (a)(2) of this section shall be open to inspection by a U.S. attorney or by an attorney of the Department of Justice where necessary in the performance of his official duties. The application for inspection shall be in writing and shall show (1) the name and address of the person for whom the return was made, (2) the kind of tax reported on the return, (3) the taxable period covered by the return, and (4) the reason why inspection is desired. The application shall, where the inspection is to be made by a U.S. attorney, be signed by such attorney, and, where the inspection is to be made by an attorney of the Department of Justice, be signed by the Attorney General, Deputy Attorney General, or an Assistant Attorney General. The application shall be addressed to the Commissioner of Internal Revenue, Washington, D.C. 20224, with a copy addressed to the internal revenue officer (the district director or the director of the service center) with whom the return was filed.

(h) *Use of returns in grand jury proceedings and in litigation.* Returns made in respect of any tax described in paragraph (a)(2) of this section, or copies thereof, may be furnished by the Secretary or the Commissioner or the delegate of either to a U.S. attorney or an attorney of the Department of Justice for official use in proceedings before a U.S. grand jury, or in litigation in any court, if the United States is interested in the result, or for use in preparation for such proceedings or litigation. The original return will be furnished only in exceptional cases, and then only if it is made to appear that the ends of justice may otherwise be defeated. Returns or copies thereof will be furnished without written application therefore to U.S. attorneys and attorneys of the Department of Justice for official use in the prosecution of claims and demands by, and offenses against, the United States, or the defense of claims and demands against the United States or officers or employees thereof, in cases arising under the internal revenue laws or related statutes which were referred by the Department of the Treasury to the Department of Justice for such prosecution or defense. In all other cases, written application for a return or copies thereof shall be made to the Commissioner of Internal Revenue, Washington, D.C. 20224, with a copy addressed to the internal revenue officer (the district director or the director of the service center) with whom the return was filed. The application shall be in writing and shall show (1) the name and address of the person for whom the return was made, (2) the kind of tax reported on the return, (3) the taxable period covered by the return, and (4) the reason why the return or a copy thereof is desired. Such application shall be signed by the U.S. attorney if the return or copy is for his use, or by the Attorney General, the Deputy Attorney General, or an Assistant Attorney General if the return or copy is for the use of an attorney of the Department of Justice. For provisions relating to the certification of copies of returns, see § 301.6103(a)-2. If a

Reg. § 301.6103(a)-1(h)

24,318 (I.R.C.) Reg. § 301.6103(a)-1(h)

return, or copy thereof, is furnished pursuant to this paragraph, it shall be limited in use to the purpose for which it is furnished and is under no condition to be made public except to the extent that publicity necessarily results from such use. Neither the original nor a copy of a return desired for use in litigation in court will be furnished if the United States is not interested in the result, but this provision is not a limitation on the use of copies of returns by the persons entitled thereto. See paragraphs (e) and (f) of this section for use, in proceedings to which the United States is a party, of information obtained by executive departments and other Federal Government establishments from inspection of returns. If a U.S. attorney or an attorney of the Department of Justice has obtained a copy of a return under paragraph (g) of this section, an application for the use of such return in a situation specified in this paragraph shall not be necessary. Returns shall not be made available to the Department of Justice for purposes of examining prospective jurors except that this shall not prohibit the answering of an inquiry, from the Department of Justice, as to whether a prospective juror has, or has not, been investigated by the Internal Revenue Service.

(i) *Disclosures by internal revenue officers for investigative purposes.* An internal revenue officer engaged in an official investigation of the liability in connection with any return or notice in respect of estate tax imposed by chapter 11, or any return in respect of gift tax imposed by chapter 12, of the Code may disclose the returned value of any item, the amount of any specific deduction, or other limited information, if the disclosure is necessary in order to verify such value, deduction, or other information, or to arrive at a correct determination of the tax. This right of disclosure, however, is limited to the purpose of the investigation, and in no case extends to such information as the amount of the estate or gift, the amount of the tax, or other general data.

(j) *Inspection of accepted offers in compromise.* Subject to such rules and under such circumstances as the Secretary or the Commissioner shall determine to be in the public interest, returns in respect of income tax imposed by chapters 1, 2, 3, or 6, estate tax imposed by chapter 11, or gift tax imposed by chapter 12, of the Code, shall be open to inspection to the extent necessary to permit examination of any accepted offer in compromise under section 7122 relative to the liability for any such tax.

○─▶ § 301.6103(a)-2 (T.D. 6546, filed 1-18-61; amended by T.D. 6700, filed 1-6-64.) Copies of returns.

Any person who may be permitted to inspect a return under section 6103 and § 301.6103 (a)-1, § 301.6103 (b)-1, or § 301.6103 (c)-1 may be furnished with a copy of such return upon request. If the request for a copy of a return is made other than at the time of inspection of such return by the applicant, the request shall be in writing, shall adequately identify the return a copy of which is desired, and shall be accompanied by satisfactory evidence that the applicant qualifies as one of the persons or governmental agencies to whom or which inspection of the return may be permitted.

Except as otherwise provided in this section, applications for copies of returns should be submitted to the Commissioner of Internal Revenue, Washington, D.C. 20224, who is authorized to furnish such copies and to certify them upon request under the official seal of his office or under the official seal of the Department of the Treasury. Where the applicant is (a) a person who may be permitted under paragraph (c) of § 301.6103(a)-1 to inspect a return, (b) an official of a State, the District of Columbia, the Commonwealth of Puerto Rico, or a possession of the United States entitled to inspect returns under paragraph (d) of § 301.6103(a)-1 or under § 301.6103 (b)-1 or (c) a shareholder entitled under § 301.6103(c)-1 to inspect returns of the corporation of which he is a shareholder, the application for a copy of the return should be submitted to, and such copy may be furnished by, the internal revenue officer (district director or the Director of International Operations) with whom the return was filed. Any copy so furnished by the district director or the Director of International Operations may, upon request, be certified by him under his official seal. The district director or the Director of International Operations is authorized, when so directed by the Commissioner, to furnish to any bureau or office of the Treasury Department or to any other department or agency of the Government copies of any returns which such bureau, office, department, or agency is permitted to inspect under paragraph (e) or (f) of § 301.6103(a)-1, and to certify such copies under the official seal of his office. Applications for copies of returns available to United States attorneys or attorneys of the Department of Justice pursuant to paragraph (g) or (h) of § 301.6103(a)-1 may be submitted to, and such copies may be furnished and certified under seal by, the Commissioner or, where desired, the district director or the Director of International Operations, as the case may be, with whom the returns were filed. Where such application is required to be in writing it shall be signed by the United States attorney if the copy is for his use, or by the Attorney General, the Deputy Attorney General, or an Assistant Attorney General if the copy is for the use of an attorney of the Department of Justice. The Commissioner may prescribe a reasonable fee for furnishing copies of returns.

○─▶ § 301.6103(a)-100 (T.D. 6135, filed 6-29-55; republished in T.D. 6498, filed 10-24-60.) Inspection by Department of Health, Education, and Welfare of individual income tax returns.

Pursuant to the provisions of section 6103(a) and of the Executive order issued thereunder, and in the interest of the internal management of the Government, any individual income tax return made in respect of a tax imposed under chapter 1 or chapter 2 of the Code shall be open to inspection by the Department of Health, Education, and Welfare as may be needed in its administration of the provisions of title II of the Social Security Act as amended (42 U.S.C. ch. 7). Upon request, the inspection of an individual income tax return may be made by any officer or employee of the Department of Health, Education, and Welfare duly authorized by the Secretary of such Department to make such inspection. The request to inspect an income tax return or returns of a particular individual shall be made, in writing, by the Secretary or any duly authorized officer or employee of the Department of Health, Education, and Welfare to the Commissioner of Internal Revenue or to any officer or employee of the Internal Revenue Service designated by the Commissioner. The written request shall be in such form and manner as may be prescribed by the Commissioner of Internal Revenue. Upon receipt of such a request, any officer or employee of the Internal Revenue Service duly authorized by the Commissioner of Internal Revenue may make the individual income tax return or returns available for inspection by any duly authorized officer or employee of the Department of Health, Education, and Welfare or may furnish such Department with a copy of the return or with any data on such return. Any information thus obtained shall be held confidential, except to the extent necessary to effectuate the purposes for which the returns are open to inspection.

○— § 301.6103(a)-101 (T.D. 6132, filed 5-3-55; republished in T.D. 6498, filed 10-24-60; amended by T.D. 7403, filed 2-6-76.) **Inspection of returns by committees of Congress other than those enumerated in section 6103(d).**

(a) Pursuant to the provisions of section 6103(a), any return with respect to income, estate, or gift tax imposed by the Code shall be open to inspection by any committee of the Congress, or any subcommittee of a committee of the Congress, specially authorized to inspect such returns by an Executive order issued under the aforementioned statutory provisions. Such inspection shall be subject to the conditions and restrictions imposed by the Executive order and, unless otherwise provided by such Executive order, the rules and regulations hereinafter prescribed.

(b) Only such of the aforementioned returns as are specified in a resolution adopted by the committee in accordance with the rules of the appropriate house of the Congress then applicable to the reporting of a measure or recommendation from such committee shall be open to inspection. Such resolution shall set forth the names and addresses of the taxpayers whose returns it is necessary to inspect and the taxable periods covered by the returns. The inspection of returns authorized in this section may be made by the committee of the Congress, or the subcommittee of a committee of the Congress, authorized as provided in paragraph (a) of this section, acting directly as a committee or as a subcommittee, or by or through such examiners or agents as such committee or subcommittee may designate or appoint in its written request hereinafter mentioned. Upon written request by the chairman of such committee or of such subcommittee to the Secretary of the Treasury, giving the names and addresses of the taxpayers whose returns it is desired to inspect and the taxable periods covered by the returns and stating that the resolution hereinbefore mentioned with respect to the inspection of such returns has been duly adopted by such committee or by the committee under which such subcommittee functions, the Secretary or any officer or employee of the Department of the Treasury, with the approval of the Secretary, shall furnish such committee or subcommittee with any data relating to or contained in any such return or shall make such return available for inspection by such committee or subcommittee or by the examiners or agents designated or appointed by such committee or subcommittee. Such data shall be furnished, or such return shall be made available for inspection, in an office of the Internal Revenue Service. Any information thus obtained by such committee or subcommittee shall be held confidential: Provided, however, That any portion thereof relevant or pertinent to the purpose of the investigation may be submitted by the investigating committee to the appropriate house of the Congress.

(c) This section shall not be applicable to any committee authorized by section 6103(d) to inspect returns.

○— § 301.6103(a)-102 (T.D. 6374, filed 4-29-59; republished in T.D. 6498, filed 10-24-60.) **Inspection by Securities and Exchange Commission of transcript cards and corporate and individual income tax returns.**

Pursuant to the provisions of section 6103(a) and of the Executive order issued thereunder, and in the interest of internal management of the Government, corporate and individual income tax returns made for taxable years ending after December 31, 1956, and statistical transcript cards prepared by the Internal Revenue Service from income tax returns of corporations made for taxable years beginning after December 31, 1953, and ending after August 16, 1954, shall be open to inspection by the Securities and Exchange Commission as may be needed in gathering statistical information in carrying out its functions under the Securities Exchange Act of 1934, (15 U.S.C. 78a—78j), as amended, or in complying with directives or recommendations of the Bureau of the Budget pursuant to section 103 of the Budget and Accounting Procedures Act of 1950 (31 U.S.C. 18b), relating to the development of programs for preparing statistical information by Executive agencies. Upon request, such inspection may be made by any officer or employee of the Securities and Exchange Commission duly authorized by the Chairman of such Commission to make it. Upon written notice by the Chairman of the Securities and Exchange Commission to the Secretary of the Treasury, stating the type of statistical transcript cards or income tax returns of which inspection is desired, the Secretary, or any officer or employee of the Treasury Department with the approval of the Secretary, may furnish the Securities and Exchange Commission with any data on such cards of returns or may make them available for inspection and the taking of such data as the Chairman of the Securities and Exchange Commission may designate. Such data shall be furnished, or such returns or cards shall be made available for inspection, in the office of the Commissioner of Internal Revenue. Any information thus obtained shall be held confidential except to the extent that it shall be published or disclosed in statistical form, provided such publication shall not disclose, directly or indirectly, the name or address of any taxpayer.

○— § 301.6103(a)-103 (T.D. 6570, filed 8-24-61.) **Inspection of returns by the Advisory**

Reg. § 301.6103(a)-103

24,320 (I.R.C.) Reg. § 301.6103(a)-103 2-17-76

Commission on Intergovernmental Relations.

(a) Pursuant to the provisions of sections 6103(a) and 6106 of the Internal Revenue Code of 1954 (68A Stat. 753, 756; 26 U.S.C. 6103(a), 6106) and of the Executive order issued thereunder, any return with respect to income tax, tax on transfers to avoid income tax, estate tax, gift tax, unemployment tax, manufacturers excise taxes, communications tax, transportation taxes, tax on safe deposit boxes, or tax on coconut and palm oil imposed by such Code shall be open to inspection by the Advisory Commission on Intergovernmental Relations for the purpose of making studies and investigations in connection with the performance of its function of recommending methods of coordinating and simplifying tax laws and administrative practices to achieve a more orderly and less competitive fiscal relationship between the levels of government and to reduce the burden of compliance for taxpayers. The inspection of returns herein authorized may be made by any member or employee of the Commission duly authorized by the Chairman of the Commission to make such inspection. Upon written notice by the Chairman to the Secretary of the Treasury stating the kinds of returns which it is desired to inspect, the Secretary of the Treasury, or any officer or employee of the Department of the Treasury with the approval of the Secretary, may furnish the Commission with any data on such returns or may make the returns available for inspection and the taking of such data as the Chairman may designate. Such data shall be furnished, or such returns shall be made available for inspection, in the office of the Commissioner of Internal Revenue. Any information thus obtained shall be held confidential except that it may be published or disclosed in statistical form provided such publication does not disclose, directly or indirectly, the name or address of any taxpayer.

(b) This section shall be effective upon its filing for publication in the Federal Register.

○━━ § 301.6103(a)-104 (T.D. 6547, filed 1-18-61.) Inspection by Department of Commerce of income tax returns made under the Internal Revenue Code of 1954.

(a) Pursuant to the provisions of section 6103(a) of the Internal Revenue Code of 1954 (68A Stat. 753; 26 U.S.C. 6103(a)) and of the Executive order issued thereunder, and in the interest of the internal management of the Government, income tax returns made under such Code shall be open to inspection by the Department of Commerce. The inspection of returns herein authorized may be made by any officer or employee of the Department of Commerce duly authorized by the Secretary of Commerce to make such inspection. Upon written notice by the Secretary of Commerce to the Secretary of the Treasury stating the classes of returns which it is desired to inspect, the Secretary of the Treasury, or any officer or employee of the Department of the Treasury with the approval of the Secretary, may furnish the Department of Commerce with any data on such returns or may make the returns available for inspection and the taking of such data as the Secretary of Commerce may designate. Such data shall be furnished, or such returns shall be made available for inspection, in the office of the Commissioner of Internal Revenue. Any information thus obtained shall be held confidential except that it may be published or disclosed in statistical form provided such publication does not disclose, directly or indirectly, the name or address of any taxpayer.

(b) This Treasury decision shall be effective upon its filing for publication in the Federal Register.

○━━ § 301.6103(a)-105 (T.D. 6544, filed 1-18-61.) Inspection by Renegotiation Board of income tax returns made under the Internal Revenue Code of 1954.

(a) Pursuant to the provisions of section 6103(a) of the Internal Revenue Code of 1954 (68A Stat. 753; 26 U.S.C. 6103(a)) and of the Executive order issued thereunder, and in the interest of the internal management of the Government, income tax returns made under such Code shall be open to inspection by the Renegotiation Board. The inspection of returns herein authorized may be made by any officer or employee of the Renegotiation Board duly authorized by the Chairman of the Board to make such inspection. Upon written notice by the Chairman to the Secretary of the Treasury stating the classes of returns which it is desired to inspect, the Secretary, or any officer or employee of the Department of the Treasury with the approval of the Secretary, may furnish the Renegotiation Board with any data on such returns or may make the returns available for inspection and the taking of such data as the Chairman of the Board may designate. Such data shall be furnished, or such returns shall be made available for inspection, in the office of the Commissioner of Internal Revenue. Any information thus obtained shall be held confidential except that it may be published or disclosed in statistical form provided such publication does not disclose, directly or indirectly, the name or address of any taxpayer.

(b) This Treasury decision shall be effective upon its filing for publication in the Federal Register.

○━━ § 301.6103(a)-106 (T.D. 6545, filed 1-18-61.) Inspection by Federal Trade Commission of income tax returns of corporations made under the Internal Revenue Code of 1954.

(a) Pursuant to the provisions of section 6103(a) of the Internal Revenue Code of 1954 (68A Stat. 753; 26 U.S.C. 6103(a)) and of the Executive order issued thereunder, and in the interest of the internal management of the Government, income tax returns of corporations made under such Code shall be open to inspection by the Federal Trade Commission as an aid in executing the powers conferred upon such Commission by the Federal Trade Commission Act of September 26, 1914 (38 Stat. 717). The inspection of returns herein authorized may be made by any officer or employee of the Federal Trade Commission duly authorized by the Chairman of the Commission to make such inspection. Upon written notice by the Chairman to the Secretary of the Treasury, the Secretary, or any officer or employee of the Department of the Treasury with the approval of the Secretary, may furnish the

Federal Trade Commission with any data on such returns or may make the returns available for inspection and the taking of such data as the Chairman of the Commission may designate. Such data shall be furnished, or such returns shall be made available for inspection, in the office of the Commissioner of Internal Revenue. Any information thus obtained shall be held confidential except that it may be published or disclosed in statistical form provided such publication does not disclose, directly or indirectly, the name or address of any taxpayer.

(b) This Treasury decision shall be effective upon its filing for publication in the Federal Register.

○→ § 301.6103(a)-107 (T.D. 6757, filed 9-4-64; amended by T.D. 6816, filed 4-5-65.) **Inspection of certain interest equalization tax information returns by the Board of Governors of the Federal Reserve System and the Federal Reserve Banks.**

(a) Pursuant to the provisions of section 6103(a) of the Internal Revenue Code of 1954 (68A Stat. 753; 26 U.S.C. 6103(a)), as amended by section 3(c) of the Interest Equalization Tax Act (Pub. L. 88-563, 78 Stat. 844), and the Executive orders issued thereunder, any information return made by a commercial bank under the Interest Equalization Tax Act shall be open to inspection by the Board of Governors of the Federal Reserve System and the Federal Reserve Banks. Such inspection may be made by—

(1) A member or employee of the Board of Governors of the Federal Reserve System duly authorized by the Board, or

(2) An officer or employee of a Federal Reserve Bank duly authorized by the president of such Bank.

Upon written notice by the Board of Governors of the Federal Reserve System or the president of a Federal Reserve Bank to the Secretary of the Treasury stating that it is desired to inspect information returns made by commercial banks under the Interest Equalization Tax Act, the Secretary of the Treasury, or any officer or employee of the Department of the Treasury with the approval of the Secretary, may furnish the Board or the Bank with any data on such returns or make the returns available for inspection and the taking of such data as the Board or the president of the Bank may designate. Such data may be furnished, or such returns may be made available for inspection, in the offices of the Board of Governors of the Federal Reserve System or in the offices of the Federal Reserve Bank, as the case may be. Any information thus obtained shall be held confidential except that it may be published or disclosed in statistical form provided such publication does not disclose, directly or indirectly, the name or address of any person filing such a return.

(b) This section shall be effective upon its filing for publication in the Federal Register.

○→ § 301.6103(a)-109 (T.D. 7205, filed 8-30-72.) **Inspection of returns by Department of the Treasury for economic stabilization purposes.**

(a) *In general.* Officers and employees of the Department of the Treasury, including the Internal Revenue Service and the Office of Chief Counsel for the Internal Revenue Service, whose official duties include the administration or enforcement of provisions of the Economic Stabilization Act of 1970 (Public Law 91-379, 84 Stat. 799), as amended by the Economic Stabilization Act Amendments of 1971 (Public Law 92-210, 85 Stat. 743), may inspect any returns made in respect of any tax described in paragraph (a)(2) of § 301.6103(a)-1 without making written application therefor. The provisions of paragraph (e) of § 301.6103(a)-1 shall not apply with respect to the head of a bureau or office in the Department of the Treasury, including the Internal Revenue Service and the Office of Chief Counsel for the Internal Revenue Service, who desires to inspect, or to have an employee of his bureau or office inspect, any such return in connection with some matter officially before him for the purpose of administering or enforcing the provisions of the Economic Stabilization Act of 1970, as amended. The information obtained from inspection pursuant to this paragraph may be—

(i) Used as evidence by the Department of the Treasury, including the Internal Revenue Service and the Office of Chief Counsel for the Internal Revenue Service, in any proceeding, conducted by or before any department or establishment of the United States, or to which the United States is a party, or

(ii) Used to the extent necessary to effectuate the purposes for which such returns are open to inspection.

(b) *Terms used*—(1) *"Return".* For the definition of the term "return" for purposes of section 6103(a) and this section, see paragraph (a)(3)(i) of § 301.6103(a)-1.

(2) *Other terms.* Any word or term used in this section, other than the word "return", which is defined in any chapter of the Code shall be given the definition contained in the chapter which is applicable to the particular return made.

○→ § 301.6103(b) **Statutory provisions;**

publicity of returns and lists of taxpayers; inspection by States. [Sec. 6103, IRC]

§ 301.6103(b)-1 (T.D. 6546, filed 1-18-61.) **Inspection by States.**

(a) *Corporation returns of income tax or unemployment tax.* Under the provisions of sections 6103(b)(1) and 6106, the proper tax officers of a State shall have access, upon application made in accordance with the provisions of this paragraph, to the returns filed by any corporation with respect to the taxes imposed by chapters 1, 3, and 6 of the Code and with respect to the unemployment tax imposed by chapter 23 of the Code, or to abstracts of such returns. Application for access to the returns of any corporation, or abstracts thereof, shall be in writing signed by the governor of the State and addressed to the Commissioner of Internal Revenue, Washington, D. C. 2022A. The application shall set forth the reason why access is desired; the names and official positions of the officers designated to have such access; and, with respect to each return to which access is desired, the name and address of the corporation filing the return, the kind of tax (income tax or unemployment tax) reported on the return, and the taxable year covered by the return.

(b) *Income tax returns*—(1) *In general.* Income tax returns filed with respect to the taxes imposed by chapters 1, 2, 3, and 6 of the Code shall, upon application made in accordance with the provisions of this paragraph, be open to inspection by any official, body, or commission, lawfully charged with the administration of any State tax law, or any properly designated representative of such official, body, or commission, if the inspection is for the purpose of such administration or for the purpose of obtaining information to be furnished to local taxing authorities as provided in section 6103(b)(2). The application shall be made in writing and signed by the governor of the State and shall be addressed to the Commissioner of Internal Revenue, Washington, D. C. 2022A. The application shall state—

(i) The title of the official, body, or commission by whom or which the inspection is to be made;

(ii) By specific reference, the State tax law which such official, body, or commission is charged with administering and the law under which he or it is so charged;

(iii) The purpose for which the inspection is to be made; and

(iv) If the inspection is for the purpose of obtaining information to be furnished to local taxing authorities, (a) the title of the official, body, or commission of each political subdivision of the State, lawfully charged with the administration of the tax laws of such political subdivision, to whom or to which the information secured by the inspection is to be furnished, and (b) the purpose for which the information is to be used by such official, body, or commission.

(2) *Returns filed in internal revenue district within or including state*—(i) General inspection. Permission may be granted by the Commissioner to any State for general inspection of returns of the taxes imposed by chapters 1, 2, 3, and 6 of the Code which are filed in an internal revenue district within or including such State. If such general inspection is desired, the application made to the Commissioner in accordance with subparagraph (1) of this paragraph shall include a statement that general inspection is desired of returns filed in the internal revenue district or districts within or including the State with respect to the taxes imposed by chapters 1, 2, 3, and 6 of the Code. Permission granted for the general inspection provided for in this subdivision shall continue in effect until such time as the Commissioner by written notice to the governor of the State provides that such inspection will be permitted only on the basis of periodic applications therefor. The governor shall supply to the district director with whom the returns to be inspected were filed a written list of the names of the individuals designated to make the inspection on behalf of the official, body, or commission named in the application to the Commissioner, and shall keep such list current by appropriate deletions or additions as may be necessary.

(ii) Inspection of specific returns. Permission for the general inspection provided in subdivision (i) of this subparagraph includes permission to inspect a specifically identified return when desired. However, a State interested only in examining the returns of particular taxpayers may inspect such returns on written application therefor to the Commissioner. The application in such case shall state, in addition to the information outlined in subparagraph (1) of this paragraph, the name and address of each taxpayer whose return or returns it is desired to inspect, the taxable year covered by each such return, and the names of the individuals designated to make the inspection on behalf of the official, body, or commission named in the application.

(3) *Returns filed in other internal revenue districts.* In the case of returns filed with the Director of International Operations or in an internal revenue district other than one within or including the State requesting the inspection, permission for the inspection provided for in subparagraph (1) of this paragraph will be granted only with respect to specifically identified returns. The application for such inspection shall be made to the Commissioner as provided in subparagraph (1) of this paragraph and, in addition to the information outlined in such subparagraph and in subparagraph (2)(ii) of this paragraph, shall specify the internal revenue district or office in which the returns to be inspected are believed to have been filed.

(c) *Time and place of inspection.* The internal revenue officer (district director or Director of International Operations) with whom the returns were filed is authorized to make such returns available in accordance with permission granted by the Commissioner pursuant to this section. Such officer shall set a convenient time and place for the inspection. The inspection will be permitted only in the presence of an internal revenue officer or employee and only in an office of the Internal Revenue Service during the regular hours of business of such office.

(d) *Definition of return.* For purposes of section 6103(b) and this section, the term "return" includes information returns, schedules, lists, and other written statements filed with the Internal Revenue Service which are designed to be supplemental to or to become a part of the return, and, in the discretion of the Commissioner, other records or reports containing information included or required by statute to be included in the return. An application for exemption from income tax under section 501(a) filed by an organization described in section 501(c) or (d) in order to establish its exemption is not a return for purposes of section 6103(b). For provisions opening to public inspection exemption applications with respect to which a determination has been made that the organization is entitled to exemption from income tax under section 501(a), see section 6104 (a) and § 301.6104-1.

(e) *Cross reference.* For additional provisions relating to inspection of returns on behalf of States, see paragraph (d) of § 301.6103(a)-1. For penalties for unauthorized disclosure of information, see section 7213.

○── § 301.6103(c) **Statutory provisions; publicity of returns and lists of taxpayers; inspection by shareholders.** [Sec. 6103, IRC]

○── § 301.6103(c)-1 (T.D. 6546, filed 1-18-61.) **Inspection of corporation returns by shareholders.**

(a) *In general.* Under the provisions of sections 6103(c) and 6106, a bona fide shareholder of record owning one percent or more of the outstanding stock of a corporation shall be allowed, upon request, to examine the annual income tax returns and unemployment tax returns of such corporation and its subsidiaries. A person is not a bona fide shareholder of record within the meaning of section 6103(c) if he acquired his shares for the purpose of obtaining the right to inspect the returns of the corporation. The privilege of inspecting returns in accordance with section 6103(c) and this section is personal to the shareholder and cannot be delegated. In the case of a corporation which has been dissolved, the returns may be examined by any shareholder who would have been entitled to examine them at the date of dissolution.

(b) *Applications.* Request for permission to inspect returns under this section shall be made in writing and verified by affidavit. The request shall be submitted to the district director or the Director of International Operations, as the case may be, with whom the return was filed. The request shall set forth (1) the name and address of the applicant, (2) the name and address of the corporation whose return or returns it is desired to inspect, (3) the kind of tax and the taxable period covered by each return it is desired to inspect, (4) the amount of the corporation's outstanding capital stock, (5) the number of shares owned by the applicant and the date or dates on which he acquired them, (6) whether the applicant has the beneficial as well as the record title to such shares, and (7) that the applicant did not acquire the shares for the purpose of obtaining the right to inspect the returns of the corporation. The request shall be accompanied by evidence establishing that the applicant is a bona fide shareholder of record of the required amount of stock of the corporation. Such evidence may be in the form of a certificate signed by the president or vice president of the corporation and countersigned by the secretary under the corporate seal.

(c) *Time and place of inspection.* The district director or the Director of International Operations, upon being satisfied from the evidence presented that the applicant meets the statutory requirements, shall grant permission to examine the returns and shall set a convenient time and place for the examination. Examination of returns by shareholders will be permitted only in the presence of an internal revenue officer or employee and only in an office of the Internal Revenue Service during the regular hours of business of such office.

(d) *Definition of return.* For purposes of section 6103(c) and this section, the term "return" includes information returns, schedules, lists, and other written statements filed with the Internal Revenue Service which are designed to be supplemental to or to become a part of the return, and, in the discretion of the Commissioner, other records or reports containing information included or required by statute to be included in the return. An application for exemption from income tax under section 501(a) filed by an organization described in section 501(c) or (d) in order to establish its exemption is not a return for purposes of section 6103(c). For provisions opening to public inspection exemption applications with respect to which a determination has been made that the organization is entitled to exemption from income tax under section 501(a), see section 6104(a) and § 301.-6104-1.

(e) *Penalties.* For penalties for unauthorized disclosure of information, see section 7213.

○── § 301.6103(d) **Statutory provisions; publicity of returns and lists of taxpayers; inspection by committees of Congress.** [Sec. 6103, IRC]

○── § 301.6103(d)-1 (T.D. 6546, filed 1-18-61.) **Inspection by committees of Congress.**

(a) *Committees on Ways and Means and Finance and joint and select committees specially authorized to investigate returns.* The Secretary and any officer or employee of the Treasury Department, upon request from the Committee on Ways and Means of the House of Representatives, the Committee on Finance of the Senate, or a select committee of the Senate or House specially authorized to investigate returns by a resolution of the Senate or House, or a joint committee so authorized by concurrent resolution, shall furnish such committee sitting in executive session with any data of any character contained in or shown by any return. Any such committee shall have the right, acting directly as a committee, or by or through such examiners or agents as it may designate or appoint, to inspect any or all of the returns at such times and in such manner as it may determine. Any relevant or useful information thus obtained may be submitted by the committee obtaining it to the Senate or the House, or to both the Senate and the House, as the case may be.

(b) *Joint Committee on Internal Reve-*

nue Taxation. The Joint Committee on Internal Revenue Taxation shall have the same right to obtain data and to inspect returns as the Committee on Ways and Means or the Committee on Finance, and the right to submit any relevant or useful information thus obtained to the Senate, the House of Representatives, the Committee on Ways and Means, or the Committee on Finance. The Committee on Ways and Means or the Committee on Finance may submit such information to the House or to the Senate, or to both the House and the Senate, as the case may be. See also section 8023 for authority of the Joint Committee to obtain additional data.

(c) *Applications for tax exemption.* The application for exemption of any organization described in section 501 (c) or (d) which is exempt from taxation under section 501 (a) for any taxable year, and any other papers which are in the possession of the Internal Revenue Service and which relate to such application, shall, in accordance with section 6104 (a) (2), be made available to any committee of Congress designated in paragraph (a) or (b) of this section as if such papers constituted returns.

§ 301.6103(e) **Statutory provisions; publicity of returns and lists of taxpayers; declarations of estimated tax.** [Sec. 6103, IRC]

§ 301.6103(f) **Statutory provisions; publicity of returns and lists of taxpayers; inspection of list of taxpayers.** [Sec. 6103, IRC]

§ 301.6103(f)-1 (T.D. 6546, filed 1-18-61.) **Public lists of persons making returns of income tax and of unemployment tax.**

In accordance with the provisions of sections 6103 (f) and 6106, the district director for each internal revenue district (including the Director of International Operations) shall prepare as soon as practicable in each year and make available to public inspection in his office during regular hours of business—

(a) Lists containing the name and post office address of each person filing an income tax return in such district; and

(b) Lists containing the name and post office address of each person filing a return in such district in respect of unemployment tax imposed by chapter 23 of the Code.

§ 301.6104 **Statutory provisions; publicity of information required from certain exempt organizations and certain trusts.** [Sec. 6104, IRC]

§ 301.6104-1 (T.D. 6331, filed 10-31-58, amended by T.D. 6391, filed 6-25-59; republished in T.D. 6498, filed 10-24-60; amended by T.D. 6565, filed 8-2-61 and T.D. 7350, filed 4-3-75.) **Public inspection of applications for tax exemption.**

(a) *Applications open to inspection*—(1) *In general.* An application for exemption together with any supporting documents, filed by an organization described in section 501(c) or (d) (or in the corresponding provisions of any prior revenue law) shall be open to public inspection on or after November 3, 1958, in accordance with section 6104(a)(1) and the provisions of this section, if the Commissioner or district director has determined on the basis of such application, that such organization is exempt from taxation for any taxable year under section 501(a) (or under the corresponding provisions of any prior revenue law). Certain applications for exemption have been destroyed pursuant to Congressional authorization and therefore will not be available for inspection.

(2) *Claim for exemption filed under section 503 or 504 and the regulations thereunder.* Claims for exemption filed to reestablish exempt status after denial thereof under the provisions of section 503 or 504 (or under the corresponding provisions of any prior revenue law), relating to denial of exemption because of certain prohibited transactions or an unreasonable accumulation of income, are considered to be applications for exemption for purposes of section 6104 (a)(1) and this section.

(3) *Requirement of exempt status.* An application for exemption and supporting documents shall not be available for public inspection before the organization filing such application has been determined, on the basis of such application, to be exempt from taxation for any taxable year. On the other hand, if the organization has been determined to be exempt for any taxable year, the application for exemption with respect to which such determination was made shall not be withheld from public inspection on the grounds that such organization is determined not to be entitled to exemption for any other taxable year or years.

(b) *Meaning of terms*—(1) *Application for exemption.* (i) For purposes of this section, the term "application for exemption" means the documents described in subdivision (ii) of this subparagraph which the organization was required to file when it applied for exemption.

(ii) *(a)* With respect to an organization for which an application for exemption form is prescribed, the application for exemption includes such form and all documents and statements required to be filed by such form.

(b) With respect to an organization described in section 501(c) or (d) for which no application for exemption form is prescribed, the application for exemption includes the application letter and a conformed copy of the articles of incorporation, declaration of trust, or other instrument of similar import, setting forth the permitted powers or activities of the organization, the bylaws or other code of regulations, and the latest financial statement showing the assets, liabilities, receipts, and disbursements of the organization, and statements showing the character of the organization, the purpose for which it was organized, its actual activities, sources of income and receipts and the disposition thereof, and whether or not any of its income or receipts is credited to surplus or may inure to the benefit of any private shareholder or individual.

(c) With respect to a mutual insurance company, the application for exemption shall, in addition to the statements and documents required to be submitted by the form, include copies of the policies or certificates of membership issued by such company.

(d) With respect to a title holding company described in section 501(c)(2), if the organization for which title is held has not been specifically notified in writing

Reg. § 301.6104-1 (b) (1)

by the Internal Revenue Service that it is held to be exempt under section 501(a), the application for exemption shall, in addition to the statements and documents required to be submitted by the form, include the statements or documents which would be considered to be included in the application for exemption of the organization for which title is held.

(e) With respect to a State chartered credit union described in section 501(c)(14), the application for exemption shall, in addition to the statements and documents indicated in (b) of this subdivision, include a statement indicating the State and date of incorporation and showing that the State credit union law with respect to loans, investments, and dividends, if any, is being complied with.

(f) With respect to an organization which is described in section 501(c)(3) and which files its application for exemption after July 26, 1959, the application for exemption shall, in addition to the statements and documents required to be submitted by the form, include a detailed statement of the proposed activities of such organization.

(iii) The term "application for exemption" does not include a request for a ruling as to whether a proposed transaction is a prohibited transaction under section 503 (or under the corresponding provisions of any prior revenue law).

(2) *Supporting document.* For purposes of this section, the term "supporting document" means any statement or document submitted by an organization in support of its application for exemption which is not specifically required by subdivision (ii) of subparagraph (1) of this paragraph. For example, a legal brief submitted in support of an application for exemption is a supporting document.

(c) *Withholding of certain information*—(1) *Trade secrets, patents, processes, styles of work, or apparatus*—(i) *In general.* Any information which is submitted by an organization whose application for exemption is open to inspection under this section and which is determined by the Commissioner to relate to any trade secret, patent, process, style of work, or apparatus of the organization submitting such information shall, upon request in writing of such organization, be withheld from public inspection under section 6104(a)(1) and this section, if the Commissioner determines that the disclosure of such information would adversely affect the organization.

(ii) *Request for withholding of information.* Requests for the withholding of information from public inspection as provided in subdivision (i) of this subparagraph shall—

(a) In the case of applications for exemption filed before November 3, 1958, be made to the Commissioner of Internal Revenue, Attention: Public Information Division, Washington 25, D.C.; or

(b) In the case of applications for exemption filed on or after November 3, 1958, be filed with the office with which the taxpayer filed the documents in which the material to be withheld is contained.
The request shall clearly identify the material desired to be withheld (the document, page, paragraph, and line) and shall include the reasons for the organization's position that the information is of the type which may be withheld from public inspection.

(iii) *Determination.* An organization which has filed a request under the provisions of this subparagraph will be notified of the determination as to whether the information to which the request relates will be withheld from public inspection.

(2) *National defense material.* The Internal Revenue Service shall withhold from public inspection any information which is submitted by an organization whose application for exemption is open to inspection under this section the public disclosure of which the Commissioner determines would adversely affect the national defense.

(d) *Place of inspection.* Applications for exemption, together with any supporting documents, which are open to public inspection under section 6104(a)(1) shall be available for inspection on or after November 3, 1958, in the Public Affairs Division, Internal Revenue Service, 1111 Constitution Avenue, NW., Washington, D.C. 20224, regardless of when or where such applications were filed except for such applications as have been destroyed pursuant to Congressional authority. In addition, in the case of an application for exemption filed on or after September 3, 1958, a copy of such application (as defined in paragraph (b)(1) of this section), but not the supporting documents, shall also be available for public inspection on or after November 3, 1958, in the office of the district director with whom the application was required to be filed.

(e) *Procedure for public inspection of applications for exemption*—(1) *Request for inspection.* Applications for exemption and the supporting documents shall be available for public inspection only upon request. If inspection at the national office is desired, the request shall be made in writing to the Commissioner of Internal Revenue, Attention: Assistant to the Commissioner (Public Affairs), 1111 Constitution Avenue, NW., Washington, D.C. 20224. Requests for inspection in the office of a district director shall be made in writing to the appropriate district director. All requests for inspection must include the name and address of the organization which filed the application for exemption the inspection of which is requested. In addition, if such organization has more than one application for exemption open to public inspection under the provisions of section 6104(a)(1), only the most recent of such applications shall be made available for inspection unless the request for inspection specifically states otherwise.

(2) *Time and extent of inspection.* A person requesting public inspection in the manner specified in subparagraph (1) of this paragraph shall be notified by the Internal Revenue Service when the material he desires to inspect will be made available for his inspection. An application for exemption will be made available for public inspection at such reasonable and proper times as not to interfere with its use by the Internal Revenue Service or to exclude other persons from inspecting it. In addition, the Commissioner or district director may limit the number of applications for exemption to be made available to any person for inspection on a given

date. The public inspection authorized by section 6104(a)(1) will be allowed only in the presence of an internal revenue officer or employee and only during the regular hours of business of the Internal Revenue Service office.

(3) *Copies.* Notes may be taken of the material opened for inspection under this section, and copies may be made manually or, if a person provides the equipment, photographically at the place of inspection, subject to reasonable supervision with regard to the facilities and equipment to be employed. Copies of such material will be furnished by the Internal Revenue Service to any person making request therefor. Requests for such copies shall be made in the same manner as requests for inspection (see subparagraph (1) of this paragraph) to the office of the Internal Revenue Service in which such material is available for inspection as provided in paragraph (d) of this section. If made at the time of inspection, the request for copies need not be in writing. Any copies furnished will be certified upon request. The Commissioner may prescribe a reasonable fee for furnishing copies of applications and supporting documents pursuant to this section.

(f) *Statement of exempt status.* A statement setting forth the following information with respect to an organization shall be furnished to any person, upon request in writing, after the application for exemption of such organization is open to public inspection under section 6104(a)(1):

(1) The subsection and paragraph of section 501 (or the corresponding provision of any prior revenue law) under which the organization has been determined, on the basis of such application, to qualify for exemption from taxation; and

(2) Whether the organization is currently held to be exempt.

Request for such information may be made in writing to the Commissioner of Internal Revenue, Attention: Assistant to the Commissioner (Public Affairs), 1111 Constitution Avenue, NW., Washington, D.C. 20224, or to the district director with whom the organization's application for exemption was required to be filed.

○—➤ § 301.6104-2 (T.D. 6331, filed 10-31-58; republished in T.D. 6498, filed 10-24-60; amended by T.D. 6565, filed 8-2-61; T.D. 6645, filed 4-1-63; T.D. 7122, filed 6-7-71; T.D. 7173, filed 3-16-72; T.D. 7290, filed 11-16-73 and T.D. 7350, filed 4-3-75.) **Publicity of information on certain information returns and annual reports.**

(a) *In general.* The following information, together with the name and address of the organization or trust furnishing such information, shall be a matter of public record:

(1) Except as otherwise provided in section 6104 and the regulations thereunder, the information required by section 6033 and the information furnished on Form 4720.

(2) The information furnished pursuant to section 6034 (relating to returns by certain trusts) on Form 1041-A.

(3) The information furnished on the annual report required by section 6056 (relating to annual reports of private foundations). The names, addresses, and amounts of contributions or bequests of contributors to an organization other than a private foundation shall not be made available for public inspection under section 6104(b). The names, addresses, and amounts of contributions or bequests of persons who are not citizens of the United States to a foreign organization described in section 4948(b) shall not be made available for public inspection under section 6104(b).

(b) *Place of inspection.* Information furnished on the public portion of returns and annual reports (as described in paragraph (a) of this section) shall be available to any person in the National Office, Public Affairs Division, Internal Revenue Service, 1111 Constitution Avenue, NW., Washington, D.C. 20224, in the Office of the Director, Mid-Atlantic Regional Service Center, Philadelphia, Pa., and in the office of the district director of the district serving the principal place of business of the organization.

(c) *Procedure for public inspection*—(1) *Requests for inspection.* The information furnished pursuant to section 6033 and 6034, the annual report required by section 6056, and Form 4720 shall be available for public inspection under section 6104(b) only upon request. If inspection at the National Office is desired, the request shall be made in writing to the Commissioner of Internal Revenue, Attention: Assistant to the Commissioner (Public Affairs), Washington, D.C. 20224. Requests for inspection in the office of a district director or Director of the Internal Revenue Service Center, Philadelphia, Pennsylvania shall be made in writing to the district director or Director of the Service Center. All requests for inspection must include the name and address of the organization which filed the return or report, the type of return or report, and the taxable year for which filed, except that requests for inspection of entire sections of the microfilm file need only designate the appropriate section desired.

(2) *Time and extent of inspection.* A person requesting public inspection in the manner specified in subparagraph (1) of this paragraph shall be notified by the Internal Revenue Service when the material he desires to inspect will be made available for his inspection. Information on returns required by sections 6033 and 6034, the annual report required by section 6056 and the information furnished on Form 4720 will be made available for public inspection at such reasonable and proper times, and under such conditions, that will not interfere with their use by the Internal Revenue Service and will not exclude other persons from inspecting them. In addition, the Commissioner, Director of the Service Center, or district director may limit the number of returns to be made available to any person for inspection on a given date. Inspection will be allowed only in the presence of an internal revenue officer or employee and only during the regular hours of business of the Internal Revenue Service office.

(3) *Returns available.* Returns filed before January 1, 1970, shall be available for public inspection only pursuant to the provisions of section 6104 in effect for such years. The information furnished on all returns and reports filed after December 31, 1969, pursuant to the requirements of section 6033, 6034, or 6056, shall be available for public inspection in accordance with the provisions of section 6104.

Reg. § 301.6104-2(c)(3)

Reg. § 301.6104-2(c)(4)

(4) *Copies.* Notes may be taken of the material opened for inspection under this section. Copies may be made manually or, if a person provides the equipment, photographically at the place of inspection, subject to reasonable supervision with regard to the facilities and equipment to be employed. Copies of the material opened for inspection will be furnished by the Internal Revenue Service to any person making request therefor. Request for such copies shall be made in the same manner as requests for inspection (see subparagraph (1) of this paragraph) to the office of the Internal Revenue Service in which such material is available for inspection as provided in paragraph (b) of this section. If made at the time of inspection, the request for copies need not be in writing. Any copies furnished will be certified upon request. The Commissioner may prescribe a reasonable fee for furnishing copies of information pursuant to this section.

§ 301.6104-3 (T.D. 7122, filed 6-7-71; amended by T.D. 7290, filed 11-16-73.) **Disclosure of certain information to State officers.**

(a) *Notification of determinations*—(1) *Automatic notification.* Upon making a determination described in paragraph (c) of this section, the Internal Revenue Service will notify the Attorney General and the principal tax officer of each of the following States of such determination without application or request by such State officers—

(i) In the case of any organization described in section 501(c)(3), the State in which the principal office of the organization is located (as shown on the last-filed return required by section 6033, or on the application for exemption if no return has been filed), and the State in which the organization was incorporated, or if a trust, in which it was created, and

(ii) In the case of a private foundation, each State which the organization was required to list as an attachment to its last-filed return pursuant to § 1.6033-2(a)(2)(iv).

(2) *Applications for notification by other State officers.* Other officers of States described in subparagraph (1) of this paragraph, and officers of States not described in such subparagraph, may request that they be notified (either generally or with respect to a particular organization or type of organization) of determinations described in paragraph (c) of this section. In such cases, these State officers must show that they are appropriate State officers within the meaning of section 6104(c)(2). The required showing may be made by presenting a letter from the Attorney General of the State setting forth (i) the functions and authority of the State officer under State law, and (ii) sufficient facts for the Internal Revenue Service to determine that such officer is an appropriate State officer within the meaning of section 6104(c)(2).

(3) *Manner of notification.* A State officer who is entitled to be notified of a determination under this paragraph will be notified by sending him a copy of the communication from the Internal Revenue Service to the organization which informs such organization of the determination.

(b) *Inspection by State officers*—(1) *In general.* After a determination described in paragraph (c) of this section has been made, appropriate State officers within the meaning of section 6104(c)(2) may inspect the material described in subparagraph (3) of this paragraph. Such material may be inspected at an office of the Internal Revenue Service which will be designated upon receipt of a request for inspection; the location of such office will be determined with due consideration of the needs of the Internal Revenue Service and the needs of the State officer entitled to inspect.

(2) *State officers who may inspect material.* Any State officer entitled to be notified of a determination without application (under paragraph (a)(1) of this section) may inspect the material described in subparagraph (3) of this paragraph upon demonstrating that he is so entitled. Any State officer who has in fact been notified by the Internal Revenue Service of a determination may inspect such material without further demonstration, unless it shall be determined by the Internal Revenue Service that such officer was not entitled to be so notified. Other State officers must demonstrate to the satisfaction of the Internal Revenue Service that they are entitled to be notified under paragraph (a)(2) of this section before they may inspect such material.

(3) *Material which may be inspected.*
(i) Except as provided in subdivision (ii) of this subparagraph, a State officer who is so entitled under subparagraphs (1) and (2) of this paragraph will be permitted to inspect and copy all returns, filed statements, records, reports, and other information relating to a determination described in paragraph (c) of this section which is relevant to a determination under State law, and which is in the hands of the Internal Revenue Service.

(ii) The following material will not be made available for inspection by State officers under section 6104(c) and this section—

(*a*) Interpretations by the Internal Revenue Service or other federal agency of federal laws (including the Internal Revenue Code of 1954 and its predecessors) which would not otherwise be made available to State officers under section 6103(b),

(*b*) Reports of informers, or any other material which would disclose the identity, or threaten the safety or anonymity, of an informer,

(*c*) Returns of persons (other than those exempt from taxation) which would not be available under section 6103(b) to the State officer requesting inspection, or

(*d*) Other material the disclosure of which the Commissioner has determined would prejudice the proper administration of the internal revenue laws.

(4) *Statement by State officer.* Before any State officer will be permitted to inspect material described in this paragraph, he must submit a statement to the Internal Revenue Service that he intends to use such material solely in fulfilling his functions under State law relating to organizations of the type described in section 501 (c)(3); material is made available to State officers under this section in reliance on such statements. For provisions relating to penalties for misuse of information which is made available under section 6104 (c) and this section, see 18 U.S.C. 1001.

(c) *Determinations defined.* For purposes of this section, a determination means a final determination by the Internal Revenue Service that—

(1) An organization is refused recognition as an organization described in section 501(c)(3), or has been operated in such a manner that it will not, or will no longer, be recognized as meeting the requirements for exemption under that section, or

(2) A deficiency of tax exists under section 507 or chapter 42.

For purposes of this paragraph, a determination by the Internal Revenue Service is not final until all administrative review with respect to such determination has been completed. For purposes of this section, a waiver of restrictions on assessment and collection of deficiency in tax is treated as a final determination that a deficiency of tax exists when such waiver has been finally accepted by the Internal Revenue Service. For example, a final determination that a deficiency of tax exists under section 507 or chapter 42 is made when the organization is sent a notice of deficiency with respect to such tax.

(d) *Effective date.* The provisions of this section apply with respect to all determinations made after December 31, 1969.

○━▶ § 301.6104-4 (T.D. 7122, filed 6-7-71.) **Public inspection of private foundations' annual reports.**

(a) *In general.* The annual report which a private foundation must file under section 6056 shall be made available by its foundation managers for inspection at its principal office during regular business hours by any citizen on request made within 180 days after the publication of notice of the availability of such report. Such notice shall be published not later than the day prescribed for filing such report (determined with regard to any extension of time for filing) in a newspaper having general circulation in the county in which the foundation's principal office is located. The notice shall state that the annual report is available at the foundation's principal office for inspection during regular business hours by any citizen who requests inspection within 180 days after the date of such publication, and shall state the address of the foundation's principal office and the name of its principal manager.

(b) *Definitions and special rules*—(1) *Principal office.* For purposes of the notice described in section 6104(d), a private foundation may designate in addition to its principal office, or (if the foundation has no principal office or none other than the residence of a substantial contributor or foundation manager) in lieu of such office, any other location at which its annual report shall be made available in the manner and at the time prescribed therefor in section 6104(d).

(2) *Newspaper having general circulation.* The term "newspaper having general circulation" in section 6104(d) shall include any newspaper or journal which is permitted to publish statements in satisfaction of State statutory requirements relating to transfers of title to real estate or other similar legal notices.

(3) *Principal manager.* A private foundation may furnish the name of its "principal manager" in the notice required by section 6104(d) by furnishing the name of the individual foundation manager who is responsible for publishing such notice or for making the annual report available for inspection under section 6104(d).

(c) *Cross-reference.* For additional rules with respect to private foundations' annual reports and their public inspection, see section 6056 and the regulations thereunder.

○━▶ § 301.6105 **Statutory provisions; compilation of relief from excess profits tax cases.** [Sec. 6105, IRC]

○━▶ § 301.6105-1 (T.D. 6546, filed 1-18-61.) **Compilation of relief from excess profits tax cases.**

Pursuant to and in accordance with the provisions of section 6105, the Commissioner shall make and publish in the Federal Register a compilation, for each fiscal year beginning after June 30, 1941, of all cases in which relief under the provisions of section 722 of the Internal Revenue Code of 1939, as amended, has been allowed during such fiscal year by the Commissioner and by the Tax Court of the United States.

○━▶ § 301.6106 **Statutory provisions; publicity of unemployment tax returns.** [Sec. 6106, IRC]

○━▶ § 301.6106-1 (T.D. 6546, filed 1-18-61.) **Publicity of unemployment tax returns.**

For provisions relating to publicity of returns made in respect of unemployment tax imposed by chapter 23 of the Code, see §§ 301.6103(a)-1, 301.6103(b)-1, 301.6103(c)-1, 301.6103(d)-1, and 301.6103(f)-1.

○━▶ § 1.6107-1 (T.D. 7519, filed 11-17-77.) **Income tax return preparer must furnish copy of return to taxpayer and must retain copy or record.**

(a) *Furnishing copy to taxpayer.* The person who is an income tax return preparer of any return of tax under subtitle A of the Internal Revenue Code of 1954 or claim for refund of tax under subtitle A of the Internal Revenue Code of 1954 shall furnish a completed copy of the original return or claim for refund to the taxpayer (or nontaxable entity) not later than the time the original return or claim for refund

Reg. § 1.6107-1(a)

24,326.2 (I.R.C.)   Reg. § 1.6107-1(a)   12-5-77

is presented for the signature of the taxpayer (or nontaxable entity). The preparer may, if it wishes, request a receipt or other evidence from the taxpayer (or nontaxable entity) sufficient to show satisfaction of the requirement of this paragraph (a).

(b) *Copy or record to be retained.* The person who is an income tax return preparer of any return or claim for refund shall—

(1)(i) Retain a completed copy of the return or claim for refund; or

(ii) Retain a record, by list, card file, or otherwise of the name, taxpayer identification number, and taxable year of the taxpayer (or nontaxable entity) for whom the return or claim for refund was prepared and the type of return or claim for refund prepared;

(2) Retain a record, by retention of a copy of the return or claim for refund, maintenance of a list or card file, or otherwise, for each return or claim for refund presented to the taxpayer (or nontaxable entity) of the name of the individual preparer required to sign the return or claim for refund pursuant to § 1.6695-1(b); and

(3) Make the copy or record of returns and claims for refund and record of the individuals required to sign available for inspection upon request by the district director.

The material described in this paragraph (b) shall be retained and kept available for inspection for the 3-year period following the close of the return period during which the return or claim for refund was presented for signature to the taxpayer (or nontaxable entity). However, in the case of a return which becomes due (with extensions, if any) during a return period following the return period during which the return was presented for signature, the material shall be retained and kept available for inspection for the 3-year period following the close of the later return period in which the return became due. For the definition of "return period" see section 6060 (c) and § 1.6060-1(c).

(c) *Preparer.* For the definition of "income tax return preparer", see section 7701 (a)(36) and § 301.7701-15. For purposes of applying this section, in the case of—

(1) An employment arrangement between two or more income tax return preparers, the person who employs (or engages) one or more other preparers to prepare for compensation any return or claim for refund other than for the person shall be considered to be the sole income tax return preparer; and

(2) A partnership arrangement for the preparation of returns and claims for refund, the partnership shall be considered to be the sole income tax return preparer.

(d) *Penalties.* (1) For the civil penalty for failure to furnish a copy of the return or claim for refund to the taxpayer (or nontaxable entity) as required under paragraphs (a) and (c) of this section, see section 6695(a) and § 1.6695-1(a).

(2) For the civil penalty for failure to retain a copy of the return or claim for refund, or to retain a record, as required under paragraphs (b) and (c) of this section, see section 6695(d) and § 1.6695-1(d).

O— § 301.6107 [Deleted]

O— § 301.6107-1 (T.D. 6546, filed 1-18-61; amended by T.D. 7087, filed 1-13-71.) [Deleted]

O— § 301.6108 Statutory provisions; publication of statistics of income. [Sec. 6108, IRC]

O— § 301.6108-1 (T.D. 6546, filed 1-18-61.) Publication of statistics of income.

Pursuant to and in accordance with the provisions of section 6108, statistics reasonably available with respect to the operation of the income tax laws shall be prepared and published annually by the Commissioner.

O— § 1.6109 [Deleted]

O— § 1.6109-1 (T.D. 6606 filed 8-24-62; amended by T.D. 7012, filed 5-14-69 and T.D. 7306, filed 3-14-74.) **Identifying numbers.**

(a) *Information to be furnished after April 15, 1974.* For provisions concerning the requesting and furnishing of identifying numbers with respect to returns, statements, and other documents which must be filed after April 15, 1974, see § 301.6109-1 of this chapter (Income Tax Regulations).

(b) *Information to be furnished before April 16, 1974.* For provisions concerning the requesting and furnishing of identifying numbers with respect to returns, statements, and other documents which must be filed before April 16, 1974, see 26 CFR § 1.6109-1 (revised as of April 1, 1973).

O— § 31.6109 Statutory provisions; identifying numbers. [Sec. 6109, IRC]

O— § 31.6109-1 (T.D. 6606, filed 8-24-62; amended by T.D. 7306, filed 3-14-74.) **Supplying of identifying numbers.**

(a) *In general.* The returns, statements, and other documents required to be filed under this subchapter shall reflect such identifying numbers as are required by each return, statement, or document and its related instructions. See § 301.6109-1 of this chapter (Regulations on Procedure and Administration).

(b) *Effective date.* The provisions of this section are effective for information which must be furnished after April 15, 1974. See 26 CFR § 31.6109-1 (revised as of April 1, 1973) for provisions with respect to information on which must be furnished before April 16, 1974.

O— § 301.6109 Statutory provisions; identifying numbers. [Sec. 6109, IRC]

O— § 301.6109-1 (T.D. 6606, filed 8-24-62; amended by T.D. 7306, filed 3-14-74.) **Identifying numbers.**

(a) *In general.* There are two types of taxpayer identifying numbers: social security numbers and employer identification numbers. Social security numbers take the form 000-00-0000, while employer identification numbers take the form 00-0000000. Social security numbers identify individual persons and estates of decedents, while employer identification numbers identify corporations, partnerships, nonprofit associations, trusts, and similar nonindividual persons. Both types of taxpayer identifying numbers are used by individuals who are employers or who are engaged in trade or business as sole proprietors, as required by returns, statements or other documents and their related instructions. Such documents often require an individual's own social security number in connection with his individual taxes, and his employer identification number in connection with his business taxes.

(b) *Use of one's own number.* Every person who files under this title a return, statement, or other document shall furnish his taxpayer identifying number as required by the forms and the instructions relating thereto. A person whose number must be included on a document filed by another person shall give the taxpayer identifying number so required to the other person on request. For provisions dealing specifically with the duty of employees with respect to their social security numbers, see paragraphs (a) and (b) of § 31.6011(b)-2 of this chapter (Employment Tax Regulations). For provisions dealing specifically with the duty of employers with respect to employer identification numbers, see § 31.6011(b)-1 of this chapter (Employment Tax Regulations).

(c) *Use of another's number.* Every person required under this title to file a return, statement, or other document shall furnish such taxpayer identifying numbers of other persons as required by the forms and the instructions relating thereto. If he does not know the taxpayer identifying number of the other person, he shall request such number of the other person. A request should state that the identifying number is required to be furnished under authority of law. When the person filing the return, statement, or other document does not know the number of the other person, and has complied with the request provision of this paragraph, he shall sign an affidavit on the transmittal document forwarding such returns, statements, or other documents to the Internal Revenue Service, so stating. A person required to file a taxpayer identifying number shall correct any errors in such filing when his attention has been drawn to them.

(d) *Obtaining a taxpayer identifying number*—(1) *Social security number.* Any individual required to furnish a social security number pursuant to paragraph (b) of this section shall apply for one, if he has not done so previously, on Form SS-5, which may be obtained from any Social Security Administration or Internal Revenue Service office. He shall make such application far enough in advance of the first required use of such number to permit issuance of the number in time for compliance with such requirement. The form, together with any supplementary statement, shall be prepared and filed in accordance with the form, instructions, and regulations applicable thereto, and shall set forth fully and clearly the data therein called for. Individuals who are ineligible for or do not wish to participate in the benefits of the social security program shall nevertheless obtain a social security number if they are required to furnish such a number pursuant to paragraph (b) of this section.

(2) *Employer identification number.* Any person required to furnish an employer identification number pursuant to paragraph (b) of this section shall apply for one, if he has not done so previously, on Form SS-4, which may be obtained from any office of the Internal Revenue Service. He shall make such application far enough in advance of the first required use of such number to permit issuance of the number in time for compliance with such requirement. The form, together with any supplementary statement, shall be prepared and filed in accordance with the form, instructions, and regulations applicable thereto, and shall set forth fully and clearly the data therein called for.

(e) *Banks, and brokers and dealers in securities.* For additional requirements relating to deposits, share accounts and brokerage accounts, see 31 CFR 103.34 and 103.35.

(f) *Penalty.* For penalty for failure to supply identifying numbers, see section 6676 and § 301.6676-1.

(g) *Nonresident alien exclusion.* This section shall not apply to nonresident aliens, foreign corporations, foreign partnerships, or foreign private foundations that do not have income effectively connected with the conduct of a trade or business within the United States and do not have an office or place of business or a fiscal or paying agent in the United States.

(h) *Effective date.* The provisions of this section are effective for information which must be furnished after April 15, 1974. See the parts of 26 CFR (revised as of April 1, 1973) which relate to the particular tax for provisions with respect to information which must be furnished before April 16, 1974 and for information which must be furnished to the Bureau of Alcohol, Tobacco and Firearms prior to the effective date of comparable procedural regulations promulgated by the Bureau in 27 CFR Part 70. Nothing contained in the regulations under section 6109 shall limit the authority of the Internal Revenue Service to obtain taxpayer identifying numbers required before or after the effective date of this paragraph after notice is served upon the taxpayer pursuant to section 6001.

○— § 1.6109-2 T.D. 7519, filed 11-17-77.)
Furnishing identifying number of income tax return preparer.

(a) *Furnishing identifying number.* Each return of tax under subtitle A of the Internal Revenue Code of 1954 or claim for refund of tax under subtitle A of the Internal Revenue Code of 1954 prepared by one or more income tax return preparers shall bear the identifying number of the preparer required by § 1.6695-1(b) to sign the return or claim for refund. In addition, if there is a partnership or employment arrangement between two or more preparers, the identifying number of the partnership or the person who employs (or engages) one or more other persons to prepare for compensation the return or claim for refund shall also appear on the return or claim for refund. If the preparer is—

(1) An individual (not described in subparagraph (2) of this paragraph (a)) who is a citizen or resident of the United States, such preparer's social security account number shall be affixed; and

(2) A person (whether an individual,

Reg. § 1.6109-2(a)(2)

corporation, or partnership) who employs (or engages) one or more persons to prepare the return or claim for refund (other than for the person), or who is not a citizen or resident of the United States and also is not employed or engaged by another preparer, such preparer's employer identification number shall be affixed.

For the definition of the term "income tax return preparer" (or "preparer") see section 7701(a)(36) and § 301.7701-15.

(b) *Furnishing address.* (1) Each return or claim for refund which is prepared by one or more income tax return preparers shall bear the street address, city, State, and postal ZIP code of that preparer's place of business where the preparation of the return or claim for refund was completed. However, if this place of business is not maintained on a year-round basis, the return or claim for refund shall bear the street address, city, State, and postal ZIP code of such preparer's principal office or business location which is maintained on a year-round basis, or if none, that preparer's residence.

(2) For purposes of satisfying the requirement of the first sentence of paragraph (b)(1) of this section, an income tax return preparer may, on returns and claims for refund, disclose only the postal ZIP code of the described place of business as a satisfactory address, but only if the preparer first by written notice advises each affected Internal Revenue Service Center that he intends to follow this practice.

(c) *Penalty.* For the civil penalty for failure to furnish an identifying number as required under paragraph (a) of this section, see section 6695(c) and § 1.6695-1(c).

○━ § 301.6110-1 (T.D. 7524, filed 12-15-77.) **Public inspection of written determinations and background file documents.**

(a) *General rule.* Except as provided in § 301.6110-3, relating to deletion of certain information, § 301.6110-5(b), relating to actions to restrain disclosure, paragraph (b)(2) of this section, relating to technical advice memoranda involving civil fraud and criminal investigations, and jeopardy and termination assessments, and paragraph (b)(3) of this section, relating to general written determinations relating to accounting or funding periods and methods, the text of any written determination (as defined in § 301.6110-2(a)) issued pursuant to a request postmarked or hand delivered after October 31, 1976, shall be open to public inspection in the places provided in paragraph (c)(1) of this section. The text of any written determination issued pursuant to a request postmarked or hand delivered before November 1, 1976, shall be open to public inspection pursuant to section 6110(h) and § 301.6110-6, when funds are appropriated by Congress for such purpose. The procedures and rules set forth in §§ 301.6110-1 through 301.6110-5 and 301.6110-7 do not apply to written determinations issued pursuant to requests postmarked or hand delivered before November 1, 1976, unless § 301.6110-6 states otherwise. There shall also be open to public inspection in each place of public inspection an index to the written determinations open or subject to inspection at such place. Each such index shall be arranged by section of the Internal Revenue Code, related statute, or tax treaty and by subject matter description within such section in such manner as the Commissioner may from time to time provide. The Commissioner shall not be required to make any written determination or background file document open to public inspection pursuant to section 6110 or refrain from disclosure of any such documents or any information therein, except as provided by section 6110 or with respect to a discovery order made in connection with a judicial proceeding. The provisions of section 6110 shall not apply to matters for which the determination of whether public inspection should occur is made pursuant to section 6104. Matters within the ambit of section 6104 include: any application filed with the Internal Revenue Service with respect to the qualification or exempt status of an organization, plan, or account described in section 6104(a)(1), whether the plan or account has more than 25 or less than 26 participants; any document issued by the Internal Revenue Service in which the qualification or exempt status of an organization, plan, or account described in section 6104(a)(1) is granted, denied or revoked or the portion of any document in which technical advice with respect thereto is given to a district director; any application filed, and any document issued by the Internal Revenue Service, with respect to the qualification or status of master, prototype, and pattern employee plans; the portion of any document issued by the Internal Revenue Service in which is discussed the effect on the qualification or exempt status of an organization, plan, or account described in section 6104(a)(1) of proposed transactions by such organization, plan, or account; and any document issued by the Internal Revenue Service in which is discussed the qualification or status of an organization described in section 509(a) or 4942(j)(3), but not including any document issued to nonexempt charitable trusts described in section 4947(a)(1).

(b) *Items that may be inspected only under certain circumstances*—(1) *Background file documents.* A background file document (as such term is defined in § 301.6110-2(g)) relating to a particular written determination issued pursuant to a request postmarked or hand delivered after October 31, 1976, shall not be subject to inspection until such written determination is open to public inspection or available for inspection pursuant to paragraph (b)(2) or (3) of this section, and then only if a written request pursuant to paragraph (c)(4) of this section is made for inspection of such background file document. Background file documents relating to written determinations issued pursuant to requests postmarked or hand delivered before November 1, 1976, shall be subject to inspection pursuant to section 6110(h) and § 301.6110-6, when funds are appropriated by Congress for such purpose. The version of the background file document which is available for inspection shall be the version originally made available for inspection, as modified by any additional disclosure pursuant to section 6110(d)(3) and (f)(4).

(2) *Technical advice memoranda involving civil fraud and criminal investigations, jeopardy and termination assessments.* Any technical advice memorandum (as such term is defined in § 301.6110-2(f)) involving any matter that is the subject of a civil fraud or criminal investigation, a jeopardy assessment (as such term is defined in sec-

tion 6861), or a termination assessment (as such term is defined in section 6851) shall not be subject to inspection until all actions relating to such investigation or assessment are completed and then only if a written request pursuant to paragraph (c)(4) of this section is made for inspection of such technical advice memorandum. A "civil fraud investigation" is any administrative step or judicial proceeding in which an issue for determination is whether the Commissioner should impose additional tax pursuant to section 6653(b). A "criminal investigation" is any administrative step or judicial proceeding in which an issue for determination is whether a taxpayer should be charged with or is guilty of criminal conduct. An action relating to a civil fraud or criminal investigation includes any such administrative step or judicial proceeding, the review of subsequent related activities and related returns of the taxpayer or related taxpayers, and any other administrative step or judicial procedure or proceeding or appellate process that is initiated as a consequence of the facts and circumstances disclosed by such investigation. An action relating to a jeopardy or termination assessment includes any administrative step or judicial proceeding that is initiated to determine whether to make such assessment, that is brought pursuant to section 7429 to determine the appropriateness or reasonableness of such assessment, or that is brought to resolve the legal consequences of the tax status or liability issue underlying the making of such assessment. Any action relating to a civil fraud or criminal investigation, a jeopardy assessment, or a termination assessment is not completed until all available administrative steps and judicial proceedings and remedies, including appeals, have been completed.

(3) *Written determinations with respect to adoption of or change in certain accounting or funding periods and methods.* Any general written determination (as defined in § 301.6110-2(c)) that relates solely to approval of any adoption of or change in—

(i) The funding method or plan year of a plan under section 412,

(ii) A taxpayer's annual accounting period under section 442,

(iii) A taxpayer's method of accounting under section 446(e), or

(iv) A partnership's or partner's taxable year under section 706

shall not be subject to inspection until such written determination would, but for this (3), be open to public inspection pursuant to § 301.6110-5(c) and then only if a written request pursuant to paragraph (c)(4) of this section is made for inspection of such written determination.

(c) *Procedure for public inspection*—(1) *Place of public inspection.* The text of any ruling (as such term is defined in § 301.6110-2(d)) or technical advice memorandum that is open to public inspection pursuant to section 6110 shall be located in the National Office Reading Room. The text of any determination letter (as such term is defined in § 301.6110-2(e)) that is open to public inspection pursuant to section 6110 shall be located in the Reading Room of the Regional Office in which is located the district office that issued such determination letter. Inspection of any written determination subject to inspection only upon written request shall be requested from the National Office Reading Room. Inspection of any background file document shall be requested only from the reading room in which the related written determination is either open to public inspection or subject to inspection upon written request. The locations and mailing addresses of the reading rooms are set forth in § 601.702(b)(3)(ii) of this chapter.

(2) *Time and manner of public inspection.* The inspection authorized by section 6110 will be allowed only in the place provided for such inspection in the presence of an internal revenue officer or employee and only during the regular hours of business of the Internal Revenue Service office in which the reading room is located. The public will not be allowed to remove any record from a reading room. A person who wishes to inspect reading room material without visiting a reading room may submit a written request pursuant to paragraph (c)(4) of this section for copies of any such material to the Internal Revenue Service reading room in which is located such material.

(3) *Copies.* Notes may be taken of any material open to public inspection under section 6110, and copies may be made manually. Copies of any material open to public inspection or subject to inspection upon written request will be furnished by the Internal Revenue Service to any person making requests therefor pursuant to paragraph (c)(4) of this section. If made at the time of inspection, the request for copies need not be in writing, unless the material is not immediately available for copying. The Commissioner may prescribe fees pursuant to section 6110(j) for furnishing copies of material open or subject to inspecion.

(4) *Requests.* Any request for copies of written determinations, for inspection of general written determinations relating to accounting or funding periods and methods or technical advice memoranda involving civil fraud and criminal investigations, and jeopardy and termination assessments, for inspection or copies of background file documents, and for copies of the index shall be submitted to the reading room in which is located the requested material. If made in person, the request may be submitted to the internal revenue employee supervising the reading room. The request shall contain—

(i) Authorization for the Internal Revenue Service to charge the person making such request for making copies, searching for material, and making deletions therein;

(ii) The maximum amount of charges which the Internal Revenue Service may incur without further authorization from the person making such request;

(iii) With respect to requests for inspection and copies of background file documents, the file number of the written determination to which such background file document relates and a specific identification of the nature or type of the background file document requested;

(iv) With respect to requests for inspection of general written determinations relating to accounting or funding periods

Reg. § 301.6110-1(c)(4)

and methods, the day, week, or month of issuance of such written determination, and the applicable category as selected from a special summary listing of categories prepared by the Internal Revenue Service;

(v) With respect to requests for copies of written determinations, the file number of the written determination to be copied, which can be ascertained in the reading room or from the index;

(vi) With respect to requests for copies of portions of the index, the section of the Internal Revenue Code, related statute or tax treaty in which the person making such request is interested;

(vii) With respect to material which is to be mailed, the name, address, and telephone number of the person making such request and the address to which copies of the requested material should be sent; and

(viii) Such other information as the Internal Revenue Service may from time to time require in its operation of reading rooms.

§ 301.6110-2 (T.D. 7524, filed 12-15-77.) Meaning of terms.

(a) *Written determination.* A "written determination" is a ruling, a determination letter, or a technical advice memorandum, as such terms are defined in paragraphs (d), (e), and (f) of this section, respectively. Notwithstanding paragraphs (d) through (f) of this section, a written determination does not include, for example, opinion letters (as defined in § 601.201(a)(4) of this chapter), information letters (as defined in § 601.201(a)(5) of this chapter), technical information responses, technical assistance memoranda, notices of deficiency, reports on claims for refund, Internal Revenue Service decisions to accept taxpayers' offers in compromise, earnings and profits determinations, or documents issued by the Internal Revenue Service in the course of tax administration that are not disclosed to the persons to whose tax returns or tax liability the documents relate.

(b) *Reference written determination.* A "reference written determination" is any written determination that the Commissioner determines to have significant reference value. Any written determination that the Commissioner determines to be the basis for a published Revenue Ruling is a reference written determination until such Revenue Ruling is obsoleted, revoked, superseded or otherwise held to have no effect.

(c) *General written determination.* A "general written determination" is any written determination that is not a reference written determination.

(d) *Ruling.* A "ruling" is a written statement issued by the National Office to a taxpayer or to the taxpayer's authorized representative (as such term is defined in § 601.201(e)(7) of this chapter) on behalf of the taxpayer, that interprets and applies tax laws to a specific set of facts. A ruling generally recites the relevant facts, sets forth the applicable provisions of law, and shows the application of the law to the facts.

(e) *Determination letter.* A "determination letter" is a written statement issued by a district director in response to a written inquiry by an individual or an organization that applies principles and precedents previously announced by the National Office to the particular facts involved.

(f) *Technical advice memorandum.* A "technical advice memorandum" is a written statement issued by the National Office to, and adopted by, a district director in connection with the examination of a taxpayer's return or consideration of the taxpayer's claim for refund or credit. A technical advice memorandum generally recites the relevant facts, sets forth the applicable law, and states a legal conclusion.

(g) *Background file document*—(1) *General rule.* A "background file document" is—

(i) The request for a written determination,

(ii) Any written material submitted in support of such request by the person by whom or on whose behalf the request for a written determination was made,

(iii) Any written communication, or memorandum of a meeting, telephone communication, or other contact, between employees of the Internal Revenue Service or Office of its Chief Counsel and persons outside the Internal Revenue Service in connection with such request or written determination which is received prior to the issuance (as such term is defined in paragraph (h) of this section) of the written determination, but not including communications described in paragraph (g)(2) of this section, and

(iv) Any subsequent communication between the National Office and a district director concerning the factual circumstances underlying the request for a technical advice memorandum, or concerning a request by the district director for reconsideration by the National Office of a proposed technical advice memorandum.

(2) *Limitations.* Notwithstanding paragraph (g)(1) of this section, a "background file document" shall not include any—

(i) Communication between the Department of Justice and the Internal Revenue Service or the Office of its Chief Counsel relating to any pending civil or criminal case or investigation,

(ii) Communication between Internal Revenue Service employees and employees of the Office of its Chief Counsel,

(iii) Internal memorandum or attorney work product prepared by the Internal Revenue Service or Office of its Chief Counsel which relates to the development of the conclusion of the Internal Revenue Service in a written determination, including, with respect to a technical advice memorandum, the Transmittal Memorandum, as defined in § 601.105(b)(5)(vi)(c) of this chapter,

(iv) Correspondence or any portion of correspondence between the Internal Revenue Service and any person relating solely to the making of or extent of deletions pursuant to section 6110(c), or a request pursuant to section 6110(g)(3) and (4) for postponement of the time at which a written determination is made open or subject to inspection,

(v) Material relating to (A) a request for a ruling or determination letter that is withdrawn prior to issuance thereof or that the Internal Revenue Service declines to answer, (B) a request for technical advice that the National Office declines to answer, or (C) the appeal of a taxpayer from the decision of a district director not to seek technical advice, or

(vi) Response to a request for technical advice which the district director declines to adopt, and the district director's request for reconsideration thereof.

(h) *Issuance.* "Issuance" of a written determination occurs, with respect to rulings and determination letters, upon the mailing of the ruling or determination letter to the person to whom it pertains. Issuance of a technical advice memorandum occurs upon the adoption of the technical advice memorandum by the district director.

(i) *Person to whom written determination pertains.* A "person to whom a written determination pertains" is the person by whom a ruling or determination letter is requested, but if requested by an authorized representative, the person on whose behalf the request is made. With respect to a technical advice memorandum, a "person to whom a written determination pertains" is the taxpayer whose return is being examined or whose claim for refund or credit is being considered.

(j) *Person to whom a background file document relates.* A "person to whom a background file document relates" is the person to whom the related written determination pertains, as such term is defined in paragraph (i) of this section.

(k) *Person who has a direct interest in maintaining confidentiality.* A "person who has a direct interest in maintaining the confidentiality of a written determination" is any person whose name and address is listed in the request for such written determination, as required by § 601.201(e)(2) of this chapter. A "person who has a direct interest in maintaining the confidentiality of a background file document" is any person whose name and address is in such background file document, or who has a direct interest in maintaining the confidentiality of the written determination to which such background file document relates.

(l) *Successor in interest.* A "successor in interest" to any person to whom a written determination pertains or background file document relates is any person who acquires the rights and assumes the liabilities of such person with respect to the transaction which was the subject matter of the written determination, provided that the successor in interest notifies the Commissioner with respect to the respect to the succession in interest.

○── § 301.6110-3 (T.D. 7524, filed 12-15-77.) **Deletion of certain information in written determinations open to public inspection.**

(a) *Information subject to deletion.* There shall be deleted from the text of any written determination open to public inspection or subject to inspection upon written request and background file document subject to inspection upon written request pursuant to section 6110 the following types of information:

(1) *Identifying details*—(i) The names, addresses, and identifying numbers (including telephone, license, social security, employer identification, credit card, and selective service numbers) of any person, other than the identifying details of a person who makes a third-party communication described in § 301.6110-4(a), and

(ii) Any other information that would permit a person generally knowledgeable with respect to the appropriate community to identify any person. The determination of whether information would permit identification of a particular person will be made in view of information available to the public at the time the written determination or background file document is made open or subject to inspection and in view of information that will subsequently become available, provided the Internal Revenue Service is made aware of such information and the potential that such information may identify any person. The "appropriate community" is that group of persons who would be able to associate a particular person with a category of transactions one of which is described in the written determination or background file document. The appropriate community may vary according to the nature of the transaction which is the subject of the written determination. For example, if a steel company proposes to enter a transaction involving the purchase and installation of blast furnaces, the "appropriate community" may include all steel producers and blast furnace manufacturers, but if the installation process is a unique process of which everyone in national industry is aware, the "appropriate community" might also include the national industrial community. On the other hand, if the steel company proposes to enter a transaction involving the purchase of land on which to construct a building to house the blast furnace, the "appropriate community" may also include those residing or doing business within the geographical locale of the land to be purchased.

(2) *Information concerning national defense and foreign policy.* Information specifically authorized under criteria established by an Executive order to be kept secret in the interest of national defense or foreign policy and which is in fact properly classified pursuant to such order.

(3) *Information exempted by other statutes and agency rules.* Information specifically exempted from disclosure by any statute other than the Internal Revenue Code of 1954 and 5 U.S.C. 552 which is applicable to the Internal Revenue Service, and any information obtained by the Internal Revenue Service solely and directly from another Federal agency subject to a nondisclosure rule of such agency. Deletion of information shall not be made solely because the same information was submitted to another Federal agency subject to a nondisclosure rule applicable only to such agency.

(4) *Trade secrets and privileged or confidential commercial or financial information.*—(i) *Deletions to be made.* Any—

(A) Trade secrets, and

(B) Commercial or financial information obtained from any person which, despite the fact that identifying details are deleted pursuant to paragraph (a)(1) of this section, nonetheless remains privileged or confidential.

(ii) *Trade secret.* For purposes of paragraph (a)(4)(i)(A) of this section, a trade secret may consist of any formula, pattern, device or compilation of information that is used in one's business, and that gives one an opportunity to obtain an advantage over competitors who do not know or use it. It may be a formula for a chemical compound, a process of manufacturing, treating or preserving materials, a pattern for a machine or other device, or a list of customers. The subject of a trade secret must be secret, that is, it must not be of public knowledge or of a general knowledge in the trade or business. Novelty, in the patent law sense, is not required for a trade secret.

(iii) *Privileged or confidential.* For purposes of paragraph (a)(4)(i)(B) of this section, information is privileged or confidential if from examination of the request and supporting documents relating to a written determination, and in consideration of the fact that identifying details are deleted pursuant to paragraph (a)(1) of this section, it is determined that disclosure of such information would cause substantial harm to the competitive position of any person. For example, while determining whether disclosure of certain information would cause substantial harm to X's competitive position, the Internal Revenue Service becomes aware that this information has previously been disclosed to the public. In this situation, the Internal Revenue Service will not agree with X's argument that disclosure of the information would cause substantial harm to X's competitive position. An example of information previously disclosed to the public is financial information contained in the published annual reports of widely held public corporations.

(5) *Information within the ambit of personal privacy.* Information the disclosure of which would constitute a clearly unwarranted invasion of personal privacy, despite the fact that identifying details are deleted pursuant to paragraph (a)(1) of this section. Personal privacy information encompasses embarrassing or sensitive information that a reasonable person would not reveal to the public under ordinary circumstances. Matters of personal privacy include, but are not limited to, details not yet public of a pending divorce, medical treatment for physical or mental disease or injury, adoption of a child, the amount of a gift, and political preferences. A clearly unwarranted invasion of personal privacy exists if from analysis of information submitted in support of the request for a written determination it is determined that the public interest purpose for requiring disclosure is outweighed by the potential harm attributable to such invasion of personal privacy.

(6) *Information concerning agency regulation of financial institutions.* Information contained in or related to reports prepared by, on behalf of, or for the use of an agency responsible for the regulation or supervision of financial institutions concerning examination, operation or condition of a financial institution, disclosure of which would damage the standing of such financial institution.

(7) *Information concerning wells.* Geological or geophysical information and data, including maps, concerning wells.

(b) *Manner of deletions.* Whenever information, which is not to be disclosed pursuant to section 6110(c), is deleted from the text of a written determination or background file document, substitutions therefor shall be made to the extent feasible if necessary for an understanding of the legal analysis developed in such written determination or to make the disclosed text of a background file document comprehensible. Wherever any material is deleted, an indication of such deletion, and of any substitution therefor, shall be made in such manner as the Commissioner deems appropriate.

(c) *Limitations on the making of deletions.* Any portion of a written determination or background file document that has been deleted will be restored to the text thereof—

(1) If pursuant to section 6110(d)(3) or (f)(4)(A) a court orders disclosure of such portion, or

(2) If pursuant to § 301.6110-5(d)(1) an agreement is reached to disclose information.

§ 301.6110-4 (T.D. 7524, filed 12-15-77.) **Communications from third parties.**

(a) *General rule.* Except as provided in paragraph (b) of this section, a record will be made of any communication, whether written, by telephone, at a meeting, or otherwise, received by the Internal Revenue Service or Office of its Chief Counsel prior to the issuance of a written determination from any person other than a person to whom the written determination pertains or the authorized representative of such person. This rule applies to any communication concerning such written determination, any communication concerning the request for such written determination, or any communication concerning other matters involving such written determination. A notation that such communication has been made shall be placed on such written determination when it is made open to public inspection or available for inspection upon written request pursuant to § 301.6110-5. The notation to be placed on a written determination shall consist of the date on which the communication was received and the category of the person making such communication, for example, Congressional, Department of Commerce, Treasury, trade association, White House, educational institution. Any person may request the Internal Revenue Service to disclose the name of any person about whom a notation has been made pursuant to this paragraph.

(b) *Limitations.* The provisions of paragraph (a) of this section shall not apply to communications received by the Internal Revenue Service from employees of the Internal Revenue Service or Office of its Chief Counsel, from the Chief of Staff of the Joint Committee on Internal Revenue Taxation, from the Department of Justice with respect to any pending civil or criminal case or investigation, or from another government agency in response to a request made by the Internal Revenue Service to such agency for assistance involving the expertise of such agency.

(c) *Action to obtain disclosure of identity of person to whom written determination pertains*—(1) *Creation of remedy.* With respect to any written determination on which a notation has been placed pursuant to paragraph (a) of this section, any person may file a petition in the United States Tax Court or file a complaint in the United States District Court for the

District of Columbia for an order requiring that the identity of any person to whom such written determination pertains be disclosed, but such petition or complaint must be filed within 36 months of the date such written determination is made open or subject to inspection.

(2) *Necessary disclosure.* Whenever an action is brought pursuant to section 6110 (d)(3), the court may order that the identity of any person to whom the written determination pertains be disclosed. Such disclosure may be ordered if the court determines that there is evidence in the record from which it could reasonably be concluded that an impropriety occurred or undue influence was exercised with respect to such written determination by or on behalf of the person to whom the written determination pertains. The court may, pursuant to section 6110(d)(3), also order the disclosure of any material deleted pursuant to section 6110(c) if such disclosure is in the public interest. The written determination or background file document with respect to which the disclosure was sought shall be revised to disclose the information which the court orders to be disclosed.

(3) *Required notice.* If a proceeding is commenced pursuant to section 6110(d)(3) and paragraph (c)(1) of this section with respect to any written determination, the Secretary shall send notice of the commencement of such proceeding to any person whose identity is subject to being disclosed and to the person about whom a third-party communication notation has been made pursuant to section 6110(d)(1). Such notice shall be sent, by registered or certified mail, to the last known address of the persons described in this (3) within 15 days after notice of the petition or complaint filed pursuant to section 6110(d)(3) is served on the Secretary.

(4) *Intervention.* Any person who is entitled to receive notice pursuant to paragraph (c)(3) of this section shall have the right to intervene in any action brought pursuant to section 6110(d)(3). If appropriate such person shall be permitted to intervene anonymously.

§ 301.6110-5 (T.D. 7524, filed 12-15-77.) **Notice and time requirements; actions to restrain disclosure; actions to obtain additional disclosure.**

(a) *Notice*—(1) *General rule.* Before a written determination is made open to public inspection or subject to inspection upon written request, or before a background file document is subject to inspection upon written request, the person to whom the written determination pertains or background file document relates shall be notified by the Commissioner of intention to disclose such written determination or background file document. The notice with respect to a written determination, other than a written determination described in § 301.6110-1(b)(2) or (3) shall be mailed when such written determination is issued. The notice with respect to any written determination relating to accounting or funding periods and methods, any technical advice memoranda involving civil fraud and criminal investigations, and jeopardy and termination assessments, and any background file document shall be mailed within a reasonable time after the receipt of the first written request for inspection thereof.

(2) *Contents of notice.* The notice required by paragraph (a)(1) of this section shall—

(i) Include a copy of the text of the written determination or background file document, which the Commissioner proposes to make open to public inspection or subject to inspection pursuant to a written request, on which is indicated (A) the material that the Commissioner proposes to delete pursuant to section 6110(c), (B) any substitutions proposed to be made therefor, and (C) any third-party communication notations required to be placed pursuant to § 301.6110-4(a) on the face of the written determination,

(ii) State that the written determination or background file document is to be open to public inspection or subject to inspection pursuant to a written request pursuant to section 6110,

(iii) State that the recipient of the notice has the right to seek administrative remedies pursuant to paragraph (b)(1) of this section and to commence judicial proceedings pursuant to section 6110(f)(3) within indicated time periods, and

(iv) Prominently indicate the date on which the notice is mailed.

(b) *Actions to restrain disclosure*—(1) *Administrative remedies.* Any person to whom a written determination pertains or background file document relates, and any successor in interest, executor or authorized representative of such person may pursue the administrative remedies described in § 601.105(b)(5)(iii)(i) and (vi)(f) and § 601.201(e)(11) and (16) of this chapter. Any person who has a direct interest in maintaining the confidentiality of any written determination or background file document or portion thereof may pursue the administrative remedies described in § 601.105(b)(5)(vi)(f) and § 601.201(e)(16) of this chapter. No person about whom a third-party communication notation has been made pursuant to § 301.6110-4(a) may pursue any administrative remedy for the purpose of restraining disclosure of the identity of such person where such identity appears with respect to the making of such third-party communication.

(2) *Judicial remedy.* Except as provided in paragraph (b)(3) of this section, any person permitted to resort to administrative remedies pursuant to paragraph (b)(1) of this section may, if such person proposes any deletion not made pursuant to § 301.6110-3 by the Commissioner, file a petition in the United States Tax Court pursuant to section 6110(f)(3) for a determination with respect to such proposed deletion. If appropriate, such petition may be filed anonymously. Any petition filed pursuant to section 6110(f)(3) must be filed within 60 days after the date on which the Commissioner mails the notice of intention to disclose required by section 6110(f)(1).

(3) *Limitations on right to bring judicial actions.* No petition shall be filed pursuant to section 6110(f)(3) unless the administrative remedies provided by paragraph (b)(1) of this section have been exhausted. However, if the petitioner has responded within the prescribed time period to the notice pursuant to section 6110(f)(1) of intention to disclose, but has not received the final administrative conclusion

Reg. § 301.6110-5(b)(3)

24,326.10 (I.R.C.)   Reg. § 301.6110-5(b)(3)   12-22-77

of the Internal Revenue Service within 50 days after the date on which the Commissioner mails the notice of intention to disclose required by section 6110(f)(1), the petitioner may file a petition pursuant to section 6110(f)(3). No judicial action with respect to any written determination or background file document shall be commenced pursuant to section 6110(f)(3) by any person who has received a notice with respect to such written determination or background file document pursuant to paragraph (b)(4) of this section.

(4) *Required notice.* If a proceeding is commenced pursuant to section 6110(f)(3) with respect to any written determination or background file document, the Secretary shall send notice of the commencement of such proceeding to any person to whom such written determination pertains or to whom such background file document relates. No notice is required to be sent to persons who have filed the petition that commenced the proceeding pursuant to section 6110(f)(3) with respect to such written determination or background file document. The notice shall be sent, by registered or certified mail, to the last known address of the persons described in this (4) within 15 days after notice of the petition filed pursuant to section 6110(f)(3) is served on the Secretary.

(5) *Intervention.* Any person who is entitled to receive notice pursuant to paragraph (b)(4) of this section shall have the right to intervene in any action brought pursuant to this section. If appropriate, such person shall be permitted to intervene anonymously.

(c) *Time at which open to public inspection*—(1) *General rule.* Except as otherwise provided in paragraph (c)(2) of this section, the text of any written determination or background file document open to public inspection or available for inspection upon written request pursuant to section 6110 shall be made open to or available for inspection no earlier than 75 days and no later than 90 days after the date on which the Commissioner mails the notice required by paragraph (a)(1) of this section. However, if an action is brought pursuant to section 6110(f)(3) to restrain disclosure of any portion of such written determination or background file document the disputed portion of such written determination or background file document shall be made open to or available for inspection pursuant to paragraph (c)(2)(i) of this section.

(2) *Limitations*—(i) *Court order.* The portion of the text of any written determination or background file document that was subject to an action pursuant to section 6110(f)(3) to restrain disclosure in which the court determined that such disclosure should not be restrained shall be made open to or available for inspection within 30 days of the date that the court order becomes final. However, in no event shall such portion of the text of such written determination or background file document be made open to or available for inspection earlier than 75 days after the date on which the Commissioner mails the notice of intention to disclose required by section 6110(f)(1) and paragraph (a)(1) of this section. Such 30-day period may be extended for such time as the court finds necessary to allow the Commissioner to comply with its decision. Any portion of a written determination or background file document which a court orders open to public inspection or subject to inspection upon written request pursuant to section 6110(f)(4) or disclosed pursuant to section 6110(d)(3) shall be made open or subject to inspection or disclosed within such time as the court provides.

(ii) *Postponement based on incomplete status of underlying transaction*—(A) *Initial period not to exceed 90 days.* The time period set forth in paragraph (c)(1) of this section within which a written determination shall be made open to public inspection or available for inspection upon written request shall be extended, upon the written request of the person to whom such written determination pertains or the authorized representative of such person, until 15 days after the date on which the transaction set forth in the written determination is scheduled to be completed, but such day shall be no later than 180 days after the date on which the Commissioner mails the notice of intention to disclose.

(B) *Additional period.* The time period determined pursuant to paragraph (c)(2)(ii)(A) of this section shall be further extended upon an additional written request, if the Commissioner determines from the information contained in such request that good cause exists to warrant such extension. This further extension shall be until 15 days after the date on which the transaction set forth in the written determination is expected to be completed, but such day shall be no later than 360 days after the date on which the Commissioner mails the notice of intention to disclose. The good cause required by this (B) exists if the person requesting the delay in inspection demonstrates to the satisfaction of the Commissioner that it is likely that the lack of such extension will cause interference with consummation of the pending transaction.

(C) *Written request for extension.* The written request for extension of the time when a written determination is to be made open to public inspection or available for inspection upon written request shall set forth the date on which it is expected that the underlying transaction will be completed, and, with respect to the additional extension described in paragraph (c)(2)(ii)(B) of this section, set forth the reason for requesting such extension. A request for extension of time may not be submitted until the notice of intention to disclose is mailed and must be received by the Internal Revenue Service office which issued such written determination no later than—

(1) In the case of the initial extension, 60 days after the date on which the Commissioner mails the notice of intention to disclose, or

(2) In the case of the additional extension, 15 days before the day on which, for purposes of paragraph (c)(2)(ii)(A) of this section, the transaction set forth in the written determination was expected to have been completed.

(D) *Notice and determination of actual completion.* If an extension of time for inspection has been granted, and the transaction is completed prior to the day on which it was expected to have been completed, the Internal Revenue Service office which issued such written determination shall be so notified by the person who requested such extension. In such event, the written determination shall be made open to public inspection or available for inspection upon written request on the earlier of (1) 30 days after the day on which the Commissioner is notified that the transaction is completed, or (2) the day on which the written determination was scheduled to be made open to public inspection or available for inspection upon written request pursuant to paragraph (c)(2)(ii) of this section. Similarly, if the Commissioner determines that the transaction was completed prior to the day on which it was expected to have been completed, even if the person requesting such extension has not so notified the Internal Revenue Service, the written determination shall be made open to public inspection or available for inspection upon written request on the earlier of (1) the day which is 30 days after the Commissioner ascertains that the transaction is completed sooner than has been expected, or (2) the day on which the written determination was scheduled to be made open to public inspection or available for inspection upon written request pursuant to paragraph (c)(2)(ii) of this section.

(d) *Actions to obtain additional disclosure*—(1) *Administrative remedies.* Under section 6110(f)(4) any person may seek to obtain additional disclosure of information contained in any written determination or background file document that has been made open or subject to inspection. A request for such additional disclosure shall be submitted to the Internal Revenue Service office which issued such written determination, or to which the request for inspection of such background file document has been submitted pursuant to § 301.6110-1(c)(4), and must contain the file number of the written determination or a description of the background file document (including the file number of the related written determination), the deleted information which in the opinion of such person should be open or subject to inspection, and the basis for such opinion. If the Internal Revenue Service determines that the request constitutes a request for disclosure of the name, address, or the identifying numbers described in § 301.6110-3(a)(1)(i) of any person, it shall within a reasonable time notify the person requesting such disclosure that disclosure will not be made. If the Internal Revenue Service determines that the request or any portion thereof constitutes a request for disclosure of information other than the name, address, or the identifying numbers described in § 301.6110-3(a)(1)(i) of any person, it shall send a notice that such additional disclosure has been requested to any person to whom the written determination or background file document relates, and to all persons who are identified by name and address in the written determination or background file document. Notice that such persons have been contacted shall be sent to the person requesting the additional disclosure. The notice that additional disclosure has been requested shall state that the Internal Revenue Service has determined that additional disclosure of information other than the name, address, or the identifying numbers described in § 301.6110-3(a)(1)(i) of any person has been requested, inform the recipient of the notice that the person seeking the additional disclosure has the right under section 6110(f)(4) to bring a judicial action to attempt to compel such disclosure, and request the recipient of the notice to reply within 20 days by submitting a statement of whether or not the recipient of the notice agrees to the requested disclosure or portion thereof. If all persons to whom a notice is sent pursuant to this (1) agree to disclose the requested information or any portion thereof, the person seeking such disclosure will be so informed; the written determination or background file document shall be accordingly revised to disclose the information with respect to which an agreement to disclose has been reached. If any of the persons to whom a notice is sent pursuant to this (1) do not agree to the additional disclosure or do not respond to such notice, the Internal Revenue Service shall within a reasonable time so notify the person requesting such disclosure, and deny the request for additional disclosure.

(2) *Judicial remedy.* Except as provided in paragraph (d)(3) of this section, any person who seeks to obtain additional disclosure of information contained in any written determination or background file document may file a petition pursuant to section 6110(f)(4) in the United States Tax Court or a complaint in the United States District Court for the District of Columbia for an order requiring that such information be made open or subject to inspection. Nothing in this paragraph shall prevent the Commissioner from disposing of written determinations and related background file documents pursuant to § 301.6110-7(a)

(3) *Limitations on right to bring judicial action*—(i) *Exhaustion of administrative remedies.* No petition or complaint shall be filed pursuant to section 6110(f)(4) unless the administrative remedies provided by paragraph (d)(1) of this section have been exhausted. However, if the Internal Revenue Service does not approve or deny the request for additional disclosure within 180 days after the request is submitted, the person making the request may file a petition pursuant to section 6110(f)(4).

(ii) *Actions to obtain identity.* No petition or complaint shall be filed pursuant to section 6110(f)(4) to obtain disclosure of the identity of any person to whom a written determination on which a third-party communication notation has been placed pursuant to § 301.6110-4(a) pertains. Such actions shall be brought pursuant to section 6110 (d)(3).

(4) *Required notice.* If a proceeding is commenced pursuant to section 6110(f)(4) with respect to any written determination or background file document, the Secretary shall send notice of the commencement if such proceeding to any person to whom the written determination pertains or background file document relates, and to all persons who are identified by name and address in the written determination or background file document. The notice shall be sent, by registered or certified mail to the last known address of the persons described in this (4) within 15 days after notice of the petition a complaint filed pursuant to section 6110(f)(4) is served on the Secretary.

(5) *Intervention.* Any person who is entitled to receive notice pursuant to paragraph (d)(4) of this section shall have the right to intervene in any action brought

Reg. § 301.6110-5(d)(5)

24,326.12 (I.R.C.)   Reg. § 301.6110-5(d)(5)   5-22-78

pursuant to this section. If appropriate, such person shall be permitted to intervene anonymously.

§ 301.6110-6 (T.D. 7524, filed 12-15-77; amended by T.D. 7548, filed 5-12-78.) **Written determinations issued in response to requests submitted before November 1, 1976.**

(a) *Inspection of written determinations and background file documents*—(1) *General rule.* Except as provided in this section, the text of any written determination issued in response to a request postmarked or hand delivered before November 1, 1976 and any related background file document shall be open or subject to inspection in accordance with the rules in §§ 301.6110-1 through 301.6110-5 and 301.6110-7. However, the rules in § 301.6110-4 do not apply to inspection under this section. The rules in § 301.6110-5(a), (b) and (c) also do not apply, except with respect to background file documents.

(2) *Exclusions.* The following written determinations are not open or subject to inspection:

(i) Written determinations with respect to matters for which the determination of whether public inspection should occur is made under section 6104. Some of these matters are listed in § 301.6110-1(a).

(ii) Written determinations issued before September 2, 1974, dealing with the qualification of a plan described in section 6104(a)(1)(B)(i) or the exemption from tax under section 501(a) of an organization forming part of such a plan.

(iii) General written determinations that relate solely to accounting or funding periods and methods, as defined in § 301.-6110-1(b)(3).

(iv) Determination letters.

(v) Written determinations issued pursuant to requests submitted before November 1, 1976 with respect to the exempt status under section 501(a) of organizations described in section 501(c) or (d), the status of organizations as private foundations under section 509(a), or the status of organizations as operating foundations under section 4942(j)(3).

(3) *Items that may be inspected only under certain circumstances*—(i) *Background file documents.* A background file document relating to a particular written determination issued in response to a request submitted before November 1, 1976 shall not be subject to inspection until the related written determination is open to public inspection or available for inspection, and then only if a written request pursuant to § 301.6110-1(c)(4) is made for inspection of the background file document. However, the following background file documents are not open or subject to inspection.

(A) Background file documents relating to general written determinations issued before July 5, 1967.

(B) Background file documents relating to written determinations described in paragraph (a)(2) of this section.

(ii) *General written determinations issued before July 5, 1967.* General written determinations issued before July 5, 1967 shall not be subject to inspection until all other written determinations issued in response to requests postmarked or hand delivered before November 1, 1976 that are open to inspection under this section have been made open to public inspection, and then only if a written request pursuant to § 301.6110-1(c)(4) is made for inspection of the written determination. In this regard, the request for inspection must also contain the section of the Internal Revenue Code in which the requester is interested and the dates of issuance of the written determinations.

(b) *Notice and time requirements, and actions to restrain disclosure*—(1) *Notice* —(i) *General rule.* Before a written determination is made open to public inspection and before a particular written determination is subject to inspection in response to the first written request therefor, the Commissioner shall publish in the Federal Register a notice that the written determination is to be made open or subject to inspection. Notices with respect to written determinations, other than those described in paragraph (a)(3)(ii) of this section, shall be published at the earliest practicable time after this regulation is adopteд as a Treasury decision. Notices with respect to written determinations subject to inspection upon written request shall be published within a reasonable time after the receipt of the first written request for inspection thereof, but no sooner than the day as of which all other written determinations open to public inspection under this section have been made open to public inspection. Notices with respect to background file documents shall be sent in accordance with the rules in § 301.6110-5(a) and will be mailed by the Internal Revenue Service to the most recent addresses of the persons to whom the background file document relates that are in the written determination file.

(ii) *Sequence of notices.* Notices with respect to written determinations, other than general written determinations issued before July 5, 1967, shall be published in the following order. The first category is notices with respect to reference written determinations issued under the Internal Revenue Code of 1954. The second category is notices with respect to general written determinations issued after July 4, 1967. The third category is notices with respect to reference written determinations issued under the Internal Revenue Code of 1939 or corresponding provisions of prior law. Within a category, the Commissioner may publish notices individually or for groups of written determinations arranged according to the jurisdictions of the ruling branches in the Offices of the Assistant Commissioner (Technical) and the Assistant Commissioner (Employee Plans and Exempt Organizations), as the Commissioner may find reasonable. To the extent practicable, notices published individually shall be published in the reverse order of the issuance of the written determinations for which they are published, starting with the most recent written determination issued. To the extent practicable, each group shall consist of consecutively issued written determinations. Notices for groups shall be published, to the extent practicable, in the reverse order of the time period of issuance of the written determinations in each group, starting with the most recent time period.

(iii) *Contents of notice.* The notice required by paragraph (b)(1)(i) of this section shall—

(A) Identify by subject matter description and dates of issuance the written determinations that the Commissioner proposes to make open or subject to inspection,

(B) State that the written determinations will be made open or subject to inspection pursuant to section 6110(h),

(C) State that the persons to whom the written determinations pertain have the right to seek administrative remedies under paragraph (b)(2)(ii) of this section and to commence judicial proceedings under section 6110(h)(4) within indicated time periods,

(D) State that there exist the possibilities that someone might request additional disclosure under section 6110(f)(4) and that someone might request inspection of a related background file document, and

(E) State that any notice that must be mailed by the Internal Revenue Service will be sent to the most recent address of the pesrson to whom the notice must be sent that is in the relevant written determination file.

(2) *Actions to restrain disclosure*—(i) *Information on written determinations described by notice.* Any person may, within 15 days after the Commissioner publishes in the Federal Register a notice of intention to disclose a written determination under section 6110(h), request the Internal Revenue Service to provide certain information. This information includes whether any of the written determinations described by the notice is one that was issued to the person requesting this information. The Internal Revenue Service will also inform the person whether any of the written determinations described by the notice is one that was issued to a person with respect to whom the person requesting this information is a successor in interest, executor or authorized representative. However, in order to do so, the Internal Revenue Service must be given the name and taxpayer identifying number of this other person and documentation of the relationship between that person and the person requesting the information. If the person requesting this information is a person to whom a written determination described by the notice pertains, or a successor in interest, executor, or authorized representative of that person, the Internal Revenue Service will also provide the person with a copy of the written determination on which is indicated the material that the Commissioner proposes to delete under section 6110 (c) and any substitution proposed to be made therefor.

(ii) *Administrative remedies.* Any person to whom a written determination described by the notice in the Federal Register pertains, and any successor in interest, executor or authorized representative of that person may pursue the administrative remedies described in this paragraph (b)(2)(ii). If, after receiving the information described in paragraph (b)(2)(i) of this section, the person pursuing these administrative remedies desires to protest the disclosure of certain information in the written determination, that person must within 35 days after the notice is published submit a written statement identifying those deletions not made by the Internal Revenue Service which the person believes should have been made. The person pursuing these administrative remedies must also submit a copy of the version of the written determination proposed to be open or subject to inspection on which that person indicates, by the use of brackets, the deletions which the person believes should have been made. The Internal Revenue Service shall, within 20 days after receipt of the response by the person pursuing these administrative remedies, mail to that person its final administrative conclusion with respect to the deletions to be made.

(iii) *Judicial remedy.* Except as provided in paragraph (b)(2)(iv) of this section, any person permitted to resort to administrative remedies under paragraph (b)(2)(ii) of this section may, if that person proposed any deletion not made under section 6110(c) by the Commissioner, file a petition in the United States Tax Court under section 6110(h)(4) for a determination with respect to the proposed deletion. If appropriate, the petition may be filed anonymously. Any petition filed under section 6110(h)(4) must be filed within 75 days after the date on which the Commissioner publishes in the Federal Register the notice of intention to disclose required under section 6110(h)(4).

(iv) *Limitations on right to bring judicial actions.* No petition shall be filed under section 6110(h)(4) unless the administrative remedies provided by paragraph (b)(2)(ii) of this section have been exhausted. However, under two circumstances the petition may be filed even though the administrative remedies have not been exhausted. The first circumstance is if the petitioner requests the information described in paragraph (b)(2)(i) of this section within 15 days after the notice of intention to disclose is published in the Federal Register, but does not receive it within 30 days after the notice is published. The other circumstance is if the petitioner submits the statement of deletions within 35 days after the notice is published, but does not receive the final administrative conclusion of the Internal Revenue Service within 65 days after the notice is published. No judicial action with respect to any written determination shall be commenced under section 6110(h)(4) by any person who has received a notice with respect to the written determination under paragraph (b)(2)(v) of this section.

(v) *Required notice.* If a proceeding is commenced under section 6110(h)(4) with respect to any written determination, the Secretary shall send notice of the commencement of the proceeding to any person to whom the written determination pertains. No notice is required to be sent to persons who have filed the petition that commenced the proceeding under section 6110(h)(4) with respect to the written determination. The notice shall be sent, by registered or certified mail, to the last known address of the persons described in this paragraph (b)(2)(v) within 15 days after notice of the petition filed under section 6110(h)(4) is served on the Secretary.

(vi) *Intervention.* Any person who is entitled to receive notice under paragraph (b)(2)(v) of this section has the right to

Reg. § 301.6110-6(b)(2)

24,326.14 (I.R.C.)   Reg. § 301.6110-6(b)(2)   5-22-78

intervene in any action brought under this paragraph (b)(2). If appropriate, this person shall be permitted to intervene anonymously.

(vii) *Background file documents.* The following qualifications of the rules in § 301.- 6110-5(b) apply with respect to the restraint of disclosure of background file documents related to written determinations to which this section applies. First, the administrative remedies described in §§ 601.105(b)(5)(iii)(i) and 601.201(e)(11) of this chapter do not apply. Second, the rule in those sections that the Internal Revenue Service will not consider the deletion of material not proposed for deletion prior to the issuance of the written determination does not apply.

(3) *Time at which open to public inspection*—(i) *General rule.* Except as otherwise provided in paragraph (b)(3)(ii) of this section, the text of any written determination open to public inpsection or available for inspection upon written request under section 6110 shall be made open to or available for inspection no earlier than 90 days and no later than 120 days after the date on which the Commissioner publishes in the Federal Register the notice of intention to disclose required under section 6110(h)(4). However, if an action is brought under section 6110(h)(4) to restrain disclosure of any portion of a written determination, the disputed portion of that written determination shall be made upon to or available for inspection under paragraph (b)(3)(ii) of this section.

(ii) *Limitation on account of court order.* The portion of the text of any written determination that was subject to an action under section 6110(h)(4) to restrain disclosure in which the court determined that the disclosure should not be restrained shall be made open to or available for inspection within 30 days of the date that the court order becomes final. However, in no event shall that portion of the text of that written determination be made open to or available for inspection earlier than 90 days after the date on which the Commissioner publishes in the Federal Register the notice of intention to disclose required by section 6110(h)(4) and paragraph (b)(1) of this section. This 30-day period may be extended for such time as the court finds necessary to allow the Commissioner to comply with its decision. Any portion of a written determination which a court orders open to public inspection or subject to inspection upon written request under section 6110(f)(4) shall be open or subject to inspection within such time as the court provides.

(iii) *Background file documents.* The rules in § 301.6110-5(c)(2)(ii) do not apply with respect to the time at which background file documents related to written determinations to which this section applies are subject to inspection.

○→ § 301.6110-7 (T.D. 7524, filed 12-15-77.) Miscellaneous provisions.

(a) *Disposition of written determinations and background file documents*—(1) *Reference written determinations.* The Internal Revenue Service shall not dispose of any reference written determination or related background file documents. The Commissioner may reclassify reference written determinations as general written determinations if the classification as reference was erroneous or if the Commissioner determines that such written determination no longer has any significant reference value. Notwithstanding the preceding sentence, the Commissioner shall not classify as a general written determination any written determination which is determined to be the basis for a published Revenue Ruling unless such Revenue Ruling is obsoleted, revoked, superseded or otherwise held to have no effect.

(2) *General written determinations* The Internal Revenue Service may dispose of general written determinations and any background file document relating to such written determination pursuant to its established records disposition procedures. Disposition of a written determination shall not occur earlier than 3 years after the date on which such written determination is made open to public inspection or available for inspection upon written request. Disposition of a background file document shall not occur earlier than 3 years after the date on which the related written determination is made open to public inspection or available for inspection upon written request.

(b) *Precedential status of written determination open to public inspection.* A written determination may not be used or cited as precedent, but the rule set forth in this paragraph shall not apply to change the precedential status, if any, of written determinations issued with respect to taxes imposed by subtitle D of the Internal Revenue Code of 1954.

(c) *Civil remedies*—(1) *Liability for failure to make deletions or to conform to time limitations*—(i) *Creation of remedy.* An exclusive remedy against the Commissioner shall exist in the Court of Claims for—

(A) The person to whom the written determination pertains whenever the Commissioner fails to act in accordance with the time requirements of section 6110(g), and

(B) The person to whom the written determination pertains and any person identified in such written determination whenever the Commissioner fails to make deletions required by section 6110(c) if as a consequence of such failure there is disclosed the identity of such person or other information with respect to such person that is required to be deleted pursuant to section 6110(c).

(ii) *Limitations.* The remedy provided in paragraph (c)(1)(i) of this section for failure to make deletions shall be available only if—

(A) The failure of the Commissioner to make the deletions required by section 6110(c) is intentional or willful,

(B) The Commissioner fails to make any deletion required by section 6110(c) which the Commissioner has agreed to make, or

(C) The Commissioner fails to make any deletion which a court has ordered to be made pursuant to section 6110(f)(3).

(iii) *Damages.* In any suit brought pursuant to paragraph (c)(1)(i) of this section in which that court determines that an employee of the Internal Revenue Service intentionally or willfully failed to make a deletion required by section 6110(c), or intentionally or willfully failed to act in accordance with the time requirements of section 6110(g), the United States shall be liable, to the person described in paragraph (c)(1)(i) of this section who brought the action, in an amount equal to the sum of—

(A) Actual damages sustained by such person but in no case shall such person be entitled to receive less than the sum of $1,000,

(B) The costs of the action, and

(C) Reasonable attorney's fees as determined by the court.

(2) *Liability for making additional disclosure of information.* The Commissioner shall not be liable for making any additional disclosure ordered pursuant to an action described in § 301.6110-5(d)(2) if the notice required by § 301.6110-5(d)(4) is sent.

(3) *Obligation to defend action for additional disclosure.* The Commissioner shall not be required to defend any action brought to obtain additional disclosure pursuant to section 6110(f)(4) if the notice required by § 301.6110-5(d)(4) is sent.

(4) *Obligation to make deletions.* The Commissioner shall be obligated to make only those deletions required by section 6110 (c) which he has agreed to make, those which a court has ordered to be made pursuant to § 301.6110-5(b)(2) and those the omission of which would be intentional or willful.

(d) *Fees*—(1) *General rule*—(i) *Copies.* The Commissioner may prescribe fees pursuant to § 601.702(f)(4) of this chapter for the costs of furnishing copies of material open to public inspection or subject to inspection upon written request pursuant to section 6110.

(ii) *Preparation of information available upon request.* The Commissioner may prescribe fees pursuant to § 601.702(f) of this chapter for the costs of searching for and making deletions from any written determinations and background file documents that are subject to inspection only upon written request pursuant to § 301.6110-1(b).

(2) *Reduction or waiver of fees*—(i) *Public interest.* The Commissioner shall reduce or waive the fees described in paragraph (d)(1) of this section if the Commissioner determines that furnishing copies of, searching for, or making deletions to any written determination or background file document primarily benefits the general public, as described in § 601.702(f)(2)(ii)(B) of this chapter.

(ii) *Previous requests.* The Commissioner may waive the fees described in paragraph (d)(1) of this section for searching for any written determination or background file document if the search for such written determination or background file document was made pursuant to a previous request for inspection thereof. The Commissioner shall waive the fees described in paragraph (d)(1) of this section for making deletions from any written determination or background file document if the making of such deletions from such written determination or background file document was made pursuant to a previous request for inspection thereof. Nothing in this (d) (2)(ii) shall prevent the Commissioner from prescribing fees for making additional deletions from such written determination or background file document pursuant to § 301.6110-5(b).

○━▶ § 301.6111 (Redesignated by T.D. 7424, filed 12-15-77.) **Statutory provisions; cross references.** [Sec. 6110, IRC]

Reg. § 301.6111

TIME AND PLACE FOR PAYING TAX
PLACE AND DUE DATE FOR PAYMENT OF TAX

§ 1.6151 Statutory provisions; time and place for paying tax shown on returns. [Sec. 6151, IRC]

§ 1.6151-1 (T.D. 6364, filed 2-13-59; republished in T.D. 6500, filed 11-25-60; amended by T.D. 6914, filed 3-7-67; T.D. 6922, filed 6-16-67; T.D. 6950, filed 4-3-68 and T.D. 7102, filed 3-23-71.) **Time and place for paying tax shown on returns.**

(a) *In general.* Except as provided in section 6152 and paragraph (b) of this section, the tax shown on any income tax return shall, without assessment or notice and demand, be paid to the internal revenue officer with whom the return is filed at the time fixed for filing the return (determined without regard to any extension of time for filing the return). For provisions relating to the time for filing income tax returns, see section 6072 and §§ 1.6072-1 to 1.6072-4, inclusive. For provisions relating to the place for filing income tax returns, see section 6091 and §§ 1.6091-1 to 1.6091-4, inclusive.

(b) *Returns on which tax is not shown.* If a taxpayer files a return and, in accordance with section 6014 and the regulations thereunder, elects not to show the tax on the return, the amount of tax determined to be due shall be paid within 30 days after the date of mailing to the taxpayer a notice stating the amount payable and making demand upon the taxpayer therefor. However, if the notice is mailed to the taxpayer more than 30 days before the due date of the return, payment of the tax shall not be required prior to such due date.

(c) *Date fixed for payment of tax.* In any case in which a tax imposed by subtitle A of the Code is required to be paid on or before a certain date, or within a certain period, any reference in subtitle A or F of the Code to the date fixed for payment of such tax shall be deemed a reference to the last day fixed for such payment (determined without regard to any extension of time for paying the tax).

(d) *Use of Government depositaries.* (1) For provisions relating to the use of Federal Reserve banks or authorized commercial banks in depositing income and estimated income taxes of certain corporations, see § 1.6302-1.

(2) For provisions relating to the use of such banks for the deposit of taxes required to be withheld under chapter 3 of the Code on nonresident aliens and foreign corporations and tax-free covenant bonds, see § 1.6302-2.

§ 31.6151 Statutory provisions; time and place for paying tax shown on returns. [Sec. 6151, IRC]

§ 31.6151-1 (T.D. 6354, filed 1-13-59; republished in T.D. 6516, filed 12-19-60; amended by T.D. 6872, filed 1-5-66; T.D. 6915, filed 3-28-67 and T.D. 7037, filed 4-27-70.) **Time for paying tax.**

(a) *In general.* The tax required to be reported on each tax return required under this subpart is due and payable to the internal revenue officer with whom the return is filed at the time prescribed in § 31.6071 (a)-1 for filing such return. See the applicable sections in Part 301 of this chapter (Regulations on Procedure and Administration), for provisions relating to interest on underpayments, additions to tax, and penalties.

(b) *Cross references.* For provisions relating to the use of Federal Reserve banks and authorized commercial banks in depositing the taxes, see §§ 31.6302(c)-1, 31.-6302(c)-2, and 31.6302(c)-3. For rules relating to the payment of taxes in nonconvertible foreign currency, see § 301.6316-7 of this chapter (Regulations on Procedure and Administration).

§ 53.6151 Statutory provisions; time and place for paying tax shown on returns. [Sec. 6151, IRC]

§ 53.6151-1 (T.D. 7368, filed 7-15-75.) **Time and place for paying tax shown on returns.**

The chapter 42 tax shown on any return shall, without assessment or notice and demand, be paid to the internal revenue officer with whom the return is filed at the time and place for filing such return (determined without regard to any extension of time for filing the return). For provisions relating to the time and place for filing such return, see §§ 53.6071-1 and 53.6091-1. For provisions relating to the extension of time for paying the tax, see § 53.6161-1.

§ 301.6151 Statutory provisions; time and place for paying tax shown on returns. [Sec. 6151, IRC]

§ 301.6151-1 (T.D. 6498, filed 10-24-60.) **Time and place for paying tax shown on returns.**

For provisions concerning the time and place for paying tax shown on returns with respect to a particular tax, see the regulations relating to such tax.

§ 1.6152 Statutory provisions; installment payments. [Sec. 6152, IRC]

§ 1.6152-1 (T.D. 6364, filed 2-13-59; republished in T.D. 6500, filed 11-25-60; amended by T.D. 6914, filed 3-7-67.) **Installment payments.**

(a) *Privilege of corporation to elect to make installment payments*—(1) *Amount to be paid.* In the case of any taxable year ending on or after December 31, 1954, a corporation subject to the taxes imposed by chapter 1 of the Code may elect, as provided in subparagraph (2) of this paragraph, to pay the unpaid amount of such tax for the taxable year in two equal installments instead of making a single payment. If such an election is made, the installments shall be paid as follows:

(i) Fifty percent on or before the date prescribed for the payment of the tax as a single payment, and

(ii) The remaining 50 percent on or before three months after the date prescribed for the payment of the first installment. For provisions relating to installment payment of estimated income tax by corporations, see section 6154 and §§ 1.6154-1 to 1.6154-3, inclusive.

(2) *Method of election.* A corporation shall be considered to have made an election to pay its tax in installments if—

(i) It files its income tax return on or before the date prescribed therefor (determined without regard to any extension

Reg. § 1.6152-1 (a) (2)

24,328 (I.R.C.) Reg. § 1.6152-1(a)(2) 7-21-75

of time) and pays 50 percent of the unpaid amount of the tax at such time, or

(ii) It files an application on Form 7004 for an automatic extension of time to file its income tax return, as provided in § 1.6081-3, and pays 50 percent of the unpaid amount of the tax at such time.

Except as provided in paragraph (c) of this section, the installment privilege is limited to the unpaid amount of tax as shown on the income tax return filed in accordance with the provisions of subdivision (i) of this subparagraph, or as shown on the Form 7004 filed in accordance with the provisions of this subdivision.

(3) *Use of Government depositaries.* For provisions relating to the use of Federal Reserve banks and authorized commercial banks in depositing the taxes see § 1.6302-1.

(b) *Privilege of estates of decedents to make installment payments.* With respect to the income tax imposed by chapter 1 of the Code upon estates of decedents, the fiduciary may elect to pay the tax in four equal installments instead of in a single payment. If the election is made, the tax shall be paid as follows:

(1) Twenty-five percent on or before the date prescribed for the payment of the tax as a single payment,

(2) Twenty-five percent on or before three months after the date prescribed for payment of the first installment,

(3) Twenty-five percent on or before six months after the date prescribed for payment of the first installment, and

(4) Twenty-five percent on or before nine months after the date prescribed for payment of the first installment.

(c) *Proration of deficiency to installments.* If an election has been made to pay the tax imposed by chapter 1 of the Code in installments, and a deficiency has been assessed, the deficiency shall be prorated equally to all the installments, whether paid or unpaid. Except as provided in section 6861, relating to jeopardy assessment, the part of the deficiency so prorated to any installment which is not yet due shall be collected at the same time as and as part of such installment. The part of the deficiency so prorated to any installment the date for payment of which has arrived shall be paid upon notice and demand from the district director.

(d) *Acceleration of payment.* If a taxpayer elects under the provisions of this section to pay the tax in installments, any installment may be paid prior to the date prescribed for its payment. If an installment is not paid in full on or before the date fixed for its payment the whole amount of the unpaid tax shall be paid upon notice and demand from the district director.

○— § 301.6152 **Statutory provisions; installment payments.** [Sec. 6152, IRC]

○— § 301.6152-1 (T.D. 6498, filed 10-24-60.) **Installment payments.**

For provisions relating to the installment payments of income taxes, see § 1.6152-1 of this chapter (Income Tax Regulations).

○— § 1.6153 **Statutory provisions; installment payments of estimated income tax by individuals.** [Sec. 6153, IRC]

○— § 1.6153-1 (T.D. 6267, filed 11-13-57; republished in T.D. 6500, filed 11-25-60; amended by T.D. 6678, filed 9-30-63.) **Payment of estimated tax by individuals.**

(a) *In general.* (1) The time for payment of the estimated tax by individuals for calendar years shall be as follows:

Date of filing declaration	Dates of payment of estimated tax
(i) On or before April 15......	In 4 equal installments— one at time of filing declaration, one on or before June 15, one on or before September 15, and one on or before January 15 of the succeeding taxable year.
(ii) After April 15 and before June 16 if not required to be filed on or before April 15.	In 3 equal installments—one at time of filing declaration, one on or before September 15, and one on or before January 15 of the succeeding taxable year.
(iii) After June 15 and before September 16 if not required to be filed on or before June 15.	In 2 equal installments—one at time of filing declaration, and the other on or before January 15 of the succeeding taxable year.
(iv) After September 15 if not required to be filed on or before September 15.	In full at time of filing declaration.

(2) If, for example, due to the nature and amount of his gross income for 1955, the taxpayer is not required to file his declaration as of April 15, but is required to file the declaration on or before June 15, 1955, the case comes within the scope of subparagraph (1)(ii) of this paragraph and the estimated tax is payable in 3 equal installments, the 1st on the date of filing, the 2d on or before September 15, 1955, and the 3d installment on or before January 15, 1956.

(3) If a declaration is filed after the time prescribed in section 6073(a) (including any extension of time granted for filing the declaration), there shall be paid at such time all installments of the estimated tax which would have been payable on or before such date of filing if the declaration had been timely filed in accordance with the provisions of section 6073(a). The remaining installments shall be paid at the times and in the amounts in which they would have been payable if the declaration had been timely filed. Thus, for example, B, a single man who makes his return on the calendar year basis, was employed from the beginning of 1955 and for several years prior thereto at an annual salary of $6,000, thus meeting the requirements of section 6015(a). B filed his declaration for 1955 on September 16,

1955. In such case, B should have filed a declaration on or before April 15, 1955, and at the time of filing his declaration he was delinquent in the payment of three installments of his estimated tax for the taxable year 1955. Hence, upon his filing the declaration on September 16, 1955, three-fourths of the estimated tax shown thereon must be paid.

(4) In the case of a decedent, payments of estimated tax are not required subsequent to the date of death. See, however, paragraph (c), of § 1.6015(b)-1, relating to the making of an amended declaration by a surviving spouse if a joint declaration was made before the death of the decedent.

(5) The payment of any installment of the estimated tax shall be considered payment on account of the tax for such taxable year. Hence, upon the return for such taxable year, the aggregate amount of the payments of estimated tax should be entered as payments to be applied against the tax shown on such return.

(b) *Farmers or fishermen.* Special provisions are made with respect to the filing of the declaration and the payment of the tax by an individual whose estimated gross income from farming or, with respect to taxable years beginning after December 31, 1962, from fishing is at least two-thirds of his total gross income from all sources for the taxable year. As to what constitutes income from farming or fishing within the meaning of this paragraph, see paragraph (b) of § 1.6073-1. The declaration of such an individual may be filed on or before January 15 of the succeeding taxable year in lieu of the time prescribed for individuals generally. Where such an individual makes a declaration of estimated tax after September 15 of the taxable year, the estimated tax shall be paid in full at the time of the filing of the declaration.

(c) *Amendment of declaration.* If any amendment of a declaration is filed, the remaining installments, if any, shall be ratably increased or decreased, as the case may be, to reflect the increase or decrease in the estimated tax by reason of the amendment. If any amendment is made after September 15 of the taxable year, any increase in the estimated tax by reason thereof shall be paid at the time of making the amendment.

(d) *Installments paid in advance.* At the election of the taxpayer any installment of the estimated tax may be paid prior to the date prescribed for its payment.

O— § 1.6153-2 (T.D. 6267, filed 11-13-57; republished in T.D. 6500, filed 11-25-60.) **Fiscal years.**

In the case of an individual on the fiscal year basis, the dates prescribed for payment of the estimated tax shall be the 15th day of the 4th month, the 15th day of the 6th month, and the 15th day of the 9th month of the taxable year and the 15th day of the 1st month of the succeeding taxable year. For example, if an individual having a fiscal year ending on June 30, 1956, first meets the requirements of section 6015 (a) on January 15, 1956, and the declaration is filed on or before March 15, 1956, the estimated tax shall be paid in 2 equal installments, one at the time of filing of such declaration and the other on or before July 15, 1956.

O— § 1.6153-3 (T.D. 6267, filed 11-13-57; republished in T.D. 6500, filed 11-25-60.) **Short taxable years.**

In the case of a short taxable year of an individual for which a declaration is required to be filed the estimated tax shall be paid in equal installments, one at the time of filing the declaration, one on the 15th of the 6th month of the taxable year and another on the 15th day of the 9th month of such year unless the short taxable year closed during or prior to such 6th or 9th month, and one on the 15th day of the 1st month of the succeeding taxable year. For example, if the short taxable year is the period of 10 months from January 1, 1955, to October 31, 1955, and the declaration is required to be filed on or before April 15, 1955, the estimated tax is payable in 4 equal installments, one on the date of filing the declaration, and one each on June 15, September 15, and November 15, 1955. If in such case the declaration is required to be filed after April 15 but on or before June 15, the tax will be payable in 3 equal installments, one on the date of filing the declaration, and one each on September 15 and November 15, 1955. The provisions of paragraph (a)(3) of § 1.-6153-1, relating to payment of estimated tax in any case in which the declaration is filed after the time prescribed in section 6073 and §§ 1.6073-1 to 1.6073-4, inclusive, are equally applicable to the payment of the estimated tax for short taxable years.

O— § 1.6153-4 (T.D. 6267, filed 11-13-57; republished in T.D. 6500, filed 11-25-60; amended by T.D. 6950, filed 4-3-68.) **Extension of time for paying the estimated tax.**

An extension of time granted an individual under section 6081 for filing the declaration of estimated tax automatically extends the time for paying the estimated tax (without interest) for the same period. See § 1.6073-4 for rules relating to extensions of time for filing declarations of estimated tax by individuals. Except as provided in paragraph (b) of § 301.6091-1 (relating to hand-carried documents), an application for an extension of time for paying a particular installment of the estimated tax shall be addressed to the internal revenue officer with whom the taxpayer files his declaration. Each application must contain a full recital of the causes for the delay. Such extension may be for a reasonable period not to exceed 6 months from the date fixed for payment thereof except in the case of a taxpayer who is abroad. Such extension does not relieve the taxpayer from the addition to the tax imposed by section 6654, and the period of the underpayment will be determined under section 6654 (c) without regard to such extension.

O— § 301.6153 **Statutory provisions; installment payments of estimated income tax by individuals.** [Sec. 6153, IRC]

O— § 301.6153-1 (T.D. 6498, filed 10-24-60.) **Installment payments of estimated income tax by individuals.**

Reg. § 301.6153-1

24,330 (I.R.C.) Reg. § 301.6153-1 4-8-68

For provisions relating to installment payments of estimated income tax by individuals, see §§ 1.6153-1 to 1.6153-4, inclusive, of this chapter (Income Tax Regulations).

§ 1.6154 Statutory provisions; installment payments of estimated income tax by corporations. [Sec. 6154, IRC]

§ 1.6154-1 (T.D. 6267, filed 11-13-57; republished in T.D. 6500, filed 11-25-60; amended by T. D. 6768, filed 11-3-64.) **Payment of estimated tax by corporations.**

(a) *Taxable years beginning on or before December 31, 1963*—(1) *Amount required to be paid.* Every corporation required to file a declaration of estimated tax for a taxable year beginning on or before December 31, 1963, shall pay the following percentage of its estimated tax:

If the taxable year ends—	The amount required to be paid is the following percentage of the estimated tax:
On or after December 31, 1955, and before December 31, 1956	10
On or after December 31, 1956, and before December 31, 1957	20
On or after December 31, 1957, and before December 31, 1958	30
On or after December 31, 1958, and before December 31, 1959	40
On or after December 31, 1959	50

(2) *Time for payment.* (i) In the case of a corporation on the calendar year basis which files its declaration on or before September 15 of the taxable year, the percentage of the estimated tax required to be paid is payable in two equal installments, one at the time of filing the declaration, and the other on or before December 15 of the taxable year. If the corporation files its declaration after September 15 of the taxable year, the percentage of the estimated tax required to be paid is payable in full on or before December 15 of the taxable year.

(ii) In the case of a corporation whose taxable year is a fiscal year, the dates prescribed for payment of the estimated tax shall be the 15th day of the 9th month and the 15th day of the 12th month of such taxable year. If the corporation files its declaration after the 15th day of such 9th month, the percentage of the estimated tax required to be paid is payable in full on or before the 15th day of such 12th month.

(3) *Amendment of declaration.* In the case of an amended declaration, filed in accordance with section 6074, the installment payable on the 15th day of the 12th month of the taxable year shall be ratably increased or decreased, as the case may be, to reflect the increase or decrease in the estimated tax by reason of the amended declaration. For example, X, a corporation on the calendar year basis, filed a declaration on September 15, 1955, reporting an estimated tax in the amount of $20,000. The first installment of $1,000 (5 percent of $20,000) accompanied the declaration. However, X filed an amended declaration on December 15, 1955, showing an estimated tax of $30,000. Since X has already paid $1,000, it must make a payment in the amount of $2,000 computed as follows:

Required amount of estimated tax which must be paid for calendar year 1955 (10% of $30,000)	$3,000
Amount paid with original estimate (5% of $20,000)	1,000
Balance to accompany amended declaration	2,000

Had the amended declaration been filed on December 10, 1955, then only the balance of the first installment ($500) otherwise due on September 15 would have been required to be paid with the declaration and the installment required to be paid on or before December 15, 1955, would be $1,500.

(b) *Taxable years beginning after December 31, 1963*—(1) *Amount and time for payment of each installment*—(i) *In general.* Paragraphs (1) through (4) of section 6154 (a) contain four tables setting forth the percentages of estimated tax for each taxable year beginning after December 31, 1963, which shall be paid as installments of estimated tax and the date on or before which each such installment shall be paid. The date on or before which the declaration of estimated tax for a taxable year is required, under the provisions of section 6074 (a), to be filed determines which of the four installment payment tables shall be used by the corporation for that taxable year. Therefore, if the declaration is required to be filed by the 15th day of the 4th, 6th, 9th, or 12th month, the estimated tax will be required to be paid in four, three, two, or one installment, respectively. However, see subdivision (iii) of this subparagraph for the rules applicable in case of the late filing of a declaration.

(ii) *Examples.* The application of the tables in section 6154 (a) may be illustrated by the following examples:

Example (1). X, a corporation reporting on a calendar year basis, is required for the calendar year 1966 to file a declaration of estimated tax on or before the 15th day of the 4th month thereof (April 15, 1966) reporting an estimated tax liability of $250,000. Assuming that the original declaration is filed on or before April 15, 1966, and is not subsequently amended, X is required to pay its estimated tax in four installments. The first and second installments, each in the amount of $22,500 (9 percent of $250,000), are to be paid on or before April 15, 1966, and June 15, 1966, respectively, and the third and fourth installments, each in the amount of $62,500 (25 percent of $250,000).

are to be paid on or before September 15, 1966, and December 15, 1966, respectively.

Example (2). Y, a corporation which reports on a calendar year basis, is required for the calendar year 1967 to file a declaration of estimated tax on or before the 15th day of the 6th month thereof (June 15, 1967) reporting an estimated tax liability of $100,000. Assuming that the original declaration is filed on or before June 15, 1967, and is not subsequently amended, Y is required to pay its estimated tax in three installments. The first installment, in the amount of $18,666.67 (18⅔ percent of $100,000), is to be paid on or before June 15, 1967, and the second and third installments, each in the amount of $29,666.67 (29⅔ percent of $100,000), are to be paid on or before September 15, 1967, and December 15, 1967, respectively.

Example (3). Z, a corporation which reports on a fiscal year basis ending with June 30 of each year, is required for the fiscal year ended June 30, 1968, to file a declaration of estimated tax on or before the 15th day of the fourth month thereof (October 15, 1967) reporting an estimated tax liability of $200,000. Assuming that the original declaration is filed on or before October 15, 1967, and is not subsequently amended, Z is required to pay its estimated tax in four installments. The first and second installments, each in the amount of $28,000 (14 percent of $200,000), are to be paid on or before October 15, 1967, and December 15, 1967, respectively, and the third and fourth installments, each in the amount of $50,000 (25 percent of $200,000), are to be paid on or before March 15, 1968, and June 15, 1968, respectively.

(iii) *Late filing of declaration of estimated tax.* If a declaration of estimated tax is filed after the date prescribed by section 6074(a) (determined without regard to any extension of time for filing the declaration under section 6081), the tables set forth in paragraphs (2), (3), and (4) of section 6154(a) do not apply except as provided in this subdivision. In such a case, there shall be paid at the time of the filing of the declaration all installments of the estimated tax which would have been payable under the appropriate table in section 6154(a) on or before such date of filing if the declaration had been timely filed in accordance with the provisions of section 6074(a). The remaining installments shall be paid at the times and in the amounts in which they would have been payable if the declaration had been timely filed. For example, Z, a corporation filing its returns on a calendar year basis, fails to file a declaration of estimated tax on April 15, 1968, even though the requirements for filing a declaration were met before April 1, 1968. However, Z does file its declaration of estimated tax on July 1, 1968, disclosing an estimated tax of $75,000. As the first two installment dates specified in paragraph (1) of section 6154(a) (the 15th days of the 4th and 6th months) have passed, Z is required to pay $28,500 (2 installments, each in the amount of 19 percent of $75,000) when the declaration is filed on July 1, 1968. If there are no subsequent amendments of the declaration for this year, Z will be required to pay installments, each in the amount of $18,750 (25 percent of $75,000), on or before September 15, 1968, and December 15, 1968, respectively.

(2) *Amendment of declaration*—(i) *In general.* If any amendment of a declaration is filed, the amount of each remaining installment (including the installment due on the date of the filing of the amendment where the amendment is filed on an installment date), if any, is the amount which would have been payable as such installment if the new estimate had been the original estimate adjusted as provided in this subdivision. The adjustment is for the difference between (a) the amount of estimated tax required to be paid before the date of the filing of the amendment and (b) the amount of estimated tax which would have been required to have been paid before such date if the new estimate had been the original estimate. The difference is divided by the number of remaining installments (including the installment due on the date of the filing of the amendment where the amendment is filed on an installment date), and the resulting amount is added to (if the amended declaration increases the amount of estimated tax) or subtracted from (if the amended declaration decreases the amount of the estimated tax) the amount which would have been payable on each remaining installment date if the new estimate had been the original estimate.

(ii) *Examples.* The application of the provisions of this subparagraph may be illustrated by the following examples:

Example (1). X, a calendar year corporation, determines that its estimated tax liability for the year 1967 is $100,000 and files a declaration of estimated tax by April 15, 1967, with an installment payment of $14,000. On June 15, 1967, the second installment payment of $14,000 is made. On July 1, 1967, X discovers that its 1967 estimated tax may reasonably be expected to be $150,000 and on September 15, 1967, files an amended declaration in that amount. The amounts to be paid on September 15, 1967, and December 15, 1967, are computed as follows:

Installment payments required to be made under the original declaration before date of filing of amendment (14% of $100,000 is $14,000 ×2)	$28,000
Installment payments which would have been required to be made before date of filing of amendment if the original declaration were in the amount of the amended declaration (14% of $150,000 is $21,000 × 2)	42,000
Difference	14,000
Amount of each installment payment due on September 15, 1967, and December 15, 1967, computed as if the original declaration were in the amount of the amended declaration (25% of $150,000)	$37,500

Reg. § 1.6154-1 (b) (2)

24,332 (I.R.C.) Reg. § 1.6154-1(b)(2) 4-8-68

Add: Amount of difference divided by number of remaining installments ($14,000 ÷ 2)	7,000
Amount of each remaining installment (September 15, 1967, and December 15, 1967)	44,500

Example (2). Assume the same facts as in example (1), except that instead of filing the amended declaration on September 15, 1967, X files an amended declaration on June 15, 1967, disclosing an estimated tax of $70,000. The installment payments for June 15, 1967, September 15, 1967, and December 15, 1967, are computed as follows:

Installment payment required to be made under the original declaration before the date of filing of amendment (14% of $100,000)	$14,000
Installment payment which would have been required to be made before date of filing of amendment if the original declaration were in the amount of the amended declaration (14% of $70,000)	9,800
Difference	4,200

June 15, 1967, installment computation:

Installment payment due on June 15, 1967, computed as if the original declaration were in the amount of the amended declaration (14% of $70,000)	$ 9,800
Less: Amount of difference divided by number of remaining installments ($4,200 ÷ 3)	1,400
Amount to be paid as an installment on June 15, 1967	8,400

September 15, 1967, and December 15, 1967, installments computation:

Amount of each installment payment due on September 15, 1967, and December 15, 1967, computed as if the original declaration were in the amount of the amended declaration (25% of $70,000)	$17,500
Less: Amount of difference divided by number of remaining installments ($4,200 ÷ 3)	1,400
Amount of each remaining installment (September 15, 1967, and December 15, 1967)	$16,100

(c) *Installments paid in advance.* A corporation may, at its election, pay any installment of its estimated tax in advance of the due date.

(d) *Considered payment of income tax.* Payments of estimated tax shall be considered payments on account of the income tax liability for the taxable year. Hence the amount of estimated tax paid shall be entered on the income tax return and applied in payment of the tax liability shown thereon.

0→ § 1.6154-2 (T.D. 6167, filed 11-13-57; republished in T.D. 6500, filed 11-25-60; amended by T.D. 6768, filed 11-3-64.) **Short taxable years.**

(a) *Taxable years beginning on or before December 31, 1963*—(1) *In general.* In the case of a corporation filing a declaration for a short taxable year beginning on or before December 31, 1963, the amount of the estimated tax required to be paid shall be paid as follows:

(i) If the short taxable year is a period of more than 9 months and the declaration is required to be filed on or before the 15th day of the 9th month, the amount of the estimated tax required to be paid shall be paid in 2 installments; the 1st on or before the 15th day of the 9th month and the 2d on or before the 15th day of the last month of the short taxable year.

(ii) If the short taxable year is a period of 9 or more months and the declaration is not required to be filed until the 15th day of the last month of the short taxable year, the amount of the estimated tax required to be paid shall be paid in full on or before the 15th day of the last month of the short taxable year.

(2) *Examples.* The application of the provisions of subparagraph (1) of this paragraph may be illustrated by the following examples:

Examples (1). If a corporation changes from a calendar year to a fiscal year beginning November 1, 1956, and ending October 31, 1957, a declaration is required on or before September 15, 1956, for the short taxable year January 1, 1956, to October 31, 1956, if such corporation otherwise meets the requirements of section 6016(a) on or before August 31, 1956. In such case the first installment of the estimated tax must be paid with the declaration filed on September 15, 1956. The second installment must be paid on or before October 15, 1956, the 15th day of the last month of the short taxable year.

Example (2). If, in the first example, the corporation did not meet the requirements of section 6016(a) until after August 31, 1956, but before October 1, 1956, the declaration would have been due on October 15, 1956. In such case the amount of the estimated tax required to be paid must be paid in full with the declaration filed on October 15, 1956.

Place and Due Date for Payment of Tax (I.R.C.) 24,332.1

(b) *Taxable years beginning after December 31, 1963*—(1) *In general.* In the case of a short taxable year which begins after December 31, 1963, and in respect of which a declaration of estimated tax is required to be filed (see paragraph (b) of § 1.6074-2), the amount of, and time for payment of, each installment of estimated tax shall be determined by paragraph (1) to (4), inclusive, of section 6154(a), except that in the case of a short taxable year ending after November 30, 1964, any estimated tax payable in installments which is not paid before the 15th day of the last month of the short taxable year (whether or not the date otherwise specified in section 6154(a) for payment has arrived) shall be paid on such 15th day of the last month of short taxable year.

(2) *Examples.* The application of the provisions of subparagraph (1) of this paragraph may be illustrated by the following examples:

Example (1). X, a corporation filing on a calendar year basis, changes to a fiscal year beginning September 1, 1965, and ending August 31, 1966, and is required to file a declaration on or before April 15, 1965, for the short taxable year January 1, 1965, to August 31, 1965. X must make two 4 percent installment payments of the estimated tax, the first on or before April 15, 1965, and the second on or before June 15, 1965, and must pay 50 percent (25 percent for the 3d installment plus 25 percent for the 4th installment) of the estimated tax on or before August 15, 1965 (the 15th day of the last month of the short taxable year), as the last installment.

Example (2). If, in the first example, X does not meet the requirements of section 6016(a) until June 15, 1965, the declaration is due on or before August 15, 1965. X is required to pay 58 percent of the estimated tax on or before August 15, 1965 (the 15th day of the last month of the short taxable year).

(3) *Late filing of declaration of estimated tax.* In the case of a declaration of estimated tax for a short taxable year beginning after December 31, 1963, filed after the date prescribed by section 6074(a) (determined without regard to any extension of time for filing the declaration under section 6081), the provisions of paragraph (b) (1) (iii) of § 1.6154-1 shall be applied in determining the amount of and time for payment of each installment. However, in the case of short taxable years beginning after December 31, 1963, and ending after November 30, 1964, where, under the provisions of paragraph (b) (1) (iii) of § 1.6154-1, installments are to be paid after the close of the short taxable year, such installments shall be paid on or before the 15th day of the last month of the short taxable year.

(4) *Amended declarations.* In the case of an amended declaration of estimated tax for a short taxable year beginning after December 31, 1963, filed in accordance with section 6074(b), the provisions of paragraph (b)(2) of § 1.6154-1 shall apply to determine the amount of each remaining installment. However, where, under the provisions of such paragraph (b)(2), installments are to be paid after the close of the short taxable year, such installments shall be paid on or before the 15th day of the last month of the short taxable year.

○── § 1.6154-3 (T.D. 6267, filed 11-13-57; republished in T.D. 6500, filed 11-25-60; amended by T.D. 6950, filed 4-3-68.) **Extension of time for paying estimated tax.**

An extension of time granted a corporation under section 6081 for filing the declaration of estimated tax automatically extends the time for paying the estimated tax (without interest) for the same period. See § 1.6074-3 for rules relating to extensions of time for filing declarations of estimated tax by corporations. Except as provided in paragraph (b) of § 301.6091-1 (relating to hand-carried documents), an application for an extension of time for paying an installment of the estimated tax shall be addressed to the internal revenue officer with whom the taxpayer files its declaration. Each application must contain a full recital of the causes for the delay. Any such extension will not relieve the taxpayer from the addition to the tax imposed by section 6655, and the period of the underpayment will be determined under section 6655 (c) without regard to such extension.

○── § 1.6154-4 (T.D. 6914, filed 3-7-67.) **Use of Government depositaries.**

For provisions relating to the use of Federal Reserve banks and authorized commercial banks in depositing the taxes see § 1.6302-1.

○── § 301.6154 **Statutory provisions; installment payments of estimated income tax by corporations.** [Sec. 6154, IRC]

○── § 301.6154-1 (T.D. 6498 filed 10-24-60.) **Installment payments of estimated income tax by corporations.**

For provisions relating to installment payments of estimated income tax by corporations, see §§ 1.6154-1 to 1.6154-3, inclusive, of this chapter (Income Tax Regulations).

○── § 301.6155 **Statutory provisions; payment on notice and demand.** [Sec. 6155, IRC]

○── § 301.6155-1 (T.D. 6498, filed 10-24-60; amended by T.D. 6585, filed 12-27-61.) **Payment on notice and demand.**

Upon receipt of notice and demand from the district director (including the Director of International Operations) or the director of the regional service center, there shall be paid at the place and time stated in such notice the amount of any tax (including any interest, additional amounts, additions to the tax, and assessable penalties) stated in such notice and demand.

EXTENSIONS OF TIME FOR PAYMENT

○── § 1.6161 **Statutory provisions; extension of time for paying tax.** [Sec. 6161, IRC]

○── § 1.6161-1 (T.D. 6364, filed 2-13-59; republished in T.D. 6500, filed 11-25-60; amended by T.D. 6950, filed 4-3-68; T.D. 7133, filed 7-21-71 and T.D. 7260, filed 2-9-73.) **Extension of time for paying tax or deficiency.**

Reg. § 1.6161-1

24,332.2 (I.R.C.)   Reg. § 1.6161-1(a)(1)   7-21-75

(a) *In general* — (1) *Tax shown or required to be shown on return.* A reasonable extension of the time for payment of the amount of any tax imposed by subtitle A of the Code and shown or required to be shown on any return, or for payment of the amount of any installment of such tax, may be granted by the district directors (including the Director of International Operations) at the request of the taxpayer. The period of such extension shall not be in excess of six months from the date fixed for payment of such tax or installment, except that if the taxpayer is abroad the period of the extension may be in excess of six months.

(2) *Deficiency.* The time for payment of any amount determined as a deficiency in respect of tax imposed by chapter 1 of the Code, or for the payment of any part thereof, may, at the request of the taxpayer, be extended by the internal revenue officer to whom the tax is required to be paid for a period not to exceed 18 months from the date fixed for payment of the deficiency, as shown on the notice and demand, and, in exceptional cases, for a further period not in excess of 12 months. No extension of the time for payment of a deficiency shall be granted if the deficiency is due to negligence, to intentional disregard of rules and regulations, or to fraud with intent to evade tax.

(b) *Undue hardship required for extension.* An extension of the time for payment shall be granted only upon a satisfactory showing that payment on the due date of the amount with respect to which the extension is desired will result in an undue hardship. The extension will not be granted upon a general statement of hardship. The term "undue hardship" means more than an inconvenience to the taxpayer. It must appear that substantial financial loss, for example, loss due to the sale of property at a sacrifice price, will result to the taxpayer from making payment on the due date of the amount with respect to which the extension is desired. If a market exists, the sale of property at the current market price is not ordinarily considered as resulting in an undue hardship.

(c) *Application for extension.* An application for an extension of the time for payment of the tax shown or required to be shown on any return, or for the payment of any installment thereof, or for the payment of any amount determined as a deficiency shall be made on Form 1127 and shall be accompanied by evidence showing the undue hardship that would result to the taxpayer if the extension were refused. Such application shall also be accompanied by a statement of the assets and liabilities of the taxpayer and an itemized statement showing all receipts and disbursements for each of the three months immediately preceding the due date of the amount to which the application relates. The application, with supporting documents, must be filed on or before the date prescribed for payment of the amount with respect to which the extension is desired. If the tax is required to be paid to the Director of International Operations, such application must be filed with him, otherwise, the application must be filed with the applicable district director referred to in paragraph (a) or (b) of § 1.6091-2, regardless of whether the return is to be filed with, or tax is to be paid to, such district director. The application will be examined, and within 30 days, if possible, will be denied, granted, or tentatively granted subject to certain conditions of which the taxpayer will be notified. If an additional extension is desired, the request therefor must be made on or before the expiration of the period for which the prior extension is granted.

(d) *Payment pursuant to extension.* If an extension of time for payment is granted, the amount the time for payment of which is so extended shall be paid on or before the expiration of the period of the extension without the necessity of notice and demand. The granting of an extension of the time for payment of the tax or deficiency does not relieve the taxpayer from liability for the payment of interest thereon during the period of the extension. See section 6601 and § 301.6601-1 of this chapter (Regulations on Procedure and Administration). Further, the granting of an extension of the time for payment of one installment of the tax does not extend the time for payment of subsequent installments.

(e) *Cross reference.* For extensions of time for payment of estimated tax, see §§ 1.6073-4 and 1.6074-3.

○━▶ § 53.6161 **Statutory provisions; extension of time for paying tax.** [Sec. 6161, IRC]

○━▶ § 53.6161-1 (T.D. 7368, filed 7-15-75.) **Extension of time for paying tax or deficiency.**

(a) *In general*—(1) *Tax shown or required to be shown on return.* A reasonable extension of the time for payment of the amount of any tax imposed by chapter 42 and shown or required to be shown on any return, may be granted by the district directors and directors of the service centers at the request of the taxpayer. The period of such extension shall not be in excess of 6 months from the date fixed for payment of such tax, except that if the taxpayer is abroad the period of the extension may be in excess of 6 months.

(2) *Deficiency.* The time for payment of any amount determined as a deficiency in respect of tax imposed by chapter 42 may, at the request of the taxpayer, be extended by the internal revenue officer to whom the tax is required to be paid for a period not to exceed 18 months from the date fixed for payment of the deficiency, as shown on the notice and demand, and, in exceptional cases for a further period not in excess of 12 months. No extension of the time for payment of a deficiency shall be granted if the deficiency is due to negligence, to intentional disregard of rules and regulations, or to fraud with intent to evade tax.

(3) *Extension of time for filing distinguished.* The granting of an extension of time for filing a return does not operate to extend the time for the payment of the tax or any part thereof unless so specified in the extension.

(b) *Undue hardship required for extension.* An extension of the time for payment shall be granted only upon a satisfactory showing that payment on the due date of the amount with respect to which the extension is desired will result in an undue hardship. The extension will not be granted upon a general statement of hardship. The term "undue hardship" means more than an inconvenience to the taxpayer. It must appear that substantial financial loss, for example, loss due to the sale of property at a sacrifice price, will result to the taxpayer from making payment on the due date of the amount with respect to which the extension is desired. If a market exists, the sale of property at the current market price is not ordinarily considered as resulting in an undue hardship.

(c) *Application for extension.* An application for an extension of the time for payment of the tax shown or required to be shown on any return, or for the payment of any amount determined as a deficiency shall be made on Form 1127 and shall be accompanied by evidence showing the undue hardship that would result to the taxpayer if the extension were refused. Such application shall also be accompanied by a statement of the assets and liabilities of the taxpayer and an itemized statement showing all receipts and disbursements for each of the three months immediately preceding the due date of the amount to which the application relates. The application, with supporting documents, must be filed on or before the date prescribed for payment of the amount with respect to which the extension is desired with the internal revenue officer to whom the tax is to be paid. The application will be examined, and within 30 days, if possible, will be denied, granted, or tentatively granted subject to certain conditions of which the taxpayer will be notified. If an additional extension is desired, the request therefor must be made on or before the expiration of the period for which the prior extension is granted.

(d) *Payment pursuant to extension.* If an extension of time for payment is granted, the amount the time for payment of which is so extended shall be paid on or before the expiration of the period of the extension without the necessity of notice and demand. The granting of an extension of the time for payment of the tax or deficiency does not relieve the taxpayer from liability for the payment of interest thereon during the period of the extension. See section 6601 and § 301.6601-1 of this chapter (Regulations on Procedure and Administration).

○— § 301.6161 **Statutory provisions; extension of time for paying tax.** [Sec. 6161, IRC]

○— § 301.6161-1 (T.D. 6498, filed 10-24-60.) **Extension of time for paying tax.**

For provisions concerning the extension of time for paying a particular tax or for paying an amount determined as a deficiency, see the regulations relating to such tax.

○— § 31.6161(a)(1) **Statutory provisions; extension of time for paying tax.** [Sec. 6161(a)(1), IRC]

○— § 31.6161(a)(1)-1 (T.D. 6472, filed 6-22-60; republished in T.D. 6516, filed 12-19-60.) **Extensions of time for paying tax.**

No extension of time will be granted for payment of any of the taxes to which the regulations in this part have application.

○— § 1.6162 **Statutory provisions; extension of time for payment of tax on gain attributable to liquidation of personal holding companies.** [Sec. 6162, IRC]

○— § 1.6162-1 (T.D. 6364, filed 2-13-59; republished in T.D. 6500, filed 11-25-60.) **Extension of time for payment of tax on gain attributable to liquidation of personal holding companies.**

(a) *In general.* (1) If it is shown to the satisfaction of the district director that undue hardship to the taxpayer will result from the payment of such portion of the amount determined as the tax under chapter 1 of the Code by the taxpayer as is attributable to the short-term or long-term capital gain derived by the taxpayer from the receipt by him of property other than money on a complete liquidation of a corporation to which section 331(a)(1) or 342 applies, the district director may grant an extension of time for the payment of such portion of the tax. For the meaning of the term "undue hardship", see paragraph (b) of § 1.6161-1.

(2) The extension of time for payment shall be for a period not in excess of five years. The extension shall only be granted for a taxable year beginning before January 1, 1956, and shall apply only if the corporation, for its taxable year preceding the year in which occurred the complete liquidation (or the first of the series of distributions in complete liquidation), was, under the law applicable to such taxable year, a personal holding company or a foreign personal holding company.

(b) *Requirement of bond.* As a condition to the granting of an extension of time for payment, the taxpayer will usually be required by the district director to furnish a bond as provided in section 6165 and the regulations thereunder. For other provisions with respect to bonds, see section 7101 and the regulations in Part 301 of this chapter (Regulations on Procedure and Administration).

○— § 301.6162 **Statutory provisions; extension of time for payment of tax on gain attributable to liquidation of personal holding companies.** [Sec. 6162, IRC]

○— § 301.6162-1 (T.D. 6498, filed 10-24-60.) **Extension of time for payment of tax on gain attributable to liquidation of personal holding companies.**

For provisions relating to the extension of time for payment of tax on gain attributable to liquidation of personal holding companies, see § 1.6162-1 of this chapter (Income Tax Regulations).

○— § 301.6163 **Statutory provisions; extension of time for payment of estate tax on value of reversionary or remainder interest in property.** [Sec. 6163, IRC]

○— § 1.6164 **Statutory provisions; extension of time for payment of taxes by corporations expecting carrybacks.** [Sec. 6164, IRC]

○— § 1.6164-1 (T.D. 6364, filed 2-13-59; republished in T.D. 6500, filed 11-25-60.) **Extensions of time for payment of taxes by corporations expecting carrybacks.**

Reg. § 1.6164-1

24,332.4 (I.R.C.) Reg. § 1.6164-1(a)

(a) *In general.* If a corporation in any taxable year files a statement with respect to an expected net operating loss carryback from such taxable year, such corporation may extend the time for the payment of all or part of any tax imposed by subtitle A of the Code for the taxable year immediately preceding such taxable year to the extent and subject to the limitations provided in section 6164. A corporation may extend the time for payment with respect to only such taxes as meet the following requirements:

(1) The tax must be one imposed by subtitle A of the Code;

(2) The tax must be for the taxable year immediately preceding the taxable year of the expected net operating loss;

(3) The tax must be shown on the return or must be assessed within the taxable year of the expected net operating loss; and

(4) The tax must not have been paid or required to have been paid prior to the filing of the statement.

(b) *Statement for purpose of extending time for payment.* (1) The time for payment of the tax is automatically extended upon the filing of a statement on Form 1138 by the corporation with the district director for the district where the tax is payable. The statement on Form 1138 must be filled out in accordance with the instructions accompanying the form, and all information required by the form and the instructions must be furnished by the taxpayer. The district director, upon request, will furnish a receipt for any statement filed. Such receipt will show the date the statement was filed.

(2) The period of extension is that provided in section 6164(d) and § 1.6164-5 unless sooner terminated by action of either the district director or the corporation.

○— § 1.6164-2 (T.D. 6364, filed 2-13-59; republished in T.D. 6500, filed 11-25-60.) **Amount of tax the time for payment of which may be extended.**

(a) *Total amount to which extension may relate.* The total amount of tax the time for payment of which may be extended under section 6164 may not exceed the amount of the reduction of the taxes previously determined attributable to the expected carryback.

(b) *Amount of tax to which extension may relate.* (1) The taxpayer shall specify on Form 1138 the kind of tax and the amount thereof the time for payment of which is to be extended. The amount of tax to which an extension may relate shall not exceed the amount of such tax shown on the return as filed, increased by any amount assessed as a deficiency (or as interest or addition to the tax) prior to the date of filing the statement and decreased by any amount paid or required to be paid prior to such date. In determining the amount of tax required to be paid prior to the date of filing the statement, only the following amounts shall be taken into consideration.

(i) The amount of the tax shown on the return as filed; and

(ii) Any amount assessed as a deficiency (or as interest or addition to the tax) if the tenth day after notice and demand for its payment occurs prior to the date of the filing of the statement.

(2) Delinquent installments are to be considered amounts required to be paid prior to the date of filing the statement. In the case of any authorized extension of time under sections 6161 and 6162, the amount of tax the time for payment of which is so extended is not to be considered required to be paid prior to the end of such extension. Similarly, any amount assessed as a deficiency (or as interest or addition to the tax) is not to be considered required to be paid prior to the date of the filing of the statement unless the tenth day after notice and demand for its payment falls prior to the date of the filing of the statement.

(3) The taxpayer may choose to extend the time for payment of all or one or more taxes, or it may choose to extend the time for payment of portions of several taxes. The taxes chosen by the taxpayer need not be those taxes which are affected by the carryback.

○— § 1.6164-3 (T.D. 6364, filed 2-13-59; republished in T.D. 6500, filed 11-25-60; amended by T.D. 6862, filed 11-17-65.) **Computation of the amount of reduction of the tax previously determined.**

(a) *Tax previously determined.* The taxpayer is to determine the amount of the reduction, attributable to the expected carryback, in the aggregate of the taxes previously determined for taxable years prior to the taxable year of the expected net operating loss. The tax previously determined is to be ascertained in accordance with the method prescribed in section 1314 (a). Thus, the tax previously determined will be the tax shown on the return as filed, increased by any amounts assessed (or collected without assessment) as deficiencies prior to the date of the filing of the statement, and decreased by any amounts abated, credited, refunded, or otherwise repaid prior to such date. Any items as to which the Internal Revenue Service and the taxpayer are in disagreement at the time of the filing of the statement shall be taken into account in ascertaining the tax previously determined only if, and to the extent that, they were reported in the return, or were reflected in any amounts assessed (or collected without assessment) as deficiencies, or in any amounts abated, credited, refunded, or otherwise repaid, prior to the date of the filing of the statement. The tax previously determined will reflect the foreign tax credit and the credit for tax withheld at source provided in section 32.

(b) *Reduction attributable to the expected carryback.* The reduction, attributable to the expected carryback or related adjustments, in any tax previously determined is to be ascertained by applying the expected carryback as if it were a determined net operating loss carryback, in accordance with the provisions of section 172 and the regulations thereunder. Items must be taken into account only to the extent that such items were included in the return, or were reflected in amounts assessed (or collected without assessment) as deficiencies, or in amounts abated, credited, refunded, or otherwise repaid, prior to the date of the filing of the statement. Thus, for example, if the taxpayer claims a deduction for depreciation of $10,000 in its return and the Internal Revenue Service asserts that only $4,000 is properly deductible, no change is to be made in the $10,000 depreciation deduction as shown by the taxpayer on his return unless a deficiency has been assessed, or an amount collected without assessment, prior to the date of filing of the statement as a result of a change in the depreciation deduction, or unless such change in the depreciation deduction was reflected in an amount abated, credited, refunded, or otherwise repaid prior to such date.

○─→ § 1.6164-4 (T.D. 6364, filed 2-13-59; republished in T.D. 6500, filed 11-25-60.) **Payment of remainder of tax where extension relates to only part of the tax.**

(a) *Time for payment.* If an extension of time relates to only part of the tax, the time for payment of the remainder of the tax shall be considered to be the dates on which payments would have been required if such remainder had been the tax and the taxpayer had elected to pay the tax in installments as provided in section 6152(a).

(b) *Example.* The provisions of this section may be illustrated by the following example:

Example. Corporation X, which keeps its books and makes its tax returns on the calendar year basis, filed its income tax return for 1956 on March 15, 1957. The corporation showed a tax of $1,000 on its return and paid 50 percent of such tax, or $500 on March 15, 1957. On June 3, 1957, corporation X, pursuant to the provisions of section 6164, extended the time for payment of $400 of such tax. The remainder of the tax the time for payment of which was not so extended, i.e., $600, is to be considered the tax for purposes of determining when it is to be paid. The remainder is considered to be due on the dates on which payment would have been required if such remainder had been the tax. Since the taxable year ended on December 31, 1956, the tax is payable in two equal installments of $300 each on March 15, 1957, and June 17, 1957. The taxpayer, having paid $500 on March 15, 1957, will have $100 to pay on June 17, 1957.

○─→ § 1.6164-5 (T.D. 6364, filed 2-13-59; republished in T.D. 6500, filed 11-25-60.) **Period of extension.**

If the time for the payment of any tax has been extended pursuant to section 6164, such extension shall expire:

(a) On the last day of the month in which falls the last date prescribed by law (including any extension of time granted the taxpayer) for the filing of the return for the taxable year of the expected net operating loss; or

(b) If an application for a tentative carryback adjustment provided in section 6411 with respect to such loss is filed before the expiration of the period specified in paragraph (a) of this section, on the date on which notice is mailed by registered mail prior to September 3, 1958, and by either registered or certified mail on and after September 3, 1958, to the taxpayer that such application is allowed or disallowed in whole or in part.

○─→ § 1.6164-6 (T.D. 6364, filed 2-13-59; republished in T.D. 6500, filed 11-25-60.) **Revised statements.**

(a) *Requirements and effect.* A corporation may file more than one statement under section 6164 with respect to any one taxable year. Each statement is to be considered a new statement and not an amendment of any prior statement. Each such new statement is to be in lieu of the last statement previously filed with respect to the taxable year. The new statement may extend the time for payment of a greater or lesser amount of tax than was extended under the prior statement or may change the kind of tax the time for payment of which is to be extended. The extension may not relate to any amount of tax which was paid or required to be paid prior to the date of filing the new statement. Any amount of tax the time for payment of which was extended under a prior statement, however, may continue to be extended under the new statement. If the amount the time for payment of which is extended under the new statement is less than the amount so extended under the last statement previously filed, the extension of time shall be terminated on the date the new statement is filed as to the difference between the two amounts. See § 1.6164-8 for the dates on which such difference must be paid. If a corporation pays any amount of tax, the time for payment of which was extended, prior to the date the extension would otherwise terminate, the extension with respect to such amount shall be deemed terminated, without regard to whether a new statement is filed, on the date such amount is paid. The corporation shall indicate on each new statement filed that it has already filed one

Reg. § 1.6164-6(a)

24,334 (I.R.C.)   Reg. § 1.6164-6(a)   1-15-73

or more prior statements with respect to the taxable year. The corporation shall likewise indicate the date each prior statement was filed and the amount of each tax the time for payment of which was extended under each prior statement.

(b) *Example.* The provisions of this section may be illustrated by the following example:

Example. Corporation Y, which keeps its books and makes its tax returns on the calendar year basis, filed its income tax return for 1956 on March 15, 1957, showing a tax of $100,000. At the same time it filed a statement under section 6164 in which it stated that it expected to have a net operating loss of $75,000 in 1957 and that the reduction in the tax previously determined for 1955 (the second taxable year preceding the year of the expected net operating loss) attributable to the expected net operating loss carryback resulting from such expected loss, would be $39,000. The corporation accordingly extended the time for payment of $39,000 of its income tax for 1956, and paid $30,500 (50 percent of the excess of $100,000 over $39,000) of such tax on March 15, 1957 (see section 6164(c) and § 1.6164-4). As a result of its operations during the next several months, the corporation filed a second statement on June 3, 1957, in which it stated that its expected net operating loss for 1957 would amount to $150,000 and that the corresponding reduction in the tax for 1955 would amount to $78,000. Corporation Y under the new statement may extend the time for payment of $30,500, the installment due on June 17, 1957, and the time for payment of the $39,000 extended under the first statement filed on March 15, 1957, may continue to be extended under the second statement. The $30,500 which was paid on March 15, 1957, will not be affected by the second statement filed on June 3, 1957.

§ 1.6164-7 (T.D. 6364, filed 2-13-59; republished in T.D. 6500, filed 11-25-60.) **Termination by district director.**

(a) *After an examination of the statement filed by the corporation is made.* The district director is authorized to make such examination of the statements filed as he deems necessary and practicable. If, upon such examination as he may make, the district director believes that, as of the time he makes the examination, all or any part of the statement is in a material respect erroneous or unreasonable, he will terminate the extension as to any part of the amount to which such extension relates which he deems should be terminated.

(b) *Jeopardy.* If the district director believes that the collection of any amount to which an extension under section 6164 relates is in jeopardy, he will immediately terminate the extension. In the case of such a termination, notice and demand shall be made by the district director for payment of such amount, and there may be no further extension of time under section 6164 with respect to such amount.

§ 1.6164-8 (T.D. 6364, filed 2-13-59; republished in T.D. 6500, filed 11-25-60.) **Payments on termination.**

(a) *In general.* If an extension of time under section 6164 is terminated with respect to any amount either (1) by the filing of a new statement by the taxpayer under section 6164(e) extending the time for payment of a lesser amount than was extended in a prior statement, or (2) by action of the district director under section 6164(f) after making an examination of the statement filed by the corporation, no further extension of time may be made under section 6164 with respect to such amount. The time for payment of such amount shall be the dates on which payments would have been required if there had been no extension with respect to such amount and the taxpayer had elected under section 6152(a) to pay the tax in installments.

(b) *Example.* The provisions of this section may be illustrated by the following example:

Example. Corporation Z, which keeps its books and makes its tax returns on the calendar year basis, filed its income tax return for 1956 on March 15, 1957, showing a tax of $100,000. At the same time it filed a statement under section 6164 extending the time for payment of the entire $100,000 on the basis of an expected net operating loss carryback from 1957. On April 10, 1957, the corporation filed a new statement indicating that the reduction, attributable to the carryback from 1957, in its income tax for 1956, would only be $80,000, and thus terminated the above extension of $20,000. The time for payment of such $20,000 may not be extended again, and such $20,000 is payable as if it were the tax for 1956 and corporation Z had elected to pay such tax in installments. That is, $10,000 is payable on March 15, 1957, and $10,000 payable on June 17, 1957. Inasmuch as the March 15 date had already passed when the corporation Z terminated the extension with respect to the $20,000, $10,000 is payable immediately upon such termination, and the other installment of $10,000 is payable on June 17, 1957. This example would also apply if the extension of time for payment of the $20,000 were terminated instead by the district director on April 10, 1957.

§ 1.6164-9 (T.D. 6364, filed 2-13-59; republished in T.D. 6500, filed 11-25-60; amended by T.D. 7244, filed 12-29-72.) **Cross references.**

For provisions with respect to interest due on amounts the payment of which is extended under section 6164, see section 6601 and paragraph (e) of § 301.6601-1 of this chapter (Regulations on Procedure and Administration). For extensions of time under section 6164 in the case of corporations making or required to make consolidated returns, see § 1.1502-77(a).

§ 301.6164 Statutory provisions; extension of time for payment of taxes by corporations expecting carrybacks. [Sec. 6164, IRC]

§ 301.6164-1 (T.D. 6498, filed 10-24-60.) **Extension of time for payment of taxes by corporations expecting carrybacks.**

For provisions relating to the extension of time for payment of taxes by corporations expecting carrybacks, see §§ 1.6164-1

§ 1.6165 **Statutory provisions; bonds where time to pay tax or deficiency has been extended.** [Sec. 6165, IRC]

§ 1.6165-1 (T.D. 6455, filed 3-1-60; republished in T.D. 6500, filed 11-25-60.) **Bonds where time to pay the tax or deficiency has been extended.**

The district director, including the Director of International Operations, may, as a condition to the granting of an extension of time within which to pay any tax or any deficiency therein, require the taxpayer to furnish a bond in an amount not exceeding double the amount of the tax with respect to which the extension is granted. Such bond shall be furnished in accordance with the provisions contained in section 7101 and the regulations in Part 301 of this chapter (Regulations on Procedure and Administration).

§ 53.6165 **Statutory provisions; bonds where time to pay tax or deficiency has been extended.** [Sec. 6165, IRC]

§ 53.6165-1 (T.D. 7368, filed 7-15-75.) **Bonds where time to pay tax or deficiency has been extended.**

If an extension of time for payment of tax or deficiency is granted under section 6161, the district director or the director of the service center may, if he deems it necessary, require a bond for the payment of the amount in respect of which the extension is granted in accordance with the terms of the extension. However, such bond shall not exceed double the amount with respect to which the extension is granted. For provisions relating to form of bonds, see the regulations under section 7101 contained in Part 301 of this chapter (Regulations on Procedure and Administration).

§ 301.6165 **Statutory provisions; bonds where time to pay tax or deficiency has been extended.** [Sec. 6565, IRC]

§ 301.6165-1 (T.D. 6498, filed 10-24-60.) **Bonds where time to pay the tax or deficiency has been extended.**

For provisions concerning bonds where time to pay a tax or deficiency has been extended, see the regulations relating to the particular tax.

§ 301.6166 **Statutory provisions; extension of time for payment of estate tax where estate consists largely of interest in closely held business.** [Sec. 6166, IRC]

ASSESSMENT

IN GENERAL

§ 301.6201 **Statutory provisions; assessment authority.** [Sec. 6201, IRC]

§ 301.6201-1 (T.D. 6119, filed 12-31-54; republished in T.D. 6498, filed 10-24-60; amended by T.D. 6585, filed 12-27-61.) **Assessment authority.**

(a) *In general.* The district director is authorized and required to make all inquiries necessary to the determination and assessment of all taxes imposed by the Internal Revenue Code of 1954 or any prior internal revenue law. The district director is further authorized and required, and the director of the regional service center is authorized to make the determinations and the assessments of such taxes. However, certain inquiries and determinations are, by direction of the Commissioner, made by other officials, such as assistant regional commissioners. The term "taxes" includes interest, additional amounts, additions to the taxes, and assessable penalties. The authority of the district/director and the director of the regional service center to make assessments includes the following:

(1) *Taxes shown on return.* The district director or the director of the regional service center shall assess all taxes determined by the taxpayer or by the district director or the director of the regional service center and disclosed on a return or list.

(2) *Unpaid taxes payable by stamp.* (i) If without the use of the proper stamp:

(a) Any article upon which a tax is required to be paid by means of a stamp is sold or removed for sale or use by the manufacturer thereof, or

(b) Any transaction or act upon which a tax is required to be paid by means of a stamp occurs;

the district director, upon such information as he can obtain, must estimate the amount of the tax which has not been paid and the district director or the director of the regional service center must make assessment therefor upon the person the district director determines to be liable for the tax. However, the district director or the director of the regional service center may not assess any tax which is payable by stamp unless the taxpayer fails to pay such tax at the time and in the manner provided by law or regulations.

(ii) If a taxpayer gives a check or money order as payment for stamps but the check or money order is not paid upon presentment, then the district director or the director of the regional service center shall assess the amount of the check or money order against the taxpayer as if it were a tax due at the time the check or money order was received by the district director.

(3) *Erroneous income tax prepayment credits.* If the amount of income tax withheld or the amount of estimated income tax paid is overstated by a taxpayer on a return or on a claim for refund, the amount so overstated which is allowed against the tax shown on the return or which is allowed as a credit or refund shall be assessed by the district director or the director of the regional service center in the same manner as in the case of a mathematical error on the return. See section 6213(b)(1), relating to exceptions to restrictions on assessment.

(b) *Estimated income tax.* Neither the district director nor the director of the regional service center shall assess any amount of estimated income tax required to be paid under section 6153 or 6154 which is unpaid.

(c) *Compensation of child.* Any income tax assessed against a child, to the extent of the amount attributable to in-

Reg. § 301.6201-1(c)

come included in the gross income of the child solely by reason of section 73(a) or the corresponding provision of prior law, if not paid by the child, shall, for the purposes of the income tax imposed by chapter 1 of the Code (or the corresponding provisions of prior law), be considered as having also been properly assessed against the parent. In any case in which the earnings of the child are included in the gross income of the child solely by reason of section 73(a) or the corresponding provision of prior law, the parent's liability is an amount equal to the amount by which the tax assessed against the child (and not paid by him) has been increased by reason of the inclusion of such earnings in the gross income of the child. Thus, if for the calendar year 1954 the child has income of $1,000 from investments and of $3,000 for services rendered, and the latter amount is includible in the gross income of the child under section 73(a) and the child has no wife or dependents, the tax liability determined under section 3 is $625. If the child had only the investment income of $1,000, his tax liability would be $62. If the tax of $625 is assessed against the child, the difference between $625 and $62, or $563, is the amount of such tax which is considered to have been properly assessed against the parent, if not paid by the child.

○━ § 301.6202 Statutory provisions; establishment by regulations of mode or time of assessment. [Sec. 6202, IRC]

○━ § 301.6203 Statutory provisions; method of assessment. [Sec. 6203, IRC]

○━ § 301.6203-1 (T.D. 6119, filed 12-31-54 as amended by T.D. 6425, filed 11-10-59; republished in T.D. 6498, filed 10-24-60; amended by T.D. 6585, filed 12-27-61.) Method of assessment.

The district director and the director of the regional service center shall appoint one or more assessment officers. The district director shall also appoint assessment officers in a Service Center servicing his district. The assessment shall be made by an assessment officer signing the summary record of assessment. The summary record, through supporting records, shall provide identification of the taxpayer, the character of the liability assessed, the taxable period, if applicable, and the amount of the assessment. The amount of the assessment shall, in the case of tax shown on a return by the taxpayer, be the amount so shown, and in all other cases the amount of the assessment shall be the amount shown on the supporting list or record. The date of the assessment is the date the summary record is signed by an assessment officer. If the taxpayer requests a copy of the record of assessment, he shall be furnished a copy of the pertinent parts of the assessment which set forth the name of the taxpayer, the date of assessment, the character of the liability assessed, the taxable period, if applicable, and the amounts assessed.

○━ § 301.6204 Statutory provisions; supplemental assessments. [Sec. 6204, IRC]

○━ § 301.6204-1 (T.D. 6119, filed 12-31-54; republished in T.D. 6498, filed 10-24-60; amended by T.D. 6585, filed 12-27-61.) Supplemental assessments.

If any assessment is incomplete or incorrect in any material respect, the district director or the director of the regional service center, subject to the restrictions with respect to the assessment of deficiencies in income, estate, and gift taxes, and subject to the applicable period of limitation, may make a supplemental assessment for the purpose of correcting or completing the original assessment.

○━ § 31.6205 Statutory provisions; special rules applicable to certain employment taxes. [Sec. 6205, IRC]

○━ § 1.6205-1 (T.D. 6472, filed 6-22-60; republished in T.D. 6516, filed 12-19-60.) Adjustments of underpayments.

(a) *In general.* (1) An employer who makes, or has made, an undercollection or underpayment of—

(i) Employee tax under section 3101, employer tax under section 3111, or the employee or employer tax under corresponding provisions of prior law,

(ii) Employee tax under section 3201, employer tax under section 3221, or the employee or employer tax under corresponding provisions of prior law, or

(iii) Income tax required under section 3402 to be withheld,

with respect to any payment of wages or compensation, shall correct such error as provided in this section. Such correction shall constitute an adjustment without interest to the extent provided in paragraph (b) or (c) of this section.

(2) Every correction under this section of an underpayment of tax with respect to a payment of wages or compensation shall be made on the return form which is prescribed for use, at the time the correction is made, in reporting tax which corresponds to the tax underpaid.

(3) Every return or supplemental return on which an underpayment is corrected pursuant to this section must have securely attached as a part thereof a statement explaining the correction, designating the return period in which the error was ascertained and the return period to which the error relates, and setting forth such other information as may be required by the regulations in this subpart and by the instructions relating to the return.

(4) For purposes of this section, an error is ascertained when the employer has sufficient knowledge of the error to be able to correct it

(5) * * *

(6) No underpayment shall be reported pursuant to this section after receipt from the district director of notice and demand for payment thereof based upon an assessment, but the amount shall be paid in accordance with such notice and demand.

(7) For provisions relating to correction of erroneous statements furnished to employees in respect of wages subject to withholding of income tax under section 3402, and of wages under the Federal Insurance Contributions Act, see paragraph (c) of § 31.6051-1.

(b) *Federal Insurance Contributions Act and Railroad Retirement Tax Act.* — * * *

(c) *Income tax required to be withheld from wages*—(1) *Undercollection ascertained before return is filed.* If no income tax, or less than the correct amount of income tax, required under section 3402 to be withheld from wages is deducted from wages paid to an employee in any return period, and if the error is ascertained before the return is filed for the period in which such wages are paid, the employer shall nevertheless report on such return the correct amount of the tax required to be withheld. However, the reporting and payment by an employer of tax in accordance with this subparagraph do not constitute an adjustment.

(2) *Underpayment ascertained after return is filed.* (i) If a return is filed for a return period, and if no income tax, or less than the correct amount of income tax, required under section 3402 to be withheld from wages paid to an employee in such period, is reported on a return and paid to the district director, the employer shall (a) report the additional amount due by reason of the underpayment on a return for any period in the calendar year in which the wages were paid, or (b) report such additional amount on a supplemental return for the return period in which such wages were paid. Such reporting constitutes an adjustment within the meaning of this section only if the return or supplemental return on which the underpayment is reported is filed on or before the last day on which the return is required to be filed for the return period in which the error was ascertained.

(ii) If a return is filed for a return period, and if no income tax, or less than the correct amount of income tax, required under section 3402 to be withheld from wages paid to an employee in such period is reported on such return and paid to the district director, and such underpayment is not reported as an adjustment within the time prescribed by subdivision (i) of this subparagraph, the amount of such underpayment shall be (*a*) reported on the employer's next return, if such next return is for any return period in the calendar year in which the wages were paid, or (*b*) reported immediately on a supplemental return.

(3) *Payment of amounts reported as undercollections or underpayments.* (i) For provisions relating to the employer's liability for an underpayment of tax unless he can show that the income tax against which the tax under section 3402 may be credited has been paid, see § 31.3402(d)-1.

(ii) Except as provided in § 31.3402(d)-1 any amount reported as an adjustment within the meaning of this paragraph shall be paid to the district director, without interest, at the time fixed for reporting the adjustment.

(iii) For interest accruing on amounts which are not paid when due, see section 6601.

(4) *Deductions from employee.* If no income tax, or less than the correct amount of income tax, required under section 3402 to be withheld from wages is deducted from wages paid to an employee in a calendar year, the employer shall collect the amount of the undercollection on or before the last day of such year by deducting such amount from remuneration of the employee, if any, under his control. Such deductions may be made even though the remuneration, for any reason, does not constitute wages. Any undercollection in a calendar year not corrected by a deduction made pursuant to the foregoing provisions of this subparagraph is a matter for settlement between the employee and the employer within such calendar year. For provisions relating to the employer's liability for the tax, whether or not he collects it from the employees, see § 31.3403-1.

§ 301.6205 **Statutory provisions; special rules applicable to certain employment taxes.** [Sec. 6205, IRC]

§ 301.6205-1 (T.D. 6119, filed 12-31-54; republished in T.D. 6498, filed 10-24-60.) **Special rules applicable to certain employment taxes.**

For regulations under section 6205, see § 31.6205-1 of this chapter (Employment Tax Regulations).

§ 301.6206 **Statutory provisions; cross references.** [Sec. 6206, IRC]

§ 301.6207 **Statutory provisions; cross references.** [Sec. 6207, IRC]

DEFICIENCY PROCEDURES IN CASE OF INCOME, ESTATE AND GIFT TAXES

§ 301.6211 **Statutory provisions; definition of a deficiency.** [Sec. 6211, IRC]

§ 301.6211-1 (T.D. 6119, filed 12-31-54; republished in T.D. 6498, filed 10-24-60; amended by T.D. 7102, filed 3-23-71; TD 7498, filed 7-12-77.) **Deficiency denied.**

(a) In the case of the income tax imposed by subtitle A of the Code, the estate tax imposed by chapter 11, subtitle B, of the Code, or the gift tax imposed by chapter 12, subtitle B, of the Code, the term "deficiency" means the excess of the tax (income, estate, or gift tax, as the case may be) over the sum of the amount shown as such tax by the taxpayer upon his return and the amounts previously assessed (or collected without assessment) as a deficiency; but such sum shall first be reduced by the amount of rebates made. If no return is made, or if the return (except a return of income tax pursuant to sec. 6014) does not show any tax, for the purpose of the definition "the amount shown as the tax by the taxpayer upon his return" shall be considered as zero. Accordingly, in any such case, if no deficiencies with respect to the tax have been assessed, or collected without assessment, and no rebates with respect to the tax have been made, the deficiency is the amount of the tax imposed by subtitle A, chapter 11, or chapter 12. Any amount shown as additional tax on an "amended return", so-called (other than amounts of additional tax which such return clearly indicates the taxpayer is protesting rather than admitting) filed after the due date of the return, shall be treated as an amount shown by the taxpayer "upon his return" for purposes of computing the amount of a deficiency.

(b) For purposes of the definition, the income tax imposed by subtitle A and the income tax shown on the return shall both be determined without regard to the credit provided in section 31 for income tax withheld at the source and without regard to so much of the credit provided in section 32 for income taxes withheld at the source as exceeds 2 percent of the interest on tax-free covenant bonds described in section 1451. Payments on account of estimated income tax, like other payments of tax by the taxpayer, shall likewise be disre-

Reg. § 301.6211-1(b)

garded in the determination of a deficiency.

(c) The computation by the Internal Revenue Service, pursuant to section 6014, of the income tax imposed by subtitle A shall be considered as having been made by the taxpayer and the tax so computed shall be considered as the tax shown by the taxpayer upon his return.

(d) If so much of the credit claimed on the return for income taxes withheld at the source as exceeds 2 percent of the interest on tax-free covenant bonds is greater than the amount of such credit allowable, the unpaid portion of the tax attributable to such difference will be collected not as a deficiency but as an underpayment of the tax shown on the return.

(e) This section may be illustrated by the following examples:

Example (1). The amount of income tax shown by the taxpayer upon his return for the calendar year 1954 was $1,600. The taxpayer had no amounts previously assessed (or collected without assessment) as a deficiency. He claimed a credit in the amount of $2,050 for tax withheld at source on wages under section 3402, and a refund of $450 (not a rebate under section 6211) was made to him as an overpayment of tax for the taxable year. It is later determined that the correct tax for the taxable year is $1,850. A deficiency of $250 is determined as follows:

Tax imposed by subtitle A	$1,850
Tax shown on return	$1,600
Tax previously assessed (or collected without assessment) as a deficiency	None
Total	1,600
Amount of rebates made	None
Balance	1,600
Deficiency	250

Example (2). The taxpayer made a return for the calendar year 1954 showing a tax of $1,250 before any credits for tax withheld at the source. He claimed a credit in the amount of $800 for tax withheld at source on wages under section 3402 and $60 for tax paid at source under section 1451 upon interest on bonds containing a tax-free covenant. The taxpayer had no amounts previously assessed (or collected without assessment) as a deficiency. The district director determines that the 2 percent tax paid at the source on tax-free covenant bonds is $40 instead of $60 as claimed by the taxpayer and that the tax imposed by subtitle A is $1,360 (total tax $1,400 less $40 paid at source on tax-free covenant bonds). A deficiency in the amount of $170 is determined as follows:

Tax imposed by subtitle A ($1,400 minus $40)	$1,360
Tax shown on return ($1,250 minus $60)	$1,190
Tax previously assessed (or collected without assessment) as a deficiency	None
Total	1,190
Amount of rebates made	None
Balance	1,190
Deficiency	170

(f) As used in section 6211, the term "rebate" means so much of an abatement, credit, refund, or other repayment as is made on the ground that the tax imposed by subtitle A or B of the Code is less than the excess of (1) the amount shown as the tax by the taxpayer upon his return increased by the amount previously assessed (or collected without assessment) as a deficiency over (2) the amount of rebates previously made. For example, assume that the amount of income tax shown by the taxpayer upon his return for the taxable year is $600 and the amount claimed as a credit under section 31 for income tax withheld at the source is $900. If the district director determines that the tax imposed by subtitle A is $600 and makes a refund of $300, no part of such refund constitutes a "rebate" since the refund is not made on the ground that the tax imposed by subtitle A is less than the tax shown on the return. If, however, the district director determines that the tax imposed by subtitle A is $500 and refunds $400, the amount of $100 of such refund would constitute a rebate since it is made on the ground that the tax imposed by subtitle A ($500) is less than the tax shown on the return ($600). The amount of such rebate ($100) would be taken into account in arriving at the amount of any deficiency subsequently determined.

o— § 301.6212 **Statutory provisions; notice of deficiency.** [Sec. 6212, IRC]

o— § 301.6212-1 (T.D. 6119 filed 12-31-54 as amended by T.D. 6425, filed 11-10-59; republished in T.D. 6498, filed 10-24-60; further amended by T.D. 7238, filed 12-28-72.) **Notice of deficiency.**

(a) *General rule.* If a district director (or an assistant regional commissioner, appellate) determines that there is a deficiency in respect of income, estate, or gift tax imposed by subtitle A or B of the Code, he is authorized to notify the taxpayer of the deficiency by registered mail prior to September 3, 1958, and by either registered or certified mail on and after September 3, 1958.

(b) *Address for notice of deficiency*—(1) *Income and gift taxes.* Unless the district director for the district in which the return in question was filed has been notified under the provisions of section 6903 as to the existence of a fiduciary relationship, notice of a deficiency in respect of income tax or gift tax shall be sufficient if mailed to the taxpayer at his last known address, even though such taxpayer is deceased, or is under a legal disability, or, in the case of a corporation, has terminated its existence.

(2) *Joint income tax returns.* If a joint income tax return has been filed by husband and wife, the district director (or assistant regional commissioner, appellate) may, unless the district director for the district in which such joint return was filed has been notified by either spouse that a separate residence has been established, send either a joint or separate notice of deficiency to the taxpayers at their last known address. If, however, the proper district director has been so notified, a separate notice of deficiency, that is, a duplicate original of the joint notice, must be sent by registered mail prior to September 3, 1958, and by either registered or certified mail on and after September 3, 1958, to each spouse at his or her last known address. The notice of separate residences should be addressed to the district director

for the district in which the joint return was filed.

(3) *Estate tax.* In the absence of notice, under the provisions of section 6903 as to the existence of a fiduciary relationship, to the district director for the district in which the estate tax return was filed, notice of a deficiency in respect of the estate tax imposed by chapter 11 of subtitle B of the Code, shall be sufficient if addressed in the name of the decedent or other person subject to liability and mailed to his last known address.

(c) *Further deficiency letters restricted.* If the district director (or assistant regional commissioner, appellate) mails to the taxpayer notice of a deficiency, and the taxpayer files a petition with the Tax Court within the prescribed period, no additional deficiency may be determined with respect to income tax for the same taxable year, gift tax for the same calendar quarter (calendar year with respect to gifts made before January 1, 1971), or estate tax with respect to the taxable estate of the same decedent. This restriction shall not apply in the case of fraud, assertion of greater deficiencies before the Tax Court as provided in section 6214(a), mathematical errors as provided in section 6213(b)(1), or jeopardy assessments as provided in section 6861(c).

§ 301.6213 Statutory provisions; restrictions applicable to deficiencies; petition to Tax Court. [Sec. 6213, IRC]

§ 301.6213-1 (T.D. 6119, filed 12-31-54 as amended by T.D. 6425, filed 11-10-59; republished in T.D. 6498, filed 10-24-60; amended by T.D. 6585, filed 12-27-61.) Restrictions applicable to deficiencies; petition to Tax Court.

(a) *Time for filing petition and restrictions on assessment*—(1) *Time for filing petition.* Within 90 days after notice of the deficiency is mailed (or within 150 days after mailing in the case of such notice addressed to a person outside the States of the Union and the District of Columbia), as provided in section 6212, a petition may be filed with the Tax Court of the United States for a redetermination of the deficiency. In determining such 90-day or 150-day period, Saturday, Sunday, or a legal holiday in the District of Columbia is not counted as the 90th or 150th day. In determining the time for filing a petition with the Tax Court in the case of a notice of deficiency mailed to a resident of Alaska prior to 12:01 p.m. (E.S.T.), January 3, 1959, and in the case of a notice of deficiency mailed to a resident of Hawaii prior to 4:00 p.m. (E.D.S.T.), August 21, 1959, the term "States of the Union" does not include Alaska or Hawaii, respectively, and the 150-day period applies. In determining the time within which a petition to the Tax Court may be filed in the case of a notice of deficiency mailed to a resident of Alaska after 12:01 p.m. (E.S.T.), January 3, 1959, and in the case of a notice of deficiency mailed to a resident of Hawaii after 4:00 p.m. (E.D.S.T.), August 21, 1959, the term "States of the Union" includes Alaska and Hawaii, respectively, and the 90-day period applies.

(2) *Restrictions on assessment.* Except as otherwise provided by this section, by section 6861(a) (relating to jeopardy assessments of income, estate, and gift taxes), by section 6871(a) (relating to immediate assessment of claims for income, estate, and gift taxes in bankruptcy and receivership cases), or by section 7485 (in case taxpayer petitions for a review of a Tax Court decision without filing bond), no assessment of a deficiency in respect of a tax imposed by subtitle A or B of the Code and no levy or proceeding in court for its collection shall be made until notice of deficiency has been mailed to the taxpayer, nor until the expiration of the 90-day or 150-day period within which a petition may be filed with the Tax Court, nor, if a petition has been filed with the Tax Court, until the decision of the Tax Court has become final. As to the date on which a decision of the Tax Court becomes final, see section 7481. Notwithstanding the provisions of section 7421 (a), the making of an assessment or the beginning of a proceeding or levy which is forbidden by this paragraph may be enjoined by a proceeding in the proper court.

(b) *Exceptions to restrictions on assessment of deficiencies*—(1) *Mathematical errors.* If a taxpayer is notified of an additional amount of tax due on account of a mathematical error appearing upon the return, such notice is not deemed a notice of deficiency, and the taxpayer has no right to file a petition with the Tax Court upon the basis of such notice, nor is the assessment of such additional amount prohibited by section 6213(a).

(2) *Tentative carryback adjustments.* (i) If the district director or the director of the regional service center determines that any amount applied, credited, or refunded under section 6411(b) with respect to an application for a tentative carryback adjustment is in excess of the overassessment properly attributable to the carryback upon which such application was based, the district director or the director of the regional service center may assess the amount of the excess as a deficiency as if such deficiency were due to a mathematical error appearing on the return. That is, the district director or the director of the regional sevice center may assess an amount equal to the excess, and such amount may be collected, without regard to the restrictions on assessment and collection imposed by section 6213(a). Thus, the district director or the director of the regional service center may assess such amount without regard to whether the taxpayer has been mailed a prior notice of deficiency. Either before or after assessing such an amount, the district director or the director of the regional service center will notify the taxpayer that such assessment has been or will be made. Such notice will not constitute a notice of deficiency, and the taxpayer may not file a petition with the Tax Court of the United States based on such notice. However, the taxpayer, within the applicable period of limitation, may file a regular claim for credit or refund based on the carryback, if he has not already filed such a claim, and may maintain a suit based on such claim if it is disallowed or if it is not acted upon by the Internal Revenue Service within 6 months from the date the claim was filed.

(ii) The method provided in subdivision (i) of this subparagraph to recover any

Reg. § 301.6213-1 (b) (2)

amount applied, credited, or refunded in respect of an application for a tentative carryback adjustment which should not have been so applied, credited, or refunded is not an exclusive method. Two other methods are available to recover such amount: *(a)* by way of a deficiency notice under section 6212; or *(b)* by a suit to recover an erroneous refund under section 7405. Any one or more of the three available methods may be used to recover any amount which was improperly applied, credited, or refunded in respect of an application for a tentative carryback adjustment.

(3) *Assessment of amount paid.* Any payment made after the mailing of a notice of deficiency which is made by the taxpayer as a payment with respect to the proposed deficiency may be assessed without regard to the restrictions on assessment and collection imposed by section 6213 (a) even though the taxpayer has not filed a waiver of restrictions on assessment as provided in section 6213(d). A payment of all or part of the deficiency asserted in the notice together with the assessment of the amount so paid will not affect the jurisdiction of the Tax Court. If any payment is made before the mailing of a notice of deficiency, the district director or the director of the regional service center is not prohibited by section 6213(a) from assessing such amount, and such amount may be assessed if such action is deemed to be proper. If such amount is assessed, the assessment is taken into account in determining whether or not there is a deficiency for which a notice of deficiency must be issued. Thus, if such a payment satisfies the taxpayer's tax liability, no notice of deficiency will be mailed and the Tax Court will have no jurisdiction over the matter. In any case in which there is a controversy as to the correct amount of the tax liability, the assessment of any amount pursuant to the provisions of section 6213(b)(3) shall in no way be considered to be the acceptance of an offer by the taxpayer to settle such controversy.

(4) *Jeopardy.* If the district director believes that the assessment or collection of a deficiency will be jeopardized by delay, such deficiency shall be assessed immediately, as provided in section 6861(a).

(c) *Failure to file petition.* If no petition is filed with the Tax Court within the period prescribed in section 6213(a), the district director or the director of the regional service center shall assess the amount determined as the deficiency and of which the taxpayer was notified by registered or certified mail and the taxpayer shall pay the same upon notice and demand therefor. In such case the district director will not be precluded from determining a further deficiency and notifying the taxpayer thereof by registered or certified mail. If a petition is filed with the Tax Court the taxpayer should notify the district director who issued the notice of deficiency that the petition has been filed in order to prevent an assessment of the amount determined to be the deficiency.

(d) *Waiver of restrictions.* The taxpayer may at any time by a signed notice in writing filed with the district director waive the restrictions on the assessment and collection of the whole or any part of the deficiency. The notice must in all cases be filed with the district director or other authorized official under whose jurisdiction the audit or other consideration of the return in question is being conducted. The filing of such notice with the Tax Court does not constitute filing with the district director within the meaning of the Code. After such waiver has been acted upon by the district director and the assessment has been made in accordance with its terms, the waiver cannot be withdrawn.

O—☛ § 301.6214 Statutory provisions; determinations by Tax Court. [Sec. 6214, IRC]

O—☛ § 301.6215 Statutory provisions; assessment of deficiency found by Tax Court. [Sec. 6215, IRC]

O—☛ § 301.6215-1 (T.D. 6119, filed 12-31-54; republished in T.D. 6498, filed 10-24-60; amended by T.D. 6585, filed 12-27-61.) Assessment of deficiency found by Tax Court.

Where a petition has been filed with the Tax Court, the entire amount redetermined as the deficiency by the decision of the Tax Court which has become final shall be assessed by the district director or the director of the regional service center and the unpaid portion of the amount so assessed shall be paid by the taxpayer upon notice and demand therefor.

O—☛ § 301.6216 Statutory provisions; cross references. [Sec. 6216, IRC]

COLLECTION
GENERAL PROVISIONS

○— § 301.6301 Statutory provisions; collection authority. [Sec. 6301, IRC]

○— § 301.6301-1 (T.D. 6119, filed 12-31-54; republished in T.D. 6498, filed 10-24-60.) **Collection authority.**

The taxes imposed by the internal revenue laws shall be collected by district directors of internal revenue. See, however, section 6304, relating to the collection of certain taxes under the provisions of the Tariff Act of 1930 (19 U.S.C. ch. 4).

○— § 1.6302 Statutory provisions; mode or time of collection, use of Government depositaries. [Sec. 6302, IRC]

○— § 1.6302-1 (T.D. 6914, filed 3-7-67; amended by T.D. 6941, filed 12-15-67 and T.D. 7293, filed 11-27-73.) **Use of Government depositaries in connection with corporation income and estimated income taxes.**

(a) *Requirement.* For taxable years ending on or after December 31, 1967, a corporation shall deposit with a Federal Reserve bank all payments of tax imposed by chapter 1 of the Code (including any payments of estimated tax) on or before the date otherwise prescribed for paying such tax. For taxable years ending after December 31, 1971, this paragraph does not apply to a foreign corporation which has no office or place of business in the United States. For taxable years ending before January 1, 1972, and on or after December 31, 1968, this paragraph does not apply to a foreign corporation which at no time during the taxable year is engaged in a trade or business in the United States. For taxable years ending before December 31, 1968, this paragraph does not apply to a foreign corporation.

(b) *Depositary forms.* A deposit required to be made by this section shall be made separately from a deposit required by any other section. A corporation may make one, or more than one, remittance of the amount required by this section to be deposited. Each remittance shall be accompanied by a Federal Tax Deposit, Corporation Income Taxes, form (Form 503) which shall be prepared in accordance with the instructions applicable thereto. The remittance, together with Form 503, shall be forwarded to a Federal Reserve bank, or at the election of the corporation, to a commercial bank authorized in accordance with Treasury Department Circular No. 1079 to accept remittances of the tax for transmission to a Federal Reserve bank. The timeliness of the deposit will be determined by the date of receipt by a Federal Reserve bank or by the authorized commercial bank, whichever is earlier. Each corporation making deposits pursuant to this section shall report on the return or declaration for the period with respect to which such deposits are made information regarding such deposits in accordance with the instructions applicable to such return or declaration. Amounts deposited under this section shall be considered as payment of the tax.

(c) *Procurement of the prescribed forms.* Copies of Form 503, the Federal Tax Deposit, Corporation Income Taxes, form will so far as possible be furnished corporations. A corporation will not be excused from making a deposit, however, by the fact that no form has been furnished to it. Corporations not supplied with the proper form should make application therefor to the district director (or director of a service center) in ample time to make the required deposits within the time prescribed. The corporation may secure the form or additional forms by applying therefor and supplying the district director or director of a service center with its name, identification number, address and the taxable year to which the deposits will relate.

(d) *Failure to deposit.* For provisions relating to the penalty for failure to make a deposit within the prescribed time, see the provisions of § 301.6656-1 of this chapter (Regulations on Procedure and Administration).

○— § 1.6302-2 (T.D. 6922, filed 6-16-67; amended by T.D. 6941, filed 12-15-67; T.D. 6957, filed 6-3-68 and T.D. 7243, filed 1-2-73.) **Use of Government depositories for payment of tax withheld on nonresident aliens and foreign corporations.**

(a) *Time for making deposits*—(1) *Deposits for 1973 and subsequent years*—(i) *Monthly deposits.* Except as provided in subdivisions (ii) and (iv) of this subparagraph, every withholding agent who, pursuant to chapter 3 of the Code, has accumulated at the close of any calendar month beginning on or after January 1, 1973, an aggregate amount of undeposited taxes of $200 or more shall deposit such aggregate amount with a Federal Reserve bank or authorized commercial bank (see paragraph (b)(1)(ii) of this section) within 15 days after the close of such calendar month. However, the preceding sentence shall not apply if the withholding agent has made a deposit of taxes pursuant to subdivision (ii) of this subparagraph with respect to a quarter-monthly period which occurred during such month.

(ii) *Quarter-monthly deposits.* If at the close of any quarter-monthly period within a calendar month beginning on or after January 1, 1973, the aggregate amount of undeposited taxes required to be withheld pursuant to chapter 3 of the Code is $2,000 or more, the withholding agent shall deposit such aggregate amount in a Federal Reserve bank or authorized commercial bank within 3 banking days after the close of such quarter-monthly period. For purposes of determining the amount of undeposited taxes at the close of a quarter-monthly period, undeposited taxes withheld with respect to items paid during a prior quarter-monthly period shall not be taken into account if the withholding agent made a deposit with respect to such prior quarter-monthly period. A withholding agent will be considered to have complied with the requirements of this subdivision with respect to the close of a quarter-monthly period if—

(a) His deposit is not less than 90 percent of the aggregate amount of the taxes required to be withheld during the period for which the deposit is made, and

Reg. § 1.6302-2(a)(1)

24,340.2 (I.R.C.) Reg. § 1.6302-2(a)(1)

(b) If such quarter-monthly period occurs in a month other than December, he deposits any underpayment with his first deposit which is otherwise required by this subparagraph to be made after the 15th day of the following month. Any underpayment of $200 or more for a quarter-monthly period closing during December must be deposited on or before the following January 31. For purposes of this subparagraph, the term "quarter-monthly period"

means the first 7 days of a calendar month, the 8th day through the 15th day of a calendar month, the 16th day through the 22nd day of a calendar month, or the portion of a calendar month following the 22nd day of such month.

(iii) *Excess deposits.* The excess (if any) of a deposit over the actual taxes for a monthly or quarter-monthly deposit period shall be applied in order of time to each of the withholding agent's succeeding deposits with respect to the same calendar year, until exhausted, to the extent that the amount by which the taxes for a subsequent deposit period exceed the deposit for such subsequent deposit period.

(iv) *Annual deposits.* If at the close of the month of December of each calendar year beginning on or after January 1, 1973, the aggregate amount of undeposited taxes required to be withheld pursuant to chapter 3 of the Code is less than $200, the withholding agent may deposit such aggregate amount in a Federal Reserve bank or authorized commercial bank on or before March 15 of the following calendar year. If such aggregate amount is not so deposited, it shall be remitted in accordance with paragraph (a)(2) of § 1.1461-3.

(2) *Deposits for years prior to 1973*—
(i) *Monthly deposits.* Except as provided in subdivision (ii) of this subparagraph, every withholding agent who, pursuant to chapter 3 of the Code, withholds during any calendar month (other than the last month of a calendar quarter) of a calendar year beginning before January 1, 1973, more than $100 in the aggregate shall deposit such aggregate amount with a Federal Reserve bank or authorized commercial bank within 15 days after the close of such calendar month, and who so withholds during March 1968, more than $100 in the aggregate shall so deposit such aggregate amount on or before April 30, 1968.

(ii) *Semimonthly deposits.* Every withholding agent who, pursuant to chapter 3 of the Code, withholds during any calendar month of a calendar quarter of a calendar year beginning before January 1, 1973, more than $2,500 in the aggregate shall deposit any tax, which is required to be withheld under such chapter during any semimonthly period of the next succeeding calendar quarter, with a Federal Reserve bank or authorized commercial bank within 3 banking days after the close of the semimonthly period during which the amounts to which such withholding relates are paid. For purposes of this subdivision, the term "semimonthly period" means the first 15 days of a calendar month or the part of a calendar month following the 15th day of such month. A withholding agent will be considered to have complied with the deposit requirements of this subdivision in respect of any semimonthly period if (a) his deposit for such semimonthly period is made within the time otherwise prescribed, (b) is not less than 90 percent of the aggregate amount of the tax required to be withheld under chapter 3 of the Code during such semimonthly period, and (c) if such semimonthly period occurs in a calendar month other than the last month in a calendar quarter, he deposits, within 3 banking days after the 15th day of the month following such calendar month, the balance of any amount withheld during such calendar month and not previously deposited, or if such semimonthly period occurs in March 1968, he deposits, on or before the last day of April 1968, the balance of any amount withheld during such calendar month and not previously deposited. In a case where an adjustment in the amount of a deposit for a semimonthly period is allowed pursuant to paragraph (b)(2) of § 1.1461-4, the 90-percent requirement of this subdivision will be considered met if the deposit for such period is not less than 90 percent of the aggregate amount of tax required to be withheld during such semimonthly period (determined without regard to such adjustment), reduced by the amount of such adjustment. See paragraph (b)(2) of § 1.1461-4 and example (2) thereunder. For determining the amount of tax required to be withheld under chapter 3 of the Code where there has been a reimbursement of overwithheld tax, see paragraph (b)(1)(ii) of § 1.1461-4.

(iii) *Quarterly deposits.* Every withholding agent who, pursuant to chapter 3 of the Code, withholds during any calendar quarter beginning after March 31, 1968, and ending on or before December 31, 1972, tax in an amount which exceeds by more than $100 the total amount deposited by him pursuant to subdivisions (i) and (ii) of this subparagraph for such calendar quarter, shall, on or before the last day of the first calendar month following the close of the calendar quarter, deposit with a Federal Reserve bank or authorized commercial bank an amount equal to the amount by which the total tax withheld during the calendar quarter exceeds the total deposits (if any) made pursuant to subdivisions (i) and (ii) of this subparagraph.

(iv) *Annual deposits.* If for any reason the total amount of tax required to be returned for a calendar year beginning after December 31, 1967, and before January 1, 1973, pursuant to paragraph (b) of § 1.1461-2 (relating to return of tax withheld) exceeds by more than $100 the sum of—

(a) Amounts deposited pursuant to subdivisions (i), (ii), and (iii) of this subparagraph (including any voluntary deposits made pursuant to paragraph (b)(3) of this section), and

(b) Amounts paid pursuant to paragraph (a)(1) of § 1.1461-3, for such calendar year, the withholding agent shall deposit the balance of tax due for such year with a Federal Reserve bank or authorized commercial bank on or before the 15th day of the third month following the close of the calendar year.

(v) *Transitional rules.* Notwithstanding the provisions of paragraph (a)(1) of § 1.1461-3 and of subdivisions (i) and (ii) of this subparagraph, the aggregate amount of tax required to be withheld under chapter 3 of the Code by any withholding agent after December 31, 1966, and before June 1, 1967, shall be deposited with a Federal Reserve bank on or before June 22, 1967. For the purpose of paragraph (b)(2) of this section any amount deposited in accordance with the requirement of this subparagraph shall be considered as if it were deposited with respect to amounts withheld during the calendar quarter beginning April 1, 1967.

Reg. § 1.6302-2(a)(2)

(3) *Cross reference.* For rules relating to the adjustment of deposits, see § 1.1461-4(b) and § 1.6414-1. For rules requiring payment of any undeposited tax, see § 1.1461-3.

(b) *Depositary forms*—(1) *Remittances*—(i) *Deposits for 1967.* Each remittance of amounts required to be deposited by paragraph (a) of this section for 1967 only, shall be accompanied by a Federal Depositary Receipt (Form 450) which shall be prepared in accordance with the instructions applicable thereto. The withholding agent shall forward such remittance, together with such depositary receipt, to a Federal Reserve bank or, at his election to a commercial bank authorized in accordance with Treasury Department Circular No. 848, 31 CFR Part 213, to accept remittances of the taxes for transmission to a Federal Reserve bank. After the Federal Reserve bank has validated the depositary receipt, such depositary receipt will be returned to the withholding agent. For purposes of this subparagraph Form 450 and Treasury Department Circular No. 848 shall be deemed to apply to the tax required to be withheld under chapter 3 of the Code.

(ii) *Deposits for 1968 and subsequent years.* Each remittance of amounts required to be deposited by paragraph (a) of this section for years subsequent to 1967 shall be accompanied by a Federal Tax Deposit, Tax Withheld at Source on Nonresident Aliens, Foreign Corporations, Tax-Free Covenant Bonds, form (Form 512) which shall be prepared in accordance with the instructions applicable thereto. The remittance, together with Form 512, shall be forwarded to a Federal Reserve bank, or at the election of the withholding agent to a commercial bank authorized in accordance with Treasury Department Circular No. 1079, 31 CFR Part 214, to accept remittances of the tax for transmission to a Federal Reserve bank. The timeliness of the deposit will be determined by the date of receipt by a Federal Reserve bank or by the authorized commercial bank, whichever is earlier. Each withholding agent making deposits pursuant to this section shall report on the return for the period with respect to which such deposits are made information regarding such deposits in accordance with the instructions applicable to such return.

(2) *Quarterly transmission of depositary receipts for 1967.* For deposits for the year 1967 only, every withholding agent making deposits pursuant to subparagraph (1)(i) of this paragraph shall forward the validated depositary receipts (Form 450) to the Director of International Operations, Internal Revenue Service, Washington D.C. 20225, on or before the last day of the first calendar month following the close of the calendar quarter during which the tax was withheld to which such receipts apply. The depositary receipts shall be forwarded with quarterly transmittal Form 4277, which shall be prepared in accordance with the instructions applicable thereto and shall identify the withholding agent for whose account such transmittal form is made. In order to secure a proper crediting of deposits or payments of tax for the account of a withholding agent against the tax liability of such withholding agent, the identification of the withholding agent on the quarterly transmittal Form 4277 must conform to the identification of the withholding agent on the annual return of tax on Form 1042 required by paragraph (b) of § 1.1461-2.

(3) *Voluntary deposits.* An amount of tax which is not required to be deposited may nevertheless be deposited if the withholding agent so desires. If such a voluntary deposit is made for 1967, the withholding agent shall make it in ample time to enable the Federal Reserve bank to return the validated receipt to the withholding agent so that it can be transmitted to the Internal Revenue Service in accordance with subparagraph (2) of this paragraph.

(4) *Separation of deposits.* A deposit required by paragraph (a) of this section for any period occurring in one calendar year shall be made separately from any deposit for any period occurring in another calendar year. In addition, a deposit required to be made by paragraph (a) of this section shall be made separately from a deposit required by any other section.

(5) *Multiple remittances.* A withholding agent may make one, or more than one, remittance of the amount required to be deposited if each remittance is accompanied by the applicable deposit form.

(6) *Time deemed paid.* In general, amounts deposited under this section shall be considered as paid on the last day prescribed for filing the return (Form 1042) in respect of such tax (determined without regard to any extension of time for filing such return), or at the time deposited, whichever is later. For purposes of section 6511 and the regulations thereunder, relating to period of limitation on credit or refund, if an amount is so deposited prior to April 15th of a calendar year immediately succeeding the calendar year in which occurs the period for which such amount was so deposited, such amount shall be considered as paid on such April 15th.

(c) *Procurement of prescribed forms.* Copies of the applicable deposit form will so far as possible be furnished withholding agents. A withholding agent will not be excused from making a deposit, however, by the fact that no form has been furnished to it. A withholding agent not supplied with the proper form should make application therefor in ample time to make the required deposits within the time prescribed. The withholding agent may secure the form or additional forms by applying therefor and supplying its name, identification number, address, and the taxable period to which the deposits will relate. Copies of Form 450, for deposits for 1967 only, may be secured by application to the district director or to a Federal Reserve bank. The address of the withholding agent as entered on such form should be the address to which the receipt should be returned following validation by the Federal Reserve bank. Copies of Form 512, for deposits only for years subsequent to 1967, may be secured by application therefor to the district director or director of a service center.

(d) *Penalties for failure to make deposits.* For provisions relating to the penalty for failure to make a deposit within the time prescribed by this section, see § 301.6656-1 of this chapter (Procedure and Administration Regulations).

(e) *Saturday, Sunday, or legal holidays.* For provisions relating to the time for performance of acts where the last day falls on Saturday, Sunday, or a legal holiday, see § 301.7503-1 of this chapter (Procedure and Administration Regulations).

(f) *Employer identification number.* For the definition of the term "employer identification number", see § 301.7701-12 of this chapter (Procedure and Administration Regulations). For provisions relating to the penalty for failure to include the employer identification number in a return, statement, or other document, see § 301.-6676-1 of such chapter.

(g) *Effective date.* Except as otherwise provided, this section shall apply to tax required to be withheld under chapter 3 of the Code after 1966.

○— § 301.6302 Statutory provisions; mode or time of collection. [Sec. 6302, IRC]

○— § 301.6302-1 (T.D. 6119, filed 12-31-54; republished in T.D. 6498, filed 10-19-60; amended by T.D. 6922, filed 6-16-67.) Mode or time of collection of taxes.—

(a) *Employment and excise taxes.* For provisions relating to the mode or time of collection of certain employment and excise taxes and the use of Federal Reserve banks and authorized commercial banks in connection with the payment thereof, see the regulations relating to the particular tax.

(b) *Income taxes.* (1) For provisions relating to the use of Federal Reserve banks or authorized commercial banks in depositing income and estimated income taxes of certain corporations, see § 1.6302-1 of this chapter (Income Tax Regulations).

(2) For provisions relating to the use of Federal Reserve banks or authorized commercial banks in depositing the tax required to be withheld under chapter 3 of the Code on nonresident aliens and foreign corporations and tax-free covenant bonds, see § 1.6302-2 of this chapter.

○— § 31.6302 (c) Statutory provisions; mode or time of collection; use of Government depositaries. [Sec. 6302(c), IRC]

○— § 31.6302 (c)-1 (T.D. 6354, filed 1-13-59; republished in T.D. 6516, filed 12-19-60; amended by T.D. 6872, filed 1-5-66; T.D. 6884, filed 5-16-66; T.D. 6903, filed 12-19-66; T.D. 6915, filed 3-28-67; T.D. 6941, filed 12-15-67; T.D. 6957, filed 6-3-68; T.D. 7078, filed 12-4-70 and T.D. 7096, filed 3-17-71.) **Use of Government depositaries in connection with taxes under Federal Insurance Contributions Act and income tax withheld.**

(a) *Requirement*—(1) *In general.* (i) In the case of a calendar month which begins after January 31, 1971—

(a) Except as provided in paragraph (b) of this section and hereinafter in this subdivision (i), if at the close of any calendar month other than the last month of a period for which a return is required to be filed (hereinafter in this subparagraph referred to as a return period), the aggregate amount of taxes (as defined in subdivision (iii) of this subparagraph) is $200 or more, the employer shall deposit the undeposited taxes in a Federal Reserve bank or authorized commercial bank (see subparagraph (3)(iii) of this paragraph)

Reg. § 31.6302(c)-1(a)(1)

24,342.2 (I.R.C.)   Reg. § 31.6302(c)-1(a)(1)   3-29-71

within 15 days after the close of such calendar month. However, the preceding sentence shall not apply if the employer has made a deposit of taxes pursuant to (b) of this subdivision (i) with respect to a quarter-monthly period which occurred during such month; or

(b) If at the close of any quarter-monthly period the aggregate amount of undeposited taxes is $2,000 or more, the employer shall deposit the undeposited taxes in a Federal Reserve bank or authorized commercial bank within 3 banking days after the close of such quarter-monthly period. For purposes of determining the amount of undeposited taxes at the close of a quarter-monthly period, undeposited taxes with respect to wages paid during a prior quarter-monthly period shall not be taken into account if the employer has made a deposit with respect to such prior quarter-monthly period. An employer will be considered to have complied with the requirements of this subdivision (i)(b) for a deposit with respect to the close of a quarter-monthly period if—

(1) His deposit is not less than 90 percent of the aggregate amount of the taxes with respect to wages paid during the period for which the deposit is made, and

(2) If such quarter-monthly period occurs in a month other than the last month of a return period, he deposits any underpayment with his first deposit which is otherwise required by this subdivision (i) to be made after the 15th day of the following month.

The excess (if any) of a deposit over the actual taxes for a deposit period shall be applied in order of time to each of the employer's succeeding deposits with respect to the same return period, until exhausted, to the extent that the amount by which the taxes for a subsequent deposit period exceed the deposit for such subsequent deposit period. For purposes of this subdivision (i), "quarter-monthly period" means the first 7 days of a calendar month, the 8th day through the 15th day of a calendar month, the 16th day through the 22nd day of a calendar month, or the portion of a calendar month following the 22nd day of such month.

(ii)(a) Except as provided in paragraph (b) of this section and (b) of this subdivision (ii), if during any calendar month which begins before February 1, 1971, other than the last month of a calendar quarter, the aggregate amount of taxes (as defined in subdivision (iii) of this subparagraph) exceeds $100 in the case of an employer, such employer shall deposit such aggregate amount within 15 days after the close of such calendar month with a Federal Reserve bank or authorized commercial bank. Notwithstanding the provisions of this subdivision (ii)(a)—

(1) Amounts required to be deposited for May 1963 may be deposited after June 15, 1966, but not later than June 20, 1966, if such amounts are combined with an amount required to be deposited under (b) of this subdivision (ii) for the first semi-monthly period in June 1966, and

(2) Amounts required to be deposited under this subdivision (ii) for January 1967 may be deposited after February 15, 1967, but not later than February 20, 1967, if such amounts are combined with an amount required to be deposited under (b) of this subdivision (ii) for the first semi-monthly period in February 1967.

(b) This subdivision (ii)(b) shall apply to taxes with respect to wages paid by an employer after January 31, 1967, and before February 1, 1971, if the aggregate of the taxes with respect to wages paid during any calendar month in the preceding calendar quarter exceeded $2,500 in the case of such employer. This subdivision (ii)(b) also applies to taxes with respect to wages paid by an employer during June 1966, during either of the last two calendar quarters in the calendar year 1966, or during January 1967, if the aggregate of the taxes with respect to wages paid during any calendar month in the preceding calendar quarter exceeded $4,000 in the case of such employer. An employer shall deposit taxes to which this subdivision (ii)(b) applies in a Federal Reserve bank or authorized commercial bank within 3 banking days after the close of the semimonthly period during which the wages to which such taxes relate are paid. For purposes of this subdivision (ii)(b) "semimonthly period" means the first 15 days of a calendar month or the portion of a calendar month following the 15th of such month. An employer will be considered to have complied with the requirements of this subdivision (ii)(b) for a semimonthly period if—

(1)(i) His deposit for such semimonthly period is not less than 90 percent of the aggregate amount of the taxes for such period, and (ii) if such period occurs in a month other than the last month in a calendar quarter, he deposits any underpayment for such month within 3 banking days after the 15th day of the following month;

(2)(i) His deposit for each semimonthly period in the month is not less than 45 percent of the aggregate amount of the taxes for the month, and (ii) if such month is other than the last month in a calendar quarter, he deposits any underpayment for such month within 3 banking days after the 15th day of the following month; or

(3)(i) His deposit for each semimonthly period in the month is not less than 50 percent of the aggregate amount of the taxes for the preceding month, and (ii) if the current month is other than the last month in a calendar quarter, he deposits any underpayment for such month within 3 banking days after the 15th day of the following month.

Items (2) and (3) of this subdivision (ii)(b) shall not apply to any employer who normally pays in the first semimonthly period in each month more than 75 percent of the total wages paid during the month.

(iii) As used in subdivisions (i) and (ii) of this subparagraph, the term "taxes" means—

(a) The employee tax withheld under section 3102,

(b) The employer tax under section 3111, and

(c) The income tax withheld under section 3402,

exclusive of taxes with respect to wages for domestic service in a private home of the employer or, if paid before April 1, 1971, wages for agricultural labor. In addition, with respect to wages paid after December 31, 1970, and before April 1, 1971, for agricultural labor, any taxes described in subparagraph (2)(ii) of this paragraph which are not required under such subparagraph to be deposited, and any income tax withheld under section 3402 with respect to such wages, shall be deemed to be "taxes" on and after April 1, 1971.

(iv) If the aggregate amount of taxes reportable on a return (other than a return on Form 942) for a return period exceeds the total amount deposited by the employer pursuant to subdivision (i) or (ii) of this subparagraph for such return period *(a)* by $200 or more in the case of a return period which ends after December 31, 1970, or *(b)* by more than $100 in the case of a return period which ends before January 1, 1971, the employer shall, on or before the last day of the first calendar month following the return period, deposit with a Federal Reserve bank or authorized commercial bank an amount equal to the amount by which the taxes reportable on the return exceed the total deposits (if any) made pursuant to subdivision (i) or (ii) of this subparagraph for such period. As used in this subdivision, the term "taxes" shall have the meaning assigned to such term in subdivision (iii) of this subparagraph, except that the term shall include the taxes referred to in *(a)*, *(b)*, and *(c)* of such subdivision (iii) of this subparagraph with respect to any wages for domestic service in a private home of the employer which the employer elects to report on a quarterly return other than a quarterly return made on Form 942.

(2) *Wages paid before April 1, 1971, with respect to agricultural labor.* (i) *Requirement for 1955.* If during any calendar month, other than the last month of a calendar quarter, in 1955 the aggregate amount of—

(a) The employee tax withheld under section 3102 with respect to wages for agricultural labor, and

(b) The employer tax under section 3111 for such month with respect to wages for agricultural labor, exceeds $100 in the case of an employer, such employer shall deposit such aggregate amount within 15 days after the close of such calendar month with a Federal Reserve bank.

(ii) *Requirement for taxes with respect to wages paid after December 31, 1955, and before April 1, 1971.* Except as provided in paragraph (b) of this section, if during any calendar month other than December, after November 1955 and before April 1971, the aggregate amount of—

(a) The employee tax withheld under section 3102 during such month with respect to wages for agricultural labor, plus any such employee tax which was previously withheld in the same calendar year with respect to such wages but which was neither deposited nor required to be deposited on or before the last day of such month, and

(b) The employer tax under section 3111 for such month with respect to wages for agricultural labor, plus any such employer tax, which was neither deposited nor required to be deposited on or before the last day of such month, for any prior month of the same calendar year with respect to wages for agricultural labor, exceeds $100 in the case of an employer, such employer shall deposit such aggregate amount within 15 days after the close of such calendar month with a Federal Reserve bank or authorized commercial bank.

(iii) *Additional requirement for 1968, 1969, and 1970.* If the aggregate amount of taxes reportable on a return on Form 943 for calendar year 1968, 1969, or 1970, exceeds by more than $100 the total amount deposited by the employer pursuant to subdivision (ii) of this subparagraph for such calendar year, the employer shall, on or before the last day of the first calendar month following the period for which the return is required to be filed, deposit with a Federal Reserve Bank or authorized commercial bank an amount equal to the amount by which the taxes reportable on the return exceed the total deposits (if any) made pursuant to subdivision (ii) of this subparagraph for such calendar year.

(3) *Depositary forms*—(i) *In general.* A deposit required to be made by an employer under subparagraph (1) of this paragraph shall be made separately from any deposit required to be made by him under subparagraph (2) of this paragraph. Similarly, a deposit required to be made by this section shall be made separately from a deposit required by any other section. An employer may make one, or more than one, remittance of the amount required to be deposited. However, a deposit for a period in one calendar quarter shall be made separately from any deposit for a period in another calendar quarter. An amount of tax which is not required to be deposited may nevertheless be deposited if the employer so desires.

(ii) *Deposits for 1967 and prior years.* Each remittance of amounts required to be deposited for periods prior to 1968 shall be accompanied by a Federal Depositary Receipt (Form 450) which shall be prepared in accordance with the instructions applicable thereto. The employer shall forward such remittance, together with such depositary receipt, to a Federal Reserve bank or, at his election, to a commercial bank authorized in accordance with Treasury Department Circular No. 848, 31 CFR Part 213, to accept remittances of the taxes for transmission to a Federal Reserve bank. After the Federal Reserve bank has validated the depositary receipt, such depositary receipt will be returned to the employer. Every employer making deposits pursuant to this section shall attach to his return for the period with respect to which such deposits are made, in part or in full payment of the taxes shown thereon, depositary receipts so validated, and shall pay the balance, if any, of the taxes due for such period. If a voluntary deposit for a period prior to 1968 is made, the employer shall make it in ample time to enable the Federal Reserve bank to return the validated receipt to the employer so that it can be attached to and filed with the employer's return.

(iii) *Deposits for 1968 and subsequent years.* Each remittance of amounts required to be deposited under subparagraph (1) of this paragraph for periods subsequent to 1967 shall be accompanied by a Federal Tax Deposit, Withheld Income and FICA Taxes, form (Form 501), or the federal tax deposit form applicable to FICA taxes and withheld income taxes with respect to agricultural workers (Form 511), or both, as the case may be. Each remittance of amounts required to be deposited under subparagraph (2) of this paragraph for years subsequent to

Reg. § 31.6302(c)-1(a)(3)

24,342.4 (I.R.C.) Reg. § 31.6302(c)-1(a)(3)

1967 and before 1971 and for January, February, and March 1971 shall be accompanied by the federal tax deposit form applicable to FICA taxes with respect to agricultural workers (Form 511). Such forms shall be prepared in accordance with the instructions applicable thereto. The remittance, together with the required form or forms, shall be forwarded to a Federal Reserve bank or, at the election of the employer, to a commercial bank authorized in accordance with Treasury Department Circular No. 1079, 31 CFR Part 214, to accept remittances of the taxes for transmission to a Federal Reserve bank. The timeliness of the deposit will be determined by the date the deposit is received (or is deemed received under section 7502(e)) by a Federal Reserve bank or by the authorized commercial bank, whichever is earlier. Each employer making deposits pursuant to this section shall report on the return for the period with respect to which such deposits are made information regarding such deposits in accordance with the instructions applicable to such return and pay therewith (or deposit by the due date of such return) the balance, if any, of the taxes due for such period.

(iv) *Time deemed paid.* In general, amounts deposited under subdivision (iii) of this subparagraph shall be considered as paid on the last day prescribed for filing the return in respect of such tax (determined without regard to any extension of time for filing such return), or at the time deposited, whichever is later. For purposes of section 6511 and the regulations thereunder, relating to period of limitation on credit or refund, if an amount is so deposited prior to April 15th of a calendar year immediately succeeding the calendar year which contains the period for which such amount was so deposited, such amount shall be considered as paid on such April 15th.

(4) *Procurement of prescribed forms.* Copies of the applicable deposit form will so far as possible be furnished employers. An employer will not be excused from making a deposit, however, by the fact that no form has been furnished to it. An employer not supplied with the proper form should make application therefor in ample time to make the required deposits within the time prescribed. The employer may secure the form or additional forms by applying therefor and supplying his name, identification number, address, and the taxable period to which the deposits will relate. Copies of Form 450 for deposits for periods prior to 1968 may be secured by application to the district director or to a Federal Reserve bank. The address of the employer as entered on such form should be the address to which the receipt should be returned following validation by the Federal Reserve bank. Copies of Form 501 and Form 511 for deposits for periods subsequent to 1967 may be secured by application therefor to the district director or director of a service center.

(b) *Exceptions* — (1) *Monthly returns.* The provisions of this section are not applicable with respect to taxes for the month in which the employer receives notice from the district director that returns are required under § 31.6011 (a)-5, or for any subsequent month for which such a return is required.

(2) *Wages paid in nonconvertible foreign currency.* The provisions of this section are not applicable with respect to taxes paid in nonconvertible foreign currency pursuant to § 301.6316-7 of this chapter (Regulations on Procedure and Administration).

○→ § 31.6302(c)-4 (T.D. 6354, filed 1-13-59; republished in T.D. 6516, filed 12-19-60; redesignated by T.D. 7037, filed 4-27-70.) Cross references.

(a) *Failure to deposit.* For provisions relating to the penalty for failure to make a deposit within the prescribed time, see the provisions of § 301.6656-1 of this chapter (Regulations on Procedure and Administration).

(b) *Saturday, Sunday, or legal holiday.* For provisions relating to the time for performance of acts where the last day falls on Saturday, Sunday, or a legal holiday, see the provisions of § 301.7503-1 of this chapter (Regulations on Procedure and Administration).

○→ § 301.6303 **Statutory provisions; notice and demand for tax.** [Sec. 6303, IRC]

○→ § 301.6303-1 (T.D. 6119, filed 12-31-54; republished in T.D. 6498, filed 10-24-60; amended by T.D. 6585, filed 12-27-61.) **Notice and demand for tax.**

(a) *General rule.* Where it is not otherwise provided by the Code, the district director or the director of the regional service center shall, after the making of an assessment of a tax pursuant to section 6203, give notice to each person liable for the unpaid tax, stating the amount and demanding payment thereof. Such notice shall be given as soon as possible and within 60 days. However, the failure to give notice within 60 days does not invalidate the notice. Such notice shall be left at the dwelling or usual place of business of such person, or shall be sent by mail to such person's last known address.

(b) *Assessment prior to last date for payment.*

If any tax is assessed prior to the last date prescribed for payment of such tax, demand that such tax be paid will not be made before such last date, except where it is believed collection would be jeopardized by delay.

○→ § 301.6304 **Statutory provisions; collection under the Tariff Act.** [Sec. 6304, IRC]

RECEIPT OF PAYMENT

○→ § 301.6311—**Statutory provisions; payment by check or money order.** [Sec. 6311, IRC]

○→ § 301.6311-1 (T.D. 6119, filed 12-31-54; republished in T.D. 6498, filed 10-24-60; amended by T.D. 6872, filed 1-5-66; T.D. 6890, filed 7-18-66 and T.D. 7188, filed 6-28-72.) **Payment by check or money order.**

(a) *Authority to receive* — (1) *In general.* (i) District directors may accept checks drawn on any bank or trust company incorporated under the laws of the United States or under the laws of any State, Territory, or possession of the United States, or money orders in payment for internal revenue taxes, provided such checks or money orders are collectible in U.S. currency at par, and subject to the further provisions contained in this section. District directors may accept such checks or money orders in payment for internal revenue stamps to the extent and under the conditions prescribed in subparagraph (2) of this paragraph. A check or money order in payment for internal revenue taxes or internal revenue stamps should be made payable to the Internal Revenue Service. A check or money order is payable at par only if the full amount thereof is payable without any deduction for exchange or other charges. As used in this section, the term "money order" means: (a) U.S. postal, bank, express, or telegraph money order; (b) money order issued by a domestic building and loan association (as defined in section 7701 (a) (19)) or by a similar association incorporated under the laws of a possession of the United States; (c) a money order issued by such other organization as the Commissioner may designate; and (d) a money order described in subdivision (ii) of this subparagraph in cases therein described. However, the district director may refuse to accept any personal check whenever he has good reason to believe that such check will not be honored upon presentment.

(ii) An American citizen residing in a country with which the United States maintains direct exchange of money orders on a domestic basis may pay his tax by postal money order of such country. For a list of such countries, see section 171.27 of the Postal Manual of the United States.

(iii) If one check or money order is remitted to cover two or more persons' taxes, the remittance should be accompanied by a letter of transmittal clearly identifying—

Reg. § 301.6311-1(a)(1)

24,344 (I.R.C.) Reg. § 301.6311-1(a)(1)

(a) Each person whose tax is to be paid by the remittance;

(b) The amount of the payment on account of each such person; and

(c) The kind of tax paid.

(2) *Payment for internal revenue stamps*—(i) *In general.* The district director may accept checks and money orders described in subparagraph (1) of this paragraph in payment for internal revenue stamps other than stamps for taxes imposed under chapter 34 of the Code (relating to documentary stamps). However, the district director may refuse to accept any personal check whenever he has good reason to believe that such check will not be honored upon presentment. For special provisions relating to documentary stamps, see subdivision (ii) of this subparagraph.

(ii) *Documentary stamps.* The district director may accept in payment for taxes imposed under chapter 34 of the Code (relating to documentary stamps) certified, cashiers' or treasurers' checks drawn on any bank or trust company incorporated under the laws of the United States or under the laws of any State, Territory, or possession of the United States or money orders described in subparagraph (1) of this paragraph. However, if an application has been submitted by a person desiring to tender personal checks for such taxes and the application has been approved by the district director, the district director may accept such personal checks as are described in subparagraph (1) (i) of this paragraph. The application shall be made to the district director and shall contain the applicant's name, address, firm name (if any), such financial information as will enable the district director to determine the amount of the credit to be extended to the applicant, and the approximate value of stamps to be purchased during the period fixed by the district director. The district director is authorized to approve or disapprove such application and, if the application is approved, to fix the maximum amount of the value of the documentary stamps for which personal checks will be accepted and to prescribe such other limitations and conditions as he deems appropriate. The district director may, for good cause, discontinue at any time the acceptance of personal checks under the provisions of this subdivision.

(3) *Payment of tax on distilled spirits, wine, beer, cigars, or cigarettes; proprietor in default.* Where a check or money order tendered in payment for taxes on distilled spirits, wines, beer, or rectified products (imposed under chapter 51 of the Code), or cigars or cigarettes (imposed under chapter 52 of the Code) is not paid on presentment, or where a taxpayer is otherwise in default in payment of such taxes, any remittance for such taxes made during the period of such default, and until the assistant regional commissioner (alcohol, tobacco and firearms) finds that the revenue will not be jeopardized by the acceptance of personal checks (if acceptable to the district director under subparagraph (1) of this paragraph), shall be in cash, or shall be in the form of a certified, cashier's, or treasurer's check, drawn on any bank or trust company incorporated under the laws of the United States, or under the laws of any State or Possession of the United States or a money order as described in subparagraph (1) of this paragraph.

(b) *Checks or money orders not paid*—(1) *Ultimate liability.* The person who tenders any check (whether certified or uncertified, cashier's, treasurer's, or other form of check) or money order in payment for taxes or stamps is not released from his liability until the check or money order is paid; and, if the check or money order is not duly paid, he shall also be liable for all legal penalties and additions, to the same extent as if such check or money order had not been tendered. For the penalty in case a check or money order is not duly paid, see section 6657 and § 301.6657-1. For assessment of the amount of a check or money order not duly paid, see section 6201(a)(2)(B) and paragraph (a)(2)(ii) of § 301.6201-1.

(2) *Liability of banks and others.* If any certified, treasurer's, or cashier's check or money order is not duly paid, the United States shall have a lien for the amount of such check upon all assets of the bank or trust company on which drawn or for the amount of such money order upon the assets of the issuer thereof. The unpaid amount shall be paid out of such assets in preference to any other claims against such bank or issuer except the necessary costs and expenses of administration and the reimbursement of the United States for the amount expended in the redemption of the circulating notes of such bank. In addition, the Government has the right to exact payment from the person required to make the payment.

(c) *Payment in nonconvertible foreign currency.* For rules relating to payment of income taxes and taxes under the Federal Insurance Contributions Act in nonconvertible foreign currency, see section 6316 and the regulations thereunder.

○── **§ 301.6312 Statutory provisions; payment by United States notes and certificates of indebtedness.** [Sec. 6312, IRC]

○── **§ 301.6312-1** (T.D. 6119, filed 12-31-54, as amended by T.D. 6292, filed 4-18-58; republished in T.D. 6498, filed 10-29-60; amended by T.D. 6914, filed 3-7-67.) **Treasury certificates of indebtedness, Treasury notes, and Treasury bills acceptable in payment of internal revenue taxes or stamps.**

(a) Treasury certificates of indebtedness, Treasury notes, or Treasury bills of any series (not including interim receipts issued by Federal reserve banks in lieu of definitive certificates, notes, or bills) may be tendered at or before maturity in payment of internal revenue taxes due on the date (or in payment for stamps purchased on the date), on which the certificates, notes, or bills mature or in payment of internal revenue taxes due on a specified prior date, but only if such certificates, notes, or bills, according to the express terms of their issue, are made acceptable in payment of such taxes or for the purchase of stamps. If the taxes for which the certificates, notes, or bills are tendered in payment become due, or the stamps are purchased, on the same date as that on which such certificates, notes, or bills mature, they will be accepted at par plus accrued interest, if any, payable with the principal (not represented by coupons attached) in payment of such taxes or stamps. If the taxes for which the certificates, notes, or bills are tendered in payment become due, or the stamps are purchased, on a date prior to that on which the certificates, notes, or bills mature, they will be accepted at the value specified in the terms under which such certificates, notes, or bills were issued. All interest coupons attached to Treasury certificates of indebtedness or Treasury notes shall be detached by the taxpayer before such certificates or notes are tendered in payment of taxes or stamps.

(b) Receipts given by a district director for Treasury certificates of indebtedness, Treasury notes, or Treasury bills received in payment of internal revenue taxes or for stamps as provided in this section shall contain an adequate description of such certificates, notes, or bills, and a statement of the value, including accrued interest, if any, payable with the principal (not represented by coupons attached), at which accepted, and shall show that the certificates, notes, or bills are tendered by the taxpayer and received by the district director, subject to no condition, qualification, or reservation whatsoever, in payment of an amount of taxes or for stamps no greater than such value. Any certificate, note, or bill offered in payment of internal revenue taxes or for stamps subject to any condition, qualification, or reservation, or for any greater amount than the value at which acceptable in payment of taxes or stamps, as specified in the terms under which such certificate, note, or bill was issued, shall not be deemed to be duly tendered and shall be returned to the taxpayer.

(c) For the purpose of saving taxpayers the expense of transmitting Treasury certificates of indebtedness, Treasury notes, or Treasury bills to the office of the district director in whose district the taxes are payable, or stamps are to be purchased, taxpayers desiring to pay taxes, or purchase stamps, with such certificates, notes, or bills acceptable in payment of taxes or for the purchase of stamps may deposit such certificates, notes, or bills with a Federal reserve bank or branch, or with the Office of the Treasurer of the United States, Treasury Building, Washington, D. C. In such cases, the Federal reserve bank or branch, or the Office of the Treasurer of the United States, shall issue a receipt in the name of the district director, describing the certificates, notes, or bills by par or dollar face amount and stating on the face of the receipt that the certificates, notes, or bills represented thereby are held by the bank or branch, or the Office of the Treasurer of the United States, for redemption at the value specified in the terms under which the certificates, notes, or bills were issued, and for application of the proceeds in payment of taxes due or for the purchase of stamps on a specified date by the taxpayer named therein.

(d) In the case of payments of tax required to be deposited with Government depositaries by regulations under section 6302 of the Code, certificates, notes, or bills referred to in paragraph (a) of this section may be deposited with a Federal Reserve bank or branch, or with the Office of the Treasurer of the United States, in part or full satisfaction of such tax liability. As in the case of all remittances of amounts so required to be deposited, each such deposit of certificates, notes, or bills shall be accompanied by the appropriate deposit form in accordance with the regulations under section 6302. In such cases, notwithstanding paragraphs (b) and (c) of this section, receipts for such certificates, notes or bills shall no longer be issued in the name of the district director.

○━ § 301.6312-2 (T.D. 6119, filed 12-31-54; republished in T.D. 6498, filed 10-24-60.) **Certain Treasury savings notes acceptable in payment of certain internal revenue taxes.**

According to the express terms of their issue, the following series of Treasury savings notes are presently acceptable in payment of income taxes (current and back, personal and corporation taxes, and excess profits taxes) and estate and gift taxes (current and back):

(a) Treasury Savings Notes, Series A,

(b) Treasury Savings Notes, Series B,

(c) Treasury Savings Notes, Series C.

○━ § 301.6313 **Statutory provisions; fractional parts of a cent.** (Sec. 6313, IRC]

○━ § 301.6313-1 (T.D. 6119, filed 12-31-54; republished in T.D. 6498, filed 10-24-60.) **Fractional parts of a cent.**

In the payment of any tax not payable by stamp, a fractional part of a cent shall be disregarded unless it amounts to one-half cent or more, in which case it shall be increased to one cent. Fractional parts of a cent shall not be disregarded in the computation of taxes.

○━ § 301.6314 **Statutory provisions; receipt for taxes.** [Sec. 6314, IRC]

○━ § 301.6314-1 (T.D. 6119, filed 12-31-54; republished in T.D. 6498, filed 10-24-60; amended by T.D. 7214, filed 10-30-72.) **Receipt for taxes.**

(a) *In general.* The district director or the director of a service center shall upon request, issue a receipt for each tax payment made (other than a payment for stamps sold an ddelivered). In addition, the district director or the director of a service center shall issue a receipt for each payment o fone dollar or more made in cash, whether or not requested. In the case of payments made by check, the cancelled check is usually a sufficient receipt. No receipt shall be issued in lieu of a stamp representing a tax, whether the payment is in cash or otherwise.

(b) *Duplicate receipt for payment of estate taxes.* Upon request, the district director or the director of a service center will issue duplicate receipts to the person

Reg. § 301.6314-1(b)

24,344.2 (I.R.C.)   Reg. § 301.6314-1(b)

paying the estate tax, either of which will be sufficient evidence of such payment and entitle the executor to be credited with the amount by any court having jurisdiction to audit or settle his accounts. For definition of the term "executor", see section 2203.

§ 301.6315 Statutory provisions; payments of estimated income tax. [Sec. 6315, IRC]

§ 301.6315-1 (T.D. 6119, filed 12-31-54; republished in T.D. 6498, filed 10-24-60.) **Payments of estimated income tax.**

The payment of any installment of the estimated income tax (see sections 6015 and 6016) shall be considered payment on account of the income tax for the taxable year for which the estimate is made. The aggregate amount of the payments of estimated tax should be entered upon the income tax return for such taxable year as payments to be applied against the tax shown on such return.

§ 301.6316 Statutory provisions; payment by foreign currency. [Sec. 6316, IRC]

§ 301.6316-1 (T.D. 6191, filed 7-18-56; republished in T.D. 6498, filed 10-24-60; amended by T.D. 6872, filed 1-5-66.) Payment of income tax in foreign currency.

Subject to the provisions of §§ 301.6316-3 to 301.6316-5, inclusive, that portion of the income tax which is attributable to amounts received by a citizen of the United States in nonconvertible foreign currency may be paid in such currency—

(a) For any taxable year beginning on or after January 1, 1955, and before January 1, 1964, if such amounts—

(1) Are disbursed from funds made available to a foundation or commission established in a foreign country pursuant to an agreement made under the authority of section 32(b) of the Surplus Property Act of 1944, as amended (50 U.S.C. App. 1641(b)(2)), or re-established under the authority of the Mutual Educational and Cultural Exchange Act of 1961, as amended (22 U.S.C. 2451);

(2) Constitute either a grant made for authorized purposes of the agreement or compensation for personal services performed in the employ of the foundation or commission;

(3) Are at least 75 percent of the entire amount of the grant or compensation; and

(4) Are treated as income from sources without the United States under the provisions of sections 861 to 864, inclusive, and §§ 1.861-1 to 1.864, inclusive, of this chapter (Income Tax Regulations); and

(b) For any taxable year beginning on or after January 1, 1964, if such amounts—

(1) Are disbursed from funds made available either to a foundation or commission, established pursuant to an agreement made under the authority of section 32(b) of the Surplus Property Act of 1944, as amended, or to a foundation or commission established or continued pursuant to an agreement made under the authority of the Mutual Educational and Cultural Exchange Act of 1961, as amended; or are paid from grants made to such citizen, or to a foundation or an educational or other institution, under the authority of the Mutual Educational and Cultural Exchange Act of 1961, as amended; or section 104(h), (j), (k), (o), or (p) of the Agricultural Trade Development and Assistance Act of 1954, as amended (7 U.S.C. 1704(h), (j), (k, (o) (p));

(2) Constitute either a grant made for a purpose authorized under any such agreement or law, or compensation for personal services performed in the employ of any organization engaged in administering any program or activity pursuant to any such agreement or law;

(3) Are at least 70 percent of the entire amount of the grant or compensation; and

(4) Are treated as income from sources without the United States under the provisions of sections 861 to 864, inclusive, and §§ 1.861-1 to 1.864, inclusive, of this chapter (Income Tax Regulations).

§ 301.6316-2 (T.D. 6191, filed 7-18-56; republished in T.D. 6498, filed 10-24-60; amended by T.D. 6872, filed 1-5-66.) Definitions.

For purposes of §§ 301.6316-1 to 301.6316-9, inclusive:

(a) The term "tax", as used in §§ 301.6316-1, 3, 4, 5, and 6 means the income tax imposed for the taxable year by chapter 1 of the Internal Revenue Code of 1954, and as used in § 301.6316-7 means the Federal Insurance Contributions Act taxes imposed by chapter 21 of the Code (or by the corresponding provisions of the Internal Revenue Code of 1939). The term "tax", as used in §§ 301.6316-8 and 9 shall relate to either of such taxes, whichever is appropriate.

(b) The term "nonconvertible foreign currency" means currency of the government of a foreign country which, owing to (1) monetary, exchange, or other restrictions imposed by the foreign country, (2) an agreement entered into with the United States of America, or (3) the terms and conditions of the United States Government grant, is not convertible into United States dollars or into other money which is convertible into United States dollars. The term shall not, however, include currency which, notwithstanding such restrictions, agreement, terms, or conditions, is in fact converted into United States dollars or into property which is readily disposable for United States dollars.

(c) If the taxpayer computes taxable income under the accrual method, then the term "received" shall be construed to mean "accrued".

§ 301.6316-3 (T.D. 6191, filed 7-18-56; republished in T.D. 6498, filed 10-24-60.) Allocation of tax attributable to foreign currency.

(a) *Adjusted gross income ratio.* The portion of the tax which is attributable to amounts received in nonconvertible foreign currency shall, for purposes of applying § 301.6316-1 to the currency of each foreign country, be the amount by which:

(1) The amount which bears the same ratio to the entire tax for the taxable year as (i) the taxpayer's adjusted gross income received in that currency bears to (ii) the adjusted gross income determined under section 62 by taking into account the entire gross income and all deductions allowable under that section without distinction as to amounts received in foreign currency, exceeds

(2) The total of the allowable credits against tax, and payments on account of tax, which are properly allocable to the account of that currency included in gross income.

(b) *Example.* (1) For the calendar year 1955 Mr. Jones and his wife filed a joint return on which the adjusted gross income is as follows, after amounts re-

24,346 (I.R.C.) Reg. § 301.6316-3(b)(1)

ceived in foreign currency had been properly translated into United States dollars for tax computation purposes:

Fulbright grant received by Mr. Jones in nonconvertible foreign currency	$ 8,000
Dividends received by Mr. Jones entitled to dividends-received credit	500
Compensation for personal services of Mrs. Jones	3,000
Net profit from business carried on by Mrs. Jones	2,500
Total adjusted gross income	14,000

(2) The following amounts are allowable as properly deductible from adjusted gross income, no determination being made as to whether or not any part of them is properly allocable to the Fulbright grant:

Deduction for personal exemptions	$ 3,000
Charitable contributions	500
Interest expense	400
Taxes	300
Total allowable deductions	4,200

(3) For the taxable year the following amounts are allowable as credits against the tax, or as payments on account of the tax:

Foreign tax credit for foreign taxes paid on Fulbright grant	$ 300.00	
Dividends-received credit	20.00	
Credit for income tax withheld upon compensation of Mrs. Jones	304.80	
Payments of estimated tax (see § 301.6316-6(b)(2) for determination of amounts):		
United States dollars $426.32		
Foreign currency 893.88		1,320.20
Total allowable credits and payments		1,945.00

(4) The portion of the tax which is attributable to amounts received in nonconvertible foreign currency is $33.49, determined as follows:

Adjusted gross income	$14,000.00
Less allowable deductions	4,200.00
Taxable income	9,800.00
Tax computed under section 2	2,148.00
Ratio of adjusted gross income received in nonconvertible foreign currency to entire adjusted gross income ($8,000 ÷ $14,000)	$ 57.14[1]
Portion of tax attributable to nonconvertible foreign currency ($2,148 × 57.14%)	1,227.37
Less: Credit for foreign taxes paid on Fulbright grant $300.00	
Payment in foreign currency of estimated tax 893.88	1,193.88
Portion of tax attributable to amounts received in nonconvertible foreign currency	33.49

[1] So in original; probably should read "57.14%"

○━▶ § 301.6316-4 (T.D. 6191, filed 7-18-56; republished in T.D. 6498, filed 10-24-60; amended by T.D. 6872, filed 1-5-66.) **Return requirements.**

(a) *Place for filing.* A return of income which includes amounts received in foreign currency on which the tax is paid in accordance with § 301.6316-1 shall be filed with the Director of International Operations, Internal Revenue Service, Washington, D. C. 20225. For the time for filing income tax returns, see sections 6072 and 6081 and §§ 1.6072-1, 1.6081-1, and 1.6081-2 of this chapter (Income Tax Regulations).

(b) *Statements required.* (1) A statement, prepared by the taxpayer, and certified by the foundation, commission, or other person having control of the payments made to the taxpayer in nonconvertible foreign currency, shall be attached to the return showing that for the taxable year involved the taxpayer is entitled to pay tax in foreign currency in accordance with section 6316 and the regulations thereunder. This statement shall disclose the total amount of grants or compensation received by the taxpayer during the taxable year under the authority of section 32 (b) of the Surplus Property Act of 1944, as amended (50 U.S.C. App. 1641 (b) (2)), or of the Mutual Educational and Cultural Exchange Act of 1961, as amended (22 U.S.C. 2451), or section 104 (h), (j), (k), (o), or (p) of the Agricultural Trade Development and Assistance Act of 1954, as amended (7 U.S.C. 1704 (h), (j), (k), (o), (p)), and the amount thereof paid in nonconvertible foreign currency. It shall also state that with respect to the grant or compensation the applicable percentage requirement of § 301.6316-1 is satisfied.

(2) The taxpayer shall also attach to the return a detailed statement showing (i) the computation, in the manner prescribed by § 301.6316-3, of the portion of the tax attributable to amounts received in nonconvertible foreign currency and (ii) the rates of exchange used in determining the tax liability in United States dollars. See paragraph (c) of § 301.6316-5.

○━▶ § 301.6316-5 (T.D. 6191, filed 7-18-56; republished in T.D. 6498, filed 10-24-60; amended by T.D. 6872, filed 1-5-66.) **Manner of paying tax by foreign currency.**

(a) *Time and place to pay.* The unpaid tax required to be shown on a return filed in accordance with § 301.6316-4, whether payable in whole or in part in foreign currency, is due and payable to the Director of International Operations, Internal Revenue Service, Washington, D. C. 20225, at the time the return is filed. However, see paragraph (d) of this section with respect to the depositing of the foreign currency with the disbursing officer of the Department of State.

(b) *Certified statement.* Every taxpayer who desires to pay tax in foreign currency under the provisions of § 301.6316-1 shall first obtain the certified statement referred to in paragraph (b)(1) of § 301.-6316-4.

(c) *Determination of the tax.* In determining the tax payable for the taxable year in United States dollars, the taxpayer, with respect to amounts described in paragraph (a) of § 301.6316-1, or amounts described in paragraph (b) of § 301.6316-1 received before November 1, 1965, shall use the rates of exchange which most clearly reflect the correct tax liability in dollars, whether it be the official rate, the open market rate, or any other appropriate rate. With respect to amounts described in paragraph (b) of § 301.6316-1 received on or after November 1, 1965, the taxpayer shall use the official rate of exchange in determining the tax payable for the taxable year in United States dollars. After determining the correct tax liability in United States dollars the taxpayer shall then ascertain, in accordance with the principles of § 301.6316-3, the portion of the tax which is attributable to amounts received in nonconvertible foreign currency.

(d) *Deposit of foreign currency with disbursing officer.* (1) After the portion of the tax which is attributable to amounts received in nonconvertible foreign currency is determined in United States dollars, the amount so determined shall be deposited in the same nonconvertible foreign currency with the disbursing officer of the Department of State for the foreign country where the fund is located from which the payments in nonconvertible foreign currency are made to the taxpayer. The amount of foreign currency to be deposited shall be that amount which, when converted at the rate of exchange used on the date of deposit by that disbursing officer for the acquisition of such currency for his official disbursements, equals the portion of the tax so determined in United States dollars.

(2) The disbursing officer may rely upon the taxpayer for the determination of the amount of tax payable in foreign currency but may not accept any such currency for deposit until the taxpayer has presented for inspection the certified statement referred to in paragraph (b)(1) of § 301.6316-4. Upon acceptance of foreign currency for deposit the disbursing officer shall give the taxpayer a receipt in duplicate showing the name and address of the depositor, the date of deposit, the amount of foreign currency deposited, and its equivalent in United States dollars on the date of deposit.

(3) Every taxpayer making a deposit of foreign currency in accordance with this paragraph shall attach to the return required to be filed in accordance with § 301.6316-4, in part or full payment of the taxes shown thereon, the original of the receipt given by the disbursing officer and shall pay to the Director of International Operations in United States dollars the balance, if any, of the tax shown to be due. Tender of such receipt to the Director of International Operations shall be considered as payment of tax in an amount equal to the United States dollars represented by the receipt.

(4) A taxpayer shall make the deposit required by this paragraph in ample time to permit him to attach the receipt to his return for filing within the time prescribed by section 6072 or 6081 and §§ 1.6072-1, 1.6081-1, and 1.6081-2 of this chapter (Income Tax Regulations).

§ 301.6316-6 (T.D. 6191, filed 7-18-56; republished in T.D. 6498, filed 10-24-60; amended by T.D. 6872, filed 1-5-66.) **Declarations of estimated tax.**

(a) *Filing of declaration.* A declaration of estimated tax in respect of amounts on which the tax is to be paid in foreign currency under the provisions of § 301.6316-1 shall be filed with the Director of International Operations, Internal Revenue Service, Washington, D.C. 20225, and shall have attached thereto the statements required by paragraph (b)(1) and (2)(i) of § 301.6316-4 in respect of the tax return except that the statement certified by the foundation, commission, or other person having control of the payments to the taxpayer in nonconvertible foreign currency may be based upon amounts expected to be received by the taxpayer during the taxable year if they are not in fact known at the time of certification. A copy of this certified statement shall be retained by the taxpayer for the purpose of exhibiting it to the disbursing officer when making installment deposits of foreign currency under the provisions of paragraph (c) of this section. For the time for filing declarations of estimated tax, see sections 6073 and 6081 and §§ 1.6073-1 to 1.6073-4, inclusive, and §§ 1.6081-1 and 1.6081-2 of this chapter (Income Tax Regulations).

(b) *Determination of estimated tax—* (1) *Allocation of tax attributable to foreign currency.* In determining the amount of estimated tax for purposes of this section, all items of income, deduction, and credit, whether or not attributable to amounts received in nonconvertible foreign currency, shall be taken into account. The portion of the estimated tax which is attributable to amounts to be received during the taxable year in nonconvertible foreign currency shall be determined consistently with the manner prescribed by § 301.6316-3.

(2) *Example.* (i) For the calendar year 1955 Mr. Jones and his wife filed a joint declaration of estimated tax in the determination of which the adjusted gross income was estimated to be as follows, after amounts to be received in foreign currency had been properly translated into United States dollars for tax computation purposes:

Fulbright grant to be received by Mr. Jones in nonconvertible foreign currency	$ 8,000
Dividends to be received by Mr. Jones entitled to dividends-received credit	375
Compensation to be received by Mrs. Jones for personal services	3,000
Net profit to be derived from business carried on by Mrs. Jones	1,625
Total estimated adjusted gross income	13,000

Reg. § 301.6316-6(b)(2)

24,348 (I.R.C.)   Reg. § 301.6316-6(b)(2)   5-15-72

(ii) The following amounts were determined to be allowable as properly deductible from estimated adjusted gross income, no determination being made as to whether or not any part of them was properly allocable to the Fulbright grant:

Deduction for personal exemptions	$3,000
Charitable contributions	300
Interest expense	400
Taxes	300
Total allowable deductions	4,000

(iii) The following estimated amounts were determined to be allowable as credits against the tax for the taxable year:

Foreign tax credit for foreign taxes to be paid on Fulbright grant	$300.00
Credit for income tax expected to be withheld upon compensation of Mrs. Jones	304.80
Dividends-received credit	15.00
Total allowable estimated credits	619.80

(iv) The portion of the estimated tax which is attributable to amounts to be received during the taxable year in nonconvertible foreign currency is $893.88, determined as follows:

Estimated adjusted gross income	$13,000.00
Less: Allowable deductions	4,000.00
Estimated taxable income	9,000.00
Tax computed under section 2	1,940.00
Ratio of estimated adjusted gross income to be received in nonconvertible foreign currency to entire estimated adjusted gross income ($8,000 ÷ $13,000) (percent)	61.54
Portion of above tax attributable to nonconvertible foreign currency ($1,940 × 61.54 percent)	$1,193.48
Less: Credit for foreign taxes expected to be paid on Fulbright grant	300.00
Portion of estimated tax which is attributable to amounts to be received during the taxable year in nonconvertible foreign currency	893.88

(b) The portion of the estimated tax which is payable in United States dollars is $426.32, determined as follows:

Tax computed under section 2	$1,940.00
Less: Total allowable estimated credits	619.80
Total estimated tax	1,320.20
Less: Portion of estimated tax payable in foreign currency	893.88
Portion of estimated tax payable in United States dollars	426.32

(c) *Payment of estimated tax.* (1) The provisions of § 301.6316-5 relating to the certified statement, determination of the tax, and the depositing of the foreign currency shall apply for purposes of this section. The full amount of estimated tax payable in foreign currency, as determined under paragraph (b) of this section, may be deposited before the date prescribed for the payment thereof.

(2) Every taxpayer making a deposit of foreign currency in accordance with this paragraph shall tender to the Director of International Operations, Internal Revenue Service, Washington, D. C. 20225, the original of the receipt from the disbursing officer as payment, to the extent of the amount represented thereby in United States dollars, of the estimated tax. For the dates prescribed for the payment of estimated tax, see sections 6153 and 6161 and §§ 1.6153-1 to 1.6153-4, inclusive, and § 1.6161-1 of this chapter (Income Tax Regulations). A taxpayer should make the deposit required by this paragraph in ample time to permit him to tender such receipt by the date prescribed for payment of the estimated tax.

(d) *Credit on return for the taxable year.* The receipt given by the disbursing officer of the Department of State and tendered in payment of estimated tax under this section shall, for purposes of paragraph (a)(2) of § 301.6316-3, be considered as payment on account of the tax for the taxable year. The amount so considered to be paid shall be the amount in United States dollars represented by the receipt.

§ 301.6316-7 (T.D. 6872, filed 1-5-66.) **Payment of Federal Insurance Contributions Act taxes in foreign currency.**

(a) *In general.* The taxes imposed on employees and employers by sections 3101 and 3111, respectively, of chapter 21 of the Code (Federal Insurance Contributions Act) or the corresponding sections of the Internal Revenue Code of 1939 may, with respect to wages (as defined in section 3121(a) of chapter 21 of the Code or the corresponding section of the Internal Revenue Code of 1939) paid in nonconvertible foreign currency (as defined in paragraph (b) of § 301.6316-2) for services performed on or after January 1, 1951, be paid in that currency if all such wages—

(1) Are paid from funds made available to a foundation or commission established in a foreign country pursuant to an agreement made under the authority of section 32(b) of the Surplus Property Act of 1944, as amended (50 U.S.C. App. 1641 (b)(2)), or established or continued pursuant to an agreement made under authority of the Mutual Educational and

Cultural Exchange Act of 1961, as amended (22 U.S.C. 2451); and

(2) Are paid to a United States citizen for services performed in the employ of such foundation or commission.

(b) *Return requirements* — (1) *Statements required.* (i) A return on which payment of Federal Insurance Contributions Act taxes is made in accordance with this section shall have attached thereto a statement, certified by the foundation or commission filing the return, stating that the foundation or commission is an organization established pursuant to an agreement made under authority of section 32 (b) of the Surplus Property Act of 1944, as amended, or established or continued pursuant to an agreement made under authority of the Mutual Educational and Cultural Exchange Act of 1961, as amended.

(ii) The taxpayer shall also attach to the return a statement showing the rates of exchange used in determining in United States dollars the wages reported on the return and the taxes due with respect thereto. See paragraph (c) (1) of this section.

(2) *Cross references.* For the place for filing returns of the Federal Insurance Contributions Act taxes, see § 31.6091-1 (c) of this chapter (Employment Tax Regulations). For the time for filing returns of the Federal Insurance Contributions Act taxes, see § 31.6071 (a)-1 of this chapter (Employment Tax Regulations).

(c) *Payment of tax*—(1) *Determination of the tax.* In determining in United States dollars the wages required to be reported on the return and the taxes due with respect thereto, the taxpayer shall use the rate of exchange which most clearly reflects the correct equivalent in dollars, whether it be the official rate, the open market rate, or any other appropriate rate.

(2) *Deposit of foreign currency with disbursing officer.* (1) After determination is made in United States dollars of the Federal Insurance Contributions Act taxes with respect to wages paid in nonconvertible foreign currency, the amount so determined shall be deposited in the same nonconvertible foreign currency with the disbursing officer of the Department of State for the foreign country where the fund is located from which such wages were paid. The amount of the foreign currency to be deposited shall be that amount which, when converted at the rate of exchange used on the date of deposit by the disbursing officer for the acquisition of such currency for his official disbursements, equals the taxes determined in United States dollars.

(ii) The disbursing officer may rely upon the taxpayer for the determination of the amount of tax payable in foreign currency but may not accept any such currency for deposit until the taxpayer has presented for inspection the certified statement referred to in paragraph (b) (1) of this section. Upon acceptance of foreign currency for deposit the disbursing officer shall give the taxpayer a receipt in duplicate showing the name and address of the depositor, the date of the deposit, the amount of foreign currency deposited and its equivalent in United States dollars on the date of deposit, and the kind of tax for which the deposit is made.

(iii) Every taxpayer making a deposit of foreign currency in accordance with this paragraph shall attach to the return required to be filed in accordance with paragraph (b) of this section the original of the receipt given by the disbursing officer. Tender of such receipt to the Director of International Operations shall be considered as payment of tax in an amount equal to the United States dollars represented by the receipt.

(iv) A taxpayer shall make the deposit required by this paragraph in ample time to permit it to attach the receipt to its return for filing within the time prescribed by § 31.6071 (a)-1 of this chapter (Employment Tax Regulations).

O— § 301.6316-8 (Originally § 301.6316-7 as added by T.D. 6191, filed 7-18-56; republished in T.D. 6498, filed 10-24-60; redesignated and amended by T.D. 6872, filed 1-5-66.)

Refunds and credits in foreign currency.

(a) *Refunds.* The refund of any overpayment of tax which has been paid under section 6316 in foreign currency may, in the discretion of the Commissioner, be made in the same foreign currency by which the tax was paid. The amount of any such refund made in foreign currency shall be the amount of the overpayment in United States dollars converted, on the date of the refund check, at the rate of exchange then used for his official disbursements by the disbursing officer of the Department of State in the country where the foreign currency was originally deposited.

(b) *Credits.* Unless otherwise in the best interest of the Internal Revenue Service, no credit of any overpayment of tax which has been paid under section 6316 in foreign currency shall be allowed against any outstanding liability of the person making the overpayment except in respect of that portion of the liability which, in accordance with § 301.6316-1 or § 301.6316-7, would otherwise be permitted to be paid in the same foreign currency.

O— § 301.6316-9 (Originally § 301.6316-8 as added by T.D. 6191, filed 7-18-56; republished in T.D. 6498, filed 10-24-60; redesignated and amended by T.D. 6872, filed 1-5-66.)

Interest, additions to tax, etc.

Any reference in §§ 301.6316-1 to 301.-6316-8, inclusive, to "tax" shall be deemed also to refer to the interest, additions to the tax, additional amounts, and penalties attributable to the tax.

LIEN FOR TAXES

O— § 301.6321 Statutory provisions; lien for taxes. [Sec. 6321, IRC]

O— § 301.6321-1 (T.D. 6119, filed 12-31-54; republished in T.D. 6498, filed 10-24-60; amended by TD 7139, filed 8-11-71.)

Lien for taxes.

If any person liable to pay any tax neglects or refuses to pay the same after demand, the amount (including any interest, additional amount, addition to tax, or assessable penalty, together with any costs that may accrue in addition thereto) shall

Reg. § 301.6321-1

24,350 (I.R.C.)   Reg. § 301.6321-1   8-30-76

be a lien in favor of the United States upon all property and rights to property, whether real or personal, tangible or intangible, belonging to such person. The lien attaches to all property and rights to property belonging to such person at any time during the period of the lien, including any property or rights to property acquired by such person after the lien arises. Solely for purposes of sections 6321 and 6331, any interest in restricted land held in trust by the United States for an individual noncompetent Indian (and not for a tribe) shall not be deemed to be property, or a right to property, belonging to such Indian. For the special lien for estate and gift taxes, see section 6324 and § 301.6324-1.

O—▸ § 301.6322 Statutory provisions; period of lien. [Sec. 6322, IRC]

O—▸ § 301.6323(a) Statutory provisions; validity and priority against certain persons; purchases, holders of security interests, mechanic's lienors, judgment lien creditors. [Sec. 6323(a), IRC]

O—▸ § 301.6323(a)-1 (T.D. 7429, filed 8-20-76.) Purchasers, holders of security interests, mechanic's lienors, and judgment lien creditors.

(a) *Invalidity of lien without notice.* The lien imposed by section 6321 is not valid against any purchaser (as defined in paragraph (f) of § 301.6323(h)-1), holder of a security interest (as defined in paragraph (a) of § 301.6323(h)-1), mechanic's lienor (as defined in paragraph (b) of § 301.6323(h)-1, or judgment lien creditor (as defined in paragraph (g) of § 301.6323(h)-1) until a notice of lien is filed in accordance with § 301.6323(f)-1. Except as provided by section 6323, if a person becomes a purchaser, holder of a security interest, mechanic's lienor, or judgment lien creditor after a notice of lien is filed in accordance with § 301.6323(f)-1, the interest acquired by such person is subject to the lien imposed by section 6321.

(b) *Cross references.* For provisions relating to the protection afforded a security interest arising after tax lien filing, which interest is covered by a commercial transactions financing agreement, real property construction or improvement financing agreement, or an obligatory disbursement agreement, see §§ 301.6323(c)-1, 301.6323(c)-2, and 301.6323(c)-3, respectively. For provisions relating to the protection afforded to a security interest coming into existence by virtue of disbursements made before the 46th day after the date of tax lien filing, see § 301.6323(d)-1. For provisions relating to priority afforded to interest and certain other expenses with respect to a lien or security interest having priority over the lien imposed by section 6321, see § 301.6323(e)-1. For provisions relating to certain other interests arising after tax lien filing, see § 301.6323(b)-1.

O—▸ § 301.6323(b) Statutory provisions; validity and priority against certain persons; protection for certain interests even though notice filed. [Sec. 6323(b), IRC]

O—▸ § 301.6323(b)-1 (T.D. 7429, filed 8-20-76.) Protection for certain interests even though notice filed.

(a) *Securities*—(1) *In general.* Even though a notice of a lien imposed by section 6321 is filed in accordance with § 301.6323(f)-1, the lien is not valid with respect to a security (as defined in paragraph (d) of § 301.6323(h)-1) against—

(i) A purchaser (as defined in paragraph (f) of § 301.6323(h)-1) of the security who at the time of purchase did not have actual notice or knowledge (as defined in paragraph (a) of § 301.6323(i)-1) of the existence of the lien;

(ii) A holder of a security interest (as defined in paragraph (a) of § 301.6323(h)-1) in the security who did not have actual notice or knowledge (as defined in paragraph (a) of § 301.6323(i)-1) of the existence of the lien at the time the security interest came into existence or at the time such security interest was acquired from a previous holder for a consideration in money or money's worth; or

(iii) A transferee of an interest protected under subdivision (i) or (ii) of this subparagraph to the same extent the lien is invalid against his transferor.
For purposes of subdivision (iii) of this subparagraph, no person can improve his position with respect to the lien by reacquiring the interest from an intervening purchaser or holder of a security interest against whom the lien is invalid.

(2) *Examples.* The application of this paragraph may be illustrated by the following examples:

Example (1). On May 1, 1969, in accordance with § 301.6323(f)-1, a notice of lien is filed with respect to A's delinquent tax liability. On May 20, 1969, A sells 100 shares of common stock in X Corporation to B, who, on the date of the sale, does not have actual notice or knowledge of the existence of the lien. Because B purchased the stock without actual notice or knowledge of the lien, under subdivision (i) of subparagraph (1) of this paragraph, the stock purchased by B is not subject to the lien.

Example (2). Assume the same facts as in example (1) except that on May 30, 1969, B sells the 100 shares of common stock in X Corporation to C who on May 5, 1969, had actual notice of the existence of the tax lien against A. Because the X stock when purchased by B was not subject to the lien, under subdivision (iii) of subparagraph (1) of this paragraph, the stock purchased by C is not subject to the lien. C succeeds to B's rights, even though C had actual notice of the lien before B's purchase.

Example (3). On June 1, 1970, in accordance with § 301.6323(f)-1, a notice of lien is filed with respect to D's delinquent tax liability. D owns twenty $1,000 bonds issued by the Y Company. On June 10, 1970, D obtains a loan from M Bank for $5,000 using the Y Company bonds as collateral. At the time the loan is made M Bank does not have actual notice or knowledge of the existence of the tax lien. Because M Bank did not have actual notice or knowledge of the lien when the security interest came into existence, under subdivision (ii) of subparagraph (1) of this paragraph, the tax lien is not valid against M Bank to the extent of its security interest.

Example (4). Assume the same facts as in example (3) except that on June 19, 1970, M Bank assigns the chose in action and its security interest to N, who had actual notice or knowledge of the existence of the lien on June 1, 1970. Because the security interest was not subject to the lien to the extent of M Bank's security interest, the security interest held by N is to the same extent entitled to priority over the tax lien because N succeeds to M Bank's rights. See subdivision (iii) of subparagraph (1) of this paragraph.

Example (5). On July 1, 1970, in accordance with § 301.6323(f)-1, a notice of lien is filed with respect to E's delinquent tax liability. E owns ten $1,000 bonds issued by the Y Company. On July 5, 1970, E borrows $4,000 from F and delivers the bonds to F as collateral for the loan. At the time the loan is made, F has actual knowledge of the existence of the tax lien and, therefore, holds the security interest subject to the lien on the bonds. On July 10, 1970, F sells the security interest to G for $4,000 and delivers the Y Company bonds pledged as collateral. G does not have actual notice or knowledge of the existence of the lien on July 10, 1970. Because G did not have actual notice or knowledge of the lien at the time he purchased the security interest, under subdivision (ii) of subparagraph (1) of this paragraph, the tax lien is not valid against G to the extent of his security interest.

Example (6). Assume the same facts as in example (5) except that, instead of purchasing the security interest from F on July 10, 1970, G lends $4,000 to F and takes a security interest in F's security interest in the bonds on that date. Because G became the holder of a security interest in a security interest after notice of lien was filed and does not directly have a security interest in a security, the security interest held by G is not entitled to a priority over the tax lien under the provisions of subparagraph (1) of this paragraph.

(b) *Motor vehicles* — (1) *In general.* Even though a notice of a lien imposed by section 6321 is filed in accordance with § 301.6323(f)-1, the lien is not valid against a purchaser (as defined in paragraph (f) of § 301.6323(h)-1) of a motor vehicle (or defined in paragraph (c) of § 301.6323(h)-1) if—

(i) At the time of the purchase, the purchaser did not have actual notice or knowledge (as defined in paragraph (a) of § 301.6323(i)-1) of the existence of the lien, and

(ii) Before the purchaser obtains such notice or knowledge, he has acquired actual possession of the motor vehicle and has not thereafter relinquished actual possession to the seller or his agent.

(2) *Examples.* The application of this paragraph may be illustrated by the following examples:

Example (1). A, a delinquent taxpayer against whom a notice of tax lien has been filed in accordance with § 301.6323(f)-1, sells his automobile (which qualifies as a motor vehicle under paragraph (c) of § 301.6323(h)-1) to B, an automobile dealer. B takes actual possession of the automobile and does not thereafter relinquish actual possession to the seller or his agent. Subsequent to his purchase, B learns of the existence of the tax lien against A. Even though notice of lien was filed before the purchase, the lien is not valid against B, because B did not know of the existence of the lien before the purchase and before acquiring actual possession of the vehicle.

Example (2). C is a wholesaler of used automobiles. A notice of lien has been filed with respect to C's delinquent tax liability in accordance with § 301.6323(f)-1. Subsequent to such filing, D, a used automobile dealer, purchases and takes actual possession of twenty automobiles (which qualify as motor vehicles under the provisions of paragraph (c) of § 301.6323(h)-1) from C at an auction and places them on his lot for sale. C does not reacquire possession of any of the automobiles. At the time of his purchase, D does not have actual notice or knowledge of the existence of the lien against C. Even though notice of lien was filed before D's purchase, the lien was not valid against D because D did not know of the existence of the lien before the purchase and before acquiring actual possession of the vehicles.

(3) *Cross reference.* For provisions relating to additional circumstances in which the lien imposed by section 6321 may not be valid against the purchaser of tangible personal property (including a motor vehicle) purchased at retail, see paragraph (c) of this section.

(c) *Personal property purchased at retail*—(1) *In general.* Even though a notice of a lien imposed by section 6321 is filed in accordance with § 301.6323(f)-1, the lien is not valid against a purchaser (as defined in paragraph (f) of § 301.6323(h)-1) of tangible personal property purchased at a retail sale (as defined in subparagraph (2) of this paragraph) unless at the time of purchase the purchaser intends the purchase to (or knows that the purchase will) hinder, evade, or defeat the collection of any tax imposed by the Internal Revenue Code of 1954.

(2) *Definition of retail sale.* For purposes of this paragraph, the term "retail sale" means a sale made in the ordinary course of the seller's trade or business, of tangible personal property of which the seller is the owner. Such term includes a sale in customary retail quantities by a seller who is going out of business, but does not include a bulk sale or an auction sale in which goods are offered in quantities substantially greater than are customary in the ordinary course of the seller's trade or business or an auction sale of goods the owner of which is not in the business of selling such goods.

(3) *Example.* The application of this paragraph may be illustrated by the following example:

Example. A purchases a refrigerator from the M Company, a retail appliance dealer. Prior to such purchase, a notice of lien was filed with respect to M's delinquent tax liability in accordance with § 301.6323(f)-1. At the time of the purchase A knows of the existence of the lien. However, A does not intend the purchase to hinder, evade, or defeat the collection of any Internal Revenue tax, and A does not have any reason to believe that the purchase will affect the collection of any Internal Revenue tax. Even though notice of lien was filed before the purchase, the lien is not valid against A because A in

Reg. § 301.6323(b)-1(c)(3)

good faith purchased the refrigerator at retail in the ordinary course of the M Company's business.

(d) *Personal property purchased in casual sale*—(1) *In general.* Even though a notice of a lien imposed by section 6321 is filed in accordance with § 301.6323(f)-1, the lien is not valid against a purchaser (as defined in § 301.6323(h)-1(f)) of household goods, personal effects, or other tangible personal property of a type described in § 301.6334-1 (which includes wearing apparel; school books; fuel, provisions, furniture, arms for personal use; livestock, and poultry (whether or not the seller is the head of a family); and books and tools of a trade, business, or profession (whether or not the trade, business, or profession of the seller)), purchased, other than for resale, in a casual sale for less than $250 (excluding interest and expenses described in § 301.6323(e)-1). For purposes of this paragraph, a casual sale is a sale not made in the ordinary course of the seller's trade or business.

(2) *Limitation.* This paragraph applies only if the purchaser does not have actual notice or knowledge (as defined in paragraph (a) of § 301.6323(i)-1)—

(i) Of the existence of the tax lien, or

(ii) That the sale is one of a series of sales.

For purposes of subdivision (ii) of this subparagraph, a sale is one of a series of sales if the seller plans to dispose of, in separate transactions, substantially all of his household goods, personal effects, and other tangible personal property described in § 301-.6334-1.

(3) *Examples.* The application of this paragraph may be illustrated by the following examples:

Example (1). A, an attorney's widow, sells a set of law books for $200 to B, for B's own use. Prior to the sale a notice of lien was filed with respect to A's delinquent tax liability in accordance with § 301.6323 (f)-1. B has no actual notice or knowledge of the tax lien. In addition, B does not know that the sale is one of a series of sales. Because the sale is a casual sale for less than $250 and involves books of a profession (tangible personal property of a type described in § 301.6334-1, irrespective of the fact that A has never engaged in the legal profession), the tax lien is not valid against B even though a notice of lien was filed prior to the time of B's purchase.

Example (2). Assume the same facts as in example (1) except that B purchases the books for resale in his second-hand bookstore. Because B purchased the books for resale, he purchased the books subject to the lien.

Example (3). In an advertisement appearing in a local newspaper, G indicates that he is offering for sale a lawn mower, a used television set, a desk, a refrigerator, and certain used dining room furniture. In response to the advertisement, H purchases the dining room furniture for $200. H does not receive any information which would impart notice of a lien, or that the sale is one of a series of sales, beyond the information contained in the advertisement. Prior to the sale a notice of lien was filed with respect to G's delinquent tax liability in accordance with § 301.6323(f)-1. Because H had no actual notice or knowledge that substantially all of G's household goods were being sold, or that the sale is one of a series of sales and because the sale is a casual sale for less than $250, H does not purchase the dining room furniture subject to the lien. The household goods are of a type described in § 301.6334-1(a)(2) irrespective of whether G is the head of a family or whether all such household goods offered for sale exceed $500 in value.

(e) *Personal property subject to possessory liens.* Even though a notice of a lien imposed by section 6321 is filed in accordance with § 301.6323(f)-1, the lien is not valid against a holder of a lien on tangible personal property which under local law secures the reasonable price of the repair or improvement of the property if the property is, and has been, continuously in the possession of the holder of the lien from the time the possessory lien arose. For example, if local law gives an automobile repairman the right to retain possession of an automobile he has repaired as security for payment of the repair bill and the repairman retains continuous possession of the automobile until his lien is satisfied, a tax lien filed in accordance with § 301.6323 (f)-1 which has attached to the automobile will not be valid to the extent of the reasonable price of the repairs. It is immaterial that the notice of tax lien was filed before the repairman undertook his work or that he knew of the lien before undertaking the work.

(f) *Real property tax and special assessment liens*—(1) *In general.* Even though a notice of a lien imposed by section 6321 is filed in accordance with § 301.6323 (f)-1, the lien is not valid against the holder of another lien upon the real property (regardless of when such other lien arises), if such other lien is entitled under local law to priority over security interests in real property which are prior in time and if such other lien on real property secures payment of—

(i) A tax of general application levied by any taxing authority based upon the value of the property;

(ii) A special assessment imposed directly upon the property by any taxing authority, if the assessment is imposed for the purpose of defraying the cost of any public improvement; or

(iii) Charges for utilities or public services furnished to the property by the United States, a State or political subdivision thereof, or an instrumentality of any one or more of the foregoing.

(2) *Examples.* The application of this paragraph may be illustrated by the following examples:

Example (1). A owns Blackacre in the City of M. A notice of lien affecting Blackacre is filed in accordance with § 301.6323 (f)-1. Subsequent to the filing of the notice of lien, the City of M acquires a lien against Blackacre to secure payment of real estate taxes. Such taxes are levied against all property in the city in proportion to the value of the property. Under local law, the holder of a lien for real property taxes is entitled to priority over a security interest in real property even though the security interest is prior in time. Because the real property tax lien held by the City of M secures payment of a tax of general application and is entitled to priority over security interests which are prior in time, the lien held by the City of M is entitled to priority over the Federal tax lien with respect to Blackacre.

Example (2). B owns Whiteacre in N County. A notice of lien affecting Whiteacre is filed in accordance with § 301.6323 (f)-1. Subsequent to the filing of the notice of lien, N County constructs a sidewalk, paves the street, and installs water and sewer lines adjacent to Whiteacre. In order to defray the cost of these improvements, N County imposes upon Whiteacre a special assessment which under local law results in a lien upon Whiteacre that is entitled to priority over security interests that are prior in time. Because the special assessment lien is (i) entitled under local law to priority over security interests which are prior in time, and (ii) imposed directly upon real property to defray the cost of a public improvement, the special assessment lien has priority over the Federal tax lien with respect to Whiteacre.

Example (3). C owns Greenacre in Town O. A notice of lien affecting Greenacre is filed in accordance with § 301.6323 (f)-1. Town O furnishes water and electricity to Greenacre and periodically collects a fee for these services. Subsequent to the filing of the notice of lien, Town O supplies water and electricity to Greenacre, and C fails to pay the charges for these services. Under local law, Town O acquires a lien to secure charges for the services, and this lien has priority over security interests which are prior in time. Because the lien of Town O (i) is for services furnished to the real property and (ii) has priority over earlier security interests, Town O's lien has priority over the Federal tax lien with respect to Greenacre.

(g) *Residential property subject to a mechanic's lien for certain repairs and improvements*—(1) *In general.* Even though a notice of a lien imposed by section 6321 is filed in accordance with § 301.6323(f)-1, the lien is not valid against a mechanic's lienor (as defined in § 301.6323(h)-1(b)) who holds a lien for the repair or improvement of a personal residence if—

(i) The residence is occupied by the owner and contains no more than four dwelling units, and

(ii) The contract price on the prime contract with the owner for the repair or improvement (excluding interest and expenses described in § 301.6323(e)-1) is not more than $1,000.

For purposes of subdivision (ii) of this subparagraph, the amounts of subcontracts under the prime contract with the owner are not to be taken into consideration for purposes of computing the $1,000 prime contract price. It is immaterial that the notice of tax lien was filed before the contractor undertakes his work or that he knew of the lien before undertaking the work.

(2) *Examples.* The application of this paragraph may be illustrated by the following examples:

Example (1). A owns a building containing four apartments, one of which he occupies as his personal residence. A notice of lien which affects the building is filed in accordance with § 301.6323(f)-1. Thereafter, A enters into a contract with B in the amount of $800, which includes labor and materials, to repair the roof of the building. B purchases roofing shingles from C for $300. B completes the work and A fails to pay B the agreed amount. In turn, B fails to pay C for the shingles. Under local law, B and C acquire mechanic's liens on A's building. Because the contract price on the prime contract with A is not more than $1,000 and under local law B and C acquire mechanic's liens on A's building, the liens of B and C have priority over the Federal tax lien.

Example (2). Assume the same facts as in example (1), except that the amount of the prime contract between A and B is $1100. Because the amount of the prime contract with the owner, A, is in excess of $1,000, the tax lien has priority over the entire amount of each of the mechanic's liens of B and C, even though the amount of the contract between B and C is $300.

Example (3). Assume the same facts as in example (1), except that A and B do not agree in advance upon the amount due under the prime contract but agree that B will perform the work for the cost of materials and labor plus 10% of such cost. When the work is completed, it is determined that the total amount due is $850. Because the prime contract price is not more than $1,000 and under local law B and C acquire mechanic's liens on A's residence, the liens of B and C have priority over the Federal tax lien.

(h) *Attorney's liens*—(1) *In general.* Even though notice of a lien imposed by section 6321 is filed in accordance with § 301.6323(f)-1, the lien is not valid against an attorney who, under local law, holds a lien upon, or a contract enforceable against, a judgment or other amount in settlement of a claim or of a cause of action. The priority afforded an attorney's lien under this paragraph shall not exceed the amount of the attorney's reasonable compensation for obtaining the judgment or procuring the settlement. For purposes of this paragraph, reasonable compensation means the amount customarily allowed under local law for an attorney's services for litigating or settling a similar case or administrative claim. However, reasonable compensation shall be determined on the basis of the facts and circumstances of each individual case. It is immaterial that the notice of tax lien is filed before the attorney undertakes his work or that the attorney knows of the tax lien before undertaking his work. This paragraph does not apply to an attorney's lien which may arise from the defense of a claim or cause of action against a taxpayer except to the extent such lien is held upon a judgment or other amount arising from the adjudication or settlement of a counterclaim in favor of the taxpayer. In the case of suits against the taxpayer, see § 301.6325-1(d)(2) for rules relating to the subordination of the tax lien to facilitate tax collection.

(2) *Claim or cause of action against the United States.* Subparagraph (1) of this section does not apply to an attorney's lien with respect to—

(i) Any judgment or other fund result-

Reg. § 301.6323(b)-1(h)(2)

24,352.2 (I.R.C.) Reg. § 301.6323(b)-1(h)(2) 8-30-76

ing from the successful litigation or settlement of an administrative claim or cause of action against the United States to the extent that the United States, under any legal or equitable right, offsets its liability under the judgment or settlement against any liability of the taxpayer to the United States, or

(ii) Any amount credited against any liability of the taxpayer in accordance with section 6402.

(3) *Examples.* The provisions of this paragraph may be illustrated by the following examples:

Example (1). A notice of lien is filed against A in accordance with § 301.6323(f)-1. Subsequently, A is struck by an automobile and retains B, an attorney to institute suit on A's behalf against the operator of the automobile. B knows of the tax lien before he begins his work. Under local law, B is entitled to a lien upon any recovery in order to secure payment of his fee. A is awarded damages of $10,000. B charges a fee of $3,000 which is the fee customarily allowed under local law in similar cases and which is found to be reasonable under the circumstances of this particular case. Because, under local law, B holds a lien for the amount of his reasonable compensation for obtaining the judgment, B's lien has priority over the Federal tax lien.

Example (2). Assume the same facts as in example (1), except that before suit is instituted A and the owner of the automobile settle out of court for $7,500. B charges a reasonable and customary fee of $1,800 for procuring the settlement and under local law holds a lien upon the settlement in order to secure payment of the fee. Because, under local law, B holds a lien for the amount of his reasonable compensation for obtaining the settlement, B has priority over the Federal tax lien.

Example (3). In accordance with § 301.6323(f)-1, a notice of lien in the amount of $8,000 is filed against C, a contractor. Subsequently C retains D, an attorney, to initiate legal proceedings to recover the amount allegedly due him for construction work he has performed for the United States. C and D enter into an agreement which provides that D will receive a reasonable and customary fee of $2,500 as compensation for his services. Under local law, the agreement will give rise to a lien which is enforceable by D against any amount recovered in the suit. C is successful in the suit and is awarded $10,000. D claims $2,500 of the proceeds as his fee. The United States, however, exercises its right of set-off and applies $8,000 of the $10,000 award to satisfy C's tax liability. Because the $10,000 award resulted from the successful litigation of a cause of action against the United States, B's contract for attorney's fees is not enforceable against the amount recovered to the extent the United States offsets its liability under the judgment against C's tax liability. It is immaterial that D had no notice or knowledge of the tax lien at the time he began work on the case.

(i) *Certain insurance contracts* — (1) *In general.* Even though a notice of a lien imposed by section 6321 is filed in accordance with § 301.6323(f)-1, the lien is not valid with respect to a life insurance, endowment, or annuity contract, against an organization which is the insurer under the contract, at any time—

(i) Before the insuring organization has actual notice or knowledge (as defined in paragraph (a) of § 301.6323(i)-1) of the existence of the tax lien,

(ii) After the insuring organization has actual notice or knowledge of the lien (as defined in paragraph (a) of § 301.6323(i)-1), with respect to advances (including contractual interest thereon as provided in paragraph (a) of § 301.6323(e)-1) required to be made automatically to maintain the contract in force under an agreement entered into before the insuring organization had such actual notice or knowledge, or

(iii) After the satisfaction of a levy pursuant to section 6332(b), unless and until the district director delivers to the insuring organization a notice (for example, another notice of levy, a letter, etc.), executed after the date of such satisfaction, that the lien exists.

Delivery of the notice described in subdivision (iii) of this subparagraph may be made by any means, including regular mail, and delivery of the notice shall be effective only from the time of actual receipt of the notification by the insuring organization. The provisions of this paragraph are applicable to matured as well as unmatured insurance contracts.

(2) *Examples.* The provisions of this paragraph may be illustrated by the following examples:

Example (1). On May 1, 1964, the X insurance company issues a life insurance policy to A. On June 1, 1970, a tax assessment is made against A, and on June 2, 1970, a notice of lien with respect to the assessment is filed in accordance with § 301.6323(f)-1. On July 1, 1970, without actual notice or knowledge of the tax lien, the X Company makes a "policy loan" to A. Under subparagraph (1)(i) of this paragraph, the loan, including interest (in accordance with the provisions of paragraph (a) of § 301.6323(e)-1), will have priority over the tax lien because X Company did not have actual notice or knowledge of the tax lien at the time the policy loan was made.

Example (2). On May 1, 1964, B enters into a life insurance contract with the Y insurance company. Under one of the provisions of the contract, in the event a premium is not paid, Y is to advance out of the cash loan value of the policy the amount of an unpaid premium in order to maintain the contract in force. The contract also provides for interest on any advances so made. On June 1, 1971, a tax assessment is made against B, and on June 2, 1971, in accordance with section 6323(f)-1, a notice of lien is filed. On July 1, 1971, B fails to pay the premium due on that date, and Y makes an automatic premium loan to keep the policy in force. At the time the automatic premium loan is made, Y had actual knowledge of the tax lien. Under subparagraph (1)(ii) of this paragraph, the lien is not valid against Y with respect to the advance (and the contractual interest thereon), because the advance was required to be made automatically under an agreement entered into before Y had actual notice or knowledge of the tax lien.

Example (3). On May 1, 1964, C enters into a life insurance contract with the Z

Insurance Company. On January 4, 1971, an assessment is made against C for $5,000 unpaid income taxes, and on January 11, 1971, in accordance with § 301.6323(f)-1, a notice of lien is filed. On January 29, 1971, a notice of levy with respect to C's delinquent tax is served on Z Company. The amount which C could have had advanced to him from Z Company under the contract on the 90th day after service of the notice of levy on Z Company is $2,000. The Z Company pays $2,000 pursuant to the notice of levy, thereby satisfying the levy upon the contract in accordance with section 6332(b). On February 1, 1973, Z Company advances $500 to C, which is the increment in policy loan value since satisfaction of the levy of January 29, 1971. On February 5, 1973, a new notice of levy for the unpaid balance of the delinquent taxes, executed after the first levy was satisfied, is served upon Z Company. Because the new notification was not received by Z Company until after the policy loan was made, under paragraph (1)(iii) of this paragraph, the tax lien is not valid against Z Company with respect to the policy loan (including interest thereon in accordance with paragraph (a) of § 301.6323(e)-1).

Example (4). On June 1, 1973, a tax assessment is made against D and on June 2, 1973, in accordance with § 301.6323(f)-1, a notice of lien with respect to the assessment is filed. On July 2, 1973, D executes an assignment of his rights, as the insured, under an insurance contract to M Bank as security for a loan. M Bank holds its security interest subject to the lien because it is not an insurer entitled to protection under section 6323(b)(9) and did not become a holder of the security interest prior to the filing of the notice of lien for purposes of section 6323(a). It is immaterial that a notice of levy had not been served upon the insurer before the assignment to M Bank was made.

(j) *Passbook loans*—(1) *In general.* Even though a notice of a lien imposed by section 6321 is filed in accordance with § 301.6323(f)-1, the lien is not valid against an institution described in section 581 or 591 to the extent of any loan made by the institution which is secured by a savings deposit, share, or other account evidenced by a passbook (as defined in subparagraph (2) of this paragraph) if the institution has been continuously in possession of the passbook from the time the loan is made. This paragraph applies only to a loan made without actual notice or knowledge (as defined in paragraph (a) of § 301.6323(i)-1) of the existence of the lien. Even though an original passbook loan is made without actual notice or knowledge of the existence of the lien, this paragraph does not apply to any additional loan made after knowledge of the lien is acquired by the institution even if it continues to retain the passbook from the time the original passbook loan is made.

(2) *Definition of passbook.* For purposes of this paragraph, the term "passbook" includes—

(i) Any tangible evidence of a savings deposit, share, or other account which, when in the possession of the bank or other savings institution, will prevent a withdrawal from the account to the extent of the loan balance, and

(ii) Any procedure or system, such as an automatic data processing system, the use of which by the bank or other savings institution will prevent a withdrawal from the account to the extent of the loan balance.

(3) *Example.* On June 1, 1970, a tax assessment is made against A and on June 2, 1970, a notice of lien with respect to the assessment is filed in accordance with § 301.6323(f)-1. A owns a savings account at the M Bank with a balance of $1,000. On June 10, 1970, A borrows $300 from the M Bank using the savings account as security therefor. The M Bank is continuously in possession of the passbook from the time the loan is made and does not have actual notice or knowledge of the lien at the time of the loan. The tax lien is not valid against M Bank with respect to the passbook loan of $300 and accrued interest and expenses entitled to priority under § 301.6323(e)-1. Upon service of a notice of levy, the M Bank must pay over the savings account balance in excess of the amount of its protected interest in the account as determined on the date of levy.

○━ § 301.6323(c) **Statutory provisions; validity and priority against certain persons; protection for certain commercial transactions financing agreements, etc.** [Sec. 6323(c), IRC]

○━ § 301.6323(c)-1 (T.D. 7429, filed 8-20-76.) **Protection for commercial transactions financing agreements.**

(a) *In general.* Even though a notice of a lien imposed by section 6321 is filed in accordance with § 301.6323(f)-1, the lien is not valid with respect to a security interest which:

(1) Comes into existence after the tax lien filing,

(2) Is in qualified property covered by the terms of a commercial transaction financing agreement entered into before the tax lien filing, and

(3) Is protected under local law against a judgment lien arising, as of the time of the tax lien filing, out of an unsecured obligation. See paragraphs (a) and (e) of § 301.6323(h)-1 for definitions of the terms "security interest" and "tax lien filing", respectively. For purposes of this section, a judgment lien is a lien held by a judgment lien creditor as defined in paragraph (g) of § 301.6323(h)-1.

(b) *Commercial transactions financing agreement.* For purposes of this section, the term "commercial transactions financing agreement" means a written agreement entered into by a person in the course of his trade or business—

(1) To make loans to the taxpayer (whether or not at the option of the person agreeing to make such loans) to be secured by commercial financing security acquired by the taxpayer in the ordinary course of his trade or business, or

(2) To purchase commercial financing security, other than inventory, acquired by the taxpayer in the ordinary course of his trade or business.

Such an agreement qualifies as a commercial transaction financing agreement only with respect to loans or purchases made under the agreement before (i) the 46th day after the date of tax lien filing or,

Reg. § 301.6323(c)-1(b)(2)

(ii) the time when the lender or purchaser has actual notice or knowledge (as defined in paragraph (a) of § 301.6323(i)-1) of the tax lien filing, if earlier. For purposes of this paragraph, a loan or purchase is considered to have been made in the course of the lender's or purchaser's trade or business if such person is in the business of financing commercial transactions (such as a bank or commercial factor) or if the agreement is incidental to the conduct of such person's trade or business. For example, if a manufacturer finances the accounts receivable of one of his customers, he is considered to engage in such financing in the course of his trade or business. The extent of the priority of the lender or purchaser over the tax lien is the amount of his disbursements made before the 46th day after the date the notice of tax lien is filed, or made before the date (before such 46th day) on which the lender or purchaser has actual notice or knowledge of the filing of the notice of the tax lien.

(c) *Commercial financing security*—(1) *In general.* The term "commercial financing security" means—

(i) Paper of a kind ordinarily arising in commercial transactions,

(ii) Accounts receivable (as defined in subparagraph (2) of this paragraph),

(iii) Mortgages on real property, and

(iv) Inventory.

For purposes of this subparagraph, the term "paper of a kind ordinarily arising in commercial transactions" in general includes any written document customarily used in commercial transactions. For example, such written documents include paper giving contract rights (as defined in subparagraph (2) of this paragraph), chattel paper, documents of title to personal property, and negotiable instruments or securities. The term "commercial financing security" does not include general intangibles such as patents or copyrights. A mortgage on real estate (including a deed of trust, contract for sale, and similar instrument) may be commercial financing security if the taxpayer has an interest in the mortgage as a mortgagee or assignee. The term "commercial financing security" does not include a mortgage where the taxpayer is the mortgagor of realty owned by him. For purposes of this subparagraph, the term "inventory" includes raw materials and goods in process as well as property held by the taxpayer primarily for sale to customers in the ordinary course of his trade or business.

(2) *Definitions.* For purposes of §§ 301.-6323(d)-1, § 301.6323(h)-1 and this section—

(i) A contract right is any right to payment under a contract not yet earned by performance and not evidenced by an instrument or chattel paper, and

(ii) An account receivable is any right to payment for goods sold or leased or for services rendered which is not evidenced by an instrument or chattel paper.

(d) *Qualified property.* For purposes of paragraph (a) of this section, qualified property consists solely of commercial financing security acquired by the taxpayer-debtor before the 46th day after the date of tax lien filing. Commercial financing security acquired before such day may be qualified property even though it is acquired by the taxpayer after the lender received actual notice or knowledge of the filing of the notice of the tax lien. For example, although the receipt of actual notice or knowledge of the filing of the notice of the tax lien has the effect of ending the period within which protected disbursements may be made to the taxpayer, property which is acquired by the taxpayer after the lender receives actual notice or knowledge of such filing and before such 46th day, which otherwise qualifies as commercial financing security, becomes commercial financing security to which the priority of the lender extends for loans made before he received the actual notice or knowledge. An account receivable (as defined in paragraph (c)(2)(ii) of this section) is acquired by a taxpayer at the time, and to the extent, a right to payment is earned by performance. Chattel paper, documents of title, negotiable instruments, securities, and mortgages on real estate are acquired by a taxpayer when he obtains rights in the paper or mortgage. Inventory is acquired by the taxpayer when title passes to him. A contract right (as defined in paragraph (c)(2)(i) of this section) is acquired by a taxpayer when the contract is made. Identifiable proceeds, which arises from the collection or disposition of qualified property by the taxpayer, are considered to be acquired at the time such qualified property is acquired if the secured party has a continuously perfected security interest in the proceeds under local law. The term "proceeds" includes whatever is received when collateral is sold, exchanged, or collected. For purposes of this paragraph, the term "identifiable proceeds" does not include money, checks and the like which have been commingled with other cash proceeds. Property acquired by the taxpayer after the 45th day following tax lien filing, by the expenditure of proceeds, is not qualified property.

(e) *Purchaser treated as acquiring security interest.* A person who purchases commercial financing security, other than inventory, pursuant to a commercial transaction financing agreement is treated, for purposes of this section, as having acquired a security interest in the commercial financing security. In the case of a bona fide purchase at a discount, a purchaser of commercial financing security who satisfies the requirements of this section has priority over the tax lien to the full extent of the security.

(f) *Examples.* The provisions of this section may be illustrated by the following examples:

Example (1). (i) On June 1, 1970, a tax is assessed against M, a tool manufacturer, with respect to his delinquent tax liability. On June 15, 1970, M enters into a written financing agreement with X, a bank. The agreement provides that, in consideration of such sums as X may advance to M, X is to have a security interest in all of M's presently owned and subsequently acquired commercial paper, accounts receivable, and inventory (including inventory in the manufacturing stages and raw materials). On July 6, 1970, notice of the tax lien is filed in accordance with § 301.6323(f)-1. On August 3, 1970, without actual notice or knowledge of the tax lien filing, X advances $10,000 to M. On August 5, 1970, M acquires additional inventory through the purchase of raw materials. On August 20, 1970, M has accounts receivable, arising from the sale of tools, amounting to $5,000. Under local law, X's security interest, arising by reason of the $10,000 advance on August 3, 1970, has priority, with respect to the raw materials and accounts receivable, over a judgment lien against M arising July 6, 1970 (the date of tax lien filing) out of an unsecured obligation.

(ii) Because the $10,000 advance was made before the 46th day after the tax lien filing, and the accounts receivable in the amount of $5,000 and the raw materials were acquired by M before such 46th day, X's $10,000 security interest in the accounts receivable and the inventory has priority over the tax lien. The priority of X's security interest also extends to the proceeds, received on or after the 46th day after the tax lien filing, from the liquidation of the accounts receivable and inventory held by M on August 20, 1970, if X has a continuously perfected security interest in identifiable proceeds under local law. However, the priority of X's security interest will not extend to other property acquired with such proceeds.

Example (2). Assume the same facts as in example (1) except that on July 15, 1970, X has actual knowledge of the tax lien filing. Because an agreement does not qualify as a commercial transactions financing agreement when a disbursement is made after tax lien filing with actual knowledge of the filing, X's security interest will not have priority over the tax lien with respect to the $10,000 advance made on August 3, 1970.

Example (3). Assume the same facts as in example (1) except that, instead of additional inventory, on August 5, 1970, M acquires an account receivable as the result of the sale of machinery which M no longer needs in his business. Even though the account receivable was acquired by taxpayer M before the 46th day after tax lien filing, the tax lien will have priority over X's security interest arising in the account receivable pursuant to the earlier written agreement because the account receivable was not acquired by the taxpayer in the ordinary course of his trade or business.

Example (4). Pursuant to a written agreement with the N Manufacturing Company entered into on January 4, 1971, Y, a commercial factor, purchases the accounts receivable arising out of N's regular sales to its customers. On November 1, 1971, in accordance with § 301.6323(f)-1, a notice of lien is filed with respect to N's delinquent tax liability. On December 6, 1971, Y, without actual notice or knowledge of the tax lien filing, purchases all of the accounts receivable resulting from N's November 1971 sales. Y has taken appropriate steps under local law so that the December 6, 1971, purchase is protected against a judgment lien arising November 1, 1971 (the date of tax lien filing) out of an unsecured obligation. Because the purchaser of commercial financing security, other than inventory, is treated as having acquired a security interest in commercial financing security, and because Y otherwise meets the requirements of this section, the tax lien is not valid with respect to Y's December 6, 1971, purchase of N's accounts receivable.

§301.6323(c)-2 (T.D. 7429, filed 8-20-76.) **Protection for real property construction or improvement financing agreements.**

(a) *In general.* Even though a notice of a lien imposed by section 6321 is filed in accordance with § 301.6323(f)-1, the lien is not valid with respect to a security interest which:

(1) Comes into existence after the tax lien filing,

(2) Is in qualified property covered by the terms of a real property construction or improvement financing agreement entered into before the tax lien filing, and

(3) Is protected under local law against a judgment lien arising, as of the time of tax lien filing, out of an unsecured obligation.

For purposes of this section, it is immaterial that the holder of the security interest had actual notice or knowledge of the lien at the time disbursements are made pursuant to such an agreement. See paragraphs (a) and (e) of § 301.6323(h)-1 for general definitions of the terms "security interest" and "tax lien filing." For purposes of this section, a judgment lien is a lien held by a judgment lien creditor as defined in paragraph (g) of § 301.6323(h)-1.

(b) *Real property construction or improvement financing agreement.* For purposes of this section, the term "real property construction or improvement financing agreement" means any written agreement to make cash disbursements (whether or not at the option of the party agreeing to make such disbursements):

(1) To finance the construction, improvement, or demolition of real property if the agreement provides for a security interest in the real property with respect to which the construction, improvement, or demolition has been or is to be made;

(2) To finance a contract to construct or improve, or demolish real property if the agreement provides for a security interest in the proceeds of the contract; or

(3) To finance the raising or harvesting of a farm crop or the raising of livestock or other animals if the agreement provides for a security interest in any property subject to the lien imposed by section 6321 at the time of tax lien filing, in the crop raised or harvested, or in the livestock or other animals raised.

For purposes of subparagraphs (1) and (2) of this paragraph, construction or improvement may include demolition. For purpose of any agreement described in subparagraph (3), the furnishing of goods and services is treated as the disbursement of cash.

(c) *Qualified property.* For purposes of this section, the term "qualified property" includes only—

(1) In the case of an agreement described in paragraph (b)(1) of this section, the real property with respect to which the construction or improvement has been or is to be made;

(2) In the case of an agreement described in paragraph (b)(2) of this section, the proceeds of the contract to construct or improve real property; or

Reg. § 301.6323(c)-2(c)-2

(3) In the case of an agreement described in paragraph (b)(3) of this section, property subject to the lien imposed by section 6321 at the time of tax lien filing, the farm crop raised or harvested, or the livestock or other animals raised.

(d) *Examples.* The provisions of this paragraph may be illustrated by the following examples:

Example (1) A, in order to finance the construction of a dwelling on a lot owned by him, mortgages the property to B. The mortgage, executed January 4, 1971, includes an agreement that B will make cash disbursements to A as the construction progresses. On February 1, 1971, in accordance with § 301.6323(f)-1, a notice of lien is filed with respect to A's delinquent tax liability. A continues the construction, and B makes cash disbursements on June 10, 1971, and December 10, 1971. Under local law B's security interest arising by virtue of the disbursements is protected against a judgment lien arising February 1, 1971 (the date of tax lien filing) out of an unsecured obligation. Because B is the holder of a security interest coming into existence by reason of cash disbursements made pursuant to a written agreement, entered into before tax lien filing, to make cash disbursements to finance the construction, of real property, and because B's security interest is protected, under local law, against a judgment lien arising as of the time of tax lien filing out of an unsecured obligation, B's security interest has priority over the tax lien.

Example (2) (i) C is awarded a contract for the demolition of several buildings. On March 3, 1969, C enters into a written agreement with D which provides that D will make cash disbursements to finance the demolition and also provides that repayment of the disbursements is secured by any sums due C under the contract. On April 1, 1969, in accordance with § 301.-6323(f)-1, a notice of lien is filed with respect to C's delinquent tax liability. With actual notice of the tax lien, D makes cash disbursements to C on August 1, September 1, and October 1, 1969. Under local law D's security interest in the proceeds of the contract with respect to the disbursements is entitled to priority over a judgment lien arising on April 1, 1969 (the date of tax lien filing) out of an unsecured obligation.

(ii) Because D's security interest arose by reason of disbursements made pursuant to a written agreement, entered into before tax lien filing, to make cash disbursements to finance a contract to demolish real property, and because D's security interest is valid under local law against a judgment lien arising as of the time of tax lien filing out of an unsecured obligation, the tax lien is not valid with respect to D's security interest in the proceeds of the demolition contract.

Example (3). Assume the same facts as in example (2) and, in addition, assume that, as further security for the cash disbursements, the March 3, 1969 agreement also provides for a security interest in all of C's demolition equipment. Because the protection of the security interest arising from the disbursements made after tax lien filing under the agreement is limited under section 6323(c)(3) to the proceeds of the demolition contract and because, under the circumstances, the security interest in the equipment is not otherwise protected under section 6323, the tax lien will have priority over D's security interest in the equipment.

Example (4). (i) On January 2, 1969, F and G enter into a written agreement whereby F agrees to provide G with cash disbursements, seed, fertilizer, and insecticides as needed by G, in order to finance the raising and harvesting of a crop on a farm owned by G. Under the terms of the agreement F is to have a security interest in the crop, the farm and all other property then owned or thereafter acquired by G. In accordance with § 301.6323(f)-1, on January 10, 1969, a notice of lien is filed with respect to G's delinquent tax liability. On March 3, 1969, with actual notice of the tax lien, F makes a cash disbursement of $5,000 to G and furnishes him seed, fertilizer, and insecticides having a value of $10,000. Under local law F's security interest, coming into existence by reason of the cash disbursement and the furnishing of goods, has priority over a judgment lien arising January 10, 1969 (the date of tax lien filing) out of an unsecured obligation.

(ii) Because F's security interest arose by reason of a disbursement (including the furnishing of goods) made under a written agreement which was entered into before tax lien filing and which constitutes an agreement to finance the raising or harvesting of a farm crop, and because F's security interest is valid under local law against a judgment lien arising as of the time of tax lien filing out of an unsecured obligation, the tax lien is not valid with respect to F's security interest in the crop even though a notice of lien was filed before the security interest arose. Furthermore, because the farm is property subject to the tax lien at the time of tax lien filing, F's security interest with respect to the farm also has priority over the tax lien.

Example (5). Assume the same facts as in example (4) and in addition that on October 1, 1969, G acquires several tractors to which F's security interest attaches under the terms of the agreement. Because the tractors are not property subject to the tax lien at the time of tax lien filing, the tax lien has priority over F's security interest in the tractors.

○→ § 301.6323(c)-3 (T.D. 7429, filed 8-20-76.) **Protection for obligatory disbursement agreements.**

(a) *In general.* Even though a notice of a lien imposed by section 6321 is filed in accordance with § 301.6323(f)-1, the lien is not valid with respect to a security interest which:

(1) Comes into existence after the tax lien filing,

(2) Is in qualified property covered by the terms of an obligatory disbursement agreement entered into before the tax lien filing, and

(3) Is protected under local law against a judgment lien arising, as of the time of tax lien filing, out of an unsecured obligation.

See paragraphs (a) and (e) of § 301.6323 (h)-1 for definitions of the terms "security interest" and "tax lien filing." For purposes of this section, a judgment lien is a lien held by a judgment lien creditor as defined in paragraph (g) of § 301.6323(h)-1.

(b) *Obligatory disbursement agreement.* For purposes of this section the term "obligatory disbursement agreement" means a written agreement, entered into by a person in the course of his trade or business, to make disbursements. An agreement is treated as an obligatory disbursement agreement only with respect to disbursements which are required to be made by reason of the intervention of the rights of a person other than the taxpayer. The obligation to pay must be conditioned upon an event beyond the control of the obligor. For example, the provisions of this section are applicable where an issuing bank obligates itself to honor drafts or other demands for payment on a letter of credit and a bank, in good faith, relies upon that letter of credit in making advances. The provisions of this section are also applicable, for example, where a bonding company obligates itself to make payments to indemnify against loss or liability and, under the terms of the bond, makes a payment with respect to a loss. The priority described in this section is not applicable, for example, in the case of an accommodation endorsement by an endorser who assumes his obligation other than in the course of his trade or business.

(c) *Qualified property.* Except as provided under paragraph (d) of this section, the term "qualified property", for purposes of this section, means property subject to the lien imposed by section 6321 at the time of tax lien filing and, to the extent that the acquisition is directly traceable to the obligatory disbursement, property acquired by the taxpayer after tax lien filing.

(d) *Special rule for surety agreements.* Where the obligatory disbursement agreement is an agreement ensuring the performance of a contract of the taxpayer and another person, the term "qualified property" shall be treated as also including—

(1) The proceeds of the contract the performance of which was ensured, and

(2) If the contract the performance of which was ensured is a contract to construct or improve real property, to produce goods, or to furnish services, any tangible personal property used by the taxpayer in the performance of the ensured contract.

For example, a surety company which holds a security interest, arising from cash disbursements made after tax lien filing under a payment or performance bond on a real estate construction project, has priority over the tax lien with respect to the proceeds of the construction contract and, in addition, with respect to any tangible personal property used by the taxpayer in the construction project if its security interest in the tangible personal property is protected under local law against a judgment lien arising, as of the time the tax lien was filed, out of an unsecured obligation.

(e) *Examples.* This section may be illustrated by the following examples:

Example (1). (i) On January 2, 1969, H, an appliance dealer, in order to finance the acquisition from O of a large inventory of appliances, enters into a written agreement with Z, a bank. Under the terms of the agreement, in return for a security interest in all of H's inventory, presently owned and subsequently acquired, Z issues an irrevocable letter of credit to allow H to make the purchase. On December 31, 1968 and January 10, 1969, in accordance with § 301.6323(f)-1, separate notices of lien are filed with respect to H's delinquent tax liabilities. On March 31, 1969, Z honors the letter of credit. Under local law, Z's security interest in both existing and after-acquired inventory is protected against a judgment lien arising on or after January 10, 1969, out of an unsecured obligation. Under local law, Z's security interest in the inventory purchased under the letter of credit qualifies as a purchase money security interest and is valid against persons acquiring security interests in or liens upon such inventory at any time.

(ii) Because Z's security interest in H's inventory did not arise under a written agreement entered into before the filing of notice of the first tax lien on December 31, 1968, that lien is superior to Z's security interest except to the extent of Z's purchase money security interest. Because Z's interest qualifies as a purchase money security interest with respect to he inventory purchased under the letter of credit, the tax liens attach under section 6321 only to the equity acquired by H, and the rights of Z in the inventory so purchased are superior even to the lien filed on December 31, 1968, without regard to this section.

(iii) Because Z's security interest arose by reason of disbursements made under a written agreement which was entered into before the filing of notice of the second tax lien on January 10, 1969, and which constitutes an agreement to make disbursements required to be made by reason of the intervention of the rights of O, a person other than the taxpayer, and because Z's security interest is valid under local law against a judgment lien arising as of the time of such tax lien filing on January 10, 1969, out of an unsecured obligation, the second tax lien is, under this section, not valid with respect to Z's security interest in inventory owned by H on January 10, 1969, as well as any after-acquired inventory directly traceable to Z's disbursements (apart from such greater protection as Z enjoys, with respect to the latter, under its purchase money security interest). No protection against the second tax lien is provided under this section with respect to a security interest in any other inventory acquired by H after January 10, 1969, because such other inventory is neither subject to the tax lien at the time of tax lien filing nor directly traceable to Z's disbursements.

Example (2). On June 1, 1971, K is awarded a contract to construct an office building. At the same time, S, a surety company, agrees in writing to ensure the performance of the contract. The agreement provides that in the event S must complete the job as the result of a default by K, S will be entitled to the proceeds of the contract. In addition, the agreement provides that S is to have a security interest in all property belonging to K. On December 1, 1971, prior to the completion of the building, K defaults. On the same date, under § 301.6323(f)-1, a notice of lien is filed with respect to K's delinquent tax liability. S completes the building on June

Reg. § 301.6323(c)-3(e)

1, 1972. Under local law S's security interest in the proceeds of the contract and S's security interest in the property of K are entitled to priority over a judgment lien arising December 1, 1971 (the date of tax lien filing) out of an unsecured obligation. Because, for purposes of an obligatory disbursement agreement which is a surety agreement, the security interest may be in the proceeds of the ensured contract, S' security interest in the proceeds of the contract has priority over the tax lien even though a notice of lien was filed before S' security interest arose. Furthermore, because the ensured contract was a contract to construct real property, S' security interest in any of K's tangible personal property used in the performance of the contract also has priority over the tax lien.

Example (3). (i) On February 2, 1970, L enters into an agreement with M, a contractor, to construct an apartment building on land owned by L. Under a separate agreement, N Bank agrees to furnish funds on a short-term basis to L for the payment of amounts due to M during the course of construction. Simultaneously, X, a financial institution, makes a binding commitment to N Bank and L to provide long-term financing for the project after its completion. Under its commitment, X is obligated to pay off the balance of the construction loan held by N Bank upon the execution by L of a new promissory note secured by a mortgage deed of trust upon the improved property. On September 4, 1970, in accordance with § 301.6323(f)-1, notice of lien is properly filed with respect to L's delinquent tax liability. On September 8, 1970, X obtains actual notice of the tax lien filing. On September 14, 1970, the documents creating X's security interest are executed and recorded, N Bank's lien for its construction loan is released, and X makes the required disbursements to N Bank. Under local law, X's security interest is protected against a judgment lien arising on September 4, 1970 (the time of tax lien filing) out of an unsecured obligation.

(ii) Because X's security interest arose by reason of a disbursement made under a written agreement entered into before tax lien filing, which constitutes an agreement to make disbursements required to be made by reason of the intervention of the rights of N Bank, a person other than the taxpayer, and because X's security interest is valid under local law against a judgment lien arising as of the time of the tax lien filing out of an unsecured obligation, the tax lien is not valid with respect to X's security interest to the extent of the disbursement to N Bank. The obligatory disbursement is protected under section 6323(c)(4) even if X is not subrogated to N Bank's rights or X's agreement is not itself a real property construction financing agreement.

○― § 301.6323(d) Statutory provisions; validity and priority against certain persons; 45-day period for making disbursements. [Sec. 6323(d), IRC]

○― § 301.6323(d)-1 (T.D. 7429, filed 8-20-76.) 45-day period for making disbursements.

(a) *In general.* Even though a notice of a lien imposed by section 6321 is filed in accordance with § 301.6323(f)-1, the lien is not valid with respect to a security interest which comes into existence, after tax lien filing, by reason of disbursements made before the 46th day after the date of tax lien filing, or if earlier, before the person making the disbursements has actual notice or knowledge of the tax lien filing, but only if the security interest is—

(1) In property which is subject, at the time of tax lien filing, to the lien imposed by section 6321 and which is covered by the terms of a written agreement entered into before tax lien filing, and

(2) Protected under local law against a judgment lien arising, as of the time of tax lien filing, out of an unsecured obligation.

For purposes of subparagraph (1) of this paragraph, a contract right (as defined in paragraph (c)(2)(i) of § 301.6323(c)-1) is subject, at the time of tax lien filing, to the lien imposed by section 6321 if the contract has been made by such time. An account receivable (as defined in paragraph (c)(2)(ii) of § 301.6323(c)-1 is subject, at the time of tax lien filing, to the lien imposed by section 6321 if, and to the extent, a right to payment has been earned by performance at such time. For purposes of subparagraph (2) of this paragraph, a judgment lien is a lien held by a judgment lien creditor as defined in paragraph (g) of § 301.6323(h)-1. For purposes of this section, it is immaterial that the written agreement provides that the disbursements are to be made at the option of the person making the disbursements. See paragraphs (a) and (e) of § 301.6323(h)-1 for definitions of the terms "security interest" and "tax lien filing," respectively. See paragraph (a) of § 301.6323(i)-1 for certain circumstances under which a person is deemed to have actual notice or knowledge of a fact.

(b) *Examples.* The application of this section may be illustrated by the following examples:

Example (1). On December 1, 1967, an assessment is made against A with respect to his delinquent tax liability. On January 2, 1968, A enters into a written agreement with B whereby B agrees to lend A $10,000 in return for a security interest in certain property owned by A. On January 10, 1968, in accordance with § 301.6323(f)-1 notice of the tax lien affecting the property is filed. On February 1, 1968, B, without actual notice or knowledge of the tax lien filing, disburses the loan to A. Under local law, the security interest arising by reason of the disbursement is entitled to priority over a judgment lien arising January 10, 1968 (the date of tax lien filing) out of an unsecured obligation. Because the disbursement was made before the 46th day after tax lien filing, because the disbursement was made pursuant to a written agreement entered into before tax lien filing, and because the resulting security interest is protected under local law against a judgment lien arising as of the date of tax lien filing out of an unsecured obligation, B's $10,000 security interest has priority over the tax lien.

Example (2). Assume the same facts as in example (1) except that when B disburses the $10,000 to A on February 10, 1968, B has actual knowledge of the tax lien filing. Because the disbursement was made with actual knowledge of tax lien filing, B's security interest does not have priority over the tax lien even though the disbursement was made before the 46th day after the tax lien filing. Furthermore, B is not protected under § 301.6323(a)-1(a) as a holder of a security interest because he had not parted with money or money's worth prior to the time the notice of tax lien was filed (January 10, 1968) even though he had made a firm commitment to A before that time.

○── § 301.6323(e)   Statutory provisions; validity and priority against certain persons; priority of interest and expenses. [Sec. 6323(e), IRC]

○── § 301.6323(e)-1 (T.D. 7429, filed 8-20-76.) Priority of interest and expenses.

(a) *In general.* If the lien imposed by section 6321 is not valid as against another lien or security interest, the priority of the other lien or security interest also extends to each of the following items to the extent that under local law the item has the same priority as the lien or security interest to which it relates:

(1) Any interest or carrying charges (including finance, service, and similar charges) upon the obligation secured,

(2) The reasonable charges and expenses of an indenture trustee (including, for example, the trustee under a deed of trust) or agent holding the security interest for the benefit of the holder of the security interest,

(3) The reasonable expenses, including reasonable compensation for attorneys, actually incurred in collecting or enforcing the obligation secured,

(4) The reasonable costs of insuring, preserving, or repairing the property to which the lien or security interest relates,

(5) The reasonable costs of insuring payment of the obligation secured (including amounts paid by the holder of the security interest for mortgage insurance, such as that issued by the Federal Housing Administration), and

(6) Amounts paid to satisfy any lien on the property to which the lien or security interest relates, but only if the lien so satisfied is entitled to priority over the lien imposed by section 6321.

(b) *Collection expenses.* The reasonable expenses described in paragraph (a)(3) of this section include expenditures incured by the protected holder of the lien or security interest to establish the priority of his interest or to collect, by foreclosure or otherwise, the amount due him from the property subject to his lien. Accordingly, the amount of the encumbrance which is protected is increased by the amounts so expended by the holder of the security interest.

(c) *Costs of insuring, preserving, etc.* The reasonable costs of insuring, preserving, or repairing described in paragraph (a)(4) of this section include expenditures by the holder of a security interest for fire and casualty insurance on the property subject to the security interest and amounts paid by the holder of the lien or security interest to repair the property. Such reasonable costs also include the amounts paid by the holder of the lien or security interest in a leasehold to the lessor of the leasehold to preserve the leasehold subject to the lien or security interest. Accordingly, the amount of the lien or security interest which is protected is increased by the amounts so expended by the holder of the lien or security interest.

(d) *Satisfaction of liens.* The amounts described in paragraph (a)(6) of this section include expenditures incurred by the protected holder of a lien or security interest to discharge a statutory lien for state sales taxes on the property subject to his lien or security interest if both his lien or security interest and the sales tax lien have priority over a Federal tax lien. Accordingly, the amount of the lien or security interest is increased by the amounts so expended by the holder of the lien or security interest even though under local law the holder of the lien or security interest is not subrogated to the rights of the holder of the state sales tax lien. However, if the holder of the lien or security interest is subrogated, within the meaning of paragraph (b) of § 301.6323(i)-1, to the rights of the holder of the sales tax lien, he will also be entitled to any additional protection afforded by section 6323(i)(2).

○── § 301.6323(f)   Statutory provisions; validity and priority against certain persons; place for filing notice; form. [Sec. 6323(f), IRC]

○── § 301.6323(f)-1 (T.D. 7429, filed 8-20-76.) Place for filing notice; form.

(a) *Place for filing.* The notice of lien referred to in § 301.6323(a)-1 shall be filed as follows:

(1) *Under State laws*—(i) *Real property.* In the case of real property, notice shall be filed in one office within the State (or the county or other governmental subdivision), as designated by the laws of the State, in which the property subject to the lien is deemed situated under the provisions of paragraph (b)(1) of this section.

(ii) *Personal property.* In the case of personal property, whether tangible or intangible, the notice shall be filed in one office within the State (or the county or other governmental subdivision), as designated by the laws of the State, in which the property subject to the lien is deemed situated under the provisions of paragraph (b)(2) of this section.

(2) *With the clerk of the United States district court.* Whenever a State has not by law designated one office which meets the requirements of subparagraph (1)(i) or (1)(ii) of this paragraph, the notice shall be filed in the office of the clerk of the United States district court for the judicial district in which the property subject to the lien is deemed situated under the provisions of paragraph (b) of this section. For example, a State has not by law designated one office meeting the requirements of subparagraph (1)(i) of this paragraph if more than one office is designated within the State, county, or other governmental subdivision for filing notices with respect to all real property located in such State, county, or other governmental subdivision. A State has not by law designated one office meeting the

Reg. § 301.6323(f)-1(a)(2)

requirements of subparagraph (1)(ii) of this paragraph if more than one office is designated in the State, county, or other governmental subdivision for filing notices with respect to all of the personal property of a particular taxpayer.

(3) *With the Recorder of Deeds of the District of Columbia.* If the property subject to the lien imposed by section 6321 is deemed situated, under the provisions of paragraph (b) of this section, in the District of Columbia, the notice shall be filed in the office of the Recorder of Deeds of the District of Columbia.

(b) *Situs of property subject to lien.* For purposes of paragraph (a) of this section, property is deemed situated as follows:

(1) *Real property.* Real property is deemed situated at its physical location.

(2) *Personal property.* Personal property, whether tangible or intangible, is deemed situated at the residence of the taxpayer at the time the notice of lien is filed.

For purposes of subparagraph (2) of this paragraph the residence of a corporation or partnership is deemed to be the place at which the principal executive office of the business is located, and the residence of a taxpayer whose residence is not within the United States is deemed to be in the District of Columbia.

(c) *Form.* The notice referred to in § 301.6323(a)-1 shall be filed on Form 668, "Notice of Federal Tax Lien under Internal Revenue Laws". Such notice is valid notwithstanding any other provision of law regarding the form or content of a notice of lien. For example, omission from the notice of lien of a description of the property subject to the lien does not affect the validity thereof even though state law may require that the notice contain a description of the property subject to the lien.

(d) *Examples.* The provisions of this section may be illustrated by the following examples:

Example (1). The law of State X provides that notices of Federal tax lien affecting personal property are to be filed in the Office of the Recorder of Deeds of the county where the taxpayer resides. The laws of State X also provide that notices of lien affecting real property are to be filed with the recorder of deeds of the county where the real property is located. On June 1, 1970, in accordance with § 301.-6323(f)-1, a notice of lien is filed in County M with respect to the delinquent tax liability of A. At the time the notice is filed, A is a resident of County M and owns real property in that county. One year later A moves to County N and one year after that A moves to County O. Because the situs of personal property is deemed to be at the residence of the taxpayer at the time the notice of lien is filed, the notice continues to be effectively filed with respect to A's personal property even though A no longer resides in County M. Furthermore, because the situs of real property is deemed to be at its physical location, the notice of lien also continues to be effectively filed with respect to A's real property.

Example (2). B is a resident of Canada but owns personal property in the United States. On January 4, 1971, in accordance with § 301.6323(f)-1, a notice of lien is filed with the Office of the Recorder of Deeds of the District of Columbia. On January 2, 1973, B changes his residence to State Y in the United States. Because the residence of a taxpayer who is not a resident of the United States is deemed to be in the District of Columbia and the situs of personal property is deemed to be at the residence of the taxpayer at the time of filing, the lien continues to be effectively filed with respect to the personal property of B located in the United States even though B has returned to the United States and taken up residence in State Y and even through B has at no time been in the District of Columbia.

Example (3). The law of State Z in effect before July 1, 1967, provides that notices of lien affecting real property are to be filed in the office of the recorder of deeds of the county in which the real property is located, but that if the real property is registered under the Torrens system of title registration the notice is to be filed with the registrar of titles rather than the recorder of deeds. The law of State Z in effect after June 30, 1967, provides that all notices of lien affecting real property are to be filed with the recorder of deeds of the county in which the real property is located. Accordingly, where the Torrens system is adopted by a county in State Z, there were before July 1, 1967, two offices designated for filing notices of Federal tax lien affecting real property in the county because one office was designated for Torrens real property and another office was designated for non-Torrens real property. Because State Z had not designated one office within the State, county, or other governmental subdivision for filing notices before July 1, 1967, with respect to all real property located in the State, county, or governmental subdivision before July 1, 1967, the place for filing notices of lien under this section, affecting property located in counties adopting the Torrens system, was with the clerk of the United States district court for the judicial district in which the real property is located. However, after June 30, 1967, the place for filing notices of lien under this section, affecting both Torrens and non-Torrens real property in counties adopting the Torrens system is with the recorder of deeds for each such county. Notices of lien filed under this section with the clerk of the United States district court before July 1, 1967, remain validly filed whether or not refiled with the recorder of deeds after the change in state law or upon refiling during the required refiling period.

Example (4). The law of State W provides that notices of lien affecting personal property of corporations and partnerships are to be filed in the office of the Secretary of State. Notices of lien affecting personal property of any other person are to be filed in the office of the clerk of court for the county where the person resides. Because the state law designates only one filing office within State W with respect to personal property of any particular taxpayer, notices of lien filed under this section, affecting personal property, shall be filed in the office designated under state law.

○━ § 301.6323(g) **Statutory provisions; validity and priority against certain persons; refiling of notice of tax lien.** [Sec. 6323(g), IRC]

○━ § 301.6323(g)-1 (T.D. 7429, filed 8-20-76.) **Refiling of notice of tax lien.**

(a) *In general*—(1) *Requirement to refile.* In order to continue the effect of a notice of lien, the notice must be refiled in the place described in paragraph (b) of this section during the required refiling period (described in paragraph (c) of this section). In the event that two or more notices of lien are filed with respect to a particular tax assessment, the failure to comply with the provisions of paragraphs (b)(1)(i) and (c) of this section in respect of one of the notices of lien does not affect the effectiveness of the refiling of any other notice of lien. Except for the filing of a notice of lien required by paragraph (b)(1)(ii) of this section (relating to a change of residence) the validity of any refiling of a notice of lien is not affected by the refiling or non-refiling of any other notice of lien.

(2) *Effect of refiling.* A timely refiled notice of lien is effective as of the date on which the notice of lien to which it relates was effective.

(3) *Effect of failure to refile.* If the district director fails to refile a notice of lien in the manner described in paragraphs (b) and (c) of this section, the notice of lien is not effective, after the expiration of the required refiling period, as against any person without regard to when the interest of the person in the property subject to the lien was acquired. However, the failure of the district director to refile a notice of lien during the required refiling period will not, following the expiration of the refiling period, affect the effectiveness of the notice with respect to:

(i) Property which is the subject matter of a suit, to which the United States is a party, commenced prior to the expiration of the required refiling period, or

(ii) Property which has been levied upon by the United States prior to the expiration of the refiling period.

However, if a suit or levy referred to in the preceding sentence is dismissed or released and the property is subject to the lien at such time, a notice of lien with respect to the property is not effective after the suit or levy is dismissed or released unless refiled during the required refiling period. Failure to refile a notice of lien does not affect the existence of the lien.

(4) *Filing of new notice.* If a notice of lien is not refiled, and if the lien remains in existence, the Internal Revenue Service may nevertheless file a new notice of lien either on the form prescribed for the filing of a notice of lien or on the form prescribed for refiling a notice of lien. This new filing must meet the requirements of section 6323(f) and § 301.6323(f)-1 and is effective from the date on which such filing is made.

(b) *Place for refiling notice of lien*—(1) *In general.* A notice of lien refiled during the required refiling period (described in paragraph (c) of this section) shall be effective only—

(i) If the notice of lien is refiled in the office in which the prior notice of lien (including a refiled notice) was filed under the provisions of section 6323; and

(ii) In any case in which 90 days or more prior to the date the refiling of the notice of lien under subdivision (i) is completed, the Internal Revenue Service receives written information (in the manner described in subparagraph (2) of this paragraph) concerning a change in the taxpayer's residence, if a notice of such lien is also filed in accordance with section 6323(f)(1)(A)(ii) in the State in which such new residence is located (or, if such new residence is located without the United States, in the District of Columbia).

A notice of lien is considered as refiled in the office in which the prior notice or refiled notice was filed under the provisions of section 6323 if it is refiled in the office which, pursuant to a change in the applicable local law, assumed the functions of the office in which the prior notice or refiled notice was filed. If on or before the 90th day referred to in subdivision (ii) more than one writen notice is received concerning a change in the taxpayer's residence, a notice of lien is required by this subdivision to be filed only with respect to the residence shown on the written notice received on the most recent date. Subdivision (ii) is applicable regardless of whether the taxpayer resides at the new residence on the date the refiling of notice of lien under subdivision (i) of this subparagraph is completed.

(2) *Notice of change of taxpayer's residence*—(i) *In general.* Except as provided in subdivision (ii) or (iii) of this subparagraph, for purposes of this section, a notice of change of a taxpayer's residence will be effective only if it (A) is received, in writing, from the taxpayer or his representative by the district director or the service center director having jurisdiction where the original notice of lien was filed, (B) relates to an unpaid tax liability of the taxpayer, and (C) states the taxpayer's name and the address of his new residence. Although it is not necessary that a written notice contain the taxpayer's identifying number authorized by section 6109, it is preferable that it include such number. For purposes of this subdivision, a notice of change of a taxpayer's residence shown on a return or an amended return (including a return of the same tax) will not be effective to notify the Internal Revenue Service.

(ii) *Notice received before August 23, 1976.* For purposes of this section, a notice of a change of a taxpayer's residence will also be effective if it (A) is received, in writing, by any office of the Internal Revenue Service before August 23, 1976, from the taxpayer or his representative, (B) relates to an unpaid tax liability of the taxpayer, and (C) states the taxpayer's name and the address of his new residence.

(iii) *By return or amended return.* For purposes of this section, in the case of a notice of lien which relates to an assessment of tax made after December 31, 1966, a notice of change of a taxpayer's residence will also be effective if it is contained in a return or amended return of the same type

Reg. § 301.6323(g)-1(b)(2)

24,352.12 (I.R.C.) Reg. § 301.6323(g)-1(b)(2) 8-30-76

of tax filed with the Internal Revenue Service by the taxpayer or his representative which on its face indicates that there is a change in the taxpayer's address and correctly states the taxpayer's name, the address of his new residence, and his identifying number required by section 6109.

(iv) *Other rules applicable.* Except as provided in subdivisions (i), (ii) and (iii) of this subparagraph, no communication (either written or oral) to the Internal Revenue Service will be considered effective as notice of a change of a taxpayer's residence under this section, whether or not the Service has actual notice or knowledge of the taxpayer's new residence. For the purpose of determining the date on which a notice of change of a taxpayer's residence is received under this section, the notice shall be treated as received on the date it is actually received by the Internal Revenue Service without reference to the provisions of section 7502.

(3) *Examples.* The provisions of this section may be illustrated by the following examples:

Example (1). A, a delinquent taxpayer, is a resident of State M and owns real property in State N. In accordance with § 301.6323(f)-1, notices of lien are filed in States M and N. In order to continue the effect of the notice of lien filed in M, the Internal Revenue Service must refile, during the required refiling period, the notice of lien with the appropriate office in M but is not required to refile the notice of lien with the appropriate office in N. Similarly, in order to continue the effect of the notice of lein filed in State N, the Internal Revenue Service must refile, during the required refiling period, the notice of lien with the appropriate office in N but is not required to refile the notice of lien with the appropriate office in M.

Example (2). B, a delinquent taxpayer, is a resident of State M. In accordance with § 301.6323(f)-1, notire of lien is properly filed in that State. One year before the beginning of the required refiling period, B establishes his residence in State N, and B immediately notifies the Internal Revenue Service of his change in residence in accordance with the provisions of paragraph (b)(2) of this section. In order to continue the effect of the notice of lien filed in M, the Internal Revenue Service must refile, during the required refiling period, notices of lien with (i) the appropriate office in M, and (ii) the appropriate office in N, because B properly notified the Internal Revenue Service of his change in residence to N more than 89 days prior to the date refiling of the notice of lien in M is completed. Even if the Internal Revenue Service had acquired actual notice or knowledge of B's change in residence by other means, if B had not properly notified the Internal Revenue Service of his change in residence, the effect of the notice of lien in State M could have been continued without any refiling in State N.

Example (3). C, a delinquent taxpayer, is a resident of State O. In accordance with § 301.6323(f)-1, notice of lien is properly filed in that State. Four years before the required refiling period, C establishes his residence in State P, and C immediately notifies the Internal Revenue Service of his change in residence in accordance with the provisions of paragraph (b)(2) of this section. Three years before the required refiling period, C establishes his residence in State R, and again C immediately notifies the Internal Revenue Service of his change in residence in accordance with the provisions of paragraph (2) of this section. In order to continue the effect of the notice of lien filed in O, the Internal Revenue Service must refile, during the required refiling period, notices of lien with (i) the appropriate office in O, and (ii) the appropriate office in R. Refiling in R is required because the notice received by the Service of C's change in residence to R was the most recent notice received more than 89 days prior to the date refiling in O is completed. The notice of lien is not required to be filed in P, even though C properly notified the Internal Revenue Service of his change in residence to P, because such notice is not the most recent one received.

Example (4). Assume the same facts as in example (3), except that C does not notify the Internal Revenue Service of his change in residence to R in accordance with the provisions of paragraph (b)(2) of this section. In order to continue the effect of the notice of lien filed in O, the Internal Revenue Service must refile, during the required refiling period, the notice of lien with (i) the appropriate office in O, and (ii) the appropriate office in P. Refiling in P is required because C properly notified the Internal Revenue Service of his change in residence to P, even though C is not a resident of P on the date refiling of the notice of lien in O is completed. The Internal Revenue Service is not required to file a notice of lien in R because C did not properly notify the Service of his change in residence to R.

Example (5). D, a delinquent taxpayer, is a resident of State M and owns real property in States N and O. In accordance with § 301.6323(f)-1, the Internal Revenue Service files notices of lien in M, N, and O States. Five years and 6 months after the date of the assessment shown on the notice of lien, D establishes his residence in P, and at that time the Internal Revenue Service received from D a notification of his change in residence in accordance with the provisions of paragraph (b)(2) of this section. On a date which is 5 years and 7 months after the date of assessment shown on the notice of lien, the Internal Revenue Service properly refiles notices of lien in M, N, and O which refilings are sufficient to continue the effect of each of the notices of lien. The Internal Revenue Service is not required to file a notice of lien in P because D did not notify the Internal Revenue Service of his change of residence to P more than 89 days prior to the date each of the refilings in M, N, and O was completed.

Example (6). Assume the same facts as in example (5) except that the refiling of the notice of lien in O occurs 100 days after D notifies the Internal Revenue Service of his change in residence to P in accordance with the provisions of paragraph (b)(2) of this section. In order to continue the effect of the notice of lien filed in O, in addition to refiling the notice of lien in O, the Internal Revenue Service must also refile, during the required refiling period, a notice of lien in P because D properly notified the Internal Revenue Service of his change of residence to P more than 89 days prior to the date the refiling in O was completed. However, the Internal Revenue Service is not required to refile the notice of lien in P to maintain the effect of the notices of lien in M and N because D did not notify the Internal Revenue Service of his change in residence to P more than 89 days prior to the date the refilings in M and N were completed.

Example (7). E, a delinquent taxpayer, is a resident of State T. Because T has not designated one office in the case of personal property for filing notices of lien in accordance with the provisions of section 6323 (f)(1)(A)(ii), the Internal Revenue Service properly files a notice of lien with the clerk of the appropriate United States district court. However, solely as a matter of convenience for those who may have occasion to search for notices of lien, and not as a matter of legal effectiveness, the Internal Revenue Service also files notice of lien with the recorder of deeds of the county in T where E resides. In addition, the Internal Revenue Service sends a copy of the notice of lien to the X Life Insurance Company to give the Company actual notice of the notice of lien. In order to continue the effect of the notice of lien, the Internal Revenue Service must refile the notice of lien with the clerk of the appropriate United States District court during the required refiling period. In order to continue the effect of the notice of the lien, it is not necessary to refile the notice of lien with the recorder of deeds of the county where E resides, because the refiling of the notice of lien with the recorder of deeds does not constitute a proper filing for the purposes of section 6323(f). In addition, to continue the effect of the notice of lien under this section it is not necessary to send a copy of the notice of lien to the X Life Insurance Company, because the sending of a notice of lien to an insurance company does not constitute a proper filing for the purposes of section 6323(f).

(c) *Required refiling period*—(1) *In general.* For the purpose of this section, except as provided in subparagraph (2) of this paragraph, the term "required refiling period" means—

(i) The 1-year period ending 30 days after the expiration of 6 years after the date of the assessment of the tax, and

(ii) The 1-year period ending with the expiration of 6 years after the close of the preceding required refiling period for such notice of lien.

(2) *Tax assessments made before January 1, 1962.* If the assessment of the tax is made before January 1, 1962, the first required refiling period shall be the calendar year 1967. Thus, to maintain the effectiveness of any notice of lien on file which relates to a lien which arose before January 1, 1962, the Internal Revenue Service will refile the notice of lien during the calendar year 1967.

(3) *Examples.* The provisions of this paragraph may be illustrated by the following examples:

Example (1). On March 1, 1963, an assessment of tax is made against B, a delinquent taxpayer, and a lien for the amount of the assessment arises on that date. On July 1, 1963, in accordance with § 301.6323 (f)-1, a notice of lien is filed. The notice of lien filed on July 1, 1963, is effective through March 31, 1969. The first required refiling period for the notice of lien begins on April 1, 1968, and ends on March 31, 1969. A refiling of the notice of lien during that period will extend the effectiveness of the notice of lien filed on July 1, 1963 through March 31, 1975. The second required refiling period for the notice of lien begins on April 1, 1974, and ends on March 31, 1975.

Example (2). Assume the same facts as in example (1), except that although the Internal Revenue Service fails to refile a notice of lien during the first required refiling period (April 1, 1968, through March 31, 1969), a notice of lien is filed on June 2, 1971 in accordance with § 301.6323(f)-1. Because of this filing, the notice of lien filed on June 2, 1971, is effective as of June 2, 1971. That notice must be refiled during the 1-year period ending on March 31, 1975, if it is to continue in effect after March 31, 1975.

Example (3). On April 1, 1960, an assessment of tax is made against B, a delinquent taxpayer, and a tax lien for the amount of the assessment arises on that date. On June 1, 1962, in accordance with § 301.6323(f)-1, a notice of lien is filed. Because the assessment of tax was made before January 1, 1962, the notice of lien filed on June 1, 1962 is effective through December 31, 1967. The first required refiling period for the notice of lien is the calendar year 1967. A refiling of the notice of lien during 1967 will extend the effectiveness of the notice of lien filed on June 1, 1962 through December 31, 1973.

○━▶ **§ 301.6323(h) Statutory provisions; validity and priority against certain persons; definitions.** [Sec. 6323(h), IRC]

○━▶ **§ 301.6323(h)-0** (T.D. 7429, filed 8-20-76.) **Scope of Definitions.**

Except as otherwise provided by § 301.6323(h)-1, the definitions provided by § 301.6323(h)-1 apply for purposes of §§ 301.-6323(a)-1 through 301.6324-1.

○━▶ **§ 301.6323(h)-1** (T.D. 7429, filed 8-20-76.) **Definitions.**

(a) *Security interest*—(1) *In general.* The term "security interest" means any interest in property acquired by contract for the purpose of securing payment or performance of an obligation or indemnifying against loss or liability. A security interest exists at any time—

(i) If, at such time, the property is in existence and the interest has become protected under local law against a subsequent judgment lien (as provided in subparagraph (2) of this paragraph) arising out of an unsecured obligation; and

(ii) To the extent that, at such time, the holder has parted with money or money's worth (as defined in subparagraph (3) of this paragraph).

For purposes of this subparagraph, a contract right (as defined in paragraph (c) (2)(i) of § 301.6323(c)-1) is in existence when the contract is made. An account receivable (as defined in paragraph (c)(2) (ii) of § 301.6323(c)-1) is in existence when, and to the extent, a right to payment is earned by performance. A security interest must be in existence, within the mean-

Reg. § 301.6323(h)-1(a)(1)

24,352.14 (I.R.C.)   Reg. § 301.6323(h)-1(a)(1)   8-30-76

ing of this paragraph, at the time as of which its priority against a tax lien is determined. For example, to be afforded priority under the provisions of paragraph (a) of § 301.6323(a)-1 a security interest must be in existence within the meaning of this paragraph before a notice of lien is filed.

(2) *Protection against a subsequent judgment lien.* (i) For purposes of this paragraph, a security interest is deemed to be protected against a subsequent judgment lien on—

(a) The date on which all actions required under local law to establish the priority of a security interest against a judgment lien have been taken, or

(b) If later, the date on which all required actions are deemed effective, under local law, to establish the priority of the security interest against a judgment lien. For purposes of this subdivision, the dates described in (a) and (b) of this subdivision (i) shall be determined without regard to any rule or principle of local law which permits the relation back of any requisite action to a date earlier than the date on which the action is actually performed. For purposes of this paragraph, a judgment lien is a lien held by a judgment lien creditor as defined in paragraph (g) of this section.

(ii) The application of this subparagraph may be illustrated by the following example:

Example. (i) Under the law of State X, a security interest in negotiable instruments, stocks, bonds or other securities may be perfected, and hence protected against a judgment lien, only by the secured party taking possession of the instruments or securities. However, a security interest in such intangible personal property is considered to be temporarily perfected for a period of 21 days from the time the security interest attaches, to the extent consideration other than past consideration is given under a written security agreement. Under the law of X, a security interest attaches to such collateral when there is an agreement between the creditor and debtor that the interest attaches, the debtor has rights in the property, and consideration is given by the creditor. Under the law of X, in the case of temporary perfection, the security interest in such property is protected during the 21-day period against a judgment lien arising, after the security interest attaches, out of an unsecured obligation. Upon expiration of the 21-day period, the holder of the security interest must take possession of the collateral to continue perfection.

(ii) Because the security interest is protected during the 21-day period against a subsequent judgment lien arising out of an unsecured obligation, and because the taking of possession before the conclusion of the period of temporary perfection is not considered, for purposes of subdivision (i) of this subparagraph, to be a requisite action which relates back to the beginning of such period, the requirements of this paragraph are satisfied. However, because taking possession is a condition precedent to continued perfection, possession of the collateral is a requiitse action to establish such priority after expiration of the period of temporary perfection. If there is a lapse of perfection for failure to take possession, the determination of when the security interest exists (for purposes of protection against the tax lien) is made without regard to the period of temporary perfection.

(3) *Money or money's worth.* For purposes of this paragraph, the term "money or money's worth" includes money, a security (as defined in paragraph (d) of this section), tangible or intangible property, services, and other consideration reducible to a money value. Money or money's worth also includes any consideration which otherwise would constitute money or money's worth under the preceding sentence which was parted with before the security interest would otherwise exist if, under local law, past consideration is sufficient to support an agreement giving rise to a security interest. A relinquishing or promised relinquishment of dower, curtesy, or of a statutory estate created in lieu of dower or curtesy, or of other marital rights is not a consideration in money or money's worth. Nor is love and affection, promise of marriage, or any other consideration not reducible to a money value a consideration in money or money's worth.

(4) *Holder of a security interest.* For purposes of this paragraph, the holder of a security interest is the person in whose favor there is a security interest. For provisions relating to the treatment of a purchaser of commercial financing security as a holder of a security interest, see § 301.6323(c)-1(e).

(b) *Mechanic's lienor*—(1) *In general.* The term "mechanic's lienor" means any person who under local law has a lien on real property (or on the proceeds of a contract relating to real property) for services, labor, or materials furnished in connection with the construction or improvement (including demolition) of the property. A mechanic's lienor is treated as having a lien on the later of—

(i) The date on which the mechanic's lien first becomes valid under local law against subsequent purchasers of the real property without actual notice, or

(ii) The date on which the mechanic's lienor begins to furnish the services, labor, or materials.

(2) *Examples.* The provisions of this paragraph may be illustrated by the following example:

Example (1). On February 1, 1968, A lets a contract for the construction of an office building on property owned by him. On March 1, 1968, in accordance with § 301.6323(f)-1, a notice of lien for delinquent Federal taxes owed by A is filed. On April 1, 1968, B, a lumber dealer delivers lumber to A's property. On May 1, 1968, B records a mechanic's lien against the property to secure payment of the price of the lumber. Under local law, B's mechanic's lien is valid against subsequent purchasers of real property without notice from February 1, 1968, which is the date the construction contract was entered into. Because the date on which B's mechanic's lien is valid under local law against subsequent purchasers is February 1, and the date on which B begins to furnish the materials is April 1, the date on which B becomes a mechanic's lienor within the meaning of this paragraph is April 1, the later of these two dates. Under paragraph (a) of § 301.6323(a)-1, B's mechanic's lien will not have priority over the Federal tax lien, even though under local law the mechanic's lien relates back to the date of the contract.

(c) *Motor vehicle.* (1) The term "motor vehicle" means a self-propelled vehicle which is registered for highway use under the laws of any State, the District of Columbia, or a foreign country.

(2) A motor vehicle is "registered for highway use" at the time of a sale if immediately prior to the sale it is so registered under the laws of any State, the District of Columbia, or a foreign country. Where immediately prior to the sale of a motor vehicle by a dealer, the dealer is permitted under local law to operate it under a dealer's tag, license, or permit issued to him, the motor vehicle is considered to be registered for highway use in the name of the dealer at the time of the sale.

(d) *Security.* The term "security" means any bond, debenture, note, or certificate or other evidence of indebtedness, issued by a corporation or a government or political subdivision thereof, with interest coupons or in registered form, share of stock, voting trust certificate, or any certificate of interest or participation in, certificate of deposit or receipt for temporary or interim certificate for, or warrant or right to subscribe to or purchase, any of the foregoing; negotiable instrument; or money.

(e) *Tax lien filing.* The term "tax lien filing" means the filing of notice of the lien imposed by section 6321 in accordance with § 301.6323(f)-1.

(f) *Purchaser*—(1) *In general.* The term "purchaser" means a person who, for adequate and full consideration in money or money's worth (as defined in subparagraph (3) of this paragraph), acquires an interest (other than a lien or security interest) in property which is valid under local law against subsequent purchasers without actual notice.

(2) *Interest in property.* For purposes of this paragraph, each of the following interests is treated as an interest in property, if it is not a lien or security interest:
  (i) A lease of property.
  (ii) A written executory contract to purchase or lease property,
  (iii) An option to purchase or lease property and any interest therein, or
  (iv) An option to renew or extend a lease of property.

(3) *Adequate and full consideration in money or money's worth.* For purposes of this paragraph, the term "adequate and full consideration in money or money's worth" means a consideration in money or money's worth having a reasonable relationship to the true value of the interest in property acquired. See paragraph (a)(3) of this section for definition of the term "money or money's worth." Adequate and full consideration in money or money's worth may include the consideration in a bona fide bargain purchase. The term also includes the consideration in a transaction in which the purchaser has not completed performance of his obligation, such as the consideration in an installment purchase contract, even though the purchaser has not completed the installment payments.

(4) *Examples.* The provisions of this paragraph may be illustrated by the following examples:

Example (1). A enters into a contract for the purchase of a house and lot from B. Under the terms of the contract A makes a down payment and is to pay the balance of the purchase price in 120 monthly installments. After payment of the last installment, A is to receive a deed to the property. A enters into possession, which under local law protects his interest in the property against subsequent purchasers without actual notice. After A has paid five monthly installments, a notice of lien for Federal taxes is filed against B in accordance with § 301.6323(f)-1. Because the contract is an executory contract to purchase property and is valid under local law against subsequent purchasers without actual notice, A qualifies as a purchaser under this paragraph.

Example (2). C owns a residence which he leases to his son-in-law, D, for a period of 5 years commencing January 1, 1968. The lease provides for payment of $100 a year, although the fair rental value of the residence is $2,500 a year. The lease is recorded on December 31, 1967. On March 1, 1968, a notice of tax lien for unpaid Federal taxes of C is filed in accordance with § 301.6323(f)-1. Under local law, D's interest is protected against subsequent purchasers without actual notice. However, because the rental paid by D has no reasonable relationship to the value of the interest in property acquired, D does not qualify as a purchaser under this paragraph.

(g) *Judgment lien creditor.* The term "judgment lien creditor" means a person who has obtained a valid judgment, in a court of record and of competent jurisdiction, for the recovery of specifically designated property or for a certain sum of money. In the case of a judgment for the recovery of a certain sum of money, a judgment lien creditor is a person who has perfected a lien under the judgment on the property involved. A judgment lien is not perfected until the identity of the lienor, the property subject to the lien, and the amount of the lien are established. Accordingly, a judgment lien does not include an attachment or garnishment lien until the lien has ripened into judgment, even though under local law the lien of the judgment relates back to an earlier date. If recording or docketing is necessary under local law before a judgment becomes effective against third parties acquiring liens on real property, a judgment lien under such local law is not perfected with respect to real property until the time of such recordation or docketing. If under local law levy or seizure is necessary before a judgment lien becomes effective against third parties acquiring liens on personal property, then a judgment lien under such local law is not perfected until levy or seizure of the personal property involved. The term "judgment" does not include the determination of a quasi-judicial body or of an individual acting in a quasi-judicial capacity such as the action of State taxing authorities.

○→ § 301.6323(i) **Statutory provisions; validity and priority against certain persons; special rules.** [Sec. 6323(i), IRC]

○→ § 301.6323(i)-1 (T.D. 7429, filed 8-20-76.) **Special rules.**

Reg. § 301.6323(i)-1

24,352.16 (I.R.C.)   Reg. § 301.6323(i)-1(a)   8-30-76

(a) *Actual notice or knowledge.* For purposes of subchapter C (section 6321 and following), chapter 64 of the Code, an organization is deemed, in any transaction, to have actual notice or knowledge of any fact from the time the fact is brought to the attention of the individual conducting the transaction, and in any event from the time the fact would have been brought to the individual's attention if the organization had exercised due diligence. An organization exercises due diligence if it maintains reasonable routines for communicating significant information to the person conducting the transaction and there is reasonable compliance with the routines. Due diligence does not require an individual acting for the organization to communicate information unless such communication is part of his regular duties or unless he has reason to know of the transaction and that the transaction would be materially affected by the information.

(b) *Subrogation* — (1) *In general* Where, under local law, one person is subrogated to the rights of another with respect to a lien or interest, such person shall be subrogated to such rights for purposes of any lien imposed by section 6321 or 6324. Thus, if a tax lien imposed by section 6321 or 6324 is not valid with respect to a particular interest as against the holder of that interest, then the tax lien also is not valid with respect to that interest as against any person who, under local law, is a successor in interest to the holder of that interest.

(2) *Example.* The application of this paragraph may be illustrated by the following example:

Example. On February 1, 1968, an assessment is made and a tax lien arises with respect to A's delinquent tax liability. On February 25, 1968, in accordance with § 301.6323(f)-1, a notice of lien is properly filed. On March 1, 1968, A negotiates a loan from B, the security for which is a second mortgage on property owned by A. The first mortgage on the property is held by C and has priority over the tax lien. Upon default by A, C begins proceedings to foreclose upon the first mortgage. On September 1, 1968, B pays the amount of principal and interest in default to C in order to protect the second mortgage against the pending foreclosure of C's senior mortgage. Under local law, B is subrogated to C's rights to the extent of the payment to C. Therefore, the tax lien is invalid against B to the extent he became subrogated to C's rights even though the tax lien is valid against B's second mortgage on the property.

(c) *Disclosure of amount of outstanding lien.* If a notice of lien has been filed (see § 301.6323(f)-1), the amount of the outstanding obligation secured by the lien is authorized to be disclosed as a matter of public record on Form 668 "Notice of Federal Tax Lien under Internal Revenue Laws". The amount of the outstanding obligation secured by the lien remaining unpaid at the time of an inquiry is authorized to be disclosed to any person who has a proper interest in determining this amount. Any person who has a right in the property or intends to obtain a right in the property by purchase or otherwise will, upon presentation by him of satisfactory evidence, be considered to have a proper interest. Any person desiring this information may make his request to the office of the Internal Revenue Service named on the notice of lien with respect to which the request is made. The request should clearly describe the property subject to the lien, identify the applicable lien, and give the reasons for requesting the information.

O—▶ § 301.6324 **Statutory provisions; special liens for estate and gift taxes.** [Sec. 6324, IRC]

O—▶ § 301.6324-1 (T.D. 6119, filed 12-31-54; republished in T.D. 6498, filed 10-24-60; amended by T.D. 7238, filed 12-28-72.) **Special liens for estate and gift taxes; personal liability of transferees and others.**

(a) *Estate tax.* (1) A lien for estate tax attaches at the date of the decedent's death to every part of the gross estate, whether or not the property comes into possession of the duly qualified executor or administrator. The lien attaches to the extent of the tax shown to be due by the return and of any deficiency in tax found to be due upon review and audit. If the estate tax is not paid when due, then the spouse, transferee, trustee (except the trustee of an employees' trust which meets the requirements of section 401(a)), surviving tenant, person in possession of the property by reason of the exercise, nonexercise, or release of a power of appointment, or beneficiary, who receives, or has on the date of the decedent's death, property included in the gross estate under sections 2034 to 2042, inclusive, shall be personally liable for the tax to the extent of the value, at the time of the decedent's death, of the property.

(2) Unless the tax is paid in full or becomes unenforceable by reason of lapse of time, and except as otherwise provided in paragraph (c) of this section, the lien upon the entire property constituting the gross estate continues for a period of 10 years after the decedent's death, except that the lien shall be divested with respect to—

(i) The portion of the gross estate used for the payment of charges against the estate and expenses of its administration allowed by any court having jurisdiction thereof;

(ii) Property included in the gross estate under sections 2034 to 2042, inclusive, which is transferred by (or transferred by the transferee of) the spouse, transferee, trustee, surviving tenant, person in possession of the property by reason of the exercise, nonexercise, or release of a power of appointment, or beneficiary to a purchaser or holder of a security interest. In such a case a like lien attaches to all the property of the spouse, transferee, trustee, surviving tenant, person in possession, beneficiary, or transferee of any such person, except the part which is transferred to a purchaser or a holder of a security interest. See section 6323(h)(1) and (6) and the regulations thereunder, respectively, for the definitions of "security interest" and "purchaser";

(iii) The portion of the gross estate (or any interest therein) which has been transferred to a purchaser or holder of a security interest if payment is made of the full amount of tax determined by the district director pursuant to a request of the fiduciary (executor, in the case of the estate of a decedent dying before January 1, 1971) for discharge from personal liability as authorized by section 2204 (relating to discharge of fiduciary from personal liability) but there is substituted a like lien upon the consideration received from the purchaser or holder of a security interest; and

(iv) Property as to which the district director has issued a certificate releasing a lien under section 6325(a) and the regulations thereunder.

(b) *Lien for gift tax.* Except as provided in paragraph (c) of this section, a lien attaches upon all gifts made during the period for which the return was filed (see § 25.6019-1) for the amount of tax imposed upon the gifts made during such period. The lien extends for a period of 10 years from the time the gifts are made, unless the tax is sooner paid in full or becomes unenforceable by reason of lapse of time. If the tax is not paid when due, the donee of any gift becomes personally liable for the tax to the extent of the value of his gift. Any part of the property comprised in the gift transferred by the donee (or by a transferee of the donee) to a purchaser or holder of a security interest is divested of the lien, but a like lien, to the extent of the value of the gift, attaches to all the property (including after-acquired property) of the donee (or the transferee) except any part transferred to a purchaser or holder of a security interest. See section 6323(h)(1) and (6) and the regulations thereunder, respectively, for the definitions of "security interest" and "purchaser".

(c) *Exceptions.* (1) A lien described in either paragraph (a) or paragraph (b) of this section is not valid against a mechanic's lienor (as defined in section 6323 (h)(2) and the regulations thereunder) and, subject to the conditions set forth under section 6323(b) (relating to protection for certain interests even though notice filed), is not valid with respect to any lien or interest described in section 6323(b) and the regulations thereunder.

(2) If a lien described in either paragraph (a) or paragraph (b) of this section is not valid against a lien or security interest (as defined in section 6323(h)(1) and the regulations thereunder), the priority of the lien or security interest extends to any item described in section 6323(e) (relating to priority of interest and expenses) to the extent that, under local law, the item has the same priority as the lien or security interest to whch it relates.

(d) *Application of lien imposed by section 6321.* The general lien under section 6321 and the special lien under subsection (a) or (b) of section 6324 for the estate or gift tax are not exclusive of each other, but are cumulative. Each lien will arise when the conditions precedent to the creation of such lien are met and will continue in accordance with the provisions applicable to the particular lien. Thus, the special lien may exist without the general lien being in force, or the general lien may exist without the special lien being in force, or the general lien and the special lien may exist simultaneously, depending upon the facts and pertinent statutory provisions applicable to the respective liens.

○━━ § 301.6325 **Statutory provisions; release of lien or discharge of property.** [Sec. 6325, IRC]

○━━ § 301.6325-1 (T.D. 6119, filed 12-31-54 as amended by T.D. 6425 filed 11-10-59; republished in T.D. 6498, filed 10-24-60; amended by T.D. 6700, filed 1-6-64; T.D. 7429, filed 8-20-76.)) **Release of lien or discharge of property.**

(a) *Release of lien*—(1) *Liability satisfied or unenforceable.* Any district director may issue a certificate of release of a lien imposed with respect to any internal revenue tax, whenever he finds that the entire liability for the tax has been satisfied or has become unenforceable as a matter of law (and not merely uncollectible or unenforceable as a matter of fact). Tax liabilities frequently are unenforceable in fact for the time being, due to the temporary nonpossession by the taxpayer of discoverable property or property rights. In all cases the liability for the payment of the tax continues until satisfaction of the tax in full or until the expiration of the statutory period for collection, including such extension of the period for collection as may be agreed upon in writing by the taxpayer and the district director.

(2) *Bond accepted.* The District Director may, in his discretion, issue a certificate of release of any tax lien if he is furnished and accepts a bond that is conditioned upon the payment of the amount assessed (together with all interest in respect thereof), within the time agreed upon in the bond, but not later than 6 months before the expiration of the statutory period for collection, including any period for collection agreed upon in writing by the district director and the taxpayer. For provisions relating to bonds, see section 7101 and 7102 and §§ 301.7101-1 and 301.7102-1.

(b) *Discharge of specific property from the lien*—(1) *Property double the amount of the liability.* (i) The district director may, in his discretion, issue a certificate of discharge of any part of the property subject to a lien imposed under chapter 64 of the Code if he determines that the fair market value of that part of the property remaining subject to the lien is at least double the sum of the amount of the unsatisfied liability secured by the lien and of the amount of all other liens upon the property which have priority over the lien. In general, fair market value is that amount which one ready and willing but not compelled to buy would pay to another ready and willing but not compelled to sell the property.

(ii) The following example illustrates a case in which a certificate of discharge may not be given under this subparagraph:

Example: The Federal tax liability secured by a lien is $1,000. The fair market value of all property which after the discharge will continue to be subject to the Federal tax lien is $10,000. There is a prior mortgage on the property of $5,000, including interest, and the property is subject to a prior lien of $100 for real estate taxes. Accordingly, the taxpayer's equity in the property over and above the amount of the mortgage and real estate taxes is $4,900, or nearly five times the amount required

Reg. § 301.6325-1 (b) (1)

24,352.18 (I.R.C.)   Reg. § 301.6325-1(b)(1)   8-30-76

to pay the assessed tax on which the Federal tax lien is based. Nevertheless, a discharge under this subparagraph is not permissible. In the illustration, the sum of the amount of the Federal tax liability ($1,000) and of the amount of the prior mortgage and the lien for real estate taxes ($5,000 + $100 = $5,100) is $6,100. Double this sum is $12,200, but the fair market value of the remaining property is only $10,000. Hence, a discharge of the property is not permissible under this subparagraph, since the Code requires that the fair market value of the remaining property be at least double the sum of two amounts, one amount being the outstanding Federal tax liability and the other amount being all prior liens upon such property. In order that the discharge may be issued, it would be necessary that the remaining property be worth not less than $12,200.

(2) *Part payment; interest of United States valueless*—(i) *Part payment.* The district director may, in his discretion, issue a certificate of discharge of any part of the property subject to a lien imposed under chapter 64 of the Code if there is paid over to him in partial satisfaction of the liability secured by the lien an amount determined by him to be not less than the value of the interest of the United States in the property to be so discharged. In determining the amount to be paid, the district director will take into consideration all the facts and circumstances of the case, including the expenses to which the Government has been put in the matter. In no case shall the amount to be paid be less than the value of the interest of the United States in the property with respect to which the certificate of discharge is to be issued.

(ii) *Interest of the United States valueless.* The district director may, in his discretion, issue a certificate of discharge of any part of the property subject to the lien if he determines that the interest of the United States in the property to be so discharged has no value.

(iii) *Valuation of interest of United States.* For purposes of this subparagraph, in determining the value of the interest of the United States in the property, or any part thereof, with respect to which the certificate of discharge is to be issued, the district director shall give consideration to the value of the property and the amount of all liens and encumbrances thereon having priority over the Federal tax lien. In determining the value of the property, the district director may, in his discretion, give consideration to the forced sale value of the property in appropriate cases.

(3) *Discharge of property by substitution of proceeds of sale.* A district director may, in his discretion, issue a certificate of discharge of any part of the property subject to a lien imposed under chapter 64 of the Code if such part of the property is sold and, pursuant to a written agreement with the district director, the proceeds of the sale are held, as a fund subject to the liens and claims of the United States, in the same manner and with the same priority as the lien or claim had with respect to the discharged property. This subparagraph does not apply unless the sale divests the taxpayer of all right, title, and interest in the property sought to be discharged. Any reasonable and necessary expenses incurred in connection with the sale of the property and the administration of the sale proceeds shall be paid by the applicant or from the proceeds of the sale before satisfaction of any lien or claim of the United States.

(4) *Application for certificate of discharge.* Any person desiring a certificate of discharge under this paragraph shall submit an application in writing to the district director responsible for collection of the tax. The application shall contain such information as the district director may require.

Applications submitted under subparagraph (1) or (3) of this paragraph do not require the submission of any sum of money for the discharge of the property from a tax lien. Since the amount to be paid for the issuance, under subparagraph (2) of this paragraph, of a certificate of discharge of property from a Federal tax lien is a matter for the determination of the District Director after consideration of the facts and law involved, no sum of money or check should be submitted with the application. The District Director shall cause a thorough investigation to be made as to the proof and accuracy of all material statements made in the application. Upon completion of such investigation, the District Director will make his determination and advise the applicant of the decision reached.

(c) *Estate or gift tax liability fully satisfied or provided for.* (1) *Certificate of discharge.* If the District Director determines that the tax liability for estate or gift tax has been fully satisfied, he may issue a certificate of discharge of any or all property from the lien imposed thereon. If the District Director determines that the tax liability for estate or gift tax has been adequately provided for, he may issue a certificate discharging particular items of property from the lien. The issuance of such a certificate is a matter resting within the discretion of the District Director, and a certificate will be issued only in case there is actual need therefor. The primary purpose of such discharge is not to evidence payment or satisfaction of the tax, but to permit the transfer of property free from the lien in case it is necessary to clear title. The tax will be considered fully satisfied only when investigation has been completed and payment of the tax, including any deficiency determined, has been made.

(2) *Application for certificate of discharge.* An application for a certificate of discharge of property from the lien for estate or gift tax should be filed with the district director, responsible for the collection of the tax. It should be made in writing under penalties of perjury and should explain the circumstances that require the discharge, and should fully describe the particular items for which the discharge is desired. (Where realty is involved each parcel sought to be discharged from the lien should be described on a separate page and each such description submitted in duplicate.) In the case of an estate tax lien, the application should show the applicant's relationship to the estate, such as executor, heir, devisee, legatee, beneficiary, transferee, or purchaser. If the estate or gift tax return has not been filed, a state-

ment under penalties of perjury may be required showing (i) the value of the property to be discharged, (ii) the basis for such valuation, (iii) in the case of the estate tax, the approximate value of the gross estate and the approximate value of the total real property included in the gross estate, (iv) in the case of the gift tax, the total amount of gifts made during the calendar year and the prior calendar years subsequent to the enactment of the Revenue Act of 1932 and the approximate value of all real estate subject to the gift tax lien, and (v) if the property is to be sold or otherwise transferred, the name and address of the purchaser or transferee and the consideration, if any, paid or to be paid by him.

(3) For provisions relating to transfer certificates in the case of nonresident estates, see § 20.6325-1 of this chapter (Estate Tax Regulations).

(d) *Subordination of lien*—(1) *By payment of the amount subordinated.* A district director may, in his discretion, issue a certificate of subordination of a lien imposed under chapter 64 of the Code upon any part of the property subject to the lien if there is paid over to the district director an amount equal to the amount of the lien or interest to which the certificate subordinates the lien of the United States. For this purpose, the tax lien may be subordinated to another lien or interest on a dollar-for-dollar basis. For example, if a notice of a Federal tax lien is filed and a delinquent taxpayer secures a mortgage loan on a part of the property subject to the tax lien and pays over the proceeds of the loan to a district director after an application for a certificate of subordination is approved, the district director will issue a certificate of subordination. This certificate will have the effect of subordinating the tax lien to the mortgage.

(2) *To facilitate tax collection*—(i) *In general.* A district director may, in his discretion, issue a certificate of subordination of a lien imposed under chapter 64 of the Code upon any part of the property subject to the lien if the district director believes that the subordination of the lien will ultimately result in an increase in the amount realized by the United States from the property subject to the lien and will facilitate the ultimate collection of the tax liability.

(ii) *Examples.* The provisions of this subparagraph may be illustrated by the following examples:

Example (1). A, a farmer, needs money in order to harvest his crop. A Federal tax lien, notice of which has been filed, is outstanding with respect to A's property. B, a lending institution is willing to make the necessary loan if the loan is secured by a first mortgage on the farm which is prior to the Federal tax lien. Upon examination, the district director believes that ultimately the amount realizable from A's property will be increased and the collection of the tax liability will be facilitated by the availability of cash when the crop is harvested and sold. In this case, the district director may, in his discretion, subordinate the tax lien on the farm to the mortgage securing the crop harvesting loan.

Example (2). C owns a commercial building which is deteriorating and in unsalable condition. Because of outstanding federal tax liens, notices of which have been filed, C is unable to finance the repair and rehabilitation of the building. D, a contractor, is willing to do the work if his mechanic's lien on the property is superior to the federal tax liens. Upon examination, the district director believes that ultimately the amount realizable from C's property will be increased and the collection of the tax liability will be facilitated by arresting deterioration of the property and restoring it to salable condition. In this case, the district director may, in his discretion, subordinate the tax lien on the building to the mechanic's lien.

Example (3). E, a manufacturer of electronic equipment, obtains financing from F, a lending institution, pursuant to a security agreement, with respect to which a financing statement was duly filed under the Uniform Commercial Code on June 1, 1970. On April 15, 1971, F gains actual notice or knowledge that notice of a federal tax lien had been filed against E on March 31, 1971, and F refuses to make further advances unless its security interest is assured of priority over the Federal tax lien. Upon examination, the district director believes that ultimately the amount realizable from E's property will be increased and the collection of the tax liability will be facilitated if the work in process can be completed and the equipment sold. In this case, the district director may, in his discretion, subordinate the tax lien to F's security interest for the further advances required to complete the work.

Example (4). Suit is brought against G by H, who claims ownership of property the legal title to which is held by G. A federal tax lien against G, notice of which has previously been filed, will be enforceable against the property if G's title is confirmed. Because section 6323(b)(8) is inapplicable, J, an attorney, is unwilling to defend the case for G unless he is granted a contractual lien on the property, superior to the Federal tax lien. Upon examination, the district director believes that the successful defense of the case by G will increase the amount ultimately realizable from G's property and will facilitate collection of the tax liability. In this case, the district director may, in his discretion, subordinate the tax lien to J's contractual lien on the disputed property to secure J's reasonable fees and expenses.

(3) *Application for certificate of subordination.* Any person desiring a certificate of subordination under this paragraph shall submit an application therefor in writing to the district director responsible for the collection of the tax. The application shall contain such information as the district director may require.

(e) *Nonattachment of lien.* If a district director determines that, because of confusion of names or otherwise, any person (other than the person against whom the tax was assessed) is or may be injured by the appearance that a notice of lien filed in accordance with § 301.6323(f)-1 refers to such person, the district director may issue a certificate of nonattachment. Such certificate shall state that the lien, notice of which has been filed, does not attach to the property of such person. Any person de-

Reg. § 301.6325-1(e)

24,352.20 (I.R.C.)   Reg. § 301.6325-1(e)   8-30-76

siring a certificate of nonattachment under this paragraph shall submit an application therefor in writing to the district director responsible for the collection of the tax. The application shall contain such information as the district director may require.

(f) *Effect of certificate*—(1) *Conclusiveness.* Except as provided in subparagraphs (2) and (3) of this paragraph, if a certificate is issued under section 6325 by a district director and the certificate is filed in the same office as the notice of lien to which it relates (if the notice of lien has been filed), the certificate shall have the following effect—

(i) In the case of a certificate of release issued under paragraph (a) of this section, the certificate shall be conclusive that the tax lien referred to in the certificate is extinguished;

(ii) In the case of a certificate of discharge issued under paragraph (b) or (c) of this section, the certificate shall be conclusive that the property covered by the certificate is discharged from the tax lien;

(iii) In the case of a certificate of subordination issued under paragraph (d) of this section, the certificate shall be conclusive that the lien or interest to which the Federal tax lien is subordinated is superior to the tax lien; and

(iv) In the case of a certificate of nonattachment issued under paragraph (e), the certificate shall be conclusive that the lien of the United States does not attach to the property of the person referred to in the certificate.

(2) *Revocation of certificate of release or nonattachment*—(i) *In general.* If a district director determines that either—

(a) A certificate of release or a certificate of nonattachment of the general tax lien imposed by section 6321 was issued erroneously or improvidently, or

(b) A certificate of release of such lien was issued in connection with a compromise agreement under section 7122 which has been breached,

and if the period of limitation on collection after assessment of the tax liability has not expired, the district director may revoke the certificate and reinstate the tax lien. The provisions of this subparagraph do not apply in the case of the lien imposed by section 6324 relating to estate and gift taxes.

(ii) *Method of revocation and reinstatement.* The revocation and reinstatement described in subdivision (i) of this subparagraph is accomplished by—

(a) Mailing notice of the revocation to the taxpayer at his last known address, and

(b) Filing notice of the revocation of the certificate in the same office in which the notice of lien to which it relates was filed (if the notice of lien has been filed).

(iii) *Effect of reinstatement*—(a) *Effective date.* A tax lien reinstated in accordance with the provisions of this subparagraph is effective on and after the date the notice of revocation is mailed to the taxpayer in accordance with the provisions of subdivision (ii)(a) of this subparagraph, but the reinstated lien is not effective before the filing of notice of revocation, in accordance with the provisions of subparagraph (ii)(b) of this subparagraph, if the filing is required by reason of the fact that a notice of the lien had been filed.

(b) *Treatment of reinstated lien.* As of the effective date of reinstatement, a reinstated lien has the same force and effect as a general tax lien imposed by section 6321 which arises upon assessment of a tax liability. The reinstated lien continues in existence until the expiration of the period of limitation on collection after assessment of the tax liability to which it relates. The reinstatement of the lien does not retroactively reinstate a previously filed notice of lien. The reinstated lien is not valid against any holder of a lien or interest described in § 301.6323(a)-1 until notice of the reinstated lien has been filed in accordance with the provisions of § 301.6323(f)-1 subsequent to or concurrent with the time the reinstated lien became effective.

(iv) *Example.* The provisions of this subparagraph may be illustrated by the following example:

Example. On March 1, 1967, an assessment of an unpaid Federal tax liability is made against A. On March 1, 1968, notice of the Federal tax lien, which arose at the time of assessment, is filed. On April 1, 1968, A executes a bona fide mortgage on property belonging to him to B. On May 1, 1968, a certificate of release of the tax lien is erroneously issued and is filed by A in the same office in which the notice of lien was filed. On June 3, 1968, the lien is reinstated in accordance with the provisions of this subparagraph. On July 1, 1968, A executes a bona fide mortgage on property belonging to him to C. On August 1, 1968, a notice of the lien which was reinstated is properly filed in accordance with the provisions of § 301.6323(f)-1. The mortgages of both B and C will have priority over the rights of the United States with respect to the tax liability in question. Because a reinstated lien continues in existence only until the expiration of the period of limitation on collection after assessment of the tax liability to which the lien relates, in the absence of any extension or suspension of the period of limitation on collection after assessment, the reinstated lien will become unenforceable by reason of lapse of time after February 28, 1973.

(3) *Certificates void under certain conditions.* Notwithstanding any other provisions of subtitle F of the Code, any lien for Federal taxes attaches to any property with respect to which a certificate of discharge has been issued if the person liable for the tax reacquires the property after the certificate has been issued. Thus, if property subject to a Federal tax lien is discharged therefrom and is later reacquired by the delinquent taxpayer at a time when the lien is still in existence, the tax lien attaches to the reacquired property and is enforceable against it as in the case of after-acquired property generally.

(g) *Filing of certificates and notices.* If a certificate or notice described in this section may not be filed in the office designated by State law in which the notice of lien imposed by section 6321 (to which the certificate or notice relates) is filed, the certificate or notice is effective if filed in the office of the clerk of the United States district court for the judicial district in which the State office where the notice of lien is filed is situated.

○━▶ § 301.6326 Statutory provision; cross references [Sec. 6326, IRC]

SEIZURE OF PROPERTY FOR COLLECTION OF TAXES

§ 301.6331 **Statutory provisions; levy and distraint.** [Sec. 6331, IRC]

§ 301.6331-1 (T.D. 6119, filed 12-31-54; republished in T.D. 6498, filed 10-24-60; amended by T.D. 7139, filed 8-11-71; T.D. 7180, filed 4-12-72 and T.D. 7253, filed 2-23-73.) **Levy and distraint.**

(a) *Authority to levy*—(1) *In general.* If any person liable to pay any tax neglects or refuses to pay such tax within 10 days after notice and demand, the district director to whom the assessment is charged or, upon his request, any other district director may proceed to collect the tax by levy upon any property, or rights to property, whether real or personal, tangible or intangible, either belonging to such person or with respect to which there is a lien provided by section 6321 or 6324 (or the corresponding provision of prior law) for the payment of such tax. As used in section 6331 and this section, the term "tax" includes any interest, additional amount, addition to tax, or assessable penalty, together with any costs and expenses that may accrue in addition thereto. For exemption of certain property from levy, see section 6334 and the regulations thereunder. Property subject to a Federal tax lien, which has been sold or otherwise transferred by the taxpayer, may be seized while in the hands of the transferee or of any subsequent transferee. However, see provisions under sections 6323 and 6324(a)(2) and (b) for protection of certain transferees against a Federal tax lien. Levy

may be made by serving a notice of levy on any person in possession of, or obligated with respect to, property or rights to property subject to levy including receivables, bank accounts, evidences of debt, securities, and accrued salaries, wages, commissions, and other compensation. A levy extends only to property possessed and obligations which exist at the time of the levy. Obligations exist when the liability of the obligor is fixed and determinable although the right to receive payment thereof may be deferred until a later date. For example, if a wage earner is paid on the Wednesday following the close of each workweek, a levy made upon his employer on Monday would reach his wages due for the prior workweek, although the employer need not satisfy the levy by paying over such amount to the district director until Wednesday. Similarly, a levy only reaches property subject to levy in the possession of the person levied upon at the time the levy is made. If, for example, a levy is made on a bank with respect to the account of a delinquent taxpayer and the bank surrenders to the district director the amount of the taxpayer's balance at the time the levy is made, the levy is satisfied. The levy has no effect upon any subsequent deposit made in the bank by the taxpayer. Subsequent deposits may be reached only by a subsequent levy on the bank.

(2) *Jeopardy cases.* If the District Director finds that the collection of any tax is in jeopardy, he may make notice and demand for immediate payment of such tax and, upon failure or refusal to pay such tax, collection thereof by levy shall be lawful without regard to the 10-day period provided in section 6331(a).

(3) *Bankruptcy or receivership cases.* During a bankruptcy proceeding or a receivership proceeding in either a Federal or a State court, the assets of the taxpayer are in general under the control of the court in which such proceeding is pending. Taxes cannot be collected by levy upon assets in the custody of a court, whether or not such custody is incident to a bankruptcy or receivership proceeding, except where the proceeding has progressed to such a point that the levy would not interfere with the work of the court or where the court grants permission to levy. Any assets which under applicable provisions of law are not under the control of the court may be levied upon, for example, property exempt from court custody under State law or the bankrupt's earnings and property acquired after the date of bankruptcy. However, levy upon such property is not mandatory and the Government may rely upon payment of taxes in the proceeding.

(4) *Certain types of compensation*—(i) *Federal employees.* Levy may be made upon the accrued salary or wages of any officer or employee (including members of the Armed Forces), or elected or appointed official, of the United States, the District of Columbia, or any agency or instrumentality of either, by serving a notice of levy on the employer of the delinquent taxpayer. As used in this subdivision, the term "employer" means (a) the officer or employee of the United States, the District of Columbia, or of the agency or instrumentality of the United States or the District of Columbia, who has control of the payment of the wages, or (b) any other officer or employee designated by the head of the branch, department, agency, or instrumentality of the United States or of the District of Columbia as the party upon whom service of the notice of levy may be made. If the head of such branch, department, agency, or instrumentality designates an officer or employee other than one who has control of the payment of the wages, as the party upon whom service of the notice of levy may be made, such head shall promptly notify the Commissioner of the name and address of each officer or employee so designated and the scope or extent of his authority as such designee.

(ii) *State and municipal employees.* Accrued salaries, wages, or other compensation of any officer, employee, or elected or appointed official of a State or Territory, or of any agency, instrumentality, or political subdivision thereof, are also subject to levy to enforce collection of any Federal tax.

(iii) *Seamen.* Notwithstanding the provisions of section 12 of the Seamen's Act of 1915 (46 U.S.C. 601), accrued wages of seamen, apprentice seamen, or fishermen employed on fishing vessels are subject to levy. See section 6334 (c).

(5) *Noncompetent Indians.* Solely for purposes of sections 6321 and 6331, any interest in restricted land held in trust by the United States for an individual noncompetent Indian (and not for a tribe) shall not be deemed to be property, or a right to property, belonging to such Indian.

(b) *Successive seizures.* Whenever any property or rights to property upon which a levy has been made are not sufficient to satisfy the claim of the United States for which the levy is made, the district director may thereafter, and as often as may be necessary, proceed to levy in like manner upon any other property or rights to property subject to levy of the person against whom such claim exists or on which there is a lien imposed by section 6321 or 6324 (or the corresponding provision of prior law) for the payment of such claim until the amount due from such person, together with all costs and expenses, is fully paid.

(c) *Notice of intent to levy on salary or wages*—(1) *In general.* Levy may be made under this section upon the salary or wages of an individual with respect to any unpaid tax only after the district director or the director of the service center has notified such individual in writing of his intention to make such levy. Such notice shall be given in person, left at the dwelling or usual place of business of such individual, or shall be sent by mail to such individual's last known address, no less than ten days before the day of levy. If a notice has been given under this paragraph with respect to an unpaid tax, no further notice is required in the case of successive levies with respect to such unpaid tax. The notice required to be given under this paragraph is in addition to, and may be given at the same time as, the notice and demand described in § 301.6303-1.

(2) *Jeopardy.* Subparagraph (1) of this paragraph shall not apply to a levy if the district director or director of the service center has made a finding under paragraph (a)(2) of this section that the collection of tax is in jeopardy.

Reg. § 301.6331-1 (c) (2)

(3) *Effective date.* This paragraph shall apply with respect to levies made after March 31, 1972.

§ 301.6332 Statutory provisions; surrender of property subject to levy [Sec. 6332 IRC]

§ 301.6332-1 (T.D. 6119, filed 12-31-54; republished in T.D. 6498, filed 10-24-60; amended by T.D. 6746, filed 7-20-64; T.D. 7180, filed 4-12-72; T.D. 7384, filed 10-21-75.) **Surrender of property subject to levy.**

(a) *Requirement*—(1) *In general.* Except as otherwise provided in § 301.6332-2, relating to levy in the case of life insurance and endowment contracts, any person in possession of (or obligated with respect to) property or rights to property subject to levy and upon which a levy has been made shall, upon demand of the district director, surrender the property or rights (or discharge the obligation) to the district director, except that part of the property or rights (or obligations) which, at the time of the demand, is actually or constructively under the jurisdiction of a court because of an attachment or execution under any judicial process.

(2) *Property held by banks.* Notwithstanding subparagraph (1) of this paragraph, if a levy has been made upon property or rights to property subject to levy which a bank engaged in the banking business in the United States or a possession of the United States is in possession of (or obligated with respect to), the Commissioner shall not enforce the levy with respect to any deposits held in an office of the bank outside the United States or a possession of the United States, unless the notice of levy specifies that the district director intends to reach such deposits. The notice of levy shall not specify that the district director intends to reach such deposits unless the district director believes—

(i) That the taxpayer is within the jurisdiction of a U.S. court at the time the levy is made and that the bank is in possession of (or obligated with respect to) deposits of the taxpayer in an office of the bank outside the United States or a possession of the United States; or

(ii) That the taxpayer is not within the jurisdiction of a U.S. court at the time the levy is made, that the bank is in possession of (or obligated with respect to) deposits of the taxpayer in an office outside the United States or a possession of the United States, and that such deposits consist, in whole or in part, of funds transferred from the United States or a possession of the United States in order to hinder or delay the collection of a tax imposed by the Code.

For purposes of this subparagraph, the term "possession of the United States" includes Guam, the Midway Islands, the Panama Canal Zone, the Commonwealth of Puerto Rico, American Samoa, the Virgin Islands, and Wake Island.

(b) *Enforcement of levy*—(1) *Extent of personal liability.* Any person who, upon demand of the district director, fails or refuses to surrender any property or right to property subject to levy is liable under the provisions of section 6332(c)(1) in his own person and estate to the United States in a sum equal to the value of the property or rights not so surrendered, but not exceeding the amount of the taxes for the collection of which the levy has been made, together with costs and interest on such sum from the date of the levy at the annual rate referred to in the regulations under section 6621. Any amount, other than costs, recovered under section 6332(c)(1) shall be credited against the tax liability for the collection of which the levy was made.

(2) *Penalty for violation.* In addition to the personal liability described in subparagraph (1) of this paragraph, any person who is required to surrender property or rights to property and who fails or refuses to surrender them without reasonable cause is liable for a penalty equal to 50 percent of the amount recoverable under section 6332(c)(1). No part of the penalty described in this subparagraph shall be credited against the tax liability for the collection of which the levy was made. The penalty described in this subparagraph is not applicable in cases where bona fide dispute exists concerning the amount of the property to be surrendered pursuant to a levy or concerning the legal effectiveness of the levy. However, if a court in a later enforcement suit sustains the levy, then reasonable cause would usually not exist to refuse to honor a later levy made under similar circumstances.

(c) *Effect of honoring levy.* Any person in possession of, or obligated with respect to, property or rights to property subject to levy and upon which a levy has been made who, upon demand by the district director, surrenders the property or rights to property, or discharges the obligation, to the district director, or who pays a liability described in paragraph (b)(1) of this section, is discharged from any obligation or liability to the delinquent taxpayer with respect to the property or rights to property arising from the surrender or payment. If an insuring organization satisfies a levy with respect to a life insurance or endowment contract in accordance with § 301.6332-2, the insuring organization is discharged from any obligation or liability to any beneficiaries of the contract arising from the surrender or payment. Also, it is discharged from any obligation or liability to the insured or other owner. Any person who mistakenly surrenders to the United States property or rights to property not properly subject to levy is not relieved from liability to a third party who owns the property. The owners of mistakenly surrendered property may, however, secure from the United States the administrative relief provided for in section 6343(b) or may bring suit to recover the property under section 7426.

(d) *Person defined.* The term "person," as used in section 6332(a) and this section, includes an officer or employee of a corporation or a member or employee of a partnership, who is under a duty to surrender the property or rights to property or to discharge the obligation. In the case of a levy upon the salary or wages of an officer, employee, or elected or appointed official of the United States, the District of Columbia, or any agency or instrumentality of either, the term "person" includes the officer or employee of the United States, of the District of Columbia, or of such agency or instrumentality who is under a duty to discharge the obligation. As to the officer or employee who is under such duty, see paragraph (a)(4)(i) of § 301.6331-1.

§ 301.6332-2 (T.D. 7180, filed 4-12-72) Surrender of property subject to levy in the case of life insurance and endowment contracts.

(a) *In general.* This section provides special rules relating to the surrender of property subject to levy in the case of life insurance and endowment contracts. The provisions of § 301.6332-1 which relate generally to the surrender of property subject to levy apply, to the extent not inconsistent with the special rules set forth in this section, to a levy in the case of life insurance and endowment contracts.

(b) *Effect of service of notice of levy*— (1) *In general.* A notice of levy served by a district director on an insuring organization with respect to a life insurance or endowment contract issued by the organization shall constitute—

(i) A demand by the district director for the payment of the cash loan value of the contract adjusted in accordance with paragraph (c) of this section, and

(ii) The exercise of the right of the person against whom the tax is assessed to the advance of such cash loan value.

It is unnecessary for the district director to surrender the contract document to the insuring organization upon which the levy is made. However, the notice of levy will include a certification by the district director that a copy of the notice of levy has been mailed to the person against whom the tax is assessed at his last known address. At the time of service of the notice of levy, the levy is effective with respect to the cash loan value of the insurance contract, subject to the condition that if the levy is not satisfied or released before the 90th day after the date of service, the levy can be satisfied only by payment of the amount described in paragraph (c) of this section. Other than satisfaction or release of the levy, no event during the 90-day period subsequent to the date of service of the notice of levy shall release the cash loan value from the effect of the levy. For example, the termination of the policy by the taxpayer or by the death of the insured during such 90-day period shall not release the levy. For the rules relating to the time when the insuring organization is to pay over the required amount, see paragraph (c) of this section.

(2) *Notification of amount subject to levy*—(i) *Full payment before the 90th day.* In the event that the unpaid liability to which the levy relates is satisfied at any time during the 90-day period subsequent to the date of service of the notice of levy, the district director will promptly give the insuring organization written notification that the levy is released.

(ii) *Notification after the 90th day.* In the event that notification is not given under subdivision (i) of this subparagraph, the district director will, promptly following the 90th day after service of the notice of levy, give the insuring organization written notification of the current status of all accounts listed on the notice of levy, and of the total payments received since service of the notice of levy. This notification will be given to the insuring organization whether or not there has been any change in the status of the accounts.

(c) *Satisfaction of levy*—(1) *In general.* The levy described in paragraph (b) of this section with respect to a life insurance or endowment contract shall be deemed to be satisfied if the insuring organization pays over to the district director the amount which the person against whom the tax is assessed could have had advanced to him by the organization on the 90th day after service of the notice of levy on the organization. However, this amount is increased by the amount of any advance (including contractual interest thereon), generally called a policy loan, made to the person on or after the date the organization has actual notice or knowledge, within the meaning of section 6323(i)(1), of the existence of the tax lien with respect to which the levy is made. The insuring organization may nevertheless, make an advance (including contractual interest thereon), generally called an automatic premium loan, made automatically to maintain the contract in force under an agreement entered into before the organization has such actual notice or knowledge. In any event, the amount paid to the district director by the insuring organization is not to exceed the amount of the unpaid liability shown on the notification described in paragraph (b)(2) of this section. The amount, determined in accordance with the provisions of this section, subject to the levy shall be paid to the district director by the insuring organization promptly after receipt of the notification described in paragraph (b)(2). The satisfaction of a levy with respect to a life insurance or endowment contract will not discharge the contract from the tax lien. However, see section 6323(b)(9)(C) and the regulations thereunder concerning the liability of an insurance company after satisfaction of a levy with respect to a life insurance or endowment contract. If the person against whom the tax is assessed so directs, the insuring organization, on a date before the 90th day after service of the notice of levy, may satisfy the levy by paying over an amount computed in accordance with the provisions of this subparagraph substituting such date for the 90th day. In the event of termination of the policy by the taxpayer or by the death of the insured on a date before the 90th day after service of the notice of levy, the amount to be paid over to the district director by the insuring organization in satisfaction of the levy shall be an amount computed in accordance with the provisions of this subparagraph substituting the date of termination of the policy or the date of death for the 90th day.

(2) *Examples.* The provisions of this section may be illustrated by the following examples:

Example (1). On March 5, 1968, notice of levy for an unpaid income tax assessment due from A in the amount of $3,000 is served on the X Insurance Company with respect ot A's life insurance policy. On March 5, 1968, the cash loan value of the policy is $1,500. On April 9, 1968, A does not pay a premium due on the policy in the amount of $200. Under an automatic premium advance provision contained in the policy originally issued in 1960, X advances the premium out of the cash value of the policy. As of June 3, 1968 (the 90th day after service of the notice of levy), pursuant to the provisions of the policy, the amount of accrued charges upon the automatic premium advance in the amount of $200 for the period April 9, 1968, through June 3, 1968, is $2. On June 5, 1968, the district director gives written notification to X indicating that A's unpaid tax assessment is $2,500. Under this section, X is required to pay to the district director, promptly after receipt of the June 5, 1968, notification, the sum of $1,298 ($1,500 less $200 less $2), which is the amount A could have had advanced to him by X on June 3, 1968.

Example (2). Assume the same facts as in example (1) except that on May 10, 1968, A requests and X grants an advance in the amount of $1,000. X has actual notice of the existence of the lien by reason of the service of the notice of levy on March 5, 1968. This advance is not required to be made automatically under the policy and reduces the amount of the cash value of the policy. For the use of the $1,000 advance during the period May 10, 1968, through June 3, 1968, X charges A the sum of $3. Under this section, X is required to pay to the district director, promptly after receipt of the June 5, 1968, notification, the sum of $1,298. This $1,298 amount is composed of the $295 amount)$1,500 less $200 less $2 less $1,000 less $3) A could have had advanced to him by X on June 3, 1968, plus the $1,000 advance plus the charges in the amount of $3 with respect thereto.

Example (3). Assume the same facts as in example (1) except that the insurance contract does not contain an automatic premium advance provision. The contract does provide that, upon default in the payment of premiums, the policy shall automatically be converted to paid-up term insurance with no cash or loan value. A fails to make the premium payment of $200 due on April 9, 1968. After expiration of a grace period to make the premium payment, the X Insurance Company applies the cash loan value of $1,500 to effect the conversion. Since the service of the notice of levy constitutes the exercise of A's right to receive the cash loan value and the amount applied to effect the conversion is not an automatic advance to A to maintain the policy in force, the conversion of the policy is not an event which will release the cash loan value from the effect of the levy. Therefore, X Insurance Company is required to pay to the district director, promptly after receipt of the June 5, 1968 notification, the sum of $1,500.

(d) *Other enforcement proceedings.* The satisfaction of the levy described in paragraph (b) of this section by insuring organization shall be without prejudice to any civil action for the enforcement of any Federal tax lien with respect to a life insurance or endowment contract. Thus, this levy procedure is not the exclusive means of subjecting the life insurance and endowment contracts of the person against whom a tax is assessed to the collection of his unpaid assessment. The United States may choose to foreclose the tax lien in any case where it is appropriate, as, for example, to reach the cash surrender value (as distinguished from the cash loan value) of a life insurance or endowment contract.

(e) *Cross references.* (1) For provisions relating to priority of certain advances with respect to a life insurance or endowment contract after satisfaction of a levy pursuant to section 6332(b), see section 6323(b)(9) and the regulations thereunder.

(2) For provisions relating to the issuance of a certificate of discharge of a life insurance or endowment contract subject to a tax lien, see section 6325(b) and the regulations thereunder.

0—☞ § 301.6333 Statutory provisions; production of books. [Sec. 6333, IRC]

0—☞ § 301.6333-1 (T.D. 6119, filed 12-31-54; republished in T.D. 6498, filed 10-24-60.) **Production of books.**

If a levy has been made or is about to be made on any property or rights to property, any person having custody or control of any books or records containing evidence or statements relating to the property or rights to property subject to levy, shall, upon demand of the internal revenue officer who has made or is about to make the levy, exhibit such books or records to such officer.

0—☞ § 301.6334 Statutory provisions; property exempt from levy. [Sec. 6334, IRC]

0—☞ § 301.6334-1 (T.D. 6119, filed 12-31-54, as amended by T.D. 6292, filed 4-18-58, and T.D. 6425, filed 11-10-59; republished in T.D. 6498, filed 10-24-60; further amended by T.D. 6870, filed 12-30-65; T.D. 7180, filed 4-12-72 and T.D. 7182, filed 4-20-72.) **Property exempt from levy.**

(a) *Enumeration.* There shall be exempt from levy—

(1) *Wearing apparel and school books.*—Such items of wearing apparel and school books as are necessary for the taxpayer or for members of his family. Expensive items of wearing apparel, such as furs, which are luxuries and are not necessary for the taxpayer or for members of his family, are not exempt from levy.

(2) *Fuel, provisions, furniture, and personal effects.* If the taxpayer is the head of a family, so much of the fuel, provisions, furniture, and personal effects in his household, and of the arms for personal use, livestock, and poultry of the taxpayer, as does not exceed $500 in value. For purposes of this provision, an individual who is the only remaining member of a family and who lives alone is not the head of a family.

(3) *Books and tools of a trade, business or profession.* So many of the books and tools necessary for the trade, business, or profession of an individual taxpayer as do not exceed in the aggregate $250 in value.

(4) *Unemployment benefits.* Any amount payable to an individual with respect to his unemployment (including any portion thereof payable with respect to dependents) under an unemployment compensation law of the United States, of any State, or of the District of Columbia or of the Commonwealth of Puerto Rico.

(5) *Undelivered mail.* Mail, addressed to any person, which has not been delivered to the addressee.

(6) *Certain annuity and pension payments.* Annuity or pension payments under the Railroad Retirement Act (45 U.S.C. ch. 9), benefits under the Railroad Unemployment Insurance Act (45 U.S.C. ch. 11), special pension payments received by a person whose name has been entered on the Army, Navy, Air Force, and Coast Guard Medal of Honor roll (38 U.S.C. 562), and annuities

based on retired or retainer pay under chapter 73 of title 10 of the United States Code.

(7) *Workmen's compensation.* Any amount payable to an individual as workmen's compensation (including any portion thereof payable with respect to dependents) under a workmen's compensation law of the United States, any State, the District of Columbia, or the Commonwealth of Puerto Rico.

(8) *Salary, wages, or other income.* If the taxpayer is required under any type of order or decree (including an interlocutory decree or a decree of support pendente lite) of a court of competent jurisdiction, entered prior to the date of levy, to contribute to the support of his minor children, so much of his salary, wages, or oher income as is necessary to comply with such order or decree. The taxpayer must establish the amount necessary to comply with the order or decree. The district director is not required to release a levy until such time as he is satisfied that the amount to be released from levy will actually be applied in satisfaction of the support obligation. The district director may make arrangements with a delinquent taxpayer to establish a specific amount of such taxpayer's salary, wage, or other income for each pay period which shall be exempt from levy. Any request for such an arrangement shall be directed to the Chief, Special Procedures Staff, for the internal revenue district in which the taxpayer resides. Where the taxpayer has more than one source of income sufficient to satisfy the support obligation imposed by the order or decree, the amount exempt from levy may at the discretion of the district director be allocated entirely to one salary, wage, or source of other income or be apportioned between the several salaries, wages, or other sources of income. This subparagraph applies with respect to levies made on or after January 30, 1970.

(b) *Appraisal.* The internal revenue officer seizing property of the type described in section 6334(a) shall appraise and set aside to the owner the amount of such property declared to be exempt. If the taxpayer objects at the time of the seizure to the valuation fixed by the officer making the seizure, such officer shall summon three disinterested individuals who shall make the valuation.

(c) *Other property.* No other property or rights to property are exempt from levy except the property specifically exempted by section 6334(a). No provision of a State law may exempt property or rights to property from levy for the collection of any Federal tax. Thus, property exempt from execution under State personal or homestead exemption laws is, nevertheless, subject to levy by the United States for collection of its taxes.

Reg. § 301.6334-1(c)

Seizure of Property for Collection of Taxes (I.R.C.) 24,357

§ 301.6335 Statutory provisions; sale of seized property. [Sec. 6335, IRC]

§ 301.6335-1 (T.D. 6119, filed 12-31-54; republished in T.D. 6498, filed 10-24-60; amended by T.D. 7180, filed 4-12-72.) **Sale of seized property.**

(a) *Notice of seizure.* As soon as practicable after seizure of property, the internal revenue officer seizing the property shall give notice in writing to the owner of the property (or, in the case of personal property, to the possessor thereof). The written notice shall be delivered to the owner (or to the possessor, in the case of personal property) or left at his usual place of abode or business if he has such within the internal revenue district where the seizure is made. If the owner cannot be readily located, or has no dwelling or place of business within such district, the notice may be mailed to his last known address. Such notice shall specify the sum demanded and shall contain, in the case of personal property, a list sufficient to identify the property seized and, in the case of real property, a description with reasonable certainty of the property seized.

(b) *Notice of sale.* (1) As soon as practicable after seizure of the property, the district director shall give notice of sale in writing to the owner. Such notice shall be delivered to the owner or left at his usual place of abode or business if located within the internal revenue district where the seizure is made. If the owner cannot be readily located, or has no dwelling or place of business within such district, the notice may be mailed to his last known address. The notice shall specify the property to be sold, and the time, place, manner, and conditions of the sale thereof, and shall expressly state that only the right, title, and interest of the delinquent taxpayer in and to such property is to be offered for sale. The notice shall also be published in some newspaper published in the county wherein the seizure is made or in a newspaper generally circulated in that county. For example, if a newspaper of general circulation in a county but not published in that county will reach more potential bidders for the property to be sold than a newspaper published within the county, or if there is a newspaper of general circulation within the county but no newspaper published within the county, the district director may cause public notice of the sale to be given in the newspaper of general circulation within the county. If there is no newspaper published or generally circulated in the county, the notice shall be posted at the post office nearest the place where the seizure is made, and in not less than two other public places.

(2) The District Director may use other methods of giving notice of sale and of advertising seized property in addition to those referred to in subparagraph (1) of this paragraph when he believes that the nature of the property to be sold is such that a wider or more specialized advertising coverage will enhance the possibility of obtaining a higher price for the property.

(3) Whenever levy is made without regard to the 10-day period provided in section 6331(a) (relating to cases in which collection is in jeopardy), a public notice of sale of the property seized shall not be made within such 10-day period unless section 6336 (relating to perishable goods) is applicable.

(c) *Time, place, manner, and conditions of sale.* The time, place, manner, and conditions of the sale of property seized by levy shall be as follows:

(1) *Time and place of sale.* The time of sale shall not be less than 10 days nor more than 40 days from the time of giving public notice under section 6335(b) (see paragraph (b) of this section). The place of sale shall be within the county in which the property is seized, except that if it appears to the district director under whose supervision the seizure was made that substantially higher bids may be obtained for the property if the sale is held at a place outside such county, he may order that the sale be held in such other place. The sale shall be held at the time and place stated in the notice of sale.

(2) *Adjournment of sale.* When it appears to the district director that an adjournment of the sale will best serve the interest of the United States or that of the taxpayer, the district director may adjourn, or cause the internal revenue officer conducting the sale to adjourn, the sale from time to time, but the date of the sale shall not be later than one month after the date fixed in the original notice of sale.

(3) *Minimum price.* The district director shall determine a minimum price, taking into account the expenses of levy and sale, for which the property shall be sold. If no person offers for such property at the sale the amount of the minimum price, the property shall be declared purchased at such price for the United States; otherwise, the property shall be declared to be sold to the highest bidder. The internal revenue officer conducting the sale shall either announce the minimum price before the sale begins or defer announcement of the minimum price until after the receipt of the highest bid, and, if the highest bid is greater than the minimum price, no announcement of the minimum price shall be made.

(4) *Offering of property*—(i) *Sale of indivisible property.* If any property levied upon is not divisible, so as to enable the district director by sale of a part thereof to raise the whole amount of the tax and expenses of levy and sale, the whole of such property shall be sold. For application of surplus proceeds of sale see section 6342(b).

(ii) *Separately, in groups, or in the aggregate.* The seized property may be offered for sale—

(a) As separate items, or

(b) As groups of items, or

(c) In the aggregate, or

(d) Both as separate items (or in groups) and in the aggregate.

In such cases, the property shall be sold under the method which produces the highest aggregate amount.

The district director shall select whichever of the foregoing methods of offering the property for sale as, in his opinion, is most feasible under all the facts and circumstances of the case, except that if the property to be sold includes both real and personal property, only the personal property may be grouped for the purpose of offering such property for sale. However,

Reg. § 301.6335-1(c)(4)

real and personal property may be offered for sale in the aggregate, provided the real property, as separate items, and the personal property as a group, or as groups, or as separate items, are first offered separately.

(iii) *Condition of title and of property.* Only the right, title, and interest of the delinquent taxpayer in and to the property seized shall be offered for sale, and such interest shall be offered subject to any prior outstanding mortgages, encumbrances, or other liens in favor of third parties which are valid as against the delinquent taxpayer and are superior to the lien of the United States. All seized property shall be offered for sale "as is" and "where is" and without recourse against the United States. No guaranty or warranty, express or implied, shall be made by the internal revenue officer offering the property for sale, as to the validity of the title, quality, quantity, weight, size, or condition of any of the property, or its fitness for any use or purpose. No claim shall be considered for allowance or adjustment or for rescission of the sale based upon failure of the property to conform with any representation, express or implied.

(iv) *Terms of payment.* The property shall be offered for sale upon whichever of the following terms is fixed by the district director in the public notice of sale:

(a) Payment in full upon acceptance of the highest bid, without regard to the amount of such bid, or

(b) If the aggregate price of all property purchased by a successful bidder at the sale is more than $200, an initial payment of $200 or 20 percent of the purchase price, whichever is the greater, and payment of the balance (including all costs incurred for the protection or preservation of the property subsequent to the sale and prior to final payment) within a specified period, not to exceed one month from the date of the sale.

(5) *Method of sale.* The district director shall sell the property either—

(i) At public auction, at which open competitive bids shall be received, or

(ii) At public sale under sealed bids. The following rules, in addition to the other rules provided in this paragraph, shall be applicable to public sale under sealed bids:

(a) Invitation to bidders. Bids shall be solicited through a public notice of sale.

(b) Form for use by bidders. A bid shall be submitted on a form which will be furnished by the district director upon request. The form shall be completed in accordance with the instructions thereon.

(c) Remittance with bid. If the total bid is $200 or less, the full amount of the bid shall be submitted therewith. If the total bid is more than $200, 20 percent of such bid or $200, whichever is greater, shall be submitted therewith. (In the case of alternative bids submitted by the same bidder for items of property offered separately, or in groups, or in the aggregate, the bidder shall remit the full amount of the highest alternative bid submitted, if that bid is $200 or less. If the highest alternative bid submitted is more than $200, the bidder shall remit 20 percent of the highest alternative bid or $200, whichever is greater.) Such remittance shall be by a certified cashier's, or treasurer's check drawn on any bank or trust company incorporated under the laws of the United States or under the laws of any State, Territory, or possession of the United States, or by a U.S. postal, bank, express, or telegraph money order.

(d) Time for receiving and opening bids. Each bid shall be submitted in a securely sealed envelope. The bidder shall indicate in the upper left hand corner of the envelope his name and address and the time and place of sale as announced in the public notice of sale. A bid will not be considered unless it is received by the internal revenue officer conducting the sale prior to the opening of the bids. The bids will be opened at the time and place stated in the notice of sale or at the time fixed in the announcement of the adjournment of the sale.

(e) Consideration of bids. The public notice of sale shall specify whether the property is to be sold separately, by groups, or in the aggregate or by a combination of these methods, as provided in subparagraph (4)(ii) of this paragraph. If the notice specifies an alternative method, bidders may submit bids under one or more of the alternatives. In case of error in the extension of prices in any bid, the unit price will govern. The internal revenue officer conducting the sale shall have the right to waive any technical defects in a bid. In the event two or more highest bids are equal in amount, the internal revenue officer conducting the sale shall determine the successful bidder by drawing lots. After the opening, examination, and consideration of all bids, the internal revenue officer conducting the sale shall announce the amount of the highest bid or bids and the name of the successful bidder or bidders. Any remittance submitted in connection with an unsuccessful bid shall be returned at the conclusion of the sale.

(f) Withdrawal of bids. A bid may be withdrawn on written or telegraphic request received from the bidder prior to the time fixed for opening the bids. A technical defect in a bid confers no right on the bidder for the withdrawal of his bid after it has been opened.

(6) *Payment of bid price.* All payments for property sold under this section shall be made by cash or by a certified, cashier's, or treasurer's check drawn on any bank or trust company incorporated under the laws of the United States or under the laws of any State, Territory, or possession of the United States, or by a U.S. postal, bank, express, or telegraph money order. If payment in full is required upon acceptance of the highest bid, the payment shall be made at such time. If deferred payment is permitted, the initial payment shall be made upon acceptance of the bid, and the balance shall be paid on or before the date fixed for payment thereof. Any remittance submitted with a successful sealed bid shall be applied toward the purchase price.

(7) *Delivery and removal of personal property.* Responsibility of the United States for the protection or preservation of seized personal property shall cease immediately upon acceptance of the highest bid. The risk of loss is on the purchaser of personal property upon acceptance of his bid. Possession of any personal property shall not be delivered to the purchaser until the purchase price has been paid in full. If payment of part of the

purchase price for personal property is deferred, the United States will retain possession of such property as security for the payment of the balance of the purchase price and as agent for the purchaser, will cause the property to be cared for until the purchase price has been paid in full or the sale is declared null and void for failure to make full payment of the purchase price. In such case, all charges and expenses incurred in caring for the property after the acceptance of the bid shall be borne by the purchaser.

(8) *Default in payment.* If payment in full is required upon acceptance of the bid and is not then and there paid, the internal revenue officer conducting the sale shall forthwith proceed again to sell the property in the manner provided in section 6335(e) and this section. If the conditions of the sale permit part of the payment to be deferred, and if such part is not paid within the prescribed period, suit may be instituted against the purchaser for the purchase price or such part thereof as has not been paid, together with interest at the rate of 6 percent per annum from the date of the sale; or, in the discretion of the district director, the sale may be declared by the district director to be null and void for failure to make full payment of the purchase price and the property may again be advertised and sold as provided in subsections (b), (c), and (e) of section 6335 and this section. In the event of such readvertisement and sale, any new purchaser shall receive such property or rights to property free and clear of any claim or right of the former defaulting purchaser, of any nature whatsoever, and the amount paid upon the bid price by such defaulting purchaser shall be forfeited to the United States.

(9) *Stay of sale of seized property pending Tax Court decision.* For restrictions on sale of seized property pending Tax Court decision, see section 6863(b)(3) and § 301.6863-2.

○━ **§ 301.6336 Statutory provisions; sale of perishable goods.** [Sec. 6336, IRC]

○━ **§ 301.6336-1** (T.D. 6119, filed 12-31-54; republished in T.D. 6498, filed 10-24-60.) **Sale of perishable goods.**

(a) *Appraisal of certain seized property.* If the district director determines that any property seized by levy is liable to perish or become greatly reduced in price or value by keeping, or that such property cannot be kept without great expense, he shall appraise the value of such property and return it to the owner if the owner complies with the conditions prescribed in paragraph (b) of this section or, if the owner does not comply with such conditions, dispose of the property in accordance with paragraph (c) of this section.

(b) *Return to owner.* If the owner of the property can be readily found, the district director shall give him written notice of his determination of the appraised value of the property. However, if the district director determines that the circumstances require immediate action, he may give the owner an oral notice of his determination of the appraised value of the property, which notice shall be confirmed in writing prior to sale. The property shall be returned to the owner if, within the time specified in the notice, the owner—

(1) Pays to the district director an amount equal to the appraised value, or

(2) Gives an acceptable bond as prescribed by section 7101 and § 301.7101-1. Such bond shall be in an amount not less than the appraised value of the property and shall be conditioned upon the payment of such amount at such time as the district director determines to be appropriate in the circumstances.

(c) *Immediate sale.* If the owner does not pay the amount of the appraised value of the seized property within the time specified in the notice, or furnish bond as provided in paragraph (b) of this section within such time, the district director shall as soon as practicable make public sale of the property in accordance with the following terms and conditions—

(1) *Notice of sale.* If the owner can readily be found, a notice shall be given to him. A notice of sale also shall be posted in two public places in the county in which the property is to be sold. The notice shall specify the time and place of sale, the property to be sold, and the manner and conditions of sale. The district director may give such other notice and in such other manner as he deems advisable under the circumstances.

(2) *Sale.* The property shall be sold at public auction to the highest bidder.

(3) *Terms.* The purchase price shall be paid in full upon acceptance of the highest bid. The payment shall be made in cash or by a certified, cashier's, or treasurer's check drawn on any bank or trust company incorporated under the laws of the United States or under the laws of any State, Territory, or possession of the United States, or by a U.S. postal, bank, express, or telegraph money order.

○━ **§ 301.6337 Statutory provisions; redemption of property.** [Sec. 6337, IRC]

○━ **§ 301.6337-1** (T.D. 6119, filed 12-31-54; republished in T.D. 6498, filed 10-24-60; amended by T.D. 7180, filed 4-12-72.) **Redemption of property.**

(a) *Before sale.* Any person whose property has been levied upon shall have the right to pay the amount due, together with costs and expenses of the proceeding, if any, to the district director at any time prior to the sale of the property. Upon such payment the district director shall restore such property to the owner and all further proceedings in connection with the levy on such property shall cease from the time of such payment.

(b) *Redemption of real estate after sale* — (1) *Period.* The owner of any real estate sold as provided in section 6335, his heirs, executors, or administrators, or any person having any interest therein, or a lien thereon, or any person in their behalf, shall be permitted to redeem the property sold, or any particular tract of such property, at any time within 120 days after the sale thereof.

PRENTICE-HALL, Inc., Englewood Cliffs, N. J.　　　**Reg. § 301.6337-1 (b) (1)**

24,360 (I.R.C.) Reg. § 301.6337-1(b)(2)

(2) *Price.* Such property or tract of property may be redeemed upon payment to the purchaser, or in case he cannot be found in the county, in which the property to be redeemed is situated, then to the district director for the internal revenue district in which the property is situated, for the use of the purchaser, his heirs, or assigns, the amount paid by such purchaser and interest thereon at the rate of 20 percent per annum. In case real and personal property (or several tracts of real property) are purchased in the aggregate, the redemption price of the real property (or of each of the several tracts) shall be determined on the basis of the ratio, as of the time of sale, of the value of the real property (or tract) to the value of the total property purchased. For this purpose the minimum price or the highest bid price, whichever is higher, offered for the property separately or in groups shall be treated as the value.

(c) *Record.* When any real property is redeemed, the district director shall cause entry of the fact to be made upon the record of sale kept in accordance with section 6340, and such entry shall be evidence of such redemption. The party who redeems the property shall notify the district director of the internal revenue district in which the property is situated of the date of such redemption and of the transfer of the certificate of sale, the amount of the redemption price, and the name of the party to whom such redemption price was paid.

○━ § 301.6338 Statutory provisions; certificate of sale; deed of real property. [Sec. 6338, IRC]

○━ § 301.6338-1 (T.D. 6119, filed 12-31-54 as amended by T.D. 6425, filed 11-10-59; republished in T.D. 6498, filed 10-24-60; amended by T.D. 7180, filed 4-12-72.) Certificate of sale; deed of real property.

(a) *Certificate of sale.* In the case of property sold as provided in section 6335 (relating to sale of seized property), the district director shall give to the purchaser a certificate of sale upon payment in full of the purchase price. A certificate of sale of real property shall set forth the real property purchased, for whose taxes the same was sold, the name of the purchaser, and the price paid therefor.

(b) *Deed to real property.* In the case of any real property sold as provided in section 6335 and not redeemed in the manner and within the time prescribed in section 6337, the district director shall execute (in accordance with the laws of the State in which the real property is situated pertaining to sales of real property under execution) to the purchaser of such real property at the sale or his assigns, upon surrender of the certificate of sale, a deed of the real property so purchased, reciting the facts set forth in the certificate.

(c) *Deed to real property purchased by the United States.* If real property is declared purchased by the United States at a sale pursuant to section 6335, the district director shall at the proper time execute a deed therefor and shall, without delay, cause the deed to be duly recorded in the proper registry of deeds.

○━ § 301.6339 Statutory provisions; legal effect of certificate of sale of personal property and deed of real property. [Sec. 6339, IRC]

○━ § 301.6339-1 (T.D. 6119, filed 12-31-54; republished in T.D. 6498, filed 10-24-60; amended by T.D. 7180, filed 4-12-72.) Legal effect of certificate of sale of personal property and deed of real property.

(a) *Certificate of sale of property other than real property.* In all cases of sale pursuant to section 6335 of property (other than real property), the certificate of such sale—

(1) *As evidence.* Shall be prima facie evidence of the right of the officer to make such sale, and conclusive evidence of the regularity of his proceedings in making the sale; and

(2) *As conveyance.* Shall transfer to the purchaser all right, title, and interest of the party delinquent in and to the property sold; and

(3) *As authority for transfer of corporate stock.* If such property consists of corporate stocks, shall be notice, when received, to any corporation, company, or association of such transfer, and shall be authority to such corporation, company, or association to record the transfer on its books and records in the same manner as if the stocks were transferred or assigned by the party holding the stock certificate in lieu of any original or prior certificate, which shall be void, whether canceled or not; and

(4) *As receipts.* If the subject of sale is securities or other evidences of debt, shall be a good and valid receipt to the person holding the certificate of sale as against any person holding or claiming to hold possession of such securities or other evidences of debt; and

(5) *As authority for transfer of title to motor vehicle.* If such property consists of a motor vehicle, shall be notice, when received, to any public official charged with the registration of title to motor vehicles, of such transfer and shall be authority to such official to record the transfer on his books and records in the same manner as if the certificate of title to such motor vehicle were transferred or assigned by the party holding the certificate of title, in lieu of any original or prior certificate, which shall be null and void, whether canceled or not.

(b) *Deed to real property.* In the case of the sale of real property pursuant to section 6335—

(1) *Deed as evidence.* The deed of sale given pursuant to section 6338 shall be prima facie evidence of the facts therein stated; and

(2) *Deed as conveyance of title.* If the proceedings of the district director as set forth have been substantially in accordance with the provisions of law, such deed shall be considered and operate as a conveyance of all the right, title, and interest the party delinquent had in and to the real property thus sold at the time the lien of the United States attached thereto.

(c) *Effect of junior encumbrances.* A certificate of sale of personal property given or a deed to real property executed pursuant to section 6338 discharges the property from all liens, encumbrances, and titles over which the lien of the United

States, with respect to which the levy was made, has priority. For example, a mortgage on real property executed after a notice of a federal tax lien has been filed is extinguished when the district director executes a deed to the real property to a purchaser thereof at a sale pursuant to section 6335 following the seizure of the property by the United States. The proceeds of such a sale are distributed in accordance with priority of the liens, encumbrances, or titles. See section 6342(b) and the regulations thereunder for provisions relating to the distribution of surplus proceeds. See section 7426(a)(2) and the regulations thereunder for judicial procedures with respect to surplus proceeds.

§ 301.6340 Statutory provisions; records of sale. [Sec. 6340, IRC]

§ 301.6340-1 (T.D. 6119, filed 12-31-54; republished in T.D. 6498, filed 10-24-60.) Records of sale.

(a) *Requirement.* Each district director shall keep a record of all sales under section 6335 of real property situated within his district and of redemptions of such property. The records shall set forth (1) the tax for which any such sale was made, the dates of seizure and sale, the name of the party assessed and all proceedings in making such sale, the amount of expenses, the names of the purchasers, the date of the deed, and, in the case of redemption of the property, (2) the date of such redemption and of the transfer of the certificate of sale, the amount of the redemption price, and the name of the party to whom such redemption price was paid.

(b) *Copy as evidence.* A copy of such record, or any part thereof, certified by the district director shall be evidence in any court of the truth of the facts therein stated.

§ 301.6341 Statutory provisions; expense of levy and sale. [Sec. 6341, IRC]

§ 301.6341-1 (T.D. 6119, filed 12-31-54; republished in T.D. 6498, filed 10-24-60.) Expense of levy and sale.

The district director shall determine the expenses to be allowed in all cases of levy and sale. Such expenses shall include the expenses of protection and preservation of the property during the period subsequent to the levy, as well as the actual expenses incurred in connection with the sale thereof. In case real and personal property (or several tracts of real property) are sold in the aggregate, the district director shall properly apportion the expenses to the real property (or to each tract).

§ 301.6342 Statutory provisions; application of proceeds of levy. [Sec. 6342, IRC]

§ 301.6342-1 (T.D. 6119, filed 12-31-54; republished in T.D. 6498, filed 10-24-60.) Application of proceeds of levy.

(a) *Collection of liability.* Any money realized by proceedings under subchapter D, chapter 64, of the Code or by sale of property redeemed by the United States (if the interest of the United States in the property was a lien arising under the provisons of the Internal Revenue Code) is applied in the manner specified in subparagraphs (1), (2), and (3) of this paragraph. Money realized by proceedings under subchapter D, chapter 64, of the Code includes money realized by seizure, by sale of seized property, or by surrender under section 6332 (except money realized by the imposition of a 50% penalty pursuant to section 6332(c)(2)).

(1) *Expense of levy and sale.* First, against the expenses of the proceedings or sale, including expenses allowable under section 6341 and amounts paid by the United States to redeem property.

(2) *Specific tax liability on seized property.* If the property seized and sold is subject to a tax imposed by any internal revenue law which has not been paid, the amount remaining after applying subparagraph (1) of this paragraph shall then be applied against such tax liability (and, if such tax was not previously assessed, it shall then be assessed);

(3) *Liability of delinquent taxpayer.* The amount, if any, remaining after applying subparagraphs (1) and (2) of this paragraph shall then be applied against the liability in respect of which the levy was made or the sale of redeemed property was conducted.

(b) *Surplus proceeds.* Any surplus proceeds remaining after the application of paragraph (a) of this section shall, upon application and satisfactory proof in support thereof, be credited or refunded by the district director to the person or persons legally entitled thereto. The delinquent taxpayer is the person entitled to the surplus proceeds unless another person establishes a superior claim thereto.

§ 301.6343 Statutory provisions; authority to release levy and return property. [Sec. 6343, IRC]

§ 301.6343-1 (T.D. 6119, filed 12-31-54 as amended by T.D. 6425, filed 11-10-59; republished in T.D. 6498, filed 10-24-60; further amended by T.D. 7180, filed 4-12-72.) Authority to release levy and return property.

(a) *Release of levy* — (1) *Authority.* The district director may release the levy upon all or part of the property or rights to property levied upon as provided in subparagraphs (2) and (3) of this paragraph. A levy may be released under subparagraph (2) of this paragraph only if the delinquent taxpayer complies with such of the conditions thereunder as the district director may require and if the district director determines that such action will facilitate the collection of the liability. A release pursuant to subparagraph (3) of this paragraph is considered to facilitate the collection of the liability. The release under this section shall not operate to prevent any subsequent levy.

(2) *Conditions for release.* The district director may release the levy as authorized under subparagraph (1) of this paragraph, if—

(i) *Escrow arrangement.* The delinquent taxpayer offers a satisfactory arrangement, which is accepted by the district director, for placing property in escrow to secure the payment of the liability (including the expenses of levy) which is the basis of the levy.

(ii) *Bond.* The delinquent taxpayer delivers an acceptable bond to the district director conditioned upon the payment of

Reg. § 301.6343-1(a)(2)

24,362 (I.R.C.)   Reg. § 301.6343-1(a)(2)

the liability (including the expenses of levy) which is the basis of the levy. Such bond shall be in the form provided in section 7101 and § 301.7101-1.

(iii) *Payment of amount of U.S. interest in the property.* There is paid to the district director an amount determined by him to be equal to the interest of the United States in the seized property or the part of the seized property to be released.

(iv) *Assignment of salaries and wages.* The delinquent taxpayer executes an agreement directing his employer to pay to the district director amounts deducted from the employee's wages on a regular, continuing, or periodic basis, in such manner and in such amount as is agreed upon with the district director, until the full amount of the liability is satisfied, and such agreement is accepted by the employer.

(v) *Installment payment arrangement.* The delinquent taxpayer makes satisfactory arrangements with the district director to pay the amount of the liability in installments.

(vi) *Extension of statute of limitations.* The delinquent taxpayer executes an agreement to extend the statute of limitations in accordance with section 6502(a)(2) and § 301.6502-1.

(3) *Release where value of interest of United States is insufficient to meet expenses of sale.* The district director may release the levy as authorized under subparagraph (1) of this paragraph if he determines that the value of the interest of the United States in the seized property, or in the part of the seized property to be released, is insufficient to cover the expenses of the sale of such property.

(b) *Return of property* —(1) *General rule.* If the district director determines that property has been wrongfully levied upon, the district director may return—

(i) The specific property levied upon,

(ii) An amount of money equal to the amount of money levied upon (without interest), or

(iii) An amount of money equal to the amount of money received by the United States from a sale of the property (without interest).

If the United States is in possession of specific property, the property may be returned at any time. An amount equal to the amount of money levied upon or received from a sale of the property may be returned at any time before the expiration of 9 months from the date of the levy. When a request described in subparagraph (2) of this paragraph is filed for the return of property before the expiration of 9 months from the date of levy, an amount of money may be returned after a reasonable period of time subsequent to the expiration of the 9-month period if necessary for the investigation and processing of such request. In cases where money is specifically identifiable, as in the case of a coin collection which may be worth substantially more than its face value, the money will be treated as specific property and, whenever possible, this specific property will be returned. For purposes of subparagraph (1)(iii) of this paragraph, if property is declared purchased by the United States at a sale pursuant to section 6335(e), the United States is treated as having received an amount of money equal to the minimum price determined by the district director before the sale or, if larger, the amount received by the United States from the resale of the property.

(2) *Request for return of property.* A written request for the return of property wrongfully levied upon shall be addressed to the district director (marked for the attention of the chief, special procedures staff) for the internal revenue district in which the levy was made. The written request shall contain the following information:

(i) The name and address of the person submitting the request,

(ii) A detailed description of the property levied upon,

(iii) A description of the claimant's basis for claiming an interest in the property levied upon, and

(iv) The name and address of the taxpayer, the originating internal revenue district, and the date of lien or levy as shown on the Notice of Tax Lien (Form 668), Notice of Levy (Form 668-A), or Levy (Form 668-B) or, in lieu thereof, a statement of the reasons why such information cannot be furnished.

(3) *Inadequate request.* Any request made prior to June 1, 1972, which apprises the Internal Revenue Service of the claimant's demand for the return of property wrongfully levied upon shall be considered adequate. A request made after May 31, 1972, shall not be considered adequate unless it is a written request containing the information required by subparagraph (2) of this paragraph. However, unless a notification is mailed by the district director to the claimant within 30 days of receipt of the request to inform the claimant of the inadequacies, any written request shall be considered adequate. If the district director timely notifies the claimant of the inadequacies of his request, the claimant shall have 30 days from the receipt of the notification of inadequacy to supply in writing any omitted information. Where the omitted information is so supplied within the 30-day period, the request shall be considered to be adequate from the time the original request was made for purposes of determining the applicable period of limitation upon suit under section 6532 (c).

○→ § 301.6344 Statutory provisions; cross references. [Sec. 6344, IRC]

ABATEMENTS, CREDITS, AND REFUNDS
PROCEDURE IN GENERAL

○→ § 301.6401-1 (T.D. 6119, filed 12-31-54; republished in T.D. 6498, filed 10-24-60; amended by T.D. 7204, filed 8-24-72; T.D. 7537, filed 3-31-78.) **Amounts treated as overpayments.**

(a) The term "overpayment" includes:

(1) Any payment of any internal revenue tax which is assessed or collected after the expiration of the period of limitation applicable thereto.

(2) Any amount allowable for a taxable year as credits under sections 31 (relating

to tax withheld on wages), 39 (relating to certain uses of gasoline, special fuels, and, lubricating oil), 43 (relating to earned income credit), and 667(b) (relating to taxes paid by certain trusts) which exceeds the tax imposed by subtitle A of the Code (reduced by the credits allowable under subpart A of part IV of subchapter A of chapter 1 of the Code, other than the credits allowable under sections 31, 39, and 43) for such year.

(b) An amount paid as tax shall not be considered not to constitute an overpayment solely by reason of the fact that there was no tax liability in respect of which such amount was paid.

○→ § 31.6402 (a) **Statutory provisions; authority to make credits or refunds.** [Sec. 6402(a), IRC]

○→ § 31.6402(a)-1 (T.D. 6472, filed 6-22-60; republished in T.D. 6516, filed 12-19-60.) **Credits or refunds.**

(a) *In general.* For regulations under section 6402 of special application to credits or refunds of employment taxes, see §§ 31.6402(a)-2, 31.6402(a)-3, and 31.6414-1. For regulations under section 6402 of general application to credits or refunds, see §§ 301.6402-1 and 301.6402-2 of this chapter (Regulations on Procedure and Administration). For provisions relating to credits of employment taxes which constitute adjustments without interest, see §§ 31.6413 (a)-1 and 31.6413(a)-2.

(b) *Period of limitation.* For the period of limitation upon credit or refund of taxes imposed by the Internal Revenue Code of 1954, see § 301.6511(a)-1 of this chapter (Regulations on Procedure and Administration). For the period of limitation upon credit or refund of any tax imposed by the Internal Revenue Code of 1939, see the regulations applicable with respect to such tax.

○→ § 301.6402 **Statutory provisions; authority to make credits or refunds.** [Sec. 6402, IRC]

○→ § 301.6402-1 (T.D. 6119, filed 12-31-54; republished in T.D. 6498, filed 10-24-60.) **Authority to make credits or refunds.**

The Commissioner, within the applicable period of limitations, may credit any overpayment of tax, including interest thereon, against any outstanding liability for any tax (or for any interest, additional amount, addition to the tax, or assessable penalty) owed by the person making the overpayment, and the balance, if any, shall be refunded to such person by the Commissioner.

○→ § 301.6402-2 (T.D. 6119, filed 12-31-54, as amended by T.D. 6292, filed 4-18-58; republished in T.D. 6498, filed 10-24-60; amended by T.D. 6585, filed 12-27-61; T.D. 6950, filed 4-3-68; T.D. 7008, filed 2-28-69; T.D. 7188, filed 6-28-72; T.D. 7410, filed 3-15-76; T.D. 7484, filed 4-29-77.) **Claims for credit or refund.**

(a) *Requirement that claim be filed.* (1) Credits or refunds of overpayments may not be allowed or made after expiration of the statutory period of limitation properly applicable unless, before the expiration of such period, a claim therefor has been filed by the taxpayer. Furthermore, under section 7422, a civil action for refund may not be instituted unless a claim has been filed within the properly applicable period of limitation.

(2) In the case of a claim filed prior to April 15, 1968, the claim together with appropriate supporting evidence shall be filed in the office of the internal revenue officer to whom the tax was paid or with the assistant regional commissioner (alcohol, tobacco and firearms) where the regulations respecting the particular tax to which the claim relates specifically require the claim to be filed with that officer. Except as provided in paragraph (b) of § 301.6091-1 (relating to hand-carried documents), in the case of a claim filed after April 14, 1968, the claim, together with appropriate supporting evidence, shall be filed (i) with the Director of International Operations if the tax was paid to him or (ii) with the assistant regional commissioner (alcohol, tobacco and firearms) where the regulations respecting the particular tax to which the claim relates specifically require the claim to be filed with that officer; otherwise, the claim with appropriate supporting evidence must be filed with the service center serving the internal revenue district in which the tax was paid. As to interest in the case of credits or refunds, see section 6611. See section 7502 for provisions treating timely mailing as timely filing and section 7503 for time for filing claim when the last day falls on Saturday, Sunday, or legal holiday.

(b) *Grounds set forth in claim.* (1) No refund or credit will be allowed after the expiration of the statutory period of limitation applicable to the filing of a claim therefor except upon one or more of the grounds set forth in a claim filed before the expiration of such period. The claim must set forth in detail each ground upon which a credit or refund is claimed and facts sufficient to apprise the Commissioner of the exact basis thereof. The statement of the grounds and facts must be verified by a written declaration that it is made under the penalties of perjury. A claim which does not comply with this paragraph will not be considered for any purpose as a claim for refund or credit.

(2) Neither the district director nor the director of the regional service center has authority to refund on equitable grounds penalties or other amounts legally collected.

(c) *Form for filing claim.* Except for claims filed after June 30, 1976 for the refunding of overpayment of income taxes, all claims by taxpayers for the refunding of taxes, interest, penalties, and additions to tax shall be made on Form 843. For special rules applicable to income taxes, see § 301.6402-3. For other provisions relating to credits and refunds of taxes other than income tax, see the regulations relating to the particular tax.

(d) *Separate claims for separate taxable periods.* In the case of income, gift, and Federal unemployment taxes, a separate claim shall be made for each type of tax for each taxable year or period.

(e) *Proof of representative capacity.* If a return is filed by an individual and, after his death, a refund claim is filed by his legal representative, certified copies of the letters testamentary, letters of administration, or other similar evidence must be annexed to the claim, to show the authority of the legal representative to file the claim. If an executor, administrator, guardian, trustee, receiver, or other fiduciary files a return and thereafter a refund claim is filed by the same fiduciary, docu-

Reg. § 301.6402-2(e)

mentary evidence to establish the legal authority of the fiduciary need not accompany the claim, provided a statement is made in the claim showing that the return was filed by the fiduciary and that the latter is still acting. In such cases, if a refund is to be paid, letters testamentary, letters of administration, or other evidence may be required, but should be submitted only upon the receipt of a specific request therefor. If a claim is filed by a fiduciary other than the one by whom the return was filed, the necessary documentary evidence should accompany the claim. A claim may be executed by an agent of the person assessed, but in such case a power of attorney must accompany the claim.

(f) *Mailing of refund check.* (1) Checks in payment of claims allowed will be drawn in the names of the persons entitled to the money and, except as provided in subparagraph (2) of this paragraph, the checks may be sent direct to the claimant or to such person in care of an attorney or agent who has filed a power of attorney specifically authorizing him to receive such checks.

(2) Checks in payment of claims which have either been reduced to judgment or settled in the course or as a result of litigation will be drawn in the name of the person or persons entitled to the money and will be sent to the Assistant Attorney General, Tax Division, Department of Justice, for delivery to the taxpayer or the counsel of record in the court proceeding.

(3) For restrictions on the assignment of claims, see section 3477 of the Revised Statutes (31 U.S.C. 203).

○—— 301.6402–3 (T.D. 6119, filed 12-31-54, as amended by T.D. 6292, filed 4-18-58 and T.D. 6425, filed 11-10-59; republished in T.D. 6498, filed 10-24-60; further amended by T.D. 6585, filed 12-27-61; T.D. 7057, filed 9-2-70; T.D. 7102, filed 3-23-71; T.D. 7234, filed 12-20-72; T.D. 7269, filed 4-12-73; T.D. 7293, filed 11-7-73; T.D. 7298, filed 12-21-73; T.D. 7410, filed 3-15-76.) **Special rules applicable to income tax.**

(a) In the case of a claim for credit or refund filed after June 30, 1976—

(1) In general, in the case of an overpayment of income taxes, a claim for credit or refund of such overpayment shall be made on the appropriate income tax return.

(2) In the case of an overpayment of income taxes for a taxable year of an individual for which a Form 1040 or 1040A has been filed, a claim for refund shall be made on Form 1040X ("Amended U.S. Individual Income Tax Return").

(3) In the case of an overpayment of income taxes for a taxable year of a corporation for which a Form 1120 has been filed, a claim for refund shall be made on Form 1120X ("Amended U.S. Corporation Income Tax Return").

(4) In the case of an overpayment of income taxes for a taxable year for which a form other than Form 1040, 1040A, or 1120 was filed (such as Form 1041 (U.S. Fiduciary Income Tax Return) or Form 990T (Exempt Organization Business Income Tax Return)), a claim for credit or refund shall be made on the appropriate amended income tax return.

(5) A properly executed individual, fiduciary, or corporation original income tax return or an amended return (on 1040X or 1120X if applicable) shall constitute a claim for refund or credit within the meaning of section 6402 and section 6511 for the amount of the overpayment disclosed by such return (or amended return). For purposes of section 6511, such claim shall be considered as filed on the date on which such return (or amended return) is considered as filed, except that if the requirements of § 301.7502-1, relating to timely mailing treated as timely filing are met, the claim shall be considered to be filed on the date of the postmark stamped on the cover in which the return (or amended return) was mailed. A return or amended return shall constitute a claim for refund or credit if it contains a statement setting forth the amount determined as an overpayment and advising whether such amount shall be refunded to the taxpayer or shall be applied as a credit against the taxpayer's estimated income tax for the taxable year immediately succeeding the taxable year for which such return (or amended return) is filed. If the taxpayer indicates on its return (or amended return) that all or part of the overpayment shown by its return (or amended return) is to be applied to its estimated income tax for its succeeding taxable year, such indication shall constitute an election to so apply such overpayment, and no interest shall be allowed on such portion of the overpayment credited and such amount shall be applied as a payment on account of the estimated income tax for such year or the installments thereof.

(6) Notwithstanding paragraph (a)(5) of this section, the Commissioner, within the applicable period of limitations, may credit any overpayment of individual, fiduciary, or corporation income tax, against any outstanding liability for any tax (or for any interest, additional amount, addition to the tax, or assessable penalty) owed by the taxpayer making the overpayment, and only the balance, if any, shall be treated in the manner so elected.

(b) In the case of a claim for credit or refund filed before July 1, 1976—

(1) In the case of income tax, claims for refund may not only be made on Form 843 but may also be made on any individual, fiduciary, or corporation income tax return, or on any amended income tax return.

(2) In the case of an overpayment for a taxable year of an individual for which a Form 1040 or Form 1040A has been filed, claim for refund may be made on Form 1040X ("Amended U.S. Individual Income Tax Return"). In cases to which this subparagraph applies, the taxpayer is encouraged to use Form 1040X.

(3) In the case of an overpayment for a taxable year of a corporation for which a corporation tax return has been filed, claim for refund may be made on Form 1120X ("Amended U.S. Corporation Income Tax Return"). In cases to which this subparagraph applies, the taxpayer is encouraged to use Form 1120X.

(4) A properly executed individual, fiduciary, or corporation income tax return shall, at the election of the taxpayer, constitute a claim for refund or credit within the meaning of section 6402 and section 6511 for the amount of the overpayment disclosed by such return. For purposes of

section 6511, such claim shall be considered as filed on the date on which such return is considered as filed, except that if the requirements of § 301.7502-1, relating to timely mailing treated as timely filing, are met the claim shall be considered to be filed on the date of the postmark stamped on the cover in which the return was mailed.

(5) An election to treat the return as a claim for refund or credit shall be evidenced by a statement on the return setting forth the amount determined as an overpayment and advising whether such amount shall be refunded to the taxpayer or shall be applied as a credit against the taxpayer's estimated income tax for the taxable year immediately succeeding the taxable year for which such return is filed. If the taxpayer elects to have all or part of the overpayment shown by his return applied to its estimated income tax for his succeeding taxable year, no interest shall be allowed on such portion of the overpayment credited and such amount shall be applied as a payment on account of the estimated income tax for such year or the installments thereof.

(6) Notwithstanding elections made under paragraph (b)(5) of this section, for taxable years ending after December 20, 1972, the Commissioner, within the applicable period of limitations, may credit any overpayment of individual, fiduciary, or corporation income tax, against any outstanding liability for any tax (or for any interest, additional amount, addition to the tax, or assessable penalty) owed by the taxpayer making the overpayment, and only the balance, if any, shall be treated in the manner so elected.

(c) The filing of a properly executed income tax return shall, in any case in which the taxpayer is not required to show his tax on such form (see section 6014 and the regulations thereunder), be treated as a claim for refund (or for claims filed before July 1, 1976, constitute an election by the taxpayer to have the return treated as a claim for refund), and such return shall constitute a claim for refund within the meaning of section 6402 and section 6511 for the amount of the overpayment shown by the computation of the tax made by the district director or the director of the regional service center on the basis of the return. For purposes of section 6511 such claim shall be considered as filed on the date on which such return is considered as filed, except that if the requirements of § 301.7502-1, relating to timely mailing treated as timely filing, are met the claim shall be considered to be filed on the date of the postmark stamped on the cover in which the return was mailed.

(d) In any case in which a taxpayer elects to have an overpayment refunded to him he may not thereafter change his election to have the overpayment applied as a payment on account of his estimated income tax.

(e) In the case of a nonresident alien individual or a foreign corporation the claim for refund must show the taxpayer's entire income subject to tax, whether or not the tax has been fully satisfied at the source upon a portion of such income. If the overpayment has resulted from the withholding of tax at source under chapter 3 of the Code, a statement shall be attached to the claim for refund declaring that the person making the claim is the beneficial owner of the income and showing (1) the amounts of tax withheld, with the names and post office addresses of withholding agents, (2) the name in which the tax was withheld if other than that of the taxpayer, and, if applicable, (3) facts sufficient to show that, at the time the income was derived, the taxpayer was entitled to the benefit of a reduced rate of, or exemption from, tax with respect to that income under the provisions of an income tax convention to which the United States is a part. Upon request of the Director of International Operations the taxpayer shall also submit such evidence as may be required to show that the taxpayer is the beneficial owner of the income. In no case may a claim for refund of overwithheld tax be made by a nonresident alien individual or foreign corporation if the taxpayer has received a repayment or reimbursement of such tax in accordance with paragraph (a) of § 1.1461-4 of this chapter (Income Tax Regulations). See also § 1.1464-1 of this chapter.

○━ § 301.6402-4 (T.D. 6119, filed 12-31-54; republished in T.D. 6498; filed 10-24-60; amended by T.D. 6585, filed 12-27-61.) **Payments in excess of amounts shown on return.**

In certain cases, the taxpayer's payments in respect of his tax liability, made before the filing of his return, may exceed the amount of tax shown on the return. For example, such payments may arise in the case of the income tax when the estimated tax or the credit for income tax withheld at the source on wages exceeds the amount of tax shown on the return, or where a corporation obtains an extension of time for filing its return and makes installment payments based on its estimate of its tax liability which exceed the tax liability shown on the return subsequently filed. In any case in which the district director or the director of the regional service center determines that the payments by the taxpayer (made within the period prescribed for payment and before the filing of the return) are in excess of the amount of tax shown on the return, he may make credit or refund of such overpayment without awaiting examination of the completed return and without awaiting filing of a claim for refund. However, the provisions of §§ 301.6402-2 and 301.6402-3 are applicable to such overpayment, and taxpayers should submit claims for refunds (if the income tax return is not itself a claim for refund, as provided in § 301.6402-3) to protect themselves in the event the district director or the director of the regional service center fails to make such determination and credit or refund. The provisions of section 6405 (relating to reports of refunds of more than $100,000 to the Joint Committee on Internal Revenue Taxation) are not applicable to the overpayments described in this section caused by timely payments of tax which exceed the amount of tax shown on a timely return.

○━ § 301.6403 **Statutory provisions; overpayment of installment.** [Sec. 6403, IRC]

○━ § 301.6403-1 (T.D. 6119, filed 12-31-54; republished in T.D. 6498, filed 10-24-60.) **Overpayment of installment.**

Reg. § 301.6403-1

24,362.4 (I.R.C.)   Reg. § 301.6403-1   4-10-78

If any installment of tax is overpaid, the overpayment shall first be applied against any outstanding installments of such tax. If the overpayment exceeds the correct amount of tax due, the overpayment shall be credited or refunded as provided in section 6402 and §§ 301.6402-1 to 301.6402-4, inclusive.

○— § 31.6404 (a) Statutory provisions; abatements [Sec. 6404(a), IRC]

○— § 31.6404 (a)-1 (T.D. 6472, filed 6-22-60; republished in T.D. 6516, filed 12-19-60.) Abatements.

For regulations under section 6404 of general application to the abatement of taxes, see § 301.6404-1 of this chapter (Regulations on Procedure and Administration). Every claim filed by an employer for abatement of employee tax under section 3101 or section 3201, or a corresponding provision of prior law, shall be made in the manner and subject to the conditions stated in paragraphs (a) (2) and (c) of § 31.6402(a)-2, as if the claim for abatement were a claim for refund.

○— § 301.6404 Statutory provisions; abatements. [Sec. 6404, IRC]

○— § 301.6404-1 (T.D. 6119, filed 12-31-54; republished in T.D. 6498, filed 10-24-60; amended by T.D. 6585, filed 12-27-61; T.D. 6950, filed 4-3-68; T.D. 7008, filed 2-28-69 and T.D. 7188, filed 6-28-72.) Abatements.

(a) The district director or the director of the regional service center may abate any assessment, or unpaid portion thereof, if the assessment is in excess of the correct tax liability, if the assessment is made subsequent to the expiration of the period of limitations applicable thereto, or if the assessment has been erroneously or illegally made.

(b) No claim for abatement may be filed with respect to income, estate, or gift tax.

(c) Except in case of income, estate, or gift tax, if more than the correct amount of tax, interest, additional amount, addition to the tax, or assessable penalty is assessed but not paid to the district director, the person against whom the assessment is made may file a claim for abatement of such overassessment. Each claim for abatement under this section shall be made on Form 843. In the case of a claim filed prior to April 15, 1968, the claim shall be filed in the office of the internal revenue officer by whom the tax was assessed or with the assistant regional commissioner (alcohol, tobacco and firearms) where the regulations respecting the particular tax to which the claim relates specifically require the claim to be filed with that officer. Except as provided in paragraph (b) of § 301.6091-1 (relating to hand-carried document), in the case of a claim filed after April 14, 1968, the claim shall be filed (1) with the Director of International Operations if the tax was assessed by him, or (2) with the assistant regional commissioner (alcohol, tobacco and firearms) where the regulations respecting the particular tax to which the claim relates specifically require the claim to be filed with that officer; otherwise, the claim shall be filed with the service center serving the internal revenue district in which the tax was assessed. Form 843 shall be made in accordance with the instructions relating to such form.

(d) The Commissioner may issue uniform instructions to district director authorizing them, to the extent permitted in such instructions, to abate amounts the collection of which is not warranted because of the administration and collection costs.

○— § 301.6405 Statutory provisions; reports of refunds and credits. [Sec. 6405, IRC]

○— § 301.6405-1 (T.D. 6119, filed 12-31-54; republished in T.D. 6498, filed 10-24-60; amended by T.D. 7224, filed 12-5-72.) Reports of refunds and credits.

Section 6405 requires that a report be made to the Joint Committee on Internal Revenue Taxation of proposed refunds or credits of any income, war profits, excess profits, estate, or gift tax in excess of $100,000. An exception is provided under which refunds and credits made after July 1, 1972, and attributable to an election under section 165(h) to deduct a disaster loss for the taxable year immediately preceding the taxable year in which the disaster occurred, may be made prior to the submission of such report to the Joint Committee on Internal Revenue Taxation.

○— § 301.6406 Statutory provisions; prohibition of administrative review of decisions. [Sec. 6406, IRC]

RULES OF SPECIAL APPLICATION

§ 301.6407 Statutory provisions; date of allowance of refund or credit. [Sec. 6407, IRC]

§ 301.6407-1 (T.D. 6119, filed 12-31-54; republished in T.D. 6498, filed 10-24-60; amended by T.D. 6585, filed 12-27-61.) **Date of allowance of refund or credit.**

The date on which the district director, or the director of the regional service center, or an authorized certifying officer designated by either of them, first certifies the allowance of an overassessment in respect of any internal revenue tax shall be considered as the date of allowance of refund or credit in respect of such tax.

§ 1.6411 Statutory provisions; tentative carryback adjustments. [Sec. 6411, IRC].

§ 1.6411-1 (T.D. 6364, filed 2-13-59; republished in T.D. 6500, filed 11-25-65; amended by T.D. 6862, filed 11-17-65; T.D. 6950, filed 4-3-68 and T.D. 7301, filed 1-3-74.) **Tentative carryback adjustments.**

(a) *In general.* Any taxpayer who has a net operating loss under section 172, a net capital loss under section 1211(a) which is a carryback under section 1212, an unused investment credit under section 46, or an unused work incentive program (WIN) credit under section 50A, may file an application under section 6411 for a tentative carryback adjustment of the taxes for taxable years prior to the taxable year of the net operating or capital loss or the unused credit, whichever is applicable, which are affected by the net operating loss carryback, the capital loss carryback, the unused investment credit carryback, or the unused WIN credit carryback, resulting from such loss or unused credit. The regulations under section 6411 shall apply with respect to investment credit carrybacks for taxable years ending after December 31, 1961, but only with respect to applications for tentative carryback adjustments for investment credit carrybacks filed after November 2, 1966. The regulations under section 6411 shall apply with respect to WIN credit carrybacks for taxable years beginning after December 31, 1971. The right to file an application for a tentative carryback adjustment is not limited to corporations, but is available to any taxpayer otherwise entitled to carry back a loss or unused credit. A corporation may file an application for a tentative carryback adjustment even though it has not extended the time for payment of tax under section 6164. In determining any decrease in tax under §§ 1.6411-1 through 1.6411-4, the decrease in tax is determined net of any increase in the tax imposed by section 56 (relating to the minimum tax for tax preferences).

(b) *Contents of application.* (1) The application for a tentative carryback adjustment shall be filed, in the case of a corporation, on Form 1139, and in the case of taxpayers other than corporations, on Form 1045. The application shall be filled out in accordance with the instructions accompanying the form, and all information required by the form and the instructions must be furnished by the taxpayer.

(2) An application for a tentative carryback adjustment does not constitute a claim for credit or refund. If such application is disallowed by the district director or director of a service center in whole or in part, no suit may be maintained in any court for the recovery of any tax based on such application. The filing of an application for a tentative carryback adjustment will not constitute the filing of a claim for credit or refund within the meaning of section 6511 for purposes of determining whether a claim for credit or refund was filed prior to the expiration of the applicable period of limitation. The taxpayer however may file a claim for credit or refund under section 6402 at any time prior to the expiration of the applicable period of limitation, and may maintain a suit based on such claim if it is disallowed or if the district director or director of a service center does not act on the claim within 6 months from the date it is filed. Such claim may be filed before, simultaneously with, or after the filing of the application for a tentative carryback adjustment. A claim for credit or refund under section 6402 filed after the filing of an application for a tentative carryback adjustment is not to be considered an amendment of such application. Such claim, however, in proper cases may constitute an amendment to a prior claim filed under section 6402.

(c) *Time and place for filing application.* Except as otherwise provided in this paragraph the application for a tentative carryback adjustment shall be filed on or after the date of the filing of the return for the taxable year of the net operating loss, net capital loss, unused investment credit, or unused WIN credit and shall be filed within a period of twelve months from the end of such taxable year. With respect to any portion of an investment credit carryback or a WIN credit carryback from a taxable year attributable to a net operating loss carryback or a capital loss carryback from a subsequent taxable year, the twelve-month period shall be measured from the end of such subsequent taxable year. In the case of an application for a tentative carryback adjustment attributable to the carryback of an unused investment credit, the twelve-month period for filing shall not expire before the close of December 31, 1966. Any application filed prior to the date on which the return for the taxable year of the loss or unused credit is filed shall be considered to have been filed on the date such return is filed. In the case of an application filed before April 15, 1968, the application shall be filed with the internal revenue officer to whom the tax was paid or by whom the assessment was made. Except as provided in paragraph (b) of § 301.6091-1 (relating to hand-carried documents), in the case of an application filed after April 14, 1968, if the tax was paid to the Director of International Operations, the application shall be filed with him; otherwise the application shall be filed with the internal revenue office with which the return was filed.

(d) *Carrybacks attributable to certifications issued under section 317 (a) of the Trade Expansion Act of 1962.* An application for a tentative carryback adjustment under the five-year carryback provision of section 172 (b) (1) (A) (ii) may be filed in

Reg. § 1.6411-1(d)

accordance with this section with respect to a net operating loss incurred in a taxable year ending on or after December 31, 1962, for which a certification has been issued under section 317 (a) of the Trade Expansion Act of 1962 (76 Stat. 889), if the taxpayer is eligible for the five-year carryback in accordance with the rules provided in § 1.172-9. If an application under this section has been filed in accordance with the three-year carryback provision of section 172 (b) (1) (A) (i), then a subsequent application for a tentative carryback adjustment under the five-year carryback provision of section 172 (b) (1) (A) (ii) may be filed under this paragraph with respect to the same net operating loss that was carried back under the three-year carryback provision only if the consent to extend the period for assessment of a deficiency required by section 172 (b) (3) (A) (ii) and paragraph (d) of § 1.172-9 is attached to such subsequent application. An application for a tentative carryback adjustment under the five-year carryback provision shall be accompanied by a statement indicating whether or not the taxpayer has previously filed an application for a tentative carryback adjustment under the three-year carryback provision with respect to the same net operating loss.

§ 1.6411-2 (T.D. 6364, filed 2-13-59; republished in T.D. 6500, filed 11-25-60; amended by T.D. 7301, filed 1-3-74.) **Computation of tentative carryback adjustment.**

(a) *Tax previously determined.* The taxpayer is to determine the amount of decrease, attributable to the carryback, in tax previously determined for each taxable year before the taxable year of the net operating loss, net capital loss, unused investment credit, or unused WIN credit. The tax previously determined is to be ascertained in accordance with the method prescribed in section 1314(a). Thus, the tax previously determined will be the tax shown on the return as filed, increased by any amounts assessed (or collected without assessment) as deficiencies before the date of the filing of the application for a tentative carryback adjustment, and decreased by any amounts abated, credited, refunded, or otherwise repaid prior to such date. Any items as to which the Internal Revenue Service and the taxpayer are in disagreement at the time of the filing of the application shall be taken into account in ascertaining the tax previously determined only if, and to the extent that, they were reported in the return, or were reflected in any amounts assessed (or collected without assessment) as deficiencies, or in any amounts abated, credited, refunded, or otherwise repaid, before the date of filing the application. The tax previously determined, therefore, will reflect the foreign tax credit and the credit for tax withheld at source provided in section 32.

(b) *Decrease attributable to carryback.* The decrease in tax previously determined which is affected by the carryback or any related adjustments, is to be determined, except for such carryback and related adjustments, on the basis of the items which entered into the computation of such tax as previously determined; the tax previously determined being ascertained in the manner described in this section. In determining any such decrease, items shall be taken into account only to the extent that they were reported in the return, or were reflected in amounts assessed (or collected without assessment) as deficiencies, or in amounts abated, credited, refunded, or otherwise repaid, before the date of filing the application for a tentative carryback adjustment. If the Internal Revenue Service and the taxpayer are in disagreement as to the proper treatment of any item, it shall be assumed for purposes of determining the decrease in the tax previously determined that such item was correctly reported by the taxpayer unless, and to the extent that, the disagreement has resulted in the assessment of a deficiency (or the collection of an amount without an assessment), or the allowing or making of an abatement, credit, refund, or other repayment, before the date of filing the application. Thus, if the taxpayer claimed a deduction on its return of $50,000 for salaries paid its officers but the district director asserts that such deduction should not exceed $20,000, and the Internal Revenue Service and the taxpayer have not agreed on the amount properly deductible before the date the application for a tentative carryback adjustment is filed, $50,000 shall be considered as the amount properly deductible for purposes of determining the decrease in tax previously determined in respect of the application for a tentative carryback adjustment. In determining the decrease in tax previously determined, any items which are affected by the carryback must be adjusted to reflect such carryback. Thus, unless otherwise provided, any deduction limited, for example, by adjusted gross income, such as the deduction for medical, dental, etc., expenses is to be recomputed on the basis of the adjusted gross income as affected by the carryback.

§ 1.6411-3 (T.D. 6364, filed 2-13-59; republished in T.D. 6500, filed 11-25-60; amended by T.D. 6950, filed 4-3-68 and T.D. 7301, filed 1-3-74.) **Allowance of adjustments.**

(a) *Time prescribed.* The district director or director of a service center (either of whom are sometimes hereinafter referred to in this section as internal revenue officer) shall act upon any application for a tentative carryback adjustment filed under section 6411 (a) within a period of 90 days from whichever of the following two dates is the later:

(1) The date the application is filed; or

(2) The last day of the month in which falls the last date prescribed by law (including any extension of time granted the taxpayer) for filing the return for the taxable year of the net operating loss, net capital loss, unused investment credit, or unused WIN credit from which the carryback results.

(b) *Examination.* Within the 90-day period described in paragraph (a) of this section, the district director or director of a service center shall make, to the extent he deems practicable in such period, an examination of the application to discover omissions and errors of computation. He shall determine within such period the decrease in tax previously determined, affected by the carryback or any related adjustments, upon the basis of the application and such examination. Such decrease shall be determined in the same manner as that provided in section 1314(a) for the determination by the taxpayer of the decrease in taxes previously determined which must be set forth in the application for a tentative carryback adjustment. Such internal revenue officer, however, may correct any errors of computation or omissions he may discover upon examination of the application. In determining the decrease in tax previously determined which is affected by the carryback or any related adjustment, he accordingly may correct any mathematical error appearing on the application and he may likewise correct any modification required by the law incorrectly made by the taxpayer in computing the net operating loss, net capital loss, unused investment credit, or unused WIN credit, the resulting carrybacks, or the net operating loss deduction, capital loss deduction, investment credit or WIN credit allowable. If the required modification has not been made by the taxpayer and such internal revenue officer has available the necessary information to make such modification within the 90-day period, he may, in his discretion, make such modification. In determining such decrease, however, such internal revenue officer will not, for example, change the amount claimed on the return as a deduction for depreciation because he believes that the taxpayer has claimed an excessive amount; likewise, he will not include in gross income any amount not so included by the taxpayer, even though such officer believes that such amount is subject to tax and properly should be included in gross income.

(c) *Disallowance in whole or in part.* If the district director or director of a service center finds that an application for a tentative carryback adjustment contains material omissions or errors of computation, he may disallow such application in whole or in part without further action. If, however, he deems that any error of computation can be corrected by him within the 90-day period, he may do so and allow the application in whole or in part. Such internal revenue officer's determination as to whether he can correct any error of computation within the 90-day period shall be conclusive. Similarly, his action in disallowing, in whole or in part, any application for a tentative carryback adjustment shall be final and may not be challenged in any proceeding. The taxpayer in such case, however, may file a claim for credit or refund under section 6402, and may maintain a suit based on such claim if it is disallowed or if such internal revenue officer does not act upon the claim within six months from the date it is filed.

(d) *Application of decrease.* (1) Each decrease determined by the district director or director of a service center in any previously determined tax which is affected by the carryback or any related adjustments shall first be applied against any unpaid amount of the tax with respect to which such decrease was determined. Such unpaid amount of tax may include one or more of the following:

(i) An amount with respect to which the taxpayer is delinquent;

(ii) An amount the time for payment of which has been extended under section 6164 and which is due and payable on or after the date of the allowance of the decrease; and

(iii) An amount (including an amount the time for payment of which has been extended under section 6162, but not including an amount the time for payment of which has been extended under section 6164) which is due and payable on or after the date of the allowance of the decrease.

(2) In case the unpaid amount of tax includes more than one of such amounts, the district director, or director of a service center in his discretion, shall determine against which amount or amounts, and in what proportion, the decrease is to be applied. In general, however, the decrease will be applied against any amounts described in subparagraph (1)(i), (ii), and (iii) of this paragraph in the order named. If there are several amounts of the type described in subparagraph (1)(iii) of this paragraph, any amount of the decrease which is to be applied against such amount will be applied by assuming that the tax previously determined minus the amount of the decrease to be so applied is "the tax" and that the taxpayer had elected to pay such tax in installments. The unpaid amount of tax against which a decrease may be applied under subparagraph (1) of this paragraph may not include any amount of tax for any taxable year other than the year of the decrease. After making such application, such internal revenue officer will credit any remainder of the decrease against any unsatisfied amount of any tax for the taxable year immediately preceding the taxable year of the net operating loss, capital loss, unused investment credit, or unused WIN credit, the time for payment of which has been extended under section 6164.

(3) Any remainder of the decrease after such application and credits may, within the 90-day period, in the discretion of the district director or director of a service center, be credited against any tax or installment thereof then due from the taxpayer, and, if not so credited, shall be refunded to the taxpayer within such 90-day period.

○──▶ § 1.6411-4 (T.D. 6364, filed 2-13-59; republished in T.D. 6500, filed 11-25-60; amended by T.D. 7244, filed 12-29-72.) **Consolidated returns.**

For further rules applicable to affiliated groups in the case of tentative carryback adjustments, see § 1.1502-78.

○──▶ § 301.6411 **Statutory provisions; tentative carryback adjustments.** [Sec. 6411, IRC]

○──▶ § 301.6411-1 (T.D. 6119, filed 12-31-54; republished in T.D. 6498, filed 10-24-60.) **Tentative carryback adjustments.**

For regulations under section 6411, see §§ 1.6411-1 to 1.6411-4, inclusive, of this chapter (Income Tax Regulations).

○──▶ § 31.6413(a) **Statutory provisions; special rules applicable to certain employment taxes; adjustment of tax.** [Sec. 6413(a), IRC]

○──▶ § 31.6413(a)-1 (T.D. 6472, filed 6-22-60; republished in T.D. 6516, filed 12-19-60.) **Repayment by employer of tax erroneously collected from employee.**

(a) *Before employer files return*—(1) *Employee tax under the Federal Insurance Contributions Act or the Railroad Retirement Tax Act.* * * *

(2) *Income tax withheld from wages.* (i) If an employer—

Reg. § 31.6413(a)-1(a)(2)

24,366 (I.R.C.)   Reg. § 31.6413(a)-1(a)(2)   7-28-75

(a) During any return period collects from an employee more than the correct amount of tax under section 3402,

(b) Repays the amount of the overcollection to the employee before the return for such period is filed with the district director and before the end of the calendar year in which the overcollection was made, and

(c) Obtains and keeps as part of his records the written receipt of the employee showing the date and amount of the repayment,

the employer shall not report on any return or pay to the district director the amount of the overcollection.

(ii) Any overcollection not repaid to and receipted for by the employee as provided in subdivision (i) of this subparagraph shall be reported and paid to the district director with the return for the return period in which the overcollection was made.

(b) *After employer files return*—(1) *Employee tax under the Federal Insurance Contributions Act or the Railroad Retirement Tax Act.* * * *

(2) *Income tax withheld from wages.* (i) If, in any return period in a calendar year, an employer collects from any employee more than the correct amount of tax under section 3402, and the employer pays the amount of such overcollection to the district director, the employer may repay or reimburse the employee in the amount thereof in any subsequent return period in such calendar year.

(ii) If the amount of the overcollection is repaid to the employee, the employer shall obtain and keep as part of his records the written receipt of the employee, showing the date and amount of the repayment. If the employer does not repay the amount of the overcollection, the employer may reimburse the employee by applying the amount of the overcollection against the tax under section 3402 which otherwise would be required to be withheld from wages paid by the employer to the employee in the calendar year in which the overcollection is made.

○━ § 31.6413(a)-2 (T.D. 6472, filed 6-22-60; republished in T.D. 6516, filed 12-19-60.) **Adjustment of overpayments.**

(a) *Taxes under the Federal Insurance Contributions Act or the Railroad Retirement Tax Act.* * * *

(b) *Income tax withheld from wages.* If, pursuant to paragraph (b)(2) of § 31.6413 (a)-1, an employer repays or reimburses an employee in the amount of an overcollection of tax under section 3402, the employer may adjust the overcollection, without interest, by entering the amount thereof as a deduction on a return of tax under section 3402, filed by the employer for any return period in the calendar year in which the employer repays or reimburses the employee. The return on which the adjustment is entered as a deduction shall have attached thereto a statement explaining the adjustment, designating the return period in which the error occurred, and setting forth such other information as is required by the regulations in this subpart and by the instructions relating to the return.

○━ § 31.6413(b) **Statutory provisions; special rules applicable to certain employment taxes; overpayments of certain employment taxes.** [Sec. 6413(b), IRC]

○━ § 31.6413(b)-1 (T.D. 6472, filed 6-22-60; republished in T.D. 6516, filed 12-19-60.) **Overpayments of certain employment taxes.**

For provisions relating to the adjustment of overpayments of tax imposed by section 3101, 3111, 3201, 3221, or 3402, see § 31.6413(a)-2. For provisions relating to refunds of tax imposed by section 3101, 3111, 3201, or 3221, see §§ 31.6402(a)-1 and 31.6402(a)-2. For provisions relating to refunds of tax imposed by section 3402, see §§ 31.6402(a)-1 and 31.6414-1.

○━ § 31.6413(c) **Statutory provisions; special rules applicable to certain employment taxes; special refunds.** [Sec. 6413(c), IRC]

○━ § 31.6413(c)-1 (T.D. 6472, filed 6-22-60; republished in T.D. 6516, filed 12-19-60; amended by T.D. 6950, filed 4-3-68; T.D. 6983, filed 12-3-68 and T.D. 7374, filed 7-23-75.) **Special refunds.**

(a) *Who may make claims*—(1) *In general.*

(i) If an employee receives wages, as defined in section 3121(a), from two or more employers in any calendar year:

(a) After 1954 and before 1959 in excess of $4,200,

(b) After 1958 and before 1966 in excess of $4,800,

(c) After 1965 and before 1968 in excess of $6,600,

(d) After 1967 and before 1972 in excess of $7,800,

(e) After 1971 and before 1973 in excess of $9,000,

(f) After 1972 and before 1974 in excess of $10,800,

(g) After 1973 and before 1975 in excess of $13,200, or

(h) After 1974 in excess of the contribution and benefit base (as determined under section 230 of the Social Security Act) which is effective with respect to such year,

the employee shall be entitled to a special refund of the amount, if any, by which the employee tax imposed by section 3101 with respect to such wages and deducted therefrom (whether or not paid) exceeds the employee tax with respect to the amount specified in (a) through (h) of this subdivision for the calendar year in question. Employee tax imposed by section 3101 with respect to tips reported by an employee to his employer and collected by the employer from funds turned over by the employee to the employer (see section 3102(c)) shall be treated, for purposes of this paragraph, as employee tax deducted from wages received by the employee. If the employee is required to file an income tax return for such calendar year (or for his last taxable year beginning in such calendar year) he may obtain the benefit of the special refund only by claiming credit as provided in § 1.31-2 of this chapter (Income Tax Regulations).

(ii) The application of this subparagraph may be illustrated by the following examples:

Example (1). Employee A in the calendar year 1968 receives taxable wages in the amount of $5,000 from each of his employers, B, C, and D, for services performed during such year (or at any time after 1936), or a total of $15,000. Employee tax (computed at 4.4 percent, the aggregate employee tax rate in effect in 1968) is deducted from A's wages in the amount of $220 by B and $220 by C, or a total of $440. Employer D pays employee tax in the amount of $220 without deducting such tax from A's wages. The employee tax with respect to the first $7,800 of such wages is $343.20. A is entitled to a special refund of $96.80 ($440 minus $343.20). The $5,000 of wages received from employer D and the $220 of employee tax paid with respect thereto have no bearing in computing A's special refund since such tax was not deducted from his wages.

Example (2). Employee E in the calendar year 1968 performs services for employers F and G, for which E is entitled to wages of $7,800 from each employer, or a total of $15,600. On account of such services, E in 1967 received an advance payment of $1,800 of wages from F; and in 1968, receives wages in the amount of $6,000 from F and $7,800 from G. Employee tax was deducted as follows: In 1967, $79.20 ($1,800 × 4.4%, the aggregate employee tax rate in effect in 1967) by employer F; and in 1968, $264.00 ($6,000 × 4.4%, the aggregate employee tax rate in effect in 1968) by employer F, and $343.20 ($7,800 × 4.4%) by employer G. Thus, E in the calendar year 1968 received $13,800 in wages from which $607.20 of employee tax was deducted. The amount of employee tax with respect to the first $7,800 of such wages received in 1968 is $343.20. E is entitled to a special refund of $264.00 ($607.20 minus $343.20). The $1,800 advance of wages received in 1967 from F, and the $79.20 of employee tax with respect thereto, have no bearing in computing E's special refund for 1968, because the wages were not received in 1968. Such amounts could not form the basis for a special refund unless E during 1967 received from F and at least one more employer wages totaling more than $6,600.

(2) *Federal employees.* For purposes of special refunds of employee tax, each head of a Federal agency or of a wholly-owned instrumentality of the United States who makes a return pursuant to section 3122 (and each agent designated by a head of a Federal agency or instrumentality who makes a return pursuant to such section) is considered a separate employer. For such purposes, the term "wages" includes the amount which each such head (or agent) determines to constitute wages paid an employee, but not in excess of the amount specified in subparagraph (1)(i)(a) through (h) of this paragraph for the calendar year in question. For example, if wages received by an employee during calendar year 1974 are reportable by two or more agents of one or more Federal agencies and the amount of such wages is in excess of $13,200 the employee shall be entitled to a special refund of the amount, if any, by which the employee tax imposed with respect to such wages and deducted therefrom exceeds the employee tax with respect to the first $13,200 of such wages. Moreover, if an employee receives wages during any calendar year from an agency or wholly-owned instrumentality of the United States and from one or more other employers, either private or governmental, the total amount of such wages shall be taken into account for purposes of the special refund provisions.

(3) *State employees.* For purposes of special refunds of employee tax, the term "wages" includes such remuneration for services covered by an agreement made pursuant to section 218 of the Social Security Act, relating to voluntary agreements for coverage of employees of State and local governments, as would be wages if such services constituted employment (see § 31.3121(a)-1 relating to wages); the term "employer" includes a State or any political subdivision thereof, or any instrumentality of any one or more of the foregoing; and the term "tax" or "tax imposed by section 3101" includes an amount equivalent to the employee tax which would be imposed by section 3101 if such services constituted employment. The provisions of subparagraph (1) of this paragraph are applicable whether or not any amount deducted from an employee's remuneration as a result of an agreement made pursuant to section 218 of the Social Security Act has been paid pursuant to such agreement. Thus, the special refund provisions are applicable to amounts equivalent to employee tax deducted from employees' remuneration by States, political subdivisions, or instrumentalities by reason of agreements made under section 218 of the Social Security Act. Moreover, if during any calendar year an employee receives remuneration for services covered by such an agreement and during the same calendar year receives wages from one or more other employers, either private or governmental, the total amount of such remuneration and wages shall be taken into account for purposes of the special refund provisions.

(4) *Employees of certain foreign corporations.* For purposes of special refunds of employee tax, the term "wages" includes such remuneration for services covered by an agreement made pursuant to section 3121 (l), relating to agreements for coverage of employees of certain foreign corporations, as would be wages if such services constituted employment (see § 31.-3121(a)-1 relating to wages); the term "employer" includes any domestic corporation which has entered into an agreement pursuant to section 3121 (l); and the term "tax" or "tax imposed by section 3101" includes, in the case of services covered by an agreement entered into pursuant to section 3121(l), an amount equivalent to the employee tax which would be imposed by section 3101 if such services constituted employment. The provisions of subparagraph (1) of this paragraph are applicable whether or not any amount deducted from the employee's remuneration by reason of such agreement has been paid to the district director. Thus, the special refund provisions are applicable to amounts equivalent to employee tax deducted from employees' remuneration by reason of agreements made under section 3121(l). A domestic corporation which enters into an agreement pursuant to section 3121(l) shall, for purposes of this paragraph, be considered an employer in its capacity as a party to such agreement separate and distinct from its identity as an employer employing individuals on its own account (see section 3121(l)(9)). If during any calendar year an employee receives re-

Reg. § 31.6413(c)-1(a)(4)

muneration for services covered by such an agreement and during the same calendar year receives wages for services in employment, the total amount of such remuneration and wages shall be taken into account for purposes of the special refund provisions. For provisions relating to agreements entered into under section 3121(l), see the regulations in Part 36 of this chapter (Regulations on Contract Coverage of Employees of Foreign Subsidiaries).

(5) *Governmental employees in American Samoa.* For purposes of special refunds of employee tax, the Governor of American Samoa and each agent designated by him who makes a return pursuant to section 3125(b) (see § 31.3125) is considered a separate employer. For such purposes, the term "wages" includes the amount which the Governor (or any agent) determines to constitute wages paid an employee, but not in excess of the amount specified in subparagraph (1)(i)(a) through (h) of this paragraph for the calendar year in question. For example, if wages received by an employee during calendar year 1974 are reportable by two or more agents pursuant to section 3125(b) and the total amount of such wages is in excess of $13,200, the employee shall be entitled to a special refund of the amount, if any, by which the employee tax imposed with respect to such wages and deducted therefrom exceeds the employee tax with respect to the first $13,200 of such wages. Moreover, if an employee receives wages during any calendar year from the Government of American Samoa, from a political subdivision thereof, or from any wholly-owned instrumentality of such government or political subdivision and from one or more other employers, either private or governmental, the total amount of such wages shall be taken into account for purposes of the special refund provisions.

(6) *Governmental employees in the District of Columbia.* For purposes of special refunds of employee tax, the Commissioner of the District of Columbia (or, prior to the transfer of functions pursuant to Reorganization Plan No. 3 of 1967 (81 Stat. 948), the Commissioners of the District of Columbia) and each agent designated by him who makes a return pursuant to section 3125(c) (see § 31.3125) is considered a separate employer. For such purposes, the term "wages" includes the amount which the Commissioner (or any agent) determines to constitute wages paid an employee, but not in excess of the amount specified in subparagraph (1)(i)(a) through (h) of this paragraph for the calendar year in question. For example, if wages received by an employee during calendar year 1974 are reportable by two or more agents pursuant to section 3125(c) and the total amount of such wages is in excess of $13,200 the employee shall be entitled to a special refund of the amount, if any, by which the employee tax imposed with respect to such wages and deducted therefrom exceeds the employee tax with respect to the first $13,200 of such wages. Moreover, if an employee receives wages during any calendar year from the Government of the District of Columbia or from a wholly-owned instrumentality thereof and from one or more other employers, either private or governmental, the total amount of such wages shall be taken into account for purposes of the special refund provisions.

(b) *Claims for special refund*—(1) *In general.* An employee who is entitled to a special refund under section 6413(c) may claim such refund under the provisions of this section only if the employee is not entitled to claim the amount thereof as a credit against income tax as provided in § 1.31-2 of this chapter (Income Tax Regulations). Each claim under this section shall be made with respect to wages received within one calendar year (regardless of the year or years after 1936 during which the services were performed for which such wages are received), and shall be filed after the close of such year.

(2) *Form of claim.* Each claim for special refund under this section shall be made on Form 843, in accordance with the regulations in this subpart and the instructions relating to such form. In the case of a claim filed prior to April 15, 1968, the claim shall be filed with the district director for the internal revenue district in which the employee resides or, if the employee does not reside in any internal revenue district, with the District Director, Baltimore, Maryland 21202. Except as provided in paragraph (b) of § 301.6091-1 (relating to hand-carried documents), in the case of a claim filed after April 14, 1968, the claim shall be filed with the service center serving such internal revenue district. However, in the case of an employee who does not reside in any internal revenue district and who is outside the United States, the claim shall be filed with the Director of International Operations, U.S. Internal Revenue Service, Washington, D.C. 20225, unless the employee resides in Puerto Rico or the Virgin Islands, in which case the claim shall be filed with the Director of International Operations, U.S. Internal Revenue Service, Hato Rey, Puerto Rico 00917. The claim shall include the employee's account number and the following information with respect to each employer from whom he received wages during the calendar year: (i) The name and address of such employer, (ii) the amount of wages received during the calendar year to which the claim relates, and (iii) the amount of employee tax collected by the employer from the employee with respect to such wages. Other information may be required but should be submitted only upon request.

(3) *Period of limitation.* For the period of limitation upon special refund of employee tax imposed by section 3101, see § 301.6511(a)-1 of this chapter (Regulations on Procedure and Administration).

(c) *Special refunds with respect to compensation as defined in the Railroad Retirement Tax Act*—(1) *In general.* In the case of any individual who, during any calendar year after 1967, receives wages (as defined by section 3121(a)) from one or more employers and also receives compensation (as defined by section 3231 (e)) which is subject to the tax imposed on employees by section 3201 or the tax imposed on employee representatives by section 3211 such compensation shall, solely for purposes of applying section 6413(c)(1) and this section with respect to the hospital insurance tax imposed by section 3101(b), be treated as wages (as defined by section 3121(a)) received from an employer with respect to which the hospital insurance tax imposed by section 3101(b) was deducted. For purposes of this section, compensation received shall be determined under the principles provided in chapter 22 of the Code and the regulations thereunder (see section 3231(e) and § 31.-3231(e)-1). Therefore, compensation paid for time lost shall be deemed earned and received for purposes of this section in the month in which such time is lost, and compensation which is earned during the period for which a return of taxes under chapter 22 is required to be made and which is payable during the calendar month following such period shall be deemed to have been received for purposes of this section during such period only. Further, compensation is deemed to have been earned and received when an employee or employee representative performs services for which he is paid, or for which there is a present or future obligation to pay, regardless of the time at which payment is made or deemed to be made.

(2) *Example.* The application of this paragraph may be illustrated by the following example.

Example. Employee A rendered services to X during 1973 for which he was paid compensation at the monthly rate of $650 which was taxable under the Railroad Retirement Tax Act. A was paid $550 by X in January 1973 which was earned and deemed received in December 1972 and $650 in January of 1974 which was earned and deemed received in December of 1973. A also earned and received wages in 1973 from employer Y, which were subject to the employee tax under the Federal Insurance Contributions Act, in the amount of $6,000. A paid hospital insurance tax on $13,800 ($7,800 compensation from X including $650 earned and deemed received in December 1973 but paid in January 1974 and not including $550 paid in January 1973 but earned and deemed received in December 1972, $6,000 compensation from Y) received or deemed received or earned in 1973. For purposes of the hospital insurance tax imposed by section 3101(b), these amounts are all wages received from an employer in 1973. Therefore, A is entitled to a special refund for 1973 under section 6413(c) and this section of $30 (1.0% × $13,800 − 1.0% × $10,800).

○— § 31.6413(d) **Statutory provisions; special rules applicable to certain employment taxes; refund or credit of Federal unemployment tax.** [Sec. 6413(d), IRC]

○— § 301.6413 **Statutory provisions; special rules applicable to certain employment taxes.** [Sec. 6413, IRC]

○— § 301.6413-1 (T.D. 6498, filed 10-24-60.) **Special rules applicable to certain employment taxes.**

For regulations under section 6413, see §§ 31.6413(a)-1 to 31.6413(c)-1, inclusive, of this chapter (Employment Tax Regulations).

○— § 1.6414 **Statutory provisions; income tax withheld.** [Sec. 6414, IRC]

○— § 1.6414-1 (T.D. 6922, filed 6-16-67.) **Credit or refund of tax withheld or nonresident aliens and foreign corporations.**

(a) *In general.* Any withholding agent who for the calendar year pays more than the correct amount of—

(1) Tax required to be withheld under chapter 3 of the Code, or

(2) Interest, addition to the tax, additional amount, or penalty with respect to such tax,

may file a claim for credit or refund of the overpayment in the manner and subject to the conditions stated in the Procedure and Administration Regulations (Part 301 of this chapter) under section 6402, or may claim credit for the overpayment as provided in paragraph (b) of this section.

(b) *Claim for credit on Form 1042.* The withholding agent may claim credit of an overpayment described in paragraph (a) of this section for any calendar year by showing the amount of overpayment on the return on Form 1042 for such calendar year, which shall constitute a claim for credit under this paragraph. The claim for credit shall be evidenced by a statement on the return setting forth the amount determined as an overpayment and showing such other information as may be required by the instructions relating to the return. The amount so claimed as a credit may be applied, to the extent it has not been applied under paragraph (b) of § 1.1461-4, by the withholding agent to reduce the amount of a payment or deposit of tax required by § 1.1461-3 or paragraph (a) of § 1.6302-2 for any payment period occurring in the calendar year following the calendar year of overwithholding. The amount so claimed as a credit shall also be entered on the annual return on Form 1042 for the calendar year following the calendar year of overwithholding and shall be applied as a payment on account of the tax shown on such form. If the withholding agent files a claim for credit or refund of the overpayment on Form 843 in accordance with § 301.6402-2 of this chapter (Procedure and Administration Regulations), or a claim for refund of the overpayment on Form 1042 in accordance with § 301.6402-3 of such chapter, he may not claim credit for the overpayment under this paragraph.

(c) *Overpayment of amounts actually withheld.* No credit or refund to the withholding agent shall be allowed for the amount of any overpayment of tax which, after taking into account paragraph (b) of § 1.1464-1, the withholding agent has actually withheld from an item of income under chapter 3 of the Code.

○— § 31.6414 **Statutory provisions; income tax withheld.** [Sec. 6414, IRC].

○— § 31.6414-1 (T.D. 6472, filed 6-22-60; republished in T.D. 6516, filed 12-19-60.) **Credit or refund of income tax withheld from wages.**

(a) *In general.* Any employer who pays to the district director more than the correct amount of—

(1) Tax under section 3402 or a corresponding provision of prior law, or

(2) Interest, addition to the tax, additional amount, or penalty with respect to such tax,

may file a claim for refund of the overpayment or may claim credit for such overpayment, in the manner and subject to the conditions stated in this section and § 301.-6402-2 of this chapter (Regulations on Procedure and Administration). If credit is claimed pursuant to this section, the

Reg. § 31.6414-1(a)(2)

amount thereof shall be claimed by entering such amount as a deductiton on a return of tax under section 3402 filed by the employer: If credit is taken pursuant to this section, a claim on Form 843 is not required, but the return on which the credit is claimed shall have attached as a part thereof a statement, which shall constitute the claim for credit, setting forth in detail the grounds and facts relied upon in support of the credit, and showing such other information as is required by the regulations in this subpart and by the instructions relating to the return. No refund or credit to the employer shall be allowed under this section for the amount of any overpayment of tax which the employer deducted or withheld from an employee.

(b) *Period of limitation.* For the period of limitation upon credit or refund of taxes imposed by the Internal Revenue Code of 1954, see § 301.6511(a)-1 of this chapter (Regulations on Procedure and Administration). For the period of limitation upon credit or refund of any tax imposed by the Internal Revenue Code of 1939, see the regulations applicable with respect to such tax.

○━━ § 301.6414 Statutory provisions; income tax withheld. [Sec. 6414, IRC]

○━━ § 301.6414-1 (T.D. 6119, filed 12-31-54; republished in T.D. 6498, filed 10-24-60; amended by T.D. 6922, filed 6-16-67.) Income tax withheld.

(a) For rules relating to the refund or credit of income tax withheld under chapter 3 of the Code on nonresident aliens and foreign corporations and tax-free covenant bonds, see § 1.6414-1 of this chapter (Income Tax Regulations).

(b) For rules relating to the refund or credit of income tax withheld under chapter 24 of the Code from wages, see § 31.6414-1 of this chapter (Employment Tax Regulations).

○━━ § 1.6425 Statutory provisions; adjustment of overpayment of estimated income tax by corporation. [See 6425, IRC]

○━━ § 1.6425-1 (T.D. 7059, filed 9-16-70.) Adjustment of overpayment of estimated income tax by corporation.

(a) *In general.* Any corporation which has made an overpayment of estimated income tax for a taxable year beginning after December 31, 1967, may file an application for an adjustment of such overpayment. The right to file an application for an adjustment of overpayment of estimated income tax is limited to corporations.

(b) *Contents of application.* (1) The application for an adjustment of overpayment of estimated income tax shall be filed on Form 4466. The application shall be filled out in accordance with the instructions accompanying the form, and all information required by the form and instructions must be furnished by the corporation. The application shall be verified in the manner prescribed by section 6065 as in the case of a return of the corporation.

(2) An application for an adjustment of overpayment of estimated income tax does not constitute a claim for credit or refund. If such application is disallowed by the district director, or director of a service center, in whole or in part, no suit may be maintained in any court for the recovery of any tax based on such application. The filing of an application for an adjustment of overpayment of estimated income tax will not constitute the filing of a claim for credit or refund within the meaning of section 6511 for the purpose of determining whether a claim for refund was filed prior to the expiration of the applicable period of limitation. The corporation, however, may file a claim for credit or refund under section 6402 at any time prior to the expiration of the applicable period of limitation and may maintain a suit based on such claim if it is disallowed or if the district director, or director of a service center, does not act on the claim within six months from the date it is filed. Such claim may be filed before, simultaneously with, or after the filing of the application for the adjustment of overpayment of estimated tax. A claim for credit or refund under section 6402 filed after the filing of an application for an adjustment of overpayment of estimated income tax is not to be considered an amendment of such application. Such claim, however, in proper cases; may constitute an amendment to a prior claim filed under section 6402.

(c) *Time and place for filing application.* (1) The application for an adjustment of overpayment of estimated income tax shall be filed after the last day of the taxable year and on or before the fifteenth day of the third month thereafter, or before the date on which the corporation first files its income tax return for such taxable year (whether or not it subsequently amends the return), whichever is earlier.

(2) Except as provided in paragraph (b)(2) of § 301.6091-1 (relating to hand-carried documents), the application on Form 4466 shall be filed with the internal revenue officer designated in instructions applicable to such form.

○━━ § 1.6425-2 (T.D. 7059, filed 9-16-70.) Computation of adjustment of overpayment of estimated tax.

(a) *Income tax liability defined.* For purposes of §§ 1.6425-1 through 1.6425-3 and § 1.6655-5, relating to excessive adjustment, the term "income tax liability" means the excess of—

(1) The tax imposed by section 11 or 1201 (a), or subchapter L of chapter 1 of the Code, whichever is applicable, over

(2) The credits against tax provided by part IV of subchapter A of chapter 1 of the Code.

(b) *Computation of adjustment.* The amount of an adjustment under section 6425 is an amount equal to the excess of the estimated income tax paid by the corporation during the taxable year over the amount which, at the time of filing Form 4466, the corporation estimates as its income tax liability for the taxable year.

○━━ § 1.6425-3 (T.D. 7059, filed 9-16-70.) Allowance of adjustments.

(a) *Limitation.* No application under section 6425 shall be allowed unless the amount of the adjustment is (1) at least 10 percent of the amount which, at the time of filing Form 4466 the corporation estimates as its income tax liability for the taxable year, and (2) at least $500.

(b) *Time prescribed.* The Internal Revenue Service shall act upon an application for an adjustment of overpayment of estimated income tax within a period of 45 days from the date on which such application is filed.

(c) *Examination.* Within the 45-day period described in paragraph (b) of this section, the Internal Revenue Service shall make, to the extent it deems practicable in such period, a limited examination of the application to discover omissions and errors therein. The Service shall verify the calculation of the adjustment, which calculation must be set forth by the corporation in the application for such adjustment, in the manner provided in Section 6425(c)(2) for the determination by the corporation of such adjustment. The Service, however, may correct any material error or omission that is discovered upon examination of the application. In determining the adjustment, the Service may correct any mathematical error appearing on the application, and it may likewise make any modification required by the law to correct the corporation's computation of the adjustment. If the required modification has not been made by the corporation and the Service has available the necessary information to make such modification within the 45-day period, it may make such modification. The examination of the application and the allowance of the adjustment shall not prejudice any right of the Service to claim later that the adjustment was improper.

(d) *Disallowance in whole or in part.* If the Internal Revenue Service finds that an application for an adjustment of overpayment of estimated tax contains material omissions or errors, the Service may disallow such application in whole or in part without further action. If, however, the Service deems that any omission or error can be corrected by it within the 45-day period, it may do so and allow the application in whole or in part. In the case of a disallowance or modification, the service shall notify the corporation of such action. The Service's determination as to whether it can correct any omission or error shall be conclusive. Similarly, its action in disallowing, in whole or in part, any application for an adjustment of overpayment of estimated income tax shall be final and may not be challenged in any proceeding. The corporation in such case, however, may file a claim for credit or refund under section 6402, and may maintain a suit based on such claim if it is disallowed or if the Service does not

Reg. § 1.6425-3(d)

act upon the claim within six months from the date it is filed.

(e) *Application of adjustment.* If the Internal Revenue Service allows the adjustment, it may first credit the amount of the adjustment against any liability in respect of an internal revenue tax on the part of the corporation which is due and payable on the date of the allowance of the adjustment before making payment of the balance to the corporation. In such a case, the Service shall notify the corporation of the credit, and refund the balance of the adjustment.

(f) *Effect of adjustment*—(1) For purposes of all sections of the Code except section 6655, relating to additions to tax for failure to pay estimated income tax, any adjustment under section 6425 is to be treated as a reduction of prior estimated tax payments as of the date the credit is allowed or the refund is paid. For the purpose of section 6655 (a) through (f) credit or refund of an adjustment is to be treated as if not made in determining whether there has been any underpayment of estimated income tax and, if there is an underpayment, the period during which the underpayment existed. However, an excessive adjustment under section 6425 shall be taken into account in applying the addition to tax under section 6655 (g).

(2) *Excessive adjustment.* For the effect of an excessive adjustment under section 6425, see § 1.6655-5.

○→ § 301.6425 **Statutory provisions; adjustment of overpayment of estimated income tax by corporation.** [Sec. 6425, IRC]

○→ § 301.6425-1 (T.D. 7059, filed 9-16-70.) **Adjustment of overpayment of estimated income tax by corporation.**

For regulations under section 6425, see §§ 1.6425-1 to 1.6425-3, inclusive, of this chapter (Income Tax Regulations).

○→ § 1.6428 **Statutory provisions; refund of 1974 individual income taxes.** [Sec. 6428, IRC]

LIMITATIONS
LIMITATIONS ON ASSESSMENT AND COLLECTION

○→ § 301.6501(a) **Statutory provisions; limitations on assessment and collection; general rule.** [Sec. 6501(a), IRC]

○→ § 301.6501(a)-1 (T.D. 6172, filed 5-2-56, as amended by T.D. 6425, filed 11-10-59; republished in T.D. 6498, filed 10-24-60.) **Period of limitations upon assessment and collection.**

(a) The amount of any tax imposed by the Code (other than a tax collected by means of stamps) shall be assessed within 3 years after the return was filed. For rules applicable in cases where the return is filed prior to the due date thereof, see section 6501(b). In the case of taxes payable by stamp, assessment shall be made at any time after the tax became due and before the expiration of 3 years after the date on which any part of the tax was paid. For exceptions and additional rules, see subsections (b) to (g) of section 6501, and for cross references to other provisions relating to limitations on assessment and collection, see sections 6501(h) and 6504.

(b) No proceeding in court without assessment for the collection of any tax shall be begun after the expiration of the applicable period for the assessment of such tax.

○→ § 301.6501(b) **Statutory provisions; limitations on assessment and collection; time return deemed filed.** [Sec. 6501(b), IRC]

○→ § 301.6501(b)-1 (T.D. 6172, filed 5-2-56; republished in T.D. 6498, filed 10-24-60; amended by T.D. 6922, filed 6-16-67.) **Time return deemed filed for purposes of determining limitations.**

(a) *Early return.* Any return, other than a return of tax referred to in paragraph (b) of this section, filed before the last day prescribed by law or regulations for the filing thereof (determined without regard to any extension of time for filing) shall be considered as filed on such last day.

(b) *Returns of social security tax and of income tax withholding.* If a return on or after November 13, 1966, of tax imposed by chapter 3 of the Code (relating to withholding of tax on nonresident aliens and foreign corporations and tax-free covenant bonds), or if a return of tax imposed by chapter 21 of the Code (relating to the Federal Insurance Contributions Act) or by chapter 24 of the Code (relating to collection of income tax at source on wages), for any period ending with or within a calendar year is filed before April 15 of the succeeding calendar year, such return shall be deemed filed on April 15 of such succeeding calendar year. For example, if quarterly returns of the tax imposed by chapter 24 of the Code are filed for the four quarters of 1955 on April 30, July 31, and October 31, 1955, and on January 31, 1956, the period of limitation for assessment with respect to the tax required to be reported on such return is measured from April 15, 1956. However, if any of such returns is filed after April 15, 1956, the period of limitation for assessment of the tax required to be reported on that return is measured from the date it is in fact filed.

(c) *Returns executed by district directors or other internal revenue officers.* The execution of a return by a district director or other authorized internal revenue officer or employee under the authority of section 6020(b) shall not start the running of the statutory period of limitations on assessment and collection.

○→ § 301.6501(c) **Statutory provisions; limitations on assessment and collection; exceptions.** [Sec. 6501(c), IRC]

○→ § 301.6501(c)-1 (T.D. 6172, filed 5-2-56; republished in T.D. 6498, filed 10-24-60.) **Exceptions to general period of limitations on assessment and collection.**

(a) *False return.* In the case of a false or fraudulent return with intent to evade any tax, the tax may be assessed, or a proceeding in court for the collection of such tax may be begun without assessment, at any time after such false or fraudulent return is filed.

(b) *Willful attempt to evade tax.* In the case of a willful attempt in any man-

Reg. § 301.6501(c)-1(b)

ner to defeat or evade any tax imposed by the Code (other than a tax imposed by subtitle A or B, relating to income, estate, or gift taxes), the tax may be assessed, or a proceeding in court for the collection of such tax may be begun without assessment, at any time.

(c) *No return.* In the case of a failure to file a return, the tax may be assessed, or a proceeding in court for the collection of such tax may be begun without assessment, at any time after the date prescribed for filing the return.

(d) *Extension by agreement.* The time prescribed by section 6501 for the assessment of any tax (other than the estate tax imposed by chapter 11 of the Code) may, prior to the expiration of such time, be extended for any period of time agreed upon in writing by the taxpayer and the district director or any assistant regional commissioner. The extension shall become effective when the agreement has been executed by both parties. The period agreed upon may be extended by subsequent agreements in writing made before the expiration of the period previously agreed upon.

○— § 301.6501(d) Statutory provisions; limitations on assessment and collection; request for prompt assessment. [Sec. 6501 (d), IRC]

○— § 301.6501(d)-1 (T.D. 6172, filed 5-2-56, as amended by T.D. 6425, filed 11-10-59; republished in T.D. 6498, filed 10-24-60.) Request for prompt assessment.

(a) Except as otherwise provided in section 6501 (c), (e), or (f), any tax for which a return is required and for which:

(1) A decedent or an estate of a decedent may be liable, other than the estate tax imposed by chapter 11 of the Code or,

(2) A corporation which is contemplating dissolution, is in the process of dissolution, or has been dissolved may be liable,

shall be assessed, or a proceeding in court without assessment for the collection of such tax shall be begun, within 18 months after the receipt of a written request for prompt assessment thereof.

(b) The executor, administrator, or other fiduciary representing the estate of the decedent, or the corporation or the fiduciary representing the dissolved corporation, as the case may be, shall, after the return in question has been filed, file the request for prompt assessment in writing with the district director for the internal revenue district in which such return was filed. The request, in order to be effective, must be transmitted separately from any other document, must set forth the classes of tax and the taxable periods for which the prompt assessment is requested, and must clearly indicate that it is a request for prompt assessment under the provisions of section 6501(d). The effect of such a request is to limit the time in which an assessment of tax may be made, or a proceeding in court without assessment for collection of tax may be begun, to a period of 18 months from the date the request is filed with the proper district director. The request does not extend the time within which an assessment may be made, or a proceeding in court without assessment may be begun, beyond 3 years from the date the return was filed. This special period of limitations will not apply to any return filed after a request for prompt assessment has been made unless an additional request is filed in the manner provided herein.

(c) In the case of a corporation the 18-month period shall not apply unless:

(1) The written request notifies the district director that the corporation contemplates dissolution at or before the expiration of such 18-month period; the dissolution is in good faith begun before the expiration of such 18-month period; and the dissolution so begun is completed either before or after the expiration of such 18-month period; or

(2) The written request notifies the district director that a dissolution has in good faith been begun, and the dissolution is completed either before or after the expiration of such 18-month period; or

(3) A dissolution has been completed at the time the written request is made.

○— § 301.6501(e) Statutory provisions; limitations on assessment and collection; substantial omission of items. [Sec. 6501, (e), IRC]

○— § 301.6501(e)-1 (T.D. 6172, filed 5-2-56; republished in T.D. 6498, filed 10-24-60; amended by T.D. 7238, filed 12-28-72). Omission from return.

(a) *Income taxes*—(1) *General rule.* (i) If the taxpayer omits from the gross income stated in the return of a tax imposed by subtitle A of the Code an amount properly includible therein which is in excess of 25 percent of the gross income so stated, the tax may be assessed, or a proceeding in court for the collection of such tax may be begun without assessment, at any time within 6 years after the return was filed.

(ii) For purposes of this subparagraph, the term "gross income", as it relates to a trade or business, means the total of the amounts received or accrued from the sale of goods or services, to the extent required to be shown on the return without reduction for the cost of such sales or services. An item shall not be considered as omitted from gross income if information, sufficient to apprise the district director of the nature and amount of such item, is disclosed in the return or in any schedule or statement attached to the return.

(2) *Constructive dividends.* If a taxpayer omits from gross income an amount properly includible therein under section 551(b) as his distributive share of the undistributed foreign personal holding company income, the tax may be assessed, or a proceeding in court for the collection of such tax may be begun without assessment, at any time within 6 years after the return was filed.

(b) *Estate and gift taxes.* (1) If the taxpayer omits from the gross estate as stated in the estate tax return, or from the total amount of the gifts made during the period for which the gift tax return was filed (see § 25.6019-1) as stated in such return, an item or items properly includible therein the amount of which is in excess of 25 percent of the gross estate as stated in the return, or 25 percent of the total amount of the gifts as stated in the returns, the tax may be assessed or a proceeding in court for the collection thereof may be begun without assessment, at any time within 6 years after the return was filed.

(2) For purposes of this paragraph, an item disclosed in the return or in any schedule or statement attached to the return in a manner sufficient to apprise the district director of the nature and amount thereof shall not be taken into account in determining items omitted from the gross estate or total gifts, as the case may be. Further, there shall not be taken into account in computing the 25 percent omission from the gross estate stated in the estate tax return or from the total gifts stated in the gift tax return, any increases in the valuation of assets disclosed on the return.

(c) *Exception.* The provisions of this section do not limit the application of section 6501(c).

O— § 301.6501(f) Statutory provisions; limitations on assessment and collection; personal holding company tax. [Sec. 6501(f), IRC]

O— § 301.6501(f)-1 (T.D. 6172, filed 5-2-56; republished in T.D. 6498, filed 10-24-60). **Personal holding company tax.**

If a corporation which is a personal holding company for any taxable year fails to file with its income tax return for such year a schedule setting forth the items of gross income described in section 543(a) received by the corporation during such year, and the names and addresses of the individuals who owned, within the meaning of section 544, at any time during the last half of such taxable year, more than 50 percent in value of the outstanding capital stock of the corporation, the personal holding company tax for such year may be assessed, or a proceeding in court for the collection thereof may be begun without assessment, at any time within 6 years after the return for such year was filed.

O— § 301.6501(g)-1 (T.D. 6172, filed 5-2-56; republished in T.D. 6498, filed 10-24-60; amended by T.D. 7533, filed 2-14-78.) **Certain income tax returns of corporations.**

(a) *Trusts or partnerships.* If a taxpayer determines in good faith that it is a trust or partnership and files a return as such under subtitle A of the Code, and if the taxpayer is later held to be a corporation for the taxable year for which the return was filed, such return shall be deemed to be the return of the corporation for the purpose of section 6501.

(b) *Exempt organizations.* If a taxpayer determines in good faith that it is an exempt organization and files a return as such under section 6033, and if the taxpayer is later held to be a taxable organization for the taxable year for which the return was filed, such return shall be deemed to be the return of the organization for the purpose of section 6501.

(c) *DISC.* If a corporation determines in good faith that it is a DISC (as defined in section 992(a)(1)) for a taxable year and files a return as such pursuant to section 6011(c)(2), and if the corporation is thereafter held to be a corporation which is not a DISC for the taxable year for which the return was filed, then—

(1) Such return shall be deemed to be the return of the corporation for the purpose of section 6501,

(2) Such return if filed within the time required by section 6072(b) for filing a DISC return shall be deemed to be filed within the time required by section 6072(b) for filing of a return by a corporation which is not a DISC, and

(3) Interest on underpayment and overpayments allowed by chapter 67 of the Code and additions to the tax, additional amounts and assessable penalties allowed by chapter 68 of the Code, when determined by reference to the time for filing of a return, shall be determined by reference to the time required by section 6072(b) for filing of a return by a DISC.

O— § 301.6501(h) Statutory provisions; limitations on assessment and collection; net operating loss carrybacks. [Sec. 6501(h), IRC]

O— § 301.6501(h)-1 (T.D. 6425, filed 11-10-59; republished in T.D. 6498, filed 10-24-60; amended by T.D. 6730, filed 5-7-64 and T.D. 7301, filed 1-3-74.) **Net operating loss or capital loss carrybacks.**

In the case of a deficiency attributable to the application to the taxpayer of a net operating loss or capital loss carryback (including deficiencies which may be assessed pursuant to the provisions of section 6213(b)(2)), such deficiency may be assessed at any time before the expiration of the period within which a deficiency for the taxable year of the net operating loss or net capital loss which results in such carryback may be assessed. In the case of a deficiency attributable to the application of a net operating loss carryback, such deficiency may be assessed within 18 months after the date on which the taxpayer files in accordance with section 172(b)(3) a copy of the certification (with respect to such taxable year) issued under section 317 of the Trade Expansion Act of 1962, if later than the date prescribed by the preceding sentence.

O— § 301.6501(i) Statutory provisions; limitations on assessment and collection; foreign tax carrybacks. [Sec. 6501(i), IRC]

O— § 301.6501(i)-1 (T.D. 6555, filed 3-14-61.) **Foreign tax carrybacks; taxable year beginning after December 31, 1957.**

With respect to taxable years beginning after December 31, 1957, a deficiency attributable to the application to the taxpayer of a carryback under section 904(d) (relating to carryback and carryover of excess foreign taxes), may be assessed at any time before the expiration of one year after the expiration of the period within which a deficiency may be assessed for the taxable year of the excess taxes described in section 904(d) which result in such carryback.

O— § 301.6501(j) Statutory provisions; limitations on assessment and collection; investment credit carrybacks. [Sec. 6501(j), IRC]

O— § 301.6501(j)-1 (T.D. 6730, filed 5-7-64; amended by T.D. 7301, filed 1-3-74.) **Investment credit carryback; taxable years ending after December 31, 1961.**

With respect to taxable years ending after December 31, 1961, a deficiency attributable to the application to the taxpayer of an investment credit carryback may be assessed at any time before the expiration of the period within which a deficiency for the taxable year of the unused investment

Reg. § 301.6501(j)-1

24,372 (I.R.C.) Reg. § 301.6501(j)-1 2-21-78

credit which results in such carryback may be assessed, or, with respect to any portion of an investment credit carryback from a taxable year attributable to a net operating loss or capital loss carryback from a subsequent taxable year, at any time before the expiration of the period within which a deficiency for such subsequent taxable year may be assessed. For purposes of this section a deficiency shall include a deficiency which may be assessed pursuant to the provisions of section 6213(b)(2), but only those arising with respect to applications for tentative carryback adjustments filed after November 2, 1966.

○━▶ **§ 301.6501(k)** Statutory provisions; limitations on assessment and collection; reductions of policyholders surplus account of life insurance companies. [Sec. 6501(k), IRC]

○━▶ **§ 301.6501(l)** Statutory provisions; limitations on assessment and collection; joint income return after separate return. [Sec. 6501(l), IRC]

○━▶ **§ 301.6501(m)** Statutory provisions; limitations on assessment and collection; tentative carryback adjustment period. [Sec. 6501(m), IRC]

○━▶ **§ 301.6501(m)-1** (T.D. 7301, filed 1-3-74.) Tentative carryback adjustment assessment period.

(a) *Period of limitation after tentative carryback adjustment.* (1) Under section 6501(m), in a case where an amount has been applied, credited, or refunded under section 6411, by reason of a net operating loss carryback, a capital loss carryback, an investment credit carryback, or a work incentive program credit carryback to a prior taxable year, the period described in section 6501(a) of the Code for assessing a deficiency for such prior taxable year is extended to include the period described in section 6501(h), (j), or (o), whichever is applicable; except that the amount which may be assessed solely by reason of section 6501(m) may not exceed the amount so applied, credited, or refunded under section 6411, reduced by any amount which may be assessed solely by reason of section 6501(h), (j), or (o), as the case may be.

(2) The application of this paragraph may be illustrated by the following example:

Example. Assume that M Corporation, which claims an unused investment credit of $50,000 for the calendar year 1968, files an application under section 6411 of the Code for an adjustment of its tax for 1965, and receives a refund of $50,000 in 1969. In 1971, it is determined that the amount of the unused investment credit for 1968 is $30,000 rather than $50,000. Moreover, it is determined that M Corporation would have owed $40,000 of additional tax for 1965 if it had properly reported certain income which it failed to include in its 1965 return. Assuming that M Corporation filed its 1968 return on March 15, 1969, and that the 3-year period described in section 6501(a) has not been extended, the period prescribed in section 6501(j) for assessing the excessive amount refunded, $20,000 (i.e., $50,000, original amount refunded, less $30,000, correct amount of unused investment credit), does not expire until March 15, 1972, and $20,000 may be assessed on or before such date under section 6501(j). Under section 6501 (m), M Corporation may be assessed on or before March 15, 1972, an amount not in excess of $30,000 ($50,000, the amount refunded under section 6411, minus $20,000, the amount which may be assessed solely by reason of section 6501(j)).

(b) *Effective date.* The provisions of paragraph (a) of this section apply only with respect to applications under section 6411 filed after November 2, 1966.

○━▶ **§ 301.6501(o)** Statutory provisions; limitation on assessment and collection; work incentive program credit carrybacks. [Sec. 6501(o), IRC]

○━▶ **§ 301.6501(o)-1** (T.D. 7301, filed 1-3-74.) Work incentive program credit carrybacks, taxable years beginning after December 31, 1971.

With respect to taxable years beginning after December 31, 1971, a deficiency attributable to the application to the taxpayer of a work incentive program credit carryback (including deficiencies which may be assessed pursuant to the provisions of section 6213(b)(2)) may be assessed at any time before the expiration of the period within which a deficiency for the taxable year of the unused work incentive program credit which results in such carryback may be assessed, or, with respect to any portion of a work incentive program credit carryback from a taxable year attributable to a net operating loss or capital loss carryback from a subsequent taxable year, at any time before the expiration of the period within which a deficiency for such subsequent taxable year may be assessed.

○━▶ **§ 301.6502 Statutory provisions; collection after assessment.** [Sec. 6502, IRC]

○━▶ **§ 301.6502-1** (T.D. 6172, filed 5-2-56; republished in T.D. 6498, filed 10-24-60; and amended by T.D. 7305, filed 3-14-74.) Collection after assessment.

(a) *Length of period* — (1) *General rule.* In any case in which a tax has been assessed within the statutory period of limitation properly applicable thereto, a proceeding in court to collect such tax may be begun, or levy for the collection of such tax may be made, within 6 years after the assessment thereof.

(2) *Extension by agreement.* (i) The 6-year period of limitation on collection after assessment of any tax may, prior to the expiration thereof, be extended for any period of time agreed upon in writing by the taxpayer and the district director. The extension shall become effective upon execution of the agreement by both the taxpayer and the district director.

(ii) The period of limitation on collection after assessment of any tax (including any extension of such period) may be extended after the expiration thereof if there has been a levy on any part of the taxpayer's property prior to such expiration and if the extension is agreed upon in writing prior to a release of the levy under the provisions of section 6343. An extension under this subdivision has the same effect as an agreement made prior to the expiration of the period of limitation on collection after assessment, and during the period of the extension collection may be enforced as to all property or rights to property owned by the taxpayer whether or not seized under the levy which was released.

(iii) Any period agreed upon under the provisions of this subparagraph may be extended by subsequent agreements in writing made before the expiration of the period previously agreed upon.

(3) The period provided by section 6502(a) and this section shall not be extended or curtailed by reason of a judgement against a taxpayer. Therefore, a personal judgment rendered against a taxpayer arising out of an unpaid assessed tax liability will not extend the period during which the liability may be collected by levy. Similarly, the period during which the liability may be collected by levy is not curtailed by the fact that the United States secures such a judgment. For example, if the United States secures a personal judgment arising out of a tax liability assessed 4 years earlier, the liability may be collected in any manner provided by section 7403 or in any manner provided for the enforcement of a judgment or, during the remaining 2 years of the 6 year statutory period, by levy as if such judgment had not been secured.

(b) *Date when levy is considered made.* The date on which a levy on property or rights to property is made is the date on which the notice of seizure provided in section 6335(a) is given.

○━▶ § 301.6503(a) Statutory provisions; suspension of running of period of limitation; issuance of statutory notice of deficiency. [Sec. 6503(a), IRC]

○━▶ § 301.6503(a)-1 (T.D. 6172, filed 5-2-56; republished in T.D. 6498, filed 10-24-60; amended by T.D. 7244, filed 12-29-72.) Suspension of running of period of limitation; issuance of statutory notice of deficiency.

(a) *General rule.* Upon the mailing of a notice of deficiency for income, estate, or gift tax under the provisions of section 6212, the period of limitation on assessment and collection of any deficiency is suspended for 90 days if the notice of deficiency is addressed to a person within the States of the Union and the District of Columbia, or 150 days if such notice is addressed to a person outside the States of the Union and the District of Columbia (not counting Saturday, Sunday, or a legal holiday in the District of Columbia as the 90th or 150th day), plus an additional 60 days thereafter in either case. If a proceeding in respect of the deficiency is placed on the docket of the Tax Court, the period of limitations is suspended until the decision of the Tax Court becomes final, and for an additional 60 days thereafter. If a notice of deficiency is mailed to a taxpayer within the period of limitation and the taxpayer does not appeal therefrom to the Tax Court, the notice of deficiency so given does not suspend the running of the period of limitation with respect to any additional deficiency shown to be due in a subsequent deficiency notice.

Example. A taxpayer filed a return for the calendar year 1954 on April 15, 1955; the notice of deficiency was mailed to him (at an address within the United States) on April 15, 1958; and he filed a petition with the Tax Court on July 14, 1958. The decision of the Tax Court became final on November 6, 1959. The running of the period of limitation for assessment is suspended from April 15, 1958 to January 5, 1960, which date is 60 days after the date (November 6, 1959) on which the decision became final. If in this example the taxpayer had failed to file a petition with the Tax Court, the running of the period of limitation for assessment would then be suspended from April 15, 1958 (the date of notice), to September 12, 1958 (that is, for the 90-day period in which he could file a petition with the Tax Court, and for 60 days thereafter).

(b) *Corporations joining in consolidated return.* If a notice under section 6212(a) with respect to a deficiency in tax imposed by subtitle A of the Code for any taxable year is mailed to a corporation, the suspension of the running of the period of limitation provided in section 6503(a)(1) shall apply in the case of corporations with which such corporation made a consolidated income tax return for such taxable year. Under § 1.1502-77(a) of this chapter (Income Tax Regulations), relating to consolidated returns, notices of deficiency are mailed only to the common parent.

○━▶ § 301.6503(b) Statutory provisions; suspension of running of period of limitation; assets of taxpayer in control or custody of court. [Sec. 6503(b), IRC]

○━▶ § 301.6503(b)-1 (T.D. 6172, filed 5-2-56; republished in T.D. 6498, filed 10-24-60; amended by T.D. 7121, filed 6-2-71.) Suspension of running of period of limitation; assets of taxpayer in control or custody of court.

Where all or substantially all of the assets of a taxpayer are in the control or custody of the court in any proceeding before any court of the United States, or of any State of the United States, or of the District of Columbia, the period of limitations on collection after assessment prescribed in section 6502 is suspended with respect to the outstanding amount due on the assessment for the period such assets are in the control or custody of the court, and for 6 months thereafter. In the case of an estate of a decedent or an incompetent, the period of limitations on collection is suspended only for periods beginning after November 2, 1966, during which assets are in the control or custody of a court, and for 6 months thereafter.

○━▶ § 301.6503(c) Statutory provisions; suspension of running of period of limitation; taxpayer outside United States. [Sec. 6503(c), IRC]

○━▶ § 301.6503(c)-1 (T.D. 6172, filed 5-2-56; republished in T.D. 6498, filed 10-24-60; amended by T.D. 7121, filed 6-2-71.) Suspension of running of period of limitation; location of property outside the United States or removal of property from the United States; taxpayer outside of United States.

(a) *Property located outside, or removed from, the United States prior to November 3, 1966.* The running of the period of limitations on collection after assessment prescribed in section 6502 is suspended for the period of time, prior to November 3, 1966, that collection is hindered or delayed because property of the taxpayer is situated or held outside the United States or

Reg. § 301.6503(c)-1(a)

24,374 (I.R.C.) Reg. § 301.6503(c)-1(a) 3-18-74

is removed from the United States. The total suspension of time under this provision shall not in the aggregate exceed 6 years. In any case in which the district director determines that collection is so hindered or delayed, he shall make and retain in the files of his office a written report which shall identify the taxpayer and the tax liability, shall show what steps were taken to collect the tax liability, shall state the grounds for his determination that property of the taxpayer is situated or held outside, or is removed from, the United States, and shall show the date on which it was first determined that collection was so hindered or delayed. The term "property" includes all property or rights to property, real or personal, tangible or intangible, belonging to the taxpayer. The suspension of the running of the period of limitations on collection shall be considered to begin on the date so determined by the district director. A copy of the report shall be mailed to the taxpayer at his last known address.

(b) *Taxpayer outside United States after November 2, 1966.* The running of the period of limitations on collection after assessment prescribed in section 6502 (relating to collection after assessment) is suspended for the period after November 2, 1966, during which the taxpayer is absent from the United States if such period is a continuous period of absence from the United States extending for 6 months or more. In a case where the running of the period of limitations has been suspended under the first sentence of this paragraph and at the time of the taxpayer's return to the United States the period of limitations would expire before the expiration of 6 months from the date of his return, the period of limitations shall not expire until after 6 months from the date of the taxpayer's return. The taxpayer will be deemed to be absent from the United States for purposes of this section if he is generally and substantially absent from the United States, even though he makes casual temporary visits during the period.

O—☞ § 301.6503(d) Statutory provisions; suspension of running of period of limitation; extensions of time for payment of estate tax. [Sec. 6503(d), IRC]

O—☞ § 301.6503(d)-1 (T.D. 6172 filed 5-2-56; as amended by T.D. 6425, filed 11-10-59; republished in T.D. 6498, filed 10-24-60.) Suspension of running of period of limitation; extension of time for payment of estate tax. Where an estate is granted an extension of time as provided in section 6161(a)(2) or (b)(2), or under the provisions of section 6166, for payment of any estate tax, the running of the period of limitations for collection of such tax is suspended for the period of time for which the extension is granted.

O—☞ § 301.6503 (e) Statutory provisions; suspension of running of period of limitation; certain powers of appointment. [Sec. 6503(e), IRC]

O—☞ § 301.6503(e)-1 (T.D. 6296, filed 6-23-58; republished in T.D. 6498, filed 10-24-60.) Suspension of running of period of limitation; certain powers of appointment.— Where the estate of a decedent is allowed an estate tax charitable deduction under the provisions of section 2055(b)(2) (with respect to property over which the decedent's surviving spouse was given a power of appointment exercisable in favor of charitable organizations) subject to the later disallowance of the deduction if all conditions set forth in section 2055(b)(2) are not complied with, the running of the period of limitation for assessment or collection of any estate tax imposed on the decedent's estate is suspended until 30 days after the expiration of the period for assessment or collection of the estate tax imposed on the estate of the decedent's surviving spouse.

O—☞ § 301.6503(f) Statutory provisions; suspension of running of period of limitation; cross references. [Sec. 6503(f), IRC]

O—☞ § 301.6503(g) Statutory provisions; suspension of running of period of limitation; wrongful seizure of property of third party. [Sec. 6503(g), IRC]

O—☞ § 301.6503(g)-1 (T.D. 7121 filed 6-2-71.) Suspension of running of period of limitation; wrongful seizure of property of third party.

The running of the period of limitations on collection after assessment prescribed in section 6502 (relating to collection after assessment) shall be suspended for a period equal to a period beginning on the date property (including money) is wrongfully seized or received by a district director and ending on the date 30 days after the date on which the district director returns the property pursuant to section 6343(b) (relating to authority to return property) or the date 30 days after the date on which a judgment secured pursuant to section 7426 (relating to civil actions by persons other than taxpayers) with respect to such property becomes final. The running of the period of limitations on collection after assessment shall be suspended under this section only with respect to the amount of such assessment which is equal to the amount of money or the value of specific property returned. This section applies in the case of property wrongfully seized or received after November 2, 1966.

Example. On June 1, 1968 (at which time 10 months remain before the period of limitations on collection after assessment will expire), the district director wrongfully seizes $1,000 in B's account in Bank X and properly seizes $500 in taxpayer A's account in Bank Y in an attempt to satisfy A's assessed tax liability of $1,500. The district director determines that the $1,000 seized in Bank X was not the property of taxpayer A and, on March 1, 1969, he returns the $1,000 to B. As a result of the wrongful seizure, the running of the period of limitations on collection after assessment of the amount owed by taxpayer A is suspended for the 9 month period (beginning June 1, 1968, when the money was wrongfully seized and ending March 1, 1969, when the money was returned to B), plus 30 days. Therefore, the period of limitations on collection after assessment prescribed in section 6502 will not expire until February 1, 1970, which is 10 months plus 30 days after the money was returned.

O—☞ § 301.6504 Statutory provisions; cross references. [Sec. 6504, IRC]

LIMITATIONS ON CREDIT OR REFUND

§ 301.6511(a) Statutory provisions; limitations on credit or refund; period of limitation on filing claim. [Sec. 6511(a), IRC]

§ 301.6511(a)-1 (T.D. 6172, filed 5-2-56, as amended by T.D. 6425, filed 11-10-59; republished in T.D. 6498, filed 10-24-60.) **Period of limitation on filing claim.**

(a) In the case of any tax (other than a tax payable by stamp):

(1) If a return is filed, a claim for credit or refund of an overpayment must be filed by the taxpayer within 3 years from the time the return was filed or within 2 years from the time the tax was paid, whichever of such periods expires the later.

Reg. § 301.6511(a)-1(a)(1)

Limitations on Credit or Refund (I.R.C.) 24,375

(2) If no return is filed, the claim for credit or refund of an overpayment must be filed by the taxpayer within 2 years from the time the tax was paid.

(b) In the case of any tax payable by means of a stamp, a claim for credit or refund of an overpayment of such tax must be filed by the taxpayer within 3 years from the time the tax was paid. For provisions relating to redemption of unused stamps, see section 6805.

(c) For limitations on allowance of credit or refund, special rules, and exceptions, see subsections (b) through (e) of section 6511. For limitations in the case of a petition to the Tax Court, see section 6512. For rules as to time return is deemed filed and tax considered paid, see section 6513.

○➔ § 301.6511(b) Statutory provisions; limitations on credit or refund; limitation on allowance of credits and refunds. [Sec. 6511(b), IRC]

○➔ § 301.6511(b)-1 (T.D. 6172, filed 5-2-56, as amended by T.D. 6425, filed 11-10-59; republished in T.D. 6498, filed 10-24-60; amended by T.D. 6585, filed 12-27-61.) Limitations on allowance of credits and refunds.

(a) *Effect of filing claim.* Unless a claim for credit or refund of an overpayment is filed within the period of limitation prescribed in section 6511(a), no credit or refund shall be allowed or made after the expiration of such period.

(b) *Limit on amount to be credited or refunded.* (1) In the case of any tax (other than a tax payable by stamp):

(i) If a return was filed, and a claim is filed within 3 years from the time the return was filed, the amount of the credit or refund shall not exceed the portion of the tax paid within the period immediately preceding the filing of the claim, equal to 3 years plus the period of any extension of time for filing return.

(ii) If a return was filed, and a claim is filed after the 3-year period described in subdivision (i) of this subparagraph but within 2 years from the time the tax was paid, the amount of the credit or refund shall not exceed the portion of the tax paid within the 2 years immediately preceding the filing of the claim.

(iii) If no return was filed, but a claim is filed, the amount of the credit or refund shall not exceed the portion of the tax paid within the 2 years immediately preceding the filing of the claim.

(iv) If no claim is filed, the amount of the credit or refund allowed or made by the district director or the director of the regional service center shall not exceed the amount that would have been allowable under the preceding subdivisions of this subparagraph if a claim had been filed on the date the credit or refund is allowed.

(2) In the case of a tax payable by stamp:

(i) If a claim is filed, the amount of the credit or refund shall not exceed the portion of the tax paid within the 3 years immediately preceding the filing of the claim.

(ii) If no claim is filed, the amount of the credit or refund allowed or made by the district director or the director of the regional service center shall not exceed the portion of the tax paid within the 3 years immediately preceding the allowance of the credit or refund.

For provisions relating to redemption of unused stamps, see section 6805.

○➔ § 301.6511(c) Statutory provisions; limitations on credit or refund; special rules applicable in case of extension of time by agreement. [Sec. 6511(c), IRC]

○➔ § 301.6511(c)-1 (T.D. 6172, filed 5-2-56; republished in T.D. 6498, filed 10-24-60.) Special rules applicable in case of extension of time by agreement.

(a) *Scope.* If, within the period prescribed in section 6511(a) for the filing of a claim for credit or refund, an agreement extending the period for assessment of a tax has been made in accordance with the provisions of section 6501(c)(4), the special rules provided in this section become applicable. This section shall not apply to any claim filed or credit or refund allowed if no claim is filed, either (1) prior to the execution of an agreement extending the period in which assessment may be made, or (2) more than 6 months after the expiration of the period within which an assessment may be made pursuant to the agreement or any extension thereof.

(b) *Period in which claim may be filed.* Claim for credit or refund of an overpayment may be filed, or credit or refund may be allowed if no claim is filed, at any time within which an assessment may be made pursuant to an agreement, or any extension thereof, under section 6501(c)(4), and for 6 months thereafter.

(c) *Limit on amount to be credited or refunded.* (1) If a claim is filed within the time prescribed in paragraph (b) of this section, the amount of the credit or refund allowed or made shall not exceed the portion of the tax paid after the execution of the agreement and before the filing of the claim, plus the amount that could have been properly credited or refunded under the provisions of section 6511(b)(2) if a claim had been filed on the date of the execution of the agreement.

(2) If no claim is filed, the amount of credit or refund allowed or made within the time prescribed in paragraph (b) of this section shall not exceed the portion of the tax paid after the execution of the agreement and before the making of the credit or refund, plus the amount that could have been properly credited or refunded under the provisions of section 6511(b)(2) if a claim had been filed on the date of the execution of the agreement.

(d) *Effective date of agreement.* The agreement referred to in this section shall become effective when signed by the taxpayer and the district director or an assistant regional commissioner.

○➔ § 301.6511(d) Statutory provisions; limitations on credit or refund; special rules applicable to income taxes. [Sec. 6511(d), IRC]

○➔ § 301.6511(d)-1 (T.D. 6172, filed 5-2-56,

Reg. § 301.6511(d)-1

24,376 (I.R.C.) Reg. § 301.6511(d)-1

as amended by T.D. 6425, filed 11-10-59; republished in T.D. 6498, filed 10-24-60.) **Overpayment of income tax on account of bad debts, worthless securities, etc.**

(a) (1) If the claim for credit or refund relates to an overpayment of income tax on account of—

(i) The deductibility by the taxpayer under section 166 or section 832(c), of a debt as a debt which became worthless, or, under section 165(g), of a loss from the worthlessness of a security, or

(ii) The effect that the deductibility of a debt or loss described in subdivision (i) of this subparagraph has on the application to the taxpayer of a carryover,

then in lieu of the 3-year period from the time the return was filed, in which claim may be filed or credit or refund allowed, as prescribed in section 6511(a) or (b), the period shall be 7 years from the date prescribed by law for filing the return (determined without regard to any extension of time for filing such return) for the taxable year for which the claim is made or the credit or refund allowed or made.

(2) If the claim for credit or refund relates to an overpayment on account of the effect that the deductibility of a debt or loss, described in subparagraph (1) of this paragraph, has on the application to the taxpayer of a net operating loss carryback provided in section 172(b), the period in which claim for credit or refund may be filed shall be whichever of the following two periods expires later:

(i) Seven years from the last date prescribed for filing the return (determined without regard to any extension of time for filing such return) for the taxable year of the net operating loss which results in such carryback, or

(ii) The period which ends with the expiration of the period prescribed in section 6511(c) within which a claim for credit or refund may be filed with respect to the taxable year of the net operating loss which resulted in the carryback.

(3) In the case of a claim for credit or refund involving items described in this section, the amount of the credit or refund may exceed the portion of the tax paid within the period provided in section 6511(b)(2) or (c), whichever is applicable, to the extent of the amount of the overpayment attributable to the deductibility of items described in subparagraph (1) of this paragraph. If the claim involves an overpayment based not only on the deductibility of items described in subparagraph (1) of this paragraph but based also on other items, the credit or refund cannot exceed the sum of the following:

(i) The amount of the overpayment which is attributable to the deductibility of items described in subparagraph (1) of this paragraph, and

(ii) The balance of such overpayment up to a limit of the portion, if any, of the tax paid within the period provided in section 6511(b)(2) or (c), or within the period provided in any other applicable provision of law.

(4) If the claim involves an overpayment based not only on the deductibility of items described in subparagraph (1) of this paragraph but based also on other items, and if the claim with respect to any items is barred by the expiration of any applicable period of limitation, the portion of the overpayment attributable to the items not so barred shall be determined by treating the allowance of such items as the first adjustment to be made in computing such overpayment.

(b) If a claim for credit or refund is not filed within the applicable period described in paragraph (a) of this section, then credit or refund may be allowed or made only if claim therefor is filed or if such credit or refund is allowed within any period prescribed in section 6511(a), (b), or (c), whichever is applicable, subject to the provisions thereof limiting the amount of credit or refund in the case of a claim filed, or, if no claim was filed, in the case of credit or refund allowed within such applicable period as prescribed in section 6511(b) or (c).

(c) The provisions of this section and section 6511(d)(1) do not apply to an overpayment resulting from the deductibility of a debt that became partially worthless during the taxable year, but only to an overpayment resulting from the deductibility of a debt which became entirely worthless during such year.

(d) The provisions of paragraph (a) of this section with regard to an overpayment caused by the deductibility of a bad debt under section 166 or section 832 (c), or of a loss from the worthlessness of a security under section 165(g), are likewise applicable to an overpayment caused by the effect that the deductibility of such bad debt or loss has on the application to the taxpayer of a carryover or of a carryback.

○— § 301.6511(d)-2 (T.D. 6172, filed 5-2-56, as amended by T.D. 6425, filed 11-10-59 and T.D. 6488, filed 8-12-60; republished in T.D. 6498, filed 10-24-60; amended by T.D. 6730, filed 5-7-64; T.D. 7196, filed 7-12-72 and T.D. 7301, filed 1-3-74.) **Overpayment of income tax on account of net operating loss or capital loss carrybacks.**

(a) *Special period of limitation.* (1) If the claim for credit or refund relates to an overpayment of income tax attributable to a net operating loss carryback (provided in section 172(b)), or a capital loss carryback (provided in section 1212(a)), then in lieu of the 3-year period from the time the return was filed in which the claim may be filed or credit or refund allowed, as prescribed in section 6511(a) or (b), the period shall be whichever of the following 2 periods expires later:

(i) The period which ends with the expiration of the fifteenth day of the fortieth month (or thirty-ninth month, in the case of a corporation) following the end of the taxable year of the net operating loss or net capital loss which resulted in the carryback; or

(ii) The period which ends with the expiration of the period prescribed in section 6511(c) within which a claim for credit or refund may be filed with respect to the taxable year of the net operating loss or net capital loss which resulted in the carryback except that—

(a) With respect to an overpayment attributable to a net operating loss carryback to any year on account of a certification issued to the taxpayer under section 317 of the Trade Expansion Act of 1962, the period shall not expire before the expiration of the sixth month following the month in which such certification is issued to the taxpayer, and

(b) With respect to an overpayment attributable to the creation of, or an increase in, a net operating loss as a result of the elimination of excessive profits by a renegotiation (as defined in section 1481(a)(1)(A)), the period shall not expire before September 1, 1959, or the expiration of the twelfth month following the month in which the agreement or order for the elimination of such excessive profits becomes final, whichever is the later.

(2) In the case of a claim for credit or refund involving a net operating loss or capital loss carryback described in subparagraph (1) of this paragraph, the amount of the credit or refund may exceed the portion of the tax paid within the period provided in section 6511(b)(2) or (c), whichever is applicable, to the extent of the amount of the overpayment attributable to the carryback. If the claim involves an overpayment based not only on a net operating loss or capital loss carryback described in subparagraph (1) of this paragraph but based also on other items, the credit or refund cannot exceed the sum of the following:

(i) The amount of the overpayment which is attributable to the net operating loss or capital loss carryback, and

(ii) The balance of such overpayment up to a limit of the portion, if any, of the tax paid within the period provided in section 6511(b)(2) or (c), or within the period provided in any other applicable provision of law.

(3) If the claim involves an overpayment based not only on a net operating loss or capital loss carryback described in subparagraph (1) of this paragraph but based also on other items, and if the claim with respect to any items is barred by the expiration of any applicable period of limitation, the portion of the overpayment attributable to the items not so barred shall be determined by treating the allowance of such items as the first adjustment to be made in computing such overpayment. If a claim for credit or refund is not filed, and if credit or refund is not allowed, within the period prescribed in this paragraph, then credit or refund may be allowed or made only if claim therefor is filed, or if such credit or refund is allowed, within the period prescribed in section 6511(a), (b), or (c), whichever is applicable, subject to the provisions thereof limiting the amount of credit or refund in the case of a claim filed, or if no claim was filed, in case of credit or refund allowed, within such applicable period. For the limitations on the allowance of interest for an overpayment where credit or refund is subject to the provisions of this section, see section 6611(f).

(b) *Barred overpayments.* (1) If the allowance of a credit or refund of an overpayment of tax attributable to a net operating loss carryback or capital loss carryback is otherwise prevented by the operation of any law or rule of law (other than section 7122, relating to compromises), such credit or refund may be allowed or made under the provisions of section 6511(d)(2)

(B) if a claim therefor is filed within the period provided by section 6511(d)(2)(A) and paragraph (a) of this section for filing a claim for credit or refund of an overpayment attributable to a carryback. Similarly, if the allowance of an application, credit, or refund of a decrease in the tax determined under section 6411(b) is otherwise prevented by the operation of any law or rule of law (other than section 7122), such application, credit, or refund may be allowed or made if an application for a tentative carryback adjustment is filed within the period provided in section 6411(a). Thus, for example, even though the tax liability (not including the net operating loss deduction or capital loss carryback (or the effect of such deduction or carryback)) for a given taxable year has previously been litigated before the Tax Court, credit or refund of an overpayment may be allowed or made despite the provisions of section 6512(a), if claim for such credit or refund is filed within the period provided in section 6511(d)(2)(A) and paragraph (a) of this section. In the case of a claim for credit or refund of an overpayment attributable to a carryback, or in the case of an application for a tentative carryback adjustment, the determination of any court, including the Tax Court, in any proceeding in which the decision of the court has become final, shall be conclusive except with respect to the net operating loss deduction, and the effect of such deduction, or with respect to the determination of a short-term capital loss, and the effect of such short-term capital loss, to the extent that such deduction or short-term capital loss is affected by a carryback which was not in issue in such proceeding.

(2) For purposes of the special period of limitation for filing a claim for credit or refund of an overpayment of tax with respect to a computation year (as defined in section 1302(c)(1)) by an individual who has chosen to compute his tax under sections 1301 through 1305 (relating to income averaging), such claim is determined to relate to an overpayment attributable to a net operating loss carryback when such carryback relates to any base period year (as defined in section 1302(c)(3)). Thus, if (i) an individual has a net operating loss for a taxable year subsequent to a taxable year for which he had chosen the benefits of income averaging, and (ii) such net operating loss carryback is wholly utilized in any one or more of his base period years (which would result in an increased amount of averagable income for such computation year), the special period of limitation with respect to such individual's computation year applies and a timely claim for credit or refund with respect to the computation year may be filed.

○→ § 301.6511(d)-3 (T.D. 6172, filed 5-2-56; republished in the T.D. 6498, filed 10-24-60.) **Special rules applicable to credit against income tax for foreign taxes.**

(a) *Period in which claim may be filed.* In the case of an overpayment of income tax resulting from a credit, allowed under the provisions of section 901 or under the provisions of any treaty to which the United States is a party, for taxes paid or accrued to a foreign country or possession of the United States, a claim for credit or

Reg. § 301.6511(d)-3(a)

refund must be filed by the taxpayer within 10 years from the last date prescribed for filing the return (determined without regard to any extension of time for filing such return) for the taxable year with respect to which the claim is made. Such 10-year period shall be applied in lieu of the 3-year period prescribed in section 6511(a).

(b) *Limit on amount to be credited or refunded.* In the case of a claim described in paragraph (a) of this section, the amount of the credit or refund allowed or made may exceed the portion of the tax paid within the period prescribed in section 6511(b) or (c), whichever is applicable, to the extent of the amount of the overpayment attributable to the allowance of a credit against income tax referred to in paragraph (a) of this section.

§ 301.6511(d)-4 (T.D. 6730, filed 5-7-64 as amended by T.D. 7301, filed 1-3-74.) **Overpayment of income tax on account of investment credit carryback.**

(a) *Special period of limitation.* (1) If the claim for credit or refund relates to an overpayment of income tax attributable to an investment credit carryback, provided in section 46(b), then in lieu of the 3-year period from the time the return was filed in which the claim may be filed or credit or refund allowed, as prescribed in section 6511(a) or (b), the period shall be whichever of the following 2 periods expires later:

(i) The period which ends with the expiration of the fifteenth day of the fortieth month (or thirty-ninth month, in the case of a corporation) following the end of the taxable year of the unused investment credit which resulted in the carryback (or, with respect to any portion of an investment credit carryback from a taxable year attributable to a net operating loss carryback or a capital loss carryback from a subsequent taxable year, the period which ends with the expiration of the fifteenth day of the fortieth month (or thirty-ninth month, in the case of a corporation) following the end of such subsequent taxable year); or

(ii) The period which ends with the expiration of the period prescribed in section 6511(c) within which a claim for credit or refund may be filed with respect to the taxable year of the unused investment credit which resulted in the carryback.

(2) In the case of a claim for credit or refund involving an investment credit carryback described in subparagraph (1) of this paragraph, the amount of the credit or refund may exceed the portion of the tax paid within the period provided in section 6511(b)(2) or (c), whichever is applicable, to the extent of the amount of the overpayment attributable to the carryback. If the claim involves an overpayment based not only on an investment credit carryback described in subparagraph (1) of this paragraph but based also on other items, the credit or refund cannot exceed the sum of the following:

(i) The amount of the overpayment which is attributable to the investment credit carryback, and

(ii) The balance of such overpayment up to a limit of the portion, if any, of the tax paid within the period provided in section 6511(b)(2) or (c), or within the period provided in any other applicable provision of law.

(3) If the claim involves an overpayment based not only on an investment credit carryback described in subparagraph (1) of this paragraph but based also on other items, and if the claim with respect to any items is barred by the expiration of any applicable period of limitation, the portion of the overpayment attributable to the items not so barred shall be determined by treating the allowance of such items as the first adjustment to be made in computing such overpayment. If a claim for credit or refund is not filed, and if credit or refund is not allowed, within the period prescribed in this paragraph, then credit or refund may be allowed or made only if claim therefor is filed, or if such credit or refund is allowed, within the period prescribed in section 6511(a), (b), or (c), whichever is applicable, subject to the provisions thereof limiting the amount of credit or refund in the case of a claim filed, or if no claim was filed, in case of credit or refund allowed, within such applicable period. For the limitations on the allowance of interest for an overpayment where credit or refund is subject to the provisions of this section, see section 6611(f).

(b) *Barred overpayments.* If the allowance of a credit or refund of an overpayment of tax attributable to an investment credit carryback is otherwise prevented by the operation of any law or rule of law (other than section 7122, relating to compromises), such credit or refund may be allowed or made under the provisions of section 6511(d)(4)(B) if a claim therefor is filed within the period provided by section 6511(d)(4)(A) and paragraph (a) of this section for filing a claim for credit or refund of an overpayment attributable to a carryback. In the case of a claim for credit or refund of an overpayment attributable to a carryback, the determination of any court, including the Tax Court, in any proceeding in which the decision of the court has become final, shall not be conclusive with respect to the investment credit, and the effect of such credit, to the extent that such credit is affected by a carryback which was not in issue in such proceeding.

§ 301.6511(d)-7 (T.D. 7301, filed 1-3-74.) **Overpayment of income tax on account of work incentive program credit carryback.**

(a) *Special period of limitation.* (1) If the claim for credit or refund related to an overpayment of income tax attributable to a work incentive program (WIN) credit carryback, provided in section 50A, then in lieu of the 3-year period from the time the return was filed in which the claim may be filed or credit or refund allowed, as prescribed in section 6511(a) or (b), the period shall be whichever of the following 2 periods expires later:

(i) The period which ends with the expiration of the fifteenth day of the fortieth month (or thirty-ninth month, in the case of a corporation) following the end of the taxable year of the unused WIN credit which resulted in the carryback (or, with respect to any portion of a WIN credit carryback from a taxable year attributable to a net operating loss carryback or a capital loss carryback from a subsequent taxable year, the period which ends with the expiration of the fifteenth day of the fortieth month (or thirty-ninth month in the case of a corporation) following the end of such subsequent taxable year); or

(ii) The period which ends with the expiration of the period prescribed in section 6511(c) within which a claim for credit or refund may be filed with respect to the taxable year of the unused WIN credit which resulted in the carryback.

(2) In the case of a claim for credit or refund involving a WIN credit carryback described in subparagraph (1) of this paragraph, the amount of the credit or refund may exceed the portion of the tax paid within the period provided in section 6511 (b)(2) or (c), whichever is applicable, to the extent of the amount of the overpayment attributable to the carryback. If the claim involves an overpayment based not only on a WIN credit carryback described in subparagraph (1) of this paragraph but based also on other items, the credit or refund cannot exceed the sum of the following:

(i) The amount of the overpayment which is attributable to the WIN credit carryback, and

(ii) The balance of such overpayment up to a limit of the portion, if any, of the tax paid within the period provided in section 6511(b)(2) or (c), or within the period provided in any other applicable provision of law.

(3) If the claim involves an overpayment based not only on a WIN credit carryback described in subparagraph (1) of this paragraph but based also on other items, and if the claim with respect to any items is barred by the expiration of any applicable period of limitation, the portion of the overpayment attributable to the items not so barred shall be determined by treating the allowance of such items as the first adjustment to be made in computing such overpayment. If a claim for credit or refund is not filed, and if credit or refund is not allowed, within the period prescribed in this paragraph, then credit or refund may be allowed or made only if claim therefor is filed, or if such credit or refund is allowed, within the period prescribed in section 6511(a), (b), or (c), whichever is applicable, subject to the provisions thereof limiting the amount of credit or refund in the case of a claim filed, or if no claim was filed, in case of credit or refund allowed, within such applicable period. For the limitations on the allowance of interest for an overpayment where credit or refund is subject to the provisions of this section, see section 6611(f).

(b) *Barred overpayments.* If the allowance of a credit or refund of an overpayment of tax attributable to a WIN credit carryback is otherwise prevented by the operation of any law or rule of law (other than section 7122, relating to compromises), such credit or refund may be allowed or made under the provisions of section 6611(d)(7)(B) if a claim therefor is filed within the period provided by section 6511(d)(7)(A) and paragraph (a) of this section for filing a claim for credit or refund of an overpayment attributable to a carryback. In the case of a claim for credit or refund of an overpayment attributable to a carryback, the determination of any court, including the Tax Court, in any proceeding in which the decision of the courts has become final, shall not be conclusive with respect to the WIN credit, and the effect of such credit, to the extent that such credit is affected by a carryback which was not in issue in such proceeding.

○━▶ § 301.6511(f) Statutory provisions; limitations on credit or refund; cross references. [Sec. 6512(f), IRC]

○━▶ § 301.6512 Statutory provisions; limitations in case of petition to Tax Court. [Sec. 6512, IRC]

○━▶ § 301.6512-1 (T.D. 6172, filed 5-2-56; republished in T.D. 6498, filed 10-24-60; amended by T.D. 7238, filed 12-28-72.) Limitations in case of petition to Tax Court.

(a) *Effect of petition to Tax Court—* (1) *General rule.* If a person, having a right to file a petition with the Tax Court with respect to a deficiency in income, estate, or gift tax imposed by subtitle A or B of the Code, has filed such petition within the time prescribed in section 6213 (a), no credit or refund of income tax for the same taxable year, or of gift tax for the same calendar year or calendar quarter, or of estate tax in respect of the taxable estate of the same decedent, in respect of which a district director (or an assistant regional commissioner, appellate) has determined the deficiency, shall be allowed or made, and no suit in any court for the recovery of any part of such tax shall be instituted by the taxpayer, except as to items set forth in subparagraph (2) of this paragraph.

(2) *Exceptions.* The exceptions to the rule stated in subparagraph (1) of this paragraph are as follows:

(i) An overpayment determined by a decision of the Tax Court which has become final;

(ii) Any amount collected in excess of an amount computed in accordance with the decision of the Tax Court which has become final; and

(iii) Any amount collected after the expiration of the period of limitation upon levying or beginning a proceeding in court for collection.

(b) *Overpayment determined by Tax Court.* If the Tax Court finds that there is no deficiency and further finds that the taxpayer has made an overpayment of income tax for the same taxable year, or of gift tax for the same calendar year or calendar quarter, or of estate tax in respect of the taxable estate of the same decedent, in respect of which a district director (or an assistant regional commissioner, appellate) has determined the deficiency, or finds that there is a deficiency but that the taxpayer has made an overpayment of such tax, the overpayment determined by the Tax Court shall be credited or refunded to the taxpayer when the decision of the Tax Court has become final. (See section 7481, relating to the date when Tax Court decision becomes final.) No such credit or refund shall be allowed or made of any portion of the tax unless the Tax Court determines as part of its decision that such portion was paid—

(1) After the mailing of the notice of deficiency, or

(2) Within the period which would be applicable under section 6511(b)(2), (c), or (d) (see §§ 301.6511(b)-1, 301.6511(c)-1, 301-

Reg. § 301.6512-1(b)(2)

.6511(d)-1, 301.6511(d)-2, and 301.6511(d)-3), if on the date of the mailing of the notice of deficiency a claim had been filed (whether or not filed) stating the grounds upon which the Tax Court finds that there is an overpayment.

(c) *Jeopardy assessments.* In the case of a jeopardy assessment made under section 6861(a), if the amount which should have been assessed as determined by a decision of the Tax Court which has become final is less than the amount already collected, the excess payment shall be credited or refunded subject to a determination being made by the Tax Court with respect to the time of payment as stated in paragraph (b) of this section.

(d) *Disallowance of deficiency by reviewing court.* If the amount of the deficiency determined by the Tax Court (in a case where collection has not been stayed by the filing of a bond) is disallowed in whole or in part by the reviewing court, then the overpayment resulting from such disallowance shall be credited or refunded without the making of claim therefor, subject to a determination being made by the Tax Court with respect to the time of payment as stated in paragraph (b) of this section. (See section 7481, relating to date Tax Court decision becomes final.)

(e) *Collection in excess of amount determined by Tax Court.* Where the amount collected is in excess of the amount computed in accordance with the decision of the Tax Court which has become final, the excess payment shall be credited or refunded within the period of limitation provided in section 6511.

(f) *Collection after expiration of statutory period.* Where an amount is collected after the statutory period of limitation upon the beginning of levy or a proceeding in court for collection has expired (see section 6502, relating to collection after assessment), the taxpayer may file a claim for refund of the amount so collected within the period of limitation provided in section 6511. In any such case, the decision of the Tax Court as to whether the statutory period upon collection of the tax expired before notice of the deficiency was mailed shall, when the decision becomes final, be conclusive.

○→ § 301.6513 **Statutory provisions; time return deemed filed and tax considered paid.** [Sec. 6513, IRC]

○→ § 301.6513-1 (T.D. 6172, filed 5-2-56; republished in T.D. 6498, filed 10-24-60; amended by T.D. 6922, filed 6-16-67.) **Time return deemed filed and tax considered paid.**

(a) *Early return or advance payment of tax.* For purposes of section 6511, a return filed before the last day prescribed by law or regulations for the filing thereof shall be considered as filed on such last day. For purposes of section 6511 (b) (2) and (c) and section 6512, payment of any portion of the tax made before the last day prescribed for payment shall be considered made on such last day. An extension of time for filing a return or for paying any tax, or an election to pay any tax in installments, shall not be given any effect in determining under this section the last day prescribed for filing a return or paying any tax.

(b) *Prepaid income tax.* For purposes of section 6511 (relating to limitations on credit or refund) or section 6512 (relating to limitations in case of petition to Tax Court)—

(1) Any tax actually deducted and withheld at the source during any calendar year under chapter 24 of the Code (relating to collection of income tax at source on wages) shall, in respect of the recipient of the income, be deemed to have been paid by him on the 15th day of the fourth month following the close of his taxable year with respect to which such tax is allowable as a credit under section 31 (relating to tax withheld on wages).

(2) Any amount paid as estimated income tax for any taxable year shall be deemed to have been paid on the last day prescribed for filing the income tax return under section 6012 for such taxable year (determined without regard to any extension of time for filing such return), and

(3) Any tax withheld at the source on or after November 13, 1966, under chapter 3 of the Code (relating to tax withheld on nonresident aliens and foreign corporations and tax-free covenant bonds) shall, in respect of the recipient of the income, be deemed to have been paid by such recipient on the last day prescribed for filing his income tax return under section 6012 for the taxable year (determined without regard to any extension of time for filing such return) with respect to which such tax is allowable as a credit under section 1462 (relating to withheld tax as credit to recipient of income).

Subparagraph (3) of this paragraph shall apply even though the recipient of the income has been granted under section 6012 and the regulations thereunder an exemption from the requirement of making an income tax return for the taxable year.

(c) *Return and payment of social security taxes and income tax withholding.* Notwithstanding paragraph (a) of this section, if a return (or payment) on or after November 13, 1966, of tax imposed by chapter 3 of the Code (relating to withholding of tax on nonresident aliens and foreign corporations and tax-free covenant bonds), or if a return (or payment) of tax imposed by chapter 21 of the Code (relating to the Federal Insurance Contributions Act) or by chapter 24 of the Code (relating to the collection of income tax at source on wages), for any period ending with or within a calendar year is filed or paid before April 15 of the succeeding calendar year, for purposes of section 6511 (relating to limitations on credit or refund) the return shall be considered filed, or the tax considered paid, on April 15 of such succeeding calendar year.

(d) *Overpayment of income tax credited to estimated tax.* If a taxpayer elects under the provisions of section 6402(b) to credit an overpayment of income tax for a taxable year against estimated tax for the succeeding taxable year, the amount so credited shall be considered a payment of income tax for such succeeding taxable year (whether or not claimed as a credit on the estimated tax return for such succeeding taxable year). If the treatment of such amount as a payment of income tax for the succeeding taxable year results in an overpayment for such succeeding taxable year, the period of limitations applicable to such overpayment is determined by reference to that taxable year. An election so to credit an overpayment of income tax precludes the allowance of a claim for credit or refund of such overpayment for the taxable year in which the overpayment arises.

○━➤ § 301.6514(a) Statutory provisions; credits or refunds after period of limitation. [Sec. 6514(a), IRC]

○━➤ § 301.6514(a)-1 (T.D. 6172, filed 5-2-56; republished in T.D. 6498, filed 10-24-60.) Credits or refunds after period of limitation.

(a) A refund of any portion of any internal revenue tax (or any interest, additional amount, addition to the tax, or assessable penalty) shall be considered erroneous and a credit of any such portion shall be considered void:

(1) If made after the expiration of the period of limitation prescribed by section 6511 for filing claim therefor, unless prior to the expiration of such period claim was filed, or

(2) In the case of a timely claim, if the credit or refund was made after the expiration of the period of limitation prescribed by section 6532(a) for the filing of suit, unless prior to the expiration of such period suit was begun.

(b) For procedure by the United States to recover erroneous refunds, see sections 6532(b) and 7405.

○━➤ § 301.6514(b) Statutory provisions; credit after period of limitation. [Sec. 6514, (b) IRC]

○━➤ § 301.6514(b)-1 (T.D. 6172, filed 5-2-56; republished in T.D. 6498, filed 10-24-60.) Credit against barred liability.

Any credit against a liability in respect of any taxable year shall be void if the collection of such liability would be barred by the applicable statute of limitations at the time such credit is made.

○━➤ § 301.6515 Statutory provisions; cross references. [Sec. 6515, IRC]

MITIGATION OF EFFECT OF PERIOD OF LIMITATIONS

○━➤ § 301.6521 Statutory provisions; mitigation of effect of limitation in case of related taxes under different chapters. [Sec. 6521, IRC]

○━➤ § 301.6521-1 (T.D. 6172, filed 5-2-56; republished in T.D. 6498, filed 10-24-60.) Mitigation of effect of limitation in case of related employee social security tax and self-employment tax.

(a) Section 6521 may be applied in the correction of a certain type of error involving both the tax on self-employment income under section 1401 and the employee tax under section 3101 if the correction of the error as to one tax is, on the date the correction is authorized, prevented in whole or in part by the operation of any law or rule of law other than section 7122, relating to compromises. Examples of such law are sections 6212(c), 6401(a), 6501, 6511, 6512(a), 6514, 6532, 6901(c), (d) and (e), 7121, and 7459(e).

(b) If the liability for either tax with respect to which the error was made has been compromised under section 7122, the provisions of section 6521 limiting the correction with respect to the other tax do not apply.

(c) Section 6521 is not applicable if, on the date of the authorization, correction of the effect of the error is permissible as to both taxes without recourse to such section.

(d) If, because an amount of wages, as defined in section 3121(a), is erroneously treated as self-employment income, as defined in section 1402(b), or an amount of self-employment income is erroneously treated as wages, it is necessary in correcting the error to assess the correct tax and give a credit or refund for the amount of the tax erroneously paid, and if either, but not both, of such adjustments is prevented by any law or rule of law (other than section 7122), the amount of the assessment, or the amount of the credit or refund, authorized shall reflect the adjustment which would be made in respect of the other tax (either the tax on self-employment income under section 1401 or the employee tax under section 3101) but for the operation of such law or rule of law. For example, assume that during 1955 A paid $10 as tax on an amount erroneously treated as "wages", when such amount was actually self-employment income, and that credit or refund of the $10 is not barred. A should have paid a self-employment tax of $15 on the amount. If the assessment of the correct tax, that is, $15, is barred by the statute of limitations, no credit or refund of the $10 shall be made without offsetting against such $10 the $15, assessment of which is barred. Thus, no credit or refund in respect of the $10 can be made.

(e) As another example, assume that during 1955 a taxpayer reports wages of $4,200 and net earnings from self-employment of $900. By reason of the limitations of section 1402(b) he shows no self-employment income. Assume further that by reason of a final decision by the Tax Court of the United States, further adjustments to the taxpayer's income tax liability are barred. The question of the amount of his wages, as defined in section 3121, was not in issue in the Tax Court litigation, but it is subsequently determined (within the period of limitations applicable under the Federal Insurance Contributions Act) that $700 of the $4,200 reported as wages was not for employment as defined in section 3121(b). Therefore, the taxpayer is entitled to the allowance of a refund of the $14 tax paid on such remuneration under section 3101. The reduction of his wages from $4,200 to $3,500 would result in the determination of $700 self-employment income, the tax on which is $21 for the year. Under section 6521, the overpayment of $14 would be offset by the barred deficiency of $21, thus eliminating the refund otherwise allowable. If the facts were changed so that the taxpayer erroneously paid tax on self-employment income of $700, having been taxed on only $3,500 as wages, and within the period of limitations applicable under the Federal Insurance Contributions Act,

Reg. § 301.6521-1(e)

it is determined that his wages were $4,200, the tax of $14 under section 3101, otherwise collectible, would be eliminated by offsetting under section 6521 the barred overpayment of $21. The balance of the barred overpayment, $7, cannot be credited or refunded.

(f) Another illustration of the operation of section 6521 is the case of a taxpayer who, for 1955, is erroneously taxed on $2,500 as wages, the tax on which is $50, and who reports no self-employment income. After the period of limitations has run on the refund of the tax under the Federal Insurance Contributions Act, it is determined that the amount treated as wages should have been reported as net earnings from self-employment. The taxpayer's self-employment income would then be $2,500 and the tax thereon would be $75. Assume that the period of limitations applicable to subtitle A of the Code has not expired, and that a notice of deficiency may properly be issued. Under section 6521, the amount of the deficiency of $75 must be reduced by the barred overpayment of $50.

§ 301.6521-2 (T.D. 6172, filed 5-2-56; republished in T.D. 6498, filed, 10-24-60.) Law applicable in determination of error.

The question of whether there was an erroneous treatment of self-employment income or of wages is determined under the provisions of law and regulations applicable with respect to the year or other taxable period as to which the error was made. The fact that the error was in pursuance of an interpretation, either judicial or administrative, accorded such provisions of law and regulations at the time the action involved was taken is not necessarily determinative of this question. For example, if a later judicial decision authoritatively alters such interpretation so that such action is contrary to the applicable provisions of the law and regulations as later interpreted, the error comes within the scope of section 6521.

PERIODS OF LIMITATION IN JUDICIAL PROCEEDINGS

§ 301.6531 Statutory provisions; periods of limitation on criminal prosecutions. [Sec. 6531, IRC]

§ 301.6532 Statutory provisions; periods of limitation on suits. [Sec. 6532, IRC]

§ 301.6532-1 (T.D. 6172, filed 4-30-56 as amended by T.D. 6425, filed 11-10-59; republished in T.D. 6498, filed 10-24-60; amended by T.D. 6827, filed 6-14-65.) Periods of limitation on suits by taxpayers.

(a) No suit or proceeding under section 7422(a) for the recovery of any internal revenue tax, penalty, or other sum shall be begun until whichever of the following first occurs:

(1) The expiration of 6 months from the date of the filing of the claim for credit or refund, or

(2) A decision is rendered on such claim prior to the expiration of 6 months after the filing thereof.

Except as provided in paragraph (b) of this section, no suit or proceeding for the recovery of any internal revenue tax, penalty, or other sum may be brought after the expiration of 2 years from the date of mailing by registered mail prior to September 3, 1958, or by either registered or certified mail on or after September 3, 1958, by a district director, a director of an internal revenue service center, or an assistant regional commissioner to a taxpayer of a notice of disallowance of the part of the claim to which the suit or proceeding relates.

(b) The 2-year period described in paragraph (a) of this section may be extended if an agreement to extend the running of the period of limitations is executed. The agreement must be signed by the taxpayer or by an attorney, agent, trustee, or other fiduciary on behalf of the taxpayer. If the agreement is signed by a person other than the taxpayer, it shall be accompanied by an authenticated copy of the power of attorney or other legal evidence of the authority of such person to act on behalf of the taxpayer. If the taxpayer is a corporation, the agreement should be signed with the corporate name followed by the signature of a duly authorized officer of the corporation. The agreement will not be effective until signed by a district director, a director of an internal revenue service center, or an assistant regional commissioner.

(c) The taxpayer may sign a waiver of the requirement that he be mailed a notice of disallowance. Such waiver is irrevocable and will commence the running of the 2-year period described in paragraph (a) of this section on the date the waiver is filed. The waiver shall set forth:

(1) The type of tax and the taxable period covered by the taxpayer's claim for refund;

(2) The amount of the claim;

(3) The amount of the claim disallowed;

(4) A statement that the taxpayer agrees the filing of the waiver will commence the running of the 2-year period provided for in section 6532(a)(1) as if a notice of disallowance had been sent the taxpayer by either registered or certified mail. The filing of such a waiver prior to the expiration of 6 months from the date the claim was filed does not permit the filing of a suit for refund prior to the time specified in section 6532(a)(1) and paragraph (a) of this section.

(d) Any consideration, reconsideration, or other action with respect to a claim after the mailing by registered mail prior to September 3, 1958, or by either registered or certified mail on or after September 3, 1958, of a notice of disallowance or after the execution of a waiver referred to in paragraph (c) of this section, shall not extend the period for bringing suit or other proceeding under section 7422(a).

§ 301.6532-2 (T.D. 6172, filed 4-30-56; republished in T.D. 6498, filed 10-24-60.) Periods of limitation on suits by the United States.

The United States may not recover any erroneous refund by civil action under section 7405 unless such action is begun within 2 years after the making of such refund. However, if any part of the refund was induced by fraud or misrepresentation of a material fact, the action to recover the erroneous refund may be brought at any time within 5 years from the date the refund was made.

§ 301.6532-3 T.D. 7305, filed 3-14-74.)

Periods of limitation on suits by persons other than taxpayers.

(a) *General rule.* No suit or proceeding, except as otherwise provided in section 6532(c)(2) and paragraph (b) of this section, under section 7426 and § 301.7426-1 relating to civil actions by persons other than taxpayers, shall be begun after the expiration of 9 months from the date of levy or agreement under section 6325(b)(3) giving rise to such action.

(b) *Period when claim is filed.* The 9-month period prescribed in section 6532 (c)(1) and paragraph (a) of this section shall be extended to the shorter of,

(1) 12 months from the date of filing by a third party of a written request under § 301.6343-1(b)(2) for the return of property wrongfully levied upon, or

(2) 6 months from the date of mailing by registered or certified mail by the district director to the party claimant of a notice of disallowance of the part of the request to which the action relates.

A request which, under § 301.6343-1(b)(3), is not considered adequate does not extend the 9-month period described in paragraph (a) of this section.

(c) *Examples.* The provisions of this section may be illustrated by the following examples:

Example (1). On June 1, 1970, a tax is assessed against A with respect to his delinquent tax liability. On July 19, 1970, a levy is wrongfully made upon certain tangible personal property of B's which is in A's possession at that time. On July 20, 1970, notice of seizure is given to A. Thus, under section 6502(b), July 20, 1970, is the date on which the levy is considered to be made. Unless a request for the return, of property is sooner made to extend the 9-month period, no suit of proceeding under section 7426 may be begun by B after April 20, 1971, which is 9 months from the date of levy.

Example (2). Assume the same facts as in the preceding example except that, on August 3, 1970, B properly files a request for the return of his property wrongfully levied upon. Assume further that the district director mails, on March 1, 1971, a notice of disallowance of B's request for the return of the property. No suit or proceeding under section 7426 may be begun by B after August 3, 1971, which is 12 months from the date of filing a request for the return of property wrongfully levied upon.

Example (3). Assume the same facts as in the preceding example except that the notice of disallowance of B's request for the return of property wrongfully levied upon is mailed to B on November 12, 1970. Since the 6-month period from the mailing of the notice of disallowance expires before the 12-month period from the date of filing the request for the return of property which ends on August 3, 1971, no suit or proceeding under section 7426 may be begun by B after May 12, 1971, which is 6 months from the date of mailing the notice of disallowance.

○━▶ § 301.6533 Statutory provisions; cross references. [Sec. 6533, IRC]

Reg. § 301.6533

INTEREST

INTEREST ON UNDERPAYMENTS

○━ § 53.6601 Statutory provisions; interest on underpayment, nonpayment, or extension of time for payment, of tax. [Sec. 6601, IRC]

○━ § 53.6601-1 (T.D. 7368, filed 7-15-75.) **Interest on underpayment, nonpayment, or extensions of time for payment, of tax.**

For regulations concerning interest on underpayment, nonpayment, or extensions of time for payment of tax, see § 301.6601-1 of this chapter (Regulations on Procedure and Administration).

○━ § 301.6601 Statutory provisions; interest on underpayment, nonpayment, or extensions of time for payment, of tax. [Sec. 6601, IRC]

○━ § 301.6601-1 (T.D. 6234, filed 5-21-57, as amended by T.D. 6425, filed 11-10-59; republished in T.D. 6498, filed 10-24-60; amended by T.D. 6585, filed 12-27-61; T.D. 6730, filed 5-7-64; T.D. 7238, filed 12-28-72; T.D. 7301, filed 1-3-74; T.D. 7384, filed 10-21-75.) **Interest on underpayments.**

(a) *General rule.* (1) Interest at the annual rate referred to in the regulations under section 6621 shall be paid on any unpaid amount of tax from the last date prescribed for payment of the tax (determined without regard to any extension of time for payment) to the date on which payment is received.

(2) For provisions requiring the payment of interest during the period occurring before July 1, 1975, see section 6601 (a) prior to its amendment by section 7 of the Act of Jan. 3, 1975 (Pub. L. 93-625, 88 Stat. 2115).

(b) *Satisfaction by credits made after December 31, 1957*—(1) *In general.* If any portion of a tax is satisfied by the credit of an overpayment after December 31, 1957, interest shall not be imposed under section 6601 on such portion of the tax for any period during which interest on the overpayment would have been allowable if the overpayment had been refunded.

(2) *Examples.* The provisions of this paragraph may be illustrated by the following examples:

Example (1). An examination of A's income tax returns for the calendar years 1955 and 1956 discloses an underpayment of $800 for 1955 and an overpayment of $500 for 1956. Interest under section 6601 (a) ordinarily accrues on the underpayment of $800 from April 15, 1956, to the date of payment. However, the 1956 overpayment of $500 is credited after December 31, 1957, against the underpayment in accordance with the provisions of section 6402(a) and § 301.6402-1. Under such circumstances interest on the $800 underpayment runs from April 15, 1956, the last date prescribed for payment of the 1955 tax, to April 15, 1957, the date the overpayment of $500 was made. Since interest would have been allowed on the overpayment, if refunded, from April 15, 1957, to a date not more than 30 days prior to the date of the refund check, no interest is imposed after April 15, 1957, on $500, the portion of the underpayment satisfied by credit. Interest continues to run, however, on $300 (the $800 underpayment for 1955 less the $500 overpayment for 1956) to the date of payment.

Example (2). An examination of A's income tax returns for the calendar years 1956 and 1957 discloses an overpayment, occurring on April 15, 1957, of $700 for 1956 and an underpayment of $400 for 1957. After April 15, 1958, the last date prescribed for payment of the 1957 tax, the district director credits $400 of the overpayment against the underpayment. In such a case, interest will accrue upon the overpayment of $700 from April 15, 1957, to April 15, 1958, the due date of the amount against which the credit is taken. Interest will also accrue under section 6611 upon $300 ($700 overpayment less $400 underpayment) from April 15, 1958, to a date not more than 30 days prior to the date of the refund check. Since a refund of the portion of the overpayment credited against the underpayment would have resulted in interest running upon such portion from April 15, 1958, to a date not more than 30 days prior to the date of the refund check, no interest is imposed upon the underpayment.

(c) *Last date prescribed for payment.* (1) In determining the last date prescribed for payment, any extension of time granted for payment of tax (including any postponement elected under section 6163(a)) shall be disregarded. The granting of an extension of time for the payment of tax does not relieve the taxpayer from liability for the payment of interest thereon during the period of the extension. Thus, except as provided in paragraph (b) of this section, interest at the annual rate referred to in the regulations under section 6621 is payable on any unpaid portion of the tax for the period during which such portion remains unpaid by reason of an extension of time for the payment thereof.

(2) (i) If a tax or portion thereof is payable in installments in accordance with an election made under section 6152(a) or 6156(a), the last date prescribed for payment of any installment of such tax or portion thereof shall be determined under the provisions of section 6152(b) or 6156(b), as the case may be, and interest shall run on any unpaid installment from such last date to the date on which payment is received. However, in the event installment privileges are terminated for failure to pay an installment when due as provided by section 6152(d) and the time for the payment of any remaining installment is accelerated by the issuance of a notice and demand therefor, interest shall run on such unpaid installment from the date of the notice and demand to the date on which payment is received. But see section 6601(e)(4).

(ii) If the tax shown on a return is payable in installments, interest will run on any tax not shown on the return from the last date prescribed for payment of the first installment. If a deficiency is prorated to any unpaid installments, in accordance with section 6152(c), interest shall run on such prorated amounts from the date prescribed for the payment of the first installment to the date on which payment is received.

(3) If, by reason of jeopardy, a notice and demand for payment of any tax is issued before the last date otherwise prescribed for payment, such last date shall nevertheless be used for the purpose of the interest computation, and no interest shall be imposed for the period commencing with the date of the issuance of the notice and demand and ending on such last date. If the tax is not paid on or before such last date, interest will automatically accrue from such last date to the date on which payment is received.

(4) In the case of taxes payable by stamp and in all other cases where the last date for payment of the tax is not otherwise prescribed, such last date for the purpose of the interest computation shall be deemed to be the date on which the liability for the tax arose. However, such last date shall in no event be later than the date of issuance of a notice and demand for the tax.

(d) *Suspension of interest; waiver of restrictions on assessment.* In the case of a deficiency determined by a direct director (or an assistant regional commissioner, (appelate) with respect to any income, estate, or gift tax, if the taxpayer files with such internal revenue officer an agreement waiving the restrictions on assessment of such deficiency, and if notice and demand for payment of such deficiency is not made within 30 days after the filing of such waiver, no interest shall be imposed on the deficiency for the period beginning immediately after such 30th day and ending on the date notice and demand is made. In the case of an agreement with respect to a portion of the deficiency, the rules as set forth in this paragraph are applicable only to that portion of the deficiency to which the agreement relates.

(e) *Income tax reduced by carryback.* (1) The carryback of a net operating loss, net capital loss, investment credit, or a work incentive program (WIN) credit shall not affect the computation of interest of any income tax for the period commencing with the last day prescribed for the payment of such tax and ending with the last day of the taxable year in which the loss or credit arises. For example, if the carryback of a net operating loss, a net capital loss, an investment credit, or a WIN credit to a prior taxable period eliminates or reduces a deficiency in income tax for that period, the full amount of the deficiency will nevertheless bear interest at the annual rate referred to in the regulations under section 6621 from the last date prescribed for payment of such tax until the last day of the taxable year in which the loss or credit arose. Interest will continue to run beyond such last day on any portion of the deficiency which is not eliminated by the carryback. With respect to any portion of an investment credit carryback or a WIN credit carryback from a taxable year attributable to a net operating loss carryback or a capital loss carryback from a subsequent taxable year, such investment credit carryback or WIN credit carryback shall not affect the computation of interest on any income tax for the period commencing with the last day prescribed for the payment of such tax and ending with the last day of such subsequent taxable year.

(2) Where an extension of time for payment of income tax has been granted under section 6164 to a corporation expecting a net operating loss carryback or a net capital loss carryback, interest is payable at the annual rate established under Section 6621 on the amount of such unpaid tax from the last date prescribed for payment thereof without regard to such extension.

(3) Where there has been an allowance of an overpayment attributable to a net operating loss carryback, a capital loss carryback, an investment credit carryback, or a WIN credit carryback and all or part of such allowance is later determined to be excessive, interest shall be computed on the excessive amount from the last day of the year in which the net operating loss, net capital loss, investment credit, or WIN credit arose until the date on which the repayment of such excessive amount is received. Where there has been an allowance of an overpayment with respect to any portion of an investment credit carryback or a WIN credit carryback from a taxable year attributable to a net operating loss carryback or a capital loss carryback from a subsequent taxable year and all or part of such allowance is later determined to be excessive, interest shall be computed on the excessive amount from the last day of such subsequent taxable year until the date on which the repayment of such excessive amount is received.

(f) *Applicable rules.* (1) Any interest prescribed by section 6601 shall be assessed and collected in the same manner as tax and shall be paid upon notice and demand by the district director or the director of the regional service center. Any reference in the Code (except in subchapter B, chapter 63, relating to deficiency procedures) to any tax imposed by the Code shall be deemed also to refer to the interest imposed by section 6601 on such tax. Interest on a tax may be assessed and collected at any time within the period of limitation on collection after assessment of the tax to which it relates. For rules relating to the period of limitation on collection after assessment, see section 6502.

(2) No interest under section 6601 shall be payable on any interest provided by such section.

(3) Interest shall not be imposed on any assessable penalty, addition to the tax, or additional amount unless such assessable penalty, addition to the tax, or additional amount is not paid within 10 days from the date of notice and demand therefor. If interest is imposed, it shall be imposed only for the period from the date of the notice and demand to the date on which payment is received.

(4) If notice and demand is made for any amount and such amount is paid within 10 days after the date of such notice and demand, interest shall not be imposed for the period after the date of such notice and demand.

(5) No interest shall be imposed for failure to pay estimated tax as required by section 59 of the Internal Revenue Code of 1939 or section 6153 or 6154 of the Internal Revenue Code of 1954.

Reg. § 301.6601-1 (f) (5)

24,382.2 (I.R.C.)   Reg. § 301.6602

§ 301.6602 Statutory provisions; interest on erroneous refund recoverable by suit. [Sec. 6602, IRC]

§ 301.6602-1 (T.D. 6234 filed 5-21-57; republished in T.D. 6498, filed 10-24-60; amended by T.D. 7384, filed 10-21-75.) **Interest on erroneous refund recoverable by suit.**

Any portion of an internal revenue tax (or any interest, assessable penalty, additional amount, or addition to tax) which has been erroneously refunded, and which is recoverable by a civil action pursuant to section 7405, shall bear interest at the annual rate referred to in the regulations under section 6621 from the date of the payment of the refund.

INTEREST ON OVERPAYMENTS

§ 301.6611 Statutory provisions; interest on overpayments. [Sec. 6611, IRC]

§ 301.6611-1 (T.D. 6234, filed 5-21-57; as amended by T.D. 6425, filed 11-10-59; republished in T.D. 6498, filed 10-24-60; amended by T.D. 6585, filed 12-27-61; T.D. 6730, filed 5-7-64; T.D. 7301, filed 1-3-74; T.D. 7384, filed 10-21-75; T.D. 7415, filed 4-2-76.) **Interest on overpayments.**

(a) *General rule.* Except as otherwise provided, interest shall be allowed on any overpayment of any tax at the annual rate referred to in the regulations under section 6621 from the date of overpayment of the tax.

(b) *Date of overpayment.* Except as provided in section 6401(a), relating to assessment and collection after the expiration of the applicable period of limitation, there can be no overpayment of tax until the entire tax liability has been satisfied.

Therefore, the dates of overpayment of any tax are the date of payment of the first amount which (when added to previous payments) is in excess of the tax liability (including any interest, addition to the tax, or additional amount) and the dates of payment of all amounts subsequently paid with respect to such tax liability. For rules relating to the determination of the date of payment in the case of an advance payment of tax, a payment of estimated tax, and a credit for income tax withholding, see paragraph (d) of this section.

(c) *Examples.* The application of paragraph (b) may be illustrated by the following examples:

Example (1). Corporation X files an income tax return on March 15, 1955, for the calendar year 1954 disclosing a tax liability of $1,000 and elects to pay the tax in installments. Subsequent to payment of the final installment, the correct tax liability is determined to be $900.

Tax liability		Record of payments	
Assessed	$1,000	March 15, 1955	$500
Correct liability	900	June 15, 1955	500
Overassessment	100		

Since the correct liability in this case is $900, the payment of $500 made on March 15, 1955, and $400 of the payment made on June 15, 1955, are applied in satisfaction of the tax liability. The balance of the payment made on June 15, 1955 ($100) constitutes the amount of the overpayment, and the date on which such payment was made would be the date of the overpayment from which interest would be computed.

Example (2). Corporation Y files an income tax return for the calendar year 1954 on March 15, 1955, disclosing a tax liability of $50,000, and elects to pay the tax in installments. On October 15, 1956, a deficiency in the amount of $10,000 is assessed and is paid in equal amounts on November 15 and November 26, 1956. On April 15, 1957, it is determined that the correct tax liability of the taxpayer for 1954 is only $35,000.

Tax liability		Record of payments	
Original assessment	$50,000	March 15, 1955	$25,000
Deficiency assessment	10,000	June 15, 1955	25,000
		November 15, 1956	5,000
Total assessed	60,000	November 26, 1956	5,000
Correct liability	35,000		
Overassessment	25,000		

Since the correct liability in this case is $35,000, the entire payment of $25,000 made on March 15, 1955, and $10,000 of the payment made on June 15, 1955, are applied in satisfaction of the tax liability. The balance of the payment made on June 15, 1955 ($15,000), plus the amounts paid on November 15, 1956 ($5,000), and November 26, 1956 ($5,000), constitute the amount of the overpayment. The dates of the overpayments from which interest would be computed are as follows:

Date	Amount of overpayment
June 15, 1955	$15,000
November 15, 1956	5,000
November 26, 1956	5,000

The amount of any interest paid with respect to the deficiency of $10,000 is also an overpayment.

(d) *Advance payment of tax, payment of estimated tax, and credit for income tax withholding.* In the case of an advance payment of tax, a payment of estimated income tax, or a credit for income tax withholding, the provisions of section 6513 (except the provisions of subsection (c) thereof), applicable in determining the date of payment of tax for purposes of the period of limitations on credit or refund, shall apply in determining the date of overpayment for purposes of computing interest thereon.

(e) *Refund of income tax caused by*

Interest on Overpayments (I.R.C.) 24,382.3

carryback. If any overpayment of tax imposed by subtitle A of the Code results from the carryback of a net operating loss, a net capital loss, an investment credit, or a work incentive program (WIN) credit, such overpayment, for purposes of this section, shall be deemed not to have been made prior to the end of the taxable year in which the loss or credit arises, or, with respect to any portion of an investment credit or a WIN credit carryback from a taxable year attributable to a net operating loss carryback or a capital loss carryback from a subsequent taxable year, such overpayment shall be deemed not to have been made prior to the close of such subsequent taxable year.

(f) *Refund of income tax caused by carryback of foreign taxes.* For purposes of paragraph (a) of this section, any overpayment of tax resulting from a carryback of tax paid or accrued to foreign countries or possessions of the United States shall be deemed not to have been paid or accrued before the close of the taxable year under subtitle F of the Code in which such taxes were in fact paid or accrued.

(g) *Period for which interest allowable in case of refunds.* If an overpayment of tax is refunded, interest shall be allowed from the date of the overpayment to a date determined by the district director or the director of the regional service center, which shall be not more than 30 days prior to the date of the refund check. The acceptance of a refund check shall not deprive the taxpayer of the right to make a claim for any additional overpayment and interest thereon, provided the claim is made within the applicable period of limitation. However, if a taxpayer does not accept a refund check, no additional interest on the amount of the overpayment included in such check shall be allowed.

(h) *Period for which interest allowable in case of credits*—(1) *General rule.* If an overpayment of tax is credited, interest shall be allowed from the date of overpayment to the due date (as determined under subparagraph (2) of this paragraph) of the amount against which such overpayment is credited.

(2) *Determination of due date*—(i) *In general.* The term "due date", as used in this section, means the last day fixed by law or regulations for the payment of the tax (determined without regard to any extension of time), and not the date on which the district director or the director of the regional service center makes demand for the payment of the tax. Therefore, the due date of a tax (other than an additional assessment subject to the special rule provided by subdivision (iv) of this subparagraph) is the date fixed for the payment of the tax or the several installments thereof.

(ii) *Tax payable in installments*—(a) *In general.* In the case of a credit against a tax, where the taxpayer had properly elected to pay the tax in installments, the due date is the date prescribed for the payment of the installment against which the credit is applied.

(b) *Delinquent installment.* If the taxpayer is delinquent in payment of an installment of tax and a notice and demand has been issued for the payment of the delinquent installment and the remaining installments, the due date of each remaining installment shall then be the date of such notice and demand.

(iii) *Tax or installment not yet due.* If a taxpayer agrees to the crediting of an overpayment against tax or an installment of tax and the schedule of allowance is signed prior to the date on which such tax or installment would otherwise become due, then the due date of such tax or installment shall be the date on which such schedule is signed.

(iv) *Additional assessment satisfied by credit before January 1, 1958.* In the case of a credit made before January 1, 1958, against an additional assessment, the due date of the tax satisfied by the credit is the date the additional assessment was made. For purposes of this subdivision, the term "additional assessment" means a further assessment of a tax of the same character previously paid in part, and includes the assessment of a deficiency as defined in section 6211.

(v) *Assessed interest.* In the case of a credit against assessed interest, the due date is the date of the assessment of such interest.

(vi) *Additional amount, addition to the tax, or assessable penalty.* In the case of a credit against an amount assessed as an additional amount, addition to the tax, or assessable penalty, the due date is the date of the assessment.

(vii) *Estimated income tax for succeeding year.* If the taxpayer elects to have all or part of the overpayment shown by his return applied to his estimated tax for his succeeding taxable year, no interest shall be allowed on such portion of the overpayment credited and such amount shall be applied as a payment on account of the estimated tax for such year or the installments thereof.

(i) [Reserved]

(j) *Refund of overpayment.* No interest shall be allowed on any overpayment of tax imposed by subtitle A of the Code if such overpayment is refunded—

(1) In the case of a return filed on or before the last date prescribed for filing the return of such tax (determined without regard to any extension of time for filing such return), within 45 days after such last date, or

(2) After December 17, 1966, in the case of a return filed after the last day prescribed for filing the return, within 45 days after the date on which the return is filed. However, in the case of any overpayment of tax by an individual (other than an estate or trust and other than a nonresident alien individual) for a taxable year beginning in 1974, "60 days" shall be substituted for "45 days" each place it appears in this paragraph.

§ 301.6612 Statutory provisions; cross references. [Sec. 6612, IRC]

DETERMINATION OF INTEREST RATE

§ 301.6621 Statutory provisions; determination of interest rate. [Sec. 6621, IRC]

§ 301.6621-1 (T.D. 7384, filed 10-21-75.) Interest rate.

Reg. § 301.6621-1

24,382.4 (I.R.C.) Reg. § 301.6621-1(a) 4-12-76

(a) *In general.* For purposes of sections 6601(a), 6602, 6611(a), 6332(c)(1), and 7426(g) and the regulations thereunder, and section 2411(a) of Title 28 of the United States Code, the interest rate under section 6621 shall be—

(1) On amounts outstanding before July 1, 1975, 6 percent per annum (or 4 percent in the case of certain extensions of time for payment of taxes as provided in sections 6601(b) and (j) prior to amendment by section 7(b) of the Act of Jan. 3, 1975 (Pub. L. 93-625, 88 Stat. 2115), and certain overpayments of the unrelated business income tax as provided in section 514(b)(3)(D), prior to its amendment by such Act).

(2) On amounts outstanding on or after July 1, 1975, 9 percent per annum, or, if an adjusted rate is established by the Commissioner under paragraph (b) of this section, such adjusted rate.

(b) *Adjustment of interest rate*—(1) *In general.* The Commissioner shall establish, not later than October 15 of any year, an adjusted rate of interest which shall become effective on February 1 of the immediately succeeding year. Such adjusted interest rate will equal the adjusted prime rate charged by banks (as defined in paragraph (b)(2) of this section) during September of such year rounded to the nearest full percent. However, no adjustment may be made to the interest rate unless—

(i) The adjusted prime rate charged by banks rounded to the nearest full percent during September of such year is at least a full percent more or less than the interest rate then in effect, and

(ii) Not less than 23 months will have expired between the date of the last previous adjustment in the interest rate pursuant to this paragraph and February 1 of the next succeeding year.

(2) *Definition of adjusted prime rate charged by banks.* For purposes of this section, the adjusted prime rate charged by banks is 90 percent of the average predominant prime rate quoted by banks to large businesses as determined by the Board of Governors of the Federal Reserve System.

(c) *Applicability of interest rate*—(1) *Computation.* Interest and additions to tax on any amount outstanding on a specific day shall be computed at the rate applicable on such day.

(2) *Addition to tax.* The addition to tax under sections 6654 and 6655 shall be computed at the same rate per annum as the interest rate set forth under paragraph (a) of this section.

(d) *Examples.* The provisions of this section may be illustrated by the following examples:

Example (1). A, an individual, files an income tax return for the calendar year 1974, on April 15, 1975, showing a tax due of $1,000. A pays the $1,000 on September 1, 1975. Pursuant to section 6601(a), interest on the underpayment of $1,000 is computed at the rate of 6 percent per annum from April 15, 1975, to June 30, 1975, a total of 76 days. Interest for 63 days, from June 30, 1975, to September 1, 1975, shall be computed at the rate of 9 percent per annum.

Example (2). An executor of an estate is granted, in accordance with section 6161 (a)(2)(A), a two-year extension of time for payment of the estate tax shown on the estate tax return, which tax was otherwise due on January 15, 1974. The tax is paid on January 15, 1976. Interest on the underpayment shall be computed at the rate of 4 percent per annum from January 15, 1974, to June 30, 1975, and at the rate of 9 percent per annum from June 30, 1975, to January 15, 1976.

Example (3). X, a corporation, files its 1973 corporate income tax return, on March 15, 1974, and pays the balance of tax due shown thereon. On August 1, 1975, an assessment of a deficiency is made against X with respect to such tax. The deficiency is paid on October 1, 1975. Interest at the rate of 6 percent per annum is due on the deficiency from March 15, 1974, the due date of the return, to June 30, 1975, and at the rate of 9 percent per annum from June 30, 1975, to October 1, 1975.

Example (4). Y, an individual, files an amended individual income tax return, on October 1, 1975, for the refund of an overpayment of income tax Y made on April 15, 1975. Interest is allowed on the overpayment to December 1, 1975. Pursuant to section 6611(a), interest is computed at the rate of 6 percent per annum from April 15, 1975, the date of overpayment, to June 30, 1975. Interest from June 30, 1975 to December 1, 1975 shall be computed at the rate of 9 percent per annum.

Example (5). A, an individual, is liable for an addition to tax under section 6654 for the underpayment of estimated tax from April 15, 1975 until January 15, 1976. The addition to tax shall be computed at the annual rate of 6 percent per annum from April 15, 1975 to June 30, 1975 and at the annual rate of 9 percent per annum from June 30, 1975 to January 15, 1976.

ADDITIONS TO THE TAX, ADDITIONAL AMOUNTS, AND ASSESSABLE PENALTIES

ADDITIONS TO THE TAX AND ADDITIONAL AMOUNTS

§ 53.6651 Statutory provisions; failure to file tax return or to pay tax.

§ 53.6651-1 (T.D. 7368, filed 7-15-75.) **Failure to file tax return or to pay tax.**

(a) *General rules.* For general rules relating to the failure to file tax return or to pay tax, see the regulations under section 6651 contained in Part 301 of this chapter (Regulations on Procedure and Administration).

(b) *Special rule where foundation files return.* (1) Except as provided in paragraph (b)(2) of this section, in the case of tax imposed by section 4941(a)(1) on any disqualified person, reasonable cause shall be presumed, for purposes of section 6651 (a)(1), where the private foundation or trust described in section 4947(a)(2) files a return in good faith and such return indicates no tax liability with respect to such tax on the part of such disqualifid person.

(2) Paragraph (b)(1) of this section shall not apply where the disqualified person knew of facts which, if known by the foundation, would have precluded the foundation from making the return, as filed, in good faith.

§ 301.6651 Statutory provisions; failure to file tax return. [Sec. 6651, IRC]

§ 301.6651-1 (T.D. 6268, filed 11-15-57; republished in T.D. 6498, filed 10-24-60; amended by T.D. 6585, filed 12-27-61; T.D. 7133, filed 7-21-71; T.D. 7160, filed 2-1-72 and T.D. 7260, filed 2-9-73.) **Failure to file tax return or to pay tax.**

(a) *Addition to the tax*—(1) *Failure to file tax return.* In case of failure to file a return required under authority of—

(i) Subchapter A, chapter 61 of the Code, relating to returns and records (other than sections 6015 and 6016, relating to declarations of estimated tax, and part III thereof, relating to information returns);

(ii) Subchapter A, chapter 51 of the Code, relating to distilled spirits, wines, and beer;

(iii) Subchapter A, chapter 52 of the Code, relating to cigars, cigarettes, and cigarette papers and tubes; or

(iv) Subchapter A, chapter 53 of the Code, relating to machine guns, destructive devices, and certain other firearms;

and the regulations thereunder, on or before the date prescribed for filing (determined with regard to any extension of time for such filing), there shall be added to the tax required to be shown on the return the amount specified below unless the failure to file the return within the prescribed time is shown to the satisfaction of the district director, the director of the service center, or, as provided in paragraph (c) of this section, the Assistant Regional Commissioner (Alcohol, Tobacco and Firearms), to be due to reasonable cause and not to willful neglect. The amount to be added to the tax is 5 percent thereof if the failure is for not more than 1 month, with an additional 5 percent for each additional month or fraction thereof during which the failure continues, but not to exceed 25 percent in the aggregate. The amount of of any addition under this subparagraph shall be reduced by the amount of the addition under subparagraph (2) of this paragraph for any month to which an addition to tax applies under both subparagraphs (1) and (2) of this paragraph.

(2) *Failure to pay tax shown on return.* In case of failure to pay the amount shown as tax on any return (required to be filed after December 31, 1969, without regard to any extension of time for filing thereof) specified in subparagraph (1) of this paragraph on or before the date prescribed for payment of such tax (determined with regard to any extension of time for payment), there shall be added to the tax shown on the return the amount specified below unless the failure to pay the tax within the prescribed time is shown to the satisfaction of the district director or the director of the service center to be due to reasonable cause and not to willful neglect. The amount to be added to the tax is 0.5 percent of the amount of tax shown on the return if the failure is for not more than 1 month, with an additional 0.5 percent for each additional month or fraction thereof during which the failure continues, but not to exceed 25 percent in the aggregate.

(3) *Failure to pay tax not shown on return.* In case of failure to pay any amount in respect of any tax required to be shown on a return specified in subparagraph (1) of this paragraph which is not so shown (including an assessment made pursuant to section 6213(b)) within 10 days from the date of the notice and demand therefor (if such notice and demand is made after December 31, 1969), there shall be added to the amount stated in the notice and demand the amount specified below unless the failure to pay the tax within the prescribed time is shown to the satisfaction of the district director or the director of the service center to be due to reasonable cause and not to willful neglect. The amount to be added to the tax is 0.5 percent of the amount stated in the notice and demand if the failure is for not more than 1 month, with an additional 0.5 percent for each additional month or fraction thereof during which the failure continues, but not to exceed 25 percent in the aggregate. The maximum amount of the addition permitted under this subparagraph shall be reduced by the amount of the addition under subparagraph (1) of this paragraph which is attributable to the tax for which the notice and demand is made and which is not paid within 10 days from the date of notice and demand.

(b) *Month defined.* (1) If the date prescribed for filing the return or paying tax is the last day of a calendar month, each succeeding calendar month or frac-

Reg. § 301.6651-1 (b) (1)

tion thereof during which the failure to file or pay tax continues shall constitute a month for purposes of section 6651.

(2) If the date prescribed for filing the return or paying tax is a date other than the last day of a calendar month, the period which terminates with the date numerically corresponding thereto in the succeeding calendar month and each successive period shall constitute a month for purposes of section 6651. If, in the month of February, there is no date corresponding to the date prescribed for filing the return or paying tax, the period from such date in January through the last day of February shall constitute a month for purposes of section 6651. Thus, if a return is due on January 30, the first month shall end on February 28 (or 29 if a leap year), and the succeeding months shall end on March 30, April 30, etc.

(3) If a return is not timely filed or tax is not timely paid, the fact that the date prescribed for filing the return or paying tax, or the corresponding date in any succeeding calendar month, falls on a Saturday, Sunday, or a legal holiday is immaterial in determining the number of months for which the addition to the tax under section 6651 applies.

(c) *Showing of reasonable cause.* (1) Except as provided in subparagraphs (3) and (4) of this paragraph, a taxpayer who wishes to avoid the addition to the tax for failure to file a tax return or pay tax must make an affirmative showing of all facts alleged as a reasonable cause for his failure to file such return or pay such tax on time in the form of a written statement containing a declaration that it is made under penalties of perjury. Such statement should be filed with the district director or the director of the service center with whom the return is required to be filed; provided, that, where special tax returns of liquor dealers are delivered to an alcohol, tobacco, and firearms officer working under the supervision of the Regional Director, Bureau of Alcohol, Tobacco, and Firearms, such statement may be delivered with the return. If the district director, the director of the service center, or, where applicable, the Regional Director, Bureau of Alcohol, Tobacco, and Firearms, determines that the delinquency was due to a reasonable cause and not to willful neglect, the addition to the tax will not be assessed. If the taxpayer exercised ordinary business care and prudence and was nevertheless unable to file the return within the prescribed time, then the delay is due to a reasonable cause. A failure to pay will be considered to be due to reasonable cause to the extent that the taxpayer has made a satisfactory showing that he exercised ordinary business care and prudence in providing for payment of his tax liability and was nevertheless either unable to pay the tax or would suffer an undue hardship (as described in § 1.6161-1(b) of this chapter) if he paid on the due date. In determining whether the taxpayer was unable to pay the tax in spite of the exercise of ordinary business care and prudence in providing for payment of his tax liability, consideration will be given to all the facts and circumstances of the taxpayer's financial situation, including the amount and nature of the taxpayer's expenditures in light of the income (or other amounts) he could, at the time of such expenditures, reasonably expect to receive prior to the date prescribed for the payment of the tax. Thus, for example, a taxpayer who incurs lavish or extravagant living expenses in an amount such that the remainder of his assets and anticipated income will be insufficient to pay his tax, has not exercised ordinary business care and prudence in providing for the payment of his tax liability. Further, a taxpayer who invests funds in speculative or illiquid assets has not exercised ordinary business care and prudence in providing for the payment of his tax liability unless, at the time of the investment, the remainder of the taxpayer's assets and estimated income will be sufficient to pay his tax or it can be reasonably foreseen that the speculative or illiquid investment made by the taxpayer can be utilized (by sale or as security for a loan) to realize sufficient funds to satisfy the tax liability. A taxpayer will be considered to have exercised ordinary business care and prudence if he made reasonable efforts to conserve sufficient assets in marketable form to satisfy his tax liability and nevertheless was unable to pay all or a portion of the tax when it became due.

(2) In determining if the taxpayer exercised ordinary business care and prudence in providing for the payment of his tax liability, consideration will be given to the nature of the tax which the taxpayer has failed to pay. Thus, for example, facts and circumstances which, because of the taxpayer's efforts to conserve assets in marketable form, may constitute reasonable cause for nonpayment of income taxes may not constitute reasonable cause for failure to pay over taxes described in section 7501 that are collected or withheld from any other person.

(3) If for a taxable year ending on or after December 31, 1971, an individual taxpayer satisfies the requirements of § 1.6081-4(a) (relating to an automatic extension of time for filing an individual income tax return), reasonable cause shall be presumed, for the period of the extension of time to file, with respect to any underpayment of tax if—

(i) The excess of the amount of tax shown on Form 1040 over, the amount of tax paid on or before the regular due date of the return by virtue of taxes withheld by the employer, payments pursuant to the declaration of estimated tax and the payment in full of estimated tax liability pursuant to § 1.6081-4, is not greater than 10 percent of the amount of tax shown on the individual's Form 1040, and

(ii) Any balance due shown on the Form 1040 is remitted with the return.

(4) If, for a taxable year ending on or after December 31, 1972, a corporate taxpayer satisfies the requirements of § 1.6081-3(a) or (b) (relating to an automatic extension of time for filing a corporation income tax return), reasonable cause shall be presumed, for the period of the extension of time to file, with respect to any underpayment of tax if—

(i) Not less than the amount of tax that would be required as the first installment under section 6152(a)(1), if the taxpayer elected to pay the tax in installments, is paid on or before the regular due date of the return and the second installment is paid on or before 3 months after such date,

(ii) The amount of tax (determined without regard to any prepayment thereof) shown on Form 7004, or the amount of tax paid on or before the regular due date of the return, is at least 90 percent of the amount of tax shown on the taxpayer's Form 1120, and

(iii) Any balance due shown on the Form 1120 is paid on or before the due date of the return, including any extensions of time for filing.

(d) *Penalty imposed on net amount due*—(1) *Credits against the tax.* The amount of tax required to be shown on the return for purposes of section 6651(a)(1) and the amount shown as tax on the return for purposes of section 6651(a)(2) shall be reduced by the amount of any part of the tax which is paid on or before the date prescribed for payment of the tax and by the amount of any credit against the tax which may be claimed on the return.

(2) *Partial payments.* (i) The amount of tax required to be shown on the return for purposes of section 6651(a)(2) shall, for the purpose of computing the addition for any month, be reduced by the amount of any part of the tax which is paid after the date prescribed for payment and on or before the first day of such month.

(ii) The amount of tax stated in the notice and demand for purposes of section 6651(a)(3) shall, for the purpose of computing the addition for any month, be reduced by the amount of any part of the tax which is paid before the first day of such month.

(e) *No addition to tax if fraud penalty assessed.* No addition to the tax under section 6651 shall be assessed with respect to an underpayment of tax if a 50 percent addition to the tax for fraud is assessed with respect to the same underpayment under section 6653(b). See section 6653(d).

(f) *Examples.* The provisions of this section may be illustrated by the following examples:

Example (1). (a) Under section 6072 (a), income tax returns of individuals on

Reg. § 301.6651-1 (f)

Additions to Tax and Additional Amounts **(I.R.C.) 24,383**

a calendar year basis must be filed on or before the 15th day of April following the close of the calendar year. Assume an individual filed his income tax return for the calendar year 1969 on July 20, 1970, and the failure to file on or before the prescribed date is not due to reasonable cause. The tax shown on the return is $800 and a deficiency of $200 is subsequently assessed, making the tax required to be shown on the return, $1,000. Of this amount, $300 has been paid by withholding from wages and $400 has been paid as estimated tax. The balance due as shown on the return of $100 ($800 shown as tax on the return less $700 previously paid) is paid on August 21, 1970. The failure to pay on or before the prescribed date is not due to reasonable cause. There will be imposed, in addition to interest, an additional amount under section 6651(a)(2) of $2.50, which is 2.5 percent (2% for the 4 months from April 16 through August 15, and 0.5% for the fractional part of the month from August 16 through August 21) of the net amount due as shown on the return of $100 ($800 shown on the return less $700 paid on or before April 15). There will also be imposed an additional amount under section 6651(a)(1) of $58, determined as follows:

20 percent (5% per month for the 3 months from April 16 through July 15 and 5% for the fractional part of the month from July 16 through July 20) of the net amount due of $300 ($1,000 required to be shown on the return less $700 paid on or before April 15)	$ 60
Reduced by the amount of the addition imposed under section 6651(a)(2) for those months	2
Addition to tax under section 6651(a)(1)	$ 58

(b) A notice and demand for the $200 deficiency is issued on January 8, 1971, but the taxpayer does not pay the deficiency until December 23, 1971. In addition to interest there will be imposed an additional amount under section 6651(a)(3) of $10, determined as follows:

Addition computed without regard to limitation:	
6 percent (5½% for the 11 months from January 19, 1971, through December 18, 1971, and 0.5% for the fractional part of the month from December 19 through December 23) of the amount stated in the notice and demand ($200)	$ 12
Limitation on addition:	
25 percent of the amount stated in the notice and demand ($200)	$ 50
Reduced by the part of the addition under section 6651(a)(1) for failure to file attributable to the $200 deficiency (20% of $200)	$ 40
Maximum amount of the addition under section 6651(a)(3)	$ 10

Example (2). An individual files his income tax return for the calendar year 1969 on December 2, 1970, and such delinquency is not due to reasonable cause. The balance due, as shown on the return, of $500 is paid when the return is filed on December 2, 1970. In addition to interest and the addition for failure to pay under section 6651 (a)(2) of $20 (8 months at 0.5% per month, 4%), there will also be imposed an additional amount under section 6651(a)(1) of $112.50, determined as follows:

Penalty at 5% for maximum of 5 months, 25% of $500	$125.00
Less reduction for the amount of the addition under section 6651(a)(2):	
Amount imposed under section 6651(a)(2) for failure to pay for the months in which there is also an addition for failure to file 2½ percent for the 5 months April 16 through September 15 of the net amount due ($500)	12.50
Addition to tax under section 6651(a)(1)	$112.50

○▶ § 301.6652 **Statutory provisions; failure to file certain information returns.** [Sec. 6552, IRC].

○▶ § 301.6652-1 (T.D. 6268, filed 11-15-57, as amended by T.D. 6425, filed 11-10-59; republished in T.D. 6498, filed 10-24-60; amended by T.D. 6585, filed 12-27-61; T.D. 6628, filed 12-27-62; T.D. 6887, filed 6-23-66; T.D. 7001, filed 1-17-69 and T.D. 7127, filed 6-14-71.) **Failure to file certain information returns.**

(a) *Returns with respect to payments made in calendar years after 1962*—(1) *Payments of dividends, interest, or patronage dividends aggregating $10 or more.* In the case of each failure to file a statement required by—

(i) Section 6042(a)(1), relating to information returns with respect to payments of dividends aggregating $10 or more in a calendar year, in effect with respect to payments made after December 31, 1962,

(ii) Section 6044 (a)(1), relating to information returns with respect to certain payments by cooperatives aggregating $10 or more in a calendar year, in effect with respect to payments made on or after the first day of the first taxable year of the cooperative beginning after December 31, 1962, with respect to patronage occurring on or after such first day, or

(iii) Section 6049(a)(1), relating to information returns with respect to payments of interest aggregating $10 or more in a calendar year, in effect with respect to payments made after December 31, 1962, and the regulations under such section, within the time prescribed for filing such statement (determined with regard to any extension of time for filing), there shall be paid by the person failing to so file the statement $10 for each such statement not so filed. However, the total amount imposed on the delinquent person for all such failures under section 6652(a) and this section during any calendar year shall not exceed $25,000.

(2) *Other payments; statements with respect to tips.* In the case of each failure—

(i) To file a statement of a payment made after December 31, 1962, to another person required under authority of section 6041, relating to information returns with respect to certain information at source, or section 6051(d), relating to information

Reg. § 301.6652-1(a)(2)

returns with respect to payments of wages as defined in section 3401(a), or

(ii) To file a statement required under authority of section 6053(b), relating to statements furnished by employers with respect to tips, and the regulations under such section, within the time prescribed for filing such statement (determined with regard to any extension of time for filing), there shall be paid by the person failing to so file the statement $1 for each such statement not so filed. However, the total amount imposed on the delinquent person for all such failures during any calendar year shall not exceed $1,000.

(b) *Returns with respect to payments made in calendar years before 1963 and to certain payments by cooperatives after 1962.* In the case of each failure to file a statement, with respect to a payment to another person, required under authority of—

(1) Section 6041, relating to information returns with respect to certain information at source, in effect with respect to payments made before 1963,

(2) Section 6042 (1), relating to information returns with respect to payments of corporate dividends, in effect with respect to payments made before 1963,

(3) Section 6044, relating to information returns with respect to payments of patronage dividends, in effect with respect to payments made by a cooperative with respect to patronage occurring before the first day of the first taxable year of the cooperative beginning after December 31, 1962, or

(4) Section 6051(d), relating to information returns with respect to payments of wages as defined in section 3401(a), in effect with respect to payments made before 1963, and the regulations under such section, within the time prescribed for filing such statement (determined with regard to any extension of time for filing), there shall be paid by the person failing to so file such statement $1 for each such statement not so filed. However, the total amount imposed on the delinquent person for all such failures during any calendar year shall not exceed $1,000.

(c) *Returns with respect to reporting payments of wages in the form of group-term life insurance provided in a calendar year after December 31, 1963.* In the case of each failure to file a return required by section 6052(a), relating to reporting payment of wages in the form of group-term life insurance provided for any employee on his life in a calendar year after December 31, 1963, and the regulations under such section, within the time prescribed for filing such return (determined with regard to any extension of time for filing), there shall be paid by the person failing to so file such return $10 for each such return not so filed. However, the total amount imposed on the delinquent person for all such failures under section 6652(a) and this section during any calendar year shall not exceed $25,000.

(d) *Returns with respect to transfer of stock or record title thereto pursuant to options exercised on or after January 1, 1964.* In the case of each failure to file a statement of the transfer of stock or of record title thereto as required by section 6039(a) and the regulations under such section within the time prescribed for filing such statement (determined with regard to any extension of time for filing), there shall be paid by the corporation failing to so file such statement, $10 for each such statement not so filed. However, the total amount imposed on the delinquent corporation for all such failures under section 6652 (a) and this section during any calendar year shall not exceed $25,000.

(e) *Manner of payment.* The amount imposed under subsection (a), (b), or (c) of section 6652 and this section on any person shall be paid in the same manner as tax upon the issuance of a notice and demand therefor.

(f) *Showing of reasonable cause.* The amount imposed by subsection (a), (b), or (c) of section 6652 shall not apply with respect to a failure to file a statement within the time prescribed if it is established to the satisfaction of the district director or the director of the internal revenue service center that such failure was due to reasonable cause and not to willful neglect. An affirmative showing of reasonable cause must be made in the form of a written statement, containing a declaration that it is made under the penalties of perjury, setting forth all the facts alleged as a reasonable cause.

(g) *Alcohol and tobacco taxes.* For penalties for failure to file certain information returns with respect to alcohol and tobacco taxes, see, generally, subtitle E of the Code.

(h) *Tips.* For regulations under section 6652 (c) in respect of failure to report tips, see § 31.6652-1 of this chapter (Employment Tax Regulations).

§ 301.6652-2 (T.D. 7127, filed 6-14-71.) **Failure by exempt organizations and certain trusts to file certain returns or annual reports or to comply with section 6104(d) for taxable years beginning after December 31, 1969.**

(a) *Exempt organization or trust.* In the case of a failure to file a return required by—

(1) Section 6033, relating to returns by exempt organizations,

(2) Section 6034, relating to returns by certain trusts, or

(3) Section 6043(b), relating to returns regarding the liquidation, dissolution, termination, or substantial contraction of an exempt organization,

within the time and in the manner prescribed for filing such return (determined with regard to any extension of time for filing), unless it is shown that such failure is due to reasonable cause, there shall be paid by the exempt organization or trust failing to file such return $10 for each day during which such failure continues. However, the total amount imposed on any exempt organization or trust under this paragraph for such failure with regard to any one return shall not exceed $5,000.

(b) *Managers.* If an exempt organization or trust fails to file under section 6652 (d)(1), the Commissioner may, by written demand, request that such organization or trust file the delinquent return within 90 days after the date of mailing of such demand, or within such additional period as the Commissioner shall determine is reasonable under the circumstances. If such organization or trust does not so file on or before the date specified in such demand, there shall be paid by the person or persons responsible for such failure to file $10 for each day after such date during which such failure continues, unless it is shown that such failure is due to reasonable cause. However, the total amount imposed under this paragraph on all persons responsible for such failure with regard to any one return shall not exceed $5,000.

(c) *Annual reports*—(1) *In general.* In the case of a failure—

(i) To file the annual report required under section 6056, relating to annual reports by private foundations, or

(ii) To comply with the requirements of section 6104(d), relating to public inspection of private foundations' annual reports, within the time and in the manner prescribed for filing such report or complying with section 6104(d) (determined with regard to any extension of time for filing), unless it is shown that such failure is due to reasonable cause, there shall be paid by the person or persons responsible for failing to file such report or to comply with section 6104(d) $10 for each day during which such failure continues. However,

the total amount imposed under this subparagraph on all persons responsible for any such failure with regard to any one annual report shall not exceed $5,000.

(2) *Amount imposed.* The amount imposed under section 6652(d)(3) is $10 per day for a failure to file the annual report and $10 per day for a failure to comply with section 6104(d). For example, assume that an annual report must be filed by X private foundation on or before May 15, 1972, for calendar year 1971. Such foundation without reasonable cause does not file the report until May 29, 1972. Further, the foundation without reasonable cause does not comply with section 6104(d) by publishing notice of the availability of the annual report until July 30, 1972. In this case, the person failing to file the report and to comply with section 6104(d) within the prescribed time is required to pay $900, $140 for filing the report 14 days late and $760 for complying with section 6104(d) 76 days late.

(3) *Cross reference.* For the penalty for willful failure to file the annual report and notice required under section 6056 or to comply with section 6104(d), see § 301.6685-1.

(d) *Special rules.* For purposes of section 6652(d) and this section—

(1) *Person.* The term "person" means any officer, director, trustee, employee, member, or other individual whose duty it is to perform the act in respect of which the violation occurs.

(2) *Liability.* If more than one person (as defined in subparagraph (1) of this paragraph) is liable for a failure to file or to comply with section 6652(d)(2) or (3), all such persons shall be jointly and severally liable with respect to such failure.

(e) *Manner of payment.* The amount imposed under section 6652(d) and this section on any exempt organization, trust, or person (as defined in paragraph (d)(1) of this section) shall be paid in the same manner as tax upon the issuance of a notice and demand therefor.

(f) *Showing of reasonable cause.* No amount imposed by section 6652(d) shall apply with respect to a failure to file or comply under this section if it is established to the satisfaction of the district director or director of the internal revenue service center that such failure was due to reasonable cause. An affirmative showing of reasonable cause must be made in the form of a written statement containing a declaration by the appropriate person (as defined in paragraph (d)(1) of this section), or, in his absence, by any officer, director, or trustee of the organization, that the statement is made under the penalties of perjury, setting forth all the facts alleged as reasonable cause.

(g) *Group returns.* If a central organization is authorized to file a group return on behalf of two or more of its local organizations for the taxable year in accordance with paragraph (d) of § 1.6033-2 (Income Tax Regulations), the responsibility for timely filing of such a return is placed upon the central organization for purposes of this section. Consequently, the amount imposed by section 6652(d)(1) for failure to file the group return shall be paid by the central organization and the

Reg. § 301.6652-2(g)

amount imposed by section 6652(d)(2) for failure to file the group return within the time prescribed by the Commissioner shall be paid by the person or persons responsible for filing the group return.

(h) *Effective date.* This section shall apply for taxable years beginning after December 31, 1969.

§ 301.6653 Statutory provisions; failure to pay tax. [Sec. 6653, IRC]

§ 301.6653-1 (T.D. 6268, filed 11-15-57; republished in T.D. 6498, filed 10-24-60; amended by T.D. 7320, filed 8-5-74; TD 7498, filed 7-12-77.) **Failure to pay tax.**

(a) *Negligence or intentional disregard of rules and regulations with respect to income or gift taxes.* If any part of any underpayment, as defined in section 6653 (c)(1) and paragraph (c)(1) of this section, of any income tax imposed by subtitle A of the Code, or gift tax imposed by chapter 12 of subtitle B of the Code, is due to negligence or intentional disregard of rules and regulations, but without intent to defraud, there shall be added to the tax an amount equal to 5 percent of the underpayment.

(b) *Fraud.* (1) If any part of any underpayment of tax, as defined in section 6653 (c) and paragraph (c) of this section required to be shown on a return is due to fraud, there shall be added to the tax an amount equal to 50 percent of the underpayment.

(2) If a 50 percent addition to the tax for fraud is assessed under section 6653 (b) with respect to an underpayment—

(i) The addition to the tax under section 6651, relating to failure to file a tax return, will not be assessed with respect to the same underpayment, and

(ii) In the case of the income taxes imposed by subtitle A and the gift tax imposed by chapter 12 of subtitle B, the 5 percent addition to the tax under section 6653 (a), relating to negligence and intentional disregard of rules and regulations, will not be assessed with respect to the same underpayment.

(c) *Definition of underpayment* — (1) *Income, estate, and gift taxes.* In the case of income, estate, and gift taxes, an underpayment for purposes of section 6653 and this section is—

(i) The total amount of all deficiencies as defined in section 6211, if a return was filed on or before the last date (determined with regard to any extension of time) prescribed for filing such return, or

(ii) The amount of the tax imposed by subtitle A or B, as the case may be, if a return was not filed on or before the last date (determined with regard to any extension of time) prescribed for filing such return.

However, for purposes of paragraph (c)(1) (i) of this section, any amount of additional tax shown on an amended return, so-called, filed after the due date of the return is a deficiency.

(2) *Other taxes.* In the case of any tax other than income, estate, and gift taxes, an underpayment for purposes of section 6653 and this section is the amount by which the tax imposed exceeds—

(i) In the case of any tax with respect to which the taxpayer is required to file a return, the sum of (a) the amount shown as tax by the taxpayer upon his return filed in respect of such tax, but only if the return is filed on or before the last date (determined with regard to any extension of time) prescribed for filing such return, plus (b) any amount not shown on a return filed by the taxpayer which is paid in respect of such tax prior to the date prescribed for filing the return. The "amount shown as tax by the taxpayer upon his return" for the purposes of this subparagraph shall be determined without regard to any credit for an overpayment for any prior tax return period, and without regard to any adjustment made under section 6205(a), or section 6413(a), relating to special rules applicable to certain employment taxes.

(ii) In the case of any tax payable by stamp, the amount paid (on or before the date prescribed for payment) in respect of such tax.

The amounts specified in subdivisions (i) and (ii) of this subparagraph shall be reduced, for purposes of determining the amount of the underpayment, by the amount of any rebates made. For purposes of this subparagraph, the term "rebates" means so much of an abatement, credit, refund or other repayment as was made on the ground that the tax imposed was less than the excess of the amount specified in subdivision (i) or (ii) of this subparagraph, whichever is applicable, over any rebates previously made.

(d) *No delinquency penalty if fraud assessed.* See paragraph (b)(2) of this section.

(e) *Failure to pay stamp tax.* Any person (as defined in section 6671 (b)) who willfully fails to pay any tax payable by stamp, coupons, tickets, books or other devices or methods prescribed by the Code or regulations promulgated thereunder, or willfully attempts in any manner to evade or defeat any such tax or the payment thereof, shall in addition to other penalties provided by law, be liable to a penalty of 50 percent of the total amount of the underpayment of the tax.

(f) *Joint returns.* No person filing a joint return shall be held liable for a fraud penalty except for his own personal fraudulent conduct. Thus, for the fraud penalty to apply to a taxpayer who files a joint return some part of the underpayment in such return must be due to the fraud of such taxpayer. A taxpayer shall not be subject to the fraud penalty solely by reason of the fraud of a spouse and his filing of a joint reutrn with such spouse.

§ 1.6654 Statutory provisions; failure by individual to pay estimated income tax. [Sec. 6654, IRC]

§ 1.6654-1 (T.D. 6267, filed 11-13-57; republished in T.D. 6500, filed 11-25-60; amended by T.D. 6678, filed 9-30-63; T.D. 7384, filed 10-21-75; T.D. 7427, filed 8-9-76.) **Addition to the tax in the case of an individual.**

(a) *In general.* (1) Section 6654 imposes an addition to the taxes under chapters 1 and 2 of the Code in the case of any underpayment of estimated tax by an individual (with certain exceptions described in section 6654(d)). This addition to the tax is in addition to any applicable criminal penalties and is imposed whether or not there was reasonable cause for the underpayment. The amount of the underpayment for any installment date is the excess of—

(i) The following percentages of the tax shown on the return for the taxable year or, if no return was filed, of the tax for such year, divided by the number of installment dates prescribed for such taxable year:

(A) 80 percent in the case of taxable years beginning after December 31, 1966, of individuals not referred to in section 6073(b) (relating to income from farming or fishing);

(B) 70 percent in the case of taxable years beginning before January 1, 1967, of such individuals; and

(C) 66⅔ percent in the case of individuals referred to in section 6073(b); over

(ii) The amount, if any, of the installment paid on or before the last day prescribed for such payment.

(2) The amount of the addition is determined at the annual rate referred to in the regulations under section 6621 upon the underpayment of any installment of estimated tax for the period from the date such installment is required to be paid until the 15th day of the fourth month following the close of the taxable year, or the date such underpayment is paid, whichever is earlier. For purposes of determining the period of the underpayment (i) the date prescribed for the payment of any installment of estimated tax shall be determined without regard to any extension of time, and (ii) a payment of estimated tax on any installment date, to the extent that it exceeds the amount of the installment determined under subparagraph (1)(i) of this paragraph for such installment date, shall be considered a payment of any previous underpayment.

(3) In determining the amount of the installment paid on or before the last day prescribed for payment thereof, the estimated tax shall be computed without any reduction for the amount which the taxpayer estimates as his credit under section 31 (relating to tax withheld at source on wages), and the amount of such credit shall be deemed a payment of estimated tax. An equal part of the amount of such credit shall be deemed paid on each installment date (determined under section 6153) for the taxable year unless the taxpayer establishes the dates on which all amounts were actually withheld. In the latter case, all amounts withheld shall be considered as payments of estimated tax on the dates such amounts were actually withheld. Under section 31 the entire amount withheld during a calendar year is allowed as a credit against the tax for the taxable year which begins in such calendar year. However, where more than one taxable year begins in any calendar year no portion of the amount withheld during the calendar year will be treated as a payment of estimated tax for any taxable year other than the last taxable year beginning in such calendar year. The rules prescribed in this subparagraph for determining the time as of which the amount withheld shall be deemed paid are applicable even though such amount was withheld during a taxable year preceding that for which the credit is allowed.

(4) The term "tax" when used in subparagraph (1)(i) of this paragraph shall mean—

(i) The tax imposed by chapter 1 of the Code (other than by section 56 or, for taxable years ending before September 30, 1968, the tax surcharge imposed by section 51), plus

(ii) For taxable years beginning after December 31, 1966, the tax imposed by chapter 2 of the Code, minus

(iii) All credits allowed by part IV, subchapter A of chapter 1, except the credit provided by section 31, relating to tax withheld at source on wages. For the disallowance of certain credits in the case of taxpayers who elect to use the standard deduction or to pay the optional tax imposed by section 3, see section 36.

(b) *Statement relating to underpayment.* If there has been an underpayment of estimated tax as of any installment date prescribed for its payment and the taxpayer believes that one or more of the exceptions described in § 1.6654-2 precludes the assertion of the addition to the tax under section 6654, he should attach to his income tax return for the taxable year a Form 2210 showing the applicability of any exception upon which he relies.

(c) *Examples.* The method prescribed in paragraph (a) of this section for computing the addition to the tax may be illustrated by the following examples:

Example (1). An individual taxpayer files his return for the calendar year 1972 on April 15, 1973 showing a tax (income and self-employment tax) of $30,000. He had paid a total of $20,000 of estimated tax in four installments of $5,000 on each of the four installment dates prescribed for such year. No other payments were made prior to the date the return was filed. Since the amount of each installment paid by the last date prescribed for payment thereof is less than one-quarter of 80 percent of the tax shown on the return, the addition to the tax is applicable in respect of the underpayment existing as of each installment date and is computed as follows:

(1)	Amount of tax shown on return	$30,000
(2)	80 percent of item (1)	24,000
(3)	One-fourth of item (2)	$ 6,000
(4)	Deduct amount paid on each installment date	5,000
(5)	Amount of underpayment for each installment date (item (3) minus item (4))	1,000
(6)	Addition to the tax:	
	1st installment — period 4/15/72 to 4/15/73	$ 60
	2nd installment—period 6/15/72 to 4/15/73	50
	3rd installment—period 9/15/72 to 4/15/73	35
	4th installment—period 1/15/73 to 4/15/73	15
	Total	$160

Example (2). An individual taxpayer files his return for the calendar year 1955 on April 15, 1956, showing a tax of $30,000. The requirements of section 6015(a) were first met after April 1 and before June 2, 1955, and a total of $18,000 of estimated tax was paid in three equal installments

Reg. § 1.6654-1(c)

24,388 (I.R.C.)   Reg. § 1.6654-1(c)

of $6,000 on each of the three installment dates prescribed for such year. Since the amount of each installment paid by the last date prescribed for payment thereof is less than one-third of 70 percent of the tax shown on the return, the addition to the tax is applicable in respect of the underpayment existing as of each installment date and is computed as follows:

(1)	Amount of tax shown on return	$30,000
(2)	70 percent of item (1) ...	21,000
(3)	⅓ of item (2)	$ 7,000
(4)	Deduct amount paid on each installment date..	6,000
(5)	Amount of underpayment for each installment date (item (3) minus item (4))	1,000
(6)	Addition to the tax:	
	1st installment—period 6/15/55 to 4/15/56	$ 50
	2nd installment—period 9/15/55 to 4/15/56	35
	3rd installment—period 1/15/56 to 4/15/56	15
	Total	$100

○━ § 301.6654 Statutory provisions; failure by individual to pay estimated income tax. [Sec. 6654, IRC]

○━ § 301.6654-1 (T.D. 6268, filed 11-15-57; republished in T.D. 6498, filed 10-24-60; amended by T.D. 7282, filed 7-16-73.) **Failure by individual to pay estimated income tax.**

For regulations under section 6654, see §§ 1.6654-1 to 1.6654-5, inclusive, of this chapter (Income Tax Regulations).

○━ § 1.6654-2 (T.D. 6267, filed 11-13-57; republished in T.D. 6500, filed 11-25-60; amended by T.D. 6678, filed 9-30-63; T.D. 6777, filed 12-15-64; T.D. 7282, filed 7-16-73; T.D. 7427, filed 8-9-76.) **Exceptions to imposition of the addition to the tax in the case of individuals.**

(a) *In general.* The addition to the tax under section 6654 will not be imposed for any underpayment of any installment of estimated tax if, on or before the date prescribed for payment of the installment, the total amount of all payments of estimated tax made equals or exceeds the least of the following amounts—

(1) The amount which would have been required to be paid on or before the date prescribed for payment if the estimated tax were the tax shown on the return for the preceding taxable year, provided that the preceding taxable year was a year of 12 months and a return showing a liability for tax was filed for such year. However, this subparagraph shall not apply with respect to any taxable year which ends on or after September 30, 1968, for which a tax is imposed by section 51 (relating to tax surcharge), in the case of a payment of estimated tax the time prescribed for payment of which is on or after September 15, 1968.

(2) The amount which would have been required to be paid on or before the date prescribed for payment if the estimated tax were an amount equal to a percentage of the tax computed by placing on an annual basis the taxable income for the calendar months in the taxable year ending before the month in which the installment is required to be paid. That percentage is 80 percent in the case of taxable years beginning after December 31, 1966, of individuals not referred to in section 6073(b) (relating to income from farming or fishing), 70 percent in the case of taxable years beginning before January 1, 1967, of such individuals, and 66⅔ percent in the case individuals referred to in section 6073(b). With respect to taxable years beginning after December 31, 1966, the adjusted self-employment income shall be taken into account in determining the amount referred to in this subparagraph if net earnings from self-employment (as defined in section 1402(a)) for the taxable year equal or exceed $400. For purposes of this subparagraph—

(i) Taxable income shall be placed on an annual basis by—

(A) Multiplying by 12 (or the number of months in the taxable year if less than 12) the taxable income (computed without the standard deduction and without the deduction for personal exemptions), or the adjusted gross income if the standard deduction is to be used, for the calendar months in the taxable year ending before the month in which the installment is required to be paid,

(B) Dividing the resulting amount by the number of such calendar months, and

(C) Deducting from such amount the standard deduction, if applicable, and the deduction for personal exemptions (such personal exemptions being determined as of the date prescribed for payment of the installment).

(ii) The term "adjusted self-employment income" means—

(A) The net earnings from self-employment (as defined in section 1402(a)) for the calendar months in the taxable year ending before the month in which the installment is required to be paid, computed as if such months constituted the taxable year, but not more than

(B) The excess of—

(1) For taxable years beginning after 1966, $6,600,

(2) For taxable years beginning after 1971, $9,000,

(3) For taxable years beginning after 1972, $10,800,

(4) For taxable years beginning after 1973, $13,200, and

(5) For taxable years beginning after 1974, an amount equal to the contribution and benefit base (as determined under section 230 of the Social Security Act) which is effective for the calendar year in which the taxable year begins,

over the amount of the wages (within the meaning of section 1402(b)) for such calendar months placed on an annual basis. For this purpose, wages are annualized in a manner consistent with subdivision (i)(A) and (B) of this subparagraph, that is, by multiplying by 12 (or the number of months in the taxable year in the case of a taxable year of less than 12 months) the wages for such calendar months and dividing the resulting amount by the number of such months.

(3) An amount equal to 90 percent of the tax computed, at the rates applicable

to the taxable year, on the basis of the actual taxable income for the calendar months in the taxable year ending before the month in which the installment is required to be paid, as if such months constituted the entire taxable year. For taxable years beginning after December 31, 1966, such computation shall include the tax imposed by chapter 2 on the actual self-employment income for such months. For purposes of this subparagraph, the term "actual self-employment income" means—

(i) The net earnings from self-employment (as defined in section 1402(a)) for such calendar months, computed as if such months constituted the taxable year, but not more than

(ii) The excess of —

(A) For taxable years beginning after 1966, $6,600,

(B) for taxable years beginning after 1971, $9,000,

(C) For taxable years beginning after 1972, $10,800,

(D) For taxable years beginning after 1973, $13,200, and

(E) For taxable years beginning after 1974, an amount equal to the contribution and benefit base (as determined under section 230 of the Social Security Act) which is effective for the calendar year in which the taxable year begins,

over the amount of wages (within the meaning of section 1402(b)) for such months.

(4) The amount which would have been required to be paid on or before the date prescribed for payment if the estimated tax were an amount equal to a tax determined on the basis of the tax rates and the taxpayer's status with respect to personal exemptions under section 151 for the taxable year, but otherwise on the basis of the facts shown on the return for the preceding taxable year and the law applicable to such year, in the case of an individual required to file a return for such preceding taxable year.

In the case of a taxpayer whose taxable year consists of 52 or 53 weeks in accordance with section 441(f), the rules prescribed by paragraph (b) of § 1.441-2 shall be applicable in determining, for purposes of subparagraph (1) of this paragraph, whether a taxable year was a year of 12 months and, for purposes of subparagraphs (2) and (3) of this paragraph, the number of calendar months in a taxable year preceding the date prescribed for payment of an installment of estimated tax. For the rules to be applied in determining taxable income for any period described in subparagraphs (2) and (3) of this paragraph in the case of a taxpayer who employs accounting periods (e.g., thirteen 4-week periods or four 13-week periods) none of which terminates with the end of the applicable period described in subparagraph (2) or (3) of this paragraph, see paragraph (a)(5) of § 1.6655-2.

(b) *Meaning of terms.* As used in this section and § 1.6654-3—

(1) The term "tax" means—

(i) The tax imposed by chapter 1 of the Code (other than by section 56), plus

(ii) For taxable years beginning after December 31, 1966, the tax imposed by chapter 2 of the Code, minus

(iii) The credits against tax allowed by part IV, subchapter A, chapter 1 of the Code, other than the credit against tax provided by section 31 (relating to tax withheld on wages), and without reduction for any payments of estimated tax.

(2) The credits against tax allowed by part IV, subchapter A, chapter 1 of the Code, are—

(i) In the case of the exception described in paragraph (a)(1) of this section, the credits shown on the return for the preceding taxable year,

(ii) In the case of the exceptions described in paragraph (a)(2) and (3) of this section, the credits computed under the law and rates applicable to the current taxable year, and

(iii) In the case of the exception described in paragraph (a)(4) of this section, the credits shown on the return for the preceding taxable year, except that if the amount of any such credit would be affected by any change in rates or status with respect to personal exemptions, the credits shall be determined by reference to the rates and status applicable to the current taxable year.

A change in rate may be either a change in the rate of tax, such as a change in the rate of tax imposed by section 1 or section 1401, or a change in a percentage affecting the computation of a credit, such as a change in the rate of withholding under chapter 3 of the Code or a change in the percentage of a qualified investment which is specified in section 46 for use in determining the amount of the investment credit allowed by section 38.

(3) The term "return for the preceding taxable year" means the income tax return for such year which is required by section 6012(a)(1) and, in the case of taxable years beginning after December 31, 1966, the self-employment tax return for such year which is required by section 6017.

(c) *Examples.* The following examples illustrate the application of the exceptions to the imposition of the addition to the tax for an underpayment of estimated tax, in the case of an individual whose taxable year is the calendar year:

Example (1). A, a married man with one child and a dependent parent, files a joint return with his spouse, B, for 1955 on April 15, 1956, showing taxable income of $44,000 and a tax of $16,760. A and B had filed a joint declaration of estimated tax on April 15, 1955, showing an estimated tax of $10,000 which was paid in four equal installments of $2,500 each on April 15, June 15, and September 15, 1955, and January 15, 1956. The balance of $6,760 was paid with the return. A and B have an underpayment of estimated tax of $433 (¼ of 70% of $16,760, less $2,500) for each installment date. The 1954 calendar year return of A and B showed a liability of $10,000. Since the total amount of estimated tax paid by each installment date equalled the amount that would have been required to be paid on or before each of such dates if the estimated tax were the tax shown on the return for the preceding

Reg. § 1.6654-2(c)

24,390 (I.R.C.)   Reg. § 1.6654-2(c)   8-16-76

year, the exception described in paragraph (a)(1) of this section applies and no addition to the tax will be imposed.

Example (2). Assume the same facts as in example (1), except that the joint return of A and B for 1954 showed taxable income of $32,000 and a tax liability of $10,400. Assume further that only two personal exemptions under section 151 appeared on the 1954 return. The exception described in paragraph (a)(1) of this section would not apply. However, A and B are entitled to four exemptions under section 151 for 1955. Taxable income for 1954 based on four exemptions, but otherwise on the basis of the facts shown on the 1954 return, would be $30,800. The tax on such amount in the case of a joint return would be $9,836. Since the total amount of estimated tax paid by each installment date exceeds the amount which would have been required to be paid on or before each of such dates if the estimated tax were $9,836, the exception described in paragraph (a)(4) of this section applies and no addition to the tax will be imposed.

Example (3). C, who is self-employed (other than as a farmer or fisherman), has annualized taxable income of $6,900 for the period January 1, 1967, through August 31, 1967, the income tax on which is $1,171. For the same period his net earnings from self-employment are $5,000 and his wages are $2,000. The estimated tax payments made by C for 1967 on or before September 15, 1967, total $1,200. For the purposes of the exception described in paragraph (a)(2) of this section, the adjusted self-employment income is $3,600, computed as follows:

(1) Net earnings from self-employment $5,000
(2) $6,600 minus annualized wages ($6,600—3,000 ($2,000 × 12 ÷ 8)) .. $3,600
(3) Lesser of (1) or (2) $3,600

The tax on C's adjusted self-employment income would be $230.40 ($3,600 × 6.4 percent). Since the total amount of estimated tax paid on or before September 15, 1967, exceeds $1,121.12, that is, 80 percent of $1,401.40 ($1,171 + 230.40), the exception described in paragraph (a)(2) of this section applies and no addition to tax will be imposed.

Example (4). D, who is self-employed (other than as a farmer or fisherman), has actual taxable income of $3,800 for the period January 1, 1967, through August 31, 1967, the income tax on which is $586. For the same period his net earnings from self-employment are $5,000 and his wages are $2,000. The estimated tax payments made by D for 1967 on or before September 15, 1967, total $840. For the purposes of the exception described in paragraph (a)(3) of this section, the actual self-employment income for this period is $4,600, computed as follows:

(1) Net earnings from self-employment $5,000
(2) $6,600 minus wages ($6,600—2,000) $4,600
(3) Lesser of (1) or (2) $4,600

The tax on D's actual self-employment income would be $294.40 ($4,600 × 6.4 percent). Since the total amount of estimated tax paid by September 15, 1967, exceeds $792.36, that is, 90 percent of $880.40 ($586 + 294.40), the exception described in paragraph (a)(3) of this section applies and no addition to tax will be imposed.

Example (5). E and F, his spouse, filed a joint return for the calendar year 1967 showing a tax liability of $10,000. The liability, attributable primarily to income received during the last quarter of the year, included both income and self-employment tax. Their aggregate payments of estimated tax on or before September 15, 1967, total $1,350, representing three installments of $450 paid on each of the first three installment dates prescribed for the taxable year. Since each installment paid, $450, was less than $2,000 (¼ of 80 percent of $10,000), there was an underpayment on each of the installment dates. Assume that the exceptions described in paragraph (a)(1) and (4) of this section do not apply. Actual taxable income for the three months ending March 31, was $2,000 and for the five months ending May 31, 1967, was $4,500. Actual self-employment income, for the same periods, was $2,000 and $4,000, respectively. Since the amounts paid by the April 15 and June 15 installment dates, $450 and $900, respectively, exceed $376.20 and $873.90, respectively (90 percent of the income tax on the actual taxable income of $2,000 and $4,500, respectively, determined on the basis of a joint return, and the self-employment tax on the actual self-employment income of $2,000 and $4,000, respectively), the exception described in paragraph (a)(3) of this section applies and no addition to the tax will be imposed for the underpayments on the April 15 and June 15 installment dates. For the eight months ending August 31, 1967, actual taxable income, assuming E and F did not elect to use the standard deduction, was $7,500; net earnings from self-employment were $6,000; and wages were $2,700. Since the total amount paid by the September 15 installment date, $1,350, was less than $1,381.14 (90 percent of the income tax on the actual taxable income of $7,500 determined on the basis of a joint return and the self-employment tax on actual self-employment income of $3,900 ($6,600 — 2,700)), the exception described in paragraph (a)(3) of this section does not apply to the September 15 installment. Furthermore, the exception described in paragraph (a)(2) of this section does not apply, as illustrated by the following computation:

(1) Income tax:
    Taxable income for the period ending August 31, 1967 (without deduction for personal exemptions) on an annual basis ($8,700 × 12 ÷ 8) $13,050.00
    Deduction for two personal exemptions 1,200.00
                                      $11,850.00
    Tax on $11,850 (on the basis of a joint return) .... $ 2,227.00
(2) Self-employment tax:
    Net earnings from self-employment .... $ 6,000.00
    Adjusted self-employment income ($6,600—4,050 annualized wages ($2,700 × 12 ÷ 8)) $ 2,550.00
    Tax on adjusted self-employment income ($2,550 × 6.4 percent) .... $ 163.20
(3) Total tax ($2,227.00 + 163.20) $ 2,390.20
(4) ¾ of 80 percent of $2,390.20 .. $ 1,434.12
Amount paid by Sept. 15, 1967 .... $ 1,350.00

Additions to Tax and Additional Amounts (I.R.C.) 24,391

An addition to the tax will thus be imposed for the underpayment of $1,550 ($2,000 — 450) on the September 15 installment.

Example (6). Assume the same facts as in example (5) and assume further that adjusted gross income for the eight months ending August 31, 1967, was $9,200 and the amount of deductions (other than the deduction for personal exemptions) not allowable in determining adjusted gross income aggregated only $500. If E and F elect, they may use the standard deduction in computing the tax for purposes of the exceptions described in paragraph (a)(2) and (3) of this section. Taxable income for purposes of the exception described in paragraph (a)(3) of this section would be reduced to $7,080 ($9,200 less $1,200 for two personal exemptions and $920 for the standard deduction). The income tax thereon is $1,205.20; income tax and self-employment tax total $1,454.80 ($1,205.20 + 249.60 ($3,900 × 6.4 percent)). Since the amount paid by the September 15 installment date, $1,350, exceeds $1,309.32 (90 percent of $1,454.80), the exception described in paragraph (a)(3) of this section applies. However, the exception described in paragraph (a)(2) of this section does not apply, as illustrated by the following computation:

Adjusted gross income for the period ending August 31, 1967	$ 9,200.00
Adjusted gross income annualized ($9,200 × 12 ÷ 8)	$13,800.00
Taxable income annualized ($13,800 minus $1,200 for two personal exemptions and $1,000 for the standard deduction)	$11,600.00
Income tax on $11,600 (on basis of a joint return)	$ 2,172.00
Self-employment tax on adjusted self-employment income ($2,550 × 6.4 percent)	$ 163.20
Total tax ($2,172.00 + 163.20)	$ 2,335.20
¾ of 80 percent of $2,335.20	$ 1,401.12
Amount paid by Sept. 15, 1967	$ 1,350.00

Example (7). G was a married individual, 73 years of age, who filed a joint return with his wife, H, for the calendar year 1956. H, who was 70 years of age, had no income during the year. G had taxable income in the amount of $7,000 for the eight-month period ending on August 31, 1956, which included $2,000 of dividend income (after excluding $50 under section 116) and $900 of rental income. The $7,000 figure also reflected a deduction of $2,400 for personal exemptions ($600 × 4), since G and H are both over 65 years of age. The application of the exception described in paragraph (a)(2) of this section to an underpayment of estimated tax on the September 15th installment date may be illustrated by the following computation:

Taxable income for the period ending August 31, 1956 (without deduction for personal exemptions) on an annual basis ($9,400 × 12 ÷ 8)	$14,100.00
Deduction for personal exemptions	2,400.00
Taxable income on an annual basis	$11,700.00
Tax (on the basis of a joint return)	$ 2,642.00
Dividends received for 8-month period $2,050	
Less: amount excluded from gross income under section 116 50	
Dividends included in gross income $2,000	
Dividend income annualized ($2,000 × 12 ÷ 8) . $3,000	
Dividends received credit under section 34 (4 percent of $3,000)	120.00
Tax less dividends received credit	$ 2,522.00
Retirement income (as defined in section 37(c)) includes:	
Dividend income (to extent included in gross income) $2,000	
Rental income 900	
Total retirement income . $2,900	
Limit on amount of retirement income under section 37(d) $1,200	
Retirement income credit under section 37 (20 percent of $1,200)	240.00
Tax less credits under section 34 and section 37	$ 2,282.00
Amount determined under the exception described in paragraph (a)(2) of this section (¾ of 70 percent of $2,282)	$ 1,198.05

(d) *Determination of taxable income for installment periods*—(1) *In general.* (i) In determining the applicability of the exceptions described in paragraph (a)(2) and (3) of this section, there must be an accurate determination of the amount of income and deductions for the calendar months in the taxable year preceding the installment date as of which the determination is made, that is, for the period terminating with the last day of the third, fifth, or eighth month of the taxable year. For example, a taxpayer distributes year-end bonuses to his employees but does not determine the amount of the bonuses until the last month of the taxable year. He may not deduct any portion of such year-end bonuses in determining his taxable income for any installment period other than the final installment period for the taxable year, since deductions are not allowable until paid or accrued, depending on the taxpayer's method of accounting.

(ii) If a taxpayer on an accrual method of accounting wishes to use either of the exceptions described in paragraph (a)(2) and (3) of this section, he must establish the amount of income and deductions for each applicable period. If his income is derived from a business in which the production, purchase, or sale of merchandise is an income-producing factor requiring the use of inventories, he will be unable to determine accurately the amount of his taxable income for the applicable period unless he can establish, with reasonable accuracy, his cost of goods sold for the applicable installment period. The cost of goods sold for such period shall be considered, unless a more exact determination is available, as such part of the cost of goods sold during the entire taxable year as the

Reg. § 1.6654-2(d)(1)

gross receipts from sales for such installment period is of gross receipts from sales for the entire taxable year.

(2) *Members of partnerships.* The provisions of this subparagraph shall apply in determining the applicability of the exceptions described in paragraph (a)(2) and (3) of this section to an underpayment of estimated tax by a taxpayer who is a member of a partnership.

(i) For purposes of determining taxable income, there shall be taken into account—

(A) The partner's distributive share of partnership items set forth under section 702,

(B) The amount of any guaranteed payments under section 707(c), and

(C) Gains or losses on partnership distributions which are treated as gains or losses on sales of property.

(ii) For purposes of determining net earnings from self-employment (for taxable years beginning after December 31, 1966) there shall be taken into account—

(A) The partner's distributive share of income or loss, described in section 702(a)(9), subject to the special rules set forth in section 1402(a) and §§ 1.1402(a)-1 to 1.1402(a)-16, inclusive, and

(B) The amount of any guaranteed payments under section 707(c), except for payments received from a partnership not engaged in a trade or business within the meaning of section 1402(c) and § 1.1402(c)-1. In determining a partner's taxable income and, for taxable years beginning after December 31, 1966, net earnings from self-employment, for the months in his taxable year which precede the month in which the installment date falls, the partner shall take into account items set forth in sections 702 and 1402(a) for any partnership taxable year ending with or within his taxable year to the extent that such items are attributable to months in such partnership taxable year which precede the month in which the installment date falls. For special rules used in computing a partner's net earnings from self-employment in the case of the termination of his taxable year as a result of death, see section 1402(f) and § 1.1402(f)-1. In addition, a partner shall include in his taxable income and, for taxable years beginning after December 31, 1966, net earnings from self-employment, for the months in his taxable year which precede the month in which the installment date falls guaranteed payments from the partnership to the extent that such guaranteed payments are includible in his taxable income for such months. See section 706(a), section 707(c), paragraph (c) of § 1.707-1 and section 1402(a).

(iii) The provisions of subdivision (i)(A) and (B) of subdivision (ii) of this subparagraph may be illustrated by the following examples:

Example (1). A, whose taxable year is the calendar year, is a member of a partnership whose taxable year ends on January 31st. A must take into account, in determining his taxable income for the installment due on April 15, 1973, all of his distributive share of partnership items described in section 702 and the amount of any guaranteed payments made to him which were deductible by the partnership in the partnership taxable year beginning on February 1, 1972, and ending on January 31, 1973. A must take into account, in determining his net earnings from self-employment, his distributive share of partnership income or loss described in section 702(a)(9), subject to the special rules set forth in section 1402(a) and §§ 1.1402(a)-1 to 1.1402(a)-16, inclusive.

Example (2). Assume that the taxable year of the partnership of which A, a calendar year taxpayer, is a member ends on June 30th. A must take into account in the determination of his taxable income and net earnings from self-employment for the installment due on April 15, 1973, his distributive share of partnership items for the period July 1, 1972, through March 31, 1973; for the installment due on June 15, 1973, he must take into account such amounts for the period July 1, 1972, through May 31, 1973; and for the installment due on September 15, 1973, he must take into account such amounts for the entire partnership taxable year of July 1, 1972, through June 30, 1973 (the date on which the partnership taxable year ends).

(3) *Beneficiaries of estates and trusts.* In determining the applicability of the exceptions described in paragraph (a)(2) and (3) of this section as of any installment date, the beneficiary of an estate or trust must take into account his distributive share of income from the estate or trust for the applicable period (whether or not actually distributed) if the trust or estate is required to distribute income to him currently. If the estate or trust is not required to distribute income currently, only the amounts actually distributed to the beneficiary during such period must be taken into account. If the taxable year of the beneficiary and the taxable year of the estate or trust are different, there shall be taken into account the beneficiary's distributable share of income, or the amount actually distributed to him as the case may be, during the months in the taxable year of the estate or trust ending within the taxable year of the beneficiary which precede the month in which the installment date falls. See subparagraph (2) of this paragraph for examples of a similar rule which is applied when a partner and the partnership of which he is a member have different taxable years.

(e) *Special rule in case of change from joint return or separate return for the preceding taxable year*—(1) *Joint return to separate returns.* In determining the applicability of the exceptions described in paragraph (a)(1) and (4) of this section to an underpayment of estimated tax, a taxpayer filing a separate return who filed a joint return for the preceding taxable year shall be subject to the following rule: The tax—

(i) Shown on the return for the preceding taxable year, or

(ii) Based on the tax rates and personal exemptions for the current taxable year but otherwise determined on the basis of the facts shown on the return for the preceding taxable year, and the law applicable to such year,

shall be that portion of the tax which bears the same ratio to the whole of the tax as the amount of the tax for which the taxpayer would have been liable bears to the sum of the taxes for which the taxpayer and his spouse would have been liable had each spouse filed a separate return for the preceding taxable year. For rules with respect to the allocation of joint payments of estimated tax, see section 6015(b) and § 1.6015(b)-1(b).

(2) *Examples.* The rule in subparagraph (1) of this paragraph may be illustrated by the following examples:

Example (1). H and W filed a joint return for the calendar year 1955 showing taxable income of $20,000 and a tax of $5,280. Of the $20,000 taxable income, $18,000 was attributable to H, and $2,000 was attributable to W. H and W filed separate returns for 1956. The tax shown on the return for the preceding taxable year, for purposes of determining the applicability of the exception described in paragraph (a)(1) of this section to an underpayment of estimated tax by H for 1956, is determined as follows:

Taxable income of H for 1955	$18,000
Tax on $18,000 (on basis of separate return)	$ 6,200
Taxable income of W for 1955	$ 2,000
Tax on $2,000 (on basis of separate return)	$ 400
Aggregate tax of H and W (on basis of separate returns)	$ 6,600
Portion of 1955 tax shown on joint return attributable to H (6200/6600 × $5280)	$ 4,960

Example (2). Assume the same facts as in example (1) and that H and W file a joint declaration of estimated tax for 1956 and pay estimated tax in amounts determined on the basis of their eligibility for three rather than two exemptions for 1956. H and W ultimately file separate income tax returns for 1956. Assume further that the exception described in paragraph (a)(1) of this section does not apply. The tax based on the tax rates and personal exemptions for 1956 but othrwise determined on the basis of the facts shown on the return for 1955 and the law applicable to 1955, for purposes of determining the applicability of the exception described in paragraph (a)(4) of this section to an underpayment of estimated tax by H for 1956, is determined as follows:

Taxable income of H and W for 1955 based on additional personal exemption for 1956	$19,400
Tax on 1955 income based on joint return rate for 1956	$ 5,076
Portion of 1955 tax attributable to H (computed as in example (1) but allowing benefit and additional exemption to H)	5900/6300
Portion of tax attributable to H based on tax rates and personal exemptions for 1956 but otherwise on facts on 1955 return (5900/6300 × $5,076)	$4,754

Example (3). Assume that H and W had the same taxable income in 1972 as in 1955, and that they filed a joint return for 1972 and separate returns for 1973. Assume further that H's taxable income for 1972 included net earnings from self-employment in excess of the $9,000 maximum base for the self-employment tax for 1972, and that the joint return filed by H and W for 1972 showed tax under chapter 1 (other than section 56) and tax under chapter 2 totaling $5,055. The tax shown on the return for 1972, for purposes of determining the applicability of the exception described in paragraph (a)(1) of this section to an underpayment of estimated tax by H for 1973, is determined as follows:

Taxable income of H for 1972	$18,000
Chapter 1 tax (other than section 56 tax) on $18,000 (on basis of separate return)	$5,170
Self-employment income of H for 1972	$ 9,000
Chapter 2 tax on $9,000	675
Total of such taxes	$5,845
Taxable income of W for 1972	$ 2,000
Chapter 1 tax (other than section 56 tax) on $2,000 (on basis of separate return)	310
Aggregate tax of H and W (on basis of separate returns)	$6,155
Portion of 1972 tax shown on joint return attributable to H (5845/6155 × $5,055)	$4,800.40

(3) *Separate return to joint return.* In the case of a taxpayer who files a joint return for the taxable year with respect to which there is an underpayment of estimated tax and who filed a separate return for the preceding taxable year—

(i) The tax shown on the return for the preceding taxable year, for purposes of determining the applicability of the exception described in paragraph (a)(1) of this section, shall be the sum of both the tax shown on the return of the taxpayer and the tax shown on the return of the taxpayer's spouse for such preceding year, and

(ii) The facts shown on both the taxpayer's return and the return of his spouse for the preceding taxable year shall be taken into account for purposes of determining the applicability of the exception described in paragraph (a)(4) of this section.

(4) *Example.* The rules described in subparagrtph (3) of this paragraph may be illustrated by the following example:

Example. H and W filed separate income tax returns for the calendar year 1944 showing tax liabilities of $2,640 and $350, respectively. In 1955 they married and participated in the filing of a joint return for that year. Thus, for the purpose of determining the applicability of the exceptions described in paragraph (a)(1) and (4) of this section to an underpayment of estimated tax for the year 1955, the tax shown on the return for the preceding taxable year is $2,990 ($2,640 plus $350).

○━▶ § 1.6654-3 (T.D. 6267, filed 11-13-57; republished in T.D. 6500, filed 11-25-60; amended by T.D. 7427, filed 8-9-76.) **Short taxable years of individuals.**

(a) *In general.* The provisions of section 6654, with certain modifications relating to the application of subsection (d) thereof, which are explained in paragraph (b) of this section, are applicable in the case of a short taxable year for which a declaration is required to be filed. (See § 1.6015(g)-1 for requirement of declaration for short taxable year.)

(b) *Rules as to application of section 6654(d).* (1) In any case in which the taxable year for which an underpayment of estimated tax exists is a short taxable year due to a change in annual accounting periods, in determining the tax—

(i) Shown on the return for the preceding taxable year (for purposes of section 6654(d)(1)), or

(ii) Based on the personal exemptions and rates for the current taxable year but otherwise on the basis of the facts shown on the return for the preceding taxable year, and the law applicable to such year (for purposes of section 6654(d)(4)), the tax will be reduced by multiplying it by the number of months in the short taxable year and dividing the resulting amount by 12.

(2) If the taxable year for which an underpayment of estimated tax exists is a short taxable year due to a change in annual accounting periods, in annualizing the taxable income for the months in the taxable year preceding an installment date, for purposes of section 6654(d)(2), the personal exemptions allowed as deductions under section 151 shall be reduced to the same extent that they are reduced under section 443(c) in computing the tax for a short taxable year.

(3) If "the preceding taxable year" referred to in section 6654(d)(4) was a short taxable year, for purposes of determining the applicability of the exception described in section 6654(d)(4), the tax, computed on the basis of the facts shown on the return for the preceding year, shall be the tax computed on the annual basis in the manner described in section 443(b)(1) (prior to its reduction in the manner described in the last sentence thereof). If the tax rates or the taxpayer's status with respect to personal exemptions for the taxable year with respect to which the underpayment occurs differs from such rates or status applicable to the preceding taxable year, the tax determined in accordance with this subparagraph shall be recomputed to reflect the rates and status applicable to the year with respect to which the underpayment occurs.

○── § 1.6654-4 (T.D. 7282, filed 7-16-73.) **Waiver of penalty for underpayment of 1971 estimated tax by an individual.**

(a) *In general.* Section 207 of the Revenue Act of 1971 provides that, in the case of individuals, the penalty prescribed by section 6654(a) and § 1.6654-1 for underpayment of estimated tax shall not apply in certain cases to taxable years beginning after December 31, 1970, and ending before January 1, 1972. The penalty shall be waived only if the taxpayer meets one of the gross income requirements contained in paragraph (b) of this section and if the limitation contained in paragraph (c) of this section is not applicable.

(b) *Gross income requirement.* Except as provided in paragraph (c) of this section, the waiver provided in paragraph (a) of this section shall be applicable only—

(1) If the gross income for the taxable year does not exceed $10,000 in the case of—

(i) a single individual who is neither a head of a household (as defined in section 2(b)) nor a surviving spouse (as defined in section 2(a)), or

(ii) a married individual not entitled under section 6013 to file a joint return for the taxable year, or

(2) If the gross income for the taxable year does not exceed $20,000 in the case of—

(i) a head of a household (as defined in section 2(b)), or

(ii) a surviving spouse (as defined in section 2(a)), or

(3) If the aggregate gross income for the taxable year does not exceed $20,000 in the case of a married individual (entitled under section 6013 to file a joint return for the taxable year) and his spouse.

(c) *Limitation.* Notwithstanding any other provision of this section, the waiver provided in paragraph (a) of this section shall not be applicable if, in the taxable year, the taxpayer has income from sources other than wages (as defined in section 3401(a)) in excess of $200 ($400 in the case of a husband and wife entitled to file a joint return for the taxable year under section 6013). Thus, for example, even if the aggregate gross income of a husband and wife (entitled under section 6013 to file a joint return for the taxable year) does not exceed $20,000, the waiver of the penalty for underpayment of estimated tax shall not apply if the husband and wife have, in the aggregate, income from sources other than wages in excess of $400.

○── § 1.6654-5 (Originally § 1.6654-4 as added by T.D. 6267, filed 11-13-57; republished in T.D. 6500, filed 11-25-60; redesignated by T.D. 7282, filed 7-16-73.) **Applicability.**

Section 6654 is applicable only with respect to taxable years beginning after December 31, 1954. Section 294(d) of the Internal Revenue Code of 1939 shall continue in force with respect to taxable years beginning before January 1, 1955.

○── § 1.6655 **Statutory provisions; failure by corporation to pay estimated tax.** [Sec. 6655, IRC]

○── § 1.6655-1 (T.D. 6267, filed 11-13-57; republished in T.D. 6500, filed 11-25-60; amended by T.D. 6768, filed 11-3-64; T.D. 7244, filed 12-29-72; amended by T.D. 7384, filed 10-21-75.) **Addition to the tax in the case of a corporation.**

(a) *In general.* (1) Section 6655 imposes an addition to the tax under chapter 1 of the Code in the case of any underpayment of estimated tax by a corporation (with certain exceptions described in section 6655(d)). This addition to the tax is in addition to any applicable criminal penalties and is imposed whether or not there was reasonable cause for the underpayment. The amount of the underpayment for any installment date is the excess of—

(i) 70 percent of the tax shown on the return for the taxable year or, if no return was filed, 70 percent of the tax for such year, multiplied by the percentage of estimated tax required to be paid on or before the installment date, over

(ii) The amount, if any, of the installment paid on or before the last day prescribed for such payment.

(2) The amount of the addition is determined at the annual rate referred to in the regulations under section 6621 upon the underpayment of any installment of estimated tax for the period from the date such installment is required to be paid

until the 15th day of the third month following the close of the taxable year, or the date such underpayment is paid, whichever is earlier. For purposes of determining the period of the underpayment (i) the date prescribed for payment of any installment of estimated tax shall be determined without regard to any extension of time, and (ii) a payment of estimated tax on any installment date, to the extent that it exceeds the amount of the installment determined under subparagraph (1)(i) of this paragraph for such date, shall be considered a payment of the previous underpayment, if any.

(3) The term "tax" as used in subparagraph (1)(i) of this paragraph means the excess of the tax imposed by section 11 or 1201(a) or subchapter L, chapter 1 of the Code, whichever is applicable, over the sum of $100,000 and the credits against tax provided by sections 32, 33, and 38. However, for the rule with respect to the limitation upon the $100,000 exemption for members of certain elected affiliated groups, see section 243(b)(3)(C)(v) and the regulations thereunder.

(4) For special rules relating to the determination of the amount of the underpayment in the case of a corporation whose income is included in a consolidated return, see § 1.1502-5(b).

(b) *Statement relating to underpayment.* If there has been an underpayment of estimated tax as of the installment date prescribed for its payment and the taxpayer believes that one or more of the exceptions described in § 1.6655-2 precludes the assertion of the addition to the tax under section 6655, it should attach to its income tax return for the taxable year a Form 2220 showing the applicability of any exception upon which the taxpayer relies.

(c) *Example.* The method prescribed in paragraph (a) of this section of computing the addition to the tax may be illustrated by the following example:

Example. A corporation using the calendar year basis reported on its declaration $50,000. It made payments of $2,500 each for 1955, estimated tax in the amount of on September 15, 1955, and December 15, 1955. On March 15, 1956, it filed its final income tax return showing a tax liability of $200,000. Since the amount of each of the two installments paid by the last date prescribed for payment thereof was less than 5 percent of 70 percent of the tax shown on the return, the addition to the tax under section 6655(a) is applicable and is computed as follows:

(1) Tax as defined in paragraph (a) of this section ($200,000 — $100,000 (no credits allowable under sections 32 and 33)) $100,000

(2) 70% of item (1) 70,000

(3) Amount of estimated tax required to be paid on each installment date (5% of $70,000) 3,500

(4) Deduct amount paid on each installment date 2,500

(5) Amount of underpayment for each installment date (item (3) minus item (4)) 1,000

(6) Addition to the tax:
First installment — period 9/15/55 to 3/15/56 ...... $30
Second installment — period 12/15/55 to 3/15/56. 15

Total 45

○━ § 1.6655-2 (T.D. 6267, filed 11-13-57, as amended by T.D. 6293, filed 5-20-58; republished in T.D. 6500, filed 11-25-60; amended by T.D. 6768, filed 11-3-64.) **Exceptions to imposition of the addition to the tax in the case of corporations.**

(a) *In general.* The addition to the tax under section 6655 will not be imposed for any underpayment of any installment of estimated tax if, on or before the date prescribed for payment of the installment, the total amount of all payments of estimated tax made equals or exceeds the amount which would have been required to be paid on or before such date if the estimated tax were the least of the following amounts—

(1) The tax shown on the return for the preceding taxable year, provided that the preceding taxable year was a year of 12 months and a return showing a liability for tax was filed for such year;

(2) An amount equal to a tax determined on the basis of the tax rates for the taxable year but otherwise on the basis of the facts shown on the return for the preceding taxable year and the law applicable to such year; in the case of a corporation required to file a return for such preceding taxable year; or

(3) An amount equal to 70 percent of the tax determined by placing on an annual basis the taxable income for—

(i) The first 3 months of the taxable year, in the case of the installment required to be paid in the 4th month,

(ii) Either the first 3 months or the first 5 months of the taxable year (whichever results in no addition being imposed), in the case of the installment required to be paid in the 6th month,

(iii) Either the first 6 months or the first 8 months of the taxable year (whichever results in no addition being imposed), in the case of the installment required to be paid in the 9th month, and

(iv) Either the first 9 months or the first 11 months of the taxable year (whichever results in no addition being imposed), in the case of the installment required to be paid in the 12th month.

The taxable income so determined shall be placed on an annual basis by first multiplying it by 12, and then dividing the resulting amount by the number of months in the taxable year for which the taxable income was so determined.

(4) In the case of a taxpayer whose taxable year consists of 52 or 53 weeks in accordance with section 441(f), the rules prescribed by paragraph (b) of § 1.441-2 shall be applicable in determining, for purposes of subparagraph (1) of this paragraph, whether a taxable year was a year of 12 months and in determining, for purposes of subparagraph (3) of this paragraph, the commencement of the 3-

Reg. § 1.6655-2(a)(4)

month period, or the 3- or 5-month period, or the 6- or 8-month period, or the 9- or 11-month period, whichever is applicable. For example, if a taxable year begins on December 26, 1956, taxable income for the first 6 months of such, year for purposes of subparagraph (3) of this paragraph, shall be taxable income for the period beginning on December 26, 1956, and ending on June 30, 1957, since such taxable year is deemed to commence on January 1, 1957, under section 441(f).

(5) If the end of any accounting period employed by the taxpayer (*e.g.*, any of either thirteen 4-week periods or four 13-week periods) does not correspond to the termination date of the applicable 3-month, or 3- or 5-month, or 6- or 8-month, or 9- or 11-month, period, taxable income shall be determined from the beginning of the taxable year to the close of the accounting period ending immediately before the termination date of the applicable 3-month, or 3- or 5-month, or 6- or 8-month, or 9- or 11-month, period and to the close of the accounting period within which such termination date falls. There shall be determined that portion of the difference between the two amounts of taxable income so determined which bears the same ratio to the total difference between such amounts as the number of days from the close of the first such accounting period to the close of such applicable 3-month, or 3- or 5-month, or 6- or 8-month, or 9- or 11-month, period bears to the total number of days between the termina-

tion dates of such two accounting periods. The portion of the difference between such amounts so determined shall then be added to (or subtracted from) taxable income determined to the close of the first such accounting period to determine taxable income for such applicable 3-month, or 3- or 5-month, or 6- or 8-month, or 9- or 11-month, period. For example, a taxpayer whose taxable year consists of 52 or 53 weeks in accordance with section 441(f) has a taxable year beginning on December 26, 1956, and thirteen 4-week accounting periods are employed in determining taxable income. Taxable income from December 26, 1956, to the close of the 4-week accounting period ending on June 11, 1957, is $200,000, and taxable income from December 26, 1956, to the close of the 4-week accounting period ending on July 9, 1957, is $228,000. Taxable income for the 6-month period ending on June 30, 1957, is $219,000 ($200,000 + (19 x 28,000 ÷ 28)).

(b) *Meaning of terms.* (1) For the purpose of the exceptions described in paragraph (a) of this section, the term "tax" means the excess of the tax imposed by section 11 or 1201(a), or subchapter L, chapter 1 of the Code, whichever is applicable, over the sum of $100,000 plus the credits against tax allowed by sections 32, 33, and 38.

(2) The credits against the tax allowed by sections 32, 33, and 38, are—

(i) In the case of the exception described in paragraph (a)(1) of this section, such credits shown on the return for the preceding taxable year,

(ii) In the case of the exception described in paragraph (a)(2) of this section, such credits shown on the return for the preceding taxable year, except that if the amount of any such credit would be affected by any change in rates, the credits shall be determined by reference to the rates applicable to the current taxable year, and

(iii) In the case of the exception described in paragraph (a)(3) of this section, such credits computed under the law and rates applicable to the current taxable year.

The provisions of subdivision (ii) of this subparagraph may be illustrated by the following example:

Example. Assume that during the taxable year within which the normal tax rate in section 11 changes from 30 percent to 25 percent, corporation X has an underpayment of estimated tax. One-fourth of the taxable income of corporation X for the taxable year preceding that in which such underpayment occurs was from sources within foreign country Y. The return of corporation X for such preceding year shows taxable income of $325,000 and a tax, without regard to any credits, of $163,500. The credit allowed by section 33 on account of taxes paid to foreign country Y may not exceed one-fourth of such amount, or $40,875 under section 904. The tax for the preceding year, computed by using the rates applicable to the year during which the underpayment occurs, would be reduced to $147,250 and the limitation under section 904 on the credit allowed under section 33 for taxes paid to foreign country Y would be reduced to $36,812.50, for purposes of determining the applicability of the exception described in paragraph (a)(2) of this section. Therefore, the exception described in paragraph (a)(2) of this section will be applicable if, on or before the date prescribed for such payment, the total amount paid by corporation X equals or exceeds the amount which would have been required to be paid by such date if the estimated tax were $10,437.50 ($147,250 less ($100,000 ÷ $36,812.50)).

(3) For the purpose of the exceptions described in paragraph (a)(1) and (2) of this section, the term "return for the preceding taxable year" means the income tax return for such year which is required by section 6012(a)(2).

(c) *Examples.* The application of the exceptions to the imposition of the addition to tax may be illustrated by examples employing the following statement of facts:

Statement of Facts

Y, a corporation reporting on a calendar year basis, filed a declaration on April 15, 1965, showing an estimated tax of $47,100 for its taxable year ending December 31, 1965. The first installment of 4 percent of the estimated tax or $1,884 was paid with the filing of the declaration, the second installment in the same amount was paid on June 15, 1965, and the third and fourth installments of $11,775 (25 percent of the estimated tax) each were paid on September 15, 1965, and December 15, 1965, respectively. Y reported a tax liability of $175,900 on its return due March 15, 1966. There was an underpayment in the amount of $241.20 on each of the first and second installment dates and $1,507.50 on each of the third and fourth installments dates determined as follows:

(1) Tax as defined in paragraph (b) of this section ($175,900-$100,000) $75,900.00
(2) 70% of item (1) 53,130.00
(3) 4% of item (2) 2,125.20
(4) Deduct amount paid on each of the first and second installment dates 1,884.00
(5) Amount of underpayment at each of the first and second installment dates (item (3) minus item (4)) 241.20
(6) 25% of item (2) $13,282.50
(7) Deduct amount paid on each of the last two installment dates 11,775.00
(8) Amount of underpayment at each of the third and fourth installment dates (item (6) minus item (7)) 1,507.50

The application of each exception described in paragraph (a) of this section is determined as follows:

(1) Assume Y reported a liability of $158,000 on its return for the taxable year ending December 31, 1964. If the estimated tax were $158,000 reduced by $100,000, or $58,000, the amount which would have been required to be paid on or before each of the first and second installment dates would be 4 percent of $58,000, or $2,320. The amount which would have been required to be paid on or before each of the third and

Reg. § 1.6655-2(c)

24,394 (I.R.C.) Reg. § 1.6655-2(c) 6-1-75

fourth installment dates would be 25 percent of $58,000, or $14,500. Since these amounts exceed the corresponding amounts actually paid on each installment date ($1,884 and $11,775, respectively), the exception described in paragraph (a)(1) of this section does not apply.

(2) As the corporation tax rates under section 11 are different for the taxable years ending December 31, 1964, and December 31, 1965, the amount of tax determined under paragraph (a)(2) of this section and the amounts required to be paid on or before each installment date must be determined. The tax liability determined on the basis of the calendar year 1965 rates but on the basis of the calendar year 1964 return is $151,900 and the estimated tax is $151,900 less $100,000, or $51,900. The amount which would have been required to be paid on or before each of the first and second installment dates would be 4 percent of $51,900, or $2,076, and the amount which would have been required to be paid on or before each of the third and fourth installment dates would be 25 percent of $51,900, or $12,975. Since these amounts exceed the corresponding amounts actually paid on each installment date ($1,884 and $11,775, respectively), the exception described in paragraph (a)(2) of this section does not apply.

(3) Y determined that its taxable income for the first 3, 5, 6, 8, 9, and 11 months was $87,500, $155,000, $185,000, $246,000, $288,000, and $341,000, respectively. The income for each period is annualized as follows:

$ 87,500 × 12 ÷ 3 = $350,000
$155,000 × 12 ÷ 5 = $372,000
$185,000 × 12 ÷ 6 = $370,000
$246,000 × 12 ÷ 8 = $369,000
$288,000 × 12 ÷ 9 = $384,000
$341,000 × 12 ÷ 11 = $372,000

To determine whether the installment payment made on April 15, 1965, equals or exceeds the amount which would have been required to be paid if the estimated tax were equal to 70 percent of the tax computed on the annualized income for the 3-month period, the following computation is necessary:

	3 months
(1) Annualized income	$350,000.00
(2) Tax on item (1) reduced by $100,000	61,500.00
(3) 70 percent of item (2)	43,050.00
(4) 4 percent of item (3)	1,722.00

To determine whether the installment payments made on or before June 15, 1965, equal or exceed the amount which would have been required to be paid if the estimated tax were equal to 70 percent of the tax computed on the annualized income for either the 3- or 5-month period, the following computation is necessary:

	3 months	5 months
(1) Annualized income	$350,000.00	$372,000.00
(2) Tax on item (1) reduced by $100,000	61,500.00	72,060.00
(3) 70 percent of item (2)	43,050.00	50,442.00
(4) 8 percent of item (3)	3,444.00	4,035.36

To determine whether the installment payments made on or before September 15, 1965, equal or exceed the amount which would have been required to be paid if the estimated tax were equal to 70 percent of the tax computed on the annualized income for either the 6-or 8-month period, the following computation is necessary:

	6 months	8 months
(1) Annualized income	$370,000.00	$369,000.00
(2) Tax on item (1) reduced by $100,000	71,100.00	70,620.00
(3) 70 percent of item (2)	49,770.00	49,434.00
(4) 33 percent of item (3)	16,424.10	16,313.22

To determine whether the installment payments made on or before December 15, 1965, equal or exceed the amount which would have been required to be paid if the estimated tax were equal to 70 percent of the tax computed on the annualized income for either the 9-or 11-month period, the following computation is necessary:

	9 months	11 months
(1) Annualized income	$384,000.00	$372,000.00
(2) Tax on item (1) reduced by $100,000	77,820.00	72,060.00
(3) 70 percent of item (2)	54,474.00	50,442.00
(4) 58 percent of item (3)	31,594.92	29,256.36

The total amounts of all payments of estimated tax actually paid on or before the installment dates of April 15, 1965, June 15, 1965, September 15, 1965, and December 15, 1965, are $1,884, $3,768, $15,543, and $27,318, respectively. Since the total amounts of estimated tax actually paid on the first and second installment dates (April 15, 1965, and June 15, 1965) exceed the amounts required to be paid on such dates if the estimated tax were 70 percent of the tax determined by placing on an annualized basis the taxable income for the first 3 months of the taxable year, the exception described in paragraph (a)(3) of this section applies and no addition to tax will be imposed for the installments paid on April 15, 1965, and June 15, 1965. However, since the total amount of all payments of estimated tax actually paid on or before the third and fourth installment dates (September 15, 1965, and December 15, 1965) does not equal or exceed the applicable alternative amounts, the addition to the tax with respect to the underpayment of the September 15, 1965, and December 15, 1965, installments must be imposed.

(d) *Determination of taxable income for portion of taxable year.* In determining the applicability of the exception described in paragraph (a)(3) of this section, there must be an accurate determination of the amount of income and deductions for the appropriate period, that is, for the first 3, 5, 6, 8, 9, or 11 months of the taxable year. See paragraph (d)(1) of § 1.6654-2 for a description of a similar requirement with respect to individuals.

○→ § 1.6655-3 (T. D. 6267, filed 11-13-57; republished in T.D. 6500, filed 11-25-60.) Short taxable years in the case of corporations.

(a) *In general.* The provisions of section 6655, with certain modifications relating to the application of subsection (d) thereof, which are explained in paragraph (b) of this section, are applicable in the case of a short taxable year for which a declaration is required to be filed. (See § 1.6016-4 for requirement of declaration for short taxable year).

(b) *Rules as to application of section 6655(d)*. In any case in which the taxable year for which an underpayment of estimated tax exists is a short taxable year due to a change in annual accounting periods, in determining the tax—

(1) Shown on the return for the preceding taxable year (for purposes of section 6655(d)(1));

(2) Based on the current year's rates but otherwise on the basis of the facts shown on the return for the preceding taxable year and the law applicable to such year (for purposes of section 6655(d)(2)); or

(3) Computed by placing taxable income for a portion of the current year on an annual basis under section 6655(d)(3); the tax will be reduced by multiplying it by the number of months in the short taxable year and dividing the resulting amount by 12. The application of the exception provided in section 6655(d)(3) shall be determined as if the estimated tax were 70 percent of the tax so reduced.

(c) *Preceding taxable year a short taxable year.* If "the preceding taxable year" referred to in section 6655(d)(2) was a short taxable year, the tax computed on the basis of the facts shown on the return for such preceding year, for purposes of determining the applicability of the exception described in section 6655(d)(2) shall be the tax computed on the annual basis in the manner described in section 443(b)(1) (prior to its reduction in the manner described in the last sentence thereof). If the tax rates for the taxable year with respect to which the underpayment occurs differ from the rates applicable to the preceding taxable year, the tax determined in accordance with the preceding sentence shall be recomputed using the rates applicable to the year with respect to which the underpayment occurs.

○— § 1.6655-4 (T.D. 7059, filed 6-16-70.) [Reserved]

○— § 1.6655-5 (T.D. 7059, filed 9-16-70; amended by T.D. 7384, filed 10-21-75.) **Addition to tax on account of excessive adjustment under section 6425.**

(a) *In general.* (1) Section 6655(g) imposes an addition to the tax under chapter 1 of the Code in the case of any excessive amount (as defined in subparagraph (3) of this paragraph) of an adjustment under section 6425 which is made before the 15th day of the third month following the close of a taxable year beginning after December 31, 1967. This addition to tax is imposed whether or not there was reasonable cause for an excessive adjustment.

(2) If the amount of an adjustment under section 6425 is excessive, there shall be added to the tax under chapter 1 for the taxable year an amount determined at the annual rate referred to in the regulations under section 6621 upon the excessive amount from the date on which the credit is allowed or the refund paid to the 15th day of the third month following the close of the taxable year. A refund is paid on the date it is allowed under section 6407.

(3) The excessive amount is equal to the lesser of the amount of the adjustment or the amount by which (i) the income tax liability (as defined in section 6425(c) of the Code) for the taxable year, as shown on the return for the taxable year, exceeds (ii) the estimated income tax paid during the taxable year, reduced by the amount of the adjustment.

(4) The computation of the addition to the tax imposed by section 6425 is made independently of, and does not affect the computation of, any addition to the tax which a corporation may otherwise owe for an underpayment of an installment of estimated tax.

(5) The provisions of section 6655 may be illustrated by the following example:

Example. Corporation A, a calendar year taxpayer, had an underpayment as defined in section 6655(b) for its fourth installment of estimated tax which was due on December 15, 1968, in the amount of $10,000. Nevertheless, on January 1, 1969, corporation A filed an application for adjustment of overpayment of estimated income tax for 1968 in the amount of $20,000. On February 15, 1969, the Internal Revenue Service in response to the application, refunded $20,000 to Corporation A. On March 15, 1969, corporation A filed its 1968 tax return and made a payment in settlement of its total tax liability. Under section 6655 (a), corporation A is subject to an addition to tax in the amount of $150 ($10,000 × 6% × 3/12) on account of corporation A's December 15, 1968 underpayment. Under section 6655 (g) corporation A is subject to an addition to tax in the amount of $100 ($20,000 × 6% × 1/12) on account of corporation A's excessive adjustment under section 6425. In determining the amount of the addition to tax under section 6655 (a) for failure to pay estimated income tax, the excessive adjustment under section 6425 is not taken into account.

(6) An adjustment is generally to be treated as a reduction of estimated income tax paid as of the date of the adjustment. However, for purposes of § 1.6655-1 through § 1.6655-3, the adjustment is to be treated as if not made in determining whether there has been any underpayment of estimated income tax and, if there is an underpayment, the period during which the underpayment existed.

○— § 301.6655 **Statutory provisions; failure by corporation to pay estimated income tax.** [Sec. 6655, IRC]

○— § 301.6655-1 (T.D. 6268 filed 11-15-57; republished in T.D. 6498, filed 10-24-60; as amended by T.D. 7059, filed 9-16-70.) **Failure by corporation to pay estimated income tax.**

For regulations under section 6655, see §§ 1.6655-1 to 1.6655-3, inclusive, and § 1.6655-5, of this chapter (Income Tax Regulations).

○— § 301.6656 **Statutory provisions; failure to make deposit of taxes.** [Sec. 6656, IRC]

○— § 301.6656-1 (T.D. 6268, filed 11-15-57; republished in T.D. 6498, filed 10-24-60; amended by T.D. 6585, filed 12-27-61; T.D. 6922, filed 6-16-67 and T.D. 7133, filed 7-21-71.) **Failure to make deposit of taxes.**

Reg. § 301.6656-1

(a) *Penalty.* (1) In case of failure by any person required by the Code or regulations prescribed thereunder to deposit any tax in a Government depositary, as is authorized under section 6302(c), within the time prescribed therefor, a penalty shall be imposed on such person unless such failure is shown to the satisfaction of the district director or the director of the service center to be due to reasonable cause and not to willful neglect. In the case of deposits, the time for making of which is after December 31, 1969, the penalty shall be 5 percent of the amount of the underpayment without regard to the period during which the underpayment continues. In the case of deposits, the time for making of which is before January 1, 1970, the penalty shall be 1 percent of the amount of the underpayment if the failure is for not more than 1 month, with an additional 1 percent for each additional month or fraction thereof during which failure continues, not to exceed 6 percent in the aggregate. For purposes of this section, the term "underpayment" means the amount of tax required to be deposited less the amount, if any, which was deposited on or before the date prescribed therefor, and the term "month" shall have the same meaning assigned to such term in paragraph (b) of 301.6651-1.

(2) A taxpayer who wishes to avoid the penalty for failure to deposit must make an affirmative showing of all facts alleged as a reasonable cause in a written statement containing a declaration that it is made under the penalties of perjury, which should be filed with the district director for the district in which the return with respect to the tax is required to be filed, or with the director of the service center. If the district director or the director of the service center determines that the delinquency was due to a reasonable cause, and not to willful neglect, the penalty will not be imposed.

(b) *Penalty not imposed after due date for return.* For the purpose of computing the amount of the penalty imposed by section 6656, the period of failure to make deposit is deemed not to continue beyond the last date (determined without regard to any extension of time) prescribed for payment of the tax required to be deposited, or beyond the date the tax is paid, whichever date is earlier. For example, during the months of January, February, and March 1955, the aggregate amount of the employee tax withheld under section 3102, the employer tax for each such month under section 3111, and the income tax withheld at source on wages under section 3402 (exclusive of the employee tax withheld under section 3102 and the employer tax under section 3111 with respect to wages of household employees), amount to $1,000 for each month. Under § 31.6302(c)-1 of this chapter (Employment Tax Regulations), the employer is required to deposit the $1,000 for January on or before February 15, 1955, and the $1,000 for February on or before March 15, 1955, but is not required to deposit the $1,000 for March 1955, prior to the date the return is due. The employer filed his quarterly return on April 30, 1955, the date prescribed for filing such return, accompanied by a remittance of $3,000. Assuming that the employer failed, without reasonable cause, to make timely deposits the penalty under section 6656 for failure to make the January deposit is $30, and the penalty for failure to make the February deposit is $20, computed as follows:

Amount required to be deposited on or before Feb. 15, 1955 ..	$1,000
Less: Amount deposited	0
Underpayment	1,000
(1 percent penalty for each month or fraction thereof, Feb. 15, 1955 to Apr. 30, 1955, 3 months)	3%
Penalty for failure to make January deposit	$30
Amount required to be deposited on or before Mar. 15, 1955	$1,000
Less: Amount deposited	0
Underpayment	1,000
(1 percent penalty for each month or fraction thereof, Mar. 15, 1955 to Apr. 30, 1955, 2 months)	2%
Penalty for failure to make February deposit	20
Total penalty	50

○→ § 301.6657 **Statutory provisions; bad checks.** [Sec. 6657, IRC]

○→ § 301.6657-1 (T.D. 6268, filed 11-15-57; republished in T.D. 6498, filed 10-24-60; amended by T.D. 6585, filed 12-27-61.) **Bad checks.**

(a) *In general.* Except as provided in paragraph (b) of this section, if a check or money order is tendered in the payment of any amount receivable under the Code, and such check or money order is not paid upon presentment, a penalty of one percent of the amount of the check or money order, in addition to any other penalties provided by law, shall be paid by the person who tendered such check or money order. If, however, the amount of the check or money order is less than $500, the penalty shall be $5 or the amount of the check or money order, whichever amount is the lesser. Such penalty shall be paid in the same manner as tax upon the issuance of a notice and demand therefor.

(b) *Reasonable cause.* If payment is refused upon presentment of any check or money order and the person who tendered such check or money order establishes to the satisfaction of the district director that it was tendered in good faith with reasonable cause to believe that it would be duly paid, the penalty set forth in paragraph (a) of this section shall not apply.

○→ § 301.6658 **Statutory provisions; addition to tax in case of jeopardy.** [Sec. 6658, IRC]

○→ § 301.6658-1 (T.D. 6268, filed 11-15-57; republished in T.D. 6498, filed 10-24-60.) **Addition to tax in case of jeopardy.**

Upon a finding by the district director that any taxpayer violated or attempted to violate, section 6851 (relating to termination of taxable year) there shall, in addition to all other penalties, be added as part of the tax 25 percent of the total amount of the tax or deficiency in the tax.

○→ § 301.6659 **Statutory provisions; applicable rules.** [Sec. 6659, IRC]

○→ § 301.6659-1 (T.D. 6268, filed 11-15-57; republished in T.D. 6498, filed 10-24-60.) **Applicable rules.**

(a) *Additions treated as tax.* Except as otherwise provided in the Code, any reference in the Code to "tax" shall be deemed also to be a reference to any addition to the tax, additional amount, or penalty imposed by chapter 68 of the Code with respect to such tax. Such additions to the tax, additional amounts, and penalties shall become payable upon notice and demand therefor and shall be asessed, collected, and paid in the same manner as taxes.

(b) *Additions to tax for failure to file return or pay tax.* Any addition under section 6651 or section 6653 to a tax shall be considered a part of such tax for the purpose of the assessment and collection of such tax. For applicability of deficiency procedures to additions to the tax, see paragraph (c) of this section.

(c) *Deficiency procedures*—(1) *Addition to the tax for failure to file tax return.* Subchapter B, chapter 63, of the Code (deficiency procedures) applies to the additions to the income, estate, and gift taxes imposed by section 6651 for failure to file a tax return to the same extent that it applies to such taxes. Accordingly, if there is a deficiency (as defined in section 6211) in the tax (apart from the addition to the tax) where a return has not been timely filed, deficiency procedures apply to the addition to the tax under section 6651. If there is no deficiency in the tax where a return has

Reg. § 301.6659-1(c)(1)

not been timely filed, the addition to the tax under section 6651 may be assessed and collected without deficiency procedures. The provisions of this subparagraph may be illustrated by the following examples:

Example (1). A filed his income tax return for the calendar year 1955 on May 15, 1956, not having been granted an extension of time for such filing. His failure to file on time was not due to reasonable cause. The return showed a liability of $1,000 and it was determined that A is liable under section 6651 for an addition to such tax of $50 (5 percent a month for 1 month). The provisions of subchapter B of chapter 63 (deficiency procedures) do not apply to the assessment and collection of the addition to the tax since such provisions are not applicable to the tax with respect to which such addition was asserted, there being no statutory deficiency for purposes of section 6211.

Example (2). Assume the same facts as in example (1) and assume further that a deficiency of $500 in tax and a further $25 addition to the tax under section 6651 is asserted against A for the calendar year 1955. Thus, the total addition to the tax under section 6651 is $75. Since the provisions of subchapter B of chapter 63 are applicable to the $500 deficiency, they likewise apply to the $25 addition to the tax asserted with respect to such deficiency (but not to the $50 addition to the tax under example (1)).

(2) *Additions to the tax for negligence or fraud.* Subchapter B of chapter 63 (deficiency procedures) applies to all additions to the income, estate, and gift taxes imposed by section 6653 (a) and (b) for negligence and fraud.

(3) *Additions to tax for failure to pay estimated income taxes*—(i) *Return filed by taxpayer.* The addition to the tax for underpayment of estimated income tax imposed by section 6654 (relating to failure by individuals to pay estimated income tax) or section 6655 (relating to failure by corporations to pay estimated income tax) is determined by reference to the tax shown on the return if a return is filed. Therefore, such addition may be assessed and collected without regard to the provisions of subchapter B of chapter 63 (deficiency procedures) if a return is filed since such provisions are not applicable to the assessment of the tax shown on the return. Further, since the additions to the tax imposed by section 6654 or 6655 are determined solely by reference to the amount of tax shown on the return if a return is filed, the assertion of a deficiency with respect to any tax not shown on such return will not make the provisions of subchapter B of chapter 63 (deficiency procedures) apply to the assessment and collection of any additions to the tax under section 6654 or 6655.

(ii) *No return filed by taxpayer.* If the taxpayer has not filed a return and his entire income tax liability is asserted as a deficiency to which the provisions of subchapter B of chapter 63 apply, such provisions likewise will apply to any addition to such tax imposed by section 6654 or 6655.

ASSESSABLE PENALTIES

Failure to collect and pay over tax, or attempt to evade or defeat tax.

Any person required to collect, truthfully account for, and pay over any tax imposed by the Code who willfully fails to collect such tax, or truthfully account for and pay over such tax, or willfully attempts in any manner to evade or defeat any such tax or the payment thereof, shall, in addition to other penalties, be liable to a penalty equal to the total amount of the tax evaded, or not collected, or not accounted for and paid over. The penalty imposed by section 6672 applies only to the collection, accounting for, or payment over of taxes imposed on a person other than the person who is required to collect, account for, and pay over such taxes. No penalty under section 6653, relating to failure to pay tax, shall be imposed for any offense to which this section is applicable.

§ 301.6671 Statutory provisions; rules for application of assessable penalties. [Sec. 6671, IRC]

§ 301.6671-1 (T.D. 6268, filed 11-15-57; republished in T.D. 6498, filed 10-24-60; amended by T.D. 6585, filed 12-27-61.) **Rules for application of assessable penalties.**

(a) *Penalty assessed as tax.* The penalties and liabilities provided by subchapter B, chapter 68 of the Code (sections 6671 to 6675, inclusive) shall be paid upon notice and demand by the district director or the director of the regional service center and shall be assessed and collected in the same manner as taxes. Except as otherwise provided, any reference in the Code to "tax" imposed thereunder shall also be deemed to refer to the penalties and liabilities provided by subchapter B of chapter 68.

(b) *Person defined.* For purposes of subchapter B of chapter 68, the term "person" includes an officer or employee of a corporation, or a member or employee of a partnership, who as such officer, employee, or member is under a duty to perform the act in respect of which the violation occurs.

§ 301.6672 Statutory provisions; failure to collect and pay over tax, or attempt to evade or defeat tax. [Sec. 6672, IRC]

§ 301.6672-1 (T.D. 6268, filed 11-15-57; republished in T.D. 6498, filed 10-24-60.)

§ 301.6673 Statutory provisions; damages assessable for instituting proceedings before the Tax Court merely for delay. [Sec. 6673, IRC]

§ 301.6673-1 (T.D. 6268, filed 11-15-57; republished in T.D. 6498, filed 10-24-60; amended by T.D. 6585, filed 12-27-61.) **Damages assessable for instituting proceedings before the Tax Court merely for delay.**

Any damages awarded to the United States by the Tax Court under section 6673 against a taxpayer for instituting proceedings before the Tax Court merely for delay shall be assessed at the same time as the deficiency and shall be paid upon notice and demand from the district director or the director of the regional service center and shall be collected as a part of the tax.

○—☞ § 31.6674 **Statutory provisions; fraudulent statement or failure to furnish statement to employee.** [See Sec. 6674, IRC]

○—☞ § 31.6674-1 (T.D. 6472, filed 6-22-60; republished in T.D. 6516, filed 12-19-60; amended by T.D. 7001, filed 1-17-69.) **Penalties for fraudulent statement or failure to furnish statement.**

Any person required to furnish a statement to an employee under the provisions of section 6051 or 6053(b) is subject to a civil penalty for willful failure to furnish such statement in the manner, at the time, and showing the information required under such section (or § 31.6051-1 or § 31.6053-2), or for willfully furnishing a false or fraudulent statement to an employee. The penalty for each such violation is $50, which shall be assessed and collected in the same manner as the tax imposed on employers under the Federal Insurance Contributions Act. See section 7204 for criminal penalty.

○—☞ § 301.6674 **Statutory provisions; fraudulent statement or failure to furnish statement to employee.** [Sec. 6674, IRC]

○—☞ § 301.6674-1 (T.D. 6268, filed 11-15-57; republished in T.D. 6498, filed 10-24-60.) **Fraudulent statement or failure to furnish statement to employee.**

For regulations under section 6674, see § 31.6674-1 of this chapter (Employment Tax Regulations).

○—☞ § 301.6676 **Statutory provisions; failure to supply identifying numbers.** [Sec. 6676, IRC]

○—☞ § 301.6676-1 (T.D. 6606, filed 8-24-62; amended by T.D. 7306, filed 3-14-74.) **Penalty for failure to supply identifying number.**

(a) *In general.* Except as provided in paragraph (c) of this section, if any person who is required by the regulations under section 6109—

(1) To include his identifying number in any return, statement, or other document,

(2) To furnish his identifying number to another person, or

(3) To include in any return, statement, or other document made with respect to another person the identifying number of such other person,

fails to comply with such requirement at the time prescribed by such regulations, such person shall pay a penalty of $5 for each such failure. Such penalty shall be paid in the same manner as tax upon the issuance of a notice and demand therefor. Under § 301.6109-1(c) a payer is required to request the identifying number of the payee. If, after such a request has been made, the payee does not furnish the payer with his identifying number, the penalty will not be assessed against the payer.

(b) *Deficiency procedures not to apply.* Subchapter B, chapter 63, of the Code (deficiency procedures) shall not apply in respect of the assessment or collection of the penalty set forth in paragraph (a) of this section.

(c) *Reasonable cause.* If any person who is required by the regulations under section 6109 to supply an identifying number fails to comply with such requirement at the time prescribed by such regulations, but establishes to the satisfaction of the district director or the director of the regional service center that such failure was due to reasonable cause, the penalty set forth in paragraph (a) of this section shall not apply.

(d) *Persons required to supply identifying numbers.* For regulations under section 6109 relating to persons required to supply an identifying number, see the regulations relating to the particular tax.

○—☞ § 301.6678 **Statutory provisions; failure to furnish certain statements.** [Sec. 6678, IRC]

○—☞ § 301.6678-1 (T.D. 6628, filed 12-27-62; amended by T.D. 6887, filed 6-23-66.) **Failure to furnish statements to payees.**

(a) *In general.* In the case of each failure to furnish a statement required—

(1) Under section 6042(c) and § 1.6042-4 to a person with respect to whom a return has been made under section 6042(a)(1), relating to information returns with respect to payments of dividends aggregating $10 or more in a calendar year,

(2) Under section 6044(e) and § 1.6044-5 to a person with respect to whom a return has been made under section 6044(a)(1), relating to information returns with respect to certain payments by cooperatives aggregating $10 or more in a calendar year,

(3) Under section 6049(c) and § 1.6049-3 to a person with respect to whom a return has been made under section 6049(a)(1), relating to information returns with respect to payments of interest aggregating $10 or more in a calendar year,

(4) Under section 6039(b) and § 1.6039-2 to a person with respect to whom a return has been made under section 6039(a), relating to information returns with respect to certain stock option transactions occurring in a calendar year, or

(5) Under section 6052(b) and § 1.6052-2 to a person with respect to whom a return has been made under section 6052(a), relating to information returns with respect to payment of wages in the form of group-term life insurance provided for an employee on his life,

within the time prescribed for furnishing such statement (determined with regard to any extension of time for furnishing), there shall be paid by the person failing to so furnish the statement $10 for each such statement not so furnished. However, the total amount imposed on the delinquent person for all such failures during a calendar year shall not exceed $25,000.

(b) *Manner of payment.* The penalty imposed under section 6678 and this section on any person shall be paid in the same manner as tax upon the issuance of a notice and demand therefor.

(c) *Showing of reasonable cause.* The penalty imposed by section 6678 shall not apply with respect to a failure to furnish a statement within the time prescribed if it is established to the satisfaction of the district director or the director of the re-

Reg. § 301.6678-1(c)

24,398 (I.R.C.) Reg. § 301.6678-1(c) 5-8-78

gional service center that such failure was due to reasonable cause and not to willful neglect. An affirmative showing of reasonable cause must be made in the form of a written statement, containing a declaration that it is made under the penalties of perjury, setting forth all the facts alleged as a reasonable cause.

○—▶ § 301.6679 Statutory provisions; failure to file returns as to organizations or reorganization of foreign corporations and as to acquisitions of their stock. [Sec. 6679, IRC]

○—▶ § 301.6679-1 (T.D. 6623, filed 11-30-62; amended by T.D. 7288, filed 9-28-73; T.D. 7542, filed 4-28-78.) Failure to file returns as to organization or reorganization of foreign corporations and as to acquisitions of their stock.

(a) *Civil penalty*—(1) *In general.* In addition to any criminal penalty provided by law, each person required to file a return under section 6046, and the regulations thereunder, who fails to file such a return within the time provided, or who files a return which does not show the required information, shall pay a penalty of $1,000, unless such failure is shown to be due to reasonable cause.

(2) *Joint return.* The penalty imposed by section 6679 and this section shall apply to each U.S. citizen, resident, or person filing a joint return pursuant to the provisions of section 6046 and § 1.6046-1, which does not show the required information.

(3) *Showing of reasonable cause.* The district director, the director of the Internal Revenue service center, and the Director of International Operations are authorized to make the determination that such failure was due to a reasonable cause and that, accordingly, the penalty imposed by section 6679 shall not apply. An affirmative showing of reasonable cause must be made in the form of a written statement, containing a declaration that it is made under the penalties of perjury, setting forth all the facts alleged as a reasonable cause. If the taxpayer exercises ordinary business care and prudence and is nevertheless unable to furnish any item of information required under section 6046 and the regulations thereunder, such failure shall be considered due to a reasonable cause. In determining the extent of a taxpayer's ability to obtain information, the percentage of stock owned by such taxpayer and the nature of the other interests in the foreign corporation will be considered.

(b) *Deficiency procedures not to apply.* The penalty imposed by section 6679 may be assessed and collected without regard to the deficiency procedures provided by subchapter B of chapter 63 of the Code.

○—▶ § 31.6682 Statutory provisions; false information with respect to withholding allowances based on itemized deductions. [Sec. 6682, IRC]

○—▶ § 31.6682-1 (T.D. 7065, filed 10-22-70.) False information with respect to withholding allowances based on itemized deductions.

(a) *Civil penalty.* (1) Except as provided in subparagraph (2) of this paragraph, if any individual claiming a withholding allowance under section 3402(f)(1)(F) (see § 31.3402(f)(1)-1) states on his withholding exemption certificate—

(i) As the amount of wages (within the meaning of section 3401(a) and the regulations thereunder) shown on his return for any taxable year an amount less than such wages actually shown, or

(ii) As the amount of itemized deductions to be taken into account in determining withholding allowances under section 3402(m) shown on the return for any taxable year an amount greater than such deductions actually shown, or both, he shall pay a penalty of $50. This penalty shall be in addition to any criminal penalty provided by law.

(2) The penalty provided in subparagraph (1) of this paragraph shall not apply if—

(i) The amount of tax deducted and withheld under chapter 24 of the Code and the regulations thereunder during the period that the withholding exemption certificate referred to in subparagraph (1) is in effect is not less than the amount of tax that would have been deducted and withheld if the amount of wages or itemized deductions referred to in subparagraph (1) had been correctly stated, or

(ii) The income taxes imposed upon the individual under subtitle A of the Code for the taxable year following the taxable year referred to in subparagraph (1) do not exceed the sum of—

(a) The credits against such taxes allowed by part IV of subchapter A of chapter 1 of the Code, and

(b) Any payments of estimated tax which are considered payments on account of such taxes.

(b) *Deficiency procedures not to apply.* The penalty imposed by section 6682 may be assessed and collected without regard to the deficiency procedures provided by subchapter B of chapter 63 of the Code.

○—▶ § 301.6682 Statutory provisions; false information with respect to withholding allowances based on itemized deductions. [Sec. 6682, IRC]

○—▶ § 301.6682-1 (T.D. 7065, filed 10-22-70.) False information with respect to withholding allowances based on itemized deductions.

For regulations under section 6682, see § 31.6682-1 of this chapter (Employment Tax Regulations).

○—▶ § 301.6684 Statutory provisions; assessable penalties with respect to liability for tax under chapter 42. [Sec. 6684, IRC]

○—▶ § 301.6684-1 (T.D. 7127, filed 6-14-71.) Assessable penalties with respect to liability for tax under chapter 42.

(a) *In general.* If any person (as defined in section 7701(a)(1)) becomes liable for tax under any section of chapter 42 (other than section 4940 or 4948(a)), relating to private foundations, by reason of any act or failure to act which is not due to reasonable cause and either—

(1) Such person has theretofore (at any time) been liable for tax under any section of such chapter (other than section 4940 or 4948(a)), or

(2) Such act or failure to act is both willful and flagrant,

then such person shall be liable for a penalty equal to the amount of such tax.

(b) *Showing of reasonable cause.* The

penalty imposed by section 6684 shall not apply to any person with respect to a violation of any section of chapter 42 if it is established to the satisfaction of the district director or director of the internal revenue service center that such violation was due to reasonable cause. An affirmative showing of reasonable cause must be made in the form of a written statement, containing a declaration by such person that it is made under the penalties of perjury, setting forth all the facts alleged as reasonable cause.

(c) *Willful and flagrant.* For purposes of this section, the term "willful and flagrant" has the same meaning as such term possesses in section 507(a)(2)(A) and the regulations thereunder.

(d) *Effective date.* This section shall take effect on January 1, 1970.

○━ § 301.6685 Statutory provisions; assessable penalties with respect to private foundation annual reports. [Sec. 6685, IRC]

○━ § 301.6685-1 (T.D. 7127, filed 6-14-71.) Assessable penalties with respect to private foundation annual reports.

(a) *In general.* In addition to the penalty imposed by section 7207, relating to fraudulent returns, statements, or other documents, any person (as defined in paragraph (b) of this section) who is required to file the annual report and the notice of availability of such report required under section 6056, relating to annual reports by private foundations, or to comply with the requirements of section 6104(d), relating to public inspection of private foundations' annual reports, and who fails so to file or comply, if such failure is willful, shall pay a penalty of $1,000 with respect to each such report or notice with respect to which there is a failure so to file or comply.

(b) *Person.* For purposes of this section, the term "person" means any officer, director, trustee, employee, member, or other individual whose duty it is to perform the act in respect of which the failure occurs.

(c) *Effective date.* This section shall take effect on January 1, 1970.

(d) *Cross reference.* For the amount imposed for failure to file the annual report required by section 6056 or to comply with section 6104(d), see paragraph (c) of § 301.6652-2.

○━ § 301.6686-1 (T.D. 7533, filed 2-14-78.) Failure of DISC to file returns.

(a) *In general.* In addition to the penalty imposed by section 7203 (relating to willful failure to file a return, supply information, or pay tax) any person who is required to supply information or to file a return under section 6011(c) (relating to records and returns of DISC's) and who fails to supply such information or file such return at the time prescribed in section 6072(b) and § 1.6072-2(e) shall pay a penalty of $100 for each failure to supply information (provided that the total amount imposed on the delinquent person for all such failures during a calendar year shall not exceed $25,000) and a penalty of $1,000 with respect to each failure to file a return, unless it is shown that such failure is due to a reasonable cause.

(b) *Showing of reasonable cause.* The penalty imposed by section 6686 shall not apply to any person with respect to a failure to supply information, or to file a return, under section 6011(c) if it is established to the satisfaction of the district director or director of the Internal Revenue Service Center that such failure was due to reasonable cause. An affirmative showing of reasonable cause must be made in the form of a written statement, which contains a declaration by such person that the statement is made under the penalties of perjury, and sets forth all the facts alleged as reasonable cause.

○━ § 301.6688 Statutory provisions; assessable penalties with respect to information required to be furnished under section 7654. [Sec. 6688, IRC]

○━ § 301.6688-1 (T.D. 7385, filed 10-28-75.) Assessable penalties with respect to information required to be furnished under section 7654 on allocation of tax to Guam or the United States.

(a) *In general.* Each individual to whom paragraph (a)(2) of § 301.7654-1 applies for a taxable year who fails to file for such year the information return required by paragraph (d) of such section within the time prescribed therein, or who files such a return but does not show the information required thereon, shall, in addition to any criminal penalty provided by law, pay a penalty of $100 for each such failure.

(b) *Manner of payment.* The penalty set forth in paragraph (a) of this section shall be paid in the same manner as tax upon the issuance of a notice and demand therefor.

(c) *Reasonable cause.* The penalty set forth in paragraph (a) of this section shall not apply if it is established, to the satisfaction of the district director (or of the Commissioner of Revenue and Taxation of Guam if the individual was required to file his return of income tax for the taxable year with Guam) that the failure to file the information return or furnish the information within the prescribed time was due to reasonable cause and not to willful neglect. An individual who wishes to avoid the penalty must make an affirmative showing of all facts alleged as a reasonable cause for his failure to file the information return on time, or furnish the information on time, in the form of a written statement containing a declaration that it is made under penalties of perjury. Such statement must be filed with the district director (or with the Commissioner of Revenue and Taxation, Agana, Guam 96910, if the individual was required to file his return of income tax for the taxable year with Guam). In determining whether there was reasonable cause for failure to furnish the required information, account will be taken of the fact that the individual was unable to furnish the required information in spite of the exercise of ordinary business care and prudence in his effort to furnish the information. An individual will be considered to have exercised ordinary business care and prudence in his effort to furnish the required information if he made reasonable efforts to furnish the information but was unable to do so because of a lack of sufficient facts on which to make a proper

Reg. § 301.6688-1(c)

determination. See paragraph (b) of § 1.935-1 of this chapter (Income Tax Regulations) for the rules which specify where returns of income tax must be filed for the taxable year by individuals to whom this section applies.

(d) *Effective date.* This section shall apply for taxable years beginning after December 31, 1972.

§ 1.6694-1 (T.D. 7519, filed 11-17-77.) **Understatement of taxpayer's liability by income tax return preparer.**

(a) *Negligent or intentional disregard of rules and regulations.* (1) If any part of an understatement of liability relating to a return of tax under subtitle A of the Internal Revenue Code of 1954 or claim for refund of tax under subtitle A of the Internal Revenue Code of 1954 is due to negligent or intentional disregard of one or more rules or regulations by one or more income tax return preparers of the return or claim for refund, each such preparer shall be subject to a separate penalty of $100. However, an employer or partnership of a preparer subject to this penalty is not also subject to the penalty, unless the employer or partnership (or one or more of its chief officers or general partners) also participated in the negligent or intentional disregard of one or more rules or regulations. A preparer is not considered to have negligently or intentionally disregarded a rule or regulation if the preparer exercises due diligence in an effort to apply the rules and regulations to the information given to the preparer to determine the taxpayer's correct liability for tax.

(2) For the definition of the term "understatement of liability", see section 6694 (e) and paragraph (d) of this section.

(3) The term "rules or regulations" includes the provisions of the Internal Revenue Code of 1954, the Treasury regulations issued under the Code, and Internal Revenue Service revenue rulings published in the Cumulative Bulletin.

(4) If a preparer in good faith and with reasonable basis takes the position that a rule or regulation does not accurately reflect the Code and does not follow it, the preparer has not negligently or intentionally disregarded the rule or regulation. This test shall be applied in the same manner as it is applied under section 6653 (a) and the regulations thereunder (relating to disregard of rules and regulations by taxpayers). For example, if a preparer reasonably takes the position in good faith that a revenue ruling does not accurately reflect the Code, the preparation of a return or claim for refund by the preparer in conflict with the revenue ruling is not a negligent or intentional disregard of the revenue ruling. For purposes of this paragraph (a), the view of the taxpayer concerning a rule or regulation is not material.

(5) In any proceeding with respect to the penalty imposed by this paragraph (a), the preparer shall bear the burden of proof on the issue whether the preparer has negligently or intentionally disregarded a rule or regulation. If the preparer presents evidence that the normal practice of the preparer concerning the treatment of a particular credit, allowance, deduction, or item of income was not negligent and that this normal practice was followed, the preparer has satisfied the burden of proof that he did not negligently disregard a rule or regulation, unless the Internal Revenue Service presents contrary evidence.

(b) *Willful understatement of liability.* (1) If any part of an understatement of liability relating to a return of tax under subtitle A of the Internal Revenue Code of 1954 or claim for refund of tax under subtitle A of the Internal Revenue Code of 1954 is due to a willful attempt in any manner to understate liability for tax by one or more income tax return preparers of the return or claim for refund, each such preparer shall be subject to a separate penalty of $500. However, an employer or partnership of a preparer subject to this penalty is not also subject to the penalty, unless the employer or partnership (or one or more of its chief officers or general partners) also participated in the willful attempt to understate liability.

(2)(i) A preparer is considered to have willfully attempted to understate liability if the preparer disregards information furnished by the taxpayer or other persons in an attempt wrongfully to reduce the tax liability of the taxpayer. For example, if a preparer disregards information concerning certain items of taxable income furnished by the taxpayer or other persons, the preparer would be subject to the penalty. Similarly, if a taxpayer states to a preparer that the taxpayer has only two dependents, and the preparer reports six dependents on the return, the preparer would be subject to the penalty.

(ii) Generally, in preparing a return, the preparer may in good faith rely without verification upon information furnished by the taxpayer. To avoid the penalty, the preparer is not required to examine or review documents or other evidence in order to verify independently the taxpayer's information. However, the preparer may not ignore the implications of information furnished. The preparer shall make reasonable inquiries if the information as furnished appears to be incorrect or incomplete. Additionally, many sections of the Code require the existence of specific facts and circumstances, such as maintenance of specific documentation, before a deduction may properly be claimed. The preparer shall make appropriate inquiries of the taxpayer to determine the existence of facts and circumstances required by a Code section or regulations incident to claiming a deduction.

(iii) For example, assume that a taxpayer, during the tax interview conducted by a preparer, stated that he had paid $2,500 in doctor bills and $4,000 in deductible travel and entertainment expenses during the tax year when in fact he had paid smaller amounts. On the basis of the information, the preparer properly calculated deductions for medical expenses and for travel and entertainment expenses which resulted in an understatement of liability for tax. The preparer had no reason to believe that the medical expense and travel and entertainment expense information presented was incorrect or incomplete. The preparer did not ask for underlying documentation of the medical expenses and, upon inquiry, was reasonably satisfied by the taxpayer's representations that the taxpayer had adequate records (or other sufficient corroborative evidence) for the deduction of $4,000 for travel and entertainment expenses. The preparer is not subject to the penalty.

(iv) In certain situations, a preparer shall be subject both to a penalty under paragraph (a) of this section for intentional disregard of rules and regulations and to a penalty under this paragraph (b) for willful understatement of liability. A penalty for willful understatement of liability may be based on an intentional disregard of rules and regulations. For example, a preparer who claims a personal exemption deduction for the taxpayer's mother with knowledge that the taxpayer is not entitled to the deduction will have both intentionally disregarded rules and regulations within the meaning of paragraph (a) of this section and willfully understated liability for tax within the meaning of this paragraph (b).

(3) For the definition of the term "understatement of liability", see section 6694 (e) and paragraph (d) of this section.

(4) If a penalty is assessed against a preparer, and collected at least in part, under paragraph (a) of this section for a return or claim for refund, then the amount of a penalty for which the preparer may be subject under this paragraph (b) for the same return or claim for refund is $500, reduced by the amount collected under paragraph (a) of this section for the return or claim for refund.

(5) In any proceeding with respect to the penalty imposed by this paragraph (b), the Internal Revenue Service shall bear the burden of proof on the issue whether the preparer has willfully attempted to un-

derstate the liability for tax. See section 7427.

(c) *Abatement of penalty where taxpayer's liability not understated.* If a penalty or penalties under section 6694(a) and paragraph (a) of this section or under section 6694(b) and paragraph (b) of this section concerning a return or claim for refund have been assessed against one or more income tax preparers, and if at any time in a final administrative determination or a final judicial decision it is established that there was no understatement of liability relating to the return or claim for refund, then—

(1) The assessment shall be abated; and

(2) If any amount of the penalty or penalties was paid, that amount shall be refunded to the person or persons who so paid, as if the payment were an overpayment of tax, without consideration of any period of limitations.

(d) *Understatement of liability defined.* For purposes of this section, an "understatement of liability" exists, if viewing the return or claim for refund as a whole, there is an understatement of the net amount payable of any tax under subtitle A of the Internal Revenue Code of 1954, or an overstatement of the net amount creditable or refundable of any tax under subtitle A of the Internal Revenue Code of 1954. Tax under subtitle A of the Internal Revenue Code of 1954 includes the additions to the tax provided by section 6654 and section 6655 (relating to underpayment of estimated tax). See section 6659(a)(2). Except as provided in paragraph (c) of this section, the determination of whether an understatement of liability exists may be made in a proceeding involving the preparer apart from any proceeding involving the taxpayer.

О— § 1.6694-2 (T.D. 7519, filed 11-17-77.) **Extension of period of collection where preparer pays 15 percent of penalty for understatement of taxpayer's liability and certain other procedural matters.**

(a) *In general.* (1) The Internal Revenue Service shall investigate the preparation by the income tax return preparer of the return of tax under subtitle A of the Internal Revenue Code of 1954 or claim for refund of tax under subtitle A of the Internal Revenue Code of 1954 and shall send a report of examination to the preparer before the assessment of either—

(i) The penalty for negligent or intentional disregard of rules and regulations under § 1.6694-1(a); or

(ii) The penalty for willful understatement of liability under § 1.6694-1(b).

Unless the period of limitation (if any) under section 6696(d) may expire without adequate opportunity for assessment, the Internal Revenue Service shall also, before the assessment of either penalty, send a 30-day letter to the preparer notifying him of the proposed penalty or penalties and offering an opportunity to the preparer to request further administrative consideration and a final administrative determination by the Internal Revenue Service concerning the assessment. If the preparer then makes a timely request, assessment may not be made until the Internal Revenue Service makes a final administrative determination adverse to the preparer.

(2) If the Internal Revenue Service assesses either of the two penalties described in paragraph (a)(1)(i) and (ii) of this section, it shall send to the preparer a statement of notice and demand, separate from any notice of a tax deficiency, for payment of the amount assessed.

(3) Within 30 days after the day on which notice and demand of either of the two penalties described in paragraph (a) (1)(i) and (ii) of this section is made against the preparer, that preparer shall either—

(i) Pay the entire amount assessed (and may file a claim for refund of the amount paid at any time not later than 3 years after the date of payment); or

(ii) Pay an amount which is not less than 15 percent of the entire amount assessed and shall file a claim for refund of the entire amount paid.

(4) If the preparer pays an amount and files a claim for refund under paragraph (a)(3)(ii) of this section, the Internal Revenue Service may not make, begin, or prosecute a levy or proceeding in court for collection of the unpaid remainder of the amount assessed until—

(i) A date which is more than 30 days after the earlier of—

(A) The day on which the preparer's claim for refund is denied; or

(B) The expiration of 6 months after the day on which the preparer filed the claim for refund; and

(ii) Final resolution of any proceeding begun as provided in paragraph (b) of this section.

Final resolution of a proceeding includes any settlement between the Internal Revenue Service and the preparer, any final determination by the court (for which the period for appeal, if any, has expired), and, generally, the types of determinations provided under section 1313(a) (relating to taxpayer deficiencies). Notwithstanding section 7421(a) (relating to suits to restrain assessment or collection), the beginning of a levy or proceeding in court by the Internal Revenue Service in contravention of this subparagraph (4) may be enjoined by a proceeding in the proper court.

(b) *Preparer must bring suit in district court to determine liability for penalty.* (1) If, within 30 days after the earlier of—

(i) The day on which the preparer's claim for refund filed under paragraph (a) (3)(ii) of this section is denied; or

(ii) The expiration of 6 months after the day on which the preparer filed the claim for refund,

the preparer fails to begin a proceeding for refund in the appropriate United States district court, then the Internal Revenue Service may proceed with collection of the amount of the penalty not paid under paragraph (a)(3)(ii) of this section.

(2)(i) If the preparer begins a proceeding for refund within the applicable 30-day period of paragraph (b)(1) of this section, then the Internal Revenue Service may not make, begin, or prosecute a levy or proceeding in court for collection of the

Reg. § 1.6694-2(b)(2)

unpaid remainder of the penalty until final resolution of the proceeding.

(ii) If the preparer begins a proceeding for refund under this paragraph (b), then the Internal Revenue Service need not bring a counterclaim in the proceeding for the unpaid remainder of the penalty, because any judicial decision on the refund will apply as well to the unpaid remainder of the penalty.

(c) *Suspension of running of period of limitations on collection.* The running of the period of limitations provided in section 6502 on the collection by levy or by a proceeding in court of the unpaid amount of a penalty or penalties described in § 1.6694-1 (a) or (b) shall be suspended for the period during which the Internal Revenue Service, under paragraphs (a)(4) and (b)(2)(i) of this section, may not collect the unpaid amount of the penalty or penalties by levy or a proceeding in court.

§ 1.6695-1 (T.D. 7519, filed 11-17-77.) **Other assessable penalties with respect to the preparation of income tax returns for other persons.**

(a) *Failure to furnish copy to taxpayer.* (1) A person who is an income tax return preparer of any return of tax under subtitle A of the Internal Revenue Code of 1954 or claim for refund of tax under subtitle A of the Internal Revenue Code of 1954 and who fails to satisfy the requirement imposed upon him by section 6107(a) and § 1.6107-1(a) and (c) to furnish a copy of the return or claim for refund to the taxpayer (or nontaxable entity) shall be subject to a penalty of $25 for the failure, unless it is shown that the failure is due to reasonable cause and not due to willful neglect. Thus, no penalty may be imposed under section 6695(a) and this paragraph (a)(1) upon a person who is an income tax return preparer solely by reason of—

(i) Section 301.7701-15(a)(2) and (b) on account of having given advice on specific issues of law; or

(ii) Section 301.7701-15(b)(3) on account of having prepared the return solely because of having prepared another return which affects amounts reported on the return.

(2) No penalty may be imposed under section 6695(a) and paragraph (a)(1) of this section upon an income tax return preparer who furnishes a copy of the return of claim for refund to a taxpayer—

(i) Who holds an elected or politically appointed position with the government of the United States or a State or political subdivision thereof; and

(ii) Who, in order faithfully to carry out his official duties, has so arranged his affairs that he has less than full knowledge of the property which he holds or of the debts for which he is responsible, if information is deleted from the copy in order to preserve or maintain this arrangement.

(b) *Failure to sign return.* (1) An individual who is an income tax return preparer with respect to a return of tax under subtitle A of the Internal Revenue Code of 1954 or claim for refund of tax under subtitle A of the Internal Revenue Code of 1954 shall manually sign the return or claim for refund (which may be a photocopy) in the appropriate space provided on the return or claim for refund after it is completed and before it is presented to the taxpayer (or nontaxable entity) for signature. Except as provided in paragraph (b)(4)(iii) of this section, an individual preparer may not satisfy this requirement by use of a facsimile signature stamp or signed gummed label. If the preparer is unavailable for signature, another preparer shall review the entire preparation of the return or claim for refund, and then shall manually sign the return or claim for refund.

(2) If more than one income tax return preparer is involved in the preparation of the return or claim for refund, the individual preparer who has the primary responsibility as between or among the preparers for the overall substantive accuracy of the preparation of such return or claim for refund shall be considered to be the income tax return preparer for purposes of this paragraph.

(3) The application of paragraph (b)(1) and (2) of this section is illustrated by the following examples:

Example (1). X law firm employs Y, a lawyer, to prepare for compensation returns and claims for refund of taxes. X is employed by T, a taxpayer, to prepare his 1977 Federal tax return. X assigns Y to prepare T's return. Y obtains the information necessary for completing the return from T and makes determinations with respect to the proper application of the tax laws to such information in order to determine T's tax liability. Y then forwards such information to C, a computer tax service which performs the mathematical computations and prints the return form by means of computers. C then sends the completed return to Y who reviews the accuracy of the return. Y is the individual preparer who is primarily responsible for the overall accuracy of T's return. Y must sign the return as preparer.

Example (2). X partnership is a national accounting firm which prepares for compensation returns and claims for refund of taxes. A and B, employees of X, are involved in preparing the 1977 tax return of T Corporation. After they complete the return, including the gathering of the necessary information, the proper application of the tax laws to such information, and the performance of the necessary mathematical computations, C, a supervisory employee of X, reviews the return. As part of this review, C reviews the information provided and the application of the tax laws to this information. The mathematical computations and carried-forward amounts are proved by D, an employee in X's comparing and proving department. The policies and practices of X require that P a partner, finally review the return. The scope of P's review includes reviewing the information provided by applying to this information his knowledge of T's affairs, observing that X's policies and practices have been followed, and making the final determination with respect to the proper application of the tax laws to determine T's tax liability. P may or may not exercise these responsibilities, or may exercise them to a greater or lesser extent, depending on the degree of complexity of the return, his confidence in C (or A and B), and other factors. P is the individual preparer who is primarily responsible for the overall accuracy of T's return. P must sign the return as preparer.

Example (3). C corporation maintains an office in Seattle, Washington, for the purpose of preparing for compensation returns and claims for refund of taxes. C makes compensatory arrangements with individuals (but provides no working facilities) in several States to collect information from taxpayers and to make determinations with respect to the proper application of the tax laws to the information in order to determine the tax liabilities of such taxpayers. E, an individual, who has such an arrangement in Los Angeles with C, collects information from T, a taxpayer, and completes a worksheet kit supplied by C which is stamped with E's name and an identification number assigned to E by C. In this process, E classifies this information in appropriate income and deduction categories for the tax determination. The completed worksheet kit signed by E, is then mailed to C. D, an employee in C's office, reviews the worksheet kit to make sure it was properly completed. D does not review the information obtained from T for its validity or accuracy. D may, but did not, make the final determination with respect to the proper application of tax laws to the information. The data from the worksheet is entered into a computer and the return form is completed. The return is prepared for submission to T with filing instructions. E is the individual preparer primarily responsible for the overall accuracy of T's return. E must sign the return as preparer.

Example (4). X employs A, B, and C to prepare income tax returns for taxpayers. After A and B have collected the information from the taxpayer and applied the tax laws to the information, the return form is completed by computer service. On the day the returns prepared by A and B are ready for their signatures, A is away from the city for 1 week on another assignment and B is on detail to another office for the day. C may sign the returns prepared by A, provided that (i) C reviews the information obtained by A relative to the taxpayer, and (ii) C reviews the preparation of each return prepared by A. C may not sign the returns prepared by B because B is available.

(4)(i) The manual signature requirement of paragraph (b)(1) and (2) of this section may be satisfied by a photocopy of a copy of the return or claim for refund which copy is manually signed by the preparer after completion of its preparation. After a copy of the return or claim for refund is signed by the preparer and before it is photocopied, no person other than the preparer may alter any entries on the copy other than to correct arithmetical errors discernible on the return or claim for refund. The employer of the preparer or the partnership in which the preparer is a partner, or the preparer (if not employed or engaged by a preparer and not a partner in a partnership which is a preparer), shall retain the manually signed copy of the return or claim for refund. A record of any arithmetical errors corrected shall be retained by the person required to retain the manually signed copy of the return or claim for refund and made available upon request.

(ii) If mechanical preparation of the return or claim for refund is accomplished by computer not under the control of the individual preparer, then the manual signature requirement of paragraph (b)(1) and (2) of this section may be satisfied by a manually signed attestation by the individual preparer attached to the return or claim for refund that all the information contained in the return or claim for refund was obtained from the taxpayer and is true and correct to the best of his knowledge, but only if that information (including any supplemental written information provided and signed by the preparer) is not altered on the return or claim for refund by another person. For purposes of the preceding sentence, the correction of arithmetical or clerical errors discernable from the information submitted by the preparer does not constitute an alteration. The information submitted by the preparer shall be retained by the employer of the preparer or by the partnership in which the preparer is a partner, or by the preparer (if not employed or engaged by a preparer and not a partner in a partnership which is a preparer). A record of any arithmetical or clerical errors corrected shall be retained by the person required to retain the information submitted by the preparer and made available upon request.

(iii) A preparer of a return or claim for refund for a nonresident alien individual taxpayer who is authorized to sign the return or claim for refund for the taxpayer may satisfy the manual signature requirement of paragraph (b)(1) and (2) of this section by a facsimile signature if the preparer is permitted to use a facsimile signature in signing the return or claim for refund for the taxpayer. This subdivision (iii) shall apply only if the preparer submits to the Internal Revenue Service with the returns or claims for refund bearing the preparer's facsimile signature a letter, manually signed by the preparer, identifying by taxpayer name and identification number each return or claim for refund bearing the facsimile signature and declaring that the facsimile signature appearing on these returns or claims for refund is the signature used by the preparer to sign these documents. After the facsimile signature is affixed, no person other than the preparer may alter any entries on the return or claim for refund other than to correct arithmetical errors discernable on the return or claim for refund. The employer of the preparer or the partnership in which the preparer is a partner, or the preparer (if not employed or engaged by a preparer and not a partner in a partnership which is a preparer) shall retain a manually signed copy of the letter submitted to the Internal Revenue Service with the returns or claims for refund. A record of any arithmetical errors corrected shall be retained by the person required to retain the manually signed letter and made available upon request.

(iv) Any items required to be retained and kept available for inspection under subdivision (i), (ii), or (iii) of this subparagraph (4) shall be retained and kept available for inspection for the same period that the material described in § 1.6107-1(b) must be retained and kept available for inspection.

(v) If the district director determines that a preparer or preparers have abused the permissive signature rules of this subparagraph (4) such as by altering the return or claim for refund after signature (in contravention of subdivision (i) of this subparagraph), by altering information on the return or claim for refund after attestation (in contravention of subdivision (ii)

Reg. § 1.6695-1 (b) (4)

of this subparagraph), or by failing to comply with the provisions of subdivision (iii) of this subparagraph, then the district director may, by written notice, prospectively deny to the preparer or preparers the right to use these permissive signature rules.

(5) An individual required by this paragraph (b) to sign a return or claim for refund shall be subject to a penalty of $25 for each failure to sign, unless it is shown that the failure is due to reasonable cause and not due to willful neglect. For purposes of this paragraph, "reasonable cause" is a cause which arises despite ordinary care and prudence exercised by the individual preparer. Thus, no penalty may be imposed under section 6695(b) and this paragraph (b) upon a person who is an income tax return preparer solely by reason of—

(i) Section 301.7701-15(a)(2) and (b) on account of having given advice on specific issues of law; or

(ii) Section 301.7701-15(b)(3) on account of having prepared the return solely because of having prepared another return which affects amounts reported on the return.

If the preparer asserts reasonable cause for failure to sign, the Service shall require a written statement in substantiation of the preparer's claim of reasonable cause.

(c) *Failure to furnish identifying number.* (1) A person who is an income tax return preparer of any return of tax under subtitle A of the Internal Revenue Code of 1954 or claim for refund of tax under subtitle A of the Internal Revenue Code of 1954 and who fails to satisfy the requirement of section 6109(a)(4) and § 1.6109-2(a) to furnish one or more identifying numbers of preparers on a return or claim for refund shall be subject to a penalty of $25 for the failure, unless it is shown that the failure is due to reasonable cause and not due to willful neglect. Thus, no penalty may be imposed under section 6695(c) and this paragraph (c)(1) upon a person who is an income tax return preparer solely by reason of—

(i) Section 301.7701-15(a)(2) and (b) on account of having given advice on specific issues of law; or

(ii) Section 301.7701-15(b)(3) on account of having prepared the return solely because of having prepared another return which affects amounts reported on the return.

(2) No penalty may be imposed under section 6695(c) and paragraph (c)(1) of this section upon—

(i) A preparer who is employed (or engaged) by a person who is also a preparer of the return or claim for refund, or

(ii) A preparer who is a partner in a partnership which is also a preparer of the return or claim for refund.

(3) No more than one penalty of $25 may be imposed under section 6695(c) and paragraph (c)(1) of this section with respect to a single return or claim for refund.

(d) *Failure to retain copy or list.* (1) A person who is an income tax return preparer of any return of tax under subtitle A of the Internal Revenue Code of 1954 or claim for refund of tax under subtitle A of the Internal Revenue Code of 1954 and who fails to satisfy the requirements imposed upon him by section 6107(b) and § 1.6107-1(b) and (c) (other than the record requirement described in both § 1.6107-1(b)(2) and (3)) to retain and make available a copy of the return or claim for refund, or to include the return or claim for refund in a record of returns and claims for refund and make the record available for inspection, shall be subject to a penalty of $50 for the failure, unless it is shown that the failure is due to reasonable cause and not due to willful neglect. Thus, no penalty may be imposed under section 6695(d) and this paragraph (d)(1) upon a person who is an income tax return preparer solely by reason of—

(i) Section 301.7701-15(a)(2) and (b) on account of having given advice on specific issues of law; or

(ii) Section 301.7701-15(b)(3) on account of having prepared the return solely because of having prepared another return which affects amounts reported on the return.

(2) A person may not, for returns or claims for refund presented to the taxpayers (or nontaxable entities) during any single return period, be subject to more than $25,000 in penalties under section 6695 (d) and paragraph (d)(1) of this section.

(e) *Failure to file correct information return.* A person who is subject to the reporting requirements of section 6060 and § 1.6060-1 and who fails to satisfy these requirements shall be subject to penalties as set forth in this paragraph, unless it is shown that the failure is due to reasonable cause and not due to willful neglect.

(1) $100, for failure to file Form 5717 as required (or to comply with an approved different reporting method), plus

(2) $5, for each failure to report as required an item on the Form 5717 (or under the approved different reporting method).

A person may not, for failure to satisfy the reporting requirements for any single return period, be subject to more than $20,000 in penalties under section 6695(e) and this section.

(f) *Negotiation of check.* (1) No person who is an income tax return preparer may endorse or otherwise negotiate, directly or through an agent, a check for the refund of tax under subtitle A of the Internal Revenue Code of 1954 which is issued to a taxpayer other than the preparer if the person was a preparer of the return or claim for refund which gave rise to the refund check.

(2) Section 6695(f) and paragraph (f)(1) and (3) of this section do not apply to a preparer-bank which—

(i) Cashes a refund check and remits all of the cash to the taxpayer or accepts a refund check for deposit in full to a taxpayer's account, so long as the bank does not initially endorse or negotiate the check (unless the bank has made a loan to the taxpayer on the basis of the anticipated refund); or

(ii) Endorses a refund check for deposit in full to a taxpayer's account pursuant to a written authorization of the taxpayer (unless the bank has made a loan to the taxpayer on the basis of the anticipated refund).

A preparer-bank may also subsequently endorse or negotiate a refund check as a part of the check-clearing process through the financial system after initial endorsement or negotiation.

(3) The preparer shall be subject to a penalty of $500 for each endorsement or negotiation of a check prohibited under section 6695(f) and paragraph (f)(1) of this section.

JEOPARDY, BANKRUPTCY AND RECEIVERSHIPS
JEOPARDY
TERMINATION OF TAXABLE YEAR

§ 1.6851 Statutory provisions; termination of taxable year. [Sec. 6851, IRC]

§ 1.6851-1 (T.D. 6426, filed 11-30-59; republished in T.D. 6500, filed 11-25-60.) **Termination of taxable period by district director.**

(a) *Income tax in jeopardy*—(1) *In general.* If a taxpayer designs by immediate departure from the United States, or otherwise, to avoid the payment of income tax for the preceding or current taxable year, the district director may, upon evidence satisfactory to him, declare the taxable period for such taxpayer immediately terminated and cause to be served upon him notice and demand for immediate payment of the income tax for the short taxable period resulting from such termination, and of the income tax for the preceding taxable year, or so much of such tax as is unpaid. In such a case, the taxpayer is entitled to a deduction for his personal exemptions (as limited in the case of certain nonresident aliens) without any proration because of the short taxable period.

(2) *Corporations in liquidation.* If the district director finds that the collection of the income tax of a corporation for the current or the preceding taxable year will be jeopardized by the distribution of all or a portion of the assets of such corporation in the liquidation of the whole or any part of its capital stock, he shall declare the taxable period for such corporation immediately terminated and cause to be served upon the corporation notice and demand for immediate payment of the income tax for the short taxable period resulting from such termination, and of the income tax for the preceding taxable year, or so much of such tax is unpaid.

(3) *Presumptive evidence of jeopardy.* In any proceeding in court brought to enforce payment of taxes made due and payable by virtue of the provisions of section 6851 and this paragraph, the finding of the district director shall be for all purposes presumptive evidence of jeopardy.

(4) *Bond.* For the provisions relating to the furnishing of a bond in lieu of making immediate payment of the taxes which become due by action pursuant to this paragraph, see § 1.6851-3.

(b) *Reopening of taxable period.* (1) *Income received after termination.* If a taxpayer whose taxable period has been terminated under section 6851 and paragraph (a) of this section receives other income subsequent to such termination within his current taxable year, the district director may reopen the period so terminated and may, in accordance with section 6851 and paragraph (a) of this section, again terminate the taxable period of such taxpayer. In such case, tax liability shall be computed for the period beginning with the first day of the current taxable year of the taxpayer and ending at the time of the later termination.

(2) *Return filed after termination.* When a taxpayer whose taxable period has been terminated under section 6851 and paragraph (a) of this section files the return required by paragraph (c) of this section, the taxable period so terminated shall be reopened.

(c) *Taxable year not affected by termination.* Notwithstanding any action by a district director under section 6851 and this section, a taxpayer shall file a return in accordance with section 6012 and the regulations thereunder for his current taxable year showing all items of gross income, deductions, and credits for such taxable year. The term "current taxable year" means the taxpayer's usual annual accounting period determined without regard to any action under section 6851 and this section. Any tax paid as a result of a termination under section 6851 and this section will be applied against the tax due for his current taxable year.

(d) *Evidence of compliance with income tax obligations.* Citizens of the United States or of possessions of the United States departing from the United States or its possessions will not be required to procure certificates of compliance or to present any other evidence of compliance with income tax obligations. However, for the rules relating to the furnishing of evidence of compliance with the income tax obligations by certain departing aliens, see § 1.6851-2.

§ 301.6851 Statutory provisions; termination of taxable year. [Sec. 6851, IRC]

§ 301.6851-1 (T.D. 6227, filed 3-29-57; republished in T.D. 6498, filed 10-24-60.) **Termination of taxable year.**

For regulations under section 6851, see §§ 1.6851-1 to 1.6851-3, inclusive, of this chapter (Income Tax Regulations).

§ 1.6851-2 (T.D. 6426, filed 11-30-59; republished in T.D. 6500, filed 11-25-60; amended by T.D. 6537, filed 1-19-61 and T.D. 6620, filed 11-29-62.) **Certificates of compliance with income tax laws by departing aliens.**

(a) *In general*—(1) *Requirement.* The rules of this section are applicable, except as otherwise expressly provided, to any alien who departs from the United States or any of its possessions after January 20, 1961. Except as provided in subparagraph (2) of this paragraph, no such alien, whether resident or nonresident, may depart from the United States unless he first procures a certificate that he has complied with all of the obligations imposed upon him by the income tax laws. In order to procure such a certificate, an alien who intends to depart from the United States (i) must file with the district director for the internal revenue district in which he is located the statements or returns required by paragraph (b) of this section to be filed before obtaining such certificate, (ii) must appear before such district director if the district director deems it necessary, and (iii) must pay any taxes required under paragraph (b) of this section to be paid before obtaining the certificate. Either such certificate of compliance, properly exe-

Reg. § 1.6851-2(a)(1)

cuted, or evidence that the alien is excepted under subparagraph (2) of this paragraph from obtaining the certificate must be presented at the point of departure. An alien who presents himself at the point of departure without a certificate of compliance, or evidence establishing that such a certificate is not required, will be subject at such departure point to examination by an internal revenue officer or employee and to the completion of returns and statements and payment of taxes as required by paragraph (b) of this section.

(2) *Exceptions*—(i) *Diplomatic representatives. (a) Diplomatic representatives, their families and servants.* — *(1)* Representatives of foreign governments bearing diplomatic passports, whether accredited to the United States or other countries, and members of their households shall not, upon departure from the United States or any of its possessions, be examined as to their liability for United States income tax or be required to obtain a certificate of compliance. If a foreign government does not issue diplomatic passports but merely indicates on passports issued to members of its diplomatic service the status of the bearer as a member of such service, such passports are considered as diplomatic passports for income tax purposes.

(2) Likewise, the servant of a diplomatic representative who accompanies any individual bearing a diplomatic passport upon departure from the United States or any of its possessions shall not be required, upon such departure, to obtain a certificate of compliance or to submit to examination as to his liability for United States income tax. If the departure of such a servant from the United States or any of its possessions is not made in the company of an individual bearing a diplomatic passport, the servant is required to obtain a certificate of compliance. However, such certificate will be issued to him on Form 2063 without examination as to his income tax liability upon presentation to the district director for the internal revenue district in which the servant is located of a letter from the chief of the diplomatic mission to which the servant is attached certifying *(i)* that the name of the servant appears on the "White List", a list of employees of diplomatic missions, and *(ii)* that the servant is not obligated to the United States for any income tax, and will not be so obligated up to and including the intended date of departure.

(b) Other employees. Any employee of an international organization or of a foreign government (other than a diplomatic representative to whom *(a)* of this subdivision applies) whose compensation for official services rendered to such organization or government is excluded from gross income under section 893 and who has received no gross income from sources within the United States, and any member of his household who has received no gross income from sources within the United States, shall not, upon departure from the United States or any of its possessions after November 30, 1962 be examined as to his liability for United States income tax or be required to obtain a certificate of compliance.

(c) Effect of waiver. An alien who has filed with the Attorney General the waiver provided for under section 247(b) of the Immigration and Nationality Act (8 U.S.C. 1257(b)) is not entitled to the exception provided by this subdivision.

(ii) Alien students and industrial trainees. A certificate of compliance shall not be required, and examination as to United States income tax liability shall not be made, upon the departure from the United States or any of its possessions of—

(a) An alien student admitted solely on an F visa who has received no gross income from sources within the United States during the period he is in the United States under such visa, other than allowances to cover the expenses incident to his study in the United States (including expenses for travel, maintenance, tuition) and the value of any services or accommodations furnished to him incident to such study; or

(b) An alien industrial trainee admitted solely on an H-3 visa who has received no gross income from sources within the United States during the period he is in the United States under such visa, other than allowances to cover the expenses incident to his training in the United States (including expenses for travel, maintenance) and the value of any services or accommodations furnished to him incident to such training.

(iii) Other aliens temporarily in the United States. A certificate of compliance shall not be required, and examination as to United States income tax liability shall not be made, upon the departure from the United States or any of its possessions of an alien hereinafter described in this subdivision, unless the district director has reason to believe that such alien has received taxable income during the taxable year up to and including the date of departure or during the preceding taxable year and that collection of income tax from such alien will be jeopardized by his departure from the United States:

(a) An alien visitor for pleasure admitted solely on a B-2 visa;

(b) An alien visitor for business admitted on a B-1 visa, or on both a B-1 visa and a B-2 visa, who does not remain in the United States or a possession thereof for a period or periods exceeding a total of 90 days during the taxable year;

(c) An alien in transit through the United States or any of its possessions on a C-1 visa or under a contract, including a bond agreement, between a transportation line and the Attorney General pursuant to section 238(d) of the Immigration and Nationality Act (8 U.S.C. 1228(d));

(d) An alien who is admitted to the United States on a border-crossing identification card or with respect to whom passports, visas, and border-crossing identification cards are not required, if such alien is a visitor for pleasure, or if such alien is a visitor for business who does not remain in the United States or a possession thereof for a period or periods exceeding a total of 90 days during the taxable year, or if such alien is in transit through the United States or any of its possessions;

(e) An alien military trainee admitted to the United States to pursue a course of instruction under the auspices of the Department of Defense who departs from the United States on official military travel orders; or

(f) An alien resident of Canada or Mexico who commutes between such country and the United States at frequent intervals for the purpose of employment and whose wages are subject to the withholding of tax.

(b) *Issuance of certificate of compliance.* (1) *In general.* (i) Upon the departure of an alien required to secure a certificate of compliance under paragraph (a) of this section, the district director shall determine whether the departure of such alien jeopardizes the collection of any income tax for the current or the preceding taxable year, but the district director may determine that jeopardy does not exist in some cases. If the district director finds that the departure of such an alien results in jeopardy, the taxable period of the alien will be terminated, and the alien will be required to file returns and make payment to tax in accordance with subparagraph (3)(iii) of this paragraph. On the other hand, if the district director finds that the departure of the alien does not result in jeopardy, the alien will be required to file the statement or returns required by subparagraph (2) or (3)(ii) of this paragraph, but will not be required to pay income tax before the usual time for payment.

(ii) The departure of an alien who is a resident of the United States or a possession thereof and who intends to continue such residence shall be treated as not resulting in jeopardy, and thus not requiring termination of his taxable period, except when the district director has information indicating that the alien intends by such departure to avoid the payment of his income tax. In the case of a nonresident alien (including a resident alien discontinuing residence), the fact that the alien intends to depart from the United States will justify termination of his taxable period unless the alien establishes to the satisfaction of the district director that he intends to return to the United States and that his departure will not jeopardize collection of the tax. The determination of whether the departure of the alien results in jeopardy will be made on examination of all the facts in the case. Evidence tending to establish that jeopardy does not result from the departure of the alien may be provided, for example, by information showing that the alien is engaged in trade or business in the United States or that he leaves sufficient property in the United States to secure payment of his income tax for the taxable year and of any income tax for the preceding year which remains unpaid.

(2) *Alien having no taxable income and resident alien whose taxable period is not terminated.* A statement on Form 2063 shall be filed with the district director by every alien required to obtain a certificate of compliance—

(i) Who is a resident of the United States and whose taxable period is not terminated either because he has had no taxable income for the taxable year up to and including the date of his departure (and for the preceding taxable year where the period for making the income tax return for such year has not expired) or because, although he has had taxable income for such period or periods, the district director has not found that his departure jeopardizes collection of the tax on such income; or

(ii) Who is not a resident of the United States and who has had no taxable income for the taxable year up to and including the date of his departure (and for the preceding taxable year where the period for making the income tax return for such year has not expired).

Any alien described in subdivision (i) or (ii) of this subparagraph who is in default in making return of, or paying, income tax for any taxable year shall, in addition, file with the district director any returns which have not been made as required and pay to the district director the amount of any tax for which he is in default. Upon compliance by an alien with the foregoing requirements of this subparagraph, the district director shall execute and issue to the alien the certificate of compliance attached to Form 2063. The certificate of compliance so issued shall be effective for all departures of the alien during his current taxable year, subject to revocation upon any subsequent departure should the district director have reason to believe that such subsequent departure would result in jeopardy. The statement required of a resident alien under this subparagraph, if made before January 21, 1961, with respect to a departure after January 20, 1961, may be

© Copyright 1963 by Prentice-Hall, Inc.

Reg. § 1.6851-2(b)(2)

made on a Form 1040C in lieu of a Form 2063.

(3) *Nonresident alien having taxable income and resident alien whose taxable period is terminated.* (i) Nonresident alien having taxable income. Every nonresident alien required to obtain a certificate of compliance (but not described in subparagraph (2) of this paragraph) who wishes to establish that his departure does not result in jeopardy shall furnish to the district director such information as may be required for the purpose of determining whether the departure of the alien jeopardizes collection of the income tax and thus requires termination of his taxable period.

(ii) Nonresident alien whose taxable period is not terminated. Every nonresident alien described in subdivision (i) of this subparagraph whose taxable period is not terminated upon departure shall file with the district director—

(a) A return in duplicate on Form 1040C for the taxable year of his intended departure, showing income received, and reasonably expected to be received, during the entire taxable year within which the departure occurs; and

(b) Any income tax returns which have not been filed as required.

Upon compliance by the alien with the foregoing requirements of this subdivision, and the payment of any income tax for which he is in default, the district director shall execute and issue to the alien the certificate of compliance on the duplicate copy of Form 1040C. The certificate of compliance so issued shall be effective for all departures of the alien during his current taxable year, subject to revocation by the district director upon any subsequent departure if the taxable period of the alien is terminated on such subsequent departure.

(iii) Alien (whether resident or nonresident) whose taxable period is terminated. Every alien required to obtain a certificate of compliance, whether resident or nonresident, whose taxable period is terminated upon departure shall file with the district director—

(a) A return in duplicate on Form 1040C for the short taxable period resulting from such termination, showing income received, and reasonably expected to be received, during the taxable year up to and including the date of departure;

(b) Where the period for filing has not expired, the return required under section 6012 and § 1.6012-1 for the preceding taxable year; and

(c) Any other income tax returns which have not been filed as required.

Upon compliance with the foregoing requirements of this subdivision, and payment of the income tax required to be shown on the returns filed pursuant to (a) and (b) of this subdivision and of any income tax due and owing for prior years, the departing alien will be issued the certificate of compliance on the duplicate copy of Form 1040C. The certificate of compliance so issued shall be effective only for the specific departure with respect to which it is issued. A departing alien may postpone payment of the tax required to be shown on the returns filed in accordance with (a) and (b) of this subdivision until the usual time of payment by furnishing a bond as provided in § 1.6851-3.

(4) *Joint return on Form 1040C.* A departing alien may not file a joint return on Form 1040C unless—

(i) Such alien and his spouse may reasonably be expected to be eligible to file a joint return at the normal close of their taxable periods for which the return is made; and

(ii) If the taxable period of such alien is terminated, the taxable periods of both spouses are so terminated as to end at the same time.

(5) *Annual return.* Nothwithstanding that Form 1040C has been filed for either the entire taxable year of departure or for a terminated period, the return required under section 6012 and § 1.6012-1 for such taxable year shall be filed. Any income tax paid on income shown on the return on Form 1040C shall be applied against the tax determined to be due on the income required to be shown on the subsequent return under section 6012 and § 1.6012-1.

O→ § 1.6851-3 (T.D. 6426, filed 11-30-59; republished in T.D. 6500, filed 11-25-60.) **Furnishing of bond to insure payment.**

If any income tax is made due and payable by virtue of the provisions of section 6851 and §§ 1.6851-1 and 1.6851-2, a taxpayer may, in lieu of making immediate payment thereof, furnish the district director a bond in an amount equal to the amount of tax (including interest thereon to the date of payment as calculated by the district director) payment of which is sought to be stayed, conditioned upon the timely filing of returns with respect to such tax and the payment of such tax at the time it would otherwise be payable without regard to the provisions of section 6851 and §§ 1.6851-1 and 1.6851-2. See section 7101 and the regulations in Part 301 of this chapter (Regulations on Procedure and Administration), relating to the form of bond and the sureties thereon.

JEOPARDY ASSESSMENTS

O→ § 301.6861 Statutory provisions; jeopardy assessments of income, estate, and gift taxes. [Sec. 6861, IRC]

O→ § 301.6861-1 (T.D. 6227, filed 3-29-57; republished in T.D. 6498, filed 10-24-60; amended by T.D. 6585, filed 12-27-61.) **Jeopardy assessments of income, estate, and gift taxes.**

(a) *Authority for making.* If a district director believes that the assessment or collection of a deficiency in income, estate, or gift tax will be jeopardized by delay, he is required to assess such deficiency immediately, together with the interest, additional amounts, and additions to the tax provided by law. A jeopardy assessment may be made before or after the mailing of the notice of deficiency provided by section 6212. However, a jeopardy assessment for a taxable year under section 6861 cannot be made after a decision of the Tax Court with respect to such taxable year has become final (see section 7481) or after the taxpayer has filed a petition for review of the decision of the Tax Court with respect to such taxable year. In the case of a deficiency determined by a decision of the Tax Court which has become final or with respect to which the taxpayer has filed a petition for review and has not filed a bond as provided in section 7485, assessment may be made in accordance with the provisions of section 6215, without regard to section 6861.

(b) *Amount of jeopardy assessment.* If a notice of a deficiency is mailed to the taxpayer before it is discovered that delay would jeopardize the assessment or collection of the tax, a jeopardy assessment may be made in an amount greater or less than that included in the deficiency notice. If a deficiency is assessed on account of jeopardy after the decision of the Tax Court is rendered, the jeopardy assessment may be made only with respect to the deficiency determined by the Tax Court.

(c) *Jurisdiction of Tax Court.* If the jeopardy assessment is made before the notice in respect of the tax to which the jeopardy assessment relates has been mailed pursuant to section 6212(a), the district director shall, within 60 days after the making of the assessment, send the taxpayer a notice of deficiency pursuant to such subsection. The taxpayer may file a petition with the Tax Court for a redetermination of the amount of the deficiency within the time prescribed in section 6213(a). If the petition of the taxpayer is filed with the Tax Court, either before or after the making of the jeopardy assessment, the Commissioner, through his counsel, is required to notify the Tax Court of such assessment or any abatement thereof, and the Tax Court has jurisdiction to redetermine the amount of the deficiency, together with all other amounts assessed at the same time in connection therewith.

(d) *Payment and collection of jeopardy assessment.* After a jeopardy assessment has been made, the district director is required to send notice and demand to the taxpayer for the amount of the jeopardy assessment. Regardless of whether the taxpayer has filed a petition with the Tax Court, he is required to make payment of the amount of such assessment (to the extent that it has not been abated) within 10 days after the sending of notice and demand by the district director, unless before the expiration of such 10-day period he files with the district director a bond as provided in section 6863. Section 6331 provides that, if the district director makes a finding that the collection of the tax is in jeopardy, he may make demand for immediate payment of the amount of the jeopardy assessment and, in such case, the taxpayer shall immediately pay such amount or shall immediately file the bond provided in section 6863. If a petition is not filed with the Tax Court within the period prescribed in section 6213(a), the district director will be so advised, and, if collection of the deficiency has been stayed by the timely filing of a bond as provided in section 6863, he should then give notice and make demand for payment of the amount assessed plus interest. After the Tax Court has rendered its decision and such decision has become final, the district director will be notified of the action taken. He will then send notice and demand for payment of the unpaid portion of the amount determined by the Tax Court, the collection of which has been stayed by the bond. If the amount of the jeopardy assessment is less than the amount determined by the Tax Court, the difference will be assessed and collected as part of the tax upon the issuance of a notice and demand therefor. If the amount of the jeopardy assessment is in excess of the amount determined by the Tax Court, the unpaid portion of such excess will be abated. If any part of the excess amount has been paid, it will be credited or refunded to the taxpayer as provided in section 6402, without the filing of claim therefor.

(e) *Abatement of excessive assessment.* The district director or the director of the regional service center may, at any time before the decision of the Tax Court is rendered, abate a jeopardy assessment in whole or in part if the district director believes that such assessment is excessive in amount.

(f) *Abatement if jeopardy does not exist.* (1) The district director or the director of the regional service center may abate a jeopardy assessment in whole or in part, if it is shown to the satisfaction of the district director that jeopardy does not exist. An abatement may not be made under this paragraph after a decision of the Tax Court in respect of the deficiency has been rendered or, if no petition is filed with such court, after the expiration of the period for filing such petition.

(2) After abatement of a jeopardy assessment in whole or in part, a deficiency may be assessed and collected in the manner authorized by law as if the jeopardy assessment or part thereof so abated had not existed. If a notice of deficiency has been sent to the taxpayer before the abatement of the jeopardy assessment in whole or in part, whether such notice was sent before or after the making of the assessment, such abatement will not affect the validity of the notice or of any proceedings for redetermination based thereon. The period of limitation on the making of assessments and the beginning of levy or a proceeding in court for collection in respect of any deficiency shall be determined as if the jeopardy assessment so abated had not been made, except that the running of such period shall in any event be suspended for the period from the date of such jeopardy assessment until the expiration of the tenth day after the date on which such jeopardy assessment is abated in whole or in part. The provisions of this subparagraph may be illustrated by the following example:

Example. On March 18, 1958, 28 days before the last day of the 3-year period of limitations on assessment, a jeopardy

Reg. § 301.6861-1 (f) (2)

24,402 (I.R.C.)

Reg. § 301.6861-1(f)(2)

assessment is made in respect of a proposed deficiency. On May 2, 1958, before the mailing of the notice of deficiency provided by section 6861(b), this assessment is abated. By virtue of this subparagraph, the last day of the period of limitations for the making of an assessment is June 9, 1958, that is, the thirty-eighth day after the date of the abatement. If the notice of deficiency provided for in section 6861(b) has been sent before the abatement, the running of the period of limitations on assessment would have been suspended pursuant to the provisions of the section 6503(a).

(3) Request for abatement of a jeopardy assessment, because jeopardy does not exist, shall be filed with the district director, shall state fully the reasons for the request, and shall be supported by such evidence as will enable the district director to determine that the collection of the deficiency is not in jeopardy. See paragraph (e) of this section with respect to the abatement of jeopardy assessments which are excessive in amount.

○── § 301.6862 Statutory provisions; jeopardy assessment of taxes other than income, estate, and gift taxes. [Sec. 6862, IRC]

○── § 301.6862-1 (T.D. 6227, filed 3-29-57; republished in T.D. 6498, filed 10-24-60.) Jeopardy assessment of taxes other than income, estate, and gift taxes.

(a) If the district director believes that the collection of any tax (other than income, estate, or gift tax) will be jeopardized by delay, he shall, whether or not the time otherwise prescribed by law for filing the return or paying such tax has expired, immediately assess such tax, together with all interest, additional amounts and additions to the tax provided by law. For example, assume that a taxpayer incurs on January 18, 1955, liability for admissions tax imposed by section 4231, that the last day on which return and payment of such tax is required to be made is April 30, 1955, and that on January 18, 1955, the district director determines that collection of such tax would be jeopardized by delay. In such case, the district director shall immediately assess the tax.

(b) The tax, interest, additional amounts, and additions to the tax will, upon assessment, become immediately due and payable, and the district director shall, without delay, issue a notice and demand for payment thereof in full. Upon failure or refusal to pay the amount demanded, collection thereof by levy shall be lawful without regard to the 10-day period provided in section 6331(a). However, the collection of the whole or any part of the amount of the jeopardy assessment may be stayed by timely filing with the district director a bond as provided in section 6863.

○── § 301.6863 Statutory provisions; stay of collection of jeopardy assessments. [Sec. 6863, IRC]

○── § 301.6863-1 (T.D. 6227, filed 3-29-57; republished in T.D. 6498, filed 10-24-60; amended by T.D. 7384, filed 10-21-75.) Stay of collection of jeopardy assessments; bond to stay collection.

(a) *General rule.* (1) The collection of a jeopardy assessment of any tax may be stayed by filing with the district director a bond on the form to be furnished by the district director upon request.

(2) The bond may be filed—

(i) At any time before the time collection by levy is authorized under section 6331(a), or

(ii) After collection by levy is authorized and before levy is made on any property or rights to property, or

(iii) In the discretion of the district director, after any such levy has been made and before the expiration of the period of limitations on collection.

(3) The bond must be in an amount equal to the portion (including interest thereon to the date of payment as calculated by the district director) of the jeopardy assessment collection of which is sought to be stayed. See section 7101 and § 301.7101-1, relating to the form of bond and the sureties thereon. The bond shall be conditioned upon the payment of the amount (together with interest thereon), the collection of which is stayed, at the time at which, but for the making of the jeopardy assessment, such amount would be due.

(4) Upon the filing of a bond in accordance with this section, the collection of so much of the assessment as is covered by the bond will be stayed. The taxpayer may at any time waive the stay of collection of the whole or any part of the amount covered by the bond. If as a result of such waiver any part of the amount covered by the bond is paid, or if any portion of the jeopardy assessment is abated by the district director, then the bond shall at the request of the taxpayer be proportionately reduced.

(b) *Additional conditions applicable to income, estate, and gift tax assessments.* In the case of a jeopardy assessment of income, estate, or gift tax, the bond must be conditioned upon the payment of so much of the amount included therein as is not abated by a decision of the Tax Court which has become final, together with the interest on such amount. If the Tax Court determines that the amount assessed is greater than the correct amount of the tax, the bond will be proportionately reduced at the request of the taxpayer after the Tax Court renders its decision. If the bond is given before the taxpayer has filed his petition with the Tax Court, it must contain a further condition that if a petition is not filed before the expiration of the period provided in section 6213(a) for the filing of such petition, the amount stayed by the bond will be paid upon notice and demand at any time after the expiration of such period, together with interest thereon at the annual rate referred to in the regulations under section 6621 from the date of the jeopardy notice and demand to the date of the notice and demand made after the expiration of the period for filing petition with the Tax Court.

○― § 301.6863-2 (T.D. 6227, filed 3-29-57; republished in T.D. 6498, filed 10-24-60.) **Collection of jeopardy assessment; stay of sale of seized property pending Tax Court decision.**

(a) *General rule.* In the case of a jeopardy assessment made after December 31, 1954, of income, estate, or gift tax imposed by the Internal Revenue Code of 1954 or the Internal Revenue Code of 1939, any property seized for the collection of such assessment shall not (except as provided in paragraph (b) of this section) be sold—

(1) Until the expiration of the period provided in section 6213(a) within which the taxpayer may file a petition for redetermination with the Tax Court, and

(2) If a petition for redetermination is filed with the Tax Court (whether before or after the making of the jeopardy assessment), until the decision of the tax Court becomes final, except that a petition for review of the Tax Court decision will not operate as a further stay of the sale of the seized property unless the taxpayer files a bond as provided in section 7485.

(b) *Exceptions.* Nothwithstanding the provisions of paragraph (a) of this section, any property seized may be sold—

(1) If the taxpayer files with the district director a written consent to the sale, or

(2) If the district director determines that the expenses of conservation and maintenance of the property will greatly reduce the net proceeds from the sale of such property, or

(3) If the property is of a type to which section 6336 (relating to sale of perishable goods) is applicable.

○― § 301.6864 Statutory provisions; termination of extended period for payment in case of carryback. [Sec. 6864, IRC]

BANKRUPTCY AND RECEIVERSHIPS

○― § 301.6871 (a) Statutory provisions; claims for income, estate, and gift taxes in bankruptcy and receivership proceedings; immediate assessments. [Sec. 6871(a), IRC]

○― § 301.6871(a)-1 (T.D. 6227, filed 3-29-57 as amended by T.D. 6425, filed 11-10-59; republished in T.D. 6498, filed 10-24-60.) **Immediate assessment of claims for income, estate, and gift taxes in bankruptcy and receivership proceedings.**

(a) Upon (1) the adjudication of bankruptcy of any taxpayer in any liquidating proceedings, (2) the filing with a court of competent jurisdiction or (where approval is required by the Bankruptcy Act, 11 U.S.C. chs. 1-14) the approval of a petition of, or the approval of a petition against, any taxpayer in any other proceeding under the Bankruptcy Act, or (3) the appointment of any receiver for any taxpayer in a receivership proceeding before any court of the United States or of any State or Territory or of the District of Columbia, the district director shall immediately assess any deficiency of income, estate, or gift tax (together with all interest, additional amounts, or additions to the tax provided by law), determined by him, if such deficiency has not heretofore been assessed in accordance with law. Such assessment shall be made immediately, whether or not a notice of deficiency has been issued, and without regard to the restrictions upon assessment under section 6213.

(b) As used in this section and §§ 301.-6871(a)-2 to 301.6873-1, inclusive, the term "proceeding under the Bankruptcy Act" includes a proceeding under chapters I to VII, inclusive, of the Bankruptcy Act, or under section 75 or 77 (11 U.S.C. 203, 205), or chapters X to XIII, inclusive, of such Act, or any other proceeding under the Act.

○― § 301.6871(a)-2 (T.D. 6227, filed 3-29-57; republished in T.D. 6498, filed 10-24-60.) **Collection of assessed taxes in bankruptcy and receivership proceedings.**

(a) During a proceeding under the Bankruptcy Act (11 U.S.C. chs. 1-14) or a receivership proceeding in either a Federal or State court, generally the assets of the taxpayer are under the control of the court in which such proceeding is pending, and the collection of taxes cannot be made by levying upon such assets. However, any assets which under applicable provisions of law are not under the control of the court may be subject to levy. See paragraph (b) of this section and § 301.6871(b)-1 with respect to claims for such taxes. See section 6873 with respect to collection of unpaid claims.

(b) District directors should, promptly after ascertaining the existence of any outstanding liability against a taxpayer in any proceeding under the Bankruptcy Act or in any receivership proceeding, and in any event within the time limited by the appropriate provisions of the Bankruptcy Act, or by the appropriate orders of the court in which such proceeding is pending, file proof of claim covering such liability in the court in which such proceeding is pending. Such proof of claim should be filed whether the unpaid taxes involved have been assessed or not, except in cases where the instructions of the Commissioner direct otherwise; for example, where the payment of the taxes is secured by a sufficient bond. At the same time proof of claim is filed with the bankruptcy or receivership court, the district director will send notice and demand for payment to the taxpayer, together with a copy of such proof of claim.

(c) Under sections 3466 and 3467 of the Revised Statutes (31 U.S.C. 191, 192) and section 64 of the Bankruptcy Act (11 U.S.C. 104), taxes are entitled to the priority over other claims therein specified, and the trustee, receiver, debtor in possession, or other person designated as in control of the assets of the debtor by the court in which the proceeding under the Bankruptcy Act or receivership proceeding is pending, may be held personally liable for failure on his part to protect the priority of the Government respecting taxes of which he has notice. Sections 75(1), 77(e), 199, 337(2), 455, and 659(6) of the Bankruptcy Act (11 U.S.C. 203(1), 205(e), 599, 737(2), 855, and 1059(6)) also contain provisions with respect to the rights of the United States relative to priority of payment. For the filing of returns by a trustee in bankruptcy or by a receiver, see section 6012(b)(3) and 28 U.S.C. 960. Bankruptcy courts have jurisdiction under the Bankruptcy Act to determine all disputes regarding the amount and validity of taxes claimed in a proceeding under the Bankruptcy Act. A proceeding under the Bankruptcy Act or a receivership proceeding does not discharge any portion of a claim of the United States for taxes except in the case of a proceeding under section 77 or chapter X of the Bankruptcy Act. However, the claim may be settled or compromised as in other cases in court.

(d) For the requirement that a receiver, trustee in bankruptcy, or other like fiduciary give notice as to his qualification as such, see section 6036 and the regulations thereunder.

○— § 301.6871(b) **Statutory provisions; claims for income, estate, and gift taxes in bankruptcy and receivership proceedings; claim filed despite pendency of Tax Court proceedings.** [Sec. 6871(b), IRC]

○— § 301.6871(b)-1 (T.D. 6227, filed 3-29-57 as amended by T.D. 6425, filed 11-10-59; republished in T.D. 6498, filed 10-24-60.) Claims for income, estate, and gift taxes in proceedings under the Bankruptcy Act and receivership proceedings; claim filed despite pendency of Tax Court proceedings.

(a) If it is determined that a deficiency is due in respect of income, estate, or gift tax and the taxpayer has filed a petition with the Tax Court before (1) the adjudication of bankruptcy in any liquidating proceeding, (2) the filing with a court of competent jurisdiction or (where approval is required by the Bankruptcy Act (11 U.S.C. chs. 1-14)) the approval of a petition of, or the approval of a petition against, any taxpayer in any other proceeding under the Bankruptcy Act, or (3) the appointment of a receiver, the trustee, receiver, debtor in possession, or other like fiduciary, may, upon his own motion, be made a party to the Tax Court proceeding and thereafter may prosecute the appeal before the Tax Court as to that particular determination. No petition shall be filed with the Tax Court for a redetermination of the deficiency after the adjudication of bankruptcy, the filing or (where approval is required by the Bankruptcy Act) the approval of a petition of, or the approval of a petition against, any taxpayer in any other bankruptcy proceeding, or the appointment of the receiver.

(b) Even though the determination of a deficiency is pending before the Tax Court for redetermination, proof of claim for the amount of such deficiency may be filed with the court in which the proceeding under the Bankruptcy Act or receivership proceeding is pending without awaiting final decision of the Tax Court. In case of a final decision of the Tax Court before the payment or the disallowance of the claim in the proceeding under the Bankruptcy Act or receivership proceeding, a copy of the Tax Court's decision may be filed by the district director with the court in which such proceeding is pending.

(c) While a district director is required by section 6871(a) and paragraph (a) of § 301.6871(a)-1 to make immediate assessment of any deficiency, such assessment is not made as a jeopardy assessment within the meaning of section 6861, and consequently the provisions of that section do not apply to any assessment made under section 6871. Therefore, the notice of deficiency provided in section 6861(b) will not be mailed. Although such notice will not be issued, a letter will be sent to the taxpayer or to the trustee, receiver, debtor in possession, or other like fiduciary, notifying him in detail how the deficiency was computed, that he may furnish evidence showing wherein the deficiency is incorrect, and that upon request he will be granted a conference by the district director with respect to such deficiency. However, such letter will not provide for such a conference where a petition was filed with the Tax Court before (1) the adjudication of bankruptcy in a liquidating proceeding, (2) the filing with a court of competent jurisdiction or (where approval is required by the Bankruptcy Act) the approval of a petition of, or the approval of a petition against any taxpayer in any other proceeding under the Bankruptcy Act, or (3) the appointment of a receiver.

○— § 301.6872 **Statutory provisions; suspension of period on assessment.** [Sec. 6872, IRC]

○— § 301.6872-1 (T.D. 6277, filed 3-29-57; republished in T.D. 6498, filed 10-24-60.) Suspension of running of period of limitations on assessment.

If any fiduciary in any proceeding under the Bankruptcy Act (11 U.S.C. chs. 1-14) including a trustee, receiver, or debtor in possession, or a receiver in any other court proceeding is required, pursuant to section 6036, to give notice in writing to the district director of his qualification as such, then the running of the period of limitations on assessment shall be suspended from the date the proceeding is instituted to the date such notice is received by the district director, and for an additional 30 days thereafter. However, the suspension under this section of the running of the period of limitation on assessment shall in no case exceed 2 years.

○— § 301.6873 **Statutory provisions; unpaid claims.** [Sec. 6873, IRC]

○— § 301.6873-1 (T.D. 6227, filed 3-29-57; republished in T.D. 6498, filed 10-24-60.) Unpaid claims in bankruptcy or receivership proceedings.

(a) If any portion of the claim allowed by the court in a receivership proceeding, or in any proceeding under the Bankruptcy Act (11 U.S.C. chs. 1-14) remains unpaid after the termination of such proceeding, the district director will send notice and demand for payment thereof to the taxpayer. Such unpaid portion with interest as provided in section 6601 may be collected from the taxpayer by levy or proceeding in court within the period of limitation for collection after assessment. For the general rule as to such period of limitation, see section 6502, and for suspension of the running of the period provided in section 6502, see for example, section 6503. For suspensions under other provisions of law, see, for example, section 11f of the Bankruptcy Act (11 U.S.C. 29(f)). Extension of time for the payment of such unpaid amount may be granted in the same manner and subject to the same provisions and limitations as provided in section 6161(c).

(b) Section 6873 is applicable only where a claim for taxes is allowed in a receivership proceeding or in a proceeding under the Bankruptcy Act. Claims for taxes, interest, additional amounts, or additions to the tax may be collectible in equity or under other provisions of law although no claim was allowed in the proceeding because, for example, such items were not included in a proof of claim filed in the proceeding or no proof of claim was filed. Except in the case of a proceeding under section 77 or chapter X of the Bankruptcy Act, a tax or a liability in respect thereof is not discharged by a proceeding under such Act, whether or not a claim is filed in such proceeding, and provisions suspending the running of the period of limitation on the collection of taxes are applicable, whether or not a claim is filed in such proceeding.

TRANSFEREES AND FIDUCIARIES

§ 301.6901 **Statutory provisions; transferred assets.** [Sec. 6901, IRC]

§ 301.6901-1 (T.D. 6246, filed 8-2-57; republished in T.D. 6498, filed 10-24-60; amended by T.D. 6585, filed 12-27-61.) **Procedure in the case of transferred assets.**

(a) *Method of Collection*—(1) *Income, estate, and gift taxes.* The amount for which a transferee of property of—

(i) A taxpayer, in the case of a tax imposed by subtitle A of the Code (relating to income taxes).

(ii) A decedent, in the case of the estate tax imposed by chapter 11 of the Code, or

(iii) A donor, in the case of the gift tax imposed by chapter 12 of the Code,

is liable, at law or in equity, and the amount of the personal liability of a fiduciary under section 3467 of the Revised Statutes, as amended (31 U.S.C. 192), in respect of the payment of such taxes, whether shown on the return of the taxpayer or determined as a deficiency in the tax, shall be assessed against such transferee or fiduciary and paid and collected in the same manner and subject to the same provisions and limitations as in the case of a deficiency in the tax with respect to which such liability is incurred, except as hereinafter provided.

(2) *Other taxes.* The liability, at law or in equity, of a transferee of property of any person liable in respect of any other tax, in any case where the liability of the transferee arises on the liquidation of a corporation or partnership, or a corporate reorganization within the meaning of section 368(a), shall be assessed against such transferee and paid and collected in the same manner and subject to the same provisions and limitations as in the case of the tax with respect to which such liability is incurred, except as hereinafter provided.

(3) *Applicable provisions.* The provisions of the Code made applicable by section 6901(a) to the liability of a transferee or fiduciary referred to in subparagraphs (1) and (2) of this paragraph include the provisions relating to:

(i) Delinquency in payment after notice and demand and the amount of interest attaching because of such delinquency;

(ii) The authorization of distraint and proceedings in court for collection;

(iii) The prohibition of claims and suits for refund; and

(iv) In any instance in which the liability of a transferee or fiduciary is one referred to in subparagraph (1) of this paragraph, the filing of a petition with the Tax Court of the United States and the filing of a petition for review of the Tax Court's decision.

For detailed provisions relating to assessments, collections, and refunds, see chapters 63, 64, and 65 of the Code, respectively.

(b) *Definition of transferee.* As used in this section, the term "transferee" includes an heir, legatee, devisee, distributee of an estate of a deceased person, the shareholder of a dissolved corporation, the assignee or donee of an insolvent person, the successor of a corporation, a party to a reorganization as defined in section 368, and all other classes of distributees. Such term also includes, with respect to the gift tax, a donee (without regard to the solvency of the donor) and, with respect to the estate tax, and person who, under section 6324(a)(2), is personally liable for any part of such tax.

(c) *Period of limitation on assessment.* The period of limitation for assessment of the liability of a transferee or of a fiduciary is as follows:

(1) *Initial transferee.* In the case of the liability of an initial transferee, one year after the expiration of the period of limitation for assessment against the taxpayer in the case of a tax imposed by subtitle A (relating to income taxes), the executor in the case of the estate tax imposed by chapter 11, or the donor in the case of the gift tax imposed by chap-

ter 12, each of which for purposes of this section is referred to as the "taxpayer" (see subchapter A, chapter 66, of the Code).

(2) *Transferee of transferee.* In the case of the liability of a transferee of a transferee, one year after the expiration of the period of limitation for assessment against the preceding transferee, or three years after the expiration of the period of limitation for assessment against the taxpayer, whichever of such periods first expires.

(3) *Court proceeding against taxpayer or last preceding transferee.* If, before the expiration of the period specified in subparagraph (1) or subparagraph (2) of this paragraph (whichever is applicable), a court proceeding against the taxpayer or last preceding transferee for the collection of the tax or liability in respect thereof, respectively, has been begun within the period of limitation for the commencement of such proceeding, then within one year after the return of execution in such proceeding.

(4) *Fiduciary.* In the case of the liability of a fiduciary, not later than one year after the liability arises or not later than the expiration of the period for collection of the tax in respect of which such liability arises, whichever is the later.

(d) *Extension by agreement*—(1) *Extension of time for assessment.* The time prescribed by section 6901 for the assessment of the liability of a transferee or fiduciary may, prior to the expiration of such time, be extended for any period of time agreed upon in writing by the transferee or fiduciary and the district director or an assistant regional commissioner. The extension shall become effective when the agreement has been executed by both parties. The period agreed upon may be extended by subsequent agreements in writing made before the expiration of the period previously agreed upon.

(2) *Extension of time for credit or refund.* (i) For the purpose of determining the period of limitation on credit or refund to the transferee or fiduciary of overpayments made by such transferee or fiduciary or overpayments made by the taxpayer to which such transferee or fiduciary may be legally entitled to credit or refund, an agreement and any extension thereof referred to in subparagraph (1) of this paragraph shall be deemed an agreement and extension thereof for purposes of section 6511(c) (relating to limitations on credit or refund in case of extension of time by agreement).

(ii) For the purpose of determining the limit specified in section 6511(c)(2) on the amount of the credit or refund, if the agreement is executed after the expiration of the period of limitation for assessment against the taxpayer with reference to whom the liability of such transferee or fiduciary arises, the periods specified in section 6511(b)(2) shall be increased by the period from the date of such expiration to the date the agreement is executed. The application of this subdivision may be illustrated by the following example:

Example. Assume that Corporation A files its income tax return on March 15, 1955, for the calendar year 1954, showing a liability of $100,000 which is paid with the return. The period within which an assessment may be made against Corporation A expires on March 15, 1958. Corporation B is a transferee of Corporation A. An agreement is executed on October 9, 1958, extending, beyond its normal expiration date of March 15, 1959, the period within which an assessment may be made against Corporation B. Under section 6511(c)(2) and section 6511(b)(2)(A) the portion of an overpayment, paid before the execution of an agreement extending the period for assessment, may not be credited or refunded unless paid within three years prior to the date on which the agreement is executed. However, as applied to Corporation B such 3-year period is increased under section 6901(d)(2) to include the period from March 15, 1958, to October 9, 1958, the date on which the agreement was executed.

(e) *Period of assessment against taxpayer.* For the purpose of determining the period of limitation for assessment against a transferee or a fiduciary, if the taxpayer is deceased, or, in the case of a corporation, has terminated its existence, the period of limitation for assessment against the taxpayer shall be the period that would be in effect had the death or termination of existence not occurred.

(f) *Suspension of running of period of limitations.* In the cases of the income, estate, and gift taxes, if a notice of the liability of a transferee or the liability of a fiduciary has been mailed to such transferee or to such fiduciary under the provisions of section 6212, then the running of the statute of limitations shall be suspended for the period during which assessment is prohibited in respect of the liability of the transferee or fiduciary (and in any event, if a proceeding in respect of the liability is placed on the docket of the Tax Court, until the decision of the Tax Court becomes final), and for 60 days thereafter.

§ 301.6902 **Statutory provisions; provisions of special application to transferees.** [Sec. 6902, IRC]

§ 301.6902-1 (T.D. 6246, filed 8-2-57; republished in T.D. 6498, filed 10-24-60.) **Burden of proof.**

In proceedings before the Tax Court the burden of proof shall be upon the Commissioner to show that a petitioner is liable as a transferee of property of a taxpayer, but not to show that the taxpayer was liable for the tax.

§ 301.6903 **Statutory provisions; notice of fiduciary relationship.** [Sec. 6903, IRC]

§ 301.6903-1 (T.D. 6246, filed 8-2-57; republished in T.D. 6498, filed 10-24-60; amended by T.D. 6585, filed 12-27-61.) **Notice of fiduciary relationship.**

(a) *Rights and obligations of fiduciary.* Every person acting for another person in a fiduciary capacity shall give notice thereof to the district director in writing. As soon as such notice is filed with the district director such fiduciary must, except as otherwise specifically provided, assume the powers, rights, duties, and privileges of the taxpayer with respect to the taxes imposed by the Code. If the person is acting as a fiduciary for a transferee or other person subject to the liability specified in section 6901, such fiduciary is required to assume the powers, rights, duties, and privileges of the transferee or other person under that section. The amount of the tax or liability is ordinarily not collectible from the personal estate of the fiduciary but is collectible from the estate of the taxpayer or from the estate of the transferee or other person subject to the liability specified in section 6901.

(b) *Manner of notice.* The notice shall be signed by the fiduciary, and shall be filed with the district director for the district where the return of the person for whom the fiduciary is acting is required to be filed. The notice must state the name and address of the person for whom the fiduciary is acting, and the nature of the liability of such person; that is, whether it is a liability for tax, and, if so, the type of tax, the year or years involved, or a liability at law or in equity of a transferee of property of a taxpayer, or a liability of a fiduciary under section 3467 of the Revised Statutes, as amended (31 U.S.C. 192), in respect of the payment of any tax from the estate of the taxpayer. Satisfactory evidence of the authority of the fiduciary to act for any other person in a fiduciary capacity must be filed with and made a part of the notice. If the fiduciary capacity exists by order of court, a certified copy of the order may be regarded as satisfactory evidence. When the fiduciary capacity has terminated, the fiduciary, in order to be relieved of any further duty or liability as such, must file with the district director with whom the notice of fiduciary relationship was filed written notice that the fiduciary capacity has terminated as to him, accompanied by satisfactory evidence of the termination of the fiduciary capacity. The notice of termination should state the name and address of the person, if any, who has been substituted as fiduciary. Any written notice disclosing a fiduciary relationship which has been filed with the Commissioner under the Internal Revenue Code of 1939 or any prior revenue law shall be considered as sufficient notice within the meaning of section 6903. Any satisfactory evidence of the authority of the fiduciary to act for another person already filed with the Commissioner or district director need not be resubmitted.

(c) *Where notice is not filed.* If the notice of the fiduciary capacity described in paragraph (b) of this section is not filed with the district director before the sending of notice of a deficiency by registered mail or certified mail to the last known address of the taxpayer (see section 6212), or the last known address of the transferee or other person subject to liability (see section 6901(g)), no notice of the deficiency will be sent to the fiduciary. In such a case the sending of the notice to the last known address of the taxpayer, transferee, or other person, as the case may be, will be a sufficient compliance with the requirements of the Code, even though such taxpayer, transferee, or other person is deceased, or is under a legal disability, or, in the case of a corporation, has terminated its existence. Under such circumstances, if no petition is filed with the Tax Court of the United States within 90 days after the mailing of the notice (or within 150 days after mailing in the case of such a notice addressed to a person outside the States of the Union and the District of Columbia) to the taxpayer, transferee, or other person, the tax, or liability under section 6901, will be assessed immediately upon the expiration of such 90-day or 150-day period, and demand for payment will be made. See paragraph (a) of § 301.6213-1 with respect to the expiration of such 90-day or 150-day period.

(d) *Definition of fiduciary.* The term "fiduciary" is defined in section 7701(a)(6) to mean a guardian, trustee, executor, administrator, receiver, conservator, or any person acting in any fiduciary capacity for any person.

(e) *Applicability of other provisions.* This section, relating to the provisions of section 6903, shall not be taken to abridge in any way the powers and duties of fiduciaries provided for in other sections of the Code.

○━ § 301.6904 Statutory provisions; prohibition of injunctions. [Sec. 6904, IRC]

○━ § 301.6905 Statutory provisions; discharge of executor from personal liability for decedent's income and gift taxes. [Sec. 6905, IRC]

○━ § 301.6905-1 (T.D. 7238, filed 12-28-72.) Discharge of executor from personal liability for decedent's income and gift taxes.

(a) *Discharge of liability.* With respect to decedents dying after December 31, 1970, the executor of a decedent's estate may make written application to the applicable internal revenue officer with whom the estate tax return is required to be filed, as provided in § 20.6091-1, for a determination of the income or gift taxes imposed upon the decedent by subtitle A or by chapter 12 of the Code, and for a discharge of personal liability therefrom. If no estate tax return is required to be filed, then such application should be filed where the decedent's final income tax return is required to be filed. The application must be filed after the return with respect to such income or gift taxes is filed. Within 9 months (1 year with respect to the estate of a decedent dying before January 1, 1974) after receipt of the application, the executor shall be notified of the amount of the income or gift tax and, upon payment thereof, he will be discharged from personal liability for any deficiency in income or gift tax thereafter found to be due. If no such notification is received, the executor is discharged at the end of such 9 month (1 year with respect to the estate of a decedent dying before January 1, 1974) period from personal liability for any deficiency thereafter found to be due. The discharge of the executor under this section from personal liability applies only to him in his personal capacity and to his personal assets. The discharge is not applicable to his liability as executor to the extent of the assets of the estate in his possession or con-

Reg. § 301.6905-1(a)

24,408 *(I.R.C.)*   Reg. § 301.6905-1(a)   7-21-75

trol. Further, the discharge does not operate as a release of any part of the property from the lien provided under section 6321 or the special lien provided under subsection (a) or (b) of section 6324.

(b) *Definition of "executor"*. For purpose of this section, the term "executor" means the executor or administrator of the decedent appointed, qualified, and acting within the United States.

(c) *Cross reference*. For provisions concerning the discharge of the executor from personal liability for estate taxes imposed by chapter 11 of the Code, see section 2204 and the regulations thereunder.

LICENSING AND REGISTRATION
LICENSING

§ 301.7001 **Statutory provisions; collection of foreign items.** [Sec. 7001, IRC]

§ 301.7001-1 (T.D. 6450, filed 2-3-60; republished in T.D. 6498, filed 10-24-60.) **License to collect foreign items.**

(a) *In general*. Any bank or agent undertaking as a matter of business or for profit the collection of foreign items must obtain a license from the district director for the district in which is located its principal place of business within the United States. For definitions of the terms "foreign item" and "collection", see paragraph (b) of this section.

(b) *Definitions*—(1) *Foreign item*. The term "foreign item", as used in this section, means any item of interest upon the bonds of a foreign country or of a nonresident foreign corporation not having a fiscal or paying agent in the United States (including Puerto Rico as if a part of the United States), or any item of dividends upon the stock of such corporation.

(2) *Collection*. The term "collection", as used in this section, includes the following:

(i) The payment by the licensee of the foreign item in cash;

(ii) The crediting by the licensee of the account of the person presenting the foreign item;

(iii) The tentative crediting by the licensee of the account of the person presenting the foreign item until the amount of the foreign item is received by the licensee from abroad; and

(iv) The receipt of foreign items by the licensee for the purpose of transmitting them abroad for deposits.

(c) *Application for license*. Application for the license required by paragraph (a) of this section shall be made in writing and shall contain the following information:

(1) The name and present business of the person, partnership (including names of all partners), or corporation applying for the license;

(2) The address of the applicant's principal place of business in the United States and of any branch offices in the United States;

(3) The date on which the applicant intends to commence the collection of foreign items; and

(4) An estimate of the aggregate amount of annual collections of foreign items (in dollars).
The application shall be signed by the applicant (a partner, in the case of a partnership, or an officer, in the case of a corporation).

(d) *Issuance of license*. The license will be issued by the district director in letter form without cost to the licensee.

(e) *Previous license holders*. Any person who has been issued a license under the corresponding provision of the Internal Revenue Code of 1939, or any prior revenue law, is not required to renew such license under this section.

(f) *Returns of information as to foreign items*. For provisions relating to the filing of returns as to foreign items, see section 6041(b) and § 1.6041-4 of this chapter (Income Tax Regulations).

BONDS

§ 53.7101 **Statutory provisions; form of bonds.** [Sec. 7101, IRC]

§ 53.7101-1 (T.D. 7368, filed 7-15-75.) **Form of bonds.**

For provisions relating to form of bonds, see the regulations under section 7101 contained in Part 301 of this chapter (Regulations on Procedure and Administration).

§ 301.7101 **Statutory provisions; form of bonds.** [Sec. 7101, IRC]

§ 301.7101-1 (T.D. 6443, filed 1-7-60; republished in T.D. 6498, filed, 10-24-60; amended by T.D. 7239, filed 12-27-72.) **Form of bond and surety required.**

(a) *In general*. Any person required to furnish a bond under the provisions of the Code (other than section 6803(a)(1), relating to bonds required of certain postmasters before June 6, 1972, and section 7485, relating to bonds to stay assessment and collection of a deficiency pending review of a Tax Court decision), or under any rules or regulations prescribed under the Code, shall (except as provided in paragraph (d) of this section) execute such bond—

(1) On the appropriate form prescribed by the Internal Revenue Service (which may be obtained from the district director), and

(2) With satisfactory surety.
For provisions as to what will be considered "satisfactory surety", see paragraph (b) of this section. The bonds referred to in this paragraph shall be drawn in favor of the United States.

(b) *Satisfactory surety*—(1) *Approved surety company or bonds or notes of the United States*. For purposes of paragraph (a) of this section, a bond shall be considered executed with satisfactory surety if:

(i) It is executed by a surety company holding a certificate of authority from the Secretary as an acceptable surety on Federal bonds; or

(ii) It is secured by bonds or notes of the United States as provided in 6 U.S.C. 15 (see 31 CFR Part 225).

(2) *Other surety acceptable in discretion of district director.* Unless otherwise expressly provided in the Code, or the regulations thereunder, a bond may, in the discretion of the district director, be considered executed with satisfactory surety if, in lieu of being executed or secured as provided in subparagraph (1) of this paragraph, it is:

(i) Executed by a corporate surety (other than a surety company) provided such corporate surety establishes that it is within its corporate powers to act as surety for another corporation or an individual;

(ii) Executed by two or more individual sureties, provided such individual sureties meet the conditions contained in subparagraph (3) of this paragraph;

(iii) Secured by a mortgage on real or personal property;

(iv) Secured by a certified, cashier's, or treasurer's check drawn on any bank or trust company incorporated under the laws of the United States or any State, Territory, or possession of the United States, or by a U.S. postal, bank, express, or telegraph money order;

(v) Secured by corporate bonds or stocks, or by bonds issued by a state or political subdivision therof, of recognized stability; or

(vi) Secured by any other acceptable collateral. Collateral shall be deposited with the district director or, in his discretion, with a responsible financial institution acting as escrow agent.

(3) *Conditions to be met by individual sureties.* If a bond is executed by two or more individual sureties, the following conditions must be met by each such individual surety:

(i) He must reside within the State in

Reg. § 301.7101-1(b)(3)

which the principal place of business or legal residence of the primary obligor is located;

(ii) He must have property subject to execution of a current market value, above all encumbrances, equal to at least the penalty of the bond;

(iii) All real property which he offers as security must be located in the State in which the principal place of business or legal residence of the primary obligor is located;

(iv) He must agree not to mortgage, or otherwise encumber, any property offered as security while the bond continues in effect without first securing the permission of the district director; and

(v) He must file with the bond, and annually thereafter so long as the bond continues in effect, an affidavit as to the adequacy of his security, executed on the appropriate form furnished by the district director.

Partners may not act as sureties upon bonds of their partnership. Stockholders of a corporate principal may be accepted as sureties provided their qualifications as such are independent of their holdings of the stock of the corporation.

(4) *Adequacy of surety.* No surety or security shall be accepted if it does not adequately protect the interest of the United States.

(c) *Bonds required by Internal Revenue Code of 1939.* This section shall also apply in the case of bonds required under the Internal Revenue Code of 1939 (other than sections 1423(b) and 1145) or under the regulations under such Code.

(d) *Bonds required under subtitle E and chapter 75 of the Internal Revenue Code of 1954.* Bonds required under subtitle E and chapter 75, subtitle F, of the Internal Revenue Code of 1954 (or under the corresponding provisions of the Internal Revenue Code of 1939) shall be in such form and with such surety or sureties as are prescribed in the regulations in Subchapter E of this chapter (Alcohol, Tobacco, and Other Excise Taxes).

§ 301.7102 Statutory provisions; single bond in lieu of multiple bonds. [Sec. 7102, IRC]

§ 301.7102-1 (T.D. 6443, filed 1-7-60; republished in T.D. 6498, filed 10-24-60.) Single bond in lieu of multiple bonds.

(a) *In general.* Except as provided in paragraph (b) of this section, a person who is required, or authorized, under the Code (other than section 6803(a)(1) and 7485), or under any rules or regulations under the Code, to execute two or more bonds may, in the discretion of the district director, furnish a single bond in lieu of such two or more bonds but only if such single bond meets all the conditions and requirements prescribed for each of the separate bonds which it replaces. This section shall also apply in the case of bonds required or authorized under the Internal Revenue Code of 1939 (other than sections 1423(b) and 1145) or under the regulations under such Code.

(b) *Bonds required under subtitle E and chapter 75 of the Internal Revenue Code of 1954.* In the case of bonds required under subtitle E and chapter 75, subtitle F, of the Internal Revenue Code of 1954 (or under the corresponding provisions of the Internal Revenue Code of 1939), a single bond will not be accepted in lieu of two or more bonds except as provided in the regulations in Subchapter E of this chapter (Alcohol, Tobacco, and Other Excise Taxes).

§ 301.7103 Statutory provisions; cross references — other provisions for bonds. [Sec. 7103, IRC]

CLOSING AGREEMENTS AND COMPROMISES

§ 301.7121 Statutory provisions; closing agreements. [Sec. 7121, IRC]

§ 301.7121-1 (T.D. 6450, filed 2-3-60; republished in T.D. 6498, filed 10-24-60.) Closing agreements.

(a) *In general.* The Commissioner may enter into a written agreement with any person relating to the liability of such person (or of the person or estate for whom he acts) in respect of any internal revenue tax for any taxable period ending prior or subsequent to the date of such agreement. A closing agreement may be entered into in any case in which there appears to be an advantage in having the case permanently and conclusively closed, or if good and sufficient reasons are shown by the taxpayer for desiring a closing agreement and it is determined by the Commissioner that the United States will sustain no disadvantage through consummation of such an agreement.

(b) *Scope of closing agreement*—(1) *In general.* A closing agreement may be executed even though under the agreement the taxpayer is not liable for any tax for the period to which the agreement relates. There may be a series of closing agreements relating to the tax liability for a single period.

(2) *Taxable periods ended prior to date of closing agreement.* Closing agreements with respect to taxable periods ended prior to the date of the agreement may relate to the total tax liability of the taxpayer or to one or more separate items affecting the tax liability of the taxpayer, as, for example, the amount of gross income, deduction for losses, depreciation, depletion, the year in which an item of income is to be included in gross income, the year in which an item of loss is to be deducted, or the value of property on a specific date. A closing agreement may also be entered into for the purpose of allowing a deficiency dividend deduction under section 547. In addition, a closing agreement constitutes a determination as defined by section 1313.

(3) *Taxable periods ending subsequent to date of closing agreement.* Closing agreements with respect to taxable periods ending subsequent to the date of the agreement may relate to one or more separate items affecting the tax liability of the taxpayer.

(4) *Illustration.* The provisions of this paragraph may be illustrated by the following example:

Example. A owns 500 shares of stock in the XYZ Corporation which he purchased prior to March 1, 1913. A is considering selling 200 shares of such stock but is uncertain as to the basis of the stock for the purpose of computing gain. Either prior or subsequent to the sale, a closing agreement may be entered into determining the market value of such stock as of March 1, 1913, which represents the basis for determining gain if it exceeds the adjusted basis otherwise determined as of such date. Not only may the closing agreement determine the basis for computing gain on the sale of the 200 shares of stock, but such an agreement may also determine the basis (unless or until the law is changed to require the use of some other factor to determine basis) of the remaining 300 shares of stock upon which gain will be computed in a subsequent sale.

(c) *Finality.* A closing agreement which is approved within such time as may be stated in such agreement, or later agreed to, shall be final and conclusive, and, except upon a showing of fraud or malfeasance, or misrepresentation of a material fact:

(1) The case shall not be reopened as to the matters agreed upon or the agreement modified by any officer, employee, or agent of the United States, and

(2) In any suit, action, or proceeding, such agreement, or any determination, assessment, collection, payment, abatement, refund, or credit made in accordance therewith, shall not be annulled, modified, set aside, or disregarded.

However, a closing agreement with respect to a taxable period ending subsequent to the date of the agreement is subject to any change in, or modification of, the law enacted subsequent to the date of the agreement and made applicable to such taxable period, and each closing agreement shall so recite.

(d) *Procedure with respect to closing agreements*—(1) *Submission of request.* A request for a closing agreement which relates to a prior taxable period may be submitted at any time before a case with respect to the tax liability involved is docketed in the Tax Court of the United States. All closing agreements shall be executed on forms prescribed by the Internal Revenue Service. The procedure with respect to requests for closing agreements shall be under such rules as may be prescribed from time to time by the Commissioner in accordance with the regulations under this section.

(2) *Collection, credit, or refund.* Any tax or deficiency in tax determined pursuant to a closing agreement shall be assessed and collected, and any overpayment determined pursuant thereto shall be credited or refunded, in accordance with the applicable provisions of law.

§ 301.7122 **Statutory provisions; compromises.** [Sec. 7122, IRC]

§ 301.7122-1 (T.D. 6450, filed 2-3-60; republished in T.D. 6498, filed 10-24-60.) **Compromises.**

(a) *In general.* Except with respect to certain criminal liabilities arising under the internal revenue laws relating to narcotics, smoking opium, and marihuana, the Commissioner may compromise any civil or criminal liability arising under the internal revenue laws prior to reference of a case involving such liability to the Department of Justice for prosecution or defense. Any such liability may be compromised only upon one or both of the following two grounds:

(1) Doubt as to liability; or

(2) Doubt as to collectibility.

No such liability will be compromised if the liability has been established by a valid judgment or is certain, and there is no doubt as to the ability of the Government to collect the amounts owing with respect to such liability.

(b) *Scope of compromise agreement.* A compromise agreement may relate to a civil or criminal liability for taxes, interest, ad valorem penalties, or specific penalties. However, a criminal liability may be compromised only if it involves a violation of a regulatory provision of the Code, or a related statute, and then only if such violation was not deliberately committed with an intent to defraud.

(c) *Effect of compromise agreement.* A compromise agreement relates to the entire liability of the taxpayer (including taxes, ad valorem penalties, and interest) with respect to which the offer in compromise is submitted and all questions of such liability are conclusively settled thereby. Specific penalties, however, shall be compromised separately and not in connection with taxes, interest, or ad valorem penalties. Neither the taxpayer nor the government shall, upon acceptance of an offer in compromise, be permitted to reopen the case except by reason of (1) falsification or concealment of assets by the taxpayer, or (2) mutual mistake of a material fact sufficient to cause a contract to be reformed or set aside. However, acceptance of an offer in compromise of a civil liability does not remit a criminal liability, nor does acceptance of an offer in compromise of a criminal liability remit a civil liability.

(d) *Procedure with respect to offers in compromise*—(1) *Submission of offers.* Offers in compromise shall be submitted on forms prescribed by the Internal Revenue Service which may be obtained from district directors of internal revenue, and should generally be accompanied by a remittance representing the amount of the compromise offer or a deposit if the offer provides for future installment payments. If the final payment on an accepted offer is contingent upon the immediate or simultaneous release of a tax lien in whole or in part, such payment must be in cash, or in the form of a certified, cashier's, or treasurer's check drawn on any bank or trust company incorporated under the laws of the United States or any State, Territory, or possession of the United States, or by a U.S. postal, bank, express, or telegraph money order.

(2) *Stay of collection.* The submission of an offer in compromise shall not automatically operate to stay the collection of any tax liability. However, enforcement of collection may be deferred if the interests of the United States shall not be jeopardized thereby.

(3) *Acceptance.* An offer in compromise shall be considered accepted only when the proponent thereof is so notified in writing. As a condition to accepting an offer in compromise, the taxpayer may be required to enter into any collateral agreement or to post any security which is deemed necessary for the protection of the interests of the United States.

(4) *Withdrawal or rejection.* An offer in compromise may be withdrawn by the proponent at any time prior to its acceptance. In the event an offer is rejected, the proponent shall be promptly notified in writing. Frivolous offers or offers submitted for the purpose of delaying the collection of tax liabilities shall be immediately rejected. If an offer in compromise is withdrawn or rejected, the amount tendered with the offer, including all installments paid, shall be refunded without interest, unless the taxpayer has stated or agreed that the amount tendered may be applied to the liability with respect to which the offer was submitted.

(e) *Record.* Except as otherwise provided in this paragraph, if an offer in compromise is accepted, there shall be placed on file the opinion of the Chief Counsel of the Internal Revenue Service with respect to such compromise, with his reasons therefor, and including a statement of—

(1) The amount of tax assessed,

(2) The amount of interest, additional amount, addition to the tax, or assessable penalty, imposed by law on the person against whom the tax is assessed, and

(3) The amount actually paid in accordance with the terms of the compromise. However, no such opinion shall be required with respect to the compromise of any civil case in which the unpaid amount of tax assessed (including any interest, additional amount, addition to the tax, or assessable penalty) is less than $500.

(f) *Requirement with respect to statute of limitations.* No other in compromise shall be accepted unless the taxpayer waives the running of the statutory period of limitations on both or either assessment or collection of the tax liability involved for the period during which the offer is pending, or the period during which any installment remains unpaid, and for one year thereafter.

(g) *Inspection with respect to accepted offers in compromise.* For provisions relating to the inspection of returns and accepted offers in compromise, see section 6103(a) and the regulations thereunder contained in this part.

§ 301.7123 Statutory provisions; cross references. [Sec. 7123, IRC]

CRIMES, OTHER CRIMES, OFFENSES, AND FORFEITURES
GENERAL PROVISIONS

§ 301.7201 Statutory provisions; attempt to evade or defeat tax. [Sec. 7201, IRC]

§ 301.7202 Statutory provisions; willful failure to collect or pay over tax. [Sec. 7202, IRC]

§ 301.7203 Statutory provisions; willful failure to file return, supply information, or pay tax. [Sec. 7203, IRC]

§ 301.7204 Statutory provisions; fraudulent statement or failure to make statement to employees. [Sec. 7204, IRC]

§ 301.7205 Statutory provisions; fraudulent withholding exemption certificate or failure to supply information. [Sec. 7205, IRC]

§ 301.7206 Statutory provisions; fraud and false statements. [Sec. 7206, IRC]

§ 301.7207 Statutory provisions; fraudulent returns, statements, or other documents. [Sec. 7207, IRC]

§ 301.7207-1 Fraudulent returns, statements, or other documents. (T.D. 6498, filed 10-24-60; amended by T.D. 6677, filed 9-16-63 and T.D. 7127, filed 6-14-71.)

Any person who willfully delivers or discloses to any officer or employee of the Internal Revenue Service any list, return, account, statement, or other document, known by him to be fraudulent or to be false as to any material matter, shall be fined not more than $1,000, or imprisoned not more than 1 year, or both. Any person required pursuant to section 6047(b) or, (c) or, after December 31, 1969, section 6056 or 6104(d), to furnish information to any officer or employee of the Internal Revenue Service or any other person who willfully furnishes to such officer or employee of the Internal Revenue Service or such other person any information known by him to be fraudulent or to be false as to any material matter shall be fined not more than $1,000, or imprisoned not more than 1 year, or both.

§ 301.7213 Statutory provisions; unauthorized disclosure of information. [Sec. 7213, IRC]

§ 301.7216 Statutory provisions; disclosure or use of information by preparers of returns. [Sec. 7216, IRC]

§ 301.7216-1 (T.D. 7310, filed 3-27-74.) Penalty for disclosure or use of tax return information.

(a) *In general.* Section 7216(a) provides in effect that, except as provided in section 7216(b), any tax return preparer (as described in paragraph (b)(2) of this section) who on or after January 1, 1972, discloses or uses any tax return informa-

Reg. § 301.7216-1(a)

tion (as described in paragraph (b)(3) of this section) other than for the specific purpose of preparing, assisting in preparing, or obtaining or providing services in connection with the preparation of, any tax return of the taxpayer by or for whom the information was made available to a tax return preparer, shall be guilty of a misdemeanor, and, upon conviction thereof, shall be fined not more than $1,000, or imprisoned not more than 1 year, or both, together with the costs of prosecution. Pursuant to section 7216(b), the provisions of section 7216(a) and this paragraph do not apply to any disclosure or use permitted under § 301.7216-2 or § 301.7216-3.

(b) *Definitions.* For purposes only of section 7216 and §§ 301.7216-1 through 301.-7216-3—

(1) *Tax return.* The term "tax return" means any return (or amended return) of the income tax imposed by chapter 1 or 2 of the Code, or any declaration (or amended declaration) of estimated tax made under section 6015.

(2) *Tax return preparer.* (i) The term tax return preparer means any person—

(A) Who is engaged in the business of preparing tax returns,

(B) Who is engaged in the business of providing auxiliary services in connection with the preparation of tax returns,

(C) Who is remunerated for preparing, or assisting in preparing, a tax return for any other person, or

(D) Any individual who, as part of his duties or employment with any person described in (A), (B), or (C) of this subdivision, performs services which assist in the preparation of, or assist in providing auxiliary services in connection with the preparation of, a tax return.

For example, assume that a bank is a tax return preparer within the meaning of (A) of this subdivision and it employs one individual to solicit the necessary tax return information for the preparation of a tax return and another individual to prepare the return on the basis of the information that is furnished. Under these circumstances, both employees are tax return preparers. Also, for example, a secretary to a tax return preparer who types or otherwise works on returns prepared by the preparer is a tax return preparer.

(ii) A person is engaged in the business of preparing tax returns as described in subdivision (i)(A) of this subparagraph if, in the course of his business, he holds himself out to taxpayers as a person who prepares tax returns, whether or not tax return preparation is his sole business activity and whether or not he charges a fee for such services.

(iii) A person is engaged in the business of providing auxiliary services in connection with the preparation of tax returns as described in subdivision (i)(B) of this subparagraph if, in the course of his business, he holds himself out to tax return preparers or to taxpayers as a person who performs such auxiliary services, whether or not providing such auxiliary services is his sole business activity and whether or not he charges a fee for such services. For example, a person part or all of whose business is to provide a computerized tax return processing service based on tax return information furnished by another person is a tax return preparer.

(iv) A tax return preparer described in subdivision (i)(C) of this subparagraph includes any person who—

(A) For remuneration but not in the course of a business prepares a tax return for another person, or

(B) For remuneration and on a casual basis helps a relative, friend, or other acquaintance to prepare the latter's tax return.

(v) A person is not a tax return preparer merely because he leases office space to a tax return preparer, furnishes credit to a taxpayer whose tax return is prepared by a tax return preparer, or otherwise performs some service which only incidentally relates to the preparation of tax returns. For example, assume that a tax return preparer contracts with a department store for the rental of space in the store, and that the store advertises that taxpayers who use the tax return preparation service may charge the cost of having their tax return prepared to their charge account with the department store. Under such circumstances, the department store is not a tax return preparer.

(3) *Tax return information.* The term "tax return information" means any information, including but not limited to a taxpayer's name, address, or identifying number, which is furnished in any form or manner by a taxpayer for, or in connection with, the preparation of a tax return of such taxpayer. Information furnished by a taxpayer includes information which is furnished on behalf of the taxpayer by any person; for example, any person required under section 6012 to make a return for such taxpayer, such as a guardian for a minor, by a duly authorized agent for his principal, by a fiduciary for an estate or trust, or by a receiver, trustee in bankruptcy, or assignee for a corporation.

○── § 301.7216-2 (T.D. 7310, filed 3-27-74.) **Disclosure or use without formal consent of taxpayer.**

(a) *Disclosure pursuant to other provisions of Internal Revenue Code.* The provisions of section 7216(a) and § 301.7216-1 shall not apply to any disclosure of tax return information if such disclosure is made pursuant to any other provision of the Code or the regulations thereunder. Thus, for example, the provisions of such sections do not apply to a disclosure pursuant to section 7269 to an officer or employee of the Internal Revenue Service of information concerning the estate of a decedent or a disclosure pursuant to section 7602 to an officer or employee of the Internal Revenue Service of books, papers, records, or other data which may be relevant to the liability of any person for the income tax.

(b) *Disclosure or use of information in the case of related taxpayers.* (1) A tax return preparer may use, in preparing a tax return of a second taxpayer, and may disclose to such second taxpayer in the form in which it appears on such return, any tax return information which the preparer obtained from a first taxpayer if—

(i) The second taxpayer is related to the first taxpayer within the meaning of subparagraph (2) of this paragraph,

(ii) The first taxpayer's tax interest in such information is not adverse to the second taxpayer's tax interest in such information, and

(iii) The first taxpayer has not expressly prohibited such disclosure or use.

(2) For purposes of subparagraph (1)(A) of this paragraph, one taxpayer is related to another taxpayer if they have any one of the following relationships: husband and wife, child and parent, grandchild and grandparent, partner and partnership, trust or estate and beneficiary, trust or estate and fiduciary, corporation and shareholder, or members of a controlled group of corporations as defined in section 1563.

(3) See § 301.7216-3(a)(3) for disclosure or use of tax return information of the taxpayer in preparing the tax return of a second taxpayer where the requirements of this paragraph are not satisfied.

(c) *Disclosure pursuant to court order.* The provisions of section 7216(a) and § 301.-7216-1 shall not apply to any disclosure of tax return information if such disclosure is made pursuant to the order of any court of record, Federal, State, or local, clearly identifying the information to be disclosed.

(d) *Disclosure for use in revenue investigations or court proceedings.* A tax return preparer may disclose tax return information (1) to his attorney, or to an employee of the Internal Revenue Service, for use in connection with an investigation of such tax return preparer conducted by the Internal Revenue Service or (2) to his attorney, or to any officer of a court, for use in connection with proceedings involving such tax return preparer before the court.

(e) *Attorneys and accountants.* A tax return preparer who is lawfully engaged in the practice of law or accountancy and prepares a tax return for a taxpayer to or for whom it renders legal or accounting services may disclose or use the tax return information of such taxpayer in the ordinary course of rendering such legal or accounting services to or for such taxpayer. Thus, for example, a lawyer who prepares a tax return for a taxpayer to or for whom he renders legal services may disclose or use the tax return information of the taxpayer for, or in connection with, the rendering of legal services, such as estate planning or administration, or preparation of trial briefs or trust instruments, to the taxpayer or his estate. In further illustration, an accountant who prepares a tax return for a taxpayer to or for whom he renders accounting services may disclose or use the tax return information of the taxpayer for, or in connection with, the preparation of books of account, working papers, or accounting statements or reports of the taxpayer and, in the normal course of rendering such accounting services to or for the taxpayer, may, with the express or implied consent of the taxpayer, make such tax return information available to stockholders, management, suppliers, lenders, or other third parties.

(f) *Corporate fiduciaries.* A trust company, trust department of a bank, or other corporate fiduciary which prepares a tax return for a taxpayer to or for whom it renders fiduciary, investment, or other custodial or management services may (1) disclose or use the tax return information of such taxpayer in the ordinary course of rendering such services to or for the taxpayer or (2), with the express or implied consent of the taxpayer, make such information available to the taxpayer's attorney, accountant, or investment advisor.

(g) *Disclosure to taxpayer's fiduciary.* If after furnishing tax return information to a tax return preparer the taxpayer dies or becomes incompetent, insolvent, or bankrupt, or his assets are placed in conservatorship or receivership, the tax return preparer may disclose such information to the duly appointed fiduciary of the taxpayer or his estate, or to the duly authorized agent of such fiduciary.

(h) *Disclosure by tax return preparer to obtain tax return processing service.* A tax return preparer may disclose tax return information of a taxpayer to another tax return preparer described in § 301.7216-1(b)(2)(i)(B) for the purpose of having the second tax return preparer transfer that information to, and compute the tax liability on, a tax return of such taxpayer by means of electronic, mechanical, or other form of tax return processing service.

(i) *Disclosure by one officer, employee, or member to another officer, employee, or member.* An officer, employee, or member of a tax return preparer may transfer any tax return information to another officer, employee, or member of the same tax return preparer for the purpose of performing services which assist in the preparation of, or assist in providing auxiliary services in connection with the preparation of, the tax return of a taxpayer by or for whom the information was furnished.

(j) *Identical information obtained from other sources.* The provisions of section 7216(a) and § 301.7216-1 shall not apply to the disclosure or use by a tax return preparer of information which is identical to any tax return information which has been furnished to him if such identical information was obtained otherwise than in connection with the preparation of, or providing auxiliary services in connection with the preparation of, a tax return.

(k) *Disclosure or use of information in preparation or audit of State returns.* The provisions of section 7216(a) and § 301.7216-1 shall not apply to the disclosure or use by any tax return preparer of any tax return information in the preparation or audit of, or in connection with the preparation or audit of, any tax return or declaration of estimated tax required of the taxpayer under the law of any State or political subdivision thereof, of the District of Columbia, or of any possession of the United States.

(l) *Retention of records.* A tax return preparer may retain tax return information of a taxpayer, including copies of tax returns or data processing tapes prepared on the basis of such tax return information, and may use such information in connection with the preparation of other tax returns of the taxpayer or in connection with an audit by the Internal Revenue Service of any tax return. The provisions of paragraph (m) of this section respecting the transfer of a taxpayer list apply also to the transfer of any records and related workpapers to which this paragraph applies.

Reg. § 301.7216-2(l)

(m) *Lists for solicitation of tax return business.* Any tax return preparer may compile and maintain a separate list containing the names and addresses of taxpayers whose tax returns he has prepared or processed. This list may be used by the compiler solely to contact the taxpayers on the list for the purpose of offering tax information or additional tax return preparation services to such taxpayers. The compiler of the list may not transfer the taxpayer list, or any part thereof, to any other person unless such transfer takes place in conjunction with the sale or other disposition of the tax return preparation business of such compiler. A person who acquires a taxpayer list, or a part thereof, in conjunction with such a sale or other disposition shall be subject to the provisions of this paragraph with respect to such list as if he had been the compiler of such list. The term "list", as used in this paragraph, includes any record or system whereby the names and addresses of taxpayers are retained.

§ 301.7216-3 (T.D. 7310, filed 3-27-74.) **Disclosure or use only with formal consent of taxpayer.**

(a) *Written consent to use or disclosure*—(1) *Solicitation of other business.* (i) If a tax return preparer has obtained from the taxpayer a consent described in paragraph (b) of this section, he may use the tax return information of such taxpayer to solicit from the taxpayer any additional current business, in matters not related to the Internal Revenue Service, which the tax return preparer provides and offers to the public. The request for such consent may not be made later than the time the taxpayer receives his completed tax return from the tax return preparer. If the request is not granted, no follow up request may be made. This authorization to use tax return information of the taxpayer does not apply, however, for purposes of facilitating the solicitation of the taxpayer's use of any services or facilities furnished by a person other than the tax return preparer, unless such other person and the tax return preparer are members of the same affiliated group within the meaning of section 1504. Thus, for example, the authorization would not apply if the other person is a corporation which is owned or controlled directly or indirectly by the same interests which own or control the tax return preparer but which is not affiliated with the tax return preparer within the meaning of section 1504(a). Moreover, this authorization does not apply for purposes of facilitating the solicitation of additional business to be furnished at some indefinite time in the future, as, for example, the future sale of mutual fund shares or life insurance, or the furnishing of future credit card services. It is not necessary, however, that the additional business be furnished in the same locality in which the tax return information is furnished.

(ii) For prohibition against solicitation of employment in matters related to the Internal Revenue Service, see 31 CFR 10.30 (Treasury Department Circular No. 230) and § 7 of Rev. Proc. 68-20, 1968-1 C.B. 812.

(2) *Permissible disclosures to third parties.* If a tax return preparer has obtained from a taxpayer a consent described in paragraph (b) of this section, he may disclose the tax return information of such taxpayer to such third persons as the taxpayer may direct. However, see § 301.7216-2 for certain permissible disclosures without formal written consent.

(3) *Disclosure or use of information in connection with another person's return.* A tax return preparer may disclose or use any tax return information, which was obtained from a first taxpayer, in preparing a tax return of a second taxpayer if the tax return preparer has obtained from the first taxpayer a written consent described in paragraph (b) of this section. See § 301.-7216-2(b) for disclosure or use in certain cases without formal consent.

(b) *Form of consent.* A separate written consent, signed by the taxpayer or his duly authorized agent or fiduciary, must be obtained for each separate use or disclosure authorized in paragraph (a)(1), (2), or (3) of this section and shall contain—

(1) The name of the tax return preparer,

(2) The name of the taxpayer,

(3) The purpose for which the consent is being furnished,

(4) The date on which such consent is signed,

(5) A statement that the tax return information may not be disclosed or used by the tax return preparer for any purpose (not otherwise permitted under § 301.-7216-2) other than that stated in the consent, and

(6) A statement by the taxpayer, or his agent or fiduciary, that he consents to the disclosure or use of such information for the purpose described in subparagraph (3) of this paragraph.

(c) *Illustrations.* The application of this section may be illustrated by the following examples:

Example (1). In order to stimulate the making of loans, a bank advertises that it is in the business of preparing tax returns. A taxpayer goes to the bank to have his tax return prepared. After the return has been completed by the bank, the employee of the bank who obtained the tax return information from the taxpayer explains that the taxpayer owes an additional $400 in taxes and that the bank's loan department may be able to offer the taxpayer a loan to pay the tax due. If the taxpayer decides to accept the opportunity offered to apply for a loan, the bank must first have the taxpayer execute a written consent described in paragraph (b) of this section for the bank to use any of such information which is required in determining whether to make the tax loan.

Example (2). An individual who sells life insurance and shares in a mutual fund is also in the business of preparing tax returns. A taxpayer who has gone to the individual to have his tax return prepared is requested, at the time he picks up his completed tax return, to give his consent to the individual's use of his tax return information in connection with such individual's solicitation of the taxpayer's purchasing a life insurance policy and shares in the mutual fund. Before the individual may use such tax return information as a basis for soliciting such additional business from the taxpayer, the taxpayer must execute separate written consents under paragraph

(b) of this section, one authorizing the use of such information as a basis for soliciting the sale of the mutual fund shares and a second authorizing the use of such information as a basis for soliciting the sale of the life insurance.

Example (3). The facts are the same as in example (2) except that the individual does not sell life insurance but does sell shares in several mutual funds. If the request is for the purpose of using the tax return information as a basis for soliciting the sale at one time of shares in mutual funds A and B, only one written consent under paragraph (b) of this section is required of the taxpayer. If, however, the request is for the purpose of using the tax return information as a basis for soliciting the sale of shares in fund A at one time, and the sale of shares in fund B at a later time, two written consents under such paragraph are required of the taxpayer.

OTHER OFFENSES

§ 301.7269 **Statutory provisions; failure to produce records.** [Sec. 7269, IRC]

§ 301.7269-1..(T.D. 6498, filed 10-24-60.) **Failure to produce records.**

Whoever fails to comply with any duty imposed upon him by section 6018, 6036 (in the case of an executor), or 6075(a), or, having in his possession or control any record, file, or paper, containing or supposed to contain any information concerning the estate of the decedent, or having in his possession or control any property comprised in the gross estate of the decedent, fails to exhibit the same upon request of any officer or employee of the Internal Revenue Service who desires to examine the same in the performance of his duties under chapter 11 of the Code (relating to estate taxes) shall be liable to a penalty of not exceeding $500, to be recovered with costs of suit, in a civil action in the name of the United States.

JUDICIAL PROCEEDINGS
CIVIL ACTIONS BY THE UNITED STATES

§ 301.7401 **Statutory provisions; authorization.** [Sec. 7401, IRC]

§ 301.7401-1 (T.D. 6498, filed 10-24-60; amended by T.D. 6746, filed 7-20-64; T.D. 6902, filed 12-13-66 and T.D. 7188, filed 6-28-72.) **Authorization.**

(a) *In general.* No civil action for the collection or recovery of taxes, or of any fine, penalty, or forfeiture, shall be commenced unless the Commissioner (or the Director, Alcohol, Tobacco and Firearms Division, with respect to the provisions of subtitle E of the Code), or the Chief Counsel for the Internal Revenue Service or his delegate authorizes or sanctions the proceedings and the Attorney General or his delegate directs that the action be commenced.

(b) *Property held by banks.* The Commissioner shall not authorize or sanction any civil action for the collection or recovery of taxes, or of any fine, penalty, or forfeiture, from any deposits held in a foreign office of a bank engaged in the banking business in the United State or a possession of the United States unless the Commissioner believes—

(1) That the taxpayer is within the jurisdiction of a U.S. court at the time the civil action is authorized or sanctioned and that the bank is in possession of (or obligated with respect to) deposits of the taxpayer in an office of the bank outside the United States or a possession of the United States; or

(2) That the taxpayer is not within the jurisdiction of a U.S. court at the time the civil action is authorized or sanctioned, the bank is in possession of (or obligated with respect to) deposits of the taxpayer in an office outside the United States or a possession of the United States, and that such deposits consist, in whole or in part, of funds transferred from the United States or a possession of the United States in order to hinder or delay the collection of a tax imposed by the Code.

For purposes of this paragraph, the term "possession of the United States" includes Guam, the Midway Islands, the Panama Canal Zone, the Commonwealth of Puerto Rico, American Samoa, the Virgin Islands, and Wake Island.

§ 301.7402 **Statutory provisions; jurisdiction of district courts.** [Sec. 7402, IRC]

§ 301.7403 **Statutory provisions; action to enforce lien or to subject property to payment of tax.** [Sec. 7403, IRC]

§ 301.7403-1 (T.D. 6498, filed 10-24-60; amended by T.D. 6902, filed 12-13-66; and T.D. 7305, filed 3-14-74.) **Action to enforce lien or to subject property to payment of tax.**

(a) *Civil actions.* In any case where there has been a refusal or neglect to pay any tax, or to discharge any liability in respect thereof, whether or not levy has been made, the Attorney General or his delegate, at the request of the Commissioner (or the Director, Bureau of Alcohol, Tobacco, and Firearms, or the Chief Counsel for the Bureau, with respect to the provisions of subtitle E of the Code), or the Chief Counsel for the Internal Revenue Service or his delegate, may direct a civil action to be filed in a district court of the United States to enforce the lien of the United States under the Code with respect to such tax or liability or to subject any property, of whatever nature, of the delinquent, or in which he has any right, title or interest, to the payment of such tax or liability. In any such proceeding, at the instance of the United States, the court may appoint a receiver to enforce the lien, or, upon certification by the Commissioner or the Chief Counsel for the Internal Revenue Service during the pendency of such proceedings that it is in the public interest, may appoint a receiver with all the powers of a receiver in equity.

(b) *Bid by the United Sates.* If property is sold to satisfy a first lien held by the United States, the United States may bid at the sale a sum which does not exceed the amount of its lien and the expenses of the sale. See also 31 U.S.C. 195.

○— § 301.7405 Statutory provisions; action for recovery of erroneous refunds. [Sec. 7405, IRC]

○— § 301.7406 Statutory provisions; disposition of judgments and moneys recovered. [Sec. 7406, IRC]

○— § 301.7406-1 (T.D. 6498, filed 10-24-60.) Disposition of judgments and moneys recovered.

All judgments and moneys recovered or received for taxes, costs, forfeitures, and penalties shall be paid to the district director as collections of internal revenue taxes.

○— § 301.7407 Statutory provisions; cross references. [Sec. 7407, IRC]

PROCEEDINGS BY TAXPAYERS AND THIRD PARTIES

○— § 301.7421 Statutory provisions; prohibition of suits to restrain assessment or collection. [Sec. 7421, IRC]

○— § 301.7422 Statutory provisions; civil actions for refund. [Sec. 7422, IRC]

○— § 301.7423 Statutory provisions; repayments to officers or employees. [Sec. 7423, IRC]

○— § 301.7423-1 (T.D. 6498, filed 10-24-60.) Repayments to officers or employees.

The Commissioner is authorized to repay to any officer or employee of the United States the full amount of such sums of money as may be recovered against him in any court, for any internal revenue taxes collected by him, with the cost and expense of suit, and all damages and costs recovered against any officer or employee of the United States in any suit brought against him by reason of anything done in the official performance of his duties under the Code.

○— § 301.7424 Statutory provisions; intervention. [Sec. 7424, IRC]

○— § 301.7424-1 (T.D. 6498, filed 10-24-60; amended by T.D. 7305, filed 3-14-74.) Civil action to clear title to property.

(a) The provisions of this section shall apply only to civil actions to clear title commenced on or before November 2, 1966. For provisions permitting the United States to be made a party defendant in a proceeding for the foreclosure of a lien upon property where the United States may have claim upon the property involved, see section 2410 of title 28 of the United States Code.

(b) Any person having a lien upon or any interest in the property referred to in section 7403, notice of which has been duly filed of record in the jurisdiction in which the property is located, prior to the filing of the notice of the lien of the United States as provided in section 6323, or any person purchasing the property at a sale to satisfy such prior lien or interest, may make a written request to the Commissioner to authorize the filing of a civil action as provided in section 7403.

(c) If the Commissioner fails to authorize the filing of such civil action within 6 months after receipt of such written request, such person or purchaser may, after giving notice to the Commissioner, file a petition in the district court of the United States for the district in which the property is located, praying leave to file a civil action for a final determination of all claims to or liens upon the property in question.

○— § 301.7424-2 (T.D. 7305, filed 3-14-74.) Intervention.

If the United States is not a party to a civil action or suit, the United States may intervene in such action or suit to assert any lien arising under title 26 of the United States Code on the property which is the subject of such action or suit. The provisions of section 2410 of title 28 of the United States Code, (except subsection (b)) and of section 1444 of title 28 of the United States Code shall apply in any case in which the United States intervenes as if the United States had originally been named a defendant in such action or suit. If the application of the United States to intervene is denied, the adjudication in such civil action or suit shall have no effect upon such lien.

○— § 301.7425 Statutory provisions; discharge of liens. [Sec. 7425, IRC]

○— § 301.7425-1 (T.D. 7430, filed 8-19-76.) Discharge of liens; scope and application; judicial proceedings.

(a) *In general.* A tax lien of the United States, or a title derived from the enforcement of a tax lien of the United States, may be discharged or divested under local law only in the manner prescribed in section 2410 of Title 28 of the United States Code or in the manner prescribed in section 7425 of the Internal Revenue Code. Section 7425(a) contains provisions relating to the discharge of a lien when the United States is not joined as a party in the judicial proceedings described in subsection (a) of section 2410 of Title 28 of the United States Code. These judicial proceedings are plenary in nature and proceed on formal pleadings. Section 7425 (b) contains provisions relating to the discharge of a lien or a title derived from the enforcement of a lien in the event of a nonjudicial sale with respect to the property involved. Section 7425(c) contains special rules relating to the notice of sale requirements contained in section 7425(b). Section 301.7425-2 contains rules with respect to the nonjudicial sales described in section 7425(b). Paragraph (a) of § 301.7425-3 contains rules with respect to the notice of sale provisions of section 7425(c)(1). Paragraph (b) of § 301.7425-3 contains rules relating to the consent to sale provisions of section 7425(c)(2). Paragraph (c) of § 301.7425-3 contains rules relating to the sale of perishable goods provisions of section 7425(c)(3). Paragraph (d) of § 301.7425-3 contains the requirements with respect to the contents of a notice of sale. Section 301.7425-4 prescribes rules with respect to the redemption of real property by the United States.

Proceedings by Taxpayers and Third Parties (I.R.C.) 24,412.5

(b) *Effective date.* The provisions of section 7425, as added by the Federal Tax Lien Act of 1966, are effective with respect to sales described in section 7425 occurring after November 2, 1966. The notice of sale provisions of section 7425(c)(1) or (3) do not apply to sales occurring after November 2, 1966, if the seller of the property performed an act before November 3, 1966, which act at the time of performance was required and effective under local law with respect to the sale. An example of such an act is publication of a notice of the sale in a local newspaper before November 3, 1966, if local law requires such publication before a sale and the publication is effective under local law. Accordingly, in such a case, it is not necessary to notify the Internal Revenue Service pursuant to the provisions of section 7425(c)(1) or (3). With respect to a notice of sale required under section 7425(c)(1) or (3)—

(1) Any notice of sale given to an office of the Internal Revenue Service or the Treasury Department during the period November 3, 1966, through December 21, 1966, shall be considered as adequate;

(2) Any notice of sale given during the period December 22, 1966, through January 31, 1968, which complies with the provisions of either—

(i) Revenue Procedure 67-25, 1967-1 C.B. 626 (based on Technical Information Release 873, dated December 22, 1966), or

(ii) Section 301.7425-3, shall be considered as adequate; and

(3) Any notice of sale given after January 31, 1968, which complies with the provisions of § 301.7425-3 shall be considered as adequate.

(c) *Judicial proceedings*—(1) *In general.* Section 7425(a) provides rules, where the United States is not joined as a party, to determine the effect of a judgment in any civil action or suit described in subsection (a) of section 2410 of title 28 of the United States Code (relating to joinder of the United States in certain proceedings), or a judicial sale pursuant to such a judgment, with respect to property on which the United States has or claims a lien under the provisions of this title. If the United States is improperly named as a party to a judicial proceeding, the effect is the same as if the United States were not joined.

(2) *Notice of lien filed when the proceeding is commenced.* Where the United States is not properly joined as a party in the court proceeding and a notice of lien has been filed in accordance with section 6323(f) or (g) in the place provided by law for such filing at the time the action or suit is commenced, a judgment or judicial sale pursuant to such a judgment shall be made subject to and without disturbing the lien of the United States.

(3) *Notice of lien not filed when the proceeding is commenced.*—(i) *General rule.* Where the United States is not joined as a party in the court proceeding and either a notice of lien has not been filed in accordance with section 6323(f) or (g) in the place provided by law for such filing at the time the action or suit is commenced, or the law makes no provision for that filing, a judgment or judicial sale pursuant to such a judgment shall have the same effect with respect to the discharge or divestment of the lien of the United States as may be provided with respect to these matters by the local law of the place where the property is situated.

(ii) *Examples.* The provisions of subparagraph (3) may be illustrated by the following examples:

Example (1). A, the first mortgagee of an apartment building located in State Y, commenced a foreclosure action on the mortgage prior to the time that a notice of a Federal tax lien, on that building, had been filed. Under the law of Y, junior liens on real property are discharged by a judicial sale pursuant to a judgment in a foreclosure action. Therefore, the Federal tax lien on the building will be discharged by the judicial sale. This result is the same whether the tax lien arose before or after the date of commencement of the foreclosure action and whether notice of the tax lien was filed at any time after commencement of the foreclosure action.

Example (2). On January 10, 1969, B dies testate and devises Blackacre to C. At B's death, Blackacre is subject to a first mortgage held by D. Realty is subject to administration as part of a decedent's estate under the laws of State X. However, C takes possession of Blackacre with the assent of E, the executor of B's estate. On January 5, 1970, D commences a foreclosure action on the mortgage. Under the law of X, junior liens on real property are discharged by a judicial sale pursuant to a judgment in a foreclosure action. After commencement of the proceedings, an assessment for estate taxes is made and, thereafter, a notice of lien is filed in accordance with section 6323. The special lien on Blackacre, arising at the date of B's death, for estate taxes under section 6324(a) will be discharged by the judicial sale because there are no provisions for filing a notice thereof under law and junior liens are discharged by the sale under local law. The lien is discharged even though the executor failed to obtain a discharge of his personal liability under section 2204. Furthermore, the general lien on Blackacre under section 6321 will be discharged by the judicial sale because the foreclosure action was commenced prior to the time that a notice of lien was filed.

(4) *Proceeds of a judicial sale.* If a judicial sale of property pursuant to a judgment in any civil action or suit to which the United States is not a party discharges a lien of the United States arising under the provisions of the Internal Revenue Code of 1954, the United States may claim the proceeds of the sale (exclusive of costs) prior to the time that distribution of the proceeds is ordered. The claim of the United States in such a case is treated as having the same priority with respect to the proceeds as the lien had with respect to the property which was discharged from the lien by the judicial sale.

§ 301.7425-2 (T.D. 7430, filed 8-19-76.) **Discharge of liens; nonjudicial sales.**

§ 301.7425-2(a)

24,412.6 (I.R.C.)   Reg. § 301.7425-2(a)   8-30-76

(a) *In general.* Section 7425(b) contains provisions with respect to the effect on the interest of the United States in property in which the United States has or claims a lien, or a title derived from the enforcement of a lien, of a sale made pursuant to—

(1) An instrument creating a lien on the property sold,

(2) A confession of judgment on the obligation secured by an instrument creating a lien on the property sold, or

(3) A statutory lien on the property sold.

For purposes of this section, such a sale is referred to as a "nonjudicial sale." The term "nonjudicial sale" includes, but is not limited to, the divestment of the taxpayer's interest in property which occurs by operation of law, by public or private sale, by forfeiture, or by termination under provisions contained in a contract for a deed or a conditional sales contract. Under section 7425(b)(1), if a notice of lien is filed in accordance with section 6323(f) or (g), or the title derived from the enforcement of a lien is recorded as provided by local law, more than 30 days before the date of sale, and the appropriate district director is not given notice of the sale (in the manner prescribed in § 301.7425-3), the sale shall be made subject to and without disturbing the lien or title of the United States. Under section 7425(b)(2)(C), in any case in which notice of the sale is given to the district director not less than 25 days prior to the date of sale (in the manner prescribed in section 7425(c)(1)), the sale shall have the same effect with respect to the discharge or divestment of the lien or title as may be provided by local law with respect to other junior liens or other titles derived from the enforcement of junior liens. A nonjudicial sale pursuant to a lien which is junior to a tax lien does not divest the tax lien, even though notice of the nonjudicial sale is given to the appropriate district director. However, under the provisions of section 6325(b) and § 301.6325-1, a district director may discharge the property from a tax lien, including a tax lien which is senior to another lien upon the property.

(b) *Date of sale.* In the case of a nonjudicial sale subject to the provisions of section 7425(b), in order to compute any period of time determined with reference to the date of sale, the date of sale shall be determined in accordance with the following rules:

(1) In the case of divestment of junior liens of property resulting directly from a public sale, the date of sale is deemed to be the date the public sale is held, regardless of the date under local law on which junior liens of the property are divested or the title to the property is transferred,

(2) In the case of divestment of junior liens on property resulting directly from a private sale, the date of sale is deemed to be the date title to the property is transferred, regardless of the date junior liens on the property are divested under local law, and

(3) In the case of divestment of junior liens on property not resulting directly from a public or private sale, the date of sale is deemed to be the date on which junior liens on the property are divested under local law.

For provisions relating to the right of redemption of the United States, see section 7425(d) and § 301.7425-4.

(c) *Examples.* The provisions of this section may be illustrated by the following examples:

Example (1). (i) Under the law of State M, upon entry of judgment, the judgment creditor obtains a statutory lien upon the real property of the judgment debtor, and certain procedures are provided by which the judgment creditor may execute by public sale upon such real property. These procedures provide, among other things, for notification by personal service or registered or certified mail to other lien creditors, if any, and publication of a notice of the sale in a local newspaper. After the expiration of a prescribed period of time after such notification and publication, the sheriff of the county where the real property is located may sell the property at public sale. After payment of the amount bid at the public sale, the sheriff issues to the purchaser a deed to the real property, and the interest of junior lienors in the property are divested.

(ii) For purposes of this section, such an execution sale is a nonjudicial sale described in section 7425(b) because the sale is made pursuant to a statutory lien on the property sold. The date of sale, for purposes of computing a period of time determined with reference to the date of sale, is the date on which the public sale is held because junior liens on the real property are divested directly as a result of the public sale. This result obtains even though the junior liens are legally divested on a later date when the sheriff issues the deed.

Example (2). (i) Under the law of State N, mortgages on real property may contain a power of sale which authorizes the mortgagee, upon breach by the mortgagor of one of the conditions of the mortgage, to have the mortgaged property sold at public sale. This public sale must be preceded by notice by advertisement in a local newspaper, and the time, place, description of the property, and other terms of the sale must be specified. The purchaser at such a public sale obtains a title to the real property which is not subject to a right of redemption by the mortgagor and which divests the interests of the junior lienors in the property.

(ii) For purposes of this section, a sale pursuant to such a power of sale is a nonjudicial sale described in section 7425(b) because the sale is made pursuant to the mortgage instrument which created a lien on the property sold. The date of the sale, for purposes of computing a period of time determined with reference to the date of sale, is the date of the public sale because junior liens on the property are divested directly as a result of the public sale.

Example (3). Assume the same facts as in example (2) except that the purchaser at the public sale obtains a title which is defeasible by the exercise of a right of redemption in the mortgagor. The purchaser's title divests the interests of junior lienors in the property as of the time of public sale. The interests of junior lienors in the property revive if the mortgagor exercises his right of redemption. The date of the sale, for purposes of computing a period of time determined with reference to the date of sale, is the date of the public sale because junior liens on the property are divested directly as a result of the public sale although such junior liens may be revived by a subsequent redemption by the mortgagor.

Example (4). (i) Under the law of State O, upon breach by a mortgagor of real property of one of the conditions of the mortgage, the mortgagee may foreclose the mortgage by securing possession of the property by one of several procedures provided by statute. These procedures are generally referred to as "strict foreclosure." In order for a foreclosure to be effective under these procedures, a certificate attesting the fact of entry must be recorded with the proper registrar of deeds within 30 days after the mortgagee enters the property. During the one-year period following the date on which the certificate of entry is recorded, the mortgagor or a junior lienor may redeem the property by paying the mortgagee the amount of the mortgage obligation. If, during such one-year period the property is not redeemed and the mortgagee's possession is continued, the interests of the mortgagor and the junior lienors in the property are divested as of the date such one-year period expires.

(ii) For purposes of this section, such a foreclosure procedure is a nonjudicial sale described in section 7425(b) because it results in the divestment of the mortgagor's interest in the property by operation of law pursuant to the mortgage which created a lien on the property. In addition, because there is no public or private sale which directly results in the divestment of junior liens on the property, the date of sale, for purposes of computing a period of time determined with reference to the date of sale, is the date on which the one-year period following the recording of the certificate of entry expires.

Example (5). The law of State P contains a procedure which permits a county to collect a delinquent tax assessment with respect to real property by the means of a tax sale of the property. First, a notice of a public auction with respect to the tax assessment on the real property is published in a local newspaper. At the public auction, the purchaser, upon payment of the delinquent taxes and interest, obtains from the county tax collector a tax certificate with respect to the real property. Because the obtaining of this tax certificate does not directly result in the divestment of either the owner's title or junior liens with respect to the property, the public auction is not a nonjudicial sale described in section 7425(b). At any time before a tax deed with respect to the property is issued by the clerk of the county court, the owner or any holder of a lien or other interest with respect to the property may obtain the tax certificate by paying the holder of the tax certificate the amount of the taxes, interest, and costs. After a date which is two years after the date on which the tax assessment became delinquent, the holder of the tax certificate may request the clerk of the county court to have the property advertised for sale. After advertisement of the sale, the clerk of the county court conducts a public sale of the real property and the purchaser obtains a tax deed. The interests of all junior lienors in the property are divested and the property is not subject to a right of redemption under the law of State P. For purposes of this section, this public sale is considered to be a nonjudicial sale described in section 7425(b) because the sale is made pursuant to a statutory lien on the property sold. The date of the sale, for purposes of computing a period of time determined with reference to the date of sale, is the date on which the public sale is held at which the purchaser obtains a tax deed as this sale directly results in the divestment of junior liens on the property.

Example (6). The law of State Q contains a provision which permits a county to collect a delinquent tax assessment with respect to real property by the means of a tax sale of the property. After public notice is given, a "tax sale" of the real property is conducted. Upon payment of the delinquent taxes and interest, a purchaser obtains a tax certificate with respect to the real property. If there is no purchaser at the tax sale, the property is deemed to be bid in by the State. Because the obtaining of this tax certificate by a purchaser or State Q does not directly result in the divestment of either the owner's title or junior liens with respect to the property, the tax sale is not a nonjudicial sale described in section 7425(b). Following the tax sale, there is a three year period during which any person having an interest in the property may redeem the property by paying the holder of the tax certificate the amount of taxes, interest, and costs. Unless redeemed, the holder of the tax certificate may obtain an absolute title at the expiration of the period of redemption provided he serves a notice of the expiration of the redemption period upon the owner at least 60 days prior to the date of expiration. Because there is no public or private sale which directly results in the divestment of junior liens on the property, the date of sale, for purposes of computing a period of time determined with reference to the date of sale, is the date on which the holder of the tax certificate obtains absolute title.

§ 301.7425-3 (T.D. 7430, filed 8-19-76.) **Discharge of liens; special rules.**

(a) *Notice of sale requirements*—(1) *In general.* Except in the case of the sale of perishable goods described in paragraph (c) of this section, a notice (as described in paragraph (d) of this section) of a nonjudicial sale shall be given, in writing by registered or certified mail or by personal service, not less than 25 days prior to the date of sale (determined under the provisions of paragraph (b) of § 301.7425-2), to the district director (marked for the attention of the chief, special procedures staff) for the internal revenue district in which the sale is to be conducted. Thus, under this section, a notice of sale is not effective if it is given to a district director other than the district director for the internal revenue district in which the sale is to be conducted. The provisions of sections 7502 (relating to timely mailing treated as timely filing) and 7503 (relating to time for performance of acts where the last day falls on Saturday, Sunday, or a legal holiday) apply in the case of notices required to be made under this paragraph.

(2) *Postponement of scheduled sale*— (i) *Where notice of sale is given.* In the event that notice of a sale is given in accordance with subparagraph (1) of this paragraph with respect to a scheduled sale which is postponed to a later time or date, the seller of the property is required to give notice of the postponement to the district director in the same manner as is required under local law with respect to other secured creditors. For example, assume that in State M local law requires that in the event of a postponement of a scheduled foreclosure sale of real property, an oral announcement of the postponement at the place and time of the scheduled sale constitutes sufficient notice to secured creditors of the postponement. Accordingly, if at the place and time of a scheduled sale in State M an oral announcement of the postponement is made, the Internal Revenue Service is considered to have notice of the postponement for the purpose of this subparagraph.

(ii) *Where notice of sale is not given.* In the event that—

(A) Notice of a nonjudicial sale would not be required under subparagraph (1) of this paragraph if the sale were held on the originally scheduled date,

(B) Because of a postponement of the scheduled sale, more than 30 days elapse between the originally scheduled date of the sale and the date of the sale, and

(C) A notice of lien with respect to the property to be sold is filed more than 30 days before the date of the sale,

notice of the sale is required to be given to the district director in accordance with the provisions of subparagraph (1) of this paragraph. In any case in which notice of sale is required to be given with respect to a scheduled sale, and notice of the sale is not given, any postponement of the scheduled sale does not affect the rights of the United States under section 7425(b).

(iii) *Examples.* The provisions of subdivision (ii) of this subparagraph may be illustrated by the following examples:

Example (1). A nonjudicial sale of Blackacre, belonging to A, a delinquent taxpayer, is scheduled for December 2, 1968. As no notice of lien is filed applicable to Blackacre more than 30 days before December 2, 1968, no notice of sale is given to the district director. On December 2, 1968, the sale of Blackacre is postponed until January 15, 1969. A notice of lien with respect to Blackacre is properly filed on January 2, 1969. The sale of Blackacre is held on January 15, 1969. Even though more than 30 days elapsed between the originally scheduled date of the sale (December 2, 1968) and the date of the sale (January 15, 1960), no notice of sale is required to be given to the district director because the notice of lien was not filed more than 30 days before the date of the sale.

Example (2). Assume the same facts as in example (1) except that a notice of lien is filed on November 29, 1968 in accordance with section 6323. Because more than 30 days elapsed between the originally scheduled date of the sale and the date of the sale, and the notice of lien is filed (on November 29, 1968) more than 30 days before the date of the sale (January 15, 1969), notice of the sale, in accordance with the provisions of subparagraph (1) of this paragraph, is required to be given to the district director.

Example (3). A nonjudicial sale of Whiteacre, belonging to B, a delinquent taxpayer, is scheduled for December 2, 1968. A notice of lien applicable to Whiteacre is filed on November 12, 1968 in accordance with section 6323. As the notice of lien was not filed more than 30 days before December 2, 1968, no notice of sale is given to the district director. On December 2, 1968, the sale of Whiteacre is postponed until December 20, 1968. The sale of Whiteacre is held on December 20, 1968. Even though more than 30 days elapsed between the date notice of lien was filed (November 12, 1968) and the date of the sale (December 20, 1968), no notice of sale is required to be given to the district director because not more than 30 days elapsed between the date of the originally scheduled sale (December 2, 1968) and the date the sale was actually held (December 20, 1968).

(b) *Consent to sale*—(1) *In general.* Notwithstanding the notice of sale provisions of paragraph (a) of this section, a nonjudicial sale of property shall discharge or divest the property of the lien or title of the United States if the district director for the internal revenue district in which the sale occurs consents to the sale of the property free of the lien or title. Pursuant to section 7425(c)(2), where adequate protection is afforded the lien or title of the United States, a district director may, in his discretion, consent with respect to the sale of property in appropriate cases. Such consent shall be effective only if given in writing and shall be subject to such limitations and conditions as the district director may require. However, a district director may not consent to a sale of property under this section after the date of sale, as determined under paragraph (b) of § 301.7425-2. For provisions relating to the authority of the district director to release a lien or discharge property subject to a tax lien, see section 6325 and the regulations thereunder.

(2) *Application for consent.* Any person desiring a district director's consent to sell property free of a tax lien or a title derived from the enforcement of a tax lien of the United States in the property shall submit to the district director for the internal revenue district in which the sale is to occur a written application, in triplicate, declaring that it is made under penalties of perjury, and requesting that such consent be given. The application shall contain the information required in the case of a notice of sale, as set forth in paragraph (d)(1) of this section, and, in addition, shall contain a statement of the reasons why the consent is desired.

(c) *Sale of perishable goods*—(1) *In general.* A notice (as described in paragraph (d) of this section) of a nonjudicial sale of perishable goods (as defined in subparagraph (2) of this paragraph) shall be given in writing, by registered or certified mail or delivered by personal service, at any time before the sale, to the district director (marked for the attention of the chief, special procedures staff) for the internal revenue district in which the sale is to be conducted. Thus, under this section, a notice of sale is not effective if it is given to a district director other than the district director for the internal revenue district in which the sale is to be conducted. If a notice of a nonjudicial sale is timely given in nonjudicial sale shall discharge or divest the manner described in this paragraph, the the tax lien, or a title derived from the enforcement of a tax lien, of the United States in the property. The provisions of section 7502 (relating to timely mailing treated as timely filing) and 7503 (relating to time for performance of acts where the last day falls on Saturday, Sunday, or a legal holiday) apply in the case of notices required to be made under this paragraph. The seller of the perishable goods shall hold the proceeds (exclusive of costs) of the sale as a fund, for not less than 30 days after the date of the sale, subject to the liens and claims of the United States, in the same manner and with the same priority as the liens and claims of the United States had with respect to the property sold. If the seller fails to hold the proceeds of the sale in accordance with the provisions of this paragraph and if the district director asserts a claim to the proceeds within 30 days after the date of sale, the seller shall be personally liable to the United States for an amount equal to the value of the interest of the United States in the fund. However, even if the proceeds of the sale are not so held by the seller, but all the other provisions of this paragraph are satisfied, the buyer of the property at the sale takes the property free of the liens and claims of the United States. In the event of a postponement of the scheduled sale of perishable goods, the seller is not required to notify the district director of the postponement. For provisions relating to the authority of the district director to release a lien or discharge property subject to a tax lien, see section 6325 and the regulations thereunder.

(2) *Definition of perishable goods.* For the purpose of this paragraph, the term "perishable goods" means any tangible personal property which, in the reasonable view of the person selling the property, is liable to perish or become greatly reduced in price or value by keeping, or cannot be kept without great expense.

(d) *Content of notice of sale*—(1) *In general.* With respect to a notice of sales described in paragraph (a) or (c) of this section, the notice will be considered adequate if it contains the information described in subdivisions (i), (ii), (iii), and (iv) of this subparagraph.

(i) The name and address of the person submitting the notice of sale;

(ii) A copy of each Notice of Federal Tax Lien (Form 668) affecting the property to be sold, or the following information as shown on each such Notice of Federal Tax Lien—

(A) The internal revenue district named thereon,

(B) The name and address of the taxpayer, and

(C) The date and place of filing of the notice;

(iii) With respect to the property to be sold, the following information—

(A) A detailed description, including location, of the property affected by the notice (in the case of real property, the street address, city, and State and the legal description contained in the title or deed to the property and, if available, a copy of the abstract of title),

(B) The date, time, place, and terms of the proposed sale of the property, and

(C) In the case of a sale of perishable property described in paragraph (c) of this section, a statement of the reasons why the property is believed to be perishable; and

(iv) The approximate amount of the principal obligation, including interest, secured by the lien sought to be enforced and a description of the other expenses (such as legal expenses, selling costs, etc.) which may be charged against the sale proceeds.

(2) *Inadequate notice.* Except as otherwise provided in this subparagraph, a notice of sale described in paragraph (a) of this section which does not contain the information described in subparagraph (1) of this paragraph shall be considered inadequate by a district director. If a district director determines that the notice is inadequate, he will give written notification of the items of information which are inadequate to the person who submitted the notice. A notice of sale which does not contain the name and address of the person submitting such notice shall be considered to be inadequate for all purposes without notification of any specific inadequacy. In any case where a notice of sale, given after December 31, 1976, does not contain the information required under subdivision (ii) of subparagraph (1) of this paragraph with respect to a Notice of Federal Tax Lien, the district director may give written notification of such omission without specification of any other inadequacy and such notice of sale shall be considered inadequate for all purposes. In the event the district director gives notification that the notice of sale is inadequate, a notice complying with the provisions of this section (including the requirement that the notice be given not less than 25 days prior to the sale in the case of a notice described in paragraph (a) of this section) must be given. However, in accordance with the provisions of paragraph (b)(1) of this section, in such a case the district director may, in his discretion, consent to the sale of the property free of the lien or title of the United States even though notice of the sale is given less than 25 days prior to the sale. In any case where the person who submitted a timely notice which indicates his name and address does not receive, more than 5 days prior to the date of the sale, written notification from the district director that the notice is inadequate, the notice shall be considered adequate for purposes of this section.

(3) *Acknowledgment of notice.* If a notice of sale described in paragraph (a) or (c) of this section is submitted in duplicate to the district director with a written request that receipt of the notice be acknowledged and returned to the person giving the notice, this request will be honored by the district director. The acknowledgment by the district director will indicate

§ 301.7425-3 (d) (4)

24,412.10 (I.R.C.) Reg. § 301.7425-3(d)(4)

the date and time of the receipt of the notice.

(4) *Disclosure of adequacy of notice.* The district director for the internal revenue district in which the sale was held or is to be held is authorized to disclose, to any person who has a proper interest, whether an adequate notice of sale was given under subparagraph (1) of this paragraph. Any person desiring this information should submit to the district director a written request which clearly describes the property sold or to be sold, identifies the applicable notice of lien, gives the reasons for requesting the information, and states the name and address of the person making the request.

○— § 301.7425-4 (T.D. 7430, filed 8-19-76.) **Discharge of liens; redemption by United States.**

(a) *Right to redeem*—(1) *In general.* In the case of a nonjudicial sale of real property to satisfy a lien prior to the tax lien or a title derived from the enforcement of a tax lien, the district director may redeem the property within the redemption period (as described in subparagraph (2) of this paragraph). The right of redemption of the United States exists under section 7425(d) even though the district director has consented to the sale under section 7425(c)(2) and § 301.7425-3(b). For purposes of this section, the term "nonjudicial sale" shall have the same meaning as used in paragraph (a) of § 301.7425-2.

(2) *Redemption period.* For purposes of this section, the redemption period shall be—

(i) The period beginning with the date of the sale (as determined under paragraph (b) of § 301.7425-2) and ending with the 120th day after such date, or

(ii) The period for redemption of real property allowable, with respect to other secured creditors, under the local law of the place where the real property is located, whichever expires later. Whichever period is applicable, section 7425 and this section shall govern the amount to be paid and the procedure to be followed.

(3) *Limitations.* In the event a sale does not ultimately discharge the property from the tax lien (whether by reason of local law or the provisions of section 7425 (b)), the provisions of this section do not apply because the tax lien will continue to attach to the property after the sale. In a case in which the Internal Revenue Service is not entitled to a notice of sale under section 7425(b) and § 302.7425-3, the United States does not have a right of redemption under section 7425(d). However, in such a case, if a tax lien has attached to the property at the time of sale, the United States has the same right of redemption, if any, which is afforded similar creditors under the local law of the place in which the property is situated.

(b) *Amount to be paid*—(1) *In general.* In any case in which a district director exercises the right to redeem real property under section 7425(d), the amount to be paid is the sum of the following amounts—

(i) The actual amount paid for the property (as determined under subparagraph (2) of this paragraph) being redeemed (which, in the case of a purchaser who is the holder of the lien being foreclosed, shall include the amount of the obligation secured by such lien to the extent legally satisfied by reason of the sale);

(ii) Interest on the amount paid (described in subdivision (i) of this subparagraph) at the sale by the purchaser of the real property computed at the rate of 6 percent per annum for the period from the date of the sale (as determined under paragraph (b) of § 301.7425-2) to the date of redemption;

(iii) The amount, if any, equal to the excess of (A) the expenses necessarily incurred to maintain such property (as determined under subparagraph (3) of this paragraph) by the purchaser (and his successor in interest, if any) over (B) the income from such property realized by the purchaser (and his successor in interest, if any) plus a reasonable rental value of such property (to the extent the property is used by or with the consent of the purchaser or his successor in interest or is rented at less than its reasonable rental value); and

(iv) With respect to a redemption made after December 31, 1976, the amount, if any, of a payment made by the purchaser or his successor in interest after the foreclosure sale to a holder of a senior lien (to the extent provided under subparagraph (4) of this paragraph).

(2) *Actual amount paid.* (i) The actual amount paid for property by a purchaser, other than the holder of the lien being foreclosed, is the amount paid by him at the sale. For purposes of this subdivision, the amount paid by the purchaser at the sale includes deferred payments upon the bid price. The actual amount paid does not include costs and expenses incurred prior to the foreclosure sale by the purchaser except to the extent such expenses are included in the amount bid and paid for the property. For example, the actual amount paid does not normally include the expenses of the purchaser such as title searches, professional fees, or interest on debt incurred to obtain funds to purchase the property.

(ii) In the case of a purchaser who is the holder of the lien being foreclosed, the actual amount paid is the sum of (A) the amount of the obligation secured by such lien to the extent legally satisfied by reason of the sale and (B) any additional amount bid and paid at the sale. For purposes of this section, a purchaser who acquires title as a result of a nonjudicial foreclosure sale is treated as the holder of the lien being foreclosed if a lien (or any interest reserved, created, or conveyed as security for the payment of a debt or fulfillment of other obligation) held by him is partially or fully satisfied by reason of the foreclosure sale. For example, a person whose title is derived from a tax deed issued under local law shall be treated as a purchaser who is the holder of the lien foreclosed in a case where a tax certificate, evidencing a lien on the property arising from the payment of property taxes, ripens into title. The amount paid by a purchaser at the sale includes deferred payments upon any portion of the bid price which is in excess of the amount of the lien being foreclosed. The actual amount paid does not include costs and expenses incurred prior to the foreclosure sale by the purchaser except to the extent such expenses are included in the amount of the lien being foreclosed which is legally satisfied by reason of the sale or in the amount bid and paid at the sale. Where the lien being foreclosed attaches to other property not subject to the foreclosure sale, the amount legally satisfied by reason of the sale does not include the amount of such lien that attaches to the other property. However, for purposes of the preceding sentence, the amount of the lien that attaches to the other property shall be considered to be equal to the amount by which the value of the other property exceeds the amount of any other senior lien on that property. Where, after the sale, the holder of the lien being foreclosed has the right to the unpaid balance of the amount due him, the amount legally satisfied by reason of the sale does not include the amount of such lien to the extent a deficiency judgment may be obtained therefor. However, for purposes of the preceding sentence, an amount, with respect to which the holder of the lien being foreclosed would otherwise have a right to a deficiency judgment, shall be considered to be legally satisfied by reason of the foreclosure sale to the extent that the holder has waived his right to a deficiency judgment prior to the foreclosure sale. For this purpose, the waiver must be in writing and legally binding upon the foreclosure lienholder as of the time the sale is concluded. If, prior to the foreclosure, payments have been made by the foreclosing lienholder to a holder of a superior lien, the payments are included in the actual amount paid to the extent they give rise to an interest which is legally satisfied by reason of the foreclosure sale.

(3) *Excess expenses incurred by purchaser.* (i) Expenses necessarily incurred in connection with the property after the foreclosure sale and before redemption by the United States are taken into account in determining if there are excess expenses payable under subparagraph (1)(iii) of this paragraph. Expenses incurred by the purchaser prior to the foreclosure sale are not considered under this subparagraph. (See subparagraph (2)(ii) of this paragraph for circumstances under which such expenses may be included in the amount to be paid.) Expenses necessarily incurred in connection with the property include, for example, rental agent commissions, repair and maintenance expenses, utilities expenses, legal fees incurred after the foreclosure sale and prior to redemption in defending the title acquired through the foreclosure sale, and a proportionate amount of casualty insurance premiums and ad valorem taxes. Improvements made to the property are not considered as an expense unless the amounts incurred for such improvements are necessarily incurred to maintain the property.

(ii) At any time prior to the expiration of the redemption period applicable under paragraph (a)(2) of this section, the district director may, by certified or registered mail or hand delivery, request a written itemized statement of the amount claimed by the purchaser or his successor in interest to be payable under subparagraph (1)(iii) of this paragraph. Unless the purchaser or his successor in interest furnishes the written itemized statement within 15 days after the request is made by the district director, it shall be presumed that no amount is payable for expenses in excess of income and the Internal Revenue Service shall tender only the amount otherwise payable under subparagraph (1) of this paragraph. If a purchaser or his successor in interest has failed to furnish the written itemized statement within 15 days after the request therefor is made by the district director, or there is a disagreement as to the amount properly payable under subparagraph (1)(iii) of this paragraph, a payment for excess expenses shall be made after the redemption within a reasonable time following the verification by the district director of a written itemized statement submitted by the purchaser or his successor in interest or the resolution of the disagreement as to the amount properly payable for excess expenses.

(4) *Payments made by purchaser or his successor in interest to a senior lienor.* (i) The amount to be paid upon a redemption by the United States made after December 31, 1976, shall include the amount of a payment made by the purchaser or his successor in interest to a holder of a senior lien to the extent a request for the reimbursement thereof (made in accordance with subdivision (ii) of this subparagraph) is approved as provided under subdivision (iii) of this subparagraph. This subparagraph applies only to a payment made after the foreclosure sale and before the redemption to a holder of a lien that was, immediately prior to the foreclosure sale, superior to the lien foreclosed. A payment of principal or interest to a senior lienor shall be taken into account. Generally, the portion, if any, of a payment which is to be held in escrow for the payment of an expense, such as hazard insurance or real property taxes, is not considered under this subparagraph. However, a payment by the escrow agent of a real property tax or special assessment lien, which was senior to the lien foreclosed, shall be considered to be a payment made by the purchaser or his successor in interest for purposes of this subparagraph. With respect to real property taxes assessed after the foreclosure sale, see subparagraph (3)(i) of this paragraph, relating to excess expenses incurred by the purchaser.

(ii) Before the expiration of the redemption period applicable under paragraph (a)(2) of this section, the district director shall, in any case where a redemption is contemplated, send notice to the purchaser (or his successor in interest of record) by certified or registered mail or hand delivery of his right under this subparagraph to request reimbursement (payable in the event the right to redeem under section 7425(d) is exercised) for a payment made to a senior lienor. No later than 15 days after the notice from the district director is sent, the request for reimbursement shall be mailed or delivered to the office specified in such notice and shall consist of—

(A) A written itemized statement, signed by the claimant, of the amount claimed with respect to a payment made to

§ 301.7425-4(b)(4)

24,412.12 (I.R.C.) § 301.7425-4(b)(4)

a senior lienor, together with the supporting evidence requested in the notice from the district director, and

(B) A waiver or other document that will be effective upon redemption by the United States to discharge the property from, or transfer to the United States, any interest in or lien on the property that may arise under local law with respect to the payment made to a senior lienor.

Upon a showing of reasonable cause, a district director may, in his discretion at any time before the expiration of the applicable period for redemption, grant an extension for a reasonable period of time to submit, amend, or supplement a request for reimbursement. Unless a request for reimbursement is timely submitted (determined with regard to any extension of time granted), no amount shall be payable to the purchaser or his successor in interest on account of a payment made to a senior lienor if the right to redeem under section 7425(d) is exercised. A waiver or other document submitted pursuant to this subdivision shall be treated as effective only to the extent of the amount included in the redemption price under this subparagraph. If the right to redeem is not exercised or a request for reimbursement is withdrawn, the district director shall, by certified or registered mail or hand delivery, return to the purchaser or his successor any waiver or other document submitted pursuant to this subdivision as soon as is practicable.

(iii) A request for reimbursement submitted in accordance with subdivision (ii) of this subparagraph shall be considered to be approved for the total amount claimed by the purchaser, and payable in the event the right to redeem is exercised, unless the district director sends notice to the claimant, by certified or registered mail or hand delivery, of the denial of the amount claimed within 30 days after receipt of the request or 15 days before expiration of the applicable period for redemption, whichever is later. The notification of denial shall state the grounds for denial. If such notice of denial is given, the request for reimbursement for a payment made to a senior lienor shall be treated as having been withdrawn by the purchaser or his successor and the Internal Revenue Service shall tender only the amount otherwise payable under subparagraph (1) of this paragraph. If a request for reimbursement is treated as having been withdrawn under the preceding sentence, payment for amounts described in this subparagraph may, in the discretion of the district director, be made after the redemption upon the resolution of the disagreement as to the amount properly payable under subparagraph (1)(iv) of this paragraph.

(5) *Examples.* The provisions of subparagraph (1)(i) of this paragraph may be illustrated by the following examples:

Example (1). A, a delinquent taxpayer, owns Blackacre located in State X upon which B holds a mortgage. After the mortgage is properly recorded, a notice of tax lien is filed under section 6323(f) which is applicable to Blackacre. Subsequently, A defaults on the mortgage and B forecloses on the mortgage which has an outstanding obligation in the amount of $100,-000. At the foreclosure sale, B bids $50,000 and obtains title to Blacacre as a result of the sale. At the time of the foreclosure sale, Blackacre has a fair market value of $75,000. Under the laws of State X, the mortgage obligation is fully satisfied by operation of the foreclosure sale per se and the mortgagee cannot obtain a deficiency judgment. Under subparagraph (1)(i) of this paragraph, the district director must pay $100,000 in order to redeem Blackacre.

Example (2). Assume the same facts as in example (1) except that under the laws of State X, the amount bid is the amount of the obligation legally satisfied as a result of the foreclosure sale, and in the case in which the amount of the obligation exceeds the amount bid, the mortgagee has the right to a judgment for the deficiency computed as the difference between the amount of the obligation and the amount bid. B does not waive, prior to the foreclosure sale, his right to a deficiency judgment. In such a case, the district director must, under subparagraph (1)(i) of this paragraph, pay $50,000 in order to redeem Blackacre, whether or not B seeks a judgment for the deficiency.

Example (3). C, a delinquent taxpayer, owns Greenacre located in State Y upon which D holds a first mortgage and E holds a second mortgage. After the mortgages are properly recorded, a notice of tax lien is filed under section 6323(f) which is applicable to Greenacre. Subsequently, C defaults on both mortgages and E pays $5,000 to D, which is the portion of D's obligation which is in default. The second mortgage held by E is an outstanding obligation in the amount of $100,000. Under the laws of State Y, E may treat the amount paid to D as an addition to his second mortgage upon foreclosure by him. E forecloses upon the security interest held by him. At the foreclosure sale, E bids $50,000 and obtains title to Greenacre subject to D's mortgage as a result of the foreclosure sale. Under the laws of State Y, the mortgage obligation legally satisfied is the amount bid and E has the right to a judgment for a deficiency in the amount of $55,000 ($100,000 plus $5,000 less $50,000). In such a case, the district director must, under subparagraph (1)(i) of this paragraph, pay $50,000 in order to redeem Greenacre, whether or not E seeks a judgment for the deficiency.

Example (4). The law of State Z contains a procedure which permits a county to collect a delinquent tax assessment with respect to real property by the means of a "tax sale" of the property. Pursuant to this procedure, a public auction is conducted on January 15, 1970, to collect the delinquent property taxes assessed against Whiteacre, which is owned by F. At the auction a bid of $1,000 (representing the tax, costs, and interest due at the time of the auction) is made by G. Subsequently, G pays the amount bid to the county and obtains a tax certificate with respect to Whiteacre. Under this tax sale procedure, the obtaining of the tax certificate does not directly result in the divestment of either F's title or any junior liens on Whiteacre. On January 15, 1973, the period under this tax sale procedure during which F could have redeemed Whiteacre expires. Further, more than 30 days before January 15, 1973, a notice of tax lien affecting Whiteacre is filed under section 6323(f) with respect to F's delinquent Federal income taxes. Under the state tax sale procedure, the amount which would be required to be paid by F to G on January 15, 1973, to redeem Whiteacre is $1,350 (the $1,000 amount bid, interest of $300, and costs of $50). However, Whiteacre is not redeemed by F under the state procedure and, on January 16, 1973, G obtains a tax deed to Whiteacre. Under the law of State Z, the issuance of the tax deed results in the divestment of F's title and junior liens on Whiteacre. Thus, under § 301.7425-2(b), the date of sale is January 16, 1973, for purposes of section 7425(b). The amount legally satisfied by reason of the sale is the amount G is entitled to receive, immediately prior to the expiration of the period for redemption under the law of State Z, if Whiteacre were redeemed at such time. Thus, the district director must, under subparagraph (1)(i) of this paragraph pay $1,350 in order to redeem Whiteacre.

(c) *Certificate of redemption*—(1) *In general.* If a district director exercises the right of redemption of the United States described in paragraph (a) of this section, he shall apply to the officer designated by local law, if any, for the documents necessary to evidence the fact of redemption and to record title to the redeemed property in the name of the United States. If no such officer has been designated by local law or if the officer designated by local law fails to issue the necessary documents, the district director is authorized to issue a certificate of redemption for the property redeemed by the United States.

(2) *Filing.* The district director shall, without delay, cause either the documents issued by the local officer or the certificate of redemption executed by the district director to be filed with the local office where certificates of redemption are generally filed. If a certificate of redemption is issued by the district director and if the State in which the real property redeemed by the United States is situated has no office with which certificates of redemption may be filed, the district director shall file the certificate of redemption in the office of the clerk of the United States district court for the judicial district in which the redeemed property is situated.

(3) *Effect of certificate of redemption.* A certificate of redemption executed pursuant to subparagraph (1) of this paragraph shall constitute prima facie evidence of the regularity of the redemption. When a certificate of redemption is recorded, it shall transfer to the United States all the rights, title, and interest in and to the redeemed property acquired by the person, from whom the district director redeemed the property, by virtue of the sale of the property. Therefore, if under local law the purchaser takes title free of liens junior to the lien of the foreclosing lienholder, the United States takes title free of such junior liens upon redemption of the property. If a certificate of redemption has been erroneously prepared and filed because the redemption was not effective, the district director shall issue a document revoking such certificate of redemption and such document shall be conclusively binding upon the United States against a purchaser of the property or a holder of a lien upon the property.

(4) *Application for release of right of redemption.* Upon application of a party with a proper interest in the real property sold in a nonjudicial sale described in section 7425(b) and § 301.7425-2 which real property is subject to the right of redemption of the United States described in this section, the district director may, in his discretion, release the right of redemption with respect to the property. The application for the release shall be submitted in writing to a district director and shall contain such information as the district director may require. If the district director determines that the right of redemption of the United States is without value, no amount shall be required to be paid with respect to the release of the right of redemption.

○━ § 301.7425 **Statutory provisions; cross references.** [Sec. 7425, IRC]

○━ § 301.7426 **Statutory provisions; civil actions by persons other than taxpayers.** [Sec. 7426, IRC]

○━ § 301.7426-1 (T.D. 7305, filed 3-14-74.) **Civil actions by persons other than taxpayers.**

(a) *Actions permitted*—(1) *Wrongful levy.* If a levy has been made on property or property has been sold pursuant to a levy, any person (other than the person against whom is assessed the tax out of which such levy arose) may bring a civil action against the United States in a district court of the United States based upon such person's claim—

(i) That he has an interest in, or a lien on, such property which is senior to the interest of the United States; and

(ii) That such property was wrongfully levied upon.

No action is permitted under section 7426 (a)(1) unless there has been a levy upon the property claimed. For example, no cause of action arises under this section where the United States sets off an amount due to the taxpayer against taxes owed by him since no levy has been made.

(2) *Surplus proceeds.* If property has been sold pursuant to levy, any person (other than the person against whom is assessed the tax out of which such levy arose) may bring a civil action against the United States in a district court of the United States based upon such person's claim that he—

(i) Has an interest in or lien on such property junior to that of the United States; and

(ii) Is entitled to the surplus proceeds of such sale.

(3) *Substituted sale proceeds.* Any person, who claims to be legally entitled

§ 301.7426-1 (a) (3)

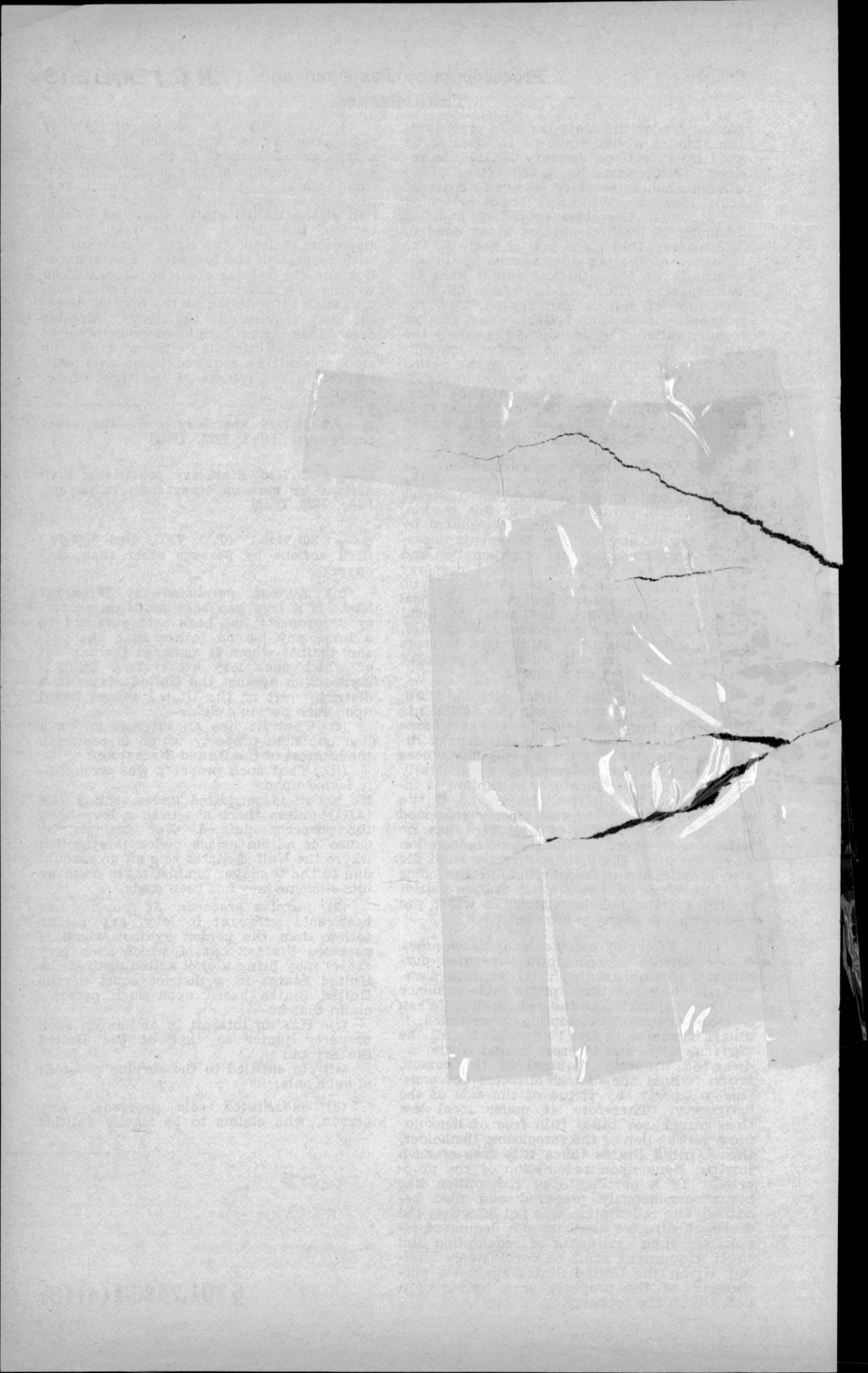

to all or any part of the amount which is held as a fund from the sale of property pursuant to an agreement described in section 6325(b)(3), may bring a civil action against the United States in a district court of the United States to obtain the relief provided by section 7426(b)(4). It is not necessary that the claimant be a party to the agreement which provides for the substitution of the sale proceeds for the property subject to the lien.

(b) *Adjudication*—(1) *Wrongful levy.* If the court determines that property has been wrongfully levied upon, the court may—

(i) Grant an injunction to prohibit the enforcement of such levy or to prohibit a sale of such property if such sale would irreparably injure rights in the property which are superior to the rights of the United States in such property; or

(ii) Order the return of specific property if the United States is in possession of such property; or

(iii) Grant a judgment for the amount of money levied upon; or

(iv) Grant a judgment for an amount not exceeding the amount received by the United States from the sale of such property (which, in the case of property declared purchased by the United States at a sale, shall be the greater of the minimum amount determined pursuant to section 6335(e) or the amount received by the United States from the resale of such property).

For purposes of this paragraph, a levy is wrongful against a person (other than the taxpayer against whom the assessment giving rise to the levy is made) if (a) the levy is upon property exempt from levy under section 6334, or (b) the levy is upon property in which the taxpayer had no interest at the time the lien arose or thereafter, or (c) the levy is upon property with respect to which such person is a purchaser against whom the lien is invalid under section 6323 or 6324(a)(2) or (b), or (d) the levy or sale pursuant to levy will or does effectively destroy or otherwise irreparably injure such person's interest in the property which is senior to the Federal tax lien. A levy may be wrongful against a holder of a senior lien upon the taxpayer's property under certain circumstances although legal rights to enforce his interest survive the levy procedure. For example, the levy may be wrongful against such a person if the property is an obligation which is collected pursuant to the levy rather than sold and nothing thereafter remains for the senior lienholder, or the property levied upon is of such a nature that when it is sold at a public sale the property subject to the senior lien is not available for the senior lienholder as a realistic source for the enforcement of his interest. Some of the factors which should be taken into account in determining whether property remains or will remain a realistic source from which the senior lienholder may realize collection are: (1) the nature of the property, (2) the number of purchasers, (3) the value of each unit sold or to be sold, (4) whether, as a direct result of the distraint sale, the costs of realizing collection from the security have or will be so substantially increased as to render the security substantially valueless as a source of collection, and (5) whether the property subject to the distraint sale constitutes substantially all of the property available as security for the payment of the indebtedness to the senior lienholder.

(2) *Example.* The provisions of subparagraph (1) of this paragraph may be illustrated by the following example:

Example. On April 10, 1972, A makes a $10,000 loan to B which is partially secured by a $5,000 obligation owed to B by C. Under local law, A's security interest in the obligation owed to B by C is protected against a subsequent judgment lien arising out of an unsecured obligation. Thus, under section 6323(h)(1), A's security interest exists as of April 10, 1972, for purposes of determining priorities against a tax lien under section 6323. On April 17, 1972, an assessment of $6,000 is made against B with respect to his delinquent Federal tax liability. Thereafter, notice of lien is filed pursuant to section 6323(f) with respect to B's delinquent tax liability. On July 10, 1972, a notice of levy is served upon C to reach the amount owed by him to B. C pays over the $5,000 obligation in satisfaction of the levy and, under local law, the obligation is discharged as to A. Because the levy effectively destroyed A's senior security interest in the obligation owed to B by C, the levy is wrongful as to A for purposes of section 7426. Under these circumstances, the levy is wrongful with respect to A even if, under local law, A may have a cause of action in contract against B for the $10,000 loan or may have a cause of action in tort against C for the amount of the $5,000 payment which defeated A's security interest in the obligation owed by C to B.

(3) *Surplus proceeds.* If the court determines that the interest or lien of any party to an action under section 7426 was transferred to the proceeds of a sale of the property, the court may grant a judgment in an amount equal to all or any part of the amount of the surplus proceeds of such sale. The term "surplus proceeds" means those proceeds realized on a sale of property remaining after application of the provisions of section 6342(a).

(4) *Substituted sale proceeds.* If the court determines that a party has an interest in or lien on the amount held as a fund pursuant to an agreement described in section 6325(b)(3), the court may grant a judgment in an amount equal to all or any part of the amount of such fund.

○— § 301.7427 Statutory provisions; cross references. [Sec. 7427, IRC]

THE TAX COURT

ORGANIZATION AND JURISDICTION

○— § 301.7441 Statutory provisions; status. [Sec. 7441, IRC]

○— § 301.7442 Statutory provisions; jurisdiction. [Sec. 7442, IRC]

Reg. § 301.7442

24,414 (I.R.C.)

○⌐ § 301.7443 Statutory provision; membership. [Sec. 7443, IRC]

○⌐ § 301.7444 Statutory provisions; organization. [Sec. 7444, IRC]

○⌐ § 301.7445 Statutory provisions; offices. [Sec. 7445, IRC]

○⌐ § 301.7446 Statutory provisions; times and places of sessions. [Sec. 7446, IRC]

○⌐ § 301.7447 Statutory provisions; retirement. [Sec. 7447, IRC]

○⌐ § 301.7448 Statutory provisions; annuities to widows and dependent children of judges. [Sec. 7448, IRC]

PROCEDURE

○⌐ § 301.7451 Statutory provisions; fee for filing petition. [Sec. 7451, IRC]

○⌐ § 301.7452 Statutory provisions; representation of parties. [Sec. 7452, IRC]

○⌐ § 301.7452-1 (T.D. 6498, filed 10-24-60.) Representation of parties.

The Commissioner shall be represented by the Chief Counsel for the Internal Revenue Service in the same manner before the Tax Court as he has heretofore been represented in proceedings before such Court. The taxpayer shall continue to be represented in accordance with the rules of practice prescribed by the Court.

○⌐ § 301.7453 Statutory provisions; rules of practice, procedure, and evidence. [Sec. 7453, IRC]

○⌐ § 301.7454 Statutory provisions; burden of proof in fraud and transferee cases. [Sec. 7454, IRC]

○⌐ § 301.7454-1 (T.D. 6498, filed 10-24-60.) Burden of proof in fraud and transferee cases.

In any proceeding involving the issue whether the petitioner has been guilty of fraud with intent to evade tax, the burden of proof in respect of such issue shall be upon the Commissioner.

○⌐ § 301.7455 Statutory provisions; service of process. [Sec. 7455, IRC]

○⌐ § 301.7456 Statutory provisions; administration of oaths and procurement of testimony. [Sec. 7456, IRC]

○⌐ § 301.7456-1 (T.D. 6498, filed 10-24-60.) Administration of oaths and procurement of testimony; production of records of foreign corporations, foreign trusts or estates and nonresident alien individuals.

Upon motion and notice by the Commissioner and upon good cause shown therefor, the Tax Court or any division thereof shall order any foreign corporation, foreign trust or estate, or nonresident alien individual, who has filed a petition with a Tax Court, to produce, or, upon satisfactory proof to the Tax Court or any of its divisions that the petitioner is unable to produce, to make available to the Commissioner, and, in either case, to permit the inspection, copying, or photographing of, such books, records, documents, memoranda, correspondence and other papers, wherever situated, as the Tax Court or any of its divisions may deem relevant to the proceedings and which are in the possession, custody or control of the petitioner, or of any person directly or indirectly under his control or having control over him or subject to the same common control.

○⌐ § 301.7457 Statutory provisions; witness fees. [Sec. 7457, IRC]

○⌐ § 307.7457-1 (T.D. 6498, filed 10-24-60.) Witness fees.

Any witness summoned for the Commissioner or whose deposition is taken under section 7456 shall receive the same fees and mileage as witnesses in courts of the United States. Such fees and mileage and the expense of taking any such deposition shall be paid by the Commissioner out of any moneys appropriated for the collection of internal revenue taxes, and may be paid in advance.

○⌐ § 301.7458 Statutory provisions; hearings. [Sec. 7458, IRC]

○⌐ § 301.7458-1 (T.D. 6498, filed 10-24-60.) Hearings.

Notice and opportunity to be heard upon any proceeding instituted before the Tax Court shall be given to the taxpayer and the Commissioner. If an opportunity to be heard upon the proceeding is given before a division of the Tax Court, neither the taxpayer nor the Commissioner shall be entitled to notice and opportunity to be heard before the Tax Court upon review, except upon a specific order of the chief judge.

○⌐ § 301.7459 Statutory provisions; reports and decisions. [Sec. 7459, IRC]

○⌐ § 301.7460 Statutory provisions; provisions of special application to divisions. [Sec. 7460, IRC]

○⌐ § 301.7461 Statutory provisions; publicity of proceedings. [Sec. 7461, IRC]

○⌐ § 301.7461-1 (T.D. 6498, filed 10-24-60.) Publicity of proceedings.

All reports of the Tax Court and all evidence received by the Tax Court and its divisions, including a transcript of the stenographic report of the hearings, shall be public records open to the inspection of the public; except that after the decision of the Tax Court in any proceeding has become final the Tax Court may, upon motion of the taxpayer or the Commissioner, permit the withdrawal by the party entitled thereto of the originals of books, documents, and records, and of models, diagrams, and other exhibits, introduced in evidence before the Tax Court or any of its divisions;

or the Tax Court may, on its own action, make such other disposition thereof as it deems advisable.

○─▶ § 301.7462 Statutory provisions; publication of reports. [Sec. 7462, IRC]

○─▶ § 301.7463 Statutory provisions; provisions of special application to transferees. [Sec. 7463, IRC]

MISCELLANEOUS PROVISIONS

○─▶ § 301.7471 Statutory provisions; employees. [Sec. 7471, IRC]

○─▶ § 301.7472 Statutory provisions; expenditures. [Sec. 7472, IRC]

○─▶ § 301.7473 Statutory provisions; disposition of fees. [Sec. 7473, IRC]

○─▶ § 301.7474 Statutory provisions; fee for transcript of record. [Sec. 7474, IRC]

DECLARATORY JUDGMENTS RELATING TO QUALIFICATION OF CERTAIN RETIREMENT PLANS

○─▶ § 1.7476 Statutory provisions; declaratory judgments. [Sec. 7476, IRC]

○─▶ § 1.7476-1 (T.D. 7421, filed 5-20-76.) Interested parties.

(a) *In general*—(1) *Notice requirement.* Before the Internal Revenue Service can issue an advance determination as to the qualified status of certain retirement plans, the applicant must provide the Internal Revenue Service with satisfactory evidence that such applicant has notified the persons who qualify as interested parties, under regulations prescribed under section 7476 (b)(1) of the Code, of the application for such determination. See section 3001(a) of the Employee Retirement Income Security Act of 1974 (88 Stat. 995). For the rules for giving notice to interested parties, see § 1.7476-2 and paragraph (o) of § 601.201 of this chapter (Statement of Procedural Rules).

(2) *Declaratory judgments.* Section 7476 provides a procedure for obtaining a declaratory judgment by the Tax Court with respect to the initial or continuing qualification under subchapter D of chapter 1 of the Code of a retirement plan defined in section 7476(d), in the case of an actual controversy involving:

(i) A determination by the Internal Revenue Service with respect to the initial qualification or continuing qualification under such subchapter of such a plan, or

(ii) A failure by the Internal Revenue Service to make a determination with respect to—

(A) Such initial qualification of such a plan, or

(B) Such continuing qualification of such a plan, if the controversy arises from a plan amendment or plan termination.

Under section 7476(d) the term "retirement plan" means a pension, profit-sharing, or stock bonus plan described in section 401 (a), or a trust which is part of such a plan, an annuity plan described in section 403(a), or a bond purchase plan described in section 405(a). This procedure is available only to the employer, the plan administrator as defined in section 414(g), an employee who qualifies as an interested party as defined in this section, or the Pension Benefit Guaranty Corporation, where such person has an actual controversy involving a determination described in paragraph (a)(2)(i) of this section, or failure to make a determination described in paragraph (a) (2)(ii) of this section. In the case of an application for such a determination, this procedure is available only if such determination or failure to make such determination is with respect to an application described in paragraph (b)(7) of this section. In addition, in the case of such an application, if a petitioner was the applicant for the determination, the Tax Court may hold, under section 7476(b)(2), the filing of a pleading for a declaratory judgment to be premature unless the petitioner establishes to the satisfaction of the Tax Court that such petitioner has caused the interested parties to be notified in accordance with this section and § 1.7476-2.

(b) *Interested parties*—(1) *In general.* If paragraphs (b)(2), (3), (4), and (5) of this section do not apply, then, except as otherwise provided in paragraphs (b)(6) (i), (ii), and (iii) of this section, the following persons shall be interested parties with respect to an application for an advance determination as to the qualified status of a retirement plan:

(i) all present employees of the employer who are eligible to participate in the plan (as defined in paragraph (d)(2) of this section), and

(ii) all other present employees of the employer whose principal place of employment (as defined in paragraph (d)(3) of this section) is the same as the principal place of employment of any employee described in paragraph (b)(1)(i) of this section.

(2) *Certain plans covering a principal owner.* Notwithstanding paragraph (b)(1) of this section, where—

(i) A principal owner (within the meaning of paragraph (d)(2) of § 11.414(c)-3 of this chapter (Temporary Income Tax Regulations under the Employee Retirement Income Security Act of 1974)) of the employer or a common parent of the employer (where the employer is a member of a parent-subsidiary group of trades or businesses under common control under section 414(b) or (c)) is eligible to participate in the plan, and

(ii) the number of employees employed by such employer (including all employees who by reason of section 414(b) or (c) are treated as employees of such employer) is 100 or less,

then except as otherwise provided in paragraphs (b)(6)(i), (ii), and (iv) of this section, all present employees of the employer shall be interested parties with respect to an application for an advance determination as to the qualified status of the retirement plan.

Reg. § 1.7476-1 (b) (2)

(3) *Certain plan amendments.* In the case of an application for an advance determination as to whether a plan amendment affects the continuing qualification of a plan, if—

(i) there is outstanding a favorable determination letter for a plan year to which section 410 applies, and

(ii) the amendment does not alter the participation provisions of the plan, then paragraphs (b)(1) and (2) of this section shall not apply, and all present employees of the employer who are eligible to participate in the plan (as defined in paragraph (d)(2) of this section), shall be interested parties. For the purpose of this paraghaph (b)(3), if qualification of the plan is dependent upon benefits under the plan integrating with those benefits provided under the Social Security Act or a similar program, and if such integration results in excluding any employee or could possibly result in any participant's benefit being reduced to zero and the amendment alters contributions to or the amount of benefits payable under the plan, then the amendment shall be considered to alter the participation provisions of the plan.

(4) *Collectively bargained plans.* In the case of an application with respect to a plan described in section 413(a) (relating to collectively bargained plans), paragraphs (b)(1), (2) and (3) of this section shall not apply and all present employees covered by a collective-bargaining agreement pursuant to which the plan is maintained shall be interested parties.

(5) *Plan terminations.* In the case of an application for an advance determination with respect to whether a plan termination affects the continuing qualification of a retirement plan, paragraphs (b)(1), (2), (3) and (4) of this section shall not apply, and all present employees with accrued benefits under the plan, all former employees with vested benefits under the plan, and all beneficiaries of deceased former employees currently receiving benefits under the plan, shall be interested parties.

(6) *Exceptions.* (i) In the case of an application to which paragraph (b)(1) or (2) of this section applies, an employee who is not eligible to participate in the plan shall not be an interested party if such employee is excluded from consideration for purposes of section 410(b)(1) by reason of section 410(b)(2)(B) or (C).

(ii) In the case of an application to which paragraph (b)(1) or (2) of this section applies, an employee who is not eligible to participate in the plan shall not be an interested party if such plan meets the eligibility standards of section 410(b)(1)(A).

(iii) In the case of an application to which paragraph (b)(1) of this section applies, an employee who is not eligible to participate in the plan shall not be an interested party with respect to such plan if such employee is eligible to participate in any other plan of the employer with respect to which a favorable determination letter is outstanding (whether or not issued pursuant to an application to which this section applies), or in such a plan of another employer whose employees, by reason of section 414(b) or (c), are treated as employees of the employer making the application.

(iv) In the case of an application to which paragraph (b)(2) of this section applies, an employee who is not eligible to participate in the plan shall not be an interested party with respect to such plan if such employee is eligible to participate in a plan described in section 413(a) (relating to collectively bargained plans) maintained by the employer with respect to which a favorable determination letter is outstanding (whether or not issued pursuant to an application to which this section applies), or in such a plan of another employer whose employees, by reason of section 414(b) or (c), are treated as employees of the employer making the application.

(7) *Applicability.* Paragraph (b) of this section shall only apply in the case of an application made to the Internal Revenue Service requesting an advance determination that a retirement plan as defined in section 7476(d) and paragraph (a) of this section meets the requirements for qualification for a plan year or years to which section 410 applies to such plan. See paragraph (c)(4) and (5) of this section for special rules in respect of years to which section 410 applies.

(c) *Special rules.* For purposes of paragraph (b) of this section and § 1.7476–2—

(1) *Time of determination.* The status of an individual as an interested party and as a present employee or former employee shall be determined as of a date determined by the applicant, which date shall not be earlier than five business days before the first date on which the notice of the application is given to interested parties pursuant to § 1.7476–2 nor later than the date on which such notice is given.

(2) *Controlled groups, etc.* An individual shall be considered to be an employee of an employer if such employee is treated as that employer's employee under section 414(b) or (c).

(3) *Self-employed individuals.* A self-employed individual shall be considered an employee.

(4) *Years to which section 410 relates.* For purposes of paragraph (b)(7) of this section, section 410 shall be considered to apply to a plan year if an election has been made under section 1017(d) of the Employee Retirement Income Security Act of 1974 to have section 410 apply to such plan year, whether or not the election is conditioned upon the issuance by the Commissioner of a favorable determination letter.

(5) *Government, church plans, etc.* In the case of an organization described in section 410(c)(1), section 410 will be considered to apply to a plan year of such organization for any plan year to which section 410(c)(2) applies to such plan.

(d) *Definitions.* For the purposes of paragraph (b) of this section and § 1.7476–2—

(1) *Employer.* The term "employer" includes all employers who maintain the plan with respect to which an advance determination applies. A sole proprietor shall be considered such person's own employer and a partnership is considered to be the employer of each of the partners.

(2) *Eligible to participate.* For purposes of this section, an employee is eligi-

ble to participate in a plan if such employee—

(i) is a participant in the plan,

(ii) would be a participant in the plan if such employee met the minimum age and service requirements of the plan or

(iii) would be a participant in the plan upon making mandatory employee contributions.

In applying this paragraph (d)(2), plan provisions (with respect to which the determination regarding qualification is to be based) not in effect on the first date on which notice is given to interested parties shall be treated as though they were in effect on such date.

(3) *Place of employment.* A place of employment includes all worksites within a plant, installation, store, office, or similar facility. Any employee who has no principal place of employment shall be treated as though such employee's principal place of employment is that place to which such employee regularly reports to the employer.

§ 1.7476-2 (T.D. 7421, filed 5-20-76.) Notice to interested parties.

(a) *In general.* Any person applying to a district director for a determination described in paragraph (b)(7) of § 1.7476-1 shall cause notice of the application to be given to persons who qualify as interested parties under § 1.7476-1 with respect to the application, whether or not such application is received by the Internal Revenue Service before the date on which section 410 applies to the plan.

(b) *Nature of notice.* The notice required by this section shall be given in writing, shall contain the information and be given within the time prescribed in paragraph (o)(3) of § 601.201 of this chapter (Statement of Procedural Rules), and shall be given in the manner prescribed in paragraph (c) of this section.

(c) *Method of giving notice*—(1) *Present employee.* In the case of a present employee who is an interested party, notice shall be given in person, by mailing, by posting, or by printing it in a publication of the employer or an employee organization which is distributed in such a manner so as to be reasonably available to such employee. Notice given by posting shall be made by posting such notice (i) at those locations within the principal places of employment of the interested parties which are customarily used for employer notices to employees with regard to labor-management relations matters, or (ii) if the plan is maintained pursuant to one or more collective-bargaining agreements, at those locations described in (i) or at those locations customarily used by the employee representatives for posting notices with regard to labor-management relations matters (such as local union meeting places) in the geographical area or areas within which the interested parties are employed. Regardless of which method is used to notify an employee, if an interested party who is a present employee is in a unit of employees covered by a collective-bargaining agreement between employee representatives and one or more employers, notice shall also be given in person or by mail to the collective-bargaining representative of such interested party.

(2) *Former employee or beneficiary.* (i) Except as otherwise provided in paragraph (c)(2)(ii) of this section, in the case of a former employee or beneficiary who is an interested party, notice shall be given in person or by mail to the last known address of such former employee or beneficiary.

(ii) In cases in which compliance with the methods for notification prescribed in paragraph (c)(2)(i) of this section will present unusual financial or administrative burdens or, by reason of the peculiar circumstances of the case, cannot reasonably be expected to result in adequate and timely notice, applicants for advance determination letters may cause notice to be given to former employees or beneficiaries by methods other than those described in such paragraph (c)(2)(i) provided such methods are reasonably calculated to provide timely notice to such employees or beneficiaries who are interested parties, or to established representatives of such interested parties who may be reasonably expected to act in their interest and on their behalf. In such a case, the application for determination shall be accompanied by a full description of the method of notification used, as well as the particular financial or administrative burdens that would have occurred if notice had been given pursuant to the methods prescribed in paragraph (c)(2)(i) of this section, or the reasons why such prescribed methods would not have resulted in adequate or timely notice.

(d) *Effective date.* (1) The provisions of § 1.7476-1 and this section shall apply to applications referred to in paragraph (b) of § 1.7476-1 made on or after June 21, 1976. Sections 11.7476-1, and 11.7476-2 of this chapter (Temporary Income Tax Regulations under the Employee Retirement Income Security Act of 1974) as promulgated by Treasury Decision 7358 (May 30, 1975) shall apply to applications made before such date. However, an applicant may elect to have the provisions of § 1.7476-1 and this section apply with respect to an application made after May 20, 1976 and before June 21, 1976. Such election may be made by attaching to the application as originally submitted, a statement that the applicant has elected to have the provisions of § 1.7476-1 and this section apply.

(2) Notwithstanding paragraph (d)(1) of this section, if—

(i) the plan or plan amendment which is the subject of an application for advance determination, is adopted on or before May 30, 1976, and,

(ii) such application for advance determination is made before September 2, 1976, the applicant may elect to have the provisions of §§ 11.7476-1 and 11.7476-2 of this chapter (Temporary Income Tax Regulations under the Employee Retirement Income Security Act of 1974) apply with respect to such application made on or after June 21, 1976 and before September 2, 1976. Such an election may be made by attaching to the application as originally submitted, a statement that the applicant has elected to have the provisions of §§ 11.7476-1 and 11.7476-2 of this chapter (Temporary Income Tax Regulations under the Em-

Reg. § 1.7476-2(d)(2)

§ 1.7476-3 (T.D. 7421, filed 5-20-76.) Notice of determination.

(a) *In general.* Under section 7476(b)(5), if a district director sends to the employer, the plan administrator, an interested party with respect to the plan, or the Pension Benefit Guaranty Corporation (or in the case of certain individuals who qualify as interested parties under paragraph (b) of § 1.7476-1, to the person described under paragraph (c) of this section as the representative of such individuals) by certified or registered mail a notice of determination with respect to the qualification of a retirement plan described in section 7476(d), no proceeding for a declaratory judgment by the United States Tax Court with respect to the qualification of such plan may be initiated by such person unless the pleading initiating such proceeding is filed by such person with such Court before the ninety-first day after the day after such notice is mailed.

(b) *Address for notice of determination*—(1) *Applicant.* In the case of the applicant for a determination, a notice of determination referred to in section 7476(b)(5) shall be sufficient if mailed to such person at the address set forth on the application for the determination.

(2) *Interested party.* In the case of an interested party or parties who, pursuant to section 3001(b) of the Employee Retirement Income Security Act of 1974 (88 Stat. 995), submitted a comment to a district director with respect to the qualification of the plan, a notice of determination referred to in section 7476(b)(5) shall be sufficient if mailed to the address designated in the comment as the address to which correspondence should be sent.

(c) *Representative of interested parties.* (1) In the case of an interested party who, in accordance with section 3001(b) of the Employee Retirement Income Security Act of 1974 (88 Stat. 995), requests the Secretary of Labor to submit a comment to a district director on matters respecting the qualification of the plan, where pursuant to such request such Secretary does in fact submit such a comment, the Administrator of Pension and Welfare Benefit Programs, Department of Labor, shall be the representative of such interested party for purposes of receiving the notice referred to in section 7476(b)(5) with respect to those matters on which the Secretary of Labor commented.

(2) In the event a single comment with respect to the qualification of the plan is submitted to a district director by two or more interested parties, the representative designated in the comment for receipt of correspondence shall be the representative of all the interested parties submitting the comment for purposes of receiving the notice referred to in section 7476(b)(5) on behalf of all of them. Such designated representative must be either one of the interested parties who submitted the comment or a person described in paragraph (e)(6)(i), (ii) or (iii) of § 601.201 of this chapter (Statement of Procedural Rules). If one person is not designated in the comment as the representative for receipt of correspondence, a notice of determination mailed to any interested party who submitted the comment shall be notice to all the interested parties who submitted the comment for purposes of section 7476(b)(5).

§ 301.7476 Statutory provisions, declaratory judgments. [Sec. 7476, IRC]

§ 301.7476-1 (T.D. 7421, filed 5-20-76.) Declaratory judgments.

See the regulations under section 7476 contained in Part 1 of this chapter (Income Tax Regulations) for provisions relating to declaratory judgments, for provisions relating to the qualification of an employee as an "interested party", and for a requirement that the applicant for an advance determination by the Internal Revenue Service of the qualification of certain retirement plans give notice of such application to interested parties.

COURT REVIEW OF TAX COURT DECISIONS

§ 301.7481 Statutory provisions; date when Tax Court decision becomes final. [Sec. 7481, IRC]

§ 301.7481-1 (T.D. 6498, filed 10-24-60.) Date when Tax Court decision becomes final; decision modified or reversed.

(a) Upon mandate of Supreme Court. Under section 7481(3)(A) of the Code, if the Supreme Court directs that the decision of the Tax Court be modified or reversed, the decision of the Tax Court rendered in accordance with the mandate of the Supreme Court shall become final upon the expiration of 30 days from the time it was rendered, unless within such 30 days either the Commissioner or the taxpayer has instituted proceedings to have such decision corrected to accord with the mandate, in which event the decision of the Tax Court shall become final when so corrected.

(b) Upon mandate of the Court of Appeals. Under section 7481(3)(B) of the Code, if the decision of the Tax Court is modified or reversed by the U.S. Court of Appeals, and if—

(i) The time allowed for filing a petition for certiorari has expired and no such petition has been duly filed, or

(ii) The petition for certiorari has been denied, or

(iii) The decision of the U.S. Court of Appeals has been affirmed by the Supreme Court, then the decision of the Tax Court rendered in accordance with the mandate of the U.S. Court of Appeals shall become final on the expiration of 30 days from the time such decision of the Tax Court was rendered, unless within such 30 days either the Commissioner or the taxpayer has instituted proceedings to have such decision corrected so that it will accord with the mandate, in which event the decision of the Tax Court shall become final when so corrected.

§ 301.7482 Statutory provisions; courts of review. [Sec. 7482, IRC]

§ 301.7482-1 (T.D. 6498, filed 10-24-60.) Courts of review; venue.

Under section 7482(b)(2) of the Code, decisions of the Tax Court may be reviewed by any U.S. Court of Appeals which may be designated by the Commissioner and the taxpayer by stipulation in writing.

○— § 301.7483 Statutory provisions; petition for review. [Sec. 7483, IRC]

○— § 301.7483-1 (T.D. 6498, filed 10-24-60.) Petition for review.

The decision of the Tax Court may be reviewed by a U.S. Court of Appeals as provided in section 7482 of the Code if a petition for such review is filed by either the Commissioner or the taxpayer within 3 months after the decision is rendered. If, however, a petition for such review is so filed by one party to the proceedings, a petition for review of the decision of the Tax Court may be filed by any other party to the proceeding within 4 months after such decision is rendered.

○— § 301.7484 Statutory provisions; change of incumbent in office. [Sec. 7484, IRC]

○— § 301.7484-1 (T.D. 6498, filed 10-24-60.) Change of incumbent in office.

When the incumbent of the office of Commissioner changes, no substitution of the name of his successor shall be required in proceedings pending before any appellate court reviewing the action of the Tax Court.

○— § 301.7485 Statutory provisions; bond to stay assessment and collection. [Sec. 7485, IRC]

○— § 301.7486 Statutory provisions; refund, credit or abatement of amounts disallowed. [Sec. 7486, IRC]

○— § 301.7487 Statutory provisions; cross reference. [Sec. 7487, IRC]

Miscellaneous Provisions

○— § 301.7501 Statutory provisions; liability for taxes withheld or collected. [Sec. 7501, IRC]

○— § 301.7502 Statutory provisions; timely mailing treated as timely filing. [Sec. 7502, IRC]

Reg. § 301.7502

○— § 301.7502-1 (T.D. 6232, filed 5-2-57, as amended by T.D. 6292, filed 4-18-58 and T.D. 6444, filed 1-14-60; republished in T.D. 6498, filed, 10-24-60.) **Timely mailing treated as timely filing.**

(a) *General rule.* Section 7502 provides that, if the requirements of such section are met, a document shall be deemed to be filed on the date of the postmark stamped on the cover in which such document was mailed. Thus, if the cover containing such document bears a timely postmark, the document will be considered filed timely although it is received after the last date, or the last day of the period, prescribed for filing such document. Section 7502 does not apply to the payment of any tax. Section 7502 is applicable only to those documents which come within the definition of such term provided by paragraph (b) of this section and only if the document is mailed in accordance with paragraph (c) of this section and is delivered in accordance with paragraph (d) of this section.

(b) *Document defined.* (1) The term "document," as used in this section, means any claim, statement, or other document required to be filed within a prescribed period or on or before a prescribed date under authority of any provision of the internal revenue laws, except as provided in the following subdivisions of this subparagraph:

(i) The term does not include any return required under authority of any internal revenue law or any other document required under authority of chapter 61 of the Code. Thus, for example, such term does not include the income tax returns required by section 6012, the declarations of estimated income tax by individuals and corporations required by sections 6015 and 6016, and the estate tax and gift tax returns required by sections 6018 and 6019. Nor does the term include any return required under authority of subtitle E of the Code, relating to alcohol, tobacco, and certain other excise taxes.

(ii) The term does not include any document filed in any court other than the Tax Court, but the term does include any document filed with the Tax Court, including a petition for redetermination of a deficiency and a petition for review of a decision of the Tax Court.

(iii) The term does not include any document which is required to be filed with a bank or other depositary pursuant to section 6302(c).

(2) A return may contain, or have attached to it, a statement which sets forth an election under the internal revenue laws. In such a case, section 7502 is applicable to the statement if the conditions of such section are met, although it does not apply to the return. Moreover, in the case of certain taxes, a return may constitute a claim for refund or credit. In such a case, section 7502 is applicable to the claim for refund or credit if the conditions of such section are met, irrespective of whether the claim is also a return.

(c) *Mailing requirements.* (1) Section 7502 is not applicable unless the document is mailed in accordance with the following requirements:

(i) The document must be contained in an envelope or other appropriate wrapper, properly addressed to the agency, officer, or office with which the document is required to be filed.

(ii) The document must be deposited within the prescribed time in the mail in the United States with sufficient postage prepaid. For this purpose, a document is deposited in the mail in the United States when it is deposited with the domestic mail service of the U.S. Post Office. The domestic mail service of the U.S. Post Office, as defined by the postal regulations, includes mail transmitted within, among, and between the United States, its Territories and possessions, and Army-Air Force (APO) and Navy (FPO) post offices (see 39 CFR 2.1). Section 7502 does not apply to any document which is deposited with the mail service of any other country.

(iii) *(a)* If the postmark on the envelope or wrapper is made by the U.S. Post Office, such postmark must bear a date on or before the last date, or the last day of the period, prescribed for filing the document. If the postmark does not bear a date on or before the last date, or the last day of the period, prescribed for filing the document, the document will be considered not to be filed timely, regardless of when the document is deposited in the mail. Accordingly, the sender who relies upon the applicability of section 7502 assumes the risk that the postmark will bear a date on or before the last date, or the last day of the period, prescribed for filing the document, but see subparagraph (2) of this paragraph with respect to the use of registered mail or certified mail to avoid this risk. If the postmark on the envelope or wrapper is not legible, the person who is required to file the document has the burden of proving the time when the postmark was made. Furthermore, in case the cover containing a document bearing a timely postmark made by the U.S. Post Office is received after the time when a document postmarked and mailed at such time would ordinarily be received, the sender may be required to prove that it was timely mailed.

(b) If the postmark on the envelope or wrapper is made other than by the U.S. Post Office, *(1)* the postmark so made must bear a date on or before the last date, or the last day of the period, prescribed for filing the document, and *(2)* the document must be received by the agency, officer, or office with which it is required to be filed not later than the time when a document contained in an envelope or other appropriate wrapper which is properly addressed and mailed and sent by the same class of mail would ordinarily be received if it were postmarked at the same point of origin by the U.S. Post Office on the last date, or the last day of the period, prescribed for filing the document. However, in case the document is received after the time when a document so mailed and so postmarked by the U.S. Post Office would ordinarily be received, such document will be treated as having been received at the time when a document so mailed and so postmarked would ordinarily be received, if the person who is required to file the document establishes *(i)* that it was actually deposited

Reg. § 301.7502-1(c)(1)

24,416 (I.R.C.) Reg. § 301.7502-1(c)(1) 4-8-74

in the mail before the last collection of the mail from the place of deposit which was postmarked (except for the metered mail) by the U.S. Post Office on or before the last date, or the last day of the period, prescribed for filing the document, *(ii)* that the delay in receiving the document was due to a delay in the transmission of the mail, and *(iii)* the cause of such delay. If the envelope has a postmark made by the U.S. Post Office in addition to the postmark not so made, the postmark which was not made by the U.S. Post Office shall be disregarded, and whether the envelope was mailed in accordance with this subdivision shall be determined solely by applying the rule of (a) of this subdivision.

(2) If the document is sent by U.S. registered mail, the date of registration of the document shall be treated as the postmark date. If the document is sent by U.S. certified mail and the sender's receipt is postmarked by the postal employee to whom such document is presented, the date of the U.S. postmark on such receipt shall be treated as the postmark date of the document. Accordingly, the risk that the document will not be postmarked on the day that it is deposited in the mail may be overcome by the use of registered mail or certified mail.

(3) As used in this section, the term "the last date, or the last day of the period, prescribed for filing the document" includes any extension of time granted for such filing. When the last date, or the last day of the period, prescribed for filing the document falls on a Saturday, Sunday, or legal holiday, section 7503 is also applicable, so that, in applying the rules of this paragraph, the next succeeding day which is not a Saturday, Sunday, or legal holiday shall be treated as the last date, or the last day of the period, prescribed for filing the document.

(d) *Delivery.* (1) Section 7502 is not applicable unless the document is delivered by U.S. mail to the agency, officer, or office with which it is required to be filed. However, if the document is sent by registered mail or certified mail, proof that the document was properly registered or that a postmarked certified mail sender's receipt was properly issued therefor, and that the envelope or wrapper was properly addressed to such agency, officer, or office shall constitute prima facie evidence that the document was delivered to such agency, officer, or office.

(2) Section 7502 is applicable only when the document is delivered after the last date, or the last day of the period, prescribed for filing the document. However, section 7502 is also applicable when a claim for credit or refund is delivered after the last day of the period specified in section 322(b)(2) of the Internal Revenue Code of 1939 or in any other corresponding provision of law relating to the limit on the amount of credit or refund that is allowable. For example, taxpayer A was required to file his income tax return for 1953 on or before March 15, 1954, but he secured an extension until June 15, 1954 to file such return. His return was filed on June 15, 1954, but no tax was paid at such time because the tax liability disclosed by the return had been completely satisfied by the income tax that had been withheld on his wages and by the payments of estimated tax. On March 14, 1957, A mailed in accordance with the requirements of this section a claim for refund of a portion of his 1953 tax. The envelope containing the claim was postmarked on such day, but it was not delivered to the district director's office until March 18, 1957. Under section 322(b)(1) of the Internal Revenue Code of 1939, A's claim for refund is timely if filed within three years from June 15, 1954. However, as a result of the limitation of section 322(b)(2) of the 1939 Code, if his claim is not filed within three years after March 15, 1954, the date on which he is deemed under section 322(e) of the 1939 Code to have paid his 1953 tax, he is not entitled to any refund. Thus, since A's claim for refund was mailed in accordance with the requirements of this section and was delivered after the last day of the period specified in such section 322(b)(2), section 7502 is applicable, and the claim is deemed to have been filed on March 14, 1957.

(e) *Applicability*—(1) *General rule.* Except as provided in subparagraph (2) of this paragraph, section 7502 and this section are applicable with respect to any document which is mailed and delivered in accordance with the requirements of this section and which is mailed in an envelope having a postmark bearing a date after August 16, 1954, irrespective of whether the postmark is made by the U.S. Post Office, and irrespective of whether the tax to which the document pertains is imposed by the Code or a prior internal revenue law.

(2) *Exception.* The provisions of section 7502 and this section which specifically apply to certified mail are applicable only if the mailing occurs on or after January 15, 1960.

○― § 301.7503 Statutory provisions; time for performance of acts where last day falls on Saturday, Sunday, or legal holiday. [Sec. 7503, IRC]

○― § 301.7503-1 (T.D. 6232, filed 5-2-57; republished in T.D. 6498, filed 10-24-60; amended by T.D. 6585, filed 12-27-61 and T.D. 7309, filed 3-27-74.) **Time for performance of acts where last day falls on Saturday, Sunday, or legal holiday.**

(a) *In general.* Section 7503 provides that when the last day prescribed under authority of any internal revenue law for the performance of any act falls on a Saturday, Sunday, or legal holiday, such act shall be considered performed timely if performed on the next succeeding day which is not a Saturday, Sunday, or legal holiday. For this purpose, any authorized extension of time shall be included in determining the last day for performance of any act. Section 7503 is applicable only in case an act is required under authority of any internal revenue law to be performed on or before a prescribed date or within a prescribed period. For example, if the 2-year period allowed by section 6532(a)(1) to bring a suit for refund of any internal revenue tax expires on Thursday, November 22, 1956 (Thanksgiving Day), the suit will be timely if filed on Friday, November 23, 1956, in the Court of Claims, or in a district court. Section 7503 applies to acts to be performed by the taxpayer (such as, the filing of any return of, and the payment of, any income, estate, or gift tax; the filing of a petition with the Tax Court for redetermination of a deficiency, or for review of a decision rendered by such Court; the filing of a claim for credit or refund of any tax) and acts to be performed by the Commissioner, a district director or the director of a regional service center (such as, the giving of any notice with respect to, or making any demand for the payment of, any tax; the assessment or collection of any tax).

(b) *Legal holidays.* (1) For the purpose of section 7503, the term "legal holiday" includes the legal holidays in the District of Columbia. Such legal holidays found in D. C. Code Ann. § 28-2701 (1967) and 5 U.S.C. 6103(a), as enacted and made effective by the Act of June 28, 1968 (82 Stat. 250), are—

(i) January 1, New Year's Day,
(ii) January 20, when such day is Inauguration Day,
(iii) Third Monday in February, Washington's Birthday,
(iv) Last Monday in May, Memorial Day,
(v) July 4, Independence Day,
(vi) First Monday in September, Labor Day,
(vii) Second Monday in October, Columbus Day,
(viii) Fourth Monday in October, Veterans' Day,
(ix) Fourth Thursday in November, Thanksgiving Day,
(x) December 25, Christmas Day.

When a legal holiday in the District of Columbia falls on a Sunday, the next day is a legal holiday in the District of Columbia (see D. C. Code Ann. § 28-2701 (1967)). For the purpose of section 7503, when a legal holiday in the District of Columbia (other than Inauguration Day) falls on a Saturday it shall be treated as falling on the preceding Friday. For calendar years prior to 1971, Washington's Birthday will be treated as falling on February 22, Memorial Day on May 30, and Veterans' Day on November 11. For calendar years 1971, 1972, 1973, and 1974, the taxpayer may, at his option (except with respect to the performance of any act relating to the jurisdiction of a court), treat Washington's Birthday as falling on either February 22 or the third Monday in February. For calendar years 1971, 1972, and 1973, the taxpayer may, at his option (except with respect to the performance of any act relating to the jurisdiction of a court), treat Memorial Day as falling on either May 30 or the last Monday in May, and Veterans' Day as falling on either November 11 or the fourth Monday in October. Columbus Day is not a legal holiday in the District of Columbia in any calendar year prior to 1971.

(2) In the case of any return, statement, or other document required to be filed, or any other act required under the authority of the internal revenue laws to be performed, at any office of the Internal Revenue Service, or any other office or agency of the United States, located outside the District of Columbia, but within an internal revenue district, the term "legal holiday" includes, in addition to the legal holidays enumerated in subparagraph (1) of this paragraph, any State-wide legal holiday of the State where the act is required to be performed. If the act is performed in accordance with law at an office of the Internal Revenue Service or any other office or agency of the United States located in a Territory or possession of the United States, the term "legal holiday" includes, in addition to the legal holidays described in subparagraph (1) of this paragraph, any legal holiday which is recognized throughout the Territory or possession in which the office is located.

(c) *Applicability.* Section 7503 and this section are applicable in any case when the last day prescribed under authority of any internal revenue law for the performance of any act falls on a Saturday, Sunday, or legal holiday, which occurs after August 16, 1954, irrespective of whether the tax in connection with which the act is required to be performed is imposed by this title or a prior internal revenue law.

o— § 301.7504 **Statutory provisions; fractional parts of a dollar.** [Sec. 7504, IRC]

o— § 301.7505 **Statutory provisions; sale of personal property purchased by the United States.** [Sec. 7505, IRC]

o— § 301.7505-1 (T.D. 6232, filed 5-2-57; republished in T.D. 6498, filed 10-24-60; and amended by T.D. 7305, filed 3-14-74.) **Sale of personal property acquired by the United States.**

(a) *Sale*—(1) *In general.* Any personal property (except bonds, notes, checks, and other securities) acquired by the United States in payment of or as security for debts arising under the internal revenue laws may be sold by the district director who acquired such property for the United States. United States savings bonds shall not be sold by the district director but shall be transferred to the appropriate office of the Treasury Department for redemption. Other bonds, notes, checks, and other securities shall be disposed of in accordance with instructions issued by the Commissioner.

(2) *Time, place, manner, and terms of sale.* The time, place, manner, and terms of sale of personal property acquired for the United States shall be as follows:

(i) Time, notice, and place of sale. The property may be sold at any time after it has been acquired by the United States. A public notice of sale shall be posted at the post office nearest the place of sale and in at least two other public places. The notice shall specify the property to be sold and the time, place, manner, and conditions of sale. In addition, the district director may use such other methods of advertising as he believes will result in obtaining the highest price for the property. The place of sale shall be within the internal revenue district where the property was originally acquired by the United States. However, if the district director believes that a substantially higher price may be obtained, the sale may be held outside his district.

(ii) *Rejection of bids and adjournment of sale.* The internal revenue officer conducting the sale reserves the right to reject any and all bids and withdraw the property from the sale. When it appears to the internal revenue officer conducting the sale that an adjournment of the sale will best serve the interest of the United States, he may order the sale adjourned from time to time. If the sale is adjourned for more than 30 days in the aggregate, public notice of

Reg. § 301.7505-1(a)(2)

the sale must again be given in accordance with subdivision (i) of this subparagraph.

(iii) *Liquidated damages.* The notice shall state whether, in the case of default in payment of the bid price, any amount deposited with the United States will be retained as liquidated damages. In case liquidated damages are provided, the amount thereof shall not exceed $200.

(3) *Agreement to bid.* The district director may, before giving notice of sale, solicit offers from prospective bidders and enter into agreements with such persons that they will bid at least a specified amount in case the property is offered for sale. In such cases, the district director may also require such persons to make deposits to secure the performance of their agreements. Any such deposit, but not more than $200, shall be retained as liquidated damages in case such person fails to bid the specified amount and the property is not sold for as much as the amount specified in such agreement.

(4) *Terms of payment.* The property shall be offered for sale upon whichever of the following terms is fixed by the district director in the public notice of sale—

(i) Payment in full upon acceptance of the highest bid, without regard to the amount of such bid, or

(ii) If the aggregate price of all property purchased by a successful bidder at the sale is more than $200, an initial payment of $200 or 20 percent of the purchase price, whichever is the greater, and payment of the balance (including all costs incurred for the protection or preservation of the property subsequent to the sale and prior to final payment) within a specified period, not to exceed one month from the date of the sale.

(5) *Method of sale.* The property may be sold either—

(i) At public auction, at which open competitive bids shall be received, or

(ii) At public sale under sealed bids.

(6) *Sales under sealed bids.* The following rules, in addition to the other rules provided in this paragraph, shall be applicable to public sales under sealed bids:

(i) *Invitation to bidders.* Bids shall be solicited through a public notice of sale.

(ii) *Form for use by bidders.* A bid shall be submitted on a form which will be furnished by the district director upon request. The form shall be completed in accordance with the instructions thereon.

(iii) *Remittance with bid.* If the total bid is $200 or less, the full amount of the bid shall be submitted therewith. If the total bid is more than $200, 20 percent of such bid or $200, whichever is greater, shall be submitted therewith. Such remittance shall be by a certified, cashier's, or treasurer's check drawn on any bank or trust company incorporated under the laws of the United States or under the laws of any State, Territory, or possession of the United States, or by a U.S. postal, bank, express, or telegraph money order.

(iv) *Time for receiving and opening bids.* Each bid shall be submitted in a securely sealed envelope. The bidder shall indicate in the upper left hand corner of the envelope his name and address and the time and place of sale as announced in the public notice of sale. A bid will not be considered unless it is received by the internal revenue officer conducting the sale prior to the opening of the bids. The bids will be opened at the time and place stated in the notice of sale, or at the time fixed in the announcement of the adjournment of the sale.

(v) *Consideration of bids.* The internal revenue officer conducting the sale shall have the right to waive any technical defects in a bid. After the opening, examination, and consideration of all bids, the internal revenue officer conducting the sale shall announce the amount of the highest bid or bids and the name of the successful bidder or bidders, unless in the opinion of the officer a higher price can be obtained for the property than has been bid. In the event the highest bids are equal in amount (and unless in the opinion of the internal revenue officer conducting the sale a higher price can be obtained for the property than has been bid), the officer shall determine the successful bidder by drawing lots. Any remittance submitted in connection with an unsuccessful bid shall be returned to the bidder at the conclusion of the sale.

(vi) *Withdrawal of bids.* A bid may be withdrawn on written or telegraphic request received from the bidder prior to the time fixed for opening the bids. A technical defect in a bid confers no right on the bidder for the withdrawal of his bid after it has been opened.

(7) *Payment of bid price.* All payments for property sold pursuant to this section shall be made by cash or by a certified, cashier's or treasurer's check drawn on any bank or trust company incorporated under the laws of the United States or under the laws of any State, Territory, or possession of the United States, or by a U.S. postal, bank, express, or telegraph money order. If payment in full is required upon acceptance of the highest bid, the payment shall be made at such time. If payment in full is not made at such time, the internal revenue officer conducting the sale may forthwith proceed again to sell the property in the manner provided in subparagraph (5) of this paragraph. If deferred payment is permitted, the initial payment shall be made upon acceptance of the bid, and the balance shall be paid on or before the date fixed for payment thereof. Any remittance submitted with a successful sealed bid shall be applied toward the purchase price.

(8) *Delivery and removal of personal property.* The risk of loss is on the purchaser of the property upon acceptance of his bid. Possession of any property shall not be delivered to the purchaser until the purchase price has been paid in full. If payment of part of the purchase price for the property is deferred, the United States will retain possession of such property as security for the payment of the balance of the purchase price and, as agent for the purchaser, will cause the property to be cared for until the purchase price has been paid in full or the sale is declared null and void for failure to make full payment of the purchase price. In such case, all charges and expenses incurred in caring for the

property after acceptance of the bid shall be borne by the purchaser.

(9) *Certificate of sale.* The internal revenue officer conducting the sale shall issue a certificate of sale to the purchaser upon payment in full of the purchase price.

(b) *Accounting.* In case of the resale of such property, the proceeds of the sale shall be paid into the Treasury as internal revenue collections, and there shall be rendered by the district director a distinct account of all charges incurred in such sale. For additional accounting rules, see section 7809 and the instructions thereunder.

○━ § 301.7506 Statutory provisions; administration of real estate acquired by the United States. [Sec. 7506, IRC]

○━ § 301.7506-1 (T.D. 6232, filed 5-2-57; republished in T.D. 6498, filed 10-24-60; amended by T.D. 7027, filed 2-26-70; and T.D. 7305, filed 3-14-74.) **Administration of real estate acquired by the United States.**

(a) *Persons charged with.* The district director for the internal revenue district in which the property is situated shall have charge of all real estate which is or shall become the property of the United States by judgment of forfeiture under the internal revenue laws, or which has been or shall be assigned, set off, or conveyed by purchase or otherwise to the United States in payment of debts or penalties arising under the laws relating to internal revenue, or which has been or shall be vested in the United States by mortgage, or other security for payment of such debts, or which has been redeemed by the United States, or which has been or shall be acquired by the United States in payment of or as security for debts arising under the internal revenue laws, and of all trusts created for the use of the United States in payment of such debts due the United States.

(b) *Sale.* The district director for the internal revenue district in which the property is situated may sell any real estate owned or held by the United States as aforesaid, subject to the following rules—

(1) *Property purchased at sale under levy.* If the property was acquired as a result of being declared purchased for the United States at a sale under section 6335, relating to sale of seized property, the property shall not be sold until after the expiration of 120 days (or 1 year in the case of such sale under levy before November 3, 1966) after such sale under levy.

(2) *Notice of sale.* A notice of sale shall be published in some newspaper published or generally circulated within the county where the property is situated, or a notice shall be posted at the post office nearest the place where the property is situated and in at least two other public places. The notice shall specify the property to be sold and the time, place, manner, and conditions of sale. In addition, the district director may use other methods of advertising and of giving notice of sale if he believes such methods will enhance the possibility of obtaining a higher price for the property.

(3) *Time and place of sale.* The time of the sale shall be not less than 20 days from the date of giving public notice of sale under subparagraph (2) of this paragraph. The place of sale shall be within the county where the property is situated. However, if the district director believes a substantially better price may be obtained, he may hold the sale outside such county.

(4) *Rejection of bids and adjournment of sale.* The internal revenue officer conducting the sale reserves the right to reject any and all bids and withdraw the property from the sale. When it appears to the internal revenue officer conducting the sale that an adjournment of the sale will best serve the interest of the United States, he may order the sale adjourned from time to time. If the sale is adjourned for more than 30 days in the aggregate, public notice of the sale must be given again in accordance with subparagraph (2) of this paragraph.

(5) *Liquidated damages.* The notice shall state whether, in the case of default in payment of the bid price, any amount deposited with the United States will be retained as liquidated damages. In case liquidated damages are provided, the amount thereof shall not exceed $200.

(6) *Agreement to bid.* The district director may, before giving notice of sale, solicit offers from prospective bidders and enter into agreements with such persons that they will bid at least a specified amount in case the property is offered for sale. In such cases, the district director may also require such persons to make deposits to secure the performance of their agreements. Any such deposit, but not more than $200, shall be retained as liquidated damages in case such person fails to bid the specified amount and the property is not sold for as much as the amount specified in such agreement.

(7) *Terms.* The property shall be offered for sale upon whichever of the following terms is fixed by the district director in the public notice of sale:

(i) Payment in full upon acceptance of the highest bid, or

(ii) If the price of the property purchased by a successful bidder at the sale is more than $200, an initial payment of $200 or 20 percent of the purchase price, whichever is the greater, and payment of the balance within a specified period, not to exceed one month from the date of the sale.

(8) *Method of sale.* The property may be sold either—

(i) At public auction, at which open competitive bids shall be received, or

(ii) At public sale under sealed bids.

(9) *Sales under sealed bids.* The following rules, in addition to the other rules provided in this paragraph, shall be applicable at public sales under sealed bids:

(i) *Invitation to bidders.* Bids shall be solicited through a public notice of sale.

(ii) *Form for use by bidders.* A bid shall be submitted on a form which will be furnished by the district director upon request. The form shall be completed in accordance with the instructions thereon.

(iii) *Remittance with bid.* If the total bid is $200 or less, the full amount of the

Reg. § 301.7506-1 (b) (9)

24,420 (I.R.C.)   Reg. § 301.7506-1(b)(9)   4-8-74

bid shall be submitted therewith. If the total bid is more than $200, 20 percent of such bid or $200, whichever is greater, shall be submitted therewith. Such remittance shall be by a certified, cashier's, or treasurer's check drawn on any bank or trust company incorporated under the laws of the United States or under the laws of any State, Territory, or possession of the United States, or by a U.S. postal, bank, express, or telegraph money order.

(iv) *Time for receiving and opening bids.* Each bid shall be submitted in a securely sealed envelope. The bidder shall indicate in the upper left hand corner of the envelope his name and address and the time and place of sale as announced in the public notice of sale. A bid shall not be considered unless it is received by the internal revenue officer conducting the sale prior to the opening of the bids. The bids will be opened at the time and place stated in the notice of sale, or at the time fixed in the announcement of the adjournment of the sale.

(v) *Consideration of bids.* The internal revenue officer conducting the sale shall have the right to waive any technical defects in a bid. After the opening, examination, and consideration of all bids, the internal revenue officer conducting the sale shall announce the amount of the highest bid or bids and the name of the successful bidder or bidders, unless in the opinion of the officer a higher price can be obtained for the property than has been bid. In the event the highest bids are equal in amount (and unless in the opinion of the internal revenue officer conducting the sale a higher price can be obtained for the property than has been bid), the officer shall determine the successful bidder by drawing lots. Any remittance submitted in connection with an unsuccessful bid shall be returned to the bidder at the conclusion of the sale.

(vi) *Withdrawal of bids.* A bid may be withdrawn on written or telegraphic request received from the bidder prior to the time fixed for opening the bids. A technical defect in a bid confers no right on the bidder for the withdrawal of his bid after it has been opened.

(10) *Payment of bid price.* All payments for property sold pursuant to this section shall be made by cash or by a certified, cashier's, or treasurer's check drawn on any bank or trust company incorporated under the laws of the United States or under the laws of any State, Territory, or possession of the United States, or by a U.S. postal, bank, express, or telegraph money order. If payment in full is required upon acceptance of the highest bid, the payment shall be made at such time. If payment in full is not made at such time, the internal revenue officer conducting the sale may forthwith proceed again to sell the property in the manner provided in subparagraph (8) of this paragraph. If deferred payment is permitted, the initial payment shall be made upon acceptance of the bid, and the balance shall be paid on or before the date fixed for payment thereof. Any remittance submitted with a successful sealed bid shall be applied toward the purchase price.

(11) *Deed.* Upon payment in full of the purchase price, the district director shall execute a quitclaim deed to the purchaser.

(c) *Lease.* Until real estate is sold, the district director for the internal revenue district in which the property is situated may, in accordance with instructions issued by the Commissioner, lease such property.

(d) *Release to debtor.* In cases where real estate has or may become the property of the United States by conveyance or otherwise, in payment of or as security for a debt arising under the laws relating to internal revenue, and such debt shall have been paid, together with the interest thereon (at the rate of one percent per month), to the United States within two years from the date of the acquisition of such real estate, the district director for the internal revenue district in which the property is located may release by deed or otherwise convey such real estate to the debtor from whom it was taken, or to his heirs or other legal representatives. If property is declared purchased by the United States under section 6335, then, for the purpose of this paragraph the date of such declaration shall be deemed to be the date of acquisition of such real estate.

(e) *Accounting.* The district director for the internal revenue district in which the property is situated shall, in accordance with section 7809 and the instructions thereunder, account for the proceeds of all sales or leases of the property and all expenses connected with the maintenance, sale, or lease of the property.

(f) *Authority of Commissioner.* Notwithstanding the other paragraphs of this section, the Commissioner may, when he deems it advisable, take charge of and assume responsibility for any real estate to which this section is applicable. In such case, the Commissioner will notify in writing the district director for the internal revenue district in which the property is situated. In any case where a single parcel of real estate is situated in more than one internal revenue district, the Commissioner may designate in writing a district director who shall have charge of and be responsible for the entire property.

○→ § 301.7507 **Statutory provisions; exemption of insolvent banks from tax.** [Sec. 7507, IRC]

§ 301.7507-1 (T.D. 6232, filed 5-2-57; republished in T.D. 6498, filed 10-24-60.) **Banks and trust companies covered.**

(a) Section 7507 applies to any national bank, or bank or trust company organized under State law, a substantial portion of the business of which consists of receiving deposits and making loans and discounts, and which has—

(1) Ceased to do business by reason of insolvency or bankruptcy, or

(2) Been released or discharged from its liability to its depositors for any part of their deposit claims, and the depositors have accepted in lieu thereof a lien upon its subsequent earnings or claims against its assets either (i) segregated and held by it for benefit of the depositors or (ii) transferred to an individual or corporate trustee or agent who liquidates, holds or operates the assets for the benefit of the depositors.

(b) As used in this section and §§ 301.7507-2 to 301.7507-11, inclusive:

(1) The term "bank," unless otherwise indicated by the context, means any national bank, or bank or trust company organized under State law, within the scope of section 7507.

(2) The terms "statute of limitations" and "limitations" mean all applicable provisions of law (including section 7507) which impose, change, or affect the limitations, conditions, or requirements relative to the allowance of refunds and abatements or the assessment or collection of tax, as the case may be.

(3) The term "segregated assets" includes transferred or trusteed assets, or assets set aside or earmarked, to all or a portion of which, or the proceeds of which, the depositors are absolutely or conditionally entitled.

§ 301.7507-2 (T.D. 6232, filed 5-2-57; republished in T.D. 6498, filed 10-24-60.) **Scope of section generally.**

(a) *Purpose.* Section 7507 is intended to assist depositors of a bank which had ceased to do business by reason of insolvency to recover their deposits, by prohibiting collection of taxes of the bank which would diminish the assets necessary for payment of its depositors and also assist depositors of banks which are in financial difficulties but which, in certain conditions, continue in business.

(b) *Requisites of application.* In order that section 7507 shall operate in a case where the bank continues business it is necessary that the depositors shall agree to accept, in lieu of all or a part of their deposit claims as such, claims against segregated assets, or a lien upon subsequent earnings of the bank, or both. When such an agreement exists, no tax diminishing such assets or earnings, or both, otherwise available and necessary for payment of depositors, may be collected therefrom. If, under such an agreement, the depositors have the right also to look to the unsegregated assets of the bank for recovery, in whole or in part, the unsegregated assets are likewise, until they exceed the amount of the depositors' claims chargeable thereto, unavailable for tax collection. Any tax of such a bank, or part of any tax, which is once uncollectible under section 7507, cannot thereafter be collected except from any residue of segregated assets remaining after claims of depositors against such assets have been paid.

(c) *Interest.* For the purposes of section 7507, depositors' claims include bona fide interest, either on the deposits as such, or on the claims accepted in lieu of deposits as such.

(d) *Limitations on immunity.* Section 7507 is not primarily intended for the relief of banks as such. It does not prevent tax collection, from assets not necessary, or not available, for payment of depositors, from a bank within section 7507(a), at any time within the statute of limitations. In other words, the immunity of such a bank is not complete, but ceases whenever, within the statutory period for collection, it becomes possible to make collection without diminishing assets necessary for payment of depositors. In the case of a bank within section 7507(b), any immunity to which the bank is entitled is absolute except as to segregated assets. Any tax coming within such immunity may never be collected. With respect to segregated assets, such a bank is subject to the same rule as a bank within section 7507(a), that is to say, after claims of depositors against segregated assets have been paid, any surplus is subject, within the statute of limitations, to collection of any tax, due at any time, the collection of which was suspended by the section. The section is not for the relief of creditors other than depositors, although it may incidentally operate for their benefit. See § 301.7507-4 and paragraph (b) of § 301.7507-9.

§ 301.7507-3 (T.D. 6232, filed 5-2-57; republished in T.D. 6498, filed 10-24-60.) **Segregated or transferred assets.**

(a) *In general.* In a case involving segregated or transferred assets, it is not necessary, for application of section 7507, that the assets shall technically constitute a trust fund. It is sufficient that segregated assets be definitely separated from other assets of the bank and that transferred assets be definitely separated both from other assets of the bank and from other assets held or owned by the trustee or agent to whom assets of the bank have been transferred; that the bank be wholly or partially released from liability for repayment of deposits as such; and that the depositors have claims against the separated assets. Any excess of segregated assets over the amount necessary for payment of such depositors will be available for tax collection after full payment of depositors' claims under the agreement against such assets. But see paragraph (a) of § 301.7507-9.

(b) *Corporate transferees.* Where the segregated assets are transferred to a separate corporate trustee or corporate agent, the assets and earnings therefrom are within the protection of the section, until full payment of depositors' claims against such assets and earnings, no matter by

Reg. § 301.7507-3(b)

24,422 (I.R.C.) Reg. § 301.7507-3(b)

whom the stock of such corporation is held, and no matter whether the assets be liquidated or operated or held for benefit of the depositors.

§ 301.7507-4 (T.D. 6232, filed 5-2-57; republished in T.D. 6498, filed 10-24-60.) **Unsegregated assets.**

(a) *Depositors' claims against assets.* (1) Claims of depositors, to the extent that they are to be satisfied out of segregated assets, will not be considered in determining the availability of unsegregated assets for tax collection. If depositors have agreed to accept payment out of segregated assets only, collection of tax from unsegregated assets will not diminish the assets available and necessary for payment of the depositors' claims. Thus, it may be possible to collect taxes from the unsegregated assets of a bank although the segregated assets are immune under the section.

(2) If the unsegregated assets of the bank are subject to any portion of the depositors' claims, such unsegregated assets will be within the immunity of the section only to the extent necessary to satisfy the claims to which such assets are subject. Taxes will still be collectible from the unsegregated assets to the extent of the amount by which the total value of such assets exceeds the liability to depositors to be satisfied therefrom. Therefore, if, for example, in the case of a bank having a tax liability, not previously immune under the section, of $50,000, the deposit claims against the bank are in the amount of $75,000, and the assets available for satisfaction of deposit claims amount to $100,000, the $50,000 tax is collectible to the extent of the $25,000 excess of assets over deposit claims. Collection is not to be postponed until the full amount of the tax is collectible.

(b) *Depositors' claims against earnings.* Even though under a bona fide agreement a bank has been released from depositors' claims as to unsegregated assets, if all or a portion of its earnings are subject to depositors' claims, all assets the earnings from which, in whole or part, are charged with the payment of depositors' claims, will be immune from tax collection. But see paragraph (a) of § 301.7507-5.

§ 301.7507-5 (T.D. 6232, filed 5-2-57; republished in T.D. 6498, filed 10-24-60.) **Earnings.**

(a) *Availability for tax collection.* Earnings of a bank within section 7507(b), whether from segregated or unsegregated assets, which are necessary for, applicable to, and actually used for, payment of depositors' claims under an agreement, are within the immunity of the section. If only a portion or percentage of income from segregated or unsegregated assets is available and necessary for payment of depositors' claims, the remaining income is available for tax collection. Earnings of the bank's first fiscal year ending after the making of the agreement not applicable to payment of depositors will be assumed to be applicable for collection of any tax due prior or subsequent to execution of the agreement. Earnings of subsequent fiscal periods from unsegregated assets not applicable to depositors' claims will be assumed to be applicable to payment of taxes as to which immunity under the section has not previously attached. Earnings from segregated assets are available for collection of tax, whether previously uncollectible under the section or not, after depositors' claims against such assets have been paid in full. See paragraph (a) of § 301.7507-3 and paragraph (a) of § 301.7507-9.

(b) *Tax computation.* The fact that earnings of a given year may be wholly or partly unavailable under section 7507 for collection of taxes does not exempt the income for that year, or any part thereof, from tax liability. The section affects collectibility only, and is not concerned with taxability. Accordingly, the taxpayer's income tax return shall correctly compute the tax liability, even though in the opinion of the taxpayer it is immune from tax collection under the section. The tax shall be determined with respect to the entire gross income and not merely with respect to the portion of the earnings out of which tax may be collected. As to establishment of immunity from tax collection see § 301.7507-7.

Example (1). An agreement, executed in the year 1954 between a bank and its depositors, provides (i) that certain assets are to be segregated for the benefit of the depositors, who have waived (as claims against unsegregated assets of the bank) a percentage of their deposits; (ii) that 40 percent of the bank's net earnings, for years beginning with 1954, from unsegregated assets, shall be paid to the depositors until the portion of their claims waived with respect to unsegregated assets of the bank has been paid; and (iii) that the unsegregated assets shall not be subject to depositors' claims. The net income of the bank for the calendar year 1954 is $10,000, $4,000 produced by the segregated, and $6,000 produced by the unsegregated assets. Such amount shall be considered the net earnings for the purpose of section 7507 in computing the portion of the earnings to be paid to depositors. The bank has an outstanding tax liability for prior years of $7,000. The income tax liability of the bank for 1954 is 30 percent of $10,000, or $3,000, making a total outstanding tax liability of $10,000. The portion of the earnings of the bank for 1954 remaining after provision for depositors is $3,600 ($6,000 less 40 percent thereof, or $2,400). It will be assumed that of the total outstanding tax liability of $10,000, $3,600 may be assessed and collected, leaving $6,400 to be collected from any excess of the segregated assets after claims of depositors against such segregated assets have been paid in full. No part of the $6,400 immune from collection from 1954 earnings may be collected thereafter from unsegregated assets of the bank or earnings therefrom, so that except for any possible surplus of the segregated assets the $6,400 is uncollectible.

(2) In the year 1955, the earnings are again $10,000, $4,000 from segregated and $6,000 from unsegregated assets, as in 1954.

However, the return filed shows income of $5,000 and a tax liability of $1,500. An investigation shows the true income to be $10,000, on which the tax is $3,000. The full $3,000 will be assumed to be collectible. The $600 difference between $3,600 (the excess of earnings from unsegregated assets over the amount going to the depositors), and the $3,000 tax for 1955, is not available for collection of the tax for prior years, which became immune as described above, but may be available for collection of tax for subsequent years.

(c) No significance attaches to the selection of the years 1954 and 1955 in the example set forth in paragraph (b) of this section. The rules indicated by the example are equally applicable to subsequent or prior years not excluded by limitations.

O— § 301.7507-6 (T.D. 6232, filed 5-2-57; republished in T.D. 6498, filed 10-24-60.) **Abatement and refund.**

(a) An assessment or collection, no matter when made, if contrary to section 7507, is subject to abatement or refund within the applicable statutory period of limitations.

(b) Collection from a bank within section 7507(b) which diminishes assets necessary for payment of depositors, if made prior to agreement with depositors, is not contrary to the section, and affords no ground for refund.

(c) Any abatement or refund is subject to existing statutory periods of limitation, which periods are not suspended or extended by sections 7507. In order to secure a refund of any taxes paid for any taxable year during the period of immunity the bank must file claim therefor.

O— § 301.7507-7 (T.D. 6232, filed 5-2-57; republished in T.D. 6498, filed 10-24-60.) **Establishment of immunity.**

(a) The mere allegation of insolvency, or that depositors have claims against segregated or other assets or earnings, will not of itself secure immunity from tax collection. It must be affirmatively established to the satisfaction of the district director that collection of tax will be contrary to section 7507. See also § 301.7507-8.

(b) Any claim, by a bank, of immunity under section 7507(b), shall be supported by a statement, under oath or affirmation, which shall show: (1) the total of depositors' claims outstanding, and (2) separately and in detail, the amount of each of the following, and the amount of depositors' claims properly chargeable against each: (i) segregated or transferred assets; (ii) unsegregated assets; (iii) estimated future average annual earnings and profits; (iv) amount collectible from shareholders; and (v) any other resources available for payment of depositors' claims. The detail shall show the full amount of depositors' claims chargeable against each of the items in subdivisions (i) to (v), inclusive, of this paragraph even though part or all of the amount chargeable against a particular item is also chargeable against some other item or items. There shall also be filed a copy of any agreement between the bank and its depositors, and any other agreement or document bearing on the claim of immunity. The statement shall show the basis, as "book," "market," etc., of valuation of the assets.

O— § 301.7507-8 (T.D. 6232, filed 5-2-57; republished in T.D. 6498, filed 10-24-60.) **Procedure during immunity.**

(a) *Statements to be filed.* As long as complete or partial immunity is claimed, a bank within section 7507(b) shall file with each income tax return a statement as required by § 301.7507-7, in duplicate, and shall also file such additional statements as the district director may require. Whether or not additional statements shall be required, and the frequency thereof, will depend on the circumstances, including the financial status and apparent prospects of the bank, and the time which is available for assessment and collection. If a copy of an agreement or document has once been filed, a copy of the same agreement or document need not again be filed with a subsequent statement, if it is shown by the subsequent statement, when and where and with what return the copy was filed. In case of amendment a copy of the amendment must be filed with the return for the taxable year in which the amendment is made.

(b) *Failure to file.* Failure of a bank to file any required statement will be treated as indicating that the bank is not entitled to immunity.

O— § 301.7507-9 (T.D. 6232, filed 5-2-57; republished in T.D. 6498, filed 10-24-60.) **Termination of immunity.**

(a) *In general.* (1) In the case of a bank within section 7507(a), immunity will end whenever, and to the extent that, taxes may be assessed and collected, within the applicable limitation periods as extended by section 7507, without diminishing the assets available and necessary for payment of depositors. Immunity of a bank within section 7507(b) is terminated, as to segregated assets, whenever claims of depositors against such assets have been paid in full. See § 301.7507-3. As to segregated assets, the termination of immunity is complete, and any balance remaining after payment of depositors is available, within statutory limitations, for collection of tax due at any time. However, taxes of the bank will be collectible from segregated assets only to the extent that the bank has a legal or equitable interest therein. Assets as to which there has been a complete conveyance for benefit of depositors, and the bank has bona fide been divested of all legal and equitable interest, are not available for collection of the bank's tax liability.

(2) As to unsegregated assets of a bank within section 7507(b), immunity terminates only as to taxes thereafter becoming due. When taxes are once immune from collection, the immunity as to unsegregated assets is absolute. But see paragraph (a) of § 301.7507-4.

(b) *General creditors.* While the immunity from tax collection is for protection of depositors, and not for benefit of general creditors, in some cases the im-

24,424 (I.R.C.) Reg. § 301.7507-9(b)

munity will not end until the assets are sufficient to cover indebtedness of creditors generally. This situation will exist where under applicable law the claims of general creditors are on a parity with those of depositors, so that to pay depositors in full it is necessary to pay all creditors in full.

(c) *Shareholder liability.* In determining the sufficiency of the assets to satisfy the depositors' claims, shareholders' liability to the extent collectible shall be treated as available assets. See § 301.7507-7.

(d) *Deposit insurance.* Deposit insurance payable to depositors shall not be treated as an asset of the bank and shall be disregarded in determining the sufficiency of the assets to meet the claims of depositors.

(e) *Notice by bank.* A bank within section 7507(b), upon termination of immunity with respect to (1) earnings, (2) segregated or transferred assets, or (3) unsegregated assets, shall immediately notify the district director of internal revenue for the internal revenue district in which the taxpayer's returns were filed of such termination of immunity. See paragraph (b) of § 301.7507-8.

(f) *Payment by bank.* As immunity terminates with respect to any assets, it will be the duty of the bank, without notice from the district director, to make payment of taxes collectible from such assets.

o— § 301.7507-10 (T.D. 6232, filed 5-2-57; republished in T.D. 6498, filed 10-24-60.) **Collection of tax after termination of immunity.**

If, in the case of a bank within section 7507(b), segregated assets (including earnings therefrom), in excess of those necessary for payment of outstanding deposits become available, such excess of segregated assets shall be applied toward satisfaction of accumulated outstanding taxes previously immune under the section, and not barred by the statute of limitations. But see § 301.7507-3. Where sufficient segregated or unsegregated assets are available, statutory interest shall be collected with the tax. When unsegregated assets or earnings therefrom previously immune become available for tax collection, they will be available only for collection of taxes (including interest and other additions) becoming due after immunity ceases. See the example in paragraph (b) of § 301.7507-5.

o— § 301.7507-11 (T.D. 6232, filed 5-2-57; republished in T.D. 6498, filed 10-24-60.) **Exception of employment taxes.**

The immunity granted by section 7507 does not apply to taxes imposed by chapter 21 or chapter 23 of the Code.

o— § 301.7508 **Statutory provisions; time for performing certain acts postponed by reason of war.** [Sec. 7508, IRC]

o— § 301.7509 **Statutory provisions; expenditures incurred by the Post Office Department.** [Sec. 7509, IRC]

o— § 301.7510 **Statutory provisions; exemption from tax of domestic goods purchased for the United States.** [Sec. 7510, IRC]

o— § 301.7510-1 (T.D. 6232, filed 5-2-57; republished in T.D. 6498, filed 10-24-60.) **Exemption from tax of domestic goods purchased for the United States.**

For any regulations under section 7510, see the applicable regulations with respect to the various taxes.

o— § 301.7511 **Statutory provisions; exemption of consular officers and employees of foreign states from payment of internal revenue taxes on imported articles.** [Sec. 7511, repealed by sec. 302(d), Tariff Classification Act 1962]

o— § 301.7512 **Statutory provisions; separate accounting for certain collected taxes, etc.** [Sec. 7512, IRC]

o— § 301.7512-1 (T.D. 6299, filed 6-30-58 as amended by T.D. 6444, filed 1-14-60; republished in T.D. 6498, filed, 10-24-60.) **Separate accounting for certain collected taxes.**

(a) *Scope.* The provisions of section 7512 and this section apply to—

(1) The following taxes imposed by subtitle C of the Code in respect of wages or compensation paid after February 11, 1958, for pay periods beginning after such date:

(i) The employee tax imposed by section 3101 of chapter 21 (Federal Insurance Contributions Act),

(ii) The employee tax imposed by section 3201 of chapter 22 (Railroad Retirement Tax Act), and

(iii) The income tax required to be withheld on wages by section 3402 of chapter 24 (Collection of Income Tax at Source on Wages); and

(2) The following taxes imposed by chapter 33 of the Code in respect of taxable payments made, except as otherwise specifically provided in this subparagraph, after February 11, 1958:

(i) The taxes imposed by section 4231 (1), (2), and (3) on amounts paid for admissions, and the tax imposed by section 4231(6) on amounts paid for admission, refreshment, service, or merchandise, at any roof garden, cabaret, or other similar place, to the extent that such tax on amounts paid on or after January 1, 1959, is required to be collected by the proprietor of the roof garden, cabaret, or similar place from a concessionaire in such establishment,

(ii) The taxes imposed by section 4241 on amounts paid as club dues,

(iii) The taxes imposed by section 4251 on amounts paid for communications services or facilities,

(iv) The tax imposed by section 4261 on amounts paid for transportation of persons and the tax imposed by section 4271 on amounts paid before August 1, 1958, for the transportation of property, and

(v) The tax imposed by section 4286 on

amounts collected for the use of safe deposit boxes.

(b) *Requirement.* If the district director determines that any person required to collect, account for, and pay over any tax described in paragraph (a) of this section has, at the time and in the manner prescribed by law or regulations, failed to collect, truthfully account for, or pay over any such tax, or make deposits, payments, or returns of any such tax, such person, if notified to do so by the district director in accordance with section 7512 and paragraph (d) of this section, shall—

(1) Collect, at the times and in the manner provided by the law and the regulations in respect of the various taxes described in paragraph (a) of this section, all of the taxes described in such paragraph which become collectible by him after receipt of such notice;

(2) Deposit the taxes so collected, not later than the end of the second banking day after collection, with a bank, as defined in section 581, in a separate account established in accordance with paragraph (c) of this section; and

(3) Keep in such account the taxes so deposited until payment thereof is made to the United States as required by the law and the regulations in respect of such taxes. The separate accounting requirements contained in subparagraphs (1), (2), and (3) of this paragraph are applicable, in the case of the taxes described in paragraph (a) (1) of this section, to taxes with respect to wages or compensation paid after receipt of the notice from the district director, irrespective of whether such wages or compensation was earned prior to or after receipt of the notice; and, in the case of the taxes described in paragraph (a) (2) of this section, to taxes with respect to taxable payments made after receipt of the notice from the district director, irrespective of whether the transactions with respect to which such payments were made occurred prior to or after receipt of the notice.

(c) *Trust fund account.* The separate bank account referred to in paragraph (b) of this section shall be established under the designation, "(Name of person required to establish account), Trustee, Special Fund in Trust for U. S. under Sec. 7512, I.R.C.". The taxes deposited in such account shall constitute a fund in trust for the United States payable only to the Internal Revenue Service on demand by the trustee.

(d) *Notice.* Notice to any person requiring his compliance with the provisions of section 7512(b) and this section shall be in writing and shall be delivered in hand to such person by an internal revenue officer or employee. In the case of a trade or business carried on other than as a sole proprietorship, such as a corporation, partnership, or trust, notice delivered in hand to an officer, partner, or trustee shall be deemed to be notice delivered in hand to such corporation, partnership, or trust and to all officers, partners, trustees, and employees thereof.

(e) *Cancellation of notice.* The district director may relieve a person to whom notice requiring separate accounting has been given pursuant to section 7512 and this section from further compliance with such separate accounting requirements whenever he is satisfied that such person will comply with all requirements of the Code and the regulations applicable, in respect of the taxes to which the notice relates, in the case of persons not required to comply with the provisions of section 7512(b). Notice of cancellation of the requirement for separate accounting shall be made in writing and shall take effect at such time as is specified in the notice of cancellation.

(f) *Penalties.* For criminal penalty for failure to comply with any provision of section 7512, see section 7215. For criminal penalties for failure to file return, supply information, or pay tax, for failure to collect or pay over tax, and for attempt to evade or defeat tax, see sections 7203, 7202, and 7201, respectively.

○—☞ § 301.7513 **Statutory provisions; reproduction of returns and other documents.** [Sec. 7513, IRC]

○—☞ § 301.7513-1 (T.D. 6444, filed 1-14-60; republished in T.D. 6498, filed 10-24-60.) **Reproduction of returns and other documents.**

(a) *In general.* The Commissioner, district directors, and other authorized officers and employees of the Internal Revenue Service may contract with any Federal agency or any person to have such agency or person process films and other photoimpressions of any return, statement, document, or of any card, record, or other matter, and make reproductions from such films and photoimpressions.

(b) *Safeguards*—(1) *By private contractor.* Any person entering into a contract with the Internal Revenue Service for the performance of any of the services described in paragraph (a) of this section shall agree to comply, and to assume responsibility for compliance by his employees, with the following requirements:

(i) The films or photoimpressions, and reproductions made therefrom, shall be used only for the purpose of carrying out the provisions of the contract, and information contained in such material shall be treated as confidential and shall not be divulged or made known in any manner to any person except as may be necessary in the performance of the contract;

(ii) All the services shall be performed under the supervision of the person with whom the contract is made or his responsible employees;

(iii) All material received for processing and all processed and reproduced material shall be kept in a locked and fireproof compartment in a secure place when not being worked upon;

(iv) All spoilage of reproductions made from the film or photoimpressions supplied to the contractor shall be destroyed, and a statement under the penalties of perjury shall be submitted to the Internal Revenue Service that such destruction has been accomplished; and

(v) All film, photoimpressions, and reproductions made therefrom, shall be transmitted to the Internal Revenue Service by

24,426 (I.R.C.) Reg. § 301.7513-1(b)(1) 11-8-71

personal delivery, first-class mail, parcel post, or express.

(2) *By Federal agency.* Any Federal agency entering into a contract with the Internal Revenue Service for the performance of any services described in paragraph (a) of this section, shall treat as confidential all material processed or reproduced pursuant to such contract.

(3) *Inspection.* The Internal Revenue Service shall have the right to send its officers and employees into the offices and plants of Federal agencies and other contractors for inspection of the facilities and operations provided for the performance of any work contracted or to be contracted for under this section.

(4) *Criminal sanctions.* For penalty provisions relating to the unauthorized use and disclosure of information in violation of the provisions of this section, see section 7213(c).

(c) *Legal status of reproductions.* Section 7513 provides that any reproduction made in accordance with such section of any return, document, or other matter shall have the same legal status as the original and requires that any such reproduction shall, if properly authenticated, be admissible in evidence in any judicial or administrative proceeding, as if it were the original, whether or not the original is in existence.

○━▶ § 301.7514 **Statutory provisions; authority to prescribe or modify seals.** [Sec. 7514, IRC]

○━▶ § 301.7514-1 (T.D. 6422, filed 10-28-59; amended by T.D. 6442, filed 1-5-60; republished in T.D. 6498, filed 10-24-60; amended by T.D. 6555, filed 3-14-61; T.D. 6585, filed 12-27-61; T.D. 6626, filed 12-26-62; T.D. 6698, filed 12-27-63 T.D. 6833, filed 7-6-65; T.D. 6974, filed 10-2-68 and T.D. 7147, filed 10-22-71.) **Seals of office.**

(a) *Establishment of seals—*(1) *Commissioner of Internal Revenue.* There is hereby established in and for the office of the Commissioner of Internal Revenue an official seal. The seal is described as follows, and illustrated below: A circle within which shall appear that part of the seal of the Treasury Department represented by the shield and side wreaths. Exterior to this circle and within a circumscribed circle in the form of a rope shall appear in the upper part the words "OFFICE OF" and in the lower part the words "COMMISSIONER OF INTERNAL REVENUE."

(2) *District directors of internal revenue* (i). There is hereby established an official seal in and for each of the offices of district director of internal revenue listed in subdivision (ii) of this subparagraph. The seal is described as follows, and one such seal is illustrated below: A circle within which shall appear that part of the seal of the Treasury Department represented by the shield and side wreaths. Exterior to this circle and within a circumscribed circle in the form of a rope shall appear in the upper part of the words "DISTRICT DIRECTOR OF INTERNAL REVENUE" and in the lower part the location of the office for which the seal is established.

(ii) The offices of district director of internal revenue for which seals are established in subdivision (i) of this subparagraph are as follows:

Ala., Birmingham	N. H., Portsmouth
Alaska, Anchorage	N. J., Newark
Ariz., Phoenix	N. Mex., Albuquerque
Ark., Little Rock	
Calif., Los Angeles	N. Y., Albany
Calif., San Francisco	N. Y., Brooklyn
Colo., Denver	N. Y., Buffalo
Conn., Hartford	N. Y., New York: Manhattan
Del., Wilmington	
Fla., Jacksonville	N. C., Greensboro
Ga., Atlanta	N. Dak., Fargo
Hawaii, Honolulu	Ohio, Cincinnati
Idaho, Boise	Ohio, Cleveland
Ill., Chicago	Okla., Oklahoma City
Ill., Springfield	Oreg., Portland
Ind., Indianapolis	Pa., Philadelphia
Iowa, Des Moines	Pa., Pittsburgh
Kans., Wichita	R. I., Providence
Ky., Louisville	S. C., Columbia
La., New Orleans	S. Dak., Aberdeen
Maine, Augusta	Tenn., Nashville
Md., Baltimore	Tex., Austin
Mass., Boston	Tex., Dallas
Mich., Detroit	Utah, Salt Lake City
Minn., St. Paul	Va., Richmond
Miss., Jackson	Vt., Burlington
Mo., St. Louis	Wash., Seattle
Mont., Helena	W.Va., Parkersburg
Nebr., Omaha	Wis., Milwaukee
Nev., Reno	Wyo., Cheyenne

(3) *Director of International Operations.* There is hereby established in and for the office of the Director of International Operations an official seal. The seal is described as follows, and illustrated below: A circle within which shall appear that part of the seal of the Treasury Department represented by the shield and side wreaths. Exterior to this circle and within a circumscribed circle in the form of a rope shall appear in the upper part the words "DI-

RECTOR OF INTERNATIONAL OPERATIONS" and in the lower part "WASHINGTON, D. C. INTERNAL REVENUE SERVICE."

REVENUE SERVICE CENTER" and in the lower part the name of the region and the name of the principal city in or near which the service center is located.

(4) *Regional commissioners of internal revenue.* (i) There is hereby established an official seal in and for each of the offices of regional commissioner of internal revenue listed in subdivision (ii) of this subparagraph. The seal is described as follows, and one such seal is illustrated below: A circle within which shall appear that part of the seal of the Treasury Department represented by the shield and side wreaths. Exterior to this circle and within a circumscribed circle in the form of a rope shall appear in the upper part the words "REGIONAL COMMISSIONER OF INTERNAL REVENUE" and in the lower part the title of the region for which the seal is established.

(ii) The offices of director of internal revenue service center for which seals are established in subdivision (i) of this subparagraph are as follows:

Director, Internal Revenue Service Center, Central Region, Covington, Ky.

Director, Internal Revenue Service Center, Mid-Atlantic Region, Philadelphia, Pa.

Director, Internal Revenue Service Center, Midwest Region, Kansas City, Mo.

Director, Internal Revenue Service Center, North-Atlantic Region, Andover, Mass.

Director, Internal Revenue Service Center, North-Atlantic Region, Brookhaven, N. Y.

Director, Internal Revenue Service Center, Southeast Region, Chamblee, Ga.

Director, Internal Revenue Service Center, Southeast Region, Memphis, Tenn.

Director, Internal Revenue Service Center, Southwest Region, Austin, Tex.

Director, Internal Revenue Service Center, Western Region, Fresno, Calif.

Director, Internal Revenue Service Center, Western Region, Ogden, Utah.

(6) *Director of Internal Revenue Service Data Center.* There is hereby established in and for the office of the Director of the Internal Revenue Service Data Center an official seal. The seal is described as follows, and illustrated below: A circle within which shall appear that part of the seal of the Treasury Department represented by the shield and side wreaths. Exterior to the circle and within a circumscribed circle in the form of a rope shall appear in the upper part the words "Director, Internal Revenue Service Data Center" and in the lower part "Detroit, Michigan".

(ii) The offices of the regional commissioner of internal revenue for which seals are established in subdivision (i) of this subparagraph are as follows:

Regional Commissioner of Internal Revenue, Central Region.

Regional Commissioner of Internal Revenue, Mid-Atlantic Region.

Regional Commissioner of Internal Revenue, Midwest Region.

Regional Commissioner of Internal Revenue, North-Atlantic Region.

Regional Commissioner of Internal Revenue, Southeast Region.

Regional Commissioner of Internal Revenue, Southwest Region.

Regional Commissioner of Internal Revenue, Western Region.

(5) *Directors of internal revenue service centers.* (i) There is hereby established an official seal in and for each of the offices of director of internal revenue service center listed in subdivision (ii) of this subparagraph. The seal is described as follows, and one such seal is illustrated below: A circle within which shall appear that part of the seal of the Treasury Department represented by the shield and side wreaths. Exterior to this circle and within a circumscribed circle in the form of a rope shall appear in the upper part the words "DIRECTOR, INTERNAL

(b) *Custody of seal.* Each seal established by this section shall be in the custody of the officer for whose office such seal is established.

(c) *Use of official seal.* Each seal of office established by this section may be affixed in lieu of the seal of the Treasury Department to any certificate or attestation

Reg. § 301.7514-1(c)

required to be made by the officer for whose office such seal is established in authentication of originals and copies of books, records, papers, writings, and documents of the Internal Revenue Service in the custody of such officer, for all purposes, including the purposes of 28 U.S.C. 1733(b), Rule 44 of the Federal Rules of Civil Procedure, and Rule 27 of the Federal Rules of Criminal Procedure, except that—

(1) No such seal shall be affixed to material to be published in the Federal Register, and

(2) The seal of the office of a district director of internal revenue or the Director of International Operations shall not be affixed to the certification of copies of books, records, papers, writings, or documents in his custody in any case in which, pursuant to Executive order, Treasury decision, or Part 601 of this chapter (Statement of Procedural Rules), such copies may be furnished to applicants only by the Commissioner.

(d) *Judicial notice.* In accordance with the provisions of section 7514, judicial notice shall be taken of the seals established under this section.

○— § 301.7515 Statutory provisions; special statistical studies and compilations and other services on request. [Sec. 7515, IRC]

○— § 301.7515-1 (T.D. 6713, filed 3-23-64.) Special statistical studies and compilations on request.

The Commissioner is authorized, within his discretion, upon written request of any person and payment by such person of the cost of the work to be performed, to make special statistical studies and compilations involving data from returns, declarations, statements, or other documents required by the Code or regulations or from records established or maintained in connection with the administration and enforcement of the Code; to engage in any such special study or compilation jointly with the party or parties requesting it; and to furnish transcripts of any such study or compilation. The requests for services should be addressed to the Commissioner of Internal Revenue, Attention: PR, Washington, D.C. 20224. The requests should describe fully the nature of the study or compilation desired, giving detailed specifications for all tables to be prepared, and should include a general statement regarding the use to be made of the data requested.

○— § 301.7516-1 (T.D. 6713, filed 3-23-64; amended by T.D. 6790, filed 1-4-65.) Training and Training Aids on Request.—

The Commissioner is authorized, within his discretion, upon written request, to admit employees and officials of any State, the Commonwealth of Puerto Rico, any possession of the United States, any political subdivision or instrumentality of any of the foregoing, the District of Columbia, or any foreign government to training courses conducted by the Internal Revenue Service, and to supply them with texts and other training aids. Requests for such training or training aids should be addressed to the Commissioner of Internal Revenue, Washington, D.C., 20224, Attention: A:T, except that requests involving officials or visitors of foreign governments should be addressed to the Commissioner of Internal Revenue, Washington, D.C., 20224, Attention: C:FA. The Commissioner may require payment from the party or parties making the request of a reasonable fee not to exceed the cost of the training and training aids supplied pursuant to such request.

DISCOVERY OF LIABILITY AND ENFORCEMENT OF TITLE
EXAMINATION AND INSPECTION

○— § 301.7601 Statutory provisions; canvass of districts for taxable persons and objects. [Sec. 7601, IRC]

○— § 301.7601-1 (T.D. 6421, filed 10-23-59; republished in T.D. 6498, filed 10-24-60; amended by T.D. 7188, filed 6-28-72 and T.D. 7297, filed 12-18-73.) Canvass of districts for taxable persons and objects.

Each district director shall, to the extent he deems it practicable, cause officers or employees under his supervision and control to proceed, from time to time, through his district and inquire after and concerning all persons therein who may be liable to pay any internal revenue tax, and all persons owning or having the care and management of any objects with respect to which any tax is imposed.

○— § 301.7602 Statutory provisions; examination of books and witnesses. [Sec. 7602, IRC]

○— § 301.7602-1 (T.D. 6421, filed 10-23-59; republished in T.D. 6498, filed 10-24-60; amended by T.D. 7188, filed 6-28-72 and T.D. 7297, filed 12-18-73.) Examination of books and witnesses.

(a) *In general.* For the purposes of ascertaining the correctness of any return, making a return where none has been made, determining the liability of any person for any internal revenue tax (including any interest, additional amount, addition to the tax, or civil penalty) or the liability at law or in equity of any transferee or fiduciary of any person in respect of any internal revenue tax, or collecting any such liability, any authorized officer or employee of the Internal Revenue Service may examine any books, papers, records or other data which may be relevant or material to such inquiry; and take such testimony of the person concerned, under oath, as may be relevant to such inquiry.

(b) *Summons.* For the purposes described in paragraph (a) of this section the Commissioner is authorized to summon the person liable for tax or required to perform the act, or any officer or employee of such person, or any person having possession, custody, or care of books of accounts containing entries relating to the business of the person liable for tax or required to perform the act, or any other person deemed proper, to appear before a designated officer or employee of the Internal Revenue Service at a time and place named in the summons and to produce such books, papers, records, or other data, and to give such testimony, under oath, as may be relevant or material to such inquiry; and take such testimony of the person concerned, under oath, as may be relevant or material to such inquiry. The Commissioner may designate any employee of the Internal Revenue Service as the individual before whom a person summoned pursuant to section 6420(e)(2), 6421(f)(2), 6424(d)(2), 6427(e)(2), or 7602 shall appear. Any such employee, when so designated in a summons, is authorized to take testimony under oath of the person summoned and to receive and examine books, papers, records, or other data produced in compliance with the summons.

§ 301.7603 Statutory provisions; service of summons. [Sec. 7603, IRC]

§ 301.7603-1 (T.D. 6421, filed 10-23-59; republished in T.D. 6498, filed 10-24-60; amended by T.D. 7188, filed 6-28-72 and T.D. 7297, filed 12-18-73.) **Service of summons.**

(a) *In general.* A summons issued under section 6420(e)(2), 6421(f)(2), 6424(d)(2), 6427(e)(2), or 7602 shall be served by an attested copy delivered in hand to the person to whom it is directed, or left at his last and usual place of abode. The certificate of service signed by the person serving the summons shall be evidence of the facts it states on the hearing of an application for the enforcement of the summons. When the summons requires the production of books, papers, records, or other data, it shall be sufficient if such books, papers, records, or other data are described with reasonable certainty.

(b) *Persons who may serve a summons.* The officers and employees of the Internal Revenue Service whom the Commissioner has designated to carry out the authority given him by § 301.7602-1(b) to issue a summons are authorized to serve a summons issued under section 6420(e)(2), 6421(f)(2), 6424(d)(2), 6427(e)(2), or 7602.

§ 301.7604 Statutory provisions; enforcement of summons. [Sec. 7604, IRC]

§ 301.7604-1 (T.D. 6421, filed 10-23-59; republished in T.D. 6498, filed 10-24-60; amended by T.D. 7297, filed 12-18-73.) **Enforcement of summons.**

(a) *In general.* Whenever any person summoned under section 6420(e)(2), 6421(f)(2), or 7602 neglects or refuses to obey such summons, or to produce books, papers, records, or other data, or to give testimony, as required, application may be made to the judge of the district court or to a U.S. commissioner for the district within which the person so summoned resides or is found for an attachment against him as for a contempt.

(b) *Persons who may apply for an attachment.* The officers and employees of the Internal Revenue Service whom the Commissioner has designated to carry out the authority given him by § 301.7602-1(b) to issue a summons are authorized to apply for an attachment as provided in paragraph (a) of this section.

§ 301.7605 Statutory provisions; time and place of examination. [Sec. 7605, IRC]

§ 301.7605-1 (T.D. 6421, filed 10-23-59; republished in T.D. 6498, filed 10-24-60; amended by T.D. 7146, filed 10-26-71.) **Time and place of examination.**

(a) *Time and place.* The time and place of examination pursuant to the provisions of section 6420(e)(2), 6421(f)(2), or 7602 shall be such time and place as may be fixed by an officer or employee of the Internal Revenue Service and as are reasonable under the circumstances. In the case of a summons under authority of section 7602(2) and § 301.7602-1, or under the corresponding authority of section 6420(e)(2) or 6421(f)(2), the date fixed for appearance before an officer or employee of the Service, shall not be less than 10 days from the date of the summons.

(b) *Restrictions on examination of taxpayer.* No taxpayer shall be subjected to unnecessary examination or investigations, and only one inspection of a taxpayer's books of account shall be made for each taxable year unless the taxpayer requests otherwise or unless an authorized internal revenue officer, after investigation, notifies the taxpayer in writing that an additional inspection is necessary.

(c) *Restriction on examination of churches*—(1) *In general.* This section imposes certain restrictions upon the examination of the books of account and religious activities of a church or convention or association of churches for the purpose of determining whether such organization may be engaged in activities the income from which is subject to tax under section 511 as unrelated business taxable income. The purposes of these restrictions are to protect such organizations from undue interference in their internal financial affairs through unnecessary examinations to determine the existence of unrelated business taxable income, and to limit the scope of examination for this purpose to matters directly relevant to a determination of the existence or amount of such income. This section also imposes additional restrictions upon other examinations of such organizations.

(2) *Books of account.* No examination of the books of account of an organization which claims to be a church or a convention or association of churches shall be made except after the giving of notice as provided in this subparagraph and except to the extent necessary (i) to determine the initial or continuing qualification of the organization under section 501(c)(3); (ii) to determine whether the organization qualifies as one, contributions to which are deductible under section 170, 545, 556, 642, 2055, 2106, or 2522; (iii) to obtain information for the purpose of ascertaining or verifying payments made by the organization to another person in determining the tax liability of the recipient, such as payments of salaries, wages, or other forms of compensation; or (iv) to determine the amount of tax, if any, imposed by the Code upon such organization. No examination of the books of account of a church or convention or association of churches shall be made unless the Regional Commissioner believes that such examination is necessary and so notifies the organization in writing at least 30 days in advance of examination. The Regional Commissioner will conclude that such examination is necessary only after reasonable attempts have been made to obtain information from the books of account by written request and the Regional Commissioner has determined that the informa-

Reg. § 301.7605-1(c)(2)

24,430 (I.R.C.) Reg. § 301.7605-1(c)(2)

tion cannot be fully or satisfactorily obtained in that manner. In any examination of a church or convention or association of churches for the purpose of determining unrelated business income tax liability pursuant to such notice, no examination of the books of account of the organization shall be made except to the extent necessary to determine such liability.

(3) *Religious activities.* No examination of the religious activities of an organization which claims to be a church or convention or association of churches shall be made except (i) to the extent necessary to determine the initial or continuing qualification of the organization under section 501(c)(3); (ii) to determine whether the organization qualifies as one, contributions to which are deductible under section 170, 545, 556, 642, 2055, 2106, or 2522; or (iii) to determine whether the organization is a church or convention or association of churches subject to the provisions of part III of subchapter F of chapter 1. The requirements of subparagraph (2) of this paragraph that the Regional Commissioner give notice prior to examination of the books of account of an organization do not apply to an examination of the religious activities of the organization for any purpose described in this subparagraph. Once it has been determined that the organization is a church or convention or association of churches, no further examination of its religious activities may be made in connection with determining its liability, if any, for unrelated business income tax.

(4) *Effective date.* The provisions of this paragraph shall apply to audits and examinations of taxable years beginning after December 31, 1969.

GENERAL POWERS AND DUTIES

○— § 301.7621 **Statutory provisions; internal revenue districts.** [Sec. 7621, IRC]

○— § 301.7621-1 (T.D. 6421, filed 10-23-59; republished in T.D. 6498, filed 10-24-60.) **Internal revenue districts.**

For delegation to the Secretary of authority to prescribe internal revenue districts for the purpose of administering the internal revenue laws, see Executive Order No. 10289, dated September 17, 1951 (16 F.R. 9499), as made applicable to the Code by Executive Order No. 10574, dated November 5, 1954 (19 F.R. 7249).

○— § 301.7622 **Statutory provisions; authority to administer oaths and certify.** [Sec. 7622, IRC].

○— § 301.7622-1 (T.D. 6421, filed 10-23-59; republished in T.D. 6498, filed 10-24-60; amended by T.D. 6585, filed 12-27-61, T.D. 7188, filed 6-28-72; T.D. 7297, filed 12-18-73 and T.D. 7359, filed 5-30-75.) **Authority to administer oaths and certify**

The officers and employees of the Internal Revenue Service whom the Commissioner has designated are authorized to administer such oaths or affirmations and to certify to such papers as may be necessary under the internal revenue laws or regulations issued thereunder, except that the authority to certify shall not be construed as applying to those papers or documents the certification of which is authorized by separate order or directive.

○— § 301.7623 **Statutory provisions; expenses of detection and punishment of frauds.** [Sec. 7623, IRC]

○— § 301.7623-1 (T.D. 6421, filed 10-23-59; republished in T.D. 6498 filed 10-24-60; amended by T.D. 7297, filed 12-18-73.) **Rewards for information relating to violations of internal revenue laws.**

(a) *In general.* A district director may approve such reward as he deems suitable for information that leads to the detection and punishment of any person guilty of violating any internal revenue law, or conniving at the same. The rewards provided for by section 7623 are limited in their aggregate to the sum appropriated therefor and shall be paid only in cases not otherwise provided for by law.

(b) *Eligibility to file claim for reward* —(1) *In general.* Any person, other than certain present or former federal employees (see subparagraph (2) of this paragraph), who submits, in the manner set forth in paragraph (d) of this section, information relating to the violation of an internal revenue law is eligible to file a claim for reward under section 7623.

(2) *Federal employees.* No person who was an officer or employee of the Department of the Treasury at the time he came into possession of information relating to violations of the internal revenue laws, or at the time he divulged such information, shall be eligible for reward under section 7623 and this section. Any other federal employee, or former federal employee, is eligible to file a claim for reward if the information submitted came to his knowledge other than in the course of his official duties.

(3) *Deceased informants.* A claim for reward may be filed by an executor, administrator, or other legal representative on behalf of a deceased informant if, prior to his death, the informant was eligible to file a claim for such reward under section 7623 and this section. Certified copies of the letters testamentary, letters of administration, or other similar evidence must be annexed to such a claim for reward on behalf of a deceased informant in order to show the authority of the legal representative to file the claim for reward.

(c) *Amount and payment of reward.* All relevant factors, including the value of the information furnished in relation to the facts developed by the investigation of the violation, shall be taken into account by a district director in determining whether a reward shall be paid, and, if so, the amount thereof. The amount of a reward shall represent what the district director deems to be adequate compensation in the particular case, normally not to exceed ten percent of the additional taxes, penalties, and fines which are recovered as a result of the information. No reward, however, shall be paid with respect to any additional interest that may be collected. Payment of a reward will be made as promptly as the circumstances of the case permit, but generally not until the taxes, penalties, or fines involved have been collected. However, the informant may waive any claim for reward with respect to an uncollected portion of the taxes, penalties, or fines involved, in which case the claim may be immediately processed. No person is authorized under these regulations to make any offer, or promise, or otherwise to bind a district director with respect to the payment of any reward or the amount thereof.

(d) *Submission of information.* Persons desiring to claim rewards under the provisions of section 7623 and this section may submit information relating to violations of the internal revenue laws, in person, to the Office of the Director of the Intelligence Division, Washington 25, D. C., or to the office of a district director, preferably to a representative of the Intelligence Division thereof. Such information may also be submitted in writing to the Commissioner of Internal Revenue, Attention: Director, Intelligence Division, Washington 25, D. C., or to any district director, Attention: Chief, Intelligence Division. If the information is submitted in person, either orally or in writing, the name and official title of the person to whom it is submitted and the date on which it is submitted must be included in the formal claim for reward.

(e) *Anonymity.* No unauthorized person shall be advised of the identity of an informant.

(f) *Filing claim for reward.* An informant who intends to claim a reward under section 7623 should notify the person to whom he submits his information of such intention, and must file a formal claim, signed with his true name, as soon after submission of the information as practicable. If other than the informant's true name was used in furnishing the information, the claimant must include with his claim satisfactory proof of his identity as that of the informant. Claim for reward under the provisions of section 7623 shall be made on Form 211, which may be obtained from the offices of the district directors, or from the Commissioner of Internal Revenue, Washington 25, D. C. A claim for reward should be transmitted to the district director, Attention: Informant's Claim Examiner, or to the Commissioner of Internal Revenue, Attention: Director, Intelligence Division, Washington 25, D. C.

POSSESSIONS

O—⇒ § 301.7654 Statutory provisions; coordination of United States and Guam individual income taxes. [Sec. 7654, IRC]

O—⇒ § 301.7654-1 (T.D. 7385, filed 10-28-75.) Coordination of U.S. and Guam individual income taxes.

(a) *Application of section*—(1) *Scope.* Section 7654 and this section set forth the general procedures to be followed by the Government of the United States and the Government of Guam in the division between the two governments of revenue derived from collections of the income taxes imposed for any taxable year beginning after December 31, 1972, with respect to any individual described in subparagraph (2) of this paragraph and paragraph (e) of this section. To the extent that section 7654 and this section are inconsistent with the provisions of section 30 of the Organic Act of Guam (48 U.S.C. 1421h), relating to duties and taxes to be covered into the treasury of Guam and held in account for the Government of Guam, such section 30 is superseded.

(2) *Individuals covered.* Paragraph (b) of this section applies only to an individual who, for a taxable year, is described in paragraph (a)(2) of § 1.935-1 of this chapter (Income Tax Regulations) and has (or in the case of a joint return, such individual and his spouse have)—

(i) Adjusted gross income of $50,000 or more, and

(ii) Gross income of $5,000 or more from sources within the jurisdiction (either the United States or Guam) other than the jurisdiction with which the individual is required to file his income tax return under paragraph (b) of § 1.935-1 of this chapter.

For the determination of gross income and adjusted gross income see sections 61 and 62, and the regulations thereunder, or, when applicable, the corresponding provisions as made applicable in Guam by the Guam Territorial income tax (48 U.S.C. 1421i). For purposes of this subparagraph, gross income consisting of compensation for military or naval service shall be taken into account not withstanding section 514 of the Soldiers' and Sailors' Civil Relief Act of 1940 (50 App. U.S.C. 574). However, see parargaph (e) of this section.

(b) *Allocation of tax.* (1) Net collections of income taxes imposed for each taxable year beginning after December 31, 1972, with respect to each individual described in paragraph (a)(2) of this section for such year shall be divided between the United States and Guam by the Commissioner of Internal Revenue and the Commissioner of Revenue and Taxation of Guam as follows:

(i) Net collections attributable to income from sources within the United States shall be covered into the Treasury of the United States,

(ii) Net collections attributable to income from sources within Guam shall be covered into the treasury of Guam, and

(iii) Net collections not described in subdivision (i) or (ii) of this subparagraph (i.e., net collection attributable to income from sources other than within the United States or Guam) shall be covered into the treasury of the jurisdiction (either the United States or Guam) with which the individual is required to file his return under paragraph (b) of § 1.935-1 of this chapter for such year.

(2) The amount of tax of any individual for a taxable year which shall be allocated to Guam for purposes of determining the portion of the net collections from such individual which shall be covered into the treasury of Guam by the United States for such year shall be that

Reg. § 301.7654-1 (b) (2)

amount which bears the same ratio to such amount of tax as the adjusted gross income of that individual for such year which is allocable to sources in Guam bears to the total adjusted gross income of such individual for such year. For purposes of such allocation by the United States, the adjusted gross income of the taxpayer shall be determined by taking into account any compensation of any member of the Armed Forces for services performed in Guam the withheld tax on which is paid into the treasury of Guam pursuant to paragraph (e) of this section. The amount of tax of any individual for any taxable year which shall be allocated to the United States for purposes of determining the portion of the net collections from such individual which shall be covered into the Treasury of the United States by Guam for such year shall be that amount which bears the same ratio to such amount of tax as the adjusted gross income of that individual for such year which is allocable to sources in the United States bears to the total adjusted gross income of such individual for such year.

(c) *Definitions and special rules.* For purposes of this section—

(1) *Net collections.* (i) In determining net collections for a taxable year, appropriate adjustment between the two jurisdictions shall be made on a proportionate basis for underpayments of income taxes for such taxable year, credits allowed against the income tax for such taxable year (other than the credit for taxes withheld under section 3402 on wages), and refunds made of income taxes paid with respect to such taxable year. Thus, if a net operating loss results in a carryback to an earlier taxable year which gives rise to a refund for that earlier year, an adjustment must be made based upon the proportion which the amount of tax covered by one jurisdiction into the treasury of the other jurisdiction for that earlier year bears to the total amount of tax paid for that earlier year, even though the loss may have resulted from activities in one jurisdiction and the income, against which the loss was offset, was earned in the other jurisdiction. Similar adjustments must be made for foreign tax credit carrybacks even though different jurisdictions are involved. If, for example, an individual pays income tax of $30,000 to the United States for 1974 and $10,000 of such tax is covered into the treasury of Guam, and if for 1975 such individual has a net operating loss attributable to a trade or business carried on in the United States which loss is carried back to 1974 and gives rise to a refund of $15,000 by the United States, Guam must cover into the Treasury of the United States the amount of $5,000 which is the adjustment based upon the refund ($15,000 × $10,000/$30,000 = $5,000).

(ii) Tax withheld from the compensation of any member of the Armed Forces described in paragraph (a)(2) of this section which is paid to Guam pursuant to section 7654(d) and paragraph (e) of this section shall be taken into account in determining the amount required to be covered into the treasury of Guam under paragraph (b)(1)(ii) of this section.

(iii) For purposes of this subparagraph, any underpayment of tax is treated as attributable on a pro rata basis to income from sources within the United States, Guam, and sources other than within the United States or Guam, respectively, and is divided between the United States and Guam under the rules in paragraph (b) of this section.

(2) *Income taxes.* The term "income taxes" means—

(i) With respect to taxes imposed by the United States, the income taxes imposed by chapter 1 of the Code, and

(ii) With respect to taxes imposed by Guam, the Guam Territorial income tax (48 U.S.C. 1421i).

(3) *Source rules.* The determination of the source of income shall be based on the principles contained in sections 861 through 863, and the regulations thereunder, or, when applicable, in those sections as made applicable in Guam by the Guam Territorial income tax. For such purposes the provisions of section 514 of the Soldiers' and Sailors' Civil Relief Act of 1940 (50 App. U.S.C. 574) relating to the determination of the source of income of members of the Armed Forces shall not be taken into account. For purposes of this subparagraph, the provisions in section 935(c) treating Guam as part of the United States, and vice versa, do not apply. For definition of the terms "United States" and "Guam" see section 7701(a)(9) of the Code and section 2 of the Organic Act of Guam (48 U.S.C. 1421).

(d) *Information return.* Each individual described in paragraph (a)(2) of this section for a taxable year who is required by paragraph (b)(1) of § 1.935-1 of this chapter to file his return of income for such year with the United States shall timely file a properly executed Form 5074 (Allocation of Individual Income Tax to Guam) by attaching such form to his income tax return. Each individual described in paragraph (a)(2) of this section for a taxable year who is required by paragraph (b)(1) of § 1.935-1 of this chapter to file his return of income for such year with Guam shall timely file such information as may be required by the Commissioner of Revenue and Taxation with respect to his income derived from sources within the United States. See section 6688 and § 301.-6688-1 for the penalty for failure to comply with this paragraph.

(e) *Military personnel in Guam.* The Commissioner of Internal Revenue shall arrange to pay to Guam the amount of the taxes deducted and withheld by the United States under section 3402 from wages paid to members of the Armed Forces who are stationed in Guam but who have no income tax liability to Guam with respect to such wages by reason of section 514 of the Soldiers' and Sailors' Civil Relief Act of 1940 (50 App. U.S.C. 574). Section 514 of that Act provides in effect that for purposes of the taxation of income by Guam a person shall not be deemed to have lost a residence or domicile in the United States solely by reason of being absent therefrom in compliance with military or naval orders and the compensation for military or naval service of such a person who is not a resident of, or domiciled in, Guam shall not be deemed income for services performed within, or from sources within, Guam. Any amount paid to Guam under this paragraph in respect of a member of the Armed Forces described in paragraph (a)(2) of this section shall be taken into account in determining the amount required to be covered into the treasury of Guam under paragraph (b)(1)(ii) of this section. For purposes of this paragraph, the term "Armed Forces of the United States" has the meaning provided by § 301.7701-8 of this chapter. This paragraph does not apply to wages for services performed in Guam by members of the Armed Forces of the United States which are not compensation for military or naval service. In determining the amount of tax to be covered into the treasury of Guam under this paragraph with respect to remuneration for services performed in Guam by members of the Armed Forces of the United States, the special procedure agreed upon with the Department of Defense in 1951 shall not apply to remuneration paid after December 31, 1974. Under that procedure the tax withheld under section 3402 upon such remuneration for services performed in Guam during April and October of each year was to be projected for the appropriate six-month period of which the base month is a part, thereby arriving at an estimated figure for semi-annual withholding tax to be covered over.

(f) *Transfers of funds.* The transfers of funds between the United States and Guam required to effectuate the provisions of this section shall be made when convenient for the two governments, but not less frequently than once in each calendar year. In complying with paragraph (b) of this section, only net balances will be transferred between the two governments. Further, amounts transferred pursuant to paragraph (b) of this section may be determined on the basis of estimates rather than the actual amounts derived from information furnished by taxpayers, except that the net collections for 1973 and every third calendar year thereafter are to be transferred on the basis of the information furnished by taxpayers pursuant to paragraph (d) of this section. In order to facilitate the transfer of funds pursuant to this section, the Commissioner of Internal Revenue and the Commissioner of Revenue and Taxation of Guam shall exchange such information, including copies of income tax returns, as will ensure that the provisions of section 7654 and this section are being properly implemented.

DEFINITIONS

§ 301.7701 **Statutory provisions; definitions.** [Sec. 7701, IRC]

§ 301.7701-1 (T.D. 6503, filed 11-15-60; amended by T.D. 6797, filed 2-2-65; T.D. 7515, filed 10-17-77.) **Classification of organizations for tax purposes.**

(a) *Person.* The term "person" includes an individual, a corporation, a partnership, a trust or estate, a joint-stock company, an association, or a syndicate, group, pool, joint venture, or other unincorporated organization or group. Such term also includes a guardian, committee, trustee, executor, administrator, trustee in bankruptcy, receiver, assignee for the benefit of creditors, conservator, or any person acting in a fiduciary capacity.

(b) *Standards.* The Internal Revenue Code prescribes certain categories, or classes, into which various organizations fall for purposes of taxation. These categories, or classes, include associations (which are taxable as corporations), partnerships, and trusts. The tests, or standards, which are to be applied in determining the classification in which an organization belongs (whether it is an association, a partnership, a trust, or other taxable entity) are determined under the Internal Revenue Code. Sections 301.7701-2 to 301.-7701-4 set forth these tests, or standards, which are to be applied in determining whether an organization is (1) an association (see § 301.7701-2), (2) a partnership (see § 301.7701-3), or (3) a trust (see § 301.7701-4).

(c) *Effect of local law.* As indicated in paragraph (b) of this section, the classes into which organizations are to be placed for purposes of taxation are determined under the Internal Revenue Code. Thus, a particular organization might be classified as a trust under the law of one State and a corporation under the law of another State. However, for purposes of the Internal Revenue Code, this organization would be uniformly classed as a trust, an association (and, therefore, taxable as a corporation), or some other entity, depending upon its nature under the classification standards of the Internal Revenue Code. Similarly, the term "partnership" is not limited to the common-law meaning of partnership, but is broader in its scope and includes groups not commonly called partnerships. See § 1.761-1 of this chapter (Income Tax Regulations) and § 301.7701-3. The term "corporation" is not limited to the artificial entity usually known as a corporation, but includes also an association, a trust classed as an association because of its nature or its activities, a joint-stock company, and an insurance company. Although it is the Internal Revenue Code rather than local law which establishes the tests or standards which will be applied in determining the classification in which an organization belongs, local law governs in determining whether the legal relationships which have been established in the formation of an organization are such that the standards are met. Thus, it is local law which must be applied in determining such matters as the legal relationships of the members of the organization among themselves and with the public at large, and the interests of the members of the organization in its assets.

§ 301.7701-2 (T.D. 6503, filed 11-15-60; amended by T.D. 6797, filed 2-2-65; T.D. 7515, filed 10-17-77.) **Associations.**

(a) *Characteristics of corporations.* (1) The term "association" refers to an organization whose characteristics require it to be classified for purposes of taxation as a corporation rather than as another type of organization such as a partnership or a trust. There are a number of major characteristics found in a pure corporation which, taken together, distinguish it from other organizations. These are: (i) Associates, (ii) an objective to carry on business and divide the gains therefrom, (iii) continuity of life, (iv) centralization of management, (v) liability for corporate debts

Reg. § 301.7701-2(a)(1)

limited to corporate property, and (vi) free transferability of interests. Whether a particular organization is to be classified as an association must be determined by taking into account the presence or absence of each of these corporate characteristics. The presence or absence of these characteristics will depend upon the facts in each individual case. In addition to the major characteristics set forth in this subparagraph, other factors may be found in some cases which may be significant in classifying an organization as an association, a partnership, or a trust. An organization will be treated as an association if the corporate characteristics are such that the organization more nearly resembles a corporation than a partnership or trust. See Morrissey et al. v. Commissioner (1935) 296 U. S. 344.

(2) Since associates and an objective to carry on business for joint profit are essential characteristics of all organizations engaged in business for profit (other than the so-called one-man corporation and the sole proprietorship), the absence of either of these essential characteristics will cause an arrangement among co-owners of property for the development of such property for the separate profit of each not to be classified as an association. Some of the major characteristics of a corporation are common to trusts and corporations, and others are common to partnerships and corporations. Characteristics common to trusts and corporations are not material in attempting to distinguish between a trust and an association, and characteristics common to partnerships and corporations are not material in attempting to distinguish between an association and a partnership. For example, since centralization of management, continuity of life, free transferability of interests, and limited liability are generally common to trusts and corporations, the determination of whether a trust which has such characteristics is to be treated for tax purposes as a trust or as an association depends on whether there are associates and an objective to carry on business and divide the gains therefrom. On the other hand, since associates and an objective to carry on business and divide the gains therefrom are generally common to both corporations and partnerships, the determination of whether an organization which has such characteristics is to be treated for tax purposes as a partnership or as an association depends on whether there exists centralization of management, continuity of life, free transferability of interests, and limited liability.

(3) An unincorporated organization shall not be classified as an association unless such organization has more corporate characteristics than noncorporate characteristics. In determining whether an organization has more corporate characteristics than noncorporate characteristics, all characteristics common to both types of organizations shall not be considered. For example, if a limited partnership has centralized management and free transferability of interests but lacks continuity of life and limited liability, and if the limited partnership has no other characteristics which are significant in determining its classification, such limited partnership is not classified as an association. Although the limited partnership also has associates and an objective to carry on business and divide the gains therefrom, these characteristics are not considered because they are common to both corporations and partnerships.

(4) The rules of this section and §§ 301.7701-3 and 301.7701-4 are applicable only to taxable years beginning after December 31, 1960. However, for any taxable year beginning after December 31, 1960, but before October 1, 1961, any amendment of the agreement establishing the organization will, in the case of an organization in existence on November 17, 1960, be treated for purposes of determining the classification of the organization as being in effect as of the beginning of such taxable year (i) if the amendment of the agreement is made before October 1, 1961, and (ii) if the amendment results in the classification of the organization under the rules of this section and §§ 301.7701-1, 301.7701-3, and 301.7701-4 in the same manner as the organization was classified for tax purposes on November 17, 1960.

(b) *Continuity of life.* (1) An organization has continuity of life if the death, insanity, bankruptcy, retirement, resignation, or expulsion of any member will not cause a dissolution of the organization. On the other hand, if the death, insanity, bankruptcy, retirement, resignation, or expulsion of any member will cause a dissolution of the organization, continuity of life does not exist. If the retirement, death, or insanity of a general partner of a limited partnership causes a dissolution of the partnership, unless the remaining general partners agree to continue the partnership or unless all remaining members agree to continue the partnership, continuity of life does not exist. See Glensder Textile Company (1942) 46 B.T.A. 176 (A., C.B. 1942-1, 8).

(2) For purposes of this paragraph, dissolution of an organization means an alteration of the identity of an organization by reason of a change in the relationship between its members as determined under local law. For example, since the resignation of a partner from a general partnership destroys the mutual agency which exists between such partner and his co-partners and thereby alters the personal relation between the partners which constitutes the identity of the partnership itself, the resignation of a partner dissolves the partnership. A corporation, however, has a continuing identity which is detached from the relationship between its stockholders. The death, insanity, or bankruptcy of a shareholder or the sale of a shareholder's interest has no effect upon the identity of the corporation and, therefore, does not work a dissolution of the organization. An agreement by which an organization is established may provide that the business will be continued by the remaining members in the event of the death or withdrawal of any member, but such agreement does not establish continuity of life if under local law the death or withdrawal of any member causes a dissolution of the organization. Thus, there may be a dissolution of the organization and no continuity of life although the business is continued by the remaining members.

(3) An agreement establishing an organization may provide that the organization is to continue for a stated period or until the completion of a stated undertaking or such agreement may provide for the termination of the organization at will or otherwise. In determining whether any member has the power of dissolution, it will be necessary to examine the agree-

ment and to ascertain the effect of such agreement under local law. For example, if the agreement expressly provides that the organization can be terminated by the will of any member, it is clear that the organization lacks continuity of life. However, if the agreement provides that the organization is to continue for a stated period or until the completion of a stated transaction, the organization has continuity of life if the effect of the agreement is that no member has the power to dissolve the organization in contravention of the agreement. Nevertheless, if, nothwithstanding such agreement, any member has the power under local law to dissolve the organization, the organization lacks continuity of life. Accordingly, a general partnership subject to a statute corresponding to the Uniform Partnership Act and a limited partnership subject to a statute corresponding to the Uniform Limited Partnership Act both lack continuity of life.

(c) *Centralization of management.* (1) An organization has centralized management if any person (or any group of persons which does not include all the members) has continuing exclusive authority to make the management decisions necessary to the conduct of the business for which the organization was formed. Thus, the persons who are vested with such management authority resemble in powers and functions the directors of a statutory corporation. The effective operation of a business organization composed of many members generally depends upon the centralization in the hands of a few of exclusive authority to make management decisions for the organization, and therefore, centralized management is more likely to be found in such an organization than in a smaller organization.

(2) The persons who have such authority may, or may not, be members of the organization and may hold office as a result of a selection by the members from time to time, or may be self-perpetuating in office. See Morrissey et al. v. Commissioner (1935) 296 U.S. 344. Centralized management can be accomplished by election to office, by proxy appointment, or by any other means which has the effect of concentrating in a management group continuing exclusive authority to make management decisions.

(3) Centralized management means a concentration of continuing exclusive authority to make independent business decisions on behalf of the organization which do not require ratification by members of such organization. Thus, there is not centralized management when the centralized authority is merely to perform ministerial acts as an agent at the direction of a principal.

(4) There is no centralization of continuing exclusive authority to make management decisions, unless the managers have sole authority to make such decisions. For example, in the case of a corporation or a trust, the concentration of management powers in a board of directors or trustees effectively prevents a stockholder or a trust beneficiary, simply because he is a stockholder or beneficiary, from binding the corporation or the trust by his acts. However, because of the mutual agency relationship between members of a general partnership subject to a statute corresponding to the Uniform Partnership Act, such a general partnership cannot achieve effective concentration of management powers and, therefore, centralized management. Usually, the act of any partner within the scope of the partnership business binds all the partners; and even if the partners agree among themselves that the powers of management shall be exclusively in a selected few, this agreement will be ineffective as against an outsider who had no notice of it. In addition, limited partnerships subject to a statute corresponding to the Uniform Limited Partnership Act, generally do not have centralized management, but centralized management ordinarily does exist in such a limited partnership if substantially all the interests in the partnership are owned by the limited partners.

(d) *Limited liability.* (1) An organization has the corporate characteristic of limited liability if under local law there is no member who is personally liable for the debts of or claims against the organization. Personal liability means that a creditor of an organization may seek personal satisfaction from a member of the organization to the extent that the assets of such organization are insufficient to satisfy the creditor's claim.

A member of the organization who is personally liable for the obligations of the organization may make an agreement under which another person, whether or not a member of the organization, assumes such liability or agrees to indemnify such member for any such liability. However, if under local law the member remains liable to such creditors notwithstanding such agreement, there exists personal liability with respect to such member. In the case of a general partnership subject to a statute corresponding to the Uniform Partnership Act, personal liability exists with respect to each general partner. Similarly, in the case of a limited partnership subject to a statute corresponding to the Uniform Limited Partnership Act, personal liability exists with respect to each general partner, except, as provided in subparagraph (2) of this paragraph.

(2) In the case of an organization formed as a limited partnership, personal liability does not exist, for purposes of this paragraph, with respect to a general partner when he has no substantial assets (other than his interest in the partnership) which could be reached by a creditor of the organization and when he is merely a "dummy" acting as the agent of the limited partners. Notwithstanding the formation of the organization as a limited partnership, when the limited partners act as the principals of such general partner, personal liability will exist with respect to such limited partners. Also, if a corporation is a general partner, personal liability exists with respect to such general partner when the corporation has substantial assets (other than its interest in the partnership) which could be reached by a creditor of the limited partnership. A general partner may contribute his services, but no capital, to the organization, but if such general partner has substantial assets (other than his interest in the partnership), there exists personal liability. Furthermore, if the organization is engaged in financial transac-

Reg. § 301.7701-2(d)(2)

tions which involve large sums of money, and if the general partners have substantial assets (other than their interests in the partnership), there exists personal liability although the assets of such general partners would be insufficient to satisfy any substantial portion of the obligations of the organization. In addition, although the general partner has no substantial assets (other than his interest in the partnership), personal liability exists with respect to such general partner when he is not merely a "dummy" acting as the agent of the limited partners.

(e) *Free transferability of interests.* (1) An organization has the corporate characteristic of transferability of interests if each of its members or those members owning substantially all of the interests in the organization have the power, without the consent of other members, to substitute for themselves in the same organization a person who is not a member of the organization. In order for this power of substitution to exist in the corporate sense, the member must be able, without the consent of the other members, to confer upon his substitute all the attributes of his interest in the organization. Thus, the characteristic of free transferability of interests does not exist in a case in which each member can, without the consent of other members, assign only his right to share in profits but cannot so assign his rights to participate in the management of the organization. Furthermore, although the agreement provides for the transfer of a member's interest, there is no power of substitution and no free transferability of interest if under local law a transfer of a member's interest results in the dissolution of the old organization and the formation of a new organization.

(2) If each member of an organization can transfer his interest to a person who is not a member of the organization only after having offered such interest to the other members at its fair market value, it will be recognized that a modified form of free transferability of interests exists. In determining the classification of an organization, the presence of this modified corporate characteristic will be accorded less significance than if such characteristic were present in an unmodified form.

(f) *Cross reference.* See paragraph (b) of § 301.7701-3 for the application to limited partnerships of the rules relating to corporate characteristics.

(g) *Examples.* The application of the rules described in this section may be illustrated by the following examples:

Example (1). [Deleted]

Example (2). A group of seven doctors forms a clinic for the purpose of furnishing, for profit, medical and surgical services to the public. They each transfer assets to the clinic and their agreement provides that except upon complete liquidation of the organization on the vote of three-fourths of its members, no member has any individual interest in its assets. Their agreement also provides that neither the death, insanity, bankruptcy, retirement, resignation, nor expulsion of a member shall cause the dissolution of the organization. However, under the applicable local law, a member who withdraws does have the power to dissolve the organization. While the agreement provides that the management of the clinic is to be vested exclusively in an executive committee of four members elected by all the members, this provision is ineffective as against outsiders who had no notice of it; and, therefore, the act of any member within the scope of the organization's business binds the organization insofar as such outsiders are concerned. While the agreement declares that each individual doctor alone is liable for acts of malpractice, members of the clinic are, nevertheless, personally liable for all debts of the clinic including claims based on malpractice. No member has the right, without the consent of all the other members, to transfer his interest to a doctor who is not a member of the clinic. The organization has associates and an objective to carry on business and divide the gains therefrom. However, it does not have the corporate characteristics of continuity of life, centralized management, limited liability, and free transferability of interests. The organization will be classified as a partnership for all purposes of the Internal Revenue Code.

Example (3). A group of twenty-five lawyers forms an organization for the purpose of furnishing, for profit, legal services to the public. Their agreement provides that the organization will dissolve upon the death, insanity, bankruptcy, retirement, or expulsion of a member. While their agreement provides that the management of the organization is to be vested exclusively in an executive committee of five members elected by all the members, this provision is ineffective as against outsiders who had no notice of it; and, therefore, the act of any member within the scope of the organization's business binds the organization insofar as such outsiders are concerned. Members of the organization are personally liable for all debts, or claims against, the organization. No member has the right, without the consent of all the other members, to transfer his interest to a lawyer who is not a member of the organization. The organization has associates and an objective to carry on business and divide the gains therefrom. However, the four corporate characteristics of limited liability, centralized management, free transferability of interests, and continuity of life are absent in this case. The organization will be classified as a partnership for all purposes of the Internal Revenue Code.

Example (4). A group of twenty-five persons forms an organization for the purpose of engaging in real estate investment activities. Each member has the power to dissolve the organization at any time. The management of the organization is vested exclusively in an executive committee of five members elected by all the members, and under the applicable local law, no one acting without the authority of this committee has the power to bind the organization by his acts. Under the applicable local law, each member is personally liable for the obligations of the organization. Every member has the right to transfer his interest to a person who is not a member of the organization, but he must first advise the organization of the proposed transfer and give it the opportunity on a vote of the majority to purchase the interest at its fair market value. The organization has associates and an objective to carry on business and divide the gains therefrom. While the organization does have the characteristics of centralized management and a modified form of free transferability of interests, it does not have the corporate characteristics of continuity of life and limited liability. Under the circumstances presented, the organization will be classified as a partnership for all purposes of the Internal Revenue Code.

Example (5). A group of twenty-five persons forms an organization for the purpose of engaging in real estate investment activities. Under their agreement, the organization is to have a life of twenty years, and under the applicable local law, no member has the power to dissolve the organization prior to the expiration of that period. The management of the organization is vested exclusively in an executive committee of five members elected by all the members, and under the applicable local law, no one acting without the authority of this committee has the power to bind the organization by his acts. Under the applicable local law, each member is personally liable for the obligations of the organization. Every member has the right to transfer his interest to a person who is not a member of the organization, but he must first advise the organization of the proposed transfer and give it the opportunity on a vote of the majority to purchase the interest at its fair market value. The organization has associates and an objective to carry on business and divide the gains therefrom. While the organization does not have the corporate characteristic of limited liability, it does have continuity of life, centralized management, and a modified form of free transferability of interests. The organization will be classified as an association for all purposes of the Internal Revenue Code.

Example (6). A group of twenty-five persons forms an organization for purposes of engaging in real estate investment activities. Each member has the power to dissolve the organization at any time. The management of the organization is vested exclusively in an executive committee of five members elected by all the members, and under the applicable local law, no one acting without the authority of this committee has the power to bind the organization by his acts. Under the applicable local law, the liability of each member for the obligations of the organization is limited to paid and subscribed capital. Every member has the right to transfer his interest to a person who is not a member of the organization, but he must first advise the organization of the proposed transfer and give it the opportunity on a vote of the majority to purchase the interest at its fair market value. The organization has associates and an objective to carry on business and divide the gains therefrom. While the organization does not have the characteristic of continuity of life, it does have limited liability, centralized management, and a modified form of free transferability of interests. The organization will be classified as an association for all purposes of the Internal Revenue Code.

Example (7). A group of twenty-five persons forms an organization for the purpose of investing in securities so as to educate the members in principles and techniques of investment practices and to share the income from such investments. While the agreement states that the organization will operate until terminated by a three-fourths vote of the total membership and will not terminate upon the withdrawal or death of any member, under the applicable local law, a member has the power to dissolve the organization at any time. The business of the organization is carried on by the members at regular monthly meetings and buy or sell action may be taken only when voted by a majority of the organization's membership present. Elected officers perform only ministerial functions such as presiding at meetings and carrying out the directions of the members. Members of the organization are personally liable for all debts of, or claims against, the organization. No member may transfer his membership. The organization has associates and an objective to carry on business and divide the gains therefrom. However, the organization does not have the corporate characteristics of limited liability, free transferability of interests, continuity of life, and centralized management. The organization will be treated as a partnership for all purposes of the Internal Revenue Code.

(ii) In determining whether a professional service organization has the major characteristics ordinarily found in a business corporation and whether any other significant factors are to be taken into account in classifying the organization, the special professional requirements of the profession engaged in by the members of the organization must be taken into consideration. Although such an organization may have associates and is engaged in business for profit, the relationships of the members of such an organization to each other as well as their relationships to employees, to clients, patients, or customers and to the public are inherently different from the relationships characteristic of an ordinary business corporation. In determining the nature of these relationships, consideration must be given to the law under which the organization is formed, the character, articles of associatiton, by-laws, or other documents relating to the formation of the organization, and all other facts and rules governing or pertaining to such relationships in the usual course of the practice of the profession of the participants.

(2) A professional service organization does not have continuity of life within the meaning of paragraph (b) of this section if the death, insanity, bankruptcy, retirement, resignation, expulsion, professional disqualification, or election to inconsistent public office of any member will (determined without regard to any agreement among the members) cause under local law the dissolution of the organization. A business corporation has a continuing identity as an entity which is not dependent upon a shareholder's active participation in any capacity in the production of the income of the corporation. Furthermore, the interest of a shareholder in an ordinary business corporation includes a right to share in the profits of the corporation, and such right is not legally dependent (determined without regard to any agreement among the shareholders) upon his participation in the production of the corporation's income. However, the interest of a member of a professional service organization generally is inextricably bound to the establishment and continuance of an employ-

Reg. § 301.7701-2(g)

ment relationship with the organization, and he cannot share in the profits of a professional service organization unless he also shares in the performance of the services rendered by the organization. For purposes of this paragraph, the term "employment relationship" is used to describe such active participation by the member and is not restricted to the common-law meaning of such term. If local law, applicable regulations, or professional ethics do not permit a member of a professional service organization to share in its profits unless an employment relationship exists between him and the organization, and if in such case, he or his estate is required to dispose of his interest in the organization if the employment relationship terminates, the continuing existence of the organization depends upon the willingness of its remaining members, if any, either to agree, by prior arrangement or at the time of such termination, to acquire his interest or to employ his proposed successor. The continued existence of such a professional service organization is similar to that of a partnership formed under the Uniform Partnership Act, whose business continues pursuant to an agreement providing that the business will be continued by the remaining members after the withdrawal or death of a partner (see paragraph (b) of this section), and is essentially different from the continuity of life possessed by an ordinary business corporation. Consequently, such a professional service organization lacks continuity of life.

(3) In applying the rules of paragraph (c) of this section, relating to centralization of management, a professional service organization does not have centralization of management where the managers of a professional service organization under local law are not vested with the continuing exclusive authority to determine any one or more of the following matters: (i) The hiring and firing of professional members of the organization and its professional and lay employees, (ii) the compensation of the members and of such employees, (iii) the conditions of employment—such as working hours, vacation periods, and sick leave, (iv) the persons who will be accepted as clients or patients, (v) who will handle each individual case or matter, (vi) the professional policies and procedures to be followed in handling each individual case, (vii) the fees to be charged by the organization, (viii) the nature of the records to be kept, their use, and their disposition, and (ix) the times and amounts of distributions of the earnings of the organization to its members as such. Moreover, although a measure of central control may exist in a professional service organization, the managers of a professional service organization in which a member retains traditional professional responsibility cannot have the continuing exclusive authority to determine all of the matters described in the preceding sentence. Instead, such measure of central control is no more than that existing in an ordinary large professional partnership which has one or more so-called managing partners and in which a member retains the traditional professional autonomy with respect to professional decisions and the traditional responsibility of a professional person to the client or patient. Such measure of central control is essentially different from the centralization of management existing in an ordinary business corporation. Therefore, centralization of management does not exist in such a professional service organization.

(4) A professional service organization has the corporate characteristic of limited liability within the meaning of paragraph (d) of this section only if the personal liability of its members, in their capacity as members of the organization, is no greater in any aspect than that of shareholder-employees of an ordinary business corporation. If under local law and the rules pertaining to professional practice, a mutual agency relationship, similar to that existing in an ordinary professional partnership, exists between the members of a professional service organization, such organization lacks the corporate characteristic of limited liability.

(5) (i) If the right of a member of a professional service organization to share in its profits is dependent upon the existence of an employment relationship between him and the organization, free transferability of interests within the meaning of paragraph (e) of this section exists only if the member, without the consent of other members, may transfer both the right to share in the profits of the organization and the right to an employment relationship with the organization.

(ii) The corporate characteristic of free transferability of interests exists in a modified form within the meaning of paragraph (e) (2) of this section when a shareholder in an ordinary business corporation can transfer his interest in such corporation only after having offered such interest to the other shareholders at its fair market value. In such a case, the so-called right of first refusal applies only to an interest which is a right to share in the profits, the assets, and the management of the enterprise. However, if the interest of a member of a professional service organization constitutes a right to share in the profits of the organization which is contingent upon and inseparable from the member's continuing employment relationship with the organization, and the transfer of such interest is subject to a right of first refusal, such interest is subject to a power in the other members of the organization to determine not only the individuals whom the organization is to employ, but also who may share with them in the profits of the organization. The possession by other members of the power to determine, in connection with the transfer of such an interest, whom the organization is to employ is so substantial a hindrance upon the free transferability of interests in the organization that such power precludes the existence of a modified form of free transferability of interests. Therefore, if a member of a professional service organization who possesses such an interest may transfer his interest to a qualified person who is not a member of the organization only after having first offered his interest to the other members of the organization at its fair market value, the corporate characteristic of free transferability of interests does not exist.

§ 301.7701-3 (T.D. 6503, filed 11-15-60.) Partnerships.

(a) *In general.* The term "partnership" is broader in scope than the common law meaning of partnership and may include groups not commonly called partnerships. Thus, the term "partnership" includes a syndicate, group, pool, joint venture, or other unincorporated organization through or by means of which any business, financial operation, or venture is carried on, and which is not a corporation or a trust or estate within the meaning of the Internal Revenue Code of 1954. A joint undertaking merely to share expenses is not a partnership. For example, if two or more persons jointly construct a ditch merely to drain surface water from their properties, they are not partners. Mere co-ownership of property which is maintained, kept in repair, and rented or leased does not constitute a partnership. For example, if an individual owner, or tenants in common, of farm property lease it to a farmer for a cash rental or a share of the crops, they do not necessarily create a partnership thereby. Tenants in common, however, may be partners if they actively carry on a trade, business, financial operation, or venture and divide the profits thereof. For example, a partnership exists if co-owners of an apartment building lease space and in addition provide services to the occupants either directly or through an agent.

(b) *Limited partnerships*—(1) *In general.* An organization which qualifies as a limited partnership under State law may be classified for purposes of the Internal Revenue Code as an ordinary partnership or as an association. Such a limited partnership will be treated as an association if, applying the principles set forth in § 301.7701-2, the organization more nearly resembles a corporation than an ordinary partnership or other business entity.

(2) *Examples.* The principles of this paragraph may be illustrated by the following examples:

Example (1). Three individuals form an organization which qualifies as a limited partnership under the laws of the State in which the organization was formed. The purpose of the organization is to acquire and operate various pieces of commercial and other investment property for profit. Each of the three individuals who are general partners invests $100,000 in the enterprise. Five million dollars of additional capital is raised through contributions of $100,000 or more by each of thirty limited partners. The three general partners are personally capable of assuming a substantial part of the obligations to be incurred by the organization. While a limited partner may assign his right to receive a share of the profits and a return of his contribution, his assignee does not become a substituted limited partner except with the unanimous consent of the general partners. The life of the organization as stated in the certificate is 20 years, but the death, insanity, or retirement of a general partner prior to the expiration of the 20-year period will dissolve the organization. The general partners have exclusive authority to manage the affairs of the organization but can act only upon the unanimous consent of all of them. The organization has associates and an objective to carry on business and divide the gains therefrom, which characterize both partnerships and corporations. While the organization has the corporate characteristic of centralized management, since substantially all of the interests in the organization are owned by the limited partners, it does not have the characteristics of continuity of life, free transferability of interests, or limited liability. The organization will be classified as a partnership for all purposes of the Internal Revenue Code.

Example (2). Three individuals form an organization which qualifies as a limited partnership under the laws of the State in which the organization was formed. The purpose of the organization is to acquire and operate various pieces of commercial and other investment property for profit. The certificate provides that the life of the organization is to be 40 years, unless a general partner dies, becomes insane, or retires during such period. On the occurrence of such death, insanity, or retirement, the remaining general partners may continue the business of the partnership for the balance of the 40-year period under a right so to do stated in the certificate. Each of the three individuals who is a general partner invests $50,000 in the enterprise and has means to satisfy the business obligations of the organization to a substantial extent. Five million dollars of additional capital is raised through the sale of freely transferable interests in amounts of $10,000 or less to limited partners. Nine hundred such interests are sold. The interests of the 900 limited partners are fully transferable, that is, a transferee acquires all the attributes of the transferor's interest in the organization. The general partners have exclusive control over management of the business, their interests are not transferable, and their liability for debts of the organization is not limited to their capital contributions. The organization has associates and an objective to carry on business and divide the gains therefrom. It does not have the corporate characteristic of limited liability and continuity of life. It has centralized management, however, since the three general partners exercise exclusive control over the management of the business, and since substantially all of the interests in the organization are owned by the limited partners. While the interests of the general partners are not transferable, the transferability test of an association is met since substantially all of the interests in the organization are represented by transferable interests. The organization will be classified as a partnership for all purposes of the Internal Revenue Code.

(c) *Partnership associations.* The laws of a number of States provide for the formation of organizations commonly known as partnership associations. Such a partnership association will be treated as an association if, applying the principles set forth in § 301.7701-2, the organization more nearly resembles a corporation than the other types of business entities.

(d) *Partner.* The term "partner" means a member of a partnership.

Reg. § 301.7701-3(d)

§ 301.7701-4 (T.D. 6503, filed 11-15-60.)
Trusts.

(a) *Ordinary trusts.* In general, the term "trust" as used in the Internal Revenue Code refers to an arrangement created either by a will or by an inter vivos declaration whereby trustees take title to property for the purpose of protecting or conserving it for the beneficiaries under the ordinary rules applied in chancery or probate courts. Usually the beneficiaries of such a trust do no more than accept the benefits thereof and are not the voluntary planners or creators of the trust arrangement. However, the beneficiaries of such a trust may be the persons who create it and it will be recognized as a trust under the Internal Revenue Code if it was created for the purpose of protecting or conserving the trust property for beneficiaries who stand in the same relation to the trust as they would if the trust had been created by others for them. Generally speaking, an arrangement will be treated as a trust under the Internal Revenue Code if it can be shown that the purpose of the arrangement is to vest in trustees responsibility for the protection and conservation of property for beneficiaries who cannot share in the discharge of this responsibility and, therefore, are not associates in a joint enterprise for the conduct of business for profit.

(b) *Business trusts.* There are other arrangements which are known as trusts because the legal title to property is conveyed to trustees for the benefit of beneficiaries, but which are not classified as trusts for purposes of the Internal Revenue Code because they are not simply arrangements to protect or conserve the property for the beneficiaries. These trusts, which are often known as business or commercial trusts, generally are created by the beneficiaries simply as a device to carry on a profit-making business which normally would have been carried on through business organizations that are classified as corporations or partnerships under the Internal Revenue Code. However, the fact that the corpus of the trust is not supplied by the beneficiaries is not sufficient reason in itself for classifying the arrangement as an ordinary trust rather than as an association or partnership. The fact that any organization is technically cast in the trust form, by conveying title to property to trustees for the benefit of persons designated as beneficiaries, will not change the real character of the organization if, applying the principles set forth in §§ 301.7701-2 and 301.7701-3, the organization more nearly resembles an association or a partnership than a trust.

(c) *Certain investment trusts.* An "investment" trust of the type commonly known as a management trust is an association, and a trust of the type commonly known as a fixed investment trust is an association if there is power under the trust agreement to vary the investment of the certificate holders. See Commissioner v. North American Bond Trust (C.C.A. 2d 1941) 122 F.2d 545, cert. denied 314 U.S. 701. However, if there is no power under the trust agreement to vary the investment of the certificate holders, such fixed investment trust shall be classified as a trust.

(d) *Liquidating trusts.* Certain organizations which are commonly known as liquidating trusts are treated as trusts for purposes of the Internal Revenue Code. An organization will be considered a liquidating trust if it is organized for the primary purpose of liquidating and distributing the assets transferred to it, and if its activities are all reasonably necessary to, and consistent with, the accomplishment of that purpose. A liquidating trust is treated as a trust for purposes of the Internal Revenue Code because it is formed with the objective of liquidating particular assets and not as an organization having as its purpose the carrying on of a profit-making business which normally would be conducted through business organizations classified as corporations or partnerships. However, if the liquidation is unreasonably prolonged or if the liquidation purpose becomes so obscured by business activities that the declared purpose of liquidation can be said to be lost or abandoned, the status of the organization will no longer be that of a liquidating trust. Bondholders' protective committees, voting trusts, and other agencies formed to protect the interests of security holders during insolvency, bankruptcy, or corporate reorganization proceedings are analogous to liquidating trusts but if subsequently utilized to further the control or profitable operation of a going business on a permanent continuing basis, they will lose their classification as trusts for purposes of the Internal Revenue Code.

§ 301.7701-5 (T.D. 6503, filed 11-15-60.)
Domestic, foreign, resident, and nonresident persons.

A domestic corporation is one organized or created in the United States, including only the States (and during the periods when not States, the Territories of Alaska and Hawaii), and the District of Columbia, or under the law of the United States or of any State or Territory. A foreign corporation is one which is not domestic. A domestic corporation is a resident corporation even though it does no business and owns no property in the United States. A foreign corporation engaged in trade or business within the United States is referred to in the regulations in this chapter as a resident foreign corporation, and a foreign corporation not engaged in trade or business within the United States, as a nonresident foreign corporation. A partnership engaged in trade or business within the United States is referred to in the regulations in this chapter as a resident partnership, and a partnership not engaged in trade or business within the United States, as a nonresident partnership. Whether a partnership is to be regarded as resident or nonresident is not determined by the nationality or residence of its members or by the place in which it was created or organized. The term "nonresident alien", as used in the regulations in this chapter, includes a nonresident alien individual and a nonresident alien fiduciary.

§ 301.7701-6 (T.D. 6503, filed 11-15-60.)
Fiduciary.

"Fiduciary" is a term which applies to persons who occupy positions of peculiar confidence toward others, such as trustees, executors, and administrators. A fiduciary is a person who holds in trust an estate to which another has the beneficial title or in which another has a beneficial interest, or receives and controls income of another, as in the case of receivers. A committee or guardian of the property of an incompetent person is a fiduciary.

§ 301.7701-7 (T.D. 6503, filed 11-15-60.)
Fiduciary distinguished from agent.

There may be a fiduciary relationship between an agent and a principal, but the word "agent" does not denote a fiduciary. An agent having entire charge of property, with authority to effect and execute leases with tenants entirely on his own responsibility and without consulting his principal, merely turning over the net profits from the property periodically to his principal by virtue of authority conferred upon him by a power of attorney, is not a fiduciary within the meaning of the Internal Revenue Code. In cases where no legal trust has been created in the estate controlled by the agent and attorney, the liability to make a return rests with the principal.

§ 301.7701-8 (T.D. 6503, filed 11-15-60.)
Military or naval forces and Armed Forces of the United States.

The term "military or naval forces of the United States" and the term "Armed Forces of the United States" each includes all regular and reserve components of the uniformed services which are subject to the jurisdiction of the Secretary of Defense, the Secretary of the Army, the Secretary of the Navy, or the Secretary of the Air Force. The terms also include the Coast Guard. The members of such forces include commissioned officers and the personnel below the grade of commissioned officer in such forces.

§ 301.7701-9 (T.D. 6503, filed 11-15-60; amended by T.D. 6585, filed 12-27-61.)
Secretary or his delegate.

(a) The term "Secretary or his delegate" means the Secretary of the Treasury, or any officer, employee, or agency of the Treasury Department duly authorized by the Secretary (directly, or indirectly by one or more redelegations of authority) to perform the function mentioned or described in the context, and the term "or his delegate" when used in connection with any other official of the United States shall be similarly construed.

(b) In any case in which a function is vested by the Internal Revenue Code of 1954 or any other statute in the Secretary or his delegate, and Treasury regulations or Treasury decisions approved by the Secretary or his delegate provide that such function may be performed by the Commissioner, assistant commissioner, regional commissioner, assistant regional commissioner, district director, director of a regional service center, or by a designated officer or employee in the office of any such officer, such provision in the regulations or Treasury decision shall constitute a delegation by the Secretary of the authority to perform such function to the designated officer or employee. If such authority is delegated to any officer or employee performing services under the supervision and control of the Commissioner, such provision in the regulations or Treasury decision shall constitute a delegation by the Secretary to the Commissioner of the authority to perform such function and a redelegation thereof by the Commissioner to the designated officer or employee.

(c) An officer or employee, including the Commissioner, authorized by regulations or Treasury decision to perform a function shall have authority to redelegate the performance of such function to any officer or employee performing services under his supervision and control, unless such power to so redelegate is prohibited or restricted by proper order or directive. The Commissioner may also redelegate authority to perform such function to other officers or employees under his supervision and control and, to the extent he deems proper, may authorize further redelegation of such authority.

(d) The Commissioner may prescribe such limitations as he deems proper on the extent to which any officer or employee under his supervision and control shall perform any such function, but, in the case of an officer or employee designated in regulations or Treasury decision is authorized to perform such function, such limitations shall not render invalid any performance by such officer or employee of the function which, except for such limitations, such officer or employee is authorized to perform by such regulations or Treasury decision in effect at the time the function is performed.

§ 301.7701-10 (T.D. 6503, filed 11-15-60.)
District director.

The term "district director" means the district director of internal revenue for an internal revenue district. The term also includes the Director of International Operations.

§ 301.7701-11 (T.D. 6604, filed 8-24-62; amended by T.D. 7306, filed 3-14-74.) Social security number.

For purposes of this chapter, the term "social security number" means the taxpayer identifying number of an individual or estate which is assigned pursuant to section 6011(b) or corresponding provisions of prior law, or pursuant to section 6109, and in which nine digits are separated by hyphens as follows: 000-00-0000. Such term does not include a number with a letter as a suffix which is used to identify an auxiliary beneficiary under the social security program. The terms "account number" and "social security number" refer to the same number.

§ 301.7701-12 (T.D. 6606, filed 8-24-62; amended by T.D. 7306, filed 3-14-74.) Employer identification number.

For purposes of this chapter, the term "employer identification number" means the taxpayer identifying number of an individual or other person (whether or not an employer) which is assigned pursuant to section 6011(b) or corresponding provisions of prior law, or pursuant to section

Reg. § 301.7701-12

24,438 (I.R.C.)   Reg. § 301.7701-12   3-18-74

6109, and in which nine digits are separated by a hyphen, as follows: 00-0000000. The terms "employer identification number" and "identification number" (defined in § 31.0-2(a)(11) of this chapter (Employment Tax Regulations)) refer to the same number.

§ 301.7701-13 (T.D. 6766, filed 11-2-64.) **Domestic building and loan association.**

(a) *In general.* For taxable years beginning after October 16, 1962, the term "domestic building and loan association" means a domestic building and loan association, a domestic savings and loan association, a Federal savings and loan association, and any other savings institution chartered and supervised as a savings and loan or similar association under Federal or State law which meets the supervisory test (described in paragraph (b) of this section), the business operations test (described in paragraph (c) of this section), and each of the various assets tests (described in paragraphs (d), (e), (f), and (h) of this section).

(b) *Supervisory test.* A domestic building and loan association must be either (1) an insured institution within the meaning of section 401(a) of the National Housing Act (12 U.S.C., sec. 1724 (a)) or (2) subject by law to supervision and examination by State or Federal authority having supervision over such associations. An "insured institution" is one the accounts of which are insured by the Federal Savings and Loan Insurance Corporation.

(c) *Business operations test*—(1) *In general.* An association must utilize its assets so that substantially all of its business consists of acquiring the savings of the public and investing in the loans described in subparagraphs (6) through (10) of paragraph (d) of this section. The requirement of this paragraph is referred to in this section as the business operations test. The business of acquiring the savings of the public and investing in the prescribed loans includes ancillary or incidental activities which are directly and primarily related to such acquisition and investment, such as advertising for savings, appraising property on which loans are to be made by the association, and inspecting the progress of construction in connection with construction loans. Even though an association meets the supervisory test in paragraph (b) and all the assets tests described in paragraph (d) through (h) of this section, it will nevertheless not qualify as a domestic building and loan association if any substantial part of its business consists of activities which are not directly and primarily related to such acquisition and investment, such as brokering mortgage paper, selling insurance, or subdividing real estate. However, an association will meet the business operations test for a taxable year if it meets the requirements of both subparagraphs (2) and (3) of this paragraph, relating respectively to acquiring the savings of the public, and investing in loans.

(2) *Acquiring the savings of the public.* The requirement that substantially all of an association's business (other than investing in loans) must consist of acquiring the savings of the public ordinarily will be considered to be met if savings are acquired in all material respects in conformity with the rules and regulations of the Federal Home Loan Bank Board or substantially equivalent rules of a State law or supervisory authority. In addition, such requirement will be considered to be met if more than 85 percent of the dollar amount of the total deposits and withdrawable shares of the association are held during the taxable year by the general public as opposed to amounts deposited by family or related business groups or persons who are officers or directors of the association. The percentage specified in this subparagraph shall be computed as of the close of the taxable year, or at the option of the taxpayer, on the basis of the average of the amounts of deposits held during the year. Such average shall be determined by computing the percentage specified either as of the close of each month, as of the close of each quarter, or semiannually during the taxable year and by using the yearly average of the monthly, quarterly, or semiannual percentages obtained.

(3) *Investing in loans*—(i) *In general.* The requirement that substantially all of an association's business (other than acquiring the savings of the public) must consist of investing in the loans described in subparagraph (6) through (10) of paragraph (d) of this section ordinarily will be considered to be met for a taxable year if the association meets both the gross income test described in subdivision (ii) of this subparagraph, and the sales activity test described in subdivision (iii) of this subparagraph. However, if an association does not meet the requirements of both subdivisions (ii) and (iii) of this subparagraph, it will nevertheless meet the investing in loans requirement if it is able to demonstrate that substantially all its business (other than acquiring the savings of the public) consisted of investing in the prescribed loans. Transactions which are necessitated by exceptional circumstances and which are not undertaken as recurring business activities for profit will not be considered a substantial part of an association's business. Thus, for example, an association would meet the investing in loans requirement if it can establish that it failed to meet the gross income test because of receipt of a nonrecurring item of income due to exceptional circumstances, or it failed to meet the sales activity test because of sales made to achieve necessary liquidity to meet abnormal withdrawals from savings accounts. For the purposes of this subparagraph, however, the acquisition of loans in anticipation of their sale to other financial institutions does not constitute "investing" in loans, even though such acquisition and sale resulted from an excess of demand for loans over savings capital in the association's area.

(ii) *Gross income test.* The gross income test is met if more than 85 percent of the gross income of an association consists of:

(a) Interest or dividends on assets defined in subparagraphs (2), (3), or (4) of paragraph (d) of this section,

(b) Interest on loans defined in subparagraphs (6) through (10) of paragraph (d) of this section,

(c) Income attributable to the portion of property used in the association's business as defined in paragraph (d)(5) of this section,

(d) Premiums, discounts, commissions, or fees (including late charges and penalties) on loans defined in subparagraphs (6)

through (10) of paragraph (d) of this section which have at some time been held by the association, or for which firm commitments have been issued,

(e) Gain or loss on the sale of governmental obligations defined in paragraph (d) (3) of this section, or

(f) Income, gain, or loss attributable to foreclosed property (as defined in paragraph (j) (1) of this section), but not including such income, gain, or loss which, pursuant to section 595 and the regulations thereunder, is not included in gross income. For the purposes of this subparagraph, gross income shall be computed without regard to gains or losses on the sale of the portion of property used in the association's business (described in paragraph (d) (5) of this section), without regard to gains or losses on the rented portion of property used as the principal or branch office of the association (described in such paragraph), and without regard to gains or losses on the sale of participations and loans (other than governmental obligations defined in paragraph (d) (3) of this section). Examples of types of income which would cause an association to fail to meet the gross income test, if in the aggregate they exceed 15 percent of gross income, are the excess of gains over losses on sale of real estate (other than foreclosed property); rental income (other than on foreclosed property and the portion of property used in the association's business); premiums, commissions, and fees (other than commitment fees) on loans which have never been held by the association; and insurance brokerage fees.

(iii) *Sales activity test: in general.* The sales activity test is met for a taxable year if the association meets both the sales of whole loans test described in subdivision (iv) of this subparagraph, and the sales of whole loans and participations test described in subdivision (v) of this subparagraph. For the purposes of this subdivision and subdivisions (iv), (v), and (vi) of this subparagraph:

(a) The term "loan" means loan as defined in paragraph (j) (1) of this section, other than foreclosed property defined in such paragraph and governmental obligations defined in paragraph (d) (3) of this section.

(b) The amount of a loan shall be determined in accordance with the rules contained in paragraph (l) (1) and (2) (ii) of this section.

(c) The term "loans acquired for investment during the taxable year" means the amount of loans outstanding as of the close of the taxable year, reduced (but not below zero) by the amount of loans outstanding as of the beginning of such year, and increased by the lesser of (1) the amount of repayments made on loans during the taxable year or (2) an amount equal to 20 percent of the amount of loans outstanding as of the beginning of the taxable year. For this purpose, repayments do not include repayments on loans to the extent such loans are refinanced by the association.

(d) The term "sales of participations" means sales by an association of interests in loans, which sales meet the requirements of the regulations of the Federal Home Loan Bank Board relating to sales of participations, or which meet substantially equivalent requirements of State law or regulations relating to sales of participations.

(e) The term "sales of whole loans" means sales of loans other than sales of participations as defined in subdivision (d) of this subdivision, but in determining the amount of sales of whole loans, the following sales shall be disregarded: sales of loans made to other financial institutions pursuant to an arrangement whereunder the association simultaneously enters into a bona fide agreement to repurchase such loans within a period of 18 months from the time of sale if such arrangement conforms to the rules and regulations of applicable supervisory authorities; sales made to the Federal Savings and Loan Insurance Corporation or to a corporation defined in paragraph (d) (4) of this section (relating to deposit insurance company securities); and sales made in the course of liquidation of the association pursuant to Federal or State law.

(iv) *Sales of whole loans test.* The sales of whole loans test is met for a taxable year if the amount of sales of whole loans during the taxable year does not exceed the greater of (a) 15 percent of the amount of loans acquired for investment during the taxable year, or (b) 20 percent of the amount of loans outstanding at the beginning of the taxable year. However, the 20 percent of beginning loans limitation specified in subdivision (b) of the previous sentence shall be reduced by the number of percentage points (rounded to the nearest one hundredth of a percentage point) which is equal to the sum of the two percentages obtained by dividing, for each of the two preceding taxable years, the amount of sales of whole loans during each such taxable year by the amount of loans outstanding at the beginning of such taxable year. For example, if the amounts of sales of whole loans made by a calendar year association in 1965 and 1966 were 3 percent and 4 percent, respectively, of loans outstanding at the beginning of each such year, the amount of sales of whole loans allowed under such subdivision (b) for 1967 would be an amount equal to 13 percent (20 percent minus 7 percentage points) of loans outstanding at the beginning of 1967. In computing the reduction to the 20 percent of beginning loans limitation specified in such subdivision (b), sales of whole loans made before January 1, 1964, shall not be taken into account.

(v) *Sales of whole loans and participations test.* The sales of whole loans and participations test is met if the sum of the amount of sales of whole loans and the amount of sales of participations during the taxable year does not exceed 100 percent of the amount of loans acquired for investment during the taxable year.

(vi) *Sales activity test: special rules—* (a) *Carryover of sales.* The amount specified in subdivision (iv) (a) of this subparagraph as the maximum amount of sales of whole loans shall be increased by the amount by which 15 percent of the amount

Reg. § 301.7701-13(c) (3)

of loans acquired for investment by the association during the two preceding taxable years exceeds the amount of sales of whole loans made during such preceding taxable years; and the amount specified in subdivision (v) of this subparagraph as the maximum amount of sales of whole loans and participations shall be increased by the amount by which the amount of loans acquired for investment by the association during the two preceding taxable years exceeds the sum of the amount of sales of whole loans and participations made during such preceding taxable years. For example, if 15 percent of the amount of loans acquired for investment in 1965 and 1966 exceeded the amount of sales of whole loans during such years by $250,000, the amount of sales of whole loans permitted in 1967 under subdivision (iv) *(a)* of this subparagraph would be increased by $250,000.

(b) Use of preceding year's base. If the amount of loans acquired for investment by the association during the preceding taxable year exceeds such amount for the current taxable year, the 15 percent limitation provided in subdivision (iv) *(a)* of this subparagraph and the 100 percent limitation provided in subdivision (v) of this subparagraph shall be based upon such preceding taxable year's amount. However, the maximum amount of sales of whole loans permitted under subdivision (iv) *(a)* and the maximum amount of sales of whole loans and participations permitted under subdivision (v) in any taxable year shall be reduced by the amount of the increase in such sales allowed for the preceding taxable year solely by reason of the application of the provisions of the previous sentence. For example, assuming no carryover of sales under subdivision *(a)* of this subdivision, if the amount of loans acquired for investment by a calendar year association was $1,000,000 in 1965, under subdivision (iv) *(a)* of this subparagraph the association could make sales of whole loans in 1966 of $150,000 (15% of $1,000,000) even though the amount of its loans acquired for investment during 1966 was only $800,000. However, the amount of sales of whole loans permitted in 1967 under subdivision (iv) *(a)* of this subparagraph would be reduced to the extent that the amount of the sales of whole loans made by the association during 1966 exceeded $120,000 (15% of $800,000).

(vii) *Examples illustrating sales activity test.* The provisions of subdivisions (iii) through (vi) of this subparagraph may be illustrated by the following examples in each of which it is assumed that the association is a calendar year taxpayer which is operated in all material respects in conformity with applicable rules and regulations of Federal or State supervisory authorities.

Example (1). X Association made sales of whole loans in 1964 and 1965 which were 10 percent and 7 percent, respectively, of the amounts of loans outstanding at the beginning of each such year, and which were 25 percent and 17 percent, respectively, of the amounts of loans acquired for investment in each such year. The amount of X's loans outstanding at the beginning of 1966 was $1,000,000, and the amount of its loans acquired for investment for such year was $300,000. The maximum amount of sales of whole loans which X may make under the percentage of beginning loans limitation for 1966 is $30,000, which is 3 percent (20 percent reduced by the sum of 10 percent and 7 percent) of $1,000,000. The maximum amount of sales of whole loans permitted under the percentage of loans acquired for investment limitation for 1966 is $45,000 (15 percent of $300,000). X may therefore sell whole loans in an amount up to $45,000 in 1966 and meet the sales of whole loans test. It is assumed that the amount of loans acquired for investment in 1965 did not exceed $300,000, so that the preceding year's base cannot be used to increase the amount of sales permitted in 1966.

Example (2). Assume the same facts as in the previous example, except that the amount of loans acquired for investment in the preceding year (1965) was $320,000. Since such amount is greater than the $300,000 amount of loans acquired for investment in 1966, X may base its 15 percent limitation for 1966 on the $320,000 amount and sell whole loans in an amount up to $48,000 (15 percent of $320,000) and still meet the sales of whole loans test. However, to the extent that the amount of sales of whole loans exceeds $45,000 (15 percent of the $300,000 amount of loans acquired for investment in 1966), the maximum amount of sales computed under the percentage of loans acquired for investment limitation (but not the 20 percent of beginning loans limitation) for 1967 must be reduced.

Example (3). Y Association made no sales of whole loans in 1964 and 1965, and made sales of participations in the two years in amounts which, in the aggregate, were $50,000 less than the amounts of loans acquired for investment for such years. At the beginning of 1966 the amount of Y's loans outstanding was $1,000,000, and the amount of its loans acquired for investment in such year was $100,000. Although the maximum amount of sales of whole loans which Y could make under the sales of whole loans test is $200,000 (20 percent of $1,000,000), nevertheless, in order to meet the sales of whole loans and participations test, the sum of the amounts of sales of whole loans and sales of participations may not exceed $150,000 (100 percent of the $100,000 amount of loans acquired for investment in 1966 plus a carryover of sales from the previous two years of $50,000). It is assumed that the amount of loans acquired for investment in 1965 did not exceed $100,000, so that the preceding year's base cannot be used to increase the amount of sales permitted in 1966.

(viii) *Reporting requirements.* In the case of income tax returns for taxable years ending after October 31, 1964, there shall be filed with the return a statement showing the amount of gross income for the taxable year in each of the categories described in subdivision (ii) of this subparagraph; and, for the taxable year and the two preceding taxable years, the amount of loans (described in subdivision (iii) *(a)* of this subparagraph) outstanding at the beginning of the year and at the end of the year, the amount of repayments on loans (not including repayments on loans to the extent such loans are refinanced by the association), the amount of sales of whole loans, and the amount of sales of participations.

(4) *Effective date.* The provisions of subparagraphs (1) through (3) of this paragraph are applicable to taxable years ending after October 31, 1964. However, at the option of the taxpayer, for a taxable year beginning before November 1, 1964, and ending after October 31, 1964, the provisions of subparagraphs (1) through (3) of this paragraph (except the 20 percent of beginning loans limitation specified in subdivision (iv) (*b*) of subparagraph (3) of this paragraph) shall apply only to the part year falling after October 31, 1964, as if such part year constituted a taxable year. In such case, the following rules shall apply:

(i) The amount of the "loans acquired for investment" for such part year shall be equal to the loans acquired for investment during the entire taxable year within which falls such part year, multiplied by a fraction the numerator of which is the number of days in such part year and the denominator of which is the number of days in such entire taxable year.

(ii) The increase in sales of whole loans and participations permitted by subdivision (vi) of subparagraph (3) of this paragraph (relating to carryover of sales and use of preceding year's base) shall be the amount of such increase computed under such subdivision, multiplied by the fraction specified in subdivision (i) of this subparagraph.

If, treating the part year as a taxable year, the association meets all the requirements of this paragraph for such part year it will be considered to have met the business operations test for the entire taxable year, providing it operated in all material respects in conformity with applicable rules and regulations of Federal or State supervisory authorities for the entire taxable year. The 20 percent of beginning loans limitation specified in subdivision (iv)(*b*) of subparagraph (3) of this paragraph shall be applied only on the basis of a taxable year and not the part year. For taxable years beginning after October 16, 1962, and ending before November 1, 1964, an association will be considered to have met the business operations test if it operated in all material respects in conformity with applicable rules and regulations of Federal or State supervisory authorities.

(d) *90 percent of assets test*—(1) *In general.* At least 90 percent of the amount of the total assets of a domestic building and loan association must consist of the assets defined in subparagraphs (2) through (10) of this paragraph. For purposes of this paragraph, it is immaterial whether the association originated the loans defined in subparagraphs (6) through (10) of this paragraph or purchased or otherwise acquired them in whole or in part from another. See paragraph (j) of this section for definition of certain terms used in this paragraph, and paragraph (k) of this section for the determination of amount and character of loans.

(2) *Cash.* The term "cash" means cash on hand, and time or demand deposits with, or withdrawable accounts in, other financial institutions.

(3) *Governmental obligations.* The term "governmental obligations" means obligations of the United States, a State or political subdivision of a State, and stock or obligations of a corporation which is an instrumentality of the United States, a State or political subdivision of a State.

(4) *Deposit insurance company securities.* The term "deposit insurance company securities" means certificates of deposit in, or obligations of, a corporation organized under a State law which specifically authorizes such corporation to insure the deposits or share accounts of member associations.

(5) *Property used in the association's business.*—(i) *In general.* The term "property used in the association's business" means land, buildings, furniture, fixtures, equipment, leasehold interests, leasehold improvements, and other assets used by the association in the conduct of its business of acquiring the savings of the public and investing in the loans defined in subparagraphs (6) through (10) of this paragraph. Real property held for the purpose of being used primarily as the principal or branch office of the association constitutes property used in the association's business so long as it is reasonably anticipated that such property will be occupied for such use by the association, or that construction work preparatory to such occupancy will be commenced thereon, within two years after acquisition of the property. Stock of a wholly owned subsidiary corporation which has as its exclusive activity the ownership and management of property more than 50 percent of the fair rental value of which is used as the principal or branch office of the association constitutes property used in such business. Real property held by an association for investment or sale, even for the purpose of obtaining mortgage loans thereon, does not constitute property used in the association's business.

(ii) *Property rented to others.* Except as provided in the second sentence of subdivision (i) of this subparagraph, property or a portion thereof rented by the association to others does not constitute property used in the association's business. However, if the fair rental value of the rented portion of a single piece of real property (including appurtenant parcels) used as the principal or branch office of the association constitutes less than 50 percent of the fair rental value of such piece of property, or if such property has an adjusted basis of not more than $150,000, the entire property shall be considered used in such business. If such rented portion constitutes 50 percent or more of the fair rental value of such piece of property, and such property has an adjusted basis of more than $150,000, an allocation of its adjusted basis is required. The portion of the total adjusted basis of such piece of property which is deemed to be property used in the association's business shall be equal to an amount which

Reg. § 301.7701-13(d)(5)

bears the same ratio to such total adjusted basis as the amount of the fair rental value of the portion used as the principal or branch office of the association bears to the total fair rental value of such property. In the case of all property other than real property used or to be used as the principal or branch office of the association, if the fair rental value of the rented portion thereof constitutes less than 15 percent of the fair rental value of such property, the entire property shall be considered used in the association's business. If such rented portion constitutes 15 percent or more of the fair rental value of such property, an allocation of its adjusted basis (in the same manner as required for real property used as the principal or branch office) is required.

(6) *Passbook loan.* The term "passbook loan" means a loan to the extent secured by a deposit, withdrawable share, or savings account in the association, or share of a member of the association, with respect to which a distribution is allowable as a deduction under section 591.

(7) *Home loan.* The term "home loan" means a loan secured by an interest in—

(i) Improved residential real property consisting of a structure or structures containing, in the aggregate, no more than 4 family units,

(ii) An individually-owned family unit in a multiple-unit structure, the owner of which unit owns an undivided interest in the underlying real estate and the common elements of such structure (so-called condominium type),

or a construction loan or improvement loan for such property. A construction loan made for the purpose of financing more than one structure (so-called tract financing) constitutes a home loan, providing no individual structure contains more than 4 family units and it is contemplated that, as soon as possible after completion of construction, the structures will become property described in subdivision (i) of this subparagraph. A construction loan secured by a structure containing more than 4 family units constitutes a home loan only if the structure has been committed to a plan of individual apartment ownership described in subdivision (ii) of this subparagraph and such plan is held out and advertised as such. A loan secured by a cooperative apartment building containing more than 4 family units does not constitute a home loan.

(8) *Church loan.* The term "church loan" means a loan secured by an interest in real property which is used primarily for church purposes, or a construction loan or improvement loan for such property. For the purposes of this subparagraph, the term "church purposes" means the ministration of sacerdotal functions, the conduct of religious worship and closely associated activities designed primarily to provide fellowship among members of the congregation, or the instruction of religion. Thus, a parish hall would normally qualify as property used primarily for church purposes, whereas a building used primarily to furnish education, other than the instruction of religion, would not.

(9) *Multi-family loan.* The term "multifamily loan" means a loan, other than one defined in subparagraph (7) of this paragraph (relating to a home loan), secured by an interest in improved residential real property or a construction loan or improvement loan for such property.

(10) *Nonresidential real property loan.* The term "nonresidential real property loan" means a loan, other than one defined in subparagraph (7), (8), or (9) of this paragraph (relating respectively to a home loan, church loan, and multifamily loan) secured by an interest in real property, or a construction loan or improvement loan for such property.

(e) *18 percent of assets test.* Not more than 18 percent of the amount of the total assets of a domestic building and loan association may consist of assets other than those defined in subparagraphs (2) through (9) of paragraph (d) of this section. Thus, the sum of the amounts of the nonresidential real property loans and the assets other than those defined in paragraph (d) of this section may not exceed 18 percent of total assets.

(f) *36 or 41 percent of assets test*—(1) *36 percent test.* Unless subparagraph (2) of this paragraph applies, not more than 36 percent of the amount of the total assets of a domestic building and loan association may consist of assets other than those defined in subparagraphs (2) through (8) of paragraph (d) of this section. Thus, unless subparagraph (2) of this paragraph applies, the sum of the amounts of multifamily loans, nonresidential real property loans, and assets other than those defined in paragraph (d) of this section may not exceed 36 percent of total assets.

(2) *41 percent test.* If this subparagraph applies, not more than 41 percent of the amount of the total assets of a domestic building and loan association may consist of assets other than those defined in subparagraphs (2) through (8) of paragraph (d) of this section. Thus, if this subparagraph applies, the sum of the amounts of multi family loans, nonresidential real property loans, and assets other than those defined in paragraph (d) of this section may not exceed 41 percent of total assets. See section 593 (b) (5) and the regulations thereunder for the effect of application of this subparagraph on the allowable addition to the reserves for bad debts.

(g) *Taxable years for which 41 percent of assets test applies*—(1) *First taxable year.* For an association's first taxable year beginning after October 16, 1962, subparagraph (2) of paragraph (f) applies.

(2) *Second taxable year.* For an association's second taxable year beginning after October 16, 1962, subparagraph (2) of paragraph (f) applies if such association met all the requirements of paragraphs (b) through (e), (h), and either subparagraph (1) or (2) of paragraph (f) for its first taxable year.

(3) *Years other than first and second taxable years.* For any taxable year of

an association beginning after October 16, 1962, other than its first and second taxable years beginning after such date, subparagraph (2) of paragraph (f) applies if such association met either—

(i) The requirements of paragraphs (b) through (e), (f)(1), and (h) of this section for the immediately preceding taxable year, or

(ii) The requirements of paragraphs (b) through (e), (f)(2), and (h) of this section for the immediately preceding taxable year, and the requirements of paragraphs (b) through (e), (f)(1), and (h) of this section for the second preceding taxable year.

Thus, in years other than its first and second taxable years beginning after October 16, 1962, an association may apply the 41 percent of assets test for two consecutive years, but only if it met the 36 percent test (and all other tests) for the year previous to the two consecutive years.

(4) *Examples.* The provisions of paragraph (f) of this paragraph may be illustrated by the following examples in each of which it is assumed that the association at all times meets all the requirements of paragraphs (b) through (e) and (h) of this section and files its returns on a calendar year basis.

Example (1). An association has 41 percent of its assets invested in assets other than those defined in subparagraphs (2) through (8) of paragraph (d) of this section as of the close of 1963 and 1964. Because 1963 is its first taxable year beginning after October 16, 1962, the 41 percent of assets test applies, and the association therefore qualifies as a domestic building and loan association for 1963. Because 1964 is its second taxable year beginning after such date and the 41 percent of assets test applied for its first taxable year, the 41 percent of assets test applies for 1964 and it therefore qualifies for such year.

Example (2). An association has 36 percent of its assets invested in assets other than those defined in subparagraphs (2) through (8) of paragraph (d) of this section as of the close of 1964, and 41 percent as of the close of 1965, 1966, and 1967. The association qualifies in 1965 because, as a result of having met the 36 percent of assets test for the immediately preceding taxable year (1964), the 41 percent of assets test applies to 1965. It qualifies in 1966 because as a result of having met the 41 percent of assets test in the immediately preceding taxable year (1965) and the 36 percent of assets test in the second preceding taxable year (1964), the 41 percent of assets test applies to 1966. The association would not qualify in 1967, however, because, although it met the 41 percent of assets test for the immediately preceding taxable year (1966), it did not meet the 36 percent of assets test in the second preceding taxable year (1965), and therefore the 41 percent of assets test does not apply to 1967.

Example (3). An association has more than 41 percent of its assets invested in assets other than those defined in subparagraphs (2) through (8) of paragraph (d) of this section as of the close of 1963, and 41 percent invested in such assets as of the close of 1964. The association does not qualify in either year. It does not qualify in 1963 because it exceeded the 41 percent limitation, and it does not qualify in 1964 because the 41 percent of assets test does not apply to 1964 since the association did not meet either the 41 percent of assets test or the 36 percent of assets test in the prior year (1963).

(h) *3 percent of assets test.* Not more than 3 percent of the amount of the total assets of a domestic building and loan association may consist of stock of any corporation, unless such stock is property which is defined in paragraph (d) of this section. The stock which constitutes property defined in such paragraph (d) is:

(1) Stock representing a withdrawable account in another financial institution;

(2) Stock of a corporation which is an instrumentality of the United States or of a State or political subdivision thereof;

(3) Stock which was security for a loan and which, by reason of having been bid in at foreclosure or otherwise having been reduced to ownership or possession of the association, is a loan within the definition of such term in paragraph (j)(i) of this section; and

(4) Stock of a wholly owned subsidiary corporation which has as its exclusive activity the ownership and management of property more than 50 percent of the fair rental value of which is used as the principal or branch office of the association.

(i) [Reserved]

(j) *Definition of certain terms.* For purposes of this section—

(1) *Loan.* The term "loan" means debt, as the term "debt" is used in section 166 and the regulations thereunder. The term "loan" also includes a redeemable ground rent (as defined in section 1055 (c)) which is owned by the taxpayer, and any property (referred to in this section as "foreclosed property") which was security for the payment of any indebtedness and which has been bid in at foreclosure, or otherwise been reduced to ownership or possession of the association by agreement or process of law, whether or not such property was acquired subsequent to December 31, 1962.

(2) *Secured.* A loan will be considered as "secured" only if the loan is on the security of any instrument (such as a mortgage, deed of trust, or land contract) which makes the interest of the debtor in the property described therein specific security for the payment of the loan, provided that such instrument is of such a nature that in the event of default, the interest of the debtor in such property could be subjected to the satisfaction of the loan with the same priority as a mortgage or deed of trust in the jurisdiction in which the property is situated.

(3) *Interest.* The word "interest" means an interest in real property which, under the law of the jurisdiction in which such property is situated, constitutes either (i) an interest in fee in such property, (ii) a leasehold interest in such property extending or renewable automatically for a period of at least 30 years, or at least 10 years beyond the date scheduled for the

Reg. § 301.7701-13(j)(3)

final payment on a loan secured by an interest in such property, (iii) a leasehold interest in property described in paragraph (d) (7) (i) of this section (relating to certain home loans) extending for a period of at least two years beyond the date scheduled for the final payment on a loan secured by an interest in such property or (iv) a leasehold interest in such property held subject to a redeemable ground rent defined in section 1055(c).

(4) *Real property.* The term "real property" means any property which, under the law of the jurisdiction in which such property is situated, constitutes real property.

(5) *Improved real property.* The term "improved real property" means—

(i) Land on which is located any building of a permanent nature (such as a house, apartment house, office building, hospital, shopping center, warehouse, garage, or other similar permanent structure), provided that the value of such building is substantial in relation to the value of such land;

(ii) Any building lot or site which, by reason of installations and improvements that have been completed in keeping with applicable governmental requirements and with general practice in the community, is a building lot or site ready for the construction of any building of a permanent nature within the meaning of subdivision (i) of this subparagraph; or

(iii) Real property which, because of its state of improvement, produces sufficient income to maintain such real property and retire the loan in accordance with the terms thereof.

(6) *Construction loan.* The term "construction loan" means a loan, the proceeds of which are to be disbursed to the borrower (either by the association or a third party) as construction work progresses on real property which is security for the loan, which property is, or from the proceeds of such loan will become, improved real property.

(7) *Improvement loan.* The term "improvement loan" means a loan which, by its terms and conditions, requires that the proceeds of the loan be used for altering, repairing, or improving real property. If more than 85 percent of the proceeds of a single loan are to be used for such purposes, the entire loan will qualify. If 85 percent or less of the proceeds of a loan are to be used for such purposes, an allocation of its adjusted basis is required. Examples of loans which constitute improvement loans are loans made for the purpose of painting a house, adding a new room to a house, remodeling the lobby of an apartment building, and purchasing and installing storm windows, storm doors, and awnings. Examples of loans which do not constitute improvement loans are loans made for the purpose of purchasing draperies, and removable appliances, such as refrigerators, ranges, and washing machines. It is not necessary that a loan be secured by the real property which is altered, repaired, or improved.

(8) *Residential real property.* The term "residential real property" means real property which consists of one or more family units. A family unit is a building or portion thereof which contains complete living facilities which are to be used on other than a transient basis by only one family consisting of one or more persons. Thus, an apartment which is to be used on other than a transient basis by one family, which contains complete facilities for living, sleeping, eating, cooking, and sanitation constitutes a family unit. Hotels, motels, dormitories, fraternity and sorority houses, rooming houses, hospitals, sanitariums, and rest homes, and parks and courts for mobile homes do not normally constitute residential real property.

(k) *Amount and character of loans*—(1) *Treatment at time of determination*—(i) *In general.* The amount of a loan, as of the time the determination required by subparagraph (3) of this paragraph is made, shall be treated for the purposes of this section as being secured:

(a) First by the portion of property, if any, defined in subparagraph (6), (7), or (8) of paragraph (d) of this section to the extent of the loan value thereof;

(b) Next by the portion of property, if any, defined in subparagraph (9) of paragraph (d) of this section to the extent of the loan value thereof; and

(c) Next by the portion of property, if any, defined in subparagraph (10) of paragraph (d) of this section to the extent of the loan value thereof.

To the extent that the amount of a loan exceeds the amount treated as being secured by property defined in subparagraphs (6) through (10) of paragraph (d) of this section, such loan shall be treated as property not defined in paragraph (d) of this section. If the loan value of any one category of property defined in paragraph (d) of this section exceeds 85 percent of the amount of the loan for which it is security then the entire loan shall be treated as a loan secured by such property.

(ii) *Loans of $40,000 or less.* Notwithstanding the provisions of subdivision (i) of this subparagraph, in the case of loans amounting to $40,000 or less as of the time of a determination, made on the security of property which is a combination of two or more categories or property defined in subparagraph (6) through (10) of paragraph (d) of this section, all such loans for any taxable year may, at the option of the association, be treated for the purposes of this section as being secured by the category of property the loan value of which constitutes the largest percentage of the total loan value of the property except to the extent that the loan is treated as property not defined in paragraph (d) of this section.

(iii) *Home loans of $20,000 or less.* Notwithstanding the provisions of subdivision (i) and (ii) of this subparagraph, if a loan amounting to $20,000 or less as of the time of a determination, is secured partly by property of a category described in subparagraph (7) of paragraph (d) of this section (relating to a home loan), the amount of the loan shall, for the purposes of this section, be treated as a loan described in such subparagraph except to the extent that the loan is treated as property not defined in paragraph (d) of this section

(2) *Treatment subsequent to time of determination.* The amount of a loan outstanding as of any time subsequent to the time of a determination shall be treated, for the purposes of this section, as being secured by each of the categories of property in the same ratio that the amount which was treated as being secured by each category bore to the total amount of the loan at the time as of which the determination was last made with respect to such loan.

(3) *Time of determination*—(i) *In general.* The determination of the amount of a loan which is treated as being secured by each of the categories of property shall be made:

(*a*) As of the time a loan is made;

(*b*) As of the time a loan is increased;

(*c*) As of the time any portion of the property which was security for the loan is released; and

(*d*) As of any time required by applicable Federal or State regulatory authorities for reappraisal or reanalysis of such loans.

(ii) *Special rule.* In the case of loans outstanding with respect to which no event described in subdivision (i) of this subparagraph has occurred in a taxable year beginning on or after October 17, 1962, the determination of the amounts of such loans which are treated as being secured by each of the categories of property may be made, at the option of the association, as of the close of the first taxable year beginning on or after such date, providing the determinations with respect to all such loans are made as of such date.

(4) *Loan value.* The loan value of property which is security for a loan is the maximum amount at the time as of which the determination is made which the association is permitted to lend on such property under the rules and regulations of applicable Federal and State regulatory authorities. Such loan value shall not exceed the fair market value of such property at such time as determined under such rules and regulations. However, in the case of loans made incidentally with and as a part of a bona fide salvage operation, the loan value of the security property shall be considered to be the face amount of the loan where the loan can be shown by the association to have been made for the primary purpose of recovering the investment of the association, and where such salvage operation is in conformity with rules and regulations of applicable Federal or State regulatory authorities.

(5) *Examples.* The following examples, in each of which it is assumed that X Savings and Loan Association files its return on a calendar year basis, illustrate the application of the rules in this paragraph:

Example (1). On July 1, 1963, X makes a single loan of $1,000,000 to M Corporation which loan is secured by real property which is a combination of homes, apartments, and stores. As of the time the loan is made X determines that the loan values of the categories of property are as follows:

Category of Property	Loan Value
Home	$400,000
Multi family	420,000
Nonresidential real property	240,000
Total	$1,060,000

As of the time the loan is made, therefore, the $1,000,000 loan is treated under subparagraph (1) (i) of this paragraph as being secured as follows:

Category of Loan	Amount of Loan	Percentage of Total
Home loan	$ 400,000	40
Multi family loan	420,000	42
Nonresidential real property loan	180,000	18
Total	$1,000,000	100

Assuming that the $1,000,000 loan to M was reduced to $900,000 as of the close of 1963, that there were no increases in the amount of the loan and no releases of property which was security for the loan, and that there was no regulatory requirement to reappraise or reanalyze the loan, such loan will be considered under subparagraph (2) of this paragraph to be secured, as of the close of 1963, as follows:

Category	Percentage as of Last Determination (7/1/63)	Amount as of 12/31/63
Home	40	$360,000 (40% × $900,000)
Multi family	42	378,000 (42% × $900,000)
Nonresidential real property	18	162,000 (18% × $900,000)
Total	100	$900,000

Example (2). X makes a loan of $40,000 secured by a building which contains a store on the first floor and four family units on the upper floors. The loan value of the part of the building used as a store is $21,000 and the loan value of the residential portion is $23,000. The loan will be treated under subdivision (i) of subparagraph (1) of this paragraph as a loan secured by residential real property containing four or fewer family units to the extent of $23,000, and by nonresidential property to the extent of $17,000, as of the time the loan is made. However, if X exercises the option to treat all loans of $40,000 or less in accordance with subdivision (ii) of subparagraph (1) of this paragraph, this loan would be treated as a home loan to the extent of the full $40,000 because the loan value of the residential portion is larger than the loan value of the nonresidential part.

(1) *Computation of percentages*—(1) *In general.* The percentages specified in paragraphs (d) through (h) of this section shall, except as provided in subparagraph (3) of this paragraph, be computed by comparing the amount of the assets described in each paragraph as of the close of the taxable year with the total amount of assets as of the close of the taxable year. The amount of the assets in any category and the total amount of assets shall be determined with reference to their adjusted basis under § 1.1011-1, or by such other method as is in accordance with sound accounting principles, provided such method is used in valuing all the assets in a taxable year.

(2) *Treatment of certain assets and reserves.* For purposes of this paragraph:

(i) Reserves for bad debts established pursuant to section 593, or corresponding provisions of prior law, and the regulations thereunder shall not constitute a reduction of total assets, but shall be treated as a surplus or net worth item.

(ii) The adjusted basis of a "loan in process" does not include the unadvanced portion of such loan.

(iii) Advances made by the association for taxes, insurance, etc., on loans shall be treated as being in the same category as the loan with respect to which the advances are made (irrespective of whether the advances are secured by the property securing the loan).

(iv) Interest receivable included in gross income shall be treated as being in the same category as the loan or asset with respect to which it is earned.

(v) The unamortized portion of premiums paid on mortgage loans acquired by the association shall be considered part of the acquisition cost of such loans.

(vi) Prepaid Federal Savings and Loan Insurance Corporation premiums shall be treated as being governmental obligations defined in paragraph (d) (3) of this section.

(vii) Accounts receivable (other than accrued interest receivable), and prepaid expenses and deferred charges other than those referred to in subdivision (v) or (vi) of this subparagraph, shall be disregarded both as separate categories and in the computation of total assets.

(viii) Foreclosed property (as defined in paragraph (j) (1) of this section) shall be treated as having the same character as the loan for which it was given as security.

(3) *Alternative method.* At the option of the taxpayer, the percentages specified in paragraphs (d) through (h) of this section may be computed on the basis of the average assets outstanding during the taxable year. Such average shall be determined by making the computation provided in subparagarph (1) of this paragraph either as of the close of each month, as of the close of each quarter, or semiannually during the taxable year and by using the yearly average of the monthly, quarterly, or semiannual percentages obtained for each category. The method selected must be applied uniformly for the taxable year to all categories of assets, but the method may be changed from year to year.

(4) *Acquisition of certain assets.* For the purpose of the annual computation of percentages under subparagraph (1) of this paragraph—

(i) Assets which, within a 60-day period beginning in one taxable year of the taxpayer and ending in the next year, are acquired directly or indirectly through borrowing and then repaid or disposed of within such period, shall be considered assets other than those defined in paragraph (d) of this section, unless both the acquisition and disposition are established to the satisfaction of the district director to have been for bona fide purposes; and

(ii) The amount of cash shall not include amounts received directly or indirectly from another financial institution (other than a Federal Home Loan Bank or a similar institution organized under State law) to the extent of the amount of cash which an association has on deposit or holds as a withdrawable account in such other financial institution.

(5) *Reporting requirements.* In the case of income tax returns for taxable years ending after October 31, 1964, there shall be filed with the return a statement showing the amount of assets as of the close of taxable year in each of the categories defined in paragraph (d), and in the category described in paragraph (h) of this section, and a brief description and amount of all other assets. If the alternative method of computing percentages under subparagraph (3) of this paragraph is selected, such statement shall show such information as of the end of each month, each quarter, or semiannually and the manner of calculating the averages. With repect to taxable years beginning after October 16, 1962, and ending before November 1, 1964, taxpayers shall maintain adequate records to establish to the satisfaction of the district director that it meets the various assets tests specified in this section.

(6) *Example.* The principles of this paragraph may be illustrated by the following example in which a description of the assets, the subparagraph of paragraph (d) in which the assets are defined, the amount of the assets, and the percentage of the total assets included in the calculation are set forth.

Z Savings and Loan Association Assets
As of December 31, 1964

Item	Described in paragraph (d), subparagraph:	Amount	Percentage
1. Cash	(2)	$ 1,000,000	1
2. Governmental obligations[1]	(3)	8,000,000	8
3. Deposit insurance company securities	(4)	1,000,000	1
Loans Outstanding:[2]			
4. Home	(7)	59,000,000	59
5. Church	(8)	1,000,000	1
6. Multifamily	(9)	20,000,000	20
7. Nonresidential real property	(10)	5,000,000	5
8. Passbook	(6)	1,000,000	1
9. Other	—	2,000,000	2
Fixed Assets: (less depreciation reserves)			
10. Used in the association's business	(5)	1,000,000	1
11. Rented to others	—	500,000	.5
12. Land held for investment	—	500,000	.5
13. Total assets included for purposes this paragraph		$100,000,000	100.0%
14. Accounts Receivable		100,000	(disregarded)
15. Prepaid Expenses (other than prepaid FSLIC premiums)		1,000,000	(disregarded)
16. Deferred Charges		1,000,000	(disregarded)
17. Total Assets		$102,100,000	

[1] Prepaid FSLIC premiums treated as governmental obligations.

[2] Not including unadvanced portion of loans in process, but including interest receivable and advances with respect to loans.

The computation of the percentages of assets in the various categories for the purpose of determining whether the percentage of assets tests in the paragraphs in this section are met as of the close of the year are as follows:

Test and Paragraph	Items Considered	Percentage
90% test (d)	$\dfrac{\text{the sum of items 1 through 8 \& 10}}{\text{item 13 (total included assets)}}$	= 97%
18% test (e)	$\dfrac{\text{the sum of items 7, 9, 11, \& 12}}{\text{item 13 (total included assets)}}$	= 8%
36% test (f)	$\dfrac{\text{the sum of items 6, 7, 9, 11, \& 12}}{\text{item 13 (total included assets)}}$	= 28%
3% test (h)	$\dfrac{0}{\text{item 13 (total included assets)}}$	= 0%

At the option of the association, the computations listed above could have been made as of the close of each month, each quarter, or semiannually, and averaged for the entire year.

(m) *Taxable years beginning before October 17, 1962.* For taxable years beginning before October 17, 1962, the term "domestic building and loan association" means a domestic building and loan association, a domestic savings and loan association, and a Federal savings and loan association substantially all the business of which is confined to making loans to members.

○━▶ § 301.7701-14 (T.D. 6766, filed 11-2-64.) **Cooperative bank.**

For taxable years beginning after October 16, 1962, the term "cooperative bank" means an institution without capital stock organized and operated for mutual purposes without profit which meets the supervisory test, the business operations test, and the various assets tests specified in paragraphs (d) through (h) of § 301.7701-13, employing the rules and definitions of paragraphs (j) through (l) of that section. In applying paragraphs (b) through (l) of such section any references to an "association" or to a "domestic building and loan association" shall be deemed to be a reference to a cooperative bank.

○━▶ § 301.7701-15 (T.D. 7519, filed 11-17-77.) **Income tax return preparer.**

(a) *In general.* An income tax return preparer is any person who prepares for compensation, or who employs (or engages) one or more persons to prepare for compensation, other than for the person, all or a substantial portion of any return of tax under subtitle A of the Internal Revenue Code of 1954 or of any claim for refund of tax under subtitle A of the Internal Revenue Code of 1954.

Reg. § 301.7701-15

24,438.10 (I.R.C.)   Reg. § 301.7701-15(a)(1)

(1) A person who furnishes to a taxpayer or other preparer sufficient information and advice so that completion of the return or claim for refund is largely a mechanical or clerical matter is considered an income tax return preparer, even though that person does not actually place or review placement of information on the return or claim for refund. See also paragraph (b) of this section.

(2) A person who only gives advice on specific issues of law shall not be considered an income tax return preparer, unless—

(i) The advice is given with respect to events which have occurred at the time the advice is rendered and is not given with respect to the consequences of contemplated actions; and

(ii) The advice is directly relevant to the determination of the existence, characterization, or amount of an entry on a return or claim for refund. For example, if a lawyer gives an opinion on a transaction which a corporation has consummated, solely to satisfy an accountant (not at the time a preparer of the corporation's return) who is attempting to determine whether the reserve for taxes set forth in the corporation's financial statement is reasonable, the lawyer shall not be considered a tax return preparer solely by reason of rendering such opinion.

(3) A person may be an income tax return preparer without regard to educational qualifications and professional status requirements.

(4) A person must prepare a return or claim for refund for compensation to be an income tax return preparer. A person who prepares a return or claim for refund for a taxpayer with no explicit or implicit agreement for compensation is not a preparer, even though the person receives a gift or return service or favor.

(5) A person who prepares a return or claim for refund outside the United States is an income tax return preparer, regardless of his nationality, residence, or the locations of his places of business, if the person otherwise satisfies the definition of income tax return preparer. Notwithstanding the provisions of § 301.6109-1(g), the person shall secure an employer identification number if he is an employer of another preparer, is a partnership in which one or more of the general partners is a preparer, or is an individual not employed (or engaged) by another preparer. The person shall comply with the provisions of section 1203 of the Tax Reform Act of 1976 and the regulations thereunder.

(6) An official or employee of the Internal Revenue Service performing his official duties is not an income tax return preparer.

(b) *Substantial preparation.* (1) Only a person (or persons acting in concert) who prepares all or a substantial portion of a return or claim for refund shall be considered to be a preparer (or preparers) of the return or claim for refund. A person who renders advice which is directly relevant to the determination of the existence, characterization, or amount of an entry on a return or claim for refund, will be regarded as having prepared that entry. Whether a schedule, entry, or other portion of a return or claim for refund is a substantial portion is determined by comparing the length and complexity of, and the tax liability or refund involved in, that portion to the length and complexity of, and tax liability or refund involved in, the return or claim for refund as a whole.

(2) For purposes of applying the rule of paragraph (b)(1) of this section, if the schedule, entry, or other portion of the return or claim for refund involves amounts of gross income, amounts of deductions, or amounts on the basis of which credits are determined which are—

(i) Less than $2,000; or

(ii) Less than $100,000, and also less than 20 percent of the gross income (or adjusted gross income if the taxpayer is an individual) as shown on the return or claim for refund,

then the schedule or other portion is not considered to be a substantial portion. If more than one schedule, entry or other portion is involved, they shall be aggregated in applying the rule of this subparagraph (2). Thus, if a person, for an individual taxpayer's return, prepares a schedule for dividend income which totals $1,500 and gives advice making him a preparer of a schedule of medical expenses which results in a deduction for medical expenses of $1,500, the person is not a preparer if the taxpayer's adjusted gross income shown on the return is more than $15,000. This subparagraph shall not apply to a person who prepares all of a return or claim for refund.

(3) A preparer of a return is not considered to be a preparer of another return merely because an entry or entries reported on the return may affect an entry reported on the other return, unless the entry or entries reported on the prepared return are directly reflected on the other return and constitute a substantial portion of the other return. For example, the sole preparer of a partnership return of income or a small business corporation income tax return is considered a preparer of a partner's or a shareholder's return if the entry or entries on the partnership or small business corporation return reportable on the partner's or shareholder's return constitute a substantial portion of the partner's or shareholder's return.

(c) *Return and claim for refund*—(1) *Return.* A return of tax under subtitle A is a return filed by or on behalf of a taxpayer reporting the liability of the taxpayer for tax under subtitle A. A return of tax under subtitle A also includes an information return filed by or on behalf of a person or entity that is not a taxable entity and which reports information which is or may be reported on the return of a taxpayer of tax under subtitle A.

(i) A return of tax under subtitle A includes an individual or corporation income tax return, a fiduciary income tax return (for a trust or estate), a regulated investment company undistributed capital gains tax return, a return of a charitable remainder trust, a return by a transferor of stock or securities to a foreign corporation, foreign trust, or foreign partnership, a partnership return of income, a small business corporation income tax return, and a DISC return.

(ii) A return of tax under subtitle A does not include an estate tax return, a gift tax return, any other return of excise taxes or income taxes collected at source on wages, an individual or corporation declaration of estimated tax, an application for an extension of time to file an individual or corporation income tax return, or an informational statement on Form 990, any Form 1099, or similar form.

(2) *Claim for refund.* A claim for refund of tax under subtitle A includes a claim for credit against any tax under subtitle A.

(d) *Persons who are not preparers.* A person shall not be considered to be a preparer of a return or claim for refund if the person performs only one or more of the following services:

(1) Typing, reproduction, or other mechanical assistance in the preparation of a return or claim for refund.

(2) Preparation of a return or claim for refund of a person, or an officer, general partner, or employee of a person, by whom the individual is regularly and continuously employed or in which the individual is a general partner.

(3) Preparation of a return or claim for refund for a trust or estate of which the person either is a fiduciary or is an officer, general partner, or employee of the fiduciary.

(4) Preparation of a claim for refund for a taxpayer in response to—

(i) A notice of deficiency issued to the taxpayer; or

(ii) A waiver of restriction after initiation of an audit of the taxpayer or another taxpayer if a determination in the audit of the other taxpayer affects, directly or indirectly, the liability of the taxpayer for tax under subtitle A.

For purposes of paragraph (d) (2) of this section, the employee of a corporation owning more than 50 percent of the voting power of another corporation, or the employee of a corporation more than 50 percent of the voting power of which is owned by another corporation, is considered the employee of the other corporation as well. For purposes of paragraph (d) (3) of this section, an estate, guardianship, conservatorship, committee, and any similar arrangement for a taxpayer under a legal disability (such as a minor, an incompetent, or an infirm individual) is considered a trust or estate.

§ 301.7701-16 (Originally § 301.7701-13 as added by T.D. 6503, filed 11-15-60; amended by T.D. 6606, filed 8-24-62 redesignated and amended by T.D. 6766, filed 11-2-64; redesignated and amended by T.D. 7519, filed 11-17-77.) **Other terms.**

Any terms which are defined in section 7701 and which are not defined in §§ 301.7701-1 to 301.7701-15, inclusive, shall, when used in this chapter, have the meanings assigned to them in section 7701.

Reg. § 301.7701-16

24,438.10-B (I.R.C.)

5-1-78

GENERAL RULES
APPLICATION OF INTERNAL REVENUE LAWS

○─► § 301.7801 Statutory provisions; authority of the Department of the Treasury. [Sec. 7801, IRC]

○─► § 301.7802 Statutory provisions; Commissioner of Internal Revenue. [Sec. 7802, IRC]

○─► § 301.7803 Statutory provisions; other personnel. [Sec. 7803, IRC]

○─► § 301.7803-1 (T.D. 6498, filed 10-24-60; amended by T.D. 7239, filed 12-27-72.) Surety bonds covering personnel of the Internal Revenue Service.

For regulations relating to the procurement of security bonds covering designated personnel of the Internal Revenue Service between January 1, 1956, and June 6, 1972, see 31 CFR Part 226.

○─► § 301.7804 Statutory provisions; effect of reorganization plans. [Sec. 7804, IRC]

○─► § 31.7805 Statutory provisions; rules and regulations. [Sec. 7805, IRC]

○─► § 31.7805-1 (T.D. 6472, filed 6-22-60; republished in T.D. 6516, filed 12-19-60.) Promulgation of regulations.

In pursuance of section 7805 of the Internal Revenue Code of 1954, the foregoing regulations are hereby prescribed. (See § 31.0-3 of Subpart A of the regulations in this part relating to the scope of the regulations.)

○─► § 301.7805 Statutory provisions; rules and regulations. [Sec. 7805, IRC]

○─► § 301.7805-1 (T.D. 6498, filed 10-24-60.) Rules and regulations.

(a) *Issuance.* The Commissioner, with the approval of the Secretary, shall prescribe all needful rules and regulations for the enforcement of the Code (except where this authority is expressly given by the Code to any person other than an officer or employee of the Treasury Department), including all rules and regulations as may be necessary by reason of any alteration of law in relation to internal revenue.

(b) *Retroactivity.* The Commissioner, with the approval of the Secretary, may prescribe the extent, if any, to which any regulation or Treasury decision relating to the internal revenue laws shall be applied without retroactive effect. The Commissioner may prescribe the extent, if any, to which any ruling relating to the internal revenue laws, issued by or pursuant to authorization from him, shall be applied without retroactive effect.

(c) *Preparation and distribution of regulations, forms, stamps, and other matters.* The Commissioner, under the direction of the Secretary, shall prepare and distribute all the instructions, regulations, directions, forms, blanks, stamps, and other matters pertaining to the assessment and collection of internal revenue.

○─► § 301.7806 Statutory provisions; construction of title. [Sec. 7806, IRC]

○─► § 301.7807 Statutory provisions; rules in effect upon enactment of this title. [Sec. 7807, IRC]

○─► § 301.7808 Statutory provisions; depositaries for collections. [Sec. 7808, IRC]

○─► § 301.7809 Statutory provisions; deposit of collections. [Sec. 7809, IRC]

EFFECTIVE DATE AND RELATED PROVISIONS

○─► § 301.7851 Statutory provisions; applicability of revenue laws. [Sec. 7851, IRC]

○─► § 301.7852 Statutory provisions; other applicable rules. [Sec. 7852, IRC]

MISCELLANEOUS PROVISIONS

○─► § 301.9000-1 (T.D. 6920, filed 6-7-67; amended by T.D. 7188, filed 6-28-72.) Procedure to be followed by officers and employees of the Internal Revenue Service upon receipt of a request or demand for disclosure of internal revenue records or information.

(a) *Authority.* The provisions of this section are prescribed under the authority of 5 U.S.C. 301; section 2 of Reorganization Plan No. 26 of 1950, 64 Stat. 1280; 18 U.S.C. 1905; section 2(g) of the Federal Alcohol Administration Act (27 U.S.C. 202(c)); and sections 5274, 6103, 6104, 6106, 6107, 7213, 7237(e), 7803, and 7805 of the Internal Revenue Code of 1954.

(b) *Definitions.* When used in this section—

(1) *Internal revenue records or information.* The term "internal revenue records or information" means any records (including copies thereof) or information, made or obtained by, furnished to, or coming to the knowledge of, any officer or employee of the Internal Revenue Service while acting in his official capacity, or because of his official status, with respect to the administration of the internal revenue laws or any other laws administered by or concerning the Internal Revenue Service.

(2) *Internal revenue officer and employee.* The term "internal revenue officer and employee" means all officers and employees of the United States, engaged in the administration and enforcement of the internal revenue laws or any other laws administered by the Internal Revenue Service, appointed or employed by, or subject to the directions, instructions or orders of, the Secretary of the Treasury or his delegate.

(3) *D e m a n d.* The term "demand" means any subpoena, notice of deposition either upon oral examination or written interrogatory, or other order, of any court, administrative agency, or other authority.

(c) *Disclosure of internal revenue records or information prohibited without prior approval of the Commissioner.* The disclosure, including the production, of internal revenue records or information to any person outside the Treasury Department or to any court, administrative agency, or other authority, in response to any request or demand for the disclosure of such records or information shall be made only with the prior approval of the Commissioner. However, nothing in this section shall restrict the disclosure of internal revenue records or information which the Commissioner has determined is authorized under any provision of statute, Executive order, or regulations, or for which a procedure has been established by the Commissioner. For example, this section does not restrict the inspection of returns and approved applications for tax exemption inspection of which is governed by sections 6103 and 6104 of the Code and the Executive orders and regulations issued thereunder, nor does it restrict the disclosure of internal revenue records or information which is requested by United States attorneys or attorneys of the Department of Justice for use in cases which arise under the internal revenue laws or related statutes and which are referred by the Department of the Treasury to the Department of Justice for prosecution or defense.

(d) *Delegation to Commissioner of authority to determine disclosure and establish procedures; procedure in the event of a request or demand for disclosure*—(1) *Delegation to Commissioner.* The Commissioner is hereby authorized to determine whether or not officers and employees of the Internal Revenue Service will be permitted to disclose internal revenue records or information in response to:

(i) A request by any court, administrative agency, or other authority, or by any person, for the disclosure of such records or information, or

(ii) A demand for the disclosure of such records or information.

The Commissioner is also authorized to establish such procedures as he may deem necessary with respect to the disclosure of internal revenue records or information by internal revenue officers and employees. Any determination by the Commissioner as to whether internal revenue records or information will be disclosed, or any procedure established by him in connection therewith, will be made in accordance with applicable statutes, Executive orders, and regulations, and such instructions as may be issued by the Secretary or his delegate. Notwithstanding the preceding provisions of this subparagraph, the Commissioner shall, where either he or the Secretary deems it appropriate, refer the opposing of a request or demand for disclosure of internal revenue records or information to the Secretary.

(2) *Procedure in the event of a request or demand for internal revenue records or information* — (i) *Request procedure.* Any officer or employee of the Internal Revenue Service who receives a request for internal revenue records or information, the disposition of which is not covered by a procedure established by the Commissioner, shall promptly communicate the contents of the request to the Commissioner through the appropriate supervisor for the district or region in which he serves. Such officer or employee shall await instructions from the Commissioner concerning the response to the request. For the procedure to be followed in the event a person making a request seeks to obtain a court order or other demand requiring the production of internal revenue records or information, see subdivision (ii) of this subparagraph.

(ii) *Demand procedure.* Any officer or employee of the Internal Revenue Service who is served with a demand for internal revenue records or information, the disposition of which is not covered by a procedure established by the Commissioner, shall promptly, and without awaiting appearance before the court, administrative agency, or other authority, communicate the contents of the demand to the Commissioner through the appropriate supervisor for the district or region in which he serves. Such officer or employee shall await instructions from the Commissioner concerning the response to the demand. If it is determined by the Commissioner that the demand should be opposed, the United States attorney, his assistant, or other appropriate legal representative shall be requested to respectfully inform the court, administrative agency, or other authority that the Commissioner has instructed the officer or employee to refuse to disclose the internal revenue records or information sought. If instructions have not been received from the Commissioner at the time when the officer or employee is required to appear before the court, administrative agency, or other authority in response to the demand, the United States attorney, his assistant, or other appropriate legal representative shall be requested to appear with the officer or employee upon whom the demand has been served and request additional time in which to receive such instructions. In the event the court, administrative agency, or other authority rules adversely with respect to the refusal to disclose the records or information pursuant to the instructions of the Commissioner, or declines to defer a ruling until instructions from the Commissioner have been received, the officer or employee upon whom the demand has been served shall, pursuant to this section, respectfully decline to disclose the internal revenue records or information sought.

(e) *Record of seizure and sale of real estate.* Record 21, "Record of seizure and sale of real estate", is open for public inspection in offices of district directors of internal revenue and copies are furnished upon application.

(f) *State liquor, tobacco, firearms, or explosives cases.* Assistant regional commissioners (alcohol, tobacco and firearms) or the Director, Alcohol, Tobacco and Firearms Division, may, in the interest of Federal and State law enforcement, upon receipt of demands or requests of State authorities, and at the expense of the State, authorize special investigators and other employees under their supervision to attend trials and administrative hearings in liquor, tobacco, firearms, or explosives cases in which the State is a party, produce records, and testify as to facts coming to their knowledge in their official capacities: Provided, That such production or testimony will not divulge information contrary to section 7213 of the Code, nor divulge information subject to the restrictions in section 5848. See also 18 U.S.C. 1905.

(g) *Penalties.* Any officer or employee of the Internal Revenue Service who disobeys the provisions of this section will be subject to dismissal and may incur criminal liability.

(h) *Effective date.* The provisions of this section are applicable to any request or demand for internal revenue records or information received by any officer or employee of the Internal Revenue Service after June 15, 1967.

Reg. § 301.9000-1(h)

PUBLIC LAW 74, 84th CONGRESS

○— § 1.9000-1 Statutory Provisions. * * *

○— § 1.9000-2 Effect of repeal in general.

(a) Section 452 (relating to prepaid income) and section 462 (relating to reserves for estimated expenses) of the Internal Revenue Code of 1954 were repealed by the Act of June 15, 1955 (Public Law 74, 84th Cong., 69 Stat. 134), with respect to all years subject to such Code. The effect of the repeal will generally be to increase the tax liability of taxpayers who elected to adopt the methods of accounting provided by sections 452 and 462. References to sections of law in §§ 1.9000-2 to 1.9000-8, inclusive, are references to the Internal Revenue Code of 1954 unless otherwise specified.

(b) The Act of June 15, 1955, provides that if the amount of any tax is increased by the repeal of sections 452 and 462 and if the last date prescribed for the payment of such tax (or any installment thereof) is before December 15, 1955, then the taxpayer shall on or before such date file a statement as prescribed in § 1.9000-3. The last date prescribed for payment for this purpose shall be determined without regard to any extensions of time and without regard to the provisions of the Act of June 15, 1955.

○— § 1.9000-3 Requirement of statement showing increase in tax liability.

(a) *Returns filed before June 15, 1955.* Where a return reflecting an election under section 452 or 462 was filed before June 15, 1955, the taxpayer must file on or before December 15, 1955, a statement on Form 2175 showing the increase in tax liability resulting from the repeal of section 452 and 462. The provisions of this paragraph may be illustrated by the following example:

Example: Corporation X filed its income tax return for the calendar year 1954 on March 15, 1955, and elected under section 6152 to pay the unpaid amount of the tax shown thereon in two equal installments. Such installment payments are due on March 15, 1955, and June 15, 1955, respectively. The corporation elected to compute its tax for such taxable year under the methods of accounting provided by sections 452 and 462. Corporation X's tax liability is increased by reason of the enactment of Public Law 74, and since the last date prescribed for paying its tax expires before December 15, 1955, it is required to submit the prescribed statement on or before December 15, 1955, showing its increase in tax liability.

(b) *Returns filed on or after June 15, 1955.* A taxpayer filing a return on or after June 15, 1955, for a taxable year ending on or before such date, may elect to apply the accounting methods provided in sections 452 and 462. The election may be exercised by either of the following methods:

(1) By computing the tax liability shown on such return as though the provisions of sections 452 and 462 had not been repealed. In such a case, the taxpayer must file on or before December 15, 1955, a statement on Form 2175 showing the increase in tax liability resulting from the repeal of sections 452 and 462.

(2) By computing his tax liability without regard to sections 452 and 462. In this case, Form 2175 must be filed with the return. However, taxable income and the tax liability computed with the application of sections 452 and 462 shall be shown on lines 8 and 14, respectively, of the form in lieu of the amounts otherwise called for on those lines. If a taxpayer does not make an election to have the provisions of sections 452 and 462 apply, the savings provisions of section 4 of the Act of June 15, 1955, are not applicable.

(c) *Taxable years ending after June 15, 1955.* A taxpayer having a taxable year ending after June 15, 1955, may not elect to apply the methods of accounting prescribed in sections 452 and 462 in computing taxable income for such taxable year. Such a taxpayer must file his return and pay the tax as if such sections had not been enacted.

(d) *Other situations requiring statements.* (1) A person who made an election under section 452 or 462 but whose tax liability was not increased by reason of the enactment of the Act of June 15, 1955, is nevertheless required to file a statement on Form 2175 if his gross income is increased or his deductions are decreased as the result of the repeal of sections 452 and 462. A partnership which makes an election under such sections must file such a statement. In addition, a partner, stockholder, distributee, etc. (whether or not such person made an election under section 452 or 462), shall file a statement showing any increase in his tax liability resulting from the effects of the repeal on the gross income or deductions of any person mentioned in the previous sentences of this subparagraph.

(2) A statement shall also be filed for a taxable year, other than a year to which an election under section 452 or 462 is applicable, if the repeal of such sections increases the tax liability of such year. Thus, a statement must be filed for any taxable year to which a net operating loss is carried from a year to which an election under section 452 or 462 is applicable, provided that the repeal of such sections affects the amount of the tax liability for the year to which such loss is carried. A separate statement must also be filed for a year in which there is a net operating loss which is changed by reason of the repeal of sections 452 and 462. Where there is a short taxable year involved, a taxpayer may have two taxable years to which elections under sections 452 and 462 are applicable and, in such a case, a statement, on Form 2175, must be filed for each such year.

§ 1.9000-4 Form and content of statement.

(a) *Information to be shown.* The statement shall be filed on Form 2175 which may be obtained from district directors. It shall be filed with the district director for the internal revenue district in which the return was filed. The statement shall be prepared in accordance with the instructions contained thereon and shall show the following information:

(1) The name and address of the taxpayer.

(2) The amounts of each type of income deferred under section 452.

(3) The amount of the addition to each reserve deducted under section 462.

(4) The taxable income and the tax liability of the taxpayer computed with the application of sections 452 and 462.

(5) The taxable income and the tax liability of the taxpayer computed without the application of sections 452 and 462.

(6) The details of the recomputation of taxable income and tax liability, including any changes in other items of income, deductions, and credits resulting from the repeal of sections 452 and 462, and

(7) If self-employment tax is increased, the computations and information required on page 3 of Schedule C, Form 1040.

(b) *Procedure for recomputing tax liability.* In determining the taxable income and the tax liability computed without the application of sections 452 and 462, such items as vacation pay and prepaid subscription income shall be reported under the law and regulations applicable to the taxable year as if such sections had not been enacted. The tax liability for the year shall be recomputed by restoring to taxable income the

Reg. § 1.9000-4(b)

amount of income deferred under section 452 and the amount of the deduction taken under section 462. Other deductions or credits affected by such changes in taxable income shall be adjusted. For example, if the deduction for contributions allowed for the taxable year was limited under section 170(b), the amount of such deduction shall be recomputed, giving effect to the increase in adjusted gross income or taxable income, as the case may be, by reason of the adjustments required by the repeal of sections 452 and 462.

§ 1.9000-5 Effect of filing statement.

(a) *Years other than years affected by a net operating loss carryback.* If the taxpayer files a timely statement in accordance with the provisions of § 1.9000-3, the amount of the increase in tax shown on such statement for a taxable year shall, except as provided in paragraph (b) of this section, be considered for all purposes of the Code, as tax shown on the return for such year. In general, such increase shall be assessed and collected in the same manner as if it had been tax shown on the return as originally filed. The provisions of this paragraph may be illustrated by the following example:

Example. A taxpayer filed his return showing a tax liability computed under the methods of accounting provided by sections 452 and 462 as $1,000 and filed the statement in accordance with § 1.9000-3 showing an increase in tax liability of $200. The tax computed as though sections 452 and 462 had not been enacted is $1,200, and the difference of $200 is the increase in the tax attributable to the repeal of sections 452 and 462. This increase is considered to be tax shown on the return for such taxable year. Additions to the tax for fraud or negligence under section 6653 will be determined by reference to $1,200 (that is, $1,000 plus $200) as the tax shown on the return.

(b) *Years affected by a net operating loss carryback.* In the case of a year which is affected by a net operating loss carryback from a year to which an election under section 452 and 462 applies, that portion of the amount of increase in tax shown on the statement for the year to which the loss is carried back which is attributable to a decrease in such net operating loss shall not be treated as tax shown on the return.

§ 1.9000-6 Provisions for the waiver of interest.

(a) *In general.* If the statement is filed in accordance with § 1.9000-3 and if that portion of the increase in tax which is due before December 15, 1955 (without regard to any extension of time for payment and without regard to the provisions of §§ 1.9000-2 to 1.9000-8, inclusive), is paid in full on or before such date, then no interest shall be due with respect to that amount. The provisions of this paragraph may be illustrated by the following example:

Example. Corporation M's return for the calendar year 1954 was filed on March 15, 1955, and the tax liability shown thereon was paid in equal installments on March 15, 1955, and June 15, 1955. M filed a statement on December 15, 1955, showing the increase in its tax liability resulting from the repeal of sections 452 and 462 and paid at that time the increase in tax shown thereon. No interest will be imposed with respect to the amount of such payment.

Interest shall be computed under the applicable provisions of the internal revenue laws on any portion of the increase in tax shown on the statement which is due after December 15, 1955, and which is not paid when due.

(b) *Limitation on application of waiver.* The provisions of paragraph (a) of this section shall not apply to any portion of the increase in tax shown on the statement if such increase reflects an amount in excess of that attributable solely to the repeal of sections 452 and 462, i.e., is attributable in whole or in part to excessive or unwarranted deferrals or accruals under section 452 or 462, as the case may be, in computing the tax liability with the application of such sections. Notwithstanding the preceding sentence, paragraph (a) of this section shall be applicable if the taxpayer can show that the tax liability as computed with the application of sections 452 and 462 is based upon a reasonable interpretation and application of such sections as they existed prior to repeal. If the taxpayer complied with the provisions of the regulations under sections 452 and 462 in computing the tax liability with the application of such sections, he will be regarded as having reasonably interpreted and applied sections 452 and 462. In this regard, it is not essential that the taxpayer submit with his return the detailed information required by such regulations in support of the deduction claimed under section 462, but such information shall be supplied at the request of the Commissioner.

(c) *Interest for periods prior to June 16, 1955.* No interest shall be imposed with respect to any increase in tax resulting solely from the repeal of sections 452 and 462 for any period prior to June 16, 1955 (the day after the date of the enactment of the Act of June 15, 1955). The preceding sentence does not apply to that part of any increase in tax which is due to the improper application of sections 452 and 462. The provisions of this paragraph shall not apply to interest imposed under section 3779 of the Internal Revenue Code of 1939. (See paragraph (d) of this section.)

(d) *Amounts deferred by corporations expecting carrybacks.* Interest shall be imposed at the rate of 6 percent on so much of the amount of tax deferred under section 3779 of the Internal Revenue Code of 1939 as is not satisfied within the meaning of section 3779(i)(1), notwithstanding the fact that a greater amount would have been satisfied, had sections 452 and 462 not been repealed. Interest will be imposed at such rate until the amount not so satisfied is paid.

§ 1.9000-7 Provisions for estimated tax.

(a) *Additions to tax under section 294 (d) of the Internal Revenue Code of 1939.* Any addition to the tax under section 294 (d) (relating to estimated tax) of the Internal Revenue Code of 1939 shall be computed as if the tax for the year for which the estimate was made were computed with sections 452 and 462 still applicable to such taxable year. For the purpose of the preceding sentence, it is not necessary for the taxpayer actually to have made an election under section 452 or 462; it is only necessary for the taxpayer to have taken such sections into account in estimating its tax liability for the year. Thus, if in determining the amount of estimated tax, the taxpayer computed his estimated tax liability by applying those sections, that portion of any additions to tax under section 294(d) resulting from the repeal of sections 452 and 462 shall be disregarded.

(b) *Additions to tax under section 6654.* In the case of an underpayment of estimated tax, any additions to the tax under section 6654, with respect to installments due before December 15, 1955, shall be computed without regard to any increase in tax resulting from the repeal of sections 452 and 462. Any additions to the tax with respect to installments due on or after December 15, 1955, shall be imposed in accordance with the applicable provisions of the Code, and as though sections 452 and 462 had not been enacted. Thus, a taxpayer whose declaration of estimated tax was based upon an estimate of his taxable income for the year of the estimate which was determined by taking sections 452 and 462 into account, must file an amended declaration on or before the due date of the next installment of estimated tax due on or after December 15, 1955. Such amended declaration shall reflect an estimate of the tax without the application of such sections. If the taxpayer bases his estimate on the tax for the preceding taxable year under section 6654(d)(1)(A), an amended declaration must be filed on or before the due date of the next installment due on or after December 15, 1955, if the tax for the preceding taxable year is increased as the result of the repeal of sections 452 and 462. Similarly, if the taxpayer bases his estimate on the tax computed under section 6654(d)(1)(B), he must file an amended declaration on or before the due date of the next installment due on or after December 15, 1955, taking into account the repeal of sections 452 and 462 with respect to the preceding taxable year. Any increase in estimated tax shown on an amended declaration filed in accordance with this paragraph must be paid in accordance with section 6153(c).

(c) *Estimated tax of corporations.* Corporations required to file a declaration of estimated tax under section 6016 for taxable years ending on and after December 31, 1955, shall estimate their tax liability for such year as if sections 452 and 462 had not been enacted. Thus, if the corporation bases its estimated tax liability under section 6655(d)(1) or (2) on its operations for the preceding taxable year, the effect of the repeal of sections 452 and 462 with respect to such year must be taken into account.

§ 1.9000-8 Extension of time for making certain payments.

(a) *Time for payment specified in Code.* (1) If the treatment of any payment (including its allowance as a deduction or otherwise) is dependent upon the making of a payment within a period of time specified in the Code the period within which the payment is to be made is extended where the amount to be paid is increased by reason of the repeal of sections 452 and 462: *Provided,* That:

(i) The taxpayer, because of a pre-existing obligation, is required to make a payment or an additional payment to another person by reason of such repeal;

(ii) The deductibility of the payment or additional payment is contingent upon its being made within a period prescribed by the Code, which period expires after the close of the taxable year; and

(iii) The payment or additional payment is made on or before December 15, 1955.

If the foregoing conditions are met, the payment or additional payment will be treated as having been made within the time specified in the Code, and, subject to any other conditions in the Code, it shall be deductible for the year to which it relates. The provision of this paragraph may be illustrated by the following examples:

Example 1. Section 267 (relating to losses, expenses and interest between related taxpayers) applies to amounts accrued by taxpayer A for salary payable to B. For the calendar year 1954, A is obligated to pay B a salary equal to 5 percent of A's taxable income for the taxable year. The amount accrued as salary payable to B for 1954 is $5,000 with the taxable income reflecting the application of section 462. As a result of the repeal of section 462 the salary payable to B for 1954 is increased to $6,000. The additional $1,000 is paid to B on December 15, 1955. In recomputing A's tax liability for 1954 the additional deduction of $1,000 for salary payable to B will be treated as having been made within two and one-half months after the close of the taxable year and will be deductible in that year.

Example 2. On March 1, 1955, Corporation X, a calendar year taxpayer using the accrual method of accounting, makes a payment described in section 404(a)(6) (relating to contributions to an employees' trust) of $10,000 which is accrued for 1954 and is determined on the basis of the amount of taxable income for that year. The taxpayer filed its return on March 15, 1955. By reason of the repeal of section 462, X's taxable income is increased so that it is required to make an additional

Reg. § 1.9000-8(a)(1)

contribution of $2,000 to the employees' trust. The additional payment is made on December 15, 1955. For purposes of recomputing X's tax liability for 1954, this additional payment is deemed to have been made on the last day of 1954.

(2) The time for inclusion in the taxable income of the payee of any additional payment of the type described in subparagraph (1) of this paragraph, shall be determined without regard to section 4(c)(3) of the Act of June 15, 1955, and §§ 1.9000-2 to 1.9000-8, inclusive.

(b) *Dividends paid under section 561.* Under section 4(c)(4) of the Act of June 15, 1955, the period during which distributions may be recognized as dividends paid under section 561 for a taxable year to which section 452 or 462 apply may be extended under the conditions set forth below.

(1) *Accumulated earnings tax or personal holding company tax.* In the case of the accumulated earnings tax or the personal holding company tax, if:

(i) The income of a corporation is increased for a taxable year by reason of the repeal of sections 452 and 462 so that it would become liable for the tax (or an increase in the tax) imposed on accumulated earnings or personal holding companies unless additional dividends are distributed;

(ii) The corporation distributes dividends to its stockholders after the 15th day of the 3d month following the close of its taxable year and on or before December 15, 1955, which dividends are attributable to an increase in its accumulated taxable income or undistributed personal holding company income, as the case may be, resulting from the repeal of sections 452 and 462, and

(iii) The corporation elects in its statement, submitted under § 1.9000-3, to have the provisions of section 4(c)(4) of the Act of June 15, 1955, apply—

then such dividends shall be treated as having been paid on the last day of the taxable year to which the statement applies.

(2) *Regulated investment companies.* In the case of a regulated investment company taxable under section 852, if—

(i) The taxable income of the regulated investment company is increased by reason of the repeal of sections 452 and 462 (without regard to any deduction for dividends paid as provided for in this subparagraph);

(ii) The company distributes dividends to its stockholders after the 15th day of the 3rd month following the close of its taxable year and on or before December 15, 1955, which dividends are attributable to an increase in its investment company income resulting from the repeal of sections 452 and 462; and

(iii) The company elects in its statement, submitted under § 1.9000-3, to have the provisions of section 4(c)(4) of the Act of June 15, 1955, apply—

then such dividends are to be treated as having been paid on the last day of the taxable year to which the statement applies. The dividends paid are to be determined under this subparagraph without regard to the provisions of section 855.

(3) *Related provisions.* An election made under subparagraph (1) or (2) of this paragraph is irrevocable. The time for inclusion in the taxable income of the distributees of any distributions of the type described in subparagraph (1) or (2) of this paragraph shall be determined without regard to section 4(c)(4) of the Act of June 15, 1955, and §§ 1.9000-2 to 1.9000-8, inclusive.

RETIREMENT-STRAIGHT LINE ADJUSTMENT ACT OF 1958

0— § 1.9001 Statutory provisions; Retirement-Straight Line Adjustment Act of 1958.

0— § 1.9001-1 (T.D. 6418, filed 10-9-59; republished in T.D. 6500, filed 12-25-60.) Change from retirement to straight-line method of computing depreciation.

(a) *In general.* The Retirement-Straight Line Adjustment Act of 1958 (72 Stat. 1669), which is contained in section 94 of the Technical Amendments Act of 1958, approved September 2, 1958, provides various adjustments to be made by certain railroads which changed from the retirement to the straight-line method of computing the allowance of deductions for the depreciation of those roadway assets which are defined in this section as retirement-straight line property. The adjustments are available to all eligible taxpayers who make an irrevocable election to have the provisions of the Retirement-Straight Line Adjustment Act of 1958, apply. This election shall be made at the time and in the manner prescribed by this section. If an election is made in accordance with this section, then the provisions of the Act and of §§ 1.9001 to 1.9001-4, inclusive, shall apply. An election made in accordance with this section shall not be considered a change in accounting method for purposes of section 481 of the 1954 Code.

(b) *Making of election.* (1) Subsection (b) of the Act provides that any taxpayer who held retirement-straight line property on its 1956 adjustment date may elect to have the provisions of the Act apply. The election shall be irrevocable and shall apply to all retirement-straight line property, including such property for periods when held by predecessors of the taxpayer.

(2) An election may be made in accordance with the provisions of this section even though the taxpayer has, at the time of election, litigated some or all of the issues covered by the provisions of the Act and has received from the courts a determination which is less favorable to the taxpayer than the treatment provided by the Act. Once an election has been made in accordance with the provisions of this section, the taxpayer may not receive the benefit of more favorable treatment, as a result of litigation, than that provided by the Act on the issues involved.

Retirement-Straight Line Adjustments Act of 1958

(3) The election to have the provisions of the Act apply shall be made by filing a statement to that effect, on or before January 11, 1960, with the district director for the internal revenue district in which the taxpayer's income tax return for its first taxable year beginning after December 31, 1955, was filed. A copy of this statement shall be filed with any amended return or claim for refund, made under the Act.

(c) *Definitions.* For purposes of the Act and §§ 1.9001 to 1.9001-4, inclusive—

(1) *The Act.* The term "the Act" means the Retirement-Straight Line Adjustment Act of 1958, as contained in section 94 of the Technical Amendments Act of 1958 (72 Stat. 1669).

(2) *Commissioner.* The term "Commissioner" means the Commissioner of Internal Revenue.

(3) *Retirement-straight line property.* The term "retirement-straight line property" means any property of a kind or class with respect to which the taxpayer (or a predecessor of the taxpayer) changed, pursuant to the terms and conditions prescribed for it by the Commissioner, from the retirement to the straight-line method of computing the allowance for any taxable year beginning after December 31, 1940, and before January 1, 1956, of deductions for depreciation. The term does not include any specific property which has always been properly accounted for in accordance with the straight-line method of computing the depreciation allowances or which, under the terms-letter, was permitted or required to be accounted for under the retirement method.

(4) *Depreciation.* The term "depreciation" means exhaustion, wear and tear, and obsolescence.

(5) *Predecessor.* The term "predecessor" means any person from whom property of a kind or class to which the Act refers was acquired, if the basis of such property is determined by reference to its basis in the hands of such person. Where a series of transfers of property has occurred and where in each instance the basis of the property was determined by reference to its basis in the hands of the prior holder, the term includes each such prior holder.

(6) *Changeover.* The term "changeover" means a change from the retirement to the straight-line method of computing the allowance of deductions for depreciation.

(7) *Changeover date.* The term "changeover date" means the first day of the first taxable year for which the changeover was effective.

(8) *1956 adjustment date.* The term "1956 adjustment date" means, in the case of any taxpayer, the first day of its first taxable year beginning after December 31, 1955.

(9) *Terms-letter.* The term "terms-letter" means the terms and conditions prescribed by the Commissioner in connection with the changeover.

(10) *Terms-letter reserve.* The term "terms-letter reserve" means the reserve for depreciation prescribed by the Commissioner in connection with the changeover.

(11) *Depreciation sustained before March 1, 1913.* The term "depreciation sustained before March 1, 1913" may be construed to mean, to the extent that it is impossible to determine the actual amount of such depreciation from the books and records, that amount which is obtained by (i) deducting the "cost of reproduction new less depreciation" from the "cost of reproduction new", as ascertained as of the valuation date by the Interstate Commerce Commission under the provisions of section 19a of part I of the Interstate Commerce Act (49 U.S.C. 19a), and then (ii) making such retroactive adjustments to the remainder as are required, in the opinion of the Commissioner of Internal Revenue, to properly reflect the depreciation sustained before March 1, 1913. For this purpose, any retirement-straight line property held on March 1, 1913, and retired on or before the valuation date shall be taken into account.

§ 1.9001-2 (T.D. 6418, filed 10-9-59; republished in T.D. 6500, filed 11-25-60.) **Basis adjustments for taxable years beginning on or after 1956 adjustment date.**

(a) *In general.* Subsection (d) of the Act provides the basis adjustments required to be made by the taxpayer as of the 1956 adjustment date in respect of all periods before that date in order to determine the adjusted basis of all retirement-straight line property held by the taxpayer on that date. This adjusted basis on the 1956 adjustment date shall be used by the taxpayer for all purposes of the Code for any taxable year beginning after December 31, 1955. In order to arrive at the adjusted basis on the 1956 adjustment date, the taxpayer shall start with the unadjusted basis of all retirement-straight line property held on the changeover date by the taxpayer or a predecessor and shall, with respect to both the asset and reserve accounts, (1) make the adjustments prescribed by this section and subsection (d) of the Act and (2) also make those adjustments required, in accordance with the method of accounting regularly used, for those additions, retirements, and other dispositions of property which occurred on or after the changeover date and before the taxpayer's 1956 adjustment date. For an illustration of adustments required in accordance with the method of accounting regularly used, see paragraph (e) (3) of this section. The adjustments required by subsection (d) of the Act shall be made in lieu of the adjustments for depreciation otherwise required by section 1016 (a) (2) and (3) of the Code. The adjustments required by subsection (d) of the Act are set forth in paragraphs (b), (c), and (d) of this section.

(b) *Adjustment for depreciation sus-*

Reg. § 1.9001-2(b)

24,444 (I.R.C.) Reg. § 1.9001-2(b)(1)

tained before March 1, 1913—(1) *In general.* Subsection (d) (1) of the Act requires an adjustment to be made as of the 1956 adjustment date for depreciation sustained before March 1, 1913, on all retirement-straight line property held on March 1, 1913, by the taxpayer or a predecessor for which cost was or is claimed as basis and which was either (i) retired before the changeover date by the taxpayer or a predecessor or (ii) held on the changeover date by the taxpayer or a predecessor. This adjustment for depreciation sustained before March 1, 1913, shall be made in accordance with the conditions and limitations described in subparagraphs (2) and (3) of this paragraph and shall be allocated, in the manner prescribed in subparagraph (4) of this paragraph, among all retirement-straight line property held by the taxpayer on its 1956 adjustment date. The term "cost", when used in this paragraph with reference to the basis of property, shall be construed to mean the amount paid for the property or, if that amount could not be determined, then such other amount as was accepted by the Commissioner as "cost" for basis purposes.

(2) *Depreciation sustained on property retired before the changeover date.* Pursuant to subsection (d) (1) (A) of the Act, an adjustment to the basis of retirement-straight line property held by the taxpayer on its 1956 adjustment date shall be made as of that date for depreciation sustained before March 1, 1913, on all retirement-straight line property held on March 1, 1913, by the taxpayer or a predecessor, for which cost was claimed as the basis and which was retired before the changeover date by the taxpayer or a predecessor, except that—

(i) The adjustment shall be made only if a deduction was allowed in computing net income by reason of the retirement and the deduction so allowed was computed on the basis of the cost of the property unadjusted for depreciation sustained before March 1, 1913, and

(ii) In the case of any such property retired during any taxable year beginning after December 31, 1929, the adjustment shall not exceed that portion of the amount attributable to depreciation sustained before March 1, 1913, which resulted, by reason of the deduction so allowed, in a reduction of taxes under the Code or under prior income, war-profits, or excess-profits tax laws.

(3) *Depreciation sustained on property held on the changeover date.* Pursuant to subsection (d) (1) (B) of the Act, an adjustment to the basis of retirement-straight line property held by the taxpayer on its 1956 adjustment date shall be made as of that date for depreciation sustained before March 1, 1913, on all retirement-straight line property held on March 1, 1913, by the taxpayer or a predecessor for which cost was or is claimed as basis and which was held on the changeover date by the taxpayer or a predecessor. This subparagraph shall not apply, however, to any such property which (i) was disposed of on or after the changeover date by reason of sale, casualty, or abnormal retirement in the nature of special obsolescence, and (ii) is property to which paragraph (c) of this section and subsection (d)(2) of the Act apply.

(4) *Manner of allocating adjustment.* Pursuant to subsection (d)(1) of the Act, the amount of the adjustment required under this paragraph for depreciation sustained before March 1, 1913, which is attributable to a particular kind or class of retirement-straight line property held by the taxpayer on its 1956 adjustment date shall be made with respect to that kind or class of property. If the adjustment required under this paragraph for depreciation sustained before March 1, 1913, is attributable to retirement-straight line property of a particular kind or class no longer held by the taxpayer on its 1956 adjustment date, then the part of such adjustment to be allocated to any retirement-straight line property held by the taxpayer on its 1956 adjustment date shall be that amount which bears the same ratio to such adjustment as the unadjusted basis of the property so held bears to the entire unadjusted basis of all retirement-straight line property held by the taxpayer on its 1956 adjustment date.

(c) *Adjustment for part of terms-letter reserve applicable to property disposed of on or after changeover date and before 1956 adjustment date.* Pursuant to subsection (d)(2) of the Act, an adjustment to the basis of retirement-straight line property held by the taxpayer on its 1956 adjustment date shall be made as of that date for that part of the terms-letter reserve which was applicable to any retirement-straight line property disposed of by sale, casualty, or abnormal retirement in the nature of special obsolescence, but only if the sale occurred in, or a deduction by reason of such casualty or abnormal retirement was allowed for Federal income-tax purposes for, a period on or after the changeover date and before the taxpayer's 1956 adjustment date. This paragraph shall apply even though, in computing the adjusted basis of the property for purposes of determining gain or loss on the sale, casualty, or abnormal retirement, the basis of the retirement-straight line property was not reduced by the part of the terms-letter reserve applicable to the property. If necessary, the adjustment required by this paragraph shall be allocated, in the manner prescribed in paragraph (b)(4) of this section, among all retirement-straight line property held by the taxpayer on its 1956 adjustment date.

(d) *Adjustment for depreciation allowable under the terms-letter for periods on and after the changeover date and before the 1956 adjustment date.* Pursuant to subsection (d)(3) of the Act, an adjustment to the basis of retirement-straight line property held by the taxpayer on its 1956 adjustment date shall be made as of that date for the entire amount of depreciation allowable under the terms-letter for all periods on or after the changeover date and before

Retirement-Straight Line Adjustments (I.R.C.) 24,445
Act of 1958

the taxpayer's 1956 adjustment date. This adjustment shall include all such depreciation allowable with respect to any retirement-straight line property which was disposed of on or after the changeover date and before the 1956 adjustment date.

(e) *Illustration of basis adjustments required for taxable years beginning on or after the 1956 adjustment date.* The application of this section may be illustrated by the following example, which is based upon the assumption that multiple asset accounts are used:

Example. (1) Assume that on its changeover date, January 1, 1943, the taxpayer or its predecessor held retirement-straight line property with an unadjusted cost basis of $10,000. The terms-letter reserve established as of January 1, 1943, with respect to such property was $3,000. Depreciation sustained before March 1, 1913, on retirement-straight line property held on that date by the taxpayer or its predecessor for which cost was or is claimed as basis amounts to $800. Of this total depreciation sustained before March 1, 1913, $200 is attributable to retirement-straight line property retired before January 1, 1943, under circumstances requiring the adjustment under paragraph (b)(2) of this section, and $600 is attributable to retirement-straight line property held on January 1, 1943, by the taxpayer or its predecessor. On December 31, 1954, retirement-straight line property costing $1,500 was permanently retired under circumstances giving rise to an abnormal retirement in the nature of special obsolescence. The terms-letter reserve applicable to this retired property was $450, of which $120 represents depreciation sustained before March 1, 1913. On December 31, 1954, retirement-straight line property costing $1,000 was also permanently retired under circumstances giving rise to a normal retirement. None of the property retired on December 31, 1954, had any market or salvage value on that date. Depreciation allowable under the terms-letter on retirement-straight line property for all periods on and after January 1, 1943, and before January 1, 1956 (the taxpayer's 1956 adjustment date), amounts to $2,155, of which $345 is applicable to the property retired as an abnormal retirement.

(2) The reserve for depreciation as of January 1, 1956, contains a credit balance of $3,360, determined as follows but without regard to the Act:

(i) Credits to reserve:
Terms-letter reserve as of January 1, 1943 .... $ 3,000
Depreciation allowable under terms-letter from January 1, 1943, to December 31, 1955 .. 2,155
Balance 5,155

(ii) Charges to reserve:
Part of terms-letter reserve applicable to property abnormally retired .... $ 450
Depreciation applicable to property abnormally retired and allowable from January 1, 1943 to December 31, 1954 345
Adjusted for normal retirement 1,000
                                                     1,795

(iii) Balance as of January 1, 1956   3,360

(3) The adjusted basis on January 1, 1956, of the retirement-straight line property held by the taxpayer on that date is $6,010, determined as follows and in accordance with this section:

(i) Asset account:
Unadjusted cost on January 1, 1943 .... $10,000
Less:
Adjustment for abnormal retirement $1,500
Adjustment for normal retirement 1,000
                                                     2,500
Balance as of January 1, 1956   7,500

(ii) Credits to reserve for depreciation:
Depreciation sustained before March 1, 1913, on—
Property retired before January 1, 1943 .... $ 200
Property held on January 1, 1943 .... $ 600
Less part of such depreciation sustained on property abnormally retired on December 31, 1954 120
                                                     480
Part of terms letter reserve applicable to abnormal retirement on December 31, 1954 (including $120 depreciation sustained before March 1, 1913) 450
Depreciation allowable under terms-letter from January 1, 1943 to December 31, 1955 2,155
Total credits 3,285

(iii) Charges to reserve for depreciation:
Part of terms-letter reserve applicable to property abnormally retired .... $ 450
Depreciation applicable to property abnormally retired and allowable from January 1, 1943, to December 31, 1954   345
Adjustment for normal retirement 1,000
Total charges 1,795

(iv) Balance in reserve for depreciation:
Total credits .... $ 3,285
Total charges 1,795

Reg. § 1.9001-2(e)

© Copyright 1963 by Prentice-Hall, Inc.

24,446 (I.R.C.) Reg. § 1.9001-2(e)

Balance as of January 1, 1956	1,490

(v) Adjusted basis of property:

Balance in asset account	$ 7,500
Balance in reserve for depreciation	1,490
Adjusted basis as of January 1, 1956	6,010

(4) The following adjustments to the reserve determined under subparagraph (2) of this paragraph may be made in order to arrive at the reserve determined under subparagraph (3)(iv) of this paragraph:

(i) Credit balance in reserve, as determined under subparagraph (2) of this paragraph	$ 3,360

(ii) Credit adjustments:

Depreciation sustained before March 1, 1913, on—		
Property retired before January 1, 1943	$ 200	
Property held on January 1, 1943	480	
Part of terms-letter reserve applicable to obnormally retired on December 31, 1954	450	
		1,130
Balance		4,490

(iii) Debit adjustment:

Terms-letter reserve as of January 1, 1943	3,000

(iv) Credit balance in reserve, as determined under subparagraph (3)(iv) of this paragraph	1,490

(5) The $6,010 adjusted basis as of January 1, 1956, of the retirement-straight line property held by the taxpayer on that date is to be recovered over the estimated remaining useful life of that property. The remaining useful life of the property will be reviewed regularly, and appropriate adjustments in the rates will be made as necessary in order to spread the remaining cost less estimated salvage over the estimated remaining useful life or the property. See § 1.167(a)-1.

○→ § 1.9001-3 (T.D. 6418, filed 10-9-59; republished in T.D. 6500, filed 11-25-60.) **Basis adjustments for taxable years between changeover date and 1956 adjustment date.**

(a) *In general.* (1) Subsection (e) of the Act provides the adjustments required to be made in determining the adjusted basis of any retirement-straight line property as of any time on or after the changeover date and before the taxpayer's 1956 adjustment date. This adjusted basis shall be used for all purposes of the Internal Revenue Code of 1939 and the Internal Revenue Code of 1954 for taxable years beginning on or after the changeover date and before the taxpayer's 1956 adjustment date, except as provided in subparagraph (4) of this paragraph. The adjustments so required, which are set forth in paragraphs (b) and (c) of this section, shall not be used in determining the adjusted basis of property for taxable years beginning before the changeover date or on or after the taxpayer's 1956 adjustment date.

(2) In order to arrive at the adjusted basis as of any specific date occurring on or after the changeover date and before the 1956 adjustment date, the taxpayer shall start with the unadjusted basis of all retirement-straight line property held on the changeover date by the taxpayer or its predecessor and shall, as of that specific date, and with respect to both the asset and reserve accounts, (i) make the adjustments prescribed by this section and subsection (e) of the Act and (ii) also make those adjustments required, in accordance with the method of accounting regularly used, for additions, retirements, and other dispositions of property. For an illustration of adjustments required in accordance with the method of accounting regularly used, see the example in paragraph (d) of this section.

(3) The adjustments required by subsection (e) of the Act shall be made in lieu of the adjustments for depreciation otherwise required by section 1016(a)(2) and (3) of the Code and by the corresponding provisions of prior revenue laws.

(4) Although this section, and subsection (e) of the Act, shall apply in determining the excess-profits tax, they shall not apply in determining adjusted basis for the purpose of computing equity capital for any day under section 437(c) (relating to the Excess Profits Tax Act of 1950) (64 Stat. 1137) of the Internal Revenue Code of 1939. For the adjustments to be made in computing equity capital under such section, see paragraph (c) of § 1.9001-4.

(b) *Adjustment for terms-letter reserve.* Pursuant to subsection (e)(1) of the Act, the basis of any retirement-straight line property shall be adjusted, as of any specific applicable date occurring on or after the changeover date and before the 1956 adjustment date, for the amount of the terms-letter reserve applicable to such property.

(c) *Adjustment for depreciation allowable under the terms-letter.* Pursuant to subsection (e)(2) of the Act, the basis of any retirement-straight line property shall be adjusted, as of any specific applicable date occurring on or after the changeover date and before the 1956 adjustment date, for depreciation applicable to such property and allowable under the terms-letter.

(d) *Illustration of basis adjustments required for taxable years beginning on or after the changeover date and before the 1956 adjustment date.* The application of this section may be illustrated by the following example, which is based upon the assumption that multiple asset accounts are used:

Example. (1) The facts are assumed to be the same as those in the example

Retirement-Straight Line Adjustments Act of 1958 (I.R.C.) 24,447 of 1958

under paragraph (e) of § 1.9001-2, except that tne adjusted basis of the retirement-straight line property is determined as of January 1, 1955, and the depreciation allowable under the terms-letter from the changeover date to December 31, 1954, is $2,100.

(2) The adjusted basis on January 1, 1955, of the retirement-straight line property held by the taxpayer on that date is $4,195, determined as follows and in accordance with this section:

(i) Asset account:
Unadjusted cost on January 1, 1943 .... $10,000
Less:
Adjustment for abnormal retirement $1,500
Adjustment for normal retirement 1,000
                                                        2,500
Balance as of January 1, 1955   7,500

(ii) Credits to reserve for depreciation:
Entire terms-letter reserve as of January 1, 1943 .... $ 3,000
Depreciation allowable under terms-letter from January 1, 1943, to December 31, 1954 ...   2,100
Total credits 5,100

(iii) Charges to reserve for depreciation:
Part of terms-letter reserve applicable to property abnormally retired on December 31, 1954 .... $ 450
Depreciation applicable to property abnormally retired and allowable from January 1, 1943, to December 31, 1954   345
Adjustment for normal retirement   1,000
Total charges 1,795

(iv) Balance in reserve for depreciation:
Total credit $5,100
Total charges 1,795
Balance as of January 1, 1955   3,305

(v) Adjusted basis of property:
Balance in asset account $7,500
Balance in reserve for depreciation   3,305
Adjusted basis as of January 1, 1955   4,195

○━▶ § 1.9001-4 (T.D. 6418, filed 10-9-59; republished in T.D. 6500, filed 11-25-60.) **Adjustments required in computing excess-profits credit.**

(a) *In general.* Subsection (f) of the Act provides adjustments required to be made in computing the excess-profits credit for any taxable year under the Excess Profits Tax Act of 1940 (54 Stat. 975) or under the Excess Profits Tax Act of 1950 (64 Stat. 1137). These adjustments are set forth in paragraphs (b) and (c) of this section, and they shall apply notwithstanding the terms-letter.

(b) *Equity invested capital.* (1) Pursuant to subsection (f)(1) of the Act, in determining equity invested capital for any day of any taxable year under section 458 (relating to the Excess Profits Tax Act of 1950) or section 718 (relating to the Excess Profits Tax Act of 1940) of the Internal Revenue Code of 1939, the accumulated earnings and profits as of the changeover date, and as of the beginning of each taxable year thereafter, shall be reduced by the depreciation sustained before March 1, 1913, on all retirement-straight line property held on March 1, 1913, by the taxpayer or a predecessor for which cost was or is claimed as basis and which was held on the changeover date by the taxpayer or a predecessor. (2) For the computation of accumulated earnings and profits in determining equity invested capital, see 26 CFR (1941 Supp.) 30.718-2, as amended by Treasury Decisions 5299, approved October 1, 1943, 8 F.R. 13451, C.B. 1943, 747 (Regulations 109; 26 CFR (1943 Cum. Supp.) 35.718-2 (Regulations 112); and 26 CFR (1939) 41.458-4 (Regulations 130).

(c) *Equity capital.* (1) Pursuant to subsection (f)(2) of the Act, in determining the adjusted basis of assets for the purpose of computing equity capital for any day under section 437(c) (relating to the Excess Profits Tax Act of 1950) of the Internal Revenue Code of 1939, the basis of the assets which enter into the computation shall also be reduced by—

(i) Depreciation sustained before March 1, 1913, on all retirement-straight line property held on March 1, 1913, by the taxpayer or a predecessor for which cost was or is claimed as basis and which was—

(a) Retired before the changeover date by the taxpayer or a predecessor, or

(b) Held on the changeover date by the taxpayer or a predecessor and also held as of the beginning of the day for which the equity capital is being determined; and

(ii) All depreciation applicable to the assets which enter into the computation and allowable under the terms-letter for all periods on and after the changeover date and before the taxable year for which the excess-profits credit is being computed.

(2) The adjustment required to be made by subparagraph (1)(i)(a) of this paragraph as of the beginning of the day for which the equity capital is being determined shall be made in accordance with the conditions and limitation described in paragraph (b)(2) of § 1.9001-2.

(3) For the determination of equity capital under section 437(c) of the Internal Revenue Code of 1939, see 26 CFR (1939) 40.437-5 (Regulations 130).

DEALER RESERVE INCOME ADJUSTMENT ACT OF 1960

○━▶ § 1.9002 **Statutory provisions; Dealer Reserve Income Adjustment Act of 1960 (74 Stat. 124).**

○━▶ § 1.9002-1 (T.D. 6490, filed 8-30-60.) **Purpose, applicability, and definitions.**

(a) *In general.* The Dealer Reserve

Reg. § 1.9002-1(a)

24,448 (I.R.C.) Reg. § 1.9002-1(a)

Income Adjustment Act of 1960 (74 Stat. 124) contains transitional provisions relating to adjustments in income resulting from a change in the income tax treatment of dealer reserve income. The purpose of the Act is to provide eligible taxpayers who elect to have its provisions apply with two alternatives for accounting for the adjustments to income resulting from a change to a proper method of reporting dealer reserve income. The Act also provides certain taxpayers with an election to pay in installments any net increase in tax. Eligible taxpayers must make any election under the provisions of the Act prior to September 1, 1960. If any election is made, then the applicable provisions of the Act and §§ 1.9002 to 1.9002-8, inclusive, shall apply.

(b) *Eligibility to elect.* In order to be eligible to make any of the elections provided by the Act, a taxpayer must have, for his most recent taxable year ending on or before June 22, 1959, (1) computed, or been required to compute, taxable income under an accrual method of accounting, and (2) treated dealer reserve income (or portions thereof) which should have been taken into account (under the accrual method of accounting) for such most recent taxable year as accruable for a subsequent taxable year. Thus, the elections provided by the Act are not available to a person who, for his most recent taxable year ending on or before June 22, 1959, reported dealer reserve income under a method proper under the accrual method of accounting or who was not required to compute taxable income under the accrual method of accounting. An election may be made even though the taxpayer is litigating his liability for income tax based upon his treatment of dealer reserve income, whether in The Tax Court of the United States or any other court, and an election filed by a taxpayer who is litigating his liability for income tax based upon his treatment of dealer reserve income does not constitute a waiver of his right to continue pending litigation until final judicial determination. He must, however, comply with the provisions of the Act and the regulations thereunder.

(c) *Definitions.* For reasons of the Act and §§ 1.9002 to 1.9002-8, inclusive—

(1) *The Act.* The term "the Act" means the Dealer Reserve Income Adjustment Act of 1960 (74 Stat. 124).

(2) *Dealer reserve income.* The term "dealer reserve income" means—

(i) That part of the consideration derived by any person from the sale or other disposition of customers' sales contracts, notes, and other evidences of indebtedness (or derived from customers' finance charges connected with such sales or other dispositions) which is—

(a) Attributable to the sale by such person to such customers, in the ordinary course of his trade or business, of real property or tangible personal property, and

(b) Held in a reserve account, by the financial institution to which such person disposed of such evidences of indebtedness, for the purpose of securing obligations of such person or of such customers, or both; and

(ii) That part of the consideration—

(a) Derived by any person from a sale described in subdivision (i) (a) of this subparagraph in respect of which part or all of the purchase price of the property sold is provided by a financial institution to or for the customer to whom such property is sold, or

(b) Derived by such person from finance charges connected with the financing of such sale, which is held in a reserve account by such financial institution for the purpose of securing obligations of such person or of such customer, or both. Thus, the term includes amounts held in a reserve account by a financial institution in transactions in which the customer becomes obligated to the institution as well as such amounts so held by a financial institution in transactions in which the taxpayer is the obligee on the contract, note, or other evidence of indebtedness. For purposes of the definition of the term "dealer reserve income" it is immaterial whether or not the taxpayer guarantees the customer's obligation in excess of the reserve retained by the financial institution. The term does not include the consideration derived from transactions relating to the sale of intangible property such as stocks, bonds, copyrights, patents, etc. Further, the term does not include consideration derived by the taxpayer from transactions relating to the sale of property by a person not the taxpayer or to casual sales of property not in the ordinary course of the taxpayer's trade or business.

(3) *Financial institutions.* The term "financial institution" means any person regularly engaged in the business of acquiring evidences of indebtedness of the kind described in section 5(a)(1) of the Act, or of financing sales of the kind described in section 5(a)(2) of the Act, or both. It thus includes banking institutions, finance companies, building and loan associations, and other similar type organizations, as well as an individual or partnership regularly engaged in the described business.

(4) *Taxpayer.* The term "taxpayer" means any person to whom the Act applies.

(5) *Other terms.* All other terms which are not specifically defined shall have the same meaning as when used in the Internal Revenue Code of 1954 except where otherwise distinctly expressed or manifestly intended.

§ 1.9002-2 (T.D. 6490, filed 8-30-60.) **Election to have the provisions of section 481 of the Internal Revenue Code of 1954 apply.**

(a) *In general.* Section 3(a) of the Act provides that if the income tax treatment of dealer reserve income by the taxpayer is changed (whether or not such change is initiated by the taxpayer) to a proper method under the accrual method of accounting, then the taxpayer may elect to have such change treated as a change in method of accounting not initiated by the

Final Regulations — Dealer Reserve Income Adjustment Act of 1960

taxpayer to which the provisions of section 481 of the Code apply. This election may be made only when the alternative election under section 4(a) of the Act has not been exercised.

(b) *Year of change.* Where an election has been made under section 3(a) of the Act to have section 481 of the Code apply, then for purposes of applying section 481 of the Code the year of change shall be determined in accordance with the provisions of section 3(b) of the Act. Section 3(b) provides that the year of change is the earlier of (1) the first taxable year ending after June 22, 1959, or (2) the earliest taxable year for which, on or before June 22, 1959,

(i) There was issued a notice of deficiency or written notice of a proposed deficiency attributable to the erroneous treatment of dealer reserve income, or

(ii) The taxpayer filed a claim for refund or credit with respect to the treatment of such income, and in respect of which the assessment of any deficiency, or the refund or credit of any overpayment, was not prevented on June 21, 1959, by the operation of any law or rule of law. The written notice of proposed deficiency includes a 15- or 30-day letter issued under established procedure or other similar written notification.

(c) *Application to pre-1954 Code years.* If the earliest year described in paragraph (b) of this section is a year subject to the Internal Revenue Code of 1939 in respect of which assessment of any deficiency or refund or credit of any overpayment was not prevented on June 21, 1959, by the operation of any law or rule of law, section 481 of the Internal Revenue Code of 1954 shall be treated as applying in the same manner as it would have applied had it been enacted as part of the Internal Revenue Code of 1939.

(d) *Examples.* The operation of this section in determining the year of change may be illustrated by the following examples:

Example (1). D, a taxpayer on the calendar year basis who employs the accrual method of accounting, voluntarily changed to the proper method of accounting for dealer reserve income for the taxable year 1959. A statutory notice of deficiency, however, was issued prior to June 23, 1959, relating to the erroneous treatment of such income for the taxable year 1956, which was the earliest taxable year in respect of which assessment of a deficiency or credit or refund of an overpayment was not prevented on June 21, 1959. Prior to September 1, 1960, D properly exercises his election under section 3 of the Act to have the change in the treatment of dealer reserve income treated as a change in method of accounting not initiated by the taxpayer to which section 481 of the Code applies. Under these facts, 1956 is the year of the change for purposes of applying section 481. Accordingly, the net amount of any adjustment found necessary as a result of the change in the treatment of dealer reserve income which is attributable to taxable years subject to the 1954 Code shall be taken into account for the year of change in accordance with section 481. The net amount of the adjustments attributable to pre-1954 Code years is to be disregarded. The income of each taxable year succeeding the year of change in respect of which the assessment of any deficiency or refund or credit of any overpayment is not prevented will be recomputed under the proper method of accounting initiated by the change.

Example (2). Assume the same facts as set forth in example (1), except that no notice of a proposed deficiency of any type has been issued, and assume further that no claim for refund has been filed. Since there was no earlier year open on June 21, 1959, for which the taxpayer either was notified of a proposed deficiency attributable to the erroneous treatment of dealer reserve income or for which he had filed a claim for refund or credit with respect to the treatment of such income, the year of change is 1959, the first taxable year ending after June 22, 1959. Accordingly, the net amount of any adjustment found necessary as a result of the change in the treatment of dealer reserve income which is attributable to taxable year subject to the 1954 Code shall be taken into account for the year of the change in accordance with section 481. The net amount of the adjustments attributable to pre-1954 Code years is to be disregarded.

Example (3). Assume the same facts as set forth in example (1), except that a refund claim specifying adjustments relative to dealer reserve income was timely filed for the taxable year 1951, which was the earliest taxable year for which a refund or credit of an overpayment or assessment of a deficiency was not prevented on June 21, 1959. Under this factual situation, the year of change for purposes of applying section 481 would be 1951. Section 481 would be applied to 1951 and be given effect for that year in the same manner as it would have applied had it been enacted as a part of the 1939 Code and as if the change to the proper method of accounting had not been initiated by the taxpayer. Any adjustment with regard to dealer reserve income attributable to pre-1951 years is disregarded. The income of each taxable year succeeding the year of change in respect of which the assessment of any deficiency or refund or credit of any overpayment is not prevented will be recomputed under the proper method of accounting initiated by the change.

§ 1.9002-3 (T.D. 6490, filed 8-30-60.) **Election to have the provisions of section 481 of the Internal Revenue Code of 1954 not apply.**

Section 4(a) of the Act provides that if the treatment of dealer reserve income by the taxpayer is changed to a method proper under the accrual method of accounting, then the taxpayer may elect to have such change treated as not a change in method of accounting to which the provisions of section 481 of the Code apply. This election shall apply to all taxable years ending on or before June 22, 1959, for which the assessment of any deficiency, or for which refund or credit of any overpayment, was not prevented on June 21, 1959, by the operation of any law or rule of law. This election may be made only if the alternative election under section 3(a) of the Act has not been exercised. If an election is made under section 4(a) of the Act, taxable income (or net income in the case of a taxable year to which the Internal Revenue Code of 1939 applies) shall be recomputed under a proper method of accounting for dealer reserve income for each taxable year to which the election applies, without regard to section 481.

§ 1.9002-4 (T.D. 6490, filed 8-30-60.) **Election to pay net increase in tax installments.**

(a) *Election.* If an election is made under section 4(a) of the Act and if the net increase in tax determined in accordance with paragraph (b) of this section exceeds $2,500, the taxpayer may also make an election under section 4(b) of the Act prior to September 1, 1960, to pay any portion of such net increase in tax, unpaid on the date of the election, in 2 or more, but not to exceed 10, equal annual installments. If the taxpayer making the election under section 4(a) of the Act is a partnership or a small business corporation electing under subchapter S, chapter 1 of the Code, the determination as to whether the net increase in tax exceeds $2,500 shall be made separately as to each partner or shareholder, respectively, with regard to his individual liability. Thus, if a partnership makes an election under section 4(a) of the Act, and partners A and B had a net increase in tax of $3,000 and $2,000, respectively, as a result of dealer reserve income adjustments to partnership income, partner A may elect under section 4(b) of the Act to pay the net increase in 2 or more, but not exceeding 10, equal annual installments to the extent that such tax was unpaid on the date of the election. Partner B may not make the election since his net increase in tax does not exceed $2,500.

(b) *Net increase in tax.* (1) The term "net increase in tax" means the amount by which the sum of the increases in tax (including interest) for all taxable years to which the election under section 4(a) of the Act applies and which is attributable to the election exceeds the sum of the decreases in tax (including interest) for all taxable years to which the election under such section applies and which is attributable to the election.

(2) In determining the net increase in tax, the tax and interest for each taxable year to which the election applies is computed by taking into account all adjustments necessary to reflect the change to the proper treatment of dealer reserve income. If the computation results in additional tax for a taxable year, then interest is computed under section 6601 of the Code (or corresponding provisions of prior law) on such additional tax for the taxable year involved from the last date prescribed for payment of the tax for such taxable year to the date the election is made. The interest so computed is then added to the additional tax determined for such taxable year. The sum of these two items (tax plus interest) represents the increase in tax for such taxable year. If the computation of the tax after taking into account the appropriate dealer reserve income adjustments results in a reduction in tax for any taxable year to which the election applies, interest under section 6611 of the Code (or corresponding provisions of prior law) is computed from the date of the overpayment of the tax for such year to the date of the election. The amount of the interest so computed is then added to the reduction in tax to determine the total decrease in tax for such year. The net increase in tax is then determined by adding together the total increases in tax for each year to which the election applies and from the resulting total subtracting the sum of the total decreases in tax for each year. If the total increases in tax for all such years do not exceed the total decreases in tax, there is no net increase in tax for purposes of section 4(b) of the Act. For purposes of determining the net increase in tax, net operating losses affecting the computation of tax for any prior taxable year not otherwise affected shall be taken into account.

(c) *Time for paying installments.* If the election under this section is made to pay the unpaid portion of the net increase in tax in installments, the first installment shall be paid on or before the date prescribed by section 6151(a) of the Code for payment of the tax for the taxable year in which such election is made. Each succeeding installment shall be paid on or before the date which is one year after the date prescribed for the payment of the preceding installment.

(d) *Termination of installment privilege*—(1) *For nonpayment of installment.* The extension of time provided by section 4(b) of the Act for payment of the net increase in tax in installments shall terminate, and any unpaid installments shall be paid upon notice and demand from the district director if any installment under such section is not paid by the taxpayer on or before the date fixed for its payment, including any extension of time for payment of any such installment.

(2) *For other reasons.* The extension of time provided by section 4(b) of the Act for payment of the net increase in tax in installments shall terminate, and any unpaid installments shall be paid upon notice and demand from the district director if—

(i) In the case of an individual, he dies or ceases to engage in any trade or business,

(ii) In the case of a partner, his entire interest in the partnership is transferred or liquidated or the partnership terminates, or

(iii) In the case of a corporation, it ceases to engage in a trade or business, unless the unpaid portion of the tax payable in installments is required to be taken into account by an acquiring corporation under section 5(d) of the Act.

Dealer Reserve Income Adjustment Act of 1960

(I.R.C.) 24,451

The installment privilege is not terminated under this subparagraph even though the taxpayer terminates the trade or business in respect of which the dealer reserve income is attributable provided the taxpayer continues in a trade or business. Further, the privilege is not terminated by a transfer of a part of a partnership interest so long as the partner retains any interest in the partnership. Also, the privilege is not terminated by a transaction falling within the provisions of section 381(a) of the Code if, under section 5(d) of the Act, the acquiring corporation is required to take into account the unpaid portion of the net increase in tax. In such a case the privilege may be continued by the acquiring corporation in the same manner and under the same conditions as though it were the distributor or transferor corporation.

(e) *Redetermination of tax subsequent to exercise of installment election.* Section 4(d) of the Act provides that where a taxpayer has elected to pay the net increase in tax in installments and thereafter it becomes necessary to redetermine the taxpayer's tax for any taxable year to which the election provided by section 4(a) of the Act applies, then the net increase in tax shall be redetermined. Where the redetermination does not involve adjustments affecting the treatment of dealer reserve income, then the net increase in tax previously computed will not be disturbed. The net increase in tax is limited to the amount of tax computed under section 4(b)(2) of the Act as a result of the change in treatment accorded dealer reserve income. If the redetermination of tax for any taxable year to which the election applies results in an addition to the net increase in tax previously computed, then such addition shall be prorated to all of the installments whether paid or unpaid. The part of the addition, prorated to installments which are not yet due, shall be collected at the same time as, and as a part of, such installments. The part of the addition prorated to installments, the time for payment of which has arrived, shall be paid upon notice and demand from the district director. Under section 4(g) of the Act, failure to make such payment within 10 days after issuance of notice and demand will terminate the installment privilege. The imposition of interest on the addition to the net increase in tax as a result of the redetermination will be determined in the same manner as interest on the previously computed net increase in tax. Thus, no interest will be imposed on the amount of the addition to the net increase in tax prorated to installments not yet due unless the installment privilege is terminated under subsection (f) or (g) of section 4 of the Act. If a reduction in the net increase in tax results from a redetermination of tax for any taxable year to which the election applies, the entire amount of such reduction shall, in accordance with the provisions of section 6403 of the Code (relating to overpayment of installments), be prorated to the installments which are not yet due, resulting in a pro rata reduction in each of such installments. Where the redetermination does not involve adjustments pertaining to dealer reserve income, then any resulting deficiency pertaining to the year to which the election applies will be assessed and collected, in accordance with the applicable provisions of the Code (or corresponding provisions of prior law) without regard to any election made under the Act.

(f) *Periods of limitation.* Section 4(h) of the Act provides that where there is an extension of time for payment of tax under the provisions of section 4(b) of the Act, the running of the periods of limitation provided by section 6502 of the Code (or corresponding provisions of prior law) for collection of such tax is suspended for the period of time for which the extension is granted.

§ 1.9002-5 (T.D. 6490, filed 8-30-60.) Special rules relating to interest.

(a) *In general.* Where an election is made under section 4(a) of the Act interest is computed under section 6601 of the Code (or corresponding provisions of prior law) on any increase in tax attributable to such election for each taxable year involved for the period from the last date prescribed for payment of the tax for such year (determined without regard to any extensions of time for filing the return) through the date preceding the date on which the election is made. Where the election under section 4(a) of the Act results in a decrease in tax for any year to which the election applies, interest is computed in accordance with section 6611 of the Code (or corresponding provisions of prior law) from the date of overpayment through the date preceding the date on which the election is made. Where there is a net increase in tax as a result of the election under section 4(a) of the Act, no interest shall be imposed on any underpayment (and no interest shall be paid on any overpayment) attributable to the dealer reserve income adjustment for any year to which the election applies for the period commencing with the date such election is made and ending on the date prescribed for filing the return (determined without regard to extensions of time) for the taxable year in which the election is made. This rule applies regardless of whether the election under section 4(b) of the Act is made. If there is no net increase in tax, interest on any underpayment or overpayment attributable to the dealer reserve income adjustment for any taxable year to which the election applies for the period commencing with the date of the election shall be determined in accordance with §§ 301.6601-1 and 301.6611-1 of this chapter (Regulations on Procedure and Administration).

(b) *Installment period*—(1) *Where payment is not accelerated.* If the election under section 4(b) of the Act is made to pay the net increase in tax in installments, no interest will be imposed on such net increase in tax for the period beginning with the due date fixed under section 4(c)

Reg. § 1.9002-5(b)(1)

24,452 (I.R.C.)   Reg. § 1.9002-5(b)(1)

of the Act for the first installment payment and ending with the date fixed under such section for the last installment payment unless payment of the unpaid installments is accelerated under other provisions of the Act. See subsections (f) and (g) of section 4 of the Act.

(2) *Where payment is accelerated.* Where payment of the unpaid installments is accelerated because of the termination of the installment privilege, interest will be computed under section 6601 of the Code on the entire unpaid net increase in tax for the applicable period set forth below:

(i) In the case of acceleration under section 4(f) of the Act for reasons other than nonpayment of an installment, from the date of the notice and demand for payment of the unpaid tax to the date of payment; or

(ii) In the case of acceleration under section 4(g) of the Act for nonpayment of an installment, from the date fixed for payment of the installment to the date of payment.

When payment is accelerated under section 4(f) of the Act, however, no interest will be charged where payment of the unpaid installments is made within 10 days of issuance of the notice and demand for such payment.

0→ § 1.9002-6 (T.D. 6490, filed 8-30-60.) Acquiring corporation.

Section 5(d) of the Act provides that for purposes of such Act in the case of the acquisition of the assets of a corporation by another corporation in a distribution or transfer described in section 381(a) of the Code the acquiring corporation shall be treated as if it were the distributor or transferor corporation.

0→ § 1.9002-7 (T.D. 6490, filed 8-30-60.) Statute of limitations.

(a) *Extension of period for assessment and refund or credit.* Under section 5(e) of the Act, if an election is made to have the Act apply, and if the assessment of any deficiency, or the refund or credit of any overpayment attributable to the election, for any taxable year to which the Act applies was not prevented on June 21, 1959, by the operation of any law or rule of law (except as provided in paragraph (b) of this section, relating to closing agreements and compromises), but would be so prevented prior to September 1, 1961, the period within which such assessment, or such refund or credit, may be made with respect to such taxable year shall not expire prior to September 1, 1961. An election under either section 3 or 4 of the Act will be considered to be a consent to the extension of the period of limitation for purposes of assessment for any year to which the Act applies. Thus, for example, if, as the result of an election under section 4(a) of the Act, assessment of a deficiency for the taxable year 1955 was not prevented by the statute of limitations, a judicial decision that had become final, or otherwise, on June 21, 1959, but would (except for section 5(e) of the Act) be prevented on a later date, as for instance September 1, 1959, then for purposes of applying section 4 of the Act assessment may be made at any time prior to September 1, 1961, with respect to such year if the taxpayer made an election under the Act prior to September 1, 1960. Section 5(e) of the Act will, in no event, operate to shorten the period of limitation otherwise applicable with respect to any taxable year.

(b) *Years closed by closing agreement or compromise.* For purposes of the Act, if the assessment of any deficiency or a refund or credit of any overpayment for any taxable year was not prevented on June 21, 1959, but is prevented on the date of an election under section 3 or 4 of the Act by the operation of the provisions of chapter 74 of the Code (relating to closing agreements and compromises), assessment, refund, or credit will, nevertheless be considered as being prevented on June 21, 1959.

0→ § 1.9002-8 (T.D. 6490, filed 8-30-60.) Manner of exercising elections.

(a) *By whom election is to be made—* (1) *In general.* Generally, the taxpayer to whom the Act applies will exercise the elections provided therein. In the case of a partnership or a corporation electing under the provisions of subchapter S, chapter 1 of the Code, the election shall be exercised by the persons specified in subparagraphs (2) and (3) of this paragraph, respectively.

(2) *Partnerships.* In the case of a partnership, the election under section 3 or 4(a) of the Act shall be exercised by the partnership. If an election is made by the partnership under section 4(a) of the Act, any election under section 4(b) of the Act to pay the net increase in tax in installments shall be made by each partner separately. The determination as to whether the net increase in tax resulting from the election under section 4(a) of the Act exceeds $2,500 shall be made with reference to the increase or decrease in the tax of each partner attributable to the adjustment to his distributive share of the partnership income resulting from the election.

(3) *Subchapter S corporations.* In the case of an electing small business corporation under subchapter S, chapter 1 of the Code, the election under section 3 or 4(a) of the Act shall be made by such corporation. An election under section 4(b) of the Act to pay the net increase in tax in installments shall, to the extent the net increase in tax resulting from the election is attributable to adjustments to income for taxable years for which the corporation was not an electing small business corporation, be made by the corporation. The determination as to whether the net increase in tax for such taxable years exceeds $2,500 shall be made with reference to the increase or decrease in tax of the corporation. Any election under section 4 (b) of the Act to pay the net increase in tax in installments shall, to the extent the increase in tax is attributable to years for which the corporation was an electing small business corporation, be made by the shareholders separately. The determination

in such a case as to whether the net increase in tax for such taxable years exceeds $2,500 shall be made with reference to the increases or decreases in the tax of each shareholder attributable to the adjustments to taxable income of the electing small business corporation resulting from the election.

(b) *Time and manner of making elections*—(1) *In general.* Any election made under the Act shall be made by the taxpayers described in paragraph (a) of this section before September 1, 1960, by filing a statement with the district director with whom such taxpayer's income tax return for the taxable year in which the election is made is required to be filed. A copy of the statement of election shall be attached to and filed with such taxpayer's income tax return for such taxable year.

(2) *Election to have section 481 apply.* An election under section 3 of the Act shall be made in the form of a statement which shall include the following:

(i) A clear indication that an election is being made under section 3 of the Act;

(ii) Information sufficient to establish eligibility to make the election; and

(iii) The year of change as defined in section 3(b) of the Act.

An amended income tax return reflecting the increase or decrease in tax attributable to the election shall be filed for the year of change together with schedules showing how the tax was recomputed under section 481 of the Code. If income tax returns have been filed for any taxable years subsequent to the year of change, amended returns reflecting the proper treatment of dealer reesrve income for such years shall also be filed. In the case of partnerships and electing small business corporations under subchapter S, chapter 1 of the Code, amended returns shall be filed by the partnership or electing small business corporation, as well as by the partners or shareholders, as the case may be. Any amended return shall be filed with the office of the district director with whom the taxpayer files his income tax return for the taxable year in which the election is made and, if practicable, on the same date the statement of election is filed, but amended returns shall be filed in no event later than November 30, 1960, unless an extension of time is granted under section 6081 of the Code. Whenever the amended returns do not accompany the statement of election, a copy of the statement shall be submitted with the amended returns.

(3) *Election not to have section 481 apply.* An election under section 4(a) of the Act shall be made in the form of a statement which shall include the following:

(i) A clear indication that an election is being made under section 4(a) of the Act;

(ii) Information sufficient to establish eligibility to make the election; and

(iii) The taxable years to which the election applies.

Amended income tax returns reflecting the increase or decrease in tax attributable to the election shall be filed for the taxable years to which the election applies. If income tax returns have been filed for any subsequent taxable years, amended returns reflecting the proper treatment of dealer reserve income for such years shall also be filed. In the case of partnerships and electing small business corporations under subchapter S, chapter 1 of the Code, amended returns shall be filed by the partnership or electing small business corporation, as well as by the partners or shareholders, as the case may be. Any amended return shall be filed with the office of the district director with whom the taxpayer files his income tax return for the taxable year in which the election is made and, if practicable, on the same date the statement of election is filed, but amended returns shall be filed in no event later than November 30, 1960, unless an extension of time is granted under section 6081 of the Code. Whenever the amended returns do not accompany the statement of election, a copy of the statement shall be submitted with the amended returns.

(4) *Election to pay tax in installments.* (i) Except as otherwise provided in subdivision (ii) of this subparagraph, if the taxpayer making the election under section 4(a) of the Act also desires to make the election under section 4(b) of the Act to pay the increase in tax in installments, then the statement of election shall include the following additional information:

(a) A clear indication that an election is also being made under section 4(b) of the Act;

(b) A summary of the total increases and decreases in tax, together with interest thereon, in sufficient detail to establish eligibility to make the election; and

(c) The number of annual installments in which the taxpayer elects to pay the net increase in tax.

(ii) Where a partnership or electing small business corporation under subchapter S, chapter 1 of the Code, has made an election under section 4(a) of the Act, and any partner or shareholder, as the case may be, desires to make an election under section 4(b) of the Act, a statement of election shall be filed by such partner or shareholder containing the following information:

(a) A clear indication that an election is being made under section 4(b) of the Act;

(b) A summary of the total increases and decreases in tax, together with interest thereon, of such partner or shareholder in sufficient detail to establish eligibility to make the election;

(c) The number of annual installments in which the partner or shareholder elects to pay the net increase in tax; and

(d) The office of the district director and the date on which the election under section 4(a) of the Act was filed by such partnership or corporation.

The statement of election under section 4(b) of the Act shall be accompanied by a copy of the statement of election under section 4(a) of the Act made by the partnership or electing small business corporation under subchapter S, chapter 1 of the Code, as the case may be.

(c) *Effect of election.* An election made

Reg. § 1.9002-8(b)(4)

24,454 (I.R.C.)   Reg. § 1.9002-8(b)(4)   6-12-78

under section 3 or 4 of the Act shall become irrevocable on September 1, 1960, and shall be binding on the taxpayer for all taxable years to which it applies.

PUBLIC DEBT AND TAX RATE EXTENSION ACT OF 1960

○― § 1.9003 (T.D. 6492, filed 9-15-60.) **Statutory provisions; section 4 of Public Law 86-781 (74 Stat. 1018), approved September 14, 1960. [Sec. 613, IRC]**

○― § 1.9003-1 (T.D. 6492, filed 9-15-60.) **Election to have the provisions of section 613(c)(2) and (4) of the 1954 Code, as amended, apply for past years.**

(a) *In general.* Section 4 of the Act of September 14, 1960 (Public Law 86-781, 74 Stat. 1018) amended section 302(c) of the Public Debt and Tax Rate Extension Act of 1960 to permit certain taxpayers for taxable years beginning before January 1, 1961, to apply the provisions of section 302(b) of that Act. Section 302(b) of the Act amended section 613(c)(2) and (4) of the Internal Revenue Code of 1954 to read in part as follows:

(2) *Mining.* The term "mining" includes not merely the extraction of the ores or minerals from the ground, but also the treatment processes considered as mining described in paragraph (4) (and the treatment processes necessary or incidental thereto), and so much of the transportation of ores or minerals (whether or not by common carrier) from the point of extraction from the ground to the plants or mills in which such treatment processes are applied thereto as is not in excess of 50 miles unless the Secretary or his delegate finds that the physical and other requirements are such that the ore or mineral must be transported a greater distance to such plants or mills.

* * * * * *

(4) *Treatment processes considered as mining.* The following treatment processes where applied by the mine owner or operator shall be considered as mining to the extent they are applied to the ore or mineral in respect of which he is entitled to a deduction for depletion under section 611:

* * * * * *

(F) In the case of calcium carbonates and other minerals when used in making cement—all processes (other than preheating of the kiln feed) applied prior to the introduction of the kiln feed into the kiln, but not including any subsequent process;

* * * * * *

(b) *Election.* Under section 302(c)(2) of the Act, the taxpayer, in the case of calcium carbonates or other minerals when used by him in making cement, may elect to apply the provisions of section 613(c)(2) and (4) of the 1954 Code as amended in lieu of the corresponding provisions of prior law. The taxpayer must make the election in accordance with § 1.9003-4 on or before November 15, 1960 (the 60th day after the publication in the Federal Register of final regulations issued under section 302(c)(2) of the Act), and the election shall become irrevocable on such 60th day.

(c) *Years to which the election is applicable.* If the election described in paragraph (b) of this section is made by the taxpayer, the provisions of section 613(c)(2) and (4) as amended by section 302(b) of the Act apply to all taxable years beginning before January 1, 1961, in respect of which—

(1) The assessment of any deficiency,

(2) Refund or credit of any overpayment,

(3) Commencement of a suit for recovery of a refund under section 7405 of the Internal Revenue Code of 1954, is not prevented on September 14, 1960, by the operation of any law or rule of law. The election also applies to taxable years beginning before January 1, 1961, in respect of which an assessment of a deficiency has been made but not collected on or before September 14, 1960.

○― § 1.9003-2 (T.D. 6492, filed 9-15-60.) **Effect of election.**

(a) *In general.* If a taxpayer makes the election described in paragraph (b) of § 1.9003-1, he shall be deemed to have consented to the application of section 302(b) of the Act with respect to all taxable years to which the election applies. Thus, subparagraph (F) of section 613(c)(4) of the Internal Revenue Code as amended must be applied in determining gross income from mining for the taxable years to which the election applies (including years subject to the Internal Revenue Code of 1939) whether or not the taxpayer is litigating the issue. Further, the election shall apply to all calcium carbonates or other minerals mined and used by the taxpaper in making cement.

(b) *Effect on gross income from mining.* The election is only determinative of what constitutes "mining" for purposes of computing percentage depletion and has no effect on the method employed in determining the amount of gross income from mining. In applying the election to the years affected there shall be taken into account the effect that any adjustments resulting from the election shall have on other items affected thereby, such as charitable contributions, foreign tax credit, net operating loss, and the effect that adjustments to any such items shall have on other taxable years. The provisions of section 302(b) of the Act are applicable with respect to taxable years subject to the Internal Revenue Code of 1939 for purposes of applying sections 450 and 453 of that Code.

○― § 1.9003-3 (T.D. 6492, filed 9-15-60.) **Statutes of limitation.**

Under section 302(c)(2) of the Act, the period within which the assessment of any deficiency or the credit or refund of any overpayment attributable to the election may be made shall not expire sooner than 1 year after November 15, 1960. Thus, if assessment of a deficiency or credit or refund of an overpayment, whichever is applicable, is not prevented on September 14, 1960, the time for making assessment or credit or refund shall not expire for at least 1 year after November 15, 1960, notwithstanding any other provisions of law to the contrary. Even though assessment of a deficiency is prevented on September 14, 1960, if commencement of a suit for recovery of a refund under section 7405 of the Code may be made on such date, then any deficiency resulting from the election may be assessed at any time within 1 year after November 15, 1960. If the taxpayer makes the election he shall be deemed to have consented to the application of the provisions of section 302(c)(2) of the Act extending the time for assessing a deficiency attributable to the election. Section 302(c)(2) of the Act does not shorten the period of limitations otherwise applicable. An agreement may be entered into under section 6501(c)(4) of the Code and corresponding provisions of prior law to extend the period for assessment.

§ 1.9003-4 (T.D. 6492, filed 9-15-60.) **Manner of exercising election.**

(a) *By whom election is to be made.* Generally, the taxpayer whose tax liability is affected by the election shall make the election. In the case of a partnership, or a corporation electing under the provisions of subchapter S, chapter 1 of the Code, the election shall be exercised by the partnership or such corporation, as the case may be.

(b) *Time and manner of making election.* The election shall be made on or before November 15, 1960, by filing a statement with the district director with whom the taxpayer's income tax return for the taxable year in which the election is made is required to be filed. The statement shall include the following:

(1) A clear indication that an election is being made under section 302(c)(2) of the Act, and

(2) The taxable years to which the election applies.

Amended income tax returns reflecting any increase or decrease in tax attributable to the election shall be filed for the taxable years to which the election applies. In the case of partnerships and electing small business corporations under subchapter S, chapter 1 of the Code, amended returns shall be filed by the partnership or electing small business corporations, as well as by the partners or shareholders, as the case may be. Any amended return shall be filed with the office of the district director with whom the taxpayer files his income tax return for the taxable year in which the election is made and, if practicable, on the same date the statement of election is filed, but amended returns shall be filed in no event later than February 28, 1961, unless an extension of time is granted under section 6081 of the Code. Whenever the amended returns do not accompany the statement of election, a copy of the statement shall be submitted with the amended returns. The amended returns shall be accompanied by payment of the additional tax (together with interest thereon) resulting from the election.

§ 1.9003-5 (T.D. 6492, filed 9-15-60.) **Terms; applicability of other laws.**

All other terms which are not otherwise specifically defined shall have the same meaning as when used in the Code (or the corresponding provisions of prior law) except where otherwise distinctly expressed or manifestly intended to the contrary. Further, all provisions of law contained in the Code (or the corresponding provisions of prior law) shall apply to the extent that they can apply. Thus, all of the provisions of subtitle F of the Code and the corresponding provisions of prior law shall apply to the extent they can apply, including the provisions of law relating to assessment, collection, credit or refund, and limitations. For purposes of this section and §§ 1.9003-1 to 1.9003-4, inclusive, the term "Act" means the Public Debt and Tax Rate Extension Act of 1960 as amended. (74 Stat. 293, 1018).

DEPLETION DEDUCTION ELECTION

§ 1.9004 (T.D. 6575, filed 10-11-61.) **Statutory provisions; the Act of September 26, 1961 (Public Law 87-312, 75 Stat. 674).**

§ 1.9004-1 (T.D. 6575, filed 10-11-61.) **Election relating to the determination of gross income from the property for taxable years beginning prior to 1961 in the case of certain clays and shale.**

(a) *In general.* The Act of September 26, 1961 (Public Law 87-312, 75 Stat. 674), provides that certain taxpayers may elect to apply the provisions thereof to all taxable years beginning before January 1, 1961, with respect to which the election is effective. The Act prescribes special rules for the application of section 613 (a) and (c) of the Internal Revenue Code of 1954 (and corresponding provisions of the Internal Revenue Code of 1939) in the case of shale and certain clays used by the mine owner or operator in the manufacture of certain clay and shale products.

(b) *Election.* The election to apply the provisions of the Act may be made only by a mine owner or operator with respect to brick and tile clay, fire clay, or shale which he mined and used in the manufacture of building or paving brick, drainage and roofing tile, sewer pipe, flower pots, and kindred products. The election must be made in accordance with § 1.9004-4 on or before December 11, 1961, and the election shall become irrevocable on December 11, 1961.

(c) *Years to which the election is applicable.* If the election described in paragraph (b) of this section is made by the taxpayer, the provisions of the Act shall be effective for all taxable years beginning before January 1, 1961, in respect of which the—

(1) Assessment of a deficiency,

(2) Refund or credit of an overpayment, or

(3) Commencement of a suit for recovery of a refund under section 7405 of the Internal Revenue Code of 1954,

is not prevented on September 26, 1961, by the operation of any law or rule of law. The election is also effective for any taxable year beginning before January 1, 1961, in respect of which an assessment of a deficiency has been made but not collected on or before September 26, 1961.

Reg. § 1.9004-1(c)(3)

○— § 1.9004-2 (T.D. 6575, filed 10-11-61.)
Effect of election.

(a) *In general.* If a taxpayer makes the election described in paragraph (b) of § 1.9004-1, he shall be deemed to have consented to the application of the Act with respect to all the clay and shale described in that paragraph for all taxable years for which the election is effective whether or not the taxpayer is litigating the issue for any of such years. Thus, in applying section 613 of the Internal Revenue Code of 1954 (and corresponding provisions of the Internal Revenue Code of 1939) to those years—

(1) The "gross income from the property" for purposes of section 613(c) of the Internal Revenue Code of 1954 (and corresponding provisions of the Internal Revenue Code of 1939) shall be 50 percent of the amount for which the mineowner or operator sold, during the taxable year, the building or paving brick, drainage and roofing tile, sewer pipe, flower pots, and kindred products manufactured from the clay and shale described in paragraph (b) of § 1.9004-1, but shall not exceed an amount equal to $12.50 multiplied by the number of short tons of all such clay or shale mined and used by the mineowner or operator in the manufacture of the products sold during the taxable year; and

(2) The "taxable income from the property" (computed without allowance for depletion) for purposes of section 613 (a) of the Internal Revenue Code of 1954 (and corresponding provisions of the Internal Revenue Code of 1939) shall be 50 percent of the taxable income from the manufactured products sold during the taxable year (computed without allowance for depletion).

(b) *Effect on depletion rates and other items.* The election shall have no effect on the applicable rate of percentage depletion for the taxable years to which the election is effective. In applying the election to the years affected there shall be taken into account the effect that any adjustments resulting from the election shall have on other items affected thereby, such as charitable contributions, foreign tax credit, net operating loss, and the effect that adjustments to any such items shall have on other taxable years. The provisions of the Act are applicable with respect to taxable years subject to the Internal Revenue Code of 1939 for purposes of applying sections 450 and 453 of that Code.

○— § 1.9004-3 (T.D. 6575, filed 10-11-61.)
Statutes of limitation.

The period within which the assessment of any deficiency or the credit or refund of any overpayment attributable to the election may be made shall not expire sooner than one year after December 11, 1961. Thus, if assessment of a deficiency or credit or refund of an overpayment, whichever is applicable, is not prevented on September 26, 1961, the time for making assessment or credit or refund shall not expire for at least one year after December 11, 1961, notwithstanding any other provision of law to the contrary. Even though assessment of a deficiency is prevented on September 26, 1961, if commencement of a suit for recovery of a refund under section 7405 of the Internal Revenue Code of 1954 may be made on such date, then any deficiency resulting from the election may be assessed at any time within 1 year after December 11, 1961. If a taxpayer makes the election, he shall be deemed to have consented to the application of the provisions of the Act extending the time for assessing a deficiency attributable to the election. The Act does not shorten the periods of limitation otherwise applicable. An agreement may be entered into under section 6501(c)(4) of the Internal Revenue Code of 1954 and corresponding provisions of prior law to extend the period for assessment.

○— § 1.9004-4 (T.D. 6575, filed 10-11-61.)
Manner of exercising election.

(a) *By whom election is to be made.* Generally, the taxpayer whose tax liability is affected by the election shall make the election. In the case of a partnership, or a corporation electing under the provisions of subchapter S, chapter 1 of the Internal Revenue Code of 1954, the election shall be exercised by the partnership or such corporation, as the case may be.

(b) *Time and manner of making election.* The election shall be made on or before December 11, 1961, by filing a statement with the district director with whom the taxpayer's income tax return for the taxable year in which the election is made is required to be filed. The statement shall include the following:

(1) A clear indication that an election is being made under the Act, and

(2) The taxable years to which the election applies.

Amended income tax returns, reflecting any increase or decrease in tax attributable to the election shall be filed for the taxable years to which the election applies. In the case of partnerships and electing small business corporations under subchapter S, chapter 1 of the Internal Revenue Code of 1954, amended returns shall be filed by the partnership or electing small business corporation, as well as by the partners or shareholders, as the case may be. Any amended return shall be filed with the office of the district director with whom the taxpayer files his income tax return for the taxable year in which the election is made and, if practicable, on the same date the statement of election is filed, but amended returns shall be filed in no event later than March 31, 1962, unless an extension of time is granted under section 6081 of the

Internal Revenue Code of 1954. Whenever the amended returns do not accompany the statement of election, a copy of the statement shall be submitted with the amended returns. The amended returns shall be accompanied by payment of the additional tax (together with interest thereon) resulting from the election.

○━► § 1.9004-5 (T.D. 6575, filed 10-11-61.) Terms; applicability of other laws.

All other terms which are not otherwise specifically defined shall have the same meaning as when used in the Internal Revenue Code of 1954 (or the corresponding provisions of prior law) except where otherwise distinctly expressed or manifestly intended to the contrary. Further, all provisions of law contained in the Code (or the corresponding provisions of prior law) shall apply to the extent that they can apply. Thus, all the provisions of subtitle F of the Code (and the corresponding provisions of prior law) shall apply to the extent they can apply, including the provisions of law relating to assessment, collection, credit or refund, and limitations. For purposes of this section and § § 1.9004-1 to 1.9004-4, inclusive, the term "Act" means the Act of September 26, 1961 (Public Law 87-312, 75 Stat. 674).

○━► § 1.9005 Statutory provisions; section 2 of the Act of September 26, 1961 (Public Law 87-321, 75 Stat. 683).

○━► § 1.9005-1 (T.D. 6583, filed 12-15-61.) Election relating to the determination of gross income from the property for taxable years beginning prior to 1961 in the case of clay and quartzite used in making refractory products.

(a) *In general.* Section 2 of the Act of September 26, 1961 (Public Law 87-321, 75 Stat. 683), provides that certain taxpayers may elect to apply the provisions of such section to all taxable years beginning before January 1, 1961, with respect to which the election is effective. Section 2 of the Act prescribes special rules for the application of section 613(c) of the Internal Revenue Code of 1954 (and corresponding provisions of the Internal Revenue Code of 1939) in the case of quartzite and clay used by the mine owner or operator in the production of refractory products.

(b) *Election.* The election to apply the provisions of section 2 of the Act may be made only in the case of quartzite and clay used in the production of products generally recognized as refractory products by the refractories industry. Examples of such products are clay firebrick, silica brick, and refractory bonding mortars. The election may be made only by a taxpayer who both mined the clay or quartzite and used it in the production of refractory products. The election must be made in accordance with § 1.9005-4 on or before February 14, 1962, and the election shall become irrevocable on that date.

(c) *Years to which the election is applicable.* If the election described in paragraph (b) of this section is made by the taxpayer, the provisions of section 2 of the Act shall be effective on and after January 1, 1951, for all taxable years beginning before January 1, 1961, in respect of which the—

(1) Assessment of a deficiency,

(2) Refund or credit of an overpayment, or

(3) Commencement of a suit for recovery of a refund under section 7405 of the Internal Revenue Code of 1954,

was not prevented on September 26, 1961, by the operation of any law or rule of law. The election is also effective on and after January 1, 1951, for any taxable year beginning before January 1, 1961, in respect of which an assessment of a deficiency has been made but not collected on or before September 26, 1961.

○━► § 1.9005-2 (T.D. 6583, filed 12-15-61.) Effect of election.

(a) *In general.* If a taxpayer makes the election described in paragraph (b) of § 1.9005-1, he shall be deemed to have consented to the application of section 2 of the Act with respect to all the clay and quartzite described in that paragraph for all taxable years for which the election is effective whether or not the taxpayer is litigating the issue for any of such years. Thus, in applying section 613 (c) of the Internal Revenue Code of 1954 (and corresponding provisions of the Internal Revenue Code of 1939) to those years—

(1) The term "ordinary treatment processes" shall include crushing, grinding, and separating the mineral from waste, but shall not include any subsequent process; and

(2) The gross income from mining for each short ton of quartzite or clay mined by the taxpayer and used by him in the production of all refractory products sold during the taxable year shall be equal to 87½ percent of the lesser of—

(i) The average lowest published or advertised price, or

(ii) The average lowest actual selling price, at which the mine owner or operator offered to sell or sold any such quartzite or clay during the taxable year.

(b) *Rules for applying paragraph (a) of this section.* (1) The price described in paragraph (a) (2) of this section and any price described in this paragraph shall be determined with reference to quartzite or clay in the form and condition of such products after the application of only the processes described in paragraph (a) (1) of this section and before transportation from the plant in which such processes were applied.

(2) If quartzite and clay were mined and used by the taxpayer in the production of refractory products, a separate price shall be used with respect to each mineral.

(3) There shall be used for each mineral the lowest price at which it was sold or offered for sale by the taxpayer during the taxable year. Thus, only one price

Reg. § 1.9005-2(b)(3)

shall be used with respect to each mineral regardless of variations in type or grade.

(4) For purposes of this paragraph, exceptional, unusual, or nominal sales of quartzite or clay shall be disregarded. Thus, for example, if the taxpayer made an accommodation sale during the taxable year at other than the regular price, such sale is to be disregarded.

(5) If the taxpayer made no sales during the taxable year of quartzite or clay in the form and condition described in subparagraph (1) of this paragraph, or if his sales were exceptional, unusual, or nominal, there shall be used the lowest recognized selling price for the taxpayer's marketing area for quartzite or clay (of the same grade and type as that used by him) which was published for the taxable year in a trade journal or other industry publication.

(6) If subparagraph (5) of this paragraph does not apply for the reason that there is no recognized selling price published in a trade journal or other industry publication for the taxpayer's marketing area, there shall be used the lowest price at which quartzite or clay comparable to that used by the taxpayer was sold or offered for sale during the taxable year in that area by other producers similarly circumstanced as the taxpayer or, if appropriate, the lowest price paid by the taxpayer for purchased quartzite or clay.

(7) If the lowest selling price otherwise applicable under the preceding provisions of this paragraph fluctuated during the taxable year, the two or more lowest selling prices shall be averaged according to the number of days during the taxable year that each such price was in effect.

(c) The provisions of paragraphs (a) and (b) of this section may be illustrated by the following examples:

Example (1) (i) *Facts.* Taxpayer A, a calendar year taxpayer, mined quartzite and clay and used them in the production of recognized refractory products. During the taxable year, the lowest price for which A sold clay after the application of crushing and grinding was $13.75 per short ton. He also sold some ground clay of a different type at $20.00 per short ton. A sold quartzite after the application of crushing and grinding for various prices, depending upon type, ranging from $14.00 per short ton to $20.00 per short ton. During the taxable year, the prices for the various types of ground clay and quartzite did not change. None of the sales by A of ground clay or quartzite were exceptional, unusual, or nominal.

(ii) *Determination of gross income from mining.* If A makes the election described in paragraph (b) of § 1.9005-1, the gross income from mining per short ton of clay mined by A and used in the production of refractory products sold during the taxable year is $12.03 (87½ percent of $13.75), and the gross income from mining per short ton of quartzite mined by A and used in the production of refractory products sold during the taxable year is $12.25 (87½ percent of $14.00). To determine his gross income from mining, A must compute the sum of—

(a) $12.03 multiplied by the number of short tons of clay which were mined by A (whether or not during the taxable year) and which were used by A in the production of refractory products (refractory bonding mortar, fire brick, etc.) sold during the taxable year; plus

(b) $12.25 multiplied by the number of short tons of quartzite which were mined by A (whether or not during the taxable year) and which were used by A in the production of refractory products sold during the taxable year.

Example (2). Assume the same facts as in example (1) except that on October 1 of the taxable year A's lowest price for clay after the application of crushing and grinding increased to $14.40 per short ton. In this case, the average lowest price for which A sold ground clay during the taxable year must be determined by taking into account the price adjustment of October 1. Under these circumstances, the average lowest price for the ground clay would be $13.91, that is $13.75 x $\frac{273}{365}$ plus $14.40 x $\frac{92}{365}$

(d) *Effect on depletion rates and other items.* The election shall have no effect on the applicable rate of percentage depletion for the taxable years for which the election is effective. In applying the election to the years affected there shall be taken into account the effect that any adjustments resulting from the election shall have on other items affected thereby, such as charitable contributions, foreign tax credit, net operating loss, and the effect that adjustments to any such items shall have on other taxable years. The provisions of section 2 of the Act are applicable with respect to taxable years subject to the Internal Revenue Code of 1939 for purposes of applying sections 450 and 453 of that Code. The election shall have no effect on the determination of the treatment processes which are to be considered as mining or on the determination of gross income from mining for any taxable year beginning after December 31, 1960.

§ 1.9005-3 (T.D. 6583, filed 12-15-61.) **Statutes of limitation.**

Notwithstanding any provision of law to the contrary, the period within which the assessment of any deficiency attributable to the election may be made, or within which the credit or refund of any overpayment attributable to the election may be made, shall not expire sooner than one year after the last day for making the election. Thus, if assessment of a deficiency or credit or refund of an overpayment, whichever is applicable, was not prevented on September 26, 1961, the time for making assessment or credit or refund shall not expire for at least one year after the last day for making the election. Even though assessment of a deficiency was prevented on September 26, 1961, if commencement of a suit for recovery of a refund under section 7405 of the Internal Revenue Code of 1954 may have been made on such date, then any deficiency resulting from the election may be assessed at any time within one year after the last day for making the election. If a taxpayer makes the election, he shall be deemed to have consented to the application of the provisions of section 2 of the Act extending the time for assessing a deficiency attributable to the election. Section 2 of the Act does not shorten the period of limitations otherwise applicable. An agreement may be entered into under section 6501(c)(4) of the Internal Revenue Code of 1954 and corresponding provisions of prior law to extend the period for assessment.

§ 1.9005-4 (T.D. 6583, filed 12-15-61.) Manner of exercising election.

(a) *By whom election is to be made.* Generally, the taxpayer whose tax liability is affected by the election shall make the election. In the case of a partnership, or a corporation electing under the provisions of subchapter S, chapter 1 of the Internal Revenue Code of 1954, the election shall be exercised by the partnership or such corporation, as the case may be.

(b) *Time and manner of making election.* The election shall be made on or before February 14, 1962, by filing a statement with the district director with whom the taxpayer's income tax return for the taxable year in which the election is made is required to be filed. The statement shall include the following:

(1) A clear indication that an election is being made under section 2 of the Act, and

(2) The taxable years to which the election applies.

Amended income tax returns reflecting any increase or decrease in tax attributable to the election shall be filed for the taxable years to which the election applies. In the case of partnerships and electing small business corporations under subchapter S, chapter 1 of the Internal Revenue Code of 1954, amended returns shall be filed by the partnership or electing small business corporation, as well as by the partners or shareholders, as the case may be. Any amended return shall be filed with the office of the district director which [with] whom the taxpayer files his income tax return for the taxable year in which the election is made, and, if practicable on the same date the statement of election is filed, but amended returns shall be filed in no event later than May 31, 1962, unless an extension of time is granted under section 6081 of the Internal Revenue Code of 1954. Whenever the amended returns do not accompany the statement of election, a copy of the statement shall be submitted with the amended returns. The amended returns shall be accompanied by payment of the additional tax (together with interest thereon) resulting from the election.

§ 1.9005-5 (T.D. 6583, filed 12-15-61.) Terms; applicability of other laws.

All other terms which are not otherwise specifically defined shall have the same meaning as when used in the Internal Revenue Code of 1954 (or the corresponding provisions of prior law) except where otherwise distinctly expressed or manifestly intended to the contrary. Further, all provisions of law contained in the Code (or the corresponding provisions of prior law) shall apply to the extent that they can apply. Thus, all the provisions of subtitle F of the Code (and the corresponding provisions of prior law) shall apply to the extent they can apply, including the provisions of law relating to assessment, collection, credit or refund, and limitations. For purposes of this section and §§ 1.9005-1 to 1.9005-4, inclusive, the term "Act" means the Act of September 26, 1961 (Public Law 87-321, 75 Stat. 683).

TAX REFORM ACT OF 1969

§ 1.9006 Statutory provisions; Tax Reform Act of 1969.

§ 1.9006-1 (T.D. 7088, filed 2-16-71.) Interest and penalties in case of certain taxable years.

(a) *Interest on underpayment.* The Internal Revenue Code of 1954 was amended in many important respects by the Tax Reform Act of 1969. Certain of these amendments affect taxable years ending prior to December 30, 1969 (the date of enactment of the Act) and thereby may cause underpayments of tax by a number of taxpayers for those years. Under section 6601 (a) of the Code, interest at the rate of 6 percent per annum is imposed upon the amount of any such underpayment. The effect of section 946 (a) of the Act is to prevent the assessment or collection of interest on an underpayment of tax for any taxable year ending before December 30, 1969, if such underpayment is attributable to any amendment made by such Act, for the period from the due date for payment until March 30, 1970. Thus, the taxpayer is afforded an interest-free period of 90 days from the date of enactment of such Act within which to account for the changes in the law affecting him and to remit the amount of such underpayment. If, on or after March 30, 1970, the amount of any underpayment (or portion thereof) attributable to an amendment made by the Act remains unpaid, then, as of such date, such underpayment (or portion thereof) shall be subject to interest as provided by section 6601 of the Code, to be computed from such date. However, if a corporation or farmers' cooperative elects to pay its final tax in two installments under section 6152 of the Code and if the second installment is due after March 30, 1970, then, in order to escape the imposition of interest under section 6601, such corporation or cooperative need pay only one-half of the additional tax arising from an amendment made by the Act before March 30, 1970, with the remaining one-half payable as part of the second installment on the regular due date for that installment. In the case of an underpayment of tax which is only partly

Reg. § 1.9006-1(a)

24,456.4 (I.R.C.)   Reg. § 1.9006-1(a)   2-22-71

attributable to an amendment made by the Act, section 946 (a) of such Act shall apply only to the extent that such underpayment is so attributable.

(b) *Declarations and payments of estimated tax.* (1) In the case of a taxable year beginning before December 30, 1969, section 946 (b) of the Tax Reform Act of 1969 provides transitional rules with respect to the payment of estimated tax and, in the case of an individual, the filing of a declaration of estimated tax. Under such section 946 (b) in the case of such a year, if any taxpayer is required to make a declaration or amended declaration of estimated tax, or to pay any amount or additional amount of estimated tax, by reason of the amendments made by the Act, such amount or additional amount shall be paid ratably on or before each of the remaining installment dates for the taxable year beginning with the first installment date on or after February 15, 1970. For purposes of section 946 (b) of such Act and this section, the term "installment date" means any date on which, under section 6153 or 6154 of the Code (whichever is applicable), an installment payment of estimated tax is required to be made by the taxpayer.

(2) With respect to any declaration or payment of estimated tax before February 15, 1970, sections 6015, 6153, 6154, 6654, and 6655 of the Code shall be applied without regard to the amendments made by such Act. Therefore, any underpayment which occurs solely by reason of the amendments made by such Act shall not be treated as an underpayment in the case of installment dates before February 15, 1970. Similarly, in the case of a taxpayer all of whose installment dates occur prior to February 15, 1970, no payment of estimated tax need be made to reflect the amendments made by such Act.

(3) The following example illustrates the application of the provisions of subparagraphs (1) and (2) of this paragraph:

Example. A, a fiscal year taxpayer with a taxable year from July 1, 1969 through June 30, 1970, had, without regard to the enactment of the Tax Reform Act of 1969, a total tax liability, which would have been shown on his return, of $500. A is not a farmer or fisherman described in section 6037 (b). A's tax liability is increased by $20 to $520, attributable to an amendment made by such Act. A makes an installment payment of estimated tax of $90 on each of the following four installment dates: October 15, 1969; December 15, 1969; March 15, 1970; and July 15, 1970. Assume that A is unaffected by the exceptions provided in section 6654 (d). Therefore, A is underpaid by $10 on both October 15 and December 15, and by $18 on both March 15 and July 15. Such underpayments are computed as follows:

(a) October 15 and December 15 installment dates

  (1) Tax without regard to Tax Reform Act of 1969 .... $500
  (2) 80% of item (1) 400
  (3) Minimum payment to avoid underpayment, determined without regard to Act:
      October 15, 1969 (25% of item (2)) 100
      December 15, 1969 (25% of item (2)) 100
  (4) Actual payment:
      October 15, 1969 90
      December 15, 1969 90
  (5) Amount of underpayment:
      October 15, 1969 ($100 — $90) 10
      December 15, 1969 ($100 — $90) 10

(b) *March 15 and July 15 installment dates*
  (1) Tax with regard to Act $520
  (2) 80% of item (1) 416
  (3) Less total of minimum payments to avoid underpayment, determined without regard to Act for October 15, 1969 and December 15, 1969 ($100 + $100) 200
  (4) Difference of items (2) and (3) $216
  (5) Minimum payment to avoid underpayment, determined with regard to Act:
      March 15 (50% of $216) 108
      July 15 (50% of $216) 108
  (6) Actual payment:
      March 15 .... $90
      July 15 90
  (7) Amount of underpayment:
      March 15 ($108 — $90) 18
      July 15 ($108 — $90) 18

(c) *Cross references.* (1) Taxpayers affected by the following sections, among others, of the Tax Reform Act of 1939 may be subject to the provisions of section 946 (a) or (b) (whichever is applicable) of such Act:

(i) Act section 201(a), which adds section 170(f)(2) to the Code and which applies to gifts made after July 31, 1969.

(ii) Act section 201(c), which repeals section 673(b) of the Code and which applies to transfers in trust made after April 22, 1969.

(iii) Act section 212(c), which amends section 1031 of the Code and which applies to taxable years to which the 1954 Code applies.

(iv) Act section 332, which amends section 677 of the Code and which applies to property transferred in trust after October 9, 1969.

(v) Act section 411(a), which adds section 279 to the Code and which applies to interest paid or incurred on an indebtedness incurred after October 9, 1969.

(vi) Act sections 412(a) and (b), which add section 453(b)(3) to the Code and which apply to sales or other dispositions occurring after May 27, 1969, which are not made pursuant to a contract entered into on or before that date.

(vii) Act section 413, which amends sections 1232(a), 1232(b)(2), and 6049 of the Code and which applies to bonds and other evidences of indebtedness issued after May 27, 1969.

(viii) Act section 414, which adds section 249 to the Code and which applies to convertible bonds or other convertible evidences of indebtedness repurchased after April 22, 1969.

(ix) Act section 421(a), which amends section 305 of the Code and which applies to distributions made after January 10, 1969.

(x) Act sections 516(a) and (d), which add section 1001(e) to the Code and which apply to sales of life estates made after October 9, 1969.

(xi) Act section 601, which amends section 103 of the Code and which applies to obligations issued after October 9, 1969.

(xii) Act section 703, which amends sections 46(b) and 47(a) of the Code and which applies to section 38 property built or acquired after April 18, 1969.

(xiii) Act section 905, which adds section 311(d) to the Code and which applies to distributions made after November 30, 1969.

(2) In addition to the references in subparagraph (1) of this paragraph, section 946(b) of the Tax Reform Act of 1969 may apply to taxpayers affected by the following sections, among others, of such Act:

(i) Act section 201(a), which adds section 170(e) to the Code and which applies to contributions paid after December 31, 1969.

(ii) Act sections 501(a) and (b), which amend section 613 of the Code and which apply to taxable years beginning after October 9, 1969.

(iii) Act sections 516(c) and (d), which add section 1253 to the Code and which apply to transfers after December 31, 1969.

(iv) Act section 701(a), which amends section 51 of the Code and which applies to taxable years ending after December 31, 1969, and beginning before July 1, 1970.

EXTENSION OF TIME FOR MAKING CERTAIN ELECTIONS

§ 1.9100-1 (T.D. 6364, filed 2-13-59; republished in T.D. 6500, filed 11-25-60; amended by T.D. 7074, filed 11-19-70.) Extension of time for making certain elections.

(a) *In general.* The Commissioner in his discretion may, upon good cause shown, grant a reasonable extension of the time fixed by the regulations in this chapter for the making of an election or application for relief in respect of tax under subtitle A of the Code provided—

(1) The time for making such election or application is not expressly prescribed by law;

(2) Request for the extension is filed with the Commissioner before the time fixed by the regulations for making such election or application, or within such time thereafter as the Commissioner may consider reasonable under the circumstances; and

(3) It is shown to the satisfaction of the Commissioner that the granting of the extension will not jeopardize the interests of the Government.

For purposes of this section, an application for an extension of time for filing a return under section 6081 is not an application for relief in respect of tax.

(b) *Exceptions applicable to elections required to be made prior to November 20, 1970.* Notwithstanding the provisions of paragraph (a) of this section, the time fixed by the regulations in this chapter shall not be extended in cases of the following types of elections and applications required by such regulations to be made prior to *November 20, 1970:*

(1) An election required to be made in or with the taxpayer's original income tax return;

(2) An election required to be exercised by the filing of a claim for credit or refund, unless the election is required to be exercised on or before a date which precedes the date of expiration of the period of limitations provided in section 6511;

(3) An election required to be filed in a petition to the Tax Court;

(4) An application for permission to change a previous election;

(5) An application for permission to change an accounting method as described in §§ 1.77-1 and 1.446-1;

Reg. § 1.9100-1(b)(5)

24,456.6 (I.R.C.)

(6) An application for permission to change an accounting period as described in § 1.442-1; or

(7) An application for permission to change the method of treating bad debts as described in § 1.166-1.

○—▶ § 1.9101-1 (T.D. 6883, filed 5-2-66.) Permission to submit information required by certain returns and statements on magnetic tape.

In any case where the use of a Form 1087, 1099, or W-2 is required by the regulations under this part for the purpose of making a return or reporting information, such requirement may be satisfied by submitting the infomation required by such form on magnetic tape or by other media, provided that the prior consent of the Commissioner or other authorized officer or employee of the Internal Revenue Service has been obtained. Applications for such consent must be filed in accordance with procedures established by the Internal Revenue Service. See paragraph (b) (2) of § 31.6011 (a)-7 of this chapter (Employment Tax Regulations) for additional rules relating to Form W-2.

MERCHANT MARINE AND FISHERIES CAPITAL CONSTRUCTION FUNDS

○—▶ § 3.0 (T.D. 7398, filed 1-23-76.) Statutory provisions; section 607, Merchant Marine Act, 1936, as amended. [Amending Acts, IRC.]

○—▶ § 3.1 (T.D. 7398, filed 1-23-76.) Scope of section 607 of the Act and the regulations in this part.

(a) *In general.* The regulations prescribed in this part provide rules for determining the income tax liability of any person a party to an agreement with the Secretary of Commerce establishing a capital construction fund (for purposes of this part referred to as the "fund") authorized by section 607 of the Merchant Marine Act, 1936, as amended (for purposes of this part referred to as the "Act"). With respect to such parties, section 607 of the Act in general provides for the nontaxability of certain deposits of money or other property into the fund out of earnings or gains realized from the operation of vessels covered in an agreement, gains realized from the sale or other disposition of agreement vessels or proceeds from insurance for indemnification for loss of agreement vessels, earnings from the investment or reinvestment of amounts held in a fund and gains with respect to amounts or deposits in the fund. Transitional rules are also provided for the treatment of "old funds" existing on or before the effective date of the Merchant Marine Act of 1970 (see § 3.10).

(b) *Cross references.* For rules relating to eligibility for a fund, deposits and withdrawals and other aspects, see the regulations prescribed by the Secretary of Commerce in titles 46 (Merchant Marine) and 50 (Fisheries) of the Code of Federal Regulations.

(c) *Code.* For purposes of this part, the term "Code" means the Internal Revenue Code of 1954, as amended.

○—▶ § 3.2 (T.D. 7398, filed 1-23-76.) Ceiling on deposits.

(a) *In general*—(1) *Total ceiling.* Section 607(b) of the Act provides a ceiling on the amount which may be deposited by a party for a taxable year pursuant to an agreement. The amount which a party may deposit into a fund may not exceed the sum of the following subceilings:

(i) The lower of (a) the taxable income (if any) of the party for such year (computed as provided in chapter 1 of the Code but without regard to the carryback of any net operating loss or net capital loss and without regard to section 607 of the Act) or (b) taxable income (if any) of such party for such year attributable under paragraph (b) of this section to the operation of agreement vessels (as defined in paragraph (f) of this section) in the foreign or domestic commerce of the United States or in the fisheries of the United States (see section 607(b)(1)(A) of the Act),

(ii) Amounts allowable as a deduction under section 167 of the Code for such year with respect to the agreement vessels (see section 607(b)(1)(B) of the Act),

(iii) The net proceeds (if not included in subdivision (i) of this paragraph) from (a) the sale or other disposition of any agreement vessels or (b) insurance or indemnity attributable to any agreement vessels (see section 607(b)(1)(C) of the Act and paragraph (c) of this section), and

(iv) Earnings and gains from the investment or reinvestment of amounts held in such fund (see section 607(b)(1)(D) of the Act and paragraphs (d) and (g) of this section).

(2) *Overdeposits.* (i) If for any taxable year an amount is deposited into the fund under a subceiling computed under subparagraph (1) of this paragraph which is in excess of the amount of such subceiling for such year, then at the party's option such excess (or any portion thereof) may—

(a) Be treated as a deposit into the fund for that taxable year under another available subceiling, or

(b) Be treated as not having been deposited for the taxable year and thus, at the party's option, may be disposed of either by it being—

(1) Treated as a deposit into the fund under any subceiling available in the first subsequent taxable year in which a subceiling is available, in which case such amount shall be deemed to have been deposited on the first day of such subsequent taxable year, or

(2) Repaid to the party from the fund.

(ii) (a) When a correction is made for an overdeposit, proper adjustment shall be made with respect to all items for all taxable years affected by the overdeposit, such as, for example, amounts in each account described in § 3.4, treatment of nonqualified withdrawals, the consequences of qualified withdrawals and the treatment of losses realized or treated as realized by the fund. Thus, for example, if the party chooses to have the fund repay to him the amount of an overdeposit, amounts in each account, basis of assets, and any affected item will be determined as though no deposit and repayment had been made. Accordingly, in such a case, if there are insufficient amounts in an account to cover a repayment of an overdeposit (as determined before correcting the overdeposit), and the party had applied the proceeds of a qualified withdrawal from such account towards the purchase of a qualified vessel (within the meaning of § 3.11(a)(2)), then such account and the basis of the vessel shall be adjusted as of the time such withdrawal was made and proceeds were applied, and repayment shall be made from such account as adjusted. If a party chooses to treat the amount of an overdeposit as a deposit under a subceiling for a subsequent year, similar adjustments to affected items shall be made. If the amount of a withdrawal would have exceeded the amount in the fund (determined after adjusting all affected amounts by reason of correcting the overdeposit), the withdrawal to the extent of such excess shall be treated as a repayment made at the time the withdrawal was made.

(b) If the accounts (as defined in § 3.4) that were increased by reason of excessive deposits contain sufficient amounts at the time the overdeposit is discovered to repay the party, the party may, at his option, demand repayment of such excessive deposits from such accounts in lieu of making the adjustments required by (a) of this subdivision (ii).

(iii) During the period beginning with the day after the date an overdeposit was actually made and ending with the date it was disposed of in accordance with subdivision (i) (b) of this subparagraph, there shall be included in the party's gross income for each taxable year the earnings attributed to any amount of overdeposit on hand during such a year. The earnings attributable to any amount of overdeposit on hand during a taxable year shall be an amount equal to the product of—

(a) The average daily earnings for each one dollar in the fund (as determined in subdivision (iv) of this subparagraph),

(b) The amount of overdeposit (as determined in subdivision (vi) of this subparagraph), and

(c) The number of days during the taxable year the overdeposit existed.

(iv) For purposes of subdivision (iii) (a) of this subparagraph, the average daily earnings for each dollar in the fund shall be determined by dividing the total earnings of the fund for the taxable year by the sum of the products of—

(a) Any amount on hand during the taxable year (determined under subdivision (v) of this subparagraph), and

(b) The number of days during the taxable year such amount was on hand in the fund.

(v) For purposes of this subparagraph—

(a) An amount on hand in the fund or an overdeposit shall not be treated as on hand on the day deposited but shall be treated as on hand on the day withdrawn, and

(b) The fair market value of such amounts on hand for purposes of this subparagraph shall be determined as provided in § 20.2031-2 of the Estate Tax Regulations of this chapter but without applying the blockage and other special rules contained in paragraph (e) thereof.

(vi) For purposes of subdivision (iii) (b) of this subparagraph, the amount of overdeposit on hand at any time is an amount equal to—

(a) The amount deposited into the fund under a subceiling computed under subparagraph (1) of this paragraph which is in excess of the amount of such subceiling, less

(b) The sum of—

(1) Amounts described in (a) of this subdivision (vi) treated as a deposit under another subceiling for the taxable year pursuant to subdivision (i) of this subparagraph,

(2) Amounts described in (a) of this subdivision (vi) disposed of (or treated as disposed of) in accordance with subdivision (i) or (ii) of this subparagraph prior to such time.

(vii) To the extent earnings attributed under subdivision (iii) of this subparagraph represent a deposit for any taxable year in excess of the subceiling described in subparagraph (1) (iv) of this paragraph for receipts from the investment or reinvestment of amounts held in the fund, such attributed earnings shall be subject to the rules of this subparagraph for overdeposits.

(3) *Underdeposit caused by audit adjustment.* [Reserved]

(4) *Requirements for deficiency deposits.* [Reserved]

(b) *Taxable income attributable to the operation of an agreement vessel*—(1) *In general.* For purposes of this section, taxable income attributable to the operation of an agreement vessel means the amount, if any, by which the gross income of a party for the taxable year from the operation of an agreement vessel (as defined in paragraph (f) of this section) exceeds the allowable deductions allocable to such operation (as determined under subparagraph (3) of this paragraph). The term "taxable income attributable to the operation of the agreement vessels" means the sum of the amounts described in the preceding sentence separately computed with respect to each agreement vessel (or share therein) or, at the party's option, computed in the aggregate.

(2) *Gross income.* (i) Gross income from the operation of agreement vessels means the sum of the revenues which are derived during the taxable year from the following:

(a) Revenues derived from the transportation of passengers, freight, or mail in such vessels, including amounts from contracts for the charter of such vessels to others, from operating differential subsidies, from collections in accordance with pooling agreements and from insurance or indemnity net proceeds relating to the loss of income attributable to such agreement vessels.

(b) Revenues derived from the operation of agreement vessels relating to commercial fishing activities, including the transportation of fish, support activities for fishing vessels, charters for commercial fishing, and insurance or indemnity net

Reg. § 3.2(b)(2)

proceeds relating to the loss of income attributable to such agreement vessels.

(c) Revenues from the rental, lease, or use by others of terminal facilities, revenues from cargo handling operations and tug and lighter operations, and revenues from other services or operations which are incidental and directly related to the operation of an agreement vessel. Thus, for example, agency fees, commissions, and brokerage fees derived by the party at his place of business for effecting transactions for services incidental and directly related to shipping for the accounts of other persons are includible in gross income from the operation of agreement vessels where the transaction is of a kind customarily consummated by the party for his own account at such place of business.

(d) Dividends, interest, and gains derived from assets set aside and reasonably retained to meet regularly occurring obligations relating to the shipping or fishing business directly connected with the agreement vessel which obligations cannot at all times be met from the current revenues of the business because of layups or repairs, special surveys, fluctuations in the business, and reasonably forseeable strikes (whether or not a strike actually occurs), and security amounts retained by reason of participation in conferences, pooling agreements, or similar agreements.

(ii) The items of gross income described in subdivision (i)(c) and (d) of this subparagraph shall be considered to be derived from the operations of a particular agreement vessel in the same proportion that the sum of the items of gross income described in subdivision (i)(a) and (b) of this subparagraph which are derived from the operations of such agreement vessel bears to the party's total gross income for the taxable year from operations described in subdivision (i)(a) and (b) of this subparagraph.

(iii) In the case of a party who uses his own or leased agreement vessels to transport his own products, the gross income attributable to such vessel operations is an amount determined to be an arm's length charge for such transportation. The arm's length charge shall be determined by applying the principles of section 482 of the Code and the regulations thereunder as if the party transporting the product and the owner of the product were not the same person but were controlled taxpayers within the meaning of § 1.482-1(a)(4) of the Income Tax Regulations of this chapter. Gross income attributable to the operation of agreement vessels does not include amounts for which the party is allowed a deduction for percentage depletion under sections 611 and 613 of the Code.

(3) *Deductions.* From the gross income attributable to the operation of an agreement vessel or vessels as determined under subparagraph (2) of this paragraph, there shall be deducted, in accordance with the principles of § 1.861-8 of the Income Tax Regulations of this chapter, the expenses, losses, and other deductions definitely related and therefore allocated and apportioned thereto and a ratable part of any expenses, losses, or other deductions which are not definitely related to any gross income of the party. Thus, for example, if a party has gross income attributable to the operation of an agreement vessel and other gross income and has a particular deduction definitely related to both types of gross income, such deduction must be apportioned between the two types of gross income on a reasonable basis in determining the taxable income attributable to the operation of the agreement vessel.

(4) *Net operating and capital loss deductions.* The taxable income of a party attributable to the operation of agreement vessels shall be computed without regard to the carryback of any net operating loss deduction allowed by section 172 of the Code, the carryback of any net capital loss deduction allowed by section 165(f) of the Code, or any reduction in taxable income allowed by section 607 of the Act.

(5) *Method of accounting.* Taxable income must be computed under the method of accounting which the party uses for Federal income tax purposes. Such method may include a method of reporting whereby items of revenue and expense properly allocable to voyages in progress at the end of any accounting period are eliminated from the computation of taxable income for such accounting period and taken into account in the accounting period in which the voyage is completed.

(c) *Net proceeds from transactions with respect to agreement vessels.* [Reserved]

(d) *Earnings and gains from the investment or reinvestment of amounts held in a fund*—(1) *In general.* (i) Earnings and gains received or accrued by a party from the investment or reinvestment of assets in a fund is the total amount of any interest or dividends received or accrued, and gains realized, by the party with respect to assets deposited in, or purchased with amounts deposited in, such fund. Such earnings and gains are therefore required to be included in the gross income of the party unless such amount, or a portion thereof, is not taken into account under section 607(d)(1)(C) of the Act and § 3.3(b)(2)(ii) by reason of a deposit or deemed deposit into the fund. For rules relating to receipts from the sale or other disposition of nonmoney deposits into the fund, see paragraph (g) of this section.

(ii) Earnings received or accrued by a party from investment or reinvestment of assets in a fund include the ratable monthly portion of original issue discount included in gross income pursuant to section 1232(a)(3) of the Code. Such ratable monthly portion shall be deemed to be deposited into the ordinary income account of the fund, but an actual deposit representing such ratable monthly portion shall not be made. For basis of a bond or other evidence of indebtedness issued at a discount, see § 3.3(b)(2)(ii)(b).

(2) *Gain realized.* (i) The gain realized with respect to assets in the fund is the excess of the amount realized (as defined in section 1001(b) of the Code and the regulations thereunder) by the fund on the sale or other disposition of a fund asset over its adjusted basis (as defined in section 1011 of the Code) to the fund. For the adjusted basis of nonmoney deposits, see paragraph (g) of this section.

(ii) Property purchased by the fund (including property considered under paragraph (g)(1)(iii) of this section as purchased by the fund) which is withdrawn from the fund in a qualified withdrawal (as defined in § 3.5) is treated as a disposition to which subdivision (i) of this subparagraph applies. For purposes of determining the amount by which the balance within a particular account will be reduced in the manner provided in § 3.6(b) (relating to order of application of qualified withdrawals against accounts) and for purposes of determining the reduction in basis of a vessel, barge, or container (or share therein) pursuant to § 3.6(c), the value of the property is its fair market value on the day of the qualified withdrawal.

(3) *Holding Period.* Except as provided in paragraph (g) of this section, the holding period of fund assets shall be determined under section 1223 of the Code.

(e) *Leased vessels.* In the case of a party who is a lessee of an agreement vessel, the maximum amount which such lessee may deposit with respect to any agreement vessel by reason of section 607(b)(1)(B) of the Act and paragraph (a)(1)(ii) of this section (relating to depreciation allowable) for any period shall be reduced by the amount (if any) which, under an agreement entered into under section 607 of the Act, the owner is required or permitted to deposit for such period with respect to such vessel by reason of section 607(b)(1)(B) of the Act and paragraph (a)(1)(ii) of this section. The amount of depreciation depositable by the lessee under this paragraph is the amount of depreciation deductible by the lessor on its income tax return, reduced by the amount described in the preceding sentence or the amount set forth in the agreement, whichever is lower.

(f) *Definition of agreement vessel.* For purposes of this section, the term "agreement vessel" (as defined in § 3.11(a)(3) and 46 CFR § 390.6) includes barges and containers which are the complement of an agreement vessel and which are provided for in the agreement, agreement vessels which have been contracted for or are in the process of construction, and any shares in an agreement vessel. Solely for purposes of this section, a party is considered to have a "share" in an agreement vessel if he has a right to use the vessel to generate income from its use whether or not the party would be considered as having a proprietary interest in the vessel for purposes of State or Federal law. Thus, a partner may enter into an agreement with respect to his share of the vessel owned by the partnership and he may make deposits of his distributive share of the sum of the four subceilings described in paragraph (a)(1) of this section. Notwithstanding the provisions of subchapter K of the Code (relating to the taxation of partners and partnerships), the Internal Revenue Service will recognize, solely for the purposes of applying this part, an agreement by an owner of a share in an agreement vessel even though the "share" arrangement is a partnership for purposes of the Code.

(g) *Special rules for nonmoney deposits and withdrawals*—(1) *In general.* (i) Deposits may be made in the form of money or property of the type permitted to be deposited under the agreement. (For rules relating to the types of property which may be deposited into the fund, see 46 CFR § 390.7(d), and 50 CFR § 259.) For purposes of this paragraph, the term "property" does not include money.

(ii) Whether or not the election provided for in subparagraph (2) of this paragraph is made—

(a) The amount of any property deposit, and the fund's basis for property deposited in the fund, is the fair market value of the property at the time deposited, and

(b) The fund's holding period for the property begins on the day after the deposit is made.

(iii) Unless such an election is made, deposits of property into a fund are considered to be a sale at fair market value of the property, a deposit of cash equal to such fair market value, and a purchase by the fund of such property for cash. Thus, in the absence of the election, the difference between the fair market value of such property deposited and its adjusted basis shall be taken into account as gain or loss for purposes of computing the party's income tax liability for the year of deposit.

(iv) For fund's basis and holding period of assets purchased by the fund, see paragraph (d)(2) and (3) of this section.

(2) *Election not to treat deposits of property other than money as a sale or exchange at the time of deposit.* A party may elect to treat a deposit of property as if no sale or other taxable event had occurred on the date of deposit. If such election is made, in the taxable year the fund disposes of the property, the party shall recognize as gain or loss the amount he would have recognized on the day the property was deposited into the fund had the election not been made. The party's holding period with respect to such property shall not include the period of time such property was held by the fund. The election shall be made by a statement to that effect, attached to the party's Federal income tax return for the taxable year to which the deposit relates, or, if such return is filed before such deposit is made, attached to the party's return for the taxable year during which the deposit is actually made.

(3) *Effect of qualified withdrawal of property deposited pursuant to election.* If property deposited into a fund, with respect to which an election under subparagraph (2) of this paragraph is made, is withdrawn from the fund in a qualified withdrawal (as defined in § 3.5) such withdrawal is treated as a disposition of such property resulting in recognition by the party of gain or loss (if any) as provided in subparagraph (2) of this paragraph with respect to nonfund property. In addition, such withdrawal is treated as a disposition of such property by the fund resulting in recognition of gain or loss by the party with respect to fund property to the extent the fair market value of the property on the date of withdrawal is greater or less (as the case may be) than the adjusted basis of the property to the fund on such date. For purposes of determining the amount by which the balance within a particular account will be reduced in the manner provided in § 3.6(b) (relating to order of application of qualified withdrawals against accounts) and for purposes of de-

Reg. § 3.2(g)(3)

24,456.10 *(I.R.C.)* Reg. § 3.2(g)(3)

termining the reduction in basis of a vessel, barge, or container (or share therein) pursuant to § 3.6(c), the value of the property is its fair market value on the day of the qualified withdrawal. For rules relating to the effect of a qualified withdrawal of property purchased by the fund (including deposited property considered under subparagraph (1)(iii) of this paragraph as purchased by the fund), see paragraph (d) (2)(ii) of this section.

(4) *Effect of nonqualified withdrawal of property deposited pursuant to election.* If property deposited into a fund with respect to which an election under subparagraph (2) of this paragraph is made, is withdrawn from the fund in a nonqualified withdrawal (as defined in § 3.7(b)), no gain or loss is to be recognized by the party with respect to fund property or nonfund property but an amount equal to the adjusted basis of the property to the fund is to be treated as a nonqualified withdrawal. Thus, such amount is to be applied against the various accounts in the manner provided in § 3.7(c), such amount is to be taken into account in computing the party's taxable income as provided in § 3.7 (d), and such amount is to be subject to interest to the extent provided for in § 3.7 (e). In the case of withdrawals to which this subparagraph applies, the adjusted basis of the property in the hands of the party is the adjusted basis on the date of deposit, increased or decreased by the adjustments made to such property while held in the fund, and in determining the period for which the party has held the property there shall be included, in addition to the period the fund held the property, the period for which the party held the property before the date of deposit of the property into the fund. For rules relating to the basis and holding period of property purchased by the fund (including deposited property considered under subparagraph (1)(ii) of this paragraph as purchased by the fund) and withdrawn in a nonqualified withdrawal see § 3.7(f).

(5) *Examples.* The provisions of this paragraph are illustrated by the following examples:

Example (1). X Corporation, which uses the calendar year as its taxable year, maintains a fund described in § 3.1. X's taxable income (determined without regard to section 607 of the Act) is $100,000, of which $80,000 is taxable income attributable to the operation of agreement vessels (as determined under paragraph (b)(1) of this section). Under the agreement, X is required to deposit into the fund all earnings and gains received from the investment or reinvestment of amounts held in the fund, an amount equal to the net proceeds from transactions referred to in § 3.2(c), and an amount equal to 50 percent of its earnings attributable to the operation of agreement vessels provided that such 50 percent does not exceed X's taxable income from all sources for the year of deposit. The agreement permits X to make voluntary deposits of amounts equal to 100 percent of its earnings attributable to the operation of agreement vessels, subject to the limitation with respect to taxable income from all sources. The agreement also provides that deposits attributable to such earnings may be in the form of cash or other property. On March 15, 1973, X deposits, with respect to its 1972 earnings attributable to the operation of agreement vessels, stock with a fair market value at the time of deposit of $80,000 and an adjusted basis to X of $10,000. Such deposit represents agreement vessel income of $80,000. At the time of deposit, such stock had been held by X for a period exceeding 6 months. X does not elect under subparagraph (2) of this paragraph to defer recognition of the gain. Accordingly, under subparagraph (1)(iii) of this paragraph, the deposit is treated as a deposit of $80,000 and X realizes a long-term capital gain of $70,000 on March 15, 1973.

Example (2). The facts are the same as in example (1), except that X elects in accordance with subparagraph (2) of this paragraph not to treat the deposit as a sale or exchange. On July 1, 1974, the fund sells the stock for $85,000. The basis to the fund of the stock is $80,000 (see subparagraph (1)(ii)(a) of this paragraph). With respect to nonfund property, X recognizes $70,000 of long-term capital gain on the sale includible in its gross income for 1974. With respect to fund property, X realizes $5,000 of long-term capital gain (the difference between the amount received by the fund on the sale of the stock, $85,000, and the basis to the fund of the stock, $80,000), an amount equal to which is required to be deposited into the fund with respect to 1974, as a gain from the investment or reinvestment of amounts held in the fund. Since the fund held the stock for a period exceeding 6 months, the $5,000 is allocated to the fund's capital gain account under § 3.4(c).

Example (3). The facts are the same as in example (2), except that the fund sells the stock on July 1, 1974, for $75,000. As the basis to the fund of the stock is $80,000, with respect to fund property, X realizes a long-term capital loss on the sale (the difference between the amount received by the fund on the sale of the stock, $75,000, and the basis to the fund of the stock, $80,000), of $5,000, an amount equal to which is required to be charged against the fund's capital gain account under § 3.4(e). Under subparagraph (2) of this paragraph, X recognizes $70,000 of long-term capital gain with respect to nonfund property on the sale which is includible in its gross income for 1974.

Example (4). The facts are the same as in example (2), except that on July 1, 1974, X makes a qualified withdrawal (as defined in § 3.5(a)) of the stock and uses it to pay indebtedness pursuant to § 3.5(b). On the disposition by X considered to occur under subparagraph (3) of this paragraph on the qualified withdrawal, X recognizes $70,000 of long-term capital gain with respect to nonfund property, which is includible in its gross income for 1974, and a long-term capital gain of $5,000 with respect to fund property, an amount equal to which is allocated to the fund's capital gain account under § 3.4(c). The fund is treated as having a qualified withdrawal of an amount equal to the fair market value of the stock on the day of withdrawal, $85,000 (see subparagraph (3) of this paragraph). In addition, $85,000 is applied against the various accounts in the order provided in § 3.6(b). The basis of the vessel with respect to which the indebtedness was incurred is to be reduced as provided in § 3.6(c).

Example (5). The facts are the same as in example (2), except that X withdraws the stock from the fund in a nonqualified withdrawal (as defined in § 3.7 (b)). Under subparagraph (4) of this paragraph, X recognizes no gain or loss with respect to fund or nonfund property on such withdrawal. An amount equal to the basis of the stock to the fund ($80,000) is applied against the various accounts in the order provided in § 3.7(c), and is taken into account in computing X's taxable income for 1974 as provided in § 3.7(d). In addition, X must pay interest on the withdrawal as provided in § 3.7(e). The basis to X of the stock is $10,000 notwithstanding the fact that the fair market value of such stock was $85,000 on the day of withdrawal (see subparagraph (4) of this paragraph).

§ 3.3 (T.D. 7398, filed 1-23-76.) **Nontaxability of deposits.**

(a) *In general.* Section 607(d) of the Act sets forth the rules concerning the income tax effects of deposits made with respect to ceilings described in section 607 (b) and § 3.2. The specific treatment of deposits with respect to each of the subceilings is set forth in paragraph (b) of this section.

(b) *Treatment of deposits* — (1) *Earnings of agreement vessels.* Section 607(d) (1)(A) of the Act provides that taxable income of the party (determined without regard to section 607 of the Act) shall be reduced by an amount equal to the amount deposited for the taxable year out of amounts referred to in section 607(b)(1) (A) of the Act and § 3.2(a)(1)(i). For computation of the foreign tax credit see paragraph (i) of this section.

(2) *Net proceeds from agreement vessels and fund earnings.* (i)(a) Section 607 (d)(1)(B) provides that gain from a transaction referred to in section 607(b)(1)(C) of the Act and § 3.2(a)(1)(iii) (relating to ceilings on deposits of net proceeds from the sale or other disposition of agreement vessels) is not to be taken into account for purposes of the Code if an amount equal to the net proceeds from transactions referred to in such sections is deposited in the fund. Such gain is to be excluded from gross income of the party for the taxable year to which such deposit relates. Thus, the gain will not be taken into account in applying section 1231 of the Code for the year to which the deposit relates.

(b) [Reserved]

(ii)(a) Section 607(d)(1)(C) of the Act provides that the earnings (including gains and losses) from the investment and reinvestment of amounts held in the fund and referred to in section 607(b)(1)(D) of the Act and § 3.2(a)(1)(iv) shall not be taken into account for purposes of the Code if an amount equal to such earnings is deposited into the fund. Such earnings are to be excluded from the gross income of the party for the taxable year to which such deposit relates.

(b) However, for purposes of the basis adjustment under section 1232(a)(3)(E) of the Code, the ratable monthly portion of original issue discount included in gross income shall be determined without regard to section 607(d)(1)(C) of the Act.

(iii) In determining the tax liability of a party to whom subparagraph (1) of this paragraph applies, taxable income, determined after application of subparagraph (1) of this paragraph, is in effect reduced by the portion of deposits which represent gain or earnings respectively referred to in subdivision (i) or (ii) of this subparagraph. The excess, if any, of such portion over taxable income determined after application of subparagraph (1) of this paragraph is taken into account in computing the net operating loss (under section 172 of the Code) for the taxable year to which such deposits relate.

(3) *Time for making deposits.* (i) This section applies with respect to an amount only if such amount is deposited in the fund pursuant to the agreement and not later than the time provided in subdivision (ii), (iii), or (iv) of this subparagraph for the making of such deposit or the date the Secretary of Commerce provides, whichever is earlier.

(ii) Except as provided in subdivision (iii) or (iv) of this subparagraph, a deposit may be made not later than the last day prescribed by law (including extensions thereof) for filing the party's Federal income tax return for the taxable year to which such deposit relates.

(iii) If the party is a subsidized operator under an operating-differential subsidy contract, and does not receive on or before the 59th day preceding such last day, payment of all or part of the accrued operating-differential subsidy payable for the taxable year, the party may deposit an amount equivalent to the unpaid accrued operating-differential subsidy on or before the 60th day after receipt of payment of the accrued operating-differential subsidy.

(iv) A deposit pursuant to § 3.2(a)(3) (i) (relating to underdeposits caused by audit adjustments) must be made on or before the date prescribed for such a deposit in § 3.2(a)(4).

(4) *Date of deposits.* (i) Except as otherwise provided in subdivisions (ii) and (iii) of this subparagraph (with respect to taxable years beginning after December 31, 1969, and prior to January 1, 1972), in § 3.2 (a)(2)(i), or in § 3.10(b), deposits made in a fund within the time specified in subparagraph (3) of this paragraph are deemed to have been made on the date of actual deposit.

(ii)(a) For taxable years beginning after December 31, 1969, and prior to January 1, 1971, where an application for a fund is filed by a taxpayer prior to January 1, 1972, and an agreement is executed and entered into by the taxpayer prior to March 1, 1972,

(b) For taxable years beginning after December 31, 1970, and prior to January 1, 1972, where an application for a fund is filed by a taxpayer prior to January 1, 1973, and an agreement is executed and entered into by the taxpayer prior to March 1, 1973, and

(c) For taxable years beginning after December 31, 1971, and prior to January 1, 1975, where an agreement is executed and entered into by the taxpayer on or prior to the due date, with extensions, for the filing

Reg. § 3.3(b)(4)

of his Federal income tax return for such taxable year, deposits in a fund which are made within 60 days after the date of execution of the agreement, or on or before the due date, with extensions thereof, for the filing of his Federal income tax return for such taxable year or years, whichever date shall be later, shall be deemed to have been made on the date of the actual deposit or as of the close of business of the last regular business day of each such taxable year or years to which such deposits relate, whichever day is earlier.

(iii) Notwithstanding subdivision (ii) of this subparagraph, for taxable years beginning after December 31, 1970, and ending prior to January 1, 1972, deposits made later than the last date permitted under subdivision (ii) but on or before January 9, 1973, in a fund pursuant to an agreement with the Secretary of Commerce, acting by and through the Administrator of the National Oceanic and Atmospheric Administration, shall be deemed to have been made on the date of the actual deposit or as of the close of business of the last regular business day of such taxable year, whichever is earlier.

(c) *Determination of earnings and profits.* [Reserved]

(d) *Accumulated earnings tax.* As provided in section 607(d)(1)(E) of the Act amounts, while held in the fund, are not to be taken into account in computing the "accumulated taxable income" of the party within the meaning of section 531 of the Code. Amounts while held in the fund are considered held for the purpose of acquiring, constructing, or reconstructing a qualified vessel or barges and containers which are part of the complement of a qualified vessel or the payment of the principal on indebtedness incurred in connection with any such acquisition, construction, or reconstruction. Thus, for example, if the reasonable needs of the business (within the meaning of section 537 of the Code) justify a greater amount of accumulation for providing replacement vessels than can be satisfied out of the fund, such greater amount accumulated outside of the fund shall be considered to be accumulated for the reasonable needs of the business. For a further example, although amounts in the fund are not taken into account in applying the tax imposed by section 531 of the Code, to the extent there are amounts in a fund to provide for replacing a vessel, amounts accumulated outside of the fund to replace the same vessel are not considered to be accumulated for the reasonable needs of the business.

(e) *Nonapplicability of section 1231.* If an amount equivalent to gain from a transaction referred to in section 607(b)(1)(C) of the Act and § 3.2(c)(1) and (5) is deposited into the fund and, therefore, such gain is not taken into account in computing gross income under the provisions of paragraph (b)(2) of this section, then such gain will not be taken into account for purposes of the computations under section 1231 of the Code.

(f) *Deposits of capital gains.* In respect of capital gains which are not included in the gross income of the party by virtue of a deposit to which section 607(d) of the Act and this section apply, the following provisions of the Code do not apply: the minimum tax for tax preferences imposed by section 56 of the Code; the alternative tax imposed by section 1201 of the Code on the excess of the party's net long-term capital gain over his net short-term capital loss; and, in the case of a taxpayer other than a corporation, the deduction provided by section 1202 of the Code of 50 percent of the amount of such excess. However, section 56 may apply upon a nonqualified withdrawal with respect to amounts treated under § 3.7(d)(2) as being made out of the capital gain account.

(g) *Deposits of dividends.* The deduction provided by section 243 of the Code (relating to the deductions for dividends from a domestic corporation received by a corporation) shall not apply in respect of dividends (earned on assets held in the fund) which are deposited into a fund, and which, by virtue of such deposits and the provisions of section 607 (d) of the Act and this section, are not included in the gross income of the party.

(h) *Presumption of validity of deposit.* All amounts deposited in the fund shall be presumed to have been deposited pursuant to an agreement unless, after an examination of the facts upon the request of the Commissioner of Internal Revenue or his delegate, the Secretary of Commerce determines otherwise. The Commissioner or his delegate will request such a determination where there is a substantial question as to whether a deposit is made in accordance with an agreement.

(i) *Special rules for application of the foreign tax credit*—(1) *In general.* For purposes of computing the limitation under section 904 of the Code on the amount of the credit provided by section 901 of the Code (relating to the foreign tax credit) the party's taxable income from any source without the United States and the party's entire taxable income are to be determined after application of section 607 (d) of the Act. Thus, amounts deposited for the taxable year with respect to amounts referred to in section 607 (b) (1) (A) of the Act and § 3.2 (a) (1) (i) (relating to taxable income attributable to the operation of agreement vessels) shall be treated as a deduction in arriving at the party's taxable income from sources without the United States (subject to the apportionment rules in subparagraph (2) of this paragraph) and the party's entire taxable income for the taxable year. Amounts deposited with respect to gain described in section 607 (d) (1) (B) of the Act and § 3.2 (c) (relating to net proceeds from the sale or other disposition of an agreement vessel and net proceeds from insurance or indemnity) and amounts deposited with respect to earnings described in section 607 (d) (1) (C) of the Act and paragraph (b) (2) (ii) (relating to earnings from the investment and reinvestment of amounts held in a fund) of this section are not taken into account for purposes of the Code and hence are not included in the party's taxable income from sources without the United States or in the party's entire taxable income for purposes of this paragraph.

(2) *Apportionment of taxable income attributable to agreement vessels.* For purposes of computing the overall limitation under section 904(a)(2) of the Code the amount of the deposit made with respect

to taxable income attributable to agreement vessels pursuant to § 3.2 (a) (1) (i) which is allocable to sources without the United States is the total amount of such deposit multiplied by a fraction the numerator of which is the gross income from sources without the United States from the operation of agreement vessels and the denominator of which is the total gross income from the operation of agreement vessels computed as provided in § 3.2(b)(2). For purposes of this paragraph gross income from sources without the United States attributable to the operation of agreement vessels is to be determined under sections 861 through 863 of the Code and under the taxpayer's usual method of accounting provided such method is reasonable and in keeping with sound accounting practice. Any computation under the per-country limitation of section 904 (a) (1) shall be made in the manner consistent with the provisions of the preceding sentences of this subparagraph.

§ 3.4 (T.D. 7398, filed 1-23-76.) Establishment of accounts.

(a) *In general.* Section 607 (e) (1) of the Act requires that three bookkeeping or memorandum accounts are to be established and maintained within the fund: The capital account, the capital gain account, and the ordinary income account. Deposits of the amounts under the subceilings in section 607 (b) of the Act and § 3.2 are allocated among the accounts under section 607 (e) of the Act and this section.

(b) *Capital account.* The capital account shall consist of:

(1) Amounts referred to in section 607 (b)(1)(B) of the Act and § 3.2(a)(1)(ii) (relating to deposits for depreciation),

(2) Amounts referred to in section 607 (b) (1) (C) of the Act and § 3.2(a) (1) (iii) (relating to deposits of net proceeds from the sale or other disposition of agreement vessels) other than that portion thereof which represents gain not taken into account for purposes of computing gross income by reason of section 607(d)(1)(B) of the Act and § 3.3 (b) (2) (relating to nontaxability of gain from the sale or other disposition of an agreement vessel),

(3) Amounts representing 85 percent of any dividend received by the fund with respect to which the party would, but for section 607 (d) (1) (C) of the Act and § 3.3 (b) (2) (ii) (relating to nontaxability of deposits of earnings from investment and reinvestment of amounts held in a fund), be allowed a deduction under section 243 of the Code, and

(4) Amounts received by the fund representing interest income which is exempt from taxation under section 103 of the Code.

(c) *Capital gain account.* The capital gain account shall consist of amounts which represent the excess of (1) deposits of long-term capital gains on property referred to in section 607 (b) (1) (C) and (D) of the Act and § 3.2(a) (1) (iii) and (iv) (relating respectively to certain agreement vessels and fund assets), over (2) amounts representing losses from the sale or exchange of assets held in the fund for more than 6 months (for purposes of this section referred to as "long-term capital losses"). For purposes of this paragraph and paragraph (d) (2) of this section, an agreement vessel disposed of at a gain shall be treated as a capital asset to the extent that gain thereon is not treated as ordinary income, including gain which is ordinary income under section 607 (g) (5) of the Act (relating to treatment of gain on disposition of a vessel with a reduced basis) and § 3.6 (e) or under section 1245 of the Code (relating to gain from disposition of certain depreciable property). For provisions relating to the treatment of short-term capital gains on certain transactions involving agreement vessels or realized by the fund, see paragraph (d) of this section. For rules relating to the treatment of capital losses on assets held in the fund, see paragraph (e) of this section.

(d) *Ordinary income account.* The ordinary income account shall consist of:

(1) Amounts referred to in section 607 (b)(1)(A) of the Act and § 3.2(a)(1)(i) (relating to taxable income attributable to the operation of an agreement vessel),

(2) Amounts representing (i) deposits of gains from the sale or exchange of capital assets held for 6 months or less (for purposes of this section referred to as "short-term capital gains") referred to in section 607(b)(1)(C) or (D) of the Act and § 3.2(a)(1)(iii) and (iv) (relating respectively to certain agreement vessels and fund assets), reduced by (ii) amounts representing losses from the sale or exchange of capital assets held in the fund for 6 months or less (for purposes of this section referred to as "short-term capital losses"). For rules relating to the treatment of certain agreement vessels as capital assets, see paragraph (c) of this section,

(3) Amounts representing interest (not including any tax-exempt interest referred to in section 607(e)(2)(D) of the Act and paragraph (b)(4) of this section) and other ordinary income received on assets held in the fund (not including any dividend referred to in section 607(e)(2)(C) of the Act and subparagraph (5) of this paragraph),

(4) Amounts representing ordinary income from a transaction (involving certain net proceeds with respect to an agreement vessel) described in section 607(b) (1)(C) of the Act and § 3.2(a)(1)(iii), including gain which is ordinary income under section 607(g)(5) of the Act and § 3.6 (e) (relating to treatment of gain on the disposition of a vessel with a reduced basis) or under section 1245 of the Code (relating to gain from disposition of certain depreciable property), and

(5) Fifteen percent of any dividend referred to in section 607(e)(2)(C) of the Act and paragraph (b)(3) of this section received on any assets held in the fund.

(e) *Limitation on deduction for capital losses on assets held in a fund.* Except on termination of a fund, long-term (and short-term) capital losses on assets held in the fund shall be allowed only as an offset to long-term (and short-term) capital gains on assets held in the fund, but only if such gains are deposited into the fund, and shall not be allowed as an offset to any capital gains on assets not held in the fund. The net long-term capital loss of the fund for the taxable year shall reduce the earliest

Reg. § 3.4(e)

long-term capital gains in the capital gain account at the beginning of the taxable year and the net short-term capital loss for the taxable year shall reduce the earliest short-term capital gains remaining in the ordinary income account at the beginning of the taxable year. Any such losses that are in excess of the capital gains in the respective accounts shall reduce capital gains deposited into the respective accounts in subsequent years (without regard to section 1212, relating to capital loss carrybacks and carryovers). On termination of a fund, any net long-term capital loss in the capital gain account and any net short-term capital loss remaining in the ordinary income account is to be taken into account for purposes of computing the party's taxable income for the year of termination as a long-term or short-term (as the case may be) capital loss recognized in the year the fund is terminated. With respect to the determination of the basis to a fund of assets held in such fund, see § 3.2(g).

O— § 3.5 (T.D. 7398, filed 1-23-76.) **Qualified withdrawals.**

(a) *In general.* (1) A qualified withdrawal is one made from the fund during the taxable year which is in accordance with section 607(f)(1) of the Act, the agreement, and with regulations prescribed by the Secretary of Commerce and which is for the acquisition, construction, or reconstruction of a qualified vessel (as defined in § 3.11(a)(2)) or barges and containers which are part of the complement of a qualified vessel (or shares in such vessels, barges, and containers), or for the payment of the principal of indebtedness incurred in connection with the acquisition, construction, or reconstruction of such qualified vessel (or a barge or container which is part of the complement of a qualified vessel).

(2) For purposes of this section the term "share" is used to reflect an interest in a vessel and means a proprietary interest in a vessel such as, for example, that which results from joint ownership. Accordingly, a share within the meaning of § 3.2(f) (relating to the definition of "agreement vessel" for the purpose of making deposits) will not necessarily be sufficient to be treated as a share within the meaning of this section.

(3) For purposes of this section, the term "acquisition" means any of the following:

(i) Any acquisition, but only to the extent the basis of the property acquired in the hands of the transferee is its cost. Thus, for example, if a party transfers a vessel and $1 million in an exchange for another vessel which qualifies for nonrecognition of gain or loss under section 1031(a) of the Code (relating to like-kind exchange), there is an acquisition to the extent of $1 million.

(ii) With respect to a lessee's interest in a vessel, expenditures which result in increasing the amounts with respect to which a deduction for depreciation (or amortization in lieu thereof) is allowable.

(iii) [Reserved]

(b) *Payments on indebtedness.* Payments on indebtedness may constitute qualified withdrawals only if the party shows to the satisfaction of the Secretary of Commerce a direct connection between incurring the indebtedness and the acquisition, construction, or reconstruction of a qualified vessel or its complement of barges and containers whether or not the indebtedness is secured by the vessel or its complement of barges and containers. The fact that an indebtedness is secured by an interest in a qualified vessel, barge, or container is insufficient by itself to demonstrate the necessary connection.

(c) *Payments to related persons.* Notwithstanding paragraph (a) of this section, payments from a fund to a person owned or controlled directly or indirectly by the same interests as the party within the meaning of section 482 of the Code and the regulations thereunder are not to be treated as qualified withdrawals unless the party demonstrates to the satisfaction of the Secretary of Commerce that no part of such payment constitutes a dividend, a return of capital, or a contribution to capital under the Code.

(d) *Treatment of fund upon failure to fulfil obligations.* Section 607(f)(2) of the Act provides that if the Secretary of Commerce determines that any substantial obligation under the agreement is not being fulfilled, he may, after notice and opportunity for hearing to the party, treat the entire fund, or any portion thereof, as having been withdrawn as a nonqualified withdrawal. In determining whether a party has breached a substantial obligation under the agreement, the Secretary will consider among other things (1) the effect of the party's action or omission upon his ability to carry out the purposes of the fund and for which qualified withdrawals are permitted under section 607(f)(1) of the Act, and (2) whether the party has made material misrepresentations in connection with the agreement or has failed to disclose material information. For the income tax treatment of nonqualified withdrawals, see § 3.7.

O— § 3.6 (T.D. 7398, filed 1-23-76.) **Tax treatment of qualified withdrawals.**

(a) *In general.* Section 607(g) of the Act and this section provide rules for the income tax treatment of qualified withdrawals including the income tax treatment on the disposition of assets acquired with fund amounts.

(b) *Order of application of qualified withdrawals against accounts.* A qualified withdrawal from a fund shall be treated as being made: first, out of the capital account; second out of the capital gain account; and third, out of the ordinary income account. Such withdrawals will reduce the balance within a particular account on a first-in-first-out basis, the earliest qualified withdrawals reducing the items within an account in the order in which they were actually deposited or deemed deposited in accordance with this part. The date funds are actually withdrawn from the fund determines the time at which withdrawals are considered to be made.

(c) *Reduction of basis.* (1) If any portion of a qualified withdrawal for the acquisition, construction or reconstruction of a vessel, barge, or container (or share therein) is made out of the ordinary income account, the basis of such vessel, barge, or container (or share therein) shall be reduced by an amount equal to such portion.

(2) If any portion of a qualified withdrawal for the acquisition, construction, or reconstruction of a vessel, barge, or container (or share therein) is made out of the capital gain account, the basis of such vessel, barge, or container (or share therein) shall be reduced by an amount equal to—

(i) Five-eighths of such portion, in the case of a corporation (other than an electing small business corporation, as defined in section 1371 of the Code), or

(ii) One-half of such portion, in the case of any other person.

(3) If any portion of a qualified withdrawal to pay the principal of an indebtedness is made out of the ordinary income account or the capital gain account, then the basis of the vessel, barge, or container (or share therein) with respect to which such indebtedness was incurred is reduced in the manner provided by subparagraphs (1) and (2) of this paragraph. If the aggregate amount of such withdrawal from the ordinary income account and capital gain account would cause a basis reduction in excess of the party's basis in such vessel, barge, or container (or share therein), the excess is applied against the basis of other vessels, barges, or containers (or shares therein) owned by the party at the time of withdrawal in the following order: (i) vessels, barges, or containers (or shares therein) which were the subject of qualified withdrawals in the order in which they were acquired, constructed, or reconstructed; (ii) agreement vessels (as defined in section 607(k)(3) of the Act and § 3.11(a)(3)) and barges and containers which are part of the complement of an agreement vessel (or shares therein) which were not the subject of qualified withdrawals, in the order in which such vessels, barges, or containers (or shares therein) were acquired by the party; and (iii) other vessels, barges, and containers (or shares therein), in the order in which they were acquired by the party. Any amount of a withdrawal remaining after the application of this subparagraph is to be treated as a nonqualified withdrawal. If the indebtedness was incurred to acquire two or more vessels, barges, or containers (or shares therein), then the basis reduction in such vessels, barges, or containers (or shares therein) is to be made pro rata in proportion to the adjusted basis of such vessels, barges, or containers (or shares therein) computed, however, without regard to this section and adjustments under section 1016(a)(2) and (3) of the Code for depreciation or amortization.

(d) *Basis for depreciation.* For purposes of determining the allowance for depreciation under section 167 of the Code in respect of any property which has been acquired, constructed, or reconstructed from qualified withdrawals, the adjusted basis for determining gain on such property is determined after applying paragraph (c) of this section. In the case of reductions in the basis of any property resulting from the application of paragraph (c)(3) of this section, the party may adopt a method of accounting whereby (1) payments shall reduce the basis of the property on the day such payments are actually made, or (2) payments made at any time during the first half of the party's taxable year shall reduce the basis of the property on the first day of the taxable year, and payments made at any time during the second half of the party's taxable year shall reduce the basis of the property on the first day of the succeeding taxable year. For requirements respecting the change of methods of accounting, see § 1.446-1(e)(3) of the Income Tax Regulations of this chapter.

(e) *Ordinary income treatment of gain from disposition of property acquired with qualified withdrawals.* [Reserved]

§ 3.7 (T.D. 7398, filed 1-23-76.) Tax treatment of nonqualified withdrawals.

(a) *In general.* Section 607(h) of the Act provides rules for the tax treatment of nonqualified withdrawals, including rules for adjustments to the various accounts of the fund, the inclusion of amounts in income, and the payment of interest with respect to such amounts.

(b) *Nonqualified withdrawals defined.* Except as provided in section 607 of the Act and § 3.8 (relating to certain corporate reorganizations, changes in partnerships, and transfers by reason of death) any withdrawal from a fund which is not a qualified withdrawal shall be treated as a nonqualified withdrawal which is subject to tax in accordance with section 607(h) of the Act and the provisions of this section. Examples of nonqualified withdrawals are amounts remaining in a fund upon termination of the fund, and withdrawals which are treated as nonqualified withdrawals under section 607(f)(2) of the Act and § 3.5(d) (relating to failure by a party to fulfill substantial obligation under agreement) or under the second sentence of section 607(g)(4) of the Act and § 3.6(c)(3) (relating to payments against indebtedness in excess of basis).

(c) *Order of application of nonqualified withdrawals against deposits.* A nonqualified withdrawal from a fund shall be treated as being made: first, out of the ordinary income account; second, out of the capital gain account; and third, out of the capital account. Such withdrawals will reduce the balance within a particular account on a first-in-first-out basis, the earliest nonqualified withdrawals reducing the items within an account in the order in which they were actually deposited or deemed deposited in accordance with this part. Nonqualified withdrawals for research, development, and design expenses incident to new and advanced ship design, machinery, and equipment, and any amount treated as a nonqualified withdrawal under the second sentence of section 607(g)(4) of the Act and § 3.6(c)(3), shall be applied against the deposits within a particular account on a last-in-first-out basis. The date funds are actually withdrawn from the fund determines the time at which withdrawals are considered to be made. For special rules concerning the withdrawal of contingent deposits of net proceeds from the installment sale of an agreement vessel, see § 3.2(c)(6).

(d) *Inclusion in income.* (1) Any portion of a nonqualified withdrawal which,

Reg. § 3.7(d)(1)

under paragraph (c) of this section, is treated as being made out of the ordinary income account is to be included in gross income as an item of ordinary income for the taxable year in which the withdrawal is made.

(2) Any portion of a nonqualified withdrawal which, under paragraph (c) of this section, is treated as being made out of the capital gain account is to be included in income as an item of long-term capital gain recognized during the taxable year in which the withdrawal is made.

(3) For effect upon a party's taxable income of capital losses remaining in a fund upon the termination of a fund (which, under paragraph (b) of this section, is treated as a nonqualified withdrawal of amounts remaining in the fund) see § 3.4(e).

(e) *Interest.* (1) For the period on or before the last date prescribed by law, including extensions thereof, for filing the party's Federal income tax return for the taxable year during which a nonqualified withdrawal is made, no interest shall be payable under section 6601 of the Code in respect of the tax on any item which is included in gross income under paragraph (d) of this section, and no addition to such tax for such period shall be payable under section 6651 of the Code. In lieu of the interest and additions to tax under such sections, simple interest on the amount of the tax attributable to any item included in gross income under paragraph (d) of this section is to be paid at the rate of interest determined for the year of withdrawal under subparagraph (2) of this paragraph. Such interest is to be charged for the period from the last date prescribed for payment of tax for the taxable year for which such item was deposited in the fund to the last date for payment of tax for the taxable year in which the withdrawal is made. Both dates are to be determined without regard to any extensions of time for payment. Interest determined under this paragraph which is paid within the taxable year shall be allowed as a deduction for such year under section 163 of the Code. However, such interest is to be treated as part of the party's tax for the year of withdrawal for purposes of collection and in determining any interest or additions to tax for the year of withdrawal under section 6601 or 6651, respectively, of the Code.

(2) For purposes of section 607(h)(3)(C)(ii) of the Act, and for purposes of certain dispositions of vessels constructed, reconstructed, or acquired with qualified withdrawals described in § 3.6(e), the applicable rate of interest for any nonqualified withdrawal—

(i) Made in a taxable year beginning in 1970 and 1971 is 8 percent.

(ii) Made in a taxable year beginning after 1971, the rate for such year as determined and published jointly by the Secretary of the Treasury or his delegate and the Secretary of Commerce. Such rate shall bear a relationship to 8 percent which the Secretaries determine to be comparable to the relationship which the money rates and investment yields for the calendar year immediately preceding the beginning of the taxable year bear to the money rates and investment yields for the calendar year 1970. The determination of the applicable rate for any such taxable year will be computed by multiplying 8 percent by the ratio which *(a)* the average yield on 5-year Treasury securities for the calendar year immediately preceding the beginning of such taxable year, bears to *(b)* the average yield on 5-year Treasury securities for the calendar year 1970. The applicable rate so determined shall be computed to the nearest one-hundredth of 1 percent. If such a determination and publication is made, the latest published percentage shall apply for any taxable year beginning in the calendar year with respect to which publication is made.

(3) No interest shall be payable in respect of taxes on amounts referred to in section 607(h)(2)(i) and (ii) of the Act (relating to withdrawals for research and development and payments against indebtedness in excess of basis) or in the case of any nonqualified withdrawal arising from the application of the recapture provision of section 606(5) of the Merchant Marine Act, 1936, as in effect on December 31, 1969.

(f) *Basis and holding period in the case of property purchased by the fund or considered purchased by the fund.* In the case of a nonqualified withdrawal of property other than money which was purchased by the fund (including deposited property considered under § 3.2(g)(1)(ii) as purchased by the fund), the adjusted basis of the property in the hands of the party is its adjusted basis to the fund on the day of the withdrawal. In determining the period for which the taxpayer has held the property withdrawn in a nonqualified withdrawal, there shall be included only the period beginning with the date on which the withdrawal occurred. For basis and holding period in the case of nonqualified withdrawals of property other than money deposited into the fund, see § 3.2(g)(4).

○━▶ § 3.8 (T.D. 7398, filed 1-23-76.) **Certain corporate reorganizations and changes in partnerships, and certain transfers on death. [Reserved]**

○━▶ § 3.9 (T.D. 7398, filed 1-23-76.) **Consolidated returns. [Reserved]**

○━▶ § 3.10 (T.D. 7398, filed 1-23-76.) **Transitional rules for existing funds.**

(a) *In general.* Section 607(j) of the Act provides that any person who was maintaining a fund or funds under section 607 of the Merchant Marine Act, 1936 prior to its amendment by the Merchant Marine Act of 1970 (for purposes of this part referred to as "old fund") may continue to maintain such old fund in the same manner as under prior law subject to the limitations contained in section 607(j) of the Act. Thus, a party may not simultaneously maintain such old fund and a new fund established under the Act.

(b) *Extension of agreement to new fund.* If a person enters into an agreement under the Act to establish a new fund, he may agree to the extension of such agreement to some or all of the amounts in the old fund and transfer the amounts in the old fund to which the agreement is to apply from the old fund to the new fund. If an agreement to establish a new fund is extended to amounts from an old fund, each item in the old fund to which such agreement applies shall be considered to be transferred to the appropriate account in the manner provided for in § 3.8 (d) in the new fund in a nontaxable transaction which is in accordance with the provisions of the agreement under which such old fund was maintained. For purposes of determining the amount of interest under section 607 (h) (3) (C) of the Act and § 3.7 (e), the date of deposit of any item so transferred shall be deemed to be July 1, 1971, or the date of the deposit in the old fund, whichever is the later.

§ 3.11 (T.D. 7398, 1-23-76.) **Definitions.**

(a) As used in the regulations in this part and as defined in section 607(k) of the Act—

(1) The term "eligible vessel" means any vessel—

(i) Constructed in the United States, and if reconstructed, reconstructed in the United States,

(ii) Documented under the laws of the United States, and

(iii) Operated in the foreign or domestic commerce of the United States or in the fisheries of the United States.

Any vessel which was constructed outside of the United States but documented under the laws of the United States on April 15, 1970, or constructed outside the United States for use in the United States foreign trade pursuant to a contract entered into before April 15, 1970, shall be treated as satisfying the requirements of subdivision (i) of this subparagraph and the requirements of subparagraph (2) (i) of this section.

(2) The term "qualified vessel" means any vessel—

(i) Constructed in the United States and, if reconstructed, reconstructed in the United States,

(ii) Documented under the laws of the United States, and

(iii) Which the person maintaining the fund agrees with the Secretary of Commerce will be operated in the United States foreign, Great Lakes, or noncontiguous domestic trade or in the fisheries of the United States.

(3) The term "agreement vessel" means any eligible vessel or qualified vessel which is subject to an agreement entered into under section 607 of the Act.

(4) The term "vessel" includes cargo handling equipment which the Secretary of Commerce determines is intended for use primarily on the vessel. The term "vessel" also includes an ocean-going towing vessel or an ocean-going barge or comparable towing vessel or barge operated in the Great Lakes.

(b) Insofar as the computation and collection of taxes are concerned, other terms used in the regulations in this part, except as otherwise provided in the Act or this part, have the same meaning as in the Code and the regulations thereunder.

Reg. § 3.11(b)

TEMPORARY RULES UNDER THE 1954 CODE

Introduction.—Temporary rules, not yet superseded by final regulations, relating to elections, etc., under 1954 Code provisions, as amended have been rearranged in Code section numbers. Texts of these rules appear at the pages noted below.

Code or Act Sec. No.	Page	Code or Act Sec. No.	Page
46(e) [now 46(f)]	24,998.3	856(g)	24,998.91
46(f)(8)	24,998.35	861(e)	24,997
57	24,998.13	911(e)	24,998.91
57(d)(2)	24,998.133	936(d)(2)	24,998.83
83(b)	24,947	954	24,998.123
103(c)	24,998.37	955	24,998.123
103(d)(5)	24,987	999(c)(1)	24,998.97
105(d)	24,998.79	1023	24,998.119
163(d)	24,998.13	1057	24,998.91
167(o)	24,998.91	1608(d)(2) '76 Tax Reform Act	24,998.91
172(b)(3)(E)	24,998.91	2103 '76 Tax Reform Act	24,998.91
183(e)	24,998.15	3402(o)	24,979
184(b)	24,957	3402(q)	24,998.111
185(d)	24,998.91	4975(d), (e)	24,998.127
190	24,998.105	4975(f)	24,998.69
191(b)	24,998.91	6013(g)	24,998.91
	24,998.107	6013(h)	24,998.91
207(c)(3) '76 Tax Reform Act	24,998.91	6039A	24,998.131
367	24,998.115	6041	24,998.89
401(d)(1)	24,998.51	6048	24,915
402(e)(4)(A)	24,998.113		24,998.121
402(e)(4)(B)	25,998.23	6103(a)	24,998.95
402(e)(4)(L)	24,998.91		24,998.129
404(a)(6)	24,998.63	6103(c)	24,998.109
408(a)(2)	25,998.59	6103(h)	24,998.93
410	24,998.45	6103(i)	24,998.93
412(c)(1)	24,998.117	6103(j)(1)—(2)	24,998.101
412(c)(2)(B)	24,998.19	6103(k)(6)	24,998.85
412(c)(8)	24,998.21	6103(l)	24,998.17
412(c)(10)	24,998.71	6103(n)	24,998.87
414(c)	24,998.55	6334(d)	24,998.99
415(c)(4)	24,998.73	7701(a)(19)	24,985
451(e)	24,998.91		
463(d)	24,998.29		
465	24,998.125		
505 '71 Revenue Act	24,998.5		
516(d)(3) '69 Tax Reform Act	24,957		
528(c)(1)(E)	24,998.91		
604 '76 Tax Reform Act	24,998.91		
664	24,998.61		
704(d)	24,998.75		
804(c)(2) '76 Tax Reform Act	24,998.103		
804(c)(3) '76 Tax Reform Act	24,998.77		
804(e)(2) '76 Tax Reform Act	24,998.91		
	24,998.104-A		
812(b)(3)	24,998.91		
819A	24,998.91		
825(d)(2)	24,998.91		
856(e)	24,998.27		
	24,998.65		

T.D. 6632

Temporary regulations relating to information returns as to creation of or transfers to certain foreign trusts. (Filed 1-9-63).

The following regulations are prescribed under section 6048 of the Internal Revenue Code of 1954, as added by section 7 (f) of the Revenue Act of 1962 (76 Stat. 987), relating to the requirement that United States persons file an information return disclosing the creation of a foreign trust or the transfer of money or property to such a trust.

The regulations set forth herein are temporary and are designed to inform persons who are required to file a return as to the information which must be furnished as well as when and where the return must be filed. More comprehensive rules with respect to these and other provisions relating to foreign trusts will be issued subsequently.

In order to prescribe temporary regulations relating to information returns as to the creation of or transfers to certain foreign trusts under section 6048 of the Internal Revenue Code of 1954, the following regulations are hereby adopted:

[Sec. 6048] § 16.3 **Statutory provisions; returns as to creation of or transfers to certain foreign trusts.** [Sec. 6048, IRC]

[Sec. 6048] § 16.3-1 (T.D. 6632, filed 1-9-63.) **Returns as to the creation of or transfers to certain foreign trusts.**

(a) *Requirement of return.* Every United States person who, on or after October 16, 1962, either creates a foreign trust or transfers money or property to a foreign trust, directly or indirectly, shall file an information return on Form 3520, except as provided in subparagraph (4) of paragraph (d) of this section. The return must be filed by the grantor or the transferor, or the fiduciary of the estate in the case of a testamentary trust. The return must be filed whether or not any beneficiary is a United States person and whether or not the grantor or any other person may be treated as the substantial owner of any portion of the trust under sections 671-678.

(b) *Meaning of terms.* For purposes of this section the following terms shall have the meaning assigned to them in this paragraph:

(1) *Foreign trust.* See section 7701 (a) (31) of the Code for the definition of foreign trust.

(2) *United States person.* See section 7701 (a) (30) of the Code for the definition of United States person.

(3) *Grantor.* The term "grantor" refers to any United States person who by an inter vivos declaration or agreement creates a foreign trust.

(4) *Transferor.* The term "transferor" refers to any United States person, other than a person who is the grantor or the fiduciary (as defined in subparagraph (5) of this paragraph), who transfers money or property to or for the benefit of a foreign trust. It does not refer to a person who transfers money or property to a foreign trust pursuant to a sale or an exchange which is made for full and adequate consideration.

(5) *Fiduciary of an estate.* In the case of a testamentary trust expressed in the will of a decedent the term "fiduciary of an estate" refers to the executor or administrator who is responsible for establishing a foreign trust on behalf of the decedent.

(c) *Information required.* The return required by section 6048 and this section shall be made on Form 3520 and shall set forth the following information:

(1) The name, address, and identifying number of the person (or persons) filing the return, a statement identifying each person named as either a grantor, fiduciary of an estate, or transferor, and the date of the transaction for which the return is being filed;

(2) In the case of a fiduciary of an estate, the name and identifying number of the decedent;

(3) The name of the trust and the name of the country under whose laws the foreign trust was created;

(4) The date the foreign trust was created and the name and address of the person (or persons) who created it;

(5) The date on which the trust is to terminate or a statement describing the conditions which will cause the trust to terminate;

(6) The name and business address of the foreign trustee (or trustees);

(7) A statement either that the trustee is required to distribute all of the trust's income currently (in which case the information required in subparagraph (9) need not be furnished) or a statement that the trust may accumulate some or all of its income;

(8) The name, address, and identifying number, if any, of each beneficiary who is either named in the instrument or whose identity is definitely ascertainable at the time the return required by this section is filed, and the date of birth for each beneficiary who is a United States person and whose rights under the trust are determined, in whole or in part, by reference to the beneficiary's age;

(9) Except as provided in subparagraph (7), a statement with respect to each beneficiary setting forth his right to receive income or corpus, or both, from the trust, his proportionate interest, if any, in the income or corpus, or both, of the trust, and any condition governing the time when a distribution to him may be made, such as a specific date or age (or in lieu of such statement a copy of the trust instrument which must be attached to the return);

(10) A detailed list of the property transferred to the foreign trust in the transaction for which the return is being filed, containing a complete description of each item transferred, its adjusted basis and its fair market value on the date transferred, and the consideration, if any, paid by the foreign trust for such transfer; and

(11) The name and address of the person (or persons) having custody of the

Reg. § 16.3-1 (c) (11)

books of account and records of the foreign trust, and the location of such books and records if different from such address.

(d) *Special provisions* — (1) *Separate return for each foreign trust and each transfer.* If a United States person creates more than one foreign trust or transfers money or property to more than one foreign trust, then separate returns must be filed with respect to each foreign trust where returns are required under section 6048 and this section. If a United States person transfers money or property to the same foreign trust at different times, then separate returns must be filed with respect to each transfer where returns are required under section 6048 and this section. However, where more than one transfer to the same foreign trust is made by a United States person during any 90-day period, such person may, at his election, file a single return, so long as the return includes the information required with respect to each transfer and is filed on or before the 90th day after the earliest transfer in any such period.

(2) *Joint returns.* Where returns are required under section 6048 and this section by two or more persons who either jointly create a foreign trust or jointly transfer money or property to a foreign trust, they may jointly execute and file one return in lieu of filing several returns.

(3) *Actual ownership of money or property transferred.* If any person referred to in this section is not the real party in interest as to the money or property transferred but is merely acting for a United States person, the information required under this section shall be furnished in the name of and by the actual owner of such money or property, except that a fiduciary of an estate shall file information relating to the decedent.

(4) *Payments to an employees' trust, etc.* In the case of contributions made to a foreign trust under a plan which provides pension, profit-sharing, stock bonus, sickness, accident, unemployment, welfare, or similar benefits or a combination of such benefits for employees, neither employers nor employees shall be required to file a return as set forth in this section.

(e) *Time and place for filing return* — (1) *Time for filing.* Any return required by section 6048 and this section shall be filed on or before the 90th day after either the creation of any foreign trust by a United States person or the transfer of any money or property to a foreign trust by a United States person. The Director of International Operations is authorized to grant reasonable extensions of time to file returns under section 6048 and this section in accordance with the applicable provisions of section 6081 (a) and § 1.6081-1.

(2) *Place for filing.* Returns required by section 6048 and this section shall be filed with the Director of International Operations, Internal Revenue Service, Washington 25, D. C.

(f) *Penalties* — (1) *Criminal.* For criminal penalties for failure to file a return see section 7203. For criminal penalties for filing or fraudulent return, see sections 7206 and 7207.

(2) *Civil.* For civil penalty for failure to file a return or failure to show the information required on a return under this section, see section 6677.

Temporary Rules
T.D. 7021

Temporary rules relating to election to include certain restricted property in gross income. (Filed 1-16-70).

The following regulations relate to the application of section 83 (b) of the Internal Revenue Code of 1954, as added by section 321 (a) of the Tax Reform Act of 1969 (81 Stat. 487), to the election to include certain restricted property in gross income in the year of transfer.

The regulations set forth herein are temporary and are designed to inform taxpayers the manner of electing to include certain restricted property in gross income in the year of transfer under section 83 (b) with respect to elections made on or after December 30, 1969, the date of enactment of such Act, and those made prior to the issuance of final regulations to be prescribed by the Commissioner and approved by the Secretary or his delegate.

In order to provide such temporary regulations under section 83 (b) of the Internal Revenue Code of 1954, the following regulations are adopted:

[Sec. 83(b)] § 13.1 (T.D. 6921, filed Jan. 16, 1970.) **Election to include in gross income in year of transfer.**

(a) In general. Under section 83 (b) of the Internal Revenue Code of 1954 any person who performs services in connection with which property is transferred which at the time of transfer is not transferable by the transferee and is subject to a substantial risk of forfeiture may elect to include in his gross income for the taxable year in which such property is transferred, the excess of the fair market value of such property at the time of transfer (determined without regard to any restriction other than a restriction which by its terms will never lapse) over the amount (if any) paid for such property. If this election is made section 83 (a) does not apply with respect to such property, and any subsequent appreciation in the value of the property is not taxable as compensation. However, if the property is later forfeited, no deduction is allowed to any person with respect to such forfeiture. This election is not necessary in the case of property which is transferred subject only to a restriction which by its terms will never lapse.

(b) Manner of making election. The election referred to in paragraph (a) is made by filing two copies of a written statement with the internal revenue officer with whom the person who performed the services files his return.

(c) Additional copies. The person who performed the services shall also submit a copy of the statement referred to in paragraph (b) of this section to the person for whom the services are performed, and, in addition, if the person who performs the services in connection with which restricted property is transferred and the transferee of such property are not the same person, the person who performs the services shall submit a copy of such statement to the transferee of the property.

(d) Content of statement. The statement shall indicate that it is being made under section 83 (b) of the Code, and shall contain the following information:

(1) The name, address, taxpayer identification number and the taxable year (For example, "Calendar year 1969" or "Fiscal year ending May 31, 1970") of the person who performed the services;

(2) A description of each property with respect to which the election is being made;

(3) The date or dates on which the property is transferred;

(4) The nature of the restriction or restrictions to which the property is subject;

(5) The fair market value at the time of transfer (determined without regard to any restriction other than a restriction which by its terms will never lapse) of each property with respect to which the election is being made; and

(6) The amount (if any) paid for such property.

(e) Time for making election. The statement referred to in paragraph (b) of this section shall be filed not later than 30 days after the date the property was transferred (or, if later, January 29, 1970). Any statement filed before February 15, 1970, may be amended not later than 30 days after the publication of this Treasury decision in the Federal Register in order to make it conform to the requirements of paragraph (d) of this section.

(f) Revocability of election. An election under section 83 (b) may not be revoked except with the consent of the Commissioner.

Temporary Rules *(I.R.C.)* 24,957
T.D. 7032; 7271

Temporary regulations relating to certain elections.

In order to prescribe temporary regulations, which shall remain in force and effect until superseded by permanent regulations, relating to the manner of making certain elections provided by the Tax Reform Act of 1969 (P.L. 91-172, 83 Stat. 487), the following regulations are hereby adopted:

O→ § 13.0 (T.D. 7032, filed 3-10-70; amended by T.D. 7271, filed 4-11-73.) **Procedure applicable to certain elections.**

(a) *Elections covered by temporary rules.* The sections of the Internal Revenue Code of 1954, or of the Tax Reform Act of 1969, to which paragraph (b) of this section applies and under which an election or notification may be made pursuant to the procedures prescribed in such paragraph are as follows:

Section	Description of Election	Availability of Election
	(1) *First category:*	
167(e)(3) of Code	[4] [See Reg. § 1.167(e)-1]	
185(c) of Code	[3] [See Reg. § 1.185-1]	
231(d)(2) of Act	[8] [See Reg. § 1.217-2]	
433(d)(2) of Act	[5] [See Reg. § 1.582-1]	
503(c)(2) of Act	[9] [See Reg. § 1.636-4]	
516(d)(3) of Act	Contingent payments by transferee of franchise, trademark, or trade name	Payments made in taxable years ending after Dec. 31, 1969, and beginning before Jan. 1, 1980, on transfers made before Jan. 1, 1970
642(c)(1) of Code	[10] [See Reg. § 1.642(c)-1(b)]	
1039(a) of Code	[7] [See Reg. § 1.1039-1]	
1251(b)(4) of Code	[11] [See Reg. § 1.1251-2]	
	(2) *Second category:*	
169(b) of Code	[1][See Reg. § 1.169-4]	
184(b) of Code	Amortization of qualified railroad rolling stock	Any taxable year beginning after Dec. 31, 1969, in which rolling stock was placed in service (or succeeding taxable year)
187(b) of Code	[2][See Reg. § 1.187-1]	
	(3) *Third category:*	
504(d)(2) of Act	[6] [See Reg. § 1.615-9]	

(1) Reg. § 1.169-4 (T.D. 7116, filed 5-17-71) superseded those provisions of Temp. Reg. § 13.0 relating to Sec. 169(b).
(2) Reg. § 1.187-1 (TD 7137, filed 8-10-71), superseded those provisions of Temp. Reg. § 13.0 relating to Sec. 187(b).
(3) Reg. § 1.185-1 (T.D. 7140, filed 9-21-71), superseded those provisions of Temp. Reg. § 13.0 relating to Sec. 185(c).
(4) Reg. § 1.167(e)-1 (T.D. 7166, filed 3-10-72), superseded those provisions of Temp. Reg. § 13.0 relating to Sec. 167(e)(3).
(5) Reg. § 1.582-1 (T.D. 7171, filed 3-16-72), superseded those provisions of Temp. Reg. § 13.0 relating to Sec. 433(d)(2) of the '69 Tax Reform Act.
(6) Reg. § 1.615-9 (T.D. 7192, filed 6-29-72) superseded those provisions of Temp. Rule § 13.0 relating to Sec. 504(d)(2) of the '69 Tax Reform Act.
(7) Reg. § 1.1039-1 (T.D. 7191, filed 6-29-72) superseded those provisions of Temp. Rule § 13.0 relating to Sec. 1039(a).
(8) Reg. § 1.217-2 (T.D. 7195, filed 7-10-72) superseded those provisions of Temp. Rule § 13.0 relating to Sec. 231(d) of the '69 Tax Reform Act.
(9) Reg. § 1.636-4 (T.D. 7261, filed 2-23-73) superseded those provisions of Temp. Reg. § 13.0, relating to Sec. 503(c)(2) of the '69 Tax Reform Act.
(10) Reg. § 1.642(c)-1(b) (T.D. 7357, filed 5-30-75) superseded those provisions of Temp. Rule § 13.0 relating to Sec. 642(c)(1).
(11) Reg. § 1.1251-2 (T.D. 7418, filed 5-6-76) superseded those provisions of Temp. Rule § 13.0 relating to Sec. 1251(b)(4).

Reg. § 13.0(a)

24,958 (I.R.C.)   Reg. § 13.0(b)(1)   5-17-76

(b) *Manner of making election or serving notice*—(1) *In general.* (i) Except as provided in subparagraph (2) of this paragraph, a taxpayer may make an election under any section referred to in paragraph (a)(1) or (2) of this section for the first taxable year for which the election is required to be made or for the taxable year selected by the taxpayer when the choice of a taxable year is optional. The election must be made not later than *(a)* the time, including extensions thereof, prescribed by law for filing the income tax return for such taxable year or *(b)* 90 days after the date on which the regulations in this part are filed with the Office of the Federal Register, whichever is later.

(ii) The election shall be made by a statement attached to the return (or an amended return) for the taxable year, indicating the section under which the election is being made and setting forth information to identify the election, the period for which it applies, and the facility, property, or amounts to which it applies.

(2) *Additional time for certain elections.* An election under section 503(c)(2) of the Act or section 642(c)(1) of the Code must be made in accordance with subparagraph (1) of this paragraph but not later than (i) the time, including extensions thereof, prescribed by law for filing the income tax return for the taxable year following the taxable year for which the election is made or (ii) 90 days after the date on which the regulations in this part are filed with the Office of the Federal Register, whichever is later.

(3) *Notification as to section 615(e) election.* (i) The notification referred to in paragraph (a)(3) of this section in respect of an election under section 615(e) which was made before the date on which the regulations in this part are filed with the Office of the Federal Register shall be made in a statement attached to the taxpayer's income tax return for the first taxable year in which expenditures are paid or incurred after December 31, 1969, which would be deductible by the taxpayer under section 617 if he so elects. The statement shall indicate the first taxable year for which such election was effective and the district director, or the director of the regional service center, with whom the election was filed.

(ii) The notification referred to in paragraph (a)(3) of this section, in respect of an election under section 615(e) which is made on or after the date on which the regulations in this part are filed with the Office of the Federal Register, shall be made in the statement of election required by paragraph (a)(2) of § 15.1-1 of this chapter (Temporary Income Tax Regulations Relating to Exploration Expenditures in the Case of Mining).

(iii) The serving of notice pursuant to this subparagraph shall not preclude the subsequent making of an election under section 617(a). A failure to serve notice pursuant to this subparagraph shall be treated as an election under section 617(a) and paragraph (a)(1) of § 15.1-1 of this chapter with respect to exploration expenditures paid or incurred after December 31, 1969, whether or not the taxpayer subsequently revokes his election under section 615(e) with respect to exploration expenditures paid or incurred before January 1, 1970.

(iv) For rules relating to the revocation of an election under section 615(e), including such an election which is treated pursuant to this subparagraph as an election under section 617(a), see paragraph (a) of § 15.1-2 of this chapter (T.D. 6907, C.B. 1967-1, 531, 535).

(c) *Effect of election*—(1) *Revocations*—(i) *Consent to revoke required.* Except as provided in subdivision (ii) of this subparagraph, an election made in accordance with paragraph (b)(1) of this section shall be binding unless consent to revoke the election is obtained from the Commissioner. An application for consent to revoke the election will not be accepted before the promulgation of the permanent regulations relating to the section of the Code or Act under which the election is made. Such regulations will provide a reasonable period of time within which taxpayers will be permitted to apply for consent to revoke the election.

(ii) *Revocation without consent.* An election made in accordance with paragraph (b)(1) of this section may be revoked without the consent of the Commissioner not later than 90 days after the permanent regulations relating to the section of the Code or Act under which the election is made are filed with the Office of the Federal Register, provided such regulations grant taxpayers blanket permission to revoke that election within such time without the consent of the commissioner. Such blanket permission to revoke an election will be provided by the permanent regulations in the event of a determination by the Secretary or his delegate that such regulations contain provisions that may not reasonably have been anticipated by taxpayers at the time of making such election.

(iii) *Election treated as tentative.* Until the expiration of the reasonable period referred to in subdivision (i) of this subparagraph or the 90-day period referred to in subdivision (ii), of this subparagraph, an election under section 433(d)(2) of the Act will be considered a tentative election, subject to revocation under the provisions of such subdivisions.

(iv) *Place for filing revocations.* A revocation under subdivision (i) or (ii) of this subparagraph shall be made by filing a statement to that effect with the district director, or the director of the regional service center, with whom the election was filed.

(2) *Termination without consent.* An election which is made in accordance with paragraph (b)(1) of this section under a section referred to in paragraph (a)(2) of this section and is not revoked pursuant to subparagraph (1) of this paragraph may, without the consent of the Commissioner, be terminated at any time after making the election by filing a statement to that effect with the district director, or the director of the regional service center, with whom the election was filed. This statement giving notice of termination must be filed before the beginning of the month specified in the statement for which the termination is to be effective. If pursuant to this subparagraph the taxpayer terminates an election made under any such section, he may not thereafter make a new election under that section with respect to the facility, property, or equipment to which the termination relates.

(d) *Furnishing of supplementary information required.* If the permanent regulations which are issued under the section of the Code or Act referred to in paragraph (a)(1) or (2) of this section to which the election relates require the furnishing of information in addition to that which was furnished with the statement of election filed pursuant to paragraph (b)(1) of this section, the taxpayer must furnish such additional information in a statement addressed to the district director, or the director of the regional service center, with whom the election was filed. This statement must clearly identify the election and the taxable year for which it was made.

(e) *Other elections.* Elections under the following sections of the Code may not be made pursuant to paragraph (b)(1) of this section but are to be made under regulations, whether temporary or permanent, which will be issued under amendments made by the Act. If necessary, such regulations will provide a reasonable period of time within which taxpayers will be permitted to make elections under the sections in this part for taxable years ending before the date on which such regulations are filed with the Office of the Federal Register:

Section	Description
167(k)(1)	Expenditures to rehabilitate low-income rental housing
167(1)(4)	Post-1969 property of certain utilities representing growth in capacity
70(b)(1)(D)(iii)	Special limitation with respect to contributions of certain capital gain property
453(c)	Revocation of election to report income on installment basis
507(b)(1)(B)(ii)	Notice of termination of private foundation status
1564(a)(2)	Allowance of certain amounts to component member of controlled group of corporations
4942(h)(2)	Deficient distributions of private foundations for prior taxable years
4943(c)(4)(E)	Determination of holdings of a private foundation in a business enterprise where substantial contributors hold more than 15 percent of voting stock

(f) *Cross reference.* For temporary regulations under sections 57(c) and 163(d)(7) of the Code, relating to elections with respect to net leases of real property, see § 12.8 of the regulations in this part (Temporary Income Tax Regulations Under the Revenue Act of 1971).

Reg.§ 13.0(f)

Temporary Rules
T.D. 7056

Temporary regulations relating to extension of income tax withholding to pension and annuity payments if requested by payee. (Filed 8-21-70.)

In order to prescribe temporary regulations, which shall remain in force and effect until superseded by permanent regulations, relating to the withholding of income tax at source upon payments of pensions and annuities under section 3402(o) of the Internal Revenue Code of 1954, as added by section 805(g) of the Tax Reform Act of 1969 (83 Stat. 708), the following regulations are hereby adopted:

○→ [Sec. 3402(o)] § 32.1 (T. D. 7056, filed 8-21-70.) **Extension of withholding of income tax at source on wages to annuity payments if requested by payee.**

(a) *In general.* Under section 3402(o) of the Internal Revenue Code of 1954 and this section, the payee (as defined in paragraph (g)(2) of this section) of an annuity (as defined in paragraph (g)(1) of this section) may request the payer (as defined in paragraph (g)(3) of this section) of the annuity to withhold income tax with respect to payments of the annuity made after December 31, 1970. If such a request is made, the payer shall deduct and withhold as requested.,

(b) *Manner of making request.* A payee who wishes a payer to deduct and withhold income tax from annuity payments shall file a request with the payer to deduct and withhold a specific whole dollar amount from each annuity payment. Such specific dollar amount requested shall be at least $5 per month and shall not reduce the net amount of any annuity payment received by the payee below $10. The request shall be made on Form W-4P (annuitant's withholding exemption certificate and request) in accordance with the instructions applicable thereto, and shall set forth fully and clearly the data therein called for. In lieu of Form W-4P, payers may prepare and use a form the provisions of which are identical with those of Form W-4P.

(c) *When request takes effect.* Upon receipt of a request under this section the payer of the annuity with respect to which such request was made shall deduct and withhold the amount specified in such request from each annuity payment commencing with the first annuity payment made on or after the date which occurs—

(1) In a case in which no previous request is in effect, three calendar months after the date on which such request is furnished to such payer, and

(2) In a case in which a previous request is in effect, the first status determination date (see section 3402(f)(3)(B) and paragraph (d) of § 31.3402(f)(3)-1) which occurs at least 30 days after the date on which such request is so furnished.

However, the payer may, at his election, commence to deduct and withhold such specified amount with respect to an annuity payment which is made prior to the annuity payment described in the preceding sentence with respect to which the payer must commence to deduct and withhold.

(d) *Duration and termination of request.* A request under this section shall continue in effect until terminated. The payee may terminate the request by furnishing the payer a signed written notice of termination. Such notice of termination shall, except as hereinafter provided, take effect with respect to the first payment of an amount in respect of which the request is in effect which is made on or after the first status determination date (see section 3402(f)(3)(B) and paragraph (d) of § 31.3402(f)(3)-1) which occurs at least 30 days after the date on which such notice is so furnished. However, at the election of such payer, such notice may be made effective with respect to any payment of an amount in respect of which the request is in effect which is made on or after the date on which such notice is so furnished and before such status determination date.

(e) *Special rules.* For purposes of chapter 24 of subtitle C of the Internal Revenue Code of 1954 (relating to collection of income tax at source on wages) and of subtitle F of such Code (relating to procedure and administration), and the regulations thereunder—

(1) An amount which is requested to be withheld pursuant to this section shall be deemed a tax required to be deducted and withheld under section 3402.

(2) An amount deducted and withheld pursuant to this section shall be deemed an amount deducted and withheld under section 3402.

(3) The term "wages" includes the gross amount of an annuity payment with respect to which there is in effect a request for withholding under this section. However, references to the definition of wages in section 3401(a) which are made in section 6014 (relating to election by the taxpayer not to compute the tax on his annual return) and section 6015(a) (relating to declaration of estimated tax by individuals) shall not be deemed to include any portion of such an annuity payment.

(4) The term "employer" includes a payer with respect to whom a request for withholding is in effect under this section.

(5) The term "employee" includes a payee with respect to whom a request for withholding is in effect under this section.

(6) The term "payroll period" includes the period of accrual with respect to which payments of an annuity which is subject to withholding under this section are ordinarily made.

(f) *Returns of income tax withheld and statements for payees.* (1) Form W-2P is to be used in lieu of Form W-2, which is required to be furnished by an employer to an employee under § 31.6051-1 and to the Internal Revenue Service under paragraph (b) of § 31.6011(a)-4. With respect to an annuity subject to withholding under this section. If an amount is required to be deducted and withheld under this section

Reg. § 32.1(f)(1)

24,980 (I.R.C.) Reg. § 32.1(f)(1)

from any or all of the payments made to a payee under an annuity contract during a calendar year, all payments with respect to that annuity contract are required to be reported on Form W-2P, in lieu of Form 1099, as prescribed in §§ 1.6041-1, 1.6041-2, and 1.6047-1; any other annuity payments made by the same payer to the same payee may, at the option of the payer, be reported on Form W-2P.

(2) Each statement on Form W-2P shall show the following:

(i) The gross amount of annuity payments made during the calendar year, whether or not income tax withholding under this section was in effect with respect to all such payments,

(ii) The total amount deducted and withheld as tax under section 3402 and this section, and

(iii) The information required to be shown by Form W-2P and the instructions applicable thereto.

(3) The provisions of § 1.9101-1 (relating to permission to submit information required by certain returns and statements on magnetic tape) shall be applicable to the information required to be furnished on Form W-2P.

(4) The provisions of § 31.6109-1 (relating to supplying of identifying numbers) shall be applicable to Form W-2P and to any payee of an annuity to whom a statement on Form W-2P is required to be furnished.

(g) *Definitions.* For purposes of this section—

(1) The term "annuity" means periodic payments which are payable over a period greater than one year and which are treated under section 72 as amounts received as an annuity, whether or not such periodic payments are variable in amount. Also, periodic payments to an individual who is retired before the normal retirement age for reasons of disability, to which the provisions of section 105(d) apply, shall be deemed to be an annuity for purposes of this section. A lump-sum payment (including a total distribution under section 72(n)) is not an annuity.

(2) The term "payee" means an individual who is a citizen or resident of the United States and who receives an annuity payment.

(3) The term "payer" means a person making an annuity payment except that, if the person making the payment is acting solely as an agent for another person, the term "payer" shall mean such other person and not the person actually making the payment. For example, if a bank makes an annuity payment only as agent for an employees' trust, the trust shall be deemed to be the "payer". Notwithstanding the preceding two sentences, any person who, under section 3401(a)(5) or (8), would not be required to deduct and withhold the tax under section 3402 if the annuity payment were remuneration for services shall not be considered a "payer".

Temporary Rules

T.D. 7070

Temporary regulations relating to the definition of the term "domestic building and loan association". (Filed 11-9-70.)

In order to prescribe temporary regulations under section 7701(a)(19) of the Internal Revenue Code of 1954, as amended by section 432(c) of the Tax Reform Act of 1969 (P.L. 91-172, 83 Stat. 622), relating to the definition of the term "domestic building and loan association", which shall remain in force and effect until superseded by permanent regulations under such section, the following regulations are hereby adopted:

[Sec. 7701(a)(19)] § 402.1-1 (T.D. 7070, filed 11-9-70.) Limitation on application of § 301.7701-13.

Section 301.7701-13 shall not apply for taxable years beginning after July 11, 1969. For rules relating to definition of the term "domestic building and loan association" for taxable years beginning after July 11, 1969, see § 402.1-2.

[Sec. 7701(a)(19)] § 402.1-2 (T.D. 7070, filed 11-9-70.) Post-1969 domestic building and loan association.

(a) *In general.* For taxable years beginning after July 11, 1969, the term "domestic building and loan association" means a domestic building and loan association, a domestic savings and loan association, a Federal savings and loan association, and any other savings institution chartered and supervised as a savings and loan or similar association under Federal or State law which meets the supervisory test (described in paragraph (b) of this section), the business operations test (described in paragraph (c) of this section), and the assets test (described in paragraph (d) of this section). For the definition of the term "domestic building and loan association" for taxable years beginning after October 16, 1962, and before July 12, 1969, see § 301.7701-13.

(b) *Supervisory test.* A domestic building and loan association must be either (1) an insured institution within the meaning of section 401(a) of the National Housing Act (12 U.S.C. 1724(a)) or (2) subject by law to supervision and examination by State or Federal authority having supervision over such associations. An "insured institution" is one the accounts of which are insured by the Federal Savings and Loan Insurance Corporation.

(c) *Business operations test*—(1) *In general.* An association must utilize its assets so that its business consists principally of acquiring the savings of the public and investing in loans. The requirement of this paragraph is referred to in this section as the business operations test. The business of acquiring the savings of the public and investing in loans includes ancillary or incidental activities which are directly and primarily related to such acquisition and investment, such as advertising for savings, appraising property on which loans are to be made by the association, and inspecting the progress of construction in connection with construction loans. Even though an association meets the supervisory test described in paragraph (b) of this section and the assets test described in paragraph (d) of this section, it will nevertheless not qualify as a domestic building and loan association if it does not meet the requirements of both subparagraphs (2) and (3) of this paragraph, relating, respectively, to acquiring the savings of the public and investing in loans.

(2) *Acquiring the savings of the public.* The requirement that an association's business (other than investing in loans) must consist principally of acquiring the savings of the public ordinarily will be considered to be met if savings are acquired in all material respects in conformity with the rules and regulations of the Federal Home Loan Bank Board or substantially equivalent rules of a State law or supervisory authority. Alternatively, such requirement will be considered to be met if more than 75 percent of the dollar amount of the total deposits, withdrawable shares, and other obligations of the association are held during the taxable year by the general public, as opposed to amounts deposited or held by family or related business groups or persons who are officers or directors of the association. However, the preceding sentence shall not apply if the dollar amount of other obligations of the association outstanding during the taxable year exceeds 25 percent of the dollar amount of the total deposits, withdrawable shares, and other obligations of the association outstanding during such year. For purposes of this subparagraph, the term "other obligations" means notes, bonds, debentures, or other obligations, or other securities (except capital stock), issued by an association in conformity with the rules and regulations of the Federal Home Loan Bank Board or substantially equivalent rules of a State law or supervisory authority. The term "other obligations" does not include an advance made by a Federal Home Loan Bank under the authority of section 10 or 10b of the Federal Home Loan Bank Act (12 U.S.C. 1430, 1430b) as amended and supplemented. Both percentages specified in this subparagraph shall be computed either as of the close of the taxable year or, at the option of the taxpayer, on the basis of the average of the dollar amounts of the total deposits, withdrawable shares, and other obligations of the association held during the taxable year. Such averages shall be determined by computing each percentage specified either as of the close of each month, as of the close of each quarter, or semiannually during the taxable year and by using the yearly average of the monthly, quarterly, or semiannual percentages obtained. The method selected must be applied uniformly for the taxable year to both percentages, but the method may be changed from year to year.

(3) *Investing on loans*—(i) *In general.* The requirement that an association's business (other than acquiring the savings of the public) must consist principally of investing in loans will be considered to be met for a taxable year only if more than 75 percent of the gross income of the association consists of—

Reg. § 402.1-2(c)(3)

24,986 (I.R.C.) Reg. § 4021.1-2(c)(3)   11-16-70

(a) Interest or dividends on assets defined in subparagraphs (1), (2), and (3) of paragraph (e) of this section,

(b) Interest on loans,

(c) Income attributable to the portion of property used in the association's business, as defined in paragraph (e)(11) of this section,

(d) So much of the amount of premiums, discounts, commissions, or fees (including late charges and penalties) on loans which have at some time been held by the association, or for which firm commitments have been issued, as is not in excess of 20 percent of the gross income of the association,

(e) Net gain from sales and exchanges of governmental obligations, as defined in paragraph (e)(2) of this section, or

(f) Income, gain or loss attributable to foreclosed property, as defined in paragraph (e)(9) of this section, but not including such income, gain or loss which, pursuant to section 595 and the regulations thereunder, is not included in gross income.

Examples of types of income which would cause an association to fail to meet the requirements of this subparagraph if, in the aggregate, they equal or exceed 25 percent of gross income, are: the excess of gains over losses from sales of real property (other than foreclosed property); rental income (other than on foreclosed property and the portion of property used in the association's business); premiums, commissions, and fees (other than commitment fees) on loans which have never been held by the association; and insurance brokerage fees.

(ii) *Computation of gross income.* For purposes of this subparagraph, gross income is computed without regard to—

(a) Gain or loss on the sale or exchange of the portion of property used in the association's business as defined in paragraph (e)(11) of this section,

(b) Gain or loss on the sale or exchange of the rented portion of property used as the principal or branch office of the association, as defined in paragraph (e)(11) of this section, and

(c) Gains or losses on sales of participations and loans, other than governmental obligations defined in paragraph (e)(2) of this section.

For purposes of this subparagraph, gross income is also computed without regard to items of income which an association establishes arise out of transactions which are necessitated by exceptional circumstances and which are not undertaken as recurring business activities for profit. Thus, for example, an association would meet the investing in loans requirement if it can establish that it would otherwise fail to meet that requirement solely because of the receipt of a non-recurring item of income due to exceptional circumstances. For this purpose, transactions necessitated by an excess of demand for loans over savings capital in the association's area are not to be deemed to be necessitated by exceptional circumstances. For purposes of (c) of this subdivision, the term "sales of participations" means sales by an association of interests in loans, which sales meet the requirements of the regulations of the Federal Home Loan Bank Board relating to sales of participations, or which meet substantially equivalent requirements of State law or regulations relating to sales of participations.

(iii) *Reporting requirement.* In the case of income tax returns for taxable years beginning after July 11, 1969, there is required to be filed with the return a statement showing the amount of gross income for the taxable year in each of the categories described in subdivision (i) of this subparagraph.

(d) *60 percent of assets test.* At least 60 percent of the amount of the total assets of a domestic building and loan association must consist of the assets defined in paragraph (e) of this section. The percentage specified in this paragraph is computed as of the close of the taxable year or, at the option of the taxpayer, may be computed on the basis of the average assets outstanding during the taxable year. Such average is determined by making the appropriate computation described in this section either as of the close of each month, as of the close of each quarter, or semiannually during the taxable year and by using the yearly average of the monthly, quarterly, or semiannual percentage obtained for each category of assets defined in paragraph (e) of this section. The method selected must be applied uniformly for the taxable year to all categories of assets, but the method may be changed from year to year. For purposes of this paragraph, it is immaterial whether the association originated the loans defined in subparagraphs (4) through (8) and (10) of paragraph (e) of this section or purchased or otherwise acquired them in whole or in part from another. See paragraph (f) of this section for definition of certain terms used in this paragraph and in paragraph (e) of this section, and for the determination of amount and character of loans.

(e) *Assets defined.* The assets defined in this paragraph are—

(1) *Cash.* The term "cash" means cash on hand, and time or demand deposits with, or withdrawable accounts in, other financial institutions.

(2) *Governmental obligations.* The term "governmental obligations" means —

(i) Obligations of the United States,

(ii) Obligations of a State or political subdivision of a State, and

(iii) Stock or obligations of a corporation which is an instrumentality of the United States, a State, or a political subdivision of a State,

other than obligations the interest on which is excludable from gross income under section 103 and the regulations thereunder.

(3) *Deposit insurance company securities.* The term "deposit insurance company securities" means certificates of deposit in, or obligations of, a corporation organized under a State law which specifically authorizes such corporation to insure the deposits or share accounts of member associations.

(4) *Passbook loan.* The term "passbook loan" means a loan to the extent se-

cured by a deposit, withdrawable share, or savings account in the association, or share of a member of the association, with respect to which a distribution is allowable as a deduction under section 591.

(5) *Residential real property loan.* [Reserved]

(6) *Church loan.* [Reserved]

(7) *Urban renewal loan.* [Reserved]

(8) *Institutional loan.* [Reserved]

(9) *Foreclosed property.* [Reserved]

(10) *Educational loan.* [Reserved]

(11) *Property used in the association's business*—(i) *In general.* The term "property used in the association's business" means land, buildings, furniture, fixtures, equipment, leasehold interests, leasehold improvements, and other assets used by the association in the conduct of its business of acquiring the savings of the public and investing in loans. Real property held for the purpose of being used primarily as the principal or branch office of the association constitutes property used in the association's business so long as it is reasonably anticipated that such property will be occupied for such use by the association, or that construction work preparatory to such occupancy will be commenced thereon, within 2 years after acquisition of the property. Stock of a wholly owned subsidiary corporation which has as its exclusive activity the ownership and management of property more than 50 percent of the fair rental value of which is used as the principal or branch office of the association constitutes property used in such business. Real property held by an association for investment or sale, even for the purpose of obtaining mortgage loans thereon, does not constitute property used in the association's business.

(ii) *Property rented to others.* Except as provided in the second sentence of subdivision (i) of this subparagraph, property or a portion thereof rented by the association to others does not constitute property used in the association's business. However, if the fair rental value of the rented portion of a single piece of real property (including appurtenant parcels) used as the principal or branch office of the association constitutes less than 50 percent of the fair rental value of such piece of property, or if such property has an adjusted basis of not more than $150,000, the entire property shall be considered used in such business. If such rented portion constitutes 50 percent or more of the fair rental value of such piece of property, and such property has an adjusted basis of more than $150,000, an allocation of its adjusted basis is required. The portion of the total adjusted basis of such piece of property which is deemed to be property used in the association's business shall be equal to an amount which bears the same ratio to such total adjusted basis as the amount of the fair rental value of the portion used as the principal or branch office of the association bears to the total fair rental value of such property. In the case of all property other than real property used or to be used as the principal or branch office of the association, if the fair rental value of the rented portion thereof constitutes less than 15 percent of the fair rental value of such property, the entire property shall be considered used in the association's business. If such rented portion constitutes 15 percent or more of the fair rental value of such property, an allocation of its adjusted basis (in the same manner as required for real property used as the principal or branch office) is required.

(f) *Special rules.* [Reserved]

Temporary rules relating to arbitrage bonds.

The following temporary regulations are intended to define the term "materially higher" as such term is used in section 103(d) of the Internal Revenue Code of 1954, and to provide special rules relating to obligations issued to carry out governmental programs which require the acquisition of certain securities or obligations. Such temporary regulations are prescribed under section 103(d)(5) of the Internal Revenue Code of 1954, as added by section 601(a) of the Tax Reform Act of 1969 (83 Stat. 656), and are to be issued under the authority contained in such section 103(d)(5) and in section 7805 of the Internal Revenue Code of 1954 (68A. Stat. 917; 26 U.S.C. 7805).

In order to provide such temporary regulations under section 103(d)(5) of the Internal Revenue Code of 1954, the following regulations are adopted:

[Sec. 103(d)(5)] § 13.4 (T.D. 7072, filed 11-12-70; amended by T.D. 7174, filed 5-26-72 and T.D. 7273, filed 4-27-73.) Arbitrage bonds; temporary rules.

(a) *In general*—(1) *Arbitrage bonds.* Section 103(d)(1) provides that any arbitrage bond (as such term is defined in section 103(d)(2)) shall be treated as an obligation not described in section 103(a)(1). Thus, the interest on an obligation which would have been excluded from gross income pursuant to the provisions of section 103(a)(1) will be included in gross income and subject to Federal income taxation if such obligation is an arbitrage bond. Under section 103(d)(2), an obligation is an arbitrage bond if it is issued by a governmental unit as part of an issue of obligations (for purposes of this section referred to as "governmental obligations") all or a major portion of the proceeds of which are (i) reasonably expected to be used directly or indirectly to acquire certain obligations or securities (for purposes of this section referred to as "acquired obligations") which may reasonably be expected, at the time of issuance of such governmental obligations, to produce a yield over the term of the issue of such governmental obligations which is materially higher (taking into account any discount or premium) than the yield on such issue, or (ii) reasonably expected to be used to replace funds which were used directly or indirectly to acquire such acquired obligations. For rules as to industrial development bonds, see section 103(c).

(2) *Definitions.* (i) For purposes of this section, the term "governmental unit" means a State, the District of Columbia, a Territory, or a possession of the United States, or any political subdivision of any of the foregoing.

(ii) For purposes of this section, the term "securities" has the same meaning as in section 165(g)(2)(A) and (B).

(3) *Materially higher.* For purposes of this section, the yield produced by acquired obligations is not "materially higher" than the yield produced by an issue of governmental obligations if it is reasonably expected, at the time of issue of such governmental obligations, that the adjusted yield (computed in accordance with subparagraphs (4) and (5) of this paragraph) to be produced by the acquired obligations will not exceed the adjusted yield (computed in accordance with subparagraphs (4) and (5) of this paragraph) to be produced by the issue of governmental obligations by more than one-eighth of 1 percentage point. In the case of an issue of governmental obligations issued on or before July 1, 1972, the percentage specified in the preceding sentence shall be one-half of 1 percentage point.

(4) *Yield.* (i) For purposes of this section, "yield" shall be computed using the "interest cost per annum" method in accordance with subdivision (ii) or (iii) of this subparagraph (as the case may be) or any other method satisfactory to the Commissioner which is consistent with generally accepted principles of computing yield. In the case of acquired obligations, the yield to be produced by such obligations shall be computed as if all acquired obligations comprised a single issue of obligations. Thus, for example, if the governmental unit acquires two blocks of Federal obligations, with different interest rates and maturity periods for each block, the yield on such acquired obligations shall be computed as if one issue of obligations with different interest rates and maturity periods had been acquired. The maturity period of each acquired obligation shall be the period that the governmental unit reasonably expects to hold such obligation.

(ii) If all the governmental or acquired obligations of an issue have a single interest rate (expressed in dollars per $1,000 of face amount of bonds), yield shall be computed using the following 4 steps:

Step (1). Compute the total number of bond years for the issue by multiplying the number of bonds (treating each $1,000 of face value as one bond for purposes of this computation) of each maturity by the length of the maturity period (expressed in years and fractions thereof) and then adding together the amounts determined for each maturity period.

Step (2). Compute the total interest payable on the issue by multiplying the total number of bond years (as computed in step (1)) by the amount payable, expressed in dollars, as interest on each $1,000 of bonds for one year.

Step (3). Compute the net interest in dollars for the issue by adding the amount, in dollars, of any discount to, or by subtracting the amount, in dollars, of any premium from, the total interest payable on the issue.

Step (4). Compute yield by dividing the net interest by the product obtained by multiplying the total number of bond years for the issue by 10.

(iii) If governmental or acquired obligations of an issue have different interest rates (expressed in dollars per $1,000 of face amount of bonds), yield shall be computed using the following 4 steps:

Step (1). Compute the total number of bond years for each group of bonds bearing the same interest rate (treating each $1,000 of face value as one bond for purposes of this computation) in the manner described in step 1 of subdivision (ii) of this subparagraph.

Step (2). Compute the total interest payable on the issue by multiplying the

Reg. § 13.4(a)(4)

24,988 (I.R.C.)   Reg. § 13.4(a)(4)   5-7-73

total number of bond years for each group of bonds bearing the same interest rate (as computed in step (1)) by the amount payable, expressed in dollars, as interest on each $1,000 of bonds for one year, and then adding together the amounts determined for each group.

Step (3). Compute net interest in the manner described in step (3) of subdivision (ii) of this subparagraph.

Step (4). Compute the yield produced by the issue in the manner described in step (4) of subdivision (ii) of this subparagraph.

(iv) For purposes of this section, the same method of computing yield shall be used to compute the yield to be produced by an issue of governmental obligations and to compute the yield to be produced by acquired obligations acquired with the proceeds of such issue of governmental obligations.

(v) The following example illustrates the provisions of this subparagraph:

Example. Assume an issue of $200,000 ($1,000 per bond) with a stated interest (expressed in dollars per bond) of $50 on bonds maturing in 1, 2, or 3 years, a stated interest of $60 on bonds maturing in 4, 5, 6, or 7 years and a stated interest of $70 on bonds maturing in 8, 9, or 10 years. Assume also that a price of $101.00 has been bid for the issue. The yield on the issue is determined in accordance with the table below:

Amount	Rate	Years to Maturity	Bond Years	Total Bond Years at Interest Rate		Interest Rate		Interest Cost
$10,000	50	1	10					
5,000	50	2	10					
25,000	50	3	75					
				95	x	$50	=	$ 4,750
10,000	60	4	40					
10,000	60	5	50					
30,000	60	6	180					
50,000	60	7	350					
				620	x.	60	=	37,200
20,000	70	8	160					
25,000	70	9	225					
15,000	70	10	150					
				535	x	70	=	37,450
Totals $200,000				1,250				$79,400
Less Premium								2,000
Net Interest Cost								$77,400
Divide by: Product of total bond years (1,250) multiplied by 10.								12,500
Yield								6.192%

(5) *Adjusted yield.* (i) For purposes of this section, "adjusted yield" shall be computed in accordance with subparagraph (4) of this paragraph, except that in the case of—

(a) Acquired obligations, an amount equal to the sum of the administrative costs reasonably expected to be incurred in purchasing, carrying, and selling or redeeming such obligations shall be treated as a premium on the purchase price of such acquired obligations,

(b) An issue of governmental obligations, an amount equal to the sum of the reasonably expected administrative costs of issuing, carrying, and repaying such issue of obligations shall be treated as a discount on the selling price of such issue of governmental obligations.

(ii) The provisions of subdivision (i) of this subparagraph may be illustrated by the following examples:

Example (1). State Z issues $15 million of obligations all of which will mature in 10 years. The obligations are sold at $1,000 each (par) to yield six percent interest. The adjusted yield produced by such issue of obligations will be determined as follows, assuming the following administrative expenses of issuing, carrying, and repaying such issue of obligations are reasonably expected:

[Table appears on page 24,988.1.]

Example (2). State Z uses the net proceeds of the issue of obligations described in Example (1) to acquire $14,922,000 of student's notes at par of $1,000 each under a student loan program. The students' notes will all mature in 10 years, and all have a stated interest of 7½ percent. Expenses of the program include printing of forms ($5,000), financial advisors' fees ($11,000), counsel fees ($12,000), trustees' fees ($5,000), fees for the collecting agents and various banks which administer the loans ($100,000), advertising expenses ($10,000), credit reference checks ($20,000), and general office overhead ($5,000). Of the expenses listed in the preceding sentence, only those indicated on the following table constitute adjustments to yield in order to determine the adjusted yield to be produced by the students' notes:

[Table appears on page 24,988.2.]

Issuing costs	
Printing $12,500	
Financial advisors 25,000	
Counsel fees 12,500	
Total	$ 50,000
Carrying costs	
Paying agent and trustees fees	10,000
Repaying costs	
Paying agent	3,000
Total administrative costs	$ 63,000
Bond years (15,000 × 10 years)	$ 150,000
Interest cost per $1000 bond per year	60
Total interest cost	$9,000,000
Discount or premium	0
Plus adjustments	63,000
Net interest cost	$9,063,000
Divide by product of bond years (150,000) multiplied by 10	1,500,000
Adjusted yield	6.042%

(b) *Rule with respect to certain governmental programs*—(1) *General rule.* Subject to the limitations of subparagraph (3) of this paragraph, any obligations which are part of an issue of governmental obligations the proceeds of which are reasonably expected to be used to finance certain governmental programs (described in subparagraph (2) of this paragraph) are not arbitrage obligations.

(2) *Governmental programs.* A governmental program is described in this subparagraph if—

(i) The program involves the acquisition of acquired purpose obligations to carry out the purposes of such program (which obligations, for purposes of this paragraph, are referred to as "acquired program obligations");

(ii) At least 90 percent of all such acquired program obligations, by amount of cost outstanding, are evidences of loans to a substantial number of persons representing the general public, loans to exempt persons within the meaning of section 103 (c)(3), or loans to provide housing and related facilities, or any combination of the foregoing;

(iii) At least 90 percent of all of the amounts received by the governmental unit with respect to acquired program obligations shall be used for one or more of the following purposes: to pay the principal or interest or otherwise to service the debt on governmental obligations relating to the governmental program; to reimburse the governmental unit, or to pay, for administrative costs of issuing such governmental obligations; to reimburse the governmental unit, or to pay, for administrative and other costs and anticipated future losses directly related to the program financed by such governmental obligations; to make additional loans for the same general purposes specified in such program; or to redeem and retire governmental obligations at the next earliest possible date of redemption; and

(iv) Requires that any person (or any related person, as defined in section 103(c)(6)(C)) from whom the governmental unit may, under the program, acquire acquired program obligations shall not, pursuant to an arrangement, formal or informal, purchase the governmental obligations in an amount related to the amount of the acquired program obligations to be acquired from such person by the governmental unit.

(3) *Limitations.* The provisions of subparagraph (1) of this paragraph shall apply only if it is reasonably expected that—

(i) A major portion of the proceeds of such issue of governmental obligations, including proceeds represented by repayments of principal and interest received by the governmental unit with respect to acquired program obligations, shall not be invested for more than a temporary period (within the meaning of section 103(d)(4)(A)), in acquired obligations (other than acquired program obligations) which produce a materially higher yield than the yield produced over the term of the issue by such governmental obligations, and

(ii)(a) The adjusted yield (computed in accordance with paragraph (a)(4) and (5) of this section) to be produced by acquired program obligations shall not exceed the adjusted yield (computed in accordance with paragraph (a)(4) and (5) of this section) to be produced by such issue of governmental obligations by more than one and one-half percentage points, or

(b) Where the difference in the adjusted yields described in subdivision (ii)(a) of this subparagraph are expected to exceed one and one-half percentage points, the amounts to be obtained as a result of the difference in such adjusted yields shall not exceed the amount necessary to pay expenses (including losses resulting from bad debts) reasonably expected to be incurred as a direct result of administering the program to be financed with the proceeds of such issue of governmental obligations, to the extent that such amounts are not payable with funds appropriated from other sources.

(4) *Examples.* The following examples illustrate governmental programs described in subparagraph (2) of this paragraph:

Example (1). State A issues obligations the proceeds of which are to be used to purchase certain home mortgage notes

Reg. § 13.4(b)(4)

24,988.2 (I.R.C.)   Reg. § 13.4(b)(4)   5-7-73

Purchasing costs		
Printing forms	$ 5,000	
Financial advisors	11,000	
Counsel fees	12,000	
Total		$ 28,000
Carrying costs		
Trustees fees		5,000
Total administrative costs		$ 33,000
Bond years (14,922 × 10 years)		$ 149,220
Interest receivable per $1,000 note per year		75
Total interest receivable		$11,191,500
Discount or premium		0
Minus adjustments		33,000
Net interest receivable		$11,158,500
Divide by product of bond years (149,220) multiplied by 10		1,492,200
Adjusted yield		7.478%

from commercial banks. The purpose of the governmental program is to encourage the construction of low income residential housing by createng a secondary market for mortgage notes and thereby increasing the availability of mortgage money for low income housing. The legislation provides that the adjusted yield produced by the mortgage notes to be acquired will not exceed the adjusted yield produced by such issue of obligations by more than one and one-half percentage points. Amounts received as interest and principal payments on the mortgage notes are to be used for one or more of the following purposes: (1) to service the debt on the governmental obligations, (2) to retire such obligations at their earliest possible date of redemption, (3) to purchase additional mortgage notes. The governmental program is one which is described in subparagraph (2) of this paragraph and the governmental obligations are not arbitrage bonds.

Example (2). State B issues obligations the proceeds of which are to be used to make loans directly to students and to purchase from commercial banks promissory notes made by students as the result of loans made to them by such banks. The legislation authorizing the student loan program provides that the purpose of the program is to enable financially disadvantaged students to continue their studies. The legislation also provides that purchases will be made from banks only where such banks agree that an amount at least equal to the purchase price will be devoted to new or additional student loans. It is reasonably expected that the difference in adjusted yields between the issue of governmental obligations by State B and the students' notes will be one and three-quarters percentage points. It is also reasonably expected that the amount necessary to pay the expenses (other than expenses taken into account in computing adjusted yield) enumerated in subparagraph (3)(ii)(b) of this paragraph, directly incurred as a result of administering State B's student loan program, such as, for example, losses resulting from bad debts, insurance costs, bookkeeping expenses, advertising expenses, credit reference checks, appraisals, title searches, general office overhead, service fees for collecting agents and various banks which administer the loans, and salaries of employees not paid from other sources, will not require a difference in adjusted yields in excess of one and one-half percentage points. The governmental program is one which is described in subparagraph (2) of this paragraph. Since, however, the difference in adjusted yields produced by the students' notes and the issue of State B obligations is reasonably expected to exceed one and one-half percentage points, and since State B cannot show that one and three-quarters percentage points is necessary to cover such expenses, the provisions of subparagraph (1) of this paragraph shall not apply to the issue of State B obligations. If, however, State B reasonably expected that one and three-quarters percentage points would be necessary to cover such expenses, the provisions of subparagraph (1) of this paragraph would apply and the governmental obligations would not be arbitrage bonds.

Example (3). Authority C issues obligations the proceeds of which are to be used to purchase land to be sold to veterans. The Governmental unit will receive purchase-money mortgage notes secured by mortgages on the land from the veterans in return for such land. The purpose of the program is to enable veterans to acquire land at reduced cost. The adjusted yield produced by the mortgage notes is not reasonably expected to exceed the adjusted yield produced by the issue of obligations issued by Authority C by more than one and one-half percentage points. Amounts received as interest and principal payments on the mortgage notes are to be used for one or more of the following purposes: (1) to pay the administrative costs directly related to the program, (2) to service the debt on the governmental obligations, (3) to retire such governmental obligations at their earliest possible call date, (4) to purchase additional land to be sold to veterans. The governmental program is one which is described in subparagraph (2) of this paragraph and the governmental obligations are not arbitrary bonds.

(e) *Effective date.* The provisions of this section will apply with respect to obligations issued after October 9, 1969, and before final regulations are promulgated.

Temporary Rules

T. D. 7158

Temporary regulations relating to income from certain aircraft and vessels. (Filed 12-30-71).

The following regulations relate to the application of section 861(e) of the Internal Revenue Code of 1954, as added by section 314 of the Revenue Act of 1971 (P.L. 92-178, 89 Stat. 497), to the election to treat income from certain aircraft and vessels as income from sources within the United States.

The regulations set forth herein are temporary and are designed to inform taxpayers of the time and manner of electing to treat income from certain aircraft and vessels as income from sources within the United States under subsection (e) of section 861 with respect to elections made after December 10, 1971, and before the issuance of regulations to be prescribed by the Commissioner and approved by the Secretary or his delegate.

In order to provide such temporary regulations under section 861(e) of the Internal Revenue Code of 1954, the following regulations are adopted:

O━━ [Sec. 861(e)] § 12.1 (T.D. 7158, filed 12-30-71.) **Election to treat income from certain aircraft and vessels as income from sources within the United States.**

(a) *In general.* Under section 861(e) a taxpayer owning certain aircraft or vessels manufactured in the United States who leases them to certain United States persons may elect to treat amounts includible in gross income with respect to such aircraft or vessels as income from sources within the United States. A vessel or aircraft with respect to which an election was made carries that election with it if it is transferred pursuant to a transaction described in section 861(e)(4).

(b) *Time and manner of making election.* The election by a taxpayer to treat income from certain aircraft and vessels as income from sources within the United States must be made not later than the time, including extensions thereof, prescribed by law for filing the income tax return for the first taxable year selected by the taxpayer for application of the rules of section 861(e) or March 31, 1972, whichever is later. The election shall be made by a statement attached to the taxpayer's return (or an amended return) for the first taxable year for which it is to be effective. The statement shall indicate that the election is made under section 861(e), shall set forth information to identify the vessel or aircraft to which it applies, and shall state that the electing taxpayer is the owner of the aircraft or vessel. In addition the statement shall represent:

(1) That the vessel is section 38 property or would be section 38 property but for section 48(a)(5),

(2) That the vessel or aircraft is leased to a United States person who is not a member of the same controlled group of corporations (as defined in section 1563) as the taxpayer and shall include the name and taxpayer identification number of the lessee, and

(3) That the vessel or aircraft was manufactured or constructed in the United States.

A copy of the statement of election shall be sent by the taxpayer to the Commissioner of Internal Revenue (Attention ACTS:A:P:), Washington, D.C. 20224.

(c) *Special rules concerning revocation of elections and permanent regulations.*—
(1) An election made in accordance with paragraph (b) of this section shall be binding unless consent to revoke is obtained from the Commissioner. An application to revoke the election will not be accepted before the promulgation of the permanent regulations under section 861(e).

(2) If the permanent regulations which are issued under section 861(e) require the furnishing of information additional to that which was furnished with the statement of election filed pursuant to paragraph (b) of this section the taxpayer must furnish such additional information in a statement addressed to the district director, or the director of the Internal Revenue service center, with whom the election was filed. This statement must clearly identify the election and the taxable year for which it was made.

* * * * * * * *

Reg. § 12.1 (c) (2)

T.D. 7161

Temporary rules relating to investment credit—public utility property elections. (Filed 2-16-71).

The following temporary regulations are adopted in order to provide rules for making elections under section 46 (e) of the Internal Revenue Code of 1954 as added by section 105 of the Revenue Act of 1971:

[Sec. 46(e)] § 12.3 (T.D. 7161, filed 2-16-72.) Investment credit—public utility property elections.

(a) *Elections*—(1) *In general.* Under section 46 (e), 3 elections may be made on or before March 9, 1972, with respect to section 46 (e) property (as defined in subparagraph (3) of this paragraph). An election made under the provisions of section 46 (e) shall be irrevocable.

(2) *Applicability of elections.* (i) Any election under section 46 (e) shall be made with respect to all of the taxpayer's property eligible for the election whether or not the taxpayer is regulated by more than one regulatory body.

(ii) (a) Paragraph (1) of section 46 (e) shall apply to all of the taxpayer's section 46 (e) property in the absence of an election under paragraph (2) or (3) of section 46 (e). If an election is made under paragraph (2) of section 46 (e), paragraph (1) of such section shall not apply to any of the taxpayer's section 46 (e) property.

(b) An election made under the last sentence of section 46 (e) (1) shall apply to that portion of the taxpayer's section 46 (e) property to which paragraph (1) of section 46 (e) applies and which is short supply property within the meaning of § 1.46-5(b)(2) of this chapter (Income Tax Regulations) as set forth in a notice of proposed rule making published in 37 F.R. 3526 on February 17, 1972.

(iii) If a taxpayer makes an election under paragraph (2) of section 46 (e), and makes no election under paragraph (3) of such section, the election under paragraph (2) of section 46 (e) shall apply to all of its section 46 (e) property.

(iv) If a taxpayer makes an election under paragraph (3) of section 46 (e), such election shall apply to all of the taxpayer's section 46 (e) property to which section 167 (l) (2) (C) applies. Paragraph (1) or (2) of section 46 (e) (as the case may be) shall apply to that portion of the taxpayer's section 46 (e) property which is not property to which section 167 (l) (2) (C) applies. Thus, for example, if a taxpayer makes an election under paragraph (2) of section 46 (e), and also makes an election under paragraph (3) of section 46 (e), paragraph (3) shall apply to all of the taxpayer's section 46 (e) property to which section 167 (l) (2) (C) applies and paragraph (2) shall apply to the remainder of the taxpayer's section 46 (e) property.

(3) *Section 46 (e) property.* "Section 46 (e) property" is section 38 property which is both property described in section 50 and is—

(i) Public utility property within the meaning of section 46 (c) (3) (B) (other than nonregulated communication property of the type described in the last sentence of 46 (c) (3) (B)), or

(ii) Property used predominantly in the trade or business of the furnishing or sale of (a) steam through a local distribution system or (b) the transportation of gas or steam by pipeline, if the rates for such furnishing or sale are established or approved by a governmental unit, agency, instrumentality, or commission described in section 46 (c) (3) (B).

(b) *Method of making elections.* A taxpayer may make the elections described in section 46 (e) by filing a statement, on or before March 9, 1972, with the district director or director of the internal revenue service center with whom the taxpayer ordinarily files its income tax return. For rules in the case of taxpayers filing consolidated returns, see § 1.1502-77 (a) of this chapter (Income Tax Regulations). Such statement shall contain the following information:

(1) The name, address, and taxpayer identification number of the taxpayer,

(2) The paragraph (or paragraphs) of section 46 (e) under which the taxpayer is making the election,

(3) If an election is made under the last sentence of section 46 (e) (1), the name and address of all regulatory bodies which have jurisdiction over the taxpayer with respect to the section 46 (e) property covered by such election and a statement setting forth the type of the public utility activity described in section 46 (e) (5) (B) in which the taxpayer engages, and

(4) If an election is made under paragraph (3) of section 46 (e), a statement indicating whether an election has been made by the taxpayer under section 167 (l) (4) (A).

Temporary Rules (I.R.C.) 24,998.5

Temporary regulations relating to transfer to a DISC of assets of export trade corporation.

In order to clarify the applicability of section 505 of the Revenue Act of 1971 (85 Stat. 551) and § 12.5 of the Income Tax Regulations (26 CFR Part 12) to certain transactions involving the transfer to a DISC of stock and assets of an export trade corporation, paragraphs (a) and (b) of § 12.5 are hereby amended to read as follows:

○→ **§ 12.5** (T.D. 7225, filed 12-4-72; amended by T.D. 7264, filed 3-7-73.) **Transfer to a DISC of assets of export trade corporation.**

(a) *In general.* (1) Section 505 of the Revenue Act of 1971 (85 Stat. 551) permits, subject to certain adjustments, certain tax-free transactions involving a transfer of property by an export trade corporation (as defined in section 971) to a DISC (as defined in section 992(a)).

(2) For purposes of this section, all statutory references are to the Internal Revenue Code of 1954 except that references to section 505 are to the Revenue Act of 1971. All terms used in this section shall have the same meaning as when used in such Code.

(b) *Direct, indirect, and other transfers.* (1) Under section 505(b)(1), if during a taxable year of an export trade corporation beginning before January 1, 1976, such export trade corporation without receiving consideration directly transfers property to a DISC, if all of the outstanding stock of each of such corporations is owned by a common parent, and if certain other conditions are met, then, among other consequences enumerated in section 505, notwithstanding section 367 or any other provision of chapter 1 of the Code, no gain or loss shall be recognized by, and no constructive dividend shall be includible in the gross income of the export trade corporation, the parent, or the DISC by reason of such transaction. If, instead of a direct transfer from the export trade corporation to the DISC, the parties enter into an indirect transfer in which the property is distributed by the export trade corporation to the parent without receiving consideration and immediately thereafter is transferred by the parent to the DISC, then for purposes of section 505(b) the transaction will be treated as a direct transfer by the export trade corporation to the DISC, but only if—

(i) It is shown to the satisfaction of the Commissioner or his delegate that such indirect transfer of the property was carried out for bona fide business reasons, and

(ii) Each United States person (as defined in section 7701(a)(30)) which is a party to the indirect transfer enters into a closing agreement under section 7121 which provides that each of the tax consequences enumerated in section 505(b) shall apply.

(2) Subparagraph (1) of this paragraph shall apply also to—

(i) Any other indirect transfer of property of the export trade corporation to the DISC if section 505 would be applicable to a direct transfer of such property by the export trade corporation to the DISC, and

(ii) Any transaction as a part of which the stock of the export trade corporation is transferred to the DISC prior to a direct transfer of the property of the export trade corporation to the DISC, if all of the parties to such indirect transfer or transaction meet the 100 percent stock ownership requirement set forth in paragraph (c) of this section.

(3) A transaction described in subparagraph (2) of this paragraph includes any transaction in which the common parent or its wholly-owned subsidiary acquires the stock of the export trade corporation without any consideration paid directly or indirectly to the export trade corporation. Thus, except as otherwise provided in this subparagraph, no gain or loss is recognized by, and no constructive dividend is includible under section 301 in the gross income of, the export trade corporation, the common parent, or the DISC by reason of such transaction. If, in exchange for such transfer of stock, a party, other than the export trade corporation, receives consideration and realizes gain, then subparagraph (1) of this paragraph and section 505 do not apply with respect to the amount realized by such party (determined without regard to section 482) and thus do not prevent recognition of such gain and, for example, the application of section 951 to the parent of such party with respect to such gain.

(c) *Special rule for stock ownership.* (1) Under section 505(b)(3), the Secretary or his delegate may prescribe rules for the application of the provisions of section 505 (b)(1) where the stock of the DISC or export trade corporation, or both, is not owned in the manner prescribed in section 505 (b)(1).

(2) Section 505(b) shall apply in any case in which 100 percent of the outstanding stock of the DISC and the export trade corporation, is owned by the common parent either directly or indirectly. For purposes of this section, if a corporation owns 100 percent of the outstanding stock of a subsidiary, such corporation shall be considered to own indirectly any stock directly or indirectly owned by the subsidiary.

(3) If (without regard to this subparagraph) the 100 percent stock ownership requirement in subparagraph (2) of this paragraph is not met with respect to a corporation solely because a person holds the minimum amount of stock in a corporation required by law (such as, for example, qualifying shares of a director), then such 100 percent of stock ownership requirement shall nevertheless be considered to be met.

(d) *Additional transfers to meet untaxed subpart F income requirement.* (1) Section 505(b)(1) applies only if the adjusted basis to the export trade corporation of the property transferred to the DISC is not less than the amount of the export trade corporation's untaxed subpart F income (as defined in section 505(b)(2)) at the time of such transfer. For purposes of computing the amount of untaxed subpart F income at the time of the transfer, the export trade corporation's taxable year shall be treated as ending upon such transfer.

(2) At the time of the initial transfer to the DISC, any reasonable method may be used to estimate the amount of untaxed subpart F income so long as the adjusted bases of all the property transferred to the DISC are not less than—

Reg. § 12.5(d)(2)

(i) The amount of untaxed subpart F income as of the beginning of the export trade corporation's taxable year in which the transfer is made plus

(ii) 75 percent of the excess of the untaxed subpart F income at the time of the transfer over the amount described in subdivision (i) of this subparagraph.

(3) Section 505 shall apply to both the initial transfer and any transfer of property by the export trade corporation to the DISC within two and one-half months after the close of the export trade corporation's taxable year (determined without regard to the last sentence of subparagraph (1) of this paragraph) in which the initial transfer of the property is made to the DISC, but only to the extent that the sum of the adjusted bases of all property additionally transferred does not exceed an amount equal to (i) the actual amount of untaxed subpart F income at the time of the transfer minus (ii) the adjusted bases of the property initially transferred under subparagraph (2) of this paragraph.

(e) *Foreign income taxes paid by export trade corporation.* Under section 505(b)(1)(H), any foreign income taxes which would have been deemed under section 902 to have been paid by the parent if the transfer had been made to the parent shall be treated as foreign income taxes paid by the DISC. If foreign law imposes an additional tax on the export trade corporation upon its transfer of property to the DISC, then such additional tax will be treated under section 505(b)(1)(H) as paid by the DISC only if such tax is imposed with respect to the earnings of the export trade corporation. If, instead, the foreign tax is imposed upon the corporation receiving (or constructively receiving) a dividend from the export trade corporation, then section 505(b)(1)(H) shall not apply even though the export trade corporation withheld and paid such tax. If the provisions of section 901 apply, a foreign tax credit shall be allowable to the corporation receiving or constructively receiving the dividend.

T.D. 7271

Temporary regulations relating to elections with respect to net leases of real property. (T.D. 7271, filed 4-11-73.)

○━ [Sec. 57,163(d)] § 12.8 (T.D. 7271, filed 4-11-73.) **Elections with respect to net leases of real property**

(a) *In general.* The elections described in this section are available for determining whether real property held by the taxpayer is subject to a net lease for purposes of section 57 (relating to items of tax preference for purposes of the minimum tax for tax preferences) or 163(d) (relating to limitation on interest on investment indebtedness). Under sections 57 (c)(1)(A) and 163(d)(4)(A)(i), property will be considered to be subject to a net lease for a taxable year where the sum of the deductions of the lessor with respect to the property for the taxable year allowable solely by reason of section 162 (other than rents and reimbursed amounts with respect to the property) is less than 15 percent of the gross income from rents produced by the property (hereinafter referred to as the "expense test"). Under sections 57(c)(2) and 163(d)(7)(A), where a parcel of real property of the taxpayer is leased under two or more leases, the taxpayer may elect to apply the expense test set forth in sections 57(c)(1)(A) and 163(d)(4)(A)(i) by treating all leased portions of such property as subject to a single lease. Under sections 57(c)(3) and 163(d)(7)(B), at the election of the taxpayer, the expense test set forth in sections 57(c)(1)(A) and 163(d)(4)(A)(i) shall not apply with respect to real property of the taxpayer which has been in use for more than 5 years.

(b) *Election with respect to multiple leases of single parcel of real property.* If a parcel of real property of the taxpayer is leased under two or more leases, the expense test referred to in paragraph (a) of this section shall, at the election of the taxpayer, be applied by treating all leased portions of such property as subject to a single lease. For purposes of this paragraph, the term "parcel of real property" includes adjacent properties each of which is subject to lease.

(c) *Election with respect to real property in use for more than five years.* At the election of the taxpayer, the expense test referred to in paragraph (a) of this section shall not apply with respect to real property of the taxpayer which has been in use for more than five years. For this purpose, real property is in use only during the period that such property is both owned and used for commercial purposes by the taxpayer. If an improvement to the property was made during the time such property was owned by the taxpayer, and if, as a result of such improvement, the adjusted basis of such property was increased by 50 percent or more, use of such property for commercial purposes shall be deemed to have commenced for purposes of this paragraph as of the date such improvement was completed. An election under this paragraph shall apply to all real property of the taxpayer which has been in use for more than five years.

(d) *Procedure for making election*—(1) *Time and scope of election.* An election under paragraph (b) or (c) of this section shall be made for each taxable year to which such election is to apply. The election must be made before the later of (i) the time prescribed by law for filing the taxpayer's return for the taxable year for which the election is made (determined with regard to any extension of time) or (ii) August 31, 1973, but the election may not be made after the expiration of the time prescribed by law for the filing of a claim for credit or refund of tax with respect to the taxable year for which the election is to apply.

(2) *Manner of making election.* Except as provided in the following sentence, an election by the taxpayer with respect to a taxable year shall be made by a statement containing the information described in subparagraph (3) of this paragraph which is—

(i) Attached to the taxpayer's return or amended return for such taxable year,

(ii) Attached to a timely filed claim by the taxpayer for credit or refund of tax for such taxable year, or

(iii) Filed by the taxpayer with the director of the Internal Revenue Service Center where the return for such taxable year was filed.

In the case of a taxable year ending before July 1, 1973, no formal statement of election is necessary if the taxpayer's return took into account an election under paragraph (b) or (c) of this section; the taxpayer will be considered to have made an election in accordance with the manner in which leases with respect to parcels of real property described in paragraph (b) of this section, or leases of property which has been in use for more than 5 years as described in paragraph (c) of this paragraph, are treated in the return.

(3) *Statement.* The statement described in subparagraph (2) of this paragraph shall contain the following information:

(i) The name, address, and taxpayer identification number of the taxpayer;

(ii) The taxable year to which the election is to apply if the statement is not attached to the return or a claim for credit or refund;

(iii) A description of any leases which are to be treated as a single lease; and

(iv) A description of any real property in use for more than five years to which the expense test is not to apply.

(4) *Revocation of election.* An election made pursuant to this paragraph may be revoked within the time prescribed in subparagraph (1) of this paragraph for making an election and may not be revoked thereafter. Any such revocation shall be made in the manner prescribed by subparagraph (2) of this paragraph for the making of an election.

(e) *Election by members of partnership.* Under section 703(b) (as amended by section 304(c) of the Revenue Act of 1971), any election under section 57(c) or

Reg. § 12.8(e)

24,998.14 *(I.R.C.)*

163(d)(7) with respect to property held by a partnership shall be made by each partner separately, rather than by the partnership. If an election made by a taxpayer under paragraph (b) of this section applies in whole or in part to property held by a partnership, the taxpayer shall, in applying the expense test referred to in paragraph (a) of this section, take into account his distributive share of the deductions of the partnership with respect to the property for the taxable year allowable solely by reason of section 162 (other than rents and reimbursed amounts with respect to the property) and also his distributive share of the partnership's rental income from such property for the taxable year.

T.D. 7308

Temporary regulations relating to activities not engaged in for profit. (Filed 3-14-74.)

The regulations set forth herein are temporary and are designed to provide rules governing the manner and time for making an election to postpone a determination of whether an activity is engaged in for profit. The regulations are effective until the issuance of final regulations to be prescribed by the Commissioner and approved by the Secretary or his delegate.

In order to provide such temporary regulations under section 183(e) of the Internal Revenue Code of 1954, the following regulations are adopted:

○━ [Sec. 183(e)] § 12.9 (T.D. 7308, filed 3-14-74.) **Election to postpone determination with respect to the presumption described in section 183(d).**

(a) *In general.* An individual, electing small business corporation, trust or estate may elect in accordance with the rules set forth in this section to postpone a determination whether the presumption described in section 183(d) applies with respect to any activity in which the taxpayer engages until after the close of the fourth taxable year (sixth taxable year, in the case of an activity described in § 1.183-1(c)(3)) following the taxable year in which the taxpayer first engages in such activity. The election must be made in accordance with the applicable requirements of paragraphs (b), (c) and (d) of this section. Except as otherwise provided in paragraphs (c) and (e) of this section, an election made pursuant to this section shall be binding for the first taxable year in which the taxpayer first engages in the activity and for all subsequent taxable years in the five (or seven) year period referred to in the first sentence of this paragraph. For purposes of this section, a taxpayer shall be treated as not having engaged in an activity during any taxable year beginning before January 1, 1970.

(b) *Period to which an election applies.* An individual, trust, estate, or small business corporation may make the election. The five year presumption period (seven year presumption period in the case of an activity described in § 1.183-1(c)(3)) to which the election shall apply shall be the five (or seven) consecutive taxable years of such taxpayer beginning with the taxable year in which such taxpayer first engages in the activity. For purposes of this section, a taxpayer who engages in an activity as a partner, engages in it in each of his taxable years with or within which ends a partnership year during which the activity was carried on by the partnership.

(c) *Time for making an election.* A taxpayer who is an individual, trust, estate or small business corporation may make the election provided in section 183(e) by filing the statement and consents required by paragraph (d) of this section within—

(1) 3 years after the due date of such taxpayer's return (determined without extensions) for the taxable year in which such taxpayer first engages in the activity, but not later than

(2) 60 days after such taxpayer receives a written notice (if any) from a district director that the district director proposes to disallow deductions attributable to an activity not engaged in for profit under section 183.

The provisions of subdivision (2) of this paragraph shall in no event be construed to extend the period described in subdivision (1) of this paragraph for making such election. Notwithstanding the time periods prescribed in subdivisions (1) and (2) of this paragraph, if no election has been made before a suit or proceeding described in section 7422(a) is maintained or a petition is filed in the Tax Court for a redetermination of a deficiency for any taxable year within the presumption period to which the election would apply, no election may be made except with the consent of the Commissioner which will not be given unless no appreciable delay in the suit or proceeding will be caused.

(d) *Manner of making election.* (1) The election shall be made by the individual, trust, estate, or electing small business corporation, as the case may be, engaged in the activity, by filing a statement which sets forth the following information—

(i) The name, address, and taxpayer identification number of such taxpayer, and, if applicable, of the partnership in which he engages in the activity,

(ii) A declaration stating that the taxpayer elects to postpone a determination as to whether the presumption described in section 183(d) applies until after the close of the taxpayer's fourth taxable year (sixth taxable year, in the case of an activity described in § 1.183-1(c)(3)) following the taxable year in which the taxpayer first engaged in such activity and identifying that first such taxable year, and,

(iii) A description of each activity (as defined in § 1.183-1(d)(1)) with respect to which the election is being made.

(2) For an election to be effective, there must be attached to the statement properly executed consents, in the form prescribed by the Commissioner, extending the period prescribed by section 6501 for the assessment of any tax to a date which is not earlier than 18 months after the due date of the return (determined without extensions) for the final year in the presumption period to which the election applies, as follows:

(i) Consents for each of the taxpayer's taxable years in the presumption period to which the election applies,

(ii) If the election is made by an electing small business corporation, a consent of each person who is a shareholder during any taxable year to which the election applies, for each of such shareholder's taxable years with or within which end each of the corporation's taxable years in the presumption period,

(iii) If a taxpayer referred to in subdivision (2)(i) of this paragraph or shareholder referred to in subdivision (2)(ii) of this paragraph is married at the time of the

Reg. § 12.9(d)(2)

24,998.16 *(I.R.C.)*   Reg. § 12.9(d)(2)

election, in the case of his present spouse, a consent for each of such spouse's taxable years which correspond to the taxable years (other than prior years of the shareholder during no part of which he was a shareholder) for which consents are required by subdivision (2)(i) or (ii) of this paragraph as the case may be. Such consents shall not be construed to shorten the period described in section 6501 for any taxable year within the presumption period to which the election applies.

(3) The statement, with the required consent attached, shall be filed—

(i) With the service center at which the taxpayer making the election is required to file his return, or

(ii) If the taxpayer is notified by a district director that, pursuant to section 183 he is proposing to disallow deductions with respect to an activity not engaged in for profit, with such district director.

(e) *Subsequent invalidations.* If, after a timely election has been made, but still within the presumption period, a suit or proceeding (as described in section 7422(a)) is maintained by the electing taxpayer, a shareholder referred to in subdivision (ii) of paragraph (d)(2) of this section, or spouse referred to in subdivision (iii) of paragraph (d)(2) of this section for any taxable year for which a consent is required by this section and the taxpayer, shareholder, or spouse has not been issued a notice of deficiency (as described in section 6212(a)) with respect to such taxable year, such election shall not be effective to postpone the determination whether the presumption applies, for such taxable year, but the consents extending the statute of limitations filed with the election shall not thereby be invalidated. The immediately preceding sentence shall not apply to a suit or proceeding maintained by the spouse of an electing taxpayer for a taxable year for which such spouse has filed a separate return, or a suit or proceeding maintained by a shareholder for a taxable year in which he was not such a shareholder. An election by an individual taxpayer or electing small business corporation, shall be subsequently invalidated for all years in the presumption period to which it had applied if—

(1) The electing taxpayer or shareholder taxpayer files a joint return for one of the first three (five, in the case of an activity described in § 1.183-1(c)(3)) taxable years in such presumption period, and

(2) The spouse with whom he files such joint return has not previously executed a consent described in subdivision (iii) of paragraph (d)(2) of this section, and

(3) Within one year after the filing of such joint return (or, if later, 90 days after March 14, 1974), such spouse has not filed a consent described in paragraph (d)(2) of this section.

An election by an electing small business corporation shall be invalidated for all years in the presumption period to which it applies if a person who was not a shareholder on the date of election becomes a shareholder during the first three (or five) years of the presumption period to which the election applies and does not, within 90 days after the date on which he becomes a shareholder (or, if later, 90 days after March 14, 1974), file a consent required by paragraph (d)(2) of this section. Invalidation of the election by operation of this paragraph will in no case affect the validity of the consents filed with such election.

(f) *Extension of time for filing election in hardship cases.* The Commissioner may, upon application by a taxpayer, consent to an extension of time prescribed in this section for making an election if he finds that such an extension would be justified by hardship occurred by reason of the time at which this section is published. The burden will be on the taxpayer to establish that under the relevant facts the Commissioner should so consent.

Because of the need for immediate guidance with respect to the provisions contained in this Treasury decision, it is found impracticable to issue it with notice and public procedure thereon under subsection (b) of section 553 of title 5 of the United States Code or subject to the effective date limitation of subsection (d) of that section.

T.D. 7325; 7546

Temporary regulations relating to disclosure to the Pension Benefit Guaranty Corporation of certain information with respect to deferred compensation plans. (T.D. 7325, filed 9-20-74; redesignated and amended by T.D. 7546, filed 5-3-78.)

Supplementary Information: Background

Section 1022(h) of ERISA added section 6103(g) to the Internal Revenue Code relating to disclosure of information with respect to deferred compensation plans, and temporary regulations under section 6103(g) were published in 1974 and 1975. Section 1202 of the Tax Reform Act of 1976 (Pub. L. 94-455) amended section 6103, effective January 1, 1977. As amended, section 6103(*l*)(2) now provides the disclosure authority formerly provided by section 6103(g)(1).

These amendments to the temporary regulations conform the regulations to the amendments to section 6103 made by Section 1202 of the Tax Reform Act of 1976 and provide additional rules regarding disclosures of returns and return information to and by officers and employees of the Department of Labor, the Pension Benefit Guaranty Corporation, and the Department of Justice for purposes of administering titles I and IV of ERISA.

In order to prescribe temporary regulations, which shall remain in force and effect until superseded by permanent regulations, relating to disclosure to the Pension Benefit Guaranty Corporation of certain information with respect to deferred compensation plans, the following regulations are hereby adopted:

○— [Sec. 6103(*l*)(2)] § 420.6103(*l*)(2)-1 (Originally § 420.6103(g)-1 as promulgated by T.D. 7325, filed 9-20-74; redesignated and amended by T.D. 7546, filed 5-3-78.) **Disclosure of returns and return information to Pension Benefit Guaranty Corporation for purposes of research and studies.**

(a) *General rule.* Pursuant to the provisions of section 6103(*l*)(2) of the Internal Revenue Code of 1954 and subject to the requirements of paragraph (b) of this section, officers and employees of the Internal Revenue Service may disclose returns and return information (as defined by section 6103(b)) to officers and employees of the Pension Benefit Guaranty Corporation for purposes of, but only to the extent necessary in, conducting research and studies authorized by title IV of the Employee Retirement Income Security Act of 1974.

(b) *Procedures and restrictions.* Disclosure of returns or return information by officers or employees of the Internal Revenue Service as provided by paragraph (a) of this section will be made only upon written request to the Commissioner of Internal Revenue by the Executor Director of the Pension Benefit Guaranty Corporation describing the returns or return information to be disclosed, the taxable period or date to which such returns or return information relates, and the purpose for which the returns or return information is needed in the administration of title IV of the Employee Retirement Income Security Act of 1974, and designating by title the officers and employees of such corporation to whom such disclosure is authorized. No such officer or employee to whom returns or return information is disclosed pursuant to the provisions of paragraph (a) shall disclose such returns or return information to any person, other than the taxpayer by whom the return was made or to whom the return information relates or other officers or employees of such corporation whose duties or responsibilities require such disclosure for a purpose described in paragraph (a), except in a form which cannot be associated with, or otherwise identify, directly or indirectly, a particular taxpayer.

T.D. 7371; 7546

Temporary regulations relating to disclosure to Department of Labor under section 6103(*l*)(2) (formerly 6103(g) with respect to the Employee Retirement Income Security Act of 1974. (T.D. 7331, filed 10-29-74; redesignated and amended by T.D. 7546, filed 5-3-78.)

In order to prescribe temporary regulations, which shall remain in force and effect until superseded by permanent regulations, relating to disclosure to the Department of Labor of certain information with respect to deferred compensation plans, the following regulations are hereby adopted and inserted immediately after § 420.6103 (g)-1 [redesignated § 420.6103 (*l*)(2)-1] of the Temporary Regulations on Procedure and Administration under the Employee Retirement Income Security Act of 1974:

○— [Sec. 6103(*l*)(2)] § 420.6103(*l*)(2)-2 (Originally § 420.6103(g)-2 as promulgated by T.D. 7331, filed 10-29-74; redesignated and amended by T.D. 7546, filed 5-3-78.) **Disclosure of returns and return information to Department of Labor for purposes of research and studies.**

(a) *General rule.* Pursuant to the provisions of section 6103(*l*)(2) of the Internal Revenue Code of 1954 and subject to the requirements of paragraph (b) of this section, officers or employees of the Internal Revenue Service may disclose returns and return information (as defined by section 6103(b)) to officers and employees of the Department of Labor for purposes of, but only to the extent necessary in, conducting research and studies authorized by section 513 of the Employee Retirement Income Security Act of 1974.

(b) *Procedures and restrictions.* Disclosure of returns or return information by officers or employees of the Internal Revenue Service as provided by paragraph (a) of this section will be made only upon written request to the Commissioner of Internal Revenue by the Administrator of the Pension and Welfare Benefit Programs of the Department of Labor describing the returns or return information to be disclosed, the taxable period or date to which such returns or return information relates, and the purpose for which the returns or return information is needed in the admin-

§ 420.6103(*l*)(2)-2(b)

24,998.18 (I.R.C.)   Reg. § 420.6103(*l*)(2)-2(b)

istration of title I of the Employee Retirement Income Security Act of 1974, and designating by title the officers and employees of such department to whom such disclosure is authorized. No such officer or employee to whom returns or return information is disclosed pursuant to the provisions of paragraph (a) shall disclose such returns or return information to any person, other than the taxpayer by whom the return was made or to whom the return was made or to whom the return information relates or other officers of employees of such department whose duties or responsibilities require such disclosure for a purpose described in paragraph (a), except in a form which cannot be associated with, or otherwise identify, directly or indirectly, a particular taxpayer.

T.D. 7371; 7546

Temporary regulations relating to disclosure to the Department of Labor and the Pension Benefit Guaranty Corporation of information relating to certain determination letters. (T.D. 7371, filed 7-21-75; redesignated and amended by T.D. 7546, filed 5-3-78.)

In order to prescribe temporary regulations relating to disclosure to the Department of Labor and the Pension Benefit Guaranty Corporation of information relating to certain determination letters, the following temporary regulations are hereby adopted and inserted immediately after § 420.6103(g)-2 [redesignated § 420.6103(*l*)(2)-2] of the Temporary Regulations on Procedure and Administration under the Employee Retirement Income Security Act of 1974:

0—☞ [Sec. 6103(*l*)(2)] § 420.6103(*l*)(2)-3 (Originally § 420.6103(g)-3 as promulgated by T.D. 7371, filed 7-21-75; redesignated and amended by T.D. 7546, filed 5-3-78.) **Disclosure to Department of Labor and Pension Benefit Guaranty Corporation of certain returns and return information.**

(a) *Disclosures following general requests.* Pursuant to the provisions of section 6103 (*l*) (2) and subject to the requirements of this paragraph, officers or employees of the Internal Revenue Service may disclose the following returns and return information (as defined by section 6103 (b)) to officers and employees of the Department of Labor or the Pension Benefit Guaranty Corporation for purposes of, but only to the extent necessary in, the administration of title I or IV of the Employee Retirement Income Security Act of 1974 (hereinafter referred to in this section as the Act)—

(1) Notification of receipt by the Service of an application by a particular taxpayer for a determination of whether a pension, profit-sharing, or stock bonus plan, a trust which is a part of such a plan, or an annuity or bond purchase plan meets the applicable requirements of part I of subchapter D of chapter 1 of the Code;

(2) Notification that a particular application described in subparagraph (1) of this paragraph alleges that certain employees may be excluded from participation by reason of section 410(b)(2)(A) and (B) for the purpose of obtaining the finding necessary for the application of such section;

(3) An application by a particular taxpayer for a determination of whether a pension, profit-sharing, or stock bonus plan, or an annuity or bond purchase plan meets the applicable requirements of part I of subchapter D of chapter 1 of the Code with respect to a termination or proposed termination of the plan or to a partial termination or proposed partial termination of the plan, and any statement filed as provided by section 6058(b);

(4) Notification that the Service has determined that a plan or trust described in subparagraph (1) or (3) of this paragraph meets or does not meet the applicable requirements of part I of subchapter D of chapter 1 of the Code and has issued a determination letter to such effect to a particular taxpayer or that an application for such a determination has been withdrawn by the taxpayer;

(5) If the Department of Labor or the Pension Benefit Guaranty Corporation has commented on an application upon which a determination letter described in subparagraph (4) of this paragraph has been issued, a copy of the letter or document issued to the applicant;

(6) Notification to a particular taxpayer that the Service intends to disqualify a pension, profit-sharing, or stock bonus plan, a trust which is a part of such plan, or an annuity or bond purchase plan because such plan or trust does not meet the requirements of section 410(a) or 411 as of the date that such notification is issued;

(7) Notification required by section 3002 (a) of the Act of the commencement of any proceeding to determine whether a particular pension, profit-sharing, or stock bonus plan, a trust which is a part of such plan, or an annuity or bond purchase plan meets the requirements of section 410 (a) or 411;

(8) Prior to issuance of a notice of deficiency to a particular taxpayer under section 6212, notification that the Service has determined that a deficiency exists under section 6211 with respect to the tax imposed by section 4971(a) or (b) on such taxpayer, except that if the Service determines that the collection of such tax is in jeopardy within the meaning of section 6861(a), such notification will be disclosed only after issuance of the notice of deficiency or jeopardy assessment;

(9) Notification that the Service has waived the tax imposed by section 4971(b) on a particular taxpayer;

(10) Prior to issuance of a notice of deficiency to a particular taxpayer under section 6212, notification that a deficiency exists under section 6211 with respect to the tax imposed by section 4975 (a) or (b) on such taxpayer, except that if the Service determines that the collection of such tax is in jeopardy within the meaning of section 6861(a), such notification will be disclosed only after issuance of the notice of deficiency or jeopardy assessment;

(11) Notification that the Service has waived the tax imposed by section 4975(b) on a particular taxpayer;

(12) Notification of applicability of section 4975 to a particular pension, profit-sharing, or stock bonus plan, a trust which is a part of such plan, or an annuity or stock purchase plan engaged in prohibited transactions within the meaning of section 4975 (c);

(13) Notification to a plan administrator that the Service has determined that a pension, profit-sharing, stock bonus, annuity, or stock purchase plan no longer meets the requirements of section 401(a) or 404(a)(2);

(14) Notification that the Service has determined that there has been a termination or partial termination of a particular pension, profit-sharing, stock bonus, annuity, or stock purchase plan within the meaning of section 411(d)(3);

(15) Notification of the occurrence of an event (other than an event described in subparagraph (13), (14), or (18) of this paragraph) which the Service has determined to indicate that a particular pension, profit-sharing, stock bonus, annuity, or stock purchase plan may not be sound under section 4043 (c) (2) of the Act;

(16) Notification that the Service has received and responded to a request on behalf of a particular pension, profit-sharing, or stock bonus plan, a trust which is a part of such plan, or an annuity or stock purchase plan for an extension of time for filing an annual return by such plan or trust;

(17) Notification that the Service has received and responded to a request on behalf of a particular pension, profit-sharing, or stock bonus plan, a trust which is a part of such plan, or an annuity or stock purchase plan to change the annual accounting period of such plan or trust;

(18) Notification that the Service has determined that a particular plan does not meet the requirements of section 412 without regard to whether such plan is one described in section 4021(a)(2) of the Act;

(19) Notification of the results of an investigation by the Service requested by the Department of Labor or the Pension Benefit Guaranty Corporation, or both, with respect to whether the tax described in section 4971 should be imposed on any employer named in such request or whether the tax imposed by section 4975 should be paid by any person named in the request;

(20) Notification of receipt by the Service of an application by a particular taxpayer for exemption under section 4975(c)(2) or of initiation by the Service of an administrative proceeding for such exemption; and

(21) Notification of receipt by the Service of an application by or on behalf of a particular taxpayer for a waiver or variance of the minimum funding standard under section 303 of the Act or section 412 (d).

Return information disclosed under this paragraph includes the taxpayer identity information (as defined in section 6103(b)(6)) of the plan or trust, the name and address of the sponsor and administrator of the plan or trustee of the trust, and the name and address of the person authorized to represent the plan or trust before the Internal Revenue Service. Disclosure of returns or return information as provided by this paragraph will be made only following receipt by the Commissioner of Internal Revenue of an annual written request for such disclosure by the Administrator of Pension and Benefit Welfare Programs of the Department of Labor or the Executive Director of the Pension Benefit Guaranty Corporation describing the categories of returns or return information to be disclosed by the Service and the particular purpose for which the returns or return information is needed in the administration of title I or IV of the Act, and designating by title the officers and employees of the Department of Labor or such corporation to whom such disclosure is authorized.

(b) *Additional returns and return information subject to disclosure*—(1) *Returns and return information relating to automatic notification.* Subject to the requirements of subparagraph (3) of this paragraph, officers or employees of the Internal Revenue Service may disclose to officers and employees of the Department of Labor or the Pension Benefit Guaranty Corporation for purposes of, but only to the extent necessary in, the administration of title I or IV of the Act additional returns and return information to any item described in paragraph (a) of this section.

(2) *Other returns and return information.* Subject to the requirements of subparagraph (3) of this paragraph, officers or employees of the Internal Revenue Service may disclose to officers and employees of the Department of Labor or the Pension Benefit Guaranty Corporation returns and return information (other than returns and return information disclosed as provided by pargaraph (a) of this section or § 420.6103 (*l*)(2)-1 or § 420.6103(*l*)(2)-2) for purposes of, but only to the extent necessary in, administration of title I or IV of the Act.

(3) *Procedures.* Disclosure of returns or return infomation by officers or employees of the Internal Revenue Service as provided by this paragraph will be made only upon written request to the Commissioner of Internal Revenue by the Administrator of Pension and Welfare Benefit Programs of the Department of Labor or his delegate or the Executive Director of the Pension Benefit Guaranty Corporation or his delegate identifying the particular taxpayer by whom such return was made or to whom such return information relates, describing the particular returns or return information to be disclosed, stating the purpose for which the returns or return information is needed in the administration of title I or IV of the Act, and designating by name and title the officers and employees of such department or corporation to whom such disclosure is authorized.

(c) *Disclosure and use of returns and return information by officers and employees of Department of Labor, Pension Benefit Guaranty Corporation, and Department of Justice*—(1) *Use by officers and employees of Department of Labor and Pension Benefit Guaranty Corporation.* Returns and return information disclosed to officers and employees of the Department of Labor and the Pension Benefit Guaranty Corporation as provided by this section may be used by such officers and employees for purposes of, but only to the extent necessary in, administration of any provision of title I or IV of the Act, including preparation for any

§ 420.6103(l)(2)-3(c)(1)

24,998.18-B (I.R.C.) Reg. § 420.6103(l)(2)-3(c)(1)

administrative or judicial proceeding (or investigation which may result in such a proceeding) authorized by, or described in, title I or IV of the Act.

(2) *Disclosure by officers and employees of Department of Labor and Pension Benefit Guaranty Corporation to, and use by, other persons, including officers and employees of the Department of Justice.* (i) Returns and return information disclosed to officers and employees of the Department of Labor or the Pension Benefit Guaranty Corporation as provided by this section may be disclosed by such officers and employees to attorneys of the Department of Justice (including United States attorneys) personally and directly engaged in, and for their necessary use in, preparation for any civil or criminal judicial proceeding (or for their necessary use in an investigation which may result in such a proceeding) authorized by, or described in, title I or IV of the Act.

(ii) Returns and return information disclosed to officers and employees of the Department of Labor and the Pension Benefit Guaranty Corporation and to attorneys of the Department of Justice as provided by this section may be disclosed by such officers, employees, and attorneys to other persons, including but not limited to, persons described in subparagraph (2)(iii) of this paragraph, but only to the extent necessary in connection with administration of the provisions of title I or IV of the Act, including proper preparation for a proceeding (or investigation) described in subparagraph (1) or (2)(i). Such disclosures may include, but are not limited to, disclosures where necessary—

(A) To properly obtain the services of persons having special knowledge or technical skills;

(B) To properly interview, consult, depose, or interrogate or otherwise obtain relevant information from, the taxpayer to whom such return or return information relates (or the legal representative of such taxpayer) or any witness who may be called to give evidence in the proceeding; or

(C) To properly conduct negotiations concerning, or obtain authorization for, settlement or disposition of the proceeding, in whole or in part, or stipulations of fact in connection with the proceeding.

Disclosure of a return or return information to a person other than the taxpayer to whom such return or return information relates (or the legal representative of such taxpayer) to properly prepare for a proceeding (or to properly conduct an investigation) described in this subparagraph should be made, however, only if such praparation (or investigation) cannot otherwise properly be accomplished without making such disclosure.

(iii) Among those persons to whom returns and return information may be disclosed by officers and employees of the Department of Labor and the Pension Benefit Guaranty Corporation and by attorneys of the Department of Justice as provided by subparagraph (2)(ii) of this paragraph are:

(A) Other officers and employees (including attorneys) of the Department of Labor, the Pension Benefit Guaranty Corporation, and the Department of Justice;

(B) Officers and employees of another Federal agency (as defined in section 6103 (b)(9)) working under the direction and control of such officers and employees of the Department of Labor, the Pension Benefit Guaranty Corporation, or the Department of Justice; and

(C) Court reporters.

Disclosure of returns or return information to other persons by officers and employees of the Department of Labor or the Pension Benefit Guaranty Corporation as provided by subparagraph (2)(ii) of this paragraph for purposes of conducting research, surveys, studies, and publications referred to in section 513(a), or authorized by title IV, of the Act shall be restricted, however, to disclosure to other officers and employees of such department or corporation to whom such disclosure is necessary in connection with such conduct or to the taxpayer by whom such return was made or to whom such return information relates if the return or return information can be associated with, or otherwise identify, directly or indirectly, a particular taxpayer.

(3) *Disclosure in judicial proceedings.* A return or return information disclosed to officers and employees (including attorneys) of the Department of Labor, the Pension Benefit Guaranty Corporation, or the Department of Justice as provided by this section may be disclosed by such officers or employees in a civil or criminal judicial proceeding authorized by, or described in, title I or IV of the Act, provided that, in the case of a judicial proceeding described in section 6103(i)(4), the requirements of section 6103(i)(4) have first been met.

(d) *Disclosure of returns and return information in connection wth certain consultations between Departments of the Treasury and Labor.* Upon general written request to the Commissioner of Internal Revenue by the Secretary of Labor, officers and employees of the Internal Revenue Service may disclose to officers and employees of the Department of Labor such returns and return information as may be necessary to properly carry out any consultation required by section 3002, 3003, or 3004 of the Act.

(e) *Return information open to public inspection under section 6104.* Nothing in these regulations shall be construed to deny officers and employees of the Department of Labor and the Pension Benefit Guaranty Corporation the right to inspect return information available to the public under section 6104.

Temporary Rules

T.D. 7335

Temporary regulations relating to an election with respect to bonds and other evidences of indebtedness when valuing assets of retirement plans. (T.D. 7335, filed 12-19-74.)

In order to prescribe temporary regulations relating to an election with respect to valuation of bonds or other evidences of indebtedness pursuant to section 412(c)(2)(B) of the Internal Revenue Code of 1954, as added by section 1013 of the Employee Retirement Income Security Act of 1974 (P.L. 93-406, 88 Stat. 914) and section 302(c)(2)(B) of the Act (88 Stat. 871) the following temporary regulations are hereby prescribed:

[Sec. 412(c)(2)(B) § 11.412(c)-11. (T.D. 7335, filed 12-19-74.) **Election with respect to bonds.**

(a) *In general.* Section 412(c)(2)(B) provides that, at the election of the administrator of a plan which includes a trust qualified under section 401(a) or of a plan which satisfies the requirements of section 403(a) or section 405(a), the value of a bond or other evidence of indebtedness which is held by the plan and which is not in default as to principal or interest may be determined on an amortized basis running from initial cost at purchase to the amount payable at maturity (or, in the case of a bond which is callable prior to maturity, the earliest call date). So long as this election is in effect, the value of any such evidence of indebtedness shall, for purposes of section 412, be determined on such an amortized basis rather than on a method taking into account fair market value as described in section 412(c)(2)(A).

(b) *Manner of making election.* The election to value evidences of indebtedness in accordance with paragraph (a) of this section shall be made by a statement to that effect attached to and filed as a part of the annual return of the plan required under section 6058 of the Code.

(c) *Effect of election.* The election provided by section 412(c)(2)(B), once made, will affect the valuation of all evidences of indebtedness, not in default as to principal or interest, which are held by the plan for the plan year for which the election is made and any evidences of indebtedness which are subsequently acquired by the plan. The value of any evidence of indebtedness which is in default as of the valuation date for the plan year must be determined on the basis of any reasonable actuarial method of valuation which takes into account fair market value in accordance with section 412(c)(2)(A) and must continue to be so valued until the indebtedness is no longer in default.

(d) *Consent to revoke required*—(1) *In general.* An election made in accordance with paragraph (a) of this section may be revoked only if consent to revoke the election is obtained from the Secretary or his delegate.

(2) *Manner of obtaining permission for revocation.* [Reserved].

Reg. § 11.412(c)-11(d)(2)

T.D. 7338

Temporary regulations relating to elections with respect to retroactive amendments. (T.D. 7338, filed 12-26-74.)

In order to prescribe temporary regulations relating to elections with respect to retroactive plan amendments pursuant to section 412(c)(8) of the Internal Revenue Code of 1954, as added by section 1013 of the Employee Retirement Income Security Act of 1974 (P.L. 93-406, 88 Stat. 917) and section 302(c)(8) of such Act (88 Stat. 872), the following temporary regulations are hereby adopted:

○━ [Sec. 412(c)(8)] § 11.412(c)-7 (T.D. 7338, filed 12-26-74.) **Election to treat certain retroactive plan amendments as made on the first day of the plan year.**

(a) *General rule.* Under section 412(c)(8), a plan administrator may elect to have any amendment which is adopted after the close of the plan year to which it applies deemed to have been made on the first day of such plan year if the amendment—

(1) Is adopted no later than 2 and one-half months after the close of such plan year (or, in the case of a multiemployer plan, no later than 2 years after the close of such plan year),

(2) Does not reduce the accrued benefit of any participant determined as of the beginning of such plan year, and

(3) Does not reduce the accrued benefit of any participant determined as of the time of adoption of the amendment, or, if it does so reduce such accrued benefit, it is shown that the plan administrator filed a notice with the Secretary of Labor notifying him of the amendment, and—

(i) The Secretary of Labor approved the amendment, or

(ii) The Secretary of Labor failed to disapprove the amendment within 90 days after the date on which the notice was filed.

(b) *Time and manner of making election.* (1) The election under section 412(c)(8) shall be made by the plan administrator by a statement of election described in subparagraph (3) of this paragraph, attached to the annual return relating to minimum funding standards required to be filed under section 6058 with respect to the plan year to which the election relates.

(2) In the event that an amendment to which paragraph (a) of this section applies is adopted after the filing of the annual return required under section 6058, the plan administrator may make the election under section 412(c)(8) by attaching a statement of election, described in subparagraph (3) of this paragraph, to a copy of such annual return, and filing such copy no later than the time allowed for the filing of such returns under section 6058. (In the case of multiemployer plans, such copy may be filed within a 24 month period beginning with the date prescribed for the filing of such returns.)

(3) The statement of election filed by or on behalf of the plan administrator shall—

(i) State the date of the close of the first plan year to which the amendment applies and the date on which the amendment was adopted;

(ii) Contain a statement that the amendment does not reduce the accrued benefit of any participant determined as of the beginning of the plan year preceding the plan year in which the amendment is adopted; and

(iii) Contain either—

(A) A statement that the amendment does not reduce the accrued benefit of any participant determined as of the time of adoption of such amendment, or

(B) A copy of the notice filed with the Secretary of Labor under section 412(c)(8) and a statement that either the Secretary of Labor has approved the amendment or he has failed to act within 90 days after notification of the amendment.

Reg. § 11.412(c)-7(b)(3)

T.D. 7339

Temporary regulations relating to election of lump sum distribution treatment under sections 402 and 403 of the Code. (T.D. 7339, filed 1-3-75.)

In order to prescribe temporary income tax regulations relating to the election to treat an amount as a lump sum distribution pursuant to section 402(e)(4)(B) of the Internal Revenue Code of 1954, as added by section 2005(a) of the Employee Retirement Income Security Act of 1974 (P.L. 93-406, 88 Stat. 987), the following temporary regulations are hereby adopted:

[Sec. 402(e)(4)(B)] § 11.402(e)(4)(B)-1 (T.D. 7339, filed 1-3-75.) **Election to treat an amount as a lump sum distribution.**

(a) *In general.* For purposes of sections 402, 403, and this section, an amount which is described in section 402(e)(4)(A) and which is not an annuity contract may be treated as a lump sum distribution under section 402(e)(4)(A) only if the taxpayer elects for the taxable year to have all such amounts received during such year so treated. Not more than one election may be made under this section with respect to an employee after such employee has attained age 59½.

(b) *Taxpayers eligible to make the election.* Individuals, estates, and trusts are the only taxpayers eligible to make the election provided by this section. In the case of a lump sum distribution made with respect to an employee to 2 or more trusts, the election provided by this section shall be made by the employee or by the personal representative of a deceased employee.

(c) *Procedure for making election*—(1) *Time and scope of election.* An election under this section shall be made for each taxable year to which such election is to apply. The election shall be made before the expiration of the period (including extension thereof) prescribed in section 6511 for making a claim for credit or refund of the assessed tax imposed by chapter 1 of subtitle A of the Code for such taxable year.

(2) *Manner of making election.* An election by the taxpayer with respect to a taxable year shall be made by filing Form 4972 as a part of the taxpayer's income tax return or amended return for the taxable year.

(3) *Revocation of election.* An election made pursuant to this section may be revoked within the time prescribed in subparagraph (1) of this paragraph for making an election, only if there is filed, within such time, an amended income tax return for such taxable year, which includes a statement revoking the election and is accompanied by payment of any tax attributable to the revocation. If an election for a taxable year is revoked, another election may be made for that taxable year under subparagraphs (1) and (2) of this paragraph.

Reg. § 11.402(e)(4)(B)-1(c)(3)

T.D. 7349

Temporary regulations relating to election with respect to foreclosure property by a real estate investment trust. (T.D. 7349, filed 3-21-75.)

In order to prescribe temporary regulations, which shall remain in force and effect until superseded by permanent regulations, relating to the manner of making an election with respect to foreclosure property under section 856(e) of the Internal Revenue Code of 1954, the following regulations are hereby adopted:

○→ [Sec. 856(e)] § 10.1 (T.D. 7349, filed 3-21-75.) **Election by real estate investment trust to treat certain property as foreclosure property.**

(a) *In general.* Under section 856(e) of the Code a real estate investment trust ("REIT") may elect to treat as foreclosure property any real property (including interests in real property), and any personal property incident to such real property, that the REIT acquires after December 31, 1973, as the result of having bid in such property at foreclosure, or having otherwise reduced such property to ownership or possession by agreement or process of law, after there was default (or default was imminent) on a lease of such property (where the REIT was the lessor) or on an indebtedness owed to the REIT which such property secured. Personal property acquired on foreclosure (including personal property not subject to a mortgage or lease of the real property) will be considered incident to a particular item of real property if the use of such personal property is an ordinary and necessary corollary of the use to which the real property is put. For example, in the case of a hotel, such items as furniture, appliances, linens, china, food, etc. would be examples of incidental personal property. Personal property eligible for the election includes personal property acquired after the acquisition of the real property, if such personal property is incident to the real property and either replaces or supplements personal property of the same or a similar nature acquired upon foreclosure. Personal property used in the continuation of a trade or business conducted on the property prior to foreclosure will be considered property eligible for the election. Also, if the REIT, through an independent contractor, completes construction of a building or other improvement on foreclosure property which was more than 10 percent complete when default was imminent, personal property (such as a refrigerator or stove) which is incident to such real property and which is placed in the building or other improvement in the course of the completion of the construction is eligible for the election to be treated as foreclosure property. Real property eligible for the election includes a building or other improvement which has been constructed on land owned and leased by the REIT and which is acquired by the REIT upon default of the lease of the land.

(b) *Special rules regarding termination of foreclosure property status*—(1) *Subsequent leases of foreclosure property.* Under section 856(e)(4)(A), foreclosure property will cease to be foreclosure property on the first day (occurring on or after the day on which the REIT acquired the property) on which the REIT enters into a lease with respect to such property which, by its terms, will give rise to income which is not described in section 856(c)(3) (other than subparagraph (F) of section 856(c)(3)) or any amount is received or accrued, directly or indirectly, pursuant to a lease entered into on or after such day which is not described in such section. If, by operation of law or by contract, the acquisition of the foreclosure property by the REIT terminates a preexisting lease of such property, or gives the REIT a right to terminate such lease, then for the purposes of section 856(e)(4)(A), a REIT, in such circumstances, will not be considered to have entered into a lease with respect to such property solely because the terms of such preexisting lease are continued in effect after foreclosure without substantial modification. Also, solely for the purposes of section 856(e)(4)(A), if a REIT enters into a lease with respect to real property on or after the day upon which the REIT acquires such real property by foreclosure, and a portion of the rent from such lease is attributable to personal property which is foreclosure property incident to such real property, such rent attributable to the incidental personal property will not be considered to terminate the status of such real property (or such incidental personal property) as foreclosure property.

(2) *Completion of construction after default is imminent.* Under section 856(e)(4)(B), property ceases to be foreclosure property if on or after the day on which the REIT acquires such property any construction takes place on such property, other than completion of a building, or completion of any other improvement, where more than 10 percent of the construction of such building or other improvement was completed before default became imminent. For purposes of section 856(e)(4)(B), if more than one default occurred with respect to an indebtedness or lease in respect of which there is an acquisition, the more-than-10-percent test will not be applied at the time a particular default became imminent if it is clear that the acquisition did not occur as the result of such default. Construction by the REIT as mortgagee in possession may not be added to the construction previously completed to satisfy the more-than-10-percent test.

(3) *Use of the property in a trade or business.* Under section 856(e)(4)(C), property ceases to be foreclosure property if, more than 90 days after the property was acquired by the REIT, the REIT uses the property in the conduct of a trade or business, other than through an independent contractor from whom the REIT does not derive or receive any income. Thus, sale of property held primarily for sale to customers in the ordinary course of a trade or business more than 90 days after the real property was acquired, other than through an independent contractor, will not be a sale of foreclosure property.

(c) *Taxable income* — (1) *Net income from foreclosure property.* Section 857(b)(4), as added by section 6(c) of Public Law

Reg. § 10.1(c)(1)

93-625, imposes a tax on the net income from foreclosure property (as defined in section 857(b)(4)(B)). For purposes of section 857(b)(4)(B), net income from foreclosure property means the aggregate of—

(i) All gains and losses from sales or other dispositions of foreclosure property described in section 1221(1), and

(ii) The difference (hereinafter called "net gain or loss from operations") between (A) the gross income derived from foreclosure property (as defined in section 856(e)) to the extent such gross income is not described in subparagraph (A), (B), (C), (D), or (E) of section 856(c)(3), and (B) the deductions allowed by chapter 1 of the Code which are directly connected with the production of such gross income.

Thus, the sum of the gains and losses from sales or other dispositions of foreclosure property described in section 1221(1) is aggregated with the net gain or loss from operations in arriving at net income from foreclosure property. Since income from the rental of personal property is not described in section 856(c)(3)(A), (B), (C), (D), or (E), such income is subject to tax under section 857(b)(4). A deduction is "directly connected" with gross income if it has a proximate and primary relationship to the earning of such income. Thus, in the case of gross income from real property, "directly connected" deductions would include depreciation on the property, interest on any obligations attributable to the carrying of the property, real estate taxes, and fees paid to an independent contractor hired to manage the property. On the other hand, general overhead and administrative expenses are not "directly connected" deductions.

(2) *Real estate investment trust taxable income.* The tax imposed by section 857(b)(4) applies only if there is net income from foreclosure property. If there is a net loss from foreclosure property (that is, if the aggregate computed under subparagraph (1) of this paragraph results in a negative amount) such loss is taken into account in computing real estate investment trust taxable income under section 857(b)(2).

(d) *Election on a property-by-property basis.* An election under section 856(e) to treat property as foreclosure property shall be made on a property-by-property basis. Thus, if the REIT acquires property eligible for the election in each of two separate foreclosures with respect to two separate obligations, the REIT may make an election with respect to the property acquired upon either, or both, of the foreclosures.

(e) *Time for making election.* The election by a REIT to treat property as foreclosure property must be made on or before either the due date (including extensions of time) for filing the REIT's income tax return for the taxable year in which the REIT acquires the property with respect to which the election is being made, or April 3, 1975, whichever is later. Thus a REIT which acquires property eligible for the election after December 31, 1973, may make an election with respect to such property on or before April 3, 1975, even though the time prescribed by law (including extensions of time) for filing the income tax return for the taxable year in which the REIT acquires such property has expired (or will expire) before April 4, 1975.

(f) *Manner of making the election.* The election shall be made by a statement attached to the REIT's income tax return for the taxable year in which the REIT acquired the property with respect to which the election is being made. If, however, the income tax return for such year has been filed before the time expires for making the election, the election may be made either by filing an amended return for such year with the statement attached, or by filing the statement with the district director, or director of the internal revenue service center, with whom the return for such year was filed. The statement shall indicate that the election is made under section 856(e) and shall indentify the property to which the election applies. The statement shall also set forth—

(1) The name, address, and taxpayer identification number of the REIT,

(2) The taxable year in which the property with respect to which the election is being made was acquired, if the statement is not attached to a return or amended return,

(3) The date the property was acquired by the REIT, and

(4) A brief description of how the real property was acquired, including the name of the person or persons from whom such real property was acquired and a description of the lease or indebtedness with respect to which default occurred or was imminent.

(g) *Election is irrevocable.* An election made in accordance with paragraph (f) of this section shall be irrevocable.

Temporary Rules
T.D. 7353

Temporary regulations relating to accrual of vacation pay. (T.D. 7353, filed 4-18-75.)

In order to provide such temporary regulations under section 463(d) of the Internal Revenue Code of 1954, the following regulations are adopted:

[Sec. 463(d)] § 10.2 (T.D. 7353, filed 4-18-75.) **Election to accrue vacation pay.**

(a) *In general.* Section 463 provides that taxpayers whose taxable income is computed under an accrual method of accounting may elect without the consent of the Commissioner, to deduct certain amounts with respect to vacation pay which, because of contingencies, would not otherwise be deductible. Such election must apply to the liability for all vacation pay accounts maintained by the taxpayer within a single trade or business if the liability is contingent when vacation pay is earned.

(b) *Time for making election.* (1) In the case of a taxpayer who established or maintained a vacation pay account pursuant to I.T. 3956 and who continued to maintain such account pursuant to section 97 of the Technical Amendments Act of 1958, as amended, for its last taxable year ending before January 1, 1973, the election must be made for each trade or business for which such account was maintained on or before the later of (i) July 21, 1975, or (ii) the due date for filing the income tax return (determined with regard to any extensions of time granted the taxpayer for filing such return) for the first taxable year beginning after December 31, 1973. The election pursuant to this paragraph shall be effective with respect to an account described in this paragraph (b)(1) for taxable years ending after December 31, 1972. Failure to file such election shall constitute a change in the method of accounting for vacation pay for the first taxable year ending after December 31, 1972. Such change in accounting method will be considered a change initiated by the taxpayer.

(2) In the case of a trade or business of a taxpayer to which paragraph (b)(1) does not apply, the election provided for in this section may be made for any taxable year beginning after December 31, 1973, by making the election not later than (i) July 21, 1975, or (ii) the due date for filing the income tax return (determined with regard to any extensions of time granted the taxpayer for filing such return) for the first taxable year for which the election is made.

(3) A taxpayer who elects under section 463 to treat vacation pay as provided in this section and who wishes to revoke such election may only do so with the consent of the Commissioner. Such revocation shall constitute a change in the method of accounting.

(c) *Manner of making election.* (1) Except as otherwise provided in paragraph (c)(2), the election provided for in this section must be made by means of a statement attached to a timely filed income tax return. The statement shall indicate that the taxpayer is electing to apply the provisions of section 463, and shall contain the following information:

(i) The taxpayer's name and a description of each vacation pay plan to which the election is to apply.

(ii) A schedule with appropriate explanations showing—

(A) In the case of a vacation pay account established or maintained pursuant to I.T. 3956 and section 97 of the Technical Amendments Act of 1958, as amended,

(1) The balance of each such vacation pay account maintained by the taxpayer, and (2) The amount, determined as if the taxpayer had maintained a vacation pay account for the last taxable year ending before January 1, 1973, representing the taxpayer's liability for vacation pay earned by employees, before the close of the taxable year and payable during such taxable year or within 12 months following the close of such taxable year.

(B) In the case of other vacation pay accounts, the amount of the closing balances the taxpayer would have had for the taxpayer's 3 taxable years immediately preceding the taxable year for which the election was made, had the taxpayer maintained an account representing the taxpayer's liability for vacation pay earned by the employees before the close of the taxable year and payable during the taxable year or within 12 months following the close of the taxable year throughout the 3 immediately preceding taxable years.

(iii) The amounts accrued and deducted for prior years for vacation pay but not paid at the close of the taxable year preceding the year for which the election is made.

(2) Where a taxpayer has filed its return for a taxable year beginning after December 31, 1973, prior to July 21, 1975, and has not made the election pursuant to this section, the election may be made by filing an amended return (showing adjustments, in any) for such year and attaching the statement required by paragraph (c)(1) on or before July 21, 1975.

(d) The time for making the election may be illustrated by the following examples:

Example (1). X, whose taxable year begins on February 1, files its return based on the accrual method of accounting. X has continuously accrued and deducted for income tax purposes contingent amounts of vacation pay, pursuant to I.T. 3956. Pursuant to section 463 and these regulations, in order for X to continue accruing and deducting its vacation pay amounts, X must elect to account for vacation pay under section 463 by attaching the election to its timely filed return for its taxable year ending on January 31, 1975 or if X has already filed such return by July 21, 1975 without such election, by filing the election statement with an amended return by July 21, 1975. If X does not make the election under section 463, X will be treated as having initiated a change in its method of accounting for vacation pay in its taxable year ending on January 31, 1973.

Example (2). Y, a calendar year taxpayer files its returns based on the accrual method of accounting. Y deducted its vacation pay amounts only when paid since

Reg. § 10.2(d)

24,998.30 (I.R.C.)   Reg. § 10.2(d)   4-28-75

such amounts were contingent when earned and Y was not entitled to the benefits of I.T. 3956. Y may elect for its taxable year ending on December 31, 1974, to deduct certain amounts with respect to contingent vacation pay which were not otherwise deductible, by filing an election pursuant to these regulations with its timely filed income tax return for such year or if such return was already filed by July 21, 1975, without such election, by filing the election with an amended return filed by July 21, 1975. If Y does not make the election for its taxable year ending on December 31, 1974, Y may make the election with respect to any subsequent taxable year by filing an election with its return for such year.

T.D. 7360

Temporary regulations relating to special elections with respect to the investment credit for certain public utilities. (T.D. 7360, filed 6-13-75.)

To prescribe the temporary regulations relating to the amendment made to the Internal Revenue Code of 1954 by section 301 (b)(3) of the Tax Reduction Act of 1975 which shall remain in effect until superseded by permanent regulations, the following regulations are hereby adopted:

○── [Sec. 46(f)(8)] § 9.1 (T.D. 7360, filed 6-13-75.) Investment credit—public utility property elections.

(a) *Applicability of prior election under section 46(f)*—(1) *In general.* Except as provided in subparagraph (2) of this paragraph, an election made before March 10, 1972 (hereinafter referred to as a 1972 election) under section 46(f) (redesignated from section 46(e) by the Tax Reduction Act of 1975) applies to the credit allowable for a taxable year with respect to public utility property described in section 46(f)(5) by reason of sections 301 and 302 of the Tax Reduction Act of 1975.

(2) *1972 immediate flow-through election.* A 1972 election under section 46(f)(3) (hereinafter referred to as an election for immediate flow-through) does not apply to the additional credit allowed under section 38 with respect to limited property (public utility property described in section 46(c)(3)(B) to which section 167(l)(2)(C) applies, other than nonregulated communication property of the type described in the last sentence of section 46(c)(3)(B)) by reason of the Tax Reduction Act of 1975. However, a 1972 election for immediate flow-through does apply to the additional credit allowed for a taxable year with respect to property described in section 46(f)(5)(B). See paragraph (b) of this section for a new election under section 46(f)(3) with regard to the additional credit with respect to limited property allowed by reason of the Tax Reduction Act of 1975. See subparagraph (3) of this paragraph for determination of additional credit. For purposes of this section the phrase "determined as if the Tax Reduction Act had not been enacted" means the following amendments shall be disregarded in determining credit allowable or allowed: (A) the increase in the amount of credit from 7 percent to 10 or 11 percent under section 46(a)(1)(A), (B), and (D), (B) the increase in the amount of qualified investment from 4/7 to 7/7 under section 46(a)(1)(C) and (c)(3)(A), (C) the increase in the dollar limitation from $50,000 to $100,000 on used property under section 48(c)(2), and (D) the increase in the limitation based on tax under section 46(a)(6) for certain public utilities. In determining the amount of credit attributable to limited property possible disallowance under section 46(f) shall be disregarded.

(3) *Additional credit allowed*—(i) *Credit earned in taxable year.* The amount of additional credit allowed for credit earned for limited property for a taxable year is an amount equal to the excess of—

(A) The credit allowed by section 38 for the taxable year (determined without regard to section 46(b)) multiplied by a fraction, the numerator of which is the amount of credit earned for limited property for the taxable year and the denominator of which is the amount of credit earned for all section 38 property for the taxable year, over

(B) The amount of normal credit allowed for limited property for the taxable year (determined without regard to section 46(b)). The amount of normal credit allowed for limited property is the amount of credit that would be allowed for the taxable year determined as if the Tax Reduction Act had not been enacted multiplied by a fraction, the numerator of which is the amount of credit earned for limited property for the taxable year determined as if the Tax Reduction Act had not been enacted and the denominator of which is the credit earned for all section 38 property for the taxable year determined as if the Tax Reduction Act had not been enacted.

(ii) *Carryover or carryback to taxable year.* The amount of additional credit allowed for limited property attributable to a carryover or a carryback of any unused credit to any taxable year is an amount equal to the excess of—

(A) The amount of credit allowed by section 38 for the taxable year by reason of section 46(b) multiplied by the fraction contained in subdivision (i)(A) of this subparagraph for the unused credit year, over

(B) The amount of unused normal credit allowed for limited property for the taxable year. The amount of unused normal credit allowed for limited property is the amount of unused credit that would be allowed for the taxable year under section 38 by reason of section 46(b), taking into account the amount of unused credit that would be allowed for any preceding year, determined as if the Tax Reduction Act had not been enacted, multiplied by the fraction contained in subdivision (i)(B) of this subparagraph for the unused credit year.

(b) *New election*—(1) *In general.* A taxpayer who made a 1972 election for immediate flow-through under section 46(f)(3) with respect to limited property may elect to apply section 46(f)(3) to the additional credit allowed by the Tax Reduction Act of 1975 with respect to such property, or, if eligible, may make the election in subparagraph (2) of this paragraph to apply section 46(f)(2) to such additional credit. The election to apply section 46(f)(2) or (3) must be made before June 28, 1975, in the manner provided in paragraph (c) of this section. If the taxpayer does not make a new election, section 46(f)(1) shall apply to additional credit for limited property. However, if the taxpayer made a 1972 election under section 46(f)(2) with respect to property to which section 46(f)(3) does not apply, then section 46(f)(2) shall apply to such additional credit notwithstanding any prohibition in section 46(f)(3) to the contrary.

(2) *Special section 46(f)(2) election.* A taxpayer who—

Reg. § 9.1 (b)(2)

(i) Made a 1972 election under section 46(f)(3),

(ii) Did not make an election to apply section 46(f)(2) with respect to property to which section 46(f)(3) does not apply, and

(iii) Did not acquire property to which section 46(f)(1) applied in any taxable year ending before January 1, 1975,

may elect to apply section 46(f)(2) to the additional credit allowed by the Tax Reduction Act of 1975 with respect to limited property notwithstanding any prohibition in section 46(f)(3) to the contrary.

(c) *Method of making election.* A taxpayer may make an election described in paragraph (b) of this section by filing a statement before June 28, 1975, with the district director or director of the internal revenue service center with whom the taxpayer ordinarily files its income tax return. For rules with respect to taxpayers filing consolidated returns, see § 1.1502-77(a) of part 1 of this chapter. The statement shall contain the following information: (1) the name, address, and taxpayer identification number of the taxpayer, and (2) the election which the taxpayer is making under paragraph (b) of this section. If a taxpayer is electing flow-through under section 46(f)(3), the statement shall also contain a written recitation that the election is made at the taxpayer's own option and without regard to any requirement imposed by an agency described in section 46(c)(3)(B) having jurisdiction over the taxpayer. The recitation shall be verified by a written declaration that is is made under the penalties of perjury.

Temporary regulations relating to solid waste disposal facilities. (T.D. 7362, filed 6-17-75.)

[Sec. 103(c)] § 17.1 TD. 7362, filed 6-17-75.) Industrial development bonds used to provide solid waste disposal facilities; temporary rules.

(a) *In general.* Section 103(c)(4)(E) provides that section 103(c)(1) shall not apply to obligations issued by a State or local governmental unit which are part of an issue substantially all the proceeds of which are used to provide solid waste disposal facilities. Section 1.103-8(f) of this chapter provides general rules with respect to such facilities and defines such facilities. In the case of property which has both a solid waste disposal function and a function other than the disposal of solid waste, only the portion of the cost of the property allocable to the function of solid waste disposal (as determined under paragraph (b) of this section) is taken into account as an expenditure to provide solid waste disposal facilities. A facility which otherwise qualifies as a solid waste disposal facility will not be treated as having a function other than solid waste disposal merely because material or heat which has utility or value is recovered or results from the disposal process. Where materials or heat are recovered, the waste disposal function includes the processing of such materials or heat which occurs in order to put them into the form in which the materials or heat are in fact sold or used, but does not include further processing which converts the materials or heat into other products.

(b) *Allocation.* The portion of the cost of property allocable to solid waste disposal is determined by allocating the cost of such property between the property's solid waste disposal function and any other functions by any method which, with reference to all the facts and circumstances with respect to such property, reasonably reflects a separation of costs for each function of the property.

(c) *Example.* The principles of this paragraph may be illustrated by the following example:

Example. Company A intends to construct a new facility to process solid waste which City X will deliver to the facility. City X will pay A a disposal fee for each ton of solid waste that City X dumps at the facility. The waste will be processed by A in a manner which separates metals, glass and similar materials. As separated, some of such items are commercially saleable; but A does not intend to sell the metals and glass until the metals are further separated, sorted, sized and cleaned and the glass is pulverized. The metals and pulverized glass will then be sold to commercial users. The waste disposal function includes such processing of the metals and glass, but no further processing is included.

The remaining waste will be burned in an incinerator. Gases generated by the incinerator will be cleaned by use of an electrostatic precipitator. To reduce the size and cost of the electrostatic precipitator, the incinerator exhaust gases will be cooled and reduced in volume by means of a heat exchange process using boilers. The precipitator is functionally related and subordinate to disposal of the waste residue and is therefore property used in solid waste disposal. The heat can be used by A to produce steam. Company B operates an adjacent electric generating facility and B can use steam to power its turbine-generator. B needs steam with certain physical characteristics and as a result A's boilers, heat exchanger and related equipment are somewhat more costly than might be required to produce steam for some other uses. The disposal function includes the equipment actually used to put the heat into the form in which it is sold.

Company A intends to construct pipes to carry the steam from A's boiler to B's facility. When converted to such steam the heat is in the form in which sold, and therefore the disposal function does not include subsequent transporting of the steam by pipes. Similarly, if A installed generating equipment and used the steam to generate electricity, the disposal function would not include the generating equipment, since such equipment transforms the commercially saleable steam into another form of energy.

Reg. § 17.1(c)

Temporary Rules *(I.R.C.)* 24,998.45

T.D. 7380; 7508

Temporary regulations relating to minimum participation standards. (T.D. 7380, filed 9-30-75; T.D. 7508, filed 9-14-77.)

In order to prescribe temporary income tax regulations (26 CFR Part 11) to reflect the addition of section 410 to the Internal Revenue Code, and in order to supersede § 11.410-1 of the Temporary Income Tax Regulations under the Employee Retirement Income Security Act of 1974 (26 CFR § 11.410-1) and § 420.0-1 of the Temporary Regulations on Procedure and Administration under the Employee Retirement Income Security Act of 1974 (26 CFR § 420.0-1), the following temporary regulations are hereby adopted: [Ed: These temporary regulations (other than § 11.410(b)-1(d)(2) which appears below) were superseded by T.D. 7508, filed 9-14-77.]

[410] § 11.410(b)-1 (T.D. 7380, filed 9-30-75; T.D. 7508, filed 9-14-77.) **Minimum coverage requirements.**

(d) *Special rules*—* * *

(2) *Discrimination.* The determination as to whether a plan discriminates in favor of employees who are officers, shareholders, or highly compensated, is made on the basis of the facts and circumstances of each case, allowing a reasonable difference between the percentage of such employees benefitted by the plan to all employees benefitted by the plan and the percentage of all such employees of the employer to all employees of the employer. A showing that a specified percentage of employees covered by a plan are not officers, shareholders, or highly compensated, without a showing that the difference (if any) between such percentage and the percentage of all employees who are not officers, shareholders, or highly compensated is reasonable, is not sufficient to establish that the plan does not discriminate in favor of employees who are officers, shareholders, or highly compensated.

* * * * * * * *

Reg. § 11.410(b)-1(d)(2)

Temporary regulations relating to nonbank trustees of pension and profit sharing trusts benefiting owner-employees. (T.D. 7383, filed 10-15-75; amended by T.D. 7448, filed 12-17-76.)

To prescribe temporary regulations relating to the amendment of the Internal Revenue Code of 1954 by section 1022(c) of the Employee Retirement Income Security Act of 1974 which shall remain in effect until superseded by permanent regulations, the following regulations are hereby adopted:

○—▶ [Sec. 401(d)] § 11.401(d)(1)-1 (T.D. 7383, filed 10-15-75; amended by T.D. 7448, filed 12-17-76.) **Nonbank trustees of trusts benefiting owner-employees.**

(a) *Effective dates*—(1) *General rule.* For a plan not in existence on January 1, 1974, this section shall apply to the first plan year commencing after September 2, 1984, and all subsequent plan years.

(2) *Existing plans.* For a plan in existence on January 1, 1974, this section shall apply to the first plan year commencing after December 31, 1975, and all subsequent plan years.

(b) *In general.* For plan years to which this section applies, the trustee of a trust described in § 1.401-12(c)(1)(i) may (notwithstanding § 1.401-12(c)) be a person other than a bank (within the meaning of section 401(d)(1)) if he demonstrates to the satisfaction of the Commissioner that the manner in which he will administer trusts will be consistent with the requirements of section 401. Such demonstration must be made by a written application to the Commissioner of Internal Revenue, Attention: E:EP, Internal Revenue Service, Washington, D.C. 20224. Such application must meet the requirements set forth in paragraphs (c) to (g) of this section.

(c) *Fiduciary ability.* The applicant must demonstrate in detail his ability to act within the accepted rules of fiduciary conduct. Such demonstration must include the following elements of proof:

(1) *Continuity.* (i) The applicant must assure the uninterrupted performance of its fiduciary duties notwithstanding the death or change of its owners. Thus, for example, there must be sufficient diversity in the ownership of the applicant to ensure that the death or change of its owners will not interrupt the conduct of its business. Therefore, the applicant cannot be an individual.

(ii) Sufficient diversity in the ownership of an incorporated applicant means that individuals each of whom owns more than 20 percent of the voting stock in the applicant own, in the aggregate, no more than 50 percent of such stock.

(iii) Sufficient diversity in the ownership of an applicant which is a partnership means that—

(A) Individuals each of whom owns more than 20 percent of the profits interest in the partnership own, in the aggregate, no more than 50 percent of such profits interest, and

(B) Individuals each of whom owns more than 20 percent of the capital interest in the partnership own, in the aggregate, no more than 50 percent of such capital interest.

(iv) For purposes of this subparagraph, the ownership of stock and of capital and profits interests shall be determined in accordance with the rules for constructive ownership of stock provided in section 1563 (e) and (f)(2). For this purpose, the rules for constructive ownership of stock provided in section 1563(e) and (f)(2) shall apply to a capital or profits interest in a partnership as if it were a stock interest.

(2) *Established location.* The applicant must have an established place of business in the United States where he is accessible during every business day.

(3) *Fiduciary experience.* The applicant must have fiduciary experience or expertise sufficient to ensure that he will be able to perform his fiduciary duties. Evidence of fiduciary experience must include proof that a significant part of the business of the applicant consists of exercising fiduciary powers similar to those he will exercise if his application is approved. Evidence of fiduciary expertise must include proof that the applicant employs personnel experienced in the administration of fiduciary powers similar to those he will exercise if his application is approved.

(4) *Fiduciary responsibility.* The applicant must assure compliance with the rules of fiduciary conduct set out in paragraph (f) of this section.

(5) *Financial responsibility.* The applicant must exhibit a high degree of solvency commensurate with the obligations imposed by this section. Among the factors to be taken into account are the applicant's net worth, his liquidity, and his ability to pay his debts as they come due.

(d) *Capacity to account.* The applicant must demonstrate in detail his experience and competence with respect to accounting for the interests of a large number of individuals (including calculating and allocating income earned and paying out distributions to payees). Examples of accounting for the interests of a large number of individuals include accounting for the interests of a large number of shareholders in a regulated investment company and accounting for the interests of a large number of variable annuity contract holders.

(e) *Fitness to handle funds*—(1) *In general.* The applicant must demonstrate in detail his experience and competence with respect to other activities normally associated with the handling of retirement funds.

(2) *Examples.* Examples of activities normally associated with the handling of retirement funds include:

(i) To receive, issue receipts for, and safely keep securities;

(ii) To collect income;

(iii) To execute such ownership certificates, to keep such records, make such returns, and render such statements as are required for Federal tax purposes;

(iv) To give proper notification regarding all collections;

(v) To collect matured or called principal and properly report all such collections;

Reg. § 11.401(d)(1)-1(e)(2)

(vi) To exchange temporary for definitive securities;

(vii) To give proper notification of calls, subscription rights, defaults in principal or interest, and the formation of protective committees;

(viii) To buy, sell, receive, or deliver securities on specific directions.

(f) *Rules of fiduciary conduct*—(1) *Administration of fiduciary powers.* The applicant must demonstrate that under applicable regulatory requirements, corporate or other governing instruments, or its established operating procedures:

(i)(A) The owners or directors of the applicant will be responsible for the proper exercise of fiduciary powers by the applicant. Thus, all matters pertinent thereto, including the determination of policies, the investment and disposition of property held in a fiduciary capacity, and the direction and review of the actions of all employees utilized by the applicant in the exercise of his fiduciary powers, will be the responsibility of the owners or directors. In discharging this responsibility, the owners or directors may assign to designated employees, by action duly recorded, the administration of such of the applicant's fiduciary powers as may be proper to assign.

(B) A written record will be made of the acceptance and of the relinquishment or closing out of all fiduciary accounts, and of the assets held for each account.

(C) At least once during each period of 12 months all the assets held in or for each fiduciary account where the applicant has investment responsibilities will be reviewed to determine the advisability of retaining or disposing of such assets.

(ii) All employees taking part in the performance of the applicant's fiduciary duties will be adequately bonded. Nothing in this subdivision shall require any person to be bonded in contravention of section 412(d) of the Employee Retirement Income Security Act of 1974 (29 U.S.C. 1112(d)).

(iii) The applicant will designate, employ or retain legal counsel who will be readily available to pass upon fiduciary matters and to advise the applicant.

(iv) In order to segregate the performance of his fiduciary duties from other business activities, the applicant will maintain a separate trust division under the immediate supervision of an individual designated for that purpose. The trust division may utilize the personnel and facilities of other divisions of the applicant, and other divisions of the applicant may utilize the personnel and facilities of the trust division, as long as the separate identity of the trust division is preserved.

(2) *Adequacy of net worth.* (i) Not less frequently than once during each calendar year the applicant will determine the value of the assets held by him in trust. Such assets will be valued at their current value, except that the assets of an employee benefit plan to which section 103(b)(3)(A) of the Employee Retirement Income Security Act of 1974 (29 U.S.C. 1023(b)(3)(A)) applies will be considered to have the value stated in the most recent annual report of the plan.

(ii) No fiduciary account will be accepted by the applicant unless his net worth (determined as of the end of the most recent taxable year) exceeds the greater of—

(A) $100,000, or

(B) Four percent of the value of all of the assets held by the applicant in trust (determined as of the most recent valuation date).

(iii) The applicant will take whatever lawful steps are necessary (including the relinquishment of fiduciary accounts) to ensure that his net worth (determined as of the close of each taxable year) exceeds the greater of—

(A) $50,000, or

(B) Two percent of the value of all of the assets held by the applicant in trust (determined as of the most recent valuation date).

(3) *Audits.* (i) The applicant will at least once during each period of 12 months cause detailed audits of the fiduciary books and records to be made by an independent qualified public accountant, and at such time will ascertain whether the fiduciary accounts have been administered in accordance with law, this section, and sound fiduciary principles. Such audits shall be conducted in accordance with generally accepted auditing standards, and shall involve such tests of the fiduciary books and records of the applicant as are considered necessary by the independent qualified public accountant.

(ii) In the case of an applicant who is regulated, supervised, and subject to periodic examination by a State or Federal agency, such applicant may adopt an adequate continuous audit system in lieu of the periodic audits required by paragraph (f)(3)(i) of this section.

(iii) A report of the audits and examinations required under this subparagraph, together with the action taken thereon, will be noted in the fiduciary records of the applicant.

(4) *Funds awaiting investment or distribution.* Funds held in a fiduciary capacity by the applicant awaiting investment or distribution will not be held uninvested or undistributed any longer than is reasonable for the proper management of the account.

(5) *Custody of investments.* (i) Except for investments pooled in a common investment fund in accordance with the provisions of paragraph (f)(6) of this section, the investments of each account will not be commingled with any other property.

(ii) Fiduciary assets requiring safekeeping will be deposited in an adequate vault. A permanent record will be kept of fiduciary assets deposited in or withdrawn from the vault.

(6) *Common investment funds.* Where not in contravention of local law the assets of an account may be pooled in a common investment fund (as defined in paragraph (f)(8)(iii) of this section) which must be administered as follows:

(i) Each common investment fund must be established and maintained in accordance with a written agreement, containing appropriate provisions as to the manner in which the fund is to be operated, including provisions relating to the investment powers and a general statement of the investment policy of the applicant with respect to the fund; the allocation of income, profits and losses; the terms and conditions governing the admission or withdrawal of participations in the fund; the auditing of accounts of the applicant with respect to the fund; the basis and method of valuing assets in the fund, setting forth specific criteria for each type of asset; the minimum frequency for valuation of assets of the fund; the period following each such valuation date during which the valuation may be made (which period in usual circumstances may not exceed 10 business days); the basis upon which the fund may be terminated; and such other matters as may be necessary to define clearly the rights of participants in the fund. A copy of the agreement must be available at the principal office of the applicant for inspection during all business hours, and upon request a copy of the agreement must be furnished to any interested person.

(ii) All participations in the common investment fund must be on the basis of a proportionate interest in all of the assets.

(iii) Not less frequently than once during each period of 3 months the applicant must determine the value of the assets in the fund as of the date set for the valuation of assets. No participation may be admitted to or withdrawn from the fund except (A) on the basis of such valuation and (B) as of such valuation date. No participation may be admitted to or withdrawn from the fund unless a written request for or notice of intention of taking such action has been entered on or before the valuation date in the fiduciary records of the applicant. No request or notice may be canceled or countermanded after the valuation date.

(iv)(A) The applicant must at least once during each period of 12 months cause an adequate audit to be made of the common investment fund by a qualified public accountant.

(B) The applicant must at least once during each period of 12 months prepare a financial report of the fund which, based upon the above audit, must contain a list of investments in the fund showing the cost and current market value of each investment; a statement for the period since the previous report showing purchases, with cost; sales, with profit or loss and any other investment changes; income and disbursements; and an appropriate notation as to any investments in default.

(C) The applicant must transmit and certify the accuracy of the financial report to the adminstrator of each plan participating in the common investment fund within 120 days after the end of the plan year.

(v) When participations are withdrawn from a common investment fund, distributions may be made in cash or ratably in kind, or partly in cash and partly in kind, provided that all distributions as of any one valuation date must be made on the same basis.

(vi) If for any reason an investment is withdrawn in kind from a common investment fund for the benefit of all participants in the fund at the time of such withdrawal and such investment is not distributed ratably in kind, it must be segregated and administered or realized upon for the benefit ratably of all participants in the common investment fund at the time of withdrawal.

(7) *Books and records.* (i) The applicant must keep his fiduciary records separate and distinct from other records. All fiduciary records must be so kept and retained for as long as the contents thereof may become material in the administration of any internal revenue law. The fiduciary records must contain full information relative to each account.

(ii) The applicant must keep an adequate record of all pending litigation to which he is a party in connection with the exercise of fiduciary powers.

(8) *Definitions.* For purposes of this paragraph and paragraph (c)(5) of this section—

(i) The term "account" or "fiduciary account" means a trust described in section 401(a) (including a custodial account described in section 401(f)), a custodial account described in section 403(b)(7), or an individual retirement account described in section 408(a) (including a custodial account described in section 408(h)).

(ii) The term "administrator" means an administrator as defined in section 3(16)(A) of the Employee Retirement Income Security Act of 1974, 29 U.S.C. 1002(16)(A).

(iii) The term "common investment fund" means a trust which satisfied the following requirements:

(A) The trust consists of all or part of the assets of several accounts which have been established with the applicant, and

(B) The trust is described in section 401(a) and exempt from tax under section 501(a), or is a common investment fund described in § 1.408-2(b)(5) (as published with notice of proposed rule making in the Federal Register on February 21, 1975, at 40 F.R. 7661), or both.

(iv) The term "employee benefit plan" means an employee benefit plan as defined in section 3(2) of the Employee Retirement Income Security Act of 1974, 29 U.S.C. 1002 (2).

(v) The term "fiduciary records" means all matters which are written, transcribed, recorded, received or otherwise come into the possession of the applicant and are necessary to preserve information concerning the acts and events relevant to the fiduciary activities of the applicant.

(vi) The term "qualified public accountant" means a qualified public accountant as defined in section 103(a)(3)(D) of the Employees Retirement Income Security Act of 1974, 29 U.S.C. 1023(a)(3)(D).

(vii) The term "net worth" means the amount of the applicant's assets less the amount of his liabilities, as determined in accordance with generally accepted accounting principles.

(g) *Special rules*—(1) *Passive trustee.* (i) An applicant who undertakes to act only as a passive trustee may be relieved of one or more of the requirements of this section upon clear and convincing proof that such requirements are not germane, under all the facts and circumstances, to the manner in which he will administer any trust. A trustee is a passive trustee only if under the written trust instrument he has no discretion to direct the investment of the trust funds or any other aspect of the business administration of the trust, but is merely authorized to acquire and hold particular investments specified by the trust instrument. Thus, for example, in the case of an applicant who undertakes merely to acquire and hold the stock of a single regulated investment company, the requirements of paragraph (f)(1)(i)(C), (1)(iv), and (6) of this section shall not apply and no negative inference

Reg. § 11.401(d)(1)-1(g)(1)

shall be drawn from the applicant's failure to demonstrate his experience or competence with respect to the activities described in paragraph (e)(2)(v) to (viii) of this section.

(ii) The determination letter issued to an applicant who is approved by reason of this subparagraph shall state that the applicant is authorized to act only as a passive trustee.

(2) *Federal or State regulation.* Evidence that an applicant is subject to Federal or State regulation with respect to one or more relevant factors shall be given weight in proportion to the extent that such regulatory standards are consonant with the requirements of section 401.

(3) *Savings account.* (i) An applicant will be approved to act as trustee under this subparagraph if the following requirements are satisfied:

(A) The applicant is a credit union, industrial loan company, savings and loan association, or other financial institution designated by the Commissioner;

(B) The investment of the trust assets will be solely in deposits in the applicant;

(C) Deposits in the applicant are insured (up to the dollar limit prescribed by applicable law) by an agency or instrumentality of the United States or a State.

(ii) Any applicant who satisfies the requirements of this subparagraph is hereby approved, and (notwithstanding paragraph (b) of this section) is not required to submit a written application. This approval takes effect on the first day after December 22, 1976, on which the applicant satisfies the requirements of this subparagraph, and continues in effect for so long as the applicant continues to satisfy those requirements.

(4) *Notification of Commissioner.* The applicant must notify the Commissioner in writing of any change which affects the continuing accuracy of any representation made in the application required by this section, whether the change occurs before or after the applicant receives a determination letter. Such notification must be addressed to Commissioner of Internal Revenue, Attention: E:EP, Internal Revenue Service, Washington, D.C. 20224.

(5) *Substitution of trustee.* No applicant shall be approved unless he undertakes to act as trustee only under trust instruments which contain a provision to the effect that the employer is to substitute another trustee upon notification by the Commissioner that such substitution is required because the applicant has failed to comply with the requirements of this section or is not keeping such records, or making such returns, or rendering such statements as are required by forms or regulations.

(6) *Revocation.* Approval of the application required by this section may be revoked for any good and sufficient reason.

Temporary regulations relating to employees of organizations under common control. (T.D. 7388, filed 10-31-75.)

To prescribe temporary regulations relating to a part of the amendment of the Internal Revenue Code of 1954 by section 1015 of the Employee Retirement Income Security Act of 1974 (88 Stat. 925) adding section 414(c), relating to employees of partnerships, proprietorships, etc., which are under common control, which also apply for purposes of section 210(d) of the Employee Retirement Income Security Act of 1974 (88 Stat. 867), and which shall remain in effect until superseded by permanent regulations, the following regulations are hereby adopted:

[Sec. 414(c)] § 11.414(c)-1 (T.D. 7388, filed 10-31-75.) **Commonly controlled trades or businesses.**

For purposes of applying the provisions of section 401 (relating to qualified pension, profit-sharing, and stock bonus plans), 410 (relating to minimum participation standards), 411 (relating to minimum vesting standards), and 415 (relating to limitations on benefits and contributions under qualified plans), all employees of two or more trades or businesses under common control within the meaning of § 11.414(c)-2 for any period shall be treated as employed by a single employer. See sections 401, 410, 411, and 415 and the regulations thereunder for rules relating to employees of trades or businesses which are under common control. See § 11.414(c)-5 for effective date.

[Sec. 414(c)] § 11.414(c)-2 (T.D. 7388, filed 10-31-75.) **Two or more trades or businesses under common control.**

(a) *In general.* For purposes of this section, the term "two or more trades or businesses under common control" means any group of trades or businesses which is either a "parent-subsidiary group of trades or businesses under common control" as defined in paragraph (b) of this section, a "brother-sister group of trades or businesses under common control" as defined in paragraph (c) of this section, or a "combined group of trades or businesses under common control" as defined in paragraph (d) of this section. For purposes of this section and §§ 11.414(c)-3 and 11.414(c)-4, the term "organization" means a sole proprietorship, a partnership (as defined in section 7701(a)(2)), a trust, an estate, or a corporation.

(b) *Parent-subsidiary group of trades or businesses under common control*—(1) *General.* The term "parent-subsidiary group of trades or businesses under common control" means one or more chains of organizations conducting trades or businesses connected through ownership of a controlling interest with a common parent organization if—

(i) A controlling interest in each of the organizations, except the common parent organization, is owned (directly and with the application of § 11.414(c)-4(b)(1), relating to options) by one or more of the other organizations; and

(ii) The common parent organization owns (directly and with the application of § 11.414(c)-4(b)(1), relating to options) a controlling interest in at least one of the other organizations, excluding, in computing such controlling interest, any direct ownership interest by such other organizations.

(2) *Controlling interest defined*—(i) *Controlling interest.* For purposes of paragraphs (b) and (c) of this section, the phrase "controlling interest" means:

(A) In the case of an organization which is a corporation, ownership of stock possessing at least 80 percent of the total combined voting power of all classes of stock entitled to vote of such corporation or at least 80 percent of the total value of shares of all classes of stock of such corporation;

(B) In the case of an organization which is a trust or estate, ownership of an actuarial interest of at least 80 percent of such trust or estate;

(C) In the case of an organization which is a partnership, ownership of at least 80 percent of the profits interest or capital interest of such partnership; and

(D) In the case of an organization which is a sole proprietorship, ownership of such sole proprietorship.

(ii) *Actuarial interest.* For purposes of this section, the actuarial interest of each beneficiary of a trust or estate shall be determined by assuming the maximum exercise of discretion by the fiduciary in favor of such beneficiary. The factors and method prescribed in § 20.2031-10 of this chapter (Estate Tax Regulations) for use in ascertaining the value of an interest in property for estate tax purposes shall be used for purposes of this subdivision in determining a beneficiary's actuarial interest.

(c) *Brother-sister group of trades or businesses under common control*—(1) *General.* The term "brother-sister group of trades or businesses under common control" means two or more organizations conducting trades or businesses if (i) the same five or fewer persons who are individuals, estates, or trusts own (directly and with the application of § 11.414(c)-4), singly or in combination, a controlling interest of each organization, and (ii) taking into account the ownership of each such person only to the extent such ownership is identical with respect to each such organization, such persons are in effective control of each organization.

(2) *Effective control defined.* For purposes of this paragraph, persons are in "effective control" of an organization if—

(i) In the case of an organization which is a corporation, such persons own stock possessing more than 50 percent of the total combined voting power of all classes of stock entitled to vote of such corporation or more than 50 percent of the total value of shares of all classes of stock of such corporation;

(ii) In the case of an organization which is a trust or estate, such persons own an aggregate actuarial interest of more than 50 percent of such trust or estate;

(iii) In the case of an organization which is a partnership, such persons own an aggregate of more than 50 percent of

Reg. § 11.414(c)-2(c)(2)

the profits interest or capital interest of such partnership; and

(iv) In the case of an organization which is a sole proprietorship, such persons own such sole proprietorship.

(d) *Combined group of trades or businesses under common control.* The term "combined group of trades or businesses under common control" means any group of three or more organizations, if (1) each such organization is a member of either a parent-subsidiary group of trades or businesses under common control or a brother-sister group of trades or businesses under common control, and (2) at least one such organization is the common parent organization of a parent-subsidiary group of trades or businesses under common control and is also a member of a brother-sister group of trades or businesses under common control.

(e) *Examples.* The definitions of parent-subsidiary group of trades or businesses under common control, brother-sister group of trades or businesses under common control, and combined group of trades or businesses under common control may be illustrated by the following examples.

Example (1). (a) The ABC Partnership owns stock possessing 80 percent of the total combined voting power of all classes of stock entitled to vote of S Corporation. ABC is the common parent of a parent-subsidiary group of trades or businesses under common control consisting of the ABC Partnership and S Corporation.

(b) Assume the same facts as in (a) and assume further that S owns 80 percent of the profits interest in the DEF Partnership. The ABC Partnership is the common parent of a parent-subsidiary group of trades or businesses under common control consisting of the ABC Partnership, S Corporation, and the DEF Partnership. The result would be the same if the ABC Partnership, rather than S, owned 80 percent of the profits interest in the DEF Partnership.

Example (2). L Corporation owns 80 percent of the only class of stock of T Corporation, and T, in turn owns 40 percent of the capital interest in the GHI Partnership. L also owns 80 percent of the only class of stock of N Corporation, and N, in turn, owns 40 percent of the capital interest in the GHI Partnership. L is the common parent of a parent-subsidiary group of trades or businesses under common control consisting of L Corporation, T Corporation, N Corporation, and the GHI Partnership.

Example (3). ABC Partnership owns 75 percent of the only class of stock of X and Y Corporations; X owns all the remaining stock of Y, and Y owns all the remaining stock of X. Since interorganization ownership is excluded (that is, treated as not outstanding) for purposes of determining whether ABC owns a controlling interest of at least one of the other organizations, ABC is treated as the owner of stock possessing 100 percent of the voting power and value of X and of Y for purposes of paragraph (b)(1)(ii) of this section. Therefore, ABC is the common parent of a parent-subsidiary group of trades or businesses under common control consisting of the ABC Partnership, X Corporation, and Y Corporation.

Example (4). Unrelated individuals A, B, C, D, E, and F own an interest in sole proprietorship A, a capital interest in the GHI Partnership, and stock of corporations W, X, Y, and Z (each of which has only one class of stock outstanding) in the following proportions:

Individuals	Organizations						Identical Ownership
	A	GHI	W	X	Y	Z	
A	100%	60%	60%	60%	60%	60%	60%
B	—	40%	—	—	—	—	—
C	—	—	40%	—	—	—	—
D	—	—	—	40%	—	—	—
E	—	—	—	—	40%	—	—
F	—	—	—	—	—	40%	—
Total	100%	100%	100%	100%	100%	100%	60%

Under these facts the following brother-sister groups of trades or businesses under common control exist: A, GHI, W, X, and Y; A, GHI, W, X and Z; A, GHI, W, Y, and Z; A, W, X, Y, and Z; and A, GHI, X, Y, and Z.

Example (5). The outstanding stock of corporations U and V, which have only one class of stock outstanding, is owned by unrelated individuals as follows:

Individuals	Organizations		Identical Ownership
	U	V	
F	5%	—	—
G	10%	—	—
H	10%	—	—
I	20%	—	—
J	55%	55%	55%
K	—	10%	—
L	—	10%	—
M	—	10%	—
N	—	10%	—
O	—	5%	—
Total	100%	100%	55%

Corporations U and V are not members of a brother-sister group of trades or businesses under common control because at least 80 percent of the stock of each corporation is not owned by the same five or fewer persons.

Example (6). A, an individual, owns a controlling interest in ABC Partnership and DEF Partnership. ABC, in turn, owns a controlling interest in X Corporation. Since ABC, DEF, and X are each members of either a parent-subsidiary group or a brother-sister group of trades or businesses under common control, and ABC is the common parent of a parent-subsidiary group of trades or businesses under common control consisting of ABC and X, and also a member of a brother-sister group of trades or businesses under common control consisting of ABC and DEF, ABC Partnership, DEF Partnership, and X Corporation are members of the same combined group of trades or businesses under common control.

○→ [Sec. 414(c) § 11.414(c)-3 (T.D. 7388, filed 10-31-75.) **Exclusion of certain interests or stock in determining control.**

(a) *In general.* For purposes of § 11.414(c)-2(b)(2)(i) and (c)(2), the term "interest" and the term "stock" do not include an interest which is treated as not outstanding under paragraph (b) of this section in the case of a parent-subsidiary group of trades or businesses under common control or under paragraph (c) of this section in the case of a brother-sister group of trades or businesses under common control. In addition, the term "stock" does not include treasury stock or nonvoting stock which is limited and preferred as to dividends. For definitions of certain terms used in this section, see paragraph (d) of this section.

(b) *Parent-subsidiary group of trades or businesses under common control*—(1) *In general.* If an organization (hereinafter in this section referred to as "parent organization") owns (within the meaning of paragraph (b)(2) of this section)—

(i) In the case of a corporation, 50 percent or more of the total combined voting power of all classes of stock entitled to vote or of the toal value of shares of all classes of stock of such corporation,

(ii) In the case of a trust or an estate, an actuarial interest (within the meaning of § 11.414(c)-2(b)(2)(ii)) of 50 percent or more of such trust or estate, and

(iii) In the case of a partnership, 50 percent or more of the profits or capital interest of such partnership,

then for purposes of determining whether the parent organization or such other organization (hereinafter in this section referred to as "subsidiary organization") is a member of a parent-subsidiary group of trades or businesses under common control, an interest in such subsidiary organization excluded under paragraph (b)(3), (4), (5), or (6) of this section shall be treated as not outstanding.

(2) *Ownership.* For purposes of paragraph (b)(1) of this section, a parent organization shall be considered to own an interest in or stock of another organization which it owns directly or indirectly with the application of paragraph (b)(1) of § 11.414(c)-4 and—

(i) In the case of a parent organization which is a partnership, a trust, or an estate, with the application of paragraph (b)(2), (3), and (4) of § 11.414(c)-4, and

(ii) In the case of a parent organization which is a corporation, with the application of paragraph (b)(4) of § 11.414(c)-4.

(3) *Plan of deferred compensation.* An interest which is an interest in or stock of the subsidiary organization held by a trust which is part of a plan of deferred compensation (within the meaning of section 406(a)(3) and the regulations thereunder) for the benefit of the employees of the parent organization or the subsidiary organization shall be excluded.

(4) *Principal owners, officers, etc.* An interest which is an interest in or stock of the subsidiary organization owned (directly and with the application of § 11.414(c)-4) by an individual who is a principal owner, officer, partner, or fiduciary of the parent organization shall be excluded.

(5) *Employees.* An interest which is an interest in or stock of the subsidiary organization owned (directly and with the application of § 11.414(c)-4) by an employee of the subsidiary organization shall be excluded if such interest or such stock is subject to conditions which substantially restrict or limit the employee's right (or if the employee constructively owns such interest or such stock, the direct or record owner's right) to dispose of such interest or such stock and which run in favor of the parent or subsidiary organization.

(6) *Controlled exempt organization.* An interest which is an interest in or stock of the subsidiary organization shall be excluded if owned (directly and with the application of § 11.414(c)-4) by an organization (other than the parent organization):

(i) To which section 501 (relating to certain educational and charitable organizations which are exempt from tax) applies, and

(ii) Which is controlled directly or indirectly (within the meaning of paragraph (d)(7) of this section) by the parent organization or subsidiary organization, by an individual, estate, or trust that is a principal owner of the parent organization, by an officer, partner, or fiduciary of the parent organization, or by any combination thereof.

(c) *Brother-sister group of trades or businesses under common control*—(1) *In general.* If five or fewer persons (hereinafter in this section referred to as "common owners") who are individuals, estates, or trusts, own (directly and with the application of § 11.414(c)-4)—

(i) In the case of a corporation, 50 percent or more of the total combined voting power of all classes of stock entitled to vote or of the total value of shares of all classes of stock of such corporation,

(ii) In the case of a trust or an estate, an actuarial interest (within the meaning of § 11.414(c)-2(b)(2)(ii)) of 50 percent or more of such trust or estate, and

(iii) In the case of a partnership, 50 percent or more of the profits or capital interest of such partnership,

then for purposes of determining whether

Reg. § 11.414(c)-3(c)(1)

24,998.56-B (I.R.C.) Reg. § 11.414(c)-3(c)(1) 11-10-75

such organization is a member of a brother-sister group of trades or businesses under common control, an interest in such organization excluded under paragraph (c)(2), (3), or (4) of this section shall be treated as not outstanding.

(2) *Exempt employee's trust.* An interest which is an interest in or stock of such organization held by an employee's trust described in section 401(a) which is exempt from tax under section 501(a) shall be excluded if such trust is for the benefit of the employees of such organization.

(3) *Employees.* An interest which is an interest in or stock of such organization owned (directly and with the application of § 11.414(c)-4) by an employee of such organization shall be excluded if such interest or stock is subject to conditions which run in favor of a common owner of such organization or in favor of such organization and which substantially restrict or limit the employee's right (or if the employee constructively owns such interest or stock, the direct or record owner's right) to dispose of such interest or stock.

(4) *Controlled exempt organization.* An interest which is an interest in or stock of such organization shall be excluded if owned (directly and with the application of § 11.414(c)-4) by an organization:

(i) To which section 501(c)(3) (relating to certain educational and charitable organizations which are exempt from tax) applies, and

(ii) Which is controlled directly or indirectly (within the meaning of paragraph (d)(7) of this section) by such organization, by an individual, estate, or trust that is a principal owner of such organization, by an officer, partner, or fiduciary of such organization, or by any combination thereof.

(d) *Definitions*—(1) *Employee.* For purposes of this section, the term "employee" has the same meaning such term is given in section 3306(i) of the Code (relating to definitions for purposes of the Federal Unemployment Tax Act).

(2) *Principal owner.* For purposes of this section, the term "principal owner" means a person who owns (directly and with the application of § 11.414(c)-4)—

(i) In the case of a corporation, 5 percent or more of the total combined voting power of all classes of stock entitled to vote in such corporation or of the total value of shares of all classes of stock of such corporation;

(ii) In the case of a trust or estate, an actuarial interest of 5 percent or more of such trust or estate; or

(iii) In the case of a partnership, 5 percent or more of the profits interest or capital interest of such partnership.

(3) *Officer.* For purposes of this section, the term "officer" includes the president, vice-presidents, general manager, treasurer, secretary, and comptroller of a corporation, and any other person who performs duties corresponding to those normally performed by persons occupying such positions.

(4) *Partner.* For purposes of this section, the term "partner" means any person defined in section 7701(a)(2) (relating to definition of partner).

(5) *Fiduciary.* For purposes of this section and § 11.414(c)-4, the term "fiduciary" has the same meaning as such term is given in section 7701(a)(6) and the regulations thereunder.

(6) *Substantial conditions* (1) *In general.* For purposes of this section, an interest in or stock of an organization is subject to conditions which substantially restrict or limit the right to dispose of such interest or stock and which run in favor of another person if the condition extends directly or indirectly to such person rights with respect to the acquisition of the direct owner's (or the record owner's) interest or stock. For a condition to be in favor of another person it is not necessary that such person be extended a discriminatory concession with respect to price. A right of first refusal with respect to an interest or stock in favor of another person is a condition which substantially restricts or limits the direct or record owner's right of disposition which runs in favor of such person. Further, any legally enforceable condition which prohibits the direct or record owner from disposing of his or her interest or stock without the consent of another person will be considered to be a substantial limitation running in favor of such person.

(ii) *Special rule.* For purposes of paragraph (c)(3) of this section only, if a condition which restricts or limits an employee's right (or direct or record owner's right) to dispose of his or her interest or stock also applies to the interest or stock in such organization held by a common owner pursuant to a bona fide reciprocal purchase arrangement, such condition shall not be treated as a substantial limitation or restriction. An example of a reciprocal purchase arrangement is an agreement whereby a common owner and the employee are given a right of first refusal with respect to stock of the employer corporation owned by the other party. If, however, the agreement also provides that the common owner has the right to purchase the stock of the employer corporation owned by the employee in the event the corporation should discharge the employee for reasonable cause, the purchase arrangement would not be reciprocal within the meaning of this subdivision.

(7) *Control.* For purposes of paragraphs (b)(6) and (c)(4) of this section, the term "control" means control in fact. The determination of whether there exists control in fact will depend upon all of the facts and circumstances of each case, without regard to whether such control is legally enforceable and irrespective of the method by which such control is exercised or exercisable.

(e) *Examples.* The provisions of this section may be illustrated by the following examples:

Example (1). ABC Partnership owns 70 percent of the capital interest and of the profits interest in the DEF Partnership. The remaining capital interest and profits interest in DEF is owned as follows: 4 percent by A (a general partner in ABC), and 26 percent by D (a limited partner in ABC). ABC satisfies the 50-percent capital interest or profits interest ownership requirement of paragraph (b)(1)(iii) of this section with respect to DEF. Since A and D are partners of ABC, under paragraph (b)(4) of this section the capital and profits interests in DEF owned by A and D are treated as not outstanding for purposes of determining whether ABC and DEF are members of a parent-subsidiary group of trades or businesses under common control under § 11.414(c)-2(b). Thus, ABC is considered to own 100 percent (70 ÷ 70) of the capital interest and profits interest in DEF. Accordingly, ABC and DEF are members of a parent-subsidiary group of trades or businesses under common control.

Example (2). Assume the same facts as in example (1) and assume further that A owns 15 shares of the 100 shares of the only class of stock of S Corporation and DEF Partnership owns 75 shares of such stock. ABC satisfies the 50-percent stock requirement of paragraph (b)(1)(i) of this section with respect to S since ABC is considered as owning 52.5 percent (70 percent x 75 percent) of the S stock with the application of § 11.414(c)-4(b)(2). Since A is a partner of ABC, the S stock owned by A is treated as not outstanding for purposes of determining whether S is a member of a parent-subsidiary group of trades or businesses under common control. Thus, DEF Partnership is considered to own stock possessing 88.2 percent (75 ÷ 85) of the voting power and value of the S stock. Accordingly, ABC Partnership, DEF Partnership, and S Corporation are members of a parent-subsidiary group of trades or businesses under common control.

Example (3). ABC Partnership owns 60 percent of the only class of stock of Corporation Y. D, the president of Y, owns the remaining 40 percent of the stock of Y. D has agreed that if she offers her stock in Y for sale she will first offer the stock to ABC at a price equal to the fair market value of the stock on the first date the stock is offered for sale. Since D is an employee of Y within the meaning of section 3306(i) of the Code and her stock in Y is subject to a condition which substantially restricts or limits her right to dispose of such stock and runs in favor of ABC Partnership, under paragraph (b)(5) of this section such stock is treated as not outstanding for purposes of determining whether ABC and Y are members of a parent-subsidiary group of trades or businesses under common control. Thus, ABC Partnership is considered to own stock possessing 100 percent of the voting power and value of the stock of Y. Accordingly, ABC Partnership and Y Corporation are members of a parent-subsidiary group of trades or businesses under common control. The result would be the same if D's husband, instead of D, owned directly the 40 percent stock interest in Y and such stock was subject to a right of first refusal running in favor of ABC Partnership.

○→ [Sec. 414(c)] § 11.414(c)-4 (T.D. 7388, filed 10-31-75.) **Rules for determining ownership.**

(a) *In general.* In determining the ownership of an interest in an organization for purposes of § 11.414(c)-2 and § 11.414(c)-3, the constructive ownership rules of paragraph (b) of this section shall apply, subject to the operating rules contained in paragraph (c). For purposes of this section the term "interest" means: in the case of a corporation, stock; in the case of a trust or estate, an actuarial interest; in the case of a partnership, an interest in the capital or profits; and in the case of a sole proprietorship, the proprietorship.

(b) *Constructive ownership*—(1) *Options.* If a person has an option to acquire any outstanding interest in an organization, such interest shall be considered as owned by such person. For this purpose, an option to acquire an option, and each one of a series of such options, shall be considered as an option to acquire such interest.

(2) *Attribution from partnerships*—(i) *General.* An interest owned, directly or indirectly, by or for a partnership shall be considered as owned by any partner having an interest of 5 percent or more in either the profits or capital of the partnership in proportion to such partner's interest in the profits or capital, whichever such proportion is greater.

(ii) *Example.* The provisions of paragraph (b)(2)(i) of this section may be illustrated by the following example:

Example. A, B, and C, unrelated individuals, are partners in the ABC Partnership. The partners' interests in the capital and profits of ABC are as follows:

Partner	Capital	Profits
A	36%	25%
B	60%	71%
C	4%	4%

The ABC Partnership owns the entire outstanding stock (100 shares) of X Corporation. Under paragraph (b)(2)(i) of this section, A is considered to own the stock of X owned by the partnership in proportion to his interest in capital (36 percent) or profits (25 percent), whichever such proportion is greater. Therefore, A is considered to own 36 shares of X stock. Since B has a greater interest in the profits of the partnership than in the capital, B is considered to own X stock in proportion to his interest in such profits. Therefore, B is considered to own 71 shares of X stock. Since C does not have an interest of 5 percent or more in either the capital or profits of ABC, he is not considered to own any shares of X stock.

(3) *Attribution from estates and trusts*—(i) *In general.* An interest in an organization (hereinafter called an "organization interest") owned, directly, or indirectly, by or for an estate or trust shall be considered as owned by any beneficiary of such estate or trust who has an actuarial interest of 5 percent or more in such organization interest, to the extent of such actuarial interest. For purposes of this subparagraph, the actuarial interest of each beneficiary shall be determined by assuming the maximum exercise of discretion by the fiduciary in favor of such beneficiary and the maximum use of the organization interest to satisfy the beneficiary's rights. A beneficiary of an estate or trust who cannot under any circumstances receive any part of an organization interest held by the estate or trust, including the proceeds from the disposition thereof, or the income therefrom, does not have an actuarial interest in such organization interest. Thus, where stock owned by a decedent's estate has been specifically bequeathed to certain beneficiaries and the remainder of the estate has been specifically bequeathed to other beneficiaries, the stock is attributable only to the beneficiaries to whom it is specifically be-

Reg. § 11.414(c)-4(b)(3)

queathed. Similarly, a remainderman of a trust who cannot under any circumstances receive any interest in the stock of a corporation which is a part of the corpus of the trust (including any accumulated income therefrom or the proceeds from a disposition thereof) does not have an actuarial interest in such stock. However, an income beneficiary of a trust does have an actuarial interest in stock if he has any right to the income from such stock even though under the terms of the trust instrument such stock can never be distributed to him. The factors and methods prescribed in § 20.2031-10 of this chapter (Estate Tax Regulations) for use in ascertaining the value of an interest in property for estate tax purposes shall be used for purposes of this subdivision in determining a beneficiary's actuarial interest in an organization interest owned directly or indirectly by or for an estate or trust.

(ii) *Special rules for estates.* (A) For purposes of this subparagraph (3) with respect to an estate, property of a decedent shall be considered as owned by his or her estate if such property is subject to administration by the executor or administrator for the purposes of paying claims against the estate and expenses of administration notwithstanding that, under local law, legal title to such property vests in the decedent's heirs, legatees, or devisees immediately upon death.

(B) For purposes of this subparagraph (3) with respect to an estate, the term "beneficiary" includes any person entitled to receive property of a decedent pursuant to a will or pursuant to laws of descent and distribution.

(C) For purposes of this subparagraph (3) with respect to an estate, a person shall no longer be considered a beneficiary of an estate when all the property to which he or she is entitled has been received by him or her, when he or she no longer has a claim against the estate arising out of having been a beneficiary, and when there is only a remote possibility that it will be necessary for the estate to seek the return of property from him or her to seek payment from him or her by contribution or otherwise to satisfy claims against the estate or expenses of administration.

(iii) *Grantor trusts, etc.* An interest owned, directly or indirectly, by or for any portion of a trust of which a person is considered the owner under subpart E, part I, subchapter J of the Code (relating to grantors and others treated as substantial owners) is considered as owned by such person.

(4) *Attribution from corporations*—(i) *General.* An interest owned, directly or indirectly, by or for a corporation shall be considered as owned by any person who owns (directly and, in the case of a parent-subsidiary group of trades or businesses under common control, with the application of paragraph (b)(1) of this section, or in the case of a brother-sister group of trades or businesses under common control, with the application of this section) 5 percent or more in value of its stock in that proportion which the value of the stock which such person so owns bears to the total value of all the stock in such corporation.

(ii) *Example.* The provisions of paragraph (b)(4)(i) of this section may be illustrated by the following example:

Example. B, an individual, owns 60 of the 100 shares of the only class of outstanding stock of corporation P. C, an individual, owns 4 shares of the P stock, and corporation X owns 36 shares of the P stock. Corporation P owns, directly and indirectly, 50 shares of the stock of S. Under this subparagraph, B is considered to own 30 shares of the S stock (60/100 × 50), and X is considered to own 18 shares of S stock (36/100 × 50). Since C does not own 5 percent or more in the value of P stock, he is not considered as owning any of the S stock owned by P. If in this example, C's wife had owned directly 1 share of the P stock, C and his wife would each own 5 shares of the P stock, and therefore C and his wife would be considered as owning 2.5 shares of the S stock (5/100 × 50).

(5) *Spouse*—(i) *General rule.* Except as provided in paragraph (b)(5)(ii) of this section, an individual shall be considered to own an interest owned, directly or indirectly, by or for his or her spouse, other than a spouse who is legally separated from the individual under a decree of divorce, whether interlocutory or final, or a decree of separate maintenance.

(ii) *Exception.* An individual shall not be considered to own an interest in an organization owned, directly or indirectly, by or for his or her spouse on any day of a taxable year of such organization, provided that each of the following conditions are satisfied with respect to such taxable year:

(A) Such individual does not, at any time during such taxable year, own directly any interest in such organization;

(B) Such individual is not a member of the board of directors, a fiduciary, or an employee of such organization and does not participate in the management of such organization at any time during such taxable year;

(C) Not more than 50 percent of such organization's gross income for such taxable year was derived from royalties, rents, dividends, interest, and annuities; and

(D) Such interest in such organization is not, at any time during such taxable year, subject to conditions which substantially restrict or limit the spouse's right to dispose of such interest and which run in favor of the individual or the individual's children who have not attained the age of 21 years. The principles of § 11.414(c)-3(d)(6)(i) shall apply in determining whether a condition is a condition described in the preceding sentence.

(iii) *Definitions.* For purposes of paragraph (b)(5)(ii)(C) of this section, the gross income of an organization shall be determined under section 61 and the regulations thereunder. The terms "interest", "royalties", "rents", "dividends", and "annuities" shall have the same meaning such terms are given for purposes of section 1244(c) and § 1.1244(c)-1(g)(1).

(6) *Children, grandchildren, parents, and grandparents*—(i) *Children and parents.* An individual shall be considered to own an interest owned, directly or indirectly, by or for the individual's children who have not attained the age of 21 years, and if the individual has not attained the age of 21 years, an interest owned, directly or indirectly, by or for the individual's parents.

(ii) *Children, grandchildren, parents, and grandparents.* If an individual is in effective control (within the meaning of § 11.414(c)-2(c)(2)), directly and with the application of the rules of this paragraph without regard to this subdivision, of an organization, then such individual shall be considered to own an interest in such organization owned, directly or indirectly, by or for the individual's parents, grandparents, grandchildren, and children, who have attained the age of 21 years.

(iii) *Adopted children.* For purposes of this section, a legally adopted child of an individual shall be treated as a child of such individual.

(iv) *Example.* The provisions of this subparagraph (6) may be illustrated by the following example:

Example—(A) *Facts.* Individual F owns directly 40 percent of the profits interest of the DEF Partnership. His son, M, 20 years of age, owns directly 30 percent of the profits interest of DEF, and his son, A, 30 years of age, owns directly 20 percent of the profits interest of DEF. The 10 percent remaining of the profits interest and 100 percent of the capital interest of DEF is owned by an unrelated person.

(B) *F's ownership.* F owns 40 percent of the profits interest in DEF directly and is considered to own the 30 percent profits interest owned directly by M. Since, for purposes of the effective control test contained in paragraph (b)(6)(ii) of this section, F is treated as owning 70 percent of the profits interest of DEF, F is also considered as owning the 20 percent profits interest of DEF owned by his adult son, A. Accordingly, F is considered as owning a total of 90 percent of the profits interest in DEF.

(C) *M's ownership.* Minor son, M, owns 30 percent of the profits interest in DEF directly, and is considered to own the 40 percent profits interest owned directly by his father, F. However, M is not considered to own the 20 percent profits interest of DEF owned directly by his brother, A, and constructively by F, because an interest constructively owned by F by reason of family attribution is not considered as owned by him for purposes of making another member of his family the constructive owner of such interest. (See paragraph (c)(2) of this section.) Accordingly, M owns and is considered as owning a total of 70 percent of the profits interest of the DEF Partnership.

(D) *A's ownership.* Adult son, A, owns 20 percent of the profits interest in DEF directly. Since, for purposes of determining whether A effectively controls DEF under paragraph (b)(6)(ii) of this section, A is treated as owning only the percentage of profits interest he owns directly, he does not satisfy the condition precedent for the attribution of the DEF profits interest from his father. Accordingly, A is treated as owning only the 20 percent profits interest in DEF which he owns directly.

(c) *Operating rules*—(1) *In general.* Except as provided in paragraph (c)(2) of this section, an interest constructively owned by a person by reason of the application of paragraph (b)(1), (2), (3), (4), (5), or (6) of this section shall, for the purposes of applying such paragraph, be treated as actually owned by such person.

(2) *Members of family.* An interest constructively owned by an individual by reason of the application of paragraph (b)(5) or (6) of this section shall not be treated as owned by such individual for purposes of again applying such subparagraphs in order to make another the constructive owner of such interest.

(3) *Precedence of option attribution.* For purposes of this section, if an interest may be considered as owned under paragraph (b)(1) of this section (relating to option attribution) and under any other subparagraph of paragraph (b) of this section, such interest shall be considered as owned by such person under paragraph (b)(1) of this section.

(4) *Examples.* The provisions of this paragraph may be illustrated by the following examples:

Example (1). A, 30 years of age, has a 90 percent interest in the capital and profits of DEF Partnership. DEF owns all the outstanding stock of corporation X and X owns 60 shares of the 100 outstanding shares of corporation Y. Under paragraph (c)(1) of this section, the 60 shares of Y constructively owned by DEF by reason of paragraph (b)(4) of this section are treated as actually owned by DEF for purposes of applying paragraph (b)(2) of this section. Therefore, A is considered as owning 54 shares of the Y stock (90 percent of 60 shares).

Example (2). Assume the same facts as in example (1). Assume further that B, who is 20 years of age and the brother of A, directly owns 40 shares of Y stock. Although the stock of Y owned by B is considered as owned by C (the father of A and B) under paragraph (b)(6)(i) of this section, under paragraph (c)(2) of this section such stock may not be treated as owned by C for purposes of applying paragraph (b)(6)(ii) of this section in order to make A the constructive owner of such stock.

Example (3) Assume the same facts assumed for purposes of example (2), and further assume that C has an option to acquire the 40 shares of Y stock owned by his son, B. The rule contained in paragraph (c)(2) of this section does not prevent the reattribution of such 40 shares to A because, under paragraph (c)(3) of this section, C is considered as owning the 40 shares by reason of option attribution and not by reason of family attribution. Therefore, since A is in effective control of Y under paragraph (b)(6)(ii) of this section, the 40 shares of Y stock constructively owned by C are reattributed to A. A is considered as owning a total of 94 shares of Y stock.

[Sec. 414(c)] § 11.414(c)-5 (T.D. 7388, filed 10-31-75.) **Effective date.**

(a) *General rule.* Except as provided in paragraph (b) or (c) of this section, the provisions of §§ 11.414(c)-1 through 11.414(c)-4 shall apply for plan years beginning after September 2, 1974.

(b) *Existing plans.* In the case of a plan in existence on January 1, 1974, unless paragraph (c) of this section applies, the provisions of §§ 11.414(c)-1 through 11.414(c)-4 shall apply for plan years beginning after December 31, 1975. For definition of

Reg. § 11.414(c)-5(b)

24,998.56-F *(I.R.C.)* Reg. § 11.414(c)-5(b)

the term "existing plan", see § 11.410(a)-2 (c).

(c) *Existing plans electing new provisions.* In the case of a plan in existence on January 1, 1974, for which the plan administrator elects pursuant to § 11.410(a)-2 (d), the provisions of §§ 11.414(c)-1 through 11.414(c)-4 shall apply to plan years as provided in § 11.410(a)-2(d).

(d) *Application.* For purposes of the Employee Retirement Income Security Act of 1974, the provisions of §§ 11.414(c)-1 through 11.414(c)-4 do not apply for any period of time before the plan years described in paragraph (a), (b), or (c) of this section, whichever is applicable.

Temporary Rules
T.D. 7390

Temporary regulations relating to certain trustees of individual retirement accounts. (T.D. 7390, filed 11-17-75.)

In order to prescribe temporary income tax regulations (26 CFR Part 11) to provide rules under section 408 (a) (2) of the Code, relating to trustees of individual retirement accounts, the following temporary regulations are hereby adopted:

[Sec. 408(a)(2)] § 11.408 (a) (2)-1 (T.D. 7390, filed 11-17-75.) **Trustee of individual retirement accounts.**

A person may demonstrate to the satisfaction of the Commissioner that the manner in which he will administer the trust will be consistent with the requirements of section 408 only upon the filing of a written application to the Commissioner of Internal Revenue, Attention: E:EP, Internal Revenue Service, Washington, D. C. 20224. Such application must meet the applicable requirements of the regulations under section 401 (d) (1) relating to non-bank trustees of pension and profit-sharing trusts benefiting owner-employees.

Temporary regulations relating to transfers for public, charitable and religious uses. (T.D. 7393, filed 12-16-75.)

In order to prescribe temporary income tax regulations (26 CFR Part 8) relating to charitable remainder trusts and temporary estate tax regulations (26 CFR Part 24) relating to transfers for public, charitable and religious uses pursuant to section 2055 of the Internal Revenue Code of 1954, as amended by section 3 of the Act of Oct. 26, 1974 (Pub. L. 93-483, 88 Stat. 1457), the following temporary regulations are hereby adopted:

[Sec. 664] § 8.1 (T.D. 7393, filed 12-16-75.) **Charitable remainder trusts.**

(a) *Certain wills and trusts in existence on September 21, 1974.* In the case of a will executed before September 21, 1974, or a trust created (within the meaning of applicable local law) after July 31, 1969, and before September 21, 1974, which is amended pursuant to section 2055(e)(3) and § 24.1 of this Chapter (Temporary Estate Tax Regulations), a charitable remainder trust resulting from such amendment will be treated as a charitable remainder trust from the date it would be deemed created under § 1.664-1(a)(4) and (5) of this chapter (Income Tax Regulations), whether or not such date is after September 20, 1974.

(b) *Certain transfers to trusts created before August 1, 1969.* Property transferred to a trust created (within the meaning of applicable local law) before August 1, 1969, whose governing instrument provides than an organization described in section 170(c) receives an irrevocable remainder interest in such trust shall be deemed transferred to a trust created on the date of such transfer, provided that the transfer occurs after July 31, 1969, and prior to October 18, 1971, and pursuant to an amendment provided in § 24.1 of this chapter (Temporary Estate Tax Regulations), the transferred property and any undistributed income therefrom is severed and placed in a separate trust as of the date of the amendment.

Reg. § 8.1(b)

Temporary Rules (I.R.C.) 24,998.63
T.D. 7402

Temporary regulations relating to time when contributions to "H.R. 10" plans deemed made. (T.D. 7402, filed 2-4-76.)

This document contains temporary income tax regulations (26 CFR Part 11) under section 404(a)(6) of the Internal Revenue Code of 1954, as amended by section 1013(c)(2) of the Employee Retirement Income Security Act of 1974 (88 Stat. 923) (hereinafter referred to as the "Act"), and is applicable for purposes of the election provided in section 1017(i) of the Act, as added by section 402 of the Tax Reduction Act of 1975 (89 Stat. 47).

In order to prescribe temporary regulations (26 CFR Part 11) to reflect the election prescribed in the Tax Reduction Act of 1975, the following temporary regulation is hereby adopted:

[Sec. 404(a)(6)] § 11.404(a)(6)-1 (T.D. 7402, filed 2-4-76.) Time when contributions to "H.R. 10" plans considered made.

(a) *In general.* Section 404(a)(6), as amended by section 1013(c)(2) of the Employee Retirement Income Security Act of 1974, provides that for purposes of paragraphs (1), (2), and (3) of section 404(a), a taxpayer shall be deemed to have made a payment on the last day of the preceding taxable year if the payment is on account of such taxable year and is made not later than the time prescribed by law for filing the return for such taxable year (including extensions thereof). Under section 1017(b) of the Employee Retirement Income Security Act of 1974 (prior to its amendment by the Tax Reduction Act of 1975), in the case of a plan which was in existence on January 1, 1974, the foregoing provision generally applies for contributions on account of taxable years of an employer ending with or within plan years beginning after December 31, 1975. In the case of a plan not in existence on January 1, 1974, the foregoing provision generally applies for contributions on account of taxable years of an employer ending with or within plan years beginning after September 2, 1974. See § 11.410(a)-2(c) for time a plan is considered in existence. See also § 11.410(a)-2 (d), which provides that a plan in existence on January 1, 1974 may elect to have certain provisions, including the amendment to section 404(a)(6) contained in section 1013 of the Employee Retirement Income Security Act of 1974, apply to a plan year beginning after September 2, 1974, and before the otherwise applicable effective date contained in that section.

(b) *"H.R. 10" plans may elect new provision.* Under section 402 of the Tax Reduction Act of 1975 (89 Stat. 47), in the case of a plan which was in existence on January 1, 1974, and which provides contributions or benefits for employees some or all of whom are employees within the meaning of section 401(c)(1) of the Code and § 1.401-10(b), the provision described in paragraph (a) of this section shall apply for taxable years of an employer ending with or within plan years beginning after December 31, 1974, but only if the employer (within the meaning of section 401(c)(4) of the Code and § 1.401-10(e)) elects to have such provisions apply as provided in paragraph (c) of this section.

(c) *Manner of election.* The election described in paragraph (b) of this section shall be considered to be made if the employer (as described in paragraph (b) of this section)—

(1) Makes a contribution which relates to his preceding taxable year within the time prescribed in paragraph (a) of this section to a plan described in paragraph (b) of this section, and

(2) Claims a deduction for such contribution on his tax return for such year (or, in the case of a contribution by a partnership on behalf of a partner, the contribution is shown on Schedule K of the partnership tax return for such year); no formal statement is necessary. In the case of an employer whose income tax return for the year on account of which the payment is made is required to be filed (determined without regard to extensions of time) on or before April 15, 1976, and who made a payment within the time prescribed in paragraph (a) of this section, the election also may be made by filing an amended return or claim for refund with respect to such year on or before September 30, 1976.

(d) *Election is irrevocable.* Any election made under paragraph (c) of this section, once made, shall be irrevocable.

(e) *Examples.* The rules of this section are illustrated by the following examples.

Example (1). On October 15, 1976, the ABC Partnership made a contribution to the ABC Profit Sharing Plan and Trust on behalf of partners and common-law employees with respect to the plan year ending December 31, 1975. The ABC Profit Sharing Trust was exempt under section 501(a) throughout 1975. The contribution for both partners and employees was reflected on the partnership return for the calendar year 1975 which was filed on October 10, 1976; proper extensions of the due date of the partnership return had been received, extending the due date to October 15, 1976. The election is valid since all requirements of this section have been met.

Example (2). The XYZ Partnership made a plan contribution on April 10, 1976, with respect to the plan year ending December 31, 1975, but the amount contributed for 1975 was not reflected in the partnership return filed for the calendar year 1975 on April 15, 1976. However, the XYZ Partnership filed an amended partnership return for the year 1975 on September 30, 1976, claiming a deduction for the employee-related contribution and setting forth on Schedule K the contribution relating to partners. The election is valid, since the contribution on account of 1975 was made within the time required, and was shown on the amended tax return of the employer for 1975 filed within the time prescribed in paragraph (c)(2) of this section.

Example (3). Mr. Smith, a sole proprietor whose taxable year is the calendar year, made a contribution to the Smith Profit Sharing Plan and Trust on April 15, 1976, for the plan year which began December 1,

Reg. § 11.404(a)(6)-1(e)

24,998.64 *(I.R.C.)*   Reg. § 11.404(a)(6)-1(e)

1974, and ended November 30, 1975. The plan was in existence on January 1, 1974. Since the contribution was made within the time prescribed by this section and was on account of a taxable year of the employer ending within a plan year which began after December 31, 1974, the contribution may be deducted on Mr. Smith's return for 1975, even though the contribution was for a plan year beginning before December 31, 1974.

Example (4). The DEF Partnership, reporting its income on the basis of a fiscal year ending June 30, made a contribution to its "H.R. 10" plan which was in existence on January 1, 1974, and whose plan year was the calendar year. The contribution was made on September 30, 1975, and was on account of the taxable year of the partnership ending June 30, 1975. The contribution was properly reflected in the partnership return for the fiscal year ending June 30, 1975. The partnership's election to have section 404(a)(6), as amended, apply to its fiscal year ending June 30, 1975, is valid since that year ended with or within a plan year beginning after December 31, 1974.

T.D. 7417

Temporary regulations relating to real estate investment trusts and extensions of the 2-year grace period with respect to foreclosure property. (T.D. 7417, filed 4-7-76.)

In order to prescribe temporary regulations, which shall remain in force and effect until superseded by permanent regulations, relating to the extension of the 2-year grace period with respect to foreclosure property under section 856(e) of the Internal Revenue Code of 1954, the following regulations are hereby adopted:

○→ [Sec. 856(e)] § 10.3 (T.D. 7417, filed 4-7-76.) **Extension of 2-year grace period with respect to foreclosure property held by a real estate investment trust.**

(a) *In general.* Under section 856(e) of the Code a real estate investment trust ("REIT") may elect to treat as foreclosure property any real property (including interests in real property), and any personal property incident to such real property, that the REIT acquires after December 31, 1973, as the result of having bid in such property at foreclosure, or having otherwise reduced such property to ownership or possession by agreement or process of law, after there was default (or default was imminent) on a lease of such property (where the REIT was the lessor) or on an indebtedness owed to the REIT which such property secured. Property that a REIT has elected to treat as foreclosure property ceases to be foreclosure property with respect to such REIT on the date which is 2 years after the date on which the REIT acquired the property, unless the REIT has been granted an extension or extensions of such 2-year period (hereinafter referred as the "grace period") in accordance with this section. In the event that the grace period is extended, the property ceases to be foreclosure property on the day immediately following the last day of the grace period, as extended.

(b) *Rules relating to date of acquisition.* Foreclosure property which secured an indebtedness owed to the REIT is acquired for purposes of section 856(e) on the date on which the REIT acquires ownership of the property for Federal income tax purposes. Foreclosure property which a REIT owned and leased to another is acquired for purposes of section 856(e) on the date on which the REIT acquires possession of the property from its lessee. A REIT will not be considered to have acquired ownership of property for purposes of section 856(e) where it takes control of such property as a mortgagee-in-possession and cannot receive any profit or sustain any loss with respect to the property except as a creditor of the mortgagor. A REIT may be considered to have acquired ownership of property for purposes of section 856(e) even though legal title to the property is held by another person. For example, where, upon foreclosure of a mortgage held by the REIT, legal title to the property is acquired in the name of a nominee for the exclusive benefit of the REIT and the REIT is the equitable owner of the property, the REIT will be considered to have acquired ownership of such property for purposes of section 856(e). Generally, the fact that under local law the mortgagor has a right of redemption after foreclosure shall not be relevant in determining whether the REIT has acquired ownership of the property for purposes of section 856(e).

(c) *Extension of grace period*—(1) If the REIT establishes to the satisfaction of the district director of the internal revenue district in which is located the principal place of business or principal office or agency of the REIT that an extension of the grace period is necessary for the orderly liquidation of the REIT's interest in foreclosure property, or for an orderly renegotiation of a lease or leases of the property, the district director may extend such 2-year period. An extension shall be for a period of not more than 1 year, and not more than two extensions shall be granted with respect to any property. An extension of the grace period may be granted by the district director either before or after the date on which the grace period, but for such extension, would expire, and shall be effective as of the date on which the grace period, but for such extension, would expire.

(2) Generally, in order to establish the necessity of an extension, the REIT must demonstrate that it has made good faith efforts to renegotiate leases with respect to, or dispose of, the foreclosure property. In certain cases, however, the REIT may establish the necessity of an extension even though it has not made such efforts. For example, if the REIT demonstrates that, for valid business reasons, construction of the foreclosure property could not be completed before the expiration of the grace period, the necessity of the extension could be established even though the REIT had made no effort to sell the property. The fact that property was acquired as foreclosure property prior to January 3, 1975 (the date of enactment of section 856(e)), generally shall be considered as a factor (but not a controlling factor) which tends to establish that an extension of the grace period is necessary.

(d) *Time for requesting an extension of the grace period.*—(1) *General rule.* A request for an extension of the grace period must be filed with the appropriate district director more than 60 days before the day on which the grace period would otherwise expire.

(2) *Exception.* In the case of a grace period which would otherwise expire before August 6, 1976, a request for an extension will be considered to be timely filed if filed on or before June 7, 1976.

(e) *Information required.* The request for an extension of the grace period shall identify the property with respect to which the request is being made and shall also include the following information:

(1) The name, address, and taxpayer identification number of the REIT,

(2) The date the property was acquired as foreclosure property by the REIT,

(3) The taxable year of the REIT in which the property was acquired,

(4) If the REIT has been previously

Reg. § 10.3(e)(4)

24,988.66 *(I.R.C.)*   Reg. § 10.3(e)(4)   4-12-76

granted an extension of the grace period with respect to the property, a statement to that effect (which shall include the date on which the grace period, as extended, expires) and a copy of the information which accompanied the request for the previous extension,

(5) A statement of the reasons why the grace period should be extended,

(6) A description of any efforts made by the REIT after the acquisition of the property to dispose of the property or to renegotiate any lease with respect to the property, and

(7) A description of any other factors which tend to establish that an extension of the grace period is necessary for the orderly liquidation of the REIT's interest in the property, or for an orderly renegotiation of a lease or leases of the property.

The REIT shall also furnish any additional information requested by the district director after the request for extension is filed.

Temporary Rules *(I.R.C.)* 24,998.69

T.D. 7425

Temporary regulations relating to the definition of certain terms in the prohibited transaction provisions. (T.D. 7425, filed 8-5-76.)

This document amends the Temporary Excise Tax Regulations under the Employee Retirement Income Security Act of 1974 (26 CFR Part 141) by adding § 141.4975-13. This new section prescribes temporary use of 26 CFR 53.4941(e)-1 (Foundation Excise Tax Regulations relating to foundation self-dealing taxes) for matters involving the terms which appear both in section 4941(e) of the Internal Revnue Code of 1954 (the Code) (relating to foundation self-dealing) and section 4975(f) of the Code (relating to employee benefit plan prohibited transactions). These terms are: "taxable period," "amount involved," "correction," and "correction period." These regulations will be effective until superseded by permanent regulations under the relevant paragraphs of section 4975(f). No inferences should be drawn from these temporary regulations concerning the contents of permanent regulations, which have not yet been proposed.

Accordingly, Part 141 of the Temporary Excise Tax Regulations under the Employee Retirement Income Security Act of 1974 are amended by adding the following new section:

[Sec. 4975(f)] § 141.4975-13 (T.D. 7425, filed 8-5-76.) **Definition of "taxable period", "amount involved", "correction", and "correction period".**

Until superseded by permanent regulations under sections 4975(f)(2), (4), (5) and (6), § 53.4941(e)-1 of this chapter (Foundation Excise Tax Regulations) will be controlling to the extent such regulations describe terms appearing both in section 4941(e) and section 4975(f).

Reg. § 141.4975-13

Temporary Rules
T.D. 7439

Temporary regulations relating to extension of time to make contributions to satisfy requirements of section 412 of the Internal Revenue Code of 1954. (T.D. 7439, filed 10-21-76.)

In order to prescribe temporary income tax regulations (26 CFR Part 11) under section 412 (c) (10) of the Internal Revenue Code of 1954, as added to such Code by section 1013 (a) of the Employee Retirement Income Security Act (Pub. L. No. 93-406, 88 Stat. 917) the following temporary regulations are hereby adopted:

[Sec. 414] § 11.412(c)-12 (T.D. 7439, filed 10-21-76.) **Extension of time to make contributions to satisfy requirements of section 412.**

(a) *In general.* Section 412(c)(10) of the Internal Revenue Code of 1954 provides that for purposes of section 412 a contribution for a plan year made after the end of such plan year but not later than two and one-half months after the last day of such plan year shall be deemed to have been made on such last day. Section 412 (c) (10) further provides that the two and one-half month period may be extended for not more than six months under regulations.

(b) *Six month extension of two and one-half month period*—(1) For purposes of section 412 a contribution for a plan year to which section 412 applies that is made not more than eight and one-half months after the end of such plan year shall be deemed to have been made on the last day of such year.

(2) The rules of this section relating to the time a contribution to a plan is deemed made for purposes of the minimum funding standard under section 412 are independent from the rules contained in section 404 (a) (6) relating to the time a contribution to a plan is deemed made for purposes of claiming a deduction for such contribution under section 404.

Reg. § 11.412(c)-12

T.D. 7442

Temporary regulations relating to special elections for certain section 403(b) annuity contracts. (T.D. 7442, filed 11-23-76; amended by T.D. 7482, filed 4-14-77; T.D. 7531, 1-5-78.)

This document contains temporary income tax regulations (26 CFR Part 11) under section 415(c)(4) of the Internal Revenue Code of 1954, as added by section 2004(a)(2) of the Employee Retirement Income Security Act of 1974 (Pub. L. No. 93-406, 88 Stat. 979) (hereinafter referred to as the "Act").

[Also,] this document amends the Temporary Income Tax Regulations Under the Employee Retirement Income Security Act of 1974 relating to section 403(b) annuity contracts and salary reduction agreements. This amendment has been prepared in response to requests by the public. This amendment affects employees of some tax-exempt organizations and provides them with somewhat easier rules for complying with the law.

Date: This amendment is applicable for a taxable year beginning in 1976 and for a limitation year ending with or within a taxable year beginning in 1976.

In order to prescribe temporary income tax regulations (26 CFR Part 11) under section 415(c)(4) of the Internal Revenue Code of 1954, as added to such Code by section 2004(a)(2) of the Employee Retirement Income Security Act of 1974 (Pub. L. No. 93-406, 88 Stat. 979) the following temporary regulations are hereby adopted [and amended]:

○── [Sec. 415(c)(4)] § 11.415(c)(4)-1 (T.D. 7442, filed 11-23-76; amended by T.D. 7482, filed 4-14-77; T.D. 7531, filed 1-5-78.) **Special elections for section 403(b) annuity contracts purchased by educational institutions, hospitals and home health service agencies.**

(a) *Limitations applicable to contributions for section 403(b) annuity contracts—*
(1) *In general.* An annuity contract described in section 403(b) which is treated as a defined contribution plan (as defined in section 414(i)) is subject to the rules regarding the amount of annual additions (as defined in section 415(c)(2)) that may be made to a participant's account in a defined contribution plan for any limitation year (as defined in subparagraph (2) of this paragraph) under section 415(c)(1) and Revenue Ruling 75-481, 1975-2 C.B. 188. An annual addition to the account of an individual under a section 403(b) annuity contract in excess of such limitation for a limitation year is includible in the gross income of the individual for the taxable year with or within which such limitation year ends and reduces the exclusion allowance under section 403(b)(2) for such taxable year to the extent of the excess. Such annuity contracts are, of course, also subject to the limitation imposed by section 403(b)(2) with respect to the amount that may be contributed by the employer for the purchase of an annuity contract described in section 403(b) and be excluded from the gross income of the employee on whose behalf such annuity contract is purchased. In general, the excludable contribution for such an annuity contract for a particular taxable year is the lesser of the exclusion allowance computed under section 403(b)(2) for such taxable year or the limitation imposed by section 415(c)(1) for the limitation year ending with or within such taxable year. For purposes of the limitation imposed by section 415(c)(1), the amount contributed toward the purchase of an annuity contract described in section 403(b) is treated as allocated to the employee's account as of the last day of the limitation year ending with or within the taxable year during which such contribution is made.

(2) *Limitation Year.* For purposes of this section—
(i) Except as provided in subdivision (ii) of this subparagraph, the limitation year applicable to an individual on whose behalf an annuity contract described in section 403(b) has been purchased by an employer shall be the calendar year unless such individual elects to change the limitation year to another 12-month period and attaches a statement to his income tax return filed for the taxable year in which such change is made.

(ii) The limitation year applicable to an individual described in subdivision (i) of this subparagraph who is in control (within the meaning of section 414(b) or (c) as modified by section 415(h)) of any employer shall be the same as the limitation year of such employer.

(3) *Special elections.* Under section 415(c)(4), special elections are permitted with respect to section 403(b) annuity contracts (including custodial accounts treated as section 403(b) annuity contracts under section 403(b)(7)) purchased by educational institutions (as defined in section 151(e)(4) and the regulations thereunder), home health service agencies (as defined in subparagraph (4) of this paragraph) and hospitals. In lieu of the limitation described in section 415(c)(1)(B) otherwise applicable to the annual addition (as defined in section 415(c)(2)) that may be made to the account of a participant in a qualified defined contribution plan for a particular limitation year, an individual for whom an annuity contract described in this subparagraph is purchased may elect, in accordance with the provisions of paragraph (b) of this section, to have substituted for such limitation the amounts described in subparagraph (5)(i) or (5)(ii) of this paragraph. In lieu of the exclusion allowance determined under section 403(b)(2) and the regulations thereunder otherwise applicable for the taxable year with or within which the limitation year ends to an individual on whose behalf an annuity contract described in this subparagraph is purchased, such an individual may elect, in accordance with the provisions of paragraph (b) of this section, to have substituted for such exclusion allowance the amount described in subparagraph (5)(iii) of this paragraph.

(4) *Definition.* For purposes of this section, a home health service agency is an organization described in section 501(c)(3) which is exempt from taxation un-

Reg. § 11.415(c)(4)-1(a)(4)

24,998.74 (I.R.C.) Reg. § 11.415(c)(4)-1(a)(4) 1-16-78

der section 501(a) and which has been determined by the Secretary of Health, Education and Welfare to be a home health agency under section 1395(x)(o) of Title 42 of the United States Code.

(5) *Elections.* (i) For the limitation year that ends with or within the taxable year in which an individual separates from the service of his employer (and only for such limitation year), the "(A) election limitation" shall be the exclusion allowance computed under section 403(b)(2)(A) and the regulations thereunder (without regard to section 415) for the taxable year in which such separation occurs taking into account such individual's years of service (as defined in section 403(b)(4) and the regulations thereunder) for the employer and contributions described in section 403(b)(2)(A)(ii) and the regulations thereunder during the period of years (not exceeding 10) ending on the date of separation. For purposes of the preceding sentence, all service for the employer performed within such period must be taken into account. However, the "(A) election limitation" shall not exceed the amount described in section 415(c)(1)(A) (as adjusted under section 415(d)(1)(B)) applicable to such individual for such limitation year.

(ii) For any limitation year, the "(B) election limitation" shall be equal to the least of the following amounts—

(A) $4,000, plus 25 percent of the individual's includible compensation (as defined in section 403(b)(3) and the regulations thereunder) for the taxable year with or within which the limitation year ends,

(B) The amount of the exclusion allowance determined under section 403(b)(2)(A) and the regulations thereunder for the taxable year with or within which such limitation year ends, or

(C) $15,000.

(iii) For any taxable year, the "(C) election limitation" shall equal the lesser of the amount described in section 415(c)(1)(A) (as adjusted under section 415(d)(1)(B)) or the amount described in section 415(c)(1)(B) applicable to the individual for the limitation year ending with or within such taxable year. For purposes of the preceding sentence, compensation described in section 415(c)(1)(B) taken into account for a particular limitation year does not include amounts contributed toward the purchase of an annuity contract described in section 403(b) during such limitation year (whether or not includable in the gross income of the individual on whose behalf such contribution is made).

(b) *Special rules for elections and salary reduction agreements for years before final regulations are published*—(1) *Election.* (i) For a limitation year which ends before or with or within the taxable year in which applicable final regulations under section 415 are first published in the Federal Register, an individual may wish to take advantage of the alternative limitations described in section 415 (c)(4). One way of doing this is to attach a statement of intention to his individual tax return for the taxable year. The statement should provide that the individual intends to elect one of those alternative limitations. It should also specify which alternative he intends to elect. No form is prescribed for the statement of intention, but it must include the individual's name, address and Social Security number. If the individual is not required to file an income tax return for the taxable year to which the statement of intention is to apply, the statement of intention may still be filed at the Internal Revenue Service Center where that individual would file the return if he were required to file. It should be filed by the time he would have filed his return. The Internal Revenue Service will treat the statement of intention as an actual election for all taxable years through the taxable year in which applicable final regulations under section 415 are first published in the Federal Register for all purposes, except that it will not be irrevocable. If, pursuant to this subdivision, an individual takes advantage of an alternative limitation for a taxable year, then, except as provided in subdivision (iii) of this subparagraph, the individual may not take advantage of any other alternative limitation pursuant to this subdivision for any taxable year. If an individual does not file a statement of intention, he will still be able to take advantage of the alternative limitations for these taxable years. He will be able to do this if he determines his income tax liability for the taxable year in a way which is consistent with one of the alternative limitations.

(ii) The actual election for all taxable years through the taxable year in which applicable final regulations under section 415 are first published in the Federal Register will be made by filing the election with the Internal Revenue Service at the time and in the manner to be described by final regulations under section 415.

(iii) When an individual makes the actual election for any taxable year through the taxable year in which applicable final regulations under section 415 are published in the Federal Register, he may choose any of the alternative limitations, even if his choice is inconsistent with the alternative limitation which he used in determining his income tax liability for that taxable year. He may also choose not to elect any of the alternative limitations, even if he used one of them in determining his income tax liability for that taxable year. However, if his choice is different from the choice which he used in determining his income tax liability for the taxable year, there may be an adjustment in his tax for that year. For purposes of section 6654 (relating to failure of an individual to pay estimated tax), a difference in tax for such a year resulting from a difference in these choices will not be treated as an underpayment. This rule applies to the extent the difference in tax is due to the actual election of one of the alternative limitations or to a final decision not to use one of the alternative limitations for the taxable year.

(2) *Salary Reduction Agreements for 1976 and 1977.* (i) An individual who is employed by an organization described in paragraph (a)(3) may make a salary reduction agreement for his taxable year beginning in 1976 or 1977 at any time before the end of the 1976 or 1977 taxable year, respectively, without the agreement's being considered a new agreement within the meaning of § 1.403 (b)-1 (b) (3) (i). The agreement for 1976 may be made on or before June 15, 1977, if that date is later than the end of the individual's 1976 taxable year. The agreement for 1977 may be

made on or before April 17, 1978, if that date is later than the end of the individual's 1977 taxable year.

(ii) This subparagraph applies only if the individual actually elects one of the alternative limitations under section 415 (c)(4) for 1976 or 1977 (as the case may be).

(iii) The salary reduction agreement for 1976 may be made effective with respect to any amount earned during the taxpayer's most recent one-year period of service (as described in § 1.403 (b)-1 (f)) ending not later than the end of the 1976 taxable year, notwithstanding § 1.403 (b)-1 (b) (3) (i). Similarly, the salary reduction agreement for 1977 may be made effective with respect to such period of service ending not later than the end of the 1977 taxable year.

(iv) If the salary reduction agreement for 1976 is entered into at any time after December 31, 1976, or if the salary reduction agreement for 1977 is entered into at any time after December 31, 1977, an amended Form W-2 must be filed on behalf of the individual.

(3) *Election is irrevocable.* The election described in paragraph (a) (3) of this section, once made in accordance with the provisions of subparagraph (1) of this paragraph, shall be irrevocable with respect to the limitation years or taxable years to which the election relates.

(4) *Limitations.* With respect to any limitation or taxable year, an election by an individual pursuant to subparagraph (1) of this paragraph to have any subdivision of paragraph (a)(5) of this section apply to contributions made on his behalf by his employer with respect to any section 403(b) annuity contract will preclude an election to have any other subdivision of paragraph (a)(5) apply for any future limitation or taxable year with respect to any section 403(b) annuity contract contributions made by any employer of such individual. With respect to any limitation year, an election by an individual to have paragraph (a)(5)(i) of this section apply to contributions made on his behalf by his employer with respect to any section 403(b) annuity contract will preclude an election to have any subdivision of paragraph (a)(5) apply for any future limitation or taxable year with respect to any section 403(b) annuity contract contributions made by any employer of such individual.

(5) *Aggregation rules — (i) Annuity contracts described in section 403(b).* For purposes of applying the limitations of this section for a particular limitation or taxable year, all contributions toward the purchase of annuity contracts described in section 403(b) made on behalf of an individual by his employer and any related employer (as defined in subdivision (ii) of this subparagraph) must be aggregated without regard to—

(A) Whether such individual makes any election pursuant to subparagraph (1) of this paragraph for such year, and

(B) Whether such individual files a statement of intention pursuant to subparagraph (1) of this paragraph, for such year.

In addition, any other aggregation required by Revenue Ruling 75-481, 1975-2 C.B. 188, must be made to the extent applicable.

(ii) *Definition.* For purposes of this section, with respect to a particular employer, a related employer is any other employer which is a member of a controlled group of corporations (as defined in section 414(b), and the regulations thereunder and as modified by section 415(h)) or a group of trades or business (whether or not incorporated) under common control (as defined in section 414(c) and the regulations thereunder and as modified by section 415(h)) in which such particular employer is a member.

(c) *Examples:* The provisions of this section may be illustrated by the following examples:

Example (1). Doctor M is an employee of H Hospital (an organization described in section 501(c)(3) and exempt from taxation under section 501(a)) for the entire 1976 calendar year. M is not in control of H within the meaning of section 414(b) or (c), as modified by section 415(h). M uses the calendar year as the taxable year and M uses the calendar year as the limitation year. M has includible compensation (as defined in section 403(b)(3) and the regulations thereunder) and compensation (as defined in section 415(c)(3) for taxable year 1976 of $30,000, and M has 4 years of service (as defined in § 1.403(b)-1(f)) with H as of December 31, 1976. During M's prior service with H, H had contributed a total of $12,000 on M's behalf for annuity contracts described in section 403(b), which amount was excludable from M's gross income for such prior years. Thus, for the limitation year ending with or within taxable year 1976, M's exclusion allowance determined under section 403(b)(2)(A) is $12,000 ((.20 x $30,000 x 4) — $12,000). The limitation imposed by section 415(c)(1) that is applicable to M for limitation year 1976 is the lesser of $26,825 (the amount described in section 415(c)(1)(A) adjusted under section 415(d)(1)(B) for limitation year 1976) or $7,500 (the amount described in section 415(c)(1)(B)). Absent the special elections provided in section 415(c)(4), $7,500 would be the maximum contribution H could make for annuity contracts described in section 403(b) on M's behalf for limitation year 1976 without increasing M's gross income for taxable year 1976. However, because H is an organization described in section 415(c)(4), M may make a special election with respect to amounts contributed by H on M's behalf for section 403(b) annuity contracts for 1976. Assume that M does not separate from the service of H during 1976 and that, therefore, the "(A) election limitation" described in section 415(c)(4)(A) is not available to M. If M elects the "(B) election limitation" for 1976, H could contribute $11,500 on M's behalf for annuity contracts described in section 403(b) for that year (the least of $11,500 (the amount described in section 415(c)(4)(B)(i)); $12,000 (the amount described in section 415(c)(4)(B)(ii)), and $15,000 (the amount described in section 415(c)(4)(B)(iii))). If M elects the "(C) election limitation" for 1976, H could only contribute up to $7,500 (the lower of the amounts described in section 415(c)(1)(A) or (B)) for section 403(b) annuity contracts on M's behalf for 1976 without increasing M's gross income for that year.

Example (2). Assume the same facts as in example (1) except that H had contributed a total of $18,000 on M's behalf for

Reg. § 11.415(c)(4)-1(c)

24,998.74-B*(I.R.C.)* Reg. § 11.415(c)(4)-1(c) 1-16-78

annuity contracts in prior years, which amount was excludable from M's gross income for such prior years. Accordingly, for 1976, M's exclusion allowance determined under section 403(b)(2)(A) is $6,000 ((.20x $30,000 x 4) — $18,000). The limitation imposed by section 415(c)(1) applicable to M for 1976 is $7,500 (the lesser of the amount described in section 415(c)(1)(A) or (B)). Absent the special elections provided in section 415(c)(4), $6,000 would be the maximum amount H could contribute for annuity contracts described in section 403(b) on M's behalf for 1976 without increasing M's gross income for that year. However, if M elects the "(C) election limitation" for 1976, H may contribute up to $7,500 without increasing M's gross income for that year.

Example (3). G, a teacher, is an employee of E, an educational institution described in section 151(e)(4). G uses the calendar year as the taxable year and G uses the 12-month consecutive period beginning July 1 as the limitation year. G has includible compensation (as defined in section 403(b)(3) and the regulations thereunder) for taxable year 1976 of $12,000 and G has compensation (as defined in section 415(c)(3)) for the limitation year ending with or within taxable year 1976 of $12,000. G has 20 years of service (as defined in § 1.403(b)-1(f)) as of May 30, 1976, the date G separates from the service of E. During G's service with E before taxable year 1976, E had contributed $34,000 toward the purchase of a section 403(b) annuity contract on G's behalf, which amount was excludable from G's gross income for such prior years. Of this amount, $19,000 was so contributed and excluded during the 10 year period ending on May 30, 1976. For the taxable year 1976, G's exclusion allowance determined under section 403(b)(2)(A) is $14,000 ((.20 × $12,000 × 20) — $34,000). Absent the special elections described in section 415(c)(4), $3,000 (the lesser of G's exclusion allowance for taxable year 1976 or the section 415(c)(1) limitation applicable to G for the limitation year ending with or within such taxable year) would be the maximum excludable contribution E could make for section 403 b) annuity contracts on G's behalf for the mitation year ending with or within taxble year 1976. However, because E is an rganization described in section 415(c)(4), may make a special election with repect to amounts contributed on G's behalf y E for section 403(b) annuity contracts or the limitation year ending with or within taxable year 1976. Because G has separated from the service of E during such taxable year, G may elect the "(A) election limitation" as well as the "(B) election limitation" or the "(C) election limitation". If G elects the "(A) election limitation" for the limitation year ending with or within taxable year 1976, E could contribute up to $5,000 ((.20 × $12,000 × 10) — $19,000) on G's behalf for section 403(b) annuity contracts for such limitation year without increasing G's gross income for the taxable year with or within which such limitation year ends. If G elects the "(B) election limitation" for such limitation year, E could contribute $7,000 (the least of $7,000 (the amount described in section 415(c)(4)(B)(i)); $14,000 (the amount described in section 415(c)(4)(B)(ii); and $15,000 (the amount described in section 415(c)(4)(B)(iii))). If G elects the "(C) election limitation" for taxable year 1976, E could contribute $3,000 (the lesser of the amounts described in section 415(c)(1)(A) or (B)).

(d) *Plan year.* For purposes of section 415 and this section, an annuity contract described in section 403(b) shall be deemed to have a plan year coinciding with the taxable year of the individual on whose behalf the contract has been purchased unless that individual demonstrates that a different 12-month period should be considered to be the plan year.

(e) *Effective date.* The provisions of this section are applicable for taxable years beginning in and for limitation years ending with or within taxable years beginning in 1976.

T.D. 7445

Temporary regulations relating to loss deductions of corporate partners in a partnership. (T.D. 7445, filed 12-17-76.)

In order to provide immediate guidance with respect to the amendment of section 704 (d), Temporary Income Tax regulations under the Tax Reform Act of 1976 (26 CFR Part 7) are added as follows:

The following section is inserted in the appropriate place:

[Sec. 704(d)] § 7.704-1 (T.D. 7445, filed 12-17-76.) **Partner's distributive share.**

(a) [Reserved]

(b) [Reserved]

(c) [Reserved]

(d) *Limitation on allowance of losses.*

(1) [Reserved]

(2) [Reserved]

(3) (i) Section 213 (e) of the Tax Reform Act of 1976 amended section 704 (d) of the Internal Revenue Code relating to the deductions by partners of losses incurred by a partnership. A partner is entitled to deduct the share of partnership loss to the extent of the adjusted basis of the partner's interest in the partnership. As amended, section 704 (d) provides, in general, that the adjusted basis of a partner's interest in the partnership for the purpose of deducting partnership losses shall not include any portion of a partnership liability for which the partner has no personal liability. This restriction, however, does not apply to any activity to the extent that section 465 of the Code applies nor to any partnership whose principal activity is investing in real property, other than mineral property. Section 465 does not apply to corporations other than a subchapter S corporation or a personal holding company.

(ii) The restrictions in the amendment to section 704 (d) will not apply to any corporate partner with respect to liabilities incurred in an activity described in section 465 (c) (1). In all other respects the restrictions in the amendment will apply to all corporate partners unless the partnership's principal activity is investment in real property, other than mineral property.

Reg. § 7.704-1 (d) (3)

T.D. 7449

Temporary regulations relating to election to have investment credit for movie and television films determined in accordance with previous litigation. (T.D. 7449, filed 12-22-76.)

Under section 804(c)(3) of the Tax Reform Act of 1976, any taxpayer who filed an action in any court of competent jurisdiction before January 1, 1976, for a determination of such taxpayer's rights to investment credit under section 38 of the Internal Revenue Code of 1954 with respect to any film placed in service in any taxable year beginning before January 1, 1975, may elect to have investment credit on all films placed in service in taxable years beginning before January 1, 1975 (except those subject to an election under section 804(e)(2) of the Act) determined as though section 804 of the Act (except section 804(c)(3) of the Act) had not been enacted.

Section 804(c)(3)(D) of the Act provides that the election shall be made by filing a notification of such election with the National Office of the Internal Revenue Service. In order to provide taxpayers who may wish to make this election assurance that they do so properly, paragraph (b) of § 7.48-1 of the regulations contained in this Treasury decision provide a permissible, but not mandatory, means of making the election.

In order to prescribe temporary income tax regulations under the Tax Reform Act of 1976 (26 CFR Part 7) relating to the means of making the election to have the investment credit for movie and television films determined in accordance with previous litigation under section 804(c)(3) of the Tax Reform Act of 1976 (P.L. 94-455, 90 Stat. 1595), the following temporary regulations are hereby adopted and added to Part 7, established at 41 F.R. 55344, December 20, 1976:

[Sec. 48] § 7.48-1 (T.D. 7449, filed 12-22-76.) **Election to have investment credit for movie and television films determined in accordance with previous litigation.**

(a) *Generally.* Under section 804(c)(3) of the Tax Reform Act of 1976 (P.L. 94-455, 90 Stat. 1595), any taxpayer who filed an action in any court of competent jurisdiction before January 1, 1976, for a determination of such taxpayer's rights to investment credit under section 38 of the Internal Revenue Code of 1954 with respect to any film placed in service in any taxable year beginning before January 1, 1975, may elect to have investment credit on all films placed in service in taxable years beginning before January 1, 1975 (except those subject to an election under section 804(e)(2) of the Act), determined as though section 804 of the Act (except section 804(c)(3) of the Act) had not been enacted.

(b) *Manner of making the election.* The election allowed by section 804(c)(3) of the Act may be made by a notification in the form of a letter signed by the taxpayer or an authorized representative of the taxpayer stating:

(1) The taxpayer's name, address, and identification number;

(2) The taxable years in which the films were placed in service with respect to which the election shall apply; and

(3) The court in which the litigation was commenced and information adequate to identify the particular litigation, for example, the names of the litigants, the date the suit was commenced, and the court case or docket number of the litigation.

The letter should be sent to the Deputy Commissioner of Internal Revenue, Attention: CC:RL:Br2, Room 4617, 1111 Constitution Avenue, N.W., Washington, D.C. 20224.

(c) *Time for making the election.* The election under section 804(c)(3) of the Act must be made not later than January 3, 1977. If mailed, the cover containing the notification of such election must be postmarked not later than January 3, 1977.

(d) *Revocation of election.* An election under section 804(c)(3) of the Act, once made, shall be irrevocable.

Temporary Rules
T.D. 7450; 7544

Temporary regulations relating to exclusion of certain disability income payments. (T.D. 7450, filed 12-22-76, T.D. 7544, filed 5-3-78.)

This document contains questions and answers relating to the exclusion of certain disability income payments received in taxable years beginning after December 31, 1975, from an employer-established plan.

Under prior law, an employee could exclude from income up to $100 a week received under wage continuation plans when such employee was absent from work on account of injury or sickness. The Tax Reform Act of 1976 eliminates the so-called sick pay exclusion for temporary absences from work and continues the exclusion of up to $5,200 a year generally for retirees under age 65 only if the disability retiree is permanently and totally disabled. In addition the Act reduces this $5,200 exclusion dollar-for-dollar for adjusted gross income (including disability income) in excess of $15,000.

These questions and answers are intended to provide guidelines which may be relied upon by taxpayers in order to resolve the issues specifically considered. However, no inferences should be drawn regarding issues not raised which may be suggested by a particular question and answer or as to why certain questions, and not others, are included. Furthermore, in applying the questions and answers, the effect of subsequent legislation, regulations, court decisions, and interpretative bulletins must be considered.

Change in Effective Date

The changes made by section 505 of the Tax Reform Act of 1976, as originally enacted, applied to taxable years beginning on or after January 1, 1976. Section 301 of the Tax Reduction and Simplification Act of 1977 delayed the effective date of most of these changes for one year. Thus, the new disability income exclusion applies only to taxable years beginning on or after January 1, 1977. However, certain taxpayers were still permitted to begin recovering their pension or annuity costs in taxable years beginning in 1976. These amendments modify § 7.105-1 to reflect these changes in the effective date.

Physician's Certificate

Under § 7.105-1, a taxpayer claiming the disability income exclusion must attach to his or her return a certificate from a qualified physician attesting to his or her permanent and total disability. This section also requires that the certificate contain an acknowledgment that the physician understands that the certificate will be used by the taxpayer to claim the exclusion for permanent and total disability on his or her income tax return. These amendments delete the requirement that the physician's certificate include this acknowledgment.

Substantial Gainful Activity

Section 105(d)(5) provides that a taxpayer is permanently and totally disabled if he is unable to engage in any substantial gainful activity by reason of a physical or mental impairment that satisfies certain requirements. However, neither section 105(d) nor § 7.105-1 defines substantial gainful activity. These amendments provide a definition of substantial gainful activity and examples of the application of this definition in specific factual situations.

In order to provide Temporary Income Tax Regulations (26 CFR Part 7) under section 105(d) of the Internal Revenue Code of 1954, as amended by section 505 (a) and (c) of the Tax Reform Act of 1976 (90 Stat. 1566), the following regulations are adopted:

○━ [Sec. 105(d)] § 7.105-1 (T.D. 7450, filed 12-22-76; amended by T.D. 7544, filed 5-3-78.) **Questions and answers relating to exclusions of certain disability income payments.**

The following questions and answers relate to the exclusion of certain disability income payments under section 105(d) of the Internal Revenue Code of 1954, as amended by section 505 (a) and (c) of the Tax Reform Act of 1976 (90 Stat. 1566):

Q-1: *What effect on the sick pay exclusion does the new law have?*

A-1: The "sick pay" provisions of prior law (which allowed a limited exclusion from gross income of sick pay received before mandatory retirement age by active employees temporarily absent from work because of sickness or injury, as well as by disability retirees) have been replaced by provisions of the new law (which provide for a limited exclusion of disability payments but restrict its application to individuals retired on disability who meet certain requirements as to permanent and total disability, age, etc.) (Q-4). As a result of the more restrictive provisions of the new law, many taxpayers who qualified for the exclusion in previous taxable years will not be eligible to claim the disability payments exclusion beginning with the effective date of the new law.

Q-2: *What is the effective date of the new law relating to disability exclusion?*

A-2: The disability income exclusion and related annuity provisions of the Tax Reform Act of 1976 are effective for taxable years beginning on or after January 1, 1977. In addition, the Tax Reduction and Simplification Act of 1977 allows certain taxpayers to begin excluding pension or annuity costs in taxable years beginning in 1976. In the case of a retiree who uses the cash receipts and disbursements method of accounting, the new law applies to payments received on or after the effective date even if the payment is for a period before the effective date. Thus, a payment for December 1976 that is received in January 1977 by a calendar-year, cash-basis taxpayer is controlled by the new law.

Q-3: *What are disability payments?*

A-3: In general, disability payments are amounts constituting wages or payments in lieu of wages made under provisions of a plan providing for the payment of such amounts to an employee for a period during which the employee is absent from work on account of permanent and total disability. Amounts paid to such an

Reg. § 7.105-1

employee after mandatory retirement age is attained are not wages or payments in lieu of wages for purposes of the disability income exclusion.

Q-4: *Who is eligible to exclude disability payments?*

A-4: A taxpayer who receives disability payments in lieu of wages under a plan providing for the payment of such amounts may qualify for the exclusion provided *all* of the following requirements are met:

1) The taxpayer has not reached age 65 (see Q-9) before the end of the taxable year,

2) The taxpayer has not reached mandatory retirement age (see Q-8) before the beginning of the taxable year,

3) The taxpayer retired on disability (see Q-10) (or if retired prior to January 1, 1977 and did not retire on disability, would have been eligible to retire on disability at the time of such retirement),

4) The taxpayer was permanently and totally disabled (see Q-11) when the taxpayer retired (or if the taxpayer retired before January 1, 1977, was permanently and totally disabled on January 1, 1976 or January 1, 1977), and

5) The taxpayer has not made an irrevocable election not to claim the disability income exclusion (see Q-17 through Q-19).

Q-5: *What limitations are placed on the amounts excludable?*

A-5: The amount of disability income that is excludable:
 a) Cannot exceed the amount of disability income payments received for any pay period,
 b) Cannot exceed a maximum weekly rate of $100 per taxpayer. Thus, the maximum disability income exclusion allowable on a joint return (see Q-7) in the usual case where one spouse receives disability payments, generally, would be $5,200, and if both spouses received disability payments the maximum exclusion, generally, would be $10,400 ($5,200 for each spouse),
 c) Cannot exceed, in the case of a disability income payment for a period of less than a week, a prorated portion of the amount otherwise excludable for that week (see Q-6), and
 d) Cannot exceed, for the entire taxable year, the total amount otherwise excludable for such taxable year reduced, dollar for dollar, by the amount by which the taxpayer's adjusted gross income (determined without regard to the disability income exclusion) exceeds $15,000. Where a disability income exclusion is claimed by either or both spouses on a joint return, the taxpayer's adjusted gross income means the total adjusted gross income of both spouses combined (determined without regard to the disability income exclusion) (see also Q-7).

Q-6: *On what occasion is a taxpayer likely to receive part-week disability payments? How do you prorate such payments?*

A-6: *Such part-week payments may be received* when one of the following events occurs after the first day of the taxpayer's normal workweek: (a) the disability retirement commences; (b) the taxpayer reaches mandatory retirement age in a taxable year prior to the taxable year in which such taxpayer attains age 65; or (c) the taxpayer dies. *To prorate a part-week disability income payment for purposes of the exclusion,* the taxpayer must:

1) Determine the "daily exclusion," which is the lesser of—
 a) the taxpayer's daily rate of disability pay, or
 b) $100 divided by the number of days in the taxpayer's normal workweek.

2) Multiply the daily exclusion by the number of days for which the part-week payment was made.

Thus, for a taxpayer whose normal workweek was Monday through Friday and whose retirement began on Wednesday, the first disability income payment would include a payment for a part-week consisting of three days. Assuming that the daily exclusion determined in 1), above, is $20, the taxpayer's exclusion for the first week would be $60 ($20 × 3).

Q-7: *What filing restrictions apply to a married taxpayer who claims a disability income exclusion?*

A-7: A taxpayer married at the close of the taxable year who lived with his or her spouse at any time during such taxable year must file a joint return in order to claim the disability income exclusion. However, a taxpayer married at the close of the taxable year who lived apart from his or her spouse for the entire taxable year may claim the exclusion on either a joint or separate return.

Q-8: *What is "mandatory retirement age"?*

A-8: Generally, mandatory retirement age is the age at which the taxpayer would have been required to retire under the employer's retirement program, had the taxpayer not become disabled.

Q-9: *Does a taxpayer reach age 65 on the day before his or her 65th birthday for purposes of the disability income exclusion, as is the case for purposes of the exemption for age and the credit for the elderly?*

A-9: No. For purposes of the disability income exclusion, a taxpayer reaches age 65 on the day of his or her 65th birthday anniversary. Thus, a taxpayer whose 65th birthday occurs on January 1, 1978, is not considered to reach age 65 during 1977, for purposes of the disability income exclusion.

Q-10: *What does "retired on disability" mean?*

A-10: Generally, it means that an employee has ceased active employment in all respects because of a disability and has retired under a disability provision of a plan for employees. However, an employee who has actually ceased active employment in all respects because of a disability may be treated as "retired on disability" even though the employee has not yet gone through formal "retirement" procedures, as for example, where an employer carries the disabled employee in a non-retired status under the disability provisions of the plan solely for the purpose of continuing such employee's eligibility for certain employer-provided fringe benefits. In addition, such an employee may be treated as "retired on disability" even though the initial period immediately following his or her ceasing of employment on account of a disability must first be used against accumulated "sick leave" or "annual leave" prior to the employee being formally placed in disability retirement status.

Q-11: *What is permanent and total disability?*

A-11: It is the inability to engage in any substantial gainful activity by reason of any medically determinable physical or mental impairment that—

a) can be expected to result in death,

b) has lasted for a continuous period of not less than 12 months, or

c) can be expected to last for a continuous period of not less than 12 months.

The substantial gainful activity referred to is not limited to the activity, or a comparable activity, in which the individual customarily engaged prior to such individual's retirement on disability. See § 7.105-2 for additional information relating to substantial gainful activity.

Q-12: *If a taxpayer retired on disability but it is not clear until the following taxable year that the disability as of the date of such retirement was permanent and total (so that the employee did not exclude any amount as disability income in the earlier taxable year), may the taxpayer file an amended return to claim the disability income exclusion for the taxable year in which such taxpayer retired on disability which was permanent and total?*

A-12: Yes.

Q-13: *What proof must a taxpayer furnish to establish the existence of permanent and total disability?*

A-13: If retired on disability before January 1, 1977: A certificate from a qualified physician attesting that—

(a) The taxpayer was permanently and totally disabled on January 1, 1976 or January 1, 1977; or

(b) The records of the Veterans Administration show that the taxpayer was permanently and totally disabled as defined in 38 CFR 3.340 or 3.342 on January 1, 1976 or January 1, 1977.

"If retired on disability during 1977 or thereafter: A certificate from a qualified physician attesting that—

(a) The taxpayer was permanently and totally disabled on the date he or she retired; or

(b) The records of the Veterans Administration show that the taxpayer was permanently and totally disabled as defined in 38 CFR 3.340 or 3.342 on the date he or she retired.

"In either case, the taxpayer must attach the certificate or a copy of the certificate to his or her income tax return. The certificate shall give the physician's name and address. No certificate from any employer is required with regard to the determination of permanent and total disability."

Q-14: *For what period does a taxpayer eligible (see Q-4) for the disability income exclusion, (without regard to the $15,000 income phaseout explained in Q-5) continue to be eligible for such exclusion?*

A-14: Unless the taxpayer earlier makes the irrevocable election not to claim the disability income exclusion described in Q-17 through Q-19, such taxpayer continues to be eligible until the earlier of:

a) the beginning of the taxable year in which the taxpayer reaches age 65,

b) the day on which the taxpayer reaches mandatory retirement age.

Q-15: *May a taxpayer while eligible (see Q-4) for the disability income exclusion under the new law, exclude any applicable pension or annuity costs?*

A-15: No. This is true even though while eligible for the disability income exclusion, such taxpayer is unable to exclude any amount of the disability income payments because of the $15,000 income phaseout (see Q-5).

Q-16: *When will a taxpayer who is eligible (see Q-4) to exclude disability income payments (without regard to the $15,000 phaseout explained in Q-5) under the new law be able to exclude any applicable pension or annuity costs?*

A-16: In general, such a taxpayer will begin to exclude any of his or her pension or annuity costs under applicable rules of the Code beginning on the first day of the taxable year in which he or she attains age 65 or, if mandatory retirement age is attained in an earlier taxable year, beginning on the day the taxpayer attains mandatory retirement age.

Q-17: *May a taxpayer who is eligible (see Q-4) to exclude disability income payments (without regard to the $15,000 phaseout explained in Q-5) under the new law begin to exclude applicable pension or annuity costs in an earlier taxable year?*

A-17: Yes, but such a taxpayer must make the election described in Q-18 and Q-19 in which case the taxpayer would no longer be eligible for the disability income exclusion.

Q-18: *What is an election not to claim the disability income exclusion?*

A-18: It is an irrevocable election for the taxable year for which the election is made, and each taxable year thereafter. If such an election is made the taxpayer will begin to recover tax-free, out of the payments, his or her annuity costs as provided under the applicable provision of the Code.

Q-19: *How does a taxpayer who is eligible to exclude disability income payments (without regard to the $15,000 phaseout explained in Q-5) under the new law make this election?*

A-19: The election is made by means of a statement attached to the taxpayer's income tax return (or amended return) for the taxable year in which the taxpayer wishes to have the applicable annuity rule apply. The statement shall set forth the taxpayer's qualifications to make the election (i.e., that the taxpayer is eligible (see Q-4) to exclude disability income payments (without regard to the $15,000 income phaseout explained in Q-5)) and that such taxpayer irrevocably elects not to claim the benefit of excluding disability income payments under section 105(d), as amended, for such taxable year and each taxable year thereafter. The election cannot be made for any taxable year beginning before January 1, 1976.

Reg. § 7.105-1

Q-20: Did the changes made by the Tax Reduction and Simplification Act provide any relief to taxpayers eligible for the sick pay exclusion in taxable years beginning in 1976?

A-20: Yes. As originally enacted, the more restrictive provisions of the disability income exclusion applied to taxable years beginning in 1976. The Tax Reduction and Simplification Act postponed the effective date of these provisions for one year. Thus, taxpayers may claim the sick pay exclusion in taxable years beginning in 1976.

○━▶ [Sec. 105(d)] § 7.105-2 (T.D. 7544, filed 5-3-78.) **Substantial gainful activity.**

(a) *Purpose.* This section defines substantial gainful activity for purposes of section 105(d) and § 7.105-1, prescribes rules for determining whether a taxpayer has the ability to engage in substantial gainful activity, and provides examples of the application of the definiton and rules in specific factual situations.

(b) *Definition.* Substantial gainful activity is the performance of significant duties over a reasonable period of time in work for remuneration or profit (or in work of a type generally performed for remuneration or profit).

(c) *General rules.* (1) Full-time work under competitive circumstances generally indicates ability to engage in substantial gainful activity.

(2) Work performed in self-care or the taxpayer's own household tasks, and non-remunerative work performed in connection with hobbies, institutional therapy or training, school attendance, clubs, social programs, and similar activities is not substantial gainful activity. However, the nature of the work performed may be evidence of ability to engage in substantial gainful activity.

(3) The fact that a taxpayer is unemployed for any length of time is not, of itself, conclusive evidence of inability to engage in substantial gainful activity.

(4) Regular performance of duties by a taxpayer in a full-time, competitive work situation at a rate of pay at or above the minimum wage will conclusively establish the taxpayer's ability to engage in substantial gainful activity. For purposes of paragraphs (c)(4) and (c)(5) of this section, the minimum wage is the minimum wage prescribed by section 6(a)(1) of the Fair Labor Standards Act of 1938, as amended, 29 U.S.C. 206(a)(1).

(5) Regular performance of duties by a taxpayer in a part-time, competitive work situation at a rate of pay at or above the minimum wage will conclusively establish the taxpayer's ability to engage in substantial gainful activity, if the duties are performed at the employer's convenience.

(6) In situations other than those described in paragraphs (c)(4) and (c)(5) of this section, other factors, such as the nature of the duties performed, may establish a taxpayer's ability to engage in substantial gainful activity.

(d) *Examples.* The following examples illustrate the application of the definition in paragraph (b) of this section and the rules in paragraph (c) of this section in specific factual situations. In examples 1 through 5, the facts establish that the taxpayers are able to engage in substantial gainful activity and, therefore, are not entitled to claim the disability income exclusion of section 105(d). In examples 6 through 9, the facts do not, of themselves, establish the taxpayers' ability or inability to engage in substantial gainful activity. In these situations, all the facts and circumstances must be examined to determine whether the taxpayers are able to engage in substantial gainful activity.

Example (1). Before retirement on disability, taxpayer worked for a hotel as night desk clerk. After retirement, the taxpayer is hired by another hotel as night desk clerk at a rate of pay exceeding the minimum wage. Since the taxpayer regularly performs duties in a full-time competitive work situation at a rate of pay at or above the minimum wage, he or she is able to engage in substantial gainful activity.

Example (2). A taxpayer who retired on disability from employment as a sales clerk is employed as a full-time babysitter at a rate of pay equal to the minimum wage. Since the taxpayer regularly performs duties in a full-time, competitive work situation at a rate of pay at or above the minimum wage, he or she is able to engage in substantial gainful activity.

Example (3). A taxpayer retired on disability from employment as a teacher because of terminal cancer. The taxpayer's physician recommended continuing employment for therapeutic reasons and taxpayer accepted employment as a part-time teacher at a rate of pay in excess of the minimum wage. The part-time teaching work is done at the employer's convenience. Even though the taxpayer's illness is terminal, the employment was recommended for therapeutic reasons, and the work is part-time, the fact that the work is done at the employer's convenience demonstrates that the taxpayer is able to engage in substantial gainful activity.

Example (4). A taxpayer who retired on disability, is employed full-time in a competitive work situation that is less demanding than his or her former position. The rate of pay exceeds the minimum wage but is about half of the taxpayer's rate of pay in the former position. It is immaterial that the new work activity is less demanding or less gainful than the work in which the taxpayer was engaged before his or her retirement on disability. Since the taxpayer regularly performs duties in a full-time, competitive work situation at a rate of pay at or above the minimum wage, he or she is able to engage in substantial gainful activity.

Example (5). A taxpayer who retired on disability from employment as a bookkeeper drives trucks for a charitable organization at the taxpayer's convenience. The taxpayer receives no compensation, but duties of this nature generally are performed for remuneration or profit. Some weeks the taxpayer works 10 hours, some weeks 40 hours, and over the year the taxpayer works an average of 20 hours per week. Even though the taxpayer receives no compensation, works part-time, and at his or her convenience, the nature of the duties performed and the average number of hours worked per week conclusively establish the taxpayer's ability to engage in substantial gainful activity.

Example (6). A taxpayer who retired on disability was instructed by a doctor that uninterrupted bedrest was vital to the treatment of his or her disability. However, because of financial need, the taxpayer secured new employment in a sedentary job. After attempting the new employment for approximately two months, the taxpayer was physically unable to continue the employment. The fact that the taxpayer attemtped to work and did, in fact, work for two months, does not, of itself, conclusively establish the taxpayer's ability to engage in substantial gainful activity.

Example (7). A taxpayer who retired on disability accepted employment with a former employer on a trial basis. The purpose of the employment was to determine whether the taxpayer was employable. The trial period continued for an extended period of time and the taxpayer was paid at a rate equal to the minimum wage. However, because of the taxpayer's disability only light duties of a nonproductive makework nature were assigned. Unless the activity is both substantial and gainful, the taxpayer is not engaged in substantial gainful activity. The activity was gainful because the taxpayer was paid at a rate at or above the minimum wage. However, the activity was not substantial because the duties were of a nonproductive, make-work nature. Accordingly, these facts do not, of themselves, establish the taxpayer's ability to engage in substantial gainful activity.

Example (8). A taxpayer who retired on disability from employment as a bookkeeper lives with a relative who manages several motel units. The taxpayer assisted the relative for one or two hours a day by performing duties such as washing dishes, answering phones, registering guests, and bookkeeping. The taxpayer can select the times during the day when he or she feels most fit to perform the tasks undertaken. Work of this nature, performed off and on during the day at the taxpayer's convenience, is not activity of a "substantial and gainful" nature even if the individual is paid for the work. The performance of these duties does not, of itself, show that the taxpayer is able to engage in substantial gainful activity.

Example (9). A taxpayer who retired on disability because of a physical or mental impairment accepts sheltered employment in a protected environment under an institutional program. Sheltered employment is offered in sheltered workshops, hospitals and similar institutions, homebound programs, and Veterans Administration domiciliaries. Typically, earnngs are lower in sheltered employment than in commercial employment. Consequently, impaired workers normally do not seek sheltered employment if other employment is available. The acceptance of sheltered employment by an impaired taxpayer does not necessarily establish his or her ability to engage in substantial gainful activity.

T.D. 7452

Temporary regulations relating to definition of qualified possession source investment income for purposes of the Puerto Rico and possession tax credit. (T.D. 7452, filed 12-29-76.)

In order to prescribe temporary income tax regulations relating to the definition of qualified possession source investment income with respect to the Puerto Rico and possession tax credit under section 936 (d) (2), as added by section 1051 of the Tax Reform Act of 1976 (Public Law 94-455, 90 Stat. 1644), the following temporary regulations are hereby adopted:

○― [Sec. 936(d)(2)] § 7.936-1 (T.D. 7452, filed 12-29-76.) Qualified possession source investment income.

For purposes of this section, interest earned after September 30, 1976 (less applicable deductions), by a domestic corporation, engaged in the active conduct of a trade or business in Puerto Rico, which elects the application of section 936 with respect to deposits with certain Puerto Rican financial institutions will be treated as qualified possession source investment income within the meaning of section 936 (d) (2) if (1) the interest qualifies for exemption from Puerto Rican income tax under regulations issued by the Secretary of the Treasury of Puerto Rico, as in effect on September 28, 1976, under the authority of section 2 (j) of the Puerto Rico Industrial Incentive Act of 1963, as amended, (2) the interest is from sources within Puerto Rico (within the meaning of section 936 (d) (2) (A)), and (3) the funds with respect to which the interest is earned are derived from the active conduct of a trade or business in Puerto Rico or from investment of funds so derived.

T.D. 7453

Temporary regulations relating to disclosures of return information by internal revenue officers and employees for investigative purposes. (T.D. 7453, filed 12-29-76.)

In order to prescribe temporary regulations on procedure and administration relating to disclosures of return information by internal revenue officers and employees for investigative purposes authorized by section 6103(k)(6) of the Internal Revenue Code of 1954, as added by section 1202 of the Tax Reform Act of 1976 (Public Law 94-455, 90 Stat. 1679), the following temporary regulations are hereby adopted and added to Part 404 of Title 26 of the Code of Federal Regulations:

[Sec. 6103(k)(6)] § 404.6103(k)(6)-1 (T.D. 7453, filed 12-29-76.) **Disclosure of return information by internal revenue officers and employees for investigative purposes.**

(a) *Disclosure of taxpayer identity information and fact of investigation in connection with official duties relating to examination collection activity, civil or criminal investigation, enforcement activity or other offense under the internal revenue laws.* In connection with the performance of official duties relating to any examination, collection activity, civil or criminal investigation, enforcement activity, or other offense under the internal revenue laws, or in connection with preparation for any proceeding (or investigation which may result in such a proceeding) described in section 6103(h)(2) of the Internal Revenue Code of 1954, an officer or employee of the Internal Revenue Service or office of the Chief Counsel therefor is authorized to disclose taxpayer identity information (as defined in section 6103(b)(6)), the fact that the inquiry pertains to the performance of official duties, and the nature of the official duties in order to obtain necessary information relating to performance of such official duties or where necessary in order to properly accomplish any activity described in subparagraph (6) of paragraph (b) of this section. Disclosure of taxpayer identity information to a person other than the taxpayer to whom such taxpayer identity information relates or such taxpayer's legal representative for the purpose of obtaining such necessary information or otherwise properly accomplishing such activities as authorized by this paragraph should be made, however, only if the necessary information cannot, under the facts and circumstances of the particular case, otherwise reasonably be obtained in accurate and sufficiently probative form, or in a timely manner, and without impairing the proper performance of the official duties, or if such activities cannot otherwise properly be accomplished without making such disclosure.

(b) *Disclosure of return information in connection with official duties relating to examination, collection activity, civil or criminal investigation, enforcement activity, or other offense under the internal revenue laws.* In connection with the performance of official duties relating to any examination, collection activity, civil or criminal investigaton, enforcement activity, or other offense under the internal revenue laws, an officer or employee of the Internal Revenue Service or office of the Chief Counsel therefor is authorized to disclose return information (as defined in section 6103(b)(2)) in order to obtain necessary information relating to the following—

(1) to establish or verify the correctness or completeness of any return (as defined in section 6103(b)(1)) or return information;

(2) to determine the responsibility for filing a return, for making a return where none has been made, or for performing such acts as may be required by law concerning such matters;

(3) to establish or verify the liability (or possible liability) of any person, or the liability (or possible liability) at law or in equity of any transferee or fiduciary of any person, for any tax, penalty, interest, fine, forfeiture, or other imposition or offense under the internal revenue laws or the amount thereof to be collected;

(4) to establish or verify misconduct (or possible misconduct) or other activity proscribed by the internal revenue laws;

(5) to obtain the services of persons having special knowledge or technical skills (such as, but not limited to, knowledge of particular facts and circumstances relevant to a correct determination of a liability described in subparagraph (3) of this paragraph or skills relating to handwriting analysis, photographic development, sound recording enhancement, or voice identification) or having recognized expertise in matters involving the valuation of property where relevant to proper performance of a duty or responsibility described in this paragraph;

(6) to establish or verify the financial status or condition and location of the taxpayer against whom collection activity is or may be directed, to locate assets in which the taxpayer has an interest, to ascertain the amount of any liability described in subparagraph (3) of this paragraph to be collected, or otherwise to apply the provisions of the Code relating to establishment of liens against such assets, or levy on, or seizure, or sale of, the assets to satify any such liability; or

(7) to prepare for any proceeding described in section 6103(h)(2) or conduct an investigation which may result in such a proceeding,

or where necessary in order to accomplish any activity described in subparagraph (6) of this paragraph. Disclosure of return information to a person other than the taxpayer to whom such return information relates or such taxpayer's legal representative for the purpose of obtaining information necessary to properly carry out the foregoing duties and responsibilities as authorized by this paragraph or for the purpose of otherwise properly accomplishing any activity described in subparagraph (6) of this paragraph should be made, however, only if such necessary information

Reg. § 404.6103(k)(6)-1(b)

24,998.86 (I.R.C.) Reg. § 404.6103(k)(6)-1(b)

cannot, under the facts and circumstances of the particular case, otherwise reasonably be obtained in accurate and sufficiently probative form, or in a timely manner, and without impairing the proper performance of such duties and responsibilities, or if the activities described in subparagraph (6) of this paragraph cannot otherwise properly be accomplished without making such disclosure.

(c) *Disclosure of return information in connection with certain personnel or claimant representative matters.* In connection with the performance of official duties relating to any investigation concerned with the enforcement of any provision of the Internal Revenue Code of 1954, including enforcement of any rules, directives, or manual issuances prescribed by the Secretary under section 7803 or any other provision of the Code, which affects or may affect the personnel or employment rights or status, or civil or criminal liability, of any employee or former or prospective employee of the Department of the Treasury or the rights of any person who is or may be a party to an administrative action or proceeding pursuant to 31 U.S.C. 1026, an officer or employee of the Internal Revenue Service or office of the Chief Counsel therefor is authorized to disclose return information (as defined in section 6103(b)(2)) for the purpose of obtaining, verifying, or establishing other information which is or may be relevant and material to such investigation. Disclosure of return information to a person other than the taxpayer to whom such return information relates or such taxpayer's legal representative for the purpose of obtaining information necessary to properly carry out the foregoing duties and responsibilities as authorized by this paragraph should be made, however, only if such necessary information cannot, under the facts and circumstances of the particular case, otherwise reasonably be obtained in accurate and sufficiently probative form, or in a timely manner, and without impairing the proper performance of such duties and responsibilities.

T.D. 7455

Temporary regulations relating to disclosures of returns and return information in connection with the procurement of property and services for tax administration purposes authorized by section 6103(n). (T.D. 7455, filed 12-30-76.)

In order to prescribe temporary regulations on procedure and administration relating to disclosures of returns and return information in connection with procurement of property and services for tax administration purposes authorized by section 6103(n) of the Internal Revenue Code of 1954, as added by section 1202 of the Tax Reform Act of 1976 (Public Law 94-455, 90 Stat. 1681), the following temporary regulations are hereby adopted:

[Sec. 6103(n)] § 404.6103(n)-1 (T.D. 7455, filed 12-30-76.) **Disclosure of returns and return information in connection with procurement of property and services for tax administration purposes.**

(a) *General rule.* Pursuant to the provisions of section 6103(n) and subject to the requirements of paragraphs (b), (c) and (d) of this section, officers or employees of the Internal Revenue Service or office of the Chief Counsel therefor are authorized to disclose returns and return information (as defined in section 6103(b)) to a person (including a person described in section 7513(a)), or to an officer or employee of such person, to the extent necessary in connection with contractual procurement by the Service or office of the Chief Counsel of—

(1) equipment or other property, or

(2) services relating to the processing, storage, transmission, or reproduction of such returns or return information or to the programming, maintenance, repair, or testing of equipment or other property, for purposes of tax administration (as defined in section 6103(b)(4)). No person, or officer or employee of such person, to whom a return or return information is disclosed by an officer or employee of the Service or office of the Chief Counsel under the authority of this paragraph shall in turn disclose such return or return information for any purpose other than as described in subparagraph (1) or (2) of this paragraph, and no such further disclosure for any such described purpose shall be made by such person, officer or employee to anyone, other than another officer or employee of such person whose duties or responsibilities require such disclosure for a purpose described in subparagraph (1) or (2), without written approval by the Service.

(b) *Limitations.* For purposes of paragraph (a) of this section, disclosure of returns or return information in connection with contractual procurement of property or services described in such paragraph will be treated as necessary only if such procurement or the performance of such services cannot otherwise be reasonably, properly or economically carried out or performed without such disclosure. Thus, for example, disclosures of returns or return information to employees of a contractor for purposes of programming, maintaining, repairing, or testing computer equipment used by the Internal Revenue Service should be made only if such services cannot be reasonably, properly, or economically performed by use of information or other data in a form which does not identify a particular taxpayer. If, however, disclosure of returns or return information is in fact necessary in order for such employees to reasonably, properly, or economically perform the computer related services, such disclosures should be restricted to returns or return information selected or appearing at random. Further, for purposes of paragraph (a), disclosure of returns or return information in connection with the contractual procurement of property or services described in such paragraph should be made only to the extent necessary to reasonably, properly, or economically conduct such procurement activity. Thus, for example, if an activity described in paragraph (c) can reasonably, properly, and economically be conducted by disclosure of only parts or portions of a return or if deletion of taxpayer identity information (as defined in section 6103(b)(6)) reflected on a return would not seriously impair the ability of the contractor or his officers or employees to conduct the activity, then only such parts or portions of the return, or only the return with taxpayer identity information deleted, should be disclosed.

(c) *Notification requirements.* Each officer or employee of any person to whom returns or return information is or may be disclosed as authorized by paragraph (a) of this section shall be notified in writing by such person that returns or return information disclosed to such officer or employee can be used only for a purpose and to the extent authorized by paragraph (a) of this section and that further disclosure of any such returns or return information for a purpose or to an extent unauthorized by such paragraph constitutes a felony, punishable upon conviction by a fine of as much as $5,000, or imprisonment for as long as 5 years, or both, together with the costs of prosecution. Such person shall also so notify each such officer and employee that any such unauthorized further disclosure of returns or return information may also result in an award of civil damages against the officer or employee in an amount not less than $1,000 with respect to each instance of unauthorized disclosure.

(d) *Safeguards.* Any person to whom a return or return information is disclosed as authorized by paragraph (a) of this section shall comply with all applicable conditions and requirements which may be prescribed by the Internal Revenue Service for the purposes of protecting the confidentiality of returns and return information and preventing disclosures of returns or return information in a manner unauthorized by paragraph (a). The terms of any contract between the Service and a person pursuant to which a return or return information is or may be disclosed by the Service for a purpose described in paragraph (a) shall provide, or shall be amended to provide, that such person, and

Reg. § 404.6103(n)-1(d)

24,998.88 *(I.R.C.)* Reg. § 404.6103(n)-1(d)

officers and employees of such person, shall comply with all such applicable conditions and restrictions as may be prescribed by the Service by regulation, published rules or procedures, or written communication to such person. If the Service determines that any person, or an officer or employee of any such person, to whom returns and return information has been disclosed as provided in paragraph (a) has failed to, or does not, satisfy such prescribed conditions or requirements, the Service may take such actions as are deemed necessary to ensure that such conditions or requirements are or will be satisfied, including suspension or termination of any duty or obligation arising under a contract referred to in this paragraph or suspension of disclosures otherwise authorized by paragraph (a), until the Service determines that such conditions and requirements have been or will be satisfied.

T.D. 7457; 7492

Temporary regulations relating to information reporting requirements on certain winnings from bingo, keno, and slot machines. (T.D. 7457, filed 1-4-77; amended by T.D. 7492, filed 6-28-77.)

In order to prescribe temporary income tax regulations relating to information reporting requirements on certain winnings from bingo, keno, and slot machines under section 6041 of the Internal Revenue Code of 1954, pursuant to section 1207(d) of the Tax Reform Act of 1976 (Public Law 94-455, 90 Stat. 1705), the following temporary regulations are hereby adopted and added to Part 7 of Title 26 of the Code of Federal Regulations:

[Sec. 6041] § 7.6041-1 (T.D. 7457, filed 1-4-77; amended by T.D. 7492, filed 6-28-77.) **Return of information as to payments of winnings from bingo, keno, and slot machines.**

(a) *In general.* On or after May 1, 1977, every person engaged in a trade or business and making a payment in the course of such trade or business of winnings (including winnings which are exempt from withholding under section 3402(q)(5)) of $1,200 or more from a bingo game or slot machine play or of $1,500 or more from a keno game shall make an information return with respect to such payment.

(b) *Special rules.* For purposes of paragraph (a) of this section, in determining whether such winnings equal or exceed the $1,200 or $1,500 amount—

(1) In the case of a bingo game or slot machine play, the amount of winnings shall not be reduced by the amount wagered;

(2) In the case of a keno game, the amount of winnings from one game shall be reduced by the amount wagered in that one game;

(3) Winnings shall include the fair market value of a payment in any medium other than cash;

(4) All winnings by the winner from one bingo or keno game shall be aggregated; and

(5) Winnings and losses from any other wagering transaction by the winner shall not be taken into account.

(c) *Prescribed form.* The return required by paragraph (a) of this section shall be made on Form W-2G and shall be filed with the Internal Revenue Service Center serving the district in which is located the principal place of business of the person making the return on or before February 28 of the calendar year following the calendar year in which the payment of winnings is made. Each Form W-2G shall contain the following:

(1) Name, address, and employer identification number of the person making the payment;

(2) Name, address, and social security number of the winner;

(3) General description of two types of identification (e.g., "driver's license", "social security card", or "voter registration card") furnished to the maker of the payment for verification of the winner's name, address, and social security number;

(4) Date and amount of the payment; and

(5) Type of wagering transaction. In addition, in the case of a bingo or keno game, Form W-2G shall show any number, color, or other designation assigned to the game with respect to which the payment is made. In the case of a slot machine play, Form W-2G shall show the identification number of the slot machine.

Reg. § 7.6041-1(c)(5)

Temporary Rules (I.R.C.) 24,998.91

T.D. 7459

Temporary regulations relating to various elections under the Tax Reform Act of 1976. (T.D. 7459, filed 1-4-77; amended by T.D. 7478, filed 4-5-77.)

In order to prescribe temporary regulations, which shall remain in force and effect until superseded by permanent regulations, relating to the manner of making certain elections provided by the Tax Reform Act of 1976, the following regulations are hereby adopted:

○→ § 7.0 (T.D. 7459, filed 1-4-77; amended by T.D. 7478, filed 4-5-77; T.D. 7526, filed 12-23-77.) **Various elections under the Tax Reform Act of 1976.**

(a) *Elections covered by temporary rules.* The sections of the Internal Revenue Code of 1954, or of the Tax Reform Act of 1976, to which this section applies and under which an election or notification may be made pursuant to the procedures described in paragraphs (b) and (d) are as follows:

Section	Description of election	Availability of election
(1) First Category		
167(o) of Code	Substantially rehabilitated historic property.	Additions to capital account occurring after June 30, 1976, and before July 1, 1981.
172(b)(3)(E) of Code	Forego of carryback period.	Any taxable year ending after December 31, 1975.
191(b) of Code	[See (1) below.]	
402(e)(4)(L) of Code	Lump sum distributions from qualified plans.	Distributions and payments made after December 31, 1975, in taxable years beginning after such date.
451(e) of Code	[See (2) below.]	
812(b)(3) of Code	Forego of carryback period by life insurance companies.	Any taxable year ending after December 31, 1975.
819A of Code	Contiguous country branches of domestic life insurance companies.	All taxable years beginning after December 31, 1975.
825(d)(2) of Code	Forego of carryback period by mutual insurance companies.	Any taxable year ending after December 31, 1975.
911(e) of Code	Foregoing of benefits of section 911.	All taxable years beginning after December 31, 1975.
(2) Second Category		
185(d) of Code	Amortization of railroad grading and tunnel bores.	All taxable years beginning after December 31, 1974.
528(c)(1)(E) of Code	Certain homeowners associations.	Any taxable year beginning after December 31, 1973.
1057 of Code	Transfer to foreign trusts etc.	Any transfer of property after October 2, 1975.
6013(g) of Code	Joint return for nonresident alien.	All taxable years ending on or after December 31, 1975.
6013(h) of Code	Joint return for year in which nonresident alien becomes resident.	Any taxable year ending on or after December 31, 1975.

(b) *Time for making election or serving notice*—(1) *Category (1).* A taxpayer may make an election under any section referred to in paragraph (a)(1) for the first taxable year for which the election is required to be made or for the taxable year selected by the taxpayer when the choice of the taxable year is optional. The election must be made by the later of the time, including extensions thereof, prescribed by law for filing income tax returns for such taxable year or March 8, 1977.

(2) *Category (2).* A taxpayer may make an election under any section referred to in paragraph (a)(2) for the first taxable year for which the election is allowed or for the taxable years elected by the taxpayer when the choice of the taxable year is optional. The election must be made (i) for any taxable year ending before December 31, 1976, for which a return has been filed before January 31, 1977, by filing an amended return, provided that the period of limitation for filing claim for credit or refund of overpayment of tax, determined from the time the return was filed, has not expired or (ii) for all other years by filing the income tax return for the year for which the election is made not later than the time, including extensions

---

(1) Reg. § 1.191(b) (T.D. 7478, filed 4-5-77) amended Temp. Reg. § 7.0(a) relating to Sec. 191(b).

(2) Reg. § 1.451-7 (T.D. 7526, filed 12-23-77) revoked Temp. Reg. § 7.0(a) to extent it applies to Sec. 451(e).

Reg. § 7.0(b)(2)

24,998.92 (I.R.C.)   Reg. § 7.0(b)(2)   12-30-77

thereof, prescribed by law for filing income tax returns for such year. However, an organization which has its exempt status under section 501(a) of the Code revoked for any taxable year and which is described in section 528 of the Code, may make an election under section 528(c)(1)(E) of the Code for such year, before the expiration of the period for filing claim for credit or refund of overpayment of tax.

(c) *Certain other elections.* The elections described in this paragraph shall be made in the manner and within the time prescribed herein and in paragraph (d).

(1) The following elections under the Tax Reform Act of 1976 shall be made:

(i) Sec. 207(c)(3) of Act	Change from static value method of accounting.	All taxable years beginning after December 31, 1976.

by filing Form 3115 with the National Office of the Internal Revenue Service before October 5, 1977.

(ii) Sec. 604 of Act	Travel expenses of State legislators.	All taxable years beginning before January 1, 1976.

by filing an amended return for any taxable year for which the period for assessing or collecting a deficiency has not expired before October 4, 1976, by the last day for filing a claim for refund or credit for the taxable year but in no event shall such day be earlier than October 4, 1977.

(iii) Sec. 804(e)(2) of Act [Ed: This election is now covered by Temp. Reg. § 7.48-3, T.D. 7509, filed 9-20-77.]	Retroactive applications of amendments to property described in section 50(a) of Code.	Certain taxable years beginning before January 1, 1975.

by filing amended returns before October 5, 1977, for all taxable years to which applicable for which the period of limitation for filing claim for credit or refund for overpayment of tax has not expired.

(iv) Sec. 1608(d)(2) of Act.	Election as a result of determination as defined in section 859(c) of the Code.	Determinations made after October 4, 1976.

by filing a statement with the district director for the district in which the taxpayer maintains its principal place of business within 60 days after such determination.

(v) Sec. 2103 of Act	Treatment of certain 1972 disaster losses.	Any taxable year in which payment is received or indebtedness is forgiven.

by filing a return for the taxable year or an amended return by the last day for making a claim for credit or refund for the taxable year but in no event shall such day be earlier than October 4, 1977.

(2) The election provided in section 37(e) of the Code relating to the credit for the elderly and section 144(a) of the Code relating to the standard deduction, available for any taxable year beginning after December 31, 1975, may be made any time before the expiration of the period of limitation for filing claim for credit or refund. Once made, such election may be revoked without the consent of the Commissioner any time before the expiration of such period by filing an amended return.

(3) The election provided for in section 167(e)(3) of the Code shall be made in accordance with § 1.167(e)-1(d) except that the election shall be applicable for the first taxable year of the taxpayer beginning after December 31, 1975.

(4) The election provided in section 501(i) of the Code relating to lobbying by public charities may be made for all taxable years beginning after December 31, 1976, by filing a statement with the Internal Revenue Service Center, 11601 Roosevelt Boulevard, Philadelphia, Pennsylvania, 19155 (for organizations in the Central Region the Internal Revenue Service Center, Cincinnati, Ohio 45298) before the close of the first taxable year for which the election is effective.

(5) The election provided in section 936(e) of the Code relating to the Puerto Rico and possession tax credit, available for all taxable years beginning after December 31, 1975, shall be made by filing Form 5712 within 90 days after the beginning of the first taxable year for which such election is made with the Internal Revenue Service Center, 11601 Roosevelt Boulevard, Philadelphia, Pennsylvania 19155. If the first taxable year for which such an election is made is a taxable year beginning before January 1, 1977, such election shall be made in the manner prescribed in the preceding sentence by May 9, 1977.

(6) The election provided in section 1033(f)(3) of the Code may be made for any taxable year beginning after December 31, 1970, by filing an amended return for any taxable year for which the period of limitation for filing a claim for credit or refund of overpayment has not expired, and for any taxable year ending on or after December 31, 1976, by filing the income tax return for the year the election is made not later than the time, including extensions thereof, prescribed by law for filing income tax returns for such taxable year.

(d) *Manner of making election.* Unless otherwise provided in the return or in a form accompanying a return for the taxable year, the elections described in paragraphs (a) and (c) (except paragraphs (c)(1)(i), (c)(4) and (c)(5)) shall be made by a statement attached to the return (or amended return) for the taxable year. The statement required when making an election pursuant to this section shall indicate the section under which the election is being made and shall set forth information to identify the election, the period for which it applies, and the taxpayer's basis or entitlement for making the election.

(e) *Effect of election*—(1) *Consent to revoke required.* Except where otherwise provided by statute or except as provided in paragraph (c)(2) and subparagraph (2) of this paragraph, an election to which this section applies made in accordance with this section shall be binding unless consent to revoke the election is obtained from the Commissioner. An application for consent to revoke the election will not be accepted before the promulgation of the permanent regulations relating to the section of the Code or Act under which the election is made. Such regulations will provide a reasonable period of time within which taxpayers will be permitted to apply for consent to revoke the election.

(2) *Revocation without consent.* An election to which this section applies, other than the elections referred to in paragraph (c)(2), made in accordance with this section, may be revoked without the consent of the Commissioner not later than 90 days after the permanent regulations relating to the section of the Code or Act under which the election is made are filed with the office of the Federal Register, provided such regulations grant taxpayers blanket permission to revoke that election within such time without the consent of the Commissioner. Such blanket permission to revoke an election will be provided by the permanent regulations in the event of a determination by the Secretary or his delegate that such regulations contain provisions that may not reasonably have been anticipated by taxpayers at the time of making such election.

(f) *Furnishing of supplementary information required.* If the permanent regulations which are issued under the section of the Code or Act referred to in this section to which the election relates require the furnishing of information in addition to that which was furnished with the statement of election filed pursuant to paragraph(d), the taxpayer must furnish such additional information in a statement addressed to the district director, or the director of the regional service center, with whom the election was filed. This statement must clearly identify the election and the taxable year for which it was made. If such information is not provided the election may, at the discretion of the Commissioner, be held invalid.

[Sec. 856(g)] § 7.856(g)-1 (T.D. 7459, filed 1-4-77.) **Special rule for real estate investment trusts.**

The election pursuant to section 856(c)(1) by a corporation, trust, or association to be treated as a real estate investment trust, may be revoked under section 856(g) for any taxable year and all succeeding taxable years by filing a statement with the district director for the district in which the taxpayer maintains its principal place of business on or before the 90th day after the first day of the first taxable year for which the revocation is to be effective.

Reg. § 7.856(g)-1

T.D. 7463

Temporary regulations relating to disclosures of returns and return information to and by officers and employees of the Department of Justice and other Federal agencies in connection with preparation for certain administrative and judicial proceedings (or investigations which may result in such proceedings). (T.D. 7463, filed 1-19-77.)

In order to prescribe temporary regulations on procedure and administration relating to disclosures of returns and return information (including taxpayer return information) to and by officers and employees of the Department of Justice and other Federal agencies in connection with preparation for certain administrative and judicial proceedings (or investigations which may result in such proceedings) under section 6103(h)(2) and (i)(1) and (2) of the Internal Revenue Code of 1954, as added by section 1202 of the Tax Reform Act of 1976 (Pub. L. 94-455, 90 Stat. 1674), the following temporary regulations are hereby adopted and added to Part 404 of Title 26 of the Code of Federal Regulations:

[Sec. 6103(h)] § 404.6103(h)(2)-1 (T.D. 7463, filed 1-19-77.) **Disclosure of returns and return information (including taxpayer return information) to and by attorneys and other officers and employees of the Depart of Justice or other Federal agencies in preparation for proceeding or investigation involving tax administration and certain other matters.**

(a) *Disclosure of returns and return information (including taxpayer return information) to and by attorneys of the Department of Justice.* (1) Returns and returns information (including taxpayer return information), as defined in section 6103(b)(1), (2), and (3) of the Internal Revenue Code, shall, to the extent provided by subparagraphs (A), (B), and (C) of paragraph (2) of section 6103(h) and subject to the requirements of section 6103(h)(3), be open to inspection by or disclosure to attorneys of the Department of Justice (including United States attorneys) personally and directly engaged in, and for their necessary use in, preparation for any proceeding (or for their necessary use in an investigation which may result in such a proceeding) before a Federal grand jury or any Federal or State court in a matter involving tax administration (as defined in section 6103(b)(4)), including any such proceeding (or any such investigation) also involving the enforcement of a related Federal criminal statute which has been referred by the Secretary to the Department of Justice.

(2) Returns and return information (including taxpayer return information) inspected by or disclosed to attorneys of the Department of Justice as provided in subparagraph (1) of this paragraph may also be used by such attorneys, or disclosed by them to other attorneys (including United States attorneys and supervisory personnel, such as Section Chiefs, Deputy Assistant Attorneys General, Assistant Attorneys General, the Deputy Attorney General, and the Attorney General) of the Department of Justice, where necessary in connection with preparation for any proceeding (or with an investigation which may result in such a proceeding) described in subparagraph (1) or any proceeding (or investigation) involving any other matter related to tax administration or involving any matter brought before a Federal grand jury or Federal court pertaining to enforcement of a specific Federal criminal statute (other than one described in subparagraph (1)) to which the United States is or may be a party, provided that such proceeding (or investigation) involves or arises out of the particular facts and circumstances giving rise to the proceeding (or investigation) described in subparagraph (1).

(b) *Disclosure of returns and return information (including taxpayer return information) by attorneys of the Department of Justice.* (1) Returns and return information (including taxpayer return information), as defined in section 6103(b)(1), (2), and (3) of the Code, inspected by or disclosed to attorneys of the Department of Justice as provided by paragraph (a) of this section may be disclosed by such attorneys to other persons, including, but not limited to, persons described in subparagraph (2) of this section, but only to the extent necessary in connection with the proper preparation for a proceeding (or in connection with an investigation which may result in such a proceeding) described in paragraph (a). Such disclosures may include, but are not limited to, disclosures where necessary—

(i) to properly accomplish any purpose or activity of the nature described in § 404.6103(k)(6)-1 which is essential to proper preparation for such proceeding (or to such investigation);

(ii) to properly interview, consult, depose, or interrogate or otherwise obtain relevant information from, the taxpayer to whom such return or return information relates (or such taxpayer's legal representative) or from any witness who may be called to give evidence in the proceeding; or

(iii) to properly conduct negotiations concerning, or obtain authorization for, settlement or disposition of the proceeding, in whole or in part or stipulations of fact in connection with the proceeding.

Disclosure of a return or return information to a person other than the taxpayer to whom such return or return information relates or such taxpayer's legal representative to properly accomplish any purpose or activity described in this paragraph should be made, however, only if such purpose or activity cannot otherwise properly be accomplished without making such disclosure.

(2) Among those persons to whom returns and return information may be disclosed by attorneys of the Department of Justice as provided by subparagraph (1) of this paragraph are—

Reg. § 404.6103(h)(2)-1

24,998.94 (I.R.C.) Reg. § 404.6103(h)(2)-1   1-31-77

(i) other officers and employees of the Department of Justice, such as, personnel of an office, board, division, or bureau of such department (for example, the Federal Bureau of Investigation or the Drug Enforcement Administration), clerical personnel (for example, secretaries, stenographers, docket and file room clerks, and mail room employees) and supervisory personnel (such as supervisory personnel of the Federal Bureau of Investigation or the Drug Enforcement Administration);

(ii) officers and employees of another Federal agency (as defined in section 6103(b)(9)) working under the direction and control of any such attorney of the Department of Justice; and

(iii) court reporters.

○━━ [Sec. 6103(i)] § 404.6103(i)-1 (T.D. 7463, filed 1-19-77.) **Disclosure of returns and return information (including taxpayer return information) to and by officers and employees of the Department of Justice or another Federal agency in preparation for proceeding or investigation involving enforcement of Federal criminal statute not involving tax administration.**

(a) *Disclosure of returns and return information (including taxpayer return information) to attorneys of the Department of Justice or another Federal agency.* Returns and return information (including taxpayer return information), as defined in section 6103(b)(1), (2), and (3) of the Internal Revenue Code, shall, to the extent provided by paragraphs (1), (2), and (3) of section 6103(i) and subject to the requirements of such paragraphs (1) and (2), be open to inspection by or disclosure to attorneys of the Department of Justice (including United States attorneys) or of another Federal agency (as defined in section 6103(b)(9)) personally and directly engaged in, and for their necessary use in, preparation for any administrative or judicial proceeding (or their necessary use in an investigation which may result in such a proceeding) pertaining to enforcement of a specifically designated Federal criminal statute not involving or related to tax administration to which the United States or such agency is or may be a party.

(b) *Disclosure of returns and return information (including taxpayer return information) by attorneys of the Department of Justice or another Federal agency.* (1) Returns and return information (including taxpayer return information), as defined in section 6103(b)(1), (2), and (3) of the Code, disclosed to attorneys of the Department of Justice or other Federal agency (as defined in section 6103(b)(9)) as provided by paragraph (a) of this section may be disclosed by such attorneys to other persons, including, but not limited to, persons described in subparagraph (2) of this paragraph, but only to the extent necessary in connection with the proper preparation for a proceeding (or in connection with an investigation which may result in such a proceeding) described in paragraph (a). Such disclosures may include, but are not limited to, disclosures where necessary—

(i) to properly obtain the services of persons having special knowledge or technical skills (such as, but not limited to, handwriting analysis, photographic development, sound recording enhancement, or voice identification);

(ii) to properly interview, consult, depose, or interrogate or otherwise obtain relevant information from, the taxpayer to whom such return or return information relates (or such taxpayer's legal representative) or any witness who may be called to give evidence in the proceeding; or

(iii) to properly conduct negotiations concerning, or obtain authorization for, disposition of the proceeding, in whole or in part, or stipulations of fact in connection with the proceeding.

Disclosure of a return or return information to a person other than the taxpayer to whom such return or return information relates or such taxpayer's legal representative to properly accomplish any purpose or activity described in this paragraph should be made, however, only if such purpose or activity cannot otherwise properly be accomplished without making such disclosure.

(2) Among those persons to whom returns and return information may be disclosed by attorneys of the Department of Justice or other Federal agency as provided by paragraph (1) of this paragraph are—

(i) other officers and employees (including attorneys) of the Department of Justice (including an office, board, division, or bureau of such department, such as the Federal Bureau of Investigation or the Drug Enforcement Administration) or other Federal agency described in paragraph (1), such as clerical personnel (for example, secretaries, stenographers, docket and file room clerks, and mail room employees) and supervisory personnel (for example, in the case of the Department of Justice, Section Chiefs, Deputy Assistant Attorneys General, Assistant Attorneys General, the Deputy Attorney General, the Attorney General, and supervisory personnel of the Federal Bureau of Investigation or the Drug Enforcement Administration);

(ii) officers and employees of another Federal agency (as defined in section 6103(b)(9)) working under the direction and control of such attorneys of the Department of Justice or other Federal agency described in paragraph (1); and

(iii) court reporters.

T.D. 7464

Temporary regulations relating to disclosures after December 31, 1976 by officers and employees of Federal agencies of returns and return information (including taxpayer return information) disclosed to such officers and employees by the Secretary before January 1, 1977 for a purpose not involving tax administration. (T.D. 7464, filed 1-19-77.)

In order to prescribe temporary regulations on procedure and administration relating to disclosures after December 31, 1976 by officers and employees of Federal agencies of returns and return information (including taxpayer return information) disclosed to such officers and employees by the Secretary before January 1, 1977, for a purpose not involving tax administration pursuant to the authority of section 6103 of the Internal Revenue Code of 1954 (or any order of the President under section 6103 or rules and regulations thereunder prescribed by the Secretary and approved by the President) before amendment of such section by Section 1202 of the Tax Reform Act of 1976 (Pub. L. 94-455, 90 Stat. 1667), the following temporary regulations are hereby adopted:

[Sec. 6103(a)] § 404.6103(a)-1 (T.D. 7464, filed 1-19-77.) **Disclosures after December 31, 1976 by officers and employees of Federal agencies of returns and return information (including taxpayer return information) disclosed to such officers and employees by the Secretary before January 1, 1977 for a purpose not involving tax administration.**

(a) *General rule.* Except as provided by paragraph (b) of this section, a return or return information (including taxpayer return information), as defined in section 6103(b)(1), (2), and (3) of the Internal Revenue Code, disclosed by the Secretary before January 1, 1977, to an officer or employee of a Federal agency (as defined in section 6103(b)(9)) for a purpose not involving tax administration (as defined in section 6103(b)(4)) pursuant to the authority of section 6103 (or any order of the President under section 6103 or rules and regulations thereunder prescribed by the Secretary and approved by the President) before amendment of such section by Section 1202 of the Tax Reform Act of 1976 (Pub. L. 94-455, 90 Stat. 1667) may be disclosed by, or on behalf of, such officer, employee, or agency after December 31, 1976, for any purpose authorized by such section (or such order or rules and regulations) before such amendment.

(b) *Exception.* Notwithstanding the provisions of paragraph (a) of this section, a return or return information (including taxpayer return information) disclosed before January 1, 1977, by the Secretary to an officer or employee of a Federal agency for a purpose unrelated to tax administration as described in paragraph (a) may, after December 31, 1976, be disclosed by, or on behalf of, such agency, officer, or employee in an administrative or judicial proceeding only if such proceeding is one described in section 6103(i)(4) and if the requirements of section 6103(i)(4) have first been met.

Reg. § 404.6103(a)-1

Temporary Rules *(I.R.C.)* 24,998.97

T.D. 7467

Temporary regulations relating to computation of international boycott factor. (T.D. 7467, filed 2-24-77.)

Certain benefits of the foreign tax credit, deferral of earnings of foreign corporations, and DISC (Domestic International Sales Corporation) are denied if a person (or a member of a controlled group that includes that person) participates in or cooperates with an international boycott. The loss of tax benefits may be determined by multiplying the otherwise allowable tax benefits by the "international boycott factor".

In order to prescribe temporary income tax regulations with respect to the computation of the international boycott factor under section 999(c)(1) of the Internal Revenue Code of 1954, as added by section 1064 of the Tax Reform Act of 1976 (Pub. L. 94-455, 90 Stat. 1643), the following temporary regulations are adopted:

[Sec. 999(c)(1)] § 7.999-1 (T.D. 7467, filed 2-24-77.) Computation of the international boycott factor.

(a) *In general.* Sections 908(a), 952(a)(3), and 995(b)(1)(F) provide that certain benefits of the foreign tax credit, deferral of earnings of foreign corporations, and DISC are denied if a person or a member of a controlled group (within the meaning of section 993(a)(3)) that includes that person participates in or cooperates with an international boycott (within the meaning of section 999(b)(3)). The loss of tax benefits may be determined by multiplying the otherwise allowable tax benefits by the "international boycott factor." Section 999 (c)(1) provides that the international boycott factor is to be determined under regulations prescribed by the Secretary. The method of computing the international boycott factor is set forth in paragraph (c) of this section. A special rule for computing the international boycott factor of a person that is a member of two or more controlled groups is set forth in paragraph (c). Transitional rules for making adjustments to the international boycott factor for years affected by the effective dates are set forth in paragraph (e). The definitions of the terms used in this section are set forth in paragraph (b).

(b) *Definitions.* For purposes of this section:

(1) *Boycotting country.* In respect of a particular international boycott, the term "boycotting country" means any country described in section 999(a)(1)(A) or (B) that requires participation in or cooperation with that particular international boycott.

(2) *Participation in or cooperation with an international boycott.* For the definition of the term "participation in or cooperation with an international boycott", see section 999(b)(3) and Parts H through M of the Treasury Department's International Boycott Guidelines.

(3) *Operations in or related to a boycotting country.* For the definitions of the terms "operations", "operations in a boycotting country", "operations related to a boycotting country", and "operations with the government, a company, or a national of a boycotting country", see Part B of the Treasury Department's International Boycott Guidelines.

(4) *Clearly demonstrating clearly separate and identifiable operations.* For the rules for "clearly demonstrating clearly separate and identifiable operations", see Part D of the Treasury Department's International Boycott Guidelines.

(5) *Purchase made from a country.* The terms "purchase made from a boycotting country" and "purchases made from any country other than the United States" mean, in respect of any particular country, the gross amount paid in connection with the purchase of, the use of, or the right to use:

(i) Tangible personal property (including money) from a stock of goods located in that country,

(ii) Intangible property (other than securities) in that country,

(iii) Securities by a dealer to a beneficial owner that is a resident of that country (but only if the dealer knows or has reason to know the country of residence of the beneficial owner),

(iv) Real property located in that country, or

(v) Services performed in, and the end product of services performed in, that country (other than payroll paid to a person that is an officer or employee of the payor).

(6) *Sales made to a country.* The terms "sales made to a boycotting country" and "sales made to any country other than the United States" mean, in respect of any particular country, the gross receipts from the sale, exchange, other disposition, or use of:

(i) Tangible personal property (including money) for direct use, consumption, or disposition in that country,

(ii) Services performed in that country,

(iii) The end product of services (wherever performed) for direct use, consumption, or disposition in that country,

(iv) Intangible property (other than securities) in that country,

(v) Securities by a dealer to a beneficial owner that is a resident of that country (but only if the dealer knows or has reason to know the country of residence of the beneficial owner), or

(vi) Real property located in that country.

To determine the country of direct use, consumption, or disposition of tangible personal property and the end product of services, see paragraph (b)(10) of this section.

(7) *Sales made from a country.* The terms "sales made from a boycotting country" and "sales made from any country other than the United States" mean, in respect of a particular country, the gross receipts from the sale, exchange, other disposition, or use of:

(i) Tangible personal property (including money) from a stock of goods located in that country,

Reg. § 7.999-1(b)(7)

(ii) Intangible property (other than securities) in that country, or

(iii) Services performed in, and the end product of services performed in, that country.

However, gross receipts from any such sale, exchange, other disposition, or use by a person that are included in the numerator of that person's international boycott factor by reason of paragraph (b)(6) of this section shall not again be included in the numerator by reason of this subparagraph.

(8) *Payroll paid or accrued for services performed in a country.* The terms "payroll paid or accrued for services performed in a boycotting country" and "payroll paid or accrued for services performed in any country other than the United States" mean, in respect of a particular country, the total amount paid or accrued as compensation to officers and employees, including wages, salaries, commissions, and bonuses, for services performed in that country.

(9) *Services performed partly within and partly without a country.* (i) *In general.* Except as provided in paragraph (b)(9)(ii) of this section, for purposes of allocating to a particular country:

(A) The gross amount paid in connection with the purchase or use of,

(B) The gross receipts from the sale, exchange, other disposition or use of, and

(C) the payroll paid or accrued for services performed, or the end product of services performed, partly within and partly without that country, the amount paid, received, or accrued to be allocated to that country, unless the facts and circumstances of a particular case warrant a different amount, will be that amount that bears the same relation to the total amount paid, received, or accrued as the number of days of performance of the services within that country bears to the total number of days of performance of services for which the total amount is paid, received, or accrued.

(ii) *Transportation, telegraph, and cable services.* Transportation, telegraph, and cable services performed partly within one country and partly within another country are allocated between the two countries as follows:

(A) In the case of a purchase of such services performed from Country A to Country B, fifty percent of the gross amount paid is deemed to be a purchase made from Country A and the remaining fifty percent is deemed to be a purchase made from Country B.

(B) In the case of a sale of such services performed from Country A to Country B, fifty percent of the gross receipts is deemed to be a sale made from Country R and the remaining fifty percent is deemed to be a sale made to Country B.

(10) *Country of use, consumption, or disposition.* As a general rule, the country of use, consumption, or disposition of tangible personal property (including money) and the end product of services (wherever performed) is deemed to be the country of destination of the tangible personal property or the end product of the services. (Thus, if legal services are performed in one country and an opinion is given for use by a client in a second country, the end product of the legal services is used, consumed, or disposed of in the second country.) The occurrence in a country of a temporary interruption in the shipment of the tangible personal property or the delivery of the end product of services shall not constitute such country the country of destination. However, if at the time of the transaction the person providing the tangible personal property or the end product of services knew, or should have known from the facts and circumstances surrounding the transaction, that the tangible personal property or the end product of services probably would not be used, consumed, or disposed of in the country of destination, that person must determine the country of ultimate use, consumption or disposition of the tangible personal property or the end product of services. Notwithstanding the preceding provisions of this subparagraph, a person that sells, exchanges, otherwise disposes of, or makes available for use, tangible personal property to any person all of whose business except for an insubstantial part consists of selling from inventory to retail customers at retail outlets all within one country may assume at the time of such sale to such person that the tangible personal property will be used, consumed, or disposed of within such country.

(11) *Controlled group taxable year.* The term "controlled group taxable year" means the taxable year of the controlled group's common parent corporation. In the event that no common parent corporation exists, the members of the group shall elect the taxable year of one of the members of the controlled group to serve as the controlled group taxable year. The taxable year election is a binding election to be changed only with the approval of the Secretary or his delegate. The election is to be made in accordance with the procedures set forth in the instructions to Form 5713, the International Boycott Report.

(c) *Computation of international boycott factor.* (1) *In general.* The method of computing the international boycott factor of a person that is not a member of a controlled group is set forth in paragraph (c)(2) of this section. The method of computing the international boycott factor of a person that is a member of a controlled group is set forth in paragraph (c)(3) of this section. For purposes of paragraphs (c)(2) and (3), purchases and sales made by, and payroll paid or accrued by, a partnership are deemed to be made or paid or accrued by a partner in that proportion that the partner's distributive share bears to the purchases and sales made by, and the payroll paid or accrued by, the partnership. Also for purposes of paragraphs (c)(2) and (3), purchases and sales made by, and payroll paid or accrued by, a trust referred to in section 671 are deemed to be made both by the trust (for purposes of determining the trust's international boycott factor), and by a person treated under section 671 as the owner of the trust (but only in that proportion that the portion of the trust that such person is considered as owning under sections 671 through 679 bears to the purchases and sales made by, and the payroll paid and accrued by, the trust).

(2) *International boycott factor of a person that is not a member of a controlled group.* The international boycott factor to be applied by a person that is not a mem-

ber of a controlled group (within the meaning of section 993(a)(3)) is a fraction.

(i) The numerator of the fraction is the sum of the—

(A) Purchases made from all boycotting countries associated in carrying out a particular international boycott,

(B) Sales made to or from all boycotting countries associated in carrying out a particular international boycott, and

(C) Payroll paid or accrued for services performed in all boycotting countries associated in carrying out a particular international boycott by that person during that person's taxable year, minus the amount of such purchases, sales, and payroll that is clearly demonstrated to be attributable to clearly separate and identifiable operations in connection with which there was no participation in or cooperation with that international boycott.

(ii) The denominator of the fraction is the sum of the—

(A) Purchases made from any country other than the United States,

(B) Sales made to or from any country other than the United States, and

(C) Payroll paid or accrued for services performed in any country other than the United States by that person during that person's taxable year.

(3) *International boycott factor of a person that is a member of a controlled group.* The international boycott factor to be applied by a person that is a member of a controlled group (within the meaning of section 993(a)(3)) shall be computed in the manner described in paragraph (c)(2) of this section, except that there shall be taken into account the purchases and sales made by, and the payroll paid or accrued by, each member of the controlled group during each member's own taxable year that ends with or within the controlled group taxable year that ends with or within that person's taxable year.

(d) *Computation of the international boycott factor of a person that is a member of two or more controlled groups.* The international boycott factor to be applied under sections 908(a), 952(a)(3), and 995(b)(1)(F) by a person that is a member of two or more controlled groups shall be determined in the manner described in paragraph (c)(3), except that the purchases, sales, and payroll included in the numerator and denominator shall include the purchases, sales, and payroll of that person and of all other members of the two or more controlled groups of which that person is a member.

(e) *Transitional rules.* (1) *Pre-November 3, 1976 boycotting operations.* The international boycott factor to be applied under sections 908(a), 952(a)(3), and 995(b)(1)(F) by a person that is not a member of a controlled group, for that person's taxable year that includes November 3, 1976, or a person that is a member of a controlled group, for the controlled group taxable year that includes November 3, 1976, shall be computed in the manner described in paragraphs (c)(2) and (c)(3), respectively, of this section. However, that the following adjustments shall be made:

(i) There shall be excluded from the numerators described in paragraphs (c)(2)(i) and (c)(3)(i) of this section purchases, sales, and payroll clearly demonstrated to be attributable to clearly separate and identifiable operations—

(A) That were completed on or before November 3, 1976, or

(B) In respect of which it is demonstrated that the agreements constituting participation in or cooperation with the international boycott were renounced, the renunciations were communicated on or before November 3, 1976, to the governments or persons with which the agreements were made, and the agreements have not been reaffirmed after November 3, 1976, and

(ii) The international boycott factor resulting after the numerator has been modified in accordance with paragraph (e)(1)(i) of this section shall be further modified by multiplying it by a fraction. The numerator of that fraction shall be the number of days in that person's taxable year (or, if applicable, in that person's controlled group taxable year) remaining after November 3, 1976, and the denominator shall be 366.

The principles of this subparagraph are illustrated in the following example:

Example. Corporation A, a calendar year taxpayer, is not a member of a controlled group. During the 1976 calendar year, Corporation A had three operations in a boycotting country under three separate contracts, each of which contained agreements constituting participation in or cooperation with an international boycott. Each contract was entered into on or after September 2, 1976. Operation (1) was completed on November 1, 1976. The sales made to a boycotting country in connection with Operation (1) amounted to $10. Operation (2) was not completed during the taxable year, but on November 1, 1976, Corporation A communicated a renunciation of the boycott agreement covering that operation to the government of the boycotting country. The sales made to a boycotting country in connection with Operation (2) amounted to $40. Operation (3) was not completed during the taxable year, nor was any renunciation of the boycott agreement made. The sales made to a boycotting country in connection with Operation (3) amounted to $25. Corporation A had no purchases made from, sales made from, or payroll paid or accrued for services performed in, a boycotting country. Corporation A had $500 of purchases made from, sales made from, sales made to, and payroll paid or accrued for services performed in, countries other than the United States. Company A's boycott factor for 1976, computed under paragraph (c)(2) of this section (before the application of this subparagraph) would be:

$$\frac{\$10 + \$40 + \$25}{\$500} = \frac{\$75}{\$500}$$

However, the $10 is eliminated from the numerator by reason of paragraph (e)(1)(i)(A) of this section, and the $40 is eliminated from the numerator by reason of paragraph (e)(1)(i)(B) of this section. Thus, before the application of paragraph (e)(1)(ii) of this section, Corporation A's international boycott factor is $25/$500. After the application of paragraph (e)(1)(ii),

Reg. § 7.999-1(e)(1)

24,998.98-B *(I.R.C.)* Reg. § 7.999-1(e)(1) 3-7-77

Corporation A's international boycott factor is:

$$\frac{\$25}{\$500} \times \frac{58}{366}$$

(2) *Pre-December 31, 1977 boycotting operations.* The international boycott factor to be applied under sections 908(a), 952(a)(3), and 995(b)(1)(F) by a person that is not a member of a controlled group, for that person's taxable year that includes December 31, 1977, or by a person that is a member of a controlled group, for the controlled group taxable year that includes December 31, 1977, shall be computed in the manner described in paragraphs (c)(2) and (c)(3), respectively, of this section. However, the following adjustments shall be made:

(i) There shall be excluded from the numerators described in paragraphs (c)(2)(i) and (c)(3)(i) of this section purchases, sales, and payroll clearly demonstrated to be attributable to clearly separate and identifiable operations that were carried out in accordance with the terms of binding contracts entered into before September 2, 1976, and—

(A) That were completed on or before December 31, 1977, or

(B) In respect of which it is demonstrated that the agreements constituting participation in or cooperation with the international boycott were renounced, the renunciations were communicated on or before December 31, 1977, to the governments or persons with which the agreements were made, and the agreements were not reaffirmed after December 31, 1977, and

(ii) In the case of clearly separate and identifiable operations that are carried out in accordance with the terms of binding contracts entered into before September 2, 1976, but that do not meet the requirements of paragraph (e)(2)(i) of this section, the numerators described in paragraphs (c)(2)(i) and (c)(3)(i) of this section shall be adjusted by multiplying the purchases, sales, and payroll clearly demonstrated to be attributable to those operations by a fraction, the numerator of which is the number of days in such person's taxable year (or, if applicable, in such person's controlled group taxable year) remaining after December 31, 1977, and the denominator of which is 365.

The principles of this subparagraph are illustrated in the following example:

Example. Corporation A is not a member of a controlled group and reports on the basis of a July 1-June 30 fiscal year. During the 1977-1978 fiscal year, Corporation A had 2 operations carried out pursuant to the terms of separate contracts, each of which had a clause that constituted participation in or cooperation with an international boycott. Neither operation was completed during the fiscal year, nor were either of the boycotting clauses renounced. Operation (1) was carried out in accordance with the terms of a contract entered into on November 15, 1976. Operation (2) was carried out in accordance with the terms of a binding contract entered into before September 2, 1976. Corporation A had sales made to a boycotting country in connection with Operation (1) in the amount of $50, and in connection with Operation (2) in the amount of $100. Corporation A had sales made to countries other than the United States in the amount of $500. Corporation A had no purchases made from, sales made from, or payroll paid or accrued for services performed in, any country other than the United States. In the absence of this subparagraph, Corporation A's international boycott factor would be:

$$\frac{\$50 + \$100}{\$500}$$

However, by reason of the application of this subparagraph, Corporation A's international boycott factor is reduced to:

$$\frac{\$50 + \$100 \left(\dfrac{181}{365}\right)}{\$500}$$

(3) *Incomplete controlled group taxable year.* If, at the end of the taxable year of a person that is a member of a controlled group, the controlled group taxable year that includes November 3, 1976 has not ended, or the taxable year of one or more members of the controlled group that includes November 3, 1976 has not ended, then the international boycott factor to be applied under sections 908(a), 952(a)(3) and 995(b)(1)(F) by such person for the taxable year shall be computed in the manner described in paragraph (c)(3) of this section. However, the numerator and the denominator in that paragraph shall include only the purchases, sales, and payroll of those members of the controlled group whose taxable years ending after November 3, 1976 have ended as the end of the taxable year of such person.

(f) *Effective date.* This section applies to participation in or cooperation with an international boycott after November 3, 1976. In the case of operations which constitute participation in or cooperation with an international boycott and which are carried out in accordance with the terms of a binding contract entered into before September 2, 1976, this section applies to such participation or cooperation after December 31, 1977.

Temporary Rules (I.R.C.) 24,998.99
T.D. 7468

Temporary regulations relating to minimum exemption from levy for wages, salary, and other income. (T.D. 7468, filed 2-25-77.)

Under sections 6331(d)(3) and 6334(a)(9), which were added by the Tax Reform Act of 1976, a levy upon wages or salary is continuous from the date the levy is first made until the liability giving rise to the levy is satisfied or becomes unenforceable by reason of lapse of time, but during such time certain amounts payable to or received by an individual as wages or salary for personal services, or as income from other sources, are exempt.

In order to prescribe temporary regulations relating to minimum exemption from levy for wages, salary, and other income pursuant to section 6334(d) of the Internal Revenue Code of 1954, as added by the Tax Reform Act of 1976 (Public Law 94-455), the following regulations are hereby adopted:

○━ [Sec. 6334(d)] 404.6334(d)-1. (T.D. 7468, filed 2-25-77.) **Minimum exemption from levy for wages, salary, or other income.**

(a) *In general.* Under section 6331(a), if an individual liable for any tax neglects or refuses to pay such tax within 10 days after notice and demand, the tax may be collected by levy upon property or rights to property belonging to such individual, including amounts payable to or received by him as wages, salary, or other income. Under section 6331(d)(3), a levy upon wages or salary is continuous from the date the levy is first made until the liability giving rise to the levy is satisfied or becomes unenforceable by reason of lapse of time. Under section 6334(a)(9), however, certain amounts payable to or received by an individual as wages or salary for personal services, or as income from other sources, are exempt from levy. Under section 6334(d), amounts so exempt are determined by taking into account (1) the individual's payroll period, i.e., the basis (whether weekly, biweekly, semimonthly, monthly or otherwise) on which the individual is paid or receives wages, salary, or other income, and (2) the number of certain other persons dependent upon the individual for their support during each such payroll period. Paragraph (b) of this section prescribes rules for determining an individual's payroll period. Paragraph (c) of this section contains rules relating to the minimum amount of wages, salary, or other income which is exempt from levy for each such payroll period, and the additional amount which is exempt for each person who is claimed as a dependent of the individual pursuant to paragraph (d) of this section.

(b) *Determination of payroll period.* For purposes of determining the amount of wages, salary, or other income exempt from levy pursuant to section 6334(a)(9) and this section—

(1) *Regularly used calendar periods.* In the case of a levy on wages, etc. paid on the basis of an established calendar period regularly used by the employer for payroll purposes (e.g., weekly, biweekly, semimonthly, or monthly), that period shall be used as the individual's payroll period.

(2) *Remuneration paid on an irregular basis.* In the case of a levy on wages, etc. not paid on the basis of an established calendar period regularly used by an employer for payroll purposes, the first day of the individual's payroll period shall be that day following the day upon which the wages, salary, or other income become payable to or are received by the individual, and the last day of the payroll period shall be that day upon which such wages, salary, or other income next become payable to or are received by him.

(c) *Determination of exempt amount.* For each payroll period determined pursuant to paragraph (b) of this section, amounts exempt from levy pursuant to section 6334(a)(9) and this section are as follows:

(1) If such payroll period is weekly: $50, plus $15 for each person who is claimed as a dependent pursuant to paragraph (d) of this section.

(2) If such payroll period is biweekly: $100, plus $30 for each person who is claimed as a dependent pursuant to paragraph (d) of this section.

(3) If such payroll period is semimonthly: $108.33, plus $32.50 for each person who is claimed as a dependent pursuant to paragraph (d) of this section.

(4) If such payroll period is monthly: $216.67, plus $65 for each person who is claimed as a dependent pursuant to paragraph (d) of this section.

(5) If such payroll period is not weekly, biweekly, semimonthly or monthly: a proportionate amount based upon the sum of an annual exemption of $2,600 plus $780 for each person who is claimed as a dependent pursuant to paragraph (d) of this section.

(d) *Dependent exemption.* (1) *Dependent defined.* For purposes of this section, a person is a dependent of an individual for any payroll period of such individual, if—

(i) Over half of such person's support for such payroll period was received from the individual, and

(ii) Such person is the spouse of the individual, or bears a relationship to the individual specified in section 152(a)(1) through (9) (relating to definition of dependent), and

(iii) Such person is not a minor child of the individual with respect to whom amounts are exempt from levy under section 6334(a)(8) (relating to exemption from levy for judgments for support of minor children) at any time during such payroll period.

For purposes of subdivision (ii) of this subparagraph, "payroll period" shall be substituted for "taxable year" each place it appears in section 152(a)(9).

(2) *Claim for dependent exemption.* No amount prescribed by paragraph (c) of this section as being exempt from levy for each person who is claimed as a dependent pursuant to this paragraph shall be so exempt unless there is delivered to the employer or other person upon whom notice

Reg. § 404.6334(d)-1(d)(2)

24,998.100 *(I.R.C.)*   Reg. § 404.6334(d)-1(d)(2)

of levy is served a written statement, signed by the individual seeking such exemption and containing a declaration that it is made under the penalties of perjury, which identifies, by name and by relationship to such individual, each person for whom a dependent exemption is claimed.

(e) *Cross references.*

(1) For the requirement for notice of intent to levy on salary or wages, see section 6331(d)(1).

(2) For the continuing effect of a levy on salary or wages, see section 6331(d)(3).

(3) For other property exempt from levy, see section 6334 and § 301.6334-1.

(f) *Effective date.* The regulations prescribed by this section shall apply with respect to levies on wages, salary, and other income made after February 28, 1977.

4-24-78   Temporary Rules   *(I.R.C.)* 24,998.101

T.D. 7471; 7521; 7539

Temporary regulations relating to disclosure of return information to certain officers and employees of the Department of Commerce and Federal Trade Commission. (T.D. 7471, filed 2-28-77; amended by T.D. 7521, filed 12-15-77; T.D. 7539, filed 4-5-78.)

This document provides temporary regulations for disclosures by the Internal Revenue Service to officers and employees of the Department of Commerce and the Federal Trade Commission for use in statistical programs and related activities authorized by law. Changes to the applicable tax law were made by the Tax Reform Act of 1976. The regulations provide Internal Revenue Service, Social Security Administration, Department of Commerce, and Federal Trade Commission personnel with guidance needed to comply with the Act.

Date: The regulations are effective as of January 1, 1977.

For Further Information Contact: Karl P. Fryzel of the Legislation and Regulations Division, Office of the Chief Counsel, Internal Revenue Service, 1111 Constitution Avenue, N.W., Washington, D.C. 20224, Attention: CC:LR:T, 202-566-3294, not a toll-free call.

Supplementary Information: Background

On Thursday, March 3, 1977, the FEDERAL REGISTER published temporary regulations on procedure and administration (26 CFR Part 404) under section 6103(j)(1) and (2) of the Internal Revenue Code of 1954 (42 FR 12181). These temporary regulations were issued to provide personnel of the Internal Revenue Service, Department of Commerce, and Federal Trade Commission with guidance needed to comply with section 1202(a) of the Tax Reform Act of 1976.

Tax Reform Act of 1976

Section 1202(a) of the Tax Reform Act of 1976 added section 6103(j)(1) and (2) to the Internal Revenue Code of 1954. Section 6103(j)(1) allows the Internal Revenue Service to disclose return or return information to officers and employees of the Bureau of Census and Economic Analysis of the Department of Commerce for specified statistical purposes and related activities authorized by law. Section 6103(j)(2) allows the Internal Revenue Service to disclose corporate income return information to officers and employees of the Division of Financial Statistics of the Bureau of Economics of the Federal Trade Commission for purposes of administering authorized economic surveys of corporations.

Congress intended that the Internal Revenue Service make these disclosures pursuant to Treasury regulations specifying the limited types of tax information (for example, name, address, etc.) to be disclosed to each agency. Temporary regulations §§ 404.6103(j)(1)-1 and 404.6103(j)(2)-1 issued on March 3, 1977 provided these rules.

Changes

Certain changes have been made to these temporary regulations. First, new provisions have been added to §§ 404.6103(j)(1)-1(b) and 404.6103(j)(2)-1(a) to permit the Social Security Administration to disclose certain employment tax return information and data to the Census Bureau and Federal Trade Commission for the statistical purposes described in section 6103(j)(1)(A) and (2). The Social Security Administration is not permitted to make these disclosures without the written authorization of the Internal Revenue Service.

Second, the restriction in § 404.6103(j)(1)-1(b), relating to the disclosure to the Census Bureau of certain individual income tax information for revenue sharing purposes, to 1975 returns has been removed. This information will be disclosed to the Census Bureau for all future taxable years.

Third, a series of technical and stylistic changes has been made to the temporary regulations.

Adoption of amendments to the regulations

Accordingly, 26 CFR Part 404 is amended as follows:

०─╼ [Sec. 6103(j)] § 404.6103(j)(1)-1 (T.D. 7471, filed 2-28-77; amended by T.D. 7521, filed 12-15-77; T.D. 7539, filed 4-5-78.) **Disclosure of return information to officers and employees of the Department of Commerce for certain statistical purposes and related activiites.**

(a) *General rule.* Pursuant to the provisions of section 6103(j)(1) of the Internal Revenue Code of 1954 and subject to the requirements of paragraph (d) of this section, officers or employees of the Internal Revenue Service will disclose return information (as defined by section 6103(b)(2)) to officers and employees of the Department of Commerce to the extent, and for such purposes as may be, provided by paragraphs (b) and (c) of this section. Further, in the case of any disclosure of return information so provided by paragraphs (b) and (c), the tax period or accounting period to which such return information relates will also be disclosed.

(b) *Disclosure of return information to officers and employees of the Bureau of Census.* (1) Officers or employees of the Internal Revenue Service will disclose the following return information reflected on returns of an individual taxpayer to officers and employees of the Bureau of the Census for purposes of conducting and preparing, as authorized by law, intercensal estimates of population and per capita income for all geographic areas included in the general revenue sharing program and demographic statistics programs, censuses and related program evaluation.

(i) Taxpayer identity information (as defined in section 6103(b)(6), other than the name of the taxpayer), validity code with respect to the taxpayer identifying number (as described in section 6109), and taxpayer identifying number of spouse, if reported;

(ii) District office and service center codes;

(iii) Marital status;

(iv) Numbers and classifications of reported exemptions;

(v) Adjusted gross income;

(vi) Wage and salary income;

(vii) Divided income;

(viii) Interest income;

(ix) Gross rent and royalty income;

(x) Entity code;

(xi) Residence information from the revenue sharing question;

Reg. § 404.6103(j)(1)-1(b)(1)

24,998.102 (I.R.C.)   Reg. § 404.6103(j)(1)-1(b)(1)   4-24-78

(xii) Code indicators for Form 1040; Schedules C, D, E, F, and SE; and

(xiii) Julian date relative to filing.

(2) Officers or employees of the Internal Revenue Service will disclose to officers and employees of the Bureau of the Census for purposes of conducting, as authorized by law, demographic, economic, and agricultural statistics programs and censuses and related program evaluation—

(i) From the business master files of the Service—

(A) Taxpayer name directory, and

(B) Entity records consisting of taxpayer identity information (as defined in section 6103(b)(6)), the principal industrial activity code, and monthly corrections of, and additions to, such entity records;

(ii) From Form SS-4, all return information reflected on such return;

(iii) From a quarterly or annual employment tax return—

(A) Taxpayer identifying number (as described in section 6109) of the employer and any employee identified on such return,

(B) Total compensation paid,

(C) Total number of employees reflected on such return,

(D) Master file tax account number,

(E) Taxable period covered by such return,

(F) Employment code,

(G) Final return indicator,

(H) Document locator number,

(I) Record code,

(J) Total number of individuals employed in the taxable period covered by the return,

(K) Taxable wages paid for purposes of chapter 21 to each such employee,

(L) Taxable tip income for purposes of chapter 21 reported on the return with respect to each such employee,

(M) Total taxable wages paid for purposes of chapter 21, and

(N) Total taxable tip income reported for purposes of chapter 21; and

(iv) From Form 1040, Schedule SE—

(A) Taxpayer identifying number of self-employed individual,

(B) Business activities subject to the tax imposed by chapter 21,

(C) Net earnings from farming,

(D) Net earnings from nonfarming activities,

(E) Total net earnings from self-employment, and

(F) Taxable self-employment income for purposes of chapter 2.

(3) Officers or employees of the Internal Revenue Service will disclose the following business related return information reflected on the return of a taxpayer to officers and employees of the Bureau of the Census for purposes of conducting and preparing, as authorized by law, demographic, economic, and agricultural statistics programs and censuses—

(i) From Form 1040, Schedule C, taxpayer identity information (as defined in section 6103(b)(6)), the principal industrial activity code, reported gross receipts, returns and allowances, cost of labor, and salaries and wages;

(ii) From Form 1120F, Section II, and Forms 1065, 1120, 1120S, 990C, and 990T, the taxpayer identifying number (as described in section 6109), the principal industrial activity code, and reported gross receipts less returns and allowances;

(iii) From Form 1040, Schedule F, taxpayer identity information and reported gross profits (cash basis) or gross sales (accrual basis) and labor hired;

(iv) From Form 1040, Schedule C, and Forms 1065, 1120, and 1120S, answers to the business activity questions;

(v) From Form 1040, Schedule C, business address and answer to the question relating to Form 941;

(vi) From Form 990PF the taxpayer identifying number, the principal industrial activity code, and reported total receipts;

(vii) From Form 1065, the names and taxpayer identifying numbers of no more than 10 members of the partnership; and

(viii) From Form 1120S the names and taxpayer identifying numbers of, and the number of shares of stock owned by, no more than 10 shareholders of that corporation.

(4) Officers and employees of the Internal Revenue Service will disclose return information relating to a taxpayer contained in the exempt organization master files of the Service to officers and employees of the Bureau of the Census for purposes of conducting and preparing, as authorized by law, economic and agricultural censuses. This return information consists of taxpayer identity information (as defined in section 6103(b)(6)), activity codes, and filing requirement code, and monthly corrections of, and additions to, such return information.

(5) Subject to the requirements of paragraph (d) of this section, officers or employees of the Social Security Administration to whom the following return information has been disclosed as provided by section 6103(l)(1)(A) may disclose such return information to officers and employees of the Bureau of the Census for purposes described in subparagraph (2) or (3) of this paragraph—

(i) From Form SS-4, all return information reflected on such return;

(ii) From a quarterly or annual employment tax return—

(A) Taxpayer identifying number (as described in section 6109) of the employer and any employee identified on such return,

(B) Total number of employees reflected on the return,

(C) Total number of individuals employed in the taxable period covered by the return,

(D) Taxable wages paid for purposes of chapter 21 to each such employee,

(E) Taxable tip income for purposes of chapter 21 reported on the return with respect to each such employee,

(F) Total taxable wages paid for purposes of chapter 21, and

(G) Total taxable tip income reported for purposes of chapter 21; and

(iii) From Form 1040, Schedule SE—

(A) Taxpayer identifying number of self-employed individual,

(B) Business activities subject to the tax imposed by chapter 21,

(C) Net earnings from farming,

(D) Net earnings from nonfarming activities,

(E) Total net earnings from self-employment, and

(F) Taxable self-employment income for purposes of chapter 2.

(c) *Disclosure of return information to officers and employees of the Bureau of Economic Analysis.* Officers or employees of the Internal Revenue Service will disclose to officers and employees of the Bureau of Economic Analysis for purposes of conducting and preparing, as authorized by law, statistical analyses return information consisting of Statistics of Income transcript-edit sheets containing return information reflected on returns of designated classes or categories of corporations with respect to the tax imposed by chapter 1 and microfilmed records of return information reflected on such returns where needed for further use in connection with such conduct or preparation.

(d) *Procedures and restrictions.* Disclosure of return information by officers or employees of the Internal Revenue Service or the Social Security Administration as provided by paragraphs (b) and (c) of this section will be made only upon written request to the Commissioner of Internal Revenue by the Secretary of Commerce describing the particular return information to be disclosed and the taxable period or date to which such return information relates and designating by name and title the officers and employees of the Bureau of the Census or the Bureau of Economic Analysis to whom such disclosure is authorized. Disclosure of return information by officers or employees of the Social Security Administration as provided by subparagraph (5) of paragraph (b) shall be made only as and to the extent authorized in writing by the Commissioner of Internal Revenue, which written authorization shall be directed to the Commissioner of Social Security and may contain such conditions or requirements on such disclosure as the Commissioner of Internal Revenue shall prescribe. No such officer or employee to whom return information is disclosed pursuant to the provisions of paragraph (b) or (c) shall disclose such return information to any person, other than the taxpayer to whom such return information relates or other officers or employees of such bureau whose duties or responsibilities require such disclosure for a purpose described in paragraph (b) or (c), except in a form which cannot be associated with, or otherwise identify, directly or indirectly, a particular taxpayer. If the Service determines that the Bureau of the Census or the Bureau of Economic Analysis, or any officer or employee thereof, has failed to, or does not, satisfy the requirements of section 6103(p)(4) or regulations or published procedures thereunder, the Service may take such actions as are deemed necessary to ensure that such requirements are or will be satisfied, including suspension of disclosures of return information otherwise authorized by section 6103(j)(1) and paragraph (b) or (c) of this section, until the Service determines that such requirements have been or will be satisfied.

○━ [Sec. 6103(j)] § 404.6103(j)(2)-1 (T.D. 7471, filed 2-28-77; amended by T.D. 7521, filed 12-15-77.) **Disclosure of return information to officers and employees of the Federal Trade Commission for certain statistical purposes and related activities.**

(a) *General rule.* (1) Pursuant to the provisions of section 6103(j)(2) of the Internal Revenue Code of 1954 and subject to the requirements of paragraph (b) of this section, officers or employees of the Internal Revenue Service will disclose the following return information (as defined by section 6103(b)(2)) reflected on the return of a corporation with respect to the tax imposed by chapter 1 to officers and employees of the Division of Financial Statistics of the Bureau of Economics of the Federal Trade Commission for purposes of developing and preparing, as authorized by law, the Quarterly Financial Report—

(i) From the business master files of the Service—

(A) Taxpayer identity information (as defined in section 6103(b)(6)),

(B) Consolidated return and final return indicators,

(C) Principal industrial activity code,

(D) Partial year indicator,

(E) Annual accounting period,

(F) Gross receipts less returns and allowances,

(G) New income or loss,

(H) Total assets; and

(ii) From Form SS-4—

(A) Month and year in which such form was executed,

(B) Taxpayer identity information; and

(C) Principal industrial activity, geographic, firm size, and reason for application codes.

(2) Subject to the requirements of paragraph (b) of this section, officers or employees of the Social Security Administration to whom the following return information reflected on Form SS-4 with respect to a corporation has been disclosed as provided by section 6103*(1)*(1)(A) may disclose such return information to officers and employees of the Division of Financial Statistics of the Bureau of Economics of the Federal Trade Commission for a purpose described in subparagraph (1) of this paragraph—

(i) Month and year in which such form was executed;

(ii) Taxpayer identity information; and

(iii) Principal industrial activity, geographic, firm size, and reason for application codes.

(b) *Procedures and restrictions.* Disclosure of return information by officers or employees of the Internal Revenue Service or the Social Security Administration as provided by paragraph (a) of this section will be made only upon written request to the Commissioner of Internal Revenue by the Chairman of the Federal Trade Commission describing the particular return information to be disclosed and the taxable period or date to which such return information relates and designating by name and title the officers and employees of the Division of Financial Statistics of the Bureau of Economics to whom such disclosure is authorized. Disclosure of return information by officers or employees of the Social Security Administration as provided by subparagraph (2) of paragraph (a) shall be made only as and to the extent authorized in writing by the Commissioner of Internal Revenue, which written authorization shall

Reg. § 404.6103(j)(2)-1(b)

24,998.102-B *(I.R.C.)*   Reg. § 404.6103(j)(2)-1(b)

be directed to the Commissioner of Social Security and may contain such conditions or requirements on such disclosure as the Commissioner of Internal Revenue shall prescribe. No such officer or employee to whom return information is disclosed pursuant to the provisions of paragraph (a) shall disclose such return information to any person, other than the taxpayer to whom such return information relates or other officers or employees of such division whose duties or responsibilities require such disclosure for a purpose described in paragraph (a), except in a form which cannot be associated with, or otherwise identify, directly or indirectly, a particular taxpayer. If the Service determines that the division, or any officer or employee thereof, has failed to, or does not, satisfy the requirements of section 6103(p)(4) or regulations or published procedures thereunder, the Service may take such actions as are deemed necessary to ensure that such requirements are or will be satisfied, including suspension of disclosures of return information otherwise authorized by section 6103(j)(2) and paragraph (a) of this section until the Service determines that such requirements have been or will be satisfied.

Temporary Rules

T.D. 7474

Temporary regulations relating to investment credit for movie and television films placed in service in a taxable year beginning before January 1, 1975, which are subject to the forty-percent election. (T.D. 7474, filed 3-29-77; amended by T.D. 7480, filed 4-12-77.)

This document contains temporary regulations providing rules for taxpayers to use in electing the forty-percent method of determining investment credit for movie and television films placed in service in a taxable year beginning before January 1, 1975. This election is provided for under section 804(c)(2) of the Tax Reform Act of 1976. These regulations affect all taxpayers desiring to make the forty-percent election and provide them with the guidance needed to make the election.

DATE: The election must be made not later than April 25, 1977.

In order to prescribe temporary income tax regulations (26 CFR Part 7) relating to election of the forty-percent method of determining investment credit for movie and television films placed in service in a taxable year beginning before January 1, 1975, under section 804(c)(2) of the Tax Reform Act of 1976 (Pub. L. 94-455), the following temporary regulations are hereby adopted:

[Sec. 48] § 7.48-2 (T.D. 7474, filed 3-29-77; amended by T.D. 7480, filed 4-12-77.) Election of forty-percent method of determining investment credit for movie and television films placed in service in a taxable year beginning before January 1, 1975.

(a) *General rule.* Under section 804(c)(2) of the Tax Reform Act of 1976 (90 Stat. 1595), taxpayers who placed movie or television films (hereinafter referred to as films and tapes) in service during taxable years beginning before January 1, 1975, may elect to have their investment credit on all such films and tapes determined under section 46(c) of the Code using an amount equal to 40 percent of aggregate production costs in lieu of the basis of such property. If the election is made, 100 percent is the applicable percentage used in determining qualified investment under section 46(c) of the Code regardless of actual useful life. The election can be made only with respect to qualified films and tapes that are new section 38 property and the investment credit is allowed only to the extent that a taxpayer has an ownership interest in the film or tape. No investment credit is allowed under section 804(c)(2) of the Act on any film or tape that is not section 38 property or that was produced and shown exclusively outside of the United States. Thus, no election may be made under this section with respect to a film or tape which is suspension period property to which section 48(h) applies or to a film or tape which is termination period property to which section 49(a) applies. Any investment credit taken on any film or tape subject to the election is not subject to recapture because of an early disposition or because a film or tape otherwise ceases to be section 38 property under section 47(a) of the Code. Thus, there will be no recapture because a film or tape is used outside the United States under section 48(a)(2) of the Code or section 804(c)(1)(C) of the Act, or because of any disposition under section 47(a)(7)(B) of the Code.

(b) *Time and manner of making an election*—(1) *Time for making the election.* The election under section 804(c)(2) of the Act must be made not later than April 25, 1977.

(2) *Manner of making the election.* An election under this section must be made by filing amended income tax returns for each taxable year beginning before January 1, 1975, in which films and tapes subject to the election were placed in service together with a statement signed by the taxpayer containing the information described below. The amended returns and the statement must be filed with the district director having audit jurisdiction over the last return filed to which the election relates. Each amended return shall contain a schedule listing by name all films and taxes placed in service during the year to which the amended return relates and setting forth all computations necessary to determine the aggregate production costs of each such film or tape listed and the ownership interest of the taxpayer in each film or tape listed. In the case of a taxpayer which is a partner, shareholder of an electing small business corporation, or beneficiary of a trust or estate, such computations must be adequate to determine the ownership interest of the partnership, electing small business corporation, or trust or estate in each such film or tape. (A taxpayer which is a partner, shareholder, or beneficiary may satisfy the requirements of the preceding sentence by attaching to his amended return a copy of an amended return, if one is filed, of the partnership, electing small business corporation, or trust or estate which sets forth computations necessary to determine the ownership interest of the entity in each such film or tape.) No amended return need be filed for a taxable year if application of the election to films and tapes placed in service during that year would not affect tax liability for any taxable year.

The statement shall contain the following information:

(i) The taxpayer's name and taxpayer identification number (under section 6109 of the Code).

(ii) A statement that the taxpayer is making the election under section 804(c)(2) of the Act.

(iii) A statement that the taxpayer agrees that the period for assessment and collection under section 6501 of the Code will remain open until December 31, 1978, solely with respect to adjustments of tax liability attributable to investment credit allowed on films and tapes placed in service in each year covered by the election. Unless the district director notifies the taxpayer within 7 days of receipt of the statement that such extension is denied, it will be presumed that the district director consents to such extension. Of course, the period covered by this statement may be extended beyond December 31, 1978 by mutual agreement. This statement does not shorten the regular statutory period for any year or take precedence over a previous or subsequent agreement with the Internal Revenue Service extending the statutory period for any year.

(iv) A list of the addresses used by the taxpayer on each return filed during each taxable year subject to the election.

Reg. § 7.48-2(b)(2)

(v) A statement that the taxpayer consents to join in judicial proceedings to determine the investment credit allowable and entitlement to investment credit on any film or tape subject to the election, which meets all of the requirements set forth in paragraph (b)(3) of this section.

(vi) A statement as to whether an election has been made by the taxpayer under section 804(e)(2) of the Act for films and tapes which are property described in section 50(a) of the Code which were placed in service in taxable years beginning before January 1, 1975.

(vii) A list by name of all films or tape placed in service during the years to which the election relates.

(viii) With respect to each film or tape listed in paragraph (b)(2)(vii) of this section, a list of all producers, distributors, and persons with a participation interest (with addresses where available).

(ix) In the case of an election made by a partner, shareholder of an electing small business corporation (as defined in section 1371(b) of the Code), or beneficiary, a statement indicating the name, taxpayer identification number, and address for tax return purposes of the respective partnership, electing small business corporation, or trust or estate.

(3) *Consent to join in judicial proceedings.* No election may be made by any taxpayer unless the statement made under paragraph (b)(2)(v) of this section provides that the taxpayer shall:

(i) Treat the determination of the investment credit allowable on each film or tape subject to an election as a separate cause of action;

(ii) Make all reasonable efforts necessary to join in or intervene in any judicial proceeding in any court for determining the person entitled to, and the amount of, the investment credit allowable with respect to any film or tape covered by the election after receiving notice from the Commissioner of Internal Revenue or his delegate indicating that a conflicting claim to the investment credit for such film or tape is being asserted in such court by another person; and

(iii) Consent to revocation of the election by the Commissioner of Internal Revenue or his delegate with respect to all films and tapes placed in service in taxable years for which the election applies, if the taxpayer fails to make all reasonable efforts necessary to join in or intervene in any judicial proceeding under paragraph (b)(3)(ii) of this section.

(4) *Who makes the election.* The election must be made separately by each person who has an ownership interest. However, where a film or tape is owned by a partnership, electing small business corporation (as defined in section 1371(b) of the Code), or trust or estate, the election must be made separately by each partner, shareholder or beneficiary. The election is not to be made by a partnership or electing small business corporation, and is to be made by a trust or estate only if the trust or estate in determining its tax liability would be allowed investment credit on a film or tape subject to the election. The election of any partner, shareholder, beneficiary or trust or estate shall be effective regardless of whether any related partner, shareholder, beneficiary, or trust or estate makes the election.

(5) *Additional time to perfect election.* A taxpayer that by April 25, 1977, files a statement containing the information described in paragraph (b)(2)(i) through (v) of this section shall be deemed to have made a timely election under paragraph (b)(2) of this section if by July 5, 1977, the taxpayer has complied with all of the requirements of paragraph (b)(2) of this section. If a taxpayer demonstrates to the satisfaction of the district director that it is unable to meet the July 5, 1977, date even though it has made a good faith effort to do so, the district director may at his discretion extend that date to no later than October 4, 1977, for that taxpayer. Requests for extensions of the July 5, 1977, date should be addressed to the district director with whom the statement was filed.

(c) *Revocation of election*—(1) *Revocation by taxpayer*—(i) Except as provided in paragraph (c)(1)(ii) of this section, an election made under section 804(c)(2) of the Act may not be revoked by a taxpayer unless consent to revoke the election is obtained from the Commissioner of Internal Revenue or his delegate. Application for consent to revoke the election will be accepted only if permanent regulations are issued which contain rules which may not reasonably have been anticipated by taxpayers at the time the election was made. Any permanent regulations will provide a reasonable period of time within which taxpayers will be permitted to apply for consent to revoke the election and will allow revocation (where revocation is not barred by the limitations on credit or refund in section 6511 of the Code) in the event of a determination by the Commissioner of Internal Revenue or his delegate that such permanent regulations contain provisions that may not reasonably have been anticipated by taxpayers at the time of making such election.

(ii) An election properly made under section 804(e)(2) of the Act, to have sections 48(k) and 47(a)(7) of the Code apply to films and tapes which are property described in section 50(a) of the Code and which were placed in service in taxable years beginning before January 1, 1975, shall automatically revoke any election under section 804(c)(2) of the Act with respect to such films and tapes. Such revocation does not require the consent of the Commissioner of Internal Revenue or his delegate.

(2) *Revocation by Commissioner.* The Commissioner of Internal Revenue or his delegate shall revoke an election made under section 804(c)(2) of the Act if a taxpayer fails to make all reasonable efforts necessary to join in or intervene in a judicial proceeding for determination of the person entitled to, and the amount of, the investment credit allowable with respect to any film or tape covered by the election after receiving notice from the Commissioner or his delegate which indicates that a conflicting claim to the investment credit for such film or tape is being asserted in court by another person.

(d) *Furnishing of supplementary information required.* If these regulations are revised to require the furnishing of information in addition to that which was furnished with the amended returns and statement of election filed pursuant to paragraph (b)(2) and (3) of this section, the taxpayer must furnish such additional information in a statement addressed to the district director with whom the amended return and statement of election were filed.

Temporary Rules
T.D. 7509

Temporary regulations relating to election under section 804(e)(2) of the Tax Reform Act of 1976. (T.D. 7509, filed 9-20-77; as corrected 10-26-77.)

This document contains temporary regulations relating to the election with respect to the investment credit for movie and television films and tapes that are property described in section 50 (a) of the Internal Revenue Code of 1954. Changes to the applicable tax law were made by the Tax Reform Act of 1976. The regulations would provide the motion picture and television industry with the guidance needed to make the election under section 804 (e)(2) of the Act. Dates: The election under section 804 (e)(2) of the Act must be made not later than October 4, 1977. For Further Information Contact: Lawrence M. Axelrod of the Legislation and Regulations Division, Office of the Chief Counsel, Internal Revenue Service, 1111 Constitution Avenue, N.W., Washington, D.C. 20224, Attention: CC:LR:T (202-566-4454, not a toll-free call).

Supplementary Information: Background

This document contains temporary regulations relating to the election under section 804 (e)(2) of the Tax Reform Act of 1976. Under section 804 (e)(2) of the Act, taxpayers may elect to apply the amendments made by section 804 (a) and (b) of the Act to movie and television films that are property described in section 50 (a) of the Internal Revenue Code of 1954 and that were placed in service in taxable years beginning before January 1, 1975. The election is to be made by filing amended returns for all taxable years to which the election relates not later than October 4, 1977. Accompanying the amended returns must be a statement containing substantially the same information required by § 7.48-2 (b)(2), (3), and (4).

Adoption of amendments to the regulations

Accordingly, 26 CFR Part 7 is amended by adding the following new section immediately after § 7.48-2.

○→ [Sec. 804(e)(2)] § 7.48-3 (T.D. 7509, filed 9-20-77.) Election to apply the amendments made by sections 804 (a) and (b) of the Tax Reform Act of 1976 to property described in section 50 (a) of the Code.

(a) *General rule.* Under section 804 (e)(2) of the Tax Reform Act of 1976 (90 Stat. 1596), taxpayers may elect to apply the amendments made by section 804 (a) and (b) of the Act to movie and television films that are property described in section 50 (a) of the Code and that were placed in service in taxable years beginning before January 1, 1975.

(b) *Time for and manner of making election*—(1) *Time for making election.* The election under section 804 (e)(2) of the Act must be made not later than October 4, 1977.

(2) *Manner of making election.* The election under section 804 (e)(2) shall be made by applying the same rules applicable under section 804 (c)(2) as described in § 7.48-2 (b)(2), (3), and (4) except that § 7.48-2 (b)(2)(ii) shall be read to require a statement that the taxpayer is making an election under section 804 (e)(2) of the Act, and § 7.48-2 (b)(2)(vi) shall not apply. An election properly made under section 804 (e)(2) of the Act may not be revoked after October 4, 1977.

T.D. 7477

Temporary regulations relating to expenditures to remove architectural and transportation barriers to the handicapped and elderly. (T.D. 7477, filed Mar. 30, 1977.)

This document contains interim income tax regulations under part VI of subchapter B of chapter 1 of the Internal Revenue Code of 1954. These amendments conform the Temporary Income Tax Regulations under the Tax Reform Act of 1976 (26 CFR Part 7) to section 2122 of the Tax Reform Act of 1976 (90 Stat. 1914). They are issued under the authority contained in sections 190 and 7805 of the Internal Revenue Code of 1954 (90 Stat. 1914 and 68A Stat. 917; 26 U.S.C. 190 and 7805). In addition, the regulations promulgated in this document are proposed to be prescribed as final Income Tax Regulations (26 CFR Part 1) under section 190 of the Internal Revenue Code of 1954. The amendments are proposed to conform the Income Tax Regulations to section 2122 of the Tax Reform Act of 1976 (90 Stat. 1914). They are also to be issued under the authority contained in sections 190 and 7805 of the Internal Revenue Code of 1954 (90 Stat. 1914 and 68A Stat. 917; 26 U.S.C. 190 and 7805).

[Sec. 190] § 7.190-1 (T.D. 7477, filed 3-30-77.) **Expenditures to remove architectural and transportation barriers to the handicapped and elderly.**

(a) *In general.* Under section 190 of the Internal Revenue Code of 1954, a taxpayer may elect, in the manner provided in § 7.190-3, to deduct certain amounts paid or incurred by him in any taxable year beginning after December 31, 1976, and before January 1, 1980, for qualified architectural and transportation barrier removal expenses (as defined in § 7.190-2(b)). In the case of a partnership, the election shall be made by the partnership. The election applies to expenditures paid or incurred during the taxable year which (but for the election) are chargeable to capital account.

(b) *Limitation.* The maximum deduction for a taxpayer (including an affiliated group of corporations filing a consolidated return) for any taxable year is $25,000. The $25,000 limitation applies to a partnership and to each partner. Expenditures paid or incurred in a taxable year in excess of the amount deductible under section 190 for such taxable year are capital expenditures and are adjustments to basis under section 1016(a). A partner must combine his distributive share of the partnership's deductible expenditures (after application of the $25,000 limitation at the partnership level) with that partner's distributive share of deductible expenditures from any other partnership plus that partner's own section 190 expenditures, if any (if he makes the election with respect to his own expenditures), and apply the partner's $25,000 limitation to the combined total to determine the aggregate amount deductible by that partner. In so doing, the partner may allocate the partner's $25,000 limitation among the partner's own section 190 expenditures and the partner's distributive share of partnership deductible expenditures in any manner. If such allocation results in all or a portion of the partner's distributive share of a partnership's deductible expenditures not being an allowable deduction by the partner, the partnership may capitalize such unallowable portion by an appropriate adjustment to the basis of the relevant partnership property under section 1016. For purposes of adjustments to the basis of properties held by a partnership, however, it shall be presumed that each partner's distributive share of partnership deductible expenditures (after application of the $25,000 limitation at the partnership level) was allowable in full to the partner. This presumption can be rebutted only by clear and convincing evidence that all or any portion of a partner's distributive share of the partnership section 190 deduction was not allowable as a deduction to the partner because it exceeded that partner's $25,000 limitation as allocated by him. For example, suppose for 1978 A's distributive share of the ABC partnership's deductible section 190 expenditures (after application of the $25,000 limitation at the partnership level) is $15,000. A also made section 190 expenditures of $20,000 in 1978 which he elects to deduct. A allocates $10,000 of his $25,000 limitation to his distributive share of the ABC expenditures and $15,000 to his own expenditures. A may capitalize the excess $5,000 of his own expenditures. In addition, if ABC obtains from A evidence which meets the requisite burden of proof, it may capitalize the $5,000 of A's distributive share which is not allowable as a deduction to A.

[Sec. 190] § 7.190-2 (T.D. 7477, filed 3-30-77.) **Definitions.**

For purposes of section 190 and the regulations thereunder—

(a) *Architectural and transportation barrier removal expenses.* The term "architectural and transportation barrier removal expenses" means expenditures for the purpose of making any facility, or public transportation vehicle, owned or leased by the taxpayer for use in connection with his trade or business more accessible to, or usable by, handicapped individuals or elderly individuals. For purposes of this section—

(1) The term "facility" means all or any portion of buildings, structures, equipment, roads, walks, parking lots, or similar real or personal property.

(2) The term "public transportation vehicle" means a vehicle, such as a bus, a railroad car, or other conveyance, which provides to the public general or special transportation service (including such service rendered to the customers of a taxpayer who is not in the trade or business of rendering transportation services).

(3) The term "handicapped individual" means any individual who has—

(i) A physical or mental disability (including, but not limited to, blindness or deafness) which for such individual constitutes or results in a functional limitation to employment, or

(ii) A physical or mental impairment (including, but not limited to, a sight or hearing impairment) which substantially limits one or more of such individual's major life activities, such as performing manual tasks, walking, speaking, breathing, learning, or working.

(4) The term "elderly individual" means an individual age 65 or over.

(b) *Qualified architectural and transportation barrier removal expense—*(1) *In*

Reg. § 7.190-2(a)(3)

24,998.106 (I.R.C.) Reg. § 7.190-2(a) (4) 4-11-77

general. The term "qualified architectural and transportation barrier removal expense" means an architectural or transportation barrier removal expense (as defined in paragraph (a) of this section) with respect to which the taxpayer establishes, to the satisfaction of the Commissioner or his delegate, that the resulting removal of any such barrier conforms a facility or public transportation vehicle to all the requirements set forth in one or more of subparagraphs (2) through (22) of this paragraph or in one or more of the subdivisions of subparagraph (20) or (21). Such term includes only expenses specifically attributable to the removal of an existing architectural or transportation barrier. It does not include any part of any expense paid or incurred in connection with the construction or comprehensive renovation of a facility or public transportation vehicle or the normal replacement of depreciable property. Such term may include expenses of construction, as, for example, the construction of a ramp to remove the barrier posed for wheelchair users by steps. Major portions of the standards set forth in this paragraph were adapted from "American National Standard Specifications for Making Buildings and Facilities Accessible to, and Usable by, the Physically Handicapped" (1971), the copyright for which is held by the American National Standards Institute, 1430 Broadway, New York, New York 10018.

(2) *Grading.* The grading of ground, even contrary to existing topography, shall attain a level with a normal entrance to make a facility accessible to individuals with physical disabilities.

(3) *Walks.* (i) A public walk shall be at least 48 inches wide and shall have a gradient not greater than 5 percent. A walk of maximum or near maximum grade and of considerable length shall have level areas at regular intervals. A walk or driveway shall have a nonslip surface.

(ii) A walk shall be of a continuing common surface and shall not be interrupted by steps or abrupt changes in level.

(iii) Where a walk crosses a walk, a driveway, or a parking lot, they shall blend to a common level. However, the preceding sentence does not require the elimination of those curbs which are a safety feature for the handicapped, particularly the blind.

(iv) An inclined walk shall have a level platform at the top and at the bottom. If a door swings out onto the platform toward the walk, such platform shall be at least 5 feet deep and 5 feet wide. If a door does not swing onto the platform or toward the walk, such platform shall be at least 3 feet deep and 5 feet wide. A platform shall extend at least 1 foot beyond the strike jamb side of any doorway.

(4) *Parking lots.* (i) At least one parking space that is accessible and approximate to a facility shall be set aside and identified for use by the handicapped.

(ii) A parking space shall be open on one side to allow room for individuals in wheelchairs and individuals on braces or crutches to get in and out of an automobile onto a level surface which is suitable for wheeling and walking.

(iii) A parking space for the handicapped, when placed between two conventional diagonal or head-on parking spaces, shall be at least 12 feet wide.

(iv) A parking space shall be positioned so that individuals in wheelchairs and individuals on braces or crutches need not wheel or walk behind parked cars.

(5) *Ramps.* (i) A ramp shall not have a slope greater than 1 inch rise in 12 inches.

(ii) A ramp shall have at least one handrail that is 32 inches in height, measured from the surface of the ramp, that is smooth, and that extends 1 foot beyond the top and bottom of the ramp. However, the preceding sentence does not require a handrail extension which is itself a hazard.

(iii) A ramp shall have a nonslip surface.

(iv) A ramp shall have a level platform at the top and at the bottom. If a door swings out onto the platform or toward the ramp, such platform shall be at least 5 feet deep and 5 feet wide. If a door does not swing onto the platform or toward the ramp, such platform shall be at least 3 feet deep and 5 feet wide. A platform shall extend at least 1 foot beyond the strike jamb side of any doorway.

(v) A ramp shall have level platforms at not more than 30-foot intervals and at any turn.

(vi) A curb ramp shall be provided at an intersection. The curb ramp shall not be less than 4 feet wide; it shall not have a slope greater than 1 inch rise in 12 inches. The transition between the two surfaces shall be smooth. A curb ramp shall have a nonslip surface.

(6) *Entrances.* A building shall have at least one primary entrance which is usable by individuals in wheelchairs and which is on a level accessible to an elevator.

(7) *Doors and doorways.* (i) A door shall have a clear opening of no less than 32 inches and shall be operable by a single effort.

(ii) The floor on the inside and outside of a doorway shall be level for a distance of at least 5 feet from the door in the direction the door swings and shall extend at least 1 foot beyond the strike jamb side of the doorway.

(iii) There shall be no sharp inclines or abrupt changes in level at a doorway. The threshold shall be flush with the floor. The door closer shall be selected, placed, and set so as not to impair the use of the door by the handicapped.

(8) *Stairs.* (i) Stairsteps shall have round nosing of between 1 and 1½ inch radius.

(ii) Stairs shall have a handrail 32 inches high as measured from the tread at the face of the riser.

(iii) Stairs shall have at least one handrail that extends at least 18 inches beyond the top step and beyond the bottom step. The preceding sentence does not require a handrail extension which is itself a hazard.

(iv) Steps shall have risers which do not exceed 7 inches.

(9) *Floors.* (i) Floors shall have a nonslip surface.

(ii) Floors on a given story of a building shall be of a common level or shall be connected by a ramp in accordance with subparagraph (5) of this paragraph.

(10) *Toilet rooms.* (i) A toilet room shall have sufficient space to allow traffic of individuals in wheelchairs.

(ii) A toilet room shall have at least one toilet stall that—

(A) Is at least 36 inches wide;

(B) Is at least 56 inches deep;

(C) Has a door, if any, that is at least 32 inches wide and swings out;

(D) Has handrails on each side, 33 inches high and parallel to the floor, 1½ inches in outside diameter, 1½ inches clearance between rail and wall, and fastened securely at ends and center; and

(E) Has a water closet with a seat 19 to 20 inches from the finished floor.

(iii) A toilet room shall have, in addition to or in lieu of a toilet stall described in (ii), at least one toilet stall that—

(A) Is at least 66 inches wide;
(B) Is at least 60 inches deep;
(C) Has a door, if any, that is at least 32 inches wide and swings out;

(D) Has a handrail on one side, 33 inches high and parallel to the floor, 1½ inches in outside diameter, 1½ inches clearance between rail and wall, and fastened securely at ends and center; and

(E) Has a water closet with a seat 19 to 20 inches from the finished floor, centerline located 18 inches from the side wall on which the handrail is located.

(iv) A toilet room shall have lavatories with narrow aprons. Drain pipes and hot water pipes under a lavatory shall be covered or insulated.

(v) A mirror and a shelf above a lavatory shall be no higher than 40 inches above the floor, measured from the top of the shelf and the bottom of the mirror.

(vi) A toilet room for men shall have wall-mounted urinals with the opening of the basin 15 to 19 inches from the finished floor or shall have floor-mounted urinals that are level with the main floor of the toilet room.

(vii) Towel racks, towel dispensers, and other dispensers and disposal units shall be mounted no higher than 40 inches from the floor.

(11) *Water fountains.* (i) A water fountain and a cooler shall have up-front spouts and controls.

(ii) A water fountain and a cooler shall be hand-operated or hand-and-foot-operated.

(iii) A water fountain mounted on the side of a floor-mounted cooler shall not be more than 30 inches above the floor.

(iv) A wall-mounted, hand-operated water cooler shall be mounted with the basin 36 inches from the floor.

(v) A water fountain shall not be fully recessed and shall not be set into an alcove unless the alcove is at least 36 inches wide.

(12) *Public telephones.* (i) A public telephone shall be placed so that the dial and the headset can be reached by individuals in wheelchairs.

(ii) A public telephone shall be equipped for those with hearing disabilities and so identified with instructions for use.

(iii) Coin slots of public telephones shall be not more than 48 inches from the floor.

(13) *Elevators.* (i) An elevator shall be accessible to, and usable by, the handicapped or the elderly on the levels they use to enter the building and all levels and areas normally used.

(ii) Cab size shall allow for the turning of a wheelchair. It shall measure at least 54 by 68 inches.

(iii) Door clear opening width shall be at least 32 inches.

(iv) All essential controls shall be within 48 to 54 inches from cab floor. Such controls shall be usable by the blind and shall be tactilely identifiable.

(14) *Controls.* Switches and controls for light, heat, ventilation, windows, draperies, fire alarms, and all similar controls of frequent or essential use, shall be placed within the reach of individuals in wheelchairs. Such switches and controls shall be no higher than 48 inches from the floor.

(15) *Identification.* (i) Raised letters or numbers shall be used to identify a room or an office. Such identification shall be placed on the wall to the right or left of the door at a height of 54 inches to 66 inches, measured from the finished floor.

(ii) A door that might prove dangerous if a blind person were to exit or enter by it (such as a door leading to a loading platform, boiler room, stage, or fire escape) shall be tactilely identifiable.

(16) *Warning signals.* (i) An audible warning signal shall be accompanied by a simultaneous visual signal for the benefit of those with hearing disabilities.

(ii) A visual warning signal shall be accompanied by a simultaneous audible signal for the benefit of the blind.

(17) *Hazards.* Hanging signs, ceiling lights, and similar objects and fixtures shall be placed at a minimum height of 7 feet, measured from the floor.

(18) *International accessibility symbol.* The international accessibility symbol (see illustration) shall be displayed on routes to and at wheelchair-accessible entrances to facilities and public transportation vehicles.

(19) *Additional standards for rail facilities.* (i) A rail facility shall contain a fare control area with at least one entrance with a clear opening at least 36 inches wide.

(ii) A boarding platform edge bordering a drop-off or other dangerous condition shall be marked with a warning device consisting of a strip of floor material differing in color and texture from the remaining floor surface. The gap between boarding platform and vehicle doorway shall be minimized.

(20) *Standards for buses.* (i) A bus shall have a level change mechanism (*e.g.*, lift or ramp) to enter the bus and sufficient clearance to permit a wheelchair user to reach a secure location.

(ii) A bus shall have a wheelchair securement device. However, the preceding sentence does not require a wheelchair securement device which is itself a barrier or hazard.

(iii) The vertical distance from a curb or from street level to the first front door step shall not exceed 8 inches; the riser

Reg. § 7.190-2(b)

height for each front doorstep after the first step up from the curb or street level shall also not exceed 8 inches; and the tread depth of steps at front and rear doors shall be no less than 12 inches.

(iv) A bus shall contain clearly legible signs that indicate that seats in the front of the bus are priority seats for handicapped or elderly persons, and that encourage other passengers to make such seats available to handicapped and elderly persons who wish to use them.

(v) Handrails and stanchions shall be provided in the entranceway to the bus in a configuration that allows handicapped and elderly persons to grasp such assists from outside the bus while starting to board and to continue to use such assists throughout the boarding and fare collection processes. The configuration of the passenger assist system shall include a rail across the front of the interior of the bus located to allow passengers to lean against it while paying fares. Overhead handrails shall be continuous except for a gap at the rear doorway.

(vi) Floors and steps shall have nonslip surfaces. Step edges shall have a band of bright contrasting color running the full width of the step.

(vii) A stepwell immediately adjacent to the driver shall have, when the door is open, at least 2 foot-candles of illumination measured on the step tread. Other stepwells shall have, at all times, at least 2 foot-candles of illumination measured on the step tread.

(viii) The doorways of the bus shall have outside lighting that provides at least 1 foot-candle of illumination on the street surface for a distance of 3 feet from all points on the bottom step tread edge. Such lighting shall be located below window level and shall be shielded to protect the eyes of entering and exiting passengers.

(ix) The fare box shall be located as far forward as practicable and shall not obstruct traffic in the vestibule.

(21) *Standards for rapid and light rail vehicles.* (i) Passenger doorways on the vehicle sides shall have clear openings at least 32 inches wide.

(ii) Audible or visual warning signals shall be provided to alert handicapped and elderly persons of closing doors.

(iii) Handrails and stanchions shall be sufficient to permit safe boarding, onboard circulation, seating and standing assistance, and unboarding by handicapped and elderly persons. On a level-entry vehicle, handrails, stanchions, and seats shall be located so as to allow a wheelchair user to enter the vehicle and position the wheelchair in a location which does not obstruct the movement of other passengers. On a vehicle that requires the use of steps in the boarding process, handrails and stanchions shall be provided in the entranceway to the vehicle in a configuration that allows handicapped and elderly persons to grasp such assists from outside the vehicle while starting to board, and to continue using such assists throughout the boarding process.

(iv) Floors shall have nonslip surfaces. Step edges on a light rail vehicle shall have a band of bright contrasting color running the full width of the step.

(v) A stepwell immediately adjacent to the driver shall have, when the door is open, at least 2 foot-candles of illumination measured on the step tread. Other stepwells shall have, at all times, at least 2 foot-candles of illumination measured on the step tread.

(vi) Doorways on a light rail vehicle shall have outside lighting that provides at least 1 foot-candle of illumination on the street surface for a distance of 3 feet from all points on the bottom step tread edge. Such lighting shall be located below window level and shall be shielded to protect the eyes of entering and exiting passengers.

(22) *Other barrier removals.* The provisions of this subparagraph apply to any barrier which would not be removed by compliance with subparagraphs (2) through (21) of this paragraph. The requirements of this subparagraph are:

(i) A substantial barrier to the access to or use of a facility or public transportation vehicle by handicapped or elderly individuals is removed;

(ii) The barrier which is removed had been a barrier for one or more major classes of such individuals (such as the blind, deaf, or wheelchair users); and

(iii) The removal of that barrier is accomplished without creating any new barrier that significantly impairs access to or use of the facility or vehicle by such class or classes.

O— **[Sec. 190]** § 7.190-3 (T.D. 7477, filed 3-30-77.) **Election to deduct architectural and transportation barrier removal expenses.**

(a) *Manner of making election.* The election to deduct expenditures for removal of architectural and transportation barriers provided by section 190(a) shall be made by claiming the deduction as a separate item identified as such on the taxpayer's income tax return for the taxable year for which such election is to apply (or, in the case of a partnership income for such year). For the election to be valid, the return must be filed not later than the time prescribed by law for filing the return (including extensions thereof) for the taxable year for which the election is to apply.

(b) *Scope of election.* An election under section 190(a) shall apply to all expenditures described in § 7.190-2 (or, in the case of a taxpayer whose architectural and transportation barrier removal expenses exceed $25,000 for the taxable year, to the $25,000 of such expenses with respect to which the deduction is claimed) paid or incurred during the taxable year for which made and shall be irrevocable after the date by which any such election must have been made.

(c) *Records to be kept.* In any case in which an election is made under section 190(a), the taxpayer shall have available, for the period prescribed by paragraph (e) of § 1.6001-1 of this chapter (Income Tax Regulations), records and documentation, including architectural plans and blueprints, contracts, and any building permits, of all the facts necessary to determine the amount of any deduction to which he is entitled by reason of the election, as well as the amount of any adjustment to basis made for expenditures in excess of the amount deductible under section 190.

T.D. 7478

Temporary regulations relating to election to amortize certain costs of rehabilitating certified historic structures. (T.D. 7478, filed 4-5-77.)

This document provides temporary income tax regulations under section 191 of the Internal Revenue Code of 1954, as added by section 2124(a) of the Tax Reform Act of 1976 (the "Act") (Public Law 94-455; 90 Stat. 1916) to provide rules for electing to amortize certain rehabilitation expenditures for certified historic structures. The temporary regulations provided by this document will remain in effect until superseded by final regulations on this subject.

○━ [Sec. 191(b)] § 7.191-1 (T.D. 7478, filed 4-5-77.) **Election to amortize certain rehabilitation expenditures for certified historic structures.**

(a) *Time and manner of election of amortization*—(1) *In general.* Under section 191(b), an election by the taxpayer to claim an amortization deduction with respect to a certified historic structure shall be made by a statement to that effect attached to its return for the taxable year in which falls the first month of the 60-month amortization period selected. The 60-month amortization period shall begin either with the month following the month in which the amortizable basis, as defined by section 191(d)(2), is acquired, or with the first month of the taxable year succeeding the taxable year in which such amortizable basis is acquired, whichever the taxpayer selects. If a taxpayer elects to begin the 60-month amortization period with the month following the month in which the amoritizable basis is acquired, a separate 60-month amortization period will be established for the amortizable basis acquired by the taxpayer in any month for which such an election is made. The statement claiming the deduction shall include the following information:

(i) A description clearly identifying each certified rehabilitation of a certified historic structure for which an amortization deduction is claimed;

(ii) The date on which the amortizable basis, as defined in section 191(d)(2), was acquired;

(iii) The date the amortization period is to begin;

(iv) The total amount of amortizable basis claimed for the rehabilitation of the historic structure, as of the first month for which the amortization deduction provided for by section 191(a) is elected;

(v) Either (A) a statement that the historic structure and rehabilitation have been certified by the Secretary of the Interior as provided for in sections 191(d)(1) and 191(d)(3) along with the dates of such certifications; or (B), if the historic structure and rehabilitation have not been certified by the Secretary of the Interior, a statement that requests for certification have been made in accordance with procedures established by such Secretary with the dates of such requests.

If subdivision (v)(B) of this subparagraph applies, the taxpayer shall submit a statement showing receipt of the certifications required by section 191 and their dates with its first income tax return filed after the receipt by the taxpayer of such certifications.

(2) *Failure to submit required certifications.* If the required certifications are not received within 30 months of the date of the commencement of the 60-month amortization period, the electing taxpayer may be requested to consent to an agreement under section 6501(c)(4) extending the period of assessment for any tax relating to the time in which amorization deductions are claimed.

(3) *Failure to elect as provided by this section.* No method of making the election provided for in section 191(a) other than that prescribed in this section shall be permitted. A taxpayer who does not elect in the manner prescribed in this section to take amortization deductions with respect to the rehabilitation of a certified historic structure shall not be entitled to such deductions.

(b) *Election to discontinue amortization.* An election to discontinue the amortization deduction provided by section 191(c) shall be made by a statement filed with the district director, or with the director of the internal revenue service center, with whom the return of the taxpayer is required to be filed for its taxable year in which falls the first month for which the election terminates. This statement shall specify the month as of the beginning of which the taxpayer elects to discontinue the amortization deductions, and it must be filed before the beginning of that month. In addition, the statement shall contain a description clearly identifying the certified historic structure and rehabilitation with respect to which the taxpayer elects to discontinue the amortization deduction. If certifications of the structure or rehabilitation have been issued, their dates shall be shown. If, at the time of the election to discontinue amortization deductions, certifications have not been issued, the taxpayer shall file the dates with its next succeeding tax return after their receipt. For purposes of this paragraph, notification to the Secretary or his delegate from the Secretary of the Interior that the historic structure or the rehabilitation no longer meet the requirements for certification shall have the same effect as notice from the taxpayer electing to terminate amortization as of the first day of the month following the month that the structure or rehabilitation ceased to meet the requirements of section 191.

Reg. § 7.191-1(b)

12-22-77 Temporary Rules *(I.R.C.)* 24,998.109
T.D. 7479; 7520

Temporary regulations relating to disclosure of returns and return information to designee of taxpayer. (T.D. 7479, filed 4-8-77 as amended by T.D. 7520, filed 12-15-77.)

This document provides temporary regulations relating to disclosures of tax returns and tax return information to certain persons. These persons are either designated in a written request for or consent to a disclosure or are requested by the taxpayer to obtain information or provide assistance concerning the taxpayer's return or other matter before the Internal Revenue Service. Changes to the applicable law were made by the Tax Reform Act of 1976. The regulations provide taxpayers and Internal Revenue Service personnel with guidance needed to comply with the Act.

Date: The regulations are effective as of January 1, 1977.

For Further Information Contact: Karl P. Fryzel of the Legislation and Regulations Division, Office of the Chief Counsel, Internal Revenue Service, 1111 Constitution Avenue, N.W., Washington, D.C. 20224 (Attention: CC:LR:T) (202-566-3294).

Supplementary Information:

Background

On Tuesday, April 12, 1977, the Federal Register published temporary regulations on procedure and administration (26 CFR Part 404) under section 6103(c) of the Internal Revenue Code of 1954 (42 FR 19144). These temporary regulations were issued to provide taxpayers and Internal Revenue Service personnel with guidance needed to comply with section 1202(a) of the Tax Reform Act of 1976.

Written Request or Consent

Section 1202(a) of the Tax Reform Act of 1976 amended section 6103 to permit disclosures of tax return and tax return information to a person designated by the taxpayer in a written request or consent. Paragraph (a) of § 404.6103(c)-1 prescribes rules governing the necessary form and content of these written requests or consents. Some stylistic changes have been made to this paragraph.

Disclosures for Information Or Assistance

A new paragraph (b) has been added to § 404.6103(c)-1. This paragraph prescribes rules for disclosures to a person who has been requested by the taxpayer to obtain information or provide assistance concerning a contact between the taxpayer and the Internal Revenue Service.

Other Changes

The language in paragraph (a) of § 404.6103(c)-1 concerning fees for reproductions of tax returns and tax return information has been deleted. This is not intended to imply that these fees will not be charged. This language was considered unnecessary because of the explicit statutory authority of section 6103(p)(2).

Adoption of amendments to the regulations

Accordingly, § 404.6103(c)-1 of the Temporary Regulations on Procedure and Administration is amended to read as follows:

○── [Sec. 6103(c)] § 404.6103(c)-1 (T.D. 7479, filed 4-8-77; amended by T.D. 7520, filed 12-15-77.) Disclosure of returns and return information (including taxpayer return information) to designee of taxpayer.

(a) *Disclosure of returns and return information (including taxpayer return information) to person or persons designated in a written request or consent.* Section 6103(c) applies to disclosures of a return or return information (including taxpayer return information) to a person designated in a written request for or consent to disclosure. A request for or consent to disclosure must be in the form of a written document pertaining solely to the authorized disclosure. The written document must be signed and dated by the taxpayer who filed the return or to whom the return information relates. The taxpayer must also indicate in the written document—

(1) The taxpayer's taxpayer identity information described in section 6103(b)(6);

(2) The identity of the person to whom disclosure is to be made;

(3) The type of return (or specified portion of the return) or return information (and the particular data) that is to be disclosed; and

(4) The taxable year covered by the return or return information.

Thus, for example, a provision included in a taxpayer's application for a loan or other benefit authorizing the Internal Revenue Service to disclose to the grantor of the loan or other benefit such returns or return information as the grantor may request for purposes of verifying information supplied on the application does not meet the requirements of this paragraph. The disclosure of a return or return information authorized by a request for or consent to the disclosure shall not be made unless the request or consent is received by the Service within 60 days following the date upon which the request or consent was signed and dated by the taxpayer.

(b) *Disclosure of returns and return information (including taxpayer return information) to designee of taxpayer to comply with request for information or assistance.* Section 6103(c) applies to requests made by the taxpayer to other persons (for example, members of Congress, friends or relatives of the taxpayer, and, when not acting as a taxpayer's representative, income tax return preparers) for information or assistance relating to the taxpayer's return or a transaction or other contact between the taxpayer and the Internal Revenue Service. The taxpayer's request for information or assistance must be in the form of a letter or other written document signed and dated by the taxpayer. The taxpayer must also indicate in the written request—

(1) The taxpayer's taxpayer identity information described in section 6103(b)(6);

(2) The identity of the person to whom disclosure is to be made; and

Reg. § 404.6103(c)-1(b)

24,998.110 (I.R.C.) Reg. § 404.6103(c)-1(b)   12-22-77

(3) Sufficient facts underlying the request for information or assistance to enable the Service to determine the nature and extent of the information or assistance requested and the returns or return information to be disclosed in order to comply with the taxpayer's request.

A return or return information will be disclosed to the taxpayer's designee as provided by this paragraph only to the extent considered necessary by the Service to comply with the taxpayer's request for information or assistance. This paragraph does not apply to disclosures to a taxpayer's representative in connection with practice before the Internal Revenue Service (as defined in Treasury Department Circular No. 230). For disclosures in these cases, see § 601.502(c) of this chapter.

(c) *Exceptions.* A disclosure of return information shall not be made under this section if the Internal Revenue Service determines that the disclosure would seriously impair Federal tax administration (as defined in section 6103(b)(4)).

T.D. 7483

Temporary regulations relating to withholding tax on certain winnings from State-conducted lotteries. (T.D. 7483, filed 4-22-77.)

This document provides temporary regulations relating to the withholding of tax on certain winnings from State-conducted lotteries. In general, these regulations require any State or State agency to withhold a tax on lottery winnings of more than $5,000.

DATE: The temporary regulations apply to winnings paid after January 2, 1977.

This document contains temporary employment tax regulations (26 CFR Part 34) under section 3402 (q) of the Internal Revenue Code of 1954. Section 3402 (q) was added to the Code by section 1207 (d) of the Tax Reform Act of 1976 (Public Law 94-455, 90 Stat. 1705) in order to require withholding on certain winnings from State-conducted lotteries.

Adoption of amendments to the regulations

Accordingly, a new part 34, Temporary Employment Tax Regulations Under the Tax Reform Act of 1976, is added to Title 26 of the Code of Federal Regulations, and the following temporary regulations are adopted:

[Sec. 3402(q) § 34.3402-1 (T.D. 7483, filed 4-22-77.) **Extension of withholding of income tax at source to certain winnings from State-conducted lotteries.**

(a) *General rule.* On or after January 3, 1977, every person, including a State or a political subdivision thereof, the District of Columbia, or any instrumentality of the foregoing, making any payment of winnings from a State-conducted lottery which are subject to withholding shall deduct and withhold from such payment a tax in an amount equal to 20 percent of such payment.

(b) *Exception.* The tax described in paragraph (a) of this section shall not apply in the case of a payment of winnings from a State-conducted lottery made to a nonresident alien individual or a foreign corporation when such payment is subject to tax under section 1441 (a) (relating to withholding on nonresident aliens) or tax under section 1442 (a) (relating to withholding on foreign corporations).

(c) *Special rules.* For purposes of paragraph (a) of this section—

(1) The term "winnings from a State-conducted lottery which are subject to withholding" means proceeds of more than $5,000 from a wager placed in a lottery conducted by an agency of a State acting under authority of State law, but only if such wager is placed with the State agency conducting such lottery, or with its authorized employees or agents. Such term shall include—

(i) Any installment payment of $5,000 or less, if the aggregate proceeds from such wager to be paid on or after January 3, 1977, exceed or will exceed $5,000;

(ii) Any periodic payment of $5,000 or less, when payments are to be made for the life of a person (or for the lives of more than one person), if it is actuarially determined that the aggregate proceeds from such wager to be paid on or after January 3, 1977, are expected to exceed $5,000; and

(iii) The total proceeds, if proceeds exceed $5,000, and not merely proceeds in excess of $5,000.

(2) The term "proceeds from a wager" means the amount determined by aggregating the amounts received by the person (or persons) making a wager and reducing such amount by the amount of the wager. For purposes of the preceding sentence, in the case of installment or periodic payments the first of such payments shall be reduced by the amount of the wager.

(3) Proceeds which are not money shall be taken into account at their fair market value.

(4) A payment of winnings is made when it is actually paid or constructively paid. Winnings are constructively paid when they are credited to or set apart for the winner without any substantial limitation or restriction as to the time or manner of payment or condition upon which payment is to be made.

(5) When a person other than the State agency conducting the lottery, or its authorized employees or agents, makes a payment of winnings, such other person shall deduct and withhold as required under paragraph (a) of this section. However, in no case shall more than 20 percent of the proceeds from a wager be deducted and withheld.

(6) Except as provided in subparagraph (7) of this paragraph, for purposes of sections 3403 and 3404 and the regulations thereunder and for purposes of so much of subtitle F (except section 7205) and the regulations thereunder as relate to chapter 24, payments to any person of winnings from a State-conducted lottery which are subject to withholding shall be treated as if they were wages paid by an employer to an employee.

(7) Solely for purposes of application of the deposit rules under section 6302 (c) and the regulations thereunder and the return requirement of section 6011 and the regulations thereunder, the withholding from winnings shall be deemed to have been made no earlier than at the time the winner's identity is known by the State. Thus, winnings from a State-conducted lottery shall be subject to withholding at the earlier of the time actually or constructively paid. However, the time for depositing the withheld taxes and filing a return with respect thereto shall be determined by reference to the date on which the State knows the winner's identity. If the State's obligation to pay lottery winnings to a particular winner is terminated other than by payment, all liabilities and requirements resulting from the requirement that the State deduct and withhold with respect to such winnings will also terminate.

(d) *Examples.* The provisions of this section may be illustrated by the following examples:

Reg. § 34.3402-1(d)

24,998.112 (I.R.C.)   Reg. § 34.3402-1(d)   5-2-77

Example (1). A purchases a lottery ticket for $1 in the State W lottery from an authorized agent of State W. On February 1, 1977, the drawing is held and A wins $5,001. Since the proceeds of the wager ($5001—$1) are not greater than $5,000, State W is not required to withhold or deduct any amount from A's winnings.

Example (2). Assume the same facts as in example (1) except that A wins $5,002. State W must deduct and withhold tax at a rate of 20% from $5,001 ($5002 less the $1 wager), or $1,000.20.

Example (3). B purchases a lottery ticket for $1 in the State X lottery from an authorized agent of State X. On June 1, 1977, the lottery drawing is held and B wins the grand prize, $50,000, payable $1,000 a month. State X must deduct and withhold tax at the rate of 20% from each of such payments. Therefore, $199.80 must be withheld from the first monthly payment to B (($1000 — $1) × 20% = $199.80) and $200 ($1000 × 20%) must be withheld from each monthly payment thereafter.

Example (4). Assume the same facts as in example (3), except that B wins an automobile rather than the grand prize. The fair market value of the automobile on the date on which it is made available to B is $10,001. State X must deduct and withhold a tax of $2,000 (($10,001 — $1) × 20%). This may be accomplished, for example, by B's paying $2,000 to State X. Alternatively, if State X, as part of the prize, pays all taxes required to be deducted and withheld, State X must deduct and withhold tax not only on the fair market value of the automobile less the wager, but also on the taxes it pays that are required to be deducted and withheld. This results in a pyramiding of taxes requiring the use of an algebraic formula. Under this formula, State X must withhold a tax of 25 percent of the fair market value of the automobile less the wager ($2,500) and, in addition, State X should indicate on Form W-2G the amount of such winnings, $12,501 ($10,001 + 25% ($10,001 — $1)).

Example (5). C purchases a lottery ticket for $1 in the State Y lottery from an authorized agent of State Y. On January 1, 1976, a drawing is held and C wins $100 a month for the rest of C's life. It is actuarially determined that, on January 3, 1977, C's life expectancy is 5 years. Based on that determination, the aggregate payments to C made on or after January 3, 1977, pursuant to his wager will exceed $5,000. Therefore, State Y must deduct and withhold $20 from each monthly payment made on or after January 3, 1977. (None of such payments is reduced by the amount of the wager because the amount of the wager was offset by the first payment of winnings which was made before January 3, 1977.)

Example (6). Assume the same facts as in example (5) except that in order to fund its own obligation to make the payments State Y purchases in its own name as owner an annuity of $100 a month for C's life from E Corporation. Although State Y remains liable for the withholding of tax, E Corporation as paying agent for State Y should deduct and withhold from each monthly payment in the manner as described in example (5).

Example (7). D purchases a lottery ticket for $1 in the State W lottery from an authorized agent of State W. D purchases the ticket on behalf of himself and on behalf of E and F, who have contributed equal amounts toward the purchase of the ticket and who have agreed to share equally in any prizes won. On February 1, 1977, the drawing is held and the ticket which D purchases wins $6,001. Since the proceeds of the wager ($6,001 — $1) are greater than $5,000 State W is required to withhold and deduct 20 percent of such proceeds.

Example (8). On February 1, 1977, a drawing is held in the State X lottery in which a winning ticket is selected. The person holding the winning ticket is entitled to proceeds of $100,000 payable either as a lump sum upon demand or $10,000 a year for ten years. Under State law, the winning ticket must be presented to an authorized agent of State X before February 1, 1978. Until the ticket is presented, State X does not know the identity of the winner. On December 1, 1977, F, the winner, presents the winning ticket to an authorized agent of the State X lottery. As a result the winnings are constructively paid to F on February 1, 1977. Since F has the option of receiving the entire proceeds upon demand, State X is required to deduct and withhold $20,000 ($100,000 × 20%) from the proceeds of F's winnings on February 1, 1977, but for purposes of determining the time at which the deposit and inclusion on Form 941 of these taxes is to be made, the withholding shall be deemed to have been made on December 1, 1977.

(e) *Statement by recipient.* Every person who is to receive a payment of winnings from a State-conducted lottery which are subject to withholding shall furnish the person making such payment a statement, made under the penalties of perjury, containing the name, address, and taxpayer identification number of the person receiving the payment and of each person entitled to any portion of such payment.

(f) *Return by payor.* Every person making any payment of winnings from a State-conducted lottery which are subject to withholding shall file a return on Form W-2G with the Internal Revenue Service Center serving the district in which is located the principal place of business of the person making the return on or before February 28 of the calendar year following the calendar year in which the payment of winnings is made. In the case of a payment to more than one winner, a separate Form W-2G shall be filed with respect to each such winner. Each Form W-2G shall contain the following:

(1) Name, address, and employer identification number of the person making the payment;

(2) Name, address, and social security number of the winner;

(3) Date and amount of the payment and amount withheld; and

(4) Type of wagering transaction.

T.D. 7488

Temporary regulations relating to lump sum distributions from qualified retirement plans in the case of an employee who has separated from service. (T.D. 7488, filed 5-26-77.)

This document provides temporary regulations relating to lump sum distributions from qualified plans in the case of an employee who separates from service and subsequently forfeits retirement benefits otherwise due him under the plan. Changes in the applicable tax law were made by the Employee Retirement Income Security Act of 1974. The temporary regulations provide rules concerning the time in which the forfeiture must occur. In general, the temporary regulations affect recipients of distributions made on account of an employee's separation from service.

DATE: The temporary regulations are effective for distributions made in taxable years of recipients beginning after December 31, 1973.

Adoption of amendments to the regulations

Accordingly, the Temporary Income Tax Regulations under the Employee Retirement Income Security Act of 1974 are amended by adding the following new section at the appropriate place:

O— [Sec. 402(e)(4)(A)] § 11.402(e)(4)(A)-1 (T.D. 7488, filed 5-26-77.) **Lump sum distributions in the case of an employee who has separated from service.**

(a) *Balance to the credit of an employee.* Section 402(e)(4)(A) provides that in order for a distribution or payment from a qualified plan to be a lump sum distribution, the distribution or payment must represent the employee's balance under the plan. The employee's balance does not include any amount which is forfeited under the plan (even though the amount may be reinstated) as of the close of the taxable year of the recipient within which the distribution is made. In addition, in the case of an employee who has separated from service, the employee's balance does not include an amount which is subject to forfeiture not later than the close of the plan year within which the employee incurs a one-year break in service (within the meaning of section 411) if—

(1) By reason of the break in service, the amount is actually forfeited at or prior to the close of that plan year, and

(2) The break in service occurs within 25 months after the employee's separation from service. In the case of a plan which uses the elapsed time method of crediting service, the break in service may occur within 25 months of the employee's severance from service. See Department of Labor regulations relating to the elapsed time method for the date an employee severs from service.

An employee may assume that an amount subject to forfeiture will be treated as forfeited by the date prescribed in subparagraphs (1) and (2) of this paragraph if, under the plan, forfeiture will occur not later than that date. Therefore, he may assume that a distribution is a lump sum distribution at the time it is made, if the other requirements for lump sum distributions are satisfied. However, if the amount is not forfeited by that date, the amount will be taken into account in determining the balance to the credit of the employee. Accordingly, the distribution will not be a lump sum distribution because it did not include the employee's entire balance under the plan.

(b) *Rollover contribution.* As described in paragraph (a) of this section, an employee may assume that a distribution is a lump sum distribution even though part of the balance of his account has not been forfeited at the time the distribution is made. He may then roll the distribution over as a contribution to an individual retirement arrangement pursuant to section 402(a)(5) or 403(a)(4). It may be subsequently determined that the distribution is not a lump sum distribution because an amount subject to forfeiture was not in fact forfeited within the time required in paragraph (a) of this section. In that case, the contribution will be an excess contribution to the individual retirement arrangement, deemed made in the first taxable year of the employee in which it can be determined that an amount subject to forfeiture will not be forfeited.

(c) *Effective date.* This section is effective for distributions made in taxable years of recipients beginning after December 31, 1973.

Reg. § 11.402(e)(4)(A)-1(c)

T.D 7494, 7530

Temporary regulations relating to ruling requests in respect of certain transfers involving a foreign corporation (T.D. 7494, filed 6-28-77, as amended by T.D. 7530, filed 12-27-77.)

This document contains temporary regulations relating to ruling requests in respect of certain transfers involving a foreign corporation. It also contains temporary regulations relating to the extent to which a foreign corporation shall be considered to be a corporation on certain exchanges with respect to which a ruling is no longer required as it was under prior law. In addition, the rules contained in the temporary regulations set forth in this document also serve as a notice of proposed rulemaking by which the rules contained therein are proposed to be prescribed as final regulations.

The major portion of the regulations set forth in this document is prescribed under changes to the applicable tax law which were made by the Tax Reform Act of 1976, but this document also contains revisions to existing regulations which are prescribed under the authority of the applicable tax law as in effect prior to the enactment of the Tax Reform Act. In addition, this document sets forth rules which are prescribed under the Act of January 17, 1971 (Pub. L. 91-681, 84 Stat. 2065). Because this document contains revisions to the existing regulations it is necessary to include the rules referred to in the previous sentence to assure that the new regulations are accurate.

Dates: Written comments and requests for a public hearing must be delivered or mailed by Feb. 28, 1978. The regulations prescribed pursuant to changes to the applicable law made by the Tax Reform Act which relate to ruling requests in respect of certain transfers involving a foreign corporation apply to transfers beginning after October 9, 1975. The regulations prescribed pursuant to changes to the applicable law made by the Act of January 17, 1971, apply to transfers made after December 31, 1967, except that in certain cases these regulations apply only with respect to transfers made after December 31, 1970. The regulations relating to exchanges for which a ruling is no longer required under the changes made to the applicable tax law by the Tax Reform Act of 1976, apply to exchanges beginning on or after January 1, 1978. *Address:* Send comments and requests for a public hearing to: Commissioner of Internal Revenue, Attention: CC: LR:T, Washington, D. C. 20224.

In order to prescribe temporary Income Tax Regulations (26 CFR Part 7) relating to requirements relating to certain exchanges involving a foreign corporation pursuant to section 367 of the Internal Revenue Code of 1954, in effect prior to the enactment of the Tax Reform Act of 1976 (the "Act"), as amended by Pub. L. 91-681 91st Cong., 2d Sess.) (84 Stat. 2065) and pursuant to section 367 of the Code, as added by section 1042 of the Tax Reform Act of 1976 (90 Stat. 1634), the following temporary regulations are hereby adopted:

Paragraph 1. Section 1.367-1 is deleted.

Para. 2. Section 7.367-1 is redesignated as § 7.367(a)-1 and is amended to read as follows:

[Sec. 367] § 7.367(a)-1 (T.D. 7494, filed 6-28-77 redesignated and amended by T.D. 7530, filed 12-27-77.) **Ruling requests under section 367 relating to certain transfers involving a foreign corporation.**

(a) *Scope.* (1) This section prescribes rules relating to the filing of ruling requests under section 367 of the Internal Revenue Code of 1954. The provisions of this section apply to any exchange to which—

(i) Section 367 as in effect prior to October 4, 1976 applies, or

(ii) Section 367 (a) (1), as amended by section 1042 (a) of the Tax Reform Act of 1976 (90 Stat. 1634), applies.

(2) Section 367 (a) (1), as amended by section 1042 (a) of the Tax Reform Act of 1976, applies in the case of any transfer which begins after October 9, 1975—

(i) Which is a "transfer described in section 367(a)(1)" (within the meaning of paragraph (b)(3) of this section), or

(ii) Which is made in connection with an exchange described in section 367(b) (within the meaning of paragraph (b)(4) of this section) if such exchange begins before January 1, 1978.

(b) *Definitions.* Except as otherwise provided, the following definitions apply for purposes of section 367, as amended by section 1042(a) of the Tax Reform Act of 1976—

(1) *Beginning of transfer.* A transfer of property shall be considered to begin on the earliest date as of which title, possession of, or right to the use of stock, securities, or property passes pursuant to the plan under which the exchange is to be made between parties to the exchange. A transfer shall not be considered to begin with a decision of a board of directors or similar action. A transfer shall be deemed to have begun even though it is made subject to a condition that, if there is a failure to obtain a determination that there is no tax avoidance purpose, the transaction will not be consummated and to the extent possible the assets transferred will be returned.

(2) *Beginning of exchange.* An exchange shall be considered to begin with the beginning of the first transfer of property (within the meaning of paragraph (b)(1) of this section) pursuant to the plan under which the exchange is to be made.

(3) *Transfer described in section 367 (a)(1).* (i) A "transfer described in section 367(a)(1)" is a transfer of property other than stock or securities of a foreign corporation which is a party to the exchange or a party to the reorganization (as defined in section 368(b)), made by a United States person (as defined in section 7701(a)(30)) directly or indirectly to a foreign corporation in connection with an exchange described in section 332, 351, 354, 355, 356, or 361.

(ii) A transfer by a United States person indirectly to a foreign corporation includes a transfer of assets by a domestic corporation to another domestic corporation in connection with a reorganization described in section 368(a)(1)(C), or in section 368(a)(1)(A) and section 368(a)(2)(D) or (E), if stock in a controlling corporation is received by any United States person who is an exchanging shareholder in such a reorganization and the controlling corporation is a foreign corporation.

(iii) A transfer by a foreign partnership, foreign trust, or foreign estate in which a United States person holds an interest, shall be considered to have been made by any such United States person who realizes gain or other income (whether or not recognized) on account of the transfer.

(iv) An election by a domestic corporation under section 1504(d) to treat a corporation organized under the laws of a contiguous foreign country as a domestic corporation shall be considered to be a transfer of property made pursuant to an exchange described in section 367(b). The revocation by a domestic corporation of an election under section 1504(d) shall be considered to be a transfer of property made pursuant to an exchange described in section 367(a)(1).

(4) *Exchange described in section 367 (b).* An "exchange described in section 367(b)" is an exchange described in section 332, 351, 354, 355, 356, or 361 with respect to which the status of a foreign corporation as a corporation is relevant for determining the extent to which gain shall be recognized, and in connection with which there is no transfer described in section 367(a)(1).

(5) *Excepted exchange.* An "excepted exchange" is an exchange made by a foreign corporation of stock in one foreign corporation (the old corporation) for stock in another foreign corporation (the new corporation) if—

(i) The exchange is made in order to effect a mere change in form of a single corporation,

(ii) The old corporation and the new corporation differ only in their form of organization,

(iii) The ownership of the old corporation immediately before the exchange is identical to the ownership of the new corporation immediately after the exchange, and

(iv) The first transfer in connection with the exchange begins after December 31, 1967.

(c) *General rule.* (1) For purposes of determining the extent to which gain shall be recognized on an exchange to which this section applies, and subject to the exception specified in paragraph (g) of this secttion, a foreign corporation shall not be considered to be a corporation unless it is established to the satisfaction of the Commissioner that such exchange is not in pursuance of a plan having as one of its principal purposes the avoidance of Federal income taxes. In the case of an exchange to which section 367 as in effect prior to October 4, 1976, applies (other than an excepted exchange), the lack of such a plan must be established prior to the exchange. In the case of an exchange to which section 367(a)(1), as amended by section 1042(a) of the Tax Reform Act of 1976, applies, the lack of such a plan must be established pursuant to a ruling request filed within the time provided in paragraph (d)(4)(iii) of this section. A determination (i) that the exchange is not in pursuance of such a plan, or (ii) of the terms and conditions pursuant to which the exchange will be determined to be not in pursuance of such a plan, shall be made pursuant to a ruling request. The ruling request must be filed in the form, time, and manner specified in paragraph (d) of this section. A ruling letter setting forth the Commissioner's determination with respect to such exchange will be forwarded to the taxpayer. If the exchange is carried out in a manner which represents a material variance from the plan submitted, or if the terms and conditions imposed under the ruling letter are not met, the Commissioner's determination will not be given effect.

(2) The taxpayer must retain a copy of the ruling letter as authority for treating a foreign corporation as a corporation in determining the extent to which gain is recognized on such exchange.

(3) If an exchange to which section 367 (a)(1) applies has begun prior to the filing of a return with respect to that exchange, and—

(i) The taxpayer receives a ruling letter regarding the exchange, the taxpayer must attach to the return a copy of the ruling letter and any decision on any protest thereto;

(ii) The taxpayer has filed a ruling request regarding the exchange but has not received a ruling letter pursuant thereto, the taxpayer must attach to the return a statement that the ruling request has been filed, and the date of such filing; or

(iii) The taxpayer has not filed a ruling request regarding the exchange, the taxpayer must attach to the return a statement indicating (A) that the exchange is one to which section 367(a)(1) applies, (B) that no ruling request has been filed regarding the exchange, (C) the date of the beginning of any transfer which is relevant for determining whether a ruling request regarding the exchange is filed within the time limits specified in paragraph (d) of this section, and (D) whether the taxpayer intends to file a ruling request within such time limits.

(d) *Form, time, and manner of filing.* A request for a ruling regarding an exchange to which this section applies must—

(1) Set forth the facts and circumstances relating to the plan under which the exchange is to be made and be accompanied by a copy, or a complete description of such plan;

(2) Be filed in accordance with all applicable procedural rules set forth in the Statement of Procedural Rules (26 CFR Part 601) and any applicable revenue procedures relating to submission of ruling requests;

(3) Be executed by the taxpayer under penalties of perjury, regardless of whether such requirement is also imposed under § 601.201(e); and

(4) Be filed in compliance with paragraph (d)(1), (2), and (3) of this section—

(i) Before the beginning of any exchange (other than an excepted exchange) to which section 367 as in effect prior to October 4, 1976 applies,

(ii) Before or after the beginning of any excepted exchange, and

(iii) At any time before or after, but not later than the 183d day after, the beginning of—

(A) In the case of an exchange described in section 367(a)(1), any transfer described in section 367(a)(1), or

(B) In the case of an exchange described in section 367(b) to which section 367(a)(1) applies by reason of section 367(d), any transfer of property made in connection with such exchange.

(e) *Timely filing.* Notwithstanding the provisions of paragraph (d) of this section, or any other provision relating to procedures for the filing of ruling requests with the Internal Revenue Service, a ruling request under section 367(a)(1) shall not be deemed filed within the time limits specified in paragraph (d)(4) of this section unless within such time limits the taxpayer files a request which meets the certain minimum standards. To meet such minimum standards a request must (1) set forth the facts and circumstances relating to the plan under which the exchange is to be made, in sufficient detail to apprise the Commissioner of the nature of the exchange and the purpose for which such request is filed, and (2) be executed under penalties of perjury as required in paragraph (d)(3) of this section. In the event of a failure to comply exactly with the provisions of paragraph (d)(1) and (2) of this section, the Service may decline to the rule until there is compliance.

(f) *Multiple transfers in connection with one exchange.* In the case of an exchange to which section 367(a)(1) applies—

(1) A foreign corporation will be treated as a corporation with respect to gain realized on any transfer pursuant to the exchange if all the following conditions are met:

(i) A ruling request is filed in the form, time, and manner specified in paragraph (d) of this section,

(ii) It is established to the satisfaction of the Commissioner that such exchange and all transfers described in the ruling request are not in pursuance of a plan having as one of its principal purposes the avoidance of Federal income taxes,

(iii) Any terms and conditions to which the Commissioner's determination are subject are satisfied, and

(iv) The exchange is consummated in accordance with all material details of the plan as described in the ruling request.

(2) If all the conditions specified in paragraph (f)(1) of this section were not met solely because there was a transfer pursuant to the exchange made more than 183 days before the ruling request was filed, and such transfer was not the subject of a ruling request filed in the form, time, and manner specified in paragraph (d) of this section, then—

(i) Except as provided in paragraph (g) of this section, gain shall be recognized on such prior transfer if a ruling request is required with respect to such prior transfer, and

(ii) The conditions specified in paragraph (f)(1) will be considered met if it is established to the satisfaction of the Commissioner that the exchange in its entirety (taking into account the gain recognized) is not in pursuance of a plan having as one of its principal purposes the avoidance of Federal income taxes.

(3) If all the conditions specified in paragraph (f)(1) of this section were not met solely because subsequent to the filing of the original ruling request there was a transfer pursuant to the exchange which was not described in the original request, then a foreign corporation shall not be considered to be a corporation with respect to gain realized on all transfers made in connection with the exchange. However, if another ruling request is timely filed with respect to the subsequent transfer in the form, time, and manner specified in paragraph (d) of this section, and if the conditions specified in paragraph (f)(1)(ii), (iii), and (iv) of this section are met with respect to the subsequent request (taking into account all transfers described in the original request), a foreign corporation will be treated as a corporation with respect to all transfers described in the requests made pursuant to the exchange (other than those as to which gain is required to be recognized pursuant to paragraph (f)(2)(i)).

(g) *Exception.* Failure of the taxpayer to request a ruling under section 367(a)(1) may not be used by the taxpayer to its advantage. In those situations which the Commissioner deems appropriate, a foreign corporation will be treated as a corporation even in the absence of a ruling request.

Par. 3. The following new sections are added immediately after § 7.367(a)-1:

[Sec. 367] § 7.367(b)-1 (T.D. 7530, filed 12-27-77.) Other transfers.

(a) *Scope.* This section and §§ 7.367(b)-2 through 7.367(b)-12 apply to exchanges to which section 367(b), as amended by section 1042(a) of the Tax Reform Act of 1976, applies. This section sets forth certain general rules regarding the extent to which a foreign corporation shall be considered to be a corporation in connection with an exchange to which section 367(b) applies. An exchange to which section 367(b) applies is any exchange described in section 367(b) and paragraph (b)(4) of § 7.367(a)-1 which begins after December 31, 1977.

(b) *General rule.* If section 367(b) applies to an exchange, a foreign corporation shall be considered to be a corporation in respect of that exchange except to the extent otherwise provided in this section and in §§ 7.367(b)-4 through 7.367(b)-12. Unless otherwise provided, if a taxpayer fails to comply with §§ 7.367(b)-1 through 7.367(b)-12, the Commissioner shall make a determination whether a foreign corporation will be considered to be a corporation based on all the facts and circumstances surrounding failure to comply. In making this determination the Commissioner may conclude that:

(1) A foreign corporation will be considered to be a corporation despite the failure to comply;

(2) A foreign corporation will be considered to be a corporation provided that the conditions imposed under §§ 7.367(b)-4 through 7.367(b)-12 are fulfilled; or

(3) A foreign corporation will not be considered to be a corporation only for pur-

Reg. § 7.367(b)-1(b)

24,998.116-B (I.R.C.) Reg. § 7.367(b)-1(b)   1-9-78

poses of determining the extent to which gain shall be recognized on such exchange but that any gain recognized by reason of the Commissioner's determination to disregard the corporate status of a foreign corporation will be taken into account for purposes of applying the provisions of section 334, 358 or 362. See, §§ 7.367(b)-5(b), 7.367(b)-6(c), 7.367(b)-7(c)(2), and 7.367(b)-10(j) for specific provisions which override the provisions of paragraph (b)(3) of this section.

(c) *Notice required*—(1) *In general.* If any person referred to in section 6012 (relating to the requirement to make returns of income) realized gain or other income (whether or not recognized) on account of any exchange to which section 367(b) applies, such person must file a notice of such exchange on or before the last date for filing a Federal income tax return (taking into account any extensions of time therefor) for the person's taxable year in which gain or other income is realized. This notice must be filed with the district director with whom the person would be required to file a Federal income tax return for the taxable year in which the exchange occurs.

(2) *Information required.* The notice shall contain—

(i) A statement that the exchange is one to which section 367(b) applies;

(ii) A complete description of the exchange;

(iii) A description of any stock or securities received in the exchange;

(iv) A statement which describes any amount required, under §§ 7.367(b)-4 through 7.367(b)-12 to be included in gross income or added to the earnings and profits or deficit of an exchanging foreign corporation for the person's taxable year in which the exchange occurs;

(v) A statement which describes any amount of earnings and profits attributed by reason of the exchange, under § 7.367(b)-4 through 7.367(b)-12, to stock owned by any United States person;

(vi) Any information which is or would be required to be furnished with a Federal income tax return pursuant to regulations under section 332, 351, 354, 355, 356, 361, or 368 (whether or not a federal income tax return is required to be filed) if such information has not otherwise been provided;

(vii) Any information required to be furnished under section 6038 or 6046 if such information has not otherwise been provided; and

(viii) If applicable, a statement that the taxpayer is making the election permitted under paragraph (d) of § 7.367(b)-3 relating to earnings and profits of a less developed country corporation.

(ix) If applicable, a statement that all relevant shareholders are making the election provided in paragraph (c)(1)(iii) of § 7.367(b)-7, in paragraph (f) of § 7.367(b)-9, in paragraph (i)(3)(ii)(C) of § 7.367(b)-10, or in paragraph (f) of § 7.367(b)-10 in order to obtain the increase in basis of stock provided in paragraph (c)(1)(iii) of § 7.367(b)-7, paragraph (i)(3)(ii)(C) of § 7.367(b)-10, paragraph (e)(1) of § 7.367(b)-9, or paragraph (e) of § 7.367(b)-10.

(3) *Failure to provide notice.* If a person required to give notice under paragraph (c)(1) of this section fails to provide, in a timely manner, information sufficient to apprise the Commissioner of the occurrence and nature of an exchange to which section 367(b) applies, the taxpayer will be considered to have failed to comply with the provisions of § 7.367(b)-1 through 7.367(b)-12 only if the taxpayer fails to establish reasonable cause for the failure.

(d) *Records to be kept*—(1) *Adjustments to earnings and profits.* Any corporation whose earnings and profits are required to be adjusted under §§ 7.367(b)-4 through 7.367(b)-12 must keep records adequate to establish the adjustment.

(2) *Amounts attributed to stock.* If, under §§ 7.367(b)-4 through 7.367(b)-12, an amount is attributed to stock in a foreign corporation which is owned by a United States person, that person must keep records to establish the amount so attributed. If the person fails to maintain such records, and an inclusion in gross income of such amount is required by reason of section 1248 or §§ 7.367(b)-4 through 7.367(b)-12, the district director shall make a reasonable determination of the amount attributed.

○━▶ [Sec. 367] § 7.367(b)-2 (T.D. 7530, filed 12-27-77.) **Definitions.**

(a) *Controlled foreign corporation.* The term "controlled foreign corporation" means a controlled foreign corporation as defined in section 957 and the regulations thereunder.

(b) *United States shareholder.* The term "United States shareholder" means any United States person who satisfies the ownership requirements of section 1248(a)(2) or of section 1248(c)(2) with respect to a foreign corporation.

(c) *Section 1246 amount.* In the case of an exchange of stock in a foreign investment company (as defined in section 1246(b)) to which section 367(b) applies, the term "section 1246 amount" means the earnings and profits, if any, of the foreign investment company, which would have been attributable under section 1246 and the regulations thereunder to the stock exchanged if the stock had been sold in a transaction to which section 1246 applied.

(d) *Section 1248 amount.* In the case of an exchange of stock in a first-tier foreign corporation to which section 367(b) applies, the term "section 1248 amount" means the earnings and profits or deficit in earnings and profits which would have been attributable under section 1248 and the regulations thereunder to the stock of the foreign corporation exchanged if the stock had been sold in a transaction to which section 1248 (a) applied.

(e) *Section 1248(c)(2) amount.* In the case of an exchange of stock in a lower-tier foreign corporation to which section 367(b) applies and which is made by another foreign corporation, the term "section 1248 (c)(2) amount" means the earnings and profits or deficit in earnings and profits which would have been attributable under section 1248 (c)(2) and the regulations thereunder to the stock of the foreign corporation exchanged (including stock in other lower-tier corporations owned by reason of ownership of the stock exchanged). The determination shall be made as if stock in any first-tier corporation by reason of the ownership of which the United States shareholder owns the stock exchanged had been sold in a transaction to which section 1248 (a) applied.

(f) *All earnings and profits amount.* The term "all earnings and profits amount" means the earnings and profits or deficit in earnings and profits for all taxable years which are attributable to the stock of the foreign corporation exchanged under the principles of section 1246 or 1248 (whichever is applicable) and the regulations thereunder. The determination shall be made by applying section 1246 or 1248 as modified by §§ 7.367 (b)-2 through 7.367 (b)-12 as if there were no distinction in those sections between earnings and profits accumulated before or after December 31, 1962.

(g) *Additional earnings and profits amount.* The term "additional earnings and profits amount" means the earnings and profits or deficit in earnings and profits for taxable years beginning before January 1, 1963, which are attributable under the principles of section 1248 and the regulations thereunder to the stock of the foreign corporation exchanged. The determination shall be made by applying section 1248 as modified by §§ 7.367 (b)-2 through 7.367 (b)-12 as if there were no distinction in those sections between earnings and profits accumulated before or after December 31, 1962.

(h) *All earnings and profits amount or additional earnings and profits amount.* In computing an "all earnings and profits amount" or "additional earnings and profits amount" under the principles of section 1248, if the stock exchanged is—

(1) Stock in a first-tier corporation, then section 1248(c)(2) (inclusion of earnings and profits of subsidiaries) does not apply.

(2) Stock in a lower-tier corporation, then section 1248(c)(2) shall be applied to determine the earnings and profits of that lower-tier corporation which are attributable to the stock exchanged but that section shall not be applied with respect to any other lower-tier corporation.

(i) *Inclusion of earnings and profits described in section 1248(d).* For purposes of computing any of the amounts defined in paragraphs (d) through (g) of this section, the exclusions from earnings and profits provided for under section 1248(d) shall not apply. See, however, paragraph (c) of § 7.367(b)-3 (relating to amounts retaining character as exclusions under section 1248 (d)).

(j) *Corporations organized under laws of Puerto Rico or United States possessions corporations.* For purposes of computing the amounts defined in paragraphs (f) and (g) of this section, if, for a taxable year, a corporation organized in or under the laws of the Commonwealth of Puerto Rico or a possession of the United States meets the requirements of section 957(c) (or would have met such requirements if the Revenue Act of 1962 had been in effect) then—

(1) Earnings and profits accumulated by the corporation during such a taxable year which begins before January 1, 1978, are not required to be taken into account, and

(2) Earnings and profits accumulated by the corporation during such a taxable year which begins after December 31, 1977, are required to be taken into account only to the extent such earnings would not qualify for the credit of section 936(a) had the corporation been a domestic corporation which met the requirements of section 936 (a)(1) and which had elected the credit under that section.

A corporation which, during its first taxable year beginning after December 31, 1962, meets the requirements of section 957(c) will be considered to have met such requirements during taxable years beginning prior to January 1, 1963.

○→ [Sec. 367] § 7.367(b)-3 (T.D. 7530, filed 12-27-77.) **Special rules.**

(a) *Character of section 1246 amount.* If, under § 7.367(b)-6, an amount attributable to stock in a foreign investment company (as defined in section 1246(b)) is required to be taken into gross income of its shareholders, such earnings and profits will be included in income as—

(1) Gain from the sale of an asset which is not a capital asset to the extent attributable to earnings and profits accumulated in taxable years beginning after December 31, 1962; and

(2) A dividend deemed paid in money to the extent attributable to earnings and profits accumulated in taxable years beginning before January 1, 1963, and required to be included as part of the "all earnings and profits amount".

(b) *Character of amounts computed under the principles of section 1248.* If, under § 7.367(b)-5 or §§ 7.367(b)-7 through 7.367(b)-12, any amount is required to be included in the gross income of a United States person, that amount shall be considered to have been distributed as a dividend paid in money immediately prior to the exchange and taxable under section 301 as a dividend formally declared in the same amount.

(c) *Amounts retaining character as exclusions under section 1248(d).* (1) Amounts described in paragraphs (d) through (g) of § 7.367(b)-2 which must be included in gross income of a United States person shall be reduced—

(i) In all cases, by earnings and profits retaining their character as exclusions under section 1248(d)(1), (2), (4), and (5), and

(ii) If the inclusion in gross income is required by a provision other than paragraph (b) of § 7.367(b)-5, paragraph (c)(2) of § 7.367(b)-7, or paragraph (j) of § 7.367 (b)-10, by earnings and profits retaining their character as exclusions under section 1248(d)(3). See, however, paragraph (d) of this section.

(2) Amounts described in paragraph (e) or (g) of § 7.367(b)-2 which must be added to the earnings and profits or deficit of an exchanging foreign corporation shall not be reduced by earnings and profits retaining their character as exclusions under section 1248(d).

(d) *Less developed country corporation election.* This paragraph applies to all

Reg. § 7.367(b)-3(d)

earnings and profits of a character described in section 1248(d)(3). Any such earnings and profits which are required to be included in gross income of a domestic corporate shareholder as part of an all earnings and profits amount may, at the election of such taxpayer, be taxed as gain from the sale of a capital asset. Such election shall be made in the notice required under paragraph (c) of § 7.367(b)-1. A corporation which during its first taxable year beginning after December 31, 1962, meets the requirements of section 902(d), as in effect before the enactment of the Tax Reduction Act of 1975, will be considered to have met such requirements during taxable years beginning prior to January 1, 1963.

(e) *Character of certain earnings and profits.* Earnings and profits or a deficit in earnings and profits to which a corporation succeeds under section 381(a)(1) or amounts which are attributed to stock under § 7.367 (b)-9, § 7.367(b)-10, and § 7.367(b)-12 shall retain their character. Earnings and profits or deficits shall be considered as if accumulated or incurred by the corporation which succeeds to such earnings and profits or deficits.

This paragraph applies for all purposes, including but not limited to sections 901 to 908, 959, 960, 1248, and §§ 7.367(b)-1 through 7.367(b)-12.

(f) *Foreign tax credit.* If an amount of earnings and profits of a foreign corporation which is considered to have been distributed as a dividend is included in gross income of a United States person, the foreign tax credit provisions (section 78, and 901 through 908) shall apply as if such earnings and profits were actually distributed by a foreign corporation as a dividend.

(g) *Treatment of section 1248 amounts and section 1248(c)(2) amounts where attribution is not made.* (1) The portion of the section 1248 amount included in gross income of a United States person which is attributable to each particular foreign corporation shall be determined as follows. First, the total gross earnings and profits (determined without regard to any deficit) attributable to each particular corporation shall be determined as if it were the only corporation included in the section 1248 amount. In situations to which § 7.367(b)-10 applies, the determination shall be made without regard to the allocation under paragraph (d) of that section. Next, that amount shall be muliplied by the amount included in gross income. Finally, the product shall be divided by the section 1248 amount. The result will be the amount of earnings and profits from that particular corporation which are included in gross income.

(2) The section 1248 amount included in gross income by a United States person which is attributable to the earnings and profits of a foreign corporation shall be considered as if distributed directly to the United States person by the foreign corporation. A section 1248(c)(2) amount which is added to the earnings and profits or deficit of an exchanging foreign corporation shall be considered as if accumulated or incurred directly by the exchanging foreign corporation.

[Sec. 367] § 7.367(b)-4 (T.D. 7530. filed 12-27-77.) **Certain exchanges described in more than one Code provision.**

(a) *Scope.* This section provides special rules for purposes of applying section 367 to certain exchanges which are described in more than one section of subchapter C of chapter 1 of subtitle A of the Code.

(b) *Precedence of section 351 or 361 over section 368(a)(1)(B).* If an exchange of stock in a foreign corporation by a United States person pursuant to a reorganization described in section 368(a)(1)(B) involving a foreign corporate transferee is described in section 351 or 361 as well as in section 354, the exchange will be considered to be described in section 351 or 361. Accordingly, such an exchange is described in section 367(b)(1), and §§ 7.367(b)-1 through 7.367(b)-12 (other than this section) do not apply to such an exchange.

(c) *Precedence of section 1036 over section 354.* If an exchange of stock in a foreign corporation pursuant to a reorganization is described both in sections 354 and 1036, the exchange will be considered to be described in section 1036, unless the stock surrendered is stock to which an amount has been attributed under §§ 7.367(b)-5 through 7.367(b)-12. In that event, the provisions of these regulations shall apply to the attributed amounts as if section 1036 did not apply to the subsequent exchange.

(d) *Special definition of reorganization described in section 368(a)(1)(F).* For purposes of section 367(b) and §§ 7.367(b)-1 through 7.367(b)-12, a reorganization will be considered to be described in section 368(a)(1)(F) only if it involves a mere change in identity, form, or place of organization, however effected, of a single corporate entity.

[Sec. 367] § 7.367(b)-5 (T.D. 7530. filed 12-27-77.) **Complete liquidation of foreign subsidiary.**

(a) *Scope.* This section applies to an exchange described in section 332 which involves receipt of a distribution in complete liquidation of a foreign corporation.

(b) *Receipt of distribution by a domestic corporation.* If a domestic corporation which receives a distribution in complete liquidation of a foreign corporation includes in its gross income the all earnings and profits amount attributable to its stock in the distributor foreign corporation, the foreign corporation will be considered to be a corporation for purposes of applying subchapter C of chapter 1 of subtitle A of the Code. The domestic corporation must include the all earnings and profits amount in gross income for the taxable year in which occurs the date of distribution (within the meaning of section 381(b)(2) and the regulations thereunder). If the domestic corporation does not include this amount in gross income, for the purpose of determining the extent to which gain is recognized on the exchange, the foreign corporation will not be considered to be a corporation. However, the provisions of the Code other than section 332 shall apply as if the foreign corporation were considered a corporation. For example, sections 334(b)(1) and 381(a)(1) shall apply where applicable.

(c) *Receipt of distribution by a foreign corporation.* If a foreign corporation receives a distribution in complete liquidation of another foreign corporation, a foreign corporation will be treated as a corporation for purposes of section 332 and other applicable sections such as section 381.

○━━ [Sec. 367] § 7.367(b)-6 (T.D. 7530, filed 12-27-77.) **Exchange of stock in a foreign investment company.**

(a) *Scope.* This section applies to an exchange of stock in a foreign investment company (as defined in section 1246(b)) if:

(1) The exchange is described in section 354, or 356 pursuant to any reorganization described in subparagraph (B), (C), (D), or (F) of section 368(a)(1) and in section 368(a)(2)(F) (if applicable), and

(2) Stock in a domestic corporation is received pursuant to the exchange.

In the case of an exchange to which stock in a foreign corporation is received see section 1246(c).

(b) *General rule.* Except as provided in paragraph (c) of this section, a taxpayer who makes an exchange to which this section applies shall include in gross income for its taxable year in which the exchange occurs the section 1246 amount attributable to the stock in the foreign investment company which was exchanged to the extent of the excess of the fair market value of such stock over its adjusted basis.

(c) *Exchange pursuant to certain asset acquisitions.* (1) If the exchange to which this section applies is made pursuant to a reorganization described in section 368(a)(1)(C), (D), or (F) involving the acquisition of assets of a foreign investment company (the "acquired corporation") by a domestic corporation, and the exchanging taxpayer is a domestic corporation, such taxpayer shall include in gross income for its taxable year in which the exchange occurs the all earnings and profits amount with respect to that stock computed in accordance with the principles of section 1246.

(2) If the domestic corporation does not include the amount referred to in paragraph (c)(1) of this section in gross income, for the purpose of determining the extent to which gain is recognized on the exchange, the foreign corporation will not be considered to be a corporation. However, the provisions of the Code other than section 354, or 356 shall apply as if the foreign corporation were considered a corporation. For example, sections 358, 362, and 381 (if applicable) shall apply as if no gain had been recognized.

(d) *Adjustment to basis.* Any amount included in gross income under paragraph (b) or (c)(1) of this section which is characterized as gain from the sale of an asset which is not a capital asset shall be treated as gain recognized for purposes of applying sections 358 and 362.

○━━ [Sec. 367] § 7.367(b)-7 (T.D. 7530, filed 12-27-77.) **Exchange of stock described in section 354.**

(a) *Scope.* This section applies to an exchange of stock in a foreign corporation (other than a foreign investment company as defined in section 1246(b)) if:

(1) The exchange is described in section 354 or 356 and is made pursuant to a reorganization described in section 368(a)(1)(B) through (F); and

(2) The exchanging person is either a United States shareholder or a foreign corporation having a United States shareholder who is also a United States shareholder of the corporation whose stock is exchanged.

(b) *Receipt of stock in a controlled foreign corporation.* If an exchanging shareholder receives stock of a controlled foreign corporation in an exchange to which this section applies (other than in an exchange pursuant to a reorganization described in section 368(a)(1)(E) or (F)), § 7.367(b)-9 applies if, with respect to such corporation, immediately after the exchange—

(1) The exchanging shareholder is a United States shareholder of that controlled foreign corporation, or

(2) All United States shareholders of the exchanging foreign corporate shareholder are United States shareholders of that controlled foreign corporation.

(c) *Receipt of other stock*—(1) *General rule.* Except as provided in paragraph (c)(2) of this section, if an exchanging shareholder receives, stock of a domestic corporation, or stock of a foreign corporation which is not a controlled foreign corporation, or stock of a controlled foreign corporation as to which the exchanging United States shareholder or any United States shareholder of the exchanging foreign corporation is not a United States shareholder, then—

(i) An exchanging United States shareholder shall include in gross income the section 1248 amount attributable to the stock exchanged, to the extent that the fair market value of the stock exchanged exceeds its adjusted basis, or

(ii) There shall be added to the earnings and profits or deficit of the exchanging foreign corporation the section 1248(c)(2) amount and the additional earnings and profits amount of the exchanging foreign corporation, computed as if all stock of the corporation whose stock is exchanged is owned by a United States shareholder. The amount added shall not be considered a dividend.

(iii) In situations to which paragraph (c)(1)(ii) of this section applies, the basis of the stock received by the exchanging shareholder shall be increased by the earnings and profits added to the earnings and profits of the exchanging foreign corporation under paragraph (c)(1)(ii) of this section. Correspondingly, the basis of such exchanging shareholder shall be decreased by any deficits added to deficits of the exchanging foreign corporation under paragraph (c)(1)(ii) of this section. Any increase in basis attributable to earnings and profits included in the section 1248(c)(2) amount referred to in paragraph (c)(1)(ii) of this section shall be made only if all United States shareholders of the exchanging corporation consent to treat amounts added to the earnings and profits of the exchanging foreign corporation as a dividend. Such consent shall be given in the notice required by paragraph (c) of § 7.367(b)-1. See paragraph (f)(1) of § 7.367(b)-9 for the effect of such election. The adjustment to basis in respect of earnings and profits or deficit accumulated or incurred in taxable years beginning before January 1, 1963, shall be taken into account only for purposes of computing an all earnings and profits amount and additional earnings

Reg. § 7.367(b)-7(c)(1)

24,998.116-F (I.R.C.) Reg. § 7.367(b)-7(c)(1)

and profits amount, where such amounts must be computed after an exchange of stock the basis of which has been adjusted under this paragraph (c)(1)(iii).

(2) *Exchange of stock by certain domestic corporations.* (i) A United States person shall include in gross income the all earnings and profits amount if:

(A) Pursuant to a reorganization described in section 368(a)(1)(C), (D), or (F), assets of a foreign corporation are acquired by a domestic corporation;

(B) The exchanging United States person is a domestic corporation; and

(C) Such United States person receives stock of a domestic corporation in exchange for its stock in the acquired corporation.

(ii) If the domestic corporation does not include this amount in gross income, for the purpose of determining the extent to which gain is recognized on the exchange, the foreign corporation will not be considered to be a corporation. However, the applicable provisions of the Code other than section 354 or 356 shall apply as if the foreign corporation were considered a corporation. For example, sections 358, 362, and 381, if applicable, shall apply as if no gain had been recognized.

○━ [Sec. 367] § 7.367(b)-8 (T.D. 7530, filed 12-27-77.) **Transfer of assets by a foreign corporation in an exchange described in section 351.**

(a) *Scope.* This section applies to a transfer of property pursuant to an exchange described in section 351, regardless of whether the transfer is also described in section 361, if:

(1) The transferor of property is a foreign corporation; and

(2) In the case of a transfer also described in section 361, the transferor remains in existence immediately after the transaction.

(b) *Section 381 inapplicable.* If this section applies to a transfer described in section 361, section 381(a)(2) shall not apply with respect to items described in section 381(c)(2).

(c) *Transfer of stock in controlled foreign corporation.* If the transferor corporation transfers stock in a foreign corporation of which there is a United States shareholder immediately before the exchange, and the transferor receives stock—

(1) Of a controlled foreign corporation as to which all United States shareholders of the transferor corporation remain United States shareholders, § 7.367(b)-9 shall apply.

(2) Of a domestic corporation, of a foreign corporation which is not a controlled foreign corporation, or of a controlled foreign corporation as to which any United States shareholder of the transferor is not a United States shareholder, paragraph (c)(1)(ii) of § 7.367(b)-7 shall apply.

○━ [Sec. 367] § 7.367(b)-9 (T.D. 7530, filed 12-27-77.) **Attribution of earnings and profits on an exchange described in section 351, 354, or 356.**

(a) *Scope.* This section applies to a transaction involving an exchange of stock in a foreign corporation to which paragraph (b) of § 7.367(b)-7 or paragraph (c)(1) of § 7.367(b)-8 applies.

(b) *General rule.* Upon an exchange of stock to which this section applies—

(1) The section 1248 amount, the section 1248(c)(2) amount, the all earnings and profits amount and the additional earnings and profits amount shall be computed with respect to each United States shareholder and to each foreign corporation as to which there is a United States shareholder who exchanges stock in the transaction. The amounts so computed shall be attributed to the stock received by each exchanging shareholder in the exchange in accordance with the principles of §§ 1.1248-2 and 1.1248-3. For the effect of attribution, see § 7.367(b)-12.

(2) Earnings and profits or deficit of the corporation whose stock is received in the exchange shall be increased as provided in paragraph (c) of this section.

(3) Earnings and profits or deficit of the corporation whose stock is exchanged and of any lower-tier corporations whose earnings and profits would be taken into account under section 1248(c)(2) shall be reduced as provided in paragraph (d) of this section.

(c) *Earnings and profits or deficits of the corporation whose stock is received.* (1) Earnings and profits or deficit of the corporation whose stock is received in the exchange shall be increased by the earnings and profits or deficit to which it would succeed if—

(i) That corporation were the acquiring corporation, within the meaning of paragraph (b)(2) of § 1.381(a)-1, in a transaction to which section 381 applies (whether or not section 381 applies or that corporation would be considered the acquiring corporation); and

(ii) The corporation whose stock is exchanged, and each lower-tier corporation whose earnings and profits would be taken into account in calculating a section 1248 or section 1248(c)(2) amount, were a transferor corporation for purposes of section 381(a)(2).

A corporation which actually is the acquiring corporation in a transaction to which section 381(a)(2) applies shall not succeed to an item of the transferor described in section 381(c)(2) by reason of section 381(a)(2). However, that corporation shall succeed to all other items described in section 381(c).

(2) To the extent that the corporation whose stock is received does not acquire, either directly or through other entities, all the stock of the corporation whose stock is exchanged or of any lower-tier corporation whose earnings and profits would be taken into account in calculating a section 1248(c)(2) amount, paragraph (c)(1) of this section shall apply only to the proportion of earnings and profits or deficits attributable to the stock acquired. Such proportion shall be determined as if the earnings and profits or deficits were section 1248 or section 1248(c)(2) amounts. The earnings and profits or deficit to which the corporation whose stock is received does not succeed by reason of this paragraph shall be considered entirely attributable to the stock not acquired by the corporation whose stock is received.

(d) *Earnings and profits of corporation whose stock is exchanged and of lower-tier corporation.* The earnings and profits or deficit of the corporation whose stock is exchanged and of any lower-tier corporation whose earnings and profits or deficit would be taken into account under section 1248 shall be reduced to the extent that the adjustment required under paragraph (c) of this section is attributable to earnings and profits or deficit of that corporation.

(e) *Adjustment to basis.* (1) This paragraph (e)(1) applies to increases and decreases to basis of stock in corporations which as to the corporation whose stock is exchanged are lower-tier corporations. To the extent that earnings and profits of corporations (other than the corporations whose stock is exchanged) are reduced under paragraph (d) of this section, the basis in stock of each corporation whose earnings and profits are so reduced shall, in the hands of its immediate shareholder, be increased. The increase shall equal the total reduction in earnings and profits in respect of all corporations which as to such immediate shareholder are lower-tier corporations. Correspondingly, the basis to such immediate shareholder of stock in a corporation (other than the corporation whose stock is exchanged) whose deficit is reduced shall be decreased by the total reduction in deficits in respect of the corporations which as to that shareholder are lower-tier corporations.

(2) This paragraph (e)(2) applies to increases and decreases to basis of stock in corporations which are not lower-tier corporations as to the corporation whose stock is exchanged but are lower-tier corporations of the corporation whose stock is received. In the case of a reorganization described in section 368 (a)(1)(B) or of a reorganization in which the acquiring corporation, within the meaning of § 1.381(a)-1(b)(2), is a lower-tier corporation as to the corporation whose stock is received, the basis of stock shall be adjusted as provided in this paragraph (e)(2). To the extent that earnings and profits of the corporation whose stock is exchanged and of its lower-tier corporations are reducted under paragraph (d) of this section, the basis to the immediate corporate shareholder

(i) Of stock in the corporation whose stock is exchanged, or

(ii) Of stock in a corporation (other than the corporation whose stock is received) which is the acquiring corporation of the corporation whose stock is exchanged,

shall be increased by the total reduction in earnings and profits under paragraph (d) of this section, except to the extent that the basis of such stock is determined by reference to the basis of the assets of the corporation whose stock is exchanged. The basis in such stock to each immediate corporate shareholder shall be similarly increased, and such increase shall in turn be made at each successive tier. The basis of the stock of the corporation whose stock is received, however, shall not be increased. Correspondingly, the basis of such stock to each immediate corporate shareholder, and at each successive higher tier, shall be decreased by the total reduction in deficits under paragraph (d) of this section, except to the extent that the basis of such stock is determined by reference to the basis of the assets of the corporation whose stock is exchanged.

(3) Any adjustment to basis in respect of earnings and profits or deficit accumulated or incurred in taxable years beginning before January 1, 1963, shall be taken into account only for purposes of computing all the earnings and profits and additional earnings and profits amounts.

(f) *Election as condition of increase in basis with respect to post-1962 earnings and profits.* (1) An increase in basis under paragraph (e)(1) of this section attributable to earnings and profits for taxable years beginning after December 31, 1962, shall be made only if all United States shareholders of the corporation whose stock is exchanged make a consent dividend election in the notice required by paragraph (c) of § 7.367(b)-1. If such consent is made, the portion of such earnings and profits attributable to each particular corporation shall be treated as if, immediately prior to the reorganization, it had been distributed as a dividend through any intervening corporations to the corporation whose stock is exchanged.

(2) An increase in basis under paragraph (e)(2) of this section attributable to earnings and profits for taxable years beginning after December 31, 1962, shall be made only if:

(i) An election has been made under paragraph (f)(1) of this section, and

(ii) All United States shareholders of the corporation whose stock is received make a consent dividend election as provided in section 565 for the taxable year in which the reorganization occurs.

If such consent is made, such earnings and profits attributable to the corporation whose stock is exchanged and of its lower-tier corporations whose earnings and profits were reduced under paragraph (d) of this section shall be treated as if immediately after the reorganization, it had been distributed as a dividend through any intervening corporations to the corporation whose stock is received.

(3) See sections 553, 951, and 959 as to the possible effect of an election under this section.

○➞ [Sec. 367] § 7.367(b)-10 (T.D. 7530, filed 12-27-77.) **Distribution of stock described in section 355.**

(a) *Scope.* This section provides rules relating to a distribution described in section 355 to which section 367(b) applies. For purposes of this section, the terms "distributing corporation" and "controlled corporation" have the meaning of those terms as used in section 355.

(b) *Distribution by domestic corporation.* If a domestic corporation distributes stock in a controlled corporation which is a controlled foreign corporation as to which the distributing corporation is a United States shareholder, section 1248(f) applies to such distribution. After earnings and profits attributable to the stock have been determined under section 1248(f), paragraphs (d) through (f) of this section apply. With respect to subsequent transactions involving the distributing group, the allocation described in paragraph (d) of this section shall not increase or decrease the amounts described in paragraphs (d) through (g) of § 7.367(b)-2.

(c) *Distribution of stock by a foreign corporation.* If a foreign corporation having a United States shareholder distributes stock in another corporation, paragraphs (d) through (j) of this section apply.

(d) *Allocation of earnings and profits.* Earnings and profits or deficit accumulated or incurred by the distributing corporation, the controlled corporation (or corporations), and by corporations which directly or indirectly are controlled by either, shall be allocated among those corporations immediately after the distribution. For purposes of making this allocation:

(1) Section 1.312-10 shall not apply.

(2) The sum of the earnings and profits accumulated prior to the distribution by each corporation shall be determined.

(3) The sum of the deficits in earnings and profits incurred prior to the distribution by each corporation shall be determined.

(4) The total gross earnings and profits and deficits shall be allocated between the distributing corporation and any corporations controlled by it after the distribution (the "distributing group") and the controlled corporation (or corporations) and any corporations controlled by them after the distribution (the "controlled group"). Such allocation shall be made in accordance with the fair market value of the assets of each group. In determining the fair market value of the assets of a group, the fair market value of stock in a corporation controlled by another corporation in a group shall not be taken into account.

(5) For purposes of allocating earnings and profit or deficits to either the distributing group or the controlled group;

(i) Earnings and profits or deficit of only the distributing corporation or of the controlled corporation shall be increased;

(ii) No allocation shall be made from one member to another member of the same group;

(iii) The earnings and profits allocated from a particular corporation shall be the proportion of total earnings and profits allocated from its group to the other group which earnings and profits of that particular corporation prior to the allocation bears to the total gross earnings and profits of all corporations in that group having earnings and profits prior to the allocation; and

(iv) The deficit in earnings and profits allocated from a particular corporation shall be the proportion of the total deficits allocated from its group to the other group which the deficit of that particular corporation prior to the allocation bears to the total gross deficit of all corporations in that group having deficits prior to the allocation.

(6) To the extent that there is not distributed all the stock of the controlled corporation, or of any lower-tier corporation of the controlled corporation whose earnings and profits would be taken into account in calculating a section 1248(c)(2) amount, paragraph (d)(1) through (5) of this section shall apply only to the proportion of the earnings and profits or deficits attributable to the stock distributed. Such proportion shall be determined as if the earnings and profits were section 1248 or section 1248(c)(2) amounts. The earnings and profits or deficits not allocated by reason of this paragraph shall be considered entirely attributable to the stock and not distributed.

(e) *Adjustment to basis.* (1) Except as provided in paragraph (f) of this section, to the extent earnings and profits are allocated from a corporation other than the distributing or controlled corporations, the basis of the stock of that corporation in the hands of its immediate shareholder shall be increased by the amount of earnings and profits allocated from it and from members of the group which as to that corporation are lower-tier corporations. Correspondingly, to the extent deficits are allocated from a corporation other than the distributing or controlled corporation, the basis of the stock of that corporation in the hands of its immediate shareholder shall be decreased by the amount of deficit allocated from it and from members of the group which as to that corporation are lower-tier corporations.

(2) Any adjustment to basis in respect of earnings and profits or deficit accumulated or incurred in taxable years beginning before January 1, 1963, shall be taken into account only for purposes of computing the all earnings and profits and additional earnings and profits amounts.

(f) *Election as condition of increase in basis.* An increase in basis attributable to allocation of earnings and profits for taxable years beginning after December 31, 1962, of a corporation to the other group shall be made only if all United States shareholders of the group from which the allocation is made (determined after the distribution) make a consent dividend election in the notice required by paragraph (c) of § 7.367(b)-1. If such consent is made, such earnings and profits, allocated from each particular corporation shall be treated as if, immediately after the distribution, they had been distributed as a dividend through any intervening corporations to the distributing corporation or controlled corporation as the case may be. See sections 553, 951, and 959 for the possible effect of an election under this section.

(g) *Computation of certain amounts.* Upon a distribution described in paragraph (c) of this section, the section 1248 or section 1248(c)(2) amount, the all earnings and profits amount, and the additional earnings and profits amount shall be computed with respect to each United States shareholder and to each foreign corporation as to which there is a United States shareholder. The computation shall be made with reference to stock owned by the shareholder in the distributing corporation prior to the distribution and shall be made regardless of whether the shareholder is an exchanging shareholder.

(h) *Attribution to stock owned after the distribution.* (1) The amounts described in paragraph (g) of this section shall be attributed to all stock owned after the distribution except stock received in the distribution and to which paragraph (i) or (j) of this section applies.

(2) Attribution of an amount shall be made to stock of a corporation in the proportion that the value of such stock bears to all stock owned after the distribution, including for this purpose stock to which paragraph (i) or (j) of this section applies and to which no attribution is made.

(3) If after the distribution the distributing foreign corporation is no longer a controlled foreign corporation as to a United States shareholder, see section 1248

(a)(2) with respect to stock disposed of within five years after a change in status.

(i) *Receipt of other stock.* Except as provided in paragraph (j) of this section, if an exchanging shareholder receives—

(1) Stock of a domestic corporation,

(2) Stock of a foreign corporation which is not a controlled foreign corporation, or

(3) Stock of a controlled foreign corporation as to which the exchanging United States shareholder or any United States shareholder of the exchanging foreign corporation is not a United States shareholder, then—

(i) An exchanging United States shareholder shall include in gross income the excess of—

(A) The section 1248 amount computed under paragraph (g) of this section, over

(B) The section 1248 amount attributed to stock under paragraph (h) of this section,

to the extent that the fair market value of stock in the distributing corporation owned by the shareholder prior to the distribution exceeds its adjusted basis; or

(ii) There shall be added to the earnings and profits or deficit of an exchanging foreign corporation the excess of

(A) The section 1248(c)(2) amount computed under paragraph (g) of this section, over

(B) The section 1248(c)(2) amount attributed to stock under paragraph (h) of this section. The amount added shall not be considered a dividend.

(C) In situations to which subdivision (B) of this subparagraph applies, the basis adjustment and election rules of § 7.367(b)-7(c)(1)(iii) shall apply.

(j) *Receipt of stock by certain domestic corporations.* A United States person shall include in its gross income the excess of the all earnings and profits amount computed under paragraph (g) of this section over the all earnings and profits amount attributed under paragraph (h) of this section if—

(1) The distribution is made pursuant to a reorganization described in section 368(a)(1)(D) and involving the acquisition of assets of the foreign distributing corporation by a domestic corporation; and

(2) The United States person is a domestic corporation.

If the domestic corporation does not include this amount in gross income, for purposes of determining the extent to which gain is recognized on the exchange, the foreign corporation will not be considered to be a corporation. However, the applicable provisions of the Code other than section 355, 356, or 361 shall apply as if the foreign corporation were considered a corporation. For example, sections 358 and 362, if applicable, shall apply as if no gain had been recognized.

O— [Sec. 367] § 7.367(b)-11 (T.D. 7530, filed 12-27-77.) **Deficit in earnings and profits.**

(a) *Scope.* This section provides rules relating to the manner in which a deficit in earnings and profits of a corporation may be used after certain exchanges to which section 367(b) applies.

(b) *Limitation on deficits allocated to a corporation.* Any deficit in earnings and profits incurred prior to the distribution which are allocated to a corporation under paragraph (c) of § 7.367(b)-9 or allocated under paragraph (d) of § 7.367(b)-10 shall be used only in the manner prescribed under section 381(c)(2)(B) and the regulations thereunder.

(c) *Deficit in earnings and profits.* If section 382 would apply to a net operating loss of a corporation in respect of a transaction to which section 367(b) applies, the percentage reduction provided in section 382 with respect to net operating losses shall reduce a deficit in earnings and profits allocated to that corporation.

(d) *Computation of allocated amounts.* If paragraph (c) of this section applies, a deficit attributed to stock under §§ 7.367(b)-5 through 7.367(b)-11 shall be adjusted in accordance with the rule of paragraph (b).

O— [Sec. 367] § 7.367(b)-12 (T.D. 7530, filed 12-27-77.) **Subsequent treatment of amounts attributed or included in income.**

(a) *Application.* This section applies to distributions with respect to, or a disposition of, stock—

(1) To which an amount has been attributed pursuant to § 7.367(b)-9, or § 7.367(b)-10; or

(2) In respect of which an amount has been included in income or added to earnings and profits pursuant to § 7.367(b)-7 or § 7.367(b)-10.

(b) *Successor in interest.* A subsequent United States shareholder of stock to which this section applies—

(1) Whose holding period is considered to include the period during which such stock was held by the prior United States shareholder, and

(2) Who acquired the stock other than by means of a transfer to which §§ 7.367(b)-1 through 7.367(b)-12 apply

shall be considered to be the "successor in interest" to the prior United States shareholder. The successor in interest will succeed to the earnings and profits or deficit which the regulations under section 367(b) attribute to the stock in the hands of the prior United States shareholder.

(c) *Distributions after attribution.* Distributions with respect to stock made after an amount has been attributed to the stock under § 7.367(b)-9 or § 7.367(b)-10 shall be considered to be made in accordance with the following rules:

(1) Distributions shall be considered to be made first out of earnings and profits accumulated since the attribution.

(2) To the extent that as of the close of a taxable year distributions have exceeded earnings and profits accumulated since the attribution, excess distributions during that year shall be considered to be made out of earnings and profits previously attributed to the stock (but will not increase a deficit attributable to the stock). Solely for this purpose, amounts which would have been attributed to stock under § 7.367(b)-9 or § 7.367(b)-10 had such stock been owned by a United States shareholder or by an exchanging foreign corporation as to which there is a United States shareholder shall be attributed to such stock.

Reg. § 7.367(b)-12(c)

(3) Distributed earnings and profits considered under paragraph (c)(2) of this section to be made out of attributed amounts shall be considered as if distributed from each of the corporations from which amounts have been attributed, in the proportions that amounts attributed from that corporation bear to amounts attributed from all corporations from which amounts have been attributed. Such amounts shall retain their character for all purposes, including sections 901 through 908 and 959.

(4) When all earnings and profits attributed have been distributed, the distributions shall be considered to have been made from earnings and profits accumulated by the distributing corporation, whether before or after the attribution.

(d) *Distributions after an inclusion in income or addition to earnings and profits.* Amounts included in gross income of a United States person pursuant to § 7.367(b)-7 or § 7.367(b)-10 shall be treated for purposes of this section in the same manner as amounts previously included in income under section 951. Thus,

(1) Subsequent distributions of amounts which would but for this section be treated as dividends shall be considered first to consist of amounts previously included in income and shall be excluded in the same manner as under section 959.

(2) In the case of an inclusion under § 7.367(b)-10, this paragraph shall apply only with respect to distributions from the corporations described in paragraph (i) or (j) of that section.

(3) Amounts to which an election applies under § 7.367(b)-7(c)(1)(iii) or § 7.367(b)-10(i)(3)(ii)(C) shall be treated in the same manner as amounts described in paragraph (d)(1) of this section but only to the extent distributed to the exchanging foreign shareholder.

(e) *Disposition after an attribution or inclusion in income.* Upon a disposition of stock to which section 1248 or § 7.367(b)-1 through 7.367(b)-12 apply, amounts described in § 7.367(b)-2(d) through (g) shall be determined in the following manner:

(1) In the case of amounts to which a corporation succeeds under section 381(a)(1), the rules of section 1248 will apply.

(2) In the case of amounts attributed under §§ 7.367(b)-9 and 7.367(b)-10:

(i) There shall first be determined earnings and profits or deficits attributed to the stock disposed of,

(ii) The earnings and profits described in paragraph (e)(2)(i) of this section shall be reduced (but deficits shall not be increased) by distributions referred to in paragraph (c)(2) of this section.

(iii) To the amount determined after applying paragraph (e)(2)(ii) of this section there shall be added amounts attributable to the stock without regard to the attribution; however, earnings and profits or deficits accumulated or incurred prior to the attribution shall not be taken into account.

Moreover, deficits incurred after the attribution shall not be taken into account to the extent they would occur by reason of distributions of previously attributed earnings and profits. For example, distributions described in paragraph (c)(2) of this section shall not be taken into account in computing a deficit under § 1.1248-3(b)(3); and no part of any deficit attributable to distributions described in paragraph (c)(2) of this section shall be allocated to stock until after the earnings and profits previously attributed have been distributed.

(iv) Amounts to which paragraph (d)(1) or (d)(3) of this section apply shall increase the basis of stock in the same manner as under section 961, and distributions attributable to those amounts shall correspondingly decrease the basis of stock.

(v) Earnings and profits distributed out of accumulated amounts shall be considered as if distributed from each of the corporations from which earnings and profits have been attributed, in the ratio that earnings and profits attributed from that corporation bear to earnings and profits attributed from the corporations from which earnings and profits have been attributed. Such distributions shall reduce the amounts previously attributed and shall retain their character for all purposes, including sections 901 through 908 and section 959.

(vi) When all attributed amounts have been distributed, the distributions shall be considered to have been made from earnings and profits accumulated by the distributing corporation, whether before or after the distribution.

○➞ [Sec. 367] § 7.367(c)-1 (T.D. 7530, filed 12-27-77.) **Section 355 distribution treated as an exchange.**

(a) *General rule.* For purposes of section 367 as in effect both before and after October 4, 1976, any distribution which is described in section 355 (or so much of section 356 as relates to section 355) shall be treated as an exchange whether or not it is an exchange.

(b) *Ruling required.* In the case of any distribution to which this section applies which begins (within the meaning of § 7.367(a)-1(b)(2)) before January 1, 1978, a foreign corporation shall not be considered to be a corporation for purposes of determining the extent to which gain shall be recognized on such distribution unless, pursuant to a ruling request timely filed in accordance with the provisions of § 7.367(a)-1(d), it is established to the satisfaction of the Commissioner at the applicable time that such distribution is not in pursuance of a plan having as one of its principal purposes the avoidance of Federal income taxes.

(c) *Application of section 367(b) regulations.* In the case of any distribution to which this section applies which begins on or after January 1, 1978, and in connection with which there is no transfer described in section 367(a)(1) (as defined in § 7.367(a)-1(b)(3)), the provisions of section 367(b), as amended by the Tax Reform Act of 1976, apply. Accordingly, a foreign corporation shall be considered to be a corporation on such distribution to the extent provided in §§ 7.367(b)-1 through 7.367(b)-12.

○➞ [Sec. 367] § 7.367(c)-2 (T.D. 7530, filed 12-17-77.) **Contribution of capital to controlled corporations.**

(a) *General rule.* For purposes of chapter 1 of subtitle A of the Internal Revenue Code of 1954, any transfer of property to a foreign corporation as a contribution to the capital of such corporation which is made after December 31, 1970, by one or more persons who, immediately after the transfer, own (within the meaning of section 318) stock possessing at least 80 percent of the total combined voting power of all classes of stock of such corporation entitled to vote shall, except as provided in paragraph (b) of this section, be treated as an exchange of such property for stock of such foreign corporation equal in value to the fair market value of the property transferred.

(b) *Treatment as contribution to capital.* In the case of a transfer of property referred to in paragraph (a) of this section which begins before October 10, 1975, such transfer shall not be treated as an exchange if, prior to the transfer, it is established that such transfer is not in pursuance of a plan having as one of its principal purposes the avoidance of Federal income taxes.

(c) *Ruling required.* In the case of a transfer of property which begins after October 9, 1975, and which is treated as an exchange under paragraph (a) of this section, a ruling is required if section 367(a)(1) applies. For example, if after October 9, 1975 and before January 1, 1978, a foreign corporation transfers property to its wholly owned foreign subsidiary as a contribution to capital, the exchange which is considered to occur is described in section 351 and section 367(a)(1) applies to such transfer.

(d) *Application of section 367(b) regulations.* In the case of a transfer of property which (i) begins after December 31, 1977, (ii) is treated as an exchange as provided in paragraph (a) of this section, and (iii) is not a transfer described in section 367(a)(1), if such a transfer is an exchange described in section 367(b) or made in connection with an exchange described in that section, a foreign corporation shall be considered to be a corporation on such transfer to the extent and upon fulfillment of any applicable conditions specified in §§ 7.-367(b)-1 through 7.367(b)-12.

○— [Sec. 367] § 7.367-2 (TD 7494, filed 6-28-77.) **Ruling requests under section 367 as in effect on December 31, 1974.**

A transfer of property to or from a United States person will be considered to have occurred in connection with a reorganization even if a United States person, as a shareholder, has not actually transferred or received stock pursuant to such reorganization, if the reorganization is described in section 368(a)(1)(D).

Reg. § 7.367-2

T.D. 7499

Temporary regulations relating to minimum funding standards for pension plans. (T.D. 7499, filed 8-3-77.)

This document provides temporary regulations relating to the determination of actuarial costs under the minimum funding standards for defined benefit pension plans. These regulations implement provisions of the Employee Retirement Income Security Act of 1974. The temporary regulations provide necessary guidance to the public for compliance with that Act, and affect many sponsors of defined benefit plans. In addition, the rules contained in the temporary regulations promulgated by this document serve as a notice of proposed rulemaking by which the rules contained therein are proposed to be prescribed as final regulations.

Dates: The temporary regulations are effective generally for plan years beginning after 1975, but earlier (or later) in the case of some plans as provided by the Employee Retirement Income Security Act of 1974. The proposed regulations are to be effective for the same period.

Written comments and requests for public hearing must be delivered or mailed by October 28, 1977.

Address: Send comments and requests for a public hearing to: Commissioner of Internal Revenue, Attention: CC:LR:T, Washington, D.C. 20224.

For Further Information Contact: J. Douglas Sorensen of the Legislation and Regulations Division, Office of the Chief Counsel, Internal Revenue Service, 1111 Constitution Avenue, N.W., Washington, D.C. 20224 (Attention: CC:LR:T) (202-566-3478).

This document contains amendments to the temporary Income Tax Regulations under the Employee Retirement Income Security Act of 1974 (26 CFR Part 11), and a notice of proposed amendments to the income tax regulations (26 CFR Part 1), under section 412(c)(1) of the Internal Revenue Code of 1954. These regulations conform the regulations to section 1013 of the Employee Retirement Income Security Act of 1974 (ERISA) (88 Stat. 914) and are issued under the authority of section 7805 of the Internal Revenue Code of 1954 (68A Stat. 917; 26 U.S.C. 7805), and section 3(31) of ERISA (88 Stat. 837; 29 U.S.C. 1002). The temporary and proposed regulations contained in this document will also apply for purposes of section 302 of ERISA (88 Stat. 869). The temporary regulations provided by this document will remain in effect until superseded by the adoption of final regulations proposed by this document.

Adoption of amendments to the temporary regulations

The temporary income tax regulations under the Employee Retirement Income Security Act of 1974, 26 CFR Part 11, are amended by adding in the appropriate place the following new sections:

[Sec. 412] § 11.412(c)(1)-1 (T.D. 7499, filed 8-3-77.) Determinations to be made under funding method—terms defined.

(a) *Actuarial cost method and funding method.* Section 3(31) of the Employee Retirement Income Security Act of 1974 ("ERISA") provides certain acceptable (and unacceptable) actuarial cost methods which may (or may not) be used by employee plans. The term "funding method" when used in section 412 has the same meaning as the term "actuarial cost method" in section 3(31) of ERISA. For shortfall method for certain collectively bargained plans, see § 11.412(c)(1)-2.

(b) *Computations included in funding method.* The funding method of a plan includes not only the overall funding method used by the plan but also each specific method of computation used in applying the overall method. However, the choice of which actuarial assumptions are appropriate to the overall method or specific method of computation is not a part of the funding method. For example, the decision to use or not use a mortality factor in the funding method of a plan is not a part of such funding method. Similarly, the specific mortality rate determined to be applicable to a particular plan year is not part of the funding method. See section 412(c)(5) for permission to change the funding method used by a plan.

[Sec. 412] § 11.412(c)(1)-2 (T.D. 7499, filed 8-3-77.) Shortfall method.

(a) *In general*—(1) *Shortfall method.* A collectively bargained plan may elect to determine the charges to the funding standard account required by section 412(b) under the shortfall method. The shortfall method is a funding method. In general, under the shortfall method, the net charge to the funding standard account is computed on the basis of an estimated number of units of service or production for a certain period (for which a certain amount per unit is to be charged). The difference between the net amount charged or credited under the shortfall method and the net amount that otherwise would have been charged or credited under section 412 for the same period is the shortfall gain or loss to be amortized. This section includes special rules for applying the method to collectively bargained plans that are maintained by more than one employer.

(2) *Collectively bargained plans.* For purposes of this section, a collectively bargained plan is a plan described in section 413(a).

(3) *Plan maintained by more than one employer.* For purposes of this section, whether a plan is maintained by more than one employer shall be determined without regard to the rules of section 414(b) and (c) (relating to related employers).

(b) *Computation of net charge*—(1) *In general.* The "net charge" to the funding standard account under the shortfall method is the estimated unit charge described in paragraph (c) of this section multiplied by the actual number of units of service or production which occurred during the plan year. When the shortfall method is used, charges and credits to the funding standard account are not made under section 412(b)(2) and (3)(B).

Reg. § 11.412(c)(1)-2(b)(1)

(2) *Example.* Paragraph (b)(1) of this section may be illustrated by the following example:

Example. A pension plan uses the calendar year as the plan year and the shortfall method. Its estimated unit charge applicable to 1980 is 80 cents per hour of covered employment. During 1980, there were 125,000 hours of covered employment. The net charge for the plan year is $100,000, (i.e., 125,000 × $.80) regardless of the amount which would be charged and credited to the funding standard account under section 412(b)(2) and (3)(B) had the shortfall method not applied. The funding standard account for 1980 will be separately credited for the amount considered contributed for the plan year under section 412(b)(3)(A). The other items which may be credited, if applicable, are a waived funding deficiency and the alternative minimum funding standard credit adjustment under section 412(b)(3)(C) and (D) because these items are not credits under section 412(b)(3)(B).

(3) *Plans maintained by more than one employer.* If a single plan maintained by more than one employer has more than one contribution rate:

(i) The plan may use as a specific method of computation under the shortfall method the computation of a separate net charge for each employer or each benefit level.

(ii) Only one actuarial valuation shall be made for the single plan on each actuarial valuation date.

(iii) The specific method of computation of the net charge must be reasonable, determined in the light of the facts and circumstances.

(c) *Estimated unit charge.* The esimated unit charge is the anticipated annual charge described in paragraph (d) of this section divided by the estimated base units of service or production described in paragraph (e) of this section.

(d) *Anticipated annual charge.* The anticipated annual charge for a plan year is the sum of the following amounts:

(1) The net anticipated charges and credits which, but for using the shortfall method, would be made under section 412 (b)(2) and (b)(3)(B).

(2) The amount described in paragraph (g)(4) of this section, if applicable, for amortization of shortfall gain or loss.

(e) *Estimated base units; in general.* The estimated base units are the expected units of service or production for the plan year (hours, days, tons, etc.) based upon the experience of the plan and reasonable expectations for such year. Except as provided in paragraph (f) of this section, the date for estimating base units (the "base unit estimation date") for a current plan year may not be earlier than the last actuarial valuation date occurring on or before the first day of the current plan year.

(f) *Base unit estimation date for plan maintained by more than one employer—*
(1) *In general.* If a plan is maintained by more than one employer, the base unit estimation date for the current plan year is determined under this paragraph (f). Such date shall be no earlier than the last actuarial valuation date occurring at least one year before the earliest date any current collectively bargained agreement in existence during the plan year came into effect.

(2) *Four-month rule.* For purposes of this paragraph (f), a current collectively bargained agreement is one in effect during at least four months of the current year.

(3) *Effective date of agreement.* For purposes of this paragraph (f), a collectively bargained agreement shall be deemed to have come into effect on the effective date of the agreement containing the currently effective provision for contributions to the plan or the benefits provided under the plan.

(4) *Long-term contract rule.* The effective date of a collectively bargained agreement shall be deemed not to occur prior to the first day of the third plan year preceding the current plan year.

(5) *Transition rule.* In no event shall the base unit estimation date be earlier than the last actuarial valuation date of the plan which occurred on or before January 1, 1976.

(6) *Example.* The rules contained in paragraphs (e) and (f) of this section are illustrated by the following table. The table shows the resulting earliest base unit estimation date with respect to the following assumed items:

V Actuarial valuation date (January 1 in each case shown)

B Beginning of a contract

E End of a contract

[Table appears on page (I.R.C.) 24,998.118-A]

(g) *Amortization of shortfall gain or loss—*(1) *Definition.* The shortfall gain for a plan is the excess for the plan year of—

(i) The net charge computed under paragraph (b) of this section over

(ii) The anticipated annual charge described in paragraph (d) of this section.

The shortfall loss for a plan is the excess for the plan year of the anticipated annual charge over the net charge.

(2) *Period of amortization; in general.* The shortfall gain or loss shall be amortized—

(i) Beginning with the first and

(ii) Ending with the 15th

plan year following the plan year it arose. For a multiemployer plan described in section 414(f), the amortization ends with the 20th plan year instead of the 15th.

(3) *Deferral of shortfall amortization period; plan maintained by more than one employer.* As a specific method of computation under the shortfall method for a plan maintained by more than one employer, the shortfall gain or loss may be amortized—

(i) Beginning with the fifth plan year following the plan year it arose, and

(ii) Ending with the plan year specified in paragraph (g)(2) of this section.

If that specific method is used, the amount of the shortfall gain or loss for a plan year must be adjusted for interest from the last day of such year to the beginning of the first plan year in which it is amortized.

(4) *Annual amortization amount.* The shortfall gain or loss must be amortized in equal annual installments. The total

COMPUTATION OF BASE UNIT ESTIMATION DATE

Example	Plan year (calendar year basis)								
	1976	1977	1978	1979	1980	1981	1982	1983	1984
Plan A 2/									
Contract A	▽		--E/B--		--E/B--				--E/B--
Base unit estimation date 1/	1976	1976	1976	1979	1979	1979	1982	1982	1982
Plan B - C 3/	▽								
Contract B	B*----						E/B*		
Contract C	---E/B	---E/B			---E/B				
Base unit estimation date 1/	1976	1976	1976	1976	1976	1976	1976		
Plan D - E 3/	▽				▽				
Contract D				E/B*---			---E/B*		
Contract E				E/B*---					---E/B
Base unit estimation date 1/	1976	1976	1976	1978	1978	1978	1978	1979	1982

1/ The base unit estimation date may be on or any time after the actuarial valuation date in the year indicated on this line.
2/ Plan A is maintained by only one employer.
3/ Plans B-C and D-E are maintained by more than one employer.
* Denotes that a prior contract ends and a new contract begins prior to the fifth month of a plan year.

---

amount to be amortized must be adjusted for interest at the rate used for determining the plan's normal cost. The adjustments are for—

(i) Interest described in paragraph (g) (3) of this section, if applicable, due to a delay of the beginning of amortization, and

(ii) Interest during the period of amortization.

(5) *Example.* This paragraph is illustrated by the following example:

Example. A multiemployer plan described in section 414(f) is maintained with the calendar year as the plan year and uses the shortfall method. A five percent interest assumption is used by the plan, with payments computed as of the first day of each plan year. The administrator chose to defer the beginning of amortization of shortfall gains and losses, as provided under paragraph (g)(3) of this section. The assumed plan costs and estimated base units for selected years, and the compu-

Reg. § 11.412(c)(1)-2(g)(5)

24,998.118-B (I.R.C.)   Reg. § 11.412(c)(1)-2(g)(5)   8-8-77

tations under this section which follow from such assumptions are shown in the following table. In the table, "(*)" denotes an assumed item. The remaining figures have been calculated on the basis of these assumptions.

(a) Computation of net charge and shortfall gain or loss.

Plan year	1976	1977	1978
1. Normal Cost*	$100,000	$100,000	$100,000
2. Amortization of unfunded liability*	50,000	50,000	50,000
3. Total anticipated charges	$150,000	$150,000	$150,000
4. Estimated base units*	100,000	100,000	100,000
5. Estimated unit charge (line 3 ÷ line 4)	$1.50	$1.50	$1.50
6. Actual units during year*	80,000	90,000	110,000
7. Net charge for year (line 5 x line 6)	$120,000	$135,000	$165,000
8. Shortfall (gain) or loss (line 3-line 7)	$30,000	$15,000	($15,000)

(b) Annual amortization amount

9. Year of shortfall gain or loss	1976	1977	1978
10. First year of amortization	1981	1982	1983
11. Last year of amortization	1996	1997	1998

12. (Gain) or loss adjusted for interest to year amortization begins (4 years)	$36,465	$ 18,233	($18,232)
13. Annual amortization (16 years)	$3,204	$1,602	($1,602)

(c) Computation of net charges for selected years (including shortfall amortization).

Plan year	1981	1982	1983
14. Normal cost*	$120,000	$125,000	$130,000
15. Amortization of unfunded liability*	50,000	50,000	50,000
16. Shortfall amortization (see line 13) from 1976	3,204	3,204	3,204
1977	-	1,602	1,602
1978	-	-	(1,602)
17. Total anticipated charges	$173,204	$179,806	$183,204
18. Estimated base units*	110,000	110,000	110,000
19. Estimated unit charge (line 17 ÷ line 18)	$1.575	$1.635	$1.665
20. Actual units during year*	105,000	110,000	105,000
21. Net charge for year (line 19 x line 20)	$165,375	$179,850	$174,825
22. Shortfall (gain) loss (line 17 - line 21)	$7,829	$(44)	$8,379

The amounts in line 22 will be amortized beginning 1986, 1987, and 1988, respectively.

Reg. § 11.412(c)(1)-2(g)(5)

(h) *Amortization of experience gain or loss*—(1) *General rule.* For purposes of determining the net anticipated annual charge under paragraph (d)(1) of this section, an experience gain or loss shall be amortized pursuant to section 412(b)(2)(B)(iv) or (b)(3)(B)(ii). This amortization begins with the first plan year commencing on or after the actuarial valuation date with respect to which such experience gain or loss is determined. For purposes of this section, a shortfall gain or loss is not an experience gain or loss.

(2) *Deferral of experience amortization period; plan maintained by more than one employer.* As a specific method of computation under the shortfall method for a plan maintained by more than one employer, the experience gain or loss may be amortized—

(i) Beginning with the fifth, and
(ii) Ending with the 15th

plan year that begins on or after the valuation date with respect to which the experience gain or loss is computed. For a multiemployer plan described in section 414(f), the amortization ends with the 20th plan year instead of the 15th. If that specific method is used, the amount of the experience gain or loss must be adjusted for interest from the valuation date to the beginning of the first plan year in which it is amortized.

(i) *Election procedure*—(1) *In general.* To elect the shortfall method, a collectively bargained plan must attach a statement to the annual report required under section 6058(a) for the first plan year to which it is applied. The statement shall state that the shortfall method is adopted, beginning with the plan year covered by such report. Advance approval from the Internal Revenue Service is not required if the shortfall method is first adopted on or before the later of—

(i) The first plan year to which section 412 applies or
(ii) The last plan year commencing before December 31, 1980.

However, approval must be received pursuant to section 412(c)(5) prior to the adoption of the shortfall method at a later time, or the discontinuance of such method, once adopted.

(2) *Use of specific computation methods by plans maintained by more than one employer.* There are specific methods of computation under the shortfall method. They are described in paragraphs (b)(3), (g)(3), and (h)(2) of this section, regarding more than one benefit level under the plan, and the delay of amortization of shortfall and experience gains and losses. These specific methods may be adopted with respect to any plan year to which the shortfall method applies. Approval from the Commissioner must be received under section 412(c)(5) prior to the adoption of one or more of the specific computation methods for a plan year subsequent to the first plan year to which the shortfall method applies, or the discontinuance of a specific computation method, once adopted.

(3) *Reporting requirements.* Each annual report required by section 6058(a) and periodic report of the actuary required by section 6059 must include all additional information relevant to the use of the shortfall method as may be required by the applicable forms and the instructions for such forms.

Temporary Rules
T.D. 7500

Temporary regulations relating to adjustment to the basis of certain carryover basis property to reflect appreciation occurring before January 1, 1977. (T.D. 7500, filed 8-1-77.)

This document provides temporary regulations for computing an adjustment to the basis of certain carryover basis property. The adjustment, made to carryover basis property which reflects the basis of marketable bonds and securities on December 31, 1976, will reflect the appreciation in value occurring before January 1, 1977. The regulations are necessary because of changes that were made to the applicable tax laws by the Tax Reform Act of 1976. The regulations provide guidance for compliance with the law. They affect executors of estates of decedents dying after December 31, 1976, and persons who receive carryover basis property from those decedents.

Date: The regulations apply to estates of decedents who die after December 31, 1976.

For Further Information Contact: William D. Gibbs of the Legislation and Regulations Division, Office of the Chief Counsel, Internal Revenue Service, 1111 Constitution Avenue, N.W., Washington, D.C. 20224 (Attention: CC:LR:T) (202-566-3293).

This document contains temporary regulations relating to the adjustment to be made to carryover basis property which reflects the adjusted basis of any marketable bond or security on December 31, 1976. This adjustment is contained in section 1023(h)(1) of the Internal Revenue Code of 1954, as added by section 2005(a)(2) of the Tax Reform Act of 1976 (Pub. L. 94-455, 90 Stat. 1875). The temporary regulations provided by this document will remain in effect until superseded by final regulations.

Adoption of amendments to the regulations

Accordingly, the Temporary Income Tax Regulations under the Tax Reform Act of 1976 (26 CFR Part 7) are amended by adding the following new section in the appropriate place:

○— [Sec. 1023] § 7.1023(h)-1 (T.D. 7500, filed 8-1-77.) **Adjustment to basis of marketable bonds and securities acquired from a decedent dying after December 31, 1976, for appreciation occurring before January 1, 1977.**

(a) *In general.* For purposes of determining gain (but not loss), the adjusted basis of carryover basis property, as defined in section 1023(b), which reflects the adjusted basis of any marketable bond or security on December 31, 1976, and which is acquired from a decedent dying after December 31, 1976, is increased by the amount of any excess of the fair market value of such bond or security on December 31, 1976, over its adjusted basis on December 31, 1976. Thereafter, this adjusted carryover basis is further adjusted as provided in sections 1023(c), (d) and (e) (relating to adjustments for estate and inheritance taxes paid and the $60,000 minimum basis). However, under section 1023(f)(1), the adjustments under section 1023(c), (d) and (e) may not increase the basis of property above its fair market value as of the date of the decedent's death (or, if the executor elects to determine the value of the gross estate as of the alternate valuation date, the value of the property determined under section 2032).

(b) *Basis for loss purposes.* For purposes of determining loss with respect to such property, its adjusted basis is the same as computed under paragraph (a), except that it is reduced by the amount of the excess described in the first sentence in paragraph (a).

(c) *Basis that reflects basis on December 31, 1976.* The adjusted basis of carryover basis property reflects the adjusted basis of any marketable bond or security on December 31, 1976, if the carryover basis property acquired from the decedent—

(1) Is the same marketable bond or security that was held by the decedent on December 31, 1976, or

(2) Has a basis that is determined in whole or in part by reference to the basis of a marketable bond or security on December 31, 1976.

(d) *Marketable bonds and securities.* For purposes of this section, marketable bonds or securities are—

(1) Bonds (including municipal bonds) or securities which are—

(i) Listed on the New York Stock Exchange, the American Stock Exchange, or any regional exchange for which quotations are published on a regular basis, including foreign securities listed on a recognized foreign national or regional exchange;

(ii) Regularly traded in the national or regional over-the-counter market, for which published quotations are available; or

(iii) Locally traded for which published quotations representing bona fide bid and asked prices are available from a registered broker or dealer;

(2) Units in a common trust fund; or

(3) Shares in a mutual fund.

(e) *Value on December 31, 1976.* The fair market value of a marketable bond or security on December 31, 1976, will be its fair market value as determined under § 20.2031-2 or § 20.2031-8(b) including the provisions relating to large blocks of securities and to securities traded sporadically at or near the valuation date. For purposes of this section, the term "reasonable period" (before or after the valuation date), as used in § 20.2031-2, will generally be 30 days. However, where it is established that the value of any bond or share of stock determined on the basis of selling or bid and asked prices as provided under paragraphs (b), (c), and (d) of § 20.2031-2 does not reflect the fair market value thereof, the principles of paragraph (e) of § 20.2031-2 will be applicable.

(f) *Examples.* The provisions of this section may be illustrated by the following examples:

Example (1). The adjusted basis of marketable securities in the hands of D,

Reg. § 7.1023(h)-1(f)

the decedent, on December 31, 1976, and on the date of his death was $75,000. The fair market value of the securities on December 31, 1976, was $90,000. D dies on July 28, 1978, when the securities are worth $80,000, and bequeaths them to his son. D's executor does not elect alternate valuation as provided in section 2032. For purposes of determining gain, if the son thereafter sells the securities, their carryover basis of $75,000 is increased by $15,000 ($90,000 − $75,000) to $90,000 under paragraph (a) of this section. Because the adjustment under section 1023(h)(1) increased the adjusted basis of the securities above the fair market value for estate tax purposes, no further adjustment is made to their basis under section 1023(c), (d) or (e), pursuant to section 1023(f)(1). For purposes of determining loss, the adjusted carryover basis of the securities, as computed under the preceding two sentences ($90,000), is reduced by the excess ($15,000) to $75,000. Therefore, if D's son realizes $100,000 on the sale of such securities, he realizes a gain of $10,000 ($100,000 − $90,000). If he realizes only $60,000 on their sale, he realizes a loss of $15,000 ($75,000 − $60,000). If he realizes between $75,000 and $90,000 on their sale, he realizes neither a gain nor a loss on them.

Example (2). The facts are the same as in Example (1) except that D received the securities on July 1, 1977, in a nontaxable distribution of principal from a trust that held such securities on December 31, 1976. In addition, the value of the securities on the date of D's death is $105,000, and the adjustment for estate taxes paid under section 1023(c), based on the remaining net appreciation of $15,000 ($105,000 − $90,000) in the securities, is $1,000. There are no other adjustments to the basis of the securities. The adjusted carryover basis of the securities for purposes of determining gain is $91,000 ($75,000 + $15,000 + $1,000). For purposes of determining loss, the adjusted carryover basis of the securities is $76,000 ($91,000 − $15,000).

T.D. 7502

Temporary regulations relating to annual return for foreign trust with United States beneficiary. (T.D. 7502, filed 8-18-77.)

This document provides temporary regulations relating to the filing of an annual return for a foreign trust having a United States beneficiary. Provisions providing for the filing of such a form were added to the tax law by the Tax Reform Act of 1976. The temporary regulations provide the time, place and manner of filing the form and affect some United States persons who are transferors to or grantors of foreign trusts having United States beneficiaries.

Date: The temporary regulations are effective for tax years ending on or after December 31, 1976.

For Further Information Contact: J. Douglas Sorensen of the Legislation and Regulations Division, Office of the Chief Counsel, Internal Revenue Service, 1111 Constitution Avenue, N.W., Washington, D.C. 20224 (Attention: CC:LR:T) (202-566-3478).

Supplementary Information:
Adoption of amendments to the temporary regulations

Accordingly, the temporary regulations on procedure and administration under the Tax Reform Act of 1976 (26 CFR Part 404) are amended by adding the following new section in the appropriate place.

[Sec. 6048] § 404.6048-1 (T.D. 7502, filed 8-18-77.) **Annual returns for foreign trusts with a United States beneficiary.**

(a) *Return required*—(1) *In general.* Each taxpayer subject to tax under section 679 with respect to a foreign trust having one or more United States beneficiaries must file Form 3520-A, Annual Return of Foreign Trust with U.S. Beneficiaries, together with any additional schedules or other information required by the form or the instructions to the form. Form 3520-A must be filed even if the taxpayer is treated as the owner of a foreign trust under both section 679 and some other provision of subpart E of Part I of Subchapter J.

(2) *Joint returns.* If the taxpayer's spouse is also subject to tax under section 679 with respect to the same foreign trust for the same taxable year, and if both taxpayer and spouse file a joint return of income tax for that year, a single Form 3520-A may be filed jointly with respect to such trust for the year.

(b) *Period covered by return.* The period covered by the return required by this section is the taxable year of the taxpayer required to file the return, regardless of the period used by the trust for accounting or any other purpose.

(c) *Time for filing*—(1) *In general.* The return required by this section must be filed no later than the 15th day of the fourth month following the end of the taxable period covered by the return.

(2) *Transitional rule.* In the case of a return required by this section for a taxable period ending on or before June 30, 1977, the return must be filed no later than—

(i) October 15, 1977, in the case of a taxpayer treated as an owner with respect to the trust under both section 679 and a provision of sections 672 through 678, or

(ii) December 31, 1977, in all other cases.

(3) *Extensions of time for filing.* For rules relating to extensions of time for filing, see section 6081 and the regulations thereunder.

(d) *Place for filing.* The return required by this section must be filed with the Director, Internal Revenue Service Center, 11601 Roosevelt Boulevard, Philadelphia, Pennsylvania, 19155.

(e) *Effective date.* This section is effective for taxable periods ending on or after December 31, 1976.

T.D. 7503

Temporary regulations relating to foreign base company shipping income. (T.D. 7503, filed 8-19-77.)

This document provides temporary regulations relating to an election permitted to United States shareholders of controlled foreign corporations by the Tax Reduction Act of 1975. These regulations provide necessary guidance for making the election.

Date: The regulations are effective for taxable years of foreign corporations beginning after December 31, 1975, and for taxable years of United States shareholders within which or with which such taxable years of such foreign corporations end.

For Further Information Contact: Benjamin J. Cohen of the Legislation and Regulations Division, Office of the Chief Counsel, Internal Revenue Service, 1111 Constitution Avenue, N.W., Washington, D.C. 20224 (Attention: CC:LR:T) (202-566-4454).

Supplementary Information: Background

On August 9, 1976, the Federal Register published proposed amendments to the Income Tax Regulations (26 CFR Part 1) under section 955 of the Internal Revenue Code of 1954, 41 F.R. 33285. The amendments were proposed to conform the regulations to section 602 of the Tax Reduction Act of 1975 (89 Stat. 58). No public hearing has been held. After consideration of all relevant comments, the rules in §§ 1.954-7(b) and 1.955A-4 are temporarily adopted by this Treasury decision.

Adoption of amendments to the regulations

Accordingly, 26 CFR Part 9 is amended by adding a new § 9.2 to read as follows:

[Sec. 954, 955] § 9.2 (T.D. 7503, filed 8-19-77.) **Election as to date of determining qualified investment in foreign base company shipping operations.**

The rules in §§ 1.954-7(b) and 1.955A-4 (as published with notice of proposed rulemaking in the Federal Register for Monday, August 9, 1976 (41 F.R. 33285)) shall apply until superseded by final regulations.

T.D. 7504

Temporary regulations relating to amounts at risk with respect to certain activities. (T.D. 7504, filed 8-19-77.)

This document provides temporary regulations relating to the determination of the amount at risk for activities begun prior to the effective date of the at risk provisions and continued after the effective date. Changes to the applicable tax law were made by the Tax Reform Act of 1976. These regulations provide necessary guidance to the public for compliance with the at risk provisions, and affect most persons who engage in activities covered by those provisions which were begun, but not completed, prior to the effective date.

Date: The regulations are effective for taxable years beginning after December 31, 1975, except as otherwise provided. For Further Information Contact: David Jacobson of the Legislation and Regulations Division, Office of the Chief Counsel, Internal Revenue Service, 1111 Constitution Avenue, N.W., Washington, D.C. 20224 (Attention: CC:LR:T) (202-566-3923).
Supplementary Information: Background

This document contains amendments to the Temporary Regulations under the Tax Reform Act of 1976 (26 CFR Part 7) under section 465 of the Internal Revenue Code of 1954. These amendments are proposed to conform the regulations to section 204 of the Tax Reform Act of 1976 (90 Stat. 1531).
Adoption of amendments to the regulations

Accordingly, 226 CFR Part 7 is amended by adding the following new sections at the appropriate place:

[Sec. 465] § 7.465-1 (T.D. 7504, filed 8-19-77.) Amounts at risk with respect to activities begun prior to effective date; in general.

Section 465 provides that a taxpayer (other than a corporation which is not a subchapter S corporation or a personal holding company) engaged in certain activities may not deduct losses from such activity to the extent the losses exceed the amount the taxpayer is at risk with respect to the activity. For the types of activities to which section 465 applies and for determining what constitutes a separate activity, see section 465(c). Section 465 generally applies to losses attributable to amounts paid or incurred in taxable years beginning after December 31, 1975. For the purposes of applying the at risk limitation to activities begun before the effective date of the provision (and which were not excepted from application of the provision), it is necessary to determine the amount at risk as of the first day of the first taxable year beginning after December 31, 1975. The amount at risk in an activity as of the first day of the first taxable year of the taxpayer beginning after December 31, 1975. The amount at risk in an activity as of the first day of the first taxable year of the taxpayer beginning after December 31, 1975, (for the purposes of § 7.465-1 through 7.465-5 such first day shall be referred to as the effective date) shall be determined according to the rules provided in sections 7.465-2 through 7.465-5.

[Sec. 465] § 7.465-2 (T.D. 7504, filed 8-19-77.) Determination of amount at risk.

(a) *Initial amount.* The amount a taxpayer is at risk on the effective date with respect to an activity to which section 465 applies shall be determined in accordance with this section. The initial amount the taxpayer is at risk in the activity shall be the taxpayer's initial basis in the activity as modified by disregarding amounts described in section 465(b)(3) or (4) (relating generally to amounts protected against loss or borrowed from related persons).

(b) *Succeeding adjustments.* For each taxable year ending before the effective date, the initial amount at risk shall be increased and decreased by the items which increased and decreased the taxpayer's basis in the activity in that year as modified by disregarding the amounts described in section 465(b)(3) or (4).

(c) *Application of losses and withdrawals.* (1) Losses described in section 465(d) which are incurred in taxable years beginning prior to January 1, 1976 and deducted in such taxable years, will be treated as reducing first that portion of the taxpayer's basis which is attributable to amounts not at risk. On the other hand, withdrawals made in taxable years beginning before January 1, 1976, will be treated as reducing the amount which the taxpayer is at risk.

(2) Therefore, if in a taxable year beginning prior to January 1, 1976 there is a loss described in section 465(d), it shall reduce the amount at risk only to the extent it exceeds the amount of the taxpayer's basis which is not at risk. For the purposes of this paragraph, the taxpayer's basis which is not at risk is that portion of the taxpayer's basis in the activity (as of the close of the taxable year and prior to reduction for the loss) which is attributable to amounts described in section 465(b)(3) or (4).

(d) *Amount at risk shall not be less than zero.* If, after determining the amount described in paragraphs (a), (b), and (c) of this section, the amount at risk (but for this paragraph) would be less than zero, the amount at risk on the effective date shall be zero.

[Sec. 465] § 7.465-3 (T.D. 7504 filed 8-19-77.) Allocation of loss for different taxable years.

If the taxable year of the entity conducting the activity differs from that of the taxpayer, the loss attributable to the activity for the first taxable year of the entity ending after the beginning of the first taxable year of the taxpayer beginning after December 31, 1975, shall be allocated in the following manner. That portion of the loss from the activity for such taxable year of the entity which bears the same ratio as the number of days in such taxable year before January 1, 1976, divided by the total number of days in the taxable year, shall be attributable to taxable years

Reg. § 7.465-3

of the taxpayer beginning before January 1, 1976. Consequently, that portion shall be treated in accordance with § 7.465-2.

○→ [Sec. 465] § 7.465-4 (T.D. 7504, filed 8-19-77.) **Insufficient records.**

If sufficient records do not exist to accurately determine under § 7.465-2 the amount which a taxpayer is at risk on the effective date, the amount at risk shall be the taxpayer's basis in the activity reduced (but not below zero) by the taxpayer's share of amounts described in section 465(b)(3) or (4) with respect to the activity on the day before the effective date.

○→ [Sec. 465] § 7.465-5 (T.D. 7504, filed 8-19-77.) **Examples.**

The provisions of § 7.465-1 and § 7.465-2 may be illustrated by the following examples:

Example (1). J. and K, as equal partners, form partnership JK on January 1, 1975. Partnership JK is engaged solely in an activity described in section 465(c)(1). On January 1, 1975, each partner contributes $10,000 in cash from personal assets to JK. On July 1, 1975, JK borrows $40,000 (of which J's share is $20,000) from a bank under a nonrecourse financing arrangement secured only by the new equipment (for use in the activity) purchased with the $40,000. On September 1, 1975, JK reduces the amount due on the loan to $36,000 (of which J's share is $18,000). On October 1, 1975, JK distributes $3,000 to each partner. For taxable year 1975, JK has no income or loss. Although J's basis in the activity is $25,000 ($10,000 + $18,000 − $3,000) J's amount at risk on the effective date is $7,000 determined as follows:

Initial amount at risk		$10,000
Plus:		
Items which increased basis other than amounts described in section 465(b)(3) or (4)	$ 0	0
		$10,000
Less:		
Distribution	3,000	3,000
J's amount at risk on effective date		$ 7,000

Example (2). Assume the same facts as in Example (1) except that JK has a loss (as described in section 465 (d)) for 1975 of which J's share is $12,000. Although J's basis in the activity is $13,000 ($10,000 + $18,000 − ($3,000 + $12,000)) J's amount at risk on the effective date is $7,000 determined as follows:

Initial amount at risk		$10,000
Plus:		
Items which increased basis other than amounts described in section 465(b)(3) or (4)	$ 0	0
		$10,000
Less:		
Distribution	$3,000	
Portion of loss ($12,000) in excess of portion of basis not at risk ($18,000)	0	3,000
J's amount at risk on effective date		$ 7,000

Example (3). Assume the same facts as in Example (1) except that JK has a loss (as described in section 465 (d)) for 1975, and J's share is $23,000. J's basis in the activity is $2,000 ($10,000 + $18,000 − ($3,000 + $23,000)). The amount at risk on the effective date is determined as follows:

Initial amount at risk		$10,000
Plus:		
Items which increased basis other than amounts described in section 465(b)(3) or (4)	$ 0	0
		$10,000
Less:		
Distribution	$3,000	
Portion of loss ($23,000) in excess of portion of basis not at risk ($18,000)	5,000	8,000
J's amount at risk on effective date		$ 2,000

Temporary Rules

T.D. 7507

Temporary regulations relating to certain requirements for employee stock ownership plans. (T.D. 7507, filed 8-30-77.)

This document provides temporary regulations relating to employee stock ownership plans ("ESOP's"). Changes in the applicable tax law were made by the Employee Retirement Income Security Act of 1974 and the Tax Reform Act of 1976. Together with final regulations published elsewhere in today's [9-2-77] FEDERAL REGISTER, these regulations are intended to provide guidance for the public in complying with the law. They affect all employees who participate in ESOP's and employers who establish ESOP's.

Date: The regulations are generally effective for plan years ending after December 31, 1974.

For Further Information Contact: Thomas Rogan of the Legislation and Regulations Division, Office of the Chief Counsel, Internal Revenue Service, 1111 Constitution Avenue, N.W., Washington, D.C. 20224 (Attention: CC:LR:T) (202-566-3478).

Supplementary Information: Background

On July 30, 1976, the FEDERAL REGISTER published proposed amendments to the Income Tax Regulations (26 CFR Part I) under section 301 of the Internal Revenue Code of 1954 and to the Pension, etc. Excise Tax Regulations (26 CFR Part 54) under section 4975(d)(3), (e)(7), and (e)(8) of the Code (41 FR 31833). Similar Department of Labor provisions appeared at the same time (41 FR 31870).

By a notice published in the FEDERAL REGISTER on October 19, 1976, the public was invited to comment orally or in writing not only upon issues addressed in the proposed amendments, but also upon issues addressed by section 803(h) of the Tax Reform Act of 1976 (90 Stat. 1590) and by the Conference Report of the Committee of Conference on H.R. 10612 (H.R. Rep. No. 94-1515, 94th Cong., 2d Sess., 539-542 (1976)), as both relate to ESOP's.

Guidelines Superseded

Questions and answers relating to ESOP's were published in Technical Information Release (TIR) 1413 on November 4, 1975, as guidelines pending the issuance of regulations. The temporary regulations under this Treasury decision supersede question and answer G-8, relating to the distribution of dividends.

Adoption of amendments to the regulations

Accordingly, 26 CFR Part 141 is amended by inserting in the appropriate place the following new section:

[Sec. 4975(d), (e)] § 141.4975-11 (T.D. 7507, filed 8-30-77.) "ESOP" requirements.

Until superseded by final regulations, the provisions under § 54.4975-11 as published with notice of proposed rule making in the FEDERAL REGISTER for Friday, Sept. 2, 1977 (42 FR 44396) apply.

Temporary Rules

T.D. 7518

Temporary regulations relating to disclosures of certain returns and return information after December 31, 1976, for tax administration purposes by Justice Department attorneys and IRS Chief Counsel personnel. (T.D. 7518, filed Nov. 11, 1977.)

This document provides temporary regulations relating to disclosures after December 31, 1976 of tax returns and tax return information by Justice Department attorneys and IRS Chief Counsel personnel for Federal tax administration purposes where such tax returns or tax return information had been originally disclosed to such attorneys or personnel prior to that date for tax administration purposes authorized by then applicable law and regulations. Changes in the applicable law were made by the Tax Reform Act of 1976. The regulations would provide Justice Department attorneys and IRS Chief Counsel personnel with guidance needed to comply with that Act and would affect disclosures of tax returns and tax return information made after December 31, 1976. DATE: The regulations are effective as of January 1, 1977.

For Further Information Contact: Karl P. Fryzel of the Office of the Chief Counsel, Internal Revenue Service, 1111 Constitution Avenue, N.W., Washington, D. C. 20224, Attention: CC:LR:T, 202-566-3294, not a toll-free call.

Supplementary Information: Prior to amendment by the Tax Reform Act of 1976, the Internal Revenue Code authorized disclosures of tax returns and tax return information to Justice Department attorneys and IRS Chief Counsel personnel for Federal tax administration purposes as provided by Presidentially approved regulations. A substantial volume of tax returns and tax return information furnished to these attorneys and personnel for tax administration purposes under prior law and regulations was in their possession on January 1, 1977, the effective date of the new statutory disclosure rules of the Act.

These regulations provide that, as a general rule, tax returns and tax return information furnished to these persons under prior law for Federal tax administration purposes may be used by them after December 31, 1976 for tax administration purposes authorized by prior law. However, if any such tax returns or tax return information is to be introduced into evidence in tax litigation after that date, the statutory relevancy tests prescribed by the new law must first be met.

Adoption of temporary regulations

Accordingly, 26 CFR Part 404 is amended as follows:

○━ [Sec. 6103(a)] § 404.6103(a)-2 (T.D. 7518, filed 11-11-77.) **Disclosures after December 31, 1976 by attorneys of the Department of Justice and officers and employees of the office of the Chief Counsel for the Internal Revenue Service of returns and return information (including taxpayer return information) disclosed to such attorneys, officers, and employees by the Secretary before January 1, 1977 for a purpose involving tax administration.**

(a) *General rule.* Except as provided by paragraph (b) of this section and subject to the requirements of this paragraph, a return or return information (including taxpayer return information), as defined in section 6103(b)(1), (2), and (3) of the Internal Revenue Code, disclosed by the Secretary before January 1, 1977, to an attorney of the Department of Justice (including a United States attorney) or to an officer or employee of the office of the Chief Counsel for the Internal Revenue Service for a purpose involving tax administration (as defined in section 6103(b)(4)) pursuant to the authority of section 6103 (or any order of the President under section 6103 or rules and regulations thereunder prescribed by the Secretary and approved by the President) before amendment of such section by Section 1202 of the Tax Reform Act of 1976 (Pub. L. 94-455, 90 Stat. 1667) may be disclosed by, or on behalf of, such attorney, officer, or employee after December 31, 1976, for any purpose authorized by such section (or such order or rules and regulations) before such amendment.

(b) *Exception.* Notwithstanding the provisions of paragraph (a) of this section, a return or return information (including taxpayer return information) disclosed before January 1, 1977, by the Secretary to an attorney of the Department of Justice or to an officer or employee of the office of the Chief Counsel for the Internal Revenue Service for a purpose related to tax administration as described in paragraph (a) may, after December 31, 1976, be disclosed by, or on behalf of, such attorney, officer, or employee in an administrative or judicial proceeding only if such proceeding is one described in section 6103(h)(4) and if the requirements of section 6103(h)(4) have first been met.

Temporary Regulations relating to information returns for carryover basis property. (T.D. 7540, filed 4-19-78.)

This document provides temporary regulations for executors of estates of decedents who died after December 31, 1976. Changes were made in the applicable tax law by the Tax Reform Act of 1976. The regulations provide instructions on how to provide information to the Internal Revenue Service and beneficiaries on carryover basis property.

DATE: The regulations generally apply to estates of persons dying after December 31, 1976.

For Further Information Contact: William D. Gibbs of the Legislation and Regulations Division, Office of the Chief Counsel, Internal Revenue Service, 1111 Constitution Avenue, N.W., Washington, D.C. 20224 (Attention: CC:LR:T) (202-566-3293) (Not a toll-free number).

This document contains temporary regulations relating to information which must be furnished to the Internal Revenue Service and to beneficiaries about carryover basis property. The furnishing of the information is required by section 6039A of the Code, as added by section 2005(d) of the Tax Reform Act of 1975 (P.L. 94-455, 90 Stat. 1877).

The regulations require those executors who must furnish information to the Service to provide to distributees of carryover basis property in writing the following information: a description of the property, the adjusted basis as computed under sections 1023(a), (c), and (d), the value of the property for Federal estate tax purposes, the amount of the increase in the basis of the property determined under section 1023(h), and a notice that the distributee should keep this information as part of permanent records. Distributees who have this information can then make the adjustment under section 1023(e) for State inheritance and similar taxes. The basis after the section 1023(e) adjustment will be the basis for purposes of determining gain. The basis for loss is computed by subtracting the amount of basis increase made to the property under section 1023(h) from the total basis as computed after the section 1023(e) adjustment.

The regulations also provide guidance as to when this information must be furnished to distributees. If an estate tax return is required to be filed, the information must be furnished on the latest of the date the property is distributed to the beneficiary, 6 months after the due date (including extensions) of the return, or October 31, 1978. If no estate tax return is required to be filed, the information must be furnished on the latest of the date the property is distributed to the beneficiary, 15 months from the date of death of the decedent, or October 31, 1978.

The regulations also contain a special rule in case subsequent adjustments are made to carryover basis property. In such a case, the executor must provide the beneficiary the same information as before, recomputed as required by these subsequent adjustments.

Adoption of amendments to the regulations

Accordingly, the Temporary Income Tax Regulations under the Tax Reform Act of 1976 (26 CFR Part 7) are amended by adding the following new section in the appropriate place:

○━▶ [Sec. 6039-A] § 7.6039A-1 (T.D. 7540, filed 4-19-78.) **Information regarding carryover basis property acquired from a decedent.**

(a) *Information for Internal Revenue Service.* In the case of a decedent who dies after December 31, 1976, the executor (as defined in section 2203) shall furnish to the Internal Revenue Service the following information, as applicable—

(1) If an estate tax return is required to be filed under section 6018 of the Internal Revenue Code of 1954, as amended, and if the return form contains questions relating to carryover basis property, the executor must answer those questions.

(2) If no estate tax return is required to be filed under section 6018 of the Internal Revenue Code of 1954, as amended, or if a return is required to be filed but the return form used does not contain questions relating to carryover basis property, the executor must file the form prescribed by the Commissioner. This form may be attached to the estate tax return or the decedent's final individual income tax return. If this form is not attached to the estate tax return or the decedent's final individual income tax return, it must be filed with the Internal Revenue Service office where the decedent's final income tax return would be filed if one were required within 9 months after the date of the decedent's death or by October 31, 1978, whichever is later.

(b) *Information to be furnished to beneficiaries.* Any executor required under paragraph (a) of this section to furnish information to the Internal Revenue Service relating to carryover basis property must furnish in writing to the distributee of each piece of carryover basis property—

(1) A description of the property,

(2) The adjusted basis of the property as computed under section 1023(a), (c), and (d),

(3) The amount of the increase in the basis of the property determined under section 1023(h),

(4) The value of the property for Federal estate tax purposes, and

(5) A notice that the beneficiary should keep this information as part of permanent records.

(c) *Time for furnishing information to beneficiaries.* The information which an executor is required to furnish to the beneficiaries under this paragraph must be furnished on or before the latest of—

(1) The date the property is distributed to the beneficiary,

(2)'(i) In the case of an executor who is required to file an estate tax return, 6 months after the due date (including extensions) of such return,

Reg. § 7.6039-A-1

(ii) In the case of an executor who is not required to file an estate tax return, 15 months from the date of death of the decedent, or

(3) October 31, 1978.

(d) *Subsequent adjustments to carryover basis.* In the event subsequent adjustments are made which relate to the carryover basis of any piece of property included in a decedent's gross estate, whether by reason of an adjustment resulting from an examination of the estate tax return or otherwise, any executor required under paragraph (a) of this section to furnish information to the Internal Revenue Service shall, within 3 months of a determination, as defined in section 1313 (a), of such adjustments, provide to the recipient of each item of carryover basis property the information set forth in paragraph (b) above, recomputed as required by such adjustments.

(e) *Effective date.* This section is effective in respect of decedents dying after December 31, 1976.

T.D. 7541

Temporary regulations relating to election with respect to recovery of intangibles under section 57(d) of the Code. (T.D. 7541, filed 4-25-78.)

This document provides temporary regulations relating to the election permitted in computing the intangible drilling costs item of tax preference. Changes to the applicable tax law were made by the Tax Reform Act of 1976. These regulations provide the public with guidance needed to make the election, and affect taxpayers who are subject to the minimum tax on the intangible drilling costs item of tax preference.

Effective Date: The regulations are effective immediately.

For Further Information Contact: John H. Parcell of the Legislation and Regulations Division, Office of Chief Counsel, Internal Revenue Service, 1111 Constitution Avenue, N.W., Washington, D. C. 20224, Attention: CC:LR:T (202-566-3287), not a toll-free call.

Supplementary Information: Background

This document amends the Temporary Income Tax Regulations under the Tax Reform Act of 1976 (26 CFR Part 7) to reflect section 57(d) of the Internal Revenue Code of 1954, as added by section 301 of the Tax Reform Act of 1976 (90 Stat. 1549). The temporary regulation provided by this document will remain in effect until superseded by final regulations on this subject.

Intangible Drilling Costs Item of Preference

Section 57(a)(11) of the Code, as added by section 301 of the Tax Reform Act of 1976, includes intangible drilling costs as an item of tax preference for taxable years beginning after December 31, 1975. Section 57(a)(11) was amended by section 308 of the Tax Reduction and Simplification Act of 1977 (91 Stat. 153), but only for taxable years beginning in 1977.

To compute the amount of the intangible drilling costs item of tax preference for any taxable year (including taxable years beginning in 1977), it is necessary to determine the amount by which certain intangible drilling and development costs exceed the straight line recovery of these costs. Section 57(d) of the Code provides that straight line recovery of intangibles can be determined through ratable amortization or, at the election of the taxpayer, through cost depletion.

Election

Section 57(d)(2) provides that the election to use cost depletion to determine straight line recovery of intangibles shall be made in the manner prescribed by regulations. Therefore, to provide immediate guidance to taxpayers, this regulation prescribes the manner in which the election is made.

The regulation provides that the election is made separately for each oil and gas well. The election is made by using cost depletion to compute straight line recovery of intangibles for purposes of determining the amount of the intangible drilling costs item of tax preference.

Adoption of amendments to the regulations

Accordingly, the Temporary Income Tax Regulations under the Tax Reform Act of 1976 (26 CFR Part 7) are amended by inserting the following temporary regulation in the appropriate place:

[Sec. 57(d)(2)] § 7.57(d)-1 (T.D. 7541, filed 4-25-78.) **Election with respect to straight line recovery of intangibles.**

(a) *Purpose.* This section prescribes rules for making the election permitted under section 57(d)(2), as added by the Tax Reform Act of 1976. Under this election taxpayers may use cost depletion to compute straight line recovery of intangibles.

(b) *Election.* The election under section 57(d) is subject to the following rules:

(1) The election is made within the time prescribed by law (including extensions thereof) for filing the return for the taxable year in which the intangible drilling costs are paid or incurred or, if later, by July 25, 1978.

(2) The election is made separately for each well. Thus, a taxpayer may make the election for only some of his or her wells.

(3) The election is made by using, for the well or wells to which the election applies, cost depletion to compute straight line recovery of intangibles for purposes of determining the amount of the preference under section 57(a)(11).

(4) The election may be made whether or not the taxpayer uses cost depletion in computing taxable income.

(5) The election is made by a partnership rather than by each partner.

(c) *Computation of cost depletion.* For purposes of computing straight line recovery of inangibles through cost depletion, both depletable and depreciable intangible drilling and development costs for the taxable year are taken into account. They are treated as if capitalized, added to basis, and recovered under § 1.611-2(a). Costs paid or incurred in other taxable years are not taken into account.

Reg. § 7.57(d)-1

PROPOSED REGULATIONS

INTRODUCTION

Introduction.—Proposed new regulations and proposed amendments to regulations are published in Code section number order on the following pages.

An existing regulation may be amended, or a new regulation issued, either to reflect a change in the law or a change in the Commissioner's interpretation of the law (which may or may not be based upon a court decision). The Commissioner gives notice of his intention to amend or issue new regulations and the proposed text is made public in advance of its adoption. The standard form of the notice generally reads as follows:

Notice is hereby given that the regulations set forth in tentative form in the attached appendix are proposed to be prescribed by the Commissioner of Internal Revenue, with the approval of the Secretary of the Treasury or his delegate. Prior to the final adoption of such regulations, consideration will be given to any comments pertaining thereto which are submitted in writing (preferably six copies) to the Commissioner of Internal Revenue, Attention: CC:LR:T, Washington, D. C. 20224, by [date specified in every proposal]. Pursuant to 26 CFR 601.601(b) designations of material as confidential or not to be disclosed, contained in such comments, will not be accepted. Thus, a person submitting written comments should not include therein material that he considers to be confidential or inappropriate for disclosure to the public. It will be presumed by the Internal Revenue Service that every written comment submitted to it in response to this notice of proposed rule making is intended by the person submitting it to be subject in its entirety to public inspection and copying in accordance with the procedures of 26 CFR 601.702(d)(9). Any person submitting written comments who desires an opportunity to comment orally at a public hearing on these proposed regulations should submit his request, in writing, to the Commissioner by [date specified in every proposal]. In such case, a public hearing will be held, and notice of the time, place, and date will be published in a subsequent issue of the Federal Register, unless the person or persons who have requested a hearing withdraw their requests for a hearing before notice of the hearing has been filed with the Office of the Federal Register. The proposed regulations are to be issued under the authority contained in section 7805 of the Internal Revenue Code of 1954 (68A Stat. 917; 26 U.S.C. 7805).

Proposed new regulations and proposed amendments to final regulations, while not binding as final regulations, reflect IRS thinking on the tax topics covered. Until promulgated under a numbered Treasury Decision, however, they are subject to changes in response to public comments. Hence, each proposed regulation or proposed amendment to a final regulation, as published below, shows the date of publication in the Federal Register. This is the date from which time is reckoned for filing protests (data, views or arguments). Thirty days or more after publication of a proposed Treasury Decision in the Federal Register, the Commissioner will issue a numbered Treasury Decision. After the issuance of the Treasury Decision, the proposed text is deleted from this division and the change is reflected in the text of the final regulations.

A final regulation has the force and effect of law in taxpayer's dealings with IRS. But if a taxpayer contests a deficiency before the Tax Court, or sues on a refund claim, he can question the validity of a regulation.

PROPOSED REGULATIONS
TABLE OF CONTENTS

	Section (§)
Political Contributions	1.41-1, 1.218-1
11-percent Investment Credit	1.46-8
Credit for Expenses of Work Incentive Programs	1.50A-1
New Jobs Credit	1.52-1, 1.280C-1
Minimum Tax for Tax Preferences	1.56-1
Nonqualified Compensation Reduction Plans	1.61-16
Annuities; Certain Proceeds of Endowment and Life Insurance Contracts	1.72-4
Group-term Life Insurance	1.79-1
Restricted Property	1.83-1
Employee Death Benefits	1.101-2
Nonqualified Stock Options	1.83-7
Interest on Governmental Obligations	1.103-1
Refunding Issues of Industrial Development Bonds	1.103-7
Arbitrage Bonds	1.103-13
Employer Contributions to Accident and Health Plans	1.106-1
Contributions in Aid of Construction	1.118-2
Deduction for Taxes	1.164-1
Deduction for Removing Architectural and Transportation Barriers for the Handicapped	7.190-1
Deduction for Retirement Savings	1.219-1
Social Clubs—Membership Organizations	1.277-1
Sec. 306 Stock	1.306-3
Collapsible Corporations	1.341-7
Certain Transfers to Foreign Corporations	7.367(a)-1
Change of Accounting Method Without the Consent of the Commissioner	1.381(c)(4)-1
Qualified Retirement Plans	1.401-8
Qualified "Keogh" or "H.R. 10" Plans	1.401(e)-1
Salary Reduction Agreements	1.402(a)-1
Rollover Amounts	1.402(a)-3, 1.403(a)-3
Treatment of Beneficiary of Nonexempt Trusts	1.402(b)-1
Tax on Certain Lump Sum Distributions	1.402(e)-2
Capital Gains Treatment for Certain Distributions	1.403(a)-2
Treatment of Beneficiary of Nonexempt Annuity Plan	1.403(c)-1
Employer Deductions	1.404(a)-9
Contributions to "Keogh" or "H.R. 10" Plans	1.404(e)-1A
Taxation of Retirement Bonds	1.405-3
Individual Retirement Accounts	1.408-1
Retirement Bonds	1.409-1
Minimum Funding Standards	1.412(i)-1
Definitions and Special Rules Under the Employee Retirement Income Security Act (ERISA '74)	1.414(b)-1
Employee Stock Options	1.421-6
Livestock Sold on Account of Drought	1.451-1
Installment Method	1.453-7
Political Organizations	1.527-1
Accumulated Earnings of Corporations	1.532-1
Personal Holding Companies	1.541-1
Bonus and Advanced Royalties	1.612-3
Small Producer Exemption	1.613A-3
Operating Mineral Interest in Mines	1.614-3
Taxation of Estates and Trusts	1.642(h)-1

Table of Contents

63,003

Section (§)

Taxation of Beneficiaries of Trusts	1.652(b)-1
Charitable Remainder Trusts	1.664-1
Alimony Trusts	1.682(b)-1
Gain or Loss on Contributions to Partnerships	1.721-1
Life Insurance Reserves	1.801-4
Regulated Investment Companies	1.851-2
Real Estate Investment Trusts	1.856-1
Income from U.S. Sources	1.861-1
Income from Certain Aircraft or Vessels	1.861-9
Nonresident Alien Individuals	1.871-1
Foreign Corporations	1.881-2
Foreign Tax Credit	1.901-1
Foreign Base Company Shipping Income	1.951-1
International Boycott Determinations	1.999-1
Foreign Personal Holding Company Stock or Securities	1.1022-1
Limitation on Capital Losses	1.1211-1
Sale or Exchange of Depreciable Property between Related Taxpayers	1.1239-1
Section 1244 Stock	1.1244(c)-1
Franchises, Trademarks and Trade Names	1.1253-1
Income Averaging	1.1304-2
Subchapter S Corporations:	
Election by Small Business Corporations	1.1372-1
Undistributed Taxable Income	1.1373-1
Special Rules on Capital Gains	1.1375-1
Certain Qualified Pensions, Etc., Plans	1.1379-1
Withholding of Tax on Nonresident Aliens	1.1441-2, 31.3401(a)(6)-1
Consolidated Returns	1.1502-3
Withholding Exemption Certificates	31.3402(f)(2)-1
Excise Taxes on Certain Retirement Savings Plans	54.4973-1, 54.5974-1
Employee Stock Ownership Plan Requirements	54.4975-11
Record-keeping Requirements	1.6001-1
Returns of Tax Withheld from Wages	31.6011(a)-4
Returns of Fiduciaries	1.6012-3
Returns by Exempt Organizations	1.6033-2
Information Returns of Trusts	1.6034-1
Information Returns for Payments to Employees	1.6034-2
Returns Upon Termination, Etc., of Exempt Organizations	1.6043-3
Returns Regarding Interest Payments	1.6049-1
Information Regarding Wages	31.6051-1
Registration of and Information Concerning Pension, Etc. Plans	301.6057-1
Mode or Time of Collection	31.6302(c)-1
Lien for Taxes	301.6321-1
Collection of State Individual Income Taxes	301.6361-1
Additions to Individual Income Taxes	1.6654-1
Failure to Collect and Pay over Tax	301.6672-1
Disclosure or Use of Information by Preparers of Returns	301.7216-2
Domestic Building and Loan Associations	301.7701-13A
Returns and Statements on Magnetic Tapes	1.9101-1
Merchant Marine and Fisheries Capital Construction Funds	3.2*

---

* These proposals (starting on page 64,378) amend regulations under Sec. 607 of the Merchant Marine Act, 1936, as amended.

Contributions to Candidates for Public Office

The following new sections are inserted immediately before § 1.46:

§ 1.41-1 (Proposed Treasury Decision, published 9-19-72.) **Credit for contributions to candidates for public office.**

(a) **In general**—(1) *Allowance of credit.* Subject to the limitations of subparagraph (2) of this paragraph, in the case of an individual who makes the election described in paragraph (c) of this section, there shall be allowed as a credit against the tax imposed by chapter 1 of the Code for the taxable year an amount equal to one-half of all political contributions, payment of which is made by such individual within such taxable year. In no event shall a political contribution qualify for the credit allowed by section 41 and this section unless such contribution is actually paid by the taxpayer within the taxable year for which the taxpayer claims such credit. For purposes of the preceding sentence, the method of accounting employed by the taxpayer and the date on which such contribution is pledged shall be irrelevant. In the case of married individuals making a joint return, a political contribution made by either spouse shall qualify for the credit under section 41. In the case of married individuals making separate returns, the contributions must have been made by the spouse claiming the credit.

(2) **Limitations**—(i) *Maximum credit.* The credit allowed by subparagraph (1) of this paragraph for a taxable year shall not exceed $12.50 (or $25, in the case of married individuals making a joint return).

(ii) *Application with other credits.* In no event shall the credit allowed by subparagraph (1) of this paragraph exceed—

(a) The amount of the tax imposed by chapter 1 of the Code for the taxable year, reduced by

(b) The sum of the credits allowable under section 33 (relating to foreign tax credit), section 35 (relating to partially tax-exempt interest), section 37 (relating to retirement income), and section 38 (relating to investment in certain depreciable property) for such taxable year.

(iii) *Verification*—(a) *In general.* The credit allowed by subparagraph (1) of this paragraph shall be allowed, with respect to any contribution, only if the taxpayer can verify that a political contribution has in fact been paid. Such verification shall consist of a written receipt from the person to whom the contribution was paid. A cancelled check, the payee of which is an individual described in paragraph (b)(1)(ii) of this section or a committee, association, or organization described in paragraph (b)(1)(iii) of this section, will normally meet the requirement for a written receipt and be accepted as proof of payment. However, in determining if a political contribution has been made to an individual or to a committee, association, or organization described in paragraph (b)(1)(iii)(a) of this section, a taxpayer may in appropriate cases be required to present additional information regarding the qualification of the individual, committee, association, or organization, unless the taxpayer provides a special authorized receipt issued by the individual, committee, association, or organization. Such receipt shall contain the information and representations set forth in (b) of this subdivision and may be issued to the contributing taxpayer at the time his contribution is made or as soon thereafter as practical. A taxpayer is not required to identify on his income tax return the name of the candidate, or of the committee, association, or organization, to whom the contribution is made.

(b) *Authorized receipt.* The receipt referred to in (a) of this subdivision shall contain the following information and representations:

Proposed Reg. § 1.41-1

(1) In the case of a contribution to an individual described in paragraph (b)(1)(ii) of this section, the full name of such individual; or, in the case of a committee, association, or organization described in paragraph (b)(1)(iii)(a) of this section, the official name of such committee, association, or organization as recited on Form 4909;

(2) The amount of the contribution;

(3) The year in which the contribution was received by such individual or such committee, association, or organization;

(4) The name of the contributor;

(5) the particular nomination or election for which the contribution has been paid, by specifying—

(i) The specific public office for which such nomination or election is sought;

(ii) The year or years in which such nomination and (or) election will be (or was) held;

(iii) Whether such office is Federal, State, or local; and

(iv) If such office is State or local, the particular State or locality involved; and

(6) In the case of an individual described in paragraph (b)(1)(ii) of this section, that Form 4908 was or will be filed in the manner prescribed in paragraph (c)(1) of § 1.41-2; or, in the case of a committee, association, or organization described in paragraph (b)(1)(iii)(a) of this section, that Form 4909 was or will be filed in the manner prescribed in paragraph (c)(1) of § 1.41-2; and that the undertakings set forth in such form will be observed.

(c) Sample receipts. The following samples illustrate the type of forms which will be deemed to satisfy the requirements of (b) of this subdivision:

SAMPLE RECEIPT—INDIVIDUAL CANDIDATE

I, John Doe of Illinois, in connection with my campaign for nomination and election to the United States Senate in 1972:

(1) acknowledge receipt during 1972 of $_____ from _____, and

(2) declare that Internal Revenue Service Form 4908 was or will have been properly filed before the end of this calendar year, and that the undertakings in such form will be observed.

_____
John Doe

SAMPLE RECEIPT—CAMPAIGN COMMITTEE FOR NAMED CANDIDATES

The Illinois Committee for John Doe, for the nomination and election of John Doe to the United States Senate in 1972:

(1) acknowledges receipt during 1972 of $_____ from _____, and

(2) declares that Internal Revenue Service Form 4909 was or will have been properly filed before the end of this calendar year, and that the undertakings in such form will be observed.

The Illinois Committee for John Doe

By _____
Authorized Agent

SAMPLE RECEIPT—CAMPAIGN COMMITTEE FOR MULTIPLE CANDIDATES

The Illinois Committee for an Effective Congress, for the nomination and election of certain individuals to the Congress of the United States in 1972:

(1) acknowleges receipt during 1972 of $——— from ——————, and

(2) declares that Internal Revenue Service Form 4909 was or will have been properly filed before the end of this calendar year, and that the undertakings in such form will be observed.

Illinois Committee for an Effective Congress

By ——————————
Authorized Agent

SAMPLE RECEIPT—CAMPAIGN COMMITTEE FOR MULTIPLE CANDIDATES IN MORE THAN ONE STATE

The Illinois Committee for Good Government, for the nomination and election of certain individuals to Federal, State, or local elective public offices in 1972:

(1) acknowledges receipt during 1972 of $——— from ——————, and

(2) declares that Internal Revenue Service Form 4909 was or will have been properly filed before the end of this calendar year, and that the undertakings in such form will be observed.

Illinois Committee for Good Government

By ——————————
Authorized Agent

(3) **Illustrations.** The application of this paragraph may be illustrated by the following examples:

Example (1). Assume that A, an unmarried individual, makes a political contribution of $10 for his taxable year ending on December 31, 1972. Assume, further, that A's total tax liability for such taxable year is $100, and that A has no allowable credit under section 33, 35, 37, or 38. Under the provisions of subparagraph (1) of this paragraph, A is allowed a credit against tax for such taxable year equal to 50 percent of the amount of such contribution, or $5.

Example (2). Assume the facts as stated in example (1), except that A makes a political contribution of $30 for his taxable year ending on December 31, 1972. Since an amount equal to 50 percent of the amount of such contribution (i.e., $15) exceeds the maximum allowable amount under subparagraph (2)(i) of this paragraph, A is allowed a credit against tax for such taxable year equal to such maximum allowable amount, or $12.50.

Example (3). Assume the facts as stated in example (1), except that A's total tax liability for the taxable year is, when reduced by the retirement income credit under section 37, equal to $3. Since an amount equal to 50 percent of the amount of such contribution (i.e., $5) exceeds the maximum allowable amount under subparagraph (2)(ii) of this paragraph (i.e., A's total tax liability for the taxable year, reduced by the sum of the credits allowable under sections 33, 35, 37, and 38), A is allowed a credit against tax for such taxable year equal to such maximum allowable amount, or $3.

Example (4). Assume that H and W, married individuals, make a joint return for their taxable year ending on December 31, 1972, and that H makes a political contribution of $50 for such taxable year. Assume, further, that the joint tax liability of H and W for such taxable year is $100 and that H and W have no allowable credit under section 33, 35, 37, or 38. Under the provisions of subpara-

Proposed Reg. §1.41-1

graph (1) of this paragraph, H and W are allowed a credit against tax for such taxable year equal to 50 percent of the amount of the contribution, or $25.

Example (5). Assume the facts as stated in example (4), except that H and W make separate returns for their taxable year ending on December 31, 1972. Assume, further, that H's total tax liability for such taxable year is $75, and that H has no allowable credit under section 33, 35, 37, or 38. Since H made the political contribution, only H may claim a credit for such contribution under section 41. In addition, since an amount equal to 50 percent of the amount of such contribution (i.e., $25) exceeds the maximum allowable amount under subparagraph (2)(i) of this paragraph, H is allowed a credit against tax for such taxable year equal to such maximum allowable amount, or $12.50.

(b) Definitions—(1) Political contribution—(i) In general. (a) For purposes of sections 41 and 218 and subject to the provisions of § 1.41-2, the term "political contribution" means any contribution, or gift, of money to one or more of the individuals described in subdivision (ii), or of the committees, associations, or organizations described in subdivision (iii), of this subparagraph.

(b) The term also includes any amount paid for the purchase of a ticket to a political dinner or function, provided that such dinner or function—

(1) In the case of a political dinner or function by or on behalf of an individual described in subdivision (ii) of this subparagraph or a committee, association, or organization described in subdivision (iii)(a) of this subparagraph, is clearly in the context of the campaign of one or more individuals who have qualified as candidates under subparagraph (2) of this paragraph by the end of the calendar year in which such ticket is purchased, and

(2) Is not primarily a device to confer private benefits in the form of meals or entertainment to the contributor. Ordinarily, a dinner or function which is incidental to the essentially political nature of the event in connection with which such dinner or function occurs will not be considered primarily a device to confer private benefits in the form of meals or entertainment to the contributor.

(c) If a political dinner or function is primarily a device to confer private benefits in the form of meals or entertainment to the contributor, then the term "political contribution" includes only the excess of the amount paid for a ticket to such dinner or function over the fair market value of all of the privileges and benefits received or receivable by the contributor as consideration for the amount paid. A reasonable, good faith estimate of the fair market value of such privileges and benefits will ordinarily be accepted for purposes of making such determination.

(d) Notwithstanding the preceding provisions of this subdivision, the term "political contribution" does not include—

(1) A contribution, or gift, of property or services;

(2) Any amount paid for a raffle ticket purchased in connection with a political campaign; or

(3) Except as provided in section 276(c) and the regulations thereunder, any amount paid for the purchase of advertising in a publication of an individual described in subdivision (ii) of this subparagraph, or of a committee, association, or organization described in subdivision (iii) of this subparagraph.

(ii) Individuals. An individual described in subdivision (i) of this subparagraph is an individual who is a candidate for nomination or election to any Federal, State, or local elective public office in any primary, general, or special election, but only if the contribution or gift is to be used by him to further his candidacy for nomination or election to that office.

(iii) Committees, associations, or organizations. A committee, association, or organization described in subdivision (i) of this subparagraph is—

(a) Any committee, association, or organization (whether or not incorporated) organized and operated exclusively for the purpose of influencing, or attempting to influence, the nomination or election of one or more individuals who are candidates for nomination or election to any Federal, State, or local elective public office, but only if the contribution or gift is to be used by such committee, association, or organization to further the candidacy of such individual or individuals for nomination or election to that office;

(b) The national committee of a national political party;

(c) The State committee of a national political party as designated by the national committee of such party; and

(d) The one local committee of each local unit of a national political party, as designated by the State committee of such party designated under (c) of this subdivision.

(iv) Limitation on committee activity. (a) A contribution or gift to a committee, association, or organization described in subdivision (iii)(a) of this subparagraph will not qualify as a political contribution if such committee, association, or organization has to any extent any purpose in addition to, or other than, the purpose of furthering the candidacy of an individual or individuals for nomination or election to a Federal, State, or local elective public office in a primary, general, or special election. Thus, for example, a contribution to a political action committee which engages in general political, educational, or legislative activities will not qualify as a political contribution.

(b) A committee, association, or organization described in subdivision (iii)(a) of this subparagraph may be run in conjunction with a political action committee, but contributions to the committee, association, or organization described in such subdivision may qualify as political contributions only if they are received directly from individual taxpayers and not from the political action committee. Contributions made by individual taxpayers to a political action committee will not qualify as political contributions even if such contributions are later contributed by the political action committee to a committee, association, or organization described in subdivision (iii)(a) of this subparagraph.

(c) If an organization which engages in general political, educational, or legislative activities operates a division which is organized and operated exclusively for the purpose of furthering the candidacy of an individual or individuals for nomination or election to a Federal, State, or local elective public office, contributions to such division may qualify as political contributions, provided that such division is, in fact, operated separately. If a labor union, business league, corporation, or other organization operates a fund or division organized and operated exclusively for the purpose of furthering the candidacy of an individual or individuals for nomination or election to a Federal, State, or local elective public office, contributions to such fund or division may qualify as political contributions, provided that such fund or division is, in fact, operated separately.

(d) Contributions to a campaign committee organized for the purpose of supporting candidates both currently and in the future, such as a congressional campaign committee, or organized for the purpose of supporting candidacies which qualify, and candidacies which do not qualify, under subparagraph (2) of this paragraph will qualify as political contributions if the requirements set forth in this section and § 1.41-2 are otherwise satisfied.

(2) **Candidate.** (i) For purposes of sections 41 and 218, the term "candidate" means, with respect to any Federal, State, or local elective public office, an individual who—

(a) Has publicly announced that he is a candidate for nomination or election to such office, and

(b) Meets the qualifications prescribed by law to hold such office.

(ii) An individual shall be considered to have made a public announcement of candidacy only if he makes a positive statement, rendered publicly, that he intends to seek nomination or election to the specified Federal, State, or local elective public office. It is not necessary that he make such statement in the State or district where he will seek nomination or election; nor is it necessary that he make the statement at a formal press conference. A qualifying announcement would be one, for example, which is made by way of an announcement on

Proposed Reg. § 1.41-1

television or radio or by way of a news release or announcement. Incumbency in the office for which an individual is seeking nomination or re-election will not of itself constitute a public announcement that he is a candidate for such nomination or re-election.

(iii) In the case of a candidate who seeks nomination for one office but ultimately runs for another, such as, for example, a candidate for President of the United States who is ultimately slated as the party nominee for Vice President, it will not be necessary to distinguish between contributions made in connection with seeking the nomination for President and contributions made in connection with the final election for Vice President. The entire activity will be treated as a single candidacy.

(3) **National political party.** For purposes of sections 41 and 218, the term "national political party" means—

(i) In the case of contributions made during a taxable year of the taxpayer in which the electors of President and Vice President of the United States are chosen, a political party presenting candidates or electors for such offices on the official election or ballot of ten or more States, or

(ii) In the case of contributions made during any other taxable year of the taxpayer, a political party which met the qualifications described in subdivision (i) of this subparagraph in the last preceding election of a President and Vice President of the United States.

(4) **State and local.** For purposes of sections 41 and 218—

(i) The term "State" means the various States and the District of Columbia, and

(ii) The term "local" means a political subdivision of a State or part of such subdivision, or two or more political subdivisions of a State or parts of such subdivisions.

(5) **Elective public office.** For purposes of sections 41 and 218, the term "elective public office" includes any office election to which requires solicitation of votes from the general public. However, such term does not include any office or position in any national, State, or local political party or similar organization, or membership in the electoral college for election of the President and Vice President of the United States.

(c) **Election to take credit.** A taxpayer may not be allowed the credit provided by section 41 and this section unless he elects to take such credit for the taxable year in which the political contributions are paid. The taxpayer shall signify on his return his election to take the credit by claiming the credit on such return instead of itemizing any deduction otherwise allowed under section 218 for such contributions for such taxable year.

(d) **Restrictions**—(1) **In general.** The credit provided by section 41 and this section may be elected only by an individual taxpayer, and not, for example, by any corporation, association, company, organization, estate, or trust. However, pursuant to section 703(b) such credit may be elected by a partnership in connection with any political contribution made by such partnership; the credit so elected shall apply to each partner's distributive share of such contribution.

(2) **Cross-reference.** For provisions relating to the disallowance to estates and trusts of the credit provided by section 41 and this section, see section 642 (a)(3).

(e) **Effective date.** The provisions of section 41 and this section apply to taxable years ending after December 31, 1971, but only with respect to political contributions, payment of which is made after such date.

§ 1.41-2 (Proposed Treasury Decision, published 9-19-72.) **Restrictions applicable to certain contributions.**

(a) **Application of section.** This section provides certain limitations which must be applied only in the case of contributions or gifts to individual candidates described in section 41(c)(1)(A) and subdivision (ii) of § 1.41-1(b)(1) and to committees, associations, or organizations described in sections 41(c)(1)(B) and subdivision (iii)(a) of § 1.41-1(b)(1). For purposes of this section, such a candidate is referred to as an "individual" and such a committee, association, or organization is referred to as a "campaign committee."

(b) **Time for qualification as a candidate.** A contribution or gift to an individual will not qualify as a political contribution unless he qualifies as a candidate under paragraph (b)(2) of § 1.41-1 by the end of the calendar year in which the contribution or gift is made. A contribution or gift to a campaign committee will not qualify as a political contribution unless the individual or individuals for whose candidacy such contribution or gift is to be used qualifies as a candidate under paragraph (b)(2) of § 1.41-1 by the end of the calendar year in which the contribution or gift is made. To qualify as political contributions, it is not necessary that contributions made to further the nomination or election of an individual who has qualified as a candidate under paragraph (b)(2) of § 1.41-1 be made before the election for which such individual is a candidate. Once the individual has qualified as a candidate, he remains a qualified candidate for the specific election involved with respect to contributions made to meet the cost of that election irrespective of when the contributions are made. Thus, if an individual who qualified as a candidate in 1972 and was elected to public office in that year sustains a campaign deficit with respect to that election, contributions to satisfy such deficit which are made in 1973 to such individual, or to a campaign committee organized and operated to further the candidacy of such individual for election to that office, may qualify as political contributions.

(c) **Requirement for filing of report**—(1) **In general.** A contribution or gift to an individual or to a campaign committee will not qualify as a political contribution unless such individual or committee makes a report on the form prescribed by subparagraph (2) or (3) of this paragraph with the service center designated in the instructions to such form. The form must be filed for each calendar year with respect to all political contributions received during the calendar year and must be filed before the end of such calendar year. The report made by an individual must be signed by him or an authorized agent; the report made by a campaign committee must be signed by an officer or authorized agent of the committee. No report is required to be made for a calendar year during which no contributions are received. For penalty for false, fraudulent, or fictitious statements see 18 U.S.C. 1001.

(2) **Form 4908 for individuals.** The report to be made by an individual shall be on Form 4908 and shall contain the following information and representations:

(i) The individual's name, address, and social security number;

(ii) The year or years in which the nomination and (or) election is to be or was held;

(iii) The specific public office involved and, if such office is not a Federal office, the particular State or locality involved;

(iv) That he is (or was, if the date of voting has occurred) a candidate for such office within the meaning of § 1.41-1(b)(2);

(v) That he had publicly announced his candidacy by the end of the calendar year for which such form is filed;

(vi) That all contributions received by him constituting restricted amounts (as defined in paragraph (d)(1) of this section) will be expended only as provided in paragraph (d)(4) or (6) of this section;

(vii) That he will maintain records adequate to identify such contributions and expenditures; and

(viii) That he will file with the Internal Revenue Service such further information as the Internal Revenue Service may require.

(3) **Form 4909 for committees.** The report to be made by a campaign committee shall be made on Form 4909 and shall contain the following information and representations:

Proposed Reg. § 1.41-2

(i) The committee's official name, address, and employer identification number;

(ii) The year or years in which the nomination and (or) election is to be or was held;

(iii) The specific public office involved and, if such office is not a Federal office, the particular State or locality involved;

(iv) If more than one individual who is a candidate is being supported by such committee, a schedule listing the names of such individuals and the offices for which they are candidates;

(v) That all contributions constituting restricted amounts (as defined in paragraph (d)(1) of this section) and received by it during the year for which such report is filed will be expended only as provided in paragraph (d)(4) or (6) of this section and will be used solely on behalf of individuals who by the end of such year have filed Form 4908;

(vi) That it will maintain records adequate to identify such contributions and expenditures; and

(vii) That it will be file with the Internal Revenue Service such further information as the Internal Revenue Service may require.

(d) Expenditure of political contributions—(1) Restricted amounts. For purposes of this section, the term "restricted amount" means every contribution or gift qualifying as a political contribution without regard to this paragraph and received during a calendar year by an individual or by a campaign committee which—

(i) Is paid by an individual taxpayer and—

(a) Does not exceed the amount of $100, or

(b) Exceeds the amount of $100, but only to the extent such contribution or gift does not exceed $100; or

(ii) Is paid by a campaign committee from restricted amounts of such committee.

(2) Unrestricted amounts. For purposes of this section, the term "unrestricted amount" means every contribution or gift received during a calendar year by an individual or by a campaign committee which—

(i) Constitutes a contribution or gift not described in subparagraph (1) of this paragraph, or

(ii) Is accounted for pursuant to procedures approved in advance by the Commissioner of Internal Revenue as being adequate to ensure that taxpayers will not claim a credit under section 41, or a deduction under section 218, with respect to such contribution or gift.

Any request for approval of procedures described in subdivision (ii) of this subparagraph must be made by submitting a letter, setting forth sufficient facts and circumstances, to the Commissioner of Internal Revenue, Attention: Income Tax Division, Washington, D.C. 20224.

(3) Record-keeping requirement. All individuals and campaign committees are required to maintain records adequate to identify restricted and unrestricted amounts described in subparagraphs (1) and (2) of this paragraph.

(4) Limitation on use of restricted amounts—(i) In general. Restricted amounts described in subparagraph (1) of this paragraph may be used only to satisfy expenditures incurred to further the candidacy of one or more individuals for nomination or election to the Federal, State, or local elective public office in the primary, general, or special election involved, provided that such expenditures are incurred during a calendar year in which such individual or individuals qualify as candidates under paragraph (b)(2) of § 1.41-1 or are incurred after the campaign in respect of which such individual or individuals are candidates and are directly related to the campaign. A campaign committee may use restricted amounts to satisfy expenditures incurred to further the candidacy of one or more individuals for nomination or election to the Federal, State, or local elective public office in the primary, general, or special election involved by making contributions for such purpose to an individual or individuals who qualify as candidates under paragraph (b)(2) of § 1.41-1 by the end of the calendar year in which such amounts are received from taxpayers or to another campaign committee which uses such contributions for an individual or individuals who so qualify.

(ii) *Qualifying expenditures defined.* (a) Expenditures incurred to further the candidacy of an individual for nomination or election to any Federal, State, or local elective public office in any primary, general, or special election include all expenditures incurred in the context of the political campaign, such as expenses for return trips home in connection with the actual campaign, expenses incurred in raising political contributions, expenses incurred for research and polling in connection with the campaign, expenses incurred to administer the campaign committee, and other general administrative expenses of the campaign.

(b) Expenses incurred in connection with a political dinner or function, such as hall rental, salaries, advertising costs, printing of tickets, and cost of food and beverages, are also included as qualifying expenditures under (a) of this subdivision if such dinner or function is given in the clear setting of the political campaign with a view to raising campaign funds for one or more individuals who qualify as candidates under paragraph (b)(2) of § 1.41-1.

(c) Any expenditure incurred by an individual who qualifies as a candidate under paragraph (b)(2) of § 1.41-1, or by a campaign committee supporting the candidacy of such an individual, which is in good faith determined by such individual or committee to be directly related to his campaign for nomination or election to the Federal, State, or local elective public office for which he is a candidate shall be presumed to be an expenditure to further his candidacy for such nomination or election.

(d) That part of the expenses incurred by a campaign committee which is incurred on behalf of one or more individuals who do not qualify as candidates under paragraph (b)(2) of § 1.41-1 must be expended from unrestricted amounts described in subparagraph (2) of this paragraph.

(e) The application of this subdivision may be illustrated by the following examples:

Example (1). C is a Congressman in the U.S. House of Representatives. In 1973, C qualifies as a candidate under § 1.41-1(b)(2) for reelection to the same office in November of 1974. In March of 1974, C travels to his home jurisdiction to confer with his constituency. C in good faith determines that the expenses incurred in connection with the trip are directly related to his campaign for re-election to the House of Representatives. Therefore, such expenses are presumed to be expenditures to further C's candidacy for re-election to that office.

Example (2). Assume the same facts as in example (1), except that for each month of 1974, C publishes and distributes to his constituency a newsletter describing his activities in the House of Representatives. C in good faith determines that the expenses incurred in connection with the newsletter are not directly related to his campaign for re-election to the House of Representatives. Accordingly, such expenses are not presumed to be expenditures to further C's candidacy for re-election to that office.

Example (3). Assume the same facts as in example (1), except that the expenses related to C's trip to his home jurisdiction are incurred before his qualification as a candidate under § 1.41-1(b)(2) for re-election to the House of Representatives in 1974. Accordingly, such expenses are not presumed to be expenditures to further C's candidacy for re-election to that office.

(5) **Determination of proper use.** In applying subparagraph (4)(i) of this paragraph, restricted amounts will be deemed to have been used for any calendar year for purposes specified in such subparagraph to the extent of the total of all expenditures incurred during such year by the individual or the campaign committee for purposes specified in such subparagraph.

(6) **Unexpired restricted amounts.** (i) That portion of the restricted amounts of an individual which is not used as provided in subparagraph (4)(i) of this paragraph may be retained by such individual at the end of the political campaign and be used in accordance with such subparagraph the next time such

individual is a candidate within the meaning of § 1.41-1(b)(2) for the same office in respect of which such portion was contributed.

(ii) That portion of the restricted amounts of a campaign committee which is not used as provided in subparagraph (4)(i) of this paragraph may be retained by such committee at the end of the political campaign and be used in accordance with such subparagraph on behalf of any individuals who qualified as candidates under paragraph (b)(2) of § 1.41-1 by the end of the calendar year in which such portion was contributed and are again candidates within the meaning of such paragraph for the same office in respect of which such portion was contributed.

(iii) That portion of the restricted amounts of an individual or campaign committee which is not used as provided in subparagraph (4)(i) of this paragraph and may not be used as provided in subdivision (i) or (ii) of this subparagraph will constitute unexpended restricted amounts and must be either—

(a) Paid to a national, State, or local committee described in subdivision (iii)(b), (c), or (d) of § 1.41-1(b)(1), or

(b) Deposited in the general fund of the U.S. Treasury or of any State or local government.

Investment Credit

Section 1.46-1 is amended by revising paragraph (c) to read as follows:

§ 1.46-1 (Proposed Treasury Decision, published 12-30-70.) Determination of amount.

* * * * * * * * * *

(c) Liability for tax. For the purpose of computing the limitation based on the amount of tax, section 46(a)(3) defines the liability for tax as the income tax imposed for the taxable year by chapter 1 (including the 2-percent tax on consolidated taxable income imposed with respect to taxable years beginning before January 1, 1964, and the 6 percent additional tax imposed by section 1562(b) with respect to taxable years ending after December 31, 1963), reduced by the sum of the credits allowable under—

(1) Section 33 (relating to taxes of foreign countries and possessions of United States),

(2) Section 34 (relating to dividends received by individuals before January 1, 1965),

(3) Section 35 (relating to partially tax-exempt interest received by individuals), and

(4) Section 37 (relating to retirement income).

For purposes of this paragraph, the tax imposed by section 56 (relating to minimum tax for tax preferences), section 531 (relating to imposition of accumulated earnings tax), section 541 (relating to imposition of personal holding company tax), or section 1378 (relating to tax on certain capital gains of subchapter S corporations) and any additional tax imposed for the taxable year by section 1351(d)(1) (relating to recoveries of foreign expropriation losses), shall not be considered tax imposed by chapter 1. Thus, the liability for tax and the credit allowed by section 38 for the taxable year are determined before computing any tax imposed by section 56, 531, 541, or 1378 and any additional tax imposed for the taxable year by section 1351(d)(1). In addition, any increase in tax resulting from the application of section 47 (relating to certain dispositions, etc., of section 38 property) shall not be treated as tax imposed by chapter 1 for purposes of computing the liability for tax. See section 47(c).

* * * * * * * * * *

Section 1.46-1 is amended by revising paragraph (c) to read as follows:

§ 1.46-1 (Proposed Treasury Decision, published 4-21-75) Determination of amount.

* * * * * * * * * *

(c) Liability for tax. For the purpose of computing the limitation based on the amount of tax, section 46(a)(3) defines the liability for tax as the income (2 imposed for the taxable year by chapter 1 (including the 2-percent tax on consolidated taxable income imposed with respect to taxable years beginning before January 1, 1964, and the 6-percent additional tax imposed by section 1562(b) with respect to taxable years ending after December 31, 1963), reduced by the sum of the credits allowable under—

(1) Section 33 (relating to taxes of foreign countries and possessions of the United States),

(2) Section 34 (relating to dividends received by individuals before January 1, 1965),

(3) Section 35 (relating to partially tax-exempt interest received by individuals), and

(4) Section 37 (relating to retirement income).

For purposes of this paragraph, the tax imposed by section 56 (relating to minimum tax for tax preferences), section 72(m)(5)(B) (relating to 10 percent tax on premature distributions to owner-employees), section 402(e) (relating to tax on lump-sum distributions), section 408(f) (relating to additional tax on income from certain retirement accounts), section 531 (relating to imposition of accumulated earnings tax), section 541 (relating to imposition of personal holding company tax) or section 1378 (relating to tax on certain capital gains of subchapter S corporations) and any additional tax imposed for the taxable year by section 1351(d)(1) (relating to recoveries of foreign expropriation losses) shall not be considered tax imposed by chapter 1. Thus, the liability for tax and the credit allowed by section 38 for the taxable year are determined before computing any tax imposed by section 56, 72(m)(5)(B), 402(e), 408(f), 531, 541, or 1378 and any additional tax imposed for the taxable year by section 1351(d)(1). In addition, any increase in tax resulting from the application of section 47 (relating to certain dispositions, etc., of section 38 property) shall not be treated as tax imposed by chapter 1 for purposes of computing the liability for tax. See section 47(c).

* * * * * * * * * *

Section 1.46-3 is amended by revising paragraph (g)(1) and (2) to read as follows:

§ **1.46-3** (Proposed Treasury Decision, published 2-17-72.) **Qualified investment.**

(g) Public utility property—(1) In general. In the case of section 38 property which is public utility property and which is described in section 50, the amount of the qualified investment with respect to such property shall be 4/7 of the amount otherwise determined under this section with respect to such property. In the case of all other section 38 property which is public utility property, the amount of the qualified investment with respect to such property shall be 3/7 of the amount otherwise determined under this section with respect to such property.

(2) Definition. (i) The term "public utility property" means property used predominantly in the trade or business of the furnishing or sale of—

(a) Electrical energy, water, or sewage disposal services,

(b) Gas through a local distribution system, or

(c) Telephone service, telegraph service by means of domestic telegraph operations (as defined in section 222(a)(5) of the Communications Act of 1934, as amended; 47 U.S.C., sec. 222(a)(5)), or, in the case of property described in section 50, other communication services (other than international telegraph service),

if the rates for such furnishing or sale, as the case may be, are regulated, i.e., have been established or approved by a regulatory body described in section 46(c)(3)(B). The term "regulatory body described in section 46(c)(3)(B)" means a State (including the District of Columbia) or political subdivision thereof, an agency or instrumentality of the United States, or a public service or public utility commission or other body of any State or political subdivision thereof similar to such a commission. The term "established or approved" includes the filing of a schedule of rates with a regulatory body which has the power to approve such rates, even though such body has taken no action on the filed schedule or generally leaves undisturbed rates filed by the taxpayer involved.

(ii) (a) In the case of property described in section 50, the term "public utility property" also means nonregulated communication property which is used

Proposed Reg. § 1.46-3

predominantly for communication purposes, if it is clearly of the type ordinarily used to provide regulated telephone or microwave communication services to which subdivision (i) (c) of this subparagraph applies. The determination whether nonregulated communication property is clearly of such type must be made on the basis of the facts and circumstances of each particular case including, for example, the state of technology and pattern of ratemaking by regulatory bodies in the communications industry.

(b) Examples of nonregulated communication property which qualifies as public utility property under (a) of this subdivision are microwave transmission equipment, private communication equipment (other than land mobile radio equipment for which the operator must obtain a license from the Federal Communications Commission), private switchboard (PBX) equipment, communications terminal equipment connected to telephone networks, data transmission equipment, and communications satellites. Examples of nonregulated communications property which does not so qualify during 1972 are computer terminals or facsimile reproduction equipment which is connected to telephone lines to transmit data. For purposes of this subdivision (ii), the term communication property does not include office furniture, stands for communication property, tools, repair vehicles, and similar property even if exclusively used in providing nonregulated telephone or microwave communications services.

(iii) For purposes of this paragraph, the term "public utility activity" means any activity described in subdivision (i) of this subparagraph, which is regulated in a manner described in such subdivision, and any activity described in subdivision (ii) of this subparagraph, but only if the property used in such activity is considered "public utility property" under such subdivision. If property is used by a taxpayer both in a public utility activity and in another activity, the characterization of such property shall be based on the predominant use of such property during the taxable year in which it is placed in service.

* * * * * * * * * * * *

The following new section is added immediately after § 1.46-4:

§ 1.46-5 (Proposed Treasury Decision, published 2-17-72.) **Limitation in case of certain regulated companies.**

(a) **In general—(1) Disallowance.** Under section 46(e), no credit shall be allowed by section 38 in certain cases with respect to certain regulated public utility property referred to as "section 46(e) property". For purposes of this section, the term "section 46(e) property" is defined in paragraph (b)(1) of this section. Section 46(e)(4) and paragraph (f) of this section refer to circumstances under which a regulatory body may put into effect a determination which will result in the disallowance of the credit otherwise allowable under section 38. Such a determination will result in a disallowance of the credit otherwise allowable under section 38 only if paragraph (1) or (2) of section 46(e) applies to such property and such determination affects the taxpayer's cost of service or rate base in a manner which is inconsistent with paragraph (1) or (2) (whichever is applicable) of section 46(e). Under the provisions of paragraph (1) of section 46(e), in general, the credit allowable by section 38 may not be flowed through to income but in certain circumstances may be used to reduce rate base (provided that such reduction is restored not less rapidly than ratably). If an election is made under paragraph (2) of section 46(e), in general, such credit may be flowed through to income (but not more rapidly than ratably) and there shall not be any reduction in rate base. If an election is made under paragraph (3) of section 46(e), none of the limitations of paragraph (1) or (2) of that section apply to certain section 46(e) property of the taxpayer. For rules as to the manner of making on or before March 9, 1972, the 3 elections enumerated in section 46(e), see paragraph (h) of this section. For rules with respect to the treatment of corporate reorganizations, asset acquisitions, and taxpayers subject to the jurisdiction of more than one regulatory body, etc., see paragraph (j) of this section.

(2) **Nonapplication of prior law.** Under section 105(e) of the Revenue Act of 1971, section 203(e) of the Revenue Act of 1964, 78 Stat. 35, shall not apply to section 46(e) property.

(b) **Definitions—(1) Section 46(e) property.** "Section 46(e) property" is section 38 property which is both property described in section 50 and is—

(i) Public utility property within the meaning of section 46(c)(3)(b) (other than nonregulated communication property of the type described in paragraph (g)(2)(ii) of § 1.46-3), or

(ii) Property used predominantly in the trade or business of the furnishing or sale of

(a) steam through a local distribution system or

(b) the transportation of gas or steam by pipeline, if the rates for such furnishing or sale are established or approved by a regulatory body described in section 46(c)(3)(B).

For purposes of determining whether property is used predominantly in the trade or business of transportation of gas by pipeline (or of transportation of gas by pipeline and of furnishing or sale of gas through a local distribution system), the rules prescribed in paragraph (g)(4) of § 1.46-3 apply except that accounts 365 through 371, inclusive (Transmission Plant), shall be added to the accounts enumerated in subdivision (i) of such paragraph (g)(4).

(2) Cost of service. (i) In determining whether or to what extent a credit allowable under section 38 (determined without regard to section 46(e)) reduces cost of service, reference shall be made to any accounting treatment that can affect cost of service. Examples of such treatment are reducing by all or a portion of such credit the amount of Federal income tax taken into account in computing the taxpayer's cost of service, reducing the depreciable bases of property by such credit for ratemaking purposes, and (for purposes of paragraph (2) of section 46(e)) requiring either such treatment on the taxpayer's regulated books of account.

(ii) For purposes of this section, a reduction in the taxpayer's rate base will be deemed not to result in a reduction in such taxpayer's cost of service for ratemaking purposes even though as a technical ratemaking term "cost of service" may include the cost of common stock investment, that is, the cost of capital rate assigned to such investment, multiplied by the amount of the investment.

(3) Rate base. For purposes of this section, the term "rate base" means the base to which the taxpayer's rate of return for ratemaking purposes is applied (i.e., the monetary amount which is used as the divisor in calculating rate of return or the amount which is multiplied by the fair rate of return to determine the allowable return in the fixing of rate levels). In determining whether or to what extent a credit allowed under section 38 (determined without regard to section 46(e)) reduces the rate base, reference shall be made to any accounting treatment of such credit that can affect the taxpayer's permitted profit on investment. Thus, for example, assigning a "cost of capital" rate to the amount of such credit which is less than the permissible overall rate of return (determined without regard to the credit) would be treated as, in effect, a rate base adjustment. What is the overall rate of return depends upon the practice of the regulatory body. Thus, for example, an overall rate of return may be a rate determined on the basis of an average or weighted average of allowable rates of return on investments by common stockholders, preferred stockholders, and creditors.

(c) General rule—(1) In general. Paragraph (1) of section 46(e) shall apply to all of the taxpayer's section 46(e) property except as otherwise provided in this section in cases where the taxpayer has made an election under paragraph (2) or (3) of section 46(e) in the manner prescribed in paragraph (h) of this section. Under paragraph (1) of section 46(e), the credit allowable by section 38 (determined without regard to section 46(e)) shall not be allowed with respect to the taxpayer's section 46(e) property if—

(i) its cost of service for ratemaking purposes is reduced by reason of any portion of such credit, or

(ii) (a) its rate base is reduced by reason of any portion of the credit and (b) such reduction in rate base is not restored or is restored less rapidly than ratably within the meaning of paragraph (g) of this section.

(2) Insufficient natural domestic supply. (i) The provisions of subparagraph (1)(ii)(b) of this paragraph shall not apply with respect to the taxpayer's "short supply property" if the taxpayer makes an election under the last sentence of paragraph (1) of section 46(e) on or before March 9, 1972, in the manner prescribed in paragraph (h) of this section. For purposes of this section, the term "short supply property" means section 46(e) property if—

Proposed Reg. § 1.46-5

(a) such property is used by the taxpayer predominantly in the trade or business of the furnishing or sale of steam through a local distribution system or transportation of gas or steam by pipeline,

(b) such gas or steam is a natural domestic product,

(c) the regulatory body described in section 46(c)(3)(B) having jurisdiction for ratemaking purposes with respect to such trade or busines is an agency or instrumentality of the United States, and

(d) such agency or instrumentality of the United States publishes in the Federal Register a determination that the natural domestic supply of gas or steam is insufficient to meet the present and future requirements of the domestic economy and such determination is in effect (within the meaning of subdivision (ii) of this subparagraph) on the date that such property is placed in service.

(ii) If a determination described in (d) of subdivision (i) of this subparagraph is made—

(a) on or before [90 days after publication in the Federal Register of permanent regulations under section 46(e)], such determination shall be considered to be in effect with respect to section 46(e) property placed in service at any time prior to the date that a revocaton of such determination is published in the Federal Register, or

(b) after [90 days after publication in the Federal Register of permanent regulations under section 46(e)], such determination shall be considered to be in effect for a period beginning on the date that such determination is published in the Federal Register and ending on the date that a revocation of such determination is published in the Federal Register.

Thus, for example, if on or before [90 days after the date of publication in the Federal Register of permanent regulations under section 46(e)] the Federal Power Commission publishes such a determination with respect to the natural domestic supply of gas, and if the taxpayer properly made an election under the last sentence of paragraph (1) of section 46(e), then, with respect to the taxpayer's short-supply property placed in service on or before [such 90th day], no credit will be allowable under section 38 if the Federal Power Commission requires the taxpayer to reduce its rate base by any portion of the credit allowable by section 38 (determined without regard to section 46(e)) with respect to section 46(e) property used predominantly in the taxpayer's business of furnishing or selling the transportation by pipeline of gas which is a natural domestic product whether or not there is a restoration to rate base.

(d) *Special rule for ratable flow-through.* If an election is made under paragraph (2) of section 46(e) on or before March 9, 1972, in the manner prescribed in paragraph (h) of this section, such paragraph (2) shall apply to all of the taxpayer's section 46(e) property except as otherwise provided in paragrah (h) of this section with respect to an election under paragraph (3) of section 46(e). Under paragraph (2) of section 46(e), the credit allowable by section 38 (determined without regard to section 46(e) shall not be allowed with respect to the taxpayer's section 46(e) property if—

(1) its cost of service for ratemaking purposes or in its regulated books of account is reduced by more than a ratable portion of such credit, or

(2) the taxpayer's rate base is reduced by reason of any portion of such credit.

(e) *Flow-through property.* If a taxpayer makes an election under paragraph (3) of section 46(e) on or before March 9, 1972, in the manner prescribed by paragraph (h) of this section, paragraph (1) and (2) of section 46(e) shall not apply to the taxpayer's section 46(e) property to which section 167(1)(2)(C) applies. Under such election, the credit is allowable under section 38 notwithstanding any determination by a regulatory body having jurisdiction over such taxpayer requiring that such credit be taken into account by adjusting in any manner the taxpayer's cost of service or rate base. In general, section 167(1)(2)(C) applies to property referred to as "post-1969 public utility property" with respect to which a "flow-through method of accounting" within the meaning of section 167(1)(3)(H) is used to take into account the allowance for depreciation under section 167(a). For example, section 167(1)(2)(C) does not apply to property with respect to which an election under section 167(1)(4)(A) applies.

Thus, such property does not qualify for an election under paragraph (3) of section 46(e).

(f) **Limitations**—(1) **Disallowance postponed.** There shall be no disallowance of the credit otherwise allowable by section 38 until the first final determination inconsistent with paragraph (1) or (2) (as the case may be) of section 46(e) is put into effect with respect to the taxpayer's section 46(e) property.

(2) **Conditions for disallowance.** Paragraph (1) or (2) (as the case may be) of section 46(e) shall apply to disallow the credit with respect to section 46(e) property placed in service (within the meaning of paragraph (d) of § 1.46-3) by the taxpayer—

(i) before the date that the first final inconsistent determination, or a subsequent inconsistent determination (whether or not final), is put into effect, and

(ii) On or after such date and before the date that a subsequent determination consistent with paragraph (1) or (2) (as the case may be) of section 46(e) (whether or not final) is thereafter put into effect.

No amount of credit for a taxable year shall be disallowed under this subparagraph if for such year assessment of a deficiency is barred by any law or rule of law.

(3) **Notification and other requirements.** The taxpayer shall notify the district director of a disallowance of a credit under subparagraph (2) of this paragraph within 30 days of the date that the applicable determination is put into effect. In the case of such a disallowance, the taxpayer shall recompute its tax liability for any affected taxable year and such recomputation shall be made in the form of an amended return where necessary.

(4) **Credit.** As used in this paragraph, the term "credit" refers to a credit allowable by section 38 (determined without regard to section 46(e)).

(5) **Determinations.** For purposes of this paragraph, the term "determination" refers to determination made with respect to section 46(e) property (other than property to which an election under paragraph (3) of section 46(e) applies) by a regulatory body described in section 46(c)(3)(B) which determines the effect of the credit—

(i) For purposes of paragraph (1) of section 46(e), on the taxpayer's cost of service or rate base for ratemaking purposes, or

(ii) In the case of a taxpayer which made an election under paragraph (2) of section 46(e), (a) on its cost of service for ratemaking purposes or in its regulated books of account or (b) on its rate base for ratemaking purposes.

(6) **Types of determinations.** For purposes of this paragraph, the term—

(i) "Inconsistent" in reference to a determination refers to a determination which is inconsistent with paragraph (1) or (2) (as the case may be) of section 46(e). Thus, for example, a determination to reduce the taxpayer's cost of service by more than a ratable portion of the credit would be a determination which is inconsistent with such paragraph (1). For a further example, such a determination would also be inconsistent if such paragraph (2) applied because in such case no reduction in cost of service is permitted.

(ii) "Consistent" in reference to a determination refers to a determination which is consistent with such paragraph (1) or (2) (as the case may be).

(iii) "Final determination" means a determination with respect to which all rights to appeal or request a review, a rehearing, or a redetermination, have been exhausted or have lapsed.

(iv) "First final determination" means the first final determination put into effect after December 10, 1971.

(v) "Subsequent determination" is any determination put into effect after a first final determination.

(7) **Put into effect.** A determination is put into effect on the later of—

(i) The date it is issued (or, if a first final determination, the date it becomes final) or

(ii) The date it becomes operative.

(8) **Examples.** The provisions of this paragraph may be illustrated by the following examples:

Proposed Reg. § 1.46-5

Example (1). Corporation X, a calendar-year taxpayer engaged in a public utility activity is subject to the jurisdiction of regulatory body A. On September 15, 1971, X purchases section 46(e) property and places it in service on that date. For 1971, X takes the credit allowable by section 38 with respect to such property. X does not make any election permitted by section 46(e). On October 9, 1972, A makes a determination that X must account for the credit allowable by section 38 in a manner inconsistent with section 46(e)(1). The determination, which was the first determination by A after December 10, 1971, becomes final on January 1, 1973, and holds that X must retroactively adjust the manner in which it accounted for the credit allowable by section 38 starting with its taxable year which began on January 1, 1972. Since, under the provisions of subparagraph (7) of this paragraph, the determination by A is put into effect on January 1, 1973 (the date it becomes final), the credit allowable by section 38 (determined without regard to section 46(e)) will be retroactively disallowed with respect to any of X's section 46(e) property placed in service prior to January 1, 1973, on any date which occurs during a taxable year with respect to which an assessment of a deficiency has not been barred by any law or rule of law. In addition, the credit will be disallowed with respect to X's section 46(e) property placed in service on or after January 1, 1973, and before the date that a subsequent determination by A, which as to X is consistent with section 46(e)(1), is put into effect. Thus, X must amend its income tax return for 1971 to reflect the retroactive disallowance of the credit allowable by section 38 (determined without regard to section 46(e)) with respect to the section 46(e) property placed in service on September 15, 1971.

Example (2). The facts are the same as in example (1), except that the first inconsistent determination by A becomes final on April 5, 1972, and requires X to account for the credit allowable by section 38 for all taxable years beginning on or after January 1, 1973, in a manner inconsistent with section 46(e)(1). Under the provisions of subparagraph (7) of this paragraph, the determination was put into effect on January 1, 1973 (the date it became operative). The result is the same as in example (1).

Example (3). The facts are the same as in example (1), except that on June 1, 1975, A issues a determination that X shall retroactively account for the credit allowable by section 38 in a manner consistent with the provisions of section 46(e)(1) for taxable years beginning on or after January 1, 1971. The determination becomes final on January 5, 1976, in the same form as originally issued. The result is the same as in example (1) with respect to property X places in service before June 1, 1975. The credit will be allowed with respect to property X places in service on or after June 1, 1975 (the date that the consistent determination is put into effect) and before a subsequent inconsistent determination is put into effect.

(g) *Ratable methods*—(1) *In general.* Under this paragraph, rules are prescribed for purposes of determining (i) whether or not under paragraph (1) of section 46(e) a reduction in the taxpayer's rate base with respect to the credit allowed by section 38 (determined without regard to section 46(e)) is restored less rapidly than ratably or (ii) whether or not under paragraph (2) of section 46(e) the taxpayer's cost of service for rate making purposes is reduced by more than a ratable portion of such credit. Whether a restoration or a reduction is ratable depends upon the factors in subparagraph (2) of this paragraph.

(2) *Regulated depreciation expense.* For purposes of subparagraph (1) of this paragraph, what is "ratable" shall be determined with reference to the period of time actually used by the taxpayer in computing its regulated depreciation expense beginning with the year which includes the date the section 46(e) property was placed in service for purposes of computing such expense. For purposes of this paragraph, the term "regulated depreciation expense" means the depreciation expense computed pursuant to the rules (if any) prescribed or required by the regulatory body having jurisdiction over the taxpayer for purposes of reflecting operating results in the taxpayer's regulated books of account. Such period of time shall be expressed in units of years (or shorter periods), of production, or of

machine hours, and shall be determined in accordance with the individual useful life system or composite (or other group asset) account system actually used by the taxpayer in computing its regulated depreciation expense. A method of restoring, or reducing, is ratable if the amount to be restored to rate base or to reduce cost of service (as the case may be) is allocated ratably in proportion to the number of such units. Thus, for example, assume that the regulated depreciation expense is computed under the straight line method by applying a composite annual percentage rate to "original cost" (as defined for purposes of computing regulated depreciation expense). See, for example, 47 CFR § 31.02-80 (relating to uniform system of accounts for Class A and Class B telephone companies). If, with respect to an item of section 46(e) property the amount to be restored annually to rate base is computed by applying such percentage to the amount by which the rate base was reduced, then the restoration is ratable. Similarly, if cost of service is reduced annually by an amount computed by applying the same percentage to the amount of the credit allowed under section 38 (determined without regard to section 46(e)), cost of service is reduced by a ratable portion. If such percentage were revised for purposes of computing regulated depreciation expense beginning with a particular accounting period, the computation of ratable restoration or ratable portion (as the case may be) must also be revised beginning with such period.

(h) **Elections**—(1) **In general.** Under section 46(e), 3 elections may be made on or before March 9, 1972, with respect to section 46(e) property. An election made under the provisions of section 46(e) shall be irrevocable.

(2) **Applicability of elections.** (i) Any election under section 46(e) shall be made with respect to all of the taxpayer's property eligible for the election whether or not the taxpayer is regulated by more than one regulatory body.

(ii)(a) Paragraph (1) of section 46(e) shall apply to all of the taxpayer's section 46(e) property in the absence of an election under paragraph (2) or (3) of section 46(e). If an election is made under paragraph (2) of section 46(e), paragraph (1) of such section shall not apply to any of the taxpayer's section 46(e) property.

(b) An election made under the last sentence of section 46(e)(1) shall apply to that portion of the taxpayer's section 46(e) property to which paragraph (1) of section 46(e) applies and which is short supply property within the meaning of paragraph (c)(2) of this section.

(iii) If a taxpayer makes an election under paragraph (2) of section 46(e), and makes no election under paragraph (3) of such section, the election under paragraph (2) of section 46(e) shall apply to all of its section 46(e) property.

(iv) If a taxpayer makes an election under paragraph (3) of section 46(e), such election shall apply to all of the taxpayer's section 46(e) property to which section 167(l)(2)(C) applies. Paragraph (1) or (2) of section 46(e) (as the case may be) shall apply to that portion of the taxpayer's section 46(e) property which is not property to which section 167(l)(2)(C) applies. Thus, for example, if a taxpayer makes an election under paragraph (2) of section 46(e) and also makes an election under paragraph (3) of section 46(e), paragraph (3) shall apply to all of the taxpayer's section 46(e) property to which section 167(l)(2)(C) applies and paragraph (2) shall apply to the remainder of the taxpayer's section 46(e) property.

(3) **Method of making elections.** A taxpayer may make the elections described in section 46(e) by filing a statement, on or before March 9, 1972, with the district director or director of the internal revenue service center with whom the taxpayer ordinarily files its income tax return. For rules with respect to taxpayers filing consolidated returns see, § 1.1502-77(a). Such statement shall contain the following nformation:

(i) The name, address, and taxpayer identification number of the taxpayer,
(ii) The paragraph (or paragraphs) of section 46(e) under which the taxpayer is making the election,
(iii) If an election is made under the last sentence of section 46(e)(1), the name and address of all regulatory bodies which have jurisdiction over the taxpayer with respect to the section 46(e) property covered by such election and a

Proposed Reg. § 1.46-5

statement setting forth the type of the public utility activity described in section 46(e)(5)(B) in which the taxpayer engages, and

(iv) If an election is made under paragraph (3) of section 46(e), a statement indicating whether an election has been made by the taxpayer under section 167(1)(4)(A).

(i) [Reserved]

(j) **Reorganizations, asset acquisitions, multiple regulation, etc.**—(1) **Taxpayers not entirely subject to jurisdiction of one regulatory body.** (i) If a taxpayer is required by a regulatory body having jurisdiction over less than all of its property to account for the credit allowable by section 38 (determined without regard to section 46 (e)) under a determination which is inconsistent with paragraph (1) or (2) (as the case may be) of section 46(e), such credit shall be disallowed only with respect to property subject to the jurisdiction of such regulatory body.

(ii) For purposes of this paragraph, a regulatory body is considered to have jurisdiction over property of a taxpayer if the property is included in the rate base for which the regulatory body determines an allowable rate of return for ratemaking purposes or if expenses with respect to the property are included in the cost of service as determined by the regulatory body for ratemaking purposes. For example, if regulatory body A, having jurisdiction over 60 percent of an item of X corporation's section 46(e) property, makes a determination which is inconsistent with section 46(e), and if regulatory body B, having jurisdiction over the remaining 40 percent of such item of property, makes a consistent determination (or if the remaining 40 percent is not subject to the jurisdiction of any regulatory body), then 60 percent of the credit allowable by section 38 (determined without regard to section 46(e)) with respect to such item will be disallowed. For a further example, if regulatory body A, having jurisdiction over 60 percent of X's section 46(e) property, has jurisdiction over 100 percent of a particular generator, 100 percent of the credit allowable by section 38 (determined without regard to section 46(e)) with respect to such generator will be disallowed.

(iii) For rules which provide that the 3 elections under section 46(e) may not be made with respect to less than all of the taxpayer's property eligible for the election, see paragraph (h)(2)(i) of this section.

(2) [Reserved]

Immediately after § 1.46-6 there are added:

§1.46-7 (Proposed Treasury Decision, published 7-30-76.) **Statutory provisions; plan requirements for taxpayers electing 11-percent investment credit.**

Section 301(d) of the Tax Reduction Act of 1975 (89 Stat. 38) provides as follows:

Sec. 301. **Increase in investment credit.** * * *

(d) **Plan requirements for taxpayers electing 11-percent credit.** In order to meet the requirements of this section—

(1) A corporation (hereinafter in this subsection referred to as the "employer") must establish an employee stock ownership plan (described in paragraph (2)) which is funded by transfers of employer securities in accordance with the provisions of paragraph (6) and which meets all other requirements of this subsection.

(2) The plan referred to in paragraph (1) must be a defined contribution plan established in writing which—

(A) Is a stock bonus plan, a stock bonus and money purchase pension plan, or a profit-sharing plan,

(B) Is designed to invest primarily in employer securities, and

(C) Meets such other requirements (similar to requirements applicable to employee stock ownership plans as defined in section 4975(e)(7) of the Internal Revenue Code of 1954) as the Secretary of the Treasury or his delegate may prescribe.

(3) The plan must provide for the allocation of all employer securities transferred to it or purchased by it (because of the requirements of section 46(a)(1)(B) of the Internal Revenue Code of 1954) to the account of each participant (who was a participant at any time during the plan year, whether or not he is a participant at the close of the plan year) as of the close of each plan year in an amount which bears substantially the same

proportion to the amount of all such securities allocated to all participants in the plan for that plan year as the amount of compensation paid to such participant (disregarding any compensation in excess of the first $100,000 per year) bears to the compensation paid to all such participants during that year (disregarding any compensation in excess of the first $100,000 with respect to any participant). Notwithstanding the first sentence of this paragraph, the allocation to participants' accounts may be extended over whatever period may be necessary to comply with the requirements of section 415 of the Internal Revenue Code of 1954.

(4) The plan must provide that each participant has a nonforfeitable right to any stock allocated to his account under paragraph (3), and that no stock allocated to a participant's account may be distributed from that account before the end of the eighty-fourth month beginning after the month in which the stock is allocated to the account except in the case of separation from service, death, or disability.

(5) The plan must provide that each participant is entitled to direct the plan as to the manner in which any employer securities allocated to the account of the participant are to be voted.

(6) On making a claim for credit, adjustment, or refund under section 38 of the Internal Revenue Code of 1954, the employer states in such claim that it agrees, as a condition of receiving any such credit, adjustment, or refund, to transfer employer securities forthwith to the plan having an aggregate value at the time of the claim of 1 percent of the amount of the qualified investment (as determined under section 46(c) and (d) of such Code) of the taxpayer for the taxable year. For purposes of meeting the requirements of this paragraph, a transfer of cash shall be treated as a transfer of employer securities if the cash is, under the plan, used to purchase employer securities.

(7) Notwithstanding any other provision of law to the contrary, if the plan does not meet the requirements of section 401 of the Internal Revenue Code of 1954—

(A) Stock transferred under paragraph (6) and allocated to the account of any participant under paragraph (3) and dividends thereon shall not be considered income of the participant or his beneficiary under the Internal Revenue Code of 1954 until actually distributed or made available to the participant or his beneficiary and, at such time, shall be taxable under section 72 of such Code (treating the participant or his beneficiary as having a basis of zero in the contract),

(B) No amount shall be allocated to any participant in excess of the amount which might be allocated if the plan met the requirements of section 401 of such Code, and

(C) The plan must meet the requirements of section 410 and 415 of such Code.

(8) If the amount of the credit determined under section 46(a)(1)(B) of the Internal Revenue Code of 1954, is recaptured in accordance with the provisions of such Code, the amounts transferred to the plan under this subsection and allocated under the plan shall remain in the plan or in participant accounts, as the case may be and continue to be allocated in accordance with the original plan agreement.

(9) For purposes of this subsection, the term—

(A) "Employer securities" means common stock issued by the employer or a corporation which is in control of the employer (within the meaning of section 368(c) of the Internal Revenue Code of 1954) with voting power and dividend rights no less favorable than the voting power and dividend rights of other common stock issued by the employer or such controlling corporation, or securities issued by the employer or such controlling corporation, convertible into such stock, and

(B) "Value" means the average of closing prices of the employer's securities, as reported by a national exchange on which securities are listed, for the 20 consecutive trading days immediately preceding the date of transfer or allocation of such securities or, in the case of securities not listed on a national exchange, the fair market value as determined in good faith and in accordance with regulations issued by the Secretary of the Treasury or his delegate.

(10) The Secretary of the Treasury or his delegate shall prescribe such regulations and require such reports as may be necessary to carry out the provisions of this subsection.

Proposed Reg. § 1.46-7

(11) If the employer fails to meet any requirement imposed under this subsection or under any obligation undertaken to comply with the requirement of this subsection, he is liable to the United States for a civil penalty of an amount equal to the amount involved in such failure. The preceding sentence shall not apply if the taxpayer corrects such failure (as determined by the Secretary of the Treasury or his delegate) within 90 days after notice thereof. For purposes of this paragraph, the term "amount involved" means an amount determined by the Secretary or his delegate, but not in excess of 1 percent of the qualified investment of the taxpayer for the taxable year under section 46(a)(1)(B) and not less than the product of one-half of one percent of such amount multiplied by the number of months (or parts thereof) during which such failure continues. The amount of such penalty may be collected by the Secretary of the Treasury in the same manner in which a deficiency in the payment of Federal income tax may be collected.

(12) Notwithstanding any provision of the Internal Revenue Code of 1954 to the contrary, no deductions shall be allowed under section 162, 212, or 404 of such Code for amounts transferred to an employee stock ownership plan and taken into account under this subsection.

§1.46-8 (Proposed Treasury Decision, published 7-30-76.) **Requirements for taxpayers electing 11-percent investment credit.**

(a) **General Rules—(1) Introduction.** For a taxable year ending after January 21, 1975, a corporation (other than an electing small business corporation within the meaning of section 1371(b) of the Code) may elect under section 46(a)(1)(B) of the Code, in the time and manner prescribed in paragraph (c)(1) of this section, to claim a credit equal to 11 percent of the qualified investment properly attributable to property and qualified progress expenditures described in section 46(c) and (d) of the Code (an "11-percent credit") to which section 46(a)(1)(B) applies by reason of section 46(a)(1)(D) if the requirements of section 301(d) of the Tax Reduction Act of 1975 (the "1975 TRA") and this section are met. To satisfy such requirements, a corporation which is an employer within the meaning of paragraph (b)(3) of this section must establish or maintain an employee stock ownership plan (a "TRASOP") meeting the general plan requirements of paragraph (d) of this section and must transfer employer securities (as defined in paragraph (b)(1) of this section) to the TRASOP in accordance with the provisions of paragraph (c)(2) of this section. The value of employer securities for purposes of determining the amount to be transferred under paragraph (c) of this section must be calculated under paragraph (b)(2) of this section. A plan which otherwise meets the requirements of this section but which is not a qualified plan under section 401(a) of the Code will nevertheless meet the requirements of the 1975 TRA and this section if such plan satisfies the requirements of paragraph (e)(2) of this section.

(2) **No deduction.** Notwithstanding any provisions of the Code to the contrary, no deduction shall be allowed under section 162, 212, or 404 of the Code for employer securities or cash transferred to a TRASOP if such amount is taken into account under this section. However, section 404 will apply to any amount transferred to the TRASOP which is not taken into account under this section. An amount is taken into account under this section if such amount is necessary in order that a credit under section 38 be allowed.

(3) **New plan not required.** A new plan need not be established if an existing plan meets the requirements of this section and section 301(d) of the 1975 TRA or is amended to meet these requirements.

(b) **Definitions—(1) Employer securities—** (i) In general. For purposes of section 301(d) of the 1975 TRA and this section, the term "employer securities" means common stock issued by the employer that meets the requirements of paragraph (b)(1)(ii) of this section and convertible securities that meet the requirements of paragraph (b)(1)(iii) of this section. No employer security may be subject to a call or right of first refusal, except that an employer security subject to a right of first refusal to the employer while held by a TRASOP before Sept. 30, 1976 may continue to be subject to such right of first refusal. All unlisted common stock or convertible securities transferred to a TRASOP after

Sept. 30, 1976 must be subject to a mandatory put to the employer that meets the requirements of paragraph (b)(1)(iv) of this section. Stock rights, warrants and options do not constitute employer securities.

(ii) Common stock. To be taken into account under this section, common stock must have voting power and unrestricted dividend rights within the meaning of paragraph (b)(4) of this section. Voting power and dividend rights must be no less favorable than the voting power and dividend rights of any other common stock issued by the employer. Common stock within the meaning of this (ii) must meet one of the following tests:

(A) The stock is part of, or identical to, a class of stock of which (prior to the transfer to the TRASOP) at least 50 percent is owned by shareholders no one of whom owns more than 10 percent of the shares in such class of stock.

(B) If there is only one class of stock, the stock issued to the TRASOP is part of, or identical to, shares in such class of stock, or if there is more than one class of stock, then shares with respect to each class must be transferred to the TRASOP, so that each class of stock transferred to the TRASOP, as compared to all classes of stock transferred to the TRASOP, is substantially in the proportion the fair market value of the total outstanding shares of the particular class bears to the aggregate fair market value of all outstanding classes of stock (both values excluding shares owned by the TRASOP). This result will be obtained if the number of shares of stock in a particular class is in proportion to the number of shares of each and every other class of stock. For example, if there are two classes of stock, Class A and Class B, and if the fair market values of the outstanding shares of Class A Stock and Class B stock are $100,000 and $200,000, respectively, and prior to the acquisition the ESOP has no interest in such stock, then such stock will meet the requirements of this (B) if the fair market value of the Class B stock it acquires is twice that of the Class A stock it acquires.

(C) The stock is part of, or identical to, that existing class of stock having the greatest number of votes per unit of fair market value. For example, if there are two classes of stock, Class A and Class B, with a fair market value per share of $1 and $.50, respectively, and if the owner of each share of each class is entitled to one vote per share, then a share of Class B stock has the greatest number of votes per dollar of value (2 votes per $1 as compared to 1 vote per $1) and stock will meet the requirements of this (C) if it is part of, or identical to, a share in Class B.

(iii) Convertible securities. To be taken into account under this section, securities must be qualifying employer securities under section 4975 (e)(8) of the Code that are immediately convertible, at a reasonable conversion ratio, into common stock (which meets the requirements of paragraphs (b)(1)(i) and (iv) of this section) by the holder of such securities after distribution and, while held by the TRASOP, at the direction of the participant to whose account the securities have been allocated.

(iv) Mandatory put. In the case of common stock or convertible securities not listed on a national exchange, in order to meet the requirements of paragraph (b)(1)(i) of this section, each share of common stock and each convertible security transferred to a TRASOP after Sept. 30, 1976 must be subject to a put to the employer that meets the requirements of this (iv). Such put must be exercisable during a two-year period which begins on the date the employer securities are distributed to a participant. If securities described in paragraph (b)(1)(iii) of this section are transferred to a participant, which are convertible into common stock which meets the requirements of paragraph (b)(1)(i) of this section, the period during which such put may be exercised expires two years after the date the convertible securities are distributed to the participant. The price at which a put meeting the requirements of this (iv) is exercisable is the fair market value of the common stock as of the date of exercise determined in accordance with paragraph (b)(2) of this section, and shall be paid in cash within a reasonable time from exercise. Such puts shall be exercisable by participants or their beneficiaries or by persons to whom such common

Proposed Reg. § 1.46-8

stock or convertible securities are transferred by gift from participants or their beneficiaries or by reason of the death of such participants and beneficiaries.

(2) **Value.** Under section 301(d) of the 1975 TRA and for purposes of paragraph (c) of this section, the term "value" means, in the case of securities listed on a national exchange, the average of closing prices of the employer's securities, as reported by such exchange for the 20 consecutive trading days immediately preceding the date of the election under paragraph (c) of this section. In the case of securities not listed on a national exchange, a good faith determination of value shall be made on the basis of all relevant factors for determining fair market value. With respect to such unlisted securities, a determination of fair market value based on two or more appraisals independently arrived at by organizations that customarily make such appraisals, all of which organizations are independent of the employer, shall in all such cases be a good faith determination of value. If the employer has knowledge of the disreputability of any appraiser making such determination, good faith will be lacking. A certificate of value with respect to unlisted securities taken into account under this section after Sept. 30, 1976 shall be filed by the employer with the TRASOP when a determination of value has been made for purposes of paragraph (c) of this section and on an annual basis thereafter. Each participant receiving a distribution of employer securities under the plan shall also receive at the time of such distribution a copy of the most recent certificate and a copy of each annual certificate thereafter until the put described in paragraph (b)(1)(iv) of this section has expired with respect to employer securities received in such distribution.

(3) **Employer.** For purposes of this section the term "employer" means the employer or a corporation which is in control of the employer within the meaning of section 368(c).

(4) **Unrestricted dividend rights.** For purposes of section 301(d) of the 1975 TRA and this section, dividend rights mean rights to receive dividends as defined by the governing law of the state of incorporation of the corporation. Such rights are unrestricted if they are limited in no way other than as positively prescribed by statute in the state of incorporation.

(c) **Election of 11-percent credit—(1) Time and manner of election.** (i) An election under section 46(a)(1)(B) to claim an 11-percent credit for a taxable year shall be made on or before the due date (including extensions of time) for filing the corporation's income tax return for the year in which the credit is earned or, if later, December 31, 1975.

(ii) The election shall be made by attaching a statement to the corporation's return for the taxable year in which the credit is earned, or in the case of a return filed prior to December 31, 1975, by attaching a statement to an amended return filed on or before December 31, 1975. The statement shall indicate that an election is being made under section 46(a)(1)(B) of the Code and that the employer agrees as a condition for receiving the 11-percent credit to transfer employer securities forthwith to a TRASOP in the manner described in paragraph (c)(2) of this section.

(iii) An election to claim the 11-percent credit for a taxable year shall apply to the total qualified investment property for such taxable year properly attributable to property and qualified progress expenditures described in section 46(c) and (d) of the Code to which section 46(a)(1)(B) applies by reason of section 46(a)(1)(D). Thus, an electing employer may not elect the 11-percent credit for one portion of such qualified investment and a 10-percent credit under section 46(a)(1)(A) of the Code for another portion.

(iv) If an election for a taxable year is not made within the time and in the manner described in paragraph (c)(1) of this section, no election may be made for such taxable year (by the filing of an amended return or otherwise).

(v) An election under section 46(a)(1)(B) for a taxable year may not be revoked without the consent of the Commissioner after the time prescribed in paragraph (c)(1) of this section for making the election has expired.

(2) **Establishment of TRASOP and transfer of employer securities.** (i) To meet the requirements of section 301(d) of the 1975 TRA, a TRASOP with accompanying trust

must be in existence on or before the last day for making an election under paragraph (c)(1) of this section. For purposes of this section a TRASOP will be considered in existence whether or not the TRASOP has been funded on such date.

(ii) The aggregate value of employer securities to be transferred under this section must at the time of the election be an amount equal to one percent of the qualified investment of the employer for the taxable year under section 46(c) and (d) of the Code to which section 46(a)(1)(B) applies by reason of section 46(a)(1)(D).

(iii) The transfer of all of the employer securities described in paragraph (c)(2)(ii) of this section must be made on or before the 30th day following the last day for making an election under paragraph (c)(1) of this section.

(iv) To meet the requirements of paragraph (c)(2) of this section, a transfer of cash in an amount equal to one percent of the qualified investment shall be treated as a transfer of employer securities if under the TRASOP the cash is used to purchase employer securities on or before the 30th day following the last day for making an election under paragraph (c)(1) of this section.

(v) The requirements of section 301(d)(6) of the 1975 TRA and paragraph (c)(2) of this section will not be satisfied merely by establishing and crediting a separate TRASOP account on the employer's books.

(vi) If a plan provides for regular contributions in addition to the contributions required under section 301(d)(6) of the 1975 TRA and paragraph (c)(2) of this section, the latter contributions must be accounted for separately from the regular contributions to the plan.

(d) **General plan requirements—(1) General rule.** A TRASOP must be a defined contribution plan established in writing which—

(i) Is a stock bonus plan, a stock bonus plan and a money purchase pension plan, or a profit-sharing plan (as described in §1.401-1(b)(1)) and

(ii) Is designed to invest primarily in employer securities as provided in paragraph (d)(2) of this section.

(2) **Designed to invest primarily in employer securities.** A plan constitutes a TRASOP only if the plan specifically states that it is designed to invest primarily in employer securities.

(3) **Employee contributions.** The receipt of benefits attributable to transfers required by the provisions of paragraph (c)(2) of this section may not be dependent upon contributions by the participants. If the employer has a plan in existence which requires employee contributions, such plan may be used to meet the requirements of this section if no employee contributions are required with respect to amounts transferred under the provisions of paragraph (c)(2) of this section and participation in the plan with respect to these amounts is not dependent upon employee contributions.

(4) **Expenses and debts of the TRASOP.** Amounts taken into account under this section cannot be used to pay the administrative expenses of the TRASOP or to satisfy a previous loan made to the TRASOP or be used as collateral for a loan to the TRASOP.

(5) **Allocation of amounts taken into account under this section.** (i) The plan must provide for the allocation of all amounts taken into account under this section. Such amounts must be allocated to the account of each participant who was a participant at any time during the plan year, whether or not he is a participant at the close of the plan year, as of a date prior to the close of each plan year. The allocation to each participant shall be in an amount which bears substantially the same proportion to the amount of all such amounts allocated to all participants in the plan for that plan year as the amount of the total annual compensation (as defined in paragraph (e)(1)(v) of this section) paid to the participant during the plan year, disregarding any compensation for such plan year in excess of a stated amount not greater than $100,000, bears to the compensation paid to all such participants during the plan year, disregarding any compensation in excess of such stated amount paid with respect to any participant. Substantial proportionality is

Proposed Reg. §1.46-8

satisfied if the participant's total annual compensation is expressed in terms of whole dollars.

(ii) If the contributions in any one year to a participant's account would exceed the limits of section 415 of the Code, the contributions shall be reallocated proportionately under paragraph (d)(5)(i) of this section to the accounts of other participants until the additions to the account of each participant reach the limits of section 415.

(iii) If, after the reallocations described in paragraph (d)(5)(ii) of this section, the amounts taken into account under this section are greater than otherwise allowed by the limits of section 415 of the Code, the portion exceeding the section 415 limits will not cause the plan to be disqualified under section 401(a) of the Code or to violate the requirements of section 301(d) of the 1975 TRA if such amount is held in an unallocated account in the TRASOP or in an escrow account and in later years such amount is allocated to the participants' accounts proportionately under paragraph (d)(5)(i) of this section with regard to the annual compensation for such later year. The beneficiary of the escrow account is to be the TRASOP. The employer may establish such an escrow account and contribute stock or cash to it. In such a case the escrow agent must transfer assets to the plan each year to the maximum extent possible without violating the limitations of section 415. Similar procedures shall apply if an unallocated account is used.

(iv) The allocation and distribution of amounts taken into account under this section may not be integrated, directly or indirectly, with contributions or benefits under Title II of the Social Security Act (42 U.S.C. 401).

(v) For purposes of this section, the term "compensation" shall have the same meaning as the term "participant's compensation" has under section 415(c)(3) and the regulations thereunder.

(vi) Participants are to be allocated fractional shares or fractional rights to shares and other employer securities.

(6) **Nonforfeitability.** The plan must provide that each participant has a nonforfeitable right to any amount taken into account under this section. For purposes of this section, forfeitures described in section 411(a)(3) of the Code are not permitted.

(7) Exercise of rights— (i) Voting rights. (A) The plan must provide that each participant is entitled to direct a designated fiduciary as to the manner in which any employer securities allocated to the amount of the participant are to be voted. The designated fiduciary shall notify participants of each occasion for the exercise of voting rights within a reasonable time (not less than 30 days) before such rights are to be exercised. This notification shall include all the information that the corporation distributes to shareholders regarding the exercise of such rights.

(B) The participants are to be allowed to vote fractional shares (or fractional rights to shares). This requirement is satisfied if the designated fiduciary votes the combined fractional shares or rights to shares to the extent possible to reflect the direction of the participants holding fractional shares or rights to shares.

(C) If a participant does not direct the designated fiduciary in whole or in part with respect to the exercise of voting rights arising under employer securities allocated to his account, such voting rights shall be exercised only to the extent directed by such participant.

(D) The plan need not permit employees to direct the voting of unallocated employer securities held by the trust.

(ii) Rights other than voting rights. The plan shall provide that each participant is entitled to direct the exercise of rights other than voting rights (such as, for example, a conversion privilege) in the manner prescribed under paragraph (d)(7)(i) of this section.

(8) **Distributions.** The plan must provide that no employer securities which have been allocated to a participant's account in accordance with section 301(d)(3) of the 1975 TRA and paragraph (d)(5) of this section may be distributed from that account before the end of the 84th month beginning after the month in which the stock is allocated to the participant's account except in the case of separation from service, death, or disability. However, a qualified money purchase pension plan can make a distribution only in

the case of separation from service, death, or disability. All TRASOP's, including qualified stock bonus TRASOP's, can distribute cash instead of fractional shares.

(9) **Controlled group of corporations**, etc. All employees who by reason of section 414 (b) and (c) of the Code are treated as employees of the electing employer shall be treated as employed by such electing employer in determining whether the participation requirements of section 410 of the Code (and section 301(d)(7)(C) of the 1975 TRA, relating to plans not meeting the requirements of section 401 of the Code) are satisfied.

(10) **Recapture of investment credit**—(i) In general. If the amount of the investment credit determined under section 46(a)(1)(B) of the Code is recaptured in accordance with the provisions of section 47 of the Code, the amount taken into account under this section shall remain in the plan or in the participants' accounts, as the case may be, and continue to be allocated in accordance with the original plan. If all or a portion of the credit attributable to the TRASOP contribution is recaptured, a deduction under section 404 of the Code, relating to deductions for contributions to an employees' trust or plan, may be allowable.

(ii) Example. The provisions of this paragraph may be illustrated by the following example:

Example. On February 1, 1975, Corporation X, which is on a calendar year basis, makes a qualified investment with a basis of $1,000,000 and a useful life of eight years. After having claimed an investment credit of $107,600 ($100,000 (10% of $1,000,000) under section 46(a)(1)(A) of the Code plus $7,600 of the additional $10,000 credit (1% of $1,000,000) permitted under section 46(a)(1)(B) of the Code) the corporation disposes of the qualified investment at the end of 1980. Corporation A contributes the full $10,000 to a TRASOP in order to qualify for the additional credit. Under section 47 of the Code, $26,900 of the qualified investment (2/8ths of $100,000 ($25,000) plus 2/8ths of $7,600 ($1,900)) must be recaptured because the section 38 property was disposed of two years before the close of its useful life. The amount recaptured with respect to the additional 1% credit ($1,900)+$2,400 ($10,000 − $7,600), the amount remaining in the plan for which no credit has been or will be allowed because of the recapture, may be deductible under section 404 of the Code. Therefore, a total of $4,300 ($1,900 + $2,400) may be deductible because of the recapture with respect to the amount taken into account under this section.

(e) **Qualified and non-qualified TRASOP's**—(1) General rule. A TRASOP may, but need not, meet the requirements of section 401(a) of the Code. See Title I of the Employee Retirement Income Security Act of 1974 ("ERISA") for additional provisions applicable to an employee pension benefit plan (whether or not qualified under section 401(a) of the Code), within the meaning of section 3(2) of ERISA.

(2) **Non-qualified TRASOP's.** Notwithstanding any other provision of law to the contrary, if the TRASOP does not meet the requirements of section 401(a) of the Code, under section 301(d)(7) of the 1975 TRA the following rules shall nevertheless apply with respect to amounts taken into account under this section:

(i) Participation. The plan must meet the requirements of section 410 of the Code. See paragraph (d)(9) of this section with regard to the application of sections 414(b) and (c) of the Code.

(ii) Contributions. The plan must meet the requirements of section 415 of the Code. However, plans qualifying under section 401(a) of the Code and plans described in section 415(e)(5) shall not be aggregated with a TRASOP in applying subsections (e), (f), and (g) of section 415 for years beginning before January 1, 1976.

(iii) Allocation. No amount shall be allocated to any participant in excess of the amount which might be allocated if the plan met the requirements of section 401(a) of the Code.

(iv) Taxability. An amount taken into account under this section and dividends thereon shall not be considered income of the participant or his beneficiary until it is ac-

Proposed Reg. § 1.46-8

tually distributed or made available to the participant or his beneficiary. These amounts shall not be considered "wages" or "compensation" for purposes of subtitle C of the Code (relating to employment taxes). The treatment of the distribution shall be determined under section 72 of the Code. For purposes of applying section 72, the investment in the contract of the participant or his beneficiary shall be treated as zero. If the TRASOP does not meet the requirements of section 301(d) of the 1975 TRA, see section 402 of the Code, relating to taxability of beneficiary of employee's trust.

(3) **Qualified TRASOP's**—(i) Introduction. To constitute a qualified plan, a TRASOP must meet the requirements of section 401(a) of the Code and paragraph (3)(ii) of this section. Such a qualified TRASOP is subject to the prohibited transaction rules of section 4975 of the Code and paragraph (e)(3)(iii) of this section.

(ii) Permanence. A TRASOP must be a permanent plan, as defined in §1.401-1(b)(2), in order to satisfy the requirements of section 401(a) of the Code. A TRASOP will not fail to be a permanent plan merely because employer contributions are not made for a year for which the 11-percent credit is not available. However, the preceding sentence will not apply if the employer fails to make contributions necessary to obtain an additional investment credit which otherwise would be available or fails to do so because such employer elected only the 10-percent credit for such year. In addition, the preceding two sentences shall not apply to any contributions to a plan not made for the express purpose of obtaining an additional investment credit. If a plan that meets the requirements of section 401(a) acquires securities under section 301(d)(6) of the 1975 TRA and paragraph (c)(2) of this section in addition to the plan's regular rate of contributions and the regular contributions continue on a permanent basis, the plan's qualification under section 401(a) will not be adversely affected merely because contributions under section 301(d)(6) of the 1975 TRA and paragraph (c)(2) of this section cease to be required, and such plan will not be considered partially terminated merely because the rate of contribution to the plan after the employer has made the contributions required under section 301(d)(6) of the 1975 TRA equals only the rate of the regular contributions provided under such plan.

(iii) Prohibited transactions—(A) In general. Because a plan that meets the requirements of section 401(a) of the Code is subject to the prohibited transaction provisions of section 4975 of the Code, a qualified TRANSOP cannot engage in certain transactions under section 4975(c)(1) unless an exemption under section 4975(c)(2) or (d) is applicable. Among such exempted transactions are certain loans under section 4975(d)(3) and the acquisition or holding of certain employer securities (otherwise limited under section 406 and 407 of ERISA) under section 4975(d)(13). Paragraph (e)(3)(iii)(B) of this section sets out a requirement for a loan to a TRASOP to qualify for the exemption under section 4975(d)(3), and paragraph (e)(3)(iii)(C) of this section allows certain TRANSOP's to qualify for the exemption under section 4975(d)(13).

(B) Certain loans to TRASOP's . For a loan to a TRASOP to meet the requirements of section 4975(d)(3) of the Code and the regulations thereunder, the TRASOP must be an employee stock ownership plan within the meaning of section 4975(e)(7) and regulations prescribed thereunder.

(C) Acquisition or holding of certain employer securities. Under section 4975(d)(13) of the Code, any transaction with a plan that is exempt from section 406 of ERISA by reason of section 408(e) of such Act (or which would be exempt if such section applied to the transaction) is exempt from the prohibitions of section 4975(c)(1). For the transaction to be exempt under section 408(e)(3)(A) of ERISA, the plan must be an eligible individual account plan for purposes of section 408(e)(3)(A) (as defined in section 407(d)(3)) of ERISA. If part of a TRASOP is a qualified money purchase plan and such TRASOP is an employee stock ownership plan under section 4975(e)(7) of the Code, such plan is an eligible individual account plan even though the money purchase plan was not in existence on September 2, 1974.

(f) **Reports.** The returns required by section 6058(a) of the Code shall be filed on behalf of the TRASOP whether or not such plan is qualified under section 401(a).

(g) **Correction of errors**—(1) Availability of 11-percent credit. (i) An employer who fails to meet the requirements of section 301(d) of the 1975 TRA and this section will still be entitled to the 11-percent credit if such employer has made a good faith effort to comply with such requirements and corrects any error within 90 days after notification by the district director of such error. The employer has the burden of establishing that a good faith effort has been made. For example, if the employer can show that he made a good faith effort to establish the fair market value of the employer securities that were transferred to the TRASOP, the employer is entitled to the 11-percent credit even if, on later examination of the return, it is determined that more stock should have been transferred. The employer must make up the deficiency within 90 days after notification of the error by contributing additional shares of stock (based on the value at the time the transfer originally was to have been made) plus the dividends paid between the time that the transfer should have been made and the actual time of the transfer.

(ii) If the employer cannot establish that an error was committed in good faith attempt to comply with the requirements of section 301(d) of the 1975 TRA and this section, the employer will not be entitled to any fraction of the 11-percent investment credit under section 46(a)(1)(B) of the Code. No attempt to comply will be treated as in good faith under this paragraph if such error is not corrected within the period stated in this paragraph.

(2) **Civil penalty**—(i) General rule. In addition to any other sanctions that may be applicable, if the employer fails to meet any requirement imposed under this section or under any obligation undertaken to comply with the requirements of this section, the employer is liable to the United States for a civil penalty of an amount equal to the amount involved in such failure. However, if the employer corrects such failure as determined by the district director within 90 days after the district director notifies the employer of such failure, the employer is not liable for the civil penalty.

(ii) Amount involved. For purposes of this paragraph, the term "amount involved" means the amount required to place the plan in the position in which it should have been if no failure had occurred. This amount shall not exceed 1 percent of the qualified investment of the employer for the taxable year under section 46(a)(1)(B) of the Code and shall not be less than the product of $\frac{1}{2}$ percent of such 1 percent of the qualified investment multiplied by the number of months, or parts of months, during which the failure continues.

(iii) Assessment and collection. The amount of such penalty shall be assessed and collected in the same manner in which a deficiency in the payment of Federal income tax may be assessed and collected.

The proposed amendments to 26 CFR Part I are as follows:

§ 1.48-8 (Proposed Treasury Decision, published 12-20-77.) **Motion picture and television films and tapes.**

(a) **Entitlement to investment credit**—(1) **In general.** Under section 48(k) an investment credit is allowable under section 38 with respect to certain motion picture films and video tapes. For the taxpayer to be entitled to the investment credit, the film or tape placed in service must be "new section 38 property", determined without regard to its useful life. The film or tape must be a qualified film within the meaning of paragraph (a)(3) of this section. In addition, the investment credit is allowable only to the extent of the taxpayer's ownership interest (within the meaning of paragraph (a)(4) of this section) in the qualified film. The investment credit is allowable only for the year in which the qualified film is placed in service except for investment credit with respect to subsequently incurred costs described in paragraph (e)(9) of this section. The refund (or credit) of any overpayment of tax that is attributable to the investment credit is subject to the provisions of section 6511. The provisions of this paragraph apply to all films and tapes regardless of the taxable year in which the film or tapes was placed in service.

(2) **Film may be divided into parts.** Once a qualified film is placed in service in any medium of exhibition in any geographical area of the world, it becomes used property and no investment credit with respect to the film is available to a taxpayer that acquires the film after that time (except for subsequently incurred costs described in paragraph (e)(9) of this section which the taxpayer incurs). Thus, for example, a film previously ex-

hibited in theaters will not be new section 38 property even when modified for television. However, where parts of a film have been sold before the film or any of its parts have been placed in service in any medium of exhibition in any geographical area of the world, each part is new section 38 property until that part is first placed in service. For purposes of this section, "a part" of a film means the exclusive right to display a film in one medium of exhibition in one geographical area over the entire period of substantial exploitation of the film in the medium in the geographical area. The period will be determined on the basis of a reasonable estimate made as of the date the film is first placed in service. For purposes of this section the term "medium of exhibition" includes, for example, free television (network telecasts and television syndications) or movie theaters. For purposes of this section, the term "geographical area" means a geographically defined commercial market recognized by the movie or television industry, but which in no case may be smaller than one country or include a portion of a country. If the owner of a qualified film transfers to another rights to display the film on a limited basis, which do not constitute a transfer of an ownership interest in a part of the film, the owner will still be treated as having "the exclusive right to display the film." For example, if the owner of a film transfers to a television network the right to display the film on network television (but does not transfer to the network syndication rights) the owner is considered to retain the "exclusive right to display the film."

(3) **Qualified film**—(i) In general. Under section 48(k)(1)(B), the term "qualified film" means a motion picture film or video tape or part thereof created primarily for use as public entertainment or for educational purposes. A film or tape is a single asset consisting of three elements: the artistic-dramatic creation, the physical films and tapes (including the original negative or tape and duplicate negatives, release prints or tapes, and original sound recordings and all other sound recordings created to simultaneously accompany the pictorial material) which embody the artistic-dramatic creation, and the world-wide copyright (common law or statutory) which is the right to exploit the completed film or tape in all mediums of exhibition in all geographical areas of the world.

(ii) Public entertainment or educational purposes. A film or tape is created primarily for use as public entertainment only if created principally for public exhibition for the amusement, enlightenment, or gratification of an audience. Thus, a dramatic or comedy show, such as "Police Woman" or "MASH" would be a film or tape created primarily for use as public entertainment. A film or tape is created primarily for educational purposes only if created principally for use by educational institutions or governmental units such as primary or secondary schools, colleges and universities, vocational and postsecondary educational institutions, public libraries, and other government agencies. Films and tapes created primarily for use by industrial or commercial organizations do not qualify for the credit. Thus, advertisements and industrial training films and tapes do not qualify for the credit.

(iii) Topical or transitory films and tapes. The term "qualified film" does not include any film or tape the market for which is primarily topical or is otherwise essentially transitory in nature. A film or tape is topical or essentially transitory in nature if it primarily deals with events and personalities of current interest at the time the film or tape is placed in service. It does not matter that a film or tape which is topical or essentially transitory in nature may be shown in subsequent years or is actually shown in subsequent years. These films or tapes include news shows such as the evening news and documentary specials relating to current affairs, interview shows such as "The Tonight Show" or "Firing Line", award shows, and shows consisting of sporting events. Similarly, variety shows, such as "Sonny and Cher" and "Bob Hope Specials," in which entertainers primarily appear as themselves, deal with personalities of current interest and do not qualify for the credit. Topical or transitory films and tapes do not include, however, dramatized recreations of recent events, for example, "Helter Skelter" or "Raid at Entebbe."

(4) **Ownership interest**—(i) In general. In order to obtain a credit with respect to a qualified film, a taxpayer must have an ownership interest in at least a part of the film. That is, the taxpayer must have a depreciable interest in the film. However, the amount of credit allowable to a taxpayer with respect to a qualified film is determined only on the basis of that taxpayer's proportionate share of any loss which may be incurred with

respect to the production costs of the qualified film. The proportionate share of any loss which may be incurred with respect to production costs by a taxpayer is the amount that the taxpayer's capital is at risk. Advance rentals received by a taxpayer prior to the date on which a qualified film is placed in service, and which are includible as ordinary income in the taxpayer's gross income will not reduce the amount that the taxpayer's capital is at risk. If a taxpayer's capital is considered at risk under the principles of section 465, the taxpayer's capital will be considered to be at risk under this paragraph. Regardless of whether he is at risk under the principles of section 465, a taxpayer's capital will be considered at risk under this paragraph if the taxpayer will suffer the economic loss if the qualified film fails to generate sufficient revenue to cover or repay production costs. For purposes of this paragraph, the amount which a taxpayer has at risk will not be considered to be reduced by a deduction for participations or residuals paid or accrued, or by a deduction under section 167 with respect to the costs of preparing prints described in paragraph (f)(1)(ii) of this section.

(ii) *Time ownership interest is determined.* An ownership interest in a qualified film is determined at the time the film is placed in service except that an ownership interest with respect to subsequently incurred costs (described in paragraph (e)(9) of this section) is determined on the last day of the taxable year in which such costs are paid or incurred. Thus, a taxpayer purchasing a part of a qualified film after the film has been placed in service acquires no ownership interest in that part for purposes of the credit. However, if a taxpayer had purchased the part before the film had been placed in service in any medium of exhibition in any geographical area of the world, the taxpayer will have acquired an ownership interest in that part of the film for purposes of the credit.

(iii) *Special rule for lenders and guarantors.* To qualify for investment credit with respect to a qualified film, the taxpayer must have a depreciable interest in the film. Solely for purposes of this paragraph, a taxpayer, who, at the time a film is first placed in service, is a lender or guarantor of all or a portion of the funds used to produce or acquire the film or part thereof, will be regarded as having a depreciable interest in the film if he can look for repayment or relief from liability solely to the proceeds generated from the exhibition of at least a part of the film. If a lender or guarantor (other than a producer who owned the film and made or guaranteed a loan to a purchaser) is regarded as having an ownership interest in the film, the lender or guarantor shall be treated as having purchased the interest under paragraph (g)(2) of this section for an amount equal to the principal amount of the loan which it made or guaranteed.

(iv) *Partnerships, electing small business corporations, and estates and trusts.* If a partnership has an ownership interest in a qualified film, the allowable credit will be apportioned pro rata among the partners on the basis of their percentage of capital at risk in the partnership at the time the film is placed in service. If an electing small business corporation has an ownership interest in a qualified film, the allowable credit will be apportioned among the shareholders on the basis of their percentage of ownership of stock of the corporation on the last day of its taxable year in which the film is placed in service. If an estate or trust has an ownership interest in a qualified film, the allowable credit will be apportioned between the estate or trust and the beneficiaries on the basis of the income of the estate or trust allocable to each in the taxable year of the trust or estate in which the film is placed in service. For purposes of determining ownership interest with respect to subsequently incurred costs (described in paragraph (e)(9) of this section), a taxpayer's proportionate share of the capital at risk in a qualified film owned by a partnership or electing small corporation is determined on the basis of the taxpayer's capital at risk in the entity on the last day of the taxable year of the entity in which the subsequently incurred costs are paid or incurred. The amount of capital which a taxpayer has at risk does not include any amount previously taken into account in determining the investment credit to which the taxpayer is entitled under section 48(k). For example, if a taxpayer has taken investment credit with respect to the entire amount which he has at risk in a partnership, no additional investment credit may be taken by the taxpayer at any time unless his amount at risk in the partnership is increased.

(v) This subparagraph may be illustrated by the following examples:

Example (1). (a) Partnership P executes a production-distribution agreement with D,

Proposed Reg. § 1.48-8

a motion picture distribution company, for P to produce a new feature-length motion picture. D agrees to provide the funds for the production by direct loans to P. The amounts borrowed by P would be repayable only out of net profits from the distribution of the picture. P assumes no liability for the repayment of any amount. In consideration for the sum advanced by D, P assigns to D the sole and exclusive right to rent, lease, exhibit, license and otherwise dispose of, or trade and deal in and with the picture. Proceeds realized from the sale or distribution of the picture would first be used to reimburse D for amounts advanced. Any amount remaining following the reimbursement to D would be distributed 50 percent to D and 50 percent to P. For purposes of this example, it is assumed that neither a partnership nor a joint venture is created.

(b) Under paragraph (a)(4)(iii) of this section, D is regarded as having a depreciable interest in the picture for purposes of the credit. P's only interest in the picture is to share in any future profits. Since only D's capital is at risk, D may claim the allowable credit with respect to the entire qualified U.S. production costs of the picture.

Example (2). (a) A and B execute a partnership agreement under which B agrees to provide the funds for the production of a motion picture in return for a 50-percent interest in the net profits of the film. A agrees to provide his services and to supply the necessary talent to produce the film in exchange for the remaining 50-percent interest. Any lease, exhibition, license, or other disposition of the film is subject to the veto of either party.

(b) The AB partnership has a depreciable interest in the film. Under paragraph (a)(4) of this section, the credit will be apportioned among the partners on the basis of their percentage of capital at risk in the partnership. A has no capital at risk and therefore is not entitled to any credit with respect to the film. Since B has supplied all the risk capital for the partnership, B may claim all the investment credit with respect to the film.

Example (3). (a) X produces a new feature-length motion picture with its own funds. Upon completion X sells the film to Y. The purchase price is payable solely out of the proceeds generated from the exhibition of the film in movie theaters in the United States. Y obtains exclusive control over the distribution of the film, and agrees to use its best efforts in promoting the distribution.

(b) Since X can look solely to the proceeds generated from the exhibition of the film to recoup its funds used to produce the film, X is treated as having a depreciable interest for purposes of the credit. Since X's capital at risk equals the production costs of the film, X may claim all of the investment credit with respect to the film.

(c) If the facts were the same except that X could look for repayment soley out of the proceeds generated from the exhibition of the film in movie theaters in the eastern portion of the United States, X would not be treated under paragraph (a)(4)(iii) of this section as having a depreciable interest in the film, and no one would be entitled to investment credit with respect to the film.

(5) **Placed in service.** A qualified film is placed in service when it is first exhibited or otherwise utilized before the primary audience for which the qualified film was created. Thus, a qualified film is placed in service when it is first publicly exhibited for entertainment purposes and a qualified educational film is placed in service when it is first exhibited for instructional purposes. Each episode of a television film or tape series is placed in service when it is first exhibited. A qualified film is not placed in service merely because it is completed and therefore in a condition or state of readiness and availability for exhibition, or merely because it is exhibited to prospective exhibitors, sponsors, or purchasers.

(b) **Applicable percentage for post-1974 qualified films.** For all qualified films placed in service in taxable years beginning after December 31, 1974, the applicable percentage under section 46(c)(2), which is used to determine the qualified investment, is 66⅔ percent unless the taxpayer elects to have the credit computed under the 90-percent rule provided in section 48(k)(3).

(c) **Election of 90-percent rule—(1) Time and manner for making the election.** A taxpayer electing under section 48(k)(3) to use the 90-percent rule in determining investment credit with respect to qualified films placed in service in taxable years beginning after December 31, 1974, shall file a written statement with the original return for the taxable year for which the 90-percent rule will first apply. The election may not be made on an amended return filed after the time prescribed for filing the original return (including extensions) for that taxable year. Notwithstanding the preceding sentences, an election with respect to taxable years beginning before January 1, 1977, will be valid if the taxpayer files a statement and amended return or returns with the district director having audit jurisdiction over the last return to which the election relates on or before [90 days after the date on which this notice is published as a Treasury decision]. A taxpayer who desires to make the election shall file with the tax return (or amended return) for the taxable year for which the election will first apply, a signed statement containing the following information:

(i) The taxpayer's name and taxpayer identification number (under section 6109 of the Code),

(ii) A statement that the taxpayer is making the election under section 48(k)(3),

(iii) A list of all qualified films placed in service in prior taxable years to which the election relates,

(iv) With respect to each qualified film listed in paragraph (c)(1)(iii) of this section, a list of all producers, distributors, and persons with a participation interest (with addresses if available), and

(v) If the election is made by a partnership, electing small business corporation (as defined in section 1371(b) of the Code), estate, or trust, a statement indicating the names, taxpayer identification numbers, and addresses for tax return purposes of the respective partners, shareholders, or beneficiaries.

(2) **Who may elect.** The election under section 48(k)(3) may be made only by a taxpayer who has a depreciable interest in a qualified film. However, where a qualified film is owned by a partnership, electing small business corporation (as defined in section 1371(b) of the Code), estate, or trust, the election must be made separately by each partner, shareholder, or beneficiary. The election is not to be made by a partnership or electing small business corporation, and is to be made by a trust or estate only if the trust or estate in determining its tax liability would be allowed investment credit on a qualified film subject to the election. The election of any partner, shareholder, beneficiary, or trust or estate will be effective regardless of whether any related partner, shareholder, beneficiary, or trust or estate makes the election.

(3) **Related business entity.** [Reserved]

(d) **Predominant use test and qualified investment—(1) Place of exhibition not relevant.** For qualified films placed in service in taxable years beginning after December 31, 1974, section 48(a)(2) (relating to property used outside the United States) does not apply. Whether a qualified film is ultimately exhibited entirely within the United States, entirely outside the United States, or partially within and partially outside the United States, is not relevant for purposes of determining the investment credit.

(2) **Qualified investment.** In determining the qualified investment under section 46(c)(1), in place of the basis of a qualified film an amount equal to the qualified United States production costs (as defined in section 48(k)(5) and paragraph (e)(1) of this section) with respect to the film must be used.

(e) **Definitions—(1) Qualified United States production costs.** For purposes of section 48(k) of the Code, the term "qualified United States production costs" means with respect to any film—

(i) Direct production costs allocable to the United States, plus

(ii) If 80 percent or more of the direct production costs are allocable to the United States, all other production costs except direct production costs allocable outside the United States.

(2) **Production costs.** The term "production costs", for purposes of section 48(k), includes the following:

(i) A reasonable allocation of general overhead costs, if capitalized,

(ii) The cost of obtaining screen rights and other material being filmed, and of developing the screenplay, if capitalized,

(iii) Residuals (as defined in paragraph (e)(3) of this section) whether or not capitalized,

Proposed Reg. § 1.48-8

(iv) Participations (as defined in paragraph (e)(4) of this section) whether or not capitalized, subject to the limitations provided in paragraph (e)(5) of this section), and

(v) All direct production costs described in paragraph (f) of this section.

The term "production costs" does not include advertising and marketing costs. It also does not include any subsequently incurred costs except for the costs described in paragraph (e)(9) of this section.

(3) **Residuals.** The term "residuals", for purposes of section 48(k) and paragraph (e) of this section, means contingent compensation payments (as opposed to fixed compensation payments) paid to creative and technical personnel, to their unions (including guilds) or to pension, health, or welfare funds, pursuant to the terms of collective bargaining agreements between the producer and the union. The collective bargaining agreements generally cover all films produced over a period of several years. For example, the conditions which fix the amount of residuals payable in any instance, may be based upon a percentage of gross receipts of the film or upon the number of times the film has been broadcast in a particular market.

(4) **Participations.** The term "participations" for purposes of section 48(k) and paragraph (e) of this section means contingent compensation payments, paid to actors, production personnel, writers, composers, directors and producers for their services in connection with the production of the film. The terms of participations generally are negotiated on a film by film basis. The amount of a participation due in any case generally is based upon the gross income or net income of the film. Participations do not include any payment which represents a distribution of profits to a person on the basis of an ownership interest. However, the mere fact that a payment is contingent on the net profits derived from the exhibition of a film does not mean that the payment is based on an ownership interest. (See Example 15, §1.1348-3(b)(4).)

(5) **Limitations.** Notwithstanding any other provision of this paragraph, the term "production costs" does not include participations, paid during the taxable year, with respect to all qualified films placed in service by the taxpayer during a particular taxable year, to the extent that such participations exceed the lesser of:

(i) The sum of 25 percent of each participation paid to each person (excluding that part of any participation payable to one person in excess of $1,000,000 for one qualified film) for each qualified film placed in service during that particular taxable year; or

(ii) Twelve and one-half percent of the aggregate qualified United States production costs determined under paragraph (e)(1) of this section (other than residuals described in paragraph (e)(3) of this section and participations described in paragraph (e)(4) of this section) of all qualified films placed in service during that particular taxable year.

(6) **Rules with respect to the 25-percent limitation.** In applying paragraph (e)(5)(i) of this section in taxable years after qualified films were placed in service, participations paid in all prior years on the films are taken into account. Thus, if films X and Y were placed in service in 1975 and participations of $100 on film X and $40 on film Y were paid in 1975 and participations of $20 on film X and $16 on film Y were paid in 1976, the 25-percent limitation would limit participations includible in production costs with respect to all films placed in service in 1975 to a maximum of $44 (25 percent of $176 ($100 + $40 + $20 + $16)). If paragraph (e)(5)(i) of this section limits total includible participations for all qualified films placed in service during a particular taxable year, the includible participations with respect to each qualified film placed in service in that year will be 25 percent of each participation paid during the taxable year (excluding that part of any participation payable to one person in excess of $1,000,000) with respect to each of these qualified films.

(7) **Rules with respect to the 12½-percent limitation.** If paragraph (e)(5)(ii) of this section limits total includible participations for all qualified films placed in service during a particular taxable year, the includible participations with respect to films placed in service in that year will be 12½ percent of the aggregate qualified United States production costs (other than residuals and participations) of those films reduced by participations includible in production costs in prior years with respect to those films. In such a case, includible participations with respect to each such qualified film shall be determined by

apportioning total includible participations pro rata among all qualified films placed in service in the particular taxable year on the basis of total participations paid with respect to each such qualified film, taking into account no more than $1,000,000 in participations for any one individual. In determining qualified participations under paragraph (e)(5)(ii) of this section in taxable years after a qualified film has been placed in service, costs of preparing prints described in paragraph (f)(1)(ii) of this section are taken into account.

(8) **Examples.** Paragraph (e)(5) of this section may be illustrated by the following examples:—

Example (1). (a) X, a corporation using a calendar taxable year, produced two motion picture films entirely within the United States during 1975, film L, placed in service on July 1, 1975, and film M, placed in service on October 1, 1975. Corporation X incurred $5,750,000 in aggregate production costs other than residuals and participations in producing film L and $565,000 in aggregate production costs other than residuals and participations in producing film M. On December 31, 1975, $1,250,000 in residuals and $2,000,000 in participations were paid in connection with film L and $25,000 in residuals and $10,000 in participations were paid in connection with film M. Participations paid in connection with film L consisted of $1,100,000 paid to the starring actor and $900,000 paid to the director.

All participations paid in connection with film M were paid to one actor.

(b) The 25-percent limitation on participations in paragraph (e)(5)(i) of this section would limit participations includible in production costs to a maximum of $475,000 with respect to film L. This amount consists of $250,000 (25 percent of $1,000,000 ($1,100,000 participation paid to the starring actor—$100,000 paid in excess of $1,000,000)) plus $225,000 (25 percent of the $900,000 participations paid to the director). The 25-percent limitation would limit participations with respect to film M to $2,500 (25 percent of the $10,000). The 25-percent limitation would limit participations includible in production costs with respect to all films placed in service in 1975 to a maximum of $477,500 ($475,000 plus $2,500).

(c) The 12½-percent limitation on participations in paragraph (e)(5)(ii) of this section would limit participations includible in production costs with respect to all films placed in service in 1975 to a maximum of $789,375 (12½ percent of $6,315,000 ($5,750,000 in aggregate production costs of film L other than residuals and participations + $565,000 in aggregate production costs of film M other than residuals and participations)).

(d) Under paragraph (e)(5) of this section, the lower limit on participations in paragraph (b) of this example applies to limit the participations includible in production costs on December 31, 1975, to $475,000 for film L and $2,500 for film M. Production costs to be taken into account in 1975 for film L are $7,475,000 ($5,750,000 in aggregate production costs other than residuals and participations plus $1,250,000 in residuals and $475,000 for includible participations). Production costs to be taken into account in 1975 for film M are $592,500 ($565,000 in aggregate production costs other than residuals and participations plus $25,000 in residuals and $2,500 for includible participations).

Example (2). (a) The facts are the same as in example (1) except that in 1976 an additional $20,000 in residuals and $10,000 in participations were paid with respect to film L. In addition, corporation X produced film N entirely within the United States and placed it in service on Novebmer 1, 1976. Corporation X incurred $750,000 in aggregate production costs other than residuals and participations in producing film N. On December 31, 1976, $25,000 in residuals and $25,000 in participations were paid in connection with film N. All participations paid in connection with film L were paid to the director and all participations paid in connection with film N were paid to the starring actor.

(b) The 25-percent limitation on participations in paragraph (e)(5)(i) of this section would limit participations includible in production costs with respect to all films placed in service in 1975 to a maximum of $480,000 ($475,000 for includible participations under paragraph (e)(5)(i) of this section in 1975 with respect to film L + $2,500 for includible participations under paragraph (e)(5)(i) of this section in 1975 with respect to film M plus $2,500 (25 percent of the $10,000 participations paid in 1976 for film L)). It would

Proposed Reg. §1.48-8

also limit participations includible in production costs with respect to all films placed in service in 1976 to a maximum of $6,250 (25 percent of the $25,000).

(c) The 12½-percent limitation on participations in paragraph (e)(5)(ii) of this section, would limit participations includible in production costs with respect to all films placed in service in 1975 (films L and M) to a maximum of $789,375. (See computation in paragraph (c) of Example (1).) It would also limit production costs with respect to the only film placed in service in 1976 (film N) to a maximum of $93,750 (12½ percent of $750,000 in aggregate production costs other than residuals and participations).

(d) Under paragraph (e)(5) of this section, the lower limit on participations in paragraph (b) of this example applies to limit the participations includible in production costs on December 31, 1976, to $2,500 for film L and $6,250 for film N. Total production costs to be taken into account by corporation X in 1976 are $22,500 ($20,000 in residuals + $2,500 in participations) for film L and $781,250 ($750,000 in aggregate production costs other than residuals and participations + $25,000 in residuals and $6,250 in allowable participations) for film N.

Example (3). (a) The facts are the same as in examples (1) and (2) except that in 1977 an additional $250,000 in residuals and $700,000 in participations were paid with respect to film N. In addition, corporation X produced films O and P entirely within the United States and placed them in service in 1977. Corporation X incurred $1,000,000 in aggregate production costs other than residuals and participations in producing film O and $500,000 in aggregate production costs other than residuals and participations in producing film P. On December 31, 1977, $200,000 in residuals and $1,000,000 in participations were paid in connection with film O and $100,000 in residuals and $300,000 in participations were paid in connection with film P. Participations paid in connection with films N, O, and P were all paid to the starring actor of each film.

(b) The 25-percent limitation on participations in paragraph (e)(5)(i) of this section would limit participations includible in production costs with respect to all films placed in service in 1976 to a maximum of $181,250 ($6,250 in participations paid in 1976 with respect to film N + $175,000 (25 percent of the $700,000 participation paid in 1977 for film N)). It would also limit participations includible in production costs with respect to all films placed in service in 1977 to a maximum of $250,000 (25 percent of the $1,000,000 participation paid to the starring actor) with respect to film O and $75,000 (25 percent of the $300,000 participation paid to the starring actor) with respect to film P.

(c) The 12½-percent limitation on participations in paragraph (e)(5)(ii) of this section, would limit participations includible in aggregate production costs with respect to all films placed in service in 1976 (film N) to a maximum of $93,750 (12½ percent of $750,000 in aggregate production costs of film N other than residuals and participations). It would also limit participations includible in production costs with respect to all films placed in service in 1977 to a maximum of $187,500 (12½ percent of $1,500,000 ($1,000,000 in aggregate production costs of film O other than residuals and particpations + $500,000 in aggregate production costs of film P other than residuals and participations)).

(d) Under paragraph (e)(5) of this section, the lower limit on participations in paragraph (c) of this example applies to limit the participations includible in aggregate production costs on December 31, 1977, to $87,500 (maximum participations allowable of $93,750—$6,250 for includible participation in 1976) for all films placed in service in 1976 and to $187,500 for all films placed in service in 1977.

(9) **Subsequently incurred costs.** The only costs incurred after a qualified film has been placed in service which are includible in production costs are the cost of preparing prints placed in service within 12 months after the film is initially released for public exhibition in any medium, residuals described in paragraph (e)(3) of this section, and participations described in paragraph (e)(4) of this section.

(f) **Direct production costs.** (1) **Definition.** The term "direct production costs", for purposes of section 48(k)(5), includes the following capitalized costs:

(i) Compensation for services performed by actors, production personnel, writers, composers, directors, and producers,

(ii) The cost of preparing prints placed in service within 12 months after the film is initially released for public exhibition in any medium (excluding the cost of distributing those prints),
(iii) The cost of equipment and supplies,
(iv) The cost of costumes, props, scenery, and all accessories,
(v) The cost of renting facilities on location, a?nd
(vi) The cost of film editing.

The term does not include any cost described in paragraph (e)(2)(i) through (e)(2)(iv) of this section.

(2) **Allocation of direct production costs.** For purposes of section 48(k)(5) of the Code and paragraph (e)(1) of this section, direct production costs are characterized as either direct production costs allocable to the United States or direct production costs allocable outside the United States, under the following rules:

(i) Compensation paid for services (including fringe benefits) is allocated to the country in which the services are performed, except that payments to United States persons (within the meaning of section 7701(a)(30) of the Code) for services performed outside the United States are allocated to the United States. For purposes of this subparagraph (2), expenses described in paragraphs (f)(2)(iii) and (iv) of this section will be treated as compensation and not subject to the allocation rules described therein, to the extent that the expenses are treated by the taxpayer as compensation to an employee on the taxpayer's return and subjected to withholding of income tax at the source under chapter 24. Payments to an electing small business corporation (within the meaning of section 1371) or to a partnership are considered payments to a United States person only to the extent that the payments are included in the gross income of a United States person other than an electing small business corporation or partnership. Payments to a domestic corporation, other than an electing small business corporation, are not considered payments to a United States person to the extent of the value of services provided by the corporation which are performed by persons who are not United States persons.

(ii) All printing costs (within the meaning of section 48(k)(B)(iii) and paragraph (f)(1)(ii) of this section) are allocated to the country in which the costs are incurred.

(iii) Per diem and other living allowances are allocated to the country in which the expenses are incurred.

(iv) Travel expenses for personnel are apportioned one-half to direct production costs allocable to the country of departure and one-half to direct production costs allocable to the country of arrival.

(v) Amounts for equipment, supplies, and related shipping costs are allocated to the country in which, with respect to the production of the film, the predominant use occurs.

In the absence of better evidence as to the actual place of predominant use, allocations may be made in accordance with the shooting days of the film.

(vi) All other items are allocated consistent with the principle set forth in section 48(k)(5)(D)(ii) and paragraph (f)(2)(v) of this section.

(g) **Entitlement to investment credit by taxpayers other than original owner—(1) Election by lessor to treat lessee as having acquired a film.** In the case of an election under section 48(d) of the Code by a lessor of a qualified film to treat the lessee as having acquired the film, the lessee's qualified United States production costs may not exceed the lowest of (1) the qualified United States production costs of the lessor, (2) the amount that the lessor has at risk with respect to the qualified film, or (3) the amount that the lessee has at risk with respect to the qualified film. For purposes of section 48(d) and section 46(e)(3), a lease with respect to a qualified film exists only when a person with an ownership interest (as defined in paragraph (a)(4) of this section) transfers full rights to exploit the film for its entire estimated useful life in one or more mediums in one or more specifically defined geographical areas (as defined in paragraph (a)(2) of this section). The election is not available where the lessee is precluded by law, regulation, or government action, from acquiring all rights to commercially exploit the film.

(2) **Purchase or sale of a qualified film.** If a taxpayer purchases an entire qualified film before it is placed in service, the purchaser's qualified United States production costs

Proposed Reg. § 1.48-8

are equal to the lesser of the total qualified United States production costs of the seller at the time of the sale or the purchase price of the film. If a taxpayer purchases part of a film before it is placed in service, the purchaser's qualified United States production costs are equal to the lesser of the qualified United States production costs of the seller at the time of the sale or the purchase price of that part of the film purchased. Notwithstanding the preceding sentences, in determining investment credit, the purchaser of a qualified film may include subsequently incurred costs (described in paragraph (e)(9) of this section) which he incurs. If a taxpayer purchases one or more parts of a film, and in the same transaction acquires an interest in the film which does not constitute a part, the purchase price for purposes of this subparagraph (2) shall be reduced by the amount of the purchase price attributable to the interest. For qualified films purchased on or before January 19, 1978, if a purchaser does not know, and after making reasonable efforts cannot obtain, the seller's qualified United States production costs, the purchaser must establish to the satisfaction of the district director, the amount of those costs on the basis of a reasonable estimate. For qualified films purchased after January 19, 1978, no credit is allowable unless the purchaser attaches to its income tax return in which the credit is claimed, a statement addressed to the district director, signed by the seller which (i) describes the nature and amount of each item qualifying as United States production costs, (ii) specifies the nature and purchase price of any part of the film previously sold, and (iii) states that the seller has not previously placed the film in service. If prior to December 20, 1977, a person has entered into a binding contract to purchase a qualified film, the qualified film will be regarded as having been purchased prior to January 19, 1978. If a taxpayer sells part of a film before the film is placed in service, his qualified United States production costs are reduced by the purchase price of that part of the qualified film sold. For example, assume a producer sells, for $75, all rights to display a film in Europe. The total qualified United States production costs for the film were $100. The producer's qualified United States production costs for that part of the film retained are $25 ($100 in total qualified United States production costs for the whole film reduced by the $75 purchase price).

Credit for Expenses of Work Incentive Programs

Section 1.50A-1 is amended by revising paragraph (c) to read as follows:

§ 1.50A-1 (Proposed Treasury Decision, published 4-21-75) **Determination of amount.**

* * * * * * * * * * *

(c) **Liability for tax.** For the purpose of computing the limitation based on amount of tax, section 50A(a)(3) defines the liability for tax as the income tax imposed for the taxable year by Chapter 1 of the Code (including the 6 percent additional tax imposed by section 1562(b)), reduced by the sum of the credits allowable under—

(1) Section 33 (relating to taxes of foreign countries and possessions of the United States),

(2) Section 35 (relating to partially tax-exempt interest received by individuals),

(3) Section 37 (relating to retirement income),

(4) Section 38 (relating to investment in certain depreciable property), and

(5) Section 41 (relating to contributions to candidates for public office).

For purposes of this paragraph, the tax imposed for the taxable year by section 56 (relating to imposition of minimum tax for tax preferences), section 72(m)(5)(B) (relating to 10 percent tax on premature distributions to owner-employees), section 402(e) (relating to tax on lump sum distributions), section 408(f) (relating to additional tax on income from certain retirement accounts), section 531 (relating to imposition of accumulated earnings tax), section 541 (relating to imposition of personal holding company tax), or section 1378 (relating to tax on certain capital gains of Subchapter S corporations), and any additional tax imposed for the taxable year by section 1351(d)(1) (relating to recoveries of foreign expropriation losses), shall not be considered tax imposed by Chapter 1 of the

Code for such year. Thus, the liability for tax for purposes of computing the limitation based on amount of tax for the taxable year is determined without regard to any tax imposed by section 56, 72(m)(5)(B), 402(e), 408(f), 531, 541, 1351(d)(1) or 1378 of the Code. In addition, any increase in tax resulting from the application of section 50A(c) and (d) and § 1.50A-3 (relating to recomputation of credit allowed due to early termination of employment by employer, or failure to pay comparable wages) shall not be treated as tax imposed by Chapter 1 of the Code for purposes of computing the liability for tax. See section 50A (c)(3) and (d)(2).

* * * * * * * * * * *

New Jobs Credit

§ 1.52-1 (Proposed Treasury Decision, published 12-14-77.) Trades or businesses that are under common control.

(a) **Apportionment of new jobs credit among members of a group of trades or businesses that are under common control—(1) General rule.** In the case of a group of trades or businesses that are under common control, the amount of the new jobs credit (computed under section 51 as if all the organizations that are under common control are one trade or business) must be apportioned among the members of the group on the basis of each member's proportionate contribution to the increase in unemployment insurance wages of the entire group. The limitations in section 53 apply to each organization individually.

(2) **Example.** Subparagraph (1) of this paragraph may be illustrated by the following example:

Example. (a) A Company and its three subsidiaries, B, C, and D Companies, are a group of businesses that are under common control. A, B, C, and D have paid out the following amounts in unemployment insurance wages during 1976 and 1977:

	1976	1977	Increase in FUTA wages in 1977 over 1976
A Co.	$1,000,000	$1,015,000	+$15,000
B Co.	500,000	650,000	+150,000
C Co.	600,000	580,000	−20,000
D Co.	40,000	100,000	+60,000
Total	$2,140,000	$2,345,000	+$205,000

(b) Since all employees of trades or businesses that are under common control are treated as employed by a single employer, the computations in section 51 are performed as if all the organizations which are under common control are one trade or business. Consequently, the amounts of the total unemployment insurance wages of the group in 1976 (i.e., $2,140,000) and 1977 (i.e., $2,345,000) are used to determine the increase in unemployment insurance wages in 1977 over the 1976 wage base. Since the amount equal to 102 percent of the 1976 unemployment insurance wages ($2,182,800) is greater than the amount equal to 50 percent of the 1977 unemployment insurance wages ($1,172,500), the increase in unemployment insurance wages in 1977 over the 1976 wage base is $162,200 ($2,345,000—$2,182,800). The limitations in section 51(c), (d), and (g) must also be computed as though all the organizations under common control are one trade or business. For purposes of this example, it is assumed that none of those limitations reduce the amount of the increase in unemployment insurance wages. As a result, the amount of the new jobs credit allowed to the group of businesses is $81,100 (50% of $162,200).

(c) The credit is apportioned among A, B, and D Companies on the basis of their proportionate contributions to the increase in unemployment insurance wages. No credit would be allowed to C Company because it did not contribute to the increase in the group's unemployment insurance wages. A Company's share of the credit would be

Proposed Reg. § 1.52-1

$5,406.66 ($81,100 × ($15,000 ÷ $225,000 (i.e., $15,000 + $150,000 + $60,000))), B Company's share would be $54,066.67 ($81,100 × ($150,000 ÷ $225,000)), and D Company's share would be $21,626.67 ($81,100 × ($60,000 ÷ $225,000)).

(b) **Trades or businesses that are under common control.** For purposes of this section, the term "trades or businesses that are under common control" means any group of trades or businesses that is either a "parent-subsidiary group under common control" as defined in paragraph (c) of this section, a "brother-sister group under common control" as defined in paragraph (d) of this section, or a "combined group under common control" as defined in paragraph (e) of this section. For purposes of this section and §§1.52-2 and 1.52-3, the term "organization" means a sole proprietorship, a partnership, a trust, an estate, or a corporation.

(c) **Parent-subsidiary group under common control.** The term "parent-subsidiary group under common control" means one or more chains of organizations conducting trades or businesses that are connected through ownership of a controlling interest with a common parent organization if—

(1) A controlling interest in each of the organizations, except the common parent organization, is owned (directly and with the application of §11.414(c)-4(b)(1), relating to options) by one or more of the other organizations; and

(2) The common parent organization owns (directly and with the application of §11.414(c)-4(b)(1), relating to options) a controlling interest in at least one of the other organizations, excluding, in computing the controlling interest, any direct ownership interest by the other organizations.

(d) **Brother-sister group under common control.** The term "brother-sister group under common control" means two or more organizations conducting trades or businesses, in which a controlling interest in each organization is owned (directly and with the application of §11.414(c)-4(b)(1), relating to options) by the same five or fewer persons. The persons may be individuals, estates, or trusts. The ownership of each person is taken into account only to the extent the ownership is identical with respect to each organization. For an illustration of a brother-sister group under common control, see Example (1) of §1.1563-1(a)(3)(ii).

(e) **Combined group under control.** The term "combined group under common control" means a group of three or more organizations, in which (1) each organization is a member of either a parent-subsidiary group under common control or brother-sister group under common control, and (2) at least one organization is the common parent organization of a parent-subsidiary group under common control and also a member of a brother-sister group under common control.

(f) **Controlling interest defined—(1) Controlling interest.** For purposes of this section, the term "controlling interest" means:

(i) In the case of a corporation, ownership of stock possessing more than 50 percent of the total combined voting power of all classes of stock entitled to vote or more than 50 percent of the total value of the shares of all classes of stock of the corporation;

(ii) In the case of a trust or estate, ownership of an actuarial interest (determined under subparagraph (2) of this paragraph) of more than 50 percent of the trust or estate;

(iii) In the case of a partnership, ownership of more than 50 percent of the profit interest or capital interest of the partnership; and

(iv) In the case of a sole proprietorship, ownership of the sole proprietorship.

(2) **Actuarial interest.** For purposes of this section, the actuarial interest of each beneficiary of a trust or estate shall be determined by assuming the maximum exercise of discretion by the fiduciary in favor of the beneficiary. The factors and method prescribed in §20.2031-10 of this chapter (Estate Tax Regulations) for use in ascertaining the value of an interest in property for estate tax purposes will be used to determine a beneficiary's actuarial interest.

(3) **Exclusion of certain interests and stock in determining control.** In determining control under this paragraph, the term "interest" and the term "stock" do not include an interest that is treated as not outstanding under §11.414(c)-3. In addition, the term "stock" does not include treasury stock or nonvoting stock that is limited and preferred regarding dividends.

(g) **Rules for determining ownership.** In determining the ownership of an interest in an organization for purposes of this section, the constructive ownership rules of §11.414(c)-4 shall apply.

§ 1.52-2 Proposed Treasury Decision, published 12-14-77.) **Adjustments for acquisitions and dispositions.**

(a) **General rule.** If, after December 31, 1975, an employer acquires the major portion of a trade or business or the major portion of a separate unit of a trade or business, then both the amount of the unemployment insurance wages and the amount of total wages considered to have been paid by the employer, for both the year in which the acquisition occurred and the preceding year, must be increased, respectively, by the amount of the unemployment insurance wages and the amount of total wages paid by the predecessor employer that are attributable to the acquired portion of the trade or business or separate unit. If the predecessor employer informs the acquiring employer in writing of the amount of the unemployment insurance wages and total wages attributable to the acquired portion of the trade or business that have been paid during the periods preceding the acquisition, then the amounts of the unemployment insurance wages and total wages considered paid by the predecessor shall be decreased by those amounts. Regardless of whether the predecessor employer so informs the acquiring employer, the predecessor employer shall not be allowed a credit for the amount of any increase in the unemployment insurance wages or the total wages in the calendar year of the acquisition attributable to the acquired portion of the trade or business over the amount of such wages in the calendar year preceding the acquisition.

(b) **Meaning of terms—(1) Acquisition.** (i) For purposes of this section, the term "acquisition" includes a lease agreement if the effect of the lease is to transfer the major portion of the trade or business or of a separate unit of the trade or business for the period of the lease. For instance, if one company leases a factory (including equipment) to another company for a two-year period, the employees are retained by the second company, and the factory is used for the same general purposes as before, then for purposes of this section the lessee has acquired the lessor's trade or business for the period of the lease.

(ii) Neither the major portion of a trade or business nor the major portion of a separate unit of a trade or business is acquired merely by acquiring physical assets. The acquisition must transfer a viable trade or business.

(iii) Subdivision (ii) of this subparagraph may be illustrated by the following examples:

Example (1). R Company, a restaurant, sells its building and all its restaurant equipment to S Company and moves into a larger, more modern building across the street. R Company purchases new equipment, retains its name and continues to operate as a restaurant. S Company opens a new restaurant in the old R Company building. S Company has merely acquired the old R Company assets; it has not acquired any portion of R Company's business.

Example (2). The facts are the same as in Example (1), except that R Company also sells its name and goodwill to S Company and ceases to operate a restaurant business. S Company operates its restaurant using the old R Company name. In this situation, S Company has acquired R Company's business.

(2) **Separate unit.** (i) A separate unit is a segment of a trade or business capable of operating as a self-sustaining enterprise with minor adjustments. The allocation of a portion of the goodwill of a trade or business to one of its segments is a strong indication that that segment is a separate unit.

(ii) The following examples are illustrations of the acquisition of a separate unit of a trade or business:

Example (1). The M Corporation, which has been engaged in the sale and repair of boats, leases the repair shop building and all the property used in its boat repair operations to the N Company for four years and gives the N Company a covenant not to compete in the boat repair business for the period of the lease. The N Company is considered to have acquired a separate unit of M Corporation's business for the period of the lease.

Proposed Reg. § 1.52-2

Example (2). (a) The P Company is engaged in the operation of a chain of department stores. There are eight divisions, each division is located in a different metropolitan area of the country, and each division operates under a different name. Although certain buying and merchandising functions are centralized, each division's day-to-day operations are independent of the others. The Q Corporation acquires all of the physical and intangible assets of one of the divisions, including the division's name. Other than making those minor adjustments necessary to give the division buying and merchandising departments, the Q Corporation allows the division to continue doing business in the same manner as it had been operating prior to the acquisition. The Q Corporation has acquired a separate unit of the P Company's business.

(b) The facts are the same as in (a) above, except that Q Corporation buys the division merely to obtain its store locations. Before the Q Corporation takes over, the division liquidates its inventory in a going-out-of-business sale. The Q Corporation has merely acquired assets in this transaction, not a separate unit of P Company's business.

Example (3). The R Company processes and distributes meat products. Both the processing division and the distributorship are self-sustaining, profitable operations. The acquisition of either the meat processing division or the distributorship would be an acquisition of a separate unit of the R Company's business.

Example (4). The S Corporation is engaged in the manufacture and sale of steel and steel products. S Corporation also owns a coal mine, which it operates for the sole purpose of supplying its coal requirements for its steel manufacturing operations. The acquisition of the coal mine would be an acquisition of a separate unit of the S Company's business.

Example (5). The T Company, which is engaged in the business of operating a chain of drug stores, sells its only downtown drug store to the V Company and agrees not to open another T Company store in the downtown area for five years. Included in the purchase price is an amount that is charged for the goodwill of the store location. The V Company has acquired a separate unit of the T Company's business.

Example (6). The W Company, which is engaged in the business of operating a chain of drug stores, sells one of its stores to the X Company, but continues to operate another drug store three blocks away. The X Company opens the store doing business under its own name. The X Company has not acquired a separate unit of the W Company's business.

Example (7). (a) The Y Corporation, which is engaged in the manufacture of mattresses, sells one of its three factories to the Z Company. At the time of the sale, the factory is capable of profitably manufacturing mattresses on its own. Z Company has acquired a separate unit of the Y Corporation.

(b) The facts are the same as in (a) above, except that a profitable manufacturing operation cannot be conducted in the factory standing on its own. Z Company has not acquired a separate unit of the Y Corporation.

Example (8). The O Construction Company is owned by A, B, and C, who are unrelated individuals. It owns equipment valued at 1.5 million dollars and construction contracts valued at 6 million dollars. A, wishing to start his own company, exchanges his interest in O Company for 2 million dollars of contracts and a sufficient amount of equipment to enable him to begin business immediately. A has acquired a separate unit of the O Company's business.

(3) **Major portion.** All the facts and circumstances surrounding the transaction shall be taken into account in determining what constitutes a major portion of a trade or business (or separate unit). Factors to be considered include:

(i) The fair market value of the assets in the portion relative to the fair market value of the other assets of the trade or business (or separate unit);

(ii) The proportion of goodwill attributable to the portion of the trade or business (or separate unit);

(iii) The proportion of the number of employees of the trade or business (or separate unit) attributable to the portion in the periods immediately preceding the transaction; and

(iv) The proportion of the sales or gross receipts, net income, and budget of the trade or business (or separate unit) attributable to the portion.

§ 1.52-3 (Proposed Treasury Decision, published 12-14-77.) **Limitations with respect to certain persons.**

(a) **Mutual savings institutions.** In the case of an organization to which section 593 applies (that is, a mutual savings bank, a cooperative bank, or a domestic building and loan association), the amount of the credit allowable under section 44B shall be 50 percent of the amount otherwise determined under section 51, or, in the case of an organization under common control, under section 52(a) or (b).

(b) **Regulated investment companies and real estate investment trusts.** In the case of a regulated investment company or a real estate investment trust subject to taxation under subchapter M, chapter 1 of the Code, the amount of the credit allowable under section 44B shall be reduced to the company's or trust's ratable share of the credit. The ratable share shall be the ratio which the taxable income of the regulated investment company or real estate investment trust for the taxable year bears to its taxable income increased by the amount of the deduction for dividends paid taken into account under section 852(b)(2)(D) in computing investment company taxable income or under section 857(b)(2)(B) in computing real estate investment trust taxable income, as the case may be.

(c) **Cooperatives.** (1) In the case of a cooperative organization described in section 1318(a), the amount of the credit allowable under section 44B shall be reduced to the cooperative's ratable share of the credit. The ratable share shall be the ratio which the taxable income of the cooperative for the taxable year bears to its taxable income increased by the amount of the deductions allowed under section 1382(b) and (c).

The proposed amendments to 26 CFR Part 1 are as follows:

§ 1.53-1 (Proposed Treasury Decision, published 4-3-78.) **Separate rule for pass-through of jobs credit.**

(a) **In general.** Under section 53(b), in the case of a credit earned under section 44B by a partnership, estate or trust, or subchapter S corporation, the amount of the credit that may be taken into account by a partner, beneficiary, or shareholder may not exceed a limitation separately computed with respect to the partner's, beneficiary's, or shareholder's interest in the entity. The separate computation is required not only for the taxable year with respect to which the credit is earned but also for each taxable year to which an unused credit attributable to an interest in such an entity is carried back or over. This section prescribes rules, under the authority of section 44B(b), relating to computation of the separate limitation.

(b) **Application of credit earned.** A credit earned under section 44B by a partnership, estate or trust, or subchapter S corporation shall be applied by a partner, beneficiary, or shareholder, to the extent allowed under section 53(b), before applying any other credit earned under section 44B. For example, if an individual has a new jobs credit from a proprietorship of $2,000 and from a partnership (after applying section 53(b)) of $1,800, but the credit must be limited under section 53(a) to $3,000, the entire $1,800 credit from the partnership would be applied before any part of the $2,000 amount is applied.

(c) **Amount of separate limitation.** The amount of the separate limitation is equal to the partner's, beneficiary's, or shareholder's limitation under section 53(a) for the taxable year multipled by a fraction. The numerator of the fraction is the portion of the taxpayer's taxable income for the year attributable to the taxpayer's interest in the entity. The denominator of the fraction is the taxpayer's total taxable income for the year reduced by the zero bracket amount, if any.

(d) **Portion of taxable income attributable to an interest in a partnership, estate or trust, or subchapter S corporation**—(1) **General rule.** The portion of a taxpayer's taxable income attributable to an interest in a partnership, estate or trust, or subchapter S corporation is the amount of income from that entity the taxpayer is required to include in gross income, reduced by—

Proposed Reg. § 1.53-1

(i) The amount of the deductions allowed to the taxpayer that are attributable to the taxpayer's interest in the entity; and

(ii) A proportionate share of the deductions allowed to the taxpayer not attributable to a specific activity (as defined in paragraph (e)).

If a deduction comprises both an item that is attributable to the taxpayer's interest in the entity and an item or items that are not attributable to the interest in the entity, and if the deduction is limited by a provision of the Code (such as section 170(b), relating to limitations on charitable contributions), the deduction must be prorated among the items taken into account in computing the deduction. For example, if an individual makes a charitable contribution of $5,000 and his distributive share of a partnership includes $2,000 in charitable contributions made by the partnership, and if the charitable contribution deduction is limited to $3,500 under section 170(b), then the portion of the deduction allowed to the taxpayer that is not attributable to a specific activity is $2,500 ($3,500 × ($5,000 ÷ $7,000)) and the portion of the deduction allowed to the taxpayer that is attributable to the interest in the partnership is $1,000 ($3,500 × ($2,000 ÷ $7,000)).

(2) **Deductions attributable to an interest in an entity.** Examples of deductions that are attributable to the taxpayer's interest in an entity include (but are not limited to) a deduction under section 1202 attributable to a net capital gain passed through the entity, and a deduction attributable to a deductible item (such as a charitable contribution) that has been passed through the entity.

(3) **Computation of the proportionate share of deductions not attributable to a specific activity.** The proportionate share of a deduction of the taxpayer not attributable to a specific activity is obtained by multiplying the amount of the deduction by a fraction. The numerator of the fraction is the income from the entity that the taxpayer is required to include in gross income, reduced by the amount of the deductions of the taxpayer that are attributable to the taxpayer's interest in the entity. The denominator is the taxpayer's gross income reduced by the amount of all the deductions attributable to specific activities.

(4) **Examples.** The method of determining the amount of taxable income attributable to an interest in a partnership, estate or trust, or subchapter S corporation is illustrated by the following examples:

Example (1). (a) A, a single individual, is a shareholder in S Corporation, a subchapter S corporation. A is required to include the following amounts from S corporation in his gross income:

Salary		$ 3,000
Undistributed taxable income:		
Ordinary income	$8,000	
Net capital gain	2,000	
	10,000	
		$13,000

A has income from other activities:

Ordinary income	$ 6,000
Net capital gain	4,000
	$10,000

(b) In order to determine the taxable income attributable to A's interest in S Corporation, it is necessary to reduce the amount of income from S Corpration that A is required to include in gross income by the amount of A's deductions attributable to the interest in S Corporation and by a proportionate share of A's deductions not attributable to a specific activity. These computations are made in paragraph (c) of this example. However, before the computation reducing A's income by a proportionate share of the deductions not attributable to a specific activity can be made, the ratio described in subparagraph (3) of this paragraph (d) must be determined. The numerator of the ratio (the amount of income from S Corporation that A is required to include in gross income, reduced by the amount of the deductions attributable to A's interest in S Corporation) is obtained in paragraph (c) of this example in the process of computing A's taxable income attributable to the interest in S Corporation. The determination of the denominator (A's gross income reduced by the amount of all deductions attributable to specific activities), however,, requires a separate computation, which follows:

Gross income:		
Income from S Corp.	$13,000	
Income from other sources	10,000	
		$23,000
Less: Deductions attributable to specific activities:		
Section 1202 deduction (50% of $6,000)		3,000
A's gross income reduced by the amount of the deductions attributable to specific activities (denominator of the ratio for determining the proportionate share of deductions not attributable to a specific activity):		$20,000

(c) Computation of the amount of A's taxable income attributable to the interest in S Corporation.

Income from S Corporation that A is required to include in gross income:		
Ordinary income	$11,000	
Net capital gain	2,000	
		$13,000
Less:		
Deductions of the taxpayer attributable to the interest in S Corporation:		
Section 1202 deduction (50% of $2,000)		1,000
(Numerator of the ratio for determining the proportionate share of deductions not attributable to a specific activity)		$12,000
Less:		
Proportionate share of the deductions of the taxpayer not attributable to a specific activity:		
Personal exemption deduction ($750 × $12,000/$20,000)	$ 450	
Zero bracket amount ($2,200 × $12,000/$20,000)	1,320	
Total		1,770
Portion of A's taxable income attributable to interest in S Corporation		$10,230

Proposed Reg. §1.53-1

Example (2). (a) C, a married individual with two children, is a partner in the CD Company. C's distributive share of the CD Company consists of the following:

Ordinary income (other than guaranteed payment)	$38,420
Guaranteed payment	20,000
Net long-term capital gain	6,000
Net short-term capital loss	2,000
Dividends qualifying for exclusion	100
Charitable contributions	500

C also has items of income from other sources and deductions, as follow:

Ordinary income	$21,680
Short-term capital gain	2,000
Dividends qualifying for exclusion	400
Deductions:	
Deductible medical expenses	16,000
Charitable contributions	4,000
Alimony	18,000
Interest and taxes on home	8,000
Loss relating to another specific activity	4,000

(b) In order to determine C's taxable income attributable to the interest in the partnership, it is necessary to reduce the amount of income from the partnership that C is required to include in gross income by the amount of C's deductions attributable to the interest in the partnership and by a proportionate share of C's deductions not attributable to a specific activity. These computations are made in paragraph (c) of this example. However, before the computation reducing C's income by a proportionate share of the deductions not attributable to a specific activity can be made, the ratio described in subparagraph (3) of this paragraph (d) must be determined. The numerator of the ratio is determined in paragraph (c) of this example in the process of computing C's taxable income attributable to the interest in the partnership. The denominator, however, requires a separate computation, reducing C's gross income by the amount of all deductions attributable to specific activities. This computation is as follows:

```
Gross income:
  Income from the partnership:
    Ordinary income .....................   $58,420
    Net long-term capital gain               6,000
    Dividends ..............   $ 100
      Less: Proportionate
        share of dividend
        exclusion ($100 x
        $100/$500 ..........        20
                              _____
                                            80
                                                       _____
                                                       $64,500
  Income from other sources
    Ordinary income .....................   $21,680
    Net short-term capital gain             2,000
    Dividends ............   $ 400
      Less: Proportionate
        share of dividend
        exclusion ($100 x
        $400/$500 ........        80
                              _____
                                            320
                                                       _____
                                                       24,000
                                                       _____
                                                       $88,500
```

Less:
Deductions attributable to specific activities:
Net short-term capital loss passed through the partnership $2,000
Loss related to another specific activity 4,000
Section 1202 deduction attributable to the interest in the partnership 2,000
Charitable contribution deduction passed through the partnership 500

                   8,500

C's gross income, reduced by the amount of the deductions attributable to specific activities (denominator of the ratio for determining the proportionate share of deductions not attributable to a specific activity): $80,000

(c) Computation of the amount of C's taxable income attributable to the interest in the partnership:

Distributive share of ordinary income (other than guaranteed payments) $38,420
Guaranteed payment 20,000
Distributive share of dividends less share of exclusion 80
Distributive share of net long-term capital gain 6,000

                   $64,500

Less:
Deductions of the partner attributable to the interest in the partnership:
Section 1202 deduction (50% of $4,000) .... $ 2,000
Charitable contribution passed through the partnership 500
Net short-term capital loss passed through the partnership 2,000

                   4,500

(Numerator of the ratio for determining the proportionate share of deductions not attributable to a specific activity) $60,000
Less:
Proportionate share of the deductions of the partner not attributable to a specific activity:
Section 1202 deduction ($1,000 × $60,000/$80,000) .... $ 750
Deductible medical expenses ($16,000 × $60,000/$80,000) 12,000
Charitable contributions ($4,000 × $60,000/$80,000) 3,000
Alimony ($18,000 × $60,000/$80,000) 13,500

Proposed Reg. § 1.53-1

Interest and taxes on home ($8,000 × $60,000/$80,000)	6,000
Personal exemption deduction ($3,000 × $60,000/$80,000)	2,250
Total	37,500
Portion of C's taxable income attributable to the interest in the partnership	$22,500

C has a deduction under section 1202 of $3,000. Of that deduction, $2,000 is attributable directly to C's interest in the partnership (50% of the net capital gain that would result from offsetting the $6,000 net long-term capital gain and the $2,000 net short-term capital loss that are attributable to C's interest in the partnership). Since the remaining $1,000 deduction under section 1202 cannot be attributed directly to either C's income from the partnership or any other specific activity, it must be treated as a deduction not attributable to a specific activity.

(e) **Deductions not attributable to a specific activity—(1) "Specific activity" defined.** A "specific activity" means a course of continuous conduct involving a particular line of endeavor, whether or not the activity is carried on for profit. Examples of a specific activity are:

(i) A trade or business carried on by the taxpayer;

(ii) A trade or business carried on by an entity in which the taxpayer has an interest;

(iii) An activity with respect to which the taxpayer is entitled to a deduction under section 212;

(iv) The operation of a farm as a hobby.

(2) **Types of deductions not attributable to a specific activity.** Examples of deductions not attributable to a specific activity include charitable contributions made by the partner, beneficiary, or shareholder; medical expenses; alimony; interest on personal debts of the partner, beneficiary, or shareholder; and real estate taxes on the personal residence of the partner, beneficiary, or shareholder. For purposes of this section, in cases in which deductions are not itemized, the zero bracket amount is considered to be a deduction not attributable to a specific activity.

Minimum Tax for Tax Preferences

The following sections are inserted immediately before § 1.61:

§ 1.56-1 (Proposed Treasury Decision, published 12-30-70, 6-24-71.) **Imposition of tax.**

(a) **In general.** Section 56(a) imposes an income tax on the items of tax preference (as defined in § 1.57-1) of all persons other than persons specifically exempt from the taxes imposed by chapter 1. The items of tax preference represent income of a person which either is not subject to current taxation by reason of temporary exclusion (such as stock options) or by reason of an acceleration of deductions (such as accelerated depreciation) or is sheltered from full taxation by reason of certain deductions (such as percentage depletion) or by reason of a special rate of tax (such as the rate of tax on corporate capital gains). The tax imposed by section 56 is in addition to the other taxes imposed by chapter 1.

(b) **Computation of tax.** The amount of such tax is 10 percent of the excess (referred to herein as "the minimum tax base") of—

(1) The sum of the taxpayer's items of tax preference for such year in excess of the taxpayer's minimum tax exemption (determined under § 1.58-1) for such year, over

(2) The sum of:

(i) The taxes imposed for such year under chapter 1 other than the taxes imposed by section 56 (relating to minimum tax for tax preferences), by section 531

(relating to accumulated earnings tax), or by section 541 relating to personal holding company tax), reduced by the sum of the credits allowable under—
  (a) Section 33 (relating to taxes of foreign countries and possessions of the United States),
  (b) Section 37 (relating to retirement income), and
  (c) Section 38 (relating to investment credit), and
  (ii) The tax carryovers to such taxable year (as described in § 1.56-5).

(c) **Special rule.** For purposes of paragraph (b) of this section where for any taxable year in which a tax is imposed under section 668 (relating to treatment of amounts deemed distributed by a trust in preceding years), that portion of the section 668 tax representing an increase in an earlier year's chapter 1 taxes as recomputed (other than taxes imposed by section 56, section 531, and section 541) is allowable as a reduction in such earlier year's minimum tax base and is not allowable as a reduction in the minimum tax base for the current taxable year. The remaining portion of the section 668 tax is not allowable as a reduction in the minimum tax base for any taxable year. Similarly, taxes imposed under section 614(c)(4) relating to increase in tax with respect to aggregation of certain mineral interests) or under section 1351(d) (relating to recoveries of foreign expropriation losses) for any taxable year are not allowed as a reduction in the minimum tax base for such taxable year to the extent they represent chapter 1 taxes which are allowable as a reduction in a minimum tax base for an earlier taxable year for purposes of the computations under section 614(c)(4) or section 1351(d) or to the extent they represent an increase in the tax imposed by section 56, section 531, or section 541 in an earlier taxable year.

(d) **Limitation on amounts treated as tax preferences.** See § 1.57-4 with respect to a limitation on the amount of the sum of the items of tax preference where there is no tax benefit from the use of an item of tax preference.

§ 1.56-2 (Proposed Treasury Decision, published 12-30-70.) **Deferral of tax liability in case of certain net operating losses.**

(a) **In general.** Section 56(b) provides for the deferral of liability for the minimum tax where, for the taxable year, the taxpayer has—
  (1) A net operating loss for such taxable year any portion of which (under section 172) remains as a net operating loss carryover to a succeeding taxable year, and
  (2) Items of tax preference in excess of the minimum tax exemption (hereinafter referred to as "excess tax preferences").

In such a case, an amount of tax equal to the lesser of the tax imposed under section 56(a) (after allowance of the retirement income credit to the extent that such credit cannot be used against the other taxes imposed by chapter 1) or 10 percent of the amount of the net operating loss carryover described in subparagraph (1) of this paragraph is deferred. Such amount is not treated as tax imposed in such taxable year, but is treated as tax imposed in the succeeding taxable year or years in which the net operating loss is used as provided in paragraphs (b) and (c) of this section. Deferral will result in the above case regardless of the character of the tax preference items. Thus, for example, if the taxpayer has $1,030,000 of items of tax preference, including the stock option item of tax preference, and a $750,000 net operating loss available for carryover to subsequent taxable years, the amount of tax imposed for the taxable year under section 56(a) is $100,000 and $75,000 is deferred by application of section 56(b). Therefore, only $25,000 is treated as tax imposed for the taxable year. The provisions of this section are applicable in the case of a net operating loss or comparable item such as an operations loss under section 812 and an unused loss as defined in section 825(b).

(b) **Year of liability.** In any taxable year in which any portion of a net operating loss carryover attributable to the amount of excess tax preferences reduces taxable income (in the form of a net operating loss deduction), section 56(b)(2) treats as tax liability imposed in such taxable year an amount equal to 10 percent of such reduction. For this purpose, the portion of such net operating loss which is considered attributable to the amount of excess tax preferences is an amount equal to the lesser of such excess or the amount of the net operating loss carryover described in paragraph (a)(1) of this section. In no case, however, shall the total amount of tax imposed by reason of section 56(b) in subsequent years exceed the amount of the tax that was deferred in the loss year.

(c) **Priority of reduction.** (1) If a portion of a net operating loss is attributable to an amount of excess tax preferences, such portion is considered to reduce taxable income in succeeding taxable years only after the other portion (if any) of such net operating loss is used to reduce taxable income. Accordingly, if the amount of a net operating loss which may be carried to succeeding taxable years is reduced because of a modification required to be made pursuant to section 172(b)(2), such reduction is to be considered to be first from that portion of the net operating loss that is attributable to excess tax preferences. If a portion of a net operating loss carryover which is attributable to an amount of excess tax preferences is not used to reduce taxable income in any succeeding taxable year, no minimum tax will be imposed with respect to such portion.

(2) In the case of taxpayers with deductions attributable to foreign sources which are suspense preferences (as defined in paragraph (c)(1)(ii) and (2)(ii) of § 1.58-7), the amount of such deductions is not included in the portion of the net operating loss not attributable to excess tax preferences. The portion of the net operating loss attributable to excess tax preferences is increased by the amount of suspense preferences which are, in accordance with the provisions of § 1.58-7 (c), converted to actual items of tax preference (and not used against the minimum tax exemption of the loss year) in subsequent taxable years. The other

portion of the net operating loss is increased by the amount of suspense preferences which reduce taxable income in subsequent taxable years but are not converted to actual items of tax preference (or are so converted but used against the minimum tax exemption of the loss year). See § 1.58-7(c)(1)(iii) Example (4).

(d) **Multiple net operating loss carryovers.** In determining whether a net operating loss is used to reduce taxable income in a taxable year to which two or more net operating losses are carried, the ordering rules of section 172(b) and the regulations thereunder are to be applied. Thus, for example, the portion of a net operating loss carried over from an earlier taxable year which is attributable to an amount of excess tax preference is used to reduce taxable income in the carryover year before any portion of any other net operating loss carried over or back from a taxable year subsequent to the earlier taxable year.

(e) **Examples:** The application of this section may be illustrated by the following examples:

Example (1). In 1970, A, a calendar year taxpayer, who is a single individual, has $180,000 of items of tax preference, a $150,000 net operating loss of which $100,000 may be carried forward, and no tax liability under chapter 1 without regard to the minimum tax. His minimum tax computed under section 56(a) is $15,000 (10% x ($180,000—$30,000)). Under section 56(b)(1) an amount equal to the lesser of the amount determined under section 56(a) ($15,000) or 10 percent of the net operating loss which may be carried forward ($10,000) is treated as a deferred liability. Thus, his minimum tax liability for 1970 is $5,000 ($15,000 minimum tax under section 56(a) minus $10,000 deferred tax liability under section 56(b)). If, in 1971, he has $80,000 of taxable income before the deduction for the 1970 net operating loss, his minimum tax liability is $8,000 (10 percent of the amount by which the net operating loss carryforward from 1970 reduces taxable income) plus any minimum tax liability resulting from items of tax preference arising in 1971. If, by reason of the modifications provided by section 172(b)(2), no portion of the 1970 net operating loss remains as a carryover from 1971, no further minimum tax liability will result from the items of tax preference arising in 1970.

Example (2). In 1970, A, a calendar year taxpayer who is a single individual, has $90,000 of items of tax preference, a $100,000 net operating loss available for carryover to future taxable years, no net operating loss carryovers from prior taxable years, and no tax liability under chapter 1 without regard to the minimum tax. His minimum tax computed under section 56(a) is $6,000 (10% $\times$ ($90,000 — $30,000)). Under section 56(b)(1) an amount equal to the lesser of the amount determined under section 56(a) ($6,000) or 10 percent of the net operating loss subject to carryforward ($10,000) is treated as a deferred liability. Thus, A owes no minimum tax in 1970 and the entire $6,000 of minimum tax liability is deferred. Under section 56(b)(2), the portion of the net operating loss attributable to the excess tax preferences described in section 56(b)(1)(B) is $60,000.

(a) In 1971, A has $25,000 of taxable income before the deduction for the 1970 net operating loss. Thus, in 1971, A has no minimum tax liability attributable to the items of tax preference arising in 1970 since, by application of section 56(b)(3), the portion of the 1970 net operating loss carryforward not attributable to the excess described in section 56(b)(1)(B), or $40,000, is considered applied against taxable income before the remaining portion.

(b) In 1972, A has $50,000 of taxable income before the deduction for the remaining 1970 net operating loss. Thus, the first $15,000 of reduction in taxable income is considered as from the portion of the 1970 net operating loss carryforward not attributable to the excess tax preferences described in section 56(b)(1)(B) and the remaining $35,000 of reduction in taxable income is considered attributable to such excess. A's 1972 minimum tax attributable to items of tax preference arising in 1970 is, therefore, $3,500 (10% $\times$ $35,000).

(c) In 1973, A has $80,000 of taxable income before the deduction for the 1970 net operating loss. The remaining $25,000 of the 1970 net operating loss carryforward is used to reduce taxable income in 1973. Thus, A's 1973 minimum

Proposed Reg. § 1.56-2

tax liability attributable to items of tax preference arising in 1970 is $2,500 (10% × $25,000).

Example (3). In 1971, M Corporation, a Western Hemisphere trade corporation (as defined in section 921), reporting on a calendar year basis has $20,000 of taxable income after all deductions including the Western Hemisphere trade deduction allowable under section 922 in the amount of $30,000. In 1970, M Corporation had a net operating loss of $100,000 all of which was available for carryover to 1971 and $60,000 of which was attributable to excess tax preferences. In computing the amount of the 1970 net operating loss carried over to 1972 pursuant to section 172(b), the 1971 Western Hemisphere trade corporation deduction is not taken into account. Thus, M Corporation's recomputed income under section 172(b) is $50,000 ($20,000 taxable income plus $30,000 Western Hemisphere trade corporation deduction). Pursuant to paragraph (c)(1) of this section, $20,000 of the $40,000 portion of the 1970 net operating loss not attributable to excess tax preferences is considered to reduce taxable income in 1971 and $30,000 of the $60,000 portion of the 1970 net operating loss attributable to excess tax preferences is considered reduced pursuant to section 172(b)(2). Thus, M Corporation has no 1971 minimum tax attributable to items of tax preference arising in 1970. Of the $50,000 remaining of the 1970 net operating loss, $30,000 is attributable to excess tax preference.

Example (4). In 1972, A, a calendar year taxpayer who is a single individual, has $25,000 of taxable income resulting from $50,000 of net long-term capital gains. In 1971, A had a net operating loss of $100,000 all of which is available to carryover to 1972 and $60,000 of which is attributable to excess tax preferences. By application of section 172(b) only $50,000 of the 1971 net operating loss is carried over to 1973. Pursuant to paragraph (c) of this section, $25,000 of the $40,000 portion of the 1971 net operating loss not attributable to excess tax preference is considered to reduce taxable income in 1972. Of the $50,000 remaining of the 1971 net operating loss, $15,000 is not attributable to excess tax preferences and $35,000 is attributable to excess tax preferences. Thus, the $25,000 section 1202 deduction, in effect, reduces the portion of the 1971 net operating loss attributable to excess tax preferences. Because a net operating loss carryover is reduced to the extent of any section 1202 deduction, section 1202 deductions do not normally produce a tax benefit in such circumstances and, pursuant to § 1.57-4, would not be treated as items of tax preference. However, in this case, to the extent the portion of the 1971 net operating loss carryover attributable to excess tax preferences is reduced by reason of the section 1202 deduction, such deduction does result in a tax benefit to the taxpayer and is, therefore, treated as an item of tax preference in 1972. See § 1.57-4(b)(2).

§ 1.56-3 (Proposed Treasury Decision, published 12-30-70.) Effective date.

(a) In general. The minimum tax is effective for taxable years ending after December 31, 1969.

(b) Taxable year beginning in 1969 and ending in 1970. In the case of a taxable year beginning in 1969 and ending in 1970, the amount of the minimum tax shall be an amount equal to the amount determined under section 56 multiplied by the following fraction:

$$\frac{\text{Number of days in the taxable year ending after December 31, 1969}}{\text{Number of days in the entire taxable year.}}$$

Where, by reason of section 56(b) and § 1.56-2, tax initially imposed in a 1969-1970 fiscal year is deferred until a subsequent taxable year or years, the amount of such tax liability in any subsequent taxable year is determined by application of the above fraction. Section 21, relating to computation of tax in years where there is a change in rates, is not applicable to the initial imposition of the minimum tax for tax preferences. The application of this paragraph may be illustrated by the following example:

Example. The taxpayer uses a June 30 fiscal year. For fiscal 1969-1970 the taxpayer has $180,000 of items of tax preference and a $50,000 net operating loss. In fiscal year 1970-1971, the taxpayer uses the full net operating loss carryover from 1969-1970 to reduce his taxable income by $50,000. Thus, without regard to the proration rules applicable under this section, the taxpayer's minimum tax liability for items of tax preference arising in 1969-1970 is $15,000 (10% x $180,000 — $30,000) of which $5,000 (10% x $50,000) is deferred until 1970-1971 under the principles of section 56(b) and § 1.56-2. By application of the above formula the taxpayer's actual minimum tax liability is $4,986.30 in 1969-1970 and $2,493.15 in 1970-1971 determined as follows:

$$1969\text{-}1970: \frac{182 \times \$10,000}{365}$$

$$1970\text{-}1971: \frac{182 \times \$5,000}{365}$$

§ 1.56-4 (Proposed Treasury Decision, published 12-30-70.) **Certain taxpayers.**

For application of the minimum tax in the case of estates and trusts, electing small business corporations, common trust funds, regulated investment companies, real estate investment trusts, and partnerships, see §§ 1.58-2 through 1.58-6.

§ 1.56-5 (Proposed Treasury Decision, published 6-24-71.) **Tax carryovers.**

(a) **In general.** Section 56 (c) provides a 7 year carryover of the excess of the taxes described in paragraph (1) of such section imposed during the taxable year over the items of tax preference described in paragraph (2) of such section for such taxable year for the purpose of reducing the amount subject to tax under section 56 (a) in subsequent taxable years.

(b) **Computation of amount of carryover.** The amount of tax carryover described in section 56 (c) is the excess (if any) of—

(1) The taxes imposed for the taxable year under chapter 1 other than taxes imposed by section 56 (relating to minimum tax for tax preferences), by section 531 (relating to accumulated earnings tax), or by section 541 (relating to personal holding company tax), reduced by the sum of the credits allowable under—

(i) Section 33 (relating to taxes of foreign countries and possessions of the United States),

(ii) Section 37 (relating to retirement income), and

(iii) Section 38 (relating to investment credit), over

(2) The sum of the taxpayer's items of tax preference for such year in excess of the taxpayer's minimum tax exemption (determined under § 1.58-1) for such year. For purposes of section 56 (c) and this section, taxes imposed in a taxable year ending on or before December 31, 1969, are not included in the taxes described in subparagraph (1) of this paragraph. In addition, the rules of paragraph (c) of § 1.56-1 are applicable in determining the taxable year for which taxes are imposed under chapter 1 for purposes of paragraph (a) (1) of this section.

(c) **Operation of carryover.** A tax carryover shall be carried over to each of the 7 taxable years succeeding the taxable year in which such amount arose as follows:

(1) To the first such succeeding taxable year to reduce (to the extent provided in paragraph (d) of this section) the amount subject to tax under section 56 (a) for such taxable year and

(2) To the extent such amount is not used to reduce the amount subject to tax under section 56 (a) for such first succeeding taxable year, to each of the succeeding 6 taxable years but only to the extent such amount is not used to reduce the amount

Proposed Reg. § 1.56-5

subject to tax under section 56 (a) in taxable years intervening between the taxable year in which such amount arose and the taxable year to which such amount may otherwise be carried over.

(d) **Priority of reduction.** If tax carryovers arising in 2 or more taxable years are carried over to a subsequent taxable year, the tax carryover arising in the earliest taxable year shall be used to reduce the amount subject to tax under section 56(a) for such subsequent taxable year before any tax carryovers arising in a later taxable year.

(e) **Special rules**—(1) *Periods of less than 12 months.* A fractional part of a year which is a taxable year under section 441(b) or 7701(a)(23) is a taxable year for purposes of section 56(c) and this section.

(2) *Electing small business corporations.* A taxable year for which a corporation is an electing small business corporation (as defined in section 1371(b)) shall be counted as a taxable year for purposes of determining the taxable years to which amounts which are available as a carryover under paragraph (a) of this section may be carried whether or not such carryovers arose in a year in which an election was in effect.

(3) *Husband and wife*—(i) **From joint to separate return.** If a joint return is filed by a husband and wife in a taxable year or years to which a tax carryover is attributable but separate returns are filed in any subsequent taxable year to which such carryover may be carried over to reduce the amount subject to tax under section 56(a), such carryover described in paragraph (b) of this section shall be allocated between husband and wife for purposes of reducing the amount subject to tax under section 56(a) for such subsequent taxable year in accordance with the principles of § 1.172-7(d).

(ii) From separate to joint return. If separate returns are filed by a husband and wife in a taxable year or years in which a tax carryover is attributable but a joint return is filed in any subsequent taxable year to which such carryover may be carried over to reduce the amount subject to tax under section 56(a), such carryover shall be aggregated for purposes of reducing the amount subject to tax under section 56(a) for such subsequent taxable year.

(4) *Estates and trusts.* In the case of the termination of an estate or trust, tax carryovers attributable to the estate or trust shall not be allowed to the beneficiaries succeeding to the property of the estate or trust.

(5) *Corporate acquisitions.* In the case of a transaction to which section 381(a) applies, the acquiring corporation shall succeed to and take into account, as of the close of the date of distribution or transfer the tax carryovers attributable to the distributor or transferor corporation. The portion of such carryovers which may be taken into account under paragraph (b) (2) (ii) of § 1.56-1 for any taxable year shall not exceed the excess of (i) the sum of the items of tax preference for such year resulting from the continuation of the business in which the distributor or transferor corporation was engaged at the time of such transaction and the items of tax preference not related to the continuation of such business which are directly attributable to the assets acquired from the distributor or transferor corporation over (ii) an amount which bears the same ratio to the acquiring corporation's minimum tax exemption for such year as the items of tax preference described in subdivision (i) of this subparagraph bears to all of the acquiring corporation's items of tax preference for such year. This item shall be taken into account by the acquiring corporation subject to the rules in section 381(b) and the regulations thereunder.

(f) **Suspense preferences.** Where an item of tax preference which is a suspense preference (as defined in § 1.58-7) arises in a taxable year in which tax carryovers may be used to reduce the minimum tax base (or in which such carryovers arise) the minimum tax liability for that year and the tax carryovers to subsequent taxable years shall be recomputed upon the conversion of the suspense preference in a subsequent year. In lieu of the above, in all cases, since there is no difference in tax consequence, the recomputation may be accomplished by recomputing the minimum tax liability of the taxable year in which the suspense preference arose without reduction of the minimum tax base for the tax carryovers which have been used as a reduction in the minimum tax base in intervening taxable years. If such method is used, the minimum tax liability of the intervening year is not recomputed and any tax carryovers carried from the taxable year in which the suspense preference arose which remain as a carryover in the year of conversion are reduced, in the priority provided in paragraph (d) of this section, to the extent used to reduce an increase in the minimum tax base for the earlier year resulting from the conversion of the suspense preference.

(g) Taxes imposed in a taxable year beginning in 1969 and ending in 1970. In the case of a taxable year beginning in 1969 and ending in 1970 the amount of the carryover determined under paragraph (b) of this section is reduced to an amount equal to the amount of such carryover (without regard to this paragraph) multiplied by the following fraction:

$$\frac{\text{Number of days in taxable year ending after December 31, 1969}}{\text{Number of days in the entire taxable year.}}$$

(h) Example. The provisions of this section may be illustrated by the following examples:

Example (1). A is a single individual who uses a June 30 fiscal year. For fiscal 1968-1969, A had income tax liability under chapter 1 in the amount of $100,000. For fiscal 1969-1970, A had items of tax preference in the amount of $212,500 and income tax liability under chapter 1 (other than taxes imposed under sections 56, 531, and 541) of $365,000.

(a) The chapter 1 tax attributable to fiscal 1968-1969 is not available as a carryover under section 56(c) to reduce the amount subject to tax under section 56(a) since this tax arose in a taxable year ending on or before December 31, 1969.

(b) A portion of the excess of chapter 1 tax over the amount subject to tax under section 56(a) attributable to fiscal year 1969-1970 is available as a carryover as provided in section 56(c) to reduce the amount subject to tax under section 56(a). The amount of this carryover is $91,000 computed as follows:

1. Carryover under paragraph (b) of this section:
    Chapter 1 taxes $365,000
    Items of tax preference in excess of exemption 182,500
                                                              _____
                                                              $182,500

2. Reduction pursuant to paragraph (g) of this section:
    $\frac{182}{365}$ × $182,500 .... $ 91,000

Example (2). A is a calendar year taxpayer who is a single individual. In 1972, A had chapter 1 income tax liability (other than taxes imposed under sections 56, 531, and 541) of $200,000 and $50,000 of items of tax preference. In 1973, A had chapter 1 income tax liability (other than taxes imposed under sections 56, 531, and 541) of $120,000 and $40,000 of items of tax preference. In 1974, A had $400,000 of items of tax preference and no liability for tax under chapter 1 other than under section 56(a). Under section 56(c), the excess of the taxes described in paragraph (1) of that section arising in an earlier taxable year not used to reduce the amount subject to tax under section 56(a) for such taxable year can be carried over as provided in section 56(c) to reduce the amount subject to tax under section 56(a).

(a) The amount of the carryover from 1972 is $180,000 computed as follows:
    Carryover under paragraph (b) of this section:
        Chapter 1 taxes $200,000
        Items of tax preference in excess of exemption 20,000
                                                                  _____
                                                                  $180,000

Proposed Reg. §1.56-5

(b) The amount of the carryover from 1973 is $110,000 computed as follows:
Carryover under paragraph (b) of this section:
Chapter 1 taxes $120,000
Items of tax preference in excess of exemption 10,000

$110,000

(c) For 1974, the excess of taxes in the preceding taxable years is used to reduce the amount subject to tax under section 56(a). The amount of carryover attributable to excess taxes arising in 1972 is used before such excess arising in 1973. The amount of tax under section 56(a) is $8,000 computed as follows:
1974 tax preferences $400,000
Less exemption 30,000

370,000
Less 1972 carryover 180,000

190,000
Less 1973 carryover 110,000

1974 minimum tax base .... $ 80,000

1974 minimum tax ($80,000 × 10%) .... $ 8,000

Example (3). The facts are the same as in example (2) except that in 1974 A had $300,000 of items of tax preference. The amount of the carryover for taxable years after 1974 is computed as follows:
1974 tax preferences $300,000
Less exemption 30,000

270,000
Less 1972 carryover 180,000

90,000
Less 1973 carryover 90,000

Minimum tax base .... — 0 —
1973 carryover 110,000
Amount used in 1974 90,000

Amount available for taxable years after 1974 .... $ 20,000

The $20,000 remaining of the 1973 carryover is available to reduce the amount subject to tax under section 56(a) in 1975 or other future taxable years as provided in section 56(c).

Example (4). M Corporation is a calendar year taxpayer. N Corporation uses a June 30 fiscal year. For the fiscal year 1970-1971, N Corporation had excess chapter 1 tax liability as described in paragraph (a) of this section in the amount of $75,000. On January 1, 1972, M Corporation acquired N Corporation in a reorganization described in section 368(a)(1)(A). N Corporation does not use any of such excess chapter 1 tax liability to reduce the amount subject to tax under section 56(a) for the short taxable year beginning on July 1, 1971, and ending on December 31, 1971. Thus, the excess chapter 1 tax liability is available to M Corporation as a carryover under paragraph (a) of this section to reduce the amount subject to tax for the next 6 succeeding taxable years beginning with taxable year 1972 as provided in this section. In applying the carryover to 1972 and succeeding taxable years, the carryover of N Corporation subject to the limitation of § 1.56-5(e)(4) is combined with any carryovers originating with M Corporation in 1970.

§ 1.57-0 (Proposed Treasury Decision, published 12-30-70.) **Scope.**
For purposes of the minimum tax for tax preferences (subtitle A, chapter I, part VI), the items of tax preference are:

(a) Excess investment interest,

(b) The excess of accelerated depreciation on section 1250 property over straight line depreciation,

(c) The excess of accelerated depreciation on section 1245 property subject to a net lease over straight line depreciation,

(d) The excess of the amortization deduction for certified pollution control facilities over the depreciation otherwise allowable,

(e) The excess of the amortization deduction for railroad rolling stock over the depreciation otherwise allowable,

(f) The excess of the fair market value of a share of stock received pursuant to a qualified or restricted stock option over the exercise price,

(g) The excess of the addition to the reserve for losses on bad debts of financial institutions over the amount which have been allowable based on actual experience,

(h) The excess of the percentage depletion deduction over the adjusted basis of the property, and

(i) The capital gains deduction allowable under section 1202 or an equivalent amount in the case of corporations.

Accelerated depreciation on section 1245 property subject to a net lease and excess investment interest are not items of tax preference in the case of a corporation, other than a personal holding company (as defined in section 542) and an electing small business corporation (as defined in section 1371(b)). In addition, excess investment interest is an item of tax preference only for taxable years beginning before January 1, 1972. Rules for the determination of the items of tax preference are contained in §§ 1.57-1 through 1.57-5. Generally, in the case of a nonresident alien or foreign corporation, the application of §§ 1.57-1 through 1.57-5 will be limited to cases in which the taxpayer has income effectively connected with the conduct of a trade or business within the United States. Special rules for the treatment of items of tax preference in the case of certain entities and the treatment of items of tax preference relating to income from sources outside the United States are provided in section 58 and in §§ 1.58-1 through 1.58-8.

§1.57-1 (Proposed Treasury Decision, published 12-30-70). Items of tax preference defined.

(a) **Excess investment interest.** Section 57(a)(1) provides that there is to be included as an item of tax preference the amount of excess investment interest for the taxable year as determined under section 57(b) and § 1.57-2.

(b) **Accelerated depreciation on section 1250 property—(1) In general.** Section 57(a)(2) provides that, with respect to each item of section 1250 property (as defined in section 1250(c)), there is to be included as an item of tax preference the amount by which the deduction allowable for the taxable year for depreciation or amortization exceeds the deduction which would have been allowable for the taxable year if the taxpayer had depreciated the property under the straight line method for each year of its useful life for which the taxpayer has held the property. The determination of the excess under section 57(a)(2) is made with respect to each separate item of section 1250 property. Accordingly, where the amount of depreciation which would have been allowable with respect to one item of section 1250 property if the taxpayer had originally used the straight line method exceeds the allowable depreciation or amortization with respect to such property, such excess may not be used to reduce the amount of the item of tax preference resulting from another item of section 1250 property.

(2) **Separate items of section 1250 property.** The determination of what constitutes a separate item of section 1250 property is to be made on the facts and circumstances of each individual case. In general, each building is a separate item of section 1250 property, but in an appropriate case more than one building may be treated as a single item. Two or more items may be treated as one item of section 1250 property for purposes of this paragraph where, with respect

Proposed Reg. §1.57-1

to each such item: (i) the period for which depreciation is taken begins on the same date, (ii) the same estimated useful life has continually been used for purposes of taking depreciation or amortization, and (iii) the same method (and rate) of depreciation or amortization has continually been used. For example, assume a taxpayer constructed a 40-unit rental townhouse development and began taking declining balance depreciation on all 40 units as of January 1, 1970, at a uniform rate and has consistently taken depreciation on all 40 units on this same basis. Although each townhouse is a separate item of section 1250 property, all 40 townhouses may be treated as one item of section 1250 property for purposes of the minimum tax since the conditions of subdivisions (i), (ii), and (iii) of this subparagraph are met. This would be true even if the 40 townhouses comprised two 20-unit developments located apart from each other. However, if the taxpayer constructed an additional development or new section on the existing development for which he began taking depreciation on July 1, 1970, at a uniform rate for all the additional units, the additional units and the original units may not be treated as one item of section 1250 property since the condition of subdivision (i) of this subparagraph is not met. Where a portion of an item of section 1250 property has been depreciated or amortized under a method (or rate) which is different from the method (or rate) under which the other portion or portions of such item have been depreciated or amortized, such portion is considered a separate item of section 1250 property for purposes of this paragraph.

(3) **Allowable depreciation or amortization.** The phrase "deduction allowable for the taxable year for exhaustion, wear and tear, obsolescence, or amortization" and references in this paragraph to "allowable depreciation or amortization" include deductions allowable for the taxable year under section 162, 167, 212, or 611 for the depreciation or amortization of section 1250 property. Such phrase does not include depreciation allowable in the year the section 1250 property is disposed of to the extent such depreciation is reflected in ordinary income. This occurs, for example, to the extent the gain resulting from such depreciation is treated by reason of section 1250 as gain from the sale or exchange of property which is neither a capital asset nor property described in section 1231 or to the extent such gain reduces the amount of any charitable contribution by the taxpayer pursuant to section 170(e)(1)(A) (relating to reduction in the amount of certain contributions of ordinary income property). For the determination of "allowable depreciation or amortization" for taxable years in which the taxpayer has taken no deduction see § 1.1016-3(a)(2).

(4) **Straight line depreciation.** (i) For purposes of computing the depreciation which would have been allowable for the taxable year if the taxpayer had depreciated the property under the straight line method for each taxable year of its useful life, the taxpayer must use the same useful life and salvage value as was used for the first taxable year in which the taxpayer depreciated or amortized the property (subject to redeterminations made pursuant to § 1.167 (a)-1(b) and (c)). If, however, for any taxable year, no useful life was used under the method of depreciation or amortization used or an artificial period was used, such as, for example, by application of section 167(k), or salvage value was not taken into account in determining the annual allowances, such as, for example, under the declining balance method, then, for purposes of computing the depreciation which would have been allowable under the straight line method for the taxable year—

(a) There is to be used the useful life and salvage value which would have been proper if depreciation had actually been determined under the straight line method (without reference to an artificial life) throughout the period the property was held, and

(b) Such useful life and such salvage value is to be determined by taking into account for each taxable year the same facts and circumstances as would have been taken into account if the taxpayer had used such method throughout the period the property was held.

(ii) Where the original use of the property does not commence with the taxpayer, but an "accelerated" method of depreciation as described in section 167 (b)(2), (3), or (4) or section 167(i)(1)(B) or (C) is permitted (see § 1.167(c)-1 (a)(4) and (5)), the depreciation which would have been allowable under the straight line method is determined as if the property had been depreciated under the straight line method since depreciation was first taken on the property by the original user of the property. In such cases, references in this paragraph to the period for which the property is held or useful life of the property are treated as including the period beginning with the commencement of the original use of the property.

(iii) For purposes of section 57(a)(2), the straight line method includes the method of depreciation described in § 1.167(b)-1 or any other method which provides for a uniform proration of the cost or other basis (less salvage value) of the property over the estimated useful life of the property to the taxpayer (in terms of years, hours of use, or other similar time units) or estimated number of units to be produced over the life of the property to the taxpayer. If a method other than the method described in § 1.167(b)-1 is used, the estimated useful life or estimated units of production shall be determined in a manner consistent with subdivision (i) of this subparagraph.

(iv) In the case of property constructed by or improvements made by a lessee, the useful life is to be determined in accordance with § 1.167(a)-4.

(5) **Application for partial period.** If an item is section 1250 property for less than the entire taxable year, the allowable depreciation or amortization includes only the depreciation or amortization for that portion of the taxable year during which the item is section 1250 property and the amount of the depreciation which would have been allowable under the straight line method is determined only with regard to such portion of the taxable year.

(6) **No section 1250 and basis adjustment.** No adjustment is to be made as a result of the minimum tax either to the basis of section 1250 property or with respect to computations under section 1250.

(7) **Example.** The principles of this paragraph may be illustrated by the following example:

Example. The taxpayer's only item of section 1250 property is an office building with respect to which operations were commenced on January 1, 1971. The taxpayer depreciates the component parts of the building on the declining balance method. The useful life and costs of the component parts for depreciation purposes are as follows:

Asset	Useful Life	Cost	Salvage Value
Building shell	50	$400,000	$50,000
Partitions and walls	10	40,000	-0-
Ceilings	10	20,000	-0-
Electrical system	25	40,000	2,500
Heating and air conditioning system	25	60,000	2,500

For purposes of computing the item of tax preference under this paragraph for the taxpayer, the partitions, walls, and ceilings may be grouped together and the electrical, heating, and air conditioning systems may be grouped together since the period for which depreciation is taken began with respect to the assets within these two groups on the same date and the assets within each group have continually had the same useful life and have continually been depreciated under the same method (and rate).

(a) The taxpayer's 1971 item of tax preference under this paragraph would be determined as follows:

Proposed Reg. § 1.57-1

(1) Item of 1250 property	(2) Declining balance depreciation	(3) Straight line depreciation	(4) Excess of (2) over (3)
1. Shell	$12,000	$7,000	$5,000
2. Partitions, walls, ceilings	9,000	6,000	3,000
3. Electrical heating and air conditioning systems	6,000	3,800	2,200
1971 preference			10,200

(b) Assuming the above facts are the same for 1974, the taxpayer's 1974 item of tax preference under this paragraph would be determined as follows:

(1) Item of 1250 property	(2) Declining balance depreciation	(3) Straight line depreciation	(4) Excess of (2) over (3)
1. Shell	$10,952	$7,000	$3,952
2. Partitions, walls, ceilings	5,529	6,000	None
3. Electrical heating and air conditioning systems	4,983	3,800	1,183
1974 preference			5,135

(c) **Accelerated depreciation on section 1245 property subject to a net lease**— (1) **In general.** Section 57(a)(3) provides that, with respect to each item of section 1245 property (as defined in section 1245(a)(3)) which is the subject of a net lease for the taxable year, there is to be included as an item of tax preference the amount by which the deduction allowable for the taxable year for depreciation or amortization exceeds the deduction which would have been allowable for the taxable year if the taxpayer had depreciated the property under the straight line method for each year of its useful life for which the taxpayer has held the property. The determination of the excess under section 57(a)(3) is made with respect to each separate item of section 1245 property. Accordingly, where the amount of depreciation which would have been allowable with respect to one item of section 1245 property if the taxpayer had originally used the straight line method exceeds the allowable depreciation or amortization with respect to such property, such excess may not be used to reduce the amount of the item of tax preference resulting from another item of section 1245 property.

(2) **Separate items of property.** The determination of what constitutes a separate item of section 1245 property must be made on the facts and circumstances of each individual case. Such determination shall be made in a manner consistent with the principles expressed in paragraph (b)(2) of this section.

(3) **Allowable depreciation or amortization.** The phrase "deduction allowable for the taxable year for exhaustion, wear and tear, obsolescence, or amortization" and references in this paragraph to "allowable depreciation or amortization" include deductions allowable for the taxable year under section 162, 167 (including depreciation allowable under section 167 by reason of section 179), 169, 184, 185, 212, or 611 for the depreciation or amortization of section 1245 property. Such phrase does not include depreciation allowable in the year the section 1245 property is disposed of to the extent such depreciation is reflected in ordinary income. This occurs, for example, to the extent the gain resulting from such depreciation is treated by reason of section 1245 as gain from the sale or exchange of property which is neither a capital asset nor property described in section 1231 or to the extent such gain reduces the amount of any charitable contribution by the taxpayer pursuant to section 170(e)(1)(A) (relating to reduction in the amount of certain contributions of ordinary income property). Amortization of certified pollution control facilities under section 169, and amortization of railroad rolling stock under section 184 are not to be treated as amortization for purposes of section 57(a)(3) to the extent such amounts are treated as an item of tax preference under section 57(a)(4) or (5) (see paragraphs (d) and (e) of this section). For the determination of "allowable depreciation or amortization" for taxable years in which the taxpayer has taken no deduction see § 1.1016-3(a)(2).

(4) **Straight line method of depreciation.** The determination of the depreciation which would have been allowable under the straight line method shall be made in a manner consistent with paragraph (b)(4) of this section. Such amount shall

include any amount allowable under section 167 by reason of section 179 (relating to additional first-year depreciation for small business).

(5) **Application for partial period.** If an item is section 1245 property for less than the entire taxable year or subject to a net lease for less than the entire taxable year the allowable depreciation or amortization includes only the depreciation or amortization for that portion of the taxable year during which the item was both section 1245 property and subject to a net lease and the amount of the depreciation which would have been allowable under the straight line method is to be determined only with regard to such portion of the taxable year.

(6) **Net lease.** Section 57(a)(3) applies only if the section 1245 property is the subject of a net lease for all or part of the taxable year. See § 1.57-3 for the determination of when an item is considered the subject of a net lease.

(7) **No section 1245 and basis adjustment.** No adjustment is to be made as a result of the minimum tax either to the basis of section 1245 property or with respect to computations under section 1245.

(8) **Nonapplicability to corporations.** Section 57(a)(3) does not apply to a corporation other than an electing small business corporation (as defined in section 1371(b)) and a personal holding company (as defined in section 542).

(d) **Amortization of certified pollution control facilities**—(1) **In general.** Section 57(a)(4) provides that, with respect to each certified pollution control facility for which an election is in effect under section 169, there is to be included as an item of tax preference the amount by which the deduction allowable for the taxable year under such section exceeds the depreciation deduction which would otherwise be allowable under section 167. The determination under section 57(a)(4) is made with respect to each separate certified pollution control facility. Accordingly, where the amount of the depreciation deduction which would otherwise be allowable under section 167 with respect to one facility exceeds the allowable amortization deduction under section 169 with respect to such facility, such excess may not be used to offset an item of tax preference resulting from another facility.

(2) **Separate facilities.** The determination of what constitutes a separate facility must be made on the facts and circumstances of each individual case. Generally, each facility with respect to which a separate election is in effect under section 169 shall be treated as a separate facility for purposes of this paragraph. However, if the depreciation or amortization which would have been allowable without regard to section 169 with respect to any part of a facility is based on a different useful life, date placed in service, or method of depreciation or amortization from the other part or parts of such facility, such part is considered a separate facility for purposes of this paragraph. For example, if a building constitutes a certified pollution control facility and various component parts of the building have different useful lives, each group of component parts with the same useful life would be treated as a separate facility for purposes of this paragraph. Two or more facilities may be treated as one facility for purposes of this paragraph where, with respect to each such facility: (i) the initial amortization under section 169 commences on the same date, (ii) the facility is placed in service on the same date, (iii) the estimated useful life which would be the basis for depreciation or amortization other than under section 169 has continually been the same, and (iv) the method of depreciation or amortization which could have been used without regard to section 169 could have continually been the same.

(3) **Amount allowable under section 169.** For purposes of the determination of the amount of the deduction allowable under section 169, see section 169 and the regulations thereunder. Such amount, however, shall not include amortization allowable in the year the pollution control facility is disposed of to the extent such amortization is reflected in ordinary income. This occurs, for example, to the extent the gain resulting from such amortization is treated by reason of section 1245 as

Proposed Reg. § 1.57-1

gain from the sale or exchange of property which is neither a capital asset nor property described in section 1231 or to the extent such gain reduces the amount of any charitable contribution by the taxpayer pursuant to section 170(e)(1)(A) (relating to reduction in the amount of certain contributions of ordinary income property).

(4) **Otherwise allowable deduction.** (i) The determination of the amount of the depreciation deduction otherwise allowable under section 167 is made as if the taxpayer had depreciated the property under section 167 for each year of its useful life for which the property has been held. For this purpose, any method which would have been permissible under section 167 for such taxable year, including accelerated methods, may be used and any additional amount which would have been allowable by reason of section 179 (relating to additional first-year depreciation for small business) may be included.

(ii) If a deduction for depreciation has not been taken by the taxpayer in any taxable year under section 167 with respect to the facility—

(a) There is to be used the useful life and salvage value which would have been proper under section 167,

(b) Such useful life and salvage value is determined by taking into account for each taxable year the same facts and circumstances as would have been taken into account if the taxpayer had used such method throughout the period the property has been held, and

(c) The date the property is placed in service is, for purposes of this section, deemed to be the first day of the first month for which the amortization deduction is taken with respect to the facility under section 169.

If, prior to the date amortization begins under section 169, a deduction for depreciation has been taken by the taxpayer in any taxable year under section 167 with respect to the facility, the useful life, salvage value, etc., used for that purpose is deemed to be the appropriate useful life, salvage value, etc., for purposes of this paragraph, with such adjustments as are appropriate in light of the facts and circumstances which would have been taken into account since the time the last such depreciation deduction was taken, unless it is established by clear and convincing evidence that some other useful life, salvage value, or date the property is placed in service is more appropriate.

(iii) For purposes of section 57(a)(4) and this paragraph, if the deduction for amortization or depreciation which would have been allowable had no election been made under section 169 would have been—

(a) An amortization deduction based on the term of a leasehold or

(b) A depreciation deduction determined by reference to section 611,

such deduction is to be deemed to be a deduction allowable under section 167.

(iv) If a facility is subject to amortization under section 169 for less than the entire taxable year, the otherwise allowable depreciation deduction under section 167 shall be determined only with regard to that portion of the taxable year during which the election under section 169 is in effect.

(v) If less than the entire adjusted basis of a facility is subject to amortization under section 169, the otherwise allowable depreciation deduction under section 167 shall be determined only with regard to that portion of the adjusted basis subject to amortization under section 169.

(5) **No section 1245 and basis adjustment.** No adjustment is to be made as a result of the minimum tax either to the basis of a certified pollution control facility or with respect to computations under section 1245.

(6) **Relationship to section 57(a)(3).** See paragraph (c)(3) with respect to an adjustment in the amount treated as amortization under that provision where both paragraphs (3) and (4) of section 57(a) are applicable to the same item of property.

(7) **Example.** The principles of this paragraph may be illustrated by the following example:

Example. A calendar year taxpayer has a certified pollution control facility on which an election is in effect under section 169 commencing with January 1, 1971. No part of the facility is section 1250 property. The original basis of the facility is $100,000 of which $75,000 constitutes amortizable basis. The useful life of the facility is 20 years. The taxpayer depreciates the $25,000 portion of the facility which is not amortizable basis under the double declining method and began taking depreciation on January 1, 1971.

(a) The taxpayer's 1971 item of tax preference under this paragraph would be determined as follows:

1. Amortization deduction	$15,000
2. Depreciation deduction on amortizable basis (double declining method)	7,500
1971 Preference (excess of 1 over 2)	$ 7,500

(b) If the taxpayer terminated his election under section 169 in 1972 effective as of July 1, 1972, the taxpayer's 1972 item of tax preference would be determined as follows:

1. Amortization deduction	$7,500
2. Depreciation deduction on amortizable basis: Full year ($75,000 (original basis) less $7,500 ("depreciation" to 1-1-72) equals adjusted basis of $67,500; multiplied by .10 (double declining rate))	$6,750
Portion of full year's depreciation attributable to amortization period (one-half)	3,375
1972 Preference (excess of 1 over 2)	$4,125

(e) **Amortization of railroad rolling stock**—(1) **In general.** Section 57(a)(5) provides that, with respect to each unit of railroad rolling stock for which an election is in effect under section 184, there is to be included as an item of tax preference the amount by which the deduction allowable for the taxable year under such section exceeds the depreciation deduction which would otherwise be allowable under section 167. The determination under section 57(a)(5) is made with respect to each separate unit of rolling stock. Accordingly, where the amount of the depreciation deduction which would otherwise be allowable under section 167 with respect to one unit exceeds the allowable amortization deduction under section 184 with respect to such unit, such excess may not be used to offset an item of tax preference resulting from another unit.

(2) **Separate units of rolling stock.** The determination of what constitutes a separate unit of rolling stock must be made on the facts and circumstances of each individual case. Such determination shall be made in a manner consistent with the manner in which the comparable determination is made with respect to separate certified pollution control facilities under paragraph (d)(2) of this section.

(3) **Amount allowable under section 184.** For purposes of the determination of the amount of the deduction allowable under section 184, see section 184 and the regulations thereunder. Such amount, however, shall not include amortization allowable in the year the rolling stock is disposed of to the extent such amortization is reflected in ordinary income. This occurs, for example, to the extent the gain resulting from such amortization is treated by reason of section 1245 as gain from the sale or exchange of property which is neither a capital asset nor property described in section 1231 or to the extent such gain reduces the amount of any charitable contribution by the taxpayer pursuant to section 170(e)(1)(A) (relating to reduction in the amount of certain contributions of ordinary income property).

(4) **Otherwise allowable deduction.** The determination of the amount of the depreciation deduction otherwise allowable under section 167 is to be made in a manner consistent with the manner in which the comparable deduction with respect to certified pollution control facilities is determined under paragraph (d)(4) of this section.

(5) **No section 1245 or basis adjustment.** No adjustment is to be made as a result of the minimum tax either to the basis of a unit of railroad rolling stock or with respect to computations under section 1245.

Proposed Reg. §1.57-1

(6) **Relationship to section 57(a)(3).** See paragraph (c)(3) of this section with respect to an adjustment in the amount treated as amortization under that provision where both paragraphs (3) and (5) of section 57(a) are applicable to the same item.

(f) **Stock options—(1) In general.** Section 57(a)(6) provides that with respect to each transfer of a share of stock pursuant to the exercise of a qualified stock option or a restricted stock option, there shall be included by the transferee as an item of tax preference the amount by which the fair market value of the share at the time of exercise exceeds the option price. The stock option item of tax preference is subject to tax under section 56(a) in the taxable year of the transferee in which the transfer is made.

(2) **Definitions.** See § 1.421-7(e), (f), and (g) for the definitions of "option price", "exercise", and "transfer", respectively. For the definition of a qualified stock option see section 422(b) and § 1.422-2. For the definition of a restricted stock option see section 424(b) and § 1.424-2. The definitions and special rules contained in section 425 and the regulations thereunder are applicable to this paragraph.

(3) **Fair market value.** The fair market value of a share of stock received pursuant to the exercise of a qualified or restricted stock option is to be determined as of the date of the exercise of the option and consistent with the principles applicable under section 83(a)(1) and the regulations thereunder.

(4) **Foreign source options.** In the case of an option attributable to sources within any foreign country or possession, see section 58(g) and § 1.58-8.

(5) **Inapplicability in certain cases.** (i) Section 57(a)(6) is inapplicable if, in the taxable year of the transfer, there is a disposition of the stock or a modification of the stock option plan which disposition or modification renders section 421(a) inapplicable or applicable solely by reason of section 423.

(ii) Section 57(a)(6) is inapplicable if, section 421(a) does not apply to the transfer because of employment requirements of section 422(a)(2) or section 424(a)(2).

(6) **Proportionate applicability.** Where, by reason of section 422(b)(7) and (c)(3) (relating to percentage ownership limitations), only a portion of a transfer qualifies for application of section 421, the fair market value and option price shall be determined only with regard to that portion of the transfer which so qualifies.

(7) **No basis adjustment.** No adjustment shall be made to the basis of the stock received pursuant to the exercise of a qualified or restricted stock option as a result of the minimum tax.

(g) **Reserves for losses on bad debts of financial institutions—(1) In general.** Section 57(a)(7) provides that, in the case of a financial institution to which section 585 or 593 (both relating to reserves for losses on loans) applies, there shall be included as an item of tax preference the amount by which the deduction allowable for the taxable year for a reasonable addition to a reserve for bad debts exceeds the amount that would have been allowable had the institution maintained its bad debt reserve for all taxable years on the basis of the institution's actual experience.

(2) **Taxpayers covered.** Section 57(a)(7) applies only to an institution (or organization) to which section 585 or 593 applies. See sections 585(a) and 593(a) and the regulations thereunder for a description of those institutions.

(3) **Allowable deduction.** For purposes of this paragraph, the amount of the deduction allowable for the taxable year for a reasonable addition to a reserve for bad debts is the amount of the deduction allowed under section 166(c) by reference to section 585 or 593.

(4) **Actual experience.** (i) For purposes of this paragraph, the determination of the amount which would have been allowable had the institution maintained its reserve for bad debts on the basis of actual experience is the amount determined under section 585(b)(3)(A) and the regulations thereunder. For this purpose, the

beginning balance for the first taxable year ending in 1970 is the amount which bears the same ratio to loans outstanding at the beginning of the taxable year as (a) the total bad debts sustained during the 5 preceding taxable years, adjusted for recoveries of bad debts during such period, bears to (b) the sum of the loans outstanding at the close of such 5 taxable years. The taxpayer may, however, select a more appropriate balance based on its actual experience subject to the approval of the district director upon examination of the return. Any such selection and approval shall be made in a manner consistent with the selection and approval of a bad debt reserve method under § 1.166-1(b). In the case of an institution which has been in existence for less than 5 taxable years as of the beginning of the first taxable year ending in 1970, the above formula for determining the beginning balance is applied by substituting the number of taxable years for which the institution has been in existence as of the beginning of the taxable year for "5" each time it appears. If any taxable year utilized in the above formula for determining the beginning balance is a short taxable year the amount of the bad debts, adjusted for recoveries, for such taxable year is modified by dividing such amount by the number of days in the taxable year and multiplying the resulting amount by 365. The beginning balance for any subsequent taxable year is the amount of the beginning balance of the preceding taxable year, decreased by bad debt losses during such year, increased by recoveries of bad debts during such year and increased by the maximum amount determined under section 585(b)(3)(A) for such year.

(ii) In the case of a new institution whose first taxable year ends after 1969, its beginning balance for its reserve for bad debts, for purposes of this paragraph, is zero and its reasonable addition to the reserve for such taxable year is determined on the basis of the actual experience of similar institutions located in the area served by the taxpayer.

(h) **Depletion**—(1) **In general.** Section 57(a)(8) provides that with respect to each property (as defined in section 614), there is to be included as an item of tax preference the amount by which the deduction allowable for the taxable year under section 611 for depletion for the property exceeds the adjusted basis of the property at the end of the taxable year (determined without regard to the depletion deduction for that taxable year). The determination under section 57(a)(8) is made with respect to each separate property. Thus, for example, if one mineral property has an adjusted basis remaining at the end of the taxable year, such basis may not be used to reduce the amount of an item of tax preference resulting from another mineral property.

(2) **Allowable depletion.** For the determination of the amount of the deduction for depletion allowable for the taxable year see section 611 and the regulations thereunder.

(3) **Adjusted basis.** For the determination of the adjusted basis of the property at the end of the taxable year see section 1016 and the regulations thereunder.

(4) **No basis adjustment.** No adjustment is to be made to the basis of property subject to depletion as a result of the minimum tax.

(i) **Capital gains**—(1) **Taxpayer other than corporations.** Section 57(a)(9)(A) provides that, in the case of a taxpayer other than a corporation, there is to be included as an item of tax preference one-half of the amount by which the taxpayer's net long-term capital gain for the taxable year exceeds the taxpayer's net short-term capital loss for the taxable year. For this purpose, for taxable years beginning after December 31, 1971, the taxpayer's net long-term capital gain does not include an amount equal to the deduction allowable under section 163 (relating to interest expense) by reason of subsection (d)(1)(C) of that section, and the excess described in the preceding sentence is reduced by an amount equal to the reduction of disallowed interest expense by reason of section 163 (d)(2)(B). Included in the computation of the taxpayer's capital gains item of tax preference are amounts reportable by the taxpayer as distributive shares of gain or loss from partnerships, estates or trusts, electing small business

Proposed Reg. § 1.57-1

corporations, common trust funds, etc. See section 58 and the regulations thereunder with respect to the above entities.

Example. For 1971, A, a calendar year individual taxpayer, recognized $50,000 from the sale of securities held for more than 6 months. In addition, A received a $15,000 dividend from X Fund, a regulated investment company, $12,000 of which was designated as a capital gain dividend by the company pursuant to section 852 (b) (3) (C). The AB partnership recognized a gain of $20,000 from the sale of section 1231 property held by the partnership. The AB partnership agreement provides that A is entitled to 50 percent of the income and gains of the partnership. A had net short-term capital loss for the year of $10,000. A's 1971 capital gains item of tax preference is computed as follows:

Capital gain recognized from securities	$50,000
Capital gain dividend from regulated investment company	12,000
Distributive share of partnership capital gain	10,000
Total net long-term capital gain	72,000
Less: net short-term capital loss	(10,000)
Excess of net long-term capital gain over net short-term capital loss	$62,000
One-half of above excess	$31,000

(2) **Corporations.** (i) Section 57 (a) (9) (B) provides that in the case of corporations there is to be included as an item of tax preference with respect to a corporation's net section 1201 gain an amount equal to the product obtained by multiplying the excess of the net long-term capital gain over the net short-term capital loss by a fraction. The numerator of this fraction is the sum of the normal tax rate and the surtax rate under section 11 minus the alternative tax rate under section 1201 (a) for the taxable year, and the denominator of the fraction is the sum of the normal tax rate and the surtax rate under section 11 for the taxable year. Included in the above computation are amounts reportable by the taxpayer as distributive shares of gain or loss from partnerships, estates or trusts, common trust funds, etc. In certain cases the amount of the net section 1201 gain which results in preferential treatment will be less than the amount determined by application of the statutory formula. Therefore, in lieu of the statutory formula, the capital gains item of tax preference for corporations may in all cases be determined by dividing—

(a) The amount of tax which would have been imposed under section 11 if section 1201 (a) did not apply minus

(b) The amount of the taxes actually imposed

by the sum of the normal tax rate plus the surtax rate under section 11. In case of foreign source capital gains and losses which are not taken into account pursuant to section 58 (g) (2) (B) and § 1.58-8, the amount determined in the preceding sentence shall be multiplied by a fraction the numerator of which is the corporation's net section 1201 gain without regard to such gains and losses which are not taken into account and the denominator of which is the corporation's net section 1201 gain. The computation of the corporate capital gains item of tax preference may be illustrated by the following examples:

Example (1) For 1971, A, a calendar year corporate taxpayer, has ordinary income of $10,000 and net section 1201 gain of $50,000, none of which is subsection (d) gain (as defined in section 1201 (d)) and none of which is attributable to foreign sources. A's 1971 capital gain item of tax preference may be computed as follows:

1. Tax under section 11:

Normal tax (.22 × $60,000)	$13,200
Surtax (.26 × $35,000)	9,100
	$22,300

2. Tax under section 1201 (a)

```
       Normal tax on ordinary income (.22 × $10,000) ....  $ 2,200
       Tax on net section 1201 gain (.30 × $50,000) ..........  15,000   17,200
                                                                        ────────
  3. Excess ......................................................  $ 5,100
                                                                        ════════
  4. Normal tax rate plus surtax rate ............................     .48
  5. Capital gains preference (line 3 divided by line 4) ............ $10,625
```

Example (2). For 1971, A, a calendar year corporate taxpayer, has a loss from operations of $30,000 and net section 1201 gain of $150,000, none of which is subsection (d) gain (as defined in section 1201 (d)) and none of which is attributable to foreign sources. A's 1971 capital gain item of tax preference may be computed as follows:

```
  1. Tax under section 11:
       Normal tax (.22 × $120,000) ...............................  $26,400
       Surtax (.26 × $95,000) ....................................   24,700
                                                                     ────────
                                                                     $51,100
  2. Tax under section 1201 (a)
       Normal tax on ordinary income ...................  None
       Tax on net section 1201 gain (.30 × $150,000) ......  45,000   $45,000
                                                                     ────────
  3. Excess ......................................................  $ 6,100
                                                                     ════════
  4. Normal tax rate plus surtax rate ............................     .48
  5. Capital gain preference (line 3 divided by line 4) .............. $12,708
```

(ii) In the case of organizations subject to the tax imposed by section 511 (a), mutual savings banks conducting a life insurance business (see section 594), life insurance companies (as defined in section 801), mutual insurance companies to which part II of subchapter L applies, insurance companies to which part III of subchapter L applies, regulated investment companies subject to tax under part I of subchapter M, real estate investment trusts subject to tax under part II of subchapter M, or any other corporation not subject to the taxes imposed by sections 11 and 1201 (a), the capital gains item of tax preference may be computed in accordance with subdivision (i) of this subparagraph except that, in lieu of references to section 11, there is to be substituted the section which imposes the tax comparable to the tax imposed by section 11 and, in lieu of references to section 1201 (a), there is to be substituted the section which imposes the alternative or special tax applicable to the capital gains of such corporation.

(iii) For purposes of this paragraph, where the net section 1201 gain is not in any event subject to the tax comparable to the normal tax and the surtax under section 11, such as in the case of regulated investment companies subject to tax under subchapter M, such comparable tax shall be computed as if it were applicable to net section 1201 gain to the extent such gain is subject to the tax comparable to the alternative tax under section 1201(a). Thus, in the case of a regulated investment company subject to tax under subchapter M, the tax comparable to the normal tax and the surtax would be the tax computed under section 852(b)(1) determined as if the amount subject to tax under section 852 (b)(3) were included in investment company taxable income. The principles of this subdivision (iii) may be illustrated by the following example:

Example. M, a calendar year regulated investment company, in 1971, has investment company taxable income (subject to tax under section 852(b)(1)) of $125,000 and net long-term capital gain of $800,000. M Company has no net short-term capital loss but has a deduction for dividends paid (determined with reference to capital gains only) of $700,000. M's 1971 capital gains item of tax preference is computed as follows:

```
  1. Section 852(b)(1) tax computed as if it were applicable
        to all income including capital gains:
        Amount subject to section 852(b)(1) ........................... $125,000
```

Proposed Reg. §1.57-1

```
Net section 1201 gain_____  $800,000
Less: Dividends paid deduction_____   700,000

Net section 1201 gain subject to tax at the company level_____   100,000
                                                                 ─────────
                                                                  225,000
Normal tax  (0.22 × $225,000)_____   $49,500
Surtax  (0.26 × 200,000)_____    52,000
                                                                       ─────────
                                                                       101,500
                                                                       ═════════
```

2. Tax comparable to section 1201(a) tax section 852(b)(1) tax:
```
Normal tax (0.22 × 125,000)_____  $27,500
Surtax  (0.26 × 100,000)_____   26,000   $53,500

Section 852(b)(3) tax  (0.30 × 100,000)_____    30,000   $83,500
                                                                         ─────────
```

3. Excess _____ 18,000
                                                                          ═════════

4. Normal tax rate plus surtax rate_____   .48
5. Capital gains preference (line 3 divided by line 4)_____ 37,500

(iv) For the computation of the capital gains item of tax preference in the case of an electing small business corporation (as defined in section 1371(b)), see § 1.58-4(c).

(3) **Nonresident aliens, foreign corporations.** In the case of a nonresident alien individual or foreign corporation, there shall be included in computing the capital gains item of tax preference under section 57(a)(9) only those capital gains and losses included in the computation of income effectively connected with the conduct of a trade or business within the United States as provided in section 871(b) or 882.

§ 1.57-2 (Proposed Treasury Decision, published 12-30-70, 6-24-71.) Excess investment interest.

(a) **In general.** Section 57(b) provides that for purposes of section 57(a)(1) (and § 1.57-1(a)), the excess investment interest item of tax preference for the taxable year is the amount by which the investment interest expense for the taxable year exceeds the net investment income for the taxable year. Excess investment interest is an item of tax preference only for taxable years beginning before January 1, 1972, and is not an item of tax preference in the case of a corporation other than a personal holding company (as defined in section 542) and an electing small business corporation as defined in section 1371(b)). Paragraph (b) of this section provides definitions of net investment income, investment income, investment expenses, and investment interest expense. A special rule for property subject to a net lease is provided in § 1.57-3. See § 1.58-7 with respect to excess investment interest attributable to foreign sources.

(b) **Definitions.** For purposes of section 57(b) and this section:

(1) **Investment interest expense.** (i) The term "investment interest expense" means interest paid or accrued on indebtedness incurred or continued to purchase or carry property held for investment. The term includes any deduction which is allowable as a deduction for the taxable year under section 163 (whether or not deducted under section 163). The term does not include, however, any expenses disallowed under any provision of the Internal Revenue Code such as sections 264(a), 265(2), 266, and 279.

(ii) For purposes of this subparagraph, the term "indebtedness" includes a loan, an advance, or any other form of debt.

(iii) (a) The determination of whether the purpose of incurring or continuing an indebtedness is to purchase or carry property held for investment must be made on the basis of the facts and circumstances of each particular case. Where it is clear that the intent of the taxpayer in incurring or continuing a particular indebtedness is solely for the purchase, improvement, or maintenance of business property, solely to engage in or continue a trade or business activity, or otherwise to use the proceeds of the indebtedness in the ordinary course of business, interest on such indebtedness is not treated as investment interest expense. Where it is clear that the intent of the taxpayer in incurring or continuing a particular indebtedness is solely for the purchase, improvement, or maintenance of property which is primarily for personal, as opposed to business or investment, use, or solely to engage in or continue an activity which is primarily personal, interest on such indebtedness is not treated as investment interest expense. Thus, indebtedness in the form of a purchase money mortgage on a personal residence, a student loan, a home improvement loan, or an installment obligation for the acquisition of consumer goods for personal use will not be investment interest expense unless it is clear that, in substance, such indebtedness was incurred to purchase or carry investment property. Similarly, interest on a purchase money mortgage or installment obligation for the acquisition of business property will not normally be investment interest expense. Where the proceeds of an indebtedness can be traced to a particular activity or property or the indebtedness constitutes all or a part of the payment for a particular activity or property, it will be inferred that such indebtedness was incurred or continued for the purpose of purchasing or carrying such property or engaging in or continuing such activity. In addition, if substantially identical amounts are borrowed and expended simultaneously it will be inferred that the resulting indebtedness was incurred for the purpose of such expenditure. Indebtedness which was originally incurred for one purpose may be continued for another purpose. Thus, if the taxpayer incurred an indebtedness to purchase business property but continued the indebtedness in order to avoid liquidation of property held for investment, the indebtedness is continued in order to carry the property held for investment. An indebtedness may be incurred or continued for multiple purposes. Where such a multiple purpose is established, including an investment purpose, a portion of the loan will be treated as incurred or continued in order to purchase or carry property held for investment. In cases where the proceeds of an indebtedness cannot be traced by application of the principles of this subdivision to a particular activity or property, it will be inferred that the indebtedness was incurred or continued in order to carry property held for investment. In some cases, however, it may be established that all or part of such indebtedness was not incurred or continued in order to carry property held for investment. Thus, where a taxpayer owns $100,000 in value of appreciated investment property, indebtedness in excess of that amount will ordinarily not be considered to be incurred or continued in order to carry investment property.

(b) The principles of this subdivision (iii) may be illustrated by the following examples:

Example (1). A taxpayer obtained an unsecured loan of $100,000 on March 16, 1970. On the same day, he purchased securities of a company in the amount of $120,000. It will be inferred that the $100,000 loan was incurred for the purpose of purchasing such securities.

Example (2). A taxpayer who owns substantial amounts of business property and investment property with a value in excess of $150,000 obtains an unsecured loan of $150,000 on June 5, 1970. The taxpayer is unable to show that the loan was for business or personal, as opposed to investment, use. It will be inferred that the loan was incurred for the purpose of purchasing or carrying investment property.

Example (3). The facts are the same as in example (2), except that the taxpayer is able to establish that he owned no more than $70,000 of investment property during the taxable year, it will be inferred that only 7/15 of the loan was incurred for the purpose of purchasing or carrying investment property.

Example (4). If, under the facts of example (3), the taxpayer obtained two different loans totaling $150,000 at different interest rates, 7/15 of each loan will be considered indebtedness incurred or continued to purchase or carry property held for investment.

Proposed Reg. § 1.57-2

(iv) For purposes of this subparagraph, interest paid or accrued on indebtedness incurred or continued in the construction of property to be used by the taxpayer in a trade or business is not treated as investment interest expense. Thus, if the taxpayer pays or accrues construction interest with respect to a building which he intends to use in his trade or business such interest is not investment interest expense. Similarly, interest paid or accrued with respect to the construction of property which is neither business nor investment property, such as the taxpayer's personal residence, is not treated as investment interest expense. On the other hand, if the taxpayer intends to hold property by leasing such property under a net lease entered into after October 9, 1969 (as defined in § 1.57-3), the resulting construction interest is investment interest expense. For this purpose, the use which the taxpayer intends is determined from the facts and circumstances of each case giving due weight to the actual use of the property and any similar property held or constructed by the taxpayer. Thus, a pattern of constructing net leased buildings is a factor to be taken into account. Similarly, if at any time prior to or during construction, the taxpayer has entered into an agreement to lease the property under an arrangement which would be considered a net lease pursuant to § 1.57-3(c), the construction interest will be investment interest expense. In determining the taxpayer's intent, however, the fact that the property is leased (regardless of when the lease is executed) under an arrangement which is subsequently considered to be a net lease pursuant to § 1.57-3(b) (but not § 1.57-3(c)) will not be considered.

(2) **Investment property.** (i) The determination whether property is held for investment must be made on the basis of the particular facts and circumstances. For purposes of this paragraph, the term "property" includes any form of property whether real, personal, tangible, or intangible. Under the facts and circumstances test, property is held for investment only if it is held for the production or collection of passive income, such as, interest, rent, dividends, royalties, or capital gain (including amounts which would be capital gain but for the application of section 1245 or section 1250) to the extent such income, gain, and amounts are not derived from properties actively used in the conduct of trade or business. Except as provided in subdivision (ii) of this subparagraph, property is not held for investment if the expenses paid or incurred by the taxpayer in connection with his use thereof are allowable as deductions under section 162. For example, real property held in the conduct of the business of renting real property is property actively used in the conduct of a trade or business. Where it can reasonably be expected that a property will generate passive income, such property will ordinarily be considered investment property. Thus, portfolio investments held in a trade or business will constitute property held for investment. Generally, stock in a corporation, other than an electing small business corporation, whether a portfolio investment or a controlling interest constitutes property held for investment since such stock is not actively used in the trade or business of the taxpayer and can reasonably be expected to generate investment income. Stock in electing small business corporations and partnership interests constitute property held for investment to the extent the assets of the corporation or partnership are held for investment.

(ii) Property which is subject to a net lease (as defined in § 1.57-3) entered into after October 9, 1969, shall be treated as property held for investment. Property subject to a lease entered into on or before October 9, 1969, shall not be considered investment property by reason of the lease being a net lease. For this purpose, a renewal or extension of a lease (unless pursuant to a right of the lessee, exercisable without consent or approval of the lessor, existing on October 9, 1969, and at all times thereafter) shall constitute a new lease entered into on the date such renewal or extension takes effect. Modifications of a lease (other than a renewal or extension thereof) shall cause the lease to be considered a new lease entered into on the date such modifications take effect unless the modifications do not cause the lease to be a net lease under § 1.57-3(c). Moreover, modifications of a lease which is a net lease on October 9, 1969, pursuant to § 1.57-3(c) shall not deem the lease to be a new lease until the expiration of such lease (determined with regard to renewals or extensions which may be effected as a matter of right by the lessee without consent or approval of the lessor on October 9, 1969, and at all times thereafter) since the modification did not cause the lease to be a net lease.

(3) **Net investment income.** The term "net investment income" means the amount (if any) by which the investment income for the taxable year exceeds the investment expenses for the taxable year.

(4) **Investment income.** The term "investment income" includes:

(i) Interest, dividends, rents, and royalties, to the extent includible in gross income;

(ii) The net short-term capital gain attributable to the disposition of property held for investment; and

(iii) Amounts treated under sections 1245 and 1250 as gain from the sale or exchange of property which is neither a capital asset nor property described in section 1231,

but only to the extent such income, gain, and amounts are not derived from the conduct of a trade or business. Income, gain, and other amounts shall be considered investment income and not derived from the conduct of a trade or business only if derived from investment property as defined in subparagraph (2) of this paragraph. Generally, dividends received by a dealer in securities, or royalties received by a manufacturer will not constitute investment income since such amounts normally constitute income from the conduct of a trade or business. However, property subject to a net lease entered into after October 9, 1969 (as defined in § 1.57-3) is, for purposes of the minimum tax, treated as property held for investment. Accordingly, rents derived from such property are, for purposes of this section, considered investment income. Where the primary purpose of holding property is for investment, net income from the incidental or temporary use of the property in the active conduct of a trade or business will be treated as investment income. Thus, for example, where a taxpayer who owns investment property which consists of a large tract of wooded country realty realizes small amounts of annual income from the sale of hunting rights, the net income will be treated as investment income. Dividends from an electing small business corporation and undistributed taxable income of such a corporation taxed to the shareholders thereof pursuant to section 1373 are investment income only to the extent of the shareholder's proportionate share of the corporation's net investment income in excess of investment interest. The balance is income derived from the conduct of a trade or business.

(5) **Investment expenses.** (i) The term "investment expenses" means the deductions allowable under section 164 (a) (1) or (2), 166, 167, 171, 212, 243, 244, 245, or 611, but only to the extent directly connected with the production of investment income, and not including any deduction allowable under section 163. Thus, taxes, depreciation, overhead, etc., not directly incurred as a result of investment property are not investment expenses. For example, if a doctor who maintains his own medical office is the lessor of section 1245 property subject to a net lease, taxes, depreciation, overhead, etc., relating to the operation of his office are directly related to the operation of his medical practice and would not be considered directly incurred as a result of the leased property, and, thus, would not be investment expenses. This would be true regardless of the fact that the lease agreement is kept at the office or that communications between lessor and lessee take place at the doctor's office. However, if the doctor pays an auditor to audit his books and the auditor spends 20 hours reviewing the doctor's books and records, 8 hours of which are spent reviewing the doctor's transactions with respect to his investment property, 8/20 of the auditor's fee would be investment expense since the additional 8 hours are directly related to the doctor's investment activity. Further, if the doctor uses his office extensively in connection with net leases or other investment transactions, a portion of the expenses relating to the operation of his office are directly connected with his investment activities to the extent that such expenses are increased as a result of his investment activities.

(ii) At the taxpayer's option, investment expenses representing depreciation or depletion may be determined as the amount of depreciation or depletion which would have been allowable had the taxpayer taken depreciation or depletion with respect to the property under the straight line method of depreciation or by use

Proposed Reg. §1.57-2

of cost depletion for each taxable year for which the taxpayer has held the property. For this purpose, depreciation under the straight line method shall be determined as provided in § 1.57-1 (b) (4). For the computation of cost depletion see § 1.611-2. However, if a taxpayer chooses to use the straight line method of depreciation pursuant to this subdivision with respect to an item of investment property for any taxable year, he must continue to use the straight line for all subsequent taxable years.

(iii) Property subject to a net lease entered into after October 9, 1969, is for purposes of the minimum tax treated as property held for investment. Accordingly, solely for purposes of this section, deductions allowable under section 162 are considered deductions allowable under section 212 to the extent such deductions would have been allowable under section 212 were that section applicable to the taxpayer and were the property considered held for the production of investment income for all purposes of the Internal Revenue Code. Thus, for example, deductions of an electing small business corporation (as defined in section 1371(b)) allowable under section 162 will be considered as investment expenses allowable under section 212 if directly connected with the production of investment income.

(iv) A taxpayer who holds property subject to a net lease and who chooses to compute his allowable depreciation or amortization under a provision of the Internal Revenue Code other than section 167 (for example, section 169 or 184), shall compute his investment expenses for purposes of this paragraph by taking into account the allowable depreciation or amortization under such provision unless such taxpayer chooses to adopt the straight line method of depreciation as described in subdivision (ii) of this subparagraph.

§ 1.57-3 (Proposed Treasury Decision, published 12-30-70.) **Net leases.**

(a) **In general.** Section 57 (c) provides a two-factor test for the determination, for purposes of section 57 (a) (3) and (b) (3), of whether property shall be considered subject to a net lease for the taxable year. Thus, property will be so considered if, and only if—

(1) The sum of the deductions with respect to such property which are allowable for the taxable year solely by reason of section 162 is less than 15 percent of the gross income from rents produced by such property, or

(2) The lessor is guaranteed a specified return or is guaranteed in whole or in part against loss of income.

(b) **Expense test.** (1) The expense test, described in paragraph (a)(1) of this section, is based on a measurement of the expenses of the taxpayer relating to or attributable to the property in relation to the gross income from rents of the taxpayer produced by the property. The test is applied separately for each taxable year. In cases where a single property is subject to more than one lease, the test is applied separately to each lease. For this purpose, the expenses relating to the property shall be allocated to each lease on a reasonable basis. Generally, an allocation of expenses in proportion to the gross rental income received under each lease or in proportion to square footage wil be considered reasonable in the absence of special factors such as vacancies or direct use of a portion of the property by the taxpayer. Further, when more than one property is subject to a single lease, and, pursuant to paragraph (d) of this section, the arrangement is considered to be a separate lease of each property, the expense test is applied separately to each such lease by making a reasonable apportionment of the payments received and expenses incurred with respect to each such property, considering all relevant factors. For example, under subparagraph (d), where a taxpayer leases an airplane which he owns to an airline along with an engine which he in turn has leased from a third party, he is treated as having made two separate leases, one covering the airplane and one covering the engine. Thus, the expense test will be applied by apportioning the related income and expenses between the two leases. Similarly, where a taxpayer leases a building erected by him on land which he holds pursuant to a ground lease, the expense test will be applied to the taxpayer as though he had leased (to the lessee) the building and ground separately. Thus, the rental income is apportioned between the land and the building, and the rental payments required under the ground lease and a portion of the general and administrative expenses also must be allocated to the lease or leases of the land.

(2) Only those expenses allowable solely by reason of section 162 are included in the expense test. Hence, depreciation allowable by reason of section 167; interest allowable by reason of section 163; taxes allowable by reason of section 164; amortization allowable by reason of section 169, 184, or 185 or similar provisions; and depletion allowable by reason of section 611 are examples of expenses which are not included in the expense test. Only those section 162 expenses paid or payable by the lessor are included. Thus, section 162 expenses paid or payable by the lessee or any party other than the lessor are not included unless the lessor is obligated to reimburse the party paying the expense. Similarly, if the lessee or some other party is obligated to reimburse the lessor for expenses paid or payable by the lessor, expenses so reimbursed are not considered paid or payable by the lessor. Further, if the lessee is obligated to pay to the lessor a charge for services which is separately stated or determinable, the expenses incurred by the lessor with respect to those services are not included.

(3) For purposes of the expense test, the gross income from rents of the lessor is the total amount which is payable to the lessor by reason of the lease agreement other than reimbursements of section 162 expenses and charges separately stated or determinable. The fact that such amount depends, in whole or in part, on the sales or profits of the lessee or the performance of significant services by the lessor shall not affect the characterization of such amounts as gross income from rents for purposes of this section. Gross income from rents, however, does not include subsidies paid by a governmental agency such as rent supplement payments pursuant to 12 U.S.C. § 1701 (National Housing Act).

(4) The principles of this paragraph may be illustrated by the following examples:

Example (1). The lease arrangement between the parties requires that the lessor pay for utilities, trash collection, and common area expenses, and that the lessee reimburse the lessor for such expenses. For purposes of the expense test, the amount of such payments to the lessor are separately stated and not considered gross income from rents and are not considered section 162 expenses of the lessor.

Example (2). The lease arrangement between the parties requires that the lessee pay a fixed rent of $200 per month and that the landlord provide utilities and trash collection services. For purposes of the expense test, since there is no separately stated or determinable charge for the utilities and trash collection services, the costs of such services are included as section 162 expenses and the full $200 per month is included as gross income from rents.

Example (3). Assume the same facts as in example (2) except that the monthly rent is redetermined annually on the basis of the Consumer Price Index. For purposes of the expense test, the costs of the utilities and trash collection services are still neither separately stated nor determinable and, therefore, are included as section 162 expenses and the full $200 per month is included as gross income from rents.

Example (4). Assume the same facts as in example (2), except that the rent increases annually by an amount equal to the increase in the utilities expense attributable to the leased property, which at the time the lease was negotiated was $25 a month. In January 1971, the amount of such increase was $10 per month. For purposes of the expense test, since the portion of the payments by the lessee that covers utilities is separately determinable, such portion is not included in the expense test and the gross income from rents is, therefore, considered to be $175 and none of the $35 utilities expense is considered to be section 162 expenses of the lessor.

Example (5). The lessor buys power at a bulk rate and submeters it to the lessee at prevailing local retail rates. For purposes of the expense test, payments from the lessee to the lessor for utilities are separately stated and are not con-

Proposed Reg. §1.57-3

sidered gross income from rents and the utilities expenses paid by the landlord are not included in the expense test.

(c). **Return test.** (1) Under the return test, described in paragraph (a)(2) of this section, property is considered to be subject to a net lease if the lessor has, in any manner, formal or informal, an assurance by the lessee or a related party that he will receive a specified return as a result of the lease, or will not suffer a loss as a result of the lease. In contrast to the expense test, the return test is not based on a year by year analysis. Rather, the return test is based upon an analysis of the leasing arrangement as a whole in order to determine whether, for any period of time covered by the lease, the lessor is guaranteed a specified return or against loss as a result of the lease. For example, the fact that the lessor may suffer a loss in the initial years of the lease period will not be determinative if the lessor is assured that he will not suffer an overall loss from the arrangement or will receive a specified return over the full duration of the lease period. Further, even if the lessor does not receive such assurances over the full duration of the lease period, the lease may be a net lease for some of the taxable years covered by the rental period. For example, if the lessor is guaranteed a specified return during 5 specific years of a 20-year lease, the lease is a net lease during such 5 years. Further, if the lessor receives no assurances about any given year, but is guaranteed a specified return with respect to a specific 5-year period of the 20-year term, the arrangement is a net lease for such 5-year period.

(2) In determining whether the lessor is assured of a specified return or that he will not suffer a loss as a result of the lease, weight will be given to all the facts and circumstances of each particular case. Thus, an arrangement whereby the lessor is assured by, or on behalf of, the lessee that, during any period, the income he will receive or accrue as a result of the lessee's use of the property during such period will exceed the expenses he will pay or accrue which are attributable to the property, or the lessee's use of the property, by a fixed or determinable amount (or that such income will equal such expense) is a net lease for such period. For purposes of this subparagraph, only that income and those expenses which economically accrue to the lessor during the lease period are taken into account. Depletion for this purpose shall be computed on the basis of cost depletion as determined under § 1.611-2 and depreciation for this purpose shall be computed on the basis of the straight-line method as determined under § 1.57-1(b)(4). A net lease of the type described in this subparagraph will result, for instance, if the lessee is obligated to pay all the expenses attributable to the property which the lessor will incur or accrue for a period covered by the lease and, in the event of complete or partial destruction of the property, the lessee is obligated either to continue to pay the full rent for such period or a lump-sum amount equivalent to the present value of such rental payments. Further, a lease will be a net lease if the lessor's liability for expenses is fixed by contracts with parties related to the lessee. On the other hand, a third party's guarantee that the lessor will receive a fixed or determinable rental payment shall not, in and of itself, result in the arrangement being a net lease. Further, the fact that the lessor is protected against increases in some but not all of the expenses attributable to the property which he will pay or accrue by means of escalator clauses or is protected against loss of income due to total or partial destruction of the premises by means of rental continuation insurance does not, in and of itself, cause the arrangement to be classified as a net lease. Further, the fact that the lessor of an equipment lease has a contract which provides all necessary repair and maintenance services for a period covered by the lease will not, in and of itself, cause the arrangement to be classified as a net lease.

(3) For purposes of determining the duration or life of the lease or the lease period, the principles for determining the term of a lease under section 178 and the regulations thereunder shall apply.

(d) **Definition of a lease.** (1) A lease, for purposes of this section, is any arrangement or agreement, formal or informal, written or oral, by which the owner of property (the "lessor") receives consideration in any form for the use of his property by another party. Whether a specific transaction constitutes a lease or a sale shall be determined on the basis of the particular facts and circumstances. For purposes of this subparagraph, two or more arrangements or agreements between the same parties for the use of the same property will be considered as a single lease where, in substance, they constitute a single unit. The determination of whether a lease covers a single property or multiple properties is based on the facts and circumstances including the property interests of the lessor in the leased properties. In addition, the determinations under this section shall be made separately with respect to each property or property interest subject to a lease unless a group of properties subject to a single lease and substantially similar in nature form a single integrated unit. For instance, a fleet of trucks subject to a single lease may be considered in the aggregate. Where, pursuant to the above, two or more properties subject to a single lease are to be considered separately, a reasonable apportionment must be made of the payments made and expenses incurred with respect to each such property considering all relevant factors. Such factors may include (but are not limited to) the basis upon which payments under the lease are computed; fair rental value of the properties; fair market value of the properties; availability, cost, and value of similar properties; and the use or uses to which the properties are to be put.

(2) Where several substantially identical units of one item of property are leased on substantially identical terms to various lessees, the various leases may, at the election of the taxpayer, be considered in the aggregate in determining whether the leases constitute a net lease. For example, all of the leases of apartments in an apartment building may be considered in the aggregate. On the other hand, if the taxpayer leases units in a shopping center and the terms of the various leases or the units differ significantly, each lease must be considered separately. An election pursuant to this subparagraph must be made at the time, including extensions thereof, prescribed by law for filing the income tax return for the first taxable year in which the taxpayer's property with respect to which the election is made is subject to a lease or leases or on or before [60 days from date of publication of notice in Federal Register], whichever is later. The election is binding on the taxpayer for such taxable year and all subsequent taxable years.

§ 1.57-4 (Proposed Treasury Decision, published 12-30-70.) **Limitation on amounts treated as items of tax preference.**

(a) **In general.** If in any taxable year, a taxpayer has deductions in excess of gross income and all or a part of any item of tax preference described in § 1.57-1 results in no tax benefit due to modifications required under section 172(c) or section 172(b)(2) in computing the amount of the net operating loss or the net operating loss to be carried to a succeeding taxable year, then, for purposes of section 56(a)(1), the sum of the items of tax preference determined under section 57(a) (and § 1.57-1) is to be limited as provided in paragraph (b) of this section.

(b) **Limitation.** The sum of the items of tax preference, for purposes of section 56(a)(1) and § 1.56-1(a), is limited to an amount determined under subparagraphs (1) and (2) of this paragraph.

(1) **Loss year.** If the taxpayer has no taxable income for the taxable year without regard to the net operating loss deduction, the amount of the limitation is equal to—

(i) In cases where the taxpayer does not have a net operating loss for the taxable year, the amount of the recomputed income (as defined in paragraph (c) of this section) or

(ii) In cases where the taxpayer has a net operating loss for the taxable year, the amount of the net operating loss (expressed as a positive amount) increased by the recomputed income or decreased by the recomputed loss for the taxable year (as defined in paragraph (c) of this section)

plus the amount of the taxpayer's stock option item of tax preference (as described in § 1.57-1(f)).

Proposed Reg. § 1.57-4

(2) **Loss carryover and carryback years.** Except in cases to which subparagraph (1)(ii) of this paragraph applies, if, in any taxable year to which a net operating loss is carried, a capital gains deduction is disallowed under section 172(b)(2) in computing the amount of such net operating loss which may be carried to succeeding taxable years, the amount of the limitation is equal to the amount, if any, by which the sum of the items of tax preference (computed with regard to subparagraph (1)(i) of this paragraph) exceeds the lesser of—

(i) The amount by which such loss is reduced because of a disallowance of the capital gains deduction in such taxable year, or

(ii) The capital gains deduction. The amount determined pursuant to the preceding sentence shall be increased by the amount, if any, that such reduction is attributable to that portion of such a net operating loss described in section 56(b)(1)(B) and § 1.56-2(a)(2) (relating to excess tax preferences).

(c) **Recomputed income or loss.** For purposes of this section, the phrase "recomputed income or loss" means the taxable income or net operating loss for the taxable year computed without regard to the amounts described in § 1.57-1 except paragraph (i)(2) of that section (relating to corporate capital gains) and without regard to the net operating loss deduction. For this purpose, the reference to the amounts described in § 1.57-1 is a reference to that portion of the deduction allowable in computing taxable income under the appropriate section equal to the amount which is determined in each paragraph of § 1.57-1. For example, the amount described in § 1.57-1(h) (relating to excess of percentage depletion over basis) is that portion of the deduction allowable for depletion under section 611 which is equal to the amount determined under § 1.57-1(h). For purposes of this paragraph, the amount described in § 1.57-1(i)(1) (relating to capital gains) is to be considered as the amount of the deduction allowable for the taxable year under section 1202.

(d) **Determination of preferences reduced.** When, pursuant to paragraph (b)(1) of this section, the sum of the items of tax preference (determined without regard to this section) are reduced, such reduction is first considered to be from the capital gains item of tax preference (described in § 1.57-1(i)(1)) and each item of tax preference relating to a deduction disallowed in computing the net operating loss pursuant to section 172(d), pro rata. The balance of the reduction, if any, is considered to be from the remaining items of tax preference, pro rata. For purposes of this subparagraph, deductions not attributable to the taxpayer's trade or business which do not relate to items of tax preference are considered as being applied in reducing gross income not derived from such trade or business before such deductions which do relate to items of tax preferences.

(e) **Examples.** The principles of this section may be illustrated by the following examples in each of which the deduction for the personal exemption is disregarded and the taxpayer is an individual who is a calendar year taxpayer.

Example (1). The taxpayer has the following items of income and deduction for 1970:

Gross income (all business income) $120,000
Deductions:
  Nonbusiness deductions 30,000
  Items of tax preference (excess accelerated depreciation on real property held in taxpayer's business) 80,000
  Other business deductions 50,000

Based on the above figures, the taxpayer has a net operating loss of $10,000 (business deductions of $130,000 less business income of $120,000, the nonbusiness deductions having been disallowed by reason of section 172(d)(4)). The limitation on the amount treated as items of tax preference is computed as follows:

Tax preferences_____ $80,000

Net operating loss_____ $10,000
Recomputed income or loss
  Gross income_____ $120,000
  Deductions other than tax preference items_____ 80,000

Recomputed income	40,000
Sum of net operating loss and recomputed income	50,000
Stock options preference	0
Limitation	50,000

Thus, the minimum tax computed under section 56 (a) would be 10 percent of $20,000 (items of tax preference of $50,000 less the minimum tax exemption of $30,000), $1,000 of which would be deferred tax liability pursuant to section 56 (b).

Example (2). Assume the same facts as in example (1) except that the other business deductions are $130,000, resulting in a net operating loss of $90,000. The limitation on the amount treated as items of tax preference is computed as follows:

Tax preferences		$80,000
Net operating loss		$90,000
Recomputed income or loss		
Gross income	$120,000	
Deductions other than tax preference items	160,000	
	(40,000)	
Disallowance of nonbusiness deductions under sec. 172(d)	30,000	
Recomputed loss		10,000
Net operating loss less recomputed loss		80,000
Stock options preference		0
Limitation		80,000

Thus, the minimum tax computed under section 56 (a) would be 10 percent of $50,000 (items of tax preference of $80,000 less the minimum tax exemption of $30,000), all of which will be deferred tax liability pursuant to section 56 (b).

Example (3). The taxpayer has the following items of income and deduction for 1970:

Gross income (all from business):		
Ordinary		$50,000
Net section 1201 gains		120,000
Deductions:		
Items of tax preference:		
Excess amortization of certified pollution control facilities	$45,000	
Capital gains deduction	60,000	105,000
Other business deductions		75,000

In addition, the taxpayer has a $55,000 item of tax preference resulting from qualified stock options. Based on the above figures the taxpayer has no taxable income and no net operating loss as the capital gains deduction is disallowed in determining the net operating loss pursuant to section 172 (d). The limitation on the amount treated as items of tax preference is computed as follows:

Tax preferences		$160,000
Net operating loss		0
Recomputed income or loss		
Gross income	$170,000	
Deductions other than tax preference items	75,000	
Recomputed income		$95,000
Plus: Stock options preference		55,000
Limitation		150,000

Thus, the minimum tax computed under section 56 would be 10 percent of $120,000 (items of tax preference of $150,000 less the minimum tax exemption of $30,000).

Proposed Reg. §1.57-4

Example (4). Assume the same facts as in example (3) except that the taxpayer has a net operating loss carryover from 1969 of $80,000. The taxpayer has $160,000 of tax preferences which are limited to $150,000 pursuant to § 1.57-4 (b) (1). In order to determine the amount of the 1969 net operating loss which remains as a carryover to 1971, the 1970 taxable income is redetermined in accordance with section 172 (b) (2) and the regulations thereunder, as follows:

Gross income — 1970		$170,000
Deductions:		
Capital gains deduction	disallowed	
Business deductions	120,000	120,000
Taxable income for section 172 (b) (2)		$ 50,000

Thus, the 1969 net operating loss which remains as a carryover to 1971 is $30,000. Pursuant to paragraph (b) (2) of this section, the limitation on the amount treated as items of tax preference is computed as follows:

Items of tax preference computed with regard to § 1.57-4 (b) (1) (per example (3))	$150,000
Less: Lesser of capital gains deduction ($60,000) or amount of reduction in carryover due to its disallowance ($50,000)	50,000
Limitation	$100,000

Thus, the minimum tax computed under section 56 would be 10 percent of $70,000 (items of tax preference of $100,000 less the minimum tax exemption of $30,000).

Example (5). The taxpayer has the following items of income and deduction for the taxable year 1970 without regard to any net operating loss deduction:

Gross income (all from business)		
Ordinary	$50,000	
Net section 1201 gain	40,000	
		$90,000
Deductions:		
Capital gains deduction	20,000	
Medical expenses ($4,100 actually paid but allowable only to the extent in excess of 3 percent of adjusted gross income of $70,000)	2,000	
Other itemized deductions	40,000	62,000
Taxable income (before net operating loss deduction)		$28,000

In addition, the taxpayer has an item of tax preference of $35,000 resulting from qualified stock options. In 1973, the taxpayer has a net operating loss of $60,000 (no portion of which is attributable to excess tax preferences pursuant to § 1.56-2) which is carried back to 1970 resulting in no taxable income in 1970. In order to determine the amount of the 1973 net operating loss which remains as a carryover to 1971, the 1970 taxable income is redetermined, in accordance with section 172 (b) (2) and the regulations thereunder, as follows:

Gross income		$90,000
Deductions:		
Capital gains deduction	disallowed	
Medical expenses ($4,100 actually paid but allowable only to the extent in excess of 3 percent of adjusted gross income of $90,000)	$ 1,400	
Other itemized deductions	40,000	41,400
Taxable income for section 172 (b) (2)		$48,600

The limitation on the amount treated as items of tax preference is treated as follows:

Items of tax preference:	
Capital gains	$20,000
Stock options	35,000
	$55,000

Less: Lesser of capital gains deduction ($20,000) or amount of reduction in carryover due to its disallowance ($20,600) .... (20,000)

Limitation $35,000

Thus, the minimum tax for 1970 under section 56 would be 10 percent of $5,000 (items of tax preference of $35,000 less the minimum tax exemption of $30,000).

Example (6). Assume the same facts as in example (5) except that the 1973 net operating loss was $45,000. In this case, the $20,600 increase in the 1970 taxable income as redetermined, results in a decrease of $17,000 (i.e., the remaining 1973 net operating loss after an initial decrease of $28,000 resulting from the 1970 taxable income before redetermination). The limitation on the amount treated as items of tax preference is computed as follows:

Items of tax preference computed without regard to this section $55,000
Less: Lesser of capital gains deduction ($20,000) or amount of reduction in carryover due to its disallowance ($17,000) .... ($17,000)

Limitation $38,000

Thus, the minimum tax for 1960 under section 56 would be 10 percent of $8,000 (items of tax preference of $38,000 less the minimum tax exemption of $30,000).

Example (7). The taxpayer has the following items of income and deduction for 1973 without regard to any net operating loss deduction:

Gross income (all from business):
  Ordinary $100,000
  Net section 1201 gains 120,000 $220,000

Deductions:
  Items of tax preference:
    Excess amortization of certified pollution control facilities 45,000
    Capital gains deduction 60,000 $105,000
  Other business deductions   75,000   180,000

Taxable income (before net operating loss deduction) .... $ 40,000

In 1972, the taxpayer had net operating loss of $70,000 which is carried forward to 1973; $20,000 of this net operating loss is attributable to excess tax preferences. In order to determine the amount of the 1972 net operating loss which remains as a carryover to 1974, the 1973 taxable income is redetermined, in accordance with section 172(b)(2) and the regulations thereunder, as follows:

Gross income $220,000
Deductions:
  Capital gains deduction .... disallowed
  Business deductions 120,000

Taxable income per sec. 172(b)(2) $100,000

In this case, the $60,000 increase in the 1972 taxable income as redetermined and the $30,000 decrease in the amount of the 1973 net operating loss remaining as a carryover to 1974 (i.e., the remaining 1972 net operating loss after an initial decrease of $40,000 resulting from the 1973 taxable income before redetermination) is entirely attributable to the disallowance of the capital gains deduction. The limitation on the amount treated as items of tax preference is computed as follows:

Items of tax preference computed without regard to this section:
  Capital gains .... $ 60,000
  Excess amortization of certified pollution control facilities 45,000
                                                                                             $105,000

Proposed Reg. §1.57-4

Less: Lesser of capital gains deduction ($60,000) or amount of reduction in carryover due to its disallowance ($30,000)	(30,000)
	$75,000
Plus: Amount of reduction of carryover (due to disallowance of capital gains deduction) attributable to excess tax preferences	$20,000
Limitation	$95,000

§ 1.57-5 (Proposed Treasury Decision, published 12-30-70.) **Records to be kept.**

(a) **In general.** The taxpayer shall have available permanent records of all the facts necessary to determine with reasonable accuracy the amounts described in § 1.57-1. Such records shall include:

(1) In the case of amounts described in paragraph (a) of § 1.57-1: the amount and nature of indebtedness outstanding for the taxable year and the date or dates on which each such indebtedness was incurred or renewed in any form; the amount expended for property held for investment during any taxable year during which such indebtedness was incurred or renewed; and the manner in which it was determined that property was or was not held for investment.

(2) In the case of amounts described in paragraphs (b), (c), (d), (e), and (h) of § 1.57-1:

(i) The dates, and manner in which, the property was acquired and placed in service,

(ii) The taxpayer's basis on the date the property was acquired and the manner in which the basis was determined,

(iii) An estimate of the useful life (in terms of months, hours of use, etc., whichever is appropriate) of the property on the date placed in service or an estimate of the number of units to be produced by the property on the date the property is placed in service, whichever is appropriate, and the manner in which such estimate was determined,

(iv) The amount and date of all adjustments by the taxpayer to the basis of the property and an explanation of the nature of such adjustments, and

(v) In the case of property which has an adjusted basis reflecting adjustments taken by another taxpayer with respect to the property or taken by the taxpayer with respect to other property, the information described in subdivisions (i) through (iv) above, with respect to such other property or other taxpayer.

(3) In the case of amounts described in paragraph (f) of § 1.57-1, the fair market value of the shares of stock at the date of exercise of the option and the option price and the manner in which each was determined.

(4) In the case of amounts described in paragraph (g) of § 1.57-1, the amount of debts written off and the amount of the loans outstanding for the taxable year and the 5 preceding taxable years or such shorter or longer period as is appropriate.

(b) **Net operating losses.** The taxpayer shall have available permanent records for the first taxable year in which a portion of a net operating loss was attributable to items of tax preference (within the meaning of § 1.56-2 (b)) and each succeeding taxable year in which there is a net operating loss or a net operating loss carryover a portion of which is so attributable. Such records shall include all the facts necessary to determine with reasonable accuracy the amount of deferred tax liability under section 56, including the amount of the net operating loss in each taxable year in which there are items of tax preference in excess of the minimum tax exemption (as determined under § 1.58-1), the amount of the items of tax preference for each such taxable year, the amount by which each such net operating loss reduces taxable income in any taxable year, and the amount by which each such net operating loss is reduced in any taxable year.

§ 1.58-1 (Proposed Treasury Decision, published 12-30-70.) **Minimum tax exemption.**

(a) **In general.** For purposes of the minimum tax for tax preferences (subtitle A, chapter 1A, part VI), the minimum tax exemption is $30,000 except as otherwise provided in this section.

(b) **Husband and wife.** In the case of a married individual filing a separate return, section 58 (a) provides that the minimum tax exemption is $15,000. This rule applies without regard to whether the married individual is living together with or apart from his spouse and without regard to whether or not his spouse has any items of tax preference.

(c) **Members of controlled groups**—(1) *Amount of exemption*—(i) *General rule.* Under section 58 (b), if a corporation is a component member of a controlled group of corporations on a December 31 (as defined in section 1563 (a) and (b) and the regulations thereunder), the minimum tax exemption for such taxable year which includes such December 31 is an amount equal to—

(a) $30,000 divided by the number of corporations which are component members of such group on December 31, or

(b) If an apportionment plan is adopted under subparagraph (3) of this paragraph, such portion of the $30,000 as is apportioned to such member in accordance with such plan.

(ii) *Consolidated returns.* The minimum tax exemption of a controlled group all of whose component members join in the filing of a consolidated return is $30,000. If there are component members of the controlled group which do not join in the filing of a consolidated return, and there is no apportionment plan effective under subparagraph (3) of this paragraph apportioning the $30,000 among the component members filing the consolidated return and the other component members of the controlled group, each component member of the controlled group (including each component member which joins in filing the consolidated return) is treated as a separate corporation for purposes of equally apportioning the $30,000 amount under subdivision (i) (a) of this subparagraph. In such case, the minimum tax exemption of the corporations filing the consolidated return is the sum of the amounts apportioned to each component member which joins in the filing of the consolidated return.

(2) *Certain short taxable years.* If the return of a corporation is for a short period which does not include a December 31, and such corporation is a component member of a controlled group of corporations with respect to such short period, then the minimum tax exemption of such corporation for such short period is an amount equal to $30,000 divided by the number of corporations which are component members of such group on the last day of such short period. The minimum tax exemption so determined is also subject to the rules of section 443 (d) (relating to reduction in the amount of the exemption for short periods) and the regulations thereunder. For purposes of this subparagraph, the term "short period" does not include any period if the income for such period is required to be included in a consolidated return under § 1.1502-76 (b). The determination of whether a corporation is a component member of a controlled group of corporations on the last day of a short period is made by applying the definition of "component member" contained in section 1563 (b) and § 1.1563-1 as if the last day of such short period were a December 31.

(3) *Apportionment of minimum tax exemption*—(i) *Apportionment plan.* (a) (In general.) In the case of corporations which are component members of a controlled group of corporations on a December 31, a single minimum tax exemption may be apportioned among such members if all such members consent, in the manner provided in subdivision (ii) of this subparagraph, to an apportionment plan with respect to such December 31. Such plan must provide for the apportionment of a fixed dollar amount to one or more of such members, but in no event may the sum of the amount so apportioned exceed $30,000. An apportionment plan is not considered as adopted with respect to a particular December 31 until each component member which is required to consent to the plan under subdivision (ii)(a) of this subparagraph files the original of a statement described in such

Proposed Reg. § 1.58-1

subdivision (or, the original of a statement incorporating its consent is filed on its behalf). In the case of a return filed before a plan is adopted, the minimum tax exemption for purposes of such return is to be equally apportioned in accordance with subparagraph (1) of this paragraph. If a valid apportionment plan is adopted after the return is filed and within the time prescribed in (b) of this subdivision (i), such return must be amended (or a claim for refund should be made) to reflect the change from equal apportionment.

(b) (Time for adopting plan.) A controlled group may adopt an apportionment plan with respect to a particular December 31 only if, at the time such plan is sought to be adopted, there is at least one year remaining in the statutory period (including any extensions thereof) for the assessment of the deficiency against any corporation the tax liability of which would be increased by the adoption of such plan. If there is less than one year remaining with respect to any such corporation, the district director or the director of the service center with whom such corporation files its income tax return will ordinarily, upon request, enter into an agreement to extend such statutory period for the limited purpose of assessing any deficiency against such corporation attributable to the adoption of such apportionment plan.

(c) (Years for which effective.) (1) The amount apportioned to a component member of a controlled group of corporations in an apportionment plan adopted with respect to a particular December 31 constitutes such member's minimum tax exemption for its taxable year including the particular December 31, and for all taxable years including succeeding December 31's, unless the apportionment plan is amended in accordance with subdivision (iii) of this subparagraph or is terminated under (c)(2) of this subdivision (i). Thus, the apportionment plan (including any amendments thereof) has a continuing effect and need not be renewed annually.

(2) If an apportionment plan is adopted with respect to a particular December 31, such plan terminates with respect to a succeeding December 31, if: the controlled group goes out of existence with respect to such succeeding December 31 within the meaning of paragraph (b) of § 1.1562-5, any corporation which was a component member of such group on the particular December 31 is not a component member of such group on such succeeding December 31, or any corporation which was not a component member of such group on the particular December 31 is a component member of such group on such succeeding December 31. An apportionment plan, once terminated with respect to a December 31, is no longer effective. Accordingly, unless a new apportionment plan is adopted, the minimum tax exemption of the component members of the controlled group for their taxable years which include such December 31 and all December 31's thereafter will be determined under subparagraph (1) of this paragraph.

(3) If an apportionment plan is terminated with respect to a particular December 31 by reason of the addition or withdrawal of a component member, each corporation which is a component member of the controlled group on such particular December 31 must, on or before the date it files its income tax return for the taxable year which includes such particular December 31, notify the district director or the director of the service center with whom it files such return of such termination. If an apportionment plan is terminated with respect to a particular December 31 by reason of the controlled group going out of existence, each corporation which was a component member of the controlled group on the preceding December 31 must, on or before the date it files its income tax return for the taxable year which includes such particular December 31, notify the district director or the director of the service center with whom it files such return of such termination.

(ii) Consents to plan—(a) General rule. (1) The consent of a component member (other than a wholly-owned subsidiary) to an apportionment plan with respect to a particular December 31 is to be made by means of a statement, signed by any person who is duly authorized to act on behalf of the consenting member, stating that such member consents to the apportionment plan with respect to such December 31. The statement must set forth the name, address, taxpayer identification number, and taxable year of the consenting component member, the amount apportioned to such member under the plan, and the internal revenue district or service center where the original of the statement is to be filed. The consent of more than one component member may be incorporated in a single statement. The original of a statement of consent is to be filed with the district director or the director of the service center with whom the component member of the group on such December 31 which has the taxable year ending first on or after such date filed its return for such taxable year. If two or more component members have the same such taxable year, a statement of consent may be filed with the district director or the director of the service center with whom the return for any such taxable year is filed. The original of a statement of consent is to have attached thereto information (referred to in this subdivision as "group identification") setting forth the name, address, taxpayer identification number, and taxable year of each component member of the controlled group on such December 31 (including wholly-owned subsidiaries) and the amount apportioned to each such member under the plan. If more than one original statement is filed, a statement may incorporate the group identification by reference to the name, address, taxpayer identification number, and taxable year of the component member of the group which has attached such group identification to the original of its statement.

(2) Each component member of the group on such December 31 (other than wholly-owned subsidiaries) must attach a copy of its consent (or a copy of the statement incorporating its consent) to the income tax return, amended return, or claim for refund filed with its district director or director of the service center for the taxable year including such date. Such copy must either have attached thereto information on group identification or must incorporate such information by reference to the name, address, taxpayer identification number, and taxable year of the component member of the group which has attached such information to its income tax return, amended return, or claim for refund filed with the same district director or director of the service center for the taxable year including such date.

(b) **Wholly-owned subsidiaries.** (1) Each component member of a controlled group which is a wholly-owned subsidiary of such group with respect to a December 31 is deemed to consent to an apportionment plan with respect to such December 31, provided each component member of the group which is not a wholly-owned subsidiary consents to the plan. For purposes of this paragraph, a component member of a controlled group is considered to be a wholly-owned subsidiary of the group with respect to a December 31, if, on each day preceding such date and during its taxable year which includes such date, all of its stock is owned directly by one or more corporations which are component members of the group on such December 31.

(2) Each wholly-owned subsidiary of a controlled group with respect to a December 31 must attach a statement containing the information which is required to be set forth in a statement of consent to an apportionment plan with respect to such December 31 to the income tax return, amended return, or claim for refund filed with its district director or director of the service center for the taxable year which includes such date. Such statement must either have attached thereto information on group identification or incorporate such information by reference to the name, address, taxpayer identification number, and taxable year of a component member of the group which has attached such information to its income tax return, amended return, or claim for refund filed with the same district director or director of the service center for the taxable year including such date.

(iii) Amendment of plan. An apportionment plan adopted with respect to a December 31 by a controlled group of corporations may be amended with respect to such December 31 or with respect to any succeeding December 31 for which the plan is effective under subdivision (i)(c) of this subparagraph. An apportionment plan must be amended with respect to a particular December 31 and the amendments to the plan are effective only if adopted in accordance with the rules prescribed in this paragraph for the adoption of an original plan with respect to such December 31.

(iv) Component members filing consolidated return. If the component members of a controlled group of corporations on a December 31 include corporations which join in the filing of a consolidated return, the corporations filing the consolidated return are treated as a single component member for purposes of this subparagraph.

Proposed Reg. § 1.58-1

Thus, for example, only one consent executed by the common parent to an apportionment plan filed pursuant to this section is required on behalf of the component members filing the consolidated return.

(d) **Estates and trusts.** Section 58(c)(2) provides that, in the case of an estate or trust, the minimum tax exemption applicable to such estate or trust is an amount which bears the same ratio to $30,000 as the portion of the sum of the items of tax preference apportioned to the estate or trust bears to the full sum before apportionment. For example, if one-third of the sum of the items of tax preference of a trust are subject to tax at the trust level after apportionment under section 58(c)(1) and § 1.58-3, the trust's minimum tax exemption is $10,000. See § 1.58-3 for rules with respect to the apportionment of items of tax preference of an estate or trust.

(e) **Short taxable year.** See section 443 (d) and § 1.443-1 (d) with respect to reduction in the amount of the minimum tax exemption in the case of a short taxable year.

§ 1.58-2 (Proposed Treasury Decision, published 12-30-70.) **General rules for conduit entities; partnerships and partners.**

(a) **General rules for conduit entities.** Section 1.58-3 through 1.58-6 provide rules under which items of tax preference of an estate, trust, electing small business corporation, common trust fund, regulated investment company, or real estate investment trust (referred to in this paragraph as the "conduit entity") are treated as items of tax preference of the beneficiaries, shareholders, participants, etc. (referred to in this paragraph as the "distributees"). Where an item of tax preference of a conduit entity is so apportioned to a distributee, the item of tax preference retains its character in the hands of the distributee and is adjusted to reflect: (1) the separate items of income and deduction of the distributee and (2) the tax status of the distributee as an individual, corporation, etc. For example, if a trust has $100,000 of capital gains for the taxable year, all of which are distributed to A, an individual, the item of tax preference apportioned to A under section 57(a) (9) (and § 1.57-1(i) (1)) is $50,000. If, however, A had a net capital loss for the taxable year of $60,000 without regard to the distribution from the trust, the trust tax preference would be adjusted in the hands of A to reflect the separate items of income and deduction passed through to the distributee, or, in this case, to reflect the net section 1201 gain to A of $40,000. Thus, A's capital gains items of tax preference would be $20,000. By application of this rule, A, in effect, treats capital gains distributed to him from the trust the same as his other capital gains in computing his capital gains item of tax preference. If A had been a corporation, the trust tax preference would be adjusted both to reflect the capital loss and to reflect A's tax status by recomputing the capital gains item of tax preference (after adjustment for the capital loss) under section 57(a)(9)(B) and § 1.57-1(i)(2). Similarly, if depreciation on section 1245 property subject to a net lease (as defined in section 57(a)(3) and § 1.57-1(c)) is apportioned from a conduit entity to a corporation (other than a personal holding company or electing small business corporation), the amount so apportioned to the corporation is not treated as an item of tax preference to such corporation since such item is not an item of tax preference in the case of a corporation (other than a personal holding company or an electing small business corporation).

(b) **Partnerships and partners.** (1) Section 701 provides that a partnership as such is not subject to the income tax imposed by chapter 1. Thus, a partnership as such is not subject to the minimum tax for tax preferences. Section 702 provides that, in determining his income tax, each partner is to take into account separately his distributive share of certain items of income, deductions, etc. of the partnership and other items of income, gain, loss, deduction, or credit of the partnership to the extent provided by regulations prescribed by the Secretary or his delegate. Accordingly, a partnership has no items of tax preference. However, each partner, in computing his items of tax preference, must take into account separately those items of income and deduction of the partnership which enter into the computation of the items of tax preference in accordance with subparagraph (2) of this paragraph.

(2) Pursuant to section 702, each partner must, solely for purposes of the minimum tax for tax preferences (to the extent not otherwise required to be taken into account separately under section 702 and the regulations thereunder), take into account separately in the manner provided in subchapter K and the regulations thereunder those items of income and deduction of the partnership which enter into the computation of the items of tax preference specified in section 57 and the regulations thereunder. A partner must, for this purpose, take into account separately his distributive share of:

(i) Investment interest expense (as defined in section 57(b) (2) (D) and § 1.57-2(b)(1)) determined at the partnership level;

(ii) Investment income (as defined in section 57(b) (2) (B) and § 1.57-2(b)(4)) determined at the partnership level;

(iii) Investment expenses (as defined in section 57(b)(2)(C) and § 1.57-2(b)(5)) determined at the partnership level;

(iv) With respect to each section 1250 property (as defined in section 1250(c)), the amount of the deduction allowable for the taxable year for exhaustion, wear and tear, obsolescence, or amortization and the deduction which would have been allowable for the taxable year had the property been depreciated under the straight line method each taxable year of its useful life (determined without regard to section 167(k)) for which the partnership has held the property;

(v) With respect to each item of section 1245 property (as defined in section 1245(a)(3)) which is subject to a net lease, the amount of the deduction allowable for exhaustion, wear and tear, obsolescence, or amortization and the deduction which would have been allowable for the taxable year had the property been depreciated under the straight line method for each taxable year of its useful life for which the partnership has held the property;

(vi) With respect to each certified pollution control facility for which an election is in effect under section 169, the amount of the deduction allowable for the taxable year under such section and the deduction which would have been allowable under section 167 had no election been in effect under section 169;

(vii) With respect to each unit of railroad rolling stock for which an election is in effect under section 184, the amount of the deduction allowable for the taxable year under such section and the deduction which would have been allowable under section 167 had no election been in effect under section 184;

(viii) In the case of a partnership which is a financial institution to which section 585 or 593 applies, the amount of the deduction allowable for the taxable year for a reasonable addition to a reserve for bad debts and the amount of the deduction that would have been allowable for the taxable year had the institution maintained its bad debt reserve for all taxable years on the basis of actual experience; and

(ix) With respect to each mineral property, the deduction for depletion allowable under section 611 for the taxable year and the adjusted basis of the property at the end of the taxable year (determined without regard to the depreciation deduction for the taxable year).

If, pursuant to section 743 (relating to optional adjustment to basis), the basis of partnership property is adjusted with respect to a transferee partner due to an election being in effect under section 754 (relating to manner of electing optional adjustment), items representing amortization, depreciation, depletion, gain or loss, and the adjusted basis of property subject to depletion, described above, shall be adjusted to reflect the basis adjustment under section 743.

(3) The minimum tax is effective for taxable years ending after December 31, 1969. Thus, subparagraph (2) of this paragraph is inapplicable in the case of items of income or deduction paid or accrued in a partnership's taxable year ending on or before December 31, 1969.

Proposed Reg. § 1.58-2

§ 1.58-3 (Proposed Treasury Decision, published 12-30-70.) **Estates and trusts.**

(a) *In general.* (1) Section 58(c)(1) provides that the sum of the items of tax preference of an estate or trust shall be apportioned between the estate or trust and the beneficiary on the basis of the income of the estate or trust allocable to each. Income for this purpose is the income received or accrued by the trust or estate which is not subject to current taxation either in the hands of the trust or estate or the beneficiary by reason of an item of tax preference. The character of the amounts distributed is determined under section 652(b) or 662(b) and the regulations thereunder.

(2) Additional computations required by reason of excess distributions are to be made in accordance with the principles of sections 665—669 and the regulations thereunder.

(3) In the case of a charitable remainder annuity trust (as defined in section 664(d)(1) and § 1.664-2) or a charitable remainder unitrust (as defined in section 664(d)(2) and § 1.664-3), the determination of the income not subject to current taxation by reason of an item of tax preference is to be made as if such trust were generally subject to taxation. Where income of such a trust is not subject to current taxation in accordance with this section and is distributed to a beneficiary in a taxable year subsequent to the taxable year in which the trust received or accrued such income, the items of tax preference relating to such income are apportioned to the beneficiary in such subsequent year (without credit for minimum tax paid by the trust with respect to items of tax preference).

(4) Items of tax preference apportioned to a beneficiary pursuant to this section are to be taken into account by the beneficiary in the same taxable year in which the income on which such apportionment is based is received or accrued by the beneficiary.

(5) Where a trust or estate has items of income or deduction which enter into the computation of the excess investment interest item of tax preference (as described in § 1.57-2), but such items do not result in an item of tax preference at the trust or estate level, each beneficiary must take into account, in computing his excess investment interest, the portion of such items distributed to him. The determination of the portion of such items distributed to each beneficiary is made in accordance with the character rules of section 652(b) or section 662(b) and the regulations thereunder.

(6) Where, pursuant to subpart E of part 1 of subchapter J (sections 671—678), the grantor of a trust or another person is treated as the owner of any portion of the trust, there shall be included in computing the items of tax preference of such person those items of income, deductions, and credits against tax of the trust which are attributable to that portion of the trust to the extent such items are taken into account under section 671 and the regulations thereunder. Any remaining portion of the trust is subject to the provisions of this section.

(b) *Examples.* The principles of this section may be illustrated by the following examples in each of which it is assumed that none of the distributions are accumulation distributions (see sections 665—669 and the regulations thereunder):

Example (1). Trust A, with one income beneficiary, has the following items of income and deduction without regard to the deduction for distributions:

Income
Business income $200,000
Investment income 20,000
                                                           $220,000

Deductions
Business deductions (nonpreference) 100,000
Investment interest expense 80,000
                                                           $180,000

Based on the above figures, the trust has $100,000 of taxable income without regard to items which enter into the computation of excess investment interest (see § 1.57-2) and the deduction for distributions. The trust also has $60,000 of excess investment interest, resulting in $40,000 of distributable net income. Thus, $60,000 of the $100,000 of noninvestment income is not subject to current taxation by reason of the excess investment interest.

(a) If $40,000 is distributed to the beneficiary, the beneficiary will normally be subject to tax on the full amount received and the "sheltered" portion of the income will remain at the trust level. Thus, none of the excess investment interest item of tax preference is apportioned to the beneficiary.

(b) If the beneficiary receives $65,000 from the trust, the beneficiary is still subject to tax on only $40,000 (the amount of the distributable net income) and, thus, is considered to have received $25,000 of business income "sheltered" by excess investment interest. Thus, $25,000 of the $60,000 of excess investment interest of the trust is apportioned to the beneficiary.

Example (2). Trust B has $150,000 of net section 1201 gain.

(a) If none of the gain is distributed to the beneficiaries, none of the capital gains item of tax preference is apportioned to the beneficiaries.

(b) If all or a part of the gain is distributed to the beneficiaries, a proportionate part of the capital gains item of tax preference is apportioned to the beneficiaries. If any of the beneficiaries are corporations the capital gains item of tax preference is adjusted in the hands of the corporations as provided in § 1.58-2(a).

Example (3). Trust C has taxable income of $200,000 computed without regard to depreciation on section 1250 property and the deduction for distributions. The depreciation on section 1250 property held by the trust is $160,000. The trust instrument provides for income to be retained by the trust in an amount equal to the depreciation on the property determined under the straight line method (which method has been used for this purpose for the entire period the trust has held the property) which, in this case, is equal to $100,000. The $60,000 excess of the accelerated depreciation of $160,000 over the straight line amount which would have resulted had the property been depreciated under that method for the entire period for which the trust has held the property is an item of tax preference pursuant to section 57(a)(2) (and § 1.57(b)). Of the remaining $100,000 of net income of the trust (after the reserve for depreciation), 80 percent is distributed to the beneficiaries. Pursuant to sections 167(h) and 642(e), 80 percent of the remaining $60,000 of depreciation deduction (or $48,000) is taken as a deduction directly by the beneficiaries and "shelters" the income received by the beneficiaries. Thus, the full $48,000 deduction taken by the beneficiaries is "excess accelerated depreciation" on section 1250 property and is an item of tax preference in the hands of the beneficiaries. None of the remaining $12,000 of "excess accelerated depreciation" is apportioned to the beneficiaries since this amount "shelters" income retained at the trust level.

Example (4). G creates a trust the ordinary income of which is payable to his adult son. Ten years from the date of the transfer, corpus is to revert to G. G retains no other right or power which would cause him to be treated as an owner under subpart E of part 1 of subchapter J (section 671 and following). Under the terms of the trust instrument and applicable local law capital gains must be applied to corpus. During the taxable year 1970 the trust has $200,000 income from dividends and interest and a net long-term capital gain of $100,000. Since the capital gain is held or accumulated for future distribution to G, he is treated under section 677(a) (2) as an owner of a portion of the trust to which the gain is attributable. Therefore, he must include the capital gain in the computation of his taxable income in 1970 and the capital gain item of tax preference is treated as being directly received by G. Accordingly, no adjustment is made to the trust's minimum tax exemption by reason of the capital gain.

Example (5). For its taxable year 1971 the trust referred to in example (4) has taxable income of $200,000 computed without regard to depreciation on

Proposed Reg. § 1.58-3

section 1250 property and the deduction for distributions. The depreciation on section 1250 property held by the trust is $160,000. The trust instrument provides for income to be retained by the trust in an amount equal to the depreciation on the property determined for purposes of the Federal income tax. If the property had been depreciated under the straight line method for the entire period for which the trust held the property the resulting depreciation deduction would have been $100,000. The $60,000 excess is, therefore, an item of tax preference pursuant to section 57(a) (2) and § 1.57-1(d). Since this amount of "income" is held or accumulated for future distributions to G, he is treated under section 677(a) (2) as an owner of a portion of the trust to which such income is attributable. Therefore, section 671 requires that in computing the tax liability of the grantor the income, deductions, and credits against tax of the trust which are attributable to such portion shall be taken into account. Thus, the grantor has received $160,000 of income and is entitled to a depreciation deduction in the same amount. The $60,000 item of tax preference resulting from the excess depreciation is treated as being directly received by G as he has directly received the income sheltered by that preference. Accordingly, no adjustment is made to the trust's minimum tax exemption by reason of such depreciation.

§ 1.58-4 (Proposed Treasury Decision, published 12-30-70.) **Electing small business corporations.**

(a) **In general.** Section 58 (d) (1) provides rules for the apportionment of the items of tax preference of an electing small business corporation among the shareholders of such corporation. Section 58(d)(2) provides rules for the imposition of the minimum tax on an electing small business corporation with respect to certain capital gains. For purposes of section 58 (d) and this section, the items of tax preference are computed at the corporate level as if section 57 generally applied to the corporation. However, the items of tax preference so computed are treated as items of tax preference of the shareholders of such corporation and not as items of tax preference of such corporation (except as provided in paragraph (c) of this section). The items of tax preference specified in section 57(a)(1) and § 1.57-1(a) (excess investment interest) and section 57(a)(3) and § 1.57-1(c) (accelerated depreciation on section 1245 property subject to a net lease), while generally inapplicable to corporations, are included as items of tax preference in the case of an electing small business corporation.

(b) **Apportionment to shareholders.** (1) The items of tax preference of an electing small business corporation, other than the capital gains item of tax preference described in paragraph (c) of this section, are apportioned pro rata among the shareholders of such corporation in a manner consistent with section 1374(c)(1). Thus, with respect to the items of tax preference of the electing small business corporation, there is to be treated as items of tax preference of each shareholder a pro rata share of such items computed as follows:

(i) Divide the total amount of such items of tax preference of the corporation by the number of days in the taxable year of the corporation, thus determining the daily amount of such items of tax preference.

(ii) Determine for each day the shareholder's portion of the daily amount of each such item of tax preference by applying to such amount the ratio which the stock owned by the shareholder on that day bears to the total stock outstanding on that day.

(iii) Total the shareholder's daily portions of each such item of tax preference of the corporation for its taxable year.

Amounts taken into account by shareholders in accordance with this paragraph are considered to consist of a pro rata share of each item of tax preference of the corporation. Thus, for example, if the corporation has $50,000 of excess investment interest and $150,000 of excess accelerated depreciation on section 1250 property and a shareholder, in accordance with this paragraph, takes into account $60,000 of the total $200,000 of tax preference items of the corporation, one-fourth ($50,000 ÷ $200,000) of the $60,000, or $15,000, taken into account by the shareholder is considered excess investment interest and three-fourths of the $60,000, or $45,000, is considered excess accelerated depreciation on section 1250 property.

(2) Items of tax preference apportioned to a shareholder pursuant to subparagraph (1) of this paragraph are taken into account by the shareholder for the shareholder's taxable year in which or with which the taxable year of the corporation ends, except that, in the case of the death of a shareholder during any taxable year of the corporation (during which the corporation is an electing small business corporation), the items of tax preference of the corporation for such taxable year are taken into account for the final taxable year of the shareholder.

(c) **Capital gains.** (1) Capital gains of an electing small business corporation, other than those capital gains subject to tax under section 1378, do not result in an item of tax preference at the corporate level since, in applying the formula specified in section 57(a)(9)(B) and § 1.57-1(i)(2), the rate of tax on capital gains (and the resulting tax) at the corporate level is zero. Under section 1375(a) shareholders of an electing small business corporation take into account the capital gains of the corporation (including capital gains subject to tax under section 1378). Therefore, the computation of the capital gains item of tax preference at the shareholder level, with respect to such capital gains, is taken into account automatically by operation of section 57(a)(9) and § 1.57-1(i). To avoid double inclusion of the capital gains item of tax preference by a shareholder with respect to capital gains subject to tax under section 1378, the capital gains item of tax preference which results at the corporate level by reason of section 58(d)(2) is not treated under section 58(d)(1) as an item of tax preference of the shareholders of the corporation.

(2) The capital gains item of tax preference of an electing small business corporation subject to the tax imposed by section 1378 is the excess of the amount of tax computed under section 1378(b)(2) over the sum of—

(i) The amount of tax that would be computed under section 1378(b)(2) if the lesser of the following amounts were excluded:

(a) That portion of the net section 1201 gain of the corporation described in section 1378(b)(1), or

(b) That portion of the net section 1201 gain to which section 1378(c) applies, and

(ii) The amount of tax imposed under section 1378

divided by the sum of the normal tax rate and the surtax rate under section 11 for the taxable year.

(3) The principles of this paragraph may be illustrated by the following example.

Example. Corporation X is a calendar year taxpayer and an electing small business corporation. For its taxable year 1971 the corporation has net section 1201 gain of $650,000 and taxable income of $800,000 (including the net section 1201 gain.) Although X's election under section 1372(a) has been in effect for its 3 immediately preceding taxable years, X is subject to the tax imposed by section 1378 for 1971 since it has net section 1201 gain (in the amount of $200,000) attributable to property with a substituted basis. The tax computed under section 1378(b)(1) is $187,500 (30% of ($650,000 − $25,000)) and under section 1378(b)(2) is $377,500 (22% of $800,000 plus 26% of $775,000). By reason of the limitation imposed by section 1378(c) the tax actually imposed by section 1378 is $60,000 (30% of $200,000, the net section 1201 gain). The tax computed under section 1378(b)(2) with the modification required under subparagraph (2)(i) of this paragraph is $281,500 (22% of $600,000 plus 26% of $575,000). Thus, the 1971 capital gains item of tax preference of X is $75,000 computed as follows:

1. Tax computed under 1378(b)(2) $377,500
2. Tax computed under 1378(b)(2) with modification 281,500

3. Excess 96,000
4. Tax actually imposed under 1378 60,000

5. Difference 36,000

Proposed Reg. § 1.58-4

6. Normal tax rate plus surtax rate	.48
7. Tax preference (line 5 ÷ line 6)	$ 75,000

In addition each shareholder of X will take into account his distributive share of the $650,000 of net section 1201 gain of X less the taxes paid by X on the gain.

§ 1.58-5 (Proposed Treasury Decision, published 12-30-70.) **Common trust funds.**

Section 58(e) provides that each participant in a common trust fund (as defined in section 584 and the regulations thereunder) is to treat as items of tax preference his proportionate share of the items of tax preference of the fund computed as if the fund were an individual subject to the minimum tax. The participant's proportionate share of the items of tax preference of the fund is determined as if the participant had realized, or incurred, his pro rata share of items of income, gain, loss, or deduction of the fund directly from the source from which realized or incurred by the fund. The participant's pro rata share of such items is determined in a manner consistent with § 1.584-2(c). Items of tax preference apportioned to a participant pursuant to this paragraph are taken into account by the participant for the participant's taxable year in which or with which the taxable year of the trust ends.

§ 1.58-6 (Proposed Treasury Decision, published 12-30-70.) **Regulated investment companies; real estate investment trusts.**

(a) **In general.** Section 58(f) provides rules with respect to the determination of the items of tax preference of regulated investment companies (as defined in section 851) and their shareholders and real estate investment trusts (as defined in section 856) and their shareholders, or holders of beneficial interest. In general, the items of tax preference of such companies and such trusts are determined at the company or trust level and the items of tax preference so determined (other than the capital gains item of tax preference (section 57(a)(9) and § 1.57-1(i)) and, in the case of a real estate investment trust, accelerated depreciation on section 1250 property (secs. 57(a)(2) and 1.57-1(b)) are treated as items of tax preference of the shareholders, or holders of beneficial interest, in the same proportion that the dividends (other than capital gains dividends) paid to each such shareholder, or holder of beneficial interest, bear to the taxable income of such company or such trust determined without regard to the deduction for dividends paid. In no case, however, is such proportion to be considered in excess of 100 percent. For example, if a regulated investment company has items of tax preference of $500,000 for the taxable year, none of which resulted from capital gains, and distributes dividends in an amount equal to 90 percent of its taxable income, each shareholder treats his share of 90 percent of the company's items of tax preference, or (a proportionate share of) $450,000, as items of tax preference of the shareholder. The remaining $50,000 constitutes items of tax preference of the company. Amounts treated under this paragraph as items of tax preference of the shareholders, or holders of beneficial interest, are deemed to be derived proportionately from each item of tax preference of the company or trust, other than the capital gains item of tax preference and, in the case of a real estate investment trust, accelerated depreciation on section 1250 property. Such amounts are taken into account by the shareholders, or holders of beneficial interest, in the same taxable year in which the dividends on which the apportionment is based are includible in income.

(b) **Capital gains.** Section 58(g)(1) provides that a regulated investment company or real estate investment trust does not treat as an item of tax preference the capital gains item of tax preference under section 57(a)(9) (and § 1.57-1(i)) to the extent that such item is attributable to amounts taken into income by the shareholders of such company under section 852(b)(3) or by the shareholders or holders of beneficial interest of such trust under section 857(b)(3). Thus, such a company or trust computes its capital gains item of tax preference on the basis of its net section 1201 gain less the sum of (1) the capital gains dividend (as defined in section 852(b)(3)(C) or section 857(b)(3)(C)) for the taxable year of the company or trust plus (2), in the case of a regulated investment company, that portion of the undistributed capital gains designated, pursuant to section 852(b)(3)(D) and the regulations thereunder, by the company to be includible in the shareholder's return as long-term capital gains for the shareholder's taxable year in which the last day of the company's taxable year falls. Amounts treated under section 852(b)(3) or 857(b)(3) as long-term capital gains of shareholders, or holders of beneficial interest, are automatically included, pursuant to section 57(a)(9) and § 1.57-1(i), in the computation of the capital gains items of tax preference of the shareholders, or holders of beneficial interest.

(c) **Accelerated depreciation on section 1250 property.** In the case of a real estate investment trust, all of the items of tax preference resulting from accelerated depreciation on section 1250 property held by the trust (section 57(a)(2) and § 1.57-1(b)) are treated as items of tax preference of the trust, and, thus, none are treated as items of tax preference of the shareholder, or holder of beneficial interest.

§ 1.58-7 (Proposed Treasury Decision, published 12-30-70, 6-24-71.) Tax preferences attributable to foreign sources; preferences other than capital gains and stock options.

(a) **In general.** Section 58(g)(1) provides that, except in the case of the stock options item of tax preference (section 57(a)(6) and § 1.57-1(f)) and the capital gains item of tax preference (section 57(a)(9) and § 1.57-1(i)), items of tax preference which are attributable to sources within any foreign country or possession of the United States shall, for purposes of section 56, be taken into account only to the extent that such items reduce the tax imposed by chapter 1 (other than the minimum tax under section 56) on income derived from sources within the United States. Items of tax preference from sources within any foreign country or possession of the United States reduce the chapter 1 tax on income from sources within the United States to the extent the deduction relating to such preferences, in combination with other foreign deductions, exceed the income from such sources and, in effect, offset income from sources within the United States. Items of tax preference, for this purpose, are determind after application of § 1.57-4 (relating to limitation on amounts treated as items of tax preference).

(b) **Preferences attributable to foreign sources—(1) Preferences other than excess investment interest.** Except in the case of excess investment interest (see subparagraph (2) of this paragraph), an item of tax preference to which this section applies is attributable to sources within a foreign country or possession of the United States to the extent such item is attributable to a deduction properly allocable or apportionable to an item or class of gross income from sources within a foreign country or possession of the United States under the principles of section 862(b), or section 863, and the regulations thereunder. Where, in the case of income partly from sources within the United States and partly from sources within a foreign country or possession of the United States, taxable income is computed before apportionment to domestic and foreign sources, and is then apportioned by processes or formulas of general apportionment (pursuant to section 863(b) and the regulations thereunder), deduction attributable to such taxable income are considered to be proportionately from sources within the United States and within the foreign country or possession of the United States on the same basis as taxable income.

(2) **Excess investment interest**—(i) Per-country limitation. (a) In the case of a taxpayer on the per-country foreign tax credit limitation under section 904(a) for the taxable year, excess investment interest (as defined in section 57(b)(1) and § 1.57-2(a)), and the resulting item of tax preference, is attributable to sources within a foreign country or a possession of the United States to the extent that investment interest expense attributable to income from sources within such foreign country or possession of the United States exceeds the net investment income from

Proposed Reg. § 1.58-7

sources within such foreign country or such possession. For this purpose, net investment income from within a foreign country or possession of the United States is the excess (if any) of the investment income from sources within such country or possession over the investment expenses attributable to income from sources within such country or such possession. For the definition of investment interest expense see section 57(b)(2)(D) and § 1.57-2(b)(4); for the definition of investment income see sction 57(b)(2)(B) and § 1.57-2(b)(2); for the definition of investment expense see section 57(b)(2)(C) and § 1.57-2(b)(3).

(b) If the taxpayer's excess investment interest computed on a worldwide basis is less than the taxpayer's total separately determined excess investment interest (as defined in this subdivision (b)), the amount of the taxpayer's excess investment interest from each foreign country or possession is the amount which bears the same relationship to the taxpayer's excess investment interest from each such country or possession, determined without regard to this subdivision (b), as the taxpayer's worldwide excess investment interest bears to the taxpayer's total separately determined excess investment interest. For purposes of this subdivision (b), the taxpayer's total separately determined excess investment interest is the sum of the total excess investment interest determined without regard to this subdivision (b) plus the taxpayer's excess investment interest from sources within the United States determined in a manner consistent with (a) of this subdivision (i).

(ii) Overall limitation. In the case of a taxpayer who has elected the overall foreign tax credit limitation under section 904(a)(2) for the taxable year, excess investment interest (as defined in section 57(b)(1) and § 1.57-2(a)), and the resulting item of tax preference, is attributable to sources within any foreign country or possession of the United States to the extent that investment interest expense attributable to income from such sources exceeds the sum of (a) the net investment income from such sources plus (b) the excess, if any, of net investment income from sources within the United States over investment interest expense attributable to sources within the United States. For this purpose, net investment income from sources within any foreign country or possession of the United States is the excess (if any) of the investment income from all such sources over the investment expenses attributable to income from such sources. For the definition of investment interest expense see section 57(b)(2)(D) and § 1.57-2(b)(4); for the definition of investment income see section 57(b)(2)(B) and § 1.57-2(b)(2); for the definition of investment expense see section 57(b)(2)(C) and § 1.57-2(b)(3).

(iii) Allocation of expenses. The determination of the investment interest expense and investment expenses attributable to a foreign country or possession of the United States is made in a manner consistent with subparagraph (1) of this paragraph.

(iv) Attribution of certain interest deductions to foreign sources. Where net investment income from sources within any foreign country or possession has the effect of offsetting investment interest expense attributable to income from sources within the United States, the deductions for the investment interest expense so offset are, for purposes of § 1.58-7(c) (relating to reduction in taxes on United States source income), treated as deductions attributable to income from sources within the foreign country or possession from which such net investment income is derived. Such an offset will occur where there is an excess of investment interest expense attributable to income from sources within the United States over net investment income from such sources and (a) in the case of a taxpayer on the per-country foreign tax credit limitation, an excess of net investment income from sources within a foreign country or possession of the United States over investment interest expense from within such foreign country or possession, or (b) in the case of a taxpayer who has elected the overall foreign tax credit limitation, there is an excess of net investment income from sources within foreign countries or possessions of the United States over investment interest expense attributable to income from within such sources.

(v) Separate limitation on interest income. Where a taxpayer has income described in section 904(f)(2) (relating to interest income subject to the separate foreign tax credit limitation) or expenses attributable to such income, the determination of the excess investment interest resulting therefrom must be determined separately with respect to such income and the expenses properly allocable or apportionable thereto in the same manner as such determination is made in the case of a taxpayer on the per-country foreign tax credit limitation for the taxable year (see subdivision (i) of this subparagraph).

(vi) *Examples.* The principles of this subparagraph may be illustrated by the following examples in each of which the taxpayer is an individual and a citizen of the United States:

Example (1). The taxpayer's only items of income and deduction relating to excess investment interest are as follows:

	United States	France	Germany	Total
Investment income from sources within	$150,000	$120,000	$180,000	$450,000
Investment expenses relating to income from sources within	(100,000)	(90,000)	(120,000)	(310,000)
Net investment income	50,000	30,000	60,000	140,000
Investment interest expense relating to income from sources within	(110,000)	(70,000)	(50,000)	(230,000)
(Excess) of investment interest expense over net investment income	(60,000)	(40,000)	*10,000	(90,000)

*Excess of net investment income over investment interest expense.

(a) If the taxpayer has elected the overall foreign tax credit limitation, his excess investment interest from sources within any foreign countries or possessions of the United States determined under subdivision (ii) of this subparagraph is computed as follows:

```
Investment interest:
  French --------------------------------------- ($70,000)
  German ---------------------------------------  (50,000)        ($120,000)

Net investment income:
  Investment income:
    French -------------------------------------  120,000
    German -------------------------------------  180,000   $300,000

Less:
  Investment expenses:
    French -------------------------------------  (90,000)
    German ------------------------------------- (120,000)  (210,000)   90,000

Excess of U.S. net income over investment interest
  expenses: .............................................         0
  Total foreign excess investment interest ..............      (30,000)
```

(b) If the taxpayer is on the per-country foreign tax credit limitation, his excess investment interest from France and Germany determined under subdivision (i)*(a)* of this subparagraph is $40,000 and zero, respectively. Since the taxpayer's worldwide excess investment interest ($90,000) is less than his total separately determined excess investment interest ($60,000 (U.S.) plus $40,000 (French) plus zero (German), or $100,000), the limitation in subdivision (i)*(b)* of this subparagraph applies and the excess investment interest attributable to France is limited as follows:

$$\frac{\text{Total worldwide excess (\$90,000)} \times \text{French excess (\$40,000)}}{\text{Total separately determined excess (\$100,000)}} = \$36,000$$

The taxpayer's total excess investment interest attributable to sources within any foreign country or possession of the United States is, thus, $36,000 ($36,000 (French) plus zero (German)). The taxpayer's excess investment interest attributable to sources within the United States is $54,000 ($\frac{\$90,000}{\$100,000} \times \$60,000$).

Proposed Reg. §1.58-7

Since, in making the latter determination, $6,000 of the $60,000 of U. S. investment interest expense in excess of U. S. net investment income is, in effect, offset by German net investment income, for purposes of § 1.58-7(c), $6,000 of interest deductions attributable to income from sources within the United States are, pursuant to subdivision (iv) of this subparagraph, treated as deductions attributable to income from sources within Germany.

Example (2). Assume the same facts as in example (1) except that the items of income and deduction in Germany and the United States are reversed. The worldwide excess investment interest, thus, remains $90,000 and the items of income and deduction relating to excess investment interest are as follows:

	United States	France	Germany	Total
Investment income from sources within	$180,000	$120,000	$150,000	$450,000
Investment expenses relating to income from sources within	(120,000)	(90,000)	(100,000)	(310,000)
Net investment income	60,000	30,000	50,000	140,000
Investment interest expense relating to income from sources within	(50,000)	(70,000)	(110,000)	(230,000)
(Excess) of investment interest expense over net investment income	10,000	(40,000)	(60,000)	(90,000)

(a) If the taxpayer has elected the overall limitation, his excess investment interest from sources within any foreign countries or possessions of the United States determined under subdivision (ii) of this subparagraph is determined as follows:

```
Foreign investment interest:
    French ............................................. ($70,000)
    German ............................................. (110,000)                    ($180,000)
Foreign net investment income:
    French .............................................  120,000
    German .............................................  150,000    $270,000
Less:
    Investment expenses:
        French ......................................... (90,000)
        German ......................................... (100,000)   (190,000)          80,000
Excess of U.S. net investment income over U.S. investment interest expense......      10,000
Excess investment interest attributable to foreign sources......................     (90,000)
```

(b) If the taxpayer has not elected the overall foreign tax credit limitation, his excess investment interest from France and Germany determined under subdivision (i) of this subparagraph (without regard to the limitation to worldwide excess investment interest) is $40,000 and $60,000, respectively, and his total separately determined excess investment interest is, thus, $100,000. Since the total separately determined excess would exceed the worldwide excess, the limitation to the worldwide excess in subdivision (i) applies and the excess investment interest is determined as follows:

France:
$$\frac{\$90,000}{\$100,000} \times \$40,000 = \$36,000$$

Germany:
$$\frac{\$90,000}{\$100,000} \times \$60,000 = \$54,000$$

Total excess investment interest attributable to sources within any foreign countries and possessions $90,000

Example (3). Assume the same facts as in example (1) except that the taxpayer, in addition has investment income, investment expenses, and investment interest subject to the separate limitation under section 904(f).

(a) If the taxpayer has elected the overall foreign tax credit limitation, his excess investment interest from sources within any foreign countries or possessions of the United States determined under subdivision (ii) of this subparagraph is the same as in (a) of example (1) of this subdivision (vi). He then treats such amount as separately determined excess investment interest attributable to a single foreign country as determined under subdivision (i) of this subparagraph and proceeds as in (b) of example (1) of this subdivision (vi) treating items of income and deduction subject to section 904(f) and from each separate foreign country or possession separately in making the additional determinations under subdivisions (i) and (iv) of this subparagraph.

(b) If the taxpayer has not elected the overall foreign tax credit limitation, his excess investment interest from sources within any foreign country or possession of the United States would be determined in the same manner as in (b) of example (1) treating items of income and deduction which are subject to section 904(f) and from each separate foreign country or possession separately in making the determinations under subdivisions (i) and (iv) of this subparagraph.

(c) **Reduction in taxes on United States source income**—(1) *Overall limitation*—(i) *In general.* If a taxpayer is on the overall foreign tax credit limitation under section 904(a)(2), the items of tax preference determined to be attributable to foreign sources under paragraph (b) of this section reduce the tax imposed by chapter 1 (other than the minimum tax imposed under section 56) on income from sources within the United States for the taxable year to the extent of the smallest of the following three amounts:

(a) Items of tax preference (other than stock options and capital gains) attributable to sources within a foreign country or possession of the United States,

(b) The excess (if any) of the total deductions properly allocable or apportionable to items or classes of gross income from sources within foreign countries and possessions of the United States over the gross income from such sources, or

(c) Taxable income from sources within the United States.

See § 1.58-7(b)(2)(iv) with respect to the attribution of certain interest deductions to foreign sources in cases involving the excess investment interest item of tax preference.

(ii) *Net operating loss.* Where there is an overall net operating loss for the taxable year, to the extent that the lesser of the amounts determined under *(a)* or *(b)* of subdivision (i) of this subparagraph exceeds the taxpayer's taxable income from sources within the United States (and, therefore do not offset taxable income from sources within the United States for the taxable year) the amount of such excess is treated as "suspense preferences." Suspense preferences are converted to actual items of tax preference, arising in the loss year and subject to the provisions of section 56, as the net operating loss is used in other taxable years, in the form of a net operating loss deduction under section 172, to offset taxable income from sources within the United States. Suspense preferences which, in other taxable years, reduce taxable income from sources within any foreign country or possession of the United States lose their character as suspense preferences and, thus, are never converted into actual items of tax preference. The amount of the suspense preferences which are converted into actual items of tax preference is equal to that portion of the net operating loss attributable to the suspense preferences which offset taxable income from sources within the United States in taxable years other than the loss year. The determination of the component parts of the net operating loss and the determination of the amount by which the portion of the net operating loss attributable to suspense preferences offsets taxable income from sources within the United States is made on a year-by-year basis in the same order as the net operating loss is used in accordance with section 172(b). Such determination is made by applying deductions attributable to U.S. source income first against such income and deductions attributable to foreign source income first against such foreign source income and in accordance with the following principles:

(a) Deductions attributable to items or classes of gross income from sources within the United States offset taxable income from sources within the United States before any remaining portion of the net operating loss;

Proposed Reg. § 1.58-7

(b) Deductions attributable to items or classes of gross income from sources within foreign countries or possessions of the United States offset taxable income from such sources before any remaining portion of the net operating loss;

(c) Deductions described in (b) of this subdivision (ii) which are not suspense preferences (referred to in this subparagraph as "other foreign deductions") offset taxable income from sources within foreign countries and possessions of the United States before suspense preferences; and

(d) Suspense preferences offset taxable income from sources within the United States before other foreign deductions.

For purposes of the above computations, taxable income is computed with the modifications specified in section 172(b)(2) or section 172(c), whichever is applicable. However, the amount of suspense preferences which are converted into actual items of tax preference in accordance with the above principles is reduced to the extent suspense preferences offset increases in taxable income from sources within the United States due to the modifications specified in section 172(b)(2) or section 172(c). For this purpose, suspense preferences are considered to offset an increase in taxable income due to the section 172(b)(2) modifications only after reducing taxable income computed before the section 172(b)(2) or section 172(c) modifications.

(iii) Examples. The principles of this subparagraph may be illustrated by the following examples. In each example the taxpayer is an individual citizen of the United States and has elected the overall foreign tax credit limitation. Personal deductions and exemptions are disregarded for purposes of these examples.

Example (1). In 1974, the taxpayer has the following items of income and deduction:

```
United States taxable income:
    Gross income ------------------------------------------------- $750,000
    Deductions  ------------------------------------------------- (250,000)    $500,000
Foreign source loss:
    Gross income ------------------------------------------------              200,000
    Deductions:
        Preference items (excess of percentage depletion
            over basis) --------------------------------- $550,000
        Other ---------------------------------------------  50,000  (600,000)  (400,000)
Overall taxable income --------------------------------------------------------  100,000
```

Pursuant to subdivision (i) of this subparagraph the smallest of (a) the items of tax preference attributable to the foreign sources ($550,000), (b) the foreign source loss ($400,000), or (c) the taxable income from sources within the United States ($500,000) reduces the tax imposed by chapter 1 (other than the minimum tax) on income from sources within the United States. Thus, $400,000 of the $550,000 of excess depletion is treated as an item of tax preference in 1974 subject to the minimum tax.

Example (2). Assume the same facts as in example (1) except that the gross income from sources within the United States is $350,000 resulting in U.S. taxable income of $100,000 and an overall net operating loss of $300,000. Pursuant to subdivision (i) of this subparagraph, $100,000 of the $550,000 excess depletion would be treated as an item of tax preference in 1974 subject to the minimum tax. In addition, pursuant to subdivision (ii) of this subparagraph, the excess of the items of tax preference from foreign sources ($550,000) or the foreign source loss ($400,000), whichever is less, over the U.S. taxable income ($100,000), or, in this example, $300,000, is treated as suspense preferences.

(a) If, in 1971, the taxpayer's total items of income and deduction result in $350,000 of taxable income all of which is from sources within the United States, the entire $300,000 net operating loss, all of which is attributable to suspense preferences, is used to offset U.S. taxable income. Accordingly, the full $300,000 of suspense preferences are converted into actual items of tax preference arising in 1974 and are subject to tax under section 56.

(b) If the $350,000 in 1971 is modified taxable income resulting from the denial of a section 1202 capital gains deduction of $175,000 by reason of section 172(b)(2), the $300,000, otherwise treated as actual items of tax preference, is reduced by

$125,000, i.e., the extent to which the suspense preferences offset U.S. taxable income attributable to the increase in taxable income resulting from the denial of the section 1202 deduction.

Example (3). In 1974, the taxpayer has the following items of income and deduction:

United States loss:
- Gross income $75,000
- Deductions .... (225,000)
  - ($150,000)

Foreign loss:
- Gross income 400,000
- Deductions:
  - Preference items (excess of accelerated depreciation on sec. 1250 property over straight-line amount) $200,000
  - Other 550,000 (750,000)
    - (350,000)

Overall net operating loss .... (500,000)

Since the nonpreference deductions reduce the foreign source income before the preference portion, the $350,000 foreign source loss consists of $200,000 of suspense preferences and $150,000 of other deductions. In 1971, 1972, and 1973 the taxpayer had taxable income from sources within the United States of $100,000, $200,000 and $300,000, respectively and taxable income from sources within foreign countries of $80,000 each year. Of the $200,000 of suspense preferences, $150,000 are converted into actual items of tax preference, subject to the minimum tax in 1974, determined as follows:

Year—Explanation	Taxable income U.S. source	Taxable income Foreign source	U.S. deductions	Foreign deductions Suspense preferences	Foreign deductions Other
1971 End of year balance before section 58(g) computations	100	80	150	200	150
1. U.S. deductions against U.S. income	(100)		(100)		
2. Other foreign deductions against foreign income		(80)			(80)
1972 End of year balance before section 58(g) computations	200	80	50	200	70
1. U.S. deductions against U.S. income	(50)		(50)		
2. Other foreign deductions against foreign income		(70)			(70)
3. Suspense preferences against foreign income		(10)		(10)	
4. Suspense preferences against U.S. income	*(150)			*(150)	
1973 End of year balance before section 58(g) computations	300	80		40	
1. U.S. deductions against U.S. income			Not applicable.		
2. Other foreign deductions against foreign income			Not applicable.		
3. Suspense preference against foreign income		(40)		(40)	
4. Suspense preferences against U.S. income			Not applicable.		
Balances	300	40			

°Suspense preferences converted to actual items of tax preference.

Example (4). In 1970, the taxpayer's total items of income and deduction, all of which are attributable to foreign sources, are as follows:

Foreign loss:
- Gross income $400,000
- Deductions:
  - Preferences (excess of accelerated depreciation on section 1250 property over straight-line) $200,000
  - Other deductions 550,000 (750,000)

Net operating loss $350,000

Pursuant to subdivision (i) of this subparagraph, none of the preferences attributable to foreign sources reduce the tax imposed by chapter 1 (other than the minimum tax) on taxable income from sources within the United States. Pursuant to subdivision (ii) of this subparagraph, the $200,000 portion of the net operating loss resulting from the excess accelerated depreciation constitutes suspense prefer-

Proposed Reg. § 1.58-7

ences. No part of the net operating loss that is carried back to previous years is reduced in such previous years. In 1971 and 1972, the taxpayer's income (before the net operating loss deduction) consists of the following:

1971 taxable income:
United States	$160,000
Foreign	70,000
Total	$230,000

1972 taxable income:
United States	$ 25,000
Foreign	105,000
Total	$130,000

(a) In 1971, the conversion of suspense preferences into actual items of tax preference under section 58(g) (and this paragraph) and the imposition of the minimum tax on 1970 items of tax preference under section 56(b) and (§ 1.56-2) are determined as follows:
Conversion of suspense preferences:

1970 NET OPERATING LOSS
[In thousands of dollars]

	U.S. taxable income	Foreign taxable income	U.S. deductions	Suspense preferences	Other foreign deductions
1. U.S. deductions against U.S. income	$160		$70	$200	$150
2. Other foreign deductions against foreign income		70	Not applicable.		(70)
3. Suspense preference against foreign income			Not applicable.		
4. Suspense preference against U.S. income	*(160)			(160)	
Balance to 1972				40	80

*Suspense preferences converted into actual items of tax preference.

Imposition of minimum tax on 1970 items of tax preference:

1970 NET OPERATING LOSS
[In thousands of dollars]

	1971 taxable income	Nonpreference portion	Preference portion	Suspense portion
1. 1971 Conversion of suspense preferences pursuant to section 58 (g)	$230	$150		$200
		[1] 30	$130	(160)
Adjusted NOL		180	130	40
2. Nonpreference portion against taxable income	(180)	(180)		
3. Preference portion against taxable income	[2] (50)		(50)	
Balance to 1972			80	40

[1] Represents the 1970 minimum tax exemption.
[2] Imposition of 1970 minimum tax (10%×$50,000=$5,000).

(b) In 1972, the conversion of suspense preferences into actual items of tax preferences under section 58(g) (and this paragraph) and the imposition of the minimum tax on 1970 items of tax preference under section 56(b) (and § 1.56-2) are determined as follows:

Conversion of suspense preferences:

1970 NET OPERATING LOSS

[In thousands of dollars]

	U.S. taxable income	Foreign taxable income	U.S. deductions	Suspense preferences	Other foreign deductions
1. U.S. deduction against U.S. income	$25	$105	Not applicable.	$40	$80
2. Other foreign deductions against foreign income		(80)			(80)
3. Suspense preferences against foreign income		(25)		(25)	
4. Suspense preferences against U.S. income	(15)			(15)	
Balance		10			

[1] Suspense preferences converted into actual items of tax preference.

Imposition of minimum tax on 1970 items of tax preference:

1970 NET OPERATING LOSS

[In thousands of dollars]

	1972 taxable income	Nonpreference portion	Preference portion	Suspense portion
1. 1972 Conversion of suspense preferences pursuant to section 58 (g)	$130		$80	$40
		$25	15	(40)
Adjusted NOL		25	95	
2. Nonpreference portion against taxable income	(25)	(25)		
3. Preference portion against taxable income	([1] 95)		(95)	
Balance		10		

[1] Imposition of 1970 minimum tax (10% × $95,000 = $9,500)

(2) **Per-country limitation.** (i) In general. If a taxpayer is on the per-country foreign tax credit limitation for the taxable year, the amount by which the items of tax preference to which this section applies reduce the tax imposed by chapter 1 (other than the minimum tax under section 56) on income from sources within the United States is determined separately with respect to each foreign country or possession of the United States. Such determination is made in a manner consistent with subparagraph (1) of this paragraph as modified by subdivision (ii) of this subparagraph. In applying subparagraph (1)(i) of this paragraph to a taxpayer on the per-country limitation, if the total potential preference amounts (as defined in this subdivision (i)) exceed the taxpayer's taxable income from sources within the United States, then, for purposes of subparagraph (1)(i)(c) of this paragraph (relating to the U.S. taxable income limitation on the amount treated as a reduction of U.S. taxable income), the taxable income from sources within the United States which is reduced by potential preference amounts with respect to each foreign country or possession is an amount which bears the same relationship to such income as the potential preference amount with respect to such foreign country or possession bears to the total of the potential preference amounts with respect to all foreign countries and possessions. For purposes of this subparagraph, the potential preference amount with respect to a foreign country or possession is the lesser of the amount of foreign source preference (described in subparagraph (1)(i)(a) of this paragraph) attributable to such country or possession or the amount of foreign source loss (described in subparagraph (1)(i)(b) of this paragraph) attributable to such country or possession.

(ii) Net operating loss. Where there is an overall net operating loss for the taxable year and the total of the potential preference amounts with respect to all foreign countries and possessions exceeds the taxpayer's taxable income from sources within the United States, the amount of such excess is treated as "suspense preferences". The suspense preferences are converted into actual items of tax preference, arising in the loss year and subject to the provisions of section 56, as the net operat-

Proposed Reg. §1.58-7

ing loss is used in other taxable years, in the form of a net operating loss deduction under section 172, to offset taxable income from sources within the United States. Suspense preferences attributable to a foreign country or possession which, in other taxable years, reduce taxable income from sources within such country or possession or offset taxable income from sources within any other foreign country or possession lose their character as suspense preferences and, thus, are never converted into actual items of tax preference. The amount of the suspense preferences which are converted into actual items of tax preference is equal to that portion of the net operating loss attributable to the suspense preferences which offsets taxable income from sources within the United States in taxable years other than the loss year. The determination of the component parts of the net operating loss and the determination of the amount by which the portion of the net operating loss attributable to the suspense preferences offset taxable income from sources within the United States is made on a year-by-year basis in the same order as the net operating loss is used in accordance with section 172(b). Such determination is made by applying deductions attributable to United States source income first against such income and applying deductions attributable to income from sources within a foreign country or possession of the United States first against income from sources within such country or possession and in accordance with the following principles:

(a) Deductions attributable to items or classes of gross income from sources within the United States offset taxable income from sources within the United States before any remaining deductions;

(b) Deductions attributable to items or classes of gross income from sources within any foreign country or possession of the United States which are not suspense preferences (referred to in this paragraph as "other foreign deductions") offset taxable income from sources within such country or possession before any remaining deductions;

(c) Suspense preferences attributable to items or classes of gross income from sources within a foreign country or possession offset any remaining taxable income from sources within such foreign country or possession after application of (b) of this subdivision (ii) before any remaining deductions;

(d) Suspense preferences from each foreign country and possession (remaining after application of (c) of this subdivision (ii)) offset taxable income from sources within the United States (remaining after application of (a) of this subdivision (ii)) before other foreign deductions pro rata on the basis of the total of such suspense preferences;

(e) Other foreign deductions from each foreign country and possession (remaining after application of (b) of this subdivision (ii)) offset taxable income from sources within the United States (remaining after application of (a) and (d) of this subdivision (ii)) pro rata on the basis of the total of such other foreign deductions;

(f) Deductions attributable to income from sources within the United States (remaining after application of (a) of this subdivision (ii)) offset taxable income from sources within any foreign country or possession before any foreign deductions;

(g) Other foreign deductions from each foreign country and possession (remaining after application of (b) and (e) of this subdivision (ii)) offset taxable income from sources within any other foreign countries or possessions (remaining after application of (f) of this subdivision (ii)) pro rata on the basis of the total of such other foreign deductions; and

(h) Suspense preferences (remaining after the application of (c) and (d) of this subdivision (ii)) offset taxable income from sources within any foreign country or possession (remaining after the application of (f) and (g) of this subdivision (ii)) pro rata on the basis of the total of such suspense preferences.

For purposes of the above computations, taxable income is computed with the modifications specified in section 172(b)(2) or section 172(c), whichever is applicable. However, the amount of suspense preferences which are converted into actual items of tax preference in accordance with the above principles is reduced to the extent the suspense preferences offset increases in taxable income from sources within the United States due to the modifications specified in section 172(b)(2) or section 172(c). For this purpose, suspense preferences are considered to offset an increase in taxable income due to section 172(b)(2) or section 172(c) modification only after reducing taxable income computed before such modifications.

(iii) *Examples.* The principles of this subparagraph may be illustrated by the following examples in each of which the per-country foreign tax credit limitation is applicable. For purposes of these examples, personal deductions and exemptions are disregarded.

Example (1). The taxpayer has the following items of income and deduction for the taxable year 1971:

	United States	France	Germany	United Kingdom
Gross income	$180,000	$165,000	$50,000	$75,000
Deductions:				
Preferences				(45,000)
Other	(120,000)	(125,000)	(80,000)	(100,000)
Taxable income (or loss)	60,000	40,000	(30,000)	(70,000)

(a) Pursuant to subdivision (i) of this subparagraph, the potential preference amount in the case of the United Kingdom is the lesser of the preferences attributable to the United Kingdom ($45,000) or the excess of deductions over gross income from sources within the United Kingdom ($70,000) and the potential preference amounts in the case of France and Germany are zero in both cases since the preferences attributable to both countries are zero. Since the total potential preference amounts ($45,000) is less than the taxable income from sources within the United States ($60,000), no modification of U.S. taxable income is required. Thus, the amount by which the U.K. preferences reduce the tax on taxable income from sources within the United States, determined in a manner consistent with subparagraph (1)(i) of this paragraph, is the smallest of (1) the items of tax preference attributable to the United Kingdom ($45,000), (2) the excess of deductions over gross income attributable to the United Kingdom ($70,000), or (3) taxable income from sources within the United States ($60,000). The full $45,000 of U.K. preference items are, therefore, taken into account as items of tax preference in 1971 and subject to the minimum tax. Since there is no net operating loss, subdivision (ii) of this subparagraph does not apply.

(b) If the French taxable income is $15,000 instead of $40,000, a $25,000 net operating loss (on a worldwide basis) results. The determination of the foreign preference items taken into account pursuant to subdivision (i) of this subparagraph is the same as in (a) of this example. Subdivision (ii) of this subparagraph again does not apply since the total potential preference amounts ($45,000) is less than the U.S. taxable income ($60,000).

Example (2). For the taxable year 1972, the taxpayer has a net operating loss of $35,000 consisting of the following items of income and deduction:

	United States	France	Germany	United Kingdom	Belgium
Gross income	$250,000	$50,000	$60,000	$5,000	$45,000
Deductions:					
Preferences		(35,000)	(70,000)	(95,000)	
Other	(100,000)	(75,000)	(30,000)		(40,000)
Taxable income (or loss)	150,000	(60,000)	(40,000)	(90,000)	5,000

(a) Pursuant to subdivision (i) of this subparagraph the potential preference amount with respect to each country is the lesser of the amount shown as preferences with respect to such country or the amount of the loss from such country. Thus, the potential preference amounts in this case are:

France	$ 35,000
Germany	40,000
U.K.	90,000
Belgium	0
Total	$165,000

Proposed Reg. § 1.58-7

Proposed Regulations

Since the total of the potential preference amounts exceeds the U.S. taxable income, in applying the principles of subparagraph (1)(i) of this paragraph, U.S. taxable income which is reduced by potential preference amounts with respect to each country is a pro-rata amount based on the total potential preference amounts as follows:

$$\text{France} \quad \left(\frac{35{,}000}{165{,}000} \times \$150{,}000\right) \quad \$31{,}818$$

$$\text{Germany} \quad \left(\frac{40{,}000}{165{,}000} \times \$150{,}000\right) \quad 36{,}364$$

$$\text{U.K.} \quad \left(\frac{90{,}000}{165{,}000} \times \$150{,}000\right) \quad 81{,}818$$

$$\text{Belgium} \quad \left(\frac{0}{165{,}000} \times \$150{,}000\right) \quad 0$$

$$\$150{,}000$$

The amount by which the foreign preference items offset U.S. taxable income pursuant to subdivision (i) of this subparagraph is then determined as follows:

	(a) Preferences	(b) Loss	(c) U.S. taxable income	(d) Smallest of (a), (b), or (c)
France	$35,000	$60,000	$31,818	$31,818
Germany	70,000	40,000	36,364	36,364
United Kingdom	95,000	90,000	81,818	81,818
Belgium				
				150,000

Thus, $150,000 of the total foreign preference items will be taken into account pursuant to subdivision (i) of this subparagraph as items of tax preference in 1972 and subject to the provisions of section 56.

(b) Pursuant to subdivision (ii) of this subparagraph, the 1972 net operating loss of $35,000 will consist of suspense preferences of $15,000 and other foreign deductions of $20,000 attributable to each foreign country as shown below and determined as follows:

			Deductions				
Explanation	United States	France Preferences	France Other	Germany Preferences	Germany Other	United Kingdom preferences	Belgium other
1. U.S. deductions against U.S. income ($250,000)	$100,000 (100,000)	$35,000	$75,000	$70,000	$30,000	$95,000	$40,000
2. Other foreign deductions against foreign income (per-country)[1]			(50,000)		(30,000)		(40,000)
3. Suspense preferences against remaining foreign income (per-country)				(30,000)		(5,000)	
4. Suspense preferences against remaining U.S. income:							
France $\left(\frac{35{,}000}{165{,}000} \times \$150{,}000\right)$		(31,818)					
Germany $\left(\frac{40{,}000}{165{,}000} \times \$150{,}000\right)$				(36,364)			
U.K. $\left(\frac{90{,}000}{165{,}000} \times \$150{,}000\right)$						(81,818)	
5. Other foreign deductions against remaining U.S. income (0)		Not applicable.					
6. U.S. deductions against other foreign income		Not applicable.					
7. Other foreign deductions against remaining foreign income ($5,000)		(5,000)					

Proposed Regulations

	Deductions					
Explanation	United States	France		Germany		United Kingdom preferences	Belgium other
		Preferences	Other	Preferences	Other		
8. Suspense preferences against remaining foreign income (0) Balance (components of NOL)		3,182	20,000	Not applicable. 3,636	....	8,182	....

[1] Foreign income amounts before step 2 are: France—$50,000; Germany—$60,000; United Kingdom—$5,000; Belgium—$45,000.

Example (3). In 1973, the taxpayer has taxable income (computed without regard to the net operating loss deduction) from the following sources and in the following amounts:

U.S.	France	Germany	U.K.
$100,000	$60,000	$20,000	$30,000

In addition, the taxpayer has a net operating loss deduction of $235,000 resulting from a 1972 net operating loss consisting of the following amounts:

Deductions attributable to income from sources within the United States $25,000
Suspense preferences attributable to income from sources within France $75,000
Deductions other than suspense preferences attributable to income from sources within France $85,000
Deductions other than suspense preferences attributable to sources within the Netherlands $50,000

(a) Pursuant to subdivision (ii) of this subparagraph, the converted suspense preferences and the remaining portions of the 1972 net operating loss carried over to 1974 are computed as follows:

[In thousands of dollars]

	1973 income				1972 net operating loss			
	United States	France	Germany	United Kingdom	United States	French suspense preferences	French other deductions	Dutch other deductions
	100	60	20	30	25	75	85	50
U.S. deductions against U.S. income	(25)				(25)			
Other foreign deductions against foreign income (per-country)		(60)					(60)	
Suspense preferences against remaining foreign income (per-country)			Not applicable.					
Suspense preferences against remaining U.S. income	([1]75)					(75)		
Other foreign deductions against remaining U.S. income			Not applicable.					
U.S. deductions against remaining foreign income			Not applicable.					
Other foreign deductions against remaining foreign income:								
French $\left(\frac{25,000}{75,000} \times \$50,000\right)$		(16.7)					(16.7)	
Dutch $\left(\frac{50,000}{75,000} \times \$50,000\right)$		(33.3)						(33.3)
Suspense preferences against remaining foreign income			Not applicable.					
Balance (1972 carryover to 1974)							8.3	16.7

[1] Suspense preferences converted to actual items of tax preference.

(b) If, in 1972, there had been no items of tax preference without regard to the suspense preferences, the conversion of the suspense preferences in 1973 would result in a 1972 minimum tax liability under section 56(a) of $4,500 (10 percent ×

Proposed Reg. § 1.58-7

($75,000 — $30,000)), all of which would have been deferred by reason of section 56(b). Further, by application of section 56(b) and § 1.56-2, $20,000 of the $45,000 preference portion of the 1972 net operating loss would be treated as having reduced taxable income in 1973 resulting in the imposition in 1973 of $2,000 of the deferred 1972 minimum tax liability.

(3) **Separate limitation under section 904(f).** In the case of a taxpayer subject to the separate limitation on interest income under section 904(f), the provisions of this paragraph shall be applied in the same manner as in subparagraph (2) of this paragraph. If the taxpayer has elected the overall foreign tax credit limitation, subparagraph (2) of this paragraph shall be applied as if all income from sources within any foreign countries or possessions of the United States and deductions relating to income from such sources other than income or deductions subject to the separate limitation under section 904(f) were from a single foreign country.

(4) **Carryover of excess taxes.** For rules relating to carryover of excess taxes described in paragraph (1) of section 56(c) when suspense preferences are converted to actual items of tax preference, see § 1.56-5(f).

(5) **Character of amounts.** Where the amounts from sources within a foreign country or possession of the United States (or all such countries or possessions in the case of a taxpayer who has elected the overall foreign tax credit limitation) which are treated as reducing chapter 1 tax on income from sources within the United States or as suspense preferences are less than the total items of tax preference described in subparagraph (1) (i) (a) of this paragraph attributable to such sources, the amounts so treated are considered derived proportionately from each such item of tax preference.

§1.58-8 (Proposed Treasury Decision, published 12-30-70; 6-24-71.) Capital gains and stock options.

(a) **In general.** Section 58(g)(2) provides that the items of tax preference specified in section 57(a)(6), and § 1.57-1(b) (stock options), and section 57(a)(9), and § 1.57-1(i) (capital gains), which are attributable to sources within any foreign country or possession of the United States shall not be taken into account as items of tax preference if, under the tax laws of such country or possession, preferential treatment is not accorded:

(1) In the case of stock options, to the gain, profit, or other income realized from the transfer of shares of stock pursuant to the exercise of an option which is under United States tax law a qualified or restricted stock option (under section 422 or section 424); and

(2) In the case of capital gains, to gain from the sale or exchange of capital assets (or property treated as capital assets under United States tax law).

Where capital gains are not accorded preferential treatment within a foreign country, capital losses as well as capital gains from such country are not taken into account for purposes of the minimum tax.

(b) **Source of capital gains and stock options.** Generally, in determining whether the capital gain or stock option item of tax preference is attributable to sources within any foreign country or possession of the United States, the principles of sections 861-863 and the regulations thereunder are applied. Thus, the stock option item of tax preference, representing compensation for personal services, is attributable, in accordance with § 1.861-4, to sources within the country in which the personal services were performed. Where the capital gain item of tax preference represents gain from the purchase and sale of personal property, such gain is attributable, in accordance with § 1.861-7, entirely to sources within the country in which the property is sold. In accordance with paragraph (c) of § 1.861-7, in any case in which the sales transaction is arranged in a particular manner for the primary purpose of tax avoidance, all factors of the transaction, such as negotiations, the execution of the agreement, the location of the property, and the place of payment, will be considered, and the sale will be treated as having been consummated at the place where the substance of the sale occurred.

(c) **Preferential treatment.** For purposes of this section, gain, profit, or other income is accorded preferential treatment by a foreign country or possession of the United States if (1) recognition of the income, for foreign tax purposes, is deferred beyond the taxpayer's taxable year or comparable period for foreign tax purposes which coincides with the taxpayer's U.S. taxable year in cases where other items of profit, gain, or other income may not be deferred; (2) it is subject to tax at a lower effective rate (including no rate of tax) than other items of profit, gain, or other income, by means of a special rate of tax, artificial deductions, exemptions, exclusions, or similar reductions in the amount subject to tax; (3) it is subject to no significant amount of tax; or (4) the laws of the foreign country or possession by any other method provide tax treatment for such profit, gain, or other income more beneficial than the tax treatment otherwise accorded income by such country or possession. For the purpose of the preceding sentence, gain, profit, or other income is subject to no significant amount of tax if the amount of taxes imposed by the foreign country or possession of the United States is equal to less than 2.5 percent of the gross amount of such income.

(d) **Examples.** The principles of this section may be illustrated by the following examples:

Example (1). The Bahamas imposes no income tax on individuals or corporations, whether resident or nonresident. Since capital gains are subject to no tax in the Bahamas, capital gains are considered to be accorded preferential treatment and will be taken into account for purposes of the minimum tax.

Example (2). In France, except in certain cases involving the sale of large blocks of stock, a nonresident individual is not subject to tax on isolated capital gains transactions. Since such capital gains are not subject to tax in France, they are considered to be accorded preferential treatment irrespective of the treatment accorded other capital gains in France and such gains will be taken into account for purposes of the minimum tax.

Example (3). In Germany, in the case of the sale within one taxable year of 1 percent or more of the shares of a corporation in which an individual taxpayer is regarded as holding a substantial interest, the gains on the sale of the large block of stock will be taxed as extraordinary income at one-half the ordinary income tax rate. Since these gains are taxed at a reduced rate of tax in comparison to other income, they are considered to be accorded preferential treatment and will be taken into account for purposes of the minimum tax.

Example (4). In Belgium, gains derived by an individual in the course of regular speculative transactions are taxed as ordinary income, but with an upper limit of 30 percent. Rates of tax on individuals in Belgium range from approximately 30 percent to approximately 60 percent. Since the gains on speculative transactions are taxed at a maximum rate which is more beneficial than the rates accorded to other income, such gains are considered to be accorded preferential treatment and will be taken into account for purposes of the minimum tax.

Example (5). In France, gains derived by a company on the sale of fixed assets held for less than 2 years are treated as short-term gains. The excess of short-term gains in any fiscal year is taxed at the full company tax rate of 50 percent. However, this tax may be paid in equal portions over the 5 years immediately following the realization of such short-term gains. Since recognition of the short-term gains for tax purposes is subject to deferral over a 5-year period, such gains are considered to be accorded preferential treatment and will be taken into account for purposes of the minimum tax.

Example (6). Also in France, in the case of the sale or exchange by a company of depreciable assets and nondepreciable assets owned for at least 2 years, the excess of long-term capital gains over long-term capital losses in a fiscal year is subject to an immediate tax at the reduced rate of 10 percent. Such excess, reduced by the 10 percent tax, is carried in a special reserve account on the taxpayer's books. If the excess is reinvested in other fixed assets within a stated period, no further tax is due. If the amounts in the special reserve are distributed, they will be treated

Proposed Reg. § 1.58-8

as ordinary income for the fiscal year in which the distribution is made. Since such gains (other than those distributed in the same fiscal year they are realized) are subject to deferral or a reduced rate of tax, they are (except to the extent distributed in the year of realization) considered to be accorded preferential treatment and are taken into account for purposes of the minimum tax.

Example (7). In Sweden, in the case of gains derived by an individual on the sale of shares or bonds held for 5 years or less, 25 percent of the gains are taxed if the holding period is 4 to 5 years, 50 percent of the gain is taxed if the holding period is 3 to 4 years, and 75 percent of the gain is taxed if the holding period is 2 to 3 years. The gain is fully taxable at ordinary income rates if held for less than 2 years. Thus, gains on shares or bonds held for 2 years or more are considered accorded preferential treatment in Sweden since they are either subject to exemption or treatment comparable to the United States capital gains deduction and are taxed at a reduced rate. Thus, such gains are taken into account for purposes of the minimum tax.

Example (8). Pursuant to Article XIV of the United States-United Kingdom Income Tax Convention, a resident of the United States is exempt from United Kingdom tax on most capital gains. Since such capital gains are exempt from United Kingdom taxation, they are considered to be accorded preferential treatment and are taken into account for purposes of the minimum tax.

Example (9). An individual resident of the United States, is desirous of selling his stock in a corporation listed on the New York Stock Exchange. He requests the stock certificates from his broker in the United States, travels to a foreign country, delivers the certificates to a broker in that country, and has the foreign broker execute the sale which takes place on the New York Stock Exchange. Since the sale was consummated in the United States, pursuant to paragraph (b) of this section and § 1.861-7, the resulting capital gain item of tax preference is attributable to sources within the United States.

Example (10). Two individuals, both residing in the United States, negotiate and reach agreement in New York City for the sale of stock of a close corporation. Prior to the transfer of the stock, in order to avoid imposition of the minimum tax, both individuals travel to a foreign country which does not accord preferential treatment to capital gains, but imposes a 5 percent rate of income tax which would be fully creditable against United States tax under sections 901 and 904 if the capital gains were sourced in that country. The stock is actually transferred and consideration paid in the foreign country. Since the primary purpose of consummating the sale in the foreign country was the avoidance of tax, pursuant to paragraph (b) of this section, and § 1.861-7(c), the resulting capital gain item of tax preference will be considered attributable to sources within the country in which the substance of sale took place or, in this case, the United States.

Compensation for Services

Paragraph (d) of §1.61-2 is amended by revising subparagraph (1), by revising subdivision (i) of subparagraph (2), by revising subparagraphs (4) and (5), and by adding new subparagraph (6) to read as follows:

§ 1.61-2 (Proposed Treasury Decision, published 6-3-71.) **Compensation for services, including fees, commissions, and similar items.**

* * * * * * * * * * *

(d) Compensation paid other than in cash—(1) In general. If services are paid for in property on or before June 30, 1969 (or if paragraph (b) of § 1.83-8 applies), the fair market value of the property taken in payment must be included in income as compensation. If services are paid for in exchange for other services, the fair market value of such other services taken in payment must be included in income as compensation. If the services were rendered at a stipulated price, such price will be presumed to be the fair market value of the compensation received in the absence of evidence to the contrary. However, for special rules relating to certain options received as compensation, see § 1.61-15 and section 421 and the regulations thereunder.

(2) **Property transferred to employee or independent contractor**—(i) Except as otherwise provided in section 421 and the regulations thereunder (relating to employee stock options) and § 1.61-15, if property is transferred on or before June 30, 1969 (or if paragraph (b) of § 1.83-8 applies), by an employer to an employee or to an independent contractor, as compensation for services for an amount less than its fair market value, then regardless of whether the transfer is in the form of a sale or exchange, the difference between the amount paid for the property and the amount of its fair market value at the time of the transfer is compensation and shall be included in the gross income of the employee or independent contractor. In computing the gain or loss from the subsequent sale of such property, its basis shall be the amount paid for the property increased by the amount of such difference included in gross income.

* * * * * * * * * * *

(4) **Stock and notes transferred to employee or independent contractor.** Except as otherwise provided by section 421 and the regulations thereunder (relating to employee stock options) and § 1.61-15, if a corporation transfers its own stock on or before June 30, 1969 (or if paragraph (b) of § 1.83-8 applies), to an employee or independent contractor as compensation for services, the fair market value of the stock at the time of transfer shall be included in the gross income of the employee or independent contractor. Notes or other evidences of indebtedness received in payment for services on or before June 30, 1969, constitute income in the amount of their fair market value at the time of the transfer. A taxpayer receiving as compensation a note regarded as good for its face value at maturity, but not bearing interest, shall treat as income as of the time of receipt its fair discounted value computed at the prevailing rate. As payments are received on such a note, there shall be included in income that portion of each payment which represents the proportionate part of the discount originally taken on the entire note.

(5) **Property transferred on or before June 30, 1969, subject to restrictions.** Notwithstanding any other provision of this paragraph, if any property is transferred as compensation for services, performed by an employee or independent contractor, and such property is subject to a restriction which has a significant effect on its value at the time of transfer, the rules of § 1.421-6(d)(2) shall apply in determining the time and the amount of compensation to be included in the gross income of the employee or independent contractor. For special rules relating to options to purchase stock or other property which are issued as compensation for services, see § 1.61-15 and section 421 and the regulations thereunder. This subparagraph is applicable only to transfers after September 24, 1959, and before July 1, 1969 (unless paragraph (b) of § 1.83-8 applies).

(6) **Property transferred to employee or independent contractor after June 30, 1969.** For rules with respect to property transferred in connection with the performance of services after June 30, 1969, see section 83 and the regulations thereunder. For rules with respect to premiums paid by an employer for an annuity contract which is not subject to section 403(a), see section 403(c) and the regulations thereunder. For the rules with respect to contributions made to an employee's trust which is not exempt under section 501(a), see section 402(b) and the regulations thereunder.

§ 1.61-2 (Proposed Treasury Decision, published 1-5-77.) **Options received as payment of income.**

Paragraph (d)(2)(ii)(*a*) of § 1.61-2 is amended by deleting "group-term life insurance on the employee's life as defined in paragraph (b)(1) of § 1.79-1" and inserting in its place "certain group-term insurance on the employee's life".

Paragraphs (a) and (d) of §1.61-15 are amended to read as follows:

Proposed Reg. § 1.61-2

§ **1.61-15** (Proposed Treasury Decision, published 6-3-71.) **Options received as payment of income.**

(a) **In general.** If any person receives an option in payment of an amount constituting compensation of such person (or of any other person) on or before June 30, 1969 (except if paragraph (b) of § 1.83-8 applies,) such option is subject to the rules contained in § 1.421-6 for purposes of determining when income is realized in connection with such option and the amount of such income. In this regard, the rules of § 1.421-6 apply to an option received in payment of an amount constituting compensation regardless of the form of the transaction. Thus, the rules of § 1.421-6 apply to an option transferred for less than its fair market value in a transaction taking the form of a sale or exchange if the difference between the amount paid for the option and its fair market value at the time of transfer is the payment of an amount constituting compensation of the transferee or any other person. This section, for example, makes the rules of § 1.421-6 applicable to options granted in whole or partial payment for services of an independent contractor. If an amount of money or property is paid for an option to which this paragraph applies, then the amount paid shall be part of the basis of such option. For the rules with respect to an option granted in connection with the performance of services after June 30, 1969, see section 83 and the regulations thereunder.

* * * * * * * * * * *

(d) **Effective date.** This section shall apply to options granted after July 11, 1963, and before July 1, 1969 (unless paragraph (d) of §1.183-8 applies), other than options required to be granted pursuant to the terms of a written contract entered into before July 11, 1963.

26 CFR Part 1 is amended by adding a new §1.61-16 immediately after §1.61-15. The new section reads as follows:

§ **1.61-16** (Proposed Treasury Decision, published 2-3-78). **Amounts payments of which are deferred under certain compensation reduction plans or arrangements.**

(a) **In general.** Except as otherwise provided in paragraph (b) of this section, if under a plan or arrangement (other than a plan or arrangement described in section 401(a), 403(a) or (b), or 405(a)) payment of an amount of a taxpayer's basic or regular compensation fixed by contract, statute, or otherwise (or supplements to such compensation, such as bonuses, or increases in such compensation) is, at the taxpayer's individual option, deferred to a taxable year later than that in which such amount would have been payable but for his exercise of such option, the amount shall be treated as received by the taxpayer in such earlier taxable year. For purposes of this paragraph, it is immaterial that the taxpayer's rights in the amount payment of which is so deferred become forfeitable by reason of his exercise of the option to defer payment.

(b) **Exception.** Paragraph (a) of this section shall not apply to an amount payment of which is deferred as described in paragraph (a) under a plan or arrangement in existence on February 3, 1978 if such amount would have been payable, but for the taxpayer's exercise of the option, at any time prior to [date 30 days following publication of this section as a Treasury decision]. For purposes of this paragraph, a plan or arrangement in existence on February 3, 1978 which is significantly amended after such date will be treated as a new plan as of the date of such amendment. Examples of significant amendments would be extension of coverage to an additional class of taxpayers or an increase in the maximum percentage of compensation subject to the taxpayer's option.

Items Specifically Included in Gross Income

Subdivision (i) of §1.72-4(a)(1) is amended by deleting "72(o)" and inserting in lieu thereof "72(n)" As amended, §1.72-4(a)(1)(i) reads as follows:

§ **1.72-4** (Proposed Treasury Decision, published 4-30-75.) **Exclusion ratio.**

(a) **General rule.** (1) (i) To determine the proportionate part of the total amount received each year as an annuity which is excludable from the gross income of a recipient in the taxable year of receipt (other than amounts received under (A) certain employee annuities described in section 72(d) and § 1.72-13, or (B) certain annuities described in section 72(n) and § 1.122-1), an exclusion ratio is to be determined for each contract. In general, this ratio is determined by dividing the investment in the contract as found under § 1.72-6 by the expected return under such contract as found under § 1.72-5. Where a single consideration is given for a particular contract which provides for two or more annuity elements, an exclusion ratio shall be determined for the contract as a whole by dividing the investment in such contract by the aggregate of the expected returns under all the annuity elements provided thereunder. However, where the provisions of paragraph (b)(3) of § 1.72-2 apply to payments received under such a contract, see paragraph (b)(3) of § 1.72-6.

Section 1.72-8(a)(1) is amended by adding a new sentence at the end thereof. As amended, this provision reads as follows:

§ **1.72-8** (Proposed Treasury Decision, published 5-6-72.) **Effect of certain employer contributions with respect to premiums or other consideration paid or contributed by an employee.**

(a) **Contributions in the nature of compensation**—(1) **Amounts includible in gross income of employee under subtitle A of the Code or prior income tax laws.** Section 72(f) provides that for purposes of section 72(c), (d), and (e), amounts contributed by an employer for the benefit of an employee or his beneficiaries shall constitute consideration paid or contributed by the employee to the extent that such amounts were includible in the gross income of the employee under subtitle A of the Code or prior income tax laws. Amounts to which this paragraph applies include, for example, contributions made by an employer to or under a trust or plan which fails to qualify under the provisions of section 401(a), provided that the employee's rights to such contributions are nonforfeitable at the time the contributions are made. See sections 402(b) and 403(c) and the regulations thereunder. This subparagraph also applies to premiums paid by an employer (other than premiums paid on behalf of an owner-employee) for life insurance protection for an employee if such premiums are includible in the gross income of the employee when paid. See § 1.72-16. However, such premiums shall only be considered as premiums and other consideration paid by the employee with respect to any benefits attributable to the contract providing the life insurance protection. See § 1.72-16. This subparagraph also applies to amounts included in the gross income of a shareholder-employee under section 1379(b) for excess contributions paid on his behalf by an electing small business corporation (see § 1.1379-2).

* * * * * * * * * * * * *

Subparagraph (3) of §1.72-13(e) is amended by deleting "72(o)" and inserting in lieu thereof "72(n)". As amended §1.72-13(e)(3) reads as follows:

§ **1.72-13** (Proposed Treasury Decision, published 4-30-75.) **Special rule for employee contributions recoverable in three years.**

* * * * * * * * * * * * *

(e) **Inapplicability of section 72(d) and this section.** Section 72(d) and this section do not apply to: * * *

(3) Amounts paid to an annuitant under chapter 73 of title 10 of the United States Code with respect to which section 72(n) and § 1.122-1 apply.

[The page following this is 63,095]

Proposed Reg. § 1.72-13

* * * * * * * * * * * * *

Section 1.72-17 is amended by adding the following new paragraph at the end thereof:

§ 1.72-17 (Proposed Treasury Decision, published 4-21-75) **Special rules applicable to owner-employees.**

* * * * * * * * * * *

(g) **Years to which this section applies.** This section applies to taxable years ending before September 3, 1974. For taxable years ending after September 2, 1974, see § 1.72-17A.

The following new section is added immediately after §1.72-17:

§ 1.72-17A (Proposed Treasury Decision, published 4-21-75) **Special rules applicable to employee annuities and distributions under deferred compensation plans to self-employed individuals and owner-employees.**

(a) **In general.** Section 72(m) and this section contain special rules for the taxation of amounts received from qualified pension, profit-sharing, or annuity plans covering an owner-employee. This section applies to such amounts for taxable years of the recipient ending after September 2, 1974, unless another date is specified. For purposes of this section, the term "employee" shall include the self-employed individual who is treated as an employee by section 401(c)(1) (see paragraph (b) of § 1.401(e)-1), and the term "owner-employee" has the meaning assigned to it in section 401(c)(3) (see paragraph (d) of § 1.401(e)-1). See also paragraph (a)(2) of § 1.401(e)-1 for the rule for determining when a plan covers an owner-employee. Paragraph (b) of this section provides rules dealing with the computation of consideration paid by self-employed individuals and paragraph (c) of this section provides rules dealing with such computation when insurance is purchased for owner-employees. Paragraph (d) of this section provides rules for constructive receipt and, for purposes of these rules, treats as an owner-employee an individual for whose benefit an individual retirement account or annuity described in section 408(a) or (b) is maintained after December 31, 1974. Paragraph (e) of this section provides rules for penalties provided by section 72(m)(5) with respect to certain distributions received by owner-employees or their successors. Paragraph (f) of this section provides rules for determining whether a person is disabled within the meaning of section 72(m)(7). See § 1.72-16, relating to life insurance contracts purchased under qualified employee plans, for rules under section 72(m)(3).

(b) **Computation of consideration paid by self-employed individuals.** Under section 72(m)(2), consideration paid or contributed for the contract by any self-employed individual shall for purposes of section 72 be deemed not to include any contributions paid or contributed under a plan described in paragraph (a), or any other plan of deferred compensation described in section 404(a) (whether or not qualified), if the contributions are—

(1) Paid under such plan with respect to a time during which the employee was an employee only by reason of sections 401(c)(1) and 404(a)(8), and

(2) Deductible under section 404 by the employer, including an employer within the meaning of sections 401(c)(4) and 404(a)(8), of such self-employed individual at the time of such payment, or subsequent to such time of payment.

For purposes of this paragraph the term "consideration paid or contributed for the contract" has the same meaning as under subparagraphs (1), (2), and (3) of paragraph (c) of this section.

(c) **Amounts paid for life, accident, health, or other insurance.** Under section 72(m)(2), amounts used to purchase life, accident, health, or other insurance protection for an owner-employee shall not be taken into account in computing the following:

Proposed Reg. § 1.72-17A

(1) The aggregate amount of premiums or other consideration paid for the contract for purposes of determining the investment in the contract under section 72(c)(1)(A) and § 1.72-6;

(2) The consideration for the contract contributed by the employee for purposes of section 72(d)(1) and § 1.72-13, which provide the method of taxing employees' annuities where the employee's contributions will be recoverable within 3 years; and

(3) The aggregate premiums or other consideration paid for purposes of section 72(e)(1)(B) and § 1.72-11, which provide the rules for taxing amounts not received as annuities prior to the annuity starting date.

The cost of such insurance protection will be considered to be a reasonable net premium cost, as determined by the Commissioner, for the appropriate period.

(d) **Amounts constructively received.** (1) Under section 72(m)(4)(A), if during any taxable year an owner-employee assigns or pledges (or agrees to assign or pledge) any portion of his interest in a trust described in section 401(a) which is exempt from tax under section 501(a), or any portion of the value of a contract purchased as part of a plan described in section 403(a), such portion shall be treated as having been received by such owner-employee as a distribution from the trust or as an amount received under the contract during such taxable year.

(2) (i) Under paragraphs (4)(A) and (6) of section 72(m), if after December 31, 1974, during any taxable year an individual for whose benefit an individual retirement account or annuity described in section 408(a) or (b) is maintained assigns or pledges (or agrees to assign or pledge) any portion of his interest in such account or annuity, such portion shall be treated as having been received by such individual as a distribution from such account or trust during such taxable year. See subsections (d) and (f) of section 408 and the regulations thereunder for the tax treatment of an amount treated as a distribution under this subparagraph.

(ii) Notwithstanding subdivision (i) of this subparagraph, if an individual retirement account or annuity, or portion thereof, is subject to the additional tax imposed by section 408(f), that amount shall be deemed not to be a distribution under section 72(m)(4)(A) and subdivision (i) of this subparagraph.

(3) Under section 72(m)(4)(B), if during any taxable year an owner-employee receives, either directly or indirectly, any amount from any insurance company as a loan under a contract purchased by a trust described in section 401(a) which is exempt from tax under section 501(a) or purchased as part of a plan described in section 403(a), and issued by such insurance company, such amount shall be treated as an amount received under the contract during such taxable year. An owner-employee will be considered to have received an amount under a contract if a premium, which is otherwise in default, is paid by the insurance company in the form of a loan against the cash surrender value of the contract. Further, an owner-employee will be considered to have received an amount to which this subparagraph applies if an amount is received from the issuer of a face-amount certificate as a loan under such a certificate purchased as part of a qualified trust or plan.

(e) **Penalties applicable to certain amounts received with respect to owner-employees under section 72(m)(5).** (1) (i) For taxable years of the recipient beginning after December 31, 1975, if any person receives an amount to which subparagraph (2) of this paragraph applies, his tax under chapter 1 for the taxable year in which such amount is received shall be increased by an amount equal to 10 percent of the portion of the amount so received which is includible in his gross income for such taxable year.

(ii) For taxable years of the recipient beginning before January 1, 1976, see subparagraph (3) of this paragraph.

(2) (i) This subparagraph is applicable to amounts, to the extent includible in gross income, received from a qualified trust described in section 401(a) or under a plan described in section 403(a) by or on behalf of an individual who is or has been an owner-employee with respect to such trust or plan—

(A) Which are received before the owner-employee reaches the age of 59½ years, and which are attributable to contributions paid on behalf of such owner-employee by his employer (that is, employer contributions within the meaning of section 401(c)(5)(A) and the increments in value attributable to such employer contributions) and the increments in value attributable to contributions made by him as an owner-employee while he was an owner-employee (that is, the increments attributable to owner-employee contributions within the meaning of section 401(c)(5)(B), but not such contributions; see subdivision (ii) of this subparagraph),

(B) Which are in excess of the benefits provided for such owner-employee under the plan formula (see subdivision (iii) of this subparagraph), or

(C) Which are subject to the transitional rules with respect to willful excess contributions made on behalf of an owner-employee in his employer's taxable years which begin before January 1, 1976 (see subdivision (v) of this subparagraph).

(ii) The amounts referred to in subdivision (i)(A) of this subparagraph do not include—

(A) Amounts received by reason of the owner-employee becoming disabled (see paragraph (f) of this section),

(B) Amounts received by the owner-employee in his capacity as a policyholder of an annuity, endowment, or life insurance contract which are in the nature of a dividend or similar distribution, or

(C) Amounts attributable to contributions (and increments in value thereon) made for years for which the recipient was not an owner-employee.

If an amount is not included in the amounts referred to in subdivision (i)(A) of this subparagraph solely by reason of the owner-employee's becoming disabled and if a penalty would otherwise be applicable with respect to all or a portion of such amount, then for the owner-employee's taxable year in which such amount is received, there must be submitted with his income tax return a doctor's statement as to the impairment, and a statement by the owner-employee with respect to the effect of such impairment upon his substantial gainful activity and the date such impairment occurred. For taxable years which are subsequent to the first taxable year with respect to which the statements referred to in the preceding sentence are submitted, the owner-employee may, in lieu of such statements, submit a statement declaring the continued existence (without substantial diminution) of the impairment and its continued effect upon his substantial gainful activity.

(iii) This subparagraph applies to amounts described in subdivision (i)(B) of this subparagraph (relating to benefits in excess of the plan formula) even though a portion of such amounts may be attributable to contributions made on behalf of an individual while he was not an owner-employee and even if he is deceased and the amounts are received by his successor.

(iv)(A) The rules described in subdivisions (i)(A) and (iii) of this subparagraph, relating to the treatment under section 72(m)(5)(A)(i) of certain premature distributions, may be illustrated by the following example:

Example. (1) A was a member of the X partnership, consisting of partners A through I, and a participant in the partnership's qualified profit-sharing plan which was established on January 1, 1972. A's taxable years, the X partnership's taxable years, the plan years, and other relevant years are all calendar years at all relevant times. For the three calendar years, 1972 through 1974, A was an owner-employee in the X partnership. On January 1, 1975, new partners J and K became partners in the X partnership, and as of that date, each of partners A through K held a 1/11 interest in the capital and profits of the X partnership. On that date, A became a partner who was not an owner-employee. A continued in this status for the 2 calendar years 1975 and 1976. On January 1, 1977, when A was 50 years old and not disabled, he liquidated his interest in the X partnership and became an employee of an unrelated employer. On that date, A received a distribution representing his entire interest in the X partnership's plan of

Proposed Reg. §1.72-17A

$54,000 cash in violation of the plan provision required by section 401(d)(4)(B). As of that date, the distribution was attributable to the following sources and times, computed by the plan in a manner consistent with this subparagraph:

Column Calendar years	A X contributions on behalf of A deductible under section 404	B A's contributions made as an employee	C Increments in value attributable to column A yearly contributions	D Increments in value attributable to column B yearly contributions
1977	$ - 0 -	$ - 0 -	$ - 0 -	$ - 0 -
1976	7,500	2,500	900	300
1975	7,500	2,500	4,000	1,300
1974	7,500	2,500	1,800	700
1973	2,500	2,500	1,200	1,200
1972	2,500	2,500	1,300	1,300
Totals	$27,500	$12,500	$9,200	$4,800

(2) The amount of the $54,000 distribution to which subdivision (i)(A) of this subparagraph applies is $20,000, computed as follows:

X contributions on behalf of A made in years A was an owner-employee:

1974	$7,500	
1973	2,500	
1972	2,500	$12,500

Increments in value attributable to such contributions:

1974	$1,800	
1973	1,200	
1972	1,300	4,300

Increments in value attributable to contributions made by A as an employee for years in which he was an owner-employee:

1974	700	
1973	1,200	
1972	1,300	3,200
		$20,000

In this example, the $20,000 amount computed above would be includible in A's gross income for 1977 and would be subject to the 10 percent tax described in subparagraph (1)(i) of this paragraph.

(3) Subdivision (i)(A) of this subparagraph does not apply to the contributions made by X on behalf of A for 1976 and 1975 ($7,500 each year, totaling $15,000) nor to the increments in value attributable to those contributions ($900 for 1976 and $4,000 for 1975, totaling $4,900), because A was not an owner-employee with respect to these two years, 1976 and 1975, on account of which these employer contributions were made. For the same reason, subdivision (i)(A) of this subparagraph does not apply to the increments in value attributable to A's contributions for 1976 and 1975 ($300 and $1,300, respectively, totaling $1,600).

See section 4972(c) for the amount of employee contributions which is permitted to be contributed by an owner-employee (as an employee) without subjecting an owner-employee to the tax on excess contributions.

(4) Subdivision (i)(A) of this subparagraph does not apply to the contributions

made by A, as an employee during the years when he was an owner-employee ($2,500 during each of the years 1972, 1973, and 1974, totaling $7,500), because the distribution was received in a taxable year of A ending after September 2, 1974; see subparagraph (3) of this paragraph. Furthermore, because the distribution of the amount of A's contributions ($12,500) constitutes consideration for the contract paid by A for purposes of section 72, the $7,500 amount described in the preceding sentence is not includible in his gross income, and that amount is not subject to the rules of this subparagraph; see subdivision (i) of this subparagraph, and paragraphs (b) and (c) of this section.

(B) The increments in value of an individual's account may be allocated to contributions on his behalf, by his employer or by such individual as an owner-employee, while he was an owner-employee either by maintaining a separate account, or an accounting, which reflects the actual increment attributable to such contributions, or by the method described in (C) of this subdivision.

(C) Where an individual is covered under the same plan both as an owner-employee and as a non-owner-employee, the portion of the increment in value of his interest attributable to contributions made on his behalf while he was an owner-employee may be determined by multiplying the total increment in value in his account by a fraction. The numerator of the fraction is the total contributions made on behalf of the individual as an owner-employee, weighted for the number of years that each contribution was in the plan. The denominator is the total contributions made on behalf of the individual, whether or not as an owner-employee, weighted for the number of years each contribution was in the plan. The contributions are weighted for the number of years in the plan by multiplying each contribution by the number of years it was in the plan. For purposes of this computation, any forfeiture allocated to the account of the individual is treated as a contribution to the account made at the time so allocated. For purposes of this computation, where the individual has received a prior distribution from such account, an appropriate adjustment must be made to reflect prior distribution.

(D) The method described in (C) of this subdivision may be illustrated by the following example:

Example. B was a member of the XYZ Partnership and a participant in the partnership's profit-sharing plan which was created in 1973. Until the end of 1977, B's interest in the partnership was less than 10 percent. On January 1, 1978, B obtained an interest in excess of 10 percent in the partnership and continued to participate in the profit-sharing plan until 1982. During 1982, prior to the time he attained the age of 59½ years and during a time when he was not disabled, B, who had not received any prior plan distributions, withdrew his entire interest in the profit-sharing plan. At the time his interest was $15,000, $9,600 contributions and $5,400 increment attributable to the contributions. The portion of the increment attributable to contributions while B was an owner-employee is $667.80, determined as follows:

	A Contribution	B Number of years contribution was in trust	C Contribution weighted for years in trust (AxB)
1982	$1,000	0	0
1981	800	1	800
1980	1,200	2	2,400
1979	600	3	1,800
1978	200	4	800
1977	400	5	2,000
1976	2,000	6	12,000
1975	1,000	7	7,000
1974	1,500	8	12,000
1973	900	9	8,100
	$9,600		46,900

Proposed Reg. §1.72-17A

Total weighted contributions as owner-employee (1978-1982)—$5,800.
Total weighted contributions—46,900.

$$\$5,400 \times \frac{5,800}{46,900} = \$667.80$$

(E) (1) The rules set forth in subdivision (iv)(E)(2) of this subparagraph shall be used to determine the amounts to which subdivision (i)(A) of this subparagraph applies in the case of a distribution of less than the entire balance of the employee's account from a plan in which he has been covered at different times as an owner-employee or as an employee other than an owner-employee.

(2) Distributions or payments from a plan for any employee taxable year shall be deemed to be attributable to contributions to the plan, and increments thereon, in the following order—

(i) Employee contributions;

(ii) Excess contributions, within the meaning of section 4972(b);

(iii) Employer contributions, other than those described in (ii), and the increments in value attributable to the employee's own contributions and his employer's contributions on the basis of the taxable years of his employer in succeeding order of time whether or not the employee was an owner-employee for any such year.

For purposes of (iii) of this subdivision, the time of contributions made on the basis of any employer taxable year shall take into account the rule specified in section 404(a)(6), relating to time when contributions deemed made.

(v) The amounts referred to in subdivision (i)(C) of this subparagraph are amounts which are received by reason of a distribution of the owner-employee's entire interest under the provisions of section 401(e)(2)(E), as in effect on September 1, 1974, relating to excess contributions on behalf of an owner-employee which are willfully made. Notwithstanding the preceding sentence, an owner-employee's entire interest in all plans with respect to which he is an owner-employee (within the meaning of subsections (d)(8)(C) and (e)(2)(E)(ii) of section 401, as in effect on September 1, 1974) does not include any distribution or payment attributable to his employer's contributions or his own contributions made with respect to his employer's taxable years beginning after December 31, 1975. However, his entire interest in all plans does include all of the distribution or payment attributable to his employer's contributions and his own contributions made with respect to all of his employer's taxable years beginning before January 1, 1976, if any portion thereof is attributable in whole or in part to such a willful excess contribution and such entire interest is received because of a willful excess contribution pursuant to section 401(e)(2)(E)(ii). A distribution or payment is described in the preceding sentence even though it is received in an owner-employee's taxable year beginning after December 31, 1975. For purposes of computing the increments in value attributable to employer taxable years which begin before January 1, 1976, and such increments attributable to such years beginning after December 31, 1975, the rules specified in subdivision (iv)(B), (C), (D), and (E) of this subparagraph shall be applied to the extent applicable. See § 1.401(e)-4(c) for transitional rules with respect to contributions described in this subdivision.

(3) (i) For taxable years of the recipient beginning before January 1, 1976, the tax with respect to amounts to which subparagraph (2) of this paragraph applies shall be computed under subparagraphs (B), (C), (D), and (E) of section 72(m)(5) as such subparagraphs were in effect prior to the amendments made by subsections (g)(1) and (2)(A) of section 2001 of the Employee Retirement Income Security Act of 1974 (88 Stat. 957) except as provided in subdivisions (ii) and (iii) of this subparagraph (see paragraph (e) of § 1.72-17). For purposes of the preceding sentence, amounts to which subparagraph (2) of this paragraph applies in the case of an amount described in section 72(m)(5)(A)(i) shall be determined under subdivisions (i)(a) and (ii) of § 1.72-17(e)(1), except as provided in subdivision (ii) of this subparagraph. For purposes of the first sentence of this subdivision, amounts to which subparagraph (2) of this paragraph applies in the case of an amount described in section 72(m)(5)(A)(ii) shall be determined under subdivisions (i)(b) and (iii) of § 1.72-17(e)(1), except as provided in subdivision

(iii) of this subparagraph.

(ii) For purposes of applying section 72(m)(5)(A)(i), after the amendment made by section 2001(h)(3) of such Act and subdivisions (i)(a) and (ii) of § 1.72-17(e)(1), to a distribution or payment received in recipient taxable years ending after September 2, 1974, and beginning before January 1, 1976, with respect to contributions made on behalf of an owner-employee which were made by him as an owner-employee (that is, employee contributions within the meaning of section 401(c)(5)(B)) the portion of any distribution or payment attributable to such contributions shall not include such contributions but shall include the increments in value attributable to such contributions.

(iii) For purposes of applying section 72(m)(5)(D) and subdivisions (2)(b) and (iii) of § 1.72-17(e)(1) to recipient taxable years beginning after December 31, 1973, and beginning before January 1, 1976, in the case of distributions or payments made after December 31, 1973, the amounts to which section 402(a)(2) or 403(a)(2) applies after the amendments made by section 2005(b)(1) and (2) of such Act (88 Stat. 990 and 991) (which are amounts to which subdivision (i)(b) of § 1.72-17(e)(1) does not apply) shall be deemed to be the amount which is treated as a gain from the sale or exchange of a capital asset held for more than 6 months under either of such sections.

(f) Meaning of disabled. (1) Section 72(m)(7) provides that an individual shall be considered to be disabled if he is unable to engage in any substantial gainful activity by reason of any medically determinable physical or mental impairment which can be expected to result in death or to be of long-continued and indefinite duration. In determining whether an individual's impairment makes him unable to engage in any substantial gainful activity, primary consideration shall be given to the nature and severity of his impairment. Consideration shall also be given to other factors such as the individual's education, training, and work experience. The substantial gainful activity to which section 72(m)(7) refers is the activity, or a comparable activity, in which the individual customarily engaged prior to the arising of the disability (or prior to retirement if the individual was retired at the time the disability arose).

(2) Whether or not the impairment in a particular case constitutes a disability is to be determined with reference to all the facts in the case. The following are examples of impairments which would ordinarily be considered as preventing substantial gainful activity:

(i) Loss of use of two limbs;

(ii) Certain progressive diseases which have resulted in the physical loss or atrophy of a limb, such as diabetes, multiple sclerosis, or Buerger's disease;

(iii) Diseases of the heart, lungs, or blood vessels which have resulted in major loss of heart or lung reserve as evidenced by X-ray, electrocardiagram, or other objective findings, so that despite medical treatment breathlessness, pain, or fatigue is produced on slight exertion, such as walking several blocks, using public transportation, or doing small chores;

(iv) Cancer which is inoperable and progressive;

(v) Damage to the brain or brain abnormality which has resulted in severe loss of judgment, intellect, orientation, or memory;

(vi) Mental diseases (e.g., psychosis or severe psychoneurosis) requiring continued institutionalization or constant supervision of the individual;

(vii) Loss or diminution of vision to the extent that the affected individual has a central visual acuity of no better than 20/200 in the better eye after best correction, or has a limitation in the fields of vision such that the widest diameter of the visual fields subtends an angle no greater than 20 degrees;

(viii) Permanent and total loss of speech;

(ix) Total deafness uncorrectible by a hearing aid.

The existence of one or more of the impairments described in this subparagraph (or of an impairment of greater severity) will not, however, in and of itself always permit a finding that an individual is disabled as defined in section 72

Proposed Reg. § 1.72-17A

(m)(7). Any impairment, whether of lesser or greater severity, must be evaluated in terms of whether it does in fact prevent the individual from engaging in his customary or any comparable substantial gainful activity.

(3) In order to meet the requirements of section 72(m)(7), an impairment must be expected either to continue for a long and indefinite period or to result in death. Ordinarily, a terminal illness because of disease or injury would result in disability. The term "indefinite" is used in the sense that it cannot reasonably be anticipated that the impairment will, in the foreseeable future, be so diminished as no longer to prevent substantial gainful activity. For example, an individual who suffers a bone fracture which prevents him from working for an extended period of time will not be considered disabled, if his recovery can be expected in the foreseeable future; if the fracture persistently fails to knit, the individual would ordinarily be considered disabled.

(4) An impairment which is remediable does not constitute a disability within the meaning of section 72(m)(7). An individual will not be deemed disabled if, with reasonable effort and safety to himself, the impairment can be diminished to the extent that the individual will not be prevented by the impairment from engaging in his customary or any comparable substantial gainful activity.

Sec. 1.79 is deleted.

A new § 1.79-0 is added and § 1.79-1 is amended. The added and amended provisions read as follows:

§ **1.79-0** (Proposed Treasury Decision, published 1-5-78). **Group-term life insurance—definitions of certain terms.**

The following definitions apply for purposes of section 79, this section, and § § 1.79-1, 1.79-2, and 1.79-3.

Carried directly or indirectly. A policy of life insurance is "carried directly or indirectly" by an employer if—

(a) The employer pays any part of the cost of the life insurance directly or through another person; or

(b) The employer or two or more employers arrange for payment of the cost of the life insurance by their employees and charge at least one employee less than the cost of his or her insurance, as determined under Table I of §1.79-3(d)(2), and at least one other employee more than the cost of his or her insurance, determined in the same way.

Employee. An "employee" is—

(a) A person who performs services if his or her relationship to the person for whom services are performed is the legal relationship of employer and employee described in §31.3401(c)-1; or

(b) A full-time life insurance salesperson described in section 7701(a)(20); or

(c) A person who formerly performed services as an employee.

A person who formerly performed services as an employee and currently performs services for the same employer as an independent contractor is considered an employee only with respect to insurance provided because of the person's former services as an employee.

Group of employees. A "group of employees" is all employees of an employer, or less than all employees if membership in the group is determined solely on the basis of age, marital status, or factors related to employment. Examples of factors related to employment are membership in a union some or all of whose members are employed by the employer, duties performed, compensation received, and length of service. Ownership of stock in the employer corporation is not a factor related to employment. However, a "group of employees" may include an employee who owns stock in the employer corporation.

Permanent benefit. A "permanent benefit" is an economic value extending beyond one policy year (for example, a paid-up or cash surrender value) that is provided under a life insurance policy. However, a permanent benefit does not include—

(a) A right to convert (or continue) life insurance after group life insurance coverage terminates; or

(b) A feature under which term life insurance is provided at a level premium for a period of five years or less.

Policy. The term "policy" includes two or more obligations of an insurer (or its affiliates) if the obligations are interrelated or are sold in conjunction. For example, a group of individual contracts under which life insurance is provided to a group of employees may be a policy. Similarly, two benefits provided to a group of employees, one term life insurance and the other a permanent benefit or life insurance that provides a permanent benefit, may be a policy. The two benefits may be a policy even if they are not provided under a single document and even if one of the benefits is provided only to employees who decline the other benefit.

§1.79-1 (Proposed Treasury Decision, published 1-5-78.) **Group-term life insurance—general rules.**

(a) **What is group-term life insurance?** Life insurance is not group-term life insurance for purposes of section 79 unless it meets the following conditions:

(1) It provides a general death benefit that is excludable from gross income under section 101(a).

(2) It is provided to a group of employees.

(3) It is provided under a policy carried directly or indirectly by the employer.

(4) The amount of insurance provided to each employee is computed under a formula that precludes individual selection. This formula must be based on factors such as age, years of service, compensation, or position. This condition may be satisfied even if the amount of insurance provided is determined under a limited number of alternative schedules that are based on the amount each employee elects to contribute. However, the amount of insurance provided under each schedule must be computed under a formula that precludes individual selection.

(b) **May group-term life insurance be combined with other benefits?** (1) No part of the life insurance provided under a policy that provides a permanent benefit is group-term life insurance unless—

(i) The policy specifies the part of the death benefit provided to each employee that is group-term life insurance;

(ii) The part of the death benefit that is provided to an employee and designated as the group-term life insurance benefit for any policy year is not less than the difference between the total death benefit provided under the policy and the paid-up death benefit that would be provided if the policy were not renewed at the end of the policy year;

(iii) Employees may elect to decline or drop the permanent benefit; and

(iv) The amount of group-term life insurance provided to an employee is identical whether the employee accepts, declines, or later drops the permanent benefit. Thus, if the amount of group-term life insurance provided to employees who elect a permanent benefit decreases, then the amount of group-term life insurance provided to employees who do not elect the permanent benefit decreases in the same manner.

(2) The condition of paragraph (b)(1)(iv) of this section is illustrated by the following examples:

Example 1. A policy permits each employee the option of having his or her employer purchase (a) $10,000 of group-term life insurance each year, or (b) declining amounts of term insurance which, when added to units of paid-up insurance purchased by the employee, amount to $10,000 each year of total insurance coverage. The amount excludible from income under either option is the cost of term insurance that would have been purchased for the employee had he or she elected option (b) if all the other requirements of section 79 are met. The additional term insurance under option (a) is not group-term life insurance within the meaning of section 79.

Example 2. A policy permits each employee to purchase units of paid-up whole life insurance but provides $10,000 of term life insurance to each employee whether or not the employee purchases the units of paid-up whole life insurance. The term life insurance is group-term life insurance for purposes of section 79 if all other requirements of section 79 are met.

Example 3. A policy permits each employee to purchase a $100 unit of paid-up, whole life insurance in each policy year. In the first policy year an employee is insured, the policy provides $10,000 of term life insurance. In each subsequent policy year, the amount of term life insurance provided is reduced by $100 whether or not the employee purchases a unit of paid-up whole life insurance. The term life insurance is group-term life insurance for purposes of section 79 if all other requirements of section 79 are met.

(c) May a group include fewer than 10 employees? (1) As a general rule, life insurance provided to a group of employees cannot qualify as group-term life insurance for purposes of section 79 unless, at some time during the calendar year, it is provided to at least 10 full-time employees who are members of the group of employees. However, this general rule does not apply if the conditions of paragraph (c)(2) or (3) of this section are met.

(2) The general rule of paragraph (c)(1) of this section does not apply if the following conditions are met:

(i) The insurance is provided to all full-time employees of the employer or, if evidence of insurability affects eligibility, to all full-time employees who provide evidence of insurability satisfactory to the insurer.

(ii) The amount of insurance provided is computed either as a uniform percentage of compensation or on the basis of coverage brackets established by the insurer. However, the amount computed under either method may be reduced in the case of employees who do not provide evidence of insurability satisfactory to the insurer. In general, no bracket may exceed 2½ times the next lower bracket and the lowest bracket must be at least 10 percent of the highest bracket. However, the insurer may establish a separate schedule of coverage brackets for employees who are over age 65, but no bracket in the over-65 schedule may exceed 2½ times the next lower bracket and the lowest bracket in the over-65 schedule must be at least 10 percent of the highest bracket in the basic schedule.

(iii) Evidence of insurability affecting an employee's eligibility for insurance or the amount of insurance provided to that employee is limited to a medical questionnaire completed by the employee that does not require a physical examination.

(3) The general rule of paragraph (c)(1) of this section does not apply if the following conditions are met:

(i) The insurance is provided under a common plan to the employees of two or more unrelated employers.

(ii) The insurance is restricted to, but mandatory for, all employees of the employer who belong to or are represented by an organization (such as a union) that carries on substantial activities in addition to obtaining insurance.

(iii) Evidence of insurability does not affect an employee's eligibility for insurance or the amount of insurance provided to that employee.

(4) For purposes of paragraphs (c)(2) and (3) of this section, employees are not taken into account if they are denied insurance for the following reasons:

(i) They are not eligible for insurance under the terms of the policy because they have not been employed for a waiting period, specified in the policy, which does not exceed six months.

(ii) They are part-time employees. Employees whose customary employment is for not more than 20 hours in any week, or 5 months in any calendar year, are presumed to be part-time employees.

(iii) They have reached the age of 65.

(5) For purposes of paragraphs (c)(1) and (2) of this section, insurance is considered to be provided to an employee who elects not to receive insurance.

(d) How much must an employee receiving permanent benefits include in income?— (1) **In general.** If an insurance policy that meets the requirements of this section provides permanent benefits to an employee, the cost of the permanent benefits reduced by the amount paid for permanent benefits by the employee is included in the employee's income. The cost of the permanent benefits is determined under the formula in paragraph (d)(2) of this section.

(2) Formula for determining cost of the permanent benefits. In each policy year the cost of the permanent benefits for any particular employee must be no less than—

$$X (DDB_2 - DDB_1)$$

where—

DDB_2 is the employee's deemed death benefit at the end of the policy year;

DDB_1 is the employee's deemed death benefit at the end of the preceding policy year; and

X is the net single premium for insurance (the premium for one dollar of paid-up, whole-life insurance) at the employee's attained age at the beginning of the policy year.

(3) Formula for determining deemed death benefit. The deemed death benefit (DDB) at the end of any policy year for any particular employee is equal to—

$$R/Y$$

where—

R is the net level premium reserve at the end of that policy year for all permanent benefits provided by the policy or, if greater, the cash value of the policy at the end of that policy year; and

Y is the net single premium for insurance (the premium for one dollar of paid-up, whole life insurance) at the employee's age at the end of that policy year.

(4) Mortality tables and interest rates used. For purposes of paragraphs (d)(2) and (d)(3) of this section, the net level premium reserve (R) and the net single premium (X or Y) shall be based on the 1958 CSO Mortality Table and 4 percent interest.

(5) Dividends. If an insurance policy that meets the requirements of this section provides permanent benefits, part or all of the dividends under the policy may be includible in the employee's income. If the employee pays nothing for the permanent benefits, all dividends under the policy that are actually or constructively received by the employee are includible in the employee's income. In all other cases, the amount of dividends included in the employee's income is equal to—

$$(D + C) - (PI + DI + AP)$$

where—

D is the total amount of dividends actually or constructively received under the policy in the current and all preceding taxable years of the employee;

C is the total cost of the permanent benefits for the current and all preceding taxable years of the employee determined under the formulas in paragraphs (d)(2) and (6) of this section;

PI is the total amount of premium included in the employee's income under paragraph (d)(1) of this section for the current and all preceding taxable years of the employee;

DI is the total amount of dividends included in the employee's income under this paragraph (d)(5) in all preceding taxable years of the employee; and

AP is the total amount paid for permanent benefits by the employee in the current and all preceding taxable years of the employee.

(6) Different policy and taxable years. (i) If a policy year begins in one employee taxable year and ends in another employee taxable year, the cost of the permanent benefits, determined under the formula in paragraph (d)(2) of this section, is allocated between the employee taxable years.

(ii) The cost of permanent benefits for a policy year is allocated first to the employee

Proposed Reg. §1.79-1

taxable year in which the policy year begins. The cost of permanent benefits allocated to that policy year is equal to—

$$F \times C$$

where—

F is the fraction of the premium for that policy year that is paid on or before the last day of the employee taxable year; and

C is the cost of permanent benefits for the policy year determined under the formula in paragraph (d)(2) of this section.

(iii) Any part of the cost of permanent benefits that is not allocated to the employee taxable year in which the policy year begins is allocated to the subsequent employee taxable year.

(iv) The cost of permanent benefits for an employee taxable year is the sum of the costs of permanent benefits allocated to that year under paragraphs (d)(6)(ii) and (iii) of this section.

(7) **Example.** The provisions of this paragraph may be illustrated by the following example:

Example. An employer provides insurance to employee A under a policy that meets the requirements of this section. Under the policy, A, who is 47 years old, received $70,000 of group-term life insurance and elects to receive a permanent benefit under the policy. A pays $2 for each $1,000 of group-term life insurance through payroll deductions and the employer pays the remainder of the premium for the group-term life insurance. The employer also pays one half of the premium specified in the policy for the permanent benefit. A pays the other one half of the premium for the permanent benefit through payroll deductions. The policy specifies that the annual premium paid for the permanent benefit is $300. However, the amount of premium allocated to the permanent benefit by the formula in paragraph (d)(2) of this section is $350. A is a calendar year taxpayer; the policy year begins on January 1. In 1980, $200 is includible in A's income because of insurance provided by the employer. This amount is computed as follows:

(1)	Cost of permanent benefits	$350
(2)	Amounts considered paid by A for permanent benefits (½ × $300)	150
(3)	Line (1) minus line (2)	$200
(4)	Cost of $70,000 of group-term life insurance under Table I of §1.79-3	$336
(5)	Cost of $50,000 of group-term insurance under Table I of §1.79-3	240
(6)	Cost of group-term life insurance in excess of $50,000 (line (4) minus line (5))	96
(7)	Amount considered paid by A for group-term life insurance (70 × $2)	140
(8)	Line (6) minus line (7) (but not less than 0)	0
(9)	Amount includible in income (line (3) plus line(8))	$200

(e) **What is the effect of state law limits?** Section 79 does not apply to life insurance in excess of the limits under applicable state law on the amount of life insurance that can be provided to an employee under a single contract of group-term life insurance.

(f) **Cross references.** (1) See section 79(b) and §1.79-2 for rules relating to group-term life insurance provided to certain retired individuals.

(2) See section 61(a) and the regulations thereunder for rules relating to life insurance not meeting the requirements of section 79, this section, or §1.79-2, such as insurance provided on the life of a non-employee (for example, an employee's spouse), insurance not provided as compensation for personal services performed as an employee, insurance not provided under a policy carried directly or indirectly by the employer, or permanent benefits.

(3) See section 106 and §1.106-1 for rules relating to certain insurance that does not provide general death benefits, such as travel insurance or accident and health insurance (including amounts payable under a double indemnity clause or rider).

(g) Effective date. Sections 1.79-0 through 1.79-3 apply to insurance provided in employee taxable years beginning on or after January 1, 1977 with the following exceptions:

(1) If the insurance is provided under a binding arrangement between an employer and an insurer in effect on November 4, 1976, or a renewal of such a binding arrangement, §§1.79-0 through 1.79-3 do not apply to the insurance provided in employee taxable years beginning before January 1, 1978. Insurance provided to additional employees or in greater amounts after November 4, 1976 is considered provided under a binding arrangement in effect on November 4, 1976 if the additional employees or greater amounts can be determined by reference to the terms of the binding arrangement.

(2) If the insurance is described in paragraph (g)(1) of this section and did not satisfy the requirement of paragraph (b)(1)(iv) of this section on November 4, 1976, paragraph (b)(1)(iv) of this section does not apply to the insurance provided in employee taxable years beginning before January 1, 1983.

See 26 CFR 1.79-1 through 1.79-3 (revised as of April 1, 1977) for rules applicable to insurance provided in taxable years beginning before January 1, 1977 (January 1, 1978, if the insurance is described in paragraph (g)(1) of this section).

§ 1.79-2 (Proposed Treasury Decision, published 1-5-77.)
Paragraph (b)(4)(ii)(a) of § 1.79-2 is amended by deleting "paragraph (a)(2) of § 1.79-1" and inserting in its place "section 79(a)".

§ 1.79-3 (Proposed Treasury Decision, published 1-5-77.)
Section 1.79-3 is amended by deleting "paragraph (a)(2) of § 1.79-1" each time it appears and inserting in its place "section 79(a)".

There are inserted after § 1.79-3 the following new sections:

§ 1.83-1 (Proposed Treasury Decision, published 6-3-71.) **Property transferred in connection with the performance of services.**

(a) In general. Section 83 provides rules for the taxation of property transferred to an employee or independent contractor (or beneficiary thereof) in connection with the performance of services by such employee or independent contractor. In general, the excess of—

(1) The fair market value of such property (determined without regard to any restriction other than a restriction which by its terms will never lapse) when the transfer of such property becomes complete, over

(2) The amount (if any) paid for such property,

shall be included as compensation in the gross income of such employee or independent contractor for the taxable year in which such transfer becomes complete. Until such transfer becomes complete, the transferor shall be regarded as the owner of such property, and any income from such property received by the employee or independent contractor (or beneficiary thereof) or the right to the use of such property by the employee or independent contractor constitutes additional compensation and shall be included in the gross income of such employee or independent contractor for the taxable year in which such income is received or such use is made available. The forfeiture of such property after its transfer becomes complete shall be treated as a disposition of such property upon which there is recognized a loss equal to the amount of the taxpayer's adjusted basis in such property, and

Proposed Reg. § 1.83-1

if such property is a capital asset in the hands of the taxpayer, such loss shall be a capital loss. This paragraph applies to a transfer of property in connection with the performance of services notwithstanding that the transferor is not the person for whom such services were performed. See section 83(h) and § 1.83-6 for rules for the treatment of employers and other transferors of property in connection with the preformance of services.

(b) **Subsequent sale or other disposition.** If property transferred in connection with the performance of services is subsequently sold or otherwise disposed of in an arm's length transaction before such transfer becomes complete, the excess of—

(i) The amount realized on such sale or other disposition, over

(ii) The amount (if any) paid for such property,

shall be included as compensation in the gross income of the person who performed such services for the taxable year of such sale or other disposition. The preceding sentence shall not apply to any exchange to the extent that the property received is not transferable and is subject to a substantial risk of forfeiture, and the property received in such an exchange shall be treated as property to which section 83 applies. If property is forfeited after a disposition to which this paragraph applies, such forfeiture shall be treated as a disposition of such property upon which there is recognized a loss equal to the amount of the taxpayer's adjusted basis in such property. If such property is a capital asset in the hands of the taxpayer, such loss shall be a capital loss.

(c) **Dispositions not at arm's length.** If property transferred in connection with the performance of services is disposed of in a transaction which is not at arm's length occurring before such transfer becomes complete, the person who performed the services in connection with which such property was transferred realizes compensation includible in his gross income in the amount of money or other property (which is transferable or not subject to a substantial risk of forfeiture) received in such disposition in accordance with his method of accounting. The amount of such compensation shall not exceed the fair market value (determined without regard to any restrictions other than a restriction which by its terms will never lapse) at the time of disposition of the property disposed of less the price originally paid for such property. Moreover, the person who performed the services realizes additional compensation at the time and in the amount determined under paragraphs (a) and (b) of this section, except that the amount of compensation determined under such paragraphs shall be reduced by any amount previously includible in gross income under this paragraph. For example, if in 1971 an employee pays $50 for a share of stock which has a fair market value of $100 and which is not transferable and is subject to a substantial risk of forfeiture, and later in 1971 (at a time when the property still has a fair market value of $100) the employee disposes of, in a transaction not at arm's length, the share of stock to his wife for $10, the employee realizes compensation of $10 in 1971. If in 1972 when the stock has a fair market value of $120 the share of stock first becomes transferable and not subject to a substantial risk of forfeiture, the employee realizes additional compensation in 1972 in the amount of $60 (the $120 fair market value of the stock less $50 price paid for the stock plus $10 taxed as compensation in 1971). For the purpose of this paragraph, if property is transferred to a person other than the person who performed the services and the transferee dies holding the property before such transfer becomes complete when the person who performed the services is still living, the transfer which results by reason of the death of such person is a transfer not at arm's length.

(d) **Certain transfers upon death.** If property is transferred in connection with the preformance of services and the person who performed such services dies before such transfer becomes complete, any income subsequently realized in respect of such property is income in respect of a decedent to which the rules of section 691 apply. In such a case the income in respect of such property shall be taxable under section 691 to the estate or beneficiary of the person who performed the services in accordance with section 83 and the regulations thereunder. If, however, such transfer becomes complete by reason of death of the person who performed the services, any income realized upon such death is not income in respect of a decedent and is includible in gross income for such person's last taxable year.

(e) **Examples.** The provisions of this section may be illustrated by the following examples:

Example (1). On November 1, 1973, X corporation sells to E, an employee, 100 shares of X corporation stock at $10 per share. At the time of such sale the fair market value of the X corporation stock is $100 per share. Under the terms of the sale, each share of stock is nontransferable and subject to a substantial risk of forfeiture which will not lapse until November 1, 1978. Evidence of these restrictions is stamped on the face of E's stock certificates. In addition, no dividends are paid on the X stock during 1973. Since E's stock is nontransferable and is subject to a substantial risk of forfeiture, such transfer is not complete, and E does not include any amount in his gross income as compensation for 1973, despite the fact that the fair market value ($100 per share) of the X corporation stock exceeds the price E paid for the stock ($10 per share).

Example (2). Assume the facts are the same as in example (1) except that on November 1, 1978, the fair market value of the X corporation stock is $250 per share. Since the transfer of the X corporation stock becomes complete in 1978, E must include $24,000 (100 shares of X corporation stock × $250 fair market value per share less $10 price paid by E for each share) as compensation in 1978.

Example (3). Assume the facts are the same as in example (2), except that on November 1, 1978, each share of stock of X corporation in E's hands could as a matter of law be transferred to a bona fide purchaser who would not be required to forfeit the stock if the risk of forfeiture materialized. In the event, however, that the risk materializes, E would be liable in damages to X. Since E's stock is transferable within the meaning of § 1.83-3(e) in 1978, the transfer is complete, and E must include $24,000 (100 shares of X corporation stock × $250 fair market value per share less $10 price paid by E for each share) as compensation in 1978.

Example (4). Assume the facts are the same as in example (1) except that, in 1974 E sells his 100 shares of X corporation stock in an arm's length sale to I, an investment company, for $120 per share. At the time of this sale each share of X corporation's stock has a fair market value of $200. Under paragraph (b) of this section, E must include $11,000 (100 shares of X corporation stock × $120 amount realized per share less $10 price paid by E per share) as compensation in 1974 notwithstanding that the stock remains nontransferable and is still subject to a substantial risk of forfeiture at the time of such sale. Under subparagraph (2) of § 1.83-4(b), I's basis in the X corporation stock is $120 per share.

§ 1.83-2 (Proposed Treasury Decision, published 6-3-71.) **Election to include in gross income in year of transfer.**

(a) **In general.** Under section 83(b), if property is transferred in connection with performance of services and such transfer is not complete at the time it is made, the person performing such services may elect to treat such transfer as a complete transfer and to include in his gross income for the taxable year in which such property is transferred, the excess of the fair market value of such property at the time of transfer (determined without regard to any restriction other than a restriction which by its terms will never lapse) over the amount (if any) paid for such property. If this election is made, section 83(a) and the regulations thereunder, do not apply with respect to such property, and except as otherwise provided in section 83(d)(2) and the regulations thereunder any subsequent appreciation in the value of the property is not taxable as compensation. In computing the gain or loss from the subsequent sale or exchange of such property, its basis shall be the amount paid for the property increased by the amount included in gross income under section 83(b). However, notwithstanding the preceding sentence if the property is later forfeited or sold in an arm's length transaction before the

Proposed Reg. § 1.83-2

transfer of such property becomes complete, such forfeiture or sale shall be treated as a disposition upon which there is recognized a loss equal to the excess (if any) of—

(1) The amount that the taxpayer actually paid for such property, over

(2) The amount realized (if any) upon such forfeiture or sale.

If such property is a capital asset in the hands of the taxpayer, such loss shall be a capital loss.

(b) **Manner of making election.** The election referred to in paragraph (a) of this section is made by filing one copy of a written statement with the internal revenue officer with whom the person who performed the services files his return. In addition, one copy of such statement shall be submitted with his income tax return for the taxable year in which such property as transferred.

(c) **Additional copies.** The person who performed the services shall also submit a copy of the statement referred to in paragraph (b) of this section to the person for whom the services are performed, and, in addition, if the person who performs the services in connection with which property is transferred and the transferee of such property are not the same person, the person who performs the services shall submit a copy of such statement to the transferee of the property.

(d) **Content of statement.** The statement shall be signed by the person making the election and shall indicate that it is being made under section 83(b) of the Code, and shall contain the following information:

(1) The name, address and taxpayer identification number of the taxpayer;

(2) A description of each property with respect to which the election is being made;

(3) The date or dates on which the property is transferred and the taxable year (for example, "calendar year 1970" or "Fiscal year ending May 31, 1970") in which such election was made;

(4) The nature of the restriction or restrictions to which the property is subject;

(5) The fair market value at the time of transfer (determined without regard to any restriction other than a restriction which by its terms will never lapse) of each property with respect to which the election is being made;

(6) The amount (if any) paid for such property; and

(7) With respect to elections made after [date of filing of the Treasury decision] a statement to the effect that copies have been furnished to other persons as provided in paragraph (c) of this section.

(e) **Time for making election.** The statement referred to in paragraph (b) of this section shall be filed not later than 30 days after the date the property was transferred (or, if later, January 29, 1970). Any statement filed before February 15, 1970, which was amended not later than February 16, 1970, in order to make it conform to the requirements of paragraph (d) of this section shall be deemed a proper election under section 83(b).

(f) **Revocability of election.** An election under section 83(b) may not be revoked except with the consent of the Commissioner. In any event, a decline in value of the property with respect to which an election under section 83(b) has been made or a failure to perform an act contemplated at the time of transfer of such property will not alone constitute grounds of revocation.

§ 1.83-3 (Proposed Treasury Decision, published 6-3-71.) **Meaning and use of certain terms.**

(a) **Transfer.** (1) For purposes of section 83 and the regulations thereunder, a transfer of property occurs when a person acquires rights in property which, without the payment of further consideration (other than the performance of substantial services), may ripen into an ownership interest in such property or when a person becomes subject to a binding commitment to purchase an ownership interest in such property. Thus, the grant of an option does not constitute a transfer of the property subject to the option, and no transfer of such property occurs until the option is exercised and the optionee pays or incurs a personal liability to pay the option price. If a person acquires an interest in property and gives an evidence of indebtedness without personal liability in exchange therefor, such person is considered to have been granted an option to purchase such property, and a transfer of such property occurs only when, and to the extent that, payments are made in discharge of such indebtedness. No transfer of property occurs upon a person's acquisition of an interest in property for the sole purpose of securing the payment of deferred compensation; see, however, section 402(b) and the regulations thereunder for rules relating to the taxability of beneficiaries of employees' trusts which are not exempt under section 501(a) and of other similar deferred compensation arrangements.

(2) The provisions of this paragraph may be illustrated by the following examples:

Example (1). On January 3, 1971, X corporation purports to transfer to E, an employee, 100 shares of stock in X corporation. The X stock is subject to the sole restriction that E must sell such stock to X on termination of employment for any reason for an amount which is equal to the excess (if any) of the book value of the X stock at termination of employment less book value on January 3, 1971. The stock is not transferable by E and the restrictions on transfer are stamped on the certificate. Under these facts and circumstances, E's rights in the X stock are more in the nature of a security interest for the payment of deferred compensation than an ownership interest in property and, accordingly, there is no transfer of property in connection with the performance of services within the meaning of section 83.

Example (2). Assume the same facts as in example (1) except that E pays for the X stock with a promissory note without personal liability with a face value equal to the book value of the X stock on January 3, 1971. In addition, X is obligated to repurchase the X stock at E's termination of employment for an amount equal to the book value of the X stock at such time. Under these facts and circumstances, for purposes of section 83, a transfer of the X stock to E occurs only when and to the extent that E makes payments of principal to X under the terms of the promissory note.

Example (3). Assume the same facts as in example (1) except that the X stock is subject to the sole restriction that it must be sold to X upon E's termination of employment for the total amount of dividends that have been declared on the X stock from January 3, 1971, to the date of E's termination of employment. Under these facts and circumstances, as in example (1), E's rights in the stock are more in the nature of a security interest for the payment of deferred compensation than an ownership interest in property and, accordingly, there is no transfer within the meaning of section 83.

Example (4). On February 28, 1971, Y corporation sells to E, an employee, stock in Z corporation, a large computer manufacturer. The purchase price for the Z stock is determined under a formula price to be an amount equal to one-half of the book value per share of the Z stock on February 28, 1971. In addition, the stock is subject to the sole restriction that E must sell the Z stock to Y when E retires or terminates employment for an amount equal to three-quarters of the book value per share of Z stock on the date of E's retirement or termination of employment. Under these facts and circumstances, E acquired a property interest on February 28, 1971, because on that date E obtained a valuable right which could increase or decrease in value dependent upon future economic success or failure of Z's computer business. Therefore, there has been a transfer of the Z stock to E within the meaning of section 83.

Example (5). G, a corporation, transfers to E, an employee, a new home in which his interest in nontransferable and is subject to a substantial risk of forfeiture for a 10-year period. However, G allows E to live rent free in the home

Proposed Reg. § 1.83-3

during the 10-year period. Since E's interest in the home is nontransferable and subject to a substantial risk of forfeiture, the transfer of the home to E is not complete. Under these facts and circumstances, E must include the fair rental value of the home in his gross income as compensation for each taxable year until the transfer of the home becomes complete. When the transfer to E of the home first becomes complete, E must include in his gross income as compensation the then existing fair market value of the home less any amount he has paid or is required to pay to complete such transfer.

(b) **Complete transfer.** For purposes of section 83 and the regulations thereunder, a transfer of property in connection with performance of services by an employee or independent contractor becomes complete when the rights of the employee or independent contractor or beneficiary thereof in such property cease to be subject to a substantial risk of forfeiture or become transferable, whichever occurs earlier.

(c) **Substantial risk of forfeiture**—(1) For purposes of section 83 and the regulations thereunder, the rights of a person in property are subject to a substantial risk of forfeiture if such person's rights to full enjoyment of such property are conditioned upon the future performance, or the refraining from the performance, of substantial services by any individual. Whether such services are substantial depends upon the particular facts and circumstances. The regularity of the performance of services and the time spent in performing such services tend to indicate whether services are substantial. In addition, the fact that the person performing such services has the right to decline to perform such services may tend to establish that services are insubstantial. Thus, for example, a requirement that an employe must return property transferred to him in connection with his performance of services for his employer if he does not complete an additional period of substantial services would cause such property to be subject to a substantial risk of forfeiture. On the other hand, a requirement that the property be returned to the employer if the employee commits a crime will not be considered to result in a substantial risk of forfeiture. An enforceable requirement that the property be returned to the employer if the employee accepts a job with a competing firm will not ordinarily be considered to result in a substantial risk of forfeiture unless the particular facts and circumstances indicate to the contrary. Factors which may be taken into account in determining whether a covenant not to compete constitutes a substantial risk of forfeiture are the age of the employee, the availability of alternative employment opportunities, the likelihood of the employee's obtaining such other employment, the degree of skill possessed by the employee, the employee's health, and the practice (if any) of the employer to enforce such covenants. Similarly, rights in property transferred to a retiring employee subject to the sole requirement that it be returned unless he renders consulting services upon the request of his former employer would not be considered subject to a substantial risk of forfeiture unless he is in fact expected to perform substantial services. Rights in property transferred to an employee (or beneficiary thereof) of a corporation who owns, directly or indirectly, more than 5 percent of the total combined voting power or value of all classes of stock of the employer corporation or of its parent or subsidiary corporation will not be considered subject to a substantial risk of forfeiture unless the possibility that the employee will not satisfy the requirement claimed to result in such risk is substantial; in determining whether the possibility is substantial, there will be taken into acccount (i) the employee's relationship to other stockholders and the extent of their control, potential control and possible loss of control of the corporation, (ii) the position of the employee in the corporation and the extent to which he is subordinate to other employees, (iii) the employee's relationship to the officers and directors of the corporation, (iv) the person or persons who must approve the employee's discharge, and (v) past actions of the employer in enforcing the provisions of the restrictions. For example, if 20 percent of the single class of stock of a corporation is owned by an employee and the remaining stock is owned by an unrelated individual and members of his immediate family, rights in property transferred to such employee by the corporation will not be considered not to be subject to a substantial risk of forfeiture by reason of his ownership of 20 percent of the stock of the employer corporation. On the other hand, if 4 percent of the voting power of all the stock of a corporation is owned by the president of such corporation and the remaining stock is so diversely held by the public that such individual in effect controls such corporation, rights in property transferred to him by such corporation will be considered not to be subject to a substantial risk of forfeiture. Where stock is transferred to an underwriter prior to a public offering and the full enjoyment of such stock is expressly or impliedly conditioned upon the successful completion of the underwriting, the stock is subject to a substantial risk of forfeiture. A substantial risk of forfeiture will not be considered to exist in connection with the performance of services where the employer is required to pay full value or substantially full value to the employee upon the return of such property. A restriction which by its terms will never lapse standing by itself will not be considered to result in a substantial risk of forfeiture.

(2) The rules stated in this paragraph may be illustrated by the following examples:

Example (1). On November 1, 1971, corporation X transfers in connection with the performance of services to E, an employee, 100 shares of corporation X stock for $90 per share. Under the terms of the transfer, E will be subject to a binding commitment to resell the stock to corporation X at $90 per share if he leaves the employment of corporation X for any reason prior to the expiration of a 10-year period from the date of such transfer. Since E must perform substantial services to corporation X, E's rights in the stock is subject to a substantial risk of forfeiture.

Example (2). On November 25, 1971, corporation X gives to E, an employee, in connection with his performance of services to corporation X, a bonus of 100 shares of corporation X stock. Under the terms of the bonus arrangement E is obligated to return the corporation X stock to corporation X if he terminates his employment for any reason. However, for each year occurring after November 25, 1971, during which E remains employed with corporation X, E ceases to be obligated to return 10 shares of the corporation X stock. Since in each year occurring after November 25, 1971, for which E remains employed he is not required to return 10 shares of corporation X's stock, E's rights in 10 shares each year for 10 years cease to be subject to a substantial risk of forfeiture for each year he remains so employed.

Example (3). Assume the same facts as in example (2) except that for each year occurring after November 25, 1971, for which E remains employed with corporation X, corporation X agrees to pay, in redemption of the bonus shares given to E if he terminates employment for any reason, 10 percent of the fair market value of each share of stock on the date of such termination of employment. Since corporation X will pay E 10 percent of the fair market value of the corporation X stock for each year E remains employed, the corporation X stock in E's hands is not subject to a substantial risk of forfeiture to the extent of such additional 10 percent amount each year which corporation X agrees to pay any amount to E in exchange for such shares.

Example (4). On January 7, 1971, corporation X, a computer service company, transfers to E, a 45-year-old employee, 100 shares of corporation X stock for $50. E is a highly compensated salesman who sold X's products in a three-state area since 1960. At the time of transfer each share of X stock has a fair market value of $100. The stock was transferred to E in connection with his termination of employment with X. Each share of X stock is subject to the sole condition that E can keep such share only if he does not engage in competition with X for a 5-year period in the three-state area where E had previously sold X's products. In order for E to establish the necessary business contacts to enable him to earn a salary in another industry comparable to his current compensation, E would have to expend considerable time and effort. In view of the substantial possibility under these

Proposed Reg. § 1.83-3

facts and circumstances that E will compete with X in the three-state area, the X stock in his hands is subject to a substantial risk of forfeiture.

(d) **Transferability of property.** For purposes of section 83 and the regulations thereunder, the rights of a person in property are transferable if such person can transfer any interest in the property to any person other than the transferor of the property, but only if the rights in such property of such transferee are not subject to a substantial risk of forfeiture. Accordingly, property is transferable if the person performing the services or receiving the property can sell, assign, or pledge as collateral for a loan or as security for the performance of an obligation or for any other purpose his interest in the property to any person other than the transferor of such property and if the transferee is not required to give up the property or its value in the event the substantial risk of forfeiture materialize. On the other hand, property is not considered to be transferable merely because the person performing the services or receiving the property may designate a beneficiary to receive the property in the event of his death.

(e) **Property.** For purposes of section 83 and the regulations thereunder, the term "property" includes both realty and personalty other than money and other than an unfunded and unsecured promise to pay deferred compensation. In the case of a transfer of a life insurance contract, retirement income contract, endowment contract, or other contract providing life insurance protection, only the cash surrender value of the contract is considered to be property. In this connection, the rules relating to the taxation of the cost of life insurance protection provided in paragraph (b) of § 1.72-16 shall apply.

(f) **Property transferred in connection with the performance of services.** In general, property transferred to an employee or an independent contractor or beneficiary thereof in recognition of the performance of services is considered transferred in connection with the performance of services within the meaning of section 83. The transfer of property is subject to section 83 whether such transfer is in respect of past, present, or future services.

§ 1.83-4 (Proposed Treasury Decision, published 6-3-71.) **Special rules.**

(a) **Holding period.** Under section 83(f), the holding period of property to which section 83(a) applies shall begin when the transfer of such property becomes complete. However, if the person who has performed the services in connection with which property is transferred has made an election under section 83(b), the holding period of such property shall begin on the date such property was transferred. If property to which section 83 and the regulations thereunder apply is transferred at arm's length, the holding period of such property in the hands of the transferee shall begin on the date of such transfer.

(b) **Basis.** (1) Except as provided in subparagraph (2) of this paragraph, if property to which section 83 and the regulations thereunder apply is acquired by any person (including a person who acquires such property in a subsequent transfer which is not at arm's length), such person's basis for the property so acquired shall be the sum of any amount paid for such property and any amount included in the gross income of the person who performed the services in connection with which such property was transferred.

(2) If property to which § 1.83-1 applies is transferred at arm's length, the basis of the property in the hands of the transferee shall be determined under section 1012 and the regulations thereunder.

(c) **Certain notes transferred to employee or independent contractor.** Notes or other evidences of indebtedness transferred in connection with the performance of services constitute compensation in accordance with section 83 and the regulations thereunder. A taxpayer receiving a note shall treat the receipt of such note as compensation in an amount and at the time determined in accordance with section 83 and the regulations thereunder at its fair market value, including any adjustment for discount or premium computed with reference to the prevailing interest rate. As payments are received on such a note, there shall be included in income that portion of each payment which represents the proportionate part of the discount originally taken on the entire note.

§ 1.83-5 (Proposed Treasury Decision, published 6-3-71.) **Certain restrictions which will never lapse.**

(a) **Definition of nonlapse restrictions.** For purposes of section 83 and the regulations thereunder, a restriction which by its terms will never lapse (hereinafter called a nonlapse restriction) is—

(1) A limitation on the subsequent transfer of property transferred in connection with the performance of services,

(2) Which allows the transferee of the property to sell such property at a price determined under a formula, and

(3) Which will continue to apply to, and to be enforced against any subsequent holder (other than the transferor).

A requirement resulting in a substantial risk of forfeiture will not be considered to result in a nonlapse restriction. Registration requirements imposed by Federal or State securities law or similar laws with respect to sales or other dispositions of stock or securities will not be considered to result in a nonlapse restriction. An obligation to resell property transferred in connection with the performance of services to the person for whom such services were performed at its fair market value at the time of such sale is not a nonlapse restriction.

(b) **Valuation.** In the case of property subject to a nonlapse restriction, the price determined under the formula price shall be deemed to be the fair market value of the property unless established to the contrary by the Commissioner, and the burden of proof shall be on the Commissioner with respect to such value. If stock in a corporation is subject to a nonlapse restriction which allows the transferee to sell such stock only at a formula price based upon book value or a reasonable multiple of earnings, the price so determined will ordinarily be regarded as determinative of the value of such property for purposes of section 83.

(c) **Cancellation—(1) In general.** Under section 83(d)(2), if a nonlapse restriction to which property is subject is cancelled, then, unless the taxpayer establishes—

(i) That such cancellation was not compensatory, and

(ii) That the person, if any, who would be allowed a deduction if the cancellation were treated as compensatory, will treat the transaction as not compensatory, as provided in subparagraph (2) of this paragraph,

the excess of the fair market value of the property (computed without regard to the restrictions) at the time of cancellation, over the sum of—

(iii) The fair market value of such property (computed by taking the restriction into account) immediately before the cancellation, and

(iv) The amount, if any, paid for the cancellation,

shall be treated as compensation for the taxable year in which such cancellation occurs. Whether there has been a noncompensatory cancellation of a nonlapse restriction depends upon the particular facts and circumstances. Ordinarily the fact that the employee is required to perform additional services or that the employee's salary is adjusted to take such cancellation into account indicates that such cancellation has a compensatory purpose. On the other hand, the fact that the original purpose of such restriction no longer exists may indicate that the purpose of such cancellation is noncompensatory. Thus, for example, if a so-called "buy-sell" restriction was imposed on a corporation's stock to limit ownership of such stock and is being cancelled in connection with a public offering of the stock, such cancellation will generally be regarded as noncompensatory. However, the mere fact that the employer is willing to forego a deduction under section 83(h) is insufficient evidence to establish a noncompensatory cancellation of a nonlapse restriction. In addition, a corporation's refusal to repurchase its own stock subject to a right of

Proposed Reg. § 1.83-5

first refusal in such corporation will generally be treated as a cancellation of such nonlapse restriction.

(2) **Evidence of noncompensatory cancellation.** In addition to the information necessary to establish the factors described in subparagraph (1) of this paragraph, the taxpayer referred to in subparagraph (1) of this paragraph shall request his employer to furnish him with a written statement indicating that the employer will not treat the cancellation of the nonlapse restriction as a compensatory event, and that no deduction will be taken with respect to such cancellation. The taxpayer shall file such written statement with his income tax return for the taxable year in which or with which such cancellation occurs.

(d) **Examples.** The provisions of this section may be illustrated by the following examples:

Example (1). On November 1, 1971, X corporation whose shares are closely held and not regularly traded, transfers to E, an employee, 100 shares of X corporation stock subject to the sole condition that, if he desires to dispose of such stock during the period of his employment, he must resell the stock to his employer at its then existing book value, and he or his estate is obligated to offer to sell the stock at his retirement or death to his employer at its then existing book value. Under these facts and circumstances, the restriction to which the shares of X corporation stock are subject is a nonlapse restriction. Consequently, the fair market value of the X stock is includible in E's gross income as compensation for taxable year 1971. However, in determining the fair market value of the X stock, the book value formula price will be regarded as being determinative of such value.

Example (2). Assume the facts are the same as in example (1), except that the X stock is subject to the sole condition that if E desires to dispose of the stock during the period of his employment he must resell the stock to his employer at a multiple of earnings per share that is in this case a reasonable approximation of value at the time of transfer to E, and he is obligated to offer to sell the stock at his retirement or death to his employer at the same multiple earnings. Under these facts and circumstances, the restriction to which the X corporation stock is subject is a nonlapse restriction. Consequently, the fair market value of the X stock is includible in E's gross income for taxable year 1971. However, in determining the fair market value of the X stock, the multiple-of-earnings formula price will be regarded as determinative of such value.

Example (3). On January 1, 1971, X corporation transfers to E, an employee, 100 shares of stock in X corporation. Each such share of stock is subject to an agreement between X and E whereby E agrees that such shares are to be held solely for investment purposes and not for resale (a so-called investment letter restriction). Since E's rights in such stock are not subject to a substantial risk of forfeiture, the fair market value of each share of X corporation stock is includible in E's gross income as compensation for taxable year 1971. Since such an investment letter restriction does not constitute a nonlapse restriction, in determining the fair market value of each share the investment letter restriction is disregarded.

§ 1.83-6 (Proposed Treasury Decision, published 6-3-71; 9-20-77.) **Deduction by employer.**

(a) **In general.** In the case of a transfer of property in connection with the performance of services or a compensatory cancellation of a restriction described in section 83(d), there is allowed as a deduction under section 162 or 212, to the person for whom such services were performed, an amount equal to the amount included, under subsection (a), (b), or (d)(2) of section 83 as compensation, in the gross income of the person who performed such services, but only to the extent such amount meets the requirements of section 162 or 212 and the regulations thereunder. Such deduction shall be allowed only for the taxable year of such person in which or with which ends the taxable year for which such amount is included as compensation in the gross income of the person who performed such services. However, no deduction is allowed under section 83(h) to the extent that property transferred in connection with the performance of services constitutes a capital expenditure. In such a case, the basis of the property to which such capital expenditure relates shall be increased at the same time and to the same extent as any amount is includible in the employee's gross income in respect of such transfer. Thus, for example, no deduction is allowed to a corporation in respect of a transfer of its stock to a promoter upon its organization, notwithstanding that such promoter must include the value of such stock in his gross income in accordance with the rules stated in section 83. For purposes of this paragraph, any amount excluded from gross income under section 101(b) or subchapter N shall be considered to have been included in gross income.

(b) **Recognition of gain or loss.** The transfer of property in connection with the performance of services constitutes, at the time a deduction is allowed under section 83(h) and paragraph (a) of this section in respect of such transfer, a disposition of such property upon which, except as provided in section 1032 and the regulations thereunder, gain or loss is recognized. For purposes of determining the amount of such gain or loss, the amount realized from such disposition is the amount allowed as a deduction under section 83(h) and paragraph (a) of this section.

(c) **Forfeitures.** If, under section 83(h) and paragraph (a) of this section, a deduction was allowed in respect of a transfer of property and such property is subsequently forfeited, the person to whom such deduction was allowed shall include in gross income as ordinary gain the excess of the fair market value of such property at the time of such forfeiture over the amount paid (if any) upon such forfeiture. If its own stock is forfeited to a corporation, the amount includible in gross income shall not exceed the amount of such deduction.

(d) **Special rules.** Where a shareholder of a corporation transfers stock to an employee of such corporation in consideration of services performed for the corporation, the transaction shall be considered to be a contribution of such stock to the capital of such corporation by the shareholder and a transfer of the stock by the corporation to the employee. Similarly, where a corporation transfers its stock to a person who has performed services for a subsidiary of such corporation, the transaction shall be considered—

(1) A contribution of money by the corporation to its subsidiary's capital,

(2) A purchase of the stock by the subsidiary from the corporation for its full value, and

(3) A transfer of the stock by the subsidiary to its employee.

(e) **Options.** A deduction is allowable according to the rules of this section for the grant of an option, in connection with the performance of services, to the person for whom such services were performed, but only if, at the time of grant, the option has a readily ascertainable fair market value (determined in accordance with the rules of §1.83-7(b)). An option granted after [insert date, 30 days after the date final regulations are filed by the Federal Register] that is not actively traded on an established market will be presumed not to have a readily ascertainable fair market value at the time of grant, unless the reporting requirements of §1.83-7(c) and paragraph (f) of this section are satisfied with respect to such option. However, if the facts show that an option does have a readily ascertainable fair market value under §1.83-7(b) when granted, failure to comply with such reporting requirements will not preclude the taxpayer from taking a deduction for the grant of such option.

(f) **Reporting requirements.** A person for whom services were performed, who claims a deduction for an option granted after [insert date, 30 days after the date final regula-

Proposed Reg. § 1.83-6

tions are filed by the Federal Register] that is not actively traded on an established market, must submit with the return on which such claim is made, the following:

(1) A statement that the option has a readily ascertainable fair market value at the time of grant for purposes of determining the deductibility of the grant of the option;

(2) An explanation of why the option has a readily ascertainable fair market value (including why the fair market value of the option privilege is readily ascertainable);

(3) A statement of the option's fair market value at the time of grant, and an explanation of the method used by the taxpayer to determine the fair market value of the option at the time of grant (including the fair market value of its option privilege) for purposes of determining the amount of the deduction;

(4) A list of the names of all employees (or independent contractors) who have been compensated by the taxpayer with the grant of an option that is deductible on this return (if includible in gross income at the time of grant) and has the same material terms (other than the exercise price) as an option for which the taxpayer is claiming a deduction on this return;

(5) A statement that each such employee (or independent contractor) agrees with the taxpayer that the option granted to such employee (or independent contractor) has a readily ascertainable fair market value, and is includible in the gross income of the employee (or independent contractor), at the time of grant; and

(6) A statement that each such employee (or independent contractor) agrees with the taxpayer as to the fair market value at the time of grant of the option granted to such employee (or independent contractor), and agrees to use such value in determining the amount includible in the gross income of the employee (or independent contractor).

§ 1.83-7 (Proposed Treasury Decision, published 6-3-71; 9-20-77.) Taxation of options not subject to sections 421-425.

(a) **In general**—(1) If there is granted, in connection with performance of services, an option to which section 421 does not apply, and which has a readily ascertainable fair market value (determined in accordance with paragraph (b) of this section) at the time the option is granted, the person who performed such services realizes compensation in accordance with the rules stated in § 1.83-1.

(2) If there is granted, in connection with the performance of services, an option to which section 421 does not apply and which does not have a readily ascertainable fair market value (determined in accordance with paragraph (b) of this section) at the time the option is granted, the person who performed such services realizes compensation when the property subject to the option is transferred upon the exercise of such option in accordance with the rules stated in § 1.83-1, even though the fair market value of such option may become readily ascertainable before such time.

(b) **Readily ascertainable defined**—(1) **Actively traded on an established market.** Options have a value at the time they are granted, but that value is ordinarily not readily ascertainable unless the option is actively traded on an established market. If an option is actively traded on an established market, the fair market value of such option is readily ascertainable for purposes of this section by applying the rules of valuation set forth in § 20.2031-2 of this chapter (the Estate Tax Regulations).

(2) **Not actively traded on an established market.** (i) When an option is not actively traded on an established market, the fair market value of the option is not readily ascertainable unless the fair market value of the option can be measured with reasonable accuracy. For purposes of this section, if an option is not actively traded on an established market, the option does not have a readily ascertainable fair market value when granted unless the taxpayer can show that all of the following conditions exist:

(a) The option is transferable by the optionee;

(b) The option is exercisable immediately in full by the optionee;

(c) The option or the property subject to the option is not subject to any restriction or condition (other than a lien or other condition to secure the payment of the purchase price) which has a significant effect upon the fair market value of the option; and

(d) The fair market value of the option privilege is readily ascertainable in accordance with subdivision (ii) of this subparagraph.

(ii) The fair market value of an option includes the value attributable to the option privilege and may include the value attributable to the right to make an immediate bargain purchase of the property subject to the option. If the option provides an option price which is less than the fair market value of the property subject to the option at the time it is granted, an immediate gain may be realized by exercising the option at the bargain price and selling the property so acquired. However, irrespective of whether there is a right to make an immediate bargain purchase of the property subject to the option, the fair market value of the option includes the value of the option privilege. The option privilege is the opportunity to benefit at any time during the period the option may be exercised from any appreciation during such period in the value of the property subject to the option without risking any capital. Therefore, the fair market value of an option is not merely the difference which may exist at a particular time between the option price and the value of the property subject to the option but also includes the value of the option privilege. Accordingly, for purposes of this section, the fair market value of the option is not readily ascertainable unless the value of the option privilege can be measured with reasonable accuracy. In determining whether the value of the option privilege is readily ascertainable, and in determining the amount of such value when such value is readily ascertainable, it is necessary to consider—

(a) Whether the value of the property subject to the option can be ascertained;

(b) The probability of any ascertainable value of such property increasing or decreasing; and

(c) The length of the period during which the option can be exercised.

(c) **Reporting requirements.** An option granted after [insert date, 30 days after the date final regulations are filed by the Federal Register] that is not actively traded on an established market will be presumed not to have a readily ascertainable fair market value when granted, unless the reporting requirements of §1.83-6(f) and this paragraph are satisfied with respect to such option. However, if the facts show that an option does have a readily ascertainable fair market value under §1.83-7(b) when granted, failure to comply with such reporting requirements will not relieve the taxpayer from having to include such option in gross income at the time of grant. An employee (or independent contractor) who includes in gross income the value of such an option must submit with the return on which such option is reported, the following:

(1) A copy of the information and statements described in §1.83-6(f)(1), (2), (3) and (5) that were submitted with a claim for a deduction for the grant of such option by the person for whom the taxpayer performed services;

(2) A statement by the taxpayer that the option has a readily ascertainable fair market value, and is includible in the taxpayer's gross income, at the time of grant; and

(3) A statement by the taxpayer that the taxpayer agrees to the determination of the option's fair market value by the person for whom the taxpayer performed services (which determination is described in §1.83-6(f)(3)) for purposes of determining the amount includible in the taxpayer's gross income at the time of grant.

§ 1.83-8 (Proposed Treasury Decision, published 6-3-71.) **Applicability of section and transitional rules.**

(a) **Scope of section 83.** Section 83 is not applicable to—

Proposed Reg. § 1.83-8

(1) A transfer of an option to which section 421 applies;

(2) Except as provided in sections 402(b) and 403(c) and the regulations thereunder, a transfer to or from a trust for the benefit of employees (whether or not qualified under section 401(a)), a transfer under an annuity plan whether or not it meets the requirements of section 404(a)(2), or a transfer under an annuity plan whether or not it meets the requirements of section 403(b);

(3) The transfer of an option without a readily ascertainable fair market value (as defined in paragraph (b)(1) of § 1.83-7); or

(4) The transfer of property pursuant to the exercise of an option with a readily ascertainable fair market value at the date of grant.

However, section 83 does apply to a transfer to or from a trust or under an annuity plan for the benefit of a person (other than an employee) who performs services for the transferor.

(b) *Transitional rules*—(1) *In general.* Except as otherwise provided in this paragraph, section 83 and the regulations thereunder shall apply to property transferred after June 30, 1969.

(2) *Binding written contracts.* Section 83 and the regulations thereunder shall not apply to property transferred pursuant to a binding written contract entered into before April 22, 1969. For purposes of this paragraph, a binding written contract means only a written contract under which the employee has an enforceable right to compel the transfer of property or to obtain damages upon the breach of such contract. A contract which provides that the individual's right to such property is contingent upon the happening of an event (including the passage of time) may satisfy the requirements of this paragraph. However, if the event itself, or the determination of whether the event has occurred, rests with the board of directors or any other individual or group acting on behalf of the employer (other than an arbitrator), the contract will not be treated as giving the employee an enforceable right for purposes of this paragraph. However, the binding nature of the contract will not be negated by a provision in such contract which allows the employee or independent contractor to terminate the contract for any year, and receive cash instead of property if such election would cause a substantial penalty, such as a forfeiture of part or all of the property received in connection with the performance of services in an earlier year.

(3) *Options granted before April 22, 1969.* Section 83 shall not apply to property received upon the exercise of an option granted before April 22, 1969.

(4) *Certain written plans.* Section 83 shall not apply to property transferred (whether or not by the exercise of an option) before May 1, 1970, pursuant to a written plan adopted and approved before July 1, 1969. A plan is to be considered as having been adopted and approved before July 1, 1969, only if prior to such date the transferor of the property undertook an ascertainable course of conduct which under applicable State law does not require further approval by the board of directors or the stockholders of any corporation. For example, if a corporation transfers property to an employee in connection with the performance of services pursuant to a plan adopted and approved before July 1, 1969, by the board of directors of such corporation, it is not necessary that the stockholders have adopted or approved such plan if State law does not require such approval. However, such approval is necessary if required by the articles of incorporation or the by-laws or if, by its terms, such plan will not become effective without such approval.

(5) *Certain options granted pursuant to a binding written contract.* Section 83 shall not apply to property transferred before January 1, 1973, upon the exercise of an option granted pursuant to a binding written contract (as defined in subparagraph (2) of this paragraph) entered into before April 22, 1969, between a corporation and the transferor of such property requiring the transferor to grant options to employees of such corporation (or a subsidiary of such corporation) to purchase a determinable number of shares of stock of such corporation, but only if the transferee was an employee of such corporation (or a subsidiary of such corporation) on or before April 22, 1969.

(6) **Certain tax free exchanges.** Section 83 shall not apply to property transferred in exchange for (or pursuant to the exercise of a conversion privilege contained in) property transferred before July 1, 1969, or for property to which section 83 does not apply (by reason of paragraphs (1), (2), (3), or (4) of section 83(i), if section 354, 355, 356, or 1036 (or so much of section 1031 as relates to section 1036)) applies, or if gain or loss is not otherwise required to be recognized upon the exercise of such conversion privilege, and if the property received in such exchange is subject to restrictions and conditions substantially similar to those to which the property given in such exchange was subject.

Employees' Death Benefits

Paragraph (d) of §1.101-2 is amended by revising subparagraph (3)(i) and examples (2), (3), and (4) of subdivision (ii), to read as follows:

§ 1.101-2 (Proposed Treasury Decision, published 4-30-75.) Employees' death benefits.

* * * * * * * * * * * *

(d) **Nonforfeitable rights.** * * *

* * * * * * * * * * * * * *

(3) (i) Notwithstanding the rule stated in subparagraph (1) of this paragraph and illustrated in subparagraph (2) of this paragraph, the exclusion from gross income provided by section 101(b) applies to a lump sum distribution (as defined in section 402(e)(4)(A) and the regulations thereunder) with respect to which the deceased employee possessed, immediately before his death, a nonforfeitable right to receive the amounts while living (see section 101(b)(2)(B)(i) and (ii)). See subparagraph (4) of this paragraph relating to the exclusion of amounts which are received under annuity contracts purchased by certain exempt organizations and with respect to which the deceased employee possessed, immediately before his death, a nonforfeitable right to receive the amounts while living.

(ii) The application of the provisions of subdivision (i) of this subparagraph may be illustrated by the following examples: * * *

Example (2). The trustee of the X Corporation noncontributory, "qualified", profit-sharing plan is required under the provisions of the plan to pay to the beneficiary of B, an employee of the X Corporation who died on July 1, 1974, the benefit due on account of the death of B. The provisions of the profit-sharing plan give each participating employee, in case of termination of employment, a 10 percent vested interest in the amount accumulated in his account for each of the first 10 years of participation in the plan, but, in case of death, the entire balance to the credit of the participant's account is to be paid to his beneficiary. At the time of B's death, he had been a participant for five years. The accumulation in his account was $8,000, and the amount which would have been distributable to him in the event of termination of employment was $4,000 (50 percent of $8,000). After his death, $8,000 is paid to his beneficiary in a lump sum. (It may be noted that these are the same facts as in example (5) of subparagraph (2) of this paragraph except that the employee has been a participant for five years instead of three and the plan is a "qualified" plan.) It is immaterial that the employee had a nonforfeitable right to $4,000, because the payment of the $8,000 to the beneficiary is the payment of a lump sum distribution to which subdivision (i) of this subparagraph applies. Assuming no other death benefits are involved, the beneficiary may exclude $5,000 of the $8,000 payment from gross income.

Example (3). The facts are the same as in example (2) except that the beneficiary is entitled to receive only the $4,000 to which the employee had a non-

Proposed Reg. § 1.101-2

forfeitable right and elects, 30 days after B's death, to receive it over a period of ten years. Because the distribution is not a lump sum distribution and because B's interest is nonforfeitable, no exclusion from gross income is allowable with respect to the $4,000.

Example (4). The X Corporation instituted a trust, forming part of a "qualified" profit-sharing plan for its employees, the cost thereof being borne entirely by the corporation. The plan provides, in part, that if an employee leaves the employ of the corporation, either voluntarily or involuntarily, before retirement, 10 percent of the account balance provided for the employee in the trust fund will be paid to the employee for each of the first 10 years of service. The plan further provides that if an employee dies before reaching retirement age, his beneficiary will receive a percentage of the account balance provided for the employee in the trust fund, on the same basis as shown in the preceding sentence. A, an employee of the X Corporation for 5 years, died before attaining retirement age while in the employ of the corporation. At the time of his death, $15,000 was the account balance provided for him in the trust fund. His beneficiary receives $7,500 in a lump sum, an amount equal to 50 percent of the account balance provided for A's retirement. The beneficiary may exclude from gross income (assuming no other death benefits are involved) $5,000 of the $7,500, since the latter amount constitutes a lump sum distribution to which subdivision (i) of this subparagraph applies.

* * * * * * * * * * * * * *

Interest on Governmental Obligations

Section 1.103-1 is amended to read as follows:

§ 1.103-1 (Proposed Treasury Decision, published 6-1-72.) **Interest upon obligations of a State, Territory, etc.**

* * * * * * * * * * *

(b) Obligations issued by or on behalf of any State or local governmental unit by constituted authorities empowered to issue such obligations are the obligations of such a unit. However, section 103 (a) (1) and this section do not apply to industrial development bonds except as otherwise provided in section 103 (c), or to arbitrage bonds except as otherwise provided in section 103 (d). See section 103 (c) and §§ 1.103-7 through 1.103-12 for the rules concerning interest paid on industrial development bonds. See section 103 (d) and § 1.103-13 and § 1.103-14 for the rules concerning interest paid on arbitrage bonds. Certificates issued by a political subdivision for public improvements (such as sewers, sidewalks, streets, etc.) which are evidence of special assessments against specific property, which assessments become a lien against such property and which the political subdivision is required to enforce, are, for purposes of this section, obligations of the political subdivision even though the obligations are to be satisfied out of special funds and not out of general funds or taxes. For purposes of this section, the term "political subdivision" denotes any division of any State or local governmental unit which is a municipal corporation, or to which has been delegated the right to exercise part of the sovereign power of the unit. As thus defined, a political subdivision of any State or local governmental unit may or may not include special assessment districts so created, such as road, water, sewer, gas, light, reclamation, drainage, irrigation, levee, school, harbor, port improvement, and similar districts and divisions of any such unit.

Section 1.103-1 is amended by revising paragraphs (a) and (b) and by adding a new paragraph (c). These revised and added provisions read as follows:

§1.103-1 (Proposed Treasury Decision, published 2-2-76.) **Interest upon obligations of a State, territory, etc.**

(a) **In general.** Interest upon obligations of a State, a territory, or a possession of the United States, or any political subdivision thereof or the District of Columbia (hereinafter collectively or individually referred to as "State or local governmental unit") is not includible in gross income except as provided under section 103(c) and (d) and the regulations thereunder. Section 103(a)(1) does not apply to industrial development bonds or to arbitrage bonds except as otherwise provided in section 103(c) and (d). See section 103(c) and §§1.103-7 through 1.103-12 for rules concerning interest paid on industrial development bonds. See section 103(d) for rules concerning interest paid on arbitrage bonds. See paragraph (b)(2) of this section for the definition of the term "political subdivision".

(b) **Obligations of a State or local governmental unit.** (1) Obligations issued by or on behalf of any State or local governmental unit by constituted authorities empowered to issue such obligations are the obligations of such unit. See paragraph (c) of this section for rules relating to obligations which are not issued directly by a State or local governmental unit but are issued by a constituted authority of a State or local governmental unit.

(2) For purposes of this section, the term "political subdivision" denotes any division of any State, territory or possession of the United States which is a municipal corporation or to which has been delegated the right to exercise part of the sovereign power of such State, territory or possession. Such term also denotes any unit which is a political subdivision of more than one State, territory, possession of the United States, or political subdivision (as described in the preceding sentence), i.e., is a municipal corporation of, or a unit to which has been delegated the right to exercise part of the sovereign power of, each of the several participating State or local governmental units. As thus defined, a political subdivision may, for purposes of this section, include special assessment districts so created, such as road, water, sewer, gas, light, reclamation, drainage, irrigation, levee, school, harbor, port improvement, and similar districts and divisions of any such unit.

(3) Certificates issued by a political subdivision for public improvements (such as sewers, sidewalks, streets, etc.) which are evidence of special assessments against specific property, which assessments become a lien against such property and which the political subdivision is required to enforce, are, for purposes of this section, obligations of the political subdivision even though the obligations are to be satisfied out of special funds and not out of general funds or taxes.

(c) **Constituted authorities—(1) In general.** This paragraph provides rules to determine whether obligations that are not issued directly by a State or local governmental unit (hereinafter in this paragraph referred to as the "unit") are nonetheless considered to be the obligations of such unit because issued by a constituted authority of such unit empowered to issue such obligations on behalf of such unit. An issuer is such a constituted authority only if the requirements of paragraph (c)(2) of this section are satisfied. Such a constituted authority may be organized as a corporation, trust, or other entity. An issuer is not such a constituted authority if it issues obligations for more than one unit. The determination that an issuer is a constituted authority under paragraph (c)(2) of this section is solely for purposes of this section and is not determinative of whether the issuer is an authority, agency, or instrumentality under any other section of this title. See paragraph (a) of this section for a definition of the term "State or local governmental unit" and see paragraph (b) of this section for a definition of the term "political subdivision".

(2) **Requirements to be a constituted authority.** The requirements of this subparagraph are satisfied if—

(i) The authority is specifically authorized pursuant to State law to issue obligations to accomplish a public purpose or purposes of the unit. Such specific authorization must either create the authority or provide that the unit may create the authority. Furthermore, such authorization must specify the public purpose or purposes of the unit for the accomplishment of which such authority is empowered to issue obligations. If the unit is a State, territory, or possession of the United States, such authorization must be specifically set forth in the Constitution, charter or other organic act creating or providing for the unit's government, or in a statute of such unit. If the unit is a political subdivision or is the District of Columbia, such authorization must be specifically set forth in its charter

Proposed Reg. § 1.103-1

or other organic act creating the unit, or in the Constitution or a statute of a State, territory or possession of which the unit is a part (including, in the case of the District of Columbia, a statute of the United States) and such authorization must also provide that the unit is authorized to utilize the authority to issue obligations to accomplish a public purpose or purposes of the unit.

(ii) The unit controls the governing board of the authority. To satisfy this requirement, the governing board of the authority must be composed in its entirety of—

(A) Public officials of the unit as members ex-officio,
(B) Persons elected by the voters of such unit for a specified term, or
(C) Persons appointed by the unit or by other members of the governing board described in (A) or (B) of this subdivision (ii) if such other members comprise a majority of the board.

In addition, if the unit does not have organizational control over the authority as described in paragraph (c)(2)(iii)(B) of this section, a majority of the members of the governing body of the authority must be members described in (A) or (B) of this subdivision (ii). Members described in (C) of this subdivision (ii) must be removable for cause or at will and must not be appointed for a term in excess of 6 years. The term of any member of the governing board described in (A) of this subdivision (ii) shall not exceed the period for which such member will be a public official of the unit.

(iii) (A) The unit has either the organizational control over the authority, described in (B) of this subdivision (iii), or the supervisory control over the activities of the authority, described in (C) of this subdivision (iii).

(B) A unit has organizational control over an authority if—

(1) The authority is created by or organized under a constitution, statute, or charter or other organic act creating or providing for the unit's government, which either creates the authority or provides that only a unit may create or organize an authority,

(2) The constitution, statute, or charter or other organic act itself provides for the organization, structure, and powers of the authority, and the authority is organized under such constitution, statute, or charter or other organic act and not under a statute providing generally for the organization of entities, such as a statute providing for the organization of nonprofit corporations, and

(3) The unit may, at its sole discretion, and at any time, alter or change the structure, organization, programs, or activities of the authority (including the power to terminate the authority), subject to any limitation on the impairment of contracts entered into by such authority.

If the unit is a political subdivision or is the District of Columbia, the power to alter or change described in paragraph (c)(2)(iii)(B)(3) of this section must be specifically set forth in the authorization described in paragraph (c)(2)(i) of this section.

(C) Supervisory control by a unit over an authority ordinarily includes (1) except to the extent otherwise fixed by the terms of the authorization described in paragraph (c)(2)(i) of this section, approval by the unit of the provisions of the governing instrument and bylaws of the authority and power to amend the same; (2) annual approval by the unit of the projected programs and projected expenditures of the authority and annual post-review of the programs and expenditures; (3) approval by the unit of each issue of obligations of the authority not more than 60 days prior to the date of issue, except that where obligations are to be issued in series at prescribed intervals over a period not exceeding 5 years, all obligations in such series may be approved at one time within 60 days prior to the date of the first issue in such series; (4) annual review of the authority's annual financial statements (including a statement of income and expenditures) by the unit; (5) access by the unit at any time to all books and records of the authority; (6) in the event of default with respect to obligations issued to finance the acquisition of property, the unit has the exclusive option to purchase such property for the amount required to discharge such obligations and is provided a reasonable time to exercise such option; and (7) agreement by the unit, in conjunction with the issuance of the obligations, to accept title to any tangible personal or real property financed by such obligations upon the retirement of such obligations. Such property must have significant value at the time that such property is conveyed to the unit. Instruments conveying title to such property must, in conjunction with the issuance of such obligations, be placed in escrow with instructions that the escrow agent deliver such instruments of title to such unit upon the retirement of the obligations. Such unit must obtain, upon retirement of the obligations, full legal title to the property with respect to which the indebtedness is incurred free of encumbrances created subsequent to the acquisition of the property by the authority. Examples of title encumbrances are options, leases which continue beyond the date of the retirement of the obligations, lease renewals or lease extensions exercisable by any person other than such unit. The requirements of paragraph (c)(2)(iii)(C)(1) through (5) of this section shall not apply if the governing board of the authority is composed in its entirety of public officials or elected persons (or both) described in paragraph (c)(2)(ii)(A) and (B) of this section.

(iv) Any net earnings of such authority (beyond that necessary for retirement of the indebtedness or to implement the public purpose or purposes or program of the unit) may not inure to the benefit of any person other than the unit.

(v) Upon dissolution of the authority, title to all property owned by such authority will vest in the unit.

(vi) The authority must be created and operated solely to accomplish one or more of the public purposes of the unit specified in the authorization described in paragraph (c)(2)(i) of this section.

The requirements of paragraph (c)(2)(i) of this section must be satisfied at the time of issuance of the obligations and the requirements of paragraph (c)(2)(ii) through (vi) of this section must be satisfied at all times during the period beginning on the date of issuance of the obligations and ending on the date of dissolution of the authority or on the date that title to all property owned by the authority is conveyed to the unit, whichever is earlier. In applying paragraph (c)(2)(ii) through (v) of this section to an authority of a political subdivision the term "unit" shall include any State, territory or possession of which the political subdivision is a part. Except as provided in paragraph (c)(2)(iii)(B) of this section, if the requirements of paragraph (c)(2)(ii) through (vi) of this section are not provided for in the authorization described in paragraph (c)(2)(i), they must be stated in the governing instruments of the entity.

(3) **Examples.** The provisions of this paragraph may be illustrated by the following examples:

Example (1). The Education Act of state A provides in part:

Section 100. *Student Loan Authorities.*

(a) *Purpose.* An incorporated municipality of the State is hereby authorized to issue obligations for the purpose of creating and maintaining a loan fund to provide loans to further the education of any resident of such municipality in accordance with the provisions of section 102 of this Act. Obligations issued pursuant to this section may be issued directly by a municipality or by a student loan authority of such municipality.

(b) *Authority.* A student loan authority of the municipality may be created by the municipality under the not-for-profit corporation act for the sole purpose of obtaining and loaning funds for the purpose described in subsection (a). Such authority is hereby authorized to issue obligations on behalf of the municipality for such purpose. An authority organized under this Act shall be governed by a board of directors comprised of elected officials of the municipality or persons appointed by the municipal council.

Pursuant to the Education Act, city B took the formal action necessary to create a corporation under the State not-for-profit corporation law for the sole purpose of having the corporation act as a student loan authority and to issue specified obligations for such purpose on behalf of the city. The formal action also provided that the authority shall be governed by a board of directors consisting of seven members, four of whom were designated elected officials serving as members ex officio and three of whom were appointed by the city council for a term not in excess of 2 years. The appointed members of the board can be removed at will by the city council. The formal action further provided that the city must approve the governing instrument and the bylaws (and any amendment thereof)

Proposed Reg. § 1.103-1

of the authority, may amend the governing instrument and bylaws, must approve, in advance, each issue of obligations, and both review and approve annually the projected programs and projected expenditures of the authority, as well as annually post-reviewing programs and expenditures. Also, annual financial statements (including a statement of income and expenditures) were required to be reviewed by the city council, and the city council was provided access to all books and records of the authority. Pursuant to the formal action, the city B student loan authority was incorporated. The articles of incorporation of the authority, in addition to providing for the supervisory authority of the city, described above, state that the authority is not organized for profit and that any of the authority's net earnings will inure only to the benefit of the city. The articles of incorporation state further that upon dissolution of the authority, title to all property owned by the authority will vest in city B. The bond resolution for the obligations issued by the authority provides that in the event of default with respect to obligations issued to finance the acquisition of the student loan notes, the city has the exclusive option to purchase the loan notes and is provided a reasonable time to exercise such option and to finance such purchase. The city B student loan authority meets the requirements of paragraph (c)(2) of this section and the obligations issued by the authority qualify under this paragraph as obligations issued on behalf of a State or local governmental unit if prior to the issuance of any such obligations the obligations are approved by the city council or voters of city B.

Example (2). The S Corporation, incorporated under the nonprofit corporation law of State T was organized for the purpose of financing and operating a hospital located in city U, a municipality of State T. S Corporation's articles of incorporation state that the corporation is not organized for profit and that none of its net earnings will inure to the benefit of any private person. The board of directors of the corporation consists of representatives of private business groups in city U elected by the members of S Corporation and approved by city U. S Corporation issued obligations to finance the construction of a new wing for the hospital. In conjunction with the issuance of the obligations, a deed conveying title to the new wing was placed in escrow by S Corporation with the instructions that the escrow agent deliver the deed to city U upon retirement of the obligations. Also, S Corporation granted city U the right at any time to purchase the new wing for an amount sufficient to retire the outstanding indebtedness on such obligations. City U, prior to the issuance of obligations by S Corporation, approved S Corporation and the issue of obligations issued by S Corporation. City U also agreed to accept title to the new wing upon retirement of the obligations. The obligations issued by S Corporation are not issued "on behalf of" city U since the following requirements for an "on behalf of" issuer have not been met:

(i) There was no specific authorization, as described in paragraph (c)(2)(i) of this section.

(ii) S Corporation was not created by such specific authorization or by city U, pursuant to any such specific authorization, as required by paragraph (c)(2)(i) of this section.

(iii) City U does not control S Corporation, within the meaning of paragraph (c)(2)(ii) of this section.

(iv) City U does not have organizational control or supervisory control over S Corporation, as required by paragraph (c)(2)(iii) of this section.

Example (3). City C, a municipal corporation located in state D, was incorporated pursuant to a statute of state D which provides in part that "municipalities incorporated under this Act may issue obligations to provide funds for any purpose related to the general welfare of the residents of such municipality". The city C Airport Agency was incorporated under state D's not-for-profit corporation law for the purpose of constructing a municipal airport with the proceeds of obligations issued by the corporation "on behalf of" city C. Neither the state statute under which city C was incorporated nor any other statute of state D provides the specific authorization described in paragraph (c)(2)(i) of this section. Thus, obligations issued by the city C Airport Agency will not qualify under this section as obligations issued "on behalf of" city C.

Example (4). Assume the same facts as in Example (3) except that the State statute provides as follows:

"Except as limited by express provision or necessary implication of general law, a municipality may take all action necessary or convenient for the government of its local affairs." Neither the state statute under which city C was incorporated nor any other statute of state D provides the specific authorization described in paragraph (c)(2)(i) of this section. Thus, obligations issued by the city C Airport Agency will not qualify under this section as obligations issued "on behalf of" city C.

Example (5). A statute of state E provides that any incorporated municipality of the state is authorized to utilize an authority to issue obligations for a public purpose of the municipality. The Municipal Parking Act of state E provides that any incorporated municipality may create an authority under the Act for the purpose of utilizing the authority to issue obligations to provide a municipal parking garage. The Act provides that the authority is to be created under provisions of the Act which govern the structure, creation, and powers of the authority. In addition the Act provides that the municipality creating the authority may alter or change the structure, organization, program, or activities of the authority and may terminate the authority. City F creates a Municipal Parking Authority under the provisions of the Act. The charter of the authority provides that the sole purpose of the authority is to construct and operate a municipal parking garage, that any net earnings of the authority will be paid to city F, that title to all property owned by the authority at the time of its dissolution will vest in city F, and that all members of the authority are to be appointed by the mayor of city F. The authority satisfies the requirements of paragraph (c)(2) of this section, and obligations issued by the authority qualify under this section as obligations issued on behalf of a State or local governmental unit.

(4) Effective date. The provisions of this paragraph apply to obligations issued on or after 180 days after the adoption of this paragraph by a Treasury decision, or, at the option of the State or local governmental unit, to obligations issued on or after Feb. 2, 1976.

Section 1.103-7 is amended by adding two new sentences at the end of paragraph (d)(1) and adding a new paragraph (e) to read as follows:

§1.103-7 (Proposed Treasury Decision, published 12-6-77.) **Industrial development bonds.**

* * * * * * * * * * * *

(d) **Refunding obligations; old rules—(1) General rule.** * * * This paragraph does not apply to refunding issues to which paragraph (e) applies. See paragraph (e)(8).

(e) **Refunding obligations; new rules—(1) Treatment as industrial development bonds.** A refunding issue satisfies the trade or business test of section 103(b)(2)(A) if the prior issue satisfied the trade or business test. If the refunding issue also satisfies the security interest test of section 103(b)(2)(B), the refunding issue is an issue of industrial development bonds.

(2) **Special transitional rule.** (i) Notwithstanding paragraph (e)(1), a refunding issue is not an issue of industrial development bonds if—

(A) The prior issue was issued before the effective date of section 103(b) (May 1, 1968, or January 1, 1969, if the transitional rules of §1.103-12 are applicable); and

(B) The refunding issue matures no later than the prior issue.

(ii) For purposes of paragraph (e)(2)(i)(B), if portions of the prior issue mature on different dates, corresponding portions of the refunding issue must mature on or before each such maturity date. Thus, for example, if one half of the prior issue matures on January 1, 1980, and the other half matures on January 1, 1985, then one half of the refunding issue must mature on or before January 1, 1980, and the other half must mature on or before January 1, 1985.

(iii) A portion of an issue is deemed to mature at the time a mandatory sinking fund redemption is made.

Proposed Reg. § 1.103-7

(iv) The issuer may treat particular obligations which are part of a multipurpose issue (defined in paragraph (e)(7)(i)) as used to refund particular prior issues. See example (5) of paragraph (e)(9).

(3) **Exempt facilities.** In general, the proceeds of a refunding issue are used to provide an exempt facility (within the meaning of section 103(b)(4)) if substantially all of the proceeds of the prior issue were used to provide an exempt facility. However, the proceeds of a refunding issue are not used to provide an exempt facility if the refunding issue is issued more than 180 days before the prior issue is redeemed.

(4) **Industrial parks.** In general, the proceeds of a refunding issue are used to acquire or develop land as the site for an industrial park (within the meaning of section 103(b)(5)) if substantially all of the proceeds of the prior issue were used for such acquisition or development. However, the proceeds of a refunding issue are not used for such acquisition or development if the refunding issue is issued more than 180 days before the prior issue is redeemed.

(5) **Small issues.** The proceeds of a refunding issue are not used as described in section 103(b)(6)(A)(i) or (ii) if the refunding issue is issued more than 180 days before the prior issue is redeemed.

(6) **Definitions.** (i) A refunding issue is an issue the proceeds of which are used to pay principal, interest, or call premium on another issue (the "prior issue") or reasonable incidental costs of the refunding (e.g., legal and accounting fees, printing costs, and rating fees). An issue is not a refunding issue for purposes of this paragraph if the prior issue had a term of less than three years and was sold in anticipation of permanent financing. However, the aggregate term of all issues sold in anticipation of the permanent financing may not exceed three years.

(ii) An issue is redeemed at the time interest ceases to accrue on the issue.

(7) **Multipurpose issues.** (i) For purposes of this paragraph, the term "multipurpose issue" means an issue the proceeds of which are used—

(A) To refund two or more prior issues, or

(B) To refund one or more prior issues and also for other purposes (e.g., to provide additional facilities or working capital).

(ii) The portion of a multipurpose issue used to refund each prior issue is treated as a separate refunding issue for purposes of this paragraph. Any remaining portion of the multipurpose issue is treated as a separate issue for purposes of section 103(b).

(8) **Effective dates.** (i) Except as provided in paragraph (e)(8)(ii), this paragraph applies to refunding issues issued after 5:00 p.m. EST on November 4, 1977.

(ii) This paragraph does not apply to a refunding issue issued on or before December 15, 1977, if substantially all of the proceeds of the prior issue were used to provide residential real property for family units within the meaning of section 103(b)(4)(A).

(9) **Examples.** The following examples illustrate the application of this paragraph:

Example (1). On February 1, 1975, State A issued $20 million of 20-year revenue bonds. The bond proceeds were used to construct a sports stadium owned and operated by X, a nonexempt person, for use by the general public. The revenues derived from the sports stadium secured payment of the principal and interest on the bonds. On January 1, 1980, State A issues $15 million of 20-year refunding bonds at par. On February 1, 1980, State A uses $14.5 million of proceeds to redeem the outstanding principal amount of the prior issue. The remaining $.5 million of proceeds is used solely to pay call premium and reasonable incidental costs of the refunding. The sports stadium revenues secure payment of the principal and interest on the refunding issue. Because the prior issue satisfied the trade or business test of section 103(b)(2)(A), under paragraph (e)(1) the refunding issue also satisfies that test. In addition, the refunding issue satisfies the security interest test. Accordingly, the refunding obligations are industrial development bonds. Since, however, substantially all of the proceeds of the original issue were used to provide an exempt sports facility within the meaning of section 103(b)(4)(B), under paragraph (e)(3) the proceeds of the refunding issue are used to provide an exempt facility. As a result, section 103(b)(1) does not apply to the refunding issue.

Example (2). The facts are the same as in example (1), except that the prior issue is not callable until February 1, 1985. During the period when both the refunding and prior issues are outstanding, the proceeds of the refunding issue are invested in United States Treasury obligations. The interest earned on the Treasury obligations is used to pay debt service on the prior issue. Because the prior issue satisfied the trade or business test of section 103(b)(2)(A), under paragraph (e)(1) the refunding issue also satisfies that test. In addition, the refunding issue satisfies the security interest test of section 103(b)(2)(B), since the revenues from the sports stadium will be used to pay the debt service on the refunding issue. Accordingly, the refunding bonds are industrial development bonds. Since the refunding issue is issued more than 180 days before the prior issue is redeemed, the proceeds of the refunding issue are not considered under paragraph (e)(3) to be used to provide an exempt facility. As a result, section 103(b)(1) applies to the refunding issue, and interest on the refunding issue is included in gross income.

Example (3). The facts are the same as in example (2), except that interest earned on the Treasury obligations is used to pay debt service on the refunding issue until the prior issue is redeemed. The sports stadium revenues are used to pay debt service on the refunding issue beginning on February 1, 1985 (the date of redemption), rather than on January 1, 1980 (the date of issuance). The refunding issue satisfies the security interest test because the sports stadium revenues will be used to pay debt service on the refunding issue after the prior issue is redeemed. Accordingly, the result is the same as in example (2).

Example (4). On January 1, 1965 (before the effective date of section 103(b)), city B issued $10 million of 30-year revenue bonds. The bond proceeds were used to construct a manufacturing facility for corporation Y, a nonexempt person. Lease payments by Y secured payment of the principal and interest on the bonds. On January 1, 1978, B issues $7 million of refunding bonds which mature on January 1, 2005. On April 1, 1978, the proceeds of the refunding issue are used to redeem the outstanding principal amount of the prior issue. The lease payments by Y secure payment of the principal and interest on the refunding issue. Because the refunding issue matures later than the prior issue, the special transitional rule of paragraph (e)(2) does not apply. Moreover, the refunding issue is treated as an issue of industrial development bonds under paragraph (e)(1). Since the proceeds of the prior issue were not used to provide an exempt facility described in section 103(b)(4) or to acquire or develop land as the site for an industrial park described in section 103(b)(5), interest on the refunding issue is included in gross income.

Example (5). (a) On January 1, 1968, state D issued $20 million of 20-year revenue bonds to construct an office building. The office building is leased to and operated by Y, a nonexempt person. Lease payments by Y secured the payment of principal and interest on the bonds. One million dollars in principal amount of the 1968 issue matures on January 1 of each year 1969 to 1988.

(b) On January 1, 1970, state D issued $15 million of 20-year revenue bonds to construct a sports stadium. The sports stadium is owned and operated by Y for use by the general public. The revenues derived from the sports stadium secured the payment of principal and interest on the 1970 issue.

(c) On February 1, 1978, state D issues a $20.5 million multipurpose issue at par. The payment of principal and interest on the multipurpose issue is secured by lease payments by Y and by revenues derived from the sports stadium. The 1978 issue matures according to the following schedule:

January 1, 1979	---	$850,000
January 1, 1980	---	850,000
January 1, 1981	---	850,000
January 1, 1982	---	850,000
January 1, 1983	---	850,000
January 1, 1984	---	850,000
January 1, 1985	---	850,000

Proposed Reg. §1.103-7

January 1, 1986	- - -	850,000
January 1, 1987	- - -	850,000
January 1, 1988	- - -	850,000
after January 1, 1988	- - -	12,000,000

On March 1, 1978, state D uses $12 million of the proceeds of the multipurpose issue to redeem the outstanding principal amount of the 1970 issue. State D uses the remaining $8.5 million of proceeds to pay principal on the 1967 issue as it comes due.

(d) Under paragraph (e)(7), the multipurpose issue is treated as two separate issues— one $12 million refunding issue and one $8.5 million refunding issue. Under paragraph (e)(2)(iv), state D treats the $8.5 million refunding issue as having the following maturities:

January 1, 1979	- - -	$850,000
January 1, 1980	- - -	850,000
January 1, 1981	- - -	850,000
January 1, 1982	- - -	850,000
January 1, 1983	- - -	850,000
January 1, 1984	- - -	850,000
January 1, 1985	- - -	850,000
January 1, 1986	- - -	850,000
January 1, 1987	- - -	850,000
January 1, 1988	- - -	850,000

(e) Under paragraph (e)(1), the $12 million refunding issue satisfies the trade or business test since the prior issue satisfied that test. Because the $12 million refunding issue also satisfies the security interest test, it is an issue of industrial development bonds. However, since substantially all of the proceeds of the 1970 issue was used to provide an exempt sports facility within the meaning of section 103(b)(4)(B), under paragraph (e)(3) the proceeds of the $12 million refunding issue are used to provide an exempt facility.

(f) One tenth of the 1968 issue (disregarding the portion of the issue retired before February 1, 1978) matures on January 1 of each year 1979 to 1988. Because one tenth of the $8.5 million refunding issue also matures on January 1 of each year 1979 to 1988, the $8.5 million refunding issue satisfies the requirement in paragraph (e)(2)(ii). Because the requirements in paragraph (e)(2)(i) are also satisfied, the $8.5 million refunding issue is not treated as an issue of industrial development bonds.

(g) Section 103(b)(1) does not apply to any portion of the multipurpose issue.

Example (6). On January 1, 1993, city D issues $40 million of revenue bonds at par. Of the $40 million of bond proceeds, $37 million is used to refund a prior issue (i.e., to pay principal and interest on the prior issue, call premium, and reasonable incidental costs of refunding). The remaining $3 million is used to provide working capital to corporation X, a nonexempt person. Under paragraph (e)(7), the issue of revenue bonds is a multipurpose issue and is treated as two separate issues—a $37 million refunding issue and a $3 million issue to provide working capital. Assume that the $3 million issue satifies the security interest test of section 103(b)(2)(B). Based on these facts, the $3 million issue is treated as an issue of industrial development bonds and does not satisfy the requirements of section 103(b)(4), (5), or (6). Accordingly, section 103(b)(1) applies to the $3 million issue.

Example (7). On January 1, 1967 (before the effective date of section 103(b)), city E issued $50 million of 25-year revenue bonds. The proceeds of the 1967 issue were used to provide a manufacturing facility for use by corporation Z, a nonexempt person, and the 1967 issue therefore satisfied the trade or business test of section 103(b)(2)(A). On January 1, 1978, city E issues $40 million of 14-year revenue bonds to refund the 1967 issue. Under paragraph (e)(1), the 1978 issue satisfies the trade or business test of section 103(b)(2)(A). However, the 1978 issue is not treated as an issue of industrial development bonds. (See paragraph (e)(2).) On January 1, 1980, city E issues $38 million of 12-year revenue bonds to refund the 1978 issue. Under paragraph (e)(1), the 1980 issue satisfies the trade or business test of section 103(b)(2)(A). Assume that the 1980 issue also satisfies the security interest test of section 103(b)(2)(B). Based on these facts, the transitional rule in paragraph (e)(2) does not apply to the 1980 issue because the 1978 issue was issued after the effective date of section 103(b). Moreover, the proceeds of the 1980 issue are not treated under paragraph (e)(3) or (4) as used to provide an exempt facility or to acquire or develop land as the site for an industrial park. Section 103(b)(1) applies to the 1980 issue, and interest on the 1980 issue is included in gross income.

Section 1.103-8 is amended by adding two new sentences at the end of paragraph (a)(1)(i) and by revising paragraph (g). The new and revised provisions read as follows:

§ 1.103-8 (Proposed Treasury Decision, published 8-20-75.) **Interest on bonds to finance certain exempt facilities.**

(g) Air or water pollution control facilities—(1) General rule. Section 103(c)(4)(F) provides that section 103(c)(1) shall not apply to obligations issued by a State or local governmental unit which are part of an issue substantially all of the proceeds of which are to be used to provide air or water pollution control facilities. Such facilities are in all events treated as serving the general public and thus satisfy the public use requirement of paragraph (a)(2) of this section. Proceeds are used to provide air or water pollution control facilities if they are used to provide property which satisfies the requirements of paragraph (g)(2) of this section. Where property has a function other than to abate or control water or atmospheric pollution or contamination (hereinafter referred to as "control of pollution"), only the incremental cost of such property is taken into account as an expenditure to provide an air or water pollution control facility. Rules to determine whether property has any function other than the control of pollution are provided in paragraph (g)(2) and (3) of this section. Rules to determine the incremental cost of such property are provided in paragraph (g)(3) of this section.

(2) Definitions. (i) Property is a pollution control facility if it is property described in paragraph (g)(2)(ii) of this section and if either (A) a Federal, State, or local agency exercising jurisdiction has certified that the facility, as designed, is in furtherance of the purpose of abating or controlling atmospheric pollutants or contaminants, or water pollution, as the case may be, or (B) the facility is designed to meet or exceed applicable Federal, State, and local requirements for the control of atmospheric contaminants, or water pollution, as the case may be, in effect at the time the obligations, the proceeds of which are to be used to provide such facilities, are issued.

(ii) Property is described in this subdivision if it (A) is either of a character subject to the allowance for depreciation provided in section 167 or land, and (B) is used in whole or in part to abate or control water or atmospheric pollution or contamination by removing, altering, disposing, or restoring pollutants, contaminants, waste or heat (hereinafter individually and collectively referred to as a pollutant). Property is not described in the preceding sentence unless it is a unit which is discrete and which performs in whole or in part one or more of the functions referred to in such sentence and which canot be further reduced in size without losing one of such characteristics. The term "pollutant" does not include any material or heat unless such material or heat is in a state or form such that its discharge or release would result in water or atmospheric pollution or contamination. Property is not described

Proposed Reg. § 1.103-8

in this subdivision to the extent that such property avoids the creation of pollutants. Property which is used solely for the processing or manufacturing of material or heat after such material or heat is no longer a pollutant is not property described in this subdivision. Property is not a pollution control facility to the extent that such property treats or processes a material in such a manner as to prevent the discharge or release of pollutants when such material is subsequently used. Property to be used in the control of water pollution includes the necessary intercepting sewers, pumping, power, and other equipment, and their appurtenances. Such property is necessary if it removes, alters, disposes of, or stores a pollutant or is functionally related and subordinate to property used to control water pollution. In the case of property which removes pollutants from fuel, see paragraph (g)(2)(iv) of this section. For inclusion, as property described in this subdivision, of property functionally related and subordinate to an exempt pollution control facility, see paragraph (a)(3) of this section.

(iii) Property is not used for the control of pollution to the extent that it—

(A) Is designed to prevent the release of pollutants in a major accident,

(B) Prevents the release of materials or heat which would endanger the employees of the trade or business in which such property is used (as determined for example by Federal, State, or local employee occupational health or safety standards),

(C) Is used to control materials or heat that traditionally have been controlled because their release would constitute a nuisance,

(D) Controls the release of hazardous materials or heat that would cause an immediate risk of substantial damage or injury to property or persons, or

(E) Controls materials or heat in essentially the same manner as the user of such property has previously controlled such material or heat as a customary practice for reasons other than compliance with pollution control requirements. If such user previously has not generated such material or heat at the location where such material or heat is controlled, such customary practice shall be determined by reference to the use of similar property by similarly situated users.

For example, property is used in the manner described in paragraph (g)(2)(C) of this section and is not used to control pollution if such property is used to control from an uncontrolled level of 200 units to a level of 100 units the release of materials that traditionally has been controlled to that level because such release would constitute a nuisance. However, if pollution control requirements limit the level of emissions to 60 units, the use of the property to reduce and control the level of emissions from 100 units to 60 units is a use for pollution control. If the method of allocation described in paragraph (g)(3)(iii) of this section is used to allocate the cost of the functions of property used to control materials from a level of 200 units to a level of 60 units, factor Y in the ratio must include the present value of gross capital costs necessary to acquire a facility that limits the release of emissions to a level of 100 units and the present value of estimated expenses necessary to operate or maintain such facility.

(iv) A facility that removes elements or compounds from fuel which would be released as pollutants when such fuels are burned is not a pollution control facility whether or not such facility is used in connection with a plan or property where such fuels are burned. Such a nonqualifying facility includes all property used to remove such elements or compounds from fuel. Related facilities for the handling and treatment of wastes and other pollutants resulting from that removal process (including the elements and compounds removed) will qualify as pollution control facilities if such facilities meet the requirements of this paragraph.

(3) **Allocation.** (i) If property described in paragraph (g)(2) of this section is used to control pollution and also has a function other than the control of pollution, only the incremental cost of such property is taken into account as an expenditure to provide air or water pollution control facilities. The incremental

Proposed Reg. § 1.103-8

cost of such property is the portion of the cost of such property which is allocable to the control of pollution (as determined under paragraph (g)(3)(ii) or (iii) of this section). Examples of functions of property other than the control of pollution are an economic benefit to the user resulting from use of the property and a function described in paragraph (g)(2)(iii) of this section. The term "economic benefit" means gross income or cost savings resulting from any increase in production or capacity, production efficiencies, the production of a byproduct, the extension of the useful life of other property which is not described in paragraph (g)(2) of this section, and any other identifiable cost savings, such as savings resulting from the use, reuse, or recycling of items recovered. For purposes of the preceding sentence, where that part of property which controls pollution makes unnecessary the use of any property which otherwise would be necessary but for the use of the property which controls pollution, the term "cost savings" includes capital expenditures and operating and maintence expenses which need not be incurred as a result of the use of the pollution control property. In the case of property which (A) controls pollution, (B) results in an economic benefit, and (C) has a non-productive function other than the control of pollution such as employee safety, which is solely related to the facility, the allocation of the cost of the property between the pollution control function and the economic benefit includes any allocation of cost to such other nonproductive function, and no other allocation of cost to such nonproductive function is necessary.

(ii) The portion of the cost of property allocable to the control of pollution is determined by an allocation of the cost of such property between the property's **pollution control function** and any other functions that clearly reflects a separation of costs for each function of the property. The method of allocation described in paragraph (g)(3)(iii) of this section is presumed to clearly reflect such a separation of the costs of such functions. Notwithstanding the preceding sentence, an allocation of costs on the basis of accounting principles may overcome such presumption if such allocation is of adequate detail and specificity to clearly reflect a separation of costs for each function of the property.

(iii) In the case of property which results in an economic benefit, the portion of the cost of such property allocable to the control of pollution is the cost of the property reduced by the amount, if any, determined by applying to such cost the following ratio:

$$\frac{Y}{C+E},$$

where Y is the present value of all estimated economic benefits, net of any selling expenses, to be realized over the useful life of such property to the person in whose trade or business such property is used; C is the present value of payments (other than interest), present and future, necessary to acquire ownership of the property, less its estimated salvage value, adjusted for the burden of Federal income taxes; and E is the present value of all estimated expenses to be paid or incurred in operating and maintaining the property, including utilities, labor, property taxes (or payments in lieu of such taxes), State and local income taxes, insurance, and interest expense. In this ratio, if the sum of $C+E$ is less than Y, such sum shall be treated as being equal to Y. Where $C+E$ is used in determining Y, because an alternative facility need not be built, $C+E$ shall not be less than zero. Present value shall be computed by use of a discount rate of 12½ percent. The sum of $C+E$, expressed as present values, is an amount equal to the gross return to capital invested by the owner of the property which is sufficient to permit payment of Federal income tax, recover the investment, receive a net rate of return on invested capital of 12½ percent, and to recover other estimated costs of operating and maintaining the property. The two terms in the denominator are defined as follows:

$$E = PV(E_t)$$

$$C = \frac{PV(O_t) - PV(a_t) - mPV(d_t)}{1-m},$$

where

$PV(\ ) = $ present value of the terms enclosed within parentheses (*i.e.*, the sum of the discounted values of the indicated quantities),

$E_t = $ estimated expenses each year, when

$t = 1, 2, 3, \ldots n$, n being the last year of the period used in the computation,

$O_t = $ outlays each year necessary to acquire ownership of the property,

$a = $ investment credit,

$m = $ tax rate, and

$d_t = $ depreciation deduction allowable each year.

This formula is to be applied to the manner set forth in example (1) of paragraph (g)(5) of this section. In the definition of C above, the outlays, O_t, are the repayments of principal of a privately financed loan which would be sufficient to enable the user to acquire the property; the associated interest payments for such a loan are included in the term "estimated expenses", E. Therefore, no other computation is made for depreciation or any rental or purchase payments on such property, since such items are already taken into account. All estimated expenses other than interest shall be computed with reference to the useful life of the property to the person in whose trade or business such property is used. The outlays necessary to acquire ownership of the property and the interest expense shall be determined on the basis of (A) acquisition of the property by a loan equal to the cost of the property discharged by equal annual amortization payments, (B) the market rate of interest (as of any date during the 90 day period preceding the date of issue) for capital construction for the owner or operator of such property, or, if such rate is not known, the prime rate on any such date, and (C) an assumed maturity equal to the lesser of the useful life of the property used in determining Y or the term of the governmental obligations. In determining m the surtax exemption shall be disregarded; in determining d_t, depreciation shall be computed by use of the straight line method based on the same useful life of the property as is used in computing Y.

(4) **Effective date.** The provisions of this paragraph apply to obligations issued after August 20, 1975, except that, at the option of the issuer, the provisions of this paragraph prescribed by T.D. 7199, as corrected August 11, 1972 (37 F.R. 16177), shall apply to obligations issued before November 19, 1975, or to obligations issued with respect to facilities the construction, reconstruction, or acquisition (including, in the case of an acquisition, a binding contract to acquire such facility) of which commences before November 19, 1975.

(5) **Examples.** The principles of this paragraph may be illustrated by the following examples:

Example (1). (a) Company A, engaged in processing ore, is required under applicable law to limit emissions causing air pollution from its plant and plans to install equipment costing $9 million that will remove the pollutants generated in the processing of the ore and convert the pollutants into ore concentrate that can be used in A's business or can be sold. The equipment is discrete property used to abate or control air pollution by removing, altering, storing, or disposing of a pollutant. The equipment also functions in part to protect the safety of employees operating the equipment. The equipment will be acquired and placed in service in 1977. Company A intends to finance the equipment with 20-year industrial development bonds. The equipment has a useful life of 20 years to A. Company A allocates the $9 million cost of the property between its pollution control function and its productive function by the method described in paragraph (g)(3)(iii) of this section.

(b) On the basis of the current market price for ore concentrate, the annual economic benefit from the recovered ore is estimated to be $588,750. The total

Proposed Reg. § 1.103-8

economic benefit over the equipment's useful life is $11,775,000, which has a present value on the date of issue, at a 12½ percent discount rate, of $4,263,346.79. The operating and maintenance expense of the equipment over its useful life is estimated on the basis of current costs to be $10,875,000, which accrues ratably over the 20-year period and which has a present value on the date of issue, at a 12½ percent discount rate, of $3,937,485.89. To apply the formula in paragraph (g)(3)(iii) of this section, it is also necessary to know the present value of the annual interest expense which would be incurred, and the present value of company A's annual investment in the facility, determined as if the $9 million facility were financed on the basis of a loan amortized by equal annual payments. Interest expense is computed by use of an interest rate of 10 percent to the user on a 20-year obligation of $9 million discharged by equal annual payments.

The equal annual payments, computed by use of the formula

$$A = P \frac{i}{1-(1+i)^{-n}}$$

are $1,057,136.62 when

A = amount of annual repayment of principal and interest payable at the end of any year,

P = $9 million, the total amount borrowed,

i = .10 (i.e., a 10 percent rate of interest), and

n = 20, the term of the loan, in years.

The following 3 step calculation is used to determine the present value of all annual payments of principal and the present value of all annual payments of interest:

(1) Compute the present value of annual payments by use of the formula

$$PV(A_t) = A \frac{1-(1+r)^{-n}}{r}$$

when r = .125 (i.e., a 12½ percent discount rate);

(2) Compute the present value of principal repayments by use of the formula

$$PV(a_t) = \frac{a_1}{1+r} \left[\frac{1-\left(\frac{1+i}{1+r}\right)^n}{1-\left(\frac{1+i}{1+r}\right)} \right]$$

when

a_1 = the first year's principal repayment and $a_1 = A - iP$

(3) Compute the present value of interest payments by use of the formula

$$PV(I_t) = PV(A_t) - PV(a_t)$$

when $PV(I_t)$ = present value of annual interest payments over the term of the loan.

By use of the 3 step calculation, the total of the present values of all annual payments of principal is determined to be $2,275,499.19 and the total of the present values of all annual payments of interest is determined to be $5,379,600.65. The equipment will not have any salvage value at the end of its useful life.

(c) Using the method of allocation described in paragraph (g)(3)(iii) of this section, including a 12½ percent discount rate, the portion of the cost of the equipment allocable to pollution control is determined as follows:

Y = $4,263,346.79, the present value of the gross economic benefit realized over the equipment's useful life.

E = $9,317,086.54, the present value of the operating expense ($3,937,485.89) plus the present value of the interest expense ($5,379,600.65).

$$C = \$156,474.74 \text{ or } \frac{PV(O_t) - a - mPV(d_t)}{1-m}$$

where the present value of the outlays of principal (O_t) is $2,275,499.19, the investment credit (a) is $630,000, the rate of tax (m) is 48 percent, and the present value of the depreciation deductions (d_t) is $3,258,609.01. Thus, C is computed as follows:

$$\frac{\$2{,}275{,}499.19 - \$630{,}000 - .48\ (\$3{,}258{,}609.01)}{1 - .48}$$

The portion of the cost of the equipment allocable to the pollution control function is:

$$\$9{,}000{,}000 - \$9{,}000{,}000 \left[\frac{\$4{,}263{,}346.79}{\$156{,}474.74 + \$9{,}317{,}086.54} \right] \text{ or}$$

$$\$9{,}000{,}000 - \$4{,}050{,}232.01 = \$4{,}949{,}767.99$$

Thus, $4,949,767.99 of the cost of the equipment is allocable to pollution control.

Example (2). Company B operates a recovery boiler to recover valuable chemicals that can be used in its manufacturing process. In the course of operating the recovery boiler gases containing particulate material are generated which, when emitted into the environment, are in violation of new local air pollution control standards. To comply with local air pollution control standards, B plans to replace the existing recovery boiler with a new recovery boiler that is based on the latest manufacturing technology. As a result of more efficient combustion, fewer gases are generated and less particulate material is discharged. Company B also plans to acquire a new electrostatic precipitator to be used in conjunction with the new recovery boiler. The new recovery boiler when operated with the electrostatic precipitator does not violate the local air pollution control standards. The electrostatic precipitator is property described in paragraph (g)(2)(i) and (ii) of this section used to remove, alter, store, or dispose of pollutants. To the extent that the cost of the electrostatic precipitator is not applicable to the recovery of any chemicals, the cost of the electrostatic precipitator qualifies as an expenditure to provide a pollution control facility. The new recovery boiler avoids the creation of pollutants by generating fewer gases and discharging less particulate material. Therefore neither the new recovery boiler nor any part of it is property described in paragraph (g)(2)(i) and (ii) of this section used to remove, alter, store, or dispose of pollutants. The recovery boiler is not an exempt facility under section 103(c)(4)(F).

Example (3). C, an oil company, intends to construct a refinery in State X. A "sour" gas stream containing hydrocarbons and hydrocarbon sulphide will result from the refining process. Pollution control laws in State X limit the amount of sulphur dioxide that C can release into the environment. To comply with the State law, C must install amine absorbers, DEA strippers, and Claus-Beavon sulphur units (or functionally equivalent facilities) at the refinery. The amine absorbers will separate the "sour" gas into an amine solution containing hydrogen sulphide and a gas containing hydrocarbons. The hydrocarbon gas will be burned as fuel in the refinery. DEA strippers will remove the hydrogen sulphide from the amine solution. The hydrogen sulphide will be converted into sulphur by the Claus-Beavon sulphur recovery units and sold. Because the amine absorbers pretreat a fuel by removing hydrogen sulphide from the "sour" gas, the amine absorbers are not exempt facilities under section 103(c)(4)(F). To the extent that the cost of the DEA strippers and the Claus-Beavon facilities is not allocable to the function of sulphur production, the cost of such facilities qualifies as an expenditure to provide pollution control facilities.

Example (4). D proposes to use water from an adjacent river to cool new machinery at its plant. Heat realized in the course of operating the new machinery will be transferred to the water. Because the heated water would destroy marine life and thus constitute a risk to the general environment, local pollution control requirements do not permit D to release heated water into the river. To comply with the local pollution control requirements D plans to install a closed-loop facility consisting of pipes, cooling towers, and related equipment which will enable D to cool the water and reuse it in manufacturing. The closed-loop facility is discrete property used to abate or control water pollution. The cost of the closed-loop facility is allocable to the control of pollution to the extent that such cost is not allocable to any cost savings resulting from the reuse or recycling of water or any cost savings resulting because an alternate facility need not be constructed which would without any pollution control restrictions, be an adequate facility to

Proposed Reg. § 1.103-8

cycle water to and from the manufacturing plant. Accordingly, if an allocation of costs is made under paragraph (g)(3)(iii) of this section to determine the portion of the cost of the closed-loop facility allocable to pollution control, factor Y in the ratio must include the present value of gross capital costs necessary to acquire the alternate facility plus the present value of estimated expenses necessary to operate or maintain the alternate facility. These capital costs and estimated expenses are determined in the same manner as C and E in the ratio. The portion of the cost of the closed-loop facility allocable to pollution control is determined by reducing the cost of the facility by an amount determined by applying to such cost the ratio

$$\frac{C^1 + E^1}{C + E},$$

where C^1 and E^1 are the present values of the capital costs necessary to acquire the alternative facility and the estimated expenses to operate and maintain such facility and C and E are the present values of the costs and expenses of the closed loop facility thus, assume that the cooling tower costs $10,000,000 and that the cost of the pipes, pumps and other equipment interconnecting with the machinery is $2,000,000. Assume further that the present value of such costs plus the present value of the operating and maintenance expenses for such property is $20,000,000. Also assume that the present value of the gross capital costs of the alternate facility necessary to bring water to the machinery and return it to the river is $5,000,000 and that the present value of the operating and maintenance expenses for such alternate facility is $7,000,000. The portion of the cost of the closed-loop facility allocable to pollution control under paragraph (g)(3)(iii) of this section is $12,000,000—

$$\left[\$12,000,000 \times \frac{\$12,000,000}{20,000,000} \right] \text{ or } \$4,800,000.$$

Example (5). E, a utility, plans to construct an electric generating plant powered by nuclear fuel. The plant will be located adjacent to city Y. The plant will have several types of facilities to prevent the release of radioactive materials into the air or water. The containment facility, the emergency core cooling system, and the emergency service water system will be designed to function in the event of a major accident, such as a loss of coolant. Under paragraph (g)(2)(iii) of this section, property designed to prevent a release of radioactive materials which would occur only in the event of a major accident is not property used for pollution control. Thus, expenditures for the containment facility, the emergency core cooling system, and the emergency service water system are not expenditures for a pollution control facility under section 103(c)(4)(F). The plant will also contain radwaste systems that will treat gas and liquid waste streams and solid waste materials containing radioactive materials which arise in the ordinary course of the plant operations. The radwaste systems are designed to prevent injury to the employees of the plant and the residents of city Y which would result if the material were released. Consequently, under paragraph (g)(2)(iii)(B) and (D) of this section, property used in the radwaste systems is not used for pollution control, and expenditures for such property are not expenditures for a pollution control facility under section 103(c)(4)(F). Water used in the generating plant will be pumped through a cooling facility the sole function of which is to cool the heated water prior to the discharge of the water into an adjacent river. The cooling facility is discrete property used to abate or control water pollution by altering the heated water into a nonpollutant. The cost of the cooling facility is an expenditure for a pollution control facility to the extent that such cost is not allocable to any cost savings resulting because an alternate facility need not be constructed which, without regard to any pollution control requirements, would be an adequate facility to cycle water to and from the manufacturing plant.

Example (6). F intends to construct a facility that generates electricity by use of a turbine which by design requires a water cooled condenser to operate at peak efficiency. The only source of water available to F is an underground spring from which F can pump limited amounts of water. In order to cool the condenser with the available water, F installs a closed-loop facility which will enable F to cool and reuse the water. The closed-loop facility is property which is used in electric generating plants as a customary practice and for reasons other than compliance with pollution control requirements to dispose of heat in water which is reused when an adequate water source is not available at the plant location. Accordingly, under the last sentence of paragraph (g)(2)(ii)(B) of this section, the closed-loop facility is not used to control pollution and is not a pollution control facility.

Example (7). G, a manufacturing company, uses a mineral in its manufacturing process which generates pollutants in violation of local pollution control requirements. To comply with local pollution control requirements, G plans to construct equipment that will wash the mineral with water so that the mineral will not generate pollutants when used in the manufacturing process. The fact that the equipment treats or processes the mineral in such a manner as to prevent the discharge or release of pollutants when the mineral is subsequently used does not qualify the equipment as a pollution control facility. Accordingly, none of the cost of the equipment qualifies as an expenditure to provide a pollution control facility. However, any additional equipment that treats water used to wash the mineral may qualify under paragraph (g)(2) of this section as property used to control pollution.

Example (8). Company H operates a manufacturing facility and is required by State pollution laws to lower the amount of waste which it emits into the environment. To satisfy this requirement H installs a series of three machines. The first machine converts the waste into a chemical which is not a pollutant. The second machine grinds the chemical into a powder and the third machine packages the powdered chemical for sale. The first machine is discrete property used to abate or control pollution. Since the chemical which leaves the first machine is not a pollutant, and the second and third machines are used solely for the processing of the chemical, none of the cost of the second and third machines qualifies as an expenditure to provide air or water pollution control facilities. The first machine is the smallest unit of property which functions to control pollution. Since the first machine functions both to control pollution and to produce an economic benefit (a chemical which when processed and packaged can be sold) only the incremental cost of the machine is taken into account as an expenditure to provide air or water pollution control facilities. If an allocation of costs is made under paragraph (g)(3)(iii) of this section to determine the portion of the cost of the first machine allocable to pollution control, factor Y in the ratio must include the present value of the unprocessed chemical resulting from the operation of the first machine.

Example (9). Company J, a mining company, intends to construct a tailings basin and an overflow treatment facility. Waste in the form of a slurry of water and tailings from the production of iron ore pellets will be pumped to the tailings basin where the tailings will settle and the water will be recycled and reused. The overflow treatment facility treats any slurry which overflows from the basin. The overflow treatment facility removes the tailings from the slurry prior to discharge of the residue into an adjacent river. Local pollution control laws prohibit the discharge of tailings into public watercourses. The basin is property which controls material in essentially the same manner as similarly situated users previously have controlled such material as a customary practice for reasons other than compliance with pollution control requirements. Accordingly, the tailings basin is not an exempt facility under section 103(c)(4)(F). The overflow treatment facility is discrete property used to abate or control water pollution, and the cost of the overflow treatment facility qualifies as an expenditure to provide pollution control facilities.

* * * * * * * * * * *

Proposed Reg. § 1.103-8

There are inserted immediately after §1.103-12 the following new sections:

§1.103-13 (Proposed Treasury Decision published 5-3-73; 12-3-75; 10-29-76; 5-31-77; 6-9-77 and 5-8-78.) **Arbitrage bonds.**

(a) **Scope—(1) In general.** Under section 103(c)(1), an arbitrage bond shall be treated as an obligation not described in section 103(a)(1) and §1.103-1. Thus, the interest on an arbitrage bond will be included in gross income and subject to Federal income taxation. In general, arbitrage bonds are obligations issued by a State or local governmental unit, the proceeds of which are reasonably expected to be used to acquire other obligations where the yield on such acquired obligations will be materially higher than the yield on the governmental obligations during the term of such governmental issue. The term "arbitrage bond" is defined in paragraph (b)(1) of this section. Under paragraph (b) of §1.103-14, the investment of all or a portion of the proceeds of an issue of obligations for a temporary period or periods will not cause such obligations to be arbitrage bonds regardless of the yield produced by such investment. Paragraph (b)(6) and (7) of §1.103-14 provides a temporary period for investment proceeds and indirect proceeds. Under paragraph (b)(1) of this section, the investment of less than a major portion of the proceeds of the issue in materially higher yield acquired obligations will not cause such obligations to be arbitrage bonds. Similarly, under paragraph (d) of §1.103-14, the investment of a portion of the proceeds as a reasonably required reserve or replacement fund will not cause such obligations to be arbitrage bonds regardless of the yield produced by such investment. Even if an obligation is not an arbitrage bond under section 103(c), such bond may nevertheless be treated as an obligation which is not described in section 103(a)(1) and §1.103-1 if it is an industrial development bond under section 103(b). For regulations as to special issues of Federal Treasury obligations offered to State and local governmental units, see 31 CFR Part 344.

(2) **Reasonable expectations.** (i) Under section 103(c)(2), the determination whether an obligation is an "arbitrage bond" depends upon the reasonable expectations, as of the date of the issue, regarding the amount and use of the proceeds of the issue. Thus, an obligation is not an arbitrage bond, if, based on the reasonable expectations on the date of issue as to the use of the proceeds of the issue, the proceeds will not be used in a manner that would cause the obligation to be an "arbitrage bond" under section 103(c)(2), this section and §§1.103-14 and 1.103-15. Reasonable expectations regarding the amount and use of the proceeds on or before September 1, 1978, may be established by the certification described in subdivision (ii) of this subparagraph. Reasonable expectations as to future events regarding a governmental obligation issued after September 1, 1978 may be established to the extent permitted by the certification described in subdivision (iii) of this subparagraph. See paragraph (b)(2)(iii) of this section for the treatment of indirect proceeds.

(ii) A State or local governmental unit may certify, in the bond indenture or a related document, that on the basis of the facts, estimates, and circumstances (including covenants of such governmental unit) in existence on the date of issue it is not expected that the proceeds of the issue of obligations will be used in a manner that would cause such obligations to be arbitrage bonds. A certification by any officer of the issuer charged either alone or with others with the responsibility for issuing the obligations may be relied upon as a certification of the issuer. The certification shall set forth such facts, estimates, and circumstances, which may be in brief and summary terms, and state that to the best of the knowledge and belief of the certifying officer there are no other facts estimates, or circumstances that would materially change such expectation. In the case of refunding issue sold on or after October 29, 1976 or issued after November 28, 1976, the certification shall specify the purpose or purposes of the refunding issue (for example, whether to defease a lien or for interest savings), including in the case of interest savings a statement of the interest to be saved and the present value thereof, and, if computation of yield will be necessary under paragraph (c) of this section, the certification shall also enumerate the administrative costs, and the amounts thereof, taken into account in computing yield and describe how and the basis on which such costs are allocated to the refunding issue or to the acquired obligations acquired with the proceeds of such issue, and shall state that the price paid for the refunding issue is reasonable under customary standards applicable in the market (see subparagraph (3) of this paragraph). The preceding sentence shall not apply if the refunding issue refunds an issue to which §1.103-14(c) applies, or a prior issue, the term of which does not exceed 3 years, which was issued in anticipation of permanent financing. For this purpose, the prior issue may itself have been a refunding issue issued in anticipation of permanent financing but the aggregate terms of all such prior issues may not exceed 3 years. In the case of an issue of governmental obligations with a face amount of $2,500,000 or more, the certification shall be accompanied by an opinion of counsel that—

(A) Based upon such investigations as counsel deemed reasonably appropriate under the circumstances, which shall be generally described, such certification is not unreasonable, or

(B) Based on such counsel's examination of law and review of the certification, the facts, estimates and circumstances are sufficiently set forth in the certification to satisfy the criteria which are necessary under section 103(c), this section, §1.103-14, and §1.103-15 to support the conclusion that the obligations of the issue will not be arbitrage bonds, and that no matters have come to such counsel's attention which make unreasonable or incorrect the representations made in the certification. The certification described in this subdivision is not affected by subsequent events, and, unless a notice under subdivision (iii) of this subparagraph is in effect with respect to the State or local governmental unit prior to the date on which an obligation of such unit is issued, holders of such obligation may conclusively rely on such certification with regard to whether the interest on such obligation is incuded in gross income.

(iii) (A) A State or local governmental unit may certify, in the bond indenture or a related document, reasonable expectations of the issuer on the date of the issue as to the future events, such as use of funds. For example, matters which may be certified include: the use to which amounts received from sale of the bonds will be put; the date on which a project financed by a sale of bonds will be completed; the amount that will be spent for construction of such a project; and that a reserve or replacement fund of a certain amount will be established. On the other hand, an issuer may not certify that a reserve or replacement fund is reasonably required because the reasonableness of a reserve fund is an opinion or judgment that can be made before the date of issuance. As such it is not a reasonable expectation as to a future event.

(B) A State or local governmental unit may not certify conclusions of law (including legal characterizations of future events). For example, an issuer may not certify the statement that an obligation is not an arbitrage bond, or the statement that a major portion of the proceeds of an issue is not reasonably expected to be used directly or indirectly to acquire securities or obligations which may be reasonably expected to produce a yield over the term of the issue which is materially higher than the yield on the obligations of such issue. Both these statements are conclusions of law. In addition, a unit may not certify the date on which a temporary period ends because that is a conclusion of law. Similarly, a unit may not certify the statement that an obligation will produce a certain yield. This is because the statement uses "yield" as a defined legal term. Thus, the statement assumes that yield has been determined in a proper manner, which is a conclusion of law. On the other hand, a unit may describe the manner in which it has computed yield and certify that the yield on an obligation (determined in the manner described) is equal to a certain amount. In this statement yield is not used as a defined legal term. Therefore, the statement does not assume any conclusions of law. Further, a unit may not certify that the original proceeds of an issue will not exceed by more than 5 percent the amount necessary for the purpose of the issue. This statement uses two defined legal terms: "original proceeds" and "issue". On the other hand, a unit may certify the amount that will be received from the sale of certain obligations and the amount necessary for a particular purpose.

(C) An officer responsible for issuing the bonds must act for the issuer.

(D) In addition to the matters certified, the certification must set forth the facts and estimates on which the issuer's expectations are based and state that, to the best of the knowledge and belief of the certifying officer, the issuer's expectations are reasonable.

Proposed Reg. §1.103-13

(E) (1) If the temporary period for a construction issue is more than 3 years but not more than 5 years, the issuer must commission an independent architect or engineer to prepare a study of the planned construction.

(2) The study prepared by the architect or engineer must accompany the certification, and must include an estimated completion date for each stage of the construction.

(F) Subsequent events do not affect a certification made in accordance with this subdivision.

(iv) (A) If a certification contains a material misrepresentation, the Commissioner may disqualify the issuer. The Commissioner will publish notice that the issuer is disqualified in the Internal Revenue Bulletin. The disqualification will not affect bonds issued before the notice is published.

(B) An issuer that is disqualified may not certify an issue under subdivision (ii) or (iii) of this subparagraph.

(C) The Commissioner will give an issuer reasonable opportunity to be heard before it is disqualified.

(D) If appropriate, the Commissioner may requalify an issuer. The Commissioner will publish notice that the issuer has been requalified in the Internal Revenue Bulletin.

(v) The provisions of this subparagraph may be illustrated by the following example:

Example (1). (i) On July 5, 1973, City A issues $2,250,000 in municipal bonds for the purpose of paying the cost of constructing and equipping a new water treatment facility. The cost of the facility is $1,900,000 and a reserve and replacement fund of $337,500 is planned. The bonds are dated July 1, 1973 and are payable in equal annual installments beginning on July 1, 1974, and ending on July 1, 1993, with interest payable on January 1 and July 1 of each year. The bonds are sold at price of par plus a premium of $5,000 and accrued interest (from July 1, 1973) of $128.00. The amounts received as premium and accrued interest are to be applied to the first payment of debt service. All additional debt service is to be paid from general revenue funds. City A determines that the yield on the issue of its obligations is 5 percent. Prior to the time that the bond proceeds are needed for the project, the city intends to use part of the proceeds to acquire Federal Treasury obligations which mature before June 30, 1976, and to deposit the remaining proceeds of the issue in noninterest bearing demand deposits. The yield on the Treasury obligations and the demand deposits when computed together is $6\frac{1}{2}$ percent. The city expects to enter into a contract for architectural services for the facility on or before October 31, 1973, and the fee to be paid to the architect is $50,000. City A expects to proceed with the project thereafter with due diligence to completion. The city expects to spend $1,900,000 on the project by July 5, 1976, which is more than 85 percent of spendable proceeds. (Spendable proceeds were $1,912,500 i.e., original proceeds of $2,255,128 minus the sum of the amount of premium and accrued interest applied to debt service ($5,128) and the amount of a reasonably required reserve fund ($337,500).) After paying the full cost of $1,900,000 for constructing the facility and applying the premium of $5,000 and accrued interest of $128 to debt service, City A will have proceeds of $350,000. (All earnings received during the construction period are to be transferred within one year of receipt to the city's general fund, as will be done with all subsequent earnings, and, consequently, such earnings are not treated as proceeds.) City A plans to invest $337,500 in acquired obligations with a yield of $6\frac{1}{2}$ percent and $12,500 in acquired obligations with a yield of $5\frac{1}{8}$ percent. The city has no plans to sell the facility.

(ii) City A includes in the bond indenture a certification which reads as follows:

"The undersigned Treasurer of City A certifies and reasonably expects that the following will occur with respect to the bonds of the city dated July 1, 1973: (1) the city will enter into a contract for architectural services for the project financed by the bonds within 6 months from the date of issue of the bonds, and the fees to be paid to the architect thereunder will exceed $2\frac{1}{2}$ percent of the total cost of the project; (2) work on the project will proceed thereunder with due diligence to completion; (3) at least 85 percent of the spendable proceeds of the bonds will be expended for project costs by July 5, 1976; (4) the yield on the municipal obligations is computed to be 5 percent, and the yield on the acquired obligations which are to be allocated to the proceeds of this bond issue except obligations in a reasonably required reserve or replacement fund and obligations held only during the temporary period is 5⅛ percent; (5) the project will not be sold or otherwise disposed of, in whole or in part, prior to the last maturity of the bonds; (6) the original proceeds of this issue will not exceed by more than 5 percent the amount necessary for the purpose of purposes of the issue.

"On the basis of the foregoing, it is not expected that the proceeds of the bonds will be used in a manner that would cause the bonds to be arbitrage bonds under section 103(c) of the Internal Revenue Code and the regulations prescribed under that section. To the best of my knowledge and belief, there are no other facts, estimates, or circumstances that would materially change the foregoing conclusion."

(iii) The certification by City A meets the requirements of this subparagraph.

Example (2). The facts are the same as in example (1) except that the bonds of a face amount of $2,500,000 are issued for that amount and the project will cost $2,150,000. The city attorney of City A chooses to write an opinion under the provisions of subdivision (ii)(A) of this subparagraph to accompany the certification. The following opinion meets the requirements of this subparagraph:

"I, City attorney for City A, have conducted an investigation regarding the issuance on July 5, 1973, of $2,500,000 in municipal water treatment facility bonds. This investigation included: (1) an examination of the proposed contract with the architect; (2) consultation with the city treasurer regarding (a) the reinvestment of investment proceeds received during the term of the issue, (b) the use of the proceeds of the issue remaining after the temporary period, (c) the amount of expenditures for the project during the temporary period, (d) the acquired obligations which are to be allocated to the proceeds of the issue, and (e) the method used to determine the yield of the obligations of the issue and acquired obligations to be allocated to the issue; (4) consultation with the city manager regarding plans for the sale or disposition of the facility; (5) an examination of the amount needed for the purpose of the issue and the amount of the issue. Based upon the above described examination, it is my opinion that the certification of the city treasurer is not unreasonable."

Example (3). (i) The facts are the same as in example (1)(i) except that the bonds are issued on July 5, 1980, and all other dates are appropriately adjusted. City A includes in the bond indenture a certification which contains a statement that 85% of the receipts from sale of the bonds will be used for construction costs by July 5, 1983.

(ii) Construction of the water treatment facility was determined by the Environmental Protection Agency to have certain adverse environmental effects. Consequently, work on the project was halted and the facility was redesigned to avoid the effects with the result that 85% of the receipts from sale of the bonds will not be expended for project costs by July 5, 1983. The certification is conclusive as to the issuer's reasonable expectations that 85% of receipts will be expended for construction costs by July 5, 1983.

(iii) Under the circumstances described in subdivision (ii), city A has not made a material misrepresentation in the certification which would permit the Commissioner to disqualify city A under subdivision (iv) of this subparagraph. If, however, city A did not actually expect that 85% of the receipts from sale of the bonds would be used for construction costs by July 5, 1983, the certification would contain a material misrepresentation. Under those circumstances, the Commissioner may disqualify city A.

Example (4). On January 1, 1980, city A sells $5 million of 6 percent refunding bonds. City A certifies the bonds in the manner provided in subdivision (iii) of this subparagraph. In addition, attorney X gives an opinion that the bonds are not arbitrage bonds. In connection with the refunding issue, city A makes use of a certain artifice or device. This artifice or device is not identified as specifically prohibited by section 103(c) or the regulations thereunder. However, as a result of the artifice or device, city A is able to exploit the difference between tax-exempt and taxable interest rates to gain a financial advantage. This financial advantage serves as a material inducement for city A to sell the refunding bonds, or to issue more refunding bonds than would otherwise be necessary, or to allow the refunding bonds to remain outstanding longer than would otherwise be necessary. Based on these facts, the artifice or device is an attempt to defeat purposes of sec-

Proposed Reg. §1.103-13

tion 103(c). Because section 103(c) and the regulations thereunder are intended to prevent the use of such an artifice or device, the legal conclusion as reached by attorney X is erroneous. Therefore, the refunding bonds are arbitrage bonds despite the certification.

(3) **Reasonable purchase price.** (i) In determining whether the purchase price of a refunding issue is reasonable for purposes of subparagraph (2)(ii) of this paragraph, each refunding issue must be judged separately and individually.

(ii) The application of this subparagraph may be illustrated by the following example:

Example. On May 13, 1977, City A sells $10.4 million principal amount of 7-percent revenue bonds and $5 million principal amount of 4-percent special obligations bonds to underwriter X. Underwriter X pays $10.6 million for the revenue bonds and $4.8 million for the special obligation bonds. Assume that $15.4 million is a reasonable price for both issues together, but also assume that the special obligation bonds could be sold separately to another underwriter for at least $4.85 million and that the revenue bonds could not be sold separately to any other underwriter for more than $10.5 million. Since each refunding issue must be judged separately and individually, neither the purchase price of the revenue bonds nor the purchase price of the special obligation bonds can be considered reasonable.

(4) **Effective date.** The provisions of section 103(c), this section, and §1.103-14 apply with respect to obligations issued after October 9, 1969. Notwithstanding the rule in the preceding sentence, obligations issued prior to June 4, 1973, will not be arbitrage bonds if such obligations are not arbitrage bonds under the provisions of the proposed regulations under section 103(c) of the Internal Revenue Code of 1954, relating to arbitrage bonds, appearing in the Federal Register for June 1, 1972 (37 FR 10946), but in determining whether obligations issued after March 8, 1973, are arbitrage bonds, the yield on governmental obligations and acquired obligations may be computed pursuant to the method described in §1.103-13(c) of such proposed regulations only if such method does not significantly distort yield. In the case of a refunding issue which is issued prior to Jan. 2, 1976, the rules of §1.103-13(b)(5)(i), (ii), and (iii), and §1.103-14(e) of the proposed regulations under section 103(c) of the Internal Revenue Code of 1954, relating to arbitrage bonds, appearing in the Federal Register for June 1, 1972 (37 FR 10946), may be applied in lieu of the rules of paragraph (b)(5)(ii) and (iii) of this section and §1.103-14(e). In the case of governmental obligations issued prior to Jan. 2, 1976, the provisions of both §1.103-13(b)(1)(ii) and §1.103-14(d)(1) of the proposed regulations under section 103(c) of the Internal Revenue Code of 1954, relating to arbitrage bonds, appearing in the Federal Register for May 3, 1973 (38 FR 10944), may be applied in lieu of the provisions of both paragraph (b)(1)(ii) of this section and §1.103-14(d)(1), and the provisions of §1.103-14(a)(2) and (3) of such proposed regulations may be applied in lieu of the provisions of paragraph (b)(9) of this section. The rules of §1.103-14(b)(8) do not apply with respect to obligations issued before Jan. 2, 1976. See paragraph (b)(6) of this section for definition of the term "date of issue." For purposes of the effective date rules in this section and §1.103-14, an issue issued before December 29, 1976 shall be deemed to be issued before November 29, 1976 if the issue must be validated by judicial proceedings and those proceedings were commenced before November 29, 1976. The amendments made by the notice of proposed rulemaking published in the FEDERAL REGISTER for May 31, 1977 (42 FR 27610) apply to issues sold after May 25, 1977.

(b) **Definitions.** For purposes of this section and §1.103-14, the following definitions and rules shall apply:

(1) **Arbitrage bonds.** (i) Under section 103(c)(2), an obligation is an arbitrage bond if it is issued by a State or local governmental unit as part of an issue of obligations (for purposes of this section §1.103-14, and §1.103-15 referred to as "governmental obligations") all or a major portion of the proceeds of which are reasonably expected to be used directly or indirectly—

(A) To acquire obligations which may reasonably be expected, on the date of issue of such governmental obligations, to produce a yield during the term of the issue of such governmental obligations which is materially higher than the yield on such issue, or.

(B) To replace funds which were used directly or indirectly to acquire such acquired obligations.

(ii) A major portion of the proceeds of an issue is any amount which at any time exceeds 15 percent of the original face amount of the issue. If the original proceeds of an issue determined without regard to issuing expenses are less than 98 percent of the original face amount of the issue, the percentage specified in the preceding sentence shall be based on the amount of such original proceeds. See §1.103-14(e) for special rules that apply to refunding issues. In determining whether acquired obligations allocable to proceeds invested as less than a major portion at a materially higher yield are so invested in the case of obligations issued after October 29, 1976, a major portion of the proceeds is invested at a materially higher yield if one or more of such obligations is acquired at a discount or results in interest payments for any annual period in excess of interest payments for any preceding annual period (thus reinvesting annually accrued interest or discount as principal) and if by taking into account the amount of such discount or excess interest (not discounted to present value) ratably each year over the term of such obligation the sum of such amounts plus the purchase price of all obligations allocable to less than a major portion at any time exceeds the amount specified in this paragraph (b)(1)(ii). The term "materially higher" is defined in subparagraph (5) of this paragraph. Yield is computed under paragraph (c) of this section. For rules with respect to bonds issued to finance certain governmental programs and with respect to exempt arbitrage bonds for educational personnel, see, respectively, paragraphs (d) and (e) of this section. Acquired obligations are defined in subparagraph (4) of this paragraph and are allocated under paragraph (f) of this section to proceeds of governmental obligations.

(2) **Proceeds.** The types of proceeds attributable to an issue of governmental obligations are defined and illustrated as follows:

(i) "Original proceeds" are net amounts (after payment of all expenses of issuing the obligations) received by the Sate or local governmental unit as a result of the sale of such issue. Examples of issuing expenses are advertising and printing costs, financial advisors' and counsel fees, initial fees of trustees, paying agents, certifying or authenticating agents, and similar expenses.

(ii) "Investment proceeds" are amounts received at any time by the issuer, such as interest and dividends, resulting from the investment of any proceeds of an issue of obligations in acquired non-purpose obligations and amounts received as interest or dividends resulting from the investment of any proceeds of such issue in acquired purpose of obligations. Thus, for example, the interest received on acquired Federal obligations purchased with the proceeds of an issue of governmental obligations constitutes investment proceeds of such issue whether or not such acquired obligations represent amounts invested for a temporary period or in a reasonably required reserve or replacement fund under §1.103-14. Investment proceeds are increased by any profits and decreased (if necessary, below zero) by any losses on such investments. Amounts received from the investment of any proceeds of an issue (other than a refunding issue issued after June 9, 1977) are not investment proceeds if, within one year of receipt, such amounts are commingled for the purpose of accounting for expenditures with substantial tax or other substantial revenues from the operations by a State or local governmental unit.

(iii) (A) "Indirect proceeds" are amounts received at any time by the issuer as repayments of principal on acquired purpose obligations and to the extent that proceeds of an issue of governmental obligations are expended to finance property, the recovery of principal from the sale or other disposition by such issuer of such property.

(B) "Indirect proceeds" are included within the definition of the term "proceeds" if such indirect proceeds are unreasonably accumulated during the term of the issue. Indirect proceeds are unreasonably accumulated if on the date of issue it is probable that such accumulated proceeds together with any accumulated original and investment proceeds would be sufficient to enable the issuer to retire substantially all of the issuer's debt on the issue at a date which is significantly earlier than the last maturity date of the issue (regardless of whether such issue is callable on such earlier date).

Proposed Reg. § 1.103-13

(C) The provisions of this subdivision may be illustrated by the following example:

Example. On January 1, 1974, City A issues $1,000,000 of 20-year serial noncallable governmental obligations with level debt service. City A plans to expend all the original proceeds of the issue to finance the construction of a municipal parking lot at a cost of $1,000,000. At the time the bonds are issued, City A plans to sell the parking lot on July 1, 1985, for $600,000 cash. As a result of the sale, City A will have on hand on July 1, 1985, indirect proceeds that are sufficient to pay substantially all of the principal, with interest to such date, of the outstanding governmental obligations. Since on the date of issue City A could reasonably have foreseen that substantially all of the governmental obligations could be retired on July 1, 1985, there is an unreasonable accumulation of indirect proceeds. Accordingly, the indirect proceeds of the issue must be taken into account as proceeds for purposes of section 103(c).

(3) **State or local governmental unit.** The term "State or local governmental unit" shall have the same meaning as in paragraph (a) of §1.103-1.

(4) **Acquired obligations.** (i) The term "acquired obligations" means securities and obligations allocated to the proceeds of an issue of governmental obligations during the period of time that such issue is outstanding.

(ii) The term "securities" has the same meaning as in section 165(g)(2)(A) and (B). Thus, the term "security" means (A) a share of stock in a corporation or (B) a right to subscribe for, or to receive, a share of stock in a corporation.

(iii) The term "obligation" means any evidence of indebtedness which is not described in section 103(a)(1). Thus, for example, if interest on a bond issued by a State or local governmental unit is not exempt in the hands of the holder because it is an industrial development bond or an arbitrage bond, the bond is an obligation within the meaning of this subdivision. For another example, a transaction which in form is a lease of property by a State or local governmental unit, but which is treated for Federal income tax purposes as a loan (or an installment sale) is an obligation for purposes of this subdivision. Time or demand deposits (whether or not such deposits are interest-bearing) are "obligations" within the meaning of this subdivision to the extent that such deposit or deposits are maintained for the purposes for which the proceeds of the issue of obligations may be expended (including as a purpose any investment in a reserve or replacement fund). Cash is not an acquired obligation. For example, cash held or received by the trustee of an issue is not taken into account as a zero-yield obligation for the period it is held before being invested in an acquired obligation or for the period that it is held after repayment of an obligation and before being reinvested in an acquired obligation. A contract between the issuer and another person is an acquired obligation if the other person is required under the contract personally (and not in his capacity as trustee or agent) to discharge any obligation of the issuer.

(iv) The classes of acquired obligations and the definitions of such classes are as follows:

(A) "Acquired purpose obligations" are obligations acquired to carry out the purpose of a governmental program for which the governmental obligations are issued. Thus, for example, a note secured by a mortgage on a facility built with the proceeds of an exempt small issue of industrial development bonds (within the meaning of section 103(c)(6) and §1.103-10) is an acquired purpose obligation in the hands of the issuer of such exempt small issue. Obligations acquired solely for the purpose of realizing an arbitrage profit are not acquired purpose obligations. Acquired obligations acquired with proceeds of a refunding issue that are to be used to discharge the prior issue or that are invested in a reasonably required reserve or replacement fund are less than a major portion are not acquired purpose obligations. However, acquired obligations acquired with transferred proceeds may be acquired purpose obligations if such obligations would have been so treated if the prior issue had not been refunded.

(B) "Acquired nonpurpose obligations" are acquired obligations other than acquired purpose obligations.

(5) **Materially higher.** (i) The yield produced by acquired obligations is "materially higher" than the yield produced by an issue of governmental obligations if the yield pro-

duced by the acquired obligations exceeds the yield produced by the issue of governmental obligations by more than (A) one-eighth of 1 percentage point, or (B) at the election of the issuer, one half of 1 percentage point if such issuer waives the provisions of subparagraphs (1) through (5) of §1.103-14(b) (relating to the temporary period). Notwithstanding an election under (B) of this subdivision, the requirements of paragraph (b)(2)(ii) of §1.103-14, relating to the expenditure test, must be satisfied. Such election may be made for any issue of governmental obligations issued after July 1, 1972, provided that in the case of an issue of obligations issued after July 4, 1973 such election shall be stated in any certification under paragraph (a)(2)(ii) of this section. See paragraph (b)(5)(ii) and (iii) of this section for rules regarding refunding proceeds and see paragraph (b)(5)(iv) of this section for rules regarding an over-issuance of obligations.

(ii) In the case of an issue of governmental obligations such as a refunding issue, the rules of paragraph (b)(5)(iii) of this section apply to such issue in lieu of the provisions of paragraph (b)(5)(i) of this section and paragraph (e)(1)(ii) of this section. The term "refunding issue" is defined in §1.103-14(e)(2)(i).

(iii) (A) Prior to the date on which the last obligation of the prior issue (as defined in §1.103-14(e)(2)(i) is discharged, the yield produced by acquired obligations allocated to the proceeds (other than transferred proceeds as defined in §1.103-14(e)(2)(ii)) of the refunding issue is materially higher than the yield produced by such issue if the yield of such acquired obligations exceeds the yield of such issue. Before the prior issue is discharged, materially higher than the yield on a refunding issue that is issued after September 1, 1978, means higher than

$$Y + \frac{(\$25{,}000 \times Y)}{(P)}, \text{ where}$$

(1) "Y" stands for the yield on the issue, and
(2) "P" stands for the amount of the original proceeds of the issue.

(B) The rules of paragraph (b)(5)(i) of this section apply to the yield produced by acquired obligations allocated to (1) transferred proceeds, and (2) on or after the date on which the last obligation of the prior issue is discharged, other proceeds of the refunding issue. The determination as to whether the yield on acquired obligations allocated to transferred proceeds is materially higher shall be made with reference to the yield of the refunding issue. The rules of paragraph (b)(5)(i)(B) and (iv) of this section and the rules of paragraph (e)(1)(ii) of this section shall apply to transferred proceeds if such rules applied to the prior issue.

(C) In the case of a refunding issue sold on or after October 29, 1976 or issued after November 28, 1976, that refunds a prior issue that is a refunding issue, proceeds of the prior refunding issue treated as transferred proceeds of the subsequent refunding issue under §1.103-14(e)(2)(ii) shall not be treated as transferred proceeds at the time they become transferred proceeds but shall be treated as proceeds of the subsequent refunding issue in applying this subdivision (iii). Thus, paragraph (b)(5)(iii)(A) applies to such proceeds prior to the date on which the last obligation of the issue which is not a refunding issue is discharged by the prior refunding issue or series of refunding issues. After such date, paragraph (b)(5)(iii)(B) applied to such proceeds.

(iv) In the case of an issue of obligations in which it is reasonably expected that the original proceeds of such issue will exceed the amount necessary for the governmental purpose or purposes of the issue by more than 5 percent of such amount, the rules of this subdivision shall apply in lieu of the provisions of subdivisions (i) and (iii) of this subparagraph. Any portion of the issue issued solely for the purpose of investing such portion at a materially higher yield as less than a major portion is not issued for a governmental purpose. If there are two or more projects (within the meaning of §1.103-14(b)(2)), such projects shall, for purposes of this subdivision, be deemed to be a single governmental purpose. The yield produced by acquired obligations acquired with the proceeds of such issue (including any acquired obligations held during the temporary

Proposed Reg. §1.103-13

periods described in §1.103-14(b), invested in the reserve or replacement fund as defined in §1.103-14(e), and any investments of less than a major portion of such proceeds as described in paragraph (b)(1) of this section) is "materially higher" than the yield produced by an issue of governmental obligations if the yield produced by the acquired obligations exceeds the yield produced by the issue of governmental obligations by more than one-eighth of 1 percentage point. However, in the case of obligations issued after Jan. 2, 1976, the yield produced by such acquired obligations is materially higher than the yield produced by such issue of governmental obligations if the yield of such acquired obligations exceeds the yield of such issue.

(v) The following example illustrates the application of paragraph (b)(5)(iv) of this section:

Example. On July 1, 1977, city A sells $10 million of 7-percent Series A revenue bonds and $5 million of 4-percent Series B special obligation bonds at par in the full cash defeasance of a prior issue. Assuming that under state law and the bond indenture agreement the amount necessary to defease the prior issue is only $10 million, paragraph (b)(5)(iv) of this section applies to both the Series A and the Series B issue. Thus, for example, if transferred proceeds of the Series A issue are invested at more than 7 percent, the Series A bonds are arbitrage bonds.

(vi) Despite anything in §1.103-13(b) or (e) to the contrary, §1.103-13(b)(5)(vii) applies to any acquired obligation that is allocated to amounts treated as proceeds under §1.103-13(g) (relating to invested sinking funds).

(vii) Materially higher than the yield on an issue means higher than—

$$Y + \frac{(\$5,000 \times Y)}{F},$$

where—

(A) "Y" stands for the yield on the issue, and

(B) "F" stands for the maximum amount that will be accumulated in a sinking fund (or funds) for the issue.

(6) **Date of issue.** The date of issue of an obligation is the date on which there is a physical delivery of the evidences of indebtedness in exchange for the amount of the issue price. For example, obligations are issued when the issuer physically exchanges the obligations for the underwriter's (or other purchaser's) check. Thus, obligations which are taken down after October 9, 1969, by purchasers pursuant to a delayed delivery agreement with the issuer are subject to the rules contained in section 103(c), this section, and §1.103-14.

(7) **Term of an issue.** The term of the issue is the period beginning on the date of issue and ending on the latest maturity date of any obligation of the issue without regard to optional redemption dates.

(8) **Bond indentures and related documents.** The term "bond indenture" includes a bond resolution or ordinance. With respect to a bond indenture, the term "related documents" includes, for example, a trust agreement, a prospectus, or a transcript of proceedings and accompanying certificates.

(9) **Multipurpose issues.** (i) In the case of an issue of governmental obligations—

(A) Issued to finance two or more projects with respect to which the temporary periods provided in paragraph (b)(1) or (5) of §1.103-14 are different (including different temporary periods resulting from an election under paragraph (b)(5)(i)(B) of this section, or

(B) Part of the proceeds of which are used for refunding to which the rules of paragraph (e) of §1.103-14 apply or for a governmental program to which the rules of paragraph (d) of this section apply,

the portion of the proceeds of such governmental obligations to be used to finance projects having different temporary periods or to be used partly for refunding or partly for a governmental program shall be treated as separate issues of governmental obligations for purposes of determining the temporary period requirements, the reasonably required reserve or replacement fund, the application of the major portion test, and the application of §1.103-15 (relating to excess proceeds) with respect to each such separate issue. A multipurpose issue described in this paragraph (b)(9)(i) sold before October 29, 1976 and issued before November 29, 1976, may be treated as separate issues for the purpose of determining whether the yield on acquired obligations is materially higher.

(ii) For purposes of this section and for purposes of §1.103-14, the term "project" means any governmental purpose financed by the issue of governmental obligations. Such purpose does not include the investment of the proceeds of such issue in acquired nonpurpose obligations.

(10) **Issue.** (i) Two or more obligations are part of the same "issue" if the obligations—
(A) Are issued at substantially the same time,
(B) Are sold pursuant to a common plan of financing, and
(C) Will be paid out of substantially the same source of funds (or will have substantially the same claim to be paid out of substantially the same source of funds).

(11) **Discharged.** An issue is "discharged" when all obligations that were part of the issue are retired.

All other facts (such as whether the obligations are offered by the same official statement or are sold under the same indenture) are irrelevant for purposes of this subparagraph.

(ii) The following examples illustrate the application of this subparagraph:

Example (1). On January 1, 1980, city T issues $10,000,000 of series A revenue bonds and on January 7, 1980, city T issues $5,000,000 of series B revenue bonds. The series A and series B bonds are sold pursuant to a common plan of financing and both will be paid solely out of revenues of the city T water works. Based on these facts, the series A and series B bonds are all part of one issue.

Example (2). The facts are the same as in example (1), except that the series B bonds are special obligation bonds and will be paid out of interest on Treasury obligations. Because the series A and series B bonds will not be paid from the same source of funds, they are treated as separate issues.

(c) **Computation of yield—(1) In general.** (i) Paragraph (c)(1)(ii) of this section provides rules to determine yield on governmental obligations and acquired obligations other than acquired nonpurpose obligations (as described in paragraph (b)(4)(iv)(A) of this section) allocable to a refunding issue issued after 5 p.m. E.D.T., September 24, 1976. Paragraph (c)(1)(iii) of this section provides rules to determine the yield on acquired nonpurpose obligations allocable to a refunding issue issued after 5 p.m. E.D.T., September 24, 1976.

(ii) For purposes of this section and §1.103-14, the term "yield" means that yield which when used in computing the present worth of all payments of principal and interest to be paid on the obligation produces an amount equal to the purchase price. The yield on both governmental obligations and acquired obligations shall be calculated by the use of the same frequency interval of compounding interest. Thus, for example, if the yield on the governmental obligations is determined on the basis of semiannual interest compounding, then the yield on acquired obligations acquired with the proceeds of such governmental obligations shall also be expressed in terms of semiannual interest compounding. In the case of governmental obligations, the computation must be made separately for each issue of obligations issued by a governmental unit, except that a single computation may be made for two or more issues if, before the issuance of the last issue, the issuer establishes to the satisfaction of the Commissioner that the single computation will not distort yield or otherwise tend to defeat the purposes of section 103(c).

In the case of acquired obligations, the computation shall be made separately with respect to each class of acquired obligations referred to in paragraph (b)(4)(iv) of this section allocated to an issue of governmental obligations. Except in the case of a refunding issue after 5 p.m. E.D.T., September 24, 1976, an amount equal to the sum of the administrative costs of issuing, carrying, and repaying an issue of governmental obligation shall

Proposed Reg. §1.103-13

be treated as a discount on the selling price of such issue, and an amount equal to the sum of the administrative costs to be incurred in purchasing, carrying, and selling or redeeming a class of acquired obligations shall be treated as a premium on the purchase price of such acquired obligations. In the case of a refunding issue issued after 5 p.m. E.D.T., September 24, 1976, the present value of the administrative costs if issuing, carrying, and repaying the issue and the present value of the administrative costs to be incurred in purchasing, carrying, and selling or redeeming acquired obligations shall be taken into account as a premium or discount, such present value to be determined by discounting such costs, based on current prices without regard to any inflation adjustment, at a yield not less than the yield of the refunding issue (determined without regard to such costs). In determining the present value of the amounts taken into account under the preceding sentence, costs paid within any period (not in excess of 1 year) corresponding to the frequency interval used in computing the yield of the refunding issue may be treated as being paid at the beginning or end of such period. In the case of a refunding issue sold on or after October 29, 1976 or issued after November 28, 1976, there shall be taken into account as administrative costs with respect to the refunding issue and the acquired obligations only amounts to be paid to the trustee of the issue, the paying agent, the escrow agent, and for custodial fees, legal fees, accounting fees, printing costs, rating fees, insurance of the obligations, and recording fees, plus fees paid for services performed as a fiscal agent or financial consultant, but fees paid for services of a fiscal agent or financial consultant shall be taken into account only to the extent that the aggregate amount of such fees does not exceed an amount equal to 3 percent of the principal face amount of the refunding issue not in excess of $1,000,000 plus 1 percent of the principal face amount of the refunding issue in excess of $1,000,000, unless prior to the date of issue of the refunding issue the issuer establishes to the satisfaction of the Commissioner that a greater amount is necessary. However, any amounts taken into account under the preceding sentence may not represent amounts designed to divert arbitrage to the recipient. In determining the administrative costs with respect to acquired obligations of a refunding issue sold on or after October 29, 1976 or issued after November 28, 1976 such costs shall be allocated pro rata between the acquired obligations subject to yield restrictions and the acquired obligations not so subject, except that any costs primarily related to the investment of or reinvestment of any obligations not subject to yield restrictions shall be allocated to such obligations. Only the costs allocated to acquired obligations subject to yield restrictions shall be taken into account in computing yield. The yield produced by an acquired obligation which is a security may be computed by any method which is consistent with the principles of the actuarial method of computing yield. For purposes of such computation, securities held beyond the last expected maturity date of the governmental obligations shall be deemed to be sold on such maturity date. In cases where the issuer has no reasonable expectations as to the amount of principal to be repaid on an acquired security at the time that such security is sold, the amount of such principal shall be deemed to be the same as the fair market value of such security on the date of issue of the governmental obligations to which such security is allocated or, if later, the date on which such security is acquired. No yield computation need be made with respect to an acquired obligation while such obligation is held during the temporary period or periods referred to in paragraph (b) or (e) of §1.103-14, since yield allocable to such temporary period or periods is disregarded in determining whether a governmental obligation is an arbitrage bond. However, in the case of an acquired obligation which is held during and after a temporary period, if the yield applicable to the temporary period exceeds the yield of a comparable obligation that could be acquired and held only during such temporary period, then the computation of yield on such acquired obligation must be made by taking into account the yield allocable to such temporary period or periods. No computation need be made with respect to acquired obligations which represent a reasonably required reserve or replacement fund under paragraph (d) or (e) of §1.103-14 or represent investments of less than a major portion of the proceeds within the meaning of paragraph (b)(1) of this section or paragraph (e) of §1.103-14. See paragraph (b)(5)(ii) of this section for rules regarding an overissuance of obligations.

(iii) (A) In the case of acquired nonpurpose obligations (as defined in paragraph (b)(4)(iv)(A) of this section) allocable to a refunding issue issued after 5 p.m. E.D.T., September 24, 1976, the term "yield" means the yield computed under paragraph (c)(1)(ii) of this section based on the market price of the acquired obligations as determined under this paragraph (c)(1)(iii). This paragraph (c)(1)(iii) applies to proceeds of the refunding issue during the period beginning on the date of issue and ending on the date the last obligation of the prior issue is discharged (i.e., retired).

(B) The market price of an acquired obligation shall be the mean of the bid and offered price on an established market where such obligation is traded on the date of issue of the refunding issue, or if earlier, on the date of a binding contract to acquire such obligation, or, if there are no bid and offered prices on such date, on the first day preceding such date for which there are bid and offered prices. Any acquired obligation for which there is not an established market shall be treated as producing a yield materially higher than the yield of the refunding issue and will cause obligations of the refunding issue to be arbitrage bonds, unless no yield computation is necessary under paragraph (c)(1)(ii) of this section with respect to such acquired obligation. Any market especially established to provide an acquired obligation to an issuer of governmental obligations will not be treated as an established market. For example, if a person sells stripped coupon bonds to issuers of governmental obligations and there is not an established market for sales of such bonds to other persons, such sales will not establish a market. The mean market price may be determined by reference to any appropriate publication, such as, for example, "Composite Closing Quotations for United States Government Securities" published by the Federal Reserve Bank of New York. Where the price of an obligation is quoted on an established market in terms of yield, the market price shall be the price necessary to produce such yield using the method of computing yield under paragraph (c)(1)(ii) of this section (determined without regard to any administative costs with respect to such obligation). The market price of an acquired obligation may be established by the borrowing practices of the issuer of the obligation, as, for example, by determining the market price based on the interest ordinarily paid by such issuer to persons other than governmental units with respect to obligations of comparable maturities. The market price of a time or demand deposit (other than a deposit acquired with transferred proceeds) shall be determined under the preceding sentence by taking into account the yield that would be paid by the obligor if the deposit were held as an interest bearing deposit for the expected period of the deposit, except that if the yield actually paid is higher than such yield the market price shall be the amount of the deposit. If the price paid for an obligation is lower than the mean market price, such lower price shall be the market price for purposes of this paragraph. If the price paid for an obligation is higher than the mean market price, such higher price may be used as the market price only if the obligation is acquired in an arm's length transaction without regard to any amount paid to reduce the yield of the obligation. For purposes of this paragraph, where a United States Treasury obligation is acquired directly from the United States Treasury, such acquisition shall be treated as establishing a market for such obligation and as establishing the market price of such obligation.

(C) Notwithstanding paragraph (c)(1)(iii)(B) of this section, in the case of a refunding issue issued before October 29, 1976, the market price of an acquired nonpurpose obligation acquired directly from the issuer of such obligation shall be the price paid for such obligation where such obligation is not secured by any underlying securities or obligations.

(D) The market price of a certificate of deposit issued by a commercial bank may be determined as the bona fide bid price quoted by a dealer who maintains an active secondary market in such certificates of deposit.

(iv) The rules in paragraph (c)(1)(iii) shall also apply to acquired obligations that are allocable to amounts treated as proceeds under paragraph (g) of this section.

(2) **Classes of acquired obligations.** The yield produced by a class of acquired obligations shall be computed as if all of the obligations of such class comprised a single is-

Proposed Reg. § 1.103-13

sue of obligations, whether or not such obligations are to be acquired or held concurrently. Thus, for example, if an issuer uses the proceeds of an issue to acquire two blocks of nonpurpose obligations (such as, for example, Federal obligations) with different interest rates and maturity periods for each block, the yield on such acquired nonpurpose obligations shall be computed as if such issuer acquired one issue of obligations with different interest rates and maturity periods. The maturity period of each acquired obligation shall be the period that the State or local governmental unit will hold such obligation.

(3) **Allocation of certain administrative costs.** (i) If two or more refunding issues are used to refund the same prior issue, then any fees paid to a lawyer, accountant, fiscal agent, or financial consultant in connection with the refunding issues must be allocated among the refunding issues in proportion to their principal amounts. The following examples illustrate the application of this subdivision:

Example (1). On January 1, 1980, State X issues $10 million of series A revenue bonds and $5 million of series B special obligation bonds in the full cash defeasance of a prior issue. On the same day, State X pays lawyer R $12,000 for legal services rendered in connection with issuing the refunding bonds and $9,000 for legal services rendered in connection with investing the proceeds of the refunding bonds. Of the $12,000 fee for services rendered in connection with issuing the refunding bonds, State X must treat $8,000

(i.e., $12,000 × $\dfrac{\$10 \text{ million}}{\$5 \text{ million} + \$10 \text{ million}}$)

as a cost of issuing the series A bonds and the remaining $4,000 as a cost of issuing the series B bonds. Similarly, of the $9,000 fee for services rendered in connection with investing the proceeds of the refunding bonds, State X must treat $6,000 as a cost of investing the proceeds of the series A bonds and $3,000 as a cost of investing the proceeds of the series B bonds.

Example (2). The facts are the same as in example (1). In addition, on November 1, 1984, State X will pay accountant K $1,500 for accounting services to be rendered in connection with carrying the refunding bonds. State X must treat $1,000 as a cost of carrying the series A bonds and the remaining $500 as a cost of carrying the series B bonds. This is the result even though some (or all) of the series B bonds will be retired before November 1, 1984.

(ii) [Reserved]

(4) **Student loans.** Payments made by the Commissioner of Education pursuant to section 127(a) of the Education Amendments of 1976 are not taken into account in determining yield on student loan notes.

(5) **Certain administrative costs.** If—

(A) An issue is issued after September 1, 1978,

(B) The original proceeds of the issue are used to purchase acquired purpose obligations, and

(C) The obligor pays administrative costs of issuing, carrying, or repaying the issue,

then such payments shall not be taken into account in determining yield. The preceding sentence applies whether or not such payments are made from bond proceeds, and whether or not such payments merely reimburse the issuer.

(6) **Example.** The provisions of this paragraph may be illustrated by the following example:

Example. (i) On January 1, 1974, City A sells for a premium of $100,000 a 5-year 1-million-dollar obligation. City A will make semi-annual interest payments beginning on July 1, 1974 of $36,425.88 and will make the 1-million-dollar principal payment on January 1, 1979. The proceeds of the issue are to be used for a municipal construction project, and City A reasonably expects on the date of issue that the project will be paid for by January 1, 1977. A portion of the proceeds of the issue are invested in a reasonably required reserve or replacement fund which will extend through the term of the issue. On January 1, 1974, $9,800 of the proceeds of the issue (other than the proceeds invested in the reasonably required reserve and replacement fund) are used to buy an acquired obligation which has a par value of $10,000, a stated interest rate of 4.7585 percent per annum and a maturity date of January 1, 1979. Interest on the acquired obligation will be paid annually at the rate of $475.85. Interest on the acquired obligation will be used when received to pay construction expenses as received.

(ii) The yield on the governmental obligations is 5 percent and is computed as follows:

Date	Payments (Interest & Principal)	Present Worth Factor	Column (1) Times Column (2)
7-1-74	36425.88	.97560976	35537.44
1-1-75	36425.88	.95181440	34670.68
7-1-75	36425.88	.92859941	33825.05
1-1-76	36425.88	.90595064	33000.05
7-1-76	36425.88	.88385429	32195.17
1-1-77	36425.88	.86229687	31409.92
7-1-77	36425.88	.84126524	30643.83
1-1-78	36425.88	.82074657	29896.42
7-1-78	36424.88	.80072836	29167.24
1-1-79	36425.88	.78119840	28455.84
1-1-79	1000000.00	.78119840	781198.40
Total			1100000.04

The present worth factor represents the present worth of a dollar payable at the specified future date based on an annual interest rate of 5 percent compounded semi-annually.

(iii) The yield on the acquired obligation is 5.124257 percent and is computed as follows:

	Payments (Interest & Principal)	Present Worth Factor	Column (1) Times Column (2)
Year 1	475.85	.9506615900	452.37
Year 2	475.85	.9037574700	430.05
	10000.00	.9037574700	9037.57
Total			9919.99

The present worth factor represents the present worth of a dollar payable at the specified future date based on an annual interest rate of 5.124257 percent compounded semi-annually. Since the yield on the acquired obligation allocable to the temporary period does not exceed the current market true yield on a comparable acquired obligation held for a 3-year period, no yield computation need be made with respect to such acquired obligation while it is held during the 3-year temporary period. Thus, the yield is computed as though the obligation matured on January 1, 1976, and as though the obligation were purchased at a discount of $80 (two-fifths of the $200 discount on the obligation).

(d) **Obligations issued after September 1, 1978**—(1) **In general.** Despite anything in paragraph (c) to the contrary, the rules in this paragraph apply to obligations issued after September 1, 1978.

(2) **Administrative costs.** Administrative costs may not be taken into account in determining yield.

(3) **Purchase price.** (i) If an issue of governmental obligations is sold to the public, the term "purchase price" means the initial offering price to the public (excluding bond houses, brokers, and other intermediaries).

(ii) If an issue of governmental obligations is privately placed, the purchase price of

Proposed Reg. § 1.103-13

each obligation is the price paid by the first buyer of the obligation. For this purpose, the term "first buyer" does not include any bond house, broker, or other intermediary.

(iii) If the purchase price of an obligation is unreasonably low, then the yield on the obligation shall be determined as if its purchase price were equal to its fair market value on the date of issue.

(4) **Illustrations.** The following examples illustrate the application of this paragraph:

Example (1). On January 1, 1979, city A sells a $10 million issue of 10-year 6-percent revenue bonds. The purchase price of the issue is $9,800,000. The yield on the revenue bonds is 6.27 percent. Administrative costs are not taken into account in determining yield.

Example (2). On January 1, 1980 city B sells $20 million of 5-percent general obligation bonds to underwriter X for $19,800,000. Underwriter X offers and sells the entire issue to the public at par. The purchase price of the issue is $20 million. The yield on the issue is 5.00 percent. The underwriter's spread is not taken into account in determining yield.

Example (3). On January 1, 1981, city C sells $12 million of revenue bonds and uses part of the proceeds to buy a 6-percent Treasury note at par. The yield on the Treasury note is 6.00 percent. Administrative costs are not taken into account in determining yield.

(e) **Exempt arbitrage bonds for personnel of educational institutions—(1) In general.** Under section 103(c)(3) except as provided in subparagraph (3) of this paragraph, interest paid on an issue of arbitrage bonds is not includable in gross income if—

(i) The bonds are issued as part of an issue 90 percent of the proceeds of which are used to provide permanent financing for real property occupied or to be occupied for residential purposes by the personnel of an educational institution (within the meaning of section 151(e)(4)) which grants baccalaureate or higher degrees, or to replace funds which are so used, and

(ii) The yield on the bonds (computed in accordance with paragraph (c) of this section) is not more than 1 percentage point lower than the yield on obligations acquired in providing such financing.

(2) **Other definitions.** The following definitions shall apply for purposes of this paragraph:

(i) The term "real property" means land or improvements thereon, such as buildings or other inherently permanent structures thereon (including items which are structural components of such buildings or structures). In addition, the term "real property" includes interests in real property. Local law definitions will not be controlling for purposes of determining the meaning of the term "real property" as used in section 103(c)(3) and this paragraph. The term includes items which are structural components of a building such as the wiring, plumbing system, central heating or central air-conditioning machinery, pipes, or ducts, and elevators or escalators installed in the building. The term also includes built-in air conditioners, stoves, refrigerators, and dishwashers, but does not include any other accessories or equipment which are not structural components of the building.

(ii) The term "personnel of an educational institution" means the personnel who are employed by the institution on a full-time basis for at least one semester even if such persons are also enrolled for a degree and take courses. The determination whether a person is employed on a full-time basis depends upon the customary practice of the educational institution.

(3) **Obligations held by substantial users or related persons.** Subparagraph (1) of this paragraph shall not apply to any bond for any period during which it is held by a person who is a substantial user of the real property financed by the proceeds of the issue of which it is a part, or by a member of the family (within the meaning of section 313(a)(1)) of any such person. A person is a substantial user of such real property if he occupies such property for any period in excess of 3 months.

(f) **Allocations of investments and expenditures—(1) In general.** A State or local governmental unit shall allocate the cost of its acquired obligations to the allocable proceeds of each issue of governmental obligations issued by such unit after October 9, 1969. Allocable proceeds for an issue are the proceeds of such issue minus expenditures made with such proceeds other than amounts expended on acquired purpose or nonpurpose obligations. In cases where any such expenditure is made from the proceeds of several issues of governmental obligations or from several types of proceeds, such expenditures shall be allocated among such proceeds. Allocations under this paragraph may be made at any time and under any reasonable method chosen by the State or local governmental unit, provided that the method of allocation satisfies the requirements in subparagraph (4) of this paragraph.

(2) **Repayments of principal.** Repayments of principal on acquired obligations are a reduction in the allocable cost of such acquired obligations. Repayments of principal on acquired purpose obligations are a reduction in the amount of allocable proceeds to which such principal was allocated. However, such reduction of proceeds may be offset by the inclusion of such repayments as indirect proceeds pursuant to paragraph (b)(2)(iii)(B) of this section.

(3) **Time or demand deposits.** The cost of a time or demand deposit may be allocated to the proceeds of an issue of governmental obligations to the extent that such time or demand deposits are maintained for the purposes for which the proceeds of such governmental obligations may be expended (including as a purpose any investments in a reserve or replacement fund). Thus, for example, if Authority A, having one issue of governmental obligations outstanding, has a checking account which on January 1, 1974, reflects a balance of $500,000, and if such authority's records show that $200,000 of such balance are proceeds of an outstanding issue of governmental obligations which are to be used to pay construction costs on the project financed with the proceeds of such issue, then Authority A may allocate $200,000 of such account to the outstanding issue of governmental obligations.

(4) **Requirements.** (i) All allocations made under this paragraph must be consistent with one another. Thus, for example, an acquired obligation cannot be allocated to more than one issue of governmental obligations at the same time.

(ii) Obligations purchased with the original proceeds of a refunding issue must be allocated to such proceeds.

(iii) Obligations not purchased with original proceeds of a refunding issue may not be allocated to such proceeds.

(iv) Obligations purchased with amounts treated as proceeds under §1.103-13(g) (relating to invested sinking funds) must be allocated to such amounts.

(v) If any obligation is allocated to two or more sources of funds, each receipt of principal or interest on the obligation must be allocated ratably among the several sources of funds. (See examples (4) and (5) of subparagraph (5) of this paragraph).

(5) **Examples.** The following examples illustrate the application of this paragraph:

Example (1). On January 1, 1974, Authority B issues a $10 million government obligation at a premium of $500,000 for the purpose of purchasing home loans. Authority B expects that prior to September 1, 1974, it will have expenditures and receipts with respect to the issue as follows:

Date	Expenditure	Receipt	Explanation
1-1-74	$ 50,000		Issuing expenses
2-1-74	1,000,000		Treasury obligations
3-1-74	8,000,000		Housing loans
6-1-74	500,000		Debt service paid with bond proceeds
8-1-74		$ 20,000	Interest on Treasury obligations
8-1-74		50,000	Repayment of principal on Treasury obligation

Proposed Reg. §1.103-13

9-1-74	200,000	Interest on loans
9-1-74	10,000	Repayment of principal on housing loans

When computing the allocable proceeds of the issue as of September 1, 1974, Authority B expects to reduce the $10,500,000 original proceeds by the following amounts:

$ 50,000	Issuing expenses
500,000	Debt service
10,000	Repayment of principal on housing loans
$560,000	Total

The following receipts result in an increase in allocable proceeds:

$ 20,000	Interest on Treasury obligations
200,000	Interest on loans
$220,000	Total

Thus, the $10,500,000 original proceeds will be decreased as of September 1, 1974, by a net amount of $340,000 and on such date the amount of allocable proceeds is $10,160,000. The investment in housing loans and Treasury obligations does not decrease allocable proceeds since the investment is for acquired purpose and acquired nonpurpose obligations. The repayment of principal on the Treasury obligations does not increase allocable proceeds. The repayment of principal on the housing loans reduces the amount of allocable proceeds. Although the amounts received as repayment of principal are indirect proceeds, such amounts are not taken into account as proceeds for purposes of section 103(c) since Authority B did not expect to unreasonably accumulate such indirect proceeds. The repayments of principal on the housing loans and the Treasury obligations reduce the allocable cost of the acquired obligations. Thus, on September 1, 1974, Authority B will have $950,000 in Treasury obligations and $7,990,000 in housing loans which may be allocated to the allocable proceeds of the governmental obligations.

Example (2). On January 1, 1974, City C issues a 10-year 5 million dollar revenue bond issue with a yield of 5 percent for the purpose of constructing a revenue producing facility. City C expects to receive, by January 1, 1978, proceeds from the issue as follows:

Proceeds from bond sales	$5,000,000
Investment proceeds	500,000
Total	$5,500,000

The city expects expenditures, by January 1, 1978, with regard to the issue as follows:

Issuing expenses	$ 25,000
Construction expenses	3,750,000
Debt service paid with bond proceeds	250,000
Total qualifying expenditures	$4,025,000
Debt service paid with revenues	$ 500,000

On January 1, 1978, City C has $1,475,000 in proceeds which have not been expended on either the project or debt service. (The debt service paid with revenues was not paid with proceeds of the issue and thus does not decrease proceeds.) On January 1, 1978, City C has a reserve or replacement fund for this issue (as described in §1.103-14(d)) in the amount of $750,000. Also $50,000 of the investment proceeds are invested for a temporary period (as described in §1.103-14(b)(6)). As of January 1, 1978, the city may allocate to the proceeds of the issue $675,000 in acquired obligations which do not have a materially higher yield. Furthermore, the city may allocate to the proceeds of the issue $800,000 in acquired obligations with a materially higher yield.

Example (3). On January 1, 1974, City C expects that on January 1, 1978, its records will show the following information regarding the city's outstanding issues of governmental obligations including the issue of obligations described in example (2):

Proposed Regulations

Governmental obligations

Date of issue	Yield	Proceeds which may be used to acquire materially higher yield acquired obligations	Proceeds which may be used to acquire obligations which do not have a materially higher yield
3-5-55	4.3		
12-13-69	7.7		
5-6-70	6.1	$ 475,000	$ 525,000
6-10-71	5.3	950,000	1,200,000
1-1-74	5.0	800,000	675,000
		$2,225,000	$2,400,000

Assume that the issue of December 13, 1969 is an issue of taxable industrial development bonds. City C may allocate its acquired obligations using any method it chooses. For January 1, 1978, City C chooses to allocate its acquired obligations as follows:

Acquired obligations

Cost of acquired obligations	Yield	Allocated to issue of 5-6-70	Allocated to issue of 6-10-71	Allocated to issue of 1-1-74
$2,500,000	8.0			
500,000	4.0			$500,000
250,000	-0-	$250,000		
1,000,000	7.5	275,000		
1,000,000	5.0		$1,000,000	
500,000	5.3		200,000	175,000
125,000	7.0			
Total $5,875,000		$525,000	$1,200,000	$675,000

City C also allocates $2,225,000 of acquired obligations to the $2,225,000 in proceeds of issues which may be used to acquire materially higher yield acquired obligations. The $250,000 acquired obligation allocated to the May 6, 1970 issue is a noninterest bearing cash deposit which the city maintains as a replacement fund for the project which was constructed with the proceeds of that issue. It is unnecessary to make any further allocations because the obligations issued on March 5, 1955 are not subject to the provisions of section 103(c), since they were not issued after October 9, 1969, and the obligations issued December 13, 1969 are taxable industrial development bonds. Pursuant to the January 1, 1978 allocation, City C determines that the yield on acquired obligations allocated to the allocable proceeds of each outstanding issue which may be used to acquire obligations that do not have a materially higher yield is not materially higher than the yield of each such issue.

Example (4). On February 1, 1980, county T issues series A revenue bonds and series B special obligation bonds in the full cash defeasance of a prior issue. $40,000 of proceeds of the Series A issue and $60,000 of proceeds of the Series B issue are used together to purchase an acquired obligation. County T allocates interest with a present value of $60,000 to the Series B issue and the remaining interest and principal to the Series A issue. THIS ALLOCATION IS IMPROPER. Instead, county T must allocate 40 percent of each payment of principal or interest on the acquired obligation to the Series A issue and 60 percent of each such payment to the Series B issue; no other allocation is permitted.

Example (5). On February 1, 1980, City A issues $10 million of revenue bonds for the purpose of constructing a water treatment facility. On the same day, City A purchases an acquired obligation for $1 million. $200,000 of the acquired obligation is allocated to proceeds of the revenue bonds that are held in a reserve fund and invested at an unrestricted yield (see §1.103-14(d)), $700,000 of the acquired obligation is allocated to proceeds of the revenue bonds that are invested at a restricted yield, and the remaining

Proposed Reg. §1.103-13

$100,000 is allocated to other funds (which are not proceeds of the revenue bonds). Of each payment of principal and interest on the acquired obligations, City A must allocate 20 percent to the bond proceeds that are invested at an unrestricted yield, 70 percent to the bond proceeds that are invested at a restricted yield, and 10 percent to the other funds.

(g) **Invested sinking funds—**

(1) **Effective date.** (i) Except as provided in §1.103-13(g)(1)(ii), this paragraph applies to bonds sold after May 2, 1978.

(ii) This paragraph does not apply to bonds sold before May 16, 1978, if—

(A) The sale of the bonds was either authorized or approved by the governing body of the governmental unit issuing the bonds or by the voters of such governmental unit,

(B) Notice of sale of the bonds was given as required by law, or

(C) A bona fide written offering statement (or preliminary offering statement) was circulated to potential purchasers,

before May 3, 1978; provided that the bonds are issued within a reasonable time after they are sold.

(2) **In general.** Amounts accumulated in a sinking fund for an issue are treated as proceeds of the issue.

(3) **Sinking fund.** The term "sinking fund" includes a debt service fund, or any similar fund, to the extent that the issuer reasonably expects to use the fund to pay principal or interest on the issue.

(4) **Withdrawals.** Amounts withdrawn from a sinking fund are not treated as proceeds under this paragraph after they are withdrawn.

(5) **Prior issue.** Proceeds of the prior issue are not treated as proceeds of a refunding issue under this paragraph. See, however, §1.103-14(e)(2)(ii) for rules relating to transferred proceeds.

(h) **Rule with respect to certain governmental programs.** [Reserved]

§1.103-14 (Proposed Treasury Decision, published 5-3-73; 12-3-75; 11-2-76; 5-31-77 and 5-8-78.) **Temporary investments; reserve fund and refunding** issues.

(a) **Temporary investments—(1) In general.** Under section 103(c)(4)(A), an obligation shall not be treated as an arbitrage bond solely by reason of the fact that all or a portion of the proceeds of the issue of which such obligation is a part may be invested in materially higher yield acquired obligations for a temporary period until such time as such proceeds are used for the purpose for which such obligations were issued. Thus, the investment for such temporary period of the proceeds of an issue of governmental obligations in acquired obligations which produce a yield materially higher than the yield produced by such issue of governmental obligations will not cause such governmental obligations to be treated as arbitrage bonds. See paragraph (d) of this section for rules with respect to a reasonably required reserve, and see §1.103-13(b)(1) for rules relating to the major portion test.

(2) **Multipurpose issues.** See §1.103-13(b)(9) for rules regarding application of the temporary period requirements to an issue which finances two or more projects with different temporary periods.

(b) **Temporary period—(1) In general.** Original proceeds and investment proceeds of an issue of governmental obligations that are invested in acquired obligations during a 3-year period (or the period determined under subparagraph (5) of this paragraph) beginning on the date of issue are invested for a temporary period if the requirements of subparagraph (2), (3), and (4) of this paragraph are satisfied. See subparagraphs (6) and (7) for rules relating to temporary periods for investment proceeds and indirect proceeds. This paragraph (b) does not apply in the case of an issue of obligations issued in anticipation of taxes or other revenues. See paragraph (c) of this section for rules relating to temporary periods for tax and other revenue anticipation notes.

(2) **Expenditure test.** (i) An amount equal to eighty-five percent of spendable proceeds must be expended on the project or projects by the end of the period described in

subparagraph (1) of this paragraph which applies to the issue.

(ii) In the case of an election under §1.103-13(b)(5)(i)(B) (relating to materially higher), eighty-five percent of spendable proceeds must be expended on the project or projects by the end of the 3-year period beginning on the date of issue and an amount equal to ninety-five percent of spendable proceeds must be expended on the project or projects by the end of the 4-year period beginning on the date of issue.

(iii) The term "spendable proceeds" means, in respect of an issue of governmental obligations, the original proceeds described in subdivision (i) of §1.103-13(b)(2) minus the sum of (A) the amount of any reasonably required reserve or replacement fund for the issue (within the meaning of paragraph (d) of this section, (B) the excess of the amount of any original proceeds which, if invested, would be treated as less than a major portion of the proceeds (within the meaning of paragraph (b)(1) of §1.103-13) over the amount determined under (A) of this subdivision, and (c) the amount of any original proceeds expended within the temporary period (or the periods described in subdivision (ii) of this subparagraph) in payment of the debt service (i.e., principal, interest, or both) on such issue of governmental obligations to the holders of such obligations (as contrasted to a sinking fund payment).

(3) **Time test.** Within 6 months after the date of issue of the governmental obligations, the State or local governmental unit must incur a substantial binding obligation to commence or acquire the project or projects, whether or not identified on the date of issue, to be financed by the issue. If, however, there are good business reasons, other than arbitrage profit, for the issuer to delay incurring such substantial binding obligation, then the issuer may have a longer period, not to exceed a one-year period from the date on which such governmental obligations are issued. A substantial binding obligation to commence exists on the date on which the issuer incurs a binding obligation to a third party involving a substantial expenditure for some part of the project, such as, for example, architectural or engineering services, land acquisition, site development, construction materials, or the purchase of equipment for the project, or, in the case of services, commits itself to make an equivalent expenditure for similar services by employees of the issuer. A contract of commitment for services which otherwise meets the requirements of this subparagraph shall be considered binding notwithstanding that it is to be performed in several stages, each subsequent stage being conditioned on a new clearance. A binding obligation to expend the lesser of (i) an amount equal to two and one half percent of that portion of the estimated total project cost financed by the issue of governmental obligations and by prior issues, or (ii) $100,000 shall be substantial.

(4) **Due diligence test.** After a substantial binding obligation to acquire or commence the project or projects is incurred (as described in subparagraph (3) of this paragraph), work on or acquisition of the project or projects must proceed with due diligence to completion.

(5) **Exception.** (i) If investments of proceeds do not qualify as investments for a temporary period because the requirement of subparagraph (2)(i) of this paragraph (relating to the expenditure test) is not satisfied, such investments shall nevertheless be considered to be for a temporary period if prior to the issuance of the governmental obligations the issuer demonstrates to the satisfaction of the Commissioner that, on the basis of facts, estimates and circumstances in existence on the date of such issue, a longer temporary period is necessary.

(ii) In the case of an issue of governmental obligations issued to finance a construction project, if investments of proceeds do not qualify as investments for a temporary period because the requirements of subparagraph (2)(i) of this paragraph (relating to the expenditure test) is not satisfied, such investments shall nevertheless be considered to be for a temporary period if the issuer certifies under §1.103-13(a)(2)(ii) that on the basis of the facts, estimates, and circumstances in existence on the date of issue, a longer temporary period not exceeding a 5-year period beginning on the date of issue is necessary. Such certificate shall be accompanied by a statement of an engineer or architect specifying that such longer period is necessary and the reasons therefor, including a statement of

Proposed Reg. §1.103-14

the estimated time required for each major category of the work and the sequence thereof (including the extent to which each such category is to be carried out concurrently with other categories). The engineer's or architect's statement may be in tabular or chart form. Examples of major work categories are: preliminary planning and design; obtaining required approvals; property acquisition (including relocation of prior occupants); final design; preparation, letting and execution of contracts; site preparation (including removal of pre-existing structures); excavation; foundations; erection of structures; finishes; and final payments after completion. For purposes of the certification required under §1.103-13(a)(2)(ii)(A) and (B), the engineer's or architect's statement shall be considered to be a part of the certification which must be reviewed by counsel.

(6) **Investment proceeds.** Investment proceeds of an issue of governmental obligations that are invested during the period described in subparagraph (1) of this paragraph or during a 1-year period beginning on the date of the receipt of such investment proceeds are invested for a temporary period.

(7) **Indirect proceeds.** Indirect proceeds of an issue of governmental obligations that are invested during a 6-month period beginning on the date of receipt of such indirect proceeds are invested for a temporary period.

(8) **Replacement issue.** (i) In the case of a replacement issue of obligations (as defined in paragraph (b)(8)(ii) of this section) that replaces an earlier issue of obligations of the issuer, the period described in paragraph (b)(1) of this section for the replacement issue shall be reduced by a period equal to the period during which the obligations of the earlier issue were outstanding. See paragraph (e)(3) of this section for rules relating to temporary periods for a refunding issue.

(ii) The term "replacement issue of obligations" means any obligations which are issued after the retirement of all or a portion of an earlier issue of obligations if the proceeds of such subsequently issued obligations—

(A) Are used to replace any proceeds of such earlier issue (or of such retired portion) which were not expended on the project for which such earlier issue was issued, and

(B) Are used for substantially the same project as was intended for such replaced and unexpended proceeds.

(9) **Invested sinking funds.** Thirty days is the temporary period for amounts treated as proceeds of an issue solely because they are accumulated in a sinking fund for the issue (see §1.103-13(g)). The temporary period begins on the date of accumulation.

(10) **Debt service fund.** Despite subparagraph (9) of this paragraph, 13 months is the temporary period for amounts contributed to a bona fide debt service fund; provided that each such amount is spent before the end of the temporary period.

(11) **Interest.** Despite subparagraph (9) of this paragraph, one year is the temporary period for amounts received from investment of a sinking fund.

(c) **Tax and other revenue anticipation notes—(1) In general.** In the case of an issue of obligations issued in anticipation of taxes or other revenues, proceeds that are invested are an investment for a temporary period if such obligations—

(i) Will not be outstanding after (A) a period ending 13 months after the date on which such obligations are issued, or (B) a period ending 60 days (but not more than 24 months after such obligations are issued) after the last date for payment without interest or penalty of the anticipated tax (or last installment thereof) imposed by an annual tax levy or the first year's tax (or last installment thereof) of the anticipated tax imposed by a levy for more than 1 year, or (C) in the case of obligations issued in anticipation of governmental grants or advances and not in anticipation of taxes or revenues from other sources, a period ending 6 months after the date on which the issuer expects to receive such grants or advances (but not more than 30 months after such obligations are issued), and

(ii) Will not be issued in an amount greater than the maximum anticipated cumulative cash flow deficit to be financed by such anticipated tax or other revenue sources for the period for which such taxes or other revenues are anticipated and during which such obligations are outstanding.

(2) Cumulative cash flow deficit. For purposes of this subparagraph, the "cumulative cash flow deficit" at any time during a period is an amount equal to:

(i) The amount that the issuing State or local governmental unit will expend from the beginning of such period to such computation date to pay expenditures which would ordinarily be paid out of or financed by the anticipated tax or other revenues, plus

(ii) The amount reasonably required by the issuer as a cash balance on hand at all times (the amount of the anticipated expenditures for a period of 1 month from such time being deemed to be reasonably required for this purpose), minus

(iii) The sum of the amounts (other than the proceeds of the issue in question), whether in the form of cash, marketable securities, or otherwise which will be available for the payment of such expenditures from the beginning of such period to such time.

(3) Amount available for payment. For purposes of subdivision (iii) of subparagraph (2) of this paragraph, amounts in accounts will be considered to be available for the payment of such expenditures to the extent that such accounts may, without legislative or judicial action, be invaded to pay such expenditures without a legislative, judicial, or contractual requirement that such accounts be reimbursed.

(4) Example. The following example illustrates the provisions of this paragraph:

Example. County B plans to issue 13-month tax anticipation notes on July 1, 1971, in anticipation of income tax revenues in the amount of $4 million to be received on March 1, 1972, and real property tax revenues in the amount of $8 million to be received on May 1, 1972. Assume that all receipts will be received on the first day of each month. The maximum amount of such notes which may be issued pursuant to the provisions of subparagraph (3) of this paragraph may be determined in accordance with the following table on the basis of the facts assumed:

	Estimated expenditures	Estimated receipts[1]	Cumulative surplus (or deficit) at end of month[2]
June			$ 2,000,000
July	$ 750,000	$ 40,000	1,290,000
August	900,000	36,450	426,450
September	1,100,000	32,132	(641,418)
October	1,250,000	26,782	(1,864,636)
November	1,000,000	20,576	(2,844,060)
December	800,000	15,779	(3,627,281)
January	1,100,000	11,858	(4,716,000)
February	1,280,994	6,417	(6,000,000)
March	1,000,000	4,020,000	(2,980,000)
April	1,535,100	15,100	(4,500,000)
May	975,000	8,475,000	3,000,000
June	1,515,000	15,000	1,500,000

[1] Tax receipts plus proceeds from investments.
[2] Does not include amount of reasonably required cash balance.

The maximum cumulative deficit is $7 million which occurs at the end of February (i.e., $6 million cumulative deficit at the end of February plus $1 million reasonably required as a cash balance on hand (the amount of the anticipated expenditures for March)). Thus, an investment of the proceeds of the County B notes will be an investment for a temporary period if such notes are not issued in an amount in excess of $7 million.

(d) Reasonably required reserve or replacement fund—(1) In general. Under section 103(c)(4)(B), an obligation shall not be treated as an arbitrage bond solely by reason of the fact that a portion of any proceeds of the issue of which such obligation is a part may be invested in materially higher yield acquired obligations which are part of a reasonably required reserve or replacement fund. As a general rule, a reserve or replacement fund will be considered to be reasonably required only if the amount so invested at any time during the term of the issue does not exceed 15 percent of the original face amount of the issue. If the original proceeds of an issue (determined without regard to issuing

Proposed Reg. § 1.103-14

expenses) are less than 98 percent of the original face amount of such issue, then the percentage specified in the preceding sentence shall be based on the amount of such original proceeds. For the purpose of determining whether the amount invested exceeds the amount specified in the preceding sentence, the rules of §1.103-13(b)(1)(ii) apply.

(2) **Exception.** If an amount in excess of the amount provided in subparagraph (1) of this paragraph is to be invested in a reserve or replacement fund, such excess will not be considered to be invested in a reasonably required reserve or replacement fund unless the State or local governmental unit seeking to issue such obligations establishes to the satisfaction of the Commissioner, prior to the issuance of such governmental obligations, that the specified reserve or replacement fund is necessary.

(3) **Relationship to major portion test.** To the extent that proceeds of an issue of governmental obligations are invested at a materially higher yield in a reasonably required reserve or replacement fund, such proceeds are included as proceeds invested in materially higher yield acquired obligations for purposes of the major portion test in §1.103-13(b)(1). Thus, if the sum of the proceeds invested in materially higher yield acquired obligations equals the maximum investment permitted under this paragraph, then the investment of any other proceeds in materially higher yield acquired obligations may cause the obligations of such issue to be arbitage bonds.

(e) **Refunding issue—(1) In general.** This paragraph applies to refunding issues. The general rules regarding the temporary period (see paragraph (b) of this section), the reasonably required reserve or replacement fund (see paragraph (d) of this section), and the major portion test (see §1.103-13(b)(1)) do not apply to a refunding issue except as provided in this paragraph. This paragraph does not apply to proceeds of a prior issue until they become "tranferred proceeds" under the rules in subparagaph (2) of this paragraph.

(1-A) Operating rules: temporary period. (i) The rules in this subparagraph apply solely for purposes of subparagraph (3) of this paragraph (relating to the temporary period).

(ii) If two or more refunding issues are used to refund the same prior issue, and if the refunding is in substance a single transaction, then the refunding issues are treated as a single issue.

(iii) If a refunding issue is used to refund a portion (but not all) of the prior issue, then the refunded and nonrefunded portions of the prior issue are treated as separate issues.

(iv) The following examples illustrate the application of this subparagraph:

Example (1). City A has outstanding $10 million of noncallable 9-percent revenue bonds (the "prior issue") due on January 1, 1990. On January 1, 1980, city A issues $6 million of series A 6½-percent general obligation bonds and $4 million of series B 7-percent revenue bonds at par in a crossover refunding of the prior issue. For purposes of the temporary period rules in subparagraph (3), the two refunding issues are treated as a single issue.

Example (2). City B has outstanding $8 million of noncallable 9-percent revenue bonds (the "prior issue") due on January 1, 1990. On January 1, 1980, city A issues $3 million of 6⅝-percent refunding bonds at par in a crossover refunding of a portion of the prior issue. The remaining $5 million of the prior issue will be paid from revenues. Based on these facts, the prior issue is treated as two separate issues—one of $3 million and one of $5 million—for purposes of the temporary period rules in subparagraph (3).

Example (3). City C has outstanding $12 million of noncallable 9-percent revenue bonds (the "prior issue") due according to the following schedule:

January 1, 1981 .... $2 million
January 1, 1982 .... $4 million
January 1, 1983 .... $6 million

On January 1, 1980, city C issues $2 million of series B 6½-percent general obligation bonds and $6 million of series A 7-percent guaranteed revenue bonds at par in a crossover refunding of two portions of the prior issue. The proceeds of the series B bonds will be used to pay the $2 million due on January 1, 1981, and the proceeds of the series A bonds will be used to pay the $6 million due on January 1, 1983. The $4 million due on January 1, 1982 will be paid from revenues. For purposes of the temporary period rules in subparagraph (3), the series A and series B issues are treated as a single issue. In addition, the $8 million refunded portion and the $4 million nonrefunded portion of the prior issue are treated as separate issues.

(1-B) Operating rules; transferred proceeds, minor portion, and 4-R fund. (i) The rules of this subparagraph apply solely for purposes of subparagraphs (2), (4), (5), and (6) of this paragraph. Subparagraphs (2), (4), (5), and (6) relate, respectively, to transferred proceeds, the major portion test, the reasonably required reserve or replacement fund, and the adjusted maturity date.

(ii) If the proceeds of a refunding issue are used to refund two or more prior issues, then the portion of the proceeds used to refund each prior issue is treated as a separate refunding issue.

(iii) If a refunding issue is used to refund a portion (but not all) of a prior issue, then—

(A) The refunded and nonrefunded portions of the prior issue are treated as separate issues,

(B) Unspent proceeds of the prior issue must be allocated ratably between the separate issues, and

(C) If any unspent proceeds of the prior issue are invested at an unrestricted yield pursuant to paragraph (d) of this section or §1.103-13(b)(1)(ii), those proceeds must be allocated ratably between the separate issues.

(iv) Notwithstanding subdivision (iii) of this subparagraph, if a Series B issue is used together with one or more Series A issues in a gross refunding of a prior issue, and if the requirements in §1.103-15(d)(2)(i), (ii), (iii) and (iv) are satisfied, then—

(A) Each portion of the prior issue that is refunded by one of the Series A issues is treated as a separate issue,

(B) All unspent proceeds of the prior issue must be allocated ratably among the separate issues,

(C) If any unspent proceeds of the prior issue are invested at an unrestricted yield pursuant to paragraph (d) of this section or §1.103-13(b)(1)(ii), those proceeds must be allocated ratably among the separate issues, and

(D) None of the unspent proceeds of the prior issue may be allocated to any portion of the prior issue that is refunded by the Series B issue.

For purposes of this subparagraph, the terms "Series B issue" and "Series A issues" have the same meaning as in §1.103-15(d).

(v) The following examples illustrate the application of this subparagraph:

Example (1). City E has outstanding $10 million of noncallable 9-percent revenue bonds and $5 million of noncallable 8-percent revenue bonds due on January 1, 1990. On January 1, 1983, city E issues $15 million of 6-percent general obligation bonds at par in a crossover refunding of both issues of revenue bonds. Under this subparagraph, the refunding issue is treated as two separate issues—one of $10 million and one of $5 million.

Example (2). The facts are the same as in example (1) of subparagraph (1-A) (iv) of this paragraph. Under this subparagraph, the prior issue is treated as two spearate issues—one $6 million issue ("issue p-1") that is refunded by the series A bonds and one $4 million issue ("issue p-2") that is refunded by the series B bonds. Assuming that $1 million of the proceeds of the prior issue remain unspent on January 1, 1980, $600,000 of these unspent proceeds must be allocated to issue p-1 and the remaining $400,000 must be allocated to issue p-2. Assuming further that $500,000 of the unspent proceeds of the prior issue are invested at an unrestricted yield in a replacement fund, $300,000 of these proceeds must be allocated to issue p-1 and the remaining $200,000 must be allocated to issue p-2.

Example (3). The facts are the same as in example (2) of this subdivision, except that the prior issue will be retired serially. The result is the same except that issues p-1 and p-2 may be further subdivided under subparagraph (6) of this paragraph (relating to adjusted maturity date).

Proposed Reg. §1.103-14

Example (4). The facts are the same as in example (2) of subparagraph (1-A) (iv) of this paragraph. Under this subparagraph, the prior issue is treated as two separate issues—one $3 million issue that is refunded and one $5 million issue that is not refunded.

Example (5). The facts are the same as in example (3) of subparagraph (1-A) (iv) of this paragraph. Under this subparagraph, the prior issue is treated as three separate issues—one $2 million issue that is refunded by the series A bonds, one $4 million issue that is not refunded, and one $6 million issue that is refunded by the series B bonds.

Example (6). The facts are the same as in example (4) of §1.103-15(j). As a result of this subparagraph, all unspent proceeds of the prior issue would become transferred proceeds of the Series A issue, and none would become transferred proceeds of the Series B issue. The result would be the same even if some of the proceeds of the Series B issue were used to pay principal on the prior issue.

(2) **Definitions.** (i) A refunding issue is an issue of governmental obligations the proceeds of which are used to pay any principal or interest of a prior issue of governmental obligations (hereinafter referred to as the "prior issue"). The term "prior issue" means (A) any outstanding issue of governmental obligations (including any governmental obligations issued for temporary financing) issued by the governmental unit or (B) any outstanding issue of governmental obligations issued by any governmental unit that is included within the governmental unit issuing the governmental obligations the proceeds of which are used to pay principal or interest of such outstanding governmental obligations. The use of proceeds of an issue of governmental obligations within 1 year after the date of issue of such issue to pay interest on other governmental obligations need not be treated as the refunding of a prior issue unless the principal of the other governmental obligations is also refunded. In addition, the use of proceeds of an issue to pay certain capitalized interest (as defined in paragraph (e)(2)(iii) of this section) on a prior governmental issue need not be treated as the refunding of such prior issue. An issue of obligations to which paragraph (c) of this section applies issued in anticipation of revenues to finance annual budget expenses of the issuer (including supplemental appropriations and other expenses) shall not be treated as a refunding issue unless issued to refund a prior issue of obligations of such issuer issued in anticipation of revenue for the same budget period.

(ii) At the time that proceeds of the refunding issue discharge the outstanding principal of the prior issue, proceeds of the prior issue become proceeds of the refunding issue (hereinafter referred to as "transferred proceeds") and cease to be proceeds of the prior issue. In the case of a discharge of a portion of such principal, the amount of proceeds of the prior issue that become transferred proceeds is an amount which bears the same relationship to the total proceeds of such prior issue at the time of such discharge as the amount of such discharged principal bears to the total principal of the prior issue outstanding immediately prior to such discharge. In the case of a refunding issue sold on or after October 29, 1976, or issued after November 28, 1976, as the proceeds of the prior issue become transferred proceeds, those proceeds of the prior issue which are invested in materially higher yield obligations pursuant to the provisions of paragraph (d) of this section or §1.103-13(b)(1)(ii) shall become transferred proceeds ratably. Generally, it is not necessary to apply the preceding two sentences for purposes of §1.103-14(e)(4) and (5). (This is because of §1.103-14(e)(6), which treats different parts of the prior issue as separate issues.) Investment proceeds resulting from the investment of transferred proceeds shall be treated as transferred proceeds. Amounts received during the term of the refunding issue and after the discharge of the prior issue which would have been indirect proceeds of the prior issue and included within the definition of proceeds of such issue if such issue had not been discharged earlier than its maturity date by the refunding issue shall be treated as transferred proceeds when received. For the purpose of determining whether any amounts received by the issuer during the term of the refunding issue are indirect proceeds under §1.103-13(b)(2)(iii)(A), any acquired purpose obligations or property acquired or financed with the proceeds of the prior issue shall be treated as also acquired or financed with the proceeds of the refunding issue. Any amounts treated as indirect proceeds solely by reason of the preceding sentence shall not be treated as proceeds of the refunding issue until the prior issue is discharged. Thus, notwithstanding that at the date of issue of the prior issue the issuer did not reasonably expect to receive a repayment of principal on an acquired purpose obligation or to recover principal from the sale or disposition of property, any amounts reasonably expected at the date of issue of the refunding issue to be received as a repayment of principal on an acquired purpose obligation acquired with the proceeds of the prior issue or as a recovery of principal from the sale or other disposition of property acquired or financed with the proceeds of the prior issue are treated as indirect proceeds of the refunding issue.

(iii) For purposes of paragraph (e)(2)(i) of this section, interest on a prior governmental obligation shall be treated as a capitalized interest if such interest accrues within the period of time necessary to complete the construction or the acquisition of the project for which such prior issue was issued plus 1 year thereafter. In lieu of the 1 year referred to in the preceding sentence, there may be substituted a period not longer than 5 years if, prior to the issuance of the obligations the proceeds of which are used to pay interest on a prior issue of obligations, the issuer demonstrates to the satisfaction of the Commissioner that because of inadequate revenues during the period of commencement of operations of the project such interest should be treated as capitalized interest. For example, if a first issue is issued on January 1, 1976, to provide funds to construct a hospital and it is necessary to issue a second issue on January 1, 1979, to provide additional funds to complete construction of the hospital, the use of any proceeds of the second issue to pay interest on the first issue during the period needed to complete construction of the hospital, plus one year thereafter, need not be treated as a refunding of the first issue. However, if the hospital had been completed on January 1, 1979, and a second issue is issued on January 1, 1981, both to provide funds for a new wing for the hospital and to pay interest on the 1976 issue, interest on the first issue is not treated as capitalized interest unless the issuer demonstrates that there are not sufficient revenues from the hospital (without regard to any revenues or losses from the new wing) to pay the interest on the first issue accruing during the period beginning January 1, 1979, and ending not later than January 1, 1984.

(3) **Temporary period.** (i) Proceeds (other than transferred proceeds) of a refunding issue that are invested for a period described in paragraph (e)(3)(ii) of this section are invested for a temporary period. Paragraph (e)(3)(ii)(B) and (C) of this section applies only if the period beginning on the date of issue and ending on the date of discharge of the last obligation of the prior issue is not longer than the period determined under such paragraph. The issuer shall certify in any certification under §1.103-13(a)(2)(ii) whether paragraph (e)(3)(ii)(A), (B) or (C) of this section applies to the issue.

(ii) The periods provided by this subdivison are—

(A) A 30-day period beginning on the date of issue;

(B) A period which is not in excess of the shortest of—

(1) A period beginning on the date of issue and ending on the date on which the last obligation of the prior issue is discharged,

(2) 2 years,

(3) A period equal to 25 percent of the term of the refunding issue,

(4) A period equal to the greater of—

(i) 50 percent of the term of the prior issue, but not more than 6 months, or

(ii) 25 percent of the term of the prior issue, or

(5) In the case of a refunding issue which is part of a series of refunding issues, where a refunding issue is refunded by a refunding issue, 2 years reduced by the sum of all temporary periods for all prior refunding issues in such series to which this subdivision (B) or paragraph (e)(3)(ii)(C) of this section applied. See paragraph (e)(3)(ii)(C)(3) of this section for the application of this subdivision (5) to a refunding issue described in paragraph (e)(3)(ii)(C)(1) of this section.

(C)(1) In the case of a refunding issue for which different temporary periods under paragraph (e)(3)(ii)(A) or (B) of this section would apply to portions of such issue because

(i) Proceeds of the refunding issue are used to pay principal or interest on two or more prior issues, or

Proposed Reg. §1.103-14

(ii) One or more portions of the issue is part of a series of refunding issues under paragraph (e)(3)(ii)(B)(5) of this section,

the period described in paragraph (e)(3)(ii)(C)(2) of this section.

(2) The period described in this subdivision is a period determined by (i) multiplying the number of months (rounded to at least one decimal point) or days in the period determined under paragraph (e)(3)(ii)(A) or (B) of this section (determined without regard to paragraph (e)(3)(ii)(B)(1) of this section and without regard to any allocation under paragraph (e)(3)(ii)(C)(3) of this section with respect to such issue) for each such portion of the refunding issue by the amount of principal and interest of the prior issue discharged by each such portion and (ii) dividing the sum of the amounts determined under paragraph (e)(3)(ii)(C)(2)(i) of this section by the total amount of principal and interest to be refunded by all portions of the refunding issue.

(3) In the case of the refunding of any prior issue to which this subdivision (C) applied, the reduction referred to in paragraph (e)(3)(ii)(B)(5) of this section for the temporary period for such prior issue shall be the temporary period of the issue determined under this subdivison (C) rather than the periods under paragraph (e)(3)(ii)(A) or (B) of this section used in determining the temporary period of the issue under this subdivision (C). Because of the application of this subdivision (C) to a refunding issue, the sum of the temporary period for a portion of such issue and all prior temporary periods under paragraph (e)(3)(ii)(B) or (C) of this section for such portion may exceed 2 years. If such sum exceeds 2 years then, for purposes of determining the amount of the reduction under paragraph (e)(3)(ii)(B)(5) of this section for the portions of such issue in which the sum of the temporary periods does not exceed 2 years, the temporary period determined under this subdivision (C) for such other portions shall be increased by a period determined by multiplying such excess by a fraction the numerator of which is the amount of principal and interest to be discharged by the portion exceeding 2 years and the denominator of which is the amount of remaining principal and interest to be discharged by all other portions of such issue. If the temporary period in paragraph (e)(3)(ii)(A) of this section is used for any portion of the issue in determining the temporary period of the issue under this subdivision (C), and the temporary period under paragraph (e)(3)(ii)(B)(5) of this section for such portion is a period shorter than 31 days, then, for purposes of the preceding sentence, the excess shall be the period by which the temporary period under this subdivision (C) for such issue exceeds 30 days. If, as a result of any increase under this subdivision (3), the cumulative temporary period for another portion exceeds 2 years, such excess shall also be allocated in accordance with this subdivision (3).

(iii) Proceeds to which any temporary period provided in paragraph (b) of this section for the prior issue applied (or to which any temporary period would apply if such prior issue had been issued after October 9, 1969) which had become transferred proceeds and are invested during the period beginning on the date of transfer and ending on the date on which the applicable temporary period for such prior issue would end (determined without regard to the discharge of the prior issue) are invested for a temporary period.

(iv) If proceeds of a prior issue are permitted to be invested in materially higher yield acquired obligations beyond any temporary period provided in paragraph (b) of this section because such proceeds were not expended as anticipated (or could be so invested if such prior issue were not discharged), and if prior to the issuance of the refunding issue the issuer demonstrates to the satisfaction of the Commissioner that, on the basis of facts, estimates and circumstances in existence on the date of issue, a reasonable extension of such investment is necessary for such proceeds, then such proceeds may be invested in materially higher yield acquired obligations when such proceeds become transferred proceeds. In determining whether an extension under this subdivison is necessary and in determining the period of any such extension, the Commissioner shall take into account (A) whether the proceeds can be expended on the project or projects in a reasonable period of time, and (B) the effect of applying such proceeds to pay all, or any portion of the principal or interest, when due, of the prior issue.

(v) The temporary periods provided in paragraph (b)(6) and (7) of this section apply to the refunding issue, except that in the case of a refunding issue sold on or after October 29, 1976 or issued after November 28, 1976 the 1-year period described in paragraph (b)(6) shall not apply to investment proceeds to be used to discharge the prior issue. For the purpose of applying the preceding sentence to investments that are not made with transferred proceeds, a reference to paragraph (e)(3)(i) and (ii) of this section shall be substituted for the reference to paragraph (b)(1) of this section appearing in paragraph (b)(6) of this section.

(vi) Where an issue of obligations to which paragraph (c) of this section applies is a refunding issue, transferred proceeds shall be deemed invested for a temporary period if the obligations of the refunding issue (A) will not be outstanding after the period applicable to the prior issue under paragraph (c)(1)(i) of this section (determined, in the case of the 6 months referred to therein, on the basis of the facts, estimates and circumstances in existence on the date of issue of the refunding issue), and (B) will not be issued in an amount greater than the amount determined under paragraph (c)(1)(ii) of this section.

(vii) Proceeds of a refunding issue are invested for a temporary period if those proceeds—

(A) Are received as accrued interest for a period not to exceed 6 months and will not be used to discharge the prior issue, and

(B) Are invested and will be expended during the 1-year period beginning on the date of issue.

(viii) Proceeds of a refunding issue that will not be used to discharge the prior issue (other than proceeds described in paragraph (e)(3)(vii) of this section) are invested for a temporary period—

(A) If those proceeds are invested during a 1-year period beginning on the date of issue but only

(B) To the extent that those proceeds either are used to pay issuance costs or do not exceed 1 percent of the original proceeds of the refunding issue.

(ix) Proceeds of a refunding issue that will not be used to discharge the prior issue (other than proceeds described in paragraph (e)(3)(vii) and (viii) of this section) are invested for a temporary period to the extent that those proceeds do not exceed the lesser of—

(A) $10,000, or

(B) One percent of the original proceeds of the refunding issue.

(x) The temporary periods provided in paragraph (e)(3)(vii), (viii), and (ix) of this section apply only to a refunding issue sold on or after October 29, 1976 or issued after November 28, 1976.

(4) Major portion test. (i) This paragraph (e)(4) applies to a refunding issue sold on or after October 29, 1976 or issued after November 28, 1976. The rules of §1.103-14(e)(4) as published with notice or proposed rule making December 3, 1975 (40 F.R. 56541) and corrected by notice published in the Federal Register for December 18, 1975 (40 F.R. 58656) shall apply to refunding issues to which this paragraph (e)(4) does not apply.

(ii) Proceeds of a refunding issue may be invested in materially higher yield obligations pursuant to §1.103-13(b)(1)(ii) (relating to major portion test), subject to the following limitations:

(A) Acquired obligations that are invested at a materially higher yield pursuant to §1.103-13(b)(1)(ii) may be acquired only with transferred proceeds.

(B) Proceeds of the refunding issue may be invested in materially higher yield acquired obligations pursuant to §1.103-13(b)(1)(ii) only to the extent that they do not exceed the amount provided in §1.103-13(b)(1)(ii) determined with reference to the prior issue.

(iii) To the extent that proceeds of an issue of governmental obligations are invested at a materially higher yield in a reasonably required reserve or replacement fund, such proceeds are included as proceeds invested in materially higher yield acquired obligations for purposes of the major portion test in §1.103-13(b)(1)(ii). See the allocation rule in paragraph (e)(1-B)(iii) and (iv) of this section if less than the outstanding principal amount of the prior issue is refunded with the proceeds of a refunding issue.

Proposed Reg. §1.103-14

(5) Reasonably required reserve or replacement fund. (i) This paragraph (e)(5) applies to a refunding issue sold on or after October 29, 1976 or issued after November 28, 1976. The rules of §1.103-14(e)(4) as published with notice of proposed rule making December 3, 1975 (40 F.R. 56451) and corrected by notice published in the Federal Register for December 18, 1975 (40 F.R. 58656) shall apply to refunding issues to which this paragraph (e)(5) does not apply.

(ii) Proceeds of a refunding issue (including transferred proceeds) may be invested in materially higher yield acquired obligations pursuant to paragraph (d) of this section (relating to a reasonably required reserve or replacement fund), subject to the following limitations:

(A) Acquired obligations that are invested at a materially higher yield pursuant to paragraph (d) of this section may be acquired only with transferred proceeds or proceeds of the refunding issue that are not to be used to discharge the prior issue.

(B) At any time before the adjusted maturity date of the prior issue, proceeds of the refunding issue may not be invested at a materially higher yield pursuant to paragraph (d) of this section.

(C) If a refundng issue is a Series B issue (within the meaning of §1.103-15(d)), and if the requirements in §1.103-15(d)(2) are satisfied, then the proceeds of the refunding issue may not be invested at a materially higher yield pursuant to paragraph (d) of this section.

(iii) See the allocation rule in paragraph (e)(1-B)(iii) and (iv) of this section if less than the outstanding principal amount of the prior issue is refunded with the proceeds of a refunding issue.

(iv) A reserve or replacement fund for a refunding issue in excess of the amount permitted under paragraph (d) of this section will be considered to be reasonably required only if the State or local governmental unit issuing the refunding issue establishes to the satisfaction of the Commissioner, prior to such issuance, that the specified reserve or replacement fund is necessary.

(6) Adjusted maturity date. (i) The adjusted maturity date of a prior issue is the earlier of—

(A) The maturity date, or

(B) The expected call date (provided that the expected call date is not unreasonably early).

(ii) If different parts of the prior issue have different adjusted maturity dates, then (solely for purposes of paragraph (e)(4) and (5) of this section) those different parts shall be treated as separate issues and the amount of any proceeds of the prior issue shall be allocated among the different parts in the same proportion as each part bears to the total outstanding principal amount of the prior issue. If parts of a prior issue are treated as separate issues under the preceding sentence, and if the proceeds of the refunding issue are used to refund two or more such parts, then (solely for purposes of paragraph (e)(4) and (5) of this section) the portion of the proceeds of the refunding issue used to refund each such part of the prior issue shall be treated as a separate refunding issue.

A new § 1.103-15 is added to read as follows:

§1.103-15 (Proposed Treasury Decision, published 5-31-77; 6-9-77 and 5-8-78.) **Excess proceeds.**

(a) **Effective date.** This section applies to refunding issues sold after May 25, 1977.

(b) **General Rule.** If the excess proceeds (as defined in paragraph (c) of this section) of a refunding issue exceed 1 percent of the original proceeds, then (except as provided in paragraph (d), (e), and (f) of this section) the refunding obligations are arbitrage bonds.

(c) **Excess proceeds—(1) In general.** For purposes of this section, the "excess proceeds" of a refunding issue are all proceeds (including investment proceeds) other than—

(i) Proceeds that will be used to pay principal, interest, or call premium on the prior issue;

(ii) Proceeds that will be used to pay not more than 6 months' accrued interest on the refunding issue;

(iii) Proceeds that will be used to pay capitalized interest (as defined in subparagraph (2) of this paragraph) on the refunding issue;

(iv) Proceeds that will be used as part of a reasonably required reserve or replacement fund for the refunding issue;

(v) Proceeds that will be used to pay the administrative costs of—

(A) Repaying the prior issue,

(B) Carrying and repaying the refunding issue, or

(C) Purchasing, carrying, and selling or redeeming obligations acquired with the proceeds of the refunding issue;

(vi) Transferred proceeds that will be used for the purpose of the prior issue;

(vii) Investment proceeds derived from the investment of a reasonably required reserve or replacement fund;

(viii) Interest on acquired purpose obligations; and

(ix) Amounts treated as proceeds solely because they are accumulated in a sinking fund for the refunding issue (see §1.103-13(g)).

(2) **Capitalized interest.** For purposes of subparagraph (1) of this paragraph, "capitalized interest" means interest on a refunding issue that accrues within—

(i) The period of time necessary to complete the construction or acquisition of the project for which the prior issue was issued, plus

(ii) (A) One year, or

(B) A period not longer than 5 years if, prior to the issuance of the refunding issue, the issuer demonstrates to the satisfaction of the Commissioner that, because of inadequate revenues during the commencement of operations of the project, interest which accrues during that period should be treated as capitalized interest.

(d) **First exception: gross refunding**—(1) **In general.** If a refunding issue (hereinafter called the "Series B issue") is used together with one or more other refunding issues (hereinafter called the "Series A issues") in a gross refunding of a prior issue, and if all five of the requirements set out in subparagraph (2) of this paragraph are satisfied, then this section shall not apply to the Series B issue or the Series A issues.

(2) **Requirements.** The requirements referred to in subparagraph (1) of this paragraph are as follows:

(i) Substantially all of the excess proceeds of the Series B issue and substantially all of the excess proceeds of each Series A issue will be used to pay principal and interest on the Series B issue. (For the meaning of "substantially all", see paragraph (e)(2) of this section.)

(ii) Substantially all of the excess proceeds of the Series B issue and substantially all of the excess proceeds of each Series A issue will be investment proceeds.

(iii) At least 99 percent of all principal and interest on the Series B issue will be paid with proceeds of the Series B and Series A issues, or with the earnings on other amounts put into escrow to discharge the prior issue.

(iv) The Series B issue will not be discharged later than the prior issue.

(v) At no time will the proceeds of the Series B issue which have been spent exceed the sum of the payments made on or before that time of—

(A) Principal and interest on the Series B issue, and

(B) Administrative costs of the Series B issue described in paragraph (c)(1)(v)(B) and (C) of this section.

(e) **Second exception: crossover refunding**—(1) **In general.** This section shall not apply to a refunding issue if both of the following requirements are satisfied:

(i) Substantially all of the excess proceeds of the refunding issue will be used to pay interest that accrues on the refunding issue before the prior issue is discharged.

(ii) No proceeds of any refunding issue will be used to pay interest on the prior issue or to replace funds that are used directly or indirectly to pay such interest.

(2) **Substantially all.** For purposes of paragraphs (d)(2) and (e)(1) of this section,

Proposed Reg. §1.103-15

"substantially all" of the excess proceeds of a refunding issue means all of the excess proceeds except for an amount not larger than 1 percent of the original proceeds.

(f) **Third exception: prior ruling—(1) In general.** This section shall not apply to a refunding issue if, prior to the issuance of the refunding issue, the issuer demonstrates to the satisfaction of the Commissioner that it will not realize any material debt service or other savings directly or indirectly from the receipt of excess proceeds amounting to more than 1 percent of the original proceeds of the issue.

(2) **Material.** For purposes of this paragraph—

(i) A debt service or other savings is material if it has a present value of more than $100 on the day the refunding issue is sold;

(ii) In determining the present value of any debt service or other savings, the yield on the refunding issue (as determined under §1.103-13(c)(2)(ii) shall be used as the discount rate.

(g) **Fourth exception; temporary period.** This section shall not apply to a refunding issue if the prior issue is discharged within 180 days after the refunding bonds are issued.

(h) **Special rule.** If the original proceeds of a refunding issue are less than $500,000, the "$5,000" shall be substituted for "1 percent of the original proceeds" in paragraphs (b) and (e)(2) of this section and for "1 percent of the original proceeds of the issue" in paragraph (f)(1) of this section.

(i) **Meaning of terms.** The terms used in this section have the same meaning as in §§1.103-13 and 1.103-14.

(j) [Reserved]

(k) **Invested sinking funds.** If a refunding issue is sold after the effective date of §1.103-13(g), then amounts accumulated in a sinking fund for the prior issue are treated as proceeds of the refunding issue for purposes of this section.

(l) **Illustrations.** For purposes of this paragraph, it is assumed that city A has outstanding $10 million of noncallable 9-percent revenue bonds (the "prior issue") due on January 1, 1990. Principal and interest on the prior issue are payable solely from revenues of the city A water works. In order to modify restrictions in the bond indenture, city A contemplates refunding the prior issue on January 1, 1983. To that end, city A takes under consideration four different advance refunding programs:

Example (1). The first refunding program contemplates a standard defeasance of the prior issue. In this first program, city A would issue $11,500,000 of 7-percent refunding bonds at par on January 1, 1983. The refunding bonds would mature on January 1, 1990 and would be paid solely from revenues of the city A water works. The original proceeds of the refunding bonds would be $11,435,000 (i.e., $11,500,000 less issuing expenses of $65,000) and the investment proceeds (derived from investment in 6.5-percent Treasury obligations) would be $4,916,820. Of the total $16,351,820 of proceeds, $10,000,000 would be used to pay principal on the prior issue, $6,300,000 would be used to pay iterest on the prior issue, $35,000 would be used to pay administrative costs of purchasing, carrying, and redeeming acquired obligations, $10,000 would be used to pay administrative costs of carrying and repaying the refunding bonds, and the remaining $6,820 would be used to pay principal on the refunding bonds. Based on these assumptions, the excess proceeds of the refunding issue (i.e., $6,820) would be less than 1 percent of the original proceeds (i.e., .01 × $11,435,000 = $114,350). Therefore, the refunding bonds would not be treated as arbitrage bonds under this section. (See paragraph (b) of this section.)

Example (2). The second refunding program contemplates a full cash defeasance of the prior issue. In this second program, city A would issue $11,135,000 of Series A revenue bonds and $5,320,000 of Series B special obligation bonds at par on January 1, 1983. The Series A bonds would bear a 7-percent coupon, would mature on January 1, 1990, and would be paid solely from revenues of the city A water works. The Series B bonds would bear a 4-percent coupon, would be paid solely out of earnings on amounts put into escrow to defease the prior issue, and would mature according to the following schedule.

July 1, 1983	$410,000
January 1, 1984	430,000
July 1, 1984	410,000
January 1, 1985	405,000
July 1, 1985	395,000
January 1, 1986	395,000
July 1, 1986	385,000
January 1, 1987	375,000
July 1, 1987	370,000
January 1, 1988	365,000
July 1, 1988	355,000
January 1, 1989	350,000
July 1, 1989	340,000
January 1, 1990	335,000

The yield on the Series B bonds (computed separately) would be approximately 4¼ percent (see §1.103-13(c)). The proceeds of both the Series A and Series B issues would be invested in United States Treasury obligations paying 6.5 percent. Even though the combined yield on the Series A and Series B issues would be somewhat greater than 6.5 percent, the Series B bonds would be arbitrage bonds.

Example (3). The third refunding program also contemplates a full cash defeasance of the prior issue. In this third refunding program, city A would issue $16,455,000 of 6⅜-percent refunding bonds at par on January 1, 1983. The 6⅜-percent refunding bonds would be amalgamation of the Series A and B refunding bonds described in example (2) of this paragraph. The 6⅜-percent refunding bonds would be paid partly from revenues of the city A water works and partly from earnings on amounts put into escrow to defease the prior issue. They would mature according to the following schedule:

July 1, 1983	$ 410,000
January 1, 1984	430,000
July 1, 1984	410,000
January 1, 1985	405,000
July 1, 1985	395,000
January 1, 1986	395,000
July 1, 1986	385,000
January 1, 1987	375,000
July 1, 1987	370,000
January 1, 1988	365,000
July 1, 1988	355,000
January 1, 1989	350,000
July 1, 1989	340,000
January 1, 1990	11,470,000

The original proceeds of the 6⅜-percent refunding issue would be $16,355,000 (i.e., $16,455,000 less issuing expenses of $100,000) and the investment proceeds (derived from investment in 6.5 percent Treasury obligations) would be $6,085,625. Of the total $22,440,625 of proceeds, $10,000,000 would be used to pay principal on the prior issue, $6,300,000 would be used to pay interest on the prior issue, $50,000 would be used to pay administrative costs of purchasing, carrying, and redeeming acquired obligations, $767,100 would be used to pay interest on the refunding bonds, and the remaining $5,323,525 would be used to pay principal on the refunding bonds. Based on these assumptions, the excess proceeds of the 6⅜-percent refunding issue would be $6,090,625 (i.e., $767,100 + $5,323,525), which is $5,927,075 more than the amount permitted under paragraph (b) of this section (i.e., 1 percent of the original proceeds = .01 × $16,355,000 = $163,550). City A would realize a debt service savings of approximately $115,000 by using the 6⅜-percent refunding bonds to refund the prior issue instead of using the 7-percent refunding bonds described in example (1) of this paragraph. More-

Proposed Reg. §1.103-15

over, at least $101 of the $115,000 savings would result from city A's receipt of $5,927,075 of impermissible excess proceeds. Therefore, the 6⅜-percent refunding bonds would not come within the exception in paragraph (f) of this section. Because the 6⅜-percent refunding bonds would also fail to come within the exceptions in paragraphs (d) and (e) of this section, they would be arbitrage bonds.

Example (4). (a) The fourth refunding program also contemplates a full cash defeasance of the prior issue. In this fourth refunding program, city A would issue $11,500,000 of Series A revenue bonds and $4,950,000 of series B special obligation bonds at par on January 1, 1983. The Series A bonds would bear a 7-percent coupon, would mature on January 1, 1990, and would be paid solely from revenues of the city A water works. The Series B bonds would bear a 4-percent coupon, would be paid solely out of earnings on amounts put into escrow to discharge the prior issue, and would mature as show in column C of Table II (see item (b) of this example).

(b) Table I shows receipts and payments of proceeds of the Serie A issue. Table II shows receipts and payments of proceeds of the Series B issue. For explanatory notes, see item (c) of this example.

Table I

A Date	B Original Proceeds Spent	C Investment Proceeds Spent	D Administrative Costs	E Remaining Proceeds	F Cash Balance
1-1-83	$ 35,000	$ 0	$35,000	$11,400,000	$ 0
7-1-83	79,500	370,500	0	11,320,500	0
1-1-84	83,084	367,916	1,000	11,237,400	16
7-1-84	84,785	365,215	0	11,152,600	31
1-1-85	88,541	362,459	1,000	11,064,000	90
7-1-85	90,420	359,580	0	10,973,600	70
1-1-86	94,358	356,642	1,000	10,879,300	12
7-1-86	96,423	353,577	0	10,782,800	89
1-1-87	100,559	350,441	1,000	10,682,300	30
7-1-87	102,825	347,175	0	10,579,500	5
1-1-88	107,166	343,834	1,000	10,472,300	39
7-1-88	109,650	340,350	0	10,362,600	89
1-1-89	114,216	336,784	1,000	10,248,400	73
7-1-89	116,927	333,073	0	10,131,500	46
1-1-90	10,131,546	329,274	4,000	0	0

Table II

A Date	B Interest Paid on Series B Issue	C Principal Paid on Series B Issue	D Investment Proceeds Spent	E Original Proceeds Spent	F Administrative Cost	G Remaining Proceeds	H Cash Balance	I Outstanding Principal Amount of Series B Issue
1-1-83	$ 0	$ 0	$ 0	$ 15,000	$15,000	$4,900,000	$ 0	$4,950,000
7-1-83	99,000	375,000	103,500	370,500	0	4,529,500	2,954	4,575,000
1-1-84	91,500	375,000	100,584	366,916	1,000	4,162,500	859	4,200,000
7-1-84	84,000	370,000	88,785	365,215	0	3,797,300	2,491	3,830,000
1-1-85	76,600	365,000	81,141	361,459	1,000	3,435,900	3,788	3,465,000
7-1-85	69,300	365,000	74,720	359,580	0	3,076,300	3,734	3,100,000
1-1-86	62,000	360,000	67,358	355,642	1,000	2,720,600	3,268	2,740,000
7-1-86	54,800	360,000	61,223	353,577	0	2,367,100	1,074	2,380,000
1-1-87	47,600	350,000	49,159	349,441	1,000	2,017,600	3,400	2,030,000
7-1-87	40,600	350,000	43,425	347,175	0	1,670,400	3,833	1,680,000
1-1-88	33,600	345,000	36,766	342,834	1,000	1,327,600	3,323	1,335,000
7-1-88	26,700	345,000	31,350	340,350	0	987,300	766	990,000
1-1-89	19,800	335,000	20,016	335,784	1,000	651,500	2,215	655,000
7-1-89	13,100	335,000	15,027	333,073	0	318,400	1,369	320,000
1-1-90	6,400	320,000	8,232	318,454	1,000	0	0	0

(c) The following notes explain Table I and II in item (b) of this example:

(1) Column B of Table I show when the original proceeds of the Series A issue would be spent. The original proceeds would be $11,435,000 (i.e., $11,500,000 less issuing expenses of $65,000). Of these original proceeds, $10,000,000 would be used to pay principal on the prior issue, $1,400,000 would be used to pay interest on the prior issue, and the remaining $35,000 would be used to pay administrative costs of investing the proceeds of the Series A issue.

(2) Column C of Table 1 shows when the investment proceeds of the Series A issue would be spent. (All these investment proceeds would be spent at the same time they were received.) Of the $4,916,820 of investment proceeds, $10,000 would be used to pay administrative costs of carrying and repaying the Series A issue, $4,900,714 (which would be excess proceeds) would be used to pay principal and interest on the Series B issue, and the remaining $6,106 would be used to pay principal on the Series A issue. These investment proceeds would be derived from investing the original proceeds of the Series A issue in 6½ percent Treasury obligations. (It is assumed that 6½ percent is the highest rate that the Treasury will pay on January 1, 1983.)

(3) Column D of Table I shows administrative costs of carrying the Series A issue and of investing the proceeds of the Series A issue. These administrative costs would be paid with proceeds of the Series A issue.

(4) Column E of Table I shows the amount of original proceeds of the Series A issue that would be invested in Treasury obligations as of the end of the corresponding day in column A.

(5) Column F of Table I shows small amounts of original proceeds that would be kept in a checking account. These amounts would be temporary investments (see §1.103-14(e)(3)(ix)).

(6) Column B of Table II shows the interest that would be paid on the Series B issue.

(7) Column C of Table II shows the principal that would be paid on the Series B issue.

(8) Column D of Table II shows when the investment proceeds of the Series B issue would be spent. (Not all these investment proceeds would be spent at the same time they were received. Some would be put into the checking account described in item (c)(12) of this example.) Of the $781,286 of investment proceeds, $7,000 would be used to pay administrative costs of carrying and repaying the Series B issue, and the remaining $774,286 (which would be excess proceeds) would be used to pay principal and interest on the Series B issue. These investment proceeds would be derived from investing the original proceeds of the Series B issue in 4.345 percent Treasury obligations. (However, the yield on the acquired obligations, taking into account $15,000 of administrative costs paid on January 1, 1983, would be only 4.252 percent. The yield on the Series B issue would also be 4.252 percent.)

(9) Column E of Table II shows when the original proceeds of the Series B issue would be spent. The original proceds would be $4,915,000 (i.e., $4,950,000 less issuing expenses of $35,000). All these original proceeds would be used to pay interest on the prior issue except for $15,000 that would be used to pay administrative costs of investing the original proceeds of the Series B issue.

(10) Column F of Table II shows administrative costs of carrying and repaying the Series B issue and investing the proceeds of the Series B issue. These administrative costs would be paid with investment proceeds of the Series B issue.

(11) Column G of Table II shows the amount of original proceeds of the Series B issue that would be invested in Treasury obligations as of the end of the corresponding day in column A.

(12) Column H of Table II shows small amounts of original and investment proceeds of the Series B issue that would be kept in a checking account. These amounts would be temporary investments (see §1.103-14(e)(3)(ix)).

(d) Based on items (a), (b), and (c) of this example, the following conclusions may be drawn:

(1) All of the excess proceeds of the Series B issue and substantially all (i.e., all but

Proposed Reg. § 1.103-15

$6,106) of the excess proceeds of the Series A issue would be used to pay principal and interest on the Series B issue.

(2) All of the excess proceeds of the Series B and Series A issues would be investment proceeds.

(3) All of the principal and interest on the Series B issue would be paid with proceeds of the Series B and Series A issues.

(4) The Series B issue would be discharged on January 1, 1990, the same day as the prior issue.

(5) The proceeds of the Series B issue would not be spent faster than principal and interest on the Series B issue and administrative costs of the Series B issue would be paid. For example, on January 1, 1984, $956,500 of proceeds of the Series B would have been spent (i.e., $752,416 of original proceeds plus $204,084 of investment proceeds), which is the same as the $956,500 of principal, interest, and administrative costs of the Series B issue that would be paid on or before January 1, 1984 (i.e., $750,000 of principal plus $190,500 of interest plus $16,000 of administrative costs).

(e) Based on the conclusions in item (d) of this example, the Series A and Series B bonds are not treated as arbitrage bonds under this section (see paragraph (d) of this section).

Employer Contributions to Accident and Health Plans

Section 1.106-1 is amended to read as follows:

§ 1.106-1 (Proposed Treasury Decision, published 5-13-71.) **Contributions by employer to accident and health plans.**

(a) **In general.** The gross income of an employee does not include contributions which his employer makes to an accident or health plan for compensation (through insurance or otherwise) to the employee for personal injuries or sickness incurred by him, his spouse, or his dependents, as defined in section 152. The employer may contribute to an accident or health plan either by paying the premium (or a portion of the premium) on a policy of accident or health insurance covering one or more of his employees, or by contributing to a separate trust or fund (including a fund referred to in section 105(e)) which provides accident or health benefits or through insurance to one or more of his employees.

(b) **Trusts or funds providing other benefits.** However, if such insurance policy, trust, or fund provides other benefits in addition to accident or health benefits, section 106 applies only to the portion of the employer's contribution which is allocable to accident or health benefits. In such cases, the amount allocable to accident and health benefits must be clearly identified. Thus, for example, if the contribution is made to an organization exempt from taxation under section 501(c)(9) (a voluntary employees' beneficiary association), the contribution will be excluded from the employee's gross income only if the organization sets aside such contributions, specifically to pay accident or health benefits, consistent with the provisions of section 512(a)(3)(B)(ii) of the Code and § 1.512(a)-3(c)(3) of the regulations.

(c) **Cross reference.** See paragraph (d) of § 1.104-1 and §§ 1.105-1 through 1.105-5, inclusive, for regulations relating to exclusion from an employee's gross income of amounts received through accident or health insurance and through accident or health plans. For rules requiring the employer to withhold tax in cases where the contribution is not excluded from the employee's gross income, see chapter 24 of the Code and the regulations thereunder (sections 3401 et seq.).

Contributions to the Capital of a Corporation

Section 1.118-2 is added to read as follows:

§ 1.118-2 (Proposed Treasury Decision, published 5-30-78.) Contributions in aid of construction.

(a) **Contribution in aid of construction—(1) Definition.** For purposes of section 118(b), the term "contribution in aid of construction" means an item or amount contributed to a regulated public utility which provides water or sewerage disposal services to the extent that the purpose of the contribution is to provide for the expansion, improvement, or replacement of the utility's water or sewerage disposal facilities.

(2) **Examples.** The application of paragraph (a)(1) of this section may be illustrated by the following examples:

Example (1). B, a developer, constructs main water lines and support facilities, including a water filtration plant and a water tower, and turns the facilities over to corporation R, a regulated public utility which provides water services. The transfer by B to R is a contribution in aid of construction.

Example (2). The facts are the same as in example (1), except that B furnishes the necessary funds to R, which uses those funds to build the facilities. The payments to R are contributions in aid of construction.

Example (3). S, a municipality, tears up a road and the water lines under it in order to build a new road. S makes payments to corporation Y, the water utility that owned the old water lines, so that it can put in new lines. The payments are contributions in aid of construction.

(3) **Customer connection fees.** Customer connection fees are not contributions in aid of construction and are includible in income. The term "customer connection fee" includes any payment made to the utility for the cost of installing a connection from the utility's main water or sewer lines (including the cost of meters and piping) and any amount paid as a service charge for stopping or starting service.

(4) **Classification by rate-making authority.** The fact that the applicable rate-making authority classifies an amount received by a utility as a contribution in aid of construction is not conclusive of its proper classification.

(b) **Expenditure rule—(1) In general.** An amount satisfies the time requirement of section 118(b)(2)(B) if the expenditure referred to in section 118(b)(2)(A) occurs before the end of the second taxable year after the taxable year in which the amount was received.

(2) **Examples.** The application of section 118(b)(2)(B) may be illustrated by the following examples:

Example (1). Corporation M, a regulated public utility which provides water services, spent $100,000 in 1976 for the construction of a water facility. It received contributions in aid of construction of $25,000 per year for the years 1977 through 1980. The purpose of the contributions was to reimburse M for its expenditure for the water facility. The requirement under section 118(b)(2)(B) is satisfied for all of the contributions because the expenditure occurred before the end of the second taxable year after the taxable year in which each contribution was received.

Example (2). In July of 1976, M received $100,000 of contributions in aid of construction for the purpose of constructing a water facility. M is a fiscal year taxpayer with its taxable year ending on June 30. In April of 1979, M constructed the water facility at a cost of $100,000. The requirement under section 118(b)(2)(B) is satisfied because the expenditure occurred before the end of the second taxable year after the taxable year in which the contributions were received.

Example (3). M, a calendar-year taxpayer, received $100,000 of contributions in aid of construction in 1977 for the purpose of constructing a water facility. To the extent that the $100,000 exceeded the actual cost of the facility, the contributions were subject to being returned. In 1978, M built the facility at a cost of $70,000 and returned $20,000 to the contributors. As of the end of 1979, M had not returned the remaining $10,000. The requirement under section 118(b)(2)(B) is satisfied for $70,000 of the contribution. Since $20,000 of the contribution was returned within the time period during which qualifying expenditures could be made, such amount is not income. However, the remaining $10,000 was income to M for the 1977 taxable year (the taxable year in which such amounts were received) since it was neither spent nor repaid during the prescribed time period.

Proposed Reg. §1.118-2

Example (4). M, a calendar-year taxpayer, received $50,000 of contributions in aid of construction in 1977 for the purpose of constructing a water facility. M built the facility in 1979 at a cost of $50,000, but none of the costs of construction were paid by M until the following year. The requirement under section 118(b)(2)(B) is not satisfied because the expenditure did not occur before the end of the second taxable year after the taxable year in which the contributions were received.

(3) **Accurate records.** (i) The taxpayer shall maintain accurate records from which it can establish the amounts contributed and expended for a particular project and the dates upon which these contributions were received and expenditures were made.

(ii) If the taxpayer fails to maintain accurate records from which it can establish the facts required by subdivision (i) of this subparagraph, then the contributions will be includible in income in the year received.

(c) **Depreciation and investment credit; adjusted basis—(1) Disallowance of deductions and investment credit.** Except as provided in paragraph (e) of this section, no deductions for depreciation shall be taken and no investment credit shall be allowed for a water or sewerage disposal facility acquired by a regulated public utility which provides water or sewerage disposal services, to the extent that—

(i) The facility is acquired as a nontaxable contribution in aid of construction,

(ii) The facility is purchased with amounts received as nontaxable contributions in aid of construction, or

(iii) The facility is constructed with amounts received as nontaxable contributions in aid of construction.

(2) **Adjusted basis.** Except as provided in paragraph (e) of this section, to the extent that the water or sewerage disposal facility described in subparagraph (1) of this paragraph is acquired as a nontaxable contribution in aid of construction or is purchased or constructed with amounts received as nontaxable contributions in aid of construction, its adjusted basis shall be zero.

(d) **Reimbursements for facilities that have been placed in service—(1) Purpose requirement.** If a water or sewerage disposal facility is placed in service before an amount is received as reimbursement for the cost of the facility, the purpose requirement of paragraph (a)(1) of this section (relating to the definition of the term "contribution in aid of construction") is not satisfied unless, at the time the facility is placed in service, there is an agreement, binding under local law between the prospective contributor and the utility, that the utility is to receive the amount as reimbursement for the cost of the facility.

(2) **Exclusion from basis.** If a contribution in aid of construction is received as reimbursement for the cost of a water or sewerage disposal facility that has been placed in service, then in order for it to be nontaxable, the utility must have excluded (at the time the facility was placed in service) an amount equal to the contribution from—

(i) The adjusted basis of the facility for the purpose of determining deductions for depreciation, and

(ii) The basis or cost of the facility for the purpose of determining investment credit.

(3) **Placed in service.** For purposes of this paragraph, a facility shall be considered placed in service in the earlier of the following taxable years:

(i) The taxable year in which, under the utility's depreciation practice, the period for depreciation with respect to such facility begins (or would begin except for the application of section 118(b) and this section), or

(ii) The taxable year in which the facility is placed in a condition or state of readiness and availability for a specifically assigned function.

(e) **Repayments of nontaxable contributions in aid of construction—(1) In general.** If a nontaxable contribution in aid of construction is repaid to the contributor either wholly or in part, then—

(i) To the extent the amount of the contribution exceeds the cost of the water or sewerage disposal facilities constructed or purchased with the contributed funds, the repayment is not a capital expenditure.

(ii) To the extent that the repayment exceeds the amount determined under subdivision (i) of this subparagraph, it is a capital expenditure in the year in which it is made.

(2) **Capital expenditure.** The amounts treated as capital expenditures under subparagraph (1) of this paragraph are to be allocated proportionately to the basis of each of the facilities constructed or purchased with the contributed funds. Where such facilities are depreciable, the allocated amounts may be depreciated over the remaining useful life of that facility. For purposes of the investment credit allowed by section 38, to the extent that the amounts treated as capital expenditures are allocated to a facility in a taxable year of the utility, the facility is considered to have been placed in service in that year.

(3) **Illustration.** The following example illustrates the application of this paragraph:

Example. Corporation M, a regulated public utility which provides water services, receives a $100,000 contribution in aid of construction in 1977 from B, a developer, for the purpose of constructing a water facility. To the extent that the $100,000 exceeds the actual cost of the facility, the contribution is subject to being returned. In addition, M agrees to pay to B a percentage of the receipts from the facility over a fixed period. In 1978, M builds the facility at a cost of $70,000 and returns $30,000 to B. In 1979, M pays $50,000 to B out of the receipts from the facility. M is a calendar year taxpayer. The $30,000 payment to B is not treated as a capital expenditure by M. The $50,000 payment to B is treated as a capital expenditure by M in 1979. The adjusted basis of the water facility is increased from zero to $50,000. If the facility is depreciable, the $50,000 basis may be depreciated over its remaining useful life. For purposes of the investment credit allowed by section 38, to the extent of the $50,000 capital expenditure, the facility is considered to have been placed in service in 1979.

(f) **Definitions—(1) Expenditure.** For purposes of section 118(b) and this section, the word "expenditure" means actual payment rather than accrual of an obligation to pay.

(2) **Water or sewerage disposal facility.** For purposes of section 118(b) and this section, the term "water or sewerage disposal facility" means tangible property described in section 1231(b) (without regard to the holding period requirements) which is used predominantly in the trade or business of furnishing water or sewerage disposal services.

(g) **Effective date.** The regulations prescribed in this section apply to contributions made after January 31, 1976.

Certain Reduced Uniformed Services Retirement Pay

Section 1.122-1 is amended by deleting "72(o)" each place it appears and inserting in lieu thereof, "72(n)". As amended, §1.122-1(b)(2)(ii) and examples (2) and (3) of §1.122-(d) read as follows:

§ **1.122-1** (Proposed Treasury Decision, published 4-30-75.) **Applicable rules relating to certain reduced uniformed services retirement pay.**

* * * * * * * * * * * * *

(b) **Rule applicable after December 31, 1965** * * *

(2) * * *

(ii) Upon the death of a member or former member of the uniformed services, where the "consideration for the contract" (as described in subdivision (iii) of this subparagraph) has not been excluded in whole or in part from gross income under section 122(b) and subdivision (i) of this subparagraph, the survivor of such member who is receiving an annuity under chapter 73 of title 10 of the United States Code shall, after December 31, 1965, exclude from gross income under section 72 (n) and this subdivision such annuity payments received after December 31, 1965, until there has been so excluded annuity payments equalling the portion of the "consideration for the contract" not previously excluded under subdivision (i) of this subparagraph.

* * * * * * * * * * * * *

Proposed Reg. § 1.122-1

(d) Examples. The rules discussed in paragraph (a) of this section may be illustrated by the following examples:

* * * * * * * * * * *

Example (2). Assume the facts in Example (1) except that A retires on disability resulting from active service and his disability is rated at 40 percent. The entire amount of disability retirement pay, prior to and including 1966, is excludable from gross income under sections 104(a)(4) and 105(d), and in 1966, section 122 (a). Assume further that A attains retirement age on December 31, 1966, dies on January 1, 1967, and his widow then begins receiving as survivor annuity under the Retired Serviceman's Family Protection Plan (10 U.S.C. 1431). A's widow may exclude from gross income in 1967 and 1968 under section 72(n) and paragraph (b)(2)(ii) of this section, the $1,800 of "consideration for the contract" i.e., the reductions in 1963, 1964, and 1965 to provide the survivor annuity. Thus, A's widow will exclude all of the survivor annuity she receives in 1967 ($1,350) and $450 of the $1,350 annuity received in 1968. In addition, if A had not attained retirement age at the time of his death, his widow would, under section 101 and paragraph (a)(2) of § 1.101-2, exclude up to $5,000 subject to the limitations of paragraph (b)(2)(ii) of this section.

Example (3). Assume, in the previous example, that A dies on January 1, 1965, and his widow then begins receiving a survivor annuity. Assume further that A's widow is entitled to exclude under section 72(b) $1,000 of the $1,350 she received in 1965. Under section 72(n) and paragraph (b)(2)(ii) of this section, A's widow for 1966 will exclude the $200 remaining consideration for the contract ($1,200—$1,000) and will include $1,150 of the survivor annuity in gross income.

* * * * * * * * * * *

Paragraph (a) of § 1.122-1 is amended by inserting "subchapter I of" immediately preceding "chapter 73 of title 10 of the United States Code".

Paragraph (b)(1) of § 1.122-1 is amended to read as follows:

§1.122-1 (Proposed Treasury Decision, published 5-18-78) Applicable rules relating to certain reduced uniformed services retirement pay.

* * * * * * * * * * *

(b) Rule applicable after December 31, 1965.—

(1) In a case of a member or former member of the uniformed services of the United States (as defined in 37 U.S.C. 101 (3)), gross income shall not include the amount of any reduction made in his or her retired or retainer pay after December 31, 1965, by reason of—

(i) An election made under the Retired Serviceman's Family Protection Plan (10 U.S.C. 1431), or

(ii) The provisions of subchapter II of chapter 73 of title 10 of the United States Code (also referred to in this section as the Survivor Benefit Plan (10 U.S.C. 1447)).

* * * * * * * * * * *

Paragraph (b)(2)(iii) of section 1.122-1 is amended by inserting in subdivision (a) "subchapter I of" immediately preceding "chapter 73 of title 10 of the United States Code"; and by substituting in subdivision (b) "sections 1438 or 1452 (d)" for "section 1438".

Paragraph (c) of section 1.122-1 is amended by inserting in subparagraphs (1), (3), and (4) "or the Survivor Benefit Plan (10 U.S.C. 1447)" immediately after "Retired Serviceman's Family Protection Plan (10 U.S.C. 1431)" and by inserting in subparagraph (4) "or Survivor Benefit Plan" after "whether or not reduced under the Retired Serviceman's Family Protection Plan".

Paragraph (d) of section 1.122-1 is amended by deleting "(as defined in § 1.79-2(b)(3))" in Example (5) and by revising the material immediately preceding "Example (1)" to read as follows:

* * * * * * * * * * *

(d) Examples with respect to the Retired Serviceman's Family Protection Plan. The rules discussed in this section relating to the Retired Serviceman's Family Protection Plan (10 U.S.C. 1431) may be illustrated by the following examples:

Section 1.122-1 is amended by adding at the end thereof a new paragraph (e) to read as follows:

* * * * * * * * * * *

(e) **Principles applicable to the Survivor Benefit Plan.** The principles illustrated by the examples set forth in paragraph (d) of this section apply to an annuity under the Survivor Benefit Plan (10 U.S.C. 1447).

Business Expenses

Section 1.162-1 is amended by revising subparagraph (2) of paragraph (b) and by adding a new subparagraph (6) at the end of amended paragraph (b). These amended and added provisions read as follows:

§ 1.162-1 (Proposed Treasury Decision, published 5-6-72.) **Business expenses.**

* * * * * * * * * * *

(b) Cross references. * * *

(2) For items not deductible, see sections 261—279, inclusive, and the regulations thereunder.

* * * * * * * * * * *

(6) For expenditures related to activities not engaged in for profit, see section 183 and the regulations thereunder.

Section 1.162-9 is amended to read as follows:

§ 1.162-9 (Proposed Treasury Decision, published 6-3-71.) **Bonuses to employees.**

Bonuses to employees will constitute allowable deductions from gross income when such payments are made in good faith and as additional compensation for the services actually rendered by the employees, provided such payments when added to the stipulated salaries do not exceed a reasonable compensation. It is immaterial whether such bonuses are paid in cash or in property or partly in cash and partly in property. For the rules with respect to when compensation paid in property, and the amount, is included in the gross income of the employees and when it is deductible by employers, see section 83 and the regulations thereunder. Donations made to employees and others, which do not have in them elements of compensation or which are in excess of reasonable compensation for services are not deductible from gross income.

Paragraph (c) of § 1.162-10 is amended to read as follows:

§ 1.162-10 (Proposed Treasury Decision, published 6-3-71.) **Certain employee benefits.**

* * * * * * * * * * *

(c) **Other plans providing deferred compensation.** For the rules relating to the deduction of amounts paid to or under a stock bonus, pension, annuity, or profit sharing plan or amounts paid or accrued under any other plan deferring the receipt of compensation, see section 404 and the regulations thereunder. For the rules relating to the deduction for property transferred in connection with the performance of services, see section 83(h) and the regulations thereunder.

Section 1.162-16 is revised to read as follows:

§ 1.162-16 (Proposed Treasury Decision, published 7-15-71.) **Cross references.**

(a) For special rules relating to expenses in connection with subdividing real property for sale, see section 1237 and the regulations thereunder.

Proposed Reg. § 1.162-16

(b) For special rules relating to the treatment of payments made by a transferee of a franchise, trademark, or trade name, see section 1253 and the regulations thereunder.

Taxes

So much of paragraph (a) of §1.164-1 as follows subparagraph (5) thereof is amended to read as follows:

§1.164-1 (Proposed Treasury Decision, published 9-29-77.) **Deduction for taxes.**

(a) In general. * * *

(5) * * *

In addition, there shall be allowed as a deduction under this section State and local, and foreign, taxes not described in subparagraphs (1) through (5) of this paragraph which are paid or accrued within the taxable year in carrying on a trade or business or an activity described in section 212 (relating to expenses for production of income). For example, dealers or investors in securities and dealers or investors in real estate may deduct State stock transfer and real estate transfer taxes, respectively, under section 164, to the extent they are expenses incurred in carrying on a trade or business or an activity for the production of income. In general, taxes are deductible only by the person upon whom they are imposed. However, see §1.164-5 in the case of certain taxes paid by the consumer. Also, in the case of a qualified State individual income tax (as defined in section 6362 and the regulations thereunder) which is determined by reference to a percentage of the Federal income tax (pursuant to section 6362(c)), an accrual method taxpayer shall use the cash receipts and disbursements method to compute the amount of his deduction therefor. Thus, the deduction under section 164 is in the amount actually paid with respect to the qualified tax, rather than the amount accrued with respect thereto, during the taxable year even though the taxpayer uses the accrual method of accounting for other purposes. In addition, see paragraph (f)(1) of §301.6361-1 of this chapter (Regulations on Procedure and Administration) with respect to rules relating to allocation and reallocation of amounts collected on account of the Federal income tax and qualified taxes.

* * * * * * * * * * * *

Section 1.167(k) is deleted.

Section 1.167(k)-1 is amended as follows:

1. Paragraph (a)(1) is amended by striking out "January 1, 1975" in the first sentence and inserting in lieu thereof "January 1, 1979".

2. The first sentence of paragraph (a)(2) is amended by striking out "December 31, 1974" and inserting in lieu thereof "December 31, 1978".

3. The second sentence of paragraph (a)(2) is amended by striking out "January 1, 1975" and inserting in lieu thereof "January 1, 1979".

4. A new paragraph (d) is added at the end to read as set forth below.

§1.167(k)-1 (Proposed Treasury Decision, published 5-8-78.) **Depreciation of property attributable to rehabilitation expenditures.**

* * * * * * * * * * * *

(d) **Expenditures deemed incurred before January 1, 1979.** For purposes of paragraph (a) of this section—

(1) Rehabilitation expenditures (including rehabilitation expenditures that are treated as paid or incurred by the taxpayer by reason of paragraph (b)(1) of this section) that are incurred pursuant to a binding contract entered into before January 1, 1979, are deemed to be incurred before January 1, 1979. The contract must require (i) the rehabilitation to be performed for the taxpayer (or the person or persons other than the taxpayer described in paragraph (b)(1) of this section) in accordance with his specifications, or (ii) the taxpayer (or the person or persons other than the taxpayer described in paragraph (b)(1) of this section) to perform the rehabilitation (or to have the work performed for

him in accordance with his specifications). The contract, as of December 31, 1978, must also specifically identify the existing building (or buildings) in connection with which the rehabilitation expenditures are to be incurred, and the expenditures must be incurred in connection with that building (or buildings). A contract may be binding, for purposes of section 167(k)(3)(D) and this section, even if it is subject to the happening of certain contingencies (such as the obtaining of financing from a third party) which have not occurred by January 1, 1979, provided that the happening of the contingencies is not within the unrestricted control of the taxpayer (or the person or persons other than the taxpayer described in paragraph (b)(1) of this section) and the contingencies in fact occur. In any event, a contract that does not represent a bona fide agreement negotiated at arms-length shall not be considered a binding contract for purposes of section 167(k)(3)(D). For purposes of section 167k)(3)(D), a binding contract includes an agreement, entered into pursuant to section 8 of the United States Housing Act of 1937, between the taxpayer (or the person or persons other than the taxpayer described in paragraph (b)(1) of this section) and the Department of Housing and Urban Development ("HUD") or a public housing agency ("PHA") providing that upon completion of rehabilitation in accordance with the taxpayer's final proposal, HUD or the PHA will enter into a housing assistance payments contract with the taxpayer (or such other person or persons). For purposes of the preceding sentence, "agreement", "final proposal", "public housing agency", and "housing assistance payments contract" have the same meaning as those terms have in 24 CFR Part 881 (relating to substantial rehabilitation under the section 8 housing assistance payments program).

(2) Rehabilitation expenditures (including rehabilitation expenditures that are treated as having been paid or incurred by the taxpayer by reason of paragraph (b)(1) of this section) incurred with respect to low-income rental housing the rehabilitation of which has begun before January 1, 1979, are deemed to be incurred before that date. For purposes of determining whether rehabilitation has begun before January 1, 1979, each dwelling unit (see §1.167(k)-3(c)) shall be considered separately. Rehabilitation begins upon the commencement of physical work at the site of the dwelling unit, as distinguished from the beginning of, or engaging in, other preliminary activities, such as the preparation of architect's sketches. The determination of whether physical work has begun shall be based upon all the facts and circumstances of a particular case. In general, where the physical work which has commenced before January 1, 1979, represents rehabilitation expenditures which are allocable under §1.167(k)-2(d) to more than one dwelling unit (such as the cost of replacing the roof of an existing structure), such work may be treated as having been done on units to which the expenditures are allocable.

Section 1.167(k)-2 is amended as follows:

1. The third sentence of paragraph (a) is amended by striking out "1974" and inserting in lieu thereof "1978"

2. The first two sentences of paragraph (c)(1) are deleted and four new sentences are inserted in lieu thereof to read as set forth below.

3. The last sentence of paragraph (c)(1) is amended by striking out "limitation" and inserting in lieu thereof "limitations"

4. Paragraph (c)(2) is amended by striking out "following example:" and *"Example."* and inserting in lieu thereof "following examples:" and *"Example* (1).", respectively.

5. A new example (2) is inserted after example (1) in paragraph (c)(2), to read as set forth below.

6. Paragraph (e) is amended as follows:

(a) Subparagraph (1) is amended by striking out "For purposes of" in the first sentence and inserting in lieu thereof "Except as provided in paragraph (e)(2) of this section, for purposes of".

(b) Subparagraph (2) is redesignated as subparagraph (3).

(c) A new subparagraph (2) is added after subparagraph (1), to read as set forth below.

Proposed Reg. §1.167(k)-1

§1.167(k)-2 (Proposed Treasury Decision, published 5-8-78.) **Limitations.**

* * * * * * * * * * * *

(c) **Maximum amount.** (1) In general, the maximum amount of rehabilitation expenditures paid or incurred by the taxpayer with respect to any dwelling unit which may be taken into account under section 167(k) is $20,000. However, in the case of rehabilitation expenditures incurred before January 1, 1976, the amount of such expenditures paid or incurred by the taxpayer with respect to any dwelling unit which may be taken into account under section 167(k) is limited to $15,000. The rules in §1.167(k)-1(a)(2) shall apply in determining whether an expenditure is incurred before January 1, 1976. Property attributable to amounts in excess of $20,000 (or, if applicable, $15,000) may qualify for the reasonable allowance provided by section 167(a). * * *

(2) * * *

Example (2). X, a calendar year taxpayer on the cash receipts and disbursements method of accounting, spends a total of $22,000 for rehabilitation of one dwelling unit in an existing building held for low-income rental housing. X would be considered, under the accrual method of accounting, to have incurred $19,000 of the expenditures in 1975 and $3,000 in 1976. The expenditures qualify as rehabilitation expenditures under §1.167(k)-3. Because of the $15,000 limitation with respect to rehabilitation expenditures incurred before January 1, 1976, property attributable to only $15,000 of the $19,000 of expenditures incurred in 1975 qualifies for an election under section 167(k). The $4,000 of expenditures incurred in 1975 with respect to which X cannot make a valid election is not taken into account in applying the $20,000 limitation. Therefore, property attributable to the entire $3,000 of expenditures incurred in 1976 qualifies for an election under section 167(k).

* * * * * * * * * * * *

(e) **Special rule.** * * *

(2) In determining, for purposes of the $15,000 limitation described in the second sentence of paragraph (c)(1) of this section, whether a rehabilitation expenditure is incurred before January 1, 1976, a rehabilitation expenditure treated as having been paid or incurred by the taxpayer by reason of §1.167(k)-1(b)(1) shall be deemed to have been incurred on the date the expenditure would be considered incurred under the accrual method of accounting by the person or persons who actually incurred the expenditure, regardless of the method of accounting used by that person or persons.

* * * * * * * * * * * *

Section 1.167(k)-3 is amended as follows:

1. Paragraph (b)(1)(i) is amended by inserting two new sentences after the first sentence to read as set forth below.

2. Paragraphs (b)(2) and (b)(3) are revised as set forth below.

3. Paragraph (b)(4) is amended by striking out "close of the certification year" each place it appears and inserting in lieu thereof "beginning of the certification year", by amending the fourth sentence as set forth below, and by deleting the fifth and sixth sentences.

4. Paragraph (b)(5) is redesignated as paragraph (b)(6) and a new paragraph (b)(5) is added to read as set forth below.

5. Example (1) and Example (2) in paragraph (b)(6), as redesignated, are revised as set forth below.

§1.167(k)-3 (Proposed Treasury Decision, published 5-8-78.) **Definitions.**

* * * * * * * * * * * *

(b) **Low-income rental housing—(1) In general.** (i) * * * A dwelling unit held for occupancy by families and individuals of low or moderate income may qualify as low-income rental housing even though other dwelling units in the same building are held for occupancy by persons who are not of low or moderate income. On the other hand, a dwelling unit held for occupancy by persons who are not of low or moderate income does not qualify as low-income rental housing, even though other dwelling units in the same building are held for occupancy by families and individuals of low or moderate income. * * *

* * * * * * * * * * * * *

(2) **Definition of low or moderate income.** The occupants of a dwelling unit are considered families and individuals of low or moderate income for purposes of section 167(k) only if their adjusted income (computed in the manner prescribed in paragraph (b)(3) of this section) does not exceed 80 percent of the median income for the area, as determined with adjustments for smaller and larger families by the Secretary of Housing and Urban Development for the purposes of applying section 8(f)(1) of the United States Housing Act of 1937, as amended (42 U.S.C. 1437f(f)(1)), except that if, for purposes of applying such section, the Secretary of Housing and Urban Development establishes an income ceiling higher or lower than 80 percent of the median for the area, the higher or lower income ceiling shall apply. Notwithstanding the preceding sentence, the occupants of a dwelling unit shall not be considered as individuals and families of low or moderate income if all the occupants are students (as defined in section 151(e)(4)), no one of whom is entitled to file a joint return under section 6013. All determinations under this subparagraph shall be made as of the first day of the certification year (as defined in paragraph (b)(3) of this section).

(3) **Adjusted income.** (i) The adjusted income of a family or individual is the anticipated total annual income of the family or individual for the certification year, determined in accordance with the criteria prescribed by the Secretary of Housing and Urban Development under section 8(f)(3) of the United States Housing Act of 1937, as amended (42 U.S.C. 1437f(f)(3)), for purposes of determining whether a family is a lower-income family within the meaning of section 8(f)(1) of the Act. The adjusted income of a family or individual shall be computed solely from the income certifications required by paragraph (b)(4) of this section and shall be computed with respect to the "certification year" of the person. Adjusted income is not affected by income earned or received during the certification year that is not included in the income certification. The "certification year" for any person is the 12-month period which begins on the later of (A) the date on which the property attributable to the expenditures allocated to the dwelling unit occupied by the person is placed in service (see §1.167(k)-1(b)(3)), or (B) the date on which the person first occupies the unit on a rental basis, or signs a lease with respect to the unit, whichever occurs first. Adjusted income must be determined with respect to the actual occupants of the dwelling unit. For purposes of the preceding sentence, if any income of a family member who is not living in the dwelling unit would be taken into account under the criteria prescribed by the Secretary of Housing and Urban Development referred to in the first sentence of this subparagraph, that person shall be considered to be an occupant of the dwelling unit. The term "family", for purposes of section 167(k), means two or more persons related by blood, marriage, or operation of law.

(ii) The principles of this subparagraph may be illustrated by the following example:

Example. Family X first signs a lease on a rehabilitated dwelling unit on January 1, 1977, which the family first occupies on January 25, 1977. All expenditures with respect to the rehabilitation of the dwelling unit were paid or incurred by the taxpayer after December 31, 1975.

The certification year for members of family X is the 12-month period beginning on January 1, 1977. All income earned by family X in 1976 is disregarded. Instead, the determination of adjusted income shall be made with respect to the total anticipated annual income of the family for the calendar year 1977, computed in accordance with the criteria prescribed by the Secretary of Housing and Urban Development referred to in the first sentence of this subparagraph.

(4) **Income certifications.** * * * The income certification shall contain a statement of the anticipated total annual income for the certification year of each person who proposes

Proposed Reg. §1.167(k)-2

to live in the dwelling unit during the certification year, the number of minors who propose to live in the dwelling unit during the certification year, the anticipated total annual income of such minors, and a description of any payments expected to be received during the certification year which are not considered to be income, all determined in accordance with the criteria prescribed by the Secretary of Housing and Urban Development referred to in paragraph (b)(3) of this section. * * *

(5) **Effective date.** Paragraph (b)(2), (3), and (4) of this section shall apply to property attributable to expenditures which are paid or incurred after December 31, 1975. (For purposes of applying this subparagraph, rehabilitation expenditures treated as having been paid or incurred by the taxpayer by reason of §1.167(k)-1(b) shall be deemed to have been paid or incurred on the date on which the expenditures were actually paid or incurred, determined in accordance with the method of accounting used by the person that actually paid or incurred the expenditures.) In the case of property attributable to expenditures paid or incurred before January 1, 1976, the rules in 26 CFR 1.167(k)-3(b)(2), (3), and (4), revised as of April 1, 1977, shall continue to apply.

(6) **Examples.** * * *

Example (1). The median family income in a particular area for a family of four, as established for the purposes of applying section 8(f)(1) of the United States Housing Act of 1937, is $12,000. During 1976, the taxpayer spends in excess of $3,000 per unit in rehabilitating three two-bedroom dwelling units, X, Y, and Z. All the units are placed in service on January 1, 1977, and are advertised for rental at $200 per month. Unit X is rented at this price to tenant A and unit Y is rented to tenant B. A and B each is married and each has two children. At the time of the signing of the lease, tenant A certifies that the family's adjusted income for the certification year (the 12-month period beginning on the date the lease is signed), computed under paragraph (b)(3) of this section, is $9,000. Tenant B, at the time of signing the lease, certifies that the family's adjusted income is $10,000 for the certification year. Assuming that the Secretary of Housing and Urban Development has not established an income ceiling higher or lower than 80 percent of median for the area for purposes of applying section 8(f)(1) of the United States Housing Act of 1937, the low or moderate income level for the purpose of this paragraph is $9,600 (80 percent of the $12,000 median income for the area). Since tenant A's adjusted income of $9,000 does not exceed this amount, rehabilitation expenditures allocated to the dwelling unit rented to tenant A could qualify under section 167(k). However, the rehabilitation expenditures allocated to the dwelling unit rented to tenant B could not qualify, since tenant B's adjusted income ($10,000) is in excess of the low or moderate income level for the area.

Example 2. The facts are the same as in example (1). Eight months after signing the lease, tenant A receives a promotion that was not anticipated when the lease was signed. Because of the unanticipated promotion, tenant A's actual income for the certification year is $9,800, which is more than the income ceiling ($9,600). Even though A's adjusted income would not have qualified if the promotion had been anticipated when the lease was signed, the original election with respect to property contained in unit X will remain valid as long as tenant A occupies the unit.

Unit Z, even though vacant throughout 1977, will be considered low-income rental housing because the rental at which the unit is offered ($2,400 per year) does not exceed $2,800, i.e., 30 percent of $9,600, the low or moderate income level for a family of four.

* * * * * * * * * * * *

Section 1.167(k)-4 is amended by adding a new paragraph (f) at the end thereof, to read as set forth below.

§1.167(k)-4 (Proposed Treasury Decision, published 5-8-78.) Time and manner of making election.

* * * * * * * * * * * *

(f) **Extension of time for election.** In the case of property attributable to expenditures paid or incurred after December 31, 1975, a taxpayer will be permitted to make an election under section 167(k) (and file the statement required for subsequent taxable years by paragraph (b)(2) of this section) on or before [the 90th day after the date this notice of proposed rulemaking is adopted as a Treasury decision], notwithstanding the fact that the period prescribed by paragraph (c) of this section for filing an election for the taxable year (or for filing the statement required for a subsequent year) has expired.

Deduction for Removing Architectural Transportation Barriers for the Handicapped

The following sections are added:

§7.190-1 (Proposed Treasury Decision, published 4-4-77.) **Expenditures to remove architectural and transportation barriers to the handicapped and elderly.**

[Proposed rules under this section are contained in the temporary regulations promulgated under T.D. 7477, filed 3-30-77, and for this reason, are not repeated here. See p. 24,998.105.]

§7.190-2 (Proposed Treasury Decision, published 4-4-77.) **Definitions.**

[Proposed rules under this section are contained in the temporary regulations promulgated under T.D. 7477, filed 3-30-77, and for this reason, are not repeated here. See p. 24,998.105.]

§7.190-3 (Proposed Treasury Decision, published 4-4-77.) **Election to deduct architectural and transportation barrier removal expenses.**

[Proposed rules under this section are contained in the temporary regulations promulgated under T.D. 7477, filed 3-30-77, and for this reason, are not repeated here. See p. 24,998.106-B.]

Proposed Reg. §7.190-3

Political Contributions

The following new sections are inserted immediately after §1.217-1:

§ 1.218-1 (Proposed Treasury Decision, published 9-19-72.) **Deduction for contributions to candidates for public office.** (a) **Allowance of deduction.** Subject to the limitations of paragraph (b) of this section, in the case of an individual, there shall be allowed as a deduction for the taxable year any political contribution, payment of which is made by such individual within such taxable year. In no event shall a political contribution qualify for the deduction allowed by section 218 and this section unless such contribution is actually paid by the taxpayer within the taxable year for which the taxpayer claims such deduction. For purposes of the preceding sentence, the method of accounting employed by the taxpayer and the date on which such contribution is pledged shall be irrelevant. In the case of married individuals making joint returns, a political contribution made by either spouse shall qualify for the deduction. In the case of married individuals making separate returns, the contribution must have been made by the spouse claiming the deduction. The provisions of paragraph (2) (relating to admission to any dinner or program) and paragraph (3) (relating to admission to an inaugural ball or similar event) of section 276(a), and the regulations thereunder, shall not apply to a deduction allowed by section 218 and this section. For definition of the term "political contribution," as used in this section, see paragraph (b)(1) of § 1.41-1.

(b) **Limitations**—(1) **Maximum deduction.** The deduction allowed by paragraph (a) of this section for a taxable year shall not exceed $50 (or $100, in the case of married individuals making a joint return).

(2) **Verification.** The deduction allowed by paragraph (a) of this section shall be allowed, with respect to any political contribution, only if the taxpayer can verify that such contribution has, in fact, been paid. Such verification shall be made in the manner prescribed by paragraph (a)(2)(iii) of § 1.41-1. The taxpayer is not required to identify on his income tax return the name of the candidate, or of the committee, association or organization, to whom the contribution is made.

(c) **Election to take credit in lieu of deduction.** The provisions of section 218 and this section shall not apply in the case of any taxpayer who, for the taxable year, elects in the manner prescribed in section 41 and § 1.41-1(c) to take the credit under such sections for any political contribution paid in such year.

(d) **Restrictions**—(1) **In general.** The deduction provided by section 218 and this section may be claimed only by individual taxpayers who do not claim the standard deduction provided by section 141. The deduction provided by section 218 shall not be allowed in computing the taxable income of any corporation, association, company, organization, estate, or trust. The deduction may be allowed in computing the taxable income of any individual partner of a partnership for his distributive share of any political contribution made by such partnership.

(2) **Cross reference.** For provisions relating to the disallowance to estates and trusts of the deduction provided by section 218 and this section, see section 642(i).

(e) **Effective date.** The provisions of section 218 and this section apply to taxable years ending after December 31, 1971, but only with respect to political contributions, payment of which is made after such date.

Deduction for Retirement Savings

Immediately after § 1.218 there is added the following new section:

Proposed Regulations

§ 1.219-1 (Proposed Treasury Decision, published 2-21-75.) **Deduction for retirement savings.**

(a) **In general.** Subject to the limitations and restrictions of paragraph (b) and the special rules of paragraph (c)(2) of this section, there shall be allowed a deduction under section 62 from gross income of amounts paid during the taxable year of an individual by or on behalf of such individual for his benefit to an individual retirement account described in § 1.408-2, for an individual retirement annuity described in § 1.408-3, or for a retirement bond described in section 409. The deduction described in the preceding sentence shall only be allowed to the individual in whose name such individual retirement account, individual retirement annuity, or retirement bond is established or purchased. The first sentence of this paragraph shall only apply in the case of a contribution of cash, and a contribution of property other than cash is not allowable as a deduction. In the case of a retirement bond, a deduction will not be allowed if the bond is redeemed within 12 months of the date of its issuance.

(b) **Limitations and restrictions**—(1) **Maximum deduction.** The amount allowable as a deduction under section 219(a) to an individual for any taxable year cannot exceed an amount equal to 15 percent of the compensation includible in his gross income for such taxable year, or $1,500, whichever is less.

(2) **Restrictions**—(i) Individuals covered by certain other plans. No deduction is allowable under section 219(a) to an individual for the taxable year if for any part of such year—

(A) He was an active participant in—

(1) A plan described in section 401(a) which includes a trust exempt from tax under section 501(a),

(2) An annuity plan described in section 403(a),

(3) A qualified bond purchase plan described in section 405(a), or

(4) A retirement plan established for its employees by the United States, by a State or political subdivision thereof, or by an agency or instrumentality of any of the foregoing, or

(B) Amounts were contributed by his employer for an annuity contract described in section 403(b) (whether or not the individual's rights in such contract are nonforfeitable).

(ii) Contributions after age 70½. No deduction is allowable under section 219(a) to an individual for the taxable year of the individual, if he has attained the age of 70½ before the close of such taxable year.

(iii) Recontributed amounts. No deduction is allowable under section 219 for any taxable year of an individual with respect to a rollover contribution described in § 1.402(a)-3, 1.403(a)-3, 1.408-1(b)(2), or 1.409-1(c).

(iv) Amounts contributed under endowment contracts. (A) For any taxable year, no deduction is allowable under section 219(a) for that portion of amounts paid under an endowment contract described in § 1.408-3(e) which is allocable under subdivision (B) to the cost of life insurance.

(B) For any taxable year, the cost of current life insurance protection under an endowment contract described in subdivision (A) is the product of the net premium cost, as determined by the Commissioner, multiplied by the excess, if any, of the death benefit payable under the contract during the taxable year over the cash value of the contract at the end of such year.

(C) The provisions of this subdivision can be illustrated by the following examples:

Example (1). A, an individual who is otherwise entitled to the maximum deduction allowed under section 219, purchases, at age 20, an endowment contract described in § 1.408-3(e) which provides for the payment of an annuity of $100 per month, at age 65, with a minimum death benefit of $10,000, and an annual premium of $220. The cash value at the end of the first year is 0. The net premium cost, as determined by the Commissioner, for A's age is $1.61 per thousand dollars of life insurance protection. The cost of current life insurance protection is $16.10. A's maximum deduction under section 219 with respect to amounts paid under the endowment contract for the first year is $203.90 ($220 − $16.10).

Example (2). Assume the same facts as in example (1), except that the cash value at the end of the second year is $200 and the net premium cost is $1.67 per thousand for A's age. The cost of current life insurance protection is $16.37. A's maximum deduction under section 219 with respect to amounts paid under the endowment contract for the second year is $203.63 ($220 − $16.37).

(c) **Definitions and special rules—(1) Definitions.** (i) For purposes of this section the term "compensation" means wages, salaries, or professional fees, and other amounts received for personal services actually rendered (including, but not limited to, commissions paid salesmen, compensation for services on the basis of a percentage of profits, commissions on insurance premiums, tips, and bonuses) and includes earned income, as defined in section 401(c)(2), but does not include amounts received as earnings or profits from property (including, but not limited to, interest and dividends) or amounts not includible in gross income such as income from sources without the United States excluded from gross income under section 911.

(ii) (A) For purposes of this section, the term "active participant" means, except as provided in (B) of this subdivision, an individual who is a participant in a plan described in paragraph (b)(2)(i)(A) of this section and for whom, at any time during the taxable year,

(1) Benefits are accrued under the plan on his behalf,

(2) The employer is obligated to contribute to or under the plan on his behalf, or

(3) The employer would have been obligated to contribute to or under the plan on his behalf if any contributions were made to or under the plan.
For purposes of the preceding sentence, a participant includes an individual regardless of whether or not his benefits under the plan are nonforfeitable (within the meaning of section 411). In applying (2) and (3) of this subdivision (A), if an employer is or would have been obligated to contribute an amount on behalf of the individual with respect to a plan year of the plan which includes any portion of the taxable year of the individual, such individual shall be considered an active participant during such taxable year. However, for any taxable year of an individual in which there have been no contributions and there has been a complete discontinuance of contributions under a plan under which such individual is covered, such individual shall not be considered an active participant.

(B) For purposes of this section, an individual is not an active participant under a plan—

(1) With respect to any prior taxable year of such individual, merely because he is given past service credit for prior years of service;

(2) With respect to any taxable year of such individual beginning after his separation from service covered under the plan and before he resumes service covered under the plan, whether or not he has a nonforfeitable right to benefits under such plan; or

(3) For any taxable year of such individual in which such individual does not elect under the plan to participate in such plan.

This subdivision shall not apply in the case of an individual who elects not to be covered under the plan and subsequently elects to be covered under the plan if, under the plan, such individual can receive benefits based upon all prior years in which such individual could have been covered under the plan had he so elected, upon the payment by him of an amount specified under the plan for such prior years. In such case, the individual shall be treated as an active participant under the plan for each such prior year with respect to which such payment is made.

(2) **Special rules.** (i) The maximum deduction allowable under section 219 (b)(1) is computed separately for each individual. Thus, if a husband and wife

each has compensation of $10,000 for the taxable year and they are each otherwise eligible to contribute to an individual retirement account and they file a joint return, then the maximum amount allowable as a deduction under section 219 is $3,000. However, if, for example, the husband alone has compensation of $20,000 and they are each otherwise eligible to contribute to an individual retirement account for the taxable year, and they file a joint return, the maximum amount allowable under section 219 is $1,500.

(ii) Section 219 is to be applied without regard to any community property laws. Thus, if, for example, a husband and wife, who are otherwise eligible to contribute to an individual retirement account, live in a community property jurisdiction and the husband alone has compensation of $20,000 for the taxable year, then the maximum amount allowable as a deduction under section 219 is $1,500.

(3) **Employer contributions.** For purposes of this chapter, any amount paid by an employer to an individual retirement account or for an individual retirement annuity or retirement bond constitutes the payment of compensation to the employee (other than a self-employed individual who is an employee within the meaning of section 401(c)(1)) includible in his gross income, whether or not a deduction for such payment is allowable under section 219 to such employee after the application of section 219(b). Thus, an employer will be entitled to a deduction for compensation paid to an employee for amounts the employer contributes on the employee's behalf to an individual retirement account, for an individual retirement annuity, or for a retirement bond if such deduction is otherwise allowable under section 162.

Allowable Deductions of Membership Organizations

New sections 1.277-1, 1.277-2 and 1.277-3 are added immediately following § 1.276-1 and read as follows:

§ **1.277-1** (Proposed Treasury Decision, published 5-6-72.) **Allowable deductions incurred by certain membership organizations.**

(a) **In general.** Section 277 provides that, in the case of a social club or other membership organization which is operated primarily to furnish services, facilities, or goods to members and which is not exempt from taxation, deductions for taxable years beginning after December 31, 1970, which are attributable to furnishing services, facilities, insurance, goods, or other items of value to members shall be allowed but only to the extent of the gross income derived during such year from members or from transactions with members. Therefore, section 277 imposes a limitation on the deductibility of items attributable to furnishing services, facilities, insurance, goods, or other items of value to members which would otherwise be allowable as items of deduction under chapter 1 of the Code (including amounts determined without regard to whether the activity giving rise to such amounts was engaged in for profit such as, for example, deductions for interest under section 163). In addition, section 277 allows such organizations a limited deduction for items attributable to furnishing services, facilities, insurance, goods, or other items of value to members which would be deductible under section 162, 167, or similar provisions of the Code if the activity giving rise to such amounts were engaged in for profit.

(b) **Definitions.** For purposes of this section—

(1) **Membership organization.** The phrase "social club or other membership organization which is operated primarily to furnish services, facilities, or goods to members" (hereinafter referred to as a "membership organization") means any taxable organization operated on a mutual, cooperative, or similar basis whose primary activity is providing members with services, facilities, or goods. For purposes of determining whether an organization is operated on a mutual, cooperative, or similar basis, it is immaterial whether the organization is incorporated or unincorporated or is regarded as a profit or a nonprofit corporation under applicable State law. An organization which is operated primarily to realize gains to be distributed among its shareholders in proportion to their capital investment

or other equity interest is not a membership organization. Thus, an organization which is a regulated investment company as defined in section 851 is not a membership organization.

(2) **Member.** The term "member" means any person (including the dependents, as defined in § 1.152-1, and guests, as defined in § 1.512(a)-3(c)(2)(iii)(b), of such a person) who has the privilege by reason of payment of dues or otherwise to obtain from the membership organization services, facilities, insurance, goods, or other items of value on a mutual, cooperative, or similar basis whether or not such person owns stock in the organization or holds a certificate of membership and whether or not such a person is entitled to participate in the management of the organization.

(3) **Membership activity.** The term "membership activity" means the furnishing of services, facilities, insurance, goods, or other items of value to members on a mutual, cooperative, or similar basis.

(4) **Nonmembership activity.** Any activity of a membership organization other than the furnishing of services, facilities, insurance, goods, or other items of value to members on a mutual, cooperative, or similar basis is a "nonmembership activity".

(c) **Examples.** The provisions of paragraph (b) of this section may be illustrated by the following examples:

Example (1). C is a nonexempt national organization composed of individuals interested in the preservation of natural resources. C's sole objective is the promotion of activities and projects which in its view, will preserve natural resources. C accomplishes its objective by advertising, by presenting its view to State and Federal elected officials, and by actively supporting candidates for public office who agree with its views. Although C and its members generally have the same opinions on conservation issues, C does not promote the specific interests of any of its members. C obtains the funds necessary to accomplish its objective by assessing each of its members annual dues of ten dollars. C is not furnishing its members services since the same services would be available to them even if they were not dues-paying members. Therefore, C is not a membership organization for purposes of section 277 and this section.

Example (2). M Corporation was established by B to own and operate a golf club for individuals living in homes built by B. B established M to facilitate the sale of houses he built. B anticipates he will earn a profit on his investment in M. M's facilities are open only to individuals who buy his homes ("its members") and their dependents and guests. Although M's "members" have a voice in the operational policies of the golf club, all decisions are subject to the approval of B, who is the sole shareholder of M. Under these circumstances, M is not providing its members with services, facilities, or goods on a mutual, cooperative, or similar basis and is not, therefore, a membership organization for purposes of section 277 and this section.

(d) **Income and deductions of a membership organization—(1) In general—** (i) Net membership income. If for any taxable year membership income (determined under subparagraph (2) of this paragraph) exceeds membership deductions (determined under subparagraph (6) of this paragraph), the taxable income of a membership organization for such taxable year is the excess of the organization's total gross income over its total deductions (determined under subparagraph (5) of this paragraph).

(ii) Net membership loss. If for any taxable year a membership organization has sustained a net membership loss (membership deductions exceed membership income), the taxable income of the organization for such taxable year is the excess of its nonmembership income (determined under subparagraph (4) of this paragraph) over its nonmembership deductions (determined under subparagraph (7) of this paragraph). A net membership loss is not deductible in the taxable year in which it is incurred, but may be carried over to succeeding taxable years in the manner provided by paragraph (e) of this section.

(2) **Membership income.** Membership income is the gross income received by a membership organization from its members in consideration for membership activities, including the interest income derived from members who pay their initial membership fee in installments. In addition, membership income also includes the gross income derived by a membership organization from institutes and trade shows conducted primarily for the education of members. The determination of whether an institute or trade show is conducted primarily for the education of members depends upon all the surrounding facts and circumstances, including such factors as the format of the exhibits, the manner in which the exhibitors are selected, the prices charged for space, and use of the exhibits as sales facilities.

(3) **Certain rental income.** For purposes of subparagraph (2) of this paragraph, the term "membership income" includes that part of the rental income received from a person in exchange for permitting him to operate a membership organization facility as determined in accordance with this subparagraph. That part of such rental income so included in "membership income" is equal to the product of the total rental income, multiplied by a fraction, the numerator of which is the gross income received from members by such operator with respect to such facility, and the denominator of which is the total gross income received by such operator with respect thereto. This subparagraph shall apply only if the operator of such facility maintains adequate records to determine what portion of the total gross income he receives is gross income from members attributable to furnishing services, facilities, insurance or goods or other items of value to members. For example, if the operation of the dining facilities of a membership organization is leased to a concessionaire, and 95 percent of the total gross income for the use of the facilities is from members, then 95 percent of the amount paid by the concessionaire to the organization shall be treated as membership income. Similarly, if a membership organization leases its golf shop to a golf professional, and 97 percent of the total gross income for the use of such facility is from members, then 97 percent of the amount paid to the membership organization by the golf professional shall be treated as membership income.

(4) **Nonmembership income.** Nonmembership income is gross income exclusive of membership income. Thus, amounts of gross income paid to a membership organization by another membership organization or an exempt social club described in section 501(c)(7) for services, facilities, insurance or goods or other items of value provided by such membership organization under a reciprocal arrangement with such other organization shall be treated as nonmembership income, even though both organizations are of like nature.

(5) **Total deductions.** For purposes of this section, the total deductions a membership organization may take into account are the sum of its membership deductions and its nonmembership deductions.

(6) **Membership deductions.** Membership deductions are the expenses, depreciation, and similar items of deduction attributable to membership activities. Such items of deduction may, however, be taken into account only to the extent that such items are otherwise allowable as deductions under chapter 1 of the Code (applied without regard to whether the activity given rise to such items was engaged in for profit).

(7) **Nonmembership deductions.** Nonmembership deductions are the expenses, depreciation, and similar items allowable as deductions under chapter 1 of the Code other than those items described in subparagraph (6) of this paragraph.

(8) **Allocation of deductions.** Items of deduction attributable in part to nonmembership activities and in part to membership activities shall be allocated between the two classes of activities on a reasonable and consistently applied basis.

(e) **Carryover of net membership loss—(1) In general.** If for any taxable year there is a net membership loss, such loss is treated as an item of deduction attributable to membership activities in the succeeding taxable year, but only if such loss is reported on the membership organization's original or amended tax return for the year in which it was sustained. Therefore, section 277 and this section do not impose a time limitation on the carryover to a succeeding taxable year of such loss.

(2) **Change of status.** If in any taxable year a membership organization ceases to operate as such an organization (as defined in paragraph (b)(1) of this section), a net membership loss sustained by such an organization in a prior taxable year may not be carried over to such a taxable year. For example, assume that a membership organization has a net membership loss in 1972 of $10,000. This loss may not be carried over to 1973, if on January 1, 1973 the organization ceases to operate as an organization whose primary activity is furnishing services, facilities, or goods to its members on a mutual, cooperative, or similar basis.

(3) **Net operating loss.** Any amount treated as a net membership loss under section 277 and this section shall not qualify as a net operating loss (as defined in section 172(c)) and shall not be allowed as a net operating loss deduction in any year.

(f) **Determination of basis.** For purposes of this section, an adjustment which would otherwise be required to be made to the basis of property used for membership activities is not affected by the denial of all or part of a deduction which might be taken into account by an organization not subject to the provisions of section 277 and this section. For example, adjustment must be made for depreciation even though the organization is allowed only a portion of the depreciation allowance because membership deductions exceed membership income.

(g) **Examples.** The application of this section may be illustrated by the following examples:

Example (1). C is a nonexempt social club organized to enrich the social and cultural life of retired persons. C's activities include the planning of social events for its members. C also owns and operates a rooming house and a home for retired persons. Accommodations in the rooming house are rented on a weekly basis to the general public with the expectation of making a profit from such rentals. Accommodations in the home for retired persons are available only to C's members. During 1972 C has the following items of gross income and deduction:

Membership income:		
Dues and assessments	$14,000	
Income from home for retired persons	15,000	$29,000
Deductions attributable to membership activities:		
Taxes on home for retired persons	1,600	
Depreciation on home for retired persons	2,000	
Maid service, food, linens, etc. for home for retired persons	15,000	
Social events for the benefit of C's members	7,400	26,000
Nonmembership income:		
Rooming house rentals		20,000
Deductions attributable to nonmembership activities:		
Depreciation of rooming house	3,500	
Taxes on rooming house	2,500	
Maid service, linens, etc. for rooming house	11,000	17,000

Since C's membership income ($29,000) exceeds its membership deduction ($26,000), C's taxable income for 1972 is $6,000, the excess of its total gross income ($49,000) over its total deductions which may be taken into account ($43,000).

Example (2). E is a nonexempt membership organization engaged in the business of supplying electricity to rural areas on a cooperative basis. Under applicable

State law and its articles of incorporation if a member lives in a rural area which becomes incorporated into a township, such member can continue to receive electricity from E on a fee basis but must transfer back to E his certificate of membership, and is no longer entitled to share in the profits of E on a patronage basis. E engages in the activity of supplying nonmembers with electricity in the expectation of making a profit. E's costs of supplying electricity to members and nonmembers is the same. For the calendar year 1972, E has gross income of $100,000 (consisting of $60,000 from members and $40,000 from nonmembers). E's deductions attributable to supplying electricity for 1972 are $85,000 (consisting of $58,000 attributable to supplying members and $27,000 attributable to supplying nonmembers). In addition, E has a $25,000 net membership loss carried over from 1971 which was reported on E's tax return for 1971. E computes its taxable income as follows:

Membership income:		$60,000
Deductions attributable to membership activities:		
for 1972	$58,000	
Carryover from 1971	25,000	83,000
Nonmembership income:		40,000
Deductions attributable to nonmembership activities:		27,000

Since E's membership deductions ($83,000) exceeds its membership income ($60,000), E's taxable income is the excess of its nonmembership income ($40,000) over its nonmembership deductions which may be taken into account ($27,000), or $13,000. In addition, E has sustained a net membership loss of $23,000 ($83,000 of deductions less $60,000 of income) which may be carried over to 1973, if E reports such loss on its tax return for 1972.

§ 1.277-2 (Proposed Treasury Decision, published 5-6-72.) **Exceptions.** Section 1.277-1 shall not apply to any organization—

(a) Which for the taxable year is subject to taxation under subchapter H or L, chapter 1 of the Code,

(b) Which has made an election before October 9, 1969, under section 456 (c) or which is affiliated with such an organization, or

(c) Which for each day of any taxable year is a national securities exchange subject to regulations under the Securities Exchange Act of 1934 or a contract market subject to regulations under the Commodity Exchange Act.

§ 1.277-3 (Proposed Treasury Decisions, published 5-6-72.) **Interrelationship with cooperatives subject to the rules contained in subchapter 1 chapter 1 of the Code.** [Reserved]

Disallowance of Certain Deductions for Wage or Salary Expenses

§ 1.280C-1 (Proposed Treasury Decision, published 12-14-77.) **Disallowance of certain deductions for wage or salary expenses.**

If an employer is entitled to a credit under section 44B, it must reduce its deduction for wage or salary expenses paid or incurred in the year the credit is earned by the amount allowable as credit (determined without regard to the provisions of section 53). In the case in which wages and salaries are capitalized, the amount subject to depreciation must be reduced by an amount equal to the amount of the credit (determined without regard to the provisions of section 53) in determining the depreciation deduction. If the employer is an organization that is under common control (as described in §1.52-1), it must reduce its deduction for wage or salary expenses by the amount of the credit that it is allowed under subsections (a) or (b) of section 52. The deduction for wage and salary expenses must be reduced in the year the new jobs credit is earned, even if the employer is unable to use the credit in that year because of the limitations imposed by section 53.

Effects on Recipients

Section 1.301-1 is amended by revising paragraph (d), by revising that part of paragraph (h)(2) which follows subdivision (i) thereof, by revising that part of paragraph (j) which follows subparagraph (2) thereof, by adding new sentences after the final one in paragraph *(l)*, and by revising paragraph (n)(l), as follows:

§ **1.301-1** (Proposed Treasury Decision, published 5-7-76.) **Rules applicable with respect to distributions of money and other property.**

* *

(d) **Distributions to corporate shareholders.** (1) If the shareholder is a corporation, the amount of any distribution to be taken into account under section 301(c) shall be—

(i) The amount of money distributed,

(ii) An amount equal to the fair market value of any property distributed which consists of any obligations of the distributing corporation, stock of the distributing corporation treated as property under section 305(b), or rights to acquire such stock treated as property under section 305(b), plus

(iii) In the case of a distribution not described in subdivision (iv) of this subparagraph, an amount equal to (a) the fair market value of any other property distributed or, if lesser, (b) the adjusted basis of such other property in the hands of the distributing corporation (determined immediately before the distribution and increased for any gain recognized to the distributing corporation under section 311(b), (c), or (d), or under section 341(f), 617(d), 1245(a), 1250(a), 1251(c), or 1252(a)), or

(iv) In the case of a distribution made after November 8, 1971, to a shareholder which is a foreign corporation, an amount equal to the fair market value of any other property distributed, but only if the distribution received by such shareholder is not effectively connected for the taxable year with the conduct of a trade or business in the United States by such shareholder.

(2) In the case of a distribution the amount of which is determined by reference to the adjusted basis described in subparagraph (1)(iii)(b) of this paragraph—

(i) That portion of the distribution which is a dividend under section 301(c)(1) may not exceed such adjusted basis, or

(ii) If the distribution is not out of earnings and profits, the amount of the reduction in basis of the shareholder's stock, and the amount of any gain resulting from such distribution, are to be determined by reference to such adjusted basis of the property which is distributed.

(3) Notwithstanding subparagraph (1)(iii) of this paragraph, if a distribution of property described in such subparagraph is made after December 31, 1962, by a foreign corporation to a shareholder which is a corporation, the amount of the distribution to be taken into account under section 301(c) shall be determined under section 301(b)(1)(C) and paragraph (n) of this section.

* *

(h) **Basis.** * * *

(2) * * *

(ii) In the case of the distribution of any other property, except as provided in subdivision (iii) (relating to certain distributions by a foreign corporation) or subdivision (iv) (relating to certain distributions to foreign corporate distributees) of this subparagraph, whichever of the following is the lesser—

(a) The fair market value of such property; or

(b) The adjusted basis (in the hands of the distributing corporation immediately before the distribution) of such property increased in the amount of gain to the distributing corporation which is recognized under section 311(b) (relating to distributions of LIFO inventory), section 311(c) (relating to distributions of property subject to liabilities in excess of basis), section 311(d) (relating to appreciated property used to redeem stock), section 341(f) (relating to certain sales of stock of consenting corporations), section 617(d) (relating to gain from dispositions of certain mining property), section 1245(a) or 1250(a) (relating to gain from dispositions of certain depreciable property), section 1251(c) (relating to gain from disposition of farm recapture property), or section 1252(a) (relating to gain from disposition of farm land);

(iii) In the case of the distribution by a foreign corporation of any other property after December 31, 1962, in a distribution not described in subdivision (iv) of this subparagraph, the amount determined under paragraph (n) of this section;

(iv) In the case of the distribution of any other property made after November 8, 1971, to a shareholder which is a foreign corporation, the fair market value of such property, but only if the distribution received by such shareholder is not effectively connected for the taxable year with the conduct of a trade or business in the United States by such shareholder.

* *

(j) **Transfers for less than fair market value.** * * *

If property is transferred in a sale or exchange after December 31, 1962, by a foreign corporation to a shareholder which is a corporation for an amount less than the amount which would have been computed under paragraph (n) of this section if such property had been received in a distribution to which section 301 applied, such shareholder shall be treated as having received a distribution to which section 301 applies, and the amount of the distribution shall be the excess of the amount which would have been computed under paragraph (n) of this section with respect to such property over the amount paid for the property. Notwithstanding the preceding provisions of this paragraph, if property is transferred in a sale or exchange after November 8, 1971, by a corporation to a shareholder which is a foreign corporation, for an amount less than its fair market value, and if paragraph (d)(1)(iv) of this section would apply if such property were received in a distribution to which section 301 applies, such shareholder shall be treated as having received a distribution to which section 301 applies and the amount of the distribution shall be the difference between the amount paid for the property and its fair market value. In all cases, the earnings and profits of the distributing corporation shall be decreased by the excess of the basis of the property in the hands of the distributing corporation over the amount received therefor. In computing gain or loss from the subsequent sale of such property, its basis shall be the amount paid for the property increased by the amount of the distribution.

* *

(n) **Distributions of certain property by foreign corporations to corporate shareholders.** (1) If a foreign corporation distributes property (other than money, the obligations of the distributing corporation, stock of the distributing corporation treated as property under section 305(b), or rights to acquire such stock treated as property under section 305(b)) after December 31, 1962, to a shareholder which is a corporation in a distribution not described in paragraph (d)(1)(iv) of this section, then, except as provided in subparagraph (2) of this paragraph, the fair market value of the property shall be taken into account under section 301(c).

* *

Section 1.306-1 is amended as follows:

1. The phrase "gain from the sale of property which is not a capital asset," is deleted from the first sentence of paragraph (a) and the phrase "ordinary income" is inserted in lieu thereof.

2. The phrase "gain from the sale of property not a capital asset" is deleted from the first sentence of paragraph (b)(1) and the phrase "ordinary income" is inserted in lieu thereof.

3. The fourth sentence of paragraph (b)(1) is amended by deleting the phrase "While the amount of earnings and profits at the time of the distribution is one of the measures of the amount to be treated as ordinary income," and by capitalizing the first letter of the word "no".

4. The phrase "gain from the sale of property which is not a capital asset" is deleted from each example of paragraph (b)(2) and the phrase "ordinary income" is inserted in lieu thereof.

5. The second sentence of paragraph (c) is deleted.

* *

Section 1.306-3 is amended as follows:

1. Paragraph (a) is revised.
2. Paragraph (b) is revised.
3. The phrase "as of" is deleted from paragraph (g)(2) each time it appears and the phrase "by reference to" is inserted in lieu thereof.
4. The phrase "gain from the sale of property which is not a capital asset" is deleted from the first sentence of paragraph (h) and the phrase "ordinary income" is inserted in lieu thereof.
5. The second sentence of paragraph (i) is deleted.

The added and revised provisions read as follows:

§1.306-3 (Proposed Treasury Decision, published 3-15-78.) **Section 306 stock defined.**

(a) For the purpose of subchapter C, chapter 1 of the Code, the term "section 306 stock" means stock which meets the requirements of section 306(c)(1). Any class of stock distributed to a shareholder in a transaction in which no amount is includible in the income of the shareholder or no gain or loss is recognized may be section 306 stock, if a distribution of money by the distributing corporation in lieu of such stock would have been a dividend in whole or in part. However, except as provided in section 306(g), if no part of a distribution of money by the distributing corporation in lieu of such stock would have been a dividend, the stock distributed will not constitute section 306 stock.

(b) For the purpose of section 306, rights to acquire stock shall be treated as stock. Such rights shall not be section 306 stock if no part of the distribution would have been a dividend if money had been distributed in lieu of the rights. When stock is acquired by the exercise of rights which are treated as section 306 stock, the stock acquired is section 306 stock. Upon the disposition of such stock (other than by redemption or within the exceptions listed in section 306(b)), the proceeds received from the disposition shall be treated as ordinary income to the extent that the fair market value of the stock rights, on the date distributed to the shareholder, would have been a dividend to the shareholder had the distributing corporation distributed cash in lieu of stock rights. Any excess of the amount realized over the sum of the amount treated as ordinary income plus the adjusted basis of the stock, shall be treated as gain from the sale of the stock.

* * * * * * * * * * * *

Collapsible Corporations

Section 1.341-1 is amended to read as follows:

§**1.341-1** (Proposed Treasury Decision, published 7-7-77.) **Collapsible corporations; in general.**

Subject to the limitations contained in §1.341-4 and the exceptions contained in §1.341-6 and §1.341-7(a), the entire gain from (a) the actual sale or exchange of stock of a collapsible corporation, (b) amounts distributed in complete or partial liquidation of a collapsible corporation which are treated, under section 331, as payment in exchange for stock, and (c) a distribution made by a collapsible corporation which, under section 301(c)(3), is treated, to the extent it exceeds the basis of the stock, in the same manner as a gain from the sale or exchange of property, shall be considered as gain from the sale or exchange of property which is not a capital asset.

There is inserted immediately after § 1.341-6 the following new section:

§**1.341-7** (Proposed Treasury Decision, published 7-7-77.) **Certain sales of stock of consenting corporations.**

Proposed Reg. §1.341-7

(a) **In general.** (1) Under section 341(f)(1), if a corporation consents (in the manner provided in paragraph (b) of this section) to the application of section 341(f)(2) with respect to dispositions by it of its subsection (f) assets (as defined in paragraph (g) of this section), then section 341(a)(1) does not apply to any sales of stock of such consenting corporation (other than a sale to such corporation) made by any of its shareholders within the 6-month period beginning on the date on which such consent is filed.

(2) For the purposes of this section the term "sale" means a sale or exchange of stock at a gain, but only if such gain would be recognized as long-term capital gain were section 341 not a part of the Code. Thus, a sale or exchange of stock is not a "sale" within the meaning of this section if there is no gain on the transaction, or if the sale or exchange gives rise to ordinary income under a provision of the Code other than section 341, or if gain on the transaction is not recognized under any provision of subtitle A of the Code.

(3) A corporation which consents to the application of section 341(f)(2) does not thereby become noncollapsible, and the fact that a corporation consents to the application of section 341(f)(2) does not affect the determination as to whether it is a collapsible corporation.

(4) For limitations on the application of section 341(f)(1), see section 341(f)(5) and (6), and paragraphs (h) and (j) of this section.

(b) **Statement of consent.** (1) The consent of a corporation referred to in paragraph (a)(1) or (j)(1) of this section shall be given by means of a statement, signed by any officer who is duly authorized to act on behalf of the consenting corporation, stating that the corporation consents to have the provisions of section 341(f)(2) apply to any dispositions by it of its subsection (f) assets. The statement shall be filed with the district director having jurisdiction over the income tax return of the consenting corporation for the taxable year during which the statement is filed.

(2) (i) The statement shall contain the name, address, and taxpayer account number of any corporation 5 percent or more in value of the outstanding stock of which is owned directly by the consenting corporation, and of any other corporation connected to the consenting corporation through a chain of stock ownership described in paragraph (j)(4) of this section. The statement shall also indicate whether such 5-percent-or-more corporation (or such "connected" corporation) has consented, within the 6-month period ending on the date on which the statement is filed, to the application of section 341(f)(2) with respect to any dispositions of its subsection (f) assets (see paragraph (j) of this section), and, if so, the district director with whom such consent was filed and the date on which such consent was filed.

(ii) If, during the 6-month period beginning on the date on which the statement is filed, the consenting corporation becomes the owner of 5-percent or more in value of the oustanding stock of another corporation or becomes connected to another corporation through a chain of stock ownership described in paragraph (j)(4) of this section, then the consenting corporation shall, within 5 days after such occurrence, notify the district director with whom it filed the statement of the name, address, and taxpayer account number of such corporation.

(3) A consent under section 341(f)(1) may be filed at any time and there is no limit as to the number of such consents that may be filed. If a consent is filed by a corporation under section 341(f)(1) and if a shareholder sells stock (i) in such corporation, or (ii) in another corporation a sale of whose stock is treated under section 341(f)(6) as a sale of stock in such corporation, at any time during the applicable 6-month period, then the consent cannot thereafter be revoked or withdrawn by the corporation. However, a consent may be revoked or withdrawn at any time prior to a sale during the applicable 6-month period. If no sale is made during such period, the consent will have no effect on the corporation. See paragraph (g) of this section.

(c) **Consenting corporation.** (1) A consenting corporation at the time that it files a consent under section 341(f)(1) shall notify its shareholders that such consent is being filed. In addition, the consenting corporation shall, at the request of any shareholder, promptly supply the shareholder with a copy of the consent.

(2) A consenting corporation shall maintain records adequate to permit identification of its subsection (f) assets.

(d) **Shareholders of consenting corporation.** (1) A shareholder who sells stock in a consenting corporation within the 6-month period beginning on the date on which the consent is filed shall—

(i) Notify the corporation, within 5 days after such sale, of the date on which such sale is made, and

(ii) Attach a copy of the corporation's consent to the shareholder's income tax return for the taxable year in which the sale is made.

(2) If the sale of stock in a consenting corporation is treated under section 341(f)(6) as the sale of stock in any other corporation, the consenting corporation shall notify such other corporation, within 5 days after receiving notification of a sale of its stock, of the date on which such sale was made.

(e) **Recognition of gain under section 341(f)(2).** (1) Under section 341(f)(2), if a subsection (f) asset (as defined in paragraph (g) of this section) is disposed of at any time by a consenting corporation, then, except as provided in section 341(f)(3) and paragraph (f) of this section, the amount by which—

(i) The amount realized (in the case of a sale, exchange, or involuntary conversion), or

(ii) The fair market value of such asset (in the case of any other disposition),

exceeds the adjusted basis of such asset is treated as gain from the sale or exchange of such asset. Such gain is recognized notwithstanding any contrary nonrecognition provision of subtitle A of the Code, but only to the extent such gain is not recognized under any other provision of subtitle A of the Code (for example, section 1245(a)(1) or 1250(a)). Gain recognized under section 341(f)(2) with respect to a disposition of a subsection (f) asset has the same character (i.e., ordinary income or capital gain) that such gain would have if it arose from a sale of such asset.

(2) The nonrecognition provisions of subtitle A of the Code which section 341(f)(2) overrides include, but are not limited to, sections 311(a), 332, 336, 337, 351, 361, 371(a), 374(a), 721, 1031, 1033, 1071, and 1081.

(3) In the case of a foreign corporation which files a statement of consent pursuant to paragraph (b) of this section, such statement, in addition to the information required in paragraph (b) of this section, shall also contain a declaration that the corporation consents that any gain upon the disposition of a subsection (f) asset which would otherwise be recognized under section 341(f)(2) will, for purposes of section 882(a)(2), be considered as gross income which is effectively connected with the conduct of a trade or business which is conducted through a permanent establishment within the United States.

(4) The provisions of subparagraphs (1) and (2) of this paragraph may be illustrated by the following examples:

Example (1). Corporation X, a consenting corporation, distributes a subsection (f) asset to its shareholders in complete or partial liquidation of the corporation. The asset, at the time of the distribution, is held by the corporation primarily for sale to customers in the ordinary course of business and has an adjusted basis of $1,000 and a fair market value of $2,000. Under section 341(f)(2), the excess of the fair market value of the asset over its adjusted basis, or $1,000, is treated as gain from the sale or exchange of property which is neither a capital asset nor property described in section 1231. Assuming the gain is not recognized by corporation X under another provision of the Code, corporation X recognizes the $1,000 gain as ordinary income under section 341(f)(2) even though, in the absence of section 341(f)(2), section 336 would preclude the recognition of such gain.

Proposed Reg. § 1.341-7

Example (2). Corporation Y, a consenting corporation, distributes a subsection (f) asset to its shareholders as a dividend. The asset at the time of the distribution is property described in section 1231 and has an adjusted basis of $6,000 and a fair market value of $8,000. Assuming that no other section of the Code would require recognition of gain, under section 341(f)(2) the excess of the fair market value of the asset over its adjusted basis, or $2,000, is recognized by corporation Y as gain from the sale or exchange of property described in section 1231 even though, in the absence of section 341(f)(2), section 311(a) would preclude the recognition of such gain.

Example (3). Assume the same facts as in example (2) except that the subsection (f) asset is section 1245 property having a "recomputed basis" (as defined in section 1245(a)(2)) of $7,200. Since the recomputed basis of the asset is lower than its fair market value, the excess of the recomputed basis over the adjusted basis, or $1,200, is recognized as ordinary income under section 1245(a)(1). The remaining amount, or $800, is recognized under section 341(f)(2) as gain from the sale or exchange of property described in section 1231.

(5) The provisions of section 341(f)(2) apply whether or not (i) on the date on which a consent is filed or at any time thereafter, the consenting corporation was in fact a collapsible corporation within the meaning of section 341(b), or (ii) on the date of any sale of stock of the consenting corporation, the purchaser of such stock was aware that a consent had been filed under section 341(f)(1) within the 6-month period ending on the date of such sale.

(6) Section 341(f)(2) does not apply to losses. Thus, section 341(f)(2) does not apply if a loss is realized upon a sale, exchange, or involuntary conversion of a subsection (f) asset nor does the section apply to a disposition other than by way of sale, exchange, or involuntary conversion if at the time of the disposition the fair market value of such property is not greater than its adjusted basis.

(7) For purposes of this paragraph, the term "disposition" includes an abandonment or retirement, a gift, a sale in a sale-and-leaseback transaction, and a transfer upon the foreclosure of a security interest. Such term, however, does not include a mere transfer of title to a creditor upon creation of a security interest or to a debtor upon termination of a security interest. Thus, for example, a disposition occurs upon a sale of property pursuant to a conditional sales contract even though the seller retains legal title to the property for purposes of security, but a disposition does not occur when the seller ultimately gives up his security interest following payment by the purchaser.

(8) The amount of gain required to be recognized by section 341(f)(2) shall be determined separately for each subsection (f) asset disposed of by the corporation. For purposes of applying section 341(f)(2), the facts and circumstances of each disposition shall be considered in determining whether the transaction involves more than one subsection (f) asset or involves both subsection (f) and nonsubsection (f) assets. In appropriate cases, several subsection (f) assets may be treated as a single asset as long as it is reasonably clear, from the best estimates obtainable on the basis of all the facts and circumstances, that the amount of gain required to be recognized by section 341(f)(2) is not less than the total gain under section 341(f)(2) which would be computed separately for each subsection (f) asset.

(9) In the case of a sale, exchange, or involuntary conversion of a subsection (f) asset and a nonsubsection (f) asset in one transaction, the total amount realized upon the disposition shall be allocated between the subsection (f) asset and the nonsubsection (f) asset in proportion to their respective fair market values. In general, if a buyer and seller have adverse interests as to the allocation of the amount realized between the subsection (f) asset and the nonsubsection (f) asset, any arm's-length agreement between the buyer and the seller will establish the allocation. In the absence of such an agreement, the allocation shall be made by taking into account the appropriate facts and circumstances. Some of the facts and circumstances which shall be taken into account to the extent appropriate include, but are not limited to, a comparison between the subsection (f) asset and all the property disposed of in such transaction of (i) the original cost and reproduction cost of

construction, erection, or production, (ii) the remaining economic useful life, (iii) state of obsolescence, and (iv) anticipated expenditures to maintain, renovate, or modernize.

(10) See subparagraph (c)(1) of §1.1502-14 for the deferral of gain recognized upon a distribution other than in complete liquidation made by one member of a group which files a consolidated return to another such member.

(f) **Exception for certain tax-free transactions.** (1) Under section 341(f)(3), no gain is taken into account under section 341(f)(2) by a transferor corporation on the transfer of a subsection (f) asset to another corporation (other than a corporation exempt from tax imposed by chapter 1 of the Code) if—

(i) The basis of such asset in the hands of the transferee corporation is determined by reference to its basis in the hands of the transferor by reason of the application of section 332 (relating to distributions in liquidation of an 80-percent-or-more controlled subsidiary corporation), section 351 (relating to transfers to a corporation controlled by the transferor), section 361 (relating to exchanges pursuant to certain reorganizations), section 371(a) (relating to exchanges pursuant to certain receivership and bankruptcy proceedings), or section 374(a) (relating to exchanges pursuant to certain railroad reorganizations), and

(ii) The transferee corporation agrees (as provided in subparagraph (3) of this paragraph) to have the provisions of section 341(f)(2) apply to any disposition by it of such asset.

(2) The provisions of subparagraph (1) of this paragraph may be illustrated by the following examples:

Example (1). Corporation M, in exchange for its voting stock worth $20,000 and $1,000 in cash, acquires the entire property of corporation N (an unencumbered apartment building) in a transaction which is described in section 368(a)(2)(B) and which, therefore, qualifies as a reorganization under section 368(a)(1)(C). The apartment building, which in the hands of corporation N, a consenting corporation, is a subsection (f) asset, has an adjusted basis of $15,000 and a fair market value of $21,000. The basis of the apartment house in the hands of corporation M is determined by reference to its basis in the hands of corporation N by reason of the application of section 361. Thus, under section 341(f)(3), if corporation M agrees to have the provisions of section 341(f)(2) apply to any disposition by it of the apartment house, then corporation N will recognize no gain under section 341(f)(2) but will recognize $1,000 gain under section 361(b) (assuming the cash it receives is not distributed in pursuance of the plan of reorganization). However, if corporation M does not so agree, the gain recognized by corporation N will be $6,000, that is, the gain of $1,000 recognized under section 361(b) plus $5,000 gain recognized under section 341(f)(2). In either case, if section 1245, 1250, or 1251 applies, some or all of the gain may be recognized under such sections in lieu of sections 341(f)(2) and 361(b).

Example (2). Corporation Y, a consenting corporation, is a wholly owned subsidiary of corporation X. In the complete liquidation of Y it distributes to X a subsection (f) asset which is section 1245 property. The asset at the time of the distribution has an adjusted basis of $10,000, a recomputed basis of $14,000, and a fair market value of $16,000. The basis of the asset in the hands of X is determined by reference to its basis in the hands of corporation Y by reason of the application of section 332. Thus, under section 341(f)(3), if corporation X agrees to have the provisions of section 341(f)(2) apply to any disposition by it of the subsection (f) asset, then Y will recognize no gain under section 341(f)(2) and will recognize no gain under section 1245(a)(1) by reason of the application of section 1245(b)(3). Under section 334(b)(1), the basis of the subsection (f) asset to corporation X will be the same as it would be in the hands of Y, or $10,000. However, if corporation X does not so agree, then under section 341(f)(2) $6,000 (the excess of the fair market value of the asset over its adjusted basis) will be treated as gain from the sale or exchange of the asset. Moreover, under section 1245(a)(1) $4,000 (the excess of the recomputed basis over the adjusted basis) of the $6,000 will be recognized

Proposed Reg. § 1.341-7

as ordinary income. The basis of the asset to corporation X is $16,000, i.e., the same as it would be in the hands of Y ($10,000) increased in the amount of gain recognized by Y on the distribution ($6,000).

(3) The agreement of a transferee corporation referred to in subparagraph (1) of this paragraph shall be filed, on or before the date on which the subsection (f) assets are transferred, with the district director having jurisdiction over its income tax return for the taxable year during which the transfer is to be made. The agreement shall be signed by any officer who is duly authorized to act on behalf of the transferee corporation (if the transaction is one to which section 371(a) or 374(a) applies, the fiduciary for the transferee corporation, in appropriate cases, may sign the agreement) and shall apply to all the subsection (f) assets to be transferred pursuant to the applicable transaction described in section 341(f)(3). The agreement shall identify the transaction by which the subsection (f) assets will be acquired, including the names, addresses, and taxpayer account numbers of the transferor and transferee corporations, and shall contain a schedule of the subsection (f) assets to be acquired. The agreement shall also state that the transferee corporation (i) agrees to have the provisions of section 341(f)(2) apply to any disposition by it of the subsection (f) assets acquired, and (ii) agrees to maintain records adequate to permit identification of such subsection (f) assets.

(4) The transferor corporation shall attach a copy of the agreement to its income tax return for the taxable year in which the subsection (f) assets are transferred.

(g) **Subsection (f) asset defined.** (1) Under section 341(f)(4), a subsection (f) asset is any property which, as of the date of any sale of stock to which paragraph (a) or (j)(3) of this section applies, is not a capital asset and is property owned by, or subject to a binding contract or an option to acquire held by, the consenting corporation. Land or any interest in real property (other than a security interest) is treated as property which is not a capital asset. Also, unrealized receivables or fees (as defined in section 341(b)(4)) are treated as property which are not capital assets.

(2) If, with respect to any property described in subparagraph (1) of this paragraph, manufacture, construction, or production has been commenced by either the consenting corporation or another person before any date of sale of stock described in subparagraph (1) of this paragraph, a consenting corporation's subsection (f) assets include any property resulting from such manufacture, construction, or production. Thus, for example, if, on the date of any sale of stock within the 6-month period, manufacture, construction, or production has been commenced on a tract of land to be used for residential housing or on a television series, the term "subsection (f) asset" includes the residential homes or the television tapes resulting from such manufacture, construction, or production by the consenting corporation (or by a transferee corporation which has agreed to the application of section 341(f)(2)). If land or any interest in real property (other than a security interest) is owned or held under an option by the consenting corporation on the date of any sale of stock described in subparagraph (1) of this paragraph, the term "subsection (f) asset" includes any improvements resulting from construction with respect to such property (by the consenting corporation or by a transferee corporation which has agreed to the application of section 341(f)(2)) if such construction is commenced within 2 years after the date of any such sale. The property or improvements resulting from any manufacture, construction, or production is a question to be determined on the basis of the particular facts and circumstances of each individual case. Thus, for example, a building which is a part of an integrated project is a subsection (f) asset if construction of the project commenced before the date of sale or within 2 years thereafter even if construction of the building commenced more than 2 years thereafter. Similarly a television tape which is part of a series is a subsection (f) asset if production of the series was commenced on the date of sale even if production of the tape commenced after the sale.

(3) The provisions of subparagraphs (1) and (2) of this paragraph may be illustrated by the following examples:

Example (1). Corporation X files a consent to the application of section 341(f)(2) on January 1, 1965. Shareholder A owns 100 percent of the outstanding stock of the consenting corporation on January 1, 1965, and sells 5 percent of the stock on January 2, 1965, 10 percent on February 10, 1965, and 1 percent on May 1, 1965. No other sales of X stock were made during the 6-month period beginning on January 1, 1965. On such date X owns an apartment building and on March 1 X purchases an office building. X's subsection (f) assets include the apartment building owned on January 1 and the office building purchased on March 1.

Example (2). Assume the same facts as in example (1) except that on January 1, 1965, X also owns a tract of raw land. On April 1, 1965, construction of a residential housing project is commenced on the tract of land. Corporation X's subsection (f) assets will include the tract of land plus the resulting improvements to the land. This result would not be changed if construction of the residential housing project were not commenced until July 1, 1966, since the construction would have been commenced within 2 years after May 1, 1965.

Example (3). Corporation Y files a consent to the application of section 341(f)(2) on January 1, 1965. Shareholder B owns 100 percent of the outstanding stock of the consenting corporation on January 1, 1965, and sells 10 percent of the stock on June 1, 1965. On April 1, 1965, Y acquires an option to purchase a motion picture when completed. On May 1, 1965, production is started on the motion picture. On February 1, 1967, production is completed, and Y exercises its option. Y holds the option and the motion picture for use in its trade or business. Y's subsection (f) assets initially include the option and ultimately include the motion picture. However, the exercise of the option is not a disposition of the option within the meaning of section 341(f)(2).

(h) **Five-year limitation as to shareholder.** Under section 341(f)(5), section 341(f)(1) does not apply to the sale of stock of a consenting corporation by a shareholder if, during the 5-year period ending on the date of such sale, such shareholder (or any person related to such shareholder within the meaning of section 341(e)(8)(A)) made a sale of any stock of another consenting corporation within any 6-month period beginning on a date on which a consent was filed under section 341(f)(1) by such other corporation. Section 341(f)(5) does not prevent a shareholder of a consenting corporation from selling additional shares of the stock of the same consenting corporation. See paragraph (a)(2) of this section for meaning of the term "sale".

(i) [Reserved]

(j) **Special rule for stock ownership in other corporations.** (1) Section 341(f)(6) provides a special rule applicable to a consenting corporation which owns 5 percent or more in value of the outstanding stock of another corporation. In such a case, a consent filed by the consenting corporation shall not be valid with respect to a sale of its stock during the applicable 6-month period unless each corporation, 5 percent or more in value of the outstanding stock of which is owned by the consenting corporation on the date of such sale, files (within the 6-month period ending on the date of such sale) a valid consent under section 341(f)(1) with respect to sales of its own stock.

(2) The provisions of subparagraph (1) of this paragraph may be illustrated by the following example:

Example. Corporation X files a consent under section 341(f)(1) on November 1, 1965. On January 1, 1966, the date on which a shareholder of corporation X sells stock of X, X owns 80 percent in value of the outstanding stock of corporation Y. In order for the consent filed by corporation X to be valid with respect to the sale of its stock on January 1, 1966, corporation Y must have filed, during the 6-month period ending on January 1, 1966, a valid consent under section 341(f)(1) with respect to sales of its stock.

(3) For purposes of applying section 341(f)(4) (relating to the definition of a subsection (f) asset) to a corporation 5 percent or more in value of the outstanding stock of which is owned by the consenting corporation, a sale of stock of the consenting corporation to which section 341(f)(1) applies shall be treated as a sale of stock of such other corporation. Thus, in the example in subparagraph (2) of this paragraph, the subsection

Proposed Reg. § 1.341-7

(f) assets of corporation Y would include property described in section 341(f)(4) owned by or held under an option by corporation Y on January 1, 1966.

(4) In the case of a chain of corporations connected by the 5-percent ownership requirement described in subparagraph (1) of this paragraph, rules similar to the rules described in subparagraphs (1) and (3) of this paragraph shall apply. Thus, in the example in subparagraph (2) of this paragraph, if corporation Y owned 5 percent or more of the stock of corporation Z on January 1, 1966, then Z must have filed a valid consent during the 6-month period ending January 1, 1966, in order for the consent filed by X to be valid with respect to the sale of its stock on January 1, 1966. In such case any sale of stock of either X or Y is treated as a sale of stock of Z for purposes of applying section 341(f)(4) to Z.

(k) **Effective date.** Paragraphs (b), (c), (e)(3), and (f)(3) of this section apply only with respect to statements and notifications filed more than 30 days after [insert date on which the regulations under section 341(f) are published by the office of the Federal Register as a Treasury decision]. Paragraph (d) applies only with respect to sales of stock made more than 30 days after [insert date on which the regulations under section 341(f) are published by the office of the Federal Register as a Treasury decision]. All other provisions of this section apply with respect to transactions after August 22, 1964.

Partial Liquidation

§1.346-1 (Proposed Treasury Decision, published 1-13-77.) Partial liquidation.

Section 1.346-1 is amended by deleting the last sentence of paragraph (c) and by inserting in lieu thereof "The term 'active conduct of a trade or business' shall have the same meaning in this section as in §1.355-3(b)(2)."

Distribution of Stock and Securities of a Controlled Corporation

Sections 1.355-1 through 1.355-4 are amended to read as follows:

§1.355-1 (Proposed Treasury Decision, published 1-13-77.) **Distribution of stock and securities of a controlled corporation.**

(a) **Application of section.** Section 355 provides for the separation, without recognition of gain or loss to the shareholders and security holders, of one or more existing businesses formerly operated, directly or indirectly, by a single corporation. It applies only to the separation of existing businesses which have been in active operation for at least 5 years (or a business which has been in active operation for at least 5 years into separate businesses), and which, in general, have been owned, directly or indirectly, for at least 5 years by the corporation making the distribution of stock or of stock and securities. For the purpose of section 355, stock rights or stock warrants are not included in the term "stock and securities".

(b) **Type of separations.** Section 355 is concerned with two general types of separations. The first is the distribution of the stock of an existing corporation. The second is the distribution of the stock of a corporation holding assets of a business previously operated by the distributing corporation. In both cases, section 355 contemplates the continued operation of the business or businesses existing prior to the separation.

§1.355-2 (Proposed Treasury Decision, published 1-13-77.) **Limitations.**

(a) **Property distributed.** In order for section 355 to apply, the property distributed must consist solely of stock, or stock and securities, of a controlled corporation. If additional property (including an excess principal amount of securities received over securities surrendered) is received, see section 356.

(b) **Business purpose and continuity of interest. (1) In general.** A distribution by a corporation of stock or securities of a controlled corporation to its shareholders with respect to its own stock or to its security holders in exchange for its own securities will not qualify under section 355 where carried out for purposes not germane to the business of the corporations. The principal reason for this requirement is to provide nonrecognition treatment only to those distributions or exchanges of stock or securities of the controlled corporation which are incident to such readjustment of corporate structures as is required by business exigencies and which effect only a readjustment of continuing interests in property under modified corporate forms. Depending upon the facts of a particular case, a shareholder purpose for a transaction may be so nearly coextensive with a corporate business purpose as to preclude any distinction between them. In such a case, the transaction is carried out for purposes germane to the business of the corporations. On the other hand, if a transaction is motivated solely by the personal reasons of a shareholder, for example, if a transaction is undertaken solely for the purpose of fulfilling the personal planning purposes of a shareholder, the distribution will not qualify under section 355 since it is not carried out for purposes germane to the business of the corporations. Section 355 contemplates a continuity of interest in all or part of the business enterprise on the part of those persons who, directly or indirectly, were the owners of the enterprise prior to the distribution or exchange. For rules with respect to the requirement of a business purpose for a transfer of assets to a controlled corporation in connection with a reorganization described in section 368(a)(1)(D), see §1.368-1(b).

(2) **Examples.** The provisions of paragraph (b)(1) of this section may be illustrated by the following examples:

Example (1). Corporation P is engaged in the production, transportation, and refining of petroleum products. In 1962, P acquired all of the properties of corporation S, which was also engaged in the production, transportation, and refining of petroleum products. In 1968, as a result of anti-trust litigation, P was ordered to divest itself of all properties acquired from S. P proposes to transfer the assets acquired from S to a new corporation and to distributee the stock of such new corporation to its shareholders. In view of the divestiture order, the distribution of the stock of the new corporation to the shareholders of P will be considered to have been carried out for a real and substantial nontax reason germane to the business of the corporations.

Example (2). Corporation R owns and operates two men's retail clothing stores. The outstanding stock of R is owned equally by two brothers, A and B, and F, their father, who does not take an active part in the retail clothing business. A and B no longer can agree on major decisions affecting the operation of the corporation. Corporation R proposes to transfer one store to a new corporation and distribute 66.7 percent of the stock of such new corporation to one brother in exchange for all of his R stock. The other 33.3 percent of the stock of such new corporation will be exchanged for one-half of F's stock of corporation R. In view of the disagreement between managing shareholders, the distribution of the stock of the new corporation will be considered to have been carried out for a real and substantial nontax reason germane to the business of the corporations.

Example (3). Corporation T is engaged in the manufacture and sale of children's novelty toys. It also manufactures and sells candy and candy products. The shareholders wish to separate the candy business from the risks and vicissitudes of the novelty toy business. It is proposed that the assets and activities associated with the toy business be transferred to a new corporation, the stock of which would then be distributed to T's shareholder. The purpose of protecting the candy business from the risks of the novelty toy business, which is fulfilled when the novelty toy assets and activities are transferred to the new corporation, does not satisfy the requirement there be a substantial nontax reason, germane to the business of the corporation, for the distribution of the stock of the new corporation to the shareholders.

Example (4). The facts are the same as in example (3) except that T also requires outside financing in order to substantially expand its candy business. As a condition of the loan, in order to prevent the potential diversion of funds to the toy business, the lender requires the separation of the candy business and the novelty toy business and the distribution of the stock of the novelty toy corporation to the shareholders. The lender's re-

Proposed Reg. §1.355-2

quirements are based upon customary business practice. In this case, the distribution of the stock of the novelty toy corporation to the shareholders will be considered to have been carried out for purposes germane to the business of the corporations.

(c) **Device for distribution of earnings and profits—(1) In general.** Section 355 does not apply to a transaction which has been used principally as a device for the distribution of the earnings and profits of the distributing corporation, of the controlled corporation, or of both. The Code recognizes that a tax-free distribution of the stock of a controlled corporation presents an extraordinary potential for tax avoidance by placing the shareholders of the distributing corporation in a position whereby, as a consequence of the subsequent sale of stock or the liquidation of either the distributing corporation or the controlled corporation, they can avoid the dividend provisions of the Code. A distribution which is pro rata or substantially pro rata among the shareholders of the distributing corporation presents the greatest potential for the withdrawal of earnings and profits and is more likely to be undertaken principally as a device for the distribution of earnings and profits. Whether a transaction which has the potential for the distribution of earnings and profits was used principally as such a device shall be determined from all the facts and circumstances. Among the factors to be considered are those factors described in paragraph (c)(2) and (3) of this section. However, in any case in which a distribution with respect to each distributee would be treated as a redemption to which section 302(a) would apply if it were taxable, the transaction is not ordinarily considered to be a device for the distribution of earnings and profits. For purposes of the preceding sentence, section 302(c)(2)(A) shall be applied without regard to clauses (ii) and (iii). Further, in any case in which neither the distributing corporation, the controlled corporation, nor the corporations controlled by such corporations immediately before the distribution have earnings and profits, the transaction is not such a device. For this purpose, earnings and profits means earnings and profits accumulated after February 28, 1913, or earnings and profits of the taxable year which includes the date of the distribution, computed without regard to any distributions during the taxable year.

(2) **Subsequent sales of stock.** If, pursuant to an arrangement negotiated or agreed upon before the distribution, 20 percent or more of the stock of either the distributing corporation or the controlled corporation is to be sold or exchanged after the distribution, the distribution will be considered to have been used principally as a device for the distribution of earnings and profits of the distributing corporation, the controlled corporation, or both. If, pursuant to such an arrangement, part or all of the securities or less than 20 percent of the stock of either corporation is to be sold or exchanged after the distribution, this fact will be considered as substantial evidence that the transaction was used principally as such a device. For purposes of this subparagraph, the term "exchange" does not include an exchange of stock or securities in a tax-free transaction in which no gain or loss is recognized or in which an insubstantial amount of gain is recognized. A sale is always pursuant to an arrangement negotiated or agreed upon before the distribution when enforceable rights to buy or sell exist before such distribution. If a sale was discussed by the buyer and the seller before the distribution and was reasonably to be anticipated by both parties, such sale shall ordinarily be considered as made pursuant to an arrangement negotiated or agreed upon before the distribution.

Whether or not a sale is negotiated or agreed upon prior to the distribution, the fact of any sale of stock or securities shall be taken into account with other evidence in determining whether a transaction was used principally as a device for the distribution of earnings and profits.

(3) **Nature and use of assets**—(i) General. In determining whether a transaction was used principally as a device for the distribution of earnings and profits of the distributing corporation, the controlled corporation, or both, consideration will be given to the nature, kind, and amount of the assets of both corporations (and corporations controlled by them) immediately after the transactions and to the use of such assets by such corporations.

(ii) New trade or business. If a substantial portion of the assets of any post-distribution corporation consists of a trade or business acquired within the 5-year period ending on the date of the distribution in a transaction in which the basis of such assets was not determined in whole or in part by reference to the transferor's basis, this will be considered as evidence that the transaction was used principally as a device for the distribution of earnings and profits.

(iii) Liquid assets. The transfer or retention of cash of liquid assets (for example, securities and accounts receivable) which is not related to the reasonable needs of the business of the transferee or retaining corporation will be considered as evidence that the transaction was used principally as a device for the distribution of earnings and profits.

(iv) Related function. In certain cases the relationship between the nature and use of the assets of the distributing corporation and the controlled corporation will be considered as evidence that a transaction was used principally as a device for the distribution of earnings and profits. For example, where the principal function of one corporation before the transaction is to perform services for or supply technical or research data to the other corporation, and after the transaction that corporation continues to function on the same basis, this would be considered as evidence that the transaction was used principally as such a device. Thus, in example (9) of §1.355-3(c), involving a controlled corporation operating a coal mine for the sole purpose of satisfying the requirements of the parent steel corporation before the transaction, if the coal mining business continued to operate on the same basis after the transaction, this fact would be considered as evidence that the distribution of the stock of the coal mining corporation in example (9) is principally a device for the distribution of earnings and profits. Similarly, in a transaction which sepa-

Proposed Reg. §1.355-2

rates the manufacturing and sales operations, as in example (8) of §1.355-3(c), if the sales corporation merely functions as the exclusive agent for the manufacturing corporation after the transaction, this fact would be considered as evidence that the transaction was principally a device for the distribution of earnings and profits.

(4) **Examples.** The provisions of this paragraph (c) may be illustrated by the following examples:

Example (1). Corporation W has engaged in the commercial banking business in state N for 20 years. The stock of W is owned equally by individuals A, B, and C. Six years ago, W organized corporation X as a wholly-owned subsidiary to offer computerized bookkeeping services to the public. W and X have substantial accumulated earnings and profits. State N has recently amended its banking laws to provide that commercial banks operating in N may not offer computerized bookkeeping services directly or through a subsidiary. D, an individual, has offered to purchase the stock of X. At a stockholders' meeting the offer was rejected and it was decided to distribute the stock of X pro rata to A, B, and C. After the meeting and before the distribution, A, B, and C agreed to sell D one-half of X stock they were to receive in the distribution. Notwithstanding the existence of a corporate business reason for the distribution of the stock of X, the distribution will be considered to have been used principally as a device for the distribution of earnings and profits of W.

Example (2). Assume the same facts as in example (1) except that A, B, and C did not agree to sell any of the X stock they were to receive to D. At the shareholders' meeting it was decided to transfer cash to X before making the pro rata distribution. The amount of cash transferred substantially exceeded the reasonable business needs of X. After the distribution A and B agreed to sell to E, an individual, one-half of their X stock. Notwithstanding the existence of a corporate business purpose for the distribution, the transaction will be considered to have been used principally as a device for the distribution of earnings and profits because of the transfer of cash to X and the subsequent sale of X stock by A and B.

(d) **Stock and securities distributed.** The distributing corporation must distribute:

(1) All of the stock and securities of the controlled corporation which it owns, or

(2) At least an amount of the stock which constitutes control as defined in section 368(c). In such case all, or any part, of the securities of the controlled corporation may be distributed.

Where a part of either the stock or securities is retained under paragraph (d)(2) of this section, it must be established to the satisfaction of the Commissioner that such retention was not in pursuance of a plan having as one of its principal purposes the avoidance of Federal income tax. Ordinarily, the business reasons (as distinguished from the desire to make a distribution of the earnings and profits) which support a distribution of stock and securities of a controlled corporation under paragraph (b) of this section will require the distribution of all of the stock and securities. If the distribution of all of the stock and securities of a controlled corporation would be treated to any extent as a distribution of "other property" under section 356, this fact does not tend to establish that the retention of any of such stock and securities is not in pursuance of a plan having as one of its principal purposes the avoidance of Federal income tax.

(e) **Principal amount of securities**—(1) **Securities received.** Section 355(a)(1) is not applicable if the principal amount of securities received exceeds the principal amount of securities surrendered or if securities are received and no securities are surrendered. In such cases, see section 356.

(2) **Only stock received.** If only stock is received in a transaction to which section 355 is applicable, the principal amount of securities surrendered, if any, and the par or stated value of stock are not relevant to the application of such section.

(f) **Period of ownership**—(1) **Other property.** For the purposes of determining whether gain or loss will be recognized upon a distribution, stock of a controlled corporation acquired in a transaction in which gain or loss in recognized, in whole or in part (other than a transaction described in §1.355-3(b)(4)(ii)) within the 5-year period ending on the date of the distribution of such stock is treated as "other property." Section 355 does not apply to a transaction which includes a distribution of such stock. See section 356. The stock so acquired is "stock", however, for the purpose of the requirements respecting the distribution of stock of such controlled corporation provided in section 355(a)(1)(D).

(2) **Example.** Paragraph (f)(1) of this section may be illustrated by the following example:

Example. Corporation A has held 85 of the 100 outstanding shares of the stock of corporation B for more than 5 years on the date of distribution. Six months before such date, it purchased 10 shares of such stock. If all of the stock of the controlled corporation owned by A is distributed, section 355 is not applicable to such distribution since the 10 shares would represent "other property." See, however, section 356. If, however, for proper business reasons it is decided to retain some of the stock of B, then the determination of the amount of such stock which must be distributed under section 355(a)(1)(D) in order to constitute a distribution to which section 355 is applicable must be made by reference to all of the stock of the controlled corporation including the 10 shares acquired 6 months before such date and the 5 shares owned by others. Similarly, if, by the use of any agency, the distributing corporation acquires any stock of the controlled corporation within the 5-year period ending on the date of distribution in a transaction in which gain or loss is recognized in whole or in part, for example, where another subsidiary purchases such stock, such stock will be treated as "other property." If A had held only 75 of the 100 outstanding shares of stock of B for more than 5 years on the date of distribution and had purchased the remaining 25 shares 6 months before such date, neither section 355 nor section 356 would be applicable.

(g) **Active conduct of a trade or business.** The rules of section 355(b) and §1.355-3 relating to the active conduct of a trade or business must be satisfied.

§1.355-3 (Proposed Treasury Decision, published 1-13-77.) **Active conduct of a trade or business.**

(a) **Requirements as to active business—(1) In general—**(i) Application of section 355. Under section 355(b)(1), a distribution of stock or securities of a controlled corporation is subject to section 355(a) only if—

(A) The distributing corporation and the controlled corporation are each engaged in the active conduct of a trade or business immediately after the distribution of stock or securities of the controlled corporation (section 355(b)(1)(A)), or

(B) Immediately before the distribution the distributing corporation had no assets other than stock or securities in the controlled corporations and each of the controlled corporations is engaged in the active conduct of a trade or business immediately after the distribution (section 355(b)(1)(B)). In connection with the requirement of "no assets" a de minimis rule is applicable.

(ii) Examples. Paragraph (a)(1)(i) of this section may be illustrated by the following examples:

Example (1). Corporation A, prior to the distribution, is engaged in the active conduct of a trade or business and owns all of the stock of corporation B which also is engaged in the active conduct of a business. A distributes all of the stock of B to its shareholders, and each corporation continues the active conduct of its business. The active business requirement of section 355(b)(1)(A) is satisfied.

Example (2). The facts are the same as in example (1), except that A transfers all of its assets except the stock of B to a new corporation in exchange for all of the new corporation's stock and transfers the stock of both controlled corporations to its shareholders. The active business requirement of section 355(b)(1)(B) is satisfied.

(b) **Active conduct of a trade or business defined—(1) In general.** Section 355(b)(2) provides rules for determining whether any corporation is treated as engaged in the active conduct of a trade or business for purposes of ascertaining whether the distributing cor-

Proposed Reg. §1.355-3

poration and the controlled corporation meet the requirements of section 355(b)(1). Under section 355(b)(2)(A), a corporation is treated as engaged in the active conduct of a trade or business if it is itself engaged in such a trade or business or if substantially all of its assets consist of the stock and securities of a corporation or corporations controlled by it (immediately after the distribution) each of which is engaged in the active conduct of a trade or business.

(2) Active conduct of trade or business immediately after distribution—(i) General. For purposes of section 355(b), a corporation shall be treated as engaged in the "active conduct of a trade or business" immediately after a distribution if the assets and activities of such corporation meet the tests and limitations described in paragraph (b)(2)(ii), (iii), and (iv) of this section.

(ii) Trade or business. A corporation shall be treated as engaged in a trade or business immediately after a distribution of stock if a specific group of activities are being carried on by such corporation for the purpose of earning income or profit from such group of activities, and the activities included in such group include every operation which forms a part of, or a step in, the process of earning income or profit from such group. Such group of activities ordinarily must include the collection of income and the payment of expenses.

(iii) Active conduct. For purposes of section 355, the determination of whether a trade or business is actively conducted is a question of fact to be determined under all the facts and circumstances. In general, the corporation must perform active and substantial management and operational functions.

(iv) Limitations. The active conduct of a trade or business does not include—

(A) The holding for investment purposes of stock, securities, land, or other property, or

(B) The ownership and operation (including leasing) of real or personal property used in a trade or business, unless the owner performs significant services with respect to the operation and management of the property.

(3) **Active conduct for 5-year period preceding distribution.** Under section 355(b)(2)(B), a trade or business must have been actively conducted for the 5-year period ending on the date of distribution of the stock and securities of the controlled corporation. For this purpose, activities which constitute a trade or business under the tests described in paragraph (b)(2) of this section, shall be treated as meeting the test contained in the preceding sentence if such activities were actively conducted throughout such 5-year period. For the purpose of determining whether such trade or business has been actively conducted throughout the 5-year period described in section 355(b)(2), the fact that during such 5-year period such trade or business underwent change (for example, by the addition of new or the dropping of old products, changes in production capacity, and the like) shall be disregarded provided the changes are not of such a character as to constitute the acquisition of a new or different business.

(4) **Special rules for acquisition of a trade or business**—(i) General. For purposes of section 355(b), a trade or business which is relied upon to meet the requirements of such section must not have been acquired by the distributing corporation, the controlled corporation, or another member of the affiliated group during the 5-year period ending on the date of distribution of the stock and securities of the controlled corporation unless it was acquired in a transaction in which no gain or loss was recognized (section 355(b)(2)(C)). For purposes of this subparagraph (4), the term "affiliated group" means an affiliated group as defined in section 1504(a) (without regard to section 1504(b)) except that the term "stock" includes nonvoting stock which is limited and preferred as to dividends. In addition, under section 355(b)(2)(D), such trade or business must not have been indirectly acquired during such 5-year period in a transaction in which gain or loss was recognized in whole or in part by means of the acquisition of control of the corporation that was engaged in such trade or business or by means of an indirect acquisition of control of such corporation through another corporation or any of its predecessors in interest. A business acquired, directly or indirectly, within the 5-year period ending on the date of the distribution in a transaction in which the basis of the assets acquired is

not determined in whole or in part by reference to the transferor's basis for such assets will not qualify under section 355(b)(2), even though no gain or loss was recognized by the transferor (for example, by reason of section 337).

(ii) Gain or loss recognized in certain transactions. The rules of section 355(b)(2)(C) and (D) are intended to prevent the direct or indirect acquisition of a trade or business by a corporation as a temporary investment of liquid assets in anticipation of a distribution by such corporation of such trade or business in a transaction to which section 355 would otherwise apply. A direct or indirect acquisition of a trade or business by one member of an affiliated group from another member of such group is not the type of transaction to which section 355(b)(2)(C) and (D) is intended to apply. Therefore, in applying section 355(b)(2)(C) or (D), such an acquisition, even though taxable, shall be disregarded.

(iii) Example. Paragraph (b)(4)(i) may be illustrated by the following example:

Example: In 1956, corporation B, having cash and other liquid assets, purchased all of the stock of corporation A which was engaged in an active business. Later, in the same year, B in a "downstream" statutory merger merges into A. In 1958, A places the assets formerly owned by B in a new subsidiary, corporation X. A's distribution of the stock of X to the stockholders of A is not within the terms of section 355, since the active business of A had, in effect, been purchased less than 5 years prior to the distribution.

(c) **Examples.** The following examples illustrate the application of the rules provided in section 355(b)(2)(A) and (B). However, a transaction which satisfies the active conduct of a trade or business requirement in these examples will qualify under section 355(a) only if the other requirements of that section are met.

Example (1). Corporation A is engaged in the manufacture and sale of soap and detergents and owns investment securities. It proposes to place the investment securities in a new corporation and distribute the stock of such new corporation to its shareholders. The new corporation's holding of investment securities does not qualify as the active conduct of a trade or business immediately after the distribution.

Example (2). Corporation B owns, manages, and derives rental income from an office building and also owns vacant land. It proposes to transfer the vacant land to a new corporation and distribute the stock of such new corporation to its shareholders. The new corporation's holding of the vacant land does not qualify as the active conduct of a trade or business immediately after the distribution.

Example (3). Corporation C owns land on which it engages in the ranching business. Oil has been discovered in the area and it is apparent that oil may be found under the land on which the ranching activities are conducted. Corporation C has engaged in no significant activities in connection with the mineral rights. It proposes to transfer the mineral rights to a new corporation and distribute the stock of the new corporation to its shareholders. The new corporation's holding of mineral rights does not qualify as the active conduct of a trade or business immediately after the distribution.

Example (4). Corporation D, a bank, has for the past 7 years owned an 11-story downtown office building, the ground floor of which has been occupied by it in the conduct of its banking business. The remaining 10 floors are rented to various tenants and the building is managed and maintained by employees of the bank. Corporation D proposes to transfer the building to a new corporation and to distribute the stock of such new corporation to the bank's shareholders. The new corporation will manage the building, negotiate leases, seek new tenants, and will repair and maintain the building. Immediately after the distribution the activities in connection with banking will constitute the active conduct of a trade or business, as will the activities in connection with the rental of the building.

Example (5). Corporation E, a bank, has for the past 9 years owned a 2-story building in a suburban area, the ground floor and one-half of the second floor of which are

Proposed Reg. § 1.355-3

occupied by it in the conduct of its banking business. The other one-half of the second floor is rented as storage space to a neighboring retail merchant. Corporation E proposes to transfer the building to a new corporation and distribute the stock of the new corporation to its shareholders. Corporation E will lease the space formerly occupied by it in the bank building from the new corporation and, under the lease, will repair and maintain its portion of the building and pay property taxes and insurance. The new corporation will not be engaged in the active conduct of a trade or business immediately after the distribution.

Example (6). Corporation F is engaged in the retail grocery business and owns all of the stock of corporation G. Corporation G has for the past 10 years derived all of its gross income from the rental of its land and building to F, under a lease in which G's principal activity consists of the collection of rent from the building. Corporation F proposes to distribute the G stock to its shareholders. Corporation G will not be engaged in the active conduct of a trade or business immediately after the distribution, since it has not actively conducted a trade or business throughout the 5-year period ending on the date of the distribution.

Example (7). Corporation H has owned and operated a men's retail clothing store in the downtown area of the City of R for 7 years and has also owned and operated a men's retail clothing store in the suburban area of the City of R for 9 years. Corporation H proposes to transfer the store building, fixtures, inventory, and other assets related to the suburban store's activity to a new corporation. However, the warehouses which formerly served both the downtown and suburban stores will be retained by H, and the new corporation will lease warehouse space from an unrelated public warehouse company. Moreover, the delivery trucks and employees which formerly served both stores will be transferred to the new corporation for its exclusive use, and corporation H will contract with a local public delivery organization to effect its deliveries. Corporation H proposes to distribute the stock of the new corporation to its shareholders. Immediately after the distribution the activities in connection with the downtown store will constitute the active conduct of a trade or business, as will the activities in connection with the suburban store.

Example (8). Corporation I has processed and sold meat products for 8 years. It has no other income. Corporation I proposes to separate the selling from the processing activities by forming a separate corporation, J, to purchase for resale the meats processed by I. Corporation I will transfer to J certain physical assets pertaining to the sales function, plus cash for working capital, in exchange for the capital stock of J which will be distributed to the shareholders of I. Immediately after the distribution corporation I will be engaged in the active conduct of a meat products processing business and corporation J will be engaged in the active conduct of a meat distribution business. The business of each corporation is deemed to have been actively conducted from the date corporation I began its meat processing and sales business.

Example (9). For 8 years corporation K has been engaged in the manufacture and sale of steel and steel products. For 6 years K's wholly-owned subsidiary, corporation L, has owned and operated a coal mine for the sole purpose of supplying K's coal requirements in the manufacture of steel. It is proposed that the stock of L be distributed to the shareholders of K. Immediately after the distribution, the activities of L in connection with the operation of the coal mine constitute the active conduct of a trade or business. The activities of K in connection with the manufacture and sale of steel products immediately after the distribution also constitute the active conduct of a trade or business.

Example (10). Corporation M has for more than 5 years been engaged in the single business of constructing sewage disposal plants and other facilities. Corporation M proposes to transfer one-half of its assets to corporation N. These assets will include a contract for the construction of a sewage disposal plant in State X, construction equipment, cash, and other tangible assets. Corporation M will retain a contract for the construction of a sewage disposal plant in State Y, construction equipment, cash and other intangible assets. The N stock is then to be distributed to one of the M shareholders in exchange for all of his M stock. Both corporations will be engaged in the active conduct of the construction business immediately after the distribution.

Example (11). Corporation O has for the past 6 years owned three factories devoted to the production of edible pork skins. The entire output of two of the factories is sold to one customer. The third factory's output is sold to a number of different customers. Corporation O proposes to transfer the two factories which produce pork skins for the single customer, together with their related activities, to a new corporation and to distribute the stock of such new corporation to its shareholders. Immediately after the distribution the activities in connection with the production and sale of edible pork skins to the one customer will constitute the active conduct of a trade or business, as will the activities in connection with the production and sale of pork skins to the other customers.

Example (12). Corporation P has owned and operated a department store in the City of W for 9 years. Three years ago P acquired a parcel of land and constructed a branch store in a suburban area of the City of W. The two stores are operated as a single unit and have common advertising, bank accounts, billing, purchasing, and management. Corporation P proposes to transfer the suburban store, together with its related activities, to a new corporation and to distribute the stock of such new corporation to its shareholders. Each store will have its own manager and will be operated independently of the other store. Immediately after the distribution the activities in connection with each of the department stores constitute the active conduct of a trade or business since each store was an integrated part of the single department store business conducted by P for 9 years.

Example (13). Corporation Q is engaged in the business of manufacturing hats in its own factory building. It proposes to transfer the factory building to corporation R and distribute the stock of R to its shareholders. After the transfer, Q will lease the factory building under a long-term lease and will operate and maintain the building and the machinery in the building. The activities of R in connection with the leased factory building immediately after the distribution will not constitute the active conduct of a trade or business.

Example (14). Corporation S has been engaged in the manufacture and sale of household products for 8 years. Throughout this period, in connection with such manufacturing, it has maintained a research department for its own use. The research department has 30 employees actively engaged in the development of new products. Corporation S proposes to transfer the research department to a new corporation and to distribute the stock of the new corporation to its shareholders. After the distribution the new corporation will continue its research operations on a contractual basis with several corporations including S. Immediately after the distribution the activities of the new corporation in connection with research will constitute the active conduct of a trade or business, as will the activities of S in connection with manufacturing.

§1.355-4 (Proposed Treasury Decision, published 1-13-77.) **Non pro rata distributions, etc.**

Section 355 provides for nonrecognition of gain or loss with respect to a distribution whether or not (a) the distribution is pro rata with respect to all of the shareholders of the distributing corporation, (b) the distribution is pursuant to a plan of reorganization (within the meaning of section 368(a)(1)(D)), or (c) the shareholder surrenders stock in the distributing corporation. Under section 355 the stock of a controlled corporation may consist of common or preferred. (See, however, section 306 and the regulations thereunder.) Section 355 does not apply, however, if the substance of a transaction is merely an exchange between shareholders or security holders of stock or securities in one corporation for stock and securities in another corporation. For example, if two individuals, A and B, each own directly 50 percent of the stock of corporation M and 50 percent of the stock of corporation N, section 355 would not apply to a transaction in which A and B transfer all of their stock of M and N to a new corporation P, for all of the stock of P,

Proposed Reg. §1.355-4

and P then distributes the stock of M to A and the stock of N to B.

* * * * * * * * * * * * *

Foreign Corporations

§1.367-1 is deleted. (Proposed Treasury Decision, 12-30-77.)

Section 7.367-1 is redesignated as §7.367(a)-1 and is amended to read as follows:

§7.367(a)-1 (Proposed Treasury Decision, published 12-30-77.) **Ruling requests under section 367 relating to certain transfers involving a foreign corporation.**

[Proposed rules under this section are contained in the temporary regulations promulgated under T.D. 7494, filed 6-28-77, as amended by T.D. 7530, filed 12-27-77, and for this reason, are not repeated here. See p. 24,998.115.]

§7.367(b)-1 (Proposed Treasury Decision, published 12-30-77.) **Other transfers.**

[Proposed rules under this section are contained in the temporary regulations promulgated under T.D. 7530, filed 12-27-77, and for this reason, are not repeated here. See p. 24,998.116-A.]

§7.367(b)-2 (Proposed Treasury Decision, published 12-30-77.) **Definitions.**

[Proposed rules under this section are contained in the temporary regulations promulgated under T.D. 7530, filed 12-27-77, and for this reason, are not repeated here. See p. 24,998.116-B.]

§7.367(b)-3 (Proposed Treasury Decision, published 12-30-77.) **Special rules.**

[Proposed rules under this section are contained in the temporary regulations promulgated under T.D. 7530, filed 12-27-77, and for this reason, are not repeated here. See p. 24,998.116-C.]

§7.367(b)-4 (Proposed Treasury Decision, published 12-30-77.) **Certain exchanges described in more than one Code provision.**

[Proposed rules under this section are contained in the temporary regulations promulgated under T.D. 7530, filed 12-27-77, and for this reason, are not repeated here. See p. 24,998.116-D.]

§7.367(b)-5 (Proposed Treasury Decision, published 12-30-77.) **Complete liquidation of foreign subsidiary.**

[Proposed rules under this section are contained in the temporary regulations promulgated under T.D. 7530, filed 12-27-77, and for this reason, are not repeated here. See p. 24,998.116-D.]

§7.367(b)-6 (Proposed Treasury Decision, published 12-30-77.) **Exchange of stock in a foreign investment company.**

[Proposed rules under this section are contained in the temporary regulations promulgated under T.D. 7530, filed 12-27-77, and for this reason, are not repeated here. See p. 24,998.116-E.]

§7.367(b)-7 (Proposed Treasury Decision, published 12-30-77.) **Exchange of stock described in section 354.**

[Proposed rules under this section are contained in the temporary regulations promulgated under T.D. 7530, filed 12-27-77, and for this reason, are not repeated here. See p. 24,998.116-E.]

§7.367(b)-8 (Proposed Treasury Decision, published 12-30-77.) **Transfer of assets by a foreign corporation in an exchange described in section 351.**

[Proposed rules under this section are contained in the temporary regulations promulgated under T.D. 7530, filed 12-27-77, and for this reason, are not repeated here. See p. 24,998.116-F.]

§7.367(b)-9 (Proposed Treasury Decision, published 12-30-77.) **Attribution of earnings and profits on an exchange described in section 351, 354, or 356.**

[Proposed rules under this section are contained in the temporary regulations promulgated under T.D. 7530, filed 12-27-77, and for this reason, are not repeated here. See p. 24,998.116-F.]

§7.367(b)-10 (Proposed Treasury Decision, published 12-30-77.) **Distribution of stock described in section 355.**

[Proposed rules under this section are contained in the temporary regulations promulgated under T.D. 7530, filed 12-27-77, and for this reason, are not repeated here. See p. 24,998.116-G.]

§ 7.367(b)-11 (Proposed Treasury Decision, published 12-30-77.) **Deficit in earnings and profits.**

[Proposed rules under this section are contained in the temporary regulations promulgated under T.D. 7530, filed 12-27-77, and for this reason, are not repeated here. See p. 24,998.116-I.]

§ 7.367(b)-12 (Proposed Treasury Decision, published 12-30-77.) **Subsequent treatment of amounts attributed or included in income.**

[Proposed rules under this section are contained in the temporary regulations promulgated under T.D. 7530, filed 12-27-77, and for this reason, are not repeated here. See p. 24,998.116-I.]

§ 7.367(c)-1 (Proposed Treasury Decision, published 12-30-77.) **Section 355 distribution treated as an exchange.**

[Proposed rules under this section are contained in the temporary regulations promulgated under T.D. 7530, filed 12-27-77, and for this reason, are not repeated here. See p. 24,998.116-J.]

§ 7.367(c)-2 (Proposed Treasury Decision, published 12-30-77.) **Contribution of capital to controlled corporations.**

[Proposed rules under this section are contained in the temporary regulations promulgated under T.D. 7530, filed 12-27-77, and for this reason, are not repeated here. See p. 24,998.116-1.]

§ 7.367-2 (Proposed Treasury Decision, published 12-30-77.) **Ruling requests under section 367 as in effect on December 31, 1974.**

[Proposed rules under this section are contained in the temporary regulations promulgated under T.D. 7494, filed 6-28077, as amended by T.D. 7530, filed 12-27-77, and for this reason, are not repeated here. See p. 24,998.116-K.]

Carryovers in Certain Corporate Acquisitions

Section 1.381(c)(1)-1(a) is amended by adding new subparagraph (3) immediately after subparagraph (2) of that section. The amended provision reads as follows:

§ 1.381(c)(1)-1 (Proposed Treasury Decision, published 12-30-70.) **Net operating loss carryovers in certain corporate acquisitions.**

(a) **Carryover requirement.** * * *
(3) For purposes of the tax imposed under section 56, the acquiring corporation succeeding to and taking into account any net operating loss carryovers of the distributor or transferor corporation shall also succeed to and take into account along with such net operating loss carryforward any deferred tax liability under section 56(b) and the regulations thereunder attributable to such net operating loss carryover.

* * * * * * * * * * * * *

Paragraph (c)(1), Example (5) of paragraph (c)(3), and paragraph (d)(1)(iii) of § 1.381(c)(4)-1 are amended to read as follows:

§ 1.381(c)(4)-1 (Proposed Treasury Decision, published 8-23-72.) **Method of accounting.**

* * * * * * * * * * * * * * * * * * *

(c) **Change of method of accounting without consent of Commissioner**—(1) **General rule.** If the acquiring corporation may not continue to use, under the provisions of paragraph (b) of this section, the method of accounting used by it or the distributor or transferor corporation or corporations on the date of distribu-

Proposed Reg. § 1.381(c)(4)-1

tion or transfer, the acquiring corporation shall use the principal method of accounting of such corporation (as determined under subparagraph (2) of this paragraph), provided that (i) such method of accounting clearly reflects the income of the acquiring corporation, and (ii) the use of such method is not inconsistent with the provisions of any closing agreement entered into under section 7121 and the regulations thereunder. If the principal method of accounting does not meet these requirements, or if there is no principal method of accounting, see subdivision (i) of paragraph (d)(1) of this section. If the acquiring corporation wishes to use a method of accounting other than the principal method of accounting, see subdivision (ii) of paragraph (d)(1) of this section. Whenever this paragraph applies, the increase or decrease in tax resulting from the change from the method of accounting previously used by any of the corporations involved shall be taken into account by the acquiring corporation. The adjustments necessary to reflect such change and such increase or decrease in tax shall be determined and computed in the same manner as if on the date of distribution or transfer each of the several corporations whose method or methods of accounting are required to be changed in accordance with this section had initiated a change in accounting method. In addition, the acquiring corporation shall take into account the portion of such adjustments which is attributable to pre-1954 Code years to the extent not taken into account by any of the other corporations in accordance with the rules provided in section 481(b)(4) and this paragraph. However, for taxable years beginning after [insert date of publication of final regulations under this subparagraph in the Federal Register], the adjustments necessary to reflect the change from the method of accounting previously used by any of the corporations involved (including any adjustments required by section 481), shall be determined and computed in the same manner as if, on the date of distribution or transfer, each of the several corporations that were not using the principal method of accounting had initiated a change in the method of accounting; however, such adjustments (as an item of income or deduction, as the case may be) shall be taken into account solely by the acquiring corporation in computing its taxable income. If the principal method of accounting is adopted under this paragraph, it will be unnecessary for the acquiring corporation to renew any election previously made by it or by any distributor or transferor corporation with respect to such principal method of accounting which is in effect on the date of distribution or transfer to the same extent as though the distribution or transfer had not occurred, and the acquiring corporation is bound by any such elections.

* *

(3) Examples. * * *

Example (5). Assume the same facts as in example (1) except that M Corporation commenced business in 1945. In addition assume that N Corporation is a calendar-year taxpayer and that of the total amount of the adjustments required by section 481 to place the accounts of M Corporation on the accrual method $40,000 is attributable to pre-1954 Code years as described in section 481(b)(4) and the regulations thereunder. Assume further than M Corporation does not elect, under section 481(b)(6), to take the $40,000 portion of the adjustments into account in the manner described in section 481(b)(1) or (2). In computing the increase in tax of M Corporation attributable to the $40,000 portion of the adjustments for the fiscal year ended June 30, 1961, only one-tenth, or $4,000, will be taken into account in 1961 by N Corporation. The remaining nine-tenths of the $40,000 portion of the adjustments, or $36,000, shall be taken into account by N Corporation in the amount of $4,000 in each of the calendar years 1962 through 1970.

(d) Change of method of accounting with consent of Commissioner—(1) General rule. * * *

(iii) The increase or decrease in tax resulting from the change from the method of accounting previously used by any of the corporations involved shall be taken into account by the acquiring corporation. The adjustments necssary to reflect such change and such increase or decrease in tax shall be determined and computed in the same manner as if, on the date of distribution or transfer, each of the several corporations that were not using the method or combination of methods of accounting adopted pursuant to subdivision (i) or (ii) of this subparagraph had initiated a change in accounting method. However, for taxable years beginning after [insert date of publication of final regulations under this subdivision in the Federal Register], the adjustments necessary to reflect the change from the method of accounting previously used by any of the corporations involved (including any adjustments required by section 481) to a method required or permitted under this paragraph shall be determined and computed in the same manner as if, on the date of distribution or transfer, each of the several corporations that were not using the method of accounting adopted pursuant to this paragraph had initiated a change in the method of accounting; however, such adjustments (as an item of income or deduction, as the case may be) shall be taken into account solely by the acquiring corporation in computing its taxable income.

* * * * * * * * * *

Net Operating Loss Carryover

Section 1.382(b)-1 is amended by adding new paragraph (h) immediately after paragraph (g). The amended provision reads as follows:

§ 1.382(b)-1 (Proposed Treasury Decision, published 12-30-70.) **Change in ownership as the result of a reorganization.**

* * * * * * * * * *

(h) **Minimum tax for tax preferences.** For purposes of the tax imposed under section 56, the acquiring corporation succeeding to and taking into account any net operating loss carryovers of the transferor corporation shall also succeed to and take into account along with such net operating loss carryover any deferred tax liability under section 56(b) and the regulations thereunder attributable to such net operating loss carryover. Any reduction of net operating loss effected pursuant to section 382 and the regulations thereunder shall, for purposes of section 56(b) and the regulations thereunder and §.1.58-7, be deemed to reduce the portions of such net operating loss described in such provisions proportionately.

* *

Effective Date of Subchapter C (Repealed)

(Proposed Treasury Decision, published 4-3-78.)
Sections 1.391 and 1.391-1 are deleted.
Sections 1.392 and 1.392-1 are deleted.
Sections 1.393 through 1.393-3 are deleted.
Sections 1.394 and 1.394-1 are deleted.
Sections 1.395 and 1.395-1 are deleted.

* *

Requirements for Qualified Retirement Plans

Section 1.401-1(a)(3) is amended by revising subdivision (ix) thereof and adding, immediately after subdivision (ix), a new subdivision (x). These revised and added provisions read as follows:

§1.401-1 (Proposed Treasury Decision, published 5-6-72.) **Qualified pension, profit-sharing, and stock bonus plans.**

(a) **Introduction.** * * *

(3) * * *

(ix) It must, if the plan benefits any self-employed individual who is an owner-employee, satisfy the additional requirements for qualification contained in section 401(a)(10) and (d);

(x) If the trust forms part of a profit-sharing plan of an electing small business corporation for a taxable year beginning after December 31, 1970, the plan

Proposed Reg. § 1.401-1

must satisfy the additional requirement for qualification provided by section 1379(a) (see § 1.1379-1).

* * * * * * * * * * * * * *

Section 1.401-4 is amended by adding, immediately after paragraph (c), a new paragraph (d) which reads as follows:

§ 1.401-4 (Proposed Treasury Decision, published 5-6-72.) **Discrimination as to contributions or benefits.**

* * * * * * * * * * * * * *

(d) For purposes of this section, contributions made on behalf of a shareholder-employee of an electing small business corporation which are included in his gross income under section 1379(b) and § 1.1379.2 are treated as contributions by the employer.

A new §1.401-8 is added immediately before §1.401-8A (as redesignated) to read as follows:

§ 1.401-8 (Proposed Treasury Decision, published 10-16-75.) **Custodial accounts and annuity contracts.**

(a) *Treatment of a custodial account or an annuity contract as a qualified trust.* Beginning on January 1, 1974, a custodial account or an annuity contract may be used, in lieu of a trust, under any qualified pension, profit-sharing, or stock bonus plan if the requirements of paragraph (b) of this section are met. A custodial account or an annuity contract may be used under such a plan, whether the plan covers common-law employees, self-employed individuals who are treated as employees by reason of section 401(c), or both. The use of a custodial account or annuity contract as part of a plan does not preclude the use of a trust or another custodial account or another annuity contract as part of the same plan. A plan under which a custodial account or an annuity contract is used may be considered in connection with other plans of the employer in determining whether the requirements of section 401 are satisfied. For regulations relating to the period before January 1, 1974, see § 1.401-8A.

(b) **Rules applicable to custodial accounts and annuity contracts.** (1) Beginning on January 1, 1974, a custodial account or an annuity contract is treated as a qualified trust under section 401 if the following requirements are met:

(i) The custodial account or annuity contract would, except for the fact that it is not a trust, constitute a qualified trust under section 401; and

(ii) In the case of a custodial account, the custodian either is a bank or is another person who demonstrates, to the satisfaction of the Commissioner, that the manner in which he will hold the assets will be consistent with the requirements of section 401. Such a demonstration must be made in accordance with the provisions of § 1.401-12(n), as if the custodial account were a trust described in § 1.401-12(c)(1)(i).

(2) If a custodial account would, except for the fact that it is not a trust, constitute a qualified trust under section 401, it must, for example, be created pursuant to a written agreement which constitutes a valid contract under local law. In addition, the terms of the contract must make it impossible, prior to the satisfaction of all liabilities with respect to the employees and their beneficiaries covered by the plan, for any part of the funds of the custodial account to be used for, or diverted to, purposes other than for the exclusive benefit of the employees or their beneficiaries as provided for in the plan (see paragraph (a) of § 1.401-2).

(3) An annuity contract would, except for the fact that it is not a trust, constitute a qualified trust under section 401 if it is purchased by an employer for an employee under a plan which meets the requirements of section 404(a)(2) and the regulations thereunder, except that the plan may be either a pension or a profit-sharing plan.

(c) **Effect of this section.** (1) (i) Any custodial account or annuity contract which satisfies the requirements of paragraph (b) of this section is treated as a qualified trust for all purposes of the Internal Revenue Code of 1954. Such a custodial account or annuity contract is treated as a separate legal person which is exempt from the income tax under section 501(a). In addition, the person holding the assets of such account or holding such contract is treated as the trustee thereof. Accordingly, such person is required to file the returns described in sections 6033 and 6047 and to supply any other information which the trustee of a qualified trust is required to furnish.

(ii) Any procedure which has the effect of merely substituting one custodian for another shall not be considered as terminating or interrupting the legal existence of a custodial account which otherwise satisfies the requirements of paragraph (b) of this section.

(2) (i) The beneficiary of a custodial account which satisfies the requirements of paragraph (b) of this section is taxed in accordance with section 402. In determining whether the funds of a custodial account are distributed or made available to an employee or his beneficiary, the rules which under section 402(a) are applicable to trusts will also apply to the custodial account as though it were a separate legal person and not an agent of the employee.

(ii) If a custodial account which has qualified under section 401 fails to qualify under such section for any taxable year, such custodial account will not thereafter be treated as a separate legal person, and the funds in such account shall be treated as made available within the meaning of section 402(a)(1) to the employees for whom they are held.

(3) The beneficiary of an annuity contract which satisfies the requirements of paragraph (b) of this section is taxed as if he were the beneficiary of an annuity contract described in section 403(a).

(d) **Definitions.** For purposes of this section—

(1) The term "bank" means a bank as defined in section 401(d)(1).

(2) The term "annuity" means an annuity as defined in section 401(g). Thus,

Proposed Reg. § 1.401-8

any contract or certificate issued after December 31, 1962, which is transferable is not treated as a qualified trust under this section.

(e) **Cross reference.** For the requirement that the assets of an employee benefit plan be placed in trust, and exceptions thereto, see section 403 of the Employee Retirement Income Security Act of 1974, 29 U.S.C. 1103, and the regulations prescribed thereunder by the Secretary of Labor.

Section 1.401-8 is redesignated as §1.401-8A and is amended by revising the title and adding a new sentence at the end of paragraph (a) to read as follows:

§ 1.401-8A (Proposed Treasury Decision, published 10-16-75.) **Custodial accounts prior to January 1, 1974.**

(a) **Treatment of a custodial account as a trust.** * * * For regulations relating to the period after December 31, 1973, see § 1.401-8.

* * * * * * * * * * *

Section 1.401-8 [redesignated §1.401-8A] is amended by revising paragraph (b)(1)(i) to read as follows:

§1.401-8A (Proposed Treasury Decision, published 5-6-72.) **Custodial accounts.**

* * * * * * * * * * *

(b) Rules applicable to custodial accounts.

(1) A custodial account shall be treated for taxable years beginning after December 31, 1962, as a qualified trust under section 401 if such account meets the following requirements described in subdivisions (i) through (iii) of this subparagraph;

(i) The custodial account must satisfy all the requirements of section 401 that are applicable to qualified trusts and, if a custodial acccount is used under a profit-sharing plan of an electing small business corporation, the additional requirement for qualification provided by section 1379(a). See subparagraph (2) of this paragraph.

* * * * * * * * * * *

Section 1.401-12 is amended as follows:
1. Paragraph (a) is amended by deleting the last sentence and inserting two new sentences in lieu thereof;
2. Paragraph (c)(1)(i) is amended;
3. Paragraph (c)(2)(iii) is amended by substituting a semicolon for the period at the end thereof;
4. Paragraph (c)(2)(iv) is added; and
5. Paragraph (n) is added.

These amended and added provisions read as follows:

§1.401-12 (Proposed Treasury Decision, published 10-16-75.) **Requirements for qualification of trusts and plans benefiting owner-employees.**

(a) **Introduction.** * * * Except as otherwise provided, paragraphs (b) through (m) of this section apply to taxable years beginning after December 31, 1962. Paragraph (n) of this section applies to plan years determined in accordance with paragraph (n)(1) of this section.

* * * * * * * * * * *

(c) **Bank trustee.** (1)(i) If a trust created after October 9, 1962, is to form a part of a qualified pension or profit-sharing plan covering an owner-employee, or if a trust created before October 10, 1962, but not exempt from tax on October 9, 1962, is to form part of such a plan, the trustee of such trust must be a bank as defined in paragraph (c)(2) of this section, unless an exception contained in paragraph (c)(4) of this section applies, or paragraph (n) of this section applies.

* * * * * * * * * * *

(2) * * *

(iv) Beginning on January 1, 1974, an insured credit union (within the meaning of section 101(6) of the Federal Credit Union Act, 12 U.S.C. 1752(6)).

* * * * * * * * * * *

(n) Nonbank trustee—(1) Effective dates—(i) General rule. For a plan not in existence on January 1, 1974, this paragraph shall apply to the first plan year commencing after September 2, 1974, and all subsequent plan years.

(ii) Existing plans. For a plan in existence on January 1, 1974, this paragraph shall apply to the first plan year commencing after December 31, 1975, and all subsequent plan years.

(2) In general. For plan years to which this paragraph applies, the trustee of a trust described in paragraph (c)(1)(i) of this section may be a person other than a bank if he demonstrates to the satisfaction of the Commissioner that the manner in which he will administer trusts will be consistent with the requirements of section 401. Such demonstration must be made by a written application to the Commissioner of Internal Revenue, Attention: E:EP, Internal Revenue Service, Washington, D.C. 20224. Such application must meet the requirements set forth in paragraph (n) (3) to (7) of this section.

(3) Fiduciary ability. The applicant must demonstrate in detail his ability to act within the accepted rules of fiduciary conduct. Such demonstration must include the following elements of proof:

(i) Continuity. (A) The applicant must assure the uninterrupted performance of its fiduciary duties notwithstanding the death or change of its owners. Thus, for example, there must be sufficient diversity in the ownership of the applicant to ensure that the death or change of its owners will not interrupt the conduct of its business. Therefore, the applicant cannot be an individual.

(B) Sufficient diversity in the ownership of an incorporated applicant means that individuals each of whom owns more than 20 percent of the voting stock in the applicant own, in the aggregate, no more than 50 percent of such stock.

(C) Sufficient diversity in the ownership of an applicant which is a partnership means that—

(1) Individuals each of whom owns more than 20 percent of the profits interest in the partnership own, in the aggregate, no more than 50 percent of such profits interest, and

(2) Individuals each of whom owns more than 20 percent of the capital interest in the partnership own, in the aggregate, no more than 50 percent of such capital interest.

(D) For purposes of this subdivision, the ownership of stock and of capital and profits interests shall be determined in accordance with the rules for constructive ownership of stock provided in section 1563(e) and (f)(2). For this purpose, the rules for constructive ownership of stock provided in section 1563(e) and (f)(2) shall apply to a capital or profits interest in a partnership as if it were a stock interest.

(ii) Established location. The applicant must have an established place of business in the United States where he is accessible during every business day.

(iii) Fiduciary experience. The applicant must have fiduciary experience or expertise sufficient to ensure that he will be able to perform his fiduciary duties.

[The page following this is 63,331]

Proposed Reg. §1.401-12

Evidence of fiduciary experience must include proof that a significant part of the business of the applicant consists of exercising fiduciary powers similar to those he will exercise if his application is approved. Evidence of fiduciary expertise must include proof that the applicant employs personnel experienced in the administration of fiduciary powers similar to those he will exercise if his application is approved.

(iv) *Fiduciary responsibility.* The applicant must assure compliance with the rules of fiduciary conduct set out in paragraph (n) (6) of this section.

(v) *Financial responsibility.* The applicant must exhibit a high degree of solvency commensurate with the obligations imposed by this paragraph. Among the factors to be taken into account are the applicant's net worth, his liquidity, and his ability to pay his debts as they come due.

(4) Capacity to account. The applicant must demonstrate in detail his experience and competence with respect to accounting for the interests of a large number of individuals (including calculating and allocating income earned and paying out distributions to payees). Examples of accounting for the interests of a large number of individuals include accounting for the interests of a large number of shareholders in a regulated investment company and accounting for the interests of a large number of variable annuity contract holders.

(5) Fitness to handle funds—(i) *In general.* The applicant must demonstrate in detail his experience and competence with respect to other activities normally associated with the handling of retirement funds.

(ii) *Examples.* Examples of activities normally associated with the handling of retirement funds include:

(A) To receive, issue receipts for, and safely keep securities;
(B) To collect income;
(C) To execute such ownership certificates, to keep such records, make such returns, and render such statements as are required for Federal tax purposes;
(D) To give proper notification regarding all collections;
(E) To collect matured or called principal and properly report all such collections;
(F) To exchange temporary for definitive securities;
(G) To give proper notification of calls, subscription rights, defaults in principal or interest, and the formation of protective committees;
(H) To buy, sell, receive, or deliver securities on specific directions.

(6) Rules of fiduciary conduct—(i) *Administration of fiduciary powers.* The applicant must demonstrate that under applicable regulatory requirements, corporate or other governing instruments, or its established operating procedures:

(A) (1) The owners or directors of the applicant will be responsible for the proper exercise of fiduciary powers by the applicant. Thus, all matters pertinent thereto, including the determination of policies, the investment and disposition of property held in a fiduciary capacity, and the direction and review of the actions of all employees utilized by the applicant in the exercise of his fiduciary powers, will be the responsibility of the owners or directors. In discharging this responsibility, the owner or directors may assign to designated employees, by action duly recorded, the administration of such of the applicant's fiduciary powers as may be proper to assign.

(2) A written record will be made of the acceptance and of the relinquishment or closing out of all fiduciary accounts, and of the assets held for each account.

(3) At least once during each period of 12 months all the assets held in or for each fiduciary account where the applicant has investment responsibilities will be reviewed to determine the advisability of retaining or disposing of such assets.

(B) All employees taking part in the performance of the applicant's fiduciary duties will be adequately bonded. Nothing in this (B) shall require any person to be bonded in contravention of section 412(d) of the Employee Retirement Income Security Act of 1974 (29 U.S.C. 1112(d)).

(C) The applicant will designate, employ or retain legal counsel who will be readily available to pass upon fiduciary matters and to advise the applicant.

Proposed Reg. § 1.401-12

(D) In order to segregate the performance of his fiduciary duties from other business activities, the applicant will maintain a separate trust division under the immediate supervision of an individual designated for that purpose. The trust division may utilize the personnel and facilities of other divisions of the applicant, and other divisions of the applicant may utlize the personnel and facilities of the trust division, as long as the separate identity of the trust division is preserved.

(ii) Adequacy of net worth. (A) Not less frequently than once during each calendar year the applicant will determine the value of the assets held by him in trust. Such assets will be valued at their current value, except that the assets of an employee benefit plan to which section 103(b)(3)(A) of the Employee Retirement Income Security Act of 1974 (29 U.S.C. 1023(b)(3)(A)) applies will be considered to have the value stated in the most recent annual report of the plan.

(B) No fiduciary account will be accepted by the applicant unless his net worth (determined as of the end of the most recent taxable year) exceeds the greater of—

(1) $100,000, or

(2) Four percent of the value of all of the assets held by the applicant in trust (determined as of the most recent valuation date).

(C) The applicant will take whatever lawful steps are necessary (including the relinquishment of fiduciary accounts) to ensure that his net worth (determined as of the close of each taxable year) exceeds the greater of—

(1) $50,000, or

(2) Two percent of the value of all of the assets held by the applicant in trust (determined as of the most recent valuation date).

(iii) Audits. (A) The applicant will at least once during each period of 12 months cause detailed audits of the fiduciary books and records to be made by an independent qualified public accountant, and at such time will ascertain whether the fiduciary accounts have been administered in accordance with law, this paragraph, and sound fiduciary principles. Such audits shall be conducted in accordance with generally accepted auditing standards, and shall involve such tests of the fiduciary books and records of the applicant as are considered necessary by the independent qualified public accountant.

(B) In the case of an applicant who is regulated, supervised, and subject to periodic examination by a State or Federal agency, such applicant may adopt an adequate continuous audit system in lieu of the periodic audits required by paragraph (n)(6)(iii)(A) of this section.

(C) A report of the audits and examinations required under this subdivision, together with the action taken thereon, will be noted in the fiduciary records of the applicant.

(iv) Funds awaiting investment or distribution. Funds held in a fiduciary capacity by the applicant awaiting investment or distribution will not be held uninvested or undistributed any longer than is reasonable for the proper management of the account.

(v) Custody of investments. (A) Except for investments pooled in a common investment fund in accordance with the provisions of paragraph (n)(6)(vi) of this section, the investments of each account will not be commingled with any other property.

(B) Fiduciary assets requiring safekeeping will be deposited in an adequate vault. A permanent record will be kept of fiduciary assets deposited in or withdrawn from the vault.

(vi) Common investment funds. Where not in contravention of local law the assets of an account may be pooled in a common investment fund (as defined in paragraph (n)(6)(viii)(C) of this section) which must be administered as follows:

(A) Each common investment fund must be established and maintained in accordance with a written agreement, containing appropriate provisions as to the manner in which the fund is to be operated, including provisions relating to the investment powers and a general statement of the investment policy of the applicant with respect to the fund; the allocation of income, profits and losses; the terms and conditions governing the admission or withdrawal of participations in the fund; the auditing of accounts of the applicant with respect to the fund; the basis and method of valuing assets in the fund, setting forth specific criteria for each type of asset; the minimum frequency for valuation of assets of the fund; the period following each such valuation date during which the valuation may be made (which period in usual circumstances may not exceed 10 business days); the basis upon which the fund may be terminated; and such other matters as may be necessary to define clearly the rights of participants in the fund. A copy of the agreement must be available at the principal office of the applicant for inspection during all business hours, and upon request a copy of the agreement must be furnished to any interested person.

(B) All participations in the common investment fund must be on the basis of a proportionate interest in all of the assets.

(C) Not less frequently than once during each period of 3 months the applicant must determine the value of the assets in the fund as of the date set for the valuation of assets. No participation may be admitted to or withdrawn from the fund except (1) on the basis of such valuation and (2) as of such valuation date. No participation may be admitted to or withdrawn from the fund unless a written request for or notice of intention of taking such action has been entered on or before the valuation date in the fiduciary records of the applicant. No request or notice may be canceled or countermanded after the valuation date.

(D) (1) The applicant must at least once during each period of 12 months cause and adequate audit to be made of the common investment fund by a qualified public accountant.

(2) The applicant must at least once during each period of 12 months prepare a financial report of the fund which, based upon the above audit, must contain a list of investments in the fund showing the cost and current market value of each investment; a statement for the period since the previous report showing purchases, with cost; sales, with profit or loss and any other investment changes; income and disbursements; and an appropriate notation as to any investments in default.

(3) The applicant must transmit and certify the accuracy of the financial report to the administrator of each plan participating in the common investment fund within 120 days after the end of the plan year.

(E) When participations are withdrawn from a common investment fund, distributions may be made in cash or ratably in kind, or partly in cash and partly in kind, provided that all distributions as of any one valuation date must be made on the same basis.

(F) If for any reason an investment is withdrawn in kind from a common investment fund for the benefit of all participants in the fund at the time of such withdrawal and such investment is not distribtued ratably in kind, it must be segregated and administered or realized upon for the benefit ratably of all participants in the common investment fund at the time of withdrawal.

(vii) Books and records. (A) The applicant must keep his fiduciary records separate and distinct from other records. All fiduciary records must be so kept and retained for as long as the contents thereof may become material in the administration of any internal revenue law. The fiduciary records must contain full information relative to each account.

(B) The applicant must keep an adequate record of all pending litigation to which he is a party in connection with the exercise of fiducary powers.

(viii) Definitions. For purposes of this subparagraph and paragraph (n) (3) (v) of this section—

(A) The term "account" or "fiduciary account" means a trust described in section 401(a) (including a custodial account described in section 401(f)), a custodial account described in section 403(b)(7), or an individual retirement account described in section 408(a) (including a custodial account described in section 408(h)).

(B) The term "administrator" means an administrator as defined in section

Proposed Reg. § 1.401-12

3(16)(A) of the Employee Retirement Income Security Act of 1974, 29 U.S.C. 1002 (16)(A).

(C) The term "common investment fund" means a trust which satisfies the following requirements:

(1) The trust consists of all or part of the assets of several accounts which have been established with the applicant, and

(2) The trust is described in section 401(a) and is exempt from tax under section 501(a), or is a common investment fund described in § 1.408-2(b)(5), or both.

(D) The term "employee benefit plan" means an employee benefit plan as defined in section 3(2) of the Employee Retirement Income Security Act of 1974, 29 U.S.C. 1002(2).

(E) The term "fiduciary records" means all matters which are written, transcribed, recorded, received or otherwise come into the possession of the applicant and are necessary to preserve information concerning the acts and events relevant to the fiduciary activities of the applicant.

(F) The term "qualified public accountant" means a qualified public accountant as defined in section 103(a)(3)(D) of the Employee Retirement Income Security Act of 1974, 29 U.S.C. 1023(a)(3)(D).

(G) The term "net worth" means the amount of the applicant's assets less the amount of his liabilities, as determined in accordance with generally accepted accounting principles.

(7) **Special rules**—(i) Passive trustee. (A) An applicant who undertakes to act only as a passive trustee may be relieved of one or more of the requirements of this paragraph upon clear and convincing proof that such requirements are not germane, under all the facts and circumstances, to the manner in which he will administer any trust. A trustee is a passive trustee only if under the written trust instrument he has no discretion to direct the investment of the trust funds or any other aspect of the business administration of the trust, but is merely authorized to acquire and hold particular investments specified by the trust instrument. Thus, for example, in the case of an applicant who undertakes merely to acquire and hold the stock of a single regulated investment company, the requirements of paragraph (n) (6) (i)(A)(3), (i)(D), and (vi) of this section shall not apply and no negative inference shall be drawn from the applicant's failure to demonstrate his experience or competence with respect to the activities described in paragraph (n)(5)(ii)(E) to (H) of this section.

(B) The determination letter issued to an applicant who is approved by reason of this subdivision shall state that the applicant is authorized to act only as a passive trustee.

(ii) Federal or State regulation. Evidence that an applicant is subject to Federal or State regulation with respect to one or more relevant factors shall be given weight in proportion to the extent that such regulatory standards are consonant with the requirements of section 401.

(iii) Savings account. (A) An applicant will be presumed to meet the requirements of this paragraph upon proof of the following:

(1) The investment of the trust assets will be solely in deposits in the applicant;

(2) Section 4975(c) will not apply to such investment by reason of section 4975(d)(4); and

(3) Such deposits will be fully insured by an agency of the United States or a State.

(B) The determination letter issued to an applicant who is approved by reason of this subdivision shall state that the applicant is authorized to act as the trustee of a trust only if the requirements of paragraph (n) (7) (iii) (A) of this section are satisfied.

(iv) Notification of Commissioner. The applicant must notify the Commissioner in writing of any change which affects the continuing accuracy of any representation made in the application required by this paragraph, whether the change occurs before or after the applicant receives a determination letter. Such notification must be addressed to Commissioner of Internal Revenue, Attention: E:EP, Internal Revenue Service, Washington, D.C. 20224.

(v) *Substitution of trustee.* No applicant shall be approved unless he undertakes to act as trustee only under trust instruments which contain a provision to the effect that the employer is to substitute another trustee upon notification by the Commissioner that such substitution is required because the applicant has failed to comply with the requirements of this paragraph or is not keeping such records, or making such returns, or rendering such statements as are required by forms or regulations.

(vi) *Revocation.* (A) Approval of the application required by this paragraph may be revoked for any good and sufficient reason in accordance with the procedures described in this subdivision.

(B) [Reserved]

Section 1.401-13 is amended by adding the following new paragraph at the end thereof:

§ 1.401-13 (Proposed Treasury Decision, published 4-21-75.) **Excess contributions on behalf of owner-employees.**

* * * * * * * * * * *

(f) Years to which this section applies. This section applies to contributions made in taxable years of employers beginning before January 1, 1976. Thus, for example, in the case of willful contributions made in taxable years of employers beginning before January 1, 1976, paragraphs (e)(1), (2), and (3) of this section apply to such taxable years beginning on or after such date. However, in such a case, because the application of paragraph (e)(4) of this section affects contributions made in taxable years of employers beginning on or after January 1, 1976, paragraph (e)(4) of this section does not apply to such taxable years; see paragraph (c) of § 1.401(e)-4 (relating to transitional rules for excess contributions).

The following new section is added immediately after § 1.401(a)-11.

§1.401(a)-12 (Proposed Treasury Decision, published 7-1-77.) **Mergers and consolidations of plans and transfers of plan assets.**

A trust will not be qualified under section 401 unless the plan of which the trust is a part provides that in the case of any merger of consolidation with, or transfer of assets or liabilities to, another plan after September 2, 1974, each participant in the plan would receive a minimum benefit if the plan terminated immediately after the merger, consolidation, or transfer. This benefit must be equal to or greater than the benefit the participant would have been entitled to receive immediately before the merger, consolidation, or transfer if the plan in which he was a participant had then terminated. This section applies to a multiemployer plan only to the extent determined by the Pension Benefit Guaranty Corporation. For additional rules concerning mergers of consolidations of plans and transfers of plan assets, see section 414(*l*) and §1.414(*l*)-1.

The following new section is added immediately before §1.401(a)-19:

§1.401(a)-18 (Proposed Treasury Decision, published 5-26-78.) Special requirements for defined benefit plans providing benefits for self-employed individuals or shareholder-employees.

For special requirements which apply to a defined benefit plan which provides benefits for an employee who is either an employee within the meaning of section 401(c)(1) or a shareholder-employee within the meaning of section 1379(d), see §§1.401(j)-1 through 1.401(j)-6.

"Keogh" or "H.R. 10" Plans

The following new sections are added immediately after § 1.401-14. These added sections read as follows:

Proposed Reg. § 1.401-14.

§1.401(e)-1 (Proposed Treasury Decision, published 4-21-75.) **Definitions relating to plans covering self-employed individuals.**

(a) **"Keogh" or "H.R. 10" plans, in general—(1) Introduction and organization of regulations.** Certain self-employed individuals may be covered by a qualified pension, annuity, or profit-sharing plan. This section contains definitions contained in section 401(c) relating to plans covering self-employed individuals and is applicable to employer taxable years beginning after December 31, 1975, unless otherwise specified. The provisions of §§ 1.401(a)-1 through 1.401(a)-20, relating to qualification requirements which are generally applicable to all qualified plans, and other provisions relating to the special rules under section 401(b), (f), (g), (h), and (i), are also generally applicable to any plan covering a self-employed individual. However, in addition to such requirements and special rules, any plan covering a self-employed individual is subject to the rules contained in §§ 1.401 (e)-2, (e)-5, and (j)-1. Section 1.401(e)-2 contains general rules, § 1.401(e)-5 contains a special rule limiting the contribution and benefit base to the first $100,000 of annual compensation, and § 1.401(j)-1 contains special rules for defined benefit plans. Section 1.401(e)-3 contains special rules which are applicable to plans covering self-employed individuals when one or more of such individuals is an owner-employee within the meaning of paragraph (d) of this section. Section 1.401(e)-4 contains rules relating to contributions on behalf of owner-employees for premiums on annuity, etc., contracts and a transitional rule for certain excess contributions made on behalf of owner-employees for employer taxable years beginning before January 1, 1976. The provisions of this section and of §§ 1.401(e)-2 through 1.401 (e)-5 are applicable to employer taxable years beginning after December 31, 1975, unless otherwise specified.

(2) [Reserved]

§ 1.401(e)-2 (Proposed Treasury Decision, published 4-21-75.) **General rules relating to plans covering self-employed individuals.**

(a) **"Keogh" or "H.R. 10" plans; introduction and organization of regulations.** This section provides certain rules which supplement, and modify, the qualification requirements of §§ 1.401(a)-1 through 1.401(a)-20 and the special rules provided by § 1.401(b)-1 and other special rules under subsections (f), (g), (h), and (i) of section 401 in the case of a qualified pension, annuity, or profit-sharing plan which covers a self-employed individual who is an employee within the meaning of section 401(c)(1). Section 1.401(e)-1(a)(1) sets forth other provisions which also supplement, and modify, these requirements and special rules in the case of a plan described in this section. The provisions of this section apply to employer taxable years beginning after December 31, 1975, unless otherwise specified.

(b) [Reserved]

§ 1.401(e)-3 (Proposed Treasury Decision, published 4-21-75.) **Requirements for qualification of trusts and plans benefiting owner-employees.**

(a) **"Keogh" or "H.R. 10" plans covering owner-employees; introduction and organization of regulations.** This section prescribes the additional requirements which must be met for qualification of a trust forming part of a pension or profit-sharing plan, or of an annuity plan, which covers any self-employed individual who is an owner-employee as defined in section 401(c)(3). These additional requirements are prescribed in section 401(d) and are made applicable to such a trust by section 401(a)(10)(B) and to an annuity plan by section 404(a)(2). However, to the extent that the provisions of §§ 1.401(e)-1 and 1.401(e)-2 are not modified by the provisions of this section such provisions are also applicable to a plan which covers an owner-employee. The provisions of this section apply to taxable years beginning after December 31, 1975, unless otherwise specified.

(b) [Reserved]

§ 1.401(e)-4 (Proposed Treasury Decision, published 4-21-75.) **Con-**

tributions for premiums on annuity, etc., contracts and transitional rule for certain excess contributions.

(a) **In general.** The provisions of this section prescribe the rules specified in section 401(e) relating to certain contributions made under a qualified pension, annuity, or profit-sharing plan on behalf of a self-employed individual who is an owner-employee (as defined in section 401(c)(3) and the regulations thereunder) in taxable years of the employer beginning after December 31, 1975. However, see also section 415 for rules applicable to limitations on contributions or benefits for years beginning after December 31, 1975. For example, if a defined contribution plan using a trust permitted an employer contribution to be made for any participant in the plan for a year beginning after December 31, 1975, in excess of the amount described in section 415(c)(1)(B), the trust established under such plan would not constitute a qualified trust under section 401(a), notwithstanding the provisions of section 401(e) and this section. Solely for the purpose of applying section 4972(b) (relating to excise tax on excess contributions for self-employed individuals) to other contributions made by an owner-employee as an employee, the amount of any employer contribution which is not deductible under section 404 for the employer's taxable year but which is described in section 401(e) and this section shall be taken into account as a contribution made by such owner-employee as an employee during the taxable year of his employer in which such contribution is made.

(b) **Contributions described in section 401(e)**—(1) An employer contribution on behalf of an owner-employee is described in section 401(e), if—

(i) Under the provisions of the plan, the contribution is expressly required to be applied (either directly or through a trustee) to pay the premiums or other consideration for one or more annuity, endowment, or life insurance contracts on the life of the owner-employee,

(ii) The employer contributions so applied meet the requirements of subparagraphs (2) through (5) of this paragraph,

(iii) The amount of the contribution exceeds the amount deductible under section 404 with respect to contributions made by the employer on behalf of the owner-employee under the plan, and

(iv) The total employer contributions required to be applied annually to pay premiums on behalf of any owner-employee for contracts described in this paragraph do not exceed $7,500. For purposes of computing such $7,500 limit, the total employer contributions include amounts which are allocable to the purchase of life, accident, health, or other insurance.

(2) (i) The employer contributions must be paid under a plan which satisfies all the requirements for qualification. Accordingly, for example, contributions can be paid under the plan for life insurance protection only to the extent otherwise permitted under sections 401 through 404 and the regulations thereunder. However, certain of the requirements for qualification are modified with respect to a plan described in this paragraph (see section 401(a)(10)(A)(ii) and (d)(5)).

(ii) A plan described in this paragraph is not disqualified merely because a contribution is made on behalf of an owner-employee by his employer during a taxable year of the employer for which the owner-employee has no earned income. On the other hand, a plan will fail to qualify if a contribution is made on behalf of an owner-employee which results in the disccrimination prohibited by section 401(a)(4) as modified by section 401(a)(10)(A)(ii) (see paragraph (f)(3) of § 1.401(e)-(3)).

(3) The employer contributions must be applied to pay premiums or other consideration for a contract issued on the life of the owner-employee. For purposes of this subparagraph, a contract is not issued on the life of an owner-employee unless all the proceeds which are, or may become, payable under the contract are payable directly, or through a trustee of a trust described in section 401(a) and exempt from tax under section 501(a), to the owner-employee or to the beneficiary named in the contract or under the plan. For example, a non-

Proposed Reg. § 1.401(e)-4

transferable face-amount certificate described in section 401(g) and the regulations thereunder is considered an annuity on the life of the owner-employee if the proceeds of such contract are payable only to the owner-employee or his beneficiary.

(4) (i) For any taxable year of the employer, the amount of contributions by the employer on behalf of the owner-employee which is applied to pay premiums under the contracts described in this paragraph must not exceed the average of the amounts deductible under section 404 by such employer on behalf of such owner-employee for the most recent three taxable years of the employer which are described in the succeeding sentence. The three employer taxable years described in the preceding sentence must be years, ending prior to the date the latest contract was entered into or modified to provide additional benefits, in which the owner-employee derived earned income from the trade or business with respect to which the plan is established. However, if such owner-employee has not derived earned income for at least three taxable years preceding such date, then, in determining the "average of the amounts deductible", only so many of such taxable years as such owner-employee was engaged in such trade or business and derived earned income therefrom are taken into account.

(ii) For the purpose of making the computation described in subdivision (i) of this subparagraph, the taxable years taken into account include those years in which the individual derived earned income from the trade or business but was not an owner-employee with respect to such trade or business. Furthermore, taxable years of the employer preceding the taxable year in which a qualified plan is established are taken into account.

(iii) For purposes of making the computations described in subdivisions (i) and (ii) of this subparagraph for any taxable year of the employer, the average of the amounts deductible under section 404 by the employer on behalf of an owner-employee for the most recent three relevant taxable years of the employer shall be determined as if section 404, as in effect for the taxable year for which the computation is to be made, had been in effect for all three such years.

(5) For any taxable year of an employer in which contributions are made on behalf of an individual as an owner-employee under more than one plan, the amount of contributions described in this section by the employer on behalf of such an owner-employee under all such plans must not exceed $7,500.

(c) **Transitional rule for excess contributions**—(1) (i) The rules of this paragraph are inapplicable to a plan which was not in existence for any taxable year of an employer which begins before January 1, 1976. For taxable years of an employer which begin before January 1, 1976, the rules with respect to excess contributions on behalf of owner-employees set forth in section 401(d)(5) and (8) and in section 401(e), as these sections were in effect on September 1, 1974, prior to their amendment by section 2001(e) of the Employee Retirement Income Security Act 1974 (hereinafter in this paragraph referred to as the "Act") (88 Stat. 954), shall apply except as provided by subparagraph (2) of this paragraph. Section § 1.401-13 generally provides the rules for excess contributions on behalf of owner-employees set forth in these sections.

(ii) Notwithstanding the provisions of subdivision (i) of this subparagraph, the rules set forth in such subsections (d)(5) and (8) and (e) of section 401 with respect to excess contributions for such taxable years beginning before January 1, 1976, apply even though the application of those rules affects a subsequent taxable year. Thus, for example, if, in 1975, a nonwillful excess contribution described in section 401(e)(1) (prior to such amendment) is made on behalf of an owner-employee, the plan will not be qualified unless the provisions required by subparagraphs (A) and (B) of such 401(d)(8) are contained in the plan and made applicable to excess contributions made for such taxable years beginning before January 1, 1976. In such case, the effect of such contribution on the plan, the employer, and the owner-employee would be determined under paragraph (2) of section 401(e), as in effect on September 1, 1974. By reason of section 401(e)(2)(F), as in effect on September 1, 1974, the period for assessing any deficiency by reason of the excess contribution will not expire until the expiration of the 6-month period described in section 401(e)(2)(C), as in effect on September 1, 1974, even if the first day of such 6-month period falls in a taxable year beginning after December 31, 1975. For the rules applicable to a willful excess contribution, which generally divide an owner-employee's interest in a plan into two parts on the basis of employer taxable years beginning before and after December 31, 1975, see § 1.72-17A(e)(2)(v). In the case of a willful excess contribution, the rule specified in section 401(e)(2)(E)'(iii), as in effect on September 1, 1974, shall not apply to any taxable year of an employer beginning on or after January 1, 1976. Thus, for example, if a willful excess contribution was made to a plan on behalf of an owner-employee with respect to his employer's taxable year beginning January 1, 1975, the plan would not meet, for purposes of section 404, the requirements of section 401(d) with respect to that owner-employee for such year, but the 5 taxable years following such year would be unaffected because those years begin on or after January 1, 1976.

(2) (i) For purposes of applying the excess contribution rules with respect to the employer taxable years specified in subparagraph (1) of this paragraph for such an employer taxable year which begins after December 31, 1973, see section 404(e) and § 1.404(e)-1A for rules increasing the limitation on the amount of allowable employer deductions on behalf of owner-employees under section 404. For purposes of applying subparagraphs (A) and (B)(i) of section 401(e)(1) prior to the amendment made by section 2001(e)(3) of the Act (88 Stat. 954), the employer deduction allowable by section 404(e)(4) with respect to an owner-employee in a defined contribution plan shall be deemed not to be an excess contribution (see § 1.404(e)-1A(c)(4)).

(ii) For purposes of applying the excess contribution rules with respect to the employer taxable years specified in subparagraph (1) of this paragrah to an employer's plan which was not in existence on January 1, 1974, or to a plan in existence on January 1, 1974, which elects under section 1017(d) of the Act (88 Stat. 934), in accordance with regulations, to have the funding provisions of section 412 apply to such an existing plan, see section 404(a)(1), (a)(6), and (a)(7), as amended by section 1013(c)(1), (2), and (3) of the Act (88 Stat. 922 and 923) for rules modifying the amount of employer deductions on behalf of owner-employees.

§ 1.401(e)-5 (Proposed Treasury Decision, published 4-21-75) **Limitation of contribution and benefit bases to first $100,000 of annual compensation in case of plans covering self-employed individuals.**

(a) **General rules.** Under section 401(a)(17), a plan maintained by an employer which provides contributions or benefits for employees some or all of whom are employees within the meaning of section 401(c)(1) is a qualified plan only if the annual compensation of each employee taken into account under the plan does not exceed the first $100,000 of such compensation. For purposes of applying section 401(a)(17) and the preceding sentence, all plans maintained by such an employer with respect to the same trade or business shall be treated as a single plan. See also sections 401(d)(9) and (10) (relating to controlled trades or businesses where a plan covers an owner-employee who controls more than one trade or business); section 404(e) (relating to special limitations for self-employed individuals); section 413(b)(7) (relating to determination of limitations provided by section 404(a) in the case of certain plans maintained pursuant to a collective bargaining agreement); section 413(c)(6) (relating to determination of limitations provided by section 404(a) in the case of certain plans maintained by more than one employer); and section 414(c) (relating to employees of partnerships, proprietorships, etc. which are under common control).

(b) **Integrated plans.** (1) In the case of a qualified plan, other than a plan described in section 414(j), which is integrated with the Social Security Act (chapter 21 of the Code), or with contributions or benefits under chapter 2 of the Code (relating to tax on self-employment income) or under any other Federal or State law, the $100,000 limitation described in subparagraph (a) shall be determined without regard to any adjustments to contributions or benefits under the plan on account of such integration. See also subsections (a)(5), (a)(15), and (d)(6) of section 401 and the regulations thereunder for other rules with respect to plans which are integrated.

(2) In the case of a qualified defined benefit plan described in section 414(j), see section 401(j)(4) for a special prohibition against integration.

(c) **Application of nondiscrimination requirement.** (1) This paragraph shall apply—

(i) In the case of a defined contribution plan which provides contributions or benefits for employees some or all of whom are employees within the meaning of section 401(c)(1) and

(ii) For a year in which the compensation of any employee covered by the plan exceeds $100,000. In the case of an employee who is an employee within the meaning of section 401(c)(1), compensation means earned income within the meaning of section 401(c)(2).

(2) In applying section 401(a)(4) under the circumstances described in subparagraph (1) of this paragraph, the determination whether the rate of contributions under the plan discriminates in favor of highly compensated employees shall be made as if the compensation for the year of each employee described in subparagraph (1)(ii) of this paragraph were $100,000, rather than the compensation actually received by him for such year.

(d) **Examples.** The provisions of this section may be illustrated by the following examples:

Example (1). A, a self-employed individual, has established the P Profit-Sharing Plan, which covers A and his two common-law employees, B and C. A's taxable year and the plan's plan year are both the calendar year. For 1976, A has earned income of $150,000, and B and C each receive compensation of less than $100,000 from A. If he wishes to contribute $7,500 to the plan on his behalf for 1976, A must also contribute to the accounts of B and C under the plan amounts at least equal to 7½ percent of their respective compensation for 1976.

Example (2). D, an owner-employee within the meaning of section 401(c)(3), is a participant in the Q Qualified Defined Contribution Plan, which, in 1975, satisfies the requirements of section 401(d)(6) and all other integration requirements applicable to qualified defined contribution plans. The taxable years of D, the employer of D within the meaning of section 401(c)(4), and the plan are all calendar years. The plan provides for an integration level of $13,200 and a contribution rate of 5 percent of compensation in excess of $13,200. For 1975, D has earned income of $115,000. The maximum amount of earned income upon which D's contribution can be determined is $86,800, and the contribution based upon this maximum amount of earned income is $4,340, computed as follows:

Maximum annual compensation which may be taken into account	$100,000
Less: Social Security Act integration level	13,200
Plan contribution base	$ 86,800
Multiplied by: Contribution rate	5%
	$ 4,340

(e) **Years to which section applies.** This section applies to taxable years of an employer beginning after December 31, 1975. However, if employer contributions made under a plan for any employee for taxable years of an employer beginning after December 31, 1973, exceed the amounts permitted to be deducted for that employee under section 404(e), as in effect on September 1, 1974, this section applies to such taxable years of an employer.

Thus, for example, a plan of a calendar year employer which was adopted on January 1, 1974, would be subject to this section in 1974, if the employer made a contribution on behalf of any employee within the meaning of section 401(c)(1) for such year in excess of the $2,500 or 10 percent earned income limit, whichever is applicable to that employee, specified in section 404(e)(1) as in effect prior to the amendment to such Code section made by section 2001(a)(1)(A) of the Employee Retirement Income Security Act of 1974 (88 Stat. 952). The plan described in the preceding sentence would also be subject to this section in 1974, if the employer made a contribution on behalf of any employee within the meaning of section 401(c)(1) which is allowable as a deduction only because of the addition of paragraph (4) to Code section 404(e) made by section 2001(a)(3) of such Act (88 Stat. 952).

§ 1.401(e)-6 (Proposed Treasury Decision, published 4-21-75) Special rules for shareholder-employees.

(a) **Limitation of contributions and benefit bases to first $100,000 of annual compensation in case of plans covering shareholder-employees.** (1) Under section 401(a)(17), a plan which provides contributions or benefits for employees, some or all of whom are shareholder-employees within the meaning of section 1379(d), is subject to the same limitation on annual compensation as a plan which provides such contributions or benefits for employees some or all of whom are self-employed individuals within the meaning of section 401(c)(1). Thus, a plan which provides contributions or benefits for such shareholder-employees is subject to the rules provided by § 1.401(e)-5, unless otherwise specified. See also section 1379 and §§ 1.1379-1 through 4.

(2) Subparagraph (1) applies to taxable years of an electing small business corporation beginning after December 31, 1975. However, if corporate contributions made under a plan on behalf of any shareholder-employee for corporate taxable years beginning after December 31, 1973, exceed the lesser of the amount of contributions specified in section 1379(b)(1)(A) or (B), as in effect on September 1, 1974, for that shareholder-employee, subparagraph (1) applies to such corporate taxable years. Thus, for example, if an electing small business corporation whose taxable year is the calendar year adopted a plan on January 1, 1974, the plan would be subject to the provisions of subparagraph (1) of this section in 1974 if the corporation made a contribution in excess of $2,500 on behalf of any shareholder-employee for such year.

(b) [Reserved]

The following new sections are added immediately after §1.401(b)-1:

§1.401(j)-1 (Proposed Treasury Decision, published 5-26-78.) Certain defined benefit plans; general rules.

(a) **Application of section 401(a)(18) and (j).** Section 401(a)(18) and (j) and the regulations thereunder apply to a defined benefit plan which provides benefits for an employee who is either an employee within the meaning of section 401(c)(1) or a shareholder-employee of an electing small business (subchapter S) corporation within the meaning of section 1379(d). In the regulations under section 401(j), such an employee is referred to, respectively, as a "self-employed individual" or a "shareholder-employee". See §1.401(j)-2(g) for a special deduction rule applicable to these plans.

(b) **Requirements; organization of regulations—(1) Requirements.** A defined benefit plan to which section 401(j) applies is not a qualified plan (and a trust forming part of such plan is not a qualified trust) unless the plan satisfies the applicable requirements of section 401(j) and the regulations thereunder (that is, §§1.401(j)-1 through 1.401(j)-6, inclusive).

(2) **General rules; definitions, etc.** This section prescribes general rules under section 401(j) for plans other than final average pay plans. These plans are commonly referred to as "career average plans". This section also provides the definitions used in applying section 401(j) and §§1.401(j)-1 through 1.401(j)-6, including the definitions set forth in section 401(j)(5). In addition, this section provides the rules under section 401(j)(2) (relating to maximum basic benefit), section 401(j)(3)(A) (relating to applicable percentages), and under 401(j)(3)(B)(i), (ii) and (iv) (relating to certain adjustments to applicable percentages).

(3) **Other requirements and special rules.** Section 1.401(j)-2 provides rules under section 401(j)(1) (relating to certain plan aggregations) and under section 401(j)(4) (relating to a requirement that a plan covering owner-employees may not be integrated with social security, etc.). Section 1.401(j)-2 also provides rules relating to fully insured plans and to the nondiscrimination requirements.

(4) **Certain changes.** Section 1.401(j)-3 provides rules under section 401(j)(3)(B)(iii) relating to changes in the rate of benefit accrual and compensation base under a plan.

Proposed Reg. §1.401(j)-1

(5) **Subchapter S corporation.** Section 1.401(j)-4 provides a special rule for plans of an electing small business corporation.

(6) **Final average pay plan.** Section 1.401(j)-5 provides rules for applying the requirements of section 401(j) and §1.401(j)-1 through 1.401(j)-4 to a final average pay plan.

(7) **Effective dates.** Section 1.401(j)-6 provides the effective dates for the application of section 401(j) to a plan and a special transitional rule.

(c) **General rule.** Section 401(j) imposes a limitation on the amount of the basic benefit, as defined in paragraph (e)(1) of this section, which may be accrued under a defined benefit plan for any plan year of participation, as defined in paragraph (e)(7) of this section, by any employee who is either a self-employed individual or a shareholder-employee. Thus, a plan to which this section applies is not a qualified plan (and a trust forming a part of such a plan is not a qualified trust) if the benefit accruing under the plan for any plan year of participation by such an employee exceeds the maximum basic benefit. Further, the plan is not qualified unless the plan contains provisions that preclude any such benefit accrual proscribed in the preceding sentence, irrespective of whether or not there is, in fact, an excess accrual for such an employee. For special benefit accrual rules which apply to a final average pay plan, see §1.401(j)-5. Section 401(j) and this section do not, however, limit the benefit which may be accrued under a plan for any plan year of participation by an employee who, during that year is neither a self-employed individual nor a shareholder-employee, nor do they require a plan to provide accrued benefits in the form of a basic benefit. For other rules and requirements which must be satisfied, see paragraph (g) of this section, and §1.401(j)-2(f), (h), (i) and (j).

(d) **Maximum basic benefit.** For purposes of section 401(j), in the case of a plan other than a final average pay plan, the maximum basic benefit of a self-employed individual or a shareholder employee for a plan year equals—

(1) The employee's annual compensation not in excess of the compensation base for such year, as defined in paragraph (e)(6) of this section, multiplied by

(2) The statutory percentage as adjusted in this section for such year (the applicable percentage).

In no event may the maximum basic benefit of such an employee for a plan year exceed 6.5 percent of $50,000, or $3,250. For adjustments to the maximum basic benefit where the compensation base is in excess of $50,000, see §1.401(j)-3(b)(2). For special rules applicable to final average pay plans, see §1.401(j)-5.

(e) **Definitions.** For purposes of section 401(j) and the regulations thereunder, the definitions in this paragraph apply.

(1) **Basic benefit.** The term "basic benefit" with respect to an employee means a benefit under a plan under the following conditions—
 (i) The benefit is in the form of a straight life annuity,
 (ii) The benefit commences at the later of age 65, or the day 5 years after the day the participant's current period of participation began,
 (iii) The plan provides no ancillary benefits, and
 (iv) The employee does not contribute to the plan.

(2) **Compensation.** The term "compensation" means—
 (i) In the case of a self-employed individual, the earned income of the individual,
 (ii) In the case of a shareholder-employee, the compensation received (or accrued in the case of an individual who computes income under the accrual method) by the individual from the electing small business corporation, or
 (iii) In the case of any employee not included in subdivision (i) or (ii) for any relevant year, the compensation includible in the individual's gross income derived from the partnership or the electing small business corporation (see the change in status rules in paragraph (g)(6) of this section for application of this provision).

(3) **Defined benefit plan.** See section 414(j) for the definition of a defined benefit plan.

(4) **Defined contribution plan.** See section 414(i) for the definition of a defined contribution plan.

(5) **Final average pay plan.** A final average pay plan is a defined benefit plan accruing benefits based on the employee's compensation over a period less than the total period of the employee's participation in the plan. Thus, for example, a plan which provides that an employee's accrued benefit is based on compensation earned over the last five years would be a final average pay plan.

(6) **Compensation base.** The term "compensation base" means the highest level of annual compensation of the employee which may be taken into account for a plan year under the plan for determining benefits.

(7) **Plan year of participation.** The term "plan year of participation" means a plan year for which a participant accrues a benefit under the terms of the plan (determined only with respect to benefits provided by the plan and without regard to any plan provision not in effect in that plan year). Thus, for example, benefits provided under the Social Security Act or past service benefits for prior years are not included.

(8) **When plan participation begins.** An employee begins his plan participation at the beginning of the first plan year in which he participates under the plan. If the plan has a past service benefit, service for which such benefits are given is not considered as participation under the plan for purposes of this subparagraph.

(9) **Current period of participation.** The term "current period of participation" means any period of consecutive plan years of participation beginning with the first day of the first plan year of participation in the period and ending with the last day of the last consecutive plan year of participation in the period. The applicable current period of participation at any relevant date is determined by the applicable period of consecutive plan years within which the relevant date falls.

(f) **Rules relating to applicable percentages—(1) Statutory percentage; applicable percentage.** For purposes of section 401(j) and the regulations thereunder, the statutory percentage for an employee for any plan year shall be the percentage shown on the following table opposite the age of the employee determined at the time the current period of participation in the plan by the employee began:

Age	Statutory percentage	Age	Statutory percentage
30 or less	6.5	46	3.5
31	6.3	47	3.4
32	6.0	48	3.2
33	5.8	49	3.1
34	5.6	50	3.0
35	5.4	51	2.9
36	5.1	52	2.8
37	4.9	53	2.7
38	4.8	54	2.6
39	4.6	55	2.5
40	4.4	56	2.4
41	4.2	57	2.3
42	4.1	58	2.2
43	3.9	59	2.1
44	3.8	60 or over	2.0
45	3.6		

The statutory percentage shall be adjusted as further provided in the regulations under section 401(j). As used hereafter, the term "applicable percentage" means the statutory percentage as so adjusted. For purposes of this subparagraph, the status of an employee at the time his current period of participation in the plan began (i.e., as a common-law employee, self-employed individual, or shareholder-employee) is not relevant.

Proposed Reg. § 1.401(j)-1

(2) **Changes in statutory percentages.** In the case of periods beginning after December 31, 1977, the statutory percentages under paragraph (f) of this section may be adjusted by the Commissioner from time to time to take into account changes in prevailing interest and mortality rates occurring after December 31, 1973.

(3) **Determination of ages.** For purposes of section 401(j), the age of an employee at a relevant date (e.g., when participation began) is the employee's age on his last birthday on or before that date.

(4) **Examples.** The provisions of this section can be illustrated by the following examples, in which, except where otherwise specified, it is assumed that the participant is not married and has continuous service and plan years of participation:

Example 1. (i) A, a self-employed individual, enters a defined benefit plan at age 30. The plan provides benefits on compensation up to $50,000 in the form of a single life annuity commencing at age 65 with no ancillary benefits. If A's compensation for the first year equals $20,000, the maximum basic benefit accruing which could be provided by the plan for A under paragraph (f) of this section equals $1,300 (6.5% of $20,000). The applicable percentage for such year is determined under paragraph (f) of this section for the age at which A's participation begins, age 30.

(ii) Assume that for the next four years, A's compensation remains at $20,000. Under this section, A's maximum benefit accruing for each of these years is still $1,300 (6.5% of $20,000). The applicable percentage is still measured by the 6.5% applicable to age 30, when his current period of plan participation began, even though he is older.

(iii) Assume that, after five years of participation, A leaves the plan and recommences participation at age 50. In the first year after his return, A earns $30,000. Under this section, A's maximum benefit for the year cannot exceed $900 (3% of $30,000). The applicable percentage is determined for age 50, when his next current period of plan participation began, and not at age 30. If A's compensation remains at $30,000 for four more years, A's maximum benefit for each of these four years remains at $900 (3% of $30,000).

(iv) Assume that, at age 55, A's compensation is $40,000. Under this section, A's maximum benefit for the year cannot exceed $1,200 (3% of $40,000). The percentage limit of paragraph (f)(1) of this section remains at 3% because the determination is made by reference to age 50, when A's current period of plan participation began. If A's compensation remains at $40,000 for four more years, A's maximum benefit for each of these four years remains at $1,200 (3% of $40,000).

(v) Assume that, at age 60, A's compensation is $50,000. Under this section, A's maximum benefit for the year cannot exceed $1,500 (3% of $50,000). The percentage limit of paragraph (f)(1) of this section remains at 3 percent. If A's compensation remains at or above $50,000 for four more years, A's maximum benefit for each of these four years remains at $1,500 (3% of $50,000).

(vi) Accordingly, the maximum basic benefit accruing which could be paid to A under the plan would be $24,500 per year, computed as follows:

Age	Compensation per year	Rate	Benefit earned per year	Total benefit
30-34	$20,000	6.5	$1,300	$6,500
50-54	30,000	3.0	900	4,500
55-59	40,000	3.0	1,200	6,000
60-64	50,000	3.0	1,500	7,500
			Total	$24,500

Example (2). A defined benefit plan covers employee F who is a self-employed individual. In 1980, F's total accrued annual benefits equal $13,000. The maximum basic benefit for F at this time equals $13,500. The plan, however, for plan year 1980 accrued an annual benefit for F equal to $1,800 when the maximum basic benefit equalled $1,625. The plan fails to satisfy the requirements of this section in 1980. Under §1.401(j)-1(c), the limitation on an employee's benefits must be satisfied in each plan year, even though his aggregate benefits may satisfy the limitations.

(g) **Certain adjustments and additional requirements—(1) Compensation base.** In order for a plan to satisfy the requirements of section 401(j), the plan must specify the compensation base under the plan. For rules applicable to plans which change compensation bases, see §1.401(j)-3(b)(2).

(2) **Nonbasic benefits.** (i) In the case of a plan which provides a benefit which is not a basic benefit, as defined in paragraph (e)(1) of this section, any nonbasic benefit shall not exceed the actuarial equivalent, as determined by the Commissioner, of the maximum basic benefit.

(ii) A defined benefit plan shall not satisfy the requirements of this section, if—

(A) Any benefit under the plan is adjusted under a cost of living formula, or

(B) The plan is funded by the purchase of variable annuity contracts.

(iii) The benefits, other than basic benefits, which a plan may provide, and for which the Commissioner shall adjust the applicable percentage, include, but are not limited to, pre-retirement death and disability benefits and benefits payable in the form of either a joint and survivor annuity or an annuity certain for a specified period.

(3) **Employee contributions.** (i) This subdivision applies to voluntary employee contributions within the meaning of section 411. The maximum basic benefit shall not be adjusted for these voluntary contributions. In such a case the plan can provide a benefit equal to the sum of the maximum basic benefit and the benefit accounted for separately. See section 411(b)(2), (c)(2)(A), and (d)(5), and §1.411(c)-1(a) for rules which require separate accounting in the case of voluntary employee contributions.

(ii) This subdivision applies to mandatory employee contributions within the meaning of section 411(c)(2)(C). Under section 411(c) and §1.411(c)-1, the employee's total accrued benefit (determined without regard to any accrued benefit attributable to voluntary employee contributions) must be allocated between the part attributable to mandatory employee contributions and the part attributable to employer contributions according to specified rules. For purposes of determining the participant's maximum basic benefit under section 401(j) the following rules apply with respect to each plan year. For each plan year, the total benefit accruing derived from all contributions and the benefit accruing from mandatory employee contributions must be computed in accordance with the rules in section 411(c)(2)(B). Then the participant's total benefit accruing for the year must be reduced by the benefit accruing derived from his mandatory contributions for the year and the remaining difference must be compared with the maximum basic benefit. The total benefit accruing for the year is determined by ascertaining the increase from the total accrued benefit (for all prior years) as of the close of the immediately preceding plan year and the benefit accruing from mandatory employee contributions is determined only with respect to those contributions made for the year.

(4) **Contributions allocable to insurance protection.** For purposes of determining the maximum basic benefit in the case of any plan which provides a benefit in the form of life, accident, health, or other insurance protection, no adjustment is required for any such plan benefit attributable to amounts considered to be contributed by the employee under the rules of section 72(f) and paragraph (b) of §1.72-16 and includible in the employee's gross income.

(5) **Change in status.** (i) In the case of a participant who is neither a self-employed individual nor a shareholder-employee and who becomes a self-employed individual or shareholder-employee during the plan year, the applicable percentage for such year is not less than the applicable percentage determined under this section for the age of the participant when he becomes a self-employed individual or shareholder-employee. A higher applicable percentage will be allowed limited to the accrual rate established by the lesser

Proposed Reg. §1.401(j)-1

of (A) the past accrual rate for the participant or (B) the applicable percentage determined under this section for the age when the participant's current period of participation commenced, and for the compensation base in effect when the participant becomes a self-employed individual or shareholder-employee.

(ii) (A) For purposes of this subparagraph, the past accrual rate equals the ratio determined by dividing (1) the employer-derived accrued benefit of the participant as of the close of plan year immediately preceding the year in which the participant becomes a self-employed individual or a shareholder-employee, by (2) the sum of the compensation earned by the participant in each year (limited to the compensation covered by the plan for each year) for all periods of plan participation ending with the close of such immediately preceding plan year. The accrued benefit of the participant as of the close of the immediately preceding plan year shall be determined by disregarding any increase in the benefit not in effect at such time. Thus, for example, a subsequent past service benefit provided retroactively for the plan year would be disregarded.

(B) If records are unavailable to compute the sum of the compensation earned by the participant, the compensation of the participant, referred to in subdivision (ii)(A), shall be determined by assuming that the participant earned compensation in each year of plan participation equal to the compensation earned in the plan year immediately preceding the plan year in which the participant becomes a self-employed individual or shareholder-employee. This assumption shall not apply to any plan years of participation ending after December 31, 1975.

§1.401(j)-2 (Proposed Treasury Decision, published 5-26-78.) Other requirements and special rules.

(a) **In general.** Paragraphs (b), (c) and (d) of this section set forth additional requirements under section 401(j)(1) applicable to an employer, and certain related employers, maintaining a plan subject to the requirements of section 401(j) and with other plans. Paragraph (e) of this section sets forth a requirement for fully insured defined benefit plans. Paragraphs (f), (g), (h), (i) and (j) set forth special rules under section 401(j)(4) and (6) and under sections 401(a)(4), 415 and 401(a), relating, respectively, to integration, deductions, nondiscrimination, other benefit limitations and definitely determinable benefits.

(b) **Multiple plans.** All plans of an employer must be taken into account in determining whether or not the requirements of section 401(j) are satisfied. In addition, in the case of a self-employed individual, all plans of all trades or businesses in which the employee is a self-employed individual must be taken into account.

(c) **Two or more defined benefit plans.** (1) If two or more defined benefit plans are required to be aggregated under paragraph (b) of this section, then the accrued benefit under all such plans for any employee subject to the limitations of this section must be aggregated in determining whether or not the limitation on benefit accruals is exceeded.

(2) In order to insure reasonable comparability of retirement benefits between qualified defined benefit plans and qualified defined contribution plans, or combinations thereof, as required by section 401(j)(1), this subparagraph sets forth certain conditions which must be satisfied in order for a defined benefit plan to be qualified. If one defined benefit plan ("first plan") is established and another defined benefit plan ("second plan") is established by the same employer subsequent to the establishment of the first plan, and if the second plan is required to be aggregated with the first plan under paragraph (b) of this section, the second plan shall be deemed not to satisfy the requirements of section 401(j) unless both plans have the same plan year. Notwithstanding the preceding sentence, in the case where two or more such plans have been adopted prior to July 25, 1978, with different plan years, the second plan shall not fail to satisfy the requirements of this section solely by reason of having a different plan year if the plans are amended to adopt, for years beginning after that date, the same plan year and to adjust plan benefits as determined by the Commissioner. Irrespective of any limitation on time of amendment, the amendment required by the preceding sentence may be adopted within the 1 year period beginning [with the date of publication of this section in the Federal Register as a Treasury decision].

(d) **Defined benefit and defined contribution plans.** (1) If a defined benefit plan and a defined contribution plan are required to be aggregated under paragraph (b) of this section, the maximum basic benefit with respect to the defined benefit plan on behalf of an employee subject to the limitations of section 401(j) shall be determined by multiplying the maximum basic benefit otherwise determined under section 401(j) for the defined benefit plan (determined without regard to this subparagraph) by 1 minus the fraction determined under subparagraph (2) of this paragraph.

(2) The fraction for any taxable year in which an employee is a participant in a defined contribution plan is a fraction—

(i) The numerator of which is the amount deductible for the participant under the defined contribution plan, and

(ii) The denominator of which is the maximum amount deductible (and not includible in gross income under section 1379(b)) under the defined contribution plan if the plan provided for the maximum deduction allowable for the participant under section 404 and the regulations thereunder.

For purposes of this paragraph, if the plan year and taxable year do not coincide, the relevant plan year is the year ending with or within such taxable year.

(e) **Special rule for certain fully insured plans.** (1) In the case of a plan which is funded exclusively by the purchase of insurance or annuity contracts, prior to any adjustments otherwise required by section 401(j), the statutory percentages determined under §1.401(j)-1(f)(1) shall be adjusted by multiplying such percentages by the ratio of the normal rate to the guaranteed rate.

(2) If the insurance or annuity contracts are based on different interest and mortality assumptions determined by the sex of the participant, the plan shall use Table A, Sex Based Table, for determining the normal rate. If the insurance or annuity contracts are not based on such different assumptions by sex, the plan shall use Table B, Unisex Table. For Table A, the normal rate is the amount shown in that table according to the sex of the participant and the age at which the basic benefit is to commence. For Table B, the normal rate is the amount shown on that table applicable to the age at which the basic benefit is to commence.

TABLE A, SEX BASED TABLE

Age When Basic Benefit Commences	Normal Rate Male	Normal Rate Female
65	$1,112	$1,305
66	1,079	1,272
67	1,046	1,238
68	1,013	1,203
69	980	1,168
70	948	1,131

TABLE B, UNISEX TABLE

Age When Basic Benefit Commences	Normal Rate
65	$1,151
66	1,118
67	1,084
68	1,051
69	1,018
70	985

Proposed Reg. §1.401(j)-2

(3) The guaranteed rate is the cash value which must be accumulated under a typical policy used by the plan to provide a guaranteed basic benefit of $10 a month commencing at the same age for a participant of the same sex (if Table A is applicable) or for a participant without regard to sex (if Table B is applicable).

(4) If a plan subject to this paragraph (e) changes either its compensation base or rate of accrual, the applicable percentages, normal rates and guaranteed rates shall all be subject to adjustment in a manner determined by the Commissioner.

(5) Nothing in section 401(j) and this paragraph precludes a plan subject to this paragraph from providing a benefit in excess of the benefit specified in the plan.

(f) **No integration for plan benefiting owner-employees.** A defined benefit plan which provides contributions or benefits for owner-employees does not satisfy the requirements of section 401(j) and this section unless such plan meets the requirements of section 401(a)(4) without taking into account contributions or benefits under chapter 2 of the Code (relating to tax on self-employment income), chapter 21 of the Code (relating to Federal Insurance Contributions Act), title II of the Social Security Act, or under any other Federal or State law. Thus, such a plan will not qualify if the plan offsets its benefits by benefits provided under Social Security or under similar laws.

(g) **Special rule for deductions and inclusions.** A defined benefit plan to which section 401(j) applies is not subject to the special limitations on deductions for self-employed individuals set forth in section 404(e) or the special deduction computations, for common-law employees and self-employed individuals, set forth in section 404(a)(9). (See §1.404(e)-1(A)). Section 404(a)(1) sets forth the rules with respect to deductions for defined benefit plans.

(h) **Other limitations.** A plan to which this section applies is also subject to the limitations on benefits set forth in section 415. Consequently, even though a plan provides benefits which are not in excess of the maximum basic benefit set forth in this section, the plan will not be qualified under section 401(a) if the plan benefits are in excess of the section 415 limitations.

(i) **Application of nondiscrimination requirements.** Section 401(a)(4) requires that a defined benefit plan not discriminate in favor of employees who are members of the prohibited group. The term "prohibited group employees" means those employees in whose favor the benefits provided under a defined benefit plan may not discriminate under section 401(a)(4). For purposes of testing discrimination under a plan which provides for full and immediate vesting, the plan will not be considered to be discriminatory merely because the accrued benefit determined under the plan for any employee is limited to the maximum basic benefit as determined under section 401(j). Thus, for example, a plan providing for full and intermediate vesting and which bases benefits on percentages of compensation determined at the age when an employee's participation in the plan commences will not be considered to be discriminatory merely because the prohibited group employees are younger than other employees at such time and consequently have benefits determined at higher percentages.

(j) **Definitely determinable benefits.** A defined benefit plan to which this section applies is also subject to the requirements under section 401(a) to provide definitely determinable benefits. Thus, for example, for a final average pay plan to satisfy both the requirements of section 401(j) and the definitely determinable requirements, the plan would have to provide for a plan benefit formula under which a self-employed individual's or shareholder-employee's accrued benefit does not exceed the lesser of the final average pay formula, determined without regard to §1.401(j)-5 but with regard to other applicable requirements (such as those set forth in section 415), or the limitation in that section.

(k) **Examples.** The provisions of this section may be illustrated by the examples set forth below. In each example the defined benefit plan is not a final average pay plan.

Example (1). Employee D is a self-employed individual in a partnership which has a defined benefit plan. D also has an unrelated sole proprietorship which has a defined benefit plan. The two plans both have the same plan years. Under paragraph (c)(1) of this section, both plans are required to be taken into account in determining whether or not the requirements of this section are satisfied.

Example (2). Employee E is covered by both a defined benefit and a defined contribution plan required to be aggregated under paragraph (b) of this section. If, for 1980, the defined contribution plan is subject to the limitation of section 404(e) and E had $50,000 of earned income in 1980, the maximum amount deductible with respect to E equals $7,500 (15% of $50,000). If, for 1980, there is a deductible contribution for E under the defined contribution plan of $1,875, the fraction referred to in pargraph (d)(2) of this section equals $1,875 or 1/4. If, for 1980, E's maximum basic benefit under the de-

$$\frac{}{\$7,500}$$

fined benefit plan, determined without regard to paragraph (d)(1) of this section, equals $2,200, E's maximum basic benefit is determined by multiplying $2,200 times 3/4 (that is, 1 minus 1/4) which equals $1,650. Consequently, if E accrues a benefit in 1980 in excess of $1,650 under the defined benefit plan, the plan fails to satisfy the requirements of section 401(j).

§ 1.401(j)-3 (Proposed Treasury Decision, published 5-26-78.) **Change in compensation base or rate of accrual.**

(a) In general. (1) Section 401(j)(1) authorizes the Secretary to prescribe regulations to insure reasonable comparability of retirement benefits between qualified defined benefit plans and qualified defined contribution plans, or combinations thereof. Further, among several provisions under which the Secretary is required to prescribe regulations is a provision stating that an increase in a plan's rate of benefit accrual or compensation base must begin a new period of participation with respect to such increase (section 401(j)(3)(B)(iii)). In order to insure such comparability and to prescribe such regulations, this section sets forth requirements applicable to a plan which changes either the compensation base or the rate of benefit accrual, or both, applicable to a participant who is either a self-employed individual or a shareholder-employee. The limitations in this section referring to a participant are applicable only to a participant who is either a self-employed individual or a shareholder-employee. If a plan never amends its compensation base or rate of benefit accrual (or amends, but makes the changes applicable only to participants who are neither self-employed individuals nor shareholder-employees), the requirements of this section will not apply. See §1.401(j)-5 for the requirements dealing with changes in compensation base and rate of benefit accrual in the case of a final average pay plan.

(2) For purposes of section 401(j) and the regulations thereunder, amendments to the compensation base or rate of accrual include both adopted plan amendments and scheduled amendments (that is, amendments which are effective at a later time). Whether a particular amendment results in a change in base or rate shall be determined by the effect of the amendment upon plan benefit accruals and not by either the particular form of the amendment or the specific plan provision amended. For example, any plan amendment which changes the definition of compensation from less than total compensation to increase that amount upon which benefit accruals are based (for example, to add overtime hours to the compensation taken into account) would constitute a change in compensation base. Additionally, an increase in a survivor annuity from 50 percent to 75 percent of the employee benefit without any actuarial reduction would constitute a change in rate of benefit accrual.

(3) If the rate of benefit accrual for any level of compensation exceeds the applicable percentage for that level determined under this section, the plan does not satisfy section

Proposed Reg. § 1.401(j)-3

401(j). Also, the general rule set forth in §1.401(j)-1(c) that a plan is not qualified unless the plan contains provisions that preclude benefit accruals in excess of permissible section 401(j) amounts is equally applicable to changes in a plan's rate of accrual or compensation base. Thus, even though there is not in fact an excess accrual for a self-employed individual or shareholder-employee by reason of such an amendment, the plan is not qualified if there could be such an excess under the plan amendment.

(4) All plan amendments which effect a change in the plan's rate of benefit accrual or compensation base, and which are effective at the same time, shall be deemed to be a single amendment for purposes of applying the rules of this section.

(b) **Definitions, etc.** (1) A plan which changes its compensation base applicable to a participant shall have its applicable percentage determined by reference to the different compensation bases. These different compensation bases result in different levels of compensation. For this purpose, the term "level of compensation" means (i) the initial compensation base and (ii) the difference between each prior compensation base (beginning with the initial base) and the next succeeding compensation base.

(2) (i) In the case of a plan which initially specifies a compensation base in excess of $50,000, the statutory percentage determined under §1.401(j)-1(f)(1) shall be adjusted by multiplying such percentage by the ratio of $50,000 to the initial compensation base of the plan.

(ii) In the case of a plan which amends its compensation base to increase such base in excess of $50,000, the statutory percentage applicable to the compensation between the prior compensation base and the new compensation base shall be adjusted by multiplying that percentage by a fraction, the numerator of which equals the excess of $50,000, if any, over the prior compensation base, and the denominator of which equals the new compensation base minus the prior compensation base. However, no adjustment is required to the statutory percentage applicable to a participant's compensation up to the prior compensation base.

(iii) In the case of a plan which has a compensation base in excess of $50,000 and which subsequently amends its compensation base to decrease such base to another base in excess of $50,000, either the adjustment specified in subdivision (ii) or (i) of this subparagraph shall be made, depending on whether there is, or is not, respectively, a prior compensation base less than $50,000.

(iv) For purposes of section 401(j) and the regulations thereunder, the adjustments in this subparagraph are referred to as the "adjustments for excess compensation base."

(3) For purposes of this section, the term "attained-age applicable percentage" means the otherwise determined applicable percentage for the age of the participant when the plan amendment to either the compensation base or the rate of accrual is effective. The attained-age applicable percentage is determined for each different level of compensation by using the compensation base in effect after the plan amendment, including any adjustment for excess compensation base referred to in paragraph (b)(2) of this section.

(4) For purposes of this section, the term "prior-benefit accrual rate" means the benefit accrual rate, if any, determined under the plan for each level of compensation under the plan prior to any change in the plan's compensation base or the benefit accrual rate. If a plan decreases its benefit accrual rate, the decreased benefit accrual rate (not the rate prior to the decrease) shall, on and after the effective date of the decrease, be deemed to be the plan's prior-benefit accrual rate.

(5) For purposes of this section, the term "entry-age applicable percentage" means, with respect to a level of compensation, the otherwise applicable percentage determined under section 401(j) for the age of the participant at which a benefit could first accrue under the plan for that level of compensation or, if later, at which that participant's current period of participation began. The entry-age applicable percentage is determined for each different level of compensation by using the compensation base in effect prior to any change in the plan's compensation base and by including any adjustment (in effect prior to such change) for excess compensation base referred to in paragraph (b)(2) of this section.

(c) **Requirements for changes in rate of benefit accrual or changes in compensation base.** If a plan changes either the rate of benefit accrual or the compensation base (or both) with respect to a participant, the applicable percentage for any level of compensation is the greater of (1) the prior-benefit accrual rate with respect to that level of compensation, or (2) the attained-age applicable percentage with respect to that level of compensation. In no event shall the prior-benefit accrual rate exceed the entry-age applicable percentage.

(d) **Other changes.** If a plan's rate of benefit accrual or compensation base is changed in a manner not dealt with in this section, the applicable percentages for the plan shall be adjusted, as determined by the Commissioner, in a manner consistent with the regulations under section 401(j).

(e) **Fresh start.** If with respect to any participant subject to the requirements of section 401(j) a plan is amended so that the participant is treated under the plan as commencing a new period of plan participation and his applicable percentage is determined on the basis of his attained age at that time, then the plan shall be deemed to be a new plan with respect to that participant. Thus, such a plan amendment would not be subject to the requirements of this section.

(f) **Examples.** The provisions of this section can be illustrated by the examples set forth below. In each of the examples (except where otherwise specified) the following assumptions have been made: (1) each participant is an unmarried self-employed individual or shareholder-employee in a career average defined benefit plan; (2) each plan is established on the first day of a coinciding plan year and employer taxable year when the entering participant is age 30 ("Time 1"); (3) each plan is amended and the amendment is effective 10 years later on the first day of the coinciding plan year and taxable year when the relevant participant is age 40 ("Time 2"); (4) each participant has continuous service and one current period of participation beginning at Time 1 and not ending before Time 2; (5) each plan provides a basic benefit for each participant; (6) at all relevant times the participant's actual compensation exceeds each plan's applicable compensation base; and (7) each plan is not a fully insured plan subject to §1.401(j)-2(e).

Example (1). Participant A begins participation at Time 1 in Plan X, which provides an accrued benefit (in the form of basic benefit) accruing at the annual rate of 3.25%. At Time 1, Plan X's compensation base is $50,000. The applicable percentage for A at Time 1 is 6.5%. At Time 2, Plan X is amended to increase its rate of benefit accrual to the maximum applicable percentage, and to provide the maximum basic benefit. The applicable percentage and maximum benefit at Time 2 are determined as follows:

(i) Under paragraph (c), the applicable percentage at Time 2 is the greater of (1) 3.25% (Plan X's prior-benefit accrual rate for A) or (2) 4.4% (Plan X's attained-age applicable percentage for A). Accordingly, the rate of benefit accrual for A in Plan X at Time 2 cannot exceed 4.4%.

(ii) Under §1.401(j)-1(d), the maximum basic benefit at Time 2 which could accrue annually for A under Plan X equals the product of $50,000 (the compensation base) times 4.4% (the applicable percentage). Accordingly, A's maximum basic benefit equals $2,200.

Example (2). Participant B begins participation at Time 1 in Plan Y, which provides an accrued benefit (in the form of a basic benefit) accruing at the annual rate of 5.0%. At Time 1, Plan Y's specified compensation base is $20,000. The applicable percentage for B at Time 1 is 6.5%. At Time 2, Plan Y is amended to increase the specified compensation base to $50,000 and to provide the maximum basic benefit. The applicable percentages for each level of compensation and maximum benefit at Time 2 are determined as follows:

(i) Under paragraph (c), the applicable percentage at Time 2 cannot exceed the limitation applicable to each level of compensation. For the initial compensation base of $20,000, the applicable percentage is the greater of (1) 5.0% (Plan Y's prior-benefit accrual rate for B) or (2) 4.4% (Plan Y's attained-age applicable percentage for B), or 5.0%.

Proposed Reg. §1.401(j)-3

(ii) The applicable percentage at Time 2 for the next level of compensation in excess of $20,000 up to the new $50,000 compensation base, or the next $30,000 of compensation, is 4.4% (Plan Y's attained-age applicable percentage for B). There is no prior-benefit accrual rate for this level of compensation.

(iii) Under §1.401(j)-1(d), the maximum basic benefit at Time 2 which could accrue annually for B under Plan Y equals the sum of $1,000 (the initial compensation base of $20,000 times the 5.0% applicable percentage) and $1,320 (the $30,000 next level of compensation times the 4.4% applicable percentage). Accordingly, B's maximum basic benefit equals $2,320.

Example (3). Assume the same facts as in example (2) for Time 1 for participant C in Plan Y except that the annual rate is 6.5%. At Time 2, Plan Y is amended to increase the specified compensation base to $75,000 and to provide the maximum basic benefit. The applicable percentages for each level of compensation and maximum benefit at Time 2 are determined as follows:

(i) Under paragraph (c), the applicable percentage at Time 2 cannot exceed a limitation applicable to each level of compensation. For the initial compensation base of $20,000, the applicable percentage is the greater of (1) 6.5% (Plan Y's prior-benefit accrual rate for C) or (2) 4.4% (Plan Y's attained-age applicable percentage for C), or 6.5%.

(ii) The applicable percentage at Time 2 for the next level of compensation in excess of $20,000 up to the new $75,000 compensation base, or the next $55,000 of compensation, is the attained-age applicable percentage (there is no prior-benefit accrual rate for this level of compensation). Under paragraph (b)(3), the attained-age applicable percentage for C is determined by making the adjustment for the excess compensation base specified in paragraph (b)(2). Accordingly, the applicable percentage is 2.4% (4.4% times ($50,000 − $20,000)/($75,000 − $20,000)).

(iii) Under §1.401(j)-1(d), the maximum basic benefit at Time 2 which could accrue annually for C under Plan Y equals the sum of $1,300 (the initial compensation base of $20,000 times the 6.5% applicable percentage) and $1,320 ($55,000, the next level of compensation, times the 2.4% applicable percentage). Accordingly, C's maximum basic benefit equals $2,620.

Example (4). Participant D begins participation at Time 1 in Plan Z, which provides an accrued benefit (in the form of a basic benefit) accruing at the annual rate of 3.25%. At Time 1, Plan Z's specified compensation base is $100,000. In order to determine the applicable percentage, the statutory percentage of 6.5% must be adjusted for the excess compensation base, as specified in paragraph (b)(2), to obtain a modified statutory percentage of 3.25% (6.5% times $50,000/$100,000). At Time 2, Plan Z is amended to decrease its specified compensation base to $50,000 and to provide the maximum basic benefit. The applicable percentage for the new compensation base and the maximum benefit at Time 2 are determined as follows:

(i) Under paragraph (c), the applicable percentage for the new $50,000 compensation base is the greater of 3.25% (Plan Z's prior-benefit accrual rate for D) or 4.4% (Plan Z's attained-age applicable percentage for D), or 4.4%.

(ii) Under §1.401(j)-1(d), the maximum basic benefit at Time 2 which could accrue annually for C under Plan Z equals the product of $50,000 (the new compensation base) times 4.4% (the applicable percentage). Accordingly, D's maximum basic benefit equals $2,200.

Example (5). Participant E begins participation at Time 1 in Plan W, which provides an accrued benefit (in the form of a basic benefit) accruing at the annual rate of 3%. At Time 1, Plan W's specified compensation base is $30,000. The applicable percentage for E at Time 1 is 6.5%. At Time 2, Plan W is amended to increase the specified compensation base to $50,000, to increase the rate of benefit accrual and to provide the maximum basic benefit. The applicable percentages for each level of compensation, the accrual rates and maximum benefit at Time 2 are determined as follows:

(i) Under paragraph (c), the applicable percentages at Time 2 cannot exceed a limitation applicable to each level of compensation. For the initial compensation base of

$30,000, the limitation determined under paragraph (c) is 4.4% (the greater of (A) 3%, Plan W's prior-benefit accrual rate for E, or (B) 4.4%, Plan W's attained-age applicable percentage for E). In this instance, Plan W can raise its benefit accrual rate to 4.4% applicable to the initial compensation base of $30,000.

(ii) The limitation on the applicable percentage at Time 2 for the next level of compensation in excess of $30,000 up to the new $50,000 compensation base (the next $20,000 of compensation) is 4.4%, the attained-age applicable percentage (there is no prior-benefit accrual rate for this level of compensation). In this instance, Plan W can raise its benefit accrual rate to 4.4% applicable to this next $20,000 level of compensation.

(iii) Under §1.401(j)-1(d), the maximum basic benefit at Time 2 which could accrue annually for E under Plan W equals the sum of $1,320 (the initial compensation base of $30,000 times the 4.4% applicable percentage) and $880 (the $20,000 next level of compensation times the 4.4% applicable percentage). Accordingly, E's maximum basic benefit equals $2,200.

§1.401(j)-4 (Proposed Treasury Decision, published 5-26-78.) Special rules for electing small business corporation.

(a) **In general; definitions.** This section sets forth special rules applicable to defined benefit plans of an electing small business corporation, as defined in section 1371(a). For purposes of this section the following definitions shall apply.

(1) **Old Sub-S plan.** The term "old Sub-S plan" means a defined benefit plan (and trust) to which section 401(j) applies and which is established prior to the first plan year to which section 401(j) applies.

(2) **New Sub-S plan.** The term "new Sub-S plan" means a defined benefit plan (and trust) to which section 401(j) applies and which is not established prior to the first plan year to which section 401(j) applies.

(3) **Pre-401(j) part.** The term "pre-401(j) part" of an old Sub-S plan (and trust) means that part attributable to benefits accrued for plan years beginning prior to the first plan year to which section 401(j) applies to the plan.

(4) **Post-401(j) part.** The term "post-401(j) part" of an old Sub-S plan (and trust) means that part attributable to benefits accrued for plan years beginning with the first plan year to which section 401(j) applies to the plan.

(b) **New Sub-S plan.** A new Sub-S plan to which section 401(j) applies is not subject to the rules on taxability of shareholder-employee beneficiaries, etc. set forth in section 1379(b) and the regulations thereunder. The other rules prescribed under section 401(j) in §§1.401(j)-1 through 1.401(j)-3, 1.401(j)-5 and 1.401(j)-6 apply to a new Sub-S plan.

(c) **Old Sub-S plan—(1) General rule.** An old Sub-S plan to which section 401(j) applies is subject to the special rules set forth in subparagraph (2).

(2) **Special rules.** (i) The pre-401(j) part of an old Sub-S plan is subject to the rules on taxability of shareholder-employees, etc. set forth in section 1379(b) and the regulations thereunder.

(ii) An old Sub-S plan may provide benefits for years to which section 401(j) and the regulations thereunder apply. In that instance, with respect to the post-401(j) part of the plan, the rules prescribed under section 401(j) in §§1.401(j)-1 through 1.401(j)-3, 1.401(j)-5 and 1.401(j)-6 apply, except as modified by the rules set forth in subdivisions (iii) and (iv).

(iii) The applicable percentage shall be determined in the same manner as is provided for a change in status under §1.401(j)-1(g)(6) and as if the time section 401(j) applies to the plan is the time of such a change in status. Thus, for example, if a plan provided for a 7.5% past accrual rate on $50,000 of compensation for Participant A, who commenced participation at age 30 in 1966, and the plan is amended for 1976 to meet the requirements of section 401(j), the applicable percentage for 1976 is determined under §1.401(j)-

Proposed Reg. §1.401(j)-4

1(g)(6)(i) and equals 6.5% (the lesser of 7.5% (past accrual rate) or 6.5% (applicable percentage in 1966); but not less than 4.4% (the applicable percentage at age 40)). Further, the past accrual rate is determined under §1.401(j)-1(g)(6)(ii)(A) by dividing the shareholder-employee's total employer-derived benefit as of the close of the plan year beginning within the employer's last taxable year (beginning before January 1, 1976) by the sum of the shareholder-employee's total compensation up to the close of that period.

(iv) A plan amendment required (with respect to the first plan year) to satisfy the requirements of section 401(a)(18) and (j) shall not be treated as a change in the plan's compensation base or rate of accrual for purposes of applying the rules of §1.401(j)-3. Thus, for example, a plan which provided a benefit accrual of 7.5% on a compensation base of $100,000 in 1975 would not be subject to the special rules of §1.401(j)-3 when the plan is amended for 1976 to provide, for example, a basic benefit accrual of 6.5% of $50,000.

§ 1.401(j)-5 (Proposed Treasury Decision, published 5-26-78.) Special rules applicable to final average pay plans.

(a) **General rule.** Except as provided in this section, the provisions of §1.401(j)-1 through 1.401(j)-4, inclusive, and §1.401(j)-6 apply to a final average pay plan, as defined in §1.401(j)-1(e)(5). If such a plan in any plan year provides for an accrual of benefits by any designated employee in excess of the limitation on amount of the basic benefit, the plan (and trust, if any) does not satisfy section 401(j) in that plan year. As indicated in §1.401(j)-1(c), the plan is also not qualified unless the plan precludes the potential of accruals in excess of the limitation on amount of basic benefit. The designated employees are self-employed individuals and shareholder-employees, and the limitation on amount is the limitation on amount determined under this section.

(b) **General limitation on amount; no amendment—(1) Application.** This paragraph (b) applies to a plan which never is amended to change the plan's compensation base or rate of benefit accrual (or is amended, but makes the changes applicable only to participants who are neither self-employed individuals nor shareholder-employees). If a participant is always subject to section 401(j) and the plan is never amended, see paragraph (b)(4). This paragraph also applies to a plan which is amended effective as of the date section 401(j) first applies to the plan to conform the plan to the requirements of section 401(j) provided that the plan is not subsequently amended. In other cases, the rules in paragraph (c) apply. In lieu of the limitation in §1.401(j)-1(c) and (d) (relating to the maximum basic benefit which can accrue for a plan year of participation under plans, other than final average pay plans) the general limitation for final average pay plans ("General Limitation"), applicable to the participant, applies.

(2) **General Limitation.** The General Limitation, with respect to a participant, is equal to the sum of (i) the limitation for the plan's pre-401(j) benefit and (ii) the limitation for the plan's post-401(j) benefit.

(3) **Limitation on pre-401(j) benefit.** The limitation with respect to a participant for the plan's pre-401(j) benefit (that is, the limitation applicable to plan years before section 401(j) becomes applicable to the participant) equals the greater of—

(i) The accrued benefit of the participant under the plan as of the close of the plan year immediately preceding the later of (A) the plan year in which the participant becomes a self-employed individual or a shareholder-employee or (B) the first plan year for which section 401(j) applies to the plan (determined as if the participant separates at such time); or

(ii) The accrued benefit of the participant obtained by multiplying (A) the applicable percentage rate, determined under §1.401(j)-1, for the time the participant's current period of plan participation commenced by (B) the sum of the compensation earned by the participant for each year for the period of plan participation beginning with his first such year and ending with the close of the immediately preceding plan year referred to in subdivision (i) of this subparagraph.

The accrued benefit of the participant determined under subdivisions (i) and (ii) of this subparagraph shall be determined in a manner consistent with the determination of the accrued benefit under §1.401(j)-1(g)(5)(ii) (relating to past accrual rates in the case of an employee's change in status). Notwithstanding §1.401(j)-1(g)(5)(ii), any plan amendment affecting the compensation base or rate of accrual occurring prior to or within the immediately preceding plan year referred to in subdivision (i) of this subparagraph shall be disregarded for purposes of determining the accrued benefit under subdivision (ii) of this subparagraph. Further, the applicable percentage in subdivision (ii)(A) and the compensation for each year described in subdivision (ii)(B) shall be determined with respect to the plan's compensation base in effect for the plan year beginning immediately after the close of the plan year referred to in subdivision (i).

(4) **Limitation on post-401(j) benefit.** The limitation with respect to a participant for the plan's post-401(j) benefit for any relevant plan year (that is, the limitation applicable to the first plan year for which section 401(j) applies to the participant and any subsequent plan year) equals the product of—

(i) The applicable percentage rate, determined under §1.401(j)-1, for the time when the participant's current period of plan participation commenced, multiplied by

(ii) The sum of the participant's compensation covered under the plan for each post-401(j) plan year within the participant's current period of plan participation including the relevant plan year (that is, the plan year for which the limitation is being determined).

(c) **General limitation on amount; amended plan—(1) Application.** This paragraph (c) applies to a plan to which paragraph (b) does not apply. In lieu of the limitation in §§1.401(j)-1(c) and (d), and 1.401(j)-3 (relating, respectively, to the maximum basic benefit, etc., and change in compensation base or rate of accrual for plans other than final average pay plans), the general limitation for amended final average pay plans ("Amended Limitation"), applicable to the participant, applies. As specified in paragraph (a) of this section, the plan does not satisfy section 401(j) in any plan year for which the plan provides for (or permits) an accrual of benefits for any designated employee which exceeds the Amended Limitation.

(2) **General limitation for amended plan.** The Amended Limitation, with respect to a participant, for any level of compensation (see §1.401(j)-3(b)(1)), equals the sum of (i) the accrued basic benefit of the participant with respect to that level of compensation under the plan as established and (ii) the accrued basic benefit of the participant under the plan on account of each subsequent amendment with respect to that level of compensation. For purposes of this subparagraph and the succeeding rules in this section, the term "under the plan as established" means, with respect to a participant's level of compensation, under the plan at the time the participant first accrues a benefit for a particular level of compensation (or could have so accrued but for his compensation being less than such level). Thus, for example, if a plan is established in year 1 and a designated employee commences participation in year 10, then the plan as established means the plan in year 10.

(3) **Accrued basic benefit under plan as established.** The accrued basic benefit of the participant under the plan as established equals the lesser of (i) the accrued benefit of the participant determined for each level of compensation based on the plan in effect on the date that the participant is first subject to section 401(j) and based on that participant's service and compensation taken into account under the plan for the participant's period of plan participation, or (ii) the participant's General Limitation determined under paragraph (b)(2) for each level of compensation.

(4) **Limitation on increases.** If the accrued benefit of the participant on account of the plan as established with respect to a level of compensation equals the participant's General Limitation (determined under subparagraph (3)(ii) above), then the accrued benefit of the participant on account of each subsequent amendment with respect to such level of compensation is zero.

(5) **Permitted increases.** If the accrued benefit of the participant on account of the plan as established with respect to a level of compensation is less than the participant's General Limitation (determined under subparagraph (3)(ii) above), then the accrued bene-

Proposed Reg. §1.401(j)-5

fit of the participant on account of each subsequent amendment with respect to such level of compensation at any relevant time affected by such amendment equals the lesser of—

(i) The increase in the accrued benefit of the participant under the plan formula as a result of such amendment, or

(ii) The future limitation for the plan's future service benefit with respect to that participant ("Averaged Cap").

(6) **Increase under plan formula; Averaged Cap.** (i) The increase in the participant's accrued benefit under the plan formula described in subparagraph (5)(i) above equals the difference between (A) the participant's accrued benefit determined under the plan in effect prior to the plan amendment and (B) the participant's accrued benefit determined under the plan in effect after the plan amendment. Both such accrued benefits are determined with respect to the participant's service and compensation taken into account under the plan and as of the relevant date (that is, the plan year for which the limitation is being determined).

(ii) The Averaged Cap described in subparagraph (5)(ii) above with respect to the participant equals the product of (A) the difference, if any, between (1) the applicable percentage rate of the participant after the amendment and (2) the prior-benefit accrual rate of the participant before the amendment, as defined in §1.401(j)-3(b)(4), and (B) the sum of the compensation earned by the participant after the amendment (and taken into account under the plan's level of compensation) for each plan year within the participant's current period of plan participation including the relevant plan year (that is, the plan year for which the limitation is being determined). The percentage rates of the participant referred to in (A)(1) and (2) of this subdivision are the otherwise determined percentages under section 401(j), including the required adjustments under §1.401(j)-3, relating to changes in compensation base and rate of accrual. Thus, for example, the participant's applicable percentage rate before the amendment for a particular level of compensation must be determined in a manner consistent with the rules in §1.401(j)-3(d), relating to requirements for changes in compensation bases.

(7) **Averaged Cap; limitation on increases.** If the accrued benefit of the participant on account of the plan as first amended with respect to a level of compensation equals the participant's Averaged Cap (determined under subparagraph (6)(ii) above), then the accrued benefit of the participant on account of each succeeding amendment, after the first such amendment, with respect to such level of compensation is zero.

(8) **Averaged Cap; permitted increases.** (i) If the accrued benefit of the participant on account of the plan's first amendment with respect to a level of compensation is less than the participant's Averaged Cap (determined under subparagraph (6)(ii) above), then the participant's accrued benefit on account of each succeeding amendment, after the first such amendment, is determined under the following procedure.

(ii) The participant's accrued benefit is determined under subparagraph (6) above by applying the rules of that subparagraph to each succeeding amendment as if the plan as established and first amended with respect to a level of compensation constituted the established plan. In that application of the rules under subparagraph (6) above, the participant's General Limitation (determined under subparagraph (3)(ii) of this paragraph) shall be deemed to be the participant's Averaged Cap (determined under subparagraph (6)(ii) above).

(d) **Other adjustments.** The Commissioner shall, in the case of a final average pay plan, determine if any other adjustments to plan accruals are required to be made in a manner consistent with section 401(j) including this section and §1.401(j)-3.

(e) **Examples.** The provisions of this section can be illustrated by the examples set forth below. In each of the examples (except where otherwise specified) the following assumptions have been made: (1) each participant is a single self-employed individual or shareholder-employee in a final average pay plan; (2) each plan is established and effective on the first day of a coinciding plan year and employer taxable year when the entering participant is age 50 ("Time 1"), (3) each plan that is amended is effectively amended on the first day of a coinciding plan year and taxable year ("Time 2"); and (4) each plan provides a basic benefit for each participant.

Example (1). Participant A begins participation in Plan M at Time 1 (age 50). Plan M provides for an annual benefit accrual of 1% of last year's compensation, not to exceed $50,000, for each year of participation (A plan would not be qualified if benefits were based on only the last year, but for illustrative purposes assume that such a formula is permissible). Plan M also limits benefit accruals to satisfy the limitations of this section. A's compensation for each of the first 10 years equals $10,000 per year. At Time 2 (age 60), A's compensation is increased and equals $40,000. A's General Limitation and benefit accrual for the 11th year is determined as follows:

(A) Because there is no pre-401(j) benefit under Plan M for A, A's General Limitation is determined under paragraph (b)(4) and equals the product of 3% (the applicable percentage at age 50) times $140,000 ((10 years times $10,000 or $100,000) plus (1 year times $40,000, or $40,000)), or $4,200.

(B) Under Plan M's benefit formula, without regard to the plan provision required to satisfy the General Limitation, A's accrued benefit would equal 1% times $40,000 times 11 years, or $4,400.

(C) Accordingly, Plan M could satisfy section 401(j) and could provide a deferred normal retirement benefit for A of $4,200, if A left the plan at the end of his 11th year of participation.

(D) If Plan M is never amended and A continues his plan participation (instead of ending his plan participation as in (C), above) for 4 more years at the same compensation of $40,000, then A's accrued normal retirement benefit under the plan equals $6,000 (1% times $40,000 times 15 years). A's General Limitation, in this instance, equals $9,000 (3% times $300,000 ($140,000 for 11 years plus $160,000 for 4 years)). Plan M would satisfy section 401(j) by providing A with a $6,000 normal retirement benefit.

Example (2). Participant B begins participation in Plan N at Time 1 (age 50). Plan N provides for an annual benefit accrual of 1% of last year's compensation, not to exceed $50,000 for each year of participation. Plan N is amended to provide for an annual benefit accrual of 2% of last year's compensation, not to exceed $50,000 when B is age 55 (6th year of B's plan participation). Plan N also limits benefit accruals to satisfy the limitation of this section. B's compensation for each of the first 10 years (age 50 to 59) equals $25,000 per year. When B is age 60, B's compensation is increased and equals $40,000 for each of the next 5 years (age 60 to age 64). Assume the Plan N's benefit formula has satisfied this section prior to the plan amendment. B's Amended Limitation and benefit accrual are determined as follows:

(A) B's Amended Limitation under Plan N is determined under paragraph (c). B's Amended Limitation for the plan's $50,000 level of compensation equals the sum of (1) B's accrued benefit under Plan N as established and (2) B's accrued benefit on account of the amendment to Plan N.

(B) B's accrued benefit under Plan N as established equals the lesser of (1) B's accrued benefit under Plan N as in effect when section 401(j) applies to B or (2) B's General Limitation. In this case these amounts, respectively, equal $6,000 (1% times $40,000 times 15 years) and $13,500 (3%, age 50, times $450,000 (10 years times $25,000, or $250,000) plus (5 years times $40,000, or $200,000)). Accordingly, B's accrued benefit under Plan N, as established, equals $6,000. Because B's General Limitation exceeds his accrued benefit under the plan as established, Plan N can amend its plan benefit accrual formula to provide B a greater accrued benefit.

(C) B's accrued benefit on account of the amendment to Plan N equals the lesser of (1) B's increased accrued benefit as a result of the amendment or (2) B's Averaged Cap. B's accrued benefit under the new plan benefit formula equals $12,000 (2% times $40,000 times 15 years). Therefore, B's increased accrued benefit equals $6,000 ($12,000 new mi-

Proposed Reg. §1.401(j)-5

nus $6,000 old). B's Averaged Cap equals (under paragraph (c)(6)(ii)) the product of a percentage and a career compensation dollar amount. B's compensation for his 10 years of plan participation since the plan amendment equals $325,000 (5 times $25,000 plus 5 times $40,000). The percentage equals the difference between the post-amendment applicable percentage and the prior-benefit accrual rate, both determined consistently with the plan amendment rules in §1.401(j)-3. In this case, B's post-amendment percentage equals the attained-age applicable percentage of 2.5% for age 55. B's prior-benefit accrual rate is determined by dividing B's accrued benefit of $6,000 under the original plan by B's $450,000 compensation for his 15 years of plan participation and equals 1.33%. The difference between the two percentages equals 1.17%. Accordingly, B's Averaged Cap under Plan N, as amended, equals $3,803 ($325,000 times 1.17%). B's accrued benefit on account of the amendment equals $3,803 (the lesser of $6,000 or $3,803).

(D) B's Amended Limitation under Plan N equals $9,803 ($6,000 plus $3,803). Because B's accrued benefit on account of the plan amendment is determined by reference to B's Averaged Cap. Plan N could not provide for additional benefit accruals for B, assuming B leaves the plan after his 15 years of participation.

Example (3). Using the facts of example (2), B's Amended Limitation and benefit accrual can be computed under the following worksheet:

FINAL AVERAGE PAY WORKSHEET
(For one level of compensation and only one period of current participation)

Step	Operation	Answer
1.	Determine accrued benefit under plan as established, using plan formula and final average pay	$6,000 (1% × 15 × $40,000)
2.	Determine General Limitation by following steps:	
	(a) Limitation on pre-401(j) benefit	
	(i) accrued benefit of participant as of close of last pre-401(j) plan year determined as of that time	0
	(ii) applicable percentage based on age as of beginning of current participation	3%
	(iii) sum of compensations within this level for years prior to 401(j)	0
	(iv) product of (ii) and (iii)	0
	(v) greater of (i) or (iv)	0
	(b) Limitation on post-401(j) benefit	
	(i) applicable percentage in (a)(ii)	3%
	(ii) sum of compensations within this level for years since 401(j)	$450,000 (10 × $25,000 + 5 × $40,000)
	(iii) product of (i) and (ii)	$13,500

Proposed Regulations

Step	Operation	Answer
	(c) General Limitation equals the sum of (a)(v) plus (b)(iii)	$13,500

If Step 1 is not less than Step 2(c), or if there are no further plan amendments, enter zero in Step 6 and proceed to Step 7. Otherwise proceed to Step 3.

		Amendment	1	2	3
3.	Determine the accrued benefit on account of each subsequent amendment, using plan formula, and final average pay as follows:				
	(a) Accrued benefit based on plan in effect after the amendment		$ 12,000 (2% × 15 × $40,000)		
	(b) Accrued benefit based on plan in effect prior to the amendment		$ 6,000		
	(c) Increase [(a) − (b)]		$ 6,000		
4.	Determine Averaged Cap steps: (a) Prior benefit accrual rate				
	(i) accrual rate for plan as established [Step 1 ÷ (Step 2(a)(iii) + Step 2(b)(ii))]		1.33% $6,000 0 + $450,000		
	(ii) greater of Step 4(a)(i) in this column or Step 4(a)(iv) in prior column		1.33%		
	(iii) from prior column [Step 5 ÷ Step 4(d)]		0		
	(iv) sum of Step 4(a) (iii) and Step 4(a)(ii)		1.33%		
	(b) Attained age applicable percentage at time of amendment		2.5%		
	(c) Excess, if any [(b) − (a)(iv)]		1.17%		
	(d) Sum of compensations within this level for years since amendment		$325,000 (5 × $40,000 + 5 × $25,000)		
	(e) Product of (c) and (d)		$ 3,803		
5.	Maximum accrued benefit attributable to this amendment (Lesser of Step 3(c) or Step 4(e))		$ 3,803		

Proposed Reg. § 1.401(j)-5

Step	Operation	Answer

If, for this amendment, Step 3(c) is not less than Step 4(e) or, if there are no subsequent amendments, proceed to Step 6. Otherwise, do Steps 3–5 for the next amendment.

6.	Maximum accrued benefit due to all amendments (sum columns of Step 5)	$3,803
7.	Maximum accrued benefit under plan as established (lesser of Steps 1 or 2 (c))	$6,000
8.	Maximum accrued benefit - Total (Sum of Step 6 and Step 7)	$9,803

§1.401(j)-6 (Proposed Treasury Decision, published 5-26-78.) Effective dates and transitional rules.

(a) **Effective dates.** Section 401(j) and the regulations thereunder apply to taxable years of an employer beginning after December 31, 1975, and to any plan year beginning with or within such taxable years.

(b) **Transitional rule.** A plan will be treated as satisfying the requirements of section 401(j) for plan years beginning prior to July 25, 1978 if, for such years, any excess of the benefit accruing under the plan over the maximum benefit permitted for a participant under section 401(j) for such year is used, to the extent reasonably possible, to reduce the maximum benefit permitted under section 401(j) for plan years beginning on or after such date. This paragraph will apply to a plan only if it is amended to satisfy the requirements of this paragraph. Irrespective of any other limitation on time of amendment, the amendment may be adopted within the 1 year period beginning [with the date of publication of this section in the Federal Register as a Treasury decision].

Taxability of Beneficiary of Employees' Trust

Section 1.402(a)-1 is amended by revising subparagraphs (1)(i) and (6)(i) of paragraph (a) to read as follows:

§ 1.402(a)-1 (Proposed Treasury Decision, published 5-6-72.) **Taxability of beneficiary under a trust which meets the requirements of section 401(a).**

(a) **In general.** (1)(i) Section 402 relates to the taxation of the beneficiary of an employees' trust. If an employer makes a contribution for the benefit of an employee to a trust described in section 401(a) for the taxable year of the employer which ends within or with a taxable year of the trust for which the trust is exempt under section 501(a), the employee is not required to include such contribution in his income except for the year or years in which such contribution is distributed or made available to him. However, see section 1379(b) and the regulations thereunder for the inclusion of excess contributions made by an electing small business corporation in the gross income of certain shareholder-employees for a year or years prior to distribution. It is immaterial in the case of contributions to an exempt trust whether the employee's rights in the contributions to the trust are forfeitable or nonforfeitable either at the time the contribution is made to the trust or thereafter.

* * * * * * * * * * * * *

(6)(i) If the total distributions payable with respect to any employee under a trust described in section 401(a) which in the year of distribution is exempt under section 501(a) are paid to, or includible in the gross income of, the distributee within one taxable year of the distributee on account of the employee's death or other separation from the service, or death after such separation from service, the amount of such distribution, to the extent it exceeds the net amount contributed by the employee, shall be considered a gain from the sale or exchange of a capital asset held for more than 6 months. Under section 402(a)(5), for taxable years ending after December 31, 1969, the amount of a distribution considered under the previous sentence to be a gain from the sale or exchange of a capital asset held for more than 6 months shall be limited as provided in § 1.402(a)-2 [36 F.R. 11443]. Section 72(n)(4) and § 1.72-19 [36 F.R. 3822] apply to the portion of the total distributions payable not treated as long-term capital gain or the net amount contributed by the employee. The total distributions payable are includible in the gross income of the distributee within one taxable year if they are made available to such distributee and the distributee fails to make a timely election under section 72(h) to receive an annuity in lieu of such total distributions. The "net amount contributed by the employee" is the amount actually contributed by the employee plus any amounts considered to be contributed by the employee under the rules of sections 72(f), 101(b), 1379(b)(2), and subparagraph (3) of this paragraph, reduced by any amounts theretofore distributed to him which were excludable from gross income as a return of employee contributions. See, however, paragraph (b) of this section for rules relating to the exclusion of amounts representing net unrealized appreciation in the value of securities of the employer corporation. In addition, all or part of the amount otherwise includible in gross income under this paragraph by a nonresident alien individual in respect of a distribution by the United States under a qualified pension plan may be excludable from gross income under section 402(a)(4). For rules relating to such exclusion, see paragraph (c) of this section. For additional rules relating to the treatment of total distributions described in this subdivision in the case of a nonresident alien individual, see sections 871 and 1441 and the regulations thereunder.

* * * * * * * * * * * * *

Section 1.402(a)-1 is amended by revising paragraphs (a)(1)(i), (a)(1)(ii), (a)(1)(iii), (a)(2), (a)(5), (a)(6), (a)(7), (a)(9), and (b)(1) to read as follows:

§ 1.402(a)-1 (Proposed Treasury Decision, published 12-6-72, 4-30-75.) **Taxability of beneficiary under a trust which meets the requirements of section 401(a).**

Proposed Reg. § 1.402(a)-1

(a) **In general.** (1)(i) Section 402 relates to the taxation of the beneficiary of an employees' trust. If an employer makes a contribution for the benefit of an employee to a trust described in section 401(a) for the taxable year of the employer which ends within or with a taxable year of the trust for which the trust is exempt under section 501(a), the employee is not required to include such contribution in his income except for the year or years in which such contribution is distributed or made available to him. However, see section 1379(b) of the Code and the regulations thereunder for the inclusion of excess contributions made by an electing small business corporation in the gross income of certain shareholder-employees for a year or years prior to distribution. It is immaterial in the case of contributions to an exempt trust whether the employee's rights in the contributions to the trust are forfeitable or nonforfeitable either at the time the contribution is made to the trust or thereafter. Whether a contribution to an exempt trust is made by the employer or the employee must be determined on the basis of the particular facts and circumstances of the individual case. An amount contributed to an exempt trust will, except as otherwise provided in this subdivision, be considered to have been contributed by the employee if at his individual option such amount was so contributed in return for a reduction in his basic or regular compensation or in lieu of an increase in such compensation. The preceding sentence shall not apply to an amount contributed to an exempt trust either (a) in a taxable year of the employee ending prior to January 1, 1972, or (b) at any time prior to December 6, 1972, where the employee has relied upon a ruling by the Commissioner to him or his employer that such amount will be treated as the contribution of the employer.

(ii) The provisions of section 402(a) relate only to a distribution by a trust which is described in section 401(a) and which is exempt under section 501(a) for the taxable year of the trust in which the distribution is made. With three exceptions, the distribution from such an exempt trust when received or made available is taxable to the distributee or recipient to the extent provided in section 72 (relating to annuities). First, for taxable years beginning before January 1, 1964, section 72(e)(3) (relating to the treatment of certain lump sums), as in effect before such date, shall not apply to such distributions. For taxable years beginning after December 31, 1963, such distributions may be taken into account in computations under sections 1301 through 1305 (relating to income averaging). Secondly, if the taxable year ends after December 31, 1969 and begins before January 1, 1974, the portion of the distribution treated as long-term capital gain is subject to the limitation under section 402(a)(5), as in effect on December 31, 1973. For treatment of such total distributions, see subparagraph (6) of this paragraph. Thirdly, for taxable years beginning after December 31, 1973, a certain portion, described in section 402(a)(2), of a lump sum distribution, as defined in section 402(e)(4), is taxable as long-term capital gain and a certain portion, described in section 402(e)(4)(E), may be taxable under section 402(e). For the treatment of such lump sum distributions, see paragraph (9) of this paragraph. Under certain circumstances, an amount representing the unrealized appreciation in the value of the securities of the employer is excludable from gross income for the year of distribution. For the rules relating to such exclusion, see paragraph (b) of this section. Furthermore, the exclusion provided by section 105(d) is applicable to a distribution from a trust described in section 401(a) and exempt under section 501(a) if such distribution constitutes wages or payments in lieu of wages for a period during which an employee is absent from work on account of a personal injury or sickness. See § 1.72-15 for the rules relating to the tax treatment of accident or health benefits received under a plan to which section 72 applies.

(iii) Except as provided in paragraph (b) of this section, a distribution of property (other than an annuity contract) by a trust described in section 401(a) and exempt under section 501(a) shall be taken into account by the recipient at its fair market value. For valuation of an annuity contract, see § 1.402(e)-2(c)(1)(ii)(F).

* * * * * * * * * *

(2) If a trust described in section 401(a) and exempt under section 501(a) purchases an annuity contract for an employee and distributes it to the employee in a year for which the trust is exempt, and the contract contains a cash surrender

value which may be available to an employee by surrendering the contract, such cash surrender value will not be considered income to the employee unless and until the contract is surrendered. For the rule as to nontransferability of annuity contracts issued after 1962, see paragraph (b)(1) of § 1.401-9. However, the distribution of an annuity contract must be treated as a lump sum distribution under section 402(e) for purposes of determining the separate tax imposed under section 402(e)(1)(A). If, however, the contract distributed by such exempt trust is a retirement income, endowment, or other life insurance contract and is distributed after October 26, 1956, the entire cash value of such contract at the time of distribution must be included in the distributee's income in accordance with the provisions of section 402(a), except to the extent that, within 60 days after the distribution of such contract, (i) all or any portion of such value is irrevocably converted into a contract under which no part of any proceeds payable on death at any time would be excludable under section 101(a) (relating to life insurance proceeds), or (ii) such contract is treated as a rollover contribution under section 402(a)(5), as in effect after December 31, 1973. If the contract distributed by such trust is a transferable annuity contract issued after 1962, or a retirement income, endowment, or other life insurance contract which is distributed after 1962 (whether or not transferable), then notwithstanding the preceding sentence the entire cash value of the contract is includible in the distributee's gross income, unless within such 60 days such contract is also made nontransferable.

*   *   *   *   *   *   *   *   *   *

(5) If pension or annuity payments or other benefits are paid or made available to the beneficiary of a deceased employee or a deceased retired employee by a trust described in section 401(a) which is exempt under section 501(a), such amounts are taxable in accordance with the rules of section 402(a) and this section. In case such amounts are taxable under section 72, the "investment in the contract" shall be determined by reference to the amount contributed by the employee and by applying the applicable rules of sections 72 and 101(b)(2)(D). In case the amounts paid to, or includible in the gross income of, the beneficiaries of the deceased employee or deceased retired employee constitute a distribution to which subparagraph (6) or (9) (whichever applies) of this paragraph is applicable, the extent to which the distribution is taxable is determined by reference to the contributions of the employee, by reference to any prior distributions which were excludable from gross income as a return of employee contributions, and by applying the applicable rules of sections 72 and 101(b).

(6) This subparagraph applies in the case of a total distribution made in a taxable year of the distributee or payee ending before January 1, 1970.

(i) If the total distributions payable with respect to any employee under a trust described in section 401(a) which in the year of distribution is exempt under section 501(a) are paid to, or includible in the gross income of, the distributee within one taxable year of the distributee on account of the employee's death or other separation from the service, or death after such separation from service, the amount of such distribution, to the extent it exceeds the net amount contributed by the employee, shall be considered a gain from the sale or exchange of a capital asset held for more than six months. The total distributions payable are includible in the gross income of the distributee within one taxable year if they are made available to such distributee and the distributee fails to make a timely election under section 72(h) to receive an annuity in lieu of such total distributions. The "net amount contributed by the employee" is the amount actually contributed by the employee plus any amounts considered to be contributed by the employee under the rules of section 72(f), 101(b), and subparagraph (3) of this paragraph, reduced by any amounts theretofore distributed to him which were excludable from gross income as a return of employee contributions. See, however, paragraph (b) of this section for rules relating to the exclusion of amounts representing net unrealized appreciation in the value of securities of the employer corporation. In addition, all or part of the amount otherwise includible in gross income under this paragraph by a nonresident alien individual in respect of a distribution by the United States under a qualified pension plan may be excludable from gross income

Proposed Reg. § 1.402(a)-1

under section 402(a)(4). For rules relating to such exclusion, see paragraph (c) of this section. For additional rules relating to the treatment of total distributions described in this subdivision in the case of a nonresident alien individual, see sections 871 and 1441 and the regulations thereunder.

* * * * * * * * * * * * *

(7) The capital gains treatment provided by section 402(a)(2), as in effect for taxable years beginning before January 1, 1974, and subparagraph (6) of this paragraph is not applicable to distributions paid during such years to a distributee to the extent such distributions are attributable to contributions made on behalf of an employee while he was a self-employed individual in the business with respect to which the plan was maintained. For the taxation of such amounts, see § 1.72-18. For the rules for determining the amount attributable to contributions on behalf of an employee while he was self-employed, see paragraphs (b)(4) and (c)(2) of such section.

* * * * * * * * * * * * *

(9) For taxable years beginning after December 31, 1973, in the case of a lump sum distribution (as defined in section 402(e)(4)(A)) made to a recipient which is an individual, estate, or trust, so much of the total taxable amount (as defined in section 402(e)(4)(D) and § 1.402(e)-2(d)(2)) of such lump sum distribution as is equal to the product of such total taxable amount multiplied by a fraction—

(i) The numerator of which is the number of calendar years of active participation (as determined under § 1.402(e)-2(d)(3)(ii)) by the employee in such plan before January 1, 1974, and

(ii) The denominator of which is the number of calendar years of active participation (as determined under § 1.402(e)-2(d)(3)(ii)) by the employee in such plan,

shall be treated as gain from the sale or exchange of a capital asset held for more than six months. For purposes of this subparagraph, in the case of an individual who at no time during his participation under the plan is an employee within the meaning of section 401(c)(1), determination of whether any distribution is a lump sum distribution shall be made without regard to the requirement that an election be made under section 402(e)(4)(B) and § 1.402(e)-3.

(b) Distributions including securities of the employer corporation—(1) In general. (i) If a trust described in section 401(a) which is exempt under section 501(a) makes a distribution to a distributee, and such distribution includes securities of the employer corporation, the amount of any net unrealized appreciation in such securities shall be excluded from the distributee's income in the year of such distribution to the following extent:

(a) If the distribution constitutes a total distribution to which the regulations of paragraph (a)(6) of this section are applicable, or if the distribution would constitute a lump sum distribution as defined in section 402(e)(4)(A) (without regard to section 402(e)(4)(H)), the amount to be excluded is the entire net unrealized appreciation attributable to that part of the distribution which consists of securities of the employer corporation; and

(b) If the distribution is other than a total distribution to which paragraph (a)(6) of this section is applicable, or if the distribution is other than a lump sum distribution as defined in section 402(e)(4)(A) (without regard to section 402(e)(4)(H)), the amount to be excluded is that portion of the net unrealized appreciation in the securities of the employer corporation which is attributable to the amount considered to be contributed by the employee to the purchase of such securities.

The amount of net unrealized appreciation which is excludable under the regulations of (a) and (b) of this subdivision shall not be included in the basis of the securities in the hands of the distributee at the time of distribution for purposes of determining gain or loss on their subsequent disposition. Further, the amount of net unrealized appreciation which is not included in the basis of the securities in the hands of the distributee at the time of distribution shall be considered as a gain from the sale or exchange of a capital asset held for more than six months to the extent that such appreciation is realized in a subsequent taxable transaction.

However, if the net gain realized by the distributee in a subsequent taxable transaction exceeds the amount of the net unrealized appreciation at the time of distribution, such excess shall constitute a long-term or short-term capital gain depending upon the holding period of the securities in the hands of the distributee.

(ii)(a) For purposes of section 402(a) and of this section, the term "securities" means only shares of stock and bonds or debentures issued by a corporation with interest coupons or in registered form, and the term "securities of the employer corporation" includes securities of a parent or subsidiary corporation (as defined in subsections (e) and (f) of section 425) of the employer corporation.

(b) For purposes of this paragraph, for taxable years beginning after December 31, 1973, the term "distributee" means "recipient".

* * * * * * * * * * * * *

After § 1.402(a)-2 there is added the following new section:

§ 1.402(a)-3 (Proposed Treasury Decision, published 2-21-75.) **Rollover amounts.**

(a) **In general.** Under section 402(a)(5), any amount distributed from an employees' trust described in section 401(a) which is exempt from tax under section 501(a) and which satisfies the requirements of paragraph (b) of this section is not includible in the gross income of the employee for the year in which paid.

(b) **General Rule.** Except as provided in paragraph (c) of this section, an amount satisfies the requirements of this paragraph if—

(1) The balance to the credit of the employee is paid or distributed to him in one or more distributions which constitute a lump sum distribution within the meaning of section 402(e)(4)(A) (determined without reference to section 402(e)(4)(B)),

(2) The employee transfers all the property he receives in such distributions to

(i) An individual retirement account described in section 408(a) and the regulations thereunder, an individual retirement annuity described in section 408(b) (other than an endowment contract) and the regulations thereunder or a retirement bond described in section 409 and the regulations thereunder, or

(ii) An employees' trust described in section 401(a) which is exempt from tax under section 501(a), or to an annuity plan described in section 403(a), on or before the 60th day after the day on which he received such property, to the extent the fair market value of the property exceeds the amounts considered contributed by the employee (determined by applying section 72(f) and paragraph (b) of § 1.72-16), reduced by any amounts theretofore distributed to him which were not includible in gross income, and

(3) The amount so transferred consists of the same property (other than cash) distributed, to the extent that the fair market value of such property does not exceed the amount required to be transferred pursuant to subparagraph (2) of this paragraph.

(c) **Special rules.** (1) Paragraph (b)(2)(ii) of this section does not apply in the case of a transfer to an employees' trust or annuity plan if any part of the lump sum distribution described in paragraph (b)(1) of this section is attributable to a trust forming part of a plan under which the employee receiving the lump sum distribution was an employee within the meaning of section 401(c)(1) at the time contributions were made on his behalf under the plan.

(2) Paragraph (b)(2)(ii) of this section does not apply unless the plan of

[The page following this is 63,523]

Proposed Reg. § 1.402(a)-3

which the employees' trust is a part or the annuity plan provides for the acceptance of such contributions.

(d) **Effective date.** (1) Except as provided in subparagraph (2) of this paragraph, the provisions of this section shall apply to all transfers described in paragraph (b)(2) of this section made after September 1, 1974.

(2) The provisions of this section shall only apply to transfers described in paragraph (b)(2)(i) of this section made to an individual retirement account, individual retirement annuity or retirement bond after December 31, 1974.

Section 1.402(b)-1 is amended to read as follows:

§ **1.402(b)-1** (Proposed Treasury Decision, published 6-3-71.) **Treatment of beneficiary of trust not exempt under section 501(a).**

(a) **Taxation by reason of employer contributions made after August 1, 1969—** (1) **Taxation of contributions.** Any contribution (other than a contribution described in paragraph (d)(1)(ii) of this section) made by an employer after August 1, 1969, on behalf of an employee to a trust during a taxable year of the employer which ends within or with a taxable year of the trust for which the trust is not exempt under section 501(a) shall be included as compensation in the gross income of the employee for his taxable year during which the contribution is made, but only to the extent to which the employee's interest in such contribution is vested at the time the contribution is made.

(2) **Meaning of vested.** An employee's beneficial interest in a contribution or premium is vested for purposes of sections 402(b), 403(c) and 404(a)(5) to the extent such employee's interest in such contribution or premium is transferable (as defined in paragraph (d) of § 1.83-3) or not subject to a substantial risk of forfeiture (as defined in paragraph (c) of § 1.83-3).

(3) **Determination of amount of employer contributions.** If, for an employee, the actual amount of employer contributions (as defined in subparagraph (1) of this paragraph) for any taxable year are not known, such amount shall be either an amount equal to the excess of—

(i) The amount determined in accordance with the formula described in subparagraph (4) of § 1.403(b)-1(d) as of the end of such taxable year, over

(ii) The amount determined in accordance with the formula described in subparagraph (4) of § 1.403(b)-1(d) as of the end of the prior taxable year, or the amount determined under any other method utilizing recognized actuarial principles which are consistent with the provisions of the plan under which such contributions are made and the method adopted by the employer for funding the benefits under the plan.

(b) **Taxability of employee when rights under nonexempt trust change from nonvested to vested**—(1) **In general.** If rights of an employee under a trust during a taxable year of the employee (ending after August 1, 1969) which ends within or with a taxable year of the trust for which the trust is not exempt under section 501(a) change from nonvested to vested, the value of the employee's interest in the trust on the date of such change shall, to the extent provided in subparagraph (3) of this paragraph, be included in his gross income for the taxable year. If an employee's rights in a trust which is exempt under section 501(a) are fully vested at a time when such trust ceases to be so exempt, then such employee must include the value of his interest in such trust in his gross income as compensation for his taxable year which ends within or with the taxable year of the trust in which it ceases to be so exempt. However, in such a case the employer shall not be allowed a deduction for any amount previously deductible in any prior taxable year in respect of the employee's interest in the trust.

(2) **Value of an employee's interest in a trust.** (i) For purposes of this sec-

Proposed Reg. § 1.402(b)-1

tion, the term "the value of an employee's interest in a trust", means the amount of the employee's beneficial interest (whether or not vested) in the net fair market value of all the assets in such trust as of any day when such employee's interest in such trust changes from nonvested to vested. The net fair market value of all the assets in a trust is the total amount of the fair market values (determined without regard to any restriction other than a restriction which by its terms will never lapse) of all the assets in the trust less the amount of all the liabilities (including taxes) to which such assets are subject or which such trust has assumed (other than the rights of any employee in such assets), as of any day when an employee's interest in such trust changes from nonvested to vested.

(ii) If a separate account in a trust for the benefit of two or more employees is not maintained for each employee, the value of an employee's interest in such trust shall be determined in accordance with the formula described in subparagraph (4) of § 1.403(b)-1(d).

(iii) If there is no valuation of a nonexempt trust's assets on the date of the change referred to in subparagraph (1) of this paragraph, the value of an employee's interest in such trust is determined by taking the weighted average of the means between the nearest valuation dates occurring before and after the date of such change. The average is to be weighted inversely by the respective number of days between the valuation dates and the date of such change. The average is to be determined in the manner described in paragraph (b) of § 20.2031-2 of this chapter (the Estate and Gift Tax Regulations).

(3) **Extent to which value of an employee's interest in trust is includible in employee's gross income.** For purposes of subparagraph (1) of this paragraph, there shall be included in the gross income of an employee for his taxable year in which his rights under an employee's trust change from nonvested to vested only an amount equal to the portion of the value of the employee's interest in such trust on the date of such change attributable to contributions made by the employer after August 1, 1969. However, the preceding sentence shall not apply—

(i) To the extent such value is attributable to a contribution made on the date of such change, and

(ii) To the extent such value is attributable to contributions described in paragraph (d)(1)(ii) of this section relating to contributions made pursuant to a binding written contract entered into before April 22, 1969.

For purposes of this subparagraph, the value of an employee's interest in a trust which is attributable to contributions made by the employer after August 1, 1969, is an amount which bears the same ratio to the value of the employee's interest as the contributions made by the employer after such date bear to the total contributions made by the employer.

(4) **Partial vesting.** If, during any taxable year of an employee, only part of his rights under an employee's trust which is not exempt under section 501(a) changes from nonvested to vested, then only the corresponding part of the value of the employee's interest in such trust is includible in the employee's gross income for such taxable year. In such a case, it is first necessary to compute, under the rules in subparagraphs (1) and (2) of this paragraph the amount which would be includible in the employee's gross income for the taxable year if his interest had changed to a fully vested interest during such year. The amount which is includible in the gross income of the employee for the taxable year in which the change occurs is an amount equal to the amount determined under the preceding sentence multiplied by the percent of the employee's interest which changed to a vested interest during the taxable year.

(5) **Basis.** The basis of an employee's interest in a trust which is not exempt under section 501(a) shall be increased by the amount included in his gross income under this section.

(6) **Treatment as owner of trust.** A beneficiary of an employee's trust shall not

be considered to be the owner under subpart E, part I, subchapter J, chapter 1 of the Code of any portion of such trust which is attributable to contributions to such trust made by the employer after August 1, 1969, or to incidental contributions made by the employee after such date. However, where contributions made by the employee are not incidental in relation to contributions made by the employer, such beneficiary shall, if the applicable requirements of such subpart E are satisfied, be considered to be the owner of the portion of the trust which is attributable to contributions made by the employee. For purposes of this suparagraph, contributions made by an employee are not incidental in relation to contributions made by his employer if the employee's total contributions as of any date exceed the employer's contributions as of such date.

(7) **Example.** The provisions in this paragraph may be illustrated by the following example:

Example. M corporation establishes an employee's trust which is not exempt under section 501(a) on January 1, 1968, for A, one of its employees, reserving the right to discontinue contributions at any time. M corporation contributes $5,000 to the trust on February 1, 1968. At the time of contribution A's rights were 50 percent vested. On January 1, 1971, and January 1, 1974, M corporation makes additional $5,000 contributions to the trust. A's interest in the trust changed from a 50 percent vested interest to a fully vested interest in the trust on December 31, 1974. The value of the employee's interest in the trust on December 31, 1974, which is attributable to employer contributions made after August 1, 1969, is calculated to be $11,000 under subparagraph (3) of this paragraph. The amount includible in A's gross income for 1971 and 1974 is computed as follows:

1971

(i) Amount of M corporation's contribution made on January 1, 1971, to the trust which is includible in A's gross income under subparagraph (1) of this paragraph (50% vested interest in the trust times $5,000 contribution) .... $ 2,500

1974

(i) Amount of M corporation's contribution made on January 1, 1974, to the trust which is includible in A's gross income under subparagraph (1) of this paragraph (50% vested interest in the trust times $5,000 contribution) .... $ 2,500

(ii) Amount which would have been includible if A's entire interest had changed to a vested interest (value of employee's interest in the trust attributable to employer contributions made after August 1, 1969) $11,000

(iii) Percent of A's interest that changed to vested interest on December 31, 1974 .... 50%

(iv) Amount includible in A's gross income for 1974 in respect of his percentage change from a nonvested to vested interest in the trust (50% of $11,000) .... $ 5,500

(v) Total amount includible in A's gross income for 1974 ((i) plus (iv)) . $ 8,000

(c) **Taxation of distributions from trust not exempt under section 501(a)—(1) In general.** Any amount actually distributed or made available to any distributee by an employees' trust which is not exempt under section 501(a) for the taxable year of the trust in which the distribution is made shall be taxable in the year in which so distributed or made available under section 72 (relating to annuities). For taxable years beginning before January 1, 1964, section 72(e)(3) (relating to the treatment of certain lump sums), as in effect before such date, shall not apply to such amounts. For taxable years beginning after December 31, 1963, such amounts may be taken into account in computations under sections 1301 through 1305 (relating to income averaging). If, for example, the distribution

Proposed Reg. §1.402(b)-1

from such a trust consists of an annuity contract, the amount of the distribution shall be considered to be the entire value of the contract at the time of distribution, and such value is includible in the gross income of the distributee at the time of the distribution to the extent that such value exceeds the investment in the contract determined by applying sections 72 and 101(b). The distributions by such an employees' trust shall be taxed as provided in section 72 whether or not the employee's rights to the contributions were nonforfeitable (within the meaning of paragraph (d)(2)(i) of this section, relating generally to employer contributions made on or before August 1, 1969) or vested (within the meaning of paragraph (a)(1) of this section) when the contributions were made or at any time thereafter. For rules relating to the treatment of employer contributions to a nonexempt trust as part of the consideration paid by the employee, see section 72(f). For rules relating to the treatment of the limited exclusion allowable under section 101(b)(2)(D) as additional consideration paid by the employee, see the regulations under that section.

(2) **Distributions before annuity starting date.** Any amount distributed or made available to any distributee before the annuity starting date (as defined in section 72(c)(4)) by an employees' trust which is not exempt under section 501(a) for the taxable year of the trust in which the distribution is made shall be treated as being made in the following order—

(i) First, from the employee's nonvested interest in the trust but only to the extent that such a distribution is treated as such under the plan of which such trust is a part,

(ii) Second, from the portion of the employee's vested interest in the trust which has not been previously includible in his gross income, and

(iii) Third, from the portion of the employee's vested interest in the trust which has been previously includible in his gross income.

(d) **Taxation by reason of employer contributions made on or before August 1, 1969.** (1) Except as provided in section 402(d), any contribution made by an employer on behalf of an employee—

(i) On or before August 1, 1969, or

(ii) After such date, if pursuant to a binding written contract (as defined in paragraph (b)(2) of § 1.83-8) entered into before April 22, 1969, or pursuant to a written plan in which the employee participated on such date and under which the obligation of the employer is essentially the same as under a binding written contract, to a trust during a taxable year of the employer which ends within or with a taxable year of the trust for which the trust is not exempt under section 501(a) shall be included in income of the employee for his taxable year during which the contribution is made if the employee's beneficial interest in the contribution is nonforfeitable at the time the contribution is made. If the employee's beneficial interest in the contribution is forfeitable at the time the contribution is made, even though his interest becomes nonforfeitable later the amount of such contribution is not required to be included in the income of the employee at the time his interest becomes nonforfeitable.

(2)(i) An employee's beneficial interest in the contribution is nonforfeitable within the meaning of sections 402(b), 403(c), and 404(a)(5) prior to the amendments made thereto by the Tax Reform Act of 1969 and section 403(b) at the time the contribution is made if there is no contingency under the plan which may cause the employee to lose his rights in the contribution. Similarly, an employee's rights under an annuity contract purchased for him by his employer change from forfeitable to nonforfeitable rights within the meaning of section 403(d) prior to the repeal thereof by the Tax Reform Act of 1969 at that time when, for the first time, there is no contingency which may cause the employee to lose his rights under the contract. For example, if under the terms of a pension plan, an employee upon termination of his services before the retirement date, whether voluntarily or involuntarily, is entitled to a deferred annuity contract to be purchased with the employer's contributions made on his behalf, or is entitled to annuity payments which the trustee is obligated to make under the terms of the trust instrument based on the contributions made by the employer on his behalf, the employee's beneficial interest in such contributions is nonforfeitable.

(ii) On the other hand, if, under the terms of a pension plan, an employee will lose the right to any annuity purchased from, or to be provided by, contributions made by the employer if his services should be terminated before retirement, his beneficial interest in such contributions is forfeitable.

(iii) The mere fact that an employee may not live to the retirement date, or may live only a short period after the retirement date, and may not be able to enjoy the receipt of annuity or pension payments, does not make his beneficial interest in the contributions made by the employer on his behalf forfeitable. If the employer's contributions have been irrevocably applied to purchase an annuity contract for the employee, or if the trustee is obligated to use the employer's contributions to provide an annuity for the employee provided only that the employee is alive on the dates the annuity payments are due, the employee's rights in the employer's contributions are nonforfeitable.

There are added immediately after §1.402(e)-1 the following new sections:

§ 1.402(e)-2 (Proposed Treasury Decision, published 4-30-75.) **Treatment of certain lump sum distributions made after 1973.**

(a) **In general.** (1) **Tax imposed; deduction allowed.** For a taxable year, at the election of the recipient of a lump sum distribution, the ordinary income portion of such distribution is subject to the tax imposed by section 402(e)(1)(A) (hereinafter referred to as the "separate tax") and, under section 402(e)(3), an amount equal to such portion is allowable as a deduction from gross income (see section 62(11), as added by sec. 2005(c)(9) of Pub. L. No. 93-406, and the regulations thereunder) to the extent such portion is included in the gross income of the taxpayer for such year. The separate tax imposed by section 402(e)(1)(A) is an addition to the tax otherwise imposed under chapter 1 of the Code and may be elected whether or not the tax otherwise imposed by such chapter is computed under part I of subchapter Q of such chapter (relating to income averaging). This section applies with respect to distributions or payments made, or made available, to a recipient after December 31, 1973, in taxable years of the recipient beginning after that date.

(2) **Cross references**—(i) Computation; ordinary method. Paragraph (b) of this section provides rules with respect to a distribution which is not a multiple distribution, and does not include an annuity contract.

(ii) Computation; special method (distribution including an annuity contract). Paragraph (c)(1) of this section provides rules with respect to a distribution which is not a multiple distribution and which includes an annuity contract.

(iii) Computation; special method (multiple distribution). Paragraph (c)(2) of this section provides rules with respect to a distribution which is a multiple distribution.

(iv) Lump sum distribution. For the definition of the term "lump sum distribution", see paragraph (d)(1) of this section.

(v) Total taxable amount. For the definition of the term "total taxable amount", see paragraph (d)(2) of this section.

(vi) Ordinary income portion. For the definition of the term "ordinary income portion", see paragraph (d)(3) of this section.

(vii) Multiple distribution. For the definition of the term "multiple distribution", see paragraph (c)(2)(ii)(E) of this section.

(viii) Election. For rules relating to the election of lump sum distribution treatment under this section, see § 1.402(e)-3.

(b) **Ordinary method**—(1) **In general.** In the case of a distribution which is not included in a multiple distribution, and which does not include an annuity contract, if the recipient elects (under § 1.402(e)-3) to treat such distribution as a lump sum distribution under this section, the tax imposed by section 402(e)(1)(A) for the recipient's taxable year is an amount equal to the initial separate tax (determined under subparagraph (2) of this paragraph) for such taxable year, multiplied by a fraction—

Proposed Reg. §1.402(e)-2

(i) The numerator of which is the ordinary income portion (determined under paragraph (d)(3) of this section) of such lump sum distribution for such taxable year, and

(ii) The denominator of which is the total taxable amount (determined under paragraph (d)(2) of this section) of such lump sum distribution for such taxable year.

(2) Computation of initial separate tax. For purposes of subparagraph (1) of this paragraph, the initial separate tax is an amount equal to 10 times the tax which would be imposed by section 1(c) (relating to unmarried individuals (other than surviving spouses and heads of households)) if the recipient were an individual referred to in such section and the taxable income referred to in such section were an amount equal to one-tenth of the excess of—

(i) The total taxable amount (determined under paragraph (d)(2) of this section) of the lump sum distribution, over

(ii) The minimum distribution allowance (determined under subparagraph (3) of this paragraph).

(3) Computation of minimum distribution allowance. For purposes of subparagraph (2)(ii) of this paragraph, the minimum distribution allowance is the lesser of—

(i) $10,000, or

(ii) one-half of the total taxable amount of the lump sum distribution for the taxable year,

reduced (but not below zero) by 20 percent of the excess (if any) of such total taxable amount over $20,000.

(4) Example. The application of this paragraph is illustrated by the following example:

Example. (i) On December 22, 1975, A separates from the service of the M Corporation and receives a lump sum distribution of $65,000 from the M Corporation's contributory qualified plan. A's contributions to the plan as an employee were $15,000. A has been an active participant in the plan since February 20, 1966. A and his wife, B, are each age 50. Neither received an annuity contract from a qualified plan in 1974 or 1975. Neither received a lump sum distribution in 1974. A and B file a joint return for the calendar year 1975. Their income for 1975 consists of A's salary of $15,000 from the M Corporation and of $5,000 from the N Corporation. Their deductions for 1975 (other than deductions attributable to the distribution) consist of itemized deductions of $3,000. Their average base period income (determined under section 1302(b)(1)) for the four preceding taxable years (1971 through 1974) is $14,000. Assuming there are no changes in the applicable tax law after 1974, A and B's income tax liability for 1975 is computed as follows.

(ii) A and B's gross income for 1975 is $70,000, computed by adding the total taxable amount of the lump sum distribution (determined under paragraph (d)(2) of this section) to their otherwise computed gross income [$15,000 + $5,000 + ($65,000 − $15,000)]. Their adjusted gross income for 1975 is $40,000 [$70,000 − ($10,000 + $20,000)] computed by reducing their gross income by the sum of the lump sum distribution deduction allowed by section 402(e)(3) with respect to the ordinary income portion of the distribution [$50,000 × 24/120] and the deduction allowed by section 1202 with respect to the capital gains portion of the distribution [($50,000 × 96/120) × 0.5]. A and B's joint taxable income is $35,500 (their itemized deductions are $3,000 and their personal exemptions total $1,500). A and B choose to apply the income averaging rules of section 1301 for 1975. Thus, A and B's income tax liability not including the separate tax on the ordinary income portion of the distribution is $8,828.

(iii) The minimum distribution allowance with respect to A's distribution is $4,000 [$10,000 −(($50,000 − $20,000) × 0.2)]. The initial separate tax on A's distribution is 10 times the tax imposed by section 1(c), computed as if the taxable income therein described were $4,600 [$50,000 − $4,000].

Thus, A's initial separate tax is $8,160. The separate tax on A's distribution is computed by multiplying the initial separate tax and the quotient of the ordinary income portion divided by the total taxable amount. Thus, the separate tax on A's distribution is $1,632 [$8,160 × $10,000/$50,000].

(iv) A and B's total income tax liability for 1975 is the sum of the income tax as otherwise determined and the separate tax. Thus, A and B's total income tax liability for 1975 is $10,460 [$8,828 + $1,632].

(c) **Special method—(1) Computation of separate tax on distribution including annuity contract and lump sum distribution.** (i) Computation. In the case of a distribution which is not included in a multiple distribution and which includes an annuity contract, if the recipient elects (under § 1.402(e)-3) to treat the portion of such distribution not consisting of an annuity contract as a lump sum distribution under this section, the separate tax imposed by section 402(e)(1)(A) of the recipient's taxable year is the excess (if any) of the adjusted separate tax over the tax attributable to the annuity contract (determined under subdivision (iii) of this subparagraph).

(ii) Definitions. For purposes of this section—

(A) Adjusted separate tax. The adjusted separate tax is an amount equal to the adjusted initial separate tax multiplied by a fraction—

(1) The numerator of which is the ordinary income portion of the distribution, and

(2) The denominator of which is the total taxable amount (determined under paragraph (d)(2) of this section) of the lump sum distribution.

(B) Adjusted initial separate tax. The adjusted initial separate tax is an amount equal to 10 times the tax which would be imposed by section 1(c) (relating to unmarried individuals (other than surviving spouses and heads of households)) if the recipient were an individual referred to in such section and the taxable income referred to in such section were an amount equal to one-tenth of the excess of—

(1) The adjusted total taxable amount of the lump sum distribution, over

(2) The adjusted minimum distribution allowance.

(C) Adjusted total taxable amount. (1) For taxable years beginning before January 1, 1975, the adjusted total taxable amount is the sum of—

(i) The excess (if any) of the current actuarial value of annuity contracts distributed to the recipient, over the portion of the net amount contributed by the employee which is allocable to the contract, and

(ii) The total taxable amount (determined under paragraph (d)(2) of this section) of the lump sum distribution for the taxable year.

For purposes of (i) of this subdivision (1), the net amount contributed by the employee which is allocable to the contract is an amount equal to the amounts considered contributed by the employee under the plan (determined by applying sections 72(f) and 101(b), and paragraph (b) of § 1.72-16) reduced by any amount theretofore distributed to the employee which were not includible in his gross income multiplied by a fraction, the numerator of which is the current actuarial value of the contract, and the denominator of which is the sum of such current actuarial value and the value of other property (including cash) distributed.

(2) For taxable years beginning after December 31, 1974, the adjusted total taxable amount is the sum of—

(i) The current actuarial value of annuity contracts distributed to the recipient, reduced by the excess, if any, of the net amount contributed by the employee (as defined in paragraph (d)(2)(ii)(A) of this section) over the cash and other property distributed, and

(ii) The total taxable amount (determined under paragraph (d)(2) of this section) of the lump sum distribution for the taxable year.

(D) Adjusted ordinary income portion. The adjusted ordinary income portion of a lump sum distribution is the amount which would be computed under subparagraph (3) of paragraph (d) of this section if "adjusted total taxable amount" is substituted for "total taxable amount" in such subparagraph.

Proposed Reg. § 1.402(e)-2

(E) Adjusted minimum distribution allowance. The adjusted minimum distribution allowance is the lesser of—

(1) $10,000, or

(2) one-half of the adjusted total taxable amount of the lump sum distribution for the taxable year,

reduced (but not below zero) by 20 percent of the excess (if any) of the adjusted total taxable amount over $20,000.

(F) Current actuarial value. The current actuarial value of an annuity contract is the greater of—

(1) The cash value of the annuity contract (determined without regard to any loans under the contract) on the date of distribution, or

(2) The amount determined under the appropriate tables contained in publication No. 861, entitled "Annuity Factors for Lump Sum Distributions".

(iii) Tax attributable to an annuity contract. For purposes of subdivision (i) of this subparagraph, the tax attributable to an annuity contract is the product of—

(A) The quotient of the adjusted ordinary income portion (determined under subdivision (ii)(D) of this subparagraph) of the lump sum distribution divided by the adjusted total taxable amount (determined under subdivision (ii)(C) of this subparagraph), and

(B) 10 times the tax which would be imposed by section 1(c) (relating to unmarried individuals (other than surviving spouses and heads of households)) if the recipient were an individual referred to in such section and the taxable income were an amount equal to one-tenth of the excess of—

(1) The current actuarial value of the annuity contract, over

(2) The adjusted minimum distribution allowance multiplied by a fraction—

(a) The numerator of which is the current actuarial value of the annuity contract, and

(b) The denominator of which is the adjusted total taxable amount (determined under subdivision (ii) of this subparagraph).

(iv) Examples. The application of this subparagraph is illustrated by the following examples:

Example (1). (i) On December 29, 1975, A separates from the service of the M Corporation and receives a distribution of the balance to the credit of his account under the M Corporation's noncontributory qualified plan. The distribution consists of cash of $44,000, and an annuity contract with a current actuarial value of $6,000. A has been a participant in the plan since March 26, 1966. A and his wife, B, are each age 50. Neither received a previous distribution from a qualified plan. A and B file a joint return for 1975. Their income for 1975, other than the distribution, consists of A's salary from the M Corporation of $15,000 and of $5,000 from the N Corporation. Their deductions (other than deductions attributable to the distribution) consist of itemized deductions of $3,000. They are not otherwise permitted to use income averaging for 1975 under section 1301. Assuming there are no changes in the applicable tax law after 1974, A and B's income tax liability for 1975 is computed as follows.

(ii) A and B's gross income for 1975 is $64,000, computed by adding the total taxable amount (determined under paragraph (d)(2) of this section) of the lump sum distribution to their otherwise computed gross income [$15,000 + $5,000 + $44,000]. Their adjusted gross income for 1975 is $37,600 [$64,000 − ($8,800 + $17,600)], computed by reducing their gross income by the sum of the lump sum distribution deduction allowed by section 402(e)(3) with respect to the ordinary income portion of the distribution [$44,000 × 24/120] and the deduction allowed by section 1202 with respect to the capital gains portion of the distribution [($44,000 × 96/120) × 0.5]. A and B's taxable income for 1975 is $33,100 (their itemized deductions are $3,000 and their personal exemptions total $1,500). Thus, A and B's income tax liability not including the separate tax on the ordinary income portion of the distribution is $9,122.

(iii) The adjusted total taxable amount of A's distribution is the sum of the current actuarial value of the annuity contract distributed and the total taxable amount of the lump sum distribution. Thus, the adjusted total taxable amount of A's distribution is $50,000 [$6,000 + $44,000]. The adjusted minimum distribution allowance with respect to A's distribution is the lesser of $10,000 or ½ of the adjusted total taxable amount, reduced by 20 percent of the excess (if any) of the adjusted total taxable amount over $20,000. Thus, the adjusted minimum distribution allowance with respect to A's distribution is $4,000 [$10,000 − (($50,000 − $20,000) × 0.2)]. The adjusted initial separate tax on A's distribution is computed by multiplying 10 times the tax imposed by section 1(c) computed as if the taxable income therein described were $4,600 [($50,000 − $4,000)/10]. Thus, A's adjusted initial separate tax is $8,160. The adjusted separate tax on A's distribution is computed by multiplying the adjusted initial separate tax by the quotient of the ordinary income portion divided by the total taxable amount. Thus, the adjusted separate tax on A's distribution is $1,632 ($8,160 × $8,800/$44,000). The tax attributable to the annuity contract is 10 times the tax that would be imposed by section 1(c) computed as if the taxable income of a person described therein were $552 [$6,000 − ($4,000 × $6,000/$50,000] multiplied by the quotient described in

10

the second preceding sentence. Thus, the tax attributable to the annuity contract is $156 [$778 × $8,800/$44,000)]. The separate tax on A's distribution is computed by reducing the adjusted separate tax by the tax attributable to the annuity contract. Thus, the separate tax on A's distribution is $1,476 [$1,632 − $156)].

(iv) A and B's total income tax liability for 1975 is the sum of their income tax liability, as otherwise determined, and the separate tax. Thus A and B's total income tax liability for 1975 is $10,598 [$9,122 + $1,476].

Example (2). (i) Assume the same facts as in example (1) except that the M Corporation's qualified plan is contributory and that A's contributions under the plan as an employee were $1,760, and the current actuarial value of the annuity contract which is distributed is $5,760.

(ii) A and B's gross income for 1975 is $62,240, computed by adding the total taxable amount (determined under paragraph (d)(2) of this section) of the lump sum distribution to their otherwise computed gross income [$15,000 + $5,000 + ($44,000 − $1,760)]. Their adjusted gross income for 1975 is $36,896 [$62,240 − ($8,448 + $16,896)], computed by reducing their gross income by the sum of the lump sum distribution deduction allowed by section 402(e)(3) with respect to the ordinary income portion of the distribution [$42,240 × 24/120] and the deduction allowed by section 1202 with respect to the capital gains portion of the distribution. [($42,240 × 96/120) × 0.5]. A and B's taxable income for 1975 is $32,396 (their itemized deductions are $3,000 and their personal exemptions total $1,500). Thus A and B's income tax liability not including the separate tax on the ordinary income portion of the distribution is $8,826.

(iii) The adjusted total taxable amount of A's distribution is the sum of the current actuarial value of the annuity contract distributed and the total taxable amount of the lump sum distribution. Thus, the adjusted total taxable amount of A's distribution is $48,000 [$5,760 + ($44,000 − $1,760)]. The adjusted minimum distribution allowance with respect to A's distribution is the lesser of $10,000 or ½ of the adjusted total taxable amount, reduced by 20 percent of the excess of the adjusted total taxable amount over $20,000. Thus, the adjusted minimum distribution allowance with respect to A's distribution is $4,400 [$10,000 − (($48,000 − $20,000) × 0.2)]. The adjusted initial separate tax on A's distribution is 10 times the tax imposed by section 1(c) computed as if the taxable income therein described were $4,360 [($48,000 − $4,440)]. Thus, A's adjusted initial separate tax is $7,656.

10

The adjusted separate tax on A's distribution is computed by multiplying the adjusted initial separate tax by the quotient of the ordinary income portion divided by the total taxable amount. Thus, the adjusted separate tax on A's distribution is $1,531

Proposed Reg. §1.402(e)-2

[$7,656 × $8,448/$42,240]. The tax attributable to the annuity contract is 10 times the tax that would be imposed by section 1(c) computed as if the taxable income of a person therein described were $523 [$5,760 − ($4,440 × ($5,760/$48,000))] multi-

$$10$$

plied by the quotient described in the second preceding sentence. Thus, the tax attributable to the annuity contract is $147 [$735 × $8,448/$42,240]. The separate tax on A's distribution is computed by reducing the adjusted separate tax by the tax attributable to the annuity contract. Thus, the separate tax on A's distribution is $1,384 [$1,531 − $147].

(iv) A and B's total income tax liability for 1975 is the sum of their income tax liability, as otherwise determined, and the separate tax. Thus A and B's total income tax liability for 1975 is $10,210 [$1,384 + $8,826].

Example (3). (i) On December 7, 1974, C separates from the service of P Corporation and receives a distribution of the balance to the credit of his account under the P Corporation's contributory qualified plan. The distribution consists of cash of $44,000, and an annuity contract with a current actuarial value of $6,000. C has been a participant in the plan since February 20, 1965. C's contributions under the plan as an employee were $2,000. C and his wife, D, are each age 50. Neither received a previous distribution from a qualified plan. C and D file a joint return for 1974. Their income for 1974, other than the distribution, consists of C's salary from the P Corporation of $20,000. Their deductions (other than deductions attributable to the distribution) consist of itemized deductions of $3,000. They are not otherwise permitted to use income averaging for 1974 under section 1301. C and D's income tax liability for 1974 is computed as follows.

(ii) C and D's gross income for 1974 is $62,240, computed by adding the total taxable amount (determined under paragraph (d)(2) of this section) of the lump sum distribution to their otherwise computed gross income [$20,000 + ($44,000 − $1,760)]. Their adjusted gross income for 1974 is $39,008 [$62,240 − ($4,224 + $19,008)], computed by reducing their gross income by the sum of the lump sum distribution deduction allowed by section 402(e)(3) with respect to the ordinary income portion of the distribution [$42,240 × 12/120] and the deduction allowed by section 1202 with respect to the capital gains portion of the distribution [($42,240 × 108/120) × 0.5]. C and D's taxable income for 1974 is $34,508 (their itemized deductions are $3,000 and their personal exemptions total $1,500). C and D's income tax liability for 1974 not including the separate tax on the ordinary income portion of the distribution is $9,713.

(iii) The adjusted total taxable amount of C's distribution is the sum of the current actuarial value of the annuity contract distributed and the total taxable amount of the lump sum distribution. Thus, the adjusted total taxable amount of C's distribution is $48,000 [($6,000 − $240) + ($44,000 − $1,760)]. The adjusted minimum distribution allowance with respect to C's distribution is the lesser of $10,000 or ½ of the adjusted total taxable amount, reduced by 20 percent of the excess of the adjusted total taxable amount over $20,000. Thus, the adjusted minimum distribution allowance with respect to C's distribution is $4,400 [$10,000 − (($48,000 − $20,000) × 0.2)]. The adjusted initial separate tax on C's distribution is 10 times the tax imposed by section 1(c) computed as if the taxable income therein described were $4,360 [($48,000 − $4,400)]. Thus, C's adjusted initial sepa-

$$10$$

rate tax is $7,656. The adjusted separate tax on C's distribution is computed by multiplying the adjusted initial separate tax by the quotient of the ordinary income portion divided by the total taxable amount. Thus, the adjusted separate tax on C's distribution is $766 ($7,656 × $4,224/$42,240). The tax attributable to the annuity contract is 10 times the tax imposed by section 1(c) computed as if the taxable income therein described were $523 [$5,760 − ($4,440 × ($5,760/$48,000))],

$$10$$

multiplied by the quotient described in the second preceding sentence. Thus, the amount attributable to the annuity contract is $74 [$735 × ($4,224/$42,240)]. The separate tax on C's distribution is computed by reducing the adjusted separate tax by the tax attributable to the annuity contract. Thus, the separate tax on C's distribution is $692 ($766 − $74).

(iv) C and D's total income tax liability for 1974 is the sum of their income tax liability, as otherwise determined, and the separate tax. Thus, C and D's total income tax liability for 1974 is $10,405 [$9,713 + $692].

(2) Computation of separate tax in case of multiple distribution—(i) Computation. In the case of a payment or distribution which is included in a multiple distribution, the separate tax imposed on such multiple distribution by section 402 (e)(1)(A) for the recipient's taxable year is the excess (if any) of the modified separate tax, over the sum of—

(A) The aggregate amount of the separate tax imposed by section 402(e)(1)(A) paid during the lookback period, and

(B) The modified tax attributable to the annuity contract.

(ii) Definitions. For purposes of this section—(A) Modified separate tax. The term "modified separate tax" means an amount equal to the modified initial separate tax multiplied by a fraction—

(1) The numerator of which is the sum of the ordinary income portions of the lump sum distributions made within the lookback period, and

(2) The denominator of which is the sum of the total taxable amounts of the lump sum distributions made within the lookback period.

(B) Modified initial separate tax. The modified initial separate tax is an amount equal to 10 times the tax which would be imposed by section 1(c) (relating to unmarried individuals (other than surviving spouses and heads of households)) if the recipient were an individual referred to in such section and the taxable income referred to in such section were an amount equal to one-tenth of the excess of—

(1) The modified total taxable amount of the lump sum distribution, over

(2) The modified minimum distribution allowance.

(C) Modified total taxable amount. The modified total taxable amount is the sum of the total taxable amounts (determined under paragraph (d)(2) of this section) of the distributions made during the lookback period and, in the case of a distribution made during such period to which subparagraph (1) of this paragraph applied, the amount specified in subparagraph (1)(ii)(C)(1)(i) or (2)(i) of this paragraph, whichever is applicable.

(D) Modified minimum distribution allowance. The modified minimum distribution allowance is the lesser of—

(1) $10,000, or

(2) one-half of the modified total taxable amount,

reduced (but not below zero) by 20 percent of the excess of the modified total taxable amount over $20,000.

(E) Multiple distributions. A distribution or payment received during a taxable year of the recipient which begins with or within a lookback period and after December 31, 1973, is included in a multiple distribution for such lookback period if—

(i) Any part of such distribution or payment (1) is treated as a lump sum distribution under this section or (2) consists of a contract which would constitute all or a part of a lump sum distribution (determined without regard to section 402 (e)(4)(B) and § 1.402(e)-3), except for the fact that it is an annuity contract, and

(ii) a distribution or payment received in another such taxable year is treated as a lump sum distribution under this section.

For purposes of this subdivision (E), if the recipient of a lump sum distribution is a trust and if a beneficiary of such trust is an employee with respect to the plan under which the distribution is made, or treated as the owner of such trust for purposes of subpart E of part I of subchapter J of chapter 1 of the Code

Proposed Reg. § 1.402(e)-2

(relating to grantors and others treated as substantial owners), then such employee or owner shall be treated as the sole recipient of the lump sum distribution. For purposes of this subdivision (E), the term "an employee with respect to the plan under which the distribution is made" means an individual who, immediately before the distribution is made, is a participant in the plan under which the distribution is made.

(F) Lookback period. The lookback period with respect to any recipient is a period of 6 consecutive taxable years ending on the last day of the taxable year of the recipient in which a payment or distribution which is a multiple distribution is made.

(iii) Modified tax attributable to an annuity contract. For purposes of subdivision (i) of this subparagraph, the modified tax attributable to an annuity contract is equal to the product of—

(A) The quotient of the sum of the ordinary income portions (determined under paragraph (d)(3)) of the lump sum distributions received during the lookback period divided by the sum of the total taxable amounts (determined under paragraph (d)(2)) of the distributions made during the lookback period, and

(B) 10 times the tax which would be imposed by section 1(c) (relating to unmarried individuals (other than surviving spouses and heads of households)) if the recipient were an individual referred to in such section and the taxable income were an amount equal to one-tenth of the excess of—

(1) The sum of the amounts described in subparagraph (1)(ii)(C)(1)(i) or (2)(i) of this paragraph in respect of the annuity contracts distributed during the lookback period, over

(2) the modified minimum distribution allowance multiplied by a fraction—

(i) the numerator of which is the sum of the amounts described in (1) of this subdivision (B), and

(ii) the denominator of which is the modified total taxable amount (determined under subdivision (ii)(C) of this subparagraph).

(iv) The application of this subparagraph is illustrated by the following examples:

Example (1). (i) On December 7, 1976, A separates from the service of N Corporation and receives a distribution of the balance to the credit of his account under the N Corporation's noncontributory qualified plan. The distribution consists of cash of $4,000 and an annuity contract with a current actuarial value of $6,000. A has been a participant in the plan since October 13, 1967. A and his wife, B, are each age 50. A and B file a joint return for 1976. Their income for 1976, other than the distribution, consists of A's salary from N Corporation of $25,000 and interest income of $3,000. Their deductions (other than deductions attributable to the distribution) consist of itemized deductions of $2,100. They are not otherwise permitted to use income averaging for 1976 under section 1301. A received a distribution in 1975 from the M Corporation and elected lump sum treatment for such distribution. The ordinary income portion of such distribution was $10,000; the total taxable amount of such distribution was $50,000; the adjusted ordinary income portion and the adjusted total taxable amount of such distribution are the same as the ordinary income portion and the total taxable amount; and they paid a separate tax on such distribution of $1,632. Assuming there are no changes in the applicable tax law after 1974, A and B's income tax liability for 1976 is computed as follows.

(ii) A and B's gross income for 1976 is $32,000, computed by adding the total taxable amount (determined under paragraph (d)(2) of this section) of the lump sum distribution to their otherwise computed gross income [$25,000 + $3,000 + $4,000]. Their adjusted gross income for 1976 is $29,400 [$32,000 − ($1,200 + $1,400)], computed by reducing their gross income by the sum of the lump sum distribution deduction allowed by section 402(e)(3) with respect to the ordinary income portion of the distribution [$4,000 × 36/120] and the deduction allowed by section 1202 with respect to the capital gains portion of the distribution [($4,000 × (84/120)) × 0.5]. A and B's taxable income for 1976 is $25,800 (their itemized deductions are $2,100 and their personal exemptions total $1,500). Thus, A and B's income tax liability for 1976, not including the separate tax on the ordinary income portion of the distribution is $6,308.

(iii) The adjusted total taxable amount of A's distribution for 1976 is the sum of the current actuarial value of the annuity contract distributed and the total taxable amount of the lump sum distribution. Thus, the adjusted total taxable amount of A's 1976 distribution is $10,000 [$6,000 + $4,000]. The modified total taxable amount is $60,000 [$50,000 + $10,000]. The modified minimum distribution allowance with respect to A's 1976 distribution is the lesser of $10,000 or ½ of the modified total taxable amount, reduced by 20 percent of the excess (if any) of the modified total taxable amount over $20,000. Thus, the modified minimum distribution allowance with respect to A's 1976 distribution is $2,000 [$10,000 − (($60,000 − $20,000) × 0.2)]. The modified initial separate tax on A's 1976 distribution is computed by multiplying 10 times the tax imposed by section 1(c) computed as if the taxable income therein described were $5,800 [($60,000 − $2,000)].

$$\overline{10}$$

Thus, A's modified initial separate tax is $10,680. The modified separate tax on A's 1976 distribution is computed by multiplying the modified initial separate tax by the quotient of the sum of the ordinary income portions of the lump sum distributions received during the lookback period divided by the sum of the total taxable amounts of each lump sum distribution made during such period. Thus, the modified separate tax on A's 1976 distribution is $2,215 [$10,680 × ($10,000 + $1,200)/($50,000 + $4,000)]. The modified tax attributable to the annuity contract is 10 times the tax imposed by section 1(c) computed as if the taxable income of a person described therein were $580 [$6,000 − (($6,000/$60,000) × $2,000)]

$$\overline{10}$$

multiplied by the quotient described in the second preceding sentence. Thus, the modified tax attributable to the annuity contract is $170 [$820 × ($10,000 + $1,200)/($50,000 + $4,000)]. The separate tax on A's 1976 distribution is computed by reducing the modified separate tax by the sum of the separate tax paid during the lookback period, and the modified tax attributable to the annuity contract. Thus, the separate tax on A's 1976 distribution is $413 [$2,215 − ($1,632 + $170)].

(iv) A and B's total income tax liability for 1976 is the sum of their income tax liability as otherwise determined, and the separate tax. Thus, A and B's total income tax liability for 1976 is $6,721 [$6,308 + $413].

Example (2). (i) Assume the same facts as in example (1) except that the N Corporation's qualified plan was contributory and that A's contributions under the plan as an employee were $800, and the current actuarial value of the annuity contract which is distributed is $4,800.

(ii) A and B's gross income for 1976 is $31,200, computed by adding the total taxable amount (determined under paragraph (d)(2) of this section) of the lump sum distribution to their otherwise computed gross income [$25,000 + $3,000 + ($4,000 − $800)]. Their adjusted gross income for 1976 is $29,120 [$31,200 − ($960 + $1,120)] computed by reducing their gross income by the sum of the lump sum distribution deduction allowed by section 402(e)(3) with respect to the ordinary income portion of the distribution [$3,200 × 36/120] and the deduction allowed by section 1202 with respect to the capital gains portion of the distribution [(($3,200 × 84/120) × 0.5]. A and B's taxable income for 1976 is $25,520 (their itemized deductions are $2,100 and their personal exemptions total $1,500). Thus, A and B's income tax liability for 1976, not including the separate tax on the ordinary income portion of the distribution, is $6,207.

(iii) The adjusted total taxable amount of A's distribution for 1976 is the sum of the current actuarial value of the annuity contract distributed and the total taxable amount of the lump sum distribution. Thus, the adjusted total taxable amount of A's 1976 distribution is $8,000 [($4,800 + ($4,000 − $800)]. The modified total taxable amount is $58,000 [$50,000 + $8,000]. The modified minimum distribution allowance with respect to A's 1976 distribution is the lesser of $10,000 or ½ of the modified total taxable amount reduced by the excess, if any, of such modified total taxable amount over $20,000. Thus, the modified minimum

Proposed Reg. § 1.402(e)-2

distribution allowance with respect to A's 1976 distribution is $2,400 [$10,000 — [(($8,000 + $50,000) — $20,000) × 0.2)]]. The modified initial separate tax on A's 1976 distribution is 10 times the tax imposed by section 1(c) computed as if the taxable income therein described were $5,560 [($58,000 − $2,400)]. Thus, A's

$$\overline{10}$$

modified initial separate tax is $10,176. The modified separate tax on A's 1976 distribution is computed by multiplying the modified initial separate tax by the quotient of the sum of the ordinary income portions of each lump sum distribution received during the lookback period divided by the sum of the total taxable amounts of each lump sum distribution made during such period. Thus, the modified separate tax on A's 1976 distribution is $2,096 [$10,176 × ($10,000 + $960)/($50,000 + $3,200)]. The modified tax attributable to the annuity contract is 10 times the tax imposed by section 1(c) computed as if the taxable income therein described were $460 [($4,800 − ($2,400 × ($4,800/$58,000))] multiplied by the quotient

$$\overline{10}$$

described in the second preceding sentence. Thus, the modified tax attributable to the annuity contract is $133 [$644 × ($10,000 + $960)/($50,000 + $3,200)]. The separate tax on A's 1976 distribution is computed by reducing the modified separate tax by the sum of the separate tax paid during the lookback period, and the modified tax attributable to the annuity contract. Thus, the separate tax on A's 1976 distribution is $331 [$2,096 − ($1,632 + $133)].

(iv) A and B's total income tax liability for 1976 is the sum of their income tax liability as otherwise determined, and the separate tax. Thus, A and B's total income tax liability for 1976 is $6,538 [$6,207 + $331].

Example (3). (i) Assume the same facts as in example (1) except that the distribution on December 7, 1976, from the N Corporation's noncontributory qualified plan consists only of an annuity contract with a current actuarial value of $6,000.

(ii) A and B's gross income for 1976 is $28,000, computed by adding the total taxable amount (determined under paragraph (d)(2) of this section) of the lump sum distribution to their otherwise computed gross income [$25,000 + $3,000 + 0]. Their adjusted gross income for 1976 is $28,000 [$28,000 − ($0 + $0)], computed by reducing their gross income by the sum of the lump sum distribution deduction allowed by section 402(e)(3) with respect to the ordinary income portion of the distribution [$0 × 36/120] and the deduction allowed by section 1202 with respect to the capital gains portion of the distribution [($0 × 84/120) × 0.5]. Their taxable income for 1976 is $24,000 (their itemized deductions are $2,100 and their personal exemptions total $1,500). Thus, A and B's income tax liability for 1976, not including the separate tax on the distribution is $5,804.

(iii) The adjusted total taxable amount of A's distribution for 1976 is the sum of the current actuarial value of the annuity contract distributed and the total taxable amount of the lump sum distribution. Thus, the adjusted total taxable amount of A's 1976 distribution is $6,000 [$6,000 + $0]. The modified total taxable amount is $56,000 [$6,000 + $50,000]. The modified minimum distribution allowance with respect to A's 1976 distribution is the lesser of $10,000 or ½ of the modified total taxable amount, reduced by 20 percent of the excess (if any) of the modified total taxable amount over $20,000. Thus, the modified minimum distribution allowance with respect to A's 1976 distribution is $2,800 [$10,000 − (($56,000 − $20,000) × 0.2)]. The modified initial separate tax on A's 1976 distribution is computed by multiplying 10 times the tax imposed by section 1(c) computed as if the taxable income therein described were $5,320 [$56,000 − $2,800].

$$\overline{10}$$

Thus, A's modified initial separate tax is $9,672. The modified separate tax on A's 1976 distribution is computed by multiplying the modified initial separate tax by the quotient of the sum of the ordinary income portions of the lump sum distributions received during the lookback period divided by the sum of the total taxable amounts of each lump sum distribution made during such period. Thus, the modified separate tax on A's 1976 distribution is $1,934 [$9,672 × ($10,000 + $0)/($50,000 + $0)]. The modified tax attributable to the annuity contract is

10 times the tax imposed by section 1(c) computed as if the taxable income of a person described therein were $570 [($6,000 − (($6,000/$56,000) X $2,800))]
———
10

multiplied by the quotient described in the second preceding sentence. Thus, the modified tax attributable to the annuity contract is $161 [$805 × ($10,000 + $0) /($50,000 + $0)]. The separate tax on A's 1976 distribution is computed by reducing the modified separate tax by the sum of the separate tax paid during the lookback period, and the modified tax attributable to the annuity contract. Thus, the separate tax on A's 1976 distribution is $141 [$1,934 − ($1,632 + $161)].

(iv) A and B's total income tax liability for 1976 is the sum of their income tax liability as otherwise determined, and the separate tax. Thus, A and B's total income tax liability for 1976 is $5,945 [$5,804 + $141].

Example (4). (i) Assume the same facts as in example (3) except that the N Corporation's qualified plan was contributory and that A's contributions under the plan as an employee were $2,000.

(ii) A and B's gross income for 1976 is $28,000, computed by adding the total taxable amount (determined under paragraph (d)(2) of this section) of the lump sum distribution to their otherwise computed gross income [$25,000 + $3,000 + 0]. Their adjusted gross income for 1976 is $28,000 [$28,000 − ($0 + $0)], computed by reducing their gross income by the sum of the lump sum distribution deduction allowed by section 402(e)(3) with respect to the ordinary income portion of the distribution [$0 × 36/120] and the deduction allowed by section 1202 with respect to the capital gains portion of the distribution [($0 × 84/120) × 0.5]. Their taxable income for 1976 is $24,400 (their itemized deductions are $2,100 and their personal exemptions total $1,500). Thus, A and B's income tax liability for 1976, not including the separate tax on the distribution is $5,804.

(iii) The adjusted total taxable amount of A's distribution for 1976 is the sum of the current actuarial value of the annuity contract distributed, reduced by the excess of the net amount contributed by the employee over the cash and other property distributed, and the total taxable amount of the lump sum distribution. Thus, the adjusted total taxable amount of A's 1976 distribution is $4,000 [($6,000 − $2,000) + $0]. The modified total taxable amount is $54,000 [$50,000 + $4,000]. The modified minimum distribution allowance with respect to A's 1976 distribution is the lesser of $10,000 or ½ of the modified total taxable amount, reduced by 20 percent of the excess (if any) of the modified total taxable amount over $20,000. Thus, the modified minimum distribution allowance with respect to A's 1976 distribution is $3,200 [$10,000 − (($54,000 − $20,000) × 0.2]. The modified initial separate tax on A's 1976 distribution is computed by multiplying 10 times the tax imposed by section 1(c) computed as if the taxable income therein described were $5,080 [$54,000 − $3,200]. Thus, A's modified initial separate tax
———
10
is $9,168. The modified separate tax on A's 1976 distribution is computed by multiplying the modified initial separate tax by the quotient of the sum of the ordinary income portions of the lump sum distribution received during the lookback period divided by the sum of the total taxable amounts of each lump sum distribution made during such period. Thus, the modified separate tax on A's 1976 distribution is $1,833 [$9,168 × ($10,000 + $0)/($50,000 + $0)]. The modified tax attributable to the annuity contract is 10 times the tax imposed by section 1(c) computed as if the taxable income therein described were $376 [$4,000 − (($4,000/$54,000) × $3,200)] multiplied by the quotient described in the second
———
10
preceding sentence. Thus, the modified tax attributable to the annuity contract is $105 [$526 × ($10,000 + $0)/($50,000 + $0)]. The separate tax on A's 1976 distribution is computed by reducing the modified separate tax by the sum of the separate tax paid during the lookback period, and the modified tax attributable to the annuity contract. Thus, the separate tax on A's 1976 distribution is $96 [$1,833 − ($1,632 + $105)].

Proposed Reg. § 1.402(e)-2

(iv) A and B's total income tax liability for 1976 is the sum of their income tax liability as otherwise determined and the separate tax. Thus, A and B's total income tax liability for 1976 is $5,900 [$5,804 + $96].

(d) **Definitions.** For purposes of this section and § 1.402(e)-3—(1) Lump sum distribution. (i) For taxable years of a recipient beginning after December 31, 1973, the term "lump sum distribution" means the distribution or payment within one taxable year of the recipient of the balance under the plan to the credit of an employee which becomes payable, or is made available, to the recipient—

(A) On account of the employee's death,

(B) After the employee attains age 59½,

(C) In the case of an employee who at no time during his participation in the plan was an employee within the meaning of section 401(c)(1), on account of the employee's separation from the service, or

(D) In the case of an employee within the meaning of section 401(c)(1), after the employee has become disabled within the meaning of section 72(m)(7) and paragraph (f) of § 1.72-17,

from a trust forming part of a plan described in section 401(a) and which is exempt from tax under section 501(a) or from a plan described in section 403(a). Although periodic payments made under an annuity contract distributed under a plan described in the preceding sentence are taxed under section 72, solely for purposes of determining the adjusted total taxable amount or the modified total taxable amount, an annuity contract distributed from a plan described in the preceding sentence shall be treated as a lump sum distribution.

(ii) (A) A distribution or payment is not a lump sum distribution unless it constitutes the balance to the credit of the employee at the time the distribution or payment commences. For purposes of the preceding sentence, the time at which a distribution or payment commences shall be the date on which the requirements of subdivision (A), (B), (C), or (D) (whichever is applicable) of subdivision (i) of this subparagraph are satisfied, disregarding any previous distribution which constituted the balance to the credit of the employee.

(B) A distribution made before the death of an employee (for example, annuity payments received by the employee after retirement) will not preclude an amount paid on account of the death of the employee from being treated as a lump sum distribution by the recipient. Further, if a distribution or payment constitutes the balance to the credit of the employee, such distribution or payment shall not be treated as other than a lump sum distribution merely because an additional amount, attributable to the last or a subsequent year of service, is credited to the account of the employee and distributed.

(C) The application of this subdivision may be illustrated by the following example:

Example. A, an individual who is a calendar year taxpayer, retires from service with the M Corporation on October 31, 1975 after attaining age 59½. A begins to receive monthly annuity payments under the M Corporation's qualified plan on November 1, 1975. On February 3, 1976, A takes the balance to his credit under the M Corporation's plan in lieu of any future annuity payments. The balance to the credit of A under the M Corporation's plan is distributed to him on February 3, 1976, and as of such date he had not previously received any amount constituting a lump sum distribution. Such payments and distributions are not to be treated as a lump sum distribution because they are not paid within 1 taxable year of the recipient.

(iii) A payment or distribution described in subdivision (i) of this subparagraph which is made to more than one person (except a payment or distribution made solely to two or more trusts), shall not be treated as a lump sum distribution, unless the entire amount paid or distributed is included in the income of the employee in respect of whom the payment or distribution is made. Thus, for example, a distribution of the balance to the credit of the employee after the death of the employee made to the surviving spouse and his children cannot be treated as a lump sum distribution by the surviving spouse and children. However, a distribution to the employee's estate can be treated as a lump sum distribution even though the estate subsequently distributes the amount received to the surviving spouse and children.

(iv) The term "balance to the credit of the employee" does not include United States Retirement Plan Bonds held by a trust to the credit of an employee. Thus, a distribution or payment by a plan described in subdivision (i) of this subparagraph may constitute a lump sum distribution with respect to an employee even though the trust retains retirement plan bonds registered in the name of such employee. Similarly, the proceeds of a retirement plan bond received as a part of the balance to the credit of an employee will not be entitled to be treated as a lump sum distribution. See section 405(e) and paragraph (a)(4) of § 1.405-3.

(v) The term "balance to the credit of the employee" includes any amount to the credit of the employee under any plan which is required to be aggregated under the provisions of section 402(e)(4)(C) and paragraph (e)(1) of this section.

(vi) The term "balance to the credit of the employee" does not include any amount which has been placed in a separate account for the funding of medical benefits described in section 401(h) as defined in paragraph (a) of § 1.401-14. Thus, a distribution or payment by a plan described in subdivision (i) of this subparagraph may constitute the "balance to the credit of the employee" with respect to an employee even though the trust retains amounts attributable to the funding of medical benefits described in section 401(h).

(vii) The term "balance to the credit of the employee" includes any amount which is not forfeited under the plan as of the close of the taxable year of the recipient within which the distribution is made except that in the case of an employee who has separated from the service and incurs a break in service (within the meaning of section 411), such term does not include an amount which is forfeited at the close of the plan year, beginning with or within such taxable year, by reason of such break in service.

(viii) The balance to the credit of the employee is includible in the gross income of the recipient if the recipient fails to make a timely election under section 72(h) to receive an annuity in lieu of such balance.

(2) **Total taxable amount.** (i) The term "total taxable amount" means, with respect to a lump sum distribution described in the first sentence of subparagraph (1)(i) of this paragraph, the amount of such lump sum distribution which exceeds the sum of—

(A) The net amount contributed by the employee, and

(B) The net unrealized appreciation attributable to that part of the distribution which consists of the securities of the employer corporation so distributed.

(ii) For purposes of (A) of subdivision (i) of this subparagraph, the term "net amount contributed by the employee" means—

(A) For taxable years beginning after December 31, 1974, the amount actually contributed by the employee plus any amounts considered to be contributed by the employee under the rules of sections 72(f) and 101(b), and paragraph (b) of § 1.72-16, reduced by any amounts theretofore distributed to him which were excludable from gross income as a return of employee contributions.

(B) For taxable years beginning before January 1, 1975, an amount equal to the product of the amounts considered contributed by the employee under the plan (determined by applying sections 72(f) and 101(b), and paragraph (b) of § 1.72-16) reduced by any amounts theretofore distributed to the employee which were not includible in his gross income, multiplied by a fraction—

(i) The numerator of which is the excess, if any, of the sum of the current actuarial value of the annuity contract distributed and the value of the other property (including cash) distributed, over such current actuarial value, and

(ii) The denominator of which is the sum of the current actuarial value of the annuity contract distributed and the value of other property (including cash) distributed.

Proposed Reg. § 1.402(e)-2

(iii) The provisions of this subparagraph may be illustrated by the following examples:

Example (1). A, age 60, receives a lump sum distribution from the M Corporation's noncontributory qualified plan on November 24, 1975. The distribution of $25,000 consists of cash and M Corporation securities with net unrealized appreciation of $15,000. The total taxable amount of the distribution to A is $10,000.

Example (2). B, age 60, receives a lump sum distribution from the N Corporation's contributory qualified plan on December 29, 1975. The distribution consists of $25,000 in cash. B's contributions under the plan as an employee are $5,000. The total taxable amount of the distribution to B is $20,000.

Example (3). W receives a lump sum distribution on April 1, 1975, from the M Corporation's noncontributory qualified plan as beneficiary of H on account of H's death. The distribution consists of $25,000 in cash. The total taxable amount of distribution to W is $20,000 if W is otherwise allowed a $5,000 exclusion under section 101(b).

(3) **Ordinary income portion.** (i) The ordinary income portion of a lump sum distribution is the product of the total taxable amount of the lump sum distribution, multiplied by a fraction—

(A) the numerator of which is the number of calendar years of active participation by the employee in the plan after December 31, 1973, under which the lump sum distribution is made, and

(B) the denominator of which is the total number of calendar years of active participation by the employee in such plan.

(ii) For purposes of computing the fraction described in subdivision (i) of this subparagraph, the number of calendar years of active participation shall be the number of calendar months during the period beginning with the first month in which the employee became a participant under the plan and ending with the earliest of—

(A) The month in which the employee receives a lump sum distribution under the plan,

(B) In the case of an employee who is not an employee within the meaning of section 401(c)(1), the month in which the employee separates from the service,

(C) The month in which the employee dies, or

(D) In the case of an employee within the meaning of section 401(c)(1) who receives a lump sum distribution on account of disability, the first month in which he becomes disabled within the meaning of section 72(m)(7) and paragraph (f) of § 1.72-17.

In computing the months of active participation, in the case of active participation before January 1, 1974, a part of a calendar year in which the employee was an active participant under the plan shall be counted as 12 months, and in the case of active participation after December 31, 1973, a part of a calendar month in which an individual is an active participant under the plan shall be counted as 1 month. Thus, for example, if A, an individual, became an active participant under a plan on December 31, 1965, and continued to be an active participant under the plan until May 7, 1976, A has 108 (12 × 9) months of active participation under the plan before January 1, 1974, and A has 29 (12 + 12 + 5) months of active participation after December 31, 1973. For special rule in case of aggregation of plans, see paragraph (e)(1)(ii) of this section.

(4) **Employee; employer.** The term "employee" includes an employee within the meaning of section 401(c)(1) and the employer of such individual is the person treated as his employer under section 401(c)(4).

(5) **Securities.** The terms "securities" and "securities of the employer corporation" shall have the meanings provided in sections 402(a)(3)(A) and 402(a) (3)(B), respectively.

(e) **Special rules—(1) Aggregation.** (i) Aggregation of trusts and plans —(A) For purposes of determining the balance to the credit of an employee, all trusts described in section 401(a) and which are exempt from tax under section

501(a) and which are part of a plan shall be treated as a single trust; all pension plans described in section 401(a) maintained by an employer shall be treated as a single plan; all profit-sharing plans described in section 401(a) maintained by an employer shall be treated as a single plan; and all stock bonus plans described in section 401(a) maintained by an employer shall be treated as a single plan. For purposes of this subdivision (i), an annuity contract shall be considered to be a trust.

(B) Trusts which are not described in section 401(a) or which are not exempt from tax under section 501(a), and annuity contracts which do not satisfy the requirements of section 404(a)(2) shall not be taken into account for purposes of subdivision (i) of this subparagraph.

(ii) *Computation of ordinary income portion.* The ordinary income portion of a distribution from two or more plans (which are treated as a single plan under subdivision (i) of this subparagraph) shall be computed by aggregating all of the amounts which would constitute the ordinary income portion of a lump sum distribution if each plan maintained by the employer were not subject to the application of subdivision (i) of this subparagraph.

(iii) *Examples.* The application of this subparagraph is illustrated by the following examples:

Example (1). M Corporation maintains a qualified profit-sharing plan and a qualified defined benefit pension plan. A, who has participated in each plan for 5 years and is age 55, separates from the service on December 5, 1975. On December 5, 1975, A receives a distribution of the balance to the credit of his account under the profit-sharing plan. Payment of his pension benefits, however, will not commence until he attains age 65. A is entitled to treat his profit-sharing distribution as a lump sum distribution.

Example (2). Assume the same facts as in example (1) except that instead of a profit-sharing plan, M Corporation maintains a qualified money purchase pension plan. A is not entitled to have the amount received from the money purchase pension plan treated as a lump sum distribution.

Example (3). Assume the same facts as in example (2) except that the trust forming part of the defined benefit pension maintained by M Corporation is not a qualified trust. A is entitled to have the amount received from the money purchase plan treated as a lump sum distribution.

Example (4). N Corporation maintains profit-sharing plan X and profit-sharing plan Y which plans are qualified and are noncontributory. A is a participant in each plan. A has been a participant in the profit-sharing plan X since October 13, 1966 and a participant in profit-sharing plan Y since its inception on May 9, 1968. A, age 55, separates from the service on December 5, 1975. He receives the balance to his credit from each plan upon separation. He receives $50,000 from profit-sharing plan X and $60,000 from profit-sharing plan Y. The ordinary income portion of his distribution from the N Corporation plans is $25,000 [($50,000 $\times$ (24/120)) + ($60,000 $\times$ (24/96))].

(2) **Community property laws.** (i) Except as provided in subdivision (ii) of this subparagraph, the provisions of this section shall be applied without regard to community property laws.

(ii) In applying the provisions of section 402(e)(3), relating to the allowance of a deduction from gross income of the ordinary income portion of a lump sum distribution, community property laws shall not be disregarded. Thus, for example, if A, a married individual subject to the community property laws of a jurisdiction, receives a lump sum distribution of which the ordinary income portion is $10,000, and he and his wife, B, file separate returns for the taxable year, generally, one half of the total taxable amount of the lump sum distribution is includible in A's gross income, and he will be entitled to a deduction under section 402(e)(3) of $5,000. In this case, the other half of the total taxable amount is includible in B's gross income, and she will be entitled to a deduction of $5,000. The entire amount of the lump sum distribution, however, must be taken into account by A in computing the separate tax imposed by section 402(e)(1)(A).

Proposed Reg. §1.402(e)-2

(3) **Minimum period of service.** For purposes of computing the separate tax imposed by section 402(e)(1)(A), no amount distributed or paid to an employee may be treated as a lump sum distribution under section 402(e)(4)(A) and this section unless he has been a participant in the plan for at least 5 full taxable years of such employee (preceding his taxable year in which such amount is distributed or paid). Thus, for example, if an amount, which would otherwise be a lump sum distribution, is distributed to A, an employee who has completed only 4 of his taxable years of participation in the plan before the first day of the taxable year in which the amount is distributed, A is not entitled to use the provisions of section 402(e) to compute the tax on the ordinary income portion of the amount distributed. If the amount were distributed to A's beneficiary on account of A's death, however, A's beneficiary could treat the distribution as a lump sum distribution under section 402(e) and this section.

(4) **Amounts subject to penalty.** Section 402(e) and this section do not apply to an amount described in section 72(m)(5)(A)(ii) and § 1.72-17(e)(1)(i)(b) to the extent the provisions of section 72(m)(5) apply to such amount.

(5) **Distributions including securities of the employer corporation.** For rules relating to distributions including securities of the employer corporation, see § 1.402(a)-1(b).

(6) **Liability for tax.** (i) Except as provided in subdivision (ii) of this subparagraph the recipient shall be liable for the tax imposed by section 402(e)(1)(A).

(ii) (A) In any case in which the recipient of a lump sum distribution is a trust, if a beneficiary of such trust is—

(1) An employee with respect to the plan under which the distribution is made, or

(2) Treated as the owner of such trust for purposes of subpart E of part I of subchapter J of chapter 1 of the Code (relating to grantors and others treated as substantial owners),

then such employee or owner shall be treated as the sole recipient of the lump sum distribution. For purposes of (1) of this subdivision, the term "an employee with respect to the plan under which the distribution is made" means an individual who, immediately before the distribution is made, is a participant in the plan under which the distribution is made.

(B) (1) In any case in which a lump sum distribution is made within a taxable year with respect to an individual only to two or more trusts, if a beneficiary of any one of such trusts is not treated as the sole recipient of the distribution by reason of the application of (A) of this subdivision (ii), the separate tax imposed by section 402(e)(1)(A) shall be computed as if the distribution were made to a single recipient consisting of all of such trusts, but the liability for such separate tax shall be allocated among the trusts according to the relative portions of the total taxable amount of the distribution received by each trust.

(2) In any case in which a lump sum distribution is made in a succeeding taxable year in a lookback period with respect to a trust described in (1) of this subdivision (B), the separate tax imposed by section 402(e)(1)(A) shall be computed as if the amount described in section 402(e)(2)(A) (relating to the amount of tax imposed by section 402(e)(1)(A) paid with respect to other distributions in a lookback period) includes the separate tax determined in (1) of this subdivision (B) (without regard to the allocation described therein).

(7) **Change in exempt status of trust.** For principles applicable in making appropriate adjustments if the trust was not exempt for one or more years before the year of distribution, see § 1.402(a)-1(a)(1)(iv).

(f) **Reporting—(1) Information required.** An employer who maintains a plan described in section 401(a) or 403(a), under which a distribution or payment which may be treated as a lump sum distribution is made in a taxable year of the recipient beginning after December 31, 1973, shall communicate (or cause to be communicated) in writing, to the recipient on Form 1099 R the following information (where applicable):

(i) The gross amount of such distribution (including the value of any United States retirement plan bonds distributed to or held for the recipient);

(ii) The total taxable amount of such distribution;

(iii) The ordinary income portion and capital gain element of such distribution;

(iv) The net amount contributed by the employee (within the meaning of paragraph (d)(2)(ii) of this section);

(v) The portions of such distribution excludable from the gross income of the recipient under paragraph (c) of § 1.72-16 and paragraph (b) of § 1.402(a)-1;

(vi) The value of any United States retirement plan bonds distributed to or held for the recipient in excess of the net amount contributed by the employee (within the meaning of paragraph (d)(2)(ii) of this section) included in the basis of such bonds;

(vii) The current actuarial value of any annuity contract distributed as part of the balance to the credit of the employee in excess of the net amount contributed by the employee (within the meaning of paragraph (d)(2)(ii) of this section) considered to be an investment in the contract;

(viii) The net unrealized appreciation on any securities of the employer corporation.

(2) **Alternate method of communication.** The obligation of the employer to communicate the information described in subparagraph (1) of this paragraph to the recipient shall be satisfied if the fiduciary of the trust or the payer of such distribution communicates the information to the recipient.

(3) **Taxable year of recipient.** The report required by this paragraph may be prepared, at the option of the employer, as if the taxable year of each employee were the calendar year.

(4) **Failure to satisfy requirements.** In the event that the requirements of this paragraph are not satisfied, the information required to be furnished under this paragraph shall be furnished as part of the return required to be filed under section 6058 and the regulations thereunder.

§ 1.402(e)-3 (Proposed Treasury Decision, published 4-30-75.) **Election to treat an amount as a lump sum distribution.**

(a) **In general.** For purposes of sections 402, 403, and this section, an amount which is described in section 402(e)(4)(A) and which is not an annuity contract may be treated as a lump sum distribution under section 402(e)(4)(A) only if the taxpayer elects for the taxable year to have all such amounts received during such year so treated. Not more than one election may be made under this section with respect to an employee after such employee has attained age 59½.

(b) **Taxpayers eligible to make the election.** Individuals, estates, and trusts are the only taxpayers eligible to make the election provided by this section. In the case of a lump sum distribution made with respect to an employee to 2 or more trusts, the election provided by this section shall be made by the employee or by the personal representative of a deceased employee.

(c) **Procedure for making election—(1) Time and scope of election.** An election under this section shall be made for each taxable year to which such election is to apply. The election shall be made before the expiration of the period (including extensions thereof) prescribed in section 6511 for making a claim for credit or refund of the assessed tax imposed by chapter 1 of subtitle A of the Code for such taxable year.

(2) **Manner of making election.** An election by the taxpayer with respect to a taxable year shall be made by filing Form 4972 as a part of the taxpayer's income tax return or amended return for the taxable year.

(3) **Revocation of election.** An election made pursuant to this section may be revoked within the time prescribed in subparagraph (1) of this paragraph for

making an election, only if there is filed, within such time, an amended income tax return for such taxable year, which includes a statement revoking the election and is accompanied by payment of any tax attributable to the revocation. If an election for a taxable year is revoked, another election may be made for that taxable year under subparagraphs (1) and (2) of this paragraph.

(4) **Effect of election on subsequent distribution.** An election made pursuant to this section shall be an election to treat an annuity contract distributed after December 31, 1973, in a lookback period (as defined in § 1.402(e)-2(c)(2)(iii)(F)) beginning after such date as a lump sum distribution in the taxable year of the recipient in which such contract is distributed.

TEMPORARY INCOME TAX REGULATIONS UNDER THE EMPLOYEE RETIREMENT INCOME SECURITY ACT OF 1974

Section 11.402(e)(4)(B)-1 is revoked.

Taxation of Employee Annuities

Section 1.403(a)-1(a) is amended to read as follows:

§ **1.403(a)-1** (Proposed Treasury Decision, published 5-6-72.) **Taxability of beneficiary under a qualified annuity plan.**

(a) An employee or retired or former employee for whom an annuity contract is purchased by his employer is not required to include in his gross income the amount paid for the contract at the time such amount is paid (except to the extent a shareholder-employee of an electing small business corporation must include excess contributions paid on his behalf in the year paid under section 1379(b)), whether or not his rights to the contract are forfeitable, if the annuity contract is purchased under a plan which meets the requirements of section 404(a)(2). For purposes of the preceding sentence, it is immaterial whether the employer deducts the amounts paid (other than certain amounts paid on behalf of a shareholder-employee by an electing small business corporation) for the contract under section 404(a)(2). See § 1.403(b)-1 for rules relating to annuity contracts which are not purchased under qualified plans but which are purchased by organizations described in section 501(c)(3) and exempt under section 501(a) or which are purchased for employees who perform services for certain public schools.

* * * * * * * * * * * *

Paragraphs (a) and (b) of §1.403(a)-1 are amended to read as follows:

§**1.403(a)-1** (Proposed Treasury Decision, published 12-6-72, 4-30-75.) **Taxability of beneficiary under a qualified annuity plan.**

(a) An employee or retired or former employee for whom an annuity contract is purchased by his employer is not required to include in his gross income the amount paid for the contract at the time such amount is paid (except to the extent a shareholder-employee of an electing small business corporation must include excess contributions paid on his behalf in the year paid under section 1379(b)), whether or not his rights to the contract are forfeitable, if the annuity contract is purchased under a plan which meets the requirements of section 404(a)(2). For purposes of the preceding sentence, it is immaterial whether the employer deducts the amounts paid (other than certain amounts paid on behalf of a shareholder-employee by an electing small business corporation) for the contract under such section 404(a)(2). Whether an annuity contract is purchased under a qualified plan by the employer or the employee must be determined on the basis of the particular facts and circumstances of the individual case. An annuity contract will, except as otherwise provided in this subdivision, be considered to have been purchased by the employee if at his individual option, and to the extent that, an amount is paid for such a contract in return for a reduction in his basic or regular compensation or in lieu of an increase in such compensation. The preceding sentence shall not apply to an amount paid for an annuity contract under a qualified plan either (a) in a taxable year of the employee ending prior to January 1, 1972, or (b) at any time prior to December 6, 1972, where the employee has relied upon a ruling by the Commissioner to him or his employer that such amount will be treated as the contribution of the employer. See § 1.403(b)-1 for rules relating to annuity contracts which are not purchased under qualified plans but which are purchased by organizations described in section 501(c)(3) and exempt under section 501(a) or which are purchased for employees who perform services for certain public schools.

(b) The amounts received by or made available to any employee referred to in paragraph (a) of this section under an annuity contract shall be included in the gross income of the employee for the taxable year in which received or made available, as provided in section 72 (relating to annuities), except that—

(1) For taxable years beginning before January 1, 1970, certain total distributions described in section 403(a)(2) (as in effect for such years) are taxable as long-term capital gains (see § 1.403(a)-2 for rules applicable to such amounts), and

(2) For taxable years beginning after December 31, 1973, a portion of a lump sum distribution (as defined by section 402(e)(4)(A)) is treated as long-term capital gains (see paragraph (d) of § 1.403(a)-2 for rules applicable to such portion and see § 1.402(e)-2 for the computation of the separate tax on the portion of a lump sum distribution not treated as long-term capital gains).

For taxable years beginning before January 1, 1964, section 72(e)(3) (relating to treatment of certain lump sums), as in effect before such date, shall not apply to an amount described in this paragraph. For taxable years beginning after December 31, 1963, such amounts may be taken into account in computations under sections 1301 through 1305 (relating to income averaging).

* * * * * * * * * * * * *

Section 1.403(a)-2 is amended by revising paragraph (a) to read as follows:

§ 1.403(a)-2 (Proposed Treasury Decision, published 5-6-72.) **Capital gains treatment for certain distributions.**

(a) If the total amounts payable with respect to any employee for whom an annuity contract has been purchased by an employer under a plan which—

(1) Is a plan described in section 403(a)(1) and § 1.403(a)-1, and

(2) Requires that refunds of contributions with respect to annuity contracts purchased under such plan be used to reduce subsequent premiums on the contracts under the plan,

are paid to, or includible in gross income of, the payee within one taxable year of the payee by reason of the employee's death or other separation from the service, or death after such separation from the service, such total payments, to the extent they exceed the net amount contributed by the employee, shall, except as limited by section 403(a)(2)(C) for taxable years ending after December 31, 1969, be considered a gain from the sale or exchange of a capital asset held for more than 6 months. The limitation on the long-term capital gain treatment under section 403(a)(2)(C) shall be determined under the rules set forth in § 1.402(a)-2, except that the rules provided by paragraphs (b)(4) and (d)(4) of § 1.402(a)-2 shall not be applied to distributions to which this section applies, and any reference in § 1.402(a)-2 to a provision of section 402 or the regulations thereunder shall be treated as a reference to the corresponding provision of section 403 or the regulations thereunder. In applying the rules provided in § 1.402(a)-2 the term "plan year" shall have the same meaning as under paragraph (a)(2) of § 1.404(a)-8. Section 72(n)(4) and § 1.72-19 apply to the portion of the total amounts payable not treated as long-term capital gain or the net amount contributed by the employee. The "net amount contributed by the employee" is the amount actually contributed by the employee plus any amounts considered to be contributed by the employee under

Proposed Reg. § 1.403(a)-2

the rules of sections 72(f), 101(b), 1379(b)(2), and paragraph (d) of § 1.403(a)-1, reduced by any amounts theretofore distributed to him which were excludable from his gross income as a return of employee contributions. For example, if under an annuity contract purchased under a plan described in this section, the total amounts payable to the employee's widow are paid to her in the year in which the employee dies, in the amount of $8,000, and if $5,000 thereof is excludable under section 101(b) and if the ordinary income element of such distribution is $4,000, the capital gain element is $3,400, and the net employee contributions $600, $2,703 ($5,000 × ($4,000 ÷ $7,400)) of the ordinary income element and $2,297 ($5,000 × ($3,400 ÷ $7,400)) of the capital gain element are excludable from her gross income. The net employee contributions, $600, are excludable from her gross income as a return of the employee's contributions.

* * * * * * * * * * * *

Section 1.403(a)-2(a)(1) and (b) is amended to read as follows:

§ 1.403(a)-2 (Proposed Treasury Decision, published 4-30-75.) Capital gains treatment for certain distributions.

(a) For taxable years beginning before January 1, 1970, if the total amounts payable with respect to any employee for whom an annuity contract has been purchased by an employer under a plan which—

(1) Is a plan described in section 403(a)(1) and § 1.403(a)-1, and

* * * * * * * * * * * *

(b) For taxable years beginning before January 1, 1970—

(1) The term "total amounts" means the balance to the credit of an employee with respect to all annuities under the annuity plan which becomes payable to the payee by reason of the employee's death or other separation from the service, or by reason of his death after separation from the service. If an employee commences to receive annuity payments on retirement and then a lump sum payment is made to his widow upon his death, the capital gains treatment applies to the lump sum payment, but it does not apply to amounts received before the time the "total amounts" become payable. However, if the total amount to the credit of the employee at the time of his death or other separation from the service or death after separation from the service is paid or includible in the gross income of the payee within one taxable year of the payee, such amount is entitled to the capital gains treatment notwithstanding that in a later taxable year an additional amount is credited to the employee and paid to the payee.

* * * * * * * * * * * *

(c) For taxable years beginning before January 1, 1970, the provisions of this section are not applicable to any amounts paid to a payee to the extent such amounts are attributable to contributions made on behalf of an employee while he was a self-employed individual in the business with respect to which the plan was established. For the taxation of such amounts, see § 1.72-18. For such years, for the rules for determining the amount attributable to contributions on behalf of an employee while he was self-employed, see paragraphs (b)(4) and (c)(2) of such section.

(d) For taxable years ending after December 31, 1969, and beginning before January 1, 1974, the portion of the total amounts described in paragraph (b)(1) of this section treated as gain from the sale or exchange of a capital asset held for more than six months is subject to the limitation of section 403(a)(2)(C), as in effect on December 31, 1973.

(e) For taxable years beginning after December 31, 1973—

(1) If a lump sum distribution (as defined in section 402(e)(4)(A) and the regulations thereunder) is received by, or made available to, the recipient under an annuity contract described in subparagraph (2)(i) of this paragraph, the ordinary income portion (as defined in section 402(e)(4)(E) and the regulations thereunder) of such distribution shall be taxable in accordance with the provisions of section 402(e) and the regulations thereunder and the portion of such distribution determined under paragraph (3) of this paragraph shall be treated in accordance with the provisions of subparagraph (2) of this paragraph.

(2) If—

(i) An annuity contract is purchased by an employer for an employee under a plan described in section 403(a)(1) and § 1.403(a)-1,

Proposed Reg. § 1.403(a)-2

(ii) Such plan requires that refunds of contributions with respect to annuity contracts purchased under the plan be used to reduce subsequent premiums on the contracts under the plan, and

(iii) A lump sum distribution (as defined in section 402(e)(4)(A) and the regulations thereunder) is paid to the recipient,

the amount described in subparagraph (3) of this paragraph shall be treated as gain from the sale or exchange of a capital asset held for more than 6 months.

(3) For purposes of subparagraph (2) of this paragraph, the portion of a lump sum distribution treated as gain from the sale or exchange of a capital asset held for more than 6 months is an amount equal to the total taxable amount of the lump sum distribution (as defined in section 402(e)(4)(D) and the regulations thereunder) multiplied by a fraction—

(i) The numerator of which is the number of calendar years of active participation (as determined under § 1.402(e)-2(d)(3)(ii)) by the employee in such plan before January 1, 1974, and

(ii) The denominator of which is the number of calendar years of active participation (as determined under § 1.402(e)-2(d)(3)(ii)) by the employee in such plan.

(4) For purposes of this paragraph—

(i) In the case of an employee who is an employee without regard to section 401(c)(1), the determination of whether or not an amount is a lump sum distribution shall be made without regard to the requirements of section 402(e)(4)(B) and § 1.402(e)-3.

(ii) No distribution to any taxpayer other than an individual, estate, or trust may be treated as a lump sum distribution under this section.

Immediately after §1.403(a)-2 there is added the following new section:

§ 1.403(a)-3 (Proposed Treasury Decision, published 2-21-75.) **Rollover amounts.**

(a) **In general.** Under section 403(a)(4), any amount distributed from an employees' annuity plan described in section 403(a)(1) which satisfies the requirements of paragraph (b) of this section is not includible in the gross income of the employee for the year in which paid.

(b) **General rule.** Except as provided in paragraph (c) of this section an amount satisfies the requirements of this paragraph if—

(1) The balance to the credit of an employee is paid to him in one or more distributions which constitute a lump sum distribution within the meaning of section 402(e)(4)(A) (determined without reference to section 402(e)(4)(B)),

(2) The employee transfers all of the property he receives in such distribution to—

(i) An individual retirement account described in section 408(a) and the regulations thereunder, an individual retirement annuity described in section 408(b) (other than an endowment contract) and the regulations thereunder, or a retirement bond described in section 409 and the regulations thereunder, or

(ii) An employees' trust described in section 401(a) which is exempt from tax under section 501(a), or to an annuity plan described in section 403(a),

on or before the 60th day after the day on which he received such property to the extent the fair market value of such property exceeds the amount considered contributed by the employee (determined by applying section 72(f) and paragraph (b) of § 1.72-16), reduced by any amount theretofore distributed to him which were not includible in gross income, and

(3) The amount so transferred consists of the same property (other than cash) distributed, to the extent that the fair market value of such property does not exceed the amount required to be transferred pursuant to subparagraph (2) of this paragraph.

(c) **Special rule.** (1) Paragraph (b)(2)(ii) of this section does not apply in the case of a transfer to an employees' trust or annuity plan if any part of the lump sum distribution described in paragraph (b)(1) of this section is attributable to a plan under which the employee receiving the lump sum distribution was an employee within the meaning of section 401(c)(1) at the time contributions were made on his behalf under the plan.

(2) Paragraph (b)(2)(ii) of this section does not apply unless the plan of which the employees' trust is a part or the annuity plan provides for the acceptance of such contributions.

(d) Effective date. (1) Except as provided in subparagraph (2) of this paragraph, the provisions of this section shall apply to all transfers described in paragraph (b)(2) of this section made after September 1, 1974.

(2) The provisions of this section shall only apply to transfers described in paragraph (b)(2)(i) of this section made to an individual retirement account, individual retirement annuity or retirement bond after December 31, 1974.

Section 1.403(b) is deleted.

Section 1.403(b)-1 is amended by adding a new paragraph (h) at the end thereof to read as follows:

§1.403(b)-1 (Proposed Treasury Decision, published 2-10-78.) **Taxability of beneficiary under annuity purchased by a section 501(c)(3) organization or public school.**

* * * * * * * * * * * *

(h) Custodial accounts—(1) Effective date. This paragraph applies to contributions made after December 31, 1973.

(2) Description of custodial account. A custodial account is described in section 403(b)(7) if all of the following requirements are satisfied:

(i) The custodial account must be established by an employer described in section 403(b)(1)(A) for an employee.

(ii) The employer must make at least one contribution to the custodial account that is excluded from the gross income of the employee under section 403(b).

(iii) The custodian must be a bank or must be a person who has been approved by the Commissioner under §1.401-12(n).

(iv) The employee's interest in the custodial account must be nonforfeitable and nontransferable.

(v) There must be a written custodial agreement, and it must be impossible under the agreement for any part of the amounts received by the custodial account or of the earnings thereon to be used for, or diverted to, purposes other than for the exclusive benefit of the employee or his beneficiaries. In particular, the assets held in the account must not be subject to the claims of the employer's creditors.

(vi) The custodial account must be established and maintained primarily to provide for the payment of benefits to the employee over a period of years, usually for life, after retirement. Thus, for example, the custodian must begin to make payments to the employee within a reasonable time after the employee retires. In addition, the custodial agreement must provide that the custodian is not to make any distributions to the employee or his beneficiaries before the employee attains age 65, unless (A) the employee becomes disabled or dies, or (B) the employee attains age 55 and leaves the service of the employer.

(vii) Section 401(f)(1) must not apply to the custodial account.

(viii) The custodial agreement must provide that the investment of the funds in the account is to be made solely in stock of one or more regulated investment companies (as defined section 403(b)(7)(C)) to be held in that account. The requirement described in the preceding sentence applies, for example, to amounts paid by the employer and to any earnings on such amounts. The requirement also applies to capital gains realized upon the sale of stock described in this subdivision, to any capital gain dividends received in connection with the stock, and to any refunds described in section 852(b)(3)(D)(ii) (relating to undistributed capital gains of a regulated investment company) that are received in connection with the stock. However, the custodian may deposit funds with a bank, in

Proposed Reg. §1.403(b)-1

either a checking or savings account, while awaiting an appropriate time to make additional investments.

(3) **Treatment of custodial account.** Except as provided in section 403(b)(7)(B), a custodial account described in section 403(b)(7) is treated as an annuity contract for all purposes of the Internal Revenue Code.

(4) **Distributions.** (i) Amounts received by or made available to an employee or his beneficiary from a custodial account described in section 403(b)(7) are treated as amounts received or made available under an annuity contract to which section 403(b) applies. (See paragraph (c) of this section.)

(ii) If a custodial account described in section 403(b)(7) purchases a nontransferable annuity contract for an employee and distributes it to the employee and if the contract contains a cash surrender value that may be available to the employee by surrendering the contract, the cash surrender value will not be considered income to the employee unless and until the contract is surrendered. If, however, the contract distributed by the custodial account is a retirement income, endowment, or other life insurance contract, the entire cash value of the contract at the time of distribution must be included in the distributee's income in accordance with the provisions of paragraph (c) of this section, except to the extent that within 60 days after the distribution of the contract, all or any portion of its value is irrevocably converted into a nontransferable contract under which no part of any proceeds payable on death at any time would be excludable under section 101(a) (relating to life insurance proceeds).

(5) **Employee contributions.** An employee is permitted to make contributions to a custodial account described in section 403(b)(7). The earnings on an employee contribution (like the earnings on any other contribution) are exempt from the income tax. However, an employee contribution is not excluded from gross income and may be subject to an excise tax on excess contributions. See section 4973.

(6) **Excess contributions.** (i) See section 4973 for rules relating to an excise tax on excess contributions.

(ii) The earnings on an excess contribution (like the earnings on any other contribution) are exempt from the income tax.

(iii) If an employer makes an excess contribution to a custodial account described in section 403(b)(7), the contribution is taxed to the employee to the extent provided under section 403(c) as if it were a premium paid for an annuity contract.

(7) **Life insurance.** The custodian of a custodial account described in section 403(b)(7) is permitted to buy life insurance for the protection of the employee. However, unless the insurance contract is distributed within 30 days after it is purchased, the contract must have no cash surrender value, the insurance protection must be merely incidental to other benefits, and the cost of the insurance must be included in the gross income of the employee. For purposes of this subparagraph, life insurance protection is merely incidental if, in each taxable year of the employer, the cost of the insurance does not exceed 25 percent of the employer's contribution to the custodial account.

(8) **Two or more employees.** A custodial account described in section 403(b)(7) may be established and maintained for the benefit of two or more employees. In such a case, the custodian must account separately for the interest of each employee.

(9) **Substitution of custodian.** Anything that has the effect of merely substituting one custodian for another is not considered as terminating or interrupting the existence of a custodial account described in section 403(b)(7).

(10) **Employee power to change investments.** A power authorizing the employee to direct the custodian to change the investment of assets held in the account solely from stock in one regulated investment company to stock in another such company will not be considered to terminate or interrupt the existence of a custodial account described in section 403(b)(7).

(11) **Other requirements.** Under section 403(b)(7)(B), the custodian of a custodial account described in section 403(b)(7) is subject to the same reporting requirements as the trustee of a qualified trust. Thus, for example, the custodian must file the returns described in sections 6033 and 6041. In addition, the custodial account is treated as an organization described in section 401(a) for purposes of subchapter F of chapter 1 (see especially sections 511 to 515).

(12) Meaning of terms. For purposes of this paragraph—
  (i) The term "bank" means a bank as defined in section 401(d)(1),
  (ii) The term "custodial account" includes a trust,
  (iii) The term "custodian" includes a trustee, and
  (iv) The term "excess contribution" means an excess contribution as defined in section 4973(c).

(13) Investment of custodial account funds in section 403(b) annuity contract. [Reserved]

Section 1.403(c)-1 is amended to read as follows:

§ 1.403(c)-1 (Proposed Treasury Decision, published 6-3-71.) **Taxability of beneficiary under a nonqualified annuity.**

(a) Taxability of vested interest in premiums. If an employer (whether or not exempt under section 501(a) or 521(a)) purchases an annuity contract (other than an annuity contract described in paragraph (d)(1)(ii) of this section), and if the premiums paid for the contract after August 1, 1969, are not subject to paragraph (a) of § 1.403(a)-1 the amount of such premiums shall, to the extent it is not excludible under paragraph (b) of § 1.403(b)-1, be included as compensation in the gross income of the employee for the taxable year during which such premiums are paid, but only to the extent to which the employee's rights in such premiums are vested at the time the premiums are paid. As to what constitutes vested rights, see paragraph (a)(2) of § 1.402(b)-1. If an employer has purchased annuity contracts and transferred them to a trust for the purpose of providing annuity contracts for his employee, the amount so paid or contributed shall be treated as a contribution to a trust described in section 402(b). For the rules relating to the taxation of the cost of life insurance protection and the proceeds thereunder, see § 1.72-16.

(b) Taxability of employee when rights under annuity contract change from nonvested to vested—(1) In general. If, during a taxable year of an employee ending after August 1, 1969, the rights of such employee under an annuity contract purchased for him by an employer (whether or not exempt under section 501(a) or 521(a)) change from nonvested to vested, the value of the annuity contract on the date of such change shall, to the extent provided in subparagraph (2) of this paragraph, be included in the employee's gross income for such taxable year. The preceding sentence shall not apply, however, to an annuity contract purchased and held as part of a plan which met at the time of such purchase and continues to meet the requirements of section 404(a)(2) or an annuity contract described in paragraph (d)(1)(ii) of this section. For purposes of this section, the value of an annuity contract on the date the employee's rights change from nonvested to vested means the cash surrender value of such contract on such date.

(2) Extent to which value of annuity contract is includible in employee's gross income. For purposes of subparagraph (1) of this paragraph, there shall be included in the gross income of an employee for his taxable year in which rights under an annuity contract change from nonvested to vested only an amount equal to the portion of the value of such contract on the date of such change attributable to premiums which were paid after August 1, 1969, and which are not excludible from the employee's gross income under paragraph (b) of § 1.403(b)-1. However, the preceding sentence shall not apply—
  (i) to the extent such value is attributable to a premium paid on the date of such change, and
  (ii) to the extent such value is attributable to premiums described in paragraph (d)(1)(ii) of this section, relating to premiums paid pursuant to a binding written contract entered into before April 22, 1969.

The value of such an annuity contract is not includible in the gross income of the employee for the year in which the change occurs to the extent that it is excludible under paragraph (b) of § 1.403(b)-1. See paragraph (b)(2) of § 1.403(b)-1 which provides that the amount otherwise includible in gross income under section 403

Proposed Reg. § 1.403(c)-1

(c) is considered to be a contribution by the employer for purposes of the exclusion provided in paragraph (b) of § 1.403(b)-1.

(3) **Partial vesting.** If, during any taxable year of an employee, only part of his beneficial interest in an annuity contract changes from a nonvested to a vested interest, then only the corresponding part of the value of the annuity contract on the date of such change is includible in the employee's gross income for such taxable year. In such a case, it is first necessary to compute, under the rules in subparagraphs (1) and (2) of this paragraph but without regard to any exclusion allowable under paragraph (b) of § 1.403(b)-1, the amount which would be includible in the employee's gross income for the taxable year if his entire beneficial interest in the annuity contract had changed to a vested interest during such year. The amount that is includible (without regard to any exclusion allowed by paragraph (b) of § 1.403(b)-1) in the gross income of the employee for the taxable year in which the change occurs is an amount equal to the amount determined under the preceding sentence multiplied by the percent of the employee's beneficial interest which changed to a vested interest during the taxable year. If at the time the employee's interest changes to a vested interest, the employer is an organization described in section 501(c)(3) and exempt from tax under section 501(a), then the amount that is includible in the employee's gross income under this subparagraph is considered as an employer contribution to which the exclusion provided in paragraph (b) of § 1.403(b)-1 applies (see paragraph (b)(2) of § 1.403(b)-1).

(c) **Amounts received or made available under an annuity contract.** The amounts received by or made available to the employee under an annuity contract shall be included in the gross income of the employee for the taxable year in which received or made available, as provided in section 72 (relating to annuities). Such amounts may be taken into account in computations under sections 1301 through 1305 (relating to income averaging). For rules relating to the treatment of employer contributions as part of the consideration paid by the employee, see section 72(f). See also section 101(b)(2)(D) for rules relating to the treatment of the limited exclusion provided thereunder as part of the consideration paid by the employee.

(d) **Taxability of beneficiary under a nonqualified annuity on or before August 1, 1969.** (1) Except as provided in section 402(d), if an employer purchases an annuity contract and if the amounts paid for the contract—

(i) On or before August 1, 1969, or

(ii) After such date, if pursuant to a binding written contract (as defined in paragraph (b)(2) of § 1.83-8) entered into before April 22, 1969, or pursuant to a written plan in which the employee participated on such date and under which the obligation of the employer is essentially the same as under a binding written contract,

are not subject to paragraph (a) of § 1.403(a)-1 or paragraph (a) of § 1.403(b)-1, the amount of such contribution shall, to the extent it is not excludible under paragraph (b) of § 1.403(b)-1, be included in the income of the employee for the taxable year during which such contribution is made if, at the time the contribution is made, the employee's rights under the annuity contract are nonforfeitable, except for failure to pay future premiums. If the annuity contract was purchased by an employer which is not exempt from tax under section 501(a) or section 521(a), and if the employee's rights under the annuity contract in such a case were forfeitable at the time the employer's contribution was made for the annuity contract, even though they became nonforfeitable later the amount of such contribution is not required to be included in the income of the employee at the time his rights under the contract become nonforfeitable. On the other hand, if the annuity contract is purchased by an employer which is exempt from tax under section 501(a) or section 521(a), all or part of the value of the contract may be includible in the employee's gross income at the time his rights under the contract become nonforfeitable (see section 403(d) prior to the repeal thereof by the Tax Reform Act of 1969 and the regulations thereunder). As to what constitutes nonforfeitable rights of an employee, see § 1.402(b)-1(d)(2). The amounts received by or made available to the employee under the annuity contract shall be included in the gross income of the employee for the taxable year in which received or made available, as provided in section 72 (relating to annuities). For taxable years beginning before January 1, 1964, section 72(e)(3) (relating to the treatment of certain lump sums), as in effect before such date, shall not apply to such amounts. For taxable years beginning after December 31, 1963, such amounts may be taken into account in computations under sections 1301 through 1305 (relating to income averaging). For rules relating to the treatment of employer contributions as part of the consideration paid by the employee, see section 72(f). See also section 101(b)(2)(D) for rules relating to the treatment of the limited exclusion provided thereunder as part of the consideration paid by the employee.

(2) If an employer has purchased annuity contracts and transferred them to a trust, or if an employer has made contributions to a trust for the purpose of providing annuity contracts for his employees as provided in section 402(d) (see paragraph (a) of § 1.402(d)-1, the amount so paid or contributed is not required to be included in the income of the employe, but any amount received by or made available to the employee under the annuity contract shall be includible in the gross income of the employee for the taxable year in which received or made available, as provided in section 72 (relating to annuities). For taxable years beginning before January 1, 1964, section 72(e)(3) (relating to the treatment of certain lump sums), as in effect before such date, shall not apply to any amount received by or made available to the employee under the annuity contract. For taxable years beginning after December 31, 1963, amounts received by or made available to the employee under the annuity contract may be taken into account in computations under sections 1301 through 1305 (relating to income averaging). In such case the amount paid or contributed by the employer shall not constitute consideration paid by the employees for such annuity contract in determining the amount of annuity payments required to be included in his gross income under section 72 unless the employee has paid income tax for any taxable year beginning before January 1, 1949, with respect to such payment or contribution by the employer for such year and such tax is not credited or refunded to the employee. In the event such tax has been paid and not credited or refunded the amount paid or contributed by the employer for such year shall constitute consideration paid by the employee for the annuity contract in determining the amount of the annuity required to be included in the income of the employee under section 72.

(3) For taxable years beginning before January 1, 1958, the provisions contained in section 403(c) prior to the amendment made thereto by the Tax Reform Act of 1969 were included in section 403(b) of the Internal Revenue Code of 1954. Therefore, the regulations contained in this paragraph shall, for such taxable years, be considered as the regulations under section 403(b) as in effect for such taxable years. For the rules with respect to contributions paid after August 1, 1969, see paragraphs (a), (b), and (c) of this section.

Section 1.403(d)-1 is amended by revising paragraph (a), paragraph (c)(2) and adding paragraph (d) to read as follows:

§ 1.403(d)-1 (Proposed Treasury Decision, published 6-3-71.) **Taxability of employee when rights under contracts purchased by exempt organizations change from forefeitable to nonforfeitable.**

(a) **In general.** If, during a taxable year of an employee beginning after December 31, 1957, the rights of such employee under an annuity contract (other than an annuity contract purchased and held as part of a plan which met at the time of such purchase and continues to meet the requirements of section 404(a)(2) or an annuity contract described in paragraph (d)(2) of this section) purchased for him by an employer which is exempt from tax under section 501(a) or 521(a) change from forefeitable to nonforfeitable rights (except if paragraph (b) of § 1.403(c)-1 applied), then the value of such annuity contract on the date of such change shall, to the extent provided in paragraph (b) of this section, be included in the employee's gross income for such taxable year. For purposes of this section, the value of an annuity contract on the date the employee's rights change from forfeitable to nonforfeitable rights means the cash surrender value of such contract on such date. As to what constitutes nonforfeitable rights of an employee, see § 1.402 (b)-1(d)(2).

Proposed Reg. § 1.403(d)-1

* * * * * * * * * * *

(c) **Partial vesting.** * * *

* * * * * * * * * * *

(2) **Example.** The provisions in subparagraph (1) of this paragraph may be illustrated by the following example:

Example. X Organization purchased an annuity contract for A, one of its employees who reports his income on a calendar year basis. X contributed ⅓ of the amount necessary to purchase the contract before January 1, 1958, and the remaining ⅔ after December 31, 1957. At the time of the contributions, X was an organization exempt from tax under section 501(a) and A's rights under the contract were forfeitable. The annuity contract was not purchased as part of a qualified plan and A made no contributions toward the purchase of the contract. On December 31, 1965, 50 percent of A's interest in the contract changed from a forfeitable to a nonforfeitable interest, and on December 31, 1968, the remaining 50 percent of A's interest in the contract changed to a nonforfeitable interest. The cash surrender value of the contract was $9,900 on December 31, 1965, and $12,000 on December 31, 1968. The amount includible in A's gross income for 1965 and 1968 is computed as follows—

1965

(i) Amount which would have been includible if A's entire interest had changed to a nonforfeitable interest (cash surrender value of contract on Dec. 31, 1965, attributable to contributions made after Dec. 31, 1957) ⅔ x $9,900 .... $6,600

(ii) Percent of A's interest that changed to a nonforfeitable interest on Dec. 31, 1965 .... 50%

(iii) Amount includible in A's gross income for 1965 ((ii) × (i)) $3,300

1968

(iv) Amount which would have been includible if A's entire interest had changed to a nonforfeitable interest (cash surrender value of contract on Dec. 31, 1968, attributable to contributions made after Dec. 31, 1957) ⅔ × $12,000 .... $8,000

(v) Percent of A's interest that changed to a nonforfeitable interest on Dec. 31, 1968 .... 50%

(vi) Amount includible in A's gross income for 1968 ((v) x (iv)) $4,000

If, on December 31, 1965, X is an organization described in section 501(c)(3) and exempt from tax under section 501(a), then only so much of the $3,300 as is not excludable under paragraph (b) of § 1.403(b)-1 is includible in A's gross income for 1965. Similarly, if, on December 31, 1968, X is an organization described in section 501(c)(3) and exempt from tax under section 501(a), then only so much of the $4,000 as is not excludable under paragraph (b) of § 1.403(b)-1 is includible in A's gross income for 1968.

(d) **Effective date.** The provisions of section 403(d), repealed by section 321(d) of the Tax Reform Act of 1969 (83 Stat. 571), applied for taxable years beginning after December 31, 1957, only with respect to premiums paid for an annuity contract—

(1) On or before August 1, 1969, or

(2) After such date, if pursuant to a binding written contract (as defined in paragraph (b)(2) of § 1.83-8) entered into before April 22, 1969, or pursuant to a written plan in which the employee participated on such date and under which the obligation of the employer is essentially the same as under a binding written contract.

For the rules with respect to premiums paid after August 1, 1969, under an annuity contract (other than an annuity contract purchased and held as part of a plan which met at the time of such purchase and continues to meet the requirements of section 404(a)(2) or an annuity contract described in subparagraph (2) of this paragraph), purchased for an employee by an employer which is exempt from tax under section 501(a) or 521(a), see section 403(c) and the regulations thereunder.

Deduction for Employer Contributions

Section 1.404(a)2A is amended by revising the section title and the first sentence of paragraph (a). As amended, §1.404(a)-2A reads as follows:

§1.404(a)-2A (Proposed Treasury Decision, published 2-10-78.) **Information to be furnished by employer; taxable years ending on or after December 31, 1971, and before December 31, 1975.**

(a) In general. For any taxable year ending on or after December 31, 1971, and before December 31, 1975, any employer who maintains a pension, annuity, stock bonus, profit-sharing, or other funded plan of deferred compensation shall file the forms prescribed by this section. * * *

* * * * * * * * * * * *

Section 1.404(a)-9 is amended by revising paragraphs (a) and (d) to read as follows:

§ 1.404(a)-9 (Proposed Treasury Decision, published 5-6-72.) **Contributions of an employer to an employees' profit-sharing or stock bonus trust that meets the requirements of section 401(a); application of section 404(a)(3)(A).**

(a) If contributions are paid by an employer to a profit-sharing or stock bonus trust for employees and the general conditions and limitations applicable to deductions for such contributions are satisfied (see § 1.404(a)-1), the contributions are deductible under section 404(a)(3)(A) if the further conditions provided therein are also satisfied. In the case of an employer who is an electing small business corporation, or a successor of such a corporation, the additional requirement contained in section 1379(a) must also be satisfied. In order to be deductible under the first, second, or third sentence of section 404(a)(3)(A), the contributions must be paid (or deemed to have been paid under section 404(a)(6)) in a taxable year of the employer which ends with or within a taxable year of the trust for which it is exempt under section 501(a) and the trust must not be designed to provide retirement benefits for which the contributions can be determined actuarially. Excess contributions paid in such a taxable year of the employer may be carried over and deducted in a succeeding taxable year of the employer in accordance with the third sentence of section 404(a)(3)(A), whether or not such succeeding taxable year ends with or within a taxable year of the trust for which it is exempt under section 501(a). This section is also applicable to contributions to a foreign situs profit-sharing or stock bonus trust which could qualify for exemption under section 501(a) except that it is not created or organized and maintained in the United States.

* * * * * * * * * * *

(d) In order that the deductions may average 15 percent of compensation otherwise paid or accrued over a period of years, where contributions in some taxable year are less than the primary limitation but contributions in some succeeding taxable year exceed the primary limitation, deductions in each succeeding year are subject to a secondary limitation instead of to the primary limitation. The secondary limitation for any year is equal to the lesser of (1) twice the primary limitation for the year, or (2) any excess of (i) the aggregate of the primary limitations for the year and for all prior years over (ii) the aggregate of the deductions allowed or allowable under the limitations provided in section 404(a)(3)(A) for all prior years. However, see section 1379(c) and § 1.1379-3 for restrictions upon the carryover amount deductible by a corporation from a year with respect to which it or its predecessor was an electing small business corporation. Because contributions paid into a profit-sharing or stock bonus trust are deductible under section 404(a)(3)(A) only if they are paid (or deemed to have been paid under section 404(a)(6)) in a taxable year of the employer which ends with or within a taxable year of the trust for which it is exempt under section 501(a), the secondary limitation described in this paragraph is not applicable with respect to determining amounts deductible for a taxable year of the employer which ends with or within a taxable year of the trust during which it is not exempt under section 501(a), or which ends after the trust has terminated. See paragraph (e) of this section for rules relating to amounts which are deductible in such a taxable year.

* * * * * * * * * * *

Section 1.404(a)-12 is amended to read as follows:

§ 1.404(a)-12 (Proposed Treasury Decision, published 6-3-71.) **Contributions of an employer under a plan that does not meet the requirements of section 401(a); application of section 404(a)(5).**

(a) **In general.** Section 404(a)(5) covers all cases for which deductions are allowable under section 404(a) but not allowable under paragraph (1), (2), (3), (4), or (7) of such section.

(b) **Contributions or payments made or accrued after August 1, 1969**—(1) **In general.** No deduction is allowable under section 404(a)(5) for any contribution paid or accrued after August 1, 1969, by an employer under a stock bonus, pension, profit-sharing, or annuity plan or for any compensation paid or accrued on account of any employee under a plan deferring the receipt of such compensation except in the taxable year in which an amount attributable to such contribution is includible as compensation in the gross income of the employees participating in the plan, and then only to the extent allowable under section 404(a). See § 1.404 (a)-1. A deduction is allowable under section 404(a)(5) even though the employee or his beneficiary excludes any part of a contribution or payment from his gross income under section 101(b) or subchapter N.

(2) **Special rule for unfunded pensions and certain death benefits.** If unfunded pensions are paid directly to former employees, such payments are includible in their gross income when paid, and accordingly, such amounts are deductible under section 404(a)(5) when paid. Similarly, if amounts are paid as a death benefit to the beneficiaries of an employee (for example, by continuing his salary for a reasonable period), and if such amounts meet the requirements of section 162 or 212, such amounts are deductible under section 404(a)(5) in any case when they are not deductible under the other paragraphs of section 404(a).

(3) **Separate accounts for plans with more than one employee.** In the case of a plan under which more than one employee participates no deduction is allowable under section 404(a)(5) with respect to any contribution meeting the requirements of subparagraph (1) of this paragraph unless separate accounts are maintained for each employee. This requirement does not apply to unfunded pensions. In addition, the requirement of separation is deemed satisfied even if separate trusts are not maintained under the plan, but only if the trust instrument provides for the allocation of each contribution made to the trust to each employee participating in the plan. If an amount is contributed during the taxable year to a trust or under a plan where separate accounts are not maintained for each employee, no deduction is allowed for such amount for any taxable year. For the rules with respect to the taxability of an employee when rights under a nonexempt trust change from nonvested to vested, see paragraph (b) of § 1.402(b)-1.

(c) **Contributions paid or accrued on or before August 1, 1969.** No deduction is allowable under section 404(a)(5) for any contribution paid or accrued on or before August 1, 1969, by an employer under a stock bonus, pension, profit-sharing, or annuity plan, or for any compensation paid or accrued on account of any employee under a plan deferring the receipt of such compensation except in the year when paid, and then only to the extent allowable under section 404(a). See § 1.404(a)-1. If payments are made under such a plan and the amounts are not deductible under the other paragraphs of section 404(a), they are deductible under paragraph (5) of such subsection to the extent that the rights of individual employees to, or derived from, such employer's contribution or such compensation are nonforfeitable at the time the contribution or compensation is paid. If unfunded pensions are paid directly to former employees, their rights to such payments are nonforfeitable, and accordingly, such amounts are deductible under section 404(a)(5) when paid. Similarly, if amounts are paid as a death benefit to the beneficiaries of an employee (for example, by continuing his salary for a reasonable period), and if such amounts meet the requirements of section 162 or 212, such amounts are deductible under section 404(a)(5) in any case where they are not deductible under the other paragraphs of section 404(a). As to what constitutes nonforfeitable rights of an employee in other cases, see § 1.402(b)-1(d)(2). If an amount is accrued but not paid during the taxable year, no deduction is allowed for such amount for such year.

§ 1.404(a)-14 (Proposed Treasury Decision, published 5-19-78.) Special rules in connection with the Employee Retirement Income Security Act of 1974.

(a) **Purpose of this section.** This section provides rules for determining the deductible limit under section 404(a)(1)(A) of the Internal Revenue Code of 1954 for defined benefit plans.

(b) **Definitions.** For purposes of this section—

(1) **Section 404(a).** The term "old section 404(a)" means section 404(a) as in effect on September 1, 1974. Any reference to section 404 without the designation "old" is a reference to section 404 as amended by the Employee Retirement Income Security Act of 1974.

(2) **Ten-year amortization base.** The term "10-year amortization base" means either the past service and other supplementary pension and annuity credits described in section 404(a)(1)(A)(iii) or any base established in accordance with paragraph (g) of this section. A plan may have several 10-year amortization bases to reflect different plan amendments, changes in actuarial assumptions, and experience gains and losses of previous years.

(3) **Limit adjustment.** The term "limit adjustment" with respect to any 10-year amortization base is the lesser of—

(i) The level annual amount necessary to amortize the base over 10 years using the valuation rate, or

(ii) The unamortized balance of the base, in each case using absolute values. To compute the level amortization amount, the base may be divided by the present value of an annuity of one dollar, obtained from standard annuity tables on the basis of a given interest rate (the valuation rate) and a known period (the amortization period).

(4) **Absolute value.** The term "absolute value" for any number is the value of that number, treating negative numbers as if they were positive numbers. For example, the absolute value of 5 is 5 and the absolute value of minus 3 is 3. On the other hand, the true value of minus 3 is minus 3. This term is relevant to the computation of the limit adjustment described in paragraph (b)(3) and the remaining amortization period of combined bases described in paragraph (i)(3) of this section.

(5) **Valuation rate.** The term "valuation rate" means the assumed interest rate used to value plan liabilities.

(c) **Use of plan year in determining deductible limit for employer's taxable year.**
Although the deductible limit applies for an employer's taxable year, the deductible limit is determined on the basis of a plan year. If the employer's taxable year coincides with the plan year, the deductible limit for the taxable year is the deductible limit for the plan year that coincides with that year. If the employer's taxable year does not coincide with the plan year, the deductible limit under section 404(a)(1)(A)(i), (ii), or (iii) for a given taxable year of the employer is one of the following alternatives:

(1) The deductible limit determined for the plan year commencing within the taxable year,

(2) The deductible limit determined for the plan year ending within the taxable year, or

(3) A weighted average of alternatives (1) and (2). Such an average may be based, for example, upon the number of months of each plan year falling within the taxable year.

The employer must use the same alternative for each taxable year unless consent to change is obtained from the Commissioner under section 446(e).

(d) **Computation of deductible limit for a plan year; general rules.** The computation

Proposed Reg. § 1.404(a)-14

of the deductible limit for a plan year is based on the funding method, actuarial assumptions, and benefit structure used for purposes of section 412, determined without regard to section 412(g) (relating to the alternative minimum funding standard), for the plan year. In making calculations required by this section which involve amortization, any consistent assumption may be made with regard to the time or times during each year that payments will be made. The method of valuing assets for purposes of section 404 must be the same method of valuing assets used for purposes of section 412. However, for purposes of applying the rules of this section (i.e., the computation of normal cost, unfunded liabilities, and the full finding limitation described in paragraph (k) of this section, where applicable) with respect to a given plan year the following adjustments must be made:

(1) There must be excluded from the total assets of the plan the amount of any plan contribution for a plan year for which the plan was qualified under section 401(a) or 403(a) that has not previously been deducted, even though that amount has been credited to the funding standard account under section 412(b)(3).

(2) There must be included in the total assets of the plan for a plan year the amount of any plan contribution that has been deducted with respect to a prior plan year, even though that amount is considered under section 412 to be contributed in a plan year subsequent to that prior plan year.

(e) **Special computation rules under section 404(a)(1)(A)(i)**—(1) **In general.** For purposes of determining the deductible limit under section 404(a)(1)(A)(i), the deductible limit with respect to a plan year is the sum of—

(i) The amount required to satisfy the minimum funding standard of section 412(a) (determined without regard to section 412(g)) for the plan year and

(ii) An amount equal to the includible employer contributions.

The term "includible employer contributions" means employer contributions which were required by section 412 for the plan year immediately preceding such plan year, and which were not deductible under section 404(a) for the prior taxable year of the employer solely because they were not contributed during the prior taxable year (determined with regard to section 404(a)(6)).

(2) **Rule for an employer using alternative minimum funding standard account and computing its deduction under section 404(a)(1)(A)(i).** This paragraph (e)(2) applies if the minimum funding requirements for the plan are determined under the alternative minimum funding standard described in section 412(g) for both the current plan year and the immediately preceding plan year. In that case, the deductible limit under section 404(a)(1)(A)(i) (regarding the minimum funding requirement of section 412) for the current year is the sum of the amount determined under the rules of paragraph (e)(1) of this section,

(i) Plus the charge under section 412(b)(2)(D), and

(ii) Less the credit under section 412(b)(3)(D),

that would be required if in the current plan year the use of the alternative method were discontinued.

(f) **Computation of deductible limit under section 404(a)(1)(A)(ii) and (iii); adjustments for 10-year amortization bases**—(1) **In general.** Subject to the full funding limitation described in paragraph (k) of this section, the deductible limit under section 404(a)(1)(A)(ii) or (iii) is the normal cost of the plan (determined in accordance with paragraph (d) of this section)—

(i) Decreased by the limit adjustments of any unamortized 10-year amortization bases required by paragraph (g) of this section that are due to a net experience gain, or to either a change in actuarial assumptions or a plan amendment which decreases the accrued liability, and

(ii) Increased by the limit adjustments of any unamortized 10-year amortization bases required by paragraph (g) or (j) of this section that are due to a net experience loss, or to either a change in actuarial assumptions or a plan amendment which increases the accrued liability.

(2) **Special limit under section 404(a)(1)(A)(ii).** If the deduction for the plan year is determined solely on the basis of section 404(a)(1)(A)(ii) (that is, without regard to

clauses (i) or (iii)), the special limitation contained in section 404(a)(1)(A)(ii), regarding the unfunded cost with respect to any three individuals, applies notwithstanding the rules contained in paragraph (f)(1) of this section.

(g) **Establishment of a 10-year amortization base**—(1) **Experience gains and losses.** In the case of a plan valued by the use of a funding method which is an immediate gain type of funding method (and therefore separately amortizes rather than includes experience gains and losses as a part of the normal cost of the plan), a 10-year amortization base must be established in any plan year equal to the net experience gain or loss required under section 412 to be determined with respect to that plan year. The base is to be maintained in accordance with paragraph (h) of this section. Such a base must not be established if the deductible limit is determined by use of a funding method which is a spread gain type of funding method (under which experience gains and losses are spread over future periods as a part of the plan's normal cost). Examples of the immediate gain type of funding method are the unit credit method, entry age normal cost method, and the individual level premium cost method. Examples of the spread gain type of funding method are the aggregate cost method, frozen initial liability cost method, and the attained age normal cost method.

(2) **Change in actuarial assumptions.** If the creation of an amortizable base is required under the rules of section 412(b)(2)(B)(v) or (3)(B)(iii) (as applied to the funding method used by the plan), a 10-year amortization base must be established at the time of a change in actuarial assumptions used to value plan liabilities. The amount of the base is the difference between the accrued liability calculated on the basis of the new assumptions and the accrued liability calculated on the basis of the old assumptions. Both computations of accrued liability are made as of the date of the change in assumptions. In the case of a plan using a funding method of the spread gain type (which type does not directly determine the accrued liability of the plan) the accrued liability determinations must be made on the basis of another funding method (of the immediate gain type) that does determine the accrued liability. In that case, the method chosen to determine the accrued liability of the plan upon the change of assumptions must not be different from the method used to establish any other 10-year amortization base maintained by the plan (if any). The base must be maintained in accordance with paragraph (h) of this section.

(3) **Past service or supplemental credits.** A 10-year base must be established when a plan is established or amended, if the creation of an amortizable base is required under the rules of section 412(b)(2)(B)(ii) or (iii), or (b)(3)(B)(i) (as applied to the funding method used by the plan. The amount of the base is the accrued liability arising from, or the decrease in accrued liability resulting from, the establishment or amendment of the plan. The base must be maintained in accordance with paragraph (h) of this section.

(h) **Maintenance of 10-year amortization base**—(1) **In general.** Each time a 10-year amortization base is established, whether by plan amendment, by change in actuarial assumptions, or by experience gains and losses, the base must, except as provided in paragraph (i) of this section, be separately maintained in order to determine when the unamortized amount of the base is zero. In the case of an immediate gain method described in paragraph (g)(1) of this section, the sum of the unamortized balances of all of the 10-year bases must equal the plan's unfunded accrued liability with the adjustment for carryovers described in paragraph (d)(1) and (2) of this section, if applicable. When the unamortized amount of a base is zero, the deductible limit is no longer adjusted to reflect the amortization of the base. Except as provided in paragraph (j) of this section (relating to the initial 10-year base for a plan in existence before the effective date of section 404(a)), the unamortized amount of the base for the plan year for which the base is established is the amount of the base. For any succeeding plan year, the unamortized amount of the base is equal to—

(i) The unamortized amount of the base as of the beginning of that plan year, plus
(ii) Interest at the valuation rate, less
(iii) The contribution made with respect to the base (adjusted for interest at the valuation rate) for that plan year.

Proposed Reg. §1.404(a)-14

(2) **Contribution with respect to each base.** The contribution made with respect to each base is equal to the product of—
 (i) The total contribution made with respect to all bases, and
 (ii) The ratio of the limit adjustment for the base to the sum (using true rather than absolute values) of the limit adjustments with respect to all bases.

The contribution made for all bases is equal to the difference between the total currently deductible contribution (including carryovers described in section 404(a)(1)(D) to the extent they are currently deductible) and the normal cost (treating a negative difference as a negative contribution). The amount of a contribution which is in excess of the total currently deductible contributions (and which thus creates an additional carryover described in section 404(a)(1)(D)) is not treated as a part of the total contribution with respect to the bases until the carryover becomes deductible under section 404(a)(1)(D). The failure to make a contribution at least equal to the sum of the normal cost plus interest on the unamortized amounts does not create a new base; instead it results in an increase in the unamortized amount of each base and consequently extends the time before the base is fully amortized. The limit adjustment for any base is not increased (in absolute terms) even if the unamortized amount computed under this subparagraph exceeds the initial 10-year amortization base. Thus, if the total unamortized amount of the plan's bases at the beginning of the plan year is $100,000 (which is also the unfunded liability of the plan), and a required $50,000 normal cost contribution is not made for the plan year, the following effects occur. The total unamortized balance of the plan's bases increases by the $50,000 normal cost for the year, plus interest on the $100,000 balance of the bases; and, because of that increase, it will take a longer period to amortize the remaining balance of the bases. (The annual amortization amount does not change).

(3) **Required adjustment to 10-year base limit adjustment if valuation rate changed.** If there is a change in the valuation rate, the limit adjustment for all unamortized 10-year amortization bases must be changed, in addition to establishing a new base as provided in paragraph (g)(2) of this section. The new limit adjustment for any base is the level amount necessary to amortize the base over the remaining amortization period using the new valuation rate. The remaining amortization period of the base is the number of years at the end of which the unamortized amount of the base would be zero if the contribution made with respect to that base equaled the limit adjustment each year. This calculation of the remaining period is made on the basis of the valuation rate used before the change. Both the remaining amortization period and the revised limit adjustment may be determined through the use of standard annuity tables. The remaining period may be computed in terms of fractional years, or it may be rounded off to a whole number. The previously amortized amount and the remaining amortization period with respect to such base shall be unchanged by any change in the valuation rate.

(i) **Combining bases—(1) General method.** For purposes of section 404 only, and not for purposes of section 412, different 10-year amortization bases may be combined into a single 10-year amortization base if such single base satisfies all of the requirements of paragraph (i)(2), (3), and (4) of this section at the time of the combining of the different bases.

(2) **Unamortized amount.** The unamortized amount of the single base equals the sum of the unamortized amount of the bases being combined (treating negative bases as having negative unamortized amounts).

(3) **Remaining amortization period.** The remaining amortization period of the single base is equal to (i) the sum of the separate products of (A) the unamortized amount of each of the bases (using absolute values) and (B) its remaining amortization period, divided by (ii) the sum of the unamortized amounts of each of the bases (using absolute values). For purposes of this paragraph (i)(3), the remaining amortization period of each base being combined is that number of years at the end of which the unamortized amount of the base would be zero if the contribution made with respect to that base equaled the limit adjustment of that base in each year. This number may be determined through the use of standard annuity tables. The remaining amortization period described

in this paragraph may be computed in terms of fractional years, or it may be rounded off to a whole number.

(4) **Limit adjustment.** The limit adjustment for the single base is the level amount necessary to amortize the combined base over the remaining amortization period described in paragraph (i)(3) of this section, using the valuation rate. This amount may be determined through the use of standard annuity tables.

(5) **Fresh start alternative.** In lieu of combining different 10-year amortization bases, a plan may replace all existing bases with one new 10-year amortization base equal to the unfunded accrued liability of the plan as of the time the new base is being established. This unfunded liability must be determined in accordance with the general rules of paragraph (d) of this section. The unamortized amount of the base and the limit adjustment for the base will be determined as though the base were newly established.

(j) **Initial 10-year amortization base for existing plan—(1) In general.** In the case of a plan in existence before the effective date of section 404(a), the 10-year amortization base on the effective date of section 404(a) is the sum of all 10 percent bases existing immediately before section 404(a) became effective for the plan, determined under the rules of old section 404(a).

(2) **Limit adjustment.** The limit adjustment for the initial base is the lesser of the unamortized amount of such base or the sum of the amounts determined under paragraph (b)(3) of this section using the original balances of the remaining bases (under old section 404(a) rules) as the amount to be amortized.

(3) **Unamortized amount.** The employer may choose either to establish a single initial base reflecting both all prior 10-percent bases and the experience gain or loss for the immediately preceding actuarial period, or to establish a separate base for the prior 10-percent bases and another for the experience gain or loss for the immediately preceding period. If the initial 10-year amortization base reflects the net experience gain or loss from the immediately preceding actuarial period, the unamortized amount of the initial base shall equal the total unfunded accrued liability on the effective date of section 404(a) determined in accordance with the general rules of paragraph (d) of this section. If, however, a separate base will be used to reflect that gain or loss, the unamortized amount of the initial base shall equal such unfunded accrued liability on the effective date of section 404(a), reduced by the net experience loss or increased by the net experience gain for the immediately preceding actuarial period. In this case, a separate 10-year amortization base must be established on the effective date equal to the net experience gain or loss. Thus, if the effective date unfunded accrued plan liability is $100,000 and an experience loss of $15,000 is recognized on that date, and if the loss is to be treated as a separate base, the unamortized balances of the two bases would be $85,000 and $15,000. If the unfunded liability were the same $100,000, but a gain of $15,000 instead of a loss were recognized on that date, the unamortized balances of the two bases would be $115,000 and a credit base of $15,000. In both cases, if only one 10-year base is to be established on the effective date, its unamortized balance would be $100,000 (the unfunded accrued liability of the plan). See paragraph (d) for rules for determining the unfunded accrued liability of the plan.

(k) . **Effect of full funding limit on 10-year-amortization bases.** The amount deductible under section 404(a)(1)(A)(i), (ii), or (iii) for a plan year may not exceed the full funding limitation for that year. See paragraph (d) of this section for rules to be used in the computation of the full funding limitation. If the total contribution for a plan year equals or exceeds the full funding limitation for the year, all 10-year amortization bases maintained by the plan will be considered fully amortized, and the deductible limit for subsequent plan years will not be adjusted to reflect the amortization of these bases.

(l) **Transitional rule.** For taxable years of employers commencing before January 1, 1979, a contribution will be deductible under section 404(a)(1)(A) if the computation of the deductible limit is based upon a reasonable interpretation of section 404(a)(1)(A),

Proposed Reg. § 1.404(a)-14

when considered in conjunction with prior published positions of the Internal Revenue Service under old section 404(a). A computation of the deductible limit may satisfy the preceding sentence even if it does not satisfy the rules contained in paragraphs (c) through (i) of this section. For taxable years of employers commencing on or after January 1, 1979, the computation of the deductible limit must reflect 10-year amortization bases retroactively established as of the first day to which this section applies and maintained in accordance with this section.

(m) **Examples.** The provisions of this section may be illustrated by the following examples:

Example (1). Initial 10-year bases. An employer whose taxable year is the calendar year maintains a calendar year plan, which was in existence on January 1, 1974. The employer computes his minimum funding requirements for the plan and his deductible limit for 1976 on the entry age normal funding method and a 5 percent interest assumption is employed. The plan is valued annually as of the first day of each plan year. The actuarial valuation produced the following data (as of January 1, 1976):

Normal Cost	$ 60,000
Accrued Liability	1,000,000
Assets	420,000
Actual Unfunded Liability	580,000
Expected Unfunded Liability	600,000
Experience Gain Recognized ($600,000 less $580,000)	20,000
10% base if section 404 were not amended by ERISA (original balance)	800,000

In computing the initial 10-year amortization bases under paragraph (j)(3) of this section, the employer chooses to treat the experience gain computed on January 1, 1976, as a separate base. Thus the plan has two initial 10-year amortization bases as of January 1, 1976. Their original balances are $800,000 (the prior 10 percent base arising from the original past service liability), and $20,000 (due to the experience gain). The limit adjustments with respect to such bases are $98,670 and -$2,467, respectively (10-year amortization of each base at 5 percent interest, assuming payments made at the beginning of each year). The unamortized amounts of such bases as determined under paragraph (j)(3) of this section are $600,000 ($580,000 unfunded liability plus the $20,000 gain determined on January 1, 1976) and -$20,000, respectively. The deductible limit for 1976 is $156,203 ($60,000 normal cost plus $98,670, the limit adjustment with respect to the $800,000 base, minus $2,467, the limit adjustment with respect to the $20,000 "negative" balance base).

Example (2). Allocation of contribution. The employer in example (1) contributed $110,000 as of January 1, 1976, and claimed $110,000 as a deduction for the 1976 taxable year. The total contribution made with respect to all bases is $50,000 ($110,000 total deductible contribution minus $60,000 normal cost). The employer did not choose to combine the 10-year amortization bases, and maintained the bases as follows through the end of 1976:

(1) Ten-Year Amortization Base	(2) Limit Adjustment With Respect to Base	(3) Contribution with Respect to Base $\frac{(2)}{\text{Total (2)}} \times \text{Total (3)}$	(4) Unamortized Amount Beginning of 1976	(5) Unamortized Amount End of 1976 $1.05((4)-(3))$
$800,000	$98,670	$51,282	$600,000	$576,154
-20,000	-2,467	-1,282	-20,000	-19,654
	$96,203	$50,000		

Example (3). Combining bases. The facts are the same as example (2) except the employer decided to combine the 10-year amortization bases as of January 1, 1976, in accordance with paragraph (i) of this section. The deductible limit for the combined base is determined on the basis of the remaining unamortized balance and the remaining amortization period of the single combined base. The remaining amortization period of the combined single base is derived from the remaining periods of the separate bases which are being combined. The computations are as follows:

(a) The remaining amortization period of the $800,000 10-year amortization base is determined as follows:
   (1) Unamortized amount of base beginning of 1976.................... $600,000
   (2) Limit adjustment with respect to base............................ $ 98,670
   (3) Present value of each $1 of the limit adjustment [(a)(1)divided by(a)(2)] $ 6.08
   (4) Remaining amortization period (equal to period certain of the amount in (a)(3) obtained from standard annuity tables reflecting first-of-year payments)... 7.0 years
(b) The remaining amortization period of the $20,000 base is: 10 years
(c) The remaining amortization period of the single base is:

$$\frac{\$600{,}000 \times 7.0 + \$20{,}000 \times 10}{\$600{,}000 + \$20{,}000} = 7.1 \text{ years}$$

(d) The limit adjustment for the combined base is computed as follows:
   (1) Present value of annuity certain for 7.1 years (using linear interpolation)... $6.15
   (2) Unamortized amount of single base $580,000
   (3) Limit adjustment with respect to single base [(d)(2) divided by (d)(1)] . $ 94,309

If the 10-year amortization bases are combined, the maximum deductible limit will be $154,309 ($60,000 normal cost + $94,309 limit adjustment with respect to the single 10-year amortization base).

(n) **Effective date.** This section applies to any taxable year of an employer to which section 404(a) applies. In the case of a plan which was in existence on January 1, 1974, section 404(a) generally applies for contributions on account of taxable years of an employer ending with or within plan years beginning after December 31, 1975. In the case of a plan not in existence on January 1, 1974, section 404(a) generally applies for contributions on account of taxable years of an employer ending with or within plan years beginning after September 2, 1974. See §1.410(a)-2(c) for rules concerning the time of plan existence. See also §1.410(a)-2(d), which provides that a plan in existence on January 1, 1974, may elect to have certain provisions, including the amendments to section 404(a) contained in section 1013 of the Employee Retirement Income Security Act of 1974, apply to a plan year beginning after September 2, 1974, and before the otherwise applicable effective date contained in that section.

Section 1.404(e)-1 is amended by adding the following new paragraph at the end thereof:

§ 1.404(e)-1 (Proposed Treasury Decision, published 4-21-75) **Contributions on behalf of a self-employed individual to or under a pension, annuity, or profit-sharing plan meeting the requirements of section 401(a); application of section 404(a)(8), (9), and (10) and section 404(e) and (f).**

* * * * * * * * * * *

(i) Years to which this section applies. This section applies to taxable years of employers beginning before January 1, 1974. For taxable years beginning after December 31, 1973, see § 1.404(e)-1A.

The following new section is added immediately after § 1.404(e)-1:

§ 1.404(e)-1A (Proposed Treasury Decision, published 4-21-75; 5-26-78.) Contributions on behalf of a self-employed individual to or under a qualified pension, annuity, or profit-sharing plan.

(a) **In general.** This section provides rules relating to employer contributions to qualified plans on behalf of self-employed individuals described in subsections (a)(8) and (9), (e), and (f) of section 404. Unless otherwise specifically provided, this section applies to taxable years of an employer beginning after

Proposed Reg. § 1.404(e)-1A

December 31, 1973. See Section 1.404(e)-1 for rules relating to plans for self-employed individuals for taxable years beginning before January 1, 1974. Paragraph (b) of this section provides general rules of deductibility, paragraph (c) provides rules relating to defined contribution plans, paragraph (d) provides rules relating to defined benefit plans, paragraph (e) provides rules relating to combinations of plans, paragraph (f) provides rules for partnerships, paragraph (g) provides rules for insurance, paragraph (h) provides rules for loans, and paragraph (i) provides definitions.

(b) **Determination of the amount deductible.** (1) If a plan covers employees, some of whom are self-employed individuals, the determination of the amount deductible is made on the basis of independent consideration of the common-law employees and of the self-employed individuals. See subparagraphs (2) and (3) of this paragraph. For purposes of determining the amount deductible with respect to contributions on behalf of a self-employed individual, such contributions shall be considered to satisfy the conditions of section 162 (relating to trade or business expenses) or 212 (relating to expenses for the production of income), but only to the extent that such contributions do not exceed the earned income of such individual derived from the trade or business with respect to which the plan is established. However, the portion of such contribution, if any, attributable to the purchase of life, accident, health, or other insurance protection shall be considered payment of a personal expense which does not satisfy the requirements of section 162 or 212. See paragraph (g) of this section.

(2) (i) If contributions are made on behalf of employees, some of whom are self-employed individuals, to a defined contribution plan described in section 414(i) and included in section 404(a)(1), (2), or (3), the amount deductible with respect to contributions on behalf of the common-law employees covered under the plan shall be determined as if such employees were the only employees for whom contributions and benefits are provided under the plan. Accordingly, for purposes of such determination, the percentage of compensation limitations of section 404(a) (3) and (7) are applicable only with respect to the compensation otherwise paid or accrued during the taxable year by the employer with respect to the common-law employees. Similarly, the costs referred to in section 404(a)(1)(A) and (B) shall be the costs of funding the benefits of the common-law employees. Also, the provisions of section 404(a)(1)(D), (3), and (7), relating to certain carryover deductions, shall be applicable only to amounts contributed, or to the amounts deductible on behalf of such employees.

(ii) [Reserved]

(3) (i) If contributions are made on behalf of individuals, some or all of whom are self-employed individuals, to a defined contribution plan described in section 414(i) and included in section 404(a)(1), (2), or (3), the amount deductible in any taxable year with respect to contributions on behalf of such individuals shall be determined as follows:

(A) The provisions of section 404(a)(1), (2), (3), and (7) shall be applied as if such individuals were the only participants for whom contributions and benefits are provided under the plan. Thus, the costs referred to in such provisions shall be the costs of funding the benefits of the self-employed individuals. If such costs are less than an amount equal to the amount determined under paragraph (c) of this section, the maximum amount deductible with respect to such individuals shall be the cost of their benefits.

(B) The provisions of section 404(a)(1)(D), the third sentence of section 404(a)(3)(A), and the second sentence of section 404(a)(7), relating to certain carryover deductions are applicable to contributions on behalf of self-employed individuals made in taxable years of an employer beginning after December 31, 1975.

(C) For any employer taxable year in applying the 15 percent limit on deductible contributions set forth in section 404(a)(3) and the 25 percent limit in section 404(a)(7) for any taxable year of the employer, the amount deductible under section 404(e)(4) and paragraph (c)(4) of this section (relating to the minimum deduction of $750 or 100 percent of earned income) shall be substituted for such limits with respect to the self-employed individuals on whose behalf contributions are deductible under section 404(e)(4) for the taxable year of the employer. However, see section 415 for rules applicable to years beginning after December 31, 1975. For example, if a defined contribution plan using a trust permitted an employer contribution to be made for any participant in the plan for a year beginning after December 31, 1975, in excess of the amount described in section 415(c)(1)(B), the trust established under such plan would not constitute a qualified trust under section 401(a), notwithstanding the provisions of section 404(e)(4). The special rule in the second sentence of paragraph (3)(A) of section 404(a) is not applicable in determining the amounts deductible on behalf of self-employed individuals.

(ii) [Reserved]

(c) **Defined contributions plans.** (1) Under section 404(e)(1) in the case of a defined contribution plan, as defined in section 414(i), the amount deductible for the taxable year of the employer with respect to contributions on behalf of a self-employed individual shall not exceed the lesser of $7,500 or 15 percent of the earned income derived by such individual for such taxable year from the trade or business with respect to which the plan is established.

(2) Under section 404(e)(2)(A) if a self-employed individual receives in any taxable year earned income with respect to which deductions are allowable to two or more employers under two or more defined contribution plans the aggregate amounts deductible shall not exceed the lesser of $7,500 or 15 percent of such earned income. This limitation does not apply to contributions made under a plan on behalf of an employee who is not self-employed in the trade or business with respect to which the plan is established.

(3) Under section 404(e)(2)(B) in any case in which the applicable limitation of subparagraph (2) of this paragraph reduces the amount otherwise deductible with respect to contributions on behalf of any employee within the meaning of section 401(c)(1), the amount deductible by each employer for such employee shall be that amount which bears the same ratio to the aggregate amount deductible for such employee with respect to all trades or businesses (as determined in subparagraph (1) of this paragraph) as his earned income derived from the employer bears to the aggregate of his earned income derived from all of the trades or businesses with respect to which plans are established.

(4) Under section 404(e)(4), notwithstanding the provisions of subparagraphs (1) and (2) of this paragraph, the limitations on the amount deductible for the taxable year of the employer with respect to contributions on behalf of a self-employed individual shall not be less than the lesser of $750 or 100 percent of the earned income derived by such individual for such taxable year from the trade or business with respect to which the plan is established. If such individual receives in any taxable year earned income with respect to which deductions are allowable to two or more employers, 100 percent of such earned income shall be taken into account for purposes of the limitations determined under this subparagraph. See, however, the special rules provided by paragraph (b)(3)(i)(C) of this section.

(d) **Defined benefit plans.** In the case of a defined benefit plan, as defined in section 401(j), the special limitations provided by section 404(e) and paragraph (c) of this section do not apply. See section 401(j) for requirements applicable to defined benefit plans.

(e) **Combination of plans.** For special rules, if a self-employed individual in any taxable year is a participant in both a defined benefit plan and a defined contribution plan, see §1.401(j)-2(d).

(f) **Partner's distributive share of contributions and deductions.** (1) For purposes of sections 702(a)(8) and 704 in the case of a defined contribution plan, a partner's distributive share of contributions on behalf of self-employed individuals under such a plan is the contribution made on his behalf, and his distributive share of deductions allowed the partnership under section 404 for contributions on behalf of a self-employed individual is that portion of the deduction which is attributable to contributions made on his behalf under the plan. The contribution on behalf of a partner and the deduction with respect thereto must be accounted for separately by such partner, for his taxable year with or within which the partnership's taxable year ends, as an item described in section 702(a)(8).

Proposed Reg. §1.404(e)-1A

(2) In the case of a defined benefit plan, a partner's distributive share of contributions on behalf of self-employed individuals and his distributive share of deductions allowed the partnership under section 404 for such contributions is determined in the same manner as his distributive share of partnership taxable income. See section 704, relating to the determination of the distributive share and the regulations thereunder.

(g) **Contributions allocable to insurance protection.** Under section 404(e)(3), for purposes of determining the amount deductible with respect to contributions on behalf of a self-employed individual, amounts allocable to the purchase of life, accident, health, or other insurance protection shall not be taken into account. Such amounts are neither deductible nor considered as contributions for purposes of determining the maximum amount of contributions that may be made on behalf of an owner-employee. The amount of a contribution allocable to insurance shall be an amount equal to a reasonable net premium cost, as determined by the Commissioner, for such amount of insurance for the appropriate period. See paragraph (b)(5) of § 1.72-16.

(h) **Rules applicable to loans.** Under section 404(f), for purposes of section 404, any amount paid, directly or indirectly, by an owner-employee in repayment of any loan which under section 72(m)(4)(B) was treated as an amount received from a qualified trust or plan shall be treated as a contribution to such trust or under such plan on behalf of such owner-employee.

(i) Definitions. Under section 401(a)(8), for purposes of section 404 and the regulations thereunder —

(1) The term "employee" includes an employee as defined in section 401(c)(1) and paragraph (b) of § 1.401(e)-1, and the term "employer" means the person treated as the employer of such individual under section 401(c)(4);

(2) The term "owner-employee" means an owner-employee as defined in section 401(c)(3) and paragraph (d) of § 1.401(e)-1;

(3) The term "earned income" means earned income as defined in section 401(c)(2) and paragraph (c) of § 1.401(e)-1; and

(4) The term "compensation" when used with respect to an individual who is an employee described in subparagraph (1) of this paragraph shall be considered to be a reference to the earned income of such individual derived from the trade or business with respect to which the plan is established.

Qualified Bond Purchase Plans

Section 1.405-3 is amended by revising paragraph (a)(1) to read as follows:

§ 1.405-3 (Proposed Treasury Decision, published 5-6-72.) **Taxation of retirement bonds.**

(a) **In general.** (1) As in the case of employer contributions under a qualified pension, annuity, profit-sharing, or stock bonus plan, employer contributions on behalf of his common-law employees under a qualified bond purchase plan are not includible in the gross income of the employees when made (except to the extent includible in the gross income of a shareholder-employee of an electing small business corporation in the year paid under section 1379(b)), and employer contributions on behalf of self-employed individuals are deductible as provided in section 405(c) and § 1.405-2. Further, an employee or his beneficiary does not realize gross income upon the receipt of a retirement bond pursuant to a qualified bond purchase plan or from a trust described in section 401(a) which is exempt from tax under section 501(a). Upon redemption of such a bond, ordinary income will be realized to the extent the proceeds thereof exceed the basis (determined in accordance with paragraph (b) of this section) of the bond. The proceeds of a retirement bond are not entitled to the special tax treatment of section 72(n) and § 1.72-18.

* * * * * * * * * * * *

Paragraph (a)(1) of § 1.405-3 is amended to read as follows:

§ 1.405-3 (Proposed Treasury Decision, published 12-6-72.) **Taxation of retirement bonds.**

(a) **In general.** (1) As in the case of employer contributions under a qualified pension, annuity, profit-sharing, or stock bonus plan, employer contributions on behalf of his common-law employees under a qualified bond purchase plan are not includible in the gross income of the employees when made (except to the extent includible in the gross income of a shareholder-employee of an electing small business corporation in the year paid under section 1379(b)), and employer contributions on behalf of self-employed individuals are deductible as provided in section 405(c) and § 1.405-2. Whether a contribution under a qualified bond purchase plan is made by the employer or the employee must be determined on the basis of the particular facts and circumstances of the individual case. An amount contributed under a qualified bond purchase plan will, except as otherwise provided in this subdivision, be considered to have been contributed by the employee if at his individual option such amount was so contributed in return for a reduction in his basic or regular compensation or in lieu of an increase in such compensation. The preceding sentence shall not apply to an amount contributed under a qualified bond purchase plan either (a) in a taxable year of the employee ending prior to January 1, 1972, or (b) at any time prior to December 6, 1972, where the employee has relied upon a ruling by the Commissioner to him or his employer that such amount will be treated as the contribution of the employer. Further, an employee or his beneficiary does not realize gross income upon the receipt of a retirement bond pursuant to a qualified bond purchase plan or from a trust described in section 401(a) which is exempt from tax under section 501(a). Upon redemption of such a bond, ordinary income will be realized to the extent the proceeds thereof exceed the basis (determined in accordance with paragraph (b) of this section) of the bond. The proceeds of a retirement bond are not entitled to the special tax treatment of section 72(n) and § 1.72-18.

* * * * * * * * * * * * * * * * * *

Subparagraph (4) of § 1.405-3(a) is revised to read as follows:

§ 1.405-3 (Proposed Treasury Decision, published 4-30-75.) **Taxation of retirement bonds.**

(a) **In general.** * * *

(4) The provisions of section 402(a)(2) and (e) are not applicable to a retirement bond. In general, section 402(a)(2) provides for capital gains treatment of a portion of a lump sum distribution as defined in section 402(e)(4)(A) and section 402(e) provides a special 10-year averaging of the ordinary income portion of such a lump sum distribution. The proceeds of a retirement bond received upon redemption will not be entitled to such capital gains treatment or 10-year averaging even though the bond is received as part of, or as the entire, balance to the credit of the employee. Nor will such a bond be taken into consideration in determining the balance to the credit of the employee. Thus, a distribution by a qualified trust may constitute a lump sum distribution for purposes of section 402(a)(2) and (e) even though the trust retains retirement bonds registered in the name of the employee.

* * * * * * * * * * * * * * * * * *

Individual Retirement Accounts and Annuities

Immediately after § 1.405-3 there are added the following new sections:

§1.408-1 (Proposed Treasury Decision, published 2-21-75. **General Rules.**

(a) **In general.** Section 408 perscribes rules relating to the individual retirement account and the individual retirement annuity. If the individual retirement account or individual retirement annuity satisfies the requirements of §§ 1.408-2 or 1.408-3, as the case may be, the following rules shall apply.

Proposed Reg. § 1.408-1

(1) **Exemption from tax.** The individual retirement account or individual retirement annuity is exempt from all taxes under subtitle A of the Code other than the taxes imposed under section 511, relating to imposition of tax on unrelated business income of charitable, etc., organizations. If (i) the individual on whose behalf an account is established or his beneficiary engages in any transaction prohibited by section 4975, or (ii) the owner of an individual retirement annuity borrows any money under or by use of such contract, such account or annuity ceases to be an individual retirement account or an individual retirement annuity.

(2) **Distributions.** The distributions received from an individual retirement account or individual retirement annuity are includible in income in accordance with the requirements of paragraph (b) of this section.

(3) **Sanctions.** If the individual retirement account or individual retirement annuity makes premature distributions (i.e., distributions or payments to the individual before he has attained age 59½ unless he has become disabled within the meaning of section 72(m)(7)) to the individual on whose behalf the account is established or who is the owner of the annuity, the individual will be subject to an additional tax (see paragraph (c) of this section). If an individual retirement account or individual retirement annuity is disqualified within the meaning of section 408(e)(2) and such individual has not attained age 59½ or become disabled (within the meaning of section 72(m)(7)) before the taxable year in which the account was disqualified, the individual on whose behalf the account is established or who is the owner of the annuity will be subject to an additional tax (see paragraph (c) of this section). If an individual retirement account or individual retirement annuity accepts and retains, beyond the time permitted for withdrawal, excess contributions, the individual on whose behalf the account is established or who is the owner of the annuity will be subject to the excise tax imposed by section 4973. If an individual retirement account or individual retirement annuity fails to distribute the minimum amount required to be distributed, the individual on whose behalf the account is established or who is the owner of the annuity, or the beneficiary of such individual, will be subject to the excise tax imposed by section 4974. If any person, described in section 4975(e)(2), other than the individual on whose behalf the account is established or his beneficiary engages, with respect to such account, in any transaction prohibited by section 4975 such person shall be subject to the excise taxes imposed by section 4975.

(4) **Reports.** The trustee of an individual retirement account or the issuer of an individual retirement annuity shall submit to the Commissioner and the individual for whose benefit the account is maintained or in whose name the annuity is purchased the reports, described in paragraph (d) of this section, regarding contributions to and distributions from the account or annuity.

(5) **Limitation on contributions and benefits.** An individual retirement account or individual retirement annuity is subject to the limitation on contributions and benefits imposed by section 415 for years beginning after December 31, 1975.

(b) **Treatment of distributions—(1) General rule.** Except as otherwise provided in this paragraph, any amount paid or distributed from an individual retirement account or individual retirement annuity shall be included in the gross income of the payee or distributee for the taxable year in which the payment or distribution is received. The basis (or investment in the contract) of any person in such an account or annuity is zero. For purposes of this section, an assignment of an individual's rights under an individual retirement account or an individual retirement annuity shall, except as provided in paragraph (f) of this section (relating to transfer incident to divorce), be deemed a distribution from such account or annuity of the amount assigned.

(2) **Rollover contribution.** (i) Except as limited by subdivision (iii) of this subparagraph, subparagraph (1) of this paragraph shall not apply to any amount paid or distributed from an individual retirement account or individual retirement annuity to the individual for whose benefit the account was established or who is the owner of the annuity if the entire amount received (including the same amount of money and any other property) is paid into an account, annuity (other than an endowment contract), or bond (described in section 409) (created for the benefit of such individual) not later than the 60th day after the day on which he receives the payment or distribution.

(ii) Subparagraph (1) of this paragraph shall not apply to any amount paid or distributed from an individual retirement account or individual retirement annuity to the individual for whose benefit the account was established or who is the owner of the annuity if—

(A) No amount in the account or no part of the value of the annuity is attributable to any source other than a rollover contribution (see section 402(a)(5) and § 1.402(a)-3) from an employees' trust described in section 401(a) which is exempt from tax under section 501(a) or a rollover contribution (see section 403(a)(4) and § 1.403(a)-3 from an annuity plan described in section 403(a) and the earnings on such sums, and

(B) The entire amount received (including the same amount of money and any other property) represents the entire amount in the account and is paid into another such trust or plan (for the benefit of such individual) not later than the 60th day after the day on which he receives the payment or distribution.

This subdivision shall not apply if any portion of the rollover contributions described in (A) of this subdivision is attributable to an employees' trust forming part of a plan or an annuity plan under which the individual was an employee within the meaning of section 401(c)(1) at the time contributions were made on his behalf under the plan.

(iii) Subdivision (i) of this subparagraph does not apply to any amount received by an individual from an account, annuity or retirement bond if at any time during the 3-year period ending on the day of receipt, the individual received any other amount from an account, annuity or retirement bond which was not includible in his gross income because of the application of this subparagraph.

(iv) An amount may be distributed to an individual on whose behalf the account is established and who has not attained age 59½ or who is not disabled within the meaning of section 72(m)(7) and paragraph (f) of § 1.72-17 only if the trustee of the account receives from such individual a statement signed by such individual indicating whether the amount distributed is to be a rollover contribution within the meaning of subdivisions (i), (ii), and (iii) of this subparagraph.

(3) **Excess contributions.** (i) Subparagraph (1) of this paragraph does not apply to the distribution of any contribution paid during a taxable year to an account or annuity to the extent the contribution exceeds the amount allowable as a deduction under section 219 if—

(A) The distribution is received on or before the day prescribed by law (including extensions) for filing the individual's return for such taxable year;

(B) No deduction is allowed under section 219 with respect to the excess contribution; and

Proposed Reg. §1.408-1

(C) The distribution is accompanied by the amount of net income attributable to the excess contribution as of the date of the distribution.
The amount of net income described in the preceding sentence is includible in the gross income of the individual for the taxable year in which it is received. Thus the amount of net income distributed may be subject to the tax imposed by section 408(f)(1).

(ii)(A) For purposes of subdivision (i)(C) of this subparagraph, the amount of net income attributable to the excess contributions is an amount equal to the amount which bears the same ratio to the net income earned by the account during the computation period as the excess contribution bears to the sum of the balance of the account as of the first day of the taxable year in which the excess contribution is made and the total contribution made for such taxable year. For purposes of this subparagraph, the term "computation period" means the period beginning on the first day of the taxable year in which the excess contribution is made and ending on the date of the distribution from the account.

(B) For purposes of subdivision (i) of this subparagraph, the net income earned by the account during the computation period is the fair market value of the balance of the account immediately after the distribution increased by the amount of distributions from the account during the computation period, and reduced (but not below zero) by the sum of—

(1) The fair market value of the balance of the account as of the first day of the taxable year in which the excess contribution is made, and

(2) The amount of contribution to the account made during the computation period.

(iii) The provisions of subparagraph (1) and this subparagraph may be illustrated by the following examples:

Example (1). On January 1, 1975, A, age 55, who is a calendar year taxpayer, contributes $1,500 to an individual retirement account established for his benefit. For 1975, A is entitled to a deduction of $1,400 under section 219. For 1975, A does not claim as deductions any other items listed in section 62. A's gross income for 1975 is $9,334. On April 1, 1976, $107 is distributed to A from his individual retirement account. As of such date, the balance of the account is $1,498 [$1,605 − $107]. There were no other distributions from the account as of such date. The net amount of income earned by the account is $105 [$1,498 + $107 − (0 + $1,500)]. The net income attributable to the excess contribution is $7. [$105 × ($100/$1,500)]. A's adjusted gross income for 1975 is his gross income for 1975 ($9,334) reduced by the amount allowable to A as a deduction under section 219 ($1,400), or $7,934. A will include the $7 of the $107 distributed on April 1, 1976, in his gross income for 1976.

Example (2) Assume the same facts as in example (1) except that there is no distribution on April 1, 1976. Assume further that the net income attributable to the excess contribution as of April 1, 1977 is $14.49; that A is entitled to deduction of $1,500 under section 219 for 1976 and contributes that amount to the account in 1976; that A is not entitled to deduct any other items enumerated in section 62 for 1976; that A's otherwise determined gross income for 1976 is $11,500; and that on April 1, 1977, $114.49 is distributed to A. A's adjusted gross income is the sum of his otherwise determined gross income ($11,500) plus the amount includible in his gross income for 1976 under subparagraph (1) of this paragraph ($114.49), reduced by the amount allowable to A as a deduction under section 219 ($1,500), or $10,114.49.

(4) **Deemed distribution.** (i) In any case in which an account ceases to be an individual retirement account by reason of the application of section 408(e)(2), subparagraph (1) of this paragraph shall apply as if there were a distribution on the first day of the taxable year in which such account ceases to be an individual retirement account of an amount equal to the fair market value on such day of all of the assets in the account on such day. In the case of a deemed distribution from an individual retirement annuity, see § 1.408-3(d).

(ii) In any case in which an individual for whose benefit an individual retirement account is established uses, directly or indirectly, all or any portion of the account as security for a loan, subparagraph (1) of this paragraph shall apply as if there were distributed on the first day of the taxable year in which the loan was made an amount equal to that portion of the account used as security for such loan.

(5) **Distribution of annuity contracts.** Subparagraph (1) of this paragraph does not apply to any annuity contract which is distributed from an individual retirement account and which satisfies the requirements of subparagraphs (1), (3), (4), and (5) of § 1.408-3(b). Amounts distributed under such contracts will be taxable to the distributee under section 72. For purposes of applying section 72 to a distribution from such a contract, the investment in such contract is zero.

(6) **Treatment of assets distributed from an individual retirement account for the purchase of an endowment contract.** Under section 408(e)(5), if all, or any portion, of the assets of an individual retirement account are used to purchase an endowment contract described in § 1.408-3(e) for the benefit of the individual for whose benefit the account is established, (i) the excess, if any, of the total amount of assets used to purchase such contract over the portion of the assets attributable to life insurance protection or waiver of premium upon disability shall be treated as a rollover contribution described in subparagraph (2)(i) of this paragraph, and (ii) the portion of the assets attributable to life insurance protection or waiver of premium upon disability shall be treated as a distribution described in subparagraph (1) of this paragraph, except that the provisions of section 408(f) and paragraph (c)(1) of this section shall not apply to such amount.

(c) **Additional taxes.** (1) **Premature distributions.** If a distribution (whether a deemed distribution or an actual distribution, including an amount described in paragraph (b)(3) of this section) is made from an individual retirement account, or individual retirement annuity, to the individual for whose benefit the account was established, or who is the owner of the annuity, before he attains the age of 59½, his tax under chapter 1 of the Code for his taxable year in which such distribution is received is increased under section 408(f)(1) by an amount equal to 10 percent of the amount of the distribution which is includible in his gross income for the taxable year. Thus, for example, if an unmarried individual, age 40, with taxable income in 1975 (determined without regard to this section) of $20,000 receives a distribution of $3,000 from an individual retirement account established and maintained by him, his income tax for 1975 would be $6,690 ($6,390 in tax on $23,000 of taxable income, plus a $300 additional tax on the premature distribution). Except in the case of the credits allowable under section 31, 39, or 42, no credit can be used to offset the tax described in the first sentence of this subparagraph.

(2) **Disqualification distributions.** If an amount is includible in gross income for a taxable year as a distribution under paragraph (b)(4) of this section and the individual has not attained the age of 59½ before the beginning of such taxable year, his tax under chapter 1 of the Code is increased under section 408 (f)(2) by an amount equal to 10 percent of the amount required to be included in his gross income as a distribution under paragraph (b)(4) of this section.

(3) **Exception for disability.** Subparagraphs (1) and (2) of this paragraph do not apply if the amount paid or distributed, or deemed paid or distributed under subparagraph (4) of paragraph (b), is attributable to the individual becoming disabled within the meaning of section 72(m)(7).

(d) **Reports**—(1) **In general.** The trustee of an individual retirement account or the issuer of an individual retirement annuity shall submit to the Commissioner and the individual on whose behalf the account is established or in whose name the annuity is purchased (or his beneficiary) annual reports regarding the amount of contributions to the account or annuity; the amount of distributions from the account or annuity; in the case of an endowment contract, the amount of the premium allocable to retirement savings; and such other information as is required by the form prescribed pursuant to subparagraph (2) of this paragraph and the instructions relating thereto in the manner and at the time required under subparagraph (2) of this paragraph.

(2) **Manner and time for filing.** (i) The trustee of an individual retirement account or the issuer of an individual retirement annuity (other than an endowment contract) shall file the form prescribed for that purpose for each individual retirement account or annuity he maintains during the taxable year of the individual on whose behalf such account was established or such annuity contract was issued. Such form shall be filed on or before the 30th day of the first month following the close of the individual's taxable year.

(ii) The issuer of an endowment contract shall provide to the individual on whose behalf the contract is purchased the information relating to the amount of the premium allocable to retirement savings on or before the 30th day after the first premium payment during the individual's taxable year but in no event later than the close of the individual's taxable year. The issuer shall also file the form prescribed for that purpose for each endowment contract he maintains during the taxable year of the individual on whose behalf the contract was issued. Such form shall be filed on or before the 30th day of the first month following the close of the individual's taxable year.

(3) *Statements to be furnished to individuals with respect to whom information is furnished.* Each trustee or issuer filing a report described in subparagraph (1) of this paragraph shall furnish to each individual for whom a report is filed under this paragraph, within the time provided in subparagraph (2) of this paragraph, a written statement showing in addition to the information described in subparagraph (1) of this paragraph the name and address of the trustee or issuer filing such report.

(e) **Community property laws.** This section, § 1.408-2, and § 1.408-3 shall be applied without regard to any community property laws.

(f) **Transfer incident to divorce**—(1) **In general.** The transfer of an individual's interest, in whole or in part, in an individual retirement account, individual retirement annuity, or a retirement bond, to his former spouse under a valid divorce decree or a written instrument incident to such divorce shall not be considered to be a distribution from such an account or annuity to such individual or his former spouse nor shall it be considered a taxable transfer by such individual to his former spouse notwithstanding any other provision of this subchapter.

(2) **Treatment of transferred interest.** The interest described in subparagraph (1) of this paragraph which is transferred to the former spouse shall be treated as an individual retirement account of such spouse if the interest is an individual retirement account; an individual retirement annuity of such spouse if such interest is an individual retirement annuity; and a retirement bond of such spouse if such interest is a retirement bond.

§1.408-2 (Proposed Treasury Decision, published 2-21-75, 11-19-75). **Individual retirement accounts.**

(a) **In general.** An individual retirement account must be a trust or a custodial account (see paragraph (i) of this section). It must satisfy the requirements of paragraph (b) of this section in order to qualify as an individual retirement account. It may be established and maintained by an individual, by an employer for the benefit of his employees (see paragraph (c) of this section), or by an employee association for the benefit of its members (see paragraph (c) of this section). It is exempt from tax (see paragraph (a)(1) of § 1.408-1) unless disqualified under paragraph (d) of this section.

(b) **Requirements.** An individual retirement account must be a trust created or organized in the United States (as defined in section 7701(a)(9)) for the exclusive benefit of an individual or his beneficiaries. Such trust must be maintained at all times as a domestic trust in the United States. The instrument creating the trust must be in writing and the following requirements must be satisfied.

(1) **Amount of acceptable contributions.** Except in the case of a rollover contribution described in § 1.402(a)-2, § 1.403(a)-3, § 1.408-1(b)(2), or § 1.409-1(c), the trust instrument must provide that contributions may not be accepted by the

trustee for the taxable year in excess of $1,500 on behalf of any individual for whom the trust is maintained.

(2) **Trustee.** (i) The trustee must be a bank (as defined in section 401(d)(1) and the regulations thereunder) or another person which demonstrates, in the manner described in subdivision (ii) of this subparagraph, to the satisfaction of the Commissioner, that the manner in which such other person will administer the trust will be consistent with the requirements of section 408 and this section.

(ii) A person may demonstrate to the satisfaction of the Commissioner that the manner in which he will administer the trust will be consistent with the requirements of section 408 only upon the filing of a written application to the Commissioner of Internal Revenue, Attention: E:EP, Internal Revenue Service, Washington, D.C. 20224. Such application must meet the applicable requirements of §1.401-12(n)(3) through (7) relating to nonbank trustees of pension and profit-sharing trusts benefiting owner employees.

(3) **Life insurance contracts.** No part of the trust funds may be invested in life insurance contracts. An individual retirement account may invest in annuity contracts which provide a death benefit, provided that such death benefit is not based upon mortality assumptions.

(4) **Nonforfeitability.** The interest of any individual on whose behalf the trust is maintained in the balance of his account must be nonforfeitable.

(5) **Prohibition against commingling.** (i) The assets of the trust must not be commingled with other property except in a common trust fund or common investment fund.

(ii) For purposes of this subparagraph, the term "common investment fund" means a group trust created for the purpose of providing a satisfactory diversification of investments or a reduction of administrative expenses for the individual participating trusts, and which group trust satisfies the requirements of section 408(c) (except that it need not be established by an employer or an association of employees and the requirements of section 401(a) in the case of a group trust in which one of the individual participating trusts is an employees' trust described in section 401(a) which is exempt from tax under section 501(a).

(iii) For purposes of this subparagraph, the term "individual participating trust" means an employees' trust described in section 401(a) which is exempt from tax under section 501(a) or a trust which satisfies the requirements of section 408(a) provided that in the case of such an employees' trust, such trust would be permitted to participate in such a group trust if all of the other individual participating trusts were employees' trusts described in section 401(a) which are exempt from tax under section 501(a).

(6) **Distribution of interest.** (i) The trust instrument must provide that the entire interest of the individual for whose benefit the trust is maintained must be distributed to him in accordance with subdivision (b)(6)(ii) or (iii) of this subparagraph.

(ii) Unless the provisions of subdivision (iii) of this subparagraph apply, the entire interest of the individual must be actually distributed to him not later than the close of his taxable year in which he attains age 70½.

(iii) In lieu of distributing the individual's entire interest as provided in subdivision (ii) of this subparagraph, the interest may be distributed commencing not later than the taxable year described in such subdivision (ii). In such case, the trust must expressly provide that the entire interest of the individual shall be distributed to him and his beneficiaries, in a manner which satisfies the requirements of subdivision (v) of this subparagraph, over any of the following periods (or any combination thereof)—

(A) The life of the individual,

(B) The joint life and last survivor expectancy of the individual and his spouse,

(C) A period certain not extending beyond the life expectancy of the individual, or

(D) A period certain not extending beyond the joint life and last survivor expectancy of the individual and his spouse.

Proposed Reg. §1.408-2

(iv) The life expectancy of the individual or the joint life and last suvivor expectancy of the individual and his spouse cannot exceed the period computed by use of the expected return multiples in § 1.72-9, or, in the case of payments under a contract issued by an insurance company, the period computed by use of the life expectancy tables of such company.

(v) If an individual's entire interest is to be distributed over a period described in subdivision (iii) of this subparagraph, beginning in the year the individual attains 70½ the amount to be distributed each year must be not less than the lesser of the balance of the individual's entire interest or an amount equal to the quotient obtained by dividing the entire interest of the individual in the trust at the beginning of such year by the life expectancy of the individual (or the joint life and last survivor expectancy of the individual and his spouse (whichever is applicable)), determined in either case as of the date the individual attains age 70½ in accordance with subdivision (iv) of this subparagraph, reduced by the number of whole years elapsed since the individual's attainment of age 70½. However, no distribution need be made in any year, or a lesser amount may be distributed, if beginning with the year the individual attains age 70½ the aggregate amounts distributed by the end of any year are at least equal to the aggregate of the minimum amounts required by this subdivision to have been distributed by the end of such year.

(vi) If an individual's entire interest is distributed in the form of an annuity contract, then the requirements of section 408(a)(6) are satisfied if the distribution of such contract takes place before the close of the taxable year described in subdivision (ii) of this subparagraph, and if the individual's interest will be paid over a period described in subdivision (iii) of this subparagraph and at a rate which satisfies the requirements of subdivision (v) of this subparagraph.

(7) **Distribution upon death.** The trust instrument must provide that if the individual for whose benefit the trust is maintained dies before his entire interest in the trust has been distributed to him, or if distribution has been commenced as provided in subparagraph (6) of this paragraph to his surviving spouse and such spouse dies before the entire interest has been distributed to such spouse, the entire interest (or the remaining part of such interest if distribution thereof has commenced) must, within 5 years after his death (or the death of the surviving spouse) be distributed, or applied to the purchase of an immediate annuity for his beneficiary or beneficiaries (or the beneficiary or beneficiaries of the surviving spouse) which will be payable for the life of such beneficiary or beneficiaries (or for a term certain not extending beyond the life expectancy of such beneficiary or beneficiaries) and which annuity contract will be immediately distributed to such beneficiary or beneficiaries. Paragraph (b)(1) of § 1.408-1 does not apply to a contract described in the preceding sentence. Amounts distributed under such a contract will be taxable under section 72. For purposes of applying section 72 to a distribution from such a contract, the investment in such contract is zero. The first sentence of this subparagraph shall have no application if distributions over a term certain commenced before the death of the individual for whose benefit the trust was maintained and the term certain is for a period permitted under subdivision (iii)(C) or (D) of subparagraph (6) of this paragraph.

(8) **Definition of beneficiaries.** The term "beneficiaries" on whose behalf an individual retirement account is established includes the estate of the individual, dependents of the individual, and any person designated by the individual to share in the benefits of the account after the death of the individual.

(c) **Accounts established by employers and certain association of employees.** (1) **In general.** A trust created or organized in the United States (as defined in section 7701(a)(9)) by an employer for the exclusive benefit of his employees or their beneficiaries, or by an association of employees for the exclusive benefit of its members or their beneficiaries, is treated as an individual retirement account established and maintained by the individual if the requirements of subparagraphs (2) and (3) of this paragraph are satisfied under the written governing instrument creating the trust. A trust described in the preceding sentence is for the exclusive benefit of employees or members even though it may maintain an account for former employees or members and employees who are temporarily on leave.

(2) **General requirements.** The trust must satisfy the requirements of subparagraphs (1) through (7) of paragraph (b).

(3) **Special requirement.** There must be a separate accounting for the interest of each employee or member.

(4) **Definitions.** (i) Separate accounting. For purposes of subparagraph (3) of this paragraph, the term "separate accounting" means that separate records must be maintained with respect to the interest of each individual for whose benefit the trust is maintained. The assets of the trust may be held in a common trust fund, common investment fund, or common fund for the account of all individuals who have an interest in the trust.

(ii) Employee Association. For purposes of this paragraph and section 408 (c), the term "employee association" means any organization composed of two or more employees including, but not limited to, an employee association described in section 501(c)(4). Such association may include employees within the meaning of section 401(c)(1).

(d) **Disqualification and effect thereof.** (1) **Disqualification.** If during any taxable year of the individual for whose benefit an individual retirement account was established such individual or his beneficiary engages in any transaction prohibited by section 4975 with respect to such account, such account will cease to be an individual retirement account as of the first day of such taxable year. For purposes of this subparagraph, the individual for whose benefit an account was established shall be treated as the creator of such account, and the interest of any individual within an individual retirement account maintained by an employer or employee association is treated as a separate individual retirement account.

(2) **Effect of disqualification.** (i) If the individual for whose benefit the account is maintained or his beneficiary engages in any transaction prohibited by section 4975 during any taxable year, the deemed distribution described in § 1.408-1(b)(4) will be includible in the gross income for such year of the person engaging in such acts. If the trust with which the individual engages in any transaction described in the preceding sentence is established by an employer or employee association under section 408(c), only that portion of such trust which is equal to such individual's interest will be disqualified. Thus, for example if an employer establishes an individual retirement account for all of his employees and one employee whose interest is 10 percent of the entire account borrows money from the account only that 10 percent interest is disqualified.

(ii) In the case of an individual who has not attained age 59½, or become disabled within the meaning of section 72(m)(7) before the first day of the taxable year in which the deemed distribution described in § 1.408-1(b)(4) is includible in his gross income, the additional tax described in § 1.408-1(c)(1) is applicable.

(e) **Custodial accounts.** For purposes of this section and section 408(a), a custodial account is treated as a trust described in section 408(a) if such account satisfies the requirement of section 408(a) except that it is not a trust and if the assets of such account are held by a bank (as defined in section 401(d)(1) and the regulations thereunder) or such other person who satisfies the requirements of paragraph (b)(2)(ii) of this section. For purposes of this chapter, in the case of a custodial account treated as a trust by reason of the preceding sentence, the custodian of such account will be treated as the trustee thereof.

§ 1.408-3 (Proposed Treasury Decision, published 2-21-75.) **Individual retirement annuities.**

(a) **In general.** An individual retirement annuity is an annuity contract or endowment contract (described in paragraph (e)(1) of this section) issued by an insurance company which is qualified to do business under the law of the jurisdiction in which the owner of the contract resides at the time of the issuance of the contract and which satisfies the requirements of paragraph (b) of this section. A distribution under the contract, other than a deemed distribution described in paragraph (d), is includible in gross income in accordance with the provisions of § 1.408-1(b). An individual retirement annuity contract which satisfies the requirements of section 408(b) need not be purchased under a trust if the requirements of paragraph (b) of this section are satisfied. An individual retirement endowment contract may not be purchased under a trust which satisfies the requirements of section 408(a). Distribution of the contract is not a taxable event. Distributions under the contract, other than a deemed distribution described in paragraph (d), are includible in gross income in accordance with the provisions of § 1.408-1(b).

(b) **Requirements**—(1) **Transferability.** The annuity or the endowment contract must not be transferable by the owner.

(2) **Annual premium.** The annual premium for the annuity or the endowment contract cannot exceed $1,500, and any refund of premiums must be applied before the close of the calendar year following the year of the refund toward the payment of future premiums or the purchase of additional benefits.

(3) **Distribution.** The entire interest of the owner must be distributed to him in the same manner and over the same period as described in § 1.408-2(b)(6).

(4) **Distribution upon death.** If the owner dies before his entire interest has been distributed to him, the remaining interest must be distributed in the same manner, over the same period, and to the same beneficiaries as described in § 1.408-2(b)(7).

(5) **Nonforfeitability.** The entire interest of the owner in the annuity or endowment contract must be nonforfeitable.

(6) **Borrowing Prohibited.** The contract must provide that the owner may not use such contract as security for a loan.

(c) **Disqualification.** If during any taxable year the owner of an annuity borrows any money under the annuity or endowment contract or by use of such contract (including, but not limited to, pledging the contract as security for any loan), such contract will cease to be an individual retirement annuity as of the first day of such taxable year. If an annuity or endowment contract which constitutes an individual retirement annuity is disqualified as a result of the preceding sentence, an amount equal to the fair market value of the contract as of the first day of the taxable year of the owner in which such contract is disqualified is deemed to be distributed to the owner. See paragraph (d) of this section for treatment of deemed distribution from an individual retirement annuity because of disqualification.

(d) **Deemed distribution.** If an individual retirement annuity is disqualified as a result of transaction described in paragraph (c) of this section and the amount described in such paragraph (c) is deemed distributed to the owner of such annnuity, then the owner of the annuity contract is to include such amount in his gross income in his taxable year in which the annuity is disqualified. If an amount is includible in the gross income of the individual under this paragraph, see § 1.408-1(c)(2) for additional tax in disqualification cases. If the individual has not attained age 59½, see § 1.408-1(c)(1) for additional tax on premature distributions.

(e) **Endowment contracts**—(1) **Additional requirements for endowment contracts.** No contract providing life insurance protection issued by a company described in paragraph (a) of this section shall be treated as an endowment contract for purposes of this section if—

(i) Such contract matures later than the taxable year of the individual in whose name the contract is purchased attains the age of 70½;

(ii) Such contract is not for the exclusive benefit of such individual or his beneficiaries;

(iii) Such contract does not provide that such individual shall notify the issuer in the event that the aggregate annual premiums due under all such contracts purchased in his name, whether or not such contracts are purchased from the same issuer, exceed $1,500;

(iv) Premiums under such contract may increase over the term of the contract;

(v) The cash value of such contract at maturity is less than the death benefit payable under the contract at any time before maturity;

(vi) The death benefit does not, at some time before maturity, exceed the greater of the cash value or the sum of premiums paid under the contract;

(vii) Such contract does not provide for a cash value;

(viii) Such contract provides that the life insurance element of such contract may increase over the term of such contract, unless such increase is merely because such contract provides for the purchase of additional benefits; or

(ix) Such contract provides insurance other than life insurance and waiver of premiums upon disability.

(2) **Treatment of proceeds under endowment contract upon death of individual.** In the case of the payment of a death benefit under an endowment contract upon the death of the individual in whose name the contract is purchased, the portion of such payment which is equal to the cash value immediately before the death of such individual is not excludable from gross income under section 101(a) and is treated as a distribution from an individual retirement annuity. The remaining portion, if any, of such payment constitutes current life insurance protection and is excludable under section 101(a). If a death benefit is paid under an endowment contract at a date or dates later than the death of the individual, section 101(d) is applicable only to the portion of the benefit which is attributable to the amount excludable under section 101(a).

Retirement Bonds

§ 1.409-1 (Proposed Treasury Decision, published 2-21-75.) **Retirement bonds.**

(a) **In general.** Section 409 authorizes the issuance of bonds under the Second Liberty Bond Act the purchase price of which would be deductible under section 219. Section 409 also prescribes the tax treatment of such bonds. See paragraph (b) of this section.

(b) **Income tax treatment of bonds—(1) General rule.** Except as provided in subparagraph (2) of this paragraph, the entire proceeds upon redemption of a retirement bond described in section 409(a) shall be included in the gross income of the taxpayer entitled to such proceeds. If a bond has not been tendered for redemption by the registered owner before the close of the taxable year in which he attains age 70½, he must include in his gross income for such taxable year the amount of the proceeds he would have received if the bond had been redeemed at age 70½. The provisions of sections 72 and 1232 do not apply to a retirement bond.

(2) **Exceptions.** (i) If a retirement bond is redeemed within 12 months after the issue date, the proceeds are excluded from gross income if no deduction is allowed under section 219 on account of the purchase of such bond. For definition of issue date, see 31 CFR § 346.1(c).

(ii) If a retirement bond is redeemed after the close of the taxable year in which the registered owner attains age 70½ the proceeds from the redemption of the bond are excludable from the gross income of the registered owner or his beneficiary to the extent that such proceeds were includible in the gross income of the registered owner for such taxable year.

(iii) If a retirement bond is surrendered for reissuance in the same or lesser face amount, the difference between current redemption value of the bond surrendered for reissuance and the current surrender value of the bond reissued is includible in the gross income of the registered owner.

Proposed Reg. § 1.409-1

(3) **Basis.** The basis of a retirement bond is zero.

(c) **Rollover.** The first sentence of paragraph (b)(1) of this section shall not apply in any case in which a retirement bond is redeemed by the registered owner before the close of the taxable year in which he attains the age of 70½ if he transfers the entire amount of the proceeds of such redemption to—

(1) An individual retirement account described in section 408(a) or an individual retirement annuity described in section 408(b) (other than an endowment contract described in § 1.408-3(e)), or

(2) An employees' trust which is described in section 401(a) which is exempt from tax under section 501(a), or an annuity plan described in section 403(a), for the benefit of the registered owner,

on or before the 60th day after the day on which he received the proceeds of such redemption. This subparagraph shall not apply in the case of a transfer to a trust or plan described in subdivision (ii) of this subparagraph unless no part of the purchase price of the retirement bond redeemed is attributable to any source other than a rollover contribution from such an employees' trust or annuity plan (other than an annuity plan or employees' trust forming part of a plan under which the individual was an employee within the meaning of section 401(c)(1) at the time contributions were made on his behalf under the plan).

(d) **Additional tax.** (1) **Early redemption.** Except as provided in subparagraph (2) of this paragraph, under section 409(c) if a retirement bond is redeemed by the registered owner before he attains age 59½, his tax under chapter 1 of the Code is increased by an amount equal to 10 percent of the proceeds of the redemption includible in his gross income for the taxable year. Except in the case of the credits allowable under sections 31, 39, or 42, no credit can be used to offset the tax described in the preceding sentence.

(2) **Limitations.** Subparagraph (1) of this paragraph shall not apply if—

(i) During the taxable year of the registered owner in which a retirement bond is redeemed, the registered owner becomes disabled within the meaning of section 72(m)(7), or

(ii) A retirement bond is tendered for redemption in accordance with paragraph (b)(2)(i) of this section.

[The page following this is 63,619]

Minimum Funding Standards

§ 11.412(c)(1)-1 (Proposed Treasury Decision, published 8-4-77.) **Determinations to be made under funding method—terms defined.**

[Proposed rules under this section are contained in the temporary regulations promulgated under T.D. 7499, filed 8-3-77, and for this reason, are not repeated here. See p. 24,998.117.]

§ 11.412(c)(1)-2. (Proposed Treasury Decision, published 8-4-77.) **Shortfall method.**

[Proposed rules under this section are contained in the temporary regulations promulgated under T.D. 7499, filed 8-3-77, and for this reason, are not repeated here. See p. 24,998.117.]

§ 1.412(i)-1 (Proposed Treasury Decision, published 2-6-75.) **Certain insurance contract plans.**

(a) **In general.** Under section 412(h)(2) of the Internal Revenue Code of 1954, as added by section 1013(a) of the Employee Retirement Income Security Act of 1974 (88 Stat. 914) (hereinafter referred to as "the Act"), an insurance contract plan described in section 412(i) for a plan year is not subject to the minimum funding requirements of section 412 for that plan year. Consequently, if an individual or group insurance contract plan satisfies all of the requirements of paragraph (b)(2) or (c)(2) of this section, whichever are applicable, for the plan year, the plan is not subject to the requirements of section 412 for that plan year. The effective date for section 412 of the Code is determined under section 1017 of the Act. In general, in the case of a plan which was not in existence on January 1, 1974, this section applies for plan years beginning after September 2, 1974, and in the case of a plan in existence on January 1, 1974, to plan years beginning after December 31, 1975.

(b) **Individual insurance contract plans.** (1) An individual insurance contract plan is described in section 412(i) during a plan year if the plan satisfies the requirements of subparagraph (2) for the plan year.

(2) The requirements of this subparagraph are:

(i) The plan must be funded exclusively by the purchase from a life insurance company (licensed under the law of a State or the District of Columbia to do business with the plan) of individual annuity or individual insurance contracts, or a combination thereof. The purchase may be made either directly by the employer or through the use of a custodial account or trust.

(ii) The individual annuity or individual insurance contracts issued under the plan must provide for level annual, or more frequent, payments to be paid for the period commencing with the date each individual participating in the plan became a participant and ending not later than the normal retirement age for that individual or, if earlier, the date the individual ceases his participation in the plan. In the case of an increase in benefits the contracts must provide for level annual payments with respect to such increase to be paid for the period commencing at the time the increase becomes effective. If payment commences on the first payment date under the contract occurring after the date an individual becomes a participant or after the effective date of an increase in benefits, the requirements of this subdivision will be satisfied even though payment does not commence on the date on which the individual's participation commenced or on the effective date of the benefit increase, whichever is applicable. If an individual accrues benefits after his normal retirement age, the requirements of this subdivision are satisfied if payment is made at the time such benefits accrue. If the provisions required by this subdivision are set forth in a separate agreement with the issuer of the individual contracts, they need not be included in the individual contracts.

(iii) The benefits provided by the plan for each individual participant must be equal to the benefits provided under his individual contracts at his normal retirement age under the plan provisions.

Proposed Reg. § 1.412(i)-1

(iv) The benefits provided by the plan for each individual participant must be guaranteed by the life insurance company, described in subdivision (i) of this subparagraph, issuing the individual contracts to the extent premiums have been paid.

(v) Except as provided in the following sentence, all premiums payable for the plan year, and for all prior plan years, under the insurance or annuity contracts must have been paid before lapse. If the lapse has occurred during the plan year, the requirements of this subdivision will be considered to have been met if reinstatement of the insurance policy, under which the individual insurance contracts are issued, occurs during such year.

(vi) No rights under the individual contracts may have been subject to a security interest at any time during the plan year. This subdivision shall not apply to contracts which have been distributed to participants if the security interest is created after the date of distribution.

(vii) No policy loans, including loans to individual participants, on any of the individual contracts may be outstanding at any time during the plan year. This subdivision shall not apply to contracts which have been distributed to participants if the loan is made after the date of distribution.

(c) **Group insurance contract plans.** (1) A group insurance contract plan is described in section 412(i) during a plan year if the plan satisfies the requirements of subparagraph (2) for the plan year.

(2) The requirements of this subparagraph are:

(i) The plan must be funded exclusively by the purchase from a life insurance company, described in paragraph (b)(2)(i) of this section, of group annuity or group insurance contracts, or a combination thereof. The purchase may be made either directly by the employer or through the use of a custodial account or trust.

(ii) In the case of a plan funded by a group insurance contract or a group annuity contract the requirements of paragraph (b)(2)(ii) of this section must be satisfied by the group contract issued under the plan. Thus, for example, each individual participant's benefits under the group contract must be provided for by level annual, or more frequent, payments equivalent to the payments required to satisfy such paragraph. The requirements of this subdivision will not be satisfied if benefits for any individual are not provided for by level payments made on his behalf under the group contract.

(iii) The group annuity or group insurance contract must satisfy the requirements of clauses (iii), (iv), (v), (vi) and (vii) of paragraph (b)(2). Thus, for example, each participant's benefits provided by the plan must be equal to his benefits provided under the group contract at his normal retirement age.

(iv)(A) If the plan is funded by a group annuity contract, the value of the benefits guaranteed by the insurance company issuing the contract under the plan with respect to each participant under the contract must not be less than the value of such benefits which the cash surrender value would provide for that participant under any individual annuity contract plan satisfying the requirements of paragraph (b) and delivered in the State where the principal office of the plan is located.

(B) If the plan is funded by a group insurance contract, the value of the benefits guaranteed by the insurance company issuing the contract under the plan with respect to each participant under the contract must not be less than the value of such benefits which the cash surrender value would provide for that participant under any individual insurance contract plan satisfying the requirements of paragraph (b) and delivered in the State where the principal office is located.

(v) Under the group annuity or group insurance contract, premiums or other consideration received by the insurance company (and, if a custodial account or trust is used, the custodian or trustee thereof) must be allocated to purchase individual benefits for participants under the plan. A plan which maintains unallocated funds in an auxiliary trust fund or which provides that an insurance company will maintain unallocated funds in a separate account, such as a group deposit administration contract, does not satisfy the requirements of this subdivision.

Definitions and Special Rules

The following new sections are added immediately after §1.405-3:

§ 1.414(b)-1 (Proposed Treasury Decision, filed 11-5-75.) **Controlled group of corporations.**

(a) **Definition of controlled group of corporations.** For purposes of this section, the term "controlled group of corporations" has the same meaning as is assigned to the term in section 1563(a) and the regulations thereunder, except that (1) the term "controlled group of corporations" shall not include an "insurance group" described in section 1563(a)(4) and (2) section 1563(e)(3)(C) (relating to stock owned by employees' trust) shall not apply. For purposes of this section, the term "members of a controlled group" means two or more corporations connected through stock ownership described in section 1563(a)(1), (2), or (3), whether or not such corporations are "component members of a controlled group" within the meaning of section 1563(b). Two or more corporations are members of a controlled group at any time such corporations meet the requirements of section 1563(a) (as modified by this paragraph). For purposes of this section, if a corporation is a member of more than one controlled group of corporations, such corporation shall be treated as a member of each controlled group.

(b) **Single plan adopted by two or more members.** If two or more members of a controlled group of corporations adopt a single plan for a plan year, then the minimum funding standard provided in section 412, the tax imposed by section 4971, and the applicable limitations provided by section 404(a) shall be determined as if such members were a single employer. In such a case, the amount of such items and the allocable portion attributable to each member shall be determined in the manner provided in regulations under sections 412, 4971, and 404(a).

(c) **Cross reference.** For rules relating to the application of sections 401, 410, 411, and 415 with respect to two or more trades or businesses which are under common control, see section 414(c) and the regulations thereunder.

§ 1.414(c)-1 (Proposed Treasury Decision, filed 11-5-75.) **Commonly controlled trades or businesses.**

For purposes of applying the provisions of sections 401 (relating to qualified pension, profit-sharing, and stock bonus plans), 410 (relating to minimum participation standards), 411 (relating to minimum vesting standards), and 415 (relating to limitations on benefits and contributions under qualified plans), all employees of two or more trades or businesses under common control within the meaning of § 1.414(c)-2 for any period shall be treated as employed by a single employer. See sections 401, 410, 411, and 415 and the regulations thereunder for rules relating to employees of trades or businesses which are under common control. See § 1.414(c)-5 for effective date.

§ 1.414(c)-2 (Proposed Treasury Decision, filed 11-5-75.) **Two or more trades or businesses under common control.**

(a) **In general.** For purposes of this section, the term "two or more trades or businesses under common control" means any group of trades or businesses which is either a "parent-subsidiary group of trades or businesses under common control" as defined in paragraph (b) of this section, a "brother-sister group of trades or businesses under common control" as defined in paragraph (c) of this section, or a "combined group of trades or businesses under common control" as defined in paragraph (d) of this section. For purposes of this section and §§ 1.414(c)-3 and 1.414(c)-4, the term "organization" means a sole proprietorship, a partnership (as defined in section 7701(a)(2)), a trust, an estate, or a corporation.

(b) **Parent-subsidiary group of trades or businesses under common control.**
(1) **General.** The term "parent-subsidiary group of trades or businesses under

Proposed Reg. §1.414(c)-2

common control" means one or more chains of organizations conducting trades or businesses connected through ownership of a controlling interest with a common parent organization if—

(i) A controlling interest in each of the organizations, except the common parent organization, is owned (directly and with the application of § 1.414(c)-4(b)(1), relating to options) by one or more of the other organizations; and

(ii) The common parent organization owns (directly and with the application of § 1.414(c)-4(b)(1), relating to options) a controlling interest in at least one of the other organizations, excluding, in computing such controlling interest, any direct ownership interest by such other organizations.

(2) **Controlling interest defined**—(i) Controlling interest. For purposes of paragraphs (b) and (c) of this section, the phrase "controlling interest" means

(A) In the case of an organization which is a corporation, ownership of stock possessing at least 80 percent of the total combined voting power of all classes of stock entitled to vote of such corporation or at least 80 percent of the total value of shares of all classes of stock of such corporation;

(B) In the case of an organization which is a trust or estate, ownership of an actuarial interest of at least 80 percent of such trust or estate;

(C) In the case of an organization which is a partnership, ownership of at least 80 percent of the profits interest or capital interest of such partnership; and

(D) In the case of an organization which is a sole proprietorship, ownership of such sole proprietorship.

(ii) *Actuarial interest.* For purposes of this section, the actuarial interest of each beneficiary of a trust or estate shall be determined by assuming the maximum exercise of discretion by the fiduciary in favor of such beneficiary. The factors and methods prescribed in § 20.2031-10 of this chapter (Estate Tax Regulations) for use in ascertaining the value of an interest in property for estate tax purposes shall be used for purposes of this subdivision in determining a beneficiary's actuarial interest.

(c) **Brother-sister group of trades or businesses under common control**—(1) *General.* The term "brother-sister group of trades or businesses under common control" means two or more organizations conducting trades or businesses if (i) the same five or fewer persons who are individuals, estates, or trusts own (directly and with the application of § 1.414(c)-4), singly or in combination, a controlling interest of each organization, and (ii) taking into account the ownership of each such person only to the extent such ownership is identical with respect to each such organization, such persons are in effective control of each organization.

(2) *Effective control defined.* For purposes of this paragraph, persons are in "effective control" of an organization if—

(i) In the case of an organization which is a corporation, such persons own stock possessing more than 50 percent of the total combined voting power of all classes of stock entitled to vote of such corporation or more than 50 percent of the total value of shares of all classes of stock of such corporation;

(ii) In the case of an organization which is a trust or estate, such persons own an aggregate actuarial interest of more than 50 percent of such trust or estate;

(iii) In the case of an organization which is a partnership, such persons own an aggregate of more than 50 percent of the profits interest or capital interest of such partnership; and

(iv) In the case of an organization which is a sole proprietorship, such persons own such sole proprietorship.

(d) **Combined group of trades or businesses under common control.** The term "combined group of trades or businesses under common control" means any group of three or more organizations, if (1) each such organization is a member of either a parent-subsidiary group of trades or businesses under common control or a brother-sister group of trades or businesses under common control, and (2) at least one such organization is the common parent organization of a parent-subsidiary group of trades or businesses under common control and is also a member of a brother-sister group of trades or businesses under common control.

(e) **Examples.** The definitions of parent-subsidiary group of trades or businesses under common control, brother-sister group of trades or businesses under common control, and combined group of trades or businesses under common control may be illustrated by the following examples.

Example (1). (a) The ABC Partnership owns stock possessing 80 percent of the total combined voting power of all classes of stock entitled to vote of S Corporation. ABC is the common parent of a parent-subsidiary group of trades or businesses under common control consisting of the ABC Partnership and S Corporation.

Proposed Reg. § 1.414(c)-2

(b) Assume the same facts as in (a) and assume further that S owns 80 percent of the profits interest in the DEF Partnership. The ABC Partnership is the common parent of a parent-subsidiary group of trades or businesses under common control consisting of the ABC Partnership, S Corporation, and the DEF Partnership. The result would be the same if the ABC Partnership, rather than S, owned 80 percent of the profits interest in the DEF Partnership.

Example (2). L Corporation owns 80 percent of the only class of stock of T Corporation, and T, in turn owns 40 percent of the capital interest in the GHI Partnership. L also owns 80 percent of the only class of stock of N Corporation and N, in turn, owns 40 percent of the capital interest in the GHI Partnership. L is the common parent of a parent-subsidiary group of trades or businesses under common control consisting of L Corporation, T Corporation, N Corporation, and the GHI Partnership.

Example (3). ABC Partnership owns 75 percent of the only class of stock of X and Y corporations; X owns all the remaining stock of Y, and Y owns all the remaining stock of X. Since interorganization ownership is excluded (that is, treated as not outstanding) for purposes of determining whether ABC owns a controlling interest of at least one of the other organizations, ABC is treated as the owner of stock possessing 100 percent of the voting power and value of X and of Y for purposes of paragraph (b)(1)(ii) of this section. Therefore, ABC is the common parent of a parent-subsidiary group of trades or businesses under common control consisting of the ABC Partnership, X Corporation, and Y Corporation.

Example (4). Unrelated individuals A, B, C, D, E, and F own an interest in sole proprietorship A, a capital interest in the GHI Partnership, and stock of corporations W, X, Y, and Z (each of which has only one class of stock outstanding) in the following proportions:

Individuals	A	GHI	W	X	Y	Z	Identical Ownership
A	100%	60%	60%	60%	60%	60%	60%
B	—	40%	—	—	—	—	—
C	—	—	40%	—	—	—	—
D	—	—	—	40%	—	—	—
E	—	—	—	—	40%	—	—
F	—	—	—	—	—	40%	—
Total	100%	100%	100%	100%	100%	100%	60%

Under these facts the following brother-sister groups of trades or businesses under common control exist: A, GHI, W, X, and Y; A, GHI, W, X, and Z; A, GHI, W, Y, and Z; A, GHI, X, Y, and Z; and A, W, X, Y, and Z.

Example (5). The outstanding stock of corporations U and V, which have only one class of stock outstanding, is owned by unrelated individuals as follows:

Individuals	U	V	Identical Ownership
F	5%	—	—
G	10%	—	—
H	10%	—	—
I	20%	—	—
J	55%	—	—
K	—	55%	55%
L	—	10%	—
	—	10%	—

Individuals	Organizations		Identical Ownership
	U	V	
M	—	10%	—
N	—	10%	—
O	—	5%	—
Total	100%	100%	55%

Corporations U and V are not members of a brother-sister group of trades or businesses under common control because at least 80 percent of the stock of each corporation is not owned by the same five or fewer persons.

Example (6). A, an individual, owns a controlling interest in ABC Partnership and DEF Partnership. ABC, in turn, owns a controlling interest in X Corporation. Since ABC, DEF, and X are each members of either a parent-subsidiary group or a brother-sister group of trades or businesses under common control, and ABC is the common parent of a parent-subsidiary group of trades or businesses under common control consisting of ABC and X, and also a member of a brother-sister group of trades or businesses under common control consisting of ABC and DEF, ABC Partnership, DEF Partnership, and X Corporation are members of the same combined group of trades or businesses under common control.

§ 1.414(c)-3 (Proposed Treasury Decision, filed 11-5-75.) **Exclusion of certain interests or stock in determining control.**

(a) **In general.** For purposes of § 1.414(c)-2(b)(2)(i) and (c)(2), the term "interest" and the term "stock" do not include an interest which is treated as not outstanding under paragraph (b) of this section in the case of a parent-subsidiary group of trades or businesses under common control or under paragraph (c) of this section in the case of a brother-sister group of trades or businesses under common control. In addition, the term "stock" does not include treasury stock or nonvoting stock which is limited and preferred as to dividends. For definitions of certain terms used in this section, see paragraph (d) of this section.

(b) **Parent-subsidiary group of trades or businesses under common control—** (1) **In general.** If an organization (hereinafter in this section referred to as "parent organization") owns (within the meaning of paragraph (b)(2) of this section)—

(i) In the case of a corporation, 50 percent or more of the total combined voting power of all classes of stock entitled to vote or of the total value of shares of all classes of stock of such corporation,

(ii) In the case of a trust or an estate, an actuarial interest (within the meaning of § 1.414(c)-2(b)(2)(ii)) of 50 percent or more of such trust or estate, and

(iii) In the case of a partnership, 50 percent or more of the profits or capital interest of such partnership,

then for purposes of determining whether the parent organization or such other organization (hereinafter in this section referred to as "subsidiary organization") is a member of a parent-subsidiary group of trades or businesses under common control, an interest in such subsidiary organization excluded under paragraph (b) (3), (4), (5), or (6) of this section shall be treated as not outstanding.

(2) **Ownership.** For purposes of paragraph (b)(1) of this section, a parent organization shall be considered to own an interest in or stock of another organization which it owns directly or indirectly with the application of paragraph (b) (1) of § 414(c)-4 and—

Proposed Reg. § 1.414(c)-3

(i) In the case of a parent organization which is a partnership, a trust, or an estate, with the application of paragraph (b)(2), (3), and (4) of § 1.414(c)-4, and

(ii) In the case of a parent organization which is a corporation, with the application of paragraph (b)(4) of § 1.414(c)-4.

(3) **Plan of deferred compensation.** An interest which is an interest in or stock of the subsidiary organization held by a trust which is part of a plan of deferred compensation (within the meaning of section 406(a)(3) and the regulations thereunder) for the benefit of the employees of the parent organization or the subsidiary organization shall be excluded.

(4) **Principal owners, officers, etc.** An interest which is an interest in or stock of the subsidiary organization owned (directly and with the application of § 1.414(c)-4) by an individual who is a principal owner, officer, partner, or fiduciary of the parent organization shall be excluded.

(5) **Employees.** An interest which is an interest in or stock of the subsidiary organization owned (directly and with the application of § 1.414(c)-4) by an employee of the subsidiary organization shall be excluded if such interest or such stock is subject to conditions which substantially restrict or limit the employee's right (or if the employee constructively owns such interest or such stock, the direct or record owner's right) to dispose of such interest or such stock and which run in favor of the parent or subsidiary organization.

(6) **Controlled exempt organization.** An interest which is an interest in or stock of the subsidiary organization shall be excluded if owned (directly and with the application of § 1.414(c)-4) by an organization (other than the parent organization):

(i) To which section 501 (relating to certain educational and charitable organizations which are exempt from tax) applies, and

(ii) Which is controlled directly or indirectly (within the meaning of paragraph (d)(7) of this section) by the parent organization or subsidiary organization, by an individual, estate, or trust that is a principal owner of the parent organization, by an officer, partner, or fiduciary of the parent organization, or by any combination thereof.

(c) **Brother-sister group of trades or businesses under common control—** (1) **In general.** If five or fewer persons (hereinafter in this section referred to as "common owners") who are individuals, estates, or trusts, own (directly and with the application of § 1.414(c)-4—

(i) In the case of a corporation, 50 percent or more of the total combined voting power of all classes of stock entitled to vote or of the total value of shares of all classes of stock of such corporation,

(ii) In the case of a trust or an estate, an actuarial interest (within the meaning of § 1.414(c)-2(b)(2)(ii)) of 50 percent or more of such trust or estate, and

(iii) In the case of a partnership, 50 percent or more of the profits or capital interest of such partnership,

then for purposes of determining whether such organization is a member of a brother-sister group of trades or businesses under common control, an interest in such organization excluded under paragraph (c)(2), (3), or (4) of this section shall be treated as not outstanding.

(2) **Exempt employee's trust.** An interest which is an interest in our stock of such organization held by an employee's trust described in section 401(a) which is exempt from tax under section 501(a) shall be excluded if such trust is for the benefit of the employees of such organization.

(3) **Employees.** An interest which is an interest in or stock of such organization owned (directly and with the application of § 1.414(c)-4) by an employee of such organization shall be excluded if such interest or stock is subject to conditions which run in favor of a common owner of such organization or in favor of such organization and which substantially restrict or limit the employee's right (or if the employee constructively owns such interest or stock, the direct or record owner's right) to dispose of such interest or stock.

(4) **Controlled exempt organization.** An interest which is an interest in or stock of such organization shall be excluded if owned (directly and with the application of § 1.414(c)-4) by an organization:

(i) To which section 501(c)(3) (relating to certain educational and charitable organizations which are exempt from tax) applies, and

(ii) Which is controlled directly or indirectly (within the meaning of paragraph (d)(7) of this section) by such organization, by an individual, estate, or trust that is a principal owner of such organization, by an officer, partner, or fiduciary of such organization, or by any combination thereof.

(d) **Definitions**—(1) **Employee.** For purposes of this section, the term "employee" has the same meaning such term is given in section 3306(i) of the Code (relating to definitions for purposes of the Federal Unemployment Tax Act).

(2) **Principal owner.** For purposes of this section, the term "principal owner" means a person who owns (directly and with the application of § 1.414(c)-4)—

(i) In the case of a corporation, 5 percent or more of the total combined voting power of all classes of stock entitled to vote in such corporation or of the total value of shares of all classes of stock of such corporation;

(ii) In the case of a trust or estate, an actuarial interest of 5 percent or more of such trust or estate; or

(iii) In the case of a partnership, 5 percent or more of the profits interest or capital interest of such partnership.

(3) **Officer.** For purposes of this section, the term "officer" includes the president, vice-presidents, general manager, treasurer, secretary, and comptroller of a corporation, and any other person who performs duties corresponding to those normally performed by persons occupying such positions.

(4) **Partner.** For purposes of this section, the term "partner" means any person defined in section 7701(a)(2) (relating to definitions of partner).

(5) **Fiduciary.** For purposes of this section and § 1.414(c)-4, the term "fiduciary" has the same meaning as such term is given in section 7701(a)(6) and the regulations thereunder.

(6) **Substantial conditions.** (i) In general. For purposes of this section, an interest in or stock of an organization is subject to conditions which substantially restrict or limit the right to dispose of such interest or stock and which run in favor of another person if the condition extends directly or indirectly to such person's rights with respect to the acquisition of the direct owner's (or the record owner's) interest or stock. For a condition to be in favor of another person it is not necessary that such person be extended a discriminatory concession with respect to price. A right of first refusal with respect to an interest or stock in favor of another person is a condition which substantially restricts or limits the direct or record owner's right of disposition which runs in favor of such person. Further, any legally enforceable condition which prohibits the direct or record owner from disposing of his or her interest or stock without the consent of another person will be considered to be a substantial limitation running in favor of such person.

(ii) Special rule. For purposes of paragraph (c)(3) of this section only, if a condition which restricts or limits an employee's right (or direct or record owner's right) to dispose of his or her interest or stock also applies to the interest or stock in such organization held by a common owner pursuant to a bona fide reciprocal purchase arrangement, such condition shall not be treated as a substantial limitation or restriction. An example of a reciprocal purchase arrangement is an agreement whereby a common owner and the employee are given a right of first refusal with respect to stock of the employer corporation owned by the other party. If, however, the agreement also provides that the common owner has the right to purchase the stock of the employer corporation owned by the employee in the event the corporation should discharge the employee for reason-

Proposed Reg. § 1.414(c)-3

able cause, the purchase arrangement would not be reciprocal within the meaning of this subdivision.

(7) **Control.** For purposes of paragraphs (b)(6) and (c)(4) of this section, the term "control" means control in fact. The determination of whether there exists control in fact will depend upon all of the facts and circumstances of each case, without regard to whether such control is legally enforceable and irrespective of the method by which such control is exercised or exercisable.

(e) **Examples.** The provisions of this section may be illustrated by the following examples:

Example (1). ABC Partnership owns 70 percent of the capital interest and of the profits interest in the DEF Partnership. The remaining capital interest and profits interest in DEF is owned as follows: 4 percent by A (a general partner in ABC), and 26 percent by D (a limited partner in ABC). ABC satisfies the 50-percent capital interest or profits interest ownership requirement of paragraph (b)(1)(iii) of this section with respect to DEF. Since A and D are partners of ABC, under paragraph (b)(4) of this section the capital and profits interests in DEF owned by A and D are treated as not outstanding for purposes of determining whether ABC and DEF are members of a parent-subsidiary group of trades or businesses under common control under § 1.414(c)-2(b). Thus, ABC is considered to own 100 percent (70 ÷ 70) of the capital interest and profits interest in DEF. Accordingly, ABC and DEF are members of a parent-subsidiary group of trades or businesses under common control.

Example (2). Assume the same facts as in example (1) and assume further that A owns 15 shares of the 100 shares of the only class of stock of S Corporation and DEF Partnership owns 75 shares of such stock. ABC satisfies the 50 percent stock requirement of paragraph (b)(1)(i) of this section with respect to S since ABC is considered as owning 52.5 percent (70 percent × 75 percent) of the S stock with the application of § 1.414(c)-4(b)(2). Since A is a partner of ABC, the S stock owned by A is treated as not outstanding for purposes of determining whether S is a member of a parent-subsidiary group of trades or businesses under common control. Thus, DEF Partnership is considered to own stock possessing 88.2 percent (75 ÷ 85) of the voting power and value of the S stock. Accordingly, ABC Partnership, DEF Partnership, and S Corporation are members of a parent-subsidiary group of trades or businesses under common control.

Example (3). ABC Partnership owns 60 percent of the only class of stock of Corporation Y. D, the president of Y, owns the remaining 40 percent of the stock of Y. D has agreed that if she offers her stock in Y for sale she will first offer the stock to ABC at a price equal to the fair market value of the stock on the first date the stock is offered for sale. Since D is an employee of Y within the meaning of section 3306(i) of the Code and her stock in Y is subject to a condition which substantially restricts or limits her right to dispose of such stock and runs in favor of ABC Partnership, under paragraph (b)(5) of this section such stock is treated as not outstanding for purposes of determining whether ABC and Y are members of a parent-subsidiary group of trades or businesses under common control. Thus, ABC Partnership is considered to own stock possessing 100 percent of the voting power and value of the stock of Y. Accordingly, ABC Partnership and Y Corporation are members of a parent-subsidiary group of trades or businesses under common control. The result would be the same if D's husband, instead of D, owned directly the 40 percent stock interest in Y and such stock was subject to a right of first refusal running in favor of ABC Partnership.

§1.414(c)-4 (Proposed Treasury Decision, filed 11-5-75.) **Rules for determining ownership.**

(a) **In general.** In determining the ownership of an interest in an organization for purposes of § 1.414(c)-2 and § 1.414(c)-3, the constructive ownership rules of paragraph (b) of this section shall apply, subject to the operating rules contained in paragraph (c). For purposes of this section the term "interest" means:

in the case of a corporation, stock; in the case of a trust or estate, an actuarial interest; in the case of a partnership, an interest in the capital or profits; and in the case of a sole proprietorship, the proprietorship.

(b) **Constructive ownership**—(1) **Options.** If a person has an option to acquire any outstanding interest in an organization, such interest shall be considered as owned by such person. For this purpose, an option to acquire an option, and each one of a series of such options, shall be considered as an option to acquire such interest.

(2) **Attribution from partnerships**—(i) General. An interest owned, directly or indirectly, by or for a partnership shall be considered as owned by any partner having an interest of 5 percent or more in either the profits or capital of the partnership in proportion to such partner's interest in the profits or capital, whichever such proportion is greater.

(ii) Example. The provisions of paragraph (b)(2)(i) of this section may be illustrated by the following example:

Example. A, B, and C, unrelated individuals, are partners in the ABC Partnership. The partners' interests in the capital and profits of ABC are as follows:

Partner	Capital	Profits
A	36%	25%
B	60%	71%
C	4%	4%

The ABC Partnership owns the entire outstanding stock (100 shares) of X Corporation. Under paragraph (b)(2)(i) of this section, A is considered to own the stock of X owned by the partnership in proportion to his interest in capital (36 percent) or profits (25 percent), whichever such proportion is greater. Therefore, A is considered to own 36 shares of X stock. Since B has a greater interest in the profits of the partnership than in the capital, B is considered to own X stock in proportion to his interest in such profits. Therefore, B is considered to own 71 shares of X stock. Since C does not have an interest of 5 percent or more in either the capital or profits of ABC, he is not considered to own any shares of X stock.

(3) **Attribution from estates and trusts**—(i) In general. An interest in an organization (hereinafter called an "organization interest") owned, directly or indirectly, by or for an estate or trust shall be considered as owned by any beneficiary of such estate or trust who has an actuarial interest of 5 percent or more in such organization interest, to the extent of such actuarial interest. For purposes of this subparagraph, the actuarial interest of each beneficiary shall be determined by assuming the maximum exercise of discretion by the fiduciary in favor of such beneficiary and the maximum use of the organization interest to satisfy the beneficiary's rights. A beneficiary of an estate or trust who cannot under any circumstances receive any part of an organization interest held by the estate or trust, including the proceeds from the disposition thereof, or the income therefrom, does not have an actuarial interest in such organization interest. Thus, where stock owned by a decedent's estate has been specifically bequeathed to certain beneficiaries and the remainder of the estate has been specifically bequeathed to other beneficiaries, the stock is attributable only to the beneficiaries to whom it is specifically bequeathed. Similarly, a remainderman of a trust who cannot under any circumstances receive any interest in the stock of a corporation which is a part of the corpus of the trust (including any accumulated income therefrom or the proceeds from a disposition thereof) does not have an actuarial interest in such stock. However, an income beneficiary of a trust does have an actuarial interest in stock if he has any right to the income from such stock even though under the terms of the trust instrument such stock can never be distributed to him. The factors and methods prescribed in § 20.2031-10 of this chapter (Estate Tax Regulations) for use in ascertaining the value of an interest in property for estate tax purposes shall be

Proposed Reg. § 1.414(c)-4

used for purposes of this subdivision in determining a beneficiary's actuarial interest in an organization interest owned directly or indirectly by or for an estate or trust.

(ii) Special rules for estates. (A) For purposes of this subparagraph (3) with respect to an estate, property of a decedent shall be considered as owned by his or her estate if such property is subject to administration by the executor or administrator for the purposes of paying claims against the estate and expenses of administration notwithstanding that, under local law, legal title to such property vests in the decedent's heirs, legatees or devisees immediately upon death.

(B) For purposes of this subparagraph (3) with respect to an estate, the term "beneficiary" includes any person entitled to receive property of a decedent pursuant to a will or pursuant to laws of descent and distribution.

(C) For purposes of this subparagraph (3) with respect to an estate, a person shall no longer be considered a beneficiary of an estate when all the property to which he or she is entitled has been received by him or her, when he or she no longer has a claim against the estate arising out of having been a beneficiary, and when there is only a remote possibility that it will be necessary for the estate to seek the return of property from him or her or to seek payment from him or her by contribution or otherwise to satisfy claims against the estate or expenses of administration.

(iii) Grantor trusts, etc. An interest owned, directly or indirectly, by or for any portion of a trust of which a person is considered the owner under subpart E, part I, subchapter J of the Code (relating to grantors and others treated as substantial owners) is considered as owned by such person.

(4) **Attribution from corporations**—(i) General. An interest owned, directly or indirectly, by or for a corporation shall be considered as owned by any person who owns (directly and, in the case of a parent-subsidiary group of trades or businesses under common control, with the application of paragraph (b)(1) of this section, or in the case of a brother-sister group of trades or business under common control, with the application of this section), 5 percent or more in value of its stock in that proportion which the value of the stock which such person so owns bears to the total value of all the stock in such corporation.

(ii) Example. The provisions of paragraph (b)(4)(i) of this section may be illustrated by the following example:

Example. B, an individual, owns 60 of the 100 shares of the only class of outstanding stock of corporation P. C, an individual, owns 4 shares of the P stock, and corporation X owns 36 shares of the P stock. Corporation P owns, directly and indirectly, 50 shares of the stock of S. Under this subparagraph, B is considered to own 30 shares of the S stock (60/100 × 50), and X is considered to own 18 shares of S stock (36/100 × 50). Since C does not own 5 percent or more in the value of P stock, he is not considered as owning any of the S stock owned by P. If in this example, C's wife had owned directly 1 share of the P stock, C and his wife would each own 5 shares of the P stock, and therefore C and his wife would be considered as owning 2.5 shares of the S stock (5/100 × 50).

(5) **Spouse**—(i) General rule. Except as provided in paragraph (b)(5)(ii) of this section, an individual shall be considered to own an interest owned, directly or indirectly, by or for his or her spouse, other than a spouse who is legally separated from the individual under a decree of divorce, whether interlocutory or final, or a decree of separate maintenance.

(ii) Exception. An individual shall not be considered to own an interest in an organization owned, directly or indirectly, by or for his or her spouse on any day of a taxable year of such organization, provided that each of the following conditions are satisfied with respect to such taxable year:

(A) Such individual does not, at any time during such taxable year, own directly any interest in such organization;

(B) Such individual is not a member of the board of directors, a fiduciary, or an employee of such organization and does not participate in the management of such organization at any time during such taxable year;

(C) Not more than 50 percent of such organization's gross income for such taxable year was derived from royalties, rents, dividends, interest, and annuities; and

(D) Such interest in such organization is not, at any time during such taxable year, subject to conditions which substantially restrict or limit the spouse's right to dispose of such interest and which run in favor of the individual or the individual's children who have not attained the age of 21 years. The principles of § 1.414(c)-3(d)(6)(i) shall apply in determining whether a condition is a condition described in the preceding sentence.

(iii) Definitions. For purposes of paragraph (b)(5)(ii)(C) of this section, the gross income of an organization shall be determined under section 61 and the regulations thereunder. The terms "interest", "royalties", "rents", "dividends", and "annuities" shall have the same meaning such terms are given for purposes of section 1244(c) and § 1.1244(c)-1(g)(1).

(6) **Children, grandchildren, parents, and grandparents**—(i) Children and parents. An individual shall be considered to own an interest owned, directly or indirectly, by or for the individual's children who have not attained the age of 21 years, and if the individual has not attained the age of 21 years, an interest owned, directly or indirectly, by or for the individual's parents.

(ii) Children, grandchildren, parents, and grandparents. If an individual is in effective control (within the meaning of § 1.414(c)-2(c)(2)), directly and with the application of the rules of this paragraph without regard to this subdivision, of an organization, then such individual shall be considered to own an interest in such organization owned, directly or indirectly, by or for the individual's parents, grandparents, grandchildren, and children, who have attained the age of 21 years.

(iii) Adopted children. For purposes of this section, a legally adopted child of an individual shall be treated as a child of such individual.

(iv) Example. The provisions of this subparagraph (6) may be illustrated by the following example:

Example—(A) Facts. Individual F owns directly 40 percent of the profits interest of the DEF Partnership. His son, M, 20 years of age, owns directly 30 percent of the profits interest of DEF, and his son, A, 30 years of age, owns directly 20 percent of the profits interest of DEF. The 10 percent remaining of the profits interest and 100 percent of the capital interest of DEF is owned by an unrelated person.

(B) F's ownership. F owns 40 percent of the profits interest in DEF directly and is considered to own the 30 percent profits interest owned directly by M. Since, for purposes of the effective control test contained in paragraph (b)(6)(ii) of this section, F is treated as owning 70 percent of the profits interest of DEF, F is also considered as owning the 20 percent profits interest of DEF owned by his adult son, A. Accordingly, F is considered as owning a total of 90 percent of the profits interest in DEF.

(C) M's ownership. Minor son, M, owns 30 percent of the profits interest in DEF directly, and is considered to own the 40 percent profits interest owned directly by his father, F. However, M is not considered to own the 20 percent profits interest of DEF owned directly by his brother, A, and constructively by F, because an interest constructively owned by F by reason of family attribution is not considered as owned by him for purposes of making another member of his family the constructive owner of such interest. (See paragraph (c)(2) of this section.) Accordingly, M owns and is considered as owning a total of 70 percent of the profits interest of the DEF Partnership.

(D) A's ownership. Adult son, A, owns 20 percent of the profits interest in DEF directly. Since, for purposes of determining whether A effectively controls DEF under paragraph (b)(6)(ii) of this section, A is treated as owning only the

Proposed Reg § 1.414 (c)-4

percentage of profits interest he owns directly, he does not satisfy the condition precedent for the attribution of the DEF profits interest from his father. Accordingly, A is treated as owning only the 20 percent profits interest in DEF which he owns directly.

(c) **Operating rules**—(1) **In general.** Except as provided in paragraph (c)(2) of this section, an interest constructively owned by a person by reason of the application of paragraph (b)(1), (2), (3), (4), (5), or (6) of this section shall, for the purposes of applying such paragraph, be treated as actually owned by such person.

(2) **Members of family.** An interest constructively owned by an individual by reason of the application of paragraph (b)(5) or (6) of this section shall not be treated as owned by such individual for purposes of again applying such subparagraphs in order to make another the constructive owner of such interest.

(3) **Precedence of option attribution.** For purposes of this section, if an interest may be considered as owned under paragraph (b)(1) of this section (relating to option attribution) and under any other subparagraph of paragraph (b) of this section, such interest shall be considered as owned by such person under paragraph (b)(1) of this section.

(4) **Examples.** The provisions of this paragraph may be illustrated by the following examples:

Example (1). A, 30 years of age, has a 90 percent interest in the capital and profits of DEF Partnership. DEF owns all the outstanding stock of corporation X and X owns 60 shares of the 100 outstanding shares of corporation Y. Under paragraph (c)(1) of this section, the 60 shares of Y constructively owned by DEF by reason of paragraph (b)(4) of this section are treated as actually owned by DEF for purposes of applying paragraph (b)(2) of this section. Therefore, A is considered as owning 54 shares of the Y stock (90 percent of 60 shares).

Example (2). Assume the same facts as in example (1). Assume further that B, who is 20 years of age and the brother of A, directly owns 40 shares of Y stock. Although the stock of Y owned by B is considered as owned by C (the father of A and B) under paragraph (b)(6)(i) of this section, under paragraph (c)(2) of this section such stock may not be treated as owned by C for purposes of applying paragraph (b)(6)(ii) of this section in order to make A the constructive owner of such stock.

Example (3). Assume the same facts assumed for purposes of example (2), and further assume that C has an option to acquire the 40 shares of Y stock owned by his son, B. The rule contained in paragraph (c)(2) of this section does not prevent the reattribution of such 40 shares to A because, under paragraph (c)(3) of this section, C is considered as owning the 40 shares by reason of option attribution and not by reason of family attribution. Therefore, since A is in effective control of Y under paragraph (b)(6)(ii) of this section, the 40 shares of Y stock constructively owned by C are reattributed to A. A is considered as owning a total of 94 shares of Y stock.

§ 1.414(c)-5 (Proposed Treasury Decision, filed 11-5-75.) **Effective date.**

(a) **General rule.** Except as provided in paragraph (b) or (c) of this section, the provisions of § 1.414(b), § 1.414(b)-1, and §§ 1.414(c) through 1.414(c)-4 shall apply for plan years beginning after September 2, 1974.

(b) **Existing plans.** In the case of a plan in existence on January 1, 1974, unless paragraph (c) of this section applies, the provisions of § 1.414(b), § 1.414(b)-1, and §§ 1.414(c) through 1.414(c)-4 shall apply for plan years beginning after December 31, 1975. For definition of the term "existing plan", see proposed § 1.410 (a)-2(c).

(c) **Existing plans electing new provisions.** In the case of a plan in existence on January 1, 1974, for which the plan administrator elects pursuant to § 11.410

(a)-2(d), the provisions of §1.414(b), §1.414(b)-1, and §§1.414(c) through 1.414(c)-4 shall apply to plan years as provided in §11.410(a)-2(d).

(d) **Application.** For purposes of the Employee Retirement Income Security Act of 1974, the provisions of §1.414(b), §1.414(b)-1 and §§1.414(c) through 1.414(c)-4 do not apply for any period of time before the plan years described in paragraph (a), (b), or (c) of this section, whichever is applicable.

The following sections are inserted in the appropriate place:

§1.414(e)-1 (Proposed Treasury Decision, published 4-8-77.) **Definition of church plan.**

(a) **General rule.** For the purposes of part I of subchapter D of chapter 1 of the Code and the regulations thereunder, the term "church plan" means a plan established and at all times maintained for its employees by a church or by a convention or association of churches (hereinafter included within the term "church") which is exempt from tax under section 501(a), provided that such plan meets the requirements of paragraphs (b) and (if applicable) (c) of this section. If at any time during its existence a plan is not a church plan because of a failure to meet the requirements set forth in this section, it cannot thereafter become a church plan.

(b) **Unrelated businesses—(1) In general.** A plan is not a church plan unless it is established and maintained primarily for the benefit of employees (or their beneficiaries) who are not employed in connection with one or more unrelated trades or businesses (within the meaning of section 513).

(2) **Establishment or maintenance of a plan primarily for persons not employed in connection with one or more unrelated trades or businesses.** (i) (A) A plan, other than a plan in existence on September 2, 1974, is established primarily for the benefit of employees (or their beneficiaries) who are not employed in connection with one or more unrelated trades or businesses if on the date the plan is established the number of employees employed in connection with the unrelated trades or businesses eligible to participate in the plan is less than 50 percent of the total number of employees of the church eligible to participate in the plan.

(B) A plan in existence on September 2, 1974, is to be considered established as a plan primarily for the benefit of employees (or their beneficiaries) who are not employed in connection with one or more unrelated trades or businesses if it meets the requirements of both paragraphs (b)(2)(ii)(A) and (B) (if applicable) in either of its first 2 plan years ending after September 2, 1974.

(ii) For plan years ending after September 2, 1974, a plan will be considered maintained primarily for the benefit of employees of a church who are not employed in connection with one or more unrelated trades or businesses if in 4 out of 5 of its most recently completed plan years—

(A) Less that 50 percent of the persons participating in the plan (at any time during the plan year) consist of, and in the same year

(B) Less that 50 percent of the total compensation paid by the employer during the plan year (if benefits or contributions are a function of compensation) to employees participating in the plan is paid to,

employees employed in connection with an unrelated trade or business. The determination that the plan is not a church plan will apply to the second year (within a 5 year period) for which the plan fails to meet paragraph (b)(2)(ii)(A) or (B) (if applicable) and to all plan years thereafter unless, taking into consideration all of the facts and circumstances as described in paragraph (b)(2)(iii) of this section, the plan is still considered to be a church plan. A plan that has not completed 5 plan years ending after September 2, 1974, shall be considered maintained primarily for the benefit of employees not employed

Proposed Reg. §1.414(e)-1

in connection with an unrelated trade or business unless it fails to meet paragraphs (b)(2)(ii)(A) and (B) in at least 2 such plan years.

(iii) Even though a plan does not meet the provisions of paragraph (b)(2)(ii) of this section, it nonetheless will be considered maintained primarily for the benefit of employees who are not employed in connection with one or more unrelated trades or businesses if the church maintaining the plan can demonstrate that based on all of the facts and circumstances such is the case. Among the facts and circumstances to be considered in evaluating each case are:

(A) The margin by which the plan fails to meet the provisions of paragraph (b)(2)(ii) of this section, and

(B) Whether the failure to meet such provisions was due to a reasonable mistake as to what constituted an unrelated trade or business or whether a particular person or group of persons were employed in connection with one or more unrelated trades or businesses.

(iv) For purposes of this section, an employee will be considered eligible to participate in a plan if such employee is a participant in the plan or could be a participant in the plan upon making mandatory employee contributions to the plan.

(3) **Employment in connection with one or more unrelated trades or businesses.** An employee is employed in connection with one or more unrelated trades or businesses of a church if a majority of such employee's duties and responsibilities in the employ of the church are directly or indirectly related to the carrying on of such trades or businesses. Although an employee's duties and responsibilities may be insignificant with respect to any one unrelated trade or business, such employee will nonetheless be considered as employed in connection with one or more unrelated trades or businesses if such employee's duties and responsibilities with respect to all of the unrelated trades or businesses of the church represent a majority of the total of such person's duties and responsibilities in the employ of the church.

(c) **Plans of two or more employers.** The term "church plan" does not include a plan which, during the plan year, is maintained by two or more employers unless—

(1) Each of the employers is a church, that is exempt from tax under section 501(a), and

(2) With respect to the employees of each employer, the plan meets the provisions of paragraph (b)(2)(ii) of this section or would be determined to be a church plan based on all the facts and circumstances described in paragraph (b)(2)(iii) of this section.

Thus, if with respect to a single employer the plan does not meet the provision of paragraph (c)(2) of this section the provisions of this paragraph are not met with respect to the entire plan.

(d) **Special rule.** (1) Notwithstanding paragraph (c)(1) of this section, a plan maintained by a church and one or more agencies of such church for the employees of such church and of such agency or agencies, that is in existence on January 1, 1974, shall be treated as a church plan for plan years ending after September 2, 1974, and beginning before January 1, 1983, provided that the plan is described in paragraph (c) of this section without regard to paragraph (c)(1) of this section, and the plan is not maintained by an agency which did not maintain the plan on January 1, 1974.

(2) For the purposes of section 414(e) and this section, an agency of a church means an organization which is exempt from tax under section 501 and which is either controlled by, or associated with, a church. For example, an organization, a majority of whose officers or directors are appointed by a church's governing board or by officials of a church, is controlled by a church within the meaning of this paragraph. An organization is associated with a church if it shares common religious bonds and convictions with that church.

(e) **Religious orders and religious organizations.** For the purpose of this section the term "church" includes a religious order or a religious organization if such order or organization (1) is an integral part of a church, and (2) is engaged in carrying out the functions of a church, whether as a civil law corporation or otherwise.

(f) **Cross reference.** (1) For rules relating to treatment of church plans, see section 410(d), 411(e), 412(h), 4975(g), and the regulations thereunder.

(2) For rules relating to church plan elections, see section 410(d) and the regulations thereunder.

§1.414(f)-1 (Proposed Treasury Decision, published 9-18-75). Defintion of multiemployer plan.

(a) **General rule.** For purposes of part I of subchapter D of chapter 1 of the Code and the regulations thereunder, a plan is a multiemployer plan for a plan year if all of the following requirements are satisfied:

(1) **Number of contributing employers.** More than one employer is required by the plan instrument or other agreement to contribute to the plan for the plan year with respect to the employees participating in the plan.

(2) **Collective bargaining agreement.** The plan is maintained for the plan year pursuant to a collective bargaining agreement between employee representatives and more than one employer.

(3) **Amount of contributions.** Except as provided by paragraph (b) of this section (relating to the special rule for contributions exceeding 50 percent), the amount of contributions made under the plan for the plan year by each employer making contributions is less than 50 percent of the total amount of contributions made under the plan for such plan year by all employers making contributions.

(4) **Benefits.** For the plan year, the plan provides that the amount of benefits payable with respect to each employee participating in the plan is determined without regard to the cessation of contributions by an employer of a participant, except to the extent such benefits accrued as a result of the participant's service with that employer during a period before such employer was a member of the plan.

(5) **Other requirements.** For the plan year, the plan satisfies such other requirements as the Secretary of Labor may by regulations prescribe under the authority of section 414(f)(1)(E) of the Code and section 3(37) of the Employee Retirement Income Security Act of 1974 (Public Law 93-406, 88 Stat. 839). See Labor Department regulations sections 2505.1 through 2505.4 proposed in the Federal Register for December 4, 1974 (39 F.R. 42234).

For purposes of subparagraph (3) of this paragraph and paragraph (b) of this section, the amount of contributions made under the plan for the plan year by each employer shall be the sum of such contributions made on or before the last day of the plan year. For purposes of determining whether contributions are made on or before the last day of the plan year, the rule of section 412(c)(10) and the regulations thereunder shall apply (relating to contributions made two and one-half months after the last day of the plan year). For purposes of subparagraph (4) of this paragraph, a benefit is deemed to have accrued as a result of the participant's service with an employer during a period before such employer was a member of the plan to the extent there is any difference between the participant's accrued benefit calculated under the plan on the date such employer ceases making contributions under the plan and the participant's accrued benefit calculated without regard to his service with such employer during a period before such employer first became a member of the plan. However, such a benefit deemed to have accrued as a result of the participant's service before his employer became a member of the plan may not exceed the benefit accrued under the plan as in effect on the date the employer first became a member of the plan. An employer shall be deemed to be a member of the plan for the period during which he employs any individual who, solely by reason of such employment, is an active participant in the plan. For purposes of section 414(f) and this section, all corporations which are members of a controlled group of corporations (within the meaning of section 1563(a) and the regulations thereunder, but determined without regard to section 1563(e)(3)(C) and the regulations thereunder) are deemed to be one employer.

Proposed Reg. §1.414(f)-1

(b) **Contributions exceeding 50 percent.** If a plan was a multiemployer plan as defined in this section for any plan year (including plan years ending prior to September 3, 1974). "75 percent" shall be substituted for "50 percent" in applying paragraph (a)(3) of this section for subsequent plan years until the first plan year following a plan year in which one employer contributed 75 percent or more of the total amount of contributions made under the plan for that plan year by all employers making contributions. In such case "75 percent" shall not again be substituted for "50 percent" until the plan has met the requirements of paragraph (a) of this section (determined without regard to this paragraph) for one plan year.

(c) **Examples.** The application of this section is illustrated by the following examples. For purposes of these examples, assume that the plan meets the requirements of paragraph (a)(1), (2), (4), and (5) of this section for each plan year.

Example (1). On January 1, 1970, U, V, and W, three employers none of which is a member of a controlled group of corporations with any of the other two employers, establish a plan with a plan year corresponding to the calendar year. U, V, and W each contribute less than one-half of the total contributions made under the plan for each of the years 1970, 1971, and 1972. For the years 1973, 1974, and 1975, U contributes 70 percent and V and W each contribute 15 percent of the total contributions made under the plan for each year. The plan is a multiemployer plan under section 414(f) and this section for 1975 because no employer has contributed 75 percent or more of the total amount contributed for each of the plan years subsequent to 1972.

Example (2). (i) First plan year. On January 1, 1975, X, Y, and Z, three employers none of which is a member of a controlled group of corporations with any of the other two employers, establish a plan with a plan year corresponding to the calendar year. X, Y, and Z each contribute less than one-half of the total contributions made under the plan for 1975. The plan is a multiemployer plan for 1975 because it meets the 50 percent contribution requirement of paragraph (a)(3) of this section.

(ii) Second plan year. For the second plan year, 1976, X contributes 70 percent and Y and Z each contribute 15 percent of the total contributions made under the plan. The plan is multiemployer plan for 1976 because it was a multiemployer plan for the preceding plan year and satisfies the 75 percent contribution requirement of paragraph (b) of this section.

(iii) Third plan year. For the third plan year, 1977, X contributes 80 percent and Y and Z each contribute 10 percent of the total contributions made under the plan. The plan is not a multiemployer plan for 1977 because it fails to satisfy the 75 percent contribution requirement of paragraph (b) of this section.

(iv) Fourth plan year. For the fourth plan year, 1978, Y contributes 60 percent and X and Z each contribute 20 percent of the total contributions made under the plan. The 75 percent contribution requirement of paragraph (b) of this section does not apply. The plan is not a multiemployer plan for 1978 because it fails to satisfy the 50 percent contribution requirement of paragraph (a)(3) of this section.

(v) Fifth plan year. For the fifth plan year, 1979, X, Y, and Z each contribute less than one-half of the total contributions made under the plan. The 75 percent contribution requirement of paragraph (b) of this section does not apply. The plan is a multiemployer plan for 1979 because it again meets the 50 percent contribution requirement of paragraph (a)(3) of this section.

(vi) Sixth plan year. For the sixth plan year, 1980, the plan will continue to be a multiemployer plan, provided that no employer contributes 75 percent or more of the total amount of contributions made under the plan for the plan year.

(d) **Retention of records.** (1) For plan years ending prior to September 3, 1974, a plan may be required to furnish proof that it met the requirements of section 414 (f) and this section for each plan year ending prior to that date to the extent necessary to show the applicability of the 75 percent test provided in paragraph (b) of this section.

(2) For plan years ending after September 2, 1974, a plan may be required to

furnish proof that it met the requirements of section 414(f) and this section for six immediately preceding plan years.

§ 1.414(g)-1 (Proposed Treasury Decision, published 9-18-75.) Definition of plan administrator.

(a) **In general.** For purposes of part I of subchapter D of chapter 1 of the Code and the regulations thereunder, if the instrument under which the plan is operated for a plan year specifically designates a person as plan administrator of the plan, such person is the plan administrator of the plan for the plan year. In the absence of a person so designated as the plan administrator of the plan by the instrument under which the plan is operated, the plan administrator of the plan for the plan year is the person described in subparagraph (1), (2), or (3) of paragraph (b) of this section (whichever applies).

(b) **Plan administrator not specifically designated.** If no person is specifically designated as the plan administrator of the plan for a plan year by the instrument under which the plan is established or operated, the plan administrator of the plan for such year is the person determined under the following rules:

(1) **Single employer.** In the case of a plan maintained by a single employer, the employer is the plan administrator.

(2) **Employee organization.** In the case of a plan maintained by an employee organization, the employee organization is the plan administrator.

(3) **Group representing the parties.** In the case of a plan maintained by two or more employers, or jointly by one or more employers and one or more employee organizations, the association, committee, joint board of trustees, or other similar group of representatives of the parties who maintain the plan, as the case may be, is the plan administrator.

(4) **Person in control of assets.** In any case where a plan administrator may not be determined by application of paragraph (a) of this section and subparagraphs (1), (2) and (3) of this paragraph, the plan administrator is the person or persons actually responsible, whether or not under the terms of the plan, for the control, disposition, or management of the cash or property received by or contributed to the plan, irrespective of whether such control, disposition, or management is exercised directly by such person or persons or indirectly through an agent or trustee designated by such person or persons.

The following new section is inserted immediately after §1.414(g)-1:

§1.414(*l*)-1 (Proposed Treasury Decision, published 7-1-77.) Mergers and consolidations of plans or transfers of plan assets.

(a) **General rule.** Under section 414(*l*),

(1) A trust which forms a part of a plan will not constitute a qualified trust under section 401, and

(2) A plan will not be treated as being qualified under section 403(a) and 405(a), unless, in the case of a merger of consolidation (as defined in paragraph (b)(2) of this section), or a transfer of assets or liabilities (as defined in paragraph (b)(3) of this section), the following condition is satisfied. This condition requires that each participant receive benefits on a termination basis (as defined in paragraph (b)(5) of this section) from the plan immediately after the merger, consolidation or transfer which are equal to or greater than the benefits the participant would receive on a termination basis immediately before the merger, consolidation, or transfer.

(b) **Definitions.** For purposes of this section:

(1) **Single plan.** A plan is a "single plan" if and only if all the plan assets are available to pay benefits to employees who are covered by the plan. For purposes of the preceding sentence, all the assets of a plan will not fail to be available to provide all the benefits of a plan merely because the plan is funded in part or in whole with allocated

Proposed Reg. §1.414(l)-1

insurance instruments. A plan will not fail to be a single plan merely because of the following:

(i) The plan has several distinct benefit structures which apply either to the same or different participants,
(ii) The plan has several plan documents,
(iii) Several employers, whether or not affiliated, contribute to the plan,
(iv) The assets of the plan are invested in several trusts or annuity contracts, or
(v) Separate accounting is maintained for purposes of cost allocation but not for purposes of providing benefits under the plan.

However, more than one plan will exist if a portion of the plan assets is not available to pay some of the benefits. This will be so even if each plan has the same benefit structure or plan document, or if all or part of the assets are invested in one trust with separate accounting with respect to each plan.

(2) **Merger or consolidation.** The terms "merger" or "consolidation" mean the combining of two or more plans into a single plan. A merger or consolidation will not occur merely because one or more corporations undergo a reorganization (whether or not taxable). Furthermore, a merger or consolidation will not occur if two plans are not combined into a single plan, such as by using one trust which limits the availability of assets of one plan to provide the benefits only of that plan.

(3) **Transfer of assets or liabilities.** A "transfer of assets or liabilities" occurs when there is a diminution of assets or liabilities with respect to one plan and the acquisition of these assets or the assumption of these liabilities by another plan. For example, the shifting of assets or liabilities pursuant to a reciprocity agreement between two plans in which one plan assumes liabilities of another plan is a transfer of assets or liabilities. However, the shifting of assets between several funding media used for a single plan (such as between trusts, between annuity contracts, or between trusts and annuity contracts) is not a transfer of assets or liabilities.

(4) **Spinoff.** The term "spinoff" means the splitting of a single plan into two or more plans.

(5) **Benefits on a termination basis.** (i) The term "benefits on a termination basis" means the benefits that would be provided exclusively by the plan assets pursuant to section 4044 of the Employee Retirement Income Security Act of 1974 ("ERISA") and the regulations thereunder if the plan terminated. Thus, the term does not include benefits that are guaranteed by the Pension Benefit Guaranty Corporation, but not provided by the plan assets.

(ii) For purposes of determining the benefits on a termination basis, the allocation of assets to various priority categories under section 4044 of ERISA must be made on the basis of reasonable actuarial assumptions. The assumptions used by the Pension Benefit Guaranty Corporation are deemed reasonable for this purpose.

(iii) If a change in the benefit structure of a plan in conjunction with a merger, consolidation or transfer of assets or liabilities alters the benefits on a termination basis, the change should be designated, at the time the merger, consolidation or transfer occurs, to be effective either immediately before or immediately after that occurrence. In the event that no designation is made, the change in the benefit structure will be deemed to occur immediately after the merger, consolidation or transfer of assets or liabilities.

(6) **Lower funded plan.** (i) The term "lower funded plan" generally means the plan which, immediately prior to the merger, would have its assets exhausted in a higher priority category than the other plan.

(ii) Where two plans, immediately prior to the merger, would have their assets exhausted in the same priority category of section 4044 of ERISA in the event of termination, the lower funded plan is the one in which the assets would satisfy a lesser proportion of the liability allocated to that priority category.

(7) **Priority category.** The term "priority category" means the category of benefits described in each paragraph of section 4044(a) of ERISA. References to higher or highest

priority categories refer to those priority categories which receive the first allocation of assets, i.e. the lowest paragraph numbers in section 4044(a).

(8) **Separate accounting of assets.** The term "separate accounting of assets" means the maintenance of an asset account with respect to a given group of participants which is:

(i) Credited with contributions made to the plan on behalf of the participants and with its allocable share of investment income, if any, and

(ii) Charged with benefits paid to the participants, and with its allocable share of investment losses or expenses.

(c) **Application of section 414(*l*)** —(1) **Two or more plans.** (i) Section 414(*l*) does not apply unless more than one plan is involved. It also does not apply unless at least one plan assumes liabilities from another plan or obtains assets from another plan (as in a merger or spinoff). For purposes of section 414(*l*), a transfer of assets or liabilities will not be deemed to occur merely because a defined contribution plan is amended to become a defined benefit plan. This rule will apply even if, under the facts and circumstances of a particular case, a termination of the defined contribution plan will be considered to have occurred for purposes of other provisions of the Code.

(ii) The requirements of this subdivision may be illustrated as follows:

Example. After acquiring Corporation B, Corporation A amends Corporation B's defined benefit plan (Plan B) to provide the same benefits as Corporation A's defined benefit plan (Plan A). The assets of Plan B are transferred to the trust containing the assets of Plan A in such a manner that the assets of each plan (1) are separately accounted for and (2) are not available to pay benefits of the other plan. Because of condition (2) there are still two plans and, therefore, a merger did not occur. As a result, section 414(*l*) does not apply. If at some later date Corporation A were to sell Corporation B and transfer the assets of Plan B that were separately accounted for to another trust or to an annuity contract solely for the purpose of providing Plan B's benefits, this transfer would also not involve section 414(*l*). This is so because Plan B was a separate plan before the entire transaction and because no plan assumed liabilities or obtained assets from another plan. If, on the other hand, Corporation A merged Plan A and Plan B at the time of the acquisition of Corporation B by deleting condition (2) above, then section 414(*l*) would apply both to the merger of Plan A and Plan B and to the spinoff of Plan B from the merged plan. The spinoff would have to satisfy the requirements of paragraph (n) of this section, even if the assets attributable to Plan A and Plan B were separately accounted for in order to allocate funding costs.

(2) **Multiemployer plans.** Except to the extent provided by regulations of the Pension Benefit Guaranty Corporation, section 414(*l*) does not apply to any transaction to the extent that participants either before or after that transaction are covered under a multiemployer plan within the meaning of section 414(f). Until these regulations are issued, section 414(*l*) does not apply to any of the following situations:

(i) A multiemployer plan is split into two plans, one or both of which are not multiemployer plans, or

(ii) A single employer plan is merged into a multiemployer plan.

Therefore, if some (but not all) of the participants in a single employer plan become participants in a multiemployer plan under an agreement in which the multiemployer plan assumes all the liabilities of the single employer plan with respect to these participants and in which some or all of the assets of the single employer plan are transferred to the multiemployer plan, section 414(*l*) applies, but only with respect to the participants in the single employer plan who did not transfer to the multiemployer plan.

(d) **Merger of defined contribution plans.** In the case of a merger of two or more defined contribution plans, the requirements of section 414(*l*) will be satisfied if all of the following conditions are met:

(1) The sum of the account balances in each plan equals the fair market value (determined as of the date of the merger) of the entire plan assets.

Proposed Reg. § 1.414(l)-1

(2) The assets of each plan are combined to form the assets of the plan as merged.

(3) Immediately after the merger, each participant in the plan as merged has an account balance equal to the sum of the account balances the participant had in the plans immediately prior to merger.

(e) **Merger of defined benefit plans**—(1) **General rule.** Section 414(l) compares the benefits on a termination basis before and after the merger. If the sum of the assets of all plans is not less than the sum of the present values of the accrued benefits (whether or not vested) of all plans, the requirements of section 414(l) will be satisfied merely by combining the assets and preserving each participant's accrued benefits. This is so because all the accrued benefits of the plan as merged are provided on a termination basis by the plan as merged. However, if the sum of the assets of all plans is less than the sum of the present values of the accrued benefits (whether or not vested) in all plans, the accrued benefits in the plan as merged are not provided on a termination basis.

(2) **Special schedule of benefits.** Generally, for some participants, the benefits provided on a termination basis for the plan as merged would be different from the benefits provided on a termination basis in the plans prior to merger if the assets were merely combined and if each participant retained his accrued benefit. Some participants would, therefore, receive greater benefits on a termination basis as a result of the merger and some other participants would receive smaller benefits. Accordingly, the requirements of section 414(l) would not be satisfied unless the distribution on termination were modified in some manner to prevent any participant from receiving smaller benefits on a termination basis as a result of the merger. This is accomplished through modifying the application of section 4044 of ERISA by inserting a special schedule of benefits.

(f) **Operational rules for the special schedule.** The application of section 4044 of ERISA as modified by the schedule of benefits is accomplished by the following steps:

(1) Section 4044 is applied in the plan as merged through the priority categories fully satisfied by the assets of the lower funded plan immediately prior to the merger.

(2) The assets in the plan as merged are then allocated to the next priority category as a percentage of the value of the benefits that would otherwise be allocated to that priority category. That percentage is the ratio of (i) the assets allocated to the first priority category not fully satisfied by the lower funded plan immediately prior to the merger to (ii) the assets that would have been allocated had that priority category been fully satisfied.

(3) A schedule of benefits is formed listing participants and scheduled accured benefits. The scheduled accrued benefit is the excess of the benefits provided on a termination basis with respect to any participant from the plans immediately prior to the merger, over the benefits provided on a termination basis in subparagraphs (1) and (2) immediately after the merger. After allocating the assets in accordance with subparagraph (2), the assets are allocated to the schedule of benefits as follows:

(i) First the assets are allocated to the scheduled benefits to the extent that the participant would have benefits provided in subparagraph (4) if there were no scheduled benefits.

(ii) Then the assets are allocated to the scheduled benefits to the extent that the participant would have benefits provided pursuant to subparagraph (5) if there were no scheduled benefits.

These assets should be allocated first to those scheduled benefits that are in the highest priority category under section 4044.

(4) The assets are then allocated to those benefits in the priority category described in subparagraph (2) with respect to which assets were not allocated. This allocation is made to the extent that these benefits are not associated with benefits in the schedule.

(5) Finally, the assets are allocated in accordance with section 4044 with respect to priority categories lower than the priority category described in subparagraph (4). This allocation is made to the extent that these benefits are not associated with benefits in the schedule.

(g) **Successive mergers**—(1) **In general.** In the case of a current merger of a defined benefit plan with another defined benefit plan which as a result of a previous merger has a special schedule, the rules of paragraphs (e) and (f) of this section apply as if the schedule were considered a category described in section 4044 of ERISA. Thus, a second schedule may be formed as a result of the current merger. The second schedule will be inserted in the priority category of section 4044 described in paragraph (f)(2) of this section as of the date of the current merger. This priority category may be higher, lower, or within the schedule of benefits existing on account of a previous merger. If this priority schedule is inserted within a schedule of benefits, a new single schedule of benefits replacing the old schedule of benefits would in effect be created.

(2) **Allocation of assets.** Assets in the new schedule of benefits are allocated as follows:

(i) First to the benefits remaining in the old schedule to the extent that there are assets immediately prior to the second merger to satisfy the original benefits,

(ii) Then to the benefits provided on a termination basis from the plans immediately prior to the second merger to the extent that they are not provided before the schedule after the second merger or in subdivision (i) of this subparagraph,

(iii) Then to benefits remaining in the original schedule not included in subdivision (i) of this subparagraph.

(h) **De minimis rule for merger of defined benefit plan—(1) In general.** In the case of a merger of a defined benefit plan ("smaller plan") whose liabilities (whether or not vested) are less than 3% of the assets of another defined benefit plan ("larger plan") as of at least one day in the larger plan's plan year in which the merger of the two plans occurs, section 414(l) will be deemed to be satisfied if the following condition is met. The condition requires that a special schedule of benefits (consisting of all the benefits that would be provided by the smaller plan on a termination basis just prior to the merger) be payable in a priority category higher than the highest priority category in section 4044 of ERISA. Assets will be allocated to that schedule in accordance with the allocation of assets to scheduled benefits in paragraph (f)(3) of this section.

(2) **Application to a series of mergers.** In the case of a series of such mergers in a given plan year of the larger plan, the rule described in subparagraph (1) will apply only if the sum of the liabilities (whether or not vested) assumed by the larger plan are less than 3% of the assets of the larger plan as of at least one day in the plan year of the larger plan in which the mergers occurred.

(3) **Application to a merger occurring over more than one plan year.** In the case of a merger of a smaller plan or a portion thereof with a larger plan designed to occur in steps over more than one plan year of the larger plan, the entire transaction will be deemed to occur in the plan year of the larger plan which contains the first of these steps.

(4) **Liabilities of the smaller plan.** (i) For purposes of subparagraphs (2) and (3), mergers satisfying paragraphs (e), (f) or (g) of this section will be ignored in determining the sum of the liabilities assumed by the larger plan.

(ii) For purposes of this paragraph, the liabilities of the smaller plan will be determined on the basis of reasonable actuarial assumptions described in paragraph (b)(5)(ii) of this section.

(i) **Data maintenance—(1) Alternative to the special schedule.** In the case of a merger which would require the creation of a special schedule in order to satisfy section 414(l), the schedule need not be created at the time of the merger if data sufficient to create the schedule is maintained. The schedule would only have to be created in the event of a subsequent plan termination or a subsequent spinoff. In that case the schedule must be determined as of the date of the merger.

(2) **Required data.** The data that must be maintained depends on the plan. Care should be taken to ensure that each element of data necessary to determine the schedule as of the date of merger is maintained, and an enrolled actuary must so certify to the plan administrator.

Proposed Reg. §1.414(l)-1

(j) Five year rule—(1) Limitation on the required use of the special schedule. A plan will not fail to satisfy the requirements of section 414(*l*) merely because the effects of the special schedule created pursuant to paragraphs (e)(2) or (h) of this section are ignored 5 years after the date of a merger. Furthermore, the data maintained pursuant to paragraph (i) of this section need not be maintained for more than 5 years after the merger, if the plan does not have a spinoff or a termination within 5 years.

(2) Illustration. If Plans A and B merge to form Plan AB and if Plan AB merges with Plan C 3 years later to form Plan ABC and if Plan ABC terminates 4 years later, the data relating to the merger of Plans A and B need not be maintained for more than 5 years after the merger of Plans A and B. In addition, after 5 years have elapsed after the merger of Plans A and B, the effect of any special schedule created by the merger of Plans A and B on the schedule created by the merger of Plans AB and C may be ignored in determining the later schedule.

(k) Examples. The provisions of paragraphs (e) through (j) of this section may be illustrated by the following examples:

Example (1). Plan A, whose assets are $220,000, is to be merged with Plan B, whose assets are $200,000. Plan A has three employees. Plan B has two employees. If Plans A and B were to terminate just prior to the merger, the benefits provided on a termination basis would be as follows:

Plan A

Priority Category of Section 4044 of ERISA	(1) Annual Accrued Benefits EE_1 EE_2 EE_3	(2) Present Value of Accrued Benefits EE_1 EE_2 EE_3	(3) Fair Market Value of Assets Allocated to Priority Category	(4) Benefits on a Termination Basis EE_1 EE_2 EE_3
3	$10,000	$120,000	$120,000	$10,000
4	2,000 $4,000	24,000 $44,000	68,000	2,000 $4,000
5	3,000 $4,000	33,000 $40,000	32,000	1,315* $1,753**
6	1,000	10,000		
			$220,000	$12,000 $5,315 $1,753

*$3,000 × $\dfrac{\$32,000}{\$73,000}$ i.e. Accrued Benefit × $\dfrac{\text{Assets available for priority category 5}}{\text{Total present value of accrued benefits in category 5}}$

**$4,000 × $\dfrac{\$32,000}{\$73,000}$

Plan B

	EE_4 EE_5	EE_4 EE_5		EE_4 EE_5
3	$15,000	$195,000	$195,000	$15,000
4	$5,000	$50,000	5,000	$500*
5	8,000	80,000		
			$200,000	$15,000 $500

*$5,000 × $\dfrac{\$5,000}{\$50,000}$

Because Plan B's assets are exhausted in a higher priority category than Plan A's assets, Plan B is the lower funded plan. A schedule will, therefore, be inserted in Priority Category 4 of the plan as merged after providing 10% of the benefits provided in category 4, i.e. the ratio of $5,000 assets in Plan B allocated to category 4 to the $50,000 liability in category 4. The schedule would be constructed as follows:

	(1)	(2)	(3)	(4)	(5)
		Benefits Provided	10% of Benefits		
	Benefits on a	from Priority	Provided in	Benefits Provided	Schedule of
	Termination Basis	Categories Higher	Priority	Before Schedule	Benefits
EE	Before Merger	Than Category 4	Category 4	(2) + (3)	(1) − (4)
1	$12,000	$10,000	$200	$10,200	$1,800
2	5,315		400	400	4,915
3	1,753				1,753
4	15,000	15,000		15,000	
5	500		500	500	

Example (2). The facts are the same as in Example (1). The plan, however, terminates one year later. Furthermore, no employee has accrued additional benefits during the year except that the $2,000 benefit of EE₁ that was originally in category 4 is now in category 3. The assets would be allocated to the priority categories to the extent that there are assets to cover the following benefits.

Priority Termination Category	EE₁	EE₂	EE₃	EE₄	EE₅
3	$12,000			$15,000	
10% of 4		$ 400			$ 500
Schedule of Benefits Included in balance of Category 4		3,600			
Schedule of Benefits Included in Category 5		1,315	$1,753		
Schedule of Benefits Included in Category 6					
Balance of Category 4 Not included in schedule					4,500
Balance of Category 5 Not included in schedule		1,685	2,247		8,000
Balance of Category 6 Not included in schedule			1,000		

(1) **Merger of defined benefit and defined contribution plan.** In the case of a merger of a defined benefit plan with a defined contribution plan, one of the plans before the merger should be converted into the other type of plan (i.e., the defined benefit converted into a defined contribution or the defined contribution converted into a defined benefit) and either paragraph (d) or paragraphs (e) through (j) of this section, whichever is appropriate, should be applied.

(m) **Spinoff of a defined contribution plan.** In the case of a spinoff of a defined contribution plan, the requirements of section 414(l) will be satisfied if after the spinoff—

(1) The sum of the account balances for each of the participants in the resulting plans equals the account balance of the participant in the plan before the spinoff, and

(2) The assets in each of the plans immediately after the spinoff equals the sum of the account balances for all participants in that plan.

(n) **Spinoff of a defined benefit plan—(1) General rule.** In the case of a spinoff of a defined benefit plan, the requirements of section 414(l) will be satisfied if—

(i) All of the accrued benefits of each participant are allocated to only one of the spun off plans, and

(ii) The value of the assets allocated to each of the spun off plans is not less than the sum of the present value of the benefits on a termination basis in the plan before the spinoff for all participants in that spunoff plan.

(2) **De minimus rule.** In the case of a spinoff, the requirements of section 414(l) will be deemed to be satisfied if the value of the assets spun off—

(i) Equals the present value of the accrued benefits spun off (whether or not vested)

Proposed Reg. §1.414(l)-1

on the basis of reasonable actuarial assumptions described in paragraph (b)(5)(ii) of this section, and

(ii) In conjunction with other assets spun off during the plan year in accordance with this subparagraph, is less than 3% of the assets as of at least one day in that year. Spinoffs occurring in previous or subsequent plan years are ignored if they are not part of a single spinoff designed to occur in steps over more than one plan year.

(3) **Special temporary rule.** In the case of a defined benefit plan maintained for different groups of employees, which is a single plan (as defined in paragraph (b)(1) of this section) and under which there has been separate accounting of assets for each group, a spinoff of the plan on or before July 1, 1978, into a separate plan for each group will be deemed to satisfy section 414(l) if—

(i) All the liabilities with respect to each group of employees are allocated to a separate plan for that group of employees, and

(ii) The assets that are separately accounted for with respect to each group of employees are allocated to the separate plan for that group of employees.

(o) **Transfers of assets or liabilities.** Any transfer of assets or liabilities will for purposes of section 414(l) be considered as a combination of separate mergers and spinoffs using the rules of paragraphs (d), (e) through (j), (l), (m) or (n) of this section, whichever is appropriate. Thus, if a block of assets and liabilities are transferred from Plan A to Plan B, each of which is a defined benefit plan, the transaction will be considered as a spinoff from Plan A and a merger of one of the spinoff plans with Plan B. The spinoff and merger described in the previous sentence would be subject to the requirements of paragraphs (n) and (e) through (j) of this section, respectively.

(p) **Effective date.** The provisions of this section apply to mergers, consolidations and transfers of assets or liabilities which occur after September 2, 1974.

Employee Stock Options

Paragraph (a)(2) of § 1.421-6 is amended to read as follows:

§ 1.421-6 (Proposed Treasury Decision, published 6-3-71.) **Options to which section 421 does not apply.**

(a) **Scope of section.** * * *

(2) This section is applicable to options granted on or after February 26, 1945, and before July 1, 1969 (except to the extent that paragraph (b) of § 1.83-8 applies), except that this section is not applicable to—

(i) Property transferred pursuant to an option exercised before September 25, 1959, if the property is transferred subject to a restriction which has a significant effect on its value, or

(ii) Property transferred pursuant to an option granted before September 25, 1959, and exercised on or after such date, if, under the terms of the contract granting such option, the property to be transferred upon the exercise of the option is to be subject to a restriction which has a significant effect on its value and if such property is actually transferred subject to such restriction. However, if an option granted before September 25, 1959, and on or after February 26, 1945, is sold or otherwise disposed of before exercise, the provisions of this section shall be fully applicable to such disposition.

* * * * * * * * * * *

Returns for Short Period

Section 1.443-1 is amended by redesignating paragraph (d) as paragraph (e) and by adding new paragraph (d) immediately after paragraph (c). These amended provisions read as follows:

§ 1.443-1 (Proposed Treasury Decision, published 12-30-70.) **Returns for period of less than 12 months.**

* * * * * * * * * * * * *

(d) Adjustment in exclusion for computing minimum tax for tax preferences. (1) If a return is made for a short period on account of any of the reasons specified in subsection (a) of section 443, the $30,000 amount specified in section 56 (relating to minimum tax for tax preferences), modified as provided by section 58 and the regulations thereunder, shall be reduced to the amount which bears the same ratio to such specified amount as the number of days in the short period bears to 365.

(2) **Example.** The provisions of this paragraph may be illustrated by the following example:

Example. A taxpayer who is an unmarried individual has been granted permission under section 442 to change his annual accounting period files a return for the short period of 4 months ending April 30, 1970. The $30,000 amount specified in section 56 is reduced as follows:

$$\frac{120 \times \$30{,}000}{365} = \$9{,}835.89.$$

(e) Cross references.* * *

General Rule for Taxable Year of Inclusion

Section 1.451-1 is amended by adding at the end thereof a new paragraph (e), to read as follows:

§1.451-1 (Proposed Treasury Decision, published 9-29-77.) **General rule for taxable year of inclusion.**

* * * * * * * * * * * *

(e) **Special rule for inclusion of qualified tax refund effected by allocation.** For rules relating to the inclusion in income of an amount paid by a taxpayer in respect of his liability for a qualified State individual income tax and allocated or reallocated in such a manner as to apply it toward the taxpayer's liability for the Federal income tax, see paragraph (f)(1) of §301.6361-1 of this chapter (Regulations on Procedure and Administration).

Installment Method

Section 1.453-7 is amended by revising subparagraphs (2) and (3) of paragraph (b). These amended provisions read as follows:

§1.453-7 (Proposed Treasury Decision, published 12-30-70.) **Change from accrual to installment method by dealers.**

* * * * * * * * * * * * * * *

(b) **Adjustment to tax.** * * *

* * * * * * * * * * * * * * *

(2) The tax determined in any of the steps provided in subparagraph (1) of this paragraph shall be the tax imposed by chapter 1, subtitle A of the Internal Revenue Code of 1954 other than the tax imposed by section 56 (relating to the minimum tax for tax preferences); or chapter 1, not including subchapter D, relating to excess profits, nor subchapter E, relating to tax on self-employment income, of the Internal Revenue Code of 1939.

(3) The computation of the adjustment provided in section 453(c)(2) may be illustrated by the following example, the principles of which are equally applicable to sales under a revolving credit plan which are reported on the installment method:

Proposed Reg. §1.453-7

ADJUSTMENTS IN TAX ON CHANGE TO INSTALLMENT METHOD

| | Taxable years (prior to change) || Adjustment years (after change) ||
	Year 1	Year 2	Year 3	Year 4
Gross profit from installment sales (receivable in periodic payments over 5 years)	$100,000	$50,000	[1] $20,000 [2] 10,000 [3] 80,000	[4] $12,000 [5] 8,000 [6] 40,000 [7] 90,000
Other income	80,000	200,000	90,000	90,000

| | Taxable years (prior to change) || Adjustment years (after change) ||
	Year 1	Year 2	Year 3	Year 4
Gross income	180,000	250,000	200,000	240,000
Deductions	60,000	50,000	50,000	60,000
Taxable income	120,000	200,000	150,000	180,000
Tax rate assumed (percentage of tax, other than tax imposed by section 56)	30	50	40	40
Tax would be	$36,000	$100,000	$60,000	$72,000

Computation of Adjustment in year 3

		Lesser tax portions
	Year 1 items	
In year 3 (portion of tax)	20,000/200,000 × 60,000 = $6,000	
In year 1 (portion of tax)	20,000/180,000 × 36,000 = $4,000	$4,000
	Year 2 items	
In year 3 (portion of tax)	10,000/200,000 × 60,000 = $3,000	
In year 2 (portion of tax)	10,000/250,000 × 100,000 = $4,000	3,000
Adjustment to tax of year 3		$7,000

Computation of Adjustment in Year 4

	Year 1 items	
In year 4 (portion of tax)	12,000/240,000 × 72,000 = $3,600	
In year 1 (portion of tax)	12,000/180,000 × 36,000 = $2,400	$2,400
	Year 2 items	
In year 4 (portion of tax)	8,000/240,000 × 72,000 = $2,400	
In year 2 (portion of tax)	8,000/250,000 × 100,000 = $3,200	2,400
Adjustment to tax of year 4		$4,800

[1] and [4] from year 1 sales.
[2] and [5] from year 2 sales.
[3] and [6] from year 3 sales.
[7] from year 4 sales.

* * * * * * * * * * * *

Year of Deduction

Section 1.461-1 is amended by revising paragraph (a)(3)(iii) to read as follows:

§ 1.461-1 (Proposed Treasury Decision, published 7-15-71.) **General rule for taxable year of deduction.**

(a) General rule. * * *

(3) Other factors which determine when deductions may be taken.

* * * * * * * * * * *

(iii) For special rules relating to certain deductions, see the following sections and the regulations thereunder: Section 165(e), relating to losses resulting from theft; section 165(h), relating to an election of the year of deduction of disaster losses; section 1253(d), relating to the deductibility of payments made by the transferee of a franchise, trademark, or trade name; section 1341, relating to the computation of tax where the taxpayer repays a substantial amount received under a claim of right in a prior taxable year; and section 1481, relating to accounting for amounts repaid in connection with renegotiation of a government contract.

* * * * * * * * * * *

Exempt Organizations

Paragraph (a) of section 1.501(c)(2)-1 is amended to read as follows:

§ 1.501(c)(2)-1 (Proposed Treasury Decision, published 5-13-71.) **Corporations organized to hold title to property for exempt organizations.**

(a) A corporation described in section 501(c)(2) and otherwise exempt from tax under section 501(a) is taxable upon its unrelated business taxable income if the income is payable to an organization which is itself subject to the tax imposed by section 511 or if the income is payable to a church or to a convention or association of churches. See part II (section 511 and following), subchapter F, chapter 1 of the Code, and the regulations thereunder.

* * * * * * * * *

§ 1.501(c)(2)-1 (Proposed Treasury Decision, published 7-8-75.) **Corporations organized to hold title to property for exempt organizations.**

(a) A corporation described in section 501(c)(2) and otherwise exempt from tax under section 501(a) is taxable upon its unrelated business taxable income. For taxable years beginning before January 1, 1970, see § 1.511-2(c)(4). Since a corporation described in section 501(c)(2) cannot be exempt under section 501(a) if it engages in any business other than that of holding title to property and collecting income therefrom, it cannot have unrelated business taxable income as defined in section 512 other than debt financed income which is treated as unrelated business taxable income solely because of section 514; or certain interest, annuities, royalties, or rents which are treated as unrelated business taxable income solely because of section 512(b)(3)(B)(ii) or (15). Similarly, exempt status under section 501(c)(2) shall not be affected where certain rents from personal property leased with real property are treated as unrelated business taxable income under section 512(b)(3)(A)(ii) solely because such rents attributable to such personal property are more than incidental when compared to the total rents received or accrued under the lease, or under section 512(b)(3)(B)(i) solely because such rents attributable to such personal property exceed 50 percent of the total rents received or accrued under the lease.

* * * * * * * * * *

The following new section is inserted immediately after § 1.501 (c)(9).

§ 1.501(c)(9)-1 (Proposed Treasury Decision, published 1-23-69.) **Voluntary employees' beneficiary associations.**

(a) *In general.* The exemption provided by section 501(a) for an organization described in section 501(c)(9) applies if all of the following requirements are met—

(1) The organization is an association of employees;

(2) The membership of the employees in the association is "voluntary",

(3) The organization is operated only for the purpose of providing for the payment of life, sick, accident, or other benefits to its members or their dependents,

(4) No part of the net earnings of the organization inures, other than by payment of the benefits described in subparagraph (3) of this paragraph, to the benefit of any private shareholder or individual, and

(5) At least 85 percent of the income of the organization consists of amounts collected from members and amounts contributed to the association by the employer of the members for the sole purpose of making such payments of benefits and meeting expenses.

(b) *Explanation of requirements necessary to constitute an organization described in section 501(c)(9).* For purposes of section 501(c)(9) and paragraph (a) of this section—

(1) *Association of employees*—(i) *In general.* An organization described in

Proposed Reg. § 1.501(c)(9)-1

section 501(c)(9) must be composed of individuals who are entitled to participate in the association by reason of their status as employees who are members of a common working unit. The members of a common working unit include, for example, the employees of a single employer, the employees of one industry, or the members of one labor union. Although membership in such an association need not be offered to all of the employees of a common working unit, membership must be offered to all of the employees of one or more classes of the common working unit and such class or classes must be selected on the basis of criteria which do not limit membership to shareholders, highly compensated employees, or other like individuals. The criteria for defining a class may be restricted by conditions reasonably related to employment, such as, a limitation based on a reasonable minimum period of service, a limitation based on a maximum compensation, or a requirement that a member be employed on a full-time basis. The criteria for defining a class may also be restricted by conditions relating to the type and amount of benefits offered, such as, a requirement that a member meet a reasonable minimum health standard in order to be eligible for life, sick, or accident benefits, or, a requirement which excludes, or has the effect of excluding, employees who are members of another organization offering similar benefits to the extent such employees are eligible for such benefits. Whether a group of employees constitutes an acceptable class is a question to be determined with regard to all the facts and circumstances, taking into account the guidelines set forth in this subdivision. Furthermore, exemption will not be barred merely because the membership of the association includes some individuals who are not employees (within the meaning of subdivision (ii) of this subparagraph) or who are not members of the common working unit, provided that these individuals constitute no more than 10 perecent of the total membership of the association.

(ii) Meaning of employee. (a) The term "employee" has reference to the legal and bona fide relationship of employer and employee. For rules applicable to the determination of whether the employer-employee relationship exists, see section 3401(c) and the regulations thereunder.

(b) The term "employee" also includes—

(1) An individual who would otherwise qualify for membership under (a) of this subdivision, but for the fact that he is retired or on leave of absence;

(2) An individual who would otherwise qualify under (a) of this subdivision but subsequent to the time he qualifies for membership he becomes temporarily unemployed. The term "temporary unemployment" means involuntary or seasonal unemployment, which can reasonably be expected to be of limited duration. An individual will still qualify as an employee under (a) of this subdivision if during a period of temporary unemployment, he performs services as an independent contractor or for another employer.

(3) An individual who qualifies as an employee under the State or Federal unemployment compensation law covering his employment, whether or not such an individual could qualify as an employee under the usual common law rules applicable in determining the employer-employee relationship.

(2) Explanation of voluntary association. An association is not a voluntary association if the employer unilaterally imposes membership in the association on the employee as a condition of his employment and the employee incurs a detriment (for example, in the form of deductions from his pay) because of his membership in the association. An employer will not be deemed to have unilaterally imposed membership on the employee if such employer requires membership as the result of a collective bargaining agreement which validly requires membership in the association.

(3) Life, sick, accident, or other benefits—(i) In general. A voluntary employees' beneficiary association must provide solely (and not merely primarily) for the payment of life, sick, accident, or other benefits to its members or their dependents. Such benefits may take the form of cash or noncash benefits.

(ii) Benefits includible in gross income. Except to the extent otherwise provided in the Code and the regulations thereunder, any cash or noncash benefit received within the meaning of subdivision (iii), (iv) or (v) of this subparagraph, as a life, sick, accident, or other benefit, by a member of a voluntary employees' beneficiary association, is includible in the gross income of such member. In the case of a noncash benefit, the amount to be included in the gross income of the member is the fair market value of the benefit on the date of receipt by the member.

(iii) Life benefits. The term "life benefits" includes life insurance benefits, or similar benefits payable on the death of the member, made available to members for current protection only. Thus, term life insurance is an acceptable benefit. However, life insurance protection made available under an endowment insurance plan or a plan providing cash surrender values to the member is not included. "Life benefits" may be payable to any designated beneficiary of a member.

(iv) Sick and accident benefits. A sick and accident benefit is, in general, an amount furnished in the event of illness or personal injury to or on behalf of a member, his spouse or an individual specified in section 152(a) (even if more than 50 percent support is not furnished). For example, a sick and accident benefit includes an amount provided under a plan to reimburse a member for amounts he expends because of illness or injury, or for premiums which he pays to a medical benefit program such as, Medicare. Sick and accident benefits may also be furnished in noncash form such as, for example, benefits in the nature of clinical care, services by visiting nurses, and transportation furnished for medical care.

(v) Other benefits. The term "other benefits" include only benefits furnished to a member, his spouse or an individual specified in section 152(a) (even if more than 50 percent support is not furnished) which are similar to life, sick, and accident benefits. A benefit is similar to a life, sick, or accident benefit if it is intended to safeguard or improve the health of the employee or to protect against a contingency which interrupts earning power. Thus, paying vacation benefits, subsidizing recreational activities such as athletic leagues, and providing vacation facilities are considered "other benefits" since such benefits protect against physical or mental fatigue and accidents or illness which may result therefrom. Severance payments or supplemental unemployment compensation benefits paid because of a reduction in force or temporary layoff are "other benefits" since they protect the employee in the event of interruption of earning power. However, severance payments at a time of mandatory or voluntary retirement and benefits of the type provided by pension, annuity, profit-sharing, or stock bonus plans are not "other benefits" since their purpose is not to protect in the event of an interruption of earning power. See section 401 and the regulations thereunder for the rules relating to the qualification of such plans for exemption; see also section 801(b)(2)(B) and the regulations thereunder for the rules relating to life insurance reserves of certain voluntary employees' beneficiary associations which do not meet the requirements of section 501(c)(9). Furthermore, the term "other benefits" does not include the furnishing of automobile or fire insurance, or the furnishing of scholarships to the member's dependents.

(4) Inurement to the benefit of any private shareholder or individual. No part of the net earnings of the organization may inure to the benefit of any private shareholder or individual other than through the payment of benefits described in subparagraph (3) of this paragraph. The disposition of property to, or the performance of services for, any person for less than its cost (including the indirect costs) to the association, other than for the purpose of providing such a benefit, will constitute inurement. Further, the payment to any member of disproportionate benefits will not be considered a benefit within the meaning of subparagraph (3) even though the benefit is of the type described in such subparagraph. For example, the payment to highly compensated personnel of benefits which are disproportionate in relation to benefits received by other members of the association will constitute inurement. However, the payment to similarly situated employees of benefits which differ in kind or amount will not constitute inurement if such benefits are paid pursuant to objective and reasonable standards. For example, two employees who are similarly situated while employed receive unemployment benefits which differ in kind and amount. These unemployment benefits will not constitute inurement if the reason for the larger payment to the one employee is to provide training for

Proposed Reg. § 1.501(c)(9)-1

that employee to qualify him for reemployment and the other employee has already received such training. Furthermore, the rebate of excess insurance premiums based on experience to the payor of the premium, or a distribution to member-employees upon the dissolution of the association, will not constitute inurement. However, the return of contributions to an employer upon the dissolution of the association will constitute inurement.

(5) *The income test*—(i) *Meaning of the term "income".* The requirement of section 501(c)(9) that 85 percent of the income of a voluntary employees' beneficiary association consists of amounts collected from members and amounts contributed by the employer for the sole purpose of making payment of the benefits described in subparagraph (3) of this paragraph (including meeting the expenses of the association) assures that not more than a limited amount (15 percent) of an association's income is from sources, such as investments, selling goods and performing services, which are foreign to what must be the principal sources of the association's income, i.e., the employees and the employer. Therefore, the term "income" as used in section 501(c)(9) means the gross receipts of the organization for the taxable year, including income from tax exempt investments (but exclusive of gifts and donations) and computed without regard to losses and expenses paid or incurred for the taxable year. The term income does not include the return to the association of an amount previously expended. Thus, for example, rebates of insurance premiums paid in excess of actual insurance costs do not constitute income for this purpose. In order to be an amount collected from a member, it must be collected as a payment, such as dues, qualifying the member to receive an allowable benefit, or as a payment for an allowable benefit actually received. For example, if the association furnishes medical care in a hospital operated by it for its members, an amount received from the member as payment of a portion of the hospital costs is an amount collected from such member. However, an amount paid by an employee as interest on a loan made by the association is not an amount collected from a member since the interest is not an amount collected as payment for an allowable benefit received. For the same reason, gross receipts collected by the association as a result of employee purchases of work clothing from an association-owned store, or employee purchases of food from an association-owned vending machine, are not amounts collected from members. Amounts collected from members or amounts contributed to the association by the employer of the members are not considered gifts or donations.

(ii) *Example.* The provisions of subdivision (i) of this subparagraph are illustrated by the following example:

Example. The books of P, a voluntary employees' beneficiary association, reflect the following information for the taxable year:

Amounts collected from members	$ 6,000
Contributions by the employer	30,000
Sales from vending machine owned by P	300
Tax-exempt interest	4,000
Interest on loans made by P	700
Long-term capital gains	1,000
Insurance rebates	500
Gifts and donations	2,000
Long-term capital losses	5,000
Administrative expenses	3,000

For purposes of the 85 percent requirement of section 501(c)(9), the "income" of P is $42,000, computed as follows:

Amounts collected from members	$ 6,000
Contributions by the employer	30,000
Sales from vending machine owned by P	300
Tax-exempt interest	4,000
Interest on loans made by P	700
Long-term capital gains	1,000
Total income of P	$42,000

The total of the amounts collected from members and contributed by the employer is $36,000 ($6,000 member collections plus $30,000 employer contributions). Since this amount ($36,000) constitutes at least 85 percent of the "income" of P (85 percent of $42,000 is $35,700), P meets the 85 percent requirement of section 501(c)(9) for the taxable year.

(c) **Record keeping requirements.** In addition to such other records which may be required, every organization described in section 501(c)(9) must maintain records indicating the amount of benefits paid by such organization to each member. If the organization is financed, in whole or in part, by amounts collected from members, the organization must maintain records indicating the amounts of each member's contributions. Further, every organization described in section 501(c)(9) which makes one or more payments totaling $600 or more in one year to an individual must file an annual information return in the manner described in paragraph (a) of § 1.6041-2.

Section 1.501(c)(13)-1 is amended to read as follows:

§ 1.501(c)(13)-1 (Proposed Treasury Decision, published 7-8-75.) **Cemetery companies and crematoria.**

(a) **Nonprofit mutual cemetery companies.** A nonprofit cemetery company may be entitled to exemption if it is owned by and operated exclusively for the benefit of its lot owners who hold such lots for bona fide burial purposes and not for the purpose of resale. A mutual cemetery company which also engages in charitable activities, such as the burial of paupers, will be regarded as operating in conformity with this standard.

(b) **Nonprofit cemetery companies and crematoria.** Any nonprofit corporation, chartered solely for the purpose of the burial, or (for taxable years beginning after December 31, 1970) the cremation of bodies, and not permitted by its charter to engage in any business not necessarily incident to that purpose, is exempt from income tax, provided that no part of its net earnings inures to the benefit of any private shareholder or individual.

(c) **Preferred stock**—(1) **In general.** (i) Any cemetery company or crematorium which fulfills the other requirements of section 501(c)(13) may be exempt, even though it issues preferred stock at par entitling the holders to dividends at a fixed rate, not exceeding the legal rate of interest in the State of incorporation or 8 percent per annum whichever is greater, on the value of the consideration for which the stock was issued, provided that its articles of incorporation require that all funds not needed either for the care and improvement of cemetery property or for the payment of dividends, shall be used currently for the retirement of such stock at par. For purposes of this paragraph (c)(1)(i), amounts set aside for the future retirement of such preferred stock shall not be treated as having been used for its "current" retirement until such stock is actually retired, except in the case of amounts set aside for the redemption of preferred stock issued before August 6, 1975 pursuant to a legal obligation requiring such set asides.

(ii) For taxable years beginning before January 1, 1978, a cemetery company or crematorium which issues preferred stock as provided in the preceding paragraph (c)(1)(i), shall not fail to be exempt solely because its articles of incorporation require:

(A) That the preferred stock shall be retired at par as soon as sufficient funds available therefor are realized from sales, and

(B) That all funds not required for the payment of dividends upon or for the retirement of preferred stock shall be used by the company for the care and improvement of the cemetery property.

(2) **Legal rate of interest.** For purposes of this paragraph, the term "legal rate of interest" shall mean the rate of interest prescribed by law in the State of

Proposed Reg. § 1.501(c)(13)-1

incorporation which prevails in the absence of an agreement between contracting parties fixing a rate.

(d) **Sales to exempt cemetery companies and crematoria.** Except as otherwise provided in pararaph (c) (with respect to preferred stock), a cemetery company or crematorium is not exempt from income tax if property is transferred to such organization in exchange for an equity interest. In determining whether property is transferred to a cemetery company or crematorium in exchange for an equity interest, as opposed to being transferred for a bona fide debt obligation, consideration will be given to all the facts and circumstances surrounding the transfer including the following factors:

(1) Whether there is a written unconditional promise to pay on demand or on a specified date a sum certain in money in return for an adequate consideration in money or money's worth, and to pay a fixed rate of interest; and

(2) Whether there is subordination to, or preference over, any indebtedness of the company.

(e) **Convertible debt obligations.** A cemetery company or crematorium is not exempt from income tax under section 501(c)(13) if it issues debt obligations after July 7, 1975 which are convertible into the preferred stock of the company.

Tax on Unrelated Business Income of Exempt Organizations

There is inserted immediately after § 1.511-3 the following new section:

§ 1.511-4 (Proposed Treasury Decision, published 12-30-70.) **Minimum tax for tax preferences.**

The tax imposed by section 56 applies to an organization subject to tax under section 511 with respect to items of tax preference which enter into the computation of unrelated business taxable income. For this purpose, only those items of income and those deductions entering into the determination of the tax imposed by this section are considered in the determination of the items of tax preference under section 57. For rules relating to the minimum tax for tax preferences, see sections 56 through 58 and the regulations thereunder.

Special Rules for Social Clubs and Employees' Associations

There is inserted immediately after § 1.512(a)-2 the following new section.

§ 1.512(a)-3. (Proposed Treasury Decision, published 5-13-71.) **Special rules applicable to organizations described in section 501(c)(7) or (9).**

(a) **Scope and purpose of section 512(a)(3)**—(1) *General rule.* For taxable years beginning after December 31, 1969, organizations described in section 501(c)(7) (referred to in this section as "social clubs") and section 501(c)(9) (referred to in this section as "employees' associations") are subject to the unrelated business tax imposed by section 511. Section 512(a)(3) sets forth special rules for determining the unrelated business taxable income of social clubs and employees' associations. In general, section 512(a)(3) is designed to impose a tax on all income from nonmember sources. Income derived from dues, fees, charges or similar amounts paid by members is not subject to the tax. Moreover, the passive income of a social club or an employees' association will generally not be taxed if it is set aside to be used for religious, charitable, scientific, literary, or educational purposes or for the prevention of cruelty to children or animals. In the case of an employees' association, passive income is generally not taxed if it is set aside to provide for the payment of life, sick, accident, or other benefits. To accomplish this result, subparagraph (A) of section 512(a)(3) provides that the unrelated business taxable income of a social club or an employees' association includes all gross income, less all allowable deductions directly connected with the production of that income, except that gross income for this purpose does not include any "exempt function income." "Exempt function income" is defined in subparagraph (B) of section 512 (a)(3) as gross income from dues, fees, charges, or similar amounts paid by members in connection with the purposes constituting the basis for the exemption of the organization. "Exempt function income" also includes income set aside for the purposes referred to above. However, income derived from an unrelated trade or business may not be set aside and thus cannot be exempt function income. Subparagraph (B) of section 512(a)(3) provides for the inclusion in income of any amounts which have been set aside if such amounts are subsequently expended for other purposes. Special rules are provided in subparagraph (C) of section 512(a)(3) for a corporation described in section 501(c)(2) which pays its income to a social club or an employees' association, and in subparagraph (D) for the nonrecognition of gain on the sale of property used in the performance of an organization's exempt function.

(2) **General computation.** The effect of the rules set forth in this paragraph may be illustrated by the following example:

Example—(a) Facts. S, a social club, derived income from only three sources for the calendar year 1971: gross income from members, gross income from debt-financed property, and gross income from investments (which income did not enter into the computation of unrelated business taxable income under section 512(a)(1) of the Code). S had no net operating loss deduction and no deduction under section 170. S had items of income and deductions for 1971 as follows:

Gross income from:	
Members	$225,000
Debt-financed property	6,500
Investments	3,000
Total	$234,500
Deductions directly connected with gross income from:	
Members	$250,000
Debt-financed property	4,000
Investments	200
Total	$254,200

For 1971 S made a net set aside under section 512(a)(3)(B) of $2,000.

(b) Computation of unrelated business taxable income. (1) From the total gross income of $234,500 and total deductions of $254,200, S excludes $225,000 and $250,000 respectively as gross income from members and the deductions directly connected therewith.

(2) S has net profit from the debt-financed property of $2500 ($6,500 − $4,000).

(3) S has investment income before reductions for set asides of $2,800 ($3,000 − $200).

(4) After reduction for the set aside, S has investment income of $800 ($2,800 − $2,000).

(5) S has unrelated business taxable income of $2,300, determined as follows:

Net profit from debt-financed property	$2,500
Unrelated investment income (after reduction for set aside)	800
Total	$3,300
Less specific deduction allowed by section 512(b)(12)	1,000
Unrelated business taxable income	$2,300

(3) **Scope of paragraph.** For more precise rules for computing the unrelated business taxable income of a social club or an employees' association, see paragraphs (b) through (e) below.

(b) **In general**—(1) **Definition.** The "unrelated business taxable income" of a

Proposed Reg. §1.512(a)-3

social club or an employees' association is its gross income (excluding exempt function income) less those deductions allowed by this chapter which are directly connected with the production of gross income (excluding exempt function income), as modified by paragraphs (6), (10), (11), and (12) of section 512(b). The gross income of a social club or an employees' association is determined by reference to section 61 but does not include those items of income excluded by part III of subchapter B of chapter 1 (sections 101 through 124). To be deductible in computing unrelated business taxable income, expenses, depreciation, and similar items not only must qualify as deductions under chapter 1 of the Code, but also must be directly connected with the production of gross income (excluding exempt function income).

(2) **Directly connected**—(i) In general. An item of deduction otherwise allowable under chapter 1 of the Code will be allowed as a deduction for purposes of computing unrelated business taxable income only if it is both directly connected with the income and incurred in the production of such income. Such determination must be based on all the facts and circumstances. The dividends received deductions otherwise allowed by sections 243, 244, and 245 are not allowable for purposes of computing unrelated business taxable income under this section since they are not expenses incurred in the production of such income.

(ii) Example. The provisions of subdivision (i) of this subparagraph may be illustrated by the following example:

Example. S, a social club, sold its golf course and club house for $300,000, and purchased new, similar facilities further from the city for $400,000. In payment for its old facilities S received a down payment of $100,000 and a purchase money mortgage in the amount of $200,000, bearing interest at six percent per annum. In payment for the new facilities, S gave the seller $100,000 in cash plus a note for $300,000, bearing interest at seven percent per annum. At the time S gave its note for $300,000, the fair market value of the purchase money mortgage was $200,000. During 1971, S had interest income from the purchase money mortgage of $12,000 (6 percent of $200,000) and paid interest on the note given to purchase the new property of $21,000 (7 percent of $300,000). Since the fair market value of the purchase money mortgage was $200,000 at the time that S incurred indebtedness with respect to its new facilities, the interest attributable to $200,000 of such indebtedness is directly connected with the production of the interest income from the purchase money mortgage. Thus, S has a directly-connected interest expense of $14,000 (7 percent of $200,000).

(3) **Income from more than one source.** In the case of a social club or an employee's association which derives gross income (excluding exempt function income) from two or more sources, its unrelated business taxable income is computed by aggregating its gross income from all such sources and by aggregating its deductions allowed with respect to such gross income.

(4) **Expenses attributable solely to unrelated business taxable income.** Expenses, depreciation, and similar items attributable solely to items of gross income (excluding exempt function income) are directly connected with such income and shall be allowable as a deduction in computing unrelated business taxable income to the extent that they qualify as deductions under chapter 1 of the Code.

(5) **Dual use of facilities or personnel.** Where facilities or personnel are used both for the exempt purpose and for the production of gross income (excluding exempt function income), expenses, depreciation, and similar items attributable to such facilities or personnel (for example, items of overhead) shall be allocated between the two uses on a reasonable basis. The portion of any such item so allocated to the production of gross income (excluding exempt function income) is directly connected with such income and shall be allowable as a deduction in computing unrelated business taxable income to the extent that it qualifies as a deduction under chapter 1 of the Code. Thus, for example, assume that X, a social club, pays its manager a salary of $10,000 a year and that it derives gross income other than exempt function income. If the manager devotes 10 percent of his time during the year to deriving X's gross income (other than exempt function income), a deduction of $1,000 (10 percent of $10,000) would be allowable for purposes of computing X's unrelated business taxable income.

(c) **Exempt function income**—(1) **General rule.** For purposes of section 512(a)(3)(A) of the Code and paragraph (b) of this section, the term "exempt function income" means the sum of an organization's gross income from members and its set aside income.

(2) **Gross income from members**—(i) **In general.** The term "gross income from members" means gross income from dues, fees, charges, or similar amounts paid by members of the organization as consideration for providing goods, facilities, or services to such members, their dependents, or guests in furtherance of the purposes constituting the basis for the exemption of the organization. The term "gross income from members" also includes, in the case of an employees' association, amounts paid by members as consideration for providing life, sick, accident, or other benefits to the members, their dependents, or designated beneficiaries. For purposes of this subparagraph, the member's spouse shall be treated as a member.

(ii) **Amounts paid by nonmembers.** "Gross income from members" does not include any amount paid to an organization by any person who is not a member, even though paid as consideration for providing goods, facilities, or services. However, amounts paid by a member's employer directly to a social club or an employees' association, or amounts paid gratuitously for the benefit of a member, are considered to have been paid by the member. Similarly, the fact that a member is reimbursed by his employer or a gratuitous donor for amounts paid to a social club or an employees' association will not prevent the amounts so paid from being considered to have been paid by the member.

(iii) **Definitions.** (a) **Dependent.** The determination of whether an individual is a dependent of a member is made by reference to section 152.

(b) **Guest.** An individual is a guest of a member only if the charges incurred by the guest are borne by the member. Charges paid gratuitously to, or on behalf of, a member are treated as having been borne by the member. For example, where a member and her friends make use of her club and her father pays the charges as a gratuitous benefit to his daughter, such payment will be considered as having

Proposed Reg. §1.512(a)-3

been made by the daughter. Similarly, the employee-member may be reimbursed by his employer, or the employer may pay the club directly, for the expenses incurred by the guest without destroying the host-guest relationship if the guest is present due to some personal or social purpose of the employee-member, or to some direct business objective or relationship of the employee-member in his work for the employer, as opposed to a purpose or objective of the employer which is primarily unrelated to the activities of the particular employee-member. In all other cases, however, if a member is reimbursed by anyone, whether directly or indirectly, for expenses incurred by the would-be guest, no true host-guest relationship exists. For example, assume that an employer has a party for all its employees at the employee-member's club and that the employer pays all the expenses of the party. Under these circumstances, the persons invited are not guests of a member because their presence is not related to a direct objective or relationship of the particular employee-member.

(c) *Employee and employer.* For purposes of this subparagraph, a partner of a partnership shall be considered to be an employee and the partnership shall be considered to be an employer.

(d) *Gratuitous payments.* A payment is gratuitous only if it is excludable from the member's gross income under section 102(a) and the regulations thereunder. Thus, a payment is gratuitous if it is made through detached and disinterested generosity. However, if the payor has reason to believe that he will benefit from the payment, or if he receives some or all the benefit for which he paid, the payment is normally not gratuitous.

(iv) *Illustration.* The provisions of this subparagraph may be illustrated by the following example:

Example. S, a social club, operates a restaurant and bar for members and their guests. Nonmembers are admitted to the restaurant and bar only if accompanied by a member. S is supported by annual dues and amounts received in consideration for food and beverages. S does not normally receive payment for food and beverages at the time they are furnished but, rather, bills its members monthly for such items. Because some members prefer not to be billed, S has facilities for receiving cash payments. Although most cash payments are made by the members and include all expenses incurred by themselves and their guests, some nonmembers insist on paying their own expenses. S did not set aside any amounts under section 512(a)(3)(B) in 1971. In 1971, S received the following amounts of gross income:

Dues	$ 55,000
Receipts from members from sale of food and beverages	195,000
Receipts from nonmembers from sale of food and beverages	5,000
Interest	500
Total	$255,500

S incurred expenses in 1971 of $180,000 from the operation of the restaurant and bar and $72,000 from the performance of other exempt function activities. The portion of the expenses directly connected with the furnishing of food and beverages to nonmembers who pay their own bills was $4,500. No expenses were incurred with respect to the interest income. S computes its unrelated business taxable income as follows:

Gross income		$255,500
Reduced by exempt function income:		
gross income from members ($55,000 + $195,000)		250,000
Gross income (excluding exempt function income)		5,500
Less:		
expenses directly connected therewith	$4,500	
specific deduction allowed by section 512(b)(12)	1,000	5,500
Unrelated business taxable income		—0—

(3) *Set aside income*—(i) *General rule.* For purposes of this section, the term "set aside income" means the net income of a social club or an employees' association which is set aside for the purposes described in subdivision (iii) of this sub-

paragraph. However, a social club or an employees' association may not set aside gross income from members or income that would enter into the computation of unrelated business taxable income (including income from debt-financed property) if the organization were subject to section 512(a)(1). Amounts may be set aside without regard to the limitation imposed by section 512(b)(10). Although set aside income may be accumulated, any accumulation which is unreasonable in amount or duration is evidence that the income was not accumulated for the purposes set forth in subdivision (iii) of this subparagraph. However, income which has been set aside may be invested temporarily, pending the action contemplated by the set aside, without being regarded as having been used for other purposes.

(ii) Computation. A social club or an employees' association which wishes to set aside income must first compute its total gross income other than (a) "gross income from members" and (b) gross income that would enter into the computation of unrelated business taxable income (including income from debt-financed property) if the organization were subject to section 512(a)(1). The remaining gross income must then be reduced by the deductions allowed by this chapter which are directly connected with the production of such remaining gross income. The difference, referred to in this section as "net investment income", may be set aside, in whole or in part, by a social club or employees' association. Deductions directly connected with the production of income which has been set aside are allowable in computing unrelated business taxable income.

(iii) Purposes for which income may be set aside. Income may be set aside for religious, charitable, scientific, literary, or educational purposes, or for the prevention of cruelty to children or animals. In the case of a national organization of college fraternities or sororities, income may be set aside for scholarships, student loans, loans on local chapter housing, leadership and citizenship schools and services, and similar purposes. In the case of an employees' association, income may be set aside to provide for the payment of life, sick, accident, or other benefits. Income also may be set aside to pay any reasonable costs of administration which are directly connected with the disbursement or other handling of income which is set aside. If a social club or an employees' association expends an amount for a purpose described in section 512(a)(3)(B), such amount may be treated as though it had been first set aside, and then expended, for such purposes. For example, assume that during the year a social club has $1,000 of net investment income and $5,000 of net income from an unrelated trade or business. If the social club contributes $3,000 during the year to a charitable organization, it may wish to treat $1,000 of the contribution as a set aside while treating the remaining $2,000 as a direct charitable contribution. Amounts treated as exempt function income by reason of being set aside are not deductible under section 170 or any other section.

(iv) Illustration. The principles of subdivision (iii) of this subparagraph may be illustrated by the following example:

Example. O, a national organization of college fraternities, received the following gross income in 1971:

Dues	$465,000
Investment income	20,000
Total	$485,000

In the same year O incurs management expenses of $2,000 directly connected with its investment activity. On November 10, 1971, O's Board of Directors votes to set aside $13,500 and to place that amount in a fund to be used for "educational purposes" as that phrase is used in section 170(c)(4) of the Code. No part of O's investment income is income which would enter into the computation of unrelated business taxable income under section 512(a)(1) of the Code. O computes its unrelated business taxable income for 1971 as follows:

Proposed Reg. §1.512(a)-3

Gross income		$485,000
Reduced by exempt function income:		
gross income from members	$465,000	
set aside income	13,500	478,500
Gross income (excluding exempt function income)		$ 6,500
Less:		
deductions allowable under this section	$ 2,000	
specific deduction allowed by section 512 (b)(12)	1,000	3,000
Unrelated business taxable income		$ 3,500

(v) *Requirements for set aside.* Net income set aside for a purpose enumerated in subdivision (iii) of this subparagraph must be specifically earmarked as such or placed in a separate account or fund. Thus, something more than a bookkeeping entry is required before income will be considered to have been set aside. Any action describing the income set aside and indicating that it is to be used for one of the designated purposes is sufficient. Income that is set aside need not be permanently committed to such use either under State law or by contract. Thus, for example, it is not necessary that the organization place these funds in an irrevocable trust.

(vi) *Withdrawals of amounts which are set aside.* If an organization withdraws any amount from its set aside fund or account, for any purpose other than those specified in subdivision (iii) of this subparagraph, such amount shall be included in unrelated business taxable income for the year in which it is withdrawn, to the extent that such amounts were previously excluded from gross income. Amounts will be considered withdrawn from a set aside if they are used in any manner— such as security for a loan—which is inconsistent with the purposes enumerated in subdivision (iii) of this subparagraph. Previously excluded amounts withdrawn from a set aside fund or account for a purpose enumerated in subdivision (iii) of this subparagraph are not deductible under section 170 or any other section of the Code. To the extent that the set aside account contains amounts which have previously been included in unrelated business taxable income or amounts which were excluded as gross income from members, withdrawals for other than the enumerated purposes will be considered to be made first out of such amounts. Such withdrawals are not includible in the organization's unrelated business taxable income.

(vii) *Time within which set asides must be made.* Income will generally be excluded from gross income only if it is set aside in the taxable year in which it is includible in gross income. However, income set aside on or before the date prescribed for filing the Exempt Organization Business Income Tax Return (Form 990-T) for the taxable year (including any extension of time) may, at the election of the taxpayer, be treated as having been set aside in such taxable year to the extent attributable to amounts that would have been includible in gross income for such year.

(4) **Example.** The provisions of this paragraph may be illustrated by the following example:

Example. T, a social club, is a calendar year taxpayer and had the following items of gross income in 1971:

Gross income from members	$753,000
Gross income from debt-financed property	13,000
Interest income	4,000
Total	$770,000

T incurred deductible expenses directly connected with the production of the income from the debt-financed property of $10,000 and deductible expenses directly connected with the production of the interest income of $100. The income from the debt-financed property was income which would have been taxable under section 512(a)(1) if T had been subject to that provision. During 1971, T's Board of Directors resolved to place $5,000 in a special bank account to be used for charitable purposes. Pursuant to that resolution, a special account was opened with a savings and loan association and $5,000 deposited therein. T computes its unrelated business taxable income for 1971 as follows:

Gross income		$770,000
Reduced by exempt function income:		
gross income from members	$753,000	
set aside income:		
limited to an amount equal to the net interest income	3,900	756,900
Gross income (excluding exempt function income)		$ 13,100
Less:		
deductions allowable under this section	$ 10,100	
specific deduction allowed by section 512(b)(12)	1,000	11,100
Unrelated business taxable income		$ 2,000

Of the $5,000 deposited in the set aside account, $1,100 ($5,000—$3,900) was previously included in unrelated business taxable income and may be withdrawn for a purpose not specified in § 1.512(a)-3(c)(3)(iii) without being again included in unrelated business taxable income. See § 1.512(a)-3(c)(3)(vi).

(d) **Applicability to certain corporations described in section 501(c)(2)**—(1) **General rule.** In the case of a corporation described in section 501(c)(2) (referred to in this paragraph as a "section 501(c)(2) corporation"), the income of which is payable to a social club or an employees' association (referred to in this paragraph as a "payee organization"), the section 501(c)(2) corporation shall be treated as though it were the payee organization. Thus, if the income of a section 501(c)(2) corporation is payable to a social club or an employees' association, the section 501 (c)(2) corporation will be subject to tax as if it were a social club or an employees' association. However, the section 501(c)(2) corporation shall not be treated as having exempt function income unless it files a consolidated return with the payee organization. See subparagraph (3) of this paragraph for rules applicable where a consolidated return is filed.

(2) **Example.** The principles of subparagraph (1) may be illustrated by the following example:

Example. All the income of S, a section 501(c)(2) corporation, is payable to P, a social club. P and S file separate returns on a calendar year basis for 1971. In 1971 S receives $105,000 in rent from an office building, and incurs expenses directly connected therewith of $85,000. Since S's income is payable to P, the rental income is included in S's unrelated business income pursuant to subparagraph (A) of section 512(a)(3). S can have no exempt function income. Therefore, S is subject to tax on $19,000 of unrelated business taxable income ($105,000 less the $85,000 of directly connected expenses and the $1,000 specific deduction allowed by section 512(b)(12)).

(3) **Consolidated returns.** Where the section 501(c)(2) corporation files a consolidated return with a payee organization, the computation of unrelated business taxable income, including exempt function income, shall be computed on a consolidated basis.

(4) **Illustration.** The principle of subparagraph (3) may be illustrated by the following example:

Example. All the income of S, a section 501(c)(2) corporation, is payable to P, a golf club exempt from taxation under section 501(c)(7). Among the properties held by S are small dressing cabanas which it rents to members on an annual basis. Each member is responsible for the care and maintenance of his own cabana. S and P file a consolidated return on a calendar year basis. In 1971, S has the following items of gross income:

Interest	$32,000
Receipts from rental of cabanas	1,000
Other rental income	7,000
Total	$40,000

Proposed Reg. § 1.512(a)-3

P has $865,000 of gross income in 1971 (excluding amounts paid by S to P), all of which is gross income from members. S incurred deductible expenses directly connected with the production of its income of $8,000. S incurred no expenses with respect to the rental of the cabanas. During 1971, P made a proper set aside of $2,000. The group computes its unrelated business taxable income as follows:

Gross income ($865,000 + $40,000)		$905,000
Reduced by exempt function income:		
gross income from members ($865,000 + $1,000)	$866,000	
set aside income	2,000	868,000
Gross income (excluding exempt function income).		$ 37,000
Less:		
deductions allowable under this section	$ 8,000	
specific deduction allowed by section 512(b)(12).	1,000	9,000
Unrelated business taxable income		$ 28,000

(e) **Nonrecognition of gain**—(1) *General rule.* If a social club or an employees' association (or a corporation described in section 501(c)(2) which files a consolidated return with, and the income of which is payable to, a social club or an employees' association) sells property which was used directly in the performance of the exempt function of the social club or employees' association and, within a period beginning 1 year before the date of such sale and ending 3 years after such date, other property is purchased and used by such organization directly in the performance of the exempt function, gain (if any) from such sale shall be recognized only to the extent that the sales price of the old property exceeds the cost of purchasing the other property. The other property need not be similar in nature or in use to the old property.

(2) **Definitions.** For purposes of this paragraph—

(i) *Old property.* The term "old property" means any property which a social club or an employees' association used directly in the performance of its exempt function and which was sold by such organization or by a section 501(c)(2) corporation holding title to such property;

(ii) *Other property.* The term "other property" means property purchased by a social club, an employees' association, or a section 501(c)(2) corporation holding title to such property and used directly in the performance of the exempt function of the social club or employees' association;

(iii) *Cost of purchasing other property.* The term "cost of purchasing other property" means the aggregate of the amounts which are attributable to the acquisition, construction, reconstruction, and improvements constituting capital expenditures made with respect to the other property and made during the period beginning 1 year before the date of the sale of the old property and ending 3 years after such date;

(iv) *Sales price.* The term "sales price" means the amount realized (as defined in subdivision (v) of this subparagraph), reduced by the aggregate of the expenses incurred for work performed on the old property in order to assist in its sale (as defined in subdivision (vi) of this subparagraph);

(v) *Amount realized.* The term "amount realized" has the same meaning as in section 1001(b) and the regulations thereunder;

(vi) *Expenses incurred to assist in its sale.* Expenses incurred for work performed on the old property in order to assist in its sale are the aggregate of all such expenses provided that such expenses—

(a) Are incurred for work performed during the 90-day period ending on the day of sale of the old property,

(b) Are paid on or before the 30th day after the date of sale of the old property, and

(c) Are neither allowable as a deduction in computing taxable income under section 63(a) nor taken into account in computing the amount realized from the sale of the old property.

(3) *Property used directly in the performance of the exempt function.* For purposes of section 512(a)(3)(D) and this paragraph, property shall be considered to be used directly in the performance of the exempt function only to the extent

it is used exclusively for a purpose which is substantially related to the purpose for which exemption was granted the organization. If property is not used exclusively for such a purpose, only that part of the gain allocable to the portion of the property used for such purpose is not to be recognized. Further, only that part of the amount realized upon sale need be reinvested in other property used for such purpose in order to avoid recognition with respect to such part of the gain. If the amount realized upon sale is reinvested in property which is used only partly for the exempt purpose, an allocation must be made to determine the portion of the reinvested proceeds that is actually used for a purpose substantially related to the exempt purpose.

(4) **Destruction, theft, seizure, requisition, or condemnation.** For purposes of section 512(a)(3)(D) and this paragraph, the destruction in whole or in part, theft, seizure, requisition, or condemnation of property used in whole or in part in the performance of the exempt function shall be treated as a sale of such property.

(5) **Sales and purchase of property.** For purposes of section 512(a)(3)(D) and this paragraph—

(i) Exchanges. An exchange of old property for other than cash consideration shall be treated as a sale of the old property. The acquisition of other property for other than cash consideration shall be treated as a purchase of such other property.

(ii) Construction or reconstruction. Property, any part of which was constructed or reconstructed by a social club, an employees' association, or a section 501(c)(2) corporation holding title to the property, shall be treated as property which was purchased. In determining the cost of purchasing such property, there shall be included only that portion of the cost which is attributable to the acquisition, construction, reconstruction, and improvements made which are properly chargeable to capital account and which are made during the period beginning one year before the date of sale of the old property and ending 3 years after such date.

(iii) Purchase and sale of other property prior to the sale of the new property. If property is purchased and is subsequently sold or otherwise disposed of before the date of the sale of the old property, the property so purchased shall not qualify as other property.

(6) **Basis.** In cases where section 512(a)(3)(D) and this paragraph require nonrecognition of gain, the adjusted basis in the other property shall be reduced by an amount equal to the amount of the gain which was not recognized upon the sale of the old property.

(7) **Statute of limitations.** Whenever an organization makes a sale of property and does not recognize gain on such sale on the basis that section 512(a)(3)(D) is applicable, the statutory period prescribed in section 6501(a) for the assessment of a deficiency attributable to any part of such gain shall not expire prior to the expiration of 3 years from the date of notification as hereinafter provided. Such notification will be deemed to occur on receipt by the internal revenue official with whom the return was filed for the taxable year or years in which the gain from the sale of the property was realized and was not recognized, of a written notice from the organization of—

(i) The organization's cost of the other property which the organization claims results in nonrecognition of any part of such gain,

(ii) The organization's subsequent decision not to purchase other property within the period when such a reinvestment would result in nonrecognition of any part of such gain, or

(iii) The organization's failure to make a purchase within such period.

Any gain from the sale of property which is required to be recognized shall be included in gross income for the taxable year or years in which such gain was realized. Any deficiency attributable to any portion of such gain may be assessed before the expiration of the 3-year period described in this paragraph, notwithstanding the provisions of any law or rule of law which might otherwise bar such assessment. The notification required by the preceding subparagraph shall contain all pertinent details in connection with the sale of the old property and, where

Proposed Reg. §1.512(a)-3

applicable, the purchase price of the new property. The notification shall be in the form of a written statement and shall be accompanied, where appropriate, by an amended return for the year in which the gain from the sale of the old property was realized, in order to reflect the inclusion in gross income for that year of gain required to be recognized in connection with such sale.

(8) **Illustration.** The principles of this paragraph may be illustrated by the following example:

Example. N, a social club, purchased a building and land for use as a golf course in 1950 for $100,000. On April 1, 1971, N sold the entire tract, in one transaction, for $250,000 and purchased another tract for $120,000. N then spent $105,000 constructing a golf course and club house on the new tract. Construction was completed in 1972. Between February 1, 1971, and April 1, 1971, N incurred $4,000 of expenses in negotiating the sale of its old property and $1,000 of noncapital expenses for work performed on the old property to assist in its sale. The club computes its recognizable gain from the sale of the property as follows:

Proceeds from sale of old property	$250,000
Less: selling expenses	4,000
Amount realized	246,000
Less: basis	100,000
Gain realized	$146,000
Amount realized	246,000
Less: fixing-up expenses	1,000
Adjusted sales price	$245,000
Cost of purchasing other property	225,000
Gain recognized	20,000
Gain realized but not recognized	126,000

N computes its adjusted basis in the other property as follows:

Cost of purchasing other property	$225,000
Less: gain realized but not recognized	126,000
Adjusted basis of other property	$ 99,000

Political Organizations

Immediately after §1.526 there are added the following new sections:

§1.527-1 (Proposed Treasury Decision, published 11-24-76.) **Tax imposed on political organizations.**

(a) **In general.** Under section 527 special tax treatment is provided for a political organization organized and operated primarily for the purpose of accepting contributions or making expenditures in furtherance of its exempt function. Generally, a political organization's exempt function involves the promotion of individuals for election to political office. (See §1.527-2(a) for a definition of a political organization and §1.527-2(b) for a description of what constitutes the organization's exempt function.) The political organization is not taxed on the receipt of exempt function income. Such income includes contributions of money or other property or the receipt of dues or assessments from members of the organization. (See §1.527-3(b) for a definition of the term "exempt function income".) The political organization is taxed on all income received by it other than exempt function income. Thus, where assets are invested or the political organization engages in a trade or business, the organization is subject to taxation on income realized from such activities under Subtitle A of the Internal Revenue Code, but only to the extent provided in section 527. (See §1.527-1(b) for rules relating to the taxation of a political organization.) Section 527 also provides that a political organization shall be considered an organization exempt from income taxes for the purpose of any law which refers to organizations exempt from income tax.

(b) **Tax imposed—(1) In general.** Section 527 imposes a tax for each taxable year on the political organization taxable income (as described in §1.527-3) of every political organization. Such tax consists of a normal tax and surtax computed as provided in section 11 (tax on corporations) as though the political organization were a corporation (whether or not the organization is in fact incorporated), and as though the "political organization taxable income" were taxable corporate income. However, in computing the tax of a political organization the surtax exemption provided by section 11(d) shall not be allowed.

(2) **Alternative tax in case of capital gains—**(i) In general. If for any taxable year a political organization has a net section 1201 gain, then the tax provided for under this section shall be the lesser of the tax computed under paragraph (b)(1) of this section or the sum of—

(A) A partial tax computed under paragraph (b)(1) on the amount which is the difference between the total political organization taxable income and the amount of the net section 1201 gain, and

(B) An amount determined as provided in section 1201(a) on such gain.

(ii) Limitation on capital losses. If for any taxable year a political organization has a net capital loss the rules of sections 1211(a) and 1212(a) shall apply.

(iii) Expenses attributable to the sale of capital assets. In determining the amount of gain or loss realized by a political organization from the sale of capital assets, the direct expenses attributable to the sale of such assets shall be treated as an addition to basis of the assets disposed of.

§1.527-2 (Proposed Treasury Decision, published 11-24-76.) **Definitions.**

(a) **Political organization—(1) In general.** For purposes of section 527 and §§1.527-1 through 1.527-7, the term "political organization" means a party, committee, association, fund, or other organization (whether or not incorporated) organized and operated primarily for the purpose of directly or indirectly accepting contributions or making expenditures, or both, for an exempt function. Accordingly, a political organization includes a committee or other group which accepts contributions or makes expenditures for the purpose of promoting the nomination of an individual for an elective public office in a primary election, or in any meeting or caucus of a political party. Where an individual establishes a segregated fund to receive contributions for the purpose of promoting the individual's nomination or election to elective public office such fund will be treated as a political organization. Similarly, a separate segregated fund meeting the requirements of 2 U.S.C. 441(b) shall be treated as a political organization. (See §1.527-5(e)). A political organization need not be formally chartered or established under articles of incorporation, nor is it necessary that such organizations operate in accordance with normal corporate formalities as ordinarily established in bylaws or under state law.

(2) **Dual purpose organizations.** Where an organization maintains a segregated fund and also has a purpose clearly distinct from the exempt function, such organization will be considered a political organization only to the extent of the segregated fund. Thus, where a committee is established to collect funds for an incumbent's next campaign and to collect funds to help offset the office expenses of the incumbent, the committee will be treated as a political organization only to the extent that it maintains a segregated fund for campaign purposes.

(3) **Segregated fund.** For purposes of these regulations, a segregated fund means a fund which is established separate and apart from the other assets of an organization and dedicated to the exempt function of the organization. Such a fund must be established for the purpose of receiving exempt function income and other amounts (including earnings on such exempt function income or other amounts) for use only for the exempt function. The segregated fund should be clearly identified as established for the purposes intended. The organization maintaining such a fund shall maintain adequate records to allow the verification of receipts into and expenditures out of such fund. A savings or checking ac-

Proposed Reg. §1.527-2

count into which all contributions to the political organization are placed and from which only expenditures for the exempt function are made shall be considered a segregated fund if properly identified as such.

(4) **Primary purpose test.** To be treated as a political organization for purposes of section 527, the organization must be organized and operated primarily to accept contributions or make expenditures, or both, for the purpose of carrying on an exempt function as defined in paragraph (b) of this section. In making the determination of whether a political organization is "organized and operated primarily to carry on an exempt function" all the facts and circumstances of each case shall be considered. For example, when a political organization provides in its articles of organization (corporate charter, trust instrument, articles of association or other instrument by which the organization is created) that its purpose is to carry on an exempt function, in the absence of other relevant factors, it will be considered to have met the organizational test. In making the determination whether an organization meets the organizational test when there are no formal documents or instruments evidencing such formation, consideration will be given to the statements that the members of such organization intend to operate it only in furtherance of one or more activities constituting an exempt function. A principal factor in determining whether a political organization is operated "primarily to carry on an exempt function" shall be the relationship of the expenditures from the segregated fund for an exempt function (including expenditures to generate exempt function income) to the total expenditures from such fund. Where an organization expends more than an insubstantial amount from its segregated fund on activities which are neither exempt function activities nor qualifying activities (as defined in paragraph (a)(6) of this section) the organization will not be considered operated primarily to carry on an exempt function. Thus, a local political club could expend exempt function income to carry on incidental social activities which are unrelated to its political activities so long as such expenditures are insubstantial in relationship to the club's total expenditures from the segregated fund. (For income tax consequences of such an expenditure, see §1.527-4.)

(5) **Relationship to sections 41 and 218.** An organization or individual receiving contributions for which a tax credit under section 41 or a deduction under section 218 is allowable must satisfy the requirements of section 527 and this section in order to qualify as a tax-exempt political organization.

(6) **Qualifying activities.** A political organization which had substantially participated in an exempt function immediately preceding or during a political election campaign may participate in qualifying activities after such election without losing its status as a section 527 political organization in a year in which it may not be supporting a specific individual for public office. Qualifying activities include activities which the political organization engages in after an election which reasonably relate to the selection, nomination, or election of individuals for the next applicable political campaign. For example, if a local political organization between elections prepares for the next party convention, engages in fundraising activities, or transacts fundraising activities, or transacts intraparty organizational business, such organization will be engaging in qualifying activities. In addition, where a political organization is established for a single campaign, it may continue to qualify as a political organization after the election to wind up the campaign, pay off its debts, or put its records in order.

(b) **Exempt function.** The term "exempt function" (for the purpose of section 527 and the regulations thereunder) means the function of influencing, or attempting to influence, the selection, nomination, election, or appointment of any individual or individuals to any Federal, State, or local public office or office in a political organization, or the election of Presidential or Vice Presidential electors, whether or not such individual or electors are selected, nominated, elected or appointed.

(c) **Expenditures.** The term "expenditures" has the meaning given to such term by section 271(b)(3). That is, the term "expenditure" includes a contract, promise, or agreement to make an expenditure whether or not legally enforceable. Expenditures which are either illegal or for a judicially determined illegal activity shall not be considered expenditures in furtherance of the exempt function even though such expenditures are expended in the process of influencing or attempting to influence the selection, nomination, election, or appointment of an individual.

§1.527-3 (Proposed Treasury Decision, published 11-24-76.) **Political organization taxable income.**

(a) **In general.** As used in this section the term "political organization taxable income" of a political organization means the excess (if any) of—

(1) The gross income for the taxable year (excluding any exempt function income as defined in paragraph (b) of this section), less

(2) The deductions allowed by chapter 1 of the Code which are directly connected with the production of gross income (other than exempt function income) computed with the modifications provided in paragraph (c)(3) of this section.

(b) **Exempt function income defined—(1) In general.** For purposes of section 527 and these regulations the term "exempt function income" means any amount received as—

(i) A contribution of money or other property;
(ii) Membership dues, fees, or assessments from a member of a political organization; and
(iii) Proceeds from a political fundraising or entertainment event, or proceeds from the sale of political campaign materials, which are not received in the ordinary course of any trade or business, to the extent such amount is segregated for use only for the exempt function of the political organization. (See also §1.527-4 regarding the treatment of expenditures for a judicially determined illegal activity).

(2) **Contributions.** In determining whether the transfer of money or other property constitutes a contribution the rules of section 271(b)(2) shall apply. That is, the term "contributions" includes a gift, subscription, loan, advance, or deposit of money or anything of value, and includes a contract, promise, or agreement to make a contribution, whether or not legally enforceable. Generally, individual contributions of money or other property, whether solicited personally, by mail or through advertising, will qualify as contributions. In addition, to the extent that political organizations receive Federal, State, or local funds under the $1 "checkoff" provision (sections 9001-9013), or any other provision for financing of campaigns, such amounts are to be treated as contributions.

(3) **Dues, fees and assessments.** For purposes of section 527 and this section amounts received as membership dues or membership fees and assessments from members of the political organization constitute exempt function income to such organization to the extent such amounts are not received in consideration for services, goods, or other items of value. Filing fees paid by an individual directly or indirectly to a political party in order that the individual may run as a candidate in a primary election of the party (or run in a general election as a candidate of that party) are to be treated as exempt function income. For example, some States provide that a certain percentage of the first year's salary of the office sought must be paid to the State as a filing (or "qualifying") fee and party assessment. The State then transfers part of this fee to the candidate's party. In such a case, the entire amount transferred to the party is to be treated as exempt function income. Amounts paid by an individual directly to the party as a qualification fee will be treated similarly.

(4) **Fundraising events—(i) In general.** For purposes of section 527 and this section, proceeds from casual and sporadic political fundraising or entertainment events (such as an annual political dinner) and the sale of campaign materials shall be considered exempt function income, but only if such events are:
(A) substantially related to the exempt function, and
(B) not carried on in the ordinary course of a trade or business.

(ii) **Substantially related—(A) In general.** Gross income derives from a trade or business within the meaning of section 527, if the conduct of the activities which produce the income is not substantially related (other than through the production of funds) to the exempt function. The presence of this requirement necessitates an examination of the

Proposed Reg. §1.527-3

relationship between the activities which generate the particular income in question and the accomplishment of the organization's exempt function.

(B) Type of relationship required. Activities are "related" to the exempt function in the relevant sense only where the conduct of the activities has a causal relationship to the achievement of the exempt function (other than through the production of funds) and is substantially related for purposes of this section only if the causal relationship is a substantial one. Thus, for the activities from which gross income is derived to be substantially related to the exempt function, the production or distribution of the goods or the performance of services from which the gross income is derived must contribute importantly to the accomplishment of those purposes. Where the activities do not contribute importantly to the exempt function the income from such activities is not substantially related to the exempt function. Whether the activities productive of gross income contribute importantly to the accomplishment of the exempt function depends in each case upon the facts and circumstances involved.

(C) Size and extent of activities. In determining whether activities contribute importantly to the accomplishment of the exempt function, the size and extent of the activities involved must be considered in relation to the nature and extent of the exempt function which they purport to serve. Thus, where the income is realized by a political organization from activities which are in part related to the performance of its exempt function but which are conducted on a larger scale than necessary for the performance of such functions, the gross income attributable to that portion of activities in excess of the needs of the exempt function constitutes gross income from the conduct of a trade or business. Such income is not derived from activities which contribute importantly to the accomplishment of the exempt function of the political organization.

(D) Activities substantially related to exempt function. Fundraising events such as breakfasts, receptions, picnics, dances and other similar activities will be considered substantially related to the exempt function where undertaken in an effort to encourage support for an individual seeking political office or for a political organization. Similarly, the sale of political memorabilia, bumper stickers, campaign buttons, hats, shirts, political posters, stationery, jewelry or cookbooks are substantially related where such items can be identified as closely relating to the other activities of the political organization, such as distributing political literature or organizing voters.

(iii) Ordinary course of a trade or business. The term "trade or business" has the same meaning it has in section 162, and generally includes any activity carried on for the production of income from the sale of goods or performance of services. However, in determining whether amounts are received in the "ordinary course" of a trade or business regard must be given to the frequency and continuity with which the activities are conducted and the manner in which they are pursued. In this regard the provisions of §1.513-1(c) (determination as to whether an unrelated business is "regularly" carried on) shall apply in principle to the determination of whether amounts are received in the "ordinary course of a trade or business".

(c) Deductions—(1) In general. Except as provided in §1.527-3(c)(3), the deductions allowed under §1.527-3(a)(2) are those allowed by chapter 1 of the Code which are directly connected with the production of gross income (excluding exempt function income). Thus, to be deductible in computing political organization taxable income expenses, depreciation, and similar items must not only qualify as deductions allowed by chapter 1 of the Code, but must also be directly connected with the production of gross income (excluding exempt function income).

(2) "Directly connected with" defined. For purposes of §1.527-3(c)(1) an item of deduction is "directly connected with" the production of gross income if such item is incurred solely as a result of the activities giving rise to such income. Thus, expenses, depreciation and similar items attributable solely to the production of gross income are directly connected to that gross income, and therefore qualify for deduction to the extent they meet the requirements of section 162, section 167, or other relevant provisions of the Internal Revenue Code. Where expenses are attributable in part to the production of exempt function income, and in part to the production of political organization taxable income, such expenses are not directly connected with the production of political organiza-

tion taxable income and are, therefore, not deductible. Thus, for example, assume a political organization subject to the provisions of section 527 derives gross income from a fundraising activity which is not substantially related, as defined in §1.527-3(b)(4)(ii), to an exempt function. The organization pays its executive officer $20,000 a year. The officer is in charge of overseeing all the activities of the organization. For purposes of this paragraph, no portion of the officer's salary expense shall be allocated to and deductible from the gross income produced from the fundraising activity.

(3) **Modifications of political organization taxable income.** In computing political organization taxable income, the excess of the gross income of the political organization less the deductions allowed by this section shall be reduced by $100, but not below zero. However, no deduction shall be allowed under:

(i) Section 172 with respect to net operating losses, and

(ii) Part VIII of subchapter B (relating to special deductions for corporations).

§1.527-4 (Proposed Treasury Decision, published 11-24-76.) **Expenditures treated as income to an individual or political organization.**

(a) **In general—(1) General rule.** Amounts expended by a political organization for its exempt function are not income to the individual or individuals on whose behalf such expenditures are made. However, where the political organization expends amounts for the personal use of any person, the person on whose behalf the funds were spent will be in receipt of income. Amounts are expended for the personal use of a person where a direct or indirect financial benefit accrues to such person. For example, where the political organization pays a private legal obligation of an individual seeking public office, such as the individual's Federal income tax liability, the individual is in receipt of gross income. Similarly, where the political organization pays for a vacation trip for the campaign manager's spouse in most cases either the campaign manager or the spouse will be in receipt of income. This paragraph also applies where the expenditure by the political organization confers a financial benefit on the organization that is not related to the organization's exempt function. Thus, where a political organization uses its exempt function income for either making improvements or additions to its facilities or for equipment which are not necessary for or used in carrying out its exempt function, the political organization will be in receipt of taxable income. However, where a political organization expends its exempt function income to make ordinary and necessary repairs on the offices from which the political organization conducts its activities or on equipment that it uses in carrying out its exempt function, such amounts are not to be included in the political organization's taxable income.

(2) **Expenditure for an illegal activity.** Expenditures by a political organization that are judicially determined to be illegal or for an activity that is judicially determined to be illegal shall be treated as amounts not segregated for use only for the exempt function and shall be included in the political organization's taxable income under §1.527-3. However, not all amounts expended by the political organization in connection with a judicially determined illegal expenditure or activity will be considered to be includible in the organization's income. For example, expenses incurred in defense of civil or criminal suits against the organization or for fines or penalties imposed on the organization as a direct result of the illegal expenditure or activity will not be treated as taxable to the organization. Similarly, voluntary reimbursement to the participants in the illegal activity for similar expenses incurred by them will not be taxable to the organization if the organization can demonstrate that such payments do not constitute a part of the inducement to engage in the illegal activity or part of the agreed upon compensation therefor. However, if the organization entered into an agreement with the participants to defray such expenses as part of the inducement, such payments would be treated as an expenditure for the illegal activity. Except where necessary to prevent the period of limitation for assessment and collection of a tax from expiring, a notice of deficiency will not generally be issued until after there has been a final determination of illegality by an appropriate court in a criminal proceeding.

Proposed Reg. §1.527-4

(b) **Certain uses not treated as income to a candidate—(1) In general.** If any political organization—

(i) Contributes any amount to or for the use of any political organization described in section 527(e),

(ii) Contributes any amount to or for the use of any organization described in paragraph (1) or (2) of section 509(a) which is exempt under section 501(a), or

(iii) Deposits any amount in the general fund of the Treasury or in the general fund of any State or local government,

such amount shall not be treated as an amount expended for the personal use of a candidate, or any other person, provided the contribution or deposit is not in satisfaction of a personal legal obligation as described in § 1.527-4(a). No deduction shall be allowed to any person under the Internal Revenue Code of 1954 for the contribution or deposit of any amount to which the preceding sentence applies.

(2) **Incidental expenditures.** Incidental amounts expended by a political organization to benefit an individual not directly related to the individual's campaign for office are not to be treated as amounts expended for the personal benefit of the individual, but only if the amounts so expended:

(i) Are minor when compared to the overall expenses of the organization; and

(ii) Have some relationship to the conduct of exempt functions.

For example, where a political organization pays the expenses incurred by a candidate in the candidate's transition to office (e.g., expenses of preparing to take office, including staff salaries), or provides the candidate and the candidate's staff with meals during a campaign, these expenses are not to be considered as expenditures for the personal benefit of the candidate if the requirements of this paragraph are satisfied.

(c) **Unexpended funds—(1) In general.** Unexpended funds held by a political organization which has ceased to engage in any exempt function, may be treated as expended for the personal use of a candidate, or any other person having control over the ultimate use of such funds, unless distributed as provided in paragraph (b)(1) of this section within a reasonable time. Where a candidate who establishes a segregated fund dies and directs such fund to go to the candidate's estate or to any other person, a reasonable period of time will be allowed for such funds to be transferred as provided in paragraph (b)(1) of this section. Any funds not transferred will constitute income of the decedent and be included in the decedent's gross estate. Where no provision is made for the disposition of such unexpended funds by the candidate and such funds go to the candidate's estate or any other person, such amounts will constitute income in respect of the decedent unless the estate disposes of the funds as provided in paragraph (b)(1) of this section within a reasonable period of time.

(2) **Interim periods.** Funds held by a political organization after a campaign, or election, will not be treated as unexpended funds for purposes of this paragraph if held in reasonable anticipation of being used by the organization for other exempt functions. For example, if funds are held by an organization following the election of its candidate, such funds will not be treated as unexpended funds if held for the candidate's re-election campaign.

§1.527-5 (Proposed Treasury Decision, published 11-24-76.) **Inclusion of certain amounts in the gross income of an exempt organization which is not a political organization.**

(a) **In general—(1) Inclusion in gross income.** If an organization described in section 501(c) which is exempt from tax under section 501(a) expends any amount during the taxable year directly (or through another organization) for an exempt function, as described in §1.527-2(b), then there shall be included in the gross income of such organization for the taxable year and shall be subject to tax as if it constituted political organization taxable income an amount equal to the lesser of—

(i) The net investment income, as defined in paragraph (b) of this section, of such organization for the taxable year, or

(ii) The aggregate amount so expended directly or indirectly during the taxable year on exempt functions within the meaning of §1.527-2(b).

(2) **Determination of tax.** The items of income included in gross income of the organization, to which paragraph (a)(1) of this section applies, shall retain their character as ordinary income or capital gain for purpose of determining the amount of tax imposed under section 527. If the amount to be included in gross income is determined by the aggregate amount expended during the taxable year for political purposes, as provided in paragraph (a)(1)(ii) of this section, the character of the items of income shall be determined by multiplying the total amount included in income under paragraph (a)(1)(ii) of this section times a fraction the numerator of which is the portion of the organization's net investment income that would be gain from the sale or exchange of a capital asset, and the denominator of which would be the organization's net investment income. For example, if $5,000 is included in the gross income of an exempt organization under paragraph (a)(1)(ii) of this section, and the organization had $100,000 of net investment income of which $10,000 is long term capital gain, then $500 would be treated as long term capital gain:

$$\frac{\text{capital gain}}{\text{net investment income}} \times \text{amount expended on political activities} = \text{portion of income subject to tax under section 1201}$$

$$\frac{\$10,000}{\$100,000} \times \$5,000 = \$500$$

(b) **Net investment income—(1) In general.** For purposes of section 527 and §1.527-5, the term "net investment income" means:

(i) The gross amount received by an organization described in section 501(c) which is exempt from tax under section 501(a), from interest, dividends, rents, and royalties, plus the excess (if any) of gains from the sale or exchange of assets over the losses from the sale or exchange of assets, over

(ii) The deductions allowed by chapter 1 of the Code which are directly connected with the production of such income. In determining the deductions directly connected with the production of income the rules of paragraph (c) of §1.527-3 shall apply.

(A) A net loss determined under section 1231(a) (property used by the trade or business and involuntary conversions) shall be allowed as a deduction in computing net investment income.

(B) Losses incurred in carrying on any trade or business described in paragraph (e) of §1.513-2, shall not be allowed as a deduction in computing net investment income.

(2) If an organization described in (b)(1)(i) of this paragraph is liable for tax under section 527 on its net investment income, in determining the amount of tax it pays, that portion of the net investment income which represents gain from the sale or exchange of capital assets, shall retain its character as capital gain.

(3) **Section 511 tax.** For purposes of this paragraph, there shall not be taken into account items taken into account for purposes of the tax imposed by section 511 (relating to tax on unrelated business income).

(c) **Modifications.** The modifications prescribed by section 527(c)(2) and §1.527-3(c)(3) shall apply in computing the tax imposed under section 527 and determined under paragraph (a) (2) of this section. Thus, no net operating loss shall be allowed under section 172 nor shall any deduction be allowed under part VIII of subchapter B. However, there shall be allowed a specific deduction of $100.

(d) **Expenditures for exempt function purposes.** An organization described in section 501(c), that is exempt from tax under section 501(a), shall be considered to have made expenditures for an exempt function (as defined in §1.527-2(b)) if it provides funds or

Proposed Reg. §1.527-5

property, by grant or otherwise, directly or indirectly, to an individual or an organization under circumstances where it might be reasonably expected that such individual or organization will expend, directly or indirectly, those amounts for political purposes. For example, where X, an organization which is described in section 501(c)(4) transfers $100 of its funds to Y, a community organization, and X knows or should know that Y among its other activities supports candidates in local political elections, X should take steps (such as obtaining written guarantees) to ensure that no portion of the $100 will be used by Y for political purposes. An organization will not be using funds for an exempt function where it publishes nonpartisan information about legislation that has been introduced in any legislative body if such organization routinely publishes such information for the general public.

(e) **Separate segregated fund.** To avoid the application of paragraph (a) of this section, an organization described in section 501(c) that is exempt under section 501(a) may establish, if consistent with its exempt status under section 501, a separate segregated fund to directly receive political contributions and make political expenditures. If the separate segregated fund is maintained independently of the section 501(c) organization that established it, expenditures from the fund will not be attributed to the section 501(c) organization. Rather, such fund will be treated as a political organization within the meaning of §1.527-2(a). Whether the segregated fund is maintained independently from the section 501(c) organization will be determined from all the facts and circumstances. Where a labor union or chamber of commerce establishes a separate segregated fund pursuant to 2 U.S.C. 441(b) or a similar State statute, such labor union or chamber of commerce may receive political contributions or dues directly and immediately transfer such funds to the separate segregated fund established by such organization without having the transfer of such funds treated as a political expenditure. Funds will not be considered immediately transferred, where prior to the transfer of such funds, the labor union or chamber of commerce deposits such funds in an interest bearing account or uses such funds for any purpose of the labor union or chamber of commerce. In addition, the fact that a labor union or chamber of commerce receives political contributions or dues and immediately transfers such funds to the separate segregated fund will not be a factor which tends to indicate that such fund is not maintained independently from the section 501(c) organization.

(f) **Effect of expenditures on exempt status.** Section 527(f) and this section do not sanction attempts to influence legislation by propaganda, or the intervention in any political campaign by an organization described in section 501(c) if such activity is inconsistent with its exempt status under section 501(a). For example, an organization described in section 501(c)(3) is precluded from engaging in any political campaign activities. The fact that section 527 imposes a tax on the political expenditures of section 501(c) organizations and permits such organizations to establish separate segregated funds to make political expenditures does not sanction these activities by section 501(c)(3) organizations.

§1.527-6 (Proposed Treasury Decision, published 11-24-76.) **Newsletter funds.**

(a) **In general.** For purposes of this section, a fund established and maintained by an individual who holds, has been elected to, or is a candidate (within the meaning of section 41(c)(2)) for nomination or election to, any Federal, State, or local elective public office for the use by such individual exclusively for the preparation and circulation of such individual's newsletter shall be treated as if such fund constituted a political organization for purposes of determining the taxable income of an organization under section 527(c) and §1.527-3 of the regulations, provided the assets of such fund are maintained in separate accounts and are used solely in preparing and circulating the newsletter. The cost of preparation is to include (but not be limited to) the cost of secretarial services and the cost of printing, addressing, and mailing the newsletter. Such a newsletter fund will be subject to tax on its political organization taxable income as provided in section 527(b) and § 1.527-1.

(b) **Modification in determining taxable income of newsletter funds.** In determining the taxable income of a newsletter fund:

(1) The "exempt function" shall be only the preparation and circulation of the newsletter; and

(2) The specific $100 deduction provided by section 527(c)(2)(A) shall not be allowed.

(c) **Expenditure for nonexempt purpose.** For purposes of this paragraph, an expenditure for a nonexempt purpose occurs when newsletter fund assets are not used exclusively for the preparation and circulation of the newsletter. Thus, newsletter fund assets may not be used for an exempt function as defined in §1.527-2(b)(1). If assets of a newsletter fund are used for any purpose other than preparing and circulating a newsletter, such amounts shall be treated as expended for the personal use of the individual who established and maintained the fund. In addition, the amounts remaining in the newsletter fund shall be included in the gross income of the individual who established and maintained the newsletter fund. For example, if newsletter funds are transferred to an organization which is not a newsletter fund, such a transfer shall be an expenditure for a nonexempt purpose since for an organization to qualify as a newsletter fund its assets must be used exclusively for newsletter (and not campaign) activities. The amount transferred shall be treated as expended for the personal use of the individual who established and maintained the fund and amounts remaining in the newsletter fund shall be included in the gross income of such individual.

(d) **Unexpended funds.** Unexpended amounts held by a newsletter fund which has ceased to engage in the preparation and circulation of the newsletter, shall be treated as expended for the personal use of the individual who established such fund unless these unexpended amounts are either:

(i) Contributed to or for the use of any organization described in paragraph (1) or (2) of section 509(a) which is exempt from tax under section 501(a), or

(ii) Deposited in the general fund of the U.S. Treasury or in the general fund of any State or local government (including the District of Columbia), or

(iii) Contributed to any other newsletter fund as described in paragraph (a) of this section, within a reasonable time. Any unexpended funds so contributed or deposited will not be treated as expended for the personal use of such individual.

§1.527-7 (Proposed Treasury Decision, published 11-24-76.) **Effective date; filing requirements; and miscellaneous provisions.**

(a) **Assessment and collections.** Since the taxes imposed by section 527 are taxes imposed by subtitle A of the Code, all provisions of law and of the regulations applicable to the taxes imposed by subtitle A are applicable to the assessment and collection of the taxes imposed by section 527. Organizations subject to the tax imposed by section 527 are subject to the same provisions, including penalties, as are provided for corporations, in general, except that the requirements of section 6154 concerning the payment of estimated tax shall not apply. See, generally section 6151, et. seq., and the regulations prescribed thereunder, for provisions relating to payment of tax.

(b) **Returns.** For requirements of filing annual returns with respect to political organization taxable income, see section 6012(a)(6) and the applicable regulations.

(c) **Taxable years, method of accounting, etc.** The taxable year (fiscal year or calendar year, as the case may be) of an organization shall be determined without regard to the fact that such organization may have been exempt from tax during any prior period. See sections 441 and 446, and the regulations thereunder in this part, and section 7701 and the regulations in Part 301 of this chapter (Regulations on Procedure and Administration). Similarly, in computing political organization taxable income, the determination of the taxable year for which an item of income or expense is taken into account shall be made under the provisions of section 441, 446, 451, 461, and the regulations thereunder, whether or not the item arose during a taxable year beginning before, on, or after the effective date of the provisions imposing a tax upon political organization taxable income. If a method for treating bad debts was selected in a return of income (other than an information return) for a previous taxable year, the taxpayer must follow such method in its returns under section 527, unless such method is changed in accordance with the pro-

Proposed Reg. §1.527-7

visions of §1.166-1. A taxpayer which has not previously selected a method for treating bad debts may, in its first return under section 527, exercise the option granted in §1.166-1.

(d) **Effective date.** Section 527 applies to taxable years beginning after December 31, 1974.

Accumulated Earnings Tax

Section 1.532-1(a) is amended by adding a new subparagraph (3) to read as follows:

§ 1.532-1 (Proposed Treasury Decision, published 7-9-68.) **Corporations subject to accumulated earnings tax.**

(a) **General rule.** * * *

(3) See § 1.533-1 (a) (3) for cases where a subsidiary corporation is deemed to have been availed of for the purpose of avoiding the income tax with respect to the shareholders of its parent corporation when the parent relies on the underlying value of its investment in the subsidiary to obtain funds for nondividend distributions to its shareholders.

* * * * * * * * * *

Section 1.533-1 (a) is amended by adding a new subparagraph (3) to read as follows:

§ 1.533-1 (Proposed Treasury Decision, published 7-9-68.) **Evidence of purpose to avoid income tax.**

(a) **In general.** * * *

(3) (i) If one corporation (hereinafter referred to as the "parent") owns, directly or indirectly, the stock of another corporation (hereinafter referred to as the "subsidiary"), the earnings and profits of the subsidiary may provide, directly or indirectly, the principal source of funds for distributions by the parent to its shareholders. Normally, the subsidiary will distribute its earnings and profits to the parent, which in turn will make distributions to its shareholders that are treated as dividends under section 301 (c) (1). However, in some cases the parent may rely upon the underlying value of its investment in the subsidiary to obtain funds for distributions to its shareholders, rather than cause the subsidiary to distribute its earnings and profits. If this occurs, the subsidiary will be deemed to have been availed of for the purpose of avoiding the income tax with respect to shareholders of the parent (including a parent whose outstanding stock is traded on a stock exchange or in an over-the-counter market), if

(a) Part or all of the distribution by the parent is treated by its shareholders in the manner provided in section 301 (c) (2) or (3), and

(b) Such distribution would have been treated as provided in section 301 (c) (1) if the subsidiary had distributed its earnings and profits to the parent.

(ii) All the circumstances which might be construed as evidence that the parent has relied upon the underlying value of its investment in the subsidiary to obtain funds for distributions to its shareholders cannot be outlined, but the following factors, among others, will be considered as evidence of such reliance:

(a) The parent borrows money and secures the loan with stock or securities of the subsidiary;

(b) The parent borrows money and the loan agreement contains conditions relating to the earnings or net assets of the subsidiary;

(c) The parent borrows money and under the loan agreement the subsidiary is required to maintain bank balances related to the amount borrowed; or

(d) Stock or securities are issued for money or property by the parent, the value of which stock or securities is based in part on the underlying asset value of the subsidiary.

(iii) In the case of an affiliated group of corporations which files or is required to file a consolidated return, see § 1.1502-43 for inapplicability of this subparagraph where the tax imposed by section 531 is based on consolidated accumulated taxable income because of an election under § 1.1502-33 (c) (4) (iii) to adjust earnings and profits to reflect increases or decreases in a member's basis or excess loss account for the stock of a subsidiary.

(iv) The application of this subparagraph may be illustrated by the following examples:

Example (1). (a) P Corporation, a publicly-held corporation, owns all the capital stock of S Corporation. P and S file separate returns for the calendar year 1967. P has no earnings and profits for 1967 and had a deficit in accumulated earnings and profits as of December 31, 1966. S has earnings and profits of $100,000 for 1967 and has accumulated earnings and profits as of December 31, 1966. A cash distribution to the shareholders of P in the amount of $25,000 is made in 1967.

(b) If during 1967 S distributes $25,000 to P, and P in turn distributes $25,000 to its shareholders and this amount is treated as a dividend under section 301 (c) (1), S will not be deemed under this subparagraph to have been availed of to avoid the income tax on the shareholders of P.

(c) If P relies upon the underlying value of its investment in S to obtain funds for the distribution to its shareholders rather than obtaining such funds by causing S to distribute its earnings and profits (for example, if P borrows $25,000 from a bank and secures the loan with the capital stock of S) and if such distribution to the P shareholders is not treated as a dividend under section 301 (c) (1), S will be deemed to have been availed of for the purpose of avoiding the income tax on the shareholders of P.

Example (2). (a) P Corporation owns all the capital stock of S Corporation. P conducts a business, as well as providing certain administrative services to S. P and S file separate returns for the calendar year 1967. P has a loss of $10,000 for 1967 and had a deficit in accumulated earnings and profits as of December 31, 1966. S has earnings and profits of $100,000 for 1967 and had accumulated earnings and profits as of December 31, 1966. No intercompany distributions are made in 1967. A cash distribution to the shareholders of P in the amount of $25,000 is made in 1967. P obtains the funds for this distribution by the sale of assets for $25,000 on which it does not realize any gain or loss.

(b) This subparagraph does not apply because P did not obtain funds for the distribution to its shareholders by relying upon the underlying value of its investment in S.

(v) This subparagraph shall apply only for taxable years beginning after July 9, 1968.

Section 1.535-1(a) is amended to read as follows:

§ 1.535-1 (Proposed Treasury Decision, published 7-9-68.) **Definition.**

(a) The accumulated earnings tax is imposed by section 531 on the accumulated taxable income. Accumulated taxable income is the taxable income of the corporation with the adjustments prescribed by section 535 (b) and § 1.535-2, minus the sum of the dividends paid deduction and the accumulated earnings credit. See section 561 and the regulations thereunder, relating to the definition of the deduction for dividends paid, and section 535 (c) and § 1.535-3, relating to the accumulated earnings credit.

* * * * * * * * *

Proposed Reg. § 1.535-1

Section 1.535-3 is amended by revising paragraph (a) and by adding a new subdivision (iii) to paragraph (b)(1). These revised and added provisions read as follows:

§1.535-3 (Proposed Treasury Decision, published 7-9-68.) **Accumulated earnings credit.**

§1.535-3 (Proposed Treasury Decision, published 7-9-78.) **Accumulated earnings credit.**

(a) In general. As provided in section 535 (a) and § 1.535-1, the accumulated earnings credit, provided by section 535 (c), reduces taxable income in computing accumulated taxable income. In the case of a corporation, not a mere holding or investment company, the accumulated earnings credit is determined as provided in paragraph (b) of this section and, in the case of a holding or investment company, as provided in paragraph (c) of this section.

(b) Corporation which is not a mere holding or investment company—(1) General rule. * * *

(iii) In a case to which subparagraph (3) of § 1.533-1 (a) applies, that is, a case in which a parent relies upon the underlying value of its investment in a subsidiary to obtain funds for nondividend distributions to its shareholders, there is a presumption that all or a part of the subsidiary's earnings and profits for the taxable year are not retained for the reasonable needs of the business. The amount to which the presumption applies is an amount equal to the sum of the distributions to the parent's shareholders during the taxable year which are treated as provided in section 301 (c) (2) or (3). The burden of overcoming such presumption and showing that earnings and profits have been retained for the reasonable needs of the business is on the taxpayer.

Personal Holding Companies

Section 1.541-1 is amended by revising paragraphs (a) and (b), and by adding new paragraphs (c) and (d). These revised and added provisions read as follows:

§ 1.541-1 (Proposed Treasury Decision, published 9-5-68.) **Imposition of tax.**

(a) **In general.** Section 541 imposes a tax upon corporations classified as personal holding companies under section 542. This tax, if applicable, is in addition to the tax imposed upon corporations generally under section 11. Unless specifically excepted under section 542(c) the tax applies to domestic and foreign corporations and, to the extent provided by section 542(b), to an affiliated group of corporations filing a consolidated return. Corporations classified as personal holding companies are exempt from the accumulated earnings tax imposed under section 531 but are not exempt from other income taxes imposed upon corporations, generally, under any other provisions of the Code. Unlike the accumulated earnings tax imposed under section 531, the personal holding company tax imposed by section 541 applies to all personal holding companies as defined in section 542, whether or not they were formed or availed of to avoid income tax upon shareholders. See section 6501(f) and § 301.6501(f)-1 of this chapter (Regulations on Procedure and Administration) with respect to the period of limitation on assessment of personal holding company tax upon failure to file a schedule of personal holding company income.

(b) **Foreign corporations.** A foreign corporation, whether resident or nonresident, which is classified as a personal holding company is subject to the tax imposed under section 541 with respect to its income from sources within the United States, even though such income is not fixed or determinable annual or periodical income specified in section 881. A foreign corporation is not classified as a personal holding company subject to tax under section 541 if it is a foreign personal holding company as defined in section 552 or if it meets the requirements of the exception provided in section 542(c)(7) (or, in the case of taxable years beginning before January 1, 1964, section 542(c)(10) prior to amendment by section 225(c)(2) of the Revenue Act of 1964 (78 Stat. 79)).

(c) **Rate of tax.** Except as otherwise provided in this paragraph, the tax imposed by section 541 is 70 percent of the undistributed personal holding company income as defined in section 545 and the regulations thereunder. For taxable years beginning before January 1, 1964, the tax imposed is 75 percent of the undistributed personal holding company income not in excess of $2,000, plus 85 percent of the undistributed personal holding company income in excess of $2,000.

(d) **Certain liquidations before January 1, 1966.** In the case of certain corporations described in section 333(g)(3) that completely liquidate and distribute all property before January 1, 1966, section 225(h) of the Revenue Act of 1964 (78 Stat. 90) provides a special rule for the application of the Internal Revenue Code of 1954. Under the special rule, the Code is applied without regard to the amendments made by section 225 (other than subsections (f) and (g) of such section) of the Revenue Act of 1964. However, an exception to the special rule is provided where section 332 applies to the liquidation.

Section 1.542-1 is amended to read as follows:

§ 1.542-1 (Proposed Treasury Decision, published 9-5-68.) **Definition of a personal holding company.**

Proposed Reg. § 1.542-1

A personal holding company is any corporation (other than one specifically excepted under section 542(c)) which—

(a) For any taxable year beginning after December 31, 1963, meets the adjusted ordinary gross income requirement specified in section 542(a)(1) and paragraph (a) of § 1.542-2, or

(b) For any taxable year beginning before January 1, 1964, meets the gross income requirement specified in paragraph (b) of § 1.542-2,

and for the taxable year meets the stock ownership requirement specified in section 542(a)(2) and § 1.542-3. Both the income and stock ownership requirements must be satisfied with respect to each taxable year. For rules relating to the exclusion of lending or finance companies, see § 1.542-5.

Section 1.542-2 is amended to read as follows:

§ **1.542-2** (Proposed Treasury Decision, published 9-5-68.) **Income requirement.**

(a) **Adjusted ordinary gross income requirement.** To meet the adjusted ordinary gross income requirement for taxable years beginning after December 31, 1963, at least 60 percent of the adjusted ordinary gross income of the corporation for the taxable year must be personal holding company income as defined in section 543 and §§ 1.543-3 through 1.543-11. For the definition of "adjusted ordinary gross income" see section 543(b)(2) and paragraph (c) of § 1.543-12.

(b) **Gross income requirement.** To meet the gross income requirement for taxable years beginning before January 1, 1964, at least 80 percent of the total gross income of the corporation must be personal holding company income as defined in §§ 1.543-1 and 1.543-2. For the definition of "gross income" see section 61 and §§ 1.61-1 through 1.61-15. Under such provisions gross income is not necessarily synonymous with gross receipts. Further, in the case of transactions in stocks and securities and in commodities transactions, gross income for purposes of this paragraph shall include only the excess of gains over losses from such transactions. See paragraph (b)(5) and (6) of §1.543-1 and §1.543-2. For determining the character of the amount includible in gross income under section 951(a), see paragraph (a) of § 1.951-1.

Section 1.542-3 is amended by revising subdvision (iv) of paragraph (a)(2) to read as follows:

§ **1.542-3** (Proposed Treasury Decision, published 9-5-68.) **Stock ownership requirement.**

(a) **General rule.** * * *

(2) **Exception.** * * *

(iv) This subparagraph is illustrated by the following example:

Example. The X Charitable Foundation (an organization described in section 501(c)(3) to which section 503 is applicable) has owned all of the stock of the Y Corporation since Y's organization in 1949. Both X and Y are calendar-year corporations. At the end of the year 1967, X has accumulated $100,000 out of income and has actually paid out only $75,000 of this amount, leaving a balance of $25,000 on December 31, 1967. X was not denied an exemption under section 504(a) for the year 1967. Y, during the calendar year 1967, has $400,000 taxable income of which $200,000 is available for distribution as dividends at the end of the year. X will be considered to have accumulated out of income during the calendar year 1967 the amount of $225,000 for the purpose of determining whether it would have been denied an exemption under section 504(a)(1). If X would have been denied an exemption under section 504(a)(1) by reason of having been deemed to have accumulated $225,000, the stock ownership requirement of section 542(a)(2) and this section will have been satisfied. If Y Corporation also satisfies the adjusted ordinary gross income requirement of section 542(a)(1) and paragraph (a) of § 1.542-2 it will be a personal holding company for the calendar year 1967.

* * * * * * * * * *

Section 1.542-4 is amended to read as follows:

§ 1.542-4 (Proposed Treasury Decision, published 9-5-68.) **Corporations filing consolidated returns.**

(a) **General rule.** A consolidated return under section 1501 shall determine the application of the personal holding company tax to the group and to any member thereof on the basis of the consolidated adjusted ordinary gross income and consolidated personal holding company income of the group, as determined under the regulations prescribed pursuant to section 1502 (relating to consolidated returns); however, this rule shall not apply to either (1) an ineligible affiliated group as defined in section 542(b)(2) and paragraph (b) of this section, or (2) an affiliated group of corporations a member of which is excluded from the definition of a personal holding company under section 542(c) (see paragraph (c) of this section). Thus, in the latter two instances the adjusted ordinary gross income requirement provided in section 542(a)(1) and paragraph (a) of § 1.542-2 shall apply to each individual member of the affiliated group of corporations.

(b) **Ineligible affiliated group.** (1) Except for certain affiliated railroad corporations, as provided in subparagraph (2) of this paragraph, an affiliated group of corporations is an ineligible affiliated group and therefore may not use its consolidated adjusted ordinary gross income and consolidated personal holding company income to determine the liability of the group or any member thereof for personal holding company tax (as provided in paragraph (a) of this section), if—

(i) Any member of such group, including the common parent, derived 10 percent or more of its adjusted ordinary gross income from sources outside the affiliated group for the taxable year, and

(ii) 80 percent or more of the adjusted ordinary gross income from sources outside the affiliated group consists of personal holding company income as defined in section 543 and §§ 1.543-3 through 1.543-11.

For purposes of subdivision (i) of this subparagraph, adjusted ordinary gross income shall not include certain dividend income received by a common parent from a corporation not a member of the affiliated group which qualifies under section 542(b)(4) and paragraph (d) of this section. See particularly the examples contained in paragraph (d)(2) of this section. Intercorporate dividends received by members of the affiliated group (including the common parent) are to be included in the adjusted ordinary gross income from all sources for purposes of the test in subdivision (i) of this subparagraph. For purposes of subdivision (ii) of this subparagraph, section 543 and §§ 1.543-3 through 1.543-11 shall be applied as if the amount of adjusted ordinary gross income derived from sources outside the affiliated group by a corporation which is a member of such group is the adjusted ordinary gross income of such corporation.

(2) An affiliated group of railroad corporations shall not be considered to be an ineligible affiliated group, notwithstanding any other provisions of section 542 (b)(2) and this paragraph, if the common parent of such group would be eligible to file a consolidated return under section 141 of the Internal Revenue Code of 1939 prior to its amendment by the Revenue Act of 1942 (56 Stat. 798).

(3) See section 562 and § 1.562-3 for dividends paid deduction in the case of a distribution by a member of an ineligible affiliated group.

Proposed Reg. § 1.542-4

(4) The determination of whether an affiliated group of corporations is an ineligible group under section 542(b)(2) and this paragraph, may be illustrated by the following examples:

Example (1). Corporations X, Y, and Z constitute an affiliated group of corporations which files a consolidated return for the calendar year 1964; corporations Y and Z are wholly-owned subsidiaries of corporation X and derive no adjusted ordinary gross income from sources outside the affiliated group; corporation X, the common parent, has adjusted ordinary gross income in the amount of $250,000 for the taxable year 1964. $200,000 of such adjusted ordinary gross income consists of dividends received from corporations Y and Z. The remaining $50,000 was derived from sources outside the affiliated group, $40,000 of which represents personal holding company income as defined in section 543. The $50,000 included in the adjusted ordinary gross income of corporation X and derived from sources outside the affiliated group is more than 10 percent of X's adjusted ordinary gross income ($50,000/$250,000) and the $40,000 which represents personal holding company income is 80 percent of $50,000 (the amount considered to be the adjusted ordinary gross income of corporation X). Accordingly, corporations X, Y, and Z would be an ineligible affiliated group and the adjusted ordinary gross income requirement under section 542(a)(1) and paragraph (a) of § 1.542-2 would be applied to each corporation individually.

Example (2). If, in the above example, only $30,000 of the $50,000 derived from sources outside the affiliated group by corporation X represented personal holding company income, this group of affiliated corporations would not be an ineligible affiliated group. Although the $50,000 representing the adjusted ordinary gross income of corporation X from sources outside the affiliated group is more than 10 percent of its total adjusted ordinary gross income, the amount of $30,000 representing personal holding company income is not 80 percent or more of the amount considered to be adjusted ordinary gross income for the purpose of this test. Under section 542(b)(2) and subparagraph (1) of this paragraph both the adjusted ordinary gross income and the personal holding company income requirements must be satisfied in determining whether an affiliated group constitutes an ineligible group. Since both these requirements have not been satisfied in this example, this group of affiliated corporations would not be an ineligible group.

(c) **Excluded corporations.** The general rule for determining liability of an affiliated group under paragraph (a) of this section shall not apply if any member thereof is a corporation which is excluded, under section 542(c), from the definition of a personal holding company.

(d) **Certain dividend income received by a common parent.** (1) Dividends received by a common parent of an affiliated group from a corporation which is not a member of the affiliated group shall not be included in adjusted ordinary gross income or personal holding company income, for the purpose of the test under section 542(b)(2)—

(i) If such common parent owned, directly or indirectly, more than 50 percent of the outstanding voting stock of the dividend paying corporation at the time such common parent became entitled to the dividend, and

(ii) If the dividend paying corporation is not a personal holding company for the taxable year in which the dividends are paid. Thus, if the tests in subdivisions (i) and (ii) of this subparagraph are met, the dividend income received by the common parent from such other corporation will not be considered adjusted ordinary gross income for purposes of the test in section 542(b)(2)(A) (paragraph (b) of this section), that is, either to determine adjusted ordinary gross income from sources outside the affiliated group or to determine adjusted ordinary gross income from all sources.

(2) The application of subparagraph (1) of this paragraph may be illustrated by the following examples:

Example (1) Corporation X is the common parent of corporation Y and corporation Z and together they constitute an affiliated group which files a consolidated return under section 1501. Corporation Y and corporation Z derived no adjusted ordinary gross income from sources outside the affiliated group. Corporation X, the common parent, had adjusted ordinary gross income of $100,000 for the calendar year 1964 of which amount $20,000 represented a dividend received from corporation W, and $4,000 represented interest from corporation T. The remaining adjusted ordinary gross income of X, $76,000, was received from corporations Y and Z. Corporation X, for its entire taxable year, owned 60 percent of the voting stock of corporation W which was not a personal holding company for the calendar year 1964. For the purpose of the adjusted ordinary gross income and personal holding company income test under section 542(b)(2) and paragraph (b) of this section, the $20,000 dividend received from corporation W would not be included in the adjusted ordinary gross income or personal holding company income of corporation X. The affiliated group would not be an ineligible group under section 542(b)(2) because no member of the group derived 10 percent or more of its adjusted ordinary gross income from sources outside the affiliated group as required by section 542 (b)(2)(A). Inasmuch as the $20,000 dividend from corporation W is not included in the adjusted ordinary gross income of corporation X for purposes of section 542(b)(2), corporation X has only $4,000 of its adjusted ordinary gross income from sources outside the affiliated group, which is only 5 percent of its adjusted ordinary gross income from all sources, $80,000.

Example (2). If, in example (1), corporation X owned 50 percent or less of the voting stock of corporation W at the time X became entitled to the dividend, or if corporation W had been a personal holding company for the taxable year in which the dividends were paid, the $20,000 dividend received by corporation X would be included in adjusted ordinary gross income and personal holding company income of corporation X for the purpose of the test under section 542(b)(2) and paragraph (b) of this section. Thus, the affiliated group would be an ineligible affiliated group under section 542(b)(2) because 24 percent of its adjusted ordinary gross income was from sources outside the affiliated group ($24,000/$100,000) and 100 percent of this $24,000 was personal holding company income.

(e) **Special rule for taxable years beginning before January 1, 1964.** In the case of taxable years beginning before January 1, 1964, the rules provided in paragraphs (a) through (d) of this section shall apply as if each reference to "adjusted ordinary gross income" were a reference to "gross income", as if each reference to paragraph (a) of § 1.542-2 were a reference to paragraph (b) of § 1.542-2, and as if each reference to §§ 1.543-3 through 1.543-11 were a reference to §§ 1.543-1 and 1.543-2.

Immediately after § 1.542-4 the following new section is inserted:

§ **1.542-5** (Proposed Treasury Decision, published 9-5-68.) **Lending or finance companies.**

(a) **General rule.** For taxable years beginning after December 31, 1963, a corporation is excluded under section 542(c)(6) from personal holding company status if each of the following tests is satisfied:

(1) **60-percent test.** At least 60 percent of the corporation's ordinary gross income (as defined in section 543(b)(1) and paragraph (b) of § 1.543-12) for the

Proposed Reg. § 1.542-5

taxable year must be derived directly from the active and regular conduct of the corporation's lending or finance business. See paragraph (b) of this section for the definition of "lending or finance business".

(2) **20-percent test.** (i) The corporation's personal holding company income for the taxable year (computed as provided in subdivision (ii) of this subparagraph) must not exceed 20 percent of its ordinary gross income (as defined in section 543 (b)(1) and paragraph (b) of § 1.543-12).

(ii) For purposes of subdivision (i) of this subparagraph, the personal holding company income of the corporation for the taxable year shall be computed under section 543(a) except that such income shall be computed—

(a) If such corporation satisfies the 60-percent test of subparagraph (1) of this paragraph, by excluding the lawful income received from a corporation which— (1) satisfies each of the tests of this paragraph, and (2) is a member of the same affiliated group (as defined in section 1504) of which such corporation is a member;

(b) By excluding income derived directly from the active and regular conduct of the corporation's lending or finance business (as defined in paragraph (b) of this section);

(c) By including the entire amount of the gross income from rents (as defined in the second sentence of section 543(b)(3) and paragraph (d)(2) of § 1.543-12);

(d) By including the entire amount of the gross income from mineral, oil, and gas royalties (as defined in paragraph (e)(2) of § 1.543-12) and from copyright royalties (as defined in section 543(a)(4) and paragraph (d) of § 1.543-7);

(e) By including the entire amount of the gross income from produced film rents (as defined in section 543(a)(5)(B) and paragraph (b) of § 1.543-8); and

(f) By including the amounts received as compensation for the use of, or right to use, property of the corporation by certain shareholders (determined in accordance with section 543(a)(6), but without regard to the last sentence of such section).

For purposes of (a) of this subdivision, the term "lawful" limits the term "income" to that income which is lawful under the applicable state law.

(3) **Deduction test.** (i) The sum of the deductions allowable for the taxable year which are directly allocable to the active and regular conduct of the corporation's lending or finance business (as defined in paragraph (b) of this section) must equal or exceed the sum of—

(a) 15 percent of so much of the ordinary gross income (as defined in section 543(b)(1) and paragraph (b) of § 1.543-12) from such business for the taxable year as does not exceed $500,000, and

(b) 5 percent of so much of such ordinary gross income for the taxable year as exceeds $500,000, but does not exceed $1,000,000. Thus, for example, in the case of a corporation which has ordinary gross income for the taxable year of $700,000 from the active and regular conduct of its lending or finance business, the sum of the deductions allowable for such year which are directly allocable to such business must be at least, but need not exceed, $85,000 ($75,000 (15 percent of $500,000) plus $10,000 (5 percent of $200,000)). In the case of a corporation which has ordinary gross income of $1,000,000 or more from the active and regular conduct of its lending or finance business, the sum of the deductions which are directly allocable to such business must be at least, but need not exceed, $100,000 ($75,000 (15 percent of $500,000) plus $25,000 (5 percent of $500,000)).

(ii) (a) For purposes of subdivision (i) of this subparagraph, the deductions which are to be taken into account shall include only—

(1) Deductions which are allowable only by reason of—(i) section 162 (relating to trade or business expenses), or (ii) section 404 (relating to deduction for contributions of an employer to an employees' trust or annuity plan and compensation under a deferred-payment plan), except that there shall be excluded any such deductions in respect of compensation for personal services rendered by shareholders (including members of a shareholder's family, as described in section 544(a)(2)); and

(2) Deductions which are allowable under—(i) section 167 (relating to depreciation), and (ii) section 164(a)(1) (relating to real property taxes), but in either case only to the extent that the property with respect to which such deductions are allowable is used directly in the active and regular conduct of the lending or finance business.

(b) For purposes of (a)(1) of this subdivision (ii)—

(1) A deduction which is specifically allowable under a section other than section 162 or 404, as, for example, the deduction for interest which is specifically allowable under section 163, shall not constitute a deduction allowable only by reason of section 162 or 404.

(2) In determining deductions in respect of compensation for personal services rendered by shareholders, the relevant date is the date when the personal services are rendered. Thus, for example, if an employee is a shareholder on the date when the personal services are rendered but is not a shareholder on the date when the compensation in respect of such services is received, the compensation is for personal services rendered by a shareholder.

(c) For purposes of subdivision (i) of this subparagraph, an expense incurred by the corporation acting merely as a conduit shall not be taken into account.

(iii) For purposes of subdivision (i) of this subparagraph, the determination of the deductions that are directly allocable to the active and regular conduct of the corporation's lending or finance business shall be made in accordance with the following rules:

(a) In a case in which a deduction that, under subdivision (ii) of this subparagraph, is to be taken into account is definitely related only to the active and regular conduct of the corporation's lending or finance business, the entire amount of the allowable deduction shall be directly allocated to such business. In a case in which such a deduction is neither in whole nor in part definitely related to the active and regular conduct of the corporation's lending or finance business, then no part of such deduction shall be allocated to such business.

(b) In a case in which the working time of an officer or employee of the corporation is divided between activities in connection with the active and regular conduct of the corporation's lending or finance business and one or more other activities of the corporation, only a portion of the deduction that is to be taken into account with respect to compensation paid to such officer or employee shall be directly allocable to the active and regular conduct of such lending or finance business. For purposes of the preceding sentence, the portion of the allowable deduction which is directly allocated to the active and regular conduct of such lending or finance business is an amount equal to such allowable deduction multiplied by a fraction, the numerator of which is a figure based on the working time of such officer or employee devoted to such lending or finance business, and the denominator of which is a figure based on the total working time of such officer or employee.

(c) In a case in which property used by the corporation in connection with the active and regular conduct of its lending or finance business is also used by

Proposed Reg. § 1.542-5

it for other purposes, then only a part of a deduction that is to be taken into account with respect to such property shall be directly allocable to the active and regular conduct of such lending or finance business. For purposes of the preceding sentence, the portion of the allowable deduction which is directly allocated to the active and regular conduct of such lending or finance business is an amount equal to such allowable deduction multiplied by a fraction, the numerator of which is a figure based on the use in connection with (or, in an appropriate case, the rental value of space devoted to) such lending or finance business, and the denominator of which is a figure based on the total use to which the property is put (or the total rental value of the property).

(d) In a case in which a deduction that is to be taken into account is definitely related to the active and regular conduct of the corporation's lending or finance business and, in addition, is definitely related to some other activity of the corporation but the rules set forth in (b) and (c) of this subdivision (iii) do not apply, the determination of the portion of the allowable deduction that is directly allocable to the active and regular conduct of the corporation's lending or finance business may be made on any reasonable basis, such as, for example, the ratio of gross income derived directly from the active and regular conduct of the corporation's lending or finance business to the entire ordinary gross income.

(iv) The application of this subparagraph, insofar as it relates to the determination of deductions directly allocable to the active and regular conduct of the corporation's lending or finance business, may be illustrated by the following example:

Example. Corporation X engages in the active and regular conduct of a lending or finance business. In addition, it carries on an investment business. It owns a three-floor building which is used in connection with both business activities. One entire floor is used solely in connection with the lending or finance business. One entire floor is used solely in connection with the investment business. The remaining floor is used in connection with both activities, the division of use being equal. Similarly, one group of employees (group A) works only in the lending or finance business. Another group of employees (group B) works only in the investment business. A third group of employees (group C) works in both business activities. The working time of the employees in group C is divided equally between the two business activities. None of the employees in groups A, B, or C are shareholders or related to shareholders in any way. For the taxable year, the allowable deductions described in subdivision (ii) of this subparagraph with respect to the building and employees are as follows:

	Deduction
Building	
Depreciation	$30,000
Real property taxes	10,000
Employees—Salaries	
Group A	80,000
Group B	50,000
Group C	60,000

The sum of such deductions which are directly allocable to the active and regular conduct of X's lending or finance business is $130,000 computed as follows:

	Directly Allocable
Building	
Depreciation (½ × $30,000)	$ 15,000
Real property taxes (½ × $10,000)	5,000
Employees—Salaries	
Group A	80,000
Group B	0
Group C (½ × $60,000)	30,000
Total	$130,000

(4) **Shareholder loan test.** (i) The loans outstanding at any time during the taxable year to a person who is a 10-percent-or-more shareholder at any time during the taxable year must not exceed $5,000 in principal amount.

(ii) For purposes of subdivision (i) of this subparagraph, a person shall be considered to be a 10-percent-or-more shareholder if such person owns, directly or indirectly, 10 percent or more in value of the corporation's outstanding stock. Stock owned, directly or indirectly, by or for a corporation, partnership, estate, or trust shall be considered as being owned proportionately by its shareholders, partners, or beneficiaries. Stock considered as owned by a corporation, partnership, estate, or trust by reason of the application of the preceding sentence shall be considered as owned by such corporation, partnership, estate, or trust for purposes of again applying such sentence. Additionally, in the case of an individual, stock owned by members of his family (as defined in section 544(a)(2)) shall be considered as owned by such individual. The amount of stock outstanding and its value shall be determined in accordance with the rules set forth in the last two sentences of paragraph (b) and in paragraph (c) of § 1.542-3.

(b) **Lending or finance business defined**—(1) **In general.** Except as provided in subparagraph (2) of this paragraph, the term "lending or finance business" means a business of—

(i) Making loans to any person;

(ii) Purchasing or discounting accounts receivable, notes, or installment obligations from any person;

(iii) Rendering services or making facilities available to any person in connection with activities, described in subdivisions (i) and (ii) of this subparagraph, carried on by the corporation rendering services or making facilities available; or

(iv) Rendering services or making facilities available to another corporation which is engaged in the lending or finance business (within the meaning of this paragraph), if—(a) such services or facilities are related to such business of such other corporation, and (b) such other corporation and the corporation rendering services or making facilities available are members of the same affiliated group (as defined in section 1504).

Except as provided in subparagraph (2)(i)(a) of this paragraph, for purposes of subdivision (i) and (ii) of this subparagraph, there is no distinction between secured obligations and obligations that are not secured.

(2) **Exceptions.** (i) For purposes of subparagraph (1) of this paragraph, the term "lending or finance business" does not include the business of—

(a) Making loans, or purchasing or discounting accounts receivable, notes, or installment obligations, if the remaining maturity exceeds 60 months, unless the loans, notes, or installment obligations are evidenced or secured by—(1) contracts of conditional sale (2) chattel mortgages, or (3) chattel lease agreements, arising out of the sale of goods or services in the course of the borrower's or transferor's trade or business; or

(b) Making loans evidenced by, or purchasing, certificates of indebtedness which are issued—(1) in a series, (2) under a trust indenture, and (3) in registered form or with interest coupons attached.

Proposed Reg. § 1.542-5

(ii) For purposes of subdivision (i)(a) of this subparagraph, the remaining maturity—(a) shall be measured as of the time the corporation makes the loan or purchases or discounts the account receivable, note, or installment obligation, and (b) shall include any period for which there may be a renewal or extension under the terms of an option which may be exercised by the obligor under such loan or such other debt obligation. In determining remaining maturity, there shall be taken into account any separate agreement which may extend the maturity of the loan or other debt obligation or result in the making of a loan in the future. The existence of an agreement or an option may be evidenced by facts and circumstances indicating that, at the time the remaining maturity is to be determined, both the taxpayer and the obligor anticipated that the maturity would be extended or a new loan would be made. Such facts and circumstances could include, for example, the fact that at the time the maturity is being determined neither party could reasonably expect the obligor to discharge his obligation within the prescribed time, or the existence of a course of prior conduct by the taxpayer indicating that it customarily extends the maturity of a loan upon request by an obligor.

(iii) If (subsequent to the time that the remaining maturity of a loan or other debt obligation is determined and prior to the time that such loan or debt obligation matures) the corporation enters into an agreement whereby it agrees to extend the term of the loan or other debt obligation or to make a loan in the future, the remaining maturity of the loan or other debt obligation shall be redetermined as of the date that the extension is granted or the agreement to make such loan is made. In redetermining the remaining maturity of the loan or other debt obligation, any option or separate agreement shall be taken into account. See subdivision (ii) of this subparagraph.

(iv) The application of this subparagraph may be illustrated by the following example.

Example. On January 1, 1968, corporation Y, a calendar year taxpayer, lends $109,500 to individual A. The loan is not secured. The note signed by A provides that the loan is to be repaid in monthly installments of $1,500 plus interest, commencing February 1, 1968, for 4 years with the balance of $37,500 becoming due on February 1, 1972. At the time of the loan, Y does not grant A a renewal or extension option, and the parties do not enter into any separate agreement as to extending the maturity of the loan or the making of a loan in the future. However, on January 1, 1969, corporation Y and individual A agree that the $1,500 monthly payments of principal shall continue until the debt is liquidated. Under the terms of the extension, the debt will be completely liquidated on February 1, 1974. On January 1, 1968, the date of the note, the loan is treated as having a remaining maturity not in excess of 60 months, since the note provides that the loan is to be completely repaid in 4 years and 1 month (49 months). Accordingly, during the period January 1, 1968, through December 31, 1968, the loan to A is considered to be a part of Y's lending or finance business. However, on January 1, 1969, the loan exceeds the 60-month maximum since, pursuant to the terms of the extension entered into on that date, the remaining maturity is 61 months (from January 1, 1969, to February 1, 1974). Accordingly, for corporation Y's taxable years 1969 through 1974, the loan to A is not considered part of its lending or finance business.

(c) **Active and regular conduct.** For purposes of this section, whether a corporation is engaged in the "active and regular" conduct of a lending or finance business shall be determined on the basis of the facts and circumstances of the particular case. However, a corporation shall be presumed to be engaged in the "active and regular" conduct of a lending or finance business if for the taxable year and at least one of the two immediately preceding taxable years at least 60 percent of its ordinary gross income consists of gross income derived directly from the conduct of a lending or finance business.

(d) **Directly.** For purposes of paragraphs (a)(1), (a)(2)(ii)(b), and (c) of this section, the use of the word "directly" in connection with the derivation of income from the conduct of a lending or finance business has the effect of excluding from such gross income any income that is not directly related to the activities of the corporation described in paragraph (b)(1) of this section. Thus, for example, income from the investment of idle funds in short-term securities, interest on a judgment obtained on a defaulted loan, and rent derived from property acquired by reason of a borrower's default on a loan do not constitute gross income derived directly from the conduct of the corporation's lending or finance business. However, subject to the exception provided in paragraph (b)(2) of this section, income from the sale or transfer of (1) notes acquired in the business of making loans, and (2) accounts receivable, notes, or installment obligations acquired in the business of purchasing or discounting accounts receivable, notes, or installment obligations, constitute gross income derived directly from the conduct of the corporation's lending or finance business.

Immediately after § 1.543 the following new section is inserted:

§ **1.543-0** (Proposed Treasury Decision published 9-5-68.) **Effective date.**

Sections 1.543-1 and 1.543-2 are applicable only to taxable years beginning before January 1, 1964, and all references therein to sections of the Code are to sections of the Internal Revenue Code of 1954 prior to the amendments made by section 225 of the Revenue Act of 1964 (78 Stat. 79). Except as otherwise expressly provided therein, §§ 1.543-3 through 1.543-12 are applicable to taxable years beginning after December 31, 1963.

Section 1.543-1 is amended by revising the section heading, paragraph (a), and subparagraphs (2) and (10) of paragraph (b) to read as follows:

§ **1.543-1** (Proposed Treasury Decision, published 9-5-68.) **Personal holding company income (taxable years beginning before January 1, 1964).**

(a) **General rule.** For taxable years beginning before January 1, 1964, the term "personal holding company income" means the portion of the gross income described in paragraph (b) of this section. See section 543(b) and § 1.543-2 for special limitations on gross income and personal holding company income in case of gains from stock, securities, and commodities transactions.

(b) **Definitions.** * * *

(2) **Interest.** The term "interest" means any amounts, includible in gross income, received for the use of money loaned, and shall include—(i) any amount treated as interest under section 483, and (ii) any annual or periodic rental payment under a redeemable ground rent (excluding amounts in redemption thereof) that is treated as interest. See section 163(c) and paragraph (b) of § 1.163-1. However, interest which constitutes "rent" shall not be classified as "interest" for purposes of section 543(a)(1) and this subparagraph, but shall be classified as "rents" (see subparagraph (10) of this paragraph). Interest on amounts set aside in a reserve fund under section 511 or 607 of the Merchant Marine Act, 1936 (46 U.S.C. 1161 or 1177), shall not be included in personal holding company income.

* * * * * * * * *

Proposed Reg. § 1.543-1

(10) **Rents (including interest constituting rents).** Rents which are to be included as personal holding company income consist of compensation (however designated) for the use, or right to use, property of the corporation. The term "rents" does not include amounts includible in personal holding company income under section 543(a)(6) and subparagraph (9) of this paragraph. The amounts considered as rents include charter fees, etc., for the use of, or the right to use, property, as well as interest on debts owed to the corporation (to the extent such debts represent the price for which real property held primarily for sale to customers in the ordinary course of the corporation's trade or business was sold or exchanged by the corporation). However, if the amount of the rents includible under section 543(a)(7) and this subparagraph constitutes 50 percent or more of the gross income of the corporation, such rents shall not be considered to be personal holding company income. For purposes of this subparagraph, an annual or periodic rental payment under a redeemable ground rent which, pursuant to section 163 (c) and paragraph (b) of § 1.163-1, is treated as interest on an indebtedness secured by a mortgage shall be treated as interest, and the redeemable ground rent shall be treated as a debt owed to the corporation.

* * * * * * * * * *

Section 1.543-2 is amended by revising the section heading and paragraph (a) to read as follows:

§ 1.543-2 (Proposed Treasury Decision, published 9-5-68) **Limitations (taxable years beginning before January 1, 1964).**

(a) For taxable years beginning before January 1, 1964, under section 543 (b)(1), the gains which are to be included in gross income, and in personal holding company income with respect to transactions described in section 543(a)(2) and paragraph (b)(5) of § 1.543-1, shall be the net gains from the sale or exchange of stock or securities. If there is an excess of losses over gains from such transactions, such excess (or net loss) shall not be used to reduce gross income or personal holding company income for purposes of the personal holding company tax. Similarly, under section 543(b)(2) the gains which are to be included in gross income, and in personal holding company income with respect to transactions described in section 543(a)(3) and paragraph (b)(6) of § 1.543-1, shall be the net gains from commodity transactions which reflect personal holding company income. Any excess of losses over gains from such transactions (resulting in a net loss) shall not be used to reduce gross income or personal holding company income. The capital loss carryover under section 1212 shall not be taken into account.

* * * * * * * * * *

There are inserted immediately after §1.543-2 the following new sections:

§ 1.543-3 (Proposed Treasury Decision, published 9-5-68.) **Personal holding company income (taxable years beginning after December 31, 1963).**

For taxable years beginning after December 31, 1963, the term "personal holding company income" means the portion of the adjusted ordinary gross income (as defined in section 543(b)(2) and paragraph (c) of § 1.543-12) which consists of the items described in §§ 1.543-4 through 1.543-11. See section 543(b) and § 1.543-12 for definitions to be used for personal holding company tax purposes.

§ 1.543-4 (Proposed Treasury Decision, published 9-5-68.) **Dividends, interest, annuities, and royalties (other than mineral, oil, or gas royalties or certain copyright royalties).**

(a) **General rule.** Under section 543(a)(1), personal holding company income includes all—

(1) Dividends (as defined in paragraph (b) of this section),
(2) Interest (as defined in paragraph (c) of this section),
(3) Annuities (as defined in paragraph (d) of this section), and
(4) Royalties (as defined in paragraph (e) of this section).

See paragraph (c)(2), (3), and (4) of this section, for certain interest amounts which shall not constitute an item of personal holding company income.

(b) Dividends. The term "dividends" includes dividends as defined in section 316 and amounts required to be included in gross income under section 551 and §§ 1.551-1 and 1.551-2 (relating to foreign personal holding company income taxed to United States shareholders).

(c) Interest. (1) The term "interest" means any amounts, includible in gross income, received for the use of money loaned, and shall include—

(i) Any amount treated as interest under section 483, and

(ii) Any annual or periodic rental payment under a redeemable ground rent (excluding amounts in redemption thereof) that is treated as interest. See section 163(c) and paragraph (b) of § 1.163-1. Interest which constitutes "rent" under paragraph (d)(2) of § 1.543-12 shall not be classified as "interest" for purposes of section 543(a)(1) and this subparagraph.

(2) Interest on amounts set aside in a reserve fund under section 511 or 607 of the Merchant Marine Act, 1936 (46 U.S.C. 1161 or 1177), shall not be an item of personal holding company income, even though such interest is includible in gross income, and is not excluded from either ordinary gross income or adjusted ordinary gross income. See section 543(b)(1) and (2) and paragraphs (b) and (c) of § 1.543-12.

(3) Interest received on a direct obligation of the United States held for sale to customers in the ordinary course of trade or business by a regular dealer who is making a primary market in such obligations shall not be an item of personal holding company income. See section 543(b)(2)(C) and paragraph (c)(5)(i) of § 1.543-12 for the exclusion of such interest from adjusted ordinary gross income.

(4) Interest on a condemnation award, a judgment, and a tax refund shall not be items of personal holding company income even though such interest is includible in gross income. See section 543(b)(2)(C) and paragraph (c)(5) of § 1.543-12 for the exclusion of such interest from adjusted ordinary gross income.

(d) Annuities. The term "annuities" includes annuities only to the extent includible in the computation of gross income. See section 72 and the regulations thereunder for rules relating to the inclusion of annuities in gross income.

(e) Royalties. The term "royalties" includes amounts received for the privilege of using patents, copyrights, secret processes and formulas, good will, trade marks, trade brands, franchises, and other like property. The term "royalties" does not include—

(1) Rents (as defined in paragraph (d)(2) of § 1.543-12),

(2) Produced film rents (as defined in paragraph (b) of § 1.543-8),

(3) Mineral, oil, and gas royalties (as defined in paragraph (e)(2) of § 1.543-12, or

(4) Copyright royalties (as defined in paragraph (d) of § 1.543-7).

Proposed Reg. § 1.543-4

§ 1.543-5 (Proposed Treasury Decision, published 9-5-68.) **Adjusted income from rents.**

(a) **In general.** Under section 543(a)(2), the adjusted income from rents (as defined in section 543(b)(3) and paragraph (d) of § 1.543-12) constitutes, generally, personal holding company income. However, if both of the requirements set forth in paragraphs (b) and (c) of this section are met, then such adjusted income from rents shall not constitute personal holding company income.

(b) **50-percent rental income requirement.** Under section 543(a)(2)(A), if the adjusted income from rents for the taxable year constitutes 50 percent or more of the corporation's adjusted ordinary gross income (as defined in section 543(b)(2) and paragraph (c) of § 1.543-12) for the taxable year and the requirement of paragraph (c) of this section is met, then such adjusted income from rents shall not constitute personal holding company income.

(c) **10-percent personal holding company income requirement.** (1) Under section 543(a)(2)(B), if—

(i) The dividends paid deduction for the taxable year (computed in accordance with subparagraph (2) of this paragraph) equals or exceeds the amount, if any, by which the personal holding company income for the taxable year (computed in accordance with the special rules set forth in subparagraph (3) of this paragraph) exceeds 10 percent of the corporation's ordinary gross income (as defined in section 543(b)(1) and paragraph (b) of § 1.543-12) for the taxable year, and

(ii) The requirement of paragraph (b) of this section is met,

then the adjusted income from rents for the taxable year shall not constitute personal holding company income.

(2) (i) For purposes of this paragraph, the dividends paid deduction shall be computed under section 561 as if the taxpayer were a personal holding company for purposes of such computation except that such deduction shall be computed without regard to—

(a) Any dividend carryover described in section 564, and

(b) Any distribution of property which, in the case of a personal holding company, would be a dividend solely on account of the application of section 316(b)(2) or section 562(b).

For purposes of this subparagraph, the taxpayer shall be treated as having elected, under section 563(b) and § 1.563-2 (relating to dividends paid after the close of the taxable year), to include (in the computation of the dividends paid deduction) dividends paid after the close of the taxable year and on or before the 15th day of the third month following the close of such taxable year, to the maximum extent permitted by such sections. If a corporation would be a personal holding company, as defined in section 542 and the regulations thereunder, but for the fact that the dividends paid deduction computed in accordance with this subparagraph meets the requirement of subparagraph (1)(i) of this paragraph, then the dividends entering into such computation shall be treated as having been made for the purpose of satisfying such requirement.

(ii) The application of this subparagraph may be illustrated as follows:

Example. Assume that corporation Y is determining whether its adjusted income from rents constitutes personal holding company income. Corporation Y has a dividend carryover to the taxable year (computed under section 564) of $10. During the taxable year, corporation Y pays a dividend (described in section 316(a)) of $30 to its shareholders. Y's undistributed personal holding company income (UPHCI) for the taxable year (computed as if Y were a personal holding company) is $10. After the close of the taxable year and on or before the 15th day of the third month following the close of such year, Y pays a dividend of $6 to its shareholders. Corporation Y's dividends paid deduction under section 561 (computed as if it were a personal holding company and in accordance with the rules of this subparagraph) is $33, computed as follows:

Dividends paid during the taxable year $30
Dividends considered under section 563 as paid on last day of the taxable year (($6) but not in excess of either UPHCI ($10) or 10 percent of dividends paid during the year ($3)) 3
                                                                                                                        33

The dividend carryover to the taxable year is not taken into account for purposes of the computation.

(3) For purposes of this paragraph, personal holding company income shall be computed under section 543(a) except that such income shall be computed—

(i) By excluding adjusted income from rents (as defined in section 543(b)(3) and paragraph (d) of § 1.543-12);

(ii) By excluding amounts received as compensation for the use of, or right to use, property of the corporation (as defined in section 543(a)(6) and § 1.543-9);

(iii) Except as provided in subdivision (v) of this subparagraph, by including copyright royalties (as defined in section 543(a)(4) and paragraph (d) of § 1.543-7);

(iv) By including adjusted income from mineral, oil, and gas royalties (as defined in section 543(b)(4) and paragraph (e) of § 1.543-12); and

(v) By excluding royalties received for the use of, or for the privilege of using, a patent, invention, model, or design (whether or not patented), secret formula or process or any other similar property right if—

(a) Such property is also used by the corporation receiving such royalties in the manufacture or production of tangible personal property held for lease to customers, and

(b) The gross income from the rental of such tangible personal property, adjusted as required by section 543(b)(2)(A) as if such income were the only gross income from rents, constitutes 50 percent or more of the corporation's adjusted ordinary gross income.

(d) The application of this section may be illustrated by the following examples:

Example (1). Assume corporation Z has gross income of $200, consisting of gross income from rent in the amount of $150, $15 of dividends, a $10 capital gain from the sale of securities, and $25 from the sale of merchandise. The total amount of the deductions for depreciation, interest, and property taxes allocable to the gross income from rents equals $100. Corporation Z's ordinary gross income equals $190 ($200 (the gross income) less $10 (capital gain)). Corporation Z's adjusted ordinary gross income equals $90 and its adjusted income from rents equals $50, computed as follows:

	Adjusted ordinary gross income	Adjusted income from rents
Gross income from rents	$150	$150
Plus: Dividends	15	
Sale of Merchandise	25	

Proposed Reg. § 1.543-5

Ordinary gross income	190	
Less: Adjustments under sec. 543(b)(2)(A)	100	100
Total	90	50

Since the adjusted income from rents ($50) constitutes 50 percent or more of the adjusted ordinary gross income ($90), the requirement of section 543(a)(2)(A) and paragraph (b) of this section is satisfied. Corporation Z's only personal holding company income, computed by excluding adjusted income from rents as provided in paragraph (c)(3) of this section, is $15 of dividends. Since $15 does not exceed 10 percent of the ordinary gross income ($190), the test of section 543(a)(2)(B) and paragraph (c) of this section is satisfied without reference to the dividends paid by corporation Z during the taxable year. Accordingly, corporation Z's adjusted income from rents does not constitute personal holding company income and corporation Z is not a personal holding company for the taxable year.

Example (2). Assume the same facts as in example (1) except that corporation Z's dividend income equals $25. In addition, corporation Z pays a dividend (described in section 316(a)) of $5 to its shareholders during the taxable year. Although the $25 of dividend income exceeds 10 percent of the ordinary gross income ($200), the dividends paid deduction for the taxable year (computed as provided in paragraph (c)(2) of this section) ($5) equals the excess of the personal holding company income (computed by excluding adjusted income from rents as provided in paragraph (c)(3) of this section) over 10 percent of the ordinary gross income, as follows:

Personal holding company income	$25
Less: 10 percent of ordinary gross income ($200)	20
Excess	$ 5

Accordingly, the test of section 543(a)(2)(B) and paragraph (c) of this section is satisfied and the adjusted income from rents does not constitute personal holding company income. Therefore, corporation Z is not a personal holding company for the taxable year.

§ 1.543-6 (Proposed Treasury Decision, published 9-5-68.) **Adjusted income from mineral, oil, and gas royalties.**

(a) **In general.** Under section 543(a)(3), the adjusted income from mineral, oil, and gas royalties (as defined in section 543(b)(4) and paragraph (e) of § 1.543-12) constitutes, generally, personal holding company income. However, if the requirements set forth in paragraph (b) of this section are met, then such adjusted income from mineral, oil, and gas royalties shall not constitute personal holding company income.

(b) **Requirements.** (1) Under section 543(a)(3)(A), (B), and (C), if—

(i) The adjusted income from mineral, oil, and gas royalties for the taxable year constitutes 50 percent or more of the corporation's adjusted ordinary gross income (as defined in section 543(b)(2) and paragraph (c) of § 1.543-12) for the taxable year;

(ii) The personal holding company income for the taxable year (computed in accordance with the special rules set forth in subparagraph (2) of this paragraph) is not more than 10 percent of the corporation's ordinary gross income (as defined in section 543(b)(1) and paragraph (b) of § 1.543-12) for the taxable year; and

(iii) The sum of the deductions allowable for the taxable year under section 162 (computed in accordance with the special rules set forth in subparagraph

(3) of this paragraph) equals or exceeds 15 percent of the adjusted ordinary gross income (as defined in section 543(b)(2) and paragraph (c) of § 1.543-12) for the taxable year,

then the adjusted income from mineral, oil, and gas royalties for the taxable year shall not constitute personal holding company income.

(2) For purposes of subparagraph (1)(ii) of this paragraph, personal holding company income shall be computed under section 543(a) except that such income shall be computed—

(i) By excluding adjusted income from mineral, oil, and gas royalties (as defined in section 543(b)(4) and paragraph (e) of §1.543-12);

(ii) By including copyright royalties (as defined in section 543(a)(4) and paragraph (d) of §1.543-7); and

(iii) By including adjusted income from rents (as defined in section 543(b)(3) and paragraph (d) of § 1.543-12).

(3) For purposes of subparagraph (1)(iii) of this paragraph, the deductions allowable under section 162 shall be computed by excluding—

(i) Deductions for compensation for personal services rendered by any shareholder of the corporation, and

(ii) Deductions which are specifically allowable under sections other than section 162, as, for example, the deduction for interest which is specifically allowable under section 163, the deduction for depreciation of the corporation's assets which is specifically allowable under sections 167 or 611, and the deduction for depletion (cost or percentage) which is specifically allowable under section 611. For purposes of subdivision (ii) of this paragraph, the deduction for intangible drilling and development costs under section 263(c) and § 1.612-4 and section 616 and the deduction for amortization of leasehold interest and leasehold improvements described in §§ 1.162-11 and 1.167(a)-4 shall be treated as deductions which are specifically allowable under a section other than section 162. An expense incurred by the corporation acting merely as a conduit shall not constitute a deduction allowable under section 162.

(4) The application of this subparagraph may be illustrated by the following example:

Example. Assume corporation N has gross income of $400, consisting of gross income from mineral royalties in the amount of $250, $40 of dividends, and $110 from the sale of merchandise. The total amount of the deductions for depletion, interest, and property and severance taxes allocable to the gross income from mineral, oil, and gas royalties equals $100. The sum of the deductions allowable under section 162 (other than deductions for compensation for personal services rendered by shareholders and deductions specifically allowable under sections other than section 162) is $45. Corporation N's adjusted ordinary gross income equals $300 and its adjusted income from mineral, oil, and gas royalties equals $150. Since the adjusted income from mineral, oil, and gas royalties constitutes 50 percent or more of the adjusted ordinary gross income, the requirement of section 543(a)(3)(A) and subparagraph (1)(i) of this paragraph is satisfied. Since the $40 of dividends is personal holding company income under section 543(a)(1), corporation N's personal holding company income, computed as provided in subparagraph (2) of this paragraph, equals $40. Since $40 is not more than 10 percent of the ordinary gross income ($400), the 10-percent test of section 543(a)(3)(B) and subparagraph (1)(ii) of this paragraph is satisfied. Since $45 (the sum of the deductions allowable under section 162 computed as provided in subparagraph (3) of this paragraph) equals

Proposed Reg. § 1.543-6

or exceeds 15 percent of the adjusted ordinary gross income ($300), the deductions requirement of section 543(a)(3)(C) and subparagraph (1)(iii) of this paragraph is satisfied. Acordingly, corporation N's adjusted income from mineral, oil, and gas royalties does not constitute personal holding company income.

§ 1.543-7 (Proposed Treasury Decision, published 9-5-68.) **Copyright royalties.**

(a) **In general.** Under section 543(a)(4), the income from copyright royalties, as defined in section 543(a)(4) and paragraph (d) of this section, constitutes, generally, personal holding company income. However, if the requirements set forth in paragraph (b) of this section are met then such income shall not constitute personal holding company income.

(b) **Requirements.** (1) Under section 543(a)(4)(A), (B), and (C), if—

(i) The copyright royalties for the taxable year (computed by excluding royalties received for the use of, or the right to use, copyrights or interests in copyrights in works created in whole, or in part, by any person who, at any time during the corporation's taxable year, is a shareholder) constitute 50 percent or more of the corporation's ordinary gross income (as defined in section 543(b)(1) and paragraph (b) of § 1.543-12) for the taxable year;

(ii) The personal holding company income (computed in accordance with the special rules set forth in subparagraph (2) of this paragraph) for the taxable year is not more than 10 percent of the corporation's ordinary gross income for such year; and

(iii) The sum of the deductions allowable for the taxable year to the corporation under section 162 (computed in accordance with the special rules set forth in subparagraph (3)(i) of this paragraph) which are properly allocable to copyright royalties (determined in accordance with subparagraph (3)(ii) of this paragraph) equals or exceeds 25 percent of the amount by which the ordinary gross income for such year exceeds the sum of the royalties paid or accrued for such year and the amounts allowable as deductions for such year under section 167 (relating to depreciation), determined under subparagraph (4) of this paragraph, then the copyright royalties for the taxable year shall not constitute personal holding company income.

(2) For purposes of subparagraph (1)(ii) of this paragraph, the personal holding company income shall be computed under section 543(a) except that such income shall be computed—

(i) By excluding copyright royalties (except that there shall be included royalties received for the use of, or the right to use, copyrights or interests in copyrights in works created, in whole or in part, by any shareholder owning, at any time during the corporation's taxable year, more than 10 percent in value of the outstanding stock of the corporation),

(ii) By excluding dividends from any corporation in which the taxpayer owns, on the date when shareholders of such corporation become entitled to dividends, at least 50 percent of all classes of stock entitled to vote and at least 50 percent of the total value of all classes of stock, provided the corporation which pays the dividends meets the requirements of section 543 (a)(4)(A), (B), and (C) and this paragraph, and

(iii) By including the adjusted income from rents (as defined in section 543 (b)(3) and paragraph (d) of § 1.543-12) and adjusted income from mineral, oil and gas royalties (as defined in section 543 (b)(4) and paragraph (e) of § 1.543-12).

(3) (i) For purposes of subparagraph (1)(iii) of this paragraph, the deductions allowable under section 162 shall be computed by excluding—

(a) Deductions for compensation for personal services rendered by a shareholder of the corporation,

(b) Deductions for copyright and other royalties paid or accrued, and

(c) Deductions which are specifically allowable under Code sections other than section 162, as, for example, the deduction for interest which is specifically allowable under section 163 and the deduction for depreciation of the corporation's assets which is specifically allowable under section 167.

An expense incurred by the corporation acting merely as a conduit shall not constitute a deduction under section 162.

(ii) In determining the deductions allowable under section 162 which are properly allocable to copyright royalties, subject to the exceptions set forth in subdivision (i) of this subparagraph, all of such deductions that are definitely related to copyright royalties shall be allocated to such royalties. In a case in which a deduction allowable under section 162 is neither in whole nor in part definitely related to copyright royalties, no part of such deduction shall be allocated to copyright royalties. In a case in which a deduction that is to be taken into account is definitely related to copyright royalties and is also definitely related to some other income or activity of the corporation, the determination of the portion of the allowable deduction that is properly allocable to copyright royalties shall be made on a reasonable basis, such as, for example, the ratio of copyright royalties for the taxable year to the entire ordinary gross income.

(4) For purposes of subparagraph (1) (iii) of this paragraph, in determining the excess of ordinary gross income over royalties and depreciation, there shall be taken into account only—

(i) Copyright and other royalties paid or accrued by the corporation, and

(ii) Depreciation allowable with respect to property acquired by the corporation, pursuant to the terms of an agreement under which certain rights existing under a copyright are assigned to the corporation, regardless of whether such contract is a sale of property or a license.

(c) **Determination of stock value and stock ownership.** For purposes of section 543 (a) (4) and this section, the following rules shall apply:

(1) The amount and value of the outstanding stock of a corporation shall be determined in accordance with the rules set forth in the last two sentences of paragraph (b) and in paragraph (c) of § 1.542-3.

(2) The ownership of stock shall be determined in accordance with the rules set forth in section 544 and §§ 1.544-1 through 1.544-7.

(3) Any person who is considered to own stock within the meaning of section 544 and §§ 1.544-1 through 1.544-7 shall be a shareholder.

(d) **Copyright royalties defined.** For purposes of section 543(a)(4) and this section, the term "copyright royalties" means compensation, however, designated, for the use of, or the right to use, copyrights in works protected by copyright issued under Title 17 of the United States Code (other than by reason of section 2 or 6 thereof) and to which copyright protection is also extended by the laws of any foreign country as a result of any international treaty, convention, or agreement to which the United States is a signatory. Thus, the term "copyright royalties" includes not only royalties from sources within the United States under protection of United States laws relating to statutory copyright but also royalties from sources within a foreign country with respect to United States statutory copyrights protected in such foreign country by an international treaty, convention, or agreement to which the United States is a signatory. In addition, the term "copyright royalties" includes—

Proposed Reg. § 1.543-7

(1) Compensation for the use of, or right to use, an interest in any such copyrighted works;

(2) Payments from any person for performing rights in any such copyrighted works; and

(3) Payments (other than produced film rents as defined in section 543(a)(5)(B) and paragraph (b) of § 1.543-8) received for the use of, or right to use, films (including television tapes).

§ 1.543-8 (Proposed Treasury Decision, published 9-5-68). **Produced film rents.**

(a) **In general.** Under section 543(a)(5) produced film rents (as defined in paragraph (b) of this section) constitute, generally, personal holding company income. However, if the total amount of such produced film rents constitutes 50 percent or more of the ordinary gross income of the corporation (as defined in section 543 (b) (1) and paragraph (b) of § 1.543-12) for the taxable year, such rents shall not be considered to be personal holding company income. In order for produced film rents to be excluded from personal holding company income, the 50-percent requirement must be met solely by reference to income which is within the definition of produced film rents.

(b) **Definition of produced film rents.** For purposes of section 543, the term "produced film rents" means payments received with respect to an interest in a film for the use of, or right to use, such film, but only to the extent that such interest was acquired before substantial completion of production of such film. What constitutes an interest in a film and whether such an interest is acquired before substantial completion of production of such film are questions to be determined on the basis of all of the facts and circumstances in each case. Thus, for example, for purposes of this section, if two corporations form a joint venture for the purpose of acquiring the motion picture rights to a book, and the joint venture proceeds to adapt such book to motion picture screenplay form, and to produce the film, then the interest in the film acquired by the joint venturers is acquired before substantial completion of production of the film. If, as a result of major revisions in the screenplay, unavailability of leading actors and actresses, or other unexpected events occurring at an early stage in the actual production of the film, substantial additional funds are required to continue production, an interest in the film acquired by a corporation at such time is acquired before substantial completion of production of the film. However, if an interest in a film is acquired by a corporation at a time when most of the major scenes have been filmed, the payments received by such corporation with respect to such interest are not "produced film rents". For the treatment of film rents other than those defined in this paragraph, see section 543(a)(4) and § 1.543-7. The term "produced film rents" does not include amounts which constitute personal holding company income under section 543 (a)(7) and § 1.543-10 (relating to personal service contracts).

§ 1.543-9 (Proposed Treasury Decision, published 9-5-68.) **Compensation for use of property.**

(a) **In general.** Under section 543(a)(6), except as provided in paragraph (b) of this section, the gross amounts received or accrued as compensation (however designated and from whomsoever received) for the use of, or right to use, property of the corporation shall be included as personal holding company income if, at any time during the taxable year, 25 percent or more in value of the outstanding stock of the corporation is owned, directly or indirectly, by or for an individual entitled to the use of the property. Thus, if a shareholder who meets the stock ownership requirement of section 543(a)(6) and this paragraph uses, or has the right to use, a yacht, residence, or other property owned by the corporation, the compensation to the corporation for such use of, or right to use, the property constitutes personal holding company income. This is true even though the shareholder may acquire the use of, or the right to use, the property by means of a sublease or under any other arrangement involving parties other than the corporation and the shareholder. For purposes of section 543(a)(6) and this paragraph, the amount of stock outstanding and its value shall be determined in accordance with the rules set forth in the last two sentences of paragraph (b) and in paragraph (c) of § 1.542-3. The stock ownership requirement of section 543(a)(6) and this paragraph relates to the stock outstanding at any time during the entire taxable year. For rules relating to the determination of stock ownership, see section 544 and §§ 1.544-1 through 1.544-7.

(b) **Exclusion from personal holding company income.** If the corporation's personal holding company income (computed in accordance with the special rules set forth in paragraph (c) of this section) for the taxable year does not exceed 10 percent of its ordinary gross income for such year, then, in a case in which a shareholder specified in paragraph (a) of this section has the use of, or right to use, property of the corporation, amounts received or accrued by the corporation as compensation for the use of, or right to use, such property shall not constitute personal holding company income. In addition, in such a case, such amounts shall not constitute "rents" (as defined in paragraph (d)(2) of § 1.543-12).

(c) **Special rules for determining personal holding company income.** For purposes of paragraph (b) of this section, personal holding company income shall be computed under section 543(a) except that such income shall be computed—

(1) By excluding amounts described in the first sentence of section 543(a)(6) and paragraph (a) of this section;

(2) By excluding adjusted income from rents (as defined in section 543(b)(3) and paragraph (d) of § 1.543-12);

(3) By including adjusted income from mineral, oil, and gas royalties (as defined in section 543(b)(4) and paragraph (e) of § 1.543-12); and

(4) By including copyright royalties (as defined in section 543(a)(4) and paragraph (d) of § 1.543-7).

§ 1.543-10 (Proposed Treasury Decision, published 9-5-68.) **Personal service contracts.**

(a) **In general.** Under section 543(a)(7), amounts received under a contract under which the corporation is to furnish personal services, as well as amounts received from the sale or other disposition of such contract, shall be included as personal holding company income if—

(1) Some person other than the corporation has the right to designate (by name or by description) the individual who is to perform the services or if the individual who is to perform the services is designated (by name or by description) in the contract; and

(2) At any time during the taxable year 25 percent or more in value of the outstanding stock of the corporation is owned, directly or indirectly, by or for the individual who has performed, is to perform, or may be designated (by name or by description) as the one to perform, such services.

For this purpose, the amount of stock outstanding and its value shall be determined in accordance with the rules set forth in the last two sentences of paragraph (b) and in paragraph (c) of § 1.542-3. It should be noted that the stock ownership

Proposed Reg. § 1.543-10

requirement of section 543(a)(7) and this section relates to the stock ownership at any time during the taxable year. For rules relating to the determination of stock ownership, see section 544 and §§ 1.544-1 through 1.544-7.

(b) **Important and essential services.** If the contract, in addition to requiring the performance of services by a 25-percent-or-more stockholder who is designated or who could be designated (as specified in section 543(a)(7) and paragraph (a) of this section), requires the performance of services by other persons which are important and essential, then only that portion of the amount received under such contract which is attributable to the personal services of the 25-percent-or-more stockholder shall constitute personal holding company income. Incidental personal services of other persons employed by the corporation to facilitate the performance of the services by the 25-percent-or-more stockholder, however, shall not constitute important or essential services. Under section 482 gross income, deductions, credits, or allowances between or among organizations, trades, or businesses may be allocated if it is determined that allocation is necessary in order to prevent evasion of taxes or clearly to reflect the income of any such organizations, trades, or businesses.

(c) **Amount attributable to personal services of 25-percent-or-more stockholder** —(1) General rule. For taxable years beginning after December 31, 1967, the portion of the amount received under a contract in any such taxable year of the corporation which is attributable to the personal services of a 25-percent-or-more stockholder shall be an amount equal to such amount received multiplied by a fraction, the numerator of which is the sum of the amounts inuring for such taxable year to the benefit of such stockholder, and the denominator of which is the sum of the amounts inuring for such taxable year to the benefit of such stockholder and all persons who are required to perform important and essential services under such contract.

(2) *Amounts inuring to the benefit of a person.* For purposes of subparagraph (1) of this paragraph, the amounts inuring to the benefit of a person for a taxable year shall be the sum of—

(i) The amounts paid (or credited) in any medium during such year, directly or indirectly, to such person by the corporation as compensation, rent, interest, royalties, and dividends (as defined in section 316 (a)), and

(ii) In the case of a person who is a stockholder, his proportionate share of the taxable income of the corporation for such year less—

(a) The amount by which the tax imposed by section 11 on such income exceeds the credits allowable under part IV (section 31 and following), subchapter A, chapter 1 of the Code, and

(b) The dividends (described in section 316(a)) paid during the taxable year.

If, by applying the rules provided in section 544, a person would be considered to own any stock which is owned (directly or indirectly) by any other person, then amounts inuring to the benefit of such other person under the first sentence of this subparagraph shall be considered as inuring to the benefit of such person.

(3) *Special rule.* For purposes of this paragraph, in any case where the corporation has gross income from more than one contract for the taxable year, the computations with respect to each contract shall be made separately. For purposes of such separate computations, the amount considered as inuring to the benefit of a person with respect to a particular contract shall be an amount equal to the total amounts inuring to the benefit of such person for the year multiplied by a fraction, the numerator of which is the gross income of the corporation from such contract, and the denominator of which is the total gross income from all contracts which require the important and essential services of such person.

(d) **Examples.** The application of section 543(a)(7) and this section may be illustrated by the following examples:

Example (1). A, whose profession is that of an actor, owns all of the outstanding capital stock of the M Corporation. The M Corporation entered into a contract with A under which A was to perform personal services for the person or persons whom the M Corporation might designate, in consideration of which A was to receive $10,000 a year from the M Corporation. The M Corporation entered into a contract with the O Corporation in which A was designated to perform personal services for the O Corporation in consideration of which the O Corporation was to pay the M Corporation $500,000 a year. The $500,000 received by the M Corporation from the O Corporation constitutes personal holding company income.

Example (2). Except as otherwise indicated, the facts are the same as in example (1). A owns only 80 percent of the M stock. In addition to A's contract with the M Corporation, B, whose profession is that of a dancer, and C, whose profession is that of a singer, were also under contract to the M Corporation to perform personal services for the person or persons whom the M Corporation might designate. The taxable year of the M Corporation involved is the calendar year 1968. B and C were each to receive $20,000 a year from the M Corporation. B owns 20 percent of the outstanding capital stock and is a member of A's family within the meaning of section 544(a)(2). Under the rules of section 544, A is considered as owning the stock owned by B, and B is considered as owning the stock owned by A. For the year 1968, M's taxable income less the excess of the tax imposed by section 11 over allowable credits, is $272,500. M Corporation pays no dividends during the taxable year. The contract entered into by the M Corporation with the O Corporation, in addition to designating that A was to perform personal services for the O Corporation, designated that B and C were also to perform personal services for the O Corporation. Because O Corporation desired the services of C, who was prominent in his field, to assist in providing a good supporting cast for the program, the services of C required under the contract are determined to be important and essential. Therefore, only that portion of the $500,000 received by the M Corporation which is attributable to the personal services of A and B (each of whom is a 25-percent-or-more stockholder and is named in the contract) constitutes personal holding company income. The sum of the amounts inuring to the benefit of A and B for the taxable year is $605,000, computed as follows:

Stockholder A

Compensation paid to 4	$ 10,000
A's share of taxable income	218,000
Compensation paid to B	20,000
B's share of taxable income	54,500

$302,500

Stockholder B

Compensation paid to B	$ 20,000
B's share of taxable income	54,500
Compensation paid to A	10,000
A's share of taxable income	218,000

$302,500

TOTAL $605,000

The sum of the amounts inuring to the benefit of A, B, and C for the taxable

Proposed Reg. § 1.543-10

year is $625,000 ($605,000 (A and B) + $20,000 (amount inuring to benefit of C)). The portion of the amount received on the contract which is attributable to the personal services of A and B and which constitutes personal holding company income is $484,000, computed as follows:

$$\frac{\$605,000 \text{ (amounts inuring to benefit of A and B)}}{625,000 \text{ (amounts inuring to benefit of A, B, and C)}} \times \$500,000 \text{ (contract amount)} = \$484,000$$

The same result would obtain even though the singer required by the contract had not been designated by name but the contract gave the M Corporation discretion to select and provide the services of a singer for the program and such services were provided.

Example (3). The N Corporation is engaged in engineering. Its entire outstanding capital stock is owned by four individuals. The N Corporation entered into a contract with the R Corporation to perform engineering services in consideration of which the R Corporation was to pay the N Corporation $50,000. The individual who was to perform the services was not designated (by name or by description) in the contract and no one but the N Corporation had the right to designate (by name or by description) such individual. The $50,000 received by the N Corporation from the R Corporation does not constitute personal holding company income.

Example (4). K, an actor, owns all of the outstanding capital stock of S Corporation. K entered into a contract with S Corporation under which K was to perform personal services for the person or persons whom S might designate in consideration of which K was to receive $400,000 a year from S Corporation. S Corporation entered into a contract with T Corporation in which K was designated to act in a film to be produced by T Corporation in consideration for a 20 percent interest in the copyright and negatives of such film when produced. The amounts received by S Corporation from its 20 percent interest in the film constitute personal holding company income under section 543(a)(7) and are not produced film rents within the meaning of section 543(a)(5).

§ 1.543-11 (Proposed Treasury Decisions, published 9-5-68.) **Estates and trusts.**

Under section 543(a)(8), personal holding company income includes amounts includible in computing the taxable income of the corporation under part I, subchapter J, chapter 1 of the Code (relating to estates, trusts, and beneficiaries). The gain from the sale or other disposition of any interest in an estate or trust is excluded from personal holding company income.

§ 1.543-12 (Proposed Treasury Decision, published 9-5-68.) **Definitions.**

(a) **Gross income.** The term "gross income" has the same meaning for personal holding company tax purposes as it does under section 61 and the regulations thereunder. Under such definition gross income is not necessarily synonymous with gross receipts, and losses incurred from dealings in property, both tangible and intangible, are disregarded. Thus, for example, if there is a loss from the sale or other disposition of a capital asset or of property described in section 1231(b), such loss shall not be used to reduce gross income for purposes of the personal holding company tax, nor shall such loss be used to reduce the amount of any gains derived from dealings in property. In the case of a mineral, oil, or gas working interest, gross income shall be determined without subtraction for depreciation and depletion based on cost. For determining the character of the amount includible in gross income under section 951(a), see paragraph (a) of § 1.951-1.

(b) **Ordinary gross income**—(1) **In general.** For personal holding company purposes, the term "ordinary gross income" means the gross income determined as provided in paragraph (a) of this section except that there shall be excluded—

(i) All gains from the sale or other disposition of capital assets, and

(ii) All gains (other than those referred to in subdivision (i) of this subparagraph) from the sale or other disposition of property described in section 1231 (b).

However, amounts which under part IV, subchapter P, chapter 1 of the Code (sections 1231 and following) are treated as gain which is not described in subdivision (i) and (ii) of this subparagraph shall not be excluded from gross income for purposes of computing ordinary gross income. Since section 631(c) has no application for personal holding company purposes, amounts which are otherwise treated as gains on the sale of coal or domestic iron ore under section 631(c) are not excluded from gross income in determining ordinary gross income.

(2) **Example.** The application of the rules provided in this paragraph may be illustrated by the following example:

Example. Assume that corporation R sells two pieces of machinery for $100 each. Machine A has an adjusted basis of $80 and machine B has an adjusted basis of $108. Assume, further, that for purposes of section 1245(a)(2) of the Code, the "recomputed basis" of machine A is $95. Corporation R's gain or loss on the sale of the two machines is computed as follows:

	Machine A	Machine B
Amount realized from sale	$100	$100
Less: Adjusted basis	80	108
Gain (loss) realized	20	(8)
Recomputed basis (sec. 1245(a))	95	
Less: Adjusted basis	80	
Amount of gain which is not treated as capital gain or sec. 1231 gain (sec. 1245(a)(1))	15	

The $8 loss on the sale of machine B is not an item of gross income and, therefore, does not enter into the computation of ordinary gross income. Of the $20 gain from the sale of machine A, $15 is treated as gain from the sale or exchange of property which is neither a capital asset nor property described in section 1231(b) of the Code, and thus is not excluded from gross income under section 543(b)(1) and this paragraph in determining ordinary gross income. The remaining $5 gain is gain from the sale of property described in section 1231(b), and is excluded from gross income under section 543(b)(1) and this paragraph for purposes of determining corporation R's ordinary gross income.

(c) **Adjusted ordinary gross income**—(1) **In general.** For personal holding company purposes, the term "adjusted ordinary gross income" means the ordinary gross income, determined as provided in paragraph (b) of this section, adjusted as provided in section 543(b)(2)(A), (B), and (C) and subparagraphs (2) through (5) of this paragraph.

(2) **Adjustments to ordinary gross income; rents**—(i) **In general.** In computing adjusted ordinary gross income for any taxable year, there shall be sub-

Proposed Reg. § 1.543-12

tracted from the gross income from rents (as defined in paragraph (d)(2) of this section), subject to the limitation provided in subdivision (iv) of this subparagraph, the amounts allowable as deductions for—

(a) Depreciation under section 167, including, where applicable, the additional first-year depreciation allowance described in section 179,

(b) Amortization of leasehold interests and leasehold improvements described in §§ 1.162-11 and 1.167(a)-4,

(c) Real property taxes and personal property taxes within the meaning of section 164(a)(1) and (2),

(d) Interest under section 163, and

(e) Rent;

to the extent that such deductions are allocable (under subdivision (iii) of this subparagraph) to such gross income from rents.

(ii) *Certain short-term leases.* For purposes of subdivision (i) of this subparagraph and notwithstanding any other provision of this subparagraph, if the gross income from rents for the taxable year includes rents derived from leases of tangible personal property of a type which is not customarily retained or used by any one lessee for a period of more than three years, such rents shall not be reduced by allowable deductions for depreciation and amortization with respect to such property. The determination of whether property is of a type which is not customarily retained or used by any one lessee for a period of more than three years shall be made by reference to the period of customary retention or use by lessees who lease from lessors in the nationwide industry of leasing such type of property. Thus, the term of the lease in a particular case will not be controlling for purposes of determining the period of customary retention or use. The special rule of this subdivision does not apply to the deductions for property taxes, interest, and rent with respect to such tangible personal property.

(iii) *Deductions allocable to rents.* For purposes of determining the deductions allocable to gross income from rents for any taxable year, the following rules shall apply:

(a) In the case of the amounts allowable as deductions for depreciation, amortization, property taxes, interest, and rent, described in subdivision (i) of this subparagraph, all such amounts which are directly or indirectly related to property held for rent during the taxable year shall be allocated to gross income from rents. For this purpose, amounts allowable as deductions which are directly or indirectly related to property held for rent include, for example, deductions for depreciation on rental property or property used in connection with rental property (such as office equipment and furniture used in a rental office), amortization of a leasehold interest in and rents paid with respect to property which is, in turn, subleased by the corporation, property taxes levied on rental property and property used in connection with rental property, interest paid or accrued on a loan the proceeds of which are used to purchase rental property or property used in connection with rental property, and interest paid or accrued on an obligation which constitutes all or part of the payment of the purchase price of rental property or property used in connection with rental property.

(b)(1) In a case in which property held for rent or property used in connection with property held for rent is also used by the corporation for other purposes, then only a part of the amounts allowable as deductions described in subdivision (i) of this subparagraph with respect to such property shall be allocable to gross income from rents. For purposes of the preceding sentence, the portion of the amounts allowable as deductions with respect to such property which is allocable to gross income from rents is an amount equal to such allowable amounts multiplied by a fraction, the numerator of which is a figure based on the use in connection with (or, in an appropriate case, the rental value of space devoted to) rental activities, and the denominator of which is a figure based on the total use to which the property is put (or the total rental value of the property).

(2) The application of this subdivision (b) may be illustrated by the following examples:

Example (1). X Corporation owns a building which has eight floors, each floor having an equal rental value. Six floors are held for rent. One floor is used exclusively in X's investment business. One-half of the remaining floor is used as a rental office and one-half is used in the investment business. X leases a business machine which is used, on the average, three hours of every eight-hour work day in connection with its rental activities. The business machine is used in connection with the investment activities for the remaining five hours of every work day. The deductions for depreciation and property taxes allowed with respect to the building for the taxable year are $10,000. The deduction for rent allowed with respect to the business machine is $800. The total amount of the deductions allocable to gross income from rents is $8,425.00, computed as follows:

Deductions	Allocable to Gross Income From Rent
$10,000 × $\frac{6.60 \text{ floors (Rental use)}}{8 \text{ floors (Total use)}}$	$8,125.00
$800 × $\frac{3 \text{ hours (Rental use)}}{8 \text{ hours (Total use)}}$	300.00
Total	8,425.00

Example (2). Assume the same facts as in example (1), except that the rental values of the floors are not equal. The rental value of each of the six floors that are held for rent is $8,000 per year. The rental value of each of the remaining floors is $1,000 per year. The total amount of the deductions allocable to gross income from rents is $10,000, computed as follows:

Deductions	Allocable to gross income from rent
$10,000 × $\frac{\$48,500 \text{ (Rental value of } 6\frac{1}{2} \text{ floors)}}{\$50,000 \text{ (Total rental value)}}$	$ 9,700
$800 × $\frac{3 \text{ hours (Rental use)}}{8 \text{ hours (Total use)}}$	300
Total	10,000

(c) In a case in which interest is paid or accrued on a loan the proceeds of which are not used to purchase property or on an obligation which does not constitute all or part of the payment of the purchase price of property, then a part of the amount allowable as a deduction for interest with respect to such loan or obligation shall be allocable to gross income from rents. For purposes of the preceding sentence, the portion of such allowable amount which is allocable to gross income from rents is an amount equal to such allowable amount multiplied by a fraction, the numerator of which is the gross income from rents, and the denominator of which is the entire ordinary gross income of the corporation.

(d) For purposes of this subdivision (iii), property will be considered held for rent whether or not such property is actually rented if such property is normally held by the taxpayer for rent or if the taxpayer intends to hold such property for

Proposed Reg. § 1.543-12

rent. Property which is held for rent on a seasonal basis shall be considered as held for rent for the entire taxable year unless the corporation establishes that the property was used for other purposes during the season when it was not held for rent.

(iv) *Limitation on adjustments.* The amounts subtracted under this subparagraph shall not exceed the corporation's entire gross income from rents. Subject to the limitation of the preceding sentence, amounts are to be subtracted even though no gross income is derived from the property to which the amounts are related. Thus, for example, assume that M Corporation owns three buildings which it holds for rent. Two of the buildings produce $150 apiece in gross income from rents. The third building produces no gross income from rents. The deductions allowable for depreciation and real property taxes with respect to building No. 1 equal $90, with respect to building No. 2 equal $110, and with respect to building No. 3 equal $105. In computing M's adjusted ordinary gross income, the amount subtracted from the gross income from rents is $300, computed as follows:

Gross income from rents

Building No. 1	$150
Building No. 2	150
Building No. 3	0
	$300

Less: Adjustments

Building No. 1	90
Building No. 2	110
Building No. 3	105
	305

Maximum amount subtracted (as limited by gross income from rents) $300

(3) **Adjustments to ordinary gross income; mineral, oil, and gas royalties—** (i) *In general.* In computing adjusted ordinary gross income for any taxable year, there shall be subtracted from the gross income from mineral, oil, and gas royalties (as defined in paragraph (e)(2) of this section), subject to the limitation provided in subdivision (iv) of this subparagraph, the amounts allowable as deductions for—

(a) Depletion under section 611,

(b) Depreciation under section 611 or section 167, including, where applicable, the additional first-year depreciation allowance described in section 179,

(c) Amortization of leasehold interests and leasehold improvements described in §§ 1.162-11 and 1.167(a)-4,

(d) Real property taxes and personal property taxes within the meaning of section 164(a)(1) and (2),

(e) Severance taxes as defined in subdivision (iii) of this subparagraph,

(f) Interest under section 163, and

(g) Rent;

to the extent that such deductions are allocable (under subdivision (ii) of this subparagraph) to such gross income from mineral, oil, and gas royalties.

(ii) *Deductions allocable to mineral, oil, and gas royalties.* For purposes of determining the deductions allocable to gross income from mineral, oil, and gas royalties for any taxable year, the following rules shall apply:

(a) In the case of the amounts allowable as deductions for depletion, depreciation, amortization, property taxes, severance taxes, interest, and rent, described in subdivision (i) of this subparagraph, all such amounts which are directly or indirectly related to mineral, oil, and gas royalties during the taxable year shall be allocated to gross income from such royalties.

(b) In a case in which property used by the corporation in connection with mineral, oil, and gas royalties is also used by the corporation for other purposes, then only a part of the amounts allowable as deductions described in subdivision (i) of this subparagraph with respect to such property shall be allocable to gross income from mineral, oil, and gas royalties. For purposes of the preceding sentence, the portion of the amounts allowable as deductions with respect to such property which is allocable to gross income from mineral, oil, and gas royalties is an amount equal to such allowable amounts multiplied by a fraction, the numerator of which is a figure based on the use in connection with (or, in an appropriate case, the rental value of space devoted to) mineral, oil, and gas royalties, and the denominator of which is a figure based on the total use to which the property is put (or the total rental value of the property). In addition, in an appropriate case, the allocation shall be made by comparing a figure based on the value of that portion of the property devoted to mineral, oil, and gas royalties and a figure based on the total value of the property.

(c) In a case in which interest is paid or accrued on a loan the proceeds of which are not used to purchase property or on an obligation which does not constitute all or part of the payment of the purchase price of property, then a part of the amount allowable as a deduction for interest with respect to such loan or obligation shall be allocable to gross income from mineral, oil, and gas royalties. For purposes of the preceding sentence, the portion of such allowable amount which is allocable to gross income from mineral, oil, and gas royalties is an amount equal to such allowable amount multiplied by a fraction, the numerator of which is the gross income from mineral, oil, and gas royalties, and the denominator of which is the entire ordinary gross income of the corporation.

(iii) Definition of severance tax. For purposes of subdivision (i)(e) of this subparagraph, a severance tax is a tax imposed either on mineral, oil, or gas severed from the ground or on the occupation or act of severing or producing mineral, oil, or gas. Thus, the characterization of such a tax under state or local law as an occupation or license tax is irrelevant for this purpose.

(iv) Limitation on adjustments. The amounts subtracted under this subparagraph shall not exceed the corporation's entire gross income from mineral, oil, and gas royalties. Subject to the limitation of the preceding sentence, amounts are to be subtracted even though no gross income is derived from the property to which the amounts are related.

(4) **Adjustments to ordinary gross income; working interests in oil or gas wells**—(i) In general. In computing adjusted ordinary gross income for any taxable year, there shall be subtracted from the gross income from working interests in oil or gas wells, subject to the limitation provided in subdivision (iii) of this subparagraph, the amounts allowable as deductions for—

(a) Depletion under section 611,

(b) Depreciation under section 611 or section 167, including, where applicable, the additional first-year depreciation allowance described in section 179,

(c) Amortization of leasehold interests and leasehold improvements described in §§ 1.162-11 and 1.167(a)-4,

(d) Real property taxes and personal property taxes within the meaning of section 164(a)(1) and (2),

Proposed Reg. § 1.543-12

(e) Severance taxes as defined in subparagraph (3)(iii) of this paragraph,
(f) Interest under section 163, and
(g) Rent;

to the extent that such deductions are allocable (under subdivision (ii) of this subparagraph) to such gross income from working interests in oil or gas wells. For purposes of this subparagraph, "working interest" shall have the same meaning as "operating mineral interest". See paragraph (b) of § 1.614-2 for the meaning of "operating mineral interest".

(ii) Deductions allocable to working interests in oil or gas wells. For purposes of determining the deductions allocable to gross income from working interests in oil or gas wells for any taxable year, the following rules shall apply:

(a) In the case of the amounts allowable as deductions for depletion, depreciation, amortization, property taxes, severance taxes, interest, and rent, described in subdivision (i) of this subparagraph, all such amounts which are directly or indirectly related to gross income from working interests in oil or gas wells shall be allocated to gross income from working interests in oil or gas wells.

(b) In a case in which property used by the corporation in connection with working interests in oil or gas wells is also used by the corporation for other purposes, then only a part of the amounts allowable as deductions described in subdivision (i) of this subparagraph with respect to such property shall be allocable to gross income from working interests in oil or gas wells. For purposes of the preceding sentence, the portion of the amounts allowable as deductions with respect to such property which is allocable to gross income from working interests in oil or gas wells is an amount equal to such allowable amounts multiplied by a fraction, the numerator of which is a figure based on the use in connection with (or, in an appropriate case, the rental value of space devoted to) the production of gross income from working interests in oil or gas wells, and the denominator of which is a figure based on the total use to which the property is put (or the total rental value of the property). In addition, in an appropriate case, the allocation shall be made by comparing a figure based on the value of that portion of the property devoted to the production of gross income from working interests in oil or gas wells and a figure based on the total value of the property.

(c) In a case in which interest is paid or accrued on a loan the proceeds of which are not used to purchase property or on an obligation which does not constitute all or part of the payment of the purchase price of property, then a part of the amount allowable as a deduction for interest with respect to such loan or obligation shall be allocable to gross income from working interests in oil or gas wells. For purposes of the preceding sentence, the portion of such allowable amount which is allocable to gross income from working interests in oil or gas wells is an amount equal to such allowable amount multiplied by a fraction, the numerator of which is the gross income from working interests in oil or gas wells, and the denominator of which is the entire ordinary gross income of the corporation.

(d) For purposes of this subdivision (ii), property will be considered held for the production of gross income from a working interest in an oil or gas well whether or not gross income is actually received from such working interest.

(iii) Limitation on adjustments. The amounts subtracted under this subparagraph shall not exceed the corporation's entire gross income from working interests in oil or gas wells. Subject to the limitation of the preceding sentence, amounts are to be subtracted even though no gross income is derived from the property to which the amounts are related.

(5) **Adjustments to ordinary gross income; interest.** In computing adjusted ordinary gross income for any taxable year there shall be subtracted from the

ordinary gross income (as defined in section 543(b)(1) and paragraph (b) of this section)—

(i) Interest received on a direct obligation of the United States held for sale to customers in the ordinary course of trade or business by a regular dealer who is making a primary market in such obligations;

(ii) Interest on a condemnation award;

(iii) Interest on a judgment; and

(iv) Interest on a tax refund (including refund of interest paid as part of any assessment).

(d) **Adjusted income from rents**—(1) **In general.** For purposes of determining personal holding company income, the term "adjusted income from rents" means the gross income from rents adjusted in the manner provided in paragraph (c)(2) of this section.

(2) **Definition of rents (including interest constituting rents).** (i) For purposes of determining personal holding company income, the term "rents" means compensation (however designated) for the use of, or right to use, property of the corporation. The term "rents" does not include:

(a) Amounts includible in personal holding company income under section 543(a)(6) and § 1.543-9;

(b) Amounts which are copyright royalties as defined in section 543(a)(4) and paragraph (d) of § 1.543-7; and

(c) Amounts which are produced film rents as defined in section 543(a)(5)(B) and paragraph (b) of § 1.543-8.

The amounts considered as rents include charter fees, etc., for the use of, or the right to use, property, as well as interest on debts owed to the corporation (to the extent such debts represent the price for which real property held primarily for sale to customers in the ordinary course of the corporation's trade or business was sold or exchanged by the corporation). For purposes of the preceding sentence, an annual or periodic rental payment under a redeemable ground rent which, pursuant to section 163(c) and paragraph (b) of § 1.163-1, is treated as interest on an indebtedness secured by a mortgage shall be treated as interest, and the redeemable ground rent shall be treated as a debt owed to the corporation. For a special rule in the case of certain amounts received or accrued as compensation for the use of, or right to use, property of the corporation, see paragraph (b) of § 1.543-9.

(ii) For taxable years beginning after December 31, 1967, the term "rents" does not include payments for the use or occupancy of rooms or other space where significant services are also rendered to the occupant, such as for the use or occupancy of rooms or other quarters in hotels, boarding houses, or apartment houses furnishing hotel services, or in tourist homes, motor courts, or motels. Generally, services are considered rendered to the occupant if they are primarily for his convenience and are other than those usually or customarily rendered in connection with the rental of rooms or other space for occupancy only. The supplying of maid service, for example, constitutes such services; whereas the furnishing of heat and light, the cleaning of public entrances, exits, stairways, and lobbies, the collection of trash, etc., are not considered as services rendered to the occupant. Payments for the use or occupancy of entire private residences or living quarters in duplex or multiple housing units, of offices in an office building, etc., are generally "rents". Payments for the parking of automobiles ordinarily do not constitute rents. Payments for the warehousing of goods or for the use of personal property do not constitute rents if significant services are rendered in connection with such payments.

Proposed Reg. § 1.543-12

(e) **Adjusted income from mineral, oil, and gas royalties—(1) In general.** For purposes of determining personal holding company income, the term "adjusted income from mineral, oil, and gas royalties" means the gross income from mineral, oil, and gas royalties adjusted in the manner provided in paragraph (c) (3) of this section.

(2) **Definition of mineral, oil, and gas royalties.** [Adopted by T.D. 7261, filed 2-26-73.]

Section 1.544-1 is amended by revising paragraphs (a) and (b), and by adding a new paragraph (e) at the end thereof. These revised and added provisions read as follows:

§ 1.544-1 (Proposed Treasury Decision, published 9-5-68.) **Constructive ownership.**

(a) Rules relating to the constructive ownership of stock are provided by section 544 for the purpose of determining whether the stock ownership requirements of the following sections are satisfied:

(1) Section 542 (a) (2), relating to ownership of stock by five or fewer individuals.

(2) Section 543 (a) (7), relating to personal holding company income derived from personal service contracts.

(3) Section 543 (a) (6), relating to personal holding company income derived from property used by shareholders.

(4) Section 543 (a) (4), relating to personal holding company income derived from copyright royalties.

(b) Section 544 provides four general rules with respect to constructive ownership. These rules are:

(1) Constructive ownership by reason of indirect ownership. See section 544 (a) (1) and § 1.544-2.

(2) Constructive ownership by reason of family and partnership ownership. See section 544 (a) (2), (4), (5), and (6), and §§ 1.544-3, 1.544-6, and 1.544-7.

(3) Constructive ownership by reason of ownership of options. See section 544(a)(3), (4), (5), and (6), and §§ 1.544-4, 1.544-6, and 1.544-7.

(4) Constructive ownership by reason of ownership of convertible securities.

See section 544(b) and § 1.544-5. Each of the rules referred to in subparagraphs (2), (3), and (4) of this paragraph is applicable only if it has the effect of satisfying the stock ownership requirement of the section to which applicable; that is, when applied to section 542(a)(2), its effect is to make the corporation a personal holding company, or when applied to section 543(a)(7), section 543(a)(6), or section 543(a)(4), its effect is to make the amounts described in such provisions includible as personal holding company income.

* * * * * * * *

(e) In the case of taxable years beginning before January 1, 1964, the rules provided in paragraphs (a) through (d) of this section shall apply as if each reference therein to section 543(a)(7) were a reference to section 543(a)(5) and each reference to section 543(a)(4) were a reference to section 543(a)(9), prior to their amendment by section 225(d) of the Revenue Act of 1964 (78 Stat. 81).

* * * * * * * * * *

Foreign Personal Holding Companies

Paragraph (c) of section 1.551-2 is amended to read as follows:

§ 1.551-2 (Proposed Treasury Decision, published 9-5-68.) **Amount included in gross income.**

* * * * * * *

(c) The amount which each United States shareholder must return is that amount which he would have received as a dividend if the above-specified portion of the undistributed foreign personal holding company income had in fact been distributed by the foreign personal holding company as a dividend on the last day of its taxable year on which the required United States group existed. Such amount is determined, therefore, by the interest of the United States shareholder in the foreign personal holding company, that is, by the number of shares of stock owned by the United States shareholder and the relative rights of his class of stock, if there are several classes of stock outstanding. Thus, if a foreign personal holding company has both common and preferred stock outstanding and the preferred shareholders are entitled to a specified dividend before any distribution may be made to the common shareholders, then the assumed distribution of the stated portion of the undistributed foreign personal holding company income must first be treated as a payment of the specified dividend on the preferred stock before any part may be allocated as a dividend on the common stock. In the case of distributions in liquidation made in taxable years of the distributing corporation beginning after December 31, 1963, the amount which would have been received as a dividend under section 551(b) and this section is determined as if any distribution in liquidation actually made in such taxable year had not been made. See section 562(b) and paragraph (b) of § 1.562-1 for rules which, for purposes of computing the deduction for dividends paid for taxable years beginning after December 31, 1963, exclude from the definition of the term "dividends" any distribution made in such taxable year in liquidation of a foreign personal holding company.

* * * * * * *

Section 1.552-3 is amended by revising paragraph (a) to read as follows:

§ 1.552-3 (Proposed Treasury Decision, published 9-5-68). **Stock ownership requirement.**

(a) To meet the stock ownership requirement, it is necessary that at some time in the taxable year more than 50 percent in value of the outstanding stock of the foreign corporation be owned, directly or indirectly, by or for not more than five individuals who are citizens or residents of the United States, herein referred to as "United States group." See section 554 and §§ 1.554-1 through 1.554-7 for rules to be applied in determining stock ownership.

* * * * * * *

Section 1.553-1 is amended to read as follows:

§ 1.553-1 Proposed Treasury Decision, published (9-5-68.) **Foreign personal holding company income.**

(a) *General rule.* The term "foreign personal holding company income" means the portion of the gross income determined in accordance with section 555 and §§ 1.555-1 and 1.555-2, which consists of the classes of gross income described in paragraph (b) of this section. See section 553(b) and § 1.553-2 for special limitations on gross income and foreign personal holding company income in cases of gains from stock, securities, and commodities transactions.

(b) *Definitions*—(1) *Dividends.* The term "dividends" includes dividends as defined in section 316 and amounts required to be included in gross income under section 551 and §§ 1.551-1 and 1.551-2 (relating to foreign personal holding company income taxed to United States shareholders).

Proposed Reg. § 1.553-1

(2) **Interest.** The term "interest" means any amounts, includible in gross income, received for the use of money loaned, and shall include—(i) any amount treated as interest under section 483, and (ii) any annual or periodic rental payment under a redeemable ground rent (excluding amounts in redemption thereof) that is treated as interest. See section 163(c) and paragraph (b) of § 1.163-1.

(3) **Royalties.** The term "royalties" includes—

(i) All amounts received for the privilege of using patents, copyrights, secret processes and formulas, good will, trade marks, trade brands, franchises, and other like property, and

(ii) All royalties, including production payments and overriding royalties, received from any interest in mineral, oil, or gas properties.

The first sentence of this subparagraph shall apply to overriding royalties received from the sublessee by the operating company which originally leased and developed the natural resource property in respect of which such overriding royalties are paid, and to mineral, oil, or gas production payments, only with respect to amounts received after September 30, 1958. The term "mineral" includes those minerals which are included within the meaning of the term "minerals" in the regulations under section 611. The term "royalties" does not include rents. For rules relating to rents see section 553(a)(7) and subparagraph (10) of this paragraph.

(4) **Annuities.** The term "annuities" includes annuities only to the extent includible in the computation of gross income. See section 72 and the regulations thereunder for rules relating to the inclusion of annuities in gross income.

(5) **Gains from the sale or exchange of stock or securities.** (i) Except in the case of regular dealers in stocks or securities as provided in subdivision (ii) of this subparagraph, gross income and foreign personal holding company income include the amount by which the gains exceed the losses from the sale or exchange of stock or securities. See section 553(b)(1) and § 1.553-2 for provisions relating to this limitation. For this purpose, there shall be taken into account all those gains includible in gross income (including gains from liquidating dividends and other distributions from capital) and all those losses deductible from gross income which are considered under chapter 1 of the Code to be gains or losses from the sale or exchange of stock or securities. The term "stock or securities" as used in section 553 (a)(2) and this subparagraph includes shares of certificates of stock, stock rights or warrants, or interests in any corporation (including any joint stock company, insurance company, associations, or other organization classified as a corpor-

ation by the Code), certificates of interest or participation in any profit-sharing agreement, or in any oil, gas, or other mineral property, or lease, collateral trust certificates, voting trust certificates, bonds, debentures, certificates of indebtedness, notes, car trust certificates, bills of exchange, and obligations issued by or on behalf of a State, Territory, or political subdivision thereof.

(ii) In the case of "regular dealers in stock or securities" there shall not be included gains or losses derived from the sale or exchange of stock or securities made in the normal course of business. The term "regular dealer in stock or securities" means a corporation with an established place of business regularly engaged in the purchase of stock or securities and their resale to customers. However, such corporations shall not be considered as regular dealers with respect to stock or securities which are held for investment. See section 1236 and § 1.1236-1.

(6) **Gains from futures transactions in commodities.** Gross income and foreign personal holding company income includes the amount by which the gains exceed the losses from futures transactions in any commodity on or subject to the rules of a board of trade or commodity exchange. See § 1.553-2 for provisions relating to this limitation. In general, for the purposes of determining such excess, there are included all gains and losses on futures contracts which are speculative. However, for the purpose of determining such excess, there shall not be included gains or losses from cash transactions, or gains or losses by a producer, processor, merchant, or handler of the commodity, which arise out of bona fide hedging transactions reasonably necessary to the conduct of its business in the manner in which such business is customarily and usually conducted by others. See section 1233 and § 1.1233-1.

(7) **Estates and trusts.** Under section 553(a)(4) foreign personal holding company income includes amounts includible in computing the taxable income of the corporation under part I, subchapter J, chapter 1 of the Code (relating to estates, trusts, and beneficiaries), and any gain derived by the corporation from the sale or other disposition of any interest in an estate or trust.

(8) **Personal service contracts**—(i) In general. Under section 553(a)(5), amounts received under a contract under which the corporation is to furnish personal services, as well as amounts received from the sale or other disposition of such contract, shall be included as foreign personal holding company income if—

(a) Some person other than the corporation has the right to designate (by name or by description) the individual who is to perform the services or if the individual who is to perform the services is designated (by name or by description) in the contract; and

(b) At any time during the taxable year 25 percent or more in value of the outstanding stock of the corporation is owned, directly or indirectly, by or for the individual who has performed, is to perform, or may be designated (by name or by description) as the one to perform, such services. For this purpose, the amount of stock outstanding and its value shall be determined in accordance with the rules set forth in paragraph (c) of § 1.552-3. It should be noted that the stock ownership requirement of section 553 (a)(5) and this subparagraph relates to the stock ownership at any time during the taxable year. For rules relating to the determination of stock ownership, see section 554 and §§ 1.554-1 through 1.554-7.

(ii) Important and essential services. If the contract, in addition to requiring the performance of services by a 25-percent-or-more stockholder who is designated or who could be designated (as specified in section 553(a)(5) and subdivision (i) of this subparagraph), requires the performance of services by other persons which are important and essential, then only that portion of the amount received under such contract which is attributable to the personal services of the 25-percent-or-more

Proposed Reg. § 1.553-1

stockholder shall constitute personal holding company income. Incidental personal services of other persons employed by the corporation to facilitate the performance of the services by the 25-percent-or-more stockholder, however, shall not constitute important or essential services. Under section 482 gross income, deductions, credits, or allowances between or among organizations, trades, or businesses may be allocated if it is determined that allocation is necessary in order to prevent evasion of taxes or clearly to reflect the income of any such organizations, trades, or businesses.

(iii) Amount attributable to personal services of 25-percent-or-more stockholder. For taxable years beginning after December 31, 1967, the portion of the amount received under a contract which is attributable to the personal services of a 25-percent-or-more stockholder shall be determined in accordance with the principles expressed in paragraph (c) of § 1.543-10.

(9) **Compensation for use of property.** (i) In general. Under section 553(a)-(6), except as provided in subdivision (ii) of this subparagraph, the gross amounts received or accrued as compensation (however designated and from whomsoever received) for the use of, or right to use, property of the corporation shall be included as foreign personal holding company income if, at any time during the taxable year, 25 percent or more in value of the outstanding stock of the corporation is owned directly or indirectly, by or for any individual entitled to the use of the property. Thus, if a shareholder who meets the stock ownership requirement of section 553(a)-(6) and this subparagraph uses, or has the right to use, a yacht, residence or other property owned by the corporation, the compensation to the corporation for such use of, or right to use, the property constitutes foreign personal holding company income. This is true even though the shareholder may acquire the use of, or the right to use, the property by means of a sublease or under any other arrangement involving parties other than the corporation and the shareholder.

(ii) Exclusion from personal holding company income. If the corporation's foreign personal holding company income for the taxable year does not exceed 10 percent of its gross income for such year, then in a case in which a shareholder specified in subdivision (i) of this subparagraph has the use of, or right to use, property of the corporation, amounts received or accrued as compensation for the use of, or right to use, such property shall not constitute foreign personal holding company income. In addition, in such a case, such amounts shall not constitute "rents" (as defined in subparagraph (10) of this paragraph). For purposes of this subdivision, foreign personal holding company income shall be computed under section 553 except that such income shall be computed by excluding—(a) such amounts received or accrued as compensation for the use of, or right to use, property of the corporation, and (b) rents (as defined in section 553(a)(7) and subparagraph (10) of this paragraph).

(iii) Determination of stock value and stock ownership. For purposes of this subparagraph, the amount of stock outstanding at any time during the taxable year and its value shall be determined in accordance with the rules set forth in paragraph (c) of § 1.552-3. For rules relating to the determination of stock ownership, see section 554 and §§ 1.554-1 through 1.554-7.

(10) **Rents**—(i) General rule. Rents which are to be included as foreign personal holding company income consist of compensation (however designated) for the use of, or right to use, property of the corporation. The term "rents" does not include amounts includible in foreign personal holding company income under section 553(a)(6) and subparagraph (9) of this paragraph. The amounts considered as rents include charter fees, etc., for the use of, or right to use, property. However, if the amount of the rents includible under section 553(a)(7) of this subparagraph constitutes 50 percent or more of the gross income of the corporation, such rents shall not be considered to be foreign personal holding company income. For a special rule in the case of certain amounts received or accrued as compensation for the use of, or right to use, property of the corporation, see subparagraph (9)(ii) of this paragraph.

(ii) Special rule. For taxable years beginning after December 31, 1967, the term "rents" does not include payments for the use or occupancy of rooms or other space where significant services are also rendered to the occupant, such as for the use or occupancy of rooms or other quarters in hotels, boarding houses, or apartment houses furnishing hotel services, or in tourist homes, motor courts, or motels. Generally, services are considered rendered to the occupant if they are primarily for his convenience and are other than those usually or customarily rendered in connection with the rental of rooms or other space for occupancy only. The supplying of maid service, for example, constitutes such services; whereas the furnishing of heat and light, the cleaning of public entrances, exits, stairways, and lobbies, the collection of trash, etc., are not considered as services rendered to the occupant. Payments for the use or occupancy of entire private residences or living quarters in duplex or multiple housing units, of offices in an office building, etc., are generally "rents". Payments for the parking of automobiles ordinarily do not constitute rents. Payments for the warehousing of goods or for the use of personal property do not constitute rents if significant services are rendered in connection with such payments.

There is inserted immediately after § 1.553-1 the following new section:

§ 1.553-2 (Proposed Treasury Decision, published 9-5-68.) **Limitation on gross income and foreign personal holding company income in transactions involving stocks, securities and commodities.**

(a) Under section 553(b)(1) the gains which are to be included in gross income, and in foreign personal holding company income with respect to transactions described in section 553(a)(2) and paragraph (b)(5) of § 1.553-1, shall be the net gains from the sale or exchange of stock or securities. If there is an excess of losses over gains from such transactions, such excess (or net loss) shall not be used to reduce gross income or foreign personal holding company income for purposes of determining whether the corporation is a foreign personal holding company. Similarly, under section 553(b)(2) the gains which are to be included in gross income, and in foreign personal holding company income with respect to transactions described in section 553(a)(3) and paragraph (b)(6) of § 1.553-1, shall be the net gains from commodity transactions which reflect foreign personal holding company income. Any excess of losses over gains from such transactions (resulting in a net loss) shall not be used to reduce gross income or foreign personal holding company income. The capital loss carryover under section 1212 shall not be taken into account.

(b) The application of section 553(b) may be illustrated by the following examples:

Example (1). The P Corporation, a foreign corporation which is not a regular dealer in stocks and securities, received rentals of $250,000 for its property from a 25-percent shareholder, and also had gains of $50,000 during the taxable year from the sale of stocks and securities. It also had losses on the sale of stocks and securities in the amount of $30,000. Accordingly, P Corporation had gross income during the taxable year of $270,000 ($250,000 plus $20,000 net gain from the sales of stocks and securities). It had foreign personal holding company income of $20,000. (The rentals of $250,000 would not be foreign personal holding company income under section 553(a)(6) since the foreign personal holding company income of the corporation, $20,000 (after excluding any such income described in section 553(a)(6)), is not more than 10 percent of its gross income.)

Example (2). The R Corporation, a foreign corporation which is not a regular dealer in stocks or securities, realized total gains during the taxable year of

Proposed Reg. § 1.553-2

$900,000 from commodity futures transactions and $200,000 from the sales of stocks and securities. It also sustained total losses of $1,000,000 on such commodity futures transactions, resulting in a net gain for the taxable year of $100,000. None of the commodity futures transactions are hedging or other types of futures transactions excluded from the application of section 553(a)(3). No part of the loss on commodity futures transactions is to be taken into account in determining foreign personal holding company income and gross income for foreign personal holding company purposes for the taxable year. The full amount of the $200,000 in gains from the sales of stocks and securities is to be included in foreign personal holding company income and in gross income for foreign personal holding company purposes for the taxable year.

Section 1.554-1 is amended to read as follows:

§ 1.554-1 (Proposed Treasury Decision 9-5-68.) **Constructive ownership.**

(a) Rules relating to the constructive ownership of stock are provided by section 554 for the purpose of determining whether the stock ownership requirements of the following sections are satisfied:

(1) Section 552(a)(2), relating to ownership of stock by five or fewer individuals.

(2) Section 553(a)(5), relating to foreign personal holding company income derived from personal service contracts.

(3) Section 553(a)(6), relating to foreign personal holding company income derived from property used by shareholders.

(b) Section 554 provides four general rules with respect to constructive ownership. These rules are:

(1) Constructive ownership by reason of indirect ownership. See section 554(a)(1) and § 1.554-2.

(2) Constructive ownership by reason of family and partnership ownership. See section 554(a)(2), (4), (5), and (6), and §§ 1.554-3, 1.554-6, and 1.554-7.

(3) Constructive ownership by reason of ownership of options. See section 554(a)(3), (4), (5), and (6), and §§ 1.554-4, 1.554-6, and 1.554-7.

(4) Constructive ownership by reason of ownership of convertible securities. See section 554(b) and § 1.554-5.

Each of the rules referred to in subparagraphs (2), (3), and (4) of this paragraph is applicable only if it has the effect of satisfying the stock ownership requirement of the section to which applicable; that is, when applied to section 552(a)(2), its effect is to make the corporation a foreign personal holding company, or when applied to section 553(a)(5) or section 553(a)(6), its effect is to make the amounts described in such provisions includible as foreign personal holding company income.

(c) All forms and classes of stock, however denominated, which represent the interests of shareholders, members, or beneficiaries in the corporation shall be taken into consideration in applying the constructive ownership rules of section 554.

(d) For rules applicable in treating constructive ownership, determined by one application of section 554, as actual ownership for purposes of a second application of section 554, see section 554(a)(5) and § 1.554-6.

There are inserted immediately after §1.554-1 the following new sections:

§ 1.554-2 (Proposed Treasury Decision, published 9-5-68.) **Constructive ownership by reason of indirect ownership.**

The following example illustrates the application of section 554(a)(1), relating to constructive ownership by reason of indirect ownership:

Example. A and B, two individuals, are the exclusive and equal beneficiaries of a trust or estate which owns the entire capital stock of the M Corporation, a foreign corporation. The M Corporation in turn owns the entire capital stock of the N Corporation, a foreign corporation. Under such circumstances the entire capital stock of both the M Corporation and the N Corporation shall be considered as being owned equally by A and B as the individuals owning the beneficial interest therein.

§ 1.554-3 (Proposed Treasury Decision, published 9-5-68.) **Constructive ownership by reason of family and partnership ownership.**

(a) The following example illustrates the application of section 554(a)(2), relating to constructive ownership by reason of family and partnership ownership.

Example. The M Corporation, a foreign corporation, at some time during the taxable year, had 1,800 shares of outstanding stock, 450 of which were held by various individuals having no relationship to one another and none of whom were partners, and the remaining 1,350 were held by 51 shareholders as follows:

Relationships		Shares		Shares		Shares		Shares		Shares
An individual	A	100	B	20	C	20	D	20	E	20
His father	AF	10	BF	10	CF	10	DF	10	EF	10
His wife	AW	10	BW	40	CW	40	DW	40	EW	40
His brother	AB	10	BB	10	CB	10	DB	10	EB	10
His son	AS	10	BS	40	CS	40	DS	40	ES	40
His daughter by former marriage (son's half-sister)	ASHS	10	BSHS	40	CSHS	40	DSHS	40	ESHS	40
His brother's wife	ABW	10	BBW	10	CBW	10	DBW	160	EBW	10
His wife's father	AWF	10	BWF	10	CWF	110	DWF	10	EWF	10
His wife's brother	AWB	10	BWB	10	CWB	10	DWB	10	EWB	10
His wife's brother's wife	AWBW	10	BWBW	10	CWBW	10	DWBW	10	EWBW	110
Individual partner	AP	10								

By applying the statutory rule provided in section 554(a)(2) five individuals own more than 50 percent of the outstanding stock as follows:

A (including AF, AW, AB, AS, ASHS, AP)	160
B (including BF, BW, BB, BS, BSHS)	160
CW (including C, CS, CWF, CWB)	220
DB (including D, DF, DBW)	200
EWB (including EW, EWF, EWBW)	170
Total, or more than 50 percent	910

Individual A represents the obvious case where the head of the family owns the bulk of the family stock and naturally is the head of the group. A's partner owns 10 shares of the stock. Individual B represents the case where he is still head of the group because of the ownership of stock by his immediate family. Individuals C and D represent cases where the individuals fall in groups headed in C's case by his wife and in D's case by his brother because of the preponderance of holdings on the part of relatives by marriage. Individual E represents the case where the preponderant holdings of others eliminate that individual from the group.

(b) For the restriction on the applicability of the family and partnership ownership rules of this section, see paragraph (b) of § 1.554-1. For rules relating to constructive ownership as actual ownership, see § 1.554-6.

Proposed Reg. § 1.554-3

§ 1.554-4 (Proposed Treasury Decision, published 9-5-68.) **Options.**
The shares of stock which may be acquired by reason of an option shall be considered to be constructively owned by the individual having the option to acquire such stock. For example: If C, an individual, on March 1, 1964, purchases an option, or otherwise comes into possession of an option, to acquire 100 shares of the capital stock of M Corporation, a foreign corporation, such 100 shares of stock shall be considered to be constructively owned by C as if C had actually acquired the stock on that date. If C has an option on an option (or one of a series of options) to acquire such stock, he shall also be considered to have constructive ownership of the stock which may be acquired by reason of the option (or the series of options). Under such circumstances, C shall be considered to have acquired constructive ownership of the stock on the date he acquired his option. For the restriction on the applicability of the rule of this section, see paragraph (b) of § 1.554-1.

§ 1.554-5 (Proposed Treasury Decision, published 9-5-68.) **Convertible securities.**
Under section 554(b) outstanding securities of a corporation such as bonds, debentures, or other corporate obligations, convertible into stock of the corporation (whether or not convertible during the taxable year) shall be considered as outstanding stock of the corporation. The consideration of convertible securities as outstanding stock is subject to the exception that, if some of the outstanding securities are convertible only after a later date than in the case of others, the class having the earlier conversion date may be considered as outstanding stock although the others are not so considered, but no convertible securities shall be considered as outstanding stock unless all outstanding securities having a prior conversion date are also so considered. For example, if outstanding securities are convertible in 1964, 1965, and 1966, those convertible in 1964 can be properly considered as outstanding stock without so considering those convertible in 1965 or 1966, and those convertible in 1964 and 1965 can be properly considered as outstanding stock without so considering those convertible in 1966. However, the securities convertible in 1965 could not be properly considered as outstanding stock without so considering those convertible in 1964 and the securities convertible in 1966 could not be properly considered as outstanding stock without so considering those convertible in 1964 and 1965. For the restriction on the applicability of the rule of this section, see paragraph (b) of § 1.554-1.

§ 1.554-6 (Proposed Treasury Decision, published 9-5-68.) **Constructive ownership as actual ownership.**
(a) **General rules.** (1) Stock constructively owned by a person by reason of the application of the rule provided in section 554(a)(1), relating to stock not owned by an individual, shall be considered as actually owned by such person for the purpose of again applying such rule or of applying the family and partnership rule provided in section 554(a)(2), in order to make another person the constructive owner of such stock, and

(2) Stock constructively owned by a person by reason of the application of the option rule provided in section 554(a)(3) shall be considered as actually owned by such person for the purpose of applying either the rule provided in section 554(a)(1), relating to stock not owned by an individual, or the family and partnership rule provided in section 554(a)(2) in order to make another person the constructive owner of such stock, but

(3) Stock constructively owned by an individual by reason of the application of the family and partnership rule provided in section 554(a)(2) shall not be considered as actually owned by such individual for the purpose of again applying such rule in order to make another individual the constructive owner of such stock.

(b) Examples. The application of this section may be illustrated by the following examples:

Example (1). A's wife, AW, owns all the stock of the M Corporation, which in turn owns all the stock of the O Corporation. The O Corporation in turn owns all the stock of the P Corporation, a foreign corporation. Under the rule provided in section 554(a)(1), relating to stock not owned by an individual, the stock in the P Corporation owned by the O Corporation is considered to be owned constructively by the M Corporation, the sole shareholder of the O Corporation. Such constructive ownership of the stock of the M Corporation is considered as actual ownership for the purpose of again applying such rule in order to make AW, the sole shareholder of the M Corporation, the constructive owner of the stock of the P Corporation. Similarly, the constructive ownership of the stock by AW is considered as actual ownership for the purpose of applying the family and partnership rule provided in section 554(a)(2) in order to make A the constructive owner of the stock of the P Corporation, if such application is necessary for any of the purposes set forth in paragraph (a) of § 1.554-1. But the stock thus constructively owned by A may not be considered as actual ownership for the purpose of again applying the family and partnership rule in order to make another member of A's family, for example, A's father, the constructive owner of the stock of the P Corporation.

Example (2). B, an individual, owns all the stock of the R Corporation which has an option to acquire all the stock of the S Corporation, a foreign corporation, owned by C, an individual, who is not related to B. Under the option rule provided in section 554(a)(3) the R Corporation may be considered as owning constructively the stock of the S Corporation owned by C. Such constructive ownership of the stock by the R Corporation is considered as actual ownership for the purpose of applying the rule provided in section 554(a)(1), relating to stock not owned by an individual, in order to make B, the sole shareholder of the R Corporation, the constructive owner of the stock of the S Corporation. The stock thus constructively owned by B by reason of the application of the rule provided in section 554(a)(1) likewise is considered as actual ownership for the purpose, if necessary, of applying the family and partnership rule provided in section 554(a)(2), in order to make another member of B's family, for example, B's wife, BW, the constructive owner of the stock of the S Corporation. However, the family and partnership rule could not again be applied so as to make still another individual the constructive owner of the stock of the S Corporation, that is, the stock constructively owned by BW could not be considered as actually owned by her in order to make BW's father the constructive owner of such stock by a second application of the family and partnership rule.

§ 1.554-7 (Proposed Treasury Decision, published 9-5-68.) **Option rule in lieu of family and partnership rule.**

(a) If, in determining the ownership of stock, such stock may be considered as constructively owned by an individual by an application of either the family and partnership rule (section 554(a)(2)) or the option rule (section 554(3)), such stock shall be considered as owned constructively by the individual by reason of the application of the option rule.

(b) The application of this section may be illustrated by the following example:

Example. Two brothers, A and B, each own 10 percent of the stock of the M Corporation, a foreign corporation, and A's wife, AW, also owns 10 percent of the stock of such corporation. AW's husband, A, has an option to acquire the stock

Proposed Reg. § 1.554-7

owned by her at any time. It becomes necessary, for one of the purposes stated in section 554(a)(4), to determine the stock ownership of B in the M Corporation. If the family and partnership rule were the only rule that applied in the case, B would be considered, under that rule, as owning 20 percent of the stock of the M Corporation, namely, his own stock plus the stock owned by his brother. In that event, B could not be considered as owning the stock held by AW since (1) AW is not a member of B's family and (2) the constructive ownership of such stock by A through the application of the family and partnership rule in his case is not considered as actual ownership so as to make B the constructive owner by a second application of the same rule with respect to the ownership of the stock. However, there is more than the family and partnership rule involved in this example. As the holder of an option upon the stock, A may be considered the constructive owner of his wife's stock by the application of the option rule and without reference to the family relationship between A and AW. If A is considered as owning the stock of his wife by application of the option rule, then such constructive ownership by A is regarded as actual ownership for the purpose of applying the family and partnership rule so as to make another member of A's family, for example, B, the constructive owner of the stock. Hence, since A may be considered as owning his wife's stock by applying either the family-partnership rule or the option rule, the provisions of section 554(a)(6) apply and accordingly A must be considered the constructive owner of his wife's stock under the option rule rather than the family-partnership rule. B thus becomes the constructive owner of 30 percent of the stock of the M Corporation, namely, his own 10 percent, A's 10 percent, and AW's 10 percent constructively owned by A as the holder of an option on the stock.

Cost Depletion

Paragraph (d) of §1.612-3 is revised to read as follows:

§1.612-3 (Proposed Treasury Decision, published 5-13-77.) **Depletion; treatment of bonus and advanced royalty.**

* * * * * * * * * * * *

(d) Percentage depletion deduction with respect to bonus and advanced royalty. In lieu of the allowance based on cost depletion computed under paragraphs (a) and (b) of this section, the payees referred to therein may be allowed a depletion deduction in respect of any bonus or advanced royalty for the taxable year in an amount computed on the basis of the percentage of gross income from the property as provided in section 613 and the regulations thereunder. However, for an exception applicable to certain bonuses and advanced royalties received in connection with oil or gas, see paragraph (f)(1) of §1.613A-7.

* * * * * * * * * * * *

[The page following this is 63,761]

Limitations on Percentage Depletion

Section 1.613-1 is amended by designating the paragraph contained therein as paragraph (a) and by adding a new paragraph (b), to read as follows:

§1.613-1 (Proposed Treasury Decision, published 5-13-77.) **Percentage depletion; general rule.**

(a) **In general.** In the case of a taxpayer computing the deduction for depletion under section 611 with respect to minerals on the basis of a percentage of gross income from the property, as defined in section 613(c) and §§1.613-3 and 1.613-4, such deduction shall be the percentage of such gross income as specified in section 613(b) and §1.613-2. The deduction shall not exceed 50 percent of the taxpayer's taxable income from the property (computed without allowance for depletion). Such taxable income shall be computed in accordance with §1.613-5. In no case shall the deduction for depletion computed under this section be less than the deduction computed upon the cost or other basis of the property provided in section 612 and the regulations thereunder. The apportionment of the deduction between the several owners of economic interests in a mineral deposit will be made as provided in paragraph (c) of §1.611-1. For rules with respect to "gross income from the property" and for definition of the term "mining", see §§1.613-3 and 1.613-4. For definitions of the terms "property", "mineral deposit" and "minerals", see paragraph (d) of §1.611-1.

(b) **Denial of percentage depletion in case of oil and gas wells.** Except as otherwise provided in section 613A and the regulations thereunder, in the case of oil or gas which is produced after December 31, 1974, and to which gross income is attributable after such date, the allowance for depletion shall be computed without regard to section 613.

Sections 1.613A-2, 1.613A-3, 1.613A-4, and 1.613A-7 are revised to read as follows:

§1.613A-2 (Proposed Treasury Decision, published 5-13-77.) **Exemption for certain domestic gas wells.**

(a) The allowance for depletion under section 611 shall be computed in accordance with section 613 with respect to:

(1) Regulated natural gas (as defined in paragraph (c) of §1.613A-7).

(2) Natural gas sold under a fixed contract (as defined in paragraph (d) of §1.613A-7), and

(3) Any geothermal deposit (as defined in paragraph (e) of §1.613A-7) in the United States or in a possession of the United States which is determined to be a gas well within the meaning of former section 613(b)(1)(A) (as in effect before enactment of the Tax Reduction Act of 1975),

and 22 percent shall be deemed to be specified in subsection (b) of section 613 for purposes of subsection (a) of that section. For special rules applicable to partnerships, trusts, and estates, see paragraphs (e) and (f) of §1.613A-3.

(b) The provisions of this section may be illustrated by the following examples:

Example (1). A is a producer of natural gas which is sold by A under a contract in effect on February 1, 1975. The contract provides for an increase in the price of the gas sold under the contract to the highest price paid to a producer for natural gas in the area. The gas sold by A qualifies under section 613A(b)(2)(B) for percentage depletion as gas sold under a fixed contract until its price increases, but does not so qualify thereafter.

Example (2). B is a producer of natural gas which is sold by B under a contract in effect on February 1, 1975. The contract provides that beginning January 1, 1980, the price of the gas may be renegotiated. Such a provision does not disqualify gas

Proposed Reg. §1.613A-2

from qualifying for the exemption under section 613A(b)(2)(B) with respect to the gas sold prior to January 1, 1980. However, gas sold on or after January 1, 1980, does not qualify for the exemption whether or not the price of the gas is renegotiated.

§1.613A-3 (Prosposed Treasury Decision, published 5-13-77.) **Exemption for independent producers and royalty owners.**

(a) **General rules.** (1) Except as provided in section 613A(d) and §1.613A-4, the allowance for depletion under section 611 with respect to oil or gas which is produced after December 31, 1974, and to which gross income from the property is attributable after that date, shall be computed in accordance with section 613 with respect to:

(i) So much of the taxpayer's average daily production (as defined in paragraph (f) of §1.613A-7) of domestic crude oil (as defined in paragraphs (a) and (g) of §1.613A-7) as does not exceed the taxpayer's depletable oil quantity (as defined in paragraph (h) of §1.613A-7), and

(ii) So much of the taxpayer's average daily production of domestic natural gas (as defined in paragraphs (a) and (b) of §1.613A-7) as does not exceed the taxpayer's depletable natural gas quantity (as defined in paragraph (i) of §1.613A-7),

and the applicable percentage (determined in accordance with the table in paragraph (c) of this section) shall be deemed to be specified in subsection (b) of section 613 for purposes of subsection (a) of that section.

(2) Except as provided in section 613A(d) and §1.613A-4, the allowance for depletion under section 611 with respect to oil or gas which is produced after December 31, 1974, and to which gross income from the property is attributable after such date and before January 1, 1984, shall be computed in accordance with section 613 with respect to:

(i) So much of the taxpayer's average daily secondary or tertiary production (as defined in paragraph (k) of §1.613A-7) of domestic crude oil as does not exceed the taxpayer's depletable oil quantity (determined without regard to section 613A(c)(3)(A)(ii), and

(ii) So much of the taxpayer's average daily secondary or tertiary production of domestic natural gas as does not exceed the taxpayer's depletable natural gas quantity (determined without regard to section 613A(c)(3)(A)(ii)),

and 22 percent shall be deemed to be specified in subsection (b) of section 613 for purposes of subsection (a) of that section.

(3) For purposes of this section, there shall not be taken into account any production with respect to which percentage depletion is allowed pursuant to section 613A(b) or is not allowable by reason of section 613A(c)(9).

(4) The provisions of this paragraph may be illustrated by the following examples:

Example (1). A, a calendar year taxpayer, owns an oil producing property with 100,000 barrels of production to which income was attributable for 1975 and a gas producing property with 1,200,000,000 cubic feet of production to which income was attributable for 1975. Under section 613A(c)(4), the oil equivalent of 1,200,000,000 cubic feet of gas is 200,000 barrels, bringing A's total production of oil and gas to which income was attributable for 1975 to the equivalent of 300,000 barrels of oil. A's average daily production was 821.92 barrels (300,000 barrels ÷ 365 days) which is less than the depletable oil quantity (2000 barrels) before reduction for any election by A under section 613A(c)(4). Accordingly, A may make such an election with respect to his entire gas production and thereby be entitled to percentage depletion with respect to his entire 1975 income from production of oil and gas. A's allowable depletion pursuant to section 613A(c) for his oil and gas properties would be the amount determined under section 613(a) computed at the 22 percent rate specified in section 613A(c)(5) for 1975.

Example (2). B, a calendar year taxpayer, owns oil producing properties with 365,000 barrels of production to which income was attributable for 1975. B was a retailer of oil and gas for only the last 3 months of 1975. B's average daily production for 1975 was 1,000 barrels (365,000 barrels ÷ 365 days).

Example (3). C, a calendar year taxpayer, owns property X with 500,000 barrels of primary production to which income was attributable for 1975 and property Y with 200,000 barrels of primary production to which income was attributable for 1975. Property Y had been transferred to C on January 1, 1975, on which date it was a proven property. Therefore, the exemption under section 613A(c)(1) does not apply to C with respect to production from property Y. C's average daily production for 1975 was 1369.86 barrels (500,000 barrels ÷ 365 days) which did not take into account the nondepletable production from property Y.

Example (4). In 1975, D received his annual payment of a recoupable advanced royalty of $100x in connection with oil property. Later in 1975, $60x (of the $100x advanced royalty) was recovered from production from the property. In 1976, D re-

Proposed Reg. §1.613A-3

ceived another advanced royalty payment of $100x. Later in 1976, $140x ($40x of the $100x advanced royalty received in 1975 and the $100x advanced royalty received in 1976) was recouped from production from the property. Neither advanced royalty payment was attributable to production in excess of D's depletable oil quantity. D is entitled to percentage depletion for 1975 only with respect to $60x of the advanced royalty received (100x dollars x $\frac{\$60x)}{\$100x)}$. D is entitled to percentage depletion for 1976 with respect to the $100x received in 1976. With respect to the $40x received in 1975 not attributable to production in 1975, D is not entitled to percentage depletion for any year. Of course, D is entitled in 1975 to determine the allowable cost depletion with respect to the entire $100x received in 1975.

Example (5). In 1975, E leased an oil property to F, receiving a lease bonus. With respect to the lease bonus, E is entitled to take cost depletion but not percentage depletion.

Example (6). G owns an oil property with producing wells X and Y on it. G converts well X into an injection well. Prior to the application of the secondary process, it is estimated that without such application the annual production from well X would have been 50x barrels of oil and from well Y would have been 100x barrels of oil. For the taxable year in which injection is commenced production from well X is 10x barrels and from well Y is 180x barrels. Forty x barrels of oil [190x barrels of oil (actual production from the property) − 150x barrels (estimate of primary production from the property)] qualifies as secondary production.

Example (7) H, a calendar year taxpayer, owns a domestic oil well which produced 100,000 barrels of oil in 1975. The proceeds from the sale of 15,000 barrels of that production are not includible in H's income until 1976. The 15,000 barrels produced in 1975 are included in H's average daily production for 1976 and excluded from such production for 1975.

(b) **Phase-out table.** For purposes of section 613A(c)(3)(A)(i) and §1.613A-7(h)(l) (relating to depletable oil quantity)—

In the case of production during the calendar year:	The tentative quantity in barrels is:
1975	2,000
1976	1,800
1977	1,600
1978	1,400
1979	1,200
1980 and thereafter	1,000

(c) **Applicable percentage.** For purposes of section 613A(c)(1) and paragraph (a) of this section—

In the case of production during the calendar year:	The applicable percentage is:
1975	22
1976	22
1977	22
1978	22
1979	22
1980	22
1981	20
1982	18
1983	16
1984 and thereafter	15

(d) **Production in excess of depletable quantity—(1) Primary production.** (i) If the taxpayer's average daily production of domestic crude oil exceeds his depletable oil quantity, the allowance pursuant to section 613A(c)(1)(A) and paragraph (a)(1)(i) of this

Proposed Reg. §1.613A-3

section with respect to oil produced during the taxable year from each property in the United States shall be that amount which bears the same ratio to the amount of depletion which would have been allowable under section 613(a) for all of the taxpayer's oil produced from such property during the taxable year (computed as if section 613 applied to all of such production at the rate specified in paragraph (c) of this section) as the amount of his depletable oil quantity bears to the aggregate number of barrels representing the average daily production of domestic crude oil of the taxpayer for such year.

(ii) If the taxpayer's average daily production of domestic natural gas exceeds his depletable natural gas quantity, the allowance pursuant to section 613A(c)(1)(B) and paragraph (a)(l)(ii) of this section with respect to natural gas produced during the taxable year from each property in the United States shall be that amount which bears the same ratio to the amount of depletion which would have been allowable pursuant to section 613(a) for all of the taxpayer's natural gas produced from such property during the taxable year (computed as if section 613 applied to all of such production at the rate specified in paragraph (c) of this section) as the amount of his depletable natural gas quantity in cubic feet bears to the aggregate number of cubic feet representing the average daily production of domestic natural gas of the taxpayer for such year.

(2) **Secondary or tertiary production.** (i) If the taxpayer's average daily secondary or tertiary production of domestic crude oil exceeds his depletable oil quantity (determined without regard to section 613A(c)(3)(A)(ii)), the allowance pursuant to section 613A(c)(6)(A)(i) and paragraph (a)(2)(i) of this section with respect to oil produced during the taxable year from each property in the United States shall be that amount which bears the same ratio to the amount of depletion which would have been allowable pursuant to section 613(a) for all taxpayer's secondary or tertiary production of oil from such property during the taxable year (computed as if section 613 applied to all of such production at the rate specified in paragraph (a)(2) of this section) as the amount of his depletable oil quantity (determined without regard to section 613A(c)(3)(A)(ii)) bears to the aggregate number of barrels representing the average daily secondary or tertiary production of domestic crude oil of the taxpayer for such year.

(ii) If the taxpayer's average daily secondary or tertiary production of domestic natural gas exceeds his depletable natural gas quantity (determined without regard to section 613A(c)(3)(A)(ii)), the allowance pursuant to section 613A(c)(6)(A)(ii) and paragraph (a)(2)(ii) of this section with respect to natural gas produced during the taxable year from each property in the United States shall be that amount which bears the same ratio to the amount of depletion which would have been allowable pursuant to section 613(a) for all of the taxpayer's secondary or tertiary production of natural gas from such property during the taxable year (computed as if section 613 applied to all of such production at the rate specified in paragraph (a)(2) of this section) as the amount of his depletable natural gas quantity in cubic feet (determined without regard to section 613A(c) (3)(A)(ii)) bears to the aggregate number of cubic feet representing the average daily secondary or tertiary production of domestic natural gas of the taxpayer for such year.

(3) **Taxable income from the property.** If both oil and gas are produced from the property during the taxable year, then for purposes of section 613A(c)(7)(A) and (B) and this paragraph the taxable income from the property, in applying the 50-percent limitation in section 613(a), shall be allocated between the oil production and the gas production in proportion to the gross income from the property during the taxable year from each. In addition, if both gas with respect to which section 613A(b) and §1.612A-2 apply and oil or gas with respect to which section 613A(c) and this section apply are produced from the property during the taxable year, then for purposes of section 613A(d)(1) and paragraph (a) of §1.613A-4 the taxable income from the property, in applying the 50-percent limitation in section 613(a), shall also be so allocated.

(4) **Examples.** The application of this paragraph may be illustrated by the following examples:

Example (1). A owns Y and Z oil producing properties. With respect to properties Y and Z, the percentage depletion allowable pursuant to section 613(a) (computed as if section 613 applied to all of such production at the rate specified in section 613A(c)(5)) for 1975 was $100x and $200x, respectively. A's average daily production for 1975 was 4,000 barrels. A's allowable depletion pursuant to section 613A(c) with respect to property Y was $50x

$$\left\{ \$100x \text{ depletion} \times \frac{2{,}000 \text{ depletable oil quantity}}{4{,}000 \text{ average daily production}} \right\}.$$

A's allowable depletion pursuant to section 613A(c) with respect to property Z was $100x

$$\left\{ \$200x \text{ depletion} \times \frac{2{,}000 \text{ depletable oil quantity}}{4{,}000 \text{ average daily production}} \right\}.$$

Example (2). B owns gas producing properties which had secondary gas production for 1975 of 3,285,000,000 cubic feet, which under section 613A(c)(4) is equivalent to 547,500 barrels of oil. B's average daily secondary production for 1975 was 1,500 barrels (547,500 barrels ÷ 365). B elected to have section 613A(c)(4) apply to such gas production. With respect to such production, the percentage depletion allowable pursuant to section 613(a) (computed at the rate specified in section 613A(c)(6)(A)) was $150x. B also owns an oil producing property which had primary oil production for 1975 of 365,000 barrels. With respect to such oil property, the percentage depletion allowable pursuant to section 613(a) (computed as if section 613 applied to all of such production at the rate specified in section 613A(c)(5)) was $100x. B's average daily production for 1975 was 1,000 barrels (365,000 barrels ÷ 365). B's depletable oil quantity for 1975 was 500 barrels (2,000 barrels tentative quantity—1,500 barrels average daily secondary production). B's allowable depletion pursuant to section 613A(c) with respect to the oil property was $50x

$$\left\{ \$100x \text{ depletion} \times \frac{500 \text{ depletable oil quantity}}{1{,}000 \text{ average daily production}} \right\}.$$

Example (3). Assume the same facts as in example (2) except that B's primary production was 6,000,000 cubic feet of natural gas daily rather than its equivalent under section 613A(c)(4) of 1,000 barrels of oil and that B elected to have that section apply to such gas. B's allowable depletion pursuant to section 613A(c) with respect to his primary production is $50x, the same as in example (2).

Example (4). C is a partner with a one-third interest in Partnerships CDE and CFG with each partnership owning a single oil property. C's percentage depletion allowable under section 613(a) (computed as if section 613 applied to all of such production at the rate specified in section 613A(c)(5)) for 1975 was $20x with respect to his allocable share of 495,000 barrels of Partnership CDE production and $40x with respect to his allocable share of 600,000 barrels of Partnership CFG production. C's average daily production is 3,000 barrels (1,095,000 total production ÷ 365 days). C's allowable depletion pursuant to section 613A(c) with respect to his share of the production or Partnership CDE is $13.33x

$$\left\{ \$20x \text{ depletion} \times \frac{2{,}000 \text{ depletable oil quantity}}{3{,}000 \text{ average daily production}} \right\}.$$

C's allowable depletion pursuant to section 613A(c) with respect to his share of the production of Partnership CFG is $26.67x

Proposed Reg. §1.613A-3

$$\left\{ \$40x \text{ depletion} \times \frac{2{,}000 \text{ depletable oil quantity}}{3{,}000 \text{ average daily production}} \right\}.$$

Example (5). H owns a property which, during his fiscal year which began on June 1, 1975, and ended on May 31, 1976, produced gas qualifying under section 613A(b) and oil qualifying under section 613A(c). For the fiscal year H's gross income from the property was $400x, of which $100x was from gas and $300x was from oil. For the oil his gross income from the property for the period beginning June 1, 1975, and ending December 31, 1975, was $100x and for the 1976 portion of the fiscal year was $200x. The percentage depletion allowance (before applying the 50 percent limitation of section 613(a) or the 65 percent limitation of section 613A(d)(1)) was $22x for the gas, $22x for the oil in 1975, and $44x for the oil in 1976. His taxable income from the property for the fiscal year was $100x. In accordance with paragraph (d)(3) of this section, the taxable income from the property is allocated $25x to the gas

$$\left\{ \$100x \text{ taxable income from the property} \times \frac{\$100x \text{ gross income from gas from the property}}{\$400x \text{ total gross income from the property}} \right\},$$

$25x to the 1975 oil

$$\left\{ \$100x \text{ taxable income from the property} \times \frac{\$100x \text{ gross income from 1975 oil from the property}}{\$400x \text{ total gross income from the property}} \right\}$$

and $50x to the 1976 oil

$$\left\{ \$100x \text{ taxable income from the property} \times \frac{\$200x \text{ gross income from 1976 oil from the property}}{\$400x \text{ total gross income from the property}} \right\}.$$

With the application of the 50 percent of taxable income from the property limitation, the allowable percentage depletion (computed without reference to section 613A) is limited to $12.50x for the gas, $12.50x for the oil in 1975, and $25x for the oil in 1976.

(e) **Partnerships.** (1) In the case of a partnership, the depletion allowance under section 611 with respect to production from domestic oil and gas properties shall be computed separately by the partners and not by the partnership. The determination of whether cost or percentage depletion is applicable is to be made at the partner level. Each partner shall be entitled to his proportionate share of the adjusted basis of each partnership domestic oil or gas property. The allocation is to be made as of the later of the date of acquisition of the oil or gas property by the partnership or January 1, 1975. A partner's proportionate share of the adjusted basis of such property shall be determined in accordance with his interest in partnership capital. However, a partner's share of the adjusted basis shall be determined in accordance with his interest in partnership income if the partnership agreement so provides, unless either written provision has been made for the share of any partner in partnership income to be reduced for any purpose other than merely to reflect the admission of a new partner or at the time of allocation any partner expects his income interest to be reduced pursuant to an understanding with another partner or partners. In the case of an agreement described in section 704(c)(2) (relating to effect of partnership agreement on contributed property), such share shall be determined by taking such agreement into account. Appropriate adjustments shall be made to the partners' adjusted bases for any partnership capital expenditures relating to such properties that are made after such allocation. Each partner must separately keep records of his share of the adjusted basis in each oil and gas property of the partnership, adjust such share of the adjusted basis pursuant to section 1016 (including adjustments for any depletion allowed or allowable with respect to such property), and use such adjusted basis each year in the computation of his cost depletion or in the computation of his gain or loss on the disposition of such property by the partnership. Moreover, the adjusted basis of a partner's interest in a partnership shall be decreased (but not below zero) pursuant to section 705 by the amount of the partner's deduction for depletion allowed or allowable with respect to domestic oil and gas wells. Upon the disposition of an oil or gas property by the partnership, each partner shall subtract his adjusted basis in such property from his allocable portion of the amount realized from the sale of such property to determine his gain or loss. For purposes of section 732 (relating to basis of distributed property other than money), the partnership's adjusted basis in oil and gas property shall be an amount equal to the sum of the partners' adjusted bases in such property as determined under this paragraph.

(2) The provisions of this paragraph may be illustrated by the following examples:

Example (1). A, B, and C have equal interests in capital in Partnership ABC. On January 1, 1970, the partnership acquired a producing domestic oil property. On January 1, 1975, the partnership's basis in the property was $90x. The partnership allocates the basis of the property to each partner in proportion to the partner's interest in partnership capital. Accordingly, each partner had a basis of $30x allocated to him. Each partner must separately compute his depletion allowance. The amount of percentage depletion allowable for each partner for 1975 was $10x. On January 1, 1976, each partner's adjusted basis in the property was $20x ($30x minus $10x). On January 1, 1976, the oil property was sold for $150x. Each partner's gain was $30x ($50x allocable share of amount realized minus his adjusted basis of $20x). Then each partner must adjust his basis in his partnership interest to reflect such gain.

Example (2). The facts are the same as in example (1) except that on January 1, 1976, the property was not sold but transferred by the partnership to partner A (in a distribution to which section 751 did not apply). A's basis in the property was $60x (sum of A, B, C's adjusted bases in property).

Example (3). The facts are the same as in example (1) with the exception that in 1975 C was a retailer of oil and gas and was only entitled to a cost depletion deduction of $5x. C's gain from the sale of the mineral property was $25x ($50x allocable share of amount realized minus his adjusted basis of $25x ($30x minus $5x)).

Example (4). D, a calendar year taxpayer, is a partner in Partnership DEF which owns a domestic producing oil property. On January 1, 1975, the partnership's adjusted basis in the property was $900x. On January 1, 1975, D's adjusted basis in his partnership interest was $300x and his adjusted basis in the partnership's oil property was $300x. D's allowable percentage depletion for 1975 with respect to production from the oil property was $50x. On January 1, 1976, D's adjusted basis in his partnership interest was $250x and his adjusted basis in the partnership's oil property was $250x ($300x minus $50x).

Example (5). On January 1, 1975, G's adjusted basis in Partnership GH's proven domestic oil property is $5x. On January 1, 1975, G sells his partnership interest to I for $100x when the election under section 754 is in effect. I has a special basis adjustment for the oil property of $95x (the difference between I's basis, $100x, and his share of the basis of partnership property, $5x). I is not entitled to percentage depletion with respect to his distributive share of the oil property income because he is a transferee of an interest in a proven oil property. However, under the cost depletion method, at an assumed rate of 10 percent, the allowance for 1975 with respect to I's interest in the oil property which has a basis to him of $100x ($5x, plus his special basis adjustment of $95x) is $10x.

Example (6). On January 1, 1960, Partnership JK acquired a domestic producing oil property. On January 1, 1975, the partnership's adjusted basis in the property was

Proposed Reg. §1.613A-3

zero. On January 1, 1975, L is admitted as a partner to the partnership which had not made an election under section 754. Since the partnership's adjusted basis in the oil property is zero, L's proportionate share of the basis in the oil property is also zero. L is not entitled to percentage depletion because he is a transferee of a proven oil property (see paragraph (g) of this section). Since the property's basis is zero, L is also not entitled to any cost depletion with respect to production from the property.

(f) **Trusts and estates.** (1) In the case of production from domestic oil and gas properties held by a trust or estate, the depletion allowance under section 611 shall be computed initially by the trust or estate. The determination of whether cost or percentage depletion is applicable shall be made at the trust or estate level, but such determination shall not result in the disallowance of cost depletion to a beneficiary of a trust or estate for whom cost depletion exceeds percentage depletion. The limitations contained in section 613A(c) and (d) shall be applied at the trust or estate level in its computation of percentage depletion pursuant to section 613A and shall also be applied by a beneficiary (the ultimate taxpayer) with respect to any percentage depletion apportioned to him by the trust or estate. For purposes of adjustments to the basis of oil or gas properties held by a trust or estate, in the absence of clear and convincing evidence to the contrary, it shall be presumed that no beneficiary is affected by any section 613A(d) limitation or by the rules contained in section 613A(c)(8) and (9) (relating to businesses under common control and members of the same family and to transfers, respectively), or has any oil or gas production from sources other than the trust or estate.

(2) The provisions of this paragraph may be illustrated by the following examples:

Example (1). A is the income beneficiary of a trust the only asset of which is a domestic producing oil property. In 1975 the property had production of 2,920,000 barrels of oil. In that year, the trustee distributed one-half of the trust's net income and accumulated the other one-half for the benefit of the remainderman. The percentage depletion computed by the trust with respect to such production (computed as if section 613 applied to all of such production at the rate specified in section 613A (c) (5)) for 1975 was $200x. The trust's average daily production for 1975 was 8,000 barrels (2,920,000 ÷ 365 days). The trust's allowable depletion pursuant to section 613A (c) with respect to such production was $50x

$$\left\{ \$200x \text{ depletion} \times \frac{2{,}000 \text{ depletable oil quantity}}{8{,}000 \text{ average daily production}} \right\}.$$

The percentage depletion of $50x was apportioned between the trustee and A so that each received $25x of such depletion. The $25x depletion received by A is attributable to one-half of the trust's depletable oil quantity, i.e., 1,000 barrels per day. A has oil production from other sources totalling 500 barrels per day. Accordingly, A's average daily production was 1,500 barrels which did not exceed his depletable oil quantity of 2,000 barrels.

Example (2). B, a retailer of oil and gas is the income beneficiary of a trust the only asset of which is a domestic producing oil property. In 1975 the trustee distributed one-half of the trust's net income and accumulated the other one-half for the benefit of the remainderman. One-half of the percentage depletion computed by the trust with respect to the production from the property was apportioned to B. Since B is a retailer of oil and gas, he is not entitled to deduct any of the percentage depletion apportioned to him. However, B is entitled to take cost depletion with respect to one-half of the production from the oil property, notwithstanding the fact that depletion was computed at the trust level on the basis of percentage depletion.

(g) **Businesses under common control; members of the same family—(1) Component members of a controlled group.** For purposes of only the depletable quantity limitations contained in section 613A(c) and this section, component members of a controlled group of corporations (as defined in paragraph (l) of §1.613A-7) shall be treated as one taxpayer. Accordingly, the group shares the depletable oil (or natural gas) quantity prescribed for a taxpayer for the taxable year and the secondary production of a member of the group will reduce the other members' share of the group's depletable quantity.

(2) **Aggregation of business entities under common control.** If 50 percent or more of the beneficial interest in two or more corporations, trusts, or estates is owned by the same or related persons (taking into account only persons who own at least 5 percent of such beneficial interest) as defined in subparagraph (2) in §1.613A-7(m), the tentative quantity determined under the table in section 613A(c)(3)(B) for a taxpayer for the taxable year shall be allocated among all such entities in proportion to the respective production of barrels of domestic crude oil (and the equivalent in barrels to the cubic feet of natural gas determined under subparagraph (4) (ii) of this paragraph).

(3) **Allocation among members of the same family.** In the case of individuals who are members of the same family, the tentative quantity determined under the table in section 613A(c)(3)(B) for a taxpayer for the taxable year shall be allocated among such individuals in proportion to the respective production of barrels of domestic crude oil (and the equivalent in barrels to the cubic feet of natural gas determined under subparagraph (4) (ii) of this paragraph) during the period in question by such individuals.

(4) **Special rules.** For purposes of section 613A(c)(8) and this section—
(i) The family of an individual includes only his spouse and minor children, and
(ii) Each 6,000 cubic feet of domestic natural gas shall be treated as 1 barrel of domestic crude oil.

(5) **Examples.** The application of this paragraph may be illustrated by the following examples:

Example (1). A owns 50 percent of the stock of Corporation M and 50 percent of the stock of Corporation N. Both corporations are calendar year taxpayers. For 1976 Corporation M's production of domestic crude oil was 8,000,000 barrels (365,000 of which was secondary production) and Corporation N's was 2,000,000 barrels (all of which was primary production). The tentative quantity (2,000 barrels per day) determined under the table in section 613A(c)(3)(B) must be allocated between the two corporations in proportion to their respective barrels of production of domestic crude oil during the taxable year. Corporation M's allocable share of the tentative quantity is

$$1{,}600 \text{ barrels} \left\{ 2{,}000 \times \frac{8{,}000{,}000}{10{,}000{,}000} \right\}$$

and Corporation N's allocable share is 400 barrels

$$\left\{ 2{,}000 \times \frac{2{,}000{,}000}{10{,}000{,}000} \right\}.$$

With respect to M's primary production, M's depletable oil quantity is 600 barrels (1,600 barrels − 1,000 barrels [365,000 secondary production ÷ 365 days]). N's depletable oil quantity, unaffected by M's secondary production, is 400 barrels.

Example (2). Corporations O and P are members of a controlled group and are treated as one taxpayer as provided in subparagraph (1) of this section. Corporation O owns oil properties A and B. Property A had primary production for 1975 of 800,000 barrels of oil. Property B had secondary production for 1975 of 365,000 barrels of oil. Corporation P owns oil property C which had primary production of 660,000 barrels for 1975. The allowable percentage depletion with respect to property B's secondary production was $360x. The controlled group's average daily production was 4,000 barrels [(800,000 plus 660,000) ÷ 365]. The controlled group's depletable oil quantity was 1,000 barrels [2,000 tentative quantity− 1,000 average daily secondary production (365,000 ÷ 365)]. The allowable percentage depletion pursuant to section 613(a) (computed as if section 613 applied to all of the production at the rate specified in section 613A(c)(5)) was $800x with respect to production from property A and $660x with respect to production from property C.

Proposed Reg. §1.613A-3

Corporation O's allowable depletion pursuant to section 613A(c) with respect to property B's secondary production (for which depletion is allowable before primary production) for 1975 was $360x. Corporation O's allowable depletion pursuant to section 613A(c) with respect to property A was $200x

$$\left\{ \text{\$800x depletion} \times \frac{1{,}000 \text{ depletable oil quantity}}{4{,}000 \text{ average daily production}} \right\}.$$

Therefore, Corporation O's allowable depletion pursuant to section 613A(c) was $560x ($360x relating to property B plus $200x relating to property A). Corporation P's allowable depletion pursuant to section 613A(c) with respect to property C was $165x

$$\left\{ \text{\$660x depletion} \times \frac{1{,}000 \text{ depletable oil quantity}}{4{,}000 \text{ average daily production}} \right\}.$$

(h) **Transfer of oil or gas property.** (1) In the case of a transfer (as defined in paragraph (n) of §1.613A-7) of an interest in any proven oil or gas property (as defined in paragraph (p) of §1.613A-7), paragraph (a)(1) of this section shall not apply to a transferee (as defined in paragraph (o) of §1.613A-7) with respect to production of crude oil or natural gas attributable to such interest, and such production shall not be taken into account for any computation by the transferee under this section. However, such a transfer shall not affect the applicability of paragraph (a)(2) (relating to secondary or tertiary production) of this section.

(2) The provisions of this paragraph may be illustrated by the following examples:

Example (1). Individual A transfers proven oil properties to Corporation M in an exchange to which section 351 applies for shares of its stock. Since there is no allocation requirement pursuant to section 613A(c)(8) between A (the transferor) and Corporation M (the transferee), the transfer of such proven properties by A is a transfer for purposes of section 613A(c)(9) and percentage depletion is not allowable to Corporation M with respect to such properties.

Example (2). Corporation N sells proven oil property to Corporation O, its wholly-owned subsidiary. Since the transfer was made between corporations which are members of the same controlled group of corporations, Corporation O is entitled to percentage depletion with respect to production from such property so long as the tentative oil quantity is allocated between the two corporations.

Example (3). B, owner of a proven oil property, died on January 1, 1975. Pursuant to the provisions of B's will, B's estate transferred the oil property on April 1, 1975, into a trust. On July 1, 1976, pursuant to a requirement in B's will, the trustee distributed the oil property to C. The transfer of the oil property by the estate to the trust and later distribution of such property by the trust to C are transfers at death. Therefore, the trust was entitled to compute percentage depletion with respect to the production from the oil property when such property was owned by the trust and C is entitled to percentage depletion with respect to production from the oil property after distribution.

Example (4). On January 1, 1975, property which produces oil resulting from secondary processes was transferred to D. The exemption under section 613A(c) applies to D because section 613A(c)(9) (relating to transfers of oil or gas property) does not apply with respect to secondary production. In addition, even if at the time of transfer the production from the property was primary and D applied secondary processes to the property transferred and obtained secondary production, D would be entitled to percentage depletion with respect to the secondary production.

Example (5). On July 1, 1975, E and F entered into a contract whereby F is to drill a well on E's unproven property and is to own the entire working interest in the property until F has recovered all the costs of drilling, equipping, and operating the well. Thereafter 50 percent of the working interest would revert to E. In accordance with the contract, 50 percent of the working interest reverted to E on July 1, 1976. F is entitled to percentage depletion because the transfer of the working interest to him occurred when the property was unproven on July 1, 1975, which is the date of the contract establishing his right to the working interest. E is entitled to percentage depletion with respect to his working interest since the reversion of such interest with respect to which E was eligible for percentage depletion is not a transfer. However, if on the date of the contract E's property was proven (although not proven when E acquired such property), F would not be entitled to claim percentage depletion with respect to any of the working interest income. Nonetheless, E would still be entitled to percentage depletion with respect to his working interest since the reversion of such interest is not a transfer.

Example (6). On January 1, 1975, G subleased an oil property to H, retaining a 1/8 royalty interest with the option to convert his royalty into a 50 percent working interest. On July 1, 1975, the property was proven and on July 1, 1976, G exercised his option. G is entitled to claim percentage depletion with respect to his working interest since the conversion of the royalty interest which is eligible for percentage depletion pursuant to section 613A(c) into an interest which constituted part of an interest previously owned by G is not a transfer pursuant to §1.613A-7(n)(8).

Example (7). I and J (both of whom are minors) are beneficiaries of a trust which owned a proven oil property. The oil property was transferred to the trust on January 1, 1975, by the father of I and J. For 1975, the trustee allocated all the income from the oil property to I. For 1976, the trustee allocated all the income from such property to J. On January 1, 1977, the trustee distributed such property to I and J as equal tenants in common. Since I, J. and their father are members of the same family within the meaning of section 613A(c)(8)(C), the transfer of the property to the trust by the father, the shifting of income between I and J, and the distribution of the oil property by the trust to I and J are not transfers for purposes of section 613A(c)(9). However, the distribution of the oil property will constitute a transfer to each distributee on the date on which he reaches majority.

Example (8). In 1975, K transferred a proven oil property productive at 5,000 feet to L. Subsequent to the transfer, L drilled new wells on the property finding another reservoir at 10,000 feet. The two zones were combined under section 614 as a single property. L is not entitled to percentage depletion on the gross income attributable to the production from the productive zone at 5,000 feet, but is entitled to percentage depletion on the gross income attributable to the production from the productive zone at 10,000 feet because that zone was not part of the proven property until the date of development expenses by L, which is after the date of the transfer. Accordingly, L's maximum allowable percentage depletion deduction for 1975 would be zero percent of gross income from the property with respect to the production from 5,000 feet, plus 22 percent of gross income from the property with respect to the production from 10,000 feet. This maximum deduction would be subject to the limitation provided for in section 613(a), i.e., 50 percent of "taxable income from the property (computed without allowance for depletion)," such taxable income being the overall taxable income resulting from the sale of production from both zones, and would also be subject to the limitations provided in section 613A.

Example (9). On July 1, 1975, M transferred an oil property with a fair market value of $100x to N. On February 1, 1976, N commenced production of oil from the property. The fair market value of the property on February 1, 1976, as reduced by actual costs incurred by N for equipment and intangible drilling and development costs, was $300x. Since the value of the property on transfer was not 50 percent or more of the value on February 1, 1976, the property transferred to N was not a proven property. However, if there had been only marginal production from the property so that the fair market value of the property on February 1, 1976, was $40x rather than $300x, the property transferred to N would have been a proven property provided the other requirements of proven property were met.

Example (10). O is the owner of a remainder interest in a trust created January 1, 1970. On such date, the trust held oil and gas properties. On January 1, 1976, O's

Proposed Reg. §1.613A-3

interest for the first time entitled him to the trust's income from oil and gas production from such properties. The transfer of the interest in oil and gas property to O is deemed to have occurred on January 1, 1970, the date O's interest was created.

Example (11). On January 1, 1976, P, Q, and R entered into a partnership for the acquisition of oil and gas leases. It was agreed that the sharing of income will be divided equally among P, Q, and R. However, it was further agreed that with respect to the first production obtained from each property acquired P will receive 80 percent thereof and Q and R each will receive 10 percent thereof until $100x has been received by P. On February 1, 1976, Partnership PQR acquired an unproven property and production therefrom was shared pursuant to the partnership agreement. P is entitled to percentage depletion with respect to the production specially allocated to him since the transfer of right to such production is deemed to have been made on the date the partnership agreement became applicable to the specific property, at which time the property was unproven. Similarly, when $100x has been obtained and Q and R each commence receiving 33 1/3 percent of the revenue, Q and R are entitled to percentage depletion with respect to their entire interests. However, if the property had been proven when acquired by the partnership, P, Q, and R would not be entitled to claim any percentage depletion with respect to production from the property.

Example (12). On December 30, 1960, S placed producing oil property in trust for the benefit of his nephew, T, and executed a trust agreement which required the trustee of the trust to transfer the oil property to T on January 1, 1975. The trustee's transfer of the oil property to T on January 1, 1975, is deemed to have occurred on December 30, 1960. Since the transfer is deemed to have occurred before January 1, 1975, section 613A (c) applies with respect to the production from the oil property. Moreover, if the trustee was not required to transfer the oil property on a specific date but was given discretion to select the date of transfer, the transfer of such property would still be deemed to have occurred on December 30, 1960. However, the result would be different if the trust agreement had provided that the trustee, at his discretion, may transfer the oil property to T on January 1, 1975, but is not under any obligation to transfer the property to T on January 1, 1975, or on any other date. Since the transfer was discretionary, the date of the actual transfer governs.

Example (13). On January 1, 1974, U acquired an oil property. On February 1, 1974, U granted V an option to purchase such oil property. V exercised his option on March 2, 1975, and subsequently the oil property is conveyed to him. The date of the transfer is March 2, 1975, the day V exercised his option (on which date both parties were bound).

Example (14). On July 1, 1974, W executed a deed conveying oil and gas property to X. W delivered the deed to X on January 1, 1975. Under state law, the mere execution of the deed without delivery did not give X any rights in the property. Title to the oil property passes to X on date of delivery. Therefore, the date of transfer is January 1, 1975.

Example (15). Y, owner of a proven oil property, transferred his interest therein on July 25, 1975, to a revocable trust of which he is treated as the owner under section 676. Y is not deemed a transferee and section 613A (c) applies to Y because immediately preceding the transfer he was entitled to percentage depletion on the production from such property.

Example (16). On January 1, 1975, a proven oil property was transferred to Z; therefore, section 613A (c)(1) did not apply with respect to the production from such property. After Z's death, neither Z's estate nor its beneficiaries are entitled to percentage depletion with respect to the decedent's oil property since Z was a transferee of proven property.

Example (17). Partnership, ABC, owner of producing oil and gas properties, admitted D as a partner in 1975 in consideration of cash. The shares of Partners A, E, and C of the partnership income were proportionately reduced so that D had a 25 percent interest in the income. D is not entitled to percentage depletion with respect to his share of partnership oil and gas income because D is a transferee for purposes of section 613A (c)(9).

Example (18). On January 1, 1975, E and F formed Partnership EF to which E contributed proven oil property. For 1975, pursuant to the partnership agreement 70 percent of the mineral income from the property was allocated to E and 30 percent of the mineral income from the property was allocated to F. F is not entitled to percentage depletion with respect to production from the property because he is a transferee of an interest in proven property. However, E is not a transferee of an interest in proven property because he was entitled to percentage depletion on the oil produced with respect to such property immediately before the transfer. Therefore, E is entitled to percentage depletion with respect to the income allocated to him. However, if in 1976 the partnership agreement were revised so that E's interest in the income was increased by 10 percent, E would not be entitled to percentage depletion with respect to the additional 10 percent interest because E is a transferee with respect thereto.

Example (19). G is the owner of a 1/3 interest in a partnership owning a proven oil property and as such is entitled to 1/3 of the income from the property. G received a distribution on July 1, 1975, from the partnership of a 1/3 interest in the proven oil property. Although the transfer of such interest is a transfer for purposes of section 613A (c)(9), G is still entitled to percentage depletion with respect to the 1/3 interest in the oil production from the property since G was entitled to percentage depletion on such production with respect to such property immediately before the transfer. If the entire property were distributed to G his percentage depletion allowance would still be based on only 1/3 of the oil produced.

Example (20). H and I contributed property X and property Y respectively to Partnership HI. The partnership agreement provides that all the gross income from property X is to be allocated to H and all the gross income from property Y is to be allocated to I. For 1975 H and I each received $100x gross income. Although the contributions of the properties by H and I are transfers for purposes of section 613A (c)(9), both H and I are entitled to percentage depletion with respect to the $100x income received since each was entitled to percentage depletion allowance with respect to the property contributed immediately before the transfer. However, if no special allocation of income were made but H and I are to share equally in the income from both properties, each would be entitled to a depletion allowance based on only one-half of the production with respect to the property he had contributed. If property X produces $100x of gross income from the property and property Y produces $200x of gross income from the property, H would be entitled to percentage depletion but only with respect to $50x (50 percent of $100x) of gross income from the property and I would be entitled to percentage depletion with respect to $100x (50 percent of $200x) of gross income from the property.

(i) **Special rule for fiscal year taxpayers.** In applying this section to a taxable year which is not a calendar year, each portion of such taxable year which occurs during a single calendar year shall be treated as if it were a short taxable year.

(j) **Information furnished by partnerships, trusts, estates, and operators.** Each partnership, trust, or estate producing domestic crude oil or natural gas, and each operator of a well from which domestic crude oil or natural gas was produced, shall provide each partner, beneficiary, or person holding a nonoperating interest, as the case may be, with all information in its possession necessary to determine the amount of his depletion deduction allowable with respect to such crude oil or natural gas. For example, a partnership will be required to provide each partner with such partnership information relating to each property as: the partner's share of gross income from the property, the partner's share of operating expenses, the partner's share of depreciation, the partner's share of allocated overhead, the partner's share of estimated reserves, the partner's share of production in barrels or cubic feet for the taxable year, the partner's original share of the partnership adjusted basis of properties producing domestic crude oil or domestic natural gas, and the partner's allocable share of any subsequent adjustments made to the basis of

Proposed Reg. §1.613A-3

such properties by the partnership. In addition, upon the disposition of an oil or gas property by the partnership, the partnership shall inform each partner of his allocable portion of the amount realized from the sale of such property.

§1.613A-4 (Proposed Treasury Decision, published 5-13-77.) **Limitations on application of §1.613A-3 exemption.**

(a) **Limitation based on taxable income.** (1) The aggregate amount of a taxpayer's deductions allowed pursuant to section 613A(c) for the taxable year shall not exceed 65 percent of the taxpayer's taxable income for the year, adjusted to eliminate the effects of:

(i) Any depletion with respect to an oil or gas property (other than a gas property with respect to which the depletion allowance for all production is determined pursuant to section 613A(b)) for which percentage depletion would exceed cost depletion in the absence of the depletable quantity limitations contained in section 613A(c)(1) and (6) or the taxble income limitation contained in section 613A(d)(1);

(ii) Any net operating loss carryback to the taxable year under section 172;

(iii) Any capital loss carryback to the taxable year under section 1212; and

(iv) In the case of a trust, any distributions to its beneficiaries, except in the case of any trust where any beneficiary of such trust is a member of the family (as defined in section 267(c)(4)) of a settlor who created inter vivos and testamentary trusts for members of the family and such settlor died within the last six days of the fifth month in 1970, and the law in the jurisdiction in which such trust was created requires all or a portion of the gross or net proceeds of any royalty or other interest in oil, gas, or other mineral representing any percentage depletion allowance to be allocated to the principal of the trust.

The amount disallowed (as defined in paragraph (q) of §1.613A-7) shall be carried over to the succeeding year and treated as an amount allowable as a deduction pursuant to section 613A(c) for such succeeding year, subject to the 65-percent limitation of section 613A(d)(1). For rules relating to corporations filing a consolidated return, see the regulations under section 1502. With respect to fiscal year taxpayers, except as provided in §1.613A-1 for taxable years beginning before January 1, 1975, and ending after that date, the limitation shall be calculated on the entire fiscal year and not applied with respect to each short period included in a fiscal year. For purposes of basis adjustments and determining whether cost depletion exceeds percentage depletion with respect to the production from a property, any amount disallowed as a deduction after the application of this paragraph shall be allocated to the respective properties from which the oil or gas was produced in proportion to the percentage depletion otherwise allowable to such properties pursuant to section 613A(c). Accordingly, the maximum amount allowable as a deduction pursuant to section 613A(c) after application of this paragraph (65 percent × adjusted taxable income) shall be allocated to properties for which percentage depletion pursuant to section 613A(c) would be allowed in the absence of the limitation contained in section 613A(d)(1) by application of the same proportion. However, once it is determined that after application of this paragraph cost depletion exceeds percentage depletion with respect to a property, the amount so allowable shall be reallocated among the remaining properties, and the portion of the amount disallowed which is allocable to such property shall be the amount by which percentage depletion pursuant to section 613A(c) before application of this paragraph exceeds cost depletion. See example (1) of subparagraph (2) of this paragraph. If the taxpayer becomes entitled to the deduction in a later year (i.e., because the disallowed depletion does not exceed 65 percent of his taxable income for that year after taking account of any percentage depletion deduction otherwise allowable for that year), then the basis of his properties must be adjusted downward (but not below zero) by the amount of the deduction in proportion to the portion of the amount disallowed to the respective properties in the year of the disallowance. However, if the property in question was disposed of by the taxpayer prior to the beginning of such later year, the amount of the deduction in such later year shall be reduced by the lesser of the taxpayer's adjusted basis in the property at the time it is disposed of or the difference between such basis and the adjusted basis which the taxpayer would have had in the property in the absence of the 65-percent limitation.

(2) The application of this paragraph may be illustrated by the following examples:

Example (1). A owns producing oil properties M, N and O. With respect to property M, the depletion allowable pursuant to section 613A(c) for 1975 without regard to section 613A(d)(1) was $60x (cost depletion would have been $40x). With respect to property N, the depletion allowable pursuant to section 613A(c) for 1975 without regard to section 613A(d)(1) was $90x (cost depletion would have been zero). With respect to property O, the depletion pursuant to 613A(c) for 1975 without regard to section 613A(d)(1) was $50x (cost depletion would have been $10x). A's taxable income (as adjusted under §1.613A-4(a)(1)) for 1975 was $100x; accordingly, A's percentage depletion pursuant to section 613A(c) for 1975 was limited to $65x (65 percent × $100x taxable income). Of that amount, $19.5x

$$\left\{ 65x \text{ dollars} \times \frac{\$60x}{\$60x + \$90x + \$50x} \right\} \text{ is tentatively allocated}$$

to property M, $29.25x

$$\left\{ 65x \text{ dollars} \times \frac{\$90x}{\$90x + \$60x + \$50x} \right\} \text{ is tentatively allocated}$$

to property N and $16.25x

$$\left\{ 65x \text{ dollars} \times \frac{\$50x}{\$50x + \$90x + \$60x} \right\} \text{ is tentatively allocated}$$

to property O. Since cost depletion of $40x with respect to property M exceeded the percentage depletion of $19.5x allowable on such property, A claimed the cost depletion. Accordingly, the only percentage depletion deduction allowable to A pursuant to section 613A(c) for 1975 is with respect to properties N anc O. Therefore, the entire $65x of amount allowable must be reallocated between properties N and O. Of that amount, $41.79x

$$\left\{ 65x \text{ dollars} \times \frac{\$90x}{\$90x + \$50x} \right\} \text{ is allocated to}$$

property N and $23.21x

$$\left\{ 65x \text{ dollars} \times \frac{\$50x}{\$50x + \$90x} \right\} \text{ is allocated to}$$

property O. The amount disallowed to A under section 613A(d)(1) is $95x ($200x aggregate depletion allowable before application of section 613A(d)(1) − $105x [$40x cost depletion allowable on property M + $41.79x percentage depletion allowable on property N after application of section 613A(d)(1) + $23.21x depletion allowable on property O after application of section 613A(d)(1)]). For purposes of basis adjustments, $20x ($60x percentage depletion before limitation − $40x cost depletion allowed) of the amount disallowed is allocated to property M. The balance of the amount disallowed of $75x is allocated $48.12x

$$\left\{ 75x \text{ dollars} \times \frac{\$90x}{\$90x + \$50x} \right\} \text{ to property N and}$$

$26.79x

$$\left\{ 75x \text{ dollars} \times \frac{\$50x}{\$50x + \$90x} \right\} \text{ to property O.}$$

Example (2). The amount disallowed to B as a deduction under this paragraph is $50x for 1975 and $125x for 1976 (including the $50x carried over from 1975). B may carry forward the $125x as a deduction to 1977 and subsequent years.

Proposed Reg. §1.613A-4

Example (3). C is a fiscal year taxpayer whose fiscal year ended on May 31, 1975. For purposes of applying the 65 percent of taxable income limitation, the period beginning January 1, 1975, and ending May 31, 1975, is treated as a short taxable year. The depletion allowable pursuant to section 613A(c) without regard to section 613A(d)(1) for such short taxable year was $80x and A's taxable income (as adjusted under §1.613A-4(a)(1)) during such short taxable year was $100x. Only $65x (65 percent × $100x adjusted taxable income) of the deduction pursuant to section 613A(c) was deductible for such portion of 1975, in addition to any percentage depletion allowable for June 1, 1974, through December 31, 1974.

Example (4). Under the trust law of State X, a trustee is required to allocate 22 percent of gross mineral income to the principal of a trust for purposes of maintaining a reserve for depletion and the depletion deduction is entirely allocated to the trustee. In 1975 the gross income of a trust in State X the only assets of which were oil properties was $1,000. The trust's allowable percentage depletion pursuant to section 613A(c) without regard to section 613A(d)(1) was $220. The trust incurred expenses of $150 for the taxable year and made distributions to beneficiaries (who are not described in the exception for family members set forth in subparagraph (1)(iv) of this paragraph) of $630 ($1,000 gross income—$220 allocated to principal—$150 expenses). For purposes of applying the 65 percent limitation, the trust's taxable income was $550 ($1,000 gross income—$150 expenses—$300 exemption). The limitation under section 613A(d)(1) was $357.50 (65% × $550 taxable income). Accordingly, the trust's percentage depletion allowance was unaffected by the 65 percent limitation.

Example (5). In 1975 D sold an oil property for which his adjusted basis was $20x. The amount disallowed for the taxable year to D under section 613A(d) was $10x. The amount of the carryover under that section to 1976 was 0 ($10x disallowed amount—$10x [$20x adjusted basis of property on sale—$10x adjusted basis which taxpayer would have had in property in absence of the 65-percent limitation]). However, if the adjusted basis of the property on disposition had been 0, the amount of the carryover to 1976 would have been $10x ($10x disallowed amount—0 adjusted basis of property on sale).

Example (6). In 1975 E owned producing oil properties M, N, O, P, Q, and R. With respect to property M, the allowable cost depletion was $100x (the allowable percentage depletion pursuant to section 613A(c) without regard to the depletable quantity and taxable income limitations contained in section 613A(c)(1), (6) and (d)(1) would have been $90x). With respect to property N, the allowable percentage depletion pursuant to section 613A(c) before applying section 613A(d)(1) was $80x (cost depletion would have been $0). With respect to property O, the allowable cost depletion was $60x (the allowable percentage depletion pursuant to section 613A(c) before applying section 613A(d)(1) would have been $70x). With respect to property P, the allowable percentage depletion pursuant to section 613A(b) was $55x (cost depletion would have been $40x). With respect to property Q which produces both gas subject to section 613A(b)(1)(B) and oil subject to section 613A(c), the allowable percentage depletion was $45x (cost depletion would have been $40x). With respect to property R, the allowable cost depletion was $40x (the allowable percentage depletion pursuant to section 613A(c) before applying section 613A(c)(7)(A) would have been $50x). Under paragraph (a)(1)(i) of this section, for purposes of applying the 65 percent limitation under section 613A(d)(1), E's taxable income shall be reduced by the allowable depletion with respect to property M (for which cost depletion exceeded percentage depletion even in the absence of section 613A(c)(1), (6), and (d)) and property P (for which all depletion is determined pursuant to section 613A(b)), but shall not be reduced by the allowable depletion with respect to properties N, O, Q, and R.

(b) **Retailers excluded.** (1) Section 613A(c) and §1.613A-3 shall not apply in the case of any taxpayer who is a retailer as defined in paragraph (r) of §1.613A-7.

(2) The application of this paragraph may be illustrated by the following examples, all of which assume that the $5,000,000 gross receipts requirement of section 613A(d)(2) is met:

Example (1). A, owner of producing oil and gas properties, also owns 5 percent in value of the stock of Corporation M, a retailer of oil and gas. None of A's production is sold through Corporation M. Since A may benefit from Corporation M's sales of oil and gas through his ownership interest in Corporation M, A is considered to be selling oil or natural gas through Corporation M, a related person. Accordingly, the exemption under section 613A(c) does not apply to A, even though none of A's production is sold through Corporation M.

Example (2). Corporation N, a retailer of oil and gas, owns 5 percent in value of the stock of Corporation O, owner of producing oil and gas properties. None of Corporation O's production is sold through Corporation N. Since Corporation O has no direct or indirect ownership interest in Corporation N, and therefore does not benefit from Corporation N's sales of oil and gas, and since none of Corporation O's production is sold through Corporation N, the exemption under section 613A(c) applies to Corporation O.

Example (3). Corporation P, a producer of oil, owns 70 percent in value of the stock of Corporation Q. Corporation Q owns 30 percent in value of the stock of Corporation R. Corporation R owns 30 percent in value of the stock of Corporation S, a retailer of oil and gas. P indirectly owns 6.3 percent (70 percent $\times$ 30 percent $\times$ 30 percent) in value of the stock of Corporation S. Since P may benefit from Corporation S's sales of oil and gas through his indirect ownership interest in Corporation S, P is not entitled to percentage depletion.

Example (4). B is the owner of certain oil and gas properties in Texas and is also the owner of a service station in Washington, D.C., which he leases to Corporation T. None of B's production is sold to Corporation T. The exemption under section 613A(c) applies to B. However, if B's production were sold to Corporation T, the exemption under section 613A(c) would not apply to B because B is selling oil or natural gas to a person given authority to occupy a retail outlet leased by the taxpayer, B.

Example (5). C has a $1/8$ royalty interest and Corporation U has a $7/8$ working interest in an oil property. Corporation V, a retailer of oil, owns 5 percent in value of the stock of Corporation U. C has no interest in either corporation. All of the production from the property is sold through Corporation V, C receiving from Corporation U $1/8$ of its receipts therefor. The exemption under section 613A(c) does not apply to Corporation U because Corporation U is selling oil or natural gas through Corporation V, a related person that is a retailer. However, the exemption applies to C because C, as owner of a nonoperating mineral interest, is not treated as an operator of a retail outlet merely because his oil or gas is sold on his behalf through a retail outlet operated by an unrelated person.

Example (6). D owns and operates retail grocery stores where refined oil may be purchased. D also owns oil and gas producing properties. If the sales of refined oil at each store location constitute less than 5 percent of the gross receipts from all sales made at that store, D is not considered a retailer by reason of such sales.

Example (7). Lessee E sells natural gas to lessor F directly from a wellhead gathering pipeline system for F's local agricultural use, in transactions incidental to the acquisition of a natural gas lease. Such sales of natural gas to F are not sales through a retail outlet.

Example (8). Corporation W produces natural gas some of which it sells at retail. For purposes of determining whether Corporation W is a retailer selling gas through a retail outlet within the meaning of §1.613A-7(r), the business office of Corporation W where a purchaser would normally contact the corporation with respect to its sales to him is considered the place at which those sales of natural gas are made.

Example (9). G, husband, is the sole owner and operator of a retail outlet which sells oil and gas. H, wife, owns producing oil and gas properties. G is not related to H for purposes of section 613A(d).

Proposed Reg. §1.613A-4

Example(10). I, husband, and J, wife, are community property owners of 10 percent in value of the stock of Corporation X which is a retailer of oil and gas. I and J are each treated as owning 5 percent of Corporation X. Therefore, neither I nor J qualify for the exemption under section 613A(c).

Example (11). Corporation Y, an electing small business corporation as defined in section 1371, owns producing oil and gas properties. K, a retailer of oil and gas, is a 50 percent interest shareholder of Corporation Y. None of Corporation Y's production is sold through K. Corporation Y is eligible for percentage depletion.

Example (12). Corporation Z, a producer of natural gas, makes bulk sales of natural gas at the wellhead to industrial users. For purposes of determining whether corporation Z is a retailer under §1.613A-7(r), such bulk sales are disregarded.

Example (13). L, a calendar year taxpayer, is the owner of a producing oil property. For 1976, L was a retailer of oil and gas for the last 122 days of the year. L's gross income from the oil property for the taxable year was $150x and his taxable income from the property was $30x. L is treated as a retailer with respect to $50x of gross income from the property.

$$\left\{150x \text{ dollars} \times \frac{122}{366}\right\} \text{ and } \$10x \text{ of taxable income from the property}$$

$$\left\{30x \text{ dollars} \times \frac{122}{366}\right\}.$$

Therefore, L is entitled to percentage depletion with respect to $100x of gross income from the property ($150x minus $50x). However, the allowable percentage depletion is limited by the 50 percent of taxable income from the property limitation to $15x (50 percent × $30x taxable income).

Example (14). Corporation M is a partner in Partnership MNO which is the owner of an operating interest in a producing oil property. Corporation P, a retailer of oil and gas, owns 5 percent in value of the stock of Corporation M. Partnership MNO sells its production to Corporation P. Corporation M is retailing oil through Corporation P, a related person, because its share of the oil is being sold on its behalf by the partnership through a retail outlet operated by a person related to Corporation M. Therefore, the exemption under section 613A(c) does not apply to Corporation M.

Example (15). M and N are beneficiaries of a trust which is a retailer of oil and gas. M has a 5 percent interest in the income of the trust for M's lifetime. N's interest in the trust entitles N to 5 percent of the income of the trust after M's death. The trust is a related person of M but not N while M is alive. Accordingly, during M's lifetime N is not disqualified from the exemption provided by section 613A(c) but M is.

Example (16). Assume the same facts as in example (15) except that M has a 4 percent interest in the income of the trust. M is disqualified from the exemption provided by section 613A(c) with respect to the income from the trust but not with respect to income from other sources.

(c) **Certain refiners excluded.** (1) Section 613A(c) and §1.613A-3 shall not apply in the case of any taxpayer who is a refiner as defined in paragraph (s) of §1.613A-7.

(2) The provisions of this paragraph may be illustrated by the following examples:

Example (1). Corporation M owns a refinery which has refinery runs in excess of 50,000 barrels on at least one day during the taxable year. Corporation M also owns 5 percent interest in Corporation N, owner of producing oil and gas properties. None of Corporation N's production is sold to Corporation M. The exemption under section 613A(c) does not apply to Corporation N because Corporation M, a related person of Corporation N, engages in the refining of crude oil.

Example (2). A and B are equal partners in Partnership AB, which owns oil and gas producing properties. A owns a refinery which has refinery runs in excess of

50,000 barrels on at least one day during the taxable year and which buys all of Partnership AB's production. B has no ownership interest in any refinery. B is not a refiner.

* * * * * * * * * * * *

§1.613A-7 (Proposed Treasury Decision, published 5-13-77.) **Definitions.**
For purposes of section 613A and the regulations thereunder—

(a) **Domestic.** The term "domestic", as applied to oil and gas wells (or to production from such wells), refers to such wells located in the United States or in a possession of the United States, as defined in section 638 and the regulations thereunder.

(b) **Natural gas.** The term "natural gas" means any product (other than crude oil as defined in paragraph (g) of this section) of an oil or gas well if a deduction for depletion is allowable under section 611 with respect to such product.

(c) **Regulated natural gas.** Natural gas is considered to be "regulated" only if all of the following requirements are met:

(1) The gas must be domestic gas produced and sold by the producer (whether for himself or on behalf of another person) before July 1, 1976,

(2) The price for which the gas is sold by the producer must not be adjusted to reflect to any extent the increase in liability of the seller for tax under chapter 1 of the Code by reason of the repeal of percentage depletion for gas,

(3) The sale of the gas must be subject to the jurisdiction of the Federal Power Commission for regulatory purposes,

(4) An order or certificate of the Federal Power Commission must be in effect (or a proceeding to obtain such an order or certificate must have been instituted), and

(5) The price at which such gas is sold must be taken into account, directly or indirectly, in the issuance of the order or certificate by the Federal Power Commission.

Price increases after February 1, 1975, shall be presumed to take increases in tax liabilities into account unless the taxpayer demonstrates to the contrary by clear and convincing evidence that the increases are wholly attributable to a purpose or purposes unrelated to the repeal of percentage depletion for gas, such as increases to reflect additional State and local real property or severance taxes, increases for additional operating costs (such as costs of secondary or tertiary processes), increases up to the highest area rate fixed by the Federal Power Commission for interstate sales (provided repeal of percentage depletion is not reflected in such rate), increases for additional drilling and related costs, or increases to reflect changes in the quality of gas sold. In the absence of a statement in writing by the Federal Power Commission that the price of the gas in question was not in fact regulated, the requirement of subparagraph (5) of this paragraph is deemed to have been met in any case in which the Federal Power Commission issues an order or certificate approving the sale to an interstate pipeline company or, in a case in which it is established by the taxpayer that the Federal Power Commission has influenced the price of such gas, an order or certificate permitting the interstate transportation of such gas. In addition, an "emergency" sale of natural gas to an interstate pipeline, which, pursuant to the authority contained in 18 CFR 2.68, 2.70, 157.22, and 157.29, may be made without prior order approving the sale, is deemed to have met the requirements of subparagraphs (3), (4), and (5) of this paragraph. For purposes of meeting the requirements under this paragraph, it is not necessary that the total gas production from a property qualify as "regulated natural gas"; the determination of whether mineral production is "regulated natural gas" shall be made with respect to each sale of the mineral or minerals produced.

(d) **Natural gas sold under a fixed contract.** The term "natural gas sold under a fixed contract" means domestic natural gas sold by the producer (whether for himself or on behalf of another person) under a contract, in effect on February 1, 1975, and at all times thereafter before such sale, under which the price for such gas during such period cannot be adjusted to reflect to any extent the increase in liabilities of the seller for tax under chapter 1 of the Code by reason of the repeal of percentage depletion for gas. The term may include gas sold under a fixed contract even though production sold under the contract had previously been treated as regulated natural gas. Price increases after Febru-

Proposed Reg. §1.613A-7

ary 1, 1975, shall be presumed to take increases in tax liabilities into account unless the taxpayer demonstrates to the contrary by clear and convincing evidence. See paragraph (c) of this section for examples of increases which do not take increases in tax liabilities into account. An additional example would be increases of a fixed percentage or fixed dollar amount pursuant to escalation clauses designed merely to reflect projected effects of inflation. However, if the adjustment provided for in the contract permits the possible increase in Federal income tax liability of the seller to be taken into account to any extent or provides for an increase in the price of the contract to the highest price paid to a producer for natural gas in the area, or if the price may be renegotiated, then gas sold under the contract after such an increase becomes permissible is not gas sold under a fixed contract. For purposes of meeting the requirements of this paragraph, it is not necessary that the total gas production from a property qualify as "natural gas sold under a fixed contract", for the determination of "natural gas sold under a fixed contract" is to be made with respect to each sale of each type of natural gas sold pursuant to each contract.

(e) **Geothermal deposit.** The term "geothermal deposit" means a geothermal reservoir consisting of heat, largely stored in rocks, and, to a lesser extent, in aqueous fluid in the form of liquid or vapor.

(f) **Average daily production.** (1) The term "average daily production" means the taxpayer's aggregate production of domestic crude oil or natural gas, as the case may be, which is produced after December 31, 1974, and to which gross income from the property is attributable during the taxable year divided by the number of days in such year. As used in the preceding sentence the term "taxpayer" includes a small business corporation as defined in section 1371 and the regulations thereunder. Notwithstanding the provisions of §1.612-3, in computing the average daily production for a taxable year only oil or gas which has been produced by the close of such taxable year shall be taken into account. For example, advanced royalties (to the extent that actual production during the taxable year is insufficient to earn such royalties) and lease bonuses, while taken into account for purposes of sections 61 and 612 (relating to the definition of gross income and cost depletion, respectively), would not be taken into account in computing the percentage depletion allowance pursuant to section 613A(c). Average daily production does not include production resulting from secondary or tertiary processes.

(2) In the case of a fiscal-year taxpayer, subparagraph (1) of this paragraph shall be applied separately to each short taxable year under section 613A(c)(10).

(3) In the case of a taxpayer holding a partial interest in the production from any property (including an interest of a partner in property of his partnership) such taxpayer's production shall be considered to be that amount of such production determined by multiplying the total production (which is produced after December 31, 1974, and to which gross income from the property is attributable during the taxable year) of such property by the taxpayer's percentage participation in the revenues from such property during such year. With respect to a holder of a net profits interest in an oil and gas property, such taxpayer's production shall be deemed to be that portion of production which produced the same fraction of the property's gross income as the fractional interest of the taxpayer in the net profits from the property.

(g) **Crude Oil.** The term "crude oil" means—
(1) A mixture of hydrocarbons which existed in the liquid phase in natural underground reservoirs and which remains liquid at atmospheric pressure after passing through surface separating facilities,
(2) Hydrocarbons which existed in the gaseous phase in natural underground reservoirs but which are liquid at atmospheric pressure after being recovered from oil well (casinghead) gas in lease separators, and
(3) Natural gas liquid recovered from gas well effluent in lease separators or field facilities before any conversion process has been applied to such production.

(h) **Depletable oil quantity.** The taxpayer's depletable oil quantity, within the meaning of section 613A(c)(1)(A), shall be equal to—

(1) The tentative quantity determined under the table contained in section 613A(c)(3)(B) and paragraph (b) of §1.613A-3, reduced (but not below zero) by

(2) The taxpayer's average daily secondary or tertiary production for the taxable year.

(i) **Depletable natural gas quantity.** The taxpayer's depletable natural gas quantity, within the meaning of section 613A(c)(1)(B), shall be equal to 6,000 cubic feet multiplied by the number of barrels of the taxpayer's depletable oil quantity to which the taxpayer elects to have section 613A(c)(4) apply. The taxpayer's depletable oil quantity for any taxable year shall be reduced (in addition to any reduction previously required to be made under paragraph (h)(2) of this section) by the number of barrels with respect to which an election under section 613A(c)(4) has been made. See §1.613A-5.

(j) **Barrel.** The term "barrel" means 42 United States gallons.

(k) **Secondary or tertiary production.** The term "secondary or tertiary production" means the increased production of crude oil or natural gas from a domestic well at any time after the application of a secondary process. The increased production is the excess of actual production over the maximum primary production which would have resulted during the taxable year if such process had not been applied. Such increased production may be due to an increase in either the rate or the duration of recovery. A secondary process is a process applied for the recovery of hydrocarbons in which substances in a liquid or gaseous state are injected into the reservoir to supplement or augment the energy required to move the hydrocarbons through the reservoir, except that no process which must be introduced early in the productive life of the mineral property in order to be reasonably effective (such as cycling of gas in the case of a gas-condensate well) is a secondary process. A process (such as fire flooding or miscible fluid injection) introduced early in the productive life of the mineral property will not be disqualified as a secondary process if a later introduction of such process in such property would still have been reasonably effective.

(*l*) **Controlled group of corporations.** The term "controlled group of corporations" has the meaning given to such term by section 1563(a), except that section 1563(b)(2) shall not apply and except that "more than 50 percent" shall be substituted for "at least 80 percent" each place it appears in section 1563(a).

(m) **Related person.** (1) A person is a "related person" to another person, within the meaning of section 613A(d)(2) and (4), paragraphs (b) and (c) of §1.613A-4, and paragraphs (r) and (s) of this section, if either a significant ownership interest in such person is held by the other, or a third person has a significant ownership interest in both such persons. For purposes of determining a significant ownership interest, an interest owned by or for a corporation, partnership, trust, or estate shall be considered as owned directly both by itself and proportionately by its shareholders, partners, or beneficiaries, as the case may be. The term "significant ownership" means—

(i) With respect to any corporation, direct or indirect ownership of 5 percent or more in value of the outstanding stock of such corporation,

(ii) With respect to a partnership, direct or indirect ownership of 5 percent or more interest in the profits or capital of such partnership, and

(iii) With respect to an estate or trust, direct or indirect ownership of 5 percent or more of the beneficial interests in such estate or trust.

(2) A person is a "related person" to another person, within the meaning of section 613A(c)(8)(B) and paragraph (g)(2) of §1.613A-3, if such persons are members of the same controlled group of corporations or if the relationship between such persons would result in a disallowance of losses under section 267 or 707(b), except that for this purpose the family of an individual includes only his spouse and minor children.

(n) **Transfer.** The term "transfer" means any change in legal or equitable ownership by sale, exchange, gift, lease, sublease, assignment, contract, or other disposition (including any contribution to or any distribution by a corporation, partnership, or trust), any change in the membership of a partnership or the beneficiaries of a trust, or any other

Proposed Reg. §1.613A-7

change by which a taxpayer's proportionate share of the income subject to depletion of an oil or gas property is increased. However, the term does not include—

(1) A transfer of property at death (including a distribution by an estate, whether or not a pro rata distribution),

(2) An exchange to which section 351 applies,

(3) A change of beneficiaries of a trust by reason of the death, birth, or adoption of any vested beneficiary if the transferee was a beneficiary of such trust or is a lineal descendant of the settlor or any other vested beneficiary of such trust, except in the case of any trust where any beneficiary of such trust is a member of the family (as defined in section 267(c)(4)) of a settlor who created inter vivos and testamentary trusts for members of the family and such settlor died within the last six days of the fifth month in 1970, and the law in the jurisdiction in which such trust was created requires all or a portion of the gross or net proceeds of any royalty or other interest in oil, gas, or other mineral representing any percentage depletion allowance to be allocated to the principal of the trust,

(4) A transfer of property between corporations which are members of the same controlled group of corporations (as defined in section 613A(c)(8)(D)(i)),

(5) A transfer of property between business entities which are under common control (within the meaning of section 613A(c)(8)(B)) or between related persons in the same family (within the meaning of section 613A(c)(8)(C)),

(6) A transfer of property between a trust and members of the same family (within the meaning of section 613A(c)(8)(C)) to the extent that both (i) the beneficiaries of that trust are and continue to be members of the family that transferred the property, and (ii) the tentative oil quantity is allocated among the members of such family,

(7) A reversion of all or part of an interest with respect to which the taxpayer was eligible for percentage depletion pursuant to section 613A(c), or

(8) A conversion of a retained interest which is eligible for such depletion into an interest which constituted all or part of an interest previously owned by the taxpayer also eligible for such depletion.

However, subparagraphs (2), (4), and (5) of this paragraph shall apply only so long as the tentative quantity determined under the table contained in section 613A(c)(3)(B) is allocated under section 613A(c)(8) between the transferor and transferee or among members of a controlled group of corporations. For purposes of subparagraphs (3) and (6), an individual adopted by a beneficiary is a lineal descendant of that beneficiary. For purposes of subparagraphs (7) and (8), a taxpayer previously ineligible for percentage depletion solely by reason of section 613A(d)(2) or (4) will be considered to have been eligible for such depletion. A transfer is deemed to occur on the day on which a contract or other commitment to transfer such property becomes binding upon both the transferor and transferee, or, if no such contract or commitment is made, on the day on which ownership of the interest in oil or gas property passes to the transferee.

(o) **Transferee.** The term "transferee", as used in section 613A(c)(9), paragraph (h) of §1.613A-3, and this section includes the original transferee of proven property and his successors in interest. A person shall not be treated as a transferee of an interest in a proven oil or gas property to the extent that such person was entitled to a percentage depletion allowance on mineral produced with respect to such property immediately before the transfer. However, a person shall be treated as a transferee of an interest in a proven property to the extent that the interest such person receives is greater than the interest in such property he held immediately before the transfer. For example, where the owner of a proven oil property transfers his entire interest therein to a partnership of which he is a member and, as a consequence, becomes entitled to a depletion allowance based on only one-third of the oil produced with respect to that property, he (the transferor) is not denied percentage depletion with respect to the one-third interest in oil production which he still possesses. if the partnership agreement had made an effective allocation (under section 704 and §1.704-1) of all the income in respect of such property to the transferor partner, he would be entitled to percentage depletion on the entire oil production from that property. For this purpose, a person who has transferred oil or gas property pursuant to a unitization or pooling agreement shall be treated as having been entitled to a depletion allowance immediately before the transfer to him of his interest in the unit or pool with respect to all of the mineral in respect of which he receives gross income from the property pursuant to the unitization or pooling agreement, except to the extent such income is attributable to consideration paid by him for such interest in addition to oil or gas property and equipment affixed thereto.

(p) **Interest in proven oil or gas property.** The term "interest in an oil or gas property" means an economic interest in oil or gas property, including working or operating interests, royalties, overriding royalties, net profits interests, and, to the extent not treated as loans under section 636, production payments from oil or gas properties. The term also includes an interest in a partnership or trust holding an economic interest in oil or gas property but does not include shares of stock in a corporation owning such an interest. An oil or gas property is "proven" if its principal value has been demonstrated by prospecting, exploration, or discovery work. The principal value of the property has been demonstrated by prospecting, exploration, or discovery work only if at the time of the transfer—

(1) Any oil or gas has been produced from a deposit, whether or not produced by the taxpayer or from the property transferred;

(2) Prospecting, exploration, or discovery work indicate that it is probable that the property will have gross income from oil or gas from such deposit sufficient to justify development of the property; and

(3) The fair market value of the property is 50 percent or more of the fair market value of the property, minus actual expenses of the transferee for equipment and intangible drilling and development costs, at the time of the first production from the property subsequent to the transfer and before the transferee himself transfers his interest.

For purposes of this paragraph, the property is to be determined by applying section 614 and the regulations thereunder to the transferee at the time of the transfer. If the transfer is of an interest in a partnership or trust, the determination shall be made with respect to each property owned by the partnership or trust. The term "prospecting, exploration, or discovery work" includes activities which produce information relating to the existence, location, extent, or quality of any deposit of oil or gas, such as seismograph surveys and drilling activities (whether for exploration or for the production of oil or gas).

(q) **Amount disallowed.** The amount disallowed, within the meaning of section 613A(d)(1) and paragraph (a) of §1.613A-4, is the excess of the amount of the aggregate of the taxpayer's allowable depletion deductions (whether based upon cost of percentage depletion) computed without regard to section 613A(d)(1) over the amount of the aggregate of such deductions computed with regard to such section. Such disallowed amount shall be carried over to the succeeding year and treated as an amount allowable as a deduction pursuant to section 613A(c) for such succeeding year, subject to the 65-percent limitation of section 613A(d)(1) and the rules contained in section 613A-4(a).

(r) **Retailer.** The term "retailer" means any taxpayer who directly, or through a related person (as defined in paragraph (m)(1) of this section), sells oil or natural gas, or any product derived from oil or natural gas—

(1) Through any retail outlet operated by the taxpayer or a related person, or

(2) To any person—

(i) Obligated under an agreement or contract with the taxpayer or a related person to use a trademark, trade name, or service mark or name owned by such taxpayer or a related person, in marketing or distributing oil or natural gas or any product derived from oil or natural gas, or

(ii) Given authority, pursuant to an agreement or contract with the taxpayer or a related person, to occupy any retail outlet owned, leased, or in any way controlled by the taxpayer or a related person.

However, such taxpayer shall not be considered a retailer in any case where, during the taxable year of the taxpayer, the combined gross receipts from sales of oil or natural gas, or products derived therefrom, of all retail outlets taken into account under the preceding sentence (including sales through a retail outlet of oil, natural gas, or a product derived

Proposed Reg. §1.613A-7

from oil or natural gas, which had previously been the subject of a sale described in subparagraph (2)(i) of this paragraph) do not exceed $5 million. For purposes of the preceding two sentences, bulk sales of oil or natural gas before it has been manufactured or converted into a refined product to commercial or industrial users shall be disregarded. In addition, sales of oil, natural gas, or any product derived from oil or natural gas, which are made outside the United States shall be disregarded if no domestic production of the taxpayer or a related person is exported during the taxable year or the immediately preceding taxable year. The term "any product derived from oil or natural gas" means gasoline, kerosene, Number 2 fuel oil, refined lubricating oils, diesel fuel, methane, butane, propane, and similar products which are recovered from petroleum refineries or field facilities. A retail outlet is any place where sales of oil, natural gas, or a product of oil or natural gas, accounting for more than 5 percent of the gross receipts from all sales made at such place during the taxpayer's taxable year, are systematically made to any person or persons for any purpose other than for resale. For purposes of this paragraph, a taxpayer shall be deemed to be selling oil or natural gas (or a product derived therefrom) through a related person in any case in which any sale of oil or natural gas (or a derivative product) by the related person produces gross income from which the taxpayer may benefit by reason of his direct or indirect ownership interest in the related person. In such cases (and in any case in which the taxpayer is himself selling through a retail outlet referred to in section 613A(d)(2)(A) or is selling such items to a person described in section 613A(d)(2)(B)), it is immaterial whether the oil or natural gas which is sold, or from which is derived a product which is sold, was produced by the taxpayer. Of course, a taxpayer shall be deemed to be selling oil or natural gas (or a derivative product) through a related person in any case in which the related person acquires for resale oil or natural gas (or a derivative product) which the taxpayer produced or caused to be made available for acquisition by the related person. An owner of a nonoperating mineral interest (such as a royalty) shall not be treated as an operator of a retail outlet merely because his oil or gas is sold on his behalf through a retail outlet operated by an unrelated person. In addition, the mere fact that a member of a partnership is a retailer shall not result in characterization of the remaining partners as retailers; however, if the partnership itself is a retailer its partners having a 5 percent or more interest in the partnership's profits or capital are treated as retailers. Similarly, if a trust is a retailer, only its beneficiaries having a 5 percent or more current income interest from the trust are treated as retailers. A person who is a retailer during a portion of the taxable year shall be treated as a retailer with respect to a fraction of his gross and taxable income from his oil or gas properties for the taxable year, the numerator of which is the number of days during the taxable year in which the taxpayer is a retailer and the denominator of which is the total number of days during the taxable year; except that a person who ceases to be a retailer during the taxable year before his first production of oil or gas during such year shall not be treated as a retailer for any portion of such year.

(s) **Refiner.** A person is a refiner if such person or a related person (as defined in paragraph (m)(1) of this section) engages in the refining of crude oil (whether or not owned by such person or related person) and if the total refinery runs of such person and any persons so related to him exceed 50,000 barrels on any day during the taxable year. Refining is any operation by which the physical or chemical characteristics of crude oil or crude oil products are changed, exclusive of such operations as passing crude oil through separators to remove gas, placing crude oil in settling tanks to recover basic sediment and water, and dehydrating crude oil.

Operating Mineral Interests in Mines

Section 1.614-3 is amended by revising subdivisions (iii), (iv), and (v) of subparagraph (3) of paragraph (g) to read as follows:

§ **1.614-3** (Proposed Treasury Decision, published 12-30-70.) **Rules relating to separate operating mineral interests in the case of mines.**

* * * * * * * * * * * *

(g) Special rule as to deductions under section 615(a) prior to aggregation. * * *

(3) Recomputation of tax. * * *

(iii) Effect of recomputation with respect to items based on amount of income. In making the recomputation of tax under this subparagraph for any taxable year, any deduction, credit, or other allowance which is based upon the adjusted gross income or taxable income of the taxpayer for such year shall be recomputed taking into account the adjustment required under subdivision (ii) of this subparagraph. For example, if a corporate taxpayer's taxable income is increased under the provisions of such subdivision, then the amount of charitable contributions which may be deducted under the limitation contained in section 170(b)(2) shall be correspondingly increased for purposes of the recomputation. Moreover, the effect that the recomputation of any deduction, credit, or other allowance for a taxable year has on the tax imposed for any other taxable year shall also be taken into account for purposes of the recomputation of tax under this subparagraph. Any change in items of tax preferences (as defined in section 57 and the regulations thereunder) must also be taken into account for purposes of the recomputation under this subparagraph.

(iv) Effect of recomputation with respect to a net operating loss and a net operating loss deduction. If the recomputation of tax under this subparagraph for the taxable year for which the recomputation is required to be made results in a reduction of a net operating loss for such year, then the taxpayer shall take into account the effect of such reduction on the tax imposed by chapter 1 of the Internal Revenue Code of 1954 (or by corresponding provisions of the Internal Revenue Code of 1939) for any taxable year affected by such reduction. If the recomputation of tax for the taxable year for which the recomputation is required to be made results in an increase in taxable income as defined in section 172(b)(2) for such year, then the taxpayer shall take into account the effect of such increase on the tax imposed by chapter 1 of the Internal Revenue Code of 1954 (or by corresponding provisions of the Internal Revenue Code of 1939) for any taxable year affected by such increase. Furthermore in making the recomputation of tax for any taxable year for which the recomputation is required to be made, the taxpayer shall take into account any change in the net operating loss deduction for such year resulting from the recomputation of tax for any other taxable year for which a recomputation is required to be made. For provisions relating to the net operating loss deduction, see section 172 and the regulations thereunder. For rules relating to the effect of the net operating loss deduction on the minimum tax for tax preferences see section 56 and the regulations thereunder and § 1.58-7.

(v) Determination of increase in tax. If the taxpayer elects to form an aggregation or aggregations for a taxable year under section 614(c)(1) and if a recomputation of tax is required to be made under this paragraph for any prior taxable year or years, then the taxpayer shall compute the difference between the tax, including the tax imposed by section 56 (relating to the minimum tax for tax preferences), as recomputed under this subparagraph for such prior taxable year or years (and other taxable years affected by the recomputation) and the tax liability previously determined (computed without regard to section 614(c)(4)) with respect to such prior taxable year or years (and other taxable years affected by the recomputation). If the taxpayer is subsequently required to make a recomputation with respect to any taxable year or years for which he has previously made a recomputation, then the taxpayer shall compute the difference between the tax as subsequently recomputed for such taxable year or years (and other taxable years affected by the subsequent recomputation) and the tax as previously recomputed for such taxable year or years (and other taxable years affected by the subsequent recomputation). For treatment of the increase in tax resulted from the recomputation of tax under this subparagraph, see subparagraph (4) of this paragraph.

* * * * * * * * * * * * *

Proposed Reg. § 1.614-3

Taxation of Estates and Trusts

Sections 1.642(a)(3)-1, 1.642(a)(3)-2, and 1.642(a)(3)-3 are deleted. (Proposed Treasury Decision, published 9-19-72.)

Section 1.642(h)-1 is amended by revising paragraph (b) to read as follows:

§ 1.642(h)-1 (Proposed Treasury Decision, published 12-30-70.) **Unused loss carryovers on termination of an estate or trust.**

* * * * * * * * * * * * *

(b) The net operating loss carryover and the capital loss carryover are the same in the hands of a beneficiary as in the estate or trust, except that the capital loss carryover in the hands of a beneficiary which is a corporation is a short-term loss irrespective of whether it would have been a long-term or short-term capital loss in the hands of the estate or trust. The net operating loss carryover and the capital loss carryover are taken into account in computing taxable income, adjusted gross income, and the tax imposed by section 56 (relating to the minimum tax for tax preferences). The first taxable year of the beneficiary to which the loss shall be carried over is the taxable year of the beneficiary in which or with which the estate or trust terminates. However, for purposes of determining the number of years to which a net operating loss, or a capital loss under paragraph (a) of § 1.1212-1, may be carried over by a beneficiary, the last taxable year of the estate or trust (whether or not a short taxable year) and the first taxable year of the beneficiary to which a loss is carried over each constitute a taxable year, and, in the case of a beneficiary of an estate or trust that is a corporation, capital losses carried over by the estate or trust to any taxable year of the estate or trust beginning after December 31, 1963, shall be treated as if they were incurred in the last taxable year of the estate or trust (whether or not a short taxable year). For the treatment of the net operating loss carryover when the last taxable year of the estate or trust is the last taxable year to which such loss can be carried over, see § 1.642(h)-2.

* * * * * * * * * * * * *

Section 1.642(h)-2 is amended by revising paragraph (a) to read as follows:

§ 1.642(h)-2 (Proposed Treasury Decision, published 12-30-70.) **Excess deductions on treatment of an estate or trust.**

(a) If, on the termination of an estate or trust, the estate or trust has for its last taxable year deductions (other than the deductions allowed under section 642(b) (relating to personal exemption) or section 642(c) (relating to charitable contributions)) in excess of gross income, the excess is allowed under section 642(h)(2) as a deduction to the beneficiaries succeeding to the property of the estate or trust. The deduction is allowed only in computing taxable income and must be taken into account in computing the items of tax preference of the beneficiary; it is not allowed in computing adjusted gross income. The deduction is allowable only in the taxable year of the beneficiary in which or with which the estate or trust terminates, whether the year of termination of the estate or trust is of normal duration or is a short taxable year. For example: Assume that a trust distributes all of its assets to B and terminates on December 31, 1954. As of that date it has excess deductions, for example, because of corpus commissions on termination, of $18,000. B, who reported on the calendar year basis, could claim the $18,000 as a deduction for the taxable year 1954. However, if the deduction (when added to his other deductions) exceeds his gross income, the excess may not be carried over to the year 1955 or subsequent years.

* * * * * * * * * *

The heading of § 1.642(i)-1 is revised to read as follows:

§ 1.642(j)-1 (Proposed Treasury Decision, published 9-19-72.) **Cross references.**

* * * * * * * * * * *

Taxation of Beneficiaries of Trusts

Section 1.652(b)-1 is amended by deleting "72(n)" and inserting in lieu thereof "402(a)(2)". As amended, §1.652(b)-1 reads as follows:

§1.652(b)-1 (Proposed Treasury Decision, published 4-30-75.) **Character of amounts.**

In determining the gross income of a beneficiary, the amounts includible under § 1.652(a)-1 have the same character in the hands of the beneficiary as in the hands of the trust. For example, to the extent that the amounts specified in § 1.652(a)-1 consist of income exempt from tax under section 103, such amounts are not included in the beneficiary's gross income. Similarly, dividends distributed to a beneficiary retain their original character in the beneficiary's hands for purposes of determining the availability to the beneficiary of the dividends received credit under section 34 (for dividends received on or before December 31 1964) and the dividend exclusion under section 116. Also, to the extent that the amounts specified in § 1.652(a)-1 consist of "earned income" in the hands of the trust under the provisions of section 1348 such amount shall be treated under section 1348 as "earned income" in the hands of the beneficiary. Similarly, to the extent the amounts specified in § 1.652(a)-1 consist of an amount received as a part of a lump sum distribution from a qualified plan and to which the provisions of section 402(a)(2) would apply in the hands of the trust, such amount shall be treated as subject to such section in the hands of the beneficiary except where such amount is deemed under section 666(a) to have been distributed in a preceding taxable year of the trust and the partial tax described in section 668(a)(2) is determined under section 668(b)(1)(B). The tax treatment of amounts determined under § 1.652(a)-1 depends upon the beneficiary's status with respect to them, not upon the status of the trust. Thus, if a beneficiary is deemed to have received foreign income of a foreign trust, the includibility of such income in his gross income depends upon his taxable status with respect to that income.

Charitable Remainder Trusts

Paragraph (f) of §1.664-1 is amended by revising the heading of subparagraph (3) and by adding a new subparagraph (4) at the end thereof. These revised and added provisions read as follows:

§1.664-1 (Proposed Treasury Decision, published 12-19-75.) **Charitable remainder trusts.**

* * * * * * * * * * * * * * * * * * *

(f) **Effective Date.** * * *

(3) **Amendment of certain trusts created after July 31, 1969.** * * *

(4) **Certain wills and trusts in existence on September 21, 1974.** (i) In the case of a will executed before September 21, 1974, or a trust created (within the meaning of applicable local law) after July 31, 1969, and before September 21, 1974, which is amended pursuant to section 2055(e)(3) and §20.2055-2(g), a charitable remainder trust resulting from such amendment will be treated as a charitable remainder trust from the date it would be deemed created under §1.664-1(a)(4) and (5), whether or not such date is after September 20, 1974.

(ii) Property transferred to a trust created (within the meaning of applicable local law) before August 1, 1969, whose governing instrument provides that an organization described in section 170(c) receives an irrevocable remainder interest in such trust shall be deemed transferred to a trust created on the date of such transfer, provided that the transfer occurs after July 31, 1969, and prior to October 18, 1971, and pursuant to an amendment provided in §20.2055-2(g), the transferred property and any undistributed income therefrom is severed and placed in a separate trust as of the date of the amendment.

Proposed Reg. §1.664-1

Alimony Payments

Section 1.682(b)-1 is amended by revising paragraph (a) to read as follows:

§ 1.682(b)-1 (Proposed Treasury Decision, published 12-30-70.) **Application of trust rules to alimony payments.**

(a) For the purpose of the application of subparts A through D (section 641 and following), part I, subchapter J, chapter 1 of the Code, the wife described in section 682 or section 71 who is entitled to receive payments attributable to property in trust is considered a beneficiary of the trust, whether or not the payments are made for the benefit of the husband in discharge of his obligations. A wife treated as a beneficiary of a trust under this section is also treated as the beneficiary of such trust for purposes of the tax imposed by section 56 (relating to the minimum tax for tax preferences). For rules relating to the treatment of items of tax preference with respect to a beneficiary of a trust, see § 1.58-3.

* * * * * * * * * * * * *

Income and Credits of Partner

Section 1.702-1 is amended by adding new paragraph (e) immediately after paragraph (d). As amended this provision reads as follows:

§ 1.702-1 (Proposed Treasury Decision, published 12-30-70.) **Income and credits of partner.**

* * * * * * * * * * * *

(e) **Cross reference.** For special rules in accordance with the principles of section 702 applicable solely for the purpose of the tax imposed by section 56 (relating to the minimum tax for tax preferences) see §1.58-2(a).

Section 1.702-1 is amended by adding a new paragraph (e) at the end thereof to read as follows:

§1.702-1 (Proposed Treasury Decision, published 5-13-77.) **Income and credits of partner.**

* * * * * * * * * * *

(e) **Cross-reference.** In the case of a disposition of an oil or gas property by the partnership, see the rules contained in section 613A(c)(7)(D) and §1.613A-3(e).

Partnership Computations

Section 1.703-1 is amended by redesignating subdivision (vii) of paragraph (a)(2) as subdivision (viii) and inserting a new subdivision (vii), to read as follows:

§1.703-1 (Proposed Treasury Decision, published 5-13-77.) **Partnership computations.**

(a) **Income and deductions.** * * *

(2) * * *

(vii) The deduction for depletion under section 611 with respect to domestic oil and gas wells.

(viii) * * *

Determination of Basis of Partner's Interest

Paragraph (a) of §1.705-1 is amended by redesignating subparagraph (4) as subparagraph (6) and inserting new subparagraphs (4) and (5) to read as follows:

§1.705-1 (Proposed Treasury Decision, published 5-13-77.) **Determination of basis of partner's interest.**

(a) **General rule.** * * *

(4) The basis shall be decreased (but not below zero) by the amount of the partner's deduction for depletion allowed or allowable under section 611 with respect to domestic oil and gas wells.

(5) The basis shall be adjusted (but not below zero) to reflect any gain or loss to the partner resulting from a disposition by the partnership of a domestic oil or gas property.

(6) * * *

Gain or Loss on Contributions to the Partnership

Paragraph (b)(1) of § 1.721-1 is amended to read as follows:

§ 1.721-1 (Proposed Treasury Decision, published 6-3-71.) **Nonrecognition of gain or loss on contributions.**

* * * * * * * * * * *

(b)(1) Normally, under local law, each partner is entitled to be repaid his contributions of money or other property to the partnership (at the value placed upon such property by the partnership at the time of the contribution) whether made at the formation of the partnership or subsequent thereto. To the extent that any of the partners gives up any part of his right to be repaid his contributions (as distinguished from a share in partnership profits) in favor of another partner as compensation (or in satisfaction of an obligation), section 721 does not apply. The transfer of such a partnership interest transferred to a partner as compensation constitutes income to the partner as follows:

(i) If the partnership interest is transferred after June 30, 1969 (except to the extent paragraph (b) of § 1.83-8 applies), then the transfer of such interest in partnership capital shall be treated as a transfer of property to which section 83 and the regulations thereunder applies.

(ii) If the partnership interest is transferred on or before June 30, 1969, then the value of the interest in such partnership capital so transferred to a partner as compensation for services shall constitute income to the partner under section 61. The amount of such income is the fair market value of the interest in capital so transferred, either at the time the transfer is made for past services, or at the time the services have been rendered where the transfer is conditioned on the completion of the transferee's future services. The time when such income is realized depends on all the facts and circumstances, including any substantial restrictions or conditions on the compensated partner's right to withdraw or otherwise dispose of such interest. To the extent that an interest in capital representing compensation for services rendered by the decedent prior to his death is transferred after his death to the decedent's successor in interest, the fair market value of such interest is an item of income in respect of a decedent under section 691.

* * * * * * * * * * * *

Life Insurance Reserves

Section 1.801-4(b)(2) is amended to read as follows:

§ 1.801-4 (Proposed Treasury Decision, published 1-23-69.) **Life insurance reserves.**

* * * * * * * * * * *

(b) **Certain reserves which need not be required by law.** * * *

(2) In the case of policies issued by an organization which meets the require-

ments of section 501(c)(9) other than the requirement of subparagraph (B) thereof. For purposes of this subparagraph, an organization which otherwise meets the requirements of section 501(c)(9) other than the requirement of subparagraph (B), and which has been ruled exempt from Federal income tax prior to June 25, 1959, the date of enactment of section 801(b)(2)(B), will be deemed to meet such requirements even though it pays benefits of the type provided by pension, annuity, profit-sharing or stock bonus plans.

Regulated Investment Companies

Paragraph (b) of §1.851-2 is amended by redesignating paragraph (b) as subparagraph (1) of paragraph (b), by adding a caption to redesignated subparagraph (1), by redesignating subparagraphs (1) and (2) of paragraph (b) as subdivisions (i) and (ii) of redesignated subparagraph (1), and by adding a new subparagraph (2) to paragraph (b). The redesignated and revised provisions read as follows:

§1.851-2 (Proposed Treasury Decision, published 5-14-76.) **Limitations.**

* * * * * * * * * * * *

(b) **Gross income requirement**—(1) **General rule.** Section 851(b)(2) and (3) provides that (i) at least 90 percent of the corporation's gross income for the taxable year must be derived from dividends, interest, and gains from the sale or other disposition of stocks or securities, and (ii) less than 30 percent of its gross income must have been derived from the sale or other disposition of stock or securities held for less than three months. * * *

(2) **Special rules.** (i) For purposes of section 851(b)(2), there shall be treated as dividends amounts which are included in gross income for the taxable year under section 951(a)(1)(A)(i) to the extent that (a) a distribution out of a foreign corporation's earnings and profits of the taxable year is not included in gross income by reason of section 959(a)(1), and (b) the earnings and profits are attributable to the amounts which were so included in gross income under section 951(a)(1)(A)(i). For allocation of distributions to earnings and profits of foreign corporations, see §1.959-3. The provisions of this subparagraph shall apply with respect to taxable years of controlled foreign corporations beginning after December 31, 1975, and to taxable years of United States shareholders (within the meaning of section 951(b)) within which or with which such taxable years of such controlled foreign corporations end.

(ii) For purposes of subdivision (i) of this subparagraph, if by reason of section 959(a)(1) a distribution of a foreign corporation's earnings and profits for a taxable year described in section 959(c)(2) is not included in a shareholder's gross income, then such distribution shall be allocated proportionately between amounts attributable to amounts included under each clause of section 951(a)(1)(A). Thus, for example, M is a United States shareholder in X Corporation, a controlled foreign corporation. M and X each use the calendar year as the taxable year. For 1977, M is required by section 951(a)(1)(A) to include $3,000 in its gross income, $1,000 of which is included under clause (i) thereof. In 1977, M received a distribution described in section 959(c)(2) of $2,700 out of X's earnings and profits for 1977, which is, by reason of section 959(a)(1), excluded from M's gross income. The amount of the distribution attributable to the amount included under section 951(a)(1)(A)(i) is $900, i.e., $2,700 multiplied by ($1,000/$3,000).

Real Estate Investment Trusts

Section 1.856-1 is amended by revising paragraphs (b)(6), (d)(4) and (5) to read as follows:

§1.856-1 (Proposed Treasury Decision, published 9-5-68, 12-7-72.) **Definition of real estate investment trust.**

* * * * * * *

(b) **Qualifying conditions.** * * *

(6) Which would not be a personal holding company (as defined in section 542) if—(i) all of its adjusted ordinary gross income (as defined in section 543(b)(2)), or (ii) in the case of taxable years beginning before January 1, 1964, all of its gross income, constituted personal holding company income, (as defined in section 543 and the regulations thereunder).

* * * * * * * * * *

(d) **Rules applicable to status requirements.** * * *

(4) Property held for sale to customers. A real estate investment trust may not hold any property primarily for sale to customers in the ordinary course of its trade or business. Whether property is held for sale to customers in the ordinary course of the trade or business of a real estate investment trust depends upon the facts and circumstances in each case. The application of the rules provided by this subparagraph may be illustrated by the following examples:

Example (1). Trust M, which otherwise qualifies as a real estate investment trust, has in its portfolio a construction loan for a condominium (a single multi-unit dwelling). The loan originated with the trust and was made in accordance with prudent lending practices. The security for the loan is a mortgage on the condominium. After completion of the construction of the condominium, the debtor defaults on the loan and the trust becomes the owner of the condominium as a result of a foreclosure sale. The condominium is listed with a broker for sale as an undivided unit. The condominium is sold to an unrelated party within a reasonable period of time after foreclosure of the mortgage. Assuming that in all other respects the condominium would not be considered as held primarily for sale to customers in the ordinary course of the trust's trade or business, solely for purposes of section 856(a)(4) and this section, the trust is not considered to have held the condominium primarily for sale to customers in the ordinary course of its trade or business merely because of the circumstances under which the foreclosure was made and the property was sold.

Example (2). The facts are the same as in Example (1), except that, at the time the trust obtains ownership of the condominium, the construction of the condominium is 80 percent completed (determined on the basis of a comparison of actual construction costs at such time with expected total construction costs) and that the trust employs an unrelated contractor to complete construction of the condominium. Solely for purposes of section 856(a)(4) and this section, the trust is not considered to have held the condominium primarily for sale to customers in the ordinary course of its trade or business merely because of the circumstances under which the foreclosure was made and the property was sold.

(5) Personal holding company. An unincorporated organization, even though it may otherwise meet the requirements of Part II of subchapter M, will not be a real estate investment trust if (i) by considering all of its adjusted ordinary income (as defined in section 543(b)(2)), or (ii) for taxable years beginning before January 1, 1964, by considering all of its gross income, as personal holding company income under section 543, it would be a personal holding company as defined in section 542. Thus if at any time during the last half of the trust's taxable year more than 50 percent in value of its outstanding stock is owned (directly or indirectly under the provisions of section 544) by or for not more than five individuals, the stock ownership requirement in section 542(a)(2) will be met and the trust would be a personal holding company. See § 1.857-6, relating to record requirements for purposes of determining whether the trust is a personal holding company.

* * * * * * * * * *

Paragraph (c)(2)(ii) of section 1.856-2 is revised to read as follows:

§ 1.856-2 (Proposed Treasury Decision, published 12-7-72.) **Limitations.**

Proposed Reg. § 1.856-2

(c) **Gross income requirements.** * * *

(2) * * *

(ii) *Interest.* In computing the percentage requirements in section 856(c)(2)(B) and (3)(B) there shall be included as interest only the amount which constitutes interest for the loan or forbearance of money. Thus, for example, a fee imposed upon a borrower which is in fact a charge for a service in addition to the charge for the use of borrowed money shall not be included as interest. In the case of loans made after December 7, 1972, an amount received or accrued with respect to an obligation shall not be included as interest for purposes of section 856(c)(2)(B) or (3)(B) if the determination of such amount depends in whole or in part on the income or profits of any person. For purposes of the preceding sentence, a loan is considered to be made if there is a binding commitment to make a loan, but not if the transaction is merely in the negotiation stage. To the extent limited by this subdivision, the 90-percent requirement in section 856(c)(2)(B) permits the inclusion of interest generally, while the 75-percent requirement in section 856(c)(3)(B) includes interest only to the extent that it relates to obligations secured by mortgages on real property. Where a mortgage covers both real and other property an apportionment of the interest income must be made for purposes of the 75-percent requirement. For purposes of such requirement, the apportionment is made as follows:

(a) If the loan value of the real property is equal to or exceeds the amount of the loan and is equal to or exceeds the loan value of the other property, then the entire interest income shall be apportioned to the real property.

(b) If the loan value of the other property exceeds both the amount of the loan and the loan value of the real property, then the entire interest income shall be apportioned to the other property.

(c) If the amount of the loan exceeds either the loan value of the real property or the total loan value of the other property, or both such values, then the interest income shall be apportioned between the real property and other property on the basis of their respective loan values.

For purposes of this subdivision, the term "other property" does not include property to the extent that its value is determined by reference to the value of property which is security for the obligation. For example, where a real estate investment trust makes a loan to a corporation which is secured by a mortgage on real property owned by the corporation and a pledge of the stock of such corporation, for purposes of this subdivision, the term "other property" does not include the stock of the corporation to the extent of the loan value of such real property.

* * * * * * * * * * * * * * * * * *

Paragraph (d) of section 1.856-3 is revised to read as follows:

§ 1.856-3 (Proposed Treasury Decision, published 12-7-72.) **Definitions.**

* * * * * * * * * * * * * * * * * *

(d) *Real property.* The term "real property" means land or improvements thereon, such as buildings or other inherently permanent structures thereon (including items which are structural components of such buildings or structures). In addition, the term "real property" includes interests in real property. Local law definitions will not be controlling for purposes of determining the meaning of the term "real property" as used in section 856 and the regulations thereunder. The term includes, for example, the wiring in a building, plumbing systems, central heating or central air-conditioning machinery, built-in air-conditioning units, built-in stoves, built-in refrigerators, permanently installed carpeting, pipes or ducts, elevators or escalators installed in the building, or other items which are structural components of a building or other permanent structure. The term does not include assets accessory to the operation of a business, such as machinery, printing presses, transportation equipment which is not a structural component of the building, office equipment, refrigerators and other appliances which are not built-in, "window" air-conditioning units, grocery counters, furnishings of a motel, hotel, or office building, etc., even though such items may be termed fixtures under local law.

* * * * * * * * * * * * * * * * * *

Paragraphs (b)(1), (b)(3)(i)(b), and (b)(3)(i)(c) of section 1.856-4 are revised to read as follows:

§ 1.856-4 (Proposed Treasury Decision, published 12-7-72.) **Rents from real property.**

* * * * * * * * * * * * * * * * * *

(b) Amounts not includible as rent. * * *

(1) *Where amount of rent depends on income or profits of any person.* Any amount received or accrued, directly or indirectly, with respect to any real property if the determination of such amount depends in whole or in part on the income or profits derived by any person from such property. However, any amount so accrued or received shall not be excluded from the term "rents from real property" solely by reason of being based on a fixed percentage or percentages of receipts or sales (whether or not receipts or sales are adjusted for returned merchandise, or Federal, State or local sales taxes). Thus, for example, "rents from real property" would include rents where the lease provides for differing percentages of receipts or sales from different departments or from separate floors of a retail store so long as each percentage is fixed at the time of entering into the lease. However, where a trust leases real property to a tenant under terms other than solely on a fixed sum rental (i.e., for example, a percentage of the tenant's gross receipts), and the tenant subleases all or a part of such property under an agreement which provides for a rental based in whole or in part on the income or profits of the sublessee, the entire amount of the rent received by the trust from the prime tenant with respect to such property is disqualified as "rents from real property". "Rents from real property" are not based in whole or in part on the income or profits derived by any person from such property if the amount of the rent is based on a fixed percentage or percentages of receipts or sales reduced by permissible escalation receipts. For purposes of this subparagraph, the term "permissible escalation receipts" means amounts received by reason of an agreement that rent shall be increased to reflect all or a portion of an increase in those costs which relate to the rental property and, in the case of a cost incurred for services, increases in costs for services which the real estate investment trust is permitted to directly furnish or render to the tenants of the property under subparagraph (3)(i)(b) of this paragraph. For purposes of the preceding sentence, costs which relate to the property include (but are not limited to) real estate taxes, personal property taxes, property insurance, and maintenance expenses, and costs which do not relate to the property include (but are not limited to) compensation to managerial and clerical personnel, office supplies, and income taxes. Where in accordance with the terms of an agreement an amount received or accrued as rent for the taxable year includes both a fixed rental and a percentage of the lessee's income or profits in excess of a specific amount (usually determined before deducting the fixed rental and sometimes called "overage rents"), neither the fixed rental nor the additional amount will qualify as "rents from real property." However, where the amount received or accrued for the taxable year under such an agreement includes only the fixed rental, the determination of which does not depend in whole or in part on the income or profits derived by the lessee, such amount may qualify as "rents from real property". Similarly, where the amount received or accrued as rent for the taxable year consists, in whole or in part, of a percentage of the lessee's receipts or sales in excess of a specific amount which amount does not depend in whole or in part on the income or profits derived by the lessee, such amount may qualify as "rents from real property". Thus, an amount received or accrued as rent which consists of a fixed rental plus a percentage of the lessee's receipts or sales in excess of a specific amount may qualify as "rents from real property". In any

Proposed Reg. § 1.856-4

event, an amount will not qualify as "rents from real property" if, considering the lease and all the surrounding circumstances, the arrangement does not conform with normal business practices but is in reality used as a means of basing the rent on income or profits. The application of the rules provided in this subparagraph may be illustrated by the following example:

Example. Trust R, which otherwise qualifies as a real estate investment trust, leases real property to PT, a prime tenant. PT subleases the real property to ST, a subtenant. The lease between PT and ST provides for rent equal to a fixed dollar amount plus an additional amount equal to any increase in property taxes, property insurance, and clerical salaries of PT above specified dollar amounts. The lease between R and PT provides for a rent equal to a fixed percentage of gross receipts of PT excluding all gross receipts attributable to rents measured by increased costs of PT. The rent received by R from PT does not qualify as "rents from real property" because the amounts excluded from gross receipts of PT include amounts which are not "permissible escalation receipts".

* * * * * * * * * * * * * * * * *

(3) **Trust furnishing services or managing property through an independent contractor**—(i) In general * * *

(b) Customary services for which no separate charge is made. Under section 856(d)(3), the trust (through its trustees or its own employees) may not directly furnish or render any services to the tenants of its property and may not directly manage or operate the property. However, for purposes of part II, subchapter M, chapter 1 of the Code, an amount will not be disqualified as "rent" if services, such as are usually or customarily furnished or rendered in connection with the mere rental of real property, are furnished or rendered to tenants of the property through an independent contractor. The independent contractor must not, however, be an employee of the trust (i.e., the manner in which he carries out his duties as independent contractor must not be subject to the control of the trust). The supplying of water, heat, air-conditioning, and light; the cleaning of windows, public entrances, exits, and lobbies; the performance of general maintenace and other janitorial services; the collection of trash; and the furnishing of elevator service, telephone answering service, incidental storage space, laundry equipment, swimming facilities and other recreation facilities which are integral parts of multiple occupancy real property provided primarily to the tenants of such real property where no services are performed other than providing a lifeguard and sanitation (but only to the extent that such recreation facilities are actually used by such tenants or their guests), a parking facility which is an integral part of multiple occupancy real property provided primarily for the convenience of the tenants of such real property where attendants perform no services other than the parking of vehicles (but only to the extent that such parking facility is actually used by such tenants or their guests or their customers), and watchman or guard services, are examples of services which are customary or incidental to the mere rental of multiple-occupancy real estate. Although the cost of such incidental services may be borne by the trust, the services must, nevertheless, be furnished or rendered through an independent contractor. Furthermore, the facilities through which such services are furnished must be maintained and operated by an independent contractor. For example, if a heating plant is located in the building, it must be maintained and operated by an independent contractor. Where no separate charge is made for such services, no apportionment is required to be made between rents from real property and compensation for these services.

(c) Services for which a separate charge is made. Under section 856(d)(3), the trust may not derive or receive any income from an independent contractor who furnishes or renders services to the tenants of the trust property or who manages or operates such property, regardless of the source from which such income was derived by the independent contractor. To the extent that services, other than those usually or customarily rendered in connection with the mere rental of real property, are rendered to the tenants of the property by the independent contractor, the cost of such services must be borne by the independent contractor,

Proposed Reg. § 1.856-4

a separate charge must be made therefor, and the amount thereof must be received and retained by the independent contractor; no amount attributable to such services shall be included in the gross income of the trust. In any event, the independent contractor must be adequately compensated for such services. Also, if a separate charge is made for the customary services described in (b) of this subdivision (i), such charge must be made and the amount thereof must be received and retained, by the independent contractor rather than by the trust. The furnishing of hotel, maid, boarding house, motel, laundry, or warehouse services are examples of services which are not usually or customarily furnished or rendered in connection with the mere rental of real estate, and the trust must not receive any income which is attributable to the furnishing or rendering of such services to tenants of the trust property. Furthermore, where electric current is purchased and then sold to the tenants at a price in excess of the purchase price (for example, submetered), such purchase and sale must be made by the independent contractor and no income therefrom may inure, directly or indirectly, to the trust.

* * * * * * * * * * * * * * * * * * * *

Income from U.S. Sources

Section 1.861-1 is amended by revising paragraph (a)(1) and (2) to read as follows:

§ 1.861-1 (Proposed Treasury Decision, published 7-24-75.) **Income from sources within the United States.**

(a) **Categories of income.** * * *

(1) **Within the United States.** The gross income from sources within the United States, consisting of the items of gross income specified in section 861(a) plus the items of gross income allocated or apportioned to such sources in accordance with section 863(a). See §§ 1.861-2 to 1.861-7, inclusive, and § 1.863-1. The taxable income from sources within the United States, in the case of such income, shall be determined by deducting therefrom, in accordance with sections 861(b) and 863(a), the expenses, losses, and other deductions properly apportioned or allocated thereto and a ratable part of any other expenses, losses, or deductions which cannot definitely be allocated to some item or class of gross income. See §§ 1.861-8 and 1-863-1. For an election to treat income from certain aircraft or vessels as income from sources within the United States for purposes of section 861(a), see § 1.861-9.

(2) **Without the United States.** The gross income from sources without the United States, consisting of the items of gross income specified in section 862(a) plus the items of gross income allocated or apportioned to such sources in accordance with section 863(a). See §§ 1.862-1 and 1.863-1. The taxable income from sources without the United States, in the case of such income, shall be determined by deducting therefrom, in accordance with sections 862(b) and 863(a), the expenses, losses, and other deductions properly apportioned or allocated thereto and a ratable part of any other expenses, losses, or deductions which cannot definitely be allocated to some item or class of gross income. See §§ 1.862-1 and 1.863-1. For an election to treat income from certain aircraft or vessels as income from sources within the United States for purposes of section 862(a), see § 1.861-9.

* * * * * * * * * * * *

The following new section is inserted immediately after §1.861-8.

§ 1.861-9 (Proposed Treasury Decision, published 7-24-75.) **Income from certain aircraft or vessels.**

(a) **General rule.** A taxpayer who owns an aircraft or vessel described in paragraph (b) of this section and who after August 15, 1971, leases such aircraft or vessel to a United States person which is not a member of a controlled group of corporations (as defined in section 1563) of which the taxpayer is a member may elect pursuant to paragraph (f) of this section, for any taxable year ending after August 15, 1971, and ending after the commencement of the lease, to treat all amounts includible in gross income with respect to such aircraft or vessel as income from sources within the United States. An election once made with respect to an aircraft or vessel will apply to the taxable year of the taxpayer for which made and to all subsequent taxable years unless it is revoked pursuant to paragraph (f)(3) of this section. A taxpayer entitled to make an election under this section is not required to be a United States person, unless otherwise required by a provision of law not contained in the Internal Revenue Code of 1954; nor is the taxpayer required to be a bank or other financial institution. The election provided by this section may not be used with the primary objective of treating losses in respect of the aircraft or vessel as losses from sources within the United States and income and gains in respect of the aircraft or vessel as income from sources without the United States. Thus, for example, if the rule in the immediately preceding sentence is violated, income in respect of the aircraft or vessel derived in a later taxable year from sources without the United States must be treated as income from sources within the United States. The term "United States person", as used in this section, shall have the meaning assigned to it by section 7701(a)(30).

(b) **Property to which the election applies**—(1) **In general.** An election under this section may be made only in the case of aircraft or vessels manufactured or constructed in the United States which are section 38 property (as defined in section 48 and the regulations thereunder) or would be section 38 property but for section 48(a)(5), relating to property used by governmental units. Except in the case of property described in section 48(a)(5), the aircraft or vessels must be property which qualifies for the investment credit under section 38. Thus, no election may be made under this section with respect to aircraft or vessels which are suspension period property as defined in section 48(h) or which are termination period property to which section 49(a) applies. If the aircraft is used predominantly outside the United States (as determined by applying the rules of § 1.48-1(g)(1)), it must be registered by the Administrator of the Federal Aviation Agency and qualify under the provisions of section 48(a)(2)(B)(i) and § 1.48-1(g)(2)(i). If the vessel is used predominantly outside the United States (as determined by applying the rules of § 1.48-1(g)(1)), it must be documented under the laws of the United States and qualify under the provisions of section 48(a)(2)(B)(iii) and § 1.48-1(g)(2)(iii).

(2) **Exclusion of certain property used outside the United States.** The term "aircraft or vessel", as used in this paragraph, does not include any property which is used predominantly outside the United States and which qualifies as section 38 property under—

(i) Section 48(a)(2)(B)(v), relating to containers used in the transportation of property to and from the United States,

(ii) Section 48(a)(2)(B)(vi), relating to certain property used for the purpose of exploring for, developing, removing, or transporting resources from the outer Continental Shelf, or

(iii) Section 48(a)(2)(B)(x), relating to certain property used in international or territorial waters.

(c) **Leases or subleases to which the election applies.** An aircraft or vessel will be considered leased to a United States person after August 15, 1971, if the aircraft or vessel is leased to a United States person pursuant to a lease entered into after August 15, 1971, for a period during which a United States person is in possession and control of such aircraft or vessel. For example, if the owner of a vessel enters into an agreement after August 15, 1971, with a United States person to bareboat charter such vessel (that is, to lease the vessel without the owner's bearing any responsibility for its operation) to such United States person and the United States person thereafter enters into a subleasing agreement to bareboat charter such vessel to a person who is not a United States person, the vessel will not be considered leased to a United States person for purposes of section 861(e) because the vessel will be in the possession and under the control of the non-United States person. However, if at any time such United States person enters into a subleasing agreement to time charter or voyage charter the vessel (that is, to contract to carry cargo for hire while bearing the responsibility of operating the vessel) to a non-United States person, the vessel will be considered

Proposed Reg. § 1.861-9

leased to a United States person and the election provided by section 861(e) will be available to the owner of the vessel because the vessel will be in the possession and under the control of the bareboat charterer who is a United States person. Section 861(e) and this section do not apply to that part occurring after August 15, 1971, of the term of a lease entered into before August 16, 1971.

(d) **Income to which the election applies.** An election under this section applies to all amounts derived by the taxpayer with respect to the aircraft or vessel which is subject to the election, including any gain from the sale or other disposition of such aircraft or vessel, but only if without regard to section 861(e) such amounts are includible in the taxpayer's gross income during or after the period of the lease. However, if by reason of the allowance of expenses and other deductions such gross income actually results in a loss from sources without the United States, the election applies so as to treat such loss as having a source within the United States. Moreover, if the sale or other disposition of the aircraft or vessel which is subject to the election results in a loss from sources without the United States, such loss will be treated as having a source within the United States. However, see paragraph (a) of this section for the prohibition against using the election to achieve U. S. source treatment for losses in respect of the aircraft or vessel but foreign source treatment for income or gains in respect of such aircraft or vessel. See also paragraph (e)(2)(iii) of this section for the application of an election under this section to the income of certain transferees or distributees.

(e) **Effect of election**—(1) **In general.** An election under this section shall apply to the taxable year for which it is made and to all subsequent taxable years for which amounts in respect of the aircraft or vessel to which the election relates are includible in gross income, unless the election is revoked pursuant to paragraph (f)(3) of this section.

(2) **Certain transfers involving carryover of basis.** (i) If an electing taxpayer transfers or distributes an aircraft or vessel which is subject to an election under this section and the basis of such aircraft or vessel in the hands of the transferee or distributee is determined by reference to its basis in the hands of the transferor or distributor, whether or not there is any amount of gain recognized to the transferor or distributor by which basis must be increased, the transferee or distributee will be treated as having made an election under this section wth respect to that aircraft or vessel. Thus, for example, if an electing corporation distributes a vessel which is subject to an election under this section to its parent corporation in a complete liquidation described in section 332(b) and the basis of the property in the hands of the parent corporation is determined under section 334(b)(1), relating to the general rule on carryover of basis, the parent corporation will be required to treat all amounts includible in gross income with respect to the vessel as income from sources within the United States, unless the election is revoked pursuant to paragraph (f)(3) of this section. In further illustration, if an electing corporation distributes a vessel which is subject to an election under this section in a distribution to which section 301(a) applies and the basis of the property received is determined under section 301(d)(2), relating to basis of corporate distributees, the corporate distributee will be treated as having made an election under this section with respect to the vessel even though the distributee's basis is the fair market value of the property, as provided in section 301(d)(2)(A). This subdivision applies even though the transferee or distributee is a nonresident alien individual or foreign corporation.

(ii) If an electing taxpayer transfers or distributes an aircraft or vessel which is subject to an election under this section and the basis of such aircraft or vessel in the hands of the transferee or distributee is determined without reference to its basis in the hands of the transferor or distributor, the election under this section with respect to such aircraft or vessel will be terminated as to the transferee or distributee.

(iii) If an aircraft or vessel which is subject to an election under this section is transferred or distributed to a nonresident alien individual or foreign corporation in a transfer or distribution described in paragraph (e)(2)(i) of this section, the transferee or distributee will not be treated as having made an election under this section with respect to any amounts which would not, by reason of section 872(a) or 882(b) without reference to section 861(e), be includible in the transferee's or distributee's gross income. Moreover, in such case the election will not cause any income (not otherwise so treated) to be treated as income which is effectively connected with the conduct of a trade or business in the United States.

(f) **Manner and time of making or revoking an election**—(1) **Time for making the election.** The election under this section must be made not later than the time, including extensions thereof, prescribed by law for filing the income tax return for the first taxable year for which the election is to apply or by March 31, 1972, whichever is later.

(2) **Manner of making the election.** An election under this section must be made by filing with the income tax return (or an amended return) for the taxable year referred to in paragraph (f)(1) of this section a statement, signed by the taxpayer, to the effect that the election under section 861(e) is being made. The statement must—

(i) Set forth sufficient facts to identify the aircraft or vessel which is the subject of the election,

(ii) State that the aircraft or vessel was manufactured or constructed in the United States,

(iii) State that the aircraft or vessel is section 38 property described in § 1.861-9(b) which was leased to a United States person (as defined in section 7701 (a)(30) of the Code) pursuant to a lease entered into after August 15, 1971,

(iv) State that the electing taxpayer is the owner of the aircraft or vessel,

(v) State the lessee of the aircraft or vessel is not a member of a controlled group of corporations (as defined in section 1563) of which the taxpayer is a member,

(vi) Give the name and taxpayer identification number of the lessee of the aircraft or vessel, and

(vii) State that, to the best of the taxpayer's knowledge and belief, the aircraft or vessel will at all times be in the possession and under the control of a United States person not described in paragraph (f)(2)(v) of this section.

(3) **Revocation**—(i) Without consent of Commissioner. A taxpayer having made an election within the time prescribed in paragraph (f)(1) of this section may, within such time, revoke the election without the consent of the Commissioner. If the taxpayer revokes the election under this paragraph (f)(3)(i) of this section without the consent of the Commissioner, he must file an amended income tax return, or claim for credit or refund, where applicable, for any taxable year to which the revocation applies.

(ii) With consent of Commissioner. Except as otherwise provided in paragraph (f)(3)(i) of this section, an election made under this section is binding unless consent to revoke is obtained from the Commissioner. A request to revoke the election must be made in writing and addressed to the Assistant Commissioner of Internal Revenue (Technical), Attention: T:C:C:3, Washington, D. C. 20224. The request must include the name and address of the taxpayer and be signed by the taxpayer or his duly authorized representative. It must specify the taxable year or years for which the revocation is to be effective and must be filed at least 90 days prior to the time, but not including extensions thereof, prescribed by law for filing the income tax return for the first taxable year for which the revocation of the election is to be effective or by [90th day following the date of publication in the Federal Register of the regulations under section 861(e)] whichever is later. The request must specify the grounds which are considered to justify the revocation. The Commissioner may require such additional information as may be necessary in order to determine whether the proposed revocation will be permitted. Consent will generally not be given to revoke an election where such revocation would result in treating gross income with respect to the aircraft or vessel (including any gain from the sale or other disposition of such aircraft or vessel) as income from sources without the United States where, during the

Proposed Reg. § 1.861-9

period the election was in effect, there were losses with respect to such aircraft or vessel treated as losses from sources within the United States. 'A copy of the consent of the Commissioner to revoke must be attached to the taxpayer's income tax return (or amended return) for each taxable year affected by the revocation.

(4) **Certain factors not causing a termination or revocation of election.** The fact that after the aircraft or vessel is leased to a United States person described in paragraph (c) of this section such lessee subleases the aircraft or vessel to a person who is not a United States person, as so described, will not cause a termination or revocation of the election made under this section with respect to such aircraft or vessel. Thus, for example, the electing taxpayer is not relieved of any of the consequences of making the election merely by reason of the fact that by reason of a sublease the aircraft or vessel comes into the possession and under the control of a person who is not a United States person. Moreover, an election under this section is not terminated or revoked by reason of the fact that after the election is made the aircraft or vessel ceases to be section 38 property described in paragraph (b) of this section.

(5) **Effect of revocation.** If an election is revoked pursuant to this paragraph, the taxpayer shall be required to recompute the tax for its taxable year or years for which the revocation is effective, determined without reference to the provisions of section 861(e)(1).

(6) **Supplementary information.** Any taxpayer who filed a statement of election pursuant to § 12.1(b) of this chapter (T.D. 7158, 1972-1 C.B. 210, 37 F.R. 16) while such section was in effect must also file an additional statement setting forth any additional information required by paragraph (f)(2) of this section which was not furnished with the earlier statement. The additional statement must be filed on or before [the day which occurs one year after the date of publication in the Federal Register of the regulations under section 861(e)] with the district director, or the director of the regional service center, with whom the election was filed and must identify the election and the taxable year for which it was made.

TEMPORARY INCOME TAX REGULATIONS
UNDER REVENUE ACT OF 1971
(26 CFR Part 12)

Section 12.1, relating to election to treat income from certain aircraft and vessels as income from sources within the United States, is deleted.

Income from Foreign Sources

Section 1.862-1 is amended by adding a new paragraph (c) to read as follows:

§1.862-1 (Proposed Treasury Decision, published 7-31-75.) **Income specifically from sources without the United States.**

*   *   *   *   *   *   *   *   *   *   *   *

(c) **Income from certain aircraft or vessels.** For provisions permitting a taxpayer to elect to treat amounts of gross income attributable to certain aircraft or vessels as income from sources within the United States which would otherwise be treated as income from sources without the United States under paragraph (a) of this section, see § 1.861-9.

Section 1.864-5(d)(2) is amended as follows:
1. Subdivision (i) is revised.
2. Subdivision (ii) is revised by changing "30 percent" to "10 percent".
3. Subdivision (ii) is revised by inserting "(30 percent in the case of taxable years of foreign corporations ending before January 1, 1976)" immediately after "10 percent".

The revised provision reads as follows:

§ 1.864-5 (Proposed Treasury Decision, published 2-9-78). **Foreign source income effectively connected with U.S. business.**

* * * * * * * * * * *

(d) Excluded foreign source income. * * *

(2) Subpart F income of a controlled foreign corporation. * * *

(i) Foreign base company shipping income which is excluded under section 954(b)(2),

(ii) Foreign base company income amounting to less than 10 percent (30 percent in the case of taxable years of foreign corporations ending before January 1, 1976) of gross income which by reason of section 954(b)(3)(A) does not become subpart F income for the taxable year,

* * * * * * * * * * *

Nonresident Alien Individuals

Section 1.871-1 is amended by revising the caption of paragraph (b) and redesignating paragraph (d) as paragraph (c), as follows:

§ 1.871-1 (Proposed Treasury Decision, published 7-12-76.) **Classification and manner of taxing alien individuals.**

* *

(b) Nonresident alien individuals. * * *

(c) Effective date. * * *

Section 1.871-7 is amended by revising paragraphs (b) and (c) to read as follows:

§ 1.871-7 (Proposed Treasury Decision, published 7-12-76.) **Taxation of nonresident alien individuals not engaged in U.S. business.**

* *

(b) Fixed or determinable annual or periodical income—(1) In general. The tax of 30 percent imposed by section 871(a)(1) applies to the gross amount received from sources within the United States as fixed or determinable annual or periodical gains, profits, or income. Specific items of fixed or determinable annual or periodical income are enumerated in section 871(a)(1)(A) as interest (other than original issue discount described in paragraph (b)(2) of this section), dividends, rents, salaries, wages, premiums, annuities, compensations, remunerations, and emoluments, but other items of fixed or determinable annual or periodical gains, profits, or income are also subject to the tax, as, for instance, royalties, including royalties for the use of patents, copyrights, secret processes and formulas, and other like property. As to the determination of fixed or determinable annual or periodical income, see paragraph (a) of § 1.1441-2. For special rules treating gain on the disposition of section 306 stock as fixed or determinable annual or periodical income for purposes of section 871(a), see section 306(f) and paragraph (h) of § 1.306-3.

(2) Original issue discount. As used in paragraph (b)(1) of this section, the term "original issue discount" means original issue discount within the meaning of section 1232(b) on any bond, debenture, note, certificate, or other evidence of indebtedness. For this purpose, it is immaterial (i) whether the evidence of indebtedness is a capital asset in the hands of the taxpayer within the meaning of section 1221, (ii) whether it was held by the taxpayer more than 6 months, or (iii) whether it was issued by a government or political subdivision thereof, or by a corporation or any other person.

(c) Other income and gains—(1) Items subject to tax. The tax of 30 percent im-

Proposed Reg. § 1.871-7

posed by section 871(a)(1) also applies to the following gains rceived during the taxable year from sources within the United States:

(i) Gains described in section 402(a)(2), relating to the treatment of total distributions from certain employees' trusts; section 403(a)(2), relating to treatment of certain payments under certain employee annuity plans; and section 631(b) or (c), relating to treatment of gain on the disposal of timber, coal, or iron ore with a retained economic interest;

(ii) In the case of—

(A) Bonds or other evidences of indebtedness issued after September 28, 1965, and before April 1, 1972, amounts which, by applying the principles of section 1232(a)(2)(B), are considered as gain from the sale or exchange of property which is not a capital asset and, in the case of corporate obligations issued after May 27, 1969, and before April 1, 1972, amounts which, by applying the principles of section 1232(a)(2)(B), would be considered as gain from the sale or exchange of property which is not a capital asset but for the fact the obligations were issued after May 27, 1969,

(B) Bonds or other evidences of indebtedness issued after March 31, 1972, which are payable more than 6 months from the date of original issue (without regard to the period held by the taxpayer), amounts which, by applying the principles of section 1232(a)(2)(B), are considered as gain from the sale or exchange of property which is not a capital asset and, in the case of corporate obligations, amounts which, by applying the principles of section 1232(a)(2)(B), would be considered as gain from the sale or exchange of property which is not a capital asset but for the fact such obligations were issued after May 27, 1969, and

(C) The payment of interest on an obligation described in paragraph (c)(1)(ii)(B) of this section, an amount equal to the original issue discount accrued on such obligation since the last payment of interest thereon, except that the tax imposed by reason of this paragraph (c)(1)(ii)(C) may not exceed the amount of such interest payment less the tax imposed thereon under the rules of paragraph (b) of this section;

(iii) Gains on transfers described in section 1235, relating to certain transfers of patent rights, made on or before October 4, 1966; and

(iv) Gains from the sale or exchange after October 4, 1966, of patents, copyrights, secret processes and formulas, good will, trademarks, trade brands, franchises, or other like property, or of any interest in any such property, to the extent the gains are from payments (whether in a lump sum or in installments) which are contingent on the productivity, use, or disposition of the property or interest sold or exchanged, or from payments which are treated under section 871(e) and §1.871-11 as being so contingent.

(2) *Nonapplication of 183-day rule.* The provisions of section 871(a)(2), relating to gains from the sale or exchange of capital assets, and paragraph (d)(2) of this section do not apply to the gains described in this paragraph; as a consequence, the taxpayer receiving gains described in paragraph (c)(1) of this section during a taxable year is subject to the tax of 30 percent thereon without regard to the 183-day rule contained in such provisions.

(3) *Determination of amount of gain.* The tax of 30 percent imposed upon the gains described in paragraph (c)(1) of this section applies to the full amount of the gains and is determined (i) without regard to the alternative tax imposed by section 1201(b) upon the excess of the net long-term capital gain over the net short-term capital loss; (ii) without regard to the deduction allowed by section 1202 in respect of capital gains; (iii) without regard to section 1231, relating to property used in the trade or business and involuntary conversions; and (iv) whether or not any property from which the gains are derived is a capital asset in the hands of the taxpayer.

(4) *Special rules applicable to original issue discount*—(i) *In general.* Section 871(a)(1)(C) and paragraph (c)(1)(ii) of this section apply, subject to the other limitations prescribed therein and in this paragraph (c)(4), to all bonds or other evidences of indebtedness which are issued at a discount within the meaning of paragraph (b)(2) of this section. Thus, in applying section 871(a)(1)(C), the provisions of section 1232(a)(2)(B) are deemed to apply to assets which are not capital assets, to obligations which are not held

by the taxpayer for more than 6 months, and to obligations not issued by a corporation or by a government or political subdivision thereof.

(ii) *Sale, exchange, or retirement of bond issued before April 1, 1972.* Section 871(a)(1)(C)(i) and paragraph (c)(1)(ii)(A) of this section apply only to amounts derived from the sale, exchange, or retirement of a bond or other evidence of indebtedness, whether or not interest-bearing, which was issued after September 28, 1965, and before April 1, 1972, and which, at the time of such sale, exchange, or retirement, had been held by the taxpayer more than 6 months. In applying section 871(a)(1)(C)(i), the provisions of section 1232(a)(2)(B) are deemed to apply to bonds or other evidences of indebtedness which were issued by a corporation after May 27, 1969, and before April 1, 1972.

(iii) *Sale, exchange, or retirement of bond issued after March 31, 1972.* Section 871(a)(1)(C)(ii) and paragraph (c)(1)(ii)(B) of this section apply only to amounts derived from the sale, exchange, or retirement of a bond or other evidence of indebtedness, whether or not interest-bearing and whether or not held by the taxpayer more than 6 months, which was issued after March 31, 1972, and is payable more than 6 months from the date of original issue. In applying section 871(a)(1)(C)(ii), the provisions of section 1232(a)(2)(B) are deemed to apply to bonds or other evidences of indebtedness which, at the time of the sale, exchange, or retirement, had been held by the taxpayer not more than 6 months and to bonds or other evidences of indebtedness which were issued by a corporation after May 27, 1969. Pursuant to section 1232(a)(2)(D) and §1.1232-3(e), section 871(a)(1)(C)(ii) and paragraph (c)(1)(ii)(B) of this section do not apply to any amount previously includible in gross income. Thus, for example, any amount treated under paragraph (c)(4)(v) of this section as included in gross income in respect of original issue discount on which tax has been imposed under section 871(a)(1)(C)(iii) and paragraph (c)(1)(ii)(C) of this section at the time of an interest payment on an obligation shall not again be subject to tax under section 871(a)(1)(C)(ii) and paragraph (c)(1)(ii)(B) of this section when such obligation is sold, exchanged, or retired.

(iv) *Interest payments on bonds issued after March 31, 1972.* Section 871(a)(1)(iii) and paragraph (c)(1)(ii)(C) of this section apply only when an interest payment is received on an interest-bearing bond or other evidence of indebtedness to which section 871(a)(1)(C)(ii) and paragraph (c)(1)(ii)(B) of this section apply. In addition to the 30-percent tax imposed on such interest under section 871(a)(1)A) and paragraph (b) of this section, an additional 30-percent tax is imposed under section 871(a)(1)(C)(iii) and paragraph (c)(1)(ii)(C) of this section on the original issue discount accrued on such bond or other evidence of indebtedness since the last payment of interest thereon, as determined under paragraph (c)(4)(vi) of this section, except that such additional tax may not exceed the amount of the interest payment less the 30-percent tax imposed on such interest under section 871(a)(1)(A) and paragraph (b) of this section.

(v) *Treatment of discount as includible in gross income.* (A) For purposes of applying paragraph (c)(4)(iii) of this section with respect to any bond or other evidence of indebtedness, an amount shall be treated as having been included in gross income which is equal to the amount obtained by dividing the amount of the additional 30-percent tax imposed under section 871(a)(1)(c)(iii) and paragraph (c)(1)(ii)(C) of this section on the accrued original issue discount on such bond or other evidence of indebtedness by 30 percent. If the additional 30-percent tax on such accrued original issue discount is reduced by an income tax convention to which the United States is a party, the amount which shall be treated as having been included in gross income shall be the amount of such reduced additional tax divided by such reduced rate of tax. If no tax is imposed under section 871(a)(1)(C)(iii) and paragraph (c)(1)(ii)(C) on the accrued original issue discount by reason of an exemption from tax under an income tax convention to which the United States is a party, the full amount of the accrued original issue discount which is so exempt from tax shall be treated as having been included in gross income.

(B) Pursuant to the principles of section 1232(a)(3)(E) and §1.1232-3A(c), the basis of the bond or other evidence of indebtedness in the hands of the holder thereof shall be increased by an amount with respect to such bond or other evidence of indebtedness

Proposed Reg. §1.871-7

63,784 Proposed Regulations 6-1-78

which is treated as having been included in gross income pursuant to this paragraph (c)(4)(v).

(vi) *Accrual of original issue discount.* For purposes of paragraph (c)(4)(iv) of this section, the original issue discount accrued on a bond or other evidence of indebtedness since the last payment of interest thereon is an amount equal to the ratable monthly portion of original issue discount, determined by applying the principles of section 1232(a)(3)(A) and §1.1232-3A(a)(2), multiplied by the sum of the number of complete months and any fractional part of a month occurring since the later of (A) the last payment of interest on the bond or other evidence of indebtedness or (B) the day on which the taxpayer purchased (within the meaning of §1.1232-3A(a)(4)) such bond or other evidence of indebtedness.

(vii) *Illustrations.* The application of this paragraph (c)(4) may be illustrated by the following examples:

Example (1). On January 1, 1973, R, a nonresident alien individual using the calendar year as the taxable year and the cash receipts and disbursements method of accounting, purchases at original issue, for cash of $7,600, M Corporation's 10-year, 5-percent bond which has a stated redemption price of $10,000 and an original issue date of January 1, 1973. Under the terms of the bond M is to make interest payments of $250 on June 30 and December 31 of each year. On July 1, 1973, R receives his first interest payment of $250, and tax of $75 ($250 × 30%) is imposed thereon under section 871(a)(1)(A) and paragraph (b) of this section. By applying the principles of section 1232(a)(3)(A) the ratable monthly portion of original issue discount is $20 ([$10,000 − $7,600] ÷ 120), and the amount accrued from the date of purchase is $120 ($20 × 6). The tax imposed under section 871(a)(1)(C)(iii) and paragraph (c)(1)(ii)(C) of this section is $36 ($120 × 30%), but not to exceed $175 ($250 − $75). Accordingly, a total tax of $111 ($75 + $36) is imposed under section 871(a)(1)(A) and (C)(iii) upon the receipt of interest by R.

Example (2). Assume the same facts as in example (1). Assume further that on December 31, 1973, M makes an interest payment of only $40. On this $40 payment of interest a tax of $12 ($40 × 30%) is imposed under section 871(a)(1)(A) and paragraph (b) of this section. By applying the principles of section 1232(a)(3)(A), the ratable monthly portion of original issue discount is $20, and the amount accrued from the last payment of interest on June 30, 1973, is $120 ($20 × 6). The tax imposed under section 871(a)(1)(C)(iii) and paragraph (c)(1)(ii)(C) of this section is $36 ($120 × 30%), but not to exceed $28 ($40 − $12). Accordingly, a total tax of $40 ($12 + $28) is imposed under section 871(a)(1)(A) and (C)(iii) upon the receipt of interest by R. The amount of original issue discount which is treated as included in R's gross income by reason of the interest payment on December 31, 1973, is $93.33 ($28 ÷ 30%). The $26.67 balance of the original issue discount ($120 − $93.33) will be subject to tax under section 871(a)(1)(C)(ii) and paragraph (c)(1)(ii)(B) of this section when the M bond is sold, exchanged, or retired.

Example (3). (a) Assume the same facts as in example (2). Assume further that on July 1, 1974, M makes an interest payment of $250 to R and that immediately thereafter R sells the bond to a U.S. citizen for $8,000. At no time during 1974 is R present in the United States. The assumption is also made that, at the time of original issue, there was no intention to call the bond before maturity. On this $250 payment of interest a tax of $75 ($250 × 30%) is imposed under section 871(a)(1)(A) and paragraph (b) of this section. By applying the principles of section 1232(a)(3)(A), the ratable monthly portion of original issue discount is $20, and the amount accrued from the last payment of interest on December 31, 1973, is $120 ($20 × 6). The tax imposed in 1974 under section 871(a)(1)(C)(iii) and paragraph (c)(1)(ii)(C) of this section is $36 ($120 × 30%), but not to exceed $175 ($250 − $75).

(b) The bond was held by R for 18 full months before it was sold. The number of complete months from the date of issue to date of maturity is 120 (10 years). The original issue discount on the bond is $2,400 ($10,000 less $7,600), as determined under section 1232(b). Accordingly, the proportionate part of the original issue discount attributable to the period of R's ownership is $360 ($2,400 × 18/120), which is the maximum amount includible by R as ordinary income. On the sale of the bond R realizes total gain of $66.67 ($8,000 − [$7,600 + $120 + $93.33 + $120]) is subject to tax under section 871(a)(1)(C)(ii) and paragraph (c)(1)(ii)(B) of this section, and the tax thereon under such provisions is $8 ($26.67 × 30%).

(c) Accordingly, in 1974 a total tax of $119 ($75 + $36 + $8) is imposed under section 871(a)(1)(A) and (C)(ii) and (iii) upon the interest, accrued original issue discount, and gain realized by R from the M bond. The remaining gain of $40 ($66.67 − $26.67) is treated as long-term capital gain which is not subject to tax under section 871(a)(1).

* *

Foreign Corporations

Section 1.881-1(e)(4)(i) is amended to read as follows:

§1.881-1 (Proposed Treasury Decision, published 2-9-78.) **Manner of taxing foreign corporations.**

* * * * * * * * * * * *

(e) Other provisions applicable to foreign corporations. * * *

(4) Controlled foreign corporations—(i) Subpart F income and increase of earnings invested in U.S. property. For the mandatory inclusion in the gross income of the U.S. shareholders of the subpart F income, of the previously excluded subpart F income withdrawn from investment in less developed countries, of the previously excluded subpart F income withdrawn from investment in foreign base company shipping operations, and of the increase in earnings invested in U.S. property, of a controlled foreign corporation, see sections 951 through 964, and the regulations thereunder.

* * * * * * * * * * * *

Section 1.881-2 is amended by revising paragraphs (b) and (c) to read as follows:

§1.881-2 (Proposed Treasury Decision, published 7-12-76.) **Taxation of foreign corporations not engaged in U.S. business.**

* *

(b) Fixed or determinable annual or periodical income—(1) In general. The tax of 30 percent imposed by section 881(a) applies to the gross amount received from sources within the United States as fixed or determinable annual or periodical gains, profits, or income. Specific items of fixed or determinable annual or periodical income are enumerated in section 881(a)(1) as interest (other than original issue discount described in paragraph (b)(2) of this section), dividends, rents, salaries, wages, premiums, annuities, compensations, remunerations, and emoluments, but other items of fixed or determinable annual or periodical gains, profits, or income are also subject to the tax, as, for instance, royalties, including royalties for the use of patents, copyrights, secret processes and formulas, and other like property. As to the determination of fixed or determinable annual or periodical income, see paragraph (a) of §1.1441-2. For special rules treating gain on the disposition of section 306 stock as fixed or determinable annual or periodical income for purposes of section 881(a), see section 306(f) and paragraph (h) of §1.306-3.

(2) Original issue discount. As used in paragraph (b)(1) of this section, the term "original issue discount" means original issue discount within the meaning of section 1232(b) on any bond, debenture, note, certificate, or other evidence of indebtedness. For this purpose, it is immaterial (i) whether the evidence of indebtedness is a capital asset in the hands of the taxpayer within the meaning of section 1221, (ii) whether it was held by the taxpayer more than 6 months, or (iii) whether it was issued by a government or political subdivision thereof, or by a corporation or any other person.

Proposed Reg. §1.881-2

(c) **Other income and gains—(1) Items subject to tax.** The tax of 30 percent imposed by section 881(a) also applies to the following gains received during the taxable year from sources within the United States:

(i) Gains described in section 631(b) or (c), relating to the treatment of gain on the disposal of timber, coal, or iron ore with a retained economic interest;

(ii) In the case of—

(A) Bonds or other evidences of indebtedness issued after September 28, 1965, and before April 1, 1972, amounts which, by applying the principles of section 1232(a)(2)(B), are considered as gain from the sale or exchange of property which is not a capital asset and, in the case of corporate obligations issued after May 27, 1969, and before April 1, 1972, amounts which, by applying the principles of section 1232(a)(2)(B), would be considered as gain from the sale or exchange of property which is not a capital asset but for the fact the obligations were issued after May 27, 1969,

(B) Bonds or other evidences of indebtedness issued after March 31, 1972, which are payable more than 6 months from the date or original issue (without regard to the period held by the taxpayer), amounts which, by applying the principles of section 1232(a)(2)(B), are considered as gain from the sale or exchange of property which is not a capital asset and, in the case of corporate obligations, amounts which, by applying the principles of section 1232(a)(2)(B), would be considered as gain from the sale or exchange of property which is not a capital asset but for the fact such obligations were issued after May 27, 1969, and

(C) The payment of interest on an obligation described in paragraph (c)(1)(ii)(B) of this section, an amount equal to the original issue discount accrued on such obligation since the last payment of interest thereon, except that the tax imposed by reason of this paragraph (c)(1)(ii)(C) may not exceed the amount of such interest payment less the tax imposed thereon under the rules of paragraph (b) of this section; and

(iii) Gains from the sale or exchange after October 4, 1966, of patents, copyrights, secret processes and formulas, good will, trademarks, trade brands, franchises, or other like property, or of any interest in any such property, to the extent the gains are from payments (whether in a lump sum or in installments) which are contingent on the productivity, use, or disposition of the property or interest sold or exchanged, or from payments which are treated under section 871(e) and §1.871-11 as being so contingent.

(2) **Determination of amount of gain.** The tax of 30 percent imposed upon the gains described in paragraph (c)(1) of this section applies to the full amount of the gains and is determined (i) without regard to the alternative tax imposed by section 1201 (a) upon the excess of the net long-term capital gain over the net short-term capital loss; (ii) without regard to section 1231, relating to property used in the trade or business and involuntary conversions; and (iii) whether or not any property from which the gains are derived is a capital asset in the hands of the taxpayer.

(3) **Special rules applicable to original issue discount.** For special rules and examples to be applied for purposes of determining the 30-percent tax on amounts described in section 881(a)(3) and paragraph (c)(1)(ii) of this section, see paragraph (c)(4) of §1.871-7.

* *

Foreign Tax Credit

Section 1.901-1 is amended by revising paragraph (f) to read as follows:

§ 1.901-1 (Proposed Treasury Decision, published 12-30-70.) **Allowance of credit for taxes.**

* * * * * * * * * * * * *

(f) **Taxes against which credit not allowed.** The credit for taxes shall be allowed only against the tax imposed by chapter 1 of the Code, but it shall not be allowed against the following taxes imposed under that chapter:

(1) The minimum tax for tax preferences imposed by section 56;

(2) The tax on accumulated earnings imposed by section 531;

(3) The personal holding company tax imposed by section 541;

(4) The additional tax relating to war loss recoveries imposed under section 1333; and

(5) The additional tax relating to recoveries of foreign expropriation losses, losses under section 1351.

* * * * * * * * * * * * *

Section 1.901-1 is amended by revising paragraph (f) to read as follows:

§ 1.901-1. (Proposed Treasury Decision, published 4-21-75) **Allowance of credit for taxes.**

* * * * * * * * * * *

(f) **Taxes against which credit not allowed.**—The credit for taxes shall be allowed only against the tax imposed by chapter 1 of the Code, but it shall not be allowed against the following taxes imposed under that chapter:

(1) The minimum tax for tax preferences imposed by section 56;

(2) The 10 percent tax on premature distributions to owner-employees imposed by section 72(m)(5)(B);

(3) The tax on lump sum distributions imposed by section 402(e);

(4) The additional tax on income from certain retirement accounts imposed by section 408(f);

(5) The tax on accumulated earnings imposed by section 531;

(6) The personal holding company tax imposed by section 541;

(7) The additional tax relating to war loss recoveries imposed by section 1333; and

(8) The additional tax relating to recoveries of foreign expropriation losses imposed by section 1351.

* * * * * * * * * * *

Controlled Foreign Corporations

Section 1.951-1 is amended as follows:

1. Paragraph (a)(2) is revised as follows:

a. Subdivision (ii) is revised by deleting "paragraph (c)" and inserting in lieu thereof "paragraph (c)(1)", and by deleting the word "and" at the end thereof.

b. Subdivision (iii) is redesignated as subdivision (iv).

c. Immediately after subdivision (ii) new subdivision (iii) is added.

2. Paragraph (b)(1) is revised by deleting "paragraph (a)(1)" and inserting in lieu thereof "paragraph (a)(2)(i)".

3. Paragraph (c) is revised.

4. Paragraph (d) is revised by deleting "paragraph (a)(3)" both times it appears and inserting in lieu thereof "paragraph (a)(2)(iv)".

5. Paragraph (e)(1) is revised.

The added and revised provisions read as follows:

§ 1.951-1 (Proposed Treasury Decision, published 2-9-78.) **Amounts included in gross income of United States shareholders.**

(a) **In general.** * * *

(2) * * *

(iii) Such shareholder's pro rata share (determined under paragraph (c)(2) of this section) of the corporation's previously excluded subpart F income withdrawn from investment in foreign base company shipping operations for such taxable year of the corporation, and

* * * * * * * * * * * *

Proposed Reg. § 1.951-1

(c) **Limitation on a United States shareholder's pro rata share of previously excluded subpart F income withdrawn from investments—(1) Investments in less developed countries.** For purposes of paragraph (a)(2)(ii) of this section, a United States shareholder's pro rata share (determined in accordance with the rules of paragraph (e) of this section) of the foreign corporation's previously excluded subpart F income withdrawn from investment in less developed countries for the taxable year of such corporation shall not exceed an amount which bears the same ratio to such shareholder's pro rata share of such income withdrawn (as determined under section 955(a)(3), as in effect before the enactment of the Tax Reduction Act of 1975, and paragraph (c) of §1.955-1) for such taxable year as the part of such year during which such corporation is a controlled foreign corporation bears to the entire taxable year. See paragraph (c)(2) of §1.955-1 for a special rule applicable to exclusions and withdrawals occurring before the date on which the United States shareholder acquires his stock.

(2) **Investments in foreign base company shipping operations.** For purposes of paragraph (a)(2)(iii) of this section, a United States shareholder's pro rata share (determined in accordance with the rules of paragraph (e) of this section) of the foreign corporation's previously excluded subpart F income withdrawn from investment in foreign base company shipping operations for the taxable year of such corporation shall not exceed an amount which bears the same ratio to such shareholder's pro rata share of such income withdrawn (as determined under section 955(a)(3) and paragraph (c) of §1.955A-1) for such taxable year as the part of such year during which such corporation is a controlled foreign corporation bears to the entire taxable year. See paragraph (c)(2) of §1.955A-1 for a special rule applicable to exclusions and withdrawals occurring before the date on which the United States shareholder acquires his stock.

* * * * * * * * * * *

(e) **"Pro rata share" defined—(1) In general.** For purposes of paragraphs (b), (c), and (d) of this section, a United States shareholder's pro rata share of a controlled foreign corporation's subpart F income, previously excluded subpart F income withdrawn from investment in less developed countries, previously excluded subpart F income withdrawn from investment in foreign base company shipping operations, or increase in earnings invested in United States property, respectively, for any taxable year is his pro rata share determined under paragraph (a) of §1.952-1, paragraph (c) of §1.955-1, paragraph (c) of §1.955A-1, or paragraph (c) of §1.956-1, respectively.

* * * * * * * * * * *

Section 1.951-3 is amended as follows:

1. Example (4) is revised as follows:
a. Paragraph (a) is revised by deleting "paragraph (b)(1) of §1.954-1" in the third sentence and inserting in lieu thereof "26 CFR 1.954-1(b)(1) (Rev. as of Apr. 1, 1975)" and by inserting in the sixth sentence, "as in effect before the enactment of the Tax Reduction Act of 1975," immediately after "section 955(a)".
b. A new paragraph (c) is added.

2. Example (5) is revised by deleting "paragraph (a)(3)" each time it appears in paragraphs (a) and (b) and inserting in lieu thereof "paragraph (a)(2)(iv)"

The added provision reads as follows:

§1.951-3 (Proposed Treasury Decision, published 2-9-78.) **Coordination of subpart F with foreign personal holding company provisions.**

* * * * * * * * * * *

Example (4). * * *

(c) The principles of this example also apply to withdrawals (determined under section 955(a), as in effect before the enactment of the Tax Reduction Act of 1975) of previously excluded subpart F income from investment in less developed countries effected after the effective date of such Act, and to withdrawals (determined under section 955(a), as amended by such Act) of previously excluded subpart F income from investment in foreign base company shipping operations.

* * * * * * * * * * *

Controlled Foreign Corporations

Section 1.952-1 is amended as follows:

1. Paragraph (a)(2) is revised by deleting "1.954-5)." and inserting in lieu thereof "1.954-7).".
2. Paragraph (b)(1) is revised.

§1.952-1 (Proposed Treasury Decision, published 2-9-78.) **Subpart F income defined.**

* * * * * * * * * * *

(b) Exclusion of U.S. income—(1) Taxable years beginning before January 1, 1967. For rules applicable to taxable years beginning before January 1, 1967, see 26 CFR 1.952-1(b)(1) (Rev. as of April 1, 1975).

* *

Section 1.952-2(c)(2)(v) and (c)(5)(i) is amended to read as follows:

§1.952-2 (Proposed Treasury Decision, published 8-9-76 and 2-9-78.) Determination of gross income and taxable income of a foreign corporation.

* * * * * * * * * * *

(c) **Special rules for purposes of this section.** * * *

(2) **Application of principles of §1.964-1.** * * *

(v) Exchange gain or loss. (a) Exchange gain or loss, determined in accordance with the principles of §1.964-1(e), shall be taken into account for purposes of determining gross income and taxable income.

(b) Exchange gain or loss shall be treated as foreign base company shipping income (or as a deduction allocable thereto) to the extent that it is attributable to foreign base company shipping operations. The extent to which exchange gain or loss is attributable to foreign base company shipping operations may be determined under any reasonable method which is consistently applied from year to year. For example, the extent to which the exchange gain or loss is attributable to foreign base company shipping operations may be determined on the basis of the ratio which the foreign base company shipping income of the corporation for the taxable year bears to its total gross income for the taxable year, such ratio to be determined without regard to this subdivision (v).

(c) The remainder of the exchange gain or loss shall be allocated between subpart F income and non-subpart F income under any reasonable method which is consistently applied from year to year. For example, such remainder may be allocated to subpart F income in the same ratio that the gross subpart F income (exclusive of foreign base company shipping income) of the corporation for the taxable year bears to its total gross income (exclusive of foreign base company shipping income) for the taxable year, such ratio to be determined without regard to this subdivision (v).

* * * * * * * * * * * *

(5) **Treatment of capital loss and net operating loss.** * * *

(i) Capital loss carryback and carryover. The capital loss carryback and carryover provided by section 1212(a) shall not be allowed.

* * * * * * * * * * *

Immediately after § 1.952-2 new § 1.952-3 is added to read as follows:

§1.952-3 (Proposed Treasury Decision, published 8-9-76.) **Order of computations.**

(a) **Scope—(1) In general.** This section describes and illustrates the computations which a United States shareholder of a controlled foreign corporation is required to make in connection with the application of section 954 and the subsequent application of section 952. However, this section does not apply to any controlled foreign corporation to which section 953 (relating to income from insurance of United States risks) applies. For rules relating to the application of section 953 and the relationship between sections 953 and 954, see the regulations under section 953.

(2) **Effective date.** This section applies to taxable years of foreign corporations beginning after December 31, 1975, and to taxable years of United States shareholders (as defined in section 951 (b)) within which or with which such taxable years of such foreign corporations end.

(b) **General rule.** Except as provided in paragraph (c) of this section, a United States shareholder must determine the subpart F income of a controlled foreign corporation to which this section applies in the following manner:

(1) **Step 1.** Determine gross income under §1.952-2, and (if applicable) §1.959-2 (relating to the exclusion of certain dividends from gross income).

(2) **Step 2.** Determine net foreign base company shipping income as follows:

(i) First. Determine foreign base company shipping income under §1.954-6;

(ii) Second. Exclude from foreign base company shipping income the items thereof which are excluded from subpart F income under §1.952-1(b)(2) (relating to the exclusion of United States income from subpart F income), or which are excluded from foreign base company income under §1.954-1(b)(2) and (3) (relating, respectively, to chain rule and to corporation not availed of to reduce tax);

(iii) Third. Reduce the balance by the deductions allocable thereto under §1.954-1(c); and

(iv) Fourth. Reduce the remaining balance by the increase in qualified investments in foreign base company shipping operations as determined under §1.954-7 (see §1.954-1(b)(1)).

(3) **Step 3.** Determine net foreign personal holding company income, net foreign base company sales income, and net foreign base company services income as follows:

(i) First. Determine foreign personal holding company income under §1.954-2, foreign base company sales income under §1.954-3, and foreign base company services income under §1.954-4;

(ii) Second. Exclude from each such type of income the items thereof which are excluded from subpart F income under §1.952-1(b)(2) or which are excluded from foreign base company income under §1.954-1(b)(2) and (3);

(iii) Third. Reduce the balance of each such type of income by the deductions allocable thereto under §1.954-1(c).

(4) **Step 4.** The foreign base company income is the sum of the net amounts determined in subparagraphs (2) and (3) of this paragraph.

(5) **Step 5.** The subpart F income is the lesser of—

(i) The sum of (A) the foreign base company income as determined under subparagraph (4) of this paragraph and (B) the exchange gain (or loss) allocable (under §1.952-2(c)(2)(v)(c)) to subpart F income; or

(ii) The earnings and profits limitation stated in section 952(c) (see §1.952-1(c)).

(6) **Step 6.** The subpart F income of an export trade corporation (as defined in section 971(a)) must be reduced as provided in §1.970-1(b).

(c) **Section 954(b)(3) ratio less than 10 percent or more than 70 percent—(1) Less than 10 percent.** Under §1.954-1(d)(1), if the foreign base company income of a controlled foreign corporation to which this section applies (determined as provided in subparagraph (3) of this paragraph) is less than 10 percent of the gross income (determined as provided in paragraph (b)(1) of this section), the subpart F income of that controlled foreign corporation is zero.

(2) **More than 70 percent.** Under §1.954-1(d)(2), if the foreign base company income of a controlled foreign corporation to which this section applies (determined as provided in subparagraph (3) of this paragraph) is more than 70 percent of the gross income (de-

termined as provided in paragraph (b)(1) of this section), a United States shareholder must determine the subpart F income of that controlled foreign corporation in the following manner:

(i) Step 1. The foreign base company income is the gross income (determined as provided in paragraph (b)(1) of this section), reduced as follows:

(A) First, exclude the items thereof which are excluded from subpart F income under §1.952-1(b)(2) or which are excluded from foreign base company income under §1.954-1(b)(3);

(B) Second, reduce the balance by the deductions allocable thereto under §1.954-1(c);

(C) Third, reduce the remaining balance by the amount of the reinvested shipping income determined as provided in subparagraph (4) of this paragraph.

(ii) Step 2. The subpart F income is the lesser of—

(A) The foreign base company income as determined under subdivision (i) of this subparagraph; or

[The page following this is 63,823]

Proposed Reg. §1.952-3

(B) The limitation stated in section 952(c) (see §1.952-1(c)).

(iii) Step 3. The subpart F income of an export trade corporation (as defined in section 971(a)) must be reduced as provided in §1.970-1(b).

(3) **Foreign base company income.** Solely for purposes of subparagraphs (1) and (2) of this paragraph, the foreign base company income of a controlled foreign corporation shall be the sum of the balances determined after applying paragraph (b)(2)(ii) and (3)(ii) of this section.

(4) **Reinvested shipping income.** Solely for purposes of subparagraph (2)(i)(C) of this paragraph, the amount of reinvested shipping income of a controlled foreign corporation shall be determined as follows:

(i) Step 1. Determine foreign base company shipping income under §1.954-6;

(ii) Step 2. Exclude from foreign base company shipping income the items thereof which are excluded from subpart F income under §1.952-1(b)(2) or which are excluded from foreign base company income under §1.954-1(b)(3);

(iii) Step 3. Reduce the balance by the deductions allocable thereto under §1.954-1(c);

(iv) Step 4. The amount of reinvested shipping income is the lesser of—
(A) The remaining balance, or
(B) The increase in qualified investments in foreign base company shipping operations as determined under §1.954-7.

(d) **Illustrations.** The application of this section may be illustrated by the following examples, in each of which it is assumed that A is a United States shareholder who owns stock in a controlled foreign corporation on December 31, 1976, the corporation uses the calendar year as the taxable year, and for 1976, the corporation has no income derived from the insurance of United States risks (within the meaning of section 953(a)) and is not an export trade corporation (within the meaning of section 971(a)):

Example (1). (a) For 1976, P Corporation has no foreign base company sales income and no foreign base company shipping income.

(b) A must apply the test prescribed by section 954(b)(3) to P's taxable year 1976 as follows, based on the facts shown in the following table

(1) Gross income $1,000

(2) (i) Foreign personal holding company income.......................... $200
    (ii) Less: items of foreign personal holding company income excluded under §§1.952-1(b)(2), 1.954-1(b)(2), and §1.954-1(b)(3) 10
    (iii) Balance 190

(3) (i) Foreign base company services income $450
    (ii) Less: items of foreign base company services income excluded under §§1.952-1(b)(2) and 1.954-1(b)(3) 100
    (iii) Balance 350

(4) Tentative foreign base company income (line (2) (iii) plus line (3) (iii)).............................. $ 540

(5) Section 954(b)(3) ratio (line 4 ÷ line (1)) .... 54 percent

(c) Since the section 954(b)(3) ratio is not less than 10 percent nor more than 70 per-

Proposed Reg. §1.952-3

cent, A must determine P's subpart F income for 1976 as follows, based on the facts shown in the following table:

(1) Gross income $1,000

(2) (i) Foreign personal holding company income 200
    (ii) Less: items of foreign personal holding company income excluded under §§1.952-1(b)(2), 1.954-1(b)(2), and 1.954-1(b)(3) 10
    (iii) Balance 190
    (iv) Less: deductions allocable to balance 170
    (v) Net foreign personal holding company income 20

(3) (i) Foreign base company services income 450
    (ii) Less: items of foreign base company services income excluded under §§1.952-1(b)(2) and 1.954-1(b)(3) 100
    (iii) Balance 350
    (iv) Less: deductions allocable to balance 250
    (v) Net foreign base company services income 100

(4) Subpart F income: (i) Foreign base company income (line (2) (v) plus line (3) (v)) 120
    (ii) Exchange gain attributable to subpart F income 7
    (iii) Tentative subpart F income (line (i) plus line (ii)) .. 127
    (iv) Earnings and profits limitation 225
    (v) Subpart F income (lesser of lines (iii) and (iv)) 127

Example (2). (a) For 1976, N Corporation has no foreign personal holding company income, no foreign base company sales income, and no foreign base company services income. However, N receives $100 of dividends from another controlled foreign corporation which is excluded from foreign base company income under §1.954-1(b)(2) as attributable to foreign base company shipping income, but which is not excluded from gross income under section 959(b).

(b) A must apply the test prescribed by section 954(b)(3) to N's taxable year 1976 as follows, based on the facts shown in the following table:

(1) Gross income $1,000

(2) (i) Foreign base company shipping income 1,000
    (ii) Less: items of foreign base company shipping income excluded under §§1.952-1(b)(2), 1.954-1(b)(2), and 1.954-1(b)(3) 100
    (iii) Balance 900

(3) Section 954(b)(3) ratio (line (2) (iii) ÷ line (1)) .... 90 percent

(c) Since the section 954(b)(3) ratio exceeds 70 percent, A must determine the amount of N's reinvested shipping income for 1976 as follows, based on the facts shown in the following table:

(1) Foreign base company shipping income $1,000
(2) Less: items of foreign base company shipping income excluded under §§1.952-1(b)(2) and 1.954-1(b)(3) 0
(3) Balance 1,000
(4) Less: deductions allocable to balance 750

(5) Remaining balance .... $ 250

(6) Increase in qualified investments in foreign base company shipping
    operations 250
(7) Reinvested shipping income (lesser of lines (5) and (6)) 250

(d) A must determine N's subpart F income for 1976 as follows, based on the facts shown in the following table:

(1) (i)   Gross income $1,000
    (ii) Less: items of gross income excluded under §§1.952-1(b)(2)
          and 1.954-1(b)(3)... 0

    (iii) Balance 1,000
    (iv) Less: deductions allocable to balance 750

    (v)   Remaining balance .... $ 250
    (vi) Less: reinvested shipping income 250

    (vii) Foreign base company income 0

(2) Earnings and profits limitation.. 1,200
(3) Subpart F income (lesser of lines (1) (vii) and (2)) 0

Example (3). (a) For 1976, M Corporation has no foreign personal holding company income, no foreign base company sales income, and no foreign base company services income.

(b) A must apply the test prescribed by section 954(b)(3) to M's taxable year 1976 as follows, based on the facts shown in the following table:

(1) Gross income $1,000

(2) (i)   Foreign base company shipping income 650
    (ii) Less: items of foreign base company shipping income
          excluded under §§1.952-1(b)(2), 1.954-1(b)(2), and
          1.954-1(b)(3) 0

    (iii) Balance 650

(3) Section 954(b)(3) ratio (line (2) (iii) ÷ line (1))................. 65 percent

(c) Since the section 954(b)(3) ratio is not less than 10 percent nor more than 70 percent, A must determine M's subpart F income for 1976 as follows, based on the facts shown in the following table:

(1) Gross income $1,000

(2) Net foreign base company shipping income: (i) Foreign base
    company shipping income... 650
    (ii) Less: items of foreign base company shipping income
          excluded under §§1.952-1(b)(2), 1.954-1(b)(2), and
          1.954-1(b)(3) 0

    (iii) Balance 650
    (iv) Less: deductions allocable to balance 550

    (v)   Remaining balance... 100
    (vi) Less: increase in qualified investments in foreign base company
          shipping operations 80

    (vii) Net foreign base company shipping income..................... 20

Proposed Reg. §1.952-3

(3) Subpart F income: (i) Foreign base company income (line (2) (vii)) .... $ 20
(ii) Exchange gain attributable to subpart F income 0

(iii) Tentative subpart F income (line (i) plus line (ii)).............. 20

(iv) Earnings and profits limitation 15
(v) Subpart F income (lesser of lines (iii) and (iv)) 15

Example (4). (a) For 1976, Q Corporation has no foreign base company sales income and no foreign base company services income.
(b) A must apply the test prescribed by section 954(b)(3) to Q's taxable year 1976 as follows, based on the facts shown in the following table:

(1) Gross income 1,000

(2) (i) Foreign base company shipping income ... $450
(ii) Less: items of foreign base company shipping income excluded under §§1.952-1(b)(2), 1.954-1(b)(2), and 1.954-1(b)(3) 100
(iii) Balance 350
(3) (i) Foreign personal holding company income .. 200
(ii) Less: items of foreign personal holding company income excluded under §§1.952-1(b)(2), 1.954-1(b)(2), and 1.954-1(b)(3) 10
(iii) Balance 190

(4) Tentative foreign base company income (line (2) (iii) plus line (3) (iii)) 540

(5) Section 954(b)(3) ratio (line (4) ÷ line (1)) .... 54 percent

(c) Since the section 954(b)(3) ratio is not less than 10 percent nor more than 70 percent, A must determine Q's subpart F income for 1976 as follows, based on the facts shown in the following table:

(1) Gross income $1,000

(2) (i) Foreign base company shipping income 450
(ii) Less: items of foreign base company shipping income excluded under §§1.952-1(b)(2), 1.954-1(b)(2), and 1.954-1(b)(3) 100
(iii) Balance 350
(iv) Less: deductions allocable to balance...................... 250
(v) Remaining balance 100
(vi) Less: increase in qualified investments in foreign base country shipping operations 135
(vii) Net foreign base company shipping income (not less than zero) ... 0

(3) (i) Foreign personal holding company income 200
(ii) Less: items of foreign personal holding company income excluded under §§1.952-1(b)(2), 1.954-1(b)(2), and 1.954-1(b)(3) 10
(iii) Balance 190
(iv) Less: deductions allocable to balance...................... 70
(v) Net foreign personal holding company income 120

(4) Subpart F income: (i) Foreign base company income (line (2) (vii) plus line (3) (v)) 120
(ii) Exchange gain attributable to subpart F income 7

6-1-77 **Proposed Regulations** 63,827

 (iii) Tentative subpart F income (line (i) plus line (ii)).............$ <u>127</u>

 (iv) Earnings and profits limitation............................ 225
 (v) Subpart F income (lesser of lines (iii) and (iv))............. <u>127</u>

Example (5). (a) For 1976, corporation R's only income is comprised of interest and dividends which are treated as foreign base company shipping income under §1.954-6(f)(1)(i). Consequently, R has no foreign personal holding company income, foreign base company sales income or foreign base company services income for 1976 (see section 954(b)(6)(A) and §1.954-1(f)(3)).

(b) A must apply the test prescribed by section 954(b)(3) to R's taxable year 1976 as follows, based on the facts shown in the following table:

(1) Gross income $1,000

(2) (i) Foreign base company shipping income 1,000
 (ii) Less: items of foreign base company shipping income excluded under §§1.952-1(b)(2), 1.954-1(b)(2), and 1.954-1(b)(3)... <u>400</u>
 (iii) Balance .... <u>600</u>

(3) Section 954(b)(3) ratio (line (2) (iii) ÷ line (1)) .... 60 percent

(c) Since the section 954(b)(3) ratio is not less than 10 percent nor more than 70 percent, A must determine R's subpart F income for 1976 as follows, based on the facts shown in the following table:

(1) Gross income $1,000
(2) Net foreign base company shipping income: (i) Foreign base company shipping income 1,000
 (ii) Less: items of foreign base company shipping income excluded under §§1.952-1(b)(2), 1.954-1(b)(2), and 1.954-1(b)(3)...... <u>400</u>
 (iii) Balance 600
 (iv) Less: deductions allocable to balance .... <u>50</u>
 (v) Remaining balance................................. 550
 (vi) Less: increase in qualified investments in foreign base company shipping operations .... <u>530</u>
 (vii) Net foreign base company shipping income .... <u>20</u>

(3) Subpart F income: (i) Foreign base company income (line (2) (vii)) 20
 (ii) Exchange gain attributable to subpart F income .... <u>0</u>
 (iii) Tentative subpart F income (line (i) plus line (ii)) .... <u>20</u>

 (iv) Earnings and profits limitation 25
 (v) Subpart F income (lesser of lines (iii) and (iv))............. <u>20</u>

Section 1.954-1 is amended as follows:

1. The heading and paragraphs (a), (b)(1), and (b)(2) are revised.

2. Paragraph (b)(3) is redesignated as paragraph (b)(4), and paragraph (b)(4) is redesignated as paragraph (b)(3).

3. Paragraph (b)(3) (as redesignated) is revised as follows:

a. The heading is revised.

b. Subdivision (i) is revised by deleting "ending after October 9, 1969", and inserting in lieu thereof "beginning after December 31, 1975".

Proposed Reg. § 1.954-1

c. Subdivision (ii) is amended by revising (a), by deleting "subparagraph (3)" in (b) and inserting in lieu thereof "subparagraph (4)", and by deleting "subparagraph (3)(viii)" in the last sentence and inserting in lieu thereof "subparagraph (4)(vii)".

d. Subdivision (iv) is revised by adding a new sentence at the end thereof.

e. Subdivision (v) is amended by deleting "Income Tax Division" and inserting in lieu thereof "Corporation Tax Division" and by deleting "paragraph (d)(6)" and inserting in lieu thereof "paragraph (d)(7)".

f. Subdivision (vi) is amended by deleting "subparagraph (3)(vi)" and inserting in lieu thereof "subparagaph (4)(v)", and by deleting "subparagraph (3)(vii)" and inserting in lieu thereof "subparagraph (4)(vi)".

g. Subdivision (vii) is amended by revising the heading, by deleting "example" in the first sentence and inserting in lieu thereof "examples", by redesignating the example as example (1), by deleting "1969" in the seventh sentence of example (1) (as redesignated) and inserting in lieu thereof "1977", and by adding new examples (2) and (3) at the end thereof.

4. Paragraph (b)(4) (as redesignated) is revised as follows:

a. The heading, subdivisions (i) and (ii), and so much of subdivision (iii) as precedes (a) thereof are revised.

b. Subdivisions (iii)(a)(1) and (2), (iii)(b), and (iv) are each revised by deleting "in respect to" and inserting in lieu thereof "in respect of".

c. Subdivision (v) is deleted.

d. Subdivisions (vi), (vii), and (viii) are redesignated as subdivisions (v), (vi), and (vii), respectively.

e. Subdivision (v) (as redesignated) is revised by deleting "the creation or organization of a controlled foreign corporation results in" and inserting in lieu thereof "there has been", by deleting "29 percent" and inserting in lieu thereof "9 percent", and by deleting "71 percent" and inserting in lieu thereof "91 percent".

f. Subdivision (vi) (as redesignated) is revised by deleting "subdivisions (i) to (vi)" and inserting in lieu thereof "subdivisions (i) to (v)".

g. Example (1) of subdivision (vii) (as redesignated) is revised by deleting "1963" and inserting "1976" in lieu thereof, and by deleting "organization of B Corporation in country Y did not have the effect of substantially reducing" and inserting in lieu thereof "there has been no substantial reduction of".

h. Example (2) of subdivision (vii) (as redesignated) is revised by deleting "organization of B Corporation in country Y did have the effect of substantially reducing" and inserting in lieu thereof "there has been a substantial reduction of".

i. Example (3) of subdivision (vii) (as redesignated) and example (4) of subdivision (vii) (as redesignated) are amended.

5. Paragraph (c) is revised by amending the first and last sentences thereof.

6. Paragraph (d) is revised as follows:

a. The heading is revised.

b. Subparagraph (1) is revised by deleting "30" in both places where it appears and inserting in lieu thereof "10".

c. Subparagraph (2) is amended by deleting "(1)," immediately after "except as provided in paragraphs", and by inserting "(1), (b)(3)," immediately after "and paragraphs (b)".

d. Subparagraph (3) is revised.

e. So much of subparagraph (4) as precedes the example is revised.

f. The example in subparagraph (4) is amended by deleting "30" in all three places where it appears and by inserting in lieu thereof "10".

7. Paragraph (e) is amended by deleting "1.954-5" and inserting in lieu thereof "1.954-7".

8. Paragraph (f) is amended by deleting "1.954-5" and inserting in lieu thereof "1.954-7", and by adding a new subparagraph (3) at the end thereof.

The added and amended provisions read as follows:

§ 1.954-1 (Proposed Treasury Decision, published 8-9-76, 3-3-77 and 2-9-78.) Foreign base company income; taxable years beginning after December 31, 1975.

(a) **In general.** The subpart F income of a controlled foreign corporation for any taxable year includes its foreign base company income for such taxable year. See section 952(a). For taxable years beginning after December 31, 1975, the foreign base company income of a controlled foreign corporation consists of the sum of its foreign personal holding company income, as defined in §1.954-2, its foreign base company sales income, as defined in §1.954-3, its foreign base company services income, as defined in §1.954-4, and its foreign base company shipping income, as defined in §1.954-6, modified and adjusted in accordance with this section. For corresponding rules applicable to taxable years beginning before January 1, 1976, see 26 CFR §1.954-1 (Rev. as of April 1, 1975). For additional rules relating to the computation of foreign base company income, see §1.952-3.

(b) **Exclusions from foreign base company income.** Foreign base company income does not include the following items:

(1) **Reinvested shipping income.** Foreign base company income does not include foreign base company shipping income to the extent that the amount of such income does not exceed the controlled foreign corporation's increase for the taxable year in qualified investments in foreign base company shipping operations. See section 954(b)(2). For definition of the term "qualified investments in foreign base company shipping operations", see section 955(b) and §1.955A-2. For rules relating to the determination of the increase for a taxable year in qualified investments in foreign base company shipping operations, see section 954(g) and §1.954-7. For rules relating to the computation of the amount excluded from foreign base company income under this subparagraph, see §1.952-3.

(2) **Chain rule for shipping income.** Except as provided in section 954(b)(3) (and notwithstanding any provision of §1.954-6), dividends distributed by a controlled foreign corporation through a chain of ownership described in section 958(a) to another controlled foreign corporation shall not be included in the foreign base company income of such other controlled foreign corporation to the extent that such dividends are attributable (under §1.954-6(f)(4)) to foreign base company shipping income. Thus, a distribution which is not excluded from gross income under section 959(b) and §1.959-2 may be excluded from foreign base company income under section 954(b)(6)(B) and this subparagraph.

(3) **Income of controlled foreign corporations not availed of to substantially reduce income or similar taxes.** * * *

(ii) Substantial reduction of income taxes. * * *

(a) Item of foreign personal holding company income described in §1.954-2 or an item of foreign base company shipping income described in §1.954-6 shall be made by applying the principles of subparagraph (4)(ii) of this paragraph, or

* * * * * * * * * * *

(iv) Application of significant purpose test. * * * The fact that an aircraft or vessel is registered in any particular foreign country does not mean that the income-producing activity in connection with which the aircraft or vessel is used is carried on in that country.

* * * * * * * * * * *

(vii) Illustrations. * * *

Example (2). Controlled foreign corporation X is incorporated under the laws of foreign country A, and uses the calendar year as the taxable year. Corporation X has conducted business for a substantial period of years prior to 1977. Before 1977, X Corpora-

Proposed Reg. § 1.954-1

tion was subject, under the laws of country A, to an effective tax rate of 46.6 percent on the income (after allocable deductions other than income or similar taxes) derived from purchasing and selling activities conducted throughout the world. A substantial part of its income for 1976 was derived from transactions in which it purchased from an unrelated person in foreign country C raw materials produced in country C and sold them to Z Corporation, a related person organized under the laws of foreign country B for use in country B. If X Corporation had been incorporated under the laws of country B it would have paid income and similar taxes to country B for 1976 in an amount effectively equal to 51.2 percent of the income (after allocable deductions other than income or similar taxes) derived from the sales to Z Corporation. If X Corporation had been incorporated under the laws of country C, it would have paid income and similar taxes to country C for years before 1977 in an amount effectively equal to 52 percent of the income (after allocable deductions other than income or similar taxes) derived from the sales to Z Corporation. In 1977, X Corporation also derives a substantial part of its income from transactions in which it purchases from an unrelated person in country C raw materials produced in country C and sells them to Z Corporation for use in country B. Effective January 1, 1977, there is a general reduction in income tax rates in country A, so that X Corporation pays an income tax to country A for 1977 in an amount effectively equal to 45 percent of the income (after allocable deductions other than income or similar taxes) from the sales to Z Corporation. The income tax laws of countries B and C applicable for 1976 remain applicable to 1977 without change. During years both before and after the reduction in country A tax, X Corporation actively conducts a trade or business of purchasing personal property from unrelated persons and selling such property to unrelated persons as well as to Z Corporation. For 1977, the percentage of total income of X Corporation derived from sales of the raw materials to Z Corporation and the nature of the raw materials so sold to Z Corporation remain substantially unchanged from that for 1976. Although the rate of income and similar taxes paid by X Corporation to country A for 1977 on the income from the sales to Z Corporation is less than 90 percent of, and as much as 5 percentage points less than, the rate (51.2 percent) of the income and similar taxes which X Corporation would have paid to country B on the income from the sales to Z Corporation, under subdivision (iv) of this subparagraph the other facts and circumstances in this example will establish to the satisfaction of the district director that (a) the organization of X Corporation in country A, and (b) the effecting through X Corporation of the sales to Z Corporation during 1977, did not have as a significant purpose a substantial reduction of income or similar taxes. Foreign base company income of X Corporation for 1977 does not include income derived from such sales. However, if the percentage of the total income of X Corporation derived from sales of raw materials to Z Corporation were substantially increased, or if the nature of the raw materials so sold to Z Corporation were significantly changed, the facts and circumstances of this example would not establish to the satisfaction of the district director that the effecting through X Corporation of the additional or unusual sales to Z Corporation during 1977 did not have as a significant purpose a substantial reduction of income or similar taxes.

Example (3). (i) Controlled foreign corporation Y, which owns and operates a fleet of foreign flag tankers, is incorporated under the laws of foreign country L. L imposes an effective rate of tax of 10 percent on the income (after allocable deductions other than income or similar taxes) from shipping operations. The sum of the normal tax rate and the surtax rate (determined without regard to the surtax exemption) prescribed by section 11 for all relevant taxable years is 48 percent. It is assumed that had Y been incorporated in the United States and owned and operated a fleet of United States flag tankers, it could have avoided payment of any taxes on its income from shipping operations because of its ability to reduce taxable income by means of deposits of amounts equal to such income into a capital construction fund under part 3 of this chapter. It is further assumed that had Y been incorporated in the United States and owned and operated a fleet of foreign flag tankers, it would have paid income taxes to the United States on its income from shipping operations at the rate prescribed by section 11.

(ii) Since the effective rate of tax on income from such shipping operations paid to country L (10 percent) does not equal or exceed 90 percent of the 48 percent rate prescribed by section 11 (43.2 percent), such income cannot be excluded from foreign base company income under subdivision (i) of this subparagraph by reason of the application of subdivision (ii)(a) of this subparagraph and subparagraph (4)(ii) of this paragraph.

(iii) Also, the fact that Y could have avoided paying any taxes in the United States on its shipping income will not establish to the satisfaction of the district director that the incorporation of Y in foreign country L did not have as a significant purpose a substantial reduction of income or similar taxes, since such avoidance of United States tax would have been possible only upon the occurrence of additional events other than incorporation in the United States (i.e., the use of United States flag tankers and the depositing of amounts into the capital construction fund), which events did not actually occur.

(4) **No substantial reduction of income or similar taxes**—(i) Scope. This subparagraph prescribes rules for the application of subparagraph (3) of this paragraph.

(ii) Foreign personal holding company income and foreign base company shipping income. For purposes of subparagraph (3)(ii)(a) of this paragraph, there will be considered to have been no substantial reduction of income, war profits, excess profits, or similar taxes with respect to an item of foreign personal holding company income described in §1.954-2 or an item of foreign base company shipping income described in §1.954-6 if the effective rate of such taxes (after allocable deductions other than such taxes) paid by a controlled foreign corporation to a foreign country for the taxable year in respect of such item of income equals or exceeds 90 percent of a percentage which equals the sum of the normal tax rate and the surtax rate (determined without regard to the surtax exemption) prescribed by section 11 for the taxable year of the United States shareholder within which or with which ends such taxable year of such controlled foreign corporation.

(iii) Foreign base company sales and services income. For purposes of this paragraph, there will be considered to have been no substantial reduction of income, war profits, excess profits, or similar taxes with respect to an item of foreign base company sales income described in §1.954-3 or an item of foreign base company services income described in §1.954-4 if the effective rate of such taxes paid to a country or countries for the taxable year in respect of such item of income by the controlled foreign corporation equals or exceeds 90 percent of, or is not as much as 5 percentage points less than—

* * * * * * * * * * * *

(vii) Illustrations. * * *

Example (3). Controlled foreign corporation A, incorporated under the laws of foreign country X, is a wholly owned subsidiary of domestic corporation M. Both corporations use the calendar year as the taxable year. In 1976, A Corporation derived interest and rent not excluded under section 954(c)(3) or (4). With respect to the item of interest, A Corporation paid an income tax to country X in an amount effectively equal to 44 percent of such item (after allocable deductions other than income or similar taxes) and, with respect to the item of rent, paid an income tax to country Y in an amount effectively equal to 40 percent of such item (after allocable deductions other than income or similar taxes). No other income or similar tax was paid by A Corporation with respect to such items. In 1976, the sum of the normal tax rate and the surtax rate (determined without regard to the surtax exemption) prescribed by section 11 for the taxable year of M Corporation is 48 percent. Therefore, with respect to the item of interest, there will be considered to have been no substantial reduction of income or similar taxes (44 percent being more than 90 percent of 48 percent), and such interest is not included in foreign base company income of A Corporation. With respect to the item of rent, however, there will be considered to have been a substantial reduction of income or similar taxes (40 percent being less than 90 percent of 48 percent), and the exclusion from foreign base company income provided by section 954(b)(4) will not apply to such item unless it is established in accordance with subparagraph (3)(i) of this paragraph that both the creation or organization of A Corporation under the laws of foreign country X and the effecting through A Corporation of the transaction which gave rise to such rental income did not have as a significant purpose a substantial reduction of such taxes.

Proposed Reg. § 1.954-1

(c) **Gross income and deductions to be taken into account.** For purposes of section 954 and this section, foreign personal holding company income as defined in §1.954-2, foreign base company sales income as defined in §1.954-3, foreign base company services income as defined in §1.954-4, and foreign base company shipping income as defined in §1.954-6 shall be taken into account in determining foreign base company income after allowance for deductions properly allocable to such categories of income. * * * However, if the foreign base company income of a controlled foreign corporation exceeds 70 percent (as determined under paragraph (d) of this section) of gross income, the entire expenses, taxes, and other deductions shall be taken into account, except expenses, taxes, and other deductions properly allocable to amounts excluded from foreign base company income under the provisions of paragraph (4) of section 954(b) and paragraph (b)(3) of this section and expenses, taxes, and other deductions properly allocable to amounts excluded from subpart F income under section 952(b) and the regulations thereunder.

(d) **Special rules where foreign base company income is less than 10 percent or more than 70 percent of gross income.** * * *

(3) **Method of computation.** See §1.952-3 for rules relating to the method of determining the percentage which foreign base company income is of gross income under subparagraphs (1) and (2) of this paragraph.

(4) **Branches of controlled foreign corporations treated as separate corporations**—(i) In general. The 10-percent and 70-percent tests described in subparagraphs (1) and (2) of this paragraph apply to the foreign base company income of each controlled foreign corporation. In addition, if a branch or similar establishment of a controlled foreign corporation is treated as a separate wholly owned subsidiary corporation of such corporation under section 954(d)(2) and paragraph (b) of §1.954-3, the 10-percent and 70-percent tests apply separately to the income allocated under such paragraph to such branch or similar establishment, to other branches and similar establishments similarly treated, and to the remainder of the controlled foreign corporation.

(ii) Illustration. The application of this subparagraph may be illustrated by the following example:

* * * * * * * * * * * *

(f) **Classification of an item of income.** * * *

(3) **Shipping classsification applies first.** Foreign base company shipping income (as determined under §1.954-6) of a controlled foreign corporation shall not also be considered foreign personal holding company income, foreign base company sales income, or foreign base company services income. See section 954(b)(6)(A).

Section 1.954-2 is amended as follows:

1. The first sentence of paragraph (a) is amended by inserting "section 954(b)(6)(A)," immediately before "section 954(c)(3) and (4)", and by striking out "(e)" and inserting "(f)" in lieu thereof.

2. Paragraph (d)(2)(iv)(b)(2) is amended as follows:
a. Subdivision (ii) is revised by deleting "and" at the end thereof.
b. Subdivision (iii) is revised by deleting the period at the end thereof and inserting in lieu thereof, "and".
c. A new subdivision (iv) is added.

3. A new paragraph (f) is added at the end thereof to read as follows:

§1.954-2 (Proposed Treasury Decision, published 8-9-76 and 2-9-78.) **Foreign personal holding company income.**

* * * * * * * * * * * *

(d) **Certain income received from unrelated persons in the active conduct of a trade or business** * * *

(2) **Dividends, interest, and gains on securities, received in banking or other financing business from unrelated persons** * * *

(iv) Income of foreign corporations owned by Edge Act or Agreement corporations * * *

(b) Foreign corporations included. * * *

(2) * * *

(iv) Foreign base company shipping income, as defined in §1.954-6.

* * * * * * * * * * * *

(f) **Shipping income for taxable years beginning after December 31, 1975.** For taxable years beginning after December 31, 1975, foreign base company shipping income of a controlled foreign corporation (as determined under §1.954-6) shall not also be considered foreign personal holding company income of that controlled foreign corporation.

* *

Subparagraph (1) of §1.954-3(a) is amended—
1. by redesignating the first five sentences thereof as subdivision (i),
2. by revising subdivision (i) as redesignated by adding a caption and by redesignating subdivisions (i), (ii), (iii), and (iv) as new inferior subdivisions (a), (b), (c), and (d),
3. by redesignating the sixth sentence of subparagraph (1) and the examples following as subdivision (iii), and
4. by adding a new subdivision (ii) immediately following redesignated subdivision (i).

The redesignated and added provisions read as follows:

§1.954-3 (Proposed Treasury Decision, published 5-14-76.) **Foreign base company sales income.**

(a) Income included—(1) In general. (i) General rules. Foreign base company sales income of a controlled foreign corporation shall, except as provided in subparagraphs (2), (3), and (4) of this paragraph, consist of gross income (whether in the form of profits, commissions, fees, or otherwise) derived in connection with (a) the purchase of personal property from a related person and its sale to any person, (b) the sale of personal property to any person on behalf of a related person, (c) the purchase of personal property from any person and its sale to a related person, or (d) the purchase of personal property from any person on behalf of a related person. * * *

(ii) Special rule—(a) In general. the term "personal property" as used in section 954(d) and this section shall not include agricultural commodities which are not grown in the United States (within the meaning of section 7701(a)(9)) in commercially marketable quantities. All of the agricultural commodities listed in Table I shall be considered grown in the United States in commercially marketable quantities. Black pepper, cocoa, coconut, and tea shall not be considered grown in the United States in commercially marketable quantities. All other agricultural commodities shall not be considered grown in the United States in commercially marketable quantities when, in consideraion of all of the facts and circumstances of the individual case, such commodities are shown to be produced in the United States in insufficient quantity and quality to be marketed commercially. The term "agricultural commodities" includes, but is not limited to, livestock, poultry, fish produced in fish farms, fruit, furbearing animals as well as the products of truck farms, ranches, nurseries, ranges, and orchards. A fish farm is an area where fish are grown or raised (artificially protected and cared for), as opposed to merely caught or harvested. However, the term "agricultural commodities" shall not include timber (either standing or felled), or any commodity at least 50 percent of the fair market value of which is attributable to manufacturing or processing, determined in a manner consistent with the regulations under section 993(c) (relating to the definition of export property). For purposes of applying such regulations, the term "processing" shall be deemed not to include handling, packing, packaging, grading, storing, transporting, slaughtering, and harvesting. Subdivision (ii) shall apply in the computation of foreign base company sales income for taxable years of controlled foreign corporations beginning after December 31,

Proposed Reg. §1.954-3

63,834   Proposed Regulations   6-1-78

1975, and to taxable years of United States shareholders (within the meaning of section 951(b)) within which or with which such taxable years of such foreign corporations end.

  (b) Table.

Table I - Agricultural Commodities Grown in the United States in Commercially Marketable Quantities.

Livestock and Products

Beeswax	Horses
Cattle and calves	Milk
Chickens	Mink
Chicken eggs	Mohair
Ducks	Rabbits
Geese	Sheep and lambs
Goats	Turkeys
Hogs	Wool
Honey	

Crops

Alfalfa	Lemons
Almonds	Lettuce
Apples	Lime
Apricots	Macadamia nuts
Artichokes	Maple syrup and sugar
Asparagus	Mint
Avocados	Mushrooms
Bananas	Nectarines
Barley	Oats
Beans	Olives
Beets	Onions
Blackberries	Oranges
Blueberries	Papayas
Brussel sprouts	Pecans
Broccoli	Peaches
Bulbs	Peanuts
Cabbage	Pears
Cantaloupes	Peas
Carrots	Peppers
Cauliflower	Plums and prunes
Celery	Potatoes
Cherries	Potted plants
Coffee	Raspberries
Corn	Rice
Cotton	Rhubarb
Cranberries	Rye
Cucumbers	Sorghum grain
Cut flowers	Soybeans
Dates	Spinach
Eggplant	Strawberries
Escarole	Sugar beets
Figs	Sugarcane
Filberts	Sweet potatoes
Flaxseed	Tangelos
Garlic	Tangerines
Grapes	Tobacco
Grapefruit	Tomatoes
Grass seed	Walnuts
Hay	Watermelons
Honeydew melons	Wheat
Hops	

(iii) Examples. The application of this subparagraph may be illustrated by the following examples: * * *

* *

1. Section 1.954-3 is amended by inserting "or foreign base company shipping income under §1.954-6" immediately after "§1.954-2" in the fourth sentence of paragraph (a)(1).

2. Paragraph (b) is amended as follows:

(a). The first sentence of subparagraph (2)(i)(d) is revised by deleting "paragraph (b)(3)(iv)" and inserting in lieu thereof "paragraph (b)(4)(iv)".

(b). The second sentence of subparagraph (3) is revised by deleting "30 percent" and inserting in lieu thereof "10 percent".

3. A new paragraph (c) is added to read as follows:

§1.954-3 (Proposed Treasury Decision, published 8-9-76 and 2-9-78.) Foreign base company sales income.

§1.954-3 (Proposed Treasury Decision, published 8-9-76.) **Foreign base company sales income.**

* * * * * * * * * * * *

(c) **Shipping income for taxable years beginning after December 31, 1975.** For taxable years beginning after December 31, 1975, foreign base company shipping income (as determined under §1.954-6) of a controlled foreign corporation shall not also be considered foreign base company sales income of that controlled foreign corporation.

Section 1.954-4(d) is amended by deleting "or" at the end of subparagraph (1), by deleting the period at the end of subparagraph (2) and inserting in lieu thereof "; or", and by adding a new subparagraph (3) at the end thereof to read as follows:

§1.954-4 (Proposed Treasury Decision, published 8-9-76.) **Foreign base company services income.**

* * * * * * * * * * * *

(d) Items excluded. * * *

(3) For taxable years beginning after December 31, 1975, foreign base company shipping income (as determined under §1.954-6).

* *

Section 1.954-5 is amended to read as follows:

§1.954-5 (Proposed Treasury Decisions, published 2-9-78.) **Increase in qualified investments in less developed countries; taxable years of controlled foreign corporations beginning before January 1, 1976.**

For rules applicable to taxable years of controlled foreign corporations beginning before January 1, 1976, see section 954(b)(1) (as in effect before the enactment of the Tax Reduction Act of 1975) and 26 CFR 1.954-5 (Rev. as of April 1, 1975).

Section 1.955 is deleted.

Immediately after §1.954-5 new §§1.954-6 and 1.954-7 are added to read as follows:

§1.954-6 (Proposed Treasury Decision, published 8-9-76.) **Foreign base company shipping income.**

(a) Scope—(1) In general. This section prescribes rules for determining foreign base company shipping income under the provisions of section 954(f), as amended by the Tax Reduction Act of 1975.

(2) **Effective date.** (i) The rules prescribed in this section apply to taxable years of foreign corporations beginning after December 31, 1975, and to taxable years of United

Proposed Reg. §1.954-6

States shareholders (as defined in section 951(b)) within which or with which such taxable years of such foreign corporations end.

(ii) Foreign base company shipping income does not include amounts earned by a foreign corporation in a taxable year of such corporation beginning before January 1, 1976. See example (1) of paragraph (g)(2) of this section for an illustration of the effect of this subparagraph on partnership income. See example (3) of paragraph (f)(4)(ii) of this section for an illustration of the effect of this subparagraph on certain dividend income. See paragraph (f)(5)(iii) of this section for the effect of this subparagraph on certain interest and gains.

(b) **Definitions**—(1) **Foreign base company shipping income.** The term "foreign base company shipping income" means—

(i) Gross income derived from, or in connection with, the use (or hiring or leasing for use) of any aircraft or vessel in foreign commerce (see paragraph (c) of this section),

(ii) Gross income derived from, or in connection with, the performance of services directly related to the use of any aircraft or vessel in foreign commerce (see paragraph (d) of this section),

(iii) Gross income incidental to income described in subdivisions (i) and (ii) of this subparagraph, as provided in paragraph (e) of this section,

(iv) Gross income derived from the sale, exchange, or other disposition of any aircraft or vessel used (by the seller or by a person related to the seller) in foreign commerce,

(v) In the case of a controlled foreign corporation, dividends, interest, and gains described in paragraph (f) of this section,

(vi) Income described in paragraph (g) of this section (relating to partnerships, trusts, etc.), and

(vii) Exchange gain, to the extent allocable to foreign base company shipping income (see §1.952-2(c)(2)(v)(b)).

(2) **Foreign base company shipping operations.** For purposes of sections 951 through 964, the term "foreign base company shipping operations" means the trade or business from which gross income described in subparagraph (1)(i) and (ii) of this paragraph is derived.

(3) **Foreign commerce.** For purposes of sections 951 through 964—

(i) An aircraft or vessel is used in foreign commerce if it is used in transportation of property or passengers—

(A) Between a port (or airport) in the United States or possession of the United States and a port (or airport) in a foreign country, or

(B) Between a port (or airport) in a foreign country and another in the same country or between a port (or airport) in a foreign country and one in another foreign country.

Thus, for example, a trawler, a factory ship, and an oil drilling ship are not considered to be used in foreign commerce. On the other hand, a cruise ship which visits one or more foreign ports is considered to be so used.

(ii) The term "vessel" includes all water craft and other artificial contrivances of whatever description and at whatever stage of construction, whether on the stocks or launched, which are used or are capable of being used or are intended to be used as a means of transportation on water.

(iii) The term "port" means any place where aircraft or vessels are accustomed to load or unload goods or to take on or let off passengers.

(iv) Any vessel (such as a lighter or beacon lightship) which serves other vessels used (within the meaning of subdivision (i) of this subparagraph) in foreign commerce shall, to the extent so used, also be considered to be used in foreign commerce.

(v) For the meaning of the term "foreign country", see section 638(2).

(4) **Use in foreign commerce.** For purposes of sections 951 through 964, the use of an aircraft or vessel in foreign commerce includes the hiring or leasing (or subleasing) of an aircraft or vessel to another for use in foreign commerce. Thus, for example, an aircraft or vessel is "used in foreign commerce" within the meaning of section 955(b)(1)(A) if such aircraft or vessel is chartered (whether pursuant to a bareboat charter, time charter, or otherwise) to another for use in foreign commerce.

(5) Related person. With respect to a controlled foreign corporation, the term "related person" means a related person as defined in §1.954-1(e)(1), and the term "unrelated person" means an unrelated person as defined in §1.954-1(e)(2).

(c) Aircraft or vessel income—(1) In general. The term "income derived from, or in connection with, the use (or hiring or leasing for use) of any aircraft or vessel in foreign commerce" as used in paragraph (b)(1)(i) of this section means—

(i) Income derived from transporting passengers or property by aircraft or vessel in foreign commerce and

(ii) Income derived from hiring or leasing an aircraft or vessel to another for use in foreign commerce.

(2) Illustrations. The application of this paragraph may be illustrated by the following examples:

Example (1). Foreign corporation C owns a foreign flag vessel which it charters under a long-term charter to foreign corporation D. The vessel is used by D as a tramp which has no fixed or regular schedule. The vessel carries bulk and packaged cargoes, as well as occasional passengers, under charter parties, contracts of affreightment, or other contracts of carriage. The carriage of cargoes and passengers is between a port in the United States and a port in a foreign country or between a port in one foreign country and another port in the same or a different foreign country. The charter hire paid to C by D constitutes income derived from the use of the vessel in foreign commerce. The charter hire and freight and passenger revenue (including demurrage and dead freight) derived by D also constitute income derived from the use of the vessel in foreign commerce.

Example (2). (a) Foreign corporation E owns a foreign flag tanker which it charters under a long-term bareboat charter to foreign corporation F for use in foreign commerce. F produces oil in a foreign country and ships the oil to other foreign countries and to the United States. The vessel, when not engaged in carrying F's oil, is used to carry bulk cargoes for unrelated persons in foreign commerce as opportunity offers. The charter hire received by E constitutes income derived from the use of the vessel in foreign commerce. The income derived by F from carrying bulk cargoes for unrelated persons also constitutes income derived from the use of the vessel in foreign commerce.

(b) F is forced to lay up the vessel as a result of adverse market developments. Pursuant to the terms of the charter, F continues to pay charter hire to E during the period of lay-up. The charter hire received by E during the period of lay-up constitutes income derived from the use of the vessel in foreign commerce.

[The page following this is 63,847]

Proposed Reg. §1.954-6

Example (3). (a) A shipment of cheese is loaded into a container owned by controlled foreign corporation S at the consignor's place of business in Hamar, Norway. The cheese is transported to Milan, Italy, by the following routings:

(1) Overland by road from Hamar, Norway, to Gothenburg, Sweden, by unrelated motor carriers via Oslo, Norway,

(2) By sea from Gothenburg to Rotterdam, Netherlands, by feeder vessel under foreign flag, time chartered to S by unrelated owner,

(3) By sea from Rotterdam to Algeciras, Spain, by feeder vessel under foreign flag, time chrtered to S by unrelated owner,

(4) By sea from Algeciras to Genoa, Italy, by line-haul vessel under U.S. flag, chartered by S from related company, and

(5) Overland from Genoa to Milan, Italy, by unrelated motor carrier.

(b) The consignor pays S total charges of $1,710, and S pays $676 to unrelated third parties, which amounts may be broken down as follows:

Description of charges	Amount billed to customer and collected by S	Revenue collected by S on behalf of an unrelated party	Costs paid to unrelated third party and absorbed by S
Ocean freight	$1,420		
Trucking charge of empty equipment to shipper's facility	50	$ 50	
Trucking charges Hamar to Oslo	60	60	
Trucking charges Oslo to Gothenburg			$315
Trucking charges Genoa to Milan	180	180	
Brokerage Commission in Europe			71
Totals	$1,710	$290	$386

(c) Of the $1,710 amount billed to the consignor and collected by S, $290 is collected by S on behalf of unrelated third parties. This $290 amount is not includible in S's gross income, and is therefore not includible in S's foreign base company shipping income. The remaining $1,420 amount (i.e., $1,710—$290) is includible in S's foreign base company shipping income. The $386 amount paid by S to unrelated third parties and absorbed by S is deductible from foreign base company shipping income under §1.954-1(c).

(d) Services directly related—(1) In general. The term "income derived from, or in connection with, the performance of services directly related to the use of an aircraft or vessel in foreign commerce", as used in paragraph (b)(1)(ii) of this section, means—

(i) Income derived from, or in connection with, the performance of services described in subparagraph (2) or (3) of this paragraph, and

(ii) Income treated as foreign base company shipping income under subparagraph (4) of this paragraph.

(2) Intragroup services. The services described in this subparagraph are services performed for a person who is the owner, lessor, or operator of an aircraft or vessel used in foreign commerce, by such person or by a person related to such person, and which fall into one or more of the following categories:

(i) Terminal services, such as dockage, wharfage, storage, lights, water, refrigeration, and similar services;

(ii) Stevedoring and other cargo handling services;

Proposed Reg. §1.954-6

(iii) Container related services (including the rental of containers and related equipment) performed in connection with the local drayage or inland haulage of cargo;
(iv) Services performed by tugs, lighters, barges, scows, launches, floating cranes, and other similar equipment;
(v) Maintenance and repairs;
(vi) Training of pilots and crews;
(vii) Licensing of patents, know-how, and similar intangible property developed and used in the course of foreign base company shipping operations,
(viii) Services performed by a booking, operating, or managing agent; and
(ix) Any service performed in the course of the actual transportation of passengers or property.

(3) **Services for passenger, consignor, or consignee.** The services described in this subparagraph are services provided by the operator (or person related to the operator) of an aircraft or vessel in foreign commerce for the passenger, consignor, or consignee, such as—

(i) Services described in one or more of the categories set out in subparagraph (2)(i) through (iv) and (ix) of this paragraph,
(ii) The rental of staterooms, berths, or living accomodations and the furnishing of meals,
(iii) Barber shop and other services to passengers aboard vessels,
(iv) Excess baggage, and
(v) Demurrage, dispatch, and dead freight.

(4) **The 70-percent test.** All the gross income for a taxable year derived by a foreign corporation from any facility used in connection with the performance of services described in one or more of the categories set out in subparagraph (2)(i) through (ix) of this paragraph is foreign base company shipping income if more than 70 percent of such gross income for either—

(i) Such taxable year, or
(ii) Such taxable year and the two preceding taxable years,

is foreign base company shipping income (determined without regard to this subparagraph). Thus, for example, if 80 percent of the gross income derived by a controlled foreign corporation at a stevedoring facility is treated as foreign base company shipping income under subparagraph (2) of this paragraph, then the remaining 20 percent is treated as foreign base company shipping income under this subparagraph.

(5) **Rules for applying subparagraph (4).** (i) Solely for purposes of applying subparagraph (4) of this paragraph, foreign base company shipping income and gross income shall be deemed to include an arm's length charge (see paragraph (h)(5) of this section) for services performed by a foreign coporation for itself.

(ii) In determining whether services performed by a foreign corporation are performed at a single facility or at two or more different facilities, all of the facts and circumstances involved will be taken into account. Ordinarily, all services performed by a foreign corporation within a single port area will be considered performed at a single facility.

(iii) The application of this subparagraph and subparagraph (4) of this paragraph may be illustrated by the following example:

Example. (a) Controlled foreign corporation X uses the calendar year as the taxable year. For 1976, X is divided into two operating divisions, A and B. Division A operates a number of vessels in foreign commerce. Division B operates a terminal facility at which it performs services described in subparagraph (2)(i) of this paragraph for vessels some of which are operated by division A, some of which are operated by persons related to X, and some of which are operated by persons unrelated to X. For 1976, the gross income derived by division B is reconstructed for purposes of subparagraph (4) of this paragraph as follows, based on the facts shown in the following table:

(1)	Gross income derived from persons unrelated to X	$20
(2)	Gross income derived from persons related to X	10
(3)	Actual gross income (line (1) plus line (2))	30

(4) Hypothetical gross income derived from division A (determined by the application of subdivision (i) of this subparagraph)	70
(5) Total reconstructed gross income (line (3) plus line (4))	$100

(b) Since 80 percent of the reconstructed gross income derived by division B would be treated as foreign base company shipping income under subparagraph (2) of this paragraph, the entire $30 amount of the gross income actually derived by division B is treated as foreign base company shipping income under subparagraph (4) of this paragraph.

(6) **Arm's length charge.** For purposes of this section, the arm's length charge for services performed by a foreign corporation for itself shall be determined by applying the principles of section 482 and the regulations thereunder as if the party for whom the services are performed and the party by whom the services are performed were not the same person, but were controlled taxpayers within the meaning of §1.482-1(a)(4).

(7) **Illustrations.** The application of this paragraph may be illustrated by the following examples:

Example (1). Controlled foreign corporation A acts as a managing agent for foreign corporation B, a related person which contracts to construct and charter a foreign flag vessel for use in foreign commerce. As managing agent for B, A performs a broad range of services relating to the use of the vessel, including arranging for, and supervising of, construction and chartering of the vessel, and handling of operating services after construction is completed. The income derived by A from its management and operating services constitutes income derived in connection with the performance of services directly related to the use of the vessel in foreign commerce.

Example (2). Controlled foreign corporation C uses the calendar year as the taxable year. During 1976, C is engaged in the trade or business of acting as a steamship agent solely for unrelated persons. C's activities as steamship agent range from "husbanding" (i.e., arranging for fuel, supplies and port services, and attending to crew and customs matters) to the solicitation and booking of cargo at a number of foreign ports. None of C's other gross income for 1976 is foreign base company shipping income. Under these circumstances, C's gross income derived from its steamship agency does not constitute foreign base company shipping income.

(e) **Incidental income—(1) In general.** Foreign base company shipping income includes all incidental income derived by a foreign corporation in the course of the active conduct of foreign base company shipping operations.

(2) **Examples.** Examples of incidental income derived in the course of the active conduct of foreign base company shipping operations are—

(i) Gain from the sale, exchange or other disposition of assets which are related shipping assets within the meaning of §1.955A-2(b),

(ii) Income derived from temporary investments described in §1.955A-2(b)(2)(i) and (iii),

(iii) Interest on accounts receivable and evidences of indebtedness described in §1.955A-2(b)(2)(ii),

(iv) Income derived from granting concessions to others aboard aircraft or vessels used in foreign commerce,

(v) Income derived from stock and currency futures described in §1.955A-2(b)(2)(vii) and (viii), and

(vi) Income derived by the lessor of an aircraft or vessel used in foreign commerce from additional rentals for the use of related equipment (such as a complement of containers).

(f) **Certain dividends, interest, and gain—(1) In general.** The foreign base company shipping income of any controlled foreign corporation which would be deemed under section 902(b) to pay taxes in respect of another foreign corporation includes—

Proposed Reg. §1.954-6

(i) Dividends and interest received from such other foreign corporation, and

(ii) Gain recognized from the sale, exchange, or other disposition of stock or obligations of such other foreign corporation,

to the extent that such dividends, interest, and gains are attributable to foreign base company shipping income. This subparagraph applies whether or not such other foreign corporation is a controlled foreign corporation.

(2) **Corporation deemed to pay taxes.** (i) For purposes of this paragraph, a controlled foreign corporation would be deemed under section 902(b) to pay taxes in respect of any other foreign corporation if such controlled foreign corporation would be deemed, for purposes of applying section 902(a) to any United States shareholder of such controlled foreign corporation, to pay taxes in respect of dividends which were received from such other foreign corporation (whether or not such other foreign corporation actually pays any taxes or dividends). Solely for purposes of this subdivision, each United States shareholder (within the meaning of section 951(b)) shall be deemed to be a domestic corporation.

(ii) The application of subdivision (i) of this subparagraph may be illustrated by the following examples:

Example (1). Domestic corporation M owns 100 percent of the one class of stock of controlled foreign corporation X, which in turn owns 40 percent of the one class of stock of foreign corporation Y. Y is not a controlled foreign corporation. For purposes of subdivision (i) of this subparagraph, X is deemed to pay taxes in respect of Y.

Example (2). The facts are the same as in example (1), except that United States shareholder A, an individual, owns 90 percent of the stock of corporation X, and United States shareholders B and C, parent and child, own the other 10 percent in equal shares. For purposes of applying this paragraph to all three United States shareholders (A, B, and C), X is deemed to pay taxes in respect of Y.

(3) **Obligation defined.** For purposes of this section, the term "obligation" means any bond, note, debenture, certificate, or other evidence of indebtedness. In the absence of legal, governmental, or business reasons to the contrary, the indebtedness must bear interest or be issued at a discount.

(4) **Dividends.** (i) For purposes of this paragraph and §1.954-1(b)(2), the portion of a dividend which is attributable to foreign base company shipping income is that amount which bears the same ratio to the total dividend received as the earnings and profits out of which such dividend is paid that are attributable to foreign base company shipping income bears to the total earnings and profits out of which such dividend is paid. For purposes of this subdivision, the source of the earnings and profits out of which a distribution is made shall be determined under section 316(a), except that the source of the earnings and profits out of which a distribution is made by a controlled foreign corporation with respect to stock owned (within the meaning of section 958(a)) by a United States shareholder of such controlled foreign corporation shall be determined under §1.959-3.

(ii) The application of this subparagraph may be illustrated by the following examples:

Example (1). Domestic corporation M owns 100 percent of the one class of stock of controlled foreign corporation X, which in turn owns 40 percent of the one class of stock of foreign corporation Y. Y, which is not a controlled foreign corporation, makes a distribution of $100 to X. Under section 316(a), such distribution is made out of Y's earnings and profits for 1978. Sixty percent of Y's earnings and profits for 1978 are attributable to foreign base company shipping income. As a result, $60 of the $100 distribution constitutes foreign base company shipping income to X under subdivision (i) of this subparagraph.

Example (2). The facts are the same as in example (1), except that under section 316(a) $20 of the $100 dividend is paid out of Y's earnings and profits for 1979, and the other $80 is paid out of Y's earnings and profits for 1978. Thirty percent of Y's earnings and profits for 1979 are attributable to foreign base company shipping income. Since 60 percent of Y's earnings and profits for 1978 are also attributable to foreign base company shipping income, $54, i.e., (.60 × $80) + (.30 × $20), of the $100 distribution constitutes foreign base company shipping income to X under subdivision (i) of this subparagraph.

Example (3). The facts are the same as in example (1), except that under section 316(a) the $100 dividend is made out of Y's earnings and profits for 1972. Since under paragraph (a)(2)(ii) of this section foreign base company shipping income does not include amounts earned by a foreign corporation in a taxable year beginning before January 1, 1976, no amount of such $100 distribution constitutes foreign base company shipping income to X under subdivision (i) of this subparagraph.

Example (4). Domestic corporation N owns 100 percent of the one class of stock of controlled foreign corporation S, which in turn owns 100 percent of the one class of stock of controlled foreign corporation T. T makes a distribution of $100 to S, of which $80 is allocable under §1.959-3 to earnings and profits for 1977 which are described in §1.959-3(c)(2), and $20 is allocable to earnings and profits for 1978 which are described in §1.959-3(c)(3). The $80 amount is excluded from S's gross income under section 959(b) and therefore is not included in S's foreign base company shipping income. One hundred percent of T's earnings and profits for 1978 described in §1.959-3(c)(3) were attributable to reinvested foreign base company shipping income. As a result, the entire $20 amount is included in S's foreign base company shipping income under this paragraph. See §1.954-1(b)(2) for the rule that such $20 amount may be excluded from the foreign base company income of S.

(5) Interest and gain. (i) Except as provided in subdivisions (ii) and (iii) of this subparagraph, the portion of any interest paid by a foreign corporation, or gain recognized from the sale, exchange, or other disposition of stock or obligations of a foreign corporation, which is attributable to the foreign base company shipping income of such foreign corporation is that amount which bears the same ratio to such interest or gain as the foreign base company shipping income of such corporation for the period described in subparagraph (6) of this paragraph bears to its gross income for such period.

(ii) Interest which is paid by a controlled foreign corporation is attributable to such corporation's foreign base company shipping income to the same extent that such interest is allocable (under the principles of §1.954-1(c)) to its foreign base company shipping income.

(iii) If interest is paid by a foreign corporation, or if stock or obligations of a foreign corporation are sold, exchanged, or otherwise disposed of, during a taxable year of such foreign corporation beginning before January 1, 1976, then no portion of such interest or gain is attributable to foreign base company shipping income.

(iv) Solely for purposes of subdivision (i) of this subparagraph, if a controlled foreign corporation (the "first corporation") owns more than 10 percent of the stock of another controlled foreign corporation (the "second corporation"), then

(A) The gross income of the first corporation for any taxable year shall be—

(1) Increased by its pro rata share of the gross income of the second corporation for the taxable year which ends with or within such taxable year of the first corporation, and

(2) Decreased by the amount of any dividends received from the second corporation; and

(B) The foreign base company shipping income of the first corporation for any taxable year shall be—

(1) Increased by its pro rata share of the foreign base company shipping income of the second corporation for the taxable year which ends with or within such taxable year of the first corporation, and

(2) Decreased by the amount of any dividends received from the second corporation which constitute foreign base company income.

(v) Solely for purposes of applying subdivision (i) of this subparagraph, the district director shall make such other adjustments to the gross income and the foreign base company shipping income of any foreign corporation as are necessary to properly deter-

Proposed Reg. §1.954-6

mine the extent to which any interest or gain is attributable to foreign base company shipping income, including proper adjustments to reflect any transaction during the test period described in subparagraph (6) of this paragraph to which section 332, 351, 354, 355, 356, or 361 applies.

(6) **Test period.** (i) Except as provided in subdivisions (ii) and (iii) of this subparagraph, the period described in this subparagraph with respect to any foreign corporation is the 3-year period ending with the close of such corporation's taxable year preceding the year during which interest was paid or stock or obligations were sold, exchanged, or otherwise disposed of, or such part of such period as such corporation was in existence.

(ii) The period described in this paragraph shall not include any part of a taxable year beginning before January 1, 1976.

(iii) If interest is paid by a foreign corporation, or if stock or obligations of a foreign corporation are sold, exchanged, or otherwise disposed of during its first taxable year, then the period described in this paragraph shall be such first taxable year.

(iv) For purposes of subdivision (iii) of this subparagraph, the first taxable year of a foreign corporation is the later of—

(A) The first taxable year of its existence, or
(B) Its first taxable year beginning after December 31, 1975.

(g) **Income from partnerships, trusts, etc.**—(1) **In general.** The foreign base company shipping income of any foreign corporation includes—

(i) Its distributive share of the gross income of any partnership, and
(ii) Any amounts includible in its gross income under section 652(a), 662(a), 671, or 691(a),

to the extent that such items would have been includible in its foreign base company shipping income had they been realized by it directly.

(2) **Illustrations.** The application of subparagraph (1) of this paragraph may be illustrated by the following examples:

Example (1). Controlled foreign corporations X and Y are equal partners in partnership P. The taxable years end on December 31 for X, June 30 for Y, and March 31 for P. In the fiscal year ending March 31, 1976, P's sole business activity is the use of a vessel in foreign commerce. P derives gross income of $200 from the use of the vessel, and incurs expenses, taxes, and other deductions of $160. Assume X's distributive share of such $200 of P's gross income is $100, all of which is includible in X's gross income. If X had realized its distributive share of $100 directly, then the amount which would have been includible in X's foreign base company shipping income under this paragraph is the portion allocable to the months of January, February, and March of 1976. Such amount, $25 (i.e., $½ \times 200×3 months/12 months), is included in X's foreign base company shipping income for its taxable year ending December 31, 1976. Similarly, X is entitled under this paragraph to a deduction from foreign base company shipping income of $20 (i.e., $½ \times 160×3 months/12 months). Since foreign base company shipping income does not include amounts earned by a foreign corporation in a taxable year beginning before January 1, 1976, Y has no foreign base company shipping income (under this paragraph or otherwise) for its taxable year beginning on July 1, 1975.

Example (2). The facts are the same as in example (1), except that P incurs expenses, taxes, and deductions of $240 in its taxable year ending on March 31, 1976. Accordingly, $25 is includible in X's foreign base company shipping income, and the amount deductible therefrom under this paragraph is $30, (i.e., $½ \times 3$ months/12 months).

(3) **Other income.** Except as expressly provided in subparagraph (1) of this paragraph, foreign base company shipping income does not include any amount includible in the gross income of a controlled foreign corporation under part I of subchapter J (section 641 and following, relating to estates, trusts, and beneficiaries), and gains from the sale or other disposition of any interest in an estate or trust.

(h) **Additional rules**—(1) **Gross income.** For purposes of this section and §1.955A-2, the gross income of a foreign corporation (whether or not a controlled foreign corporation) shall be determined in accordance with the provisions of section 952 and §1.952-2.

Thus, for example, section 883 (relating to exclusions from gross income of foreign corporations) is inapplicable under §1.952-2(a)(1) and (c)(1). In addition, the gross income of a controlled foreign corporation shall be determined, with respect to a United States shareholder of such controlled foreign corporation, by excluding distributions received by such corporation which are excluded from gross income from section 959(b) with respect to such shareholder.

(2) **Earnings and profits.** For purposes of this section, the earnings and profits of a foreign corporation (whether or not a controlled foreign corporation) shall be determined in accordance with the provisions of section 964 and the regulations thereunder.

(3) **No double counting.** No item of gross income shall be counted as foreign base company shipping income under more than one provision of this section. For example, if $200 of gross income derived from the use of a lighter is treated as foreign base company shipping income under both paragraph (b)(1)(i) and paragraph (b)(1)(ii) of this section, then such $200 is counted only once as foreign base company shipping income.

(4) **Losses.** (i) Generally, if a controlled foreign corporation has losses which are properly allocable to foreign base company shipping income, the extent to which such losses are deductible from such income shall be determined by treating such foreign corporation as a domestic corporation and applying the principles of section 63. See §§1.954-1(c) and 1.952-2(b). Thus, for example, losses from sales or exchanges of capital assets are allowable only to the extent of gains from such sales or exchanges.

(ii) If gain from the sale, exchange, or other disposition of any stock or obligation would be treated (to any extent) as foreign base company shipping income, then loss from such sale, exchange, or other disposition is properly allocable to foreign base company shipping income (to the same extent).

(iii) In determining the extent to which any loss on the disposition of a qualified investment in foreign base company shipping operations is deductible from foreign base company shipping income, it is immaterial that such loss is taken into account under §1.955A-1(b)(1)(ii) as a reduction in the amount of the decrease in qualified investments in foreign base company shipping operations.

(5) **Hypothetical charges.** Under paragraph (d)(5)(i) of this section and §1.955A-2(a)(4)(ii)(A), gross income may be deemed to include hypothetical arm's length charges for services performed by a controlled foreign corporation for itself. Under paragraph (d)(2) of this section, certain of these hypothetical charges may be treated as foreign base company shipping income. Such hypothetical charges are deemed to be income solely for purposes of applying the "extent of use" tests prescribed by paragraph (d)(4) of this section and §1.955A-2(a)(4). Charges for services performed by a controlled foreign corporation for itself shall in no event be included in income for any other purpose.

§1.954-7 (Proposed Treasury Decision, published 8-9-76.) **Increase in qualified investments in foreign base company shipping operations.**

(a) **Determination of investments at close of taxable year—(1) In general.** Under section 954(g), the increase in qualified investments in foreign base company shipping operations, for purposes of section 954(b)(2) and paragraph (b)(1) of §1.954-1, of any controlled foreign corporation for any taxable year is, except as provided in paragraph (b) of this section, the amount by which—

(i) The controlled foreign corporation's qualified investments in foreign base company shipping operations at the close of the taxable year, exceed

(ii) Its qualified investments in foreign base company shipping operations at the close of the preceding taxable year.

(2) **Preceding taxable year.** For purposes of this section, a taxable year which begins before January 1, 1976, may be a preceding taxable year.

(3) **Cross-reference.** See section 955(b) and §1.955A-2 for the definition of the term "qualified investments in foreign base company shipping operations".

(b) **Election to determine investments at close of following taxable year—(1) General rule.** In lieu of determining an increase in qualified investments in foreign base

Proposed Reg. §1.954-7

company shipping operations for a taxable year in the manner provided in paragraph (a) of this section. A United States shareholder of a controlled foreign corporation may make an election under section 955(b)(3) to determine the increase for the corporation's taxable year by ascertaining the amount by which—

(i) Such corporation's qualified investments in foreign base company shipping operations at the close of the taxable year immediately following such taxable year, exceed

(ii) Its qualified investments in foreign base company shipping operations at the close of the taxable year immediately preceding such following taxable year.

(2) **Election with respect to first taxable year.** Notwithstanding subparagraph (1) of this paragraph, if an election is made without consent by a United States shareholder under §1.955A-4(b)(1) with respect to a controlled foreign corporation the increase in such controlled foreign corporation's qualified investments in foreign base company shipping operations for the first taxable year to which such election applies shall be the amount by which—

(i) Such corporation's qualified investments in foreign base company shipping operations at the close of the taxable year immediately following such first taxable year, exceed

(ii) Its qualified investments in foreign base company shipping operations at the close of the taxable year immediately preceding such first taxable year.

(3) **Manner of making election.** For the manner of making an election under section 955(b)(3), and for rules pertaining to the revocation of such an election, see §1.955A-4.

(4) **Coordination with prior law.** If a United States shareholder makes an election without consent under §1.955A-4(b)(1) with respect to a controlled foreign corporation, then such corporation's increase in qualified investments in foreign base company shipping operations for the first taxable year to which such election applies shall be determined by disregarding any change which occurs during such taxable year in the amount of such corporation's investments in stock or obligations of a less developed country shipping company described in §1.955-5(b) if both of the following conditions exist:

(i) Such taxable year is the first taxable year of such corporation which begins after December 31, 1975, and

(ii) Such United States shareholder has elected to determine the change in such corporation's qualified investments in less developed countries for its last taxable year beginning before January 1, 1976, under §1.954-5(b) or §1.955-3.

(5) **Illustrations.** The application of this paragraph may be illustrated by the following examples:

Example (1). (a) Controlled foreign corporation X is a wholly-owned subsidiary of domestic corporation M. X uses the calender year as the taxable year. The amounts of X's qualified investments in foreign base company shipping operations at the close of 1975 through 1979 are as follows:

Qualified investments at 12-31-75	$16,000
Qualified investments at 12-31-76	$17,000
Qualified investments at 12-31-77	$23,000
Qualified investments at 12-31-78	$28,000
Qualified investments at 12-31-79	$30,000

(b) Assume that M properly files without consent a timely election under §1.955A-4(b)(1) to determine X's increase for 1976 in qualified investments in foreign base company shipping operations pursuant to this paragraph, and that the election remains in force through 1978. Then X's increases for 1976 through 1978 in qualified investments in foreign base company shipping operations are as follows:

Increase for 1976 ($23,000 minus $16,000)	$7,000
Increase for 1977 ($28,000 minus $23,000)	$5,000
Increase for 1978 ($30,000 minus $28,000)	2,000

Example (2). Assume the same facts as in example (1), except that M never files an election under §1.955A-4(b)(1). X's increases for 1976 through 1978 in qualified investments in foreign base company shipping operations are as follows:

Increase for 1976 ($17,000 minus $16,000) $1,000
Increase for 1977 ($23,000 minus $17,000) $6,000
Increase for 1978 ($28,000 minus $23,000) $5,000

Example (3). The facts are the same as in example (1), except that X's qualified investments in foreign base company shipping operations include an investment in less developed country shipping companies described in §1.955-5(b) of $500 on December 31, 1975, and $750 on December 31, 1976. Assume further that M has made an election under section 955(b)(3) (as in effect before the enactment of the Tax Reduction Act of 1975) with respect to X's taxable year 1975. Then X's increase in qualified investments in foreign base company shipping operations for 1976 is $6,750 (i.e., $7,000 − $250).

(c) Illustration. The application of this section may be illustrated by the following example:

Example. (a) Controlled foreign corporation X uses the calendar year as the taxable year. On December 31, 1975, X's qualified investments in foreign base company shipping operations (determined as provided in §1.955A-2(g)) consist of the following amounts:

Cash	$ 6,000
Readily marketable securities	1,000
Stock of related controlled foreign corporations	4,000
Traffic and other receivables	14,000
Foreign income tax refunds receivable	1,000
Prepaid shipping expenses and shipping inventories ashore	1,000
Vessel construction funds	0
Vessels	123,000
Vessels plans and construction in progress	3,000
Containers and chassis	0
Terminal property and equipment	2,000
Shipping office (land and building)	1,000
Vessel spare parts ashore	1,000
Performance deposits	2,000
Deferred charges	2,000
Stock of less developed country shipping company described in §1.955-5 (b)	10,000
	$171,000

(b) On December 31, 1976, X's qualified investments in foreign base company shipping operations (determined as provided in §1.955A-2(g)) consist of the following amounts:

Cash	$ 5,000
Readily marketable securities	2,000
Stock of related controlled foreign corporations	4,000
Traffic and other receivables	16,000
Foreign income tax refunds receivable	3,000
Prepaid shipping expenses and shipping inventories ashore	2,000
Vessel construction funds	1,000
Vessels	117,000
Vessel plans and construction in progress	12,000
Containers and chassis	4,000
Terminal property and equipment	2,000
Shipping office (land and building)	1,000
Vessel spare parts ashore	1,000
Performance deposits	2,000
Deferred charges	2,000
Stock of less developed country shipping company described in §1.955-5(b)	0
	$174,000

Proposed Reg. §1.954-7

(c) For 1976, X's increase in qualified investments in foreign base company shipping operations is $3,000, which amount is determined as follows:

Qualified investments at 12-31-76	$174,000
Qualified investments at 12-31-75	171,000
Increase for 1976	$ 3,000

A new §1.955-0 is added immediately after §1.955.

§1.955-0 (Proposed Treasury Decision, published 8-9-76 and 2-9-78.) **Effective dates.**

(a) **Section 955 as in effect before the enactment of the Tax Reduction Act of 1975—(1) In general.** In general, §§ 1.955-1 through 1.955-6 are applicable with respect to withdrawals of previously excluded subpart F income from qualified investment in less developed countries for taxable years of foreign corporations beginning after December 31, 1962, and to taxable years of United States shareholders (as defined in section 951(b)) within which or with which such taxable years of such foreign corporations end. However, such sections are effective with respect to withdrawals of amounts invested in less developed country shipping companies described in section 955(c)(2) (as in effect before the enactment of the Tax Reduction Act of 1975) only for taxable years of foreign corporations beginning before January 1, 1976, and for taxable years of United States shareholders (as defined in section 951(b)) within which or with which such taxable years of such foreign corporations end. For rules applicable to withdrawals of amounts invested in less developed country shipping companies described in section 955(c)(2) (as in effect before such enactment), in taxable years of foreign corporations beginning after December 31, 1975, see section 955(b)(5) (as amended by such Act) and §§1.955A-1 through 1.955A-4.

(2) **References.** Except as otherwise provided therein, all references contained in §§1.955-1 through 1.955-6 to section 954 or 955 or to the regulations under section 954 are to those sections and regulations as in effect before the enactment of Tax Reduction Act of 1975. For regulations under section 954 (as in effect before such enactment), see 26 CFR 1.954-1 through 1.954-5 (Rev. as of April 1, 1975). For taxable years of foreign corporations beginning after December 31, 1975, and for taxable years of United States shareholders (as described in section 951(b)) within which or with which such taxable years of such foreign corporations end, the definitions of less developed countries and less developed country corporations contained in section 902(d) (as amended by such Act) and §1.902-2 apply for purposes of determining the credit for corporate stockholders in foreign corporations under section 902.

(b) **Section 955 as amended by the Tax Reduction Act of 1976.** Except as otherwise provided therein, §§1.955A through 1.955A-4 are applicable to taxable years of foreign corporations beginning after December 31, 1975, and to taxable years of United States shareholders (as defined in section 951(b)) within which or with which such taxable years of such foreign corporations end.

1. Paragraph (a) of §1.955-1 is amended; and
2. Paragraph (b) is amended as follows:

(a). Subparagraph (2)(i)(a) is revised by inserting "(including prior taxable years beginning after December 31, 1975)" immediately after "1962"

(b). Subparagraph (2)(ii)(a) is amended.

(c). A new subparagraph (3) is added.

The added and amended provisions read as follows:

§1.955-1 (Proposed Treasury Decision, published 2-9-78; 8-9-76.) **Shareholder's pro rata share of amount of previously excluded subpart F income withdrawn from investment in less developed countries.**

(a) **In general.** Pursuant to section 951(a)(1)(A)(ii) and the regulations thereunder, a United States shareholder of a controlled foreign corporation must include in its gross income its pro rata share (as determined in accordance with paragraph (c) of this section) of the amount of such controlled foreign corporation's previously excluded subpart F income which is withdrawn for any taxable year from investment in less developed countries. Section 955 provides rules for determining the amount of a controlled foreign corporation's previously excluded subpart F income for any taxable year of the corporation beginning after December 31, 1962 that is withdrawn from investment in less developed countries for any taxable year of the corporation beginning before January 1, 1976. Except for investments in less developed country shipping companies, section 955 also provides rules for determining the amount of a controlled foreign corporation's previously excluded subpart F income for any taxable year of the corporation beginning after December 31, 1962 which is withdrawn from investment in less developed countries in taxable years of the corporation beginning after December 31, 1975. To determine the amount of a controlled foreign corporation's previously excluded subpart F income withdrawn from investment in less developed country shipping companies described in section 955(c)(2) in taxable years of a controlled foreign corporation beginning after December 31, 1975, see section 955(b)(5) (as in effect after amendment by the Tax Reduction Act of 1975) and §§1.955A-1 through 1.955A-4. For effective dates, see §1.955-0.

(b) Amount withdrawn by controlled foreign corporation. * * *

(2) Limitations applicable in determining decreases. * * *

(ii) Treatment of earnings and profits. * * *

(a)(1) Amounts which, for the current taxable year, are included in the gross income of a United States shareholder of such controlled foreign corporation under section 951(a)(1)(A)(i) or (iii), or

(2) Amounts which, for any prior taxable year, have been included in the gross income of a United States shareholder of such controlled foreign corporation under section 951(a) and have not been distributed; or

* * * * * * * * * * * *

(3) Taxable years beginning after December 31, 1975. (i) In the case of a taxable year of a controlled foreign corporation beginning after December 31, 1975, §1.955-2(b)(5) must be applied in determining the amount of its qualified investments in less developed countries on both of the determination dates applicable to such taxable year.

(ii) The application of this subparagraph may be illustrated by the following examples:

Example (1). (a) Controlled foreign corporation M uses the calendar year as the taxable year. Throughout 1974 through 1976, M owns 100 percent of the only class of stock of foreign corporation N, a less developed country shipping company described in §1.955-5(b), and M owns no other stock or obligations. The amount taken into account under §1.955-2(d) with respect to the stock of N is $10,000 at the close of 1974, 1975, and 1976. The amount of M's previously excluded subpart F income which is withdrawn for 1975 (a year to which §1.955-2(b)(5) does not apply) from investment in less developed countries is zero, determined as follows:

(1)	Qualified investments in less developed countries at the close of 1974	$10,000
(2)	Less: qualified investments in less developed countries at the close of 1975	10,000
(3)	Balance	$ 0

(Further computations similar to those set out in lines (iv) through (ix) of example (1) of paragraph (d) of this section are unnecessary because the balance in line (3) of this example is zero).

(b) As a result of §1.955-2(b)(5)(ii), the amount of M's previously excluded subpart F

Proposed Reg. §1.995-1

income which is withdrawn for 1976 from investment in less developed countries is zero, determined as follows:

(1)	Qualified investments in less developed countries at the close of 1975	$ 0
(2)	Less: qualified investments in less developed countries at the close of 1976	0
(3)	Balance	$ 0

Example (2). The facts are the same as in example (1), except that foreign corporation N is a less developed country corporation described in §1.955-5(a). The amount of M's previously excluded subpart F income withdrawn for 1976 from investment in less developed countries is zero, determined as follows:

(1)	Qualified investments in less developed countries at the close of 1975	$10,000
(2)	Less: qualified investments in less developed countries at the close of 1976	10,000
(3)	Balance	$ 0

* *

Section 1.955-2 is amended by revising paragraph (b)(4) and adding new paragraphs (b)(5), (b)(6), and (d)(4) thereto to read as follows:

§1.955-2 (Proposed Treasury Decision, published 8-9-76. **Amount of a controlled foreign corporation's qualified investments in less developed countries.**

* * * * * * * * * * * *

(b) **Special rules.** * * *

(4) **Date of acquisition.** For purposes of paragraphs (a)(2) and (b)(5)(i) of this section, stock or an obligation shall be considered acquired by a foreign corporation as of the date such corporation acquires an adjusted basis in the stock or obligation. For this purpose, in a case in which a foreign corporation acquires stock or an obligation in a transaction (other than a reorganization of the type described in section 368(a)(1)(E) or (F)) in which no gain or loss would be recognized had the transaction been between two domestic corporations, such corporation will be considered to have acquired an adjusted basis in such stock or obligation as of the date such transaction occurs.

(5) **Taxable years beginning after December 31, 1975.** For taxable years beginning after December 31, 1975, qualified investments in less developed countries do not include—

(i) Any property acquired after the latest determination date applicable to a taxable year beginning before December 31, 1975,

(ii) Stock or obligations of a less developed country shipping company described in §1.955-5(b), and

(iii) Stock or obligations which were not treated as qualified investments in less developed countries on the later of the two determination dates applicable to the preceding taxable year.

See §1.955-1(b)(3) for rules relating to the application of this subparagraph. See §1.955A-2(h) for rules relating to the treatment of investments in stock or obligations described in subdivision (ii) of this subparagraph as qualified investments in foreign base company shipping operations.

(6) **Determination dates.** For purposes of subparagraph (5) of this paragraph and §1.955-1(b)(3), the determination dates applicable to a taxable year of a controlled foreign corporation are—

(i) Except as provided in subdivision (ii) of this subparagraph, the close of such taxable year and the close of the preceding taxable year, and

(ii) With respect to a United States shareholder who has made an election under section 955(b)(3) to determine such corporation's increase in qualified investments in less developed countries at the close of the following taxable year, the close of such taxable year and the close of the taxable year immediately following such taxable year.

* * * * * * * * * * * *

(d) Amount attributable to property. * * *

(4) Taxable years beginning after December 31, 1975. For taxable years beginning after December 31, 1975, the amount taken into account under subparagraph (1) of this paragraph with respect to any property which constitutes a qualified investment in less developed countries shall not exceed the amount taken into account with respect to such property at the close of the preceding taxable year.

* *

Section 1.955-3 is amended as follows:

1. The first sentence of paragraph (a) is revised by deleting "In lieu of determining the increase under" and inserting in lieu thereof "In lieu of determining the increase for a taxable year of a foreign corporation beginning before January 1, 1976, under".

2. Immediately after the last sentence of paragraph (b)(1) a new sentence is added.

3. Paragraph (b)(2) is revised by adding a new sentence after the second sentence thereof.

4. Paragraph (c)(3) is revised by adding a new sentence after the fifth sentence thereof.

5. Paragraph (c)(3)(i) is amended by inserting "name, address, and taxpayer identification number" in lieu of "name and address".

The added provisions read as follows:

§1.955-3 (Proposed Treasury Decision, published 8-9-76 and 2-9-78.) **Election as to date of determining qualified investments in less developed countries.**

* * * * * * * * * * * *

(b) Time and manner of making election—(1) Without consent. * * * For taxable years of a foreign corporation beginning after December 31, 1975, no election under this section with respect to a controlled foreign corporation may be made without the consent of the Commissioner.

* * * * * * * * * * * *

(2) With consent. * * * Consent will not be granted if the first taxable year of the controlled foreign corporation with respect to which the shareholder desires to compute an amount described in section 954(b)(1) in accordance with the election provided in this section begins after December 31, 1975.

(c) Effect of election. * * *

(3) Revocation. * * * The application may also be filed in a taxable year beginning after December 31, 1975.

* * * * * * * * * * * *

The following new sections are added immediately after §1.955-6:

§1.955A-1 (Proposed Treasury Decision, published 8-9-76.) **Shareholder's pro rata share of amount of previously excluded subpart F income withdrawn from investment in foreign base company shipping operations.**

(a) In general. Section 955 provides rules for determining the amount of a controlled foreign corporation's previously excluded subpart F income which is withdrawn for any taxable year beginning after December 31, 1975, from investment in foreign base company shipping operations. Pursuant to section 951(a)(1)(A)(iii) and the regulations thereunder, a United States shareholder of such controlled foreign corporation must include in his gross income his pro rata share of such amount as determined in accordance with paragraph (c) of this section.

(b) **Amount withdrawn by controlled foreign corporation—(1) In general.** For purposes of sections 951 through 964, the amount of a controlled foreign corporation's previously excluded subpart F income which is withdrawn for any taxable year from investment in foreign base company shipping operations is an amount equal to the decrease for such year in such corporation's qualified investments in foreign base company shipping operations. Such decrease is, except as provided in §1.955A-4—

(i) An amount equal to the excess of the amount of its qualified investments in foreign base company shipping operations at the close of the preceding taxable year over the amount of its qualified investments in foreign base company shipping operations at the close of the taxable year, minus

(ii) The amount (if any) by which recognized losses on sales or exchanges by such corporation during the taxable year of qualified investments in foreign base company shipping operations exceed its recognized gains on sales or exchanges during such year of qualified investments in foreign base company shipping operations,

but only to the extent that the net amount so determined does not exceed the limitation determined under subparagraph (2) of this paragraph. See §1.955A-2 for determining the amount of qualified investments in foreign base company shipping operations.

(2) **Limitation applicable in determining decreases—**(i) In general. The limitation referred to in subparagraph (1) of this paragraph for any taxable year of a controlled foreign corporation shall be the lesser of the following two limitations:

(A) The sum of (1) the controlled foreign corporation's earnings and profits (or deficit in earnings and profits) for the taxable year, computed as of the close of the taxable year without diminution by reason of any distribution made during the taxable year, (2) the sum of its earnings and profits (or deficits in earnings and profits) accumulated for prior taxable years beginning after December 31, 1975, and (3) the amount described in subparagraph (3) of this paragraph; or

(B) The sum of the amounts excluded under section 954(b)(2) (see subparagraph (4) of this paragraph) from the foreign base company income of such corporation for all prior taxable years beginning after December 31, 1975, minus the sum of the amounts (determined under this paragraph) of its previously excluded subpart F income withdrawn from investment in foreign base company shipping operations for all such prior taxable years.

(ii) Certain exclusions from earnings and profits. For purposes of determining the earnings and profits of a controlled foreign corporation under subdivision (i)(A)(1) and (2) of this subparagraph, such earnings and profits shall be considered not to include any amounts which are attributable to—

(A) (1) Amounts which, for the current taxable year, are included in the gross income of a United States shareholder of such controlled foreign corporation under section 951(a)(1)(A)(i), or

(2) Amounts which, for any prior taxable year, have been included in the gross income of a United States shareholder of such controlled foreign corporation under section 951(a) and have not been distributed; or

(B) (1) Amounts which, for the current taxable year, are included in the gross income of a United States shareholder of such controlled foreign corporation under section 551(b) or would be so included under such section but for the fact that such amounts were distributed to such shareholder during the taxable year, or

(2) Amounts which, for any prior taxable year, have been included in the gross income of a United States shareholder of such controlled foreign corporation under section 551(b) and have not been distributed.

The rules of this subdivision apply only in determining the limitation on a controlled foreign corporation's decrease in qualified investments in foreign base company shipping

Proposed Reg. §1.955A-1

operations. See section 959 and the regulations thereunder for rules relating to the exclusion from gross income of previously taxed earnings and profits.

(3) Carryover of amounts relating to investments in less developed country shipping companies—(i) In general. The amount described in this subparagraph for any taxable year of a controlled foreign corporation beginning after December 31, 1975, is the lesser of—

(A) The excess of the amount described in subdivision (ii) of this subparagraph, over the amount described in subdivision (iii) of this subparagraph, or

(B) The limitation determined under subdivision (iv) of this subparagraph.

(ii) Previously excluded subpart F income invested in less developed country shipping companies. The amount described in this subdivision for all taxable years of a controlled foreign corporation beginning after December 31, 1975, is the lesser of—

(A) The amount of such corporation's qualified investments (determined under §1.955-2 other than paragraph (b)(5) thereof) in less developed country shipping companies described in §1.955-5(b) at the close of the last taxable year of such corporation beginning before January 1, 1976, or

(B) The limitation determined under §1.955-1(b)(2)(i)(b) (relating to previously excluded subpart F income) for the first taxable year of such corporation beginning after January 1, 1976.

(iii) Amounts previously carried over. The amount described in this subdivision for any taxable year of a controlled foreign corporation shall be the sum of the excesses determined for each prior taxable year beginning after December 31, 1976, of—

(A) The amount (determined under this paragraph) of such corporation's previously excluded subpart F income withdrawn from investment in foreign base company shipping operations, over

(B) The sum of the earnings and profits determined under subparagraph (2)(i)(A)(1) and (2) of this paragraph.

(iv) Extent attributable to accumulated earnings and profits. The limitation determined under this subdivision for any taxable year of a controlled foreign corporation is the sum of such controlled foreign corporation's earnings and profits (or deficits in earnings and profits) accumulated for taxable years beginning after December 31, 1962, and before January 1, 1976. For purposes of the preceding sentence, earnings and profits shall be determined by excluding the amounts described in subparagraph (2)(ii)(A) and (B) of this paragraph.

(v) Illustration. The application of this subparagraph may be illustrated by the following example:

Example. (a) Throughout the period here involved A is a United States shareholder of controlled foreign corporation M, M is not a foreign personal holding company, and M uses the calendar year as the taxable year.

(b) The amount described in this subparagraph for M's taxable year 1978 with respect to A is determined as follows, based on the facts shown in the following table:

(1)	Investment in less developed country shipping companies on December 31, 1975 (subdivision (ii) (A) amount)	$10,000
(2)	§1.955-1(b)(2)(i)(b) limitation for 1976 (previously excluded subpart F income not withdrawn from investment in less developed countries) (subdivision (ii) (B) amount)	$50,000
(3)	Subdivision (ii) amount (lesser of lines (1) and (2))	$10,000
(4)	Subdivision (iii) amount: Excess for 1977 of M's previously excluded subpart F income withdrawn from investment in foreign base country shipping operations, $3,000, over the sum of the amounts determined under subparagraphs (2) (i) (a)(1) and (2) of this paragraph, $1,000	2,000
(5)	Excess of line (3) over line (4)	$ 8,000
(6)	Sum of M's earnings and profits accumulated for 1962 through 1975, determined on December 31, 1978	$26,000
(7)	Amount described in this subparagraph for 1978 (lesser of line (5) and line (6))	$ 8,000

(c) For 1978, M's earnings and profits (reduced as provided in §1.955-1(b)(2)(ii)(a)(1)) are $19,000, and the amount of M's previously excluded subpart F income withdrawn from investment in less developed countries (determined under §1.955-1(b)) is $42,000. Consequently, $23,000 of M's earnings and profits accumulated for 1962 through 1975 are attributable to such $42,000 amount, and will therefore be excluded under subparagraph (2)(ii)(A)(2) of this paragraph from M's earnings and profits accumulated for 1962 through 1975, determined as of December 31, 1979. No other portion of M's earnings and profits accumulated for 1962 through 1975 is distributed or included in the gross income of a United States shareholder in 1978.

(d) The amount described in this subparagraph for M's taxable year 1979 with respect to A is determined as follows, based on the additional facts shown in the following table:

(1)	Subdivision (ii) amount (line (3) from paragraph (b) of this example)	$10,000
(2)	Subdivision (iii) amount: (i) Excess for 1977 from line (4) of paragraph (b) of this example	$ 2,000
	(ii) Plus: excess for 1978 of M's previously excluded subpart F income withdrawn from investment in foreign base country shipping operations, $6,000 over the sum of the amounts determined under subparagraphs (2) (i) (A) (1) and (2) of this paragraph, $25,000	$0
	(iii) Subdivision (iii) amount	$ 2,000
(3)	Excess of line (3) over line (4) (iii)	$ 8,000
(4)	Sum of M's earnings and profits accumlated for 1962 through 1975, determined on December 31, 1979 ($26,000 minus $23,000)	$ 3,000
(5)	Amount described in this subparagraph for 1979 (lesser of line (5) and line (6))	$ 3,000

(4) **Amount excluded.** For purposes of subparagraph (2)(i)(B) of this paragraph, the amount excluded under section 954(b)(2) from the foreign base company income of a controlled foreign corporation for any taxable year beginning after December 31, 1975, is the excess of—

(i) The amount which would have been equal to the subpart F income of such corporation for such taxable year if such corporation had had no increase in qualified investments in foreign base company shipping operations for such taxable year, over

(ii) The subpart F income of such corporation for such taxable year.

(c) **Shareholder's pro rata share of amount withdrawn by controlled foreign corporation—(1) In general.** A United States shareholder's pro rata share of a controlled foreign corporation's previously excluded subpart F income withdrawn for any taxable year from investment in foreign base company shipping operations in his pro rata share of the amount withdrawn for such year by such corporation, as determined under paragraph (b) of this section. See section 955(a)(3). Such pro rata share shall be determined in accordance with the principles of §1.951-1(e).

(2) **Special rule.** A United States shareholder's pro rata share of the net amount determined under paragraph (b)(2)(i)(B) of this section with respect to any stock of the controlled foreign corporation owned by such shareholder shall be determined without taking into account any amount attributable to a period prior to the date on which such shareholder acquired such stock. See section 1248 and the regulations thereunder for rules governing treatment of gain from sales or exchanges of stock in certain foreign corporations.

(d) **Illustrations.** The application of this section may be illustrated by the following examples:

Proposed Reg. §1.955A-1

Example (1). A, a United States shareholder, owns 60 percent of the only class of stock of M Corporation, a controlled foreign corporation throughout the entire period here involved. Both A and M use the calender year as a taxable year. The amount of M's previously excluded subpart F income withdrawn for 1978 from investment in foreign base company shipping operations is $40,000, and A's pro rata share of such amount is $24,000, determined as follows based on the facts shown in the following table:

(a)	Qualified investments in foreign base company shipping operations at the close of 1977	$125,000
(b)	Less: qualified investments in foreign base company shipping operations at the close of 1978	75,000
(c)	Balance	50,000
(d)	Less: excess of recognized losses ($15,000) over recognized gains ($5,000) on sales during 1978 of qualified investments in foreign base company shipping operations	10,000
(e)	Tentative decrease in qualified investments in foreign base company shipping operations for 1978	40,000
(f)	Earnings and profits for 1976, 1977, and 1978	45,000
(g)	Plus: amount determined under paragraph (b)(3) of this section	0
(h)	Earnings and profits limitation	$ 45,000
(i)	Excess of amount excluded under section 954(b)(2) from foreign base company income for 1976 ($75,000) over amount of previously excluded subpart F income withdrawn for 1977 from investment in foreign base company shipping operations ($25,000)	50,000
(j)	M's amount of previously excluded subpart F income withdrawn for 1978 from investment in foreign base company shipping operations (item (e), but not to exceed the lesser of item (h) or item (i))	40,000
(k)	A's pro rata share of M Corporation's amount of previously excluded subpart F income withdrawn for 1978 from investment in foreign base company shipping operations (60 percent of $40,000)	$ 24,000

Example (2). The facts are the same as in example (1), except that M's earnings and profits (determined under paragraph (b)(2) of this section) for 1976, 1977, and 1978 (item (f)) are $30,000 instead of $45,000. M's amount of previously excluded subpart F income withdrawn for 1978 from investment in foreign base company shipping operations is $30,000. A's pro rata share of such amount is $18,000 (60 percent of $30,000).

Example (3). The facts are the same as in example (1), except that the excess of the amount excluded under section 954(b)(2) for 1976 from M Corporation's foreign base company income over the amount of its previously excluded subpart F income withdrawn for 1977 from investment in foreign base company shipping operations (item (i)) is $20,000 instead of $50,000. M's amount of previously excluded subpart F income withdrawn for 1978 from investment in foreign base company shipping operations is $20,000. A's pro rata share of such amount is $12,000 (60 percent of $20,000).

§1.955A-2 (Proposed Treasury Decision, published 8-9-76.) **Amount of a controlled foreign corporation's qualified investments in foreign base company shipping operations.**

(a) *Qualified investments*—(1) *In general.* Under section 955(b), for purposes of sections 951 through 964, a controlled foreign corporation's "qualified investments in foreign base company shipping operations" are investments in—

(i) Any aircraft or vessel, to the extent that such aircraft or vessel is used (or hired or leased for use) in foreign commerce.

(ii) Related shipping assets (within the meaning of paragraph (b) of this section),

(iii) Stock or obligations of a related controlled foreign corporation, to the extent provided in paragraph (c) of this section,

(iv) A partnership, to the extent provided in paragraph (d) of this section, and

(v) Stock or obligations of a less developed country shipping company described in §1.955-5(b), as provided in paragraph (h) of this section.

(2) **Coordination of provisions.** No amount shall be counted as a qualified investment in foreign base company shipping operations under more than one provision of this section. Thus, for example, if a $10,000 investment in stock of a controlled foreign corporation is treated as a qualified investment in foreign base company shipping operations under both subparagraph (1)(iii) and (v) of this paragraph, then such $10,000 is counted only once as a qualified investment in foreign base company shipping operations.

(3) **Definitions.** If the meaning of any term is defined or explained in §1.954-6, then such term shall have the same meaning when used in this section.

(4) **Extent of use.** (i) For purposes of subparagraph (1)(i) of this paragraph and paragraph (b)(1) of this section, the extent to which an asset of a controlled foreign corporation is used during a taxable year in foreign base company shipping operations shall be determined on the basis of the proportion for such year which the foreign base company shipping income derived from the use of such asset bears to the total gross income derived from the use of such asset.

(ii) For purposes of determining under subdivision (i) of this subparagraph the amounts of foreign base company shipping income and gross income of a controlled foreign corporation—

(A) Such amounts shall be deemed to include an arm's length charge (see §1.954-6(h)(5)) for services performed by such corporation for itself.

(B) Such amounts shall be deemed to include an arm's length charge for the use of an asset (such as a vessel under construction or laid up for repairs) which is held for use in foreign base company shipping operations, but is not actually so used,

(C) Foreign base company shipping income shall be deemed to include amounts earned in taxable years beginning before January 1, 1976, and

(D) The district director shall make such other adjustments to such amounts as are necessary to properly determine the extent to which any asset is used in foreign base company shipping operations.

(b) **Related shipping assets—(1) In general.** For purposes of this section, the term "related shipping asset" means any asset which is used (or held for use) for or in connection with the production of income described in §1.954-6(b)(1)(i) or (ii), but only to the extent that such asset is so used (or is so held for use).

(2) **Examples.** Examples of assets of a controlled foreign corporation which are used (or held for use) for or in connection with the production of income described in subparagraph (1) of this paragraph include—

(i) Money, bank deposits, and other temporary investments which are reasonably necessary to meet the working capital requirements of such corporation in its conduct of foreign base company shipping operations,

(ii) Accounts receivable and evidences of indebtedness which arise from the conduct of foreign base company shipping operations by such corporation or by a related person,

(iii) Amounts (other than amounts described in subdivision (i) of this subparagraph) deposited in bank accounts or invested in readily marketable securities pursuant to a specific, definite, and feasible plan to purchase any tangible asset for use in foreign base company shipping operations,

(iv) Amounts paid into escrow to secure the payment of (A) charter hire for an aircraft, vessel, or other asset used in foreign base company shipping operations or (B) a debt which constitutes a specific charge against such an asset,

(v) Capitalized expenditures (such as progress payments) made under a contract to purchase any asset for use in foreign base company shipping operations,

(vi) Prepaid expenses and deferred charges incurred in the course of foreign base company shipping operations,

(vii) Stock acquired and retained to insure a source of supplies or services used in the conduct of foreign base company shipping operations, and

Proposed Reg. §1.955A-2

(viii) Currency futures acquired and retained as a hedge against international currency fluctuations in connection with foreign base company shipping operations.

(3) **Limitations.** (i) Notwithstanding any other provision of this paragraph, the term "related shipping assets" does not include any money or other intangible assets of a controlled foreign corporation, to the extent that such assets are permitted to accumulate in excess of the reasonably anticipated needs of the business.

(ii) If a controlled foreign corporation accumulates money or other intangible assets pursuant to a plan to purchase one or more vessels for use in foreign commerce, and if—
 (A) The amount so accumulated, plus
 (B) The sum of the amounts accumulated by other controlled foreign corporations which are related persons (within the meaning of section 954(d)(3)) pursuant to similar plans,

at any time exceeds 110 percent of a reasonable down payment on the first vessel so planned to be purchased, then such plan will not normally be considered to be feasible. For purposes of the preceding sentence, a reasonable down payment shall not exceed 25 percent of the total cost of acquisition.

(iii) In determining whether a plan to purchase any asset other than a vessel for use in foreign base company shipping operations is feasible, principles similar to those stated in subdivision (ii) of this subparagraph shall be applied.

(4) **Cross-reference.** See §1.954-7(c) for additional illustrations bearing on the application of this paragraph.

(c) **Stock and obligations—(1) In general.** Investments by a controlled foreign corporation (the "first corporation") in stock or obligations of a second controlled foreign corporation which is a related person (within the meaning of section 954(d)(3)) are considered to be qualified investments in foreign base company shipping operations only if each asset held by such second corporation is either (i) an aircraft or vessel used (at least to some extent) in foreign commerce, or (ii) a related shipping asset, and then only to the extent that the assets of such second corporation are used in foreign base company shipping operations. See subparagraph (2) of this paragraph.

(2) **Extent of use.** On any determination date applicable to a taxable year of the first corporation, the extent to which the assets of the second corporation are used in foreign base company shipping operations shall be determined on the basis of the proportion which the amount of such second corporation's qualified investments in foreign base company shipping operations bears to its net worth, such proportion to be determined at the close of the second corporation's last taxable year which ends on or before such determination date. For purposes of the preceding sentence—

(i) A controlled foreign corporation's net worth is the total adjusted basis of the corporate assets reduced by the total outstanding principal amount of the corporate liabilities, and

(ii) The determination dates applicable to a taxable year of a controlled foreign corporation are—

(A) Except as provided in (B) of this subdivision, the close of such taxable year and the close of the preceding taxable year, and

(B) With respect to a United States shareholder who has made an election under section 955(b)(3) to determine such corporation's increase in qualified investments in foreign base company shipping operations at the close of the following taxable year, the close of such taxable year and the close of the taxable year immediately following such taxable year.

(3) **Illustrations.** The application of this paragraph may be illustrated by the following examples:

Example (1). On December 31, 1976, controlled foreign corporation X owns 100 percent of the single class stock of controlled foreign corporation Y. X and Y both use the calendar year as the taxable year. On December 31, 1976, Y's assets consist entirely of a vessel used in foreign commerce and related shipping assets. On such date Y has qualified investments in foreign base company shipping operations (determined under paragraph (g) of this section) of $60,000, and a net worth of $100,000. If X's investment in the stock of Y is $50,000, then $30,000 of such amount, i.e.,

$$\frac{\$60{,}000}{\$100{,}000} \times \$50{,}000,$$ is a qualified investment in foreign base company shipping operations.

Example (2). The facts are the same as in example (1), except that on December 31, 1976, Y has qualified investments in foreign base company shipping operations (determined under paragraph (g) of this section) of $16,000 and a net worth of $20,000. If X's investment in the stock of Y is $50,000, then $40,000, i.e.,

$$\frac{\$16{,}000}{\$20{,}000} \times \$50{,}000,$$ is a qualified investment in foreign base company shipping operations.

(d) **Partnerships—(1) In general.** A controlled foreign corporation's investment in a partnership at the close of any taxable year of such corporation shall be considered a qualified investment in foreign base company shipping operations to the extent of the proportion which such corporation's foreign base company income for such taxable year would bear to its gross income for such taxable year if—

(i) Such corporation had realized no income other than its distributive share of the partnership gross income, and

(ii) Such corporation's income were adjusted in accordance with the rules stated in paragraph (a)(4)(ii)(B) and (D) of this section.

(2) **Transitional rule.** For purposes of subparagraph (1)(i) of this paragraph, the controlled foreign corporation's distributive share of the partnership gross income shall not include any amount attributable to income earned by the partnership before the first day of such corporation's first taxable year beginning after December 31, 1975.

(3) **Cross-reference.** See paragraph (g)(4) of this section for rules relating to the determination of the amount of a controlled foreign corporation's investment in a partnership.

(e) **Trusts—(1) In general.** An investment in a trust is not a qualified investment in foreign base company shipping operations.

(2) **Grantor trusts.** Notwithstanding subparagraph (1) of this paragraph, if a controlled foreign corporation is treated as the owner of any portion of a trust under Subpart E of Part I of Subchapter J (relating to grantors and others treated as substantial owners), then for purposes of this section such controlled foreign corporation is deemed to be the actual owner of such portion of the assets of the trust. Accordingly, its investments in such assets (as determined under paragraph (g)(5) of this section) may be treated as a qualified investment in foreign base company shipping operations.

(3) **Definitions.** For purposes of this section, the term "trust" means a trust as defined in §301.7701-4.

(f) **Excluded property.** For purposes of paragraph (b) of this section, property acquired principally for the purpose of artificially increasing the amount of a controlled foreign corporation's qualified investments in foreign base company shipping operations will not be recognized; whether an item of property is acquired principally for such purpose will depend upon all the facts and circumstances of each case. One of the factors that will be considered in making such a determination with respect to an item of property is whether the item is disposed of within 6 months after the date of its acquisition.

(g) **Amount attributable to property—(1) General rule.** For purposes of this section, the amount taken into account under section 955(b)(4) with respect to any property which constitutes a qualified investment in foreign base company shipping operations shall be its adjusted basis as of the applicable determination date, reduced by the outstanding principal amount of any liability (other than a liability described in subparagraph (2) of this paragraph) to which such property is subject on such date, including a liability secured only by the general credit of the controlled foreign corporation. Liabilities shall be taken into account in the following order:

Proposed Reg. §1.955A-2

(i) The adjusted basis of each and every item of corporate property shall be reduced by any specific charge (nonrecourse or otherwise) to which such item is subject. For this purpose, if a liability constitutes a specific charge against several items of property and cannot definitely be allocated to any single item of property, the specific charge shall be apportioned against each of such items of property in that ratio which the adjusted basis of such item on the applicable determination date bears to the adjusted basis of all such items on such date. The excess of a liability which constitutes a specific charge against property over the adjusted basis of such property shall be taken into account as a liability secured only by the general credit of the coporation.

(ii) A liability which is evidenced by an open account or which is secured only by the general credit of the controlled foreign corporation shall be apportioned against each and every item of corporate property in that ratio which the adjusted basis of such item on the applicable determination date (reduced as provided in subdivision (i) of this subparagraph) bears to the adjusted basis of all the corporate property on such date (reduced as provided in subdivision (i) of this subparagraph); provided that no liability shall be apportioned under this subdivision against any stock or obligations described in paragraph (h)(1) of this section.

(2) **Excluded charges.** For purposes of subparagraph (1) of this paragraph, a liability created principally for the purpose of artificially increasing or decreasing the amount of a controlled foreign corporation's qualified investments in foreign base company shipping operations will not be recognized. Whether a liability is created principally for such purpose will depend upon all the facts and circumstances of each case. One of the factors that will be considered in making such a determination with respect to a loan is whether the loan is from a related person, as defined in section 954(d)(3) and paragraph (e) of §1.954-1. Another such factor is whether the liability was created after March 29, 1975, in a taxable year beginning before January 1, 1976.

(3) **Statement required.** If for purposes of this section the adjusted basis of property which constitutes a qualified investment in foreign base company shipping operations by a controlled foreign corporation is reduced on the ground that such property is subject to a liability, each United States shareholder shall attach to his return a statement setting forth the adjusted basis of the property before the reduction and the amount and nature of the reduction.

(4) **Partnership interest.** If a controlled foreign corporation is a partner in a partnership, its investment in the partnership taken into account under section 955(b)(4) shall be its adjusted basis in the partnership determined under section 722 or 742, adjusted as provided in section 705, and reduced as provided in subparagraph (1) of this paragraph. (However, if the partnership is not engaged solely in the conduct of foreign base company shipping operations, such amount shall be taken into account only to the extent provided in paragraph (d)(1) of this section.)

(5) **Grantor trust.** If a controlled foreign corporation is deemed to own a portion of the assets of a trust under paragraph (e)(2) of this section, then the amount taken into account under section 955 (b)(4) with respect to such assets shall be determined as provided in subparagraph (1) of this paragraph by the application of the following rules:

(i) Such controlled foreign corporation's adjusted basis in such assets shall be deemed to be a proportionate share of the trust's adjusted basis in such assets, and

(ii) A proportionate share of the liabilities of the trust shall be deemed to be liabilities of such controlled foreign corporation and to constitute specific charges against such assets.

(6) **Translation into United States dollars.** The amounts determined in accordance with this paragraph shall be translated into United States dollars in accordance with the principles of §1.964-1(e)(4).

(h) **Investments in shipping companies under prior law—(1) In general.** If an amount invested in stock or obligations of less developed country shipping company described in §1.955-5(b) is treated as a qualified investment in less developed countries under §1.955-2 (applied without regard to paragraph (b)(5)(ii) thereof) on the applicable determination date for purposes of section 954(g) or section 955(a)(2) with respect to a taxable year beginning after December 31, 1975, then such amount shall be treated as a qualified investment in foreign base company shipping operations on such determination date. See section 955(b)(5).

(2) **Effect on prior law.** See §1.955-2(b)(5)(ii) for the rule that investments which are treated as qualified investments in foreign base company shipping operations under subparagraph (1) of this paragraph shall not be treated as qualified investments in less developed countries for purposes of section 951(a)(1)(A)(ii).

(3) **Illustration.** The application of this paragraph may be illustrated by the following example:

Example. (a) Throughout the period here involved controlled foreign corporation X owns 100 percent of the single class of stock of controlled foreign corporation Y. X and Y each use the calendar year as the taxable year. At the close of 1975, X's $50,000 investment in the stock of Y is treated as a qualified investment in less developed countries under §1.955-2 (applied without regard to §1.955-2(b)(5)(ii)), and Y is a less developed country shipping company described in §1.955-5(b).

(b) On December 31, 1976, Y is still a less developed country shipping company and X's $50,000 investment in the stock of Y is still treated as a qualified investment in less developed countries under §1.955-2 (applied without regard to §1.955-2(b)(5)(ii)). Under subparagraph (1) of this paragraph, X's entire $50,000 investment in the stock of Y is treated as a qualified investment in foreign base company shipping operations.

(c) For 1977, Y's gross income is $10,000 and Y's foreign base company shipping income is $7,500. Since Y fails to meet the 80-percent income test of §1.955-5(b)(1), Y is no longer a less developed country shipping company described in §1.955-5(b), and X's investment in the stock of Y is no longer treated as a qualified investment in less developed countries under §1.955-2 (applied without regard to §1.955-2(b)(5)(ii)). However, assume that on December 31, 1977, Y's assets consist entirely of a vessel used in foreign commerce and related shipping assets, that Y's net worth (as defined in paragraph (c)(2)(i) of this section) is $100,000, that Y's qualified investments in foreign base company shipping operations (determined under this section) on December 31, 1977, are $75,000, and that X's investment in the stock of Y (as determined under paragraph (g) of this section) continues to be $50,000. Then $37,500, i.e.,

$$\frac{\$75,000}{\$100,000} \times \$50,000,$$ of X's $50,000 investment in the stock of Y is treated as a qualified investment in foreign company shipping operations under paragraph (c) of this section.

(d) For 1978, all of Y's gross income is foreign base company shipping income. Although Y is again a less developed country shipping company described in §1.955-5(b), X's investment in the stock of Y is no longer treated as a qualified investment in less developed countries under §1.955-2(b)(5)(iii). Thus, X's investment in the stock of Y is not treated as a qualified investment in foreign base company shipping operations under subparagraph (1) of this paragraph. However, X's investment in the stock of Y may be so treated under another provision of this section, as was the case in item (c) of this example.

§1.955A-3 (Proposed Treasury Decision, published 8-9-76.) **Election as to qualified investments by related persons.**

(a) **In general.** If a United States shareholder elects the benefits of section 955(b)(2) with respect to a related group (as defined in paragraph (b)(1) of this section) of controlled foreign corporations, then an investment in foreign base company shipping operations made by one member of such group will be treated as having been made by another member to the extent provided in paragraph (c)(4) of this section, and each member will be subject to the other provisions of paragraph (c) of this section. For the manner of making an election under section 955(b)(2), and for rules relating to the revocation of such an election, see paragraph (d) of this section. For rules relating to the coordination of sections 955(b)(2) and 955(b)(3), see paragraph (e) of this section.

(b) **Related group—(1) Related group defined.** The term "related group" means

Proposed Reg. §1.955A-3

two or more controlled foreign corporations, but only if all of the following requirements are met:

(i) All such corporations use the same taxable year,

(ii) The same United States shareholder controls each such corporation within the meaning of section 954(d)(3) at the end of such taxable year, and

(iii) Such United States shareholder elects to treat such corporations as a related group for such taxable year.

(2) **Group taxable years defined.** The "group taxable year" is the common taxable year of a related group.

(3) **Limitation.** If a United States shareholder elects to treat two or more corporations as a related group for a group taxable year (the "first group taxable year"), then such United States shareholder may not also elect to treat two or more other corporations as a related group for a group taxable year any day of which falls within the first group taxable year.

(4) **Illustrations.** The application of this paragraph may be illustrated by the following examples:

Example (1). Domestic corporation M owns 100 percent of the only class of stock of controlled foreign corporations A, B, C, D, and E. A, B, and C use the calendar year as the taxable year. D and E use the fiscal year ending on June 30 as the taxable year. M may elect to treat A, B, and C as a related group. However, M may not elect to treat C, D, and E as a related group.

Example (2). The facts are the same as in example (1). In addition, M elects to treat A, B, and C as a related group for the group taxable year which ends on December 31, 1976. M may not elect to treat D and E as a related group for the group taxable year ending on June 30, 1977.

Example (3). United States shareholder A owns 60 percent of the only class of stock of controlled foreign corporation X and 40 percent of the only class of stock of controlled foreign corporation Y. United States shareholder B owns the other 40 percent of the stock of X and the other 60 percent of the stock of Y. Neither A or B (nor both together) may elect to treat X and Y as a related group.

(c) **Effect of election.** If a United States shareholder elects to treat two or more controlled foreign corporations as a related group for any group taxable year then, for purposes of determining the foreign base company income (see §1.954-1) and the increase or decrease in qualified investments in foreign base company shipping operations (see §§1.954-7, 1.955A-1, and 1.955A-4) of each member of such group for such year, the following rules shall apply:

(1) **Intragroup dividends.** The gross income of each member of the related group shall be deemed not to include dividends received from any other member of such group, to the extent that such dividends are attributable (within the meaning of §1.954-6(f)(4)) to foreign base company shipping income.

(2) **Group excess deduction.** (i) The deductions allocable under §1.954-1(c) to the foreign base company shipping income of each member of the related group shall be deemed to include such member's pro rata share of the group excess deduction.

(ii) The group excess deduction for the group taxable year is the sum of the excesses for each member of the related group (having an excess) of—

(A) The member's deductions (determined without regard to this subparagraph) allocable to foreign base company shipping income for such year, over

(B) The member's foreign base company shipping income for such year.

(iii) A member's pro rata share of the group excess deduction is the amount which bears the same ratio to such group excess deduction as—

(A) The excess of such member's foreign base company shipping income over the deductions (so determined) allocable thereto, bears to

(B) The sum of such excesses for each member of the related group having an excess.

(iv) For purposes of this subparagraph, "foreign base company shipping income" means foreign base company shipping income (as defined in §1.954-6), reduced by excluding therefrom all amounts which are—

(A) Excluded from subpart F income under section 952(b) (relating to exclusion of United States income) or

(B) Excluded from foreign base company income under section 954(b)(4) (relating to exception for foreign corporation not availed of to reduce taxes).

(v) The application of this subparagraph may be illustrated by the following example:

Example. Controlled foreign corporations X, Y, and Z are a related group for calendar year 1976. The excess group deduction for 1976 is $9, X's pro rata share of the group excess deduction is $6, and Y's pro rata share is $3, determined as follows on the basis of the facts shown in the following table:

		X	Y	Z	Group
(1)	Gross shipping income	$100	90	80	
(2)	Shipping deductions	60	70	89	
(3)	Net shipping income	40	20	(9)	
(4)	Group excess deduction				9
(5)	X's pro rata share of group excess deduction ($9 x $40 / $60)	6			
(6)	Y's pro rata share of group excess deduction ($9 x $20 / $60)		3		

(3) **Intragroup investments.** On both of the determination dates applicable to the group taxable year for purposes of section 954(g) or section 955(a)(2), the qualified investments in foreign base company shipping operations of each member of the related group shall be deemed not to include stock or obligations of any other member of the related group. In addition, neither the gains nor the losses on dispositions of such stock or obligations during the group taxable year shall be taken into account under §1.955A-1(b)(1)(ii) in determining the decrease in qualified investments in foreign base company shipping operations of any member of such related group.

(4) **Group excess investment.** (i) On the later (and only the later) of the two determination dates applicable to the group taxable year for purposes of section 954(g) or section 955(a)(2), the qualified investments in foreign base company shipping operations of each member of the related group shall be deemed to include such member's pro rata share of the group excess investment.

(ii) The group excess investment for the group taxable year is the sum of the excess for each member of the related group (having an excess) of—

(A) The member's increase in qualified investments in foreign base company shipping operations (determined under §1.954-7 after the application of subparagraph (3) of this paragraph) for such year, over

(B) The member's foreign base company shipping income for such year.

(iii) A member's pro rata share of the group excess investment is the amount which bears the same ratio to such group excess investment as—

(A) Such member's shortfall in qualified investments, bears to

(B) The sum of the shortfalls in qualified investments of each member of such related group having a shortfall.

(iv) If a member has an increase in qualified investments in foreign base company shipping operations (determined as provided in §1.954-7 after the application of subparagraph (3) of this paragraph) for the group taxable year, then such member's "shortfall in qualified investments" is the excess of—

(A) Such member's foreign base company shipping income for such year, over

(B) Such increase.

(v) If a member has a decrease in qualified investments in foreign base company shipping operations (determined under §1.955A-1(b)(1) or §1.955A-4(a), whichever is applica-

Proposed Reg. §1.955A-3

ble, after the application of subparagraph (3) of this paragraph) for the group taxable year, then such member's "shortfall in qualified investments" is the sum of—

(A) Such member's foreign base company shipping income for such year and
(B) Such decrease.

(vi) For purposes of this subparagraph, "foreign base company shipping income" means foreign base company shipping income (as defined in subparagraph(2)(iv) of this paragraph), reduced by the deductions allocable thereto under §1.954-1(c) (including the additional deductions described in subparagraph(2) of this paragraph).

(vii) The application of this subparagraph may be illustrated by the following examples:

Example (1). (a) Controlled foreign corporations R, S, and T are a related group for calendar year 1977. S's pro rata share of the group excess investment is $15, and T's pro rata share is $5, determined as follows on the basis of the facts shown in the following table:

		R	S	T	Group
(1)	Net shipping income	$100	95	85	
(2)	Increase (decrease) in qualified investments	120	(55)	35	
(3)	Excess investment	20			20
(4)	Shortfall		150	50	200
(5)	S's pro rata share of group excess investment ($20 x $150/$200)		15		
(6)	T's pro rata share of group excess investment ($20 x $50/$200)			5	

(b) On December 31, 1977, T has qualified investments in foreign base company shipping operations of $105 (determined without regard to this section), of which $15 consists of obligations of S. For purposes of determining T's increase or decrease in qualified investments in foriegn base company shipping operations for 1977, the amount of T's qualified investments in foreign base company shipping operations on December 31, 1977, is deemed to be $95, determined as follows:

(1)	Qualified investments (determined without regard to this section) at 12-31-77	$105
(2)	Less: Investments in obligations of another member of related group	15
(3)	Balance	90
(4)	Plus: Pro rata share of group excess investments	5
(5)	Total qualified investments	95

(5) **Collateral effect.** (i) An election under this section by a United States shareholder to treat two or more controlled foreign corporations as a related group for a group taxable year shall have no effect on—

(A) Any other United States shareholder (including a minority shareholder of a member of such related group),

(B) Except as provided in subdivision (ii) of this subparagraph, any other controlled foreign corporation,

(C) The foreign personal holding company, foreign base company sales income, and foreign base company services income, and the deductions allocable under §1.954-1(c) thereto, of any member of such related group, and

(D) Any other taxable year.

(ii) If—

(A) A United States shareholder elects to treat two or more controlled foreign corporations as a related group,

(B) Any member of the group holds an asset not described in §1.955A-2(c)(1)(i) or (ii), and

(C) Another controlled foreign corporation owns stock or obligations of any member of such related group,

then with respect to such shareholder such stock or obligations will not be considered qualified investments in foreign base company shipping operations under §1.955A-2(c).

(iii) The application of this subparagraph may be illustrated by the following examples:

Example (1). United States shareholder A owns 80 percent of the only class of stock of controlled foreign corporations X and Y. United States shareholder B owns the other 20 percent of the stock of X and Y. X and Y both use the calendar year as the taxable year. A elects to treat X and Y as a related group for 1977. For purposes of determining the amounts includible in B's gross income under section 951(a) in respect of X and Y, the election made by A shall be disregarded.

Example (2). The facts are the same as in example (1). In addition, the amount of X's qualified investments in foreign base company shipping operations on December 31, 1977, determined as provided in §1.955A-2 and modified as provided in paragraph (c)(3) and (4) of this section, is $1,000. A does not elect to treat X and Y as a related group for 1978. The amount of X's qualified investments in foreign base company shipping operations on December 31, 1978, determined without regard to paragraph (c)(3) and (4) of this section, is $1,200. The amount of X's qualified investments in foreign base company shipping operations on December 31, 1977, determined without regard to paragraph (c)(3) and (4) of this section, is $900. X's increase in qualified investments in foreign base company shipping operations for 1978 is $300.

Example (3). Controlled foreign corporations X, Y, and Z are all wholly-owned subsidiaries of domestic corporation M, and all use the calendar year as the taxable year. M elects to treat X and Y as a related group for 1977. On December 31, 1977, Z owns $1,000 of obligations of X. Assume that Y owns assets including a hotel on December 31, 1977. The obligations owned by Z are not treated as qualified investments in foreign base company shipping operations.

(d) **Procedure—(1) Time and manner of making election.** A United States shareholder shall make an election under this section to treat two or more controlled foreign corporations as a related group for a group taxable year by filing a statement to such effect with his return for the taxable year within which or with which such group taxable year ends. The statement shall include the following information:

(i) The name, address, taxpayer identification number, and taxable year of the United States shareholder;

(ii) The name, address, and taxable year of each controlled foreign corporation which is to be a member of the related group; and

(iii) A schedule showing the calculations by which the amounts described in this section have been determined.

(2) **Revocation.** (i) Except as provided in subdivision (ii) of this subparagraph, an election under this section by a United States shareholder shall be binding for the group taxable year for which it is made.

(ii) Upon application by the United States shareholder, an election made under this section may, subject to the approval of the Commissioner, be revoked. Approval will not be granted unless a material and substantial change in circumstances occurs which could not have been anticipated when the election was made. The application for consent to revocation shall be made by mailing a letter for such purpose to Commissioner of Internal Revenue, Attention: T:C:C, Washington, D.C. 20224, containing a statement of the facts which justify such consent.

(e) **Coordination with section 955(b)(3).** If a United States shareholder elects under this section to treat two or more controlled foreign corporations as a related group for any taxable year, and if such United States shareholder is required under §1.955A-4(c)(2)

Proposed Reg. §1.955A-3

63,872   Proposed Regulations   6-1-77

for purposes of filing any return to estimate the qualified investments in foreign base company shipping operations of any member of such group, then such United States shareholder shall, for purposes of filing such return, determine the amount includible in his gross income in respct of each member of such related group on the basis of such estimate. If the actual amount of such investments is not the same as the amount of the estimate, the United States shareholder shall immediately notify the Commissioner. The Commissioner will thereupon redetermine the amount of tax of such United States shareholder for the year or years with respect to which the incorrect amount was taken into account. The amount of tax, if any, due upon such redetermination shall be paid by the United States shareholder upon notice and demand by the district director. The amount of tax, if any, shown by such redetermination to have been overpaid shall be credited or refunded to the United States shareholder in accordance with the provisions of sections 6402 and 6511 and the regulations thereunder.

(f) **Illustrations.** The application of this section may be illustrated by the following examples:

Example (1). (a) Controlled foreign corporations X and Y are wholly owned subsidiaries of domestic corporation M. X and Y use the calendar year as the taxable year. For 1977, X and Y are not export trade corporations (as defined in section 971(a)), nor have they any income derived from the insurance of United States risks (within the meaning of section 953(a)). M does not elect to treat X and Y as a related group for 1977.

(b) For 1977, X and Y each have gross income (determined as provided in §1.954-6(h)(1)) of $1,000, X's foreign base company income is $20 and Y's foreign base company shipping income is $0, determined as follows, based on the facts shown in the following table:

		X	Y
(1)	Foreign base company shipping income	$1,000	$1,000
(2)	Less: amounts excluded from subpart F income under section 952(b) (relating to United States income) and amounts excluded from foreign base company income under section 954(b)(4) (relating to corporation not availed of to reduce taxes)	0	0
(3)	Balance	1,000	1,000
(4)	Less: deductions allocable under §1.954-1(c) to balance	800	1,040
(5)	Remaining balance	200	0
(6)	Less: increase in qualified investments in foreign base company shipping operations	180	
(7)	Foreign base company income	20	

(c) For 1977, Y has a withdrawal of previously excluded subpart F income from investment in foreign base company shipping operations of $20, determined as follows, on the basis of the facts shown in the following table:

(1)	Qualified investments in foreign base company shipping operations at 12-31-76	$1,210
(2)	Less: qualified investments in foreign base company shipping operations at 12-31-77	1,170
(3)	Balance	40
(4)	Less: excess of recognized losses over recognized gains on sales during 1977 of qualified investments in foreign base company shipping operations	20
(5)	Tentative decrease in qualified investments in foreign base company shipping operations for 1977	20
(6)	Limitation described in §1.955A-1(b)(2)	160

(7) Y's amount of previously excluded subpart F income withdrawn from investment in foreign base company shipping operations (lesser of lines (5) and (6))................. 20

Example (2). (a) The facts are the same as in example (1), except that M does elect to treat X and Y as a related group for 1977.

(b) The group excess deduction, which is solely attributable to Y's net shipping loss, is $40 (i.e., $1,040 − $1,000). Since X is the only member of the related group with net shipping income, X's pro rata share of the group excess deduction is the entire $40 amount.

(c) X's foreign base company income for 1977 is zero, determined as follows:

(1)	Preliminary net foreign base company shipping income (line (b) (5) of example (1))	$200
(2)	Less: X's pro rata share of group excess deduction	40
(3)	Remaining balance	160
(4)	Less: increase in qualified investments in foreign base company shipping operations	180
(5)	Foreign base company income	0

(d) The group excess investment, which is solely attributable to X's excess investment, is $20 (i.e., $180 minus $160). Since Y is the only member of the related group with a shortfall in qualified investments, Y's share of the group excess investment is the entire $20 amount.

(e) During 1976 and 1977, Y owns no obligation of X. Y's withdrawal of previously excluded subpart F income from investment in foreign base company shipping operations for 1977 is zero, determined as follows:

(1)	Qualified investments at 12-31-76			$1,210
(2)	(i)	Qualified investments at 12-31-77 (determined without regard to paragraph (c) (4) of this section)	1,170	
	(ii)	Y's pro rata share of group excess investment	20	
	(iii)	Total qualified investments at 12-31-77 (line (i) plus line (ii))		1,190
(3)	Balance (line (1) minus line (2) (iii))			20
(4)	Less: excess of recognized losses over recognized gains on sales during 1977 of qualified investments in foreign base company shipping operations			20
(5)	Decrease in qualified investments for 1977			0

§1.955A-4 (Proposed Treasury Decision, published 8-9-76.) **Election as to date of determining qualified investments in foreign base company shipping operations.**

(a) **Nature of election.** In lieu of determining the increase under the provisions of section 954(g) and §1.954-7(a) or the decrease under the provisions of section 955(a)(2) and §1.955A-1(b) in a controlled foreign corporation's qualified investments in foreign base company shipping operations for a taxable year in the manner provided in such provisions, a United States shareholder of such controlled foreign corporation may elect, under the provisions of section 955(b)(3) and this section to determine such increase in accordance with the provisions of §1.954-7(b) and to determine such decrease by ascertaining the amount by which—

(1) Such controlled foreign corporation's qualified investments in foreign base company shipping operations at the close of such taxable year exceed its qualified investments

Proposed Reg. §1.955A-4

in foreign base company shipping operations at the close of the taxable year immediately following such taxable year, and reducing such excess by

(2). The amount determined under §1.955A-1(b)(1)(ii) for such taxable year, subject to the limitation provided in §1.955A-1(b)(2) for such taxable year. An election under this section may be made with respect to each controlled foreign corporation with respect to which a person is a United States shareholder within the meaning of section 951(b), but the election may not be exercised separately with respect to the increases and the decreases of such controlled foreign corporation. If an election is made under this section to determine the increase of a controlled foreign corporation in accordance with the provisions of §1.954-7(b) subsequent decreases of such controlled foreign corporation shall be determined in accordance with this paragraph and not in accordance with §1.955A-1(b).

(b) **Time and manner of making election**—(1) **Without consent.** An election under this section with respect to a controlled foreign corporation shall be made without the consent of the Commissioner by a United States shareholder's filing a statement to such effect with his return for his taxable year in which or with which ends the first taxable year of such controlled foreign corporation in which—

(i) Such shareholder is a United States shareholder, and

(ii) Such controlled foreign corporation realizes foreign base company shipping income, as defined in §1.954-6.

The statement shall contain the name and address of the controlled foreign corporation and identification of such first taxable year of such corporation.

(2) **With consent.** An election under this section with respect to a controlled foreign corporation may be made by a United States shareholder at any time with the consent of the Commissioner. Consent will not be granted unless the United States shareholder and the Commissioner agree to the terms, conditions, and adjustments under which the election will be effected. The application for consent to elect shall be made by the United States shareholder's mailing a letter for such purpose to the Commissioner of Internal Revenue, Washington, D.C., 20224. The application shall be mailed before the close of the first taxable year of the controlled foreign corporation with respect to which the shareholder desires to compute an amount described in section 954(b)(2) in accordance with the election provided in this section. The application shall include the following information:

(i) The name, address, taxpayer identification number, and taxable year of the United States shareholder;

(ii) The name and address of the controlled foreign corporation;

(iii) The first taxable year of the controlled foreign corporation for which income is to be computed under the election;

(iv) The amount of the controlled foreign corporation's qualified investments in foreign base company shipping operations at the close of its preceding taxable year; and

(v) The sum of the amounts excluded under section 954(b)(2) and §1.954-1(b)(1) from the foreign base company income of the controlled foreign corporation for all prior taxable years during which such shareholder was a United States shareholder of such corporation and the sum of the amounts of its previously excluded subpart F income withdrawn from investment in foreign base company shipping operations for all prior taxable years during which such shareholder was a United States shareholder of such corporation.

(c) **Effect of election**—(1) **General.** Except as provided in subparagraphs (3) and (4) of this paragraph, an election under this section with respect to a controlled foreign corporation shall be binding on the United States shareholder and shall apply to all qualified investments in foreign base company shipping operations acquired, or disposed of, by such controlled foreign corporation during the taxable year following its taxable year for which income is first computed under the election and during all succeeding taxable years of such corporation.

(2) **Returns.** Any return of a United States shareholder required to be filed before the completion of a period with respect to which determinations are to be made as to a controlled foreign corporation's qualified investments in foreign base company shipping operations for purposes of computing such shareholder's taxable income shall be filed on the basis of an estimate of the amount of the controlled foreign corporation's qualified investments in foreign base company shipping operations at the close of the period. If the actual amount of such investments is not the same as the amount of the estimate, the United States shareholder shall immediately notify the Commissioner. The Commissioner will thereupon redetermine the amount of tax of such United States shareholder for the year or years with respect to which the incorrect amount was taken into account. The amount of tax, if any, due upon such redetermination shall be paid by the United States shareholder upon notice and demand by the district director. The amount of tax, if any, shown by such redetermination to have been overpaid shall be credited or refunded to the United States shareholder in accordance with the provisions of sections 6402 and 6511 and the regulations thereunder.

(3) **Revocation.** Upon application by the United States shareholder, the election made under this section may, subject to the approval of the Commissioner, be revoked. Approval will not be granted unless the United States shareholder and the Commissioner agree to the terms, conditions, and adjustments under which the revocation will be effected. Unless such agreement provides otherwise, the change in the controlled foreign corporation's qualified investments in foreign base company shipping operations for its first taxable year for which income is computed without regard to the election previously made will be considered to be zero for purposes of effectuating the revocation. The application for consent to revocation shall be made by the United States shareholder's mailing a letter for such purpose to the Commissioner of Internal Revenue, Washington, D.C., 20224. The application shall be mailed before the close of the first taxable year of the controlled foreign corporation with respect to which the shareholder desires to compute the amounts described in section 954(b)(2) or 955(a) without regard to the election provided in this section. The application shall include the following information:

(i) The name, address, and taxpayer identification number of the United States shareholder;

(ii) The name and address of the controlled foreign corporation;

(iii) The taxable year of the controlled foreign corporation for which such amounts are to be so computed;

(iv) The amount of the controlled foreign corporation's qualified investments in foreign base company shipping operations at the close of its preceding taxable year;

(v) The sum of the amounts excluded under section 954(b)(2) and §1.954-1(b)(1) from the foreign base company income of the controlled foreign corporation for all prior taxable years during which such shareholder was a United States shareholder of such corporation and the sum of the amounts of its previously excluded subpart F income withdrawn from investment in foreign base company shipping operations for all prior taxable years during which such shareholder was a United States shareholder of such corporation; and

(vi) The reasons for the request for consent to revocation.

(4) **Transfer of stock.** If during any taxable year of a controlled foreign corporation—

(i) A United States shareholder who has made an election under this section with respect to such controlled foreign corporation sells, exchanges, or otherwise disposes of all or part of his stock in such controlled foreign corporation, and

(ii) The foreign corporation is a controlled foreign corporation immediately after the sale, exchange, or other disposition,

then, with respect to the stock so sold, exchanged, or disposed of, the change in the controlled foreign corporation's qualified investments in foreign base company shipping operations for such taxable year shall be considered to be zero. If the United States shareholder's successor in interest is entitled to and does make an election under paragraph (b)(1) of this section to determine the controlled foreign corporation's increase in quali-

Proposed Reg. §1.955A-4

fied investments in foreign base company shipping operations for the taxable year in which he acquires such stock, such increase with respect to the stock so acquired shall be determined in accordance with the provisions of §1.954-7(b)(1). If the controlled foreign corporation realizes no foreign base company income from which amounts are excluded under section 954(b)(2) and §1.954-1(b)(1) for the taxable year in which the United States shareholder's successor in interest acquires such stock and such successor in interest makes an election under paragraph (b)(1) of this section with respect to a subsequent taxable year of such controlled foreign corporation, the increase in the controlled foreign corporation's qualified investments in foreign base company shipping operations for such subsequent taxable year shall be determined in accordance with the provisions of §1.954-7(b)(2).

(d) **Illustrations.** The application of this section may be illustrated by the following examples:

Example (1). Foreign corporation A is a wholly owned subsidiary of domestic corporation M. Both corporations use the calendar year as a taxable year. In a statement filed with its return for 1977 M makes an election under section 955(b)(3) and the election remains in force for the taxable year 1978. At December 31, 1978, A's qualified investments in foreign base company shipping operations amount to $100,000; and, at December 31, 1979, to $80,000. For purposes of paragraph (a)(1) of this section, A Corporation's decrease in qualified investments in foreign base company shipping operations for the taxable year 1978 is $20,000 and is determined by ascertaining the amount by which A Corporation's qualified investments in foreign base company shipping operations at December 31, 1978 ($100,000) exceed its qualified investments in foreign base company shipping operations at December 31, 1979 ($80,000).

Example (2). The facts are the same as in example (1) except that A experiences no changes in qualified investments in foreign base company shipping operations during its taxable years 1980 and 1981. If M's election were to remain in force, A's acquisitions and dispositions of qualified investments in less developed countries during A's taxable year 1982 would be taken into account in determining whether A has experienced an increase or a decrease in qualified investments in foreign base company shipping operations for its taxable year 1981. However, M duly files before the close of A's taxable year 1981 an application for consent to revocation of M Corporation's election under section 955(b)(3), and, pursuant to an agreement between the Commissioner and M, consent is granted by the Commissioner. Assuming such agreement does not provide otherwise, A's change in qualified investments in foreign base company shipping operations for its taxable year 1981 is zero because the effect of the revocation of the election is to treat acquisitions and dispositions of qualified investments in foreign base company shipping operations actually occurring in 1982 as having occurred in such year rather than in 1981.

Example (3). The facts are the same as in example (2) except that A's qualified investments in foreign base company shipping operations at December 31, 1982, amount to $70,000. For purposes of paragraph (b)(1)(i) of §1.955A-1, the decrease in A's qualified investments in foreign base company shipping operations for the taxable year 1982 is $10,000 and is determined by ascertaining the amount by which A's qualified investments in foreign base company shipping operations at December 31, 1981 ($80,000) exceed its qualified investments in foreign base company shipping operations at December 31, 1982 ($70,000).

Example (4). The facts are the same as in example (1). Assume further that on September 30, 1979, M sells 40 percent of the only class of stock of A to N Corporation, a domestic corporation. N uses the calendar year as a taxable year. A remains a controlled foreign corporation immediately after such sale of its stock. A's qualified investments in foreign base company shipping operations at December 31, 1980 amount to $90,000. The changes in A Corporation's qualified investments in foreign base company shipping operations occurring in its taxable year 1979 are considered to be zero with respect to the 40-percent stock interest acquired by N Corporation. The entire $20,000 reduction in A Corporation's qualified investments in foreign base company shipping operations which occurs during the taxable year 1979 is taken into account by M for purposes of paragraph (c)(1) of this section in determining its tax liability for the taxable year 1978. A's increase in qualified investments in foreign base company shipping operations for the taxable year 1979 with respect to the 60-percent stock interest retained by M is $6,000 and is determined by ascertaining M's pro rata share (60 percent) of the amount by which A's qualified investments in foreign base company shipping operations at December 31, 1980 ($90,000) exceed its qualified investments in foreign base company shipping operations at December 31, 1979 ($80,000). N does not make an election under section 955(b)(3) in its return for its taxable year 1980. Corporation A's increase in qualified investments in foreign base company shipping operations for the taxable year 1980 with respect to the 40-percent stock interest acquired by N is $4,000.

* * * * * * * * * * * *

The first sentence of §1.958-1(a) is amended to read as follows:

§1.958-1 (Proposed Treasury Decision, published 2-9-78.) Direct and indirect ownership of stock.

(a) In general. Section 958(a) provides that, for purposes of sections 951 to 964 (other than sections 955(b)(1)(A) and (B) and 955(c)(2)(A)(ii) (as in effect before the enactment of the Tax Reduction Act of 1975), and 960(a)(1)), stock owned means—

(1) Stock owned directly; and
(2) Stock owned with the application of paragraph (b) of this section.

* * * * * * * * * * * *

Section 1.959-1 is amended as follows:

1. The second and third sentences of paragraph (a) are revised.
2. The third sentence of paragraph (b) is revised.
3. The second sentence of paragraph (c) is revised.
4. Paragraph (d)(2) is revised.

The revised provisions read as follows:

§1.959-1 (Proposed Treasury Decision, published 2-9-78.) Exclusion from gross income of United States persons of previously taxed earnings and profits.

(a) In general. * * * The amounts so taxed to certain United States shareholders are described as subpart F income, previously excluded subpart F income withdrawn from investment in less developed countries, previously excluded subpart F income withdrawn from investment in foreign base company shipping operations, and increases in earnings invested in United States property. Section 959 provides that amounts taxed as subpart F income, as previously excluded subpart F income withdrawn from investment in less developed countries, or as previously excluded subpart F income withdrawn from investment in foreign base company shipping operations are not taxed again as increases in earnings invested in United States property. * * *

(b) Actual distributions to United States persons. * * * Thus, earnings and profits attributable to amounts which are, or have been, included in the gross income of a United States shareholder of a foreign corporation under section 951(a)(1)(A)(i) as subpart F income, under section 951(a)(1)(A)(ii) as previously excluded subpart F income withdrawn from investment in less developed countries, under section 951(a)(1)(A)(iii) as previously excluded subpart F income withdrawn from investment in foreign base company shipping operations, or under section 951(a)(1)(B) as earnings invested in United States property, shall not be again included in the gross income of such shareholder when such amounts are actually distributed, directly or indirectly, to such shareholder. * * *

* * * * * * * * * * * *

(c) Excludable investment of earnings in United States property. * * * Thus, earnings and profits attributable to amounts which are, or have been, included in the gross

Proposed Reg. §1.959-1

income of a United States shareholder of a foreign corporation under section 951(a)(1)(A)(i) as subpart F income, under section 951(a)(1)(A)(ii) as previously excluded subpart F income withdrawn from investment in less developed countries, or under section 951(a)(1)(A)(iii) as previously excluded subpart F income withdrawn from investment in foreign base company shipping operations may be invested in United States property without being again included in such shareholder's income under section 951(a). * * *

* * * * * * * * * * *

(d) Application of exclusions to shareholder's successor in interest. * * *

(2) The name, address, and taxpayer identification number of the person from whom the stock interest was acquired;

* * * * * * * * * * *

Section 1.959-3 is amended as follows:

1. Paragraph (a) is amended by inserting "previously excluded subpart F income withdrawn from investment in foreign base company shipping operations," immediately after "countries,".

2. Paragraph (b) is amended by deleting "Earnings" the first time it appears in the fourth sentence of the flush material following subparagraph (3) and inserting in its place "For example, earnings".

3. Paragraph (b) is amended further by inserting "or foreign base company shipping operations" immediately after "assets" in the fourth sentence of the flush material following subparagraph (3).

§1.959-3 (Proposed Treasury Decision, published 2-9-78.) **Allocation of distributions to earnings and profits of foreign corporations.**

* *

Section 1.964-1 is amended as follows:

1. The second sentence of the flush material following paragraph (b)(2)(ii) is revised by inserting a comma after "section 957)", and by inserting a comma after "or (3)(B)", and by inserting before the period ", or pays a dividend that is included in the foreign base company shipping income of a controlled foreign corporation under §1.954-6(f)".

2. The first sentence of example (2) of paragraph (b)(3) is revised by deleting "Corporation N" and inserting in lieu of thereof "In 1973, Corporation N"

3. The first sentence of paragraph (c)(2) is revised by inserting a comma after "section 957)", by inserting a comma after "or (3)(B)", and by deleting "section 952(d)," and inserting in lieu thereof "section 952(d), or pays a dividend that is included in the foreign base company shipping income of a controlled foreign corporation under §1.954-6(f)".

4. Paragraph (c)(3)(ii) is revised.

5. Paragraph (c)(5) is revised by adding at the end thereof a new sentence.

6. Paragraph (c)(6) is revised as follows:

a. Subdivision (ii) is revised by deleting "section 955(c))" and inserting in lieu thereof "section 955(c), as in effect before the enactment of the Tax Reduction Act of 1975)"

b. Subdivision (iii) is revised by deleting the word "or" from the end thereof.

c. Subdivision (iv) is revised by deleting the period from the end thereof and inserting in lieu thereof "; or".

d. A new subdivision (v) is added.

e. The second sentence of the flush material following new subdivision (v) is revised by inserting immediately before the period "or pays a dividend that is included in the foreign base company shipping income of a controlled foreign corporation under §1.954-6(f)".

The revised and added provisions read as follows:

§1.964-1 (Proposed Treasury Decision, published 2-9-78.) **Determination of the earnings and profits of a foreign corporation.**

* * * * * * * * * * * *

(c) **Tax adjustments.** * * *
(3) **Action on behalf of a corporation** * * *

(ii) *Written statement.* The written statement required by subdivision (i) of this subparagraph shall be jointly executed by the controlling United States shareholders, shall be filed with the Director of the Internal Revenue Service Center, 11601 Roosevelt Blvd., Philadelphia, Pennsylvania 19155, within 180 days after the close of the taxable year of the foreign corporation with respect to which the election is made or the adoption or change of method effected, or before May 1, 1965, whichever is later, and shall set forth the name and country of organization of the foreign corporation, the names, addresses, taxpayer identification numbers, and stock interests of the controlling United States shareholders, the nature of the action taken, the names, addresses, and taxpayer identification numbers of all other United States shareholders notified of the election or adoption or change of method, and such other information as the Commissioner may by forms require.

* * * * * * * * * * *

(5) **Controlling United States shareholders.** * * *

In the event that a foreign corporation is not a controlled foreign corporation but pays a dividend to a controlled foreign corporation that is attributable to foreign base company shipping income under §1.954-6(f), the controlling United States shareholders (as defined in this subparagraph) of the controlled foreign corporation shall be considered the controlling United States shareholders of the foreign corporation.

* * * * * * * * * * *

(6) **Action not required until significant.** * * *

(v) It is sought to be established that the corporation has foreign base company shipping income (within the meaning of section 954(f)).

* * * * * * * * * * *

Section 1.964-2(a) and (b)(1) are revised by inserting "(as in effect both before and after the enactment of the Tax Reduction Act of 1975)" immediately after "section 955,".

Section 1.964-2(c)(1)(i)(b) and (ii) are revised to read as follows:

§1.964-2 (Proposed Treasury Decision, published 2-9-78.) **Treatment of blocked earnings and profits.**

* * * * * * * * * * *

(c) **Removal of restriction or limitation—(1) In general.** * * *
(i) *Treatment of deferred income.* * * *
(b) The applicable limitations under paragraph (c) of §1.952-1, paragraph (b)(2) of §1.955-1, paragraph (b)(2) of §1.955A-1, or paragraph (b) of §1.956-1, determined as of the last day of the immediately preceding taxable year, taking into account the provisions of subdivision (ii) of this subparagraph.

(ii) *Treatment of earnings and profits.* For purposes of sections 952, 955 (as in effect both before and after the enactment of the Tax Reduction Act of 1975), and 956, the earnings and profits which are no longer subject to a currency or other restriction or limitation shall be treated as included in the corporation's earnings and profits for the year in which such earnings and profits were derived.

* * * * * * * * * * *

Section 1.964-3 is amended as follows:

1. Paragraph (b) is revised as follows:
a. Subparagraphs (3) and (4) are redesignated subparagraphs (4) and (5) respectively.
b. A new subparagraph (3) is inserted immediately after subparagraph (2).
2. Paragraph (c)(1)(i) is revised.

Proposed Reg. §1.964-2

The added and revised provisions read as follows:

§1.964-3 (Proposed Tresury Decision, published 2-9-78.) **Records to be provided by United States shareholders.**

* * * * * * * * * * * *

(b) Records to be provided. * * *

(3) The previously excluded subpart F income of such corporation withdrawn from investment in foreign base company shipping operations,

* * * * * * * * . * * * *

(c) Special rules. * * *

(1) * * *

(i) The locus and nature of such corporation's activities were such as to make it unlikely that the foreign base company income of such corporation (determined in accordance with paragraph (c)(3) of §1.952-3) exceeded 5 percent of its gross income (determined in accordance with paragraph (b)(1) of §1.952-3) for the taxable year (For taxable years to which §1.952-3 does not apply, such amounts shall be determined under 26 CFR 1.954-1(d)(3)(i) and (ii) (Rev. as of April 1, 1975).), and * * *

Section 1.964-4 is amended as follows:

1. Paragraph (d) is revised as follows:
a. Subparagraphs (4) and (5) are revised.
b. Subparagraphs (6) and (7) are redesignated subparagraphs (7) and (10), respectively.
c. New subparagraphs (6), (8), and (9) are added
d. Subparagraph (10) as redesignated is revised by changing "(1) through (6)" to "(1) through (9)".

2. Paragraph (g) is redesignated paragraph (g-1) and revised as follows:
a. The heading is revised by inserting "in less developed countries" immediately after "investment".
b. Subparagraph (1) is revised by inserting "(both as in effect for taxable years beginning before January 1, 1976, see 26 CFR 1.954 and 1.954-1(b)(1) (Rev. as of April 1, 1975))" immediately after "§1.954-1".
c. Subparagraph (2) is revised by inserting "(as in effect before the enactment of the Tax Reduction Act of 1975)" immediately after "section 955(a)".
d. Subparagraph (3) is revised by inserting "(as in effect before the enactment of the Tax Reduction Act of 1975)" immediately after "section 955(a)".

3. A new paragraph (g-2) is added immediately after redesignated paragraph (g-1).

The revised and added provisions read as follows:

§1.964-4 (Proposed Treasury Decision, published 2-9-78.) **Verification of certain classes of income.**

* * * * * * * * * * * *

(d) Foreign base company income and exclusions therefrom * * *

(4) **Qualified investments in less developed countries.** For rules in effect for taxable years of foreign corporations beginning before January 1, 1976, see 26 CFR 1.964-4(d)(4) (Rev. as of April 1, 1975).

(5) **Income derived from aircraft or ships.** For rules in effect for taxable years of foreign corporations beginning before January 1, 1976, see 26 CFR 1.964-4(d)(5) (Rev. as of April 1, 1975).

(6) **Foreign base company shipping income.** The foreign base company shipping income to which section 954(f) and §1.954-6 apply, for which purpose there must be established—

(i) Gross income derived from, or in connection with, the use (or hiring or leasing for use) of any aircraft or vessel in foreign commerce, as determined under §1.954-6(c),

(ii) Gross income derived from, or in connection with, the performance of services directly related to the use of any aircraft or vessel in foreign commerce, as determined under §1.954-6(d),

(iii) Gross income incidental to income described in subdivisions (i) and (ii) of this subparagraph, as determined under §1.954-6(e),

(iv) Gross income derived from the sale, exchange, or other disposition of any aircraft or vessel used (by the seller or by a person related to the seller) in foreign commerce,

(v) Dividends, interest, and gains described in §1.954-6(f),

(vi) Income described in §1.954-6(g) (relating to partnerships, trusts, etc.), and

(vii) Exchange gain, to the extent allocable to foreign base company shipping income, as determined under §1.952-2(c)(2)(v)(b),

If the controlled foreign corporation has income derived from or in connection with, the use (or hiring or leasing for use) of any aircraft or vessel in foreign commerce, or derived from, or in connection with, the performance of services directly related to the use of any aircraft or vessel in foreign commerce, it shall be necessary to establish, from the books and records of the controlled foreign corporation, that such aircraft or vessel was used in foreign commerce within the meaning of subparagraphs (3) and (4) of §1.954-6(b).

* * * * * * * * * * * *

(8) **Qualified investments in foreign base company shipping operations.** The foreign base company shipping income that is excluded from foreign base company income under section 954(b)(2) and §1.954-1(b)(1).

(9) **Special rule for shipping income.** The distributions received through a chain of ownership described in section 958(a) which are excluded from foreign base company income under section 954(b)(6)(B) and §1.954-1(b)(2).

* * * * * * * * * * * *

(g-2) **Withdrawal of previously excluded subpart F income from investment in foreign base company shipping operations.** Books or records sufficient to verify the previously excluded subpart F income of the controlled foreign corporation withdrawn from investment in foreign base company shipping operations for the taxable year must establish—

(1) The sum of the amounts of income excluded from foreign base company income under section 954(b)(2) and paragraph (b)(1) of §1.954-1 for all prior taxable years,

(2) The sum of the amounts of previously excluded subpart F income withdrawn from investment in foreign base company shipping operations for all prior taxable years, as determined under section 955(a) and paragraph (b) of §1.955A-1,

(3) The amount withdrawn from investment in foreign base company shipping operations for the taxable year as determined under section 955(a) and paragraph (b) of §1.955A-1, and

(4) If the carryover (as described in §1.955A-1(b)(3)) of amounts relating to investments in less developed country shipping companies (as described in §1.955-5(b)) is applicable, (i) the amount of the corporation's qualified investments (determined under §1.955-2 other than paragraph (b)(5) thereof) in less developed country shipping companies at the close of the last taxable year of the corporation beginning before January 1, 1976, and (ii) the amount of the limitation with respect to previously excluded subpart F income (determined under §1.955-1(b)(2)(i)(b)) for the first taxable year of the corporation beginning after December 31, 1975.

* * * * * * * * * * * *

Export Trade Corporations

Section 1.970-1(c)(1) is amended by inserting "(as in effect before the enactment of the Tax Reduction Act of 1975)" immediately after "section 955".

§1.970-1 (Proposed Treasury Decision, published 2-9-78.) **Export Trade Corporations.**

* * * * * * * * * * * *

Section 1.972-1(b)(3) is amended by inserting "(as in effect before the enactment of the Tax Reduction Act of 1975)" immediately after "section 955".

§1.972-1 (Proposed Treasury Decision, published 2-9-78.) **Consolidation of group of export trade corporations.**

* * * * * * * * * * * *

[The page following this is 63,931]

International Boycott Determinations

Sec. 1.999-1 is added as follows:

§1.999-1 (Proposed Treasury Decision, published 3-1-77.) **Computation of the International Boycott Factor.**

(a) **In general.** Sections 908(a), 952(a)(3), and 995(b)(1)(F) provide that certain benefits of the foreign tax credit, deferral of earnings of foreign corporations, and DISC are denied if a person or a member of a controlled group (within the meaning of section 993(a)(3)) that includes that person participates in or cooperates with an international boycott (within the meaning of section 999(b)(3)). The loss of tax benefits may be determined by multiplying the otherwise allowable tax benefits by the "international boycott factor." Section 999(c)(1) provides that the international boycott factor is to be determined under regulations prescribed by the Secretary. The method of computing the international boycott factor is set forth in paragraph (c) of this section. A special rule for computing the international boycott factor of a person that is a member of two or more controlled groups is set forth in paragraph (d). Transitional rules for making adjustments to the international boycott factor for years affected by the effective dates are set forth in paragraph (e). The definitions of the terms used in this section are set forth in paragraph (b).

(b) **Definitions.** For purposes of this section:

(1) **Boycotting country.** In respect of a particular international boycott, the term "boycotting country" means any country described in section 999(a)(1)(A) or (B) that requires participation in or cooperation with that particular international boycott.

(2) **Participation in or cooperation with an international boycott.** For the definition of the term "participation in or cooperation with an international boycott", see section 999(b)(3) and Parts H through M of the Treasury Department's International Boycott Guidelines.

(3) **Operations in or related to a boycotting country.** For the definitions of the terms "operations", "operations in a boycotting country", "operations related to a boycotting country", and "operations with the government, a company, or a national of a boycotting country", see Part B of the Treasury Department's International Boycott Guidelines.

(4) **Clearly demonstrating clearly separate and identifiable operations.** For the rules for "clearly demonstrating clearly separate and identifiable operations", see Part D of the Treasury Department's International Boycott Guidelines.

(5) **Purchase made from a country.** The terms "purchase made from a boycotting country" and "purchases made from any country other than the United States" mean, in respect of any particular country, the gross amount paid in connection with the purchase of, the use of, or the right to use:

(i) Tangible personal property (including money) from a stock of goods located in that country,

(ii) Intangible property (other than securities) in that country,

(iii) Securities by a dealer to a beneficial owner that is a resident of that country (but only if the dealer knows or has reason to know the country of residence of the beneficial owner),

(iv) Real property located in that country, or

(v) Services performed in, and the end product of services performed in, that country (other than payroll paid to a person that is an officer or employee of the payor).

(6) **Sales made to a country.** The terms "sales made to a boycotting country" and "sales made to any country other than the United States" mean, in respect of any particular country, the gross receipts from the sale, exchange, other disposition, or use of:

(i) Tangible personal property (including money) for direct use, consumption, or disposition in that country,

Proposed Reg. §1.999-1

(ii) Services performed in that country,

(iii) The end product of services (wherever performed) for direct use, consumption, or disposition in that country,

(iv) Intangible property (other than securities) in that country,

(v) Securities by a dealer to a beneficial owner that is a resident of that country (but only if the dealer knows or has reason to know the country of residence of the beneficial owner), or

(vi) Real property located in that country.

To determine the country of direct use, consumption, or disposition of tangible personal property and the end product of services, see paragraph (b)(10) of this section.

(7) **Sales made from a country.** The terms "sales made from a boycotting country" and "sales made from any country other than the United States" mean, in respect of a particular country, the gross receipts from the sale, exchange, other disposition, or use of:

(i) Tangible personal property (including money) from a stock of goods located in that country,

(ii) Intangible property (other than securities) in that country, or

(iii) Services performed in, and the end product of services performed in, that country.

However, gross receipts from any such sale, exchange, other disposition, or use by a person that are included in the numerator of that person's international boycott factor by reason of paragraph (b)(6) of this section shall not again be included in the numerator by reason of this subparagraph.

(8) **Payroll paid or accrued for services performed in a country.** The terms "payroll paid or accrued for services performed in a boycotting country" and "payroll paid or accrued for services performed in any country other than the United States" mean, in respect of a particular country, the total amount paid or accrued as compensation to officers and employees, including wages, salaries, commissions, and bonuses, for services performed in that country.

(9) **Services performed partly within and partly without a country.** (i) In general. Except as provided in paragraph (b)(9)(ii) of this section, for purposes of allocating to a particular country—

(A) The gross amount paid in connection with the purchase or use of,

(B) The gross receipts from the sale, exchange, other disposition or use of, and

(C) The payroll paid or accrued for services performed, or the end product of services performed, partly within and partly without that country, the amount paid, received, or accrued to be allocated to that country, unless the facts and circumstances of a particular case warrant a different amount, will be that amount that bears the same relation to the total amount paid, received, or accrued as the number of days of performance of the services within that country bears to the total number of days of performance of services for which the total amount is paid, received, or accrued.

(ii) **Transportation, telegraph, and cable services.** Transportation, telegraph, and cable services performed partly within one country and partly within another country are allocated between the two countries as follows:

(A) In the case of a purchase of such services performed from Country A to Country B, fifty percent of the gross amount paid is deemed to be a purchase made from Country A and the remaining fifty percent is deemed to be a purchase made from Country B.

(B) In the case of a sale of such services performed from Country A to Country B, fifty percent of the gross receipts is deemed to be a sale made from Country A and the remaining fifty percent is deemed to be a sale made to Country B.

(10) **Country of use, consumption, or disposition.** As a general rule, the country of use, consumption, or disposition of a tangible personal property (including money) and the end product of services (wherever performed) is deemed to be the country of destination of the tangible personal property or the end product of the services. (Thus, if legal services are performed in one country and an opinion is given for use by a client in a second country, the end product of the legal services is used, consumed, or disposed of in

the second country.) The occurrence in a country of a temporary interruption in the shipment of the tangible personal property or the delivery of the end product of services shall not constitute such country the country of destination. However, if at the time of the transaction the person providing the tangible personal property or the end product of services knew, or should have known from the facts and circumstances surrounding the transaction, that the tangible personal property or the end product of services probably would not be used, consumed, or disposed of in the country of destination, that person must determine the country of ultimate use, consumption or disposition of the tangible personal property or the end product of services. Notwithstanding the preceding provisions of this subparagraph, a person that sells, exchanges, otherwise disposes of, or makes available for use, tangible personal property to any person all of whose business except for an insubstantial part consists of selling from inventory to retail customers at retail outlets all within one country may assume at the time of such sale to such person that the tangible personal property will be used, consumed, or disposed of within such country.

(11) **Controlled group taxable year.** The term "controlled group taxable year" means the taxable year of the controlled group's common parent corporation. In the event that no common parent corporation exists, the members of the group shall elect the taxable year of one of the members of the controlled group to serve as the controlled group taxable year. The taxable year election is a binding election to be changed only with the approval of the Secretary or his delegate. The election is to be made in accordance with the procedures set forth in the instructions to Form 5713, the International Boycott Report.

(c) **Computation of international boycott factor.** (1) In general. The method of computing the international boycott factor of a person that is not a member of a controlled group is set forth in paragraph (c)(2) of this section. The method of computing the international boycott factor of a person that is a member of a controlled group is set forth in paragraph (c)(3) of this section. For purposes of paragraphs (c)(2) and (3), purchases and sales made by, and payroll paid or accrued by, a partnership are deemed to be made or paid or accrued by a partner in that production that the partner's distributive share bears to the purchases and sales made by, and the payroll paid or accrued by, the partnership. Also for purposes of paragraphs (c)(2) and (3), purchases and sales made by, and payroll paid or accrued by, a trust referred to in section 671 are deemed to be made both by the trust (for purposes of determining the trust's international boycott factor), and by a person treated under section 671 as the owner of the trust (but only in that proportion that the portion of the trust that such person is considered as owning under sections 671 through 679 bears to the purchases and sales made by, and the payroll paid and accrued by, the trust).

(2) **International boycott factor of a person that is not a member of a controlled group.** The international boycott factor to be applied by a person that is not a member of a controlled group (within the meaning of section 993(a)(3), is a fraction.

(i) The numerator of the fraction is the sum of the—

(A) Purchases made from all boycotting countries associated in carrying out a particular international boycott,

(B) Sales made to or from all boycotting countries associated in carrying out a particular international boycott, and

(C) Payroll paid or accrued for services performed in all boycotting countries associated in carrying out a particular international boycott

by that person during that person's taxable year, minus the amount of such purchases, sales, and payroll that is clearly demonstrated to be attributable to clearly separate and identifiable operations in connection with which there was no participation in or cooperation with that international boycott.

(ii) The denominator of the fraction is the sum of the—

(A) Purchases made from any country other than the United States,

Proposed Reg. § 1.999-1

(B) Sales made to or from any country other than the United States, and

(C) Payroll paid or accrued for services performed in any country other than the United States

by that person during that person's taxable year.

(3) **International boycott factor of a person that is a member of a controlled group.** The international boycott factor to be applied by a person that is a member of a controlled group (within the meaning of section 993(a)(3)) shall be computed in the manner described in paragraph (c)(2) of this section, except that there shall be taken into account the purchases and sales made by, and the payroll paid or accrued by, each member of the controlled group during each member's own taxable year that ends with or within the controlled group taxable year that ends with or within that person's taxable year.

(d) **Computation of the international boycott factor of a person that is a member of two or more controlled groups.** The international boycott factor to be applied under sections 908(a), 952(a)(3), and 995(b)(1)(F) by a person that is a member of two or more controlled groups shall be determined in the manner described in paragraph (c)(3), except that the purchases, sales, and payroll included in the numerator and denominator shall include the purchases, sales, and payroll of that person and of all other members of the two or more controlled groups of which that person is a member.

(e) **Transitional rules. (1) Pre-November 3, 1976 boycotting operations.** The international boycott factor to be applied under sections 908(a), 952(a)(3), and 995(b)(1)(F) by a person that is not a member of a controlled group, for that person's taxable year that includes November 3, 1976, or a person that is a member of a controlled group, for the controlled group taxable year that includes November 3, 1976, shall be computed in the manner described in paragraphs (c)(2) and (c)(3), respectively, of this section. However, that the following adjustments shall be made—

(i) There shall be excluded from the numerators described in paragraphs (c)(2)(i) and (c)(3)(i) of this section purchases, sales, and payroll clearly demonstrated to be attributable to clearly separate and identifiable operations—

(A) that were completed on or before November 3, 1976, or

(B) in respect of which it is demonstrated that the agreements constituting participation in or cooperation with the international boycott were renounced, the renunciations were communicated on or before November 3, 1976, to the governments or persons with which the agreements were made, and the agreements have not been reaffirmed after November 3, 1976, and

(ii) The international boycott factor resulting after the numerator has been modified in accordance with paragraph (e)(1)(i) of this section shall be further modified by multiplying it by a fraction. The numerator of that fraction shall be the number of days in that person's taxable year (or, if applicable, in that person's controlled group taxable year) remaining after November 3, 1976, and the denominator shall be 366.

The principles of this subparagraph are illustrated in the following example:

Example. Corporation A, a calendar year taxpayer, is not a member of a controlled group. During the 1976 calendar year, Corporation A had three operations in a boycotting country under three separate contracts, each of which contained agreements constituting participation in or cooperation with an international boycott. Each contract was entered into on or after September 2, 1976. Operation (1) was completed on November 1, 1976. The sales made to a boycotting country in connection with Operation (1) amounted to $10. Operation (2) was not completed during the taxable year, but on November 1, 1976, Corporation A commmunicated a renunciation of the boycott agreement covering that operation to the government of the boycott country. The sales made to a boycotting country in connection with Operation (2) amounted to $40. Operation (3) was not completed during the taxable year, nor was any renunciation of the boycott agreement made. The sales made to a boycotting country in connection with Operation (3) amounted to $25. Corporation A had no purchases made from, sales made from, or payroll paid or accrued for services performed in, a boycotting country. Corporation A had $500 of purchases made from, sales made from, sales made to, and payroll paid or accrued for services performed in, countries other than the United States. Company A's boycott factor for 1976, computed under paragraph (c)(2) of this section (before the application of this subparagraph) would be:

$$\frac{\$10+\$40+\$25}{\$500} = \frac{\$75}{\$500}$$

However, the $10 is eliminated from the numerator by reason of paragraph (e)(1)(i)(A) of this section, and the $40 is eliminated from the numerator by reason of paragraph (e)(1)(i)(B) of this section. Thus, before the application of paragraph (e)(1)(ii) of this section, Corporation A's international boycott factor is $25/$500. After the application of paragraph (e)(1)(ii), Corporation A's international boycott factor is:

$$\frac{\$25}{\$500} \times \frac{58}{366}$$

(2) Pre-December 31, 1977 boycotting operations. The international boycott factor to be applied under sections 908(a), 952(a)(3), and 995(b)(1)(F) by a person that is not a member of a controlled group, for that person's taxable year that includes December 31, 1977, or by a person that is a member of a controlled group, for the controlled group taxable year that includes December 31, 1977, shall be computed in the manner described in paragraphs (c)(2) and (c)(3), respectively, of this section. However, the following adjustments shall be made—

(i) There shall be excluded from the numerators described in paragraphs (c)(2)(i) and (c)(3)(i) of this section purchases, sales, and payroll clearly demonstrated to be attributable to clearly separate and identifiable operations that were carried out in accordance with the terms of binding contracts entered into before September 2, 1976, and—

(A) That were completed on or before December 31, 1977, or

(B) In respect of which it is demonstrated that the agreements constituting participation in or cooperation with the international boycott were renounced, the renunciations were communicated on or before December 31, 1977, to the governments or persons with which the agreements were made, and the agreements were not reaffirmed after December 31, 1977, and

(ii) In the case of clearly separate and identifiable operations that are carried out in accordance with the terms of binding contracts entered into before September 2, 1976, but that do not meet the requirements of paragraph (e)(2)(i) of this section, the numerators described in paragraphs (c)(2)(i) and (c)(3)(i) of this section shall be adjusted by multiplying the purchases, sales, and payroll clearly demonstrated to be attributable to those operations by a fraction, the numerator of which is the number of days in such person's taxable year (or, if applicable, in such person's controlled group taxable year) remaining after December 31, 1977, and the denominator of which is 365.

The principles of this subparagraph are illustrated in the following example:

Example. Corporation A is not a member of a controlled group and reports on the basis of a July 1-June 30 fiscal year. During the 1977-1978 fiscal year, Corporation A had 2 operations carried out pursuant to the terms of separate contracts, each of which had a clause that constituted participation in or cooperation with an international boycott. Neither operation was completed during the fiscal year, nor were either of the boycotting clauses renounced. Operation (1) was carried out in accordance with the terms of a contract entered into on November 15, 1976. Operation (2) was carried out in accordance with the terms of a binding contract entered into before September 2, 1976. Corporation A had sales made to a boycotting country in connection with Operation (1) in the amount of $50, and in connection with Operation (2) in the amount of $100. Corporation A had sales made to countries other than the United States in the amount of $500. Corporation A had no purchases made from, sales made from, or payroll paid or accrued for services performed in, any country other than the United States. In the absence of this subparagraph, Corporation A's international boycott factor would be

Proposed Reg. § 1.999-1

$$\frac{\$50 + \$100}{\$500}$$

However, by reason of the application of this subparagraph, Corporation A's international boycott factor is reduced to

$$\frac{\$50 + \$100 \left(\dfrac{181}{365}\right)}{\$500}$$

(3) **Incomplete controlled group taxable year.** If, at the end of the taxable year of a person that is a member of a controlled group, the controlled group taxable year that includes November 3, 1976 has not ended, or the taxable year of one or more members of the controlled group that includes November 3, 1976 has not ended, then the international boycott factor to be applied under sections 908(a), 952(a)(3) and 995(b)(1)(F) by such person for the taxable year shall be computed in the manner described in paragraph (c)(3) of this section. However, the numerator and the denominator in that paragraph shall include only the purchases, sales, and payroll of those members of the controlled group whose taxable years ending after November 3, 1976 have ended as the end of the taxable year of such person.

(f) **Effective date.** This section applies to participation in or cooperation with an international boycott after November 3, 1976. In the case of operations which constitute participation in or cooperation with an international boycott and which are carried out in accordance with the terms of a binding contract entered into before September 2, 1976, this section applies to such participation or cooperation after December 31, 1977.

Foreign Personal Holding Company Stock or Securities

Section 1.1016-5 is amended by adding at the end thereof the following new paragraph (s):

§ 1.1016-5 (Proposed Treasury Decision, published 9-5-68.) **Miscellaneous adjustments to basis.**

* * * * * * * * * *

(s) **Stock or securities in foreign personal holding companies acquired from certain decedents.** In the case of a person acquiring stock or securities of a foreign personal holding company from a decedent dying after December 31, 1963, the basis of such stock or securities shall be adjusted to the extent provided in section 1022 and the regulations thereunder.

Immediately after § 1.1021-1 the following new section is inserted:

§ 1.1022-1 (Proposed Treasury Decision, published 9-5-68.) **Increase in basis with respect to certain foreign personal holding company stock or securities.**

(a) **General rule.** Under section 1022, the basis (determined under section 1014(b)(5)) of certain stock or securities of a corporation which was a foreign personal holding company for its most recent taxable year ending before the date of the decedent's death is subject to the special adjustment described in paragraph (b) of this section. This special adjustment applies only to stocks or securities acquired from a decedent dying after December 31, 1963. Section 1022 shall not apply to any stock or securities of a foreign corporation described in section 342(a)(2), relating to certain corporations which in 1937 were foreign personal holding companies. If section 1022 and this section apply, the basis of the stock or securities is increased as of the date of the decedent's death regardless of the date of payment of the Federal estate tax. For purposes of this section the term "acquired" shall have the same meaning as it has in section 1014(b)(5).

(b) **Amount of adjustment—(1) In general.** The basis of each share of stock or security to which paragraph (a) applies shall be increased by its proportionate share (as determined under subparagraph (2) of this paragraph) of the Federal estate tax attributable to the net appreciation in value of all such stock and securities (as determined under subparagraph (3) of this paragraph).

(2) **Proportionate share.** The proportionate share of a share of stock or a security referred to in subparagraph (1) of this paagraph is the amount determined by multiplying the amount determined under subparagraph (3) of this paragraph by a fraction, the numerator of which is the appreciation in value of such share or security, and the denominator of which is the aggregate appreciation in value of all such shares and securities having appreciation in value. For purposes of the preceding sentence, the appreciation in value of a share of stock or a security shall be the excess of—

(i) The fair market value of such share or security, over

(ii) The adjusted basis of such share or security in the hands of the decedent.

See paragraph (c) (2) of this section for the meaning of "fair market value".

(3) **Federal estate tax attributable to net appreciation in value.** The Federal estate tax attributable to the net appreciation in value of all shares of stock and securities to which paragraph (a) of this section applies is the amount determined by multiplying the Federal estate tax (as defined in paragraph (c) (1) of this section) imposed on the transfer of the decedent's taxable estate by a fraction, the numerator of which is the net appreciation in value of all such shares and securities (as defined in paragraph (c) (3) of this section), and the denominator of which is the value of the decedent's gross estate as determined under chapter 11 of the Code (section 2001 and following including section 2032, relating to alternate valuation).

(c) **Definitions.** For purposes of this section, the following definitions shall apply:

(1) **Federal estate tax.** The term "Federal estate tax" means the tax imposed by section 2001 or 2101 reduced by any credit allowable with respect to a tax on prior transfers by section 2013 or 2102. Thus, for this purpose, the tax imposed by section 2001 or 2101 shall not be reduced by the credits for state death taxes (section 2011), foreign death taxes (section 2014), or any other credit properly allowable with respect to such tax other than the credit for tax on prior transfers.

(2) **Fair market value.** The term "fair market value" means fair market value determined under chapter 11 of the Code (section 2001 and following, including section 2032, relating to alternate valuation). Thus, for example, if the executor elects under section 2032 to value the property included in the gross estate as of a date other than the date of the decedent's death, then the fair market value of the stock or security shall be determined at such other date.

(3) **Net appreciation in value of all shares and securities.** The "net appreciation in value of all shares and securities to which paragraph (a) of this section applies" shall be the amount by which the sum of the fair market values (as defined in subparagraph (2) of this paragraph) of all such shares and securities exceeds the sum of the adjusted basis of all such shares and securities in the hands of the decedent. Thus, for example, if—(i) the decedent owned 100 shares of stock described in paragraph (a) of this section, (ii) his adjusted basis in each such share was $500, and (iii) each such share is valued for Federal estate tax purposes at $750, then the net appreciation in value of such shares is $25,000.

(d) **Example.** The application of this section may be illustrated by the following example:

Example. A dies in 1964 owning 200 shares of stock in corporation M, a calendar year taxpayer, which was a foreign personal holding company for the taxable year 1963. M is not a corporation referred to in section 342(a)(2). The 200 shares of M

Proposed Reg. § 1.1022-1

stock are included in A's gross estate for Federal estate tax purposes and are bequeathed to B. In A's hands, each share of stock had an adjusted basis of $30. The fair market value of each share for Federal estate tax purposes is $60. The basis of each share of M stock determined under section 1014(b)(5) is $30. The value of the gross estate is $300,000 and the Federal estate tax reduced by the credit for tax on prior transfers but computed without regard to any other credit is $8,000. The net appreciation in value of the 200 shares of M stock is $6,000 (the excess of the fair market value of such stock for estate tax purposes ($12,000), over the basis of such stock in the hands of A ($6,000)). The Federal estate tax attributable to the net appreciation in value of the 200 shares of M stock is $160, computed as follows:

$$\frac{\$6{,}000 \text{ (net appreciation in value of 200 shares of M stock)}}{\$300{,}000 \text{ (value of gross estate)}} \times \$8{,}000 \text{ Federal estate tax} = \$160$$

Each share's proportionate share of the $160 Federal estate tax attributable to the net appreciation in value of the M stock is $.80, computed as follows:

$$\frac{\$30 \text{ (excess of fair market value of share (\$60), over A's basis (\$30))}}{\$6{,}000 \text{ (aggregate appreciation in value of 200 shares of M stock)}} \times \$160 = \$.80$$

Thus, the basis of each of the 200 shares of M stock is increased by $.80 and the basis of each such share in the hands of B or in the hands of the estate is $30.80.

Limitation on Capital Losses

Par. 2. Paragraph (b) of §1.1211-1 is amended by striking out "net capital gain" each place it appears in subparagraph (3)(ii) and (iv) and inserting in lieu thereof "capital gain net income (net capital gain for taxable years beginning before January 1, 1977)", by striking out "net capital gains and losses" as it appears in subparagraph (3)(v) and inserting in lieu thereof "capital gain net income (net capital gains for taxable years beginning before January 1, 1977) and net capital losses", by revising subparagraphs (2), (3)(i), (6)(ii), and (7), and by adding new material at the end of each example in subparagraph (8). The revised provisions and added material read as follows:

§1.1211-1 (Proposed Treasury Decision, published 5-31-78.) **Limitation on capital losses.**

* * * * * * * * * * * * *

(b) **Taxpayers other than corporations.** * * *

(2) **Additional Allowance.** Except as otherwise provided by subparagraph (3) of this paragraph, the additional allowance deductible under section 1211(b) for taxable years beginning after December 31, 1969, shall be the least of—

(i) The taxable income for the taxable year reduced, but not below zero, by the zero bracket amount (in the case of taxable years beginning before January 1, 1977, the taxable income for the taxable year);

(ii) $3,000 ($2,000 for taxable years beginning in 1977; $1,000 for taxable years beginning before January 1, 1977); or

(iii) The sum of the excess of the net short-term capital loss over the net long-term capital gain, plus one-half of the excess of the net long-term capital loss over the net short-term capital gain.

(3) **Transitional additional allowance—(i) In general.** If, pursuant to the provisions

of §1.1212-1(b) and subdivision (iii) of this subparagraph, there is carried to the taxable year from a taxable year beginning before January 1, 1970, a long-term capital loss, and if for the taxable year there is an excess of net long-term capital loss over net short-term capital gain, then, in lieu of the additional allowance provided by subparagraph (2) of this paragraph, the transitional additional allowance deductible under section 1211(b) shall be the least of—

(a) The taxable income for the taxable year reduced, but not below zero, by the zero bracket amount (in the case of taxable years beginning before January 1, 1977, the taxable income for the taxable year);

(b) $3,000 ($2,000 for taxable years beginning in 1977; $1,000 for taxable years beginning before January 1, 1977); or

(c) The sum of the excess of the net short-term capital loss over the net long-term capital gain; that portion of the excess of the net long-term capital loss over the net short-term capital gain computed as provided in subdivision (ii) of this subparagraph; plus one-half of the remaining portion of the excess of the net long-term capital loss over the net short-term capital gain.

* * * * * * * * * * * *

(6) **Special Rules.** * * *

(ii) For taxable years beginning before January 1, 1976, in case the tax is computed under section 3 and the regulations thereunder (relating to optional tax tables for individuals), the term "taxable income" as used in section 1211(b) and this paragraph shall be read as "adjusted gross income."

* * * * * * * * * * * *

(7) **Married taxpayers filing separate returns**—(i) In general. In the case of a husband or a wife who files a separate return for a taxable year beginning after December 31, 1969, the $3,000, $2,000, and $1,000 amounts specified in subparagraphs (2)(ii) and (3)(i)(b) of this paragraph shall instead be $1,500, $1,000, and $500, respectively.

(ii) Special rule. If, pursuant to the provisions of §1.1212-1(b) and subparagraph (3)(iii) or (iv) of this paragraph, there is carried to the taxable year from a taxable year beginning before January 1, 1970, a short-term capital loss or a long-term capital loss, the $1,500, $1,000, and $500 amounts specified in subdivision (i) of this subparagraph shall instead be maximum amounts of $3,000, $2,000, and $1,000, respectively, equal to $1,500, $1,000, and $500, respectively, plus the total of the transitional net long-term capital loss component for the taxable year computed as provided by subparagraph (3)(ii) of this paragraph and the transitional net short-term capital loss component for the taxable year computed as provided by subparagraph (3)(iv) of this paragraph.

(8) **Examples.** The provisions of section 1211(b) may be illustrated by the following examples:

Example (1). * * * If A had the same taxable income for purposes of section 1211(b) (after reduction by the zero bracket amount) and the same transactions in 1977, the additional allowance would be $2,000, and a net long-term capital loss of $100 would be carried over. For a taxable year beginning in 1978 or thereafter, these facts would give rise to a $2,050 additional allowance and no carryover.

Example (2). * * * Assuming the same taxable income for purposes of section 1211(b) (after reduction by the zero bracket amount) and the same transactions for taxable years beginning in 1977 or thereafter, the same result would be reached.

Example (3). * * * Assuming the same taxable income for purposes of section 1211(b) (after reduction by the zero bracket amount) and the same transactions for taxable years beginning in 1977 or thereafter, the result would remain unchanged.

Example (4). * * * Assuming the same taxable income for purposes of section 1211(b) (after reduction by the zero bracket amount) and the same transactions for taxable years beginning in 1977 or thereafter, the result would remain unchanged.

Example (5). * * * Assuming the same taxable income for purposes of section

Proposed Reg. § 1.1211-1

1211(b) (after reduction by the zero bracket amount) and the same transactions for taxable years beginning in 1977 or thereafter, the additional allowance would be $2,000, and there would be no carryover.

Example (6). * * * Assuming the same taxable income for purposes of section 1211(b) (after reduction by the zero bracket amount) and the same transactions for taxable years beginning in 1977 or thereafter, the transitional additional allowance would be $1,800. No amount would remain to be carried over to the succeeding taxable year.

Example (7). * * * Assuming the same taxable income for purposes of section 1211(b) (after reduction by the zero bracket amount) and the same transactions for taxable years beginning in 1977 or thereafter, the transitional additional allowance would be $1,900. No amount would remain to be carried over to the succeeding taxable year.

Example (8). * * * Assuming the same taxable income for purposes of section 1211(b) (after reduction by the zero bracket amount) and the same transactions as in example (7) for a married individual filing a separate return for a taxable year beginning in 1977 or thereafter, the transitional additional allowance would be $1,900. No amount would remain to be carried over to the succeeding taxable year.

Example (9). * * * Assuming the same taxable income for purposes of section 1211(b) (after reduction by the zero bracket amount) and the same transactions for a taxable year beginning in 1977, the transitional additional allowance would be $2,000. A net long-term capital loss of $800 would remain to be carried over. Of this amount $100 would be treated as carried over from 1969. Assuming the original facts for a taxable year beginning in 1978, the transitional additional allowance would be $2,800. No amount would remain to be carried over to the succeeding taxable year.

Special Rules for Determining Capital Gains and Losses

A new § 1.1239-1 is added, to read as follows:

Proposed Reg. § 1.1239-1 (Proposed Treasury Decision, published 5-31-78.) Gain from sale or exchange of depreciable property between certain related taxpayers after October 4, 1976.

(a) **In general.** In the case of a sale or exchange of property, directly or indirectly, between related persons after October 4, 1976 (other than a sale or exchange made under a binding contract entered into on or before that date), any gain recognized by the transferor shall be treated as ordinary income if such property is, in the hands of the transferee, subject to the allowance for depreciation provided in section 167. This rule also applies to property which would be subject to the allowance for depreciation provided in section 167 except that the purchaser has elected a different form of deduction, such as those allowed under sections 169, 188, and 191.

(b) **Related persons.** For purposes of paragraph (a), the term "related persons" means—

(1) A husband and wife,

(2) An individual and a corporation 80 percent or more in value of the outstanding stock of which is owned, directly or indirectly, by or for such individual, or

(3) Two or more corporations 80 percent or more in value of the outstanding stock of each of which is owned, directly or indirectly, by or for the same individual.

(c) **Rules of construction—(1) Husband and wife.** For purposes of paragraph (b)(1), if on the date of the sale or exchange a taxpayer is legally separated from his spouse under an interlocutory decree of divorce, the taxpayer and his spouse shall not be treated as husband and wife, provided the sale or exchange is made pursuant to the decree and the decree subsequently becomes final. Thus, if pursuant to an interlocutory decree of divorce, an individual transfers depreciable property to his spouse and, because of this section, the gain recognized on the transfer of the property is treated as ordinary income, the individual may, if the interlocutory decree becomes final after his tax return has been filed, file a claim for a refund.

(2) **Sales between commonly controlled corporations.** In general, in the case of a sale or exchange of depreciable property between related corporations (within the mean-

ing of paragraph (b)(3) of this section), gain which is treated as ordinary income by reason of this section shall be taxable to the transferor corporation rather than to a controlling shareholder. However, such gain shall be treated as ordinary income taxable to a controlling shareholder rather than the transferor corporation if the transferor corporation is used by a controlling shareholder as a mere conduit to make a sale to another controlled corporation, or the entity of the corporate transferor is otherwise properly disregarded for tax purposes. Sales between two or more corporations that are related within the meaning of paragraph (b)(3) of this section may also be subject to the rules of section 482 (relating to allocation of income between or among organizations, trades, or businesses which are commonly owned or controlled), and to rules requiring constructive dividend treatment to the controlling shareholder in appropriate circumstances.

Section 1.1239-1 is redesignated as § 1.1239-2 and is amended by revising the heading and first two sentences thereof to read as follows:

§1.1239-2 (Proposed Treasury Decision, published 5-31-78.) **Gain from sale or exchange of depreciable property between certain related taxpayers on or before October 4, 1976.**

Section 1239 provides in general that any gain from the sale or exchange of depreciable property between a husband and wife or between an individual and a controlled corporation on or before October 4, 1976 (and in the case of a sale or exchange occurring after that date if made under a binding contract entered into on or before that date), shall be treated as ordinary income. Thus, any gain recognized to the transferor from a sale or exchange after May 3, 1951, and on or before October 4, 1976 (or thereafter if pursuant to a binding contract entered into on or before that date), directly or indirectly, between a husband and wife or between an individual and a controlled corporation, of property which, in the hands of the transferee, is property of a character subject to an allowance for depreciation provided in section 167 (including such property on which a deduction for amortization is allowable under section 168 and 169) shall be considered as gain from the sale or exchange of property which is neither a capital asset nor property described in section 1231. * * *

(3) **Ownership of stock.** For purposes of determining the ownership of stock under this section, the constructive ownership rules of section 318 shall be applied, except that section 318(a)(2)(C) (relating to attribution of stock ownership from a corporation) and section 318(a)(3)(C) (relating to attribution of stock ownership to a corporation) shall be applied without regard to the 50-percent limitation contained therein. The application of the constructive ownership rules of section 318 to section 1239 is illustrated by the following examples:

Example (1). A, an individual, owns 79 percent of the stock (by value) of Corporation X, and a trust for A's children owns the remaining 21 percent of the stock. A's children are deemed to own the stock owned for their benefit by the trust in proportion to their actuarial interests in the trust (section 318(a)(2)(B)). A, in turn, constructively owns the stock so deemed to be owned by his children (section 318(a)(1)(A)(ii)). Thus, A is treated as owning all the stock of Corporation X, and any gain A recognizes from the sale of depreciable property to Corporation X is treated under section 1239 as ordinary income.

Example (2). Y Corporation owns 80% in value of the stock of Z Corporation. Y Corporation sells depreciable property at a gain to Z Corporation. P and his daughter, D, own 80 percent in value of the Y Corporation stock. Under the constructive ownership rules of section 318, as applied to section 1239, P and D are each considered to own the stock in Z Corporation owned by Y Corporation. Also, P and D are each considered to own the stock in Y Corporation owned by the other. As a result, both P and D constructively own 80 percent or more in value of the stock of both Y and Z Corporations. Thus, the sale between Y and Z is governed by section 1239 and produces ordinary income to Y.

Proposed Reg. § 1.1239-2

Section 1.1244(c)-1 is amended by revising subdivisions (ii) and (iii) of paragraph (g) (1) to read as follows:

§ 1.1244(c)-1   (Proposed Treasury Decision, published 9-5-68.) **Section 1244 stock defined.**

* * * * * * *

(g) **Gross receipts.** (1) * * *

(ii) The term "royalties" as used in subdivision (i) of this subparagraph means all royalties, including mineral, oil, and gas royalties, and amounts received for the privilege of using patents, copyrights, secret processes and formulas, good will, trademarks, trade brands, franchises, and other like property. The term "royalties" does not include amounts received upon the disposal of timber, coal, or domestic iron ore with a retained economic interest with respect to which the special rules of section 631(b) and (c) apply or amounts received from the transfer of patent rights to which section 1235 applies. For the definition of "mineral, oil and gas royalties", see paragraph (e)(2) of § 1.543-12. For purposes of this subdivision, the gross amount of royalties shall not be reduced by any part of the cost of the rights under which they are received or by any amount allowable as a deduction in computing taxable income. Whether or not any portion of the corporation's adjusted ordinary gross income or, in the case of taxable years beginning before January 1, 1964, the corporation's gross income is personal holding company income as defined in section 543 and the regulations thereunder is irrelevant for purposes of this subdivision.

(iii) The term "rents" as used in subdivision (i) of this subparagraph means amounts received for the use of, or right to use, property (whether real or personal) of the corporation. The term "rents" does not include payments for the use or occupancy of rooms or other space where significant services are also rendered to the occupant, such as for the use or occupancy of rooms or other quarters in hotels, boarding houses, or apartment houses furnishing hotel services, or in tourist homes, motor courts, or motels. Generally, services are considered rendered to the occupant if they are primarily for his convenience and are other than those usually or customarily rendered in connection with the rental of rooms or other space for occupancy only. The supplying of maid service, for example, constitutes such services; whereas the furnishing of heat and light, the cleaning of public entrances, exits, stairways, and lobbies, the collection of trash, etc., are not considered as services rendered to the occupant. Payments for the use or occupancy of entire private residences or living quarters in duplex or multiple housing units, of offices in an office building, etc., are generally "rents" under section 1244(c)(1)(E). Payments for the parking of automobiles ordinarily do not constitute rents. Payments for the warehousing of goods or for the use of personal property do not constitute rents if significant services are rendered in connection with such payments. Whether or not any portion of the corporation's adjusted ordinary gross income or, in the case of taxable years beginning before January 1, 1964, the corporation's gross income is personal holding company income as defined in section 543 and the regulations thereunder is irrelevant for purposes of this subdivision.

Section 1.1245-2 is amended by revising subparagraph (7) of paragraph (a) to read as follows:

§ 1.1245-2   (Proposed Treasury Decision, published 12-30-70.) **Definition of recomputed basis.**

(a) **General rule.** * * *

(7) **Depreciation or amortization allowed or allowable.** For purposes of determining recomputed basis, generally all adjustments (for periods after December 31, 1961, or June 30, 1963, as the case may be) attributable to allowed or allowable depreciation or amortization must be taken into account. See section 1016(a) (2) and the regulations thereunder for the meaning of "allowed" or "allowable".

However, if a taxpayer can establish by adequate records or other sufficient evidence that the amount allowed for depreciation or amortization for any period was less than the amount allowable for such period, the amount to be taken into account for such period shall be the amount allowed. No adjustment is to be made on account of the tax imposed by section 56 (relating to the minimum tax for tax preferences). See paragraph (b) of this section (relating to records to be kept and information to be filed). For example, assume that in the year 1967 it becomes necessary to determine the recomputed basis of property, the $500 adjusted basis of which reflects adjustments of $1,000 with respect to depreciation deductions allowable for periods after December 31, 1961. If the taxpayer can establish by adequate records or other sufficient evidence that he had been allowed deductions amounting to only $800 for the period, then in determining recomputed basis the amount added to adjusted basis with respect to the $1,000 adjustments to basis for the period will be only $800.

* *

Franchises, Trademarks and Trade Names

Immediately before § 1.1301, the following new sections are inserted:

§ 1.1253-1 (Proposed Treasury Decision, published 7-15-71.) Transfers of franchises, trademarks, and trade names.

(a) **General rule.** The transfer of a franchise, trademark, or trade name shall not be treated as the sale or exchange of a capital asset for purposes of the tax imposed by chapter 1 of the Code if the transferor retains any significant power, right, or continuing interest with respect to the subject matter of the franchise, trademark, or trade name transferred. Section 1253 and this section do not apply to amounts received during the taxable year with respect to the transfer of a franchise, trademark, or trade name by a nonresident alien individual or a foreign corporation which are not effectively connected for the taxable year with the conduct of a trade or business within the United States. Such amounts received by a nonresident alien individual or a foreign corporation shall be taxable as provided in section 871(a)(1) or 881(a), and the regulations thereunder. For the definition of terms used in this section, see § 1.1253-2.

(b) **Transferor's treatment of contingent payments.** All amounts received or accrued by the transferor on account of the transfer of a franchise, trademark, or trade name which are contingent on the productivity, use, or disposition of the franchise, trademark, or trade name transferred are includible in gross income as ordinary income. However, treatment of such amounts as ordinary income is not determinative as to whether such amounts will be treated as royalty income for purposes of any section of the Code specifically relating to royalties. Such determination shall be made pursuant to such section of the Code.

(c) **Transferee's treatment of payments—(1) Contingent payments.** Amounts paid or incurred during the taxable year on account of the transfer of a franchise, trademark, or trade name which are contingent on the productivity, use, or disposition of the franchise, trademark, or trade name transferred are deductible by the transferee as a trade or business expense pursuant to section 162(a) and the regulations thereunder, even though the transfer is treated as a sale or other disposition of property or the property transferred has a useful life which can be estimated with reasonable accuracy. A payment which is deductible under this subparagraph is not to be treated as an amount properly chargeable to capital account for purposes of section 1016(a)(1). See § 1.1253-3 for special provisions relating to the election under section 516(d)(3) of the Tax Reform Act of 1969 (83 Stat. 648) to apply section 1253(d)(1) and this subparagraph to certain contingent payments made on account of transfers of franchises, trademarks, or trade names occurring before January 1, 1970.

(2) **Initial payments by transferee in case of a sale or exchange.** If a transfer of a franchise, trademark, or trade name is treated as a sale or exchange of property, any noncontingent payment (that is, any amount not described in subparagraph (1) of this paragraph) made in discharge of a principal sum agreed upon in the

Proposed Reg. § 1.1253-1

transfer agreement shall be treated as an amount properly chargeable to capital account for purposes of section 1016(a)(1). If the property acquired in such transfer has a useful life to the transferee which can be estimated with reasonable accuracy, it may be the subject of a depreciation allowance, as provided in § 1.167(a)-3. This subparagraph applies both when the transfer giving rise to such principal sum is treated, by applying the provisions of paragraph (a) of this section, as a sale or exchange of a capital asset and when, without reference to this section, the transfer is treated as a sale or exchange of property which is not a capital asset.

(3) *Initial payments by transferee in case of a license.* If a transfer of a franchise, trademark, or trade name is treated as a transaction which is not a sale or exchange of property, any noncontingent payment made by the transferee in discharge of a principal sum agreed upon in the transfer agreement is allowed as a

deduction under section 1253(d)(2) and the following subdivisions of this subparagraph, provided that such principal sum is treated by the transferee as an amount properly chargeable to capital account for purposes of section 1016(a)(1):

(i) *Single payment.* In the case of a single payment made in discharge of such principal sum, the payment is deductible ratably over the shorter of—

(a) The 10 consecutive taxable years which begin with the taxable year in which such payment is made, or

(b) Those consecutive taxable years which begin with the taxable year in which such payment is made and end with the last taxable year beginning in the period of the transfer agreement.

(ii) *Series of equal payments payable over the period of transfer agreement or more than 10 years.* If the payment is one of a series of approximately equal payments (whether or not in consecutive taxable years) made in discharge of such principal sum, which are payable over—

(a) The period of the transfer agreement, whether a period of more or less than 10 consecutive taxable years, or

(b) A period of more than 10 consecutive taxable years, whether such period ends before or after the end of the period of the transfer agreement,
the payment is deductible in the taxable year in which it is made.

(iii) *Series of equal payments payable over a period of not more than 10 years.* In the case of a series of approximately equal payments (whether or not in consecutive taxable years) made in discharge of such principal sum and payable over a period of not more than 10 consecutive taxable years (whether such period ends before or after the end of the period of the transfer agreement) the payments are deductible ratably over the shorter of—

(a) The 10 consecutive taxable years which begin with the taxable year in which the first such payment is made, or

(b) Those consecutive taxable years which begin with the taxable year in which such first payment is made and end with the last taxable year beginning in the period of the transfer agreement, provided that the amount so allowable as a deduction in the taxable year, when added to amounts allowable as a deduction under this subdivision in previous taxable years in respect of such principal sum, shall not exceed the total payments which by the end of such taxable year have been made in discharge of such principal sum. If there is such an excess, see subdivision (vi) of this subparagraph.

(iv) *Series of unequal payments payable over the period of transfer agreement or more than 10 years.* If the payment is one of a series of unequal payments (whether or not in consecutive taxable years) made in discharge of such principal sum, which are payable over—

(a) The period of the transfer agreement, whether a period of more or less than 10 consecutive taxable years, or

(b) A period of more than 10 consecutive taxable years, whether such period ends before or after the end of the transfer agreement, the payment is deductible in the taxable year in which it is made, provided that no such payment exceeds 20 percent of such principal sum and provided that no more than 75 percent of such principal sum is paid in the first half of the period of the transfer agreement or in the period of 10 consecutive taxable years which begin with the taxable year in which the first such payment is made, whichever such period is shorter. If the payment is not deductible by reason of either of the above-mentioned provisos, see subdivision (vi) of this subparagraph.

(v) *Series of unequal payments payable over a period of not more than 10 years.* In the case of a payment which is one of a series of unequal payments (whether or not in consecutive taxable years) made in discharge of such principal sum and payable over a period of not more than 10 consecutive taxable years which is less than the period of the transfer agreement, the payments are deductible ratably over the shorter of—

(a) The 10 consecutive taxable years which begin with the taxable year in which the first such payment is made, or

Proposed Reg. §1.1253-1

(b) Those consecutive taxable years which begin with the taxable year in which such first payment is made and end with the last taxable year beginning in the period of the transfer agreement, provided that the amount so allowable as a deduction in the taxable year, when added to amounts allowable as a deduction under this subdivision in previous taxable years in respect of such principal sum, shall not exceed the total payments which by the end of such taxable year have been made in discharge of such principal sum. If there is such an excess, see subdivision (vi) of this subparagraph.

(vi) *Other payments.* In the case of any payment not described in subdivisions (i) through (v) of this subparagraph, the payment is deductible in the taxable year or years specified by the Commissioner upon written request of the taxpayer sent to the Commissioner of Internal Revenue, Washington, D. C. 20224, setting forth

[The page following this is 64,153]

sufficient information to identify the transfer involved, the period of the transfer agreement, the terms of the agreement, the amount of each payment to be made by the transferee in discharge of the principal sum agreed upon in the transfer agreement, and the dates on which such payments are to be made.

(4) **Illustrations.** The application of subparagraph (3) of this paragraph may be illustrated by the following examples:

Example (1). On January 1, 1970, M Corporation, a national franchisor of sparerib drive-ins, which uses the calendar year as its taxable year, transfers to A one of its sparerib franchises. Under the terms of the franchise agreement M Corporation retains a number of significant rights and powers in the franchise. As a result, the transfer is not treated as a sale or exchange of property. The franchise agreement is for a term of 20 years, and A agrees to pay M Corporation an initial payment of $24,000 on the date of signature. Under subparagraph (3)(i) of this paragraph, A is allowed a $2,400 deduction for each of the years 1970 through 1979.

Example (2). Assume the same facts as in example (1), except that A is to pay the initial payment to M Corporation in equal installments of $1,600 each for 15 years beginning in 1970. Under subparagraph (3)(ii) of this paragraph, A is allowed a $1,600 deduction for each of the years 1970 through 1984.

Example (3). Assume the same facts as in example (1), except that A is to pay the initial payment to M Corporation in installments of $3,000 in each even numbered year, beginning with 1970, until the initial payment of $24,000 is fully discharged. Under subparagraph (3)(ii) of this paragraph, A is allowed a $3,000 deduction for each year in which such an installment is paid to M Corporation.

Example (4). Assume the same facts as in example (1), except that A is to pay the initial payment to M Corporation in installments of $3,000 in each of the 8 consecutive years beginning with 1970. Under subparagraph (3)(iii) of this paragraph, A is allowed a $2,400 deduction for each of the years 1970 through 1979.

Example (5). Assume the same facts as in example (1), except that A is to pay the initial payment to M Corporation in installments of $1,500 for each of the first 14 years beginning with 1970, and $3,000 in 1984. Since none of such installments exceeds 20 percent of the initial payment of $24,000 and since the total payments of $15,000 made in the first 10 consecutive years of payment are less than $18,000 (75 percent of $24,000), A is allowed a $1,500 deduction for each of the years 1970 through 1983 and a $3,000 deduction for 1984, under the rules contained in subparagraph (3)(iv) of this paragraph.

Example (6). Assume the same facts as in example (1), except that A is to pay the initial payment to M Corporation in installments of $2,800 in each even numbered year, beginning with 1970 and ending with 1982, and $4,400 in 1984. Since none of such installments exceeds 20 percent of the initial payment of $24,000 and since the total payments of $14,000 made in the first 10 consecutive years of payment are less than $18,000 (75 percent of $24,000), A is allowed a $2,800 deduction for each of the years in which such an installment is paid and a $4,400 deduction for 1984, under the rules contained in subparagraph (3)(iv) of this paragraph.

Example (7). Assume the facts as in example (1), except that A is to pay the initial payment to M Corporation in installments of $3,000 in 1970, $7,000 in 1971, $6,000 in 1973, and $8,000 in 1976. Under subparagraph (3)(v) of this paragraph, A is allowed a $2,400 deduction for each of the years 1970 through 1979, since the amount so allowable in each such year, when added to amounts allowable in previous taxable years, does not exceed the total installment payments which by the end of such year have been made in discharge of the initial payment.

(d) **Transfer of a franchise, trademark, or trade name incident to the transfer of a trade or business—(1) In general.** Section 1253 and this section apply to amounts which are attributable to the transfer of a franchise, trademark, or trade name incident to the transfer of a trade or business. The amount attributable to the transfer of the franchise, trademark, or trade name is to be determined on the basis of the facts and circumstances involved in each case, including any written

Proposed Reg. § 1.1253-1

agreement entered into by the parties to the contract. However, to the extent the facts and circumstances do not show otherwise, that portion of the amount attributable to the transfer of a trade or business which is not attributable to the transfer of specific tangible assets, such as, for example, inventory, fixtures, and equipment, is to be treated as being attributable to the transfer of intangible assets, including goodwill, or any franchise, trademark, or trade name transferred as part of the transaction. In such case, that portion (whether represented by contingent or noncontingent payments) which is attributable to the transfer of intangible assets must be allocated on a reasonable basis among such intangible assets, including any franchise, trademark, or trade name transferred incident to the transaction. Generally, absent facts and circumstances indicating that another method of allocation would be more appropriate, contingent payments will be deemed attributable to intangible assets and will be allocated to such franchise, trademark, or trade name.

(2) **Illustrations.** The application of subparagraph (1) of this paragraph may be illustrated by the following examples:

Example (1). A sells his restaurant, which is famous for its fruit pies, to B for $500,000. As part of the transaction, A grants B the right to continue using A's name as the name of the restaurant. In consideration for such right, B grants A the "significant right" to prescribe the ingredients that may be used in making the pies and to inspect the restaurant weekly to make sure that the food being served is of the same high quality that A previously served. As a consquence, the transfer of the trade name to B is not treated as the sale or exchange of a capital asset. However, A establishes that a major factor in B's deciding to purchase A's restaurant, and in establishing the price to be paid therefor, was the fact that State X planned to build a new highway in the vicinity of the restaurant. Both A and B anticipated that the new highway would substantially increase the sales volume of the restaurant. Of the $500,000 received by A, it can reasonably be determined that $400,000 is attributable to land, building, fixtures and other tangible assets. Accordingly, the remaining $100,000 is to be treated as being attributable to the transfer of intangible assets. It is further determined that $40,000 of such $100,000 is attributable to the anticipated increase in sales volume attributable to the proposed highway construction and $60,000 is attributable to the continued use by B of A's name (the only other intangible asset transferred by A). Pursuant to subparagraph (1) of this paragraph, the $60,000 attributable to the transfer of the trade name is to be included in A's gross income as ordinary income.

Example (2). D sells his cleaning business to E for $500,000 and 5 percent of the gross income of the business for the next 5 years. As part of the transaction, D grants E the right to continnue to use D's name as the name of the business. In the absence of any other facts indicating that a contrary allocation would be more appropriate, contingent payments will be deemed attributable to the transfer of intangible assets and will be treated as being attributable to the transfer of the trade name. Consequently, whether or not the transfer of the trade name is treated as the sale of a capital asset, the portion of the contingent payments which is attributable to the transfer of the trade name is to be treated as ordinary income to D under section 1253(c) and paragraph (b) of this section.

(e) **Exception as to professional sports.** Section 1253 and this section do not apply to the transfer of a franchise to engage in professional football, basketball, baseball, or any other professional sport. However, this exception applies only to franchises for teams to participate in a professional sports league and does not apply to other franchised sports enterprises, such as a franchise to operate a golfing, bowling, or other sporting enterprise as a trade or business.

(f) **Effective date.** Except as provided in § 1.1253-3, this section and § 1.1253-2 apply only to transfers of franchises, trademarks, or trade names which occur after December 31, 1969.

§ 1.1253-2 (Proposed Treasury Decision, published 7-15-71.) **Definition of terms.**

For the purposes of §§ 1.1253-1 to 1.1253-3, inclusive—
(a) **Franchise.** The term "franchise" includes an agreement which gives the transferee the right to distribute, sell, or provide goods, services, or facilities within a specific area, such as a geographical area to which the business activity of the

transferee is limited by the agreement. The term includes distributorships or other similar exclusive-type contractual arrangements pursuant to which the transferee is permitted or licensed to operate or conduct a trade or business within a specific area.

(b) **Trademark.** The term "trademark" includes any word, name, symbol, or device, or any combination thereof, adopted and used by a manufacturer or merchant to identify his goods and distinguish them from those manufactured or sold by others. See 15 U.S.C. 1127.

(c) **Trade name.** The term "trade name" includes any name used by a manufacturer or merchant to identify or designate a particular trade or business or the name or title lawfully adopted and used by a person or organization engaged in a trade or business. See 15 U.S.C. 1127.

(d) **Significant power, right or continuing interest.** The term "significant power, right, or continuing interest" includes, but is not limited to, the following rights (whether expressly stated in the agreement or implied in fact from the conduct of the parties) with respect to the franchise, trademark, or trade name which is transferred:

(1) A right to disapprove any assignment of the transferred interest, or of any part thereof;

(2) A right to terminate the transferred interest at will;

(3) A right to prescribe the standards of quality of products used or sold, or of services furnished, and of the equipment and facilities used to promote such products or services;

(4) A right to require that the transferee sell or advertise only the products or services of the transferor;

(5) A right to require that the transferee purchase substantially all of his supplies and equipment from the transferor or from suppliers designated by the transferor;

(6) A right to payments contingent on the productivity, use, or disposition of the subject matter of the transferred interest where the estimated amount of such payments constitutes more than 50 percent of the total estimated amount the transferee has agreed to pay the transferor in consideration for the transfer;

(7) A right to prevent the transferee from removing equipment outside of th territory in which the transferee is permitted to operate;

(8) A right to participate in a continuing manner in the commercial or economic activities of the transferred interest, such as, for example, by conducting activities with respect to a transferred franchise such as sales promotion (including advertising), sales and management training, employee training programs, holding national meetings for the transferee, or providing the transferee with blue prints or formulae; or

(9) Any other right which permits the transferor to exercise continuing, active, and operational control over the transferee's trade or business activities.

(e) **Contingent payments.** The term "contingent payments" includes continuing payments, other than installment payments of a principal sum agreed upon in the transfer agreement, measured by a percentage of the selling price of the products marketed, or based on the units manufactured or sold, or based in a similar manner upon production, sale or use, or disposition of the franchise, trademark, or trade name transferred.

(f) **Transfer.** The term "transfer" includes—

(1) The sale, exchange, or other disposition of any interest, or any part of an interest, in a franchise, trademark, or trade name; and

(2) The renewal of an existing transfer agreement in respect of a franchise, trademark, or trade name. An existing transfer agreement is renewable where the provisions of the agreement continue to be binding on both parties to the agreement after the stated term of the agreement has elapsed subject to the termination by either party. The beginning of the period of the transfer agreement for purposes of paragraph (c)(3) of § 1.1253-1 and the date of transfer for the purposes of para-

Proposed Reg. § 1.1253-2

graph (f) of such section shall be—

(i) In the case of a renewable agreement which has not been terminated, the day following the date on which the stated term elapsed,

(ii) In the case of a new agreement entered into after the termination of a prior agreement, whether such prior agreement was renewable or non-renewable, the date of such new agreement, and

(iii) In the case of a termination of prior agreement where payments are continued pursuant to an express or implied agreement (terminable at will or otherwise) pending execution of a new agreement, the day following the termination of such prior agreement.

(3) The application of this paragraph may be illustrated by the following examples:

Example (1). M Corporation, a nationwide franchisor of M sparerib drive-ins, transfers to A the right to establish M drive-ins in state X including the right to franchise others to establish M drive-ins in state X. M Corporation also transfers to B the right to establish M drive-ins in state Y. A then establishes 25 M drive-ins in state X and franchises ten other persons to establish M drive-ins in state X. All of these transfers, both those between the national franchisor, M Corporation, and the middle level franchisors, A and B, and those between the middle level franchisor, A, and the local franchisees, are transfers for purposes of § 1.1253-1.

Example (2). Assume the same facts as in example (1) and that one of the franchises transferred by A in state X was transferred to C, an individual who uses the calendar year as the taxable year, on January 1, 1965. In the transfer agreement between A and C it is provided that the agreement is to be in effect for a term of 10 years commencing on January 1, 1965. After 10 years either party may terminate the agreement by giving 6 months' written notice to the other. The agreement provides for a $10,000 initial payment to be made in 10 equal installments commencing on January 1, 1965, and for contingent payments of 3 percent of the gross sales of M spareribs by C. The provisions of § 1.1253-1 do not apply to any payments made pursuant to this transfer agreement, except that, pursuant to an election made under § 1.1253-3, C may deduct under paragraph (c)(1) of § 1.1253-1 the contingent payments which he makes in taxable years ending after December 31, 1969, on account of the original transfer. If neither A nor C gives notice after December 31, 1974, of termination of the agreement, all contingent payments made pursuant to the renewal on January 1, 1975, shall be included in A's gross income as ordinary income under paragraph (b) of § 1.1253-1 and shall be allowed as a deduction to C under paragraph (c)(1) of such section.

Example (3). Assume the same facts as in example (2) except that the agreement is in effect for only 10 years. On January 1, 1975, A and C negotiate a new agreement to establish an M drive-in in state X for a term of 10 years commencing on that date. This new agreement provides for a $10,000 initial payment to be made on January 1, 1975, and for contingent payments of 4 percent of the gross sales of M Spareribs by C. Assume also that under the terms of the new agreement M Corporation retains a number of significant rights and powers in the franchise. In accordance with paragraph (a) of § 1.1253-1, the initial payment of $10,000 is included in A's gross income as ordinary income. Under the provisions of paragraph (c)(3)(i) of § 1.1253-1, C is allowed a $1,000 deduction for each of the years 1975 through 1984 in respect of the initial payment of $10,000. All contingent payments made pursuant to the transfer on January 1, 1975, shall be included in A's gross income as ordinary income under paragraph (b) of § 1.1253-1 and shall be allowed as a deduction to C under paragraph (c)(1) of such section.

§ 1.1253-3 (Proposed Treasury Decision, published 7-15-71.) **Election with respect to contingent payments on pre-1970 transfers.**

(a) **Election.** Section 516(d)(3) of the Tax Reform Act of 1969 (83 Stat. 648) provides that the transferee may elect to apply section 1253(d)(1) and paragraph (c)(1) of § 1.1253-1 to contingent payments made on account of transfers before January 1, 1970, of franchises, trademarks, or trade names, but only with respect to payments made in taxable years ending after December 31, 1969, and beginning before January 1, 1980. An election under such section must be made not later than (1) the time, including extensions thereof, prescribed by law for filing the income tax return for the first taxable year ending after December 31, 1969, in which contingent payments are made on account of any such transfer or (2) June 8, 1970, whichever is later. The election shall apply to all payments made in taxable years ending after December 31, 1969, and beginning before January 1, 1980, on account of the transfer in respect of which the election is made. If there are contingent payments in such years on account of more than one such transfer occurring before January 1, 1970, the transferee may elect as to one, more than one, or all of such transfers.

(b) **Manner of making election.** The election shall be made by a statement attached to the return (or an amended return) for the taxable year and shall, with respect to each transfer in respect of which the election is made—

(1) State the name and address of the transferee and of the transferor;

(2) Indicate that the transferee elects to take a deduction under section 1253 (d)(1) for all contingent payments on account of such transfer which are made in taxable years ending after December 31, 1969, and beginning before January 1, 1980;

(3) Identify the franchise, trademark, or trade name and the date of the agreement pursuant to which the transfer is made;

(4) State the period of the transfer agreement;

(5) State the amount the transferee is deducting for such taxable year pursuant to the election;

(6) State the total amount of contingent payments which were made in previous taxable years on account of such transfer, identifying the amounts and years in which such payments were made; and

(7) Show the formula agreed upon by the transferor and transferee for determining the amount of contingent payments.

(c) **Revocation—(1) With consent.** Except as provided in subparagraph (2) of this paragraph, an election made in accordance with paragraph (a) of this section shall be binding unless consent of the Commissioner is obtained under section 446(e) and § 1.446-1(e) to change the method of treating contingent payments to which such election applies. This paragraph shall not apply to an election made pursuant to paragraph (d) of this section.

(2) **Without consent.** If on or before [the date of publication in the Federal Register of the regulations under section 1253] an election has been made under paragraph (a) of this section for a taxable year for which the last day for filing an income tax return (including extensions thereof) falls before [the 90th day after such date], consent is hereby given for the taxpayer to revoke such election without the consent of the Commissioner. A revocation under this subparagraph shall be made by filing, on or before [such 90th day], a statement to that effect with the district director, or with the director of the internal revenue service center, with whom the election was filed. For any taxable year for which such revocation is applicable, an amended return reflecting such revocation shall be filed on or before [such 90th day].

(d) **Controlled foreign corporations—(1) In general.** The controlling United States shareholders (as defined in paragraph (c) (5) of § 1.964-1) of a foreign corporation (other than a resident foreign corporation required to file a return under section 6012 and the regulations thereunder) may make the election described in paragraph (a) of this section by (i) filing a written statement to such effect with the Director of International Operations, Washington, D.C. 20225, within 180 days after the close of the first taxable year of the foreign corporation ending after December 31, 1969, in which contingent payments are made on account of any transfer described in paragraph (a) of this section or on or before December 31, 1971, whichever is later, and (ii) providing the written notice in the time and manner prescribed in paragraph (c) (3) (iii) of § 1.964-1. The written statement shall furnish the information required by paragraph (b) of this section and paragraph (c) (3) (ii) of § 1.964-1 and shall be jointly executed by the controlling United States shareholders. The filing of a written statement pursuant to this subparagraph shall constitute an election for purposes of paragraph (c) (1) (iv) of § 1.964-1.

(2) **Exception.** Subparagraph (1) of this paragraph shall not apply with respect to any foreign corporation for which an election may by made pursuant to paragraph (c) (6) or (f) of § 1.964-1.

Proposed Reg. § 1.1253-3

Income Averaging

Paragraph (a) of § 1.1304-2 is amended to read as follows:

§ 1.1304-2 (Proposed Treasury Decision, published 4-30-75.) **Provisions inapplicable if income averaging is chosen.**

(a) **Provisions inapplicable.** If a taxpayer chooses the benefits of income averaging for any taxable year, pursuant to section 1304(a) and § 1.1304-1, the following sections of the Code will not apply for such year: * * *

(2) In taxable years beginning before January 1, 1974, section 72(n)(2) (relating to limitation of tax in case of certain distributions with respect to contributions by self-employed individuals).

* * * * * * * * * * * * *

Claim of Right

Section 1.1341-1(b) is amended by revising subdivision (ii) of subparagraph (1) to read as follows:

§ 1.1341-1 (Proposed Treasury Decision, published 12-30-70.) **Restoration of amounts received or accrued under claim of right.**

* * * * * * * * * * * *

(b) **Determination of tax.** (1) * * *

(ii) The tax for the taxable year computed under section 1341(a)(5), that is, without taking such deduction into account, minus the decrease in tax (net of any increase in tax imposed by section 56, relating to the minimum tax for tax preferences) (under chapter 1 of the Internal Revenue Code of 1954, under chapter 1 (other than subchapter E) and subchapter E of chapter 2 of the Internal Revnue Code of 1939, or under the corresponding provisions of prior revenue laws) for the prior taxable year (or years) which would result solely from the exclusion from gross income of all or that portion of the income included under a claim of right to which the deduction is attributable. For the purpose of this subdivision, the amount of the decrease in tax is not limited to the amount of the tax for the taxable year. See paragraph (i) of this section where the decrease in tax for the prior taxable year (or years) exceeds the tax for the taxable year.

* * * * * * * * * * * *

Election of Certain Partnerships and Proprietorships as to Taxable Status

Section 1.1361-2 is amended by revising subparagraphs (1) and (3) of paragraph (e) to read as follows:

§ 1.1361-2 (Proposed Treasury Decision, published 9-5-68.) **Qualifications.**

* * * * * * * *

(e) **Nature of income.** (1) An election may not be made with respect to an

[The page following this is 64,173]

enterprise unless, during the period described in paragraph (a)(1) of this section, (i) the enterprise is one in which capital is a material income-producing factor, or (ii) 50 percent or more of the gross income of the enterprise consists of gains, profits, or income derived from trading as a principal or from either buying or selling real property, stock, securities or commodities for the account of others. Income derived from trading as a principal (but not, in the case of taxable years beginning before January 1, 1964, such income which is personal holding company income as defined in §§ 1.543-1 and 1.543-2) shall be combined with income derived from buying or selling for the account of others in determining whether the 50-percent requirement is satisfied.

* * * * * * * * * *

(3) The 50-percent determination described in subparagraph (1) of this paragraph is made by reference to gross income, other than those items of gross income which are excluded from gross income of the enterprise by section 1361(i)(1), relating to personal holding company income. The determination is made by reference to the gross income of the entire period described in paragraph (a)(1) of this section; it is not necessary that the 50-percent test be satisfied on each day during such period.

Section 1.1361-8 is amended by revising paragraph (a), by adding a new subparagraph (3) to paragraph (b) and a new subparagraph (5) to paragraph (c), and by revising paragraph (d). These revised and added provisions read as follows:

§ 1.1361-8 (Proposed Treasury Decision, published 9-5-68.) **Personal holding company income.**

(a) **General rule.** Personal holding company income received or accrued by a section 1361 corporation shall not be included in its gross income. For this purpose, the term "personal holding company income" means any item of gross income (computed without regard to the adjustments provided in section 543(b)(3) or (4)) if such item (adjusted, where applicable, as provided in section 543(b)(3) or (4)) would constitute personal holding company income under section 543 (a) and §§ 1.543-3 through 1.543-11. However, for taxable years beginning before January 1, 1964, the term "personal holding company income" means personal holding company income, as defined in section 543 (prior to its amendment by section 225 (d) of the Revenue Act of 1964 (78 Stat. 81)) and §§ 1.543-1 and 1.543-2, other than income received or accrued from either buying or selling real property, stock, securities, or commodities for the account of others.

(b) **Income and deductions of owners.** * * * (3) In the case of a section 1361 corporation which is, in a transaction occurring after April 14, 1966, a party to a reorganization described in section 368(a)(1)(F) as a result of a transfer of assets to an actual corporation during a taxable year (see paragraph (b)(2) of § 1.1361-5), the personal holding company income for the portion of such year, and the deductions attributable to such income, which are treated as the income and deductions of the owner or owners of the section 1361 corporation shall be determined by allocating such income and deductions between (i) the period beginning on the first day of such taxable year and ending with the close of the date of transfer, and (ii) the balance of such taxable year. However, such income and deductions shall be taken into account by an owner for his taxable year ending with, or within which ends, the taxable year of the corporation.

(c) **Distributions.** * * *

(5) For purposes of this paragraph, in the case of a section 1361 corporation which is, in a transaction occurring after April 14, 1966, a party to a reorganization

Proposed Reg. § 1.1361-8

described in section 368(a)(1)(F) as a result of a transfer of assets to an actual corporation during a taxable year (see paragraph (b)(2) of § 1.1361-5), such full taxable year shall be considered the taxable year of the section 1361 corporation in determining the taxable year of the corporation during which a distribution is made.

(d) Special rule. For purposes of determining whether a particular item of income is personal holding company income under section 543 for any taxable year, income otherwise excluded from the gross income of the enterprise by reason of section 1361 (i)(1) shall enter into the determination of gross income, ordinary gross income, adjusted ordinary gross income, and personal holding company income. Thus, if a section 1361 corporation has gross income for each of the calendar years 1963 and 1964 of $100,000, consisting of $35,000 from a mercantile business, $25,000 from dividends, and $40,000 from rents, the gross income from rents is personal holding company income in 1963 for purposes of section 1361(i) because it does not constitute 50 percent or more of the gross income received or accrued by the corporation in such year. In addition, assuming that the corporation makes no distributions which are treated as dividends for purposes of section 543(a)(2)(B) for 1964, then (even if the adjusted income from rents constituted 50 percent or more of the corporation's adjusted ordinary gross income for 1964) the gross income from rents in 1964 is personal holding company income for purposes of section 1361(i) because the amount of the dividends (zero) does not equal or exceed $15,000, the amount by which the corporation's other personal holding company income ($25,000 from dividends) exceeds 10 percent of the ordinary gross income ($100,000) for such year.

Election of Certain Small Business Corporations as to Taxable Status

Section 1.1371-1 is amended by revising paragraph (e) to read as follows:

§ 1.1371-1 (Proposed Treasury Decision, published 5-6-72.) **Definition of small business corporation.**

* * * * * * * * * * *

(e) **Shareholders must be individuals or estates.** A corporation in which any shareholder is a corporation, trust, or partnership does not qualify as a small business corporation. The word "trust" as used in this paragraph includes all trusts subject to the provisions of subchapter D (including a trust forming part of a stock bonus plan), F, H, or J (including subpart E thereof), chapter 1 of the Code and voting trusts. Thus, even though the grantor is treated as the owner of all or any part of a trust, the corporation in which such trust is a shareholder does not meet the qualifications of a small business corporation.

* * * * * * * * * * *

Section 1.1372-1 is amended by revising paragraph (a) and subparagraph (1) of paragraph (b). These amended provisions read as follows:

§ 1.1372-1 (Proposed Treasury Decision, published 12-30-70.) **Election by small business corporation.**

(a) **Eligibility.** Under section 1372, an eligible small business corporation may elect not to be subject to the taxes imposed by chapter 1 of the Code (other than the tax imposed by section 1378 for taxable years beginning after April 14, 1966, and the tax imposed by section 56 for taxable years ending after December 31, 1969). The qualifications of a small business corporation must be met as of the first day of the first taxable year of the corporation for which the election is to be effective and on the date of election, unless the election is made after such first day, in which case the qualifications need not exist prior to the date of election. For example, the existence of a corporate shareholder or a nonresident alien as a shareholder prior to the date of election does not preclude qualification. However, if the election is made for a taxable year beginning before September 3, 1958, the qualifications must be met on such date and on each day after such date and before the date of the election. The election by a small business corporation is valid only if all the shareholders in the corporation on the first day of the first taxable year for which the election is to be effective, or on the day of election, whichever is later, consent to such election. See § 1.1372-3, relating to shareholders' consent.

(b) **Effect of election**—(1) **Effect on corporation.** The effect on a small business corporation of a valid election under section 1372 is to exempt such corporation from the taxes imposed by chapter 1 of the Code (other than the tax imposed by section 1378 for taxable years beginning after April 14, 1966, and the tax imposed by section 56 for taxable years ending after December 31, 1969 with respect to taxable years of the corporation for which the election is in effect and to subject the corporation with respect to such taxable years and all of its subsequent taxable years to section 1377, relating to special rules for computing the earnings and profits of an election small business corporation.

* * * * * * * * * * * * *

Section 1.1373-1 is amended by revising paragraph (b) to read as follows:

§ **1.1373-1** (Proposed Treasury Decision, published 12-30-70.) **Corporation undistributed taxable income taxed to shareholders.**

* * * * * * * * * * * * *

(b) **Determination of amount included by shareholders.** To determine the amount each shareholder must include in his gross income as provided in paragraph (a) of this section it is necessary to—

(1) Compute the taxable income of the electing small business corporation for its taxable year in accordance with the provisions of paragraph (c) of this section.

(2) Determine in accordance with paragraph (d) of this section the amount of money distributed as dividends during the taxable year out of earnings and profits of such year.

(3) Determine in accordance with §§ 1.56-1 through 1.56-4 the amount of tax imposed by section 56 for the taxable year.

(4) Determine in accordance with §§ 1.1378-1 through 1.1378-3 the amount of tax imposed by section 1378 for the taxable year.

(5) Subtract the sum of the amounts determined in subparagraph (2), (3), and (4) of this paragraph from the amount computed in subparagraph (1) of this paragraph. The result is the undistributed taxable income for the taxable year.

(6) Determine in accordance with paragraph (e) of this section the amount that would be treated as a dividend to such shareholder if an amount of money equal to such undistributed taxable income were distributed pro rata to the shareholders of the corporation on the last day of the taxable year of the corporation in a distribution which is not an exchange of stock.

* * * * * * * * * * * * *

Section 1.1375-1 is amended by revising paragraph (a), subparagraph (1) of paragraph (b), and subdivision (i) of example (2) of paragraph (e). These amended provisions read as follows:

§ **1.1375-1** (Proposed Treasury Decision, published 12-30-70.) **Special rules applicable to capital gains.**

(a) **In general.** The amount includable by a shareholder in gross income as dividends received from an electing small business corporation during any taxable year of such corporation shall be treated as long-term capital gain to the extent, if any, of such shareholder's pro rata share of the excess of the corporation's net long-term capital gain over its net short-term capital loss for such taxable year. For this purpose, such excess shall be reduced by the amount of the taxes imposed by sections 56 and 1378 on the income of the corporation for the taxable year, and the amount of such excess so reduced shall not exceed the taxable income (as

© 1976 by Prentice-Hall, Inc.

Proposed Reg. § 1.1375-1

defined in section 1373(d)) of the corporation for the taxable year. This capital gain treatment applies both to actual distributions of dividends and to amounts treated as dividends pursuant to section 1373(b); however, it applies only to the extent that a dividend is out of earnings and profits of the current taxable year of the corporation. Furthermore, this capital gain treatment applies whether or not the shareholder held any stock in the corporation at the close of the taxable year of the corporation.

(b) **Determination of pro rata share.** * * *
(1) The excess of the corporation's net long-term capital gain over its net short-term capital loss for the taxable year, reduced by the amount of tax, if any, imposed by section 56 and 1378 on the income of the corporation for such year;

* * * * * * * * * * * * *

(e) **Examples.** The application of this section may be illustrated by the following examples:

* * * * * * * * * * * * *

Example (2). (i) An electing small business corporation which has four equal shareholders has taxable income (as defined in section 1373(d)) and current earnings and profits of $80,000 for the taxable year 1959. It has an excess of $100,000 of net long-term capital gain over net short-term capital loss for the taxable year. (The corporation is not subject to the tax imposed by section 1378 for the taxable year.) The corporation distributes $100,000 in money during the taxable year, $25,000 to each shareholder, all of which is treated as a dividend since the corporation had a substantial amount of accumulated earnings and profits at the beginning of the taxable year. However, since the amount which will be treated as long-term capital gain in the hands of the shareholders cannot exceed the corporation's taxable income for the taxable year, and is limited to distributions out of earnings and profits of the taxable year, the amount which can be treated as a long-term capital gain by each shareholder is $20,000.

* * * * * * * * * * * * *

Certain Qualified Pensions, Etc., Plans

There are inserted immediately after § 1.1378-3 the following new sections:

§ **1.1379-1** (Proposed Treasury Decision, published 5-6-72; 5-26-78.) Additional requirement for qualification of profit-sharing plans of electing small business corporations.

(a) **Introduction.** Section 1379(a) and this section prescribe an additional requirement which must be met for qualification under section 401 of a trust forming part of a profit-sharing plan which does not provide that each employee's rights to the contributions, or to the benefits derived from the contributions, of the employer are nonforfeitable at the time the contributions are paid to, or under, the plan and—

(1) Which is maintained (i) by a corporation which is an electing small business corporation (as defined in section 1371(b) and §1.1371-2) with respect to any taxable year beginning after December 31, 1970, during which such plan was maintained, or (ii) by the successor of such a corporation, and

(2) Which covers any individual who is a shareholder-employee (as defined in section 1379(d) §1.1379-4) of such corporation or a predecessor of such corporation for any taxable year referred to in subparagraph (1) of this paragraph.

Thus, this requirement must be met even though a corporation ceases to be an electing small business corporation or the plan ceases to be a profit-sharing plan as long as the plan covers an individual who was a shareholder-employee of such corporation or a predecessor of such corporation while it was an electing small business corporation which maintained the profit-sharing plan. With respect to stock bonus plans, see paragraph (e) of §1.1371-1 for rules relating to the ownership of the stock of a small business corporation. The provisions of section 1379(a) and this section apply to such trusts for taxable years beginning after December 31, 1970. For special requirements which apply to a defined benefit plan for taxable years beginning after December 31, 1975, see section 401(j) and the regulations thereunder.

(b) General rule. A trust described in paragraph (a) of this section does not constitute a qualified trust under section 401 unless the plan of which such trust is

[The page following is 64,179]

Proposed Reg. §1.1379-1

a part provides that funds in such plan arising from forfeitures may not be allocated to the account of an employee to the extent that—

(1) Such funds are attributable to a restricted contribution; and

(2) The employee is a shareholder-employee for the taxable year of the corporation in which the restricted contribution is deducted.

For purposes of this section, the term "restricted contribution" means a contribution which is deducted or deductible under section 404(a)(3) for a taxable year beginning after December 31, 1970, by an employer which is an electing small business corporation for such a taxable year. A trust meets the requirements of section 1379(a) and this section if the plan of which such trust is a part provides that funds arising from a forfeiture which are attributable to a restricted contribution shall be determined in a manner consistent with paragraph (c) of this section and shall be applied in a manner consistent with paragraph (d) of this section.

(c) **Funds attributable to restricted contributions**—(1) **In general.** The funds arising from a forfeiture which are attributable to a restricted contribution for a particular taxable year of an electing small business corporation consist of so much of its contribution for such year (including the income derived thereon) as is forfeited by an employee. For purposes of this section, a forfeiture which is attributable to a restricted contribution for a taxable year of the employer shall be determined under a method which is specified in the plan and which meets the requirements of subparagraph (2) or subparagraph (3) of this paragraph.

(2) **Apportionment method.** Under the apportionment method, the portion of a forfeiture which is attributable to a restricted contribution for a particular taxable year of the corporation shall be determined by dividing the amount of such forfeiture by the number of years the forfeiting employee participated in the plan. For this purpose, the number of years an employee's participation includes years for which no contribution was made under the plan and years for which no contribution to the plan was deductible by the corporation under section 404(a)(3).

(3) **Direct tracing method.** Under the direct tracing method, the portion of a forfeiture which is attributable to a restricted contribution for a particular year is an amount which bears the same ratio to the amount of such forfeiture as the forfeiting employee's annual account balance for such year bears to the sum of all annual account balances for such employee. For purposes of the preceding sentence, the annual account balance for an employee shall be determined by the maintenance of a separate account which reflects with respect to a taxable year of the employer—

(i) The amount of contribution allocated to the employee's account in any year, which is deductible by the employer under section 404(a)(3) for such taxable year;

(ii) The amount of contribution deductible by the employer for such taxable year which is included in a forfeiture allocated to the employee's account in any year;

(iii) The amount of net income and net gain or loss for all years from the investment and reinvestment of the employer contribution described in subdivisions (i) and (ii) of this subparagraph for such taxable year; and

(iv) The adjustments made with respect to each amount determined under the preceding subdivisions on account of any distributions made before termination of services.

For purposes of subdivisions (i) and (ii) of this subparagraph, if, for any taxable year, an employer pays contributions to both a profit-sharing plan and a pension or annuity plan in excess of the limitation of section 404(a)(7), the amount of such contributions which are deductible under section 404(a)(3) is an amount which bears the same ratio to the limitation of section 404(a)(7) as the amount otherwise deductible under section 404(a)(3) bears to the sum of such amount and the amount otherwise deductible under section 404(a)(1) or (2). For such purposes, where all or a portion of an employer contribution allocated to an employee's account is deductible, if at all, as a carryover to a taxable year subsequent to the taxable year in which the forfeiture occurs, the funds attributable to the contribution carryover shall be treated as a restricted contribution with respect to any employee who is a shareholder-employee for the year in which the forfeiture occurs. For purposes of this

Proposed Reg. § 1.1379-1

subparagraph, all taxable years beginning before January 1, 1971, may be treated as a single taxable year.

(d) Acceptable treatment of forfeitures. For purposes of this section, funds attributable to a restricted contribution are not considered to inure to the benefit of an employee who was a shareholder-employee for the taxable year for which such contribution was deductible if—

(1) In the case of a plan containing a definite formula (within the meaning of paragraph (d) of § 1.401-12) for determining the contributions to be made by the employer on behalf of employees, (i) such funds are to be used solely to reduce the employer's contribution for the taxable year in which such funds arise, and (ii) any excess of the funds so arising in any taxable year over the amount determined under such formula for such year is to be allocated in accordance with plan provisions satisfying the requirement of subparagraph (2) of this paragraph; or

(2) (i) The plan provides that such funds are to be allocated solely to employees other than such shareholder-employees or (ii) if there are no such other employees participating in the plan, such funds are to be repaid to the employer not later than the 15th day of the third month following the close of the taxable year of the employer in which such funds arose.

A trust forming part of a profit-sharing plan shall not be considered not to meet the requirement of section 401(a)(2) and § 1.401-2, relating to impossibility of diversion under the trust instrument, merely because such plan permits funds to be repaid to the employer in accordance with subparagraph (2)(ii) of this paragraph. Such requirement shall not be deemed to be satisfied with respect to any amount repaid to the employer unless such amount is contributed to the trust, immediately upon receipt thereof by the employer, as a contribution by the employer for its taxable year in which such funds arose.

(e) Treatment of amounts repaid to employer. Any amount repaid to an employer under paragraph (d)(2) of this section shall be included in the gross income of the employer for its taxable year in which such funds arose but shall not be treated as passive investment income for purposes of section 1372(e)(5).

(f) Timely amendment. A trust shall be considered to satisfy the requirement of section 1379(a) and this section for the period beginning with the first day of a taxable year and ending with the 15th day of the third month following the close of such taxable year if, as of the end of such period, the plan of which such trust is a part provides that all funds in such plan, to the extent attributable to a restricted contribution, arising since the beginning of such period from forfeitures will be treated in a manner which meets such requirement. Further, for any taxable year begining after December 31, 1970, and ending on or before the 90th day after the date regulations under section 1379(a) are first published in the Federal Register as a Treasury decision, a trust shall be considered to satisfy the requirement of section 1379(a) and this section if, as of such 90th day, the plan of which such trust is a part provides that all such funds arising during any taxable year beginning after December 31, 1970, will be treated in a manner which meets such requirement.

§ 1.1379-2 (Proposed Treasury Decision, published 5-6-72.) **Taxability of shareholder-employee beneficiaries.**

(a) **In general.** Under section 1379(b)(1), if an electing small business corporation maintains a qualified pension, annuity, profit-sharing, or bond purchase plan, a participant in such plan who is a shareholder-employee of such corporation for a taxable year of such corporation for which it is allowed a deduction under section 404(a)(1), (2), or (3) on account of contributions to such plan must include as compensation in his gross income, for his taxable year in which or with which such taxable year of such corporation ends, the portion of such contributions determined under paragraph (c) of this section, which is paid on his behalf and which exceeds the limitation provided in paragraph (b) of this section. Section 1379(b)(1) and this section apply notwithstanding the provisions of section 402 (relating to taxability of beneficiary of employees' trust), section 403 (relating to taxation of employee annuities), or section 405(d) (relating to taxability of beneficiaries under qualified bond purchase plan). Section 1379(b)(1) and this section apply notwithstanding the fact that a shareholder-employee's rights in a contribution paid on his behalf are forfeitable (within the meaning of paragraph (d)(2) of § 1.402(b)-1) in whole or in part. Section 1379(b)(1) and this section apply to contributions on account of which a deduction is allowed under section 404(a)(1), (2), or (3) for taxable years of an electing small business corporation which began after December 31, 1970.

(b) **Limitation on excludable contributions**—(1) **In general.** The limitation on excludable contributions on behalf of a shareholder-employee of an electing small business corporation for any taxable year of such corporation is the lesser of—

(i) Except as provided in subparagraph (2) of this paragraph, $2,500, or

(ii) 10 percent of the compensation received by such shareholder-employee from such corporation during such year, or if he computes his income under the accrual method, 10 percent of the compensation accrued by him from such corporation during such year.

For purposes of subdivision (ii) of this subparagraph, the term "compensation" means all compensation for personal services actually rendered except that for which a deduction is allowable under a plan that qualifies under section 401(a), including a plan that qualifies under section 404(a)(2). Thus, amounts includible in gross income under section 1379(b)(1) are not compensation for purposes of subdivision (ii) of this subparagraph.

(2) **Multiple corporations.** If an individual is a shareholder-employee of two or more electing small business corporations and participates in qualified pension, annuity, profit-sharing, or bond purchase plans maintained by more than one of such corporations, the excludable portion of the contributions paid on his behalf by all such corporations for their taxable years ending in or with one of his taxable years shall not exceed $2,500. If such contributions exceed $2,500, the excludable contributions paid on his behalf by each such corporation shall be determined by substituting for the $2,500 amount specified in subparagraph (1)(i) of this paragraph an amount which bears the same ratio to $2,500 as the compensation received or accrued from each such corporation bears to the total compensation received or accrued from all such corporations.

(c) **Deductible contributions paid on behalf of a shareholder-employee**—(1) **In general.** This paragraph provides rules for determining the portion of the contributions to a qualified pension, annuity, profit-sharing, or bond purchase plan by an electing small business corporation on account of which it is allowed a deduction under section 404(a)(1), (2), or (3) which are paid on behalf of a shareholder-employee of such corporation. Subparagraph (2) of this paragraph provides rules for making this determination in the case of contributions to defined contribution plans (as defined in paragraph (b)(1) of § 1.402(a)-2 [36 F.R. 11443]) and to certain defined benefit plans (as defined in paragraph (d)(1) of § 1.402(a)-2 [36 F.R. 11447]). Subparagraph (3) of this paragraph provides rules for making this determination in the case of contributions to defined benefit plans if separate accounts are not maintained with respect to contributions made on behalf of each employee.

(2) **Defined contribution plans and certain defined benefit plans**—(i) **General rule.** For purposes of this section, the portion of the contributions for a taxable year to a defined contribution plan (or a defined benefit plan as provided by subdivision (iii) of this subparagraph) by an electing small business corporation on account of which it is allowed a deduction under section 404(a)(1), (2), or (3) which are paid on behalf of a shareholder-employee of such corporation are the amounts actually contributed to the plan for such taxable year by such corporation which are (a) credited to the account of the shareholder-employee or (b) are not so credited but are applied as consideration for, or against any indebtedness on, an annuity, retirement income, endowment, or other life insurance contract for the shareholder-employee. The amount considered as employer contributions credited to the account of the shareholder-employee under this subdivision shall at his option be reduced by the excess (if any) of the gross annual premium paid under an annuity, retirement income, endowment, or other life insurance contract purchased for

Proposed Reg. § 1.1379-2

him over the adjusted premium under such contract. For purposes of this subdivision, the adjusted premium for any year is the amount of premium considered by the insurer in computing the cash surrender value of an insurance contract for such year. No amount shall be treated as consideration for any such contract for any period for which the gross premiums are waived. For purposes of this subdivision (i), the amount of employer contributions actually contributed to the plan does not include any amounts considered to be contributed by a shareholder-employee under the rules of section 72(f) or paragraph (b) of § 1.72-16.

(ii) Excess contributions. If the amount actually contributed to a defined contribution plan for a taxable year of the corporation exceeds the deduction allowable for such year under section 404(a) on account of such contributions, the amount determined under subdivision (i) of this subparagraph shall be reduced (but not below zero) by an amount equal to such excess, multiplied by a fraction (a) the numerator of which is the amount determined under subdivision (i) of this subparagraph without regard to this subdivision, and (b) the denominator of which is the amount actually contributed to such plan for such year. The amount of any reduction under the preceding sentence shall be treated as an amount actually contributed to such plan for any succeeding taxable year of the corporation in the same proportion that such excess is deductible under paragraph (e) of § 1.404(a)-9.

(iii) **Defined benefit plans with separate accounts.** If separate accounts are maintained with respect to contributions made on behalf of each employee, the portion of the contributions for a taxable year to a defined benefit plan by an electing small business corporation on account of which it is allowed a deduction under section 404(a)(1) or (2) which are paid on behalf of a shareholder-employee may be determined under the rules provided under this subparagraph. The determination of such portion for a taxable year under the rules provided by this subparagraph shall be treated as the adoption of a method of accounting by the shareholder-employee for purposes of section 446.

(3) **Defined benefit plans**—(i) **In general.** If a shareholder-employee has not adopted the method of accounting described in subparagraph (2) of this paragraph, the portion of the contributions for a taxable year to a defined benefit plan by an electing small business corporation, on account of which it is allowed a deduction under section 404(a)(1) or (2), which are paid on behalf of a shareholder-employee of such corporation shall be considered to be an amount determined on the basis of level funding of the benefits to be provided under such plan during the shareholder-employee's participation in such plan, payment of employer contributions at the end of the plan year, and a growth rate of 6 percent per annum compounded annually. The determination of such portion for a taxable year under the rules provided under this subparagraph shall be treated as the adoption of a method of accounting by the shareholder-employee for purposes of section 446.

(ii) Deductible employer contributions paid on behalf of a shareholder-employee for a taxable year. If this subparagraph applies, the portion of the contributions for a taxable year which is deductible under section 404(a)(1) or (2) which are paid on behalf of a shareholder-employee shall be equal to the adjusted annual contribution (determined under subdivision (iii) of this subparagraph) to a plan for such shareholder-employee for such taxable year.

(iii) Adjusted annual contribution. For purposes of this subparagraph, the amount of the adjusted annual contribution to a plan for a shareholder-employee for a taxable year is the excess (if any) of the sum of—

(a) The amount of the unadjusted annual contribution (determined under subdivision (iv) of this paragraph) for such taxable year, and

(b) The amount, if any, of the pre-retirement death benefit adjustment (determined under subdivision (v) of this paragraph) for such taxable year,

over the amount, if any, of his mandatory contributions to the plan (as defined in paragraph (d)(2)(ii)(a) of § 1.402(a)-2) for such taxable year.

(iv) Unadjusted annual contribution. The amount of the unadjusted annual contribution on behalf of a shareholder-employee for a taxable year is the amount by which the reserve for the shareholder-employee as of the end of such taxable year (determined under subdivision (vi) of this paragraph) exceeds 106 percent of the reserve for such shareholder-employee as of the end of the preceding taxable year (determined under subdivision (vi) of this paragraph). For this purpose, the reserve for a shareholder-employee as of the end of the preceding taxable year shall be zero in the case where the unadjusted annual contribution is computed for the first taxable year in which such shareholder-employee is a participant under the plan.

(v) *Pre-retirement death benefit adjustment.* If a plan provides benefits in case of death before retirement and paragraph (b) of § 1.72-16 does not apply, the excess (if any) of the value of such benefits over 103 percent of the reserve for a shareholder-employee as of the end of the preceding taxable year (determined under subdivision (vi) of this subparagraph) shall be considered current life insurance protection, and the cost thereof (determined in accordance with the rules of paragraph (b) of § 1.72-16) shall be treated as a contribution made on behalf of the shareholder-employee by the corporation for the taxable year for purposes of subdivision (iii) of this subparagraph.

(vi) *Reserve for shareholder-employee.* The reserve for a shareholder-employee as of the end of a taxable year is (a) the product of—

(1) The level contribution to retirement (determined under subdivision (vii) of this subparagraph), and

(2) The factor from Table IV of subdivision (ix) of this subparagraph for the number of years of participation in the plan by the shareholder-employee at such time,

or (b) 106 percent of the reserve for the shareholder-employee as of the end of the previous taxable year, if greater. However, if the shareholder-employee does not treat certain disability benefits under the plan as an early retirement benefit under subdivision (vii) of this subparagraph, the amount of the reserve for a shareholder-employee as of the end of a taxable year shall be considered to be 1% of the amount determined under the preceding sentence.

(vii) *Level contribution to retirement.* Except as hereinafter provided with respect to benefits payable under the plan before normal retirement age, the amount of the level contribution to retirement is the product of (a) the single sum equivalent at retirement age (determined under subdivision (viii) of this subparagraph) and (b) the factor from Table III of subdivision (ix) of this subparagraph (representing the present value of contributions which will accumulate to $1 at normal retirement age) for the number of years of anticipated participation in the plan until normal retirement age. If benefits, including disability benefits, are payable under the plan before normal retirement age and the level contribution to such early retirement age (computed in a manner consistent with the provisions of the preceding sentence) exceeds the level contribution to normal retirement age, the level contribution to retirement shall be considered to be the greatest amount determined with respect to each retirement age prior to normal retirement age. For this purpose, if the disability payments under the plan are payable only for the period of time when an employee is eligible for and receives disability benefits under section 223 of the Social Security Act, as amended and supplemented (49 Stat. 620) and the reserve for the shareholder-employee is determined in accordance with the second sentence of subdivision (vi) of this subparagraph, such disability benefits shall not be treated as benefits payable under the plan before normal retirement age.

(viii) *Single sum equivalent at retirement age.* The single sum equivalent at retirement age for a shareholder-employee is the product of—

(a) The projected annual amount of his pension (as of such time) to be provided at retirement age which is not attributable to his voluntary contributions to the plan (as defined in paragraph (d)(2)(ii)(b) of § 1.402(a)-2), based upon the provisions of the plan in effect at such time and upon the assumption of his continued employment with his present employer at his then current compensation rate,

(b) The factor from Table I of subdivision (ix) of this subparagraph (representing the value at retirement age of an annuity of $1 per annum payable in equal monthly installments during the life of the employee) based upon the employee's sex and retirement age, and

(c) If the form of retirement benefit under the plan is other than a straight

Proposed Reg. § 1.1379-2

life annuity, the appropriate factor from Table II of subdivision (ix) of this subparagraph.

If a plan contains provisions for the commutation of an annuity to a single sum at retirement and the amount determined by applying such provisions is greater than the single sum equivalent at retirement age otherwise determined under this subdivision, the single sum equivalent at retirement age shall be such greater amount. The single sum equivalent shall be determined with respect to each retirement age provided under the plan.

(ix) Tables.*

TABLE I

[Value at retirement age of an annuity of $1 per annum payable in monthly installments during the life of the employee, based upon the employee's sex and retirement age.]

Age	Male	Female
20	15.6483	16.0963
21	15.5871	16.0456
22	15.5241	15.9922
23	15.4580	15.9361
24	15.3882	15.8769
25	15.3130	15.8147
26	15.2320	15.7492
27	15.1452	15.6804
28	15.0528	15.6079
29	14.9548	15.5321
30	14.8517	15.4524
31	14.7432	15.3692
32	14.6292	15.2822
33	14.5096	15.1911
34	14.3843	15.0957
35	14.2532	14.9960
36	14.1163	14.8918
37	13.9736	14.7829
38	13.8252	14.6695
39	13.6710	14.5516
40	13.5116	14.4289
41	13.3468	14.3014
42	13.1768	14.1692
43	13.0017	14.0320
44	12.8214	13.8897
45	12.6359	13.7420
46	12.4453	13.5888
47	12.2497	13.4302
48	12.0499	13.2660
49	11.8467	13.0964
50	11.6412	12.9215
51	11.4336	12.7413
52	11.2239	12.5557
53	11.0116	12.3641
54	10.7959	12.1657
55	10.5761	11.9599
56	10.3518	11.7463
57	10.1233	11.5252
58	9.8916	11.2971
59	9.6586	11.0633
60	9.4249	10.8242
61	9.1912	10.5807
62	8.9574	10.3323
63	8.7234	10.0787
64	8.4890	9.8192
65	8.2539	9.5535

Age	Male	Female
66	8.0183	9.2810
67	7.7824	9.0023
68	7.5460	8.7183
69	7.3084	8.4300
70	7.0695	8.1389

TABLE II

Type of Benefit	Factor
Annuity for 5 years certain and life thereafter[1]	1.04387
Annuity for 10 years certain and life thereafter[1]	1.15354
Annuity for 15 years certain and life thereafter[1]	1.29708
Annuity for 20 years certain and life thereafter[1]	1.44956
Life annuity with installment refund	1.14067
Life annuity with one-half continued to surviving spouse of employee	1.21493
Life annuity with two-thirds continued to surviving spouse of employee	1.28657
Life annuity with entire amount continued to surviving spouse of employee	1.42985

[1] In the case of annuities for periods certain other than those provided in the foregoing table, the factor shall be computed by interpolation between the nearest given factors in the table.

TABLE III

[Level annual contribution which will accumulate to $1 at end of number of years]

Number of Years:	Factor	Number of Years:	Factor
1	1.00000	26	.01690
2	.48544	27	.01570
3	.31411	28	.01459
4	.22859	29	.01358
5	.17740	30	.01265
6	.14336	31	.01179
7	.11914	32	.01100
8	.10104	33	.01027
9	.08702	34	.00960
10	.07587	35	.00897
11	.06679	36	.00839
12	.05928	37	.00786
13	.05296	38	.00736
14	.04758	39	.00689
15	.04296	40	.00646
16	.03895	41	.00606
17	.03544	42	.00568
18	.03236	43	.00533
19	.02962	44	.00501
20	.02718	45	.00470
21	.02500	46	.00441
22	.02305	47	.00415
23	.02128	48	.00390
24	.01968	49	.00366
25	.01823	50	.00344

TABLE IV

[Amount of annuity of $1 at end of such period]

Years	Factor	Years	Factor
1	1.0000	3	3.1836
2	2.0600	4	4.3746

Proposed Reg. §1.1379-2

Number of Years:	Factor	Number of Years:	Factor
5	5.6371	28	68.5281
6	6.9753	29	73.6398
7	8.3938	30	79.0582
8	9.8975	31	84.8017
9	11.4913	32	90.8898
10	13.1808	33	97.3432
11	14.9716	34	104.1838
12	16.8699	35	111.4348
13	18.8821	36	119.1209
14	21.0151	37	127.2681
15	23.2760	38	135.9042
16	25.6725	39	145.0585
17	28.2129	40	154.7620
18	30.9056	41	165.0477
19	33.7600	42	175.9505
20	36.7856	43	187.5076
21	39.9927	44	199.7580
22	43.3923	45	212.7435
23	46.9958	46	226.5081
24	50.8156	47	241.0986
25	54.8645	48	256.5645
26	59.1564	49	272.9584
27	63.7058	50	290.3359

(x) *Examples.* The application of this subparagraph may be illustrated by the following examples:

Example (1). (i) A is a male employee of, and owns all the stock of, X Corporation, an electing small business corporation. A and X Corporation are calendar-year taxpayers. X Corporation has a qualified pension plan which it adopted on January 1, 1968, and which provides at age 65 a straight life annuity payable at the end of each month of 50 percent of a participant's average monthly compensation during the last five years of service. He began participation in the plan on January 1, 1968. The plan does not provide any benefits in case of death or disability before retirement or for a lump sum distribution in lieu of the straight life annuity. A's annual compensation for calendar years 1973 and 1974 is $50,000. A was born on October 4, 1927. The plan is noncontributory.

(ii) A's projected annual pension as of the end of 1973 and 1974 is $25,000 (50 percent of $50,000). The factor from Table I for the value of a straight life annuity at age 65 of $1 payable in monthly installments at the end of each month is 8.2539. The single sum equivalent as of the end of 1974 is $206,347.50 ($25,000 × 8.2539). The factor from Table III, representing the present value of contributions which will accumulate to $1.00 at retirement age, for 25 years of anticipated participation in the plan by A is .01823. The level contribution to retirement is $3,761.71 ($206,347.50 × .01823). The factor from Table IV for the number of years of participation in the plan is 6.9753 for 1973 and 8.3938 for 1974. The reserve for A is $26,239.06 ($3,761.71 × 6.9753) at the end of 1973 and $31,575.04 ($3,761.71 × 8.3938) at the end of 1974. The unadjusted annual contribution for A is $3,761.64 ($31,575.04—($26,239.06 × 1.06)). Because no adjustment is necessary for mandatory employee contributions or pre-retirement death benefits, the adjusted annual contribution for A is equal to the unadjusted annual contribution for A. Accordingly, the portion of the contribution for 1974 to the plan by X Corporation on account of which it is allowed a deduction under section 404(a)(1) which are paid on A's behalf is $3,761.64.

Example (2). The facts are the same as in example (1) except that the plan provides that if an employee dies before retirement, his spouse or his estate will receive an amount equal to his annual compensation at the time of his death. The death benefit is uninsured and thus paragraph (b) of § 1.72-16 does not apply. A reasonable net premium cost for A's age (47) is $7.32 per $1,000. Accordingly, the portion of the contributions for 1974 to the plan by X Corporation on account of which it is allowed a deduction under section 404(a)(1) which are paid on behalf of A is $3,929.81 ($3,761.64 [the amount determined in example (1)] + $168.17 [$50,000 − ($26,239.06 × 1.03)) × 0.00732)].

Example (3). The facts are the same as in exemple (1) except that A's annual compensation for calendar year 1974 is $55,000). Accordingly, A's projected annual pension as of the end of 1974 is $27,500 (50 percent of $55,000). The single sum equivalent as of the end of 1974 is $226,982.25 ($27,500 × 8.2539). The level contribution to retirement is $4,137.89 ($226,982.25 × 0.01823). The reserve for A as of the end of 1974 is $34,732.62 ($4,137.89 × 8.3938). Thus, the portion of the contributions for 1974 to the plan by X corporation on account of which it is allowed a deduction under section 404(a)(1) which are paid on behalf of A is $6,919.22 ($34,732.62 − ($26,239.06 × 1.06)).

Example (4). (i) The facts are the same as in example (1) except that the plan is amended January 1, 1974, effective as of such date, to provide early retirement benefits beginning at age 60 equal to the benefit at age 65 reduced 3 percent per annum for each year by which the employee's age is less than 65.

(ii) The age under the plan for which the level contribution to retirement is the greatest is age 60, computed as follows:

(a) Potential Retirement Age	(b) Projected Annual Retirement Benefit	(c) Single Sum Equivalent At Retirement Age [(a) × (b)]	(d)	(e) Level Contribution to Retirement [(c) × (d)]
		Table I Factor	Table III Factor	
65	$25,000	8.2539	$206,347.50	.01823	$3,761.71
64	24,250	8.4890	205,858.25	.01968	4,051.29
63	23,500	8.7234	204,999.90	.02128	4,362.40
62	22,750	8.9574	203,780.85	.02305	4,697.15
61	22,000	9.1912	202,206.40	.02500	5,055.16
60	21,250	9.4249	200,279.13	.02718	5,443.59

(iii) The reserve for A is $45,692.41 ($5,443.59 × 8.3938) as of the end of 1974. Accordingly, the portion of the contributions for 1974 to the plan by X Corporation on account of which it is allowed a deduction under section 404(a)(1) which are paid on behalf of A is $17,879.01 ($45,692.41 − ($26,239.06 × 1.06)).

(d) *Treatment of amounts included in gross income.* Any amount included in the gross income of a shareholder-employee under section 1379(b)(1) and this section shall be treated as consideration for the contract contributed by the shareholder-employee for purposes of section 72 (relating to annuities). See § 1.72-8 (a)(1). If an individual is a participant in two or more plans maintained by one or more electing small business corporations with respect to which such individual is a shareholder-employee, the amount treated as consideration paid or contributed by such individual to a particular plan for a year shall be a ratable portion of the total amount included, under section 1379(b) and this section, by him in his gross income for that year.

(e) **Deduction for excess contributions not received as benefits—(1)** *General rule.* If, immediately after the termination of the rights of a shareholder-employee or his beneficiaries under the plan, the sum of the amounts included in the gross income of the shareholder-employee under paragraph (a) of this section exceeds the sum of the distributions and payments which are excludable from gross income, or will be excluded by a beneficiary in the case of a survivorship annuity with term certain, such excess shall be allowable as a deduction from gross income. For purposes of the preceding sentence, all distributions and payments which are excluded from gross income are considered to consist entirely of amounts treated as consideration for the contract contributed by a shareholder-employee under paragraph (d) of this section until such excludable distributions and payments equal the total amount includible in gross income by the shareholder-employee under paragraph (a) of this section. Except as provided in subparagraph (2) of this paragraph, such deduction shall be allowable to the shareholder-employee for

Proposed Reg. § 1.1379-2

his taxable year in which the termination of rights under the plan occurs. In the case of a termination of rights by reason of the death of the shareholder-employee, the deduction shall be allowable in computing his taxable income for the taxable year ending with the date of his death. For purposes of this paragraph, a termination of rights occurs when, in all events, the entire amount of benefits payable under a plan with respect to a shareholder-employee has been distributed or paid except so much as remains to be paid to a beneficiary under a survivorship annuity with term certain.

(2) **Special rule.** If, immediately prior to the termination of benefits with respect to a shareholder-employee, such shareholder-employee is not alive, a portion of the deduction referred to in subparagraph (1) of this paragraph is allowable to each person who, immediately prior to such termination, was a beneficiary of the shareholder-employee under the plan and whose interest as a beneficiary at such time was not a future interest. The deduction is allowable to each such person for his taxable year in which the termination of benefits occurs. The portion of the deduction referred to in subparagraph (1) of this paragraph allowable to each such person is obtained by multiplying the amount of such deduction by a fraction—

(i) The numerator of which is the amount of benefits under the plan received by such person with respect to the shareholder-employee, and

(ii) The denominator of which is the total amount of benefits under the plan received by all persons to whom a portion of the deduction is allowable.

If, however, no such person has received benefits under the plan, the portion of the deduction referred to in subparagraph (1) of this paragraph which is allowable to each such person is obtained by dividing the amount of such deduction by the number of persons to whom a portion of the deduction is allowable.

§ 1.1379-3 (Proposed Treasury Decision, published 5-6-72.) **Carryover of amounts deductible.**

For taxable years beginning after December 31, 1970, no amount deductible shall be carried forward under the second sentence of section 404(a)(3)(A) (relating to limits on deductible contributions under stock bonus and profit-sharing trusts) or § 1.404(a)-9(d) to a taxable year of a corporation with respect to which it is not an electing small business corporation.

§ 1.1379-4 (Proposed Treasury Decision, published 5-6-72.) **Shareholder-employee.**

For purposes of § 1.1379-1 and § 1.1379-2, under section 1379(d), an individual is a shareholder-employee for a taxable year of an electing small business corporation beginning after December 31, 1970, if he is an employee or officer of such corporation who owns (or is considered as owning within the meaning of section 318(a)(1) and the regulations thereunder), on any day during such taxable year of such corporation, more than 5 percent of the total number of shares of the outstanding stock of the corporation.

* * * * * * * * * * *

Withholding of Tax on Nonresident Aliens

Section 1.1441-2 is amended by revising paragraph (a)(1) and by adding a new paragraph (b)(2)(ii), as follows:

§1.1441-2 (Proposed Treasury Decision, published 7-12-76.) **Income subject to withholding.**

(a) **Fixed or determinable annual or periodical income.** (1) The gross amount of fixed or determinable annual or periodical income is subject to withholding. Section 1441(b) specifically includes in such income interest, dividends, rent, salaries, wages, premiums, annuities, compensations, remunerations, and emoluments; but other kinds of income are included, as, for instance, royalties.

For purposes of the preceding sentence, the term "interest" includes interest on certain deferred payments, as provided in section 483 and the regulations thereunder. Effective with respect to payments occurring after March 31, 1972, the term "interest", as used in section 1441(b) and this paragraph (a)(1), does not include any original issue discount on any bond, debenture, note, certificate, or other evidence of indebtedness, as described in §1.871-7(b)(2). The term "fixed or determinable annual or periodical" income is merely descriptive of the character of a class of income. If an item of income falls within the class of income contemplated by the statute, it is immaterial whether payment of that item is made in a series of payments or in a single lump sum. Thus, for example, $5,000 in royalty income would come within the meaning of the term, whether paid in 10 payments of $500 each or in one payment of $5,000.

* *

(b) **Other income subject to withholding.** * * *

(2) **Payments in taxable years of recipients beginning after December 31, 1966.*** * *

(ii) Amounts subject to the 30-percent tax under section 871(a)(1)(C) and §1.871-7(c)(1)(ii), or section 881(a)(3) and §1.881-2(c)(1)(ii), relating to—

(A) Gains realized on the sale, exchange, or retirement of certain bonds or other evidences of indebtedness which are issued after September 28, 1965, and

(B) Original issue discount ratably accrued on certain interest-bearing bonds or other evidences of indebtedness which are issued after March 31, 1972, and are payable more than 6 months from the date of original issue,

but only to the extent and in the manner provided by §1.1441-3(c)(6);

* *

Section 1.1441-3 is amended by revising the caption of paragraph (c), by adding a new subparagraph (6) to paragraph (c), and by revising paragraph (e)(2), as follows:

§1.1441-3 (Proposed Treasury Decision, published 7-12-76.) **Exceptions and rules of special application.**

* *

(c) **Interest and original issue discount.** * * *

(6) **Original issue discount**—(i) *In general.* (A) In the case of payments occurring before [the 31st day following publication of the Treasury decision], withholding is required under §1.1441-1 by the original issuer of any bond or other evidence of indebtedness issued after September 28, 1965, and before April 1, 1972, upon any gain realized by the holder on the sale, exchange, or retirement of such bond or other indebtedness, whether or not interest-bearing, to the extent that such gain is subject to tax under section 871(a)(1)(C)(i) and §1.871-7(c)(1)(ii)(A), or under section 881(a)(3)(A) and §1.881-2(c)(1)(ii)(A),

(B) In the case of payments occurring after [the 30th day following publication of the Treasury decision], withholding is required under §1.1441-1 by a United States person upon any gain realized by the holder on the sale, exchange, or retirement of any bond or other evidence of indebtedness, whether or not interest-bearing, issued after September 28, 1965, and before April 1, 1972, to the extent that such gain is subject to tax under section 871(a)(1)(C)(i) and §1.871-7(c)(1)(ii)(A), or under section 881(a)(3)(A) and §1.881-2(c)(1)(ii)(A),

(C) In the case of payments occurring after March 31, 1972, withholding is required under §1.1441-1 by a United States person upon any gain realized by the holder on the sale, exchange, or retirement of any bond or other evidence of indebtedness, whether or not interest-bearing, issued after March 31, 1972, and payable more than 6 months from the date of original issue, to the extent that such gain is subject to tax under section 871(a)(1)(C)(ii) and §1.871-7(c)(1)(ii)(B), or under section 881(a)(3)(B) and §1.881-2(c)(1)(ii)(B), and

(D) In the case of payments occurring after March 31, 1972, withholding is required

Proposed Reg. §1.1441-3

under §1.1441-1 upon interest paid on any bond or other evidence of indebtedness issued after March 31, 1972, and payable more than 6 months from the date of original issue, to the extent that tax may be withheld from such interest upon accrued original issue discount subject to tax under section 871(a)(1)(C)(iii) and §1.871-7(c)(1)(ii)(C), or under section 881(a)(3)(C) and §1.881-2(c)(1)(ii)(C).

(ii) *Evidences of indebtedness subject to withholding.* Withholding is required under paragraph (c) (6) (i) of this section on any bond, debenture, note, certificate, or other evidence of indebtedness taxable under section 871(a)(1)(C) and §1.871-7(c) (1)(ii) and section 881(a)(3) and §1.881-2(c)(1)(ii), except for payments occurring before [the 31st day following publication of the Treasury decision] on evidences of indebtedness issued by a person other than a government or political subdivision thereof, or by a corporation. Withholding is required under paragraph (c) (6) (i) of this section on any bond, debenture, note, certificate, or other evidence of indebtedness issued by a person other than a government or political subdivision thereof, or by a corporation only with respect to payments occurring after [the 30th day following publication of the Treasury decision]. Thus, withholding is required in all cases whether the evidence of indebtedness is a capital asset in the hands of the taxpayer within the meaning of section 1221 or whether it was held by the taxpayer more than 6 months, and withholding is also required with respect to payments occurring after [the 30th day following publication of the Treasury decision] whether the evidence of indebtedness was issued by a government or political subdivision thereof, or by a corporation or any other person.

(iii) *Statement by bond holder.* In the case of an amount described in paragraph (c) (6) (i) of this section, if the withholding agent does not know the amount subject to tax under section 871(a)(1)(C) or 881(a)(3), or the amount of tax under such section, he is required to deduct and withhold such amount as may be necessary to assure that the tax withheld will not be less than the tax imposed under such Section. The withholding agent may, unless he has reason to believe to the contrary, rely on the statement of the person entitled to the income as to the amount which is subject to withholding or as to the amount of tax required to be withheld. The statement of such person must be filed with the withholding agent in duplicate and must show the name, address, and identifying number, if any, of the taxpayer, and contain a computation, in accordance with §1.871-7(c)(4), of the amount of tax imposed under section 871(a)(1)(C) or 881(a)(3). The statement must be signed by the taxpayer with a written declaration that it is made under the penalties of perjury. No particular form is prescribed for this statement. The duplicate copy of each statement filed during any calendar year pursuant to this paragraph (c) (6) (ii) must be forwarded by the withholding agent with, and attached to, the Forms 1042S required by paragraph (c) of §1.1461-2 with respect to such amount for such calendar year. Appropriate adjustment, if any, will be made by the payee's filing of a claim for refund, together with appropriate supporting evidence, in accordance with paragraph (h) of this section.

(iv) *Definition of United States person.* The term "United States person", as used in this paragraph (c) (6), has the meaning assigned to it by section 7701(a)(30) except that it also includes any withholding agent (within the meaning of section 1465 and the regulations thereunder) required to deduct and withhold tax under chapter 3 upon interest on any obligation of the United States, a State or any political subdivision thereof, the District of Columbia, or any agency or instrumentality of any such government.

* *

(e) **Personal exemption.** * * *

(2) (i) In the determination of the tax to be withheld at the source under §1.1441-1 from remuneration paid for labor or personal services performed within the United States by a nonresident alien individual, the benefit of the deduction for personal exemptions provided in section 151, to the extent allowable under section 873(b)(3) and the regulations thereunder, shall be allowed, prorated upon a daily basis for the period during which labor or personal services are performed within the United States by the alien individual. The benefit of the deduction for such personal exemptions shall also be allowed in the determination of the tax of 14 percent to be withheld at the source under §1.1441-1

and paragraph (c) of §1.1441-2 from amounts paid after March 4, 1964, to nonresident alien individuals who are temporarily present in the United States as nonimmigrants under subparagraph (F) (relating to the admission of students into the United States) or subparagraph (J) (relating to the admission of teachers, trainees, specialists, etc., into the United States) of section 101(a)(15) of the Immigration and Nationality Act, as amended, 8 U.S.C. 1101(a)(15) (F) or (J), and such personal exemptions shall be prorated upon a daily basis for the period during which the described nonresident alien student or scholar receives the payments. In the case of taxable years beginning before January 1, 1970, the proration is on a basis of $1.70 per day for each exemption to which the nonresident alien individual is entitled. In the case of taxable years beginning after December 31, 1969, the proration of one personal exemption on a daily basis shall be the amount of the personal exemption provided in section 151 for the taxpayer's taxable year divided by 360.

(ii) Thus, if A, a married nonresident alien individual without dependents is paid remuneration in 1966 subject to withholding under §1.1441-1 for performing personal services during a stay of 100 days in the United States in such year, the amount of $170 will be allocated as the portion of the deduction to be allowed against the remuneration for personal services performed within the United States during that period; and withholding at 30 percent shall be applied against the balance, if any, of the remuneration. If, for example, the total remuneration paid to A for that period is $2,000, a total tax in the amount of $549 ([$2,000 − $170] × 0.30) is required to be withheld under §1.1441-1. However, if A is a resident of Canada or Mexico, and his spouse has no gross income which is subject to income tax under chapter 1 of the Code, and is not the dependent of another taxpayer subject to such tax, an amount of $340 will be allocated as the portion of the deduction to be allowed against the remuneration for personal services performed within the United States. Thus, in such case, a total tax in the amount of $498 ([$2,000 − $340] × 0.30) is required to be withheld under §1.1441-1.

(iii) As to what constitutes remuneration for labor or personal services performed within the United States see section 861(a)(3) and the regulations thereunder.

Consolidated Returns

Section 1.1502-3 is amended as follows:

1. A new sentence is added as flush material at the end of paragraph (c)(2).
2. New subparagraph (3) is added to paragraph (c).
3. New examples (4) and (5) are added to paragraph (d).
4. A new sentence is added as flush material at the end of paragraph (e)(2).
5. New subparagraph (3) is added to paragraph (e).

The new and revised provisions are set forth below:

§ 1.1502-3 (Proposed Treasury Decision, published 1-4-73.) **Consolidated investment credit.**

* * * * * * * * * * * * * * *

(c) **Limitation on investment credit carryovers and carrybacks from separate return limitation years.** * * *

(2) **Computation of limitation.** * * * In the case of an unused credit arising in a separate return limitation year ending before January 1, 1971, which is an investment credit carryover to a consolidated return year beginning after December 31, 1970, the amount determined under this subparagraph shall be computed without regard to subdivision (ii)(a) of this subparagraph.

(3) **Treatment as unused credit arising in separate return limitation year.** If the amount of an investment credit carryover from a separate return limitation year of a member ending before January 1, 1971, which is added to the amount allowable as a credit for a consolidated return year beginning after December 31, 1970, exceeds the amount of such carryover which could be so added were it not for the last sentence of subparagraph (2) of this paragraph, then an

Proposed Reg. § 1.1502-3

amount of credit earned by such member for the taxable year equal to such excess shall not be taken into account for purposes of computing the consolidated credit earned. Instead, such amount shall be treated as an unused credit of such member arising in a separate return limitation year of such member.

(d) **Examples.** * * *

Example (4). (i) Corporation P acquires all the outstanding stock of corporation S on January 1, 1972, and the P-S group files a consolidated return for the calendar year 1972. S has an unused credit of $40 for 1970 which is an investment credit carryover to 1972. P has no unused credits for 1970 and prior years, and neither P nor S has a credit earned or tax liability in 1971. In 1972, P and S each has a credit earned of $50. The limitation based on amount of tax of the group for 1972 is $100 and such limitation recomputed by excluding the items of income, deductions, and foreign tax credit of S is $25.

(ii) Under section 46(b), the amount of S's unused credit from 1970 which may be added to the amount allowable as a credit for 1972 is determined without regard to the credit earned by P and S for 1972. However, since 1970 is a separate return limitation year of S, the amount of the 1970 carryover of S which may be added to the amount allowable as a credit for 1972 is limited to the amount determined under paragraph (c)(2) of this section. The amount determined under such paragraph for 1972 is $75 (the excess of (a) the limitation based on amount of tax of the group, $100, minus such limitation recomputed by excluding the items of income, deductions, and foreign tax credit of S, $25, over (b) the unused credits attributable to S which may be carried to 1972 arising in years prior to 1970, zero). Thus, all $40 of S's carryover from 1970 may be added to the amount allowable in 1972.

(iii) If the last sentence of paragraph (c)(2) of this section did not apply, the amount determined under such paragraph would be $25 (the excess of the subdivision (i) amount, $75, over the subdivision (ii) amount, $50). Thus, as a result of the application of the last sentence of paragraph (c)(2) of this section, an additional $15 of the 1970 carryover of S is added to the amount allowable for 1972. Consequently, the amount of credit earned by S for 1972 ($50) which may be taken into account in computing the consolidated credit earned is only $35. The $15 not taken into account as part of the consolidated credit earned for 1972 is treated as an unused credit of S arising in a separate return limitation year and therefore in subsequent years will be subject to the limitation of paragraph (c) of this section.

(iv) The credit earned by the group which may be taken into account in computing consolidated credit earned for 1972 is $85 ($50 from P and $35 from S). Of this amount, only $60, the excess of $100 (the limitation based on amount of tax for 1972) over $40 (the unused credit for 1970 which may be added to the amount allowable for 1972) may be added to the amount allowable for 1972. Therefore, the consolidated unused credit for 1972 is $25.

Example (5). The facts are the same as in example (4) except that in addition P has an unused credit of $120 in 1970 which is an investment credit carryover to 1972. Under paragraph (b)(2) of this section, $75 of P's carryover and $25 of S's carryover is absorbed in 1972. Since the amount of S's carryover which is added to the amount allowable for 1972 does not exceed the amount which could be so added without regard to the last sentence of paragraph (c)(2), all of the credit earned by S for 1972 is taken into account in computing the consolidated credit earned for 1972.

* * * * * * * * * * * * * * * * *

(e) **Limitation on investment credit carryovers where there has been a consolidated return change of ownership.** * * *

(2) **Computation of limitation.** * * * In the case of an unused credit arising in a taxable year ending before January 1, 1971, which is an investment credit carryover to a taxable year beginning after December 31, 1970, the amount determined under this subparagraph shall be computed without regard to subdivision (i) of this subparagraph.

(3) **Treatment as unused credit arising prior to year of change.** If the aggre-

gate amount of investment credit carryovers from a taxable year ending before January 1, 1971, which is added to the amount allowable as a credit for any year of change beginning after December 31, 1970, or any subsequent year, exceeds the amount of such carryovers which could be so added were it not for the last sentence of subparagraph (2) of this paragraph, then an aggregate amount of the credit earned by the old members for such taxable year beginning after December 31, 1970, equal to such excess shall not be taken into account for purposes of computing the consolidated credit earned for such taxable year. Instead, such amount shall be treated as an unused credit of the old members for such year and, solely for the purpose of applying the limitation of subparagraph (2) of this paragraph, as arising in a taxable year prior to the year of change. The amount of credit earned by each of the old members which is not taken into account is a pro rata share of the aggregate amount of the credit earned by old members which is not taken into account.

* * * * * * * * * * * * * * * * * * *

Section 1.1502-4(d) (1) is amended by revising subdivisions (ii) and (iv) thereof to read as follows:

§ 1.1502-4 (Proposed Treasury Decision, published 1-4-73.) **Consolidated foreign tax credit.**

* * * * * * * * * * * * * * * * * * *

(d) **Computation of limitation on credit.** * * *
(1) **Computation of taxable income from foreign sources.** * * *

Proposed Reg. § 1.1502-4

(ii) Any such foreign source net capital gain (determined without regard to any net capital loss carryover or carryback);

* * * * * * * * * * * * * * * * *

(iv) The portion of any consolidated net capital loss carryover or carryback attributable to such foreign source income which is absorbed in the taxable year.

* * * * * * * * * * * * * * * * *

Section 1.1502-5 is amended by adding a sentence at the end of paragraph (a)(2) and by revising examples (1), (2), and (3) of paragraph (c). The new and revised provisions read as follows:

§ 1.1502-5 (Proposed Treasury Decision, published 1-4-73.) Estimated tax.

(a) **General rule.** * * *

(2) **Estimated tax on a separate basis.** * * * Notwithstanding the first sentence of this subparagraph, in the case of a taxable year ending before [the date of publication of this regulation as a Treasury decision] the group may file its declaration of estimated tax on a consolidated basis for the first and second taxable years for which it files a consolidated return and in such case shall be treated as a single corporation for purposes of sections 6016 and 6154.

* * * * * * * * * * * * * * * * *

(c) **Examples.** * * *

Example (1). Corporations P and S-1 file a consolidated return for the first time for calendar year 1973. P and S-1 also file consolidated returns for 1974 and 1975. For 1973 and 1974 P and S-1 must file separate declarations of estimated tax, and they are entitled to separate $100,000 exemptions. For 1975, however, the group must compute its estimated tax on a consolidated basis, and it is limited to a single $100,000 exemption. In determining whether P and S-1 come within the exception provided in section 6655(d)(1) for 1975, the "tax shown on the return" is the tax shown on the consolidated return for 1974.

Example (2). Assume the same facts as in example (1). Assume further that corporation S-2 was a member of the group during 1974, and joined in the filing of the consolidated return for such year, but ceased to be a member of the group on September 15, 1975. In determining whether the group (which no longer includes S-2) comes within the exception provided in section 6655(d)(1) for 1975, the "tax shown on the return" is the tax shown on the consolidated return for 1974.

Example (3). Assume the same facts as in example (1). Assume further that corporation S-2 becomes a member of the group on June 1, 1975, and joins in the filing of the consolidated return for 1975. In determining whether the group (which now includes S-2) comes within the exception provided in section 6655(d)(1) for 1975, the "tax shown on the return" is the tax shown on the consolidated return for 1974. Any tax of S-2 for any separate return year is not included as a part of the "tax shown on the return" for purposes of applying section 6655(d)(1).

* * * * * * * * * * * * * * * * *

Section 1.1502-22 is amended as follows:

(1) Paragraph (a)(1)(i) and (iii) is revised.
(2) Paragraph (b)(1) is revised.
(3) The title of paragraph (c) is revised.
(4) Paragraph (c)(2)(i) is revised.

The revised provisions are set forth below:

Proposed Reg. § 1.1502-5

§ 1.1502-22 (Proposed Treasury Decision, published 1-4-73.) **Consolidated net capital gain or loss.**

(a) **Computation—(1) Consolidated net capital gain.** * * *

(i) The aggregate of the capital gains and losses (determined without regard to gains or losses to which section 1231 applies or net capital loss carryovers or carrybacks) of the members of the group for the consolidated return year.

* * * * * * * * * * * * * *

(iii) The consolidated net capital loss carryovers or carrybacks to such year (as determined under paragraph (b) of this section).

* * * * * * * * * * * * * *

(b) **Consolidated net capital loss carryovers and carrybacks—(1) In general.** The consolidated net capital loss carryovers and carrybacks to the taxable year shall consist of any consolidated net capital losses of the group, plus any net capital losses of members of the group arising in separate return years of such members, which may be carried over or back to the taxable year under the principles of section 1212(a). However, such consolidated carryovers and carrybacks shall not include any consolidated net capital loss apportioned to a corporation for a separate return year pursuant to paragraph (b) of § 1.1502-79 and shall be subject to the limitations contained in paragraphs (c) and (d) of this section. For purposes of section 1212(a)(1), the portion of any consolidated net capital loss for any taxable year attributable to a foreign expropriation capital loss is the amount of the foreign expropriation capital losses of all the members for such year (but not in excess of the consolidated net capital loss for such year).

* * * * * * * * * * * * * *

(c) **Limitation on net capital loss carryovers and carrybacks from separate return limitation years.** * * *

(2) **Computation of limitation.** * * *

(i) The consolidated net capital gain for the taxable year (computed without regard to any net capital loss carryovers or carrybacks), minus such consolidated net capital gain for the taxable year recomputed by excluding the capital gains and losses and the gains and losses to which section 1231 applies of such member, over

* * * * * * * * * * * * * *

Section 1.1502-24(c) is amended to read as follows:

§ 1.1502-24 (Proposed Treasury Decision, published 1-4-73.) **Consolidated charitable contributions deduction.**

* * * * * * * * * * * * * *

(c) **Adjusted consolidated taxable income.** For purposes of this section, the adjusted consolidated taxable income of the group for any consolidated return year shall be the consolidated taxable income computed without regard to this section, section 242, section 243(a)(2) and (3), § 1.1502-25, § 1.1502-26, and § 1.1502-27, and without regard to any consolidated net operating or net capital loss carrybacks to such year.

Section 1.1502-25(c)(2) is amended by revising subdivisions (ii) and (iv) thereof to read as follows:

§ 1.1502-25 (Proposed Treasury Decision, published 1-4-73.) **Consolidated section 922 deduction.**

* * * * * * * * * * * * * *

(c) **Portion of consolidated taxable income attributable to Western Hemisphere trade corporations.** * * *

(2) **Taxable income.** * * *

(ii) Such member's net capital gain (determined without regard to any net capital loss carryover or carryback attributable to such member);

* * * * * * * * * * * * * *

(iv) The portion of any consolidated net capital loss carryover or carryback attributable to such member which is absorbed in the taxable year.

* * * * * * * * * * * * * * * *

Section 1.1502-27(b) is amended by revising subparagraphs (2) and (4) to read as follows:

§ 1.1502-27 (Proposed Treasury Decision, published 1-4-73.) **Consolidated section 247 deduction.**

* * * * * * * * * * * * * * * *

(b) **Computation of taxable income.** * * *

(2) Such member's net capital gain (determined without regard to any net capital loss carryover or carryback attributable to such member);

* * * * * * * * * * * * * * * *

(4) The portion of any consolidated net capital loss carryover or carryback attributable to such member which is absorbed in the taxable year.

Section 1.1502-32 is amended as follows:
1. Paragraph (b)(2)(iii)(b) is revised.
2. New subdivision (c) is added to paragraph (b)(2)(iii).
3. Paragraph (c)(2)(ii) is revised.
4. New subdivision (iii) is added to paragraph (c)(2).

The new and revised provisions read as follows:

§ 1.1502-32 (Proposed Treasury Decision, published 1-4-73.) **Investment adjustment.**

* * * * * * * * * * * * * * * *

(b) **Stock which is not limited and preferred as to dividends.** * * *

(2) **Negative adjustment.** * * *
(iii) * * *

(b) Accumulated in preaffiliation years of the subsidiary, if the distribution occurs on or before [the date of publication of this regulation as a Treasury decision]; or

(c) Accumulated in separate return limitation years of the subsidiary, if the distribution occurs after [the date of publication of this regulation as a Treasury decision]; and

* * * * * * * * * * * * * * * *

(c) **Limited and preferred stock.** * * *

(2) **Negative adjustment.** * * *
(ii) Accumulated in preaffiliation years of the subsidiary, if the distribution occurs on or before [the date of publication of this regulation as a Treasury decision]; or

(iii) Accumulated in separate return limitation years of the subsidiary, if the distribution occurs after [the date of publication of this regulation as a Treasury decision].

* * * * * * * * * * * * * * * *

Section 1.1502-41(b) is amended to read as follows:

§ 1.1502-41 (Proposed Treasury Decision, published 1-4-73.) **Determination of consolidated net long-term capital gain and consolidated net short-term capital loss.**

* * * * * * * * * * * * * * * *

Proposed Reg. § 1.1502-41

(b) **Consolidated net short-term capital loss.** The consolidated net short-term capital loss shall be determined by taking into account (1) those gains and losses to which paragraph (a)(1) of § 1.1502-22 applies which are treated as short term under section 1222, and (2) the consolidated net capital loss carryovers and carrybacks to the taxable year (as determined under paragraph (b) of § 1.1502-22).

Section 1.1502-42 is amended to read as follows:

§ 1.1502-42 (Proposed Treasury Decision, published 1-4-73.) **Mutual savings banks, domestic building and loan associations, and cooperative banks.**

(a) **In general.** The provisions of this section shall apply to mutual savings banks, domestic building and loan associations, and cooperative banks.

(b) **Total deposits.** In computing for purposes of section 593(b)(1)(B)(ii) total deposits or withdrawable accounts at the close of the taxable year, the total deposits or withdrawable accounts of other members shall be excluded.

(c) **Taxable income.** (1) In the case of a taxable year the due date for the return of which is on or before [the date of publication of this regulation as a Treasury decision], a member's taxable income for purposes of section 593(b)(2) shall be the amount computed under § 1.1502-27(b) (computed without regard to the amount of any addition to the reserve for bad debts of any member determined under section 593(b)(2)). In the case of a taxable year beginning before July 12, 1969, such amount shall be computed without regard to any net operating loss carryback.

(2) In the case of a taxable year the due date for the return of which is after [the date of publication of this regulation as a Treasury decision], a member's taxable income for purposes of section 593(b)(2) shall be the portion of consolidated taxable income attributable to such member. For purposes of this subparagraph, the portion of the consolidated taxable income attributable to a member is an amount equal to the consolidated taxable income (computed without regard to the amount of any additions to reserves for bad debts under section 593(b)(2)) multiplied by a fraction, the numerator of which is the taxable income of the member and the denominator of which is the sum of the taxable incomes of all members of the group. For purposes of the preceding sentence, the taxable income of a member shall be the separate taxable income determined under § 1.1502-12, adjusted for the following items taken into account in the computation of consolidated taxable income:

(i) The portion of the consolidated net operating loss deduction, the consolidated charitable contributions deduction, and the consolidated dividends received deduction, attributable to such member;

(ii) Such member's net capital gain (determined without regard to any net capital loss carryover or carryback attributable to such member);

(iii) Such member's net capital loss and section 1231 net loss, reduced by the portion of the consolidated net capital loss attributable to such member; and

(iv) The portion of any consolidated net capital loss carryover or carryback attributable to such member which is absorbed in the taxable year.

If the computation of the taxable income of a member under this subparagraph results in an excess of deductions over gross income, then for purposes of this subparagraph such member's taxable income shall be zero.

Section 1.1502-79 is amended by revising paragraph (b)(1) and (2)(i) to read as follows:

§ 1.1502-79 (Proposed Treasury Decision, published 1-4-73.) **Separate return years.**

* * * * * * * * * * * *

(b) **Carryover and carryback of consolidated net capital loss to separate return years.**—(1) **In general.** If a consolidated net capital loss can be carried under the principles of section 1212(a) and paragraph (b) of § 1.1502-22 to a separate return year of a corporation (or could have been so carried if such corporation were in existence) which was a member of the group in the year in which such consolidated net capital loss arose, then the portion of such consolidated net capital loss attributable to such corporation (as determined under subparagraph (2) of this paragraph) shall be apportioned to such corporation (and any successor to such corporation in a transaction to which section 381(a) applies) under the principles of paragraph (a)(1), (2), and (3) of this section and shall be a net capital loss carryback or carryover to such separate return year.

(2) **Portion of consolidated net capital loss attributable to a member.** * * *
(i) Such member's net capital gain or loss (determined without regard to any net capital loss carryover or carryback); and

* * * * * * * * * * * * * *

Collection of Income Tax at Source

Section 31.3401(a)(6)-1 is amended by adding a new paragraph (f) to read as follows:

§31.3401(a)(6)-1 (Proposed Treasury Decision, published 7-12-76.) **Remuneration for services of nonresident alien individuals paid after December 31, 1966.**

* *

(f) **Remuneration for services of aliens performed in a previous taxable year.** Remuneration paid to a nonresident alien individual during a taxable year for services performed within the United States during a previous taxable year is excepted from wages and hence is not subject to withholding if such individual is not engaged in a trade or business in the United States in such succeeding taxable year and uses the cash receipts and disbursements method of accounting. Thus, for example, assume that R, a nonresident alien individual who uses the calendar year as the taxable year and the cash receipts and disbursements method of accounting is present in the United States from June 1, 1972, to December 20, 1972, performing personal services therein for which he receives in 1972 remuneration of $13,000 which constitutes wages within the meaning of §31.3401(a)-1. Assume further that R leaves the United States on December 20, 1972, and that in 1973, during which R is not engaged in trade or business in the united States, he receives $2,000 additional remuneration for the services performed in the United States during 1972. Under the circumstances, the $2,000 received in 1973 does not constitute wages within the meaning of §31.3401(a)-1 but is subject to withholding under section 1441 and §1.1441-1 of this chapter (Income Tax Regulations). See §1.1441-4(b) of this chapter. See also example (3) in §1.864-3(b) of this chapter.

Section 31.3402(f)(2)-1 is amended by adding at the end thereof of a new paragraph (e), to read as follows:

§31.3402(f)(2)-1 (Proposed Treasury Decision, published 9-29-77.) **Withholding exemption certificates.**

* * * * * * * * * *

(e) **Applicability of withholding exemption certificate to qualified State individual income taxes.** The withholding exemption certificate shall be used for purposes of withholding with respect to qualified State individual income taxes as well as Federal tax. For provisions relating to the withholding exemption certificate with respect to such State taxes, see paragraph (d)(3)(i) of §301.6361-1 of this chapter (Regulations on Procedure and Administration).

So much of §31.3402(n)-1 as follows paragraph (b) and precedes example (1) is amended to read as follows:

§31.3402(n)-1 (Proposed Treasury Decision, published 9-29-77.) **Employees incurring no income tax liability.**

* * * * * * * * * * *

Proposed Reg. §31.3402(n)-1

For purposes of section 3402(n) and this section, an employee is not considered to incur liability for income tax imposed under subtitle A if the amount of such tax is equal to or less than the total amount of credits against such tax which are allowable to him under part IV of subchapter A of chapter 1 of the Code, other than those allowable under section 31 or 39. For purposes of section 3402(n) and this section, "liability for income tax imposed under subtitle A" shall include liability for a qualified State individual income tax which is treated pursuant to section 6361(a) as if it were imposed by chapter 1 of the Code. An employee is not considered to incur liability for such a State income tax if the amount of such tax does not exceed the total amount of the credit against such tax which is allowable to him under section 6362(b)(2)(B) or (C) or section 6362(c)(4). For purposes of this section, an employee who files a joint return under section 6013 is considered to incur liability for any tax shown on such return. An employee who is entitled to file a joint return under such section shall not certify that he anticipates that he will incur no liability for income tax imposed by subtitle A for his current taxable year if such statement would not be true in the event that he files a joint return for such year, unless he filed a separate return for his preceding taxable year and anticipates that he will file a separate return for his current taxable year.

* * * * * * * * * * *

Paragraph (b)(1)(ii)(c) of § 31.3402(p)-1 is amended to read as follows:

§31.3402(p)-1 (Proposed Treasury Decision, published 9-29-77.) **Voluntary withholding agreements**

* * * * * * * * * * *

(b) Form and duration of agreement. (1) * * *
(ii) * * *

(c) A statement that the employee desires withholding of Federal income tax, and, if applicable, of qualified State individual income tax (see paragraph (d)(3)(i) of §301.6361-1 of this chapter (Regulations on Procedure and Administration)), and

* * * * * * * * * * *

Qualified Pension, Etc., Plans

These regulations are prescribed as part of a new Part 54:

§ 54.4973-1 (Proposed Treasury Decision, published 2-21-75.) Excess contributions to certain accounts, contracts and bonds.

(a) **In general. (1) General rule.** Under section 4973, in the case of an individual retirement account (as described in section 408(a)), an individual retirement annuity (as described in section 408(b)), a custodial account treated as an annuity contract under section 403(b)(7)(A), or a retirement bond described in section 409, a tax equal to 6 percent of the amount of excess contributions (as defined in paragraph (b) of this section) to such account, annuity, or bond is imposed on the individual for whose benefit such account, annuity, or bond is established.

(2) **Special rules.** (i) The tax imposed by section 4973 cannot exceed 6 percent of the value (determined as of the close of the individual's taxable year) of the account, annuity, or bond.

(ii) In the case of an endowment contract described in section 408(b), the tax imposed by section 4973 is not applicable to any amount allocable under § 1.219-1(b)(2)(iv)(B) to life insurance under the contract.

(b) **Excess contributions defined. (1) Sections 408 and 409 excess contributions.** For purposes of this section, in the case of an individual retirement account (described in section 408(a)), an individual retirement annuity (described in section 408(b)), or a retirement bond described in section 409, the term "excess contribution" means the sum of—

(i) The excess (if any) of the amount contributed for the taxable year to an account or for an annuity or bond (other than a rollover contribution described in section 402(a)(5), 403(a)(4), 408(d)(3), or 409(b)(3)(C)), over the amount allowable for such taxable year as a deduction under section 219 for such contributions, and

(ii) The amount determined under this subparagraph for the preceding taxable year, reduced by the excess (if any) of the maximum amount allowable as a deduction under section 219 for the taxable year over the amount contributed to the account or for the annuity or bond for the taxable year and reduced by the sum of the distributions out of the account (for all prior taxable years) which were included in the gross income of the payee under section 408(d)(1) or 409(b)(1).

For purposes of subdivision (ii) of this subparagraph any contribution which is distributed out of the account or annuity in a distribution to which section 408 (d)(4) or 409(b)(3)(A) applies is treated as an amount not contributed.

(2) **Section 403(b)(7)(A) excess contributions.** For purposes of this section, in the case of a custodial account treated as an annuity contract under section 403(b)(7)(A), the term "excess contributions" means the sum of—

(i) The excess (if any) of the amount contributed for the taxable year to such account, over the lesser of the amount excludable from the gross income of the employee under section 403(b) or the amount permitted to be contributed under the limitations contained in section 415 (or under whichever such section is applicable, if only one is applicable), and

(ii) The amount determined under this subparagraph (b)(2) of this section for the preceding taxable year, reduced by—

(A) The excess (if any) of the lesser of (1) the amount excludable from the gross income of the employee under section 403(b) or (2) the amount permitted to be contributed under the limitations contained in section 415 (or under whichever such section is applicable, if only one is applicable), over the amount contributed to the account for the taxable year, and

(B) The sum of the distributions out of the account (for all prior years) which are included in the gross income of the employee under section 72(e).

(C) Examples. The provisions of this section may be illustrated by the following examples:

Example (1). On January 1, 1975, A, an individual, establishes an individual retirement account and contributes $1,500. On December 31, 1975, the value of A's account is $1,500. On January 31, 1976, A determines he has compensation for 1975 within the meaning of section 219(c) and the regulations thereunder of $9,334. Under section 219, the maximum amount allowable as a deduction for retirement savings available to A is $1,400. On April 15, 1976, A files his income tax return for 1975 taking a deduction of $1,400 for his contribution to his individual retirement account, and as of such date there had been no distribution from the account. Under section 4973, A would have $100 of excess contribution to his account for 1975 [($1,500−$1,400)+0] and A would be liable for an excise tax of $6 on such excess contribution.

Example (2). Assume the same facts as in Example (1). Assume further that on June 1, 1976, A contributes $1,500 to his account. On January 31, 1977, he determines that he has compensation for 1976 of $10,000. Under section 219, the maximum amount allowable to A as a deduction for retirement savings is $1,500 for 1976. On April 15, 1977, A files his income tax return for 1976 taking a deduction of $1,500 for his contribution to his individual retirement account, and as of such date there has been no distribution from the account. Under section 4973, A would have $100 of excess contribution in his account for 1976 [($1,500 − $1,500) + $100] and A would be liable for an excise tax of $6 on such excess contribution.

Example (3). Assume the same facts as in Examples (1) and (2). Assume further that on June 1, 1977, A contributes $1,500 to his account. On January 31, 1978, A determines he has compensation for 1977 of $11,000. Under section 219, the maximum amount allowable to A as a deduction for retirement savings is $1,500 for 1977. On March 26, 1978, A receives a distribution of $100 from his account. On April 15, 1978, A files his income tax return for 1977 taking a deduction for retirement savings of $1,500. Under section 4973, A would have $100 of excess contributions for 1977 [(0 + $100)] and A would be liable for

Proposed Reg. §54.4973-1

an excise tax of $6 on such excess contribution. For additional tax, see section 408(f).

Example (4). Assume the same facts as in Examples (1), (2), and (3). Assume further that on June 1, 1978, A contributes $1,500 to his account. On January 31, 1979, A determines he has compensation for 1978 of $11,000. Under section 219, the maximum amount allowable to A as a deduction for retirement savings is $1,500 for 1978. On April 15, 1979, A files his income tax return for 1978 taking a deduction for retirement savings of $1,500 and including the $100 distribution of March 26, 1978, in his gross income for 1978. Under section 4973, A would have no excess contribution in his individual retirement account [0 + ($100 − $100)] and would have no excise tax liability for excess contributions.

Example (5). Assume the same facts as in example (3), except that instead of contributing $1,500 to his account A contributes $1,400 and is allowed a deduction for retirement savings under section 219 of $1,400. Under section 4973, A would have no excess contribution in his individual retirement account [0 + ($100 − ($1,500 − $1,400))] and would have no excise tax liability for excess contributions.

Example (6). On May 7, 1975, B establishes an individual retirement account and contributes $1,000 to such account. On October 13, 1975, B purchases an individual retirement annuity for $900. B has compensation of $10,000 for 1975. Under section 219, the maximum amount allowable to B as a deduction for retirement savings is $1,500. On April 15, 1976, B files his income tax return for 1975 and there has been no distribution from the account nor has there been any refund of premiums under the annuity. Under section 4973, B would have $400 of excess contribution [($1,900 − $1,500) + 0] and would be liable for an excise tax of $24.

Example (7). Assume the same facts as in example (1) except the value of A's account as of the end of 1975 is $90. Under section 4973, A would have $100 of excess contribution in his account for 1975 but A would only be liable for an excise tax of $5.40 (6% of $90).

Example (8). On January 1, 1977, a custodial account under section 403(b)(7)(A) is established for the benefit of A who is otherwise eligible to have such an account established and a contribution of $7,000 is made to such account by A's employer which is a tax-exempt organization described in section 501(c)(3). The amount excludable from A's gross income in 1977 under section 403(b) is $4,000 and the amount permitted to be contributed for 1977 under section 415 is $5,000. Under section 4973, A would have an excess contribution of $3,000 [($7,000 − $4,000) + 0] in his account for 1977 and would be liable for an excise tax of $180.

Example (9). Assume the same facts as in example (8). Assume further that on June 22, 1978, a contribution of $1,000 is made by A's employer. The amount otherwise excludable from A's income in 1978 under section 403(b) is $4,000 and the amount permitted to be contributed for 1978 under section 415 is $5,000. Under section 4973, A would have no excess contribution in his account for 1978 [0 + ($3,000 − ($4,000 − $1,000))] and would have no excise tax liability for 1978.

§ 54.4974-1 (Proposed Treasury Decision, published 2-21-75.) **Excise tax on accumulations in individual retirement accounts or annuities.**

(a) **General rule.** A tax equal to 50 percent of the amount by which the minimum amount required to be distributed from an individual retirement account or annuity described in section 408 during the taxable year of the payee under paragraph (b) of this section exceeds the amount actually distributed during the taxable year is imposed by section 4974 on the payee.

(b) **Minimum amount required to be distributed.** For purposes of this section, the minimum amount required to be distributed is the amount required under § 1.408-2(b)(6)(v) to be distributed in the taxable year described in paragraph (a) of this section.

(c) **Examples.** The application of this section may be illustrated by the following examples.

Example (1). In 1975, the minimum amount required to be distributed under § 1.408-2(b)(6)(v) to A under his individual retirement account is $100. Only $60 is actually distributed to A in 1975. Under section 4974, A would have an excise tax liability of $20 [50% of ($100 − $60)].

Example (2). Although no distribution is required under § 1.408-2(b)(6)(v) to be made in 1986, H, a married individual born on February 1, 1921, who has established and maintained an individual retirement account decides to begin receiving distributions from the account beginning in 1986. H's wife, W, was born on March 6, 1921. H and W are calendar year taxpayers. H decides to receive his interest in the account over the joint life and last survivor expectancy of himself and his wife. On January 1, 1986, the balance in H's account is $10,000; H and W, based on their nearest birthdates, are 65; and the joint life and last survivor expectancy of H and his wife is 22.0 years (see Table II of § 1.72-9). His annual payments during the following years (none of which were required) were determined by dividing the balance in the account on the first day of each year by the joint life and last survivor expectancy reduced by the number of whole years elapsed since the distributions were to commence.

Date	Life expectancy minus whole years elapsed	Account Balance at beginning of each year	Annual payment
1-1-86	22.0	$10,000	$455
1-1-87	21.0	$10,118	$482
1-1-88	20.0	$10,214	$511
1-1-89	19.0	$10,285	$541
1-1-90	18.0	$10,329	$574
1-1-91	17.0	$10,340	$608

For 1986, 1987, 1989, and 1990, the amount required to be distributed under § 1.408-2(b)(6)(v) is zero. Thus, H would have no excise tax liability under section 4974 for these years. In 1991, the year H attains age 70½, the amount required to be distributed from the account under § 1.408-2(b)(6)(v) is $565, determined by dividing $10,340 (the account balance as of January 1, 1991) by 18.3 years (the joint life and last survivor expectancy of H and W, assuming they are both still living, as of January 1, 1991). If W should die after December 31, 1990, the joint life and last survivor expectancy determined on January 1, 1991 (18.3 years) would not be redetermined. Because the amount distributed from the account in 1991 ($608) exceeds the amount required to be distributed from the account in 1991 ($565), H has no excise tax liability under section 4974 for 1991.

Example (3). Assume the same facts as in example (2) except that W dies in 1988. For 1988, 1989, and 1990, the amount required to be distributed under § 1.408-2(b)(6)(v) is zero. Thus, H would have no excise tax liability under section 4974 for these years. In 1991, the amount required to be distributed under § 1.408-2(b)(6)(v) is $855, determined by dividing $10,340 (the account balance as of January 1, 1991) by 12.1 years (the life expectancy of H as of January 1, 1991). Because the amount distributed from the account in 1991 ($608) is less than the amount required to be distributed from the account in 1991 ($855), H has an excise tax liability of $123.50 under section 4974 for 1991 [50% of ($855 − $608)].

Section 54.4975-11 is amended by—
1. Revising paragraph (a)(3), (7)(ii), (8)(iii), and (10).
2. Adding a new sentence at the end of paragraph (d)(3),
3. Revising paragraph (e)(2), and
4. Revising paragraph (f)(3).

These revised and added provisions read as follows:

§54.4975-11 (Proposed Treasury Decision, published 9-2-77.) **"ESOP" requirements.**

Proposed Reg. §54.4975-11

(a) **In general.** * * *

(3) **Nonterminable provisions.** An ESOP must provide that, notwithstanding the fact that it ceases to be an ESOP, qualifying employer securities acquired with proceeds of an exempt loan will continue after the loan is paid to be subject to §54.4975-7(b)(4), (10), (11), and (12) relating to put, call or other options and to buy-sell or similar arrangements. Thus, for example, and ESOP must provide that publicly traded securities acquired with exempt loan proceeds must, if the plan ceases to be an ESOP after their acquisition, satisfy the put option provisions in the event that the securities cease to be publicly traded within 15 months after their distribution.

* * * * * * * * * * * *

(7) **Certain arrangements barred.** * * *

(ii) *Integrated plans.* An ESOP established after Nov. 1, 1977 must not be integrated directly or indirectly with contributions or benefits under Title II of the Social Security Act (42 U.S.C. 401) or under the Railroad Retirement Act of 1937 (45 U.S.C. 228a). ESOP's established and integrated before such date may remain integrated. However, such plans must not be amended to increase the integration level or the integration percentage. Such plans may in operation continue to increase the level of integration if under the plan such increase is limited by reference to a criterion existing apart from the plan.

(8) **Effect of certain ESOP provisions on section 401(a) status.** * * *

(iii) *Income pass-through.* An ESOP will not fail to meet the requirements of section 401(a) merely because it provides for the current payment of income under paragraph (f)(3) of this section.

* * * * * * * * * * * *

(iv) *Additional transitional rules.* Notwithstanding paragraph (a)(9) of this section, a plan established before Nov. 1, 1977 that otherwise satisfies the provisions of this section constitutes an ESOP if by December 31, 1977, it is amended to comply from Nov. 1, 1977 with this section even though before such date the plan did not satisfy the following provisions of this section:

(i) Paragraph (a)(3) and (8)(iii);
(ii) The last sentence of paragraph (d)(3); and
(iii) Paragraph (f)(3).

* * * * * * * * * * * *

(d) **Allocations to accounts of participants.** * * *

(3) **Income.** * * * Certain income may be distributed currently under paragraph (f)(3) of this section.

* * * * * * * * * * * *

(e) **Multiple plans** * * *

(2) **Special rule for combined ESOP's.** Two or more ESOP's, one or more of which does not exist on Nov. 1, 1977, may be considered together for purposes of applying section 401(a)(4) and (5) or section 410(b) only if the proportion of qualifying employer securities to total plan assets is substantially the same for each ESOP and—

(i) The qualifying employer securities held by all ESOP's are all of the same class; or
(ii) The ratios of each class held to all such securities held is substantially the same for each plan.

(3) **Amended coverage, contribution, or benefit structure.** For purposes of paragraph (e)(1)(i) of this section, if the coverage, contribution, or benefit structure of a plan that exists on Nov. 1, 1977 is amended after that date, as of the effective date of the amendment, the plan is no longer considered to be a plan that exists on Nov. 1, 1977.

(f) **Distribution.** * * *

(3) **Income.** Income paid with respect to qualifying employer securities acquired by an ESOP in taxable years beginning after December 31, 1974, may be distributed at any time after receipt by the plan to participants on whose behalf such securities have been

allocated. However, under an ESOP that is a stock bonus plan, income held by the plan for a 2-year period or longer must be distributed under the general rules described in paragraph (f)(1) of this section. (See the last sentence of section 803(h), Tax Reform Act of 1976.)

Proposed Reg. §54.4975-11

Returns and Records

Paragraphs (a) and (d) of § 1.6001-1 are amended to read as follows:

§1.6001-1 (Proposed Treasury Decision, published 9-29-77.) **Records.**

(a) **In general.** Except as provided in paragraph (b) of this section, any person subject to tax under subtitle A of the Code (including a qualified State individual income tax which is treated pursuant to section 6361(a) as if it were imposed by chapter 1 of subtitle A), or any person required to file a return of information with respect to income, shall keep such permanent books of account or records, including inventories, as are sufficient to establish the amount of gross income, deductions, credits, or other matters required to be shown by such person in any return of such tax or information.

* * * * * * * * * * * *

(d) **Notice by district director requiring returns, statements, or the keeping of records.** The district director may require any person, by notice served upon him, to make such returns, render such statements, or keep such specific records as will enable the district director to determine whether or not such person is liable for tax under subtitle A of the Code, including qualified State individual income taxes, which are treated pursuant to section 6361(a) as if they were imposed by chapter 1 of subtitle A.

* * * * * * * * * * * * * * *

There is inserted immediately after § 1.6001-1 the following new section:

§1.6001-2 (Proposed Treasury Decision, published 9-29-77.) **Returns.**

For rules relating to returns required to be made by every individual, estate, or trust which is liable for one or more qualified State individual income taxes, as defined in section 6362, for a taxable year, see paragraph (b) of §301.6361-1 of this chapter (Regulations on Procedure and Administration).

* * * * * * * * * * * * * *

Income Tax Returns

Paragraph (a) of §31.6011(a)-4 is amended, paragraph (b) is deleted, and paragraph (c) is redesignated paragraph (b). The amended provision reads as follows:

§ 31.6011(a)-4 (Proposed Treasury Decision, published 9-29-77; 5-10-78.) Returns of income tax withheld from wages.

(a) **In general.** (1) Except as otherwise provided in subparagraph (3) of this paragraph and in §31.6011(a)-5, every person required to make a return of income tax withheld from wages pursuant to section 1622 of the Internal Revenue Code of 1939 for the calendar quarter ended December 31, 1954, shall make a return for each subsequent calendar quarter (whether or not wages are paid therein) until he has filed a final return in accordance with §31.6011(a)-6. Except as otherwise provided in subparagraph (3) of this paragraph and in §31.6011(a)-5, every person not required to make a return for the calendar quarter ended December 31, 1954, shall make a return of income tax withheld from wages pursuant to section 3402 for the first calendar quarter thereafter in which he is required to deduct and withhold such tax and for each subsequent calendar quarter (whether or not wages are paid therein) until he has filed a final return in accordance with §31.6011(a)-6. Except as otherwise provided in §31.6011(a)-8 and in subparagraphs (2) and (3) of this paragraph, Form 941 is the form prescribed for making the return required under this paragraph. For the requirements relating to Form 941 with respect to qualified State individual income taxes, see paragraph (d)(3)(iv) of §301.6361-1 of this chapter (Regulations on Procedure and Administration).

(2) Form 942 is the form prescribed for making the return required under subparagraph (1) of this paragraph with respect to income tax withheld, pursuant to an agreement under section 3402 (p), from wages paid for domestic service in a private home of

Proposed Reg. §31.6011(a)-4

the employer not on a farm operated for profit. The preceding sentence shall not apply in the case of an employer who has elected under paragraph (a)(3) of §31.6011(a)-1 to use Form 941 as his return with respect to such payments for purposes of the Federal Insurance Contributions Act. For the requirements relating to Form 942 with respect to qualified State individual income taxes, see paragraph (d)(3)(iv) of §301.6361-1.

(3) Every person shall make a return of income tax withheld, pursuant to an agreement under section 3402(p), from wages paid for agricultural labor for the first calendar year in which he is required (by reason of such agreement) to deduct and withhold such tax and for each subsequent calendar year (whether or not wages for agricultural labor are paid therein) until he has filed a final return in accordance with §31.6011(a)-6. Form 943 is the form prescribed for making the return required under this subparagraph. For the requirements relating to Form 943 with respect to qualified State individual income taxes, see paragraph (d)(3)(iv) of §301.6361-1.

* * * * * * * * * * * * * * *

Section 31.6011(a)-5(b)(2) is amended to read as follows:

§31.6011(a)-5 (Proposed Treasury Decision, published 5-10-78.) **Monthly returns.**

* * * * * * * * * * *

(b) **Information returns.** * * *

(2) **Information returns on Form W-3 and Social Security Administration copies of Form W-2.** See §31.6051-2 for requirements with respect to information returns on Form W-3 and Social Security Administration copies of Form W-2.

* * * * * * * * * * * *

Section 31.6011(a)-7(b)(2) is amended to read as follows:

§31.6011(a)-7 (Proposed Treasury Decision, published 5-10-78.) **Execution of returns.**

* * * * * * * * * * * *

(b) **Use of prescribed forms.** * * *

(2) **Permission for use of magnetic tape.**

In any case where the use of Form W-2 is required for the purpose of making a return or reporting information, such requirement may be satisfied by submitting the information required by such form on magnetic tape or other approved media, provided that the prior consent of the Commissioner of Social Security (or other authorized officer or employee thereof) has been obtained.

* * * * * * * * * * * *

Paragraph (a)(2) of §1.6012-1 is amended by adding at the end thereof a new subdivision (vi), and new subparagraph (9) immediately after subparagraph (8) of paragraph (a). The amended provisions read as follows:

§1.6012-1 (Proposed Treasury Decision, published 12-30-70, 9-29-77.) Individuals required to make returns of income.

(a) **Individual citizen or resident.** * * *

(2) **Special rules.** * * *

(vi) For rules relating to returns required to be made by every individual who is liable for one or more qualified State individual income taxes, as defined in section 6362, for a taxable year, see paragraph (b) of §301.6361-1 of this chapter (Regulations on Procedure and Administration).

(9) **Items of tax preference.** For taxable years ending after December 31, 1969, an individual with items of tax preference (described in section 57 and the regulations thereunder) in excess of $15,000 during any such taxable year, shall attach the required form to the return required under this paragraph.

* * * * * * * * * * * * *

Section 1.6012-2 is amended by redesignating paragraph (i) as paragraph (j) and by adding new paragraph (i) immediately after paragraph (h). The amended provision reads as follows:

§ **1.6012-2** (Proposed Treasury Decision, published 12-30-70.) **Corporations required to make returns of income.**

* * * * * * * * * * * * *

(i) Items of tax preference—(1) In general. Every corporation required to make a return under this section and having items of tax preference (described in section 57 and the regulations thereunder) in any amount shall file the required form relating to such items as part of such return.

(2) **Organizations with unrelated business income and foreign corporations.** Regardless of the provisions of paragraphs (e) and (g) of this section, any organization described in either such paragraph having items of tax preference (described in section 57 and the regulations thereunder) in any amount entering into the computation of unrelated business income is required to make a return on Form 990-T or Form 1120F, respectively, and to attach the required form as part of such return.

(j) **Other provisions.** * * *

Section 1.6012-3 is amended by revising subparagraph (1) of paragraph and by adding at the end thereof a new subparagraph (8), to read as follows:

§ **1.6012-3** (Proposed Treasury Decision, published 12-30-70, 9-29-77.) **Returns of fiduciaries.**

(a) **For estates and trusts**—(1) **In general.** Every fiduciary, or at least one of joint fiduciaries, must make a return of income on Form 1041 and attach the required form if the estate or trust has items of tax preference (as defined in section 57 and the regulations thereunder) in any amount—

* * * * * * * * * * * * *

(8) **Estates and trusts liable for qualified tax.** In the case of an estate or trust which is liable for one or more qualified State individual income taxes, as defined in section 6362, for a taxable year, see paragraph (b) of §301.6361-1 of this chapter (Regulations on Procedure and Administration) for rules relating to returns required to be made.

* * * * * * * * * * * * *

Section 1.6015(c)-1 is amended by revising such section to read as follows:

§ **1.6015(c)-1** (Proposed Treasury Decision, published 12-30-70.) **Definition of estimated tax.**

In the case of an individual, the term "estimated tax" means the amount which the individual estimates as the amount of the income tax imposed by chapter 1 of the Code (other than the tax imposed by section 56) for the taxable year, minus the amount which he estimates as the sum of the credits against tax provided by part IV, subchapter A of such chapter. These credits are those provided by section 31 (relating to tax withheld on wages), section 32 (relating to tax withheld at source on nonresident aliens and foreign corporations and on tax-free convenant bonds), section 33 (relating to foreign taxes), section 34 (relating to the credit for dividends received on or before December 31, 1964), section 35 (relating to partially tax-exempt interest), and section 37 (relating to retirement income). An individual who expects to elect to pay the optional tax imposed by section 3, or one who expects to elect to take the standard deduction allowed by section 144, should disregard any credits otherwise allowable under sections 32, 33, and 35 in computing his estimated tax since, if he so elects, these credits are not allowed in computing his tax liability. See section 36.

Section 1.6015(c)-1 is amended to read as follows:

§**1.6015(c)-1** (Proposed Treasury Decision, published 9-29-77.) **Definition of estimated tax.**

Proposed Reg. § 1.6015(c)-1

(a) **In general.** In the case of an individual, the term "estimated tax" means—

(1) The amount which the individual estimates as the amount of the income tax imposed by chapter 1 (other than the tax imposed by section 56 or, for taxable years ending before September 30, 1968, the tax surcharge imposed by section 51) for the taxable year (and including the amount which he estimates as the amount of any qualified State individual income taxes which are treated pursuant to section 6361(a) as if they were imposed by chapter 1 for the taxable year), plus

(2) For taxable years beginning after December 31, 1966, the amount which the individual estimates as the amount of the self-employment tax imposed by chapter 2 for the taxable year, minus

(3) The amount which the individual estimates as the sum of any credits against tax provided by part IV of subchapter A of chapter 1. These credits are those provided by section 31 (relating to tax withheld on wages), section 32 (relating to tax withheld at source on nonresident aliens and foreign corporations and on tax-free covenant bonds), section 33 (relating to foreign taxes), section 34 (relating to the credit for dividends received on or before December 31, 1964), section 35 (relating to partially tax-exempt interest), section 37 (relating to the elderly), section 38 (relating to the investment credit), section 39 (relating to certain uses of gasoline, special fuels, and lubricating oil), section 40 (relating to expenses of work incentive programs), section 41 (relating to contributions to candidates), section 42 (relating to general tax credit), section 43 (relating to earned income), section 44 (relating to purchase of new principal residence), section 44A (relating to expenses for household and dependent care services necessary for gainful employment), section 44B (relating to credit for employment of certain new employees), and section 45 (relating to overpayments of tax), and also minus

(4) In the case of an individual who is subject to one or more qualified State individual income taxes, the amount which he estimates as the sum of the credits allowed against such taxes pursuant to section 6362(b)(2)(B) or (C) or section 6362(c)(4) and paragraph (c) of §301.6362-4 of this chapter (Regulations on Procedure and Administration) (relating to the credit for income taxes of other States or political subdivisions thereof) and paragraph (c)(2) of §301.6361-1 (relating to the credit for tax withheld from wages on account of qualified State individual income taxes).

(b) **Example.** A, a self-employed individual not subject to any qualified State individual income tax, estimates that his liabilities for income tax and self-employment tax for 1973 will be $1,600 and $400, respectively. A is required to declare and pay an estimated tax of $2,000 for that year.

Information Returns of Partnerships

Section 1.6031-1 is amended by revising paragraph (a) to read as follows:

§ 1.6031-1 (Proposed Treasury Decision, published 12-30-70.) **Return of partnership income.**

(a) **In general.** Except as provided in paragraphs (b) and (d) of this section with respect to certain organizations excluded from the application of subchapter K, chapter 1 of the Code, and certain partnerships having no United States business, an unincorporated organization defined as a partnership in section 761(a), through or by means of which any business, financial operation, or venture is carried on, shall make a return for each taxable year on Form 1065. For purposes of filing a partnership return, an unincorporated organization will not be considered, within the meaning of section 761(a), to carry on a business, financial operation, or venture as a partnership before the first taxable year in which such organization receives income or incurs any expenditures treated as deductions for Federal income tax purposes. Such return shall state specifically the items of partnership gross income, and deductions allowable by subtitle A of the Code and shall include the names and addresses of all the partners and the amount of the distributive shares of income, gain, loss, deduction, or credit (including any items which enter into the determination of the tax imposed by section 56) allocated to each partner. Such return shall be made for the taxable year of the partnership, irrespective of the taxable years of the partners. For taxable years of a partnership and of a partner, see section 706 and § 1.706-1. For signing of a partnership return, see § 1.6063-1.

* * * * * * * * * * * *

Returns of Banks with Common Trust Funds

Section 1.6032-1 is amended by revising such section to read as follows:

§ 1.6032-1 (Proposed Treasury Decision, published 12-30-70.) Returns of banks with respect to common trust funds.

Every bank (as defined in section 581) maintaining a common trust fund shall make a return of income of the common trust fund, regardless of the amount of its taxable income. If a bank maintains more than one common trust fund, a separate return shall be made for each. No particular fund is prescribed for making the return under this section, but Form 1065 may be used if it is designated by the bank as the return or common trust fund. The return shall be made for the taxable year of the common trust fund and shall be filed on or before the fifteenth day of the fourth month following the close of such taxable year with the district director for the district in which the income tax return of the bank is filed. Such return shall state specifically with respect to the fund the items of gross income and the deductions allowed by subtitle A of the Code, shall include each participant's name and address, the participant's proportionate share of taxable income or net loss (exclusive of gains and losses from sales or exchanges of capital assets), the participant's proportionate share of gains and losses from sales or exchanges of capital assets, and the participant's share of items which enter into the determination of the tax imposed by section 56. See § 1.584-2 and § 1.58-5. A copy of the plan of the common trust fund must be filed with the return. If, however, a copy of such plan has once been filed with a return, it need not again be filed if the return contains a statement showing when and where it was filed. If the plan is amended in any way after such copy has been filed, a copy of the amendment must be filed with the return for the taxable year in which the amendment was made. For the signing of a return of a bank with respect to common trust funds, see § 1.6062-1, relating to the manner prescribed for the signing of a return of a corporation.

Returns by Exempt Organizations

Section 1.6033-2 is amended by revising paragraphs (a)(3)(ii) and (h)(3) to read as follows: to read as follows:

§ 1.6033-2 (Proposed Treasury Decision, published 2- -78.) **Returns by exempt organizations; taxable years beginning after December 31, 1969.**

(a) In general. * * *

(3) * * *

(ii) For taxable years ending on or after December 31, 1971, and before December 31, 1975, every employee's trust described in section 401(a) which is exempt from taxation under section 501(a) shall file an annual return on Form 990-P. The trust shall furnish such information as is required by such form and the instructions issued with respect thereto.

* * * * * * * * * * *

(h) **Records, statements, and other returns of tax-exempt organizations.** * * *

(3) An organization which has established its exemption from taxation under section 501(a), including an organization which is relieved under section 6033 and this section from filing annual returns of information, is not relieved of the duty of filing other returns of information. See, for example, sections 6041, 6043, 6051, 6057, and 6058 and the regulations thereunder.

* * * * * * * * * * *

Proposed Reg. § 1.6033-2

Information Returns of Trusts

Section 1.6034-1 is amended by revising so much thereof that precedes paragraph (a) (2) and by revising paragraphs (c) and (d). These amended provisions read as follows:

§ 1.6034-1 (Proposed Treasury Decision, published 4-13-71.) **Information returns required of trusts described in section 4947 (a) or claiming charitable or other deductions under section 642 (c).**

(a) **In general.** Every trust (other than a trust described in paragraph (b) of this section) claiming a charitable or other deduction under section 642 (c) for the taxable year shall file, with respect to such taxable year, a return of information on Form 1041-A. In addition, for taxable years beginning after December 31, 1969, every trust (other than a trust described in paragraph (b) of this section) described in section 4947 (a) (including trusts described in section 664) shall file such return for each taxable year, unless (with respect to a trust described in section 4947 (a) (2)) all transfers in trust occurred before May 27, 1969. The return shall set forth the name and address of the trust and the following information concerning the trust in such detail as is prescribed by the form or in the instructions issued with respect to such form:

(1) The amount of the charitable or other deduction taken under section 642 (c) for the taxable year (and, for taxable years beginning prior to January 1, 1970, showing separately for each class of activity for which disbursements were made (or amounts were permanently set aside) the amounts which, during such year, were paid out (or which were permanently set aside) for charitable or other purposes under section 642 (c));

* * * * * * * * * * *

(c) **Time and place for filing return.** The return on Form 1041-A shall be filed on or before the fifteenth day of the fourth month following the close of the taxable year of the trust, with the internal revenue officer designated by the instructions applicable to such form. For extensions of time for filing returns under this section, see § 1.6081-1.

(d) **Other provisions.** For publicity of information on Form 1041-A, see section 6104 and the regulations thereunder in Part 301 of this chapter. For provisions relating to penalties for failure to file a return required by this section, see section 6652 (d). For the criminal penalties for a willful failure to file a return and filing a false or fraudulent return, see sections 7203, 7206, and 7207.

Section 301.6034-1 is amended to read as follows:

§ 301.6034-1 (Proposed Treasury Decision, published 4-13-71.) **Returns by trusts described in section 4947(a) or claiming charitable or other deductions under section 642(c).**

For provisions relating to the requirement of returns by trusts described in section 4947(a) or claiming charitable or other deductions under section 642(c), see § 1.6034-1 of this chapter (Income Tax Regulations).

Information Concerning Transactions with Other Persons

Section 1.6041-1(a)(2) is amended by deleting the second sentence.

Section 1.6041-2(a) is amended as follows:

1. Subparagraph (2) is deleted and subparagraphs (3), (4), and (5) are redesignated as subparagraphs (2), (3), and (4), respectively.

2. Subparagraph (1) is amended by deleting the third sentence and inserting in lieu thereof the following: "All other payments of compensation, including the cash value of payments made in any medium other than cash, to an employee by his employer in the course of the trade or business of the employer must also be reported on Form W-2 if the total of such payments and the amount of the employee's wages (as defined in section 3401), if any, required to be reported on Form W-2 aggregates $600 or more in a calendar year."

§ 1.6041-2 (Proposed Treasury Decision, published 1-23-69; 5-10-78.) **Return of information as to payments to employees.**

(a) **In general.** Wages, as defined in section 3401, paid to an employee are required to be reported on Form W-2. All other payments of compensation, including the cash value of payments made in any medium other than cash, to an employee by his employer in the course of the trade or business of the employer must be reported on Form 1099 if the total of such payments and the amount of the employee's wages, if any, required to be reported on Form W-2 equals $600 or more in a calendar year. For example, if a payment of $700 was made to an employee and $400 thereof represents wages subject to withholding under section 3402 and the remaining $300 represents compensation not subject to withholding, the $400 must be reported on Form W-2 and the $300 must be reported on Form 1099. In addition, every organization described in section 501(c)(9) which makes one or more payments totaling $600 or more in one year to an individual must file an annual information return on Form 1096, accompanied by a statement on Form 1099, for each such inidividual. Payments made by an employer or by another organization should not be considered in determining whether the $600 amount has been paid by the organization.

* * * * * * * * * * * * *

There is inserted immediately after § 1.6043-2 the following new section:

§ 1.6043-3 (Proposed Treasury Decision, published 4-13-71.) **Return regarding liquidation, dissolution, termination, or substantial contraction of organizations exempt from taxation under section 501 (a).**

(a) **In general.** Except as provided in paragraph (b) of this section, for taxable years beginning after December 31, 1969, every organization which for any of its last 5 taxable years preceding its liquidation, dissolution, termination, or substantial contraction was exempt from taxation under section 501 (a) shall file, with respect to such liquidation, dissolution, termination, or substantial contraction, a return of information on Form 966-E. The return shall set forth the name and address of the organization and such information concerning the organization as is prescribed by the form or in the instructions issued with respect to such form.

(b) **Exceptions.** The following organizations are not required to file the return described in paragraph (a) of this section:

(1) Churches, their integrated auxiliaries, or conventions or associations of churches;

(2) Any organization which is not a private foundation (as defined in section 509 (a)) and the gross receipts of which in each taxable year are normally not more than $5,000;

(3) Any organization which has terminated its private foundation status under section 507 (b) (1) (B); and

(4) Any organization described in section 401(a) if the employer who established such organization files such a return.

The Commissioner may relieve any organization or class of organizations from filing the return required by section 6043 (b) and this section, where he determines that such returns are not necessary for the efficient administration of the internal revenue laws.

(c) **When to file—(1) Corporations and associations.** The return required by this paragraph shall be filed on or before the later of:

(i) The 30th day after publication of final regulations under this section in the Federal Register; or

(ii) The 30th day after the adoption of a resolution or plan for the dissolution or liquidation in whole or in part of the corporation or association, or the 30th day after the occurrence of any substantial contraction of the corporation or association. If there is an amendment or supplement to such resolution or plan, a Form 966-E based on the resolution or plan as amended or supplemented shall be filed on or before the later of the 30th day after publication of final regulations under this section in the Federal Register, or the 30th day after the adoption of such amendment or supplement. If a prior return with respect to such resolution or plan has been filed, a return with respect to an amendment or supplement of such resolution or plan shall be sufficient if it provides the taxpayer's identification number and the date on which such prior return was filed, and contains a certified copy of such amendment or supplement and all other information required by Form 966-E which was not given on such prior return.

(2) **Trusts.** With respect to a trust, the return required by this section shall be filed on or before the later of the 30th day after the publication of final regulations under this section in the Federal Register, or the 30th day after the termination or any substantial contraction of the trust.

(d) **Where to file.** The returns required by this section shall be filed with the internal revenue officer designated by the instructions applicable to such form.

(e) **Penalties.** For provisions relating to the penalty provided for failure to furnish any return required by this section, see section 6652 (d) and the regulations thereunder.

(f) **Definitions.** (1) (i) The term "substantial contraction", as used in this section, shall include any partial liquidation or any other significant disposition of assets, other than transfers for full and adequate consideration or distributions out of current income. For purposes of this subparagraph, the term "significant disposition of assets" shall not include any disposition for a taxable year where the aggregate of—

(a) The dispositions for the taxable year and

(b) Where any disposition for the taxable year is part of a series of related dispositions made during prior taxable years, the total of the related dispositions made during such prior taxable years,

is less than 25 percent of the fair market value of the net assets of the organization at the beginning of the taxable year (in the case of (a) of this subdivision) or at the beginning of the first taxable year in which any of the series of related dispositions was made (in the case of (b) of this subdivision). A "significant disposition of assets" may result from the transfer of assets to a single organization or to several organizations, and it may occur in a single taxable year (as in (a) of this subdivision) or over the course of two or more taxable years (as in (b) of this subdivision). The determination whether a significant disposition has occurred through a series of related dispositions (within the meaning of (b) of this subdivision) will be determined from all the facts and circumstances of the particular case. Ordinarily, a distribution described in section 170 (b) (1) (E) (ii) shall not be taken into account as a significant disposition of assets within the meaning of this subparagraph.

(ii) The provisions of this subparagraph may be illustrated by the following examples:

Example (1). M, an organization described in section 501(c)(4) is on the calendar year basis. It has net assets worth $100,000 as of January 1, 1971. In 1971, in addition to distributions out of current income, M transfers $10,000 to N, $10,000 to O, and $10,000 to P. Such dispositions to N, O, and P are not distributions described in section 170(b)(1)(E)(ii). N, O, and P are all organizations described in section 501(c)(4). Under subdivision (i)(a) of this subparagraph, M has made a significant disposition of its assets in 1971 since M has disposed of more than 25 percent of its net assets (with respect to the fair market value of such assets as of January 1, 1971). Thus, M is subject to the provisions of section 6043(b) and this section for the year 1971.

Example (2). U, a tax-exempt private foundation on the calendar year basis, has net assets worth $100,000 as of January 1, 1971. As part of a series of related dispositions in 1971 and 1972, U transfers in 1971, in addition to distributions out of current income, $10,000 to private foundation X and $10,000 to private foundation Y, and in 1972, in addition to distributions out of current income, U transfers $10,000 to private foundation Z. Such dispositions to X, Y, and Z are not distributions described in section 170(b)(1)(E)(ii). Under subdivision (i) of this subparagraph, U is treated as having made a series of related dispositions in 1971 and 1972. The aggregate of the 1972 disposition (under subdivision (i)(a) of this subparagraph) and the series of related dispositions (under subdivision (i)(b) of this subparagraph) is $30,000, which is more than 25 percent of the fair market value of U's net assets as of the beginning of 1971 ($100,000), the first year in which any such disposition was made.

Thus, U has made a significant disposition of its assets and is subject to the provisions of section 6043(b) and this section for the year 1972.

(2) For the definition of the term "normally" as used in paragraph (b)(2) of this section, see section 1.6033-2(g)(3).

(3) For examples of the term "integrated auxiliaries" as used in paragraph (b)(1) of this section, see section 1.6033-2(g)(1)(i)(a).

* * * * * * * * * * * * * * *

Section 301.6043-1 is amended to read as follows:

§ 301.6043-1 (Proposed Treasury Decision, published 4-13-71.) **Returns regarding liquidation, dissolution, termination, or contraction.**

For provisions relating to the requirement of returns of information regarding liquidations, dissolutions, terminations, or contractions, see §§ 1.6043-1, 1.6043-2, and 1.6043-3 of this chapter (Income Tax Regulations).

Paragraph (c) of § 1.6047-1 is amended to read as follows:

§1.6047-1 (Proposed Treasury Decision, published 2-10-78.) **Information to be furnished with regard to employee retirement plan covering an owner-employee.**

* * * * * * * * * * * *

(c) **Penalties.** For civil penalty for failure to file a return required by this section, and for criminal penalty for furnishing fraudulent information under this section, see §§301.6652-3 and 301.7207-1, respectively.

* * * * * * * * * * * *

Paragraph (a)(1) of § 1-6049-1 is amended by inserting immediately after subdivision (v) the following new subdivision:

§1.6049-1 (Proposed Treasury Decision, published 3-13-78.) **Returns of information as to interest paid in calendar years after 1962 and original issue discount includible in gross income for calendar years after 1970.**

(a) **Requirement of reporting—(1) In general.** * * *

(vi) Every person carrying on the banking business who makes payments of interest to another person (whether or not aggregating $10 or more during a calendar year) with respect to certificates of deposit issued in bearer form (other than such certificates issued in an amount of $100,000 or more) shall make an information return on Forms 1096 and 1099-CD for such calendar year. The information return required by this subdivision for the calendar year shall show the following:

(a) The aggregate amount of interest paid with respect to the certificate of deposit;

(b) The name, address, and taxpayer identification number of the person to whom the interest is paid;

(c) The name, address, and taxpayer identification number of the person to whom the certificate was originally issued;

(d) The amount of interest with respect to the certificate attributable to each calendar year falling within the term of such certificate; and

(e) Such other information as is required by the form.

* * * * * * * * * * * *

Paragraphs (a)(2) and (c)(2) of § 1.6049-2 are amended to read as follows:

Proposed Reg. § 1.6049-1

§1.6049-2 (Proposed Treasury Decision, published 3-13-78.) **Interest and original issue discount subject to reporting.**

(a) Interest in general. * * *

(2) Interest on deposits (except deposits evidenced by negotiable time certificates of deposit issued in an amount of $100,000 or more) paid (or credited) by persons carrying on the banking business. In the case of a certificate of deposit issued in bearer form, the term "interest", as used in the preceding sentence and in paragraph (a)(1)(vi) of §1.6049-1, has the same meaning as in §1.61-7 (regardless of whether taxable to the payee in the year the information return is made).

* * * * * * * * * * * *

(c) Original issue discount—(1) In general. * * *

(2) Coordination with interest reporting. In the case of an obligation issued after May 27, 1969 (other than an obligation issued pursuant to a written commitment which was binding on May 27, 1969, and at all times thereafter), original issue discount which is not subject to the reporting requirements of paragraph (a)(1)(ii) of §1.6049-1 is interest within the meaning of paragraph (a) of this section. Original issue discount which is subject to the reporting requirements of paragraph (a)(1)(ii) of §1.6049-1 is not interest within the meaning of paragraph (a) of this section.

* * * * * * * * * * * *

Par. 4. Paragraph (a) of §1.6049-3 is amended by adding the following sentence at the end thereof: "References in this section to Form 1099 shall be construed to include Form 1099-CD, except that in applying paragraph (b)(2) of this section no information relating to the person to whom the certificate of deposit was originally issued shall be disclosed to another person to whom the payment of interest is made."

Information Regarding Wages

Section 31.6051-1 is amended as follows:

1. Paragraph (a)(1)(i) is amended by deleting the word "and" in inferior subdivision (e); so much of paragraph (a)(1)(i) as follows (f) thereof is amended; deleting the period at the end of inferior subdivision (f) and inserting in lieu thereof ", and"; and adding, immediately after inferior subdivision (f), new inferior subdivision (g) to read as set forth below.

2. Paragraph (b)(1) is amended by deleting the word "and" in subdivision (iii); deleting the period at the end of subdivision (iv) and inserting in lieu thereof ", and"; and adding, immediately after subdivision (iv), new subdivision (v) to read as set forth below.

§ 31.6051-1 (Proposed Treasury Decision, published 9-29-77; 5-10-78.) Statements for employees.

(a) **Requirement if wages are subject to withholding of income tax—(1) General rule.** (i) * * *

(f) * * *

See paragraph (d) of this section for provisions relating to the time for furnishing the statement required by this subparagraph. See paragraph (f) of this section for an exception for employers filing composite returns from the requirement that statements for employees be on Form W-2. For the requirements relating to Form W-2 with respect to qualified State individual income taxes, see paragraph (d)(3)(ii) of §301.6361-1 of this chapter (Regulations on Procedure and Administration).

* * * * * * * * * * * *

(g) Such information relating to coverage the employee has earned under the Federal Insurance Contributions Act as may be required by Form W-2 or its instructions.

* * * * * * * * * * * *

(b) **Requirement if wages are not subject to withholding of income tax—(1) General rule.** * * *

(v) Such information relating to coverage the employee has earned under the Federal Insurance Contributions Act as may be required by Form W-2 or its instructions.

* * * * * * * * * * *

Section 31.6051-2(a) and (b) are amended to read as follows:

§31.6051-2 (Proposed Treasury Decision, published 5-10-78.) **Information returns on Form W-3 and Social Security Administration copies of Forms W-2.**

(a) In general. Every employer who is required to make a return of tax under §31.6011(a)-1 (relating to returns under the Federal Insurance Contributions Act), §31.6011(a)-4 (relating to returns of income tax withheld from wages), or §31.6011(a)-5 (relating to monthly returns) for a calendar year or any period therein shall file the Social Security Administration copy of each Form W-2 required under §31.6051-1 to be furnished by the employer with respect to wages paid during the calendar year. Each Form W-2 and the transmittal Form W-3 shall together constitute an information return to be filed with the Social Security Administration office indicated on the instructions to such forms. However, in the case of an employer who elects to file a composite return pursuant to §31.6011(a)-8, the information return required by this section shall consist of magnetic tape (or other approved media) containing all information required to be on the employee statement, together with transmittal Form 4804.

(b) Corrected returns. The Social Security Administration copies of corrected Forms W-2 (or magnetic tape or other approved media) for employees for the calendar year shall be submitted with Form W-3 (or Form 4804), on or before the date on which information returns for the period in which the correction is made would be due under paragraph (a)(3)(ii) of §31.6071(a)-1, to the Social Security Administration office with which Forms W-2 are required to be filed.

* * * * * * * * * * *

Paragraph (a)(1)(i) of §1.6052-1 is amended by deleting "set forth in paragraph (a)(2) of §1.79-1" and inserting in its place "provided in section 79(a)".

Paragraph (a)(2) of §1.6052-1 is amended to read as follows:

§1.6052-1 (Proposed Treasury Decision, published 1-5-77.) **Information returns regarding payment of wages in the form of group-term life insurance.**

(a) Requirement of reporting—* * *

(2) **Definitions.** Terms used in paragraph (a)(1) of this section and in section 79 and the regulations thereunder have the meaning ascribed to them in section 79 and the regulations thereunder.

* * * * * * * * * * * * *

Paragraph (e) of §1.6052-2 is amended to read as follows:

§1.6052-2 (Proposed Treasury Decision, published 1-5-78.) **Statements to be furnished employees with respect to wages paid in the form of group-term life insurance.**

* * * * * * * * * * * * *

(e) **Definitions.** Terms used in this section and in section 79 and the regulations thereunder have the meaning ascribed to them in section 79 and the regulations thereunder.

* * * * * * * * * * * * *

Registration of and Information Concerning Pension, Etc. Plans

There is inserted in the appropriate place the following new sections:

§301.6057-1 (Proposed Treasury Decision, published 1-20-78.) **Employee retirement benefit plans; identification of participant with deferred vested retirement benefit.**

(a) **Annual registration statement—(1) In general.** Under section 6057(a), the plan

Proposed Reg. §301.6057-1

administrator (within the meaning of section 414(g)) of an employee retirement benefit plan must file with the Internal Revenue Service information relating to each plan participant who separates from service covered by the plan and is entitled to a deferred vested retirement benefit under the plan, but is not paid this retirement benefit. Plans subject to this filing requirement are described in subparagraph (3) of this paragraph. Subparagraph (4) describes how the information is to be filed with the Internal Revenue Service. In the case of a plan to which only one employer contributes, the time for filing the information with respect to each separated participant is described in subparagraph (5). In the case of a plan to which more than one employer contributes the time for filing the information with respect to a participant is described in paragraph (b)(2). Paragraph (b) also provides other rules applicable only to plans to which more than one employer contributes.

(2) **Deferred vested retirement benefit.** For purposes of this section, a plan participant's deferred retirement benefit is considered a vested benefit if it is vested under the terms of the plan at the close of the plan year described in paragraph (a)(5) or (b)(4) (whichever is applicable) for which information relating to any deferred vested retirement benefit of the participant must be filed. A participant's deferred retirement benefit need not be a nonforfeitable benefit within the meaning of section 411(a) for the filing requirements described in this section to apply. Accordingly, information relating to a participant's deferred vested retirement benefit must be filed as required by this section notwithstanding that the benefit is subject to forfeiture by reason of an event or condition occurring subsequent to the close of the plan year described in paragraph (a)(5) or (b)(4) (whichever is applicable) for which information relating to any deferred vested retirement benefit of the participant must be filed.

(3) **Plans subject to filing requirement.** The term "employee retirement benefit plan" means a plan to which the vesting standards of section 203 of part 2 of subtitle B of Title I of the Employee Retirement Income Security Act of 1974 (88 Stat. 854) apply for any day in the plan year. (For purposes of this section, "plan year" means the plan year as determined for purposes of the annual return required by section 6058(a)). Accordingly, a plan need not be a qualified plan within the meaning of section 401(a) to be subject to these filing requirements. A plan to which more than one employer contributes must file the report of deferred vested retirement benefits described in this section, but see paragraph (b) for special rules applicable to such a plan.

(4) **Filing requirements.** Information relating to the deferred vested retirement benefit of a plan participant must be filed on Schedule SSA as an attachment to the Annual Return/Report of Employee Benefit Plan (Form 5500 series). Schedule SSA shall be filed on behalf of an employee retirement benefit plan for each plan year for which information relating to the deferred vested retirement benefit of a plan participant if filed under paragraph (a)(5) or (b)(2) of this section. There shall be filed on Schedule SSA the name and Social Security number of the participant, a description of the nature, form and amount of the deferred vested retirement benefit to which the participant is entitled, and such other information as is required by section 6057(a) or Schedule SSA and the accompanying instructions. The form of the benefit reported on Schedule SSA shall be the normal form of benefit under the plan, or, if the plan administrator (within the meaning of section 414(g)) considers it more appropriate, any other form of benefit.

(5) **Time for reporting deferred vested retirement benefit**—(i) In general. In the case of a plan to which only one employer contributes, information relating to the deferred vested retirement benefit of a plan participant must be filed no later than on the Schedule SSA filed for the plan year following the plan year within which the participant separates from service covered by the plan. Information relating to a separated participant may, at the option of the plan administrator, be reported earlier (that is, on the Schedule SSA filed for the plan year in which the participant separates from service covered by the plan). For purposes of this paragraph a participant is not considered to separate from service covered by the plan solely because the participant incurs a break in service under the plan. In addition, for purposes of this paragraph, in the case of a plan which uses the elapsed time method described in Department of Labor regulations for crediting service for benefit accrual purposes, a participant is considered to separate from

service covered by the plan on the date the participant severs from service covered by the plan.

(ii) Exception. Notwithstanding subdivision (i), no information relating to the deferred vested retirement benefit of a separated participant is required to be reported on Schedule SSA if, after the participant separates from service covered by the plan, but before the end of the plan year following the plan year during which the participant so separates from service covered by the plan, the participant (A) is paid retirement benefits under the plan, (B) returns to service covered by the plan, or (C) forfeits the deferred vested retirement benefit under the plan.

(b) **Plans to which more than one employer contributes—(1) Application.** Section 6057 and this section apply to a plan to which more than one employer contributes with the modifications set forth in this paragraph. For purposes of section 6057 and this section, whether or not more than one employer contributes to a plan shall be determined by the number of employers who are required to contribute to the plan. Thus, for example, this paragraph applies to plans maintained by more than one employer which are collectively bargained as described in section 413(a), multiple-employer plans described in section 413(c) and the regulations thereunder, multiemployer plans described in section 414(f), and plans adopted by more than one employer of certain controlled and common control groups described in section 414(b) and (c).

(2) **Time for reporting deferred vested retirement benefit—**(i) In general. In the case of a plan to which more than one employer contributes, information relating to the deferred vested retirement benefit of a plan participant must be filed no later than on the Schedule SSA filed for the plan year within which the participant completes the second of two consecutive one-year breaks in service (as defined in the plan for vesting percentage purposes) in service computation periods (as defined in the plan for vesting percentage purposes) beginning after December 31, 1974. For the definition of the term "one-year break in service" in the case of a plan which uses the elapsed time method described in Department of Labor Regulations for crediting service for vesting percentage purposes, see §1.411(a)-6(c)(2). At the option of the plan administrator, information relating to a participant's deferred vested retirement benefit may be filed earlier (that is, on the Schedule SSA filed for the plan year in which the participant incurs the first one-year break in service or, in the case of a separated participant, on the Schedule SSA filed for the plan year in which the participant separates from service).

(ii) Exception. Notwithstanding subdivision (i) of this subparagraph, no information relating to a participant's deferred vested retirement benefit is required to be filed on Schedule SSA if, before the end of the plan year in which the participant incurs the second consecutive one-year break in service, the participant (A) is paid some or all of such deferred vested retirement benefit under the plan, (B) accrues additional retirement benefits under the plan, or (C) forfeits the deferred vested retirement benefit under the plan.

(iii) Special transitional rule. Notwithstanding subdivision (i), if the second consecutive one-year break in service described in subdivision (i) is incurred in a plan year beginning before January 1, 1977, information relating to the participant's deferred vested retirement benefit is to be reported on the Schedule SSA filed for the first plan year beginning after December 31, 1976. Further, no information relating to a participant's deferred vested retirement benefit is required to be reported on Schedule SSA if, before the end of the first plan year beginning after December 31, 1976, the participant (A) is paid some or all of such deferred vested retirement benefit under the plan, (B) accrues additional retirement benefits under the plan, or (C) forfeits the deferred vested retirement benefit under the plan.

(3) **Information relating to deferred vested retirement benefit—**(i) Incomplete records. Section 6057(a) and paragraph (a)(4) of this section require the filing on Schedule SSA of a description of the deferred vested retirement benefit to which the participant is entitled. If the plan administrator of a plan to which more than one employer contributes maintains records of a participant's service covered by the plan which are incomplete as

Proposed Reg. §301.6057-1

of the close of the plan year with respect to which the plan administrator files information relating to the participant on Schedule SSA, the plan administrator may elect to file the information required by Schedule SSA based only upon these incomplete records. The plan administrator is not required, for purposes of completing Schedule SSA, to compile from sources other than such records a complete record of a participant's years of service covered by the plan. Similarly, if retirement benefits under the plan are determined by taking into account a participant's service with an employer which is not service covered by the plan, but the plan administrator maintains records only with respect to periods of service covered by the plan, the plan administrator may complete Schedule SSA taking into account only the participant's period of service covered by the plan.

(ii) Inability to determine correct amount of participant's deferred vested retirement benefit.

If the amount of a participant's deferred vested retirement benefit which is filed on Schedule SSA is computed on the basis of plan records maintained by the plan administrator which—

(A) Are incomplete with respect to the participant's service covered by the plan (as described in subdivision (i)), or

(B) Fail to account for the participant's service not covered by the plan which is relevant to a determination of the participant's deferred vested retirement benefit under the plan (as described in subdivision (i)),

then the plan administrator must indicate on Schedule SSA that the amount of the deferred vested retirement benefit shown therein may be other than that to which the participant is actually entitled because the amount is based upon incomplete records.

(iii) Inability to determine whether participant vested in deferred retirement benefit. Where, as described in subdivision (i), information to be reported on Schedule SSA is to be based upon records which are incomplete with respect to a participant's service covered by the plan or which fail to take into account relevant service not covered by the plan, the plan administrator may be unable to determine whether or not the participant is vested in any deferred retirement benefit. There may be reason to believe, however, that, because plan records are incomplete, the participant may in fact be vested in a deferred retirement benefit. In such a case, information relating to the participant must be filed on Schedule SSA with the notation that the participant may be entitled to a deferred vested retirement benefit under the plan, but information relating to the amount of the benefit may be omitted. This subdivision (iii) does not apply in a case in which it can be determined from plan records maintained by the plan administrator that the participant is vested in a deferred retirement benefit. Subdivision (ii), however, may apply in such a case.

(c) **Voluntary reports.** The plan administrator of an employee retirement benefit plan described in paragraph (a)(3) of this section, or any other employee retirement benefit plan, may at its option, file on Schedule SSA information relating to the deferred vested retirement benefit of any plan participant who separates at any time from service covered by the plan, including plan participants who separate from such service in plan years beginning prior to 1976.

(d) **Individual statement to participant.** The plan administrator of an employee retirement benefit plan defined in paragraph (a)(3) of this section must provide each participant with respect to whom information is required to be filed on Schedule SSA a statement describing the deferred vested retirement benefit to which the participant is entitled. The description provided the participant must include the information filed with respect to the participant on Schedule SSA, and any other information the Internal Revenue Service may require. The statement is to be delivered to the participant or forwarded to the participant's last known address no later than the date on which any Schedule SSA reporting information with respect to the participant is required to be filed.

(e) **Penalties.** For amounts imposed in the case of failure to file the report of deferred vested retirement benefits required by section 6057(a) and paragraph (a) or (b) of this section, see section 6652(e)(1). For the penalty relating to a failure to provide the participant the individual statement of deferred vested retirement benefit required by section 6057(e) and paragraph (d) of this section, see section 6690.

(f) Effective dates—(1) Plans to which only one employer contributes. In the case of a plan to which only one employer contributes, this section is effective for plan years beginning after December 31, 1975, and with respect to a participant who separates from service covered by the plan in plan years beginning after that date.

(2) Plans to which more than one employer contributes. In the case of a plan to which more than one employer contributes, this section is effective for plan years beginning after December 31, 1976.

§ 301.6057-2 (Proposed Treasury Decision, published 1-20-78.) **Employee retirement benefit plans; notification of change in plan status.**

(a) Change in plan status. The plan administrator (within the meaning of section 414(g)) of an employee retirement benefit plan defined in §301.6057-1(a)(3) (including a plan to which more than one employer contributes, as described in §301.6057-1(b)(1)), must notify the Internal Revenue Service of the following changes in plan status—

(1) A change in the name of the plan,
(2) A change in the name or address of the plan administrator,
(3) The termination of the plan, or
(4) The merger or consolidation of the plan with another plan or the division of the plan into two or more plans.

(b) Notification. A notification of a change in status described in paragraph (a) must be filed on the Annual Return/Report of Employee Benefit Plan (Form 5500 series) for the plan year in which the change in status occurred. The notification must be filed at the time and place and in the manner prescribed in the form and any accompanying instructions.

(c) Penalty. For amounts imposed in the case of failure to file a notification of a change in plan status required by section 6057(b) and this section, see section 6652(e)(2)

(d) Effective date. This section is effective for changes in plan status occurring within plan years beginning after December 31, 1975.

There is inserted in the appropriate place the following new section:

§ 301.6058-1 (Proposed Treasury Decision, published 2-10-78.) **Information required in connection with certain plans of deferred compensation.**

(a) Reporting of information—(1) Annual return. For each funded plan of deferred compensation an annual return must be filed with the Internal Revenue Service. The annual return of the plan is the appropriate Annual Return/Report of Employee Benefit Plan (Form 5500 series) as determined under these forms. The annual period for the annual return of the plan shall be either the plan year or the taxable year of the employer maintaining the plan as determined under these forms. These forms are hereinafter referred to as the "forms prescribed by section 6058(a)."

(2) Plans subject to requirements. For purposes of this section, the term "funded plan of deferred compensation" means each pension, annuity, stock bonus, profit-sharing, or other funded plan of deferred compensation described in part 1 of subchapter D of chapter 1. Accordingly, the term includes qualified plans under sections 401(a), 403(a), and 405(a); individual retirement accounts and annuities described in sections 408(a) and 408(b); and custodial accounts under section 403(b)(7). The term also includes funded plans of deferred compensation which are not qualified plans and such plans which are governmental plans, church plans, and plans maintained outside the united States primarily for nonresident aliens (as defined, respectively, in subsection (b)(1), (2) and (4) of section 4 of part 2 of subtitle B of Title I of the Employee Retirement Income Security Act of 1974 (88 Stat. 839)). The term does not include annuity contracts described in section 403(b)(1) or individual retirement accounts (an individual participant or surviving benefi-

Proposed Reg. § 301.6058-1

ciary in such account must file under paragraph (d)(2) of this section) and bonds described in sections 408(c) and 409.

(3) **Required Information.** The information required to be furnished on the forms prescribed by section 6058(a) shall include such information concerning the qualification of the plan, the financial condition of the trust, fund, or custodial or fiduciary account which is a part of the plan, and the operation of the plan as shall be required by the forms, accompanying schedules and related instructions applicable to the annual period.

(4) **Time of filing.** The forms prescribed by section 6058(a) shall be filed in the manner and at the time as required by the forms and related instructions applicable to the annual period.

(b) **Who must file—(1) In general.** The annual return required to be filed under section 6058(a) and paragraph (a) of this section for the annual period shall be filed by either the employer maintaining the plan or the plan administrator (as defined in section 414(g)) of the plan for that annual period. Whether the employer or plan administrator files shall be determined under the forms prescribed by section 6058(a) and related instructions applicable to the annual period. Nothing in these forms shall preclude an employer from filing the return on behalf of the plan administrator, or the plan administrator from filing on behalf of the employer.

(2) **Definition of employer.** For purposes of subparagraph (1) of this paragraph, the term "employer" includes a sole proprietor and a partnership.

(c) **Other rules applicable to annual returns—(1) Extensions of time for filing.** For rules relating to the extension of time for filing, see section 6081 and the regulations thereunder and the instructions on the forms prescribed by section 6058(a).

(2) **Amended filing.** Any form prescribed by this section may be filed as an amendment to a form previously filed under this section with respect to the same annual period pursuant to the instructions for such forms.

(3) **Additional information.** In addition to the information otherwise required to be furnished by this section, the district director may require any further information that is considered necessary to determine allowable deductions under section 404, qualification under section 401, or the financial condition and operation of the plan.

(4) **Records.** Records substantiating all data and information required by this section to be filed must be kept at all times available for inspection by internal revenue officers at the principal office or place of business of the employer or plan administrator.

(5) **Relief from filing.** Notwithstanding paragraph (a) of this section, the Commissioner may, in his discretion, relieve an employer, or plan administrator, from reporting information on the forms prescribed by section 6058(a) which is reported on other returns filed with the Service. This discretion includes the ability to relieve an employer, or plan administrator, from filing the applicable form.

(d) **Special rules for individual retirement arrangements—(1) Application.** This paragraph, in lieu of paragraph (a) of this section, applies to an individual retirement account described in section 408(a) and an individual retirement annuity described in section 408(b), including such accounts and annuities for which a deduction is allowable under section 220 (spousal individual retirement arrangements).

(2) **General rule.** For each taxable year beginning after December 31, 1974, every individual who during such taxable year—

(i) Establishes or maintains an individual retirement account described in section 408(a) (including an individual who is a participant in an individual retirement account described in section 408(c)),

(ii) Purchases or maintains an individual retirement annuity described in section 408(b), or

(iii) Is a surviving beneficiary with respect to an account or annuity referred to in this subparagraph which is in existence during such taxable year,

shall file Form 5329 (or any other form designated by the Commissioner for this purpose), as an attachment to or part of the Form 1040 filed by such individual for such taxable year, setting forth in full the information required by that form and the accompanying instructions.

(3) **Special information returns.** If an individual described in subparagraph (2) of this paragraph is not required to file a Form 1040 for such taxable year, such individual shall file a Form 5329 (or any other designated form) with the Internal Revenue Service by the 15th day of the 4th month following the close of such individual's taxable year setting forth in full the information required by that form and the accompanying instructions.

(4) **Relief from filing.** The Commissioner may, in his discretion, relieve an individual from filing the form prescribed by this paragraph.

(5) **Retirement bonds.** An individual who purchases, holds, or maintains a retirement bond described in section 409 may be required to file a return under other provisions of the Code.

(e) **Actuarial statement in case of mergers, etc.** For requirements with respect to the filing of actuarial statements in the case of a merger, consolidation, or transfer of assets or liabilities, see section 6058(b) and section 414(l) and the regulations thereunder.

(f) **Effective dates—(1) Section 6058(a) requirements.** The rules with respect to annual returns required under section 6058(a) (the rules in this section, other than paragraph (e) thereof) are effective for plan years beginning after September 2, 1974.

(2) **Section 6058(b) requirements.** The requirements of section 6058(b), relating to mergers, etc., and paragraph (e) of this section are effective on September 2, 1974, with respect to events described in section 6058(b) occurring on or after such date.

Section 31.6081(a)-1(a)(3) is amended as follows:

1. By deleting "district director or director of a service center" and inserting in lieu thereof "director of a Social Security Administration data operations center (or other authorized officer or employee thereof)".

2. By deleting "internal revenue office" both times it appears and inserting in lieu thereof "Social Security Administration office.".

§ 31.6081(a)-1(a)(3) (Proposed Treasury Decision, published 5-10-78.) Extensions of time for filing returns and other documents.

Section 31.6091-1(d) is amended to read as follows:

§31.6091-1 (Proposed Treasury Decision, published 5-10-78.) **Place for filing returns.**

* * * * * * * * * * * *

(d) **Returns filed with internal revenue service centers or Social Security Administration offices.** Notwithstanding paragraphs (a), (b), and (c) of this section, whenever instructions applicable to such returns provide that the returns shall be filed with an internal revenue service center or an office of the Social Security Administration, such returns shall be filed in accordance with such instructions.

* * * * * * * * * * * *

Notice of Deficiency

Paragraph (c) of § 301.6212-1 is amended to read as follows:

§301.6212-1 (Proposed Treasury Decision, published 9-29-77.) **Notice of deficiency.**

* * * * * * * * * * * *

(c) **Further deficiency letters restricted.** If the district director (or assistant regional commissioner, appellate) mails to the taxpayer notice of a deficiency, and the taxpayer files a petition with the Tax Court within the prescribed period, no additional deficiency may be determined with respect to income tax for the same taxable year, gift tax for the same calendar quarter (calendar year with respect to gifts made before January 1, 1971), or estate tax with respect to the taxable estate of the same decedent. This restriction shall

Proposed Reg. § 301.6212-1

not apply in the case of fraud, assertion of deficiencies with respect to any qualified tax (as defined in paragraph (b) of §301.6361-4) in respect of which no deficiency was asserted for the taxable year in the notice, assertion of deficiencies with respect to the Federal tax when deficiencies with respect to only a qualified tax (and not the Federal tax) were asserted for the taxable year in the notice, assertion of greater deficiencies before the Tax Court as provided in section 6214(a), mathematical errors as provided in section 6213(b)(1), or jeopardy assessments as provided in section 6861(c).

Mode or Time of Collection

Paragraph (a)(1)(i) and (ii) and paragraph (b)(1) of §31.6302(c)-1 are amended, effective with respect to wages paid after September 30, 1975, to read as follows:

§ 31.6302(c)-1 (Proposed Treasury Decision, published 6-27-75.) **Use of Government depositaries in connection with taxes under Federal Insurance Contributions Act and income tax withheld.**

(a) **Requirement—(1) In general.** (i) In the case of a calendar quarter which begins after September 30, 1975—

(a) Except as provided in paragraph (b) of this section and hereinafter in this subdivision (i), if on any day during the calendar quarter the aggregate amount of undeposited taxes is $2,000 or more, the employer shall deposit the undeposited taxes as of such day in a Federal Reserve bank or authorized commercial bank within 7 calendar days after such day.

(b) Except as provided in paragraph (b) of this section, if—

(1) During the calendar quarter preceding the current calendar quarter the employer's aggregate taxes with respect to wages paid during such preceding calendar quarter were $25,000 or more, and

(2) At the close of any quarter-monthly period the aggregate amount of undeposited taxes is $2,000 or more,

the employer shall deposit the undeposited taxes in a Federal Reserve bank or authorized commercial bank within 3 banking days after the close of such quarter-monthly period. For purposes of determining the amount of undeposited taxes at the close of a quarter-monthly period, undeposited taxes with respect to wages paid during a prior quarter-monthly period shall not be taken into account if the employer has made a deposit with respect to such prior quarter-monthly period. The excess (if any) of a deposit over the actual taxes for a deposit period shall be applied in order of time to each of the employer's succeeding deposits with respect to the same period for which a return is required to be filed, until exhausted, to the extent that the amount by which the taxes for a subsequent deposit period exceed the deposit for such subsequent deposit period. For purposes of this subdivision (i)(b), "quarter-monthly period" means the first 7 days of a calendar month, the 8th day through the 15th day of a calendar month, the 16th day through the 22d day of a calendar month, or the portion of a calendar month following the 22d day of such month.

The aggregate amount of additions to tax imposed under section 6656 (by reason of failure to deposit in accordance with this subdivision (i)) with respect to any deposits of taxes required to be made during the first month of the current calendar quarter shall be the lesser of the aggregate amount of such additions to tax determined with respect to the requirements of (a) of this subdivision (i) or the requirements of (b) of this subdivision (i), regardless of which requirements govern the determination of the amounts of additions to tax for the other months of the calendar quarter.

(ii) In the case of a calendar month which begins after January 31, 1971, and before October 1, 1975—

(a) Except as provided in paragraph (b) of this section and hereinafter in this subdivision (ii), if at the close of any calendar month other than the last month of a period for which a return is required to be filed (hereinafter in this subparagraph referred to as a return period), the aggregate amount of taxes (as defined in subdivision (iii) of this subparagraph) is $200 or more, the employer shall deposit the undeposited taxes in a Federal Reserve bank or authorized commercial bank (see subparagraph (3)(iii) of this paragraph) within 15 days after the close of such calendar month. However, the preceding sentence shall not apply if the employer has made a deposit of taxes pursuant to (b) of this subdivision (ii) with respect to a quarter-monthly period which occurred during such month; or

(b) If at the close of any quarter-monthly period the aggregate amount of undeposited taxes is $2,000 or more, the employer shall deposit the undeposited taxes in accordance with the provisions of subdivision (i)(b) of this subparagraph, without regard to (1) thereof. An employer will be considered to have complied with the requirements of this subdivision (ii)(b) for a deposit with respect to the close of a quarter-monthly period if—

(1) His deposit is not less than 90 percent of the aggregate amount of the taxes with respect to wages paid during the period for which the deposit is made, and

(2) If such quarter-monthly period occurs in a month other than the last month of a return period, he deposits any underpayment with his first deposit which is otherwise required by this subdivision (ii) to be made after the 15th day of the following month.

* * * * * * * * * * *

(b) Exceptions—(1) Separate accounting. The provisions of this section are not applicable with respect to taxes required to be deposited under the separate accounting procedures provided in § 301.7512-1 of this chapter (Regulations on Procedure and Administration), which are applicable if notification is given by the district director of failure to comply with certain employment tax requirements.

* * * * * * * * * * *

Paragraph (a)(1)(iii) of § 31.6302(c)-1 is amended to read as follows:

§31.6302(c)-1 (Proposed Treasury Decision, published 9-29-77.) **Use of Government depositaries in connection with taxes under Federal Insurance Contributions Act and income tax withheld.**

(a) **Requirement—(1) In general.** * * *

(iii) As used in subdivisions (i) and (ii) of this subparagraph, the term "taxes" means—

(a) The employee tax withheld under section 3102,

(b) The employer tax under section 3111, and

(c) The income tax withheld under section 3402, including amounts withheld with respect to qualified State individual income taxes,

exclusive of taxes with respect to wages for domestic service in a private home of the employer or, if paid before April 1, 1971, wages for agricultural labor. In addition, with respect to wages paid after December 31, 1970, and before April 1, 1971, for agricultural labor, any taxes described in subparagraph (2)(ii) of this paragraph which are not required under such subparagraph to be deposited, and any income tax (including qualified State individual income tax) withheld under section 3402 with respect to such wages, shall be deemed to be "taxes" on and after April 1, 1971. For the requirements relating to the deposit and payment of withheld tax with respect to qualified State individual income taxes, see paragraph (d)(3)(iii) of §301.6361-1 of this chapter (Regulations on Procedure and Administration).

* * * * * * * * * * *

Lien for Taxes

Section 301.6321-1 is amended to read as follows:

§301.6321-1 (Proposed Treasury Decision, published 9-29-77.) **Lien for Taxes.**

If any person liable to pay any tax neglects or refuses to pay the same after demand, the amount (including any interest, additional amount, addition to tax, or assessable penalty, together with any costs that may accrue in addition thereto) shall be a lien in favor of the United States upon all property and rights to property, whether real or personal, tangible or intangible, belonging to such person. For purposes of section 6321 and this section, the term "any tax" shall include a State individual income tax which is a "quali-

Proposed Reg. § 301.6321-1

fied tax", as defined in paragraph (b) of §301.6361-4. The lien attaches to all property and rights to property belonging to such person at any time during the period of the lien, including any property or rights to property acquired by such person after the lien arises. Solely for purposes of sections 6321 and 6331, any interest in restricted land held in trust by the United States for an individual noncompetent Indian (and not for a tribe) shall not be deemed to be property, or a right to property, belonging to such Indian. For the method of allocating amounts collected pursuant to a lien between the Federal Government and a State or States imposing a qualified tax with respect to which the lien attached, see paragraph (f) of §301.6361-1. For the special lien for estate and gift taxes, see section 6324 and §301.6324-1.

Collection of State Individual Income Taxes

The following new section is inserted immediately after § 1.6302-2:

§1.6361-1 (Proposed Treasury Decision, published 9-29-77.) **Collection and administration of qualified State individual income taxes.**

Except as otherwise provided in §§301.6361-1 to 301.6365-2, inclusive, of this chapter (Regulations on Procedure and Administration), the provisions of this part under subtitle F of the Internal Revenue Code of 1954 relating to the collection and administration of the taxes imposed by chapter 1 of such Code on the incomes of individuals (or relating to civil or criminal sanctions with respect to such collection and administration) shall apply to the collection and administration of qualified State individual income taxes (as defined in section 6362 of such Code and the regulations thereunder) as if such taxes were imposed by chapter 1.

The following new section is inserted immediately after §31.6317:

§31.6361-1 (Proposed Treasury Decision, published 9-29-77.) **Collection and administration of qualified State individual income taxes.**

Except as otherwise provided in §§301.6361-1 to 301.6365-2, inclusive, of this chapter (Regulations on Procedure and Administration), the provisions of this part under subtitle F or chapter 24 of the Internal Revenue Code of 1954 relating to the collection and administration of the taxes imposed by chapter 1 of such Code on the incomes of individuals (or relating to civil or criminal sanctions with respect to such collection and administration) shall apply to the collection and administration of qualified State individual income taxes (as defined in section 6362 of such Code and the regulations thereunder) as if such taxes were imposed by chapter 1 or chapter 24.

* * * * * * * * * * * * *

The following new sections are inserted immediately after §301.6344:

§301.6361-1 (Proposed Treasury Decision, published 9-29-77.) **Collection and administration of qualified taxes.**

(a) **In general.** In the case of any State which has in effect a State agreement (as defined in paragraph (a) of §301.6361-4), the Commissioner of Internal Revenue shall collect and administer each qualified tax (as defined in paragraph (b) of §301.6361-4) of such State. No fee or other charge shall be imposed upon any State for the collection or administration of any qualified tax of such State or any other State. In any such case of collection and administration of qualified taxes, the provisions of subtitle F (relating to procedure and administration), subtitle G (relating to the Joint Committee on Taxation), and chapter 24 (relating to the collection of income tax at source on wages), and the provisions of regulations thereunder, insofar as such provisions relate to the collection and administration of the taxes imposed on the income of individuals by chapter 1 (and the civil and criminal sanctions provided by subtitle F, or by title 18 of the United States Code (relating to crimes and criminal procedure), with respect to such collection and administration) shall apply to the collection and administration of qualified taxes as if such taxes were imposed by chapter 1, except to the extent that the application of such provisions (and sanctions) are modified by regulations issued under subchapter E (as defined in paragraph (d) of §301.6361-4). Any extension of time which is granted for the making of a payment, or for the filing of any return, which relates to any Federal tax imposed by subtitle A (or by subtitle C with respect to filing a return) shall constitute automatically an extension of the same amount of time for the making of the corresponding payment or for the filing of the corresponding return relating to any qualified tax.

(b) **Returns of qualified taxes.** Every individual, estate, or trust which has liability for one or more qualified taxes for a taxable year—

(1) Shall file a Federal income tax return at the time prescribed pursuant to section 6072(a) (whether or not such return is required by section 6012), and shall file therewith on the prescribed form a return under penalties of perjury for each tax which is—

(i) A qualified resident tax imposed by a State of which the taxpayer was a resident, as defined in §301.6362-6, for any part of the taxable year;

(ii) A qualified nonresident tax imposed by a State within which was located the source or sources from which the taxpayer derived, while not a resident of such State and while not exempt from liability for the tax by reason of a reciprocal agreement between such State and the State of which he is a resident, 25 percent or more of his aggregate wage and other business income, as defined in paragraph (c) of §301.6362-5, for the taxable year; or

(iii) A qualified resident or nonresident tax with respect to which any amount was currently collected from the taxpayer's income (including collection by withholding on wages or by payment of estimated income tax), as provided in paragraph (f) of §301.6362-6, for any part of the taxable year; and

(2) Shall declare (in addition to the declaration required with respect to the return of the Federal income tax and in the place and manner prescribed by form or instructions thereto) under penalties of perjury that, to the best of the knowledge and belief of the taxpayer (or, in the case of an estate or trust, of the fiduciary who executes the Federal income tax return), he has no liability for any qualified tax for the taxable year other than any such liabilities returned with the Federal income tax return (pursuant to subparagraph (1) of this paragraph). Such declaration shall constitute a return indicating no liability with respect to each qualified tax other than any such tax for which liability is so returned. A Federal income tax return form which is filed but which does not contain such declaration shall constitute a Federal income tax return only if the taxpayer in fact has no liability for any qualified State tax for the taxable year.

(c) **Credits—(1) Credit for tax of another State or political subdivision—**(i) In general. A credit allowable under a qualified tax law against the tax imposed by such law for a taxpayer's tax liability to another State or a political subdivision of another State shall be allowed if the requirements of subdivision (ii) of this subparagraph are met, and if the credit meets the requirements of paragraph (c) of §301.6362-4. Such credit shall be allowed without regard to whether the tax imposed by the other State or subdivision thereof is a qualified tax, and without regard to whether such tax has been paid.

(ii) Substantiation of tax liability for which a credit is allowed. If the liability which gives rise to a credit of the type described in subdivision (i) of this subparagraph is with respect to a qualified tax, then the fact of such liability shall be substantiated by filing the return on which such liability is reported. If such liability is not with respect to a qualified tax, then the Commissioner may require a taxpayer who claims entitlement to such a credit to complete a form to be submitted with his return of the qualified tax against which the credit is claimed. On such form the taxpayer shall identify each of the other States (the liabilities to which were not substantiated as provided in the first sentence of this subdivision) or political subdivisions to which the taxpayer reported a liability for a tax giving rise to the credit, furnish the name or description of each such tax, state the amount of the liability so reported with respect to each such tax and the beginning and ending dates of the taxable period for which such liability was reported, and provide such other information as is requested in the form or in the instructions thereto. In addition, the taxpayer shall agree on such form to notify the Commissioner in the event that the amount of any tax liability (or portion thereof) which is claimed as giving rise to a credit of the type described in subdivision (i) of this subparagraph is changed or

Proposed Reg. §301.6361-1

adjusted, whether as a result of an amended return filed by the taxpayer, a determination by the jurisdiction imposing the tax, or in any other manner.

(2) **Credit for withheld qualified tax.** An individual from whose wages an amount is withheld on account of a qualified tax shall receive a credit for such amount against his aggregate liability for all such qualified taxes and the Federal income tax for the taxable year, whether or not such tax has been paid over to the Federal Government by the employer. The credit shall operate in the manner provided by section 31(a) of the Code and the regulations thereunder with respect to Federal income tax withholding.

(d) **Collection of qualified taxes at source on wages—(1) In general.** Except as otherwise provided in subparagraph (2) of this paragraph, every employer making payment of wages to an employee described in such subparagraph shall deduct and withhold upon such wages the amount prescribed with respect to the qualified tax designated in such subparagraph. The amounts prescribed for withholding with respect to each such qualified tax shall be published in Circular E (Employer's Tax Guide) or other appropriate Internal Revenue Service publications. See paragraph (f)(1) of §301.6362-7 with respect to civil and criminal penalties to which an employer shall be subject with respect to his responsibilities relating to qualified taxes.

(2) **Specific withholding requirements.** An employer shall deduct and withhold upon an employee's wages the amount prescribed with respect to a qualified tax with respect to which such employee is subject to the current collection provisions pursuant to paragraph (f) of §301.6362-6, unless:

(i) In the case of a qualified resident tax, the employee's services giving rise to the wages are performed in another State, and such other State or a political subdivision thereof imposes a nonresident tax on such employee with respect to which the withholding amount exceeds the prescribed withholding amount with respect to such qualified resident tax, and the State imposing such qualified resident tax grants a credit against it for such nonresident tax.

(ii) In the case of a qualified nonresident tax, either:

(A) Residents of the State in which the employee resides are exempt from liability for the qualified nonresident tax imposed by the State from sources within which his wage income is derived, by reason of an interstate compact or agreement to which the two States are parties, or

(B) The State in which the employee resides imposes a qualified resident tax on such employee with respect to which the prescribed withholding amounts exceed the prescribed withholding amounts with respect to the qualified nonresident tax imposed by the State from sources within which his wage income is derived, and the State in which he resides grants a credit against its qualified resident tax for such qualified nonresident tax.

If the nonresident tax described in subdivision (i) of this subparagraph is a qualified nonresident tax imposed by a State, then the reference in such subdivision to the State in which the services are performed shall be construed as a reference to the State from sources within which the wage income is derived, within the meaning of paragraph (d)(1) of §301.6362-5.

(3) **Forms, procedures, and returns relating to withholding with respect to qualified taxes—**

(i) Forms W-4 and W-4P. Forms W-4 (Employee's Withholding Allowance Certificate) and W-4P (Annuitant's Request for Income Tax Withholding), shall include information as to the State in which the employee resides, and shall be used for purposes of withholding with respect to both Federal and qualified taxes. An employee shall show on his Form W-4 the State in which he resides for purposes of this paragraph, and shall file a new Form W-4 within 10 days after he changes his State of residence. An employee who fails to meet either of the requirements set forth in the preceding sentence, with the intent to evade the withholding tax imposed with respect to a qualified tax, shall be subject to the penalty provided in section 7205 of the Code. An employer shall be responsible for determining the State within which are located the sources from which the employee's wage income is derived for purposes of this paragraph; and, if the employee does not file a Form W-4, the employer shall assume for such purposes that the employee resides in that State. When an employer and an employee enter into a voluntary withholding agreement pursuant to §31.3402(p)-1, the employer shall withhold the amount prescribed with respect to the qualified resident tax imposed by the State in which the employee resides, as indicated on Form W-4. Similarly, if an annuitant requests withholding with respect to his annuity payments pursuant to section 3402(o)(1)(B) of the Code, the payer shall withhold the whole dollar amount specified by the annuitant with respect to a qualified resident tax, provided that the combined withholding with respect to Federal and qualified taxes on each annuity payment shall be a whole dollar amount not less than $5, and that the net amount of any annuity payment received by the payee shall not be reduced to less than $10.

(ii) Forms W-2 and W-2P. Forms W-2 (Wage and Tax Statement) and W-2P (the corresponding form for annuities) shall show:

(A) The total amount withheld with respect to the Federal income tax;
(B) The total amount withheld with respect to qualified taxes;
(C) The name of each State imposing a qualified tax in which the employee (or annuitant) resided during the taxable year, as shown on Form W-4 (or W-4P);
(D) The name of each State imposing a qualified nonresident tax within which were located sources from which the employee's wage income was derived during a period of the taxable year in which he was not shown as a resident of such State on Form W-4, and the amount of the employee's wage income so derived; and
(E) The name of each State or locality that imposes an income tax which is not a qualified tax and with respect to which the employer withheld on the employee's wage income for the taxable year, and the amount of wage income with respect to which the employer so withheld.

(iii) Requirements relating to deposit and payment of withheld tax. Rules relating to the deposit and remittance of withheld Federal income and FICA taxes, including those prescribed in section 6302 of the Code and the regulations thereunder, shall apply also to amounts withheld with respect to qualified taxes. Thus, an employer's liability with respect to the deposit and payment of withheld taxes shall be for the combined amount of withholding with respect to Federal and qualified taxes. The Federal Tax Deposit form shall separately indicate:

(A) The combined total amount of Federal income, FICA, and qualified taxes withheld;
(B) The combined total amount of qualified taxes withheld and
(C) The total amount of qualified taxes withheld with respect to each electing State.

Data indicating the total amount of tax deposits processed by the Internal Revenue Service with respect to the qualified taxes of an electing State will be available to that State upon request on as frequent as a weekly basis. These data will be available no later than 10 working days after the end of the calendar week in which the deposits were processed by the Service.

(iv) Employment tax returns. Forms 941 (Employer's Quarterly Federal Tax Return), 941-E (Quarterly Return of Withheld Income Tax), 941-M (Employer's Monthly Federal Tax Return), 942 (Employer's Quarterly Tax Return for Household Employees), and 943 (Employer's Annual Tax Return for Agricultural Employees), shall indicate the total amount withheld with respect to each qualified tax, as directed by such forms or their instructions.

(e) **Criminal penalties.** A criminal offense committed with respect to a qualified tax shall be treated as a separate offense from a similar offense committed with respect to the Federal tax. Thus, for example, if a taxpayer willfully attempts to evade both the Federal tax and a qualified tax by failing to report a portion of his income, he shall be considered as having committed two criminal offenses, each subject to separate penalty under section 7201. See also §301.6362-7(f) with respect to criminal penalties.

(f) **Allocation of amounts collected with respect to tax and criminal fines—(1) In general.** The aggregate amount that has been collected from a taxpayer (including

Proposed Reg. §301.6361-1

amounts collected by withholding) in respect to liability fo both one or more qualified taxes and the Federal income tax for a taxable year shall be allocated among the Federal Government and the States imposing qualified taxes for which the taxpayer is liable in the proportion which the taxpayer's liability for each such tax bears to his aggregate liability for such year to all of such taxing jurisdictions with respect to such taxes. A reallocation shall be made either when an amount is collected from the taxpayer or his employer or is credited or refunded to the taxpayer, subsequent to the making of the initial allocation, or when a determination is made by the Commissioner that an error was made with respect to a previous allocation. However, any such allocation or reallocation shall not affect the amount of a taxpayer's or employer's liability to either jurisdiction, or the amount of the assessment and collection which may be made with respect to a taxpayer or employer. Accordingly, such allocations and reallocations shall not be taken into consideration for purposes of the application of statutes of limitation or provisions relating to interest, additions to tax, penalties, and criminal sanctions. See example (4) in subparagraph (4) of this paragraph. In addition, any such allocation or reallocation shall not affect the amount of the deduction to which a taxpayer is entitled under section 164 for a year in which he made a payment (including payments made by withholding) of an amount which was designated as being in respect of his liability for a qualified tax. However, to the extent that an amount which was paid by a taxpayer and designated as being in respect of his liability for a qualified tax is allocated or reallocated in such a manner as to apply it toward the taxpayer's liability for the Federal income tax, such allocation or reallocation shall be treated as a refund to the taxpayer of an amount paid in respect of a State income tax, and shall be included in the gross income of the taxpayer to the extent appropriate under section 111 and the regulations thereunder in the year in which the allocation or reallocation is made. See section 451 and the regulations thereunder. Similarly, to the extent that an amount which was paid by a taxpayer and designated as being in respect of his Federal income tax liability is allocated or reallocated in such a manner as to apply it toward his liability for a qualified tax, such allocation or reallocation shall be treated as a payment made by the taxpayer in respect of a State income tax, and shall be deductible under section 164 in the year in which the allocation or reallocation is made. The Internal Revenue Service shall notify the taxpayer in writing of any allocation or reallocation of tax liabilities in a proportion other than that of the respective tax liabilities shown on the taxpayer's returns.

(2) **Amounts of collections and liabilities.** For purposes of this paragraph, the aggregate amount that has been collected from a taxpayer or his employer in respect of tax liability shall include the amounts of interest provided in chapter 67, and additions to tax and assessable penalties provided in chapter 68, which are collected with respect to such tax; but shall not include criminal fines provided in chapter 75, or in title 18 of the United States Code, which are collected with respect to offenses relating to such tax. (See subparagraph (3) of this paragraph with respect to the treatment of such criminal fines.) However, for purposes of this paragraph, the amount of the taxpayer's liability for each tax shall exclude his liability for such interest, additions to tax, and assessable penalties with respect to such tax, and his liability for criminal fines imposed with respect to offenses relating to such tax. For purposes of this paragraph, the amount of the taxpayer's liability for each tax shall be computed by taking credits into account, except that there shall be no reduction for any amounts paid on account of such liability, whether by means of withholding, estimated tax payment, or otherwise.

(3) **Special rules relating to criminal fines.** (i) Except as otherwise provided in subdivision (ii) of this subparagraph, when a criminal charge is brought against a taxpayer with respect to a taxable year pursuant to chapter 75, or to title 18 of the United States Code, or to a corresponding provision of a qualified tax law, alleging that an offense was committed against the United States with respect to the Federal income tax or against a State with respect to a qualified tax, and an amount of money is collected by the Federal Government as a fine as a result of such charge, then the Federal Government shall remit an amount to each State, if any, which is an affected jurisdiction. The amount remitted to each such State shall bear the same proportion to the total amount collected as a fine as the taxpayer's liability with respect to the qualified taxes on that State bears to

the aggregate of the taxpayer's income tax liabilities to all affected jurisdictions for the taxable year, as determined under subparagraphs (1) and (2) of this paragraph. For purposes of this subparagraph, an affected jurisdiction is (A) a jurisdiction with respect to the tax of which a criminal charge described in the preceding sentence was brought for the taxable year, or (B) a jurisdiction with respect to the Federal income tax or the qualified tax of which the acts or omissions alleged in such a criminal charge would constitute the basis for the bringing of a criminal charge for the same taxable year. However, in no case shall the amount received by an affected State, or the amount of the excess of the amount received by the Federal Government over the amount of its remissions to States, with respect to a fine exceed the maximum fine prescribed by statute for the offense against that jurisdiction with respect to which a criminal charge was brought, or with respect to which the bringing of a criminal charge could have been supported on the basis of the acts or omissions alleged in a criminal charge brought. For purposes of this subparagraph, the amount collected as a fine as a result of a criminal charge shall include amounts paid in settlement of an actual or potential liability for a fine, amounts paid pursuant to a conviction and amounts paid pursuant to a plea of guilty or nolo contendere.

(ii) If a criminal charge described in the first sentence of subdivision (i) of this subparagraph is actually brought with respect to the income tax of every affected jurisdiction with respect to the taxable year, and if a Court adjudicates on the merits the taxpayer's liability for a fine to each such jurisdiction, and includes in its decree a direction of the amount, if any, to be paid as a fine to each such jurisdiction, then that decree shall govern the allocation of the amount of money collected by the Federal Government as a fine with respect to the taxable year.

(4) **Examples.** The application of this paragraph may be illustrated by the following examples:

Example (1). The total combined amount of State X qualified tax and Federal income tax collected from A, a resident of State X, for the taxable year is $5,100. The amounts of A's liabilities for such taxes for that year are $800 to State X and $4,000 to the Federal Government. Since A's tax liability to State X is one-sixth of the combined tax liability ($4,800), one-sixth ($50) of the amount to be refunded to A ($300) is chargeable against State X's account, and five-sixths ($250) is chargeable against the Federal Government's account.

Example (2). Assume the same facts as in example (1) except that the total amount collected from A is $4,500. Since A's liabilities for the State X tax and the Federal tax are one-sixth and five-sixths, respectively, of the combined tax liability, the Federal Government shall pay over to State X one-sixth ($750) of the amount actually collected from A, and the Federal Government shall retain five-sixths ($3,750).

Example (3). The total amount of State X qualified tax, State Y qualified tax, and Federal income tax collected from B, a resident of State X who is employed in State Y, for the taxable year is $5,500. The amounts of B's liabilities for such taxes for that year are: $250 for the State X tax (after allowance of a credit for State Y's qualified tax), $750 for the State Y tax, and $4,000 for the Federal tax. Since B's liability for the State X tax ($250) is 5 percent of the combined tax liability ($5,000), his liability for the State Y tax ($750) is 15 percent of such combined liability, and his liability for the Federal tax ($4,000) is 80 percent of such combined liability, the total amount to be refunded to B ($500) shall be chargeable in the following manner: 5 percent ($25) against State X's account, 15 percent ($75) against State Y's account, and 80 percent ($400) against the Federal Government's account.

Example (4). C is liable for $2,000 in Federal income tax and $500 in State X qualified tax (a resident tax) for the taxable year. However, on his Federal income tax return for such year, C erroneously described himself as a resident of State Y (which does not have a qualified tax), and he filed with such return his declaration to the effect that he had no qualified tax liability for the year. Accordingly, C paid only $2,000 for his Fed-

Proposed Reg. § 301.6361-1

eral tax liability, and such amount was retained in the account of the Federal Government. Subsequently, C's error is discovered. The amount collected by the Federal Government from C for such year must be allocated between the Federal Government and State X in proportion to C's tax liability to both. Accordingly, the Federal Government must pay over to State X the amount of $400 (which is $1/5$ ($500/$2,500) of the $2,000 collected. If the Federal Government collects from C the additional $500 owed, it will retain $400 of such amount and pay the remaining $100 to State X. Similarly, if the Federal Government collects from C any interest, or any additions to tax or assessable penalties under chapter 68, $4/5$ of the amount of such collections shall be retained by the Federal Government, and $1/5$ of such amount shall be paid over to State X. However, notwithstanding the allocation of the funds between the taxing jurisdictions, C's liability for the $500 retains its character as a liability for State X tax. Therefore, any interest, additions to tax, or assessable penalties imposed with respect to the State X tax shall be imposed with respect to C's full $500 liability for such tax, notwithstanding the fact that amounts collected with respect to such items shall be allocated $4/5$ to the Federal Government.

Example (5). A criminal charge is brought against D pursuant to chapter 75, alleging that he willfully evaded the payment of Federal income tax by failing to report interest income derived from obligations of the United States. D enters a plea of nolo contendere to the charge and pays $2,500 as a fine to the Federal Government. The act alleged in the criminal charge would not support the bringing of a criminal charge under a State law corresponding to chapter 75, or to title 18 of the United States Code, with respect to the qualified tax of any State; accordingly, the United States is the only affected jurisdiction, and no remittances shall be made to any State with respect to the amount collected by the Federal Government as a fine.

Example (6). A criminal charge is brought against E pursuant to chapter 75, alleging that he willfully attempted to evade the assessment of liability for both Federal income tax and the qualified tax of State X by filing false and fraudulent income tax returns. E's case is settled upon the condition that he pay a fine in the amount of $5,000. As determined pursuant to subparagraph (2) of this paragraph, E's liabilities for the taxable year are in the amounts of $7,200 to the Federal Government and $800 to State X. Accordingly, after the Federal Government collects the fine, $500 ($5,000 × $800/$8,000) is remitted to State X.

Example (7). Assume the same facts as in example (6), except that E is tried and convicted on both charges, and pursuant to court decree he pays to the United States a fine of $6,000 with respect to each charge, or a total of $12,000. Because a criminal charge was brought with respect to each affected jurisdiction, and the allocation of the total amount paid as a fine was specifically imposed by a court decree, the direction of the Court shall govern the allocation. Accordingly, after the Federal Government collects the fines it pays over $6,000 to the account of State X.

§301.6361-2 (Proposed Treasury Decision, published 9-29-77.) **Judicial and administrative proceedings; Federal representation of State interests.**

(a) **Civil proceedings—(1) General rule.** Any person shall have the same right to bring or contest a civil action, and to obtain review thereof, with respect to a qualified tax (including the current collection thereof) in the same court or courts which would be available to him, and pursuant to the same requirements and procedures to which he would be subject, under chapter 76 (relating to judicial proceedings), and under title 28 of the United States Code (relating to the judiciary and judicial procedure), if the tax were imposed by section 1 or chapter 24 of the Internal Revenue Code. For purposes of this section, the term "person" includes the Federal Government. Except as provided in subparagraph (2) of this paragraph, to the extent that the preceding sentence provides judicial procedures (including review procedures) with respect to any matter, such procedures shall replace civil judicial procedures under State law.

(2) **Exception.** The right or power of the courts of any State to pass on matters involving the constitution of such State is unaffected by any provision of this paragraph; however, the jurisdiction of a State court in such matters shall not extend beyond the

issue of constitutionality. Thus, if in a case involving the validity of a qualified tax statute under the State constitution, the State court holds such statute constitutional, such court shall not proceed to decide the amount of the tax liability.

(b) **Criminal proceedings.** Only the Federal Government shall have the right to bring a criminal action with respect to a qualified tax (including the current collection thereof). Such an action shall be brought in the same court or courts which would be available to the Federal Government, and pursuant to the same requirements and procedures to which the Federal Government would be subject, if the tax were imposed by section 1 or chapter 24 of the Internal Revenue Code.

(c) **Administrative proceedings.** Any person shall have the same rights in administrative proceedings of the Internal Revenue Service with respect to a qualified tax (including the current collection thereof) which would be available to him, and shall be subject to the same administrative requirements and procedures to which he would be subject, if the tax were imposed by section 1 or chapter 24 of the Internal Revenue Code.

(d) **United States representation of State interests—(1) General rule.** Except as provided in subparagraphs (2) and (3) of this paragraph, the Federal Government shall appear on behalf of any State the qualified tax of which it collects (or did collect for the year in issue), and shall represent such State's interests in any administrative or judicial proceeding, either civil or criminal in nature, which relates to the administration and collection of such qualified tax, in the same manner as it represents the interests of the United States in corresponding proceedings involving Federal income tax matters.

(2) **Exceptions.** The Federal Government shall not so represent a State's interests either—

(i) In proceedings in a State court involving the constitution of such State, to the extent of such constitutional issue, or

(ii) In proceedings in any court involving the relationship between the United States and the State, to the extent of the issue pertaining to such relationship, if either:

(A) The proceeding is one which is initiated by the United States against the State, or by the State against the United States, and no individual (except in his official capacity as a governmental official) is an original party to the proceeding, or

(B) The proceeding is not one described in (A), but the State elects to represent its own interests to the extent permissible under this subdivision.

(3) **Finality of Federal administrative determinations.** State and local government officials and employees may not review Federal administrative determinations concerning tax liabilities of, refunds owed to, or criminal prosecutions of, individuals with respect to qualified taxes. See, however, §301.6363-3 relating to State administration of a qualified tax with respect to transition years. If requested by an electing State, the Commissioner or his delegate may, under terms and conditions set forth in an agreement with such State, permit such State to carry on operations supplementary to the Federal administration of the State's qualified tax (including supplemental audits or examinations of tax returns by State audit personnel), but all administrative determinations shall be made by the Federal Government without review by the State. An agreement which permits supplemental audits or examinations of tax returns by State audit personnel shall provide that the audits and examinations shall be conducted under the supervision and control of the Commissioner or his delegate, who shall have the authority to determine which returns shall be audited and when the audits shall occur. Also, such agreements shall provide that the results of any such supplemental audit shall be referred to the Commissioner or his delegate for final administrative determination. The Commissioner or his delegate shall, to the extent permitted by law, allow an electing State reasonable access to tax returns and other appropriate records and information relating to its qualified tax for the purpose of conducting any such supplemental operations. In addition, the Secretary or his delegate shall permit an electing State to inspect the workpapers which are compiled in the course of verification by the Treasury Department of the correctness of the

Proposed Reg. §301.6361-2

accounting by which the amounts of the actual net collections attributable to the electing State's qualified taxes are determined.

§301.6361-3 (Proposed Treasury Decision, published 9-29-77.) **Transfers to States.**

(a) **Periodic transfers.** In general, amounts collected by the Federal Government which are allocable to qualified taxes (including criminal fines which are required to be paid to a State, as determined under paragraph (f)(3) of §301.6361-1) shall be promptly transferred to each State imposing such a tax. Transfers of such amounts, based on percentages of estimated Federal collections, shall be made not less frequently than every third business day unless the State agrees to accept transfers at less frequent intervals.

(b) **Determination of amounts of transfers.** The amounts allocable to the qualified taxes of each State for purposes of periodic transfer shall be determined as a percentage of the estimated aggregate net individual income tax collections made by the Federal Government. For purposes of this paragraph, the "aggregate net individual income tax collections" shall include amounts collected on account of the Federal individual income tax and all qualified taxes by all means (including withholding, tax returns, and declarations of estimated tax), and shall be reduced to the extent of any liability to taxpayers for credits or refunds by reason of overpayments of such taxes. The percentage of the estimated amount of such collections which is allocated to each State shall be based on an estimate which is to be made by the Office of Tax Analysis prior to the beginning of each calendar year as to what portion of the estimated aggregate net individual income tax collections for the forthcoming year will be attributable to the qualified taxes of that State. Each State will be notified prior to the beginning of each calendar year of the amount which it is estimated that the State will receive by application of that percentage for the year. However, the Office of Tax Analysis shall, from time to time throughout the calendar year, revise the percentage estimates when such a revision is, in the opinion of that office, necessary to conform such estimates to the actual receipts. When such a revision is made, the payments to the State will be adjusted accordingly.

(c) **Adjustment of difference between actual collections and periodic transfers.** At least once annually the Secretary or his delegate shall determine the difference between the aggregate amount of the actual net collections made (taking into account credits, refunds, and amounts received by withholding with respect to which a tax return is not filed) which is attributable to each State's qualified taxes during the preceding year and the aggregate amount actually transferred to such State based on estimates during such year. The amount of such difference, as so determined, shall be a charge against, or an addition to, the amounts otherwise determined to be payable to the State.

(d) **Recipient of tranferred funds.** All funds transferred pursuant to section 6361(c) and paragraph (a) of this section shall be transferred by the Federal Government to the State official designated by the Governor to receive such funds in the State agreement pursuant to paragraph (d)(5) of §301.6363-1, unless the Governor notifies the Secretary or his delegate in writing of the designation of a different State official to receive the funds.

§301.6361-4 (Proposed Treasury Decision, published 9-29-77.) **Definitions.**

For purposes of the regulations in this part under subchapter E of chapter 64 of the Internal Revenue Code of 1954, relating to collection and administration of State individual income taxes—

(a) **State agreement.** The term "State agreement" means an agreement between a State and the Federal Government which was entered into pursuant to section 6363 and the regulations thereunder, and which provides for the Federal collection and administration of the qualified tax or taxes of that State.

(b) **Qualified tax.** The term "qualified tax" means a tax which is a "qualified State individual income tax", as defined in section 6362 (including subsection (f)(1) thereof, which requires that a State agreement be in effect) and the regulations thereunder.

(c) **Chapters and subtitles.** References in regulations in this part under subchapter E to chapters and subtitles are to chapters and subtitles of the Internal Revenue Code of 1954, unless otherwise indicated.

(d) **Subchapter E.** The term "subchapter E" means subchapter E of chapter 64 of the Internal Revenue Code of 1954, relating to collection and administration of State individual income taxes, as amended from time to time.

§301.6361-5 (Proposed Treasury Decision, published 9-29-77.) **Effective date of section 6361.**

Section 6361 shall take effect on the first January 1 which is more than 1 year after the first date on which at least one State has filed a notice of election with the Secretary or his delegate to enter into a State agreement. For purposes of this section, a notice of election shall be deemed to have been filed by a State only if there is no defect in either the State's notice of election or the State's tax law of which the Secretary notified the Governor pursuant to paragraph (c) of §301.6363-1, and which has not been retroactively cured under the provisions of such paragraph.

§301.6362-1 (Proposed Treasury Decision, published 9-29-77.) **Types of qualified tax.**

(a) **In general.** A qualified tax may be either a "qualified resident tax" within the meaning of paragraph (b) of this section, or a "qualified nonresident tax" within the meaning of paragraph (c) of this section.

(b) **Qualified resident tax.** A tax imposed by a State on the income of individuals, estates, and trusts which are residents of such State within the meaning of section 6362(e) and §301.6362-6 shall be a "qualified resident tax" if it is either:

(1) A tax based on Federal taxable income which meets the requirements of section 6362(b), (e), and (f), and of §§301.6362-2, 301.6362-6, and 301.6362-7; or

(2) A tax which is a percentage of the Federal tax and which meets the requirements of section 6362(c), (e), and (f), and of §§301.6362-3, 301.6362-6, and 301.6362-7.

(c) **Qualified nonresident tax.** A tax imposed by a State on the wage and other business income of individuals who are not residents of such State within the meaning of section 6362(e)(1) and paragraph (b) of §301.6362-6 shall be a "qualified nonresident tax" if it meets the requirements of section 6362(d), (e), and (f), and of §§301.6362-5, 302.6362-6, and 301.6362-7.

§301.6362-2 (Proposed Treasury Decision, published 9-29-77.) **Qualified resident tax based on taxable income.**

(a) **In general.** A tax meets the requirements of section 6362(b) and this section only if it is imposed on the amount of the taxable income, as defined in section 63, of the individual, estate, or trust, adjusted—

(1) By subtracting an amount equal to the amount of the taxpayer's interest on obligations of the United States which was included in his gross income for the taxable year;

(2) By adding an amount equal to the amount of the taxpayer's net State income tax deduction, as defined in paragraph (a) of §301.6362-4, for the taxable year;

(3) By adding an amount equal to the amount of the taxpayer's net tax-exempt income, as defined in paragraph (b) of §301.6362-4, for the taxable year; and

(4) If a credit is allowed against the tax in accordance with paragraph (b)(3) of this section for sales tax imposed by the State or a political subdivision thereof, by adding an amount equal to the amount of the taxpayer's deduction under section 164(a)(4) for such sales tax.

The tax may provide for either a single rate or multiple rates which vary with the amount of taxable income, as adjusted.

(b) **Permitted adjustments.** A tax which otherwise meets the requirements of paragraph (a) of this section shall not be deemed to fail to meet such requirements solely because it provides for one or more of the following adjustments:

(1) A credit meeting the requirements of paragraph (c) of §301.6362-4 is allowed

Proposed Reg. §301.6362-2

against the tax for the taxpayer's income tax liability to another State or a political subdivision thereof.

(2) A tax is imposed on the amount taxed under section 56 (relating to the minimum tax for tax preferences).

(3) A credit is allowed against the tax for all or a portion of any general sales tax imposed by the State or a political subdivision thereof with respect to sales either to the taxpayer or to one or more of his dependents.

(c) **Method of making mandatory adjustments.** The mandatory adjustments provided in paragraph (a) of this section shall be made directly to taxable income. Except as provided in paragraph (c)(2) of §301.6362-4, no account shall be taken of any reduction or increase in the Federal adjusted gross income which would result from the exclusion from, or inclusion in, gross income of the items which are the subject of the adjustments. Thus, for example, when for purposes of the calculation the taxpayer's Federal taxable income is adjusted to reflect the exclusion from gross income of interest on obligations of the United States, no change shall be made in the amount of the taxpayer's deduction for medical expenses, or in the amount of his charitable contribution base, even though such amounts would ordinarily depend upon the amount of adjusted gross income.

§301.6362-3 (Proposed Treasury Decision, published 9-29-77.) **Qualified resident tax which is a percentage of Federal tax.**

(a) **In general.** A tax meets the requirements of section 6362(c) and this section only if:

(1) The tax is imposed as a single specified percentage of the excess of the taxes imposed by chapter 1 over the sum of the credits allowable under part IV of subchapter A of chapter 1 (other than the credits allowable under sections 31 and 39), and

(2) The amount of the tax is decreased by the amount of the decrease in such liability which would result from excluding from the taxpayer's gross income an amount equal to the amount of interest on obligations of the United States which was included in his gross income for the taxable year.

(b) **Permitted adjustments.** A tax which otherwise meets the requirements of paragraph (a) of this section shall not be deemed to fail to meet such requirements solely because it provides for one or more of the following three adjustments:

(1) The amount of a taxpayer's liability for tax is increased by the amount of the increase in such liability which would result from including in such taxpayer's gross income all of the following:

(i) An amount equal to the amount of his net State income tax deduction, as defined in paragraph (a) of §301.6362-4, for the taxable year;

(ii) An amount equal to the amount of his net tax-exempt income, as defined in paragraph (b) of §301.6362-4, for the taxable year, and

(iii) If a credit is allowed against the tax under paragraph (b)(3) of this section for sales tax imposed by the State or a political subdivision thereof, an amount equal to the amount of his deduction under section 164(a)(4) for such sales tax.

(2) A credit meeting the requirements of paragraph (c) of §301.6362-4 is allowed against the tax for the income tax of another State or a political subdivision thereof.

(3) A credit is allowed against the tax for all or a portion of any general sales tax imposed by the State or a political subdivision thereof with respect to sales either to the taxpayer or to one or more of his dependents.

(c) **Method of making adjustments.** Except as specifically provided in paragraphs (a)(2) and (b)(1) of this section and in paragraph (c)(2) if §301.6362-4, no account shall be taken of any reduction or increase in the Federal adjusted gross income which would result from the exclusion from, or inclusion in, gross income of the items which are the subject of the adjustments provided in those paragraphs. Thus, for example, when for purposes of the calculation the taxpayer's Federal income tax liability is adjusted to reflect the exclusion from gross income of interest on obligations of the United States, no change shall be made in the amount of the taxpayer's deduction for medical expenses, or in the amount of his charitable contribution base, even though such amounts would ordinarily depend upon the amount of adjusted gross income. Also, when calculating the adjusted Federal tax liability to which the rate of the State tax is to be applied, no adjustment shall be made in the amount of any credit against Federal tax to which a taxpayer is entitled.

§301.6362-4 (Proposed Treasury Decision, published 9-29-77.) **Rules for adjustments relating to qualified resident taxes.**

(a) Net State income tax deduction. For purposes of section 6362(b)(1)(B) and (c)(3)(B), and §§301.6362-2 and 301.6362-3, the "net State income tax deduction" shall be the excess (if any) of (1) the amount deducted from income under section 164(a)(3) as taxes paid to a State or to a political subdivision thereof, over (2) the amounts included in income as recoveries of prior income taxes which were paid to a State or to a political subdivision thereof and which had been deducted under section 164(a)(3).

(b) Net tax-exempt income. For purposes of section 6362(b)(1)(C) and (c)(3)(A) and §§301.6362-2 and 301.6362-3, the "net tax-exempt income" shall be the excess (if any) of:

(1) The sum of (i) the interest on obligations described in section 103(a)(1) other than obligations of the State imposing the tax and the political subdivisions thereof, and (ii) the interest on obligations described in such section of such State and the political subdivisions thereof which under the law of the State is subject to the tax; over

(2) The sum of (i) the amount of deductions allocable to the interest described in subparagraph (1)(i) or (ii) of this paragraph which is disallowed pursuant to section 265 and the regulations thereunder, and (ii) the amount of the adjustment to basis allocable to such obligations which is required to be made for the taxable year under section 1016(a)(5) or (6).

For purposes of subparagraph (1)(ii) of this paragraph, a State may, at its option, subject to the tax the interest from all, none, or some of its section 103(a)(1) obligations and those of its political subdivisions. For example, a State may subject to tax all of such obligations other than those which it or its political subdivisions issued prior to a specified date, which may be the date that subchapter E became applicable to the State.

(c) Credits for taxes of other jurisdictions—(1) In general. A State tax law that provides for a credit, purusant to section 6362(b)(2)(B) or (C) or section 6362(c)(4), and paragraph (b)(1) of §301.6362-2 or paragraph (b)(2) of §301.6362-3, for income tax of another State or a political subdivision thereof shall provide that, in the case of each taxpayer, the amount of the credit shall equal the amount of his liability with respect to such other jurisdiction's tax for the taxable year which runs concurrently with, or which ends in, the taxable year used by the taxpayer for purposes of the State tax which provides for the credit. Such a credit may be allowed with respect to every income tax (whether or not qualified) imposed on the taxpayer by another State or a political subdivision thereof, or only with respect to certain of such taxes. However, for purposes of this paragraph, the amount which is treated as being the amount of the taxpayer's liability with respect to any such tax imposed by another jurisdiction shall not exceed the amount of liability for such tax which is both—

(A) Reported to the taxing authorities responsible for collecting such other jurisdiction's tax, and

(B) Substantiated pursuant to the requirements of paragraph (c)(1)(ii) of §301.6361-1.

(2) Limitation. The amount of any credit allowed for the taxable year pursuant to this paragraph shall not exceed the product of the amount of the resident tax against which the credit is allowed, as computed without subtracting any such credit, multiplied by a fraction the numerator of which is the amount of income subject to tax by both the State imposing the resident tax against which the credit is allowed and the other jurisdiction whose tax is being credited, and the denominator of which is the amount of income subject to tax by the State imposing the resident tax against which the credit is allowed. For purposes of the preceding sentence, "income subject to tax" means the amount of the taxpayer's adjusted gross income which is taken into account for purposes of comput-

Proposed Reg. §301.6362-4

ing tax liability; in the case of a qualified resident tax, an appropriate modification shall be made to take into account any adjustments which are made pursuant to paragraph (a)(1) and (3) of §301.6362-2, or pursuant to paragraph (a)(2) or (b)(1)(ii) of §301.6362-3.

(3) **Examples.** The application of this paragraph may be illustrated by the following examples:

Example (1). (i) A, a calendar-year, cash-basis taxpayer, is a resident of State X throughout the taxable year. For such year, his adjusted gross income for Federal income tax purposes consists of $24,000, consisting of $3,000 derived from employment in State X, $5,000 derived from employment in State Y, $15,000 derived from employment in State Z, and $1,000 in interest income from United States savings bonds. In addition, he received net tax-exempt income in the amount of $2,000. For the taxable year, he incurs liabilities of $200 for the State Y nonresident income tax, and $1,400 for the State Z nonresident income tax. State X, which has in effect a State agreement for the taxable year, imposes a resident tax against which credits are allowed for the nonresident taxes imposed by States Y and Z. Without taking any such credits into account, however, the amount of A's liability for such resident tax would be $1,500. A properly reports his nonresident income tax liabilities to States Y and Z at the same time that he files his return with respect to the State X tax, and he substantiates on such return his liabilities to States Y and Z.

(ii) The amount of A's income subject to tax in State X is $25,000 (his adjusted gross income of $24,000, minus the United States savings bond income of $1,000, plus the net tax-exempt income of $2,000). The amount of the credit allowable against the State X resident tax for the amount of A's liability with respect to the State Y nonresident tax is calculated as follows: The maximum amount of credit is the actual amount of his liability to Y, or $200. Under subparagraph (2) of this paragraph, the amount of the credit is limited to $300 ($1,500 × $5,000/$25,000). Thus, such limit has no effect, and the full $200 is allowable as a credit against A's liability for the resident tax of State X. The amount of the credit allowable against the State X resident tax for the amount of A's liability with respect to the State Z nonresident tax is calculated as follows: The maximum amount of the credit is the actual amount of his liability to Z, or $1,400. Under subparagraph (2) of this paragraph, the amount of the credit is limited to $900 ($1,500 × $15,000/$25,000). Thus, such limit has the effect of reducing to $900 the amount of the credit allowable for tax of State Z against A's liability for the resident tax of State X.

Example (2). (i) B, a calendar-year, cash-basis taxpayer, is a resident of State X employed in State Y through March 14, 1977. On March 15, 1977, B becomes a resident of State Z and remains a resident of such State through the remainder of 1977. For 1977, the amount of B's adjusted gross income for Federal income tax purposes is $20,000, consisting of $6,000 derived from employment in State Y which B held during the period of his residence in State X, $12,000 derived from employment in State Z which B held during the period of his residence in State Z, and $2,000 in interest income from various bank accounts. During 1977, B has no interest income from United States obligations, and no tax-exempt income. For 1977, B incurs a liability of $200 to State Y on account of its nonresident income tax imposed with respect to his $6,000 of income derived from sources within that State. State Z, which has in effect a State agreement for 1977, imposes a resident income tax on B which, if B had been a resident of State Z for all 1977, would amount to $1,200 prior to the allowance of any credits under this paragraph. However, by reason of paragraph (e)(1) of §301.6362-6, B's liability for the resident tax of State Z, before taking into account credits allowed under this paragraph, is reduced to $960 ($1,200 × 292/365, or 4/5). Furthermore, State Z allows a credit for the nonresident tax imposed by State Y.

(ii) The amount of the credit allowable against the State Z resident tax for the amount of B's liability with respect to the State Y nonresident tax is calculated as follows: The maximum amount of the credit is the amount of his actual liability to State Y, or $200. Under subparagraph (2) of this paragraph, the amount of the credit is limited to $288 ($960 × $6,000/$20,000). Thus, such limit has no effect, and the full $200 is allowable as a credit for tax of State Y against B's liability for the resident tax of State Z.

§301.6362-5 (Proposed Treasury Decision, published 9-29-77.) **Qualified nonresident tax.**

(a) **In general.** A tax meets the requirements of section 6362(d) and this section only if:

(1) The tax is imposed by a State which simultaneously imposes a resident tax meeting the requirements of section 6362(b) and §301.6362-2 or of section 6362(c) and §301.6362-3;

(2) The tax is required to be computed in accordance with either the method prescribed in paragraph (b) of this section or another method of which the Secretary or his delegate approves upon submission by the State of the laws pertaining to the tax;

(3) The tax is imposed only on the wage and other business income derived from sources within such State (as defined in paragraph (d) of this section), of all individuals each of whom derives 25 percent or more of his aggregate wage and other business income for the taxable year from sources within such State while he is neither (i) a resident of such State within the meaning of section 6362(e) and §301.6362-6, nor (ii) exempt from liability for the tax by reason of a reciprocal agreement between such State and the State of which he is a resident within the meaning of those provisions;

(4) The amount of the tax imposed with respect to any individual does not exceed the amount of tax for which such individual would be liable under the qualified resident tax imposed by such State if he were a resident of the State for the period during which he earned wage or other business income from sources within the State, and if his taxable income for such period were an amount equal to the sum of the zero bracket amount (within the meaning of section 63(d) and determined as if he had been a resident of the State for such period) and the excess of:

(i) The amount of his wage and other business income derived from sources within the State, over

(ii) That portion of the sum of the zero bracket amount and the nonbusiness deductions (i.e., all deductions from adjusted gross income allowable in computing taxable income) taken into account for purposes of the State's qualified resident tax which bears the same ratio to such sum as the amount described in subdivision (i) of this subparagraph bears to his total adjusted gross income for the year; and

(5) For purposes of the tax, wage or other business income is considered as being the income of the individual whose income it is for purposes of section 61.

(b) **Approved method of computing liability for qualified nonresident tax.** A tax satisfies the requirement of paragraph (a)(2) of this section if the amount of the tax is computed either as a percentage of the excess of the amount described in paragraph (a)(4)(i) of this section over the amount described in paragraph (a)(4)(ii) of this section, or by application of progressive rates to such excess.

(c) **Definition of wage and other business income.** For purposes of section 6362(d) and this section, the term "wage and other business income" means the following types of income:

(1) Wages, as defined in section 3401(a) and the regulations thereunder, but for these purposes:

(i) The amount of wages shall exclude amounts which are treated as wages under section 3402(o) or (p) (relating to supplemental unemployment compensation benefits, annuity payments, and voluntary withholding agreements), and amounts which are treated as disability payments to the extent that they are excluded from gross income for Federal income tax purposes, pursuant to section 105(d), and

(ii) The amount of wages shall be reduced by those expenses which are directly related to the earning of such wages and with respect to which deductions are properly claimed from gross income in computing adjusted gross income;

(2) Net earnings from self-employment, as defined in section 1402(a); and

(3) The distributive share of income of any trade or business carried on by a trust,

Proposed Reg. §301.6362-5

estate, or electing small business corporation (as defined in section 1371(a) and the regulations thereunder), to the extent that such share:

(i) Is includible in the gross income of the taxpayer for the taxable year, and

(ii) Would constitute net earnings from self-employment if the trade or business were carried on by a partnership.

For purposes of this subparagraph, "distributive share" includes the income of a trust or estate which is taxable to the taxpayer as a beneficiary under applicable Federal income tax rules, and the undistributed taxable income of an electing small business corporation which is taxable to the taxpayer as a shareholder under section 1373.

(d) **Income derived from sources within a State**—(1) **Income attributable primarily to services.** Except as otherwise provided by Federal statute (see paragraphs (h), (i), and (j) of §301.6362-7), wage income and other business income (net earnings from self-employment or distributive shares) which is attributable more to services performed by the taxpayer than to a capital investment of the taxpayer shall be considered to have been derived from sources within a State only if the services of the taxpayer which give rise to the income are performed in such State. If for a taxable year only a portion of the taxpayer's services giving rise to the income from one employment, trade, or business is performed within a State, then it shall be presumed that the amount of income from such employment, trade, or business which is derived from sources within that State equals that portion of the total income derived from such employment, trade, or business for the year which the amount of time spent by the taxpayer for such year performing services with respect to that employment, trade, or business in that State bears to the aggregate amount of time spent by the taxpayer for such year performing all of such services. However, the presumption stated in the preceding sentence may be rebutted in the event that the taxpayer proves, by use of detailed records, that the correct allocation of his income is otherwise.

(2) **Income attributable primarily to investment.** Except as otherwise provided by Federal statute (see paragraph (j) of §301.6362-7), business income (net earnings from self-employment or distributive shares) which is attributable more to a capital investment of the taxpayer than to services performed by the taxpayer shall be considered to have been derived from sources within the State, if any, in which the significant activities of the trade or business are conducted. If for the taxable year only a portion of the significant activities conducted with respect to one trade or business is conducted within a certain State, then the portion of the taxpayer's total income for the year from such trade or business which is considered to be derived from sources within that State shall be computed as follows:

(i) **Allocation by records.** The portion of the taxpayer's total income from the trade or business which is considered to be derived from sources within the State shall be the portion which is allocable to such sources according to the records of the taxpayer or of the partnership, trust, estate, or electing small business corporation from which his income is derived, provided that the taxpayer establishes to the satisfaction of the district director, when requested to do so, that those records fairly and equitably reflect the income which is allocable to sources within the State. An allocation made pursuant to this subdivision shall be based on the location of the significant activities of the trade or business, and not on the location at which the taxpayer's personal services are performed.

(ii) **Allocation by formula.** If the taxpayer (or the trade or business) does not keep records meeting the requirements of subdivision (i) of this subparagraph, or if the taxpayer fails to meet the burden of proof set forth therein, then the amount of the taxpayer's income from the trade or business which is considered to be derived from sources within the State shall be determined by multiplying the total of his income (as defined in paragraphs (c)(2) and (3) of this section) from the trade or business for the taxable year by the percentage which is the average of these three percentages:

(A) **Property percentage.** The percentage computed by dividing the average of the value, at the beginning and end of the taxable year, of real and tangible personal property connected with the taxpayer's trade or business and located within the State, by the average of the value, at the beginning and end of the taxable year, of all such property located both within and without the State. For this purpose, real property shall include real property rented to the taxpayer in connection with the trade or business, or rented to the trade or business.

(B) **Payroll percentage.** The percentage computed by dividing the total wages, salaries, and other compensation for personal services which is paid or incurred during the taxable year to employees in connection with the taxpayer's trade or business, and which would be treated as derived by such employees from sources within the State pursuant to subparagraph (1) of this paragraph, by the total of all such wages, salaries, and other compensation for personal services which is so paid or incurred without regard to whether such payments would be treated as derived by the employees from sources within the State. For purposes of this subdivision (ii), no amount paid as deferred compensation pursuant to a retirement plan to a former employee shall be taken into consideration.

(C) **Gross income percentage.** The percentage computed by dividing the gross sales or charges for services performed by or through an agency located within the State by the total of all gross sales or charges for services performed both within and without the State. The sales or charges to be allocated to the State shall include all sales which are negotiated, and charges which are for services performed, by an employee, agent, agency, or independent contractor chiefly situated at, or working principally out of an office located within, the State.

(3) **Income attributable to real estate investment.** Notwithstanding subparagraph (2) of this paragraph, income and deductions from the rental of real property, and gain and loss from the sale, exchange, or other disposition of real property, shall not be subject to allocaton under subparagraph (2), but shall be considered as entirely derived from sources located within the State in which such property is located.

(4) **Treatment of losses.** A loss attributable to the taxpayer's employment, or to his conduct of, participation in, or investment in a trade or business, shall be allocated in the same manner as the income attributable to such employment or trade or business would be allocated pursuant to this paragraph.

(5) **Examples.** The application of this paragraph may be illustrated by the following examples:

Example (1). A, an employee who earns $10,000 in wage income attributable to services, and who has no other wage or other business income, spends 60 percent of his working time performing services for his employer in State X, 30 percent in State Y, and 10 percent in State Z. In the absence of the requisite proof to the contrary, A's wage income is considered to have been derived 60 percent from sources located within State X, 30 percent within State Y, and 10 percent within State Z. Assuming that A is a nonresident with respect to all three States, and that they all impose qualified nonresident taxes, then the qualified nonresident tax of State X is imposed on $6,000, the qualified nonresident tax of State Y is imposed on $3,000, and the qualified nonresident tax of State Z is not imposed on any of the income because A did not derive at least 25 percent of his wage and other business income from sources located within State Z.

Example (2). B, who earns no wage income but who has a total of $10,000 of other business income for the taxable year, all of which is net income from self-employment attributable primarily to services, spends 45 percent of his working time performing services in State X, 30 percent in State Y, and 25 percent in State Z. However, the rates that B is able to charge for his services and the business expenses which he incurs vary in the different States, and he is able to prove by detailed records that his net income from self-employment was in fact derived 50 percent from sources located within State X, 35 percent from sources located within State Y, and 15 percent from sources located within State Z. Assuming that B is a nonresident with respect to all three States, and that they all impose qualified nonresident taxes, then the qualified nonresident tax of State X is imposed on $5,000, the qualified nonresident tax of State Y is imposed on $3,500, and the qualified nonresident tax of State Z is not imposed on any of the income because B

Proposed Reg. §301.6362-5

did not derive at least 25 percent of his wage and other business income from sources located within State Z.

Example (3). C is a partner in a profitable business concern, in which he has a substantial capital investment. His net earnings from self-employment attributable to his partnership interest are $75,000 for the taxable year. The fair market value of the services which C performs for the partnership during the taxable year is $30,000. C's income is therefore attributable primarily to his capital investment. The partnership business is carried on partially within and partially without State X. Neither C nor the partnership maintains records from which the portion of C's $75,000 income which is considered to be derived from sources within State X can be satisfactorily proven. As determined under subparagraph (2) of this paragraph, the partnership's "property percentage" in State X is 70, its "payroll percentage" therein is 60, and its "gross income percentage" therein is 56. The amount of C's partnership income considered to be derived from sources within State X is $46,500 ($75,000 × 62 percent). This result would obtain even if C's services for the partnership are performed entirely within State X.

Example (4). Assume the same facts as in example (3), except that the records of the partnership of which C is a member indicate that the net profits of the partnership are derived 40 percent from business activities conducted in State X, and 60 percent from business activities conducted in State Y. C is requested to prove that those records fairly and equitably reflect the income which is allocable to sources within State X. The documentary evidence which he adduces in support of the allocation made by the records shows how such allocation results from a careful step-by-step tracing of the profitability of each phase and aspect of the partnership's operations, and shows the State in which each such phase and aspect of the operations is conducted. C's proof is satisfactory to show the percentage allocation, and the amount of his partnership income considered to be derived from sources within State X is $30,000, or $75,000 multiplied by 40 percent. This result would obtain even if B's services for the partnership are performed entirely within State X.

§301.6362-6 (Proposed Treasury Decision, published 9-29-77.) **Requirements relating to residence.**

(a) **In general.** A tax imposed by a State meets the requirements of section 6362(e) and this section if in effect it provides that:

(1) The State of residence of an individual, estate, or trust is determined according to paragraphs (1), (2), or (3), respectively, of section 6362(e), and according to paragraphs (b), (c), or (d), respectively, of this section.

(2) The liability for a resident tax imposed by such State upon an individual or trust which changes residence to another State in the taxable year is determined according to section 6362(e)(4) and paragraph (e) of this section.

(3) The rules relating to current collection of tax apply as provided in section 6362(e)(5) and paragraph (f) of this section.

(b) **Residence of an individual—(1) In general.** Except as otherwise provided in subparagraph (5) of this paragraph, an individual is treated as a resident of a State with respect to a taxable year only if:

(i) His principal place of residence (as defined in subparagraph (2) of this paragraph) is within such State for a period of at least 135 consecutive days, at least 30 days of which are in such taxable year; or

(ii) In the case of a citizen or resident of the United States who is not a resident of any State (determined as provided in subdivision (i) of this subparagraph) with respect to such taxable year, his domicile (as defined in subparagraph (3) of this paragraph) is in such State for at least 30 days during such taxable year.

With respect to an individual who is a resident (determined as provided in subdivision (i) of this subparagraph) of more than one State during a taxable year, see paragraph (e) of this section.

(2) **Principal place of residence—(i) Definition.** For purposes of subparagraph (1)(i) of this paragraph and paragraph (d)(4) of this section, the term "principal place of

residence" shall mean the place which is an individual's primary home. An individual's temporary absence from his primary home shall not effect a change with respect thereto. On the other hand, if an individual moves to another State, other than as a mere transient or sojourner, he shall be treated as having changed the location of his primary home.

(ii) *Examples.* The application of this subparagraph may be illustrated by the following examples:

Example (1). A has a city home and a country home. He resides in the city home for 7 months of the year and uses the address of that home as his legal residence for purposes of driver's license, automobile registration, and voter registration. He resides in the country home for 5 months of the year. His city home is considered his principal place of residence.

Example (2). During the taxable year, B, a construction worker, is employed at several different locations in different States. The duration of each job on which he is employed ranges from a few weeks to several months, and he knows when he accepts a job what its approximate duration will be. He owns a house in State X which he uses as his legal residence for purposes of driver's license, automobile registration, and voter registration. In addition, his family lives there during the entire year, and B lives there during periods between jobs. However, the duration of the jobs and the distance between the job-sites and his house require him to live in the localities of the respective job-sites during the period of his employment, although occasionally he returns to his house in State X on weekends. B's house in State X is his principal place of residence during all of the taxable year.

Example (3). C, a dependent of his parents who are residents of State X, is a full-time student in a 4-year degree program at a college in State Y. During the 9-month academic year, C lives on the college campus, but he returns to his parents' home in State X for the summer recess. C gives State Y as his residence for purposes of his driver's license and voter registration, but lists the address of his parents' home in State X as his "permanent address" on the records of the college which he attends. Although C's domicile remains at his parents' home in State X, his presence in State Y cannot be regarded as that of a mere transient or sojourner; accordingly, C's principal place of residence is in State Y for that portion of the taxable year during which he attends college.

Example (4). D loses his job in State X, where he lived and worked for many years. After a series of unsuccessful attempts to find other employment in State X, he accepts a job in State Y. D gives up his apartment in State X and moves to State Y upon commencing his new job; however, he intends to continue to explore available employment opportunities in State X so that he may return there as soon as any opportunity to do so arises. D changes his principal place of residence when he moves to State Y.

(3) **Domicile defined.** For purposes of subparagraph (1)(ii) of this paragraph and paragraph (d)(4) of this section, the term "domicile" shall mean an individual's fixed or permanent home. An individual acquires a domicile in a place by living there, even for a brief period of time, with no definite present intention of later removing therefrom. Residence without the requisite intention to remain indefinitely will not suffice to change domicile, nor will intention to change domicile effect such a change until accompanied by actual removal. A domicile, once acquired, is maintained until a new domicile is acquired.

(4) **Period of residence**—(i) *General rule.* An individual who becomes a resident of a State pursuant to subparagraph (1) of this paragraph, or who is at the beginning of a taxable year a resident of a State pursuant to such provision, shall be treated as continuing to be a resident of such State through the end of the taxable year, unless, prior thereto, such individual becomes a resident, under the principles of subparagraph (1), of another State or a possession or foreign country. In the event that the individual becomes a resident of such another jurisdiction prior to the end of the taxable year, his residence in such State shall be treated as ending on the day prior to the day on which he becomes a resident of such other jurisdiction pursuant to subparagraph (1).

Proposed Reg. §301.6362-6

(ii) *Examples.* The application of this subparagraph may be illustrated by the following examples:

Example (1). A, a calendar-year taxpayer, has his principal place of residence in State X from the beginning of 1976 through August 1, 1976, when he gives up permanently such principal place of residence. He spends the remainder of 1976 traveling outside of the United States, but does not become a resident of any other country. A is considered to be a resident of State X for the entire year 1976.

Example (2). Assume the same facts as in example (1), except that A ceases his traveling and establishes his principal place of residence in State Y on November 15, 1976. Assume, also, that A maintains that principal place of residence for more than 135 consecutive days. Under these circumstances, for his taxable year 1976, A is considered to be a resident of State X from January 1 through November 14, and a resident of State Y from November 15 through December 31.

(5) *Special rules.* (i) No provision of subchapter E or the regulations thereunder shall be construed to require or authorize the treatment of a Senator, Representative, Delegate, or Resident Commissioner as a resident of a State other than the State which he represents in Congress.

(ii) For special rules relating to members of the Armed Forces, see paragraph (h) of §301.6362-7.

(6) *Examples.* The application of this paragraph may be illustrated by the following examples:

Example (1). A, a calendar-year taxpayer, maintains his principal place of residence in State X from December 1, 1976, through April 15, 1977. Assuming that A was not a resident of any other jurisdiction at any time during 1976, A is treated as a resident of State X for the entire year 1976. Such result would obtain even if A was absent from State X on vacation for some portion of December 1976. Moreover, such result would obtain even if it is assumed that A was a domiciliary of State Y from January 1, 1976, through April 15, 1977, because an individual's domicile does not determine his residence so long as residence in one State for the taxable year can be determined from the general rule stated in the first sentence of paragraph (b)(1) of this section.

Example (2). Assume the same facts as in example (1) (including the fact of A's domicile in State Y), except that A maintained his principal place of residence in State Z from September 15, 1975, through January 31, 1976, inclusive. With respect to the year 1976. A is treated as a resident of State Z from January 1 through November 30, and as a resident of State X from December 1 through December 31. A's liability for the qualified taxes of the respective States for 1976 shall be determined pursuant to the provisions in paragraph (e) of this section.

(c) *Residence of an estate.* An estate of an individual is treated as a resident of the last State of which such individual was a resident, as determined under the rules of paragraph (b) of this section, prior to his death. However, the estate of an individual who was not a resident of any State (as determined without regard to the 30-day requirement in paragraph (b)(1) of this section) immediately prior to his death, and who was not a resident of any State at any time during the 3-year period ending on the date of his death, is not treated as a resident of any State. For purposes of determining the decedent's last State of residence, the rules of paragraph (b) shall be applied irrespective of whether subchapter E was in effect at the time the period of 135 consecutive days of residence began, or whether the decedent's last State of residence is a State electing to enter into an agreement pursuant to subchapter E. The determination of the State of residence of an estate pursuant to this paragraph shall not be governed by any determination under State law as to which State is treated as the residence or domicile of the decedent for purposes other than its individual income tax (such as liability for State inheritance tax or jurisdiction of probate proceedings).

(d) *Residence of a trust*—(1) *In general.* (i) The State of residence of a trust shall be determined by reference to the circumstances of the individual who, by either an inter-vivos transfer or a testamentary transfer, is deemed to be the "principal contributor" to the trust under the provisions of subdivision (ii) of this subparagraph.

(ii) If only one individual has ever contributed assets to the trust, including the assets which were transferred to the trust at its inception, then such individual is the principal contributor to the trust. However, if on any day subsequent to the initial creation of the trust, such trust receives assets having a value greater than the aggregate value of all assets theretofore contributed to it, then the trust shall be deemed (for the limited purpose of determining the State of residence) to have been "created" anew, and the individual who on the day of such creation contributed more (in value) than any other individual contributed on that day shall become the principal contributor to the trust. When a trust is created anew, all references in this paragraph to the creation of the trust shall be construed as referring to the most recent creation. For purposes of this paragraph, the value of any asset shall be its fair market value on the day that it was contributed to the trust; any subsequent appreciation or depreciation in the value of the asset shall be disregarded.

(2) **Testamentary trust.** A trust with respect to which a deceased individual is the principal contributor by reason of property passing on his death is treated as a resident of the last State of which such individual was a resident, as determined under the rules of paragraph (b) of this section, before his death. However, if such deceased individual was not a resident of any State (as determined without regard to the 30-day requirement in paragraph (b)(1) of this section) immediately prior to his death, and was not a resident of any State at any time during the 3-year period ending on the date of his death, then a testamentary trust of which he is the principal contributor by reason of property passing on his death is not treated as a resident of any State. All property passing on the transferor's death is treated for this purpose as a contribution made to the trust on the date of death, regardless of when the property is actually paid over to the trust.

(3) **Nontestamentary trust.** A trust which is not a trust described in subparagraph (2) of this paragraph is treated as a resident of the State in which the principal contributor to the trust, during the 3-year period ending on the date of the creation of the trust, had his principal place of residence for an aggregate number of days longer than the aggregate number of days he had his principal place of residence in any other State. However, if the principal contributor to such a trust was not a resident of any State at any time during such 3-year period, then the trust is not treated as a resident of any State.

(4) **Special rules.** If the application of the provisions of the foregoing subparagraphs of this paragraph results in a determination of more than one State of residence for a trust, or does not provide a rule by which the residence or nonresidence of the trust can be determined, then the determination of the State of residence of such trust shall be made according to the rules of the applicable subdivision of this subparagraph.

(i) If, at the time of creation of the trust, 50 percent or more in value of the trust corpus consists of real property, then the trust shall be treated as a resident of the State in which more of the real property (in value) which was in the trust at such time was located than any other State.

(ii) If, at the time of creation of the trust, less than 50 percent in value of the trust corpus consists of real property, then the trust shall be treated as a resident of the State in which, at such time, the trustee, if an individual, had his principal place of residence, or, if a corporation, had its principal place of business. If there were two or more trustees, then the foregoing sentence shall be applied by reference to the principal places of residence, or of business, of the majority of trustees who had authority to make investment and other management decisions for the trust.

(iii) If, after application of the provisions of subdivisions (i) and (ii) of this subparagraph, the State of residence of the trust still cannot be ascertained, then the Commissioner of Internal Revenue shall determine the State of residence of such trust for purposes of qualified taxes. Such determination shall be made by reference to the number of significant contacts each State had with the trust at the time of its creation. Significant contacts shall include the principal place of residence of the principal contributor or contributors to the trust, the principal place of residence or business of the trustee (or trustees), the situs of the assets of which the trust corpus was composed, and the location

Proposed Reg. §301.6362-6

from which management decisions emanated with respect to the business and investment interests of the trusts.

(5) **Examples.** The application of this paragraph may be illustrated by the following examples:

Example (1). A created a trust in 1950 by transferring to it certain stock in a corporation. At the time of such transfer, the stock had a fair market value of $1,000. A at all relevant times had his principal place of residence in State X, and accordingly the trust is treated as a resident of such State for qualified tax purposes. As of January 1, 1977, the stock originally contributed by A, which was at all times the only property in the trust, has a fair market value of $3,000. On such date, B, who has had his principal place of residence in State Y for more than 3 years, contributes to the trust property having a fair market value of $1,200. For purposes of determining the identity of the principal contributor to the trust and the State of residence of the trust, the stock contributed by A in 1950 continues to be valued for such purposes at $1,000. Thus, the trust is treated as being created anew on January 1, 1977, with B as the principal contributor, and with State Y as its State of residence.

Example (2). C has his principal place of residence in State X continuously for many years, until August 1, 1978, when he establishes his principal place of residence in State Y. The change of residence is intended to be permanent, and C has no further contact with State X after such change. On January 1, 1980, C creates a nontestamentary trust. During the 3-year period ending on such date C had his principal place of residence in State X for 576 days, and in State Y for 519 days. Therefore, the trust is treated as a resident of State X.

(e) **Liability for tax on change of residence during taxable year—(1) In general.** If, under the principles contained in paragraph (b) or (d) of this section, an individual or trust becomes a resident, or ceases to be a resident, of a State, and is also a resident of another jurisdiction outside of such State during the same taxable year, the liability of such individual or trust for the resident tax of such State shall be determined by multiplying the amount which would be his or its liability for tax (computed after allowing the nonrefundable credits (i.e., credits not corresponding to the credits referred to in section 6401(b) available against the tax)) if he or it had been a resident of such State for the entire taxable year by a fraction, the numerator of which is the number of days he or it was a resident of such State during the taxable year, and the denominator of which is the total number of days in the taxable year. The preceding sentence shall not apply by reason of the fact that an individual is born or dies during the taxable year, or by reason of the fact that a trust comes into existence or ceases to exist during the taxable year.

(2) **Residence determined by domicile.** When an individual is treated as a resident of a State by reason of being domiciled in such State, pursuant to paragraph (b)(1)(ii) of this section, then the numerator of the fraction provided in subparagraph (1) of this paragraph shall be the number of days the individual was domiciled in the State during the taxable year.

(3) **Example.** The application of this paragraph may be illustrated by the following example.

Example. A, a calendar-year taxpayer, is a resident of State X continuously for many years prior to March 15, 1977. On such date, A retires and establishes a new principal place of residence in State Y. A earns $6,000 in 1977 prior to March 15, but receives no taxable income for the remainder of such year. If A had been a resident of State X for the entire taxable year 1977, his liability with respect to the qualified tax of such State (computed after allowing the nonrefundable credits available against the tax) would be $600. If he had been a resident of State Y for the entire taxable year 1977, his liability with respect to the qualified tax of that State (computed similarly) would be $400. Pursuant to the provisions in paragraph (e) of this section, A's liabilities for State qualified taxes for 1977 are as follows:

Liability for State X tax = $600 × $\frac{73}{365}$ = $120

Liability for State Y tax = $400 × $\frac{292}{365}$ = $320

(f) **Current collection of tax.** The State tax laws shall contain provisions for methods of current collection with respect to individuals which correspond to the provisions of the Internal Revenue Code of 1954 with respect to such current collection, including chapter 24 (relating to the collection of income tax at source on wages) and sections 6015, 6073, 6153, and other provisions of the Code relating to declarations (and amendments thereto) and payments of estimated income tax. Except as otherwise provided by Federal statute (see paragraphs (h), (i), and (j) of §301.6362-7), in applying such provisions of the State tax laws:

(1) In the case of a resident tax, an individual shall be subject to the current collection provisions if either—

(i) He is a resident of the State within the meaning of paragraph (b) of this section, or

(ii) He has his principal place of residence (as defined in paragraph (b)(2) of this section) within the State,

and it is reasonable to expect him to have it within the State for 30 days or more during the taxable year.

(2) In the case of a nonresident tax, an individual shall be subject to the current collection provisions if he does not meet either description relating to an individual in subparagraph (1) of this paragraph, if he is not exempt from liability for the tax by reason of a reciprocal agreement between the State of which he is a resident and the State imposing the tax, and if it is reasonable to expect him to receive wage or other business income derived from sources within the State imposing the tax (as defined in paragraph (d) of §301.6362-5) for services performed on 30 days or more of the taxable year.

For additional rules relating to withholding see paragraph (d) of §301.6361-1.

§301.6362-7 (Proposed Treasury Decision, published 9-29-77.) **Additional requirements.**

A State tax meets the additional requirements of section 6362(f) and this section only if:

(a) **State agreement must be in effect for period concerned.** A State agreement, as defined in paragraph (a) of §301.6361-4, is in effect with respect to such tax for the taxable period in question.

(b) **State laws must contain certain provisions.** Under the laws of such State, the provisions of subchapter E and the regulations thereunder, as in effect from time to time, are applicable for the entire period for which the State agreement is in effect. Any change made by the State in such tax (other than an adjustment in the State law which is made solely in order to comply with a change in the Federal law or regulations) shall not apply to taxable years beginning in any calendar year for which the State agreement is in effect unless the change is enacted before November 1 of such year.

(c) **State individual income tax laws can be only of certain kinds.** Such State does not impose any tax on the income of individuals other than (1) a qualified resident tax, and (2) either or both a qualified nonresident tax and a separate tax on income which is not wage and other business income (as defined in paragraph (c) of §301.6362-5) and which is received or accrued by individuals who are domiciled in the State, but who are not residents of the State (as defined in paragraph (b) of §301.6362-6). For purposes of this paragraph, a tax imposed on the amount taxed under section 56 (as permitted under §301.6362-2(b)(2)) shall be treated as an adjustment to and a part of the qualified resident tax. Also, tax laws which were in effect prior to the effective date of a State agree-

Proposed Reg. §301.6362-7

ment and which are not repealed, but which are made inapplicable for the period during which the State agreement is in effect, shall be disregarded.

(d) **Taxable years must coincide.** The taxable years of all individuals, estates, and trusts under such tax are required to coincide with their taxable years used for purposes of the taxes imposed by chapter 1. Accordingly, when subchapter E begins to apply to a State, a taxpayer whose taxable year for purposes of the Federal income tax is different from his taxable year for purposes of the State income tax which precedes the qualified tax may have one short taxable year for purposes of such State income tax, so that thereafter his taxable year for purposes of the qualified tax will coincide with the Federal taxable year.

(e) **Married individuals.** Individuals who are married within the meaning of section 143 of the Code are prohibited from filing (1) a joint return for purposes of such State tax if they file separate Federal income tax returns, or (2) separate returns for purposes of such State tax if they file a joint Federal income tax return.

(f) **Penalties; no double jeopardy.** Under the laws of such State:

(1) Civil and criminal sanctions identical to those provided by subtitle F, and by title 18 of the United States Code (relating to crimes and criminal procedure), with respect to the taxes imposed on the income of individuals by chapter 1 and on the wages of individuals by chapter 24, apply to individuals and their employers who are subject to such State tax (and the collection and administration thereof, including the corresponding withholding tax imposed to implement the current collection of such State tax) as if such tax were imposed by chapter 1 (or chapter 24, in the case of the withholding tax), except to the extent that the application of such sanctions is modified by regulations issued under subchapter E; and

(2) No other sanctions or penalties apply with respect to any act or omission to act in respect of such State tax.

See also paragraph (e) of §301.6361-1 with respect to criminal penalties.

(g) **Partnerships, trusts, subchapter S corporations, and other conduit entities.** Under the laws of such State, the State tax treatment of—

(1) Partnerships and partners,

(2) Trusts and their beneficiaries,

(3) Estate and their beneficiaries,

(4) Electing small business corporations (within the meaning of section 1371(a)) and their shareholders, and

(5) Any other entity and the individuals having beneficial interests therein (such as a cooperative corporation and its shareholders), to the extent that such entity is treated as a conduit for purposes of the taxes imposed by chapter 1,

corresponds to the tax treatment provided therefor with respect to the taxes imposed by chapter 1. For example, a subchapter S corporation shall not be subject to the State's corporate income tax on amounts which are includible in shareholders' incomes which are subject to that State's individual income tax, except to the extent that the subchapter S corporation is subject to tax under Federal law. Similarly, a partnership shall not be subject to the State's unincorporated business income tax on amounts which are includible in partners' incomes which are subject to that State's individual income tax. However, the laws of the State which set forth the provisions of such State individual income tax shall authorize the Commissioner of Internal Revenue to require that the conduit entities described in this paragraph (or some of them) supply information to the Federal Government with respect to the source of income, the State of residence, or the amount of income of a particular type, of an individual, estate, or trust holding a beneficial interest in such conduit entity.

(h) **Members of Armed Forces.** The relief provided to any member of the Armed Forces by section 514 of the Soldiers' and Sailors' Civil Relief Act (50 U.S.C. App. sec. 574) is in no way diminished. Accordingly, for purposes of such State tax, an individual shall not be considered to have become a resident of a State solely because of his absence from his original State of residence under military orders. Moreover, compensation for military service shall not be considered as income derived from a source within a State of which the individual earning such compensation is not a resident, within the meaning of paragraph (d) of §301.6362-5. The preceding sentence shall not apply to nonmilitary compensation. Thus, for example, if an individual who is serving in State X as a member of the Armed Forces, and who is regarded as a resident of State Y under the Soldiers' and Sailors' Civil Relief Act, earns nonmilitary income in State X from a part-time job, such nonmilitary income may be subject to a qualified nonresident tax imposed by State X.

(i) **Withholding on compensation of employees of railroads, motor carriers, airlines, and water carriers.** There is no contravention of the provisions of section 26, 226A, or 324 of the Interstate Commerce Act, or of section 1112 of the Federal Aviation Act of 1958, with respect to the withholding of compensation to which such sections apply for purposes of the nonresident tax.

(j) **Income derived from interstate commerce.** There is no contravention of the provisions of the Act of September 14, 1959 (73 Stat. 555), with respect to the taxation of income derived from interstate commerce to which such statute applies.

§301.6363-1 (Proposed Treasury Decision, published 9-29-77.) **State agreements.**

(a) **Notice of election.** If a State elects to enter into a State agreement it shall file notice of such election with the Secretary or his delegate. The notice of election shall include the following:

(1) **Statement by the Governor.** A written statement by the Governor of the electing State:

(i) Requesting that the Secretary enter into a State agreement, and

(ii) Binding the Governor and his successors in office to notify the Secretary or his delegate immediately of the enactment, between the time of the filing of the notice of election and the time of the execution of the State agreement, of any law of that State which meets the description given in any of the subdivisions of subparagraph (2) of this paragraph, whether or not such law is intended to be administered by the United States pursuant to subchapter E.

(2) **Copy of State laws.** Certified copies of all laws of that State described in any of the following subdivisions of this subparagraph, and a specification of laws described in subdivision (i) of this subparagraph as "subchapter E laws", of laws described in subdivision (ii) as "other tax laws", of laws described in subdivision (iii) as "non-tax laws", and of laws described in subdivision (iv) as "interstate cooperation laws":

(i) All of the State individual income tax laws (including laws relating to the collection or administration of such taxes or to the prosecution of alleged civil or criminal violations with respect to such taxes) which the State would expect the United States to administer pursuant to subchapter E if the State agreement is executed as requested. In order to have a valid notice, the State must have a tax which would meet the requirements for qualification specified in section 6362 and the regulations thereunder if a State agreement were in effect with respect thereto, with no conditions attached to the effectiveness of such tax other than the execution of a State agreement. Such tax must be effective no later than the January 1 specified in the State's notice of election as the date as of which subchapter E is desired to become applicable to the electing State, except that such effective date shall be deferred to the date provided in the State agreement for the beginning of applicability of subchapter E to the State, if the latter date is different from the date specified in the notice of election..

(ii) All of the State income tax laws applicable to individuals (including laws relating to the collection or administration of such taxes or to the prosecution of alleged civil or criminal violations with respect to such taxes) which the State would not expect the United States to administer but which may be in effect simultaneously (for any period of time) with the State agreement.

(iii) All of the State laws other than individual income tax laws which provide for the

Proposed Reg. §301.6363-1

making of any payments by the State based on one or more criteria which the State may desire to verify by reference to information contained in returns of qualified taxes.

(iv) All of the State laws which may be in effect simultaneously (for any period of time) with the State agreement and which provide for cooperation or reciprocal agreement between the electing State and another State with respect to income taxes applicable to individuals.

(3) **Approval by legislature or authorization by constitutional amendment.** A certified copy of an Act or Resolution of the legislature of the electing State in which the legislature affirmatively expresses its approval of the State's entry into a State agreement, or a certified copy of an amendment to the constitution of such State by which the voters of the State affirmatively authorize such entry.

(4) **Opinion by State Attorney General or judgment of highest court.** A written statement by the State Attorney General to the effect that, in his opinion, no provision of the State's Constitution would be violated by the State law's incorporation by reference of the Federal individual income tax laws and regulations, as amended from time to time, by the Federal prosecution and trial of individuals who are alleged to have committed crimes with respect to the State's qualified tax (when it goes into effect as such), or by any other provision relating to such tax, considered as of the time it is being collected and administered by the Federal Government pursuant to subchapter E. However, if such a statement is not included in the notice of election, a judgment of the highest court of the State to the same effect may be submitted in its place.

(5) **Effective date.** A written specification of the January as of which subchapter E is desired to become applicable to the electing State.

(b) **Rules relating to time for filing notice of election.** An electing State must file its notice of election more than 6 months prior to the January 1 as of which the notice specifies that the provisions of subchapter E are desired to become applicable to such State. Thus, for example, if the date specified in the notice is January 1, 1979, the notice must be filed no later than June 30, 1978. However, because under the provisions of section 204(b) of the Federal-State Tax Collection Act of 1972 (86 Stat. 945), as amended by section 2116(a) of the Tax Reform Act of 1976 (90 Stat. 1910), the provisions of subchapter E will initially take effect on the first January 1 which is more than 1 year after the first date on which at least one State has filed a notice of its election (see §301.6361-5), the notice of an election which causes subchapter E to initially take effect must be filed with the Secretary or his delegate more than 1 year prior to the January 1 as of which such notice specifies that the provisions of subchapter E are desired to become applicable to such State. Thus, for example, if such an initially electing State desires to elect subchapter E as of January 1, 1979, its notice must be filed no later than December 31, 1977. For purposes of this section, if the notice of election is sent by either registered or certified mail to the Secretary of the Treasury, Washington, D.C. 20220, then it shall be deemed to be filed on the date of mailing; otherwise, the notice of election shall be deemed to be filed when it is received by the Secretary or his delegate.

(c) **Procedures relating to defects in notice or tax laws.** If a State has filed a notice of election, then the Secretary shall, within 90 days after the notice is filed, notify the Governor of such State in writing of any defect in the notice of election which prevents it from being valid, and of any defect in the State's tax laws which causes the tax submitted to fail to meet the requirements for qualification specified in section 6362 and the regulations thereunder, other than the fact that no State agreement is in effect with respect thereto.

Any such defect of which the Secretary does not notify the Governor within such 90-day period is waived. The Secretary or his delegate may, in his discretion, permit any of such defects of which the Governor is timely notified to be cured retroactively to the date of the filing of the notice of election, by amendment of the notice or the State law. Judicial review of the Secretary's determination that the notice of election or the tax laws, or both, contain defects, may be obtained as set forth in section 6363(d) and §301.6363-4.

(d) **Execution and contents of State agreement.** If the Secretary does not timely notify the Governor of a defect in the notice of election or in the State's tax laws, as provided in paragraph (c) of this section, or if, as provided in such paragraph, all such defects have been cured retroactively, then the Secretary shall enter into a State agreement. The agreement shall include the following elements:

(1) Effective date. The agreement shall specify the January 1 as of which subchapter E will commence to be applicable to the State. Such date shall be the same as that specified in the notice of election pursuant to paragraph (a)(5) of this section, unless the parties agree to a different January 1, except that in no event shall a State agreement executed after November 1 specify the next January 1.

(2) Obligation of Governor to notify the United States of changes in pertinent State laws. The agreement shall require the Governor of the State, and his successors in office, to notify the Secretary or his delegate within 30 days of the enactment of any law of the State, after the execution of the agreement, of a type described in paragraph (a)(2) of this section.

(3) Obligation of Governor to furnish to the United States information needed to administer State tax laws. The agreement shall require the Governor and his successors to furnish to the Secretary or his delegate any information needed by the Federal Government to administer the State tax laws. Such information shall include, for example, a list (which shall be maintained on a current basis) of those obligations of the State or its political subdivisions described in section 103(a)(1) from which the interest is not subject to the qualified taxes of the State.

(4) Identification of State official to act as liaison with Federal Government. The agreement shall include a designation by the Governor of the State official or officials with whom the Secretary or his delegate should coordinate in connection with any questions or problems which may arise during the period for which the State agreement is effective, including those which may result from changes or contemplated changes in pertinent State laws.

(5) Identification of State official to receive transferred funds. The agreement shall include a designation by the Governor of the State official who shall initially receive the funds on behalf of the State when they are transferred pursuant to section 6361(c) and §301.6361-3.

(6) Other obligations. If the Secretary and the Governor both so agree, the agreement shall provide for additional obligations.

(e) State agreement superseding certain other agreements. For the period of its effectiveness, a State agreement shall supersede an otherwise effective agreement entered into by the State and the Secretary for the withholding of State income taxes from the compensation of Federal employees pursuant to 5 U.S.C. 5517 (or pursuant to 5 U.S.C. 5516, in the case of the District of Columbia).

§301.6363-2 (Proposed Treasury Decision, published 9-29-77.) **Withdrawal from State agreements.**

(a) By notification. If a State which has entered into a State agreement desires to withdraw from the agreement, its Governor shall file a notice of withdrawal with the Secretary or his delegate. A notice of withdrawal shall include the following documents:

(1) Request by the Governor. A request by the Governor of the State that the State agreement cease to be effective with respect to taxable years beginning on or after a specified January 1, except as provided in paragraph (b)(2) of §301.6365-2 with respect to withholding in the case of fiscal-year taxpayers.

(2) Legislative approval of withdrawal. A certified copy of an Act or Resolution of the legislature of the State in which the legislature affirmatively expresses its approval of the State's withdrawal from the State agreement.

(3) Identification of State official. A written identification of the State official or officials with whom the Secretary or his delegate should coordinate in connection with the State's withdrawal from the State agreement.

Proposed Reg. §301.6363-2

(b) **By change in State law.** If any law of a State which has entered into a State agreement is enacted pertaining to individual income taxes (including the collection or administration of such taxes, and the prosecution of alleged civil or criminal violations with respect to such taxes), and if the Secretary or his delegate determines that as a result of such law the State no longer has a qualified tax, then such change in the State law shall be treated as a notification of withdrawal from the agreement. The Secretary shall notify the Governor in writing when a change is to be so treated. Such notification shall have the same effect as if, on the effective date of the disqualifying change in the law, the Governor had filed with the Secretary or his delegate a valid and sufficient notice of withdrawal requesting that the State agreement cease to be effective with respect to taxable years beginning on or after the first January 1 which is more than 6 months thereafter, subject to the exception with respect to withholding in the case of fiscal-year taxpayers. However, the cessation of effectiveness may be deferred to a subsequent January 1 if the Governor so requests and if the Secretary or his delegate in his discretion determines that the date of cessation provided in the preceding sentence would subject the State or its taxpayers to undue hardship. In addition, the Governor may request the Secretary or his delegate to permit the State's early withdrawal from the agreement, pursuant to paragraph (c)(2) of this section. Until the date of cessation of effectiveness of the State agreement, the change in State law which was treated as a notification of withdrawal, and any other such subsequent change that would be similarly treated, shall not be given effect for purposes of the Federal collection and administration of the State taxes. Similarly, such changes shall not be given effect for such purposes during the period of litigation if the State seeks judicial review of the action of the Secretary or his delegate pursuant to section 6363(d) or §301.6363-4, even if such changes are ultimately found by the court not to disqualify the State's qualified tax. However, a change in State law which would be treated as a notice of withdrawal in the absence of this sentence shall not be so treated if, prior to the last November 1 preceding the January 1 on which the cessation of effectiveness of the State agreement is to occur, either such change in State law is retroactively repealed, or the State law is retroactively modified and the Secretary or his delegate determines that with such modification the State has a qualified tax.

(c) **Rules relating to time of withdrawal—(1) General rule.** Except as provided in subparagraph (2) of this paragraph, a notice of withdrawal shall not be valid unless the January 1 specified therein is not earlier than the first January 1 which is more than 6 months subsequent to the date on which the notice is received by the Secretary or his delegate. Thus, for example, if the notice specifies January 1, 1980, for withdrawal, the notice must be received no later than June 30, 1979.

(2) **Early withdrawal.** The Secretary or his delegate may, in his discretion and upon written request by a Governor of a State who has filed a notice of withdrawal, waive the 6-months requirement of section 6363(b)(1) and subparagraph (1) of this paragraph if the Secretary determines that:

(i) The State will suffer a hardship if required to meet such requirement, and

(ii) The early withdrawal requested by the Governor would be practicable from the standpoint of orderly collection of the qualified tax and administration of the State law by the Federal Government.

§301.6363-3 (Proposed Treasury Decision, published 9-29-77.) **Transition years.**

The State may by law provide for the transition to or from a qualified tax to the extent necessary to prevent double taxation or other unintended hardships, or to prevent unintended benefits, under State law. Generally, such provisions shall be administered by the State; but, if requested to do so by the Governor of the State, the Secretary or his delegate may, in his discretion, agree to administer such provisions either solely or jointly with the State.

§301.6363-4 (Proposed Treasury Decision, published 9-29-77.) **Judicial review.**

(a) **General rule.** If the Secretary or his delegate determines pursuant to paragraph (c) of §301.6363-1 that a State did not file a valid notice of election or does not have a tax which would meet the requirements for qualification specified in section 6362 and the regulations thereunder if a State agreement were in effect with respect thereto, or if he determines pursuant to paragraph (b) of §301.6363-2 that a participating State has enacted a law as a result of which the State no longer has a qualified tax, such State may, within 60 days after its Governor has received notification of such determination, file a petition for the review of such determination with either the United States Court of Appeals for the circuit in which the State is located or the United States Court of Appeals for the District of Columbia. If a State files such a petition, the clerk of the court shall forthwith transmit a copy of the petition to the Secretary or his delegate, who in turn shall thereupon file in the court the record of proceedings on which the determination adverse to the State was based, as provided in section 2112 of title 28, United States Code.

(b) **Court of Appeals' Jurisdiction.** The Court of Appeals may affirm or set aside, in whole or in part, the action of the Secretary or his delegate; and (subject to the rules delaying the effectiveness of the change in State law provided in paragraph (b) of §301.6363-2) the court may issue such other orders as may be appropriate with respect to taxable years which include any part of the period of litigation.

(c) **Review of Court of Appeals' judgment.** The judgment of the Court of Appeals shall be subject to review by the Supreme Court of the United States upon certiorari or certification sought by either party as provided in section 1254 of title 28, United States Code.

(d) **Effect of final judgment.** If a final judgment, rendered with respect to litigation involving a State's petition to review a determination of the Secretary or his delegate to the effect that the State's individual income tax laws included in its notice of election would not meet the requirements for qualification specified in section 6362 and the regulations thereunder if a State agreement were in effect with respect thereto, includes a determination that the State's tax would in fact meet such requirements, then the provisions of subchapter E shall apply to the State with respect to taxable years beginning on or after the first January 1 which is more than 6 months after the date of such final judgment. If a final judgment, rendered with respect to litigation involving a State's petition to review a determination of the Secretary or his delegate to the effect that the State's previously-qualified tax ceases to qualify because of a change in the State's law, includes a determination that the State's tax does in fact cease to qualify, then the provisions of subchapter E (other than section 6363) shall cease to apply to the State with respect to taxable years beginning on or after the first January 1 which is more than 6 months after the date of such final judgment. See paragraph (b) of §301.6365-2 for special rules with respect to withholding in the case of fiscal-year taxpayers.

(e) **Expeditious treatment of judicial proceedings.** Under section 6363(d)(4), any judicial proceedings to which a State and the United States are parties, and which are brought pursuant to section 6363, are entitled to receive a preference, and to be heard and determined as expeditiously as possible, upon request of the Secretary or the State.

§301.6365-1 (Proposed Treasury Decision, published 9-29-77.) **Definitions.**

(a) **State.** For purposes of subchapter E and the regulations thereunder, the term "State" shall include the District of Columbia, but shall not include the Commonwealth of Puerto Rico or any possession of the United States.

(b) **Governor.** For purposes of subchapter E and the regulations thereunder, the term "Governor" shall include the Mayor of the District of Columbia.

§301.6365-2 (Proposed Treasury Decision, published 9-29-77.) **Commencement and cessation of applicability of subchaper E to individual taxpayers.**

(a) **General rule.** Except for purposes of chapter 24 (relating to the collection of income tax at source on wages), whenever subchapter E begins or ceases to apply to any State (i.e., a State agreement begins or ceases to be effective) as of any January 1, such commencement or cessation of applicability shall apply to taxable years of individuals beginning on or after such date. For example, if subchapter E begins to apply to a partic-

Proposed Reg. §301.6365-2

ular State on January 1, 1980, it would become applicable for calendar year 1980 for calendar-year taxpayers in that State; but if a taxpayer in the State is using a fiscal year running from July 1 to June 30, the subchapter would begin to apply (except for purposes of chapter 24) to that taxpayer on July 1, 1980, for his taxable year ending June 30, 1981. Similarly, if the subchapter ceases to apply to such State on January 1, 1982, it would cease to apply to calendar-year taxpayers after the end of calendar year 1981; but it would cease to apply (except for purposes of chapter 24) to fiscal-year taxpayers at the end of their fiscal years which are in progress on January 1, 1982. The cessation of applicability of subchapter E to a State does not affect rights, duties, and liabilities with respect to any taxable year for which subchapter E does apply with respect to any taxpayer (or his employer).

(b) **Special rules pertaining to withholding—(1) Subchapter E beginning to apply.** The Federal withholding system provided in chapter 24 shall go into effect for State individual income tax purposes with respect to wages paid on or after the January 1 as of which subchapter E begins to apply to a State. If an employee is subject to a qualified tax imposed by the State, such withholding system shall apply to his wages paid on or after that January 1, without regard to whether he is a calendar-year or fiscal-year taxpayer. See §301.6363-3 with respect to transition-year rules.

(2) **Subchapter E ceasing to apply.** The Federal withholding system provided in chapter 24 shall cease to be effective for State tax purposes with respect to wages paid on or after the January 1 as of which subchapter E ceases to apply to the State, although fiscal-year taxpayers of that State continue to be subject to the other provisions of subchapter E for the remainder of their fiscal years then in progress. See §301.6363-3 with respect to transition-year rules.

Reports of Refunds and Credits

Section 301.6405-1 is amended to read as follows:

§301.6405-1 (Proposed Treasury Decision, published 9-29-77.) **Reports of refunds and credits.**

Section 6405 requires that a report be made to the Joint Committee on Taxation of proposed refunds or credits in excess of $100,000 of any income tax (including any qualified State individual income tax collected by the Federal Government), war profits tax, excess profits tax, estate tax, or gift tax. An exception is provided under which refunds and credits made after July 1, 1972, and attributable to an election under section 165(h) to deduct a disaster loss for the taxable year in which the disaster occurred, may be made prior to the submission of such report to the Joint Committee on Taxation.

Tentative Carryback Adjustments

Section 1.6411-1 is amended by revising paragraph (a) to read as follows:

§ 1.6411-1 (Proposed Treasury Decision, published 12-30-70.) **Tentative carryback adjustments.**

(a) **In general.** Any taxpayer who has a net operating loss under section 172 may file an application under section 6411 for a tentative carryback adjustment of the taxes for taxable years prior to the taxable year of the loss which are affected by the net operating loss carryback resulting from such loss. The right to file an application for a tentative carryback adjustment is not limited to corporations, but is available to any taxpayer. A corporation may file an application for a tentative carryback adjustment even though it has not extended the time for payment of tax under section 6164. In determining any decrease in tax under § 1.6411-1 through § 1.6411-4, the decrease in tax is determined net of any increase in the tax imposed by section 56 (relating to the minimum tax for tax preferences).

* * * * * * * * * * * * *

Additions to the Tax and Additional Amounts

There is added immediately after § 301.6652-2 the following new section:

§ **301.6652-3** (Proposed Treasury Decision, published 1-20-78 and 2-10-78.) **Failure to file information with respect to employee retirement benefit plan.**

(a) **Amount imposed—(1) Annual registration statement.** The plan administrator (within the meaning of section 414(g)) of an employee retirement benefit plan defined in §301.6057-1(a)(3) is liable for the amount imposed by section 6652(e)(1) in each case in which there is a failure to file information relating to the deferred vested retirement benefit of a plan participant, as required by section 6057(a) and §301.6057-1, at the time and place and in the manner prescribed therefor (determined without regard to any extension of time for filing). The amount imposed by section 6652(e)(1) on the plan administrator is $1 for each participant with respect to whom there is a failure to file the required information, multiplied by the number of days during which the failure continues. However, the total amount imposed by section 6652(e)(1) on the plan administrator with respect to a failure to file on behalf of a plan for a plan year shall not exceed $5,000.

(2) **Notification of change in status.** The plan administrator (within the meaning of section 414(g)) of an employee retirement benefit plan defined in section 301.6057-1(a)(3) is liable for the amount imposed by section 6652(e)(2) in each case in which there is a failure to file a notification of a change in plan status, as described in section 6057(b) and §301.6057-2, at the time and place and in the manner prescribed therefor (determined without regard to any extension of time for filing). The amount imposed by section 6652(e)(2) on the plan administrator is $1 for each day during which the failure to so file a notification of a change in plan status continues. However, the total amount imposed by section 6652(e)(2) on the plan administrator with respect to a failure to file a notification of a change in plan status shall not exceed $1,000.

(3) **Annual return of funded plan of deferred compensation.** Under section 6652(f) the amount described in this subparagraph is imposed in each case in which there is a failure to file the annual return described in section 6058(a) on behalf of a plan described in §301.6058-1(a) at the time and in the manner prescribed therefore (determined with regard to any extension of time for filing). The employer maintaining the plan is liable for the amount imposed with respect to a failure to so file the annual return in each case in which the employer must file the return under §301.6058-1(a). The plan administrator (within the meaning of section 414(g)) is liable for the amount imposed in each case in which the plan administrator must file the return under §301.6058-1(a). In the case of an individual retirement account or annuity described in section 408, the individual described in §301.6058-1(d)(2) who must file the annual return under §301.6058-1(d) is liable for the amount imposed with respect to a failure to so file the annual return. The amount imposed is $10 for each day during which the failure to file the annual return on behalf of a plan for a year continues. However, the total amount imposed with respect to a failure to file on behalf of a plan for any year shall not exceed $5,000

(4) **Actuarial statement in case of mergers.** The plan administrator (within the meaning of section 414(g)) is liable for an amount imposed by section 6652(f) in each case in which there is a failure to file the actuarial statement described in section 6058(b) at the time and in the manner prescribed therefor (determined without regard to any extension of time for filing). The amount imposed by section 6652(f) on the plan administrator is $10 for each day during which the failure to file the statement with respect to a merger, consolidation or transfer of assets or liabilities continues. However, the amount imposed by section 6652(f) on the plan administrator with respect to a failure to file the statement with respect to a merger, consolidation or transfer shall not exceed $5,000.

(5) **Information relating to certain trusts and annuity and bond purchase plans.** Under section 6652(f) the amount described in this subparagraph is imposed in each case in which there is a failure to file a return or statement required by section 6047 at the time

Proposed Reg. § 301.6652-3

and in the manner prescribed therefor in §1.6047-1 (determined without regard to any extension of time for filing). The amount is imposed upon the trustee of a trust described in section 401(a), custodian of a custodial account or issuer of an annuity contract, as the case may be (see §1.6047-1(a)(1)(i) and (ii)). The amount imposed by section 6652(f) is $10 for each day during which the failure to file with respect to a payee for a calendar year continues. However, the amount imposed with respect to a failure to file with respect to a payee for a calendar year shall not exceed $5,000.

(b) **Showing of reasonable cause**—(1) No amount imposed by section 6652(e) shall apply with respect to a failure to file information relating to the deferred vested retirement benefit of a plan participant under section 6057(a), or a failure to give notice of a change in plan status under section 6057(b), if it is established to the satisfaction of the director of the internal revenue service center at which the information or notice is required to be filed that the failure was due to reasonable cause.

(2) No amount imposed by section 6652(f) shall apply with respect to a failure to file a return or statement required by section 6058 or 6047, or a failure to provide material items of information called for on such a return or statement, if it is established to the satisfaction of the appropriate district director or the director of the internal revenue service center at which the return or statement is required to be filed that the failure was due to reasonable cause.

(3) An affirmative showing of reasonable cause must be made in the form of a written statement setting forth all the facts alleged as reasonable cause. The statement must contain a declaration by the appropriate individual that the statement is made under the penalties of perjury.

(c) **Joint liability.** If more than one person is responsible for a failure to comply with sections 6057(a) or (b) or section 6058(a) or (b) or section 6047, all such persons shall be jointly and severally liable with respect to the failure.

(d) **Manner of payment.** An amount imposed under section 6652(e) or (f) and this section shall be paid in the same manner as a tax upon the issuance of notice and demand therefor.

(e) **Effective dates**—(1) **Annual registration statement.** With respect to the annual registration statement described in section 6057(a), this section is effective—

(i) In the case of a plan to which only one employer contributes, for plan years beginning after December 31, 1975, with respect to participants who separate from service covered by the plan in plan years beginning after that date, and

(ii) In the case of a plan to which more than one employer contributes, for plan years beginning after December 31, 1976.

(2) **Notification of change in status.** With respect to the notification of change in plan status required by section 6057(b), this section is effective with respect to a change in status occurring within plan years beginning after December 31, 1975.

(3) **Annual return of employee benefit plan.** With respect to the annual return of employee benefit plan required by section 6058(a), this section is effective for plan years beginning after September 2, 1974.

(4) **Actuarial statement in case of mergers.** With respect to the actuarial statement required by section 6058(b), this section is effective with respect to mergers, consolidations or transfers of assets or liabilities occurring after September 2, 1974.

(5) **Information relating to certain trusts and annuity and bond purchase plans.** With respect to reports or statements required to be filed by section 6047 and the regulations thereunder, this section is effective with respect to calendar years ending after September 2, 1974.

Section 1.6654-1 is amended by revising paragraph (a)(1) and (4) to read as follows:

§1.6654-1 (Proposed Treasury Decision, published 9-29-77.) **Addition to the tax in the case of an individual.**

(a) **In general.** (1) Section 6654 imposes an addition to the taxes under chapters 1 and 2 of the Code in the case of any underpayment of estimated tax by an individual (with certain exceptions described in section 6654(d)), including any underpayment of estimated qualified State individual income taxes which are treated pursuant to section 6361(a) as if they were imposed by chapter 1. This addition to the tax is in addition to any applicable criminal penalties and is imposed whether or not there was reasonable cause for the underpayment. The amount of the underpayment for any installment date is the excess of—

(i) The following percentages of the tax shown on the return for the taxable year or, if no return was filed, of the tax for such year, divided by the number of installment dates prescribed for such taxable year:

(A) 80 percent in the case of taxable years beginning after December 31, 1966, of individuals not referred to in section 6073(b) (relating to income from farming or fishing);

(B) 70 percent in the case of taxable years beginning before January 1, 1967, of such individuals; and

(C) 66 2/3 percent in the case of individuals referred to in section 6073(b); over

(ii) The amount, if any, of the installment paid on or before the last day prescribed for such payment.

* * * * * * * * * * *

(4) The term "tax" when used in subparagraph (1)(i) of this paragraph shall mean—

(i) The tax imposed by chapter 1 of the Code (other than by section 56 or, for taxable years ending before September 30, 1968, the tax surcharge imposed by section 51), including any qualified State individual income taxes which are treated pursuant to section 6361(a) as if they were imposed by chapter 1, plus

(ii) For taxable years beginning after December 31, 1966, the tax imposed by chapter 2 of the Code, minus

(iii) All credits allowed by part IV, subchapter A of chapter 1, except the credit provided by section 31, relating to tax withheld at source on wages, and also minus

(iv) In the case of an individual who is subject to one or more qualified State individual income taxes, the sum of the credits allowed against such taxes pursuant to section 6362(b)(2)(B) or (C) or section 6362(c)(4) and paragraph (c) of §301.6362-4 of this chapter (Regulations on Procedure and Administration) (relating to the credit for income taxes of other States or political subdivisions thereof) and paragraph (c)(2) of §301.6361-1 (relating to the credit for tax withheld from wages on account of qualified State individual income taxes).

* * * * * * * * * * * * * * * *

Section 1.6654-1 is amended by revising subparagraph (4) of paragraph (a) to read as follows:

§ 1.6654-1 (Proposed Treasury Decision, published 12-30-70.) **Addition to tax in the case of an individual.**

(a) In general * * *

(4) The term "tax" when used in subparagraph (1)(i) of this paragraph shall mean the tax imposed by chapter 1 of the Code (other than by section 56) reduced by all credits allowed by part IV, subchapter A of that chapter, except the credit provided by section 31, relating to tax withheld at source on wages. For the disallowance of certain credits in the case of taxpayers who elect to use the standard deduction or to pay the optional tax imposed by section 3, see section 36.

* * * * * * * * * * * * *

Section 1.6654-2 is amended by revising paragraph (b)(1) to read as follows:

§ 1.6654-2 (Proposed Treasury Decision, published 12-30-70.) **Exceptions to imposition of the addition to the tax in the case of individuals.**

* * * * * * * * * * * * *

Proposed Reg. §1.6654-2

(b) Meaning of terms. * * *

(1) The term "tax" means the tax imposed by chapter 1 of the Code (other than by section 56) reduced by the credits against tax allowed by part IV, subchapter A, of such chapter, other than the credit against tax provided by section 31 (relating to tax withheld on wages), and without reduction for any payments of estimated tax.

* * * * * * * * * * * * *

Paragraph (b)(1) of section 1.6654-2 is amended to read as follows:

§ 1.6654-2 (Proposed Treasury Decision, published 9-29-77.) **Exceptions to imposition of the addition to the tax in the case of individuals.**

* * * * * * * * * * * *

(b) Meaning of terms. * * *

(1) The term "tax" means—

(i) The tax imposed by chapter 1 of the Code (other than by section 56), including any qualified State individual income taxes which are treated pursuant to section 6361 (a) as if they were imposed by chapter 1, plus

(ii) For taxable years beginning after December 31, 1966, the tax imposed by chapter 2 of the Code, minus

(iii) The credits against tax allowed by part IV, subchapter A, chapter 1 of the Code, other than the credit against tax provided by section 31 (relating to tax withheld on wages), and without reduction for any payments of estimated tax, and also minus

(iv) In the case of an individual who is subject to one or more qualified State individual income taxes, the sum of the credits allowed against such taxes pursuant to section 6362(b)(2)(B) or (C) or section 6362(c)(4) and paragraph (c) of §301.6362-4 of this chapter (Regulations on Procedure and Administration) (relating to the credit for income taxes of other States or political subdivisions thereof) and paragraph (c)(2) of §301.6361-1 (relating to the credit for tax withheld from wages on account of qualified State individual income taxes).

Assessable Penalties

Section 301.6672-1 is amended to read as follows:

§ 301.6672-1 (Proposed Treasury Decision, published 7-28-72.) **Failure to collect and pay over tax, or attempt to evade or defeat tax.**

(a) **In general.** Any person required to collect, truthfully account for, and pay over any tax imposed by the Code who willfully fails to collect such tax, or truthfully account for and pay over such tax, or willfully attempts in any manner to evade or defeat any such tax or the payment thereof, shall in addition to other penalties, be liable to a penalty equal to the total amount of the tax evaded, or not collected, or not accounted for and paid over. The penalty imposed by section 6672 applies only to the collection, accounting for, or payment over of taxes imposed on a person other than the person who is required to collect, account for, and pay over such taxes. No penalty under section 6653, relating to failure to pay tax, shall be imposed for any offense to which this section is applicable.

(b) **Presumption of willful failure to collect in certain cases.** (1) In the case of the taxes imposed by sections 4251, 4261, and 4271 upon payments for the rendering of services, if payment for the services is made before the services are rendered and if at the time the services are rendered the tax due on the payment has not been collected, there is a presumption that the person rendering the services has willfully failed to collect such tax. Thus, if an air carrier renders prepaid transportation services without having collected the tax imposed by section 4261 or 4271 on the payment for such services, the carrier will be presumed to have willfully failed to collect such tax.

(2) In the case of the taxes imposed by sections 4251, 4261, and 4271 upon payments for the rendering of services, if the services are rendered on credit and the

tax is not collected at the time of payment, the person rendering the services will be presumed to have willfully failed to collect the tax unless such person terminates the credit privileges of the payor within a reasonable period after having received the payment for services. In the case of the tax imposed by section 4251 on communication services, credit privileges will be considered as terminated within a reasonable period after receipt of payment for particular services if such privileges are terminated no later than 60 days after the first day on which, under applicable local law or the rules and regulations of any Federal or State regulatory agency, the person rendering the services would have been permitted to discontinue rendering communication services to the payor if the payor has failed to pay for the particular services.

(3) In the case of the tax imposed by section 4271 upon payments for the transportation of property by air, if the payment subject to tax is made outside the United States for air transportation which begins and ends in the United States and if the tax is not collected at the time of payment, the person furnishing the last segment of the taxable transportation is obligated to collect the tax from the person to whom the property is delivered in the United States. See section 4271(b)(2). In such case, if the property is delivered without collection of the tax and if, under applicable local law or the rules and regulations of any Federal or State regulatory agency, the person rendering the last segment of taxable transportation in the United States would have been permitted to refuse delivery to the consignee of the property if the consignee had failed to pay for the transportation service, such person will be presumed to have willfully failed to collect the tax.

(4) The presumption of willful failure to collect tax on any payment for services may be overcome only upon a showing that the person receiving the payment reasonably believed that such payment was not subject to tax.

* * * * * * * * * * *

There is added in the appropriate place the following new section.

§ 301.6690-1 (Proposed Treasury Decision, published 1-20-78.) **Penalty for fraudulent statement or failure to furnish statement to plan participant.**

(a) Penalty. Any plan administrator required by section 6057(e) and §301.6057-1(d) to furnish a statement of deferred vested retirement benefit to a plan participant is subject to a penalty of $50 in each case in which the administrator (1) willfully fails to furnish the statement to the participant in the manner, at the time, and showing the information required by section 6057(e) and §301.6057-1(d), or (2) willfully furnishes a false or fraudulent statement to the participant. The penalty shall be assessed and collected in the same manner as the tax imposed on employers under the Federal Insurance Contribution Act.

(b) Effective date. This section shall take effect on September 2, 1974.

Allowable Disclosure or Use of Information By Preparers of Returns

Section 301.7216-2 is amended by revising paragraphs (c) and (e) and by adding a new paragraph (n), as follows:

§ 301.7216-2 (Proposed Treasury Decision, published 12-12-74.) **Disclosure or use without formal consent of the taxpayer.**

* * * * * * * * * * *

(c) Disclosure pursuant to an order of a court or of a Federal regulatory agency. The provisions of section 7216(a) and § 301.7216-1 shall not apply to any disclosure of tax return information if such disclosure is made pursuant to—

(1) The order of any court of record, Federal, State, or local, or

(2) An administrative order, demand, summons, or subpoena issued by any

Proposed Reg. §301.7216-2

Federal regulatory agency in the performance of its duties, which clearly identifies the information to be disclosed.

* * * * * * * * * * * * *

(e) **Attorneys and accountants.** (1) A tax return preparer who is lawfully engaged in the practice of law or accountancy and prepares a tax return for a taxpayer may use the tax return information of the taxpayer, or disclose such information to another employee or member of his law or accounting firm who may use it, to render other legal or accounting services to or for such taxpayer. Thus, for example, a lawyer who prepares a tax return for a taxpayer may use the tax return information of the taxpayer for, or in connection with, rendering legal services, such as estate planning or administration, or preparation of trial briefs or trust instruments, for the taxpayer or his estate; or if another member of the same firm renders the other legal services for the taxpayer, the lawyer who prepared the tax return may disclose the tax return information to that other member for use by him in rendering those services for the taxpayer. In further illustration, an accountant who prepares a tax return for a taxpayer may use the tax return information, or disclose it to another member of the firm for use by him, for, or in connection with, the preparation of books of account, working papers, or accounting statements or reports to or for the taxpayer. Further, in the normal course of rendering such legal or accounting services to or for the taxpayer, the attorney or accountant may, with the express or implied consent of the taxpayer, make such tax return information available to third parties, such as stockholders, management, suppliers, or lenders.

(2) A tax return preparer who is lawfully engaged in the practice of law or accountancy and prepares a tax return for a taxpayer may (i) take such tax return information into account, and may act upon it, in the course of performing legal or accounting services for a client other than the taxpayer or (ii) disclose such information to another employee or member of his law or accounting firm to enable him to take the information into account, and act upon it, in the course of performing legal or accounting services for a client other than the taxpayer, when such information is or may be relevant to the subject matter of such legal or accounting services for the other client and its consideration by those performing the services is necessary for the proper performance by them of such services; provided, however, that in no event may such tax return information be disclosed to a person who is not an employee or member of the law or accounting firm unless such disclosure is exempt from the application of section 7216(a) and § 301.7216-1 by reason of another provision, other than this subparagraph, of § 301.7216-2 or § 301.7216-3.

(3) The application of this paragraph may be illustrated by the following examples:

Example (1). A, a member of an accounting firm, renders an opinion on a financial statement of M Corporation that is part of a registration statement filed with the Securities and Exchange Commission. After the filing of such registration statement, but before its effective date, B, a member of the same accounting firm, prepares an income tax return for N Corporation. In the course of preparing such income tax return, B discovers that N does business with M and concludes that information he is given by N should be considered by A to determine whether the financial statement reported on by A contains an untrue statement of material fact or omitted to state a material fact required to keep the statement from being misleading. B discloses to A the tax return information of N for this purpose. A determines that there is an omission of material fact and that an amended statement should be filed. He so advises M and the Securities and Exchange Commission. He explains that the omission was revealed as a result of confidential information which came to his attention after the statement was filed, but he does not disclose the identity of the taxpayer or the tax return information itself. Section 7216(a) and § 301.7216-1 do not apply to the foregoing disclosure of N's tax return information by B to A and the use of such information by A in advising M and the Securities and Exchange Commission of the necessity for filing an amended statement. Section 7216(a) and § 301.7216-1 would apply to a disclosure of N's tax return information to M or to the Securities and Exchange Commission unless such disclosure is exempt from the application of section 7216(a) and § 301.7216-1 by reason of another provision of either § 301.7216-2 or § 301.7216-3.

Example (2). A, a member of an accounting firm, is conducting an audit of M Corporation, and B, a member of the same accounting firm, prepares an income tax return for D, an officer of M. In the course of preparing such return, B obtains information from D indicating that D, pursuant to an arrangement with a supplier doing business with M, has been receiving from the supplier, a percentage of the amounts which the supplier invoices to M. B discloses this information to A who, acting upon it, searches in the course of the audit for indications of such a kickback scheme. As a result, A discovers information from audit sources which also, but independently, indicates the existence of such a scheme. Without revealing the tax return information he has received from B, A brings to the attention of officers of M the audit information indicating the existence of the kickback scheme. Section 7216(a) and § 301.7216-1 do not apply to the foregoing disclosure of D's tax return information by B to A, the use by A of such information in the course of the audit, and the disclosure by A to M of the audit information indicating the existence of the kickback scheme. See also § 301.7216-2(j). Section 7216(a) and § 301.7216-1 would apply to a disclosure to M, or to any other person not an employee or member of the accounting firm, of D's tax return information furnished to B.

* * * * * * * * * * * * *

(n) **Disclosure to report the commission of a crime.** The provisions of section 7216(a) and § 301.7216-1 shall not apply to the disclosure of any tax return information to the proper Federal or State official in order, and to the extent necessary, to inform such official of the commission of a crime.

[The page following this is 64,375]

Proposed Reg. § 301.7216-2

Domestic Building and Loan Associations

Section 301.7701-13 is amended by revising so much thereof as precedes paragraph (b) to read as follows:

§ 301.7701-13 (Proposed Treasury Decision, published 11-10-70.) **Pre-1970 domestic building and loan association.**

(a) **In general.** For taxable years beginning after October 16, 1962, and before July 12, 1969, the term "domestic building and loan association", a domestic savings and loan association, a Federal savings and loan association, and any other savings institution chartered and supervised as a savings and loan or similar association under Federal or State law which meets the supervisory test (described in paragraph (b) of this section), the business operations test (described in paragraph (c) of this section), and each of the various assets tests (described in paragraphs (d), (e), (f), and (h) of this section). For the definition of the term "domestic building and loan association" for taxable years beginning after July 11, 1969, see § 301.7701-13A.

* * * * * * * * * * *

The following provisions are added immediately after § 301.7701-13:

§ 301.7701-13A (Proposed Treasury Decision, published 11-10-70.) **Post-1969 domestic building and loan association.**

(a) **In general.** For taxable years beginning after July 11, 1969, the term "domestic building and loan association" means a domestic building and loan association, a domestic savings and loan association, a Federal savings and loan association, and any other savings institution chartered and supervised as a savings and loan or similar association under Federal or State law which meets the supervisory test (described in paragraph (b) of this section), the business operations test (described in paragraph (c) of this section), and the assets test (described in paragraph (d) of this section). For the definition of the term "domestic building and loan association" for taxable years beginning after October 16, 1962, and before July 12, 1969, see § 301.7701-13.

(b) **Supervisory test.** A domestic building and loan association must be either (1) an insured institution within the meaning of section 401(a) of the National Housing Act (12 U.S.C. 1724(a)) or (2) subject by law to supervision and examination by State or Federal authority having supervision over such associations. An "insured institution" is one the accounts of which are insured by the Federal Savings and Loan Insurance Corporation.

(c) **Business operations test—(1) In general.** An association must utilize its assets so that its business consist principally of acquiring the savings of the public and investing in loans. The requirement of this paragraph is referred to in this section as the business operations test. The business of acquiring the savings of the public and investing in loans includes ancillary or incidental activities which are directly and primarily related to such acquisition and investment, such as advertising for savings, appraising property on which loans are to be made by the association, and inspecting the progress of construction in connection with construction loans. Even though an association meets the supervisory test described in paragraph (b) of this section and the assets test described in paragraph (d) of this section, it will nevertheless not qualify as a domestic building and loan association if it does not meet the requirements of both subparagraphs (2) and (3) of this paragraph, relating, respectively, to acquiring the savings of the public and investing in loans.

(2) **Acquiring the savings of the public.** The requirement that an association's business (other than investing in loans) must consist principally of acquiring the savings of the public ordinarily will be considered to be met if savings are acquired in all material respects in conformity with the rules and regulations of the Federal Home Loan Bank Board or substantially equivalent rules of a State law or supervisory authority. Alternatively, such requirement will be considered to be met if more than 75 percent of the dollar amount of the total deposits, withdrawable shares, and other obligations of the association are held during the taxable year

Proposed Reg. § 301.7701-13A

by the general public, as opposed to amounts deposited or held by family or related business groups or persons who are officers or directors of the association. However, the preceding sentence shall not apply if the dollar amount of other obligations of the association outstanding during the taxable year exceeds 25 percent of the dollar amount of the total deposits, withdrawable shares, and other obligations of the association outstanding during such year. For purposes of this subparagraph, the term "other obligations" means notes, bonds, debentures, or other obligations, or other securities (except capital stock), issued by an association in conformity with the rules and regulations of the Federal Home Loan Bank Board or substantially equivalent rules of a State law or supervisory authority. The term "other obligations" does not include an advance made by a Federal Home Loan Bank under the authority of section 10 or 10b of the Federal Home Loan Bank Act (12 U.S.C. 1430, 1430b) as amended and supplemented. Both percentages specified in this subparagraph shall be computed either as of the close of the taxable year or, at the option of the taxpayer, on the basis of the average of the dollar amounts of the total deposits, withdrawable shares, and other obligations of the association held during the taxable year. Such averages shall be determined by computing each percentage specified either as of the close of each month, as of the close of each quarter, or semiannually during the taxable year and by using the yearly average of the monthly, quarterly, or semiannual percentages obtained. The method selected must be applied uniformly for the taxable year to both percentages, but the method may be changed from year to year.

(3) **Investing in loans**—(i) In general. The requirement that an association's business (other than acquiring the savings of the public) must consist principally of investing in loans will be considered to be met for a taxable year only if more than 75 percent of the gross income of the association consists of—

(a) Interest or dividends on assets defined in subparagraphs (1), (2), and (3) of paragraph (e) of this section,

(b) Interest on loans,

(c) Income attributable to the portion of property used in the association's business, as defined in paragraph (e) (11) of this section,

(d) So much of the amount of premiums, discounts, commissions, or fees (including late charges and penalties) on loans which have at some time been held by the association, or for which firm commitments have been issued, as is not in excess of 20 percent of the gross income of the association,

(e) Net gain from sales and exchanges of governmental obligations, as defined in paragraph (e) (2) of this section, or

(f) Income, gain or loss attributable to foreclosed property, as defined in paragraph (e) (9) of this section, but not including such income, gain or loss which, pursuant to section 595 and the regulations thereunder, is not included in gross income.

Examples of types of income which would cause an association to fail to meet the requirements of this subparagraph if, in the aggregate, they equal or exceed 25 percent of gross income, are: the excess of gains over losses from sales of real property (other than foreclosed property); rental income (other than on foreclosed property and the portion of property used in the association's business); premiums, commissions, and fees (other than commitment fees) on loans which have never been held by the association; and insurance brokerage fees.

(ii) Computation of gross income. For purposes of this subparagraph, gross income is computed without regard to—

(a) Gain or loss on the sale or exchange of the portion of property used in the association's business as defined in paragraph (e)(11) of this section,

(b) Gain or loss on the sale or exchange of the rented portion of property used as the principal or branch office of the association, as defined in paragraph (e)(11) of this section, and

(c) Gains or losses on sales of participations and loans, other than governmental obligations defined in paragraph (e)(2) of this section.

For purposes of this subparagraph, gross income is also computed without regard to items of income which an association establishes arise out of transactions which are necessitated by exceptional circumstances and which are not undertaken as recurring business activities for profit. Thus, for example, an association would meet the investing in loans requirement if it can establish that it would otherwise fail to meet that requirement solely because of the receipt of a non-recurring item of income due to exceptional circumstances. For this purpose, transactions necessitated by an excess of demand for loans over savings capital in the association's area are not to be deemed to be necessitated by exceptional circumstances. For purposes of (c) of this subdivision, the term "sales of participations" means sales by an association of interests in loans, which sales meet the requirements of the regulations of the Federal Home Loan Bank Board relating to sales of participations, or which meet substantially equivalent requirements of State law or regulations relating to sales of participations.

(iii) Reporting requirement. In the case of income tax returns for taxable years beginning after July 11, 1969, there is required to be filed with the return a statement showing the amount of gross income for the taxable year in each of the categories described in subdivision (i) of this subparagraph.

(d) **60 percent of assets test.** At least 60 percent of the amount of the total assets of a domestic building and loan association must consist of the assets defined in paragraph (e) of this section. The percentage specified in this paragraph is computed as of the close of the taxable year or, at the option of the taxpayer, may be computed on the basis of the average assets outstanding during the taxable year. Such average is determined by making the appropriate computation described in this section either as of the close of each month, as of the close of each quarter, or semiannually during the taxable year and by using the yearly average of the monthly, quarterly, or semiannual percentage obtained for each category of assets defined in paragraph (e) of this section. The method selected must be applied uniformly for the taxable year to all categories of assets, but the method may be changed from year to year. For purposes of this paragraph, it is immaterial whether the association originated the loans defined in subparagraphs (4) through (8) and (10) of paragraph (e) of this section or purchased or otherwise acquired them in whole or in part from another. See paragraph (f) of this section for definition of certain terms used in this paragraph and in paragraph (e) of this section, and for the determination of amount and character of loans.

(e) **Assets defined.** The assets defined in this paragraph are—

(1) **Cash.** The term "cash" means cash on hand, and time or demand deposits with, or withdrawable accounts in, other financial institutions.

(2) **Governmental obligations.** The term "governmental obligations" means—

(i) Obligations of the United States,

(ii) Obligations of a State or political subdivision of a State, and

(iii) Stock or obligations of a corporation which is an instrumentality of the United States, a State, or a political subdivision of a State,
other than obligations the interest on which is excludable from gross income under section 103 and the regulations thereunder.

(3) **Deposit insurance company securities.** The term "deposit insurance company securities" means certificates of deposit in, or obligations of, a corporation organized under a State law which specifically authorizes such corporation to insure the deposits or share accounts of member associations.

(4) **Passbook loan.** The term "passbook loan" means a loan to the extent secured by a deposit, withdrawable share, or savings account in the association, or share of a member of the association, with respect to which a distribution is allowable as a deduction under section 591.

(5) **Residential real property loan.** [Reserved]

(6) **Church loan.** [Reserved]

(7) **Urban renewal loan.** [Reserved]

(8) **Institutional loan.** [Reserved]

Proposed Reg. § 301.7701-13A

(9) **Foreclosed property.** [Reserved]

(10) **Educational loan.** [Reserved]

(11) **Property used in the association's business**—(i) In general. The term "property used in the association's business" means land, buildings, furniture, fixtures, equipment, leasehold interests, leasehold improvements, and other assets used by the association in the conduct of its business of acquiring the savings of the public and investing in loans. Real property held for the purpose of being used primarily as the principal or branch office of the association constitutes property used in the association's business so long as it is reasonably anticipated that such property will be occupied for such use by the association, or that construction work preparatory to such occupancy will be commenced thereon, within 2 years after acquisition of the property. Stock of a wholly owned subsidiary corporation which has as its exclusive activity the ownership and management of property more than 50 percent of the fair rental value of which is used as the principal or branch office of the association constitutes property used in such business. Real property held by an association for investment or sale, even for the purpose of obtaining mortgage loans thereon, does not constitute property used in the association's business.

(ii) Property rented to others. Except as provided in the second sentence of subdivision (i) of this subparagraph, property or a portion thereof rented by the association to others does not constitute property used in the association's business. However, if the fair rental value of the rented portion of a single piece of real property (including appurtenant parcels) used as the principal or branch office of the association constitutes less than 50 percent of the fair rental value of such piece of property, or if such property has an adjusted basis of not more than $150,000, the entire property shall be considered used in such business. If such rented portion constitutes 50 percent or more of the fair rental value of such piece of property, and such property has an adjusted basis of more than $150,000, an allocation of its adjusted basis is required. The portion of the total adjusted basis of such piece of property which is deemed to be property used in the association's business shall be equal to an amount which bears the same ratio to such total adjusted basis as the amount of the fair rental value of the portion used as the principal or branch office of the association bears to the total fair rental value of such property. In the case of all property other than real property used or to be used as the principal or branch office of the association, if the fair rental value of the rented portion thereof constitutes less than 15 percent of the fair rental value of such property, the entire property shall be considered used in the association's business. If such rented portion constitutes 15 percent or more of the fair rental value of such property, an allocation of its adjusted basis (in the same manner as required for real property used as the principal or branch office) is required.

(f) **Special rules.** [Reserved]

Returns and Statements on Magnetic Tapes

Section 1.9101-1 is amended by deleting the words "Form 1087, 1099, or W-2" and inserting in lieu thereof "Form 1087 or 1099"; and by deleting the last sentence and inserting in lieu thereof the following: "In any case where the use of Form W-2 is required for the purpose of making a return or reporting information, such requirement may be satisfied by submitting the information required by such form on magnetic tape or other approved media, provided that the prior consent of the Commissioner of Social Security (or other authorized officer or employee thereof) has been obtained."

§ 1.9101-1 (Proposed Treasury Decision, published 5-10-78.) **Permission to submit information required by certain returns and statements on magnetic tape.**

Capital Construction Funds

Section 3.2, as adopted by Treasury Decision 7398, is amended by revising paragraphs (a)(3) and (4), (c), and (g)(2). These revised provisions read as follows:

§3.2 (Proposed Treasury Decision, published 1-29-76.) **Ceiling on deposits.**

(a) **In general.** * * *

(3) **Underdeposit caused by audit adjustment.** (i) If, upon an audit of a party's Federal income tax return, the district director, or director of an Internal Revenue Service center, makes an adjustment which increases the amount of a subceiling (as defined in subparagraph (1) of this paragraph) in a taxable year over the amount of such subceiling as determined when such return was filed, and if the party complies with the requirements of subparagraph (4) of this paragraph, then the party may make a deficiency deposit which will reduce the party's taxable income or be excluded from gross income (as the case may be) for purposes of determining the tax on the party's taxable income for that taxable year.

(ii) Such deficiency deposit shall not exceed the excess (if any) between (a) the subceiling allowable under section 607(b) of the Act and paragraph (a)(1) of this section, as

Proposed Reg. §3.2

determined on audit, or under the agreement of the party with the Secretary of Commerce, whichever is lower, and (b) the subceiling determined when the party's return was filed.

(iii) A deficiency deposit will be related to the fund's subceiling in the manner provided in subparagraphs (1) and (2) of this paragraph in the taxable year to which it relates. The reduction in the party's taxable income or the exclusion from gross income (as the case may be) occasioned by a deficiency deposit will not, however, be allowed for the purpose of determining interest, additional amounts, or assessable penalties, computed with respect to the tax on the party's taxable income prior to the allowance of such reduction or exclusion. For example, in the case of a calendar year taxpayer, if a deposit is made in 1972 of an amount equal to an amount of earnings from shipping operations in 1971, and in 1974 a deficiency deposit is made which represents the portion of taxable income from 1971 that resulted from adjustments made upon an audit by the Internal Revenue Service, then the amounts deposited in 1972 and 1974 would both reduce taxable income for 1971. In such a case, interest, additional amounts, or assessable penalties will be due in the manner and under the conditions specified in the Code, applied by treating payment of the tax as having been made on the date the tax is paid or the deficiency deposit is actually made in the fund, whichever is earlier. No interest shall be allowed on a credit or refund arising from the application of this subparagraph.

(iv) For purposes of determining the order of withdrawals under §3.6(b) and §3.7(c) and interest on nonqualified withdrawals under §3.7(e), these deposits will be treated under §3.3(b)(4)(i) as having been made on the date they were actually made.

(4) Requirements for deficiency deposits. (i) In order for the deficiency deposit under subparagraph (3) of this paragraph to be allowed—

(a) There must be a determination described in subdivision (ii) of this subparagraph of the party's income tax liability determined without regard to any deficiency deposit,

(b) The adjustment made by the district director, or director of an Internal Revenue Service center, referred to in subparagraph (3)(i) of this paragraph, must not have resulted from an underpayment described in section 6653(a) (relating to negligence or intentional disregard of rules and regulations) or section 6653(b) (relating to fraud) of the Code,

(c) The deficiency deposit must be made by the party on, or within 90 days after, the date of such determination and prior to the filing of a claim under subdivision (iii) of this subparagraph for deduction for deficiency deposits,

(d) The claim under subdivision (iii) of this subparagraph must be filed within 120 days after such determination, and

(e) The adjustment to the party's tax liability occasioned by the reduction in the party's taxable income or the exclusion from the party's gross income (as the case may be) under subparagraph (3) of this paragraph must not be prohibited by section 6215 or 6512 of the Code (with respect to Tax Court decision), the statute of limitations, or any other law or rule of law.

(ii) A determination of the party's income tax liability shall, for purposes of this subparagraph, be established in the following manner:

(a) A closing agreement made under section 7121 of the Code. For purposes of subdivision (i)(c) of this subparagraph, the date such agreement is approved by the Commissioner shall be the date of determination.

(b) An agreement signed by the district director, director of the service center with which the party files its annual return, or by such other official to whom authority to sign the agreement is delegated, and by or on behalf of the party, which agreement sets forth the total amount of the party's income tax liability for the taxable year or years and has been sent to the party at his last known address by either registered or certified mail. For purposes of subdivision (i)(c) of this subparagraph, if such agreement is sent by registered mail, the date of registration is considered the date of determination; if sent by certified mail, the date of postmark on the sender's receipt for such mail is considered the

Proposed Reg. §3.2

date of determination. If the party makes a deficiency deposit before such registration or postmark date but on or after the date the district director, director of the service center or other official has signed the agreement, the date of signature by the district director or director of the service center or other official is considered the date of final determination,

(c) A decision of the United States Tax Court which has become final, as prescribed in section 7481 of the Code,

(d) A decision of a court of the United States (other than the United States Tax Court) which has become final. The date upon which a judgment of a court becomes final, which is the date of the determination in such cases, must be determined upon the basis of the facts in the particular case. For example, a judgment of a United States District Court becomes final upon the expiration of the time allowed for taking an appeal, if no such appeal is duly taken within such time; and a judgment of the United States Court of Claims becomes final upon the expiration of the time allowed for filing a petition for certiorari if no such petition is duly filed within such time.

(iii) A claim for deduction for a deficiency deposit shall be made in duplicate, shall be dated and signed by the party and shall contain or be verified by, a written declaration that it is made under the penalties of perjury. The claim shall also contain the following information:

(a) The name and address of the party;

(b) The amount of the deficiency determined with respect to the party's income tax and the taxable year or years involved; the amount of the unpaid deficiency or, if the deficiency has been paid in whole or in part, the date of payment and the amount thereof; a statement as to how the deficiency was established, if unpaid; or if paid in whole or in part, how it was established that any portion of the amount paid was a deficiency at the time when paid and, in either case whether it was by an agreement under subdivision (ii)(b) of this subparagraph, by a closing agreement under section 7121, or by a decision of the Tax Court or court judgment and the date thereof; if established by a final judgment in a suit against the United States for refund, the date of payment of the deficiency, the date the claim for refund was filed, and the date the suit was brought; if established by a Tax Court decision or court judgment, a copy thereof shall be attached, together with an explanation of how the decision became final; if established by an agreement under subdivision (ii)(b) of this subparagraph, a copy of such agreement shall be attached;

(c) The amount and date of the deposit with respect to which the claim for the deduction or exclusion for the deficiency deposit is filed and a copy of the deposit receipt for such deposit;

(d) The amount claimed as a deduction or exclusion for deficiency deposit; and

(e) Such other information as may be required by the Commissioner or his delegate.

* *

(c) Net proceeds from transactions with respect to agreement vessels—(1) Gross proceeds from disposition of agreements vessels. (i) Except as provided in subparagraph (6) of this paragraph, with respect to installment sales, the gross proceeds from the sale or other disposition (including certain mortgages treated for purposes of this part as a disposition) of an agreement vessel is the total amount realized or to be realized by the party from the sale or other disposition of such vessel, including any property (whether or not a vessel) and evidences of indebtedness and contract rights received, whether or not they constitute an amount realized under section 1001(b) of the Code and the regulations thereunder, but only to the extent not included in taxable income under paragraph (b) of this section. Notwithstanding the preceding sentence, gross proceeds does not include any property to the extent received without recognition of gain under both the Act and the Code. For purposes of this paragraph, sale or other disposition does not include any transaction between persons related within the meaning of subparagraph (3)(ii) of this paragraph which has as its primary purpose the creation of an allowable subceiling under section 607(b)(1)(C) of the Act and paragraph (a)(1)(iii) of this section.

(ii) Gross proceeds does not include interest on obligations received by the party from the sale or other disposition of an agreement vessel, but does include amounts received as the result of the forfeiture of collateral for the payment of purchase-money obligations and amounts received from the mortgaging of a qualified vessel. (For rules requiring the deposit of net proceeds from the mortgaging of a qualified vessel into the capital account of the fund, see 46 CFR §390.11(b) and 50 CFR §259.)

(2) **Net proceeds.** Net proceeds from the sale or other disposition of an agreement vessel is the greater of—
  (i) The sum of—
  (a) The gain recognized (before application of this part) upon a sale or other disposition and
  (b) The gain recognized under section 607(g)(5) of the Act upon such sale or other disposition which is not taken into account under (a) of this subdivision, or
  (ii) The excess of the gross proceeds (as defined in subparagraph (1) of this paragraph) over the sum of—
  (a) Amounts necessarily paid or incurred in connection with the sale or other disposition and
  (b) The amounts of any indebtedness assumed by the purchaser of such vessel, subject to which the purchaser acquires the vessel, or secured by such vessel which the party must satisfy out of the proceeds of the sale or other disposition.

(3) **Deposits of net proceeds.** (i) For purposes of this part, any net proceeds deposited for the year of sale or other disposition shall be treated as an amount realized that year. In the case of the sale or other disposition of properties which include at least one agreement vessel, or share therein, for a lump sum, the gross proceeds shall be allocated between agreement vessels and other property in proportion to the aggregate fair market values of each of the two types of property on the date of the sale or other disposition. For purposes of determining the amount of net proceeds permitted to be deposited pursuant to this paragraph as a result of such a sale or other disposition, the party may use the aggregate gross proceeds that were allocated to the agreement vessels or, if less than the entire aggregate net proceeds is deposited, may further allocate the gross proceeds among each vessel or share therein. In order not to take gain into account, as provided by section 607(d)(1)(B) of the Act, the party must deposit an amount equal to the entire net proceeds realized or to be realized with respect to the agreement vessel sold or otherwise disposed of. Such deposit must be in the form of money and securities and stock of a type specified in section 607(c) of the Act other than securities or stock issued by the party or a person related to the party (as described in subdivision (ii) of this subparagraph); however, if the purchaser or transferee is not related to the party (as described in subdivision (ii) of this subparagraph), the deposit may include any intangible property received on such sale or other disposition.

(ii) For purposes of the preceding sentence a person is a related person to another person if—
  (a) The relationship between such persons would result in disallowance of losses under section 267 or 707(b) of the Code, or
  (b) Such persons are members of the same controlled group of corporations (as defined in section 1563(a) of the Code, except that "more than 50 percent" shall be substituted for "at least 80 percent" each place it appears therein).

(4) **Related purchaser.** In the event the party and the purchaser are owned or controlled directly or indirectly by the same interests within the meaning of section 482 of the Code and the regulations thereunder, the amount realized or to be realized shall be the fair market value of the vessels sold or otherwise disposed of. In such case, the party shall furnish evidence sufficient, in the opinion of the Secretary of Commerce, to establish that the amount realized or to be realized is the fair market value.

(5) **Net proceeds from insurance or indemnity.** Where the net proceeds of insurance or indemnity are received in more than one payment, the deposit of such net proceeds shall relate to the taxable year of receipt. The net proceeds from insurance or indemnity attributable to an agreement vessel under a contract of insurance or indemnity as compensation for damages done to the vessel (other than amounts intended to compensate for loss of profits) is the greater of—
  (i) The sum of—
  (a) The gain recognized (before application of this part) under such a contract and

Proposed Reg. §3.2

(b) The gain recognized under section 607(g)(5) of the Act upon such contract which is not taken into account under (a) of this subdivision, or

(ii) The excess of the gross proceeds the party received under such contract over the sum of—

(a) The amounts necessarily paid or incurred purely for the collection of such compensation and

(b) The amount of any indebtedness secured by such vessel which the party was required to satisfy out of the amount of such insurance of indemnity received.

(6) Installment sale of agreement vessel. (i) If the party deposits in a fund net proceeds from the sale or other disposition of an agreement vessel, gain from the disposition of the vessel may be reported under the installment method if such method is otherwise available under section 453 of the Code. If an installment obligation is not deposited into the fund, the ceiling on deposits described in paragraph (a) of this section is not increased by the income which consists of interest on each installment payment.

(ii) If the party properly elects the installment method under section 453 of the Code with respect to the sale or other disposition of an agreement vessel, then—

(a) The evidences of indebtedness of the purchaser (within the meaning of section 453(b) of the Code) which are not deposited into the fund shall not be considered to be gross proceeds or net proceeds,

(b) For purposes of this subparagraph, for each taxable year the amount of net proceeds realized and required to be deposited shall be the amount determined under subdivision (iii) of this subparagraph or, if the "short-cut" method is permitted, under subdivision (v) of this subparagraph,

(c) If the net proceeds so determined for a year are not timely deposited, the provisions of subdivision (vi) of this subparagraph shall apply, and

(d) The income (other than interest) on each installment payment shall be deemed to consist of any gain which is treated as ordinary income by reason of the application of section 1245(a)(1) of the Code until all such gain is reported, then any gain which is treated as ordinary income by reason of the application of section 607(g)(5) of the Act and §3.6(e) until all such gain has been reported, and the remaining portion (if any) of such income shall be deemed to consist of gain to which neither section 1245(a)(1) nor section 607(g)(5) of the Act and §3.6(e) applies.

(iii) With respect to the sale or other disposition of an agreement vessel, the amount of net proceeds for any taxable year which must be timely deposited is equal to the greater of (a) the gain which would be recognized in that taxable year if the deposit were not made or (b) an amount equal to (1) the installment payment (within the meaning of §1.453-4(c) of the Income Tax Regulations of this chapter) received during the taxable year minus (2) the sum of the expenses necessarily paid or incurred (or so treated under subdivision (iv) of this subparagraph) during such taxable year in connection with the installment sale and amounts of any indebtedness which the party must satisfy out of the proceeds of the sale in such taxable year. For purposes of this subdivision (iii), but not subdivision (iv) of this subparagraph, the amount in (b) of this subdivision shall not be less than zero.

(iv) If for any taxable year the amount in subdivision (iii)(a) of this subparagraph exceeds the amount in subdivision (iii)(b) of this subparagraph, then such excess is an unabsorbed portion of expenses and indebtedness, which shall be treated as an expense or indebtedness described in subdivision (iii)(b)(2) of this subparagraph in the subsequent taxable year. Thus, for example, if the amount in subdivision (iii)(b) of this subparagraph is less than zero, such excess is the sum of such amount and the amount in subdivision (iii)(a) of this subparagraph.

(v) The "short-cut" method of this subdivision is permitted if the purchaser takes the vessel subject to, or assumes, a liability which was a lien on the vessel, and the amount of such liability at the time of the sale was in excess of the party's adjusted basis in such vessel. In such a case, the amount of net proceeds for any taxable year which must be timely deposited is equal to the gain recognized for the taxable year under section 453 of the Code and the regulations thereunder.

(vi) With respect to any sale or other disposition of an agreement vessel, deposits of net proceeds realized (determined under subdivision (iii) or (v) of this subparagraph) shall be contingent deposits until there is deposited the entire net proceeds to be realized (determined without regard to this paragraph) from such sale or other disposition or from the earlier disposition or satisfaction of installment obligations received pursuant to such sale or other disposition. If for any taxable year such net proceeds are not timely deposited pursuant to subdivision (iii) or (v) of this subparagraph, all amounts previously deposited with respect to such sale or other disposition shall be withdrawn in a nonqualified withdrawal under §3.7, and such withdrawal shall be considered to have taken place on the last day of the party's first taxable year during which the net proceeds (which were not deposited) were received. See 46 C.F.R. §390 and 50 C.F.R. §259.

(vii) The provisions of this subparagraph are illustrated by the following examples:

Example (1). X Corporation, which uses the calendar year as its taxable year and maintains a fund described in §3.1, contracts to sell an agreement vessel (with an adjusted basis of $20,000) used in its shipping business for $200,000 plus a sufficient amount of interest so that section 483 does not apply. Thus, the gain realized is $180,000. The terms of the sale are that the purchaser is to assume the outstanding amount ($90,000) of a purchase-money mortgage, followed by 10 equal semi-annual principal payments of $11,000 for the 5 consecutive taxable years after the year of sale. Under §1.453-4(c) of the Income Tax Regulations of this chapter, the excess of the mortgage ($90,000) over X's adjusted basis ($20,000), or $70,000, is included as a payment received in the year of sale. Since under section 453(b)(2)(A) of the Code payments in the taxable year of sale may not exceed 30 percent of the selling price (30% of $200,000 = $60,000), X may not elect under section 453 of the Code to report the gain under the installment method and the provisions of this subparagraph do not apply to such sale.

Example (2). (a) Assume the same facts as in example (1) except that X sells the vessel in 1972 when it has an adjusted basis of $100,000 and the terms of payment of the selling price of $200,000 are the assumption of an outstanding amount of a purchase-money mortgage of $50,000, a cash downpayment of $50,000 in 1972 (the year of the sale), and principal payments of $20,000 per year for the next 5 years. Thus, since the outstanding amount of the purchase-money mortgage ($50,000) is not greater than the vessel's adjusted basis ($100,000), the "contract price" within the meaning of §1.453-4(c) of the Income Tax Regulations of this chapter is $150,000, i.e., downpayment, $50,000, plus 5 payments of $20,000 each, $100,000. Assume further that X incurred $10,000 in selling expenses of the type described in subdivision (iii)(b)(2) of this subparagraph. Thus, X's gain on the sale is $90,000 (i.e., selling price, $200,000 minus adjusted basis, $100,000, minus selling expenses, $10,000) and the gross profit realized or to be realized when the property is paid for (within the meaning of §1.453-1(b) of the Income Tax Regulations of this chapter) is also $90,000.

(b) X properly elects to report the sale under the installment method under section 453 of the Code since payments in the year of sale ($50,000) do not exceed 30 percent of the selling price of $200,000, or $60,000.

(c) Since X has elected under section 453 of the Code to report gain on the installment method, in order to defer the gain on the sale as provided by section 607(d)(1)(B) of the Act and §3.3(b)(2)(i), subdivision (ii)(c) of this subparagraph requires that X must timely deposit into the fund the net proceeds for each taxable year in which received.

(d) For each taxable year, the net proceeds which must be timely deposited under subdivision (iii) of this subparagraph are determined as follows:

		1972	Next 5 years
(1)	Installment payment	$50,000	$20,000
(2)	Multiply by gross profit percentage: Gross profit ($90,000) ÷ contract price ($150,000)	60%	60%
(3)	Gain recognized	$30,000	$12,000

Proposed Reg. §3.2

(4) Selling expenses	$10,000		$0
(5) Indebtedness which party must satisfy	0		0
(6) Sum of lines (4) and (5)	10,000		0
(7) Line (1) minus line (6)	40,000		20,000
(8) Required deposit: greater of line (3) or (7)	$40,000		$20,000

In the above computation, there is no unabsorbed portion of expenses and indebtedness under subdivision (iv) of this subparagraph since for no taxable year does line (3) exceed line (7).

(e) For purposes of subdivision (vi) of this subparagraph, the entire net proceeds determined under subparagraph (2) of this paragraph which must be deposited before any deposits will no longer be contingent deposits is the excess of the gross proceeds to be realized of $200,000 (i.e., the sum of the mortgage assumed, $50,000, the cash downpayment, $50,000, and the 5 annual $20,000 payments, $100,000) over the sum of selling expenses ($10,000) and the amount of the mortgage assumed ($50,000), or $140,000.

(f) Of the $90,000 gain to be recognized upon sale of the vessel, assume that $60,000 would be recognized as ordinary income by reason of the application of section 1245(a)(1) of the Code (relating to depreciation recapture), $20,000 would be recognized as ordinary income under section 607(g)(5) of the Act and §3.6(e)(1) (relating to ordinary income treatment of certain gains), and $10,000 would be recognized as gain from the sale or exchange of property to which section 1231 of the Code applies. Under §1.1245-6(d) of the Income Tax Regulations of this chapter and §3.6(e)(1), the $80,000 of ordinary income (i.e., $60,000 plus $20,000) is treated as recognized first. Thus, under section 607(e) of the Act and §3.4, the deposit of the entire net proceeds of $140,000 will result in the following additions to the fund accounts in the years indicated in the table below:

	(1)	(2)	(3)	(4)	(5)	(6)
Year	Payment	Net proceeds	Gain	Ordinary income account	Capital gain account	Capital account
1972	$50,000	$40,000	$30,000	$30,000		$10,000
1973	20,000	20,000	12,000	12,000		8,000
1974	20,000	20,000	12,000	12,000		8,000
1975	20,000	20,000	12,000	12,000		8,000
1976	20,000	20,000	12,000	12,000		8,000
1977	20,000	20,000	12,000	2,000	$10,000	8,000
Totals	$150,000	$140,000	$90,000	$80,000	$10,000	$50,000

Example (3). (a) Assume the same facts as in example (2) except that X's adjusted basis in the vessel at the time of sale is $30,000, the sale price is $150,000, and the terms of payment are the assumption of the outstanding amount of a purchase-money mortgage of $45,000, cash down-payment of $25,000, and principal payments of $40,000 per year for the next 2 years. Under §1.453-4(c) of the Income Tax Regulations of this chapter, the excess ($15,000) of the outstanding amount of the purchase-money mortgage assumed ($45,000) over X's adjusted basis in the vessel ($30,000) is treated as a payment received in the year of sale, and thus, the payments in the year of sale are the sum of such excess, $15,000, and the downpayment, $25,000, or $40,000. Accordingly, the "contract price" is $120,000, i.e., the payments in the year of sale, $40,000, plus two payments of $40,000 each. Selling expenses remain at $10,000 in the year of sale. Thus, X's gain on the sale is $110,000 (i.e., selling price, $150,000, minus adjusted basis, $30,000, minus selling expenses $10,000) and the gross profit realized or to be realized when the property is paid for (within the meaning of §1.453-1(b) of the Income Tax Regulations of this chapter) is also $110,000.

(b) X properly elects to report the sale under the installment method under section 453 of the Code since payments in the year of sale ($40,000) do not exceed 30 percent of the selling price of $150,000, or $45,000.

(c) Since X has elected under section 453 of the Code to report gain on the installment method, in order to defer the gain on the sale as provided by section 607(d)(1)(B) of the Act and §3.3(b)(2)(i), subdivision (ii)(b) of this subparagraph requires that X must timely deposit into the fund the net proceeds for each taxable year in which received.

(d) For each taxable year, the net proceeds which must be timely deposited under subdivision (iii) of this subparagraph are determined as follows:

		1972	1973	1974
(1)	Installment payment	$40,000	$40,000	$40,000
(2)	Multiply by gross profit percentage: gross profit ($110,000) ÷ contract price ($120,000)	91 2/3%	91 2/3%	91 2/3%
(3)	Gain recognized	$36,667	$36,667	$36,667
(4)	Selling expenses	10,000	0	0
(5)	Indebtedness which the party must satisfy	0	0	0
(6)	Unabsorbed portion of expenses and indebtedness under subdivision (iv) of this subparagraph: line (10)(e) from from preceding year	-	6,667	3,333
(7)	Sum of lines (4), (5), and (6)	10,000	6,667	3,333
(8)	Excess of line (1) over (7)	30,000	33,333	36,667
(9)	Required deposit greater of line (3) or line (8)	36,667	36,667	36,667
(10)	Unabsorbed portion carried forward to subsequent year:			
	(a) Line (3)	36,667	36,667	36,667
	(b) Line (1)	40,000	40,000	40,000
	(c) Line (7)	10,000	6,667	3,333
	(d) Line (b) minus line (c)	30,000	33,333	36,667
	(e) If line (a) exceeds line (d), the excess	6,667	3,333*	--

Proposed Reg. §3.2

(e) Since the outstanding amount of the purchase-money mortgage ($45,000) exceeds X's adjusted basis in the vessel ($30,000), X is permitted to use the "short-cut" method under subdivision (v) of this subparagraph, requiring the deposit of X's gain from the sale in each year ($36,667, as determined under line (3) of (d) of this example), which gives the same result as the determination under subdivision (iii) of this subparagraph.

Example (4). (a) Assume the same facts as in example (1) except that X sells the vessel in 1972 when it has an adjusted basis of $106,000 and the terms of payment of the selling price of $150,000 are the assumption of an outstanding amount of a purchase-money mortgage of $90,000, no payment in the year of sale, and principal payments of $19,000, $21,000, and $20,000, respectively, for the next 3 years. Thus, since the outstanding amount of the purchase-money mortgage ($90,000) is not greater than the vessel's adjusted basis ($106,000), the "contract price" within the meaning of §1.453-4(c) of the Income Tax Regulations of this chapter is $60,000, i.e., the sum of the 3 annual payments. Assume further that X incurred $20,000 in selling expenses of the type described in subdivision (iii)(b)(2) of this subparagraph. Thus, X's gain on the sale is $24,000 (i.e., selling price, $150,000, minus adjusted basis, $106,000, minus selling expenses, $20,000) and the gross profit realized or to be realized when the property is paid for (within the meaning of §1.453-1(b) of the Income Tax Regulations of this chapter) is also $24,000.

(b) X properly elects to report the sale under the installment method under section 453 of the Code since payments in the year of sale ($0) do not exceed 30 percent of the selling price of $150,000, or $45,000.

---

*Difference due to rounding.

(c) Since X has elected under section 453 of the Code to report gain on the installment method, in order to defer the gain on the sale as provided by section 607(d)(1)(B) of the Act and §3.3(b)(2)(i), subdivision (ii)(b) of this subparagraph requires that X must timely deposit into the fund the net proceeds for each taxable year in which received.

(d) For each taxable year, the net proceeds which must be timely deposited under subdivision (iii) of this subparagraph are determined as follows:

	1972	1973	1974	1975
(1) Installment payment	$0	$19,000	$21,000	$20,000
(2) Multiply by gross profit percentage: Gross profit ($24,000) ÷ contract price ($60,000)	40%	40%	40%	40%
(3) Gain recognized	0	7,600	8,400	8,000
(4) Selling expenses	20,000	0	0	0
(5) Indebtedness which party must satisfy	0	0	0	0
(6) Unabsorbed portion of expenses and indebtedness under subdivision (iv) of this subparagraph: line (10)(e) from preceding year	--	20,000	8,600	0
(7) Sum of lines (4), (5), and (6)	20,000	20,000	8,600	0
(8) Excess of line (1) over line (7)	0	0	12,400	20,000
(9) Required deposit: greater of line (3) or line (8)	0	7,600	12,400	20,000

	1972	1973	1974	1975
(10) Unabsorbed portion carried forward to subsequent year:				
(a) Line (3)	0	7,600	8,400	8,000
(b) Line (1)	0	19,000	21,000	20,000
	1972	1973	1974	1975
(c) Line (7)	20,000	20,000	8,600	0
(d) Line (b) minus line (c)	(20,000)	(1,000)	12,400	20,000
(e) If line (a) exceeds line (d), the excess	20,000	8,600	--	--

* *

(g) **Special rules for nonmoney deposits and withdrawals.** * * *

(2) **Election not to treat deposits of property other than money as a sale or exchange at the time of deposit.** A party may elect to treat a deposit of property as if no sale or other taxable event had occurred on the date of deposit. If such election is made, in the taxable year the fund disposes of the property, or the party disposes of the fund in a transaction which is treated as not constituting a nonqualified withdrawal by reason of the application of §3.8(b)(2) or (c), then the party shall recognize as gain or loss with respect to nonfund property the amount he would have recognized on the day the property was deposited into the fund had the election not been made. The party's holding period with respect to such property shall not include the period of time such property was held by the fund. If the party disposes of a fund which contains property subject to the election provided by this subparagraph in a transaction which is treated as not constituting a nonqualified withdrawal by reason of the application of §3.8(b)(1), then for purposes of determining the basis of property received by the party in such transaction, the basis of property in the fund subject to such election is the party's, not the fund's, adjusted basis for such property. The election shall be made by a statement to that effect, attached to the party's Federal income tax return for the taxable year to which the deposit relates, or, if such return is filed before such deposit is made, attached to the party's return for the taxable year during which the deposit is actually made. Such statement shall also contain, or shall be considered as containing, an agreement by the party to be bound by the rules of this paragraph.

* *

Section 3.3, as adopted by Treasury Decision 7398, is amended by revising paragraph (b)(2)(i)(b) and paragraph (c). These revised provisions read as follows:

§3.3 (Proposed Treasury Decision, published 1-29-76.) **Nontaxability of deposits.**

* *

(b) **Treatment of deposits.** * * *

(2) **Net proceeds from agreement vessels and fund earnings.** (i) (a) * * *

(b) However, if (1) a party transfers a vessel, (2) the basis of the property the party receives is determined by reference to the basis of such vessel or such vessel's basis in the hands of the transferee is determined by reference to its basis in the hands of the party, (3) the party deposits the net proceeds of the transfer into the fund, and (4) by reason of applying section 607(d)(1)(B) of the Act the party's gain is not taken into account, then for the purpose of determining the basis of such property received, of such vessel in the hands of the transferee, or both (as the case may be) such gain shall be treated as if it were recognized. The provisions of this subdivision (b) are illustrated in example (4) of §3.6(e)(7)(ii).

* *

Proposed Reg. §3.3

(c) **Determination of earnings and profits.** Under section 607(d)(1)(D) of the Act, in general the earnings and profits of any corporation (within the meaning of section 316 of the Code) shall be determined without regard to this part. Thus, for example—

(1) Although certain amounts deposited into the fund reduce taxable income and certain other amounts deposited into the fund result in an exclusion from gross income, earnings and profits of the corporation are not reduced by the amount of such deposits.

(2) Earnings and profits are not increased when amounts withdrawn from the fund are included in income under §3.7(d).

(3) For purposes of the third sentence of section 312(f)(1) of the Code (see §1.312-7(c) of the Income Tax Regulations of this chapter), the reduction in basis provided by §3.6(c) of a qualified vessel purchased with fund assets or, in certain circumstances, of a vessel other than a qualified vessel is not a proper adjustment for earnings and profits purposes and thus, the depreciation deduction with respect to, and the gain or loss on the sale of, such a vessel shall, for earnings and profits purposes, be determined as if such reduction had not been made.

(4) The earnings (including gains and losses) from the investment and reinvestment of amounts held in the fund is a proper adjustment for earnings and profits purposes.

(5) Interest determined under §3.7 which is allowed as a deduction under section 163 of the Code is allowed as a deduction in computing earnings and profits.

(6) The gain or loss recognized by a party on the disposition by the fund of property subject to an election under §3.2(g)(2) not to recognize gain or loss upon the deposit is a proper adjustment for earnings and profits purposes.

(7) Deposits of property considered to be a sale under §3.2(g)(1)(iii) increase or decrease earnings and profits by the amount of gain or loss included in the party's income for the taxable year.

* *

Section 3.5, as adopted by Treasury Decision 7398, is amended by revising paragraph (a)(3)(iii) to read as follows:

§3.5 (Proposed Treasury Decision, published 1-29-76.) **Qualified withdrawals.**

(a) **In general.** * * *

(3) * * *

(iii) The receipt of property (which is a qualified vessel or barges and containers which are part of the complement of a qualified vessel (or shares therein)) by a parent corporation in liquidation of an 80-percent-or-more controlled subsidiary corporation in which the parent's basis for the property is determined under section 334(b)(2) of the Code by reference to its basis for the subsidiary's stock, but only if (a) the subsidiary adopts a plan of liquidation not more than 30 days after the date of the transaction described in section 334(b)(2)(B) of the Code (or, in the case of a series of transactions, the date of the first such transaction) and (b) the property is actually distributed within 120 days of such transaction (or first transaction), provided, however, that the amount of the qualified withdrawal for such purpose shall be limited to the lower of the fair market value of such property on the date of such transaction (or of the first such transaction) reduced by the amount of any liability secured by such property and the allocable amount of any unsecured liability of the subsidiary or the parent's basis for the stock of the subsidiary allocable to such property. For purposes of the preceding sentence, an allocable amount of liability or basis of stock shall be determined by reference to the relative gross fair market values of the assets of the subsidiary.

* * * * * * * * * * * * *

Section 3.6, as adopted by Treasury Decision 7398, is amended by revising paragraph (e) to read as follows:

§3.6 (Proposed Treasury Decision, published 1-29-76.) **Tax treatment of qualified withdrawals.**

* *

(e) Ordinary income treatment of gain from disposition of property acquired with qualified withdrawals. (1) (i) Under section 607(g)(5) of the Act and this paragraph, if any property the basis of which was reduced under paragraph (c) of this section is disposed of, then except as otherwise provided in this paragraph any gain realized on such disposition (after application of section 1245 of the Code) to the extent provided in subparagraph (2) of this paragraph shall be recognized and treated as an amount referred to in section 607(h)(3)(A) of the Act and §3.7 (relating to nonqualified withdrawals) which was withdrawn on the date of such disposition. Accordingly, notwithstanding any provision of the Code, the amount of such gain shall be included in the gross income of the party as an item of ordinary income for the taxable year in which the disposition occurred. In the case of a partnership holding any such property, see subparagraph (8) of this paragraph. In the case of a sale of such property which is reported under the installment method, see subparagraph (9) of this paragraph.

(ii) Interest on gain referred to in subdivision (i) of this subparagraph shall not attach under section 607(h)(3)(C) of the Act and §3.7(e) unless the disposition occurred within 1 year of final delivery from the shipyard or within 1 year of first loading of the vessel, and the Secretary of Commerce determines that such disposition was not for a purpose for which the fund is established. Interest shall not attach in the case of an involuntary conversion.

(iii) If an amount representing the net proceeds (as defined in §3.2(c)(2)) from the disposition is deposited into the fund pursuant to §3.2(c)(3), the agreement, and the regulations prescribed by the Secretary of Commerce, such gain referred to in subdivision (i) of this subparagraph is to be excluded from gross income (and interest shall not be payable on such amount) and is to be treated as gain to which section 607(d)(1)(B) of the Act and §3.3(b)(2) apply. The portion of such deposit which represents amounts that if not deposited would be treated as ordinary income under section 1245(a)(1) of the Code or as gain attributable to the reduction in basis under paragraph (c) of this section is considered a deposit in accordance with section 607(b)(1)(C) of the Act (relating to net proceeds from the sale of an agreement vessel) and must be allocated to the ordinary income account of the fund in accordance with §3.4(d)(4).

(2) (i) The amount of gain included in gross income of the party as an item of ordinary income by reason of section 607(g)(5) of the Act and subparagraph (1)(i) of this paragraph shall be determined pursuant to section 1245 of the Code (including the exceptions and limitations in subsection (b) (other than paragraph (5) thereof)), applied in the manner and only to the extent prescribed in subparagraphs (3) and (4) of this paragraph, except that for purposes of this determination the exceptions and limitations in section 1245(b)(3) and (4) of the Code shall not apply unless a closing agreement is properly entered into under section 7121 of the Code which meets the requirements of subdivisions (ii) and (iii) of this subparagraph.

(ii) For a closing agreement to meet the requirements of this subdivision, it must (a) provide that the provisions of this paragraph shall apply for purposes of determining the consequences of the exchange, (b) be signed by the Assistant Commissioner (Technical) or his delegate and by the party disposing of the vessel and, in the case of a transaction to which subparagraph (5) of this paragraph applies, the transferee of such vessel, and (c) be consistent with the examples set out in subparagraph (7)(i) of this paragraph.

(iii) For a closing agreement to meet the requirements of this subdivision, the party must make application therefor on or before the later of the applicable following dates:

(a) April 28, 1976, or

(b) The last day prescribed by law (including extensions thereof) for filing the party's Federal income tax return for the taxable year in which the exchange occurs, or the date on which such return is actually filed, whichever is earlier.

For purposes of this subdivision (iii), a party makes application for a closing agreement by mailing a signed proposed agreement which meets the requirements of subdivision (ii) of this subparagraph to the Commissioner of Internal Revenue, Attention: T:FP:T, Wash-

Proposed Reg. §3.6

ington, D.C. 20224. If the execution of such agreement by the Service prior to any particular date is desired, the party should make such application prior to 90 days before such date.

(3) The amount of gain to which section 1245 of the Code actually applies shall be determined first and without regard to section 607(g)(5) of the Act and subparagraph (1)(i) of this paragraph. Then the amount of gain to which section 607(g)(5) and subparagraph (1) of this paragraph apply shall be determined pursuant to the rules of section 1245 of the Code, applied in the manner and to the extent described in subparagraph (2) of this paragraph.

(4) For the purposes of determining the amount of gain to which section 607(g)(5) of the Act and subparagraph (1)(i) of this paragraph apply, the following rules are prescribed:

(i) For such purposes, any reduction in basis under paragraph (c) of this section (whether in respect of the same or other property) allowed to the party or any other person shall be treated as an adjustment reflected in adjusted basis on account of deductions for depreciation within the meaning of section 1245(a)(2) of the Code (relating to definition of recomputed basis).

(ii) For such purposes, the rules of subparagraph (5) of this paragraph shall apply with respect to transfers to which section 1245(b)(3) of the Code applies (relating to certain transfers where the transferee's basis is determined with reference to the transferor's basis) and, in the case of a distribution from a partnership, the rules of subparagraph (8) of this paragraph shall also apply.

(iii) For such purposes, the rules of subparagraph (6) of this paragraph shall apply with respect to a disposition described in section 1031 of the Code (relating to like-kind exchanges) and rules consistent with the principles of such subparagraph shall apply to a conversion with respect to which section 1033(a)(1) of the Code applies (relating to involuntary conversion into similar property). However, for such purpose, section 1245(b)(4) of the Code shall not apply to a conversion with respect to which an election under section 1033(a)(3) of the Code has been made.

(iv) (a) For such purposes, if there is reflected in the adjusted basis of a vessel reductions in basis made (whether in respect of such vessel or another vessel) under section 607(g)(2), (3), or (4) of the Act (1) by reason of paragraph (c)(3)(i), (ii), or (iii) of this section and (2) not by such reason, then any such gain recognized shall be treated as reducing any such reductions in basis in the order in which they were made, the earliest first. For any taxable year in which reductions of a character described in both (1) and (2) of this subdivision (a) were made, those described in (1) of this subdivision (a) shall be deemed to have occurred first.

(b) Notwithstanding (a) of this subdivision (iv), a party may, at his option, treat all reductions of a character described in (a)(1) of this subdivision (iv) as having occurred first.

(5) If the basis of a vessel in the hands of a transferee is determined (without regard to section 607(g)(5) of the Act and this paragraph) by reference to its basis in the hands of the transferor by reason of the application of section 332, 351, 361, 371(a), 374(a), 721, or 731 of the Code, and if a closing agreement is properly entered into pursuant to subparagraph (2) of this paragraph, then—

(i) The amount of gain recognized under section 607(g)(5) of the Act and subparagraph (1)(i) of this paragraph shall not exceed the excess of the amount of gain recognized to the transferor on the transfer of such vessel (determined without regard to section 607(g)(5) of the Act and subparagraph (1)(i) of this paragraph) over the amount of such gain to which section 1245(a)(1) of the Code actually applies.

(ii) Immediately after the transfer the amount of the reduction in basis under paragraph (c) of this section treated as an adjustment reflected in the adjusted basis of the vessel in the hands of the transferee shall be an amount equal to—

(a) The amount of such reduction treated as an adjustment reflected in the adjusted basis of the vessel in the hands of the transferor immediately before the disposition, minus

(b) The amount of gain recognized under section 607(g)(5) of the Act and subparagraph (1)(i) of this paragraph (determined without regard to section 607(d)(1)(B) of the Act and §3.3(b)(2)(i)(a)).

(iii) Immediately after the transfer, the character of the reduction in basis under paragraph (c) of this section treated as an adjustment reflected in the adjusted basis of the vessel in the hands of the transferee shall be the same as it was in the hands of the transferor, reduced by, under subparagraph (4)(iv) of this paragraph, the amount of gain described in subdivision (ii)(b) of this subparagraph.

(iv) Immediately after the transfer, the basis of the property received shall be determined in accordance with the Code, but without taking into account any gain which would have been recognized by the party under section 607(g)(5) of the Act had the closing agreement not been signed but which was not recognized by reason of subdivision (i) of this subparagraph.

(v) In the case of any distribution from a partnership, the provisions of this subparagraph shall apply in the manner, and only to the extent, prescribed in subparagraph (8)(iii) of this paragraph.

(6) If a vessel is exchanged for a vessel and gain (determined without regard to section 607(g)(5) of the Act and this paragraph) is not recognized in whole or in part under section 1031 of the Code (relating to like-kind exchanges), and if a closing agreement is properly entered into pursuant to subparagraph (2) of this paragraph, then—

(i) The amount of gain recognized under section 607(g)(5) of the Act and subparagraph (1)(i) of this paragraph shall not exceed the sum of—

(a) The excess of the amount of gain recognized on such disposition (determined without regard to section 607(g)(5) of the Act and subparagraph (1)(i) of this paragraph) over the amount of such gain to which section 1245(a)(1) of the Code actually applies, plus

(b) The fair market value of the vessel acquired which is not a qualified vessel, but (1) only if there was reflected in the adjusted basis of the vessel exchanged reductions in basis made (whether in respect of such vessel or another vessel) under section 607(g)(2), (3), or (4) of the Act other than reductions in basis applied to any vessel by reason of paragraph (c)(3)(i), (ii), or (iii) of this section, and (2) only to the extent of such reductions in basis, and (3) then only to the extent of amounts not taken into account under (a) of this subdivision, plus

(c) The fair market value of property acquired which is not a vessel and which is not taken into account under (a) of this subdivision.

(ii) Immediately after the exchange the amount of the reduction in basis under paragraph (c) of this section treated as an adjustment reflected in the adjusted basis of the vessel acquired shall be an amount equal to—

(a) The amount of such reduction treated as an adjustment reflected in the adjusted basis of the vessel exchanged immediately before the disposition, minus

(b) The amount of gain recognized under section 607(g)(5) of the Act and subparagraph (1)(i) of this paragraph (determined without regard to section 607(d)(1)(B) of the Act and §3.3(b)(2)(i)(a)).

(iii) Immediately after the transfer, the character of the reduction in basis under paragraph (c) of this section treated as an adjustment reflected in the adjusted basis of the vessel acquired shall be the same as it was in the vessel exchanged, reduced by, under subparagraph (4)(iv) of this paragraph, the amount of gain described in subdivision (ii)(b) of this subparagraph.

(iv) Immediately after the exchange, the basis of the property received shall be determined in accordance with section 1031(d) of the Code, without taking into account any gain which would have been recognized by the party under section 607(g)(5) of the Act had the closing agreement not been signed but which was not recognized by reason of subdivision (i) of this subparagraph.

Proposed Reg. §3.6

(7) (i) Closing agreements that will satisfy the requirements of subparagraph (2)(ii) of this paragraph can be illustrated by the following sample closing agreements.

Example (1). Proposed exchange to which section 1031 of the Code (relating to like-kind exchanges) will apply.

CLOSING AGREEMENT AS TO FINAL DETERMINATION COVERING SPECIFIC MATTERS

THIS CLOSING AGREEMENT, made in triplicate under and in pursuance of section 7121 of the Internal Revenue Code of 1954 by and between _____ and the Commissioner of Internal Revenue:

WHEREAS, taxpayer proposes to exchange a ____(type)____ vessel named _____ U.S. Coast Guard Registry number _____ (hereinafter "first vessel"), to _____ for a ____(type)____ vessel named _____, U.S. Coast Guard Registry number _____ (hereinafter "second vessel") [and other consideration]*,

*Do not identify other consideration. Delete if inapplicable.

WHEREAS, the taxpayer and Commissioner desire to finally determine the effect of such proposed exchange under section 607 of the Merchant Marine Act, 1936, as amended (hereinafter "Act"), the Treasury Regulations thereunder (26 CFR Part 3), and the Internal Revenue Code of 1954 (hereinafter "Code"), and

WHEREAS, if the proposed exchange qualifies under the provisions of section 1031 of the Code, then

IT HAS BEEN DETERMINED for Federal income tax purposes that the provisions of Treasury Regulations 26 CFR §3.6(e) as in force this date shall apply for purposes of determining—

1. The amount of gain to be taken into account by the taxpayer under section 607(g)(5) of the Act,

2. The amounts of adjusted basis, and adjustments reflected in the adjusted basis, of the second vessel in the hands of the taxpayer immediately after the exchange,

3. The treatment of such amounts of the adjustments reflected in the adjusted basis of the second vessel immediately after the exchange as attributable to reductions in basis of the second vessel in the hands of the taxpayer under section 607(g)(2), (3), and (4) of the Act by reason of qualified withdrawals by the taxpayer from a capital construction fund (whether or not it has such a fund), and

4. All other consequences of the proposed exchange.

WHEREAS, the determinations as set forth above are hereby agreed to by said taxpayer.

NOW, THIS CLOSING AGREEMENT WITNESSETH, that the said taxpayer and said Commissioner of Internal Revenue hereby mutually agree that the determinations as set forth above shall be final and conclusive, subject, however, to reopening in the event of fraud, malfeasance, or misrepresentation of material fact, and provided that any change or modification of applicable statutes will render this agreement ineffective to the extent that it is dependent upon such statutes.

IN WITNESS WHEREOF, the above parties have subscribed their names to these presents, in triplicate.

Signed this _____ day of _____, 19 ____

_____
(Taxpayer)

By _____

(Title)

Commissioner of Internal Revenue
By _____
                    Assistant Commissioner (Technical)
Date _____

Example (2). Proposed transfer of vessel in an exchange to which subparagraph (5) of this paragraph will apply (relating to certain transfers where the transferee's basis is determined with reference to the transferor's basis).

CLOSING AGREEMENT AS TO FINAL DETERMINATION
COVERING SPECIFIC MATTERS

THIS CLOSING AGREEMENT, made in quadruplicate under and in pursuance of section 7121 of the Internal Revenue Code of 1954 by and between _____ (hereinafter "transferor"), _____ (hereinafter "transferee"), and the Commissioner of Internal Revenue:

WHEREAS, transferor proposes to transfer a _____ vessel named _____, U.S. Coast Guard Registry number _____ type to transferee for [stock] [stock and securities] [partnership interest]* [of, in]** transferee [and other consideration],**

WHEREAS, the transferor, transferee, and Commissioner desire to finally determine the effect, of such proposed exchange, under section 607 of the Merchant Marine Act, 1936, as amended (hereinafter "Act"), the Treasury Regulations thereunder (26 CFR Part 3), and the Internal Revenue Code of 1954 (hereinafter "Code"), and

WHEREAS, if the proposed exchange qualifies under the provisions of section _____ of the Code, then

IT HAS BEEN DETERMINED for Federal income tax purposes that the provisions of Treasury Regulations 26 CFR §3.6(e) as in force this date shall apply for purposes of determining—

_____

*Delete inapplicable terms or insert other appropriate term. Do NOT further identify consideration, such as number of shares or class of stock.

**Insert proper term or delete if inapplicable, but do not further identify other consideration.

1. The amount of gain to be taken into account by the transferor under section 607(g)(5) of the Act,
2. The amounts of adjusted basis, and adjustments reflected in the adjusted basis, of the vessel in the hands of the transferee immediately after the exchange, including for purposes of applying section 607(g)(5) to a subsequent transaction involving such vessel by the transferee,
3. The treatment of such amounts, of the adjustments reflected in the adjusted basis of the vessel immediately after the exchange, as attributable to reductions in basis of the vessel in the hands of the transferee under section 607(g)(2), (3), and (4) of the Act by reason of qualified withdrawals by the transferee from a capital construction fund (whether or not it has such a fund),
4. The adjusted basis in the hands of the transferor of the stock, securities, or partnership interest in the transferee received in exchange for the vessel, and
5. All other consequences of the proposed exchange.

WHEREAS, the determinations as set forth above are hereby agreed to by said transferor and transferee.

Proposed Reg. §3.6

NOW, THIS CLOSING AGREEMENT WITNESSETH, that the said transferor, said transferee, and said Commissioner of Internal Revenue hereby mutually agree that the determinations as set forth above shall be final and conclusive, subject, however, to reopening in the event of fraud, malfeasance, or misrepresentation of material fact, and provided that any change or modification of applicable statutes will render this agreement ineffective to the extent that it is dependent upon such statutes.

IN WITNESS WHEREOF, the above parties have subscribed their names to these presents, in quadruplicate.

Signed this _____ day of _____ , 19 ____

_____
(Transferor)
By _____

_____
(Title)

_____
(Transferee)
By _____

_____
(Title)
Commissioner of Internal Revenue
By _____

Assistant Commissioner (Technical)
Date _____

(ii) The provisions of subparagraphs (1) through (6) of this paragraph are illustrated by the following examples:

Example (1). X Corporation, which maintains a fund described in §3.1, exchanges qualified vessel A for qualified vessel B in a transaction in which no gain or loss is recognized under section 1031 (relating to like-kind exchange) of the Code, determined without regard to the Act and section 1245 of the Code. Prior to the exchange, a closing agreement is properly entered into under section 7121 of the Code which meets the requirements of subparagraph (2) of this paragraph. Vessel A had been purchased for $2 million, of which $1.5 million was attributable to a qualified withdrawal from the ordinary income account of the fund. Depreciation of $100,000 had been allowed (the amount allowable) on vessel A and, before any depreciation is allowed or allowable on vessel B, X sells vessel B for cash of $2.1 million. Under section 1245(b)(4) of the Code (relating to dispositions of property without recognition of gain or loss by reason of section 1031 of the Code) no gain is recognized under section 1245(a)(1) of the Code upon the exchange notwithstanding the depreciation of $100,000 allowed with respect to vessel A. Since the only property received in the exchange is a qualified vessel, and since the closing agreement was properly entered into, under subparagraph (6)(i) of this paragraph no gain is recognized under section 607(g)(5) of the Act and subparagraph (1)(i) of this subparagraph. Under subparagraph (6)(iii) of this paragraph, X's basis in vessel B just before the sale is the same as that of vessel A, or $400,000, i.e., cost of $2 million reduced by $1.5 million qualified withdrawal (see paragraph (c)(1) of this section) and by $100,000 allowed as depreciation. Immediately after the exchange, the amount of depreciation adjustments reflected in adjusted basis under §1.1245-2(c)(4) of the Income Tax Regulations of this chapter (determined without regard to this section) is $100,000, and the amount of the reduction in basis under paragraph (c) of this section treated as an adjustment reflected in adjusted basis under subparagraph (6)(ii) of this paragraph is $1.5 million. Gain recognized on the sale is $1.7 million, i.e., amount realized, $2.1 million, minus adjusted basis, $400,000. The first $100,000 of gain on the sale is gain to which section 1245(a)(1) of the Code applies, and the next $1.5 million of gain on the sale is gain to which subparagraph(1)(i) of this paragraph applies. Thus, $1.6 million of gain is included as ordinary income in X's gross income for the taxable year of the sale. The remaining $100,000 of gain may be treated as gain from the sale or exchange of property described in section 1231 of the Code.

Example (2). Assume the same facts as in example (1), except that X deposits the net proceeds from the sale into the fund in the manner described in subparagraph (1)(iii) of this paragraph. Under §3.3(b)(2), X recognizes no gain on the sale, and the net proceeds of $2.1 million on the sale (see §3.2(c)(2)) are allocated to the following accounts in the following amounts: $100,000 to the ordinary income account as gain to which section 1245 of the Code applies (see §3.4(d)(4)), $1.5 million to the ordinary income account in accordance with subparagraph (1)(iii) of this paragraph (see §3.4(d)(4)), $100,000 to the capital gain account (see §3.4(c)), assuming X had purchased vessel A more than 6 months before its sale of vessel B (see section 1223(1) of the Code), and $400,000 to the capital account (see §3.4(b)(2)).

Example (3). Assume the same facts as in example (1), except that X received vessel B, with a fair market value of $1 million, and $1 million in cash in exchange for vessel A and did not sell vessel B. Since section 1031(b) of the Code limits the amount of gain recognized to $1 million, subparagraph (6)(i) of this paragraph limits application of subparagraph (1) of this paragraph, but only after application of section 1245 of the Code. Under section 1245(a)(1) of the Code, the first $100,000 of recognized gain is treated as ordinary income. Under subparagraph (6)(i) of this paragraph, the amount of gain recognized under subparagraph (1)(i) of this paragraph is limited to $900,000, i.e., the $1 million of gain recognized under section 1031(b) of the Code less the $100,000 of such gain to which section 1245 of the Code applies. Accordingly, the amount of the reduction in basis under paragraph (c) of this section treated as an adjustment reflected in adjusted basis under subparagraph (6)(ii) of this paragraph of vessel B is $600,000, i.e., the amount of adjustments reflected in the adjusted basis of vessel A immediately before the disposition ($1.5 million) less the amount of gain recognized under subparagraph (1)(i) of this paragraph ($900,000). The basis of vessel B is equal to $400,000, computed in accordance with section 1031(d) of the Code, i.e., the basis in vessel A of $400,000 less cash received of $1 million plus gain recognized of $1 million.

Example (4). Assume that in example (3) X deposits the net proceeds from the exchange into the fund in the manner described in subparagraph (1)(iii) of this paragraph. Assume further that there were no selling expenses connected with the exchange and, at the time of the exchange, vessel A was not security for any mortgage. Since by reason of the application of subparagraph (6)(i) of this paragraph vessel B was received without recognition of gain under section 607(g)(5) of the Act, and since under §3.2(c)(1)(i) gross proceeds does not include any property to the extent received without recognition of gain under the Act and the Code, the gross proceeds is equal to the amount of cash received, i.e., $1 million. Since X had no expenses described in §3.2(c)(2)(ii) to reduce gross proceeds, and since the sum of the gain recognized on the exchange (before application of this part), $1 million, plus the gain recognized under section 607(g)(5) of the Act and subparagraph (6)(i) of this paragraph not taken into account in computing the gain of $1 million, zero, is not greater than the net proceeds, the net proceeds is also $1 million. By reason of the deposit, X recognizes no gain on the exchange and the entire $1 million of net proceeds is allocated to the ordinary income account in accordance with subparagraph (1)(iii) of this paragraph, i.e., $100,000 as gain to which section 1245(a)(1) of the Code would have applied and $900,000 as gain to which subparagraph (1)(i) of this paragraph would have applied had there been no deposit (see §3.4(d)(4)). The amount of adjustments reflected in the adjusted basis of vessel B is determined in the same manner as in example (3). Since under §3.3(b)(2)(i)(b) the $1 million of gain not recognized by reason of the deposit into the fund is treated as recognized for purposes of determining vessel B's basis, vessel B's basis is $400,000 as determined in example (3).

Example (5). (1) Assume the same facts as in example (1), except that X did not sell vessel B and vessel B is not a qualified vessel. Assume further that the fair market value of vessel B is $2.2 million. As stated in example (1), the limitation provided by section 1245(b)(4) of the Code prevents recognition of any gain under section 1245 of the Code notwithstanding the $100,000 of depreciation allowed with respect to vessel A. Since the only property received in the exchange is vessel B, which is not a qualified ves-

Proposed Reg. §3.6

sel, and since no gain is recognized under section 1245 of the Code, under subparagraph (6)(i) of this paragraph the amount of gain recognized under section 607(g)(5) of the Act and subparagraph (1)(i) of this paragraph is limited to the amount in subparagraph (6)(i)(b) of this paragraph. Since the fair market value of vessel B, $2.2 million, exceeds the reduction in basis of vessel A by virtue of paragraph (c) of this section, $1.5 million, subparagraph (6)(i)(b) of this paragraph limits the amount of gain recognized under section 607(g)(5) of the Act and subparagraph (1)(i) of this paragraph to $1.5 million, which is included in X's gross income as an item of ordinary income in the taxable year of the exchange. Further, since under subparagraph (3) of this paragraph the determination of gain under section 1245(b)(4) of the Code is made without regard to section 607(g)(5) of the Act and this paragraph, no part of this gain of $1.5 million is considered gain to which section 1245 of the Code applies.

(ii) If the entire $1.5 million of adjustments reflected in the adjusted basis of vessel A under paragraph (c) of this section were amounts applied under paragraph (c)(3)(i), (ii), or (iii) of this section by reason of qualified withdrawals to pay the principal of indebtedness incurred with respect to vessels other than vessel A, then the amount in subparagraph (6)(i)(b) of this paragraph would be zero and, accordingly, by reason of the application of subparagraph (6)(i) of this paragraph no gain would be recognized under section 607(g)(5) of the Act.

(iii) The results would be the same as stated in subdivision (i) of this example if there had been no closing agreement whether or not vessel B is a qualified vessel.

(8) If a partnership holds any property the basis of which was reduced under paragraph (c) of this section, then—

(i) For purposes of subparagraph (1)(i) of this paragraph, the term "disposition" includes a distribution by the partnership.

(ii) If a partner sells or exchanges all or a part of his interest in the partnership or receives a distribution from the partnership, then for purposes of applying section 751(c) of the Code (relating to unrealized receivables of a partnership) the amount of such gain to which section 607(g)(5) of the Act and subparagraph (1)(i) of this paragraph would apply if the property were sold by a partnership at its fair market value shall be treated as gain to which section 1245(a) of the Code would have applied.

(iii) [Reserved]

(9) Gain from a disposition to which subparagraph (1) of this paragraph applies may be reported under the installment method if such method is otherwise available under section 453 of the Code. In such case, the income (other than interest) on each installment payment shall be deemed to consist of any gain which is treated as ordinary income by reason of the application of section 1245(a)(1) of the Code until all such gain is reported, then any gain to which this paragraph applies until all such gain has been reported, and the remaining portion (if any) of such income shall be deemed to consist of gain to which this paragraph does not apply.

Par. 5. Section 3.8, as adopted by Treasury Decision 7398, is revised to read as follows:

§3.8 (Proposed Treasury Decision, published 1-29-76.) **Certain corporate reorganizations and changes in partnerships, and certain transfers on death.**

(a) **In general.** Section 607(i) of the Act and this section provide rules for certain corporate reorganizations, changes in partnerships, and certain transfers on death. Except as provided in paragraphs (b) and (c) of this section, any transfer of a fund from one taxpayer to another is a nonqualified withdrawal of the entire fund whether or not the transfer is voluntary, involuntary, or by operation of law.

(b) **Certain transfers to corporations and partnerships.** (1) If (i) a party which is a corporation transfers property (including property held in a fund) in a transaction to which section 381 of the Code applies, or a party which is a partnership transfers property (including property held in a fund) to a partnership which is treated as a continuation of the transferor partnership under the provisions of subchapter K of the Code, and (ii) the transfer of the fund has been approved by the Secretary of Commerce, then such transfer will be treated as if it did not constitute a nonqualified withdrawal and, if the fund included property subject to an election under §3.2(g)(2), the transferee shall, for purposes of this part, be treated as if it had made such election. For purposes of determining the basis of property received in a transaction described in this subparagraph which involves the transfer of a fund including property subject to an election under §3.2(g)(2), see §3.2(g)(2).

(2) If a party transfers property (including property held in a fund) to a corporation solely in an exchange for stock or securities in which no gain or loss is recognized by reason of section 351(a) of the Code, the transfer of the fund will be treated as if it did not constitute a nonqualified withdrawal, but only if on or before the last day prescribed by law (including extensions thereof) for filing the party's Federal income tax return for the taxable year in which the transfer occurs, or the date on which such return is actually filed, whichever is earlier (or, if later, on or before April 28, 1976)—

(i) The transfer of the fund to, and maintenance of the fund by, the corporation has been approved by the Secretary of Commerce, and

(ii) A closing agreement under section 7121 of the Code which meets the requirements of paragraph (e) of this section has been applied for by the party and the corporation.

For purposes of this paragraph, a closing agreement has been applied for when a signed proposed agreement which meets the requirements of paragraph (e) of this section is mailed to the Commissioner of Internal Revenue, Attention: T:FP:T, Washington, D.C. 20224. If the execution of such agreement by the Service prior to any particular date is desired, such application should be made prior to 90 days before such date.

(3) If by reason of subparagraph (2) of this paragraph, a transfer of a fund does not constitute a nonqualified withdrawal, then—

(i) The consequences to the transferee shall be determined under paragraph (d) of this section,

(ii) If the fund includes property covered by an election under §3.2(g)(2) (relating to an election not to treat deposits of property other than money as a sale or exchange at the time of deposit), then with respect to such property the party shall under §3.2(g)(2) recognize on the date of such transfer the amount of gain or loss it would have recognized under §3.2(g)(1)(iii) (had the election not been made) on the day the property was deposited into the fund,

(iii) For purposes of determining the party's basis for the stock or securities of the transferee received by the party in the exchange—

(a) The basis of the assets in the fund that were transferred shall be considered to be the fund's basis for the property (see §3.2(g)(1)(ii) for manner of determining such basis with respect to contributed property), and

(b) With respect to property in the fund to which subdivision (ii) of this subparagraph applies, the party's basis (as determined under (a) of this subdivision) for stock or securities received in the exchange for such property shall not be increased by the amount of gain (or decreased by the amount of loss) under §3.2(g)(2) referred to in such subdivision (ii), and

(iv) The party's basis of the stock or securities of the transferee received by him in the exchange shall be the party's basis of the properties transferred (determined by taking into account the provisions of subdivision (iii) of this subparagraph) reduced by the sum of—

(a) The amount in the ordinary income account (see §3.4(d)), and

(b) Five-eighths (in the case of a corporation (other than an electing small business corporation, as defined in section 1371 of the Code)) or one-half (in the case of any other person) of the amount in the capital gain account (see §3.4(c)).

(c) **Transfers on death.** (1) If a party who is an individual dies, the transfer of a fund and property held therein to an executor or administrator of the decedent's estate, or to any other person by reason of his death, will be treated as if it did not constitute a

Proposed Reg. §3.8

nonqualified withdrawal, but only if on or before the last day prescribed by law (including extensions thereof) for filing the party's Federal income tax return for the taxable year in which the transfer occurs, or the date on which such return is actually filed, whichever is earlier (or, if later, on or before April 28, 1976)—

(i) Such executor, administrator, or other person receives approval for his maintenance of the fund from the Secretary of Commerce, and

(ii) A closing agreement under section 7121 of the Code which meets the requirements of paragraph (e) of this section has been applied for by such executor, administrator, or other person.

For purposes of this subparagraph, a closing agreement has been applied for when a signed proposed agreement which meets the requirements of paragraph (e) of this section is mailed to the Commissioner of Internal Revenue, Attention: T:FP:T, Washington, D.C. 20224. If the execution of such agreement by the Service prior to any particular date is desired, such application should be made prior to 90 days before such date.

(2) If—

(i) By reason of the application of subparagraph (1) of this paragraph, the transfer of a fund from the individual who died to the executor or administrator of the decedent's estate was treated as if it did not constitute a nonqualified withdrawal,

(ii) The fund passes from the decedent's estate to another person or persons, and

(iii) Such passing of the fund does not constitute in whole or in part a sale or exchange (see §1.1014-4(a)(3) of the Income Tax Regulations of this chapter), then the passing of such fund from the decedent's estate to such other person will also be treated as if it did not constitute a nonqualified withdrawal, but only if the requirements of subparagraph (3) of this paragraph are satisfied.

(3) The requirements of this subparagraph are satisfied with respect to the passing of a fund from a decedent's estate to another person if on or before the last day prescribed by law (including extensions thereof) for filing the estate's Federal Income tax return for the taxable year in which the passing occurs, or the date on which such return is actually filed, whichever is earlier (or, if later, on or before April 28, 1976)—

(i) The passing of the fund to, and maintenance of the fund by, such other person has been approved by the Secretary of Commerce, and

(ii) A closing agreement under section 7121 of the Code which meets the requirements of paragraph (e) of this section has been applied for by such other person and the executor or administrator of the decedent's estate.

For purposes of this subparagraph, a closing agreement has been applied for when a signed proposed agreement which meets the requirements of paragraph (e) of this section is mailed to the Commissioner of Internal Revenue, Attention: T:FP:T, Washington, D.C. 20224. If the execution of such agreement by the Service prior to any particular date is desired, such application should be made prior to 90 days before such date.

(4) If a fund is transferred from an individual by reason of his death to his estate or from his estate to another person and the fund includes property covered by an election under §3.2(g)(2) (relating to an election not to treat deposits of property other than money as a sale or exchange at the time of deposit), then with respect to such property the individual or estate shall under §3.2(g)(2) recognize on the date of death or transfer the amount of gain or loss it would have recognized under §3.2(g)(1)(iii) (had the election not been made) on the date the property was deposited into the fund.

(d) **Special rules.** In the case of a transfer which is not a nonqualified withdrawal by reason of the application of paragraph (b) or (c) of this section, all attributes of the fund and of the assets in the fund (as determined after the application of §3.2(g)(2) and paragraphs (b)(3)(ii) and (c)(4) of this section) shall carry over from the transferor to the transferee. If the transferee is a party to an existing fund, the assets of the funds and the respective accounts within the funds, shall be combined. Thus, for example, each item in the combined fund shall retain its character as an item which was deposited into the capital account, the capital gain account, or the ordinary income account, as the case may be, on the date on which they were deposited into each original fund.

(e) **Closing agreement.** (1) For a closing agreement to meet the requirements of paragraph (b)(2), (c)(1), or (c)(3) of this section, it must (a) provide that the provisions of this section shall apply for purposes of determining the consequences of the transfer of the fund, (b) be signed by the Assistant Commissioner (Technical) or his delegate, the person transferring the fund (other than a decedent), and the person receiving the fund, and (c) be consistent with the examples set out in subparagraph (2) of this paragraph.

(2) The provisions of subparagraph (1) of this paragraph can be illustrated by the following sample closing agreements:

Example (1). Proposed transfer of fund in an exchange to which section 351(a) of the Code (relating to transfer to controlled corporation) will apply.

CLOSING AGREEMENT AS TO FINAL DETERMINATION
COVERING SPECIFIC MATTERS

THIS CLOSING AGREEMENT, made in quadruplicate under and in pursuance of section 7121 of the Internal Revenue Code of 1954 by and between _____ (hereinafter "transferor"), _____ (hereinafter "transferee"), and Commissioner of Internal Revenue.

WHEREAS, transferor proposes to transfer property (including property held in its capital construction fund as described in Treasury Regulations 26 CFR §3.1(a), hereinafter "fund") to transferee for stock or securities, or both*, of transferee,

WHEREAS the transfer of the fund to, and maintenance of the fund by, transferee was approved by the Secretary of Commerce on _____, 19__,

WHEREAS, the transferor, transferee, and Commissioner desire to finally determine the effect, of such proposed exchange, under section 607 of the Merchant Marine Act, 1936, as amended (hereinafter "Act"), the Treasury Regulations thereunder (26 CFR Part 3), and the Internal Revenue Code of 1954 (hereinafter "Code"), and

---

*Do NOT further identify stock or securities.

WHEREAS, if the proposed exchange qualifies under the provisions of section 351(a) of the Code, then

IT HAS BEEN DETERMINED for Federal income tax purposes that the provisions of Treasury Regulations 26 CFR §3.8 as in force this date shall apply for purposes of determining—

1. If the fund includes property covered by an election under §3.2(g)(2), the amount of gain to be taken into account by the transferor under 26 CFR §§3.2(g)(2) and 3.8(b)(3)(ii),

2. The transferor's basis of the stock or securities, or both, received in the exchange from the transferee,

3. The tax attributes of the fund and property in the fund in the hands of the transferee, and

4. All other consequences of the proposed exchange.

WHEREAS, the determinations as set forth above are hereby agreed to by said transferor and transferee.

NOW, THIS CLOSING AGREEMENT WITNESSETH, that the said taxpayer and said Commissioner of Internal Revenue hereby mutually agree that the determinations as set forth above shall be final and conclusive, subject, however, to reopening in the event of fraud, malfeasance, or misrepresentation of material fact, and provided that any change or modification of applicable statutes will render this agreement ineffective to the extent that it is dependent upon such statutes.

IN WITNESS WHEREOF, the above parties have subscribed their names to these presents, in quadruplicate.

Proposed Reg. §3.8

Signed this _____ day of _____, 19___

By _____
                    (Transferor)
_____
                      (Title)

By _____
                    (Transferee)
_____
                      (Title)

Commissioner of Internal Revenue
By _____
              Assistant Commissioner (Technical)
Date _____

Example (2). Maintenance of fund by decedent's estate.

CLOSING AGREEMENT AS TO FINAL DETERMINATION
COVERING SPECIFIC MATTERS

THIS CLOSING AGREEMENT, made in triplicate under and in pursuance of section 7121 of the Internal Revenue Code of 1954 by and between_____ and the Commissioner of Internal Revenue:

WHEREAS property was held in a capital construction fund as described in Treasury Regulations 26 CFR §3.1(a) (hereinafter "fund") maintained by_____ (hereinafter "decedent") who died on_____ , 19__,

WHEREAS by reason of the death of the decedent the fund passed from decedent to the taxpayer as _____ of decedent's estate,
                    executor or administrator

WHEREAS the maintenance of the fund by the taxpayer was approved by the Secretary of Commerce on _____, 19__, and

WHEREAS, the taxpayer and Commissioner desire to finally determine the effect of the passing of the fund from decedent to taxpayer, under section 607 of the Merchant Marine Act, 1936, as amended (hereinafter "Act"), the Treasury Regulations thereunder (26 CFR Part 3), and the Internal Revenue Code of 1954 (hereinafter "Code"), then

IT HAS BEEN DETERMINED for Federal income tax purposes that the provisions of Treasury Regulations 26 CFR §3.8 as in force this date shall apply for purposes of determining—

1. If the fund includes property covered by an election under §3.2(g)(2), the amount of gain to be taken into account by the decedent under 26 CFR §§3.2(g)(2) and 3.8(c)(4),

2. The tax attributes of the fund and property in the fund in the hands of the taxpayer, and

3. All other consequences of the transaction.

WHEREAS, the determinations as set forth above are hereby agreed to by said taxpayer.

NOW, THIS CLOSING AGREEMENT WITNESSETH, that the said taxpayer and said Commissioner of Internal Revenue hereby mutually agree that the determinations as set forth above shall be final and conclusive, subject, however, to reopening in the event of fraud, malfeasance, or misrepresentation of material fact, and provided that any change or modification of applicable statutes will render this agreement ineffective to the extent that it is dependent upon such statutes.

IN WITNESS WHEREOF, the above parties have subscribed their names to these presents, in triplicate.

Signed this _____ day of _____, 19____
_____
(Taxpayer)
By _____
_____
(Title)
Commissioner of Internal Revenue
By _____
Assistant Commissioner (Technical)
Date _____

Example (3). Proposed transfer of fund from a decedent's estate to another person.

CLOSING AGREEMENT AS TO FINAL DETERMINATION
COVERING SPECIFIC MATTERS

THIS CLOSING AGREEMENT, made in quadruplicate under and in pursuance of section 7121 of the Internal Revenue Code of 1954 by and between _____ (hereinafter "transferor"), _____ (hereinafter "transferee") and the Commissioner of Internal Revenue:

WHEREAS, transferor proposes to transfer property held in its capital construction fund as described in Treasury Regulations 26 CFR §3.1(a) (hereinafter "fund") to transferee,

WHEREAS the transfer of the fund to, and maintenance of the fund by, transferee was approved by the Secretary of Commerce on_____, 19__,

WHEREAS, the transferor, transferee, and Commissioner desire to finally determine the effect, of such proposed exchange, under section 607 of the Merchant Marine Act, 1936, as amended (hereinafter "Act"), the Treasury Regulations thereunder (26 CFR Part 3), and the Internal Revenue Code of 1954 (hereinafter "Code"), and

WHEREAS, if the proposed transfer qualifies as meeting the conditions of subdivisions (i), (ii), and (iii) of Treasury Regulations 26 CFR §3.8(c)(2), then

IT HAS BEEN DETERMINED for Federal income tax purposes that the provisions of Treasury Regulations 26 CFR §3.8 as in force this date shall apply for purposes of determining—

1. If the fund includes property covered by an election under §3.2(g)(2), the amount of gain to be taken into account by the transferor under 26 CFR §§3.2(g)(2) and 3.8(c)(4),
2. The tax attributes of the fund and property in the fund in the hands of the transferee, and
3. All other consequences of the proposed exchange.

WHEREAS, the determination as set forth above are hereby agreed to by said transferor and transferee.

NOW, THIS CLOSING AGREEMENT WITNESSETH, that the said taxpayer and said Commissioner of Internal Revenue hereby mutually agree that the determinations as set forth above shall be final and conclusive, subject, however, to reopening in the event of fraud, malfeasance, or misrepresentation of material fact, and provided that any change or modification of applicable statutes will render this agreement ineffective to the extent that it is dependent upon such statutes.

IN WITNESS WHEREOF, the above parties have subscribed their names to these presents, in quadruplicate.

Signed this _____ day of _____, 19____
_____
(Transferor)

Proposed Reg. §3.8

64,402 Proposed Regulations 3-1-76

By _____
   _____
                          (Title)
   _____
                       (Transferee)
By _____
   _____
                          (Title)
Commissioner of Internal Revenue
By _____
              Assistant Commissioner (Technical)
Date _____

6-1-78   *(Fed. Reg.)* 69,001

INDEX
TO FINAL REGULATIONS UNDER '54 CODE

Index references are to Sections (§) in the final Regulations.

Check Page 23,003 for latest developments and Page 23,075 for Regulations that do not reflect current law.

Index to Proposed Regulations starts on page 69,101.

— A —

Abandonment, property..1.165-2; 1.167(a)-(9)
Abatement of tax..31.6404(a)-1; 301.6404-1
. Armed Forces..1.692-1
. insolvent banks..301.7507-6
Accident and health plans..1.104-1—1.106-1
. absence from work..1.105-3
. annuities under..1.72-15; 7.105-1; 7.105-2
. contributions by employer..1.106-1
. defined..1.105-1; 1.105-5
. mandatory retirement age, payments before..1.105-6
. medical care reimbursement..1.105-2
. permanent injuries..1.105-3; 7.105-2
. wage continuation payments..1.105-4
Account numbers..301.7701-1
Accounting methods..1.446-1—1.472-8
. accrual basis..1.446-1
. adjustments required by change in ..1.381(c)(21)-1; 1.481-1—1.483-2
. advance payments..1.451-5
. carryovers in certain corporate acquisitions..1.381(c)(4)-1
. cash basis..1.446-1
. change of, adjustments for..1.446-1; 1.481-1—1.481-6
. dealers in personal property..1.453-7
. decedent's deductions..1.461-1(b)
. decedent's income..1.451-1(b)
. earnings and profits..1.312-6
. election to return to former method ..1.481-6
. foreign tax credit..1.901-1—1.905-5
. inventories..1.471-1—1.471-11
.. LIFO..1.472-1—1.472-7
. research and experimental expenditures ..1.174-3

Accounting periods..1.441-1—1.443-1
. affiliated group..1.1502-14
. change in..1.442-1
.. accumulated earnings tax..1.536-1
. partner and partnership..1.706-1
Accounts receivable:
. partnership distribution of..1.735-1; 1.751-1
Accrual basis:
. change to installment..1.453-7
. contributions to employees' trust 1.404(a)-1
. foreign tax credit..1.905-1
. real property taxes..1.461-1
Accumulated earnings tax..1.531-1—1.537-3
. adjustments to taxable income..1.535-2
. controlled corporations..1.1561-0—1.1561-2
. credit allowance..1.535-3
. disallowance of credit..1.1551-1
. dividends-paid deductions..1.563-1

Accumulated taxable income:
. computation..1.535-2
. defined..1.535-1

Acquiring corporation:
. accounting method changed by transferor ..1.381(c)(1)-1
. carryovers..1.381(a)-1; 1.381(c)(5)-1
. deduction of acquiring corporation ..1.381(c)(16)-1
. inventory methods changed..1.381(c)(5)-1
Acquisitions to evade or avoid tax..1.269-1—1.269-6; 1.1551-1
Activities not engaged in for profit..1.183-1 —1.183-4
. election to postpone determination of ..12.9
. taxable years affected..1.183-4
Acts, time for, last day Saturday, Sunday, or holiday..301.7503-1
Additions to tax..301.6651-1—301.6659-1
. assessment and collection..301.6659-1
. interest on..301.6601-1
Adjudication, bankruptcy..301.6871(b)-1
Adjusted basis..1.1011-1
. new residence, tax credit application ..1.44-3(d)
Adjusted gross income:
. defined..1.62-1
. less than $5,000..1.3-1; 1.4-1
. standard deduction..1.141-1
Adjustments:
. basis of partnership property..1.754-1
. closed taxable year..1.1314(a)-2
. deferred payments, interest..1.483-1; 1.483-2
. depreciation..1.1016-3; 1.1016-4
. limitation period:
.. prior years' errors affecting current year..1.1311(a)-1
. method of..1.1314(b)-1
. prior years' errors..1.1314(a)-1
. tentative carryback..1.6411-1—1.6411-4
Adjustments to basis..1.1016-1
Administration and procedure..1.6001-1 et seq.; 31.6001-1 et seq; 301.6001-1 et seq.
Administration expenses:
. deductibility..1.642(g)-1, 1.642(g)-2
Adopted children, as dependents..1.152-2
ADR System..1.167(a)-11; 1.167(a)-12; 1.167(*l*)-5
Advance payments:
. interest on overpayments..301.6611-1
. taxes..1.6151-1(c)
"Adverse party", defined..1.672(a)-1
Advertising expenditures..1.162-20; 1.263 (b)-1
. political conventions..1.276-1
Affiliated corporations:
. basis of property acquired during affiliation..1.1051-1
. change in group..1.1502-13
. consolidated returns..1.1501-1—1.1552-1
. definition of affiliated group..1.1502-2
. dividends-paid deduction..1.562-1—1.562-3
. earnings and profits..1.1552-1

69,002 (Fed. Reg.)   AFFILIATED—ASSESSMENTS   5-25-78

Affiliated corporations (continued):
. foreign tax credit..1.902-1
. investment credit..1.46-1—1.46-4
. period of affiliation defined..1.1051-1

Affiliated group, defined..1.1502-1

Age 65 or over:
. general tax credit..1.42A-1
. personal exemptions..1.42-1

Agency contracts canceled..1.1241-1

Agents:
. distinguished from fiduciary..301.7701-7
. employment taxes..31.3504-1
. nonresident aliens..1.871-6; 1.6012-1(b)(3)
. return by..1.6012-1(a)(5), (b)(3)
. withholding tax on wages..31.3402(g)-3

Agricultural labor, exemption from withholding..31.3401(a)(2)-1

Agricultural organizations, exemption ..1.501(c)(5)-1

Air Force: See "Armed Forces of U.S."

Aircraft, foreign, reciprocal exemption ..1.872-2; 1.883-1

Aliens:
. classified..1.871-1
. departing, certificate of compliance ..1.6851-2
. dependents..1.152-2
. determination of residence..1.871-2
. gross income..1.872-1
. nonresident: See "Nonresident aliens"
. proof of residence..1.871-4
. status change during year..1.871-13
. taxation of..1.871-1

Alimony and separate maintenance payments:
. deductibility..1.215-1
. gross income..1.61-10; 1.71-1
. periodic payments..1.71-1
. taxable years..1.71-2
. trusts..1.682(a)-1—1.682(c)-1
. written instrument..1.71-2

Allocation:
. basis:
. . depreciable and nondepreciable property ..1.167(a)-5
. carryovers on termination of estate or trust..1.642(h)-4; 1.642(h)-5
. cooperatives:
. . taxability to patrons..1.61-5
. deduction, foreign corporations and nonresident aliens..1.861-8
. earnings and profits:
. . nontaxable transactions..1.312-10
. excess deductions on termination of estate or trust..1.642(h)-4; 1.642(h)-5
. income and deductions..1.482-1—1.482-2
. unused loss carryover on termination of estate or trust..1.642(h)-4; 1.642(h)-5

Alternative taxes:
. capital gains and losses..1.1201-1
. mutual savings banks' life insurance business..1.594-1

American Red Cross, sports programs for ..1.114-1

Amortization:
. adjusting basis due to..1.1016-3—1.1016-10
. bond premium..1.171-1—1.171-4
. coal mine safety equipment..1.187-1—1.187-2
. emergency facilities..1.168-1—1.168-7
. exceeding depreciation, sale of property ..1.1238-1
. improvements on leased property; cost of acquiring a lease..1.178-1—1.178-3
. organizational expenditures..1.248-1
. railroad grading and tunnel bores ..1.185-1—1.185-3
. research and experimental expenditures ..1.174-1—1.174-4
. trademark and trade name expenditures ..1.177-1

Animals, organizations for prevention of:
. cruelty to, exemption..1.501(a)-1; 1.501(c)(3)-1

Annualizing income..1.443-1
. accumulated earnings tax..1.536-1

Annuities..1.72—1.72-18; 1.691(d)-1
. contracts..1.72-2
. employees: See "Employees' trusts"
. exchange of contracts..1.1035-1
. gross income..1.61-10; 1.72-1
. interest paid to purchase..1.264-3
. investment in the contract..1.72-6
. beneficiaries..1.72-15(1)(3)
. payments..1.72-12; 1.72-14; 7.105-1
. . substantial gainful activity, defined ..7.105-2
. remainders to charity..1.170A-6
. retirement: See "Employees' trusts"
. sale of, adjusted basis..1.1021-1
. self-employed individuals..1.72-11; 1.72-18
. starting date..1.72-4(b), (c)
. tables..1.72-9
. transfer of contracts..1.72-10

Annuity plan: See "Employees' trusts"

Anti-cruelty societies: See "Humane societies"

Anti-trust laws:
. treble damage payments..1.162-22

Arbitrage bonds..13.4

Arbitrage transactions..1.1233-1(d)(2)

Architectural and transportation barriers to handicapped and elderly persons, removal costs..7.190-1—7.190-3

Armed Forces of U.S.:
. abatement of tax upon death..1.692-1
. allowances:
. . scholarship or fellowship grant status ..1.117-4
. combat pay..1.112-1
. . withholding tax..31.3401(a)(1)-1
. compensation:
. . exempt income..1.112-1
. contracts, limitations on profits..1.1471-1
. defined..301.7701-8
. disability pay..1.104-1(e)
. gain on sale of residence..1.1034-1
. gross income, defined..1.61-2
. hospitalized as result of combat-zone services..1.112-1; 31.3401(a)(1)-1
. mustering-out pay..1.113-1
. refunds and credits:
. . deceased members..1.692-1
. retirement pay..1.122-1
. veterans' organizations..1.501(c)(19)-1; 1.512(a)-4
. withholding statements..31.6051-1

Assessable penalties..301.6671-1—301.6685-1

Assessment of tax..301.6201-1—301.6205-1
. additional, defined..301.6611-1
. additions treated as tax..301.6659-1
. authority..301.6201-1
. bankruptcy and receivership..301.6871(a)-1—301.6872-1
. collection after..301.6502-1
. deficiency, change of election of standard deduction..1.444-2
. excessive abatement..301.6404-1
. foreign tax credit carrybacks and carryovers..301.6501(1)-1
. injunction..301.6213-1
. jeopardy..301.6861-1—301.6863-2
. limitation period..301.6501(a)-1—301.6503(d)-1
. method of..301.6203-1
. request for prompt..301.6501(d)-1
. supplemental..301.6204-1
. transferred assets..301.6901-1

Assessments against local benefits, deductibility..1.164-4

5-25-78   **ASSET—BASIS**   *(Fed. Reg.)* **69,003**

———References are to SECS. (§) in the Regs.   Check Page 23,003 for latest developments———

Asset depreciation range (ADR) system
..1.167(a)-11; 1.167(a)-12; 1.167(*l*)-5
Assignee, return for corporation, signature
..1.6012-3(b)(4); 1.6062-1(a)(2)
Associate company, defined..1.1083-1
Assumption of liability:
. partners and partnerships..1.752-1
. reorganization exchange..1.357-1; 1.357-2
At risk amounts, loss deduction..7.465-1—7.465-5
Atomic Energy Commission, municipal services..1.164-8
Attorneys, Government, inspection of returns..404.6103(a)-1—404.6103(k)(6)-1
Averageable income..1.1301-0—1.1304-6
. base period income..1.1302-2; 1.1304-3
. definition..1.1302-1; 1.1302-3
. eligible individuals..1.1303-1
. inapplicable provisions..1.1304-2
. limitation on tax..1.1301-1; 1.1304-4
. short taxable year..1.1304-6
. taxable years affected..1.1301-0
Avoidance of tax: See "Evasion or avoidance of tax"
Awards..1.74-1
. anti-trust suits..1.61-14

— B —

Bad checks in payment of taxes, etc.
..301.6657-1
Bad debts..1.166-1—1.166-8
. banks..1.582-1; 1.585-1—1.585-4; 1.593-1—1.593-11
. deduction..1.166-1—1.166-8
. evidence of worthlessness..1.166-2
. life insurance companies..1.809-6
. mortgage foreclosures..1.595-1
. overpayments on account of..301.6511(d)-1
. partial deductions..1.166-3
. nonbusiness debts..1.166-5
. recovery..1.111-1
.. corporate acquisitions..1.381(c)(12)-1
. reserve for..1.166-6
.. building and loan associations..1.593-1—1.593-11
.. cooperative banks..1.593-1—1.593-11
.. mutual savings banks, etc...1.593-1—1.593-11
.. small business investment companies..1.586-1; 1.586-2
. reserve method of accounting..1.166-4
"Bail-out" preferred stock..1.306-1—1.306-3
Bank affiliates, special deduction..1.601-1
Bank Holding Company Act of 1956:
. distributions..1.1101—1.1102-3
Banking institutions..1.581-1—1.601-1
Bankruptcy and receivership..301.6871(a)-1—301.6873-1
. adjustments under Bankruptcy Act..1.1016-7; 1.1016-8
. basis of property..1.372-1
. collection of taxes..301.6871(a)-2
. debts discharged by:
.. basis affected by..1.1016-7; 1.1016-8
. deficiency assessment..301.6871(a)-1
. reorganization..1.371-1—1.373-3
.. adjustment of capital structure before Sept. 22, 1938..1.1018-1
.. railroads..1.373-1
. returns..1.6012-3(b)(4), (5); 1.6062-1(a)(2)
Banks..1.581-1—1.601-1
. acquisition of security property..1.595-1
. affiliate:
.. special deduction..1.601-1
. bad debt deduction..1.582-1; 1.585-1—1.585-4

Banks (continued):
. cooperative:
.. adjusted basis of property..1.1016-9
.. government loans repaid by..1.592-1
.. reserves..1.593-1—1.593-11
.. taxation of..1.581-2
. depositors' guaranty fund..1.162-13
. deposits:
.. interest on:
... deduction..1.591-1
. dividend deduction by..1.591-1
. foreign central bank of issue..1.895-1
. holding companies..1.1101-1—1.1102-3
. insolvent..301.7507-1—301.7507-11
. mutual savings banks..1.591-1—1.594-1
.. adjusted basis of property..1.1016-9
.. life insurance departments of:
... status..1.594-1
.. returns of common trust funds..1.6032-1
.. taxation of..1.581-1
.. worthless stock owned by..1.582-1
Basis for gain or loss..1.1011-1—1.1021-1
. adjusted..1.1011-1
. affiliation, property acquired during..1.1051-1
. after disallowed loss..1.267(d)-1; 1.267(d)-2
. aggregation of separate interests for depletion purposes..1.614-6
. amortization adjustments..1.1016-3; 1.1016-4
. annuity contracts..1.1021-1
. assumption of liabilities affecting..1.358-3
. bankruptcy and receiverships..1.372-1
. bad debt deduction..1.166-1
. bargain sale to a charitable organization..1.1011-2
. cancellation of debt affecting..1.1016-7; 1.1016-8
. contributions to capital..1.362-2
. cost..1.1012-1
. depletion adjustments..1.614-6; 1.1016-3; 1.1016-4
. depreciation adjustments..1.1016-3; 1.1016-4
. discharge of debt affecting..1.1017-1; 1.1017-2
. employee stock options..1.421-5; 1.421-6
. errors, prior years:
.. adjustment in barred year under mitigation rule..1.1312-6
. established by 1932 Act..1.1052-1
. established by 1934 Act..1.1052-2
. established by 1939 Code..1.1052-3
. exchanged property..1.1031(a)-1—1.1039-1
. FCC orders..1.1071-3
. gifts..1.1015-1—1.1015-5
. government payments for defense purposes..1.621-1
. installment obligations..1.453-9
. inventories..1.471-2; 1.472-1
. liquidating distribution..1.334-1; 1.334-2
. March 1, 1913, property acquired before..1.1053-1
. nontaxable distributions..1.307-1; 1.307-2
. nontaxable exchanges..1.358-1—1.358-4, 1.1031(a)-1—1.1039-1
. obsolescence adjustments..1.1016-3; 1.1016-4
. paid-in surplus..1.362-1; 1.362-2
. partner's interest..1.705-1, 1.722-1; 1.733-1; 1.742-1
. partnerships:
.. distributed property..1.732-1; 1.732-2; 1.734-1; 1.743-1; 1.754-1; 1.755-1
.. property contributed..1.723-1
.. rules for allocation..1.755-1

69,004 (Fed. Reg.)   BASIS—BUILDING   5-25-78

Basis for gain or loss (continued):
- property acquired by issuance of stock or as paid-in surplus..1.362-1; 1.362-2
- property acquired from decedent..1.1014-2
- property dividends..1.301-1
- property improved by lessee..1.1019-1
- railroad reorganizations..1.373-1—1.373-2; 1.374-2
- remainders..1.1014-8
- reorganization..1.358-1—1.358-4
- retirement-straight line property..1.372-1
- sale or other disposition of property ..1.1012-1
- SEC orders..1.1082-1—1.1082-6
- section 38 property..1.48-5—1.48-7
- stock of foreign personal holding companies..1.551-1—1.551-5
- stock on which stock dividends or rights received..1.307-1
- stocks and securities:
  - carryover basis..7.1023(h)-1
  - redemption through related corporation ..1.304-2
- Subchapter S corporation stock..1.1376-1; 1.1376-2
- substituted..1.1016-10
- tax-free exchanges:
  - SEC orders..1.1082-1—1.1082-6
- transfers in part sale and in part gift ..1.1015-4
- transfers in trust..1.1015-2; 1.1015-3
- uniformity, decedent's property..1.1014-4
- war loss recoveries..1.1336-1
- wash sales..1.1091-2

Beneficiaries, insurance, defined..1.264-1

Beneficiaries of estates or trusts..1.641(a)-(O)—1.692-1
- alimony trust..1.682(a)-1; 1.682(b)-1
- carryover basis property, information returns..7.6039A-1
- control over trusts..1.678(a)-1—1.678(d)-1
- credits against tax..1.642(a)(1)-1—1.642(a)(3)-3
- defined..1.318-3; 1.643(c)-1
- depreciation..1.167(g)-1
- DISC stock, basis..1.1014-1(b); 1.1014-9
- dividends received credit and exclusion ..1.683-2
- employees' trusts..1.402(a)-1—1.402(e)-1
- life insurance proceeds or employees' death benefits..1.101-1—1.101-6
- nonresident aliens..1.875-2
- personal holding company stock owned by..1.544-2
- taxability:
  - nonqualified annuity plan..1.403(b)-1; 1.403(c)-1
  - qualified annuity plan..1.403(a)-1; 1.403(a)-2
- **wife as beneficiary of alimony trust ..1.682(a)-1; 1.682(b)-1**

Benevolent associations, exemption..1.501(c)(8)-1; 1.501(c)(12)-1

Bequests:
- basis for gain or loss..1.1014-1—1.1014-8
- exemption..1.102-1

Biweekly withholding table..31,3402(c)-1

Blind individuals:
- defined..1.151-1
- general tax credit..1.42A-1
- medical expense maximum deduction ..1.213-1; 1.213-2
- personal exemptions..1.42-1; 1.42A-1; 1.151-1; 1.151-2
- taxable income credit..1.42A-1

Board and lodging..1.119-1; 1.120-1; 1.162-2

Board of Tax Appeals: See "Tax Court, U.S."

Board of Trade, exemption..1.501(c)(6)-1

Bond discount:
- issued on or before May 27, 1969..1.163-3
- original issued after May 27, 1969..1.163-4

Bond for payment of taxes:
- extension granted..1.6165-1
- forms..301.7101-1
- jeopardy assessments..301.6863-1
- single in lieu of multiple..301.7102-1
- surety..301.7101-1
- termination of taxable year..1.6851-1—1.6851-3

Bond purchase plans, pension funds..1.410(a)-1—1.410(d)-1; 1.411(a)-1—1.411(d)-3; See also "Employees' trusts"
- age requirements..1.410(a)-3
- collectively bargained plans..1.413-1
- declaratory judgments as to qualification ..1.7476-1—1.7476-3
- participation standards..1.410(a)-1—1.410(d)-1
- service requirements..1.410(a)-3

Bonds:
- capital gain or loss..1.1232-1—1.1232-4
- carryover basis..7.1023(h)-1
- convertible, repurchase..1.249-1
- defined..1.171-4
- discount:
  - corporate acquisitions..1.381(c)(9)-1
  - unamortized upon discharge of debt ..1.108(a)-1
- exempt: See "Exempt income"; "Exempt securities"
- posting by taxpayer..301.7101-1; 301.7102-1
- premium:
  - amortizable..1.171-1—1.171-4
  - corporate acquisitions..1.381(c)(9)-1
  - determination of..1.171-2
- purchased with unmatured coupons detached..1.1232-4
- tax-free covenant..1.1451-1—1.1451-2
- U.S.: See "United States, obligations"
- worthless, loss..1.582-1

Bonuses:
- gross income, defined..1.61-2
- deductibility..1.162-9
- withholding..31.3402(g)-1

Books and records:
- controlled corporation, transfers to ..1.351-3
- distraint proceedings..301.6333-1
- distributions of stock or securities of controlled corporation..1.355-5
- election of reorganization tax treatment under 1939 or 1954 Code..1.393-3
- employee expense reporting..1.162-17
- employees, relating to..31.6001-1—31.6001-5
- employment taxes—31.6001-1—31.6001-5
- failure to keep, accounting period ..1.441-1(g)
- failure to produce, penalties..301.7269-1
- IRS disclosure of..301.9000-1
- liquidation in calendar month..1.333-5
- railroad reorganization..1.374-3
- reorganization..1.368-3
- requirements..1.6001-1; 31.6001-5
- research and experimental expenditures ..1.174-4
- SEC exchanges..1.1081-11
- seized property..301.6340-1
- summons to produce..301.7603-1

Boot, nontaxable exchanges..1.356-1—1.356-5
- reorganizations..1.361-1

Bridges, income from operation of..1.115-1

Brother-sister controlled group, retirement benefit plans..11.414(c)-1—11.414(c)-5

Building and loan associations..1.591-1—1.593-2
- adjusted basis of property..1.1016-9
- dividends, deductibility..1.591-1
- domestic, defined..301.7701-13

Building and loan associations (continued):
- government loans repaid by..1.592-1
- mortgage foreclosures..1.595-1
- organizations providing reserve funds for and insurance of, shares in..1.501(c)(14)-1
- taxation of..1.581-2

Buildings, improvements, deductibility ..1.263(a)-1

Burden of proof:
- accumulated earnings..1.534-1; 1.534-2
- transferee liability .301.6902-1

Business development corporations, bad debt reserves..1.586-1; 1.586-2

Business expenses:
See also specific items
- deduction of..1.162-1
- employees..1.162-17
- unpaid 2½ months after close of year ..1.267(a)-1

Business income:
- exempt organizations..1.501(a)-1—1.501(e)-1, 1.511-1—1.514(c)-1
- foreign sources..1.901-1—1.905-5; 1.911-1—1.943-1

Business leagues, exemption..1.501(c)(6)-1
Business needs, corporation, defined..1.537-1
Business outside U.S., foreign corporations ..1.881-1; 1.881-2
Business trusts, defined..301.7701-4

— C —

Calendar year:
- change to or from..1.442-1
- defined..1.441-1

Calls, puts and..1.1234-1
Campaign:
- return designating $1 toward presidential fund..301.6096-1; 301.6096-2

Canada, residents, withholding tax on wages..31.3401(a)(7)-1
Cancellation of debt: See "Discharge of Indebtedness"
Cancellation of lease, capital gain or loss ..1.1241-1

Capital accounts:
- adjusted basis..1.1016-2
- carrying charges applied to..1.266-1

Capital asset, defined; see also "Capital gains and losses"..1.1221-1

Capital contributions:
- basis..1.362-2
- consent dividends..1.565-3
- exempt income..1.118-1
- partnerships..1.721-1—1.723-1
- transfer of stock or securities to foreign corporation as, tax on..1.1491-1; 1.1492-1

Capital expenditures:
- advertising..1.162-14
- basis, adjustments..1.1016-5
- deductibility..1.263(a)-1
- defined..1.263(a)-2
- Federal Natl. Mortgage Assn...1.162-19
- planting and developing citrus and almond groves..1.278-1
- railroad rolling stock..1.263(e)-1

Capital gains and losses..1.1201-1—1.1250-5
- alternative tax..1.1201-1
- bonds and other debt..1.1232-1—1.1232-4
- cancellation of lease or distributor's agreement..1.1241-1
- capital asset defined..1.1221-1
- carryover..1.381(c)(3)-1; 1.1212-1
- - life insurance companies..1.817-4

Capital gains and losses (continued):
- coal royalties..1.631-3
- collapsible corporations..1.341-1
- dealers in securities..1.1236-1
- deduction for capital gains..1.1202-1
- definitions..1.1222-1
- depreciable realty..1.1250-1—1.1250-5
- earnings and profits computation..1.312-7; 1.1377-2
- emergency facilities sold..1.1238-1
- employee annuities..1.403(a)-1—1.403(b)-1
- employee's termination payments..1.240-1
- employees' trust distributions..1.402(a)-1
- estates and trusts..1.1202-1
- farmers' cooperatives..1.522-1—1.522-3
- foreign investment companies..1.1247-3
- holding period..1.1223-1
- - aggregated mineral interests..1.614-6
- - collapsible corporations..1.341-4
- - partnership distributed property..1.735-1
- - short sales..1.1233-1
- - timber-cutting..1.631-2
- involuntary conversions..1.1231-1; 1.1231-2
- limitation on capital losses..1.1211-1
- - earnings and profits computation ..1.312-7
- liquidating dividend..1.333-4
- long-term..1.1222-1
- deductibility..1.1202-1
- net capital gain defined..1.1222-1
- net capital loss defined..1.1222-1
- net short-term and long-term..1.1222-1
- options..1.1234-1
- partnership distributions..1.731-1
- partnership interest transferred..1.741-1
- patents..1.1235-1; 1.1235-2
- property used in trade or business ..1.1231-1; 1.1231-2
- realty subdivided for sale..1.1237-1
- redemption of stock to pay death taxes ..1.303-1—1.303-3
- related-taxpayer transactions..1.1239-1
- retirement of bonds..1.1232-2
- short sales..1.1233-1
- short-term..1.1222-1
- straddles, grantors of..1.1234-2
- termination payments to employees ..1.1240-1
- timber..1.631-1; 1.631-2
- worthless securities..1.165-5

Capital loss carryover: See "Capital gains and losses"

Carrybacks and carryovers:
- adjustments required by changes in accounting method..1.381(c)(1)-1; 1.381(c)(21)-1
- capital loss: See "Capital gains and losses"
- contributions to employees' trusts ..1.404(d)-1
- corporate acquisitions..1.381(a)-1—1.382(c)-1; 1.383-1—1.383-3
- dividends, personal holding companies ..1.564-1
- expected..1.6164-1—1.6164-9
- foreign tax credit..1.904-2
- investment credit..1.46-2
- mutual life insurance companies other than life, unused loss..1.825-1—1.825-3
- net operating loss: See "Net operating loss carrybacks and carryovers"
- payment of tax extended due to..1.6164-1—1.6164-9

69,006 (Fed. Reg.) CARRYBACKS—COMMON 5-25-78

Carrybacks and carryovers (continued):
. tentative adjustments..301.6411-1
. tentative refund adjustments..1.6411-1—1.6411-4

Carrying charges:
. deductibility..1.266-1
. election to capitalize..1.266-1
. installment sales..1.163-1; 1.163-2

Cash basis..1.446-1

Casual laborers, exemption from withholding..31.3401(a)(4)-1

Casualty losses..1.165-1; 1.165-7; 1.165-8

Cemetery companies, exemption..1.501(c)(13)-1

Cent, fractional part..301.6313-1

Certificate of compliance, departing aliens ..1.6851-2

Certificate of sale for tax collection ..301.6339-1

Certificates, employees' withholding..31.3402(f)(2)-1; 31.3402(f)(3)-1

Certification of papers..301.7622-1

Chambers of Commerce, exemption..1.501(c)(6)-1

Changes in rates during taxable year ..1.21-1

Charitable contributions: See "Contributions"

Charitable organizations:
. exemption..1.501(c)(3)-1
. feeder organizations..1.502-1
. sales to, loss..1.267(b)-1

Charitable remainder trusts..1.664-1—1.664-4; 8.1; 53.4947-1; 53.4947-2

Charitable trusts, private foundation treatment for..53.4947-1; 53.4947-2

Check in payment of tax..301.6311-1
. bad..301.6657-1

Child-care expenses..1.214-1

Children:
. compensation..1.73-1
. organizations for prevention of cruelty to, exemption..1.501(c)(3)-1
. returns..1.6012-1(a)(4)

China Trade Act corporations..1.941-1—1.943-1
. dividends from:
.. deduction for..1.246-1
. foreign tax credit..1.901-1
. returns..1.6072-3
. withholding tax..1.943-1

Christian Science practitioners, self-employment tax..1.1402(e)-1

Christmas trees, timber status..1.631-1, 1.631-2

Circulation expenditures..1.173-1

Citizens:
. credit, foreign taxes..1.901-1—1.905-5
. income from U.S. possessions..1.931-1
. nonresident: See "Nonresident citizens"
. persons subject to income tax..1.1-1
. possession of United States..1.931-1—1.933-1

Civic leagues, exemption..1.501(c)(4)-1

Claim of right:
. income received under:
.. repayment..1.1341-1
. recovery of previously deducted patent infringement damages..1.1342-1

Claims—see also "Refunds and Credits":
. abatement..1.6404-1
. against U.S...1.1347-1
. U.S., acquisition of property..1.1347-1
. unpaid, bankruptcy and receiverships ..301.6873-1

Class Life Asset Depreciation Range System (ADR):
. election to compute..1.167(a)-11; 1.167(a)-12

Classification of taxpayers:
. associations..301.7701-2
. organizations..301.7701-1
. partnerships..301.7701-3
. trusts..301.7701-4

Clearance of aliens departing from U.S. ..1.6851-2

Clergymen:
. compensation..1.61-2
. rental value of parsonage..1.107-1
. withholding..31.3401(a)(9)-1

"Clifford" type trusts..1.671-1—1.678(d)-1
. as determination..1.1313(a)-2
. Commissioner's authority..301.7121-1

Closing agreements:
. as determination..1.1313(a)-2
. Commissioner's authority..301.7121-1

Closing taxable year..1.6851-1; 1.6851-2; 301.6851-1

Clubs, college, domestic employees, exemption from withholding..31.3401(a)(3)-1

Clubs, social, exemption..1.501(c)(7)-1

Coal, coal lands and coal companies:
. expenditures in disposal of coal..1.272-1
. percentage depletion..1.613-2
. royalties..1.631-3
. safety equipment, amortization of ..1.187-1—1.187-2

Coast and Geodetic Survey:
. disability pay..1.104-1(e)

Coast Guard: See "Armed Forces of U.S."

Collapsible corporations:
. defined..1.341-2
. gain to shareholders of..1.341-1—1.341-6

Collapsible partnership..1.751-1

Collection at source: See "Withholding tax at source"

Collection of foreign items, information returns..1.6041-4

Collection of taxes..301.6301-1—301.6343-1
. accounting for..301.7512-1
. at source from wages: See "Withholding tax at source"
. bankruptcy and receiverships..301.6503(b)-1
. employment taxes..31.6302(c)-1—31.6302(c)-4
. government depositaries..31.6302(c)-1—31.6302(c)-4; 301.6302-1
. injunction..301.6213-1
. liens..301.6321-1—301.6325-1
. limitation period..301.6501(a)-1—301.6503(d)-1
. receipt of payment..301.6311-1—301.6315-1
. suit for:
.. authorization..301.7401-1
. lien for taxes enforced by..301.7403-1
. transferees..301.6901-1
. transfers to foreign entities..1.1494-1

Collectively bargained retirement plans ..1.410(b)-1(c); 1.413-1; 11.412(c)(1)-2

Combat pay..1.112-1
. withholding..31.3401(a)(1)-1

Commissioner, closing agreements with ..301.7121-1
. special studies and compilations ..301.7515-1

Commissions: See "Compensation"

Commodity Credit Corporation:
. loans..1.77-1, 1.77-2
. property pledged to..1.1016-5

Commodity futures transactions..1.1233-1
. personal holding company..1.543-1, 1.543-2
.. foreign..1.553-1

Common investments funds, self-employed retirement plans..11.401(d)(1)-1

5-25-78   **COMMON—CONTROLLED**   *(Fed. Reg.)* 69,007

──────References are to SECS. (§) in the Regs. Check Page 23,003 for latest developments──────

Common parent corporation:
. agent for subsidiaries..1.1502-16
. consolidated return..1.1503-1—1.1504-1
Common trust funds..1.584-1—1.584-6
. returns..1.6032-1
Communistic organization, exemption
  ..1.501(e)-1
Community chest, fund or foundation, exemption..1.170A-9; 1.501(c)(3)-1
Community property:
. basis of property acquired from decedent
  ..1.1014-2
. retirement income credit..1.37-2
Compensation:
. business expense..1.162-2
. children..1.73-1
. deduction as business expense..1.162-7
. deferred-payment plan..1.421-1—1.421-6
. disability..1.72-15; 1.104-1—1.106-1; 7.105-1
. . substantial gainful activity, defined
  ..7.105-2
. employee stock options..1.421-1—1.421-8
. excessive..1.162-8
. foreign government employees..1.893-1
. gross income..1.61-1; 1.61-2
. income from sources within U.S...1.861-4
. information returns..1.6041-1—1.6041-3; 1.6041-6; 31.6051-1
. injuries or sickness..1.72-15; 1.104-1—1.106-1; 7.105-1
. international organizations' employee
  ..1.893-1
. levy upon, exemption..404.6334(d)-1
. meals and lodging..1.119-1; 1.120-1
. more than one year, withholding tax
  ..31.3402(g)-2
. nonresident citizens, exemption..1.911-1
. partners..1.707-1
. restoration of amount held under claim of right..1.1341-1
. termination payments..1.1240-1
. unpaid 2½ mos. after close of year
  ..1.267(a)-1
"Complex" estates and trusts..1.661(a)-1—1.663(c)-4
Compromise of tax cases, authorization
  ..301.7122-1
Computation of tax:
. changes in rates during year..1.1-3
. IRS, by..1.6014-1; 1.6014-2
. optional tax on individuals..1.3-1
. period for..1.441-1
. sources within U.S...1.861-8
Condemnation of property:
. amounts received from U.S...1.1347-1
. gain or loss..1.1033(a)-1—1.1033(h)-1; 1.1034-1; 1.1231-1
. residence, treated as sale..1.1034-1(h)
Congressional committees, inspection of returns..301.6103(a)-101
Consent:
. adjustment of basis..1.108(a)-2
. soil and water conservation expenditures as expenses..1.175-6
Consent dividends..1.565-1—1.565-6
Consent stock, defined..1.565-6
Conservation expenses..1.175-1—1.175-6
Consolidated returns:
. taxable years beginning after Dec. 31, 1965..1.1501-1; 1.1502-0—1.1502-100
Consolidations: See "Reorganization"
Construction, residence, tax credit purposes
  ..1.44-2
Constructive ownership of stock:
. controlled group of corporations, retirement benefit plan purposes..11.414(c)-4

Constructive ownership (continued):
. corporate distributions and adjustments
  ..1.318-1—1.318-4
. nondeductible losses..1.267(c)-1
. personal holding companies..1.544-1—1.544-7
Constructive receipt of income..1.451-2
Continental shelf areas..1.638-1—1.638-2
Contributions..1.170A-1—1.170A-11; 1.170-0—1.170-3
. accident and health plans of employer
  ..1.106-1
. appreciated property..1.170A-4
. bargain sales to a charitable organization
  ..1.1011-2
. business expense..1.162-15
. . revocation of exempt status of organization..1.681(a)-1—1.682(b)-2
. carryovers by corporations..1.170A-11
. carryovers by individuals..1.170A-10
. charitable contributions in trust..1.170A-6
. charitable, religious, etc.:
. . carryovers in certain acquisitions
  ..1.381(c)(19)-1
. . estates and trusts..1.642(c)-1—1.642(c)-6; 1.681(a)-1—1.682(b)-2
. . exempt organization's prohibited transactions..1.503(e)-4; 1.681(a)-1—1.682(b)-2
. . hospitals..1.170A-9(c)(2)
. . remainders..1.170A-12
. . revocation of exempt status of organization..1.681(a)-1—1.682(b)-2
. community chest, fund or foundation
  ..1.170-A
. definition of section 170(b)(1)(A) organization..1.170A-9
. future interests in tangible personal property..1.170A-5
. interest on certain indebtedness..1.170A-3
. limitations on corporate deductions..1.170A-11
. limitations on individual deductions..1.170A-8; 1.170-2
. . medical research organizations..1.170A-9(c)(2)
. nondeductible..1.162-15
. partial interests in property..1.170A-7
. students as members of household..1.170A-2
Contributions to capital: See "Capital contributions"
Contributions to partnership..1.721-1—1.723-1
Control by beneficiaries, trust income taxable to whom..1.678(a)-1—1.678(d)-1
Control, controlled, defined:
. regulated investment company purpose
  ..1.851-3
. retirement benefit plans..11.414(c)-2(b)(2); 11.414(c)-3(d)(7)
Controlled corporations:
. accumulated earnings tax..1.1561-0—1.1561-2
. basis to distributees..1.358-1
. distribution of stock and securities
  1.355-1—1.355-5
. . receipt of additional consideration
  ..1.356-1—1.356-5
. earnings and profits affected by distributions and exchanges..1.312-10
. foreign..1.951-1—1.964.5
. . less developed countries, investments in
  ..1.963-0
. . minimum distributions to domestic corporations..1.963-1—1.963-7
. tax credit..1.960-1—1.960-6

69,008 (Fed. Reg.)   **CONTROLLED—COURT**   5-25-78

Controlled corporations (continued):
- nontaxable exchanges..1.351-1—1.351-3
- redemption of stock through..1.304-1
- sales and exchanges between stockholders and, gains..1.1239-1
- spin-offs, split-offs, split-ups..1.355-1—1.355-5
- surtax exemption..1.1551-1; 1.1561-0—1.1564-1
- transfers to..1.351-1—1.351-3
- . earnings or profits, effect on..1.312-11

Controlled group of corporations, retirement benefit plans..1.410(b)-1(d)(8); 1.411(a)-5; 11.414(c)-1—11.414(c)-5
- brother-sister controlled group, defined ..11.414(c)-2(c)
- combined group, defined..11.414(c)-2(d)
- control, determination of, exclusions ..11.414(c)-3
- parent-subsidiary group, defined..11.414(c)-2(b)

Controlled taxpayer:
- allocation of income, deductions, etc. ..1.482-1—1.482-2

Convertible securities, personal holding company..1.544-5

Cooperative associations:
- exemptions..1.501(c)(12)-1, 1.501(c)(16)-1, 1.521-1
- farmers: See "Farmers' cooperatives"
- patronage dividends..1.61-5
- per-unit retain certificates..1.61-5
- taxation of..1.522-1—1.522-4

Cooperative banks..1.591-1—1.593-2
- defined..301.7701-14
- organizations providing reserve funds for, and insurance of, deposits in ..1.501(c)(14)-1

Cooperative housing corporations:
- depreciation..1.216-2
- gain from sale of stock in..1.1034-1
- taxes and interest..1.216-1

Cooperatives:
- definitions..1.1388-1
- exempt farmers' cooperatives..1.1382-3
- patronage dividends, tax treatment ..1.1382-2, 1.1385-1
- pooling arrangements, treatment of ..1.1382-5
- tax treatment..1.1381-1—1.1383-1

Corporate distributions: See "Distributions by corporations"; "Dividends"

Corporate reorganizations: See "Reorganization"

Corporations:
- accumulated earnings tax..1.531-1—1.537-3
- affiliated: See "Affiliated corporations"
- avoidance of tax on shareholders:
- . improperly accumulating surplus ..1.531-1—1.537-3
- . personal holding companies..1.541-1—1.565-6
- carryovers in certain acquisitions ..1.381(a)-1—1.381(c)(16)-1
- characteristics of..301.7701-2
- collapsible, gain to shareholders of 1.341-1—1.341-5
- consent dividends..1.565-1
- consolidated returns..1.1501-1—1.1552-1
- controlled: See "Controlled corporations"
- convertible obligations, repurchase..1.249-1
- dealing in own stock..1.1032-1
- declaration of estimated tax..1.6016-1—1.6016-4; 1.6074-1—1.6074-3
- dissolution:
- . information returns..1.6043-1; 1.6043-2
- . transferee liability..301.6901-1—301.6903-1

Corporations (continued):
- distributions: See "Distributions by corporations"; "Dividends"
- dividends: See "Dividends"
- domestic defined..301.7701-5
- election to be taxed as partnership ..1.1371-1—1.1377-3
- estimated tax..1.6016-1—1.6016-4; 1.6074-1—1.6074-3; 1.6154-1—1.6154-3; 1.6425-1—1.6425-3; 1.6655-1—1.6655-5
- exempt: See "Exempt organizations"
- feeder organizations..1.502-1
- foreign: See "Foreign corporations"
- income:
- . . sources within possessions of U.S. ..1.931-1
- insurance on lives of officers:
- . deductibility of premiums..1.264-1
- interest on acquisition indebtedness ..1.279-1—1.279-7
- liquidation..1.331-1—1.346-3
- . information returns..1.6043-1; 1.6043-2
- . installment obligations..1.453-9
- . sales during 1954..1.392-1
- officers:
- . withholding tax from..31.3401(c)-1
- partnerships electing to be taxed as ..1.1361-1—1.1361-15
- . revocation of election..1.1361-15
- payment of tax..1.6152-1; 1.6154-1—1.6154-3
- proprietorships electing to be taxed as
- purchase and change of business ..1.382(a)-1
- rates of tax..1.11-1
- related, redemption of stock through ..1.304-2
- reorganization: See "Reorganization"
- returns..1.6012-2
- . amended, as refund claims..301.6402-3
- . consolidated..1.1501-1—1.1552-1
- . extensions..1.6081-1—1.6081-3
- . filing..1.6041-6; 1.6071-1; 1.6072-2
- . information..1.6038-1; 1.6038-2; 1.6041-1 et seq.
- . partnership returns as, limitations on assessment and collection purposes ..301.6501(g)-1
- . place to file..1.6091-1—1.6091-4; 31.6091-1(b)
- . required..1.6012-2
- . signing of..1.6062-1; 31.6061-1
- . time to file..1.6072-2; 1.6072-3
- . trust returns as, limitations on assessment and collection purposes ..301.6501(g)-1
- sale of property:
- . liquidation..1.337-1—1.337-5
- sale or exchange of stock..1.1248-6
- special deductions for..1.241-1—1.248-1
- surtax exemption..1.11-1; 1.1551-1
- tax on..1.11-1
- unrelated business income, charitable organizations..1.511-1—1.514(c)-1

Corpus of estate or trust:
- control of grantor over..1.671-1—1.678(d)-1
- distribution affecting simple trust status ..1.651(a)-3

Correction of error..1.1311(a)-1—1.1311(b)-3

Cost as basis of property..1.1012-1; 1.1015-4

Cost of depletion..1.612-1—1.612-4

Cost-of-living allowances..1.912-1; 1.912-2

Court of Appeals:
- review of TC decisions:
- . change of Secretary or his delegate ..301.7484-1
- . jurisdiction..301.7482-1
- . time to file petition..301.7483-1

COURTS—DEPENDENTS *(Fed. Reg.)* **69,009**

———References are to SECS. (§) in the Regs. Check Page 23,003 for latest developments———

Courts:
- decisions:
  - as a determination..1.1313(a)-1
- estates in control of:
  - limitations on assessment and collection..301.6503(b)-1

Credit unions, exemption..1.501(c)(14)-1

Creditors, validity of tax lien against ..301.6323-1

Credits against estimated tax..301.6402-4

Credits against tax..1.31-1—1.37-6
- disallowance, acquisition made to evade or avoid tax..1.269-1
- estates and trusts..1.642(a)(1)-1—1.642(a)(3)-3
- general tax credit..1.42A-1
- investment in certain depreciable property..1.46-1—1.46-3; 1.48-1—1.48-7
- new residence, purchase or construction ..1.44-1—1.44-5
- partially tax-exempt interest..1.35-1—1.35-2
- personal exemptions..1.42-1; 1.42A-1
- retirement income..1.37-1—1.37-5
- "special refund", employee social security tax..1.31-2
- taxable income credit..1.42A-1
- withheld taxes..1.31-1; 1.31-2; 1.1462-1; 301.6201-1

Credits and refunds: See "Refunds and credits"

Crop-financing cooperatives..1.501(c)(16)-1

Crop insurance proceeds:
- inclusion in gross income..1.451-6

Crop unharvested sold with land..1.268-1

Cruelty, society for prevention of, exemption..1.501(c)(3)-1

Currently distributable income, complex trusts..1.662(a)-1; 1.662(a)-2

Customs duties, deductibility..1.164-3

— **D** —

Damages:
- exemption..1.104-1(c)
- Tax Court proceeding instituted merely for delay..301.6673-1

Damages for antitrust violations, recoveries of..1.186-1

Date, liquidation plan adopted..1.337-2

Dealers in securities:
- capital gains and losses..1.1236-1
- tax-exempt securities..1.75-1

Death benefits, exempt income..1.101-1—1.101-6

Death, members of armed forces, tax upon ..1.692-1

Death taxes, redemption of stock to pay ..1.303-1—1.303-3

Debentures, sale or exchange by bank losses..1.582-1

Debts: See "Indebtedness"
- bad: See "Bad debts"
- discharge of: See "Discharge of indebtedness"

Decedents:
- accrued deductions and credits..1.691(b)-1
- credits against tax—1.691(b)-1; 1.691(c)-1; 1.691(c)-2
- deductions:
  - accrual basis..1.461-1
  - allowable to whom..1.691(b)-1
- discharge of executor from personal liability..301.6905-1
- income of..1.691(a)-1—1.692-1; 1.753-1

Decedents *(continued)*:
- *income of (continued)*:
  - inclusion in gross income of recipients ..1.61-13; 1.691(a)-2
  - time taxable..1.451-1
- medical expenses..1.213-1
- property acquired from:
  - basis..1.1014-1
  - carryover basis property, information returns..7.6039A-1
- returns, time for filing..1.6072-1

Declaration of estimated tax: See "Estimated tax"

Declaratory judgments, retirement plans, qualification..1.7476-1—1.7476-3

Deductions:
- adjusted gross income purposes..1.62-1
- allowance of..1.161-1; 1.211-1; 1.241-1
- income averaging..1.144-3
- nondeductible items..1.261-1—1.276-1
- standard..1.141-1—1.144-2
- time to take..1.461-1
- withheld taxes..31.3502-1

Deeds:
- seized property sold..301.6338-1; 301.6339-1

Deferred compensation..1.401-1—1.404(e)-1; 1.421-1—1.421-8

Deferred payment sales, real estate..1.453-6

Deficiency..301.6211-1—301.6215-1
- assessment..301.6213-1—301.6215-1
- bankruptcy and receivership..301.6871(a)-1—301.6873-1
- defined..301.6211-1
- extension of time for payment..1.6161-1
- interest on..301.6601-1
- limitations on assessment and collection ..301.6501(a)-1
- notice and demand for payment ..301.6303-1
- notice of..301.6212-1
- suspension of limitation on assessment and collection..301.6503(a)-1
- payment:
  - extension..1.6161-1(a)(2)
  - bond required..1.6165-1
  - installments..1.6152-1(c)
- redetermination:
  - petition for..301.6213-1

Deficiency dividends, personal holding companies..1.547-1—1.547-7

Definitions..301.7701-1—301.7701-16
See also specific items

Delinquency amounts:
- recovery exclusion..1.111-1

Delinquency penalty..301.6651-1
- fraud involved..301.6653-1

Delinquent taxes, interest on..301.6601-1

Demolition of buildings..1.165-3

Dental expenses..1.213-1; 1.213-2

Department of Justice, disclosure of returns and return information ..404.6103(a)-1—404.6103(k)(6)-1

Department of Labor:
- disclosure of returns and return information..420.6103(*l*)(2)-2; 420.6103(*l*)(2)-3

Dependents:
- defined..1.152-1—1.152-4; 1.214-1
- earnings of..1.73-1
- exemptions for..1.151-1—1.151-4
- expenses for care of..1.214-1
- students..1.151-2; 1.151-3
- support test, child of divorced or separated parents..1.152-4

Depletion:
- adjusting basis due to..1.1016-3—1.1016-10
- charitable remainder interest..1.170A-12
- deduction for..1.611-0—1.614-8
- earnings and profits affected by..1.312-6
- elections..1.9004-1—1.9005-5
- information required with return..1.611-2; 1.611-3; 1.613-5
- percentage:
  - corporate acquisitions..1.381(c)(18)-1
  - list of mineral groups..1.613-2
  - property defined..1.614-1
- reserve:
  - distributions..1.316-2

Depositaries for Government:
- payment of taxes to..1.6302-1—1.6302-2; 31.6302(c)-1—31.6302(c)-4; 301.6302-1

Depreciable property, records..1.167(a)-7

Depreciation..1.167(a)-1—1.167(i)-1
- ADR system..1.167(a)-11; 1.167(a)-12
- additional first-year allowance, election ..1.179-1—1.179.4
- adjusting basis due to..1.1016-3—1.1016-10
- amortization in excess of, sale of property..1.1238-1
- asset depreciation range (ADR)..1.167-(a)-11; 1.167(a)-12; 1.167(l)-5
- basis:
  - conversion of personal-use property ..1.167(f)-1
  - exempt organization that became taxable..1.1016-4
- change from retirement to straight-line method..1.9001-1—1.9001-4
- change in method..1.167(e)-1
- charitable remainder interest..1.170A-12
- Class Life Asset Depreciation Range System (ADR)..1.167(a)-11; 1.167(a)-12
- corporate acquisitions..1.381(c)(6)-1
- declining balance method..1.167(b)-2
- deductibility..1.167(a)-1—1.167(k)-4
  - section 1250 property ..1.167(j)-1—1.167(j)-7
- earnings or profits affected by..1.312-6
- election as to, period before 1952..1.1020-1
- improvements, oil and mineral..1.611-5
- life or terminable interests..1.273-1
- low-income housing..1.167(k)-1—1.167(k)-4
- public utility property..1.167(l)-4
- recapture of, as to realty..1.1250-1—1.1250-5
- repair allowance..1.167(a)-11; 1.263(f)-1
- reserves:
  - distributions..1.316-2
- sinking fund method..1.167(b)-4
- straight-line method..1.167(b)-1
- sum of the years-digits methods ..1.167(b)-3
- time to deduct..1.167(a)-10
- useful life..1.167(d)-1

Determinations:
- amount of gain or loss..1.1001-1
- sources of income..1.861-1—1.863-6
- tax, closing agreement as..1.1313(a)-4
- tax liability..1.1-1—1.37-5

Development expenditures:
- carryover of deferred..1.381(c)(10)-1
- deduction..1.616-1
- election to defer..1.616-2
- mines or deposits..1.616-1; 1.616-2
- oil and gas wells..1.612-4

Devises:
- basis for gain or loss..1.1014-1—1.1014-8
- exemption..1.102-1

Director of International Operations:
- district director status..301.7701-10

Disability benefits..1.72-15; 1.104-1—1.106-1; 1.214A-1—1.214-1; 7.105-1
- substantial gainful activity, defined ..7.105-2

Disaster loss..1.165-11

DISC (Domestic International Sales Corporation): See "Domestic International Sales Corporation"

Discharge of indebtedness:
- adjustments to basis..1.1016-7; 1.1016-8
- basis adjusted for..1.1017-1; 1.1017-2
- exempt income..1.108(a)-1—1.108(b)-1
- income..1.61-12
- stockholder-corporation:
  - dividend status..1.301-1

Disclosure of returns and return information..301.7216-1—301.7216-3; 404.6103(a)-1—404.6103(n)-1; 420.6103(l)(2)-1 —420.6103(l)(2)-3
- written determinations..301.6110-1—301.6110-7

Discount:
- obligations issued at..1.454-1
- capital gain or loss..1.1232-3
  - gross income inclusion..1.6049-1

Distraint: See "Seizure of property"

Distributee of corporate exchanges..1.358-1—1.358-4

Distributions by corporations..1.301-1—1.305-1
- appreciated property used to redeem stock..1.311-2
- Bank Holding Company Act of 1956 ..1.1101-1—1.1102-3
- basis of stock reduced by..1.301-1
- carryovers..1.381(a)-1—1.381(c)(1)-2
- cash in lieu of fractional shares..1.305-3(c)
- common and preferred stock..1.305-4
- convertible preferred stock..1.305-6
- definitions relating to..1.316-1—1.317-1
- depletion or depreciation reserves..1.316-2
- earnings and profits computation..1.312-1—1.312-15
- fair market value date..1.301-1
- gain or loss to corporation..1.311-1
- insolvency reorganizations..1.371-1—1.373-3
- liquidations..1.331-1—1.346-3
- organizations and reorganizations..1.351-1—1.373-3
- preference dividends on stock, discharge of..1.305-3
- proceeds of loan insured by U.S...1.312-12
- redemption of stock..1.302-1—1.304-3
  - earnings and profits as affected by ..1.312-1—1.312-12
- SEC orders..1.1081-1—1.1081.11
- source of..1.316-1; 1.316-2
- spin-offs, split-offs, split-ups..1.355-1—1.355-5
- stock and stock rights..1.305-1—1.307-2
- stock ownership rule..1.318-1—1.318-4
- tax-free:
  - adjustment of basis..1.1016-5
  - adjustment of basis of stock..1.307-1, 1.307-2
  - basis to distributees..1.358-1; 1.358-2
  - conversion ratio, adjustment ..1.305-3(d)
  - earnings and profits computation..1.312-1—1.312-12
- transactions treated as..1.305-7

Distributions by partnership..1.731-1—1.736-1

Distributive shares of partners..1.704-1

Distributor's agreement, cancellation ..1.1241-1

DISTRICT—DOMESTIC *(Fed. Reg.)* **69,011**

———————References are to SECS. (§) in the Regs. Check Page 23,003 for latest developments———————

District directors of internal revenue:
. abatement of taxes by..301.6404-1
. defined..301.7701-10
. notice requiring returns, etc..31.6001-6
. returns, authority to execute..301.6020-1

District of Columbia:
. employees, withholding tax..31.3401(c)-1
. obligations of, interest exemption..1.103-1

Dividend carryover:
. personal holding companies..1.564-1

Dividends..1.301-1—1.395-1
. appreciated values before Mar. 1, 1913
  ..1.316-2
. China Trade Act corporations..1.246-1
.. consent dividends..1.565-1—1.565-6
. cooperatives..1.521-1—1.522-3
.. information returns..1.6044-1
. credits against tax..1.34-1—1.34-6
. date considered paid..1.561-2; 1.563-3
. deductibility by corporations..1.243-1—1.247-1
. deficiency, personal holding companies
  ..1.547-2
. defined..1.316-1
.. dividends paid deduction purposes
  ..1.562-1
. exempt..1.34-1; 1.116-1
.. Subchapter S corporation shareholders
  ..1.1375-2
. foreign corporations..1.245-1—1.246-3
. gross income..1.61-9
. income from sources within or without
  U.S...1.861-3
. information returns..1.6041-1—1.6044-1
. instrumentalities of U.S...1.103-2
. inventory assets..1.312-2—1.312-4
. liquidating..1.302-1; 1.331-1.346-3
.. basis..1.334-1, 1.334-2
... calendar-month..1.333-1—1.333-5; 1.334-2
.. collapsible corporation..1.341-1—1.341-5
.. dividends-paid deduction..1.562-1—
   1.562-3
.. earnings and profits as affected by
   ..1.312-5; 1.312-11
.. information returns..1.6043-2
.. installment obligations..1.453-9
.. minority stockholders..1.337-5; 1.337-6
.. partial..1.302-2
.. partial, defined..1.346-1—1.346-3
. medium of payment, election of stockholders..1.305-2
. patronage..1.522-1—1.522-3; 1.1388-1
. personal holding companies..1.316.1
. preferential:
.. distributions in discharge of..1.305-3
.. dividends-paid deduction..1.562-1—
   1.562-3
. property..1.316-1
.. appreciation in value while held by
   corporation..1.301-1
.. corporate shareholders..1.301-1
.. gain or loss to corporation..1.311-1;
   1.311-2
.. liabilities connected with..1.312-3;
   1.312-4
. property sold at less than market..1.301-1
. public utilities' preferred stock..1.244-1
. regulated investment companies..1.854-1
  —1.855-1
. reorganizations..1.301-1
. rights to subscribe to stock..1.305-1
. securities in payment:
.. earnings and profits computation
   ..1.312-1—1.312-12

Dividends (continued):
. *securities in payment (continued):*
.. gain or loss to corporation..1.311-1;
   1.311-2
. source of distribution..1.316-2
. stock..1.305-1—1.307-2
.. basis..1.307-1, 1.307-2
.. common and preferred distributed
   ..1.305-4
.. earnings and profits, effect on..1.312-8
.. gain or loss to corporation..1.311-1;
   1.311-2
.. preference dividends, in discharge of
   ..1.305-3
.. preferred on common..1.306-2
. stock rights..1.305-1
. taxability..1.301-1

Dividends-paid deduction..1.561-1—1.565-6
. foreign personal holding companies
  ..1.556-1
. personal holding companies..1.381(c)
  (14)-1; 1.545-1; 1.547-1—1.547-7
. preferred stock of public utilities..1.247-1

Dividends-received credit:
. common trust funds..1.584-1
. estates and trusts..1.642(a)(3)-2
. individuals..1.34-1—1.34-5
. intercorporate..19.4-1
. limitations..1.34-2
. partners..1.702-1
. regulated investment company shareholders..1.854-1—1.854-3
. Subchapter S corporation shareholders
  ..1.1375-2
. who entitled to..1.34-3—1.34-5

Dividends-received deduction..1.78-1; 1.243-1
  —1.246-3
. limitation on..1.596-1

Divorce: See "Alimony and separate
   maintenance payments"

Documents, reproduction of..301.7513-1

Dollar, fractional..301.6102-1

Domestic building and loan associations
  ..402.1-1; 402.1-2; 301.7701-13

Domestic corporation, defined..301.7701-5

Domestic International Sales Corp. (DISC)
  ..1.991-1—1.997-1
. acquiring corporation, carryovers
  ..1.996-7
. actual..1.996-1
. allocation of income..1.995-5(g)
. assets test..1.992-1(c)
. controlled group..1.995-5
. corporate acquisitions and reorganizations
  ..1.995-5(d)
. corporate distributee..1.997-1
. decedent's stock, basis..1.1014-1(b);
  1.1014-9
. deemed distributions..1.995-2; 1.996-1
. deficiency distributions..1.992-3; 1.995-1
  (c)
. defined..1.992-1
. disqualification as, distributions upon
  ..1.995-3; 1.996-4
. distributions to stockholders:
.. accounts charged..1.996-1
.. adjustments..1.996-4; 1.996-5
.. dividends-received deduction..1.246-4
.. failure to make..1.992-3(c)
.. foreign tax credit..1.901-1(i)
.. tax treatment..1.995-1
. earnings and profits, divisions of..1.996-3
. election as..1.992-1(e); 1.992-2; 12.7
. export property..1.993-3
.. assets qualifying as..1.993-2
... sale of..1.993-1

69,012 (Fed. Reg.)   DOMESTIC—EMPLOYEES   5-25-78

Domestic International Sales Corp (DISC) (continued):
- export property (continued):
  - destination test..1.993-3(d)
  - film rentals..1.992-4
- foreign corporations and trusts..1.996-6
- foreign export corporation, related..1.993-5
- foreign tax credit, limitations..1.904-4
- gross receipts..1.993-6
- gross receipts test..1.992-1(b)
- ineligible corporations..1.992-1(f)
- loss carrybacks..1.996-8
- losses..1.996-2
- personal holding company income..1.995-1(d)
- possessions' corporation..1.931-1(j)
- producer's loans..1.993-4; 1.995-5
- qualified export assets..1.993-2
- qualified export receipts..1.993-1
- redemption of stock..1.996-4(b)
- returns..1.992-1(g); 1.6011-2; 301.6501(g)-1
  - failure to file..301.6686-1
  - time for filing..1.6072-2(e)
- royalties and fees..1.995-5(b)(6)
- stock of, sale or exchange..1.995-4
- taxation of..1.991-1
- transfer of property by export trade corporation..12.5
- transfers of shares upon disqualification..1.995-3(c)
- United States, defined..1.993-7

Domestic service employees exemption from withholding..31.3401(a)(3)-1

Double deductions:
- basis adjusted for..1.1016-6
- estate of decedent..1.642(g)-1
- limitation statute causing adjustment..1.1312-2

Double disallowance of deduction or credit..1.1312-4

Drilling costs, oil and gas wells..1.612-4; 7.57(d)-1

Drought, livestock sold..1.451-7; 1.1033(f)-1

Drugs, expense of..1.213-1

Due date..1.6071-1—1.6074-1
- employment taxes..31.6071(a)-1
- extended, bond required..1.6165-1
- holiday..301.7503-1
- timely mailing..301.7502-1

—E—

Earned income:
- defined..1.911-1
- maximum tax rate..1.1348-1—1.1348-3
- nonresident citizens, exemption..1.911-1; 1.911-2
- retirement income credit purposes..1.37-1

Earnings and profits:
- accounting methods..1.312-6
- accumulated:
  - grounds for..1.537-2
  - tax on..1.531-1—1.537-3
- affiliated corporations..1.1552-1
- carryovers by acquiring corporation..1.381(c)(2)-1
- depreciation, effect on..1.312-15
- distribution of property affecting..1.312-1—1.312-12
- net operating loss deduction..1.1377-3
- undistributed taxable income..1.1377-1

Education:
- expenses for..1.162-5

Educational institutions:
- defined..1.151-3
- dependents attending..1.151-2; 1.151-3
- exemption..1.501(c)(3)-1
- feeder organizations..1.502-1

Effective dates:
- Code of 1954..1.395-1
- distributions by corporations..1.391-1
- liquidation of corporations..1.392-1
- withholding exemption certificates..31.3402(f)(3)-1; 31.3402(f)(4)-1

Elections:
- accounting methods, return to old..1.481-6
- aggregation of separate interests, depletion purposes..1.614-2
- amortization of organizational expenditures..1.248-1
- amortization of trademark and trade name expenditures..1.177-1
- bad debts..1.166-1
- basis of stock rights..1.307-2
- Commodity Credit loans..1.77-1
- condemnation of residence..1.1034-1
- contested liabilities..1.461-1; 1.461-2
- disaster losses..1.165-11
- extension of time for making..1.9100-1
- farm fertilizer expenses..1.180-1—1.180-2
- foreign corporations..1.962-1—1.962-4; 1.963-7; 1.964-1
- 52-53-week year..1.441-2
- installment method..1.453-1; 1.453-7; 1.453-8
- involuntary conversion, FCC orders..1.1071-4
- life insurance company transfers, policyholders surplus account to shareholders..1.815-6
- life insurance reserve computed on preliminary term basis..1.818-4
- net leases of real property..12.8
- percentage depletion rates..1.613-7
- realty income, nonresident aliens..1.871-8; 1.871-10
- reorganization tax treatment under 1939 or 1954 Code..1.393-3
- sales or exchanges on orders of FCC..1.1071-2
- single interest as more than one property, depletion purposes..1.614-3
- 65-day rule by fiduciary of trust..1.663(b)-2
- passive investment income..14.1-1
- soil and water conservation expenditures..1.175-6
- standard deduction..1.141-1; 1.144-1
- stockholder's, medium of dividend payment..1.305-2
- Subchapter S corporations..1.1372-1—1.1372-6
  - capital gains, special rules..1.1375-1
  - definitions..1.1371-1—1.1371-2
  - net operating loss deduction..1.1374-1—1.1374-4
- Tax Reform Act of 1969, under..13.0
- timber-cutting as sale or exchange..1.631-1
- war loss recoveries treatment..1.1335-1

Electric railway reorganization..1.373-3

Emergency facilities:
- amortization..1.168-1—1.168-7
- estates and trusts..1.642(f)-1
- sale of property..1.1238-1

Employee stock options..1.421-1—1.421-8; 1.1014-1

Employee stock ownership plans (ESOPs)..54.4975-7—54.4975-12

Employees:
- accident and health benefits..1.72-15; 1.104-1—1.106-1; 7.105-1
- annuities: See "Employees' trusts"
- death benefits..1.101-2
- defined:
  - withholding tax purposes..31.3401(c)-1
- disability benefits..1.72-15, 1.104-1—1.106-1; 7.105-1

EMPLOYEES—EMPLOYEES' *(Fed. Reg.)* **69,013**

References are to SECS. (§) in the Regs. Check Page 23,003 for latest developments

Employees (continued):
. *disability benefits (continued):*
. . substantial gainful activity, defined..7.105-2
. insurance on lives of:
. . premiums, deductibility..1.264-1
. meals and lodging..1.119-1; 1.162-2
. receipts for withheld taxes: See "Withholding tax statements"
. stock options received by..1.421-1—1.421-8; 1.1014-1
. termination payments..1.1240-1
. withholding on wages: See "Withholding tax on wages"

Employees' Annuities:
. accident and health plans..7.105-1
. . substantial gainful activity, defined..7.105-2
. contributions to:
. . limitations..11.415(c)(4)-1
. foreign subsidiaries..1.406-1; 1.407-1

Employees' associations:
. accident and health benefits..1.105-5
. exemption..1.501(c)(4)-1

Employees' trusts..1.401-1—1.404(e)-1; 1.405-1—1.405-3; 1.410(a)-1—1.410(d)-1; 1.411(a)-1—1.411(d)-3
. accident or health benefits..1.72-15
. accrued benefit requirement..1.411(a)-7(a)
. . allocation between employer and employee contributions..1.411(c)-1
. . cash-outs of..1.411(a)-7(d)
. . computation..1.411(b)-1
. age requirements..1.410(a)-3; 1.410(a)-4
. amendment to plan..1.411(a)-3(a)(3)
. annuities..1.401-9; 1.401(a)-11; 1.403(b)-1; 1.403(c)-1
. . contributions to..11.401(a)(6)-1
. assignment or alienation of benefits..1.401(a)-13
. beneficiaries, taxability..1.402(a)-1 et seq.
. capital gain..1.403(a)-2
. change in plans, retroactive..1.401(b)-1
. class-year plans..1.411(d)-3
. classification of employees..1.410(b)-1
. contributions to..1.404(a)-1—1.404(e)-1
. . carryovers of predecessor corp...1.381(c)(11)-1
. . computing employee's amount..1.72-8
. . extension of time..11.412(c)-12
. . recoverable in 3 years..1.72-13
. . refunds of premiums..1.404(a)-8
. . time deemed made..11.404(a)(6)-1
. controlled group of corporations: See "Controlled group of corporations"
. coverage requirements..1.410(b)-1
. custodian accounts..1.401-8
. declaratory judgment as to qualification..1.7476-1—1.7476-3
. deductibility..1.404(a)-1; 1.404(a)-13
. defined benefit plan:
. . accrued benefit requirement..1.411(a)-7(a)(1); 1.411(b)-1
. . break in service..1.411(a)-6(c)
. defined contribution plan:
. . accrued benefit requirement..1.411(a)-7(a)(2); 1.411(b)-1(e)(2)
. . break in service..1.411(a)-6(c)
. . limitations on..11.415(c)(4)-1
. Dept. of Labor, information to..420.6103(*l*)(2)-2; 420.6103(*l*)(2)-3
. disclosure of plans and reports..420.6103(*l*)(1)—420.6103(*l*)(3)

Employees' trusts (continued):
. distributions, retirement income credit..1.37-1—1.37-5
. early retirement..1.401(a)-14; 11.401(a)-11(d)
. . benefits..1.411(a)-7(c)
. employee requirement..11.410(b)-1
. exemption from tax..1.501(a)-1
. fiduciary of plan defined..54.4975-9
. foreign subsidiaries' employees..1.406-1; 1.407-1
. forfeitures..1.401-7; 1.411(a)-4; 11.402(e)(4)(A)-1
. gross income..1.72-1—1.72-15
. highly compensated employees..1.410(b)-1(b)(2), (d)(1)
. information returns..1.6033-1; 1.6041-2(b); 1.6047-1
. life insurance contracts..1.72-16—1.72-17
. . loans on..1.401(a)-13(d)(2)
. lump-sum distributions..11.402(e)(4)(A)-1
. medical benefits..1.401-14
. minimum funding standards..11.412(c)(1); 11.412(c)(1)-2
. more than one employer..1.413-2
. multiple trusts under one plan..1.410(b)-1(d)(3)
. nonforfeitable beneficial interest..1.401(a)-19
. . percentage determination:
. . . service requirements..1.411(a)-5
. normal retirement benefit..1.411(a)-7(c)
. owner-employees..1.72-17; 11.401(d)(1)-1
. participation standards..1.410(a)-1—1.410(d)-1
. partners and partnerships..1.1361-4; 11.414(c)-1—11.414(c)-5
. Pension Benefit Guaranty Corporation, information to..420.6103(*l*)(2)-1
. predecessor employers and plans..1.411(a)-5(b)(3)(iv)(v)
. prohibited transactions..1.503(a)-1—1.503(i)-1; 54.4975-6; 141.4975-13
. qualified bond purchase plans..1.405-1—1.405-3
. qualified plans and trusts defined..1.401-0
. repayment of distributions..1.411(a)-7(d)
. retirement age..1.411(a)-7(b)
. retirement income credit..1.37-1—1.37-5
. retroactive payments..1.401(a)-14
. self-employed individuals..1.72-18; 1.401-10—1.401-13; 1.404(e)-1; 11.401(d)(1)-1
. service requirements..1.410(a)-3; 1.411(a)-5
. . break in service..1.410(a)-5; 1.411(a)-6(c); 1.411(a)-9
. Social Security benefits, effect on..1.401(a)-15
. taxation of..1.403(a)-1—1.403(a)-2; 1.403(c)-1
. termination..1.401-6; 1.411(a)-5(b)(3); 1.411(d)(2)
. discriminatory effects..1.411(d)-3
. time payments begin..1.401(a)-14
. union-industry plan..1.410(b)-1
. vesting rights, minimum standards 1.411(a)-1—1.411(d)-3
. . change in schedule..1.411(a)-8
. . collectively bargained plans..1.413-1
. . combination of trusts and plans..1.413-2
. . more than one employer..1.413-2
. . withdrawals..1.401(a)-19; 1.411(a)-4(b)
. withholding..31.3401(a)(12)-1

69,014 (Fed. Reg.) EMPLOYEES'—EVERGREEN 5-25-78

Employees' trusts (continued):
. years of service..1.411(a)-6
. years of service factor..1.411(a)-5

Employers:
. acts to be performed by agents..31.3504-1
. defined, withholding on wages ..31.3401(d)-1
. duty as to taxes of aliens..1.871-6
. identification numbers..31.6011(b)-1; 301.6109-1; 301.7701-12
. liability for withholding tax..31.3403-1
. withholding statements: See "Withholding tax statements"

Employment taxes:
. adjustments..31.6205-1
. agents..31.3504-1
. books and records..31.6001-1—31.6001-4
. deductibility..31.3502-1
. employers' identification numbers ..31.6011(b)-1; 301.6109-1
. erroneous payments..31.3503-1
. Federal Insurance Contributions Act ..31.6011(a)-6
. government depositaries..31.6302(c)-1— 31.6302(c)-3
. mitigation of effect of statute of limitations..301.6521-1; 301.6521-2
. overpayments..31.6413(a)-1—31.6414-1
. returns..31.6011(a)-1; 301.6011(b)-2
. undercollection..31.6205-1
. underpayments..31.6205-1

Endowment contracts:
. defined..1.1035-1
. exchange of..1.1035-1
. income from..1.72-1—1.72-15
. interest paid to purchase..1.264-2; 1.264-3

Endowment insurance policy:
. dividends..1.316-1
. income from..1.61-10
. lump-sum settlement:
. . option to receive annuity..1.72-12
. single premium, interest paid to purchase ..1.264-3

Entertainment expenses..1.162-17; 1.274-1— 1.274-7
Erosion prevention costs..1.175-1—1.175-6
Erroneous payments, employment tax ..31.3503-1
Errors, adjustments in tax..1.1311(a)-1— 1.1314(c)-1

Estate tax:
. deductibility..1.164-2; 1.691(c)-1; 1.691(c)-2
. redemption of stock to pay..1.303-1— 1.303-3

Estates and trusts..1.641(a)-0—1.683-3: See also "Trusts"
. administration expenses..1.642(g)-1; 1.642(g)-2
. amortization deduction..1.642(f)-1
. capital gains and losses..1.1202-1
. . contributions out of..1.642(c)-3
. . distributable net income computation ..1.643(a)-3
. carryover basis property, information returns..7.6039A-1
. casualty losses..1.642(g)-1
. charitable contributions..1.681(a)-1— 1.681(d)-1
. charitable remainders..1.664-1—1.664-4; 8.1
. "Clifford" type trusts..1.671-1—1.678(d)-1
. "complex"..1.661(a)-1—1.663(c)-4
. credits against tax..1.901-1
. declaration of estimated tax..1.6015(h)-1
. deductions..1.642(b)-1—1.642(i)-1
. . correlative, adjustments under mitigation rule..1.1312-5
. distributable net income..1.643(a)-0— 1.643(a)-7

Estates and trusts (continued):
. dividends received by..1.642(a)(3)-1; 1.642(a)(3)-2
. . credit and exclusion..1.683-2
. employees' trusts: See "Employees' trusts"
. gross income..1.61-13
. income:
. . accumulation..1.661(a)-1—1.663(c)-4
. . adjustment in barred year under mitigation rule..1.1312-5
. . defined..1.643(b)-1
. . distributable..1.643(a)-1—1.643(a)-7
. . taxability..1.641(a)-0—1.643(d)-2
. pension trusts: See "Employees' trusts"
. personal holding company stock owned by..1.544-2
. pooled income funds..1.642(c)-5—1.642(c)-7
. . profit-sharing trusts: See "Employees' trusts"
. redemption of stock to pay death taxes ..1.303-1—1.303-3
. returns..1.6012-3(a)
. . place to file..1.6091-2
. . signature..31.6061-1
. . time to file..1.6072-1
. simple trusts, allocation of income ..1.652(b)-2
. stock bonus trusts: See "Employees' trusts"
. stock ownership rule:
. . corporate distribution and adjustments ..1.318-3
. work incentive program expenses, credit for..1.50A-6; 1.50B-3

Estimated tax:
. assessment..301.6201-1
. credits against..301.6402-1
. declarations:
. . corporations..1.6016-1—1.6016-4; 1.6074-1 —1.6074-3; 1.6154-1—1.6154-3; 1.6655-1 —1.6655-3
. . individuals..1.6015(a)-1—1.6015(i)-1; 1.6073-1—1.6073-4
. . . Fulbright grants..301.6316-6
. defined..1.6015(c)-1; 1.6016-1(b)
. excessive adjustment by corporation ..1.6655-5
. extension of time to pay..1.6154-3— 1.6154-4
. failure to pay..1.6654-1—1.6654-5; 1.6655-1; 1.6655-3
. fiscal year..1.6153-2
. nonresident aliens..1.6015(i)-1
. overpayment by corporation, adjustment of..1.6425-1—1.6425-3
. overstatement of amount paid as ..301.6201-1
. payment..1.6153-1; 1.6154-1
. penalties..1.6654-1; 1.6655-1
. . waiver of for 1971..1.6654-4
. publicity..301.6103(a)-100; 301.6103(a)-101
. short taxable year..1.6153-3; 1.6154-2
. underpayments..1.6654-1; 1.6654-2; 1.6655-1; 1.6655-2
. . '69 Tax Reform Act..1.9006-1

Estoppel, basis for gain or loss..1.1016-6

Evasion or avoidance of tax:
. acquisitions to effect..1.1551-1
. corporations used to avoid income tax on shareholders..1.531-1—1.537-3, 1.541-1—1.565-6
. defined..1.269-1—1.269-6
. penalties..301.6672-1
. transfers to foreign entities..1.1491-1— 1.1494-2; 7.367(a)-1—7.367-2

Evergreen trees, timber status..1.631-1; 1.631-2

EVIDENCE—EXPENSES *(Fed. Reg.)* 69,015

———References are to SECS. (§) in the Regs. Check Page 23,003 for latest developments———

Evidence, accumulated earnings for tax avoidance..1.533-1
Examination of books and records, time and place..301.7605-1
Excess deduction account, farm losses ..1.1251-1; 1.1251-2
Excess profits tax, compilation of relief cases..301.6105-1
Excessive profits on Government contracts ..1.1471-1
Exchanges:
. annuity contracts..1.1035-1
. assumption of liabilities..1.357-1; 1.357-2
. basis for gain or loss:
. . liquidation of subsidiary..1.334-1; 1.334-2
. controlled corporation..1.351-1—1.351-3
. defined, holding period purposes..1.223-1
. endowment contracts..1.1035-1
. FCC orders..1.1071-1—1.1071-4
. gain or loss..1.61-6; 1.1001-1; 1.1002-1
. insolvency reorganization..1.371-1
. insurance policies..1.1035-1
. investment property..1.1031(a)-1
. livestock of different sexes..1.1031(e)-1
. liquidation in one calendar month:
. . basis of property received..1.334-2
. nontaxable..1.1031(a)-1—1.1039-1
. productive-use property..1.1031(a)-1
. property of like kind..1.1031(a)-1
. radio broadcasting stations involved ..1.1071-1—1.1071-4
. railroad reorganization..1.354-1; 1.373-1—1.373-3
. reorganization: See "Reorganization"
. residence..1.1034-1
. SEC orders..1.1081-1—1.1083-1
. Sec. 306 stock involved..1.356-4
. security holders of insolvent corporation ..1.371-2
. solely in kind..1.1031(a)-1—1.1031(d)-1
. spin-offs, split-offs, split-ups..1.355-1—1.355-5
. stock for property..1.1032-1
. stock for stock of same corporation ..1.1036-1
. tax-free..1.1031(a)-1—1.1039-1
. . boot..1.361-1
. . earnings and profits affected by ..1.312-7—1.312-11
. . property for other property and money ..1.1031(b)-1
. . railroad reorganization..1.1374-1
Excise taxes:
. deductibility..1.164-3
. exemption..316.24—316.27
Exclusions: See "Exempt income"
Executors and administrators:
. liability..301.6901-1—301.6903-1
. . discharge of..301.6905-1
Exempt corporations: See "Exempt organizations"
Exempt income..1.101-1—1.121
. compensation for injuries or sickness ..1.104-1
. contributions to capital..1.118-1
. cost-of-living allowances..1.912-1; 1.912-2
. discharge of indebtedness..1.108(a)-1—1.108(b)-1
. distribution from..1.312-6
. earned income of nonresident citizen ..1.911-1
. expenses allocable to..1.265-1
. fellowships..1.117-1—1.117-4
. foreign corporations..1.883-1
. foreign government employees..1.893-1
. foreign governments..1.892-1
. foreign service employees..1.912-2

Exempt income (continued):
. Government payments for defense purposes..1.621-1
. improvements by lessee..1.109-1
. interest..1.103-1—1.103-12
. international organizations..1.892-1
. . employees of..1.893-1
. Philippine government employees..1.893-1
. post allowances..1.912-2
. proceeds of life insurance policy at death..1.101-1
. Puerto Rican source income..1.933-1
. scholarships..1.117-1—1.117-4
. treaty obligations..1.894-1
Exempt organizations..1.501(a)-1—1.522-3
. application for..1.501(a)-1
. books and records..1.6001-1(c)
. business income..1.511-1—1.514(c)-1
. business lease, defined..1.514(f)-1
. business lease indebtedness..1.514(g)-1
. claim for exemption, inspection of ..301.6104-1
. debt-financed income and deductions, unrelated..1.514(a)-1—1.514(g)-1
. debt-financed property, defined..1.514(b)-1
. dividends from, deduction for..1.246-1
. feeder organizations..1.502-1; 1.511-1—1.514(c)-1
. foreign, withholding..1.1443-1
. information returns..1.6033-1; 1.6033-2
. . failure to file..301.6652-2
. . public inspection..301.6104-2
. list of..1.501(c)(2)-1—1.501(d)-1
. loans as prohibited transactions ..1.503(h)-1—1.503(i)-1
. loss of exemption..1.503(a)-1—1.503(i)-1; 1.504-1
. . basis of property..1.1016-3
. . charitable contributions after..1.681(a)-1—1.682(b)-2
. . future status..1.503(c)-1
. proof of..1.501(a)-1
. prohibited transactions..1.503(a)(1)—1.503(i)-1
. . charitable contributions deduction ..1.681(a)-1—1.682(b)-2
. returns..1.6012-2(e), (f); 1.6012-3; 1.6033-1; 1.6033-2
. . disclosure of certain information to State officers..301.6104-3
. . inspection..301.6104-2
. . transfers..1.6060-1; 301.6050-1
. sale to or by person controlling..1.267(b)-1
. unrelated business taxable income ..1.501(c)(2)-1; 1.511-1—1.514(d)
Exempt securities..1.103-1—1.103-12
. dealers in..1.75-1
. interest to purchase or carry..1.265-2
Exempt wages, withholding tax purposes ..31.3401(a)-2—31.3401(a)(12)-1
Exemption:
. nonresidents..1.874-1; 1.1441-3
. personal..1.151-1—1.153-1
. surtax purposes, corporations..1.11-1; 1.1551-1
. withholding..31.3402(f)(1)-1
Exemption certificates:
. withholding tax on wages..31.3402(f)(2)-1
Exemption from levy..301.6334-1
Exemption from tax:
. common trust funds..1.584-1
Exemption from withholding ..31.3401(a)-2—31.3401(a)(12)-1
Expenses:
. allocable to exempt income..1.265-1
. deductible..1.62-1; 1.162-1—1.162-16

69,016 (Fed. Reg.)   EXPENSES—FIVE YEARS   5-25-78

Expenses (continued):
. determination, collection or refund of taxes, connected with..1.212-1
. education..1.162-5
. employees, reporting of...1.162-17
. income-producing..1.212-1
. nondeductible..1.261-1—1.273-1
. sports programs for Red Cross..1.114-1
. unpaid 2½ mos. after close of year..1.267(a)-1

Experimental expenditures..1.174-1—1.174-4

Exploration expenditures..1.615-1—1.615-9; 1.617-1—1.617-4
. carryover of deferred..1.381(c)(10)-1
. limitation on deduction..1.617-2
. payments to encourage..1.621-1
. recapture..1.617-3

Export trade corporation..1.970-1—1.972-1
. transfer of property to a disc..12.5

Extension of time:
. declaration of estimated tax..1.6073-3; 1.6074-3; 1.6153-4; 1.6154-3
. elections, to make..1.9100-1
. file returns..1.6081-1—1.6081-3
.. employment taxes..31.6081(a)-1
. pay tax..1.6161-1—1.6164-9; 31.6161(a)(1)-1
.. bond required..1.6165-1
. withholding statements..31.6051-1(d)

— F —

Family:
. defined:
.. personal holding company stock ownership..1.544-3
. expenses..1.262-1
. losses..1.267(c)-1
. partnerships..1.704-1
. stock ownership rule:
.. collapsible corporations..1.341-4
.. corporate distributions and adjustments ..1.318-1—1.318-4

Farm:
. accounting methods..1.61-4
. as a business, defined..1.175-3
. crop unharvested, sold with land..1.268-1
. depreciation..1.167(a)-6
. drought, livestock sold..1.451-7; 1.1033(f)-1
. excess deduction account..1.1251-1; 1.1251-2
. fertilizing expenditures..1.180-1; 1.180-2
. hobby losses..1.270-1
. inventories..1.471-6
. livestock diseased..1.1033(e)-1
. losses..1.165-6
.. nonfarm income offset by..1.1251-1—1.1251-4
. "on-farm" training, as school attendance ..1.151-3
. recapture of conservation expenses ..1.1252-1; 1.1252-2
. soil and water conservation expenditures ..1.175-1; 1.175-2
. workers, exemption from withholding ..31.3401(a)(2)-1

Farmers:
. as employers, withholding taxes..31.3402(e)-1
. books and records..1.6001-1(b)
. declaration of estimated tax..1.6015(f)-1; 1.6073-1(b); 1.6073-2(b); 1.6073-3(b)
. excess deduction accounts..1.1251-1; 1.1251-2
. expenditures for clearing land..1.182-1—1.182-6
. expenses..1.162-12
. gross income..1.61-4
. losses
.. nonfarm income offset by..1.1251-1—1.1251-4
. recapture of conservation expenses ..1.1252-1; 1.1252-2

Farmers' cooperatives..1.521-1—1.522-4; 1.1381-2
. allocation defined..1.522-3
. crop financing..1.501(c)(16)-1
. dividends paid on its stock..1.521-1—1.522-4
. exemption..1.521-1
. patronage dividends..1.522-3
.. deduction by recipient corporation ..1.246-1
.. information returns..1.6044-1
. returns..1.6012-2
. taxable years affected..1.522-4

Federal bonds: See "United States, obligations"

Federal Communications Commission:
. sales or exchanges to effectuate policies of..1.1071-1—1.1071-4

Federal Exchange Commission policy ..1.1071-1—1.1071-4

Federal excise tax:
. deduction..1.164-3
. exemption..316.24—316.27

Federal Housing Authority, insured loan ..1.312-12

Federal instrumentalities: See "Instrumentalities of U.S."

Federal Insurance Contributions Act: See "Employment Taxes."

Federal officers and employees:
. cost-of-living allowances..1.912-1
. disclosure of returns and return information..404.6103(a)-1—404.6103(k)(6)-1
. offenses by..301.7214-1
. repayments to..301.7423-1
. withholding tax..31.3401(c)-1

Federal taxes, deductibility..1.164-2

Federal Unemployment Tax Act: See "Employment Taxes."

Feeder organizations..1.502-1; 1.511-2

Fees:
. gross income..1.61-2
. paid public officials, withholding..31.3401(a)-2

Fellowships..1.117-1—1.117-4

Fiduciaries:
. defined..301.7701-6
. distinguished from agent..301.7701-7
. employees' trusts purposes..54.4975-9
. liability..301.6901-1—301.6903-1
. notice of relationship..301.6903-1
. returns by..1.6012-3
.. refund claim status..301.6402-3
.. signature..31.6061-1
. withholding tax at source
.. wages..31.3402(g)-3

52-53 week year..1.441-2

Filing of returns:
. extension of time..1.6081-1—1.6081-4
. place for..1.6091-1—1.6091-4; 31.6091-1
. time for..1.6071-1—1.6074-1

Finance company, cooperative, exempt status..1.501(c)(16)-1

Fire insurance companies, mutual..1.831-1—1.832-2

Fire losses:
. deduction from gross income..1.165-7
. residential property..1.1034-1

Fiscal year:
. change to or from..1.442-1
. changes in rates during..1.21-1
. defined..1.441-1

Five-year throwback rule, excess distributions by trusts..1.665(a)-0A—1.668(b)-2

Five years, losses for..1.270-1

FOREIGN—FOREIGN *(Fed. Reg.)* **69,017**

———References are to SECS. (§) in the Regs. Check Page 23,003 for latest developments———

Foreign community income:
- ..1.981-1—1.981-3
- partnerships, distributive share..1.981-1(b)(4)
- trade or business..1.981-1(b)(3)

Foreign corporations..1.881-1—1.894-1
- accumulated earnings tax..1.532-1
- adjustments for overwithholding of tax..1.1461-4
- classified..301.7701-5
- consent dividends..1.565-5
- controlled..1.951-1—1.964-5
- . foreign tax credit..1.960-1—1.960-6
- . insurance on U.S. risks..1.953-1—1.953-6
- . less developed countries, investments in ..1.963-0
- . subpart F income..1.952-1
- credit, foreign taxes..1.882-1
- credit or refund of tax withheld..1.6414-1
- credits against tax..1.32
- deductions..1.882-4
- defined..301.7701-5
- dividends from, deduction for..1.245-1—1.246-3
- dividends paid by:
- . dividends received deduction..1.245-1
- . foreign tax credit..1.902-1
- earnings and profits..1.964-1—1.964-4; 1.1248-1—1.1248-3; 1.1248-7
- effectively connected income..1.882-2
- engaged in trade or business in U.S. ..1.882-1
- exchange or sale of stock, gain from ..1.1248-1—1.1248-7
- exemption:
- . earnings of ships or aircraft..1.883-1
- extension of time for filing returns ..1.6081-2
- foreign base income..1.952-1; 1.954-1—1.954-5
- Government depositaries..1.6302-2
- gross income..1.882-3
- income effectively connected with U.S. business..1.882-2
- income from insurance..1.953-1—1.953-6
- insurance of U.S. risks..1.952-1
- investment companies..1.1247-1—1.1247-5
- minimum distribution during surcharge period..1.963-8
- nonresident:
- . deductions..1.882-3; 1.882-4
- . taxation of..1.881-2
- reorganization involving..7.367(a)-1—7.367-2
- returns..1.6012-2(g)
- . as to formation..1.6046-1
- . less developed country corporations..1.1248-5
- . place to file..1.6091-3
- stock basis..1.961-1; 1.961-2
- stock ownership..1.958-1; 1.958-2
- taxes of, credit for..1.902-1
- transfers to:
- . to avoid income tax, tax on..1.1491-1; 1.1492-1
- . recognition of gain..7.367(a)-1—7.367-2
- . rulings, request for..7.367(a)-1; 7.367-2
- withholding tax at source..1.1441-2; 1.1442-1; 1.1451-1

Foreign countries and governments:
- improper payments to employees of ..1.162-18
- income of..1.892-1
- officers and employees of:

Foreign countries and governments (continued):
- officers and employees of (continued):
- . . compensation..1.893-1
- . . withholding tax..31.3401(a)(5)-1
- taxes imposed by, credit..1.642(a)(2)-1; 1.702-1; 1.841-1; 1.874-1; 1.882-1; 1.901-1—1.905-5; 1.931-1

Foreign currencies and exchange:
- nonconvertible, defined..301.6316-2
- payment of tax..301.6316-3
- refunds and credits..301.6316-8

Foreign estates and trusts:
- defined..1.1493-1
- distributable net income..1.643(a)-6
- returns..1.6091-3
- transfers to, information returns ..404.6048-1

Foreign exempt organizations, rents, withholding..1.1443-1

Foreign income..1.901-1—1.943-1
- return of..1.6012-1(a)(3)

Foreign international sales corporations ..1.993-5

Foreign investment companies..1.1247-1—1.1247-5

Foreign items:
- information returns..1.6041-4
- license to collect..301.7001-1(c)

Foreign life insurance companies..1.819.2

Foreign partnership, extension of time for filing return..1.6081-2

Foreign personal holding companies ..1.551-1—1.556-3
- accumulated earnings tax..1.532-1
- deductions..1.561-1; 1.561-2; 1.562-1
- dividends paid deduction..1.561-1—1.565-6
- foreign income..1.954-2
- information returns..1.6035-1; 1.6035-2; 1.6046-1
- liquidation:
- . distributions..1.342-1
- . extension of time to pay tax..1.6162-1
- returns..1.6035-1—1.6035-3
- . formation of..1.6046-1
- undistributed income..1.556-1—1.556-3

Foreign Service officers and employees, allowances..1.912-2

Foreign situs trusts..1.402(c)-1; 1.404(a)-11

Foreign students and exchange visitors:
- U.S. business status..1.871-8; 1.871-9

Foreign subsidiary, credit for taxes of ..1.902-1

Foreign tax credit..1.901-1—1.905-5
- carrybacks and carryovers..1.383-1—1.383-3
- conditions for allowance..1.905-2
- controlled foreign corporations..1.960-1—1.960-6
- decedent's estate..1.691(b)-1
- Domestic International Sales Corp. (DISC)..1.904-4
- estates and trusts..1.642(a)(2)-1
- foreign investment companies..1.1247-4
- husband and wife..1.904-3
- less developed country corporation ..1.902-4
- refunds resulting from..301.6511(d)-3
- regulated investment companies..1.853-1—1.853-4

Foreign taxes:
- credit: See "Foreign tax credit"
- deductibility..1.164-1; 1.164-2; 1.905-1
- interest on refund of..1.905-3

Foreign trusts, defined..1.1493-1
- information returns..16.3.1

69,018 (Fed. Reg.)   FORMS—GAS   5-25-78

Forms:
- composite returns..31.6011(a)-8; 31.6051-1 (f); 31.6051-2
- filing of:
  - 843..301.6402-3
  - 926..1.1494-1
  - 942..31.6051-2
  - 957, 958..1.6035-1; 1.6035-3
  - 959..1.6046-1—1.6046-3
  - 964..1.333-3
  - 966..1.6043-1
  - 990, 990-A, 990-C, 990-P..1.6012-2; 1.6033-1
  - 1000, 1001..1.1461-1
  - 1012, 1013, 1042..1.1461-3
  - 1040..1.6012-1; 1.6017-1
  - 1040A..1.6012-1; 1.6151-1
  - 1040C..1.6851-2
  - 1040NR..1.6012-1(b)
  - 1040SS..1.6017-1
  - 1040W..1.6012-1(a)(8)
  - 1041..1.6012-3
  - 1041-A..1.6034-1
  - 1042, 1042-S..1.1461-2
  - 1045..1.6411-1
  - 1065..1.6031-1
  - 1087..1.6041-5; 1.6042-1
  - 1096, 1099..1.1301-14; 1.6041-1—1.6041-6; 1.6042-1; 1.6043-2; 1.6044-1
  - 1099L..1.6043-2
  - 1116..1.905-2
  - 1118..1.853-4; 1.905-2
  - 1120..1.541-1; 1.1361-3; 1.6012-2
  - 1120F..1.6012-2
  - 1120L..1.802-1; 1.802-3; 1.6012-2
  - 1120M..1.821-1; 1.6012-2
  - 1120NB..1.6012-2
  - 1120-POL..1.6012-6
  - 1127..1.6161-1
  - 1128..1.442-1; 1.1502-14
  - 1138..1.1502-19; 1.6164-1
  - 1139..1.1502-19; 1.6411-1
  - 2063..1.6851-2
  - 2350..1.911-1
  - 2438..1.852-9
  - 2439..1.852-9
  - 2553..1.1372-2
  - 2688..1.6081-1
  - 2848..1.6012-1(b)
  - 2950..1.404(a)-2
  - 2952..1.6038-1; 1.6038-2
  - 3115..1.446-1
  - 4804..31.6051-2
  - 7004..1.6081-3
  - SS-5..1.6017-1
  - W-2..1.6041-2; 31.6051-1(f); 31.6051-2
  - W-3..31.6051-2
  - T-Timber..1.611-3

Foster children, unadopted..1.152-1
Fractional cent..301.6313-1
Fractional dollar..301.6102-1
Fractional year returns..1.443-1
Franchised corporations..1.1563-4
Fraternal associations, exemption..1.501(c)(8)-1; 1.501(c)(10)-1
Fraternities, college, domestic employees, exemption from withholding..31.3401(a)(3)-1

Fraud:
- damages received due to:
  - as income..1.61-14
- deficiency dividend deduction..1.547-5
- penalties..301.6653-1; 301.6674-1; 301.7207-1

Fringe benefits..1.162-10
Fruit growers' associations:
- exemption..1.521-1
- taxation of..1.522-1—1.522-3

Funded pension trusts..1.501(c)(18)-1
Futures..1.1233-1

— G —

Gain or loss:
- basis: See "Basis for gain or loss"
- Commodity Credit loans..1.77-2
- computation..1.1001-1; 1.1002-1
- condemnation of property..1.1231-1; 1.1231-2
- cooperative housing corporation stock..1.1034-1
- corporation:
  - disposition of own stock..1.1032-1
- determination of amount..1.1001-1
- earnings and profits affected by..1.312-7
- election, corporate liquidation..1.333-1—1.333-5
- emergency facilities sold..1.1238-1
- exchanges: See "Exchanges"
- reorganization: See "Reorganization"
- installment obligations..1.453-9
- installment sales..1.453-1; 1.453-5; 1.453-9; 1.1001-1
- involuntary conversions..1.1033(a)-1—1.1033(h)-1; 1.1231-1; 1.1231-2
- issuance of stock..1.1032-1
- life interests, sale of..1.1014-5
- liquidation:
  - calendar month..1.331-1—1.333-5
  - corporation:
    - minority stockholders..1.337-5; 1.337-6
- liquidation of corporation..1.331-1—1.346-3
- liquidation of subsidiary..1.332-1—1.332-7
- natural resources..1.631-1—1.632-1
- options to buy or sell..1.1234-1
- partner's capital contribution..1.721-1
- partnership distributions..1.731-1
  - disposition of..1.735-1; 1.751-1
- partnership interest transferred..1.741-1
- patents...1.1235-1; 1.1235-2
- preferred stock "bail-out"..1.306-1—1.306-3
- property on which loss previously disallowed because of related taxpayers..1.267(d)-1
- radio broadcasting properties..1.1071-1—1.1071-4
- realty subdivided for sale..1.1237-1
- recognition..1.1002-1
  - earnings and profits computation..1.312-7
- redemption of stock to pay death taxes..1.303-1—1.303-3
- related taxpayers..1.267(d)-1
- remainder interests, sale of..1.1014-5
- reorganization exchanges: See "Reorganization"
- residence sold or exchanged..1.1034-1
  - aged persons..1.121-1—1.121-5
- retirement of bonds..1.1232-2
- sales and exchanges of property..1.61-6; 1.1001-1; 1.1002-1
- short sales..1.1233-1
- stock of collapsible corporation..1.341-1—1.341-5
- straddles, grantors of..1.1234-2
- timber..1.631-1; 1.631-2
- transfers to controlled corporation..1.351-1—1.351.3
- transfers to foreign corporations..7.367(a)-1—7.367-2
- treasury stock..1.1032-1
- wash sales..1.1091-1; 1.1091-2

Gambling:
- losses from..1.165-10
- winnings, information returns..7.6041-1

Gas property:
- depletion..1.611-1; 1.611-2; 1.613-1; 1.613-2; 1.613-5
- sale of..1.632-1

5-25-78   **GAS—INCOME**   *(Fed. Reg.)* **69,019**

———————References are to SECS. (§) in the Regs. Check Page 23,003 for latest developments———————

Gas royalties, personal holding company income..1.543-1; 1.543-12

Gasoline tax:
. state, deductibility..1.164-5

General tax credit..1.42A-1

Gift:
. basis for gain or loss..1.1015-1—1.1015-5
. charitable..1.170A-1—1.170A-11; 1.170-0—1.170-3: See also "Contributions"
. exclusion from gross income..1.102-1
. trade or business expense..1.274-2; 1.274-3

Gift expenses..1.162-15; 1.274-1—1.274-7

Gift tax, deductibility..1.164-2

Goodwill expenditures..1.263(b)-1

Government contracts, excessive profits on ..1.1471-1

Government corporations: See "Instrumentalities of U.S."

Government depositaries:
. nonresident aliens and foreign corporations..1.6302-2
. payment of taxes to..1.6302-1; 31.6302(c)-1—31.6302(c)-3; 301.6302-1

Government employer, return and payment of withheld tax..31.3404-1

Government loans repaid, deductibility ..1.592-1

Government obligations, interest on..1.103-1—1.103-12

Government pensions and annuities..1.410(a)-1(c)

Grain storage facilities:
. amortization:
.. estates and trusts..1.642(f)-1

Grantor of trust, income taxable to..1.671-1-—1.678(d)-1

Grants for defense purposes..1.621-1

Gross income..1.71-1—1.77-2
See also specific items
. adjusted..1.62-1
. defined..1.61-1—1.61-15
.. depletion purposes..1.613-1—1.613-4
. nonresident aliens..1.872-1
. time to report..1.451-1—1.454-1
. crop insurance proceeds..13.3

Ground rents, deductibility..1.163-1
. redeemable..1.1055-1—1.1055-4

Group life insurance..1.61-2; 1.162-10

Group term life insurance..1.79-1—1.79-3; 31.3401(a)(14)-1

Guam:
. taxes, coordination with U.S. individual taxes..1.935-1; 301.7654-1
.. failure to furnish information ..301.6688-1
. United States income tax laws in..1.932-1

Guaranteed annuity interest, contributions of..1.170A-6

Guardians, estates or trusts..1.641-1 et seq.

— H —

Handicapped individuals, architectural and transportation barriers to, removal costs..7.190-1—7.190.3

Head of household:
. defined..1.2-2
. medical expense maximum deduction ..1.213-1; 1.213-2
. optional tax..1.3-1
. rates of tax..1.1-1
. wage earner's return..1.6012-1(a)(7); 1.6014-1

Health benefits..1.72-15; 1.104-1—1.106-1

Health insurance, employee plans..1.105-1

Heir, included as transferee..301.6901-1(b)

Historic structures, amortization of rehabilitation expenses..7.191-1

Hobby expenses and losses..1.270-1
. presumption against hobby status..12.9

Holding companies, exemption..1.501(c)(2)-1

Holding period..1.1223-1

Holiday last day..301.7503-1

Home health service agency, employee annuities..11.415(c)(4)-1

Horticultural organizations, exemption ..1.501(c)(5)-1

Hospital, employee annuities..11.415(c)(4)-1

Housing credit, purchase or construction of new residence..1.44-1—1.44-5

Husband and wife:
. alimony: See "Alimony and separate maintenance payments"
. credit for foreign taxes..1.904-3
. declaration of estimated tax, joint ..1.6015(b)-1
. income splitting..1.2-1
. personal exemptions..1.42A-1
. returns:
.. joint..1.2-1; 1.6013-1—1.6013.4
... death..1.6013-3
... dividends received credit and exclusion ..1.116-1; 1.116-2
... net operating loss..1.172-7
... self-employment tax..1.6017-1(b)
.. separate..1.4-3
... change to joint..1.6013-2
... optional tax..1.4-3
... standard deduction..1.142-1
... surviving spouse..1.2-1
... wage earner's return..1.6014-1(c)
. sales or exchanges between..1.1239-1
. self-employment tax..1.1402(a)-1; 1.6017-1(b)
. separated:
.. maintenance payments..1.71-1
.. status..1.6013-4
. taxable income credit..1.42A-1

— I —

Identification number of employer..31.6011(b)-1; 301.6109-1; 301.7701-12

Identifying numbers..1.6109-1; 31-6109-1; 301.6109-1
. failure to supply..301.6676-1
. social security benefit numbers as ..301.6109-1(d); 301.7701-11

Illness, compensation for..1.72-15; 1.104-1; 7.105-1

Improper accumulation of surplus, See "Accumulated earnings tax"

Improper payments, to foreign country employees..1.162-18

Improvements:
. amortization by lessee..1.178-1—1.178-3
. by lessee..1.109-1
.. basis adjusted for..1.1019-1
. deductibility..1.263(a)-1—1.263(a)-3
. depreciation:
.. lessee..1.178-1—1.178-3
.. natural resources..1.611-5

Income..1.71-1
. attributable to several years..1.1301-0—1.1304-1
. expenses for production of..1.212-1
. illegal business..1.61-14
. prepaid subscriptions..1.455-1—1.455-6
. restoration of amount held under claim of right..1.1341-1

69,020 (Fed. Reg.) INCOME—INSURANCE 5-25-78

Income (continued):
- source of:
- .. connected with U.S. business..1.864-3—1.864-7
- .. partly within and partly without U.S...1.863-1—1.863-3
- .. sale, meaning of..1.864-1
- .. within U.S...1.861-1—1.861-8
- .. aircraft and vessels..12.1
- .. trade or business..1.864-2
- .. without U.S...1.862-1; 1.901-1—1.905-5; 1.911-1—1.943-1
- .. nonresident citizens: See "Nonresident citizens, earned income"
- time to report..1.451-1—1.454-1

Income averaging..1.1301-0—1.1304-6 See also "averagable income"

Income splitting..1.2-1

Income tax:
- deductibility..1.164-1
- lessee paying for lessor..1.110-1
- paid by another, as income..1.61-14
- return..1.6012-1—1.6017-1

Inconsistent position..1.1311(b)-1

Indebtedness:
- assumption of..1.357-1; 1.357-2; 1.358-3
- .. corporate acquisitions..1.381(c)(16)-1
- .. partners and partnerships..1.752-1
- .. property dividends..1.301-1; 1.312-3; 1.312-4
- at risk amounts..7.465-1—7.465-5
- bad debts: See "Bad debts"
- discharge of..1.108(a)-1—1.108(b)-1; 1.1017-1; 1.1017-2
- property dividends involving..1.312-3; 1.312-4
- retirement, personal holding companies ..1.381(c)(15)-1

Individual retirement savings plans:
- disclosure statements..1.408(i)-1
- participants in plan, information to ..1.408(i)-1

Individuals:
- alternative taxes, capital gain or loss ..1.1201-1
- credit, foreign taxes..1.901-1; 1.903-1—1.905-4
- credit, investment..1.46-1—1.46-4
- declaration of estimated tax..1.6015(a)-1—1.6015(i)-1; 1.6073-1—1.6073-4
- deductions itemized..1.161-1—1.169-4; 1.211-1—1.216-1; 31.3402(m)-1
- dividend received credit..1.34-1—1.34-5; 1.116-1
- general tax credit..1.42A-1
- gross income at $10,000 or less..1.3-1
- limitation on amount of tax..1.1-2
- limitation on deduction..1.270-1
- limitation on foreign tax credit..1.904-1
- losses by, deductibility..1.165-1—1.166-8
- personal exemptions, credit..1.42-1; 1.42A-1
- rates of tax..1.1-1—1.4-4
- returns: See "Returns"
- standard deduction..1.141-1—1.144-2
- taxable income credit..1.42A-1

Industrial development bonds..1.103-7—1.103-12

Industrial park bonds..1.103-9

Industry-union pension plan..1.410(b)-1(c)(1)

Information, reorganization exchanges ..1.368-3

Information returns..1.6031-1—1.6056-1
- amended..31.6051-2
- electing small business corporations ..1.6037-1; 301.6037-1
- employees' trusts..1.6041-2(b)
- estates and trusts, carryover basis property..7.6039A-1
- exempt organizations..1.6033-1

Information returns (continued):
- failure to file..301.6652-1; 301.6652-2
- foreign subsidiaries..1.6038-1
- foreign trusts..16.3-1; 404.6048-1
- gambling winnings, information returns ..7.6041-1
- group-term insurance..1.6052-1; 1.6052-2; 301.6052-1
- liquidation in calendar month..1.333-5
- magnetic tape..31.6011(a)-8; 31.6051-2; 1.6041-7; 1.9101-1
- partnerships..1.6031-1
- payments for which no return required ..1.6041-3
- payments of $600 or more..1.6041-1—1.6041-4
- publicity..301.6104-2
- self-employed retirement plans ..1.6041-2(b)
- stock option transactions..1.6039-1; 1.6039-2; 301.6039-1
- tax return preparers..404.6060-1
- .. disclosure of information..301.7216-1—301.7216-3
- tips, reporting..31.6053-1

Informers, rewards..301.7623-1

Inheritance taxes:
- deductibility..1.164-2
- redemption of stock to pay..1.303-1—1.303-3

Inheritances:
- basis for gain or loss..1.1014-5
- exemption..1.102-1

Inherited property, exclusion from income ..1.102-1

Injunction against assessment and collection..301.6213-1

Insolvency reorganizations..1.371-1—1.373-3

Insolvent banks, exemption..301.7507-1—301.7507-11

Insolvent corporations, reorganization of ..1.371-1

Inspection of returns..301.6103(a)-1—301.6104-4

Installment obligations:
- basis..1.453-1; 1.453-9
- corporate acquisitions..1.381(c)(8)-1
- gain or loss on disposition..1.453-9
- liquidation of corporation..1.337-3
- transmission at death of holder ..1.691(a)-5

Installment payment of tax..1.6152-1—1.6154-3
- estimated tax:
- .. penalties..1.6654-1; 1.6654-2; 1.6655-1; 1.6655-2
- overpayment..301.6403-1

Installment sales..1.453-1—1.453-10
- carrying charges..1.163-1, 1.163-2
- formula for interest deduction where not separately stated..1.163-2
- gain or loss..1.1001-1
- interest..1.163-1; 1.163-2
- life insurance companies..1.453-1
- revocation of election..13.11
- revolving credit plan..1.453-1; 1.453-2

Instrumentalities of U.S.:
- date stock or shares issued..1.103-4
- dividends from..1.103-2
- employees
- .. withholding tax..31.3401(c)-1
- obligations, interest..1.103-3
- .. controlled foreign corporations..1.953-1—1.953-6
- .. corporations deduction..1.242-1

Insurance, exemption:
- accident and health..1.104-1—1.106-1
- life..1.101-1—1.101-5

INSURANCE—INSURANCE (Fed. Reg.) 69,021

———References are to SECS. (§) in the Regs. Check Page 23,003 for latest developments———

Insurance companies..1.801-1—1.832-6
. defined..1.801-3
. election of multiple line companies ..1.831-4
. fire, mutual..1.831-1—1.832-6
. foreign..1.953-1—1.953-6
. interinsurers..1.821-1
. life: See "Life insurance companies"
. marine, mutual..1.831-1—1.832-6
. mutual other than life, marine or fire ..1.821-1—1.823-2
. other than life or mutual..1.831-1—1.832-6
. percentage for computing tax..1.819-2
. returns..1.6012-2(c)
Insurance policies, exchange of..1.1035-1
Insurance premiums, deductibility..1.264-1—1.264-3
Insurance, United States risks, controlled foreign corporation..1.953-1—1.953-6
Intangible drilling and development costs:
. oil and gas wells..1.612-4
Intercompany transactions and agreements:
. earnings and profits, effect on..1.312-11
Interest:
. **annuity loans**..1.264-2—1.264-4
. assessments for local benefits..1.164-4
. corporate acquisition indebtedness..1.279-1—1.279-7
. deduction for..1.163-1—1.163-4
. deferred payments..1.483-1—1.483-2
. deficiency in tax..301.6601-1; 301.6621-1
. delinquent payment of taxes..301.6601-1
. disallowance if unpaid 2½ months after close of year..1.267(a)-1
. **endowment contract loans**..1.264-2—1.264-4
. erroneous refund recoveries..301.6602-1; 301.6621-1
. estimated tax underpaid..301.6316-8
. extension of time to pay tax..301.6601-1
. foreign tax credit adjustments..1.905-3
. governmental obligations..1.103-1—1.103-12; 1.242-1
. information returns..1.6041-1; 1.6041-3—1.6041-6
. income..1.61-7
. **installment purchases**..1.163-2
. **life insurance loans**..1.264-2—1.264-4
. life insurance proceeds..1.101-3
. nonpayment of tax..301.6601-1; 301.6621-1
. original issue discount..1.1232-3A; 1-.6049-1
. overpayment of tax..301.6611-1
. paid:
. . defined..1.803-3
. . **to purchase or carry exempt securities** ..1.265-2
. **partner's capital contributions**..1.707-1
. penalties..301.6601-1; 301.6621-1
. **postal savings accounts**..1.103-4
. received from sources within or without U.S...1.861-2
. refunds and credits..301.6611-1; 301.6621-1
. . erroneous refunds recovered..301.6602-1
. tax-free covenant bonds..1.1451-1
. U.S. obligations: See "United States, obligations"
. underpayment of tax..301.6601-1
. underpayments under '69 Tax Reform Act ..1.9006-1

Interest (continued):
. unpaid 2½ mos. after close of year ..1.267(a)
. wrongful levy recovery..301.6621-1
Interinsurance organization, mutual, exemption..1.501(c)(15)-1
Interinsurers, rates of tax..1.821-1
Internal Revenue Code of 1939, repeal and continuance..1.395-1
Internal Revenue Districts, canvass of ..301.7601-1
Internal Revenue Service, seals of ..301.7514-1
International boycotts, participation in:
. international boycott factor, computation ..7.999-1
International organizations:
. employees of, exemptions..1.893-1
. income of, exemption..1.892-1
. withholding tax..31.3401(a)(5)-1
Interurban railway corporation, acquisition of property by..1.373-3
Inventories..1.471-1—1.472-8
. acquiring corporation..1.381(c)-5; 1.381(c)(5)-1; 1.471-9
. basis..1.1013-1
. change of method..1.381(c)(5)-1
. dealers in tax-exempt securities..1.75-1
. dividends paid out of..1.311-1; 1.312-2—1.312-4
. involuntary liquidation and replacement ..1.1321-1; 1.1321-2
. LIFO..1.472-1—1.472-7
. . distributions of..1.311-1; 1.312-5
. . involuntary liquidation and replacement ..1.1321-1; 1.1321-2
. liquidation of corporation..1.337-3
. manufacturers..1.471-7; 1.471-11
. miners..1.471-7
. partnership distribution out of..1.735-1; 1.751-1
. retail merchants..1.471-8
. sale during corporate liquidation..1.337-3
. substantial appreciation defined..1.751-1
"Inventory items", defined..1.751-1(d)(2)
Investment companies..1,851-1—1.855-1
. foreign..1.1247-1—1.1247-5
Investment credit..1.38-1—1.50-1
. acquiring corporation..1.381(c)(23)-1
. assessment and collection
. . tentative carryback adjustments..301-.6501(m)-1
. basis, adjustment to..1.48-7
. carryback and carryover..1.46-2
. . corporate acquisitions..1.383-1—1.383-3
. . limitation on assessment..301.6501(j)-1
. determination of amount..1.46-1
. electing small business corporations ..1.48-5
. estates and trusts..1.48-6
. limitations with respect to certain persons ..1.46-4
. motion picture and television films ..7.48-1—7.48-3
. public utility property..12.3
. qualified investment..1.46-3
. recapture of..1.47-1—1.47-6
. restoration of..1.50-1
. section 38 property..1.48-1—1.48-4
Investment expenses..1.212-1
Investment in annuity contract:
. accident and health plans..1.72-15
. transfers affecting..1.72-10

Investment property, exchange of..1.1031(a)-1
Investment trusts, defined..301.7701-4
Investors, at risk amounts..7.465-1—7.465-5
Involuntary conversions..1.1033(a)-1—1.1033(h)-1
. basis of property acquired through ..1.1033(c)-1
. capital gains and losses..1.1231-1
. carryovers, corporate acquisitions..1.381-(c)(13)-1
. election as to gain:
. . FCC orders..1.1071-1
. livestock..1.451-7; 1.1033(e)-1; 1.1033(f)-1
. nonrecognition of gain..1.1033(a)-1
. residence..1.1033(b)-1, 1.1034-1
Involuntary liquidation of LIFO inventories ..1.1321-1; 1.1321-2
IRA: See "Individual retirement savings plans"
Iron ore; special rules..1.631-3

— J —

Jeopardy:
. addition to tax in case of..301.6658-1
. bond..1.6851-1—1.6851-3; 301.6863-1
. interest..301.6601-1
. termination of taxable year because of ..1.6851-1; 301.6851-1
Jeopardy assessments...301.6861-1—301.6863-2
Joint and survivor annuities..1.72-1—1.72-15; 1.691(d)-1
. employees' trusts—1.401(a)-11
Joint declaration..1.6015(b)-1
Joint employers, withholding tax..31.3402(g)-3
Joint fiduciaries, returns..1.6012-3(c)
Joint returns: See "Returns"
Judgment, disposition of, suits by U.S. ..301.6502-1(a)(3); 301.6532-1; 301.6532-2
Judgment creditors, lien for taxes as against..301.6323-1
Judicial proceedings, limitation periods ..301.6532-1—301.6532-3
Jury fees, withholding tax..31.3401(a)-2

— L —

Labor:
. organizations:
. . exemptions..1.501(c)(5)-1
. . pension plan with industry..1.410(b)-1(c)(1)
Land:
. erosion, conservation expenditures ..1.175-1—1.175-6
. used in farming..1.175-4
Leases:
. cancellation..1.1241-1
. renewable:
. . amortization of cost..1.178-1—1.178-3
Legacies: See "Bequests"
Legal holiday, due date falling on..301.7503-1
Legislation:
. organizations attempting to influence exemption..1.501(c)(3)-1
Less developed countries, investments in ..1.963-0
Less developed country corp., foreign tax credit..1.902-4
Lessee and lessor:
. depreciation..1.167(a)-4
. improvements by lessee:
. . basis adjusted for..1.1019-1
. . depreciation..1.178-3
. . exempt income..1.109-1
. related, amortizing improvements..1.178-2
. taxes of lessor paid by lessee..1.110-1

Levy and distraint: See "Seizure of property"
Liabilities assumed: See "Indebtedness, assumption"
Liabilities, compromise of..301.7122-1
License, termination payment..1.1241-1
Lien for taxes..301.6321-1—301.6325-1
. civil action by person other than taxpayer..301.6532-3; 301.7426-1
. discharge of...400.2-1; 301.7425-1—301.7425-4
. intervention by U.S...301.7424-2
. nonjudicial sale..301.7425-1—301.7425-4
. . notice required..400.4-1
. . perishable goods..301.7425-1—301.7425-4
. redemption of real property by U.S. ..301.7425-1—301.7425-4; 400.5-1
. subordination of..400.2-1
. third party rights..301.6532-3; 301.7426-1
. U.S. bid price at sale of property..301.7403-1(b)
Life insurance:
. exchange of policies..1.1035-1
. exemption..1.101-1
. income from..1.61-10; 1.72-1—1.72-17
. interest paid to purchase..1.264-2; 1.264-3
. lump-sum settlement..1.72-12
. premiums, deductibility..1.264-1—1.264.3
. premiums paid by employer on employee's life..1.61-2
. proceeds, death of insured..1.101-1—1.101-5
Life insurance companies..1.801-1—1.820-3
. accounting provisions..1.818-1—1.818-7
. adjusted basis of property..1.817-3
. adjusted reserves..1.805-5; 1.805-6
. benevolent, exemption..1.501(c)(12)-1
. capital gains and losses..1.817-1—1.817-4
. carryovers by successor..1.381(c)(22)-1
. consolidated returns:
. . policyholders' investment yield, computation..1.818-8
. defined..1.801-1; 1.801-3
. exemption..1.501(c)(12)-1
. foreign companies..1.819-1—1.819-2
. gain or loss from operations..1.809-1—1.809-8
. mutual savings banks' life insurance departments as..1.594-1
. 1955 formula:
. . tax imposed..1.803-4; 1.805-2
. policyholders surplus account..1.815-4; 1.815-6
. premiums..1.820-3
. reinsurance..1.820-2; 1.820-3
. reserves..1.801-3—1.801-6; 1.806-4; 1.810-2—1.810-4; 1.818-4
. tax imposed on..1.802-3
. taxable income defined..1.802-4
. taxable investment income..1.804-2
. taxable years 1959 and 1960..1.802-5
. variable annuities..1.801-7
Life insurance contract, defined..1.1035-1
Life tenant:
. depreciation..1.167(g)-1
. shrinkage of interest..1.273-1
LIFO inventories: See "Inventories"
Limitation on tax..1.1-2
Limitations:
. exploration expenditures..1.615-4; 1.617-2
. rate of tax, claims against U.S. involving acquisition of property..1.1347-1
Liquidating distributions: See "Dividends, liquidating"
Liquidating trusts, defined..301.7701-4

LIQUIDATION—MINERALS *(Fed. Reg.)* **69,023**

—References are to SECS. (§) in the Regs. Check Page 23,003 for latest developments—

Liquidation:
- corporations..1.331-1—1.346-3
- LIFO inventories..1.1321-1; 1.1321-2
- termination of taxable period..1.6851-1

Literary organizations, exemption..1.501(c)(3)-1

Livestock:
- draft, breeding or dairy purposes, when held for..1.231-2
- involuntary conversion..1.451-7; 1.1033(a)-1; 1.1033(e)-1; 1.1033(f)-1; 1.1033(h)-1

Living expenses..1.262-1
- insurance proceeds, exclusion of..1.123-1

Loans:
- Commodity Credit Corporation..1.77-1; 1.77-2
- from government repaid..1.592-1
- insured by U.S. exceeding adjusted basis of property..1.312-12
- production payments of mineral interest as..1.636-1
- prohibited transaction of:
  - employee stock ownership plans (ESOPs)..54.4975-7
  - exempt organization..1.503(h)-1; 1.503(i)-1

Lobbying:
- expense deduction..1.162-15(c)(1); 1.162-20
- organization engaged in, exemption..1.501(c)(3)-1

Local benefits, taxes assessed against..1.164-4

Lodges, exemption..1.501(c)(8)-1

Lodging expenses..1.119-1; 1.120-1; 1.162-2; 1.162-5

Long-term capital gain and loss: See "Capital gains and losses"

Long-term contracts, defined..1.451-3

Losses:
- capital: See "Capital Gains and Losses"
- casualty: See "Casualty losses"
- deductibility..1.165-1—1.166-8
- disaster loss..1.165-11
- earnings and profits computation..1.312-6
- exchanges..1.1001-1; 1.1002-1
- family..1.267(c)-1
- farmers..1.165-6; 1.1251-1—1.1251-4
- five consecutive years..1.270-1
- foreign expropriation..19.1-1
- hobby..1.270-1
- net operating: See "Net operating losses"
- railroad reorganization..1.373-1—1.373-3
- related-taxpayer transactions..1.267(a)-1
- small business investment company stock..1.1242-1
- stocks and securities:
  - decline in value..1.165-4
  - wash sales..1.1091-1
  - worthlessness..1.165-5
- war: See "War losses"

Lots, sale of..1.1237-1

Low-income housing..1.1039-1
- depreciation..1.167(k)-1—1.167(k)-4

Lump-sum employee distributions..1.402(a)-1; 1.403(a)-2

— M —

Magazines:
- circulation costs..1.173-1
- vendors withholding..31.3401(a)(10)-1

Manufacturers, inventories of..1.471-7; 1.471-11

March 1, 1913:
- basis..1.1053-1
- earnings or profits before, distribution..1.316-2
- value:
  - earnings and profits, effect on..1.312-9

Marine Corps: See "Armed Forces of U.S."

Marine insurance companies: See "Insurance companies"

Marital status:
- determination..1.143-1
- exemptions for..1.151-1; 1.153-1
- standard deduction..1.144-1; 1.144-2

Maryland, ground rent..1.163-1

Materials, cost of..1.162-3

Maximum tax on earned income..1.1348-1—1.1348-3

Meals and lodging:
- deduction for..1.162-2; 1.162-5
- employer's convenience..1.119-1
- policemen..1.120-1

Medical care, defined..1.213-1

Medical expenses..1.213-1; 1.213-2
- age 65 and disabled..1.213-2
- allowable as child-care expenses..1.214-1
- maximum deduction..1.213-2

Medicines, expense of..1.213-1

Merchant Marine Act of 1936:
- capital construction funds..3.1—3.11

Mergers: See "Reorganization"

Metal mines, percentage depletion..1.613-2

Mexico, resident of:
- withholding tax on wages..31.3401(a)(7)-1

Military and naval forces of U.S.: See "Armed Forces of U.S."

Mineral production payments..1.636-1—1.636-4

Mineral royalties, personal holding company income..1.543-1

Minerals, mines and mining:
- abandonment loss..1.614-6
- aggregated interest..1.614-6
- basis..1.614-6
- development and exploration expenses, adjustments..1.1016-5
- capital additions..1.612-2
- combined interest..1.614-6
- continental shelf areas..1.638-1—1.638-2
- defined..1.613-3(b); 1.613-4
- depletion:
  - cost basis..1.612-1
  - deduction, general rule..1.611-1
  - nonoperating mineral interests..1.614-5
  - operating mineral interests..1.614-4
- depreciation:
  - improvements..1.167(h)-1
- development expenditures..1.616-1—1.616-3
- exploration expenditures..1.074-2; 1.615-1—1.615-9; 1.617-1—1.617-4
- Government payments to encourage..1.621-1
- holding period..1.614-6
- improvements:
  - depreciation..1.611-5; 1.612-2
- inventories of miners..1.471-7
- percentage depletion..1.613-1—1.613-7
- production payments..1.636-1—1.636-4
- rules applicable to..1.611-2
- separate interest..1.614-8

69,024 (Fed. Reg.) MINIMUM—NONRESIDENT 5-25-78

Minimum tax on preference income:
. net leases of real property..12.8
. oil and gas wells, drilling and development costs..7.57(d)-1

Ministers of the gospel: See "Clergymen"

Minors, taxability of earnings..1.73-1

Mitigation of effect of:
. limitations and other provisions..1.1311(a)-1—1.1314(c)-1
.. self-employment tax and FICA taxes

Money order, payment of tax by..301.6311-1
. bad check..301.6657-1

Monthly withholding table..31.3402(c)-1

Mortgages:
. executed to U.S. instrumentalities ..1.103-3
. loan guaranteed by U.S...1.312-12
. property dividend subject to..1.312-5

Motion picture films, investment credit ..7.48-1—7.48-3

Motor vehicles, seized for taxes, transfer of title..301.6339-1

Moving expenses..1.217-1
. deduction for:
.. taxable years beginning after 12-31-69 ..1.217-2
.. taxable years beginning before 1-1-70 ..1.217-1
. reimbursement for..1.82-1; 31.3401(a)(15)-1

Multiple interest, basis:
. decedent's property..1.1014-7

Multiple support agreement..1.52-3

Municipal services in atomic energy communities..1.164-8

Municipalities:
. income of, exclusion..1.115-1
. obligations:
.. interest exemption..1.103-1
.. interest to purchase or carry..1.265-2
.. short-term, issued at discount..1.454-1
. officers and employees:
.. withholding tax..31.3401(c)-1

Mustering-out pay..1.113-1

Mutual ditch or irrigation companies, exemption..1.501(c)(12)-1

Mutual fire insurance companies..1.831-1—1.832-2

Mutual Funds: See "Real estate investment trusts"; "Regulated investment companies"

Mutual insurance companies other than life, marine or fire..1.821-1—1.826-7
. exemption..1.501(c)(15)-1

Mutual insurance funds, exemption ..1.501(c)(14)-1

Mutual marine insurance companies ..1.831-1—1.832-2

Mutual savings bank..1.591-1—1.594-1
. investment credit..1.46-4
. organizations, providing reserve funds for, and insurance of deposits in ..1.501(c)(14)-1

— N —

National banks: See "Banks"

Natural deposits: See "Minerals, mines and mining"

Naval forces: See "Armed Forces of U. S."

Navy contracts, profit limitations..1.1471-1

Negligence penalty..301.6653-1

Net capital gain, defined..1.1222-1

Net capital loss, defined..1.1222-1

Net earnings from self-employment, defined ..1.1402(a)-1

Net long-term capital gain, defined..1.1222-1

Net long-term capital loss, defined..1.1222-1

Net operating loss..1.172-1—1.172-11
. common trust funds..1.584-6
. defined..1.172-1
. dividends received deduction..1.246-2
. estates and trusts..1.642(d)-1; 1.642(h)-1
. foreign expropriation loss..1.72-11
. Subchapter S corporations..1.1374-2

Net operating loss carrybacks and carryovers..1.172-4
. computation..1.172-6
. corporate acquisitions..1.381(a)-1; 1.381(c)(1)-2; 1.382(a)-1; 1.383-1—1.383-3
. deficiency resulting from:
.. limitations on assessment and collection..301.6501(h)-1
. estates and trusts..1.642(h)-(1)
. excess profits tax purposes..1.172-8
. expected:
.. extension of time for payment of tax ..1.6164-1—1.6164-9
. investment credit..1.383-1—1.383-3
. modifications..1.172-5
. overpayment due to carryback..301.6511(d)-2; 301.6511(d)-4; 301.6511(d)-7
. regulated transportation corporations ..1.172-10
. soil and water conservation expenditures ..1.175-5
. Subchapter S corporations..1.1374-3; 1.1374-4
. successor corporations..1.381(a)-1
. tentative adjustments..1.6411-1—1.6411-4; 301.6411-1
. Trade Expansion Act of 1962..1.172-9
. years to which carried..1.172-4

Net short-term capital loss, carry-over ..1.1212-1

Newsboys, withholding tax..31.3401(a)(10)-1

Newspaper, circulation costs..1.173-1

"Nonadverse party", defined..1.672(b)-1

Nonbusiness debt, defined..1.166-5

Nonbusiness expenses..1.212-1
. allocable to exempt income..1.265-1
. unpaid 2½ mos. after close of year ..1.267(a)-1

Nondeductible items:
. carrying charges..1.266-1
. disposal of coal or domestic iron ore ..1.272-1
. general rules..1.261-1—1.262-1
. insurance contracts, payment in connection with..1.264-1—1.264-4
. life or terminable interests..1.273-1
. political parties, debts owed by..1.271-1
. political parties, indirect contributions to ..1.276-1
. tax-exempt income, expenses and interest relating to..1.265-1; 1.265-2

Nonexempt property, defined..1.1083-1

Nonresident aliens..1.871-1—1.894-1
. adjustments for overwithholding of tax ..1.1461-4
. agents for..1.871-6
. business, change in status of..1.871-8(c)
. change of status..1.871-13
. community income..1.981-1—1.981-3
. consent dividends..1.565-5
. credit or refund of tax withheld..1.6414-1
. credits against tax..1.32; 1.871-8(d)
. deductions..1.35-2; 1.873-1; 1.874-1
. definition..301.7701-5
. engaged in trade or business in U.S. ..1.871-8; 1.875-1
.. beneficiaries of estates or trusts ..1.875-2

NONRESIDENT—PARTNERS (Fed. Reg.) 69,025

————References are to SECS. (§) in the Regs. Check Page 23,003 for latest developments————

Nonresident aliens (continued):
. estimated tax..1.6015(i)-1
. fixed or determinable income..1.871-7
. Government depositaries..1.6302-2
. gross income..1.872-1
. intangible property sold or exchanged ..1.871-7; 1.871-11
. pension, etc. distributions..1.871-7(c); 1.872-2
. realty in U. S...1.871-8; 1.871-10
. remuneration for services..31.3401(a)(6)-1; 31.3401(a)(6)-1A
. returns..1.6012-1(b)
. scholarships and fellowships..1.871-8; 1.871-9
. standard deduction..1.142-2
. temporarily in U. S...1.871-7(d)
. treaty income..1.871-12; 1.872-2
. withholding tax at source..1.1441-1—1.1441-6; 1.6012(b)(3); 31.3401(a)(7)-1

Nonresident citizens:
. community income..1.981-1—1.981-3
. defined..1.911-1
. dependency exemptions..1.152-2
. earned income..1.911-1
. pension and profit-sharing trusts..1.406-1; 1.407-1
. returns..1.6091-3; 1.6091-4; 301.7654-1
. withholding tax..31.3401(a)(8)(A)-1

Nonresident, defined..301.7701-5
Nontaxable exchanges..1.1031(a)-1—1.1039-1
Nontaxable income; See "Exempt income"
Normal tax; corporations..1.11-1

Notes:
. payment of tax by..301.6312-1; 301.6312-2
. sale or exchange by bank, losses..1.582-1
Notice, deficiency..301.6212-1
Notice and demand for payment..301.6303-1

— O —

Oath, authority to administer..301.7622-1
Obligations:
. issued at discount..1.454-1
.. gross income inclusion..1.6049-1
. U.S.: See "United States, obligations"

Obsolescence:
. adjusting basis due to..1.1016-3—1.1016-10
. deductibility..1.167(a)-9
. nondepreciable property..1.165-2

Oil and gas wells:
. depletion..1.611-1—1.614-5
. drilling and development costs..1.612-4; 7.57(d)-1
. exploration expenditures..1.174-1—1.174-4
. gross income from the property ..1.613-3(a)
. sale, surtax..1.632-1

Oil royalties, personal holding company income..1.543-1; 1.543-2
Old-age exemptions..1.151-1—1.151-3
Old persons, credit for retirement income ..1.37-1—1.37-5
Omissions from gross income, limitations on assessment and collection ..301.6501(e)-1
Optional adjustment to basis of partnership property..1.734-1; 1.743-1; 1.754-1; 1.755-1
Optional standard deduction: See "Standard Deduction"
Optional tax on individuals..1.3-1; 1.4-1—1.4-4; 1.6014-1

Options:
. employees' stock..1.421-1—1.421-8; 1-.1014-1
. personal holding company stock..1.544-4
. sale or exchange of..1.1234-1
. stock purchase:
.. constructive ownership..1.318-3
Organizational expenditures..1.248-1
Organizations, classification for tax purposes..301.7701-1
Organizations exempt from taxation: See "Exempt organizations"
Original issue discount:
. obligations issued after May 27, 1969 ..1.163-4; 1.1232-3A
Overlapping pay periods..31.3402(g)-1; 31.3402(g)-2
Overpayments of tax..301.6401-1—301.6407-1
. interest on..301.6611-1
Overtime, withholding tax..31.3402(g)-1

— P —

Paid-in surplus, basis of property acquired as..1.362-1; 1.362-2
Parent, defined..1.73-1(c)
Parsonage, exemption..1.107-1
Partial liquidation, defined..1.346-1—1.346-3
Partially tax-exempt interest:
. corporations..1.242-1
. individuals..1.35-1—1.35-2
Partners and partnerships..1.701-1—1.771-1
. accounting methods..1.453-7; 1.481-2
. assumption of liabilities between..1.752-1
. basis:
.. contributed property..1.723-1
.. distributed property..1.732-1; 1.732-2
.. optional adjustment..1.722-1; 1.733-1; 1.734-1; 1.742-1
.. partner's interest..1.722-1; 1.733-1; 1.742-1
.. rules for allocation..1.755-1
.. transfers of interests..1.742-1; 1.743-1
.. undistributed property..1.734-1
. capital contributions..1.721-1—1.723-1
. collapsible partnership..1.751-1
. compensation attributable to several years..1.707-1; 1.1301-1; 1.1301-2
. continuation of partnership..1.708-1
. credits..1.702-1
. deceased partner, payments to successor in interest of..1.736-1
. defined..1.761-1; 301.7701-3
. determination of tax liability..1.701-1—1.708-1
. distributions..1.731-1—1.736-1
. distributive share..1.61-13; 1.702-1; 1.704-1
.. losses..7.704-1
. effective dates..1.771-1
. elections of..1.703-1
.. to be taxed as corporations..1.1361-1—1.1361-16
. family..1.704-1
. foreign community income..1.981-1(b)(4)
. income:
.. computation..1.703-1
.. time taxable..1.706-1
. income in respect of decedent..1.753-1
. information returns..1.6031-1
. interest in:
.. basis..1.705-1; 1.722-1; 1.733-1; 1.742-1
.. sale of, capital gain or loss..1.741-1
.. transfer of..1.736-1; 1.741-1—1.743-1
. interest on capital..1.707-1

69,026 (Fed. Reg.)   PARTNERS—PERSONAL   5-25-78

Partners and partnerships (continued):
. inventory items distributed..1.735-1; 1.751-1
. liabilities between..1.752-1
. liability for tax..1.701-1
. net operating loss deduction..1.702-2
. nonresident alien members, doing business in United States..1.875-1
. nonresident partnership defined ..301.7701-5
. pension or profit-sharing plan..1.1361-4
. personal holding company stock owned by..1.544-3
. resident partnership defined..301.7701-5
. retirement benefit plans..11.414(c)-1—11.414(c)-5
. retiring partner, payments to..1.736-1
. returns..1.6031-1
.. signature..1.6063-1; 31.6061-1
. self-employment tax..1.1402(a)-2; 1.1402(f)-1
. stock ownership rule:
.. corporate distributions and adjustments ..1.318-2
. Subchapter S corporations taxed as ..1.1371-1—1.1377.3
. taxable income computation..1.703-1
. taxable years of..1.706-1
. termination..1.708-1
. transactions between..1.707-1
. unrealized receivables distributed ..1.751-1
. work incentive program expenses, credit for..1.50A-7; 1.50B-4
Party to reorganization, defined..1.368-2
Patents:
. defined..1.1235-2
. depreciation..1.167(a)-6
. sale or exchange..1.1235-1; 1.1235-2
.. to foreign corporations..1.1249-1
Patronage dividends..1.522-1—1.522-3
. deduction by recipient corporation ..1.246-1
. gross income inclusion..1.61-5
. information returns..1.6044-1
Pay-as-you-go tax..31.3401(a)-1—31.3404-1
Payment of tax..1.6151-1 et seq.; 31.6151-1
. advance, interest on overpayments ..301.6611-1
.. check..301.6311.1
.. bad..301.6657-1
. date due..1.6151-1
. estimated tax..1.6153-1; 1.6154-1; 301.6315-1
. extension..1.6161-1—1.6164-9; 31.6161(a)(1)-1
.. bond required..1.6165-1
.. expected carrybacks..1.6164-1—1.6164-9
.. interest..301.6601-1
.. personal holding company liquidation ..1.6162-1
. failure to make..301.6653-1; 301.6659-1; 301.6672-1
. foreign funds..301.6316-1
. fraction of cent..301.6313-1
. Fulbright grants..301.6316-5
. government depositaries..1.6302-1; 31.6302(c)-1—31.6302(c)-3; 301.6302-1
. interest on delinquency..301.6601-1
. money order..301.6311-1
. notice and demand..301.6303-1
. receipt for..301.6314-1
. time for..1.6151-1
. transfers to foreign entities..1.1494-1
. U.S. securities used for..301.6312-1; 301.6312-2
. withheld taxes on wages, governmental employer..31.3404-1
. withholding tax at source..1.1461-2—1.1461-3

Payroll period:
. defined..31.3401(b)-1
. overlapping..31.3402(g)-1; 31.3402(g)-2
Penalties..301.6651-1—301.6674-1
. assessable..301.6671-1—301.6685-1
. bad checks in payment of taxes ..301.6657-1
. disclosure of tax return information ..301.7216-1—301.7216-3
. estimated tax..1.6654-1—1.6654-5; 1.6655-1—1.6655-3
.. waiver of, for 1971..1.6654-4
. evasion of tax..301.6672-1
. failure to:
.. account for tax..301.7512-1
.. collect or pay over tax..301.6672-1
.. file foreign corporation returns ..301.6679-1
.. file return..301.6651-1; 301.6652-1; 301.6659-1
.. furnish statements to payees..301.6678-1
.. furnish withholding statement ..301.6674-1
.. make deposit of taxes..301.6656-1
.. pay estimated tax...1.6654-1; 1.6654-2; 1.6655-1; 1.6655-2
.. pay tax..301.6653-1; 301.6659-1; 301.6672
.. supply identifying number..301.6676-1
.. surrender property subject to levy ..301.6332-1
.. U.S.-Guam taxes, furnish information as to..301.6688-1
. fraud..301.6653-1
. interest on..301.6601-1(f); 301.6621-1
. negligence:
.. fraud penalties also involved..301.6653-1
.. new creditable residence, false certification..1.44-3
. perjury..1.6065-1; 31.6065(a)-1
. Tax Court proceeding instituted merely for delay..301.6673-1
. underpayments under '69 Tax Reform Act..1.9006-1
Pennsylvania, ground rent..1.163-1
Pension Benefit Guaranty Corporation:
. disclosure of returns and return information..420.6103(l)(2)-3
. identification and statistical information to..420.6103(l)(2)-1; 420.6103(l)(2)-3
Pension plan, defined..1.401-1—1.401-14
Pension trusts: See "Employees' trusts"
Pensions:
. business expense..1.162-10
. disability..1.72-15; 1.105-4; 1.105-6; 7.105-1
.. substantial gainful activity, defined ..7.105-2
. gross income..1.61-11
. retirement income credit..1.37-1—1.37-5
Percentage depletion..1.613-1—1.613-7
. gross income from the property ..1.613-3; 1.613-4
. taxable income from the property ..1.613-5
Percentage method withholding..31.3402(b)-1
Period of limitation—see "Statute of Limitations"
Periodicals, circulation expenditures, deductibility..1.173-1
Perishable goods, seizure and sale ..301.6336-1
Perjury..1.6065-1; 31.6065(a)-1
Person, defined..301.7701-1
. United States person..1.957-4
Personal exemptions..1.151-1—1.153-1
. child-care-expense deduction..1.214-1
. credit for..1.42-1; 1.42A-1
. estates and trusts..1.642(b)-1
. short-period returns..1.443-1
Personal expenses..1.262-1

PERSONAL—PRIVATE *(Fed. Reg.)* **69,027**

References are to SECS. (§) in the Regs. Check Page 23,003 for latest developments

Personal holding companies..1.541-1—1.547-7
. adjustments to taxable income..1.545-2
. commodity transactions..1.543-2
. consolidated returns..1.542-4
. convertible securities..1.544-5
. corporate acquisitions, carryovers..1.381-(c)(14)-1; 1.381(c)(15)-1
. deficiency dividends..1.547-1; 1.547-2
.. corporate acquisitions..1.381(c)(17)-1
. DISC dividends..1.995-1(d)
. distributions by..1.316-1(b)
. dividend carryover..1.564-1
. dividends paid by:
.. after close of taxable year..1.563-2
. limitations on assessment and collection ..301.6501(f)-1
. liquidation, extension of time to pay tax ..1.6162-1
. mineral, oil and gas royalties..1.543-12(e)(2)

Personal injuries, compensation..1.104-1; 1.105-4; 1.105-6

Personal property: See also "Property":
. casual sales of..1.453-3
. dealers, installment plan..1.453-2
. income from sources partly within and partly without U.S...1.863-3
. purchased without U.S. and sold within U.S., income from..1.861-7

Personal service contracts, personal holding company..1.543-1

Personal service income..1.861-1—1.862-1

Petitions, Tax Court..301.6213-1; 301.6215-1

Philippine Islands, compensation of employees of Commonwealth..1.893-1

Plans, reorganization..1.393-2

Pledgees, lien for taxes as against ..301.6323-1

Policemen, subsistence allowance..1.120-1

Political campaign, organizations participating in, exemption..1.501(c)(3)-1

Political conventions:
. advertising in program of..1.276-1

Political expenditures..1.162-15(b); 1.162-20; 1.271-1; 1.276-1

Political organizations, returns..1.6012-6

Political parties:
. debts owed by..1.271-1
. indirect contributions, disallowance of ..1.276-1

Political subdivisions:
. bridges acquired by..1.115-1
. obligations of, interest exemption..1.103-1
. officers and employees, withholding tax ..31.3401(c)-1

Pollution control facilities:
. amortization of..1.169-1—1.169-4

Pooled income funds..1.642(c)-5—1.642(c)-7

Possessions of the United States:
. citizens of:
.. place to file returns..1.6091-3
.. status..1.932-1
. defined..1.931-1
. income from:
.. determination where sources partly within and partly without..1.863-6
.. interest..7.936-1
. income from sources within..1.931-1—1.932-1
.. DISC corporations..1.931-1(j)
.. dividends-received deduction..1.246-1
. obligations:
.. interest exemption..1.103-1
.. short-term, issued at discount..1.454-1
. taxes of:

Possessions of the United States (continued):
. taxes of (continued):
.. deductibility..1.164-1—1.164-7
.. withholding tax..31.3401(a)(8)(B)-1
. taxes paid to:
.. credit against U.S. tax..1.901-1—1.905-5

Post allowances..1.912-1—1.912-2

Postal savings accounts, interest..1.103-4

Postmarks as timely filing..301.7502-1

Power of appointment, beneficial interest status..1.672(d)-1

Predecessor, net operating loss of..1.381-(a)-1

Preferential dividends:
. defined..1.565-6
. dividends-paid deduction..1.562-1—1.562-3

Preferred stock:
. bail-out..1.306-1—1.306-3
. credit for dividends paid on..1.247-1

Premiums, life insurance, deductibility ..1.264-1—1.264-3

Prepaid items:
. dues, certain membership organizations ..1.456-1—1.456-7

Prepaid subscriptions..1.455-1—1.455-6

Preparers of returns: See "Tax return preparers"

Presidential Election Campaign Fund:
. designation by individuals..301.6096-1; 301.6096-2

Presumptions, collapsible corporation status..1.341-3; 1.341-5

Price certification, housing credit..1.44-3

Prime rate of interest, obligations owed to or by U.S...301.6621-1

Prior year deductions, subsequent recovery..1.111-1

Private foundations..1.507-1—1.509(e)-1; 53.4940-1—53.4948-1
. annual reports..1.6056-1
.. public inspection..301.6104-4
. attribution rules..1.509(a)-5
. business holdings, excessive..53.4943-1—53.4943-11
. continuation of status as..1.509(b)-1
. definitions..1.509(a)-1
. definitions and special rules..53.4946-1
. exclusions from status of..1.509(a)-2—1.509(a)-4
. foreign organizations..1.4443-1; 53.4948-1
. "gross investment income" defined ..1.509(e)-1
. net investment income..53.4940-1
. operating foundation..53.4942(b)-1; 53.4942(b)-3
. organizations described in section 170(b)(1)(A)..1.509(a)-2
. penalty as to excise taxes..301.6684-1
. penalty for failure to file or publicize annual report..301.6685-1
. permitted holdings..143.6
. publicly supported organizations ..1.509(a)-3
. section 501(c)(3) organizations..1.508-1—1.508-4
. scholarship and fellowship grants..143.2
. self-dealing, taxes on..53.4941(a)-1—53.4941(f)-1
. status after termination..1.509(c)-1
. "substantial contributor" defined..1.507-6
. "support" defined..1.509(d)-1
. supporting organizations..1.509(a)-4

69,028 (Fed. Reg.)   PRIVATE—REAL   5-25-78

Private foundations (continued):
- tax on jeopardizing investments..53.4944-1—53.4944-6
- taxable expenditures..53.4945-1—53.4945-6
- - individuals, grants to..53.4945-4
- - influencing elections..53.4945-3
- - noncharitable purposes, expenditures for..53.4945-6
- - organizations, grants to..53.4945-5
- - propaganda influencing legislation ..53.4945-2
- termination of status..1.507-1—1.507-9
- transfer to, or operation as public charity..1.507-2
- transferee foundations..1.507-3
- trusts treated as..53.4947-1; 53.4947-2
- undistributed income..53.4942(a)-1—53.4942(a)-3

Prizes..1.74-1
- withholding tax..31.3402(j)-1

Procedure and administration..1.6001-1 et seq.; 31.6001-1 et seq.

Production of income, expenses..1.212-1

Productive-use property, exchange of..1.1031(a)-1

Professional persons, business expenses..1.162-6

Profits:
- declared as dividends, information return ..1.6042-1
- regulated investment companies..1.852-1—1.852-9

Profit-sharing plans: See "Employees' Trusts"

Prohibited transactions:
- employee stock ownership plans..54.4975-7
- trusts..1.503(a)-1—1.503(i)-1; 54.4975-6

Propaganda, organizations disseminating:
- exemption..1.501(c)(3)-1

Property:
- defined..1.317-1
- - depletion purposes..1.614-1—1.614-4
- - used in trade or business..1.1231-1—1.1232-2
- - - life insurance companies..1.817-2
- dividends in..1.301-1; 1.316-1
- - earnings and profits computation ..1.312-1—1.312-12
- - gain or loss to corporation..1.311-1
- - exchanged for stock..1.1032-1
- - income-producing, expenses..1.212-1
- - location outside U.S.
- - limitations on assessment and collection ..301.6503(c)-1
- money as..1.317-1
- taxes:
- - cooperative housing corporations ..1.216-1
- - deductibility..1.164-1—1.164-7
- - purchaser and seller..1.164-6
- - transfer of:
- - farm recapture property..1.1251-1—1.1251-4
- - partly sale and partly gift..1.1015-4
- - transferred in connection with performance of services..13.1
- **transmitted at death:**
- - basis for gain or loss..1.1014-2—1.1014-3

Proprietorships, election to be taxed as corporation..1.1361-1—1.1361-15

Public cemeteries, trusts for..1.642(c)-1

Public Health Service:
- disability pay..1.104-1(e)

Public inspection, written determinations ..301.6110—301.6110-7

Public safety testing organizations, exemption..1.501(c)(3)-1

Public utilities:
- dividends-paid deduction..1.247-1
- dividends received from, deduction for 1.244-1—1.244-2; 1.246-1
- normalization method of accounting ..13.13
- preferred stock, dividends on:
- - dividends paid deduction..1.247-1
- - dividends received deduction computation..1.244-2

Public utility property:
- asset depreciation range system..1.167(a)-11; 1.167(a)-12(a)(4)(iii); 1.167(l)-5
- investment credit..12.3

Publication, statistics..301.6108-1

Publicity:
- exempt organizations, application ..301.6104-1
- refunds and credits..301.6405-1
- returns..301.6103(a)-100 et seq.; ..301.6104-2

Publicly supported organizations:
- community chest, fund or foundation, qualification as..1.170A-9
- supporting organizations, beneficiary requirement..1.509(a)-5

Puerto Rico:
- alien residents:
- - taxation of..1.876-1
- bona fide residents, defined..1.933-1
- citizens of:
- - income from U.S. possessions..1.932-1
- income from sources within..1.933-1; 7.936-1
- possession of U.S...1.931-1(a)
- residents, withholding..31,3401(a)(6)-1; 31.3401(a)(8)(C)-1

Purchasers, lien for taxes as against ..301.6323-1

Puts and calls..1.1234-1

— Q —

Qualified electing shareholder, defined ..1.333-2

Qualified pension, profit-sharing or stock-bonus plans: See "Employees' trusts"

Qualified stock options..1.422-1—1.422-2

— R —

Radio broadcasting properties, gain on sale 1.1071-1—1.1071-4

Railroad grading and tunnel bores:
- amortization..1.185-1—1.185-3

Railroad Retirement Tax Act: See "Employment Taxes"

Railroads:
- consolidated returns..1.1502-2(g)
- depreciation, change from retirement to straight-line..1.9001-1—1.9001-4
- discharge of debts, income from..1.108(b)-1
- reorganizations..1.354-1; 1.373-1—1.373-3
- retirement-straight line property depreciation..1.372-1
- rolling stock:
- - capital expenditures..1.263(e)-1

Real estate:
- accrual of taxes, accounting methods ..1.461-1
- acquired by U.S., administration of ..301.7506-1
- business property..1.1033(g)-1; 1.1231-1
- cost as basis..1.1012-1
- deferred payment sales..1.453-4

Real estate (continued):
. improvements by lessee..1.109-1
.. basis adjusted for..1.1019-1
. installment sales..1.453-5
. nonresident alien income..1.871-8; 1.871-10
. **sale of:**
.. income from sources within U.S. ..1.861-6
. subdivision:
.. capital gains and losses..1.1237-1
. taxes:
.. accrual..1.461-1
.. apportionment, seller and purchaser ..1.164-6
.. cooperative housing corporations ..1.216-1
.. deductibility..1.164-1; 1.164-4; 1.164-6
.. purchaser and seller..1.164-6
. trusts: See "Real estate investment trusts"

Real estate boards, exemption..1.501(c)(6)-1

Real estate investment trusts..1.856-1—1.858-1; 7.856(g)-1; 10.3

Real property:
. repossession of..1.1038-1—1.1038-3

Reasonable needs of business, accumulated earnings tax..1.537-1

Rebates, defined..301.6653-1

Recapitalization, as reorganization..1.368-2

Recapture:
. farm:
.. conservation expenses..1.1252-1; 1.1252-2
.. sale or other disposition..1.1251-1—1.1251-4

Receivables or fees, partners and partnerships..1.751-1

Receivers, returns by, signature..1.6012-3(b)(4); 1.6062-1(a)(2)

Receiverships: See "Bankruptcy and receivership"

Reciprocal underwriters, rates of tax ..1.821-1

Reclamation laws, property sold pursuant to..1.1033(d)-1

Recognition of gain or loss..1.1002-1

Records: See "Books and Records"

Recovery:
. excessive profits on Government contracts..1.1471-1
. exclusions..1.111-1
. unconstitutional Federal taxes..1.1346-1

Recovery exclusion, corporate acquisitions ..1.381(c)(12)-1

Red Cross, sports programs for..1.114-1

Redemption, trading stamps and coupons ..1.451-4

Refunds and credits..301.6401-1 et seq.
. after limitation period..301.6514(a)-1
. application for tentative carryback adjustment as..1.6411-1
. Armed Forces, deceased members..1.692-1
. authorization..301.6402-1
. barred, adjustment under mitigation rule ..1.1311(b)-2; 1.1314(c)-1
. carrybacks:
.. limitations..301.6511(d)-2; 301.6511(d)-4
.. Work incentive program..301.6511(d)-7
. claims for..301.6402-2
. date of allowance..301.6407-1
. deficiency dividends, personal holding companies…1.547-3
. erroneous..301.6514(a)-1; 301.6514(b)-1
.. recovery of..301.6532-2; 301.6621-1

Refunds and credits (continued):
. excessive tax withheld..31.6413(a)-1—31.6414-1
. final disposition as a determination ..1.1313(a)-3
. foreign currency..301.6316-8
. foreign tax credit adjustments..1.905-1—1.905-4; 301.6511(d)-3
. insolvent banks..301.7507-6
. installment payments of tax..301.6403-1
. interest on..301.6611-1
. limitation in case of petition to TC ..301.6512-1
. limitation period..301.6511(a)-1—301.6514(b)-1
. overpayment credited against taxes due ..301.6402-0
. payments in excess of amounts shown on return..301.6402-4
. publicity..301.6405-1
. reports of..301.6405-1
. requirement that claim be filed ..301.6402-2
. return not filed..301.6511(a)-1; 301.6511(b)-1
. "special refunds" of employee social security tax..1.31-2
. suits for refund..301.6532-1—301.6532-3
. tentative carrybacks..1.6411-1—1.6411-4
. time for filing
.. bad debts..301.6511(d)-1
.. waiver as extending..301.6511(c)-1

Registered holding company, defined ..1.1083-1

Registration, requirements..301.7011-1(b)

Regulated investment companies..1.851-1—1.855-1
. investment trust..1.46-4
. unit investment trusts..1.851-7

Regulated public utility, consolidated return..1.1502-13(j)

Related corporations, redemption of stock through..1.304-1

Related or subordinate party, defined ..1.672(c)-1

Related taxpayer:
. adjustment in barred year under mitigation rule..1.1311(b)-3
. defined..1.1313(c)-1
. employee expense reporting..1.162-17
. gains from sales or exchanges..1.1239-1
. losses from sales or exchanges..1.267(a)-1; 1.267(d)-1
. unpaid expenses and interest..1.267(a)-1

Religious organizations:
. employee retirement plans..1.410(a)-1(c); 1.410(d)-1
. exemption..1.501(c)(3)-1; 1.501(d)-1
. feeder organizations..1.502-1

Remainder interest, charitable..1.170A-12

Remainderman, valuation of interest of ..1.1014-8

Rent:
. business expense..1.162-1
. income from..1.61-8; 1.861-5
. taxes paid by lessee..1.110-1

Reorganization..1.354-1—1.373-3
. active business requirements..1.355-4
. adjustment of capital structure before Sept. 22, 1938..1.1018-1
. assumption of liability..1.357-1—1.357-2
. bankruptcy and receiverships..1.371-1—1.373-3
. basis in case of bankruptcy and receivership acquisitions..1.372-1

69,030 (Fed. Reg.) REORGANIZATION—RETURNS 5-25-78

Reorganization (continued):
- basis of property received..1.358-1; 1.1018-1
- basis to corporations..1.362-1
- business or corporate purpose..1.355-2
- . railroads..1.373-2
- carryovers..1.381(a)-1—1.381(c)(1)-2; 1.381(c)(22)-1; 1.383-3
- change of ownership..1.382(b)-1
- consolidation of group or export trade corporations..1.972-1
- control defined..1.368-2
- defined..1.368-2
- distribution of stock and securities of controlled corporation..1.355-1
- effective date, 1954 Code..1.393-1
- effects on corporation..1.361-1—1.362-2
- effects on shareholders and security holders..1.354-1—1.358-4
- election to have 1939 or 1954 Code apply ..1.393-3
- exchange of stock and securities..1.354-1
- . receipt of additional consideration ..1.356-1; 1.356-2
- exchanges:
- . information..1.371-1; 1.371-2
- . purpose and scope of exception of ..1.368-1
- . receipt of additional consideration ..1.356-1
- foreign corporations..7.367(a)-1—7.367-2
- information to be filed..1.368-3
- insolvency..1.371-1—1.373-3
- liabilities..1.357-1; 1.357-2
- party to..1.368-2
- plan of:
- . adopted after Dec. 31, 1953 and before June 22, 1954..1.392-1
- . date filed..1.393-2
- . receipt of additional consideration ..1.356-2
- records to be kept..1.368-3
- spin-offs, split-offs, split-ups..1.355-1—1.355-5
- stock, defined..1.382(c)-1

Repairs, deductibility..1.162-1; 1.162-4; 1.212-1

Repayment of income held under claim of right..1.1341; 1.1341-2

Repeal of 1939 Code, effect of..1.395-1

Replacement fund, involuntary conversion ..1.1033(a)-4

Request for prompt assessment..301.6501 (d)-1

Requisitioned property..1.1033(a)-1; 1.1231-1; 1.1231-2

Research expenditures..1.174-1—1.174-4

Research work, exempt organization's income from..1.512(b)-1

Reserves:
- bad debts..1.166-6; 1.585-1—1.585-4; 1.593-1—1.593-11
- cooperative associations, effect on exemption..1.501(c)(16)-1; 1.521-1
- deductions..1.462-5; 1.462-6
- reasonable additions..1.462-1; 1.462-7

Residence:
- alien seamen..1.871-3
- condemnation..1.1034-1
- determination of alien's..1.871-2
- loss of, by alien..1.871-5
- new, tax credit for purchase or construction of..1.44-4
- sale or exchange of..1.1034-1

Resident, defined..301.7701-5

Resident foreign corporations tax..1.882-1 —1.882-4

Residential property:
- converted to business or income-producing use:
- . depreciation..1.167(f)-1
- . exchange of..1.1034-1
- . involuntary conversion..1.1033(b)-1—1.1034-1
- new residence, tax credit for purchase or construction..1.44-1—1.44-5
- . definitions..1.44-5
- . recapture upon disposition of..1.44-4
- sale of:
- . defined..1.1034-1
- . gain or loss..1.165-9
- . nonrecognition of gain..1.1034-1

Residents:
- alien..1.901-1
- . change of status..1.871-13
- corporation..1.882-1—1.882-4
- nonresident alien..1.871-1—1.876-1

Restoration, war losses, recoveries of investments..1.1334-1

Restricted stock option..1.424-1—1.424-2

Retail commission salesmen, noncash remuneration..31.3402(j)-1

Retail merchants, inventories of..1.471-8

Retail sales tax, deductibility..1.164-5

Retirement age, wage continuation purposes..1.105-4(a)(3); 1.105-6

Retirement income credit..1.37-1—1.37-5

Retroactive regulations or rulings ..301.7805-1

Return preparers: See "Tax return preparers"

Returns..1.6001-1 et seq., 31.6001-1 et seq.
- accounting period changed..1.443-1
- amended..31.6051-2
- . claim for refund status..301.6402-3
- . W-2 corrected..31.6051-2
- common trust funds..1.6032-1
- composite, in lieu of specified form ..31.6011(a)-8; 31.6051-1(f)
- computation of tax by IRS..1.6014-1; 1.6014-2; 1.6151-1(b)(1)
- computations on..1.6102-1; 301.6102-1
- consolidated:
- . taxable years beginning after Dec. 31, 1965..1.1501-1; 1.1502-0—1.1502-100
- . copies of 301.6103(a)-2
- . tax return preparers..1.6107-1
- corporate acquisitions..1.381(b)-1
- delinquency penalty..301.6651-1
- depletion and depreciation..1.613-6
- disclosure of information by preparer ..301.7216-1—301.7216-3
- elections..1.6012-1(a)(7)
- employee expense reporting..1.162-17
- employment taxes..31.6011(a)-1—31.6011(b)-2
- estates and trusts..1.641(b)-1; 1.6012-3
- exempt organizations..1.6033-1; 1.6033-2
- . transfers to..1.6050-1; 301.6050-1
- . unrelated business income..1.6012-2(e), (f); 1.6012-3(a)(5)
- extension of time for filing..1.6081-1—1.6081-2
- failure to file:
- . deficiency dividend deduction..1.547-5
- . limitations on refunds..301.6511(a)-1; 301.6511(b)-1
- . penalties..301.6651-1
- . false or fraudulent..301.7207-1
- foreign personal holding companies ..1.6035-1; 1.6035-2
- Guamanian income involved..301.7654-1
- failure to furnish information..301.6688-1
- identifying numbers..1.6109-1; 301.6109-1

Returns (continued):
- income tax..1.6012-1—1.6017-1
- individuals..1.1—1.1-3
- . automatic extension..1.6081-4
- information: See "Information returns"
- inspection..301.6103(a)-1; 301.6103(a)-2; 301.6103(a)-100—301.6103(a)-109; 301.6103(b)-1—301.6103(d)-1
- Dept. of Labor..402.6103(*l*)(2)-2; 402.6103(*l*)(2)-3
- Internal Revenue Service Centers ..1.6091-4
- joint..1.2-1; 1.2-2; 1.6013-1—1.6013-4
- mailing time as timely filing..301.7502-1
- mathematical errors..301.6201-1; 301.6213-1
- miscellaneous..1.6012-4
- notice requiring..31.6001-6
- partnerships..1.6031-1; 31.6061-1
- period covered..1.441-1; 31.6101-1
- person required to make..1.6012-1—1; 1.6012-6
- place for filing..1.6091-1—1.6091-4; 31-.6091-1; 301.6091-1
- . . foreign currencies involved..301.6316-4
- . . information returns..1.6041-6
- . . other than required district..1.6091-4
- political organizations..1.6012-6
- publicity..301.6103(a)-100—301.6103(a)-109
- receivers, signature..1.6012-3(b)(4)
- reproduction of..301.7513-1
- requirements..1.6011-1; 1.6012-6
- self-employment tax..1.6017-1
- short period..1.443-1; 1.536-1
- signatures..1.6061-1—1.6063-1; 31.6061-1; 301.6064-1
- surviving spouse..1.2-1; 1.2-2; 1.6013-3
- time deemed filed..301.6501(b)-1; 301.6513-1
- . . as declaration or amendment thereof ..1.6015(f)-1
- . . foreign personal holding companies ..1.6035-1—1.6035-3
- . . information returns..1.6041-6
- . . refund limitation from date of filing ..301.6511(a)-1; 301.6511(b)-1
- . . withheld taxes..1.1461-2—1.1461-3
- time to file..1.6071-1—1.6074-2; 31.6071(a)-1
- . . extension..1.6081-1—1.6081-3; 31.6081(a)-1
- timely mailing as timely filing..301.7502-1
- trustee in bankruptcy, signature..1.6012-3(b)(4); 1.6062-1(a)(2)
- verification..1.6065-1; 31.6065(a)-1
- who must file..1.6011-1; 1.6012-6

Revenue agents and officers
- entry of premises..301.7606-1
- examination of books and witnesses ..301.7602-1
- oaths, authority to administer..301.7622-1

Revocable trusts..1.676(a)-1; 1.676(b)-1

Reversionary interest, grantor having income taxable to whom ..1.671-1—1.678(d)-1

Rights to subscribe to stock, dividends ..1.305-1

Royalties:
- advance, depletion..1.612-3
- coal..1.631-3
- credit for United Kingdom income tax ..1.905-5

Rules and regulations, authority..301.7805-1

— S —

Salaries: See "Compensation"
Sale of property:
- collapsible corporation..1.341-1—1.3415
- gain from, as income from sources within U.S...1.861-7
- gain or loss..1.61-6; 1.1001-1; 1.1002-1
- installment basis..1.453-1—1.453-10
- land with unharvested crop..1.268-1
- life tenant and remainderman..1.1014-5
- liquidation of corporation..1.337-1—1.337-5
- natural resources..1.631-1—1.632-1
- radio broadcasting stations..1.1071—1.1071-4
- related taxpayers..1.267(a)-1; 1.267(d)-1; 1.1239-1
- residence..1.1034-1
- seized for taxes..301.6863-1; 301.6863-2; 301.7403-1(b)
- short sales..1.1233-1
- wash sales..1.1091-1; 1.1091-2

Sales tax, retail, deductibility..1.164-5
Saturday last day..301.7503-1
Savings and loan associations..1.581-2
- information return..1.6042-1(a)(2)
Scholarships and fellowship grants..1.117-1—1.117-4
- nonresident aliens..1.871-8; 1.871-9
Scientific organizations, exemption..1501(c)(3)-1
Sec. 38 property, defined..1.48-1—1.48-3
Sec. 179 property, defined..1.179-3
Sec. 306 stock..1.306-1—1.306-3
Sec. 341 assets, defined..1.341-2
Sec. 501(c)(3) organizations..1.508-1—1.508-4
Sec. 1245 property, defined..1.1245-3
Sec. 1250 property, depreciation of ..1.167(j)-1—1.167(j)-7
Sec. 1361 corporations..1.1361-1—1.1361-15
Secretary or his delegate, defined..301.7701-9
Securities:
- as other property, tax-free exchanges ..1.356-3
- carryover basis..7.1023(h)-1
- dividends paid with:
- . . earnings and profits computation ..1.312-1 et seq.
- . . gain or loss to corporation..1.311-1
- exempt: See "Exempt securities"; "Exempt income"
- lien for taxes..301.6323-1
- seized for taxes, sale of..301.6339-1
- wash sales..1.1091-1; 1.1091-2
- worthless:
- . . bad debts..1.165-5
- . . banks..1.582-1
- . . overpayments on account of..301.6511(d)-1
- . . war losses..1.1337-1

Securities and Exchange Commission:
- exchanges, sales and distributions ..1.1081-1—1.1081-11
- . . basis..1.1082-1—1.1082-6
- . . definitions of various terms used ..1.1083-1
- inspection of returns..301.6103(a)-102
- tax-free exchanges..1.1081-1—1.1081-11

69,032 (Fed. Reg.)   SEIZURE—STATUTE   5-25-78

Seizure of property..301.6331-1—301.6343-1
- gain or loss..1.1231-1; 1.1231-2
- levy and distraint..301.6331-1; 301.6502-1; 301.6503(a)-1
- limitation period..301.6502-1—301.6503(g)-1
- sale of seized property..301.6335-1; 301.-6336-1; 301.6863-1; 301.6863-2; 301.7505-1; 301.7506-1
- stay of sale pending TC decision ..301.6863-1; 301.6863-2
- third party rights..301.6532-3; 301.7426-1
- wrongful, third party suits..301.7426-1; 301.6621-1

Self-employed:
- annuities..1.72-17—1.72-18
- qualified pension trusts..1.401-10—1.401-13

Self-Employed Retirement Plans:
- common investment funds..11.401(d)(1)-1
- contributions to:
  - time deemed made..1.404(a)(6)-1
- information requirement..1.6041-2(b)
- trustees, qualifications..11.401(d)(1)-1

Self-employment income, defined ..1.1402(b)-1

Self-employment tax..1.1401-1—1.1403-1
- computation of earnings..1.1402(a)-2
- correction of errors involving employee social security tax..301.6521-1
- husband and wife..1.6017-1(b)
- law applicable in determination of error ..301.6521-2
- returns..1.6017-1

Semimonthly withholding table..31.3402(c)-1

Senior citizens, architectural and transportation barriers to, removal costs ..7.190-1—7.190-3

Separate maintenance payments: See "Alimony and separate maintenance payments"

Separate return followed by joint return ..1.6013-2

Servants, domestic exemption from withholding..31.3401(a)(3)-1

Servicemen: See "Armed Forces of U. S."

Services of children..1.73-1

Shareholders: See "Stockholders"

Ships, foreign, earnings derived from ..1.872-2; 1.883-1

Shipwreck losses:
- deduction from gross income..1.165-7

Shopping news, delivery withholding tax ..31.3401(a)(10)-1

Short sales..1.1233-1

Short taxable year:
- accumulated earnings tax..1.536-1
- caused by death..1.4-4
- computation of tax..1.443-1
- declaration of estimated tax..1.6015(g)-1; 1.6016-4
- returns..1.443-1

Short-term capital gain, defined..1.1222-1

Short-term capital loss, defined..1.1222-1

Sick benefits..1.72-5; 1.104-1—1.106-1

Sick pay exclusion, annuity contracts ..1.72-15

Signing of returns, etc..1.6061-1—1.6063-1; 31.6061-1

"Simple" trusts..1.651(a)-1—1.652(c)-4

Single premium life insurance, endowment or annuity contract..1.264-2
- interest..1.101-3

Small business corporations: See "Subchapter S corporations"

Small business deduction, life insurance companies..1.1561-0—1.1564-1

Small business investment companies:
- accumulated earnings tax..1.533-1
- bad debt reserves..1.586-1; 1.586-2
- dividends-received deduction..1.1242-1
- losses..1.1242-1; 1.1243-1
- returns..1.6037-1

Small business stock..1.1244(a)-1—1.1244(e)-1

Social Club, exemption..1.501(c)(7)-1

Social Security benefit number as identifying number..301.6109-1(d); 301.-7701-11

Social Security Benefits:
- employees' trusts benefits affected by increases in..1.401(a)-15

Social security taxes: See "Employment taxes"

Social welfare organizations, exemption ..1.501(c)(4)-1

Soil and conservation expenditures..1.175-1—1.175-6

Soldiers and sailors: See "Armed Forces of U.S."

Sororities, college, domestic employees, exemption from withholding..31,3401(a)(3)-1

Source:
- distributions..1.316-2
- within and without U.S., income from ..1.863-6

Spin-offs, split-offs, split-ups..1.355-1—1.355-5

Split-interest trusts, private foundation restrictions..53.4947-1; 53.4947-2

Splitting corporations:
- surtax exemption..1.1551-1

Splitting income..1.2-1

Sports programs for Red Cross..1.114-1

Standard deduction..1.141-1—1.144-2

Standards, for determining classification ..301.7701-1

States:
- bridges acquired by..1.115-1
- disability benefits, exemption..1.105-5
- gasoline tax, deductibility..1.164-5
- income of, exclusion..1.115-1
- loans from, repayment of..1.592-1
- obligations:
  - interest exemption..1.103-1
  - interest to purchase or carry..1.265-2
  - short-term, issued at discount..1.454-1
- officers and employees:
  - withholding tax..31.3401(c)-1
- police, subsistence allowance..1.120-1
- retail sales tax, deductibility..1.164-5

Status determination date:
- exemptions..1.153-1
- standard deduction..1.143-1

Statute of limitations:
- adjustment, prior years' errors affecting current year..1.1311(a)-1
- assessment and collection..301.6501(a)-1—301.6503(d)-1
- investment credit carryback..301.6501-(j)-1
- claim for refund..301.6511(a)-1
- credits after..301.6514(b)-1
- judicial proceedings..301.6532-1—301.6532-3
- levy and distraint..301.6502-1; 301.6503(a)-1

Statute of limitations (continued):
. mitigation of effect of..1.1311(a)-1—
  1.1314(c)-1
.. self-employment tax and FICA taxes
   ..301.6521-1
. petition to TC..301.6213-1
. refunds and credits..301.6511(a)-1—
  301.6514(b)-1
.. adjustment in barred year under mitigation rule..1.1311(a)-2
.. third party suits..301.6532-3
. suspension..301.6503(a)-1—301.6503(g)-1
Stock:
. carryover basis..7.1023(h)-1
. consent stock defined..1.565-6
. constructive ownership:
.. corporate distributions and adjustments
   ..1.318-1
.. nondeductible losses..1.267(c)-1
.. personal holding company..1.544-1—
   1.544-7
. convertible preferred, distributions of
  ..1.305-6
. dividends..1.305-1—1.307-2
. exchange of:
.. for property..1.1032-1
.. for stock and cash, gain or loss..1.361-1
.. reorganization: See "Reorganization"
.. same corporation..1.1036-1
. gain or loss on sale by corporation
  ..1.1032-1
. March 1, 1913 value..1.1053-1
. options received by employees..1.421-1—
  1.421-8; 1.1014-1
. ownership rule:
.. corporate distributions and adjustments
   ..1.318-1—1.318-4
.. foreign personal holding companies
   ..1.552-3
.. nondeductible losses..1.267(c)-1
.. personal holding companies..1.544-1—
   1.544-7
. preferred, "bail-out"..1.306-1—1.306-3
. property acquired by issuance of, basis
  ..1.362-1; 1.362-2
. redemption..1.302-1—1.304-3
.. as liquidating distributions..1.346-2
.. defined..1.317-1
.. earnings and profits, effect on..1.312-5
. Sec. 306 stock..1.306-1—1.306-3; 1.312-1;
  1.391-1
. seized for taxes, transfer of..301.6339-1
. short sales..1.1233-1
. small business, loss on..1.1244(a)—1.1244
  (e)-1
. tax-free exchange:
.. reorganizations..1.354-1
. transactions treated as distributions..1-
  .305-7
. wash sales..1.1091-1
. worthless, war losses..1.1337-1
Stock bonus trust: See "Employees'
  trusts"
Stock dividends..1.305-1—1.307-2
Stock in trade, partners and partnerships
  ..1.751-1
Stock life insurance companies:
. distributions to shareholders..1.815-2;
  1.815-5
. policyholders surplus account..1.815-6
. shareholders surplus account..1.815-6
Stock purchase plans..1.423-1—1.423-2

Stock rights..1.305-1—1.307-2
. earnings and profits, effect on..1.312-1
. gain or loss to corporation..1.311-1
. stock acquired through, basis..1.307-1;
  1.307-2
Stockholders:
. consent dividends..1.565-1—1.565-6
. election as to gain in corporate liquidation..1.333-1—1.333-5
. election as to medium of dividend payment..1.305-2
. foreign corporations..1.902-1—1.902-5
.. information returns..1.964-4; 1.6035-2
.. records..1.964-3
. gross income of United States shareholders..1.951-1—1.951-3, 1.959-1—
  1.959-4
. minority:
.. liquidation of corporation..1.337-5;
  1.337-6
. regulated investment companies..1.852-4
. taxes, paid by corporation:
.. bank or other stock..1.164-7
Storm losses:
. deduction from gross income..1.165-7
Straddles, grantors of..1.1234-2
Strategic minerals or metals:
. Government payments to encourage
  ..1.621-1
Street railway corporation, acquisition on
  property, gain or loss..1.373-3
Students, defined..1.151-3
Subchapter S corporations:
. capital gains, special rules..1.1375-1
. definitions..1.1371-1—1.1371-2
. distributions by..1.1375-1—1.1375-6
. earnings and profits..1.1377-1—1.1377-3
. election by..1.1372-1—1.1372-6
. election to be taxed as partnership
  ..1.1371-1—1.1377-3
. imposition of tax on capital gains
  ..1.1378-1—1.1378-3
. net operating loss deduction..1.1374-1—
  1.1374-4
. stock and indebtedness owing shareholders:
.. adjustment to basis of..1.1376-1—
   1.1376-2
. undistributed taxable income..1.1373-1
. work incentive program expenses, credit
  for..1.50A-5; 1.50B-2
Subdivided lots..1.1237-1
Subscriptions:
. prepaid income..1.455-1—1.455-6
Subsidiaries:
. foreign:
.. credit for taxes of..1.902-1
.. employees' trusts..1.406-1; 1.407-1
.. information returns..1.6038-1
.. liquidation..1.332-1—1.332-7
.. basis of property received..1.334-1
.. earnings and profits..1.312-11
. redemption of stock through use of
  ..1.304-3
Subsidies, defense purposes..1.621-1
Subsistence allowance, policemen..1.120-1
Substituted basis..1.1016-10
Suburban railway corporation, acquisition
  of property, gain or loss..1.373-3
Subversive organizations, exemption
  ..1.501(e)-1
Succession taxes:
. gross income, deducted from..1.164-2
Successor corporations, carrybacks and
  carryovers of predecessor..1.381(a)-1
  —1.381(c)(23)-1; 1.383-1—1.383-3

69,034 (Fed. Reg.)   SUITS—TIMBER   5-25-78

Suits:
- recovery of erroneous refunds..301.6532-2
- . limitation period..301.6532-1
- recovery of taxes..1.6532-1
- . . limitation period..301.6532-1—301.6532-2
- restraining assessment and collection of tax..301.6213-1
- third parties..301.6532-3; 301.7426-1

Summons:
- enforcement of..301.7604-1
- service of..301.7603-1

Sundays and holidays, last day..301.7503-1
Surcharge, imposition of..1.51-1
Surplus accumulations, tax on..1.531-1—1.537-3

Surtax:
- corporations..1.11-1
- oil or gas properties, sale of..1.632-1

Surtax exemption:
- controlled corporations..1.1561-0—1.1564-1
- corporations..1.11-1
- . . disallowance of..1.1551-1

Surviving spouse:
- defined..1.2-2
- income splitting..1.2-1; 1.2-2
- wage earner's return..1.6014-1(c)

Suspension of statute of limitations
..301.6503(a)-1; 301.6503(d)-1

System group:
- defined..1.1083-1
- transfers within..1.1081-6
- . . gain or loss, determination..1.1082-6

— T —

Tables:
- annuity..1.72-9
- withholding..31.3402(c)-1

Tax benefit rule..1.111-1

Tax Court, U.S.
- burden of proof
- . . accumulated earnings..1.534-2
- . . fraud cases..301.7454-1
- date decision becomes final..301.7481-1
- decisions, as a determination..1.1313(a)-1
- deficiencies disallowed by..301.6215-1
- foreign entities' records, production of ..301.7456-1
- hearings before..301.7458-1
- nonresident alien's records, production of ..301.7456-1
- oaths, administration of..301.7456-1
- petition to..301.6213-1
- . . instituted merely for delay..301.6673-1
- publicity of proceedings..301.7461-1
- representation of parties..301.7452-1
- transferee proceeding..301.6902-1
- witnesses' fees..301.7457-1

Tax preference income:
- net leases of real property..12.8

Tax return preparers..1.6107-1; 1.6109-1; 1.6694-1; 1.6694-2; 1.6695-1
- defined..301.7701-15

Tax shelters, at risk amounts..7.465-1—7.465-5

Tax surcharge..1.51-1

Taxable income:
- defined, depletion purposes..1.613-4
- period for computation of..1.441-1
- sources within U.S...1.861-1
- sources without U.S...1.862-1

Taxable income credit..1.42A-1

Taxable year:
- change in..1.442-1
- changes in rates during..1.21-1
- defined..1.441-1
- partner and partnership..1.706-1
- termination by district director..1.6851-1—1.6851-2
- . termination by Secretary..301.6851-1

Taxes:
- additions treated as..301.6659-1
- capitalization..1.266-1
- deduction for..1.164-1—1.164-8; 1.266-1
- . . employment taxes..31.3502-1
- . time for..1.461-1
- defined, for levy and distraint purposes ..301.6331-1
- failure to make deposit of..301.6656-1
- lessee paying for lessor..1.110-1
- penalties as part of..301.6659-1
- rates of..1.1-1; 1.11-1
- recovery of..1.111-1
- unconstitutional, recovery..1.1346-1
- when deemed paid..301.6513-1

Tax-exempt income, expenses and interest, deductibility..1.265-1—1.265-2

Tax-exempt organizations..1.501(a)-1—1.504-1
- information requirements..1.6033-1
- unrelated business income..1.511-1—1.514(c)-1

Tax-exempt securities, dealers in...1.75-1

Tax-free covenenant bonds..1.1451-1
- credit for taxes withheld..1.32
- ownership certificates for interest ..1.1461-1

Tax-free distributions, earnings and profits 1.312-11

Tax-free exchanges..1.1031(a)-1—1.1036-1

Tax-free interest:
- life insurance company..1.803-4
- mutual insurance company other than life..1.822-1

Taxpayers, list of, publication..301.6107-1

Teachers, annuities..1.403(b)-1; 1.415(c)(4)-1

Telephone and telegraph:
- foreign companies' income from sources partly within and partly without U.S...1.863-5

Telephone companies, mutual or cooperative, exemption..1.501(c)(12)-1

Television films, investment credit..7.48-1—7.48-3

Tenants by entirety, dividends received credit and exclusion..1.116-1—1.116-2

Tenants in common, dividends received credit and exclusion..1.116-1—1.116-2

Tentative carryback adjustments..1.6411-1—1.6411-4; 301.6411-1
- limitation on assessment..301.6501(m)-1

Terminable interests, shrinkage..1.273-1

Terminal railroad corporations, taxable income..1.281-1—1.281-4

Termination of taxable year..1.6851-1; 1.6851-2; 301.6851-1

Termination payments to employees ..1.1240-1
- employees:
- . . withholding tax..31.3401(c)-1
- obligations, interest, exempt income 1.103-1

Testing for public safety, organizations devoted to, exemption..1.501(c)(3)-1

Theft, losses..1.165-8

Third parties, property belonging to, levy against..301.6532-3; 301.7426-1

Throw-back rule, excess distributions by trusts..1.665(a)-0A—1.668(b)-2

Timber and timberland:
- capital gains and losses..1.631-1—1.632-2
- cost depletion..1.612-1
- cutting of..1.631-1
- depletion:
- . . bonus and royalty..1.612-3
- disposal under cutting contract..1.631-2
- rules applicable to..1.611-3

Time:
- dividends received for credit and exclusion purposes..1.116-1—1.116-2
- reorganization plan filed..1.393-2

Time for deductions, depreciation..1.167(a)-10

Time for filing:
- consents to dividends..1.565-1
- elections:
  - consolidated return..1.1502-10
  - development expenditures..1.616-3
  - exploration expenditures..1.615-5
  - gain in corporate liquidation..1.333-3
  - LIFO inventory..1.472-3
- returns or documents..1.6071-1—1.6074-1

Time income taxable:
- accrual basis..1.451-1
- treasure trove..1.61-14

Tips: 31.3401(a)(16)-1; 31.3401(f)-1; 31.3402(k)-1
- employer statements..31.6053-2

Title holding corporations, exemption ..1.501(c)(2)-1

Title to property, suit to clear, tax lien ..301-7424-1

Trade or business:
- defined, self-employment tax purposes ..1.1402(c)-1
- employee expense reporting..1.162-17
- exempt organizations..1.502-1; 1.511-1—1.514(c)-1
- expenses..1.162-1—1.162-16
- foreign community income..1.981-1(b)(3)
- income effectively connected with U.S. ..1.864-3—1.864-7
- net operating loss deduction..1.172-3
- property used in, defined..1.1231-1; 1.1231-2

Trademark and trade name expenditures, amortization..1.177-1

Transferees..301.6901-1—301.6903-1
- basis for gain or loss, substituted..1-.1016-10

Transferor property transferred to corporation controlled by..1.351-1

Transfers in contemplation of death, basis ..1.1014-6

Transfers to avoid income tax
- foreign corporations..7.367(a)-1—7.367-2
- tax..1.1491—1.1494-2

Transportation expenses of employee..1.62-1

Transportation services, foreign corporations..1.863-4

Traveling expenses..1.162-2
- disallowance..1.274-1—1.274-6
- proof..1.162-17
- substantiation requirements..1.274-5

Treasury bonds: See "United States obligations"

Treasury stock, sold or exchanged..1.1032-1

Treaty, income exempt under..1.894-1
- nonresident aliens..1.871-12

Treble damages..1.162-22

Trust companies, bank as..1.581-1

Trustees in bankruptcy, returns, signature ..1.6012-3(b)(4); 1.6062-1(a)(2)

Trusts..1.641(a)-0—1.683-3
- accumulation distributions..1.665(b)-1A et seq.
- alimony..1.682(a)-1—1.682(c)-1

Trusts (continued):
- amortization deduction..1.642(f)-1
- annuity interests to charity..1.170A-6
- basis of property..1.1015-1—1.1015-4
- charitable contributions..1.170A-6; 1.681-(a)-1—1.681(d)-1
  - information required..1.6034-1
- charitable remainder..1.664-1—1.664-4; 8.1; 53.4947-1; 53.4947-2
- "Clifford" type..1.671-1—1.678(d)-1
- "complex"..1.661(a)-1—1.663(c)-4
- control by beneficiaries..1.678(a)-1—1.678(d)-1
- control of grantor over corpus..1.671-1—1.678(d)-1
- credits against tax..1.641(b)-1; 1.642(a)(1)-1—1.642(a)(3)-3
- currently distributable income..1.651(a)-1—1.652(c)-4; 1.661(a)-1; 1.662(a)-1; 1.662(a)-2; 1.663(c)-4
- deductions..1.642(b)-1—1.642(i)-1
- defined..301.7701-4
- depletion..1.642(e)-1
- depreciation..1.642(e)-1
- discretionary distributions..1.661(a)-2; 1.662-3
- dividends-received credit..1.642(a)(3)-1; 1.683-2
- employees: See "Employees' Trusts"
- excess distributions..1.665(a)-0A—1.669(f)-2A; 1.665(a)-0—1.669(b)-2
  - accumulation distribution allocated to preceding years..1.666(a)-1A—1.666(d)-1A
  - amounts deemed distributed in preceding years..1.668(a)-1A—1.668(b)-4A
  - capital gain deemed distributed in preceding years..1.669(a)-1A—1.669(f)-2A
  - credit to beneficiaries..1.667(b)-1A
  - definitions..1.665(a)-0A—1.665(g)-2A
  - denial of refund to trusts..1.667(a)-1A
- foreign tax credit..1.642(a)(2)-1
- gifts..1.663(a)-1
- grantors and others treated as owners ..1.671-1—1.678(d)-1
- income..1.641(a)-2
  - accumulation..1.661(a)-1—1.663(c)-4
  - alimony and separate maintenance payments..1.682(a)-1—1.682(c)-1
  - allocation..1.666(a)-1—1.666(c)-2
  - currently distributable..1.651(a)-1—1.652(c)-4; 1.661(a)-1; 1.662(a)-1; 1.662(a)-2; 1.663(c)-4
  - distributable..1.643(a)-0—1.643(a)-7
  - grantor as owner..1.671-1—1.678(d)-1
  - grantor's benefit..1.677(a)-1
  - legal obligation discharged through 1.662(a)-4
  - properly paid or credited..1.661(a)-1—1.663(c)-4
  - revocable trusts..1.676(a)-1
  - taxability..1.641(a)-1
  - taxable to person other than grantor ..1.678(a)-1—1.678(d)-1
- net operating loss..1.642(d)-1
- nonexempt, private foundation restrictions..53.4947-1; 53.4947-2
- payment of tax..1.641(b)-2
- pension: see "Employees' trusts"[2]
- personal exemption..1.642(b)-1
- personal holding company stock owned by..1.544-2
- power of grantor to control beneficial enjoyment..1.674(a)-1
- profit-sharing: See "Employees' trusts"
- profits set aside for charity..1.642(c)-3

69,036 (Fed. Reg.) TRUSTS—WITHHOLDING 5-25-78

Trusts (continued):
. rates of tax..1.641(a)-1
. returns..1.641(b)-2
. reversionary interest of grantor..1.167-1—1.678(d)-1
. revocable..1.676(a)-1
. separate shares as separate trusts..1.663-(c)-1—1.663(c)-4; 1.665(e)-2
. "simple"..1.651(a)-1—1.652(c)-4
. split-interest, private foundation restrictions..53.4947-1; 53.4947-2
. stock-bonus: See "Employees' trusts"
. stock ownership rule:
.. corporate distributions and adjustments ..1.318-3
. termination..1.641(b)-3
. transfer in:
.. basis..1.1015-2; 1.1015-3

— U —

Unconstitutional Federal taxes, recovery ..1.1346-1
Underpayment of tax:
. defined..301.6653-1
. estimated tax..1.6654-1—1.6654-5; 1.6655-1—1.6655-3
.. waiver of penalties..1.6654-4
.. interest..301.6601-1
Underpayment of withholding tax..31.6205-1
Undistributed foreign personal holding company income..1.556-1—1.556-3
Undistributed personal holding company income, defined..1.545-1—1.545-2
Unincorporated business enterprises, election to be taxed as corporation ..1.1361-1—1.1361-15
Unit investment trusts..1.851-7
United Kingdom, credit for income taxes paid..1.905-5
United States:
. claims against:
.. limitations on tax..1.1347-1
. instrumentalities of: See "Instrumentalities of U. S."
. obligations:
.. exchanges of..1.1037-1
.. interest:
... corporation deduction..1.242-1
... exemption..1.103-2—1.103-6
... paid to purchase or carry..1.265-2
... payment of taxes with..1.6312-1—1.6312-2
.. short-term, issued at discount..1.454-1
. removal of property from:
.. limitations on assessment and collection ..301.6503(c)-1
. savings bonds retained after maturity ..1.454-1
Unreasonable accumulation of income by exempt organization..1.504-1
Unrelated business taxable income, defined ..1.512(a)-1—1.512(c)-1
Unrelated trade or business, defined..1.513-1—1.513-2
U.S. possessions: See "Possessions of U.S."
Utilities, defined—see also "Public utilities"..1.247-1(b)

— V —

Value, defined..1.851-3
Verification of returns..1.6065-1; 31.6065(a)-1
Veterans: See "Armed Forces of U. S."

Vinson Act contracts..1.1471-1
Virgin Islands:
. income tax liability, reduction..1.934-1
. possession of U.S...1.931-1(a)

— W —

Wage bracket withholding..31.3402(c)-1
Wage continuation plans..1.72-15; 1.105-4
. mandatory retirement age, payments before..1.105-4(a)(3); 1.105-6
Wage earners:
. books and records..1.6001-1(b); 31.6001-5
. returns..1.6012-1(a)(7); 1.6014-1; 1.6151-1(b)
Wagering:
. losses, deductibility..1.165-10
. winnings, information returns..7.6041-1
Wages: See also "Compensation"
. defined, withholding tax purposes..31.3401(a)-1
Waiver:
. restrictions on assessment and collection of deficiency..301.6213-1
.. refund limitation extended by..301.6511-(c)-1
War loss recoveries..1.1331-1—1.1337-1
War-profits tax, foreign deductibility ..1.164-1—1.164-2
War veterans: See "Armed Forces of U.S."
Wash sales..1.1091-1; 1.1091-2
. losses, effect on earnings and profits ..1.312-7
Water conservation expenditures..1.175-1; 1.175-2
Weekly withholding table..31.3402(c)-1
Western Hemisphere Trade Corporations
. defined..1.921-1
. DISC status..1.922-1(c)
. special deduction..1.922-1
Widow or widower:
. expenses for care of dependents..1.214-1
. income splitting..1.2-1
Wife beneficiary of alimony trust..1.682(a)-1; 1.682(b)-1
Withholding exemptions..31.3402(f)(1)-1—31.3402(f)(6)-1
Withholding, nonresidents..1.1461-1—1.1465-1
Withholding statements: See "Withholding tax statements"
Withholding tables..31.3402(c)-1
Withholding tax at source..1.144-1—1.1464-1
. adjustment for overwithholding..1.1461-4
. agent for:
.. defined..1.1465-1
.. payment of tax..1.1461-2—1.1461-3
. annuity payments..32.1
. credit for tax withheld..1.1462-1
. employee receipts..31.6051-1
. foreign corporations..1.1441-1—1.1443-1
. nonresident aliens..1.1441-1—1.1443-1
.. scholarship or fellowship grants ..1.1441-2
. ownership certificates..1.1461-1
. payment and return of tax..1.1461-2—1.1461-3
. refunds and credits..1.1464-1; 1.6414-1; 301.6414-1
. returns..1.6072-4
. supplemental wage payments..31.3402(g)-1
. tax paid by recipient..1.1463-1
. tax-free covenant bonds..1.32; 1.1451-1; 1.1451-2

WITHHOLDING—YEAR

———References are to SECS. (§) in the Regs. Check Page 23,003 for latest developments———

Withholding tax on wages..31.3401(a)-1—31.3404-1
. additional withholding..31.3402(i)-1
. adjustments..301.6205-1; 31.6413(a)-2
. agents..31.3504-1
. allowance for itemized deductions ..31.3402(m)-1
. false information..31.6682-1
. alternative methods of computing ..31.3402(h)(1)-1—31.3402(h)(4)-1
. assessment and collection..31.6205-1
. certification of nontaxability..31.3402(n)-1
. commission salesmen..31.3402(j)-1
. deductibility of tax..31.3502-1
. definitions..31.3401(a)-1—31.3401(e)-1
. excessive..301.6401-1; 31.6413(a)-1—31.6414-1
. exemption certificates..31.3402(f)(2)-1—31.3402(f)(6)-1
. exemption from withholding..31.3401(a)-1—31.3401(a)(12)-1
. exemptions..31.3402(f)(1)-1
. extension of, to payments other than wages..31.3402(o)-1
. failure to collect and pay over tax..301.-6672-1
. final returns..31.6011(a)-6
. government depositaries..31.6302(c)-1
. government employer..31.3404-1
. group term life insurance..31.3401(a)(14)-1
. included and excluded wages..31.3401(a)-1—31.3401(a)(12)-1; 31.3402(e)-1
. liability for tax..31.3403-1
. . acts performed by agents..31.3504-1
. marital status, disclosure of..31.3402(l)-1
. monthly returns..31.6011(a)-5
. noncash remuneration..31.3401(a)(11)-1; 31.3402(j)-1
. overlapping pay periods..31.3402(g)-1; 31.3402(g)-2
. payment of tax withheld..31.3404-1; 31.6011-(a)-5; 31.6151-1
. . extension..31.6161(a)(i)-1
. penalties..31.6674-1
. percentage method..31.3402(b)-1
. . wages paid before 1-1-70..31.3402(b)-2
. rates..31.3402(a)-2; 31.3402(b)-1; 31.3402(c)-1
. receipts to employees: See "Withholding tax statements"
. records..31.6001-1; 31.6001-5
. refunds and credits..1.31-1; 31.6414-1; 301.6414-1
. . interest on overpayments..301.6611-1
. . overstated credits..301.6201-1
. reimbursed expenses..31.3401(a)(15)
. returns of tax withheld..31.3404-1; 31.6011(a)-4; 31.6011(a)-5
. . execution of..31.6011(a)-7
. . extensions..31.6081(a)-1
. . identification of taxpayers..31.6011(a)-4—31.6011(a)-5; 31.6011(b)-1
. . period covered..31.6101-1
. . place to file..31.6091-1
. . time to file..31.6071(a)-1
. separate accounting..301.7512-1
. services not in course of employer's trade or business..31.3401(a)(4)-1; 31.3401(a)(11)-1
. signing of returns..31.6061-1
. statement to employees: See "Withholding tax statements"
. tables..31.3402(c)-2
. tax paid by recipient..31.3402(d)-1

Withholding tax on wages (continued):
. tips..31.3401(a)(16)-1; 31.3401(f)-1 31.3402(k)-1
. undercollection..31.6205-1
. underpayments..31.6205-1
. verification of returns..31.6065(a)-1
. voluntary agreements..31.3402(p)-1
. wage brackets..31.3402(c)-1
. who required to withhold..31.3402(a)-1
Withholding tax statements..31.6051-1
. failure to furnish..31.6674-1
. false or fraudulent..31.6674-1
. requirements..31.6051-1; 31.6051-2
. requirement where composite return used..31.6051-1(f); 31.6053-2
Work Incentive Program expenses:
. carrybacks and carryovers..1.381(c)(24)-1; 1.383-1—1.383-3
. credit..1.40-1; 1.50A-1; 1.50B-5
. . carrybacks..301.6501(m)-1; 301.6501(o)-1
. . definitions and special rules..1.50B-1—1.50B-5
. . estates and trusts..1.50A-6; 1.50B-3
. . partnerships..1.50A-7; 1.50B-4
. . Subchapter S corporations..1.50A-5; 1.50B-2
. overpayment of tax due to carrybacks ..301.6511(d)-7
Working women, expenses for care of dependents..1.214-1
Workmen's compensation act awards ..1.104-1(b)
Written determinations, disclosure ..301.6110-1—301.6110-7

— Y —

Year:
. change in..1.442-1
. deductions reported..1.461-1
. errors affecting prior, adjustment..1.1311(a)-1
. gross income reported..1.451-1—1.454-1
. . crop insurance proceeds..13.3

INDEX

To Proposed Regulations Under '54 Code

Index references are to Sections (§) in the Proposed Regulations.
Index for Final Regulations starts on page 69,001.

A-B-C

Accident and health plans:
. employer contributions..1.106-1
Accumulated earnings tax..1.532-1—1.535-3
Additions to tax..1.6654-1; 1.6654-2
Affiliated corporations:
. investment credit..1.1502-3
. returns..1.5424-4; 1.1502-3—1.1502-79
Arbitrage bonds..1.103-13—1.103-15
Architectural and transportation barriers to the handicapped and elderly, removal costs..7.190-1—7.190-3
Armed Forces of U.S.:
. retirement pay..1.122-1
Banks:
. consolidated returns..1.1502-42
. information returns..1.6049-1; 1.6049-2
. new jobs credit..1.52-3
Basis for gain or loss:
. adjusted:
.. stock acquired by foreign personal holding companies..1.1022-1
. partner's interest..1.705-1
. property dividends..1.301-1
. Section 1245 property..1.1245-2
Bond purchase plans, pension funds ..1.405-3; 1.409-1
. excess contributions..54.4973-1
Bonds:
. arbitrage..1.103-13—1.103-15
. original issue discount, information returns..1.6049-1; 1.6049-2
Boycotts, international: See "International boycott factor"
Building and loan associations:
. consolidated returns..1.1502-42
. defined..301.7701-13; 301.7701-13A
Capital construction funds, Merchant Marine Act of 1936..3.2—3.8
Capital losses, limitation on..1.1211-1
Carrybacks and carryovers:
. capital gains and losses..1.1502-22(b)(c); 1.1502-79
. corporate acquisitions..1.381(c)(4)-1; 1.382(b) 1
. minimum tax on preference income ..1.56-5; 1.57-4
. tentative refund adjustments..1.6411-1
Cemetery associations..1.501(c)(13)-1
Charitable contributions, consolidated returns..1.1502-24
Charitable remainder trusts..1.664-1
Charitable trusts, information returns ..1.6034-1
Claim of right, restoration of income held under..1.1341-1
Common trust funds:
. preference income..1.58-2(a); 1.58-5
. returns..1.6032-1
Compensation:
. agreements to defer, payments under ..1.61-16
. bonuses..1.162-9
. claim of right, restoration of amounts held under..1.1341-1
. constructive receipt..1.61-16

Compensation (continued):
. information returns..1.6041-2(a); 31.6051-1
. property in payment..1.61-2; 1.61-15; 1.83-1—1.83-8
Constructive receipt of income:
. compensation..1.61-16
Controlled corporations:
. distributions..1.355-1—1.355-4
. sale or exchange between stockholders and..1.1239-1; 1.1239-2
Controlled foreign corporations:
. carrybacks and carryovers..1.954-2(c)
. earnings and profits, previously taxed ..1.959-1
. foreign base company income..1.954-1—1.954-7
. foreign base company shipping operations..1.955A-1—1.955A-4
.. less developed countries..1.954-5; 1.955-0 —1.955-3
. investments:
.. qualified..1.955A-2—1.955A-4
.. U.S. property..1.881-1
. stock ownership defined..1.958-1
. taxable and gross income determination ..1.881-1; 1.952-2; 1.952-3
Controlled group of corporations:
. international boycott factor..1.999-1
. new jobs credit..1.52-1
Cooperative associations:
. new jobs credit..1.52-3
Corporations:
. accumulated earnings tax..1.532-1—1.535-3
. acquisitions:
.. accounting method..1.381(c)(4)-1
.. net operating loss carryovers..1.381(c)(1)-1; 1.382(b)-1
. distributions to foreign corporations ..1.301-1
. information returns..1.16041-2(a)
. returns, consolidated..1.1502-5
Credits against tax: See specific item

D-E-F

Dealers in personal property, accounting methods..1.453-7
Deductions: See specific item
Depletion:
. oil and gas wells..1.613A-2—1.613A-7
. operating mineral interests..1.614-3
. percentage..1.613-1—1.613A-7
. royalties, advance..1.612-3
Depreciation:
. low-income housing..1.167(k)-1—1.167(k)-4
Disability benefits, employer contributions ..1.106-1
Dividends:
. consolidated returns..1.1502-32
. property..1.301-1
. Subchapter S corporations..1.1375-1
Electing small business corporations: See "Subchapter S corporations"
Employee stock options..1.421-6

69,102 (Fed. Reg.) Index—Proposed Regulations 6-1-78

Employee stock ownership plans (ESOPs)..1.46-7; 1.46-8; 54.4975-11

Employees' annuities:
. contributions to..1.72-8; 1.72-13
. exclusion ratio..1.72-4
. self-employed retirement plans..1.72-17A

Employees' beneficiary associations..1.501(c)(9)-1; 1.512(a)-3

Employees' trusts:
. actuarial reports, requirement..301.6058-1
. administrator of plan..1.414(g)-1
. annual information reports..301.6057-1; 301.6058-1
. . deferred retirement benefits..301.6057-1
. . failure to file..301.6652-3
. . participants' statements, fraudulent or failure to furnish..301.6690-1
. beneficiaries, taxation of..1.402(a)-1—1.403(d)-1
. change in plan, notification..301.6652-3
. church plans..1.414(e)-1
. commonly controlled trades or businesses..1.414(c)-1—1.414(c)-5
. contributions to:
. . accident and health plans..1.106-1
. . deduction limitation..1.404(a)-14
. . employer making..1.404(a)-9; 1.404(a)-12
. controlled group of corporations, defined..1.414(b)-1
. custodial accounts..1.401-8; 1.401-8A; 1.403(b)-1
. death benefits..1.101-2
. defined benefit plans..1.404(a)-14
. discriminatory benefits or contributions..1.401-4
. distributions..1.402(e)-2; 1.403(a)-2; 1.403(a)-3; 1.6041-2(b)
. IRA's: See "Individual retirement savings plans"
. information returns..1.6033-2; 1.6041-2(b); 301.6652-3
. insurance contract plans..1.412(i)-1
. life insurance, group-term..1.79-0
. lump-sum distributions..1.402(e)-2; 1.402(e)-3
. multi-employer plans..1.414(f)-1
. owner-employee: See "Self-employed retirement plans"
. qualification requirements..1.401-1
. registration of plan..301.6057-1; 301.6652-3
. rollover contributions..1.402(a)-3; 1.403(a)-3
. self-employed retirement plans: See "Self-employed retirement plans"
. Subchapter S corporations..1.1379-1—1.1379-4
. trustees..1.401-12

Employers, information returns..1.6041-2

Estates and trusts:
. alimony payments..1.682(b)-1
. beneficiaries, gross income determination..1.652(b)-1
. charitable remainder trusts..1.664-1
. excess deductions..1.642(h)-2
. fiduciaries, returns by..1.6012-3
. information returns..1.6034-1
. net operating loss carrybacks and carryovers..1.642(h)-1
. new jobs credit..1.53-1
. personal holding company income..1.543-11
. preference income..1.58-1(d); 1.58-3

Estimated tax:
. corporations, consolidated returns..1.1502-5

Exempt organizations: See also specific item
. annuity contracts purchased by..1.403(d)-1
. minimum tax on preference income..1.511-4
. returns..1.6043-3
. termination..1.6043-3
. unrelated business taxable income..1.511-4; 1.512(a)-3

Evasion or avoidance of tax, penalties..301.6672-1

Federal collection of state individual income taxes..1.6361-1; 31.6361-1; 301.6361-1—301.6365-2

Fiduciaries, returns by..1.6012-3

Finance companies, personal holding company status..1.542-5

Foreign corporations:
. distributions..1.301-1(n)
. earnings and profits..1.964-1—1.964-3
. no U.S. business..1.881-1; 1.881-2
. shareholders, books and records..1.964-3; 1.964-4

Foreign personal holding companies..1.541-1—1.542-5; 1.551-2—1.553-1
. constructive ownership of stock..1.554-1—1.554-7
. foreign base company income..1.954-2
. income..1.954-2
. stock and securities:
. . acquisition of..1.1016-5
. . basis, adjustments..1.1022-1
. . ownership requirements..1.552-3

Franchise, transfer of..1.1253-1—1.1253-3

G-H-I

Handicapped individuals, architectural and transportation barriers to, removal costs..7.190-1—7.190-3

Holding companies, exemption..1.501(c)(2)-1

Income:
. source of, within or without U.S...1.861-1
. . aircraft or ships leased for foreign use..1.861-9; 1.862-1

Individual retirement savings plans..1.408-1—1.408-3
. accumulations in accounts, penalties..54.4974-1
. annual information reports..301.6058-1
. contributions to, deduction limitation..1.219-1
. distributions, minimum, failure to make..54.4973-1
. excess contribution..54.4973-1
. rollover amounts..1.402(a)-3; 1.403(a)-3

Industrial development bonds..1.103-7(d)(e); 1.103-8

Information returns:
. magnetic tape..1.9101-1; 31.6011(a)-7
. who must file..1.6033-2; 1.6034-1; 1.6041-2; 1.6047-1; 1.6049-1; 1.6049-2; 301.6652-3
. withholding taxes..31.6051-1; 31.6051-2; 31.6011(a)-5; 31.6011(a)-7; 31.6091-1

Interest:
. arbitrage bonds..1.103-13—1.103-15
. foreign personal holding companies..1.553-1
. governmental obligations..1.103-1
. industrial development bonds..1.103-7(d)(e)
. information returns..1.6049-1; 1.6049-2

International boycott factor, computation..1.999-1

Investment credit:
. affiliated corporations..1.1502-3
. ESOPs additional for funding..1.46-7; 1.46-8
. liability for tax..1.46-1(c)
. motion picture films and video tapes ..1.48-8
. public utility property..1.46-3(g); 1.46-5
. qualified investment..1.46-3
. TRASOPs..1.46-8

J-K-L

Keogh plans: See "Self-employed retirement plans"
Leases, aircraft and ships for foreign use ..1.861-9; 1.862-1
Lending institutions, personal holding company status..1.542-5
Life insurance companies:
. group-term:
.. employees' trusts..1.79-0
. reserves..1.801-4
Lump-sum distributions: See "Employees' trusts, lump-sum distributions"

M-N-O

Membership organizations..1.277-1—1.277-3
Merchant Marine Act of 1936, capital construction funds..3.2—3.8
Minimum tax on preference income..1.56-1—1.56-5
. books and records..1.57-5
. carrybacks and carryovers..1.56-5; 1.57-4
. conduit entities..1.58-1—1.58-6
. exempt organizations..1.511-4
. exemption..1.58-1
. net operating losses..1.56-2; 1.57-4; 1.57-5(b); 1.382(b)-1
. preference items..1.57-0—1.57-5
.. excess, deferral of tax..1.56-2
.. foreign sources..1.58-7; 1.58-8
. returns..1.6012-1(a)(9); 1.6012-2(i)
.. short period..1.443-1(d)
Municipalities:
. obligations, interest exemption..1.103-1
Net operating loss carrybacks and carryovers:
. estates and trusts..1.642(h)-1
. minimum tax on preference income..1.57-5(b); 1.382(b)-1
. successor corporations..1.381(c)1-1; 1.382(b)-1
New jobs credit 1.52-1—1.53-1
Nonresident aliens:
. taxation of..1.871-7
. withholding tax..1.1441-2; 1.1441-3; 31.-3401(a)(b)-1

P-Q-R

Partners and partnerships:
. capital contributions..1.721-1
. depletion..1.703-1; 1.705-1
. new jobs credit..1.53-1
. preference income..1.58-2(b)
. returns..1.6031-1(a)
Percentage depletion..1.612-3; 1.613-1—1.613A-4
Personal holding companies..1.541-1—1.542-5
. compensation for use of property by shareholder..1.543-9
. constructive ownership..1.544-1
. copyright royalties..1.543-7

Personal holding companies (continued):
. definitions..1.543-12
. estates and trusts..1.543-11
. finance companies..1.542-5
. income..1.543-1; 1.543-12
. income requirements..1.542-2
. lending institutions..1.542-5
. limitations..1.543-2
. mineral, oil or gas royalties..1.543-6
. personal service contracts..1.543-10
. produced film rents..1.543-8
. real estate investment trusts..1.856-1(d)(5)
. rentals and royalties..1.543-1—1.543-7
. returns, consolidated..1.542-4
Political contributions:
. credit for..1.41-1
. deduction for..1.218-1
. requirements on receipt of..1.41-2
Political organizations..1.527-1—1.527-7
Political subdivisions:
. obligations of, interest exemption..1.103-1
Preference income: See "Minimum tax on preference income"
Preparers of returns: See "Tax return preparers"
Property:
. sale or exchange, related taxpayers ..1.1239-1; 1.1239-2
. transferred in connection with services ..1.61-2; 1.83-1; 1.83-8
Real estate investment trusts:
. defined..1.856-1
. gross income requirements..1.856-2(c)
. independent contractors..1.856-4
. new jobs credit..1.52-3
. preference income..1.58-2(a); 1.58-6
. property held primarily for sale to customers..1.856-1(d)(4)
. real property defined..1.856-3(d)
. rents from real property..1.856-4
Refunds and credits:
. reports of..301.6405-1
. tentative carryback adjustments..1.6411-1
Regulated investment companies:
. gross income requirement..1.851-2
. new jobs credit..1.52-3
. preference income..1.58-2(a); 1.58-6
Rehabilitation expenses, low income housing..1.167(k)-1—1.167(k)-4
Related taxpayers, sales or exchanges ..1.1239-1; 1.1239-2
Returns:
. common trust funds..1.6032-1
. consolidated..1.1502-3—1.1502-79
.. personal holding companies..1.542-4
. corporations..1.6012-2(i)
. disclosure, tax return preparers..301.7216-2
. place to file..31.6091-1
. preference income..1.6012-1(a)(9); 1.6012-2(i)
. short period, minimum tax for preference income..1.443-1(d)
. who must file..1.6012-1(a)(9); 1.6012-3; 1.6031-1(a); 1.6043-3

S-T-U

Salary reduction plans..1.61-16
Sale of property, related taxpayers..1.1239-1; 1.1239-2
Section 306 stock..1.306-1; 1.306-3
Section 1244 stock, gross receipts..1.1244(c)-1
Section 1245 property,recomputed basis..1.-1245-2(a)(7)

Self-employed retirement plans:
. annuities..1.72-17A
. contributions to..1.404(e)-1; 1.404(e)-1A
. income averaging..1.1304-2
. information returns..1.6047-1
. owner-employees..1.401-12; 1.401-13; 1.6047-1

Sick benefits:
. employer contributions..1.106-1

Small business corporations: See "Subchapter S Corporations"

Social clubs..1.277-1—1.277-3; 1.512(a)-3

State:
. obligations of, interest exemption..1.103-1

Stock:
. foreign personal holding companies ..1.1022-1
. option to purchase:
.. compensation paid in..1.61-2; 1.61-15
.. employees..1.421-6
.. preference item..1.58-8
. Section 306 stock..1.306-1; 1.306-3
. Section 1244 stock..1.1244(c)-1

Subchapter S corporations:
. capital gains and losses..1.1375-1
. election..1.1372-1
. employees' trusts..1.404(a)-9; 1.1379-1—1.1379-4
. exemption from taxes..1.1372-1
. new jobs credit..1.53-1
. preference income..1.58-2(a); 1.58-4
. stockholders..1.1371-1
. undistributed taxable income..1.1373-1

Supplemental unemployment benefit plans:
. distributions, information returns..1.6041-2(b)

Tax preference income: See "Minimum tax on preference income"

Tax return preparers, disclosure of returns ..301.7216-2

Teachers, annuities..1.403(b)-1

Tentative carryback adjustments, net operating loss..1.6411-1.

Territories:
. obligations, interest exemption..1.103-1

Title holding corporations, exemption ..1.501(c)(2)-1

Trade name, transfer of..1.1253.1—1.1253-3

Trade or business, income effectively connected with U.S...1.864-5

Trademark, transfer of..1.1253-1—1.1253-3

Trusts: See "Estates and trusts"

V-W-X

Western Hemisphere Trade Corporations, consolidated returns..1.1502-25

Withholding tax:
. exemption..31.3401(a)(6)-1
. failure to collect and pay over..301.6672-1
. government depositaries..31.6302(c)-1
. information returns..31.6011(a)-5; 31.6011(a)-7; 31.6051-1; 31.6051-2; 31.6091-1
. nonresident alien..1.1441-2; 1.1441-3; 31.3401(a)(6)-1
. statements, requirements..31.6051-1; 31.6051-2

Work incentive program expenses, credit for..1.50A-1